Collins

CW01648393

Collins COBUILD

ILLUSTRATED STUDENT'S DICTIONARY

HEINLE
CENGAGE Learning™

Australia • Brazil • Japan • Korea • Mexico • Singapore • Spain • United Kingdom • United States

HEINLE
CENGAGE Learning

Collins | COBUILD

Collins COBUILD Illustrated Student's Dictionary

Heinle Cengage Learning

President: Dennis Hogan
Publisher: Sherrise Roehr
Director of Content Development: Anita Raducanu
Development Editor: Katherine Carroll
Editorial Assistant: Victoria Forrester
Director of Product Marketing: Amy T. Mabley
Marketing Manager: Stefanie Walters
International Marketing Manager: Ian Martin
Director of Content and Media Production: Michael Burggren
Product Marketing Manager: Katie Kelley
Content Project Manager: Dawn Marie Elwell
Asset Development Coordinator: Noah Vincelette
Sr. Frontlist Buyer: Mary Beth Hennebury
Editors: Angela Adcock, Niki Alford, Samantha Buchan, Laura Bowkley Craggs, Robert Grossmith, Orin Hargraves, Vanessa Harrison, Maria Leedham, Tim Matthew, David McKenzie, Alex Parker, Robert Parker, Chris Taylor, Mark Tondeur, Catherine Weller
Front and End Matter Typeset: Parkwood Composition Service, Inc.
Illustrators: See pg. 937 for illustration and photo credits.
Printer: China Translation and Printing Services Ltd

Collins COBUILD

Founding Editor-in-Chief: John Sinclair
Publishing Management: Elaine Higgleton
Project Management: Lisa Sutherland
Editors: Sandra Anderson, Katharine Coates, Penny Hands
Shakespeare Supplement: Martin Toseland, Simon Toseland
Computing support by Thomas Callan
A–Z Typeset by Wordcraft
Shakespeare Supplement typeset: Davidson Pre-Press, Glasgow

Harper Collins Publishers
Westerhill Road
Bishopbriggs
Glasgow
G64 2QT
Great Britain

www.collins.co.uk

This edition for sale in sub-Saharan Africa only.

Paperback Book + CD-ROM ISBN: 978-0-00-737792-3

Photo and illustration credits can be found on page 937, which constitutes a continuation of this copyright page.

Reprinted edition for sub-Saharan Africa 2010

Printed in India by Gopsons Papers Ltd
1 2 3 4 5 6 7 8 9 10

Contents

ACKNOWLEDGEMENTS

The publishers would like to acknowledge the following for their invaluable contribution to the original COBUILD concept:

John Sinclair
Patrick Hanks
Gwyneth Fox
Richard Thomas

Stephen Bullion, Jeremy Clear, Rosalind Combley, Susan Hunston, Ramesh Krishnamurthy, Rosamund Moon, Elizabeth Potter

Jane Bradbury, Joanna Channell, Alice Deignan, Andrew Delahunty, Sheila Dignen, Gill Francis, Helen Liebeck, Elizabeth Manning, Carole Murphy, Michael Murphy, Jonathan Payne, Elaine Pollard, Christina Rammell, Penny Stock, John Todd, Jenny Watson, Laura Wedgeworth, John Williams

We would like to acknowledge the assistance of the many hundreds of individuals and companies who have kindly given permission for copyright material to be used in the Bank of English™. The written sources include many national and regional newspapers in Britain and overseas; magazines and periodical publishers; and book publishers in Britain, the United States, and Australia. Extensive spoken data has been provided by radio and television broadcasting companies; research workers at many universities and other institutions; and numerous individual contributors. We are grateful to them all.

Consultant
Paul Nation

JOHN SINCLAIR

Founding Editor-in-Chief, Collins COBUILD Dictionaries
1933-2007

John Sinclair was Professor of Modern English Language at the University of Birmingham for most of his career; he was an outstanding scholar, one of the very first modern corpus linguists, and one of the most open-minded and original thinkers in the field. The COBUILD project in lexical computing, funded by Collins, revolutionized lexicography in the 1980s, and resulted in the creation of the largest corpus of English language texts in the world.

Professor Sinclair personally oversaw the creation of this very first electronic corpus, and was instrumental in developing the tools needed to analyze the data. Having corpus data allowed Professor Sinclair and his team to find out how people really use the English language, and to develop new ways of structuring dictionary entries. Frequency information, for example, allowed him to rank senses by importance and usefulness to the learner (thus the most common meaning should be put first); and the corpus highlights collocates (the words which go together), information which had only been sketchily covered in previous dictionaries. Under his guidance, his team also developed a full-sentence defining style, which not only gave the user the sense of a word, but showed that word in grammatical context.

When the first *Collins COBUILD Dictionary of English* was published in 1987, it revolutionized dictionaries for learners, completely changed approaches to dictionary-writing, and led to a new generation of corpus-driven dictionaries and reference materials for English language learners.

Professor Sinclair worked on the Collins COBUILD range of titles until his retirement, when he moved to Florence, Italy and became president of the Tuscan Word Centre, an association devoted to promoting the scientific study of language. He remained interested in dictionaries until his death, and the Collins COBUILD range of dictionaries remains a testament to his revolutionary approach to lexicography and English language learning. Professor Sinclair will be sorely missed by everyone who had the great pleasure of working with him.

Guide to Key Features

Through a collaborative initiative, Collins COBUILD and Heinle is co-publishing a dynamic new line of dictionaries offering unparalleled pedagogy and resources for students.

BANK *of* ENGLISH

The Bank of English™ is the original and the most current computerised corpus of authentic English. This robust research tool was used to create each definition with language appropriate for intermediate level students. All sample sentences are drawn from the rich selection that the corpus offers which also allows for level appropriate sentences.

Packed with everyday examples from spoken and written English, the *Collins COBUILD Illustrated Student's Dictionary* makes words easy to find, easy to understand, and easy to use.

Promote learning through *Definitions PLUS:*

- Full sentence definitions use the most common context in which target words are most typically found in real life.
- Grammatical patterns shown in context help the student to use English accurately and naturally.
- Natural English definitions guide the user to discover words as they appear in everyday English.

GRAMMATICAL INFORMATION AND PATTERNS

NATURAL ENGLISH

FULL SENTENCE DEFINITIONS

mine /maɪn/ **(mines, mining, mined)** 1 PRON **Mine** is the first person singular possessive pronoun. A speaker or writer uses **mine** to indicate that something belongs or relates to himself or herself. ❑ *She was seated at the table next to mine.* ❑ *That wasn't his fault; it was mine.* 2 N-COUNT A **mine** is a place where deep holes or tunnels are dug under the ground in order to extract minerals. ❑ *...a coal mine.* 3 V-T When a mineral **is mined**, it is obtained from the ground by digging deep holes and tunnels. ❑ *He started mining coal at the age of ten.* ● **miner** **(miners)** N-COUNT ❑ *My father was a miner.* ● **mining** N-UNCOUNT ❑ *...traditional industries such as coal mining.* 4 N-COUNT A **mine** is a bomb hidden in the ground or in water which explodes when something touches it.

Vocabulary Builders

Over 3,000 pedagogical features encourage curiosity and exploration, which in turn build the student's bank of active and passive vocabulary knowledge. The 'Vocabulary Builders' outlined here enhance vocabulary acquisition, increase language fluency, and improve accurate communication. They provide the student with a greater depth and breadth of knowledge of the English language. The *Collins COBUILD Illustrated Student's Dictionary* offers a level of content and an overall learning experience unmatched in other dictionaries.

'Picture Dictionary' boxes illustrate vocabulary and concepts. The words are chosen for their usefulness in an academic setting, frequently showing a concept or process that benefits from a visual presentation.

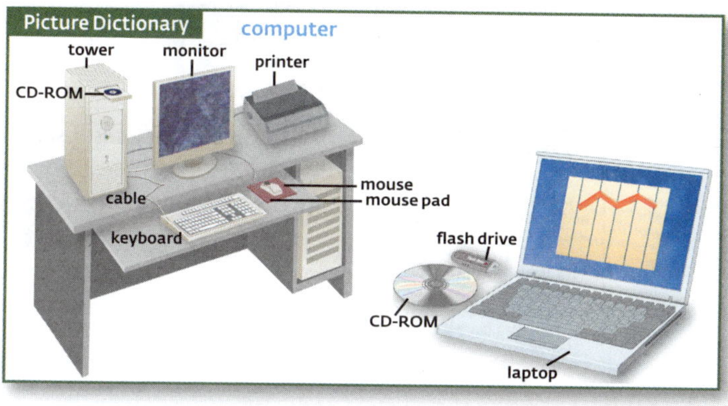

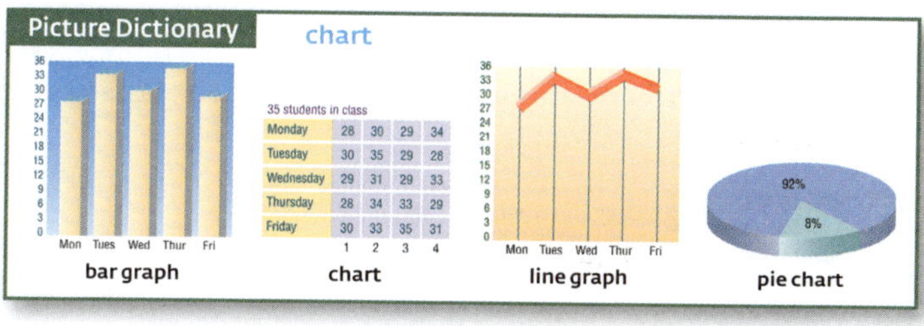

'Word Webs' present topic-related vocabulary through encyclopedia-like readings combined with stunning art, creating opportunities for deeper understanding of the language and concepts. All key words in bold are defined in the dictionary. Upon looking up one word, students discover other related words that draw them further into the dictionary and the language. The longer students spend exploring words, the greater and richer their language acquisition is. The 'Word Webs' encourage language exploration.

Word Web spice

While studying the use of **spices** in cooking, scientists found that many spices can help prevent disease. Bacteria can grow quickly on food and cause serious illnesses in humans. The researchers found that many spices kill bacteria. For example, **garlic**, **onion**, allspice, and oregano kill almost all common **germs**. **Cinnamon**, tarragon, cumin, and chili **peppers** also stop about 75% of bacteria. And even common, everyday **black pepper** kills about 25% of all germs. The scientists also found that food is connected to climate. Spicy food is common in hot climates. Bland food is common in cold climates.

Word Web wave

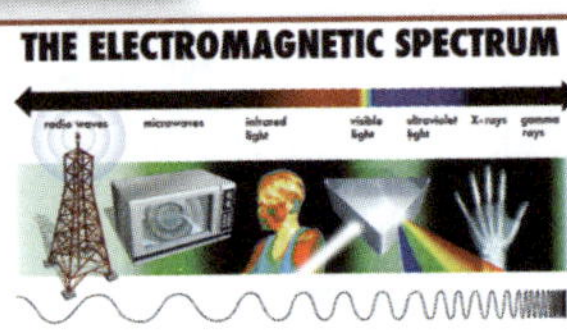

As **wind** blows across water, it makes **waves**. It does this by transferring energy to the water. If the waves meet an object, they bounce off it. Light also moves in waves and acts the same way. We can see an object only if light waves bounce off it. Light waves differ in **frequency**. Wave frequency is usually the measure of the number of waves per second. **Radio waves** and **microwaves** are examples of low-frequency light waves. **Visible light** is made of medium-frequency light waves. **Ultraviolet radiation** and **X-rays** are high-frequency light waves.

Chosen based on frequency in the Bank of English™, **'Word Partnerships'** show high-frequency word patterns, giving the complete collocation with the headword in place to clearly demonstrate use. The numbers refer the student to the correct meaning within the definition of the word that collocates with the headword.

Word Partnership Use *trust* with:

V. **build** trust, **create** trust, **learn to** trust, **place** trust **in** ***someone*** 1
ADJ. **mutual** trust 1
charitable trust 7
N. trust ***your*** **instincts**, trust ***someone's*** **judgment** 6
investment trust 7

Word Partnership Use *moment* with:

ADV. a moment **ago**, **just a** moment 1
N. moment **of silence**, moment **of thought** 1
V. **stop for a** moment, **take a** moment, **think for a** moment, **wait a** moment 1
ADJ. **an awkward** moment, **a critical** moment, **the right** moment 2

'Word Links' exponentially increase language awareness by showing how words are built in English, something that will be useful for students in all areas of academic work as well as in daily communication. Focusing on prefixes, suffixes, and word roots, each 'Word Link' provides a simple definition of the building block and then gives three examples of it used in a word. Providing three examples encourages students to look up these words to develop their understanding.

Word Link	*port ≈ carrying : export, import, portable*

Word Link	*geo ≈ earth : geography, geology, geologist*

'Thesaurus' entries offer both synonyms and antonyms for high-frequency words. An extra focus on synonyms offers students an excellent way to expand vocabulary knowledge and usage by directing them to other words they can research in the dictionary. The numbers refer the student to the correct meaning within the definition of the headword.

Thesaurus	*talk* Also look up:
V.	chat, discuss, gossip, say, share, speak, tell; *(ant.)* listen 1
N.	argument, chat, conversation, dialogue, discussion, interview, negotiation; *(ant.)* silence 1

Thesaurus	*difficult* Also look up:
ADJ.	challenging, demanding, hard, tough; *(ant.)* easy, simple, uncomplicated 1 irritable; *(ant.)* accommodating 2

CD-ROM

A valuable enhancement to the learning experience, the *Collins COBUILD Illustrated Student's Dictionary* CD-ROM offers students a fast and simple way to explore words and their meanings while working on a computer.

- **Search** definitions, sample sentences, word webs, and picture dictionary boxes.
- **'PopUp' Dictionary:** Find the definition of a word while working in any computer application.
- **Audio pronunciation with record and playback** provides pronunciation practice.
- **'My Dictionary'** allows students to create a personalised tool by adding their own words, definitions, and sample sentences.
- **Bookmarks** allow students to save and organise vocabulary.

By using the resources found in this volume, students will discover that the *Collins COBUILD Illustrated Student's Dictionary* is something that they want to delve into and spend time exploring, not just something to flip through for a quick answer. As they investigate options for words that will best serve their individual communicative needs at any given point, students will find more opportunities for learning than they have ever seen in a traditional reference tool. This will become their ultimate resource as they progress within the English language.

Introduction

Welcome to the *Collins Cobuild Illustrated Student's Dictionary*.

It is now over 20 years since the first Collins COBUILD dictionary was published. To celebrate, we are proud to launch this new edition, which contains a brand new supplement of key words and phrases that are used in the works of Shakespeare. In addition to the new supplement, this edition includes several innovative and colourful features that not only help users understand the meanings of words, but also how to use them properly, and how to make the words their own.

Like all COBUILD dictionaries, the *Collins COBUILD Illustrated Student's Dictionary* is based on a huge database of text, both written and spoken, called The Bank of English®. At this printing, The Bank of English® contains over 650 million words, and it is the basis of all the statements that COBUILD makes about the language. It allows the dictionary editors to study the way the language works, and shows the patterns and systems of the English language.

The Bank of English® gives fast and accurate access to all sorts of information about the language. One major area is word frequency. This information is very important in helping to prepare dictionary entries, both because it helps in the choice of words that are suitable for dictionary definitions, and because it provides a sensible list of words that need to be included.

The words explained in this dictionary account for over 90% of the language that is written and spoken. That is because there is a relatively small number of words which are used over and over again, while there is a large number of words which are not used very often. For example, in this introduction, there are 694 words in total. Of these, the word 'the' occurs 67 times, while 132 words occur only once. In fact, there are only 223 different words in this introduction. In a much larger amount of text, the words that do not occur very often are much less important. That is why this dictionary concentrates on the words that occur over and over again, and why the entries represent the language that you really do need to know and to use.

One of the main aims of a COBUILD dictionary is to provide information about those words that the user already 'knows', as well as to provide information that the user does not know. Many words have several uses and meanings, and we do not really 'know' a word until we are familiar with its full range of meaning and grammatical behaviour.

The entries contain a detailed account of the main uses and meanings of each word. Each of the forms is listed at the start of each entry, along with information about alternative spellings, if any exist. Explanations are written in full sentences, and show typical grammatical behaviour. The explanations also give a clear description of meaning. And of course, the thousands of examples are taken directly from The Bank of

English®, showing typical patterns of use and grammatical structure. The information in this dictionary has been carefully chosen in order to allow the dictionary user to be a confident language user.

The *Collins COBUILD Illustrated Student's Dictionary* is printed in full colour, which helps the entries to stand out on the page. Over 3,000 of the most frequent English words in the dictionary are clearly shown by having the headword highlighted in magenta. These have been identified by using the frequency information in the Bank of English®.

Entries which are very long or complex are treated differently to make it easier to find exactly what you are looking for. A menu shows the sections the entry is divided into, and how they are ordered, so that you can immediately go to the correct section to find the meaning you want. For example, **hand** is divided into two sections, showing its noun and verb uses. The entry for **fire** has three sections showing different groups of meaning.

There are a number of language and usage notes which supplement the information already provided in the dictionary entries. In many cases, these language notes draw together information that helps to clarify the differences that exist between some items.

Guide to the Dictionary Entries

Entries and letter index

The main text of the dictionary is made up of entries from A to Z. An **entry** is a complete explanation of a word and all its meanings. For example, the first entries on page 51 are *babble*, *babe*, and *baby*. Entries are shown under the letter that they begin with. On left-hand pages, the letter is shown as a capital letter, and on right-hand pages, it is shown as a small letter.

Running heads

At the top of every page you will see a word. This is called a **running head.** On left-hand pages, the running head is the same as the first complete entry on that page. For example, on page 2 the first complete entry is *abject* and this is the running head at the top of the page. On right-hand pages, the running head is the same as the last entry that begins on that page. On page 3, for example, the running head is *abuse* because that is the last entry which begins on the page.

Entry order

Entries are ordered alphabetically and spaces, hyphens, apostrophes, and accents do not make any difference to this. For example, *up-to-date* comes after *uptight* and before *uptown*, and *director general* comes after *directorate* and before *directory*. In the same way, abbreviations and entries beginning with capital letters are treated like ordinary words, so *B & B* comes after *bandage* and before *bandit*, and *April* comes between *apricot* and *apron*.

Headwords and superheadwords

Every entry begins with a **headword,** starting at the left-hand edge of the colmun. Most of the headwords are printed in blue. Words which are closely related in meaning to the headword are also printed in blue, with a black circle before them. For example, on page 1 of the main text, *abandoned* appears as part of the entry for *abandon*.

Some entries are very long or have very different meanings. These entries are called **superheadwords.** They are divided into numbered sections, with a menu at the beginning of the entry to guide you to the correct section for the meaning you are looking for. For example, *close* on page 130 is divided into two sections; section 1 is verb uses and section 2 is adjective uses.

Inflected forms and alternative spellings

Inflected forms are the different grammatical forms that a word can have. Different forms are shown after the pronunciation. Verbs are shown with the 3rd person singular, the *-ing* form, the past tense, and, where it is different from the past tense, the past participle. Adjectives and adverbs are shown with their comparative forms and nouns are shown with their plural forms. Where a noun does not change its form in the plural, this information is also given. Where there are **alternative spellings** for the headword, these are given in blue before the pronunciation.

Definitions, meanings, and set structures

Definitions are written in full sentences using simple words and show the common ways in which the headword is used. When there is more than one **meaning,** the different meanings are numbered. If a word or expression is used to show approval or disapproval, this information is also given in the definition.

Many words are used in particular grammatical patterns. The definitions show you these important patterns by highlighting these **set structures** in bold (black) print.

For example, if you look at the entry for the verb *agree* on page 17, you can see that the preposition *with* is also bold to show that it is used with this verb.

Examples

The **examples** follow the definitions and are written in *italics*. They are all examples of real language taken from the Bank of English®. They show how the word or phrase is generally used, and give more information about the grammatical patterns in which it is most often used.

Grammatical labels

Before a definition, there is a **grammatical label.** These labels are explained on pages xvi–xxi. Where a word has more than one meaning, there is a grammatical label at the beginning of each numbered meaning.

Style and usage

Some words are used by particular groups of people or in particular contexts. This is shown in the dictionary by a label in square brackets and in small capitals after the definition.

Geographical labels:

[AM] and [mainly AM]: used only, or mainly, by speakers and writers in the U.S. and in other places where American English is taught or used.

[BRIT] and [mainly BRIT]: used only, or mainly, by speakers and writers in Britain and in other places where British English is taught or used. The American equivalent, if there is one, is given.

Style labels:

[BUSINESS]: used mainly when talking about the field of business, e.g. *asset*

[COMPUTING]: used mainly when talking about the field of computing, e.g. *chat room*

[DATED]: no longer in common general use, e.g. *motor car*

[FORMAL]: used mainly in official situations such as politics and business, e.g. *allege*

[INFORMAL]: used mainly in informal situations, conversations, and personal letters, e.g. *pal*

[JOURNALISM]: used mainly in newspapers, television, and radio, e.g. *spearhead*

[LEGAL]: used mainly in legal documents, in law courts, and by the police in official situations, e.g. *accused*

[LITERARY]: used mainly in novels, poetry, and other forms of literature, e.g. *aloft*

[MEDICAL]: used mainly in medical texts, and by doctors in official situations, e.g. *psychosis*

[SPOKEN]: used mainly in speech rather than in writing, e.g. *pardon*

[TECHNICAL]: used mainly when talking or writing about specialist subjects, such as science or music, e.g. *biotechnology*

[WRITTEN]: used mainly in writing rather than in speech, e.g. *avail*

PRONUNCIATION

In this dictionary the International Phonetic Alphabet (IPA) is used to show how the words are pronounced. The symbols used in the International Phonetic Alphabet are shown in the table below.

In written English, the same sound can be shown by more than one letter or combination of letters. This can make spelling difficult in English.

IPA Symbols

Vowel	Sounds	Consonant	Sounds
ɑː	calm, ah	b	bed, rub
æ	act, mass	d	done, red
aɪ	dive, cry	f	fit, if
aɪə	fire, tyre	g	good, dog
aʊ	out, down	h	hat, horse
aʊə	flour, sour	j	yellow, you
e	met, lend, pen	k	king, pick
eɪ	say, weight	l	lip, bill
eə	fair, care	m	mat, ram
ɪ	fit, win	n	not, tin
i	seem, me	p	pay, lip
ɪə	near, beard	r	run, read
ɒ	lot, spot	s	soon, bus
əʊ	note, coat	t	talk, bet
ɔː	claw, more	v	van, love
ɔɪ	boy, joint	w	win, wool
ʊ	could, stood	x	loch
uː	you, use	z	zoo, buzz
ʊə	lure, pure	ʃ	ship, wish
ɜː	turn, third	ʒ	measure, leisure
ʌ	fund, must	ŋ	sing, working
ə	*the first vowel in* about	tʃ	cheap, witch
i	*the second vowel in* very	θ	thin, myth
		ð	then, bathe
		dʒ	joy, bridge

Notes

Primary and secondary stress are shown by marks above and below the line, in front of the stressed syllable. For example, in the word *abbreviation*, represented /əbriviːʃən/, the second syllable has secondary stress and the fourth syllable has primary stress.

Compound words, that is words which are made up of more than one word with either a space or a hyphen between them, are not usually given pronunciations. Pronunciations for the individual words that make up the compounds are usually found at their entries at other parts of the dictionary. However, compounds words are given stress markers.

Where appropriate, American pronunciations are given immediately after the British English pronunciations and are preceded by the abbreviation AM.

/ɑː/ or /æ/

A number of words are shown in the dictionary with alternative pronunciations with /ɑː/ and /æ/, such as 'path' /pɑːθ, pæθ/. In this case, /pɑːθ/ is the standard British pronunciation. However, in many other accents of English, including standard American English, the pronunciation is /pæθ/.

Grammatical Labels Used in the Dictionary

Nearly all the words that are explained in this dictionary have grammar information given about them. For each word or meaning, its word class is shown in capital letters, just before the definition. Examples of word classes are N-COUNT, VERB, PRON, and ADV.

The sections below contain further information about each word class.

Verbs

A verb is a word which is used to say what someone or something does or what happens to them, or to give information about them.

V-I

An **intransitive verb** is one which takes an indirect object or no object, e.g.:

sleep: *She slept till noon.*

V-T

A **transitive verb** is one which takes a direct object, e.g.:

eat: *I ate my chicken quickly.*

V-T/V-I

Some verbs may be **transitive** or **intransitive** depending on how they are used, e.g.:

open: *He opened the window.* (transitive) *The doors opened.* (intransitive)

V-T PASSIVE

V-T PASSIVE means **passive verb.** A passive verb is a verb that is formed using a form of *be* followed by the past participle of the main verb. Passive verbs focus on the person or thing that is affected by the action, e.g.:

born: *My mother was 40 when I was born.*

PHR-VERB

PHR-VERB means **phrasal verb.** A phrasal verb is a combination of a verb and an adverb (e.g. *catch up*) or a verb and a preposition (e.g. *call for*), which together have a particular meaning. Some phrasal verbs have both an adverb and a preposition (for example *add up to*).

catch up: *I stopped and waited for her to catch up.*

call for: *I shall be calling for you at seven o'clock.*

add up to: *Profits can add up to millions of dollars.*

LINK-VERB

A **link verb** is a verb such as *be*, *feel*, or *seem*. These verbs connect the subject of a sentence to a complement. Most link verbs do not occur in the passive, e.g.:

be: *She is my mother.*

feel: *It feels good to finish a piece of work.*

seem: *Everyone seems busy.*

MODAL

A **modal** is a **modal verb** such as *may*, *must*, or *would*. A **modal** is used before the infinitive form of a verb, e.g. *You must see a doctor.* In questions, it comes before the subject, e.g. *May we come in?* In negatives, it comes before the negative word, e.g. *Anne wouldn't mind going to Italy to live.* It does not inflect, for example, it does not take an *-s* in the third person singular, e.g. *I can take care of myself.*

Nouns

N-COUNT

N-COUNT means a **count noun.** Count nouns refer to things which can be counted, and they have both the singular and plural forms. When a count noun is used in the singular, it must normally have a word such as *a*, *an*, *the*, or *her* in front of it, e.g.:

head: *She turned her head away.*

room: *Go to my room and bring down my handbag, please.*

N-UNCOUNT

N-UNCOUNT means an **uncount noun.** Uncount nouns refer to things that are not normally counted or which we do not think of as individual items.

Uncount nouns do not have a plural form, and are used with a singular verb, e.g.:

help: *He shouted for help.*

rain: *We got very wet in the rain.*

bread: *She bought a loaf of bread.*

N-VAR

N-VAR means a **variable noun.** Variable nouns are uncount when they refer to something in general, and count nouns when they refer to a particular instance of something, e.g.:

night: *He didn't leave the house all night.*

Night finally fell.

Other variable nouns refer to substances. They are uncount when they refer to a mass of the substance, and count nouns when they refer to types or brands, e.g.:

coffee: *Would you like some coffee?*

We had a coffee.

N-SING

N-SING means a **singular noun.** A singular noun is always singular and must have a word such as *a*, *an*, *the*, or *my* in front of it, e,g,:

sun: *The sun was low in the sky.*

fault: *It was all his fault.*

N-PLURAL

N-PLURAL means a **plural noun.** A plural noun is always plural and is used with plural verbs, e.g.:

dislikes: *Consider your likes and dislikes about your job.*

finances: *Here are some tips on how to manage your finances.*

N-TITLE

N-TITLE means a noun that is used to refer to someone who has a particular role or position. Titles come before the name of the person and begin with a capital letter, e.g. *President Bush, Queen Elizabeth.*

N-VOC

N-VOC means a **vocative noun.** A vocative noun is a noun that is used when speaking directly to someone or writing to them, e.g.:

darling: *Thank you, darling.*

dear: *You're a lot like me, dear.*

N-PROPER

N-PROPER means a **proper noun.** A proper noun refers to one person, place, thing, or institution, and begins with a capital letter, e.g.:

Earth: *We don't know everything about the Earth.*

Customs: *Customs discovered the goods in his suitcase.*

Other Word Classes

ADJ

ADJ means an **adjective.** An adjective is a word which is used to tell you more about a person or thing, such as its appearance, colour, size, or other qualities, e.g.:

angry: *An angry crowd gathered.*

brown: *She has brown eyes.*

wet: *My gloves were wet.*

ADJ BEFORE N

This means an adjective that is normally used only in front of a noun. For examples, you can talk about an *indoor market*, but you cannot say 'The market was indoor.'

ADJ AFTER LINK-V

This means an adjective that is normally used only after a link verb. For example, you can say *they are glad to see you*, but you cannot say 'a glad woman'.

ADV

ADV means an **adverb.** An adverb is a word that gives more information about when, how, or where something happens, e.g.:

tomorrow: *Bye, see you tomorrow.*

slowly: *He spoke slowly and clearly.*

home: *She wanted to go home.*

CONJ

CONJ means a **conjunction.** Conjunctions are words such as *and*, *but*, *although*, or *since*, which are used to link two words or two clauses in a sentence, e.g.:

although: *Although I was only six, I remember it.*

but: *I'm sorry, but it's true.*

since: *So much has changed since I was a teenager.*

CONVENTION

A **convention** is a word or fixed phrase which is used in conversation, for example when greeting someone, apologizing, or replying. Examples of conventions are *hello*, *sorry*, and *I'm afraid*, e.g.:

hello: *Hello, this is Susan. Could I speak to Nancy please?*

sorry: *Sorry I took so long.*

I'm afraid: *I'm afraid I don't agree.*

DET

DET means a **determiner.** A determiner is a word such as *a*, *the*, *my*, or *every* which is used at the beginning of a noun group, e.g.:

an: *Her holiday came to an end when she broke her foot.*

the: *Daily walks are the best exercise.*

every: *We had meetings every day.*

EXCLAM

EXCLAM means an **exclamation.** An exclamation is a word or phrase which is spoken suddenly or loudly in order to express a strong emotion, e.g.:

oh: *'Oh!' Kenny said. 'Has everyone gone?'*

wow: *Wow, this is so exciting!*

QUANT

QUANT means a **quantifier.** A quantifier is a word or phrase like *plenty* or *a lot* which allowed you to say in a general way how many there are of something, or how much there is of something. Quantifiers are often followed by *of*, e.g.:

all: *He was talking to all of us.*

enough: *They had enough money for a one-way ticket.*

whole: *We spent the whole summer in Italy.*

NUM

NUM means **number,** e.g.:

ten: *It took almost ten years.*

billion: *...3 billion dollars.*

ORD

ORD means **ordinal.** An ordinal is a number that is used like an adjective or an adverb, e.g.:

hundredth: *the hundredth anniversary of his birth.*

second: *It is the second time I have met him.*

PHRASE

A **phrase** is a group of words which have a particular meaning when they are used together. This meaning is not always understandable from the separate parts, e.g.:

out of the blue: *His resignation came out of the blue.*

sit tight: *Sit tight, I'll be right back.*

PREDET

PREDET means a **predeterminer.** A predeterminer is a word such as *all* or *half* which can come before a determiner, e.g.:

all: *She's worked all her life.*

half: *She's half his age*

PREFIX

A **prefix** is a group of letters which are added to the beginning of a word in order to make a different word. The same prefix added to different words changes the meaning of the word in the same way. For example, adding *un-* to the beginning of a word makes it mean the opposite, e.g. *unfriendly* and *unhappy* are the opposite of *friendly* and *happy.*

PREP

PREP means a **preposition.** A preposition is a word such as *by*, *with*, or *from* which is always followed by a noun group or the *-ing* form of a verb, e.g.:

near: *He stood near the door.*

of: *She is a young woman of twenty-six.*

PRON

PRON means a **pronoun.** A pronoun is used to refer to someone or something that has already been mentioned or whose identity is already known, e.g.:

her: *Liz travelled round the world with her boyfriend.*

theirs: *I don't know whose book it is. Somebody must have left theirs.*

this: *I have seen many films, but never one like this.*

Some meanings in entries have more than one word class. For example:

control 2: V-T & N-UNCOUNT

This means that *control* is both a transitive verb and an uncount noun for meaning 2:

You can't control what other people think.

He lost control of his car.

behind 1: PREP & ADV

This means that *behind* is both a preposition and an adverb for meaning 1:

Put the cushion behind his head.

She led the way upstairs, with Terry following behind.

Infinitive	Past Tense	Past Participle
arise	arose	arisen
be	was, were	been
beat	beat	beaten
become	became	become
begin	began	begun
bend	bent	bent
bet	bet	bet
bind	bound	bound
bite	bit	bitten
bleed	bled	bled
blow	blew	blown
break	broke	broken
bring	brought	brought
build	built	built
burn	burned *or* burnt	burned *or* burnt
burst	burst	burst
buy	bought	bought
can	could	–
cast	cast	cast
catch	caught	caught
choose	chose	chosen
cling	clung	clung
come	came	come
cost	cost *or* costed	cost *or* costed
creep	crept	crept
cut	cut	cut
deal	dealt	dealt
dig	dug	dug
dive	dived	dived
do	did	done
draw	drew	drawn
dream	dreamed *or* dreamt	dreamed *or* dreamt
drink	drank	drunk
drive	drove	driven
eat	ate	eaten
fall	fell	fallen
feed	fed	fed
feel	felt	felt
fight	fought	fought
find	found	found
fly	flew	flown
forbid	forbade	forbidden
forget	forgot	forgotten
freeze	froze	frozen
get	got	gotten, got

give	gave	given
go	went	gone
grind	ground	ground
grow	grew	grown
hang	hung	hung
have	had	had
hear	heard	heard
hide	hid	hidden
hit	hit	hit
hold	held	held
hurt	hurt	hurt
keep	kept	kept
kneel	kneeled *or* knelt	kneeled *or* knelt
know	knew	known
lay	laid	laid
lead	led	led
lean	leaned *or* leant	leaned *or* leant
leap	leaped *or* leapt	leaped *or* leapt
learn	learned *or* learnt	learned *or* learnt
leave	left	left
lend	lent	lent
let	let	let
lie	lay	lain
light	lit *or* lighted	lit *or* lighted
lose	lost	lost
make	made	made
may	might	–
mean	meant	meant
meet	met	met
pay	paid	paid
put	put	put
quit	quit	quit
read	read	read
rid	rid	rid
ride	rode	ridden
ring	rang	rung
rise	rose	risen
run	ran	run
say	said	said
see	saw	seen
seek	sought	sought
sell	sold	sold
send	sent	sent
set	set	set
shake	shook	shaken
shed	shed	shed

shine	shone	shone
shoe	shod	shod
shoot	shot	shot
show	showed	shown
shrink	shrank	shrunk
shut	shut	shut
sing	sang	sung
sink	sank	sunk
sit	sat	sat
sleep	slept	slept
slide	slid	slid
smell	smelled *or* smelt	smelled *or* smelt
speak	spoke	spoken
speed	sped *or* speeded	sped *or* speeded
spell	spelled *or* spelt	spelled *or* spelt
spend	spent	spent
spill	spilled *or* spilt	spilled *or* spilt
spit	spat	spat
spoil	spoiled *or* spoilt	spoiled *or* spoilt
spread	spread	spread
spring	sprang	sprung
stand	stood	stood
steal	stole	stolen
stick	stuck	stuck
sting	stung	stung
stink	stank	stunk
strike	struck	struck *or* stricken
swear	swore	sworn
sweep	swept	swept
swell	swelled	swollen
swim	swam	swum
swing	swung	swung
take	took	taken
teach	taught	taught
tear	tore	torn
tell	told	told
think	thought	thought
throw	threw	thrown
wake	woke	woken
wear	wore	worn
weep	wept	wept
win	won	won
wind	wound	wound
write	wrote	written

SUFFIXES AND PREFIXES

Suffixes are word endings which can be added to words, usually to make a new word with a similar meaning but different part of speech. In this dictionary some words have a black circle in front of them and have an example but no definition. These words are formed by adding a suffix.

The list of suffixes is followed by a list of the most frequent prefixes. Prefixes are beginnings of words, which have a regular meaning. Adding a prefix to a word changes its meaning, and adding the same prefix to different words changes their meaning in the same way.

Suffixes

-ability and **-ibility** replace *-able* and *-ible* at the end of adjectives to form nouns which refer to a particular state or quality. For example, *reliability* is the state or quality of being reliable.

-able forms adjectives which indicate what someone or something can have done to them. For example, if something is *readable*, it is possible to read it.

-al forms adjectives which indicate what something is connected with. For example, *environmental* problems are problems connected with the environment.

-ally is added to adjectives ending in *-ic* to form adverbs which indicate how something is done or what something relates to. For example, if something is done *enthusiastically*, it is done in an enthusiastic way.

-ance and **-ence** form nouns which refer to a particular action, state, or quality. For example, *brilliance* is the state or quality of being brilliant, and *reappearance* is the action of reappearing.

-ation, -ication, -sion, and **-tion** form nouns which refer to a state or process, or to an instance of that process. For example, the *protection* of something is the process of protecting it.

-cy forms nouns which refer to a particular state or quality. For example, *accuracy* is the state or quality of being accurate.

-ed is added to verbs to make the past tense and past participle. Past participles formed are often used as adjectives which indicate that something has been affected in some way. For example, *cooked* food is food that has been cooked.

-ence see **-ance**

-er and **-or** form nouns which refer to a person who performs a particular action, often because it is their job. For example, a *teacher* is someone who teaches. **-er** and **-or** also form nouns which refer to tools and machines that perform a particular action. For example, a *boiler* is a machine that boils things.

-ful forms nouns which refer to the amount of a substance that something contains or can contain. For example, a *handful* of sand is the amount of sand that you can hold in your hand.

-ibility see **-ability**

-ic forms adjectives which indicate that something or someone is connected with a particular thing. For example, *photographic* equipment is equipment connected with photography.

-ication, see **-ation**

-ing is added to verbs to make the *-ing* form, or present participle. Present participle forms are often used as adjectives describing a person or thing who is doing something. For example, a *sleeping* baby is a baby that is sleeping and an *amusing* joke is a joke that amuses people. Present participle forms are also used as nouns which refer to activities. For example, if you say you like *dancing*, you mean that you like to dance.

-ish forms adjectives which indicate that someone or something has a quality to a small extent. For example, if you say that something is *largish*, you mean it is fairly large, and something that is *yellowish* is slightly yellow in colour.

-ish also forms words that indicate that a particular time or age mentioned is approximate. For example, if someone is *fortyish*, they are about forty years old.

-ism forms nouns which refer to particular beliefs, or to behaviour based on these beliefs. For example, *professionalism* is behaviour that is professional and *racism* is the beliefs and behaviour of a racist.

-ist replaces *-ism* at the end of nouns to form nouns and adjectives. The nouns refer to the people who have particular beliefs. For example, a *fascist* is someone who supports *fascism*. The adjectives indicate that something is related to or is based on particular beliefs.

-ist also forms nouns which refer to people who do a particular kind of work. For example, a *scientist* is someone whose work is connected with science.

-ist also forms nouns which refer to people who play a particular musical instrument, often as their job. For example, a *violinist* is someone who plays the violin.

-ity forms nouns which refer to a particular state or quality. For example, *solidity* is the state or quality of being solid.

-less forms adjectives which indicate that someone or something does not have a particular thing. For example, someone who is *childless* does not have any children.

-ly forms adverbs which indicate how something is done. For example, if someone speaks *cheerfully*, they speak in a cheerful way.

-ment forms nouns which refer to the process of making or doing something, or to the result of this process. For example, *replacement* is the process of replacing something or the thing which replaces it.

-ness forms nouns which refer to a particular state or quality. For example, *gentleness* is the state or quality of being gentle.

-or see **-er**

-ous forms adjectives which indicate that someone or something has a particular quality. For example, an person who is *humorous* has a lot of humour.

-sion, -tion, see **-ation**

-y forms adjectives which indicate that something is full of something else or covered in it. For example, if something is *dirty*, it is covered with dirt.

-y also forms adjectives which mean that something is like something else. For example, if something tastes *chocolatey*, it tastes like chocolate, although it is not actually chocolate.

Prefixes

a- forms adjectives which have *not*, *without*, or *opposite* in their meaning. For example, *atypical* behaviour is not typical of someone.

anti- forms nouns and adjectives which refer to some sort of opposition. For example, if something moves *anti-clockwise*, it moves in the opposite direction to clockwise.

auto- forms words which refer to someone doing something to, for, or about themselves. For example, your *autobiography* is an account of your life, which you write yourself.

bi- forms nouns and adjectives which have *two* as part of their meaning. For example, if someone is *bilingual*, they speak two languages.

bi- also forms adjectives and adverbs which refer to something happening twice in a period of time, or once in two consecutive periods of time. A **bimonthly** event happens twice a month, or once every two months.

co- forms verbs and nouns which refer to people sharing things or doing things together. For example, if two people *co-write* a book, they write it together. The *co-author* of a book is one of the people who have written it.

counter- forms words which refer to actions or activities that oppose another action or activity. For example, a *counter-measure* is an action you take to weaken the effect of another action or situation.

de- is added to some verbs to make verbs which mean the opposite. For example, to *deactivate* a mechanism means to switch it off so that it cannot work.

dis- can be added to some words to form words which have the opposite meaning. For example, if someone is *dishonest*, they are not honest.

eco- forms nouns and adjectives which refer to something related to the environment. For example, *eco-friendly* products do not harm the environment.

ex- forms words which refer to people who are no longer a particular thing. For example, an *ex-police officer* is someone who is no longer a police officer.

extra- forms adjectives which refer to something being outside or beyond something else. For example, something which is *extraordinary* is more than ordinary, that is, very special.

extra- also forms adjectives which refer to something having a large amount of a particular quality. For example, if something is *extra-strong*, it is very strong.

hyper- forms adjectives which refer to people or things which have a large amount of, or too much, of a particular quality. For example, *hyperinflation* is very extreme inflation.

il-, **im-**, **in-**, and **ir-** can be added to some words to form words which have the opposite meaning. For example, if an activity is *illegal*, it is not legal. If someone is *impatient*, they are not patient.

inter- forms adjectives which refer to things that move, exist, or happen between two or more people or things. For example, *inter-city* trains travel between cities.

ir- see **il-**

kilo- forms words which refer to things which have a thousand parts. For example, a *kilometre* is a thousand metres.

mal- forms words which refer to things that are bad or unpleasant, or that are unsuccessful or imperfect. For example, if a machine *malfunctions*, it does not work properly.

mega- forms words which refer to units which are a million times bigger. For example, a *megawatt* is a million watts.

micro- forms nouns which have *small* as part of their meaning. For example, a *micro-organism* is a very small living thing that you cannot see with your eyes alone.

mid- forms nouns and adjectives which refer to the middle part of a particular period of time, or the middle part of a particular place. For example, *mid-June* is the middle of June.

milli- forms nouns which refer to units which are a thousand times smaller. For example, a *millimetre* is a thousandth of a metre.

mini- forms nouns which refer to things which are a smaller version of something else. For example, a *minibus* is a small bus.

mis- forms verbs and nouns which refer to something being done badly or wrongly. For example, if you *misbehave*, you behave badly.

mono- forms nouns and adjectives which have *one* or *single* as part of their meaning. For example, *monogamy* is the custom of being married to one person.

multi- forms adjectives which refer to something that consists of many things of a particular kind. For example, a *multi-coloured* object has many different colours.

neo- forms nouns and adjectives which refer to modern versions of styles and particular groups of the past. For example, *neo-classical* architecture is based on ancient Greek or Roman architecture.

non- forms nouns and adjectives which refer to people or things that do not have a particular quality or characteristic. For example, a *non-fatal* accident is not fatal.

non- also forms nouns which refer to situations where a particular action has not taken place. For example, someone's *non-attendance* at a meeting is the fact that they did not go to the meeting.

out- forms verbs which refer to an action as being done better by one person than by another. For example, if you can *outswim* someone, you can swim further or faster than they can.

over- forms words which refer to a quality of action that exists or is done to to great an extent. For example, if someone is being *over-cautious*, they are being too cautious.

part- forms words which refer to something that is partly but not completely a particular thing. For example, *part-baked bread* is only partly baked.

poly- forms nouns and adjectives which have *many* as part of their meaning. For example, a *polysyllabic* word contains many syllables.

post- forms words that refer to something that takes place after a particular date, period, or event. For example, a *postscript* (PS) to a letter is extra information that you write at the end, after you have signed it.

pre- forms words that refer to something that takes place before a particular date, period, or event. For example, a *prenatal* examination is one which a woman will have while she is pregnant.

pro- forms adjectives which refer to people who strongly support a particular person or thing. For example, if you are *pro-democracy*, you support democracy.

pseudo- forms nouns and adjectives which refer to something which is not really what is seems or claims to be. For example, a *pseudo-science* is something that claims to be a science, but is not.

re- forms verbs and nouns which refer to an action or process being repeated. For example, if you *re-read* something, you read it again.

semi- forms nouns and adjectives which refer to people and things that are partly, but not completely, in a particular state. For example, if you are *semi-conscious*, you are partly, but not wholly, conscious.

sub- forms nouns which refer to things that are part of a larger thing. For example, a *subcommittee* is a small committee made up of members of a larger committee.

sub- also forms adjectives which refer to people or things that are inferior. For example, *substandard* living conditions are inferior to normal living conditions.

super- forms nouns and adjectives which refer to people and things that are larger, better, or more advanced than others. For example, a *super-fit* athlete is extremely fit, and a *supertanker* is a very large tanker.

tri- forms nouns and adjectives which have 'three' as part of their meaning. For example, a *tricycle* is a cycle with three wheels.

ultra- forms adjectives which refer to people and things that possess a quality to a very large degree. For example, an *ultra-light* fabric is extremely light.

un- can be added to some words to form words which have the opposite meaning. For example, if something is *unacceptable*, it is not acceptable.

under- forms words which refer to an amount or value being too low or not enough. For example, if someone is *underweight*, their weight is lower than it should be.

Activity Guide Contents

1. USING YOUR BRAIN

Word Web Activities (p. 83) Choosing the Right Definition (p. 83)	Word Link Activities (p. 245) Practice with Pragmatics (p. 83)

1. **Word Web Activities**

   Use the Word Web feature entitled *brain* to answer the following questions about the brain.

   a. Which part tells you it's time to eat? ____________________
   b. Which part helps you learn to speak? ____________________
   c. Which part makes sure you stand up straight? ____________________
   d. Which part controls your heartbeat? ____________________
   e. Which part is wrapped around the outside of the brain? ____________________

2. **Choosing the Right Definition**

   Study the numbered definitions for *brain*. Then write the number of the definition that relates to each sentence below.

   a. _____ Angela mastered the new computer programme in one day. She has some brain!
   b. _____ Some studies show that people with larger brains are more intelligent than people with smaller brains.
   c. _____ They say that Martin is the brains behind the success of the company.
   d. _____ If you'll just use your brain, you'll make the right decision.
   e. _____ In proportion to the size of its body, the elephant's brain is very small.

3. Word Link Activities

a. The definition of *brain* says that it 'enables you to think.'
The prefix in the word *enable* is ______________________.

b. Find the Word Link for this prefix.
What does the prefix mean? ______________________

c. What two other words with this prefix do you find?

______________________ ______________________

Guess what each word means. Then check your answers by looking up the words.

4. Practice with Pragmatics

Study the information about the fourth meaning of the definition of *brain*. Read the four sentences below. Write *Yes* if the sentence uses the term appropriately, and *No* if the usage is inappropriate.

a. ______ I think Anna was the brains behind the kids' plan to miss school on Friday.

b. ______ History states that Einstein was the brains behind the discovery of the theory of relativity.

c. ______ The Prime Minister said that the Chancellor was the brains behind the economic recovery.

d. ______ I supplied the money, but Mike was the brains behind the surprise party.

ANSWER KEY:

1. **a.** medulla oblongata; **b.** cerebrum; **c.** cerebellum; **d.** medulla oblongata; **e.** cerebrum
2. **a.** 3, **b.** 1, **c.** 4; **d.** 2; **e.** 1
3. **a.** en; **b.** making or putting; **c.** enact, encode
4. **a.** Yes; **b.** No; **c.** No; **d.** Yes

2. GOING IN CIRCLES

Grammar Activities (p. 122-123) Picture Dictionary Activities (p. 699, 37)	Word Link Activities (p. 122)

1. **Grammar Activities**

Many different words are based on the word *circle*. Write the part of speech of each underlined word—noun, verb, or adjective. Use your dictionary to check your answers.

a. The moon was perfectly circular last night. ______

b. The students arranged the chairs in a circle. ______

c. Vitamin E improves the circulation of the blood. ______

d. Aeroplanes sometimes circle several times before landing. ______

e. Please open the window so the air can circulate. ______

f. What is the circulation of *The Times*? ______

g. Did the teacher circle your mistakes? ______

h. I like circular glasses, not square ones. ______

2. **Picture Dictionary Activities—A**

a. How many other shapes can you think of besides the circle? Write your list below.

______

Look at the Picture Dictionary feature *shapes* and check your answers.

b. Which two shapes most closely resemble the circle?

______ ______

3. **Picture Dictionary Activities—B**

Look at the Picture Dictionary feature entitled *area*. Pay special attention to how to find the area of a circle.

a. What do you call the distance from the centre of the circle to the outside edge? ______

b. What do you call the line that runs around the outside of the circle? ______

c. What do you call the line that runs across the circle from one side to the other? ______

d. What is the formula for finding the area of a circle? ______

e. If a circle has a radius of 3 inches, what is its area? Use $\pi = 3.14$. ______

4. Word Link Activities

a. The first four letters of the word *circle* form a Word Link. What is that link? ________

b. Look up the words *circle*, *circuit*, and *circulate*. Notice the Word Link *circ-* in those words. Write each word below.

Then look it up in the dictionary and identify it as *verb*, *noun*, or *both*.

______________________, ______________

(word) (part of speech)

______________________, ______________

(word) (part of speech)

______________________, ______________

(word) (part of speech)

c. Complete each sentence below with the correct word from item **b**.

1. Blood __________ around the body.
2. A __________ is a shape with all points the same distance from the centre.
3. A tree fell on the power lines and broke the electrical __________.

ANSWER KEY:

1. **a.** adjective; **b.** noun; **c.** noun; d. verb; **e.** verb; **f.** noun; **g.** verb; **h.** adjective
2. **a.** Answers will vary; **b.** ellipse, oval
3. **a.** radius; **b.** circumference; **c.** diameter; **d.** πr^2; **e.** 28.26 inches
4. **a.** circ; **b.** circle, both; circuit, noun; circulate, verb; **c1.** circulate; **c2.** circle; **c3.** circuit

3. TRANSPORT

Choosing the Right Definition (p. 820) Word Web Activities (p. 820, 702)	Dictionary Research (p. 332) Word Link Activities (p. 819)

1. Choosing the Right Definition

Study the numbered definitions for *transport*. Then write the number of the definition that relates to each sentence below.

a. _____ The transport of nuclear waste through large cities can be dangerous.

b. _____ Using mass transport helps the environment.

c. _____ Many schools provide transport for children in the form of school buses.

d. _____ Trains provide rapid transport.

e. _____ Bad weather slows down most forms of transport.

2. Word Web Activities—A

Use the Word Web feature entitled *transport* to answer the following questions.

What are the three names for underground transport systems?

s__________________ m__________________ t__________________

3. Word Web Activities—B

Use the Word Web feature entitled *ship* to answer the following questions.

Look up these words in the dictionary to check your answers.

a. What do you call things other than people that are carried on ships? __________________

b. What do you call the place where a ship stops? __________________

c. What do you call the person who steers a large ship? __________________

d. What do you call the place where a plane can land on a large ship? __________________

4. **Dictionary Research**

a. Reread the definition of *transport*. Write your own definition of the word *goods* as it is used in the definition.

____

b. Look up the word *goods* in the dictionary and complete these sentences.

Goods are things that people make and then later _________.

Goods are things that people _________ and can move from one place to another.

5. **Word Link Activities**

The first five letters of the word *transport* form a Word Link.

a. What is the Word Link? _________

b. What does the Word Link *trans* mean? _________

c. Look up the words *transfer*, *transition*, and *translate*. Notice the Word Link *trans* in those words. Read the definitions.

d. Complete each sentence below with the correct word from item **c.** Check your answers by looking up each word in the dictionary.

1. I don't know how to read Chinese. Can you _________ this letter for me?
2. After the director of the firm left, there was a period of _________ before a new one was appointed.
3. You'll have to take two buses to get there. You can _________ from the 101 to the 145 at Main Street.

ANSWER KEY:

1. **a.** 2, **b.** 1, **c.** 1; **d.** 1; **e.** 2
2. subway, metro, tube
3. **a.** cargo; **b.**port; **c.** captain; d. flight deck
4. **a.** Answers will vary; **b.** sell, own, or make
5. **a.** trans; **b.** across; **d1.** translate; **d2.** transition; **d3.** transfer

4. TRIAL BY JURY

Dictionary Research (p. 822) Word Web Activities (p. 823) Word Partnership Activities (p. 419)	Word Link Activities (p. 383) Choosing the Right Definition (p. 822-823)

1. **Dictionary Research**

   Study the first numbered definition for *trial*. Think about the meaning of the four words listed below. Then match each word with the correct definition below. Look up these words in the dictionary if you are not sure.

   _____ **a.** judge
   _____ **b.** guilty
   _____ **c.** jury
   _____ **d.** evidence

   1. something you see that causes you to believe something is true
   2. a person who decides how a law is applied
   3. responsible for a crime
   4. group of people who decide if a person is guilty or not

2. **Word Web Activities**

   Study the Word Web feature entitled *trial*. Then use bold words from this Word Web feature to complete the following sentences. Look up any words you aren't sure of.

   a. The defendant will get a trial by _________.
   b. The defendant may or may not _________ guilty.
   c. The person who accused the defendant is the _________.
   d. The _________ will tell what they know about the crime.
   e. The words the witnesses say is called their _________.
   f. In the end, the jury will deliver a _________.

3. **Word Partnership Activities**

Study the Word Partnership feature for *jury*. Pay special attention to the phrases below. Then match each phrase with the correct definition. Look up the words in the dictionary if you are not sure.

_____ **a.** jury convicts
_____ **b.** hung jury
_____ **c.** jury duty

1. a jury that can't agree on a verdict
2. a jury finds someone guilty
3. a citizen's obligation to serve on a jury

4. **Word Link Activities**

Study the Word Link feature for the words *illegal*, *illiterate*, and *illogical*. Read the definitions.

a. What is the meaning of the Word Link *il*? __________

Which of these words (*illegal*, *illiterate*, *illogical*) names or describes the following? Read the definitions again if you are not sure.

b. a person who is unable to read __________
c. something that does not make sense __________
d. something that is against the law __________

5. **Choosing the Right Definition**

Study the definition of *trial*. Then write the number of the definition that relates to each sentence below.

a. _____ Elena learned to bake bread by trial and error.
b. _____ You should give aspirin a trial before you ask for anything stronger.
c. _____ The murderer's trial lasted for six weeks.
d. _____ The boss gave me a three-week trial to see if I could handle the responsibilities.

ANSWER KEY:

1. **a.** 2; **b.** 3; **c.** 4; **d.** 1
2. **a.** jury; **b.** plead; **c.** plaintiff; **d.** witnesses; **e.** testimony; **f.** verdict
3. **a.** 2; **b.** 1; **c.** 3
4. **a.** not; **b.** illiterate; **c.** illogical; **d.** illegal
5. **a.** 3; **b.** 2; **c.** 1; **d.** 2

5. ORCHESTRA

Word Web Activities (p. 538) Word Partnership Activities (p. 565)	Word Link Activities (p. 565, 781) Choosing the Right Definition (p. 144, 403)

1. **Word Web Activities**

Study the information in the Word Web feature entitled *orchestra*. Then answer the questions below. Write T for *true* or F for *false*.

_____ **a.** A symphony orchestra usually has more than 100 players.
_____ **b.** The largest section of the orchestra is the string section.
_____ **c.** The double bass plays in the string section.
_____ **d.** The brass section needs to play very loud.
_____ **e.** The timpani is part of the brass section.

2. **Word Partnership Activities**

The job of a symphony orchestra is to *perform* for the public. Look up the word *perform* in the dictionary.

a. Write the number of the definition that applies to music. _____________

Study the Word Partnership feature for *perform*. Then complete the four sentences below using the word *perform* before or after one of these words or phrases: *tasks, able to, miracles, well*. Use each of these words or phrases one time.

b. Some people believe holy people can ___________ ___________.
c. The violinist felt ill and was not ___________ ___________.
d. The new tyres ___________ ___________ on the icy roads.
e. Doctors believe the brains of adults and children ___________ ___________ in different ways.

3. Word Link Activities

The *percussion* section is an important part of a *symphony* orchestra.

- Percussion. Look up *percussion* and read the Word Links *per* and *cuss*.
  - **a.** What does *per* mean? ______________
  - **b.** What does *cuss* mean? ______________
  - **c.** So the percussion instruments make sounds ______________ ______________ one thing against another.
- Symphony. Look up *symphony* and read the Word Links *sym* and *phon*.
  - **d.** What does *sym* mean? ______________
  - **e.** What does *phon* mean? ______________
  - **f.** So *symphony* means to make ______________ ______________.

4. Choosing the Right Definition

Reread the Word Web feature for *orchestra*. Several of the bold words in this feature have multiple meanings.

Study the numbered definitions for *composition*. Then write the number of the definition that relates to each sentence below.

_____ **a.** The composition of furniture in the store window was very attractive.

_____ **b.** Have you written any new compositions lately?

Study the numbered definitions for *instrument*. Then write the number of the definition that relates to each sentence below.

_____ **c.** The piano is my favorite instrument.

_____ **d.** The dentist placed the instruments on the shelf.

ANSWER KEY:

1. **a.** F; **b.** T; **c.** T; **d.** F; **e.** F
2. **a.** 3; **b.** perform miracles; **c.** able to perform; **d.** perform well; **e.** perform tasks
3. **a.** through; **b.** striking; **c.** through striking; **d.** together; **e.** sound; **f.** sound together
4. **a.** 1; **b.** 2 or 3; **c.** 2; **d.** 1

6. COOKING

Word Web Activities (p. 161, 739, 552) Picture Dictionary Activities (p. 160, 239)	Thesaurus Activities (p.160) Grammar Activities (p. 160) Dictionary Research (p.160)

1. Word Web Activities

As you complete this activity, look up any words you aren't sure of.

Read the definitions for *cook* and *cooking*. Then use the Word Web feature entitled *cooking* to answer the following questions.

a. Which bold word means the opposite of *tough?* ________

b. Which bold word means *absorb food into your body?* ________

Now use the Word Web feature entitled *spice* to answer the following questions.

c. Which spice is the least effective in killing germs? ________

d. What kind of food do people in cold climates usually like? ________

Now use the Word Web feature entitled *pan* to answer the following questions.

e. Cooking pans are very heavy when made of what material? ________

f. Copper pans are usually covered with a thin layer of what metal? ________

2. Picture Dictionary Activities—A

Look at the Picture Dictionary feature for *cook*. Then complete the sentences correctly.

a. If you want to make tea, you have to ________ the water.

b. You need an oven if you want to ________, ________, or ________ food.

c. When you put food in a wire container with boiling water under it, you ________ the food.

d. When you make a slice of bread brown by cooking it you ________ it.

e. When you cook food in an oven very close to the flame, you ________ it.

3. Picture Dictionary Activities—B

Look at the Picture Dictionary feature for *egg*. Then answer the questions below. Look up any words you aren't sure of. Write T for *true* or F for *false*.

______ **a.** The scrambled eggs have peppers in them.

______ **b.** The hard-boiled egg has a round yolk.

______ **c.** The fried egg is in a frying pan.

4. **Thesaurus Activities**

Find the Thesaurus feature with the word *cook*. Then complete the sentences using words from the feature. Look up any words you aren't sure of.

a. A _________ works in a restaurant.

b. Yeast is the ingredient that _______ bread rise.

c. If the meal cooked but it has gone cold, you might __________ _________ the food.

d. Busy people tend to eat meals that are simple to __________.

5. **Grammar Activities**

Write the part of speech of each underlined word—noun or verb.

a. Denise's favourite programmes are about <u>cooking</u>. ____________

b. My sister's <u>cooking</u> is fantastic. ____________

c. Janet's aunt taught her how to <u>cook</u>. ____________

d. On Sunday I <u>cooked</u> dinner for my family. ____________

e. My husband is a very good <u>cook</u>. ____________

6. **Dictionary Research**

Look at other words and phrases that follow the word *cook* in the dictionary.

a. Which one describes a collection of recipes? ____________

b. Which one describes something in the kitchen? ____________

c. Which one describes how someone plans to do something? ____________

d. Which one describes preparing food? ____________

ANSWER KEY:

1. **a.** tender; **b.** digest; **c.** black pepper; **d.** bland; **e.** cast iron; **f.** tin
2. **a.** boil; **b.** roast, bake, grill; **c.**steam; **d.** toast; **e.** grill
3. **a.** F; **b.** T; **c.** T
4. **a.** chef; **b.** makes; **c.**heat up; **d.** prepare
5. **a.** noun; **b.** noun; **c.**verb; **d.** verb; **e.** noun
6. **a.** cookbook; **b.** cooker; **c.** cook up; **d.**cookery

7. ENERGY

Choosing the Right Definition (p.247) Word Web Activities (p. 248)	Word Link Activities Grammar Activities (p. 247)

1. Choosing the Right Definition

Study the numbered definitions for *energy*. Then write the number of the definition that relates to each sentence below.

a. _____ She's putting all her energies into her school work.
b. _____ My children have more energy than I do.
c. _____ One problem with nuclear energy is that it produces radioactive waste.
d. _____ You should put more energy into your homework.
e. _____ Which energy source do you think is the cleanest?
f. _____ Conserve your energy. Go to bed early.

2. Word Web Activities

Use the Word Web feature entitled *energy* to answer the following questions. Answer each question with one of the bold words in the Word Web feature.

a. What kind of power plants were built in the 1970s? __________
b. What kind of gas is still used for home heating? __________
c. What was the primary energy source for American settlers? __________
d. What was the source of electrical power in the early 1900s? __________

3. Word Link Activities

Look up the words below to find the Word Link in the word. Write the Word Link.

a. hydraulic _____
b. carefree _____
c. electricity _____
d. complicate _____
e. seller _____

Match the Word Link with the correct definition.

Word Link	Definition
f. hydr	1. without
g. free	2. cause to be
h. electr	3. one who acts as
i. ate	4. water
j. er	5. electric

Now look back at the Word Web feature for *energy*. Write the three words from this feature that are formed from these Word Links.

k. g________ **l.** h________ **m.** e________

4. **Grammar Activities**

Review the dictionary entry for *energy* and *energetic*. Then complete each sentence with the correct form of a word starting with the letters *energ-*. Identify the part of speech of each word you use—noun, verb, adjective, or adverb.

	Part of Speech
a. Celia is very ________ today.	________
b. I don't know what happened to all my ________. I'm really tired.	________
c. David washed the car ________.	________

ANSWER KEY:

1. **a.** 2; **b.** 1; **c.** 3; **d.** 2 **e.** 3; **f.** 1
2. **a.** nuclear; **b.** natural; **c.** wood; **d.** coal
3. **a.** hydr; **b.** free; **c.** electr; **d.** ate; **e.** er; **f.** 4; **g.** 1; **h.** 5; **i.** 2; **j.** 3; **k.** (g)enerate; **l.** (h)ydroelectric ; **m.** (e)lectrical
4. **a.** energetic, adjective; **b.** energy, noun; **c.** energetically, adverb

8. SEEDS AND PLANTS

Choosing the Right Definition (p. 577, 689) Picture Dictionary Activities	Dictionary Research (p. 577) Word Link Activities (p. 29)

1. Choosing the Right Definition

Study the numbered definitions for *plant*. Then write the number of the definition that relates to each sentence below.

_____ **a.** The child shouted 'No' and planted her feet firmly on the ground.

_____ **b.** I brought a plant as a housewarming present.

_____ **c.** My brother works in a power plant in Manchester.

Study the definition of *seed*. Then write the number of the definition that relates to each sentence below.

_____ **d.** I bought a package of flower seeds to plant in the garden.

_____ **e.** I didn't have all the details worked out, but I did have the seed of an idea.

2. Picture Dictionary Activities

Use the Picture Dictionary feature entitled *plants* to answer the following questions. Look up the meaning of any words you don't know.

a. What tree loses its leaves? ____________________

b. What tree is always green? ____________________

3. Dictionary Research

Study the first numbered definitions for *plant*. Think about the meaning of the four words listed below. Then match each word with the correct definition. Look up these words in the dictionary if you are not sure.

_____ **a.** root

_____ **b.** exotic

_____ **c.** assembly

_____ **d.** stem

1. very unusual
2. the long thin part of a plant that is above ground
3. the part of a plant that is underground
4. putting things together

4. **Word Link Activities**

a. Some plants are *annual* plants. These plants bloom for only one year or season. Notice the root word *ann* in the word *annual*. Look up *annual* and find the Word Link. What does *ann* mean ? ________

b. What other words with the root *ann* do you find?

____________________ ____________________

c. Which word in item **b** means money you receive every year? ________

d. Which word in item **b** means a certain amount of money paid each year? ________

ANSWER KEY:

1. **a.** 6; **b.** 1; **c.** 4; **d.** 1; **e.** 2
2. **a.** deciduous; **b.** evergreen
3. **a.** 3; **b.** 1; **c.** 4; **d.** 2
4. **a.** year; **b.** anniversary, annum; **c.** annuity; **d.** anniversary

9. STARS AND ASTRONOMERS

Word Web Activities (p. 749) Choosing the Right Definition (p. 748)	Word Partnership Activities (p. 524) Thesaurus Activities (p. 526) Word Link Activities (p. 44, 321)

1. Word Web Activities

Use the Word Web feature entitled *star* to answer the following questions. Look up each word in the dictionary to check your answers.

a. What is a group of stars called? a ________

b. What do people call the idea that the stars control our lives? ________

c. What is the scientific study of the stars called? ________

d. Which star is used to guide ships on the sea? the ________

Use the Word Web feature entitled *astronomer* to answer this question:

e. Copernicus was an astronomer who thought that the centre of the universe was the ________.

2. Choosing the Right Definition

Study the five numbered definitions for *star*. Then write the number of the definition that relates to each sentence below.

a. ______ Eric is starring in a new TV comedy called *Just for You*.

b. ______ It was cloudy last night, and we couldn't see any stars.

c. ______ Madonna is my favourite singing star.

d. ______ The flag of the United States has 50 stars on it.

3. Word Partnership Activities

Reread the Word Web feature for *star*. Find the word *object* in the second sentence. Look up the word *object* in the dictionary and read the definitions.

a. The first meaning of *object* is *something that has a fixed* ________ or ________.

b. The second meaning of *object* is ________ or ________.

Study the Word Partnership feature for the noun form of *object*. Then complete the four sentences below using the word *object* and one of these words: *foreign, moving, solid*. Use each of these words one time. Look up any words you aren't sure of.

c. We watched as the magician passed a ________ ________ through a mirror.

d. A fast-________ ________ has a high speed.

e. If a child swallows a ________ ________ call a doctor for advice.

4. Thesaurus Activities

Reread the Word Web feature entitled *astronomer*. Notice the word *study* in the second sentence of the feature. A synonym for *study* is *observe*. Look up *observe* in the dictionary and study the Thesaurus feature that accompanies it. Which of the words in the box goes with each sentence below?

notice	watch	study

a. Medical students study and observe the behaviour of babies. ________

b. I checked the level of the water every hour, but I didn't observe any change. ________

c. Jane Goodall would observe the chimps carefully for hours without moving. ________

5. Word Link Activities

The first five letters of the word *astronomer* form a Word Link. Look at the information in the Word Link for *astro*.

a. What does the Word Link *astro* mean? ________

b. What are the three Word Links for *astro*?

________ ________ ________

c. Complete each sentence below with the correct word from item b. Check your answers by looking up each word in the dictionary.

1. This symbol (*) is called the ________.
2. You need a telescope to study ________.
3. You have to know how to fly a plane before you can study to become an ________.

d. Reread the Word Web feature for *star*. Find the word *astrology*. It contains two Word Links. You have studied the Word Link *astro*. Now look up *geology* and find the Word Link *logy*.

1. What does *logy* mean? ________
2. So the literal meaning of *astrology* is the ________ of ________.

ANSWER KEY:

1. **a.** constellation; **b.** astrology; **c.** astronomy; **d.** North Star; **e.** Sun
2. **a.** 4; **b.** 1; **c.** 3; **d.** 2
3. **a.** shape, form; **b.** aim, purpose; **c.** solid object; **d.** moving object; **e.** foreign object
4. **a.** study; **b.** notice; **c.** observe
5. **a.** star; **b.** asterisk, astronaut, astronomy; **c.** **1.** asterisk, **2.** astronomy, **3.** astronaut; **d.** **1.** study of, **2.** study, stars

10. FOOD

Word Web Activities (p. 298) Thesaurus Activities (p. 814) Picture Dictionary Activities (p. 200)	Choosing the Right Definition (p. 280) Dictionary Research (p. 522)

1. **Word Web Activities**

Study the information in the Word Web feature entitled *food*. Then answer the questions below. Write T for *true* or F for *false*.

_____ **a.** Snakes are herbivores.
_____ **b.** Mice are predators.
_____ **c.** Green plants store energy from the sun.

2. **Thesaurus Activities**

The Word Web feature for *food* says that a hawk is a *top predator*. Look at the Thesaurus feature for the word *top*. Then complete the sentences using words from the feature. Look up any words you aren't sure of.

a. The adjective meanings for *top* are _________ and _________.
b. Which adjective best describes the hawk's position as a top predator? _________

3. **Picture Dictionary Activities**

Look at the Picture Dictionary feature for *dessert*. Then answer the questions below. Look up any words you aren't familiar with.

a. Which two desserts don't have to be cooked?
_________ and _________
b. Which two desserts are usually very cold? _________ and _________
c. Which dessert is made mostly of eggs? _________
d. Which dessert is made mostly of a white grain? _________

4. **Choosing the Right Definition**

The word *feed* is related to the word *food*. Look up the word *feed* and study the numbered definitions. Then write the number of the definition that relates to each sentence below.

a. _____ My mother always feeds the children dinner early on Friday nights.

b. _____ The squirrels in our yard like to feed on the seed we leave for the birds.

c. _____ Newborn babies usually feed every three hours.

d. _____ We collected money to feed the tsunami victims in Asia.

5. **Dictionary Research**

a. Look up the word *nutrient*. Write your own definition of the word *nutrient* as it is used in the definition.

____

b. Use the definition of *nutrient* to complete this sentence.
Nutrients are things that plants and animals __________ .

c. Study the words on the page after *nutrient* in the dictionary. Which words also contain the prefix *nutri* ?

________________ ________________ ________________

ANSWER KEY:

1. **a.** F; **b.** F; **c.** T
2. **a.** highest, better; **b.** highest
3. **a.** ice cream, fruit salad; **b.** ice cream, jelly; **c.** custard; **d.** rice pudding
4. **a.** 1; **b.** 3; **c.** 4; **d.** 2
5. **a.** Answers will vary; **b.** need; **c.** nutrition, nutritional, nutritious

11. ART

Word Web Activities (p. 40) Thesaurus Activities (p. 445)	Word Link Activities Choosing the Right Definition (p. 764)

1. Word Web Activities

Use the Word Web feature entitled *art* to answer the following questions.

a. What inspired the term 'Impressionism'? a painting by ________
b. In what part of the world did impressionism start? in ________
c. What did the impressionists usually paint? ________
d. What elements did they emphasize in their paintings? ________ and colour
e. The art of what country influenced the impressionists? ________

2. Thesaurus Activities

The Word Web feature for *art* says that the impressionists were interested in light and colour. Find the Thesaurus feature with the word light. Then complete the sentences using words from the feature. Look up any words you aren't sure of.

a. The noun meanings for *light* are ________, ________, ________, ________, and ________.
b. Which noun meaning best describes the soft light of a fire when there are no flames? ________
c. Which noun meaning describes the happiness on a person's face? ________
d. Which adjective describes a room with a lot of windows facing south? ________

3. Word Link Activities

Review the Word Web feature for *art* noting the words *realistic* and *depiction*. Look up the words below and study the Word Links. Then answer the questions.
Look up *reality, realize, really*

a. What does the Word Link *real* mean? ________
b. Which word in this link means 'to make something happen'? ________
c. Which word in this link means 'actually'? ________

Look up *biologist, chemist, journalist*

d. What does *ist* mean? ____________

e. Which word in this link means someone who is a writer? ____________

f. Which word describes someone who works in a chemists' shop? ____________

Look up *depict, picture, picturesque*

g. What does the Word Link *pict* mean? ____________

h. Which word in this link means 'charming and pretty'? ____________

i. Which word in this link means 'show or illustrate'? ____________

4. Choosing the Right Definition

The Word Web feature for *art* says that the impressionists stopped painting in their *studios*. Study the numbered definitions for *studio*. Then write the number of the definition that relates to each sentence below.

a. ______ The TV show originated in a studio in New York City.

b. ______ The photographer has a large studio with large windows.

ANSWER KEY:

1. **a.** Monet; **b.** Europe; **c.** landscapes; **d.** light; **e.** Japan
2. **a.** brightness, gleam, glow, radiance, shine; **b.** glow; **c.** radiance/glow; **d.** sunny
3. **a.** actual; **b.** realize; **c.** really; **d.** one who practises; **e.** journalist; **f.** pharmacist; **g.** painting; **h.** picturesque; **i.** depict
4. **a.** 2; **b.** 1

12. TELEVISION

Word Web Activities (p. 793) Thesaurus Activities (p. 127, 572) Word Link Activities (p. 792, 858)	Choosing the Right Definition (p. 683, 750) Grammar Activities (p. 602)

1. **Word Web Activities**

   Use the Word Web feature entitled *television* to answer the following questions. Look up any words you don't know in the dictionary.

   a. What kind of tube was used in old-fashioned televisions? ______________

   b. What are the tiny dots of light on a TV screen called? ______________

   c. What are the three sources of TV signals?

   ______________, ______________, and ______________

2. **Thesaurus Activities**

   The Word Web feature for *television* says that high-definition televisions have a very *clear picture*.

   a. Read the dictionary definition for *clear*. *Clear* is used to describe a TV picture that is easy to __________.

   Find the Thesaurus feature for *clear*. Then complete the sentences using words from the feature. Look up any words you aren't sure of.

   b. These words describe something that is easy to understand.

   __________ __________ __________

   Read the dictionary definition for *picture*. Then study the Thesaurus feature for this word and answer the questions below.

   c. Which meaning of the word *picture* applies to a television picture?

   ____

   d. Look at the verb meanings of *picture* in the Thesaurus entry. They describe a picture that exists only in a person's __________.

3. **Word Link Activities**

   - Television

     a. Look up the Word Link for *tele*. What does *tele* mean? __________

     b. Look up the word *visible*. Read the Word Link above *visible*. What is the meaning of the prefix *vis*? __________

     c. So television is something that lets you __________ things at a __________.

4. Choosing the Right Definition

Reread the Word Web feature for *television*. Pay special attention to the words *screen* and *station*. Then look up these words in the dictionary. Study the numbered definitions for *screen*. Then write the number of the definition that relates to each sentence below.

_____ **a.** At the cinema a tall person sat in front of me and it was hard to see the screen.

_____ **b.** Blood samples are screened in a laboratory

Study the numbered definitions for *station*. Then write the number of the definition that relates to each sentence below.

_____ **c.** We live down the road from a Tube station.

_____ **d.** Which station is showing the football match tonight?

5. Grammar Activities

The Word Web feature says that cathode ray tubes are used to *produce* a television picture. Many different words are based on the word *produce*. Write the part of speech of each underlined word—noun, verb, adjective, or adverb. Use your dictionary to check your answers.

a. I always buy my produce from the fruit market on the corner. _____

b. There are so many new products on the market, I don't know which to buy. _____

c. A lot of film production takes place on the streets of New York. _____

d. I am the most productive early in the morning. _____

e. The thief produced a gun from his pocket. _____

f. The students work most productively in small groups. _____

ANSWER KEY:

1. **a.** cathode ray; **b.** pixels; **c.** ground stations, satellites, cables
2. **a.** see; **b.** obvious, plain, straightforward; **c.** 4; **d.** mind
3. **a.** distance; **b.** seeing; **c.** see, distance
4. **a.** 1; **b.** 5; **c.** 1; **d.** 4
5. **a.** noun; **b.** noun; **c.** noun; **d.** adjective; **e.** verb; **f.** adverb

13. MONEY

Word Web Activities (p. 494) Word Partnership Activities (p. 97) Thesaurus Activities (p. 494)	Choosing the Right Definition (p. 69) Dictionary Research (p. 488)

1. Word Web Activities

Use the Word Web feature entitled *money* to answer the following questions.

a. Which word in the feature means the same as *trade*? ________

b. What form of ocean life was used as money at one time? ________

c. Were the first coins round? ________

d. What country had the first circular coins? ________

e. Which two metals were used by the Lydians to make coins? ________ and ________

2. Word Partnership Activities

Look up the word *buy* in the dictionary.

a. What is the past tense of the verb *buy*? ________

b. Which meaning of *buy* is found in this sentence?
I bought myself a few minutes to think of the answer to the question.
sense number ________

Study the Word Partnership feature for *buy*. Then complete the four sentences below using the word *buy* before or after one of these words or phrases: *online, and sell, afford to*. Use each of these items once.

c. I can't ________ ________ a flat screen TV. I haven't got enough money.

d. If you ________ ________ shares at the right time, you can get rich.

e. Is it safe to ________ ________?

3. Thesaurus Activities

Find the Thesaurus feature with the word *money*. Then complete the sentences using words from the feature. Look up any words you aren't sure of.

a. A single ________ is now in use in all European Union countries.

b. I never use ________. I prefer to pay by credit card or cheque.

c. I don't have the amount of ________ I need to start my own business.

d. The group decided to raise ________ to help people with AIDS.

e. The discovery of oil brought great ________ to the Middle East.

4. **Choosing the Right Definition**

Study the numbered definitions for *bill*. Then write the number of the definition that relates to each sentence below.

_____ **a.** Please ask the waiter to bring the bill.

_____ **b.** My electric bill this month was over £100.

_____ **c.** The mechanic billed us for some work he didn't do.

_____ **d.** Parliament passed a bill that prohibited smoking in hospitals.

5. **Dictionary Research**

The Word Web feature for *money* says that the Lydians *minted* three types of coins. Look up the word *mint* in the dictionary.

Meaning number

a. Which numbered meaning of *mint* is used in the Word Web feature? _____

b. Which meaning names an herb people cook with? _____

c. Which meaning names a type of sweet? _____

d. Which meaning tells where money is manufactured? _____

ANSWER KEY:

1. **a.** barter; **b.** cowrie shells; **c.** no; **d.** China; **e.** gold, silver
2. **a.** bought; **b.** 3; **c.** afford, to buy; **d.** buy, and sell; **e.** buy, online
3. **a.** currency; **b.** cash; **c.** capital; **d.** funds; **e.** wealth
4. **a.** 2; **b.** 1; **c.** 3; **d.** 5
5. **a.** 4; **b.** 1; **c.** 2; **d.** 3

14. POLLUTION AND THE GREENHOUSE EFFECT

Word Web Activities (p. 584) Word Partnership Activities (p. 109) Word Link Activities (p. 265)	Choosing the Right Definition (p. 318)

1. **Word Web Activities**

   Use the Word Web feature entitled *pollution* to answer the following questions. Look up any words you aren't sure of.

   a. *Smog* is a combination of smoke and _________.

   b. Factories in the Northwest cause _________ that falls in Scotland.

   c. A substance used to kill insects is called a _________.

   Use the Word Web feature entitled the *greenhouse effect* to answer these questions.

   d. Energy that comes from the sun is called _________ radiation.

   e. Petrol is an example of a _________ fuel.

2. **Word Partnership Activities**

   Notice how the word *cause* is used in the Word Web features for *pollution* and the *greenhouse effect*. Next study the Word Partnership feature for *cause*. Use the correct Word Partnership phrase to complete each sentence below. If necessary, look up new words in the dictionary.

   a. Scientists are looking for answers. They want to _____________ of global warming.

   b. My cold isn't serious at all. There's no _____________.

   c. They want to know why their dog died. The vet is looking for the _____________.

3. **Word Link Activities**

   a. The prefix in the word *explode* is _________.

   b. Find the Word Link at the entry for *explode*. What does the prefix mean? _____________

   Which of the words in the *ex* Word Link means the same as the following? Look up the words in the dictionary if you are not sure.

   c. to leave _________

   d. to break into many pieces _________

   e. to go beyond _________

4. **Choosing the Right Definition**

The Word Web feature for *the greenhouse effect* mentions carbon dioxide and other *gases*. Study the numbered definitions for *gas*. Then write the number of the definition that relates to each sentence below.

_____ **a.** The soldiers were gassed by a small group of enemy troops.
_____ **b.** Our new stove uses gas instead of electricity.
_____ **c.** Cigarette smoke contains poisonous gases.
_____ **d.** Oxygen is a gas that plants give off.

5. **Dictionary Research**

The Word Web feature for *greenhouse effect* says that global average *temperature* has risen over the past 100 years. Search the Word Webs to find the answers to the following questions about temperature.

	Word Web	Question	Answer
a.	sun	The temperature of the sun is _________.	_______
b.	climate	In the last 100 years, the earth's temperature has increased by _________.	_______
c.	wind	Air flows from one place to another because of the _________ in temperature from one area to another.	_______
d.	cooking	Heating food to a high temperature kills _________.	_______

ANSWER KEY:

1. **a.** fog; **b.** acid rain; **c.** pesticide; **d.** solar; **e.** fossil
2. **a.** determine the cause; **b.** cause for concern; **c.** cause of death
3. **a.** ex; **b.** away, from, out; **c.** exit; **d.** explode; **e.** exceed
4. **a.** 4; **b.** 1; **c.** 1; **d.** 1
5. **a.** 15 million degrees Celsius; **b.** about 1° Fahrenheit; **c.** difference; **d.** bacteria

15. BRIDGES AND DAMS

Word Web Activities (p. 87) Thesaurus Activities (p. 429)	Grammar Activities (p. 777) Word Partnership Activities (p. 92)

1. Word Web Activities

Study the Word Web feature for *bridge*. Then match each number below with the correct description.

_____ **a.** over 1 mile
_____ **b.** 1883
_____ **c.** 120,000
_____ **d.** 1,000 feet
_____ **e.** 8.5
_____ **f.** 12,828 feet

1. The height in feet of the Akashi Kaikyo Bridge
2. When the Brooklyn Bridge was built
3. The length of the Evergreen Point Floating Bridge
4. How many vehicles cross the Brooklyn Bridge every day
5. The strength of an earthquake that the Akashi Kaikyo Bridge can withstand
6. The length of the Akashi Kaikyo Bridge

Study the Word Web feature for *dam*. Then answer the questions below. Write T for *true* or F for *false*.

_____ **g.** The world's first dam was built near Memphis, Egypt.
_____ **h.** The world's first dam prevented flooding.
_____ **i.** Hydroelectric dams provide 20% of the world's electricity.
_____ **j.** The Itapu Dam took 10 years to build.

2. Thesaurus Activities

The Word Web feature for *dam* states that dams sometimes damage valuable forest *lands*. Find the Thesaurus feature with the word *land*. Then complete the sentences below using words from the feature. Look up any words you aren't sure of.

a. Someday I will return to the _________ of my birth.
b. Harry doesn't own a house, but he does own some _________ _________ outside of town.
c. We weren't sure when the plane would _________.
d. Do you live in a safe _________?

3. Grammar Activities

The Word Web feature for *dam* describes the world's longest *suspension* bridge. Study the words that are formed from the root word *suspend*. Write the part of speech of each underlined word—noun or verb. Use your dictionary to check your answers.

a. Julie was suspended from her job shortly after the incident. ________

b. I drove over a large rock and damaged the car's suspension. ________

c. The airline suspends flights during storms. ________

d. I use suspenders instead of a belt. ________

e. I couldn't stand the suspense, so I asked the teacher what my grade was. ________

4. Word Partnership Activities

Study the Word Partnership feature for *build*. Use one of the phrases in this feature to complete each sentence below. If necessary, look up new words in these phrases in the dictionary.

a. Students need to speak English as much as possible to ________.

b. Leo works out at the gym and has a very ________.

c. Many female ballet dancers have a ________.

d. The government will ________ to connect all the major cities in the country.

e. Tax revenue often helps to ________ and ________.

ANSWER KEY:

1. **a.** 3; **b.** 2; **c.** 4; **d.** 1; **e.** 5; **f.** 6; **g.** T; **h.** F; **i.** T; **j.** F
2. **a.** country; **b.** real estate; **c.** arrive *or* touch down; **d.** area
3. **a.** verb; **b.** noun; **c.** verb; **d.** noun; **e.** noun
4. **a.** build confidence; **b.** athletic/strong build; **c.** slender build; **d.** build roads; **e.** build bridges, build schools

16. CLONE

Word Web Activities (p. 130) Thesaurus Activities (p. 509)	Word Link Activities (p. 381, 221) Choosing the Right Definition (p. 248)

1. **Word Web Activities**

   Use the Word Web feature entitled *clone* to answer the following questions. Answer each question with one of the bold words in the Word Web feature Look up any words you aren't sure of.

   a. Maria and her sister are _________.

   b. I need to give them a _________ of my driving licence.

   c. The girls look like _________, but they were born a year apart.

   d. Each _________ in your body contains DNA.

   e. Scientists use _________ to create new types of plants.

2. **Thesaurus Activities**

   Find the Thesaurus feature for the word *natural*. Then complete the sentences using words from the feature. Look up any words you aren't sure of.

   a. It is _________ for new students to be a little nervous at first.

   b. This doesn't look like _________ leather to me. I think it's plastic.

   c. Please accept my _________ apology for what I said.

   d. Farm-grown strawberries are good, but _________ strawberries are better.

3. Word Link Activities

Find the word *identical* in the Word Web feature for *clone*. Look up *identical*. Study the Word Link feature for the root *ident*.

a. What does the Word Link *ident* mean? ____________

Write the word in this Word Link that matches each definition below. Look up the words in the dictionary if you are not sure.

b. your passport or driving licence ______

c. exactly the same ______

d. unknown or nameless ______

Find the word *donor* in the Word Web feature for *clone*. Look up *donor*. Study the Word Link feature for the root *don*.

e. What does the Word Link *don* mean? ____________

Write the word in this Word Link that matches each definition below. Look up the words in the dictionary if you are not sure.

f. to forgive someone ______

g. someone who gives something away ______

h. to give money or goods to an organization ______

4. Choosing the Right Definition

Scientists produce clones by *genetic engineering*. Study the numbered definitions for *engineer*. Then write the number of the definition that relates to each sentence below.

_____ **a.** The building engineer repaired the water heater.

_____ **b.** A famous civil engineer designed that bridge.

_____ **c.** They engineered the car in such a way that it would get good mileage.

ANSWER KEY:

1. **a.** twins; **b.** copy; **c.** twins; **d.** cell; **e.** genetic engineering
2. **a.** normal; **b.** genuine; **c.** sincere; **d.** wild
3. **a.** same; **b.** identification; **c.** identical; **d.** unidentified; **e.** giving; **f.** pardon; **g.** donor; **h.** donate
4. **a.** 3; **b.** 1; **c.** 2

Aa

a /ə, STRONG eɪ/ or **an** /ən, STRONG æn/

> The form **an** is used in front of words that begin with vowel sounds.

1 DET You use **a** or **an** when you are referring to someone or something for the first time, or when you do not want to be specific. ❑ *Today you've got a new teacher.* ❑ *A waiter entered with a tray.* ❑ *He refused to work with an orchestra ever again.* **2** DET You can use **a** or **an** in front of nouns when the noun is followed by other words that describe it more fully. ❑ *There's a feeling that we have been cheated.* **3** DET You can use **a** or **an** instead of the number 'one' in front of some numbers and measurements. ❑ *...a hundred miles.* **4** DET You use **a** or **an** in expressions such as **eight hours a day** to express a rate or ratio. ❑ *Prices start at £13.95 a metre.*

aback /əˈbæk/ PHRASE If you are **taken aback**, you are very surprised or shocked by something. ❑ *People were taken aback by his resignation.*

abandon /əˈbændən/ (**abandons, abandoning, abandoned**) **1** V-T If you **abandon** a thing, place, or person, you leave them permanently or for a long time. ❑ *His parents had abandoned him.* ● **abandoned** ADJ ❑ *...an abandoned village.* ● **abandonment** N-UNCOUNT ❑ *...her father's complete abandonment of her.* **2** V-T If you **abandon** an activity or idea, you stop doing it or thinking about it before it is finished. ❑ *He abandoned his studies after two years.* ● **abandonment** N-UNCOUNT ❑ *Rain forced the abandonment of the competition.* **3** N-UNCOUNT If you do something **with abandon**, you do it in a carefree way. ❑ *He danced with abandon.*

Thesaurus *abandon* Also look up:

V.	desert, leave, quit; *(ant.)* stay **1** break off, give up, quit, stop; *(ant.)* continue **2**

abate /əˈbeɪt/ (**abates, abating, abated**) V-I When something **abates**, it becomes much less strong or widespread. [FORMAL] ❑ *The crime wave shows no sign of abating.*

abbey /ˈæbi/ (**abbeys**) N-COUNT An **abbey** is a church with buildings attached to it in which monks or nuns live or used to live.

Word Link ***brev** ≈ **short** : ab**brev**iate, ab**brev**iated, ab**brev**iation*

abbreviate /əˈbriːvieɪt/ (**abbreviates, abbreviating, abbreviated**) V-T If a word or a phrase **is abbreviated**, it is made shorter. ❑ *'Compact disc' is often abbreviated to 'CD'.* ● **abbreviated** ADJ ❑ *...a very abbreviated description of the project.*

abbreviation /əˌbriːviˈeɪʃən/ (**abbreviations**) N-COUNT An **abbreviation** is a short form of a word or phrase. ❑ *The postal abbreviation for Kansas is KS.*

abdicate /ˈæbdɪkeɪt/ (**abdicates, abdicating, abdicated**) **1** V-I If a king or queen **abdicates**, he or she resigns. ❑ *King Constantine was forced to abdicate.* ● **abdication** N-UNCOUNT ❑ *...the abdication of Edward VIII.* **2** V-T If you **abdicate responsibility** for something, you refuse to accept the responsibility for it any longer. ❑ *Their parents have abdicated their responsibilities.* ● **abdication** N-UNCOUNT ❑ *...an outrageous abdication of their duties.*

abdomen /ˈæbdəmən/ (**abdomens**) N-COUNT Your **abdomen** is the part of your body below your chest where your stomach is. ● **abdominal** /æbˈdɒmɪnəl/ ADJ BEFORE N ❑ *...the abdominal muscles.*
→ see **insect**

abduct /æbˈdʌkt/ (**abducts, abducting, abducted**) V-T If someone **is abducted**, he or she is taken away illegally. ❑ *He was charged with abducting a taxi driver.* ● **abduction** (**abductions**) N-VAR ❑ *...the abduction of British tourists.*

aberration /ˌæbəˈreɪʃən/ (**aberrations**) N-VAR An **aberration** is an incident or way of behaving that is not normal. [FORMAL] ❑ *I think this attack was an aberration, an incident that does not occur on a regular basis.*

abide /əˈbaɪd/ (**abides, abiding, abided**) PHRASE If you say that you **can't abide** someone or something, you mean that you dislike them intensely. ❑ *I can't abide people who can't make decisions.* ▶ **abide by** PHR-VERB If you **abide by** a law, agreement, or decision, you do what it says.

abiding /əˈbaɪdɪŋ/ **1** ADJ BEFORE N An **abiding** feeling or memory is one that you have for a very long time. ❑ *He acquired an abiding interest in history.* **2** → see also **law-abiding**

ability /əˈbɪlɪti/ (**abilities**) N-VAR Your **ability** is the quality or skill that you have which makes it possible for you to do something. ❑ *Her drama teacher noticed her ability.* ❑ *...his leadership abilities.* ❑ *...the human ability to communicate using language.*

Thesaurus *ability* Also look up:

N.	capability, competence, skill, technique

Word Partnership Use *ability* with:

V.	ability **to handle**, **have the** ability, **lack the** ability
N.	**lack of** ability
ADJ.	**natural** ability

A

abject /'æbdʒekt/ ADJ You use **abject** to emphasize that a situation or quality is shameful or depressing. ❑ *...abject poverty.* ❑ *The scheme was an abject failure.*

ablaze /ə'bleɪz/ ADJ AFTER LINK-V Something that is **ablaze** is burning fiercely. ❑ *Within seconds, curtains and woodwork were ablaze.* ❑ *Two houses were set ablaze.*

able /'eɪbəl/ (**abler, ablest**) **1** PHRASE If you **are able to** do something, you have the skills, freedom, or other means which make it possible for you to do it. ❑ *I was never able to play any sports.* **2** ADJ An **able** person is clever or good at doing something. ● **ably** ADV ❑ *He was ably assisted by Robert James.*

abnormal /æb'nɔːməl/ ADJ Someone or something that is **abnormal** is unusual or exceptional in a way that is worrying. ❑ *She has an abnormal fear of strangers.* ● **abnormally** ADV ❑ *...abnormally high levels of fat.*

abnormality /ˌæbnɔː'mælɪti/ (**abnormalities**) N-VAR An **abnormality** is an unusual part or feature of something that is worrying or dangerous. ❑ *...a genetic abnormality.*

aboard /ə'bɔːd/ PREP & ADV If you are **aboard** a ship or plane, you are on or in it. ❑ *No-one else was aboard the plane.* ❑ *It took two hours to load all the people aboard.*

abolish /ə'bɒlɪʃ/ (**abolishes, abolishing, abolished**) V-T If someone in authority **abolishes** a practice or organization, they put an end to it. ❑ *Parliament voted to abolish fox-hunting.* ● **abolition** /ˌæbə'lɪʃən/ N-UNCOUNT ❑ *...the abolition of slavery.*

Thesaurus *abolish* Also look up:

v. eliminate, end; *(ant.)* continue

abominable /ə'bɒmɪnəbəl/ ADJ Something that is **abominable** is very unpleasant or very bad. ❑ *Their treatment of him was abominable.* ❑ *...this abominable war.*

Aboriginal /ˌæbə'rɪdʒɪnəl/ (**Aboriginals**) N-COUNT An **Aboriginal** is a member of one of the tribes which were living in Australia when Europeans arrived. ❑ *...health and housing for Aboriginals.*

Aborigine /ˌæbə'rɪdʒɪni/ (**Aborigines**) N-COUNT **Aborigine** means the same as **Aboriginal**. Some people consider **Aborigine** to be a racist word.

abort /ə'bɔːt/ (**aborts, aborting, aborted**) **1** V-T If an unborn baby **is aborted**, the pregnancy is ended deliberately and the baby is not born alive. **2** V-T If a process, plan, or activity **is aborted**, it is stopped before it is finished. ❑ *The take-off was aborted.*

abortion /ə'bɔːʃən/ (**abortions**) N-VAR An **abortion** is a medical operation in which a pregnancy is deliberately ended and the baby is not born alive. ❑ *This drug is not yet accepted as a method of abortion in the US.*

abortive /ə'bɔːtɪv/ ADJ An **abortive** attempt or action is unsuccessful. ❑ *...three abortive attempts to light a fire.*

abound /ə'baʊnd/ (**abounds, abounding, abounded**) V-I If things **abound**, or if a place **abounds with** things, there are very large numbers of them. [FORMAL] ❑ *Stories abound about when he was in charge.* ❑ *San Francisco abounds with lawyers.*

about /ə'baʊt/ **1** PREP You use **about** to introduce who or what something relates to or concerns. ❑ *Helen's told me about you.* ❑ *...advice about exercise.* ❑ *He couldn't do anything about it.* **2** PREP When you say that there is a particular quality **about** someone or something, you mean that they have this quality. ❑ *There was something special about her.* **3** ADV **About** in front of a number means approximately. ❑ *The child is about eight years old.* **4** ADV & PREP If someone or something moves **about**, they keep moving in different directions. ❑ *The kids ran about in the garden.* ❑ *From 1879 to 1888 he wandered about Germany.* **5** ADJ AFTER LINK-V If someone or something is **about**, they are present or available. ❑ *There's lots of money about.* **6** PHRASE If you **are about to** do something, you are going to do it soon. ❑ *The film was about to start.* **7** **how about** → see **how** **8** **what about** → see **what** **9** **just about** → see **just**

Usage

When you are talking about movement in no particular direction, you can use **around** and **round** as well as **about**. ❑ *It's so romantic up there, flying around in a small plane.* ❑ *I spent a couple of hours driving round Richmond.* ❑ *Policemen walk about with guns on their hips.* When you are talking about something being generally present or available, you can use **around** or **about**, but not **round**, as adverbs. ❑ *There is a lot of talent around at the moment.* ❑ *There are not that many jobs about.* **Round** has a lot of other meanings, as a noun, verb, and adjective which you can see at the entry for **round**. You cannot use **about** in these cases.

above /ə'bʌv/ **1** PREP & ADV If one thing is **above** another one, it is directly over it or higher than it. ❑ *He lifted his hands above his head.* ❑ *...the flat above mine.* ❑ *A long scream sounded from somewhere above.* **2** ADV & N-SING & ADJ BEFORE N You use **above** in writing to refer to something that has already been mentioned. ❑ *...the results described above.* ❑ *For additional information, contact any of the above.* ❑ *I may be reached at the above address.* **3** PREP & ADV If an amount or measurement is **above** a particular level, it is greater than that level. ❑ *The temperature rose to just above 40 degrees.* ❑ *...above average levels of rainfall.* ❑ *...people of 18 years and above.* **4** PREP & ADV If someone is **above** you, they are in a position of authority over you. ❑ *...the people above you in the positions of power.* ❑ *I had orders from above.* **5** PREP If someone thinks that they are **above** something, they think that they are too good or too important for it; used showing disapproval. ❑ *He considered himself above such childish behaviour.* **6** PREP If someone is **above** criticism or suspicion, they cannot be criticized or suspected because of their good qualities or their position. ❑ *Everyone in the Military Council was completely above suspicion.* **7** **over and above** → see **over**.
→ see **location**

abrasive /ə'breɪsɪv/ **1** ADJ If you describe someone's manner as **abrasive**, you think they are rude and unkind. ❑ *His abrasive style upset one member of Congress.* **2** ADJ An **abrasive** substance is rough and can be used to clean hard surfaces.

a

abreast /əˈbrest/ 1 ADV If people or things walk or move **abreast**, they are side by side. ❑ *They walked three abreast.* 2 PREP If you **keep abreast of** a subject, you know all the most recent facts about it. ❑ *He always keeps abreast of the news.*

abroad /əˈbrɔːd/ ADV If you go **abroad**, you go to a foreign country. ❑ *I would love to go abroad this year.*

abrupt /əˈbrʌpt/ 1 ADJ An **abrupt** action is very sudden and often unpleasant. ❑ *Her holiday came to an abrupt end when she broke her foot.* ● **abruptly** ADV ❑ *He stopped abruptly.* 2 ADJ Someone who is **abrupt** is rather rude and unfriendly. ● **abruptly** ADV ❑ *'Good night, then,' she said abruptly.*

absence /ˈæbsəns/ (**absences**) N-VAR The **absence** of someone or something is the fact that they are not there. ❑ *The letters had arrived in my absence.* ❑ *...her husband's frequent absences.* ❑ *In the absence of a manager, staff must make their own decisions.*

absent /ˈæbsənt/ 1 ADJ If someone or something is **absent from** a place or situation, they are not there. ❑ *He was absent from work for 35 days.* 2 ADJ If someone appears **absent**, they are not paying attention. ● **absently** ADV ❑ *He nodded absently.*

absentee /ˌæbsənˈtiː/ (**absentees**) N-COUNT An **absentee** is a person who should be in a particular place but who is not there. ❑ *...absentees from work.* ❑ *The agency will force absentee fathers to pay for their children.*

ˌabsent-ˈminded ADJ An **absent-minded** person is very forgetful or does not pay attention to what they are doing. ● **absent-mindedly** ADV ❑ *He did it automatically, almost absent-mindedly.*

absolute /ˈæbsəluːt/ (**absolutes**) 1 ADJ BEFORE N **Absolute** means total and complete. ❑ *...absolute beginners.* ❑ *It's absolute nonsense.* 2 N-COUNT & ADJ BEFORE N **Absolutes** or **absolute** principles are believed to be true or right for all situations.

absolutely /ˌæbsəˈluːtli/ 1 ADV **Absolutely** means totally and completely. ❑ *Jill is absolutely right.* ❑ *It's an absolutely brilliant book.* ❑ *I absolutely refuse to get married.* 2 ADV **Absolutely** is an emphatic way of saying yes or agreeing with someone. **Absolutely not** is an emphatic way of saying no or disagreeing with someone. ❑ *'Was it worth it?'—'Absolutely.'* ❑ *'Did he approach you?'—'No, absolutely not.'*

absorb /əbˈzɔːb/ (**absorbs, absorbing, absorbed**) 1 V-T To **absorb** a substance means to soak it up or take it in. ❑ *Plants absorb carbon dioxide from the air.* ❑ *Some sugars are absorbed into the bloodstream very quickly.* ● **absorption** N-UNCOUNT ❑ *...the absorption of iron from food.* 2 V-T If a group **is absorbed into** a larger group, it becomes part of the larger group. ❑ *The Colonial Office was absorbed into the Foreign Office.* ❑ *...the ability of a bigger bank to absorb a smaller one.* ● **absorption** N-UNCOUNT ❑ *This eventually led to Serbia's absorption into the Ottoman Empire.* 3 V-T If you **absorb** information, you understand and remember it. ❑ *Sometimes he only absorbs half the information.* ❑ *Try to give employees time to absorb bad news.* 4 V-T If something **absorbs** you, it interests you and gets all your attention. 5 V-T If something **absorbs** a force, it reduces its effect. ❑ *These shoes are not designed to absorb the impact of running.*

absorbed /əbˈzɔːbd/ ADJ AFTER LINK-V If you are **absorbed** in a person, activity, or subject, they get all your attention. ❑ *She was totally absorbed in her partner.*

absorbing /əbˈzɔːbɪŋ/ ADJ An **absorbing** activity interests you a great deal and takes up all your attention. ❑ *...an absorbing hobby.*

absorption /əbˈzɔːpʃən/ → see **absorb**

abstain /æbˈsteɪn/ (**abstains, abstaining, abstained**) 1 V-I If you **abstain from** something you like doing, you deliberately do not do it. ❑ *You can't totally abstain from eating.* ● **abstention** /æbˈstenʃən/ N-UNCOUNT ❑ *...abstention from alcohol.* 2 V-I If you **abstain** during a vote, you do not vote. ● **abstention** (**abstentions**) N-VAR ❑ *The voting was twenty in favour, six against, and sixteen abstentions.*

abstinence /ˈæbstɪnəns/ N-UNCOUNT **Abstinence** is the practice of not having something you enjoy, often for health or religious reasons. ❑ *...lifelong abstinence from alcohol.*

abstract /ˈæbstrækt/ (**abstracts**) 1 ADJ & PHRASE An **abstract** idea or way of thinking is based on general ideas rather than on particular things. You can also talk or think about something **in the abstract**. ❑ *It's too easy to talk about these things in the abstract.* 2 ADJ BEFORE N & N-COUNT **Abstract** art makes use of shapes and patterns rather than showing people or things as they actually are. An **abstract** is an abstract work of art. 3 N-COUNT An **abstract** of an article or speech is a short piece of writing that summarizes the main points.

absurd /æbˈsɜːd/ ADJ & N-SING If you say that something is **absurd**, you think that it is ridiculous or does not make sense. **The absurd** means things that are absurd. ❑ *The thought of being a movie star was absurd to her.* ❑ *...a highly developed sense of the absurd.* ● **absurdly** ADV ❑ *Prices were still absurdly low.* ● **absurdity** (**absurdities**) N-VAR ❑ *...the absurdity of all wars.*

Thesaurus	*absurd* Also look up:
ADJ.	crazy, foolish

abundance /əˈbʌndəns/ N-SING & PHRASE If there is an **abundance of** something, or if something is **in abundance** there is a large quantity of it. ❑ *...an abundance of safe beaches.* ❑ *Food was in abundance.*

abundant /əˈbʌndənt/ ADJ Something that is **abundant** is present in large quantities. ❑ *There was an abundant supply of energy.*

abuse (**abuses, abusing, abused**)

noun /əˈbjuːs/, verb /əˈbjuːz/.

1 V-T & N-VAR If someone **is abused**, or if they are victims of **abuse**, they are treated cruelly and violently. ❑ *...parents who might abuse their children.* ❑ *...human rights abuses.* 2 V-T & N-UNCOUNT You can say that someone **is abused** if rude and insulting things are said to them. **Abuse** is rude and insulting things that people say when they are angry. ❑ *He was verbally abused by other soldiers.* ❑ *I was left shouting abuse as the car sped off.* 3 V-T & N-UNCOUNT If you **abuse** something, you use it in a wrong way or for a bad purpose. **Abuse** of something is the use of it in this way. ❑ *The rich and*

A

powerful can abuse their position. ❑ ...an abuse of power. ❑ ...alcohol abuse.

Thesaurus *abuse* Also look up:

N. damage, harm, injury, violation 1
V. damage, harm, injure; *(ant.)* care for, protect, respect 1
insult, offend, pick on, put down; *(ant.)* compliment, flatter, praise 2

abusive /əˈbjuːsɪv/ 1 ADJ **Abusive** language is extremely rude and insulting. ❑ *He is accused of using abusive language towards staff.* 2 ADJ Someone who is **abusive** is cruel and violent towards someone else. ❑ *...her cruel and abusive parents.*

abysmal /əˈbɪzməl/ ADJ **Abysmal** means very bad or poor in quality. ❑ *My knowledge of the subject was abysmal.* ● **abysmally** ADV ❑ *Standards of education are abysmally low.*

abyss /æˈbɪs/ (**abysses**) 1 N-COUNT An **abyss** is a hole in the ground which is so deep that it is impossible to measure. ❑ *He looked over the edge of the abyss.* 2 N-COUNT You can refer to a frightening situation which could have terrible consequences as an **abyss**. [WRITTEN] ❑ *He took his country to the abyss of war.*

academic /ˌækəˈdemɪk/ (**academics**) 1 ADJ BEFORE N **Academic** means relating to life or work in schools, colleges, and universities, especially work which involves studying and reasoning rather than practical or technical skills. ❑ *...the academic year.* ❑ *Their academic standards are high.* ● **academically** ADV ❑ *He is academically gifted.* 2 ADJ Someone who is **academic** is good at studying. 3 N-COUNT An **academic** is a member of a university or college who teaches or does research. 4 ADJ If you say that something is **academic**, you mean that it has no real relevance or effect. ❑ *The match result is academic for this team, who automatically qualify for the European cup.*

academy /əˈkædəmi/ (**academies**) N-COUNT A school or college specializing in a particular subject is sometimes called an **academy**. ❑ *...the Royal Academy of Music.*

accelerate /ækˈseləreɪt/ (**accelerates, accelerating, accelerated**) V-T/V-I When the rate or speed of something **accelerates**, it increases. ❑ *We need to accelerate the pace of change.* ❑ *The car accelerated.* ● **acceleration** N-UNCOUNT ❑ *...acceleration to 60 mph.*
→ see **motion**

accelerator /ækˈseləreɪtə/ (**accelerators**) N-COUNT In a vehicle, the **accelerator** is the pedal you press to go faster.

accent /ˈæksənt/ (**accents**) 1 N-COUNT Someone who speaks with a particular **accent** pronounces the words of a language in a way that indicates their country, region, or social class. ❑ *He had a slight American accent.* 2 N-COUNT An **accent** is a mark written above or below certain letters in some languages to show how they are pronounced. 3 N-SING If you put the **accent on** a particular feature of something, you give it special importance or emphasis.

Word Partnership Use *accent* with:

ADJ. **American/French** accent, **regional** accent, **thick** accent 1
ADV. **heavily** accented 1
V. **do an** accent, **have an** accent 1
put the accent **on** 3

accentuate /ækˈsentʃueɪt/ (**accentuates, accentuating, accentuated**) V-T To **accentuate** something means to emphasize it or make it more noticeable. ❑ *His shaven head accentuates his large round face.*

accept /ækˈsept/ (**accepts, accepting, accepted**) 1 V-T/V-I If you **accept** something that you have been offered, you say yes to it or agree to take it. ❑ *I accepted his offer of employment.* ❑ *All those invited to the conference have accepted.* ● **acceptance** N-UNCOUNT ❑ *...acceptance of the invitation to Moscow.* 2 V-T If you **accept** a fact, you believe that it is true or valid. ❑ *He could never accept that he had been wrong.* ❑ *Her parents accepted her decision.* ● **acceptance** N-UNCOUNT ❑ *...a theory that is steadily gaining acceptance.* 3 V-T To **accept** a difficult or unpleasant situation means to recognize that it cannot be changed. ❑ *Urban dwellers often accept noise as part of city life.* ❑ *We also accept that some marriages do not survive.* ● **acceptance** N-UNCOUNT ❑ *...his calm acceptance of whatever comes his way.* 4 V-T If you **accept** the blame or responsibility for something, you admit that you are responsible for it. 5 V-T When an organization or group **accepts** someone, they give them a job or allow them to join their group. ❑ *They refused to accept women as bus drivers.* ❑ *Stephen was accepted into the family.* ● **acceptance** N-UNCOUNT ❑ *Would he be popular enough to gain acceptance?* 6 → see also **accepted**

Thesaurus *accept* Also look up:

V. receive, take; *(ant.)* refuse, reject 1
acknowledge, recognize 2
endure, live with, tolerate; *(ant.)* disallow, reject 3

acceptable /ækˈseptəbəl/ 1 ADJ If a situation or action is **acceptable**, people generally approve of it or allow it to happen. ❑ *It is not acceptable for any country to attack Red Cross buildings during war.* ❑ *The air pollution exceeds acceptable levels.* ● **acceptability** N-UNCOUNT ❑ *...increasing the social acceptability of divorce.* ● **acceptably** ADV ❑ *We teach children to behave acceptably.* 2 ADJ If something is **acceptable**, it is good enough or fairly good. ❑ *We've made an acceptable start.*

accepted /ækˈseptɪd/ ADJ **Accepted** ideas are agreed by most people to be correct or reasonable. ❑ *It is a generally accepted fact that men dislike shopping.*

access /ˈækses/ (**accesses, accessing, accessed**) 1 N-UNCOUNT If you have **access to** a building or other place, you are able or allowed to go into it. [FORMAL] ❑ *...unlimited access to the swimming pool.* 2 N-UNCOUNT Your **access to** someone is the opportunity or right you have to see them. ❑ *They denied him access to his children.* 3 V-T & N-UNCOUNT If you **access** information, or if you have **access to** it, you are able to see or get it. ❑ *...to give patients right of access to their medical records.*

a

accessible /æk'sesɪbəl/ **1** ADJ If a place is **accessible**, you are able to reach it or get into it. ❑ *Put it in a low cupboard that's easily accessible.* ● **accessibility** /æk͵sesɪ'bɪlɪti/ N-UNCOUNT ❑ *...accessibility to the city centre.* **2** ADJ If something is **accessible to** people, they can easily use it or obtain it. ❑ *...making computers truly accessible to people.* ● **accessibility** N-UNCOUNT ❑ *...the cost, quality and accessibility of health care.*
→ see **disability**

accessory /æk'sesəri/ (**accessories**) **1** N-COUNT **Accessories** are extra parts added to something to make it more efficient, useful, or decorative. ❑ *...bathroom accessories.* **2** N-COUNT An **accessory to** a crime is someone who helps the person who committed it, but does not tell the police. [TECHNICAL]

accident /'æksɪdənt/ (**accidents**) **1** N-VAR An **accident** is an event which happens by chance. You can also say that something happens **by accident**. ❑ *He has aged well, but that is no accident.* ❑ *She discovered the problem by accident.* **2** N-COUNT An **accident** is something unpleasant that happens and that often causes injury or death. ❑ *He's had a serious car accident.*

Word Partnership Use *accident* with:

ADJ.	**bad** accident, **a tragic** accident **1** **2**
V.	**cause an** accident, **insure against** accident, **killed in the** accident, **report an** accident **1** **2**
N.	**car** accident **1** **2**, **the cause of an** accident **1** **2**
PREP.	**by** accident **1**

accidental /͵æksɪ'dentəl/ ADJ An **accidental** event happens by chance or as the result of an accident. ❑ *The fire was accidental.* ● **accidentally** ADV ❑ *Names were accidentally erased from computer disks.*

Word Link *claim, clam ≈ shouting : acclaim, exclaim, proclamation*

acclaim /ə'kleɪm/ (**acclaims, acclaiming, acclaimed**) V-T & N-UNCOUNT If someone or something **is acclaimed**, or **wins acclaim**, they are praised publicly and enthusiastically. [FORMAL] ❑ *She has been acclaimed for the TV drama 'Prime Suspect'.* ❑ *He was acclaimed as England's greatest modern painter.* ❑ *She won critical acclaim for her performance.* ● **acclaimed** ADJ ❑ *He's written six highly acclaimed novels.*

acclimatize [BRIT also **acclimatise**] /ə'klaɪmətaɪz/ (**acclimatizes, acclimatizing, acclimatized**) V-T/V-I When you **acclimatize** or **are acclimatized to** a new situation, place, or climate, you become used to it. ❑ *The athletes are acclimatising to the heat.* ❑ *He has left for St Louis early to acclimatise himself.* ❑ *It would take her two years to get acclimatized.*

accolade /'ækəleɪd/ (**accolades**) N-COUNT An **accolade** is something that is done or said about someone which shows how much people admire them. [FORMAL] ❑ *...the ultimate international accolade, the Nobel Peace Prize.*

accommodate /ə'kɒmədeɪt/ (**accommodates, accommodating, accommodated**) **1** V-T If a building or space can **accommodate** someone or something, it has enough room for them. ❑ *The school was not big enough to accommodate all the children.* **2** V-T To **accommodate** someone means to provide them with a place to stay. ❑ *We were accommodated overnight in tents.* **3** V-T To **accommodate** someone means to help them. ❑ *The beauty salon accommodates both men and women.* ● **accommodating** ADJ ❑ *Lindi seemed a nice, accommodating girl.*

accommodation /ə͵kɒmə'deɪʃən/ N-UNCOUNT **Accommodation** is used to refer to rooms or buildings where people live, stay, or work. ❑ *Travel and overnight accommodation are included.*

accompaniment /ə'kʌmpnɪmənt/ (**accompaniments**) **1** N-UNCOUNT The **accompaniment** to a singer or instrument is the music that is played at the same time, forming a background to it. ❑ *...a lively musical accompaniment.* **2** N-VAR An **accompaniment to** something is another thing that happens or exists at the same time, usually something that complements the first thing. ❑ *Biscuits make an ideal accompaniment to morning coffee.* ❑ *The procession moved through the streets to the accompaniment of excited shouting.*

accompany /ə'kʌmpəni/ (**accompanies, accompanying, accompanied**) **1** V-T If you **accompany** someone, you go somewhere with them. [FORMAL] ❑ *Children must be accompanied by an adult.* **2** V-T If one thing **accompanies** another, the two things happen or exist at the same time. ❑ *...sauces that accompany chicken dishes.* **3** V-T When you **accompany** a singer or a musician, you play one part of a piece of music while they sing or play the main tune.

accomplice /ə'kʌmplɪs, AM ə'kɒm-/ (**accomplices**) N-COUNT An **accomplice** is a person who helps to commit a crime.

accomplish /ə'kʌmplɪʃ, AM ə'kɒm-/ (**accomplishes, accomplishing, accomplished**) V-T If you **accomplish** something, you succeed in doing it. ❑ *She managed to accomplish the journey in five weeks.* ● **accomplishment** N-UNCOUNT ❑ *...the accomplishment of his highly important mission.*

Thesaurus *accomplish* Also look up:

V. achieve, complete, gain, realise, succeed

accomplished /ə'kʌmplɪʃt, AM ə'kɒm-/ ADJ If someone is **accomplished**, they are very good at something. ❑ *He is an accomplished linguist.*

accomplishment /ə'kʌmplɪʃmənt, AM ə'kɒm-/ (**accomplishments**) **1** N-COUNT Your **accomplishments** are the things you have achieved or the things that you do well. [FORMAL] ❑ *The list of her accomplishments is impressive.* **2** → see also **accomplish**

accord /ə'kɔːd/ (**accords, according, accorded**) **1** V-T If you **are accorded** a particular kind of treatment, people treat you in that way. [FORMAL] ❑ *...the military honours accorded to all visiting heads of state.* **2** N-COUNT An **accord** between countries or groups of people is a formal agreement, for example to end a war. ❑ *...the 1991 peace accords.* **3** PHRASE If one person, action, or fact is **in accord with** another, there is no conflict between them. You can also say that two people or things are **in accord**. [FORMAL] **4** PHRASE When you do

A

something **of** your **own accord**, you do it freely and because you want to. If something happens **of** its **own accord**, it seems to happen automatically, without anybody making it happen. ❑ *He had left her of his own accord.*

accordance /əˈkɔːdəns/ PHRASE If something is done **in accordance with** a rule or system, it is done in the way that the rule or system says it should be done. ❑ *Act in accordance with the law.*

accordingly /əˈkɔːdɪŋli/ ADV You use **accordingly** to say that one thing happens as a result of another thing. ❑ *It is a difficult job and they should be paid accordingly.*

acˈcording to **1** PREP If something is true **according to** a particular person or book, that person or book claims that it is true. ❑ *Philip stayed at the hotel, according to Mr Hemming.* **2** PREP If something is done **according to** a particular principle or plan, this principle or plan is used as the basis for the way it is done. ❑ *Things really did work out according to plan.*

account /əˈkaʊnt/ (**accounts, accounting, accounted**) **1** N-COUNT If you have an **account** with a bank, you leave money with the bank and take it out when you need it. ❑ *Have you got a savings account?* **2** N-COUNT In business, a regular customer of a company can be referred to as an **account**. ❑ *The marketing agency has won two Edinburgh accounts.* **3** N-PLURAL **Accounts** are detailed records of all the money that a person or business receives and spends. ❑ *He kept detailed accounts of his spending.* **4** N-COUNT An **account** is a written or spoken report of something that has happened. ❑ *She gave a detailed account of what happened.* ❑ *He is, by all accounts, a superb teacher.* **5** PHRASE If someone **is called, held,** or **brought to account** for something they have done wrong, they are made to explain why they did it, and are often criticized or punished for it. **6** PHRASE If you **take** something **into account**, you consider it when you are thinking about a situation. **7** PHRASE If you tell someone not to do something **on** your **account**, you mean that they should do it only if they want to, and not because they think it will please you. ❑ *Don't leave on my account.* **8** PHRASE If you say that something should **on no account** be done, you are emphasizing that it should not be done under any circumstances. ❑ *When asked for your opinion, on no account must you be negative.*
→ see **history**

▶ **account for** **1** PHR-VERB If you can **account for** something, you can explain it or give the necessary information about it. ❑ *How do you account for the missing money?* **2** PHR-VERB If something **accounts for** a particular proportion of a whole thing, it is what that proportion consists of. ❑ *Computers account for 5% of the country's commercial electricity consumption.*

accountable /əˈkaʊntəbəl/ ADJ If you are **accountable for** something that you do, you are responsible for it. ❑ *Public officials can finally be held accountable for their actions.* ● **accountability** N-UNCOUNT ❑ *We want full accountability for every penny.*

accountancy /əˈkaʊntənsi/ N-UNCOUNT **Accountancy** is the work of keeping financial accounts.

accountant /əˈkaʊntənt/ (**accountants**) N-COUNT An **accountant** is a person whose job is to keep financial accounts.

accumulate /əˈkjuːmjʊleɪt/ (**accumulates, accumulating, accumulated**) V-T/V-I When you **accumulate** things or when they **accumulate**, they collect or are gathered over a period of time. ❑ *Chemicals can accumulate in processed foods.* ● **accumulation** (**accumulations**) N-COUNT ❑ *...accumulation of wealth.* ❑ *...accumulations of dirt.*

accurate /ˈækjʊrət/ **1** ADJ Something that is **accurate** is correct to a detailed level. ❑ *That's a fairly accurate description of the man.* ❑ *Quartz watches are very accurate.* ● **accuracy** N-UNCOUNT ❑ *...the accuracy of the story.* ● **accurately** ADV ❑ *The questions have been accurately recorded.* **2** ADJ A person, device, or machine that is **accurate** is able to perform a task without making a mistake. ❑ *The rifle was extremely accurate.* ● **accuracy** N-UNCOUNT ❑ *The bank pays close attention to the accuracy of its staff.* ● **accurately** ADV ❑ *Players don't focus enough on placing the ball accurately.*

Thesaurus *accurate* Also look up:

ADJ. right, true; *(ant.)* inaccurate **1**
correct, precise, rigorous **2**

accusation /ˌækjʊˈzeɪʃən/ (**accusations**) N-COUNT If you make an **accusation** against someone, you express the belief that they have done something wrong.

accuse /əˈkjuːz/ (**accuses, accusing, accused**) V-T If you **accuse** someone **of** something, you say that you believe they did something wrong or dishonest. ❑ *He accused her of having an affair.* ❑ *They accused him of stealing $26 million.*

Thesaurus *accuse* Also look up:

V. blame, charge, implicate; *(ant.)* vindicate

accused /əˈkjuːzd/

Accused is both the singular and the plural form.

N-COUNT **The accused** refers to the person or people charged with a crime or on trial for it. ❑ *The accused were all members of the same gang.* ❑ *The accused is out on bail.*

accustom /əˈkʌstəm/ (**accustoms, accustoming, accustomed**) V-T If you **accustom yourself to** something, you experience it or learn about it, so that it becomes familiar or natural. ❑ *His team accustomed itself to the climate.* ❑ *Shakespeare has accustomed us to a mixture of humour and tragedy.* ● **accustomed** ADJ AFTER LINK-V ❑ *He was accustomed to hard work.*

ace

ace /eɪs/ (**aces**) **1** N-COUNT An **ace** is a playing card with a single symbol on it. ❑ *...the ace of hearts.* **2** N-COUNT In tennis, an **ace** is a serve which is so good that the other player cannot return the ball.

ache /eɪk/ (**aches, aching, ached**) **1** V-I & N-COUNT If part of your body **aches**, or if you have an **ache**, you feel a steady, fairly strong pain. ❑ *He was aching, tired, and hungry.* ❑ *...an effective remedy for aches and pains.* **2** V-T/V-I If you **ache for** something or **ache to** do something, you want it very much. ❑ *She ached for somebody to hold her.* ❑ *...a country aching to get away from its past.*

Thesaurus	*ache* Also look up:
N.	hurt, pain, pang **1**
V.	throb **1**

achieve /əˈtʃiːv/ (**achieves, achieving, achieved**) V-T If you **achieve** a particular aim or effect, you succeed in doing it or causing it to happen, usually after a lot of effort. ❑ *Achieving our goals makes us feel good.*

Thesaurus	*achieve* Also look up:
V.	accomplish, bring about; (*ant.*) fail, lose, miss

achievement /əˈtʃiːvmənt/ (**achievements**) **1** N-COUNT An **achievement** is something which someone has succeeded in doing, especially after a lot of effort. **2** N-UNCOUNT **Achievement** is the process of achieving something. ❑ *The achievement of these goals will bring peace.*

achiever /əˈtʃiːvə/ (**achievers**) N-COUNT A high **achiever** is someone who is successful in their studies or their work, usually as a result of their efforts. A low **achiever** is someone who is unsuccessful.

acid /ˈæsɪd/ (**acids**) **1** N-VAR An **acid** is a liquid or substance with a pH value of less than 7. Strong acids can damage your skin and clothes. ❑ *...citric acid.* ❑ *Acids in the stomach destroy the virus.* **2** ADJ An **acid** substance contains acid. ❑ *These plants must have an acid soil.* **3** ADJ An **acid** fruit or drink has a sour or sharp taste. ❑ *These wines may taste rather hard and somewhat acid.* **4** ADJ An **acid** remark is unkind or critical.

acidic /əˈsɪdɪk/ ADJ Something that is **acidic** contains acid or has a pH value of less than 7.

acidity /æˈsɪdɪti/ N-UNCOUNT **Acidity** is the quality of having a pH value lower than 7.

ˌacid ˈrain N-UNCOUNT **Acid rain** is rain that damages plants, rivers, and buildings because it contains acid released into the atmosphere from factories and other industrial processes.
→ see **pollution**

acknowledge /ækˈnɒlɪdʒ/ (**acknowledges, acknowledging, acknowledged**) **1** V-T If you **acknowledge** a fact, you accept that it is true. [FORMAL] ❑ *He acknowledged that his team had not performed well.* ❑ *This is now acknowledged as an urgent national problem.* **2** V-T If you **acknowledge** someone, you show that you have seen and recognized them. ❑ *She never even acknowledged the man who opened the door.* **3** V-T If you **acknowledge** a message or letter, you tell the person who sent it that you have received it. ❑ *They sent me a postcard acknowledging my request.*

acknowledgement also **acknowledgment** /ækˈnɒlɪdʒmənt/ (**acknowledgements**) **1** N-SING An **acknowledgement** of something is a statement or action that recognizes that it is true. ❑ *His resignation was an acknowledgment that he had lost hope.* **2** N-VAR If you receive an **acknowledgement** of something you have sent to someone, you are told officially that it has arrived. **3** N-PLURAL The **acknowledgements** in a book are the parts in which the author thanks the people who have helped.

acne /ˈækni/ N-UNCOUNT **Acne** is a skin disease which causes spots on the face and neck.

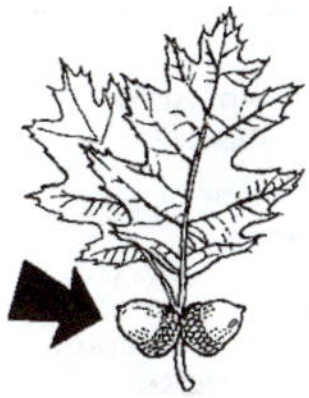
acorn

acorn /ˈeɪkɔːn/ (**acorns**) N-COUNT An **acorn** is a pale oval nut that is the fruit of an oak tree.

acoustic /əˈkuːstɪk/ (**acoustics**) **1** ADJ BEFORE N An **acoustic** musical instrument is one which is not electric. **2** N-PLURAL The **acoustics** of a room are the structural features which determine how well you can hear sound in it. ❑ *The acoustics of the theatre are still superb.* **3** ADJ **Acoustic** means relating to sound or hearing. ❑ *...acoustic signals.*
→ see **string**

acquaint /əˈkweɪnt/ (**acquaints, acquainting, acquainted**) V-T If you **acquaint** someone **with** something, you tell them about it, so that they know it or become familiar with it. [FORMAL] ❑ *This chapter will acquaint you with some standard business writing styles.*

acquaintance /əˈkweɪntəns/ (**acquaintances**) **1** N-COUNT An **acquaintance** is someone who you have met but do not know particularly well. ❑ *Rose and Jim Gordon were old acquaintances.* **2** N-VAR If you have an **acquaintance with** someone, you have met them and you know them. ❑ *So began my acquaintance with the gardener's daughter.* **3** N-SING Your **acquaintance with** a subject is your knowledge or experience of it. ❑ *They had little acquaintance with Chinese history.*

acquainted /əˈkweɪntɪd/ **1** ADJ AFTER LINK-V If you are **acquainted with** something, you know about it because you have learned it or experienced it. [FORMAL] ❑ *He was well acquainted with the literature of France.* **2** ADJ AFTER LINK-V If you are **acquainted with** someone, you know them but they are not a close friend. You can also say that two people are **acquainted**.

acquire /əˈkwaɪə/ (**acquires, acquiring, acquired**) **1** V-T If you **acquire** something, you obtain it. ❑ *We have acquired 20 properties over the last 10 years.* **2** V-T If you **acquire** a skill or habit, you learn it or develop it. ❑ *He had acquired the habit of observing people.* ❑ *Salt is an acquired taste.*

acquisition /ˌækwɪˈzɪʃən/ (**acquisitions**) **1** N-COUNT An **acquisition** is something that you have obtained. ❑ *His latest acquisition is a Mercedes Benz.* **2** N-UNCOUNT The **acquisition of** something is the process of getting it or being given it. ❑ *...the acquisition of land by force.* **3** N-UNCOUNT The **acquisition** of a skill or habit is the process of learning it or developing it. ❑ *...language acquisition.*

acquit /əˈkwɪt/ (**acquits, acquitting, acquitted**) **1** V-T If someone **is acquitted of** a crime, it is formally declared in court that they did not commit it. ❑ *Mr Ling was acquitted of disorderly behaviour.* ❑ *All the accused were acquitted.* **2** V-T If

A

you **acquit yourself** in a particular way, other people feel that you behave in that way. [FORMAL] ❑ *Most officers and men acquitted themselves well.*

acquittal /əˈkwɪtəl/ (**acquittals**) N-VAR The **acquittal** of someone who has been accused of a crime is a formal declaration that they are innocent. ❑ *The judge ordered their acquittal.*

acre /ˈeɪkə/ (**acres**) N-COUNT An **acre** is a unit of area equal to 4840 square yards or approximately 4047 square metres.

acrimonious /ˌækrɪˈməʊniəs/ ADJ **Acrimonious** words or quarrels are bitter and angry. [FORMAL]

Word Link	*onym ≈ name : acronym, anonymous, synonym*

acronym /ˈækrənɪm/ (**acronyms**) N-COUNT An **acronym** is a word made of the initial letters of the words in a phrase, especially when this is the name of an organization such as NATO.

across /əˈkrɒs, AM əˈkrɔːs/ **1** PREP & ADV If you go or look **across** somewhere, you go or look from one side of it to the other. ❑ *He watched Karl run across the street.* ❑ *He looked across at his sleeping wife.* **2** PREP & ADV Something that is situated **across** a street, river, or area is on the other side of it, or stretches from one side to the other. ❑ *I saw you across the room.* ❑ *They parked across from the Castro Theatre.* ❑ *...the floating bridge across Lake Washington.* **3** ADV **Across** is used to indicate the width of something. ❑ *This hand-decorated plate measures 30cm across.* **4** PREP When something happens **across** a place or organization, it happens equally everywhere within it. ❑ *The film opens across America on December 11.* **5** **across the board** → see **board**

acrylic /æˈkrɪlɪk/ ADJ **Acrylic** material is man-made, and manufactured by a chemical process. ❑ *...acrylic jumpers.*

act /ækt/ (**acts, acting, acted**) **1** V-I When you **act**, you do something for a particular purpose. ❑ *The police acted quickly to deal with the situation.* ❑ *We have acted properly and responsibly in this case.* **2** N-COUNT An **act** is a single action or thing that someone does. ❑ *...the act of reading.* ❑ *My insurance excludes acts of terrorism.* **3** V-I If someone **acts** in a particular way, they behave in that way. ❑ *A gang of youths were acting suspiciously.* ❑ *He acted as if he hadn't heard.* **4** V-I If someone or something **acts as** a particular thing, they have that role or function. ❑ *He acted as the ship's surgeon.* **5** N-SING If you say that someone's behaviour is an **act**, you mean that it does not express their real feelings. **6** V-I If you **act** in a play or film, you have a part in it. ❑ *Every time I see her act I am filled with admiration.* **7** N-COUNT An **act** in a play, opera, or ballet is one of the main parts into which it is divided. **8** N-COUNT An **act** in a show is one of the short performances in the show. ❑ *...the best new comedy acts.* **9** N-COUNT An **Act** is a law passed by the government. ❑ *...the Tax Reform Act of 1986.*

acting /ˈæktɪŋ/ **1** N-UNCOUNT **Acting** is the activity or profession of performing in plays or films. ❑ *The acting was superb.* ❑ *...her acting career.* **2** ADJ BEFORE N You use **acting** before the title of a job to indicate that someone is doing that job temporarily. ❑ *...the new acting President.*

action /ˈækʃən/ (**actions**) **1** N-UNCOUNT **Action** is doing something for a particular purpose. ❑ *They want to see tough action taken against the criminals.* **2** N-COUNT An **action** is something that you do on a particular occasion. ❑ *Peter had a reason for his action.* **3** N-SING **The action** refers to all the important and exciting things that are happening in a situation. ❑ *Hollywood is where the action is now.* **4** N-UNCOUNT **Action** is fighting in a war. ❑ *He'd been listed as missing in action.* **5** PHRASE If you **put** an idea or policy **into action**, you begin to use it. **6** PHRASE If someone is **out of action**, they are injured and cannot work. You can also say that something is **out of action**. ❑ *The lifts were out of action.*
→ see **genre**

Word Partnership Use *action* with:

N.	**course of** action, **plan of** action **1**
V.	**take** action **1**
ADJ.	**disciplinary** action **1**
	military action **4**
	legal action **1**

activate /ˈæktɪveɪt/ (**activates, activating, activated**) V-T If a device or process **is activated**, something causes it to start working. ❑ *Video cameras can be activated by movement.*

active /ˈæktɪv/ **1** ADJ An **active** person is energetic and always busy. ❑ *Johnson is still active today, in his late eighties.* **2** ADJ If someone is **active** in an organization or cause, they are involved in it and work hard for it. ❑ *...an active member of the Conservative Party.* • **actively** ADV ❑ *They actively campaigned for the vote.* **3** ADJ BEFORE N **Active** is used to emphasize that someone is taking action in order to achieve something, rather than just waiting for it to happen. ❑ *They are taking active steps to reduce stress.* • **actively** ADV ❑ *They have never been actively encouraged to take such risks.* **4** ADJ An **active** volcano has erupted recently.

Word Partnership Use *active* with:

N.	active **imagination** **1**
	active **role** **2**
	active **ingredient** **4**
ADV.	**politically** active **2**

activist /ˈæktɪvɪst/ (**activists**) N-COUNT An **activist** is a person who works to bring about political or social changes. ❑ *...political activists.*

activity /ækˈtɪvɪti/ (**activities**) **1** N-UNCOUNT **Activity** is a situation in which a lot of things are happening. ❑ *The Black Country was famous for its industrial activity.* **2** N-COUNT An **activity** is something that you spend time doing. ❑ *...outdoor activities.* **3** N-PLURAL The **activities** of a group are the things they do to achieve their aims. ❑ *...terrorist activities.*

actor /ˈæktə/ (**actors**) N-COUNT An **actor** is someone whose job is acting in plays or films.
→ see **drama, theatre**

Usage

Note that many women who act prefer to be called **actors** rather than **actresses**. ❑ *She wants to be an actor when she grows up.*

Word Link	*ess ≈ female : actress, empress, heiress*

a

actress /'æktrəs/ (**actresses**) N-COUNT An **actress** is a woman whose job is acting in plays or films.

actual /'æktʃuəl/ **1** ADJ BEFORE N **Actual** is used to emphasize that you are referring to something real or genuine. ❑ *The actual number of victims is higher than statistics suggest.* **2** ADJ BEFORE N You use **actual** to contrast the important aspect of something with a less important aspect. ❑ *We can help you, but it will be up to you to do the actual work.* **3** **in actual fact** → see **fact**

actually /'æktʃuəli/ **1** ADV You use **actually** to indicate that a situation exists or that it is true. ❑ *I grew bored and actually fell asleep for a few minutes.* ❑ *Interest is only payable on the amount actually borrowed.* **2** ADV You use **actually** as a way of being more polite, especially when you are correcting or contradicting someone, advising them, or when you are introducing a new topic of conversation. ❑ *No, I'm not a student. I'm a doctor, actually.* ❑ *Well actually, John, I rang you for some advice.*

Usage

Actual and **actually** are not used to mean 'happening now, at the present time'. For this meaning, you need to use adjectives such as **current** or **present**, or adverbs such as **currently** or **now**. **Actual** and **actually** are used to emphasize what is true or genuine in a situation, often when this is surprising, or a contrast with what has just been said.

acumen /'ækjʊmen, AM ə'kju:mən/ N-UNCOUNT **Acumen** is the ability to make good judgments and quick decisions. ❑ *...business acumen.*

acupuncture /'ækjʊpʌŋktʃə/ N-UNCOUNT **Acupuncture** is the treatment of a person's illness or pain by sticking small needles into their body.

acute /ə'kju:t/ **1** ADJ An **acute** situation or feeling is very intense or unpleasant. ❑ *...a very acute infection.* ● **acutely** ADV ❑ *It was an acutely uncomfortable journey.* **2** ADJ If a person's or animal's senses are **acute**, they are sensitive and powerful. ❑ *Cats have very acute hearing.* ● **acutely** ADV ❑ *He was acutely aware of the smell of cooking oil.* **3** ADJ In geometry, an **acute** angle is less than 90°.

ad /æd/ (**ads**) N-COUNT An **ad** is an advertisement. [INFORMAL]

AD /,eɪ 'di:/ You use **AD** in dates to indicate a number of years or centuries since the year in which Jesus Christ is believed to have been born. ❑ *...the Great Fire of 1136 AD.*

adamant /'ædəmənt/ ADJ If you are **adamant about** something, you are determined not to change your mind. ❑ *Sue was adamant about going for that job in Australia.* ● **adamantly** ADV ❑ *She adamantly refused to put the book back.*

adapt /ə'dæpt/ (**adapts, adapting, adapted**) **1** V-I If you **adapt to** a new situation, you change your ideas or behaviour in order to deal with it. ❑ *MPs have quickly adapted to the cameras.* **2** V-T If you **adapt** something, you change it to make it suitable for a new purpose or situation. ❑ *They've adapted the library for use as an office.* **3** V-T If you **adapt** a book or play, you change it so that it can be made into a film or a television programme. ❑ *He has adapted his novel for the screen.* **4** → see also **adapted**

Thesaurus *adapt* Also look up:

v. adjust, conform **1**
modify, revise **2**

adaptable /ə'dæptəbəl/ ADJ Someone or something that is **adaptable** is able to change or be changed in order to suit new situations. ❑ *Children are very adaptable. They get used to anything.* ❑ *...an adaptable piece of summer clothing.* ● **adaptability** N-UNCOUNT ❑ *Pine trees are well known for their adaptability.*

adaptation /,ædæp'teɪʃən/ (**adaptations**) **1** N-COUNT An **adaptation** of a story is a play or film based on it. ❑ *...his screen adaptation of Shakespeare's Henry V.* **2** N-UNCOUNT **Adaptation** is the act of changing something to make it suitable for a new purpose or situation. ❑ *Most living creatures are capable of adaptation.*

adapted /ə'dæptɪd/ ADJ AFTER LINK-V If something is **adapted to** a particular situation or purpose, it is especially suitable for it. ❑ *Our brains are not perfectly adapted to modern life.*

add /æd/ (**adds, adding, added**) **1** V-T If you **add** one thing **to** another, you put it with the other thing, to complete or improve it. ❑ *Add the grated cheese to the sauce.* ❑ *He wants to add an extra floor to the current house.* **2** V-T & PHR-VERB If you **add** numbers or amounts, or **add** them **up**, you calculate their total. ❑ *Add the three numbers together and divide by three.* **3** V-I If one thing **adds to** another, it makes the other thing greater in degree or amount, or it gives it a particular quality. ❑ *Cheerful faces added to the general gaiety.* ● **added** ADJ BEFORE N ❑ *For added protection choose a lipstick with a sun screen.* **4** V-T If you **add** something when you are speaking, you say something more. ❑ *Hunt added his congratulations.*

▸ **add in** PHR-VERB If you **add in** something, you include it as a part of something else. ❑ *Once the vegetables start to cook, add in two tablespoons of water.*

▸ **add on** **1** PHR-VERB If something **is added on**, it is attached to or made part of something else. ❑ *A service charge is added on to all meals.* **2** PHR-VERB If you **add on** an extra item or amount to a list or total, you include it in the list or total. ❑ *Add on £3 for postage and packing.*

▸ **add up** **1** → see **add** (meaning **2**) **2** PHR-VERB If facts or events do not **add up**, they make you confused about the true nature of the situation. ❑ *This charge of burglary just doesn't add up.* **3** PHR-VERB If small amounts of something **add up**, they gradually increase. ❑ *It's the little problems that add up.*

▸ **add up to** PHR-VERB If amounts **add up to** a particular total, they result in that total when they are put together. ❑ *Profits can add up to millions of dollars.*

Thesaurus *add* Also look up:

v. put on, throw in **1**
calculate, tally, total; *(ant.)* reduce, subtract **2**
increase; *(ant.)* lessen, reduce **3**

addict /'ædɪkt/ (**addicts**) **1** N-COUNT An **addict** is someone who cannot stop taking harmful

A

drugs. ❑ *...a drug addict.* 2 N-COUNT You can say that someone is an **addict**, when they like a particular activity very much. ❑ *She is a TV addict.*

addicted /əˈdɪktɪd/ 1 ADJ Someone who is **addicted to** a harmful drug cannot stop taking it. ❑ *Many of the women are addicted to heroin.* 2 ADJ If you are **addicted to** something, you like it very much. ❑ *She had become addicted to golf.*

addiction /əˈdɪkʃən/ (**addictions**) 1 N-VAR **Addiction** is the condition of being addicted to harmful drugs. ❑ *...drug addiction.* 2 N-VAR An **addiction to** something is a very strong desire or need for it. ❑ *...his addiction to gambling.*

addictive /əˈdɪktɪv/ 1 ADJ If a drug is **addictive**, people who start taking it find that they cannot stop. ❑ *Cigarettes are highly addictive.* 2 ADJ Something that is **addictive** is so enjoyable that it makes you want to do it or have it a lot. ❑ *Video movie-making can quickly become addictive.*

addition /əˈdɪʃən/ (**additions**) 1 PHRASE You use **in addition** or **with the addition of** to mention another item connected with the subject you are discussing. ❑ *There's a postage fee in addition to the repair charge.* 2 N-COUNT An **addition to** something is a thing which is added to it. ❑ *...recent additions to the range of 4x4 cars.* ● **additional** ADJ ❑ *The US is sending additional troops to the region.* 3 N-UNCOUNT **Addition** is the process of calculating the total of two or more numbers. → see **mathematics**

additionally /əˈdɪʃənəli/ 1 ADV You use **additionally** to introduce an extra fact. [FORMAL] ❑ *All teachers are qualified to teach their native language. Additionally, we select our teachers for their engaging personalities.* 2 ADV **Additionally** is used to say that something happens to a greater extent than before. ❑ *The birds are additionally protected in the reserves here.*

additive /ˈædɪtɪv/ (**additives**) N-COUNT An **additive** is a substance which is added to food by the manufacturer for a particular purpose, such as colouring it. ❑ *Strict safety tests are carried out on food additives.* ❑ *...additive-free baby foods.*

address /əˈdres, AM ˈædres/ (**addresses, addressing, addressed**) 1 N-COUNT Your **address** is the number of the house, the name of the street, and the town where you live or work. ❑ *The address is 2025 Main Street, Northwest, Washington, DC, 20036.* 2 V-T If a letter **is addressed to** you, your name and address has been written on it. ❑ *Applications should be addressed to the business editor.* 3 N-COUNT The **address** of a website is its location on the Internet, for example http://www.cobuild.collins.co.uk. ❑ *Internet addresses are also known as URLs.* 4 V-T & N-COUNT If you **address** a group of people or if you give an **address**, you give a speech to them. ❑ *He turned to address the crowd.* ❑ *...an address to the American people.* 5 V-T If you **address** someone or **address** a remark **to** someone, you say something to them. ❑ *The two foreign ministers did not address each other directly.* 6 V-T If you **address** someone by a name or a title such as 'sir', you call them that name or title. ❑ *I heard him address her as darling.* 7 V-T If you **address** a problem or if you **address yourself to** it, you try to understand it or deal with it. ❑ *Mr King tried to address those fears when he spoke at the meeting.* ❑ *Throughout the book we have addressed ourselves to the problem of ethics.*

Thesaurus *address* Also look up:

N.	lecture, speech, talk 4

Word Partnership Use *address* with:

ADJ.	**permanent** address 1
	public address, **inaugural** address 4
N.	**name and** address, **street** address 1
	address **remarks to** 5

adept /æˈdept/ ADJ Someone who is **adept at** something does it skilfully. ❑ *He was adept at persuading others to finance his projects.* ❑ *He is an adept guitar player.*

adequate /ˈædɪkwət/ ADJ If something is **adequate**, there is enough of it or it is good enough for a particular purpose. ❑ *...an amount adequate to purchase another house.* ● **adequacy** N-UNCOUNT ❑ *...the adequacy of the diet.* ● **adequately** ADV ❑ *I speak the language adequately.*

adhere /ædˈhɪə/ (**adheres, adhering, adhered**) 1 V-I If you **adhere to** a rule, you act in the way that it says you should. ❑ *All members adhere to a strict code of practice.* ● **adherence** N-UNCOUNT ❑ *...strict adherence to the constitution.* 2 V-I If you **adhere to** an opinion or belief, you support or hold it. ❑ *...those who adhered to more traditional views.* 3 V-I If a substance **adheres to** a surface or object, it sticks to it. [FORMAL] ❑ *Small particles adhere to the seed.*

adhesive /ædˈhiːsɪv/ (**adhesives**) N-VAR & ADJ An **adhesive** or an **adhesive** substance is used to make things stick together. ❑ *...adhesive tape.*

ad hoc /ˌæd ˈhɒk/ ADJ An **ad hoc** activity or organization is done or formed only when it becomes necessary, rather than being planned in advance. ❑ *I accept opportunities in TV on an ad hoc basis.* ❑ *...ad hoc committees.*

adjacent /əˈdʒeɪsənt/ ADJ If two things are **adjacent**, they are next to each other. ❑ *He sat in an adjacent room.* ❑ *...offices adjacent to the museum.*

adjective /ˈædʒɪktɪv/ (**adjectives**) N-COUNT In grammar, an **adjective** is a word such as 'big', 'dead', or 'financial' that describes a person or thing, or gives extra information about them. Adjectives usually come before nouns or after link verbs.

adjoin /əˈdʒɔɪn/ (**adjoins, adjoining, adjoined**) V-T If one room, place, or object **adjoins** another, they are next to each other. [FORMAL] ❑ *We waited in an adjoining office.*

adjourn /əˈdʒɜːn/ (**adjourns, adjourning, adjourned**) V-T/V-I If a meeting or trial **is adjourned** or if it **adjourns**, it is stopped for a short time. ❑ *The meeting has now been adjourned until next week.* ● **adjournment** (**adjournments**) N-COUNT ❑ *The court ordered a four-month adjournment.*

adjust /əˈdʒʌst/ (**adjusts, adjusting, adjusted**) 1 V-I When you **adjust to** a new situation, you get used to it by changing your behaviour or your ideas. ❑ *I felt I had adjusted to the idea of being a mother very well.* ❑ *It has been hard to adjust.* ● **adjustment** (**adjustments**) N-COUNT ❑ *He will have to make major adjustments to his thinking.* 2 V-T If you **adjust** something, you change it so that it is more effective or appropriate. ❑ *Panama has adjusted its* *tax and labour laws.* ● **adjustment** N-COUNT ❑ *The figure is 5.7%, after adjustment for inflation.* **3** V-T If you **adjust** something, you correct or alter its position or setting. ❑ *You can manually adjust the camera.* ● **adjustment** N-COUNT ❑ *...a workshop for repairs and adjustments.*

adjustable /ə'dʒʌstəbəl/ ADJ If something is **adjustable**, it can be changed to different positions or sizes. ❑ *The bags have adjustable shoulder straps.* ❑ *The seats are fully adjustable.*

Thesaurus	*adjustable* Also look up:
ADJ.	adaptable; *(ant.)* fixed

administer /æd'mɪnɪstə/ (**administers, administering, administered**) **1** V-T If someone **administers** something such as a country, the law, or a test, they take responsibility for organizing and supervising it. ❑ *The UN will administer the country until the elections.* **2** V-T If a doctor or a nurse **administers** a drug, they give it to a patient. [FORMAL]

administration /æd,mɪnɪ'streɪʃən/ **1** N-UNCOUNT **Administration** is the range of activities connected with organizing and supervising the way that an organization functions. ❑ *Too much time is spent on administration.* ❑ *...business administration.* **2** N-SING The **administration** of a company or institution is the group of people who organize and supervise it. ❑ *The college administration has banned video games.* **3** → See note at **government**

administrative /æd'mɪnɪstrətɪv, AM -streɪt-/ ADJ **Administrative** work involves organizing and supervising an organization. ❑ *...administrative costs.*

administrator /æd'mɪnɪstreɪtə/ (**administrators**) N-COUNT An **administrator** is a person whose job involves helping to organize and supervise the way that an organization functions.

admirable /'ædmɪrəbəl/ ADJ An **admirable** quality or action deserves to be praised and admired. ❑ *He was a very admirable person.* ● **admirably** ADV ❑ *Peter dealt admirably with the sudden questions.*

admiral /'ædmərəl/ (**admirals**) N-COUNT & N-TITLE An **admiral** is a naval officer of the highest rank.

admiration /,ædmɪ'reɪʃən/ N-UNCOUNT **Admiration** is a feeling of great liking and respect. ❑ *I have always had the greatest admiration for him.*

admire /əd'maɪə/ (**admires, admiring, admired**) **1** V-T If you **admire** someone or something, you like and respect them. ❑ *All those who know him admire him for his work.* ● **admirer** (**admirers**) N-COUNT ❑ *He was an admirer of her grandfather's paintings.* **2** V-T If you **admire** someone or something, you look at them with pleasure. ❑ *We took time to stop and admire the view.*

Thesaurus	*admire* Also look up:
V.	adore, esteem, honour, look up to, respect **1**

admission /æd'mɪʃən/ (**admissions**) **1** N-VAR If you gain **admission to** a place or organization, you are allowed to enter it or join it. ❑ *Students apply for admission to a particular college.* ❑ *...increases in hospital admissions.* **2** N-UNCOUNT **Admission** is the amount of money you pay to enter a place such as a park or museum. **3** N-VAR An **admission** is a statement that something bad or embarrassing is true. ❑ *She wanted some admission of guilt from her father.*
→ see **hospital**

admit /æd'mɪt/ (**admits, admitting, admitted**) **1** V-T/V-I If you **admit** that something bad or embarrassing is true, you agree, often reluctantly, that it is true. ❑ *He rarely admits to making errors.* ❑ *None of these people will admit responsibility.* **2** V-T If someone **is admitted to** hospital, they are taken into hospital for treatment. **3** V-T If someone **is admitted to** a place or organization, they are allowed to enter it or join it. ❑ *He was admitted to university after the war.* ❑ *Journalists are rarely admitted to the region.*

Word Partnership	Use *admit* with:
V.	**ashamed to** admit, **be the first to** admit, **must** admit, **willing to** admit **1**
N.	admit **defeat** **1**
CONJ.	admit **that** **1**

admittedly /æd'mɪtɪdli/ ADV You use **admittedly** when you are saying something which weakens the force of your statement. ❑ *It's only a theory, admittedly, but it seems to make sense.*

adolescent /,ædə'lesənt/ (**adolescents**) ADJ & N-COUNT **Adolescent** is used to describe young people who are no longer children but who have not yet become adults. An **adolescent** is a young person. ❑ *...an adolescent boy.* ● **adolescence** N-UNCOUNT ❑ *...children who have reached adolescence.*
→ see **age, child**

Word Link	*opt ≈ choosing : adopt, opt, optional*

adopt /ə'dɒpt/ (**adopts, adopting, adopted**) **1** V-T If you **adopt** someone else's child, you take it into your own family and make it legally your own. ❑ *...an adopted child.* ● **adoption** (**adoptions**) N-VAR ❑ *They gave their babies up for adoption.* **2** V-T If you **adopt** a new attitude or plan, you begin to have it. ❑ *The ambassador tried to persuade each side to adopt a new international peace plan.* ● **adoption** N-UNCOUNT ❑ *...the adoption of Japanese management practices.*

Thesaurus	*adopt* Also look up:
V.	care for, raise, take in **1**; approve, endorse, support; *(ant.)* refuse, reject **2**

adoptive /ə'dɒptɪv/ ADJ BEFORE N Someone's **adoptive** family is the family that adopted them. ❑ *He was brought up by adoptive parents in London.*

adorable /ə'dɔːrəbəl/ ADJ If you say that someone or something is **adorable**, you are emphasizing that they are very attractive and you feel great affection for them. ❑ *We had three adorable children.*

adore /ə'dɔː/ (**adores, adoring, adored**) **1** V-T If you **adore** someone, you love and admire them. ● **adoration** N-UNCOUNT ❑ *He was used to female*

A

adoration. 2 V-T If you **adore** something, you like it very much. [INFORMAL] ❑ *My mother adores bananas.*
→ see **emotion**

adoring /əˈdɔːrɪŋ/ ADJ An **adoring** person loves and admires someone else very much. • **adoringly** ADV ❑ *She looks adoringly at her husband.*

adorn /əˈdɔːn/ (**adorns, adorning, adorned**) V-T If something **adorns** a place or an object, it makes it look more beautiful. ❑ *Several magnificent oil paintings adorn the walls.* • **adornment** (**adornments**) N-VAR ❑ *...a building without any adornment or decoration.*

adrenalin also **adrenaline** /əˈdrenəlɪn/ N-UNCOUNT **Adrenalin** is a substance produced by your body which makes your heart beat faster and gives you more energy.

adrift /əˈdrɪft/ 1 ADJ AFTER LINK-V If a boat is **adrift**, it is floating on the water without being controlled. ❑ *They were spotted after three hours adrift in a motor boat.* 2 ADJ AFTER LINK-V If something or someone has gone **adrift**, they no longer seem to have any purpose or direction. ❑ *...a policy that has gone adrift.*

adult /ˈædʌlt, AM əˈdʌlt/ (**adults**) N-COUNT & ADJ BEFORE N An **adult** is a mature, fully developed person or animal. **Adult** means relating to the time when you are an adult, or typical of adults. ❑ *...a pair of adult birds.* ❑ *I've lived most of my adult life in London.*
→ see **age**

Thesaurus	*adult* Also look up:
N.	grown-up, man, woman

adultery /əˈdʌltəri/ N-COUNT If a married person **commits adultery**, they have sex with someone that they are not married to.

Word Link	***hood*** ***≈ state, condition :*** ***adulthood, childhood, manhood***

adulthood /ˈædʌlthʊd, AM əˈdʌlt-/ N-UNCOUNT **Adulthood** is the state of being an adult. ❑ *...children coming into adulthood.*

advance /ædˈvɑːns, -ˈvæns/ (**advances, advancing, advanced**) 1 V-I & N-VAR To **advance** or to make an **advance** means to move forward, often in order to attack someone. ❑ *Rebel forces are advancing on the capital.* ❑ *The defences are intended to obstruct any advance by tanks.* 2 V-I & N-VAR If you **advance** or make an **advance** in something you are doing, you make progress in it. ❑ *Allison advanced from sales manager to director of sales and services.* ❑ *...the dramatic advances of the 1970s.* 3 V-T & N-COUNT If you **advance** someone a sum of money, or if you give them an **advance**, you give them money earlier than arranged. ❑ *The bank advanced him $1.2 billion.* ❑ *She was paid a £100,000 advance for her next two novels.* 4 V-T To **advance** an event, or its time or date, means to bring it forward to an earlier time or date. ❑ *Too much protein in the diet may advance the ageing process.* 5 ADJ BEFORE N **Advance** booking or warning is done or given before an event happens. ❑ *The event received little advance publicity.* 6 PHRASE If you do something **in advance**, you do it before a particular date or event. If one thing happens or is done **in advance of** another, it happens or is done before the other thing. ❑ *I asked everyone to submit questions in advance.*

advanced /ædˈvɑːnst, -ˈvænst/ 1 ADJ An **advanced** system, method, or design is modern and has been developed from an earlier version of the same thing. ❑ *...the most advanced optical telescope in the world.* 2 ADJ A country that is **advanced** has reached a high level of industrial or technological development. ❑ *...the educational levels reached in other advanced countries.* 3 ADJ An **advanced** student has learned the basic facts of a subject and is doing more difficult work.

Thesaurus	*advanced* Also look up:
ADJ.	cutting edge, foremost, latest, sophisticated 1

advancement /ædˈvɑːnsmənt, -ˈvæns-/ 1 N-UNCOUNT **Advancement** is promotion in your job, or to a higher social class. ❑ *He cared little for social advancement.* 2 N-UNCOUNT The **advancement** of something is the process of helping it to progress. ❑ *...the advancement of education.*

advantage /ædˈvɑːntɪdʒ, -ˈvæn-/ (**advantages**) 1 N-VAR An **advantage** is something that puts you in a better position than other people. **Advantage** is the state of being in a better position than others who are competing against you. ❑ *A good audience will be a definite advantage to me.* ❑ *Men have created a position of advantage for themselves.* 2 N-COUNT An **advantage** is a way in which one thing is better than another. ❑ *The great advantage of this system is that it's safe.* 3 PHRASE If you **take advantage of** something, you make good use of it while you can. ❑ *I intend to take full advantage of this trip to buy the things we need.* 4 PHRASE If someone **takes advantage of** you, they treat you unfairly for their own benefit. 5 PHRASE If you **use** something **to** your **advantage** or **turn** something **to** your **advantage**, you exploit it in order to benefit from it.

Word Partnership	Use *advantage* with:
ADJ.	**competitive** advantage, **unfair** advantage 1
V.	**have an** advantage 1
	take advantage **of** ***someone/something*** 4
	use to ***someone's*** advantage 5

advantageous /ˌædvənˈteɪdʒəs/ ADJ Something that is **advantageous to** you is likely to benefit you. ❑ *The new system is advantageous to the workers.* ❑ *...very advantageous prices.*

advent /ˈædvent/ N-UNCOUNT **The advent of** something is the fact of it starting or coming into existence. [FORMAL] ❑ *...the advent of the computer.*

adventure /ædˈventʃə/ (**adventures**) N-VAR An **adventure** is a series of events that you become involved in that are unusual, exciting, and perhaps dangerous. ❑ *I set off for a new adventure in the United States.* ❑ *...a feeling of adventure.* • **adventurer** (**adventurers**) N-COUNT ❑ *...a true adventurer's paradise.*

adventurous /ædˈventʃərəs/ ADJ An **adventurous** person is willing to take risks and eager to have new experiences. Something that is **adventurous** involves new things or ideas. ❑ *The* menu seemed more adventurous before.

Word Link *verb ≈ word : adverb, proverb, verbal*

adverb /'ædvɜːb/ (**adverbs**) N-COUNT In grammar, an **adverb** is a word such as 'slowly' or 'very' which adds information about time, place, or manner.

adversary /'ædvəsəri, AM -seri/ (**adversaries**) N-COUNT Your **adversary** is someone you are competing with or fighting against. ❑ *...political adversaries.*

adverse /'ædvɜːs, AM æd'vɜːrs/ ADJ **Adverse** effects or conditions are unfavourable to you. ❑ *Stress can have an adverse effect on your health.* ● **adversely** ADV ❑ *...countries adversely affected by the increase in the price of oil.*

adversity /æd'vɜːsɪti/ N-UNCOUNT **Adversity** is a very difficult situation. ❑ *...ways in which people manage to enjoy life despite adversity.*

advert /'ædvɜːt/ (**adverts**) N-COUNT An **advert** is the same as an **advertisement**. [INFORMAL]

advertise /'ædvətaɪz/ (**advertises, advertising, advertised**) **1** V-T/V-I If you **advertise** or **advertise** something such as a product, event, or job, you tell people about it in newspapers, on television, or on posters. ❑ *Religious groups are not allowed to advertise on television.* ● **advertiser** (**advertisers**) N-COUNT ❑ *...campaigns by the advertiser in support of the film.* **2** V-I If you **advertise for** someone to do something for you, you place an advertisement for it in a newspaper, on television, or on a poster, saying that you need someone to do it. ❑ *We advertised for staff in a local newspaper.*

advertisement /æd'vɜːtɪsmənt, AM ˌædvə'taɪz-/ (**advertisements**) N-COUNT An **advertisement** is an announcement in a newspaper, on television, or on a poster that tells people about a product, event, or job vacancy. ❑ *...job advertisements.*

advertising /'ædvətaɪzɪŋ/ N-UNCOUNT **Advertising** is the business activity of encouraging people to buy products, go to events, or apply for jobs. ❑ *...a ban on tobacco advertising.*

advice /æd'vaɪs/ N-UNCOUNT If you give someone **advice**, you tell them what you think they should do. ❑ *Take my advice and stay away from him!*

Usage

Note that **advice** is only ever used as an uncount noun. You can say *a piece of advice* or *some advice*, but you cannot say 'an advice' or 'advices'.

Thesaurus *advice* Also look up:

N. counsel, encouragement, guidance, help, information, input, opinion, recommendation, suggestion

Word Partnership Use *advice* with:

PREP. **against** advice
V. **ask for** advice, **give** advice, **need some** advice, **take** advice
ADJ. **bad/good** advice, **expert** advice

advisable /æd'vaɪzəbəl/ ADJ AFTER LINK-V If you tell someone that it is **advisable to** do something, you are suggesting that they should do it. ❑ *It's advisable to book early for city-centre restaurants.*

advise /æd'vaɪz/ (**advises, advising, advised**) **1** V-T If you **advise** someone **to** do something, you tell them what you think they should do. ❑ *Could you advise me how to use this camera?* **2** V-T If you **advise** people **on** a particular subject, you give them help and information on it. ❑ *...a booklet advising the public on financial problems.* **3** V-T If you **advise** someone **of** a fact or situation, you tell them the fact or explain what the situation is. [FORMAL] ❑ *A counsellor will advise you of your rights.*

adviser also **advisor** /æd'vaɪzə/ (**advisers**) N-COUNT An **adviser** is an expert whose job is to advise people on a particular subject. ❑ *...a careers adviser.*

Word Link *ory ≈ relating to : advisory, contradictory, sensory*

advisory /æd'vaɪzəri/ ADJ An **advisory** committee gives people help and information on a particular subject. ❑ *...the advisory committee on nuclear power.*

Word Link *voc ≈ speaking: advocate, vocabulary, vocal*

advocate (**advocates, advocating, advocated**)

verb /'ædvəkeɪt/, noun /'ædvəkət/.

1 V-T & N-COUNT If you **advocate** a particular action or plan, or if you are an **advocate of** it, you support it publicly. [FORMAL] ❑ *He advocates fewer government controls on business.* **2** N-COUNT An **advocate** is a lawyer who speaks in favour of someone or defends them in a court of law. [TECHNICAL]

Word Link *aer ≈ air : aerial, aeroplane, aerosol*

aerial /'eəriəl/ (**aerials**) **1** ADJ BEFORE N You use **aerial** to talk about things which happen in the air or are done from the air, particularly from an aeroplane. ❑ *...aerial photographs.* **2** N-COUNT In British English, an **aerial** is a piece of metal equipment that receives television or radio signals. The American word is **antenna**.

aerobics /eə'rəʊbɪks/ N-PLURAL **Aerobics** is a form of exercise which increases the amount of oxygen in your blood and strengthens your heart and lungs. **Aerobics** can take the singular or plural form of the verb. ❑ *...an aerobics class.*

aeroplane /'eərəpleɪn/ (**aeroplanes**) N-COUNT An **aeroplane** is a vehicle with wings and engines that enable it to fly through the air. The usual American word is **airplane**.

aerosol /'eərəsɒl, AM -sɔːl/ (**aerosols**) N-COUNT An **aerosol** is a container in which a liquid such as paint is kept under pressure. When you press a button, the liquid is forced out as a spray.

aesthetic also **esthetic** /iːs'θetɪk, AM es-/ ADJ **Aesthetic** is used to talk about beauty or art, and people's appreciation of beautiful things. ❑ *...products chosen for their aesthetic qualities.* ● **aesthetically** ADV ❑ *...aesthetically pleasing furniture.*

A

affable /ˈæfəbəl/ ADJ **Affable** people are pleasant and friendly. ❏ *...his gentle, affable nature.*

affair /əˈfeə/ (**affairs**) **1** N-COUNT You refer to an event as an **affair** when you are talking about it in a general way. ❏ *The whole affair has caused great confusion.* **2** N-PLURAL In politics and journalism, **affairs** is used to refer to a particular type of activity or to the activities in a particular place. ❏ *...our foreign affairs correspondent.* **3** → see also **current affairs, state of affairs** **4** N-PLURAL Your **affairs** are your personal concerns. ❏ *He is unable to manage his own affairs.* **5** N-SING If you say that a decision or situation is someone's **affair**, you mean that other people should not interfere. ❏ *If you wish to behave like a fool, that is your own affair.* **6** N-COUNT If two people who are married, but not to each other have an **affair**, they have a sexual relationship.

affect /əˈfekt/ (**affects, affecting, affected**) **1** V-T When something **affects** someone or something, it influences them or causes them to change. ❏ *...decisions that would affect me for the rest of my life.* ❏ *More than seven million people have been affected by floods.* **2** V-T If a disease **affects** you, it makes you ill. ❏ *The disease affects men and women in equal numbers.*

affection /əˈfekʃən/ (**affections**) **1** N-UNCOUNT If you regard someone or something with **affection**, you care about them. **2** N-PLURAL Your **affections** are your feelings of love or liking for someone. ❏ *She had focused her affections on her father.* → see **love**

Word Link	***ate ≈ filled with : affectionate, compassionate, considerate***

affectionate /əˈfekʃənət/ ADJ If you are **affectionate**, you show your fondness for another person in your behaviour. ❏ *They were more affectionate towards the younger child.* ● **affectionately** ADV ❏ *He looked affectionately at his niece.*

affidavit /ˌæfɪˈdeɪvɪt/ (**affidavits**) N-COUNT An **affidavit** is a written statement which you swear is true and which may be used as evidence in a court of law.

affiliate (**affiliates, affiliating, affiliated**) **1** N-COUNT /əˈfɪliət/ An **affiliate** is an organization which is officially connected with another, larger organization or is a member of it. **2** V-I /əˌfɪliˈeɪt/ If an organization **affiliates to** or **with** another larger organization, it forms a close connection with it or becomes a member of it. ❏ *Is your society affiliated to the Labour Party?* ● **affiliation** (**affiliations**) N-COUNT ❏ *The group has no affiliation to any political party.*

affinity /əˈfɪnɪti/ (**affinities**) **1** N-SING If you have an **affinity with** someone or something, you feel that you belong with them and understand them. ❏ *The staff show a natural affinity with children.* **2** N-COUNT If people or things have an **affinity with** each other, they are similar in some ways. ❏ *We discussed the affinities between Caribbean writers and the authors of the American South.*

Word Link	***firm ≈ making strong : affirm, confirm, reaffirm***

affirm /əˈfɜːm/ (**affirms, affirming, affirmed**) **1** V-T If you **affirm** that something is true, you state firmly and publicly that it is true. [FORMAL] ❏ *...a speech in which he affirmed a commitment to lower taxes.* ● **affirmation** /ˌæfəˈmeɪʃən/ (**affirmations**) N-VAR ❏ *...affirmation that Mr Green was a man of courage.* **2** V-T If an event **affirms** something, it shows that it is true or exists. [FORMAL] ● **affirmation** N-UNCOUNT ❏ *The book is an affirmation of the band's 28-year-old friendship.*

affirmative /əˈfɜːmətɪv/ ADJ An **affirmative** word or gesture indicates that you agree with someone or that the answer to a question is 'yes'. [FORMAL] ❏ *She gave an affirmative nod.*

afflict /əˈflɪkt/ (**afflicts, afflicting, afflicted**) V-T If you **are afflicted with** something, it affects you badly. ❏ *Both people who died were afflicted with a rare disease.* ❏ *The country has been afflicted by corruption for years.*

Word Link	***flict ≈ striking : affliction, conflict, inflict***

affliction /əˈflɪkʃən/ (**afflictions**) N-VAR An **affliction** is something which causes suffering. [FORMAL] ❏ *Loneliness is a dreadful affliction.*

affluent /ˈæfluənt/ ADJ **Affluent** people have a lot of money. ❏ *...Philadelphia's affluent suburbs.* ● **affluence** N-UNCOUNT ❏ *This was an era of new affluence for the working class.*

afford /əˈfɔːd/ (**affords, affording, afforded**) **1** V-T If you cannot **afford** something, you do not have enough money to pay for it. ❏ *We can't afford to pay the rent.* **2** V-T If you cannot **afford to** do something or allow it to happen, you must not do it or you must prevent it from happening because it would be harmful or embarrassing to you. ❏ *We can't afford to wait.* ❏ *I can't afford the luxury of a weekend off.*

Word Partnership	Use *afford* with:
ADJ.	**able/unable to** afford **1** **2**
V.	afford **to buy/pay** **1**
	can/could afford,
	can't/couldn't afford **1** **2**
	afford **to lose** **2**

Word Link	***able ≈ able to be : affordable, incurable, portable***

affordable /əˈfɔːdəbəl/ ADJ If something is **affordable**, people have enough money to buy it. ❏ *...affordable housing.* ● **affordability** N-UNCOUNT ❏ *...advertisements that emphasized affordability.*

affront /əˈfrʌnt/ (**affronts, affronting, affronted**) V-T & N-COUNT If something **affronts** you, or if it is an **affront to** you, it makes you feel insulted. ❏ *...results which would affront people's good sense.* ❏ *It's an affront to human dignity to keep someone alive like this.*

afield /əˈfiːld/ **1** PHRASE **Further afield** or **farther afield** mean in places other than the nearest or most obvious one. ❏ *Lucerne is a good base for travelling further afield.* **2** PHRASE If people come from **far afield**, they come from a long way away.

afloat /əˈfləʊt/ **1** ADV When someone or something is **afloat**, they remain partly above the surface of water and do not sink. **2** ADV If a person or business manages to stay **afloat**, they have just enough money to pay their debts. ❏ *He and his family kept afloat by doing odd jobs.*

afoot /ə'fʊt/ ADJ AFTER LINK-V If something such as a plan is **afoot**, it is already happening or being planned, often secretly. ❑ *Workers claim plans are afoot to move work abroad.*

aforementioned /ə'fɔːmenʃənd/ ADJ BEFORE N When you refer to **the aforementioned** person or subject, you mean the person or subject that has already been mentioned. [FORMAL]

afraid /ə'freɪd/ **1** ADJ AFTER LINK-V If you are **afraid of** someone or **afraid to** do something, you are frightened because you think that something horrible is going to happen. ❑ *I was afraid of the other boys.* **2** ADJ AFTER LINK-V If you are **afraid that** something unpleasant will happen, you are worried that it may happen. ❑ *The Government is afraid of losing the election.* **3** ADJ AFTER LINK-V If you are **afraid for** someone else, you are worried that they are in danger. ❑ *She's afraid for her family back home.* **4** CONVENTION When you want to disagree with someone or apologize to them in a polite way, you can say **'I'm afraid'**. ❑ *I'm afraid I can't agree with you on that John.*

Thesaurus	*afraid* Also look up:
ADJ.	alarmed, fearful, frightened, petrified, scared, terrified, worried **1**

afresh /ə'freʃ/ ADV If you do something **afresh**, you do it again in a different way.

African /'æfrɪkən/ (**Africans**) **1** ADJ **African** means belonging or relating to the continent of Africa. ❑ *...African art.* **2** N-COUNT An **African** is someone who comes from Africa.

ˌAfrican-A'merican (**African-Americans**) N-COUNT & ADJ An **African-American** is an American whose family originally came from Africa. **African-American** means relating to African-Americans.

ˌAfrican-Cari'bbean (**African-Caribbeans**) N-COUNT & ADJ An **African-Caribbean** is someone from the Caribbean whose family originally came from Africa. **African-Caribbean** means relating to African-Caribbeans.

after /'ɑːftə, 'æftə/

> In addition to the uses below, **after** is used in phrasal verbs such as 'ask after' or 'look after'.

1 PREP & CONJ If something happens or is done **after** a particular event or date, it happens or is done during the period of time that follows it. ❑ *I went for a walk after lunch.* ❑ *After completing and signing it, please return the form to us.* ❑ *She's leaving the day after tomorrow.* **2** PREP In American English, **after** is used when telling the time. **3** PREP If you are **after** someone, you follow or chase them. ❑ *He knew the police were after him.* **4** PREP If you shout or stare **after** someone, you shout or stare at them as they move away from you. **5** PREP If you are **after** something, you are trying to get it. ❑ *I'm not after Rick's job.* **6** PREP To be named **after** someone or something means to be given the same name as them. ❑ *Phillimore Island is named after Sir Robert Phillimore.* **7** PREP You use **after** in order to give the most important aspect of something when comparing it with something else. ❑ *After Germany, America is Britain's second-biggest customer.* **8** CONVENTION If you say **'after you'** to someone, you are being polite and allowing them to go in front of you. **9** **after all** → see **all**

aftermath /'ɑːftəmɑːθ, 'æftəmæθ/ N-SING The **aftermath** of an important or serious event is the situation that results from it. ❑ *Several jobs were lost in the aftermath of the disaster.*

afternoon /ˌɑːftə'nuːn, ˌæf-/ (**afternoons**) N-COUNT The **afternoon** is the part of each day which begins at 12 o'clock lunchtime and ends at about six o'clock.
→ see **time**

afterwards /'ɑːftəwədz, 'æf-/

> The form **afterward** is also used, mainly in American English.

ADV If something is done or happens **afterwards**, it is done or happens later than a particular event or time that has already been described. ❑ *James was taken to hospital but died soon afterwards.*

again /ə'gen, ə'geɪn/ **1** ADV You use **again** to indicate that something happens a second time, or after it has already happened before. ❑ *He kissed her again.* ❑ *I don't ever want to go through anything like that again.* **2** PHRASE You can use **again and again** or **time and again** to emphasize that something happens many times. ❑ *Time and again we have failed to deal with this problem.* **3** ADV You use **again** to indicate that something has returned to the particular state or place that it used to be in. ❑ *She opened the door and closed it again.* **4** **every now and again** → see **now**

against /ə'genst, ə'geɪnst/ **1** PREP If something is leaning or pressing **against** something else, it is touching it. ❑ *She leaned against him.* ❑ *...the rain beating against the window panes.* **2** PREP & ADV If you are **against** an idea, policy, or system, you think it is wrong. ❑ *...a march to protest against job losses.* ❑ *...12 votes in favour, 2 votes against.* **3** PREP If you take action **against** someone or something, you try to harm them. ❑ *...the crime of violence against women.* **4** PREP If you do something **against** someone's wishes, advice, or orders, you do it although they tell you not to. ❑ *He stopped the treatment against the advice of doctors.* **5** PREP If you compete **against** someone in a game, you try to beat them. ❑ *The tour will include games against the Australians.* **6** PREP If you do something to protect yourself **against** something unpleasant, you do something which will make its effects on you less serious. ❑ *This cream protects against damage from sunlight.* **7** PREP Something that is **against** the law is forbidden by law. **8** PREP & ADV The odds **against** something happening are the chance that it will not happen.

age /eɪdʒ/ (**ages, ageing** or **aging, aged**) **1** N-VAR Your **age** is the number of years that you have lived. ❑ *She has a nephew who is just ten years of age.* ❑ *At the age of sixteen he went to college.* **2** N-UNCOUNT **Age** is the state of being old. ❑ *This cologne, like wine, improves with age.* ❑ *At 67, he is showing signs of age.* **3** V-T/V-I When someone **ages**, they become or seem much older. ❑ *He seemed to have aged in the last few months.* ❑ *Worry had aged him.* ● **ageing** N-UNCOUNT ❑ *Inadequate fluid intake and poor diet all contribute to ageing.* **4** N-COUNT An **age** is a period in history. ❑ *We're living in the age of television.* ❑ *...the Bronze Age.* **5** → see also **aged, middle age** **6** PHRASE Someone who is **under age** is not legally old enough to do something. ❑ *Many of the drinkers in the town's pubs are under age.* ❑ *...under-age smoking.* **7** PHRASE When someone

Picture Dictionary age

comes of age, they legally become an adult.
→ see Picture Dictionary: **age**

aged 1 ADJ /eɪdʒd/ You use **aged** followed by a number to say how old someone is. ❑ *They have a son aged five.* 2 ADJ BEFORE N & N-PLURAL /ˈeɪdʒɪd/ An **aged** person is very old. You can refer to people who are very old as **the aged**. ❑ *...his aged parents.* ❑ *...a home for the aged.* 3 → see also **middle-aged**

agency /ˈeɪdʒənsi/ (**agencies**) 1 N-COUNT An **agency** is a business which provides services for a person or another business. ❑ *...a dating agency.* ❑ *...an advertising agency.* 2 N-COUNT An **agency** is an administrative organization run by a government. ❑ *...the Central Intelligence Agency.*

agenda /əˈdʒendə/ (**agendas**) 1 N-COUNT An **agenda** is a list of items to be discussed at a meeting. ❑ *This will be an item on the agenda next week.* 2 N-COUNT You can refer to the political issues which are important at a particular time as an **agenda**. ❑ *He has set out an agenda for peace in his country.*

Word Partnership Use *agenda* with:

ADJ.	**domestic/legislative/political** agenda, **hidden** agenda 1
PREP.	**on the** agenda 2
V.	**set the** agenda 2

agent /ˈeɪdʒənt/ (**agents**) 1 N-COUNT An **agent** is someone who arranges work or business for someone else. ❑ *You are buying direct, rather than through an agent.* 2 → see also **estate agent, travel agent** 3 N-COUNT An **agent** is someone who works for a country's secret service.
→ see **concert**

ˌage of conˈsent N-SING **The age of consent** is the age at which a person can legally marry or agree to have a sexual relationship.

age-old ADJ BEFORE N An **age-old** story, tradition, or problem has existed for a very long time.

aggravate /ˈægrəveɪt/ (**aggravates, aggravating, aggravated**) 1 V-T If someone or something **aggravates** a situation, they make it worse. ❑ *The army could further aggravate the situation.* 2 V-T If someone or something **aggravates** you, they make you annoyed. [INFORMAL] ❑ *It's been aggravating me for months.* ● **aggravating** ADJ ❑ *Children can be sometimes aggravating and other times delightful.* ● **aggravation** (**aggravations**) N-VAR ❑ *The sounds were a constant aggravation.*

aggregate /ˈægrɪgət/ (**aggregates**) 1 N-COUNT & ADJ BEFORE N An **aggregate** or **aggregate** amount is an amount made up of several smaller amounts. ❑ *...an aggregate of twelve hundred acres spread over four separate parks.* ❑ *...an aggregate loss of £353 million.* 2 PHRASE If one team beats another team **on aggregate**, it wins by getting the higher total over a series of games. [BRIT] ❑ *We were not the better team in that match, but we won on aggregate.*

aggression /əˈgreʃən/ N-UNCOUNT **Aggression** is angry or violent behaviour towards someone. ❑ *...an act of aggression.*
→ see **anger**

Word Partnership Use *aggression* with:

N.	**act of** aggression
PREP.	aggression **against**
ADJ.	**military** aggression, **physical** aggression

aggressive /əˈgresɪv/ 1 ADJ An **aggressive** person behaves angrily or violently towards other people. ❑ *Some children are much more aggressive than others.* ❑ *...aggressive behaviour.* ● **aggressively** ADV ❑ *...rumours she always aggressively denies.* 2 ADJ If you are **aggressive** in your work or other activities, you behave in a forceful way because you are eager to succeed. ❑ *...a very aggressive and competitive executive.*

aggressor /ə'gresə/ (**aggressors**) N-COUNT The **aggressor** is the person or country that starts a fight.

Word Link *griev ≈ heavy, serious : aggrieved, grievance, grieve*

aggrieved /ə'gri:vd/ ADJ If you feel **aggrieved**, you feel upset and angry because of the way you have been treated.

aghast /ə'gɑ:st, ə'gæst/ ADJ If you are **aghast**, you are filled with horror and surprise. [FORMAL]

agile /'ædʒaɪl, AM -dʒəl/ **1** ADJ Someone who is **agile** can move with ease and speed. ❑ *He is very agile for a big man.* • **agility** /ə'dʒɪlɪti/ N-UNCOUNT ❑ *He lacks Bruce's natural agility.* **2** ADJ If you have an **agile** mind, you think quickly and intelligently. • **agility** N-UNCOUNT ❑ *...exercises in mental agility.*

agitate /'ædʒɪteɪt/ (**agitates, agitating, agitated**) V-I If people **agitate for** something, they protest or take part in political activity in order to get it. ❑ *The women had begun to agitate for better conditions.* • **agitation** N-UNCOUNT ❑ *...continuing agitation against the decision.*

agitated /'ædʒɪteɪtɪd/ ADJ If someone is **agitated**, they are very worried or upset, and show this in their behaviour or voice. ❑ *Susan seemed agitated about something.*

agitation /ˌædʒɪ'teɪʃən/ **1** N-UNCOUNT **Agitation** is worry. ❑ *Sheila tried to hide her agitation.* **2** → see also **agitate**

ago /ə'gəʊ/ ADV You use **ago** to refer to past time. ❑ *She died one year ago.*

Usage

You only use **ago** when you are talking about a period of time measured back from the present. If you are talking about a period measured back from some earlier time, you use **before** or **previously**. ❑ *She had died a month before.*

Word Link *agon ≈ struggling : agony, agonize, protagonist*

agonize [BRIT also **agonise**] /'ægənaɪz/ (**agonizes, agonizing, agonized**) V-I If you **agonize over** something, you feel anxious and spend a long time thinking about it. ❑ *I agonize over what to give my wife for Christmas.*

agonizing [BRIT also **agonising**] /'ægənaɪzɪŋ/ ADJ Something that is **agonizing** causes you to feel great physical or mental suffering. ❑ *The wait was agonizing.* ❑ *It was an agonising decision.*

agony /'ægəni/ (**agonies**) N-VAR **Agony** is great physical or mental suffering. ❑ *She called out in agony.* ❑ *...the agonies of parenthood.*

agree /ə'gri:/ (**agrees, agreeing, agreed**) **1** V-T/V-I If you **agree with** someone, you have the same opinion about something. ❑ *I agree with you entirely.* ❑ *We agreed that she was not to be told.* **2** V-T If you **agree to** do something, you say that you will do it. ❑ *He agreed to meet me at my hotel.* **3** V-T/V-I If people **agree on** something or **agree** something, they all decide to have or do something. ❑ *We never agreed a date.* **4** V-I If you **agree with** an action or a suggestion, you approve of it. ❑ *The Cabinet agreed with his plan.* **5** V-I If two stories or totals **agree**, they are the same as each other. ❑ *His statement agrees with the other witnesses' stories.*

agreeable /ə'gri:əbəl/ **1** ADJ If something or someone is **agreeable**, they are pleasant and people like them. ❑ *...an agreeable surprise.* ❑ *He was a very agreeable guest.* **2** ADJ AFTER LINK-V If you are **agreeable to** something or if it is **agreeable to** you, you are willing to do it or to allow it. [FORMAL] ❑ *...a solution that would be agreeable to all.*

Word Link *ment ≈ state, condition : agreement, management, movement*

agreement /ə'gri:mənt/ (**agreements**) **1** N-COUNT An **agreement** is a decision that two or more people, groups, or countries have made together. ❑ *...a legal agreement.* **2** N-UNCOUNT & PHRASE **Agreement** with someone means having the same opinion as they have. You can also say that you are **in agreement with** someone. ❑ *The unions had reached broad agreement on the resolution.* ❑ *Not all scholars are in agreement with her.*

Word Partnership Use *agreement* with:

N.	**peace** agreement, **terms of an** agreement, **trade** agreement **1**
V.	**enter into an** agreement, **sign an** agreement **1**
	reach an agreement **1** **2**

agriculture /'ægrɪkʌltʃə/ N-UNCOUNT **Agriculture** is farming and the methods used to look after crops and animals. • **agricultural** /ˌægrɪ'kʌltʃərəl/ ADJ ❑ *...agricultural research.* → see **farm, grassland, industry**

aground /ə'graʊnd/ ADV If a ship or boat runs **aground**, it gets stuck on the ground in a shallow area of water.

ahead /ə'hed/ **1** ADV Something that is **ahead** is in front of you. If you look **ahead**, you look directly in front of you. ❑ *The road ahead was now blocked.* ❑ *Ahead, he saw the bridge.* ❑ *Brett looked straight ahead.* **2** ADV If you are **ahead** in your work or achievements, you have made more progress than you expected. ❑ *Children in small classes were 1.5 months ahead in reading.* **3** ADV If a person or a team is **ahead** in a competition, they are winning. ❑ *The goal put Dublin 6-1 ahead.* ❑ *Clinton was ahead in the polls.* **4** ADV If you go on **ahead**, you leave for a place before other people. ❑ *I'd have to send Tina on ahead with Rachael.* **5** ADV **Ahead** means in the future. ❑ *A bigger battle is ahead for the president.* ❑ *Book ahead as the restaurant is very popular.* ❑ *...the days ahead.*

Word Partnership Use *ahead* with:

ADV.	**straight** ahead **1**
V.	**get** ahead **4**
	go ahead **1**
	look ahead, **move** ahead **1** **2**
	lie ahead, **plan** ahead **2**
PREP.	**in the days/months/years** ahead **2**
	ahead **of schedule/time** **3**

a'head of **1** PREP If someone or something is **ahead of** you, they are in front of you. ❑ *I saw the* man thirty metres ahead of me. ❑ *She walked ahead of Helene up the steps.* **2** PREP If an event or period of time lies **ahead of** you, it is going to happen or come soon or in the future. ❑ *We have a very busy day ahead of us.* **3** PREP If something happens **ahead of** an event, it happens before that event. If something happens **ahead of** time, it happens earlier than was planned. ❑ *The Prime Minister was speaking ahead of today's meeting.* ❑ *The election was held six months ahead of schedule.* **4** PREP If one person is **ahead of** another, they have made more progress and are more advanced in what they are doing. ❑ *Henry generally stayed ahead of the others in maths.* **5** **ahead of** one's **time** → see **time**

aid /eɪd/ (**aids, aiding, aided**) **1** V-T & N-UNCOUNT To **aid** a person, country, or organization, or to give them **aid**, means to help them by giving them money, equipment, or services. ❑ *...international efforts to aid refugees.* ❑ *They have already promised billions of dollars in aid.* ● **-aided** ❑ *...state-aided schools.* **2** V-T & N-UNCOUNT To **aid** someone or to give them **aid** means to help or assist them. ❑ *...a software system to aid managers in project-planning.* ❑ *He was forced to ask us for aid.* **3** V-T & N-COUNT If something **aids** a process, it makes it easier or more likely to happen. An **aid** is something that makes things easier to do. ❑ *...a medicine designed to relieve pain and aid recovery.* ❑ *...slimming aids.* **4** → see also **first aid** **5** PHRASE If an activity or event is **in aid of** a particular cause, it raises money for that cause. ❑ *...a charity performance in aid of Great Ormond Street Children's Hospital.* **6** PHRASE If you come or go **to** someone's **aid**, you try to help them when they are in danger or difficulty. ❑ *Neighbours rushed to his aid as he fell.*

aide /eɪd/ (**aides**) N-COUNT An **aide** is an assistant to a person with an important job. ❑ *...a presidential aide.*

AIDS /eɪdz/ N-UNCOUNT **AIDS** is an illness which destroys the natural system of protection that the body has against disease. **AIDS** is an abbreviation for 'acquired immune deficiency syndrome'.

Word Partnership Use *AIDS* with:

N.	AIDS **activists**, AIDS **epidemic**, AIDS **patient**, AIDS **research**, **spread of** AIDS, AIDS **victims**
V.	**infected with** AIDS

ailing /ˈeɪlɪŋ/ **1** ADJ If someone is **ailing**, they are ill and not getting better. **2** ADJ An **ailing** business is in difficulty.

ailment /ˈeɪlmənt/ (**ailments**) N-COUNT An **ailment** is an illness, especially one that is not very serious.

aim /eɪm/ (**aims, aiming, aimed**) **1** V-T/V-I If you **aim for** something or **aim to** do it, you plan or hope to achieve it. ❑ *He said he would aim for the 100 metres world record.* ❑ *The appeal aims to raise money for children with special needs.* **2** N-COUNT The **aim** of something that you do is the purpose for which you do it. ❑ *The aim of the festival is to increase awareness of Hindu culture.* **3** V-T PASSIVE If an action or plan **is aimed at** achieving something, it is intended to achieve it. ❑ *The plan is aimed at improving services.* **4** V-T If your action **is aimed at** a particular person, you intend it to affect and influence them. ❑ *Most of their advertisements are aimed at women.* **5** V-T & N-SING If you **aim** a weapon **at** someone or something, you point it towards them before firing. Your **aim** is the act of pointing a weapon at a target or your ability to hit the target. ❑ *He was aiming the rifle at Wade.* **6** PHRASE If you **take aim at** someone or something, you point a loaded weapon at them.

aimless /ˈeɪmləs/ ADJ A person or activity that is **aimless** has no clear purpose or plan. ❑ *...aimless chatter about last night's TV.* ● **aimlessly** ADV ❑ *I wandered around aimlessly.*

ain't /eɪnt/ **Ain't** is used in some dialects of English instead of 'am not', 'aren't', or 'isn't'. Some people consider this use to be incorrect. [SPOKEN]

air /eə/ (**airs, airing, aired**) **1** N-UNCOUNT **Air** is the mixture of gases which forms the earth's atmosphere and which we breathe. ❑ *Keith opened the window and leaned out into the cold air.* **2** N-SING **The air** is the space around things or above the ground. ❑ *...firing their guns in the air.* **3** N-UNCOUNT **Air** is used to refer to travel in aircraft. ❑ *Amy had never travelled by air before.* ❑ *...help towards paying the air fare.* **4** N-SING If someone or something has a particular **air**, they give this general impression. ❑ *She regarded him with an air of amusement.* ❑ *The meal gave the occasion a festive air.* **5** V-T If you **air** your opinions, you make them known to people. ❑ *Both sides aired all their differences.* ● **airing** N-SING ❑ *Their views would at long last get an airing.* **6** V-T If you **air** a room, you let fresh air circulate around it. When

Word Web air

The **air** we breathe has seventeen different **gases**. It is made up mostly of **nitrogen**, not **oxygen**. Recently, human activities have changed the balance in the earth's **atmosphere**. Atmosphere is the air that surrounds the earth. The widespread burning of coal and oil increases the levels of **carbon monoxide** gas. Scientists believe this air **pollution** may cause **global warming**. Certain chemicals used in air conditioners, farming, and manufacturing are the problem. They break down the **ozone layer** around the earth. With less protection from the sun, the air temperature rises and makes the earth warmer. This leads to harmful effects on people, farming, animals, and the natural environment.

Composition of Air

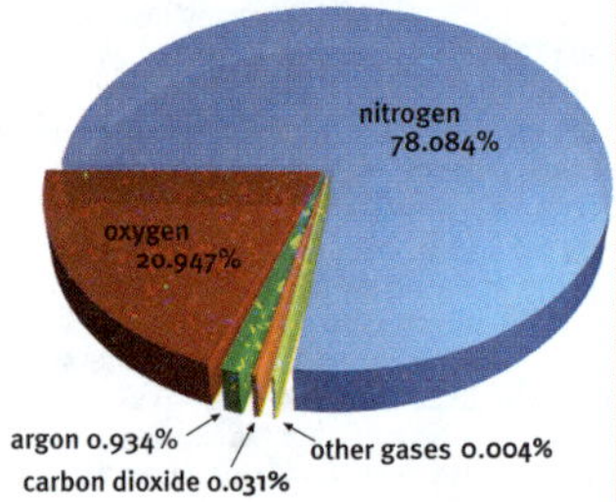

you **air** clothes, you put them in a place where warm air can circulate around them, helping to dry them. **7** PHRASE If you do something to **clear the air**, you do it in order to remove any misunderstandings that there might be. ❑ *An inquiry will clear the air and settle the facts.* **8** PHRASE If a person or programme is **on the air**, they are broadcasting or being broadcast on radio or television. ❑ *I was on the air for two hours.* ❑ *The show first went on the air in 1964.*

→ see Word Web: **air**

→ see **erosion, respiration, wind**

'air base also **airbase** (**air bases**) N-COUNT An **air base** is a military airport.

airborne /'eəbɔːn/ ADJ **Airborne** means flying in the air or coming from the air. ❑ *The aircraft was soon airborne again.* ❑ *...airborne troops.*

→ see **pollution**

ˌair-con'ditioned ADJ If a room is **air-conditioned**, the air in it is kept cool and dry by means of a special machine.

ˌair-con'ditioning also **air conditioning** N-UNCOUNT **Air-conditioning** is a method of providing buildings and vehicles with cool air.

aircraft /'eəkrɑːft, -kræft/

Aircraft is both the singular and the plural form.

N-COUNT An **aircraft** is a vehicle which can fly, for example an aeroplane or a helicopter.

→ see **fly, ship**

airfield /'eəfiːəld/ (**airfields**) N-COUNT An **airfield** is a place where small planes or military aircraft take off and land.

'air force also **airforce** (**air forces**) N-COUNT An **air force** is the part of a country's military organization that is concerned with fighting in the air.

'air hostess (**air hostesses**) N-COUNT An **air hostess** is a woman whose job is to look after passengers in an aircraft. [BRIT, DATED]

airlift /'eəlɪft/ (**airlifts, airlifting, airlifted**) V-T & N-COUNT If people or goods **are airlifted** somewhere, they are carried by air, especially in a war or when land routes are closed. An **airlift** is an operation to do this. ❑ *The injured were airlifted to hospital in Prestwick.* ❑ *...an airlift of food, medicines and blankets.*

airline /'eəlaɪn/ (**airlines**) N-COUNT An **airline** is a company which provides regular services carrying people or goods in aeroplanes.

airliner /'eəlaɪnə/ (**airliners**) N-COUNT An **airliner** is a large aeroplane used for carrying passengers.

airman /'eəmæn/ (**airmen**) N-COUNT An **airman** is a man who serves in his country's air force.

airplane /'eəpleɪn/ (**airplanes**) N-COUNT An **airplane** is the same as an **aeroplane**. [AM]

→ see **fly**

airport /'eəpɔːt/ (**airports**) N-COUNT An **airport** is a place where aircraft land and take off, usually with a lot of buildings and facilities.

'air raid (**air raids**) N-COUNT An **air raid** is an attack in which military aircraft drop bombs on people or places.

airspace /'eəspeɪs/ N-UNCOUNT A country's **airspace** is the part of the sky that is over that country and is considered to belong to that country.

airtight /'eətaɪt/ ADJ If a container is **airtight**, its lid fits so tightly that no air can get in or out.

airwaves /'eəweɪvz/ N-PLURAL If someone says something **over the airwaves** or **on the airwaves**, they say it on the radio or television. [JOURNALISM]

airy /'eəri/ ADJ If a building or room is **airy**, it is large and has plenty of fresh air inside. ❑ *The bathroom has a light and airy feel.*

aisle /aɪl/ (**aisles**) N-COUNT An **aisle** is a long narrow gap that people can walk along between rows of seats in a public building such as a church, or between rows of shelves in a supermarket.

aka **aka** is an abbreviation for 'also known as'; it is used especially when referring to a nickname or stage name. ❑ *...Anna Mae Bullock, aka Tina Turner.*

akin /ə'kɪn/ ADJ AFTER LINK-V If one thing is **akin to** another, it is similar to it in some way. [FORMAL] ❑ *The journey will be more akin to air travel than to a normal train.*

alarm /ə'lɑːm/ (**alarms, alarming, alarmed**) **1** V-T & N-UNCOUNT If something **alarms** you, it makes you afraid or anxious that something unpleasant might happen. This feeling is called **alarm**. ❑ *We could not see what had alarmed him.* ❑ *She sat up in alarm.* • **alarmed** ADJ ❑ *Ministers were alarmed at the new crime figures.* • **alarming** ADJ ❑ *The statistics were even more alarming.* • **alarmingly** ADV ❑ *...the alarmingly high rate of heart disease.* **2** N-COUNT An **alarm** is an automatic device that warns you of danger, for example by ringing a bell. ❑ *He heard the alarm go off.*

Word Partnership	Use *alarm* with:
V.	**cause** alarm **1**
	raise/sound the alarm, **set** the alarm **2**
N.	**alarm** system **2**

a'larm clock (**alarm clocks**) N-COUNT An **alarm clock** is a clock that you can set to make a noise so that it wakes you up at a particular time.

alas /ə'læs/ ADV **Alas** is used to express sadness or regret about something that has happened. [FORMAL] ❑ *...many wonderful people who are, alas, no longer here.*

albeit /ɔːl'biːɪt/ ADV You use **albeit** to introduce a fact or comment which reduces the force or significance of what you have just said. [FORMAL] ❑ *He has a majority, albeit a small one.*

album /'ælbəm/ (**albums**) **1** N-COUNT An **album** is a CD, record, or cassette with music on it, usually several different tracks. ❑ *This new single is taken from their latest album.* **2** N-COUNT An **album** is a book in which you put things such as photographs or stamps that you have collected.

alcohol /'ælkəhɒl, AM -hɔːl/ **1** N-UNCOUNT Drinks that can make people drunk, such as beer, wine, and whisky, can be referred to as **alcohol**. **2** N-UNCOUNT **Alcohol** is a colourless liquid which is found in drinks such as beer, wine, and whisky. It is also used in products such as perfumes and cleaning fluids.

alcoholic /ˌælkə'hɒlɪk, AM -'hɔːl-/ (**alcoholics**) **1** N-COUNT An **alcoholic** is someone who is addicted to alcohol. • **alcoholism** N-UNCOUNT ❑ *His sister died two years ago as a result of alcoholism.*

A

2 ADJ **Alcoholic** drinks contain alcohol.

ale /eɪl/ (**ales**) N-VAR **Ale** is the same as beer.

alert /əˈlɜːt/ (**alerts, alerting, alerted**) 1 ADJ If you are **alert**, you are paying full attention to things around you and are ready to deal with anything that might happen. ❑ *We all have to stay alert.* • **alertness** N-UNCOUNT ❑ *A doctor's alertness saved her son.* 2 ADJ AFTER LINK-V & V-T If you are **alert to** a problem, you are fully aware of it. You can also **alert** someone **to** a dangerous or unpleasant situation. ❑ *The bank is alert to the danger.* ❑ *He wanted to alert people to the activities of the group.* 3 N-COUNT An **alert** is a situation in which people prepare themselves for something dangerous that may happen soon. ❑ *...a security alert.* 4 PHRASE When soldiers, police, or other authorities are **on alert**, they are ready to deal with anything that may happen.

ˈA level (**A levels**) N-VAR **A levels** are British educational qualifications which schoolchildren take when they are about eighteen years old.

algae /ˈældʒi, ˈælgaɪ/ N-UNCOUNT **Algae** is a type of plant with no stems or leaves that grows in water or on damp surfaces.
→ see **plant**

algebra /ˈældʒɪbrə/ N-UNCOUNT **Algebra** is a type of mathematics in which letters are used to represent quantities.
→ see **mathematics**

Word Link	*ali ≈ other : alias, alibi, alien*

alias /ˈeɪliəs/ (**aliases**) N-COUNT & PREP An **alias** is a false name, especially one used by a criminal or actor. ❑ *He was travelling under an alias.* ❑ *...Richard Thorp, alias Alan Turner.*

alibi /ˈælɪbaɪ/ (**alibis**) N-COUNT If you have an **alibi**, you can prove that you were somewhere else when a crime was committed.

alien /ˈeɪliən/ (**aliens**) 1 ADJ **Alien** is used to describe someone or something that belongs to a different country, race, group, or culture. This use is considered offensive by some people. ❑ *...alone in an alien culture.* 2 N-COUNT An **alien** is someone who is not a legal citizen of the country in which they live. [TECHNICAL] 3 ADJ AFTER LINK-V If something is **alien to** you, it is not the way you would normally feel or behave. ❑ *Such an attitude is alien to most businessmen.* 4 N-COUNT In science fiction, an **alien** is a creature from outer space.

alienate /ˈeɪliəneɪt/ (**alienates, alienating, alienated**) 1 V-T If you **alienate** someone such as a friend, you cause them to lose their friendly relationship with you. ❑ *The government cannot afford to alienate either group.* 2 V-T If you **are alienated from** something, you are emotionally or intellectually separated from it. ❑ *They are rejected by their families and alienated from society.* • **alienated** ADJ ❑ *...alienated young people.* • **alienation** N-UNCOUNT ❑ *...her sense of alienation from the world.*

alight /əˈlaɪt/ (**alights, alighting, alighted**) 1 ADJ AFTER LINK-V If something is **alight**, it is burning. ❑ *Several buildings were set alight.* 2 ADJ AFTER LINK-V If you describe someone's face or expression as **alight**, you mean it shows that they are feeling a strong emotion such as excitement or happiness. ❑ *Her eyes were alight with enjoyment of life.* 3 V-I When you **alight from** a train or bus, you get out of it after a journey. [FORMAL]

align /əˈlaɪn/ (**aligns, aligning, aligned**) 1 V-T If you **align yourself with** a particular group, you support their political aims. • **alignment** (**alignments**) N-VAR ❑ *This could affect political alignment in the region.* 2 V-T If objects **are aligned with** each other, they are placed in a precise position in relation to each other. ❑ *Keep your hips and knees aligned with your toes.* • **alignment** N-UNCOUNT ❑ *...the alignment of the planets.*

Word Link	*like ≈ similar : alike, likeness, likewise*

alike /əˈlaɪk/ 1 ADJ AFTER LINK-V & ADV If two or more people or things are **alike**, they are similar. ❑ *We looked very alike.* ❑ *They assume that all men and women think alike.* 2 ADV You use **alike** after mentioning two or more people, groups, or things in order to emphasize that you are referring to both or all of them. ❑ *The techniques are used by big and small firms alike.*

Thesaurus	*alike* Also look up:
ADJ.	comparable, equal, equivalent, matching, parallel, similar; *(ant.)* different 1

ˈA-list 1 ADJ An **A-list** celebrity is a celebrity who is very famous indeed. ❑ *...an A-list Hollywood actress.* ❑ *Quinn's connections are strictly A-list.* 2 N-SING An **A-list** of celebrities is a group of celebrities who are very famous indeed. ❑ *...the A-list of Hollywood stars.*

alive /əˈlaɪv/ 1 ADJ AFTER LINK-V If people or animals are **alive**, they are living. ❑ *The treatment kept her alive for over a year.* 2 ADJ AFTER LINK-V If an activity, organization, or situation is **alive**, it continues to exist or to function. ❑ *The big factories are trying to stay alive by cutting costs.* 3 ADJ If you say that someone seems **alive**, you mean that they seem to be lively and to enjoy everything that they do. ❑ *I never expected to feel so alive in my life again.* 4 ADJ & PHRASE If a place is **alive with** something, a lot of people or things are there and it seems busy or exciting. You can say people, places, or events **come alive** when they start to be active or lively. ❑ *The forest was alive with the sounds of many different animals.*

Word Partnership	Use *alive* with:
ADJ.	**dead** or alive 1
ADV.	alive **and well** 1
	still alive 1 2
V.	**found** alive, **keep** ***someone/something*** alive 1
	stay alive 1 2
	feel alive 3
	come alive 4

all /ɔːl/ 1 QUANT You use **all** to indicate that you are referring to the whole of a group or thing or to everyone or everything of a particular kind. ❑ *He was talking to all of us.* ❑ *I spent all I had, every* *last penny.* ❑ *We all admire your dedication.* **2** DET & PREDET You use **all** to refer to the whole of a period of time. ❑ *George had to cut grass all afternoon.* ❑ *She's worked all her life.* **3** PRON You use **all** to refer to a situation or to life in general. ❑ *All is silent on the island now.* **4** ADV You use **all** to emphasize the extent to which something happens or is true. ❑ *I got scared and left her all alone.* ❑ *...universities all round the world.* **5** ADV **All** is used in expressions such as **all the more** or **all the better** to mean even more or even better than before. ❑ *The living room is decorated in pale colours that make it all the more airy.* **6** ADV You use **all** when you are talking about an equal score in a game. **7** PHRASE You say **above all** to emphasize that the thing you are mentioning is the most important point. ❑ *Above all, chairs should be comfortable.* **8** PHRASE You use **after all** when introducing a statement which supports or helps explain something you have just said. ❑ *They know that there is a lot to lose. After all, health care is a $900 billion industry.* **9** PHRASE You use **after all** when you are saying that something that you thought might not be true is in fact true. ❑ *There wasn't much wrong after all.* **10** PHRASE You use **all in all** to introduce a summary or generalization. ❑ *I think, all in all, my life's been great.* **11** PHRASE You use **at all** to emphasize a negative or a question. ❑ *She never really liked him at all.* **12** PHRASE You use **for all** to say that a particular fact does not affect or contradict what you are saying, although it may seem to do so. ❑ *For all his faults, he was kind and considerate.* **13** PHRASE **In all** means in total. ❑ *In all some 15 million people live in the selected areas.* **14** PHRASE You use **of all** to emphasize the words 'first' or 'last', or a superlative adjective or adverb. ❑ *First of all, answer these questions.* ❑ *Now she faces her hardest task of all.*

Usage

All is often used to mean the same as **whole** but when used in front of plurals, **all** and **whole** have different meanings. For example, if you say, **'All the buildings have been destroyed'**, you mean that every building has been destroyed. If you say **'Whole buildings have been destroyed'**, you mean that some buildings have been destroyed completely.

Allah /ˈælə, ˈælɑː/ N-PROPER **Allah** is the name of God in Islam.

ˌall-Aˈmerican ADJ BEFORE N If you describe someone as an **all-American** boy or girl, you mean that they seem to have all the typical qualities that are valued by ordinary Americans, such as patriotism and healthy good looks.

ˌall-aˈround → see **all-round**

allay /əˈleɪ/ (**allays, allaying, allayed**) V-T If you **allay** someone's fears or doubts, you stop them feeling afraid or doubtful. [FORMAL] ❑ *He did what he could to allay his wife's fears.*

allegation /ˌælɪˈgeɪʃən/ (**allegations**) N-COUNT An **allegation** is a statement saying that someone has done something wrong. ❑ *...allegations of theft.*

allege /əˈledʒ/ (**alleges, alleging, alleged**) V-T If you **allege** that someone has done something wrong, you say it but do not prove it. [FORMAL] ❑ *The accused is alleged to have killed a man.* ❑ *It is alleged that he was threatened.* ❑ *...protests at the alleged beatings.* ● **allegedly** ADV ❑ *His van allegedly struck them as they were crossing a street.*

allegiance /əˈliːdʒəns/ (**allegiances**) N-VAR Your **allegiance** is your support for and loyalty to a group, person, or belief. ❑ *...his allegiance to his country of birth.*

allergic /əˈlɜːdʒɪk/ ADJ If you are **allergic to** something, or have an **allergic** reaction **to** it, you become ill or get a rash when you eat it, smell it, or touch it.
→ see **peanut**

allergy /ˈælədʒi/ (**allergies**) N-VAR If you have a particular **allergy**, you become ill or get a rash when you eat, smell, or touch something that does not normally make people ill. ❑ *Allergy to cats is one of the commonest causes of asthma.* ❑ *...food allergies.*

alleviate /əˈliːvieɪt/ (**alleviates, alleviating, alleviated**) V-T If you **alleviate** pain, suffering, or an unpleasant condition, you make it less intense or severe. ❑ *...the problem of alleviating mass poverty.* ● **alleviation** N-UNCOUNT ❑ *...the alleviation of the refugees' misery.*

alley /ˈæli/ (**alleys**) N-COUNT An **alley** or **alleyway** is a narrow passage or street with buildings or walls on both sides.

alliance /əˈlaɪəns/ (**alliances**) N-VAR An **alliance** is a relationship in which different countries, political parties, or organizations work together for some purpose. You can also refer to the group that is formed in this way as an **alliance.** ❑ *He is sure that the alliance will hold together.*

allied /ˈælaɪd, AM əˈlaɪd/ **1** ADJ BEFORE N **Allied** countries, political parties, or groups are united by a formal agreement. ❑ *...forces from three allied nations.* **2** ADJ If one thing or group is **allied to** another, the two things are related because they have particular qualities or characteristics in common. ❑ *...lectures on subjects allied to health, beauty and fitness.* ❑ *...doctors, and allied medical professionals.* **3** → see also **ally**

alligator /ˈælɪgeɪtə/ (**alligators**) N-COUNT An **alligator** is a large reptile with short legs, a long tail and very powerful jaws.

alligator

allocate /ˈæləkeɪt/ (**allocates, allocating, allocated**) V-T If one item or share of something **is allocated to** a particular person or **for** a particular purpose, it is given to that person or used for that purpose. ❑ *The budget allocated $7.3 billion for development programmes.* ❑ *Our plan is to allocate one member of staff to handle appointments.* ● **allocation** N-UNCOUNT ❑ *...the allocation of land for new homes.*

allot /əˈlɒt/ (**allots, allotting, allotted**) V-T If something **is allotted to** someone, it is given to them as their share. ❑ *We were allotted half an hour to discuss the issue.* ❑ *I was allotted just £2000 for a part-time secretary or a driver.* ● **allotment** (**allotments**) N-COUNT ❑ *...their full allotment of $300 million.*

allotment /əˈlɒtmənt/ (**allotments**) N-COUNT In Britain, an **allotment** is a small area of land which a person rents to grow vegetables on.

ˌall-ˈout ADJ BEFORE N & ADV You use **all-out** to talk about actions that are carried out in a very

A

energetic and determined way, using all the resources available. ❑ *...an all-out effort to bring the fire under control.* ❑ *We will be going all out to ensure it doesn't happen again.*

allow /əˈlaʊ/ (**allows, allowing, allowed**) **1** V-T If someone **is allowed to** do something, it is all right for them to do it. ❑ *The children are not allowed to watch violent TV programmes.* **2** V-T If you **are allowed** something, you are given permission to have it or are given it. ❑ *Gifts like chocolates or flowers are allowed.* ❑ *He should be allowed the occasional treat.* **3** V-T If you **allow** something **to** happen, you do not prevent it. ❑ *If the soil is allowed to dry out the tree could die.* **4** V-T If something **allows** a particular thing **to** happen, it makes it possible. ❑ *The money they saved allowed them to help others.* **5** V-T If you **allow** a length of time or an amount of something **for** a particular purpose, you include it in your planning. ❑ *Please allow 28 days for delivery.*

▶ **allow for** PHR-VERB If you **allow for** certain problems or expenses, you include some extra time or money in your planning so that you can deal with them if they occur. ❑ *Allow for taxes being 15 to 20 per cent higher.*

Thesaurus *allow* Also look up:

V. approve, consent, tolerate; *(ant.)* disallow, forbid, prohibit, prevent **3**
let, support **4**

allowance /əˈlaʊəns/ (**allowances**) **1** N-COUNT An **allowance** is money that is given regularly to someone. **2** PHRASE If you **make allowances for** certain circumstances in a situation, you take them into consideration when making your plans. ❑ *Schools need to make allowances for children with special needs.* **3** PHRASE If you **make allowances for** someone who is behaving badly, you deal with them less severely than you would normally, usually because of a problem that they have. ❑ *You make allowances for your children when they are feeling ill.*

ˌall ˈright also **alright** **1** ADJ AFTER LINK-V If you say that someone or something is **all right**, you mean that you find them satisfactory but not especially good. ❑ *Most of the teachers are all right.* ❑ *The red wine sauce was all right.* **2** ADJ AFTER LINK-V If someone is **all right**, they are well or safe. ❑ *I'm all right now.* ❑ *Are you feeling all right?* **3** CONVENTION You say **'all right'** when you are agreeing to something. ❑ *'I think you should go now.'—'All right.'*

ˌall-ˈround [AM also **all-around**] **1** ADJ BEFORE N An **all-round** person is good at a lot of different things. ❑ *He is a great all-round player* **2** ADJ BEFORE N **All-round** means doing or relating to all aspects of a job or activity. ❑ *...an excellent all-round guide on shopping for the best foods.*

ˈall-time ADJ **All-time** is used when you are comparing all the things of a particular type that there have ever been. ❑ *...her all-time favourite film.*

allude /əˈluːd/ (**alludes, alluding, alluded**) V-I If you **allude to** something, you mention it in an indirect way. [FORMAL] ❑ *She alluded to his absence in vague terms.*

allure /əˈljʊə, AM əˈlʊr/ N-UNCOUNT The **allure of** something is a pleasing or exciting quality that it has. ❑ *The antique cars had lost their allure.*

allusion /əˈluːʒən/ (**allusions**) N-VAR An **allusion to** something is an indirect or vague reference to it. ❑ *She made an allusion to the events in Los Angeles.* ❑ *His poetry is dense with literary allusions.*

ˈall-ˌweather ADJ **All-weather** sports take place on an artificial surface instead of on grass. ❑ *...all-weather racing.* ❑ *...an all-weather tennis court.*

ally (**allies, allying, allied**) **1** N-COUNT /ˈælaɪ/ An **ally** is a country, organization, or person that helps and supports another. ❑ *...the Western allies.* **2** V-T /əˈlaɪ/ If you **ally yourself with** someone, you support them. ❑ *Ten years later he allied himself with the British.* **3** → see also **allied**

almighty /ɔːlˈmaɪti/ **1** N-PROPER **The Almighty** is another name for God. ❑ *...a hymn to the Almighty.* **2** ADJ BEFORE N An **almighty** row, problem, or mistake is a very serious one. ❑ *Apparently they had an almighty row.*

almond /ˈɑːmənd/ (**almonds**) N-COUNT An **almond** is a kind of pale oval nut.

Word Link *most ≈ superlative degree : almost, foremost, utmost*

almost /ˈɔːlməʊst/ ADV **Almost** means very nearly, but not completely. ❑ *The camps are almost full.* ❑ *I stood up and almost fell.*

Thesaurus *almost* Also look up:

ADV. about, most, practically, virtually

Word Link *loft ≈ air : aloft, loft, lofty*

aloft /əˈlɒft, AM əˈlɔːft/ ADV Something that is **aloft** is in the air or off the ground. [LITERARY] ❑ *After the result was announced, Mr Peres was raised aloft by his supporters.*

alone /əˈləʊn/ **1** ADJ AFTER LINK-V When you are **alone**, you are not with any other people. ❑ *She wanted to be alone.* **2** ADJ AFTER LINK-V A person who is **alone** is someone who has no family or friends. ❑ *Never in her life had she felt so alone, so abandoned.* **3** ADJ AFTER LINK-V If one person is **alone with** another, they are together, with nobody else present. ❑ *I couldn't imagine why he would want to be alone with me.* ❑ *We'll be alone together, quite like old times.* **4** ADV If you do something **alone**, you do it without help from other people. ❑ *Do you prefer working with groups or do you prefer working alone?* **5** ADV You say that one person or thing **alone** does something when you are emphasizing that only one person or thing is involved. ❑ *The cost of the damage alone amounted to billions of dollars.* **6** to **leave** someone **alone** → see **leave**

Thesaurus *alone* Also look up:

ADJ. solitary **1** **2**

along /əˈlɒŋ, AM əˈlɔːŋ/ **1** PREP If you move or look **along** something, you move or look towards one end of it. ❑ *Newman walked along the street.* ❑ *The young man led Mark along a corridor.* ❑ *I looked along the length of the building.* **2** PREP & ADV If something is situated **along** a road, river, or corridor, it is situated in it or beside it. ❑ *Half the houses along the road were for sale.* ❑ *Two thirds of the way along, turn right.* **3** ADV If something is coming **along** in a particular way, it is progressing in that way.

a

❑ *Everything was coming along fine after all.* **4** ADV If you **take** someone **along** when you go somewhere, you take them with you. If someone **comes along**, they come to a particular place. ❑ *My parents went to all the musicals and plays and always took me along.* ❑ *Bring along your friends and colleagues.* **5** PHRASE You use **all along** to say that something has existed or been the case throughout a period of time. ❑ *She had been planning to leave Hungary all along.* **6** PHRASE If you do something **along with** someone else, you both do it. If you take one thing **along with** another, you take both things. ❑ *The baby's mother escaped along with two other children.*

alongside /əˌlɒŋˈsaɪd, AM -ˌlɔːŋ-/ **1** PREP & ADV If something is **alongside** something else, it is next to it. ❑ *He walked alongside Central Park.* ❑ *I rode the bicycle and he ran alongside.* **2** PREP If people or systems work or exist **alongside** each other, they work or exist in the same place or in the same situation. ❑ *Volunteers work alongside local staff.*

aloof /əˈluːf/ **1** ADJ If you say that someone is **aloof**, you think they are not very friendly and that they try to keep away from other people. **2** ADJ AFTER LINK-V If you stay **aloof from** something, you do not become involved with it. ❑ *The Government is keeping aloof from the situation.*

aloud /əˈlaʊd/ ADV When you speak or read **aloud**, you speak so that other people can hear you. ❑ *When we were children, our father read aloud to us, usually after supper.*

alphabet /ˈælfəbet/ (**alphabets**) N-COUNT The **alphabet** is the set of letters in a fixed order which is used for writing the words of a language.

alphabetical /ˌælfəˈbetɪkəl/ ADJ BEFORE N **Alphabetical** means arranged according to the normal order of the letters in the alphabet. ❑ *...arranged in strict alphabetical order.*

alpine /ˈælpaɪn/ ADJ **Alpine** means existing in or relating to mountains. ❑ *...alpine plants.*

already /ˌɔːlˈredi/ **1** ADV If something has **already** happened, it has happened before the present time. ❑ *I have already started making baby clothes.* ❑ *They've spent nearly a billion dollars on it already.* ❑ *She had already told me that it was none of our business.* **2** ADV You use **already** to say that a situation exists at this present moment or that it exists at an earlier time than expected. You use **already** after the verb 'be' or an auxiliary verb, or before a verb if there is no auxiliary. ❑ *He was already late for his appointment.* ❑ *Is it five o'clock already?* ❑ *Various insurance schemes already exist for this purpose.*

Usage

In British English, **already** and **yet** are usually used with the present perfect tense. ❑ *I have already started knitting baby clothes.* ❑ *Have they said sorry or not yet?* In American English, a past tense is commonly used. ❑ *She already told the neighbours not to come.* ❑ *I didn't get any sleep yet.*

alright /ˌɔːlˈraɪt/ → see **all right**

also /ˈɔːlsəʊ/ **1** ADV You use **also** when you are giving more information about a person or thing. ❑ *The designer, Linley, also owns a restaurant.* ❑ *We've got a big table and also some stools and benches.* **2** ADV You can use **also** to say that the same fact applies to someone or something else. ❑ *The UN says six other civilians were also injured.*

Usage

Also and **too** are similar in meaning. **Also** never comes at the end of a clause, whereas **too** usually comes at the end. ❑ *He was also an artist and lived at Compton.* ❑ *He's a singer and an actor too.*

Thesaurus *also* Also look up:

ADV. additionally, furthermore, plus, still **1**
and, likewise, too **2**

Word Link *alt ≈ high : altar, altitude, alto*

altar /ˈɔːltə/ (**altars**) N-COUNT An **altar** is a holy table in a church or temple.

alter /ˈɔːltə/ (**alters, altering, altered**) V-T/V-I If something **alters**, or if you **alter** it, it changes. ❑ *Not much had altered in the village.* ❑ *The government has altered the rules.* ● **alteration** (**alterations**) N-VAR ❑ *There were a few minor alterations to the cast.*

alternate (**alternates, alternating, alternated**) **1** V-I /ˈɔːltəneɪt/ When you **alternate between** two things, you regularly do or use one thing and then the other. ❑ *I alternated between feeling freezing cold and boiling hot.* **2** V-I When one thing **alternates with** another, the two things regularly occur, one after the other. ❑ *Her aggressive moods alternated with more gentle states.* **3** ADJ BEFORE N /ɔːlˈtɜːnət/ **Alternate** actions, events, or processes regularly occur after each other. ❑ *They were decorated with alternate bands of colour.* ● **alternately** ADV ❑ *He lived alternately in Florence and Naples.* **4** ADJ BEFORE N If something happens on **alternate** days, it happens on one day, then happens on every second day after that. In the same way, something can happen in **alternate** weeks or years. ❑ *Some government offices open on alternate Saturdays.* **5** ADJ BEFORE N In American English, **alternate** is used to describe something that can exist or that you can do instead of something else. The British word is **alternative**. ❑ *He sent Congress an alternate version of the bill.* ● **alternately** ADV ❑ *Alternately, the coconut can be toasted.*

alternative /ɔːlˈtɜːnətɪv/ (**alternatives**) **1** N-COUNT & ADJ BEFORE N An **alternative** is something that can exist or you can do instead of something else. ❑ *How about natural gas? Is that an alternative?* ❑ *There were alternative methods of travel available.* **2** ADJ BEFORE N **Alternative** is used to describe things which are different from traditional or established things of their kind. ❑ *...alternative medicine.*

alternatively /ɔːlˈtɜːnətɪvli/ ADV You use **alternatively** to introduce a suggestion or to mention something different from what has just been stated. ❑ *It takes eight hours to drive from Calais. Alternatively, you can fly there.*

although /ɔːlˈðəʊ/ **1** CONJ You use **although** to introduce a statement which contrasts with something else that you are saying. ❑ *Although I was only six, I can remember seeing it on TV.* ❑ *Their system worked, although no one was sure how.* **2** CONJ **Although** is used to introduce clauses that modify what is being said or that add further information. ❑ *The restaurant was closed for the night, although lights were still lit in the dining-room.*

A

Thesaurus *although* Also look up:

CONJ. despite, though, while 1 2

Word Link *alt ≈ high : altar, altitude, alto*

altitude /ˈæltɪtjuːd, AM -tuːd/ (**altitudes**) N-VAR If something is at a particular **altitude**, it is at that height above sea level. ❑ *As we lost altitude, the wind became stronger.*

alto /ˈæltəʊ/ (**altos**) N-COUNT An **alto** is a woman with a low singing voice, or a man with a high singing voice.

altogether /ˌɔːltəˈgeðə/ 1 ADV You use **altogether** to emphasize that something has stopped, been done, or finished completely. ❑ *His tour had to be cancelled altogether.* 2 ADV You use **altogether** in front of an adjective or adverb to emphasize that adjective or adverb. ❑ *This wine has an altogether stronger flavour.* ❑ *The choice of language is altogether different.* 3 ADV You use **altogether** to indicate that the amount you are mentioning is a total. ❑ *There were 11 of us altogether.*

altruism /ˈæltruɪzəm/ N-UNCOUNT **Altruism** is unselfish concern for other people's happiness and welfare. • **altruistic** ADJ ❑ *The company was not being entirely altruistic.*

aluminium /ˌæluːˈmɪniəm/ [AM **aluminum**] /əˈluːmɪnəm/ N-UNCOUNT **Aluminium** is a lightweight metal used for making things such as cooking equipment and aircraft parts.

always /ˈɔːlweɪz/ 1 ADV If you **always** do something, you do it regularly, whenever a particular situation arises. ❑ *Always lock your garage.* ❑ *David always collects Alistair from school.* 2 ADV If you **always** do a particular thing, you do it all the time, continuously. ❑ *He has always been the family solicitor.* ❑ *He was always cheerful.* 3 ADV You use **always** in expressions such as **can always** or **could always** when you are making suggestions or giving advice. ❑ *I guess I can always ring Jean.*

Thesaurus *always* Also look up:

ADV. consistently, constantly, regularly 1
continuously, endlessly, repeatedly; (*ant.*) never, rarely 2

am /əm, STRONG æm/ **Am** is the first person singular of the present tense of **be**.

a.m. /ˌeɪ ˈem/ **a.m.** after a number indicates that the number refers to a particular time between midnight and noon. ❑ *Visitor Centre and shop open 9 a.m.–5 p.m.*

amalgamate /əˈmælgəmeɪt/ (**amalgamates, amalgamating, amalgamated**) V-T/V-I When two or more organizations **amalgamate**, or when they **are amalgamated**, they become one large organization. ❑ *The two firms have amalgamated.* • **amalgamation** N-UNCOUNT ❑ *...an amalgamation of the two parties.*

amass /əˈmæs/ (**amasses, amassing, amassed**) V-T If you **amass** something such as money, you gradually get a lot of it. ❑ *She has amassed a personal fortune of £8 million.*

Word Link *eur ≈ one who does : amateur, chauffeur, entrepreneur*

amateur /ˈæmətə, AM -tʃɜːr/ (**amateurs**) N-COUNT An **amateur** is someone who does a particular activity as a hobby, not as a job. ❑ *He continued racing for another year as an amateur.* ❑ *...amateur dramatic productions.*

amaze /əˈmeɪz/ (**amazes, amazing, amazed**) V-T If something **amazes** you, it surprises you very much. ❑ *He amazed us with his knowledge of Welsh history.* • **amazed** ADJ ❑ *I was amazed to learn she was still writing her stories.*

Word Partnership Use *amaze* with:

V. **continue to** amaze, **never cease to** amaze
N. amaze **your friends**

amazement /əˈmeɪzmənt/ N-UNCOUNT **Amazement** is what you feel if you are very surprised by something. ❑ *Both men stared at her in amazement.* ❑ *To my amazement, Peterson disagreed.*

amazing /əˈmeɪzɪŋ/ ADJ If something is **amazing**, it is very surprising and makes you feel pleasure or admiration. ❑ *It's the most amazing thing to watch.* ❑ *It's amazing how people collect so much stuff.* • **amazingly** ADV ❑ *She was an amazingly good cook.*

Thesaurus *amazing* Also look up:

ADJ. astonishing, astounding, extraordinary, incredible, stunning, wonderful

ambassador /æmˈbæsədə/ (**ambassadors**) N-COUNT An **ambassador** is an important official living in a foreign country who represents the government of his or her own country.

amber /ˈæmbə/ ADJ Something that is **amber** in colour is orange or yellowish-brown.

ambience also **ambiance** /ˈæmbiəns/ N-SING The **ambience** of a place is its character and atmosphere. [LITERARY] ❑ *The overall ambience of the room is cosy.*

ambiguity /ˌæmbɪˈgjuːɪti/ (**ambiguities**) N-VAR You say that there is **ambiguity** when something can be understood in more than one way.

ambiguous /æmˈbɪgjʊəs/ ADJ Something that is **ambiguous** can be understood in more than one way. ❑ *They made a few ambiguous remarks.* • **ambiguously** ADV ❑ *...an ambiguously worded document.*

ambition /æmˈbɪʃən/ (**ambitions**) 1 N-COUNT If you have an **ambition** to achieve something, you want very much to achieve it. ❑ *His ambition is to sail round the world.* 2 N-UNCOUNT **Ambition** is the desire to be successful, rich, or powerful. ❑ *He is brilliant, talented and full of ambition.*

ambitious /æmˈbɪʃəs/ 1 ADJ Someone who is **ambitious** wants to be successful, rich, or powerful. 2 ADJ An **ambitious** idea or plan is on a large scale and needs a lot of work to be successful.

ambivalent /æmˈbɪvələnt/ ADJ If you are **ambivalent about** something, you are not sure exactly what you think about it. ❑ *She remained ambivalent about her marriage.*

amble /ˈæmbəl/ (**ambles, ambling, ambled**) V-I When you **amble** somewhere, you walk there slowly and in a relaxed manner. ❑ *They slowly ambled back to the car.*

ambulance /ˈæmbjʊləns/ (**ambulances**)

N-COUNT An **ambulance** is a vehicle for taking people to and from hospital.

ambush /ˈæmbʊʃ/ (**ambushes, ambushing, ambushed**) V-T & N-COUNT If people **ambush** their enemies, they attack them after hiding and waiting for them. The attack is called an **ambush**. ❑ *...rebels ambushed and killed 10 patrolmen.*

amen /ˌɑːˈmen, ˌeɪ-/ CONVENTION **Amen** is said or sung by Christians at the end of a prayer.

amend /əˈmend/ (**amends, amending, amended**) **1** V-T If you **amend** something that has been written or said, you change it. ❑ *They voted to amend the constitution.* **2** PHRASE If you **make amends** when you have harmed someone, you show you are sorry by doing something to please them. ❑ *He wanted to make amends for causing their marriage to fail.*

amendment /əˈmendmənt/ (**amendments**) N-COUNT An **amendment** is a section that is added to a law or rule in order to change it.

amenity /əˈmiːnɪti, AM -ˈmen-/ (**amenities**) N-COUNT **Amenities** are things such as shopping centres or sports facilities that are for people's convenience or enjoyment. ❑ *The hotel amenities include a health club and spa.*
→ see **hotel**

American /əmˈerɪkən/ (**Americans**) ADJ & N-COUNT **American** means belonging or relating to the United States of America. An **American** is someone who comes from the United States of America. ❑ *...the American economy.* ❑ *...an American living in London.*

Aˌmerican ˈfootball → see **football**

amiable /ˈeɪmiəbəl/ ADJ Someone who is **amiable** is friendly and pleasant. ❑ *...an educated, amiable and decent man.* • **amiably** ADV ❑ *We chatted amiably about old friends.*

amicable /ˈæmɪkəbəl/ ADJ When people have an **amicable** relationship, they are pleasant to each other and solve their problems without quarrelling. ❑ *Our discussions were amicable and productive.* ❑ *...an amicable agreement.* • **amicably** ADV ❑ *Mr Taylor divorced amicably from his wife.*

amid /əˈmɪd/ **1** PREP If something happens **amid** other things, it happens while the other things are happening. [LITERARY] ❑ *Amid the excitement, she jumped into her car.* **2** PREP If something is **amid** other things, it is surrounded by them. [LITERARY] ❑ *She lived in a tiny cottage amid clusters of trees.*

amidst /əˈmɪdst/ PREP **Amidst** means the same as **amid**.

amiss /əˈmɪs/ ADJ AFTER LINK-V If you say that something is **amiss**, you mean there is something wrong.

ammonia /əˈməʊniə/ N-UNCOUNT **Ammonia** is a colourless liquid or gas with a strong smell.

ammunition /ˌæmjʊˈnɪʃən/ **1** N-UNCOUNT **Ammunition** consists of bullets and rockets that are made to be fired from guns. **2** N-UNCOUNT If you use information as **ammunition**, you use it against someone. ❑ *It helps to have details as ammunition.*

amnesty /ˈæmnɪsti/ (**amnesties**) **1** N-COUNT If a prisoner is granted an **amnesty**, they are officially pardoned. ❑ *He announced a general amnesty for political prisoners.* **2** N-COUNT An **amnesty** is a period of time during which people can confess to a crime or give up weapons without being punished.

among /əˈmʌŋ/ **1** PREP A person or thing that is **among** a group of people or things is surrounded by them or is with them. ❑ *They walked among the crowds.* ❑ *The houses are set among tidy gardens.* ❑ *I was brought up among people who read and wrote a lot.* **2** PREP If someone or something is **among** a group, they are a member of that group. ❑ *A British man was among the people killed.* ❑ *Among his purchases were several books.* **3** PREP If an opinion or situation exists **among** a group of people, they have it or experience it. If something happens **among** a group of people, they do it. ❑ *There is concern among book and magazine sellers.* ❑ *We discussed it among ourselves.* **4** PREP If something is divided **among** three or more people, they all get a part of it.

> **Usage**
>
> If there are more than two people or things, you should use **among**. If there are only two people or things, you should use **between**. **Amongst** is slightly old-fashioned.

amongst /əˈmʌŋst/ PREP **Amongst** means the same as **among**.

amount /əˈmaʊnt/ (**amounts, amounting, amounted**) **1** N-COUNT An **amount of** something is how much of it you have, need, or get. ❑ *He needs that amount of money to survive.* ❑ *I still do a certain amount of work.* **2** V-I If something **amounts to** a particular total, all the parts of it add up to that total. ❑ *The total rain and snowfall amounted to 50mm.* **3** PHRASE If you say that there are **any amount of** things or people, you mean that there are a lot of them. ❑ *There are any amount of clubs you could join.*
▶ **amount to** PHR-VERB If you say that one thing **amounts to** something else, you mean the first thing is the same as the second. ❑ *The banks have what amounts to a monopoly.*

amp /æmp/ (**amps**) N-COUNT An **amp** is a unit which is used for measuring electric current. ❑ *...a 3 amp fuse.*

> **Word Link** *ampl ≈ large : ample, amplifier, amplify*

ample /ˈæmpəl/ ADJ If there is an **ample** amount of something, there is enough of it and some extra. ❑ *There'll be ample opportunity to relax.* ❑ *There's ample space for a good-sized kitchen.* • **amply** ADV ❑ *Its 160 pages are amply illustrated.*

amplifier /ˈæmplɪfaɪə/ (**amplifiers**) N-COUNT An **amplifier** is an electronic device in a radio or stereo system, which causes sounds or signals to become louder.

amplify /ˈæmplɪfaɪ/ (**amplifies, amplifying, amplified**) **1** V-T To **amplify** a sound means to make it louder. ❑ *Most hearing aids amplify sounds to the eardrum.* • **amplification** /ˌæmplɪfɪˈkeɪʃən/ N-UNCOUNT ❑ *...an electronic amplification system.* **2** V-T To **amplify** an idea, feeling, or statement means to increase its strength or intensity. ❑ *Her anxiety about the world was amplifying her personal fears.*

amputate /ˈæmpjʊteɪt/ (**amputates, amputating, amputated**) V-T If a surgeon **amputates** someone's arm or leg, he or she cuts it off in an operation. ❑ *He had to have one leg* amputated. ● **amputation** (**amputations**) N-VAR ❑ *...the amputation of limbs.*

amuse /ə'mju:z/ (**amuses, amusing, amused**) 1 V-T If something **amuses** you, it makes you want to laugh or smile. ❑ *The thought seemed to amuse him.* 2 V-T If you **amuse yourself**, you do something in order to pass the time and not become bored. ❑ *I always invented stories to amuse myself.*

amused /ə'mju:zd/ ADJ If you are **amused** by something, it makes you want to laugh or smile. ❑ *He was amused to learn that he and O'Brien had similar ideas.*

amusement /ə'mju:zmənt/ (**amusements**) 1 N-UNCOUNT **Amusement** is the feeling that you have when you think that something is funny. ❑ *He stopped and watched with amusement.* 2 N-UNCOUNT **Amusement** is the pleasure that you get from being entertained or from doing something interesting. ❑ *He wrote for the amusement of his friends.* 3 N-COUNT **Amusements** are ways of passing the time pleasantly. ❑ *People had very few amusements to choose from.*

amusing /ə'mju:zɪŋ/ ADJ An **amusing** person or thing makes you laugh or smile. ❑ *He was a capable and amusing companion.* ● **amusingly** ADV ❑ *It must be amusingly written.*

an /ən, STRONG æn/ DET **An** is used instead of 'a' in front of words that begin with vowel sounds.

anaemia also **anemia** /ə'ni:miə/ N-UNCOUNT **Anaemia** is a medical condition in which there are too few red cells in your blood, so that you feel tired and look pale. ● **anaemic** ADJ ❑ *Losing a lot of blood makes you tired and anaemic.*

Word Link	*a, an ≈ not, without : anaesthetic, anorexia, atheism*

anaesthetic also **anesthetic** /ˌænɪs'θetɪk/ (**anaesthetics**) N-VAR **Anaesthetic** is a substance used to stop you feeling pain during an operation. ❑ *...while they are under the anaesthetic.*

anaesthetist also **anesthetist** /ə'ni:sθətɪst/ (**anaesthetists**) N-COUNT In British English, an **anaesthetist** is a doctor or nurse who gives anaesthetics to patients. The usual American word is **anesthesiologist**.

anal /'eɪnəl/ ADJ **Anal** means relating to the anus.

analogue /'ænəlɒg/

> The spelling **analog** is used in American English, and also in British English for meaning 2.

1 ADJ An **analogue** watch or clock shows the time with two pointers called hands, rather than with a number display. Compare **digital**. 2 ADJ **Analogue** technology involves measuring, storing, or recording information by using physical quantities such as voltage. Compare **digital**.

analogy /ə'nælədʒi/ (**analogies**) N-COUNT If you **draw an analogy** between two things, you show that they are similar. ❑ *He drew an analogy between sport and business.* ● **analogous** /ə'næləgəs/ ADJ ❑ *Swimming has no event that is analogous to the 100 metres in athletics.*

Word Partnership	Use *analogy* with:
PREP.	analogy **between**
V.	**draw an** analogy, **make an** analogy
ADJ.	**false** analogy

analyse → see **analyze**

analysis /ə'nælɪsɪs/ (**analyses** /ə'nælɪsi:z/) 1 N-VAR **Analysis** is the process of considering something or examining it in order to understand it or to find out what it consists of. ❑ *...a careful analysis of the situation.* ❑ *They collect blood samples for analysis.* 2 PHRASE You say **in the final analysis** or **in the last analysis** to indicate that the statement you are making is about the basic facts of a situation. ❑ *In the final analysis, it is the quality of our lives that matters.*

analyst /'ænəlɪst/ (**analysts**) 1 N-COUNT An **analyst** is a person whose job is to analyze a subject and give opinions about it. ❑ *...a political analyst.* 2 N-COUNT An **analyst** is someone who is trained to examine and treat people who have emotional problems. ❑ *My analyst has helped me not to feel guilty.*

analytic /ˌænə'lɪtɪk/ ADJ **Analytic** means the same as **analytical**.

analytical /ˌænə'lɪtɪkəl/ ADJ **Analytical** skills or methods involve the use of logical reasoning. ❑ *...your analytical and leadership skills.*

analyze [BRIT also **analyse**] /'ænəlaɪz/ (**analyzes, analyzing, analyzed**) V-T If you **analyze** something, you consider it or examine it in order to understand it or to find out what it consists of. ❑ *Analyze what is causing the stress in your life.* ❑ *They had their tablets analyzed.*

Thesaurus	*analyze* Also look up:
V.	consider, examine, inspect

anarchist /'ænəkɪst/ (**anarchists**) N-COUNT An **anarchist** is someone who believes the laws and power of governments should be replaced by people working together freely. ● **anarchism** N-UNCOUNT ❑ *...fervent political anarchism.*

Word Link	*arch ≈ rule : anarchy, hierarchy, monarch*

anarchy /'ænəki/ N-UNCOUNT **Anarchy** is a situation where nobody obeys rules or laws. ❑ *...an attempt to stop the country slipping into anarchy.* ● **anarchic** /æ'nɑ:kɪk/ ADJ ❑ *...the near anarchic level of violence.*

anatomy /ə'nætəmi/ (**anatomies**) N-VAR **Anatomy** is the study of the bodies of people or animals. The **anatomy** of a person or animal is the structure of its body. ❑ *...a professor of anatomy.* ❑ *...the female anatomy.* ● **anatomical** /ˌænə'tɒmɪkəl/ ADJ ❑ *...minute anatomical differences between insects.*
→ see **medicine**

ancestor /'ænsestə/ (**ancestors**) N-COUNT Your **ancestors** are the people from whom you are descended. ❑ *...our daily lives, so different from those of our ancestors.* ● **ancestral** /æn'sestrəl/ ADJ ❑ *...the family's ancestral home.*

ancestry /'ænsestri/ (**ancestries**) N-COUNT Your **ancestry** consists of the people from whom

a

you are descended. ❑ *They've traced their ancestry back to the sixteenth century.*

anchor /'æŋkə/ (**anchors, anchoring, anchored**) 1 N-COUNT An **anchor** is a heavy hooked object at the end of a chain that is dropped from a boat into the water to make the boat stay in one place. 2 V-T/V-I When a boat **anchors**, or when you **anchor** it, its anchor is dropped into the water to make it stay in one place. ❑ *We could anchor off the pier.* 3 V-T If you **anchor** an object, you fix it to something so that it will not move. ❑ *The roots anchor the plant in the earth.*

anchor

ancient /'eɪnʃənt/ ADJ **Ancient** means very old, or having existed for a long time. ❑ *...ancient Greece and Rome.* ❑ *...ancient Jewish traditions.*
→ see **history**

and /ənd, STRONG ænd/ 1 CONJ You use **and** to link two or more words, groups, or clauses. ❑ *She and Simon had already gone.* ❑ *I'm 53 and I'm very happy.* 2 CONJ You use **and** to link two identical words or phrases to emphasize their degree or to suggest that something continues or increases over a period of time. ❑ *We talked for hours and hours.* ❑ *Learning becomes more and more difficult.* 3 CONJ **And** links two statements about events which follow each other. ❑ *I waved goodbye and went down the stone harbour steps.* ❑ *I looked up and found her staring at me.* 4 CONJ You use **and** to link two statements when the second statement continues the point that has been made in the first statement. ❑ *You could only tell the effects of the disease in the long term, and five years wasn't long enough.* ❑ *'He used to be so handsome.'—'And now?'.* 5 CONJ **And** indicates that two numbers are to be added together. ❑ *What does two and two make?*

anecdote /'ænɪkdəʊt/ (**anecdotes**) N-COUNT An **anecdote** is a short entertaining account of something that has happened. ❑ *Then he switched to an anecdote from his time as a lecturer in literature.* • **anecdotal** /ˌænɪk'dəʊtəl/ ADJ ❑ *...anecdotal accounts of journeys and encounters.*

anemia /ə'ni:miə/ → see **anaemia**

anemic /ə'ni:mɪk/ → see **anaemia**

anesthetic /ˌænɪs'θetɪk/ → see **anaesthetic**

anesthetist /ə'ni:sθətɪst/ → see **anaesthetist**

anew /ə'nju:, AM ə'nu:/ ADV If you do something **anew**, you do it again, often in a different way. [LITERARY] ❑ *She's ready to start anew.*

angel /'eɪndʒəl/ (**angels**) 1 N-COUNT **Angels** are spiritual beings that some people believe are God's messengers and servants in heaven. 2 N-COUNT If you refer to someone as an **angel**, you mean that they are good, kind, and gentle. ❑ *Thank you so much. You're an angel.*

angelic /æn'dʒelɪk/ ADJ You can describe someone as **angelic** when they are very good, kind, and gentle. ❑ *...an angelic face.*

anger /'æŋgə/ (**angers, angering, angered**) 1 N-UNCOUNT **Anger** is the strong emotion that you feel when you think someone has behaved in an unfair, cruel, or unacceptable way. ❑ *He cried with anger and frustration.* 2 V-T If someone or something **angers** you, they make you angry. ❑ *His coldness angered her.*
→ see Word Web: **anger**
→ see **emotion**

ˌanger 'management N-UNCOUNT **Anger management** is a set of guidelines that are designed to help people control their anger. ❑ *...anger management courses.*

angle /'æŋgəl/ (**angles, angling, angled**) 1 N-COUNT If something is **at an angle**, it is leaning in a particular direction so that it is not straight, horizontal, or vertical. ❑ *The boat is now leaning at a 30 degree angle.* ❑ *Press here to adjust the angle of the sofa.* 2 N-COUNT An **angle** is the direction from which you look at something. ❑ *From the angle he was standing at, he could just see the sunset.* 3 N-COUNT You can refer to a way of presenting something or thinking about it as a particular **angle**. ❑ *He was considering the idea from all angles.* 4 V-I If you are **angling for** something, you are trying to make someone offer it to you without asking for it directly. ❑ *It sounds as if he's just angling for sympathy.* 5 → see also **right angle**.
→ see **mathematics**

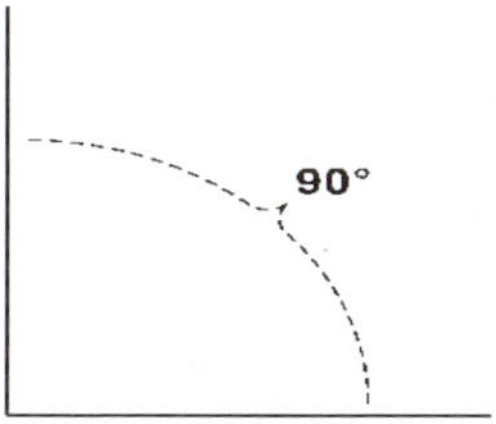

angle

angler /'æŋglə/ (**anglers**) N-COUNT An **angler** is someone who fishes with a fishing rod as a hobby.

angling /'æŋglɪŋ/ N-UNCOUNT **Angling** is the activity of fishing with a fishing rod.

Anglo- /'æŋgləʊ-/ PREFIX **Anglo-** is added

Word Web anger

Anger can be a positive thing. Until we feel anger, we may not know how **upset** we are about a situation. Anger can give us a sense of our own power. Showing someone how **annoyed** we are with them may lead them to change. Anger also helps us to let go of **tension** in **frustrating** situations. This allows us to move on with our lives. But anger has its downside. It's hard to think clearly when we're **furious**. We may use bad judgment. **Rage** can also keep us from seeing the truth about ourselves. And when anger turns into **aggression**, people get hurt.

A

Word Web animation

TV **cartoons** are one of the most popular forms of **animation**. Each **episode**, or show, begins with a **storyline**. Once the **script** is final, cartoonists make up **storyboards**. The director uses them to plan how the **artists** will **illustrate** the episode. First the illustrators **draw** some **sketches**. Next they draw a few important **frames** for each **scene**. **Animators** turn these into moving storyboards. This form of the cartoon looks unfinished. The producers then look at the storyboard and suggest changes. After they make these changes, the artists fill in the missing frames. This makes the movements of the characters look smooth and natural.

to adjectives indicating nationality to form adjectives describing something which involves relations between Britain and another country. ❑ *...Anglo-American relations.*

angry /'æŋgri/ (**angrier, angriest**) ADJ When you are **angry**, you feel strong emotion about something that you consider unfair, cruel, or insulting. ❑ *She was angry at her husband.* ❑ *An angry crowd gathered outside the court.* ● **angrily** ADV ❑ *France and Italy reacted angrily to the decision.*

Usage

Angry is normally used to talk about someone's mood or feelings on a particular occasion. If someone is often angry, you can describe them as **bad-tempered.** ❑ *She's a bad-tempered young lady.* If someone is very angry, you can describe them as **furious.** ❑ *Senior police officers are furious about the mistake.* If they are less angry, you can describe them as **annoyed** or **irritated.** ❑ *The Premier looked annoyed but calm.* ❑ *...a man irritated by the barking of his neighbour's dog.* Typically, someone is **irritated** by something because it happens constantly or continually.

Thesaurus *angry* Also look up:

ADJ. bitter, enraged, mad; *(ant.)* content, happy, pleased

angst /æŋst/ N-UNCOUNT **Angst** is a feeling of anxiety and worry. ❑ *Many teenage kids suffer from angst.*

anguish /'æŋgwɪʃ/ N-UNCOUNT **Anguish** is great mental or physical suffering. ❑ *For a few brief minutes we forgot the anxiety and anguish.*

anguished /'æŋgwɪʃt/ ADJ **Anguished** means feeling or showing great mental or physical suffering. [WRITTEN] ❑ *She let out an anguished cry.*

angular /'æŋgjʊlə/ ADJ **Angular** things have shapes that contain a lot of straight lines and sharp points. ❑ *She has a very angular face.*

Word Link ***anim** ≈ alive, mind : **anim**al, **anim**ated, un**anim**ous*

animal /'ænɪməl/ (**animals**) **1** N-COUNT Any living creature other than a human being can be referred to as an **animal**. ❑ *He was attacked by wild animals.* **2** N-COUNT An **animal** is any living thing that is not a plant, including people. ❑ *...members of the animal kingdom.* **3** ADJ **Animal** qualities or feelings relate to your physical nature and instincts rather than your mind. ❑ *...an animal panic to run and hide.* **4** N-COUNT If you say that someone is an **animal**, you find their behaviour disgusting or very unpleasant. ❑ *This man is an animal, a beast.*
→ see **earth**

Word Partnership Use *animal* with:

N.	**plant and** animal **1** **cruelty to** animals, animal **hide**, animal **kingdom**, animal **noises**, animal **shelter** **1** **2**
ADJ.	**domestic** animal, **stuffed** animal, **wild** animal **2**

animate /'ænɪmət/ ADJ Something that is **animate** has life, in contrast to things like stones and machines which do not. ❑ *He loved the whole of the natural world, animate and inanimate.*

animated /'ænɪmeɪtɪd/ **1** ADJ Someone or something that is **animated** is lively and interesting. ❑ *She was in animated conversation with the singer.* **2** ADJ BEFORE N An **animated** film is one in which puppets or drawings appear to move. ❑ *...Disney's animated film 'Lady and the Tramp'.*

animation /ˌænɪ'meɪʃən/ **1** N-UNCOUNT **Animation** is the quality of being lively and interesting. ❑ *They both spoke with animation.* **2** N-UNCOUNT **Animation** is the use of puppets or drawings that appear to move in films. ❑ *...traditional cartoon animation.*
→ see Word Web: **animation**

animosity /ˌænɪ'mɒsɪti/ (**animosities**) N-VAR **Animosity** is a feeling of strong dislike and anger. ❑ *The animosity between the two men grew.*

ankle /'æŋkəl/ (**ankles**) N-COUNT Your **ankle** is the joint where your foot joins your leg.
→ see **body**, **foot**

annex also **annexe** (**annexes, annexing, annexed**) **1** N-COUNT /'æneks/ An **annex** is a building which is joined to or is next to a larger main building. **2** V-T /æ'neks/ If a country **annexes** another country or an area of land, it seizes it and takes control of it. ❑ *Rome annexed the Nabatean kingdom in 106 AD.* ● **annexation** N-UNCOUNT ❑ *...the annexation of occupied territories.*

annihilate /ə'naɪɪleɪt/ (**annihilates, annihilating, annihilated**) V-T If something **is annihilated**, it is destroyed completely. ❑ *The fire annihilated everything in its path.* ● **annihilation** N-UNCOUNT ❑ *Leaders fear the annihilation of their people.*

Word Link ***ann** ≈ **year** : **anniversary, annual, annum***

anniversary /ˌænɪ'vɜːsəri/ (**anniversaries**) N-COUNT An **anniversary** is a date which is remembered or celebrated because a special event happened on that date in a previous year. ❑ *...their third wedding anniversary.*

Word Link ***nounce** ≈ **reporting** : **announce, denounce, pronounce***

announce /ə'naʊns/ (**announces, announcing, announced**) **1** V-T If you **announce** something, you tell people about it publicly or officially. ❑ *She was planning to announce her engagement.* ❑ *He will announce tonight that he is resigning.* **2** V-T If you **announce** something, you say it in a deliberate way. ❑ *He announced that he was leaving.* ❑ *'I'm having a bath and going to bed,' she announced.*

Thesaurus *announce* Also look up:

V. advertise, declare, reveal; (*ant.*) withhold **1** **2**

announcement /ə'naʊnsmənt/ (**announcements**) **1** N-COUNT An **announcement** is a public statement which gives information about something that has happened or that will happen. ❑ *...an announcement of a cut in the bank loan rate.* **2** N-SING The **announcement of** something is the act of telling people about it. ❑ *...the announcement of Jeanne's engagement.*

Word Partnership Use *announcement* with:

V.	**make an** announcement **1** **2**
ADJ.	**formal** announcement, **official** announcement, **public** announcement, **surprise** announcement **1** **2**

announcer /ə'naʊnsə/ (**announcers**) N-COUNT An **announcer** is someone who introduces programmes on radio or television.

annoy /ə'nɔɪ/ (**annoys, annoying, annoyed**) V-T If someone **annoys** you, they make you quite angry and impatient. ❑ *Make a note of the things which annoy you.* ❑ *It annoyed me that he didn't help with the children.*
→ see **anger**

annoyance /ə'nɔɪəns/ N-UNCOUNT **Annoyance** is the feeling that you get when someone annoys you. ❑ *To her annoyance the stranger did not go away.*

annoyed /ə'nɔɪd/ **1** ADJ If you are **annoyed**, you are quite angry about something. ❑ *Eleanor was annoyed at having to wait so long.* **2** → See note at **angry**

annoying /ə'nɔɪɪŋ/ ADJ An **annoying** person or action makes you feel quite angry and impatient. ❑ *It's very annoying when this happens.*

annual /'ænjʊəl/ **1** ADJ BEFORE N **Annual** means happening or done once every year. ❑ *...our annual holiday.* ● **annually** ADV ❑ *Interest will be paid annually.* **2** ADJ BEFORE N **Annual** quantities or rates relate to a period of one year. ❑ *...annual sales of about $80 million.* ● **annually** ADV ❑ *El Salvador produces 100,000 tons of refined copper annually.*
→ see **plant**

annum /'ænəm/ → see **per annum**

anomaly /ə'nɒməli/ (**anomalies**) N-COUNT If something is an **anomaly**, it is different from what is normal or usual. [FORMAL]

Word Link ***onym** ≈ **name** : **acronym, anonymous, synonym***

anonymous /ə'nɒnɪməs/ **1** ADJ If you remain **anonymous** when you do something, you do not let people know that you were the person who did it. Something that is **anonymous** does not reveal who you are. ❑ *You can remain anonymous if you wish.* ❑ *...anonymous phone calls.* ● **anonymously** ADV ❑ *Reports can be made anonymously.* ● **anonymity** /ˌænɒ'nɪmɪti/ N-UNCOUNT ❑ *The official requested anonymity.* **2** ADJ Something that is **anonymous** has no interesting features. ❑ *...an anonymous holiday villa.*

anorak /'ænəræk/ (**anoraks**) N-COUNT An **anorak** is a warm waterproof jacket, usually with a hood.

Word Link ***a, an** ≈ **not, without** : **anaesthetic, anorexia, atheism***

anorexia /ænə'reksiə/ N-UNCOUNT **Anorexia** or **anorexia nervosa** is an illness in which a person refuses to eat enough because they have a fear of becoming fat.

another /ə'nʌðə/ **1** DET & PRON **Another** thing or person means one more in addition to those that already exist or are known about. ❑ *We're going to have another baby.* ❑ *Drink up, there's time for another.* **2** DET & PRON **Another** can be used to mean a different thing or person from the one just mentioned. ❑ *Her doctor referred her to another therapist.* ❑ *He said one thing and has done quite another.* **3** PHRASE You use **one another** to indicate that each member of a group does something to or for the other members. ❑ *...women learning to help themselves and one another.* **4** PHRASE If you talk about **one** thing **after another**, you are referring to a series of repeated or continuous events. ❑ *They kept going, destroying one store after another.*

Word Partnership Use *another* with:

ADV.	**yet** another **1**
N.	another **chance**, another **day**, another **one** **1**
	another **man/woman**, another **thing** **2**
V.	**tell one from** another **2**
PRON.	**one** another **3**

answer /'ɑːnsə, 'æn-/ (**answers, answering, answered**) **1** V-T When you **answer** someone who has asked you something, you say something back to them. ❑ *Just answer the question.* ❑ *'When?' asked Alba, calmly. 'Tonight', answered Hunter.* **2** V-T If you **answer** a letter or advertisement, you write to the person who wrote it. ❑ *She answered an advert for a job.* **3** N-COUNT An **answer** is something that you say or write when you answer someone. ❑ *I wrote to him but I never had an answer back.* **4** V-T & N-COUNT When you **answer** the telephone, you pick it up when it rings. When you **answer** the door, you open it when you hear a knock or the bell. If no-one picks up the phone or opens the door, you can say there is **no answer**. ❑ *She answered her phone on the first ring.* **5** N-COUNT An **answer** to a problem

A

Picture Dictionary answer

Tick
Check the correct answer.

"Small" is an ___.
___noun
✓ adjective
___verb

Choose
Choose the correct answer.

b Q: Is he a waiter?
A: Yes, he ___.
a. am
b. is
c. are

Circle
Circle the best answer.

She isn't tall. She's
(thin / short / little).

Cross out
Cross out the word
that doesn't belong.

chicken
dog
~~table~~
cow

Match
Match the words
that go together.

savings dispenser
cash guard
security account

Fill in the oval
Fill in the oval.

Ann ___ with her family.
○ live
○ living
● lives

Fill in the blank
Fill in the blank.

Q: Have you met Bill?
A: Yes, I have.

Underline
Underline the adjectives.

The young woman was talking
with a tall man.

Unscramble
Unscramble the words.

(been / you / where / have)
Where have you been?

is a possible solution to it. ❑ *Legislation is only part of the answer.* **6** V-T & N-COUNT When you **answer** a question in a test, or give an **answer** to it, you write or say something in an attempt to give the facts that are asked for. ❑ *She answered 81 questions.* ❑ *Simply marking an answer wrong will not help the pupil.*
→ see Picture Dictionary: **answer**

▶ **answer back** PHR-VERB If someone, especially a child, **answers** you **back**, or if they **answer back**, they speak rudely to you when you speak to them. ❑ *She was punished by her teacher for answering back.*

▶ **answer for** PHR-VERB If you have to **answer for** something bad you have done, you are punished for it. ❑ *He must be made to answer for his crimes.*

Thesaurus	*answer* Also look up:
V.	reply, respond **1** **2**

Word Partnership	Use *answer* with:
V.	**refuse to** answer **1** **2**
	have an answer, **wait for an** answer **3**
	find the answer **5**
N.	answer **a question** **1** **6**
	answer **the door/telephone** **4**
DET.	**no** answer **4**
ADJ.	**correct/right** answer, **straight** answer, **wrong** answer **5**

'answering machine (**answering machines**) N-COUNT An **answering machine** is a device which records telephone messages while you are out.

ant /ænt/ (**ants**) N-COUNT **Ants** are small crawling insects that live in large groups.
→ see **insect**

antagonism /æn'tægənɪzəm/ N-UNCOUNT **Antagonism** is hatred or hostility. ❑ *...a history of antagonism between the two sides.*

antagonist /æn'tægənɪst/ (**antagonists**) N-COUNT Your **antagonist** is your opponent or enemy.

antagonize [BRIT also **antagonise**] /æn'tægənaɪz/ (**antagonizes, antagonizing, antagonized**) V-T If you **antagonize** someone, you make them feel hostile towards you. ❑ *She didn't want to antagonize him further.*

antenna /æn'tenə/ (**antennae** /æn'teniː/ or **antennas**)

For meaning 2 the plural is usually **antennas**.

1 N-COUNT The **antennae** of an insect are the two long thin parts attached to its head that it uses to feel things with. **2** N-COUNT An **antenna** is a device that sends and receives television or radio signals.
→ see **insect**

anthem /'ænθəm/ (**anthems**) **1** N-COUNT An **anthem** is a song or hymn written for a special occasion. ❑ *...the Olympic anthem.* **2** → see also **national anthem**

anthology /æn'θɒlədʒi/ (**anthologies**) N-COUNT An **anthology** is a collection of writings by different writers published together in one book.

Word Link	*anthrop ≈ mankind : anthropology, misanthropy, philanthropy*

anthropology /,ænθrə'pɒlədʒi/ N-UNCOUNT **Anthropology** is the study of people, society, and culture. • **anthropologist** (**anthropologists**) N-COUNT ❑ *...an anthropologist who had been*

in China.
→ see **evolution**

Word Link *bio ≈ life : antibiotic, biography, biology*

antibiotic /ˌæntibaɪˈɒtɪk/ (**antibiotics**) N-COUNT **Antibiotics** are drugs that are used in medicine to kill bacteria and to cure infections.
→ see **medicine**

antibody /ˈæntiˌbɒdi/ (**antibodies**) N-COUNT **Antibodies** are substances which your body produces in order to fight diseases.

anticipate /ænˈtɪsɪpeɪt/ (**anticipates, anticipating, anticipated**) **1** V-T If you **anticipate** an event, you realize in advance that it may happen and you are prepared for it. ❑ *We never anticipated this result.* ● **anticipation** N-UNCOUNT ❑ *They store food in anticipation of future shortages.* **2** V-T If you **anticipate** a question, request, or need, you do what is necessary or required before the question, request, or need occurs. ❑ *Do you expect your partner to anticipate your needs?* **3** V-T If you **anticipate** something pleasant or exciting that is going to happen, you look forward to it with pleasure. ● **anticipation** N-UNCOUNT ❑ *His hands were shaking in anticipation.*

Word Link *anti ≈ against : anti-clockwise, antidote, antiseptic*

anticlockwise

anti-clockwise /ˌæntiˈklɒkwaɪz/ ADV & ADJ In British English, if something is moving **anti-clockwise**, it is moving in a circle in the opposite direction to the hands of a clock. The usual American word is **counterclockwise**.

antics /ˈæntɪks/ N-PLURAL **Antics** are funny, silly, or unusual ways of behaving.

antidote /ˈæntidəʊt/ (**antidotes**) N-COUNT An **antidote** is a chemical substance that controls the effect of a poison.

Word Link *antiq ≈ old : antiquated, antique, antiquity*

antiquated /ˈæntɪkweɪtɪd/ ADJ **Antiquated** things seem very old or old-fashioned. ❑ *Many factories are so antiquated they are not worth saving.*

antique /ænˈtiːk/ (**antiques**) N-COUNT An **antique** is an old object which is valuable because of its beauty or rarity. ❑ *...a genuine antique.*

antiquity /ænˈtɪkwɪti/ (**antiquities**) **1** N-UNCOUNT **Antiquity** is the distant past, especially the time of the ancient Egyptians, Greeks, and Romans. ❑ *...famous monuments of classical antiquity.* **2** N-COUNT **Antiquities** are interesting old things, such as buildings and statues, that you can visit.

antiseptic /ˌæntiˈseptɪk/ (**antiseptics**) N-VAR **Antiseptic** kills harmful bacteria.
→ see **medicine**

ˌanti-ˈsocial **1** ADJ **Anti-social** people are unwilling to meet and be friendly with other people. ❑ *...an anti-social loner.* **2** ADJ **Anti-social** behaviour is annoying or upsetting to others.

ˌanti-ˈvirus or **antivirus** ADJ **Anti-virus** software is software that protects a computer against viruses.

anus /ˈeɪnəs/ (**anuses**) N-COUNT A person's **anus** is the hole between their buttocks, from which faeces leave their body.

anxiety /æŋˈzaɪɪti/ (**anxieties**) N-VAR **Anxiety** is a feeling of nervousness or worry. ❑ *Her voice was full of anxiety.* ❑ *...anxieties about money.*

anxious /ˈæŋkʃəs/ **1** ADJ AFTER LINK-V If you are **anxious to** do something or **anxious that** something should happen, you very much want to do it or want it to happen. ❑ *I was anxious to get here on time.* ❑ *He is anxious that there should be no delay.* **2** ADJ If you are feeling **anxious**, you are worried about something. ❑ *She had become very anxious and alarmed.* ❑ *They had to wait 10 anxious days.* ● **anxiously** ADV ❑ *They waited anxiously for news.*

any /ˈeni/ **1** QUANT You use **any** in negative statements to mean none of a particular thing. ❑ *I never make any big decisions.* ❑ *You don't know any of my friends.* ❑ *The children need new clothes and Kim can't afford any.* **2** ADV You can use **any** to emphasize a comparative adjective or adverb in a negative statement. ❑ *I can't see things getting any easier.* **3** QUANT You use **any** in questions and conditional clauses to ask if there is some of a particular thing or to suggest that there might be. ❑ *Do you speak any foreign languages?* ❑ *Do you use any of the following?* ❑ *I'll be happy to answer any questions if there are any.* **4** QUANT You use **any** in positive statements when you are referring to something or someone without saying exactly what, who, or which kind you mean. ❑ *I'm prepared to take any advice.* ❑ *...the biggest mistake any of them could remember.* **5** PHRASE If something does not happen or is not true **any more** or **any longer**, it has stopped happening or is no longer true. ❑ *I don't want to see her any more.* ❑ *I couldn't hide the tears any longer.*

Usage

Any is mainly used in questions and negative sentences. You use **not any** instead of **some** in negative sentences. ❑ *There isn't any money.* You only use **some** in questions when you expect the answer yes. ❑ *Did you buy some wine?* Otherwise you say **any**. ❑ *Did you buy any wine?*

anybody /ˈenibɒdi/ → see **anyone**

Usage

Anybody is mainly used in questions and negative sentences. You use **not anybody** instead of **somebody** in negative sentences. ❑ *There isn't anybody here.* You only use **somebody** in questions when you expect the answer yes. ❑ *Is somebody there?* Otherwise you say **anybody**. ❑ *Is anybody there?*

anyhow /ˈenihaʊ/ → see **anyway**

anymore /ˌeniˈmɔː/ also **any more** ADV If something does not happen or is not true **anymore**, it has stopped happening or is no longer true. Some people think this spelling is incorrect and prefer to use **any more**. ❑ *People are not interested in movies anymore.*

anyone /ˈeniwʌn/ or **anybody** /ˈenibɒdi/

A

1 PRON You use **anyone** in negative statements to indicate that nobody is present or involved in an action. ❑ *You needn't talk to anyone if you don't want to.* ❑ *He was too scared to tell anybody.* **2** PRON You use **anyone** in questions and conditional clauses to ask or talk about someone who might be involved in a particular situation or action. ❑ *Did you tell anyone?* ❑ *If anybody wants me, I'll be in my office.* **3** PRON You use **anyone** before words which indicate the kind of person you are talking about. ❑ *It's not a job for anyone who is slow with numbers.* **4** PRON You use **anyone** to say that a particular thing would be true of any person out of a very large number of people. ❑ *Al Smith could make anybody laugh.*

Usage

Do not confuse **anyone** with **any one. Anyone** always refers to people. In the phrase **any one**, '**one**' is a pronoun or a determiner that can refer to either a person or a thing, depending on the context. It is often followed by the word **of.** ❑ *Parting from any one of you for even a short time is hard.* ❑ *None of us stays in any one place for a very long time.* In these examples, **any one** is a more emphatic way of saying **any. Anyone** is mainly used in questions and negative sentences. You use **not anyone** instead of **someone** in negative sentences. ❑ *There isn't anyone here.* You only use **someone** in questions when you expect the answer yes. ❑ *Is someone there?* Otherwise you say **anyone.** ❑ *Is anyone there?*

anyplace /ˈenipleɪs/ ADV **Anyplace** means the same as **anywhere.** [AM]

anything /ˈeniθɪŋ/ **1** PRON You use **anything** in negative statements to say that nothing is present or an action or event does not happen. ❑ *She couldn't see or hear anything.* ❑ *I couldn't manage anything.* **2** PRON You use **anything** in questions and conditional clauses to ask or talk about whether something is present or happening. ❑ *Did you find anything?* ❑ *Is there anything I could do to help?* **3** PRON You use **anything** to emphasize that a particular thing could be true about any one of a very large number of things. ❑ *Anything could happen.* ❑ *He can have anything.* ❑ *...anything from 25 to 40 litres of milk.* **4** PRON You use **anything** before words which indicate the kind of thing you are talking about. ❑ *She collects anything that is purple.* **5** PRON You use **anything** in expressions such as **anything near, anything close to,** and **anything like** to emphasize a statement that you are making. ❑ *This is the only way he can live anything like a normal life.*

Usage

Anything is mainly used in questions and negative sentences. You use **not anything** instead of **something** in negative sentences. ❑ *There isn't anything here.* You only use **something** in questions when you expect the answer yes. ❑ *Is something wrong?* Otherwise you say **anything.** ❑ *Is anything wrong?*

anytime /ˌeniˈtaɪm/ ADV You use **anytime** to mean at an unspecified point in time. ❑ *The college admits students anytime during the year.* ❑ *He can leave anytime he wants.*

anyway /ˈeniweɪ/ or **anyhow** /ˈenihaʊ/ **1** ADV You use **anyway** to indicate that a statement explains or supports a previous point. ❑ *Be careful with the salt because the fish is salty anyway.* **2** ADV You use **anyway** to suggest that a statement is true or relevant in spite of other things that have been said. ❑ *I wasn't qualified for the job but I got it anyhow.* **3** ADV You use **anyway** to correct or modify a statement. ❑ *Ann doesn't want to have children. Not right now, anyway.* **4** ADV You use **anyway** to change the topic or return to a previous topic. ❑ *'I've got a terrible cold.'—'Have you? Oh dear. Anyway, so you're not going to go away this weekend?'.*

anywhere /ˈeniweə/ **1** ADV You use **anywhere** in negative statements, questions, and conditional clauses to refer to a place without saying exactly where you mean. ❑ *Did you try to get help from anywhere?* ❑ *I haven't got anywhere to live.* **2** ADV You use **anywhere** in positive statements to emphasize an expression that refers to a place or area. ❑ *...jokes that are so funny they work anywhere.* ❑ *He'll meet you anywhere you want.* **3** ADV When you do not want to be exact, you use **anywhere** to refer to a particular range of things. ❑ *His shoes cost anywhere from $200 up.*

Usage

Anywhere is mainly used in questions and negative sentences. You use **not anywhere** instead of **somewhere** in negative sentences. ❑ *He isn't going anywhere.* You only use **somewhere** in questions when you expect the answer yes. ❑ *Are you going somewhere tonight?* Otherwise you say **anywhere.** ❑ *Are you going anywhere tonight?*

apart /əˈpɑːt/ **1** ADV When someone or something is positioned **apart from** a person or thing, they are some distance from them. ❑ *She was standing apart from the rest of us.* ❑ *He was standing, feet apart.* ❑ *She tried in vain to keep the two dogs apart.* **2** ADV If two people are **apart**, they are no longer living together or spending time together. ❑ *Mum and Dad live apart.* **3** ADV If something comes **apart**, its parts separate from each other. ❑ *The handle of his new racket came apart.* **4** PREP You use **apart from** when you are giving an exception to a general statement. ❑ *The room was empty apart from one man sitting beside the fire.* **5** PREP You use **apart from** to indicate that you are aware of one aspect of a situation, but that you are going to focus on another aspect. ❑ *The Queen remains above criticism, apart from the tax issue.*

Word Partnership Use *apart* with:

ADV.	**far** apart **1**
N.	**miles** apart **1**
V.	**drive** apart, **fall** apart, **tear** apart **1**
	take apart **3**
	set *someone/something* apart **5**

apartheid /əˈpɑːthaɪt/ N-UNCOUNT **Apartheid** was a political system in South Africa in which people were divided into racial groups and kept apart by law.

apartment /əˈpɑːtmənt/ (**apartments**) N-COUNT An **apartment** is a set of rooms for living in, usually on one floor of a large building. This word can be used in British and American English, although **flat** is the more common word

in Britain.
→ see **city**

Word Link *path ≈ feeling : apathy, empathy, sympathy*

apathy /ˈæpəθi/ N-UNCOUNT **Apathy** is a state of mind in which you are not interested in or enthusiastic about anything. ❑ *...the political apathy of young Americans.* ● **apathetic** /ˌæpəˈθetɪk/ ADJ ❑ *The voters seem so apathetic about European issues.*

ape /eɪp/ (**apes, aping, aped**) 1 N-COUNT **Apes** are animals such as chimpanzees or gorillas. 2 V-T If you **ape** someone's behaviour, you imitate it. ❑ *...French films which only aped Hollywood.*
→ see **primate**

ape

aperture /ˈæpətʃə/ (**apertures**) N-COUNT An **aperture** is a narrow hole or gap. [FORMAL] ❑ *Through the aperture he could see daylight.*

apex /ˈeɪpeks/ (**apexes**) 1 N-SING The **apex** of an organization or system is the highest and most important position in it. ❑ *At the apex of the party was its central committee.* 2 N-COUNT The **apex** of something such as a pyramid is its pointed top.

apiece /əˈpiːs/ ADV If people have a particular number of things **apiece**, they have that number each. ❑ *He and I had two fish apiece.*

apologetic /əˌpɒləˈdʒetɪk/ ADJ If you are **apologetic**, you show or say that you are sorry that you have hurt someone or caused trouble for them. ❑ *He was apologetic about his activities.* ● **apologetically** ADV ❑ *MaryAnn smiled at her apologetically.*

apologize [BRIT also **apologise**] /əˈpɒlədʒaɪz/ (**apologizes, apologizing, apologized**) V-I When you **apologize to** someone, you say that you are sorry that you have hurt them or caused trouble for them. You can say **'I apologize'** as a formal way of saying sorry. ❑ *He apologized to the people who had been affected.* ❑ *I apologize for being late.*

Word Link *log ≈ reason, speech : apology, dialogue, logic*

apology /əˈpɒlədʒi/ (**apologies**) N-VAR An **apology** is something that you say or write in order to tell someone that you are sorry that you have hurt them or caused trouble for them. ❑ *I make no apologies for the way we played.* ❑ *...a letter of apology.*

Word Partnership Use *apology* with:

V.	**demand an** apology, **make an** apology, **owe *someone* an** apology
ADJ.	**formal/public** apology
N.	**letter of** apology

apostrophe /əˈpɒstrəfi/ (**apostrophes**) N-COUNT An **apostrophe** is the mark ', written to indicate that one or more letters have been omitted from a word, as in 'isn't'. It is also added to nouns to form possessives, as in 'Mike's car'.
→ see **punctuation**

appal [AM **appall**] /əˈpɔːl/ (**appals, appalling, appalled**) V-T If something **appals** you, it shocks you because it is so bad. ❑ *My wife now looks like her mother, which appals me.* ● **appalled** ADJ ❑ *I am absolutely appalled at what this man has done.*

appalling /əˈpɔːlɪŋ/ ADJ Something that is **appalling** is so bad that it shocks you. ❑ *They have been living under appalling conditions.* ● **appallingly** ADV ❑ *...an appallingly bad speech.*

apparatus /ˌæpəˈreɪtəs, -ˈræt-/ (**apparatuses**) 1 N-VAR The **apparatus** of an organization or system is its structure and method of operation. ❑ *...the technical apparatus of management.* 2 N-UNCOUNT **Apparatus** is the equipment which is used to do a particular job or activity. ❑ *...firefighters wearing breathing apparatus.*

apparent /əˈpærənt/ 1 ADJ BEFORE N An **apparent** situation seems to be the case, although you cannot be certain that it is. ❑ *The apparent failure of the mission is a serious disappointment.* 2 ADJ AFTER LINK-V If something is **apparent**, it is clear and obvious. ❑ *It was apparent that he was very confused.*

apparently /əˈpærəntli/ ADV You use **apparently** to refer to something that seems to be the case although it may not be. ❑ *The news apparently came as a complete surprise.*

appeal /əˈpiːl/ (**appeals, appealing, appealed**) 1 V-I & N-COUNT If you **appeal for** something that you need, or make an **appeal for** it, you make a serious and urgent request for it. ❑ *The UN has appealed for help from the international community.* ❑ *...a last-minute appeal to him to cancel his trip.* 2 V-I & N-COUNT If you **appeal to** someone in authority against a decision, or if you make an **appeal**, you formally ask them to change it. ❑ *The government has appealed against the court's decision.* ❑ *Maguire has appealed to the Supreme Court.* 3 V-I & N-UNCOUNT If something **appeals to** you, or if it has **appeal**, you find it attractive or interesting. ❑ *The idea appealed to him.* ❑ *...tiny dolls with great appeal to young girls.*
→ see **trial**

Word Partnership Use *appeal* with:

PREP.	appeal **for *something*** 1
	appeal **to a court**, appeal **to *someone*** 2
V.	**make an** appeal 1 2
	appeal **a case/decision** 2

appealing /əˈpiːlɪŋ/ ADJ Someone or something that is **appealing** is pleasing and attractive. ❑ *She had a sense of humour that I found very appealing.*

appear /əˈpɪə/ (**appears, appearing, appeared**) 1 LINK-VERB If you say that something **appears to** be the case or **appears to** have a certain quality, you mean that you have the impression that it is the case or that it has that quality. ❑ *He appeared to be depressed.* ❑ *The aircraft appears to have crashed.* ❑ *There appeared to be a problem with the baby's breathing.* ❑ *He is anxious to appear a gentleman.* 2 V-I When something or someone **appears**, it becomes possible to see them or obtain them. ❑ *A woman appeared at the far end of the street.* ❑ *It has white flowers, which appear in early summer.* ❑ *New diet books appear every week.* 3 V-I When someone **appears**

A

in a play, a show, or a television programme, they take part in it. 4 V-I When someone **appears** before a court of law, they go there to answer charges or to give information.

Thesaurus *appear* Also look up:

V. seem 1
arrive, show up, turn up; *(ant.)* disappear, vanish 2

appearance /ə'pɪərəns/ (**appearances**) 1 N-COUNT When someone makes an **appearance** at a public event or in a broadcast, they take part in it. ❑ *...the president's second public appearance.* ❑ *...a brief appearance on television.* 2 N-SING The **appearance of** someone or something in a place is the fact of their arriving or becoming visible there. ❑ *...the welcome appearance of Cousin Fred.* ❑ *Flowering plants were making their first appearance.* 3 N-SING Your **appearance** is what you look like or how you present yourself. ❑ *She used to be so careful about her appearance.* ❑ *It adds nothing to the appearance of the house.*

Word Partnership Use *appearance* with:

N. **court** appearance 1
ADJ. **public** appearance 1
sudden appearance 2
physical appearance 3
V. **give/have an** appearance **of, make an** appearance 1
change ***your*** appearance 3

appease /ə'pi:z/ (**appeases, appeasing, appeased**) V-T If you try to **appease** someone, you try to maintain a peaceful situation by giving them what they want; often used showing disapproval. ❑ *The government tried to appease angry workers.* ● **appeasement** N-UNCOUNT ❑ *Appeasement didn't work with him.*

appendix /ə'pendɪks/ (**appendices** /ə'pendɪsi:z/) 1 N-COUNT Your **appendix** is a small tube inside your body at the end of your digestive system. 2 N-COUNT An **appendix to** a book is extra information that is placed at the end of it.

appetite /'æpɪtaɪt/ (**appetites**) 1 N-VAR Your **appetite** is your desire to eat. ❑ *He has a healthy appetite.* ❑ *...loss of appetite.* 2 N-COUNT If you have an **appetite for** something, you have a strong desire for it. ❑ *...his appetite for success.*

appetizing [BRIT also **appetising**] /'æpɪtaɪzɪŋ/ ADJ **Appetizing** food looks and smells nice, so that you want to eat it.

applaud /ə'plɔ:d/ (**applauds, applauding, applauded**) 1 V-T/V-I When a group of people **applaud** or **applaud** someone, they clap their hands to show that they have enjoyed a performance. ❑ *I didn't applaud him because it was a very bad speech.* 2 V-T When a person or their behaviour **is applauded**, people praise it. ❑ *He should be applauded for his courage.* ❑ *We applaud her determination.*

applause /ə'plɔ:z/ N-UNCOUNT **Applause** is the noise made by a group of people clapping their hands to show approval. ❑ *They greeted him with thunderous applause.*

apple /'æpəl/ (**apples**) N-VAR An **apple** is a round fruit with a smooth skin and firm white flesh.
→ see **fruit**

appliance /ə'plaɪəns/ (**appliances**) N-COUNT An **appliance** is a device such as a vacuum cleaner that does a particular job in your home. ❑ *...electrical appliances.*

applicable /'æplɪkəbəl, ə'plɪkə-/ ADJ Something that is **applicable to** a particular situation is relevant to it. ❑ *...standards applicable to all police officers.* ❑ *Write down your name and, where applicable, your professional post.*

applicant /'æplɪkənt/ (**applicants**) N-COUNT An **applicant for** a job or position is someone who applies for it.

application /ˌæplɪ'keɪʃən/ (**applications**) 1 N-VAR An **application for** something such as a job or a place at a college is a formal written request to be given it. ❑ *His application for membership of the organisation was rejected.* ❑ *Tickets are available on application.* 2 N-VAR The **application of** a rule or piece of knowledge is the use of it in a particular situation. ❑ *...the practical application of the theory.* ❑ *...artificial intelligence and its application to robotics.*

Word Partnership Use *application* with:

V. **accept/reject an** application, **file/submit an** application, **fill out an** application 1
N. **college** application, application **form**, **grant/loan** application, **job** application, **membership** application 1
application **software** 2
ADJ. **practical** application 2

applied /ə'plaɪd/ ADJ An **applied** subject of study is practical rather than theoretical. ❑ *...applied linguistics.*
→ see **science**

apply /ə'plaɪ/ (**applies, applying, applied**) 1 V-I If you **apply for** something or **to** something, you write asking formally to be allowed to have it or do it. ❑ *I am continuing to apply for jobs.* ❑ *Charity groups may apply to the government for funding.* 2 V-T If you **apply yourself to** something, you concentrate hard on it. ❑ *Faulks has applied himself to this task with considerable energy.* ❑ *They had to apply their minds to many questions.* 3 V-I If something **applies to** a person or a situation, it is relevant to them. ❑ *The rule does not apply to us.* 4 V-T If you **apply** a rule or piece of knowledge, you use it in a situation or activity. ❑ *We apply technology to practical business problems.* 5 V-T If you **apply** something **to** a surface, you put it onto the surface or rub it into it. [FORMAL] ❑ *Apply direct pressure to the wound.* ❑ *Applying the dye can be messy.*

Word Partnership Use *apply* with:

PREP. apply **for admission**, apply **for a job** 1
N. **laws/restrictions/rules** apply 3
apply **make-up**, apply **pressure** 5

appoint /ə'pɔɪnt/ (**appoints, appointing, appointed**) V-T If you **appoint** someone **to** a job or post, you formally choose them for it. ❑ *They have* *appointed a consultant to carry out the investigation.* ● **appointment** N-UNCOUNT ❑ *...his appointment as foreign minister.*

appointed /əˈpɔɪntɪd/ ADJ BEFORE N If something happens at the **appointed time**, it happens at the time that was decided in advance. [FORMAL]

appointment /əˈpɔɪntmənt/ (**appointments**) **1** N-COUNT An **appointment** is a job or position of responsibility. ❑ *Mr Fay has taken up an appointment as a teacher.* **2** N-VAR If you **have an appointment with** someone, you have arranged to see them at a particular time. If something can be done **by appointment**, you can make an appointment to do it. **3** → see also **appoint**

Thesaurus	*appointment*	Also look up:
N.	date, engagement, meeting **2**	

appraisal /əˈpreɪzəl/ (**appraisals**) N-VAR If you make an **appraisal of** something, you consider it carefully and form an opinion about it. ❑ *I tried to make a calm appraisal of the situation.*

appraise /əˈpreɪz/ (**appraises, appraising, appraised**) V-T If you **appraise** something or someone, you consider them carefully and form an opinion about them. ❑ *I carefully appraised the situation.*

appreciate /əˈpriːʃieɪt/ (**appreciates, appreciating, appreciated**) **1** V-T If you **appreciate** something, you like it because you recognize its good qualities. ❑ *Anyone can appreciate our music.* ● **appreciation** N-UNCOUNT ❑ *...children's understanding and appreciation of art.* **2** V-T If you **appreciate** a situation or problem, you understand it and know what it involves. ❑ *We appreciate how tough it is in business.* ❑ *You'll appreciate the reason for secrecy.* ● **appreciation** N-UNCOUNT ❑ *They lacked appreciation of social and political issues.* **3** V-T If you say that you **appreciate** something, you mean that you are grateful for it. ❑ *I'd appreciate it if you wouldn't mention it.* ● **appreciation** N-UNCOUNT ❑ *...gifts presented to them in appreciation of their work.* **4** V-I If something **appreciates** over a period of time, its value increases. ❑ *Houses will appreciate in value.* ● **appreciation** N-UNCOUNT ❑ *...long-term price appreciation.*

appreciative /əˈpriːʃətɪv/ ADJ If you are **appreciative**, you are grateful. ❑ *We are very appreciative of their support.* ● **appreciatively** ADV ❑ *Michael smiled appreciatively.*

apprehension /ˌæprɪˈhenʃən/ (**apprehensions**) N-VAR **Apprehension** is a feeling of fear that something bad may happen. [FORMAL] ❑ *...her apprehensions about the big risks she was taking.*

apprehensive /ˌæprɪˈhensɪv/ ADJ Someone who is **apprehensive** is afraid that something bad may happen.

apprentice /əˈprentɪs/ (**apprentices**) N-COUNT An **apprentice** is a person who works with someone in order to learn their skill.

apprenticeship /əˈprentɪsʃɪp/ (**apprenticeships**) N-VAR Someone who has an **apprenticeship** works for a fixed period of time for someone who teaches them a particular skill. **Apprenticeship** is the system of learning a skill like this. ❑ *He served an apprenticeship as an engineer.*

approach /əˈprəʊtʃ/ (**approaches, approaching, approached**) **1** V-T/V-I & N-COUNT When someone **approaches** or **approaches** you, they come nearer to you. You can also talk about their **approach**. ❑ *He didn't approach the front door at once.* ❑ *...the approaching car.* ❑ *At their approach the little boy ran away.* **2** N-COUNT The **approach to** a place is the road or path that leads to it. ❑ *The path serves as an approach to the boat house.* **3** V-T & N-COUNT If you **approach** someone **about** something or if you make an **approach to** them, you speak to them because you want them to do something for you. ❑ *Chappel approached me about the job.* ❑ *Anna approached several builders.* **4** V-T & N-COUNT When you **approach** a situation in a particular way, you think about it or deal with it in that way. You can call this your **approach to** it. ❑ *The Bank has approached the issue in a practical way.* ❑ *...different approaches to gathering information.* **5** V-T/V-I & N-SING As a future time or event **approaches**, or as you **approach** it, it gradually comes nearer. You can also talk about **the approach of** a future time or event. ❑ *...the approaching crisis.* ❑ *The weather will improve with the approach of spring.* **6** V-T If something **approaches** a particular level or state, it almost reaches that level or state. ❑ *...speeds approaching 200mph.*

Thesaurus	*approach*	Also look up:
V.	close in, near; *(ant.)* go away, leave **1**	
N.	attitude, method, technique **4**	

Word Link	***propr** ≈ **owning** : **appropriate**, **proprietary**, **proprietor***

appropriate (**appropriates, appropriating, appropriated**) **1** ADJ /əˈprəʊpriət/ Something that is **appropriate** is suitable or acceptable for a particular situation. ❑ *Wear an outfit appropriate to the job.* ❑ *The teacher can then take appropriate action.* ❑ *It is appropriate that the exhibition should be sponsored by BMW.* ● **appropriately** ADV ❑ *Dress appropriately.* **2** V-T /əˈprəʊprieɪt/ If you **appropriate** something which does not belong to you, you take it for yourself. [FORMAL] ❑ *Several other newspapers have appropriated the idea.* ● **appropriation** N-UNCOUNT ❑ *...illegal appropriation of land.*

Thesaurus	*appropriate*	Also look up:
ADJ.	correct, fitting, relevant, right; *(ant.)* improper, inappropriate, incorrect **1**	

approval /əˈpruːvəl/ **1** N-UNCOUNT If a plan or request gets someone's **approval**, they agree to it. ❑ *He gave his personal approval to the security arrangements.* ❑ *...the royal seal of approval.* **2** N-UNCOUNT If someone has your **approval**, you like and admire them.

approve /əˈpruːv/ (**approves, approving, approved**) **1** V-I If you **approve of** something or someone, you like them or think they are good. ❑ *Not everyone approves of the festival.* ❑ *You don't approve, do you?* **2** V-T If someone in authority **approves** a plan or idea, they formally agree to it.

approved /əˈpruːvd/ ADJ An **approved** method or person is generally or officially recommended or acceptable for a particular job. ❑ *...an approved driving instructor.*

approving /əprˈuːvɪŋ/ ADJ An **approving**

A

reaction shows support for something, or satisfaction with it. • **approvingly** ADV ❑ *He nodded approvingly.*

Word Link *proxim ≈ near : approximate, approximation, proximity*

approximate (**approximates, approximating, approximated**) 1 ADJ /ə'prɒksɪmət/ **Approximate** figures are close to the correct figure, but are not exact. ❑ *The times are approximate only.* ❑ *Could you tell me its approximate age?* • **approximately** ADV ❑ *The conservatory measures approximately 4m x 5m.* 2 V-I /ə'prɒksɪmeɪt/ If something **approximates to** something else, it is similar to it but not exactly the same. ❑ *...something approximating to a hospital.*

approximation /ə,prɒksɪ'meɪʃən/ (**approximations**) N-COUNT An **approximation** is a fact, description, or calculation that is not exact. ❑ *This story is a rough approximation of the truth.*

apricot /'eɪprɪkɒt/ (**apricots**) N-COUNT An **apricot** is a small, soft, round fruit with yellow-orange flesh and a stone inside.

April /'eɪprɪl/ (**Aprils**) N-VAR **April** is the fourth month of the year. ❑ *Felix was born in April 2001.*

apron /'eɪprən/ (**aprons**) N-COUNT An **apron** is a piece of clothing that you put on over the front of your clothes to prevent them from getting dirty.

apt /æpt/ 1 ADJ If someone is **apt to** behave in a particular way, they often behave in that way. ❑ *She was apt to raise her voice.* 2 ADJ **Apt** means suitable. • **aptly** ADV ❑ *We went to the beach in the aptly named town of Oceanside.*

aptitude /'æptɪtju:d, AM -tu:d/ (**aptitudes**) N-VAR If you have an **aptitude for** something, you are able to learn it quickly and do it well. ❑ *Alan has no aptitude for music.*

aquatic /ə'kwætɪk/ ADJ **Aquatic** means existing or happening in water. ❑ *...aquatic plants.*

arable /'ærəbəl/ ADJ **Arable** farming involves growing crops rather than keeping animals. **Arable** land is land that is used for arable farming.

arbitrary /'ɑ:bɪtri, AM -treri/ ADJ An **arbitrary** decision or action is not based on any principle or plan, and therefore may seem unfair. ❑ *...arbitrary arrests and imprisonment.* • **arbitrarily** ADV ❑ *Prisoners-of-war are being arbitrarily killed.*

arbitrate /'ɑ:bɪtreɪt/ (**arbitrates, arbitrating, arbitrated**) V-I When someone **arbitrates between** two people who are in dispute, they consider all the facts and decide who is right. ❑ *The tribunal had been set up to arbitrate in the dispute.* • **arbitration** N-UNCOUNT ❑ *Both sides hope to settle through arbitration.*

arc /ɑ:k/ (**arcs**) N-COUNT An **arc** is a smoothly curving line or movement.

arcade /ɑ:'keɪd/ (**arcades**) N-COUNT An **arcade** is a covered passageway where there are shops. ❑ *...a shopping arcade.*

arch /ɑ:tʃ/ (**arches, arching, arched**) 1 N-COUNT An **arch** is a structure which is made when two columns join at the top in a curve. ❑ *...railway arches.* 2 V-T/V-I If something **arches** or if you **arch** it, it forms a curved shape or line. ❑ *Don't arch your back.*
→ see **architecture, foot**

archaeology also **archeology** /,ɑ:ki'ɒlədʒi/ N-UNCOUNT **Archaeology** is the study of the past by examining the remains of things such as buildings and tools. • **archaeological** /,ɑ:kiə'lɒdʒɪkəl/ ADJ BEFORE N ❑ *...archaeological sites.* • **archaeologist** (**archaeologists**) N-COUNT ❑ *Archaeologists have uncovered treasures from ancient Egypt.*
→ see **history**

archaic /ɑ:'keɪɪk/ ADJ **Archaic** means very old or very old-fashioned. ❑ *The existing law is archaic.*

archbishop /,ɑ:tʃ'bɪʃəp/ (**archbishops**) N-COUNT In the Roman Catholic church, and in some other churches, an **archbishop** is a bishop of the highest rank.

arched /ɑ:tʃt/ → see **arch**

archeology /,ɑ:ki'ɒlədʒi/ → see **archaeology**

archetype /'ɑ:kɪtaɪp/ (**archetypes**) N-COUNT The **archetype** of a particular kind of person or thing is a perfect or typical example of it. • **archetypal** ADJ ❑ *Cricket is the archetypal English game.*
→ see **myth**

architect /'ɑ:kɪtekt/ (**architects**) N-COUNT An **architect** is a person who designs buildings.

architecture /'ɑ:kɪtektʃə/ 1 N-UNCOUNT **Architecture** is the art of designing and constructing buildings. • **architectural** /,ɑ:kɪ'tektʃərəl/ ADJ ❑ *...architectural drawings.* • **architecturally** ADV ❑ *...sites which are architecturally interesting.* 2 N-UNCOUNT The **architecture** of a building is the style in which it is constructed. ❑ *This is a fine example of Moroccan architecture.*
→ see Word Web: **architecture**

archive /'ɑ:kaɪv/ (**archives**) N-COUNT **Archives** are collections of documents that contain information about the history of an organization or group of people. ❑ *...Soviet military archives.*

ardent /'ɑ:dənt/ ADJ Someone who is **ardent** about something is very enthusiastic or passionate about it. ❑ *...ardent fans.* • **ardently** ADV ❑ *He believed ardently in fairness.*

arduous /'ɑ:dʒʊəs/ ADJ Something that is **arduous** is difficult and involves a lot of physical effort. ❑ *...a long, arduous journey.*

are /ə, STRONG ɑ:/ **Are** is the plural and the second person singular of the present tense of **be**. **Are** is often abbreviated to **'re** after pronouns.

area /'eəriə/ (**areas**) 1 N-COUNT An **area** is a particular part of a city, a country, or the world. ❑ *Half the French population still lived in rural areas.* 2 N-COUNT A particular **area** of a room or other place is a part that is used for a particular activity. ❑ *...Gatwick airport's luggage area.* 3 N-COUNT The **area** of a shape or piece of land is the amount that it covers, expressed as a measurement. ❑ *The islands cover a total area of 625.6 square kilometres.* 4 N-COUNT You can use **area** to refer to a particular subject or to a particular part of a general situation or activity. ❑ *Awards were presented to writers in every area of the arts.*
→ see Picture Dictionary: **area**

a

Word Web architecture

The Colosseum (sometimes spelled Coliseum) in Rome is a great **architectural** success of the ancient world. This amphitheatre, built in the first century BC, could hold 50,000 people. It was used for animal fights, human executions, and staged battles. The oval shape allowed people to be closer to the action. It also prevented participants from hiding in the corners. The **arches** are an important part of the **building**. They are an example of a Roman improvement to the simple arch. Each arch is supported by a **keystone** in the top center. The **design** of the Colosseum has influenced the design of thousands of other public places. Many modern day sports stadiums are the same shape.

Word Partnership Use *area* with:

ADJ. **local** area, **metropolitan** area, **remote** area, **residential** area, **restricted** area, **rural/suburban/urban** area, **surrounding** area 1

N. **downtown** area, **tourist** area 1 2

PREP. **throughout the** area 1 2
area **of expertise** 4

arena /ə'riːnə/ (**arenas**) 1 N-COUNT An **arena** is a place where public events such concerts take place. ❑ *...a spectacular sports arena.* 2 N-COUNT You can refer to a particular field of activity, especially one where there is a lot of conflict, as an **arena**. ❑ *He entered the political arena in 1987.*

aren't /ɑːnt, AM 'ɑːrənt/ 1 **Aren't** is the usual spoken form of 'are not'. 2 **Aren't** is used instead of 'am not' in negative questions.

arguably /'ɑːgjʊəbli/ ADV You can use **arguably** when you are stating your opinion or belief, as a way of giving more authority to it. ❑ *We now have arguably the best bookshops in the world.*

argue /'ɑːgjuː/ (**argues, arguing, argued**) 1 V-I If you **argue with** someone, you disagree with them about something, often angrily. ❑ *They spent most of the time arguing with each other.* ❑ *They argued about the cost of a taxi.* 2 V-T/V-I If you **argue** that something is true, you give the reasons why you think it is true. If you **argue for** or **against** an idea or policy, you state the reasons why you support or oppose it. ❑ *His lawyers are arguing that he is not well enough to stand trial.* ❑ *The report argues against tax increases.*

Thesaurus *argue* Also look up:

V. bicker, disagree, fight, quarrel; *(ant.)* agree 1

argument /'ɑːgjʊmənt/ (**arguments**) 1 N-COUNT If people have an **argument**, they disagree with each other, often angrily. ❑ *She had an argument with one of the marchers.* 2 N-VAR An **argument** is a set of statements that you use to try to convince people that your opinion is correct.

Picture Dictionary area

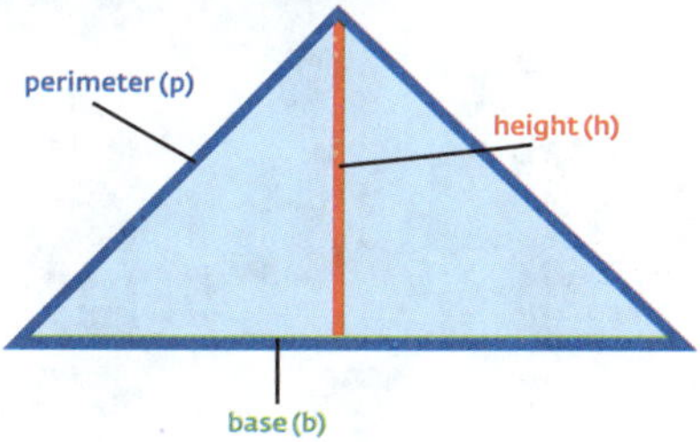

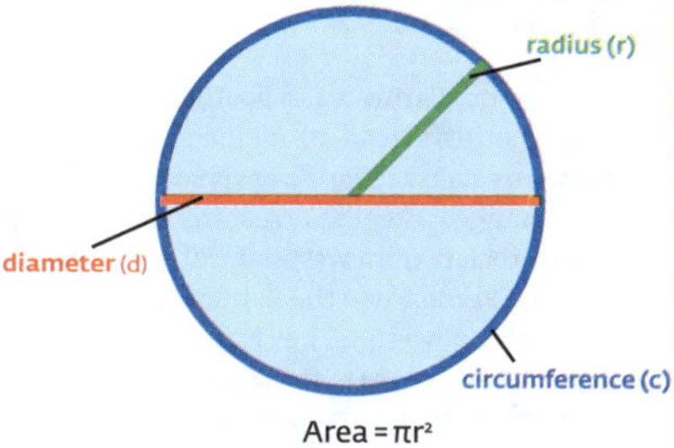

(The Greek letter π or pi is the ratio of the circumference of a circle to its diameter, roughly equivalent to 3.14 or 22/7.)

A

❑ *There's a strong argument for lowering the price.*

Word Partnership Use *argument* with:

ADJ.	**heated** argument, **persuasive** argument 1
V.	**get into an** argument, **have an** argument 1 **support an** argument 2
PREP.	**without** argument 1 argument **against/for** 2

arid /ˈærɪd/ ADJ **Arid** land is so dry that very few plants can grow on it.

arise /əˈraɪz/ (**arises, arising, arose** /əˈroʊz/, **arisen** /əˈrɪzən/) 1 V-I If a situation or problem **arises**, it begins to exist or people start to become aware of it. ❑ *Language problems arose when their families moved from England.* 2 V-I If something **arises from** a particular situation, or **arises out of** it, it is created or caused by the situation. ❑ *The claim was for damages arising from the disaster.* ❑ *Depression may arise out of loneliness.*

Word Link *cracy ≈ rule by : aristocracy, bureaucracy, democracy*

aristocracy /ˌærɪˈstɒkrəsi/ (**aristocracies**) N-COUNT The **aristocracy** is a class of people in some countries who have a high social rank and special titles.

Word Link *crat ≈ power : aristocrat, bureaucrat, democrat*

aristocrat /ˈærɪstəkræt, əˈrɪst-/ (**aristocrats**) N-COUNT An **aristocrat** is someone whose family has a high social rank, especially someone with a title. • **aristocratic** ADJ ❑ *...aristocratic values.*

arithmetic /əˈrɪθmɪtɪk/ N-UNCOUNT **Arithmetic** is the part of mathematics that deals with adding, subtracting, multiplying, and dividing numbers.
→ see **mathematics**

arm /ɑːm/ (**arms, arming, armed**) 1 N-COUNT Your **arms** are the parts of your body between your hands and your shoulders. 2 N-COUNT The **arm** of a piece of clothing is the part of it that covers your arm. 3 N-COUNT The **arm** of a chair is the part on which you rest your arm. 4 N-PLURAL **Arms** are weapons, especially bombs and guns. ❑ *...nuclear arms reductions.* 5 V-T To **arm** someone **with** a weapon means to provide them with it. ❑ *She armed herself with a loaded gun.* ❑ *Governments are reluctant to arm all police officers.*
→ see **body, war**

Word Partnership Use *arms* with:

PREP.	arms **around** 1
ADJ.	**open/outstretched** arms 1
V.	arms **crossed/folded; hold/take in *your*** arms, **join/link** arms 1 **bear** arms 4
N.	arms **control**, arms **embargo**, arms **sales** 4

armaments /ˈɑːməmənts/ N-PLURAL A country's **armaments** are its weapons and military equipment.

armchair /ˈɑːmtʃeə/ (**armchairs**) N-COUNT An **armchair** is a comfortable chair with a support on each side for your arms.

armed /ɑːmd/ ADJ Someone who is **armed** is carrying a weapon. You can also use **armed** to describe crimes or conflicts involving weapons. ❑ *He may be armed.* ❑ *...armed robbery.*

ˌarmed ˈforces N-PLURAL The **armed forces** or the **armed services** of a country are its army, navy, and air force.

armour [AM **armor**] /ˈɑːmə/ 1 N-UNCOUNT **Armour** is a metal covering that protects a military vehicle against attack. ❑ *The missile can penetrate the armour of most tanks.* 2 N-UNCOUNT In former times, **armour** was the protective metal clothing worn by soldiers.
→ see **army**

armoured [AM **armored**] /ˈɑːʳməʳd/ ADJ An **armoured** vehicle has a metal covering that protects it from gunfire and other missiles.

armoury [AM **armory**] /ˈɑːməri/ (**armouries**) 1 N-COUNT An **armoury** is a place where weapons, bombs, and other military equipment are stored. You can also refer to all a country's weapons and military equipment as its **armoury**. 2 N-COUNT You can refer to a large number of things which someone can use to achieve a particular goal as their **armoury**. ❑ *There is a large armoury of drugs for the treatment of mental illness.*

armpit /ˈɑːmpɪt/ (**armpits**) N-COUNT Your **armpits** are the areas of your body under your arms where your arms join your shoulders.

Word Web army

The first Roman **army** was a poorly organized **militia band**. Its members had no **weapons** such as **swords** or **spears**. Things changed after the Etruscans, an advanced society from west-central Italy, **conquered** Rome. Then the Roman army became more powerful. They learned how to **deploy** their **troops** to **fight** better in **battles**. By the first century BC, the Roman army learned the importance of protective equipment. They started using bronze **helmets**, **armour**, and wooden **shields**. They fought many **military campaigns** and won many **wars**.

army /'ɑːmi/ (**armies**) 1 N-COUNT An **army** is a large organized group of people who are armed and trained to fight. 2 N-COUNT An **army of** people, animals, or things is a large number of them together. ❑ *...an army of volunteers.*
→ see Word Web: **army**

aroma /ə'rəʊmə/ (**aromas**) N-COUNT An **aroma** is a strong pleasant smell. ❑ *...the wonderful aroma of freshly baked bread.*

aromatic /ˌærə'mætɪk/ ADJ **Aromatic** plants, food, or oil have a strong pleasant smell.

arose /ə'rəʊz/ **Arose** is the past tense of **arise**.

around /ə'raʊnd/ 1 **Around** means the same as the preposition and adverb uses of **round**. 2 ADV & PREP If someone or something is **around**, they are near, present, or available. ❑ *The idea has been around for ages.* ❑ *Most people around here no longer care.* 3 ADV **Around** means approximately. ❑ *My salary was around £25,000.* ❑ *He expects the elections to be held around November.*

Usage

Around and **round** are used in various ways as prepositions and adverbs, often as part of phrasal verbs. In most cases, you can use either word without any difference of meaning. In American English, **around** is much more common than **round**. When you are talking about movement in no particular direction, you can use **about** as well as **around** and **round**. ❑ *It's so romantic up there, flying around in a small plane.* ❑ *I spent a couple of hours driving round Richmond.* ❑ *Police constables walk about with guns on their hips.* When you are talking about something being generally present or available, you can use **around** or **about**, but not **round**, as adverbs. ❑ *There is a lot of talent around at the moment.* ❑ *There's not that many jobs about.* **Round** has a lot of other meanings, as a noun, verb, and adjective. You cannot use **around** in these cases.

arousal /ər'aʊzᵊl/ N-UNCOUNT If you are in a state of **arousal**, you are excited or alert.

arouse /ə'raʊz/ (**arouses, arousing, aroused**) 1 V-T If something **arouses** a particular reaction or feeling in you, it causes you to have that reaction or feeling. ❑ *She had a gift for arousing strong emotions.* 2 V-T To **arouse** someone means to make them feel sexually excited.

arrange /ə'reɪndʒ/ (**arranges, arranging, arranged**) 1 V-T/V-I If you **arrange** something such as an event or meeting or **arrange** to do something, you make the plans and preparations that are necessary for it to happen. ❑ *We arranged a social event once a year.* ❑ *I've arranged to see him on Friday morning.* ❑ *I will arrange for someone to take you.* 2 V-T If you **arrange** objects, you place them in a particular position. ❑ *She enjoys arranging dried flowers.*

arrangement /ə'reɪndʒmənt/ (**arrangements**) 1 N-PLURAL **Arrangements** are plans and preparations which you make so that something can happen. ❑ *I must make all the arrangements for the wedding.* 2 N-COUNT An **arrangement** of things is a group of them displayed in a particular way. ❑ *...beautiful flower arrangements.*

array /ə'reɪ/ N-COUNT An **array of** different things is a large number of them. ❑ *She felt an overwhelming array of emotions.*

arrears /ə'rɪəz/ N-PLURAL **Arrears** are amounts of money that someone owes. If someone is **in arrears with** regular payments, they have not paid them. ❑ *The arrears have been increasing in recent months.*

arrest /ə'rest/ (**arrests, arresting, arrested**) V-T & N-VAR When the police **arrest** someone or make an **arrest**, they take them to a police station in order to decide whether they should be charged with an offence. ❑ *Police arrested five young men in connection with the attacks.* ❑ *Detectives placed him under arrest.*

arrival /ə'raɪvəl/ (**arrivals**) 1 N-VAR Your **arrival** at a place is the act of arriving there. 2 N-SING If you talk about **the arrival of** something new, you are referring to the fact that it has begun to exist or become available. ❑ *...the arrival of modern technologies.* 3 N-COUNT An **arrival** is someone who has just arrived at a place. ❑ *Each day there are new arrivals in the camp.*

arrive /ə'raɪv/ (**arrives, arriving, arrived**) 1 V-I When you **arrive** at a place, you reach it at the end of a journey. ❑ *Several groups of guests arrived.* ❑ *I've just arrived from England.* 2 V-I When something **arrives**, it is brought to you or it becomes available to you. ❑ *Your letter arrived yesterday.* 3 V-I When you **arrive at** an idea, decision, or conclusion, you reach it or decide on it. ❑ *Payton said he had arrived at a personal decision in the past week.*

Thesaurus *arrive* Also look up:

v. enter, land, reach; *(ant.)* depart 1

arrogant /'ærəgənt/ ADJ If you say that someone is **arrogant**, you disapprove of them because they behave as if they are better than other people. • **arrogance** N-UNCOUNT ❑ *The arrogance of those in power is quite shocking.* • **arrogantly** ADV ❑ *The doctor arrogantly dismissed their cry for help.*

arrow /'ærəʊ/ (**arrows**) 1 N-COUNT An **arrow** is a long, thin weapon with a sharp point at one end which is shot from a bow. 2 N-COUNT An **arrow** is a written sign which points in a particular direction to indicate where something is.

arsenal /'ɑːsənəl/ (**arsenals**) N-COUNT An **arsenal** is a large collection of weapons and military equipment. ❑ *...reductions in Britain's nuclear arsenal.*

arson /'ɑːsən/ N-UNCOUNT **Arson** is the crime of deliberately setting fire to a building or vehicle.

art /ɑːt/ (**arts**) 1 N-UNCOUNT **Art** is paintings, drawings, and sculpture which are beautiful or which express an artist's ideas. **Art** is also the activity of creating these things. ❑ *...contemporary American art.* ❑ *...an art class for children.* 2 N-VAR The **arts** are activities such as music, painting, literature, cinema, and dance. ❑ *...people working in the arts.* ❑ *...the art of cinema.* 3 N-PLURAL At a university or college, **arts** are subjects such as history or languages in contrast to scientific subjects. ❑ *...arts and social science graduates.* 4 N-COUNT If you describe an activity as an **art**, you mean that it requires a lot of skill. ❑ *...the art of acting.* 5 → see also **fine art, martial art, state-of-the-art, work of art**
→ see Word Web: **art**
→ see **blog, culture**

A

Word Web art

The **Impressionist** movement in **painting** began in Europe during the second half of the 19th century. The Impressionists no longer used traditional **realistic depictions** of people and objects painted in **studios.** They often painted **landscapes**, with more light and colour in their **interpretations** of everyday life. Among these painters were French artists Paul Cézanne, Pierre Renoir, and Claude Monet. The word "Impressionist" comes from the name of a Monet painting, "Impression, Sunrise." Japanese prints also had an effect on the Impressionist movement. The Impressionists liked the use of contrasting dark and bright colours found in these prints.

Word Link *fact, fic ≈ making : artefact, artificial, factor*

artefact [AM **artifact**] /'ɑːtɪfækt/ (**artefacts**) N-COUNT An **artefact** is an ornament, tool, or other object made by a human being, especially one that has archaeological or cultural interest. → see **history**

artery /'ɑːtəri/ (**arteries**) N-COUNT Your **arteries** are the tubes that carry blood from your heart to the rest of your body.

Word Link *itis ≈ inflammation : arthritis, hepatitis, meningitis*

arthritis /ɑː'θraɪtɪs/ N-UNCOUNT **Arthritis** is a condition in which the joints in someone's body are swollen and painful. ● **arthritic** /ɑː'θrɪtɪk/ ADJ ❑ *...arthritic hands.*

artichoke /'ɑːtɪtʃəʊk/ (**artichokes**) **1** N-VAR An **artichoke** or a **globe artichoke** is a round vegetable with thick green leaves arranged like the petals of a flower. **2** N-VAR An **artichoke** or a **Jerusalem artichoke** is a small, yellow-white vegetable similar to a potato.

Word Link *cle ≈ small : article, cubicle, particle*

article /'ɑːtɪkəl/ (**articles**) **1** N-COUNT An **article** is a piece of writing in a newspaper or magazine. **2** N-COUNT You can refer to objects as **articles of** some kind. [FORMAL] ❑ *...articles of clothing.* **3** N-COUNT An **article of** a formal document is a section dealing with a particular point. ❑ *...Article 50 of the UN charter.* **4** → see also **definite article, indefinite article**

articulate (**articulates, articulating, articulated**) **1** ADJ /ɑː'tɪkjʊlət/ If you are **articulate**, you are able to express yourself well. ❑ *...an articulate description.* **2** V-T /ɑː'tɪkjʊleɪt/ When you **articulate** your ideas or feelings, you express them clearly in words. [FORMAL] ❑ *Encourage her to articulate her views.*

articulated /ɑː'tɪkjʊleɪtɪd/ ADJ An **articulated** vehicle, especially a lorry, is made in two sections with a moving joint between them. [BRIT]

artifact /'ɑːtɪfækt/ → see **artefact**

artificial /ˌɑːtɪ'fɪʃəl/ **1** ADJ **Artificial** objects, materials, or situations do not occur naturally and are created by people. ❑ *...artificial limbs.* ❑ *...the artificial environment of an office.* ● **artificially** ADV ❑ *...artificially sweetened lemonade.* ❑ *...artificially high prices.* **2** ADJ If you describe someone's behaviour as **artificial**, you disapprove of them because they are pretending to have attitudes and feelings which they do not really have. ❑ *...a fixed, artificial smile.*

Thesaurus *artificial* Also look up:

ADJ. manufactured, synthetic, unnatural; (*ant.*) natural **1**

artificial in'telligence N-UNCOUNT **Artificial intelligence** is a type of computer technology concerned with making machines work in a similar way to the human mind. [COMPUTING]

artillery /ɑː'tɪləri/ N-UNCOUNT & N-SING **Artillery** consists of large, powerful guns which are transported on wheels. **The artillery** is the section of the army which uses these guns.

artist /'ɑːtɪst/ (**artists**) **1** N-COUNT An **artist** is someone who draws, paints, or produces other works of art. **2** N-COUNT You can refer to a musician, actor, dancer, or other performer as an **artist**. ❑ *She's a popular artist who has sold millions of records.* → see **animation**

artistic /ɑː'tɪstɪk/ **1** ADJ Someone who is **artistic** is good at drawing or painting, or arranging things in a beautiful way. ❑ *They encourage boys to be sensitive and artistic.* **2** ADJ **Artistic** means relating to art or artists. ❑ *...the campaign for artistic freedom.* ● **artistically** ADV ❑ *...artistically gifted children.*

artistry /'ɑːtɪstri/ N-UNCOUNT **Artistry** is great skill. ❑ *...his artistry as a cellist.*

as /əz, STRONG æz/ **1** CONJ If something happens **as** something else happens, it happens at the same time. ❑ *We shut the door behind us as we entered.* **2** PREP You use **as** when you are referring to the appearance or function of something. ❑ *I only told them that as a joke.* ❑ *He has worked as a diplomat.* **3** CONJ You use **as** when you are saying how something is done. ❑ *I'll behave toward them as I would like to be treated.* **4** PREP You use the structure **as...as** when you are comparing things, or emphasizing how large or small something is. ❑ *This was not as easy as we imagined.* ❑ *...as many as eight thousand letters.* **5** CONJ You can use **as** to mean 'because'. ❑ *Lighting is important as it creates warmth in a room.* **6** PREP You use **as** in expressions like **as a result** and **as a consequence** to indicate how two situations or events are related to each other. ❑ *Large numbers of fish are dying as a result of pollution in the oceans.* 7 CONJ You use **as if** and **as though** when you are comparing one situation to another. ❑ *He looked as though he'd seen a ghost.* 8 PREP You use **as for** and **as to** to introduce a slightly different subject. ❑ *There's a lot of pressure on policemen. And as for giving them guns, I don't think that's a very good idea at all.* 9 PREP You use **as to** to indicate what something refers to. ❑ *They make decisions as to whether the student needs more help.* 10 PREP If you say that something will happen **as of** or **as from** a particular date or time, you mean that it will happen from that time onwards. ❑ *She is to retire as from 1 October.*

asbestos /ˌæs'bestɒs/ N-UNCOUNT **Asbestos** is a grey material which does not burn. It was used in the past to protect against fire or heat.

Word Link ***scend** ≈ **climbing** : **ascend**, **condescend**, **descend***

ascend /ə'send/ (**ascends, ascending, ascended**) 1 V-T If you **ascend** a hill or a staircase, you go up it. [WRITTEN] ❑ *Mrs Clayton had to hold Lizzie's hand as they ascended the steps.* 2 V-I If something **ascends**, it leads or goes upwards. [WRITTEN] ❑ *They ascended 55,900 feet in their balloon.* ❑ *A number of staircases ascend from the cobbled streets.*

ascending /ə'sendɪŋ/ ADJ BEFORE N If a group of things is arranged in **ascending order**, each thing is greater in size, amount, or importance than the thing before it. ❑ *The batteries are arranged in ascending order of size.*

ascent /ə'sent/ (**ascents**) N-COUNT An **ascent** is a steep upward slope, or a journey up a steep slope. ❑ *...the first ascent of the world's highest peak.*

Word Link ***cert** ≈ **determined, true** : **ascertain**, **certificate**, **certify***

ascertain /ˌæsə'teɪn/ (**ascertains, ascertaining, ascertained**) V-T If you **ascertain** the truth about something, you find out what it is. [FORMAL] ❑ *They had ascertained that he was not a spy.* ❑ *They were unable to ascertain the extent of the damage.*

ascribe /ə'skraɪb/ (**ascribes, ascribing, ascribed**) V-T If you **ascribe** something **to** a person, thing, or event, you believe that they cause it or have it. [FORMAL] ❑ *They ascribe every setback to some kind of conspiracy.* ❑ *It is obvious now that Philip never had the qualities that were ascribed to him.*

ash /æʃ/ (**ashes**) 1 N-UNCOUNT & N-PLURAL **Ash** or **ashes** is the grey powder-like substance that is left after something is burnt. ❑ *...volcanic ash.* ❑ *He ordered their villages to be burned to ashes.* 2 N-VAR An **ash** is a kind of tree. **Ash** is the wood of this tree.
→ see **fire, glass, volcano**

ashamed /ə'ʃeɪmd/ ADJ AFTER LINK-V If someone is **ashamed of** something or someone, they feel embarrassed about it or guilty because of it. ❑ *I felt incredibly ashamed of myself for getting so angry.* ❑ *She was ashamed that she looked so shabby.* ❑ *Women are often ashamed to admit they are being abused.*

ashore /ə'ʃɔː/ ADV Something that comes **ashore** comes from the sea onto the shore. ❑ *Oil from the tanker has come ashore at two beaches in Devon.*

ashtray /'æʃtreɪ/ (**ashtrays**) N-COUNT An **ashtray** is a small dish in which people put the ash from their cigarettes and cigars.

Asian /'eɪʃən, 'eɪʒən/ (**Asians**) 1 ADJ **Asian** means belonging or relating to Asia. ❑ *...Asian music.* 2 N-COUNT An **Asian** is a person who comes from a country or region in Asia.

aside /ə'saɪd/ 1 ADV If you move something **aside**, you move it to one side of you. If you move **aside**, you move to one side. ❑ *Sarah closed the book and laid it aside.* ❑ *He stood aside and allowed Hillsden to enter.* 2 ADV If you take someone **aside**, you take them away from a group of people in order to talk to them in private. ❑ *She took us aside and told us everyone was okay.* 3 PREP **Aside from** means the same as **apart from**. [AM] ❑ *Aside from that one detail, he didn't give us much information.*

ask /ɑːsk, æsk/ (**asks, asking, asked**) 1 V-T If you **ask** someone something, you say something in the form of a question because you want some information. ❑ *'How is Frank?' he asked.* ❑ *I asked him his name.* ❑ *I wasn't the only one asking questions.* ❑ *She asked me if I'd enjoyed my dinner.* 2 V-T If you **ask** someone **to** do something, you tell them that you want them to do it. If you **ask to** do something, you tell someone that you want to do it. ❑ *We had to ask him to leave.* ❑ *I asked to see the Director.* 3 V-I If you **ask for** something, you say that you would like it. If you **ask for** someone, you say that you want to see them or speak to them. ❑ *I went to the next house and asked for food.* ❑ *There's a man at the gate asking for you.* 4 V-T If you **ask** someone's permission or forgiveness, you try to obtain it. ❑ *He asked permission to leave.* 5 V-T If you **ask** someone somewhere, you invite them there. ❑ *Couldn't you ask Jon to the party?* 6 PHRASE You can say **'if you ask me'** to emphasize that you are stating your personal opinion. ❑ *He was too rude, if you ask me.*

Thesaurus *ask* Also look up:

V.	demand, interrogate, question, quiz; (*ant.*) answer, reply, respond 1
	beg, plead, request; (*ant.*) command, insist 4

Word Partnership Use *ask* with:

ADJ.	**afraid to** ask 1
DET.	ask **how/what/when/where/who/why** 1
CONJ.	ask **if/whether** 1
PREP.	ask **about** 1
	ask **for** 3 4
	ask **to** 2 5
N.	ask **a question** 1
	ask **for help** 3
	ask **forgiveness**, ask ***someone's* opinion**, ask **permission** 4
V.	**come to** ask, **have to** ask 1
	don't ask **me** 6

asleep /ə'sliːp/ 1 ADJ AFTER LINK-V Someone who is **asleep** is sleeping. ❑ *He was asleep on Mum's bed.* 2 PHRASE When you **fall asleep**, you start sleeping. 3 PHRASE Someone who is **fast asleep** or **sound asleep** is sleeping deeply.
→ see **sleep**

A

asparagus /ə'spærəgəs/ N-UNCOUNT **Asparagus** is a vegetable with green shoots that you cook and eat.
→ see **vegetable**

aspect /'æspekt/ (**aspects**) 1 N-COUNT An **aspect** of something is one of the parts of its character or nature. ❑ *Climate and weather affect every aspect of our lives.* ❑ *He was interested in all aspects of the work here.* 2 N-COUNT A room or a window with a particular **aspect** faces in that direction. [FORMAL] ❑ *The house had a south-west aspect.*

aspiration /ˌæspər'eɪʃən/ (**aspirations**) N-VAR Someone's **aspirations** are their ambitions to achieve something. ❑ *The girl had aspirations to a movie career.*

Word Link	spir ≈ breath : aspire, inspire, respiratory

aspire /ə'spaɪə/ (**aspires, aspiring, aspired**) V-I If you **aspire to** something such as an important job, you have a strong desire to have it. ❑ *He aspired to a career in diplomacy.*

aspirin /'æspɪrɪn/ (**aspirins**) N-VAR **Aspirin** is a mild drug which reduces pain and fever.

aspiring /ə'spaɪərɪŋ/ ADJ BEFORE N **Aspiring** describes someone who is trying to become successful in a particular career. ❑ *...aspiring young artists.*

ass /æs/ (**asses**) 1 N-COUNT An **ass** is the same as a **donkey**. [DATED] 2 N-COUNT If you call someone an **ass**, you mean that they are behaving in a silly way. [INFORMAL]

assailant /ə'seɪlənt/ (**assailants**) N-COUNT Someone's **assailant** is a person who has physically attacked them. [FORMAL]

assassin /ə'sæsɪn/ (**assassins**) N-COUNT An **assassin** is a person who assassinates someone.

assassinate /ə'sæsɪneɪt/ (**assassinates, assassinating, assassinated**) 1 V-T If someone important **is assassinated**, they are murdered as a political act. ❑ *Robert Kennedy was assassinated in 1968.* • **assassination** (**assassinations**) N-VAR ❑ *...an assassination plot.* 2 → See note at **kill**

assault /ə'sɔːlt/ (**assaults, assaulting, assaulted**) 1 V-T & N-VAR To **assault** someone means to attack them physically. An **assault on** a person is a physical attack on them. ❑ *The gang assaulted him with iron bars.* ❑ *...a series of savage assaults.* 2 N-COUNT An **assault on** someone is a strong criticism of them. ❑ *...a fierce personal assault on John Major.* 3 N-COUNT An **assault** by an army is a strong attack made against an enemy.

assemble /ə'sembəl/ (**assembles, assembling, assembled**) 1 V-T/V-I When people **assemble**, or when someone **assembles** them, they come together in a group. ❑ *...a convenient place for students to assemble between classes.* 2 V-T To **assemble** something means to fit the different parts of it together. ❑ *Workers were assembling planes*
→ see **industry**

assembly /ə'sembli/ (**assemblies**) 1 N-COUNT An **assembly** is a group of people gathered together for a particular purpose. ❑ *...an assembly of party members from the Russian republic.* 2 N-VAR The **assembly** of a machine or device is the process of fitting its parts together.

as'sembly line (**assembly lines**) N-COUNT An **assembly line** is an arrangement of workers and machines in a factory where the product passes from one worker to another until it is finished.
→ see **mass production**

assent /ə'sent/ (**assents, assenting, assented**) 1 N-UNCOUNT If someone gives their **assent to** something, they formally agree to it. ❑ *He gave his assent to the proposed legislation.* 2 V-I To **assent to** something means to agree to it. [FORMAL] ❑ *They reluctantly assented to having their picture taken.*

assert /ə'sɜːt/ (**asserts, asserting, asserted**) 1 V-T If you **assert** a fact or belief, you state it firmly. [FORMAL] ❑ *The company asserts that it will not be held responsible.* ❑ *He asserted his innocence.* • **assertion** (**assertions**) N-VAR ❑ *Police accepted his assertion that the men had threatened him.* 2 V-T If you **assert yourself** or **assert your** authority, you speak and act in a firm, forceful way. ❑ *He's speaking up and asserting himself.*

assertive /ə'sɜːtɪv/ ADJ Someone who is **assertive** speaks and acts in a firm, forceful way. ❑ *Assertive behaviour gets positive results.* • **assertiveness** N-UNCOUNT ❑ *...assertiveness training.*

assess /ə'ses/ (**assesses, assessing, assessed**) V-T If you **assess** something or someone, you consider them carefully and make a judgement about their quality or value. ❑ *I looked around and assessed the situation; I was safe.* ❑ *You can ask the court to assess whether the request is fair.* • **assessment** (**assessments**) N-VAR ❑ *...the assessment of future senior managers.*

asset /'æset/ (**assets**) 1 N-COUNT If something that you have is an **asset**, it is useful to you. ❑ *He is a great asset to the company.* 2 N-PLURAL The **assets** of a company or a person are the things that they own.

assign /ə'saɪn/ (**assigns, assigning, assigned**) 1 V-T If you **assign** a task or function **to** someone, you give it to them. ❑ *I would assign a topic to children which they would write about.* ❑ *...when teachers assign homework.* 2 V-T If you **are assigned to** a place or group, you are sent to work in the place or with the group. ❑ *I was assigned to Troop A of the 10th Cavalry.*

assignment /ə'saɪnmənt/ (**assignments**) N-VAR An **assignment** is a piece of work that you are given to do, as part of your job or studies. ❑ *...written assignments and practical tests.* ❑ *...a photographer on assignment for Life magazine.*

Thesaurus	assignment	Also look up:
N.	chore, duty, job, task	

Word Link	simil ≈ similar : assimilate, similarity, similarly

assimilate /ə'sɪmɪleɪt/ (**assimilates, assimilating, assimilated**) 1 V-T/V-I When immigrants **are assimilated into** a community, or when that community **assimilates** them, they become an accepted part of it. ❑ *His family tried to assimilate into the white and Hispanic communities.* ❑ *Most of them are trying to assimilate themselves into society.* • **assimilation** N-UNCOUNT ❑ *...assimilation of minority ethnic groups.* 2 V-T If you **assimilate** ideas, customs, or methods, you learn them and make use of them. ❑ *...someone who assimilates facts*

well. ● **assimilation** N-UNCOUNT ❑ *...assimilation of knowledge.*
→ see **culture**

assist /ə'sɪst/ (**assists, assisting, assisted**) V-T If someone or something **assists** you, they help you. [FORMAL] ❑ *The family decided to assist me with my chores.* ❑ *...information to assist you in making the best selection.*

assistance /ə'sɪstəns/ N-UNCOUNT If you give someone **assistance**, you help them. Someone or something that is **of assistance** is helpful or useful. [FORMAL] ❑ *I would be grateful for any assistance.*

Word Partnership Use *assistance* with:

V.	**need/require** assistance, **provide** assistance
ADJ.	**emergency** assistance, **medical** assistance, **financial** assistance, **technical** assistance

assistant /ə'sɪstənt/ (**assistants**) 1 ADJ BEFORE N **Assistant** is used in front of titles or jobs to indicate a slightly lower rank. ❑ *...the assistant minister of defence.* 2 N-COUNT Someone's **assistant** is a person who helps them in their work. ❑ *...a research assistant.* 3 N-COUNT An **assistant** is a person who sells things in a shop. ❑ *...a sales assistant.*

Word Link *soci ≈ companion : associate, social, sociology*

associate (**associates, associating, associated**) 1 V-T /ə'səʊsieɪt/ If you **associate** one thing **with** another, the two are connected or you think of them as connected. ❑ *I associate chocolate with feelings of well-being.* ❑ *Older students are very often associated with a more serious attitude to college.* 2 V-T If you **are associated with** an organization, cause, or point of view, you support it publicly. ❑ *I really couldn't associate myself with the military.* 3 V-I If you **associate with** a person or group of people, you spend a lot of time with them. ❑ *I began associating with different people.* 4 N-COUNT /ə'səʊsiət/ Your **associates** are your business colleagues.

association /əˌsəʊsi'eɪʃən/ (**associations**) 1 N-COUNT An **association** is an official group of people who have the same occupation, aim, or interest. ❑ *...the British Astronomical Association.* 2 N-UNCOUNT Your **association with** a person, group, or organization is the connection that you have with them. If someone does something **in association with** someone else, they do it together. ❑ *His biography was written in association with Tony Williams.* 3 N-COUNT If something has particular **associations** for you, it is connected in your mind with a particular memory or feeling. ❑ *...a flood of unhappy associations.*

assorted /ə'sɔːtɪd/ ADJ A group of **assorted** things of a particular kind have different sizes, colours, or qualities. ❑ *...paper in assorted sizes.*

assortment /ə'sɔːtmənt/ (**assortments**) N-COUNT An **assortment** is a group of similar things that have different sizes, colours, or qualities.

Word Link *sume ≈ taking : assume, consume, presume*

assume /ə'sjuːm, AM ə'suːm/ (**assumes, assuming, assumed**) 1 V-T If you **assume** that something is true, you suppose that it is true, sometimes wrongly. ❑ *I assume the eggs will be fresh.* ❑ *Mistakes were assumed to be the fault of the commander.* 2 V-T If someone **assumes** power or responsibility, they take power or responsibility. ❑ *It is usually the woman who assumes overall care of the baby.* 3 V-T If you **assume** a particular expression, quality, or way of behaving, you start to look or behave in this way. ❑ *His face assumed a weary expression.*

Word Partnership Use *assume* with:

V.	**let's** assume ***that***, **tend to** assume 1
ADV.	**automatically** assume, assume **so** 1
N.	assume **the worst** 1
	assume **control/power**, assume **responsibility**, assume **a role** 2

assuming /ə'sjuːmɪŋ, AM -'suːm-/ CONJ You use **assuming** or **assuming that** when you are supposing that something is true, so that you can think about what the consequences would be. ❑ *Assuming he's still alive, what is he doing now?*

Word Link *sumpt ≈ taking : assumption, consumption, presumption*

assumption /ə'sʌmpʃən/ (**assumptions**) N-COUNT If you make an **assumption**, you suppose that something is true, sometimes wrongly. ❑ *Their assumption is that all men and women think alike.*

assurance /ə'ʃʊərəns/ (**assurances**) 1 N-VAR If you give someone an **assurance** about something, you say that it is the case, in order to make them less worried. ❑ *He gave written assurance that he would start work at once.* 2 N-UNCOUNT If you do something **with assurance**, you do it with confidence and certainty. ❑ *Adams led the orchestra with assurance.*

assure /ə'ʃʊə/ (**assures, assuring, assured**) 1 V-T If you **assure** someone that something is true or will happen, you tell them that it is the case, to make them less worried. ❑ *I can assure you that the animals are well cared for.* 2 V-T To **assure** someone **of** something means to make certain that they will get it. ❑ *He is assured of success in the championship.*

assured /ə'ʃʊəd/ ADJ Someone who is **assured** is very confident and relaxed. ❑ *He gave an assured performance.*

Word Link *aster, astro ≈ star : asterisk, astronaut, astronomy*

asterisk /'æstərɪsk/ (**asterisks**) N-COUNT An **asterisk** is the symbol *.

asthma /'æsmə, AM 'æz-/ N-UNCOUNT **Asthma** is an illness which affects the chest and makes breathing difficult.

asthmatic /æs'mætɪk, AM æz-/ (**asthmatics**) N-COUNT & ADJ An **asthmatic** or someone who is **asthmatic** suffers from asthma.

astonish /ə'stɒnɪʃ/ (**astonishes, astonishing, astonished**) V-T If someone or something

A

astonishes you, they surprise you very much. • **astonished** ADJ ❑ *I was astonished by his stupidity.*

astonishing /əˈstɒnɪʃɪŋ/ ADJ Something that is **astonishing** is very surprising. • **astonishingly** ADV ❑ *...an astonishingly beautiful young woman.*

astonishment /əˈstɒnɪʃmənt/ N-UNCOUNT **Astonishment** is a feeling of great surprise. ❑ *She looked at her husband in astonishment.*

astound /əˈstaʊnd/ (**astounds, astounding, astounded**) V-T If something **astounds** you, you are amazed by it. • **astounding** ADJ ❑ *...an astounding discovery.*

astray /əˈstreɪ/ **1** PHRASE If you **are led astray** by someone or something, they make you behave badly or foolishly. ❑ *He was led astray by this older woman.* **2** PHRASE If something **goes astray**, it gets lost. ❑ *Many items of mail go astray every day.*

astride /əˈstraɪd/ PREP If you sit or stand **astride** something, you sit or stand with one leg on each side of it. ❑ *Three youths stood astride their bicycles.*

astrology /əˈstrɒlədʒi/ N-UNCOUNT **Astrology** is the study of the movements of the planets, sun, moon, and stars in the belief that they can influence people's lives. • **astrologer** (**astrologers**) N-COUNT ❑ *He consulted an astrologer.*
→ see **star**

astronaut

astronaut /ˈæstrənɔːt/ (**astronauts**) N-COUNT An **astronaut** is a person who travels in a spacecraft.

astronomical /ˌæstrəˈnɒmɪkəl/ ADJ If you describe an amount as **astronomical**, you are emphasizing that it is very large. ❑ *The cost will be astronomical.*

Word Link	*aster, astro ≈ star : asterisk, astronaut, astronomy*

Word Link	*er, or ≈ one who does, that which does: astronomer, author, writer*

astronomy /əˈstrɒnəmi/ N-UNCOUNT **Astronomy** is the scientific study of the stars, planets, and other natural objects in space.

• **astronomer** (**astronomers**) N-COUNT ❑ *...an amateur astronomer.*
→ see Word Web: **astronomer**
→ see **galaxy, star, telescope**

astute /əˈstjuːt, AM əˈstuːt/ ADJ Someone who is **astute** is clever and skilful at understanding behaviour and situations. ❑ *She was politically astute.* ❑ *...astute business decisions.*

asylum /əˈsaɪləm/ (**asylums**) **1** N-COUNT An **asylum** is a mental hospital. **2** N-UNCOUNT **Asylum** is protection given to foreigners who have left their own country for political reasons. ❑ *He applied for asylum in 1987.*

at /ət, STRONG æt/ **1** PREP You use **at** to say where something happens or is situated. ❑ *We had dinner at a restaurant.* ❑ *I've damaged the muscles at the back of the thigh.* ❑ *Graham was already at the door.* ❑ *I studied psychology at Hunter College.* **2** PREP If you look **at** something or someone, you look towards them. If you direct something **at** someone, you direct it towards them. ❑ *He looked at Michael and laughed.* ❑ *They threw petrol bombs at the police.* **3** PREP You use **at** to say when something happens. ❑ *We closed our offices at 2:00 p.m.* ❑ *He only sees her at Christmas.* **4** PREP You use **at** to express a rate, frequency, level, or price. ❑ *I drove back down the highway at normal speed.* ❑ *Oil prices were closing at $19.76 a barrel.* **5** PREP If you are working **at** something, you are dealing with it. If you are aiming **at** something, you are trying to achieve it. ❑ *She has worked hard at her marriage.* ❑ *...a $1.04m grant aimed at improving student performance.* **6** PREP If something is done **at** someone's command or invitation, it is done as a result of it. ❑ *I went to Japan at the invitation of the Foreign Minister.* **7** PREP You use **at** to say that someone or something is in a particular state or condition. ❑ *Their countries had been at war for nearly six weeks.* **8** PREP You use **at** to say how something is done. ❑ *...shots fired at random from a minibus.* ❑ *Mr Martin was taken out of his car at gunpoint.* **9** PREP If you are good **at** something, you do it well. If you are bad **at** something, you do it badly. **10** PREP If you are delighted, pleased, or appalled **at** something, that is the effect it has on you.

ate /et, eɪt/ **Ate** is the past tense of **eat**.

Word Web astronomer

The Italian **astronomer** Galileo Galilei did not invent the telescope. However, he was the first person to use it to study **celestial** bodies. He recorded his findings. What Galileo saw through the telescope supported the theory that the **planet** Earth is not the centre of the universe. This theory was written by Polish astronomer Nicolaus Copernicus in 1530. Copernicus said that all of the planets in the universe revolve around the **sun**. In 1609, Galileo used a telescope to see the **craters** on the Earth's **moon**. He also discovered the four largest **satellites** of the planet Jupiter. These four bodies are called the Galilean moons.

Word Link *a, an ≈ not, without : anaesthetic, anorexia, atheism*

atheism /'eɪθiɪzəm/ N-UNCOUNT **Atheism** is the belief that there is no God. ● **atheist** (**atheists**) N-COUNT ❑ *...a confirmed atheist.*

athlete /'æθliːt/ (**athletes**) N-COUNT An **athlete** is a person who takes part in athletics competitions.

athletic /æθ'letɪk/ 1 ADJ BEFORE N **Athletic** means relating to athletes and athletics. 2 ADJ An **athletic** person is fit, healthy, and active.

athletics /æθ'letɪks/ N-UNCOUNT **Athletics** consists of sports such as running, the high jump, and the javelin.

atlas /'ætləs/ (**atlases**) N-COUNT An **atlas** is a book of maps.

Word Link *sphere ≈ ball : atmosphere, hemisphere, sphere*

atmosphere /'ætməsfɪə/ (**atmospheres**) 1 N-COUNT A planet's **atmosphere** is the layer of air or other gas around it. ● **atmospheric** /ˌætməs'ferɪk/ ADJ ❑ *...atmospheric pressure.* 2 N-COUNT The **atmosphere** of a place is the air that you breathe there. ❑ *...the smoky atmosphere of the gaming room.* 3 N-SING The **atmosphere** of a place is the general impression that you get of it. ❑ *We try and provide a homely atmosphere.*
→ see **air, core, earth, greenhouse effect, meteor, moon, ozone, water**

atom /'ætəm/ (**atoms**) N-COUNT An **atom** is the smallest possible amount of a chemical element.
→ see **element**

atomic /ə'tɒmɪk/ ADJ BEFORE N **Atomic** means relating to atoms or to the power produced by splitting atoms. ❑ *...atomic particles.* ❑ *...an atomic bomb.*

atrocious /ə'trəʊʃəs/ ADJ If you describe something as **atrocious**, you mean it is extremely bad or unpleasant. ❑ *The food here is atrocious.* ❑ *...atrocious weather conditions.*

atrocity /ə'trɒsɪti/ (**atrocities**) N-VAR An **atrocity** is a very cruel, shocking action. ❑ *Those people who committed atrocities should be punished.*

attach /ə'tætʃ/ (**attaches, attaching, attached**) 1 V-T If you **attach** something **to** an object, you join it or fasten it to the object. ❑ *Attach the sticker to your car window.* ❑ *Don't forget to attach the completed entry form.* 2 V-T If you **attach** a quality **to** something or someone, you consider that they have that quality. ❑ *We attach great importance to the food at all our hotels.* 3 V-T If you **attach** a file **to** a message that you send to someone, you send it with the message but separate from it. [COMPUTING]

attached /ə'tætʃt/ ADJ AFTER LINK-V If you are **attached to** someone or something, you care deeply about them. ❑ *She is very attached to her family.*

attachment /ə'tætʃmənt/ (**attachments**) 1 N-VAR An **attachment to** someone or something is a love or liking for them. ❑ *Mother and child form a close attachment.* ❑ *...a feeling of attachment to the land.* 2 N-COUNT An **attachment** is a device that can be fixed onto a machine in order to enable it to do different jobs. ❑ *...a close-up lens attachment for your camera.* 3 N-COUNT An **attachment** is an extra document that is added to another document. 4 N-COUNT An **attachment** is a file which is attached separately to a message that you send to someone. [COMPUTING]

attack /ə'tæk/ (**attacks, attacking, attacked**) 1 V-T/V-I & N-VAR To **attack** a person or place, or to launch an **attack on** them, means to try to hurt or damage them using physical violence. ❑ *I thought he was going to attack me.* ❑ *He commanded his troops to attack.* ❑ *...a vicious attack on a police officer.* ❑ *The soldiers came under attack.* ● **attacker** (**attackers**) N-COUNT ❑ *She struggled with her attacker.* 2 N-COUNT An **attack of** an illness is a short period in which you suffer badly from it. ❑ *...an attack of asthma.* 3 V-T & N-VAR If you **attack** a person, belief, or idea, or if you launch an **attack on** them, you criticize them strongly. ❑ *The union has attacked the plan.* ❑ *He attacked bosses for giving themselves big pay rises.* ❑ *...his response to attacks on his work.* 4 V-T If you **attack** a job or a problem, you start to deal with it in an energetic way. ❑ *Parents shouldn't attack the problem on their own.* 5 V-I In a game such as football, when players **attack**, they try to score. 6 → see also **counter-attack, heart attack.**
→ see **war**

attain /ə'teɪn/ (**attains, attaining, attained**) V-T If you **attain** something, you gain it, often after a lot of effort. [FORMAL] ❑ *Jim is halfway to attaining his pilot's licence.* ● **attainment** N-UNCOUNT ❑ *...the attainment of independence.*

Word Link *tempt ≈ trying : attempt, temptation, tempted*

attempt /ə'tempt/ (**attempts, attempting, attempted**) 1 V-T & N-COUNT If you **attempt to** do something or **attempt** it, or if you **make** an **attempt to** do it, you try to do it. ❑ *He is accused of attempting to murder his neighbour.* ❑ *He attempted a brave smile.* ❑ *...a deliberate attempt to mislead people.* ● **attempted** ADJ BEFORE N ❑ *...a case of attempted murder.* 2 N-COUNT If someone makes an **attempt on** a person's life, they try to kill that person. ❑ *There were several attempts on her life.*

Thesaurus *attempt* Also look up:

N.	effort, try, venture 1
V.	strive, tackle, take on, try 1

Word Partnership Use *attempt* with:

V.	attempt **to control/find/prevent/solve** 1
	make an attempt 1 2
ADJ.	**any** attempt, **desperate** attempt, **failed/successful** attempt 1 2
N.	attempt **suicide, assassination** attempt 2

attend /ə'tend/ (**attends, attending, attended**) 1 V-T/V-I If you **attend** a meeting or other event, you are at it. [FORMAL] ❑ *Thousands of people attended the funeral.* ❑ *They had been invited but were not expected to attend.* ● **attendance** N-UNCOUNT ❑ *...his lack of attendance at classes.* 2 V-T If you **attend** an institution such as a school or church, you go to it

A

regularly. [FORMAL] ❑ *They attended college together.* **3** V-I If you **attend to** something, you deal with it. ❑ *The staff will helpfully attend to your needs.*

attendance /ə'tendəns/ (**attendances**) N-VAR The **attendance** at an event is the number of people who are present there. ❑ *...falling church attendances.*

attendant /ə'tendənt/ (**attendants**) **1** N-COUNT An **attendant** is someone whose job is to serve people, for example in a petrol station or a cloakroom. **2** ADJ You use **attendant** to describe something that results from or is connected to a thing already mentioned. ❑ *...Mr Brady's victory, and all the attendant publicity.*

attention /ə'tenʃən/ **1** N-UNCOUNT If something has your **attention** or if you are **paying attention to** it, you have noticed it and are interested in it. ❑ *The light attracted his attention.* ❑ *They have tried to draw attention to human rights abuses.* ❑ *He never paid much attention to his audience.* **2** N-UNCOUNT If something needs **attention**, it needs care or action. ❑ *If you are badly burnt, seek medical attention.*

Word Partnership Use *attention* with:

N.	**center of** attention **1**
PREP.	attention **to detail** **1**
V.	**call/direct *someone's*** attention, **catch *someone's*** attention, **focus** attention, **turn** attention, **to *something/someone*** **1** **attract** attention, **draw** attention, **pay** attention **1** **2**
ADJ.	**careful/close/undivided** attention, **unwanted** attention **1** **special** attention **1** **2** **medical** attention **2**

attentive /ə'tentɪv/ **1** ADJ If you are **attentive**, you watch or listen carefully. ❑ *...an attentive audience.* ● **attentively** ADV ❑ *He listened attentively.* **2** ADJ Someone who is **attentive** is helpful and polite. ❑ *He is attentive to his wife.*

attic /'ætɪk/ (**attics**) N-COUNT An **attic** is a room at the top of a house, just below the roof.
→ see **house**

attitude /'ætɪtju:d, AM -tu:d/ (**attitudes**) N-VAR Your **attitude to** something is the way you think and feel about it. ❑ *My attitude to life in general comes from my mother.* ❑ *...negative attitudes to work.*

Word Partnership Use *attitude* with:

PREP.	attitude **about/toward**
ADJ.	**bad** attitude, **new** attitude, **negative/positive** attitude, **progressive** attitude
V.	**change your** attitude

attorney /ə'tɜ:ni/ (**attorneys**) N-COUNT In American English, an **attorney** is a lawyer.
→ see **trial**

attract /ə'trækt/ (**attracts, attracting, attracted**) **1** V-T If someone or something **attracts** you, they have qualities which make it easy for you to like or admire them. ❑ *The theory attracted him by its logic.* ❑ *What first attracted me to her was her wide experience of life.* ● **attracted** ADJ ❑ *I wasn't deeply attracted to him.* **2** V-T If something **attracts** attention, publicity, or support, it gets it. ❑ *He wants to attract investment from private companies.* **3** V-T If something **attracts** people or animals, it has features that make them want to go to it. ❑ *The gallery is attracting many visitors.* **4** V-T If something magnetic **attracts** an object, it causes the object to move towards it.
→ see **magnet**

attraction /ə'trækʃən/ (**attractions**) **1** N-COUNT An **attraction** is a feature which makes something interesting or desirable. ❑ *...America's top tourist attraction, Disney World.* ❑ *What's the attraction of trains and train books?* **2** N-UNCOUNT **Attraction** is a feeling of liking someone. ❑ *...our level of attraction to the opposite sex.*

attractive /ə'træktɪv/ **1** ADJ An **attractive** person or thing is pleasant to look at. ❑ *He was immensely attractive to women.* ❑ *The flat was small but attractive.* ● **attractiveness** N-UNCOUNT ❑ *...the attractiveness of the region.* **2** → See note at **beautiful** **3** ADJ You say that something is **attractive** when it seems desirable. ❑ *Making money has always been attractive.*

Thesaurus *attractive* Also look up:

ADJ.	appealing, charming, good-looking, pleasant; *(ant.)* repulsive, ugly, unattractive **1**

Word Link *tribute ≈ giving: attribute, contribute, distribute*

attribute (**attributes, attributing, attributed**) **1** V-T /ə'trɪbju:t/ If you **attribute** something **to** a person, thing, or event, you believe that they cause it or have it. [FORMAL] ❑ *Women tend to attribute their success to luck.* ❑ *She actually had none of the qualities he attributed to her.* **2** V-T If a piece of writing or a remark **is attributed to** someone, people say that that person created it or said it. ❑ *...a play attributed to William Shakespeare.* **3** N-COUNT /'ætrɪbju:t/ An **attribute** is a quality or feature. ❑ *Imagination is an attribute of human beings.*

aubergine /'əʊbəʒi:n/ (**aubergines**) N-VAR An **aubergine** is a vegetable with a smooth purple skin.
→ see **vegetable**

auburn /'ɔ:bən/ ADJ **Auburn** hair is reddish brown.

auction /'ɔ:kʃən/ (**auctions, auctioning, auctioned**) **1** N-VAR An **auction** is a sale where goods are sold to the person who offers the highest price. ❑ *Lord Salisbury bought the picture at auction.* **2** V-T If something **is auctioned**, it is sold in an auction. ❑ *We'll auction them for charity.*
▸ **auction off** PHR-VERB If you **auction off** a number of things, you sell them at an auction. ❑ *They're coming to auction off my farm.*

Word Link *eer ≈ one who does: auctioneer, engineer, volunteer*

auctioneer /,ɔ:kʃə'nɪə/ (**auctioneers**) N-COUNT An **auctioneer** is a person in charge of an auction.

audacious /ɔ:'deɪʃəs/ ADJ Something or someone that is **audacious** is very daring and takes a lot of risks. ❑ *...an audacious plan to win the* presidency. • **audacity** /ɔːˈdæsɪti/ N-UNCOUNT ❑ *He had the audacity to make a 200-1 bet on himself to win.*

Word Link *ible ≈ able to be : audible, flexible, possible*

audible /ˈɔːdɪbəl/ ADJ An **audible** sound can be heard. • **audibly** ADV ❑ *Hugh sighed audibly.*

Word Link *audi ≈ hearing : audience, audition, auditorium*

audience /ˈɔːdiəns/ (**audiences**) 1 N-COUNT The **audience** is all the people who are watching or listening to a play, concert, film, or programme. ❑ *The entire audience applauded loudly.* 2 N-COUNT You can use **audience** to refer to the people who read someone's books or hear about their ideas. ❑ *...books that are accessible to a general audience.*
→ see **concert**

Word Partnership Use *audience* with:

PREP.	**before/in front of an** audience 1
N.	audience **participation**, **studio** audience 1, **television** audience 1 2
ADJ.	**captive** audience, **live** audience 1, **large** audience 1 2, **general** audience, **target** audience, **wide** audience 2
V.	**reach an** audience 2

audio /ˈɔːdiəʊ/ ADJ BEFORE N **Audio** equipment is used for recording and reproducing sound. ❑ *...audio tapes.*

audit /ˈɔːdɪt/ (**audits, auditing, audited**) V-T & N-COUNT When an accountant **audits** an organization's accounts or conducts an **audit** on them, he or she examines them to make sure that they are correct. • **auditor** (**auditors**) N-COUNT ❑ *...the group's internal auditors.*

audition /ɔːˈdɪʃən/ (**auditions, auditioning, auditioned**) N-COUNT & V-T/V-I If someone does an **audition**, or if they **audition**, they give a short performance so that a director or conductor can decide if they are good enough to be in a play, film, or orchestra. You can also say that a director or conductor **auditions** someone. ❑ *He failed his audition.* ❑ *She wrote to Paramount Studios and asked if she could audition for the part.*
→ see **theatre**

auditorium /ˌɔːdɪˈtɔːriəm/ (**auditoriums** or **auditoria** /ˌɔːdɪˈtɔːriə/) N-COUNT In a theatre or concert hall, the **auditorium** is the part of the building where the audience sits.

augment /ɔːgˈment/ (**augments, augmenting, augmented**) V-T To **augment** something means to make it larger by adding something to it. [FORMAL] ❑ *...searching for a way to augment the family income.*

August /ˈɔːgəst/ (**Augusts**) N-VAR **August** is the eighth month of the year. ❑ *He got married in August.*

aunt /ɑːnt, ænt/ (**aunts**) N-COUNT Your **aunt** is the sister of your mother or father, or the wife of your uncle. ❑ *...Aunt Vera.*
→ see **family**

auntie also **aunty** /ˈɑːnti, ˈænti/ (**aunties**) N-COUNT **Auntie** means the same as **aunt**. [INFORMAL]

au pair /ˌəʊ ˈpeə, AM ˌɔː -/ (**au pairs**) N-COUNT An **au pair** is a young person who lives with a family in a foreign country in order to learn their language and help around the house.

aura /ˈɔːrə/ (**auras**) N-COUNT An **aura** is a quality or feeling that appears to surround a person or place. ❑ *She had an aura of authority.*

aural /ˈɔːrəl, ˈaʊrəl/ ADJ **Aural** means related to the sense of hearing. ❑ *...astonishing visual and aural effects.*

auspices /ˈɔːspɪsɪz/ PHRASE If something is done **under the auspices of** a person or organization or **under** someone's **auspices**, it is done with their support. [FORMAL] ❑ *...a conference held in 1961 under British auspices.*

austere /ɔːˈstɪə/ 1 ADJ Something that is **austere** is plain and not decorated. • **austerity** /ɔːˈsterɪti/ N-UNCOUNT ❑ *...the austerity of the priest's coat.* 2 ADJ An **austere** person is strict and serious. ❑ *...a rather austere, distant, somewhat cold person.* 3 ADJ An **austere** way of life is rather harsh, with no luxuries. ❑ *The life of the troops was still rather austere.* • **austerity** N-UNCOUNT ❑ *They suffered greatly during the years of austerity which followed the war.*

authentic /ɔːˈθentɪk/ ADJ If something is **authentic**, it is genuine or accurate. ❑ *...authentic Italian food.* • **authenticity** /ˌɔːθenˈtɪsɪti/ N-UNCOUNT ❑ *Many experts doubted the painting's authenticity.*

Word Link *er, or ≈ one who does, that which does: astronomer, author, writer*

author /ˈɔːθə/ (**authors**) 1 N-COUNT The **author of** a piece of writing is the person who wrote it. ❑ *...Rick Rogers, the author of the report.* 2 N-COUNT An **author** is a person whose occupation is writing books. ❑ *Tolstoy's my favourite author.*

authorise /ˈɔːθəraɪz/ → see **authorize**

authoritarian /ɔːˌθɒrɪˈteəriən, AM -ˈtɔːr-/ (**authoritarians**) N-COUNT & ADJ An **authoritarian** or an **authoritarian** person wants to control other people rather than letting them decide things themselves; used showing disapproval. ❑ *...authoritarian governments.*

authoritative /ɔːˈθɒrɪtətɪv, AM əˈθɔːrɪteɪtɪv/ 1 ADJ An **authoritative** statement or piece of writing is based on a complete knowledge of the subject. ❑ *...the first authoritative study of depression.* • **authoritatively** ADV ❑ *I can't speak authoritatively on that.* 2 ADJ An **authoritative** person seems powerful and in control; used showing approval. ❑ *...a calm and authoritative voice.*

authority /ɔːˈθɒrɪti, AM -ˈtɔːr-/ (**authorities**) 1 N-COUNT An **authority** is an official organization that has the power to make decisions. You can refer generally to these organizations, especially government ones, as **the authorities**. ❑ *...the Health Authority.* ❑ *That was just a pretext for the authorities to cancel the elections.* 2 N-UNCOUNT If you have **authority to** do something, you have been given the power or permission to do it. ❑ *Only the king himself had the authority to order such an investigation.* ❑ *The bank charged my account a fee without my authority.* 3 N-COUNT Someone who is an **authority on** a subject knows a lot about it. ❑ *...a world authority on heart disease.*

A

authorize [BRIT also **authorise**] /ˈɔːθəraɪz/ (**authorizes, authorizing, authorized**) V-T If someone **authorizes** something, they give their official permission for it to happen. ❑ *Only the President could authorize its use.* ❑ *The police have been authorized to break up any large gatherings.* • **authorization** (**authorizations**) N-VAR ❑ *We didn't have authorization to go.*

autobiography /ˌɔːtəbaɪˈɒgrəfi/ (**autobiographies**) N-COUNT Your **autobiography** is an account of your life, which you write yourself. • **autobiographical** /ˌɔːtəʊbaɪəˈgræfɪkəl/ ADJ ❑ *...a highly autobiographical novel.*

Word Link	*graph ≈ writing : autograph, biography, graph*

autograph /ˈɔːtəgrɑːf, -græf/ (**autographs, autographing, autographed**) N-COUNT & V-T If a famous person puts their **autograph** on something, or if they **autograph** it, they write their signature on it for you. ❑ *They asked for his autograph.* ❑ *...an autographed photo.*

automated /ˈɔːtəmeɪtɪd/ ADJ An **automated** factory, office, or process uses machines to do the work instead of people.

Word Link	*auto ≈ self : automatic, automobile, autonomy*

automatic /ˌɔːtəˈmætɪk/ (**automatics**) 1 ADJ & N-COUNT An **automatic** machine can keep running without someone operating its controls. You can refer to an automatic gun, car, or washing machine as an **automatic**. ❑ *Modern trains have automatic doors.* ❑ *The weapons were automatics.* • **automatically** ADV ❑ *...equipment to automatically bottle the wine.* 2 ADJ An **automatic** action is one that you do without thinking about it. ❑ *His response was automatic.* • **automatically** ADV ❑ *He switched automatically into interview mode.* 3 ADJ If something such as an action or a punishment is **automatic**, it happens as the normal result of something else. ❑ *The winners will gain an automatic place in the final.* • **automatically** ADV ❑ *Many loan application forms automatically add on insurance.*

automation /ˌɔːtəˈmeɪʃən/ N-UNCOUNT **Automation** is the use of machines to do work instead of people. ❑ *Automation has reduced the work force by half.*
→ see **factory**

Word Link	*mobil ≈ moving : automobile, mobile, mobilize*

automobile /ˈɔːtəməbiːl, AM -məʊˈbiːl/ (**automobiles**) N-COUNT In American English, cars are sometimes called **automobiles**.
→ see **car**

autonomy /ɔːˈtɒnəmi/ N-UNCOUNT If a country, person, or group has **autonomy**, they control themselves rather than being controlled by others. ❑ *Activists stepped up their demands for local autonomy.* • **autonomous** ADJ ❑ *...the autonomous regional government of Andalucia.*

autopsy /ˈɔːtɒpsi/ (**autopsies**) N-COUNT An **autopsy** is an examination of a dead body by a doctor in order to discover the cause of death.

autumn /ˈɔːtəm/ (**autumns**) N-VAR In British English, **autumn** is the season between summer and winter. The American word is **fall**. ❑ *The best time to visit is in autumn.* ❑ *She died last autumn.*

auxiliary /ɔːgˈzɪljəri, AM -ləri/ (**auxiliaries**) 1 N-COUNT & ADJ BEFORE N An **auxiliary**, or an **auxiliary** staff member, is a person who is employed to assist other people, often in the health service or the armed forces. ❑ *...nursing auxiliaries.* 2 ADJ BEFORE N **Auxiliary** equipment is extra equipment that is available for use when necessary. ❑ *...auxiliary fuel tanks.* 3 N-COUNT In grammar, the **auxiliary verbs** are 'be', 'have', and 'do'. They are used with a main verb to form tenses, negatives and questions.

avail /əˈveɪl/ PHRASE If an action is **to no avail**, it does not achieve what you want. ❑ *His efforts were to no avail.* ❑ *Matt fought back but to little avail.*

available /əˈveɪləbəl/ 1 ADJ If something is **available**, you can use it or obtain it. ❑ *Breakfast is available from 6 a.m.* ❑ *There are three small boats available for hire.* ❑ *...the best available information.* • **availability** N-UNCOUNT ❑ *...the easy availability of guns.* 2 ADJ AFTER LINK-V Someone who is **available** is free to talk to you or spend time with you. ❑ *Mr Leach is not available for comment.*

Thesaurus	*available* Also look up:
ADJ.	accessible, handy, usable 1
	free 2

avalanche /ˈævəlɑːntʃ, -læntʃ/ (**avalanches**) 1 N-COUNT An **avalanche** is a large mass of snow or rock that falls down the side of a mountain. 2 N-SING You can refer to a large quantity of things that arrive or happen at the same time as an **avalanche of** them. ❑ *The star was greeted with an avalanche of publicity.*
→ see **snow**

avant-garde /ˌævɒŋˈgɑːd/ ADJ **Avant-garde** theatre or writing is modern and experimental.

avenge /əˈvendʒ/ (**avenges, avenging, avenged**) V-T If you **avenge** a wrong or harmful act, you hurt or punish the person who did it. [FORMAL] ❑ *He was trying to avenge the death of his friend.*

avenue /ˈævɪnjuː, AM -nuː/ (**avenues**) 1 N-COUNT An **avenue** is a wide road, with shops or houses on each side. ❑ *...the most expensive stores on Park Avenue.* 2 N-COUNT An **avenue** is a way of getting something done. ❑ *...possible avenues of investigation.*

average /ˈævərɪdʒ/ (**averages, averaging, averaged**) 1 N-COUNT & ADJ BEFORE N An **average**, or an **average** amount, is the result you get when you add several amounts together and divide the total by the number of amounts. ❑ *The boats remain at sea for an average of ten days.* ❑ *The average age was 63.* 2 PHRASE You say **on average** to indicate that a number is the average of several numbers. ❑ *Women are, on average, paid 25 per cent less than men.* 3 V-T To **average** a particular amount means to be that amount as an average over a period of time. ❑ *We averaged 42 miles per hour.* 4 ADJ & N-SING Something that is **average** or **the average** is normal in quality or amount for a particular group of things or people. ❑ *His first novel is much better than the average novel.* ❑ *...what is found in an average British dustbin.*

aversion /əˈvɜːʃən, AM -ʒən/ (**aversions**) N-VAR If you have an **aversion to** someone or something, you dislike them very much. [FORMAL] ❑ *I've always*

a

had an aversion to being part of a group.

avert /əˈvɜːt/ (**averts, averting, averted**) 1 V-T If you **avert** something unpleasant, you prevent it from happening. ❑ *Talks with the teachers' union have averted a strike.* 2 V-T If you **avert** your eyes, you look away from something.

aviary /ˈeɪvjəri/ (**aviaries**) N-COUNT An **aviary** is a large cage in which birds are kept.

aviation /ˌeɪviˈeɪʃən/ N-UNCOUNT **Aviation** is the operation and production of aircraft.
→ see **oil**

avid /ˈævɪd/ ADJ You use **avid** to describe someone who is very enthusiastic about something. ❑ *He's an avid reader.* ● **avidly** ADV ❑ *Clare read each of the old magazines avidly.*

avocado /ˌævəˈkɑːdəʊ/ (**avocados**) N-VAR An **avocado** is a fruit in the shape of a pear with a dark green skin and a large stone inside it.

avoid /əˈvɔɪd/ (**avoids, avoiding, avoided**) 1 V-T If you **avoid** something unpleasant that might happen, you take action in order to prevent it from happening. ❑ *...emergency action to avoid a disaster.* ❑ *Drink lots of water to avoid becoming dehydrated.* 2 V-T If you **avoid** doing something, you make a deliberate effort not to do it. ❑ *I avoid working in places which are too public.* ❑ *He ran away to Costa Rica to avoid military service.* ● **avoidance** N-UNCOUNT ❑ *...tips regarding health maintenance and stress avoidance.* 3 V-T If you **avoid** someone or something, you try not to have contact with them. ❑ *She thought he was trying to avoid her.* 4 V-T If a person or vehicle **avoids** someone or something, they change the direction they are moving in, so that they do not hit them. ❑ *We managed to avoid the main roads and the holiday traffic.*

Usage

When you try not to do something, you say that you **avoid doing it**, not that you 'avoid to do it'. ❑ *This leaflet tells you how to avoid getting ill.* If you want to suggest that you cannot stop yourself from doing something, you should use the expression **can't help**. ❑ *I'm sorry, I can't help being suspicious.* ❑ *Nobody liked her to cough, but she couldn't help it.*

await /əˈweɪt/ (**awaits, awaiting, awaited**) 1 V-T If you **await** someone or something, you wait for them. [FORMAL] ❑ *We awaited the arrival of the chairman.* 2 V-T Something that **awaits** you is going to happen to you in the future. [FORMAL] ❑ *A nasty surprise awaited them.*

Word Link — **wak ≈ being awake : awake, awakening, wake**

awake /əˈweɪk/ (**awakes, awaking, awoke, awoken**) 1 ADJ AFTER LINK-V If you are **awake**, you are not sleeping. If you are **wide awake**, you are fully awake. 2 V-T/V-I When you **awake**, or when something **awakes** you, you wake up. [LITERARY] ❑ *The sound of many voices awoke her.*
→ see **sleep**

Word Partnership — Use *awake* with:

V.	**keep** *someone* awake, **lie** awake, **stay** awake 1
ADV.	**fully** awake, **half** awake, **wide** awake 1

awaken /əˈweɪkən/ (**awakens, awakening, awakened**) 1 V-T To **awaken** a feeling in a person means to cause them to have this feeling. [FORMAL] ❑ *...struggling to awaken people's interest in local issues.* ● **awakening** (**awakenings**) N-COUNT ❑ *Janet sensed in herself the awakening of something quite special.* 2 V-T/V-I When you **awaken**, or when something **awakens** you, you wake up. [LITERARY]

award /əˈwɔːd/ (**awards, awarding, awarded**) 1 N-COUNT An **award** is a prize or certificate you get for doing something well. ❑ *...the Booker Prize, Britain's top award for fiction.* 2 V-T If you are **awarded** something, you get a prize or certificate for doing something well. ❑ *The Mayor awarded him a medal of merit.* 3 V-T If a judge or referee **awards** someone something, they decide that a sum of money should be given to the person. ❑ *The court awarded them £17,124 for costs and expenses.* 4 N-COUNT An **award** is a sum of money that a judge or referee decides should be given to someone. ❑ *...workmen's compensation awards.*

Word Link — **war ≈ watchful : aware, beware, unaware**

Word Link — **ness ≈ state, condition : awareness, consciousness, kindness**

aware /əˈweə/ 1 ADJ AFTER LINK-V If you are **aware of** a fact or situation, you know about it. ❑ *Smokers are well aware of the dangers to their own health.* ❑ *We are aware that we might lose our jobs.* ● **awareness** N-UNCOUNT ❑ *...general awareness about healthy eating.* 2 ADJ AFTER LINK-V If you are **aware of** something, you realize that it is present or is happening because you hear it, see it, smell it, or feel it. ❑ *She was acutely aware of the noise of the city.* 3 ADJ AFTER LINK-V Someone who is **aware** notices events that are happening around them. ❑ *They are politically very aware.*

Word Partnership — Use *aware* with:

ADV.	**acutely/vaguely** aware, **fully** aware, **painfully** aware, **well** aware 1 2
PREP.	aware **of** *something/someone*, aware **that** 1 2
V.	**become** aware 1 2

awash /əˈwɒʃ/ ADJ AFTER LINK-V If an area or a floor is **awash**, there is a lot of water on it. ❑ *The fuel tanks had burst and the whole boat was awash with diesel.*

away /əˈweɪ/ 1 ADV If you move **away from** a place, you move so that you are no longer there. If you are **away**, you are not in the usual place. ❑ *He walked away from his car.* ❑ *Jason was away on a business trip.* 2 ADV If you put something **away**, you put it in a safe place. ❑ *All her letters were carefully filed away.* ❑ *I have $100m hidden away.* 3 PREP & ADV If something is **away from** a person or place, it is at a distance from that person or place. ❑ *The two women were sitting as far away from each other as possible.* ❑ *The nearest river was four miles away.* 4 → See note at **far** 5 ADJ BEFORE N & ADV When a sports team plays an **away** game, or when it plays **away**, it plays at its opponents' ground. 6 ADV You can use **away** to say that something slowly disappears, or changes so that

A

it is no longer the same. ❑ *So much snow has already melted away.* ❑ *The Liberal Democrats' support fell away.* 7 ADV You use **away** to talk about future events. For example, if an event is a week **away**, it will happen in a week. 8 ADV **Away** is used to emphasize that an action is continuous or repeated. ❑ *He would often be working away on his computer.* 9 **right away** → see **right** 10 **far and away** → see **far**

Word Partnership Use *away* with:

N.	away **from home** 1
V.	**back** away, **blow** away, **break** away, **chase** ***someone*** away, **drive** away, **hide** away, **move** away, **walk** away 1 **put** away, **throw** away 2 **get** away, **go** away, **stay** away 3
ADJ.	**far** away 3

awe /ɔː/ (**awes, awed**) N-UNCOUNT & V-T **Awe** is the respect and amazement that you feel when you are faced with something wonderful and rather frightening. When you have this feeling you are **in awe of** it or **awed** by it. ❑ *She gazed in awe at the great stones.* ❑ *I am still awed by David's courage.*

Word Link ***some*** ≈ ***causing: awesome, fearsome, troublesome***

awesome /'ɔːsəm/ ADJ Something that is **awesome** is very impressive and often frightening. ❑ *The responsibility is awesome.*

awful /'ɔːfʊl/ 1 ADJ If you say that something is **awful**, you mean that it is very bad. ❑ *...the same awful jokes.* ❑ *Her injuries were massive. It was awful.* ❑ *I hardly slept at all and felt pretty awful.* 2 ADJ BEFORE N You can use **awful** to emphasize how large an amount or how long a time is. [INFORMAL] ❑ *I've got an awful lot of work to do.*

Thesaurus *awful* Also look up:

ADJ.	bad, dreadful, horrible, terrible; *(ant.)* good, nice, pleasing 1

awfully /'ɔːfʊli/ ADV You use **awfully** to emphasize how much of a quality someone or something has. [INFORMAL] ❑ *The caramel looks awfully good.* ❑ *I'm awfully sorry.*

awhile /ə'waɪl/ ADV **Awhile** means for a short time. [AM] ❑ *He worked awhile as a pharmacist.*

awkward /'ɔːkwəd/ 1 ADJ An **awkward** situation is embarrassing and difficult to deal with. If you feel **awkward**, you feel embarrassed and shy. ❑ *It was a bit awkward for me.* ❑ *...awkward questions.* ● **awkwardly** ADV ❑ *Awkwardly, we took our places.* 2 ADJ Something that is **awkward to** use or carry is difficult to use or carry because of its design. An **awkward** job is difficult to do. ❑ *It was small but heavy enough to make it awkward to carry.* ● **awkwardly** ADV ❑ *...an awkwardly shaped room.* 3 ADJ An **awkward** movement or position is uncomfortable or clumsy. ❑ *Amy made an awkward movement with her hands.* ● **awkwardly** ADV ❑ *He fell awkwardly.* 4 ADJ Someone who is **awkward** deliberately causes problems for other people. ❑ *Don't be awkward.*

Thesaurus *awkward* Also look up:

ADJ.	delicate, embarrassing, sticky, uncomfortable 1 cumbersome, difficult 2 blundering 3

awoke /ə'wəʊk/ **Awoke** is the past tense of **awake**.

awoken /ə'wəʊkən/ **Awoken** is the past participle of **awake**.

axe [AM **ax**] /æks/ (**axes, axing, axed**) 1 N-COUNT An **axe** is a tool used for chopping wood. It consists of a blade attached to the end of a long handle. 2 V-T If someone's job or something such as a service or programme **is axed**, it is ended suddenly.

axis /'æksɪs/ (**axes** /'æksiːz/) 1 N-COUNT An **axis** is an imaginary line through the middle of something. ❑ *...the daily rotation of the earth upon its axis.* 2 N-COUNT An **axis** of a graph is one of the two lines on which the scales of measurement are marked.
→ see **graph, moon**

Bb

babble /'bæbəl/ (**babbles, babbling, babbled**) V-I & N-SING If you **babble**, you talk in a confused or excited way. You can refer to people's voices as a **babble of** sound when they babble. ❑ *Mum babbled on and on.* ❑ *...the high babble of voices.*

babe /beɪb/ (**babes**) 1 N-VOC Some people use **babe** as an affectionate way of addressing someone. [INFORMAL] ❑ *I'm sorry, babe.* 2 N-COUNT A **babe** is the same as a **baby**. [DATED]

baby /'beɪbi/ (**babies**) 1 N-COUNT A **baby** is a very young child that cannot yet walk or talk. 2 N-VOC & N-COUNT You can use **baby** as an affectionate way of addressing someone. [INFORMAL] ❑ *He was confused, poor baby.*
→ see **child**

Word Partnership Use *baby* with:

N.	baby **boy/girl/sister**, baby **clothes**, baby **food**, baby **names**, baby **talk** 1
V.	**deliver a** baby, **have a** baby 1
ADJ.	**new/newborn** baby, **unborn** baby 1

babysit also **baby-sit** /'beɪbisɪt/ (**babysits, babysitting, babysat**) V-I If you **babysit** for someone, you look after their children while they are out. ❑ *I'd be happy to babysit any time.*
• **babysitter** (**babysitters**) N-COUNT

bachelor /'bætʃələ/ (**bachelors**) N-COUNT A **bachelor** is a man who has never married.

back

❶ ADVERB USES
❷ OPPOSITE OF FRONT; NOUN AND ADJECTIVE USES
❸ VERB USES

back /bæk/
❶ 1 ADV If you move **back**, you move in the opposite direction to the way you are facing. ❑ *She stepped back from the door.* 2 ADV You use **back** to say that someone or something returns to a particular place or state. ❑ *I went back to bed.* ❑ *I'll be back as soon as I can.* ❑ *Denise hopes to be back at work soon.* 3 ADV If you give or put something **back**, you return it to the person who had it or to the place where it was before you took it. If you get or take something **back**, you then have it again after not having it for a while. ❑ *She handed the knife back.* ❑ *Put it back in the freezer.* ❑ *You'll get your money back.* 4 ADV You use **back** to indicate that you are talking or thinking about something that happened in the past. ❑ *The story starts back in 1950.* ❑ *...that big earthquake a few years back.* 5 ADV If you do something **back**, you do to someone what they have done to you. ❑ *If the phone rings, say you'll call back.* ❑ *Lee looked at Theodora. She stared back.* 6 ADV If someone or something is kept or situated **back** from a place, they are at a distance from it. ❑ *Keep back from the edge of the platform.* 7 PHRASE If you move **back and forth**, you repeatedly move in one direction and then in the opposite direction. ❑ *He paced back and forth.* ❑ *...throwing a ball back and forth.* 8 PHRASE If two or more things are done **back to back**, one follows immediately after the other without any interruption. ❑ *...two half-hour shows, which will be screened back to back.*

back /bæk/ (**backs**)
❷ 1 N-COUNT Your **back** is the part of your body from your neck to your waist that is on the opposite side to your chest. 2 N-COUNT & ADJ BEFORE N The **back** or the **back** part of something is the part of it that is behind or farthest from the front. ❑ *...the back of her neck.* ❑ *...the index at the back of the book.* ❑ *...the back door.* 3 N-COUNT The **back** of a chair is the part that you lean against. 4 PHRASE If you do something **behind** someone's **back**, you do it without them knowing about it. 5 PHRASE If you **turn** your **back on** someone or something, you ignore them or refuse to help them. 6 PHRASE If you are wearing something **back to front**, you are wearing it with the back of it on the front of your body.
→ see **body**, **horse**

back /bæk/ (**backs, backing, backed**)
❸ 1 V-I If a building **backs onto** something, the back of it faces in the direction of that thing or touches the edge of that thing. ❑ *...a ground floor flat which backs onto a busy street.* 2 V-T/V-I When you **back** a vehicle somewhere, or when it **backs** somewhere, it moves backwards. ❑ *He backed his car out of the drive.* 3 V-T If you **back** a person or a plan, you support them. ❑ *...the decision to back nuclear power.* 4 V-T If you **back** someone in a competition, you hope that they will win.
5 → see also **backing**

▶ **back away** PHR-VERB If you **back away**, you move away because you are nervous or frightened. ❑ *Jim backed away from the door.*

▶ **back down** PHR-VERB If you **back down**, you stop arguing that you are right.

▶ **back off** PHR-VERB If you **back off**, you move away in order to avoid problems or a fight.

▶ **back out** PHR-VERB If you **back out**, you decide not to do something that you previously agreed to do. ❑ *The Hungarians backed out of the project in 1989.*

▶ **back up** 1 PHR-VERB If someone or something **backs up** a statement, they show that it is true. 2 PHR-VERB If you **back** someone **up**, you help and support them. 3 PHR-VERB If you **back up** a computer file, you make a copy of it to use if the original file is damaged or lost. 4 → see also **back-up**

backbench /'bækbentʃ/ ADJ BEFORE N A **backbench** MP is a Member of Parliament who is not a minister and who does not hold an official position in his or her political party. [BRIT]

backbone /ˈbækbəʊn/ (**backbones**) **1** N-COUNT Your **backbone** is the column of small linked bones along the middle of your back. **2** N-SING The **backbone** of an organization or system is the part of it that gives it its main strength. ❑ *Small businesses are the backbone of this country.*

backer /ˈbækə/ (**backers**) N-COUNT A **backer** is someone who gives support or money to a person or project.

backfire /ˌbækˈfaɪə, AM -ˈfaɪr/ (**backfires, backfiring, backfired**) **1** V-I If a plan **backfires,** it has the opposite result to the one that was intended. **2** V-I When a motor vehicle or its engine **backfires,** it produces an explosion in the exhaust pipe.

Word Link *ground ≈ bottom : background, groundwork, underground*

background /ˈbækgraʊnd/ (**backgrounds**) **1** N-COUNT Your **background** is the kind of family you come from and the kind of education you have had. ❑ *She came from a working-class Yorkshire background.* **2** N-COUNT The **background to** an event or situation consists of the facts that explain what caused it. ❑ *...the background to these troubles.* **3** N-SING The **background** refers to things, shapes, colours, or sounds that are around or behind the main ones. ❑ *...the sound of applause in the background.* ❑ *It had a pattern of white flowers on a green background.* ❑ *...background music.*

Word Partnership Use *background* with:

N.	background **check** 1 background **information/knowledge** 1 2 background **story** 2 background **music/noise** 3
ADJ.	**cultural/ethnic/family** background, **educational** background 1
PREP.	**against a** background, **in the** background 3
V.	**blend into the** background 3

backing /ˈbækɪŋ/ N-UNCOUNT **Backing** is money, resources, or support given to a person or organization. ❑ *Mr Bach set up his own business with the backing of his old boss.*

backlash /ˈbæklæʃ/ N-SING A **backlash against** a trend or development in society or politics is a sudden strong reaction against it. ❑ *There is a backlash against the long working hours of the 1980s.*

backlog /ˈbæklɒg, AM -lɔːg/ (**backlogs**) N-COUNT A **backlog** is a number of things which have not yet been done, but which need to be done. ❑ *The company has a backlog of orders amounting to nearly $1 million.*

backside /ˌbækˈsaɪd/ (**backsides**) N-COUNT Your **backside** is the part of your body that you sit on. [INFORMAL]

backstage /ˌbækˈsteɪdʒ/ ADV In a theatre, **backstage** refers to the areas behind the stage. ❑ *He went backstage and asked for her autograph.*

backstroke /ˈbækstrəʊk/ N-UNCOUNT **Backstroke** is a swimming stroke that you do on your back.

ˌback-to-ˈback ADJ **Back-to-back** wins are gained one after another without any defeats between them. ❑ *...their first back-to-back victories of the season.*

ˈback-up also **backup** (**back-ups**) **1** N-VAR **Back-up** consists of extra equipment or people that you can get help or support from if necessary. ❑ *Does the company have a 24-hour backup service?* **2** N-VAR If you have a second copy of something as **back-up**, you keep it to use in case the first one does not work. ❑ *Computer users should make regular back-up copies.*

Word Link *ward ≈ in the direction of : backward, forward, inward*

backward /ˈbækwəd/ or **backwards** /ˈbækwədz/

In American English and in formal British English, **backward** is often used as an adverb instead of **backwards.**

1 ADV & ADJ BEFORE N If you move or look **backwards,** you move or look in the direction that your back is facing. A **backward** movement or look is in the direction that your back is facing. ❑ *The diver stepped backwards into the water.* ❑ *He took two steps backward.* ❑ *...a backward glance.* **2** ADV If you do something **backwards,** you do it in the opposite way to the usual way. ❑ *He works backwards, building a house from the top downwards.* **3** ADJ A **backward** country or society does not have modern industries and machines; used showing disapproval. **4** PHRASE If someone or something moves **backwards and forwards,** they move repeatedly first in one direction and then in the opposite direction. ❑ *...people travelling backwards and forwards.*

backwater /ˈbækwɔːtə/ (**backwaters**) N-COUNT A **backwater** is a place or an institution that has not been influenced by modern ideas; used showing disapproval. ❑ *The city was a backwater for more than seven centuries.*

backyard /ˌbækˈjɑːd/ (**backyards**) N-COUNT A **backyard** is an area of land at the back of a house.

bacon /ˈbeɪkən/ N-UNCOUNT **Bacon** is salted or smoked meat taken from the back or sides of a pig.

bacteria /bækˈtɪəriə/ N-PLURAL **Bacteria** are very small organisms which can cause disease. • **bacterial** ADJ BEFORE N ❑ *Cholera is a bacterial infection.*

bad /bæd/ (**worse, worst**) **1** ADJ Something that is **bad** is unpleasant, harmful, or of poor quality. ❑ *...a bad day at work.* ❑ *The floods are the worst in nearly fifty years.* **2** ADJ You can say that something is **not bad** to mean that it is quite good. ❑ *The food wasn't bad.* **3** ADJ If you are **bad at** doing something, you are not very skilful at it. ❑ *Dad was really bad at arriving on time.* ❑ *He was a bad driver.* **4** ADJ If you feel **bad** about something, you feel sorry or guilty about it. ❑ *I feel bad that he's doing most of the work.* **5** ADJ If you have a **bad** back, heart, leg, or eye, there is something wrong with it. **6** ADJ **Bad** language is language that contains rude or offensive words. **7** ADJ If you are in a **bad** mood, you do not feel cheerful and you behave unpleasantly to people. **8** PHRASE If you say **'too bad'**, you mean that nothing can be done to change the situation. ❑ *Too bad our trip was so short.*

Thesaurus *bad* Also look up:

ADJ. damaging, dangerous, harmful
inferior, poor, unsatisfactory; *(ant.)* acceptable, good, satisfactory 1

badge /bædʒ/ (**badges**) N-COUNT A **badge** is a small piece of metal or cloth showing a design or words, which you attach to your clothes.

badger /ˈbædʒə/ (**badgers, badgering, badgered**) 1 N-COUNT A **badger** is a wild animal with a white head with two wide black stripes on it. 2 V-T If you **badger** someone, you repeatedly tell them to do something or repeatedly ask them questions.

badly /ˈbædli/ (**worse, worst**) 1 ADV If you do something **badly**, you do it with very little success or effect. ❑ *The project was badly managed.* 2 ADV **Badly** is used to say that something bad happens to a great degree. ❑ *Twelve people were badly injured.* ❑ *This crisis has affected this region badly.* 3 ADV If you need or want something **badly**, you need or want it very much. 4 → see also **worse, worst**

ˌbadly ˈoff (**worse off, worst off**) ADJ If you are **badly off**, you are in a bad situation or condition, especially financially. ❑ *The dirtiest factories are in badly-off communities.* ❑ *There are people much worse off than me, ill, or in pain.*

badminton /ˈbædmɪntən/ N-UNCOUNT **Badminton** is a game played on a rectangular court by two or four players. They hit a feathered object called a shuttlecock across a high net.

ˌbad-ˈtempered 1 ADJ If you are **bad-tempered**, you are not cheerful and get angry easily. ❑ *I became bad-tempered and tearful with my boyfriend.* 2 → See note at **angry**

baffle /ˈbæfəl/ (**baffles, baffling, baffled**) V-T If something **baffles** you, you cannot understand it or explain it. ❑ *Scientists are baffled by the find.* • **baffling** ADJ ❑ *...the baffling descriptions on food labels.*

bag /bæg/ (**bags**) 1 N-COUNT A **bag** is a container made of paper, plastic, or leather which you use to carry things. ❑ *...a clear polythene bag.* ❑ *...a bag of sweets.* 2 N-PLURAL If you have **bags** under your eyes, you have folds of skin there, usually because you have not had enough sleep.

baggage /ˈbægɪdʒ/ 1 N-UNCOUNT Your **baggage** consists of the suitcases and bags that you take with you when you travel. 2 N-UNCOUNT You can use **baggage** to refer to someone's problems. ❑ *He's carrying a lot of old emotional baggage.*

Usage

Baggage is an uncount noun. You can have **a piece of baggage** or **some baggage** but you cannot have 'a baggage' or 'some baggages'.

baggy /ˈbægi/ ADJ **Baggy** clothes hang loosely on your body.

bail /beɪl/ (**bails, bailing, bailed**)

Bail is also spelled **bale** for meaning 2, and for meaning 1 of the phrasal verb.

1 V-T & N-UNCOUNT If someone who is awaiting trial **is bailed**, or if they are released **on bail**, they are set free until they have to appear in court, provided someone agrees to pay an amount of money if they fail to appear. ❑ *Schwarz is now on bail, waiting for a new trial.* 2 V-T/V-I If you **bail** water from a boat, you remove it using a container. ❑ *We kept the boat afloat for a couple of hours by bailing madly.*

▸ **bail out** 1 PHR-VERB If you **bail** someone **out**, you help them out of a difficult situation, often by giving them money. 2 PHR-VERB If you **bail** someone **out**, you pay bail on their behalf.

bailiff /ˈbeɪlɪf/ (**bailiffs**) N-COUNT A **bailiff** is a law officer who makes sure that the decisions of a court are obeyed. [BRIT]

bait /beɪt/ (**baits, baiting, baited**) 1 N-UNCOUNT & V-T **Bait** is food which you put on a hook or in a trap in order to catch fish or animals. When you **bait** a hook or trap, you put bait on it. 2 N-UNCOUNT If someone or something is being used as **bait**, they are being used to tempt someone to do something. ❑ *The general said his soldiers had been used as bait.* 3 V-T If someone **baits** you, they deliberately try to make you angry by teasing them. ❑ *The defense lawyers may be able to bait him and get him to act aggressively.*

bake /beɪk/ (**bakes, baking, baked**) 1 V-I When food **bakes**, it cooks in the oven without any extra liquid or fat. ❑ *...baked potatoes.* 2 V-T/V-I When you **bake** food, you prepare and mix together ingredients, especially to make cakes, biscuits, or bread. You then put them in the oven to cook. ❑ *Who has enough time to bake at home these days?* ❑ *How did you learn to bake cakes?* • **baking** N-UNCOUNT ❑ *Christine describes her job as 'cooking, cleaning, ironing and baking'.* 3 → See note at **cook** 4 → see also **baking**

→ see **cook**

baker /ˈbeɪkə/ (**bakers**) N-COUNT A **baker** is a person whose job is to bake and sell bread and cakes. You also refer to the shop where bread and cakes are sold as a **baker** or a **baker's**.

Word Link *ery ≈ place where something happens : bakery, brewery, refinery*

bakery /ˈbeɪkəri/ (**bakeries**) N-COUNT A **bakery** is a building where bread and cakes are baked, or the shop where they are sold.

baking /ˈbeɪkɪŋ/ ADJ & ADV You can use **baking** to describe weather or a place that is very hot indeed. ❑ *...a baking July day.* ❑ *...a baking-hot island off Borneo.*

balance /ˈbæləns/ (**balances, balancing, balanced**) 1 V-T/V-I If something or someone **balances** somewhere, or if you **balance** them there, they remain steady and do not fall over. ❑ *I balanced on the edge.* ❑ *She had balanced a glass on her head.* 2 N-UNCOUNT **Balance** is the steadiness that someone or something has when they are balanced on something. ❑ *He lost his balance as his foot slipped on the ice.* 3 N-SING A **balance** is a situation or combination of things in which all the different parts are equal or correct in strength or importance. ❑ *...the ecological balance of the forest.* 4 V-T/V-I If you **balance** one thing **with** something different, or if one thing **balances with** another, each of the things has the same strength or importance. ❑ *I found it difficult to balance my job with my family.* 5 V-T To **balance** a budget or **balance the books** means to make

B

sure that the amount of money that is spent is not greater than the amount that is received. **6** N-COUNT The **balance** in your bank account is the amount of money in it. **7** N-SING **The balance** to be paid on something is the amount of money which remains to be paid for it. ❑ *They would pay the balance on delivery.* **8** PHRASE If something is **in the balance**, its future is uncertain. **9** PHRASE You can say **on balance** to indicate that you are stating an opinion only after considering all the relevant facts or arguments. ❑ *On balance he agreed with Christine.*
→ see **brain**

Word Partnership Use *balance* with:

V.	**keep/lose your** balance, **restore** balance **1** **2**
	check a balance, **maintain a** balance **6**
	pay a balance **7**
ADJ.	**delicate** balance **1** **3**
	balance **due**, **outstanding** balance **7**
N.	balance **a budget** **5**
	account balance, balance **transfer** **6**

balanced /ˈbælənst/ **1** ADJ A **balanced** account or report is fair and reasonable. **2** ADJ Something that is **balanced** is pleasing or sensible because its different parts are in the correct proportions. ❑ *...a balanced diet.*

balcony /ˈbælkəni/ (**balconies**) **1** N-COUNT A **balcony** is a platform on the outside of a building with a wall or railing around it. **2** N-COUNT The **balcony** in a theatre or cinema is an upstairs seating area.

bald /bɔːld/ (**balder, baldest**) **1** ADJ Someone who is **bald** has little or no hair on the top of their head. ● **baldness** N-UNCOUNT ❑ *He wears a cap to cover his baldness.* **2** ADJ A **bald** tyre has become worn down and it is no longer safe or legal to use. **3** ADJ BEFORE N A **bald** statement has no unnecessary words in it. ● **baldly** ADV ❑ *Put so baldly, the point seems obvious.*

balding /ˈbɔːldɪŋ/ ADJ If you are **balding**, you are beginning to lose the hair on the top of your head.

bale /beɪl/ (**bales, baling, baled**) **1** N-COUNT A **bale of** something such as hay or paper is a large quantity tied up tightly. **2** V-T When hay or paper **is baled**, it is tied together in a tight bundle. **3** → see also **bail**

balk also **baulk** /bɔːlk, AM bɔːk/ (**balks, balking, balked**) V-I If you **balk at** something, you are very reluctant to do it. ❑ *Even biology students may balk at animal experiments.*

ball /bɔːl/ (**balls**) **1** N-COUNT A **ball** is a round object used in games such as football. **2** N-COUNT A **ball** is something that has a round shape. ❑ *They heard an explosion and saw a ball of fire go up.* **3** N-COUNT The **ball of** your foot or the **ball** of your thumb is the rounded part where your toes join your foot or where your thumb joins your hand. **4** N-COUNT A **ball** is a large formal dance. **5** PHRASE If you **are having a ball**, you are having a very enjoyable time. [INFORMAL] **6** PHRASE If you **start the ball rolling**, you start something happening.
→ see **foot, golf**

Word Partnership Use *ball* with:

N.	**bowling/golf/tennis** ball, **crystal** ball, ball **field**, ball **game** **1**
	snow ball **2**
V.	**bounce/catch/hit/kick/throw a** ball **1**
	roll into a ball **2**
PREP.	ball **of *something*** **2**

ballad /ˈbæləd/ (**ballads**) **1** N-COUNT A **ballad** is a slow, romantic, popular song. **2** N-COUNT A **ballad** is a long song or poem which tells a story using simple language.

ballet /ˈbæleɪ, AM bæˈleɪ/ (**ballets**) **1** N-UNCOUNT **Ballet** is a type of artistic dancing with carefully planned movements. **2** N-COUNT A **ballet** is an artistic work performed by ballet dancers.
→ see **dance**

balloon /bəˈluːn/ (**balloons, ballooning, ballooned**) **1** N-COUNT A **balloon** is a small, thin, rubber bag that becomes larger when you blow air into it. **2** N-COUNT A **balloon** is a large strong bag filled with gas or hot air, which can carry passengers in a compartment underneath it. **3** V-I When something **balloons**, it quickly becomes bigger. ❑ *Her weight ballooned from 8 to 11 stone.*

ballot /ˈbælət/ (**ballots, balloting, balloted**) **1** N-COUNT A **ballot** is a secret vote in which people choose someone in an election, or express their opinion about something. **2** V-T If you **ballot** a group of people, you find out what they think about something by organizing a secret vote. ❑ *The union will ballot members on whether to strike.*

balm /bɑːm/ (**balms**) N-VAR **Balm** is a sweet-smelling oil that is obtained from some tropical trees and is used to make ointments that heal wounds or lessen pain.

bamboo /bæmˈbuː/ (**bamboos**) N-VAR **Bamboo** is a tall tropical plant with hard hollow stems.

ban /bæn/ (**bans, banning, banned**) **1** V-T & N-COUNT If you **ban** something or place a **ban on** it, you state officially that it must not be done, shown, or used. ❑ *A law that bans smoking in all public places.* ❑ *The General also lifted a ban on political parties.* **2** V-T If you **are banned from** doing something, you are officially prevented from doing it. ❑ *He was banned from driving for three years.*

banal /bəˈnɑːl, -ˈnæl/ ADJ If you describe something as **banal**, you mean that it is so ordinary that it is not at all effective or interesting. ❑ *...a banal conversation.* ● **banality** N-UNCOUNT ❑ *...the banality of daytime TV.*

banana /bəˈnɑːnə, -ˈnæn-/ (**bananas**) N-VAR A **banana** is a long curved fruit with a yellow skin.
→ see **fruit**

band /bænd/ (**bands, banding, banded**) **1** N-COUNT A **band** is a group of musicians who play jazz, rock, or pop music, or who play brass instruments together. **2** N-COUNT A **band of** people is a group of people who have joined together because they share an interest or belief. ❑ *...her growing band of followers.* **3** N-COUNT A **band** is a flat narrow strip of cloth which you wear round your head or wrists, or round a piece of clothing. ❑ *...a black arm-band.* **4** N-COUNT A **band**

is a strip or loop of metal or other strong material which strengthens something, or which holds several things together. **5** N-COUNT A **band** is a range of numbers or values within a system of measurement. ❑ *...a new tax band of 20p in the pound.*
→ see **concert**, **theatre**
▶ **band together** PHR-VERB If people **band together**, they act as a group in order to try to achieve something.

bandage /ˈbændɪdʒ/ (**bandages, bandaging, bandaged**) **1** N-COUNT A **bandage** is a long strip of cloth that is tied around a wounded part of someone's body in order to protect or support it. **2** V-T If you **bandage** a wound or part of someone's body, you tie a bandage round it. ❑ *...a man with a bandaged head.*

ˌB&ˈB (**B&Bs**) → see **bed and breakfast**

bandit /ˈbændɪt/ (**bandits**) N-COUNT A **bandit** is an armed robber, especially one who robs travellers.

bandwagon /ˈbændwægən/ (**bandwagons**) N-COUNT If you say that someone has **jumped on the bandwagon**, you mean that they are doing something only because it has become fashionable to do it. ❑ *Many farms are jumping on the bandwagon and growing organic foods.*

bandwidth /ˈbændwɪdθ/ (**bandwidths**) N-VAR A **bandwidth** is the range of frequencies used for a particular telecommunications signal, radio transmission, or computer network.

bang /bæŋ/ (**bangs, banging, banged**) **1** N-COUNT A **bang** is a sudden loud noise such as an explosion. **2** V-T/V-I If you **bang** something such as a door, or if it **bangs**, it closes suddenly with a loud noise. ❑ *The door banged shut behind them.* **3** V-T/V-I If you **bang on** something, or if you **bang** it, you hit it so that it makes a loud noise. ❑ *I banged on the wall.* ❑ *There is no point in shouting or banging the table.* ❑ *Daryl banged his fist on the desk.* **4** V-T & N-COUNT If you **bang** part of your body **against** something, you accidentally knock into it and hurt yourself. A **bang** is a knock or blow. ❑ *He hurried away, banging his leg against a chair.* ❑ *...a sharp bang on the head.*

banish /ˈbænɪʃ/ (**banishes, banishing, banished**) **1** V-T If someone or something **is banished from** a place or activity, they are sent away from it. ❑ *John was banished from England.* **2** V-T If you **banish** something, you get rid of it. ❑ *...diseases like malaria that have now been banished.*

bank /bæŋk/ (**banks, banking, banked**) **1** N-COUNT A **bank** is a place where you can keep your money in an account. **2** N-COUNT You use **bank** to refer to a large amount of something, stored for use. For example, a blood **bank** is a store of blood. **3** N-COUNT The **banks** of a river, canal, or lake are the raised areas of ground along its edge. **4** N-COUNT A **bank** of ground is a raised area of it with a flat top and one or two sloping sides. ❑ *...a grassy bank.* **5** N-COUNT A **bank of** something is a long high row or mass of it. ❑ *...a bank of fog.*
▶ **bank on** PHR-VERB If you **bank on** something happening, you expect it to happen. ❑ *The French are banking on 13 million tourists arriving from Britain this year.*

banker /ˈbæŋkə/ (**bankers**) N-COUNT A **banker** is someone involved in banking at a senior level.

ˌbank ˈholiday (**bank holidays**) N-COUNT A **bank holiday** is a public holiday. [BRIT]

banking /ˈbæŋkɪŋ/ N-UNCOUNT **Banking** is the business activity of banks and similar institutions.
→ see **industry**

banknote also **bank note** /ˈbæŋknəʊt/ (**banknotes**) N-COUNT A **banknote** is a piece of paper money.

bankrupt /ˈbæŋkrʌpt/ (**bankrupts, bankrupting, bankrupted**) **1** ADJ People or organizations that go **bankrupt** do not have enough money to pay their debts. ❑ *He was declared bankrupt after not repaying a £114m loan.* **2** V-T To **bankrupt** a person or organization means to make them go bankrupt. ❑ *The cost of the court case bankrupted him.*

bankruptcy /ˈbænkrʌptsi/ (**bankruptcies**) **1** N-UNCOUNT **Bankruptcy** is the state of being bankrupt. ❑ *Many old firms were facing bankruptcy.* **2** N-COUNT A **bankruptcy** is an instance of an organization or person going bankrupt.

Word Partnership	Use *bankruptcy* with:
V.	**force into** bankruptcy **1**
	avoid bankruptcy **1 2**
	declare bankruptcy, **file for** bankruptcy **2**
N.	bankruptcy **law**, bankruptcy **protection** **1 2**

banner /ˈbænə/ (**banners**) N-COUNT A **banner** is a long strip of cloth with a message on it.

ˈbanner ˌad (**banner ads**) N-COUNT A **banner ad** is a large advertisement on a website that stretches across the top or down the side of the window. [COMPUTING]

banquet /ˈbæŋkwɪt/ (**banquets**) N-COUNT A **banquet** is a grand formal dinner.

banter /ˈbæntə/ N-UNCOUNT **Banter** is friendly, joking talk.

baptism /ˈbæptɪzəm/ (**baptisms**) N-VAR A **baptism** is a ceremony in which a person is baptized.

baptize [BRIT also **baptise**] /bæpˈtaɪz/ (**baptizes, baptizing, baptized**) V-T When someone **is baptized**, drops of water are put on their head or they are dipped in water as a sign that they have become a member of the Christian Church.

bar /bɑː/ (**bars, barring, barred**) **1** N-COUNT A **bar** is a place where people buy and drink alcoholic drinks. **2** N-COUNT A **bar** is a counter on which alcoholic drinks are served. ❑ *He leaned across the bar.* **3** N-COUNT A **bar** is a long, straight piece of metal. ❑ *...an iron bar.* **4** N-COUNT A **bar of** something is a rectangular piece of it. ❑ *...a bar of soap.* **5** V-T If you **bar** someone from going somewhere or doing something, you prevent them from going there or doing it. ❑ *She stood in the doorway, barring his way out.* ❑ *Amnesty workers have been barred from Sri Lanka since 1982.* **6** PREP You can use **bar** to mean 'except'. For example, all the work **bar** the washing means all the work except the washing. [FORMAL] **7** N-PROPER **The Bar** is used to refer to the profession of a barrister in England, or of any kind of lawyer in the United States. ❑ *Robert was planning to read for the Bar.* **8** N-COUNT In music, a **bar** is one of the several short parts

B

Picture Dictionary barn

of the same length into which a piece of music is divided. **9** → see also **barring** **10** PHRASE If someone is **behind bars**, they are in prison.
→ see **chart**, **gymnastics**, **soap**

barbaric /bɑːˈbærɪk/ ADJ **Barbaric** behaviour is extremely cruel. ❑ *This barbaric crime must be punished.* • **barbarism** /ˈbɑːbərɪzəm/ N-UNCOUNT ❑ *...an act of barbarism.* • **barbarity** /bɑːˈbærɪti/ (**barbarities**) N-VAR ❑ *...the barbarities of early medicine.*

barbecue /ˈbɑːbɪkjuː/ (**barbecues, barbecuing, barbecued**) **1** N-COUNT A **barbecue** is a grill used to cook food outdoors. **2** N-COUNT A **barbecue** is an outdoor party at which people eat food cooked on a barbecue. **3** V-T If you **barbecue** food, you cook it on a barbecue. ❑ *Tuna can be grilled, fried or barbecued.* ❑ *...barbecued chicken.*
→ see **cook**

ˌbarbed ˈwire N-UNCOUNT **Barbed wire** is strong wire with sharp points sticking out of it, which is used to make fences.

barber /ˈbɑːbə/ (**barbers**) **1** N-COUNT A **barber** is a man whose job is cutting men's hair. **2** N-SING The shop where a barber works is called the **barber's**.

bard /bɑːd/ (**bards**) N-COUNT A **bard** is a poet. [LITERARY]

bare /beə/ (**barer, barest, bares, baring, bared**) **1** ADJ If a part of your body or a surface is **bare**, it is not covered by anything. ❑ *Her feet were bare.* ❑ *...bare wooden floors.* **2** ADJ If a room, cupboard, or shelf is **bare**, it is empty. ❑ *His fridge was bare apart from a tomato.* **3** ADJ You use **bare** to talk about a very small amount of something or its most basic elements. ❑ *She gave them the barest details of her illness.* **4** V-T If you **bare** something, you uncover it and show it. [WRITTEN] ❑ *She bared her teeth like a dog.* **5** PHRASE If you do something with your **bare hands**, you do it without using any weapons or tools. ❑ *They slowly collected the broken glass in their bare hands.*

barefoot /ˈbeəfʊt/ ADJ If you are **barefoot** or **barefooted**, you are wearing nothing on your feet.

barely /ˈbeəli/ ADV You use **barely** to say that something is only just true or possible. ❑ *Anastasia could barely remember going to the hospital.* ❑ *The water had barely boiled when she cracked four eggs into it.*

bargain /ˈbɑːgɪn/ (**bargains, bargaining, bargained**) **1** V-I When people **bargain with** each other, they discuss what each of them will do, pay, or receive. ❑ *We are not prepared to bargain with you.* ❑ *Shop in small local markets and don't be afraid to bargain.* • **bargaining** N-UNCOUNT ❑ *The government has called for sensible pay bargaining.* **2** N-COUNT A **bargain** is a formal agreement on what two people will do, pay, or receive. ❑ *The treaty was based on a bargain between the French and German governments.* **3** N-COUNT A **bargain** is something which is good value for money, usually because it has been sold at a lower price than normal. ❑ *At this price the wine is a bargain.* **4** PHRASE You use **into the bargain** when mentioning an additional quantity, feature, fact, or action, to emphasize that it is also involved. ❑ *You could lose money and a friend into the bargain.*

▶ **bargain for** PHR-VERB If you get something you had not **bargained for**, or if you get more than you **bargained for**, something happens that you did not expect or something happens to a greater degree than you had expected.

Thesaurus	*bargain* Also look up:
V.	barter, haggle, negotiate **1**
N.	agreement, deal, understanding **2**
	deal, discount **3**

b

Word Partnership

Use *bargain* with:

V.	**make/strike a** bargain 2
	find/get a bargain 3
N.	bargain **hunter**, bargain **price**, bargain **rates** 3
	part of the bargain 2
PREP.	bargain **with *someone*** 1

barge /bɑːdʒ/ (**barges, barging, barged**) 1 N-COUNT A **barge** is a narrow boat with a flat bottom, used for carrying heavy loads. 2 V-I If you **barge into** a place or person, you rush into it or push past them in a rude or rough way. [INFORMAL] ❑ *He barged past her.* ❑ *Students tried to barge into the buildings.*
→ see **ship**

baritone /ˈbærɪtəʊn/ (**baritones**) N-COUNT A **baritone** is a man with a fairly deep singing voice.

bark /bɑːk/ (**barks, barking, barked**) 1 V-I & N-COUNT When a dog **barks** or gives a **bark**, it makes a short, loud noise. ❑ *A small dog barked at a seagull.* 2 N-UNCOUNT **Bark** is the tough material that covers the outside of a tree.

barley /ˈbɑːli/ N-UNCOUNT **Barley** is a crop which has seeds that are used in the production of food, beer, and whisky.

barmaid /ˈbɑːmeɪd/ (**barmaids**) N-COUNT In British English, a **barmaid** is a woman who serves drinks in a bar or pub. The American word is **bartender**.

barman /ˈbɑːmən/ (**barmen**) N-COUNT In British English, a **barman** is a man who serves drinks in a bar or pub. The American word is **bartender**.

barn /bɑːn/ (**barns**) N-COUNT A **barn** is a building on a farm in which crops or animal food are kept.
→ see Picture Dictionary: **barn**

Word Link

meter ≈ measuring : barometer, diameter, perimeter

barometer /bəˈrɒmɪtə/ (**barometers**) N-COUNT A **barometer** is an instrument that measures air pressure and shows when the weather is changing.

baron /ˈbærən/ (**barons**) 1 N-COUNT & N-TITLE A **baron** is a man who is a member of the nobility. 2 N-COUNT You use **baron** to refer to someone who controls a large amount of an industry and who is therefore extremely powerful. ❑ *She married an oil baron.*

Word Link

ess ≈ female : baroness, heiress, mistress

baroness /ˈbærənes/ (**baronesses**) N-COUNT & N-TITLE A **baroness** is a woman who has the same rank as a baron, or who is the wife of a baron.

barracks /ˈbærəks/ (**barracks**) N-COUNT A **barracks** is a building or group of buildings where members of the armed forces live.

barrage /ˈbærɑːʒ, AM bəˈrɑːʒ/ (**barrages**) 1 N-COUNT If you get a lot of questions or complaints about something, you can say that you are getting a **barrage of** them. ❑ *He faced a barrage of angry questions.* 2 N-COUNT A **barrage** is continuous firing on an area with a large number of weapons such as heavy guns and tanks. ❑ *...a barrage of anti-aircraft fire.*

barrel /ˈbærəl/ (**barrels**) 1 N-COUNT A **barrel** is a large round container for liquids or food. Barrels are usually wider in the middle than at the top or bottom. ❑ *...12 million barrels of oil.* 2 N-COUNT The **barrel** of a gun is the long metal tube through which the bullet moves when the gun is fired.

barren /ˈbærən/ ADJ **Barren** land has soil of such bad quality that plants cannot grow on it. ❑ *...a hot, barren desert.*

barricade /ˈbærɪkeɪd/ (**barricades, barricading, barricaded**) 1 N-COUNT A **barricade** is a line of vehicles or other objects placed across a road or passage to stop people getting past. 2 V-T If people **barricade** a road or passage, they put something across it to stop other people passing. ❑ *Police barricaded the entrance to the court.* 3 V-T If you **barricade yourself** inside a room or building, you put something heavy against the door so that other people cannot get in. ❑ *The students have barricaded themselves into their dormitory building.*

barrier

barrier /ˈbæriə/ (**barriers**) 1 N-COUNT A **barrier** is a fence or wall that prevents people or things from moving from one area to another. 2 N-COUNT A **barrier** is something such as a law or policy that makes it difficult or impossible for something to happen. ❑ *Taxes are the most obvious barrier to free trade.*

Word Partnership

Use *barrier* with:

V.	**break down a** barrier, **cross a** barrier 1
N.	barrier **islands/reef**, **police** barrier 1
	language barrier 2
PREP.	barrier **between** 1 2
ADJ.	**psychological** barrier, **racial** barrier 2

barring /ˈbɑːrɪŋ/ PREP You use **barring** to indicate that the person, thing, or event that you are mentioning is an exception to the point that you are making. ❑ *Barring accidents, you'll live until your early seventies.*

barrister /ˈbærɪstə/ (**barristers**) N-COUNT A **barrister** is a lawyer who represents people in the higher courts of law. [BRIT]

bartender /ˈbɑːtendə/ (**bartenders**) N-COUNT In American English, a **bartender** is a person who serves drinks in a bar. The British word is **barman** or **barmaid**.

barter /ˈbɑːtə/ (**barters, bartering, bartered**) V-T/V-I & N-UNCOUNT If you **barter** goods, you exchange them for other goods, rather than selling them. **Barter** is the act of exchanging goods in this way. ❑ *They have been bartering wheat for cotton.* ❑ *...streetmarkets where you can barter for leather and silverware.* ❑ *...the old barter system.*
→ see **money**

base /beɪs/ (**bases, basing, based**) 1 N-COUNT The **base** of something is its lowest edge or part, or the part at which it is attached to something

B

else. ❑ *...a cake tin with a removable base.* ❑ *...the base of the cliffs.* **2** N-COUNT A position or thing that is a **base** for something is one from which that thing can be developed or achieved. ❑ *Puerto Andraitx is an ideal base for touring the west coast.* **3** V-T If you **base** one thing **on** another thing, or if one thing **is based on** another, the first thing is developed from the second one. ❑ *He based his conclusions on the evidence.* ❑ *The new products are based on traditional herbal medicines.* **4** N-COUNT & ADJ Your **base** is the main place where you work, stay, or live. If you **are based** in a particular place, that is the place where you live or do most of your work. ❑ *Her base was her home in Scotland.* ❑ *Both firms are based in Kent.* **5** N-VAR A military **base** is a place which part of an army, navy, or air force works from. ❑ *...a British army base near Hanover.*

→ see **area**

Word Partnership Use *base* with:

N.	**client/customer** base, **fan** base, **knowledge** base, **tax** base **2**
	base **camp**, base **of operation** **4**
ADJ.	**military/naval** base **5**

baseball /ˈbeɪsbɔːl/ N-UNCOUNT **Baseball** is a game played by two teams of nine players. Each player from one team hits a ball with a bat and then tries to run round all four bases before the other team can get the ball back.

basement /ˈbeɪsmənt/ (**basements**) N-COUNT The **basement** of a building is an area partly or completely below ground level, with a room or rooms in it. ❑ *...a basement flat.*

→ see **house**

bases **1** /ˈbeɪsɪz/ **Bases** is the plural and the third person singular of **base**. **2** /ˈbeɪsiːz/ **Bases** is the plural of **basis**.

bash /bæʃ/ (**bashes, bashing, bashed**) **1** N-COUNT A **bash** is a party or celebration. [INFORMAL] ❑ *...one of the biggest showbiz bashes of the year.* **2** V-T If you **bash** someone or something, you hit them hard in a rough way. ❑ *I bashed him on the head.* ❑ *Too many golfers try to bash the ball out of sand.*

basic /ˈbeɪsɪk/ (**basics**) **1** ADJ & N-PLURAL You use **basic** or **the basics** to describe the most important or the simplest aspects of something. ❑ *There are four basic principles to follow to keep warm.* ❑ *Let's get down to basics.* ❑ *...teaching the basics of reading, writing and arithmetic.* **2** ADJ **Basic** goods and services are very simple ones which every human being needs. ❑ *...shortages of even the most basic foods.* ❑ *...the basic needs of food and water.* **3** ADJ AFTER LINK-V An activity, situation, or plan that is **basic to** the achievement or success of something else is necessary for it. ❑ *These principles are basic to all the great religions.* **4** ADJ You describe something as **basic** when it has only the most important features and no luxuries. ❑ *...basic cooking and camping equipment.*

Thesaurus *basic* Also look up:

ADJ.	essential, fundamental, key, main, necessary, principle, vital; *(ant.)* secondary **1**-**4**

Word Partnership Use *basic* with:

ADJ.	**most** basic, basic **types of *something*** **1**-**4**
N.	basic **right** **1**
	basic **idea**, basic **principles/values**, basic **problem**, basic **questions**, basic **skills**, basic **understanding** **1** **3**
	basic **(health) care**, basic **needs** **2** **4**

basically /ˈbeɪsɪkli/ **1** ADV You use **basically** to give a general description of something. ❑ *He is basically healthy.* **2** ADV You use **basically** to indicate what the most important feature of something is. ❑ *The building basically looks the same as it did in 1950.*

basin /ˈbeɪsən/ (**basins**) **1** N-COUNT A **basin** is a deep bowl that you use for holding liquids, or for mixing food in. **2** N-COUNT A **basin** is the same as a **washbasin**. **3** N-COUNT The **basin** of a large river is the area of land around it from which water runs down into it. ❑ *...the Amazon basin.*

→ see **bathroom, lake**

basis /ˈbeɪsɪs/ (**bases** /ˈbeɪsiːz/) **1** N-COUNT The **basis** of something is the central and most important part of it, from which it can be developed. ❑ *They hope they will reach the basis for an agreement by May.* **2** N-COUNT The **basis** for something is the thing that provides a reason for it. ❑ *The idea has its basis in fact.* **3** PHRASE If something happens or is done **on a** particular **basis**, it happens or is done in that way. ❑ *We're going to meet there on a regular basis.* ❑ *They work on a voluntary basis.*

Word Partnership Use *basis* with:

V.	**serve as a** basis, **provide a** basis **1**
PREP.	**on the** basis **of *something*** **1**
	basis **for *something*** **1** **2**
ADJ.	**equal** basis, **on a daily/regular/weekly** basis, **on a voluntary** basis **3**

bask /bɑːsk, bæsk/ (**basks, basking, basked**) **1** V-I If you **bask in** the sunshine, you lie in it and enjoy its warmth. **2** V-I If you **bask in** someone's approval, favour, or admiration, you thoroughly enjoy it. ❑ *For now, the company can bask in its success.*

basket /ˈbɑːskɪt, ˈbæs-/ (**baskets**) N-COUNT A **basket** is a container made of thin strips of cane, metal or plastic woven together. ❑ *He put the toothpaste in his basket.*

basketball /ˈbɑːskɪtbɔːl, ˈbæs-/ N-UNCOUNT **Basketball** is a game in which two teams of five players each try to score points by throwing a large ball through a circular net fixed to a metal ring at each end of the court.

bass /beɪs/ (**basses**) **1** N-COUNT A **bass** is a man with a deep singing voice. **2** ADJ BEFORE N A **bass** instrument has a range of notes of low pitch. ❑ *...a bass guitar.*

bastion /ˈbæstiən, AM -tʃən/ (**bastions**) N-COUNT If you describe a system or organization as a **bastion of** a particular way of life, you mean that it is important and effective in defending that way of life. [LITERARY] ❑ *St Xavier's College was a male bastion until 1978 when it began admitting women.*

bat /bæt/ (**bats, batting, batted**) **1** N-COUNT A

b

Word Web bat

Bats fly like birds, but they are **mammals**. Female bats give birth to their young and produce milk to feed them. Bats are **nocturnal**. They search for food at night and sleep during the day. They **roost** upside down in dark, quiet places such as caves and lofts. People think that bats drink blood, but only **vampire bats** do this. Most bats eat fruit or insects. As bats fly they make high-pitched sounds that bounce off objects. This **echolocation** is a kind of **radar** that guides them as they fly.

bat is a specially shaped piece of wood that is used for hitting the ball in cricket, baseball, or table tennis. ❑ *...a baseball bat.* 2 V-I When you **bat**, you have a turn at hitting the ball with a bat in cricket or baseball. ❑ *Penney also batted well to make 57.* 3 N-COUNT A **bat** is a small flying animal that looks like a mouse with wings. Bats fly at night.
→ see Word Web: **bat**
→ see **cave**

batch /bætʃ/ (**batches**) N-COUNT A **batch of** things or people is a group of them, especially one that is dealt with at the same time. ❑ *Bread is baked in batches throughout the day.* ❑ *...a new batch of students.*

bath /bɑːθ, bæθ/ (**baths, bathing, bathed**) 1 N-COUNT In British English, a **bath** is a container which you fill with water and sit in while you wash your body. The American word is **bathtub**. 2 N-COUNT When you **have** a **bath** or **take** a **bath**, you wash your body while sitting in a bath filled with water. ❑ *I took a long hot bath.* 3 V-T & N-COUNT If you **bath** a child or other person, or if you **give** them a **bath**, you wash them in a bath. ❑ *You don't have to bath your child every day.*
→ see **bathroom**

bathe /beɪð/ (**bathes, bathing, bathed**) 1 V-I When you **bathe** in a sea, river, or lake, you swim or play there. [BRIT, FORMAL] ❑ *The water's 45 degrees centigrade, so it's nice to bathe in.* • **bathing** N-UNCOUNT ❑ *...bathing beaches.* 2 V-I When you **bathe**, you have a bath. [AM] ❑ *At least 60% of us bathe or shower once a day.* 3 V-T When you **bathe** a wound, you wash it gently. ❑ *Bathe the infected area in salty water.* 4 V-T If a place **is bathed in** light, it is very bright. ❑ *I was led to a small room bathed in sunlight.*

bathroom /ˈbɑːθruːm, ˈbæθ-/ (**bathrooms**) 1 N-COUNT A **bathroom** is a room in a house that contains a bath or shower, a washbasin, and sometimes a toilet. 2 N-SING In American English, a **bathroom** is a room in a house or public building that contains a toilet. The usual British word is **toilet**.
→ see Picture Dictionary: **bathroom**
→ see **house**

Thesaurus	*bathroom*	Also look up:
N.	lavatory, toilet 2	

bathtub /ˈbɑːθtʌb, ˈbæθ-/ (**bathtubs**) N-COUNT In American English, a **bathtub** is a container which you fill with water and sit in while you wash your body. The British word is **bath**.

baton /ˈbætɒn, AM bəˈtɑːn/ (**batons**) 1 N-COUNT A **baton** is a stick, for example one which is used

Picture Dictionary bathroom

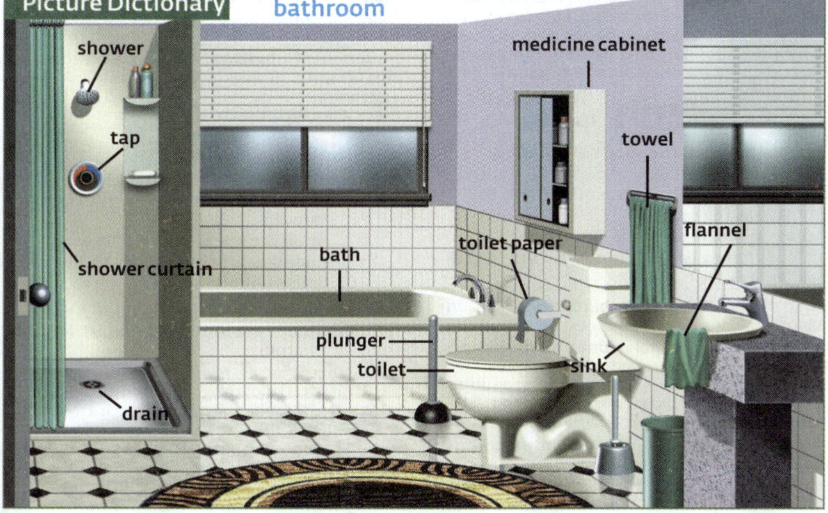

by the conductor of an orchestra, or by athletes in a relay race. **2** N-COUNT A **baton** is a short heavy stick which is sometimes used as a weapon by the police.

batsman /ˈbætsmən/ (**batsmen**) N-COUNT In a game of cricket, the **batsman** is the person who is batting.

battalion /bəˈtæljən/ (**battalions**) N-COUNT A **battalion** is a large group of soldiers consisting of three or more companies.

batter /ˈbætə/ (**batters, battering, battered**) **1** V-T To **batter** someone or something means to hit them many times. ❑ *They'd been waiting ten years to batter me and now they had their chance.* ❑ *I felt battered and exhausted.* ❑ *Batter the steaks flat.* **2** N-UNCOUNT **Batter** is a mixture of flour, eggs, and milk used to make pancakes.

battered /ˈbætəd/ ADJ Something that is **battered** is old, worn, and damaged. ❑ *...a battered leather suitcase.*

battering /ˈbætərɪŋ/ (**batterings**) N-COUNT If something **takes** a **battering**, it suffers very badly as a result of a particular event or action. ❑ *Hotels have been closed after a battering from the hurricane.*

battery /ˈbætəri/ (**batteries**) **1** N-COUNT **Batteries** are the devices that you put in electrical items to provide the power that makes them work. **2** N-COUNT A **battery of** things, people, or events is a large number of them. ❑ *...a battery of journalists and television cameras.*
→ see **cellphone**

battle /ˈbætəl/ (**battles, battling, battled**) **1** N-VAR In a war, a **battle** is a fight between armies or between groups of ships or planes. ❑ *...a gun battle.* ❑ *...men who die in battle.* **2** N-COUNT & V-I A **battle** is a conflict in which different people or groups compete for power or try to achieve opposite things. Opposing groups can also **battle with** one another. ❑ *...a long legal battle.* ❑ *2,000 fans battled with police.* ❑ *The sides must battle again for a quarter-final place.* **3** V-T/V-I If you **battle**, you try hard to be successful in spite of very difficult circumstances. ❑ *Doctors battled through the night to save her life.* ❑ *He is battling with a leg injury.* **4** PHRASE If one person or group **does battle with** another, they take part in a battle or contest against them.
→ see **army**

Word Partnership Use *battle* with:

ADJ.	**bloody** battle, **major** battle 1
	legal battle 2
	constant battle, **uphill** battle 2 3
	losing battle 2 4
V.	**prepare for** battle 1
	fight a battle, **lose/win a** battle 1 2 4
N.	battle **of wills** 2

battlefield /ˈbætəlfiːld/ (**battlefields**) N-COUNT A **battlefield** is a place where a battle is fought.

battleground /ˈbætəlgraʊnd/ (**battlegrounds**) **1** N-COUNT A **battleground** is the same as a **battlefield**. **2** N-COUNT You can refer to a subject over which people disagree or compete as a **battleground**. ❑ *...the battleground of education.*

battleship /ˈbætəlʃɪp/ (**battleships**) N-COUNT A **battleship** is a very large, heavily armoured warship.

baulk /bɔːlk, AM bɔːk/ → see **balk**

bawl /bɔːl/ (**bawls, bawling, bawled**) **1** V-T/V-I If you **bawl**, you shout or sing something loudly and harshly. ❑ *Laura and Peter were shouting and bawling at each other.* ❑ *He bawled the opening line of his song.* **2** V-I If a child **is bawling**, it is crying loudly. ❑ *...a bawling baby.*

bay /beɪ/ (**bays**) **1** N-COUNT A **bay** is a part of a coastline where the land curves inwards. ❑ *...San Francisco Bay.* **2** N-COUNT A **bay** is a partly enclosed area used for a particular purpose. ❑ *The car reversed into the loading bay.* **3** PHRASE If you **keep** something or someone **at bay**, or **hold** them **at bay**, you prevent them from reaching or affecting you. ❑ *Eating oranges keeps colds at bay.*
→ see **land**

bayonet /ˈbeɪənət/ (**bayonets**) N-COUNT A **bayonet** is a long sharp blade that can be fixed to the end of a rifle and used as a weapon.

bazaar /bəˈzɑː/ (**bazaars**) **1** N-COUNT A **bazaar** is an area with many small shops and stalls, especially in the Middle East and India. **2** N-COUNT A **bazaar** is a sale to raise money for charity.

BC /ˌbiː ˈsiː/ You use **BC** in dates to indicate a number of years or centuries before the year in which Jesus Christ is believed to have been born. ❑ *...the fourth century BC.*

be /bi, STRONG biː/ (**am, are, is, being, was, were, been**) **1** LINK-VERB You use **be** to introduce more information about the subject, such as its identity, nature, qualities, or position. ❑ *She's my mother.* ❑ *Cheney was in Madrid.* ❑ *He's still alive isn't he?* **2** LINK-VERB You use **be**, with 'it' as the subject, in clauses where you are describing something or giving your judgement of a situation. ❑ *Now it is necessary to say no.* ❑ *It's nice having friends here.* ❑ *It's a good idea to eat fresh food.* **3** LINK-VERB You use **be** as a link between a subject and a clause, as exemplified below. ❑ *It was me she liked.* ❑ *Our problem is persuading them.* **4** LINK-VERB You use **be** with 'there' in expressions like **there is** and **there are** to say that something exists or happens. ❑ *Clearly there is a problem.* ❑ *There are few cars on this street.*

beach /biːtʃ/ (**beaches**) N-COUNT A **beach** is an area of sand or pebbles by the sea. ❑ *...a beautiful sandy beach.*
→ see Word Web: **beach**

Word Partnership Use *beach* with:

PREP.	**along the** beach, **at/on the** beach
N.	beach **chair**, beach **club/resort**, beach **vacation**
V.	**lie on the** beach, **walk on the** beach
ADJ.	**nude** beach, **private** beach, **rocky** beach, **sandy** beach

beacon /ˈbiːkən/ (**beacons**) N-COUNT A **beacon** is a light or a fire on a hill or tower, which acts as a signal or a warning.

bead /biːd/ (**beads**) **1** N-COUNT **Beads** are small pieces of coloured glass, wood, or plastic with a hole through the middle which are used for jewellery or decoration. ❑ *...a string of colourful beads.* **2** N-COUNT A **bead of** liquid or moisture is a small drop of it. ❑ *There were beads of sweat on his forehead.*
→ see **glass**

b

Word Web beach

Beaches have a natural cycle of build-up and **erosion**. **Ocean currents**, **wind**, and **waves** move **sand** along the **coast**. In certain spots, some of the sand gets left behind. The **surf** deposits it on the beach. Then the wind blows it into **dunes**. As currents change, they **erode** sand from the beach. High waves carry beach sand **seaward**. This process raises the **seafloor**. As the water gets shallower, the waves become smaller. Then they begin depositing sand on the beach. At the same time, small **pebbles** smash into each other. They break up and form new sand.

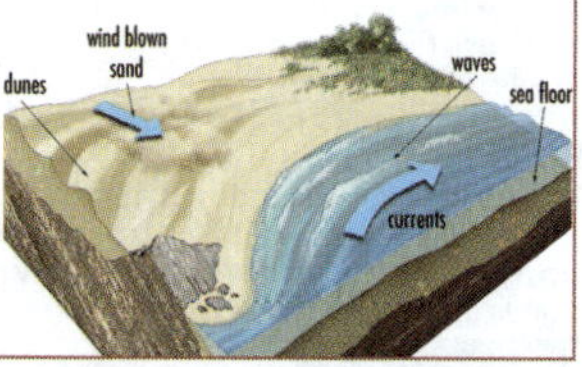

beak

beak /biːk/ (**beaks**) N-COUNT A bird's **beak** is the hard curved or pointed part of its mouth.
→ see **bird**

beaker /ˈbiːkə/ (**beakers**) 1 N-COUNT A **beaker** is a plastic cup. 2 N-COUNT A **beaker** is a glass or plastic jar which is used in chemistry.
→ see **laboratory**

beam /biːm/ (**beams, beaming, beamed**) 1 V-I If you **are beaming**, you are smiling because you are happy. [WRITTEN] ❑ *The teacher was beaming at him.* 2 V-T/V-I If something such as radio signals or television pictures **are beamed** somewhere, or if they **beam** somewhere, they are sent there by means of electronic equipment. ❑ *Soon, CMTV will be beaming into British homes.* 3 N-COUNT A **beam of** light is a line of light that shines from an object such as a torch or the sun. 4 V-I If something such as the sun or a lamp **beams down**, it sends light to a place and shines on it. ❑ *A white spotlight beamed down on the stage.* 5 N-COUNT A **beam** is a long thick bar of wood, metal, or concrete which is used to support the roof of a building.
→ see **gymnastics, laser**

bean /biːn/ (**beans**) 1 N-COUNT **Beans** are the pods of a climbing plant, or the seeds that the pods contain, which are eaten as a vegetable. 2 N-COUNT **Beans** are the seeds of plants such as coffee or cocoa, which can be dried and used in making drinks or chocolate.

bear /beə/ (**bears, bearing, bore, borne**) 1 N-COUNT A **bear** is a large strong wild animal with thick fur and sharp claws. 2 V-T If you **bear** something somewhere, you carry it there. [LITERARY] ❑ *They bore the huge box into the kitchen.* 3 V-T If something **bears** the weight of something else, it supports the weight of that thing. ❑ *The ice was not thick enough to bear their weight.* 4 V-T If you **bear** something difficult, you accept it and are able to deal with it. ❑ *They have to bear living in constant fear.* ❑ *He can't bear to talk about it.* 5 V-T If you **bear** someone a feeling such as love or hate, you feel that emotion towards them. [FORMAL] ❑ *We do not bear a grudge against anyone for what has happened.* 6 to **bear the brunt of** → see **brunt** 7 to **bear in mind** → see **mind**

bear

▶ **bear out** PHR-VERB If something **bears** someone **out** or **bears out** what they are saying, it supports what they are saying. ❑ *The facts do not bear out the theory.*

▶ **bear with** PHR-VERB If you ask someone to **bear with** you, you are asking them to be patient. ❑ *Bear with me, Frank, just let me explain.*

Thesaurus	*bear*	Also look up:
V.	carry, lug, move, transport 2	
	endure, put up with, stand, tolerate 4	

bearable /ˈbeərəbəl/ ADJ If something is **bearable**, you can accept it, although it is rather unpleasant. ❑ *...the small luxuries that made life bearable.*

beard /bɪəd/ (**beards**) N-COUNT A man's **beard** is the hair that grows on his chin and cheeks.
→ see **hair**

bearded /bɪədɪd/ ADJ A **bearded** man has a beard.

bearer /ˈbeərə/ (**bearers**) N-COUNT The **bearer of** something such as a document or a piece of news is the person who has it, or the person who brings it to you. ❑ *Spanish identity documents state the bearer's profession.* ❑ *I hate to be the bearer of bad news.*

bearing /ˈbeərɪŋ/ (**bearings**) 1 PHRASE If something **has a bearing on** a situation or event, it is relevant to it. ❑ *Diet has an important bearing on your general health.* 2 PHRASE If you **get** your **bearings** or **find** your **bearings**, you find out where you are or what you should do next. If you **lose** your **bearings**, you do not know where you are or what you should do next.

beast /biːst/ (**beasts**) N-COUNT A **beast** is an animal, especially a large one. [LITERARY]

beat /biːt/ (**beats, beating, beat, beaten**) 1 V-T To **beat** someone or something means to hit them very hard. ❑ *He is chased by Monica, who beats him with a frying pan.* ❑ *The rain was beating on the window.* ● **beating** (**beatings**) N-COUNT ❑ *Prisoners showed signs of severe beatings.* ❑ *...the beating of the rain.* 2 V-I & N-COUNT When your heart or pulse **beats**, it continually makes regular rhythmic movements. The **beat** of your heart or pulse is a single movement of it. ❑ *My heart beat faster.* ❑ *...more than 70 beats per minute.* ● **beating** N-SING ❑ *...the beating of my heart.* 3 N-COUNT The **beat** of a piece of music is the main rhythm that it has.

B

❑ *...the heavy beat of rock music.* 4 V-T If you **beat** eggs, cream, or butter, you mix them thoroughly. 5 V-T If you **beat** someone in a competition, you do better than them. ❑ *She was beaten into third place.* ● **beating** N-SING ❑ *The right-wingers took a beating in the debate.*
→ see **drum**

▶ **beat down** 1 PHR-VERB When the sun **beats down**, it is very hot and bright. 2 PHR-VERB When the rain **beats down**, it rains very hard.

▶ **beat up** PHR-VERB If someone **beats** a person **up**, they hit or kick the person many times. ❑ *I was beaten up and lost a lot of blood.*

Thesaurus *beat* Also look up:

V. hit, pound, punch; *(ant.)* caress, pat, pet 1
mix, stir, whip 4

Word Partnership Use *beat* with:

N. beat **a drum**, beat **a rug** 1
heart beat 2
beat **eggs** 4
beat **a deadline** 5
PREP. beat **against**, beat **on** 1
on/to a beat 3
PRON. beat **its/their wings** 2

Word Link *ful ≈ filled with : beautiful, careful, dreadful*

beautiful /ˈbjuːtɪfʊl/ 1 ADJ **Beautiful** means attractive to look at. ❑ *...the most beautiful child on earth.* ❑ *New England is beautiful.* ● **beautifully** ADV ❑ *...a beautifully clear, sunny day.* 2 ADJ You can describe something that someone does as **beautiful** when they do it very skilfully. ❑ *...the finest and most beautiful display of bowling.* ● **beautifully** ADV ❑ *He writes beautifully.*

Usage

When you are describing someone's appearance, you usually use **beautiful** and **pretty** to describe women, girls, and babies. **Beautiful** is a much stronger word than **pretty**. The equivalent word for a man is **handsome**. **Good-looking** and **attractive** can be used to describe people of either sex.

Thesaurus *beautiful* Also look up:

ADJ. gorgeous, lovely, pretty, stunning; *(ant.)* grotesque, hideous, homely, ugly 1

beauty /ˈbjuːti/ (**beauties**) 1 N-UNCOUNT **Beauty** is the state or quality of being beautiful. ❑ *...an area of outstanding natural beauty.* ❑ *...the idea of feminine beauty.* 2 N-COUNT A beautiful woman is sometimes described as a **beauty**. 3 N-PLURAL The **beauties of** something are its attractive qualities or features. [LITERARY] ❑ *...the beauties of the countryside.* 4 N-COUNT If you say that a particular feature is **the beauty of** something, you mean that this feature is what makes the thing so good. ❑ *The beauty of this is that any fool can make it.*

beaver /ˈbiːvə/ (**beavers**) N-COUNT A **beaver** is a furry animal like a large rat with a big flat tail.

beaver

became /bɪˈkeɪm/ **Became** is the past tense of **become**.

because /bɪˈkʌz, bɪˈkɒz/ 1 CONJ You use **because** when stating the reason or explanation for something. ❑ *He is called Mitch, because his name is Mitchell.* ❑ *Maybe they won because they had the best players?* 2 PREP If an event or situation occurs **because of** something, that thing is the reason or cause. ❑ *Many families break up because of a lack of money.*

beckon /ˈbekən/ (**beckons, beckoning, beckoned**) 1 V-T/V-I If you **beckon to** someone, you signal to them to come to you. ❑ *He beckoned to the waiter.* ❑ *I beckoned her over.* 2 V-I If something **beckons**, it is so attractive that you want to become involved in it. ❑ *...the warm bars and restaurants now beckoned.*

become /bɪˈkʌm/ (**becomes, becoming, became, become**) 1 LINK-VERB If someone or something **becomes** a particular thing, they start being that thing. ❑ *He became a professional footballer.* ❑ *The wind became stronger.* 2 PHRASE If you wonder **what has become of** someone, you wonder where they are and what has happened to them.

bed /bed/ (**beds**) 1 N-VAR A **bed** is a piece of furniture that you lie on when you sleep. ❑ *We went to bed at about 4am.* ❑ *Sam and Robina put the children to bed.* 2 PHRASE To **go to bed with** someone means to have sex with them. 3 N-COUNT A **flower bed** is an area of earth in which you grow plants. 4 N-COUNT The **sea bed** or a **river bed** is the ground at the bottom of the sea or of a river.
→ see Picture Dictionary: **bed**
→ see **lake, sleep**

Word Partnership Use *bed* with:

ADJ. **asleep in** bed, **double/single/twin** bed, **ready for** bed 1
V. **be sick in** bed, **get into** bed, **go to** bed, **lie (down) in** bed, **put *someone* to** bed 1
PREP. **in/out of** bed, **under the** bed 1
bed **of *something*** 3

bed and ˈbreakfast N-UNCOUNT **Bed and breakfast** is a system of accommodation in a hotel or guest house in which you pay for a room for the night and for breakfast the following morning. The abbreviation **B&B** is also used.

bedclothes /ˈbedkləʊðz/ N-PLURAL **Bedclothes** are the sheets and covers which you put on a bed.

bedding /ˈbedɪŋ/ N-UNCOUNT **Bedding** consists of sheets, blankets, and other covers used on beds.

bedrock /ˈbedrɒk/ N-UNCOUNT The **bedrock of** something refers to all the principles on which it is based. ❑ *Trust is the bedrock of a relationship.*

bedroom /ˈbedruːm/ (**bedrooms**) N-COUNT A **bedroom** is a room which is used for sleeping in.
→ see **house**

Picture Dictionary **bed**

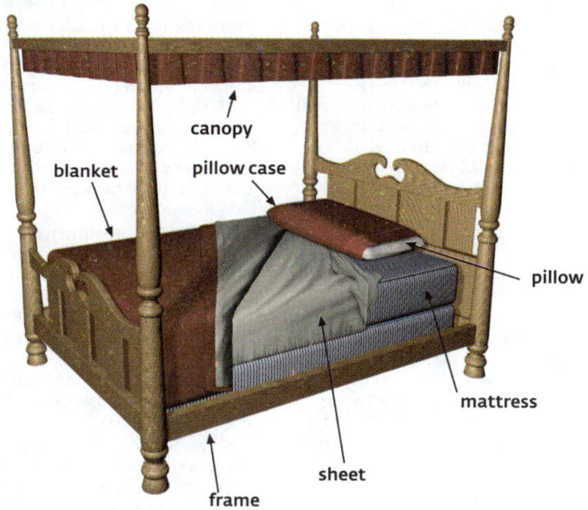

bedside /ˈbedsaɪd/ **1** N-SING Your **bedside** is the area beside your bed. ❑ *He drew a chair up to the bedside and sat down.* **2** N-SING If you talk about being at someone's **bedside**, you are talking about being near them when they are ill in bed. ❑ *She was called to her brother's bedside.*

bee /biː/ (**bees**) N-COUNT A **bee** is an insect with a yellow-and-black striped body that makes a buzzing noise as it flies. Bees make honey.

beef /biːf/ N-UNCOUNT **Beef** is the meat of a cow, bull, or ox.
→ see **meat**

▸ **beef up** PHR-VERB If you **beef** something **up**, you increase, strengthen, or improve it. ❑ *These companies are planning to beef up their workforce with new staff.*

been /bɪn, biːn/ **1** **Been** is the past participle of **be**. **2** V-I If you have **been to** a place, you have gone to it or visited it. ❑ *He's already been to Tunisia.*

beer /bɪə/ (**beers**) N-VAR **Beer** is a bitter alcoholic drink made from grain. A **beer** is a glass of beer.

beet /biːt/ (**beets**) **1** N-UNCOUNT **Beet** is a root vegetable that is used as food for animals. **2** N-VAR In American English, **beets** are **beetroot**.
→ see **sugar**

beetle /ˈbiːtəl/ (**beetles**) N-COUNT A **beetle** is an insect with a hard covering to its body.

beetroot /ˈbiːtruːt/ (**beetroots**) N-VAR In British English, **beetroot** is a dark red root vegetable which can be cooked or pickled. The American word is **beets**.

befall /bɪˈfɔːl/ (**befalls, befalling, befell** /bɪˈfel/, **befallen**) V-T If something bad or unlucky **befalls** you, it happens to you. [LITERARY] ❑ *A disaster befell the island of Flores.*

befit /bɪˈfɪt/ (**befits, befitting, befitted**) V-T If something **befits** a person or thing, it is suitable or appropriate for them. ❑ *He writes beautifully, as befits a poet.*

before /bɪˈfɔː/ **1** PREP & CONJ & ADV If something happens **before** a time or event, it happens earlier than that time or event. ❑ *My husband rarely comes to bed before 3am.* ❑ *Where did Mary live before she moved to Newtown?* ❑ *He phoned just before you came.* ❑ *I earned more than I did the year before.* **2** ADV If you have done something **before**, you have done it on a previous occasion. ❑ *'Have you been to York before?'* ❑ *...people she had never met before.* **3** PREP If you are **before** something, you are in front of it. [FORMAL] ❑ *They stopped before a large white villa.* **4** PREP When you have a task or difficult situation **before** you, you have to deal with it. ❑ *...the duty which lay before me.*

> **Thesaurus** *before* Also look up:
>
> ADV. already, earlier, previously; *(ant.)* after **1** **3**

beforehand /bɪˈfɔːhænd/ ADV If you do something **beforehand**, you do it earlier than a particular event. ❑ *Make a list of your questions beforehand.*

befriend /bɪˈfrend/ (**befriends, befriending, befriended**) V-T If you **befriend** someone, you make friends with them.

beg /beg/ (**begs, begging, begged**) **1** V-T/V-I If you **beg** someone **to** do something, you ask them anxiously or eagerly to do it. ❑ *I begged to be taken home.* ❑ *We are not going to beg for help.* ❑ *'Please leave,' I begged.* **2** V-T/V-I If you **beg** or **beg** food or money from someone, you ask them to give it to you. ❑ *I was surrounded by people begging.* ❑ *She was living alone, begging food from neighbours.* **3** **I beg your pardon** → see **pardon**

began /bɪˈgæn/ **Began** is the past tense of **begin**.

beggar /ˈbegə/ (**beggars**) N-COUNT A **beggar** is someone who lives by asking people for money or food.

begin /bɪˈgɪn/ (**begins, beginning, began** /bɪˈgæn/, **begun** /bɪˈgʌn/) **1** V-T/V-I When

B

someone or something **begins to** do something, they start doing it. ❑ *He stood up and began to move around.* ❑ *Snow began falling again.* ❑ *'Professor Theron,' he began, 'I'm very pleased to see you.'* **2** V-T/V-I When something **begins** or when you **begin** it, it takes place from a particular time onwards. ❑ *The concert begins at 5 p.m.* ❑ *He had begun his career as a painter.* **3** PHRASE You use the phrase **to begin with** when you are talking about the first stage of a situation, event, or process, or to introduce the first of several things that you want to say. ❑ *He was one of a staff of six to begin with.* ❑ *This is more than wrong. To begin with, the link is not a logical one.*

Thesaurus *begin* Also look up:

V. commence, kick off, start; *(ant.)* end, stop **1** **2**

beginner /bɪ'gɪnə/ (**beginners**) N-COUNT A **beginner** is someone who has just started learning to do something and cannot do it well yet.

beginning /bɪ'gɪnɪŋ/ (**beginnings**) N-COUNT **The beginning of** something is the first part of it. ❑ *This was the beginning of her career.* ❑ *She contacted me at the beginning of August.* ❑ *I had the beginnings of a headache.*

begun /bɪ'gʌn/ **Begun** is the past participle of **begin**.

behalf /bɪ'hɑːf, -'hæf/ PHRASE If you do something **on** someone's **behalf**, you do it as their representative. ❑ *His sisters applied on his behalf, without his knowledge.*

behave /bɪ'heɪv/ (**behaves, behaving, behaved**) **1** V-I The way that you **behave** is the way that you do and say things, and the things that you do and say. ❑ *He'd behaved badly.* **2** V-T/V-I If you **behave yourself**, you act in the way that people think is correct and proper. ❑ *You're going to behave and do what you're told.* ❑ *They were expected to behave themselves.*

behaviour [AM **behavior**] /bɪ'heɪvjə/ N-UNCOUNT A person's **behaviour** is the way they behave. ❑ *...anti-social behaviour.* ❑ *It was interesting to observe how his behaviour changed from cheeky to polite, then timid.*

Word Partnership Use *behaviour* with:

ADJ. **aggressive/criminal** behaviour, **bad/good** behaviour, **learned** behaviour
V. **change** ***someone's*** behaviour
N. **human** behaviour, behaviour **pattern**, behaviour **problems**

behavioural [AM **behavioral**] /bɪ'heɪvjərəl/ ADJ BEFORE N **Behavioural** means relating to the behaviour of a person or animal, or to the study of their behaviour. ❑ *...emotional and behavioural problems.*

behind /bɪ'haɪnd/ (**behinds**) **1** PREP & ADV If someone or something is **behind** another person or thing, they are facing the back of that person or thing. ❑ *Put the cushion behind his head.* ❑ *They were parked behind the truck.* ❑ *She led the way upstairs, with Terry following behind.* **2** ADV If you stay **behind**, you remain in a place after other people have gone. **3** ADV If you leave something or someone **behind**, you do not take them with you when you go. **4** PREP & ADV When someone or something is **behind**, they are delayed or are making less progress than they should. ❑ *The train was seven minutes behind schedule.* **5** PREP The people or events **behind** a situation are the causes of it or the things that are responsible for it. ❑ *It is not clear who was behind the killing.* **6** PREP If something or someone is **behind** you, they support and help you. ❑ *His family are completely behind him.* **7** N-COUNT Your **behind** is the part of your body that you sit on. [INFORMAL] **8** to do something **behind** someone's **back** → see **back** **9** **behind bars** → see **bar** **10** **behind the scenes** → see **scene**
→ see **location**

being /'biːɪŋ/ (**beings**) **1** **Being** is the present participle of **be**. **2** N-UNCOUNT **Being** is existence. Something that **comes into being** begins to exist. ❑ *The committee came into being in 1993.* **3** N-COUNT You can refer to any real or imaginary creature as a **being**. ❑ *...beings from outer space.*

belated /bɪ'leɪtɪd/ ADJ A **belated** action happens later than it should have done. ❑ *They decided to hold a belated celebration.* • **belatedly** ADV ❑ *In the morning, I belatedly reported the accident to the police.*

belch /beltʃ/ (**belches, belching, belched**) **1** V-I & N-COUNT If someone **belches**, they make a sudden noise, called a **belch**, in their throat because air has risen up from their stomach. **2** V-T/V-I If an engine or factory **belches** smoke, or if smoke **belches from** it, large amounts of smoke come from it. ❑ *Steam started to belch from the engine.*

beleaguered /bɪ'liːgəd/ ADJ **Beleaguered** people or places are being attacked or criticized. [FORMAL] ❑ *...the beleaguered city of Vukovar.*

belie /bɪ'laɪ/ (**belies, belying, belied**) V-T If one thing **belies** another, it creates a false idea or image of someone or something. ❑ *His energy belies his years.*

belief /bɪ'liːf/ (**beliefs**) N-VAR **Belief** is a feeling of certainty that something exists, is true, or is good. ❑ *...a belief in reincarnation.*

believable /bɪ'liːvəbəl/ ADJ Something that is **believable** makes you think that it could be true or real. ❑ *This book is full of believable characters.*

believe /bɪ'liːv/ (**believes, believing, believed**) **1** V-T If you **believe** that something is true, you think that it is true. ❑ *Experts believe that the drought will be extensive.* **2** V-T If you **believe** someone, you accept that they are telling the truth. ❑ *He sounded as if he believed her.* ❑ *Don't believe what you read in the papers.* **3** V-I If you **believe in** things such as God, fairies, or miracles, you are sure that they exist or happen. **4** V-I If you **believe in** a way of life or an idea, you think it is good or right. ❑ *I believe in prevention rather than cure.*

Usage

Note that when you are using the verb **believe** with a **that** clause in order to state a negative opinion or belief, you normally make **believe** negative, rather than the verb in the **that** clause. For instance, it is more usual to say '*He didn't believe she could do it*' than 'He believed she couldn't do it'. The same pattern applies to other verbs with a similar meaning, such as **consider**, **suppose**, and **think**. ❑ *I don't consider that you kept your promise.* ❑ *I don't suppose he ever saw it.* ❑ *I don't think he saw me.*

believer /bɪ'liːvə/ (**believers**) **1** N-COUNT If you are a **believer in** something, you think that it is good or right. ❑ *Mum was a great believer in herbal medicines.* **2** N-COUNT A **believer** is someone who is sure that God exists or that the teachings of their religion are true.

bell /bel/ (**bells**) **1** N-COUNT A **bell** is a device that makes a ringing sound which attracts people's attention. ❑ *I've been ringing the door bell.* **2** N-COUNT A **bell** is a hollow metal object with a loose piece hanging inside it that hits the sides and makes a sound. ❑ *...church bells.*

belligerent /bɪ'lɪdʒərənt/ ADJ A **belligerent** person is hostile and aggressive. ● **belligerence** N-UNCOUNT ❑ *He could be accused of passion, but never belligerence.*

bellow /'beləʊ/ (**bellows, bellowing, bellowed**) V-T/V-I & N-COUNT If you **bellow**, you shout angrily in a loud deep voice. You call a sound like this a **bellow**. ❑ *'I didn't ask to be born!' she bellowed.* ❑ *The owner bellowed orders at the teenager.* ❑ *Alfred let out a bellow.*

belly /'beli/ (**bellies**) N-COUNT A person's or animal's **belly** is their stomach or abdomen. → see **horse**

belong /bɪ'lɒŋ, AM -'lɔːŋ/ (**belongs, belonging, belonged**) **1** V-I If something **belongs to** you, you own it. ❑ *The jeep belonged to the army.* ❑ *This handwriting belongs to a male.* **2** V-I If someone or something **belongs to** a particular group, they are a member of it. ❑ *I used to belong to a youth club.* **3** V-I If a person or thing **belongs in** a particular category, group, or place, they are of that category or group, or usually found in that place. ❑ *Today, however, the two countries belong in very different categories.*

belongings /bɪ'lɒŋɪŋz, AM -'lɔːŋ-/ N-PLURAL Your **belongings** are the things that you own.

beloved /bɪ'lʌvɪd/

Also pronounced /bɪ'lʌvd/ when used after a noun or after the verb 'be'.

ADJ A **beloved** person, thing, or place is one that you feel great love or affection for. ❑ *His beloved wife died last year.*

below /bɪ'ləʊ/ **1** PREP & ADV If something is **below** something else, it is in a lower position. ❑ *To the west, the sun dipped below the horizon.* ❑ *The path runs below a long brick wall.* ❑ *Spread out below was a great crowd.* ❑ *Please write to me at the address below.* **2** PREP & ADV If something is **below** a particular amount or level, it is less than it. ❑ *Rainfall has been below average.* ❑ *...temperatures at zero or below.* **3** **below par** → see **par**

Word Partnership Use *below* with:

ADV.	**directly** below, **far/significantly/substantially/well** below, **just/slightly** below **1** **2**
N.	below **the belt/waist**, below **ground**, below **the surface** **1** below **cost**, below **freezing**, below **the poverty level/line**, below **zero** **2**
V.	**described** below, **dip/drop/fall** below, **listed** below, **see** below **1**
ADJ.	below **average**, below **normal** **2**

belt /belt/ (**belts, belting, belted**) **1** N-COUNT A **belt** is a strip of leather or cloth that you fasten round your waist. **2** N-COUNT A **belt** is a circular strip of rubber used in machines to drive moving parts or to move objects along. **3** N-COUNT A **belt of** land or sea is a long, narrow area of it that has some special feature. ❑ *Behind him was a belt of trees.* ❑ *...Zambia's northern copper belt.* **4** V-T & N-COUNT If someone **belts** you or gives you a **belt**, they hit you very hard. [INFORMAL] **5** → see also **safety belt, conveyor belt** **6** PHRASE If you have to **tighten** your **belt**, you must manage without things because you have less money than you used to have. **7** PHRASE If you have something **under** your **belt**, you have already achieved it or done it. ❑ *Colvin already has two albums under her belt.* → see **button**

bemused /bɪ'mjuːzd/ ADJ If you are **bemused**, you are slightly puzzled or confused. ❑ *Mary looked at her with a bemused expression.*

bench /bentʃ/ (**benches**) **1** N-COUNT A **bench** is a long seat of wood or metal. **2** N-COUNT A **bench** is a long narrow table in a factory, laboratory, or workshop. **3** N-SING In a court of law, **the bench** consists of the judge or magistrates. ❑ *Allgood served on the bench for 50 years.*

bend /bend/ (**bends, bending, bent** /bent/) **1** V-I When you **bend**, you move the top part of your body downwards and forwards. ❑ *I bent over and kissed her cheek.* **2** V-T/V-I When you **bend** a part of your body such as your arm or leg, or when it **bends**, you change its position so that it is no longer straight. ❑ *Stand up straight, then bend one leg.* ❑ *As you walk faster, you will find the arms bend naturally.* ● **bent** ADJ ❑ *Keep your knees slightly bent.* **3** V-T When you **bend** something that is flat or straight, you use force to make it curved or angular. ❑ *Bend the bar into a horseshoe.* ● **bent** ADJ ❑ *...a length of bent wire.* **4** V-I When a road or river **bends**, it changes direction to form a curve or angle. ❑ *The road bent sharply to the left.* **5** N-COUNT A **bend** in a road, river, or pipe is a curved part in it. **6** V-T If you **bend the rules**, you do something which is not allowed, either to gain an advantage or to help someone else. **7** → see also **bent** **8** to **bend double** → see **double**

Thesaurus *bend* Also look up:

V.	arch, bow, hunch, lean; *(ant.)* straighten **1** contort, curl, twist **3**
N.	angle, curve, deviation, turn **5**

beneath /bɪ'niːθ/ PREP & ADV Something that is **beneath** another thing is under it. ❑ *She could see his muscles move beneath his T-shirt.* ❑ *On a shelf beneath he saw a photo album.*

benefactor /'benɪfæktə/ (**benefactors**) N-COUNT Your **benefactor** is a person who helps you by giving you money.

beneficial /ˌbenɪ'fɪʃəl/ ADJ Something that is **beneficial** helps people or improves their lives. ❑ *Any regular exercise is beneficial, including gardening.*

beneficiary /ˌbenɪ'fɪʃəri, AM -ʃieri/ (**beneficiaries**) N-COUNT Someone who is a **beneficiary of** something is helped by it. ❑ *He was not the only beneficiary of his father's will.*

benefit /'benɪfɪt/ (**benefits, benefiting,**

B

benefited or **benefitting, benefitted**) 1 V-T/V-I & N-VAR If you **benefit from** something, if it **benefits** you, or if you **have the benefit of** it, it helps you or improves your life. ❑ *He hopes to benefit from the tax cuts.* ❑ *...government programmes benefiting children.* ❑ *Steve didn't have the benefit of a college education.* 2 N-UNCOUNT **Benefit** is money given by the government to people who are poor, ill, or unemployed. ❑ *...unemployment benefit.* 3 PHRASE If you give someone **the benefit of the doubt**, you accept what they say as true, because you cannot prove that it is not true.

Word Link	*vol ≈ will : benevolent, involuntary, volunteer*

benevolent /bɪ'nevələnt/ ADJ A **benevolent** person is kind, helpful, and tolerant. ● **benevolence** N-UNCOUNT ❑ *The ruler ran his country with benevolence and compassion.*

benign /bɪ'naɪn/ 1 ADJ You use **benign** to describe someone who is kind, gentle, and harmless. ❑ *...a nice chap with a benign expression.* ● **benignly** ADV ❑ *I just smiled benignly.* 2 ADJ A **benign** disease or substance will not cause death or serious harm. [TECHNICAL]

bent /bent/ 1 **Bent** is the past tense and past participle of **bend**. 2 ADJ AFTER LINK-V If you are **bent on** doing something, you are determined to do it. ❑ *The Education Secretary is bent on helping our young people.* 3 N-SING If you have a **bent for** something, you have a natural ability to do it or a natural interest in it. ❑ *...his bent for history.*

bequeath /bɪ'kwi:ð/ (**bequeaths, bequeathing, bequeathed**) V-T If you **bequeath** something **to** someone, you formally state that they should have it when you die, usually in your will. ❑ *Fielding bequeathed them twenty thousand dollars.* ❑ *He bequeathed all his silver to his children.*

bereaved /bɪ'ri:vd/ ADJ & N-PLURAL A **bereaved** person has a relative or close friend who has recently died. Bereaved people are sometimes called **the bereaved**. [FORMAL] ❑ *Mr Dinkins visited the bereaved family to offer comfort.* ❑ *He wanted to show his sympathy for the bereaved.* ● **bereavement** (**bereavements**) N-VAR ❑ *Those people have suffered a bereavement.*

bereft /bɪ'reft/ ADJ If a person or thing is **bereft of** something, they no longer have it. [FORMAL] ❑ *The place seemed to be utterly bereft of human life.* ❑ *They were bereft of ideas.*

berry /'beri/ (**berries**) N-COUNT **Berries** are small round fruit that grow on a bush or a tree.

berth /bɜ:θ/ (**berths, berthing, berthed**) 1 N-COUNT A **berth** is a space in a harbour where a ship stays for a period of time. 2 V-I When a ship **berths**, it sails into harbour and stops at the quay. ❑ *As soon as they berthed, the fish would be unloaded.* ❑ *Where is the ferry berthed?* 3 N-COUNT A **berth** is a bed on a boat or train, or in a caravan.

beset /bɪ'set/ (**besets, besetting, beset**) V-T If someone or something **is beset** by problems or fears, they have many problems or fears which affect them severely. ❑ *...the problems now besetting the country.*

beside /bɪ'saɪd/ 1 PREP Something that is **beside** something else is at the side of it or next to it. ❑ *Beside his plate was a pile of books.* ❑ *I moved from my desk to sit beside her.* 2 PHRASE If you are **beside yourself with** anger or excitement, you are extremely angry or excited. 3 **beside the point** → see **point**

besides /bɪ'saɪdz/ 1 PREP & ADV **Besides** or **beside** something means in addition to it. ❑ *I think she has many good qualities besides being beautiful.* ❑ *Brunel designed railways, bridges, ships and much else besides.* 2 ADV You use **besides** to make an additional point or give an additional reason. ❑ *'I don't need any help. Besides, I'm nearly finished.'*

besiege /bɪ'si:dʒ/ (**besieges, besieging, besieged**) 1 V-T If you **are besieged** by people, many people want something from you and continually bother you. ❑ *She was besieged by reporters.* 2 V-T If soldiers **besiege** a place, they surround it and wait for the people in it to surrender.

best /best/ 1 ADJ **Best** is the superlative of **good**. 2 ADV **Best** is the superlative of **well**. 3 N-SING Your **best** is the greatest effort or the highest achievement that you are capable of. ❑ *Miss Blockey was at her best when she played the piano.* 4 N-SING **The best** is used to refer to things of the highest quality or standard. ❑ *He'll have the best care.* 5 ADV If you like something **best** or like it **the best**, you prefer it. ❑ *What music do you like best?* ❑ *What was the role you loved the best?* 6 PHRASE You use **at best** to indicate that even if you describe something as favourably as possible, it is still not very good. ❑ *At best Nella would be an invalid; at worst she would die.* 7 PHRASE If you **make the best of** an unsatisfactory situation, you accept it and try to be cheerful about it. ❑ *I'll try to make the best of what I've got.* 8 **the best part of** something → see **part** 9 **the best of both worlds** → see **world**

bestow /bɪ'stəʊ/ (**bestows, bestowing, bestowed**) V-T If you **bestow** something **on** someone, you give it to them. [FORMAL] ❑ *The Mayor bestowed medals on the police.*

ˌbest-'seller also **bestseller** (**best-sellers**) N-COUNT A **best-seller** is a book of which a very large number of copies have been sold.

ˌbest-'selling also **bestselling** 1 ADJ BEFORE N A **best-selling** product is very popular and a large quantity of it has been sold. 2 ADJ BEFORE N A **best-selling** author is an author who has sold a very large number of copies of his or her book.

bet /bet/ (**bets, betting, bet**) 1 V-T/V-I & N-COUNT If you **bet on** the result of a horse race, football match, or other event, or if you put a **bet on** it, you give someone a sum of money which they give you back with extra money if the result is what you predicted, or which they keep if it is not. ❑ *Viewers can bet on sports events via their TV screens.* ❑ *He bet them 500 pounds they would lose.* ❑ *He placed a bet on one of the horses.* ● **betting** N-UNCOUNT ❑ *...on-line betting.* 2 PHRASE You say **'You bet'** or **'You bet your life'** as an emphatic way of saying 'yes' or of emphasizing a statement. [INFORMAL] ❑ *'It's settled, then?'—'You bet.'* 3 PHRASE If you use a phrase such as **'I bet'**, **'I'll bet'**, or **'you can bet'**, you mean that you are sure something is true. ❑ *I bet you were good at games at school.*

betray /bɪ'treɪ/ (**betrays, betraying, betrayed**) 1 V-T If you **betray** someone who trusts you, you do something which hurts and disappoints them. ❑ *He is the only one who did not betray his people and co-operate with the enemy.* 2 V-T If someone **betrays** their country or their comrades, they give information to an enemy, putting their country's security or their comrades' safety at risk. ❑ *He could never bring himself to betray his country.* **3** V-T If you **betray** your feelings or thoughts, you show them without intending to. ❑ *Jeremy's voice betrayed little emotion.*

betrayal /bɪˈtreɪəl/ (**betrayals**) N-VAR A **betrayal** is an action that betrays someone or something. ❑ *Our supporters see this vote as an act of betrayal.*

better /ˈbetə/ **1** ADJ **Better** is the comparative of **good**. **2** ADV **Better** is the comparative of **well**. **3** ADV If you like one thing **better than** another, you like it more. ❑ *I always liked you better than Sandra.* ❑ *They liked it better when it rained.* **4** ADJ AFTER LINK-V If you are **better** after an illness or injury, you are less ill. If you feel **better**, you no longer feel so ill. **5** → See note at **recover** **6** ADV You can tell someone that they **are better** doing one thing **than** another, or **it is better** doing one thing **than** another when you are advising them about what they should do. ❑ *You are better eating just a small snack than hurrying a main meal.* **7** PHRASE If you say that you **had better** do something, you mean that you ought to do it. ❑ *I think we had better go home.* **8** PHRASE If you **are better off**, you are in a more pleasant situation than before. ❑ *A child is better off in its country of birth.* **9** PHRASE If something changes **for the better**, it improves. **10** PHRASE If something **gets the better of** you, you are unable to resist it. **11** **the better part of**
→ see **part**

Word Partnership Use *better* with:

N.	better **idea**, **nothing** better **1**
V.	**make** ***something*** better **1**
	deserve better **1** **3**
	look better **1** **4**
	feel better, **get** better **4**
ADV.	**any** better, **even** better, better **than** **1** **3**
	much better **1** **3** **4**

between /bɪˈtwiːn/ **1** PREP & ADV If something is **between** two things or is **in between** them, it has one of the things on one side of it and the other thing on the other side. ❑ *There was a cigarette between his lips.* ❑ *...raised flower beds that have paths in between.* **2** PREP If people or things travel **between** two places, they travel regularly from one place to the other and back again. ❑ *I often travel between Britain, France and Germany.* **3** PREP A relationship, discussion, or difference **between** two people, groups, or things is one that involves them both or relates to them both. ❑ *...the relationship between patients and doctors.* **4** PREP If something stands **between** you and what you want, it prevents you from having it. **5** PREP If something is **between** or **in between** two amounts or ages, it is greater or older than the first one and smaller or younger than the second one. ❑ *A third of its population is aged between 18 and 30.* **6** PREP & ADV If something happens **between** or **in between** two times or events, it happens after the first time or event and before the second one. ❑ *The canal was built between 1793 and 1797.* ❑ *...pain lasting a few minutes, with periods of calm in between.* **7** PREP If you must choose **between** two things, you must choose one thing or the other one. **8** PREP If people have a particular amount of something **between** them, this is the total amount that they have. ❑ *These books have about 5000 pages between them.* **9** PREP When something is divided or shared **between** people, they each have a share of it. ❑ *All the tasks are shared between us.*
→ see **location**

Usage

If there are only two people or things, you should use **between**. If there are more than two people or things, you should use **among**. **Amongst** is slightly old-fashioned.

Word Partnership Use *between* with:

N.	**line** between, **link** between **1**
	between **countries/nations**, **difference** between, **relationship** between **3**
	choice between **7**
ADV.	***somewhere*** **in** between **1** **6**
V.	**caught** between **1**
	choose/decide/distinguish between **7**

beverage /ˈbevərɪdʒ/ (**beverages**) N-COUNT A **beverage** is a drink. [FORMAL] ❑ *...hot beverages.*
→ see **sugar**

Word Link ***war*** ≈ ***watchful*** **:** ***aware, beware, unaware***

beware /bɪˈweə/

Beware is only used as an imperative or infinitive. It does not have any other forms.

V-I If you tell someone to **beware of** a person or thing, you are warning them that the person or thing may harm them. ❑ *Beware of being too impatient with others.* ❑ *Motorists were warned to beware of wet conditions.*

bewildered /bɪˈwɪldəd/ ADJ If you are **bewildered**, you are very confused and cannot understand something or decide what you should do. ❑ *Some shoppers looked bewildered by the variety.* ● **bewildering** ADJ ❑ *The choice of trips was bewildering.*

bewilderment /bɪˈwɪldəmənt/ N-UNCOUNT **Bewilderment** is the feeling of being bewildered. ❑ *He shook his head in bewilderment.*

bewitch /bɪˈwɪtʃ/ (**bewitches, bewitching, bewitched**) V-T If someone or something **bewitches** you, you find them so attractive that you cannot think about anything else. ❑ *The doctor is bewitched by Maya's beauty.* ● **bewitching** ADJ ❑ *...bewitching brown eyes.*

beyond /bɪˈjɒnd/ **1** PREP & ADV If something is **beyond** a place or barrier, it is on the other side of it. ❑ *They heard footsteps in the main room, beyond a door.* ❑ *...industry throughout Europe and beyond.* **2** PREP & ADV If something extends **beyond** a particular thing, it affects or includes other things. If something happens **beyond** a particular time or date, it continues after that time or date has passed. ❑ *His interests extend beyond the fine arts to international politics and philosophy.* ❑ *...through the 1990s and beyond.* **3** PREP If something is, for example, **beyond** understanding or **beyond** belief, it is so extreme in some way that it cannot be understood or believed. ❑ *By the year 2007, business computing will have changed beyond recognition.* **4** PREP If you say that something is **beyond** you, you mean that you are incapable of dealing with it. ❑ *Any practical help would be beyond him.*

bias /baɪəs/ (**biases**) **1** N-VAR **Bias** is prejudice against one group and favouritism towards another, which may badly affect someone's judgment. ❑ *...the bias in favour of new road schemes.* ❑ *Is there a bias against private schools?* **2** N-VAR **Bias** is a concern with or interest in one thing more than others. ❑ *The Department has a strong bias towards neuroscience.*

biased /baɪəst/ **1** ADJ AFTER LINK-V Someone or something that is **biased towards** one thing is more concerned with it than with other things. ❑ *University funding was tremendously biased towards scientists.* **2** ADJ If someone or something is **biased**, they show prejudice against one group and favouritism towards another, or are influenced so much by something that any judgment they make is likely to be unfair. ❑ *She claimed that judges were biased against women victims.*

bible /ˈbaɪbəl/ (**bibles**) **1** N-PROPER **The Bible** is the sacred book of the Christian religion. ● **biblical** /ˈbɪblɪkəl/ ADJ ❑ *...the biblical story of creation.* **2** N-COUNT A **bible** is a copy of the Bible.

bibliography /ˌbɪbliˈɒgrəfi/ (**bibliographies**) N-COUNT A **bibliography** is a list of books on a particular subject or a list of the books and articles referred to in a particular book.

bicker /ˈbɪkə/ (**bickers, bickering, bickered**) V-I If you **bicker**, you argue about unimportant things. ❑ *We bickered all through supper.* ● **bickering** N-UNCOUNT ❑ *...months of political bickering.*

Word Link *bi ≈ two : bicycle, bilingual, binoculars*

bicycle /ˈbaɪsɪkəl/ (**bicycles**) N-COUNT A **bicycle** is a vehicle with two wheels which you ride by sitting on it and pushing two pedals with your feet.
→ see Word Web: **bicycle**

bid /bɪd/ (**bids, bidding, bade, bidden**) **1** N-COUNT A **bid for** something or a **bid to** do something is an attempt to obtain it or do it. ❑ *...Sydney's successful bid for the 2000 Olympic Games.* ❑ *She recently went on a strict diet in a bid to lose weight.* **2** N-COUNT & V-T/V-I If you make a **bid for** something or if you **bid** a particular amount of money **for** it, you offer to pay that amount to buy it. **Bid** is the past tense and past participle in this meaning. ❑ *Hanson made an agreed takeover bid of £351 million.* ❑ *He certainly wasn't going to bid $18 billion for this company.* ❑ *It's now easier for small firms to bid for government business.* ● **bidder** (**bidders**) N-COUNT ❑ *The sale will be made to the highest bidder.*

Word Link *er ≈ more : bigger, louder, taller*

big /bɪg/ (**bigger, biggest**) **1** ADJ Something that is **big** is large in size or great in degree, extent, or importance. ❑ *Australia's a big country.* ❑ *Her husband was a big man.* ❑ *...the big backlog of applications.* ❑ *...one of the biggest companies in Italy.* ❑ *Her problem was just too big for her to solve alone.* **2** ADJ BEFORE N Children often refer to their older brother or sister as their **big** brother or sister. [INFORMAL]

Usage

Big, **large**, and **great** are all used to talk about size. In general, **large** is more formal than **big**, and **great** is more formal than **large**. **Big** and **large** are normally used to describe objects. If you use **great** to describe an object, you are suggesting that it is impressive because of its size. ❑ *The great bird of prey was a dark smudge against the sun.* You can use **large** or **great**, but not **big**, to describe amounts. ❑ *He noticed a large amount of blood on the floor.* ❑ *The coming of tourists in great numbers changes things.* **Great** is often used with nouns referring to things such as feelings or ideas. It is the only one of the three words that can be used in front of an uncount noun. ❑ *It gives me very great pleasure to welcome you to Kings Norton.* Remember that **great** has several other meanings, when it does not refer to size, but to something that is remarkable, very good, or enjoyable.

Thesaurus *big* Also look up:

ADJ. enormous, huge, large, massive; *(ant.)* little, small, tiny **1**

ˌbig ˈbusiness N-UNCOUNT Something that is **big business** has become an important commercial activity. ❑ *Sport has become big business.*

ˌbig ˈdeal **1** N-SING If you say that something is a **big deal**, you mean that it is important or significant. ❑ *Winning was such a big deal for the whole family.* **2** CONVENTION If you say **'big deal'** to

Word Web **bicycle**

A Scotsman named Kirkpatrick MacMillan invented the first **bicycle** with **pedals** around 1840. Early bicycles had wooden or metal **wheels**. However, by the mid-1800s **tyres** with tubes appeared. Modern **racing bikes** are very lightweight and aerodynamic. The wheels have fewer **spokes** and the tyres are very thin and smooth. **Mountain bikes** allow riders to ride up and down steep hills on dirt trails. These bikes have fat, knobby tyres for extra traction. The **tandem** is a bicycle for two people. It has about the same **wind resistance** as a one-person bike. But with twice the power, it goes faster.

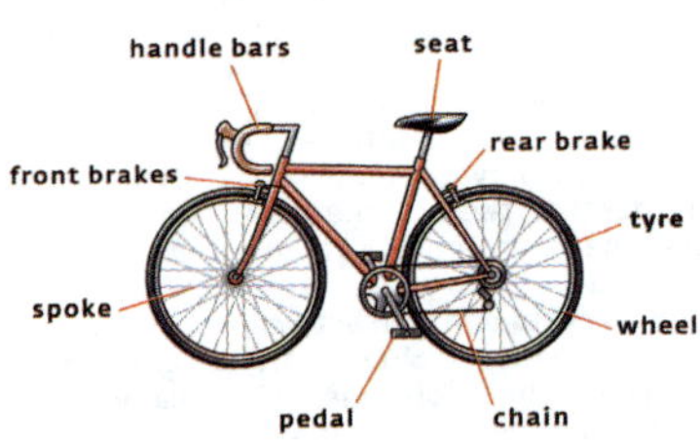

someone, you mean that you are not impressed by something or someone that they consider important or impressive. [INFORMAL] ❑ *There is only one woman in the government. Big deal. Why only one?*

bigot /'bɪgət/ (**bigots**) N-COUNT If you describe someone as a **bigot**, you disapprove of them because they have strong unreasonable prejudices or opinions. ❑ *...a narrow-minded bigot.*

bigotry /'bɪgətri/ N-UNCOUNT **Bigotry** is the fact of having or expressing strong unreasonable prejudices or opinions. ❑ *He hated religious bigotry.*

bike /baɪk/ (**bikes**) N-COUNT A **bike** is a bicycle or a motorcycle. [INFORMAL] ❑ *I used to ride a bike.* ❑ *...to encourage motorists to go by bike.*

bikini /bɪ'kiːni/ (**bikinis**) N-COUNT A **bikini** is a two-piece swimming costume worn by women.

Word Link	*lingu ≈ language : bilingual, linguist, linguistics*

bilingual /ˌbaɪ'lɪŋgwəl/ ADJ **Bilingual** means involving or using two languages. ❑ *...bilingual education.* ❑ *...the Collins bilingual dictionaries.* ❑ *He is bilingual in an Asian language and English.*

bill /bɪl/ (**bills, billing, billed**) **1** N-COUNT In British English, a **bill** is a written statement of money that you owe for goods or services; the American word is **check**. ❑ *He paid his bill for the newspapers.* ❑ *...phone bills.* **2** N-SING In British English, **the bill** in a restaurant is a piece of paper on which the price of the meal you have just eaten is written and which you are given before you pay. The American word is **check**. **3** V-T If you **are billed for** something, you are given or sent a bill for it. ❑ *Are you going to bill me for this?* **4** N-COUNT In American English, a **bill** is a piece of paper money. The usual British word is **note**. **5** N-COUNT In parliament, a **bill** is a formal statement of a proposed new law that is discussed and then voted on. ❑ *...the toughest crime bill that has been passed in a decade.*

Word Partnership	Use *bill* with:
N.	**electricity/gas/telephone** bill, **hospital/hotel** bill **1**
	dollar bill **4**
V.	**pay a** bill **1**
	pass a bill, **sign a** bill, **vote on a** bill **5**

billboard /'bɪlbɔːd/ (**billboards**) N-COUNT A **billboard** is a very large board on which posters and advertisements are displayed.

billiards /'bɪljədz/

The form **billiard** is used as a modifier.

N-UNCOUNT **Billiards** is a game played on a large table, in which you use a long stick called a cue to hit small heavy balls against each other or into pockets around the sides of the table. ❑ *...a game of billiards.*

billion /'bɪljən/ (**billions**) **1** NUM In British English, a **billion** is a million million. In American English, a billion is a thousand million. ❑ *...3 billion dollars.* **2** QUANT You can use **billions** to mean an extremely large amount. ❑ *They've sold billions of them.* ❑ *It must be worth billions.*

billionaire /ˌbɪljə'neə/ (**billionaires**) N-COUNT A **billionaire** is an extremely rich person who has money or property worth at least a thousand million pounds or dollars.

billow /'bɪləʊ/ (**billows, billowing, billowed**) V-I When something **billows**, it swells out and moves slowly in the wind. ❑ *Her pink dress billowed out around her.*

bin /bɪn/ (**bins**) N-COUNT A **bin** is a container that you put rubbish in.

bind /baɪnd/ (**binds, binding, bound**) **1** V-T If something **binds** people together, it makes them feel as if they are all part of the same group. ❑ *...the social and political ties that bind the USA to Britain.* **2** V-T If you **are bound** by something such as a rule or agreement, you are forced or required to act in a certain way. ❑ *We will be legally bound to arrest any suspects.* ❑ *The treaty binds them to respect their neighbour's independence.* **3** V-T If you **bind** something, you tie string or rope tightly round it. ❑ *Bind the ends of the cord together with thread.* **4** V-T When a book **is bound**, the pages are joined together and the cover is put on. ❑ *Each volume is bound in bright-coloured leather.* **5** → see also **bound**

binding /'baɪndɪŋ/ (**bindings**) **1** ADJ A **binding** agreement or decision must be obeyed or carried out. ❑ *...a legally binding commitment.* **2** N-VAR The **binding** of a book is its cover. ❑ *Its books are noted for the quality of their bindings.*

binge /bɪndʒ/ (**binges, binging, binged**) N-COUNT & V-I If you **go on a binge**, or if you **binge**, you do too much of something, such as drinking or eating. [INFORMAL] ❑ *I binged on pizzas.*

bingo /'bɪŋgəʊ/ N-UNCOUNT **Bingo** is a game in which players aim to match the numbers that someone calls out with the numbers on a card that they have been given. ❑ *Do you play bingo?*

Word Link	*bi ≈ two : bicycle, bilingual, binoculars*

binoculars

binoculars /bɪ'nɒkjʊləz/ N-PLURAL **Binoculars** consist of two small telescopes joined together side by side, which you look through in order to see things that are a long way away. You can also say **a pair of binoculars**.

Word Link	*chem ≈ chemical : biochemical, chemical, chemistry*

biochemical /ˌbaɪəʊ'kemɪkəl/ ADJ BEFORE N **Biochemical** processes are the chemical processes that happen in living things.

biochemistry /ˌbaɪəʊ'kemɪstri/ N-UNCOUNT **Biochemistry** is the study of the chemical processes that happen in living things. • **biochemist** (**biochemists**) N-COUNT ❑ *Other enzymes were identified by biochemists.*

biographer /baɪ'ɒgrəfə/ (**biographers**) N-COUNT Someone's **biographer** is a person who writes an account of their life.

Word Link	*bio ≈ life : antibiotic, biography, biology*

Word Link	*graph ≈ writing : autograph, biography, graph*

b

biography /baɪ'ɒgrəfi/ (**biographies**) N-COUNT A **biography** of a person is an account of their life, written by someone else. ● **biographical** /ˌbaɪə'græfɪkəl/ ADJ ❑ *...a biographical film.*
→ see **library**

biological /ˌbaɪə'lɒdʒɪkəl/ **1** ADJ **Biological** is used to describe processes and states that occur in the bodies and cells of living things. ❑ *...a natural biological response.* ● **biologically** ADV ❑ *Humans are biologically programmed to eat.* **2** ADJ BEFORE N **Biological** studies are connected with research in biology. ❑ *...biological sciences.* **3** ADJ **Biological** weapons and **biological** warfare involve the use of organisms which damage living things. ❑ *...biological weed control.*
→ see **war, zoo**

Word Link	*logy, ology ≈ study of : anthropology, biology, geology*

Word Link	*ist ≈ one who practices : biologist, journalist, pharmacist*

biology /baɪ'ɒlədʒi/ N-UNCOUNT **Biology** is the science concerned with the study of living things. ● **biologist** (**biologists**) N-COUNT ❑ *Biologists are studying the fruit fly.*

biometric /ˌbaɪə'metrɪk/ ADJ **Biometric** tests and devices use biological information about a person to create a detailed record of their personal characteristics. ❑ *...the use of biometric information such as fingerprints.*

biotechnology /ˌbaɪəʊtek'nɒlədʒi/ N-UNCOUNT **Biotechnology** is the use of living parts such as cells or bacteria in industry and medicine. [TECHNICAL]
→ see **technology**

bioweapon or **bio-weapon** /'baɪəʊˌwepən/ (**bioweapons**) N-COUNT **Bioweapons** are biological weapons.

bi'polar disˌorder (**bipolar disorders**) N-VAR **Bipolar disorder** is a mental illness in which a person's state of mind changes between extreme happiness and extreme depression.

birch /bɜːtʃ/ (**birches**) N-VAR A **birch** is a tall tree with thin branches. **Birch** is the wood of this tree.

bird /bɜːd/ (**birds**) N-COUNT A **bird** is a creature with feathers and wings.
→ see Word Web: **bird**

'bird ˌflu N-UNCOUNT **Bird flu** is a virus which can be transmitted from chickens, ducks, and other birds to people.

Biro /'baɪərəʊ/ (**Biros**) N-COUNT A **biro** is a pen with a small metal ball at its tip. **Biro** is a trademark.

birth /bɜːθ/ (**births**) **1** N-VAR When a baby is born, you refer to this event as its **birth**. When a woman **gives birth**, she produces a baby from her body. ❑ *The twins were separated at birth.* **2** N-UNCOUNT You can refer to the beginning or origin of something as its **birth**. ❑ *...the birth of democracy.*
→ see **reproduction**

Word Partnership Use *birth* with:

PREP.	**at** birth, **before** birth, **by** birth **1**
V.	**give** birth **1**
ADJ.	**premature** birth **1**
N.	birth **of a baby/child**, birth **certificate**, birth **control**, birth **and death**, birth **defect**, birth **rate** **1**
	date of birth **1**
	birth **of a** nation **2**

'birth control N-UNCOUNT **Birth control** means planning whether to have children and using contraception to prevent unwanted pregnancy.

birthday /'bɜːθdeɪ, -di/ (**birthdays**) N-COUNT Your **birthday** is the anniversary of the date on which you were born. ❑ *...his 24th birthday.* ❑ *I'm getting a bike for my birthday.* ❑ *Happy Birthday!*

birthplace /'bɜːθpleɪs/ (**birthplaces**) **1** N-COUNT Your **birthplace** is the place where you were born. [WRITTEN] **2** N-COUNT The **birthplace of** something is the place where it began or originated. ❑ *Athens was the birthplace of the Olympics.*

'birth rate (**birth rates**) N-COUNT The **birth rate** is the number of babies born for every 1000 people during a particular period.

biscuit /'bɪskɪt/ (**biscuits**) N-COUNT In British English, a **biscuit** is a small flat cake that is crisp and usually sweet. The usual American word is **cookie**.
→ see **dessert**

bisexual /ˌbaɪ'sekʃuəl/ (**bisexuals**) ADJ & N-COUNT A **bisexual** person or a **bisexual** is sexually attracted to both men and women.

bishop /'bɪʃəp/ (**bishops**) N-COUNT A **bishop** is a clergyman of high rank.
→ see **chess**

bistro /'biːstrəʊ/ (**bistros**) N-COUNT A **bistro** is a small restaurant or bar.

bit /bɪt/ (**bits**) **1** QUANT A **bit of** something is a small amount of it, or a small piece or part of it. [INFORMAL] ❑ *...a little bit of money.* ❑ *...bits of paper.* ❑ *Now comes the really important bit.* **2** PHRASE **A bit** means to a small extent or degree. [INFORMAL]

Word Web bird

Many scientists today believe that birds evolved from **avian** dinosaurs. Recently many links have been found. Like birds, these dinosaurs laid their **eggs** in **nests**. Some had **wings**, **beaks**, and **claws** similar to modern birds. But perhaps the most dramatic link was found in 2001. Scientists in China discovered a well-preserved *Sinornithosaurus*, a bird-like dinosaur with **feathers**. This dinosaur is believed to be related to a prehistoric bird, the *Archaeopteryx*.

❏ *This girl was a bit strange.* ❏ *I have a bit more to offer.* **3** PHRASE You can use **a bit of** to make a statement less extreme. ❏ *It's all a bit of a mess.* **4** N-COUNT In computing, a **bit** is the smallest unit of information that is held in a computer's memory. **5** **Bit** is the past tense of **bite**. **6** PHRASE You can say that someone's behaviour is **a bit much** when you are annoyed about it. [INFORMAL] ❏ *It was a bit much that we were disconnected for such a long time.* **7** PHRASE You say that something is **every bit as** good or interesting **as** another to emphasize that they are just as good or interesting as each other. ❏ *My dinner jacket is every bit as good as his.* **8** PHRASE If you do something **for a bit**, you do it for a short period of time. [INFORMAL] ❏ *That'll keep you busy for a bit.* **9** PHRASE **Quite a bit** means a lot. [INFORMAL] ❏ *He's quite a bit older than me.*

bitch /bɪtʃ/ (**bitches**) N-COUNT A **bitch** is a female dog.

bite /baɪt/ (**bites, biting, bit, bitten**) **1** V-T/V-I & N-COUNT When a person or animal **bites** something, they use their teeth to cut into it or through it. A **bite** is an act of biting something. ❏ *He bit the apple.* ❏ *Llamas won't bite or kick.* ❏ *You can't eat that in one bite!* **2** V-T/V-I & N-COUNT If an insect or a snake **bites** you, it makes a mark or hole in your skin, called a **bite**. ❏ *A snake bit his ankle.* ❏ *This is when the mosquitoes bite.* ❏ *Try not to scratch insect bites.* **3** V-I When an action or policy begins to **bite**, it begins to have a serious or harmful effect. ❏ *The recession started biting deeply into British industry.* **4** PHRASE If you **bite** your **lip**, or if you **bite** your **tongue**, you stop yourself from saying something that you want to say, because it would be wrong in the circumstances.

bite

Usage

Note that animals, snakes and mosquitoes **bite** you, but wasps and bees **sting** you.

biting /ˈbaɪtɪŋ/ **1** ADJ A **biting** wind is extremely cold. **2** ADJ **Biting** criticism is very unkind. ❏ *This was the most biting criticism made against her.*

bitten /ˈbɪtən/ **Bitten** is the past participle of **bite**.

bitter /ˈbɪtə/ (**bitterest, bitters**) **1** ADJ In a **bitter** argument, people argue very angrily. ❏ *It was a bitter attack on the Government.* **2** ADJ If you are **bitter**, you feel angry and resentful. ❏ *She is very bitter about the way she was treated.* ● **bitterly** ADV ❏ *He was married, but always complained bitterly about his wife.* ● **bitterness** N-UNCOUNT ❏ *He left feeling some bitterness towards the club.* **3** ADJ You can use **bitter** to emphasize feelings of disappointment. ● **bitterly** ADV ❏ *I was bitterly disappointed to have lost.* **4** ADJ A **bitter** wind or **bitter** weather is extremely cold. ● **bitterly** ADV ❏ *It's bitterly cold here in Moscow.* **5** ADJ A **bitter** taste is sharp, not sweet, and often slightly unpleasant. **6** N-VAR **Bitter** is a kind of British beer. ❏ *...a pint of bitter.*
→ see **taste**

bizarre /bɪˈzɑː/ ADJ Something that is **bizarre** is very odd and strange. ❏ *What a bizarre story!* ● **bizarrely** ADV ❏ *She dressed bizarrely.*

black /blæk/ (**blacker, blackest, blacks, blacking, blacked**) **1** ADJ & N-VAR Something that is **black** is of the darkest colour that there is. ❏ *...a black coat.* ❏ *He was dressed all in black.* ● **blackness** N-UNCOUNT ❏ *...the blackness of night.* **2** ADJ & N-COUNT A **black** person belongs to a race of people with dark skins, for example a race from Africa. You can refer to black people as **blacks**, but some people find this use offensive. ❏ *...black musicians.* **3** ADJ **Black** coffee or tea has no milk or cream added to it. ❏ *Black coffee for me please.* **4** ADJ If you describe a situation as **black**, you are emphasizing that it is very bad indeed. ❏ *It was one of the blackest days of his career.* **5** ADJ **Black** humour involves jokes about things that are actually sad. ❏ *...a black comedy.*
▶ **black out** **1** PHR-VERB If you **black out**, you lose consciousness for a short time. **2** → see also **blackout**

ˌblack and ˈwhite **1** ADJ & N-UNCOUNT In a **black and white** photograph or film, everything is shown in black, white, and grey. ❏ *The pictures were in black and white.* **2** PHRASE You say that something is **in black and white** when it has been written or printed, and not just spoken. ❏ *He'd seen the proof in black and white.*

blackberry /ˈblækbəri, AM -beri/ (**blackberries**) **1** N-COUNT A **blackberry** is a small dark purple fruit. **2** N-COUNT A **Blackberry** is a mobile computing device that allows you to send and receive e-mail. Blackberry is a trademark. [COMPUTING]

blackboard /ˈblækbɔːd/ (**blackboards**) N-COUNT In British English, a **blackboard** is a dark-coloured board which teachers write on with chalk. The usual American word is **chalkboard**.

blackcurrant /ˌblækˈkʌrənt, AM -ˈkɜːrənt/ (**blackcurrants**) N-COUNT **Blackcurrants** are very small, dark purple fruits that grow in bunches.

blacken /ˈblækən/ (**blackens, blackening, blackened**) V-T To **blacken** something means to make it black or very dark in colour. ❏ *Smoke from the fire has blackened the kitchen walls.*

ˌblack ˈeye (**black eyes**) N-COUNT A **black eye** is a dark-coloured bruise around the eye. ❏ *Smith gave him a black eye.*

blackmail /ˈblækmeɪl/ (**blackmails, blackmailing, blackmailed**) N-UNCOUNT & V-T **Blackmail** is the action of threatening to do something unpleasant to someone unless they do what you want them to do. If one person **blackmails** another person, they use blackmail against them. ❏ *She was a perfect target for blackmail.* ❏ *He was trying to blackmail me into saying what he wanted.* ● **blackmailer** (**blackmailers**) N-COUNT ❏ *...a blackmailer's threat to poison supermarket food.*

ˌblack ˈmarket (**black markets**) N-COUNT If something is bought or sold on **the black market**, it is bought or sold illegally. ❏ *There are plenty of guns on the black market.*

blackout /ˈblækaʊt/ (**blackouts**) **1** N-COUNT A **blackout** is a period of time during a war in which the buildings in an area are made dark for safety reasons. ❏ *The last show had to be over before the blackout began.* **2** N-COUNT If you **have a blackout**, you temporarily lose consciousness.

blacksmith /ˈblæksmɪθ/ (**blacksmiths**)

N-COUNT A **blacksmith** is someone whose job is making things out of metal, for example horseshoes.

B

bladder /ˈblædə/ (**bladders**) N-COUNT Your **bladder** is the part of your body where urine is held until it leaves your body.

blade /bleɪd/ (**blades**) 1 N-COUNT The **blade** of a knife, axe, or saw is the sharp edge of it that is used for cutting. 2 N-COUNT The **blades** of a propeller are the parts that turn round.

blade

blame /bleɪm/ (**blames, blaming, blamed**) 1 V-T & PHRASE If you **blame** a person or thing **for** something bad, or if you think or say they are **to blame**, you think or say that they are responsible for it. ❑ *He resigned, blaming himself for the team's defeat.* ❑ *Miller could have blamed others, but he took responsibility.* ❑ *...who is to blame?* 2 N-UNCOUNT **The blame for** something bad that has happened is the responsibility for causing it or letting it happen. ❑ *I'm not going to take the blame for that.* 3 V-T If you say that you do not **blame** someone **for** doing something, you mean that it was a reasonable thing to do in the circumstances. ❑ *I do not blame them for trying to make some money.*

Word Partnership Use *blame* with:

N.	blame **the victim** 1
V.	**tend to** blame 1
	lay blame, **share the** blame 2
	can hardly blame ***someone*** 3

blanch /blɑːntʃ, blæntʃ/ (**blanches, blanching, blanched**) V-I If you **blanch**, you suddenly become very pale. ❑ *She felt herself blanch at the memory.*

bland /blænd/ (**blander, blandest**) ADJ If you describe someone or something as **bland**, you mean that they are dull, uninteresting, and very ordinary. ❑ *...a bland beige carpet.* ❑ *...a bland hamburger.*
→ see **spice**

blank /blæŋk/ (**blanker, blankest**) 1 ADJ Something that is **blank** has nothing on it. ❑ *...a blank page.* ❑ *...blank cassettes.* 2 ADJ If you look **blank**, your face shows no feeling or understanding. ❑ *He gave her a blank look.* • **blankly** ADV ❑ *She stared at him blankly.* 3 PHRASE If your mind or memory **goes blank**, you cannot think of anything or remember anything. 4 → see also **point-blank**

blanket /ˈblæŋkɪt/ (**blankets, blanketing, blanketed**) 1 N-COUNT A **blanket** is a large piece of thick cloth, especially one which you put on a bed to keep you warm. 2 N-SING & V-T If there is a **blanket of** something such as snow, or if snow **blankets** an area, it covers it. ❑ *Heavy cloud blanketed the valley.* 3 ADJ You use **blanket** to describe something which affects or refers to every person or thing in a group. ❑ *Christian people cannot give this action blanket support.*

blare /bleə/ (**blares, blaring, blared**) V-I & N-SING When something such as a radio **blares** or **blares out**, it makes a loud, unpleasant noise called a **blare**. ❑ *Music blared from the flat behind me.* ❑ *...the blare of a passing car radio.*

blasphemy /ˈblæsfəmi/ (**blasphemies**) N-VAR You can describe something that shows disrespect for God or a religion as **blasphemy**. • **blasphemous** ADJ ❑ *The film had been attacked in Christian circles as blasphemous.*

blast /blɑːst, blæst/ (**blasts, blasting, blasted**) 1 N-COUNT A **blast** is a big explosion. ❑ *250 people were killed in the blast.* 2 V-T If people or things **blast** something, they destroy or damage it with a bomb or an explosion. ❑ *Police used explosives to blast a hole in a back wall.* 3 N-COUNT A **blast of** air or wind, or a **blast of** a sound, is a sudden strong rush of it. ❑ *Blasts of cold air came down from the mountains.* ❑ *...the loud blast of a horn.* 4 V-T To **blast** someone or something means to shoot at them with a gun. [JOURNALISM] ❑ *Gunmen blasted their car with a shower of bullets.*
▶ **blast off** PHR-VERB When a space rocket **blasts off**, it leaves the ground at the start of its journey.

blatant /ˈbleɪtənt/ ADJ If you describe something you think is bad as **blatant**, you mean that it is very obvious. ❑ *He made up blatant lies to my father about me.* • **blatantly** ADV ❑ *I'm making it blatantly clear here and now.*

blaze /bleɪz/ (**blazes, blazing, blazed**) 1 V-I When a fire or a light **blazes**, it burns or shines strongly and brightly. ❑ *The fire blazed for hours.* 2 N-COUNT A **blaze** is a large fire in which things are damaged. ❑ *The blaze swept through the tower block.* 3 N-COUNT A **blaze of** light or colour is a large amount of it. 4 N-SING A **blaze of** publicity or attention is a great amount of it. ❑ *His presidency ended in a blaze of glory.*

blazer

blazer /ˈbleɪzə/ (**blazers**) N-COUNT A **blazer** is a kind of jacket.

blazing /ˈbleɪzɪŋ/ 1 ADJ BEFORE N You use **blazing** or **blazing hot** to describe the weather when it is very hot and sunny. ❑ *...blazing hot summers.* 2 ADJ BEFORE N When people have a **blazing row**, they quarrel in a very noisy and excited way.

bleach /bliːtʃ/ (**bleaches, bleaching, bleached**) 1 V-T/V-I If you **bleach** material, you use a chemical to make it white or pale. The sun can also **bleach** things, especially someone's hair. ❑ *Do you have bleached hair?* ❑ *They put cloth out to bleach in the sun.* 2 N-UNCOUNT **Bleach** is a chemical that is used to make cloth white, or to clean things thoroughly. ❑ *...a strong smell of bleach.*

bleak /bliːk/ (**bleaker, bleakest**) 1 ADJ If a situation is **bleak**, it is bad, and seems unlikely to improve. ❑ *The immediate outlook remains bleak.* • **bleakness** N-UNCOUNT ❑ *...the bleakness of the postwar period.* 2 ADJ If you describe something as **bleak**, you mean it looks cold or unpleasant. ❑ *...bleak inner-city streets.* ❑ *The weather can be quite bleak on the coast.* 3 ADJ If someone looks or sounds **bleak**, they seem depressed or unfriendly. ❑ *Julian's face took on a bleak look.* • **bleakly** ADV ❑ *'There is nothing left,' she says bleakly.*

bleed /bliːd/ (**bleeds, bleeding, bled**) V-I When you **bleed**, you lose blood from your body as a result of injury or illness. ❑ *She's going to bleed to death.* ❑ *His head had hit the sink and was bleeding.*

● **bleeding** N-UNCOUNT ❑ *...internal bleeding.*

blemish /ˈblemɪʃ/ (**blemishes, blemishing, blemished**) **1** N-COUNT A **blemish** is a mark that spoils the appearance of something. ❑ *If there is the slightest blemish it is rejected.* **2** V-T & N-COUNT If something **blemishes** your reputation, or if it is a **blemish on** it, it spoils it. ❑ *The only blemish on his record came in 1999.* ❑ *A few minor blemishes spoilt this performance.*

blend /blend/ (**blends, blending, blended**) **1** V-T & N-COUNT When you **blend** substances together, you mix them together so that they become one substance. A **blend of** substances is a mix of them. ❑ *Blend the butter with the sugar.* ❑ *...a blend of spices.* **2** V-I When colours or sounds **blend**, they combine in a pleasing way. ❑ *Paint the walls and ceiling the same colour so they blend together.*

▶ **blend into** or **blend in** PHR-VERB If something **blends into** the background or **blends in**, it is so similar to the background in appearance or sound that it is difficult to see or hear it separately. ❑ *The toad changed its colour to blend in with its new environment.*

bless /bles/ (**blesses, blessing, blessed**) **1** V-T When a priest **blesses** people or things, he or she asks for God's favour and protection for them. **2** V-T PASSIVE If you **are blessed with** a good quality or skill, you have it. ❑ *He is blessed with strength and power.*

blessed /ˈblesɪd/ ADJ BEFORE N You use **blessed** to describe something that you are thankful for or relieved about. ❑ *Rainy weather brings blessed relief to hay fever victims.* ● **blessedly** ADV ❑ *Most British election campaigns are blessedly brief.*

blessing /ˈblesɪŋ/ (**blessings**) **1** N-COUNT A **blessing** is something good that you are thankful for. ❑ *...the blessings of freedom and democracy.* **2** N-COUNT If something is done **with** your **blessing**, you approve of it. **3** PHRASE If you say that a situation is a **mixed blessing**, you mean that it has disadvantages as well as advantages. ❑ *...the mixed blessing of modern technology.*

blew /bluː/ **Blew** is the past tense of **blow**.

blight /blaɪt/ (**blights, blighting, blighted**) **1** N-COUNT You can refer to something as a **blight** when it causes great difficulties or damage to something. ❑ *Wednesday night was a blight on Irish football.* **2** V-T If something **blights** something else, it damages it. ❑ *An embarrassing error nearly blighted his career.*

blind /blaɪnd/ (**blinds, blinding, blinded**) **1** ADJ & N-PLURAL If you are **blind**, you cannot see because your eyes are damaged. You can refer to people who are blind as **the blind**. ❑ *...a blind person.* ❑ *He went blind.* ● **blindness** N-UNCOUNT ❑ *Early diagnosis and treatment can usually prevent blindness.* **2** V-T If something **blinds** you, you become unable to see, either for a short time or permanently. ❑ *The strong sunlight blinded him.* **3** ADJ AFTER LINK-V & V-T If you are **blind to** a fact or situation or if something **blinds** you **to** it, you take no notice of it or are unaware of it. ❑ *All the time I was blind to your suffering.* **4** ADJ If you describe someone's beliefs or actions as **blind**, you think that they do not question or think about what they are doing. ❑ *We must place blind trust in these doctors.* **5** PHRASE If you say that someone **is turning a blind eye to** something bad or illegal, you mean that they are pretending not to notice that it is happening so that they will not have to do anything about it. ❑ *The referee turned a blind eye and let the fight continue.* **6** ADJ BEFORE N A **blind** corner is one that you cannot see round. **7** N-COUNT In British English, a **blind** is a roll of material which you pull down over a window to keep out the light. The American word is **shade**.

→ see **disability**

Word Partnership Use *blind* with:

ADJ.	blind **and deaf** **1**
ADV.	**legally** blind, **partially** blind **1**
N.	blind **person** **1**
	blind **faith** **4**

blindfold /ˈblaɪndfəʊld/ (**blindfolds, blindfolding, blindfolded**) **1** N-COUNT A **blindfold** is a strip of cloth that is tied over someone's eyes so that they cannot see. **2** V-T If you **blindfold** someone, you tie a blindfold over their eyes. ❑ *He had been blindfolded and his hands were tied.*

blinding /ˈblaɪndɪŋ/ ADJ A **blinding** light is extremely bright.

blindly /blaɪndli/ **1** ADV If you do something **blindly**, you do it when you cannot see properly. ❑ *He was squinting blindly as he moved from the bright sunlight.* **2** ADV You use **blindly** to say that someone does something without having enough information, or without thinking about it. ❑ *Don't just blindly do what the banker says.*

bling /blɪŋ/ or **bling-bling** N-UNCOUNT Some people refer to expensive or fancy jewellery as **bling** or **bling-bling**. [INFORMAL] ❑ *Jewellers are battling it out to get celebrities to wear their bling.* ❑ *There was plenty of bling-bling, with diamonds adorning wrists, necks and fingers.*

blink /blɪŋk/ (**blinks, blinking, blinked**) **1** V-T/V-I & N-COUNT When you **blink**, or **blink** your eyes, or when you give a **blink**, you shut your eyes and very quickly open them again. ❑ *She was blinking her eyes rapidly.* ❑ *Her father gave a blink and shook his head.* **2** V-I When a light **blinks**, it flashes on and off. ❑ *A warning light blinked on.*

bliss /blɪs/ N-UNCOUNT **Bliss** is a state of complete happiness. ❑ *...90 minutes of pure bliss.*

blissful /ˈblɪsfʊl/ ADJ A **blissful** time or state is a very happy one. ❑ *We spent a blissful week together.* ● **blissfully** ADV ❑ *We're blissfully happy.*

blister /ˈblɪstə/ (**blisters, blistering, blistered**) **1** N-COUNT A **blister** is a painful swelling containing clear liquid on the surface of your skin. **2** V-I When your skin **blisters**, blisters appear on it as a result of burning or rubbing. ❑ *The affected skin turns red and may blister.*

blistering /ˈblɪstərɪŋ/ **1** ADJ **Blistering** heat is very great heat. ❑ *...a blistering summer day.* **2** ADJ A **blistering** remark expresses great anger or sarcasm. ❑ *...a blistering attack on his critics.*

blithe /blaɪð/ ADJ You use **blithe** to indicate that something is done casually, without serious thought. ❑ *He has inherited his blithe optimism from his grandfather.* ● **blithely** ADV ❑ *Your editorial blithely ignores the hard facts.*

blitz /blɪts/ (**blitzes**) N-COUNT If you have a **blitz on** something, you make a big effort to deal with it or to improve it. [INFORMAL] ❑ *There is to be a blitz on incorrect grammar.*

B

blizzard /ˈblɪzəd/ (**blizzards**) N-COUNT A **blizzard** is a storm in which snow falls heavily and there are strong winds.
→ see **snow, storm, weather**

bloated /ˈbləʊtɪd/ ADJ Something that is **bloated** is much larger than normal, usually because it has a lot of liquid or gas inside it. ❑ *Drinking a lot during a meal can make you feel bloated.*

blob /blɒb/ (**blobs**) N-COUNT A **blob of** thick or sticky liquid is a small amount of it. ❑ *Add a blob of cream.*

bloc /blɒk/ (**blocs**) N-COUNT A **bloc** is a group of countries who act together because they have similar political aims and interests. ❑ *...the former Soviet bloc.*

block /blɒk/ (**blocks, blocking, blocked**) **1** N-COUNT A **block of** flats or offices is a large building containing them. ❑ *She lives in a modern block of six flats in London.* **2** N-COUNT In a town, a **block** is a group of buildings with streets on all four sides. ❑ *She walked four blocks down High Street.* **3** N-COUNT A **block of** a substance is a large rectangular piece of it. **4** V-T To **block** a road or channel means to put something across or in it so that nothing can go through it or along it. ❑ *Police blocked the entrance to Westminster Bridge.* ❑ *...a blocked drain.* **5** V-T If something **blocks** your view, it prevents you from seeing something by being between you and that thing. ❑ *A row of trees blocked his view.* **6** V-T When people **block** something, they do not allow it to happen. ❑ *The country has tried to block imports of various cheap foreign products.*

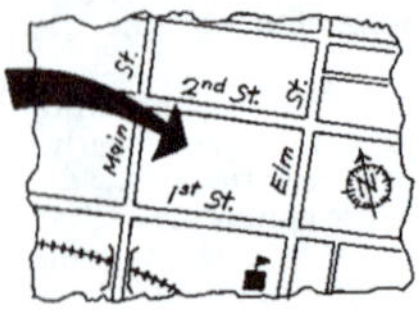

block

▶ **block out** PHR-VERB If you **block out** a thought, you try not to think about it. ❑ *She accuses me of blocking out the past.*

▶ **block up** PHR-VERB If you **block** something **up** or if it **blocks up**, it becomes completely blocked so that nothing can get through it. ❑ *I've blocked up any holes in the kitchen where the mice are getting through.*

blockade /blɒˈkeɪd/ (**blockades, blockading, blockaded**) N-COUNT & V-T A **blockade** is an action that is taken to prevent goods from entering or leaving a place. You can also say that people **blockade** a place. ❑ *...a blockade of the harbour.* ❑ *Warships are blockading the port.*

blockage /ˈblɒkɪdʒ/ (**blockages**) N-COUNT A **blockage** in a pipe or tunnel is something that is blocking it. ❑ *...a fatal blockage in the lung.*

blockbuster /ˈblɒkbʌstə/ (**blockbusters**) N-COUNT A **blockbuster** is a very popular and successful film or book. [INFORMAL]

blog /blɒg/ (**blogs**) N-COUNT A **blog** is a website containing a diary or journal on a particular subject. [COMPUTING] ❑ *When Barbieux started his blog, he simply hoped to communicate with a few people.* ● **blogger** (**bloggers**) N-COUNT ❑ *While most bloggers comment on news reported elsewhere, some do their own reporting.* ● **blogging** N-UNCOUNT ❑ *...the popularity of blogging.*
→ see Word Web: **blog**

bloke /bləʊk/ (**blokes**) N-COUNT A **bloke** is a man. [BRIT, INFORMAL]

blonde also **blond** /blɒnd/ (**blondes**) ADJ & N-COUNT A **blonde** person or a **blonde** has pale yellow-coloured hair. The form **blonde** is used to refer to women, and **blond** to refer to men. ❑ *Do blondes really have more fun?* ❑ *The boy had blond curls.*

blood /blʌd/ **1** N-UNCOUNT **Blood** is the red liquid that flows inside your body. **2** N-UNCOUNT You can use **blood** to refer to the race or social class of someone's parents or ancestors. ❑ *There was Greek blood in his veins.* **3** PHRASE If something violent and cruel is done **in cold blood**, it is done deliberately and in an unemotional way. **4** PHRASE New people who are introduced into an organization and whose fresh ideas are likely to improve it are referred to as **new blood, fresh blood,** or **young blood.** ❑ *Some experts criticised the company for failing to bring in new blood.* **5** **own flesh and blood** → see **flesh**
→ see **donor**

Word Partnership Use *blood* with:

V.	**donate/give** blood **1**
N.	**(red/white)** blood **cells**, blood **clot**, blood **disease**, blood **loss**, **pool of** blood, blood **sample**, blood **stream**, blood **supply**, blood **test**, blood **transfusion** **1**
ADJ.	**covered in** blood, blood **stained** **1** **related by** blood **2**
PREP.	**in *someone's*** blood **2**

ˈblood pressure N-UNCOUNT Your **blood pressure** is a measure of the force with which blood is pumped around your body.
→ see **diagnosis**

Word Web blog

The word **blog** is a combination of the words **web** and **log**. It is a **website** that has many dated **entries**. A blog can focus on one subject of interest. Most blogs are written by one person. A group of people may write a blog. Political committees, corporations, or other groups may keep a blog. Many blogs ask readers to leave comments on the site. This often results in a group of readers who write back and forth to each other. The total group of web logs is the blogosphere. A blogstorm occurs when there are many people using blogs about the same topic.

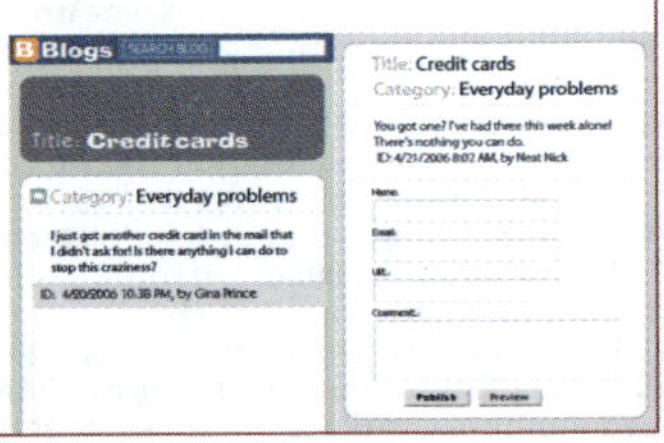

bloodshed /ˈblʌdʃed/ N-UNCOUNT **Bloodshed** is violence in which people are killed or wounded. ❑ *...another week of bloodshed.*

bloodstream /ˈblʌdstriːm/ (**bloodstreams**) N-COUNT Your **bloodstream** is your blood as it flows around your body. ❑ *The hormone goes straight into the bloodstream.*

ˈblood test (**blood tests**) N-COUNT A **blood test** is a medical examination of a sample of your blood.

ˈblood vessel (**blood vessels**) N-COUNT **Blood vessels** are the narrow tubes through which your blood flows.

bloody /ˈblʌdi/ (**bloodier, bloodiest**) **1** **Bloody** is a swear word. Some people use 'bloody' to emphasize what they are saying, especially when they are angry about something someone has said or done. [BRIT] **2** ADJ A situation or event that is **bloody** is one in which there is a lot of violence and people are killed. ❑ *...the bloody street riots of 1981.*

bloom /bluːm/ (**blooms, blooming, bloomed**) **1** N-COUNT A **bloom** is the flower on a plant. **2** PHRASE A plant or tree that is **in bloom** has flowers on it. **3** V-I When a plant or tree **blooms**, it produces flowers. When a flower **blooms**, the flower bud opens.

blossom /ˈblɒsəm/ (**blossoms, blossoming, blossomed**) **1** N-VAR **Blossom** is the flowers that appear on a tree before the fruit. ❑ *...cherry blossom.* **2** V-I When a tree **blossoms**, it produces blossom. **3** V-I If someone or something **blossoms**, they develop good, attractive, or successful qualities. ❑ *What began as a local festival has blossomed into an international event.*

blot /blɒt/ (**blots, blotting, blotted**) N-COUNT A **blot** is a drop of liquid that has been spilled on a surface and has dried. ❑ *...an ink blot.*

▶ **blot out** **1** PHR-VERB If one thing **blots out** another thing, it is in front of the other thing and prevents it from being seen. ❑ *Clouds blotted out the sun.* **2** PHR-VERB If you try to **blot out** a memory, you try to forget it. ❑ *She's trying to blot out all thoughts of the accident.*

blotch /blɒtʃ/ (**blotches**) N-COUNT A **blotch** is a small area of colour, for example on someone's skin. ❑ *His face was covered in red blotches.*

blouse /blaʊz, AM blaʊs/ (**blouses**) N-COUNT A **blouse** is a kind of shirt worn by girls or women.
→ see **clothing**

blow /bləʊ/ (**blows, blowing, blew, blown**) **1** V-I When a wind or breeze **blows**, the air moves. ❑ *A cold wind blew at the top of the hill.* **2** V-T/V-I If the wind **blows** something somewhere, or if something **blows** there, it is moved there by the wind. ❑ *The wind blew her hair back from her forehead.* ❑ *Sand blew in our eyes.* **3** V-I If you **blow**, you send out a stream of air from your mouth. ❑ *Danny blew on his fingers to warm them.* **4** V-T/V-I When a whistle or horn **blows**, or when someone **blows** it, they make a sound by blowing into it. **5** V-T When you **blow** your **nose**, you force air out of it through your nostrils in order to clear it. **6** V-T To **blow** something **out**, **off**, or **away** means to violently remove or destroy it with an explosion. ❑ *The can exploded, blowing out windows.* ❑ *The gunmen blew the city to bits.* **7** N-COUNT If someone receives a **blow**, they are hit by someone or something. ❑ *He went off to hospital after a blow to the face.* **8** N-COUNT A **blow** is something that happens which makes you very disappointed or unhappy. ❑ *It was a terrible blow when he was sacked.* **9** V-T If you **blow** a chance or an attempt to do something, you make a mistake which wastes the chance or causes the attempt to fail. [INFORMAL] ❑ *I had probably blown my chances for this job.* ❑ *Oh you fool! You've blown it!* **10** V-T If you **blow** a large amount of money, you spend it quickly on things you don't need. [INFORMAL]
→ see **glass, wind**

▶ **blow away** PHR-VERB If you say that you **are blown away** by something, or if it **blows** you **away**, you mean that you are very impressed by it. [INFORMAL] ❑ *I was blown away by the tone and the quality of the story.* ❑ *Everyone I met overwhelmed me and kind of blew me away.*

▶ **blow out** PHR-VERB If you **blow out** a flame or a candle, you blow at it so that it stops burning.

▶ **blow over** PHR-VERB If something such as trouble or an argument **blows over**, it comes to an end. ❑ *Wait, and it'll all blow over.*

▶ **blow up** **1** PHR-VERB If someone **blows** something **up**, or if it **blows up**, it is destroyed by an explosion. ❑ *Their boat blew up.* **2** PHR-VERB If you **blow up** something such as a balloon or a tyre, you fill it with air.

Word Partnership Use *blow* with:

N.	blow **bubbles**, blow **smoke** 3
	blow **a whistle** 4
	blow ***your* nose** 5
ADV.	blow **away** 6
V.	**deliver/strike a** blow 7
	cushion/soften a blow, **suffer a** blow 8
PREP.	blow **to the head** 7
	blow **to *someone*** 8
ADJ.	**crushing/devastating/heavy** blow 7 8

blown /bləʊn/ **Blown** is the past participle of **blow**.

blue /bluː/ (**bluer, bluest, blues**) **1** ADJ & N-VAR Something that is **blue** is the colour of the sky on a sunny day. **2** PHRASE Something that happens **out of the blue** happens suddenly and unexpectedly. ❑ *Turner's resignation came out of the blue.* **3** N-PLURAL **The blues** is a type of music which is similar to jazz, with a slow tempo and a strong rhythm.
→ see **colour, rainbow**

ˌblue-ˈcollar ADJ **Blue-collar** workers work in industry, doing physical work, rather than in offices.

blueprint /ˈbluːprɪnt/ (**blueprints**) N-COUNT A **blueprint for** something is an original plan or description of how it is expected to work. ❑ *...his blueprint for the country's future.*

bluff /blʌf/ (**bluffs, bluffing, bluffed**) **1** N-VAR A **bluff** is an attempt to make someone believe that you will do something when you do not really intend to do it. ❑ *The letter was a bluff.* ❑ *...a game of bluff.* **2** PHRASE If you **call** someone's **bluff**, you tell them to do what they have been threatening to do, because you are sure that they will not really do it. **3** V-T/V-I If you **bluff**, you try to make someone believe that you will do something although you do not really intend to do it, or that you know something when you really do not know it.

B

❑ *Either side, or both, could be bluffing.* ❑ *He tried to bluff his way through another test.*

blunder /ˈblʌndə/ (**blunders, blundering, blundered**) **1** N-COUNT & V-I If you **make a blunder**, or if you **blunder**, you make a stupid mistake. ❑ *It was a blunder to give him the assignment.* ❑ *The company admitted it had blundered.* **2** V-I If you **blunder** somewhere, you move there in a clumsy way. ❑ *He blundered into the table.*

blunt /blʌnt/ (**blunter, bluntest, blunts, blunting, blunted**) **1** ADJ If you are **blunt**, you say exactly what you think without trying to be polite. ❑ *His blunt answer surprised them.* ● **bluntly** ADV ❑ *'I don't believe you!' Jean said bluntly.* ● **bluntness** N-UNCOUNT ❑ *His bluntness got him into trouble.* **2** ADJ BEFORE N A **blunt** object has a rounded or flat end rather than a sharp one. ❑ *He was beaten to death with a blunt instrument.* **3** ADJ A **blunt** knife is no longer sharp and does not cut well. **4** V-T If something **blunts** an emotion or feeling, it weakens it. ❑ *Our appetite was blunted by the beer.*

blur /blɜː/ (**blurs, blurring, blurred**) **1** N-COUNT A **blur** is a shape or area which you cannot see clearly because it has no clear outline or because it is moving very fast. ❑ *Her face is a blur.* **2** V-T/V-I If an image **blurs**, or if something **blurs** it, it becomes a blur. ❑ *Tears ran into my eyes and blurred my vision.* ● **blurred** ADJ ❑ *...slightly blurred photos.* **3** V-T If something **blurs** a distinction between things, the differences between them are no longer clear. ❑ *Television is blurring the distinction between sport and show business.* ● **blurred** ADJ ❑ *Fiction and reality became blurred.*

blurt /blɜːt/ (**blurts, blurting, blurted**)
▶ **blurt out** PHR-VERB If you **blurt** something **out**, you say it suddenly, after trying hard to keep quiet. ❑ *'You're mad,' the driver blurted out.* ❑ *Richard blurted out what was on his mind.*

blush /blʌʃ/ (**blushes, blushing, blushed**) V-I & N-COUNT When you **blush**, or when a **blush** spreads over your face, your face becomes redder than usual because you are ashamed or embarrassed. ❑ *I felt myself blush.* ❑ *Ann accepted it with a blush.*

bluster /ˈblʌstə/ (**blusters, blustering, blustered**) V-I & N-UNCOUNT If you say that someone is **blustering** or that what they say is **bluster**, you mean that they are speaking aggressively or proudly but without authority. ❑ *'I'm sorry,' he blustered.* ❑ *At the heart of Tom's bluster was a great shyness.*

BMI /ˌbiːemˈaɪ/ **BMI** is an abbreviation for **body mass index.** [MEDICAL] ❑ *The average BMI in women is around 23.*

boar /bɔː/

The plural is **boar** or **boars**.

1 N-COUNT A **boar** or a **wild boar** is a wild pig. **2** N-COUNT A **boar** is a male pig.

board /bɔːd/ (**boards, boarding, boarded**) **1** N-COUNT A **board** is a flat piece of wood, plastic, or cardboard which is used for a particular purpose. ❑ *...a chopping board.* ❑ *...a chess board.* ❑ *They laid new carpets on top of the wooden boards.* **2** N-COUNT You can refer to a blackboard or a noticeboard as a **board.** ❑ *He wrote a few more notes on the board.* **3** N-COUNT The **board** of a company or organization is the group of people who control it. ❑ *I'm on the board of directors.* ❑ *...board meetings.* **4** V-T/V-I & PHRASE When you **board** a train, ship, or aircraft, when it **is boarding**, or when you go **on board**, you get on it. ❑ *From there she will board a ferry to Dover.* ❑ *...Flight BA4325, now boarding at Gate 10.* ❑ *There were four people on board the aircraft.* **5** N-UNCOUNT **Board** is the food which is provided when you stay somewhere, for example in a hotel. ❑ *Free room and board are provided for all hotel staff.* **6** PHRASE If a policy or a situation applies **across the board**, it affects everything or everyone in a particular group. ❑ *...to increase salaries across the board.* **7** PHRASE If you **take on board** an idea or suggestion, you begin to accept it. ❑ *I hope the council will take that message on board.*
▶ **board up** PHR-VERB If you **board up** a door or window, you fix pieces of wood over it so that it is covered up. ❑ *The shops are all boarded up.*

Word Partnership	Use *board* with:
N.	board **game**, **cutting** board, **diving** board **1**
	bulletin board, **message** board **2**
	chair/member of the board, board **of directors**, board **meeting** **3**
	board **a flight/plane/ship** **4**
	room and board **5**

ˈboarding school (**boarding schools**) N-VAR A **boarding school** is a school where the pupils live during the term. ❑ *Now she is away at boarding school.*

boardroom /ˈbɔːdruːm/ (**boardrooms**) N-COUNT The **boardroom** is a room where the board of a company meets.

boast /bəʊst/ (**boasts, boasting, boasted**) V-I & N-COUNT If someone **boasts about** something that they have done or that they own, they talk about it proudly in a way that other people may find irritating or offensive. A **boast** is what someone says when they boast. ❑ *Carol boasted about her expensive costume.* ❑ *Furci boasted that he helped to kill them.* ❑ *His boast was that he'd done no research at all.*

boat /bəʊt/ (**boats**) **1** N-COUNT A **boat** is something in which people can travel across water. ❑ *...a small fishing boat.* ❑ *You can reach the island by boat.* **2** N-COUNT You can refer to a passenger ship as a **boat.** ❑ *My father met me off the boat.* **3** PHRASE If you say that someone **is rocking the boat**, you mean that they are upsetting a calm situation and causing trouble. **4** PHRASE If two or more people are **in the same boat**, they are in the same unpleasant situation. ❑ *She's in the same boat as me. She's unemployed herself.*
→ see Word Web: **boat**
→ see **ship**

boating /ˈbəʊtɪŋ/ N-UNCOUNT **Boating** is travelling on a lake or river in a small boat for pleasure. ❑ *...a boating accident.* ❑ *I wanted to go boating.*

bob /bɒb/ (**bobs, bobbing, bobbed**) V-I If something **bobs**, it moves up and down, like something does when it is floating on water. ❑ *Huge balloons bobbed about in the sky above.*

bode /bəʊd/ (**bodes, boding, boded**) V-I If something **bodes well**, it makes you think that something good will happen. If something **bodes ill**, it makes you think that something bad will

Word Web boat

People once used **boats** only for transportation. But today millions of people enjoy boating as a hobby. Weekend **captains** enjoy quietly **sailing** their **small boats** along the shore. However, other boaters like to ride around in **motorboats**. Any **rowing boat** can become a motorboat just by attaching an **outboard motor** to the back. **Inboard** motors are quieter, but they're more expensive. Fishermen usually like to use a rowing boat with **oars** instead of a boat with a motor. That way they won't scare the fish away. For an even more peaceful ride, some people **paddle** around in **canoes**. But really adventurous folks like the thrill of white-water rafting.

happen in the future. [LITERARY] ❑ *Their 100 per cent record so far bodes well.*

bodily /ˈbɒdɪli/ **1** ADJ BEFORE N Your **bodily needs** and **functions** are the needs and functions of your body. **2** ADV You use **bodily** to indicate that an action involves the whole of someone's body. ❑ *I was thrown bodily to the ground.*

body /ˈbɒdi/ (**bodies**) **1** N-COUNT Your **body** is all your physical parts, including your head, arms, and legs. ❑ *My whole body hurt.* **2** N-COUNT You can refer to the main part of your body, excluding your arms, head, and legs, as your **body**. ❑ *Gently pull your leg towards your body.* **3** N-COUNT A **body** is a dead person's body. ❑ *Police later found a body.* **4** N-COUNT A **body** is an organized group of people who deal with something officially. ❑ *FIFA is football's governing body.* **5** N-COUNT The **body** of a car or plane is its main part, excluding its engine, wheels, and wings.
→ see Picture Dictionary: **body**

bodyguard /ˈbɒdigɑːd/ (**bodyguards**) N-COUNT Someone's **bodyguard** is the person or group of people employed to protect them.

ˈbody language N-UNCOUNT Your **body language** is the way you show your feelings or thoughts using the movements of your body.

ˌbody mass ˈindex N-SING A person's **body mass index** is a measurement that represents the relationship between their weight and their height. [MEDICAL] ❑ *...those with a body mass index of 30 and over.*

bog /bɒg/ (**bogs**) N-COUNT A **bog** is a wet muddy area of land.

ˌbogged ˈdown ADJ If you are **bogged down in** something, it prevents you from making progress or getting something done. [INFORMAL] ❑ *Why get bogged down in legal details?*

boggle /ˈbɒgəl/ (**boggles, boggling, boggled**) V-I If you say that **the mind boggles at** something, you mean that it is so strange or amazing that it is difficult to imagine or understand. [INFORMAL] ❑ *The mind boggles at how much work they have to do.*

bogus /ˈbəʊgəs/ ADJ If you describe something as **bogus**, you mean that it is not genuine. ❑ *...their bogus insurance claim.*

bohemian /bəʊˈhiːmiən/ (**bohemians**) ADJ & N-COUNT You can describe someone as **bohemian**, or as a **bohemian**, if they are artistic and live in an unconventional way.

boil /bɔɪl/ (**boils, boiling, boiled**) **1** V-T/V-I When a hot liquid **boils**, or when you **boil** it, bubbles appear in it and it starts to change into steam. ❑ *Boil the water in the saucepan.* ❑ *...a large pan of boiling water.* **2** PHRASE When you **bring** a liquid **to the boil**, you heat it until it boils. **3** V-T/V-I When you **boil** a kettle, or when you put it on **to boil**, you heat the water inside it until it boils. ❑ *Marianne put the kettle on to boil.* **4** V-T/V-I When you **boil** food, or when you put it on **to boil**, you cook it in boiling water. ❑ *Boil the potatoes for 10 minutes.* **5** → See note at **cook** **6** N-COUNT A **boil** is a red painful swelling on your skin.
→ see **cook, egg, thermometer**

▸ **boil down to** PHR-VERB If you say that a

Picture Dictionary body

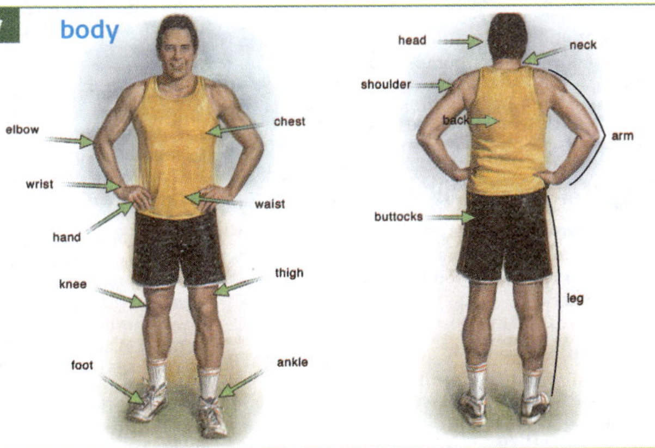

situation or problem **boils down to** a particular thing, you mean that this is the most important aspect of it. ❑ *It all boils down to money again.*
▶ **boil over** PHR-VERB When a liquid that is being heated **boils over**, it rises and flows over the edge of the container.

boiler /ˈbɔɪlə/ (**boilers**) N-COUNT A **boiler** is a device which burns fuel to provide hot water.

boiling /ˈbɔɪlɪŋ/ **1** ADJ Something that is **boiling** or **boiling hot** is very hot. ❑ *It's boiling in here.* ❑ *...boiling hot food.* **2** → See note at **hot**

boisterous /ˈbɔɪstərəs/ ADJ Someone who is **boisterous** is noisy, lively, and full of energy. ❑ *...a boisterous but good-natured crowd.*

bold /bəʊld/ (**bolder, boldest**) **1** ADJ Someone who is **bold** is brave or confident. ❑ *We should be bolder.* ❑ *...bold economic reforms.* ● **boldly** ADV ❑ *You can and must act boldly.* ❑ *'You should do it,' the girl said, boldly.* ● **boldness** N-UNCOUNT ❑ *She called on her leaders to show boldness.* **2** ADJ **Bold** colours or designs are painted or drawn in a clear strong way. ❑ *...bold handwriting.*

bolster /ˈbəʊlstə/ (**bolsters, bolstering, bolstered**) V-T If you **bolster** someone's confidence or courage, you make them more confident or more courageous. ❑ *This will bolster his self-belief.*

bolt /bəʊlt/ (**bolts, bolting, bolted**) **1** V-T & N-COUNT If you **bolt** one thing **to** another, you fasten them firmly together, using a **bolt**, which is a long metal object which screws into a nut. ❑ *...nuts and bolts that haven't been tightened.* ❑ *The wooden bench which was bolted to the floor.* ❑ *Simply bolt these two parts together.* **2** N-COUNT A **bolt** on a door or window is a metal bar that you slide across in order to fasten the door or window. ❑ *All I've got at the moment is a bolt on the front door.* **3** V-T If you **bolt** a door or window, you slide the bolt across to fasten it. ❑ *Lock and bolt the kitchen door.* **4** V-I If a person or animal **bolts**, they suddenly start to run very fast, often because something has frightened them. ❑ *I made some excuse and bolted for the exit.*

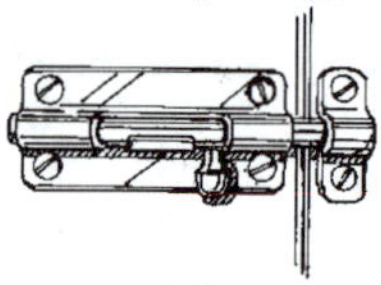
bolt

→ see **lightning**

bomb /bɒm/ (**bombs, bombing, bombed**) **1** N-COUNT A **bomb** is a device which explodes, damaging a large area or killing people. **2** V-T When a place **is bombed**, it is attacked with bombs. ❑ *Airforce jets bombed the airport.* ● **bombing** (**bombings**) N-VAR ❑ *...the bombing of Dresden.*

Word Partnership Use *bomb* with:

ADJ.	**atomic/nuclear** bomb, **live** bomb **1**
N.	bomb **blast**, **car** bomb, **pipe** bomb, bomb **shelter**, bomb **squad**, bomb **threat** **1**
V.	**drop/plant a** bomb, **set off a** bomb **1**

bombard /ˌbɒmˈbɑːd/ (**bombards, bombarding, bombarded**) **1** V-T If someone **bombards** you **with** something, they make you face a great deal of it. ❑ *We have been bombarded with requests for information.* ❑ *He began bombarding her with love letters.* **2** V-T When soldiers **bombard** a place, they attack it with continuous gunfire or bombs. ● **bombardment** N-UNCOUNT ❑ *...a night of heavy bombardment.*

bomber /ˈbɒmə/ (**bombers**) **1** N-COUNT A **bomber** is an aeroplane that drops bombs. **2** N-COUNT **Bombers** are people who plant bombs in public places.

bombshell /ˈbɒmʃel/ (**bombshells**) N-COUNT A **bombshell** is a sudden piece of bad or unexpected news. ❑ *Then Grandfather dropped his bombshell.*

bonanza /bəˈnænzə/ (**bonanzas**) N-COUNT You can refer to a time or situation when people suddenly become much richer as a **bonanza**. ❑ *...a sales bonanza for computer makers.*

bond /bɒnd/ (**bonds, bonding, bonded**) **1** N-COUNT A **bond between** people is a close link between them, for example feelings of love, or a special agreement. ❑ *...the bond between mothers and babies.* ❑ *The republic is successfully breaking its bonds with Moscow.* **2** V-I When people **bond with** each other, they form a relationship based on love or shared experiences. ❑ *Belinda had trouble bonding with the baby.* **3** V-I When things **bond together**, they stick to each other or become joined in some way. ❑ *Here we see how carbon atoms bond together in rings.* **4** N-COUNT A **bond** is a certificate issued by a government or company which shows that you have lent them money and that they will pay you interest.
→ see **love**

bondage /ˈbɒndɪdʒ/ N-UNCOUNT **Bondage** is the condition of being a slave. [LITERARY] ❑ *Masters sometimes allowed slaves to buy their way out of bondage.*

bone /bəʊn/ (**bones, boning, boned**) **1** N-VAR Your **bones** are the hard parts inside your body which together form your skeleton. ❑ *Stephen broke his thigh bone.* ❑ *The body is made up primarily of bone, muscle, and fat.* **2** V-T If you **bone** a piece of meat or fish, you remove the bones from it before cooking it.

bonfire /ˈbɒnfaɪə/ (**bonfires**) N-COUNT A **bonfire** is a fire built outdoors, usually to burn rubbish.

bonnet /ˈbɒnɪt/ (**bonnets**) **1** N-COUNT In British English, the **bonnet** of a car is the metal cover over the engine at the front. The American word is **hood**. **2** N-COUNT A **bonnet** is a hat worn by babies which has ribbons that are tied under the chin.
→ see **hat**

bonus /ˈbəʊnəs/ (**bonuses**) **1** N-COUNT A **bonus** is an amount of money that is added to someone's pay, usually because they have worked very hard. **2** N-COUNT A **bonus** is something good that you get in addition to something else, usually something which is unexpected. ❑ *As a bonus, each child receives a Zoo Crew T-shirt.*

bony /ˈbəʊni/ (**bonier, boniest**) ADJ If someone has, for example, a **bony** face or **bony** hands, their face or hands are too thin.

boo /buː/ (**boos, booing, booed**) V-T & N-COUNT If you **boo** a speaker or performer, you shout 'boo' or make other loud sounds to indicate that you do not like them. The sounds you make are called **boos**. ❑ *They were booed by their own supporters.* ❑ *She was greeted with boos and hisses.* ● **booing** N-UNCOUNT ❑ *The prime minister remained silent during the booing.*

b

book /bʊk/ (**books, booking, booked**)
1 N-COUNT A **book** consists of pieces of paper, usually with words printed on them, which are fastened together and fixed inside a cover of strong paper or cardboard. **2** N-COUNT A **book of** something such as stamps is a small number of them fastened together between thin cardboard or plastic covers. **3** N-PLURAL An organization's **books** are written records of money that has been spent and earned, or of the names of people who belong to it. ❑ *An accountant has checked the books.* ❑ *Many of the people on our books are in the computing industry.* **4** V-T When you **book** something such as a hotel room or a ticket, you arrange to have it or use it at a particular time. [BRIT] ❑ *I have booked a table in the restaurant.* **5** PHRASE If a hotel, restaurant, or theatre is **fully booked**, **booked solid**, or **booked up**, it has no rooms, tables, or tickets left.
→ see **concert, library**
▶ **book into** or **book in** PHR-VERB In British English, when you **book into** a hotel or when you **book in**, you officially state that you have arrived to stay there, usually by signing your name in a register. The American term is **check in**.

Word Partnership	Use *book* with:
N.	**address** book, book **award**, **children's** book, book **club**, **comic** book, **copy of a** book, book **cover**, **library** book, **phone** book, book **review**, **subject of a** book, **title of a** book **1**
ADJ.	**latest/new/recent** book **1**
V.	**publish a** book, **read a** book, **write a** book **1**

bookcase /ˈbʊkkeɪs/ (**bookcases**) N-COUNT A **bookcase** is a piece of furniture with shelves for books.
bookie /ˈbʊki/ (**bookies**) N-COUNT A **bookie** is the same as a **bookmaker**. [INFORMAL]

Word Link	*let ≈ little : booklet, droplet, leaflet*

booklet /ˈbʊklət/ (**booklets**) N-COUNT A **booklet** is a small paperback book, containing information on a particular subject.
bookmaker /ˈbʊkmeɪkə/ (**bookmakers**) N-COUNT A **bookmaker** is a person whose job is to take your money when you bet and to pay you money if you win.

Word Link	*mark ≈ boundary, sign : bookmark, landmark, unmarked*

bookmark /ˈbʊkmɑːk/ (**bookmarks, bookmarking, bookmarked**) **1** N-COUNT A **bookmark** is a narrow piece of card or cloth that you put between the pages of a book so that you can find that particular page easily. **2** N-COUNT A **bookmark** is the address of an Internet site that you put into a list on your computer so that you can return to it easily. [COMPUTING] **3** V-T If you **bookmark** an Internet site, you put it into a list on your computer so that you can return to it easily. [COMPUTING]
boom /buːm/ (**booms, booming, boomed**)
1 N-COUNT & V-I If there is a **boom** in something such as the economy, or if it **is booming**, it increases or develops very quickly. ❑ *...the 1980s property boom.* ❑ *Sales are booming.* **2** V-I & N-COUNT When something such as a cannon or someone's voice **booms** or **booms out**, it makes a loud, deep, echoing sound called a **boom**. ❑ *'Ladies,' boomed Helena, 'we all know why we're here tonight'.* ❑ *The stillness was broken by the boom of a cannon.*

Thesaurus	*boom* Also look up:
V.	flourish, prosper, succeed, thrive; *(ant.)* fail **1**
N.	explosion, roar **2**

boon /buːn/ (**boons**) N-COUNT You say that something is a **boon to** people or **for** people when it makes their life better or easier. ❑ *Fans that follow the games will provide a boon to local hotels.*
boost /buːst/ (**boosts, boosting, boosted**)
1 V-T & N-COUNT If one thing **boosts** another, or if it gives it a **boost**, it causes the second thing to increase or be more successful. ❑ *Advertising had boosted sales.* ❑ *That would provide an important boost to education.* **2** V-T & N-COUNT If something **boosts** your confidence or morale, or if it gives it a **boost**, it improves it. ❑ *It gave me a boost to win the race.*
boot /buːt/ (**boots, booting, booted**) **1** N-COUNT **Boots** are strong heavy shoes that cover your whole foot and the lower part of your leg. **2** V-T If you **boot** something such as a ball, you kick it hard. [INFORMAL] **3** N-COUNT In British English, the **boot** of a car is a covered space at the back or front that is used for luggage. The usual American word is **trunk**. **4** PHRASE If you **get the boot**, you are forced to leave your job. [INFORMAL] **5** PHRASE You can say **to boot** after the last item in a list of things in order to emphasize that particular thing. ❑ *He was a liar, a cheat and a bad businessman to boot.*
→ see **clothing, shoe**
booth /buːð/ (**booths**) **1** N-COUNT A **booth** is a small area separated from a larger public area by screens or thin walls where, for example, you can make a telephone call. **2** N-COUNT A **booth** is a small tent or stall, usually at a fair, in which you can buy goods or watch some entertainment.
booze /buːz/ (**boozes, boozing, boozed**)
1 N-UNCOUNT **Booze** is alcoholic drink. [INFORMAL] **2** V-I When people **booze**, they drink a lot of alcohol. [INFORMAL]
border /ˈbɔːdə/ (**borders, bordering, bordered**)
1 N-COUNT The **border** between two countries is the dividing line between them. ❑ *They escaped across the border.* **2** V-T If one thing **borders** another, it is next to it. ❑ *These countries border the Mediterranean.* ❑ *...miles of white beach bordered by palm trees.* **3** N-COUNT A **border** is a strip or band around the edge of something. ❑ *The wall of plain tiles has a bright border.* **4** V-I When you say that something **borders on** a particular state, you mean that it has almost reached that state. ❑ *He admitted that his feelings bordered on despair.*

border

B

Thesaurus *border* Also look up:
V. surround, touch 2

bore /bɔː/ (**bores, boring, bored**) 1 V-T & N-COUNT If someone or something **bores** you, you find them dull and uninteresting. You can refer to them as a **bore**. ❑ *Dick bored him all the way through the meal.* ❑ *Her husband Jim is a terrible bore.* 2 N-SING You can describe a situation as **a bore** when you find it annoying or a nuisance. ❑ *'Old age is a bore,' she says.* 3 V-T If you **bore** a hole in something, you make a deep round hole in it using a drilling tool. 4 **Bore** is the past tense of **bear**.

bored /bɔːd/ ADJ If you are **bored**, you feel tired and impatient because you are not interested in something or because you have nothing to do. ❑ *I got bored with my job as a travel agent.* ❑ *I'm so bored at the moment.*

Word Link *dom ≈ state of being : boredom, freedom, wisdom*

boredom /ˈbɔːdəm/ N-UNCOUNT **Boredom** is the state of being bored. ❑ *She's terrified of boredom – she wants to see new places all the time.*

boring /ˈbɔːrɪŋ/ ADJ If you say that someone or something is **boring**, you think that they are very dull and uninteresting. ❑ *...a boring job.*

Thesaurus *boring* Also look up:
ADJ. dull, tedious; *(ant.)* exciting, fun, interesting, lively

born /bɔːn/ 1 V-T PASSIVE When a baby **is born**, it comes out of its mother's body. You can refer to a baby's parents by saying that he or she **is born of** or **born to** those people. ❑ *My mother was 40 when I was born.* ❑ *He was born of German parents and lived most of his life abroad.* 2 ADJ BEFORE N You use **born** to describe someone who has a natural ability to do a particular activity or job. For example, a **born** cook has a natural ability to cook well.

-born **-born** is added to the name of a place or nationality to indicate where a person was born. ❑ *...a German-born photographer.*

borne /bɔːn/ **Borne** is the past participle of **bear**.

borough /ˈbʌrə, AM ˈbɜːrəʊ/ (**boroughs**) N-COUNT A **borough** is a town or district, which has its own council. ❑ *...the London Borough of Merton.*

borrow /ˈbɒrəʊ/ (**borrows, borrowing, borrowed**) V-T If you **borrow** something that belongs to someone else, you take it, usually with their permission, intending to return it. ❑ *Can I borrow a pen please?* ❑ *He borrowed $200 from his wife.* ● **borrowing** N-UNCOUNT ❑ *The borrowing must be privately arranged.*

borrower /ˈbɒrəʊə/ (**borrowers**) N-COUNT A **borrower** is a person or organization that borrows money. ❑ *Borrowers repay a fixed amount each month.* → see **library**

bosom /ˈbʊzəm/ (**bosoms**) 1 N-COUNT A woman's breasts are sometimes referred to as her **bosom** or her **bosoms**. [DATED] 2 N-SING If you are in **the bosom of** your family or **of** a community, you are among people who love and protect you. [LITERARY] ❑ *I do enjoy being in the bosom of a family.* 3 ADJ BEFORE N A **bosom** friend is a very close friend.

boss /bɒs/ (**bosses, bossing, bossed**) 1 N-COUNT Your **boss** is the person in charge of the organization or department where you work. ❑ *He cannot stand his boss.* 2 PHRASE If you **are** your **own boss**, you work for yourself or do not have to ask other people for permission to do something. ❑ *I'm very much my own boss and no one interferes with me.* 3 V-T & PHR-VERB If someone **bosses** you, or if they **boss** you **around**, they keep telling you what to do. ❑ *We cannot boss them into doing more.*

Thesaurus *boss* Also look up:
N. chief, director, employer, foreman, manager, owner, superintendent, supervisor 1

bossy /ˈbɒsi/ (**bossier, bossiest**) ADJ A **bossy** person enjoys telling other people what to do; used showing disapproval. ❑ *...a rather bossy little girl.*

botany /ˈbɒtəni/ N-UNCOUNT **Botany** is the scientific study of plants. ● **botanical** ADJ BEFORE N ❑ *The area is of great botanical interest.* ● **botanist** (**botanists**) N-COUNT ❑ *He trained as a botanist.*

botch /bɒtʃ/ (**botches, botching, botched**) V-T & PHR-VERB If you **botch** a piece of work, or if you **botch** it **up**, you do it badly or clumsily. [INFORMAL] ❑ *She had already botched it.* ❑ *I hate it when builders botch up repairs on my house.*

both /bəʊθ/ 1 QUANT You use **both** when you are referring to two people or things and saying that something is true about each of them. ❑ *Put both vegetables into a bowl.* ❑ *Both of us had tears in our eyes.* ❑ *Well, I'll leave you both then.* 2 CONJ You use the structure **both...and** when you are giving two facts or alternatives and emphasizing that each of them is true or possible. ❑ *Now women work both before and after having their children.*

Usage
Notice that all these sentences mean the same thing: **'Both boys have been ill', 'Both the boys have been ill', 'Both of the boys have been ill', 'The boys have both been ill'.** You cannot say 'Both of boys have been ill'. When a pronoun is used, you can say **'Both of us have been ill'.**

bother /ˈbɒðə/ (**bothers, bothering, bothered**) 1 V-T/V-I If you do not **bother to** do something or if you do not **bother with** it, you do not do it, consider it, or use it because you think it is unnecessary or because you are too lazy. ❑ *Lots of people don't bother to go through a marriage ceremony.* ❑ *The papers didn't even bother reporting it.* ❑ *He does not bother with a helmet.* 2 PHRASE If you say that you **can't be bothered to** do something, you mean that you are not going to do it because you think it is unnecessary or because you are too lazy. ❑ *I just can't be bothered to clean the house.* 3 N-UNCOUNT **Bother** is trouble, fuss, or difficulty. ❑ *I usually buy sliced bread – it's less bother.* ❑ *It's never a bother, talking to you.* 4 V-T/V-I If something **bothers** you it worries, annoys, or upsets you. ❑ *It bothered me when I heard that.* ❑ *Never bother about other people's opinions.* ● **bothered** ADJ AFTER LINK-V ❑ *I was bothered about the cut on my hand.* 5 V-T If you **bother** someone, you talk to them or interrupt them when they are busy. ❑ *I concentrate, talk to nobody, and nobody bothers me.*

bottle /ˈbɒtəl/ (**bottles, bottling, bottled**) N-COUNT & V-T A **bottle** is a glass or plastic container for keeping liquids in. You **bottle** liquid when you put it in a bottle. ❑ *...two empty milk bottles.* ❑ *Bring your own bottle of water to the meeting.* ❑ *The oil is bottled in small hard plastic bottles.* ● **bottled** ADJ ❑ *...bottled water.*
→ see **container, glass**
▶ **bottle up** PHR-VERB If you **bottle up** feelings, you do not express them or show them. ❑ *Teenagers tend to bottle up their feelings.* ❑ *I prefer to bottle it up, even though it's not good for me.*

bottom /ˈbɒtəm/ (**bottoms, bottoming, bottomed**) **1** N-COUNT The **bottom** of something is the lowest part of it. ❑ *He sat at the bottom of the stairs.* ❑ *Go to the bottom of page 8.* **2** ADJ BEFORE N The **bottom** thing in a series of things is the lowest one. ❑ *...the bottom drawer.* ❑ *...the bottom shelf.* **3** N-SING If someone is **bottom** or at **the bottom** in a survey, test, or league, their performance is worse than that of all the other people involved. ❑ *He was always bottom of the class.* **4** N-COUNT Your **bottom** is the part of your body that you sit on. **5** PHRASE If you **get to the bottom of** something, you discover the real cause of it. ❑ *Now you can get to the bottom of this mystery.*
▶ **bottom out** PHR-VERB If a trend such as a fall in prices **bottoms out**, it stops getting worse or decreasing. ❑ *He expects the recession to bottom out.*

Thesaurus *bottom* Also look up:

N.	base, floor, foundation, ground; *(ant.)* peak, top **1**

Word Partnership Use *bottom* with:

N.	bottom **of a hill**, bottom **of the page/screen** **1**
	bottom **drawer**, bottom **lip**, bottom **of the sea**, bottom **of the pool**, **river** bottom, bottom **rung** **1** **2**
V.	**reach the** bottom, **sink to the** bottom **3**
PREP.	**along the** bottom, **at/near the** bottom, **on the** bottom **1** **2** **3**

ˌbottom ˈline (**bottom lines**) N-SING **The bottom line** in a decision or situation is the most important factor that you have to consider. ❑ *The bottom line is that you work as fast as you can.*

bought /bɔːt/ **Bought** is the past tense and past participle of **buy**.

boulder /ˈbəʊldə/ (**boulders**) N-COUNT A **boulder** is a large rounded rock.

boulevard /ˈbuːləvɑːd, AM ˈbʊl-/ (**boulevards**) N-COUNT A **boulevard** is a wide street in a city, usually with trees along each side.

bounce /baʊns/ (**bounces, bouncing, bounced**) **1** V-T/V-I & N-COUNT When something such as a ball **bounces**, or when you **bounce** it, it moves upwards or away immediately after hitting a surface. This movement is called a **bounce**. ❑ *The ball bounced right in front of them.* ❑ *I bounced a ball against the house.* ❑ *...two bounces of the ball.* **2** V-I If you **bounce on** something, you jump up and down on it repeatedly. ❑ *She even lets us bounce on our beds.* **3** V-I If something **bounces**, it swings or moves up and down. ❑ *Her long black hair bounced as she walked.* **4** V-T/V-I If a cheque **bounces** or if a bank **bounces** it, the bank refuses to accept it and pay out the money.

bouncer /ˈbaʊnsə/ (**bouncers**) N-COUNT A **bouncer** is a person who is employed to prevent unwanted people from entering a nightclub or causing trouble in it.

bouncy /ˈbaʊnsi/ (**bouncier, bounciest**) ADJ Someone or something that is **bouncy** is very lively and enthusiastic. ❑ *...good, bouncy pop songs.* ❑ *She was bouncy and full of energy.*

bound /baʊnd/ (**bounds, bounding, bounded**) **1** **Bound** is the past tense and past participle of **bind**. **2** PHRASE If one thing is **bound up with** another, it is closely connected with it. ❑ *My fate was bound up with hers.* **3** PHRASE If something is **bound to** happen or be true, it is certain to happen or be true. ❑ *There are bound to be price increases next year.* ❑ *He's bound to know.* **4** ADJ AFTER LINK-V If a vehicle is **bound for** a particular place, it is travelling towards it. ❑ *The ship was bound for Italy.* **5** N-PLURAL **Bounds** are limits which restrict what can be done. ❑ *Visitors are kept firmly within bounds – no noise, no photographs.* **6** PHRASE If a place is **out of bounds**, people are not allowed to go there. **7** V-I When animals or people **bound**, they move quickly with large leaps. ❑ *He bounded up the steps.*

Word Partnership Use *bound* with:

V.	bound **and gagged** **1**
	bound **to fail** **3**
N.	**feet/hands/wrists** bound, **leather** bound, **spiral** bound, bound **with tape** **1**
	a flight/plane/ship/train bound **for** **4**
PREP.	bound **together**, bound **up with** **1** **2**
ADV.	**legally** bound, **tightly** bound **1** **2**
N.	bound **by duty** **2**

boundary /ˈbaʊndəri/ (**boundaries**) N-COUNT The **boundary** of an area of land is an imaginary line that separates it from other areas. ❑ *...the disputed boundary between the two countries.*

Word Partnership Use *boundary* with:

N.	boundary **dispute**, boundary **line**
PREP.	boundary **around places/things**, boundary **between places/things**, **beyond a** boundary, boundary **of *someplace/something*,**
V.	**cross a** boundary, **mark/set a** boundary

bounty /ˈbaʊnti/ (**bounties**) N-VAR You can refer to something that is provided in large amounts as **bounty**. [LITERARY] ❑ *...autumn's bounty of fruits, seeds and berries.*

bouquet /bəʊˈkeɪ, buː-/ (**bouquets**) N-COUNT A **bouquet** is a bunch of flowers arranged in an attractive way. ❑ *...a bouquet of red roses.*

bourgeois /ˈbʊəʒwɑː/ ADJ **Bourgeois** means typical of fairly rich middle-class people; used showing disapproval. ❑ *Let's face it, we're all bourgeois now.*

bout /baʊt/ (**bouts**) **1** N-COUNT If you have a

B

bout of something such as an illness, you have it for a short period. ❑ *...a bad bout of flu.* **2** N-COUNT A **bout of** activity is a short time during which it happens a great deal or in which you do it a great deal. ❑ *...the latest bout of violence.*

boutique /buːˈtiːk/ (**boutiques**) N-COUNT A **boutique** is a small shop that sells fashionable clothes, shoes, or jewellery.

bow
❶ BENDING OR SUBMITTING
❷ OBJECTS

bow /baʊ/ (**bows, bowing, bowed**)
❶ **1** V-I & N-COUNT When you **bow to** someone, or if you give them a **bow**, you briefly bend your body towards them as a formal way of greeting them or showing respect. ❑ *He bowed low as the queen approached.* ❑ *At the end of the play, John came on stage and took a bow.* **2** V-T If you **bow** your head, you bend it downwards so that you are looking towards the ground. ❑ *He bowed his head, ashamed.* **3** V-I If you **bow to** pressure or **to** someone's wishes, you agree to do what they want you to do. ❑ *Should he bow to popular opinion and sack the minister?*
▶ **bow out** PHR-VERB If you **bow out of** something, you stop taking part in it. ❑ *He will bow out of politics after the next election.* ❑ *He bowed out gracefully.*

bow /bəʊ/ (**bows**)
❷ **1** N-COUNT A **bow** is a knot with two loops and two loose ends that is used in tying shoelaces and ribbons. ❑ *Tie a length of ribbon in a bow.*

bow

2 N-COUNT A **bow** is a weapon for shooting arrows, consisting of a long curved piece of wood with a string attached to both its ends. **3** N-COUNT The **bow** of a violin or other stringed instrument is a long, thin piece of wood with horse hair stretched along it, which you move across the strings of the instrument in order to play it.

bowed **1** ADJ /bəʊd/ Something that is **bowed** is curved. ❑ *...an old lady with bowed legs.* **2** ADJ /baʊd/ If a person's body is **bowed**, it is bent forward. ❑ *She was praying with her head bowed.*

bowels /baʊəlz/ N-PLURAL Your **bowels** are the tubes in your body through which digested food passes from your stomach to your anus.

bowl /bəʊl/ (**bowls, bowling, bowled**)
1 N-COUNT A **bowl** is a circular container with a wide uncovered top that is used for mixing and serving food. ❑ *He gave her two copper bowls.* **2** N-COUNT The contents of a bowl can be referred to as a **bowl of** something. ❑ *...a bowl of soup.* **3** N-COUNT You can refer to the hollow rounded part of an object as its **bowl**. ❑ *...the toilet bowl.* **4** V-I In cricket, when a bowler **bowls**, they throw the ball down the pitch towards the batsman. **5** N-UNCOUNT **Bowls** is a game in which the players try to roll large wooden balls as near as possible to a small ball.
→ see **dish, kitchen**
▶ **bowl over** **1** PHR-VERB To **bowl** someone **over** means to push into them and make them fall to the ground. **2** PHR-VERB If you **are bowled over** by something, you are very impressed or surprised by it. ❑ *I was bowled over by the beauty of Cornwall.*

bowler /ˈbəʊlə/ (**bowlers**) **1** N-COUNT In cricket, the **bowler** is the person who is bowling. **2** N-COUNT A **bowler** or a **bowler hat** is a round stiff hat with a narrow curved brim.

bowling /ˈbəʊlɪŋ/ N-UNCOUNT **Bowling** is a game in which you roll a heavy ball down a narrow track towards a group of wooden objects and try to knock down as many of them as possible. ❑ *I go bowling for relaxation.*

box /bɒks/ (**boxes, boxing, boxed**) **1** N-COUNT A **box** is a square or rectangular container with stiff sides and sometimes a lid. ❑ *...a small wooden box.* ❑ *...a box of chocolates.* **2** N-COUNT A **box** on a form is a square or rectangular space in which you have to write something. **3** N-COUNT In a theatre or at a sports ground, a **box** is a small enclosed area where a small number of people can sit to watch the performance or game. **4** V-I To **box** means to fight someone according to the rules of the sport of boxing. ❑ *At school I boxed and played rugby.* ● **boxer** (**boxers**) N-COUNT ❑ *...a professional boxer.*
→ see **container**
▶ **box in** PHR-VERB If you **are boxed in**, you are unable to move because you are surrounded by other people or cars. ❑ *The jet was boxed in by other aircraft at the gate.*

boxing /ˈbɒksɪŋ/ N-UNCOUNT **Boxing** is a sport in which two people wearing padded gloves fight, using only their hands.

ˈbox office (**box offices**) **1** N-COUNT The **box office** in a theatre or cinema is the place where the tickets are sold. **2** N-SING People talk about **the box office** when they are referring to the success of a film or play in terms of the number of people who go to see it. ❑ *The movie looks set to be the biggest box office success of all time.*

boy /bɔɪ/ (**boys**) **1** N-COUNT A **boy** is a male child. **2** N-COUNT You can refer to a young man as a **boy**, especially when talking about relationships between young men and women.

ˈboy band (**boy bands**) N-COUNT A **boy band** is a band consisting of young men who sing popular music and dance.

boycott /ˈbɔɪkɒt/ (**boycotts, boycotting, boycotted**) V-T & N-COUNT When people **boycott** a product they disapprove of, or organize a **boycott** against it, they refuse to buy it. People also **boycott** events and organizations by refusing to have anything to do with them. ❑ *The main opposition parties are boycotting the elections.* ❑ *The students began a boycott of classes last week.*

boyfriend /ˈbɔɪfrend/ (**boyfriends**) N-COUNT Someone's **boyfriend** is the man or boy with whom they are having a romantic or sexual relationship.

boyhood /ˈbɔɪhʊd/ N-UNCOUNT **Boyhood** is the period of a man's life during which he is a boy. ❑ *He has been a football supporter since boyhood.*

boyish /ˈbɔɪɪʃ/ ADJ If you describe a man as **boyish**, you mean that his appearance or behaviour is like that of a boy, and you find this attractive. ❑ *...a boyish grin.* ❑ *...a boyish enthusiasm for life.* ● **boyishly** ADV ❑ *John grinned boyishly.*

Br. **Br.** is a written abbreviation for **British**.

bra /brɑː/ (**bras**) N-COUNT A **bra** is a piece of underwear that a woman wears to support her breasts.

b

brace /breɪs/ (**braces, bracing, braced**) **1** V-T If you **brace yourself for** something unpleasant or difficult, you prepare yourself for it. ❑ *Diego braced himself for bad news.* **2** V-T If you **brace yourself against** something, you press against it in order to steady yourself or to avoid falling. ❑ *Elaine braced herself against the dresser.* **3** N-COUNT A **brace** is a device attached to a person's leg to strengthen or support it. **4** N-COUNT A **brace** is a metal device fastened to a child's teeth to help them grow straight. **5** N-PLURAL In British English, **braces** are a pair of straps that you wear over your shoulders to prevent your trousers from falling down. The American word is **suspenders**.
→ see **teeth**

bracelet /'breɪslɪt/ (**bracelets**) N-COUNT A **bracelet** is a piece of jewellery that you wear round your wrist.
→ see **jewellery**

bracing /'breɪsɪŋ/ ADJ If you describe a place, climate, or activity as **bracing**, you mean that it makes you feel fit and full of energy.

bracket /'brækɪt/ (**brackets**) **1** N-COUNT If you say that someone or something is in a particular **bracket**, you mean that they are within a particular range. ❑ *...a low income bracket.* **2** N-COUNT **Brackets** are pieces of metal, wood, or plastic that are fastened to a wall in order to support something such as a shelf. **3** N-COUNT **Brackets** are a pair of written marks such as ( ) that you place round a word or sentence in order to indicate that you are giving extra information.

brag /bræg/ (**brags, bragging, bragged**) V-I If someone **brags**, they talk very proudly about what they have done or what they own; used showing disapproval. ❑ *He's always bragging about his ability as a cricketer.* ❑ *They like to brag that Texas is the only state that was once a nation.*

braid /breɪd/ (**braids, braiding, braided**) **1** N-UNCOUNT **Braid** is a narrow piece of decorated cloth or twisted threads, used to decorate clothes or curtains. **2** V-T In American English, if you **braid** hair, you twist three or more lengths of it over and under each other to make one thick length. The usual British word is **plait**. **3** N-COUNT In American English, a **braid** is a length of hair which has been plaited and tied. The usual British word is **plait**.

brain /breɪn/ (**brains**) **1** N-COUNT Your **brain** is the organ inside your head that controls your body's activities and enables you to think and to feel things. **2** N-COUNT Your **brain** is your mind and the way that you think. ❑ *Force yourself to use your brain.* **3** N-COUNT If you say that someone has **brains** or a **good brain**, you mean that they are intelligent and have the ability to make good decisions. ❑ *You've got brains, you've got ideas, get on with it.* **4** N-SING The person who plans the activities of an organization can be referred to as **the brains** behind it. [INFORMAL] ❑ *Some investigators see her as the brains of the gang.*
→ see Word Web: **brain**
→ see **nervous system**

brainchild /'breɪntʃaɪld/ N-SING The **brainchild of** a person is an idea or invention that they have thought up or created.

brake /breɪk/ (**brakes, braking, braked**) **1** N-COUNT A vehicle's **brakes** are devices that make it go slower or stop. **2** V-I When the driver of a vehicle **brakes**, or when the vehicle **brakes**, the driver presses the vehicle's brake, to make it slow down or stop. ❑ *She braked sharply to avoid another car.*

bran /bræn/ N-UNCOUNT **Bran** consists of small brown flakes that are left when wheat grains have been used to make white flour.

branch /brɑːntʃ, bræntʃ/ (**branches, branching, branched**) **1** N-COUNT The **branches** of a tree are the parts that grow out from its trunk. **2** N-COUNT A **branch of** a business or other organization is one of the offices, shops, or local groups which belong to it. ❑ *The local branch of Bank of America is handling the accounts.* **3** N-COUNT A **branch of** a subject is a part or type of it. ❑ *...a new branch of mathematics known as complexity theory.*
▸ **branch off** PHR-VERB A road or path that **branches off** from another one starts from it and goes in a slightly different direction. If you **branch off** somewhere, you change the direction in which you are going. ❑ *After a few miles, a small road branched off to the right.*
▸ **branch out** PHR-VERB If you **branch out**, you do something different from your normal activities or work. ❑ *Telephone companies are branching out into new information services.*

brand /brænd/ (**brands, branding, branded**) **1** N-COUNT A **brand of** a product is the version made by one particular manufacturer. ❑ *...another brand of cola.* ❑ *...a supermarket's own brand.* **2** V-T If someone **is branded as** something bad, many people decide that they are that thing. ❑ *They have been branded poor students by their teachers.* ❑ *They recently branded him a war criminal.* **3** V-T When someone **brands** an animal, they burn a permanent mark onto its skin in order to show who it belongs to.

brandish /'brændɪʃ/ (**brandishes, brandishing, brandished**) V-T If you **brandish** something, especially a weapon, you hold it in a threatening

Word Web **brain**

The human **brain** weighs about three pounds. It has seven different parts. The largest are the cerebrum, the cerebellum, and the medulla oblongata. The cerebrum wraps around the outside of the brain. It handles **learning**, **communication**, and voluntary **movement**. The cerebellum controls **balance**, **posture**, and movement. The medulla oblongata joins the **spinal cord** with other parts of the brain. This part of the brain controls those actions that happen without us knowing, such as breathing, heartbeat, and swallowing. It also tells us when we are hungry and when we need to sleep.

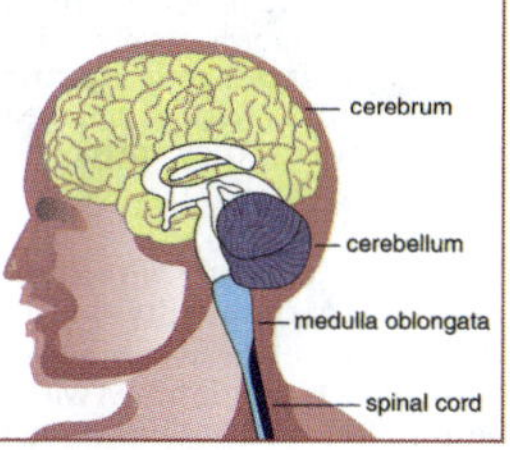

Picture Dictionary **bread**

way. ❑ *He appeared in the lounge brandishing a knife.*

ˈbrand name (**brand names**) N-COUNT A product's **brand name** is the name the manufacturer gives it and under which it is sold.

ˌbrand-ˈnew ADJ Something that is **brand-new** is completely new.

brandy /ˈbrændi/ (**brandies**) N-VAR **Brandy** is a strong alcoholic drink.

brash /bræʃ/ (**brasher, brashest**) ADJ If you describe someone as **brash**, you disapprove of them because you think that they are too confident. ● **brashly** ADV ❑ *The young man had brashly challenged his leadership.* ● **brashness** N-UNCOUNT ❑ *She inherited her mother's brashness.*

brass /brɑːs, bræs/ 1 N-UNCOUNT **Brass** is a yellow metal made from copper and zinc. ❑ *...shining brass buttons.* 2 N-PLURAL The **brass** is the section of an orchestra which consists of brass wind instruments such as trumpets and horns.

brat /bræt/ (**brats**) N-COUNT If you call a child a **brat**, you disapprove of their bad or annoying behaviour.

bravado /brəˈvɑːdəʊ/ N-UNCOUNT **Bravado** is an appearance of courage that someone shows in order to impress other people.

brave /breɪv/ (**braver, bravest, braves, braving, braved**) 1 ADJ Someone who is **brave** is willing to do dangerous things, and does not show fear in difficult or dangerous situations. ❑ *She became an extremely brave horsewoman.* ❑ *Are you brave enough to face up to this challenge?* ● **bravely** ADV ❑ *The enemy fought bravely.* 2 V-T If you **brave** a difficult or dangerous situation, you deliberately experience it, in order to achieve something. ❑ *Thousands have braved icy rain to demonstrate their support.* 3 PHRASE If you say that someone is **putting a brave face on** a difficult situation, you mean that they are pretending that they are happy or coping with a problem when they are not.
→ see **hero**

bravery /ˈbreɪvəri/ N-UNCOUNT **Bravery** is brave behaviour or the quality of being brave.

brawl /brɔːl/ (**brawls, brawling, brawled**) V-I & N-COUNT If people **brawl with** each other, or become involved in a **brawl**, they fight in a rough disorganized way. ❑ *He was sent off again for brawling with fellow players.*

brazen /ˈbreɪzən/ ADJ If you describe someone as **brazen**, you mean that they are very bold and do not care if other people think that they are behaving wrongly. ❑ *It was a brazen challenge to the security forces.* ● **brazenly** ADV ❑ *This man is brazenly breaking the law.*

breach /briːtʃ/ (**breaches, breaching, breached**) 1 N-VAR & V-T If there is a **breach of** an agreement or a law, or if you **breach** an agreement or a law, you break it. ❑ *He was fined for breach of contract.* 2 N-COUNT A **breach in** a relationship is a serious disagreement which often results in the relationship ending. ❑ *Is this a serious breach in relations between the two countries?* 3 V-T If someone or something **breaches** a barrier, they make an opening in it, usually leaving it weakened or destroyed. ❑ *The bomb apparently breached a fire wall.* 4 N-COUNT A **breach** in a barrier is a wide gap in it. 5 V-T & N-COUNT If someone **breaches** security or defences, or if there is a **breach** in security or defences, they manage to get through and attack an area that is heavily guarded and protected.

bread /bred/ N-UNCOUNT **Bread** is a food made from flour, water, and often yeast. The mixture is baked in an oven. ❑ *...a loaf of bread.*
→ see Picture Dictionary: **bread**

breadth /bretθ, AM bredθ/ 1 N-UNCOUNT The **breadth** of something is the distance between its two sides. ❑ *The breadth of the whole camp was 400 metres.* 2 N-UNCOUNT **Breadth** is the quality of consisting of or involving many different things. ❑ *Older people have a bigger breadth of experience.*

breadwinner /ˈbredwɪnə/ (**breadwinners**) N-COUNT In a family, the **breadwinner** is the person who earns the money that the family needs.

break /breɪk/ (**breaks, breaking, broke, broken**) 1 V-T/V-I When an object **breaks** or when you **break** it, it suddenly separates into two or more pieces, often because it has been hit or dropped. ❑ *The plane broke into three pieces.* ❑ *He fell through the window, breaking the glass.* ❑ *Break the chocolate into a bowl.* 2 V-T/V-I When a tool or a piece of machinery **breaks** or when you **break** it, it is damaged and no longer works. ❑ *He accused her of breaking the stereo.* ❑ *...broken washing machines.*

3 V-T If you **break** a rule or agreement, you do something that the rule or agreement indicates you should not do. ❑ *We didn't know we were breaking the law.* ❑ *...broken promises.* 4 V-I If you **break free** or **break loose**, you free yourself from something or escape from it. ❑ *The man fought the officer, broke free and drove off.* 5 V-T To **break** a difficult or unpleasant situation that has existed for some time means to end it suddenly. ❑ *We must do more to break the link between addiction and crime.* 6 V-T To **break** someone means to destroy their determination, their success, or their career. ❑ *He never let his jailers break him.* 7 N-COUNT & V-I If you **have a break** or if you **break**, you stop what you are doing and do something else or have a rest. ❑ *Do you want to have a little break?* ❑ *They broke for lunch.* 8 V-T To **break** the force of something such as a blow or fall means to weaken its effect. ❑ *Here the trees probably broke his fall.* 9 V-T If you **break** a piece of bad news to someone, you tell it to them. ❑ *Then Louise broke the news that she was leaving me.* 10 N-COUNT A **break** is a lucky opportunity. [INFORMAL] ❑ *Her big break came when she appeared on TV.* 11 V-T If you **break** a record, you beat the previous record for a particular achievement. 12 V-I When day or dawn **breaks**, it starts to grow light after the night has ended. 13 V-I When a wave **breaks**, it passes its highest point and turns downwards. 14 V-T If you **break** a secret code, you work out how to understand it. 15 V-I When a boy's voice **breaks**, it becomes permanently deeper. 16 → see also **broke, broken** 17 to **break even** → see **even**
→ see **crash, factory**

▶ **break down** 1 PHR-VERB If a machine or a vehicle **breaks down**, it stops working. 2 PHR-VERB When a discussion, relationship, or system **breaks down**, it fails because of a problem or disagreement. ❑ *Talks with business leaders broke down last night.* 3 PHR-VERB If you **break down**, you start crying. 4 PHR-VERB When a substance **breaks down** or when something **breaks** it **down**, it changes into a different form because of a chemical process. ❑ *It breaks down fully and disappears completely.* 5 PHR-VERB If you **break down** a door or barrier, you hit it so hard that it falls down. ❑ *His father failed to break the door down.* 6 → see also **breakdown**

▶ **break in** 1 PHR-VERB If someone **breaks in**, they get into a building by force. ❑ *The robbers broke in and stole $8,000.* 2 → see also **break-in** 3 PHR-VERB If you **break in** on someone's conversation, you interrupt them. ❑ *'She told you to stay here,' Mike broke in.*

▶ **break into** 1 PHR-VERB If someone breaks into a building, they get into it by force. 2 PHR-VERB You can use **break into** to indicate that someone suddenly starts doing something. ❑ *I feel like breaking into song.* 3 PHR-VERB If you **break into** a new area of activity, you become involved in it. ❑ *She finally broke into films.*

▶ **break off** 1 PHR-VERB When part of something **breaks off** or when you **break** it **off**, it is snapped off or torn away. ❑ *Luke broke off a small piece of orange.* 2 PHR-VERB If you **break off** when you are doing or saying something, you suddenly stop doing it or saying it. ❑ *Llewelyn broke off in mid-sentence.* 3 PHR-VERB If you **break off** a relationship, you end it. ❑ *...the courage to break it off with her.*

▶ **break out** 1 PHR-VERB If something such as a fight or disease **breaks out**, it begins suddenly. ❑ *He was 29 when war broke out.* 2 PHR-VERB If you **break out in** a rash or a sweat or if it **breaks out**, it appears on your skin.

▶ **break through** 1 PHR-VERB If you **break through** a barrier, you succeed in forcing your way through. ❑ *About fifteen prisoners broke through onto the roof.* 2 → see also **breakthrough**

▶ **break up** 1 PHR-VERB When something **breaks up** or when you **break** it **up**, it separates or is divided into several smaller parts. ❑ *Break up the chocolate and melt it.* ❑ *He broke the bread up into chunks.* 2 PHR-VERB If you **break up with** your partner, you end your relationship with them. [INFORMAL] ❑ *My girlfriend had broken up with me.* ❑ *The marriage broke up.* 3 PHR-VERB If an activity **breaks up** or if you **break** it **up**, it is brought to an end. ❑ *She was trying to break up a fight between two boys.* 4 PHR-VERB When schools or their pupils **break up**, the term ends and the pupils start their holidays. [BRIT] ❑ *...the last week before they break up.* 5 → see also **break-up**

Word Partnership Use *break* with:

N.	break **a bone**, break ***your* arm/leg/neck** 1
	break **the law**, break **a promise**, break **a rule** 3
	break **a habit**, break **the silence** 5
	coffee/lunch break 7
	break **a record** 11
V.	**need a** break, **take a** break 7

breakaway /ˈbreɪkəweɪ/ ADJ BEFORE N A **breakaway** group is a group of people who have separated from a larger group. ❑ *...Yugoslavia's breakaway republic of Croatia.*

breakdown /ˈbreɪkdaʊn/ (**breakdowns**) 1 N-COUNT The **breakdown** of a system, plan, or discussion is its failure or ending. ❑ *...the breakdown of trade talks between the US and EU officials.* 2 N-COUNT If you suffer a **breakdown**, you become so depressed that you cannot cope with life. ❑ *'I had a breakdown and I am still fighting it,' she said.* 3 → see also **nervous breakdown** 4 N-COUNT A **breakdown** of a car or piece of machinery is when it stops working. 5 N-COUNT A **breakdown of** something is a list of its separate parts. ❑ *The organisers were given a breakdown of the costs.*
→ see **traffic**

breakdown

breakfast /ˈbrekfəst/ (**breakfasts**) 1 N-VAR **Breakfast** is the first meal of the day, which is usually eaten early in the morning. ❑ *He likes two eggs for breakfast.* ❑ *I have breakfast at 9am.* 2 → See note at **meal**.
→ see **meal**

ˈbreak-in (**break-ins**) N-COUNT When there is a **break-in**, someone gets into a building by force.

ˈbreaking point N-UNCOUNT If something or someone has reached **breaking point**, they have so many problems that they may soon be unable to continue. ❑ *His parents were almost at breaking point.*

breakneck /ˈbreɪknek/ ADJ BEFORE N Something that happens or travels at **breakneck** speed happens or travels very fast. ❑ *The company has expanded at a breakneck pace.*

breakout also **break-out** /ˈbreɪkaʊt/ (**breakouts**) N-COUNT If there has been a **breakout**, someone has escaped from prison. ❑ *High Point prison had the highest number of breakouts.*

breakthrough /ˈbreɪkθruː/ (**breakthroughs**) N-COUNT A **breakthrough** is an important development or achievement. ❑ *The company looks ready to make a significant breakthrough in China.*

ˈbreak-up (**break-ups**) N-COUNT The **break-up of** a group, relationship, or system is its end. ❑ *...since the break-up of his marriage.*

breast /brest/ (**breasts**) **1** N-COUNT A woman's **breasts** are the two soft round pieces of flesh on her chest that can produce milk to feed a baby. **2** N-COUNT A person's chest can be referred to as his or her **breast.** [LITERARY] ❑ *He struck his breast.* **3** N-COUNT A bird's **breast** is the front part of its body. **4** N-VAR A piece of **breast** is a piece of meat that is cut from the front of a bird or lamb. ❑ *...grilled chicken breast.*

breaststroke /ˈbreststrəʊk/ N-UNCOUNT **Breaststroke** is a swimming stroke which you do lying on your front, and making circular movements with your arms and legs.

breath /breθ/ (**breaths**) **1** N-VAR Your **breath** is the air which you take into and let out of your lungs when you breathe. ❑ *I could smell the garlic on his breath.* **2** N-VAR When you take a **breath**, you breathe in once. ❑ *He took a deep breath.* ❑ *She spoke for an hour, almost without a pause for breath.* **3** PHRASE If you are **out of breath**, you are breathing very quickly and with difficulty because you have been doing something energetic. **4** PHRASE If you **hold** your **breath**, you make yourself stop breathing for a few moments. **5** PHRASE If you say something **under** your **breath**, you say it in a very quiet voice. **6** PHRASE If you describe something new or different as **a breath of fresh air**, you mean that you approve of it as it makes a situation or subject more interesting or exciting. ❑ *His album hit the dance music scene like a breath of fresh air.* **7** PHRASE If you say that something **takes** your **breath away**, you mean that it is extremely beautiful or amazing. ❑ *I heard this song on the radio and it just took my breath away.*

Word Partnership	Use *breath* with:
ADJ.	**bad** breath, **fresh** breath **1**
	deep breath **2**
V.	**hold *your*** breath **1**
	catch *your* breath, **gasp for** breath, **take a** breath **2**

breathalyze [BRIT also **breathalyse**] /ˈbreθəlaɪz/ (**breathalyzes, breathalyzing, breathalyzed**) V-T If the driver of a car **is breathalyzed** by the police, they ask him or her to breathe into a special device in order to test whether he or she has drunk too much alcohol.

breathe /briːð/ (**breathes, breathing, breathed**) **1** V-T/V-I When people or animals **breathe**, they take air into their lungs and let it out again. ❑ *The air was so hot, it was really hard to breathe.* ❑ *A thirteen year old girl is in hospital after breathing in smoke.* ● **breathing** N-UNCOUNT ❑ *Her breathing became slow and heavy.* **2** V-T If you do not **breathe** a word about something, you say nothing about it, because it is a secret. ❑ *He never breathed a word about our conversation.*
→ see **respiration**
▶ **breathe in** PHR-VERB When you **breathe in**, you take some air into your lungs.
▶ **breathe out** PHR-VERB When you **breathe out**, you send air out of your lungs through your nose or mouth.

breather /ˈbriːðə/ (**breathers**) N-COUNT If you **take a breather**, you stop what you are doing for a short time and have a rest. [INFORMAL]

ˈbreathing space N-UNCOUNT A **breathing space** is a short period of time in which you can recover from one activity and prepare for a second one. ❑ *We hope that it will give us some breathing space.*

breathless /ˈbreθləs/ ADJ If you are **breathless**, you have difficulty in breathing properly, for example because you have been running. ● **breathlessly** ADV ❑ *'I'll go in,' he said breathlessly.* ● **breathlessness** N-UNCOUNT ❑ *They may then develop breathlessness.*

breathtaking also **breath-taking** /ˈbreθteɪkɪŋ/ ADJ If you say that something is **breathtaking**, you mean that it is extremely beautiful or amazing. ❑ *The house has breathtaking views from every room.* ● **breathtakingly** ADV ❑ *The idea was breathtakingly simple.*

breed /briːd/ (**breeds, breeding, bred** /bred/) **1** N-COUNT A **breed of** animal is a particular type of it. **2** V-T If you **breed** animals or plants, you keep them for the purpose of producing more animals or plants. ❑ *He used to breed dogs for the police.* ❑ *New varieties of rose are bred each year.* ● **breeder** (**breeders**) N-COUNT ❑ *...horse breeders.* ● **breeding** N-UNCOUNT ❑ *...centuries of careful breeding.* **3** V-I When animals **breed**, they mate and produce offspring. ● **breeding** N-UNCOUNT ❑ *...the breeding season.* **4** V-T If something **breeds** a situation or feeling, it causes it to develop. ❑ *The act of work breeds a sense of responsibility.* **5** PHRASE Someone who was **born and bred** in a particular place was born there and spent their childhood there. ❑ *...a Londoner born and bred.* **6** N-COUNT A particular **breed of** person is a type of person, with special qualities or skills. ❑ *...a new breed of British women squash players.*
→ see **zoo**

breeze /briːz/ (**breezes, breezing, breezed**) **1** N-COUNT A **breeze** is a gentle wind. ❑ *I imagined a breeze blowing against my face.* ❑ *...a cool sea breeze.* **2** V-I If you **breeze into** a place, you enter it in a casual and carefree way. ❑ *He was late, but eventually he breezed in.*
→ see **wind**

breezy /ˈbriːzi/ (**breezier, breeziest**) **1** ADJ Someone who is **breezy** behaves in a brisk, casual, cheerful, and confident way. ❑ *...his bright and breezy personality.* **2** ADJ When the weather is **breezy**, there is a fairly strong but pleasant wind blowing. ❑ *The day was breezy and warm.*

brew /bruː/ (**brews, brewing, brewed**) **1** V-T When you **brew** tea or coffee, you make it by pouring hot water over tea leaves or ground coffee. **2** N-COUNT A **brew** is a pot of tea or coffee. It can also be a particular kind of tea or coffee. ❑ *...a mild*

b

Word Web bridge

The world's longest and tallest **suspension bridge** is the Akashi Kaikyo Bridge. It is 12,828 feet long and almost 1,000 feet tall. It can stand up against an 8.5 magnitude earthquake. Another famous **span**, the Brooklyn Bridge in New York City, dates from 1883. It was the first suspension bridge to use **steel** for its **cable** wire. Over 120,000 cars and trucks still use the bridge every day. The Evergreen Point Floating Bridge near Seattle, Washington, floats on **pontoons**. It's over a mile long. During windy weather the **drawbridge** in the middle must stay open to protect the bridge from damage.

herbal brew. 3 V-T If someone **brews** beer, they make it. 4 V-I If an unpleasant situation **is brewing**, it is starting to develop. ❑ *A crisis was brewing.*
→ see **tea**

brewer /'bru:ə/ (**brewers**) N-COUNT A **brewer** is a person or company that makes beer.

Word Link *ery ≈ place where something happens : bakery, brewery, refinery*

brewery /'bru:əri/ (**breweries**) N-COUNT A **brewery** is a place where beer is made.

bribe /braɪb/ (**bribes, bribing, bribed**) N-COUNT & V-T If you are offered a **bribe** or if you **are bribed**, you are offered a sum of money or something valuable in order to persuade you to do something. ❑ *He was investigated for receiving bribes.* ❑ *He bribed the workers to keep quiet.*

bribery /'braɪbəri/ N-UNCOUNT **Bribery** is the action of giving someone a bribe. ❑ *He was jailed on charges of bribery.*

brick /brɪk/ (**bricks**) N-VAR **Bricks** are rectangular blocks of baked clay used for building walls. ❑ *...a huge brick building.*

bride /braɪd/ (**brides**) N-COUNT A **bride** is a woman who is getting married or who has just got married. ❑ *The guests crowded around the bride and groom.* ● **bridal** ADJ BEFORE N ❑ *...a bridal shop.*
→ see **wedding**

bridegroom /'braɪdgru:m/ (**bridegrooms**) N-COUNT A **bridegroom** is a man who is getting married.

bridesmaid /'braɪdzmeɪd/ (**bridesmaids**) N-COUNT A **bridesmaid** is a woman or a girl who helps a bride on her wedding day.
→ see **wedding**

bridge /brɪdʒ/ (**bridges, bridging, bridged**) 1 N-COUNT A **bridge** is a structure built over a river, road, or railway so that people or vehicles can cross from one side to the other. ❑ *I walked across the bridge.* 2 V-T & N-COUNT If something **bridges** the gap between two people or things, or if it acts as a **bridge** between them, it makes it easier for the differences or disagreements between them to be reduced or overcome. ❑ *Will the two sides be able to bridge their differences?* 3 N-UNCOUNT **Bridge** is a card game for four players.
→ see Word Web: **bridge**
→ see **ship**

bridle /'braɪdəl/ (**bridles, bridling, bridled**) N-COUNT & V-T A **bridle** is a set of straps that is put around a horse's head and mouth so that the person riding or driving the horse can control it. When you **bridle** a horse, you put a bridle on it.

brief /bri:f/ (**briefer, briefest, briefs, briefing, briefed**) 1 ADJ Something that is **brief** lasts for only a short time. ❑ *She once made a brief appearance on television.* ❑ *...a brief statement.* 2 ADJ AFTER LINK-V If you are **brief**, you say what you want to say in as few words as possible. ❑ *I hope to be brief and to the point.* 3 N-PLURAL Men's or women's underpants can be referred to as **briefs**. 4 V-T If someone **briefs** you, they give you information or instructions that you need. ❑ *The Prime Minister has been briefed by her parliamentary aides.*

Word Partnership Use *brief* with:

N. brief **appearance**, brief **conversation**, brief **description**, brief **explanation**, brief **history**, brief **pause**, brief **speech**, brief **statement** 1

briefcase /'bri:fkeɪs/ (**briefcases**) N-COUNT A **briefcase** is a case for carrying documents.

briefing /'bri:fɪŋ/ (**briefings**) N-VAR A **briefing** is a meeting at which information or instructions are given to people. ❑ *They're holding a press briefing tomorrow.*

briefly /'bri:fli/ 1 ADV Something that happens **briefly** happens for a very short period of time. ❑ *He smiled briefly.* ❑ *The couple chatted briefly on the doorstep.* 2 ADV If you say something **briefly**, you use very few words or give very few details. ❑ *She told them briefly what had happened.* ❑ *Briefly, these are some of my main findings.*

brigade /brɪ'geɪd/ (**brigades**) 1 N-COUNT A **brigade** is one of the groups which an army is divided into. 2 → see also **fire brigade**

brigadier /ˌbrɪgə'dɪə/ (**brigadiers**) N-COUNT & N-TITLE A **brigadier** is an army officer of high rank.

bright /braɪt/ (**brighter, brightest**) 1 ADJ A **bright** colour is strong and noticeable, and not dark. ❑ *...a bright red dress.* ● **brightly** ADV ❑ *...brightly coloured wallpaper.* 2 ADJ A **bright** light, object, or place is shining strongly or is full of light. ❑ *...a bright October day.* ● **brightly** ADV ❑ *...a warm, brightly lit room.* ❑ *The sun shone brightly.* ● **brightness** N-UNCOUNT ❑ *...the brightness of each star.* 3 ADJ **Bright** people or ideas are clever and original. ❑ *Were you always fairly bright at school?* 4 ADJ If you look or sound **bright**, you look or sound cheerful. ❑ *'May I help you?' said a bright American voice.* ● **brightly** ADV ❑ *He smiled brightly.* 5 ADJ If the future is **bright**, it is likely to be pleasant and successful. ❑ *They were both successful and the future looked bright.*

B

brighten /ˈbraɪtən/ (**brightens, brightening, brightened**) **1** V-I If you **brighten**, or if you **brighten up**, you suddenly look happier. ❑ *They brightened up at the mention of leaving.* **2** V-T/V-I If someone or something **brightens** a situation, or if the situation **brightens**, it becomes more pleasant or favourable. ❑ *It might be a brightening picture for teachers.* **3** V-T & PHR-VERB If something **brightens** a place, or if it **brightens** it **up**, the place becomes brighter or lighter. ❑ *Here's a fun idea to brighten up a corner of the room.*

brilliant /ˈbrɪliənt/ **1** ADJ If you describe people or ideas as **brilliant**, you mean that they are extremely clever. ❑ *He was a brilliant musician.* ❑ *She had a brilliant mind.* ● **brilliantly** ADV ❑ *...a great production, brilliantly written and acted.* ● **brilliance** N-UNCOUNT ❑ *...his brilliance as a director.* **2** ADJ You can say something is **brilliant** when it is very successful. ❑ *She knew he could have a brilliant future.* **3** ADJ BEFORE N A **brilliant** light or colour is extremely bright. ❑ *The woman had brilliant green eyes.* ● **brilliantly** ADV ❑ *...brilliantly coloured flowers.*

brim /brɪm/ (**brims, brimming, brimmed**) **1** N-COUNT The **brim** of a hat is the wide part that sticks outwards at the bottom. **2** V-I If something **is brimming with** things of a particular kind, it is full of them. ❑ *Her eyes were brimming with tears now.*

bring /brɪŋ/ (**brings, bringing, brought**) **1** V-T If you **bring** someone or something **with** you when you come to a place, they come with you or you have them with you. ❑ *Remember to bring a pencil.* ❑ *Someone went upstairs and brought down a huge kettle.* ❑ *Come to my party and bring a girl with you.* **2** V-T If you **bring** something somewhere, you move it there. ❑ *She reached into her pocket and brought out a coin.* ❑ *Her mother brought her hands up to her face.* ❑ *He poured some water for Dena and brought it to her.* **3** V-T To **bring** something or someone to a place means to cause them to come to that place. ❑ *I told you what brought me here.* **4** V-T If you **bring** something or someone into a particular state or condition, you cause them to be in it. You can also say that something **brings** a particular feeling, situation, or quality. ❑ *He brought the car to a stop.* ❑ *They have brought down some taxes.* ❑ *Her three children brought her joy.* **5** V-T If you cannot **bring yourself to** do something, you cannot make yourself do it. ❑ *I cannot bring myself to talk about it.*

▶ **bring about** PHR-VERB If you **bring** something **about**, you cause it to happen. ❑ *...the only way to bring about political change.*

▶ **bring along** PHR-VERB If you **bring** someone or something **along**, you bring them with you when you come to a place. ❑ *Dad brought a notebook along.* ❑ *Bring along your friends.*

▶ **bring back** **1** PHR-VERB If something **brings back** a memory, it makes you start thinking about it. ❑ *Your article brought back sad memories for me.* **2** PHR-VERB When people **bring back** a fashion or practice that existed at an earlier time, they introduce it again. ❑ *The government wants to bring back bilingual signs.*

▶ **bring down** PHR-VERB To **bring down** a government or ruler means to cause them to lose power. ❑ *You don't bring down a government at a time of international crisis.*

▶ **bring forward** **1** PHR-VERB If you **bring forward** an event, you arrange for it to take place at an earlier time than had been planned. ❑ *He had to bring forward an 11 o'clock meeting.* ❑ *We decided to bring the wedding forward.* **2** PHR-VERB If you **bring forward** an argument or proposal, you state it so that people can consider it. ❑ *They must bring forward practical solutions that offer greater choice.*

▶ **bring in** **1** PHR-VERB When an organization **brings in** a new law or system, they introduce it. ❑ *Hewson wants to bring in a system like they have in America.* **2** PHR-VERB If you **bring in** money, you earn it. [INFORMAL] ❑ *I have three jobs, which bring in about £14,000 a year.*

▶ **bring off** PHR-VERB If you **bring off** something difficult, you succeed in doing it. [INFORMAL] ❑ *It's the trickiest of all operas to bring off in the theatre.* ❑ *Can he do it? Can he actually bring it off?*

▶ **bring out** **1** PHR-VERB When a person or company **brings out** a new product, they produce it and sell it. ❑ *He's now brought out a book.* **2** PHR-VERB Something that **brings out** a particular kind of behaviour **in** you causes you to behave in that way. ❑ *A challenge brought out the best in him.*

▶ **bring up** **1** PHR-VERB If you **bring up** a child, you look after it until it is grown up. ❑ *She brought up four children.* ❑ *I bring my children up to be trusting, honest and helpful.* **2** PHR-VERB If you **bring up** a particular subject, you introduce it into a discussion or conversation. ❑ *Why are you bringing it up now?* **3** PHR-VERB If you **bring up** food, you vomit. [INFORMAL]

Usage

Bring and **take** are both used to talk about carrying something or accompanying someone somewhere, but **bring** is used to suggest movement towards the speaker and **take** is used to suggest movement away from the speaker. ❑ *We could not bring it here because it is rather heavy.* ❑ *Anna took the book to bed with her.* In the first sentence, **bring** suggests that we are coming to the same place as the speaker, that is, the speaker is here too. In the second sentence, **took** suggests that Anna moved away from the speaker when she went to bed, or alternatively that the speaker is merely reporting something that he or she was not involved in. The difference between **bring** and **take** is equivalent to that between **come** and **go**. **Bring** and **come** suggest movement towards the speaker, while **take** and **go** suggest movement away.

Thesaurus *bring* Also look up:

V. accompany, carry, take; *(ant.)* drop, leave **1**
move, take, transfer **2**

Word Partnership Use *bring* with:

N. bring **bad/good luck** **1**
bring ***something/someone*** **home** **2**
bring **to *someone's* attention**, bring **to a boil**, bring **to justice**, bring **to life**, bring **to mind**, bring **together** **4**

brink /brɪŋk/ N-SING If you are **on the brink of** something important, terrible, or exciting, you are just about to do it or experience it. ❑ *He was on the brink of madness.*

brisk /brɪsk/ (**brisker, briskest**) 1 ADJ A **brisk** action is done quickly and in an energetic way. ❑ *...a brisk walk.* • **briskly** ADV ❑ *Eve walked briskly down the corridor.* 2 ADJ If someone's behaviour is **brisk**, they behave in a busy confident way which shows that they want to get things done quickly. ❑ *Her voice was brisk and professional.* • **briskly** ADV ❑ *'Anyhow,' she added briskly, 'it's none of my business'.* 3 ADJ If the weather is **brisk**, it is cold and refreshing. ❑ *...a brisk winter's day.*

bristle /ˈbrɪsəl/ (**bristles, bristling, bristled**) 1 N-COUNT **Bristles** are short thick hairs that feel hard and rough. 2 N-COUNT The **bristles** of a brush are the thick hairs attached to the handle. 3 V-I If the hair on your body **bristles**, it rises away from your skin because you are cold, frightened, or angry. ❑ *It makes the hairs on your arm bristle.* 4 V-I If you **bristle at** something, you react to it angrily. ❑ *Some bristle at the suggestion that their data could be false.*

▸ **bristle with** PHR-VERB If a place **bristles with** objects or people, there are a lot of them there. ❑ *The island was bristling with soldiers.*

British /ˈbrɪtɪʃ/ 1 ADJ **British** means belonging or relating to Great Britain. ❑ *...the British government.* 2 N-PLURAL **The British** are the people who come from Great Britain.

Briton /ˈbrɪtən/ (**Britons**) N-COUNT A **Briton** is a person who comes from Great Britain. ❑ *...seventeen-year-old Briton Jane March.*

brittle /ˈbrɪtəl/ ADJ A **brittle** object or substance is hard but easily broken. ❑ *...the dry, brittle ends of the hair.*

broach /brəʊtʃ/ (**broaches, broaching, broached**) V-T When you **broach** a subject, you mention it in order to start a discussion on it. ❑ *I broached the subject of her early life.*

broad /brɔːd/ (**broader, broadest**) 1 ADJ Something that is **broad** is wide. ❑ *His shoulders were broad.* ❑ *...the broad river.* 2 ADJ You use **broad** to describe something that involves many different things or people, or when a description is general, rather than detailed. ❑ *A broad range of issues was discussed.* ❑ *It's a broad outline of the Society's development.* 3 ADJ BEFORE N A **broad hint** is a very obvious one. ❑ *They've been giving broad hints about what to expect.* 4 ADJ A **broad accent** is strong and noticeable. ❑ *He has a broad Yorkshire accent.*

Word Partnership	Use *broad* with:
N.	broad **expanse**, broad **shoulders**, broad **smile** 1 broad **definition**, broad **range**, broad **spectrum**, broad **strokes**, broad **view** 2

broadband /ˈbrɔːdbænd/ N-UNCOUNT **Broadband** is a method of sending many electronic messages at the same time by using a wide range of frequencies.

broadcast /ˈbrɔːdkɑːst, -kæst/ (**broadcasts, broadcasting, broadcasted** or **broadcast**) 1 N-COUNT A **broadcast** is something that you hear on the radio or see on television. ❑ *A broadcast of the speech was heard in San Francisco.* 2 V-T To **broadcast** a programme means to send it out by radio waves, so that it can be heard on the radio or seen on television. ❑ *The concert will be broadcast live on television.* • **broadcasting** N-UNCOUNT ❑ *...the BBC Weather Service celebrated 70 years of broadcasting.*

broadcaster /ˈbrɔːdkɑːstə, -kæst-/ (**broadcasters**) N-COUNT A **broadcaster** is someone who gives talks or takes part in discussions on radio or television.

broaden /ˈbrɔːdən/ (**broadens, broadening, broadened**) 1 V-I When something **broadens**, it becomes wider. ❑ *The smile broadened to a grin.* ❑ *As we drove towards Chamdo, the river broadened.* 2 V-T/V-I If you **broaden** something, or if it **broadens**, you make it involve or affect more things or people. ❑ *We need to broaden our services throughout the country.* ❑ *The range of restaurants here has broadened.*

broadly /ˈbrɔːdli/ 1 ADV You use **broadly** to indicate that something is generally true. ❑ *The idea that software is capable of any task is broadly true.* 2 ADV You use **broadly** to say that something is true to a large extent. ❑ *The new law has been broadly welcomed.* 3 ADV If you smile **broadly**, your mouth is stretched very wide.

ˌbroad-ˈminded ADJ Someone who is **broad-minded** does not disapprove of actions or attitudes that many other people disapprove of; used showing approval. ❑ *...a broad-minded man of high intelligence.*

broccoli /ˈbrɒkəli/ N-UNCOUNT **Broccoli** is a vegetable with green stalks and green or purple flower buds.
→ see **vegetable**

brochure /ˈbrəʊʃə, AM brəʊˈʃʊr/ (**brochures**) N-COUNT A **brochure** is a booklet with pictures that gives you information about a product or service. ❑ *...holiday brochures.*

broil /brɔɪl/ (**broils, broiling, broiled**) 1 V-T In American English, if you **broil** food, you cook it using strong heat directly above or below it. The British word is **grill**. 2 → See note at **cook**

broke /brəʊk/ 1 **Broke** is the past tense of **break**. 2 ADJ If you are **broke**, you have no money. [INFORMAL] ❑ *He was broke when I married him.* 3 PHRASE If a company or person **goes broke**, they lose money and are unable to continue in business or to pay their debts.

Thesaurus	*broke* Also look up:
ADJ.	bankrupt, destitute, impoverished, penniless, poor; (*ant.*) rich, wealthy, well-to-do 2

broken /ˈbrəʊkən/ 1 **Broken** is the past participle of **break**. 2 ADJ BEFORE N A **broken** line is not continuous but has gaps in it. 3 ADJ BEFORE N You use **broken** to describe a marriage that has ended in divorce, or a home in which the parents of the family are divorced, when you think this is a sad thing. ❑ *...children from broken homes.* 4 ADJ BEFORE N If someone talks in **broken** English or in **broken** French, for example, they speak slowly and make a lot of mistakes because they do not know the language very well.

broker /ˈbrəʊkə/ (**brokers, brokering, brokered**) 1 N-COUNT A **broker** is a person whose job is to buy and sell shares, foreign money, or goods for other people. 2 V-T If a country or government **brokers** an agreement, they try to negotiate or arrange it. ❑ *The United Nations brokered a peace in Mogadishu.*

B

bronze /brɒnz/ (**bronzes**) 1 N-UNCOUNT **Bronze** is a yellowish-brown metal made from copper and tin. 2 N-COUNT A **bronze** is a sculpture made of bronze. ❑ *...a bronze of Napoleon on horseback.* 3 ADJ Something that is **bronze** is yellowish-brown in colour. ❑ *Her hair shone bronze and gold.*

ˌbronze ˈmedal (**bronze medals**) N-COUNT If you win a **bronze medal**, you come third in a competition, especially a sports contest, and are often given a medal made of bronze as a prize.

brooch /brəʊtʃ/ (**brooches**) N-COUNT A **brooch** is a small piece of jewellery which can be pinned on a dress, blouse, or coat.
→ see **jewellery**

brood /bruːd/ (**broods, brooding, brooded**) 1 N-COUNT A **brood** is a group of baby birds belonging to the same mother. 2 V-I If you **brood over** or **about** something, you think about it a lot, unhappily. ❑ *She constantly broods about her family.*

brooding /ˈbruːdɪŋ/ 1 ADJ **Brooding** is used to describe an atmosphere or feeling that causes you to feel disturbed or slightly afraid. [LITERARY] ❑ *...a heavy, brooding silence.* 2 ADJ If you describe someone's expression as **brooding**, you mean that they look as if they are thinking deeply about something. ❑ *...his dark, brooding eyes.*

brook /brʊk/ (**brooks**) N-COUNT A **brook** is a small stream.

broom /bruːm/ (**brooms**) N-COUNT A **broom** is a long-handled brush which is used to sweep the floor.

broth /brɒθ, AM brɔːθ/ N-UNCOUNT **Broth** is a kind of soup. It usually has vegetables or rice in it.

brothel /ˈbrɒθəl/ (**brothels**) N-COUNT A **brothel** is a building where men pay to have sex with prostitutes.

brother /ˈbrʌðə/ (**brothers**) 1 N-COUNT Your **brother** is a boy or a man who has the same parents as you. ❑ *...my younger brother.* 2 → see also **half-brother** 3 N-COUNT Some people describe a man as their **brother** when he belongs to the same group as them. ❑ *All players are brothers; we are a private club.* 4 N-TITLE **Brother** is a title given to a man who belongs to a religious institution such as a monastery. ❑ *...Brother Otto.*
→ see **family**

Usage

Note that there is no common English word that can refer to both a brother and a sister. You simply have to use both words. ❑ *She has 13 brothers and sisters.* The word **sibling** exists, but it is rare and very formal.

brotherhood /ˈbrʌðəhʊd/ (**brotherhoods**) 1 N-UNCOUNT **Brotherhood** is the affection and loyalty that you feel for people who you have something in common with. ❑ *He believed in socialism and the brotherhood of man.* 2 N-COUNT A **brotherhood** is an organization whose members all have the same political aims and beliefs or the same job or profession.

ˈbrother-in-law (**brothers-in-law**) N-COUNT Someone's **brother-in-law** is the brother of their husband or wife, or the man who is married to their sister.
→ see **family**

brought /brɔːt/ **Brought** is the past tense and past participle of **bring**.

brow /braʊ/ (**brows**) 1 N-COUNT Your **brow** is your forehead. ❑ *He wiped his brow with the back of his hand.* 2 N-COUNT Your **brows** are your eyebrows. 3 N-COUNT The **brow of** a hill is the top part of it.

brown /braʊn/ (**browner, brownest, browns, browning, browned**) 1 ADJ & N-VAR Something that is **brown** is the colour of earth or wood. ❑ *...her deep brown eyes.* 2 ADJ You can describe a white-skinned person as **brown** when they have been sitting in the sun until their skin is darker than usual. ❑ *You don't have to burn to go brown.* 3 V-T/V-I If you **brown** in the sun or if the sun **browns** you, you become brown in colour. When food **browns** or when you **brown** food, you cook it, usually for a short time on a high flame. ❑ *Cook for ten minutes until the sugar browns.*

browse /braʊz/ (**browses, browsing, browsed**) 1 V-I & N-COUNT If you **browse** or have a **browse** in a shop, you look at things in a casual way, without intending to buy anything. ❑ *I stopped in several bookshops to browse.* ❑ *I'm just browsing around.* ❑ *...a browse around the shops.* 2 V-I If you **browse through** a book or magazine, you look through it in a casual way. ❑ *...browsing through brochures.* 3 V-I If you **browse** on a computer, you search for information in files or on the Internet. [COMPUTING] ❑ *Allen spends an average of four hours a weekend browsing the Internet.*

browser /ˈbraʊzə/ (**browsers**) 1 N-COUNT A **browser** is a piece of computer software that you use to search for information on the Internet. [COMPUTING] 2 N-COUNT A **browser** is someone who browses in a shop. ❑ *...a casual browser.*

bruise /bruːz/ (**bruises, bruising, bruised**) 1 N-COUNT A **bruise** is an injury which appears as a purple or dark mark on your body. 2 V-T If you **bruise** a part of your body, a bruise appears on it, for example because something hits you. ❑ *I had only bruised my knee.* • **bruised** ADJ ❑ *...a badly bruised leg.*

brunt /brʌnt/ PHRASE If someone or something **bears the brunt** or **takes the brunt of** something unpleasant, they suffer the main part or force of it. ❑ *Young people are bearing the brunt of unemployment.*

brush /brʌʃ/ (**brushes, brushing, brushed**) 1 N-COUNT A **brush** is an object with a large number of bristles fixed to it. You use brushes for painting, for cleaning things, and for tidying your hair. ❑ *...a hair brush.* 2 V-T & N-SING When you **brush** something or when you give it a **brush**, you clean it or tidy it using a brush. ❑ *Do this just after you brush your teeth.* 3 V-T If you **brush** something somewhere, you remove it with quick light movements of your hands. ❑ *He brushed the snow off the windscreen.* 4 V-T/V-I If one thing **brushes against** another or if you **brush** one thing **against** another, the first thing touches the second thing lightly while passing it. ❑ *Something brushed against her leg.* ❑ *He brushed my hand away.*
→ see **teeth**

▶ **brush aside** or **brush away** PHR-VERB If you **brush aside** or **brush away** an idea, remark, or feeling, you refuse to consider it because you think it is not important or useful, even though it may be. ❑ *Eddie brushed aside his feeling of embarrassment.*

▶ **brush up** PHR-VERB If you **brush up** something or if you **brush up on** it, you practise it or improve your knowledge of it. ❑ *Eleanor spent the summer brushing up on her driving.*

brusque /brʌsk/ ADJ If you describe a person as **brusque**, you mean that they deal with people quickly and abruptly, without showing much consideration for their feelings. ❑ *The doctors are brusque and busy.* ● **brusquely** ADV ❑ *'It's only a scratch,' Paula said brusquely.*

ˌbrussels 'sprout also **Brussels sprout** (**brussels sprouts**) N-COUNT **Brussels sprouts** or **sprouts** are vegetables that look like tiny cabbages.

brutal /ˈbruːtəl/ 1 ADJ A **brutal** act or person is cruel and violent. ❑ *This is a brutal and senseless war.* ● **brutally** ADV ❑ *He brutally killed a woman for her watch.* 2 ADJ If someone expresses something unpleasant with **brutal** honesty or frankness, they express it in a clear and accurate way, without attempting to reduce its unpleasant effect. ❑ *She spoke with a brutal honesty.* ● **brutally** ADV ❑ *The talks had been brutally frank.*

brutality /bruːˈtælɪti/ (**brutalities**) N-VAR **Brutality** is cruel and violent treatment or behaviour. A **brutality** is an instance of cruel and violent treatment or behaviour. ❑ *...police brutality.* ❑ *...the brutalities of civil war.*

brute /bruːt/ (**brutes**) 1 N-COUNT If you call a man a **brute**, you mean that he is rough and insensitive. ❑ *Giovanni is a brute and a bore.* 2 ADJ BEFORE N When you refer to **brute** strength or force, you are contrasting it with gentler methods or qualities. ❑ *He used brute force to take control.*

BSE /ˌbiː es ˈiː/ N-UNCOUNT **BSE** is a fatal disease which affects the nervous system of cows. **BSE** is an abbreviation for 'bovine spongiform encephalopathy'.

BTW **BTW** is the written abbreviation for 'by the way', mainly used in e-mail. [COMPUTING]

bubble /ˈbʌbəl/ (**bubbles, bubbling, bubbled**) 1 N-COUNT **Bubbles** are small balls of air or gas in a liquid. ❑ *...a bubble of gas.* 2 N-COUNT A **bubble** is a hollow delicate ball of soapy liquid floating in the air or standing on a surface. ❑ *...soap bubbles.* 3 V-I When a liquid **bubbles**, bubbles move in it, for example because it is boiling or moving quickly. ❑ *The water bubbled to the surface.* 4 V-I If you **are bubbling with** a good feeling, you are full of it. ❑ *She came to the phone bubbling with excitement.*
→ see **soap**

bubbly /ˈbʌbli/ (**bubblier, bubbliest**) 1 ADJ If something is **bubbly**, it has a lot of bubbles in it. ❑ *...warm, bubbly water.* 2 N-UNCOUNT Champagne is sometimes called **bubbly**. [INFORMAL] 3 ADJ Someone who is **bubbly** is very lively and cheerful. ❑ *She's a bubbly girl who loves to laugh.*

buck /bʌk/ (**bucks, bucking, bucked**) 1 N-COUNT A **buck** is a US or Australian dollar. [INFORMAL] ❑ *That would probably cost you about fifty bucks.* 2 PHRASE When someone makes **a fast buck** or makes **a quick buck**, they earn a lot of money quickly and easily, often by doing something which is considered to be dishonest. [INFORMAL] 3 N-COUNT A **buck** is the male of various animals, including the deer and rabbit. 4 V-I If a horse **bucks**, it jumps into the air wildly with all four feet off the ground. 5 PHRASE If you **pass the buck**, you refuse to accept responsibility for something. ❑ *The doctors are trying to pass the buck to the government.*

▶ **buck up** 1 PHR-VERB If you **buck** someone **up** or if you **buck up** their spirits, you say or do something to make them more cheerful. [INFORMAL] 2 PHR-VERB If you tell someone to **buck up** or to **buck up** their ideas, you are telling them to start behaving in a more positive and efficient manner. [INFORMAL] ❑ *If we don't buck up we'll be in trouble.*

bucket /ˈbʌkɪt/ (**buckets**) N-COUNT A **bucket** is a deep round metal or plastic container with a handle. ❑ *...a blue bucket.* ❑ *...a bucket of water.*

buckle /ˈbʌkəl/ (**buckles, buckling, buckled**) 1 N-COUNT & V-T A **buckle** is a piece of metal or plastic attached to one end of a belt or strap and used to fasten it. When you **buckle** a belt or strap, you fasten it with a buckle. ❑ *...a big silver belt buckle.* ❑ *He always buckles his seat belt.* 2 V-T/V-I If an object **buckles** or if something **buckles** it, it becomes bent as a result of strong heat or force. ❑ *We watched as the buckling bridge crashed into the water below.* 3 V-I If your legs **buckle**, they bend because they have become very weak. ❑ *His knees buckled and he fell backwards.*
→ see **button, crash**

▶ **buckle down** PHR-VERB If you **buckle down to** something, you start working seriously at it. ❑ *We decided to watch a movie before buckling down to our studies.*

bud /bʌd/ (**buds, budding, budded**) 1 N-COUNT A **bud** is a small pointed lump that appears on a tree or plant and develops into a leaf or flower. 2 V-I When a tree or plant **is budding**, buds are appearing on it or are beginning to open. 3 PHRASE If you **nip** something **in the bud**, you stop it before it can develop very far. [INFORMAL] ❑ *It is important to nip jealousy in the bud before it gets out of hand.*
→ see **flower**

Buddhist /ˈbʊdɪst/ (**Buddhists**) N-COUNT & ADJ **Buddhists** believe in a religion which teaches that the way to end suffering is by overcoming your desires. **Buddhist** means relating to this religion. ❑ *She has been a Buddhist since 1976.* ❑ *...a Buddhist temple.* ● **Buddhism** N-UNCOUNT ❑ *The Cardinal invited representatives of Judaism, Islam, Hinduism, Buddhism and Sikhism to pray with him.*

budding /ˈbʌdɪŋ/ ADJ BEFORE N You use **budding** to describe someone who is just beginning to succeed or become interested in a certain activity. You also use **budding** to describe a situation that is just beginning. ❑ *...a budding actress.* ❑ *...our budding romance.*

buddy /ˈbʌdi/ (**buddies**) 1 N-COUNT A **buddy** is a close friend, usually a male friend of a man. [INFORMAL] ❑ *We became great buddies.* 2 N-VOC Men sometimes call each other **buddy**. [AM, INFORMAL]

budge /bʌdʒ/ (**budges, budging, budged**) 1 V-T/V-I If someone will not **budge** on a matter, or if nothing **budges** them, they refuse to change their mind or to compromise. ❑ *Both sides say they will not budge.* ❑ *Sir Geoffrey could not budge him.* 2 V-T/V-I If someone or something will not **budge**, or if you cannot **budge** them, they will not move. ❑ *Her mother refused to budge from London.* ❑ *I got a grip on the boat and pulled but I couldn't budge it.*

budget /ˈbʌdʒɪt/ (**budgets, budgeting,**

b

B

budgeted) 1 N-COUNT A **budget** is a plan showing how much money a person or organization has available and how it will be spent. The **budget for** something is the amount of money that a person, organization, or country has available to spend on it. ❑ *I do try and buy within my budget.* ❑ *I said the budget for the food was not enough.* 2 V-T/V-I If you **budget** certain amounts of money for particular things, you decide that you can afford to spend those amounts on those things. ❑ *The movie is only budgeted at $10 million.* ❑ *I'm learning how to budget.* ● **budgeting** N-UNCOUNT ❑ *...our budgeting for the current year.* 3 ADJ BEFORE N **Budget** is used to suggest that something is being sold cheaply. ❑ *...a budget-priced CD.*

Word Partnership Use *budget* with:

N.	budget **crisis**, budget **crunch**, budget **cuts**, budget **deficit** 1 2
ADJ.	**tight** budget 1
V.	**balance a** budget 1 2
PREP.	**over** budget, **under** budget 1 2

buff /bʌf/ (**buffs, buffing, buffed**) 1 N-COUNT You can use **buff** to talk about people who know a lot about a particular subject. [INFORMAL] ❑ *...a film buff.* 2 V-T If you **buff** the surface of something, you rub it with a piece of soft material in order to make it shine.

buffalo /ˈbʌfələʊ/

The plural is **buffalo** or **buffaloes**.

buffalo

N-COUNT A **buffalo** is a wild animal like a large cow with long curved horns. → see **grassland**

buffer /ˈbʌfə/ (**buffers**) 1 N-COUNT A **buffer** is something that prevents something else from being harmed. ❑ *Keep savings as a buffer against unexpected cash needs.* 2 N-COUNT The **buffers** on a train or at the end of a railway line are two metal discs on springs that reduce the shock when they are hit.

buffet (**buffets, buffeting, buffeted**) 1 N-COUNT /ˈbʌfeɪ, AM bʊˈfeɪ/ A **buffet** is a meal of cold food at a special occasion. Guests usually help themselves to the food. 2 N-COUNT On a train, the **buffet** or the **buffet car** is the carriage where food is sold. [BRIT] 3 V-T /ˈbʌfɪt/ If something **is buffeted** by rough winds or seas, it is repeatedly struck or blown around by them. ❑ *Their plane was severely buffeted by storms.*

bug /bʌg/ (**bugs, bugging, bugged**) 1 N-COUNT A **bug** is a tiny insect, especially one that causes damage. [INFORMAL] 2 N-COUNT A **bug** is a minor illness such as a cold. ❑ *...a stomach bug.* ❑ *There was a bug going around.* 3 N-COUNT If there is a **bug** in a computer program, there is an error in it. [COMPUTING] 4 N-COUNT A **bug** is a tiny hidden microphone that transmits what people are saying. ❑ *There is a bug on the phone.* 5 V-T If a place **is bugged**, tiny microphones are hidden there to secretly record what people are saying. 6 V-T If something or someone **bugs** you, they worry or annoy you. [INFORMAL] ❑ *I only did it to bug my parents.*

Thesaurus *bug* Also look up:

N.	disease, germ, infection, virus 2 breakdown, defect, error, hitch, malfunction 3

build /bɪld/ (**builds, building, built** /bɪlt/) 1 V-T If you **build** a structure, you make it by joining things together. ❑ *Developers are proposing to build a hotel on the site.* ❑ *45 per cent wanted the government to build more motorways.* 2 V-T If you **build** something **into** a wall or object, you make it in such a way that it is in the wall or object, or is part of it. ❑ *The TV was built into the ceiling.* 3 V-T If people **build** an organization or a society, they gradually form it. ❑ *Their purpose is to build a fair society and a strong economy.* 4 V-T If you **build** an organization, system, or product **on** something, you base it on it. ❑ *...a foundation of fact on which to build theories.* 5 V-T If you **build** something **into** a policy, system, or product, you make it a part of it. ❑ *We have to build IT into the school curriculum.* 6 N-COUNT Your **build** is the shape that your bones and muscles give to your body. ❑ *He is of medium build.* 7 → see also **built**

→ see **muscle**

▶ **build up** 1 PHR-VERB If an amount of something **builds up**, or if you **build** it **up**, it gradually gets bigger as a result of more being added to it. ❑ *A thick layer of fat built up on the pan's surface.* 2 PHR-VERB If you **build** someone **up**, you help them to feel stronger or more confident. ❑ *You can't build up your strength unless you eat.* 3 → see also **build-up, built-up**

Thesaurus *build* Also look up:

V.	assemble, make, manufacture, produce, put together, set up; *(ant.)* demolish, destroy, knock down 1

Word Partnership Use *build* with:

V.	**plan to** build 1
N.	build **bridges**, build **roads**, build **schools** 1 build **confidence**, build **momentum** 3
ADJ.	**athletic** build, **slender** build, **strong** build 6

builder /ˈbɪldə/ (**builders**) N-COUNT A **builder** is a person whose job is to build or repair buildings.

building /ˈbɪldɪŋ/ (**buildings**) N-COUNT A **building** is a structure with a roof and walls, such as a house.

→ see **architecture**

ˈbuilding society (**building societies**) N-COUNT In Britain, a **building society** is a business in which people can invest their money, and which lends people money to buy houses.

ˈbuild-up or **buildup** or **build up** (**build-ups**) 1 N-COUNT A **build-up** is a gradual increase in something. ❑ *There has been a build-up of troops on both sides of the border.* 2 N-COUNT The **build-up to** an event is the way that people talk about it a lot in the period immediately before it. ❑ *...the build-up to Christmas.*

built /bɪlt/ 1 **Built** is the past tense and past participle of **build**. 2 ADJ If you say that someone is **built** in a particular way, you are describing the kind of body they have. ❑ *He is heavily built.*

ˌbuilt-ˈin ADJ BEFORE N **Built-in** features are included in something as an essential part of it. ❑ *...built-in cupboards in the bedrooms.*

ˈbuilt-up ADJ A **built-up** area is one where there are many buildings.

bulb /bʌlb/ (**bulbs**) **1** N-COUNT A **bulb** is the glass part of an electric lamp which gives out light when electricity passes through it. **2** N-COUNT A **bulb** is an onion-shaped root that grows into a plant.
→ see **flower**

bulge /bʌldʒ/ (**bulges, bulging, bulged**) **1** V-I If something **bulges**, it sticks out. ❑ *His eyes were bulging.* **2** V-I If something **is bulging with** things, it is very full of them. ❑ *They returned home with the car bulging with boxes.* ❑ *...a bulging briefcase.* **3** N-COUNT A **bulge** is a lump on an otherwise flat surface. ❑ *...those bulges on your hips and thighs.*

bulimia /buːˈlɪmiə/ N-UNCOUNT **Bulimia** or **bulimia nervosa** is a mental illness in which a person eats very large amounts and then makes themselves vomit. ● **bulimic** ADJ ❑ *Nobody knew I was bulimic.*

bulk /bʌlk/ (**bulks, bulking, bulked**) **1** N-SING You can refer to the **bulk** of a person or thing when you want to indicate that they are very large and heavy. ❑ *Despite his bulk he moved lightly on his feet.* **2** QUANT **The bulk of** something is most of it. ❑ *...the bulk of the world's great poetry.* ❑ *Diamonds come from other places, but the bulk is produced in South Africa.* **3** N-UNCOUNT If you buy or sell something **in bulk**, you buy or sell it in large quantities. ❑ *I've got a big freezer and buy everything in bulk.*
▶ **bulk up** PHR-VERB If someone **bulks up** or if they **bulk up** their body, they put on weight in the form of extra muscle. ❑ *I need to bulk up, and improve my upper body strength.* ❑ *My friend is obsessed with going to the gym and has really bulked up her arms.*

bulky /ˈbʌlki/ (**bulkier, bulkiest**) ADJ Something that is **bulky** is large and heavy. ❑ *...a bulky sweater.*

bull /bʊl/ (**bulls**) **1** N-COUNT A **bull** is a male animal of the cow family. **2** N-COUNT Male elephants and whales are called **bulls**.

bulldog /ˈbʊldɒg, AM -dɔːg/ (**bulldogs**) N-COUNT A **bulldog** is a type of dog with a large square head and powerful jaws.

bulldoze /ˈbʊldəʊz/ (**bulldozes, bulldozing, bulldozed**) V-T To **bulldoze** something means to knock it down with a bulldozer.

bulldozer /ˈbʊldəʊzə/ (**bulldozers**) N-COUNT A **bulldozer** is a large tractor with a broad metal blade at the front, used for moving earth or knocking down buildings.

bullet /ˈbʊlɪt/ (**bullets**) N-COUNT A **bullet** is a small piece of metal which is fired from a gun.

bulletin /ˈbʊlɪtɪn/ (**bulletins**) **1** N-COUNT A **bulletin** is a short news report on radio or television. ❑ *...NBC's evening news bulletin.* **2** N-COUNT A **bulletin** is a regular newspaper or leaflet produced by a group or organization.

ˈbullet point (**bullet points**) N-COUNT A **bullet point** is one of a series of important items for discussion or action in a document, marked by a square or round symbol.

ˈbullet-proof also **bulletproof** ADJ Something that is **bullet-proof** is made of a strong material that bullets cannot pass through. ❑ *...bullet-proof glass.*
→ see **glass**

bullion /ˈbʊliən/ N-UNCOUNT **Bullion** is gold or silver in the form of bars.

bullock /ˈbʊlək/ (**bullocks**) N-COUNT A **bullock** is a young bull that has been castrated.

bully /ˈbʊli/ (**bullies, bullying, bullied**) **1** V-T & N-COUNT If someone **bullies** you, or if someone is a **bully**, they use their strength or power to hurt or frighten you. ● **bullying** N-UNCOUNT ❑ *...an anti-bullying programme at the school.* **2** V-T If someone **bullies** you **into** doing something, they make you do it by using force or threats. ❑ *She should not have bullied us into going.*

bum /bʌm/ (**bums**) **1** N-COUNT A **bum** is a person who has no permanent home or job and who gets money by doing a little work or by begging. This use is considered offensive. [AM, INFORMAL] **2** N-COUNT Your **bum** is the part of your body which you sit on. [INFORMAL]

bump /bʌmp/ (**bumps, bumping, bumped**) **1** V-T/V-I & N-COUNT If you **bump** something, or **bump into** or **against** something, you accidentally hit it while you are moving. You can also talk about a **bump**. ❑ *The boat bumped against something.* ❑ *He bumped his head.* ❑ *Small children often cry after a minor bump.* **2** N-COUNT A **bump** is a minor swelling that you get on your body if you hit something or if something hits you. ❑ *He had a huge bump on his head.* **3** V-I If a vehicle **bumps over** a surface, it travels in a rough, bouncing way because the surface is very uneven. ❑ *We left the road, and bumped over the mountainside.* **4** N-COUNT A **bump** on a road is a raised, uneven part.
▶ **bump into** PHR-VERB If you **bump into** someone you know, you meet them by chance. [INFORMAL] ❑ *I bumped into a friend of yours today.*

bumper /ˈbʌmpə/ (**bumpers**) **1** N-COUNT **Bumpers** are bars at the front and back of a vehicle which protect it if it bumps into something. **2** ADJ BEFORE N A **bumper** crop or harvest is larger than usual.

bumpy /ˈbʌmpi/ (**bumpier, bumpiest**) **1** ADJ A **bumpy** road or path has a lot of bumps on it. **2** ADJ A **bumpy** journey is uncomfortable and rough. ❑ *...a hot and bumpy ride across the desert.*

bun /bʌn/ (**buns**) **1** N-COUNT A **bun** is a small round cake. **2** N-COUNT If a woman has her hair in a **bun**, it is fastened into a round shape at the back of her head.
→ see **bread**

bunch /bʌntʃ/ (**bunches, bunching, bunched**) **1** N-COUNT A **bunch of** people or things is a group of them. ❑ *The players were a great bunch.* ❑ *We did a bunch of songs together.* **2** N-COUNT A **bunch of** flowers or fruit is a group of them held or tied together, or growing on the same stem.
▶ **bunch up** or **bunch together** PHR-VERB If people or things **bunch up** or **bunch together**, they move close to each other so that they form a small tight group. ❑ *A group of prisoners appeared, bunched together on a truck.*

bundle /ˈbʌndəl/ (**bundles, bundling, bundled**) **1** N-COUNT A **bundle** is a number of things tied together or wrapped in a cloth so that they can be carried or stored. ❑ *...a bundle of five pound notes.*

B

❑ ...*bundles of clothing.* **2** N-SING If you describe someone as, for example, a **bundle of** fun, you are emphasizing that they are full of fun. ❑ *He's a bundle of energy.* **3** V-T If you **bundle** someone somewhere, you push them there in a rough and hurried way. ❑ *He was bundled into a car.*

bungalow /'bʌŋgələʊ/ (**bungalows**) N-COUNT A **bungalow** is a house with only one storey.

bungle /'bʌŋgəl/ (**bungles, bungling, bungled**) V-T If you **bungle** something, you fail to do it properly, because you make mistakes. ❑ *A senior surgeon bungled a simple operation.* • **bungled** ADJ ❑ ...*a bungled kidnap attempt.*

bunk /bʌŋk/ (**bunks**) N-COUNT A **bunk** is a bed fixed to a wall, especially in a ship or caravan. **Bunk beds** are two beds fixed one above the other in a frame.

bunker /'bʌŋkə/ (**bunkers**) **1** N-COUNT A **bunker** is an underground shelter, built with strong walls to protect it against gunfire and bombs. **2** N-COUNT A **bunker** is a container for coal or other fuel. **3** N-COUNT On a golf course, a **bunker** is a large hollow filled with sand that golfers must try and avoid.
→ see **golf**

bunny /'bʌni/ (**bunnies**) N-COUNT Small children call a rabbit a **bunny** or a **bunny rabbit**.

buoy /bɔɪ, AM 'bu:i/ (**buoys, buoying, buoyed**) N-COUNT A **buoy** is a floating object that shows ships and boats where they can go and warns them of danger.
▶ **buoy up** PHR-VERB If someone in a difficult situation **is buoyed up** by something, it makes them feel more cheerful. ❑ *They are buoyed up by a sense of hope.*

buoyant /'bɔɪənt/ **1** ADJ If you are **buoyant**, you feel lively and cheerful. ❑ *He sounded buoyant once again.* • **buoyancy** N-UNCOUNT ❑ ...*a mood of buoyancy and optimism.* **2** ADJ Something that is **buoyant** floats on a liquid or in the air. • **buoyancy** N-UNCOUNT ❑ *Air is pumped into the diving suit to increase buoyancy.*

burden /'bɜ:dən/ (**burdens, burdening, burdened**) **1** N-COUNT Something that is a **burden** causes you a lot of worry or hard work. ❑ *I don't want to be a burden to you.* **2** V-T If someone **burdens** you **with** something that is likely to worry you, they tell you about it. ❑ *We decided not to burden him with the news.* **3** N-COUNT A **burden** is a heavy load that is difficult to carry. [FORMAL]

burdened /'bɜ:dənd/ ADJ If you are **burdened with** something, it causes you a lot of worry or hard work. ❑ *Developing countries are already burdened with debt.*

bureau /'bjʊərəʊ/ (**bureaux** or **bureaus**) **1** N-COUNT A **bureau** is an office, organization, or government department that collects and distributes information. ❑ ...*the Australian Bureau of Statistics.* **2** N-COUNT A **bureau** is a desk with drawers and a lid that opens to form a writing surface. [BRIT]

Word Link	*cracy ≈ rule by : aristocracy, bureaucracy, democracy*

bureaucracy /bjʊ'rɒkrəsi/ (**bureaucracies**) **1** N-COUNT A **bureaucracy** is an administrative system operated by a large number of officials. ❑ *They hold positions in the bureaucracies of some African states.* **2** N-UNCOUNT **Bureaucracy** is all the rules and procedures followed by government departments and similar organizations; often used showing disapproval. ❑ *People usually complain about too much bureaucracy.*

Word Link	*crat ≈ power : aristocrat, bureaucrat, democrat*

bureaucrat /'bjʊərəkræt/ (**bureaucrats**) N-COUNT A **bureaucrat** is an official who works in a bureaucracy, especially one who seems to follow rules and procedures too strictly.

bureaucratic /ˌbjʊərə'krætɪk/ ADJ **Bureaucratic** rules and procedures are complicated and can cause long delays. ❑ *The department has become a bureaucratic nightmare.*

bureaux /'bjʊərəʊz/ **Bureaux** is a plural of **bureau**.

burgeon /'bɜ:dʒən/ (**burgeons, burgeoning, burgeoned**) V-I If something **burgeons**, it grows or develops quickly. [LITERARY] ❑ ...*Japan's burgeoning satellite-TV industry.*

burger /'bɜ:gə/ (**burgers**) N-COUNT A **burger** is a flat round mass of meat or vegetables, which is grilled or fried.

burglar /'bɜ:glə/ (**burglars**) N-COUNT A **burglar** is a thief who breaks into houses and steals things.

burglary /'bɜ:gləri/ (**burglaries**) N-VAR If someone commits **burglary**, they enter a building by force and steal things. ❑ *He's been arrested for burglary.*
→ see **crime**

burgle /'bɜ:gəl/ (**burgles, burgling, burgled**) V-T In British English, if a house **is burgled**, someone breaks in and steals things. The usual American word is **burglarize**. ❑ *My flat had been burgled.*

burial /'beriəl/ (**burials**) N-VAR A **burial** is the ceremony that takes place when a dead body is put into a grave. ❑ *The priest prepared the body for burial.*

burly /'bɜ:li/ (**burlier, burliest**) ADJ A **burly** man has a broad body and strong muscles. ❑ ...*a burly security guard.*

burn /bɜ:n/ (**burns, burning, burned** or **burnt**) **1** V-I If there is a fire or a flame somewhere, you say that there is a fire or flame **burning** there. ❑ *Fires were burning out of control.* **2** V-I If something **is burning**, it is on fire. ❑ *One of the vehicles was still burning.* • **burning** N-UNCOUNT ❑ ...*a terrible smell of burning.* • **burnt** ADJ ❑ ...*the smell of burnt toast.* **3** V-T If you **burn** something, you destroy it with fire. ❑ *Protesters set cars on fire and burned a building.* **4** V-T & N-COUNT If you **burn yourself**, or if you suffer **burns**, you are injured by fire or by something very hot. ❑ *How long can you stay in the sun without burning?* ❑ *She suffered terrible burns to her back.* **5** V-I If you **are burning with** an emotion, you feel it very strongly. ❑ *Shannon was burning with impatience.*
→ see **calories, fire**
▶ **burn down** PHR-VERB If a building **burns down** or if someone **burns** it **down**, it is completely destroyed by fire. ❑ *Anarchists burnt down a restaurant.*

b

Thesaurus *burn* Also look up:

V. ignite, incinerate, scorch, singe; *(ant.)* extinguish, put out 1 2

Word Partnership Use *burn* with:

N. **fires** burn 1
burn **victim** 4
V. **watch *something*** burn 1 2

burner /ˈbɜːnə/ (**burners**) N-COUNT A **burner** is a device which produces heat or a flame.
→ see **laboratory**

burning /ˈbɜːnɪŋ/ ADJ If something is extremely hot, you can say that it is **burning** or **burning hot**. ❑ *...the burning desert of Central Asia.*

burnt /bɜːnt/ **Burnt** is a past tense and past participle of **burn**.

ˌburnt-ˈout also **burned-out** ADJ **Burnt-out** vehicles or buildings have been very badly damaged by fire.

burqa or **burka** /ˈbɜːkə/ (**burqas**) N-COUNT A **burqa** is a long garment that covers the head and body and is traditionally worn by women in Islamic countries.

burrow /ˈbʌrəʊ, AM ˈbɜː-/ (**burrows, burrowing, burrowed**) V-I & N-COUNT When an animal **burrows**, or digs a **burrow**, it digs a tunnel or hole in the ground.

burst

burst /bɜːst/ (**bursts, bursting, burst**) 1 V-T/V-I When something **bursts** or when you **burst** it, it suddenly splits open, and air or some other substance comes out. ❑ *A tyre burst.* ❑ *It is not a good idea to burst a blister.* 2 V-I If you **burst into** or **through** something, you suddenly go into it or through it with a lot of energy. ❑ *Gunmen burst into his home and opened fire.* 3 N-COUNT A **burst of** something is a sudden short period of it. ❑ *...a burst of gunfire.*
→ see **crash**
▶ **burst into** 1 PHR-VERB If you **burst into** tears or laughter, you suddenly begin to cry or laugh. 2 to **burst into flames** → see **flame**
→ see **cry**
▶ **burst out** PHR-VERB If you **burst out** laughing or crying, you suddenly begin laughing or crying loudly.
→ see **laugh**

Thesaurus *burst* Also look up:

V. blow, explode, pop, rupture 1

Word Partnership Use *burst* with:

N. burst **appendix**, **bubble** burst, **pipe** burst 1
burst **of air**, burst **of energy**, burst **of laughter** 2
ADJ. **ready to** burst 1
sudden burst 3

bursting /ˈbɜːstɪŋ/ 1 ADJ AFTER LINK-V If a place is **bursting with** people or things, it is full of them. ❑ *The wardrobes were bursting with clothes.* 2 ADJ AFTER LINK-V If you are **bursting with** a feeling, you are full of it. ❑ *I was bursting with curiosity.* 3 ADJ If you are **bursting to** do something, you are very eager to do it. ❑ *She was bursting to tell everyone.*

bury /ˈberi/ (**buries, burying, buried**) 1 V-T If you **bury** something, you put it into a hole in the ground and cover it up, often in order to hide it. ❑ *The squirrels buried the seeds.* 2 V-T When a dead person **is buried**, their body is put into a grave and covered with earth. 3 V-T If you **are buried** under something that falls on top of you, you are completely covered and may not be able to get out. ❑ *Many people were buried under the collapsed buildings.* 4 V-T If you **bury yourself in** your work, you concentrate hard on it.

bus /bʌs/ (**buses**) N-COUNT A **bus** is a large motor vehicle which carries passengers.
→ see **transportation**

bush /bʊʃ/ (**bushes**) 1 N-COUNT A **bush** is a plant which is like a very small tree. 2 N-SING The wild parts of some hot countries are referred to as **the bush**. ❑ *I managed to escape into the bush.*
→ see **plant**

bushy /ˈbʊʃi/ (**bushier, bushiest**) ADJ **Bushy** hair or fur grows very thickly. ❑ *...bushy eyebrows.*

busily /ˈbɪzɪli/ ADV If you do something **busily**, you do it in a very active way. ❑ *He was busily taking notes.*

business /ˈbɪznɪs/ (**businesses**) 1 N-UNCOUNT **Business** is work relating to the production, buying, and selling of goods or services. ❑ *Looking for a career in business?* ❑ *...Harvard Business School.* 2 N-COUNT A **business** is an organization which produces and sells goods or provides a service. ❑ *...small businesses.* 3 N-UNCOUNT **Business** is used when talking about how many products or services a company is able to sell. ❑ *...German companies would lose business.* ❑ *Business is good.* 4 PHRASE If a shop or company goes **out of business**, it has to stop trading because it is not making enough money. 5 N-UNCOUNT You can use **business** to refer to any activity, situation, or series of events. ❑ *I've got some unfinished business here.* 6 N-SING If you say that something is your **business**, you mean that it concerns you personally and that other people should not get involved in it. ❑ *It's her business if she doesn't want the police involved.* ❑ *My marriage is none of your business, David.* 7 → see also **big business** 8 PHRASE If you say that someone **has no business to** do something, you mean that they have no right to do it. ❑ *I had no business to be there at all.* 9 PHRASE If someone **means business**, they are serious and determined about what they are doing. [INFORMAL]
→ see **city**

Thesaurus *business* Also look up:

N. company, corporation, firm, organization 2

B

Word Partnership Use *business* with:

N. business **administration**, **close of** business, business **decision**, business **expenses**, business **hours**, business **opportunity**, business **owner**, business **partner**, business **practices**, business **school** 1 2
V. **go out of** business, **run a** business 2 4
ADJ. business **casual**, **family** business, **online** business, **small** business 1 2 **unfinished** business 5 **your own** business 6

businesslike /ˈbɪznəslaɪk/ ADJ Someone who is **businesslike** deals with things in an efficient way.

businessman /ˈbɪznɪsmæn/ (**businessmen**) N-COUNT A **businessman** is a man who works in business.

businesswoman /ˈbɪznɪswʊmən/ (**businesswomen**) N-COUNT A **businesswoman** is a woman who works in business.

busk /bʌsk/ (**busks, busking, busked**) V-I People who **busk** play music or sing for money in public places. [BRIT] ● **busking** N-UNCOUNT ❑ *You find busking on every street corner.* ● **busker** (**buskers**) N-COUNT ❑ *He earned a living as a busker.*

bust /bʌst/ (**busts, busting, busted**) 1 V-T When you **bust** something, you break it or damage it so badly that it cannot be used. [INFORMAL] ❑ *They will have to bust the door to get him out.* 2 PHRASE If a company **goes bust**, it loses so much money that it is forced to close down. [INFORMAL] 3 N-COUNT A **bust** is a statue of someone's head and shoulders. ❑ *...a bronze bust of the Queen.* 4 N-COUNT You can refer to a woman's breasts as her **bust**. ❑ *Start by having your bust measured.*

bust

bustle /ˈbʌsəl/ (**bustles, bustling, bustled**) 1 V-I If you **bustle** somewhere, you move there in a hurried and determined way. ❑ *My mother bustled around the kitchen.* 2 V-I A place that **is bustling with** people or activity is full of people who are very busy or lively. ❑ *The harbour bustled with activity.* ❑ *...the bustling market.* 3 N-UNCOUNT **Bustle** is busy noisy activity. ❑ *There was plenty of cheerful bustle.*

ˈbust-up (**bust-ups**) N-COUNT If you have a **bust-up** with someone, you have a serious quarrel, often resulting in the end of a relationship. [INFORMAL]

busy /ˈbɪzi/ (**busier, busiest, busies, busying, busied**) 1 ADJ If you are **busy**, you are working hard at something, so that you are not free to do anything else. ❑ *They are busy preparing for the day's activity.* ❑ *She's too busy to come.* 2 V-T If you **busy yourself with** something, you occupy yourself by dealing with it. ❑ *He busied himself with the camera.* ❑ *She busied herself getting towels ready.* 3 ADJ A **busy** street or place is full of traffic and people moving about.

but /bət, STRONG bʌt/ 1 CONJ You use **but** to introduce something which contrasts with what you have just said. ❑ *'You said you'd stay till tomorrow.'—'I know, Bel, but I think I would rather go back.'* 2 CONJ You use **but** when you are adding something or changing the subject. ❑ *I can't figure out why he did it – but anyway, he succeeded.* 3 CONJ You use **but** to link an excuse or apology with what you are about to say. ❑ *I'm sorry, but it's nothing to do with you.* 4 ADV **But** can mean 'only'. [FORMAL] ❑ *This is but one of the methods used.* 5 PREP **But** means 'except'. ❑ *He didn't speak anything but Greek.* 6 PHRASE You use **but for** to introduce the only factor that causes a particular thing not to happen or not to be completely true. ❑ *...the small square below was empty but for a delivery van.*

butcher /ˈbʊtʃə/ (**butchers, butchering, butchered**) 1 N-COUNT A **butcher** is a shopkeeper who sells meat. You can refer to a shop where meat is sold as a **butcher** or a **butcher's**. 2 V-T You say that someone **has butchered** people when they have killed a lot of them in a very cruel way, and you want to express your horror and disgust. ❑ *Guards butchered 1,350 prisoners.*

butler /ˈbʌtlə/ (**butlers**) N-COUNT A **butler** is the chief male servant in the house of a wealthy family.

butt /bʌt/ (**butts, butting, butted**) 1 N-COUNT The **butt** of a weapon is the thick end of its handle. 2 N-COUNT The **butt** of a cigarette or cigar is the small part that is left when you have finished smoking it. 3 N-SING If you are **the butt of** teasing or criticism, people keep teasing you or criticizing you. ❑ *He is the butt of countless jokes.* 4 V-T If a person or animal **butts** you, they hit you with the top of their head. 5 N-COUNT Someone's **butt** is their bottom. [AM, INFORMAL]
▶ **butt in** PHR-VERB If you **butt in**, you rudely join in a private conversation without being asked to. ❑ *'I should think not,' Sarah butted in.*

butter /ˈbʌtə/ (**butters, buttering, buttered**) 1 N-UNCOUNT **Butter** is a yellowish substance made from cream which you spread on bread or use in cooking. 2 V-T When you **butter** bread, you spread butter on it.

butterfly /ˈbʌtəflaɪ/ (**butterflies**) N-COUNT A **butterfly** is an insect with large colourful wings and a thin body.
→ see **insect**

buttock /ˈbʌtək/ (**buttocks**) N-COUNT Your **buttocks** are the two rounded fleshy parts of your body that you sit on.
→ see **body**

button /ˈbʌtən/ (**buttons, buttoning, buttoned**) 1 N-COUNT **Buttons** are small hard objects sewn on to pieces of clothing, which you use to fasten the clothing. 2 V-T & PHR-VERB If you **button** or **button up** a shirt, coat, or other piece of clothing, you fasten it by pushing its buttons through the buttonholes. ❑ *I buttoned up my mink coat.* 3 N-COUNT A **button** is a small object that you press in order to operate something. ❑ *He pressed the 'play' button on the remote control.* 4 N-COUNT In American English, a **button** is a small piece of metal or plastic which you pin onto your clothes to show your support for someone or something. The British word is **badge**.
→ see Picture Dictionary: **button**
→ see **photography**
▶ **button up** → see **button** (meaning **2**).

Picture Dictionary — button

button, buttonhole

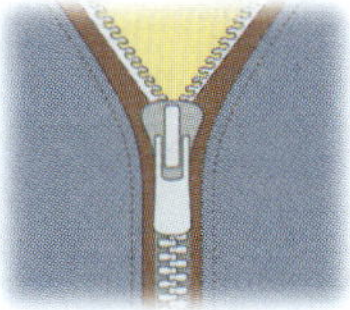
zip

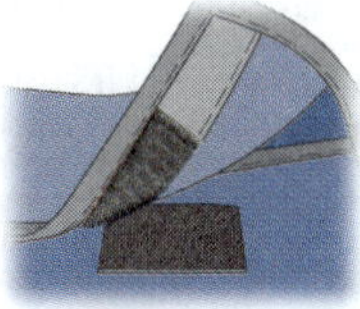
Velcro™

press stud / popper

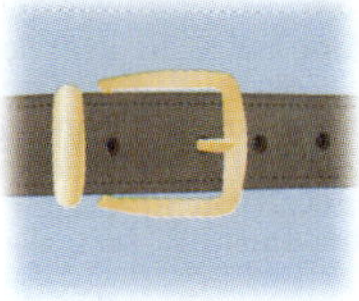
belt, buckle

shoelace

Word Partnership Use *button* with:

N. **shirt** button 1
V. **sew on a** button 1
press a button, **push a** button 3
PREP. button **up** ***something*** 2

buttonhole /ˈbʌtənhəʊl/ (**buttonholes, buttonholing, buttonholed**) 1 N-COUNT A **buttonhole** is a hole that you push a button through in order to fasten a piece of clothing. 2 N-COUNT A **buttonhole** is a flower that you wear on your lapel. [BRIT]
→ see **button**

Word Link *ar, er ≈ one who acts as : buyer, liar, seller*

buy /baɪ/ (**buys, buying, bought**) 1 V-T If you **buy** something, you obtain it by paying money for it. ❑ *He could not afford to buy a house.* ❑ *Lizzie bought herself a mountain bike.* ❑ *I'd like to buy him lunch.* ● **buyer** (**buyers**) N-COUNT ❑ *Car buyers are more interested in safety.* 2 N-COUNT If something is a good **buy**, it is of good quality and not very expensive. ❑ *Good buys this week include broccoli and tomatoes.* 3 V-T If you **buy** something such as time or freedom, you obtain it but only by offering or giving up something in return. ❑ *It was a risky operation, but might buy more time.*
▶ **buy out** PHR-VERB If you **buy** someone **out**, you buy their share of something that you previously owned together. ❑ *The bank had to pay to buy out most of the other partners.*
▶ **buy up** PHR-VERB If you **buy up** land, property, or a commodity, you buy large amounts of it, or all that is available. ❑ *His officials were yesterday buying up huge stocks of corn.*
▶ **buy into** PHR-VERB If someone **buys into** a company or an organization, they buy part of it, often in order to gain some control of it.

Thesaurus *buy* Also look up:

V. acquire, bargain, barter, get, obtain, pay, purchase 1

Word Partnership Use *buy* with:

V. **afford to** buy, buy **and/or sell** 1
N. buy **in bulk**, buy **clothes**, buy **food**, buy **a house**, buy **shares/stocks**, buy **tickets** 1
ADV. buy **direct**, buy **online**, buy **retail**, buy **wholesale** 1

buyout also **buy-out** /ˈbaɪaʊt/ (**buyouts**) N-COUNT A **buyout** is the buying of a company, especially by its managers or employees. ❑ *...a management buyout.*

buzz /bʌz/ (**buzzes, buzzing, buzzed**) 1 N-SING A **buzz** is a continuous sound, like the sound of a bee when it is flying. ❑ *...the continuous buzz of insects.* ❑ *...the excited buzz of conversation.* 2 V-I If something **buzzes**, it makes a long continuous sound, like a bee. ❑ *A fly buzzed on the window-pane.* ❑ *Helicopter gunships buzzed overhead.* 3 V-I If a place **is buzzing with** activity or conversation, there is a lot of activity or conversation there, especially because something important or exciting is about to happen. ❑ *The capital is buzzing with rumours.* 4 N-COUNT If a place or event has a **buzz**, it has a lively, interesting and modern atmosphere. ❑ *There's a buzz about Dublin.*

buzzer /ˈbʌzə/ (**buzzers**) N-COUNT A **buzzer** is a device that makes a buzzing sound, for example in an alarm clock.

buzzword also **buzz word** /ˈbʌzwɜːd/ (**buzzwords**) N-COUNT A **buzzword** is a word or expression that has become fashionable in a particular field. ❑ *Specialisation is the new buzzword.*

by /baɪ/ 1 PREP If something is done **by** a person or thing, that person or thing does it. ❑ *The boys were rescued by firemen.* ❑ *He was fascinated by her beauty.* 2 PREP **By** is used to say how something is done. ❑ *You should travel by car.* ❑ *We'll eat by candlelight.* ❑ *Make the sauce by boiling the cream.* ❑ *I'll pay by cheque.* 3 PREP If you say that a book, a piece of music, or a painting is **by** someone, you mean that they wrote it or created it. ❑ *...detective stories by American writers.* 4 PREP If you hold someone or something **by** a particular part of them, you hold

B

that part. ❑ *He caught her by the shoulder.* **5** PREP & ADV Someone or something that is **by** something else is beside it and close to it. ❑ *Put the rocking-chair by the window.* ❑ *Large numbers of security police stood by.* **6** PREP & ADV If a person or vehicle goes **by** you, it moves past without stopping. ❑ *A few cars passed close by me.* ❑ *A police patrol went by.* **7** PREP If something happens **by** a particular time, it happens at or before that time. ❑ *He had arrived by eight o'clock.* **8** PREP Things that are made or sold **by** the million or **by** the dozen are made or sold in those quantities. ❑ *Parcels arrived by the dozen from America.* **9** PREP If something increases or decreases **by** a particular amount, that amount is gained or lost. ❑ *Crime has increased by 10 percent.* **10** PREP You use **by** in expressions such as 'day by day' to say that something happens gradually. **11** PREP If you are **by** yourself, you are alone. If you do something **by** yourself, you do it without any help.

bye /baɪ/ CONVENTION **'Bye'** and **'bye-bye'** are informal ways of saying goodbye.

'by-election (**by-elections**) N-COUNT A **by-election** is an election that is held to choose a new member of parliament when a member has resigned or died.

bygone /ˈbaɪgɒn, AM -gɔːn/ ADJ BEFORE N **Bygone** means happening or existing a very long time ago. ❑ *...bygone generations.*

bypass /ˈbaɪpɑːs, -pæs/ (**bypasses, bypassing, bypassed**) **1** V-T If you **bypass** someone in authority, you avoid asking their permission to do something. **2** N-COUNT A **bypass** is a main road which takes traffic round the edge of a town rather than through its centre. **3** V-T If you **bypass** a place, you go round it rather than through it. **4** N-COUNT A **bypass** is an operation in which the flow of blood is redirected so that it does not flow through a part of the heart which is diseased or blocked. ❑ *...heart bypass surgery.*

'by-product (**by-products**) N-COUNT A **by-product** is something which is made during the manufacture of another product. ❑ *Glycerine is a by-product of soap-making.*

bystander /ˈbaɪstændə/ (**bystanders**) N-COUNT A **bystander** is a person who sees something happen but does not take part in it.

byte /baɪt/ (**bytes**) N-COUNT In computing, a **byte** is a unit of storage approximately equivalent to one printed character.

Cc

cab /kæb/ (**cabs**) **1** N-COUNT A **cab** is a taxi. ❑ *They went home in a cab.* **2** N-COUNT The **cab** of a lorry is the part in which the driver sits.

cabaret /ˈkæbəreɪ, AM -ˈreɪ/ (**cabarets**) N-VAR **Cabaret** is live entertainment which is performed in the evening in restaurants or nightclubs. ❑ *He sings in bars and cabarets.* ❑ *...a cabaret act.*

cabbage /ˈkæbɪdʒ/ (**cabbages**) N-VAR A **cabbage** is a round vegetable with green leaves.
→ see **vegetable**

cabin /ˈkæbɪn/ (**cabins**) **1** N-COUNT A **cabin** is a small room in a ship or boat, or one of the areas inside a plane. ❑ *...a first-class cabin.* **2** N-COUNT A **cabin** is a small wooden house.

cabinet /ˈkæbɪnɪt/ (**cabinets**) **1** N-COUNT A **cabinet** is a cupboard used for storing things or for displaying objects in. ❑ *...a medicine cabinet.* **2** N-COUNT **The Cabinet** is a group of the most senior ministers in a government. **3** → See note at **government**.
→ see **bathroom**

cable /ˈkeɪbəl/ (**cables, cabled, cabling**) **1** N-VAR A **cable** is a thick wire, or a bundle of wires inside a rubber or plastic covering, which is used to carry electricity or electronic signals. ❑ *...overhead power cables.* **2** N-UNCOUNT **Cable** is used to refer to television systems in which the signals are sent along underground wires rather than by radio waves. ❑ *...the national sports cable channel.* **3** V-T If an area or building **is cabled**, cables and other equipment are put in place so that the people there can receive cable television.
→ see **bridge, computer, laser, television**

cactus

cache /kæʃ/ (**caches**) N-COUNT A **cache** is a quantity of things such as weapons that have been hidden.

cactus /ˈkæktəs/ (**cactuses** or **cacti** /ˈkæktaɪ/) N-COUNT A **cactus** is a desert plant with a thick stem, often with spikes.
→ see **desert**

cadet /kəˈdet/ (**cadets**) N-COUNT A **cadet** is a young person who is being trained in the armed forces or police.

café /ˈkæfeɪ, AM kæˈfeɪ/ (**cafés**) N-COUNT A **café** is a place where simple meals, snacks, and drinks are sold.

Usage

In Britain, a **café** serves tea, coffee, soft drinks, and light meals, but not usually alcohol. If you want an alcoholic drink, you can go to a **pub**. In American English, a **pub** is more usually called a **bar**. Many pubs serve food, but for a larger or more special meal, you can go to a **restaurant**.

cafeteria /ˌkæfɪˈtɪəriə/ (**cafeterias**) N-COUNT A **cafeteria** is a self-service restaurant in a large shop or workplace.

caffeine /ˈkæfiːn, AM kæˈfiːn/ N-UNCOUNT **Caffeine** is a chemical substance found in coffee, tea, and cocoa, which makes you more active.

cage /keɪdʒ/ (**cages**) N-COUNT A **cage** is a structure of wire or metal bars in which birds or animals are kept.

caged /keɪdʒd/ ADJ A **caged** bird or animal is inside a cage.

cajole /kəˈdʒəʊl/ (**cajoles, cajoling, cajoled**) V-T If you **cajole** someone, you get them to do something through persuasion. ❑ *We cajoled him into bringing us here.*

cake /keɪk/ (**cakes**) **1** N-VAR A **cake** is a sweet food made by baking a mixture of flour, eggs, sugar, and fat. ❑ *...a piece of chocolate cake.* **2** N-COUNT Food that is formed into flat round shapes before it is cooked can be referred to as **cakes**. ❑ *...fish cakes.*
→ see **dessert**

cakewalk /ˈkeɪkwɔːk/ N-SING If you say that something is **a cakewalk**, you mean that it is very easy to do or achieve. ❑ *Fittipaldi's victory was a cakewalk.*

calamity /kəˈlæmɪti/ (**calamities**) N-COUNT A **calamity** is an event that causes great damage or distress. [FORMAL] ❑ *...the calamity of war.*

calcium /ˈkælsiəm/ N-UNCOUNT **Calcium** is a soft white element found in bones and teeth, and also in limestone, chalk, and marble.

calculate /ˈkælkjʊleɪt/ (**calculates, calculating, calculated**) **1** V-T If you **calculate** a number or amount, you work it out by doing some arithmetic. ❑ *They have calculated that 57 per cent of Britons work on Saturdays and 37 per cent on Sundays.* ● **calculation** /ˌkælkjʊˈleɪʃən/ (**calculations**) N-VAR ❑ *The machine does the calculations.* **2** V-T If you **calculate** the effects of something, you consider what they will be. ❑ *Scientists are beginning to calculate the long-term effects of the floods.* ● **calculation** N-VAR ❑ *...political calculation.*

calculated /ˈkælkjʊleɪtɪd/ ADJ If something is **calculated**, it is deliberately planned to have a particular effect. ❑ *Her words were calculated to make him feel guilty.* ❑ *...a calculated attempt to cover up her crime.*

calculating /ˈkælkjʊleɪtɪŋ/ ADJ If you describe someone as **calculating**, you think they are planning to get what they want, probably by harming other people. ❑ *...a cool, calculating and clever criminal.* ● **calculation** /ˌkælkjʊˈleɪʃən/ N-UNCOUNT ❑ *...unspeakably cruel calculation.*

calculation → see **calculate, calculating**
→ see **mathematics**

calculator /ˈkælkjʊleɪtə/ (**calculators**) N-COUNT A **calculator** is a small electronic device used for doing mathematical calculations.
→ see **office**

calendar /ˈkælɪndə/ (**calendars**) 1 N-COUNT A **calendar** is a chart or device which displays the date and the day of the week, and often the whole of a particular year. 2 ADJ A **calendar month** is one of the twelve periods of time that a year is divided into. 3 N-COUNT A **calendar** is a list of dates within a year that are important for a particular organization or activity. ❑ *This is the biggest game on the football calendar in this country.*
→ see **year**

calf /kɑːf, AM kæf/ (**calves**) 1 N-COUNT A **calf** is a young cow. 2 N-COUNT The young of some animals, such as elephants, giraffes, and whales, are called **calves**. 3 N-COUNT Your **calves** are the backs of your legs between your ankles and knees.

calibre [AM **caliber**] /ˈkælɪbə/ N-UNCOUNT The **calibre of** someone or something is their qualities, abilities, or high standards. ❑ *The calibre of teaching was very high.*

call /kɔːl/ (**calls, calling, called**) 1 V-T If you **call** someone or something **by** a particular name or title, you give them that name or title. ❑ *Everybody called each other by their surnames.* ❑ *There are two men called Bob in my office.* 2 V-T If you **call** a person or situation something, that is how you describe them. ❑ *They called him a liar and a cheat.* ❑ *She calls me lazy.* 3 V-T & PHR-VERB If you **call** something, or if you **call** it **out**, you say it in a loud voice. ❑ *I heard someone calling my name.* ❑ *He called out, 'Quiet please!'* 4 V-T & N-COUNT If you **call** someone, or make a telephone **call**, you telephone them. ❑ *He called me at my office.* ❑ *I think we should call the doctor.* ❑ *I made a phone call to the United States.* 5 PHRASE If someone is **on call**, they are ready to go to work at any time if they are needed. ❑ *...a doctor on call.* 6 V-T If you **call** a meeting, you arrange for it to take place. 7 V-I & N-COUNT If you **call** somewhere, or pay a **call** there, you make a short visit there. ❑ *The police called at the house.* ❑ *He decided to pay a call on Tommy.* 8 N-COUNT If there is a **call for** something, someone demands that it should happen. ❑ *...a call for all businessmen to work together.* 9 to **call it a day** → see **day**

▶ **call back** PHR-VERB If you **call** someone **back**, you telephone them again or in return for a telephone call that they have made to you earlier. ❑ *OK, I'll call you back around three o'clock.*

▶ **call for** 1 PHR-VERB If you **call for** someone or something, you go to collect them. ❑ *I shall be calling for you at seven o'clock.* 2 PHR-VERB If you **call for** an action, you demand that it should happen. ❑ *The committee angrily called for Robinson's resignation.* 3 PHR-VERB If something **calls for** a particular action or quality, it needs it. ❑ *Does the situation call for military action?*

▶ **call in** 1 PHR-VERB If you **call** someone **in**, you ask them to come and do something for you. ❑ *Call in a professional decorator to do the work.* 2 PHR-VERB If you **call in** somewhere, you make a short visit there. ❑ *He called in at the office the other day.*

▶ **call off** PHR-VERB If you **call off** an event, you cancel it. ❑ *The wedding was called off.*

▶ **call on** or **call upon** 1 PHR-VERB If you **call on** someone **to** do something, you say publicly that you want them to do it. ❑ *He has called on the government to resign.* 2 PHR-VERB If you **call on** someone, you pay them a short visit.

▶ **call out** 1 PHR-VERB If you **call** someone **out**, you order them to come to help, especially in an emergency. ❑ *I got so worried, I called out the doctor.* 2 → see also **call** (meaning 3)

▶ **call up** 1 PHR-VERB If you **call** someone **up**, you telephone them. ❑ *I called her up to invite her to lunch.* 2 PHR-VERB If someone **is called up**, they are ordered to join the armed forces.

▶ **call upon** → see **call on**

ˈ**call centre** [AM **call center**] (**call centres**) N-COUNT A **call centre** is an office where people work answering or making telephone calls for a company.

caller /ˈkɔːlə/ (**callers**) 1 N-COUNT A **caller** is a person who is making a telephone call. 2 N-COUNT A **caller** is a person who comes to see you for a short visit.

callous /ˈkæləs/ ADJ A **callous** person or action is cruel and shows no concern for other people. ❑ *...a callous attack on innocent people.* • **callously** ADV ❑ *...callously ill-treating his wife.* • **callousness** N-UNCOUNT ❑ *...the callousness of the murder.*

calm /kɑːm/ (**calmer, calmest, calms, calming, calmed**) 1 ADJ & N-UNCOUNT A **calm** person does not show or feel any worry, anger, or excitement. You can refer to someone's feeling of **calm**. ❑ *...a calm and diplomatic woman.* ❑ *Try to keep calm.* ❑ *He felt a sudden sense of calm.* • **calmly** ADV ❑ *She speaks slowly and calmly.* 2 N-UNCOUNT **Calm** is a state of being quiet and peaceful. ❑ *Shouting disturbed the calm of the peaceful little street.* 3 ADJ If the weather is **calm**, there is little or no wind. If the sea is **calm**, the water is not moving very much. 4 V-T If you **calm** someone, you do something to make them less upset or excited. ❑ *Isabella helped to calm his fears.* • **calming** ADJ ❑ *Yoga can have a very calming effect on the mind.*

▶ **calm down** PHR-VERB If you **calm down** or if someone **calms** you **down**, you become less upset or excited. ❑ *I'll try a herbal remedy to calm him down.*

Thesaurus	*calm* Also look up:
ADJ.	laid-back, peaceful, placid, relaxed serene, tranquil; *(ant.)* excited, upset 1

calorie /ˈkæləri/ (**calories**) N-COUNT A **calorie** is a unit of measurement for the energy value of food.
→ see Word Web: **calorie**
→ see **diet**

calves /kɑːvz, AM kævz/ **Calves** is the plural of **calf**.

camcorder /ˈkæmkɔːdə/ (**camcorders**) N-COUNT A **camcorder** is a portable video camera.

camel

came /keɪm/ **Came** is the past tense of **come**.

camel /ˈkæməl/ (**camels**) N-COUNT A **camel** is a desert animal with one or two humps on its back.

cameo /ˈkæmiəʊ/ (**cameos**) 1 N-COUNT A **cameo** is a small

Word Web calories

Calories are a measure of **energy**. One calorie of heat raises the **temperature** of 1 gram of water by 1°C*. However, we usually think of calories in relation to food and exercise. A person eating a cup of vanilla ice cream takes in 270 calories. Walking a mile **burns** 66 calories. Different types of foods store different amounts of energy. **Proteins** and **carbohydrates** contain 4 calories per gram. However **fat** contains 9 calories per gram. Our bodies store extra calories in the form of fat. For every 3,500 extra calories we take in, we gain a pound of fat.

0°Celsius = 32° Fahrenheit

C

part in a film or play acted by a famous actor. ❑ *Schwarzenegger will make a cameo appearance in the film 'The Rundown' later this year.* **2** N-COUNT A **cameo** is a brooch with a raised stone design on a flat stone of another colour.

camera /'kæmrə/ (**cameras**) **1** N-COUNT A **camera** is a piece of equipment for taking photographs or for making a film. ❑ *...a video camera.* **2** PHRASE If someone or something is **on camera**, they are being filmed.
→ see **photography**

cameraman /'kæmrəmæn/ (**cameramen**) N-COUNT A **cameraman** is a person who operates a television or film camera.

'camera ˌphone (**camera phones**) N-COUNT A **camera phone** is a cellphone that can also take photographs.

Word Link *age ≈ state of, related to : camouflage, courage, marriage*

camouflage /'kæməflɑːʒ/ (**camouflages, camouflaging, camouflaged**) **1** N-UNCOUNT **Camouflage** consists of things such as leaves, branches, or paint, used to make military forces or their equipment difficult to see. ❑ *...a camouflage jacket.* **2** V-T When military forces **camouflage themselves** or their weapons, they use camouflage to make themselves or their weapons difficult to see. ● **camouflaged** ADJ ❑ *You won't see them from the air. They'll be very well camouflaged.* **3** N-UNCOUNT **Camouflage** is the way in which some animals are coloured and shaped to look as though they are part of their natural surroundings.

camp /kæmp/ (**camps, camping, camped**) **1** N-VAR A **camp** is a place where people live or stay in tents or caravans. **2** V-I If you **camp** somewhere, you stay there in a tent or caravan. ❑ *We camped near the beach.* ❑ *For six months they camped out in a caravan.* ● **camping** N-UNCOUNT ❑ *They recently went on a camping trip to Africa.* **3** N-COUNT A **camp** is a collection of buildings for people such as soldiers, refugees, or prisoners. ❑ *...refugee camps.* **4** N-COUNT You can use **camp** to refer to a group of people with a particular idea or belief. ❑ *He's the right person to lead the conservative camp.*

campaign /ˌkæm'peɪn/ (**campaigns, campaigning, campaigned**) N-COUNT & V-I A **campaign** is a planned set of actions aimed at achieving a particular result. To **campaign** means to carry out a campaign. ❑ *...an advertising campaign to attract more people.* ❑ *...a bombing campaign.* ❑ *They have been campaigning to improve the legal status of women.* ● **campaigner** (**campaigners**) N-COUNT ❑ *...peace campaigners.*
→ see **army**

camper /'kæmpə/ (**campers**) **1** N-COUNT A **camper** is a person who goes camping. **2** N-COUNT A **camper** is a van fitted with beds and cooking equipment.

Word Link *site, situ ≈ position, location : campsite, situation, website*

campsite /'kæmpsaɪt/ (**campsites**) N-COUNT A **campsite** or a **camping site** is a place where people who are on holiday can stay in tents.

campus /'kæmpəs/ (**campuses**) N-COUNT A **campus** is the area of land containing the main buildings of a college or university.

can
❶ MODAL USES
❷ CONTAINER

can /kən, STRONG kæn/
❶ **1** MODAL If you **can** do something, you have the ability or opportunity to do it. ❑ *I can take care of myself.* ❑ *See if you can find Karl.* ❑ *You can't be with your baby all the time.* **2** MODAL If you **can** do something, you are allowed to do it. ❑ *You must pay the mechanic before you can take your car away from the garage.* ❑ *I can't tell you what he said: he made me promise not to say anything.* **3** MODAL You use **can** to indicate that something is true sometimes or in some circumstances. ❑ *Long-term therapy can last five years or more.* ❑ *Exercising on your own can be boring.* **4** MODAL You use **cannot** or **can't** to state that you are certain that something is not true or will not happen. ❑ *This man can't be Douglas.* **5** MODAL You use **can** in order to make suggestions or requests, or to offer to do something. ❑ *If you need money, you can always ask me.* ❑ *Can I have a look at that?* ❑ *Can I help you?*

can /kæn/ (**cans, canning, canned**)
❷ **1** N-COUNT A **can** is a sealed metal container for food, drink, or paint. ❑ *...empty beer cans.* **2** V-T When food or drink **is canned**, it is put into a metal container and sealed.
→ see **container**

canal /kə'næl/ (**canals**) N-COUNT A **canal** is a long, narrow, man-made stretch of water.

C

Word Web cancer

The traditional **treatments** for **cancer** are **surgery**, **radiation therapy**, and **chemotherapy**. However, there is a new type of treatment called targeted therapy. This treatment uses new drugs that target specific types of cancer cells. Targeted therapy does not have many of the **toxic** effects on healthy **tissue** that traditional chemotherapy can have. One of these drugs helps stop blood vessels that feed a tumor from growing. Another drug kills cancer cells.

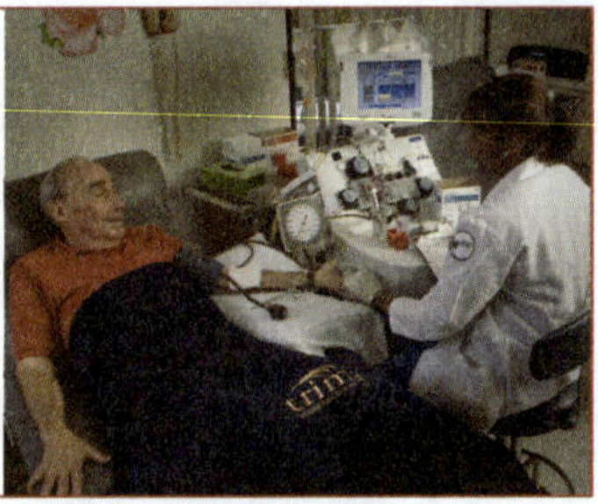

cancel /'kænsəl/ (**cancels, cancelling, cancelled** or [AM] **canceling, canceled**) **1** V-T/V-I If you **cancel** an order or an arrangement, you stop it from happening. ❑ *Many trains have been cancelled today.* ❑ *If you cancel, a fee may be charged.* ● **cancellation** (**cancellations**) N-VAR ❑ *The cancellation of his visit has disappointed many people.* **2** V-T If someone in authority **cancels** a document or a debt, they officially declare that it is no longer valid or that it no longer legally exists. ❑ *...a government order cancelling his passport.* ● **cancellation** N-UNCOUNT ❑ *...cancellation of Third World debt.* ▸ **cancel out** PHR-VERB If one thing **cancels out** another thing, the two things have opposite effects which combine to produce no real effect. ❑ *Gary Bannister's goal was cancelled out by Chris Waddle's.* ❑ *The pluses and minuses have cancelled each other out.*

Thesaurus	*cancel* Also look up:
v.	break, call off, scrap, trash, undo **1**

cancer /'kænsə/ (**cancers**) N-VAR **Cancer** is a serious illness in which abnormal body cells increase, producing growths. ❑ *Ninety per cent of lung cancers are caused by smoking.* ● **cancerous** ADJ ❑ *Nine out of ten lumps are not cancerous.*
→ see Word Web: **cancer**

candid /'kændɪd/ ADJ If you are **candid with** someone or **about** something, you speak honestly. ❑ *I wasn't completely candid with him.* ❑ *...a candid interview.* ● **candidly** ADV ❑ *He says candidly that he is in love with her.*

candidacy /'kændɪdəsi/ N-UNCOUNT Someone's **candidacy** is their position of being a candidate in an election. ❑ *Today he formally announced his candidacy for President.*

candidate /'kændɪdeɪt/ (**candidates**) **1** N-COUNT A **candidate** is someone who is being considered for a position. ❑ *She is the best candidate for the job.* **2** N-COUNT A **candidate** is someone taking an examination.

candle /'kændəl/ (**candles**) N-COUNT A **candle** is a stick of hard wax with a piece of string called a wick through the middle. You light the wick so the candle produces light.

candour [AM **candor**] /'kændə/ N-UNCOUNT **Candour** is the quality of speaking honestly and openly about things. ❑ *He spoke with unusual candour.*

candy /'kændi/ (**candies**) N-VAR In American English, sweet foods such as toffees, chocolates, and mints are referred to as **candy**. The British word is **sweets**. ❑ *...a box of candies.*

cane /keɪn/ (**canes, caning, caned**) **1** N-UNCOUNT **Cane** is the long hollow stems of a plant such as bamboo. ❑ *...cane baskets and furniture.* **2** N-COUNT A **cane** is a long narrow stick. ❑ *He leaned heavily on his cane.* **3** V-T & N-SING When schoolchildren **were caned** or were given **the cane**, they were hit with a cane as a punishment. ❑ *If you misbehaved you would get the cane.*
→ see **disability, sugar**

canine /'keɪnaɪn/ ADJ **Canine** means relating to or resembling a dog.

canister /'kænɪstə/ (**canisters**) N-COUNT A **canister** is a metal container.

cannabis /'kænəbɪs/ N-UNCOUNT **Cannabis** is a drug which some people smoke. It is illegal in many countries.

cannibal /'kænɪbəl/ (**cannibals**) N-COUNT A **cannibal** is a person who eats human flesh. ● **cannibalism** N-UNCOUNT ❑ *...tales of cannibalism.*

cannon /'kænən/

The plural is **cannon** or **cannons**.

1 N-COUNT A **cannon** is a large gun on wheels, formerly used in battles. **2** N-COUNT A **cannon** is a heavy automatic gun, especially one fired from an aircraft.

cannot /'kænɒt, kə'nɒt/ **Cannot** is the negative form of **can**.

canoe /kə'nuː/ (**canoes**) N-COUNT A **canoe** is a small narrow boat that you row using a paddle.
→ see **boat**

canoe

canon /'kænən/ (**canons**) N-COUNT A **canon** is one of the clergy on the staff of a cathedral.

canopy /'kænəpi/ (**canopies**) N-COUNT A **canopy** is a decorated cover which hangs above something such as a bed or throne.
→ see **bed**

can't /kɑːnt, AM kænt/ **Can't** is the usual spoken form of **cannot**.

canteen /kæn'tiːn/ (**canteens**) N-COUNT A **canteen** is a place in a factory, office, or shop where the workers can have meals.

canter /'kæntə/ (**canters, cantering, cantered**) V-I & N-SING When a horse **canters** or when it moves **at a canter**, it moves at a speed between a gallop and a trot.

canvas /ˈkænvəs/ (**canvases**) **1** N-UNCOUNT **Canvas** is strong heavy cloth used for making tents, sails, and bags. **2** N-VAR A **canvas** is a piece of cloth on which an oil painting is done, or the painting itself. ❑ *...canvases by masters like Carpaccio, Canaletto and Guardi.*
→ see **painting**

canvass /ˈkænvəs/ (**canvasses, canvassing, canvassed**) **1** V-I If you **canvass for** a person or political party, you try to persuade people to vote for them. ❑ *I'm canvassing for the Labor Party.* **2** V-T If you **canvass** public opinion, you find out how people feel about something. ❑ *They canvassed the views of almost eighty economists.*

canyon /ˈkænjən/ (**canyons**) N-COUNT A **canyon** is a long narrow valley with very steep sides.

cap /kæp/ (**caps, capping, capped**) **1** N-COUNT A **cap** is a soft flat hat usually worn by men or boys. **2** N-COUNT The **cap** of a bottle is its lid. **3** V-T You can say that the last event in a series of events **caps** the others. ❑ *Fans were delighted when the band capped the night with their new song.*
→ see **clothing, hat**

capable /ˈkeɪpəbəl/ **1** ADJ AFTER LINK-V If you are **capable of** doing something, you are able to do it. ❑ *He was hardly capable of standing up.* ❑ *I realised he was capable of murder.* ● **capability** /ˌkeɪpəˈbɪlɪti/ (**capabilities**) N-VAR ❑ *He has great capabilities as an actor.* **2** ADJ Someone who is **capable** has the ability to do something well. ❑ *She's a very capable speaker.* ● **capably** ADV ❑ *It was all dealt with very capably.*

Thesaurus	*capable* Also look up:
ADJ.	able, competent, skillful, talented; *(ant.)* incapable, incompetent **2**

capacity /kəˈpæsɪti/ (**capacities**) **1** N-VAR & ADJ BEFORE N The **capacity** of something is the maximum amount that it can hold or produce. A **capacity** crowd completely fills a theatre or stadium. ❑ *The theatre has a seating capacity of 350.* ❑ *The restaurant was packed to capacity.* ❑ *This feature gives the vehicles a much greater fuel capacity.* **2** N-COUNT Your **capacity for** something is your ability to do it. ❑ *...our capacity for giving care, love and attention.* **3** N-COUNT If someone does something **in** a particular **capacity**, they do it as part of their duties. ❑ *He was visiting the country in his capacity as an official.*

cape /keɪp/ (**capes**) **1** N-COUNT A **cape** is a short cloak. **2** N-COUNT A **cape** is a large piece of land that sticks out into the sea.

Word Link	***cap*** ≈ ***head*** : ***capital, capitulate, captain***

capital /ˈkæpɪtəl/ (**capitals**) **1** N-UNCOUNT **Capital** is a sum of money used to start or expand a business or invested to make more money. **2** N-COUNT The **capital** of a country is the city where its government meets. **3** N-COUNT & ADJ BEFORE N A **capital** or a **capital letter** is the large form of a letter used at the beginning of sentences and names. **4** ADJ BEFORE N A **capital offence** is one that is punished by death.
→ see **city, country**

Usage

Note that you must always use a capital letter with days of the week, months of the year, and festivals. ❑ *...on Monday the 13th of January.* ❑ *...at Christmas.* Names of seasons, however, usually begin with a small letter. ❑ *...in spring.* Capitals must also be used with the names of countries and other places, as well as with the adjectives and nouns derived from them, such as those which refer to their inhabitants or languages. ❑ *...in Portugal.* ❑ *...the Swiss police.* ❑ *Thousands of Germans filled the streets of Berlin.* ❑ *He spoke fluent Arabic.*

capitalise /ˈkæpɪtəlaɪz/ → see **capitalize**

capitalism /ˈkæpɪtəlɪzəm/ N-UNCOUNT **Capitalism** is an economic and political system in which property, business, and industry are owned by private individuals and not by the state. ● **capitalist** (**capitalists**) N-COUNT ❑ *...the industrialized capitalist countries.* ❑ *...Western capitalists.*

capitalize [BRIT also **capitalise**] /ˈkæpɪtəlaɪz/ (**capitalizes, capitalizing, capitalized**) V-I If you **capitalize on** a situation, you use it to gain some advantage. ❑ *To succeed in life, you have to capitalize on every opportunity.*

ˌcapital ˈpunishment N-UNCOUNT **Capital punishment** is the legal killing of a person who has committed a serious crime.

capitulate /kəˈpɪtʃʊleɪt/ (**capitulates, capitulating, capitulated**) V-I If you **capitulate**, you stop resisting and do what someone else wants you to do. [FORMAL] ❑ *The club eventually capitulated and now grants equal rights to women.* ● **capitulation** N-UNCOUNT ❑ *Acceptance of the plan would mean capitulation.*

capsize /kæpˈsaɪz, AM ˈkæpsaɪz/ (**capsizes, capsizing, capsized**) V-T/V-I If you **capsize** a boat or if it **capsizes**, it turns upside down in the water. ❑ *The sea got very rough and the boat capsized.*

capsule /ˈkæpsjuːl, AM ˈkæpsəl/ (**capsules**) **1** N-COUNT A **capsule** is a small container with powdered or liquid medicine inside, which you swallow whole. **2** N-COUNT The **capsule** of a spacecraft is the part in which the astronauts travel.

captain /ˈkæptɪn/ (**captains, captaining, captained**) **1** N-COUNT & N-TITLE A **captain** is a military officer of middle rank. ❑ *...a captain in the army.* **2** N-COUNT The **captain** of an aeroplane or ship is the officer in charge of it. **3** N-COUNT The **captain** of a sports team is its leader. **4** V-T If you **captain** a ship or team, you are the captain of it. ❑ *The team was captained by celebrity Brian Kelley.*
→ see **boat, ship**

captaincy /ˈkæptɪnsi/ N-UNCOUNT The **captaincy** of a team is the position of being captain. ❑ *Under his captaincy, Leeds lost twice to Rangers.*

caption /ˈkæpʃən/ (**captions**) N-COUNT The **caption** of a picture consists of the words printed underneath.

Word Link	***cap*** ≈ ***seize*** : ***captivate, captive, capture***

captivate /ˈkæptɪveɪt/ (**captivates, captivating,**

C

Word Web car

The first mass-produced **automobile** in the U.S. was the Model T. In 1909, Ford sold over 10,000 of these **vehicles**. They all had the same basic **engine** and **chassis**. For years the only color choice was black. Three different bodies were available—**roadster, saloon,** and **coupé**. Today car makers offer many more choices. These include **convertibles**, **sports cars, estates, vans, pick-up trucks** and **SUVs**. Laws now require **seat belts** and **airbags** to make **driving** safer. Some car makers now offer **hybrid** vehicles. They combine an electrical engine with an **internal combustion engine** to improve **fuel** economy.

captivated) V-T If you **are captivated by** someone or something, you find them fascinating and attractive. ❑ *For 40 years she has captivated the world with her beauty.* ● **captivating** ADJ ❑ *...her captivating smile.*

captive /ˈkæptɪv/ (**captives**) **1** ADJ BEFORE N A **captive** animal or person is being kept in a particular place and is not allowed to escape. ❑ *...captive monkeys.* **2** PHRASE If someone **takes** or **holds** you **captive**, they take or keep you as a prisoner. **3** N-COUNT A **captive** is a prisoner. [LITERARY]

captivity /kæpˈtɪvɪti/ N-UNCOUNT **Captivity** is the state of being kept as a captive. ❑ *...animals that have been reared in captivity.*

capture /ˈkæptʃə/ (**captures, capturing, captured**) **1** V-T & N-UNCOUNT If you **capture** someone or something, you catch them or take possession of them. You can also talk about the **capture of** someone or something. ❑ *Most of the soldiers were captured.* ❑ *This final battle led to the army's capture of the town.* **2** V-T To **capture** something means to gain control of it. ❑ *In 1987, McDonald's captured 19 percent of all fast-food sales.* **3** V-T If someone **captures** the atmosphere or quality of something, they represent it successfully in pictures, music, or words. ❑ *They took out their cameras to capture the moment.*

Word Partnership Use *capture* with:

V. **avoid** capture, **escape** capture, **fail to** capture **1**
N. capture **territory** **1**
capture **your *attention***, capture ***your*** **imagination** **3**

car /kɑː/ (**cars**) **1** N-COUNT A **car** is a motor vehicle with room for a small number of passengers. ❑ *They arrived by car.* **2** N-COUNT In American English, a **car** is one of the separate sections of a train that carries passengers. The usual British word is **carriage**. **3** N-COUNT In Britain, railway carriages are called **cars** when they are used for a particular purpose. ❑ *...the dining car.*
→ see Word Web: **car**
→ see **train**

caramel /ˈkærəmel/ (**caramels**) **1** N-COUNT A **caramel** is a kind of toffee. **2** N-UNCOUNT **Caramel** is burnt sugar used for colouring and flavouring food.

carat /ˈkærət/ (**carats**) **1** N-COUNT A **carat** is a unit equal to 0.2 grams used for measuring the weight of diamonds and other precious stones. ❑ *...a huge eight-carat diamond.* **2** N-COUNT A **carat** is a unit for measuring the purity of gold. The purest gold is 24-carat gold. ❑ *...a 14-carat gold fountain pen.*

caravan /ˈkærəvæn/ (**caravans**) **1** N-COUNT In British English, a **caravan** is a vehicle in which people live or spend their holidays. The usual American word is **trailer**. ❑ *...a caravan holiday in France.* **2** N-COUNT A **caravan** is a group of people and animals that travel together, especially in deserts. ❑ *...a caravan of horses.*

ˈcaravan site (**caravan sites**) N-COUNT In British English, a **caravan site** is an area of land where people can stay in a caravan on holiday, or where people live in caravans. The American term is **trailer park**.

Word Link ***hydr ≈ water : dehydrate, carbohydrate, hydraulic***

carbohydrate /ˌkɑːbəʊˈhaɪdreɪt/ (**carbohydrates**) N-VAR **Carbohydrates** are energy-giving substances found in foods such as sugar and bread.
→ see **calories, diet**

carbon /ˈkɑːbən/ N-UNCOUNT **Carbon** is a chemical element that diamonds and coal are made of.
→ see **fossil**

carbon dioxide /ˌkɑːbən daɪˈɒksaɪd/ N-UNCOUNT **Carbon dioxide** is a gas that animals and people breathe out.
→ see **greenhouse effect, ozone, respiration**

carbon monoxide /ˌkɑːbən məˈnɒksaɪd/ N-UNCOUNT **Carbon monoxide** is a poisonous gas produced for example by cars.
→ see **air, ozone**

carcass also **carcase** /ˈkɑːkəs/ (**carcasses**) N-COUNT A **carcass** is the body of a dead animal.

card /kɑːd/ (**cards**) **1** N-COUNT A **card** is a piece of stiff paper or thin cardboard on which something is written or printed, such as a picture and a message to celebrate a special occasion. ❑ *She always sends me a card on my birthday.* **2** N-UNCOUNT **Card** is strong stiff paper or thin cardboard. **3** N-COUNT **Cards** are thin pieces of cardboard decorated with numbers or pictures, used to play various games. ❑ *...a pack of cards.* ❑ *I taught Rachel how to play cards.*

cardboard /'kɑːdbɔːd/ N-UNCOUNT **Cardboard** is thick stiff paper used to make boxes and other containers. ❑ *...a thin cardboard folder.*

cardiac /'kɑːdiæk/ ADJ BEFORE N **Cardiac** means relating to the heart. [TECHNICAL] ❑ *...a top cardiac surgeon.*
→ see **muscle**

cardigan /'kɑːdɪgən/ (**cardigans**) N-COUNT A **cardigan** is a knitted woollen garment that fastens at the front.

cardinal /'kɑːdnəl/ (**cardinals**) **1** N-COUNT A **cardinal** is a priest of high rank in the Catholic church. **2** N-COUNT A **cardinal number** is a whole number such as one, three, or ten, that tells you how many people or things are being talked about. Compare **ordinal**.

care /keə/ (**cares, caring, cared**) **1** V-T/V-I If you **care about** something, you are concerned about it or interested in it. ❑ *This company cares about the environment.* ❑ *I really don't care what he thinks.* **2** V-I If you **care for** or **about** someone, you feel a lot of affection for them. ❑ *He still cared for me.* ❑ *These people are your friends, and they care about you.* **3** V-T/V-I If you **care to** do something or **care for** something it means you want or choose to do it. [FORMAL] ❑ *He asked if we would care to join him.* ❑ *Would you care for some orange juice?* **4** V-I & N-UNCOUNT If you **care for** someone or something, or if you **take care of** them, you look after them and keep them in a good state or condition. ❑ *They hired a nurse to care for her.* ❑ *There was no one else to take care of their children.* ❑ *Sensitive teeth need special care.* **5** N-UNCOUNT Children who are **in care** are looked after by the state. ❑ *...a home for children in care.* ❑ *She was taken into care as a baby.* **6** N-UNCOUNT If you do something **with care**, you do it with great attention to avoid mistakes or damage. ❑ *The crimes were planned with care.* ❑ *Take great care when using matches.* **7** CONVENTION You can say **'Take care'** when saying goodbye to someone. [INFORMAL] **8** N-COUNT Your **cares** are your worries, anxieties, or fears. ❑ *She didn't seem to have a care in the world.* **9** → see also **caring**

Word Partnership Use *care* with:

ADJ.	**good** care, **loving** care **4**
V.	**provide** care, **receive** care **4**

career /kə'rɪə/ (**careers, careering, careered**) **1** N-COUNT Your **career** is your job or profession or the part of your life that you spend working. ❑ *...a career in journalism.* ❑ *During his career, he wrote more than fifty plays.* **2** V-I If a person or vehicle **careers** somewhere, they move fast and in an uncontrolled way. ❑ *His car careered into a river.*

Thesaurus *career* Also look up:

N.	field, job, profession, speciality, vocation, work **1**

Word Partnership Use *career* with:

N.	career **advancement**, career **goals**, career **opportunities**, career **path** **1**
ADJ.	**political** career, **professional** career **1**
V.	**pursue a** career **1**

Word Link *free ≈ without : carefree, duty-free, hands-free*

carefree /'keəfriː/ ADJ A **carefree** person or period of time does not have any problems or responsibilities. ❑ *...carefree summers at the beach.*

Word Link *ful ≈ filled with : beautiful, careful, dreadful*

careful /'keəfʊl/ **1** ADJ If you are **careful**, you pay attention to what you are doing in order to avoid damage or mistakes. ❑ *Be very careful with this stuff: it can be dangerous.* ❑ *We were careful not to be seen.* ● **carefully** ADV ❑ *Drive carefully.* ❑ *He chose his words carefully.* **2** ADJ **Careful** work, thought, or examination is thorough and shows a concern for details. ❑ *The trip needs careful planning.* ❑ *...keeping careful records.* ● **carefully** ADV ❑ *All her letters were carefully organized.*

Word Partnership Use *careful* with:

ADV.	**better be** careful **1**
	extremely careful, **very** careful **1** **2**
N.	careful **attention**, careful **consideration**, careful **observation**, careful **planning** **2**

Word Link *less ≈ without : careless, endless, wireless*

careless /'keələs/ ADJ If you are **careless**, you do not pay enough attention to what you are doing, and so you make mistakes. ❑ *The company was careless about safety.* ● **carelessly** ADV ❑ *She was fined £100 for driving carelessly.* ● **carelessness** N-UNCOUNT ❑ *The fire resulted from carelessness.*

Thesaurus *careless* Also look up:

ADJ.	absent-minded, forgetful, irresponsible, reckless, sloppy; (*ant.*) attentive, careful, cautious

caress /kə'res/ (**caresses, caressing, caressed**) V-T & N-COUNT If you **caress** someone, you stroke them gently and affectionately. A **caress** is an act of caressing someone. ❑ *He was gently caressing her golden hair.* ❑ *Her voice was like a caress.*

caretaker /'keəteɪkə/ (**caretakers**) N-COUNT A **caretaker** is a person who looks after a large building such as a school or a block of flats.

cargo /'kɑːgəʊ/ (**cargoes**) N-VAR The **cargo** of a ship or plane is the goods that it is carrying. ❑ *...a cargo of bananas.* ❑ *...cargo planes.*
→ see **ship**, **train**

caricature /'kærɪkətʃʊə, AM -tʃər/ (**caricatures, caricaturing, caricatured**) **1** N-VAR A **caricature** is a drawing or description of someone that exaggerates their appearance or behaviour. ❑ *My brother drew a caricature of Steve.* **2** V-T If you

caricature someone, you draw or describe them in an exaggerated way in order to make people laugh. ❑ *Their leader was often caricatured as a fool.*

caring /ˈkeərɪŋ/ ADJ A **caring** person is affectionate, helpful, and sympathetic. ❑ *...a loving, caring husband.*

C

Word Link	*carn ≈ flesh : carnage, incarnation, reincarnation*

carnage /ˈkɑːnɪdʒ/ N-UNCOUNT **Carnage** is the violent killing of a lot of people. [LITERARY] ❑ *...scenes of panic and carnage.*

carnation /kɑːˈneɪʃən/ (**carnations**) N-COUNT A **carnation** is a plant with white, pink, or red flowers.

carnival /ˈkɑːnɪvəl/ (**carnivals**) N-COUNT A **carnival** is a public festival with music, processions, and dancing.

carol /ˈkærəl/ (**carols**) N-COUNT **Carols** are Christian religious songs that are sung at Christmas.

ˈcar park (**car parks**) N-COUNT In British English, a **car park** is an area or building where people can leave their cars. The American word is **parking lot**.

carpenter /ˈkɑːpɪntə/ (**carpenters**) N-COUNT A **carpenter** is a person whose job is making and repairing wooden things.

carpet /ˈkɑːpɪt/ (**carpets**) **1** N-COUNT A **carpet** is a thick covering for a floor or staircase, made of wool or a similar material. **2** N-COUNT A **carpet of** something is a layer of it covering the ground. ❑ *...the carpet of leaves in my garden.*

carpeted /ˈkɑːpɪtɪd/ **1** ADJ If a floor or room is **carpeted**, it has a carpet on the floor. ❑ *...the grey-carpeted dining room.* **2** ADJ If the ground is **carpeted with** something, there is a layer of it covering the ground. ❑ *The ground was thickly carpeted with snow.*

carriage /ˈkærɪdʒ/ (**carriages**) **1** N-COUNT In British English, a **carriage** is one of the separate sections of a train that carries passengers. The usual American word is **car**. **2** N-COUNT A **carriage** is an old-fashioned vehicle pulled by horses.

carriageway /ˈkærɪdʒweɪ/ (**carriageways**) N-COUNT A **carriageway** is one of the two sides of a motorway or major road. [BRIT]

carrier /ˈkæriə/ (**carriers**) **1** N-COUNT A **carrier** is a vehicle that is used for moving people or things. ❑ *...a stylish people carrier.* **2** N-COUNT A **carrier** or a **carrier bag** is a paper or plastic bag with handles. [BRIT]
→ see **ship**

carrot /ˈkærət/ (**carrots**) **1** N-VAR **Carrots** are long, thin, orange-coloured vegetables that grow under the ground. **2** N-COUNT Something that you offer to someone in order to persuade them to do something can be referred to as a **carrot**. ❑ *There is a carrot of extra cash if they achieve their targets.*
→ see **vegetable**

carry /ˈkæri/ (**carries, carrying, carried**) **1** V-T If you **carry** something, you take it with you, holding it so that it does not touch the ground. ❑ *He was carrying a briefcase.* ❑ *She carried her son to the car.* **2** V-T To **carry** something means to have it with you wherever you go. ❑ *He always carried a notebook.* **3** V-T To **carry** someone or something means to take them somewhere. ❑ *He carried a message of thanks to the president.* ❑ *The ship can carry seventy passengers.* **4** V-T If someone **is carrying** a disease, they are infected with it and can pass it on to other people. ❑ *They were carrying the virus.* **5** V-T If an action or situation **carries** a particular quality or consequence, it has it. ❑ *The injury carries the risk of paralysis.* ❑ *The charges carry a maximum sentence of 65 years.* **6** V-T If you **carry** an idea or a method further, you use or develop it or apply it in new circumstances. ❑ *It's not such a new idea, but I carried it to extremes.* **7** V-T If a newspaper **carries** a picture or an article, it contains it. **8** V-T If a proposal or motion **is carried** in a debate, a majority of people vote for it. **9** V-I If a sound **carries**, you can hear it a long way away. ❑ *She screamed and the sound carried all over the house.* **10** PHRASE If you **get carried away**, you are so eager or excited about something that you do something hasty or foolish.

▶ **carry on** **1** PHR-VERB If you **carry on** doing something, you continue to do it. ❑ *The assistant carried on talking.* **2** PHR-VERB If you **carry on** an activity, you take part in it. ❑ *They carried on a conversation all morning.*

▶ **carry out** PHR-VERB If you **carry out** a threat, task, or instruction, you do it or act according to it. ❑ *The police carried out the arrests.*

▶ **carry through** PHR-VERB If you **carry** something **through**, you do it, often in spite of difficulties. ❑ *We'll support the government in carrying through these changes.*

Thesaurus	*carry* Also look up:
V.	bear, bring, cart, haul, lug, move, truck **1**

cart /kɑːt/ (**carts, carting, carted**) **1** N-COUNT A **cart** is an old-fashioned wooden vehicle, usually pulled by an animal. **2** V-T If you **cart** things somewhere, you carry or transport them there, often with difficulty. [INFORMAL] ❑ *They carted off the entire contents of the house.*
→ see **golf**

cartel /kɑːˈtel/ (**cartels**) N-COUNT A **cartel** is an association of companies or countries involved in the same industry who act together to control competition and prices.

cartilage /ˈkɑːtɪlɪdʒ/ N-UNCOUNT **Cartilage** is a strong flexible substance which surrounds the joints in your body.
→ see **shark**

carton /ˈkɑːtən/ (**cartons**) **1** N-COUNT A **carton** is a plastic or cardboard container in which food or drink is sold. ❑ *...a carton of milk.* **2** N-COUNT A **carton** is a large strong cardboard box. [AM]
→ see **container**

cartoon /kɑːˈtuːn/ (**cartoons**) **1** N-COUNT A **cartoon** is a humorous drawing in a newspaper or magazine. **2** N-COUNT A **cartoon** is a film in which all the characters and scenes are drawn rather than being real people or objects.
→ see **animation**

cartoonist /kɑːˈtuːnɪst/ (**cartoonists**) N-COUNT A **cartoonist** is a person whose job is to draw cartoons for newspapers and magazines.

cartridge /ˈkɑːtrɪdʒ/ (**cartridges**) **1** N-COUNT

In a gun, a **cartridge** is a tube containing a bullet and an explosive substance. **2** N-COUNT A **cartridge** is a part of a machine that can be easily removed and replaced when it is worn out or empty.

carve /kɑːv/ (**carves, carving, carved**) **1** V-T If you **carve** an object, you cut it out of stone or wood. You **carve** wood or stone in order to make the object. ❑ *One of the prisoners has carved a beautiful wooden chess set.* **2** V-T If you **carve** writing or a design on an object, you cut it into the surface. ❑ *He carved his name on his desk.* **3** V-T If you **carve** meat, you cut slices from it. **4** V-T & PHR-VERB If you **carve** a **career** or a **niche** for yourself, or if you **carve out** a career or niche, you succeed in getting the career or the position that you want by your own efforts. ❑ *She has carved a niche for herself as an actor.*

▶ **carve up** PHR-VERB If someone **carves** something **up**, they divide it into smaller areas or pieces; used showing disapproval. ❑ *European nations decided in 1885 to carve Africa up among themselves.*

carving /ˈkɑːvɪŋ/ (**carvings**) **1** N-COUNT A **carving** is an object or design that has been cut out of stone or wood. **2** N-UNCOUNT **Carving** is the act of carving objects or designs.

cascade /kæsˈkeɪd/ (**cascades, cascading, cascaded**) **1** N-COUNT A **cascade of** something is a large amount of it. [LITERARY] ❑ *...a cascade of laughter.* **2** V-I When water **cascades**, it pours downwards very fast and in large quantities. ❑ *The freezing water cascaded past her.*

Word Link *cas ≈ box, hold : case, encase, suitcase*

case /keɪs/ (**cases**) **1** N-COUNT A **case** is a particular situation or instance, especially one that you are using as an example of something more general. ❑ *He has a family to support – in his case, nine people.* ❑ *In extreme cases, death can result.* **2** N-COUNT A **case** is a person that a professional such as a doctor is dealing with. ❑ *Social workers were meeting to discuss her case.* **3** N-COUNT A crime, or a trial that takes place after a crime, can be called a **case**. ❑ *The burglary case never came to court.* ❑ *He won a court case against the newspaper.* **4** N-COUNT In an argument, the **case for** or **against** something consists of the facts and reasons used to support or oppose it. ❑ *He listened while I made the case for his inclusion.* **5** N-COUNT A **case** is a container that is designed to hold or protect something. ❑ *He carried a black case for his spectacles.* **6** N-COUNT A **case** is the same as a **suitcase**. **7** PHRASE You say **in any case** when you are adding another reason for something you have said or done. ❑ *The concert was fully booked, and in any case, most of us couldn't afford a ticket.* **8** PHRASE You say **in case** to indicate that you have something or are doing something because a particular thing might happen or might have happened. ❑ *All exits must be kept clear in case of fire.* ❑ *I'm waiting for Mary, in case you're wondering.* ❑ *She carried her pills in her purse, just in case.* **9** PHRASE You say **in that case** or **in which case** to indicate that you are assuming that a previous statement is correct or true. ❑ *You may, of course, disagree, in which case, please let me know.* **10** PHRASE When you say that a job or task **is a case of** doing a particular thing, you mean that the job or task consists of doing that thing. ❑ *Every team has a weakness; it's just a case of finding it.*
→ see **hospital**

case-ˈsensitive ADJ If a word is **case-sensitive**, it must be written in a particular form, for example using all capital letters or all small letters, in order for the computer to recognize it. [COMPUTING]

ˈcase study (**case studies**) N-COUNT A **case study** is a written account that gives detailed information about a person, group, or thing and their development over a period of time. ❑ *...a large case study of malaria in West African children.*

cash /kæʃ/ (**cashes, cashing, cashed**) **1** N-UNCOUNT **Cash** is money, especially money in the form of notes and coins. ❑ *We were desperately short of cash.* ❑ *...two thousand pounds in cash.* **2** V-T If you **cash** a cheque, you exchange it at a bank for the amount of money that it is worth.

▶ **cash in** PHR-VERB If someone **cashes in on** a situation, they use it to gain an advantage for themselves. ❑ *Publishers are eager to cash in on schools' demand for books.*

cashier /kæˈʃɪə/ (**cashiers**) N-COUNT A **cashier** is the person that customers pay money to or get money from in a shop or bank.

cashmere /ˌkæʃˈmɪə, AM ˈkæʒmɪr/ N-UNCOUNT **Cashmere** is a kind of very fine soft wool.

casino /kəˈsiːnəʊ/ (**casinos**) N-COUNT A **casino** is a place where people play gambling games.

casserole /ˈkæsərəʊl/ (**casseroles**) **1** N-VAR A **casserole** is a meal made by cooking food in liquid in an oven. ❑ *...lamb casserole.* **2** N-COUNT A **casserole** or **casserole dish** is a large heavy container with a lid used for cooking casseroles.

Word Link *ette ≈ small : cassette, cigarette, gazette*

cassette /kəˈset/ (**cassettes**) N-COUNT A **cassette** is a small, flat, rectangular, plastic container with magnetic tape inside, which is used for recording and playing back sounds.

cast /kɑːst, kæst/ (**casts, casting, cast**) **1** N-COUNT The **cast** of a play or film is all the people who act in it. In the singular **cast** may be followed by a singular or plural verb. ❑ *Most of the cast was amazed by the play's success.* **2** V-T To **cast** an actor means to choose them to act a particular role. ❑ *He was cast as a college professor.* **3** V-T If you **cast** something somewhere, you throw it there. [LITERARY] ❑ *He cast the stone away.* **4** V-T If you **cast** your eyes or **cast** a look somewhere, you look there. [WRITTEN] ❑ *He cast a look at the two men.* **5** V-T If you **cast** doubt or suspicion on something, you make other people unsure about it. ❑ *New tests have cast doubt on the cause of the explosion.* **6** V-T When you **cast** your vote in an election, you vote. **7** V-T To **cast** an object means to make it by pouring hot liquid metal into a container and leaving it until it becomes hard.
→ see **theatre**

▶ **cast about** or **cast around** PHR-VERB If you **cast about** or **cast around for** something, you try to find it. ❑ *She was casting around for a good excuse not to go to the party.*

▶ **cast aside** PHR-VERB If you **cast** someone or something **aside**, you get rid of them. ❑ *In America we seem to cast aside our elderly people.*

C

▸ **cast off** PHR-VERB If you **cast** something **off**, you get rid of it or no longer use it. [WRITTEN] ❑ *We have cast off an inefficient economic system.*

caste /kɑːst, kæst/ (**castes**) N-VAR A **caste** is one of the social classes into which people in a Hindu society are divided. ❑ *India is divided in many ways: by caste, religion, language, and region.*

castigate /ˈkæstɪgeɪt/ (**castigates, castigating, castigated**) V-T If you **castigate** someone, you scold or criticize them severely. [FORMAL]

ˈcast-iron **1** ADJ **Cast-iron** objects are made of a special type of iron containing carbon. ❑ *...a cast-iron bath.* **2** ADJ A **cast-iron** excuse, guarantee, or solution is absolutely certain to be effective.
→ see **pan**

castle /ˈkɑːsəl, ˈkæsəl/ (**castles**) N-COUNT A **castle** is a large building with thick high walls, built by important people, such as kings, in former times, for protection during wars and battles.

castrate /kæˈstreɪt, AM ˈkæstreɪt/ (**castrates, castrating, castrated**) V-T To **castrate** a male animal means to remove its testicles. • **castration** (**castrations**) N-VAR ❑ *...the castration of male farm animals.*

casual /ˈkæʒʊəl/ **1** ADJ If you are **casual**, you are relaxed and not very concerned about what is happening. • **casually** ADV ❑ *'No need to hurry,' Ben said casually.* **2** ADJ BEFORE N Something that is **casual** happens by chance or without planning. ❑ *...a casual remark.* **3** ADJ BEFORE N **Casual** clothes are ones that you normally wear at home or on holiday, and not for formal occasions. • **casually** ADV ❑ *They were smartly but casually dressed.* **4** ADJ BEFORE N **Casual** work is done for short periods and is not permanent. ❑ *Restaurants often employ people on a casual basis.*

casualty /ˈkæʒʊəlti/ (**casualties**) **1** N-COUNT A **casualty** is a person who is injured or killed in a war or accident. ❑ *The casualties on our side were high.* **2** N-COUNT A **casualty of** an event or situation is a person or a thing that has suffered badly as a result of it. ❑ *Small companies were early casualties of the recession.* **3** N-UNCOUNT **Casualty** is an informal name for the department of a hospital where people are taken for emergency treatment. [BRIT]

cat /kæt/ (**cats**) **1** N-COUNT A **cat** is a small furry animal with a tail, whiskers, and sharp claws. **2** N-COUNT **Cats** are a group of animals which includes lions, tigers, and domestic cats. **3** PHRASE In a fight or contest, if the stronger person or group **plays cat and mouse with** the other, they choose to defeat their opponent slowly, using skill and deceit, rather than force or violence.

catalogue [AM **catalog**] /ˈkætəlɒg/ (**catalogues, cataloguing, catalogued**) **1** N-COUNT A **catalogue** is a list of things, such as the goods you can buy from a company. **2** V-T To **catalogue** things means to make a list of them. **3** N-COUNT A **catalogue of** similar things, especially bad things, is a number of them happening one after another. ❑ *Mr Taylor tried to explain the catalogue of errors.*
→ see **library**

catalyst /ˈkætəlɪst/ (**catalysts**) **1** N-COUNT You can describe a person or thing as a **catalyst** when they cause a change or event to happen. ❑ *The report acted as a catalyst to bring all of the groups together.* **2** N-COUNT In chemistry, a **catalyst** is a substance that causes a reaction to take place more quickly.

catapult /ˈkætəpʌlt/ (**catapults, catapulting, catapulted**) **1** N-COUNT A **catapult** is a device for shooting small stones. It consists of a Y-shaped stick with a piece of elastic tied between the two top parts. **2** V-T/V-I If someone or something **catapults** through the air, they move or are thrown very suddenly and violently through it. ❑ *His car catapulted across the road.* ❑ *Georgina was catapulted through the windscreen.*

cataract /ˈkætərækt/ (**cataracts**) N-COUNT A **cataract** is a layer that has grown over a person's eye that prevents them from seeing properly.

catastrophe /kəˈtæstrəfi/ (**catastrophes**) N-COUNT A **catastrophe** is an unexpected event that causes great suffering or damage. ❑ *From our point of view, war would be a catastrophe.*

catastrophic /ˌkætəˈstrɒfɪk/ ADJ **Catastrophic** means extremely bad or serious, often causing great suffering or damage. ❑ *Even a small oil spill would be catastrophic.* ❑ *...a catastrophic mistake.*

catch /kætʃ/ (**catches, catching, caught**) **1** V-T If you **catch** a person or animal, you capture them. ❑ *The police are confident of catching the gunman.* ❑ *...an animal caught in a trap.* **2** V-T If you **catch** an object which is moving through the air, you seize it with your hands. ❑ *I jumped up to catch the ball.* **3** V-T If something which is moving **catches** something else, it hits it. ❑ *One of the horse's hooves caught Sally's head.* **4** V-I If something **catches on** or **in** an object, or if it **is caught on** or **in** it, it becomes trapped by it. ❑ *Her heel caught on a rusty nail.* **5** V-T If you **catch** a bus, train, or plane, you get on it to travel somewhere. **6** V-T If you **catch** someone doing something wrong, you discover them doing it. ❑ *He caught a youth breaking into a car.* ❑ *They caught him with $30,000 in a briefcase.* **7** V-T PASSIVE If you **are caught** in a storm or other unpleasant situation, it happens when you cannot avoid its effects. ❑ *Visitors to the area were caught in the explosion.* **8** V-T If something **catches** your attention or your eye, you notice it or become interested in it. **9** V-T If you cannot **catch** what someone says, you cannot manage to hear it. ❑ *Sorry, I didn't catch your name.* **10** V-T If you **catch** a cold or a disease, you become ill with it. **11** V-T If something **catches** the **light**, or if the light **catches** it, it reflects the light and looks bright or shiny. **12** N-COUNT A **catch** on a window or door is a device that fastens it. **13** N-SING A **catch** is a hidden problem or difficulty in a plan or course of action. ❑ *'It's your money. You deserve it.'—'What's the catch?'*

▸ **catch on** **1** PHR-VERB If you **catch on to** something, you understand it, or realize that it is happening. ❑ *I was slow to catch on to what she was trying to tell me.* **2** PHR-VERB If something **catches on**, it becomes popular. ❑ *Photography began to catch on as a respectable activity.*

▸ **catch out** PHR-VERB To **catch** someone **out** means to cause them to make a mistake that reveals that they are lying about something. ❑ *His attempt to catch her out failed.*

▸ **catch up** **1** PHR-VERB If you **catch up with** someone, you reach them by walking faster than them. ❑ *I ran faster to catch up with him.* ❑ *I stopped and waited for her to catch up.* **2** PHR-VERB To **catch up with** someone means to reach the same standard or level that they have reached. ❑ *She'll soon catch up with the other students.* **3** PHR-VERB If you **catch up on** an activity that you have not had much time to do, you spend time doing it. ❑ *I was catching up on a bit of reading.* **4** PHR-VERB If you **are caught up in** something, you are involved in it, usually unwillingly. ❑ *Innocent people were caught up in the fighting.*

▶ **catch up with** **1** PHR-VERB When people **catch up with** someone who has done something wrong, they succeed in finding them. ❑ *The police caught up with Tony eventually.* **2** PHR-VERB If something **catches up with** you, you find yourself in an unpleasant situation which you have been able to avoid but which you are now forced to deal with. ❑ *His criminal past caught up with him.*

Thesaurus	*catch* Also look up:
V.	arrest, capture, grab, seize, snatch, trap; *(ant.)* free, let go, let off, release **1**

catchy /'kætʃi/ (**catchier, catchiest**) ADJ A **catchy** tune, name, or phrase is attractive and easy to remember.

categorical /ˌkætɪ'gɒrɪkəl, AM -'gɔːr-/ ADJ If you are **categorical** about something, you state your views with certainty and firmness. ❑ *...his categorical denial that there is any danger.* • **categorically** ADV ❑ *I categorically refused to leave.*

categorize [BRIT also **categorise**] /'kætɪgəraɪz/ (**categorizes, categorizing, categorized**) V-T If you **categorize** people or things, you say which set they belong to. ❑ *They categorized me as a rock 'n' roll player.* • **categorization** (**categorizations**) N-VAR ❑ *...the labelling and categorization of people in news reports.*

category /'kætɪgri, AM -gɔːri/ (**categories**) N-COUNT If people or things are divided into **categories**, they are divided into groups according to their qualities and characteristics. ❑ *There was one winner in each category.*

Thesaurus	*category* Also look up:
N.	class, classification, grouping, kind, rank, sort, type

cater /'keɪtə/ (**caters, catering, catered**) V-I In British English, to **cater for** people means to provide them with the things they need. In American English, you **cater to** people. ❑ *...clubs that cater for all ages.*

caterer /'keɪtərə/ (**caterers**) N-COUNT A **caterer** is a person or a company that provides food in a particular place or on a special occasion.

catering /'keɪtərɪŋ/ N-UNCOUNT **Catering** is the activity or business of providing food for people. ❑ *...a catering company.*

caterpillar /'kætəpɪlə/ (**caterpillars**) N-COUNT A **caterpillar** is a small worm-like animal that eventually develops into a butterfly or moth.

cathedral /kə'θiːdrəl/ (**cathedrals**) N-COUNT A **cathedral** is a large important church which has a bishop in charge of it.

Catholic /'kæθlɪk/ (**Catholics**) ADJ & N-COUNT The **Catholic** Church is the branch of the Christian Church that accepts the Pope as its leader. A **Catholic** is a member of the Catholic Church. ❑ *...Catholic priests.* ❑ *...a very devout Catholic.* • **Catholicism** /kə'θɒlɪsɪzəm/ N-UNCOUNT ❑ *...her conversion to Catholicism.*

C

cattle /'kætəl/ N-PLURAL **Cattle** are cows and bulls.
→ see **dairy**

catwalk /'kætwɔːk/ (**catwalks**) N-COUNT At a fashion show, **the catwalk** is a narrow platform that models walk along to display clothes.

caught /kɔːt/ **Caught** is the past tense and past participle of **catch**.

cauldron /'kɔːldrən/ (**cauldrons**) N-COUNT A **cauldron** is a very large round metal pot used for cooking over a fire. [LITERARY]

cauliflower /'kɒliflaʊə, AM 'kɔː-/ (**cauliflowers**) N-VAR A **cauliflower** is a large, round, white vegetable surrounded by green leaves.
→ see **vegetable**

cause /kɔːz/ (**causes, causing, caused**) **1** N-COUNT & V-T The **cause of** an event or the thing that **causes** it is the thing that makes it happen. ❑ *The cause of death is not yet known.* ❑ *...the factors that caused prices to rise.* ❑ *They never really caused us problems.* **2** N-UNCOUNT If you **have cause for** a particular feeling or action, you have good reasons for it. ❑ *It seems that you have cause for celebration.* ❑ *Have you ever had cause to be angry at a computer?* **3** N-COUNT A **cause** is an aim which a group of people supports or is fighting for. ❑ *...present-day supporters of the cause.* **4** PHRASE If you say that something is **in a good cause** or **for a good cause**, you mean that it is worth doing because it will help other people. ❑ *I'm happy to help raise money for a good cause.*

Thesaurus	*cause* Also look up:
V.	generate, make, produce, provoke; *(ant.)* deter, prevent, stop **1**

Word Partnership	Use *cause* with:
N.	cause **an accident**, cause **cancer**, cause **for concern**, cause **of death**, cause **problems**, cause **a reaction** **1**
V.	**determine the** cause **1**
	support a cause **3**

Word Link	*caut* ≈ *taking care* : *caution, cautious, precaution*

caution /'kɔːʃən/ (**cautions, cautioning, cautioned**) **1** N-UNCOUNT **Caution** is great care taken in order to avoid danger. ❑ *The animals must be treated with extreme caution.* **2** V-T/V-I & N-UNCOUNT If someone **cautions** you, or if they give you a **caution**, they warn you. ❑ *Tony cautioned against becoming impatient.* ❑ *They caution that the process is long and difficult.* ❑ *One word of caution. It is not wise to become dependent on others.*

cautionary /'kɔːʃənri, AM -neri/ ADJ A **cautionary** story is intended to give a warning. ❑ *...cautionary tales.*

cautious /'kɔːʃəs/ ADJ A **cautious** person acts very carefully in order to avoid danger. ❑ *I am* *a cautious driver.* • **cautiously** ADV ❑ *David moved cautiously forward.*

Thesaurus *cautious* Also look up:	
ADJ.	alert, careful, guarded, watchful; *(ant.)* careless, rash, reckless

C

cavalier /ˌkævəˈlɪə/ ADJ If you describe a person as **cavalier**, you disapprove of them because you think that they do not consider other people's feelings or take account of the seriousness of a situation. ❑ *She has a cavalier attitude to her finances.*

cavalry /ˈkævəlri/ N-SING **The cavalry** used to be the soldiers who rode horses in an army. Nowadays, it is usually the soldiers who use armoured vehicles in an army.

Word Link *cav ≈ hollow : cave, cavity, excavate*

cave /keɪv/ (**caves, caving, caved**) N-COUNT A **cave** is a large hole in the side of a cliff or hill, or under the ground.

▶ **cave in** 1 PHR-VERB When a roof or wall **caves in**, it collapses inwards. 2 PHR-VERB If you **cave in**, you suddenly stop arguing or resisting. ❑ *The Government has caved in to the demands of other western leaders.*

cavern /ˈkævən/ (**caverns**) N-COUNT A **cavern** is a large deep cave.

cavernous /ˈkævənəs/ ADJ A **cavernous** room or building is very large inside.

caviar also **caviare** /ˈkæviɑː/ (**caviars**) N-VAR **Caviar** is a food that consists of the salted eggs of a fish called the sturgeon.

cavity /ˈkævɪti/ (**cavities**) N-COUNT A **cavity** is a small space or hole in something solid. ❑ *Decay causes cavities in your teeth.*
→ see **smell, teeth**

cc /ˌsiː ˈsiː/ 1 **cc** is an abbreviation for 'cubic centimetres', used when referring to the volume or capacity of something. ❑ *...1,500 cc sports cars.* 2 **cc** is used in an email or business letter to indicate that a copy is being sent to another person. ❑ *...cc J. Chater, S. Cooper.*

CCTV /ˌsiː siː tiː ˈviː/ N-UNCOUNT **CCTV** is an abbreviation for 'closed-circuit television'. ❑ *...a CCTV camera.* ❑ *The girls were filmed on CCTV.*

CD /ˌsiː ˈdiː/ (**CDs**) N-COUNT A **CD** is a small shiny disc on which music or information is stored. **CD** is an abbreviation for 'compact disc'.
→ see **DVD, laser**

CˈD burner (**CD burners**) N-COUNT A **CD burner** is the same as a **CD writer**.

CˈD player (**CD players**) N-COUNT A **CD player** is a machine on which you can play CDs.

CD-ROM /ˌsiː diː ˈrɒm/ (**CD-ROMs**) N-COUNT A **CD-ROM** is a disc which can be read by a computer, and on which a large amount of data is stored. [COMPUTING]
→ see **computer**

CˈD writer (**CD writers**) N-COUNT A **CD writer** is a piece of computer equipment that you use for copying data from a computer onto a CD.

cease /siːs/ (**ceases, ceasing, ceased**) 1 V-I If something **ceases**, it stops happening. [FORMAL] ❑ *At one o'clock the rain ceased.* 2 V-T To **cease to** do something means to stop doing it. [FORMAL] ❑ *He never ceases to amaze me.* ❑ *A small number of firms have ceased trading.*

Thesaurus *cease* Also look up:	
V.	end, finish, halt, quit, stop; *(ant.)* begin, continue, start 1

ceasefire /ˈsiːsfaɪə/ (**ceasefires**) N-COUNT A **ceasefire** is an arrangement in which countries at war agree to stop fighting for a time.

cedar /ˈsiːdə/ (**cedars**) N-VAR A **cedar** is a kind of evergreen tree. **Cedar** is the wood of this tree.

cede /siːd/ (**cedes, ceding, ceded**) V-T If someone in a position of authority **cedes** land or power to someone else, they let them have it. [FORMAL] ❑ *The General had promised to cede power by January.*

ceiling /ˈsiːlɪŋ/ (**ceilings**) 1 N-COUNT A **ceiling** is the top inside surface of a room. ❑ *...a small air vent in the ceiling.* 2 N-COUNT A **ceiling** is an official upper limit on prices or wages. ❑ *...an agreement to put a ceiling on salaries.*

celebrate /ˈselɪbreɪt/ (**celebrates, celebrating, celebrated**) 1 V-T/V-I If you **celebrate** something, you do something enjoyable because of a special occasion. ❑ *The England football team have been celebrating their victory.* ❑ *I was in a mood to celebrate.* • **celebration** (**celebrations**) N-VAR ❑ *Their supporters had little cause for celebration.* ❑ *...his eightieth birthday celebrations.* 2 V-T When priests **celebrate** Holy Communion or Mass, they officially perform the actions and ceremonies that are involved.

celebrated /ˈselɪbreɪtɪd/ ADJ A **celebrated** person or thing is famous and much admired. ❑ *...his most celebrated film.*

celebrity /sɪˈlebrɪti/ (**celebrities**) N-COUNT A **celebrity** is someone who is famous. ❑ *At the age of 30, Hersey suddenly became a celebrity.*

celery /ˈseləri/ N-UNCOUNT **Celery** is a vegetable with long pale green stalks.

celestial /sɪˈlestiəl/ ADJ **Celestial** is used to describe things connected with heaven or the sky. [LITERARY]
→ see **astronomer**

celibate /ˈselɪbət/ ADJ Someone who is **celibate** does not marry or have sex. [FORMAL] • **celibacy** N-UNCOUNT ❑ *...a monk who took the vow of celibacy.*

cell /sel/ (**cells**) 1 N-COUNT A **cell** is the smallest part of an animal or plant. Animals and plants are made up of millions of cells. 2 N-COUNT A **cell** is a small room in which a prisoner is locked. ❑ *...police cells.*
→ see **cellphone, clone, skin**

cellar /ˈselə/ (**cellars**) N-COUNT A **cellar** is a room underneath a building.

cello /ˈtʃeləʊ/ (**cellos**) N-VAR A **cello** is a musical instrument that looks like a large violin. You hold it upright and play it sitting down. • **cellist** (**cellists**) N-COUNT ❑ *...the world's greatest cellist.*
→ see **orchestra, string**

cellphone /ˈselfəʊn/ (**cellphones**) N-COUNT In American English, a **cellphone** is a telephone that you can carry with you and use to make or receive calls wherever you are. The usual British word is **mobile phone**.
→ see Word Web: **cellphone**

C

Word Web cellphone

The word **"cell"** is not something inside the **cellular phone** itself. It describes the area around the **wireless transmitter** that your phone uses to make a call. The electrical system and **battery** in today's **mobile** phones are tiny. This makes their electronic **signals** weak. They can't travel very far. Therefore today's **cellular** phone systems need a lot of cells close together. When you make a call, your cellular phone connects to the wireless transmitter with the strongest signal. Then it chooses a radio **channel** and connects you to the number you dialed. If you are riding in a car, **stations** in several different cells may handle your call.

cellular /'seljʊlə/ ADJ **Cellular** means relating to the cells of animals or plants. ❑ *...cellular damage.*
→ see **cellphone**

cellulite /'seljʊlaɪt/ N-UNCOUNT **Cellulite** is lumpy fat which people may get under their skin, especially on their thighs.

Celsius /'selsiəs/ 1 ADJ **Celsius** is a scale for measuring temperature, in which water freezes at 0° and boils at 100°. Another word for this is 'centigrade'. ❑ *Night temperatures can drop below 15 degrees Celsius.* 2 → See note at **temperature**.
→ see **thermometer**

cement /sɪ'ment/ (**cements, cementing, cemented**) 1 N-UNCOUNT **Cement** is a grey powder which is mixed with sand and water in order to make concrete. 2 V-T If things **are cemented** together, they are stuck or fastened together. ❑ *A plaque was cemented to the wall.* 3 V-T Something that **cements** a relationship, situation or agreement makes it stronger. ❑ *He has cemented his position as Scotland's highest-paid boss.*

cemetery /'semətri, AM -teri/ (**cemeteries**) N-COUNT A **cemetery** is a place where dead people are buried.

censor /'sensə/ (**censors, censoring, censored**) 1 V-T If someone **censors** a letter or the media, they officially examine it and cut out any parts that they consider unacceptable. ❑ *Television companies tend to censor bad language in feature films.* 2 N-COUNT A **censor** is a person who has been officially appointed to censor things.

Word Link *ship ≈ condition or state : censorship, citizenship, friendship*

censorship /'sensəʃɪp/ N-UNCOUNT When there is **censorship**, letters or the media are censored. ❑ *I am totally against censorship.*

censure /'senʃə/ (**censures, censuring, censured**) V-T & N-UNCOUNT If someone **is censured** or if they attract **censure**, they are criticized strongly. [FORMAL] ❑ *He refuses to censure his son.* ❑ *This policy has attracted international censure.*

census /'sensəs/ (**censuses**) N-COUNT A **census** is an official survey of the population of a country.

cent /sent/ (**cents**) 1 N-COUNT A **cent** is a small unit of money in many countries, for example in the United States and Australia. 2 → see also **per cent**

centenary /sen'ti:nəri, AM -'ten-/ (**centenaries**) N-COUNT A **centenary** is the one hundredth anniversary of an event. [BRIT] ❑ *...the centenary of the French Revolution.*

center /'sentə/ → see **centre**

Word Link *cent ≈ hundred : centigrade, centimetre, percentage*

Centigrade /'sentɪgreɪd/ 1 ADJ **Centigrade** means the same as **Celsius**. ❑ *Daytime temperatures reached forty degrees centigrade.* 2 → See note at **temperature**
→ see **thermometer**

centimetre [AM **centimeter**] /'sentɪmi:tə/ (**centimetres**) N-COUNT A **centimetre** is a unit of length equal to ten millimetres or one-hundredth of a metre.
→ see **measurement**

Word Link *centr ≈ middle : centre, central, decentralized*

central /'sentrəl/ 1 ADJ BEFORE N A **central** group or organization makes all the important decisions for a larger organization or country. ❑ *...the central committee of the Cuban communist party.* ● **centrally** ADV ❑ *...a centrally planned economy.* 2 ADJ Something that is **central** is in the middle of a place or area. ❑ *...central London.* ● **centrally** ADV ❑ *The hotel is centrally placed in the city.* 3 ADJ The **central** person or thing in a particular situation is the most important one. ❑ *...a central part of their culture.*

Word Partnership Use *central* with:

N. central **government** 1
central **location** 2

,central 'heating N-UNCOUNT **Central heating** is a heating system in which water or air is heated and passed round a building through pipes and radiators.

centralize [BRIT also **centralise**] /'sentrəlaɪz/ (**centralizes, centralizing, centralized**) V-T To **centralize** a country or organization means to create a system in which one central authority gives instructions to regional groups. ❑ *The firm wants to centralize its operations.* ● **centralized** ADJ ❑ *...a centralized economy.* ● **centralization** N-UNCOUNT ❑ *...the centralization of political power.*

Word Link *centr ≈ middle : centre, central, decentralized*

centre [AM **center**] /'sentə/ (**centres, centring, centred**) 1 N-COUNT The **centre** of something

C

is the middle of it. ❑ *...the centre of the room.* 2 N-COUNT A **centre** is a place where people have meetings, get help of some kind, or take part in a particular activity. ❑ *...the medical centre.* ❑ *...the National Exhibition Centre.* 3 N-COUNT If an area or town is a **centre** for an industry or activity, that industry or activity is very important there. ❑ *London is a major international insurance centre.* 4 N-COUNT If someone or something is **the centre of** attention or interest, people are giving them a lot of attention. ❑ *I enjoy being the centre of attention.* 5 V-T PASSIVE Someone or something that **is centred** in a particular place is based there. ❑ *The silk industry was centred in Valencia.* 6 V-T/V-I If something **centres on** or **is centred on** a particular thing or person, that thing or person is the main subject of attention. ❑ *The plan centres on academic achievement.* ❑ *All his concerns were centred around himself.* ● **-centred** ❑ *...a child-centred approach to teaching.*
→ see **football**

Word Partnership Use *centre* with:

N. centre **of a circle** 1
adult education centre, **city/town** centre, **research** centre 2
centre **of attention** 4

century /'sentʃəri/ (**centuries**) 1 N-COUNT A **century** is a period of a hundred years that is used when stating a date. For example, the 19th century was the period from 1801 to 1900. 2 N-COUNT A **century** is any period of a hundred years.

ceramic /sɪ'ræmɪk/ (**ceramics**) 1 N-VAR **Ceramic** is clay that has been heated to a very high temperature so that it becomes hard. 2 N-COUNT **Ceramics** are ceramic ornaments or objects. 3 N-UNCOUNT **Ceramics** is the art of making ceramic objects.
→ see **pottery**

cereal /'sɪəriəl/ (**cereals**) 1 N-VAR **Cereal** is a food made from grain, usually mixed with milk and eaten for breakfast. 2 N-COUNT **Cereals** are plants such as wheat or rice that produce grain. ❑ *...cereal crops.*

cerebral /'serɪbrəl/ 1 ADJ **Cerebral** means relating to thought or reasoning rather than to emotions. [FORMAL] ❑ *Their father was a distant, cerebral man.* 2 ADJ BEFORE N **Cerebral** means relating to the brain. [TECHNICAL] ❑ *...a cerebral haemorrhage.*

ceremonial /ˌserɪ'məʊniəl/ ADJ BEFORE N Something that is **ceremonial** is used in a ceremony or relates to a ceremony. ❑ *He represented the nation on ceremonial occasions.*

Word Link *mony ≈ resulting state : ceremony, harmony, testimony*

ceremony /'serɪməni, AM -məʊni/ (**ceremonies**) 1 N-COUNT A **ceremony** is a formal event such as a wedding or a coronation. 2 N-UNCOUNT **Ceremony** consists of the special things that are said and done on very formal occasions. ❑ *Great ceremony surrounded the Pope's visit.*
→ see **graduation**, **wedding**

certain /'sɜːtən/ 1 ADJ If you are **certain of** or **about** something or if it is **certain**, you firmly believe it is true and have no doubt about it. ❑ *She's absolutely certain she's going to win.* ❑ *It wasn't David – I'm certain of that.* ❑ *The scheme is certain to meet opposition.* 2 ADJ You use **certain** to indicate that you are referring to one particular thing or person, although you are not saying exactly which it is. ❑ *There will be certain people who say 'I told you so!'.* ❑ *You owe a certain person a sum of money.* 3 PHRASE If you know something **for certain**, you have no doubt about it. ❑ *She didn't know for certain what time he had left.* 4 PHRASE When you **make certain** that something happens, you take action to ensure that it happens. ❑ *He made certain all the doors were locked.*

Thesaurus *certain* Also look up:

ADJ. definite, known, positive, sure, true, unmistakeable 1

certainly /'sɜːtənli/ 1 ADV You can use **certainly** to emphasize what you are saying. ❑ *The public is certainly getting tired of it.* ❑ *Certainly, pets can help children develop friendship skills.* 2 ADV You use **certainly** when you are agreeing or disagreeing strongly with what someone has said. ❑ *'You try to avoid them, don't you?'—'I certainly do.'* ❑ *'Perhaps it would be better if I left.'—'Certainly not!'*

certainty /'sɜːtənti/ (**certainties**) 1 N-UNCOUNT **Certainty** is the state of having no doubts at all. ❑ *'He'll lose the match,' she said, with absolute certainty.* 2 N-COUNT **Certainties** are things that nobody has any doubts about. ❑ *In politics there are never any certainties.*

Word Link *cert ≈ determined, true : ascertain, certificate, certify*

certificate /sə'tɪfɪkət/ (**certificates**) N-COUNT A **certificate** is an official document which states that particular facts are true, or which you receive when you have successfully completed a course of study or training. ❑ *...birth certificates.* ❑ *...the University of Cambridge First Certificate in English.*
→ see **wedding**

certify /'sɜːtɪfaɪ/ (**certifies, certifying, certified**) 1 V-T If someone in an official position **certifies** something, they officially state that it is true or genuine. ❑ *The president certified that the project would receive at least $650m.* ❑ *The National Election Council certifies the results.* ● **certification** /səˌtɪfɪ'keɪʃən/ (**certifications**) N-VAR ❑ *...written certification of the election results.* 2 V-T If someone **is certified as** a particular kind of worker, they are given a certificate stating that they have successfully completed a course of training in their profession. ❑ *They wanted to get certified as divers.* ● **certification** N-UNCOUNT ❑ *...training leading to the certification of their skill.*

cervix /'sɜːvɪks/

The plural is **cervixes** or **cervices**.

N-COUNT The **cervix** is the entrance to the womb. [TECHNICAL] ● **cervical** /'sɜːvɪkəl, sə'vaɪkəl/ ADJ BEFORE N ❑ *...cervical cancer.*

CFC /ˌsiː ef 'siː/ (**CFCs**) N-COUNT **CFCs** are chemicals that are used in aerosols, refrigerators, and cooling systems, and in the manufacture of various plastics. **CFC** is an abbreviation for 'chlorofluorocarbon'.

CGI /ˌsiːdʒiː'aɪ/ N-UNCOUNT **CGI** is a type of

computer technology that is used to make special effects in cinema and on television. **CGI** is an abbreviation for 'computer-generated imagery'. ❑ *Dramatic use of CGI was seen in the film 'Jurassic Park'.*

chain /tʃeɪn/ (**chains, chaining, chained**) **1** N-COUNT A **chain** consists of metal rings connected together in a line. ❑ *He wore a gold chain around his neck.* **2** V-T If a person or thing **is chained to** something, they are attached to it with a chain. ❑ *The dog was chained to a gate post.* ❑ *She chained her bike to the railings.* **3** N-COUNT A **chain of** things is a group of them arranged in a line. ❑ *...a chain of islands.* **4** N-COUNT A **chain** of shops or hotels is a number of them owned by the same company. ❑ *...a large supermarket chain.* **5** N-COUNT A **chain of** events is a series of them happening one after another.
→ see **food**

chair /tʃeə/ (**chairs, chairing, chaired**) **1** N-COUNT A **chair** is a piece of furniture for one person to sit on, with a back and four legs. **2** N-COUNT At British universities, a **chair** is the post of professor. **3** V-T If you **chair** a meeting, you are the person in charge of it. ❑ *...a meeting chaired by Dr Robert McDonald.* **4** N-COUNT The **chair** of a meeting is the chairperson.

chairman /ˈtʃeəmən/ (**chairmen**) N-COUNT The **chairman** of a meeting or organization is the person in charge of it.

chairperson /ˈtʃeəpɜːsən/ (**chairpersons**) N-COUNT The **chairperson** of a meeting or organization is the person in charge of it.

chairwoman /ˈtʃeəwʊmən/ (**chairwomen**) N-COUNT The **chairwoman** of a meeting or organization is the woman in charge of it.

chalet /ˈʃæleɪ, AM ʃæˈleɪ/ (**chalets**) N-COUNT A **chalet** is a small wooden house, especially in a mountain area or holiday camp.

chalk /tʃɔːk/ (**chalks, chalking, chalked**) **1** N-UNCOUNT **Chalk** is soft white rock. ❑ *...the highest chalk cliffs in Britain.* **2** N-COUNT **Chalk** refers to small pieces of chalk used for writing or drawing. ❑ *...coloured chalks.*
▶ **chalk up** PHR-VERB If you **chalk up** a success, you achieve it. ❑ *The team has chalked up another victory.*

chalkboard /ˈtʃɔːkbɔːd/ (**chalkboards**) N-COUNT In American English, a **chalkboard** is a dark-coloured board that you can write on with chalk. The British word is **blackboard**.

challenge /ˈtʃælɪndʒ/ (**challenges, challenging, challenged**) **1** N-VAR A **challenge** is something new and difficult which requires great effort and determination. ❑ *The new government's first challenge is the economy.* **2** PHRASE If you **rise to the challenge**, you successfully act in response to a difficult situation. ❑ *They rose to the challenge of entertaining 80 schoolchildren.* **3** V-T & N-COUNT If you **challenge** someone or if you present them with a **challenge**, you invite them to fight or compete with you. ❑ *He left a note at the scene of the crime, challenging the police to catch him.* ❑ *These groups pose a serious challenge to the President.* **4** V-T & N-VAR To **challenge** ideas or people means to question their truth, value, or authority. A **challenge** is an act of challenging someone or something. ❑ *Rose challenged him to explain his opinion.* ❑ *The details are open to challenge.* ❑ *...a direct challenge to the authority of the government.* **5** ADJ If you say that someone is **challenged** in a particular way, you mean that they have a disability in that area. **Challenged** is often used for humorous effect, but is only used after an adverb for this meaning. ❑ *She married an intellectually-challenged footballer.*

Word Partnership Use *challenge* with:

V.	**accept a** challenge, **present a** challenge **1** **dare to** challenge **3**
ADJ.	**biggest** challenge, **new** challenge **1** **legal** challenge **3**

challenger /ˈtʃælɪndʒə/ (**challengers**) N-COUNT A **challenger** is someone who competes for a position or title. ❑ *...a challenger for the 1995 Americas Cup.*

challenging /ˈtʃælɪndʒɪŋ/ **1** ADJ A **challenging** job or activity requires great effort and determination. ❑ *I've always worked in a difficult, challenging profession.* **2** ADJ **Challenging** behaviour seems to be inviting people to argue or compete. ❑ *Mona gave him a challenging look.*

chamber /ˈtʃeɪmbə/ (**chambers**) **1** N-COUNT A **chamber** is a large room that is used for formal meetings, or that is designed and equipped for a particular purpose. ❑ *...the Council chamber.* ❑ *...a burial chamber.* **2** N-COUNT You can refer to a country's parliament or to one section of it as a **chamber**.

ˌchamber of ˈcommerce (**chambers of commerce**) N-COUNT A **chamber of commerce** is a group of business people who work together to improve business and industry in their area.

champ /tʃæmp/ (**champs**) N-COUNT A **champ** is the same as a **champion**. [INFORMAL]

champagne /ʃæmˈpeɪn/ N-UNCOUNT **Champagne** is an expensive French sparkling white wine. It is often drunk to celebrate something.

champion /ˈtʃæmpiən/ (**champions, championing, championed**) **1** N-COUNT A **champion** is someone who has won the first prize in a competition. ❑ *...a former Olympic champion.* ❑ *...champion boxer Lennox Lewis.* **2** N-COUNT & V-T If you are a **champion of** a person, a cause or a principle, or if you **champion** them, you support or defend them. ❑ *He was a champion of social reform.* ❑ *She passionately championed the poor.*

championship /ˈtʃæmpiənʃɪp/ (**championships**) **1** N-COUNT A **championship** is a competition to find the best player or team in a particular sport. ❑ *...the world chess championship.* **2** N-SING **The championship** refers to the title or status of being a sports champion. ❑ *He went on to win the championship.*

chance /tʃɑːns, tʃæns/ (**chances**) **1** N-VAR If there is a **chance of** something happening, it is possible that it will happen. ❑ *His chances of winning are slim.* ❑ *There seems little chance of the situation improving.* **2** N-SING If you have a **chance to** do something, you have the opportunity to do it. ❑ *Flanagan is angry that he was not given a chance to reply to the charges.* ❑ *I felt I had to give him a chance.* **3** N-UNCOUNT & ADJ BEFORE N Something that

C

C

happens **by chance** was not planned. ❑ *He was found by chance on Tuesday by a relative.* ❑ *...a chance meeting.* 4 PHRASE If you say that someone **stands a chance of** achieving something, you mean that they are likely to achieve it. If you say that they do not **stand a chance**, you mean that they cannot possibly achieve it. 5 PHRASE When you **take a chance**, you try to do something although there is a large risk of danger or failure. ❑ *You take a chance on the weather if you holiday in the UK.*

Word Partnership Use *chance* with:

N.	chance **of success**, chance **of survival**, chance **of winning** 1
	chance **encounter**, chance **meeting** 3
ADJ.	**fair** chance, **good** chance, **slight** chance 1 2
V.	**give *someone/something* a** chance, **have a** chance, **miss a** chance 1 2
	get a chance 2

chancellor /ˈtʃɑːnslə, ˈtʃæns-/ (**chancellors**) 1 N-TITLE In several European countries, **the Chancellor** is the head of government. ❑ *...Chancellor Schröder of Germany.* 2 N-COUNT The heads of British universities and some American universities are called **Chancellors**.

ˌChancellor of the Exˈchequer (**Chancellors of the Exchequer**) N-COUNT The **Chancellor of the Exchequer** or the **Chancellor** is the minister in the British government who makes decisions about finance and taxes.

chandelier /ʃændəˈlɪə/ (**chandeliers**) N-COUNT A **chandelier** is an ornamental frame hanging from a ceiling, which holds light bulbs or candles.

change /tʃeɪndʒ/ (**changes, changing, changed**) 1 N-VAR If there is a **change in** something, it becomes different. ❑ *...a change in US policy.* ❑ *What they need is a change of attitude.* ❑ *Political change is on its way.* 2 V-T/V-I When something **changes** or when you **change** it, it becomes different. ❑ *She has now changed into a happy, self-confident woman.* ❑ *They should change the law.* 3 PHRASE If you say that something **is a change** or **makes a change**, you mean that it is enjoyable because it is different from what you are used to. ❑ *A dinner party on a Spanish theme would make a delicious change.* 4 PHRASE If you say that something is happening **for a change**, you mean that you are glad that it is happening because usually it does not. ❑ *Now let me ask you a question, for a change.* 5 V-T & N-COUNT To **change** something means to replace it with something new or different. A **change of** something is an act of replacing something. ❑ *He can't even change a light bulb.* ❑ *A change of leadership alone will not be enough.* 6 V-T/V-I When you **change** your clothes, you take them off and put on different ones. ❑ *She showered and changed.* ❑ *I changed into a tracksuit.* ❑ *I've got to get changed first.* 7 → See note at **wear** 8 V-T When you **change** a baby or **change** its nappy, you take off its dirty nappy and put on a clean one. 9 V-T/V-I When you **change** or **change** buses or trains, you get off one and get on to another to continue your journey. ❑ *Depart Manchester at 10.25; change at Crewe.* 10 V-T When you **change** a bed or **change** the sheets, you take off the dirty sheets and put on clean ones. 11 N-UNCOUNT Your **change** is the money that you receive when you pay for something with more money than it costs. 12 N-UNCOUNT **Change** is coins, rather than notes. ▶ **change over** PHR-VERB If you **change over from** one thing **to** another, you stop doing one thing and start doing the other. ❑ *The mistake occurred when we were changing over to new computer systems.*

Thesaurus *change* Also look up:

N.	adjustment, alteration 1
V.	adapt, modify, transform, vary 2

Word Partnership Use *change* with:

V.	**adapt to** change, **resist** change 1
	make a change 1 2
N.	**policy** change 1
	change **direction** 2
	change **of pace** 3
	change **of address**, change **color**, change **the subject** 5
	change **clothes** 6
ADJ.	**gradual** change, **social** change, **sudden** change 1
	loose change, **spare** change 10

channel /ˈtʃænəl/ (**channels, channelling, channelled** or [AM] **channeling, channeled**) 1 N-COUNT A **channel** is a wavelength on which television programmes are broadcast. ❑ *...movie channels.* 2 N-COUNT If something has been done through particular **channels**, a particular group of people have arranged for it to be done. ❑ *What if you can't get a ticket through official channels?* 3 V-T If you **channel** money into something, you arrange for it to be used for that purpose. ❑ *A system was set up to channel funds to poor countries.* 4 V-T If you **channel** your energies into something, you concentrate on that one thing, rather than a range of things. ❑ *He channels his energies into campaigning against racism.* 5 N-COUNT A **channel** is a passage along which water flows. ❑ *...a drainage channel.* 6 N-PROPER **The Channel** or **the English Channel** is the narrow area of water between England and France. → see **cellphone**

chant /tʃɑːnt, tʃænt/ (**chants, chanting, chanted**) 1 N-COUNT A **chant** is a word or group of words that is repeated over and over again. ❑ *The crowd shouted down both presidents with chants of 'No more lies.'* 2 N-COUNT A **chant** is a religious song or prayer that is sung on only a few notes. ❑ *...a Gregorian chant.* 3 V-T/V-I If you **chant** or **chant** something, you repeat the same words over and over again. ❑ *They chanted his name throughout the match.* ● **chanting** N-UNCOUNT ❑ *A lot of the chanting was in support of the deputy Prime Minister.*

chaos /ˈkeɪɒs/ N-UNCOUNT **Chaos** is a state of complete disorder and confusion. ❑ *The meeting ended in chaos.*

Word Partnership Use *chaos* with:

V.	**bring** chaos, **cause** chaos
N.	chaos **and confusion**
ADJ.	**complete** chaos, **total** chaos

Word Link *otic ≈ affecting, causing : chaotic, erotic, neurotic*

chaotic /keɪˈɒtɪk/ ADJ If a situation is **chaotic**, it is in a state of disorder and confusion.

chap /tʃæp/ (**chaps**) N-COUNT A **chap** is a man or boy. [BRIT, INFORMAL]

chapel /ˈtʃæpəl/ (**chapels**) 1 N-COUNT A **chapel** is a part of a church which has its own altar and which is used for private prayer. 2 N-COUNT A **chapel** is a small church in a school, hospital, or prison.

chaplain /ˈtʃæplɪn/ (**chaplains**) N-COUNT A **chaplain** is a member of the Christian clergy who does religious work in places such as hospitals, schools, or prisons.

chapped /tʃæpt/ ADJ If your skin is **chapped**, it is dry, cracked, and sore.

chapter /ˈtʃæptə/ (**chapters**) 1 N-COUNT A **chapter** is one of the parts that a book is divided into. ❑ *Turn to Chapter 1.* 2 N-COUNT You can refer to a part of your life or a period in history as a **chapter**. [WRITTEN] ❑ *This had been a difficult chapter in the country's recent history.* 3 N-COUNT A **chapter** is a branch of a society, club, or union.

character /ˈkærɪktə/ (**characters**) 1 N-COUNT The **character** of a person or place consists of all the qualities they have that make them distinct. ❑ *There is an unpleasant side to his character.* ❑ *...the spectacular beauty and character of the region.* 2 PHRASE If someone behaves **in character**, they behave in the way you expect them to. If they behave **out of character**, they do not behave as you expect. 3 N-VAR Someone's **character** is their reputation. ❑ *...her opponent's attack on her character.* ❑ *...his previous good character.* 4 N-COUNT The **characters** in a film, book, or play are the people in it. 5 N-COUNT You can refer to a person as a **character**, especially when describing their qualities. ❑ *He's a very strange character.* 6 N-COUNT A **character** is a letter, number, or other symbol that is written or printed.
→ see **printing**

Word Partnership Use *character* with:

N.	character **flaw**, character **trait** 1
	character **in a book/film**, **cartoon** character, character **development** 4
ADJ.	**moral** character 1 3
	fictional character, **main** character, **minor** character 4

characteristic /ˌkærɪktəˈrɪstɪk/ (**characteristics**) 1 N-COUNT A **characteristic** is a quality or feature that is typical of someone or something. ❑ *These new drugs share the same basic characteristics.* 2 ADJ If something is **characteristic of** a person, thing, or place, it is typical of them. ❑ *Refusal to admit defeat was characteristic of Davis.* ● **characteristically** ADV ❑ *He replied in characteristically confident style.*

characterize [BRIT also **characterise**] /ˈkærɪktəraɪz/ (**characterizes, characterizing, characterized**) 1 V-T If something **is characterized** by a particular feature or quality, that feature or quality is very evident in it. [FORMAL] ❑ *...the greed that characterized the 1980s.* 2 V-T If you **characterize** someone or something **as** a particular thing, you describe them as that thing. [FORMAL] ❑ *Both companies have characterized the relationship as 'friendly'.* ● **characterization** (**characterizations**) N-VAR ❑ *...his characterisation of other designers as 'thieves'.*

C

charade /ʃəˈrɑːd, AM -ˈreɪd/ (**charades**) N-COUNT A **charade** is a pretence which is so obvious that nobody is deceived.

charcoal /ˈtʃɑːkəʊl/ N-UNCOUNT **Charcoal** is a black substance used as a fuel and for drawing, obtained by burning wood without much air.
→ see **blog**, **firework**

charge /tʃɑːdʒ/ (**charges, charging, charged**) 1 V-T If you **charge** someone an amount of money, you ask them to pay that amount for something. ❑ *Local nurseries charge £100 a week.* ❑ *He charged us a fee of seven hundred pounds.* 2 N-COUNT A **charge** is an amount of money that you have to pay for a service. ❑ *We can arrange this for a small charge.* 3 PHRASE If something is **free of charge**, it does not cost anything. 4 N-COUNT A **charge** is a formal accusation that someone has committed a crime. ❑ *He faces criminal charges.* 5 V-T When the police **charge** someone, they formally accuse them of having done something illegal. ❑ *Police have charged Mr Smith with murder.* 6 N-UNCOUNT If you have **charge of** or are **in charge of** something or someone, you have responsibility for them. ❑ *The coach will take charge of Lazio after the World Cup finals.* ❑ *You will be in charge of the smaller children.* 7 V-I If you **charge** towards someone or something, you move quickly and aggressively towards them. ❑ *He charged into my office, shouting.* 8 V-T To **charge** a battery means to pass an electrical current through it to make it more powerful or to make it last longer.
→ see **lightning**, **magnet**, **trial**

Word Partnership Use *charge* with:

N.	charge **a fee** 1
	charge **a battery** 8
V.	**deny** a charge 4
	lead a charge 7
ADJ.	**criminal** charge, **guilty of a** charge 4
	electrical charge 8

charisma /kəˈrɪzmə/ N-UNCOUNT If someone has **charisma**, they can attract, influence, and inspire people by their personal qualities. ● **charismatic** /ˌkærɪzˈmætɪk/ ADJ ❑ *...a charismatic politician.*

charitable /ˈtʃærɪtəbəl/ 1 ADJ Someone who is **charitable** is kind and tolerant. 2 ADJ BEFORE N A **charitable** organization or activity helps and supports people who are ill, disabled, or poor.

charity /ˈtʃærɪti/ (**charities**) 1 N-COUNT A **charity** is an organization which raises money to help people who are ill, disabled, or poor. 2 N-UNCOUNT People who live on **charity** live on money or goods which are given to them because they are poor. ❑ *She wouldn't accept charity.* 3 N-UNCOUNT **Charity** is kindness and tolerance towards other people. ❑ *...acts of charity.*

C

Picture Dictionary chart

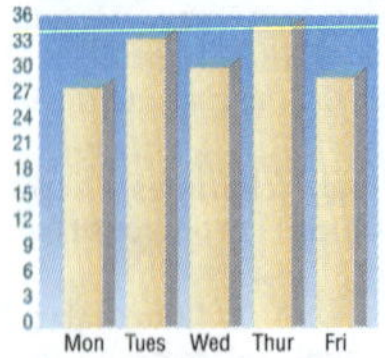

bar graph

35 students in class

Monday	28	30	29	34
Tuesday	30	35	29	28
Wednesday	29	31	29	33
Thursday	28	34	33	29
Friday	30	33	35	31
	1	2	3	4

chart

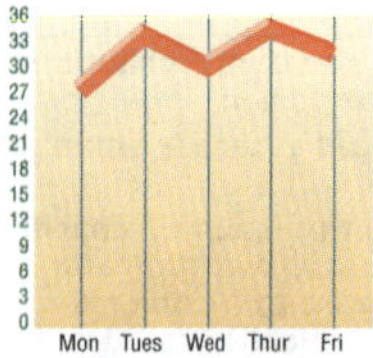

line graph

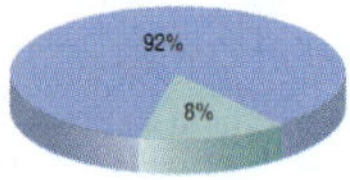

pie chart

Word Partnership Use *charity* with:

ADJ. **local** charity, **private** charity 1
N. charity **organization** 1
donation to charity, charity **event**, **money for** charity, charity **work** 2
V. **collect for** charity, **donate to** charity, **give to** charity 2

charm /tʃɑːm/ (**charms, charming, charmed**) 1 N-VAR **Charm** is the quality of being attractive and pleasant. ❑ *This classic Disney film has lost none of its original charm.* ❑ *He finds it hard to resist any woman's charms.* 2 V-T If you **charm** someone, you please them by using your charm. ❑ *He charmed all of us.* 3 N-COUNT A **charm** is an action, saying, or object that is believed to have magic powers. ❑ *They gave me a ring as a good luck charm.*
→ see **jewellery**

charming /ˈtʃɑːmɪŋ/ ADJ If someone or something is **charming**, they are very pleasant and attractive. ❑ *What a charming man!* ❑ *...a charming little village.* ● **charmingly** ADV ❑ *Moira smiled charmingly.*

charred /tʃɑːd/ ADJ Something that is **charred** is black as a result of being badly burnt. ❑ *...charred sausages.*

chart /tʃɑːt/ (**charts, charting, charted**) 1 N-COUNT A **chart** is a diagram or graph which displays information. ❑ *...a wall chart showing the parts of the body.* 2 N-COUNT A **chart** is a map of the sea or stars. 3 V-T If you **chart** the development or progress of something, you observe and record it carefully. ❑ *The book charts the history of four generations of his family.* 4 N-PLURAL **The charts** are the official lists that show which pop records have sold the most copies each week.
→ see Picture Dictionary: **chart**

charter /ˈtʃɑːtə/ (**charters, chartering, chartered**) 1 N-COUNT A **charter** is a formal document describing the rights, aims, or principles of an organization. ❑ *...the United Nations Charter.* 2 ADJ BEFORE N A **charter** plane or boat is hired for use by a particular person or group. ❑ *...charter flights to Spain.* 3 V-T If someone **charters** a plane or boat, they hire it for their own use. ❑ *He chartered a jet to fly his injured wife home.*

chartered /ˈtʃɑːtəd/ ADJ BEFORE N **Chartered** is used to show that someone such as an accountant or surveyor has formally qualified in their profession. [BRIT]

chase /tʃeɪs/ (**chases, chasing, chased**) 1 V-T & N-COUNT If you **chase** someone, you run after them or follow them in order to catch them or force them to leave a place. A **chase** is an act of chasing someone. ❑ *She chased the thief for 100 yards.* ❑ *The farmer will probably chase you off his land.* ❑ *He finally gave up the chase.* 2 V-T/V-I If you **are chasing** something you want, such as work or money, you are trying hard to get it. ❑ *14 people are chasing every job.* ❑ *...booksellers chasing after profits.*

chasm /ˈkæzəm/ (**chasms**) 1 N-COUNT A **chasm** is a very deep crack in rock or ice. 2 N-COUNT If there is a **chasm** between two things or between two groups, there is a very large difference between them. ❑ *...the chasm that separates the two cultures.*

chat /tʃæt/ (**chats, chatting, chatted**) V-I & N-COUNT When people **chat**, or when they **have** a **chat**, they talk in an informal and friendly way. ❑ *I was chatting to him the other day.* ❑ *We chatted about old times.* ❑ *I had a chat with John.*
▶ **chat up** PHR-VERB If you **chat** someone **up**, you talk to them in a friendly way because you are sexually attracted to them. [BRIT, INFORMAL] ❑ *He spent most of the evening chatting up one of my friends.*

château also **chateau** /ˈʃætəʊ/ (**châteaux** /ˈʃætəʊz/) N-COUNT A **château** is a large country house in France.

chatline /ˈtʃætlaɪn/ (**chatlines**) N-COUNT People phone in to **chatlines** to have conversations with other people who have also phoned in.

ˈchat room (**chat rooms**) N-COUNT A **chat room** is a site on the Internet where people can exchange messages about a particular subject. [COMPUTING]

ˈchat show (**chat shows**) N-COUNT In British English, a **chat show** is a television or radio show in which an interviewer and his or her guests talk in a friendly informal way about different topics. The usual American expression is **talk show**.

chatter /ˈtʃætə/ (**chatters, chattering, chattered**) 1 V-I & N-COUNT If you **chatter**, you talk quickly and continuously about unimportant things. **Chatter** is this kind of talk. ❑ *...chattering away in different languages.* ❑ *Erica was friendly and chattered about Andrew's children.* ❑ *...idle chatter.* 2 V-I If your teeth **chatter**, they rattle together because you are cold.

Word Link
eur ≈ one who does : amateur, chauffeur, entrepreneur

chauffeur /ˈʃəʊfə, ʃəʊˈfɜː/ (**chauffeurs, chauffeuring, chauffeured**) 1 N-COUNT A **chauffeur** is a person whose job is to drive and look after another person's car. 2 V-T If you **chauffeur**

someone somewhere, you drive them there in a car, often as part of your job. ❑ *She was always chauffeuring him around.*

chauvinism /ˈʃəʊvɪnɪzəm/ **1** N-UNCOUNT If you accuse a man of **chauvinism**, you are criticizing him because he believes that men are naturally better and more important than women. ● **chauvinist** (**chauvinists**) N-COUNT ❑ *He was a male chauvinist who treated his wife very badly.* **2** N-UNCOUNT **Chauvinism** is a strong and unreasonable belief that your own country is better and more important than other people's. ● **chauvinist** ADJ ❑ *...extreme nationalist and chauvinist forces.*

cheap /tʃiːp/ (**cheaper, cheapest**) **1** ADJ **Cheap** goods or services cost less money than usual or than you expected. ❑ *Tickets are still very cheap.* ● **cheaply** ADV ❑ *We can help you to plan your holiday more cheaply.* **2** ADJ BEFORE N **Cheap** goods cost less money than similar products but their quality is poor. ❑ *...some cheap material.* ❑ *...cheap clothes shops.* **3** ADJ BEFORE N **Cheap** remarks are unkind and unnecessary. ❑ *I accused him of making cheap remarks.*

Thesaurus *cheap* Also look up:

ADJ.	budget, economical, reasonable; *(ant.)* costly, expensive **1** second-rate, shoddy **2**

cheat /tʃiːt/ (**cheats, cheating, cheated**) **1** V-I & N-COUNT If someone **cheats**, or if they are a **cheat**, they do not obey a set of rules which they should be obeying, for example in a game or exam. ❑ *Students may be tempted to cheat.* ❑ *His wife knew he was a cheat and a liar.* ● **cheating** N-UNCOUNT ❑ *He was accused of cheating.* **2** V-T If someone **cheats** you **out of** something, they get it from you by behaving dishonestly. ❑ *This was a clear attempt to cheat them out of their prize money.* **3** PHRASE If you **feel cheated**, you feel that you have been let down or treated unfairly. ❑ *They feel cheated when the actual holiday doesn't match their dreams.*

▸ **cheat on** PHR-VERB If someone **cheats on** their husband, wife, or partner, they have a sexual relationship with another person. [INFORMAL]

check /tʃek/ (**checks, checking, checked**) **1** V-T/V-I & N-COUNT If you **check** something, or if you make a **check on** it, you make sure that it is satisfactory, safe, or correct. ❑ *I don't know whether that's true or not. I'd have to check.* ❑ *She hadn't checked whether she had a clean shirt.* ❑ *Stephen checked on the baby several times during the night.* ❑ *...regular checks on his blood pressure.* **2** V-T To **check** something, usually something bad, means to stop it from continuing or spreading. ❑ *It is almost impossible to check the spread of the disease.* **3** PHRASE If something or someone **is held** or **kept in check**, they are prevented from becoming too great or powerful. ❑ *The heat was held in check by a strong breeze.* **4** N-SING In American English, **the check** in a restaurant is a piece of paper on which the price of the meal you have just eaten is written and which you are given before you pay. The British word is **bill**. **5** N-COUNT A pattern of squares, usually of two colours, can be referred to as **checks** or a **check**. ❑ *...check trousers.* **6** → see also **cheque**

▸ **check in** or **check into** **1** PHR-VERB When you **check into** a hotel or clinic, or when you **check in**, you arrive and go through the necessary procedures before staying there. ❑ *He checked in at the hotel and asked to see the manager.* ❑ *The footballer has checked into a clinic to receive the treatment.* **2** PHR-VERB When you **check in** at an airport, you arrive and show your ticket before going on a flight. ● **check-in** (**check-ins**) N-VAR ❑ *Ask at the check-in if families can board early.* ❑ *There were long queues at check-in.*

→ see **hotel**

▸ **check out** **1** PHR-VERB When you **check out of** a hotel, you pay the bill and leave. **2** PHR-VERB If you **check** someone or something **out**, you find out about them. ❑ *The police had to check out the call.* **3** → see also **checkout**

▸ **check up** **1** PHR-VERB If you **check up on** someone or something, you find out information about them. **2** → see also **check-up**

Thesaurus *check* Also look up:

V.	confirm, find out, make sure, verify; *(ant.)* ignore, overlook **1**

Word Partnership Use *check* with:

PREP.	**background** check, **credit** check, **security** check **1**
N.	check **for/that *something***, check **with *someone*** **1**

checked /tʃekt/ ADJ Something that is **checked** has a pattern of small squares, usually of two colours. ❑ *...a checked shirt.*

→ see **pattern**

checkout /ˈtʃekaʊt/ (**checkouts**) N-COUNT In a supermarket, a **checkout** is a counter where you pay for your goods.

checkpoint /ˈtʃekpɔɪnt/ (**checkpoints**) N-COUNT A **checkpoint** is a place where traffic has to stop and be checked.

ˈcheck-up (**check-ups**) N-COUNT A **check-up** is a routine examination by a doctor or dentist.

cheek /tʃiːk/ (**cheeks**) **1** N-COUNT Your **cheeks** are the sides of your face below your eyes. **2** N-SING You say that someone has a **cheek** when you are annoyed at something unacceptable they have done. [INFORMAL] ❑ *I'm amazed they had the cheek to ask.*

→ see **face**, **kiss**

cheekbone /ˈtʃiːkbəʊn/ (**cheekbones**) N-COUNT Your **cheekbones** are the two bones in your face just below your eyes.

cheeky /ˈtʃiːki/ (**cheekier, cheekiest**) ADJ Someone who is **cheeky** is rude to someone they ought to respect, but often in a charming or amusing way. ❑ *He is a very cheeky boy.* ❑ *...a cheeky grin.*

cheer /tʃɪə/ (**cheers, cheering, cheered**) **1** V-I & N-COUNT When people **cheer**, they shout loudly to show approval or encouragement. A **cheer** is the sound made when people do this. ❑ *Swiss fans cheered Jakob Hlasek during yesterday's match.* ❑ *...a loud cheer.* **2** V-T If you **are cheered** by something, it makes you feel happier. ❑ *He has been cheered by the hundreds of letters of support.* **3** CONVENTION People say **'Cheers'** just before they drink an alcoholic drink.

C

▶ **cheer on** PHR-VERB If you **cheer** someone **on**, you shout loudly in order to encourage them. ❑ *500,000 spectators cheered on the runners.*

▶ **cheer up** PHR-VERB When you **cheer up**, you stop feeling depressed and become more cheerful. ❑ *I wrote that song just to cheer myself up.* ❑ *Cheer up! Better times may be ahead.*

cheerful /'tʃɪəfʊl/ **1** ADJ A **cheerful** person is happy. ❑ *They are both very cheerful in spite of their colds.* ● **cheerfully** ADV ❑ *'We've come with good news,' Pat said cheerfully.* ● **cheerfulness** N-UNCOUNT ❑ *...his unfailing cheerfulness.* **2** ADJ **Cheerful** things are pleasant and make you feel happy. ❑ *The nursery is bright and cheerful.*

cheery /'tʃɪəri/ ADJ **Cheery** means cheerful and happy. ● **cheerily** ADV ❑ *'Come on in,' she said cheerily.*

cheese /tʃi:z/ (**cheeses**) N-VAR **Cheese** is a solid food made from milk.

chef /ʃef/ (**chefs**) N-COUNT A **chef** is a cook in a restaurant or hotel.

Word Link *chem ≈ chemical : chemical, chemist, chemistry*

chemical /'kemɪkəl/ (**chemicals**) **1** ADJ BEFORE N **Chemical** means involving or resulting from a reaction between two or more substances, or relating to the substances that something consists of. ❑ *...chemical reactions.* ❑ *...the chemical composition of the blood.* ● **chemically** ADV ❑ *...chemically treated foods.* **2** N-COUNT **Chemicals** are substances that are used in or made by a chemical process.
→ see **farm, firework, war**

chemist /'kemɪst/ (**chemists**) **1** N-COUNT In Britain, a **chemist** or a **chemist's** is a shop where medicines are sold or given out. You can also refer to the specially qualified person who prepares and sells the medicines in this shop as a **chemist**. **2** N-COUNT A **chemist** is a person who studies chemistry.

Usage

In British English, the usual way of referring to a shop where medicines are sold or given out is **chemist** or **chemist's**. ❑ *She went into a chemist's and bought some aspirin.* **Pharmacy** is also used, but is not as common. In American English, the word **drugstore** is used, but this usually refers to a shop where you can buy drinks, snacks, and other small items, as well as medicines. ❑ *At the drugstore I bought a Coke and the local papers.*

chemistry /'kemɪstri/ N-UNCOUNT **Chemistry** is the scientific study of the characteristics and composition of substances.

chemo /'ki:məʊ/ N-UNCOUNT **Chemo** is the same as **chemotherapy**. [INFORMAL] ❑ *The first time I had chemo I was quite scared.*

chemotherapy /ˌki:məʊ'θɛrəpi/ N-UNCOUNT **Chemotherapy** is the treatment of disease using chemicals. It is often used in treating cancer.
→ see **cancer**

cheque [AM **check**] /tʃek/ (**cheques**) N-COUNT A **cheque** is a printed form on which you write an amount of money and say who it is to be paid to. Your bank then pays the money to that person from your account. ❑ *He wrote them a cheque for £10,000.* ❑ *I'd like to pay by cheque.*

cherish /'tʃerɪʃ/ (**cherishes, cherishing, cherished**) **1** V-T If you **cherish** something such as a hope or a pleasant memory, you keep it in your mind for a long period of time. ❑ *We will cherish the memory of our visit to Ohio.* ● **cherished** ADJ ❑ *...the cherished dream of a world without wars.* **2** V-T If you **cherish** someone or something, you take good care of them because you love them. ● **cherished** ADJ BEFORE N ❑ *...his most cherished possession.* **3** V-T If you **cherish** a right or a privilege, you regard it as important and try hard to keep it. ❑ *They cherish their independence.* ● **cherished** ADJ BEFORE N ❑ *...some deeply cherished beliefs.*

cherry /'tʃeri/ (**cherries**) **1** N-COUNT **Cherries** are small, round fruit with red or black skins. **2** N-COUNT A **cherry** or a **cherry tree** is a tree that cherries grow on.

chess /tʃes/ N-UNCOUNT **Chess** is a game for two people played on a board with 64 black and white squares. Each player has 16 pieces including a King. The aim is to trap your opponent's King.
→ see Word Web: **chess**

chest /tʃest/ (**chests**) **1** N-COUNT Your **chest** is the top part of the front of your body. ❑ *He was shot in the chest.* ❑ *...mild chest pain.* **2** N-COUNT A **chest** is a large heavy box, used for storing things.
→ see **body**

chestnut /'tʃesnʌt/ (**chestnuts**) **1** N-COUNT A **chestnut** or **chestnut tree** is a tall tree with broad leaves. **2** N-COUNT The nuts that grow on chestnut trees are called **chestnuts**. **3** ADJ Something that is **chestnut** is dark reddish-brown. ❑ *...a woman with chestnut hair.*

chew /tʃu:/ (**chews, chewing, chewed**) V-T/V-I When you **chew** food, you break it up with your teeth and make it easier to swallow. ❑ *You should chew each mouthful fifteen times before you swallow.* ❑ *Polly took a bite of the apple, chewed and swallowed.*

chic /ʃi:k/ ADJ Something or someone that is **chic** is fashionable and sophisticated. ❑ *...chic bars and restaurants.*

chick

chick /tʃɪk/ (**chicks**) N-COUNT A **chick** is a baby bird.

chicken /'tʃɪkɪn/ (**chickens, chickening, chickened**) **1** N-COUNT **Chickens** are birds which are kept on a farm for their eggs and their meat. **2** N-UNCOUNT **Chicken** is the meat of a chicken eaten for food.
→ see **meat**

▶ **chicken out** PHR-VERB If someone **chickens out of** something, they do not do it because they are afraid. [INFORMAL] ❑ *I chickened out of telling her the bad news.*

chief /tʃi:f/ (**chiefs**) **1** N-COUNT The **chief** of an organization or department is its leader or the person in charge of it. ❑ *...the chief test pilot.* ❑ *...the police chief.* **2** ADJ BEFORE N The **chief** cause, part, or member of something is the most important one. ❑ *What was the chief reason for the company's closure?*

C

Word Web chess

Scholars disagree on the origin of the game of **chess**. Some say it started in China around 570 AD. Others say it was invented later in India. In early versions of the **game**, the **king** was the most powerful **chess piece**. But when the game was brought to Europe in the Middle Ages, a new form appeared. It was called Queen's Chess. Modern chess is based on this game. The king is the most important piece, but the **queen** is the most powerful. Chess **players** use **rooks**, **bishops**, **knights**, and **pawns** to protect their king and to put their **opponent** in **checkmate**.

Thesaurus *chief* Also look up:

N. boss, director, head, leader 1
ADJ. key, main, major; *(ant.)* minor, unimportant 2

chiefly /'tʃi:fli/ ADV You use **chiefly** to indicate that a particular reason, emotion, method, or feature is the main or most important one. ❑ *The band is chiefly remembered for one song.* ❑ *He painted chiefly portraits.*

chiffon /'ʃɪfɒn, AM ʃɪ'fɑ:n/ N-UNCOUNT **Chiffon** is a kind of very thin silk or nylon cloth.

child /tʃaɪld/ (**children**) 1 N-COUNT A **child** is a human being who is not yet an adult. ❑ *...when I was a child.* ❑ *The show is suitable for children aged six upwards.* 2 N-PLURAL Someone's **children** are their sons and daughters. ❑ *His children have left home.*
→ see Word Web: **child**
→ see **age**

Word Partnership Use *child* with:

V. **adopt a** child, **have a** child, **raise a** child 1
N. child **abuse**, child **care** 1
ADJ. **difficult** child, **happy** child, **small/young** child, **unborn** child 1

childbirth /'tʃaɪldbɜ:θ/ N-UNCOUNT **Childbirth** is the act of giving birth to a child. ❑ *She died in childbirth.*

Word Link ***hood** ≈ state, condition : adult**hood**, child**hood**, man**hood***

childhood /'tʃaɪldhʊd/ (**childhoods**) N-VAR A person's **childhood** is the time when they are a child. ❑ *She had a happy childhood.* ❑ *...a story heard in childhood.*
→ see **child**

childish /'tʃaɪldɪʃ/ 1 ADJ **Childish** means relating to or typical of a child. ❑ *...childish enthusiasm.* 2 ADJ If you describe someone, especially an adult, as **childish**, you mean their behaviour is silly and more like that of a child than an adult. ❑ *...very childish behaviour.*
● **childishly** ADV ❑ *Mark could be childishly silly at times.*

childless /'tʃaɪldləs/ ADJ Someone who is **childless** has no children.

childlike /'tʃaɪldlaɪk/ ADJ You describe someone as **childlike** when they seem like a child in their appearance or behaviour.

children /'tʃɪldrən/ **Children** is the plural of **child**.

chili /'tʃɪli/ → see **chilli**

chill /tʃɪl/ (**chills, chilling, chilled**) 1 V-T To **chill** something means to make it cold. ❑ *Chill the tarts for two hours before serving.* ❑ *The wind chilled our wet bodies to the bone.* ❑ *...a glass of chilled fruit juice.* 2 V-T & N-COUNT If something that you see, hear, or feel **chills** you, it frightens you. If something sends a **chill** through you, it gives you a sudden feeling of fear or anxiety. [WRITTEN] ❑ *This film will chill you to the bone.* ❑ *...a chill of fear.* ● **chilling** ADJ ❑ *...a chilling reminder of the destruction.* 3 N-COUNT A **chill** is a mild illness which can give you a slight fever.
→ see **illness**
▶ **chill out** PHR-VERB If you **chill out**, you relax after doing something tiring or stressful. [INFORMAL] ❑ *...music to chill out to.*

Word Web child

In the Middle Ages, only **infants** and **toddlers** enjoyed the freedoms of **childhood**. A **child** of seven or eight helped the family by working. In the countryside, **sons** started working on the family's farm. **Daughters** did important housework. In cities, children became labourers and worked along with adults. Today **parents** treat children with special care. **Babies** play with toys to help them learn. There are educational programs for nursery school aged children. The idea of **adolescence** as a separate stage of life appeared about 100 years ago. Today **teenagers** often have part-time jobs while they go to school.

chilli also **chili** /'tʃɪli/ (**chillies**) N-COUNT **Chillies** are small red or green seed pods with a hot, spicy taste.

chilly /'tʃɪli/ (**chillier, chilliest**) **1** ADJ **Chilly** means uncomfortably cold. ❑ *It was a chilly afternoon.* ❑ *The house felt a bit chilly.* **2** ADJ You say that relations between people are **chilly** or that a person's response is **chilly** when they are not at all friendly or enthusiastic. ❑ *The students received a chilly welcome.*

chime /tʃaɪm/ (**chimes, chiming, chimed**) **1** V-T/V-I When a bell or clock **chimes**, it makes ringing sounds. ❑ *The clock chimed three o'clock.* ❑ *Far away a bell chimed.* **2** N-COUNT A **chime** is a ringing sound made by a bell, especially when it is part of a clock. ❑ *The chimes of midnight struck.*
→ see **percussion**
▸ **chime in** PHR-VERB If someone **chimes in**, they say something just after someone else has spoken. ❑ *'Why?' Pete asked impatiently.—'Yes, why?' Bob chimed in.*

chimney

chimney /'tʃɪmni/ (**chimneys**) N-COUNT A **chimney** is a pipe above a fireplace or furnace through which smoke can go up into the air.

chimpanzee /ˌtʃɪmpæn'ziː/ (**chimpanzees**) N-COUNT A **chimpanzee** is a kind of small African ape.
→ see **primate, zoo**

chin /tʃɪn/ (**chins**) N-COUNT Your **chin** is the part of your face below your mouth and above your neck.

china /'tʃaɪnə/ **1** N-UNCOUNT **China** or **china clay** is a very thin clay used to make cups, plates, and ornaments. **2** N-UNCOUNT Cups, plates, and ornaments made of china are referred to as **china**. ❑ *Judy collects blue and white china.*
→ see **pottery**

chink /tʃɪŋk/ (**chinks, chinking, chinked**) **1** N-COUNT A **chink** is a very narrow opening. ❑ *...a chink in the curtains.* **2** V-I When objects **chink**, they touch each other, making a light ringing sound. ❑ *The ice chinked in his glass.*

chip /tʃɪp/ (**chips, chipping, chipped**) **1** N-COUNT In British English, **chips** are long thin pieces of fried potato eaten hot. The American expression is **French fries**. **2** N-COUNT In American English, **chips** or **potato chips** are very thin slices of potato that have been fried until they are hard and crunchy and that are eaten cold as a snack. The British word is **crisps**. **3** N-COUNT A silicon **chip** is a very small piece of silicon with electronic circuits on it. **4** V-T/V-I If you **chip** something, a small piece is broken off it. ❑ *A singer chipped a tooth on his microphone.* ❑ *The plastic looks as if it would chip easily.* • **chipped** ADJ ❑ *...a chipped tooth.* **5** N-COUNT A **chip** is a small piece of something, especially a piece which has been broken off something. ❑ *...chocolate chips.* ❑ *...wood chips.* **6** PHRASE If you say that someone has **a chip on** their **shoulder**, you mean they behave aggressively, because they believe they have been treated unfairly. [INFORMAL]
▸ **chip in** PHR-VERB When a number of people **chip in**, each person gives some money so that they can pay for something together. [INFORMAL] ❑ *The brothers chip in a certain amount of money each month.*

ˌchip and 'PIN N-UNCOUNT **Chip and PIN** is a method of paying for goods you have bought by using both a bank card and a PIN number. ❑ *...the new chip and PIN cards.*

chisel /'tʃɪzəl/ (**chisels, chiselling, chiselled** or [AM] **chiseling, chiseled**) **1** N-COUNT A **chisel** is a tool that has a long metal blade with a sharp edge at the end. It is used for cutting and shaping wood and stone. **2** V-T If you **chisel** wood or stone, you cut and shape it using a chisel. ❑ *They chisel the stone to size.*

chlamydia /klə'mɪdiə/ N-UNCOUNT **Chlamydia** is a sexually transmitted disease.

chlorine /'klɔːriːn/ N-UNCOUNT **Chlorine** is a gas that is used to disinfect water and to make cleaning products.

chocolate /'tʃɒklɪt, AM 'tʃɔːk-/ (**chocolates**) **1** N-VAR **Chocolate** is a sweet food made from cocoa beans. **2** N-COUNT **Chocolates** are small sweets or nuts covered with a layer of chocolate. **3** N-UNCOUNT **Chocolate** or **hot chocolate** is a hot drink made from a powder containing chocolate.

choice /tʃɔɪs/ (**choices, choicer, choicest**) **1** N-COUNT If there is a **choice of** things, there are several of them and you can choose the one you want. ❑ *It's available in a choice of colours.* ❑ *At lunchtime, there's a choice between sandwiches or a cooked meal.* **2** N-COUNT Your **choice** is the thing or things that you choose. ❑ *Her choice of words made Robert angry.* ❑ *...tickets to see the football team of your choice.* **3** PHRASE If you **have no choice but to** do something, or **have little choice but to** do it, you cannot avoid doing it. ❑ *He had no choice but to accept the decision.* **4** N-COUNT The item **of choice** is the one that most people prefer. ❑ *Diamonds remain the gift of choice.* **5** ADJ BEFORE N **Choice** means of very high quality. [FORMAL] ❑ *...his choicest cuts of meat.*

Word Partnership	Use *choice* with:
N.	choice **of** ***something***, **freedom of** choice **1**
V.	**given a** choice, **have a** choice, **make a** choice **1** **2**
ADJ.	**best/good** choice, **wide** choice **1**

choir /kwaɪə/ (**choirs**) N-COUNT A **choir** is a group of people who sing together.

choke /tʃəʊk/ (**chokes, choking, choked**) **1** V-I If you **choke on** something, it prevents you from breathing properly. ❑ *A small child could choke on the doll's hair.* ❑ *The girl choked to death after breathing in smoke.* ❑ *His rising anger almost choked him.* **2** V-T To **choke** someone means to squeeze their neck until they are dead. **3** V-T If a place **is choked with** things or people, it is full of them and they prevent movement in it. ❑ *The village's roads are choked with traffic.* ❑ *The garden was choked by weeds.* **4** N-COUNT A vehicle's **choke** is a device that reduces the amount of air going into the engine and makes it easier to start.

cholera /'kɒlərə/ N-UNCOUNT **Cholera** is a serious disease that affects your digestive organs.

cholesterol /kə'lestərɒl, AM -rɔːl/ N-UNCOUNT **Cholesterol** is a substance that exists in the fat, tissues, and blood of all animals. Too much cholesterol in a person's blood can cause heart disease.

choose /tʃu:z/ (**chooses, choosing, chose, chosen**) 1 V-T/V-I If you **choose** someone or something from all the people or things that are available, you decide to have that person or thing. ❑ *It would be nice to buy all of these things, but most of us have to choose.* ❑ *We went shopping and I chose a beautiful white wedding dress.* 2 V-T If you **choose to** do something, you do it because you want to or because you feel that it is right. ❑ *The government chose not to inform the public about the risks.*
→ see **answer**

Thesaurus	*choose* Also look up:
v.	decide on, opt for, prefer, settle on; *(ant.)* pass over, refuse, reject 1

chop /tʃɒp/ (**chops, chopping, chopped**) 1 V-T If you **chop** something, you cut it into pieces with a knife or axe. ❑ *Finely chop the onion.* 2 N-COUNT A **chop** is a small piece of meat cut from the ribs of a sheep or pig. ❑ *...lamb chops.*
→ see **cut**

▶ **chop down** PHR-VERB If you **chop down** a tree, you cut through its trunk with an axe so that it falls to the ground.

▶ **chop off** PHR-VERB To **chop off** something such as a part of someone's body means to cut it off. ❑ *They both chopped off their hair.*

▶ **chop up** PHR-VERB If you **chop** something **up**, you chop it into small pieces. ❑ *Chop up three firm tomatoes.*

chopper /'tʃɒpə/ (**choppers**) N-COUNT A **chopper** is a helicopter. [INFORMAL]

choral /'kɔ:rəl/ ADJ **Choral** music is sung by a choir.

chord /kɔ:d/ (**chords**) N-COUNT A **chord** is a number of musical notes played or sung together with a pleasing effect. ❑ *The whole song is based on four chords.*

chore /tʃɔ:/ (**chores**) N-COUNT A **chore** is an unpleasant task. ❑ *Making pasta by hand can be a real chore.* ❑ *...household chores.*

choreograph /'kɒriəgrɑ:f, AM 'kɔ:riəgræf/ (**choreographs, choreographing, choreographed**) V-T When someone **choreographs** a ballet or other dance, they invent the steps and movements and tell the dancers how to perform them. ❑ *...one of the first dance pieces to be choreographed by Morris.* ● **choreographer** /ˌkɒri'ɒgrəfə, AM ˌkɔ:-/ (**choreographers**) N-COUNT ❑ *...dancer and choreographer Rudolph Nureyev.*

choreography /ˌkɒri'ɒgrəfi, AM ˌkɔ:-/ N-UNCOUNT **Choreography** is the inventing of steps and movements for ballets and other dances. ● **choreographic** /ˌkɒriə'græfɪk, AM ˌkɔ:-/ ADJ ❑ *...his choreographic work for The Birmingham Royal Ballet.*

chorus /'kɔ:rəs/ (**choruses, chorusing, chorused**) 1 N-COUNT A **chorus** is a large group of people who sing together. 2 N-COUNT The **chorus** of a song is the part which is repeated after each verse. 3 N-SING When there is a **chorus of** criticism, disapproval, or praise, that attitude is expressed by a lot of people at the same time. ❑ *...the growing chorus of complaint.* 4 V-T When people **chorus** something, they say or sing it together. ❑ *'Hi,' they chorused.*

chose /tʃəʊz/ **Chose** is the past tense of **choose**.

chosen /'tʃəʊzən/ **Chosen** is the past participle of **choose**.

christen /'krɪsən/ (**christens, christening, christened**) 1 V-T When a baby **is christened**, he or she is given Christian names during a christening. ❑ *She was christened Susan.* 2 V-T You say that you **christen** a person, place, or object if you choose a name for them and start calling them by that name. ❑ *He has christened his car Lola.*

christening /'krɪsənɪŋ/ (**christenings**) N-COUNT A **christening** is a ceremony in which a baby is made a member of the Christian church and is given his or her Christian names.

Word Link	***an, ian** ≈ one of, relating to : Christian, European, pedestrian*

Christian /'krɪstʃən/ (**Christians**) N-COUNT & ADJ A **Christian** or a **Christian** person follows the teachings of Jesus Christ. ❑ *...the Christian Church.*

Christianity /ˌkrɪsti'ænɪti/ N-UNCOUNT **Christianity** is a religion based on the teachings of Jesus Christ.

'Christian name (**Christian names**) N-COUNT A person's **Christian name** is the name given to them when they were born or christened.

Christmas /'krɪsməs/ (**Christmases**) N-VAR **Christmas** is the period around the 25th of December when Christians celebrate the birth of Jesus Christ. ❑ *Merry Christmas.* ❑ *It happened two Christmases ago.*

ˌChristmas 'Day N-UNCOUNT **Christmas Day** is the 25th of December.

ˌChristmas 'Eve N-UNCOUNT **Christmas Eve** is the 24th of December.

'Christmas tree (**Christmas trees**) N-COUNT A **Christmas tree** is a real or artificial fir tree, which people put in their houses at Christmas and decorate with lights and balls.

chrome /krəʊm/ N-UNCOUNT **Chrome** is a hard silver-coloured metal, used to coat other metals.

chromium /'krəʊmiəm/ N-UNCOUNT **Chromium** is the same as chrome.

chromosome /'krəʊməsəʊm/ (**chromosomes**) N-COUNT A **chromosome** is a part of a cell in an animal or plant. It contains genes which determine what characteristics the animal or plant will have.

Word Link	***chron** ≈ time : chronic, chronicle, chronological*

chronic /'krɒnɪk/ 1 ADJ A **chronic** illness lasts for a very long time. ❑ *...chronic depression.* ● **chronically** ADV ❑ *Most of them were chronically ill.* 2 ADJ A **chronic** situation is very severe and unpleasant. ❑ *...chronic housing shortages.* ● **chronically** ADV ❑ *...chronically poor service.*

chronicle /'krɒnɪkəl/ (**chronicles, chronicling, chronicled**) 1 V-T If you **chronicle** a series of events, you describe them in the order in which they happened. ❑ *The book chronicles his sudden rise to fame.* 2 N-COUNT A **chronicle** is an account or record of a series of events. ❑ *...a chronicle of Napoleonic times.*
→ see **diary**

C

chronological /ˌkrɒnəˈlɒdʒɪkəl/ ADJ If things are described or shown in **chronological** order, they are described or shown in the order in which they happened. ❑ *The photographs are not arranged in chronological order.* ● **chronologically** ADV ❑ *The exhibition is organized chronologically rather than thematically.*

chrysanthemum /krɪˈzænθɪməm/ (**chrysanthemums**) N-COUNT A **chrysanthemum** is a large garden flower with many long, thin petals.

chubby /ˈtʃʌbi/ **1** ADJ A **chubby** person is rather fat. **2** → See note at **fat**

chuck /tʃʌk/ (**chucks, chucking, chucked**) V-T When you **chuck** something somewhere, you throw it there in a casual way. [INFORMAL] ❑ *He screwed the paper up and chucked it in the bin.*
▶ **chuck away** or **chuck out** PHR-VERB If you **chuck** something **away** or **chuck** it **out**, you throw it away. [INFORMAL]

chuckle /ˈtʃʌkəl/ (**chuckles, chuckling, chuckled**) V-I & N-COUNT When you **chuckle**, you laugh quietly. A quiet laugh is called a **chuckle**. ❑ *He gave a little chuckle.*

chug /tʃʌg/ (**chugs, chugging, chugged**) V-I When a vehicle **chugs** somewhere, it goes there slowly with its engine making short thudding sounds. ❑ *The train chugs down the track.*

chum /tʃʌm/ (**chums**) N-COUNT In British English, your **chums** are your friends. [INFORMAL] ❑ *...his old chum Anthony.*

chunk /tʃʌŋk/ (**chunks**) **1** N-COUNT A **chunk of** something is a thick solid piece of it. ❑ *...chunks of ice.* **2** N-COUNT A **chunk of** something is a large amount or part of it. [INFORMAL] ❑ *...a chunk of farmland near Gatwick Airport.*

chunky /ˈtʃʌŋki/ ADJ A **chunky** person or thing is large and heavy. ❑ *...a plain, chunky girl.* ❑ *...a chunky sweater.*

church /tʃɜːtʃ/ (**churches**) **1** N-VAR A **church** is a building in which Christians worship. ❑ *I didn't see you in church on Sunday.* **2** N-COUNT A **Church** is one of the groups of people within the Christian religion that have their own beliefs, clergy, and forms of worship. ❑ *...the Catholic Church.*

churn /tʃɜːn/ (**churns, churning, churned**) **1** N-COUNT A **churn** is a container used for making butter. **2** V-T & PHR-VERB If something **churns** mud, water, or dust, or **churns** it **up**, it moves it about violently. ❑ *Winds churned the sea to giant waves.* ❑ *...dust churned up by the passing trucks.* **3** V-T/V-I If you say that your stomach **is churning**, you mean that you feel sick. You can also say that something **churns** your stomach. ❑ *My stomach churned as I stood up.*
▶ **churn out** PHR-VERB To **churn** something **out** means to produce large quantities of it very quickly. [INFORMAL] ❑ *He churned out those novels in the 1960s.*
▶ **churn up** → see **churn** (meaning **2**)

chute /ʃuːt/ (**chutes**) **1** N-COUNT A **chute** is a steep narrow slope down which people or things can slide. ❑ *...a water chute.* **2** N-COUNT A **chute** is a parachute. [INFORMAL] ❑ *The chute failed to open.*

chutney /ˈtʃʌtni/ (**chutneys**) N-VAR **Chutney** is a strong-tasting mixture of fruit, vinegar, sugar, and spices.

cider /ˈsaɪdə/ (**ciders**) N-VAR **Cider** is an alcoholic drink made from apples.

cigar /sɪˈgɑː/ (**cigars**) N-COUNT **Cigars** are rolls of dried tobacco leaves which people smoke.

Word Link *ette ≈ small : cassette, cigarette, gazette*

cigarette /ˌsɪgəˈret/ (**cigarettes**) N-COUNT **Cigarettes** are small tubes of paper containing tobacco which people smoke.

cinder /ˈsɪndə/ (**cinders**) N-COUNT **Cinders** are the pieces of blackened material that are left after wood or coal has burned.

cinema /ˈsɪnɪmɑː/ (**cinemas**) **1** N-COUNT In British English, a **cinema** is a place where people go to watch films. The American term is **movie theater** or **movie house**. **2** N-UNCOUNT **Cinema** is the business and art of making films. ❑ *...the greatest director in the history of cinema.* ● **cinematic** /ˌsɪnɪˈmætɪk/ ADJ ❑ *...the cinematic industry.*

cinnamon /ˈsɪnəmən/ N-UNCOUNT **Cinnamon** is a spice used for flavouring sweet food.
→ see **spice**

circa /ˈsɜːkə/ PREP If you write **circa** in front of a year, you mean that the date is approximate. ❑ *...circa 1850.*

Word Link *circ ≈ around : circle, circuit, circulate*

circle /ˈsɜːkəl/ (**circles, circling, circled**) **1** N-COUNT A **circle** is a round shape. Every part of its edge is the same distance from the centre. ❑ *...a red flag with a large white circle in the center.* ❑ *Cut out 4 circles of pastry.* **2** V-T/V-I To **circle** someone or something, or to **circle around** them, means to move around them in a circle. ❑ *The plane circled the field once before landing.* ❑ *Emily kept circling around her mother.* ❑ *A police helicopter circled overhead.* **3** N-COUNT You can refer to a group of people as a

Word Web circle

During the 1970s crop **circles** began to appear in England and the U.S. Something creates these mysterious **rings** in fields of crops such as wheat or corn. Are they messages left by visitors from other worlds? Most people think they are made by humans. The **diameter** of each crop circle ranges from a few inches to a few hundred feet. Sometimes the patterns have **shapes** that are not **circular**, such as **ovals**, **triangles**, and **spirals**. Occasionally the shapes seem to represent something, such as a face or a flower. One pattern even had a written message: *We are not alone.*

circle. ❑ *He has a small circle of friends.* ❑ *This is a well-known fact in financial circles.* 4 N-SING **The circle** in a theatre is an area of seats on the upper floor. 5 → see also **vicious circle**
→ see Word Web: **circle**
→ see **shape**

Word Partnership Use *circle* with:

ADJ.	**big/large/small** circle 1
V.	**draw a** circle, **form a** circle, **make a** circle 1
PREP.	circle **around, inside/outside/within a** circle 1 2

Word Link *circ ≈ around : circle, circuit, circulate*

circuit /'sɜːkɪt/ (**circuits**) 1 N-COUNT An electrical **circuit** is a complete route which an electric current can flow around. 2 → see also **closed-circuit** 3 N-COUNT A **circuit** is a series of places that are visited regularly by a person or group. ❑ *...the Australian comedy circuit.* 4 N-COUNT A racing **circuit** is a track on which cars, motorbikes, or cycles race. [BRIT] 5 N-COUNT A **circuit of** a place or area is a journey all the way round it. [FORMAL] ❑ *She made a slow circuit of the room.*

circular /'sɜːkjʊlə/ (**circulars**) 1 ADJ Something that is **circular** is shaped like a circle. ❑ *...a circular hole twelve feet wide.* ❑ *...a circular motion.* ❑ *...a long, circular route.* 2 N-COUNT A **circular** is a letter or advertisement which is sent to a large number of people at the same time.
→ see **circle**

circulate /'sɜːkjʊleɪt/ (**circulates, circulating, circulated**) 1 V-T/V-I When something **circulates** or **is circulated**, it is passed round or spread among a group of people. ❑ *Copies of the accounts were circulated before the meeting.* ❑ *Rumours began to circulate about his health.* ● **circulation** N-UNCOUNT ❑ *The research involves the circulation of 10,000 questionnaires.* 2 V-I When something **circulates**, it moves easily and freely within a closed place or system. ❑ *Hot air circulates all round the food to cook it evenly.* ● **circulation** N-UNCOUNT ❑ *...free circulation of goods.*

circulation /ˌsɜːkjʊ'leɪʃən/ (**circulations**) 1 N-COUNT The **circulation** of a newspaper or magazine is the number of copies sold each time it is produced. ❑ *The Daily News once had the highest circulation of any daily newspaper in the country.* 2 N-SING Your **circulation** is the movement of blood around your body. ❑ *...cold spots in the fingers caused by poor circulation.* 3 PHRASE If something such as money is **in circulation**, it is being used by the public. ❑ *There are 208 million £5 notes in circulation.* 4 → see also **circulate**

Word Link *circum ≈ around : circumcise, circumference, circumstance*

circumcise /'sɜːkəmsaɪz/ (**circumcises, circumcising, circumcised**) V-T If a boy or man **is circumcised**, the loose skin at the end of his penis is cut off. ● **circumcision** /ˌsɜːkəm'sɪʒən/ N-UNCOUNT ❑ *...the practice of circumcision.*

circumference /sə'kʌmfrəns/ (**circumferences**) N-COUNT The **circumference** of a circle, place, or round object is the distance around its edge. ❑ *The island is 3.5 km in circumference.*
→ see **area**

circumstance /'sɜːkəmstæns/ (**circumstances**) 1 N-COUNT **Circumstances** are the conditions which affect what happens in a particular situation. ❑ *Under certain circumstances, it may be possible to get your money back.* ❑ *I wish we could have met under happier circumstances.* ❑ *They would not increase their offer under any circumstances.* 2 PHRASE You can use **in the circumstances** or **under the circumstances** before or after a statement to indicate that you have considered the conditions affecting the situation before making the statement. ❑ *In the circumstances, he seemed remarkably cheerful.* 3 N-PLURAL Your **circumstances** are the conditions of your life, especially the amount of money that you have. ❑ *We offer help and support for the single mother, whatever her circumstances.*

Word Partnership Use *circumstances* with:

PREP.	**under the** circumstances 1 2
ADJ.	**certain** circumstances, **different/similar** circumstances, **difficult** circumstances, **exceptional** circumstances 1 3

circus /'sɜːkəs/ (**circuses**) N-COUNT A **circus** is a travelling show performed in a large tent, with performers such as clowns and trained animals.

citation /saɪ'teɪʃən/ (**citations**) 1 N-COUNT A **citation** is an official document or speech which praises a person for something brave or special that they have done. 2 N-COUNT A **citation** from a book or piece of writing is a quotation from it. [FORMAL]

cite /saɪt/ (**cites, citing, cited**) V-T If you **cite** something, you quote it or mention it, especially as an example or proof of what you are saying. [FORMAL] ❑ *She cited a favourite poem by George Herbert.* ❑ *In my reply, I cited the time and details of the incident.*

citizen /'sɪtɪzən/ (**citizens**) 1 N-COUNT If someone is a **citizen** of a country, they are legally accepted as belonging to that country. ❑ *...American citizens living in Canada.* 2 N-COUNT The **citizens of** a town are the people who live there. ❑ *...the citizens of Buenos Aires.* 3 → see also **senior citizen**
→ see **citizenship**

Word Link *ship ≈ condition or state : censorship, citizenship, friendship*

citizenship /'sɪtɪzənʃɪp/ N-UNCOUNT If you have **citizenship** of a country, you are legally accepted as belonging to it.
→ see Word Web: **citizenship**

citrus /'sɪtrəs/ ADJ BEFORE N A **citrus fruit** is a sharp-tasting fruit such as an orange, lemon, or grapefruit.

city /'sɪti/ (**cities**) 1 N-COUNT A **city** is a large town. ❑ *...a busy city centre.* 2 N-PROPER **The City** is the part of London where many financial institutions have their main offices. ❑ *The City fears that profits could fall.*
→ see Word Web: **city**

C

Word Web city

For the past 6,000 years people have been moving from the **countryside** to **urban** centres. The world's oldest **capital** is Damascus, Syria. People have lived there for over 2,500 years. Cities are usually economic, commercial, cultural, political, social, and transportation centres. **Tourists** travel to cities for shopping and **sightseeing**. In some big cities, **skyscrapers** contain **apartments**, **businesses**, **restaurants**, **theatres**, and **retail stores**. People never have to leave their building. Sometimes cities become **overpopulated** and **crime rates** soar. Then people move to the **suburbs**. In recent decades this trend has been reversed in some places and **inner cities** are being rebuilt.

Word Link *civ ≈ citizen : civic, civil, civilian*

civic /ˈsɪvɪk/ ADJ BEFORE N **Civic** means having an official status in a town. ❑ *...the businessmen and civic leaders of Manchester.*

civil /ˈsɪvəl/ **1** ADJ You use **civil** to describe things that relate to the people of a country, and their rights and activities, often in contrast with the armed forces. ❑ *...civil war.* ❑ *...the US civil aviation industry.* ❑ *...civil and political rights.* **2** ADJ A **civil** person is polite in a formal way, but not particularly friendly. [FORMAL] ● **civility** /sɪˈvɪlɪti/ (**civilities**) N-VAR ❑ *She treats the press with civility.*

Word Partnership Use *civil* with:

N. civil **court (law)suit/trial**, civil **disobedience**, civil **liberties/rights**, civil **unrest** **1**

civilian /sɪˈvɪliən/ (**civilians**) N-COUNT A **civilian** is anyone who is not a member of the armed forces. ❑ *...the country's civilian population.*
→ see **war**

civilization [BRIT also **civilisation**] /ˌsɪvɪlaɪˈzeɪʃən/ (**civilizations**) **1** N-VAR A **civilization** is a human society with its own social organization and culture. ❑ *...the ancient civilizations of Central and Latin America.* **2** N-UNCOUNT **Civilization** is the state of having an advanced level of social organization and a comfortable way of life. ❑ *...our advanced state of civilisation.*
→ see **history**

civilize [BRIT also **civilise**] /ˈsɪvɪlaɪz/ (**civilizes, civilizing, civilized**) V-T To **civilize** a person or society means to educate them and improve their way of life. ❑ *My mother did her best to civilize me.*

civilized [BRIT also **civilised**] /ˈsɪvɪlaɪzd/ **1** ADJ A **civilized** society is one that has an advanced level of social organization. ❑ *I believed that in civilized countries, torture had ended long ago.* **2** ADJ If you describe a person or their behaviour as **civilized**, you mean that they are polite and reasonable.

ˌcivil ˈrights N-PLURAL **Civil rights** are the rights that people have to equal treatment and equal opportunities, whatever their race, sex, or religion.

ˌcivil ˈservant (**civil servants**) N-COUNT A **civil servant** is a person who works in the Civil Service.

ˌCivil ˈService N-SING **The Civil Service** of a country consists of the government departments and the people who work in them.

ˌcivil ˈwar (**civil wars**) N-COUNT A **civil war** is a war which is fought between different groups of people living in the same country.

CJD /ˌsiː dʒeɪ ˈdiː/ N-UNCOUNT **CJD** is an incurable brain disease that affects human beings and is believed to be caused by eating beef from cows with BSE. **CJD** is an abbreviation of 'Creutzfeld Jacob disease'.

clad /klæd/ ADJ AFTER LINK-V If you are **clad in** particular clothes, you are wearing them. [LITERARY] ❑ *...the figure of a woman, clad in black.*

claim /kleɪm/ (**claims, claiming, claimed**) **1** V-T & N-COUNT If someone **claims** that something is true, or if they make a **claim** that it is true, they say that it is true but they have not proved it and it may be false. ❑ *The man claimed to be a journalist.* ❑ *He claims a 70 to 80 per cent success rate.*

Word Web citizenship

Citizenship gives people important **rights**. In most countries **citizens** have the right to **vote** in **elections**. Citizens can hold government jobs and travel with a **passport**. They are also free to **demonstrate** to show disagreement with the government. In addition, citizens have **duties** and **responsibilities**. Two main duties of citizens are obeying the law and paying **taxes**. They may also be asked to be a **juror** in a court case. In some countries citizens have to do **military service**.

❑ *He repeated his claim that the people supported his action.* **2** V-T If you **claim** responsibility, or **claim** the credit for something, you say that you are responsible for it. ❑ *He is trying to claim the credit for this year's success.* **3** V-T & N-COUNT If you **claim** something such as money, property, or land, or if you make a **claim for** it, you ask for it because you have a right to it. ❑ *Now they are returning to claim what was theirs.* ❑ *This office has been dealing with their insurance claim.* **4** V-T If a fight or disaster **claims** someone's life, they are killed in it. [WRITTEN] ❑ *Heart disease claims 180,000 lives a year.* **5** N-COUNT If you have a **claim on** someone or their attention, you have a right to demand things from them or to demand their attention. ❑ *Everyone made strong claims on his attention.* **6** PHRASE Someone's **claim to fame** is something quite important or interesting that they have done or that is connected with them. ❑ *His claim to fame is that he climbed Mount Everest.* **7** PHRASE If you **lay claim to** something, you say that it is yours. [FORMAL] **8** PHRASE If you **stake** your **claim**, you show or say that you have a right to be something or to have something. ❑ *Jane is determined to stake her claim as an actress.*

claimant /'kleɪmənt/ (**claimants**) N-COUNT A **claimant** is someone who has applied for something such as compensation, an insurance payment, or unemployment benefit which they think they should receive.

clam /klæm/ (**clams**) N-COUNT A **clam** is a kind of shellfish.
→ see **shellfish**

clamber /'klæmbə/ (**clambers, clambering, clambered**) V-I If you **clamber** somewhere, you climb there with difficulty. ❑ *They clambered up the stone walls.*

clamour [AM **clamor**] /'klæmə/ (**clamours, clamouring, clamoured**) **1** V-I & N-UNCOUNT If people **are clamouring for** something, or if there is a **clamour for** it, people are demanding it noisily or angrily. [JOURNALISM] ❑ *Fans are clamouring for tickets for Friday's game.* ❑ *...the clamour for his resignation.* **2** N-SING **Clamour** is used to describe the loud noise of a large group of people talking or shouting together. ❑ *She could hear a clamour in the road outside.*

clamp /klæmp/ (**clamps, clamping, clamped**) **1** N-COUNT A **clamp** is a device that holds two things firmly together. **2** V-T When you **clamp** one thing **to** another, you fasten them together with a clamp. ❑ *Clamp the microphone to the pole.* **3** V-T To **clamp** something in a particular place means to put it there firmly and tightly. ❑ *He clamped his lips together.*
→ see **laboratory**
▶ **clamp down** PHR-VERB To **clamp down on** something means to stop it or control it. [JOURNALISM] ❑ *The government has failed to clamp down on crime.*

clan /klæn/ (**clans**) N-COUNT A **clan** is a group of families related to each other.

clandestine /klæn'destɪn/ ADJ Something that is **clandestine** is hidden or secret, and often illegal. [FORMAL] ❑ *...their clandestine meetings.*

clap /klæp/ (**claps, clapping, clapped**) **1** V-T/V-I & N-SING When you **clap** or **clap** your hands, you hit your hands together to express appreciation or attract attention. This action is called a **clap**. ❑ *Rosamond clapped her hands with delight.* ❑ *As long as the crowd gives them a clap, they're quite happy.* **2** V-T If you **clap** an object or your hand onto something, you put it there quickly and firmly. ❑ *I clapped a hand over her mouth.* **3** N-COUNT A **clap of thunder** is a sudden loud noise of thunder.

claret /'klærət/ (**clarets**) N-VAR **Claret** is a type of red French wine.

Word Link	*clar ≈ clear : clarify, clarity, declare*

Word Link	*ify ≈ making : clarify, diversify, intensify*

clarify /'klærɪfaɪ/ (**clarifies, clarifying, clarified**) V-T To **clarify** something means to make it easier to understand. ❑ *She asked him to clarify the situation.* ● **clarification** /ˌklærɪfɪ'keɪʃən/ N-UNCOUNT ❑ *He wrote to them asking for clarification of the situation.*

clarinet /ˌklærɪ'net/ (**clarinets**) N-COUNT A **clarinet** is a wind instrument with a single reed in its mouthpiece.
→ see **orchestra**

clarity /'klærɪti/ N-UNCOUNT **Clarity** is the quality of being clear and easy to understand. ❑ *...a fascinating book, written with clarity.*

clash /klæʃ/ (**clashes, clashing, clashed**) **1** V-I & N-COUNT When people **clash**, or when they are involved in a **clash**, they disagree, argue, or fight with each other. ❑ *The two countries clashed over human rights.* ❑ *...clashes between police and demonstrators.* **2** V-I & N-COUNT Beliefs, ideas, or qualities that **clash** are very different from each other and are therefore opposed. You can also talk about a **clash of** these things. ❑ *...decisions which clash with company policy.* ❑ *...a clash of views.* **3** V-I If one event **clashes with** another, they happen at the same time and so you cannot go to both of them. ❑ *His wedding clashed with a golf tournament.* ❑ *We'll go to both events if the times don't clash.* **4** V-I If one colour **clashes with** another, they look ugly together. ❑ *His pink shirt clashed with his red hair.*

clasp /klɑːsp, klæsp/ (**clasps, clasping, clasped**) **1** V-T & N-COUNT If you **clasp** someone or something, you hold them tightly. A **clasp** is an act of clasping someone or something. ❑ *She clasped the children to her.* ❑ *With one last clasp of his hand, she left him.* **2** N-COUNT A **clasp** is a small metal fastening.

class /klɑːs, klæs/ (**classes, classing, classed**) **1** N-COUNT A **class** is a group of pupils or students who are taught together. **2** N-COUNT A **class** is a course of teaching in a particular subject. ❑ *He got a law degree by taking classes at night.* **3** N-UNCOUNT If you do something **in class**, you do it during a lesson in school. ❑ *There is a lot of reading in class.* **4** N-VAR **Class** is used to refer to the division of people in a society according to their social status. ❑ *...the British class structure.* ❑ *...the relationship between social classes.* **5** N-COUNT A **class of** things is a group of them with similar characteristics. ❑ *...the largest class of warship ever built.* **6** N-UNCOUNT If you say that someone has **class**, you mean that they are elegant and sophisticated. **7** V-T If someone or something **is classed as** a particular thing, they are considered as belonging to that group of things. ❑ *Why is this film classed as political?* **8** PHRASE If you say that

C

someone is **in a class of** their **own**, you mean that they have more of a particular skill or quality than anyone else. **9** → see also **middle class, upper class, working class**

Word Partnership	Use *class* with:
N.	class **for beginners**, **graduating** class, class **size**, **students in a** class **1** **leisure** class, class **struggle**, **working** class **4**
V.	**take a** class, **teach a** class **2**
ORD.	**first/second** class **4**
ADJ.	**social** class **4**

classic /ˈklæsɪk/ (**classics**) **1** ADJ A **classic** example of something has all the features which you expect that kind of thing to have. ❑ *His first two goals were classic cases of being in the right place at the right time.* ● **classically** ADV ❑ *He's not classically handsome.* **2** ADJ BEFORE N & N-COUNT A **classic** piece of writing or film, or a **classic**, is a piece of writing or film of high quality that has become a standard against which similar things are judged. ❑ *...the classic study of the Civil Rights Movement in the United States.* ❑ *...a film classic.* **3** N-UNCOUNT **Classics** is the study of ancient Greek and Roman civilizations, especially their languages, literature, and philosophy.

classical /ˈklæsɪkəl/ **1** ADJ You use **classical** to describe something that is traditional in form, style, or content. ❑ *...classical, rock and jazz music.* ● **classically** ADV ❑ *...classically trained dancers.* **2** ADJ **Classical** is used to describe things relating to ancient Greek or Roman civilization. ❑ *...ancient Egypt and classical Greece.*
→ see **genre**

classified /ˈklæsɪfaɪd/ ADJ **Classified** information is officially secret. ❑ *...a classified British Army document.*

ˌclassified adˈvertisement (**classified advertisements**) N-COUNT **Classified ads** or **classified advertisements** are small advertisements in a newspaper or magazine. They are usually from a person or small company.

classified ad

classify /ˈklæsɪfaɪ/ (**classifies, classifying, classified**) V-T To **classify** things means to divide them into groups or types so that things with similar characteristics are in the same group. ❑ *They classified his death as a suicide.* ● **classification** /ˌklæsɪfɪˈkeɪʃən/ (**classifications**) N-VAR ❑ *...a new system for the classification of schools.*

classless /ˈklɑːsləs, ˈklæs-/ ADJ If politicians refer to a **classless society**, they mean a society in which people are not affected by differences in social status; used showing approval.

classmate /ˈklɑːsmeɪt, ˈklæs-/ (**classmates**) N-COUNT Your **classmates** are students in the same class as you at school or college.

classroom /ˈklɑːsruːm, ˈklæs-/ (**classrooms**) N-COUNT A **classroom** is a room in a school where lessons take place.

classy /ˈklɑːsi, ˈklæsi/ (**classier, classiest**) ADJ If you describe someone or something as **classy**, you mean they are stylish and sophisticated. [INFORMAL] ❑ *...a classy restaurant.*

clatter /ˈklætə/ (**clatters, clattering, clattered**) **1** V-I If you say that people or things **clatter** somewhere, you mean that they move there noisily. ❑ *He clattered down the stairs.* **2** V-I & N-SING When something hard **clatters**, or when it makes a **clatter**, it makes repeated short noises as it hits against another hard thing. [LITERARY] ❑ *Her cup clattered against its saucer.* ❑ *...the clatter of cutlery.*

clause /klɔːz/ (**clauses**) **1** N-COUNT A **clause** is a section of a legal document. **2** N-COUNT In grammar, a **clause** is a group of words containing a verb.

claw /klɔː/ (**claws, clawing, clawed**) **1** N-COUNT The **claws** of a bird or animal are the thin curved nails on its feet. **2** V-T/V-I When people or animals **claw** something, or when they **claw at** it, they damage it or try to get hold of it with their nails or claws. ❑ *His fingers clawed at Blake's wrist.*
→ see **bird**

claw

clay /kleɪ/ N-UNCOUNT **Clay** is a type of earth that is soft when it is wet and hard when it is baked dry.
→ see **pottery**

clean /kliːn/ (**cleaner, cleanest, cleans, cleaning, cleaned**) **1** ADJ Something that is **clean** is free from dirt or unwanted marks. ❑ *This is the cleanest beach in Europe.* ❑ *Kitchen floors are not easy to keep clean.* **2** V-T & N-SING If you **clean** something, or if you give it a **clean**, you make it free from dirt and unwanted marks. ❑ *It took ages to clean the marks off the bath.* ❑ *Give the cooker a good clean.* ● **cleaning** N-UNCOUNT ❑ *I do the cleaning myself.* **3** ADJ If something such as a book, joke, or lifestyle is **clean**, it is not sexually immoral or offensive; used showing approval. ❑ *It's a good, clean, family movie.* **4** ADJ If someone's reputation or record is **clean**, they have never done anything illegal or wrong. ❑ *Yes, I have a clean driving licence.* **5** ADJ BEFORE N If you **make a clean** break or start, you end a situation completely and start again in a different way. ❑ *Walesa insisted on a clean break with Poland's communist past.* **6** PHRASE If you **come clean about** something that you have been keeping secret, you admit it. [INFORMAL]
→ see **soap**
▶ **clean out** PHR-VERB If you **clean out** a cupboard or room, you clean and tidy it thoroughly.
▶ **clean up** PHR-VERB If you **clean up** something, you clean it thoroughly. ❑ *Remember to clean up garden tools when you are putting them away.*

Thesaurus	*clean* Also look up:
ADJ.	neat, pure; *(ant.)* dirty, filthy **1**
V.	launder, rinse, wash; *(ant.)* dirty, soil, stain **2**

cleaner /ˈkliːnə/ (**cleaners**) **1** N-COUNT A **cleaner** is someone who is employed to clean the rooms and furniture inside a building or someone whose job is to clean a particular type of thing.

❑ *He's a window cleaner.* 2 N-VAR A **cleaner** is a substance or device for cleaning things. ❑ *A can of oven cleaner.* ❑ *...a carpet cleaner.* 3 N-COUNT A **cleaner** or a **cleaner's** is a shop where things such as clothes are dry-cleaned. 4 → see also **vacuum cleaner**

cleanliness /ˈklenlɪnəs/ N-UNCOUNT **Cleanliness** is the degree to which people keep themselves and their surroundings clean. ❑ *...standards of cleanliness in hospitals.*

cleanse /klenz/ (**cleanses, cleansing, cleansed**) 1 V-T To **cleanse** a person, place, or organization **of** something dirty, unpleasant, or evil means to make them free of it. ❑ *He tried to cleanse the house of bad memories.* 2 V-T If you **cleanse** your skin or a wound, you clean it.

cleanser /klenzə/ (**cleansers**) N-VAR A **cleanser** is a liquid or cream that you use for cleaning something, especially your skin.

clear /klɪə/ (**clearer, clearest, clears, clearing, cleared**) 1 ADJ Something that is **clear** is easy to understand, see, or hear. ❑ *It is a clear account of what happened.* ❑ *This television transmits much clearer pictures.* • **clearly** ADV ❑ *It is important to learn to express yourself clearly.* 2 ADJ Something that is **clear** is obvious. ❑ *It was a clear case of murder.* ❑ *It became clear that I was losing the argument.* • **clearly** ADV ❑ *Clearly, the police cannot break the law.* 3 ADJ If you are **clear about** something, you understand it completely. ❑ *She sat and thought, trying to be clear about her feelings.* 4 ADJ If you have a **clear** mind or way of thinking, you are able to think sensibly and logically. ❑ *She needed a clear head for this job.* • **clearly** ADV ❑ *I can think clearly when I'm alone.* 5 ADJ If a substance is **clear**, it has no colour and you can see through it. ❑ *...a clear glass window.* ❑ *...a clear liquid.* 6 ADJ **Clear** skin or eyes look healthy. 7 ADJ If it is a **clear day**, there is no mist, rain, or cloud. 8 V-I When fog or mist **clears**, it gradually disappears. 9 ADJ If a surface or place is **clear**, it is free from obstructions or unwanted objects. ❑ *The runway is clear – go ahead and land.* 10 V-T When you **clear** a place, you remove unwanted things from it. ❑ *They've cleared the bushes to widen the road.* ❑ *The girls were clearing the table.* 11 ADJ If your conscience is **clear**, you do not feel guilty about anything. ❑ *I can look back with a clear conscience.* 12 ADJ AFTER LINK-V If one thing is **clear of** another, the two things are not touching. ❑ *Try to keep your feet clear of the water.* 13 V-T If an animal or person **clears** a fence, wall, or hedge, they jump over it without touching it. 14 V-T If a course of action **is cleared**, people in authority give permission for it to happen. ❑ *The helicopter was cleared for take-off.* 15 V-T If someone **is cleared of** a crime or mistake, they are proved to be not guilty of it. 16 → see also **clearing** 17 PHRASE If you **stay clear of** or **steer clear of** a person or place, you do not go near them. 18 PHRASE If someone is **in the clear**, they are free from blame, suspicion, or danger. [INFORMAL] ❑ *The police told him the he was in the clear.* 19 to **clear** your **throat** → see **throat**

▶ **clear away** PHR-VERB When you **clear** things **away**, or when you **clear away**, you put away things that you have been using. ❑ *The waitress cleared away the plates.* ❑ *Tania cooked, served, and cleared away.*

▶ **clear off** PHR-VERB If you tell someone to **clear off**, you are telling them in a rude way to go away. [INFORMAL]

▶ **clear out** 1 PHR-VERB If you tell someone to **clear out of** a place or to **clear out**, you are telling them rather rudely to leave the place. [INFORMAL] ❑ *'Clear out!' he shouted. 'Private property!'* 2 PHR-VERB If you **clear out** a cupboard or room, you tidy it and throw away unwanted things.

▶ **clear up** 1 PHR-VERB When you **clear up**, or when you **clear** a place **up**, you tidy a place and put things away. ❑ *I cleared up my room.* 2 PHR-VERB To **clear up** a problem, misunderstanding, or mystery means to settle it or find a satisfactory explanation for it. 3 PHR-VERB When bad weather **clears up**, it stops raining or being cloudy.

Thesaurus	*clear* Also look up:
ADJ.	obvious, plain, straightforward 1

Word Partnership	Use *clear* with:
V.	**be** clear, **make it** clear, **seem** clear 1 2
ADJ.	**crystal** clear 1 2 3
N.	clear **the way** 3
	clear **understanding**, clear **idea** 3 4
	clear **picture**, clear **goals/purpose** 4

clearance /ˈklɪərəns/ (**clearances**) 1 N-VAR **Clearance** is the removal of old or unwanted buildings, trees, or other things from an area. ❑ *...the clearance of the forests.* 2 N-VAR If you get **clearance** to do or have something, you get official approval or permission to do or have it. ❑ *The plane was given clearance to land.*

ˌclear-ˈcut ADJ Something that is **clear-cut** is easy to understand and definite. ❑ *These questions do not have clear-cut answers.*

clearing /ˈklɪərɪŋ/ (**clearings**) N-COUNT A **clearing** is a small area in a forest where there are no trees.

clench /klentʃ/ (**clenches, clenching, clenched**) 1 V-T When you **clench** your **fist**, you curl your fingers up tightly, usually because you are very angry. ❑ *The angry protestors clenched their fists.* 2 V-T When you **clench** your **teeth**, you squeeze them together firmly, usually because you are angry or upset. ❑ *Slowly, he breathed out through clenched teeth.*

clergy /ˈklɜːdʒi/ N-PLURAL The **clergy** are the religious leaders of a particular group of believers. ❑ *...Catholic clergy.*

clergyman /ˈklɜːdʒimən/ (**clergymen**) N-COUNT A **clergyman** is a male member of the clergy.

cleric /ˈklerɪk/ (**clerics**) N-COUNT A **cleric** is a member of the clergy.

clerical /ˈklerɪkəl/ 1 ADJ BEFORE N **Clerical** jobs, skills, and workers are concerned with work that is done in an office. ❑ *...a clerical error.* 2 ADJ BEFORE N **Clerical** means relating to the clergy. ❑ *...Iran's clerical leadership.*

clerk /klɑːk, AM klɜːrk/ (**clerks**) N-COUNT A **clerk** is a person who works in an office, bank, or law court and whose job is to look after records or accounts. ❑ *...an accounts clerk.*
→ see **hotel**

clever /ˈklevə/ (**cleverer, cleverest**) 1 ADJ A **clever** person is intelligent and able to understand things easily or to plan things well. ❑ *My sister was always a lot cleverer than I was.* • **cleverly** ADV ❑ *He* did that very cleverly. • **cleverness** N-UNCOUNT ❑ *He sat back, smiling at his own cleverness.* **2** ADJ A **clever** idea, book, or invention is extremely effective and shows the skill of the people involved. ❑ *It is quite a clever novel.* ❑ *...this clever new machine.* • **cleverly** ADV ❑ *She wore a cleverly designed swimsuit.*

C

Thesaurus	*clever* Also look up:
ADJ.	bright, ingenious, smart; *(ant.)* dumb, stupid **1** **2**

cliché also **cliche** /'kli:ʃeɪ, AM kli:'ʃeɪ/ (**clichés**) N-COUNT A **cliché** is an idea or phrase which has been used so much that it is no longer interesting or effective; used showing disapproval. ❑ *I'm afraid it's an old musician's cliché, but music is my life.*

click /klɪk/ (**clicks, clicking, clicked**) **1** V-T/V-I & N-COUNT If something **clicks**, or if you **click** it, it makes a short sharp sound, called a **click**. ❑ *Cameras clicked all around.* ❑ *Blake clicked his fingers at the waiter.* ❑ *...a click of a button.* **2** V-I & N-COUNT If you **click on** an area of a computer screen, you point the cursor at that area and press one of the buttons on the mouse in order to make something happen. This action is called a **click**. [COMPUTING] ❑ *For more information, click here.* ❑ *Check your email with a click of your mouse.* **3** V-I When you suddenly understand something, you can say that it **has clicked**. [INFORMAL] ❑ *It suddenly clicked that this was fantastic fun.*

client /klaɪənt/ (**clients**) N-COUNT A **client** is someone for whom a professional person or organization is providing a service or doing some work. ❑ *The company took the clients' fees in advance.*
→ see **trial**

Usage

If you use the professional services of someone such as a lawyer or an accountant, you are one of their **clients**. When you buy goods from a particular shop or company, you are one of its **customers**. Doctors and hospitals have **patients**, while hotels have **guests**. People who travel on public transport are referred to as **passengers**.

clientele /ˌkli:ɒn'tel, ˌklaɪən-/ N-SING The **clientele** of a place or business are the type of customers or clients it attracts. ❑ *The hotel appeals to an older clientele.*

cliff /klɪf/ (**cliffs**) N-COUNT A **cliff** is a high area of land with a very steep side, especially one next to the sea.
→ see **land, mountain**

climate /'klaɪmət/ (**climates**) **1** N-VAR The **climate** of a place is the general weather conditions that are typical of it. ❑ *Cyprus has a hot and humid climate.* **2** N-COUNT You can use **climate** to refer to the atmosphere or situation somewhere. ❑ *...the existing climate of violence.*
→ see Word Web: **climate**

climax /'klaɪmæks/ (**climaxes, climaxing, climaxed**) V-I & N-COUNT If something **climaxes with** a particular event, that is the most exciting or important moment in it, usually near the end. This part of an event is called the **climax**. ❑ *Taking part in the Olympics was the climax of her career.* ❑ *The performance climaxed with a spectacular firework display.*

climb /klaɪm/ (**climbs, climbing, climbed**) **1** V-T & N-COUNT If you **climb** something such as a tree, mountain, or ladder, or if you **climb up** it, you move towards the top of it. Climbing something is called a **climb**. ❑ *Climb the steps to the bridge.* ❑ *Children love to climb.* ❑ *...an hour's gentle climb up the hill.* **2** V-I If you **climb** somewhere, you move there carefully and often awkwardly, for example because you are moving into a small space. ❑ *The girls climbed into the car.* **3** V-I When something like an aeroplane **climbs**, it moves upwards. ❑ *The plane climbed to 370 feet.* **4** V-I When something **climbs**, it increases in value or amount. ❑ *Prices have climbed by 21%.*
▸ **climb down** **1** PHR-VERB If you **climb down** something such as a tree, mountain, or ladder, you move towards the bottom of it. **2** PHR-VERB If you **climb down** in an argument or dispute, you admit that you are wrong, or change your intentions or demands.

Word Partnership	Use *climb* with:
N.	climb **the stairs** **1**
	prices climb **4**
PREP.	climb **down/up**, climb **in/on** **1** **2**
V.	**begin/continue to** climb **3** **4**

climber /'klaɪmə/ (**climbers**) N-COUNT A **climber** is someone who climbs rocks or mountains as a sport.

climbing /'klaɪmɪŋ/ N-UNCOUNT **Climbing** is the activity of climbing rocks or mountains.

clinch /klɪntʃ/ (**clinches, clinching, clinched**) V-T To **clinch** an agreement or argument means to settle it. [INFORMAL] ❑ *He is about to clinch a deal with an American engine manufacturer.*

cling /klɪŋ/ (**clings, clinging, clung**) **1** V-I If you **cling to** or **onto** something or someone, you hold onto them tightly. ❑ *She had to cling onto the door handle.* ❑ *They hugged each other, clinging together.* **2** V-I Clothes that **cling to** you stay pressed against your body when you move. ❑ *Her wet clothing clung to her body.* **3** V-I If you **cling to** an idea or way of behaving, you continue to believe in its value or importance, even though it may no longer be valid or useful. ❑ *She clings to a romantic idea of marriage.*

clinic /'klɪnɪk/ (**clinics**) N-COUNT A **clinic** is a building where people receive medical advice or treatment.

clinical /'klɪnɪkəl/ **1** ADJ BEFORE N **Clinical** means involving or relating to the medical treatment or testing of patients. ❑ *...a clinical psychologist.* • **clinically** ADV ❑ *The plant has been clinically proven to heal and protect the skin.* **2** ADJ **Clinical** thought or behaviour is very logical and does not involve any emotion; used showing disapproval. ❑ *He didn't like the clinical way she talked about their love.*

clink /klɪŋk/ (**clinks, clinking, clinked**) V-T/V-I & N-COUNT When glass or metal objects **clink**, or when you **clink** them, they touch each other and make a short light sound, called a **clink**. ❑ *She clinked her glass against his.* ❑ *...the clink of a spoon in a cup.*

clip /klɪp/ (**clips, clipping, clipped**) **1** N-COUNT A **clip** is a small metal or plastic device that is used for holding things together. ❑ *She took the clip out of*

Word Web climate

During the past 100 years, the air **temperature** of the earth has increased by about 1° **Fahrenheit** (F). Alaska has warmed by about 4° F. At the same time, **precipitation** over the northern hemisphere increased by 10%. This suggests that the increase of rain and snow has caused the sea level to rise 4-8 inches around the world. The years 1998, 2001, and 2002 were the three hottest ever recorded. This warm period followed what some scientists call the "Little Ice Age." Researchers found that from the 1400s to the 1800s the Earth cooled by about 6° F. Air and water temperatures were lower, **glaciers** grew quickly, and **ice caps** came further south than usual.

St. Mark's Square in Venice flooded 111 times in 2002.

her hair. **2** V-T/V-I If you **clip** one thing **to** another, you fasten it there with a clip. You can also say that one thing **clips** ***to*** another. ❑ *He clipped his tie neatly in place.* ❑ *The pen clips to the side of your screen.* **3** N-COUNT A **clip** from a film or a radio or television programme is a short piece of it that is broadcast separately. ❑ *...a film clip of Lenin speaking.* **4** V-T If you **clip** something, you cut small pieces from it. ❑ *I saw an old man clipping his roses.*

clipped /klɪpt/ **1** ADJ **Clipped** means neatly trimmed. ❑ *...a quiet street of clipped lawns.* **2** ADJ If you have a **clipped** way of speaking, you speak with quick short sounds. ❑ *'Come in,' a clipped voice said.*

clipping /ˈklɪpɪŋ/ (**clippings**) N-COUNT A **clipping** is an article, picture, or advertisement that has been cut from a newspaper or magazine. ❑ *...newspaper clippings.*

clique /kliːk/ (**cliques**) N-COUNT If you describe a group of people as a **clique**, you mean that they spend a lot of time together and seem unfriendly towards people who are not in the group; used showing disapproval. ❑ *...a clique of first-year students.*

cloak /kləʊk/ (**cloaks, cloaking, cloaked**) **1** N-COUNT A **cloak** is a wide loose coat that fastens at the neck and does not have sleeves. **2** V-T & N-SING To **cloak** something, or to put a **cloak** around it, means to hide the truth about it or cover it up. ❑ *The subject remains cloaked in mystery.* ❑ *We prepared for the wedding under a cloak of secrecy.*

cloakroom /ˈkləʊkruːm/ (**cloakrooms**) N-COUNT A **cloakroom** is a small room in a public building where people can leave their coats.

clobber /ˈklɒbə/ (**clobbers, clobbering, clobbered**) V-T If you **clobber** someone, you hit them. [BRIT, INFORMAL]

clock /klɒk/ (**clocks, clocking, clocked**) **1** N-COUNT A **clock** is an instrument, for example in a room or on the outside of a building, that shows you what the time is. **2** → see also **o'clock** **3** PHRASE If you work **round** or **around the clock**, you work all day and all night without stopping. ❑ *She will be guarded round the clock.* ❑ *...an around-the-clock service.* **4** PHRASE If you want to **turn the clock back** or **put the clock back**, you want to return to a situation that used to exist, but which has now changed.
→ see **time**

▶ **clock up** PHR-VERB To **clock up** a large total means to reach that total. [BRIT] ❑ *Neil has clocked up 18 points so far.*

Word Partnership Use *clock* with:

N.	clock **radio, hands of a** clock **1**
V.	**look at a** clock, **put/turn the** clock **back/forward,** **set a** clock, clock **strikes**, clock **ticks** **1**

Word Link *wise ≈ in the direction or manner of : clockwise, likewise, otherwise*

clockwise /ˈklɒkwaɪz/ ADV & ADJ BEFORE N When something is moving **clockwise** or when it is moving in a **clockwise** direction, it is moving in a circle, in the same direction as the hands on a clock.

clockwise

clockwork /ˈklɒkwɜːk/ **1** ADJ BEFORE N A **clockwork** toy or device has machinery inside it which makes it move or operate when it is wound up with a key. **2** PHRASE If something happens **like clockwork**, it happens without problems or delays. ❑ *The Queen's holiday is arranged to go like clockwork.*

clog /klɒg/ (**clogs, clogging, clogged**) **1** V-T/V-I & PHR-VERB When something **clogs** a hole or place, or when a hole or place **clogs up**, it becomes blocked so that nothing can pass through. ❑ *The traffic clogged the Thames bridges.* ❑ *The lungs clog up with liquid.* ● **clogged** ADJ ❑ *The streets were clogged with people.* **2** N-COUNT **Clogs** are heavy leather or wooden shoes with thick wooden soles.
→ see **shoe**

clone /kləʊn/ (**clones, cloning, cloned**) **1** V-T & N-COUNT If you **clone** an animal or plant, you produce it artificially from a cell of another animal or plant, so that it is exactly the same as the original. An animal or plant that has been

C

Word Web clone

Clones have always existed. For example, a plant can be duplicated by using a leaf cutting to create an identical new plant. Identical **twins** are also natural clones of each other. Recently however, scientists have started using **genetic engineering** to produce man-made clones of animals. The first step involves removing the genetic information called **DNA** from a **cell**. Next, the genetic information is placed into an egg cell. The egg then grows into a **copy** of the donor animal. The first animal experiments in the 1970s involved tadpoles. In 1997 a sheep named Dolly became the first successfully cloned mammal.

produced like this is called a **clone**. 2 N-COUNT If you say that someone is a **clone** of someone else, you disapprove of them because they try to look and behave exactly like that person. ❑ *We don't all want to be Barbie clones.*
→ see Word Web: **clone**

close
❶ VERB USES
❷ ADJECTIVE USES

close /kləʊz/ (**closes, closing, closed**)
❶ 1 V-T/V-I When you **close** a door, window, or lid, or when it **closes**, it moves so that a hole, gap, or opening is covered. ❑ *If you are cold, close the window.* ❑ *Zak heard the door close.* 2 V-T/V-I When a place **closes**, or when it **is closed**, people cannot use it, or all work stops there. ❑ *The shops close on Christmas Day.* ❑ *The hospital was closed soon after the deaths.* 3 V-T To **close** a matter or event means to bring it to an end. ❑ *He needs another $30,000 to close the deal.* ❑ *...the closing ceremony of the Olympic Games.* 4 N-SING **The close of** a period of time or an activity is the end of it. To **bring** something **to a close** or to **draw** something **to a close** means to end it. ❑ *Orders will be received until the close of business tomorrow.* 5 V-I If you **are closing on** someone or something that you are following, you are getting nearer and nearer to them. ❑ *I was near the runner in second place, and closing on him.* 6 → see also **closing**
▶ **close down** PHR-VERB If a factory or a business **closes down**, or if it **is closed down**, all work or activity stops there, usually for ever. ❑ *The Government has closed down two newspapers.*
▶ **close in** PHR-VERB If people **close in on** a person or place, they come nearer and gradually surround them. ❑ *Troops were closing in on Berlin.*

close /kləʊs/ (**closer, closest**)
❷ 1 ADJ AFTER LINK-V Something that is **close to** something else is near to it. ❑ *The house is close to the station.* ❑ *The dog moved closer.* ❑ *The tables were pushed close together.* ● **closely** ADV ❑ *They were closely followed by security men.* 2 ADJ People who are **close** know each other well and like each other a lot. ❑ *She and Linda became very close.* ❑ *...a close friend from school.* ● **closeness** N-UNCOUNT ❑ *...her closeness to her mother.* 3 ADJ BEFORE N Your **close relatives** are the members of your family most directly related to you, for example your parents, brothers, or sisters. 4 ADJ BEFORE N **Close** contact or co-operation involves seeing or communicating with someone often. ❑ *He kept in close contact with his three grown-up sons.* ● **closely** ADV ❑ *We work closely with the careers officers.* 5 ADJ If there is a **close** connection between two things, they are strongly connected. ❑ *There is a close connection between pain and stress.* ● **closely** ADV ❑ *Religion and politics are closely linked in this part of the country.* 6 ADJ When a competition or election is **close**, it is only won or lost by a small amount. ❑ *It is still a close contest between the two teams.* 7 ADJ BEFORE N **Close** inspection or observation of something is careful and thorough. ❑ *Let's have a closer look.* ● **closely** ADV ❑ *Let's look closely at some of the problems in society.* 8 ADJ AFTER LINK-V If you are **close to** something, or if it is **close**, it is likely to happen or come soon. ❑ *She sounded close to tears.* ❑ *An official said the agreement is close.* ❑ *He's close to signing a contract.* 9 ADJ If the atmosphere in a place is **close**, it is uncomfortably warm and does not have enough fresh air. 10 PHRASE Something that is **close by** or **close at hand** is near to you. 11 PHRASE If you describe an event as **a close shave** or **a close call**, you mean that an accident nearly happened. 12 PHRASE If something is **close to** or **close on** a particular amount or distance, it is slightly less than that amount or distance. ❑ *Sisulu spent close to 30 years in prison.* 13 PHRASE If you look at something **close up** or **close to**, you look at it when you are very near to it. ❑ *They always look smaller close up.* 14 → see also **close-up**

Thesaurus *close* Also look up:
V. fasten, shut, slam, seal; *(ant.)* open ① 1

Word Partnership Use *close* with:
N. close **a door**, close ***your* eyes** ① 1
close **friend**, close **to *someone*** ② 2
close **family/relative** ② 2 3
close **election**, close **race** ② 6
close **attention/scrutiny** ② 7
ADV. close **enough, so/too/very** close ② 2 5 6

closed /kləʊzd/ ADJ A **closed** group of people does not welcome new people or ideas from outside. ❑ *It is a completely closed society: they have no experience of foreigners.*

ˌclosed-ˈcircuit ADJ **Closed-circuit television** is a television system used to film people, for example in shops so thieves can be identified. ❑ *...closed-circuit cameras.*

closet /ˈklɒzɪt/ (**closets**) 1 N-COUNT In

American English, a **closet** is a piece of furniture with doors at the front and shelves inside, which is used for storing things. The usual British word is **cupboard.** 2 ADJ BEFORE N **Closet** is used to describe a person who has beliefs, habits, or feelings which they keep secret. ❑ *He is a closet Fascist.*
→ see **house**

close-up /ˈkləʊs ʌp/ (**close-ups**) N-COUNT A **close-up** is a photograph or a picture in a film that shows a lot of detail because it is taken very near to the subject.

closing /ˈkləʊzɪŋ/ 1 ADJ BEFORE N The **closing** part of an activity or period of time is its final part. ❑ *...in the closing stages of the war.* 2 → see also **close**

closure /ˈkləʊʒə/ (**closures**) 1 N-VAR The **closure** of a business or factory is the permanent shutting of it. ❑ *They are protesting against the closure of the main post office.* 2 N-COUNT The **closure** of a road or border is the blocking of it to prevent people from using it.

clot /klɒt/ (**clots, clotting, clotted**) V-I & N-COUNT When blood **clots**, it thickens and forms a thick lump inside the body, called a **clot.** ❑ *The cold weather causes blood to clot more easily.* ❑ *They removed a blood clot from his brain.*

cloth /klɒθ, AM klɔːθ/ (**cloths**) 1 N-VAR **Cloth** is fabric which is made by weaving or knitting a substance such as cotton or wool. 2 N-COUNT A **cloth** is a piece of cloth used for a particular purpose, such as cleaning. ❑ *Clean the surface with a damp cloth.*

clothed /kləʊðd/ ADJ AFTER LINK-V If you are **clothed** in a certain way, you are dressed in that way. ❑ *He lay down on the bed fully clothed.*

clothes /kləʊðz/ N-PLURAL **Clothes** are the things that people wear, such as shirts, coats, trousers, and dresses.

Usage

There is no singular form of **clothes.** You cannot talk about 'a clothe'. In formal English, you can talk about a **garment**, a **piece of clothing**, an **article of clothing**, or an **item of clothing**, but in ordinary conversation, you usually name the piece of clothing you are talking about. For the different verbs associated with clothes, see the note at **wear.**

clothing /ˈkləʊðɪŋ/ N-UNCOUNT **Clothing** is the clothes people wear. ❑ *You'll need protective clothing.*
→ see Picture Dictionary: **clothing**

cloud /klaʊd/ (**clouds, clouding, clouded**) 1 N-VAR A **cloud** is a mass of water vapour that is seen as a white or grey mass in the sky. ❑ *The helicopter crashed in thick cloud.* ❑ *Dark clouds formed overhead.* 2 N-COUNT A **cloud of** smoke or dust is a mass of it floating in the air. 3 V-T If you say that something **clouds** your view of a situation, you mean that it makes you unable to understand the situation or judge it properly. ❑ *Anger clouded his thinking.* 4 V-T If something **clouds** an event or situation, it makes it less pleasant. ❑ *The situation is clouded with problems.*
→ see **water**

▶ **cloud over** PHR-VERB If your face or eyes **cloud over**, you suddenly look sad or angry.

cloudy /ˈklaʊdi/ (**cloudier, cloudiest**) 1 ADJ If it is **cloudy**, there are a lot of clouds in the sky. 2 ADJ A **cloudy** liquid is less clear than it should be.

clout /klaʊt/ (**clouts, clouting, clouted**) 1 V-T & N-COUNT If you **clout** someone, or if you give them a **clout**, you hit them. [INFORMAL] ❑ *She clouted him on the head.* ❑ *I wanted to give one of them a clout.* 2 N-UNCOUNT A person or institution that has **clout** has influence and power. ❑ *The two firms have enormous clout in financial markets.*

clove /kləʊv/ (**cloves**) 1 N-VAR **Cloves** are small

Picture Dictionary clothing

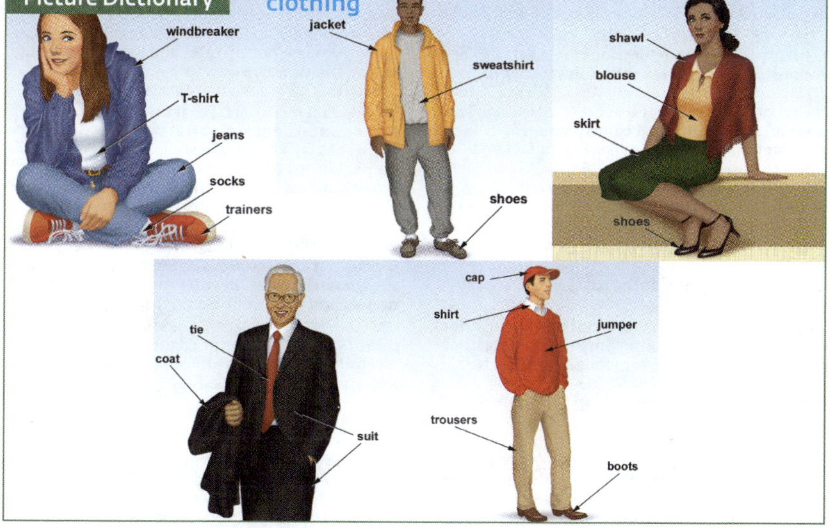

C

C

dried flower buds used as a spice. **2** N-COUNT A **clove of** garlic is one of the small sections of a garlic bulb.

clown /klaʊn/ (**clowns, clowning, clowned**) N-COUNT A **clown** is a performer who wears funny clothes and bright make-up, and does silly things to make people laugh.
▶ **clown around** PHR-VERB If you **clown around**, you do silly things to make people laugh.

club /klʌb/ (**clubs, clubbing, clubbed**) **1** N-COUNT A **club** is an organization of people who are all interested in a particular activity. ❑ *...a chess club.* **2** N-COUNT A **club** is a team which competes in professional or amateur sporting competitions. ❑ *...the Italian football club, AC Milan.* **3** N-COUNT A **club** is a place where the members of a particular club or organization meet. **4** N-COUNT A **club** is the same as a **nightclub**. ❑ *...a night of dancing at a club.* **5** V-T & N-COUNT To **club** a person or animal means to hit them hard with something such as a thick heavy stick called a **club**. ❑ *He had been clubbed to death with a metal bar.* **6** N-COUNT A golf **club** is a long thin metal stick with a piece of wood or metal at one end. **7** N-VAR **Clubs** is one of the four suits in a pack of playing cards. Each card in the suit is called a **club** and is marked with one or more black symbols: ♣.
→ see **golf**

clubhouse also **club house** /ˈklʌbhaʊs/ (**clubhouses**) N-COUNT A **clubhouse** is the place where the members of a sports club meet.
→ see **golf**

clue /kluː/ (**clues**) **1** N-COUNT A **clue to** a problem, mystery, or puzzle is something that helps you find the answer. ❑ *...a crossword puzzle clue.* ❑ *...clues to the girl's killer.* **2** PHRASE If you **haven't a clue** about something, you know nothing about it. ❑ *I haven't a clue what to give Carl for his birthday.*

clump /klʌmp/ (**clumps**) N-COUNT A **clump of** things is a small group of them growing together or collected together in one place. ❑ *...a clump of trees.* ❑ *Her hair fell out in clumps.*

clumsy /ˈklʌmzi/ (**clumsier, clumsiest**) **1** ADJ A **clumsy** person moves or handles things in an awkward way. ● **clumsily** ADV ❑ *She rose clumsily.* ● **clumsiness** N-UNCOUNT ❑ *His clumsiness embarrassed him.* **2** ADJ A **clumsy** action or statement is not skilful or is without tact and likely to upset people. ❑ *He apologised for his clumsy language.* ● **clumsily** ADV ❑ *The report was clumsily written.* ● **clumsiness** N-UNCOUNT ❑ *...clumsiness of expression.* **3** ADJ A **clumsy** object is ugly and awkward to use. ❑ *The keyboard is a large and clumsy instrument.*

clung /klʌŋ/ **Clung** is the past tense and past participle of **cling**.

cluster /ˈklʌstə/ (**clusters, clustering, clustered**) V-I & N-COUNT If people or things **cluster** together, they gather together or are found together in small groups, called **clusters**. ❑ *The children clustered around me.* ❑ *Small cottages are clustered together here.* ❑ *The shrub has clusters of tiny flowers in summer.*

clutch /klʌtʃ/ (**clutches, clutching, clutched**) **1** V-T/V-I If you **clutch** something, you hold it very tightly. ❑ *Michelle clutched my arm.* **2** N-PLURAL If you are in another person's **clutches**, that person has control over you. **3** N-COUNT In a car, the **clutch** is the pedal that you press before you change gear, and the mechanism that it operates.

clutter /ˈklʌtə/ (**clutters, cluttering, cluttered**) **1** N-UNCOUNT **Clutter** is a lot of unnecessary or useless things in an untidy state. ❑ *Carolyn lives surrounded by clutter.* **2** V-T If things **clutter** a place, they fill it untidily. ❑ *Every surface was cluttered with toys.* ● **cluttered** ADJ ❑ *...a cluttered desk.*

cm. **cm.** is the written abbreviation for **centimetre**. ❑ *He has grown 2.5 cm.*

co- /kəʊ-/ **Co-** is used to form words that refer to people sharing things or doing things together. ❑ *He co-produced the album with Bowie.* ❑ *His co-workers hated him.*

coach /kəʊtʃ/ (**coaches, coaching, coached**) **1** N-COUNT A **coach** is a large comfortable bus that carries passengers on long journeys. ❑ *From Bangkok you travel by coach to the beach resort of Pattaya.* **2** N-COUNT A **coach** is one of the separate sections of a train that carries passengers. [BRIT] **3** N-COUNT A **coach** is an enclosed four-wheeled vehicle pulled by horses, in which people used to travel. **4** V-T & N-COUNT If you **coach** someone or a team, you help them to become better at a particular sport or subject. A person who does this is called a **coach**. ❑ *He coached the local basketball team.* ❑ *...a drama coach.* ❑ *...a football coach.*

coal /kəʊl/ (**coals**) **1** N-UNCOUNT **Coal** is a hard black substance taken from underground and burned as fuel. **2** N-PLURAL **Coals** are burning pieces of coal.
→ see **energy**

coalition /ˌkəʊəˈlɪʃən/ (**coalitions**) **1** N-COUNT A **coalition** is a government consisting of people from two or more political parties. ❑ *...a coalition government.* **2** N-COUNT A **coalition** is a group consisting of people from different political or social groups. ❑ *He formed a political coalition with the support of 83 members.*

coarse /kɔːs/ (**coarser, coarsest**) **1** ADJ **Coarse** things have a rough texture. ❑ *...a beach of coarse sand.* ● **coarsely** ADV ❑ *...coarsely ground black pepper.* **2** ADJ A **coarse** person talks and behaves in a rude and offensive way. ● **coarsely** ADV ❑ *Some of the characters speak coarsely in the play.*

coast /kəʊst/ (**coasts, coasting, coasted**) **1** N-COUNT The **coast** is an area of land next to the sea. ● **coastal** ADJ BEFORE N ❑ *...coastal areas.* **2** V-I If a person or a team **is coasting**, they are doing something easily and without effort. ❑ *Charles was coasting at school.* ❑ *Murray coasted to an easy victory.*
→ see **beach**

coastguard /ˈkəʊstgɑːd/ (**coastguards**) N-COUNT A **coastguard** is an official who watches the sea near a coast, in order to get help when it is needed and to prevent smuggling.

coastline /ˈkəʊstlaɪn/ (**coastlines**) N-VAR A country's **coastline** is the edge of its coast. ❑ *The country has over a thousand miles of coastline.*

coat /kəʊt/ (**coats, coating, coated**) **1** N-COUNT A **coat** is a piece of clothing with long sleeves worn over your other clothes when you go outside. **2** N-COUNT An animal's **coat** is its fur or hair. **3** V-T If you **coat** something **with** a substance, you cover it with a thin layer of the substance. ❑ *The birds died, coated with oil.* ● **-coated** ❑ *...chocolate-coated sweets.* **4** N-COUNT A **coat of** paint or

varnish is a thin layer of it.
→ see **clothing, painting**

coating /'kəʊtɪŋ/ (**coatings**) N-COUNT A **coating** of a substance is a thin layer of it. ❑ *Brush the pan with a light coating of olive oil.*

coax /kəʊks/ (**coaxes, coaxing, coaxed**) V-T If you **coax** someone **to** do something, you gently try to persuade them to do it. ❑ *I coaxed him to tell me what was wrong.*

cobble /'kɒbəl/ (**cobbles, cobbling, cobbled**)
▶ **cobble together** PHR-VERB If you say that someone has **cobbled** something **together**, you mean that they have made or produced it roughly or quickly. ❑ *The group cobbled together a few songs.*

cobra /'kəʊbrə/ (**cobras**) N-COUNT A **cobra** is a kind of poisonous snake.

cobweb /'kɒbweb/ (**cobwebs**) N-COUNT A **cobweb** is the fine net that a spider makes in order to catch insects.

cocaine /kəʊ'keɪn/ N-UNCOUNT **Cocaine** is an addictive drug which people take for pleasure.

cock /kɒk/ (**cocks, cocking, cocked**) **1** N-COUNT A **cock** is an adult male chicken. **2** V-T If you **cock** a part of your body in a particular direction, you lift it or point it in that direction. ❑ *He paused and cocked his head.*

cockpit /'kɒkpɪt/ (**cockpits**) N-COUNT The **cockpit** in a small plane or racing car is the part where the pilot or driver sits.

cockroach /'kɒkrəʊtʃ/ (**cockroaches**) N-COUNT A **cockroach** is a large brown insect that is often found in dirty or damp places.
→ see **insect**

cocktail /'kɒkteɪl/ (**cocktails**) **1** N-COUNT A **cocktail** is an alcoholic drink containing several ingredients. ❑ *...a champagne cocktail.* **2** N-COUNT A mixture of a number of different things can be called a **cocktail**. ❑ *...a fruit cocktail.* ❑ *He promises a cocktail of dance, theatre, and opera.*

cocky /'kɒki/ (**cockier, cockiest**) ADJ A **cocky** person is very self-confident and pleased with themselves. [INFORMAL] ❑ *He had a confident, even cocky, look.*

cocoa /'kəʊkəʊ/ **1** N-UNCOUNT **Cocoa** is a brown powder used in making chocolate. **2** N-UNCOUNT **Cocoa** is a hot drink made with cocoa powder and milk.

coconut /'kəʊkənʌt/ (**coconuts**) N-VAR A **coconut** is a very large nut with a hairy shell, white flesh, and milky juice inside. **Coconut** is the white flesh of a coconut.

cocoon /kə'ku:n/ (**cocoons**) **1** N-COUNT A **cocoon** is a covering of silky threads made by the larvae of moths and other insects before they grow into adults. **2** N-COUNT You can use **cocoon** to describe a safe and protective place. ❑ *She was glad to get back to the warm cocoon of her sleeping bag.*

cod /kɒd/

Cod is both the singular and the plural form.

N-VAR A **cod** is a large sea fish with white flesh. **Cod** is the flesh of this fish eaten as food.

Word Link	*cod ≈ writing : code, decode, encode*

code /kəʊd/ (**codes**) **1** N-COUNT A **code** is a set of rules about how people should behave. ❑ *...a strict code of practice.* ❑ *...the school dress code.* **2** N-VAR A **code** is a system of replacing the words in a message with other words or symbols, so that people who do not know the system cannot understand it. ❑ *Remember your number by writing it down in code.* **3** N-COUNT A **code** is a group of numbers or letters used to identify something such as a postal address. ❑ *I dialled the wrong area code.* **4** N-COUNT A **code** is any system of signs or symbols that has a meaning. ❑ *...computer code.*

coded /'kəʊdɪd/ ADJ **Coded** messages have words or symbols which represent other words, so that the message is secret unless you know the system behind the code. ❑ *The police officers were waiting for coded instructions.*

coding /'kəʊdɪŋ/ N-UNCOUNT **Coding** is a method of making it easy to see the difference between several things, for example by marking them in different colours.

coerce /kəʊ'ɜ:s/ (**coerces, coercing, coerced**) V-T If you **coerce** someone **into** doing something, you make them do it against their will. [FORMAL] ❑ *Clark had managed to coerce Jenny into signing the document.* ● **coercion** N-UNCOUNT ❑ *Nobody likes doing things by coercion.*

coffee /'kɒfi, AM 'kɔ:fi/ (**coffees**) **1** N-VAR **Coffee** is the roasted beans of the coffee plant. **2** N-VAR **Coffee** is a drink made from boiling water and ground roasted coffee beans. ❑ *Would you like a coffee?*

'coffee shop (**coffee shops**) N-COUNT A **coffee shop** is a restaurant that sells coffee, tea, cakes, and sometimes sandwiches and snacks.

coffers /'kɒfəz/ N-PLURAL The **coffers** of an organization consist of the money that it has to spend.

coffin /'kɒfɪn, AM 'kɔ:fɪn/ (**coffins**) N-COUNT A **coffin** is a box in which a dead body is buried or cremated.

cognac /'kɒnjæk, AM 'kəʊn-/ (**cognacs**) N-VAR **Cognac** is a kind of brandy.

Word Link	*cogn ≈ knowing : cognitive, recognition, recognize*

cognitive /'kɒgnɪtɪv/ ADJ BEFORE N **Cognitive** means relating to the mental process involved in knowing, learning, and understanding things. [TECHNICAL] ❑ *...physical, emotional and cognitive growth.*

coherent /kəʊ'hɪərənt/ **1** ADJ If something is **coherent**, it is well planned, so that it is clear and sensible. ❑ *We need a coherent short-term plan.* ● **coherence** N-UNCOUNT ❑ *...political coherence.* **2** ADJ If someone is **coherent**, they express their thoughts in a clear and calm way. ❑ *She was not able to have a coherent conversation.* ● **coherently** ADV ❑ *He has lost the ability to express himself coherently.*

cohesion /kəʊ'hi:ʒən/ N-UNCOUNT If there is **cohesion** within a society, organization, or group, the different members fit together well and form a united whole. ❑ *The cohesion of the armed forces was breaking down.*

cohesive /kəʊ'hi:sɪv/ ADJ Something that is **cohesive** consists of parts that fit together well and form a united whole. ❑ *Experts agree that a cohesive effort needs to be made.*

coil /kɔɪl/ (**coils, coiling, coiled**) **1** N-COUNT A **coil of** rope or wire is a length of it that has been

C

wound into a series of loops. ❑ *He had a coil of rope over his shoulder.* **2** V-T/V-I & PHR-VERB If something **coils**, or if you **coil** it **up**, it curves into a series of loops or into the shape of a ring. ❑ *Her brown hair coiled around her head.* ❑ *We take the wire and we coil it up.*

coin /kɔɪn/ (**coins, coining, coined**) **1** N-COUNT A **coin** is a small piece of metal used as money. **2** V-T If you **coin** a word or a phrase, you are the first person to say it. ❑ *Jaron Lanier coined the term 'virtual reality'.*
→ see **English, money**

coinage /'kɔɪnɪdʒ/ **1** N-UNCOUNT **Coinage** consists of the coins used in a country. **2** N-UNCOUNT **Coinage** is the system of money used in a country.

coincide /ˌkəʊɪn'saɪd/ (**coincides, coinciding, coincided**) **1** V-I If one event **coincides with** another, they happen at the same time. ❑ *The film's release coincided with the school holidays.* **2** V-I If the opinions or ideas of two or more people **coincide**, they are the same. ❑ *Ideally, the beliefs of patient and doctor should coincide.* ❑ *These were people whose interests coincided with his own.*

coincidence /kəʊ'ɪnsɪdəns/ (**coincidences**) N-VAR A **coincidence** happens when two or more things occur at the same time by chance. ❑ *We are both, by coincidence, wearing red sweaters.* ❑ *...a series of amazing coincidences.*

coincidentally /ˌkəʊɪnsɪ'dentli/ ADV You say **coincidentally** when you want to draw attention to a coincidence. ❑ *Coincidentally, I had once been in a similar situation.*

coke /kəʊk/ (**cokes**) **1** N-VAR **Coke** is a sweet, brown, non-alcoholic fizzy drink. **Coke** is a trademark. **2** N-UNCOUNT **Coke** is **cocaine**. [INFORMAL]

cola /'kəʊlə/ N-UNCOUNT **Cola** is a sweet, brown, non-alcoholic fizzy drink.

> **Word Link** *est ≈ most : coldest, highest, largest*

cold /kəʊld/ (**colder, coldest, colds**) **1** ADJ & N-UNCOUNT If something or someone is **cold**, they have a very low temperature. **The cold** is cold weather or a low temperature. ❑ *...cold running water.* ❑ *This is the coldest winter I can remember.* ❑ *It was windy and Jake felt cold.* ❑ *He came inside to get out of the cold.* ● **coldness** N-UNCOUNT ❑ *...the coldness of the night.*

> **Usage**
>
> If you want to emphasize how cold the weather is, you can say that it is **freezing**, especially in winter when there is ice or frost. In summer, if the temperature is below average, you can say that it is **cool**. In general, **cold** suggests a lower temperature than **cool**, and **cool** things may be pleasant or refreshing. ❑ *A cool breeze came off the sea; it was pleasant out there.*

2 ADJ **Cold** food, such as salad or meat that has been cooked and cooled, is not intended to be eaten hot. **3** ADJ A **cold** person does not show much emotion or affection and therefore seems unfriendly. ❑ *She was a cold woman.* ● **coldly** ADV ❑ *'I'll see you in the morning,' Hugh said coldly.* ● **coldness** N-UNCOUNT ❑ *His coldness angered her.* **4** N-COUNT & PHRASE If you have a **cold**, you have a mild, very common illness which makes you sneeze a lot and gives you a sore throat or a cough. If you **catch cold**, or if you **catch a cold**, you become ill with a cold. **5 in cold blood** → see **blood**

> **Thesaurus** *cold* Also look up:
>
> ADJ. bitter, chilly, cool, freezing, frozen, raw; *(ant.)* hot, warm **1**
> cool, distant; *(ant.)* friendly, warm **3**

> **Word Partnership** Use *cold* with:
>
> ADV. **bitterly** cold, **freezing** cold **1** **2**
> N. cold **air**, **dark and** cold, cold **night**, cold **rain**, cold **water**, cold **weather**, cold **wind** **1** **2**
> V. **feel** cold, **get** cold **1**
> **catch/get a** cold **4**

ˌcold 'calling N-UNCOUNT **Cold calling** is phoning or visiting someone without their agreement in order to try to sell them something.

> **Word Link** *co ≈ together : collaborate, co-operate, co-ordinate*

> **Word Link** *labor ≈ working : collaborate, elaborate, laboratory*

collaborate /kə'læbəreɪt/ (**collaborates, collaborating, collaborated**) **1** V-I When people **collaborate**, they work together on a particular project. ❑ *Students collaborate in group exercises.* ❑ *He collaborated with his son on the project.* ● **collaboration** (**collaborations**) N-VAR ❑ *Drummond was working on a book in collaboration with the band.* ● **collaborator** (**collaborators**) N-COUNT ❑ *He completed the film with his collaborator, Hugh Lynn.* **2** V-I If someone **collaborates with** an enemy which has occupied their country, he or she helps them; used showing disapproval. ● **collaboration** N-UNCOUNT ❑ *There were rumours of his collaboration with the enemy.* ● **collaborator** N-COUNT ❑ *...a collaborator with the secret police.*

collaborative /kə'læbərətɪv, AM -reɪt-/ ADJ BEFORE N A **collaborative** piece of work is done by two or more people working together. [FORMAL] ❑ *...a collaborative research project.*

collage /'kɒlɑːʒ, AM kə'lɑːʒ/ (**collages**) N-VAR A **collage** is a picture made by sticking pieces of paper or cloth onto paper. **Collage** is the method of making these pictures.

> **Word Link** *lapse ≈ falling : collapse, elapse, lapse*

collapse /kə'læps/ (**collapses, collapsing, collapsed**) **1** V-I & N-UNCOUNT If something **collapses**, or if there is a **collapse** of it, it suddenly falls down or falls inwards. ❑ *The roof had collapsed.* **2** V-I & N-UNCOUNT If you **collapse**, or if you have a **collapse**, you suddenly fall down because you are ill or tired. ❑ *Jimmy collapsed on the floor.* ❑ *A few days after his collapse he was sitting up in bed.* **3** V-I & N-UNCOUNT If a system or institution **collapses**, or if there is a **collapse**, it fails completely and suddenly. ❑ *The company collapsed in 1992 with debts of £1.4 million.* ❑ *The medical system is facing collapse.*

collar /'kɒlə/ (**collars, collaring, collared**)

collar

1 N-COUNT The **collar** of a shirt or coat is the part which fits round the neck and is usually folded over. 2 N-COUNT A **collar** is a leather band which is put round the neck of a dog or cat. 3 V-T If you **collar** someone who has done something wrong or who is running away, you catch them and hold them so that they cannot escape. [INFORMAL] ❑ *Boycott collared Kerr as he ran for the train.*

collate /kəˈleɪt/ (**collates, collating, collated**) V-T When you **collate** pieces of information, you gather them all together and examine them. ❑ *The 2001 figures have not yet been collated.*

collateral /kəˈlætərəl/ N-UNCOUNT **Collateral** is money or property which is used as a guarantee that someone will repay a loan. [FORMAL] ❑ *You can use your home as collateral for a small business loan.*

colleague /ˈkɒliːg/ (**colleagues**) N-COUNT Your **colleagues** are the people you work with, especially in a professional job. ❑ *...a business colleague.*

collect /kəˈlekt/ (**collects, collecting, collected**) 1 V-T If you **collect** a number of things, you bring them together from several places. ❑ *Two girls were collecting firewood.* ❑ *1.5 million signatures have been collected.* 2 V-T If you **collect** things as a hobby, you get a large number of them over a period of time because you are interested in them. ❑ *He collected antique furniture.* ● **collecting** N-UNCOUNT ❑ *...stamp collecting.* ● **collector** (**collectors**) N-COUNT ❑ *...a collector of Indian art.* 3 V-T When you **collect** someone or something, you go and get them from a place where they are waiting for you or have been left for you. ❑ *David always collects Alistair from school.* ❑ *I went to collect the car and paid the bill.* ● **collection** N-UNCOUNT ❑ *...services such as rubbish collection.* 4 V-T/V-I If a substance **collects** somewhere, or if something **collects** it, it keeps arriving over a period of time and is held in that place or thing. ❑ *Methane gas collects in the mines.* ❑ *The water tanks collect rainwater.* 5 V-T/V-I If you **collect for** a charity or **for** a present, you ask people to give you money for it. ❑ *They collected money to help military families.* ❑ *The children were collecting for a local school choir.* ● **collection** (**collections**) N-COUNT ❑ *There was a collection for flowers.* 6 V-T If you **collect yourself** or **collect** your thoughts, you make an effort to calm or prepare yourself. ❑ *I needed to relax and collect my thoughts.*

Thesaurus	*collect* Also look up:
v.	accumulate, compile, gather; *(ant.)* scatter 1

collection /kəˈlekʃən/ (**collections**) 1 N-COUNT A **collection of** things is a group of similar or related things. ❑ *This is the world's largest collection of sculptures by Henry Moore.* ❑ *...a collection of essays.* 2 → see also **collect**

collective /kəˈlektɪv/ (**collectives**) 1 ADJ BEFORE N **Collective** means shared by or involving every member of a group of people. ❑ *It was a collective decision.* ● **collectively** ADV ❑ *These men have collectively given over 600 years' service.* 2 N-COUNT A **collective** is a business or farm whose employees share the decision-making and the profits.

collector /kəˈlektə/ (**collectors**) 1 N-COUNT A **collector** is someone whose job is to take something such as money or tickets from people. ❑ *He's a rent collector.* ❑ *...rubbish collectors.* 2 → see also **collect**
→ see **solar**

college /ˈkɒlɪdʒ/ (**colleges**) 1 N-VAR A **college** is an institution where students study after they have left school. ❑ *Joanna is doing business studies at a local college.* ❑ *I'm going to college in September.* 2 N-COUNT A **college** in a university is one of the institutions which some British universities are divided into. ❑ *...Balliol College, Oxford.* 3 N-COUNT A **college** of a particular kind is an organized group of people who have special duties and powers. [FORMAL] ❑ *...the Royal College of Nursing.*
→ see **graduation**

collide /kəˈlaɪd/ (**collides, colliding, collided**) V-I If people or vehicles **collide**, they bump into each other. ❑ *Two trains collided head-on.* ❑ *Racing up the stairs, he almost collided with Daisy.*

Thesaurus	*collide* Also look up:
v.	bump, clash, crash, hit, smash; *(ant.)* avoid 1

colliery /ˈkɒljəri/ (**collieries**) N-COUNT A **colliery** is a coal mine. [BRIT]

collision /kəˈlɪʒən/ (**collisions**) N-VAR A **collision** occurs when a moving object hits something. ❑ *Their van was involved in a collision with a car.* ❑ *...a head-on collision between two aeroplanes.*

collude /kəˈluːd/ (**colludes, colluding, colluded**) V-I If one person **colludes with** another, they co-operate secretly or illegally. ❑ *The colleges are colluding with the government over the plans.* ● **collusion** N-UNCOUNT ❑ *Schemes like this are run in collusion with the local council.*

colon /ˈkəʊlən/ (**colons**) 1 N-COUNT Your **colon** is the lower part of your intestines. ❑ *...cancer of the colon.* 2 N-COUNT A **colon** is the punctuation mark (:).
→ see **punctuation**

colonel /ˈkɜːnəl/ (**colonels**) N-COUNT & N-TITLE A **colonel** is a senior military officer.

colonial /kəˈləʊniəl/ ADJ BEFORE N **Colonial** means relating to countries that are colonies, or to colonialism. ❑ *...independence from British colonial rule.*

colonialism /kəˈləʊniəlɪzəm/ N-UNCOUNT **Colonialism** is the practice by which a powerful country directly controls less powerful countries. ❑ *We can see the lasting effects of colonialism.*

colonist /ˈkɒlənɪst/ (**colonists**) N-COUNT **Colonists** are people who start a colony. ❑ *...early American colonists.*

colonize [BRIT also **colonise**] /ˈkɒlənaɪz/ (**colonizes, colonizing, colonized**) V-T When large numbers of people, plants or animals **colonize** a place, they go to live there and make it their home. ❑ *The first British attempt to colonize Ireland was in the twelfth century.* ❑ *This plant is colonising many London gardens.* ● **colonization** N-UNCOUNT ❑ *...the European colonization of America.*

colony /ˈkɒləni/ (**colonies**) 1 N-COUNT A

C

Picture Dictionary colour

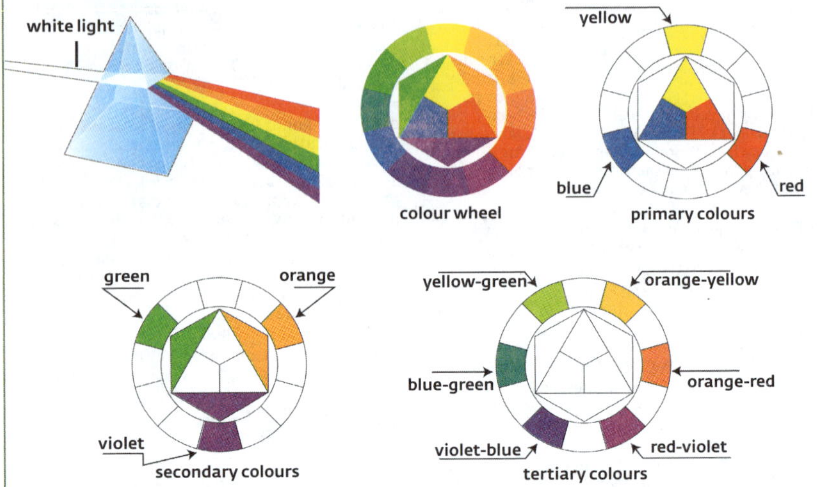

colony is a country which is controlled by a more powerful country. 2 N-COUNT A **colony** is a group of people or animals of a particular sort living together. ❑ *...an artists' colony.* ❑ *...a seal colony.*

color /'kʌlə/ → see **colour**

colorless /'kʌlələs/ → see **colourless**

colossal /kə'lɒsəl/ ADJ Something that is **colossal** is very large. ❑ *...a colossal waste of money.*

colour [AM **color**] /'kʌlə/ (**colours, colouring, coloured**) 1 N-COUNT The **colour** of something is the appearance that it has as a result of reflecting light. Red, blue, and green are colours. ❑ *What colour is the car?* ❑ *Her dress was sky-blue, the colour of her eyes.* 2 N-COUNT Someone's **colour** is the colour of their skin. People often use **colour** in this way to refer to a person's race. ❑ *Colour was just not important.* 3 ADJ A **colour** television, film, or photograph shows things in all their colours, and not just in black and white. ❑ *...colour illustrations.* 4 N-UNCOUNT **Colour** is a quality that makes something interesting or exciting. ❑ *A checked shirt adds colour to a work suit.* 5 V-T If something **colours** your opinion, it affects your opinion.
→ see Picture Dictionary: **colour**
→ see **painting**
▶ **colour in** PHR-VERB If you **colour in** a drawing, you give it different colours using crayons or paints.

Word Partnership
Use *colour* with:

ADJ.	**bright** colour, **favourite** colour 1
N.	colour **blind** 1
	eye/hair colour 1
	skin colour 2
	colour **film/photograph**, colour **television** 3

coloured [AM **colored**] /'kʌləd/ 1 ADJ **Coloured** means having a particular colour or combination of colours. ❑ *...a cheap gold-coloured bracelet.* ❑ *...brightly coloured silks.* 2 ADJ A **coloured** person belongs to a race of people with dark skins. [OFFENSIVE]

colourful [AM **colorful**] /'kʌləfʊl/ 1 ADJ Something that is **colourful** has bright colours. ❑ *...colourful flowers.* 2 ADJ **Colourful** means interesting and exciting. ❑ *Boxing has a colourful history.* ❑ *...the island's colourful past.*

Thesaurus
colourful Also look up:

ADJ.	bright, lively, vibrant, vivid; *(ant.)* bland, colourless, dull 1
	animated, dramatic, interesting 2

colouring [AM **coloring**] /'kʌlərɪŋ/ 1 N-UNCOUNT Someone's **colouring** is the colour of their hair, skin, and eyes. ❑ *None of the girls had their father's dark colouring.* 2 N-UNCOUNT **Colouring** is a substance that is used to give colour to food.

colourless [AM **colorless**] /'kʌlələs/ 1 ADJ A **colourless** substance is clear or invisible. ❑ *...a colourless liquid.* 2 ADJ **Colourless** people or places are dull and uninteresting. ❑ *We hurried through the colourless little town.*

colt /kəʊlt/ (**colts**) N-COUNT A **colt** is a young male horse.

column /'kɒləm/ (**columns**) 1 N-COUNT A **column** is a tall solid cylinder, especially one supporting part of a building. 2 N-COUNT A **column** is something that has a tall narrow shape. ❑ *...a column of smoke.* 3 N-COUNT A **column of** people, animals, or vehicles is a group of them moving in a line. ❑ *...a column of tanks.* 4 N-COUNT In a newspaper or magazine, a **column** is a vertical section of writing, or a regular section written by the same person. ❑ *He writes a column for The Wall Street Journal.*

columnist /'kɒləmɪst/ (**columnists**) N-COUNT

A **columnist** is a journalist who writes a regular article in a newspaper or magazine.

coma /ˈkəʊmə/ (**comas**) N-COUNT If someone is **in a coma**, they are deeply unconscious.

comb /kəʊm/ (**combs, combing, combed**) 1 V-T & N-COUNT When you **comb** your hair, you tidy it using a flat piece of plastic or metal with long thin pointed parts called a **comb**. 2 V-T If you **comb** a place **for** something, you search thoroughly for it. ❑ *Officers combed the woods for the murder weapon.*

combat (**combats, combating, combated**) 1 N-VAR /ˈkɒmbæt/ **Combat** is fighting that takes place in a war. ❑ *Over 16 million men had died in combat.* 2 V-T /kəmˈbæt/ If people in authority **combat** something, they try to stop it happening. ❑ *What are we doing to combat crime?*
→ see **war**

Word Partnership Use *combat* with:

ADJ.	**heavy** combat 1
N.	combat **forces/troops/units**, combat **gear** 1
	combat **crime**, combat **disease**, combat **terrorism** 2

combatant /ˈkɒmbətənt, AM kəmˈbæt-/ (**combatants**) N-COUNT A **combatant** is someone who takes part in a fight or a war.

combative /ˈkɒmbətɪv, AM kəmˈbætɪv/ ADJ A **combative** person is aggressive and eager to fight or argue.

combination /ˌkɒmbɪˈneɪʃən/ (**combinations**) 1 N-COUNT A **combination** is a mixture of things. ❑ *...a fantastic combination of colours.* 2 N-COUNT The **combination** of a lock is the series of letters or numbers used to open it. ❑ *Only the manager knows the combination to the safe.*

Word Link *com* ≈ *with, together* : *combine, compact, companion*

combine (**combines, combining, combined**) 1 V-T/V-I /kəmˈbaɪn/ If you **combine** two or more things, or if they **combine**, they exist or join together. ❑ *Combine the flour with 3 tablespoons of water.* ❑ *Disease and starvation combine to kill thousands.* ● **combined** ADJ BEFORE N ❑ *Their combined wealth totals £20 billion.* 2 V-T If someone or something **combines** two qualities or features, they have both of them. ❑ *Their system combines two main elements.* ❑ *His menu combines classic cooking with imaginative presentation.* 3 V-T If someone **combines** two activities, they do them both at the same time. ❑ *It is possible to combine a career with being a mother.* ❑ *He will combine the two jobs.* 4 N-COUNT /ˈkɒmbaɪn/ A **combine** is a group of people or organizations that are working together.

Thesaurus *combine* Also look up:

V.	blend, fuse, incorporate, join, mix, unite; *(ant.)* detach, disconnect, divide, separate 1 2 3

combustion /kəmˈbʌstʃən/ N-UNCOUNT **Combustion** is the act of burning something or the process of burning. [TECHNICAL]
→ see **engine**

come /kʌm/ (**comes, coming, came, come**) 1 V-I You use **come** to say that someone or something arrives somewhere, or moves towards you. ❑ *Two police officers came into the hall.* ❑ *He came to a door.* ❑ *Beryl came round to apologize.* 2 V-I If something **comes** to a particular point, it reaches it. ❑ *I wore a large shirt which came down to my knees.* 3 V-I You use **come** in expressions which state what happens to someone or something. ❑ *The door handle came off.* ❑ *The Communists came to power in 1944.* ❑ *Their worst fears may be coming true.* 4 V-T If someone **comes to** do something, they gradually start to do it. ❑ *She said it so many times that she came to believe it.* 5 V-I When a particular time or event **comes**, it arrives or happens. ❑ *The announcement came after a meeting at the Home Office.* ❑ *The time has come for us to move on.* 6 V-I If a thought or idea **comes to** you, you suddenly realize it. 7 V-I If something such as a sum **comes to** a particular amount, it adds up to it. ❑ *Lunch came to £80.* 8 V-I If someone or something **comes from** a particular place or thing, that place or thing is their origin or source. ❑ *Half the students come from abroad.* ❑ *Chocolate comes from the cacao tree.* 9 V-I Something that **comes from** something else or **comes of** it is the result of it. ❑ *His feeling of power came from driving fast.* 10 V-I If someone or something **comes** first, next, or last, they are first, next, or last in a series, list, or competition. 11 V-I If a type of thing **comes in** a range of colours, styles, or sizes, it can have any of those colours, styles, or sizes. ❑ *The wallpaper comes in black and white only.* 12 PHRASE You can use expressions like **I know where you're coming from** or **you can see where she's coming from** to say that you understand someone's attitude or point of view. ❑ *Do you see where I'm coming from?* 13 → See note at **bring** 14 → see also **coming**

▶ **come about** PHR-VERB When you say how or when something **came about**, you say how or when it happened. ❑ *This situation came about when I suggested that he give up his job.*

▶ **come across** 1 PHR-VERB If you **come across** someone or something, or **come upon** them, you meet or find them by chance. ❑ *This is the worst place I've come across.* 2 PHR-VERB The way that someone **comes across** is the impression they make on other people. ❑ *He comes across as an extremely pleasant young man.*

▶ **come along** 1 PHR-VERB If you ask someone to **come along** to a place or event where you are going to be, you are inviting them to come with you or go there. 2 PHR-VERB When something **comes along**, it arrives or happens, perhaps by chance. ❑ *It was lucky you came along.* 3 PHR-VERB If something **is coming along**, it is developing or making progress. ❑ *How's your research coming along?*

▶ **come around** or **come round** 1 PHR-VERB If you **come around to** an idea, you eventually change your mind and accept it. ❑ *They're finally coming around to our way of thinking.* 2 PHR-VERB When something **comes around**, it happens as a regular or predictable event. ❑ *The World Cup comes around again next year.* 3 PHR-VERB When someone who is unconscious **comes around** or **comes to**, they recover consciousness.

▶ **come at** PHR-VERB If a person or animal **comes at** you, they move towards you in a threatening way and try to attack you.

▶ **come back** 1 PHR-VERB If someone **comes back** to a place, they return to it. ❑ *I came back to*

C

London and decided to be a photographer. **2** PHR-VERB If something that you had forgotten **comes back to** you, you remember it. ❑ *His name will come back to me in a moment.* **3** PHR-VERB When something **comes back**, it becomes fashionable again. ❑ *I'm glad hats are coming back.* • **comeback** (**comebacks**) N-COUNT ❑ *Tight t-shirts are making a comeback.*

▶ **come by** PHR-VERB To **come by** something means to find or obtain it.

▶ **come down** **1** PHR-VERB If the cost, level, or amount of something **comes down**, it becomes less than it was before. ❑ *The price of petrol is coming down.* **2** PHR-VERB If something **comes down**, it falls to the ground.

▶ **come down on** **1** PHR-VERB If you **come down on** one side of an argument, you declare that you support that side. **2** PHR-VERB To **come down on** someone means to criticize them or treat them harshly.

▶ **come down to** PHR-VERB If a problem or decision **comes down to** a particular thing, that thing is the most important factor involved. ❑ *The problem comes down to money.*

▶ **come down with** PHR-VERB If you **come down with** an illness, you get it.

▶ **come for** PHR-VERB If people such as soldiers **come for** you, they come to find you.

▶ **come forward** PHR-VERB If someone **comes forward**, they offer to do something in response to a request for help. ❑ *A witness has come forward; she says she saw Tanner wearing the boots.*

▶ **come in** **1** PHR-VERB If information or a report **comes in**, you receive it. ❑ *Reports are now coming in of trouble at the jail.* **2** PHR-VERB If you have money **coming in**, you receive it regularly as your income. **3** PHR-VERB If someone or something **comes in**, or **comes into** a situation, they are involved in it. ❑ *Finally, he could do no more, which is where Jacques came in.* **4** PHR-VERB When a new idea, fashion, or product **comes in**, it becomes popular or available.

▶ **come in for** PHR-VERB If someone or something **comes in for** criticism or blame, they receive it.

▶ **come into** **1** PHR-VERB If someone **comes into** money or property, they inherit it. **2** → see also **come in** (meaning 3)

▶ **come off** PHR-VERB If something **comes off**, it is successful or effective. ❑ *It was a good try but it didn't quite come off.*

▶ **come on** **1** PHR-VERB You say **'Come on'** to someone to encourage them to do something. ❑ *Come on Doreen, let's dance.* **2** PHR-VERB When a machine **comes on**, it starts working. **3** PHR-VERB If you have an illness or a headache **coming on**, you can feel it starting. **4** PHR-VERB If something **is coming on**, it is developing or making progress. ❑ *My knee's coming on fine, I'm walking comfortably already.*

▶ **come on to** PHR-VERB When you **come on to** a particular topic, you start discussing it. ❑ *We're going to make some changes, but I'll come on to that later.*

▶ **come out** **1** PHR-VERB When a new product **comes out**, it becomes available to the public. ❑ *Cameron Diaz has a new movie coming out.* **2** PHR-VERB If a fact **comes out**, it becomes known to people. ❑ *The truth is beginning to come out about what happened.* **3** PHR-VERB If you **come out for** or **against** something, you declare that you support it or that you do not support it. **4** PHR-VERB If a photograph does not **come out**, it is blank or unclear when it is developed and printed. **5** PHR-VERB When the sun, moon, or stars **come out**, they appear in the sky.

▶ **come over** PHR-VERB If a feeling **comes over** you, it affects you. ❑ *A strange feeling came over me.*

▶ **come round** → see **come around**

▶ **come through** **1** PHR-VERB To **come through** a dangerous or difficult situation means to survive it. ❑ *The city has faced a crisis and come through it.* **2** PHR-VERB If something **comes through**, you receive it. ❑ *The news came through at about five o'clock.* **3** PHR-VERB If a quality or impression **comes through**, it is clearly shown in what is said or done. ❑ *I hope my love for the subject came through.*

▶ **come to** → see **come around** (meaning 3)

▶ **come under** **1** PHR-VERB If you **come under** attack or pressure, for example, people attack you or put pressure on you. **2** PHR-VERB If something **comes under** your authority, you control how it is managed.

▶ **come up** **1** PHR-VERB If someone **comes up to** you, they walk over to you. **2** PHR-VERB If an event **is coming up**, it is about to take place. ❑ *We have elections coming up.* **3** PHR-VERB If something **comes up**, it happens unexpectedly. ❑ *I was delayed – something came up at home.* **4** PHR-VERB If a topic **comes up** in a conversation, it is mentioned. **5** PHR-VERB If a job **comes up** or if something **comes up for sale**, it becomes available. **6** PHR-VERB When the sun or moon **comes up**, it rises.

▶ **come up against** PHR-VERB If you **come up against** a problem or difficulty, you have to deal with it. ❑ *Then they came up against the quickest team in the world.*

▶ **come upon** → see **come across** (meaning 1)

comeback /ˈkʌmbæk/ (**comebacks**) → see **come back** (meaning 3)

comedian /kəˈmiːdiən/ (**comedians**) N-COUNT A **comedian** is an entertainer whose job is to make people laugh by telling jokes.

comedy /ˈkɒmədi/ (**comedies**) **1** N-UNCOUNT **Comedy** consists of types of entertainment that are intended to make people laugh. ❑ *His career was in comedy.* ❑ *It's a TV comedy series.* **2** N-COUNT A **comedy** is a play, film, or television programme that is intended to make people laugh.
→ see **genre**

comet /ˈkɒmɪt/ (**comets**) N-COUNT A **comet** is an object that travels around the sun leaving a bright trail behind it.
→ see **solar system**

comfort /ˈkʌmfət/ (**comforts, comforting, comforted**) **1** N-UNCOUNT **Comfort** is the state of being physically or mentally relaxed. ❑ *Wear two pairs of socks for extra comfort.* **2** N-UNCOUNT If you are living **in comfort**, you have enough money to have everything you need. **3** N-COUNT **Comforts** are things that make your life easier and more pleasant. ❑ *She enjoys the comforts of married life.* **4** V-T & N-UNCOUNT If you **comfort** someone, or if you offer them **comfort**, you make them feel less worried or unhappy. ❑ *Ned put his arm around her, trying to comfort her.* ❑ *She could offer her friend no words of comfort.*

comfortable /ˈkʌmftəbəl/ **1** ADJ You describe things such as furniture as **comfortable** when they make you feel physically relaxed. When you are physically relaxed you can also say that you are **comfortable**. ❑ *...a comfortable chair.* ❑ *Lie down* and make yourself comfortable. • **comfortably** ADV ❑ *Are you sitting comfortably?* 2 ADJ If someone is **comfortable**, they have enough money to be able to live without financial problems. • **comfortably** ADV ❑ *Cayton describes himself as comfortably well-off.* 3 ADJ AFTER LINK-V If you feel **comfortable with** a particular situation or person, you feel confident and relaxed with them. ❑ *I felt comfortable with him.* ❑ *I'll tell them, but I won't feel comfortable about it.*

Thesaurus *comfortable* Also look up:

ADJ. well-off 2
cozy, soft; (*ant.*) uncomfortable 1
relaxed 3

comforting /'kʌmfətɪŋ/ ADJ If something is **comforting**, it makes you feel less worried or unhappy. ❑ *It's comforting to know that some things never change.*

comic /'kɒmɪk/ (**comics**) 1 ADJ Something that is **comic** makes you want to laugh. ❑ *The novel is comic and tragic.* ❑ *...a fine comic actor.* 2 N-COUNT A **comic** is an entertainer who tells jokes in order to make people laugh. 3 N-COUNT In British English, a **comic** is a magazine that contains stories told in pictures. The usual American term is **comic book**.

comical /'kɒmɪkəl/ ADJ If something is **comical**, it makes you want to laugh because it seems funny or silly. ❑ *Her expression was comical.*

'comic book (**comic books**) N-COUNT A **comic book** is the same as a **comic**. [AM]

coming /'kʌmɪŋ/ ADJ BEFORE N A **coming** event or time will happen soon. ❑ *Prices are likely to rise in the coming months.*

comma /'kɒmə/ (**commas**) N-COUNT A **comma** is the punctuation mark (,).
→ see **punctuation**

command /kə'mɑːnd, -'mænd/ (**commands, commanding, commanded**) 1 V-T & N-COUNT If you **command** someone **to** do something, or if you give them a **command to** do it, you order them to do it. ❑ *'Follow me,' he commanded.* ❑ *The dog owner will then give the command 'Forward'.* 2 V-T If you **command** something such as obedience or attention, you obtain it as a result of being popular or important. ❑ *This doctor commands the respect of all his colleagues.* 3 V-T & N-UNCOUNT An officer who **commands** part of an army, navy, or air force or has **command of** it, is in charge of it. ❑ *Who would command these troops in a war?* ❑ *In 1942 he took command of 108 Squadron.* 4 N-UNCOUNT Your **command of** something is your knowledge of it and ability to use it. ❑ *...his excellent command of English.*

commandant /'kɒməndænt/ (**commandants**) N-COUNT A **commandant** is an army officer in charge of a particular place or group of people.

commander /kə'mɑːndə/ (**commanders**) 1 N-COUNT & N-TITLE A **commander** is an officer in charge of a military operation. 2 N-COUNT & N-TITLE A **commander** is an officer in the navy.

commanding /kə'mɑːndɪŋ/ 1 ADJ If you are in a **commanding** position, you are in a strong or powerful position. ❑ *The company holds a commanding position in Southern England.* 2 ADJ If you have a **commanding** voice or manner, you seem powerful and confident.

commando /kə'mɑːndəʊ/ (**commandos** or **commandoes**) N-COUNT **Commandos** are soldiers specially trained to carry out surprise attacks in enemy areas.

Word Link *memor ≈ memory : commemorate, memorial, memory*

commemorate /kə'meməreɪt/ (**commemorates, commemorating, commemorated**) V-T If you **commemorate** a person or event, you remember them by means of a special action or ceremony, or a specially created object. ❑ *Australia Day commemorates the landing by Captain Arthur Philip in 1788.* • **commemoration** (**commemorations**) N-VAR ❑ *...a service of commemoration.*

commemorative /kə'memərətɪv/ ADJ BEFORE N A **commemorative** object or event is intended to make people remember an event or person. ❑ *...a commemorative coin.*

commence /kə'mens/ (**commences, commencing, commenced**) V-T/V-I When something **commences**, or when you **commence** it, it begins. [FORMAL] ❑ *Work is due to commence on July 16.* • **commencement** N-UNCOUNT ❑ *...the commencement of oil production.*

commend /kə'mend/ (**commends, commending, commended**) V-T If you **commend** someone or something, you praise them formally to other people. ❑ *I commended her for that action.* • **commendation** (**commendations**) N-VAR ❑ *...a letter of commendation.*

commendable /kə'mendəbəl/ ADJ If you describe someone's behaviour as **commendable**, you approve of it. [FORMAL] ❑ *Mr Spratt acted with commendable speed.* • **commendably** ADV ❑ *The police officer remained commendably cool.*

comment /'kɒment/ (**comments, commenting, commented**) V-T/V-I & N-VAR If you **comment on** something, or if you make a **comment on** it, you give your opinion about it or make a statement about it. ❑ *Police have refused to comment on the case.* ❑ *Stuart commented that this was very true.* ❑ *He made his comments at a news conference.*

commentary /'kɒməntri, AM -teri/ (**commentaries**) 1 N-VAR A **commentary** is a spoken description of an event that is broadcast on radio or television while it is taking place. ❑ *He turned on his radio to listen to the commentary.* 2 N-COUNT A **commentary** is a book or article which explains or discusses something. ❑ *...a commentary on the situation in India.*

commentate /'kɒmənteɪt/ (**commentates, commentating, commentated**) V-I To **commentate** means to give a radio or television commentary on an event. ❑ *They are in Sweden to commentate on the European Championships.*

commentator /'kɒmənteɪtə/ (**commentators**) 1 N-COUNT A **commentator** is a broadcaster who gives a commentary on an event. 2 N-COUNT A **commentator** is someone who often writes or broadcasts about a particular subject. ❑ *Harris was a political commentator with the Economist.*

Word Link *merc ≈ trading: commerce, merchandise, merchant*

commerce /'kɒmɜːs/ N-UNCOUNT **Commerce**

C

is the activity of buying and selling things on a large scale. ❑ *They made their wealth from industry and commerce.*

commercial /kəˈmɜːʃəl/ (**commercials**) **1** ADJ **Commercial** means relating to the buying and selling of goods. ❑ *...English commercial law.* **2** ADJ **Commercial** activities, organizations, and products are concerned with making a profit. ❑ *The airline will restart commercial flights next month.* ● **commercially** ADV ❑ *The fruit trees are grown commercially in Queensland.* **3** ADJ **Commercial television** and **radio** are paid for by advertising. **4** N-COUNT A **commercial** is an advertisement broadcast on television or radio.

C

commission /kəˈmɪʃən/ (**commissions, commissioning, commissioned**) **1** V-T & N-COUNT If you **commission** a piece of work, or if you give someone a **commission** to do it, you formally arrange to pay for someone to do it for you. ❑ *A Japanese publisher commissioned a book from me.* **2** N-VAR **Commission** is a sum of money paid to a salesperson for every sale that they make. ❑ *The adviser gets commission on every new policy sold.* **3** N-COUNT A **commission** is a group of people appointed to find out about something or to control something. **Commission** can take the singular or plural form of the verb. ❑ *...the Press Complaints Commission.* **4** V-T & N-COUNT If a member of the armed forces is **commissioned**, or if they receive a **commission**, they are made an officer.

commissioner /kəˈmɪʃənə/ (**commissioners**) N-COUNT A **commissioner** is an important official in a government department or other organization. ❑ *...the European Commissioner for External Affairs.*

commit /kəˈmɪt/ (**commits, committing, committed**) **1** V-T If someone **commits** a crime or a sin, they do something illegal or bad. ❑ *They know who committed the murder.* **2** V-T To **commit** money or resources **to** something means to use them for a particular purpose. ❑ *The agencies refused to commit funds to the hospital.* **3** V-T If you **commit yourself to** a way of life or course of action, you accept it fully or definitely decide to do it. ❑ *Mary committed herself to becoming a teacher.* ● **commitment** (**commitments**) N-VAR ❑ *They made a commitment to peace.* **4** V-T If someone **is committed to** a hospital or prison, they are officially sent there. ❑ *He was committed to a psychiatric hospital.*

commitment /kəˈmɪtmənt/ (**commitments**) N-COUNT A **commitment** is a regular task which takes up some of your time. ❑ *I've got a lot of commitments.*

committee /kəˈmɪti/ (**committees**) N-COUNT A **committee** is a group of people who represent a larger group or organization and make decisions for them. **Committee** can take the singular or plural form of the verb. ❑ *...the Committee for Safety in Medicine.*

commodity /kəˈmɒdɪti/ (**commodities**) N-COUNT A **commodity** is something that is sold for money. [TECHNICAL] ❑ *...basic commodities like bread and meat.*

common /ˈkɒmən/ (**commoner, commonest, commons**) **1** ADJ If something is **common**, it is found in large numbers or it happens often. ❑ *Hansen is a common name in Norway.* ❑ *It's a common mistake.* ● **commonly** ADV ❑ *Parsley is the herb we most commonly use.* **2** ADJ If something is **common to** two or more people or groups, it is possessed, done, or used by them all. ❑ *Such behaviour is common to all young people.* ❑ *Moldavians and Romanians share a common language.* **3** PHRASE If two or more people or things have something **in common**, they have the same interests, experiences, characteristics or features. **4** ADJ BEFORE N **Common** is used to indicate that something is ordinary and not special. ❑ *The scientific name for common salt is sodium chloride.* **5** ADJ If you describe someone as **common**, you mean they behave in a way that shows lack of taste, education, and good manners. **6** N-COUNT A **common** is an area of grassy land where the public is allowed to go.

Thesaurus *common* Also look up:

ADJ.	frequent, typical, usual **1**
	accepted, standard, universal **2**
	commonplace, everyday; *(ant.)* special **4**

Word Partnership Use *common* with:

ADV.	**fairly/increasingly/more/most** common **1**
N.	common **belief**, common **language**, common **practice**, common **problem** **1**
V.	**have *something* in** common **3**

ˌcommon ˈlaw **1** N-UNCOUNT **Common law** is the system of law which is based on judges' decisions and on custom rather than on written laws. **2** ADJ BEFORE N A **common law** relationship is regarded as a marriage because it has lasted a long time, although no official marriage contract has been signed. ❑ *...his common law wife.*

commonplace /ˈkɒmənpleɪs/ ADJ If something is **commonplace**, it happens often or is often found. ❑ *This kind of event has become commonplace.*

ˌcommon ˈsense also **commonsense** N-UNCOUNT **Common sense** is the natural ability to make good judgements and behave sensibly.

Commonwealth /ˈkɒmənwelθ/ N-PROPER **The Commonwealth** is an association of countries that used to belong to the British Empire.

commotion /kəˈməʊʃən/ (**commotions**) N-VAR A **commotion** is a lot of noise and confusion. ❑ *I heard a commotion in the street.*

communal /ˈkɒmjʊnəl, AM kəˈmjuːnəl/ ADJ Something that is **communal** is shared by a group of people. ❑ *Guests share a communal lounge and kitchen.*

commune /ˈkɒmjuːn/ (**communes**) N-COUNT A **commune** is a group of people who live together and share everything.

Word Link ***commun*** **≈ *sharing* :** *communicate, communism, community*

communicate /kəˈmjuːnɪkeɪt/ (**communicates, communicating, communicated**) **1** V-I If you **communicate with** someone, you give them information, for example by speaking, writing, or sending radio signals. ❑ *My natural* mother has never communicated with me. ❑ They communicated in sign language. ● **communication** N-UNCOUNT ❑ She has no means of communication. 2 V-T If you **communicate** an idea or a feeling **to** someone, you make them aware of it. ❑ I was having trouble communicating my feelings. 3 V-I If you say that people are able to **communicate**, you mean they talk to each other openly, which allows them to understand each other's feelings or attitudes. ❑ This is one way that husbands and wives communicate.

communication /kə,mju:nɪ'keɪʃən/ (**communications**) 1 N-PLURAL **Communications** are the systems and processes that are used to communicate or broadcast information. ❑ ...a communications satellite. 2 N-COUNT A **communication** is a message that is sent to someone by, for example, sending a letter. [FORMAL] 3 → see also **communicate**
→ see **brain, radio**

communion /kə'mju:njən/ 1 N-UNCOUNT **Communion** is the Christian ceremony in which people eat bread and drink wine as a symbol of Christ's death and resurrection. 2 N-UNCOUNT **Communion with** nature or some other power or spirit, or **communion with** a person, is the feeling that you are sharing thoughts or feelings with them.

communiqué /kə'mju:nɪkeɪ, AM -'keɪ/ (**communiqués**) N-COUNT A **communiqué** is an official statement. ❑ ...a joint communiqué, issued by China and Saudi Arabia.

Word Link	ism ≈ action or state : communism, optimism, patriotism

communist /'kɒmjʊnɪst/ (**communists**) N-COUNT & ADJ A **communist** is someone who supports a political system in which the state controls the means of production, and everyone is supposed to be equal. ❑ ...communist rebels. ● **communism** N-UNCOUNT ❑ ...Karl Marx, the father of modern-day communism.

community /kə'mju:nɪti/ (**communities**) 1 N-SING & N-COUNT A **community** is a group of people who live in a particular area or are alike in some way. **Community** can take the singular or plural form of the verb. ❑ The event was supported by the local community. ❑ ...the business community. 2 N-UNCOUNT **Community** is friendship between different people or groups, and a sense of having something in common. ❑ These people have no sense of community.

Thesaurus	community	Also look up:
N.	neighbourhood, public, society 1	

com'munity centre [AM **community center**] (**community centres**) N-COUNT A **community centre** is a place where the people, groups, and organizations in a particular area can go and meet one another and do things.

com,munity 'service N-UNCOUNT **Community service** is unpaid work that criminals sometimes do as a punishment instead of being sent to prison. ❑ He was sentenced to 140 hours' community service.

Word Link	mut ≈ changing : commute, mutant, mutate

commute /kə'mju:t/ (**commutes, commuting, commuted**) 1 V-I If you **commute**, you travel a long distance to work every day. ● **commuter** (**commuters**) N-COUNT ❑ The number of commuters to London has dropped by 100,000. 2 V-T If a prisoner's sentence **is commuted**, it is changed to a less serious sentence.
→ see **traffic, transportation**

Word Link	com ≈ with, together : combine, compact, companion

compact /kəm'pækt/ (**compacts, compacting, compacted**) 1 ADJ Something that is **compact** is small or takes up very little space. ❑ ...a compact camera. 2 V-T To **compact** something means to press it so that it becomes more dense. [FORMAL] ❑ Walking on the paths compacts the soil.

compact disc /,kɒmpækt 'dɪsk/ (**compact discs**) N-COUNT **Compact discs** are small discs on which sound, especially music, is recorded. The abbreviation **CD** is also used.
→ see **DVD**

companion /kəm'pænjən/ (**companions**) N-COUNT A **companion** is someone who you spend time with or travel with. ❑ He has been her constant companion recently.

companionship /kəm'pænjənʃɪp/ N-UNCOUNT **Companionship** is having someone you know and like with you, rather than being on your own. ❑ I was glad of her companionship.

company /'kʌmpəni/ (**companies**) 1 N-COUNT A **company** is a business organization that makes money by selling goods or services. ❑ ...an insurance company. 2 N-COUNT A **company** is a group of opera singers, dancers, actors, or other performers who work together. 3 N-UNCOUNT **Company** is the state of having companionship. ❑ Please stay for a while. I need the company. 4 PHRASE If you **keep** someone **company**, you spend time with them and stop them feeling lonely or bored.

Word Partnership	Use company with:
ADJ.	**foreign** company, **parent** company 1
V.	**buy/own/sell/start a** company, company **employs**, company **makes** 1 **have** company, **keep** company, **part** company 3 4

comparable /'kɒmpərəbəl/ 1 ADJ Something that is **comparable to** something is roughly similar, for example in amount or importance. ❑ This lady's experience was not comparable to mine. ● **comparably** ADV ❑ ...comparably qualified students. 2 ADJ If two or more things are **comparable**, they are similar and so can be reasonably compared. ❑ In Ashford, comparable properties cost £60,000.

comparative /kəm'pærətɪv/ (**comparatives**) 1 ADJ BEFORE N You use **comparative** to show that your description of something is accurate only when it is compared to something else, or to what is usual. ❑ We carried the soldier back to comparative safety. ● **comparatively** ADV ❑ ...a comparatively small nation. 2 ADJ BEFORE N A **comparative** study involves the comparison of two or more things of the same kind. ❑ ...the comparative study of English *and Latin authors.* 3 N-COUNT & ADJ BEFORE N In grammar, **the comparative** or the **comparative** form of an adjective or adverb is used to indicate that something has more of a quality than it used to have or than something else has. For example, 'bigger' is the comparative form of 'big'. Compare **superlative**.

C

Word Link ***par* ≈ *equal* : *compare, disparate, part***

compare /kəm'peə/ (**compares, comparing, compared**) 1 V-T If you **compare** things, you consider them and discover the differences or similarities between them. ❑ *Compare the two illustrations on page 60.* 2 V-T If you **compare** one person or thing **to** another, you say that they are like the other person or thing. ❑ *His work has been compared to that of James Joyce.*

Thesaurus *compare* Also look up:

V.	analyze, consider, contrast, examine 1
	equate, match 2

compared /kəm'peəd/ PREP You can use **compared with** and **compared to** when you want to contrast two things or situations. For example, if you say that one thing is large compared with another or compared to another, you mean that it is larger than the other thing.

comparison /kəm'pærɪsən/ (**comparisons**) 1 N-VAR When you make a **comparison** between two or more things, you discover the differences or similarities between them. ❑ *...a comparison of the British and German governments.* ❑ *By comparison with previous years, this year was very relaxed.* 2 N-VAR When you make a **comparison**, you say that one thing is like another in some way. ❑ *...the comparison of her life to a sea voyage.*

compartment /kəm'pɑːtmənt/ (**compartments**) 1 N-COUNT A **compartment** is one of the separate sections of a railway carriage. 2 N-COUNT A **compartment** is one of the separate parts of an object that is used for keeping things in. ❑ *I put the champagne in the freezer compartment.*

compass

compass /'kʌmpəs/ (**compasses**) 1 N-COUNT A **compass** is an instrument that you use for finding directions. It has a dial and a magnetic needle that always points to the north. 2 N-PLURAL **Compasses** are an adjustable V-shaped instrument that you use for drawing circles. ❑ *We'll need a pair of compasses.*
→ see **magnet, navigation**

compassion /kəm'pæʃən/ N-UNCOUNT **Compassion** is a feeling of pity, sympathy, and understanding for people who are suffering. ❑ *He felt compassion for this helpless woman.*

Word Link ***ate* ≈ *filled with* : *affectionate, compassionate, considerate***

compassionate /kəm'pæʃənət/ ADJ A **compassionate** person feels pity, sympathy, and understanding for people who are suffering. ❑ *...a deeply compassionate man.* • **compassionately** ADV ❑ *He smiled compassionately.*

compatible /kəm'pætɪbəl/ 1 ADJ If things, systems, or ideas are **compatible**, they work well together or can exist together successfully. ❑ *His story is fully compatible with the facts.* • **compatibility** N-UNCOUNT ❑ *...compatibility with VHS video recorders.* 2 ADJ If you are **compatible with** someone, you have a good relationship with them because you have similar opinions and interests. • **compatibility** N-UNCOUNT ❑ *The basis of friendship is compatibility.*

compatriot /kəm'pætriət, AM -'peɪt-/ (**compatriots**) N-COUNT Your **compatriots** are people from your own country.

Word Link ***pel* ≈ *driving, forcing* : *compel, expel, propel***

compel /kəm'pel/ (**compels, compelling, compelled**) V-T If a situation, a rule, or a person **compels** you **to** do something, they force you to do it. ❑ *Should cyclists be compelled to wear a helmet?*

compelling /kəm'pelɪŋ/ ADJ A **compelling** argument or reason for something convinces you that something is true or that something should be done. ❑ *...a compelling reason to spend money.*

compensate /'kɒmpənseɪt/ (**compensates, compensating, compensated**) 1 V-T If someone **is compensated for** something unpleasant which has happened to them, they receive compensation for it. ❑ *Farmers will be compensated for their losses.* 2 V-I To **compensate for** something, especially something harmful or unwanted, means to do something which balances it or makes it ineffective. ❑ *Nothing fully compensates for a mother's absence.*

compensation /ˌkɒmpən'seɪʃən/ (**compensations**) 1 N-UNCOUNT **Compensation** is money that someone who has undergone loss or suffering claims from the person or organization responsible. ❑ *He received one year's salary as compensation.* 2 N-VAR If something is a **compensation**, it reduces the effects of something bad that has happened. ❑ *Sweet puddings are one of the compensations for the colder winter weather.*

compete /kəm'piːt/ (**competes, competing, competed**) 1 V-I If one person or organization **competes with** another **for** something, they try to get that thing for themselves and stop the other getting it. ❑ *Students are competing with foreigners for summer jobs.* 2 V-I If you **compete** in a contest or a game, you take part in it. ❑ *Eight entrants competed for prizes totalling $1000.*

competent /'kɒmpɪtənt/ ADJ Someone who is **competent** is efficient and effective. ❑ *He is a very competent worker.* • **competently** ADV ❑ *The company performs competently.* • **competence** N-UNCOUNT ❑ *They have a high level of competence.*

competition /ˌkɒmpɪ'tɪʃən/ (**competitions**) 1 N-UNCOUNT **Competition** is a situation in which two or more people or groups are trying to get something which not everyone can have. ❑ *There's been a lot of competition for the title.* 2 N-VAR A **competition** is an event in which people take part in order to find out who is best at a particular activity. ❑ *...a drawing competition.*

competitive /kəm'petɪtɪv/ 1 ADJ **Competitive** situations or activities are ones in which people compete with each other. ❑ *...the competitive* world of magazine publishing. ● **competitively** ADV ❑ ...skiing competitively. 2 ADJ A **competitive** person is eager to be more successful than other people. ❑ *I'm a very competitive person; I like to be the best.* ● **competitively** ADV ❑ *Recently, he has played more competitively.* ● **competitiveness** N-UNCOUNT ❑ *I can't stand competitiveness in the office.* 3 ADJ You can say goods or services are at a **competitive** price or rate when they are less expensive than other goods of the same kind. ● **competitively** ADV ❑ *...competitively priced vehicles.*

Word Partnership Use *competitive* with:

N.	competitive **sport** 1
	competitive **advantage** 1 3
	competitive **person** 2
ADV.	**fiercely** competitive, **highly** competitive, **more** competitive 1 2

competitor /kəm'petɪtə/ (**competitors**) 1 N-COUNT A company's **competitors** are other companies that sell similar kinds of goods or services. ❑ *The bank isn't doing as well as some of its competitors.* 2 N-COUNT A **competitor** is a person who takes part in a competition.

compilation /ˌkɒmpɪ'leɪʃən/ (**compilations**) N-COUNT A **compilation** is a record containing music from many different artists or music from different periods of one artist's career. ❑ *...a compilation of his jazz works.*

compile /kəm'paɪl/ (**compiles, compiling, compiled**) V-T If you **compile** something such as a book, report, or TV programme, you produce it by putting together pieces of information. ❑ *Eleven photographers took ten years to compile the book.* ● **compilation** /ˌkɒmpɪ'leɪʃən/ N-UNCOUNT ❑ *...the compilation of data.*

Word Link *plac ≈ pleasing : complacent, placate, placid*

complacent /kəm'pleɪsənt/ ADJ If someone is **complacent** about something like a threat or danger, they behave as if there is nothing to worry about. ❑ *We must not be complacent about our health.* ● **complacency** N-UNCOUNT ❑ *The professor said complacency about the disease was the biggest problem.* ● **complacently** ADV ❑ *He smiled complacently at his own cleverness.*

complain /kəm'pleɪn/ (**complains, complaining, complained**) 1 V-T/V-I If you **complain about** something, you say you are not satisfied with it. ❑ *The Americans complained about the high cost of visiting Europe.* ❑ *People always complain that big banks are unfriendly.* ❑ *Spencer wanted to complain to somebody.* 2 V-I If you **complain of** a pain or illness, you say you have it.

complaint /kəm'pleɪnt/ (**complaints**) 1 N-VAR A **complaint** is a statement of dissatisfaction about a situation or a reason for it. ❑ *There were nearly 1 million passenger complaints last year.* 2 N-COUNT A **complaint** is an illness. ❑ *I told the doctor about my skin complaint.*

complement (**complements, complementing, complemented**) 1 V-T /'kɒmplɪment/ If people or things **complement** each other, they have different qualities which go well together. ❑ *Choose a dessert to complement your meal.* ❑ *A written examination complements the practical test.* 2 N-COUNT /'kɒmplɪmənt/ Something that is a **complement to** something else has qualities which make the two things go well together. ❑ *Green wallpaper is the perfect complement to the light wood.* 3 N-COUNT In grammar, the **complement** of a link verb is an adjective group or noun group which comes after the verb and describes or identifies the subject. For example, in the sentence 'They felt very tired', 'very tired' is the complement.

complementary /ˌkɒmplɪ'mentri/ ADJ If two different things are **complementary**, they form a complete unit when they are brought together, or they combine well with each other. ❑ *The two groups had complementary skills.*

Word Link *ple ≈ filling : complement, complete, deplete*

complete /kəm'pliːt/ (**completes, completing, completed**) 1 ADJ If something is **complete**, it contains all the parts that it should contain. ❑ *A garden is not complete without a bed of roses.* ❑ *...a complete set of keys to the shop.* 2 ADJ You use **complete** to emphasize that something is as great in degree or amount as it possibly can be. ❑ *The party came as a complete surprise.* ● **completely** ADV ❑ *Many homes were completely destroyed.* 3 V-T If you **complete** something, you finish doing or producing it. ❑ *Peter Mayle has just completed his first novel.* ● **completion** N-UNCOUNT ❑ *The project is nearing completion.* 4 ADJ AFTER LINK-V If a task is **complete**, it is finished. ❑ *Our work on the farmhouse is complete.* 5 V-T To **complete** a set or group means to provide the last item that is needed to make it a full set or group. ❑ *Put a word in each space to complete the sentence.* 6 V-T To **complete** a form means to write the necessary information on it. 7 PHRASE If one thing comes **complete with** another, it has that thing as an extra or additional part. ❑ *The diary comes complete with a gold-coloured pen.*

Thesaurus *complete* Also look up:

ADJ.	entire, whole; *(ant.)* partial 1
	total, utter 2

complex /'kɒmpleks/ (**complexes**) 1 ADJ **Complex** things have many different parts and are hard to understand. ❑ *...a complex system of voting.* ❑ *...her complex personality.* ❑ *...complex machines.* 2 N-COUNT A **complex** is a group of buildings used for a particular purpose. ❑ *...a new shopping complex.* 3 N-COUNT If someone has a **complex** about something, they have a mental or emotional problem relating to it, often because of an unpleasant experience in the past. ❑ *I have never had a complex about my height.*

complexion /kəm'plekʃən/ (**complexions**) N-COUNT Your **complexion** is the natural colour or condition of the skin on your face. ❑ *...a pale complexion.*

complexity /kəm'pleksɪti/ (**complexities**) N-VAR **Complexity** is the state of having many different parts connected or related to each other in a complicated way. ❑ *...the increasing complexity of modern weapon systems.* ❑ *...legal complexities.*

compliance /kəm'plaɪəns/ N-UNCOUNT **Compliance with** something, for example a law or agreement, means doing what you are required or

C

expected to do. [FORMAL] ❑ *Compliance with the new law is likely to be very expensive.*

Word Link	**ate ≈ causing to be : complicate, humiliate, motivate**

C

complicate /'kɒmplɪkeɪt/ (**complicates, complicating, complicated**) V-T To **complicate** something means to make it more difficult to deal with or understand. ❑ *I don't want to complicate matters for you.*

complicated /'kɒmplɪkeɪtɪd/ ADJ Something that is **complicated** has many parts and is therefore difficult to understand. ❑ *The rules of cricket are complicated.*

complication /ˌkɒmplɪ'keɪʃən/ (**complications**) N-COUNT A **complication** is a problem or difficulty. ❑ *Luckily, she recovered without complications.*

complicity /kəm'plɪsɪti/ N-UNCOUNT **Complicity** is involvement with other people in an illegal activity. [FORMAL] ❑ *The men admitted complicity in the murders.*

compliment (**compliments, complimenting, complimented**)

verb /'kɒmplɪment/, noun /'kɒmplɪmənt/.

1 V-T & N-COUNT If you **compliment** someone, or if you **pay** them a **compliment**, you say something nice about them. ❑ *They complimented me on my dress.* 2 N-PLURAL **Compliments** is used in expressing good wishes or respect. [FORMAL] ❑ *My compliments to the chef.*

complimentary /ˌkɒmplɪ'mentəri/ 1 ADJ If you are **complimentary** about something, you express admiration for it. ❑ *We often get complimentary remarks about our garden.* 2 ADJ A **complimentary** seat, ticket, drink, etc. is given to you free.

comply /kəm'plaɪ/ (**complies, complying, complied**) V-I If you **comply with** a demand or rule, you do what you are required to do. [FORMAL] ❑ *They refused to comply with the rules.*

component /kəm'pəʊnənt/ (**components**) N-COUNT The **components** of something are its parts. ❑ *The plan has four main components.*
→ see **mass production**

Word Partnership	Use *component* with:
ADJ.	**key** component, **main** components, **separate** components
N.	component **parts**

compose /kəm'pəʊz/ (**composes, composing, composed**) 1 V-T The things that something **is composed of** are its parts or members. The separate things that **compose** something are the parts or members that form it. ❑ *The force will be composed of troops from NATO countries.* ❑ *These are the basic elements that compose the human nervous system.* 2 V-T/V-I When someone **composes**, or **composes** music, a speech, or a letter, they write it. 3 V-T If you **compose yourself**, you become calm after being angry or excited. • **composed** ADJ ❑ *Laura stood beside him, very calm and composed.*
→ see **music**

composer /kəm'pəʊzə/ (**composers**) N-COUNT A **composer** is a person who writes music.
→ see **music**

composite /'kɒmpəzɪt, AM kəm'pɑːzɪt/ (**composites**) ADJ & N-COUNT A **composite** object or item is made up of several different things, parts, or substances. A **composite** is a composite object or item. ❑ *...composite pictures.*

composition /ˌkɒmpə'zɪʃən/ (**compositions**) 1 N-UNCOUNT The **composition of** something is the things that it consists of and the way that they are arranged. ❑ *Look at the composition of Saturday's team.* ❑ *The oils vary greatly in composition.* 2 N-COUNT A **composition** is a piece of written work, especially one that children write at school. 3 N-COUNT A composer's **compositions** are the pieces of music he or she has written.
→ see **orchestra**

compost /'kɒmpɒst, AM -pəʊst/ N-UNCOUNT **Compost** is a mixture of decaying plants and manure which is used to improve soil. ❑ *Don't let the compost dry out.*

composure /kəm'pəʊʒə/ N-UNCOUNT Someone's **composure** is their appearance or feeling of calm and their control of their feelings, often in a difficult situation. [FORMAL]

compound (**compounds, compounding, compounded**)

noun and adjective /'kɒmpaʊnd/, verb /kəm'paʊnd/.

1 N-COUNT A **compound** is an enclosed area of land used for a particular purpose. ❑ *...a military compound.* 2 N-COUNT In chemistry, a **compound** is a substance consisting of two or more elements. 3 ADJ BEFORE N In grammar, a **compound** noun, adjective, or verb is made up of two or more words, for example 'fire engine'. 4 V-T To **compound** a problem means to make it worse by increasing it in some way. [FORMAL] ❑ *More violence will only compound the problem.*
→ see **element, rock**

comprehend /ˌkɒmprɪ'hend/ (**comprehends, comprehending, comprehended**) V-T If you cannot **comprehend** something, you cannot understand it. [FORMAL] ❑ *I cannot begin to comprehend what it must be like.*

comprehension /ˌkɒmprɪ'henʃən/ (**comprehensions**) 1 N-UNCOUNT **Comprehension** is the ability to understand something or the process of understanding something. ❑ *This situation was beyond her comprehension.* ❑ *They have no comprehension of why they are fighting.* 2 N-VAR A **comprehension** is an exercise to find out how well you understand a piece of text.

comprehensive /ˌkɒmprɪ'hensɪv/ (**comprehensives**) 1 ADJ Something that is **comprehensive** includes everything necessary or relevant. ❑ *...a comprehensive guide to the region.* • **comprehensively** ADV ❑ *The book is comprehensively illustrated.* 2 ADJ BEFORE N & N-COUNT In Britain, a **comprehensive school** or a **comprehensive** is a secondary school where children of all abilities are taught together.

compress /kəm'pres/ (**compresses, compressing, compressed**) V-T/V-I If you **compress** something, or if it **compresses**, it is pressed or squeezed so that it takes up less space. ❑ *Compressing a gas heats it up.* • **compression** N-UNCOUNT ❑ *The compression of the wood is easily achieved.*

comprise /kəm'praɪz/ (**comprises, comprising,**

comprised) V-T If something **comprises** or **is comprised of** a number of things or people, it has them as its parts or members. [FORMAL] ❑ *The exhibition comprises 50 works of art.*

compromise /ˈkɒmprəmaɪz/ (**compromises, compromising, compromised**) 1 N-VAR & V-I If you reach a **compromise with** someone or if you **compromise with** them, you reach an agreement whereby you both give up something that you originally wanted. ❑ *A compromise will have to be found.* ❑ *Would he compromise on his demands?* ❑ *Make an effort to compromise with colleagues.* 2 V-T If someone **compromises themselves** or their beliefs, they do something which causes people to doubt their honesty, loyalty, or moral principles. ❑ *He is not prepared to compromise his beliefs.*

compromising /ˈkɒmprəmaɪzɪŋ/ ADJ If you describe information or a situation as **compromising**, you mean that it reveals an embarrassing or guilty secret about someone. ❑ *...compromising photographs.*

Word Link	*puls ≈ driving, pushing : compulsion, expulsion, impulse*

compulsion /kəmˈpʌlʃən/ (**compulsions**) 1 N-COUNT A **compulsion** is a strong desire to do something. ❑ *Nancy felt a strong compulsion to spend some time in England.* 2 N-UNCOUNT If someone uses **compulsion** to make you do something, they force you to do it. ❑ *There is no compulsion to go sight-seeing.*

compulsive /kəmˈpʌlsɪv/ 1 ADJ BEFORE N You use **compulsive** to describe people who cannot stop doing something. ❑ *...a compulsive liar.* ● **compulsively** ADV ❑ *John is compulsively neat and clean.* 2 ADJ If you say a book is **compulsive** reading or a film is **compulsive** viewing, you find it so interesting that you do not want to stop reading the book or watching the film. [BRIT]

compulsory /kəmˈpʌlsəri/ ADJ If something is **compulsory**, you must do it because a law or someone in authority says you must. ❑ *Learning Latin is no longer compulsory here.*

Word Link	*put ≈ thinking : computer, dispute, undisputed*

computer /kəmˈpjuːtə/ (**computers**) N-COUNT A **computer** is an electronic machine which makes quick calculations and deals with large amounts of information.
→ see Picture Dictionary: **computer**
→ see **office**

computerize [BRIT also **computerise**] /kəmˈpjuːtəraɪz/ (**computerizes, computerizing, computerized**) V-T To **computerize** a system or type of work means to introduce computers into it. ● **computerized** ADJ ❑ *There was a debate about computerized identity cards.*

computing /kəmˈpjuːtɪŋ/ N-UNCOUNT **Computing** is the activity of using a computer and writing programs for it.

comrade /ˈkɒmreɪd, AM -ræd/ (**comrades**) N-COUNT Someone's **comrades** are their friends or companions. [LITERARY]

con /kɒn/ (**cons, conning, conned**) 1 V-T & N-COUNT If someone **cons** you, or if what they do is a **con**, they trick you into doing or believing something by saying things that are not true. [INFORMAL] ❑ *The businessman had conned him out of £5,000.* ❑ *It was all a con.* 2 **pros and cons** → see **pro**

conceal /kənˈsiːl/ (**conceals, concealing, concealed**) V-T To **conceal** something means to hide it or keep it secret. ❑ *The hat concealed her hair.* ❑ *He was concealing something from her.* ● **concealment** N-UNCOUNT ❑ *...the concealment of weapons.*

concede /kənˈsiːd/ (**concedes, conceding, conceded**) V-T If you **concede** something, you admit it or accept that it is true, often unwillingly. ❑ *Bess finally conceded that Nancy was right.* ❑ *'Well,' he conceded, 'I am a bit deaf.'*

conceivable /kənˈsiːvəbəl/ ADJ If something is **conceivable**, you can imagine it or believe it. ❑ *It is just conceivable that survivors might be found.* ● **conceivably** ADV ❑ *The project could conceivably be finished this week.*

conceive /kənˈsiːv/ (**conceives, conceiving,**

Picture Dictionary computer

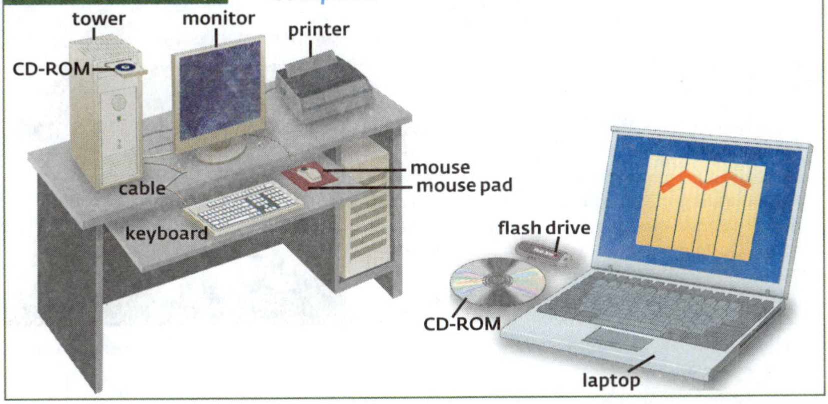

C

C

conceived) 1 V-I If you cannot **conceive of** something, you cannot imagine it or believe it. ❑ *He couldn't conceive of anyone disagreeing with him.* 2 V-T If you **conceive** a plan or idea, you think of it and work out how it can be done. ❑ *Calder conceived the idea of a Writers' Conference.* ● **conception** /kən'sepʃən/ N-UNCOUNT ❑ *He's attended every World Cup since its conception.* 3 V-T/V-I When a woman **conceives**, or **conceives** a baby, she becomes pregnant. ● **conception** **(conceptions)** N-VAR ❑ *Six weeks after conception your baby is the size of your little fingernail.* 4 → see also **conception**

concentrate /'kɒnsəntreɪt/ **(concentrates, concentrating, concentrated)** 1 V-I If you **concentrate on** something, you give it all your attention. ❑ *He sat back and concentrated on his driving.* ❑ *At work you need to be able to concentrate.* 2 V-T When something **is concentrated** in one place, it is all there rather than being spread around. ❑ *The most expensive houses are concentrated in London.*

concentrated /'kɒnsəntreɪtɪd/ 1 ADJ A **concentrated** liquid has been increased in strength by having water removed from it. 2 ADJ A **concentrated** activity is done with great intensity in one place. ❑ *We had to make a concentrated effort to keep going.*

concentration /ˌkɒnsən'treɪʃən/ **(concentrations)** 1 N-UNCOUNT **Concentration** on something involves giving all your attention to it. ❑ *We lost concentration and missed the goal.* 2 N-VAR A **concentration of** something is a large amount of it or large numbers of it in a small area. ❑ *Here is one of the world's greatest concentrations of wildlife.*

ˌconcen'tration camp **(concentration camps)** N-COUNT A **concentration camp** is a prison where non-military prisoners are kept in very bad conditions, usually in wartime.

concept /'kɒnsept/ **(concepts)** N-COUNT A **concept** is an idea or abstract principle. ❑ *She couldn't accept the concept of arranged marriage.* ● **conceptual** /kən'septʃuəl/ ADJ BEFORE N ❑ *He was quick at understanding the conceptual structure of a song.*

conception /kən'sepʃən/ **(conceptions)** 1 N-VAR A **conception** is an idea that you have in your mind. ❑ *They have no conception of a world before the Internet.* 2 → see also **conceive**

concern /kən'sɜːn/ **(concerns, concerning, concerned)** 1 V-T & N-UNCOUNT **Concern** is worry about a situation. If something **concerns** you, it worries you. ❑ *There is no cause for concern.* ❑ *It concerns me that nobody told us about this.* ● **concerned** ADJ ❑ *I've been concerned about you lately.* 2 N-COUNT A **concern** is a fact or situation that worries you. ❑ *Unemployment was the country's main concern.* 3 V-T If you **concern yourself with** something, you give attention to it because you think that it is important. ❑ *I didn't concern myself with politics.* 4 N-UNCOUNT Your **concern for** someone is a feeling that you want them to be happy, safe, and well. ❑ *He went there out of concern for his grandsons.* 5 V-T If a book, speech, or piece of information **concerns** a particular subject, it is about that subject. ❑ *Chapter 2 concerns the practical problems of living abroad.* ● **concerned** ADJ AFTER LINK-V ❑ *Randolph's work was concerned with the effects of pollution.* 6 V-T If a situation, event, or activity **concerns** you, it affects you or involves you. ❑ *'That doesn't concern you,' Zlotin said sharply.* ● **concerned** ADJ ❑ *It's a very stressful situation for everyone concerned.* 7 N-SING If a situation or problem is your **concern**, it is your duty or responsibility. ❑ *Road safety is the concern of everyone.* 8 N-COUNT A **concern** is a company or business. ❑ *The Minos Beach Hotel is a family concern.* 9 PHRASE You say **as far as** something **is concerned** to indicate the subject that you are talking about. ❑ *As far as my career was concerned, the affair was very helpful.* 10 PHRASE You say **as far as I'm concerned** to indicate that you are giving your own opinion. ❑ *The only problem, as far as I'm concerned, is Jenny.*

concerning /kən'sɜːnɪŋ/ PREP You use **concerning** to indicate what a question or piece of information is about. ❑ *Your doctor will give you important information concerning this product.*

concert /'kɒnsət/ **(concerts)** N-COUNT A **concert** is a performance of music. ❑ *...live rock concerts.*
→ see Word Web: **concert**

concerted /kən'sɜːtɪd/ 1 ADJ A **concerted** action is done by several people or groups working together. ❑ *...a concerted attack on crime.* 2 ADJ If you **make** a **concerted effort** to do something, you try very hard to do it. ❑ *I'm going to make a concerted effort to write more letters.*

concerto /kən'tʃeətəʊ/ **(concertos)** N-COUNT A **concerto** is a piece of music for a solo instrument and an orchestra.
→ see **music**

concession /kən'seʃən/ **(concessions)** N-COUNT

Word Web **concert**

A **rock concert** is much more than a group of **musicians** playing **music** on a **stage**. It is a full-scale **performance**. Each **band** must have a **manager** and an **agent** who **books** the **venue** and **promotes** the **show** in each new location. The band's assistants, called roadies, set up the stage, test the **microphones**, and tune the **instruments**. **Sound engineers** make sure the band sounds as good as possible. There's always **lighting** to **spotlight** the **lead singer** and backup singers. The bright, moving lights help to build excitement. The **fans** scream and yell when they hear their favorite **songs**. The **audience** never wants the show to end.

If you make a **concession to** someone, you agree to let them do or have something, especially in order to end an argument or conflict. ❑ *He has refused to make any concessions to the kidnappers.*

conciliation /kən,sɪli'eɪʃən/ N-UNCOUNT **Conciliation** is trying to end a disagreement. ❑ *...a mood of conciliation.*

conciliatory /kən'sɪliətri, AM -tɔːri/ ADJ If you are **conciliatory** in your actions or behaviour, you show you are willing to end a disagreement with someone. ❑ *Conciliatory talks are expected this summer.*

concise /kən'saɪs/ ADJ Something that is **concise** gives all the necessary information in a very brief form. ❑ *Burton's text is concise and informative.* ● **concisely** ADV ❑ *He delivered his report clearly and concisely.*

conclude /kən'kluːd/ (**concludes, concluding, concluded**) 1 V-T If you **conclude that** something is true, you decide that it is true using the facts you know. ❑ *He concluded that Oswald was guilty.* ❑ *So what can we conclude from this discussion?* 2 V-T/V-I When you **conclude** something, or when it **concludes**, it finishes. [FORMAL] ❑ *I concluded the meeting with a few suggestions.* ❑ *The evening concluded with dinner and speeches.* 3 V-T If people or groups **conclude** a treaty or business deal, they arrange it or agree it. [FORMAL]

conclusion /kən'kluːʒən/ (**conclusions**) 1 N-COUNT When you **come to** a **conclusion**, you decide that something is true after you have thought about it carefully. ❑ *I've come to the conclusion that she's a very great musician.* ❑ *Other people will draw their own conclusions.* 2 N-SING The **conclusion** of something is its ending. 3 PHRASE You can describe something that seems certain to happen as a **foregone conclusion**. 4 PHRASE You say **'in conclusion'** to introduce the last thing that you want to say. ❑ *In conclusion, walking is a cheap, safe and easy form of exercise.*

Word Partnership Use *conclusion* with:

V.	**come to a** conclusion, **draw a** conclusion, **reach a** conclusion 1
N.	conclusion **of** ***something*** 1 2
PREP.	**in** conclusion 4

conclusive /kən'kluːsɪv/ ADJ **Conclusive evidence** shows that something is definitely true. ❑ *There is no conclusive proof that this product is harmful.* ● **conclusively** ADV ❑ *He proved conclusively that the treatment is successful in 85% of cases.*

concoct /kən'kɒkt/ (**concocts, concocting, concocted**) 1 V-T If you **concoct** an excuse, you invent one. ❑ *He had concocted the story to avoid going to prison.* 2 V-T If you **concoct** something, especially something unusual, you make it by mixing several things together. ❑ *Luke was concocting some kind of fruit drink.*

concoction /kən'kɒkʃən/ (**concoctions**) N-COUNT A **concoction** is something that has been made out of several things mixed together. ❑ *It's a concoction of honey, yogurt, oats, and apples.*

concrete /'kɒŋkriːt/ 1 N-UNCOUNT **Concrete** is a substance used for building. It is made from cement, sand, small stones, and water. 2 ADJ Something that is **concrete** is definite and specific. ❑ *He had no concrete evidence.*

concur /kən'kɜː/ (**concurs, concurring, concurred**) V-I If two or more people **concur**, they agree. [FORMAL] ❑ *Many will concur with his opinion.*

Word Link ***curr, curs ≈ running, flowing : concurrent, current, excursion***

concurrent /kən'kʌrənt, AM -'kɜːr-/ ADJ If two things are **concurrent**, they happen at the same time. ❑ *He will serve three concurrent five-year prison sentences.* ● **concurrently** ADV ❑ *Three races were running concurrently.*

Word Link ***cuss ≈ striking : concussion, percussion, repercussions***

concussion /kən'kʌʃən/ N-UNCOUNT If you suffer **concussion** after you hit your head, you lose consciousness or feel sick or confused.

condemn /kən'dem/ (**condemns, condemning, condemned**) 1 V-T If you **condemn** something, you say that it is bad and unacceptable. ❑ *Mr Davies condemned the price increase.* ● **condemnation** /,kɒndem'neɪʃən/ (**condemnations**) N-VAR ❑ *There was general condemnation of Saturday's killings.* 2 V-T If someone **is condemned to** a punishment, they are given it. ❑ *He was condemned to life imprisonment.* 3 V-T If authorities **condemn** a building, they officially decide that it is not safe and must be pulled down.

condemned /kən'demd/ ADJ A **condemned** prisoner is going to be executed. ❑ *...a condemned man's last request.*

condense /kən'dens/ (**condenses, condensing, condensed**) 1 V-T If you **condense** a piece of writing or speech, you make it shorter. ❑ *His job was to condense newspaper reports for the magazine.* 2 V-I/V-T When a gas or vapour **condenses**, or when you **condense** it, it changes into a liquid. → see **matter, water**

Word Link ***scend ≈ climbing : ascend, condescend, descend***

condescend /,kɒndɪ'send/ (**condescends, condescending, condescended**) 1 V-T If you say that someone **condescends to** do something, you disapprove of them because they agree to do it in a way which shows that they think they are superior to other people and should not have to do it. ❑ *He wouldn't condescend to talk to the nurse.* 2 V-I If you say that someone **condescends to** other people, you disapprove of them because they behave in a way which shows that they think they are superior to other people. ❑ *Don't condescend to me.* ● **condescending** ADJ ❑ *He has a condescending attitude.* ● **condescension** N-UNCOUNT ❑ *...a smile of condescension.*

condition /kən'dɪʃən/ (**conditions, conditioning, conditioned**) 1 N-SING The **condition** of someone or something is the state they are in. ❑ *He remains in a serious condition in hospital.* ❑ *The boat is in good condition.* 2 N-PLURAL The **conditions** in which people live or do things are the factors that affect their comfort, safety, or success. ❑ *People are living in shocking conditions.* ❑ *We drove through changing weather conditions.* 3 N-COUNT A **condition** is something which must happen in order for something else to be possible. ❑ *One condition of the job was that he had to go to college.* 4 PHRASE When you agree to do something **on condition that** something else

happens, you mean that you will only do it if this other thing happens or is agreed to first. ❑ *He spoke to reporters on condition that he was not named.* **5** N-COUNT You can refer to an illness or medical problem as a particular **condition**. ❑ *She has a heart condition.* **6** V-T If someone **is conditioned to** think or do something in a particular way, they do it as a result of their upbringing or training. ❑ *Men are conditioned to believe that it is weak to be afraid.* ● **conditioning** N-UNCOUNT ❑ *...social conditioning.*
→ see **factory**

C

conditional /kən'dɪʃənəl/ ADJ If a situation or agreement is **conditional on** something, it will only happen if this thing happens. ❑ *The deal is conditional on agreement from publishers.* ❑ *...a conditional offer.*

condolence /kən'dəʊləns/ (**condolences**) N-PLURAL & N-UNCOUNT When you offer your **condolences**, or when you send a message of **condolence**, you express sympathy for someone whose friend or relative has died recently.

condom /'kɒndɒm/ (**condoms**) N-COUNT A **condom** is a rubber covering which a man wears on his penis as a contraceptive.

condone /kən'dəʊn/ (**condones, condoning, condoned**) V-T If someone **condones** behaviour that is wrong, they accept it and allow it to happen. ❑ *I cannot condone violence.*

conducive /kən'dju:sɪv, AM -'du:sɪv/ ADJ If one thing is **conducive to** another, it makes the other thing likely to happen. ❑ *Make your bedroom as conducive to sleep as possible.*

conduct (**conducts, conducting, conducted**)

verb /kən'dʌkt/, noun /'kɒndʌkt/.

1 V-T & N-SING When you **conduct** an activity or task, you organize it and do it. You can also talk about the **conduct** of an activity or task. ❑ *I decided to conduct an experiment.* ❑ *...the conduct of fair elections.* **2** N-UNCOUNT & V-T Your **conduct**, or the way you **conduct yourself**, is the way you behave. ❑ *We cannot allow this kind of conduct.* ❑ *He conducts himself in a similar way on and off the tennis court.* **3** V-T/V-I When someone **conducts** an orchestra or choir, they stand in front of it and direct its performance. ❑ *Solti continued to conduct here and abroad.* ❑ *I've always wanted to conduct an orchestra.* ● **conductor** (**conductors**) N-COUNT ❑ *Several hundred musicians need a conductor.* **4** V-T If something **conducts** heat or electricity, it allows heat or electricity to pass through it.
→ see **metal**

Thesaurus *conduct* Also look up:

V.	control, direct, manage **1**
N.	attitude, behaviour, manner **2**

Word Partnership Use *conduct* with:

N. conduct **business**, conduct **an experiment** **1**
code of conduct **2**

cone /kəʊn/ (**cones**) **1** N-COUNT A **cone** is a shape with a circular base and smooth curved sides ending in a point at the top. **2** N-COUNT A **cone** is the fruit of a pine or fir tree.
→ see **solid, volcano, volume**

cone

confederation /kən,fedə'reɪʃən/ (**confederations**) N-COUNT A **confederation** is an organization of groups or states, especially one that exists for political or business purposes. ❑ *...the Confederation of British Industry.*

confer /kən'fɜ:/ (**confers, conferring, conferred**) **1** V-I When you **confer with** someone, you discuss something with them in order to make a decision. ❑ *He conferred with Phil.* ❑ *His doctors conferred by telephone.* **2** V-T If someone or something **confers** power or honour **on** you, they give it to you. ❑ *On such occasions the Queen often confers an honour on her host.*

conference /'kɒnfrəns/ (**conferences**) N-COUNT A **conference** is a meeting, often lasting a few days, which is organized on a particular subject. ❑ *...a conference on education.* ❑ *...the Conservative Party conference.*

confess /kən'fes/ (**confesses, confessing, confessed**) V-T/V-I If you **confess to** doing something wrong or something that you are ashamed of, you admit that you did it. ❑ *He confessed to seventeen murders.* ❑ *Ed confessed that he was worried.*

confession /kən'feʃən/ (**confessions**) **1** N-VAR **Confession** is the act of admitting that you have done something that you are ashamed of or embarrassed about. ❑ *I have a confession to make.* **2** N-COUNT A **confession** is a signed statement by someone in which they admit that they have committed a particular crime. ❑ *They forced him to sign a confession.*

confide /kən'faɪd/ (**confides, confiding, confided**) V-I If you **confide in** someone, you tell them a secret. ❑ *She had confided in me a year earlier.* ❑ *He once confided to me that he felt very guilty.*

confidence /'kɒnfɪdəns/ (**confidences**) **1** N-UNCOUNT If you have **confidence in** someone, you feel you can trust them. ❑ *I have every confidence in you.* **2** N-UNCOUNT If you have **confidence**, you feel sure about your abilities, qualities, or ideas. ❑ *The team was full of confidence.* **3** N-UNCOUNT If you tell someone something **in confidence**, you tell them a secret. ❑ *We told you all these things in confidence.* **4** N-COUNT A **confidence** is a secret that you tell someone. **5** PHRASE If you take someone **into** your **confidence**, you tell them a secret.

confident /'kɒnfɪdənt/ **1** ADJ If you are **confident** about something, you are certain that it will happen in the way you want it to. ❑ *I'm confident that we will succeed.* ● **confidently** ADV ❑ *I can confidently promise that things will change.* **2** ADJ People who are **confident** feel sure of their own abilities, qualities, or ideas. ❑ *He became more confident and relaxed.* ● **confidently** ADV ❑ *She walked confidently across the hall.*

confidential /,kɒnfɪ'denʃəl/ ADJ Information that is **confidential** is meant to be kept secret. ❑ *This was confidential information about her private life.* ● **confidentially** ADV ❑ *Any information you give will be treated confidentially.* ● **confidentiality**

N-UNCOUNT ❑ *We guarantee complete confidentiality to our clients.*

Thesaurus *confidential* Also look up:
ADJ. private, restricted; *(ant.)* public

Word Link *fig ≈ form, shape : configuration, disfigure, figure*

configuration /kən,fɪgʊ'reɪʃən, AM -,fɪgjə-/ (**configurations**) N-COUNT A **configuration** is an arrangement of a group of things. [FORMAL] ❑ *...an ancient configuration of giant stones.*

Word Link *fig ≈ form, shape : configure, disfigure, figure*

configure /kən'fɪgə, AM -'fɪgjər/ (**configures, configuring, configured**) V-T If you **configure** a piece of computer equipment, you set it up so that it is ready for use. ❑ *How easy was it to configure the software?*

confine (**confines, confining, confined**) **1** V-T /kən'faɪn/ To **confine** something or someone **to** a particular place or group means to prevent them from spreading beyond it or from leaving it. ❑ *The US will take steps to confine the conflict.* ❑ *The dog was confined to the kitchen again.* ● **confinement** N-UNCOUNT ❑ *...confinement to a wheelchair.* **2** V-T If you **confine yourself** or your activities **to** something, you do only that thing. ❑ *Yoko confined her activities to the world of big business.* **3** N-PLURAL /'kɒnfaɪnz/ The **confines of** a building or area are its boundaries. [FORMAL] ❑ *The movie is set within the confines of an old factory.*

confined /kən'faɪnd/ **1** ADJ AFTER LINK-V If something is **confined to** a particular place or group, it exists only there. ❑ *The problem is not confined to Germany.* **2** ADJ A **confined space** or **area** is small and enclosed by walls.

Word Link *firm ≈ making strong : affirm, confirm, reaffirm*

confirm /kən'fɜːm/ (**confirms, confirming, confirmed**) **1** V-T If something **confirms** what you believe, it shows that it is definitely true. ❑ *X-rays have confirmed that he has not broken any bones.* ❑ *This news confirms our worst fears.* ● **confirmation** /,kɒnfə'meɪʃən/ N-UNCOUNT ❑ *The bomb was confirmation that the daily attacks have returned.* **2** V-T If you **confirm** something that has been stated or suggested, you say that it is definitely true. ❑ *The police have confirmed that a man has died at the prison.* ● **confirmation** N-UNCOUNT ❑ *She looked over at James for confirmation.* **3** V-T If you **confirm** an arrangement or appointment, you make it definite. ❑ *You make the reservation, and I'll confirm it in writing.* ● **confirmation** N-UNCOUNT ❑ *You will receive a booking confirmation number.*

confiscate /'kɒnfɪskeɪt/ (**confiscates, confiscating, confiscated**) V-T If you **confiscate** something from someone, you take it away from them, often as a punishment. ❑ *The police confiscated his passport.*

Word Link *flict ≈ striking : affliction, conflict, inflict*

conflict (**conflicts, conflicting, conflicted**) **1** N-UNCOUNT /'kɒnflɪkt/ **Conflict** is serious disagreement and argument. If two people or groups are **in conflict**, they have had a serious disagreement and have not yet reached agreement. ❑ *Try to avoid conflict and establish a good working relationship.* ❑ *He found himself in conflict with his colleagues.* **2** N-VAR **Conflict** is fighting between countries or groups of people. ❑ *...a military conflict.* **3** V-I /kən'flɪkt/ If ideas, beliefs, or accounts **conflict**, they are very different from each other and it seems impossible for them to exist together. ❑ *Most of his opinions conflicted with my own.* ● **conflicting** ADJ ❑ *She received a lot of conflicting advice.*
→ see **war**

conform /kən'fɔːm/ (**conforms, conforming, conformed**) **1** V-I If something **conforms to** or **with** a law or someone's wishes, it is what is required or wanted. ❑ *The lamp conforms to new safety requirements.* ❑ *These activities do not conform with international law.* **2** V-I If you **conform**, you behave in the way that you are expected to behave. ❑ *People feel they have failed if they don't conform.*

conformity /kən'fɔːmɪti/ N-UNCOUNT **Conformity** is behaviour, thought, or appearance that is the same as that of most other people.

confound /kən'faʊnd/ (**confounds, confounding, confounded**) V-T If someone or something **confounds** you, they make you confused or surprised. ❑ *His behaviour has certainly confounded us.*

confront /kən'frʌnt/ (**confronts, confronting, confronted**) **1** V-T If you **are confronted with** a problem or task, you have to deal with it. ❑ *She was confronted with severe money problems.* ❑ *The difficulties confronting them were immense.* **2** V-T If you **confront** someone, you stand or sit in front of them, especially when you are going to fight or argue with them. ❑ *The men confronted each other during a televised debate.* **3** V-T If you **confront** someone **with** evidence, you present it to them in order to accuse them of something. ❑ *How do managers react when we confront them with this fact?*

confrontation /,kɒnfrʌn'teɪʃən/ (**confrontations**) N-VAR A **confrontation** is an argument, fight, or battle. ❑ *...confrontation with the enemy.* ● **confrontational** ADJ ❑ *He took a confrontational approach from the start.*

confuse /kən'fjuːz/ (**confuses, confusing, confused**) **1** V-T If you **confuse** two things, you get them mixed up, so that you think one is the other. ❑ *I can't see how anyone could confuse you two!* ● **confusion** N-UNCOUNT ❑ *Use different colours of ink to avoid confusion.* **2** V-T To **confuse** someone means to make it difficult for them to know what is happening or what to do. ❑ *German politics confused him.* **3** V-T To **confuse** a situation means to make it complicated or difficult to understand. ❑ *Talking about it would just confuse things even more.*

confused /kən'fjuːzd/ **1** ADJ If you are **confused**, you do not know what to do or you do not understand what is happening. ❑ *People are confused about what they should eat to stay healthy.* **2** ADJ Something that is **confused** does not have any order or pattern and is difficult to understand. ❑ *After a time, the system became confused.*

confusing /kən'fjuːzɪŋ/ ADJ Something that is **confusing** makes it difficult for people to know

C

what to do or what is happening. ❑ *This new system must be confusing for you.*

confusion /kən'fjuːʒən/ **1** N-UNCOUNT If there is **confusion about** something, it is not clear what the true situation is. ❑ *There's still confusion about how many people died.* **2** N-UNCOUNT **Confusion** is a situation in which everything is in disorder, especially because there are lots of things happening at the same time. ❑ *There was confusion when a man fired the shots.* **3** N-UNCOUNT If your mind is in a state of **confusion**, you do not know what to believe or what you should do. **4** → see also **confuse**

congenial /kən'dʒiːniəl/ ADJ A **congenial** person, place, or environment is pleasant. [FORMAL]

congested /kən'dʒestɪd/ ADJ A **congested** road or area is extremely crowded and blocked with traffic or people.

congestion /kən'dʒestʃən/ N-UNCOUNT If there is **congestion** in a place, the place is extremely congested. ❑ *...problems of traffic congestion.* → see **traffic**

conglomerate /kən'glɒmərət/ (**conglomerates**) N-COUNT A **conglomerate** is a large business consisting of several different companies. ❑ *Fiat is Italy's largest industrial conglomerate.*

Word Link	***grat** ≈ pleasing : **congratulate**, **gratify**, **gratitude***

congratulate /kən'grætʃʊleɪt/ (**congratulates, congratulating, congratulated**) V-T If you **congratulate** someone, you express pleasure for something good that has happened to them, or you praise them for something they have achieved. ❑ *She congratulated him on the birth of his son.* • **congratulation** N-UNCOUNT ❑ *...letters of congratulation.*

congratulations /kən,grætʃʊ'leɪʃənz/ CONVENTION You say **'congratulations'** to someone in order to congratulate them. ❑ *Congratulations, you have a healthy baby girl.*

congregate /'kɒŋgrɪgeɪt/ (**congregates, congregating, congregated**) V-I When people **congregate**, they gather together. ❑ *Young people congregate here in the evenings.*

congregation /,kɒŋgrɪ'geɪʃən/ (**congregations**) N-COUNT The people who attend a church service are the **congregation**. **Congregation** can take the singular or plural form of the verb.

congress /'kɒŋgres/ (**congresses**) N-COUNT A **congress** is a large meeting held to discuss ideas and policies. **Congress** can take the singular or plural form of the verb.

Congress /'kɒŋgres/ **1** N-PROPER **Congress** is the elected group of politicians that is responsible for making the law in the USA. • **congressional** /kən'greʃənəl/ ADJ BEFORE N ❑ *...a congressional report.* **2** → See note at **government**

congressman /'kɒŋgrɪsmən/ (**congressmen**) **1** N-COUNT & N-TITLE A **congressman** is a male member of the US Congress. **2** → See note at **government**

congresswoman /'kɒŋgrɪswʊmən/ (**congresswomen**) **1** N-COUNT & N-TITLE A **congresswoman** is a female member of the US Congress. **2** → See note at **government**

conjecture /kən'dʒektʃə/ (**conjectures**) N-VAR **Conjecture** is a guess based on incomplete or doubtful information. [FORMAL] ❑ *What will happen next is a matter of conjecture.*

conjoined twin /kən,dʒɔɪnd 'twɪn/ (**conjoined twins**) N-COUNT **Conjoined twins** are twins who are born with their bodies joined.

conjunction /kən'dʒʌŋkʃən/ (**conjunctions**) **1** PHRASE If one thing is done or used **in conjunction with** another, the two things are done or used together. [FORMAL] ❑ *The army operated in conjunction with the navy.* **2** N-COUNT In grammar, a **conjunction** is a word that joins together words, groups, or clauses. For example, 'and' and 'or' are conjunctions.

conjure /'kʌndʒə, AM 'kɑːn-/ (**conjures, conjuring, conjured**) V-T & PHR-VERB If you **conjure** something out of nothing, or if you **conjure up** something, you produce it as if by magic. ❑ *Every day a different chef will be conjuring up delicious dishes.*
▶ **conjure up** PHR-VERB To **conjure up** a memory, picture, or idea means to create it in your mind. ❑ *The hotel's name alone conjures up images of the Italian Riviera.*

connect /kə'nekt/ (**connects, connecting, connected**) **1** V-T To **connect** one thing **to** another means to join them together. ❑ *Connect the wires.* ❑ *The trailer was connected to the car.* ❑ *The long hallway connects the rooms.* **2** V-T If a piece of equipment or a place **is connected to** a source of power or water, it is joined to that source. ❑ *The island is now connected to the mainland water supply.* **3** V-T If a telephone operator **connects** you, he or she enables you to speak to another person by telephone. **4** V-I If one train or plane **connects with** another, it arrives at a time which allows passengers to change to the other one in order to continue their journey. ❑ *The train connects with a ferry to Ireland.* **5** V-T If you **connect** a person or thing **with** something, you realize that there is a link between them. ❑ *I hoped he would not connect me with the article.* ❑ *I never connected the two things.*

connected /kə'nektɪd/ ADJ If one thing is **connected with** another, there is a link between them. ❑ *Skin problems are often connected with too much sun.* ❑ *This incident can be connected to the recent killings.*

connection /kə'nekʃən/ (**connections**) **1** N-COUNT A **connection** is a relationship between two people, groups, or things. ❑ *I have no connection with the police.* **2** N-COUNT A **connection** is the joint where two wires or pipes are joined together. **3** N-COUNT If you **get a connection** at a station or airport, you continue your journey by catching another train, bus, or plane. ❑ *My flight was late and I missed the connection.* **4** PHRASE If you talk to someone **in connection with** something, you talk to them about that thing. ❑ *I am writing in connection with Michael Stower's letter.*

connoisseur /,kɒnə'sɜː/ (**connoisseurs**) N-COUNT A **connoisseur** is someone who knows a lot about the arts, food, or drink. ❑ *...connoisseurs of good food.*

connotation /,kɒnə'teɪʃən/ (**connotations**) N-COUNT The **connotations** of a word are the ideas or qualities that it makes you think of. ❑ *The words 'sneaky' and 'sly' both have negative connotations.*

conquer /'kɒŋkə/ (**conquers, conquering, conquered**) 1 V-T If one country or group of people **conquers** another, they take complete control of their land. ❑ *During 1936, Mussolini conquered Abyssinia.* ● **conqueror** (**conquerors**) N-COUNT ❑ *...the attitudes of European conquerors.* 2 V-T If you **conquer** something such as a problem, you succeed in ending it or dealing with it. ❑ *Has he conquered his fear of fire?*
→ see **army, empire**

conquest /'kɒŋkwest/ N-UNCOUNT **Conquest** is the act of conquering a country or group of people. ❑ *He led the conquest of southern Poland.*

Word Link	*sci ≈ knowing : conscience, conscious, science*

conscience /'kɒnʃəns/ (**consciences**) 1 N-COUNT Your **conscience** is the part of your mind that tells you if what you are doing is wrong. If you have a **guilty conscience**, or if you have something **on** your **conscience**, you feel guilty because you know you have done something wrong. ❑ *I started paying attention to my conscience.* 2 N-UNCOUNT **Conscience** is doing what you believe is right even though it might be unpopular or difficult. ❑ *Prisoners of conscience were kept in the castle here.*

conscientious /ˌkɒnʃi'enʃəs/ ADJ Someone who is **conscientious** is very careful to do their work properly. ❑ *She's a conscientious mother.* ● **conscientiously** ADV ❑ *He studied conscientiously.*

Word Link	*sci ≈ knowing : conscience, conscious, science*

conscious /'kɒnʃəs/ 1 ADJ AFTER LINK-V If you are **conscious of** something, you notice it or are aware of it. ❑ *He was conscious of the faint smell of aftershave.* 2 ADJ **Conscious** is used in expressions such as 'politically conscious' to describe someone who believes that a particular aspect of life is important. ❑ *She was very health-conscious.* 3 ADJ BEFORE N A **conscious** decision or effort is one that you are aware of making. ❑ *We never made a conscious decision to have a big family.* ● **consciously** ADV ❑ *Sophie was not consciously looking for a husband.* 4 ADJ Someone who is **conscious** is awake rather than asleep or unconscious. ❑ *She was fully conscious.*

Thesaurus	*conscious* Also look up:
ADJ.	calculated, deliberate, intentional, rational 3
	awake, aware, responsive; *(ant.)* unaware, unconscious 4

Word Link	*ness ≈ state, condition : awareness, consciousness, kindness*

consciousness /'kɒnʃəsnəs/ 1 N-UNCOUNT Your **consciousness** consists of your mind, thoughts, beliefs and attitudes. ❑ *Ideas came flowing into his consciousness.* ❑ *Cinema can change the consciousness of a nation.* 2 N-UNCOUNT If you **lose consciousness**, you become unconscious. When you **regain consciousness**, you become conscious again.

conscript (**conscripts, conscripting, conscripted**) 1 V-T /kən'skrɪpt/ If someone **is conscripted**, they are officially made to join the armed forces of a country. ❑ *He was conscripted into the army.* ● **conscription** N-UNCOUNT ❑ *In 1939 Britain introduced conscription for the first time.* 2 N-COUNT /'kɒnskrɪpt/ A **conscript** is a person who has been made to join the armed forces of a country.

consecrate /'kɒnsɪkreɪt/ (**consecrates, consecrating, consecrated**) V-T When a building, place, or object **is consecrated**, it is officially declared to be holy. ● **consecration** N-UNCOUNT ❑ *...the consecration of the new Coventry Cathedral.*

consecutive /kən'sekjʊtɪv/ ADJ **Consecutive** periods of time or events happen one after the other without interruption. ❑ *This is his second consecutive win.*

Word Link	*con ≈ together, with : consensus, contemporary, convene*

consensus /kən'sensəs/ N-SING A **consensus** is general agreement amongst a group of people. ❑ *There is a growing consensus in Europe that more action is needed.*

consent /kən'sent/ (**consents, consenting, consented**) 1 N-UNCOUNT **Consent** is permission given to someone to do something. ❑ *Can the doctor examine my child without my consent?* 2 N-UNCOUNT **Consent** is agreement about something between people. ❑ *By common consent it was the best game of the championship.* 3 V-I If you **consent to** something, you agree to do it or agree to it being done.

consequence /'kɒnsɪkwens/ (**consequences**) 1 N-COUNT The **consequences of** something are the results or effects of it. ❑ *If we do not take the right actions now, we will suffer the consequences later.* 2 PHRASE If one thing happens and then another thing happens **in consequence**, the second thing happens as a result of the first. ❑ *He could no longer continue farming, and in consequence, his life had to change.* 3 N-UNCOUNT Someone or something that is **of consequence** is important or valuable. Someone or something that is **of** no **consequence** is not important or valuable.

consequent /'kɒnsɪkwənt/ ADJ **Consequent** means happening as a direct result of something. [FORMAL] ❑ *...the warming of the Earth and the consequent climate changes.* ● **consequently** ADV ❑ *They have been studying continuously since September, and are consequently tired and unhappy.*

conservation /ˌkɒnsə'veɪʃən/ 1 N-UNCOUNT **Conservation** is the preservation and protection of the environment. ❑ *...wildlife conservation.* 2 → see also **conserve**

conservationist /ˌkɒnsə'veɪʃənɪst/ (**conservationists**) N-COUNT A **conservationist** is someone who works and campaigns for the conservation of the environment.

conservative /kən'sɜːvətɪv/ (**conservatives**) 1 N-COUNT & ADJ A **Conservative** or a **Conservative** politician or voter is a member of or votes for the Conservative Party. ❑ *...Conservative MPs.* ● **conservatism** N-UNCOUNT ❑ *He presented his new image of caring Conservatism.* 2 ADJ & N-COUNT Someone who is **conservative** or who is a **conservative** has right-wing views. 3 ADJ Someone who is **conservative** is unwilling to accept changes and new ideas. ❑ *Older people*

C

tend to be more conservative than younger ones.
● **conservatism** N-UNCOUNT ❑ *Designers blame the conservatism of UK manufacturers.* 4 ADJ A **conservative** estimate is very cautious. ❑ *Conservative estimates put her wealth at £5 million.* ● **conservatively** ADV ❑ *This player is conservatively valued at £500,000.*

C

Thesaurus *conservative* Also look up:

ADJ. conventional, right-wing, traditional; *(ant.)* left-wing, liberal, radical 2 3

Word Link ***ory ≈ place where something happens: conservatory, factory, territory***

conservatory /kən'sɜːvətri, AM -tɔːri/ (**conservatories**) N-COUNT A **conservatory** is a glass room built onto a house.

Word Link ***serv ≈ keeping : conserve, observe, preserve***

conserve /kən'sɜːv/ (**conserves, conserving, conserved**) 1 V-T If you **conserve** a supply of something, you use it carefully so that it lasts longer than it normally would. ❑ *We're trying to conserve as much money as possible.* ● **conservation** /ˌkɒnsə'veɪʃən/ N-UNCOUNT ❑ *...energy conservation.* 2 V-T To **conserve** something means to protect it from harm, loss, or change. ❑ *We want to conserve this natural beauty for ever.*

consider /kən'sɪdə/ (**considers, considering, considered**) 1 V-T If you **consider** a person or thing to be something, this is your opinion of them. ❑ *I consider him a coward.* ❑ *Others consider the move foolish.* ❑ *Sidney considers that Mitchel has ruined his life.* 2 V-T If you **consider** something, you think about it carefully. ❑ *You have to consider the feelings of those around you.* ● **consideration** /kənˌsɪdə'reɪʃən/ N-UNCOUNT ❑ *He said the idea needed further consideration.* 3 → see also **considering**

Usage

Note that when you are using the verb **consider** with a **that** clause in order to state a negative opinion or belief, you normally make **consider** negative, rather than the verb in the **that** clause. For instance, it is more usual to say '*I don't consider that you kept your promise*' than 'I consider that you didn't keep your promise'. The same pattern applies to other verbs with a similar meaning, such as **believe, suppose**, and **think**. ❑ *He didn't believe she could do it.* ❑ *I don't suppose he ever saw it.* ❑ *I don't think he saw me.*

Thesaurus *consider* Also look up:

V. contemplate, examine, study, think about, think over; *(ant.)* dismiss, forget, ignore 2

considerable /kən'sɪdərəbəl/ ADJ **Considerable** means great in amount or degree. ❑ *He has considerable wealth.* ❑ *Vets' fees can be considerable.* ● **considerably** ADV ❑ *His ideas have changed considerably over the years.*

Word Link ***ate ≈ filled with : affectionate, compassionate, considerate***

considerate /kən'sɪdərət/ ADJ A **considerate** person pays attention to the needs, wishes, or feelings of other people.

consideration /kənˌsɪdə'reɪʃən/ (**considerations**) 1 N-UNCOUNT Someone who shows **consideration** pays attention to the needs, wishes, or feelings of other people. ❑ *Show consideration for other travellers.* 2 N-COUNT A **consideration** is something that should be thought about when you are planning or deciding something. ❑ *Another important consideration is the weather.* 3 → see also **consider** 4 PHRASE If you **take** something **into consideration**, you think about it because it is relevant to what you are doing. ❑ *Would the President take public opinion into consideration?* 5 PHRASE If something is **under consideration**, it is being discussed. ❑ *Several proposals are under consideration.*

considering /kən'sɪdərɪŋ/ CONJ & PREP You use **considering** to indicate that you are taking a particular fact into account when giving an opinion. ❑ *Considering how ill he was, he made an amazing recovery.* ❑ *She was in excellent health, considering her age.*

consign /kən'saɪn/ (**consigns, consigning, consigned**) V-T If you **consign** someone or something **to** a particular place or situation, you put or place them there. ❑ *Most of his drawings were consigned to the dustbin long ago.*

consignment /kən'saɪnmənt/ (**consignments**) N-COUNT A **consignment of** goods is a load that is being delivered to a place or person.

consist /kən'sɪst/ (**consists, consisting, consisted**) V-I Something that **consists of** particular things is formed from them. ❑ *His diet consisted of bread, cheese and water.*

consistency /kən'sɪstənsi/ N-UNCOUNT The **consistency** of a substance is the extent to which it is thick or smooth. ❑ *Add water until the paint is the consistency of milk.*

consistent /kən'sɪstənt/ 1 ADJ A **consistent** person always behaves or responds in the same way. ❑ *Becker has never been a very consistent player.* ● **consistency** N-UNCOUNT ❑ *He has shown remarkable consistency.* ● **consistently** ADV ❑ *The company has consistently denied that there are any problems.* 2 ADJ If facts or ideas are **consistent**, there is no contradiction between or within them. ❑ *This result is consistent with the findings.*

consolation /ˌkɒnsə'leɪʃən/ (**consolations**) N-VAR If something is a **consolation**, it makes you feel more cheerful when you are unhappy. ❑ *He now knew that he was right, but it was no consolation.*

console (**consoles, consoling, consoled**) 1 V-T /kən'səʊl/ If you **console** someone who is unhappy, you try to make them more cheerful. ❑ *I could say nothing to console him.* 2 N-COUNT /'kɒnsəʊl/ A **console** is a panel with switches or knobs that is used to operate a machine.

consolidate /kən'sɒlɪdeɪt/ (**consolidates, consolidating, consolidated**) V-T If you **consolidate** something such as your power or success, you strengthen it so that it becomes more effective or secure. ❑ *This new product will consolidate the company's success in Europe.* ● **consolidation**

N-UNCOUNT ❑ *The report recommends some consolidation of police powers.*

consonant /'kɒnsənənt/ (**consonants**) N-COUNT A **consonant** is a sound such as 'p' or 'f' which you pronounce by stopping the air flowing freely through your mouth.

consortium /kən'sɔːtiəm/ (**consortiums** or **consortia** /kən'sɔːtiə/) N-COUNT A **consortium** is a group of people or firms who have agreed to work together. **Consortium** can take the singular or plural form of the verb.

conspicuous /kən'spɪkjʊəs/ ADJ If someone or something is **conspicuous**, people can see or notice them very easily. ❑ *I felt very conspicuous.* ● **conspicuously** ADV ❑ *Johnston's name was conspicuously absent from the list.*

conspiracy /kən'spɪrəsi/ (**conspiracies**) N-VAR **Conspiracy** is the secret planning by a group of people to do something wrong or illegal. ❑ *He is guilty of conspiracy to cause criminal damage.*

conspirator /kən'spɪrətə/ (**conspirators**) N-COUNT A **conspirator** is a person who joins a conspiracy.

conspire /kən'spaɪə/ (**conspires, conspiring, conspired**) **1** V-T If two or more people **conspire to** do something illegal or harmful, they make a secret agreement to do it. ❑ *The five men were found guilty of conspiring to commit the robberies.* **2** V-T If events **conspire to** produce a particular result, they seem to cause this result. ❑ *Illness and age have conspired to make my memory unreliable.*

constable /'kʌnstəbəl, 'kɒn-/ (**constables**) N-COUNT & N-TITLE In Britain, a **constable** is a police officer of the lowest rank.

constant /'kɒnstənt/ **1** ADJ Something that is **constant** happens all the time or is always there. ❑ *...constant interruptions.* ❑ *...constant noise.* ● **constantly** ADV ❑ *The direction of the wind is constantly changing.* **2** ADJ An amount or level that is **constant** stays the same over a particular period of time. ❑ *The temperature remains more or less constant.*

constellation /ˌkɒnstə'leɪʃən/ (**constellations**) N-COUNT A **constellation** is a group of stars which form a fixed pattern.
→ see **star**

consternation /ˌkɒnstə'neɪʃən/ N-UNCOUNT **Consternation** is a feeling of anxiety or fear. [FORMAL] ❑ *The news has caused consternation.*

constipation /ˌkɒnstɪ'peɪʃən/ N-UNCOUNT **Constipation** is a medical condition which causes people to have difficulty getting rid of waste matter from their bowels.

constituency /kən'stɪtʃʊənsi/ (**constituencies**) N-COUNT A **constituency** is an area for which someone is elected as the representative in parliament.

constituent /kən'stɪtʃʊənt/ (**constituents**) **1** N-COUNT A **constituent** is someone who lives in a particular constituency. **2** N-COUNT & ADJ BEFORE N A **constituent** or a **constituent** part of something is one of the things that it is made from. ❑ *Caffeine is one of the major constituents of coffee.*

constitute /'kɒnstɪtjuːt, AM -tuːt/ (**constitutes, constituting, constituted**) **1** LINK-VERB If something **constitutes** a particular thing, it can be regarded as being that thing. ❑ *What constitutes normal behaviour?* **2** LINK-VERB If a number of things or people **constitute** something, they are the parts or members that form it. ❑ *Hindus constitute 83% of India's population.*

constitution /ˌkɒnstɪ'tjuːʃən, AM -'tuː-/ (**constitutions**) **1** N-COUNT The **constitution** of a country or organization is the system of laws which formally states people's rights and duties. ❑ *...the French constitution.* ● **constitutional** /ˌkɒnstɪ'tjuːʃənəl, AM -'tuː-/ ADJ ❑ *The committee suggested a constitutional change.* **2** N-COUNT Your **constitution** is your health. ❑ *He has a strong constitution.*

constrain /kən'streɪn/ (**constrains, constraining, constrained**) V-T To **constrain** someone or something means to limit their development or activities. [FORMAL] ❑ *He is constrained by lack of money.* ● **constrained** ADJ ❑ *...constrained choices.*

constraint /kən'streɪnt/ (**constraints**) **1** N-COUNT A **constraint** is something that limits or controls what you can do. ❑ *...time constraints.* **2** N-UNCOUNT **Constraint** is control over the way you behave which prevents you from doing what you want to do. ❑ *Their country wants freedom after years of constraint.*

constrict /kən'strɪkt/ (**constricts, constricting, constricted**) **1** V-T/V-I If a part of your body **constricts** or **is constricted**, something causes it to become narrower. ❑ *Don't scream as this constricts the throat.* ❑ *The skin constricts in response to cold.* ● **constriction** N-UNCOUNT ❑ *...constriction of the blood vessels.* **2** V-T If something **constricts** you, it limits your actions so that you cannot do what you want to do. ❑ *She could still walk using a stick but her life was fairly constricted.* ● **constriction** (**constrictions**) N-COUNT ❑ *...the constrictions of small-town life.*

Word Link ***struct ≈ building : construct, destructive, instruct***

construct (**constructs, constructing, constructed**) **1** V-T /kən'strʌkt/ If you **construct** something, you build, make, or create it. ❑ *He plans to construct a hotel here.* ❑ *This building was constructed in 1852.* **2** N-COUNT /'kɒnstrʌkt/ A **construct** is a complex idea. [FORMAL]

construction /kən'strʌkʃən/ (**constructions**) **1** N-UNCOUNT **Construction** is the building or creating of something. ❑ *A new school is under construction.* ❑ *This is the best type of wood for boat construction.* **2** N-COUNT A **construction** is an object that has been made or built. ❑ *...an enormous steel and glass construction.*

constructive /kən'strʌktɪv/ ADJ A **constructive** discussion, comment, or approach is useful and helpful. ❑ *...constructive criticism.* ● **constructively** ADV ❑ *Use your time constructively.*

construe /kən'struː/ (**construes, construing, construed**) V-T If something **is construed** in a particular way, its nature or meaning is interpreted in that way. [FORMAL] ❑ *The police construed the accident as murder.*

consul /'kɒnsəl/ (**consuls**) N-COUNT A **consul** is a government official who lives in a foreign city and looks after all the people there who are from his or her own country. ● **consular** /'kɒnsjʊlə, AM

C

-sə-/ ADJ BEFORE N ❑ *...British Consular officials.*

consulate /ˈkɒnsjʊlət, AM -sə-/ (**consulates**) N-COUNT A **consulate** is the place where a consul works. ❑ *...the British consulate in Lyons.*

consult /kənˈsʌlt/ (**consults, consulting, consulted**) 1 V-T/V-I If you **consult** someone or something, you refer to them for advice or information. You can also **consult** with someone. ❑ *If you still feel ill, consult your doctor.* ❑ *They will consult with their advisers.* • **consultation** /ˌkɒnsəlˈteɪʃən/ (**consultations**) N-VAR ❑ *...a consultation with a lawyer.* 2 → see also **consultation**

consultancy /kənˈsʌltənsi/ (**consultancies**) 1 N-COUNT A **consultancy** is a company that gives expert advice on a particular subject. ❑ *...an international health consultancy.* 2 N-UNCOUNT **Consultancy** is expert advice which a person or group is paid to provide. ❑ *The company provides both consultancy and training.*

consultant /kənˈsʌltənt/ (**consultants**) 1 N-COUNT A **consultant** is an experienced doctor specializing in one area of medicine. [BRIT] ❑ *...a consultant heart surgeon.* 2 N-COUNT A **consultant** is a person who gives expert advice on a particular subject. ❑ *He was a consultant to the Swedish government.*

consultation /ˌkɒnsəlˈteɪʃən/ (**consultations**) 1 N-VAR **Consultations** are meetings which are held to discuss something. **Consultation** is discussion about something. ❑ *...consultations with the president.* 2 → see also **consult**

consultative /kənˈsʌltətɪv/ ADJ A **consultative committee** or **document** gives advice or makes proposals about a particular problem or subject.

> **Word Link** *sume ≈ taking : assume, consume, presume*

consume /kənˈsjuːm, AM -ˈsuːm/ (**consumes, consuming, consumed**) 1 V-T If you **consume** something, you eat or drink it. [FORMAL] ❑ *She consumes a large amount of chocolate every day.* 2 V-T To **consume** an amount of fuel, energy, or time means to use it up. ❑ *North America consumes 24 million barrels of oil per day.* • **-consuming** ❑ *...a time-consuming job.*

consumed /kənˈsjuːmd, AM -ˈsuːmd/ ADJ AFTER LINK-V If you are **consumed with** a feeling or idea, it affects you very strongly. ❑ *He was consumed with jealousy.*

consumer /kənˈsjuːmə, AM -ˈsuː-/ (**consumers**) N-COUNT A **consumer** is a person who buys things or uses services. ❑ *Consumers are ready to keep spending.*

consuming /kənˈsjuːmɪŋ, AM -ˈsuː-/ ADJ A **consuming** passion or interest is more important to you than anything else. ❑ *He has a consuming passion for chess.*

> **Word Link** *summ ≈ highest point : consummate, summary, summit*

consummate (**consummates, consummating, consummated**) 1 ADJ /ˈkɒnsjəmət/ You use **consummate** to describe someone who is extremely skilful. [FORMAL] ❑ *...a consummate politician.* ❑ *He plays football with consummate skill.* 2 V-T /ˈkɒnsəmeɪt/ If two people **consummate** a marriage or relationship, they make it complete by having sex. • **consummation** /ˌkɒnsəˈmeɪʃən/ N-UNCOUNT ❑ *...the consummation of their marriage.* 3 V-T To **consummate** an agreement means to complete it. [FORMAL] ❑ *They were unable to consummate the deal.*

> **Word Link** *sumpt ≈ taking : assumption, consumption, presumption*

consumption /kənˈsʌmpʃən/ 1 N-UNCOUNT The **consumption** of fuel or energy is the amount of it that is used, or the act of using it. ❑ *Fuel consumption is down 10%.* 2 N-UNCOUNT The **consumption** of food or drink is the act of eating or drinking something. [FORMAL] ❑ *I'm not happy about the high consumption of fizzy drinks in this country.* 3 N-UNCOUNT **Consumption** is the act of buying and using things. [TECHNICAL] ❑ *...the consumption of goods and services.*

> **Word Link** *tact ≈ touching : contact, intact, tactic*

contact /ˈkɒntækt/ (**contacts, contacting, contacted**) 1 N-VAR **Contact** involves meeting or communicating with someone. ❑ *I have very little contact with children.* ❑ *I shall be in contact with my family by telephone.* ❑ *He made contact with me yesterday.* 2 V-T If you **contact** someone, you telephone them or write to them. ❑ *Have you contacted him?* 3 ADJ Your **contact** details or number are information such as a telephone number where you can be contacted. ❑ *You must leave your full name and contact details when you phone.* 4 N-UNCOUNT If you come **into contact with** something, you have some experience of it in the course of your work or other activities. ❑ *My job brings me into contact with a lot of different people.* 5 N-COUNT A **contact** is someone you know in an organization who helps you or gives you information. ❑ *My contact in the company is called Phil.* 6 N-UNCOUNT If people or things are **in contact**, they are touching each other. ❑ *Lie face down so that your entire body is in contact with the floor.*

ˈcontact lens (**contact lenses**) N-COUNT **Contact lenses** are small lenses that you put on your eyes to help you to see better.
→ see **eye**

contact lens

contagious /kənˈteɪdʒəs/ 1 ADJ A **contagious disease** can be caught by touching people or things that are infected with it. 2 ADJ A **contagious** feeling or attitude spreads quickly among a group of people. ❑ *Laughter can be contagious.*

contain /kənˈteɪn/ (**contains, containing, contained**) 1 V-T If something such as a box or a room **contains** things, those things are in it. ❑ *The bag contained a present.* 2 V-T If something **contains** a particular substance, that substance is part of it. ❑ *Lemons contain lots of vitamin C.* 3 V-T To **contain** something such as a feeling, problem, or activity means to control it and prevent it from increasing. ❑ *Edward could not contain his delight.* ❑ *Firemen are still trying to contain the fire.*

container /kənˈteɪnə/ (**containers**) 1 N-COUNT A **container** is something such as a box or bottle

Picture Dictionary container

that is used to hold things. **2** N-COUNT A **container** is a very large metal or wooden box used for transporting goods so that they can be loaded easily onto ships and lorries. ❑ *...a large container lorry.*
→ see Picture Dictionary: **container**
→ see **ship**

contaminate /kən'tæmɪneɪt/ (**contaminates, contaminating, contaminated**) V-T If something **is contaminated** by dirt, chemicals, or radiation, it becomes impure or harmful. ❑ *The water was contaminated by chemicals.* ● **contamination** N-UNCOUNT ❑ *...the contamination of the sea.*

contemplate /'kɒntəmpleɪt/ (**contemplates, contemplating, contemplated**) **1** V-T If you **contemplate** something, you consider it as a possibility. ❑ *He contemplated a career as a doctor.* ❑ *They are contemplating selling their farm.* **2** V-T If you **contemplate** an idea or subject, you think about it for a long time. ❑ *He cried as he contemplated his future.* ● **contemplation** N-UNCOUNT ❑ *Her garden is a place of quiet contemplation.* **3** V-T To **contemplate** something or someone means to look at them for a long time. ❑ *He contemplated his hands.*

Word Link *con ≈ together, with : consensus, contemporary, convene*

Word Link *tempo ≈ time : contemporary, temporal, temporary*

contemporary /kən'tempərəri, AM -pəreri/ (**contemporaries**) **1** ADJ **Contemporary** means existing now or at the time you are talking about. ❑ *...contemporary music.* **2** N-COUNT Someone's **contemporaries** are people who are or were alive at the same time as them. ❑ *...Shakespeare and his contemporaries.*

contempt /kən'tempt/ N-UNCOUNT If you have **contempt for** someone or something, you have no respect for them. ❑ *He has contempt for most politicians.* ❑ *They were regarded with contempt.*

contemptuous /kən'temptʃuəs/ ADJ If you are **contemptuous of** someone or something, you have no respect for them. ❑ *They are contemptuous of such old-fashioned ideas.* ● **contemptuously** ADV ❑ *'Food?' he said contemptuously, 'You call that food?'*

contend /kən'tend/ (**contends, contending, contended**) **1** V-I If you **have to contend with** a problem or difficulty, you have to deal with it or overcome it. ❑ *They had a very unhappy child to contend with.* **2** V-I If you **contend** with someone **for** something, you compete with them to try to get it. ❑ *The two leaders were contending for power.* ● **contender** (**contenders**) N-COUNT ❑ *He's a strong contender for an Olympic gold medal.* **3** V-T If you **contend that** something is true, you state or argue that it is true. [FORMAL] ❑ *His lawyers contend that he was attacked.*

content
❶ NOUN USES
❷ ADJECTIVE AND VERB USES

content /'kɒntent/ (**contents**)
❶ **1** N-PLURAL The **contents of** a container such as a bottle, box, or room are the things inside it. ❑ *...the contents of her handbag.* ❑ *The house and its contents belong to Edward.* **2** N-VAR The **content of** a piece of writing, speech, or television programme is its subject and the ideas expressed in it. ❑ *You must know the content of a film before your children see it.* ❑ *...the letter's contents.* **3** N-PLURAL The **contents** of a book are its different chapters and sections. ❑ *The book has a list of contents at the beginning.* **4** N-SING You can use **content** to refer to the amount or proportion of something that a substance contains. **Content** is always used after a noun for this meaning. ❑ *Fruit juice has a high sugar content.*

content /kən'tent/ (**contents, contenting, contented**)
❷ **1** ADJ AFTER LINK-V If you are **content to** do something or **content with** something, you are willing to accept it, rather than wanting something more or better. ❑ *He is content to stay in Berlin.* ❑ *She is content with their beautiful home in France.* **2** V-T If you **content yourself with** something, you accept it and do not try to do or have other things. ❑ *She has a quiet life and contents herself with gardening and housework.* **3** ADJ AFTER LINK-V If you are **content**, you are happy and satisfied with your way of life. **4** → see also **contentment**

contented /kən'tentɪd/ ADJ If you are **contented**, you are satisfied with your life or the situation you are in. • **contentedly** ADV ❑ *She smiled contentedly.*

contention /kənˈtenʃən/ (**contentions**) **1** N-COUNT Someone's **contention** is the opinion that they are expressing. ❑ *The lawyer's contention is that his client will not get a fair trial.* **2** N-UNCOUNT **Contention** is disagreement or argument about something. ❑ *What happened next is a matter of contention.* **3** PHRASE If you are **in contention** in a contest, you have a chance of winning it. ❑ *Four actors are in contention for the award.*

contentious /kənˈtenʃəs/ ADJ A **contentious** issue causes disagreement and arguments. ❑ *The plan is highly contentious.*

contentment /kənˈtentmənt/ N-UNCOUNT **Contentment** is the feeling of being content.

contest (**contests, contesting, contested**) **1** N-COUNT /ˈkɒntest/ A **contest** is a competition or game. ❑ *...a writing contest.* **2** N-COUNT A **contest** is a struggle to win power or control. ❑ *...next year's presidential contest.* **3** V-T /kənˈtest/ If someone **contests** an election or competition, they take part in it in order to win. **4** V-T If you **contest** a statement or decision, you disagree with it formally. ❑ *He is contesting her claims.*

Thesaurus *contest* Also look up:

N. competition, game, match **1**
fight, struggle **2**

contestant /kənˈtestənt/ (**contestants**) N-COUNT A **contestant** in a competition or quiz is a person who takes part in it.

context /ˈkɒntekst/ (**contexts**) **1** N-VAR The **context of** an idea or event is the general situation in which it occurs. ❑ *This event must be seen in context.* **2** N-VAR The **context** of a word or sentence consists of the words or sentences before it and after it. ❑ *Without a context, I would guess it was written by a man.*

continent /ˈkɒntɪnənt/ (**continents**) **1** N-COUNT A **continent** is a very large area of land, such as Africa or Asia, that consists of several countries. **2** N-PROPER In Britain, the mainland of Europe is sometimes referred to as **the Continent**. • **continental** /ˌkɒntɪˈnentəl/ ADJ BEFORE N ❑ *...the economies of Britain and continental Europe.*
→ see Word Web: **continents**
→ see **earth, meal**

contingency /kənˈtɪndʒənsi/ (**contingencies**) N-COUNT A **contingency** is something that might happen in the future. ❑ *I need to examine all possible contingencies.* ❑ *...contingency plans.*

contingent /kənˈtɪndʒənt/ (**contingents**) **1** N-COUNT A **contingent** is a group of people representing a country or organization. ❑ *A contingent of politicians from Japan has arrived.* ❑ *This meeting of European scientists includes a British contingent.* **2** ADJ If an event is **contingent on** something, it can only happen if that thing happens or exists. [FORMAL] ❑ *The deal is contingent on several factors.*

continual /kənˈtɪnjuəl/ ADJ BEFORE N **Continual** means happening without stopping, or happening again and again. ❑ *...continual pain.* ❑ *...continual criticism.* • **continually** ADV ❑ *Malcolm continually changes his mind about things.*

Usage

Both **continual** and **continuous** can be used to say that something continues without interruption, but only **continual** can correctly be used to say that something keeps happening repeatedly. ❑ *There have been continual demands to cut costs.* ❑ *Chris became aware of a continuous background noise.*

Thesaurus *continual* Also look up:

ADJ. constant, ongoing

continuation /kənˌtɪnjuˈeɪʃən/ **1** N-UNCOUNT The **continuation** of something is the fact that it continues to happen or exist. ❑ *...the continuation of the war.* **2** N-SING Something that is a **continuation of** something else is closely connected with it and develops it in some way. ❑ *This chapter is a continuation of Chapter 8.*

continue /kənˈtɪnjuː/ (**continues, continuing, continued**) **1** V-T/V-I If something **continues**, it does not stop. If you **continue to** do something, you do not stop doing it. ❑ *Talks continued last night between the leaders of the two sides.* ❑ *House prices*

Word Web continents

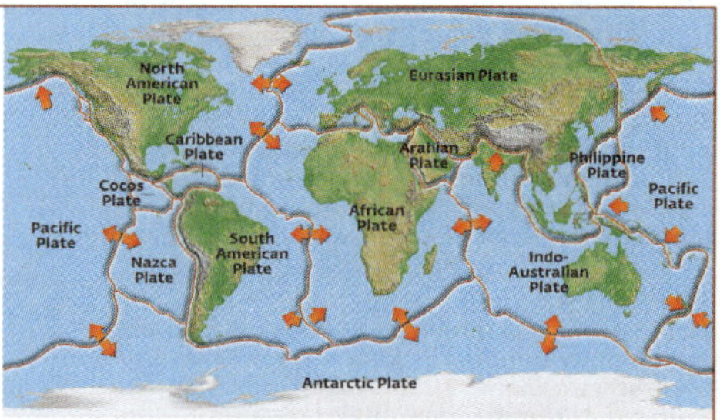

Major Plates of the Earth's Crust

In 1912, Alfred Wegener* made an important discovery. The shapes of the **continents** seemed to fit together like the pieces of a puzzle. He decided they had once been a single **land mass**, which he called **Pangaea**. He thought the continents had slowly moved apart. Wegener called this theory **continental drift**. He said the earth's **crust** is not a single, solid piece. It's full of cracks which allow huge pieces to move around on the earth's **mantle**. The movement of these **tectonic plates** increases the distance between Europe and North America by about 20 millimeters every year.

Alfred Wegener (1880-1930): a German scientist.

continue to rise. ❑ *She wants to continue working for the company.* **2** V-T/V-I If something **continues**, or if you **continue** it, it starts again after stopping for a period of time. ❑ *The trial continues today.* ❑ *I went up to my room to continue my work.* **3** V-T/V-I To **continue** means to begin speaking again after a pause or interruption. ❑ *'Anyway, that is my idea,' she continued.* **4** V-I If you **continue** in a particular direction, you keep going in that direction. ❑ *He continued quickly up the path.*

Thesaurus *continue* Also look up:

V. go on, persist; *(ant.)* stop **1**
carry on, resume **3**

continuity /ˌkɒntɪˈnjuːɪti, AM -ˈnuː-/ (**continuities**) N-VAR The **continuity** of something is the fact that it happens, exists, or develops without stopping or changing suddenly. ❑ *...political continuity.*

continuous /kənˈtɪnjuəs/ **1** ADJ A **continuous** process or event continues for a period of time without stopping. ❑ *...a continuous stream of phone calls.* ● **continuously** ADV ❑ *The machinery should go on working continuously for twelve hours.* **2** ADJ A **continuous** line or surface has no gaps in it. **3** ADJ In English grammar, **continuous** tenses are formed using the auxiliary 'be' and the present participle of a verb, as in 'I'm feeling a bit tired'. Compare **simple**.

contort /kənˈtɔːt/ (**contorts, contorting, contorted**) V-T/V-I When something **contorts** or **is contorted**, it changes into an unnatural and unattractive shape. ❑ *His face contorted with pain.* ● **contortion** (**contortions**) N-VAR ❑ *...the contortions of the gymnasts.*

contour /ˈkɒntuə/ (**contours**) **1** N-COUNT The **contours of** something are its shape or outline. ❑ *...the contours of the body.* **2** N-COUNT On a map, a **contour** is a line joining points of equal height.

Word Link *contra ≈ against : contraception, contradict, contravene*

contraception /ˌkɒntrəˈsepʃən/ N-UNCOUNT Methods of preventing pregnancy are called **contraception**.

contraceptive /ˌkɒntrəˈseptɪv/ (**contraceptives**) N-COUNT A **contraceptive** is a device or pill used to prevent pregnancy.

Word Link *tract ≈ dragging, drawing : contract, subtract, tractor*

contract (**contracts, contracting, contracted**) **1** N-COUNT /ˈkɒntrækt/ A **contract** is a legal agreement, usually between two companies or between an employer and employee, which involves doing work for a stated sum of money. ❑ *They were given the contract to build Europe's tallest building.* **2** V-I /kənˈtrækt/ If you **contract with** someone **to** do something, you legally agree to do it for them or for them to do it for you. [FORMAL] ❑ *They contracted with us to deliver the car.* **3** V-I When something **contracts**, it becomes smaller or shorter. ❑ *As we move our bodies, muscles contract and relax.* ● **contraction** (**contractions**) N-VAR ❑ *...the contraction of blood vessels.* **4** V-T If you **contract** a serious illness, you become ill with it. [FORMAL] → see **illness, muscle**

Word Partnership Use *contract* with:

N. **terms of a** contract **1**
contract **with *someone*** **2**
contract **a disease** **4**
V. **sign a** contract **1** **2**

contractor /ˈkɒntræktə, kənˈtræk-/ (**contractors**) N-COUNT A **contractor** is a person or company that works for other people or companies.

contractual /kənˈtræktʃuəl/ ADJ A **contractual** arrangement or relationship involves a legal agreement between people. [FORMAL] ● **contractually** ADV ❑ *The company was contractually obliged to pay him $30 million.*

Word Link *contra ≈ against : contraception, contradict, contravene*

Word Link *dict ≈ speaking : contradict, dictate, predict*

contradict /ˌkɒntrəˈdɪkt/ (**contradicts, contradicting, contradicted**) **1** V-T If you **contradict** someone, you say or suggest that what they have just said is wrong. ❑ *She dared not contradict her.* **2** V-T If one statement or action **contradicts** another, the first one makes the second appear to be wrong. ❑ *Her story contradicts the Government's report.*

contradiction /ˌkɒntrəˈdɪkʃən/ (**contradictions**) **1** N-VAR A **contradiction** is an aspect of a situation which appears to conflict with other aspects, so that they cannot all exist or be successful. ❑ *...the contradictions between her private life and public life.* **2** PHRASE If you say that something is **a contradiction in terms**, you mean that it is described as having a quality that it cannot have. ❑ *A public service run for profit is a contradiction in terms.*

Word Link *ory ≈ relating to : advisory, contradictory, sensory*

contradictory /ˌkɒntrəˈdɪktəri, AM -tɔːri/ ADJ If two or more facts, ideas, or statements are **contradictory**, they state or imply that opposite things are true. ❑ *Her friends' advice was contradictory and confusing.*

contrary /ˈkɒntrəri, AM -treri/ **1** ADJ **Contrary** ideas or opinions are completely different from each other. ❑ *He holds a contrary view to mine.* ❑ *Contrary to popular belief, a little exercise actually makes you feel less hungry.* **2** PHRASE You use **on the contrary** when you are contradicting what has just been said. ❑ *'People just don't do things like that.'—'On the contrary, they do them all the time.'*

Usage

Do not confuse **on the contrary** with **on the other hand. On the contrary** is used to contradict someone or something, to say that they are wrong. **On the other hand** is used to state a different, often contrasting aspect of the situation you are considering. ❑ *Food prices fell. Wages on the other hand increased.*

3 PHRASE Evidence or statements **to the contrary** contradict what you are saying or what someone

C

else has said. ❑ *There has been no fighting in the city, despite reports to the contrary.*

contrast (**contrasts, contrasting, contrasted**) **1** N-VAR /'kɒntrɑːst, -træst/ A **contrast** is a great difference between two or more things. ❑ *...the contrast between town and country.* ❑ *His behaviour has always been in marked contrast to that of his son.* **2** PHRASE You use **contrast** in expressions such as **by contrast** or **in contrast**, to show that you are mentioning a very different situation from the one you have just mentioned. ❑ *All this criticism is in contrast to his popularity a few years ago.* **3** V-I /kən'trɑːst, -'træst/ If one thing **contrasts with** another, it is very different from it. ❑ *The latest news contrasts significantly with earlier reports.* ❑ *Paint the wall in a colour that contrasts with the furniture.* **4** V-T If you **contrast** one thing **with** another, you show the differences between them. ❑ *She contrasted her lifestyle in the past with her current situation.* ❑ *In this book we contrast four possible solutions to the problem.*

Word Link *contra ≈ against : contraception, contradict, contravene*

contravene /ˌkɒntrə'viːn/ (**contravenes, contravening, contravened**) V-T To **contravene** a law or rule means to do something that is forbidden by it. [FORMAL] ● **contravention** /ˌkɒntrə'venʃən/ (**contraventions**) N-VAR ❑ *Attacking the city would be in contravention of international law.*

Word Link *tribute ≈ giving: attribute, contribute, distribute*

contribute /kən'trɪbjuːt/ (**contributes, contributing, contributed**) **1** V-I If you **contribute to** something, you say or do something to help make it successful. ❑ *The children at this school contribute to community work.* **2** V-T If a person, organization, or country **contributes** money or resources **to** something, they help to pay for it or achieve it. ❑ *France will contribute $3 billion.* ● **contributor** (**contributors**) N-COUNT ❑ *...contributors to the national economy.* **3** V-I If something **contributes to** a situation, it is one of its causes. ❑ *A bad diet contributed to their health problems.* ❑ *Stress can be a contributing factor to this illness.* ● **contributor** N-COUNT ❑ *Old buses are major contributors to pollution.* **4** V-I If you **contribute to** a magazine or book, you write things that are published in it. ❑ *She contributes regularly to Vogue magazine.* ● **contributor** N-COUNT ❑ *...a regular contributor to this magazine.*

Thesaurus *contribute* Also look up:

V.	aid, assist, chip in, commit, donate, give, grant, help, support; *(ant.)* neglect, take away **2**

contribution /ˌkɒntrɪ'bjuːʃən/ (**contributions**) **1** N-COUNT If you make a **contribution to** something, you do something to help make it successful or to produce it. ❑ *He won a prize for his contribution to world peace.* **2** N-COUNT A **contribution** is a sum of money that you give in order to help pay for something. ❑ *This company makes contributions to charity every month.*

Word Partnership Use *contribution* with:

V.	**make a** contribution, **send a** contribution **1** **2**
ADJ.	**important** contribution, **significant** contribution **1** **2**

contrive /kən'traɪv/ (**contrives, contriving, contrived**) **1** V-T If you **contrive to** do something difficult, you manage to do it. [FORMAL] ❑ *He contrived to see her most days.* **2** V-T If you **contrive** an event or situation, you succeed in making it happen. [FORMAL] ❑ *Dimitrijevic Pasic contrived the murder of King Alexander of Serbia in 1903.*

contrived /kən'traɪvd/ ADJ If you say that something is **contrived**, you think it is false or unconvincing; used showing disapproval. ❑ *The plot of the novel is contrived.*

control /kən'trəʊl/ (**controls, controlling, controlled**) **1** V-T & N-UNCOUNT If someone **controls** an organization, place, or system, or if they have **control of** it, they have the power to take all the important decisions about the way it is run. You can also say they are **in control of** it or it is **under** their **control**. ❑ *Mr Ronson gave up control of the company.* ❑ *People like to feel in control of their own lives.* ● **-controlled** ❑ *The company is French-controlled.* ● **controller** (**controllers**) N-COUNT ❑ *...an air traffic controller.* **2** V-T & N-UNCOUNT If you **control** a person or machine, or if you have **control of** them, you are able to make them do what you want them to do. ❑ *You can't control what other people think.* ❑ *He lost control of his car.* ❑ *Teachers should be able to control their pupils.* **3** V-T & N-UNCOUNT If you **control yourself** or your feelings, or show **control**, you make yourself behave calmly even though you are feeling angry, excited, or upset. ❑ *I couldn't control my temper.* ❑ *Sometimes he completely loses control.* ● **controlled** ADJ ❑ *She was quiet and very controlled.* **4** V-T & N-UNCOUNT To **control** prices, wages, or undesirable activities means to restrict them to an acceptable level. **Control** is the act of controlling something in this way. If something is **out of control**, it cannot be restricted by anyone. If it is **under control**, it is being dealt with successfully. ❑ *Our main aim is to control prices.* ❑ *Pollution must be controlled.* ❑ *The fire is burning out of control.* **5** N-PLURAL **Controls** are the methods an organization uses to restrict something. ❑ *The controls announced yesterday will help to lower prices.* **6** N-COUNT A **control** is a device such as a switch or lever which you use in order to operate a machine or other piece of equipment. ❑ *He was at the controls of the plane when it crashed.*
→ see **experiment**

Usage

You do not use **control** as a verb to talk about inspecting documents. The word you use is **check**. ❑ *Police searched cars and checked identity documents.* However, at an airport or port, the place where passports are checked is called **passport control**.

controversial /ˌkɒntrə'vɜːʃəl/ ADJ Someone or something that is **controversial** causes intense public argument, disagreement, or disapproval. ❑ *...the controversial new book.*

controversy /'kɒntrəvɜːsi, kən'trɒvəsi/

(**controversies**) N-VAR **Controversy** is a lot of discussion and disagreement about something, often involving strong anger or disapproval. ❑ *...fierce controversy over the new Olympic Stadium.*

convalesce /ˌkɒnvəˈles/ (**convalesces, convalescing, convalesced**) V-I If you **are convalescing**, you are resting and regaining your health after an illness or operation. ❑ *He is convalescing in hospital.* • **convalescent** ADJ ❑ *...his convalescent wife.* • **convalescence** N-UNCOUNT ❑ *I visited him during his convalescence.*

Word Link	*con ≈ together, with : consensus, contemporary, convene*

convene /kənˈviːn/ (**convenes, convening, convened**) V-T/V-I If you **convene** a meeting, you arrange for it to take place. You can also say that people **convene** at a meeting. ❑ *Government officials convened in October.*

convenience /kənˈviːniəns/ (**conveniences**) **1** N-UNCOUNT If something is done **for** your **convenience**, it is done in a way that is useful or suitable for you. ❑ *They left a map of the city on the table for her convenience.* **2** N-COUNT If you describe something as a **convenience**, you mean it is useful. ❑ *The Internet is a convenience for shoppers who are too busy to go into town.* **3** N-COUNT **Conveniences** are pieces of equipment designed to make your life easier. ❑ *...an apartment with all the modern conveniences.*

convenient /kənˈviːniənt/ **1** ADJ Something that is **convenient** is easy, useful, or suitable for a particular purpose. ❑ *Internet banking is very convenient.* ❑ *Sometimes it's more convenient to have a snack than a three-course meal.* • **conveniently** ADV ❑ *Break your journey at our conveniently located hotel.* • **convenience** N-UNCOUNT ❑ *...the convenience of a non-stop flight.* **2** ADJ A place that is **convenient** is near to where you are, or near to another place where you want to go. ❑ *Martin drove along until he found a convenient parking place.* • **conveniently** ADV ❑ *The hotel is conveniently close to the beach.* **3** ADJ A **convenient** time to do something is a time when you are free to do it or would like to do it. ❑ *Is this evening convenient for you?*

convent /ˈkɒnvənt/ (**convents**) N-COUNT A **convent** is a building in which a community of nuns live.

convention /kənˈvenʃən/ (**conventions**) **1** N-VAR A **convention** is an accepted way of behaving or of doing something. ❑ *It's just a social convention that men don't wear skirts.* **2** N-COUNT A **convention** is an official agreement between countries or organizations. ❑ *...a convention on the rights of the child.* **3** N-COUNT A **convention** is a large meeting of an organization or group. ❑ *...the annual convention of the World Boxing Council.*

conventional /kənˈvenʃənəl/ **1** ADJ **Conventional** people behave in a way that is accepted as normal in their society. ❑ *She's a married woman with conventional opinions.* • **conventionally** ADV ❑ *She dresses conventionally.* **2** ADJ A **conventional** method or product is the one that is usually used. ❑ *...a conventional computer floppy disk.* • **conventionally** ADV ❑ *...conventionally produced food.* **3** ADJ **Conventional** wars and weapons do not involve nuclear explosives.

Word Link	*verg, vert ≈ turning : converge, diverge, subvert*

converge /kənˈvɜːdʒ/ (**converges, converging, converged**) **1** V-I When roads or lines **converge**, they meet or join. ❑ *The five rivers converge, just south of the city.* **2** V-I When people or vehicles **converge on** a place, they move towards it from different directions. ❑ *Hundreds of buses converged on the capital.* **3** V-I If different ideas or societies **converge**, they gradually become similar to each other. ❑ *The views of the richest people converged with those of the poorest people.* • **convergence** (**convergences**) N-VAR ❑ *...economic convergence between European countries.*

conversation /ˌkɒnvəˈseɪʃən/ (**conversations**) **1** N-VAR If you **have** a **conversation** with someone, you talk to each other, usually in an informal situation. ❑ *I had a conversation with him.* • **conversational** ADJ ❑ *The author has an easy, conversational style.* • **conversationally** ADV ❑ *'Tell me,' he said conversationally. 'Just why did you call the police?'* **2** PHRASE When you **make conversation**, you talk to someone in order to be polite rather than because you want to.

converse (**converses, conversing, conversed**) **1** V-I /kənˈvɜːs/ If you **converse with** someone, you talk to each other. [FORMAL] ❑ *Luke conversed with the pilot.* ❑ *They were conversing in German.* **2** N-SING /ˈkɒnvɜːs/ **The converse** of a statement or fact is its opposite or reverse. ❑ *If great events produce great men, the converse is also true.* • **conversely** /ˈkɒnvɜːsli, kənˈvɜːsli/ ADV ❑ *Some people mistake politeness for weakness, and conversely, they think that rudeness is a sign of strength.*

Word Link	*vert ≈ turning : convert, invert, revert*

convert (**converts, converting, converted**) **1** V-T/V-I /kənˈvɜːt/ To **convert** one thing **into** another means to change it into a different shape or form. ❑ *The table converts into an ironing board.* ❑ *He wants to convert the town hall into a hotel.* • **conversion** (**conversions**) N-VAR ❑ *...the conversion of the stables into a house.* **2** V-T/V-I If you **convert**, or if someone **converts** you, they persuade you to change your religious or political beliefs. ❑ *He converted to Catholicism in 1917.* • **conversion** N-VAR ❑ *...his conversion to Christianity.* **3** N-COUNT /ˈkɒnvɜːt/ A **convert** is someone who has changed their religious or political beliefs. ❑ *...new converts to democracy.*

Thesaurus	*convert*	Also look up:
V.	adapt, alter, change, modify, transform **1**	

convertible /kənˌvɜːtɪbəl/ (**convertibles**) **1** N-COUNT A **convertible** is a car with a soft roof that can be folded down or removed. **2** ADJ **Convertible** money can be easily exchanged for other forms of money. [TECHNICAL]
→ see **car**

convey /kənˈveɪ/ (**conveys, conveying, conveyed**) **1** V-T To **convey** facts or feelings means to cause them to be known or understood. ❑ *She tried to convey her fears to her husband.* **2** V-T To **convey** someone or something to a place means

C

C

to transport them there. [FORMAL] ❑ *Most people convey goods from the supermarket to the car in plastic bags.*

conveyor belt /kən'veɪəbelt/ (**conveyor belts**) N-COUNT A **conveyor belt** or a **conveyor** is a continuously moving strip which is used in factories to move objects along.

convict (**convicts, convicting, convicted**) 1 V-T /kən'vɪkt/ If someone **is convicted of** a crime, they are found guilty of it in a law court. ❑ *He was convicted of murder.* ❑ *There was not enough evidence to convict him.* 2 N-COUNT /'kɒnvɪkt/ A **convict** is someone who is in prison, convicted of committing a crime.

conviction /kən'vɪkʃən/ (**convictions**) 1 N-COUNT A **conviction** is a strong belief or opinion. ❑ *The United States of America was founded on the conviction that everyone is created equal.* 2 N-COUNT If someone has a **conviction**, they have been found guilty of a crime. ❑ *He will appeal against his conviction.*

Word Link *vict, vinc ≈ conquering : convince, invincible, victorious*

convince /kən'vɪns/ (**convinces, convincing, convinced**) 1 V-T If someone or something **convinces** you **of** something, they make you believe that it is true or that it exists. ❑ *I convinced him of my innocence.* ● **convinced** ADJ ❑ *He became convinced that she was lying.* 2 V-T If someone or something **convinces** you **to** do something, they persuade you to do it. ❑ *I convinced him to take the job.*

Thesaurus *convince* Also look up:

V. argue, persuade, sell, talk into, win over; (*ant.*) discourage 1 2

convincing /kən'vɪnsɪŋ/ ADJ If someone or something is **convincing**, you believe them. ❑ *He sounded very convincing.* ● **convincingly** ADV ❑ *He argued convincingly.*

convoy /'kɒnvɔɪ/ (**convoys**) N-COUNT A **convoy** is a group of vehicles or ships travelling together. ❑ *The army vehicles travelled in convoy.*

convulsion /kən'vʌlʃən/ (**convulsions**) N-COUNT If someone has **convulsions**, they suffer uncontrollable movements of their muscles.

cook /kʊk/ (**cooks, cooking, cooked**) 1 V-T/V-I When you **cook**, or **cook** a meal, you prepare and heat food so it can be eaten. ❑ *Let the vegetables cook for about 10 minutes.* ❑ *Chefs at this restaurant have cooked for the Queen.* ❑ *We'll cook my parents a nice Italian meal.* ● **cooking** N-UNCOUNT ❑ *You do a lot of cooking, don't you?* 2 N-COUNT A **cook** is a person whose job is to prepare and cook food. 3 → see also **cooking**

→ see Picture Dictionary: **cook**

▶ **cook up** PHR-VERB If someone **cooks up** a dishonest scheme, they plan it. [INFORMAL] ❑ *They cooked up the plan between them.*

Usage

You often use a more specific verb instead of **cook** when you are talking about preparing food using heat. For example, you **roast** meat in an oven, but you **bake** bread and cakes. You can **boil** vegetables in hot water, or you can **steam** them over a pan of boiling water. You can **fry** meat and vegetables in oil or fat. You can also **grill** them directly under or over a flame. In American English, **broil** is used instead of **grill**. You do not normally talk about **grilling** bread. Instead, you **toast** it.

Thesaurus *cook* Also look up:

V. heat up, make, prepare 1
N. chef 2

cookbook /'kʊkbʊk/ (**cookbooks**) N-COUNT A **cookbook** is a book that contains recipes for preparing food.

cooker /'kʊkə/ (**cookers**) N-COUNT A **cooker** is a large metal device used for cooking food using gas or electricity.

cookery /'kʊkəri/ N-UNCOUNT **Cookery** is the activity of preparing and cooking food.

cookie /'kʊki/ (**cookies**) 1 N-COUNT In American English, a **cookie** is a small, sweet, flat cake. The usual British word is **biscuit**. 2 N-COUNT A **cookie** is a piece of computer software which enables a website you have visited to recognize you if you visit it again. [COMPUTING]

cooking /'kʊkɪŋ/ 1 N-UNCOUNT **Cooking** is cooked food. ❑ *I like your cooking.* 2 → see also **cook**

→ see Word Web: **cooking**

Picture Dictionary cook

Word Web cooking

Scientists that study humans believe our ancestors began to experiment with **cooking** about 1.5 million years ago. Cooking made some poisonous or **inedible** plants safe to **eat**. It made tough meat **tender** and easier for our bodies to **digest**. It also improved the flavor of the food they ate. **Heating up food** to a high **temperature** killed dangerous bacteria. **Cooked** food could be stored longer. This all helped increase the amount of food available to our ancestors.

C

cool /kuːl/ (**cooler, coolest, cools, cooling, cooled**) **1** ADJ Something that is **cool** has a low temperature but is not cold. ❑ *There was a cool breeze.* ❑ *The drinks were kept cool in the fridge.* ● **coolness** N-UNCOUNT ❑ *...the coolness of the stone floor.* **2** → See note at **cold** **3** V-T/V-I & PHR-VERB When something **cools** or when you **cool** it, it becomes lower in temperature. You can also say it **cools down** or you **cool** it **down**. ❑ *They use air conditioning to cool the air inside their homes.* ❑ *She waited for the car engine to cool down.* **4** ADJ If you stay **cool** in a difficult situation, you remain calm. ● **coolly** ADV ❑ *We must think this situation through calmly and coolly.* ● **coolness** N-UNCOUNT ❑ *The police praised him for his coolness.* **5** ADJ If you say that a person or their behaviour is **cool**, you mean that they are unfriendly or lack enthusiasm. ● **coolly** ADV ❑ *'Hello, Adam,' she said coolly.* ● **coolness** N-UNCOUNT ❑ *...the coolness of her friend's manner.* **6** ADJ If you say that someone is **cool**, you mean that they are fashionable and attractive. [INFORMAL]

▶ **cool down** **1** → see **cool** (meaning **3**) **2** PHR-VERB If someone **cools down** or if you **cool** them **down**, they become less angry. ❑ *He had time to cool down.*

▶ **cool off** PHR-VERB If someone or something **cools off** or if you **cool** them **off**, they become cooler after being hot. ❑ *Cool off in the pool.*

Thesaurus *cool* Also look up:

ADJ. chilly, cold; *(ant.)* warm **1**
easy-going, serene, tranquil **3**
distant, unfriendly **4**

Word Partnership Use *cool* with:

N. cool **air**, cool **breeze** **1** **2**
V. **lose** ***your*** cool, **play it** cool, **stay** cool **3**

Word Link ***oper*** **≈ work :** ***co-operate, opera, operation***

Word Link ***co*** **≈ together :** ***collaborate, co-operate, co-ordinate***

co-operate /kəʊ-ˈɒpəreɪt/ (**co-operates, co-operating, co-operated**) **1** V-I If you **co-operate with** someone, you work with them or help them. ❑ *The UN is co-operating with the British government.* ● **co-operation** /kəʊ-ˌɒpəˈreɪʃən/ N-UNCOUNT ❑ *...the friendship and co-operation between Senegal and the United States.* **2** V-I If you **co-operate**, you do what someone asks you to do. ❑ *He agreed to co-operate with the police investigation.* ● **co-operation** N-UNCOUNT ❑ *The public's co-operation in the hunt for the killer is very important.*

Word Partnership Use *co-operate* with:

V. **agree to** co-operate, **continue to** co-operate, **fail to** co-operate, **refuse to** co-operate **1** **2**
ADV. co-operate **fully** **1** **2**
N. **willingness to** co-operate **1** **2**

co-operative /kəʊ-ˈɒpərətɪv/ (**co-operatives**) **1** N-COUNT A **co-operative** is a business or organization run by the people who work for it, who share its benefits and profits. **2** ADJ A **co-operative** activity is done by people working together. ❑ *The project is a co-operative effort involving various groups.* ● **co-operatively** ADV ❑ *They agreed to work co-operatively.* **3** ADJ Someone who is **co-operative** does what you ask them to. ❑ *I tried to be co-operative.*

Thesaurus *co-operative* Also look up:

ADJ. combined, shared, united; *(ant.)* independent, private, separate **2**
accommodating; *(ant.)* **3**

Word Link ***co*** **≈ together :** ***collaborate, co-operate, co-ordinate***

co-ordinate also **coordinate** (**co-ordinates, co-ordinating, co-ordinated**) **1** V-T /kəʊˈɔːdɪneɪt/ If you **co-ordinate** an activity, you organize it. ❑ *The committee co-ordinates police work.* ❑ *...a well co-ordinated rescue team.* ● **co-ordination** N-UNCOUNT ❑ *...better co-ordination of air and land operations.* ● **co-ordinator** (**co-ordinators**) N-COUNT ❑ *...a project co-ordinator.* **2** V-T If you **co-ordinate** the parts of your body, you make them work together efficiently. ● **co-ordination** N-UNCOUNT ❑ *He was clumsy and had no co-ordination.* **3** N-COUNT /kəʊˈɔːdɪnət/ The **co-ordinates** of a point on a map or graph are the two sets of numbers or letters that you need in order to find that point.

Thesaurus *co-ordinate* Also look up:

V. direct, manage, organize **1**

cop /kɒp/ (**cops**) N-COUNT A **cop** is a policeman or policewoman. [INFORMAL]

cope /kəʊp/ (**copes, coping, coped**) V-I If you **cope with** a problem, task, or difficult situation, you deal with it successfully. ❑ *She had to cope with losing all her money.* ❑ *Don't worry, Carrie. I'll cope.*

Word Partnership Use *cope* with:

N.	**ability to** cope, cope **with loss**
V.	**learn to** cope, **manage to** cope
ADJ.	**unable to** cope
ADV.	**how to** cope

C

copious /ˈkəʊpiəs/ ADJ A **copious** amount is a large amount. ❑ *...copious amounts of food.* ● **copiously** ADV ❑ *She wept copiously.*

copper /ˈkɒpə/ (**coppers**) **1** N-UNCOUNT **Copper** is a soft reddish-brown metal. **2** N-COUNT A **copper** is a policeman or policewoman. [BRIT, INFORMAL] **3** N-COUNT **Coppers** are brown metal coins of low value. ❑ *I gave him a few coppers.*
→ see **metal, mineral, pan**

copy /ˈkɒpi/ (**copies, copying, copied**) **1** N-COUNT If you make a **copy of** something, you produce something that looks like the original thing. ❑ *I found a copy of Steve's letter.* **2** V-T & PHR-VERB If you **copy** something which has been written or **copy** it **out**, you write it again exactly. ❑ *He copied her address from my notebook.* ❑ *Concentrating hard, the pupils copied out the text.* **3** V-T If you **copy** a person or their ideas, you behave like them. ❑ *Children copy the behaviour of people around them.* **4** N-COUNT A **copy of** a book, newspaper, or record is one of many identical ones that have been printed or produced. ❑ *...a copy of 'The Times'.*
→ see **clone, draw**
▸ **copy down** PHR-VERB If you **copy down** what someone says or writes, you write it down yourself. ❑ *The secretary copied down his words.*
▸ **copy out** → see **copy** (meaning **2**).

Thesaurus *copy* Also look up:

N.	likeness, photocopy, replica, reprint; *(ant.)* master, original **1**
V.	reproduce; *(ant.)* create **2** imitate, mimic **3**

copyright /ˈkɒpiraɪt/ (**copyrights**) N-VAR If someone has the **copyright** on a piece of writing or music, it is illegal to reproduce or perform it without their permission. ❑ *Who owns the copyright on the film?*

coral /ˈkɒrəl, AM ˈkɔː-/ N-UNCOUNT **Coral** is a hard substance formed from the skeletons of very small sea animals.

cord /kɔːd/ (**cords**) **1** N-VAR **Cord** is strong thick string. ❑ *We tied it up with a length of cord.* **2** N-VAR **Cord** is electrical wire covered in rubber or plastic. ❑ *...electrical cord.*

cordial /ˈkɔːdiəl, AM -dʒəl/ ADJ **Cordial** means warm and friendly. ❑ *They have a cordial relationship.* ● **cordiality** /ˌkɔːdiˈælɪti, AM -ˈdʒæl-/ N-UNCOUNT ❑ *...an atmosphere of cordiality.* ● **cordially** ADV ❑ *They greeted me cordially.*

cordon /ˈkɔːdən/ (**cordons, cordoning, cordoned**) N-COUNT A **cordon** is a line of police, soldiers, or vehicles preventing people from entering or leaving an area. ❑ *Police formed a cordon between the two crowds.*
▸ **cordon off** PHR-VERB If police or soldiers **cordon off** an area, they prevent people from entering or leaving it.

core /kɔː/ (**cores**) **1** N-COUNT The **core** of a fruit is the central part containing seeds or pips. ❑ *...an apple core.* **2** N-COUNT The **core of** something is the central or most important part. ❑ *This is the core of the problem.*
→ see Picture Dictionary: **core**

Word Partnership Use *core* with:

N.	**apple** core **1** core **beliefs**, core **curriculum**, core **group** **2**

cork /kɔːk/ (**corks**) **1** N-UNCOUNT **Cork** is a soft light substance which forms the bark of a Mediterranean tree. **2** N-COUNT A **cork** is a piece of cork or plastic that is pushed into the opening of a bottle to close it.

Picture Dictionary core

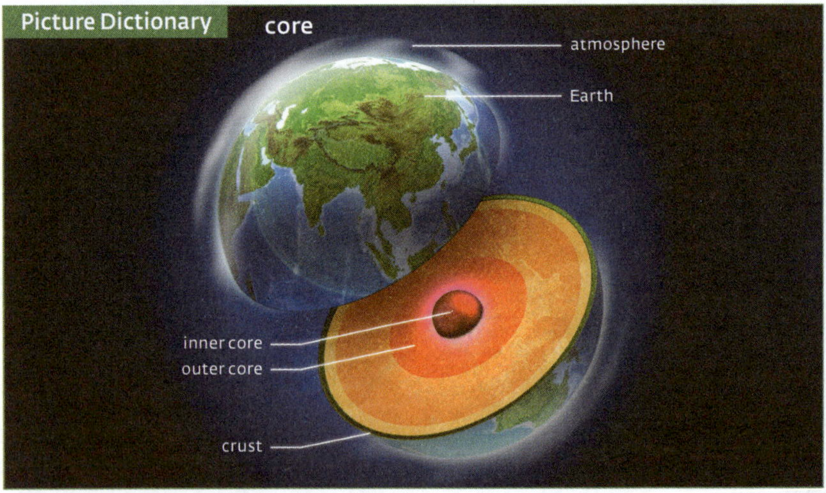

corkscrew /ˈkɔːkskruː/ (**corkscrews**) N-COUNT A **corkscrew** is a device for pulling corks out of bottles.

corn /kɔːn/ **1** N-UNCOUNT **Corn** refers to crops such as wheat and barley, or their seeds. [BRIT] ❑ *...fields of corn.* **2** N-UNCOUNT **Corn** is the same as **maize.** [AM] ❑ *...freshly baked corn bread.*
→ see **grain, vegetable**

corner /ˈkɔːnə/ (**corners, cornering, cornered**) **1** N-COUNT A **corner** is a place where two sides or edges of something meet, or where a road meets another road. ❑ *There is a table in the corner of the living room.* ❑ *He waited until the man had turned a corner.* **2** V-T If you **corner** a person or animal, you force them into a place they cannot escape from. ❑ *The gang was cornered by police.* ❑ *...a cornered animal.* **3** V-T If a company or place **corners** an area of trade, they gain control over it so that no one else can have any success in it. ❑ *This company has cornered the market in high-quality food.* **4** PHRASE If you say that something is **around the corner**, you mean that it will happen very soon. ❑ *The world championship is just around the corner.*

Word Partnership Use *corner* with:

ADJ.	**far** corner, **sharp** corner **1**
V.	**round/turn a** corner, **sit in a** corner **2**
N.	**corner of a** room, **street** corner **2**
PREP.	**in a** corner **1**
	around the corner **4**

cornerstone /ˈkɔːnəstəʊn/ (**cornerstones**) N-COUNT The **cornerstone of** something is the basis of its existence or success. [FORMAL] ❑ *Mr Carter made human rights the cornerstone of his presidency.*

corny /ˈkɔːni/ ADJ If you describe something as **corny**, you mean that it is obvious or sentimental and not at all original. ❑ *I love corny films such as 'White Christmas'.*

Word Link *coron ≈ crown : coronary, coronation, coroner*

coronary /ˈkɒrənri, AM ˈkɔːrəneri/ (**coronaries**) **1** ADJ BEFORE N **Coronary** means relating to the heart; technical. ❑ *...the coronary arteries.* **2** N-COUNT If someone **has a coronary**, blood cannot reach their heart because of a blood clot.

coronation /ˌkɒrəˈneɪʃən, AM ˌkɔːr-/ (**coronations**) N-COUNT A **coronation** is the ceremony at which a king or queen is crowned.

coroner /ˈkɒrənə, AM ˈkɔːr-/ (**coroners**) N-COUNT A **coroner** is an official who is responsible for investigating sudden or unusual deaths.

Word Link *corp ≈ body : corporal, corpse, incorporate*

corporal /ˈkɔːprəl/ (**corporals**) N-COUNT & N-TITLE A **corporal** is a non-commissioned officer in the army.

ˌcorporal ˈpunishment N-UNCOUNT **Corporal punishment** is the punishment of people by hitting them.

corporate /ˈkɔːprət/ ADJ BEFORE N **Corporate** means relating to business corporations. ❑ *...a corporate lawyer.*

Word Partnership Use *corporate* with:

N.	corporate **clients**, corporate **culture**, corporate **hospitality**, corporate **image**, corporate **solicitor**, corporate **sector**, corporate **structure**

corporation /ˌkɔːpəˈreɪʃən/ (**corporations**) N-COUNT A **corporation** is a large business or company.

corps /kɔː/

Corps is both the singular and the plural form.

1 N-COUNT A **corps** is a part of the army which has special duties. ❑ *...the Army Medical Corps.* **2** N-COUNT A **corps** is a small group of people who do a special job. ❑ *...the diplomatic corps.*

corpse /kɔːps/ (**corpses**) N-COUNT A **corpse** is a dead body.

Word Link *rect ≈ right, straight : correct, rectangle, rectify*

correct /kəˈrekt/ (**corrects, correcting, corrected**) **1** ADJ Something that is **correct** is accurate and has no mistakes. ❑ *Check the address is correct.* ● **correctly** ADV ❑ *Did I pronounce your name correctly?* **2** ADJ AFTER LINK-V If you are **correct**, what you have said or thought is true. ❑ *If Casey is correct, the total cost will be $110 billion.* **3** ADJ BEFORE N The **correct** thing or method is the one that is most suitable in a particular situation. ❑ *That is not the correct way to deal with this problem.* ● **correctly** ADV ❑ *The exercises, correctly performed, will stretch the muscles.* **4** V-T If you **correct** a mistake, problem, or fault, you put it right. ❑ *The restaurant corrected the mistake and offered me a free lunch.* **5** V-T When someone **corrects** a piece of writing, they mark the mistakes in it. **6** V-T If you **correct** someone, you say something which is more accurate or appropriate than what they have just said. ❑ *I must correct him on a minor point.* **7** ADJ **Correct** behaviour is considered socially acceptable. ● **correctly** ADV ❑ *He behaved correctly.* ● **correctness** N-UNCOUNT ❑ *...political correctness.*
→ see **answer**

Thesaurus *correct* Also look up:

ADJ.	accurate, precise, right, true; *(ant.)* false, inaccurate, incorrect, wrong **1**
V.	fix, rectify, repair; *(ant.)* damage, hurt **4**

Word Partnership Use *correct* with:

N.	correct **answer**, correct **response** **1** **7**
	correct **a mistake**, correct **a situation** **4**
	correct ***someone*** **6**

correction /kəˈrekʃən/ (**corrections**) **1** N-VAR A **correction** is something which puts right something that is wrong. ❑ *We will make the necessary corrections.* **2** N-COUNT **Corrections** are marks or comments made on a piece of written work which indicate where there are mistakes and what are the right answers.

corrective /kəˈrektɪv/ ADJ **Corrective** measures are intended to put right something that is wrong. ❑ *...corrective surgery.*

C

C

correlate /'kɒrəleɪt, AM 'kɔːr-/ (**correlates, correlating, correlated**) V-I If one thing **correlates with** another, there is a close similarity or connection between them. ❑ *Mobile phone use correlates with age.*

correlation /ˌkɒrə'leɪʃən, AM ˌkɔːr-/ (**correlations**) N-COUNT A **correlation between** things is a link between them. [FORMAL] ❑ *...the correlation between family income and education.*

correspond /ˌkɒrɪ'spɒnd, AM ˌkɔːr-/ (**corresponds, corresponding, corresponded**) **1** V-I If one thing **corresponds to** another, there is a close similarity or connection between them. ❑ *Reflexology is based on the idea that areas on the feet correspond to other parts of the body.* ❑ *The two maps of London correspond closely.* ● **corresponding** ADJ BEFORE N ❑ *March sales this year are up 8% on the corresponding period last year.* ● **correspondingly** ADV ❑ *The average course length is two weeks, but a longer course allows students to make correspondingly greater progress.* **2** V-I If you **correspond with** someone, you write letters to them. ❑ *She still corresponds with her American friends.* ❑ *We corresponded regularly.*

correspondence /ˌkɒrɪ'spɒndəns, AM ˌkɔːr-/ (**correspondences**) **1** N-UNCOUNT **Correspondence** is the act of writing letters to someone. ❑ *...a long correspondence with a college friend.* **2** N-UNCOUNT Someone's **correspondence** is the letters that they receive or send. **3** N-COUNT If there is a **correspondence between** two things, there is a similarity between them. ❑ *...correspondences between Eastern religions and Christianity.*

correspondent /ˌkɒrɪ'spɒndənt, AM ˌkɔːr-/ (**correspondents**) N-COUNT A **correspondent** is a television or newspaper reporter.

corridor /'kɒrɪdɔː, AM 'kɔːrɪdər/ (**corridors**) N-COUNT A **corridor** is a long passage in a building or train, with rooms on one or both sides.

corroborate /kə'rɒbəreɪt/ (**corroborates, corroborating, corroborated**) V-T To **corroborate** something that has been said means to provide evidence that supports it. [FORMAL] ❑ *These documents corroborate the story.* ● **corroboration** N-UNCOUNT ❑ *...independent corroboration.*

corrode /kə'rəʊd/ (**corrodes, corroding, corroded**) V-T/V-I When metal or stone **corrodes** or **is corroded**, it is gradually destroyed by rust or by a chemical. ❑ *The bridge has been corroded by rust.* ● **corroded** ADJ ❑ *The pipes were badly corroded.* ● **corrosion** N-UNCOUNT ❑ *Zinc is used to protect other metals from corrosion.*

corrugated /'kɒrəgeɪtɪd, AM 'kɔːr-/ ADJ **Corrugated** metal or cardboard has been folded into a series of small parallel folds to make it stronger.

corrupt /kə'rʌpt/ (**corrupts, corrupting, corrupted**) **1** ADJ A **corrupt** person behaves in a way that is morally wrong, especially by doing illegal things for money. **2** V-T If someone **is corrupted** by something, it causes them to become dishonest and unable to be trusted. ❑ *He was corrupted by the desire for money.*

corruption /kə'rʌpʃən/ N-UNCOUNT **Corruption** is dishonest and illegal behaviour by people in positions of power. ❑ *The President was charged with corruption.*

cosmetic /kɒz'metɪk/ (**cosmetics**) **1** N-COUNT **Cosmetics** are substances such as lipstick or face powder. **2** ADJ **Cosmetic** measures or changes improve the appearance of something without changing its basic character or without solving a basic problem. ❑ *The changes in the country are still largely cosmetic.*

cosmic /'kɒzmɪk/ ADJ **Cosmic** means occurring in, or coming from, the part of space that lies outside Earth and its atmosphere. ❑ *...cosmic phenomena.*

Word Link *poli ≈ city : cosmopolitan, metropolis, politics*

cosmopolitan /ˌkɒzmə'pɒlɪtən/ ADJ **Cosmopolitan** means influenced by many different countries and cultures. ❑ *London is a cosmopolitan city.*

cosmos /'kɒzmɒs, AM -məs/ N-SING **The cosmos** is the universe. [TECHNICAL]

cost /kɒst, AM kɔːst/ (**costs, costing, cost**) **1** N-COUNT The **cost of** something is the amount of money needed to buy, do, or make it. ❑ *Pens are available at a cost of £2.50.* **2** V-T If something **costs** a particular amount of money, you can buy, do, or make it for that amount. ❑ *It cost £100,000 to buy new trucks for the company.* **3** N-SING The **cost of** achieving something is the loss, damage or injury involved in achieving it. ❑ *The factories are to be closed at a cost of 150 jobs.* **4** V-T If an event or mistake **costs** you something, you lose that thing because of it. ❑ *The accident cost him his leg.* **5** PHRASE If you say that something must be avoided **at all costs**, you are emphasizing that it must not be allowed to happen under any circumstances.

Thesaurus *cost* Also look up:

N.	fee, price **1**	
	harm, loss, sacrifice **4**	

Word Partnership Use *cost* with:

N.	cost **of living** **1**
ADJ.	**additional** costs **1**
V.	**cover the** cost, **cut** costs, **keep** costs **down** **1** **2**

'co-star (**co-stars, co-starring, co-starred**) **1** N-COUNT An actor or actress who is a **co-star** of a film has one of the most important parts in it. **2** V-I If an actor or actress **co-stars with** another actor or actress, the two of them have the main parts in a film. ❑ *She co-starred in the film with her father.*

ˌcost-ef'fective ADJ Something that is **cost-effective** saves or makes more money than it costs to make or maintain.

costly /'kɒstli, AM 'kɔːst-/ (**costlier, costliest**) **1** ADJ Something that is **costly** is very expensive. **2** ADJ If you describe someone's action or mistake as **costly**, you mean that it results in a serious disadvantage for them. ❑ *This scandal has been politically costly for the government.*

ˌcost of 'living N-SING **The cost of living** is the average amount of money that people need to spend on food, housing, and clothing.

costume /'kɒstjuːm, AM -tuːm/ N-UNCOUNT

A particular type of **costume** is a set or style of clothes worn by people at a certain time in history, or in a particular country.
→ see **drama, theatre**

cosy [AM **cozy**] /ˈkəʊzi/ (**cosier, cosiest**) **1** ADJ A **cosy** house or room is comfortable and warm. **2** ADJ You use **cosy** to describe activities that are pleasant and friendly. ❑ *...a cosy chat between friends.*

cot

cot /kɒt/ (**cots**) N-COUNT In British English, a **cot** is a bed for a baby, with bars or panels round it so that the baby cannot fall out. The American word is **crib**.

cottage /ˈkɒtɪdʒ/ (**cottages**) N-COUNT A **cottage** is a small house, usually in the country.

cotton /ˈkɒtən/ (**cottons, cottoning, cottoned**) **1** N-VAR **Cotton** is cloth made from the soft fibres from the cotton plant. ❑ *Sheets are often made of cotton.* ❑ *...a cotton shirt.* **2** N-UNCOUNT **Cotton** is a plant which produces the soft fibres used in making cotton cloth. **3** N-VAR **cotton** is sewing thread. [BRIT] ❑ *...a needle and cotton.*
▶ **cotton on** PHR-VERB If you **cotton on to** something, you understand it or realize it. [INFORMAL] ❑ *She cottoned on to the fact that he had been lying to her.*

ˌcotton ˈwool N-UNCOUNT **Cotton wool** is soft fluffy cotton, often used for applying creams to your skin. [BRIT]

couch /kaʊtʃ/ (**couches, couching, couched**) **1** N-COUNT A **couch** is a long soft piece of furniture for sitting or lying on. **2** V-T If a statement **is couched in** a particular style of language, it is expressed in that style of language. [WRITTEN] ❑ *The statement was couched in polite language.*

cough /kɒf, AM kɔːf/ (**coughs, coughing, coughed**) **1** V-I & N-COUNT When you **cough**, you force air out of your throat with a sudden harsh noise. A **cough** is an act of coughing. ❑ *Graham began to cough.* ❑ *She heard a loud cough behind her.* ● **coughing** N-UNCOUNT ❑ *...a terrible fit of coughing.* **2** N-COUNT A **cough** is an illness in which you cough. ❑ *Contact your doctor if the cough persists.* **3** V-T If you **cough** blood, it comes up out of your throat or mouth when you cough.
→ see **illness**
▶ **cough up** PHR-VERB If you **cough up** money, you give someone money, usually when you would prefer not to. [INFORMAL] ❑ *I'll have to cough up $10,000 a year for college fees.*

could /kəd, STRONG kʊd/ **1** MODAL If you **could** do something, you were able to do it. ❑ *I could see that something was terribly wrong.* ❑ *The children couldn't read or write.* **2** MODAL You use **could** after 'if' when you are imagining what would happen if something was the case. ❑ *If I could afford it, I'd buy a new car.* **3** MODAL You use **could** to indicate that something sometimes happened. ❑ *He could be very pleasant when he wanted to.* **4** MODAL You use **could have** to indicate that something was a possibility in the past, although it did not actually happen. ❑ *He could have made a lots of money as a lawyer.* **5** MODAL You use **could** to indicate that something is possibly true, or that it may possibly happen. ❑ *Food which is high in fat could cause health problems.* **6** MODAL You use **could** when making offers and suggestions. ❑ *I could call the doctor.* ❑ *Couldn't you have a talk with your brother?* **7** MODAL You use **could** in questions to make polite requests. ❑ *Could I stay tonight?* ❑ *He asked if he could have a cup of coffee.*

C

couldn't /ˈkʊdənt/ **Couldn't** is the usual spoken form of 'could not'.

could've /kʊdəv/ **Could've** is the usual spoken form of 'could have', when 'have' is an auxiliary verb.

council /ˈkaʊnsəl/ (**councils**) **1** N-COUNT A **council** is a group of people elected to govern a town or other area. ❑ *...Edinburgh County Council.* **2** ADJ BEFORE N **Council** houses or flats are owned by the local council and people pay rent to live in them. [BRIT]

councillor [AM **councilor**] /ˈkaʊnsələ/ (**councillors**) N-COUNT A **councillor** is a member of a local council.

counsel /ˈkaʊnsəl/ (**counsels, counselling, counselled** or [AM] **counseling, counseled**) **1** N-UNCOUNT **Counsel** is careful advice. [FORMAL] ❑ *If you have a problem, it is a good idea to seek help and counsel.* **2** V-T If you **counsel** someone **to** do something, you advise them to do it. [FORMAL] ❑ *My advisers counselled me to talk to the police.* **3** V-T If you **counsel** people, you give them advice about their problems. ❑ *...a psychologist who counsels people with anorexia.* ● **counselling** N-UNCOUNT ❑ *...marriage counselling.* ● **counsellor** (**counsellors**) N-COUNT ❑ *Talk to a trained counsellor.* **4** N-COUNT Someone's **counsel** is the lawyer who gives advice on a legal case and speaks for them in court.

count /kaʊnt/ (**counts, counting, counted**) **1** V-I When you **count**, you say all the numbers in order up to a particular number. ❑ *Brian counted slowly to twenty.* **2** V-T & PHR-VERB If you **count** all the things in a group, or if you **count** them **up**, you add them up to see how many there are. ❑ *I counted the money.* ❑ *They counted up all the extra hours the staff had worked.* **3** N-COUNT A **count** is the action of counting, or the number that you get after counting. ❑ *At the last count, 26.8% of houses in the United Kingdom had only one person living in them.* **4** V-I If something or someone **counts for** something, or if they **count**, they are important or valuable. ❑ *Personal happiness counts for a lot.* ❑ *Their opinions don't count.* **5** V-I If something **counts as** a particular thing, it is regarded as being that thing. ❑ *He wants to be counted as a good man.* **6** N-COUNT & N-TITLE A **Count** is a male member of the nobility. **7** PHRASE If you **keep count of** a number of things, you keep a record of how many have occurred. If you **lose count of** a number of things, you cannot remember how many have occurred. ❑ *She's lost count of the number of jobs she's had.*
→ see **mathematics, zero**
▶ **count against** PHR-VERB If something **counts against** you, it may cause you to be punished or rejected. ❑ *The footballer's history of injury counts against him.*
▶ **count on** or **count upon** PHR-VERB If you **count on** someone or something, you rely on them to support you. ❑ *I can always count on you to cheer me up.*
▶ **count out** PHR-VERB If you **count out** a sum of money, you count it as you put the notes or coins

in a pile.

▶ **count up** → see **count** (meaning 2)

▶ **count upon** → see **count on**.

countable noun /ˌkaʊntəbəl 'naʊn/ (**countable nouns**) N-COUNT A **countable noun** is the same as a **count noun**.

C

countdown /'kaʊntdaʊn/ (**countdowns**) N-COUNT A **countdown** is the counting aloud of numbers in reverse order before something happens.

countenance /'kaʊntɪnəns/ (**countenances, countenancing, countenanced**) 1 V-T If someone will not **countenance** something, they do not agree with it and will not allow it to happen. [FORMAL] ❑ *They do not countenance failure.* 2 N-COUNT Someone's **countenance** is their face. [LITERARY]

counter /'kaʊntə/ (**counters, countering, countered**) 1 N-COUNT In a shop, a **counter** is a long flat surface at which customers are served. ❑ *...the meat counter.* 2 V-T & N-SING If you **counter** something that is being done, or do something as **a counter to** it, you take action to make it less effective. ❑ *The bank must counter these problems.* ❑ *The organisation was set up as a counter to nationalist groups.* 3 V-T If you **counter** something that has been said, you say something in reaction to it or in opposition to it. ❑ *Both of them had to counter fierce criticism.* 4 PHRASE If one thing **runs counter to** another, or if one thing **is counter to** another, the first thing is the opposite of the second thing or conflicts with it. ❑ *The idea runs counter to government plans.* 5 N-COUNT A **counter** is a small, flat, round object used in a board game.

counteract /ˌkaʊntər'ækt/ (**counteracts, counteracting, counteracted**) V-T To **counteract** something means to reduce its effect by doing something that has the opposite effect. ❑ *These pills counteract high blood pressure.*

'counter-attack (**counter-attacks, counter-attacking, counter-attacked**) V-I & N-VAR When an army **counter-attacks**, or when it makes a **counter-attack**, it attacks an enemy that has just attacked it.

counterclockwise /ˌkaʊntə'klɒkwaɪz/ ADV & ADJ **Counterclockwise** means the same as **anti-clockwise**. [AM]

counterfeit /'kaʊntəfɪt/ (**counterfeits, counterfeiting, counterfeited**) 1 N-COUNT & ADJ **Counterfeits**, or **counterfeit** money, goods, or documents, are not genuine, but have been made to look exactly like real ones in order to deceive people. ❑ *You can buy counterfeits of the watches everywhere.* ❑ *...counterfeit currency.* 2 V-T To **counterfeit** something means to make a counterfeit version of it. • **counterfeiting** N-UNCOUNT ❑ *...the crime of counterfeiting.*

counterpart /'kaʊntəpɑːt/ (**counterparts**) N-COUNT Someone's or something's **counterpart** is another person or thing that has a similar function in a different place. ❑ *The Prime Minister telephoned his German counterpart.*

ˌcounter-pro'ductive also **ˌcounterproductive** ADJ Something that is **counter-productive** has the opposite effect from what you intend. ❑ *Attempts to stop him are likely to be counter-productive.*

countess /'kaʊntɪs/ (**countesses**) N-COUNT & N-TITLE A **Countess** is a female member of the nobility.

countless /'kaʊntləs/ ADJ BEFORE N **Countless** means very many. ❑ *She brought joy to countless people.*

'count noun (**count nouns**) N-COUNT A **count noun** is a noun such as 'bird', 'chair', or 'year' which has a singular and a plural form and is always used after a determiner in the singular.

country /'kʌntri/ (**countries**) 1 N-COUNT A **country** is one of the political areas which the world is divided into, covering a particular area of land. You can refer to the people who live in a particular country as **the country.** ❑ *Brazil is the largest country in South America.* ❑ *The country voted for a new president.* 2 N-SING **The country** is land away from towns and cities. ❑ *...a healthy life in the country.* 3 N-UNCOUNT **Country** is used to refer to an area with particular characteristics or connections. ❑ *...the mountainous country east of Genoa.* 4 N-UNCOUNT **Country** music is a style of popular music from the USA.

→ see Word Web: **country**

> **Usage**
>
> **Country** is the most usual word to use when you are talking about the major political units that the world is divided into. **State** is used when you are talking about politics or government institutions. ❑ *...the new German state created by the unification process.* ❑ *...Italy's state-controlled telecommunications company.* **State** can also refer to a political unit within a particular country. ❑ *...the American state of California.* **Nation** is often used when you are talking about a country's inhabitants, and their cultural or ethnic background. ❑ *Wales is a proud nation with its own traditions.* ❑ *A senior government spokesman will be coming to address the nation.* **Land** is a less precise and more literary word, which you can use, for example, to talk about the feelings you have for a particular country. ❑ *She was fascinated to learn about this strange land at the edge of Europe.*

countryman /'kʌntrimən/ (**countrymen**) N-COUNT Your **countrymen** are people from your own country.

countryside /'kʌntrisaɪd/ N-UNCOUNT The **countryside** is land away from towns and cities.

→ see **city**

> **Usage**
>
> Do not confuse **countryside, landscape, scenery,** and **nature. Countryside** is land which is away from towns and cities. ❑ *...3,500 acres of flat countryside.* With **landscape,** the emphasis is on the physical features of the land, while **scenery** includes everything you can see when you look out over an area of land, usually in the country. ❑ *...the landscape of woods and distant mountains.* ❑ *...unattractive urban scenery.* **Nature** includes the landscape, the weather, animals, and plants. ❑ *He writes songs about the beauty of nature.*

county /'kaʊnti/ (**counties**) N-COUNT A **county** is a region of Britain, Ireland, or the USA with its own local government.

Word Web country

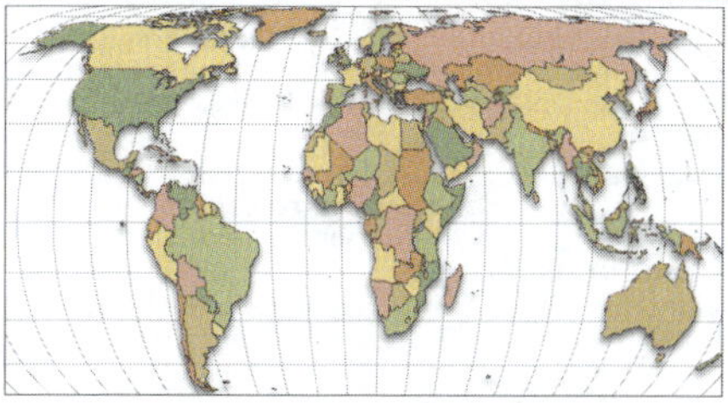

The largest **country** in the world geographically is Russia. It has an area of six million square miles and a **population** of more than 142 million people. Russia is a federal state with a republican form of **government**. The government is based in Russia's **capital** city, Moscow.

One of the smallest countries in the world is Nauru. This tiny island **nation** in the South Pacific Ocean is 8.1 square miles in size. Many of Nauru's more than 13,000 **residents** live in Yaren, which is the largest city, but not the capital. The Republic of Nauru is the only nation in the world without an official capital.

coup /kuː/ (**coups**) 1 N-COUNT A **coup** is the same as a **coup d'état**. 2 N-COUNT A **coup** is an achievement thought to be especially brilliant because of its difficulty. ❑ *Getting the top job in the company at his young age was quite a coup.*

coup d'état /ˌkuː deɪˈtɑː/ (**coups d'état**)

> The plural is pronounced the same as the singular.

N-COUNT When there is a **coup d'état**, a group of people take power in a country.

couple /ˈkʌpəl/ (**couples, coupling, coupled**) 1 QUANT If you refer to **a couple of** people or things, you mean two or approximately two of them. ❑ *I think the trouble will be over in a couple of days.* 2 N-COUNT A **couple** is two people who are married, or having a sexual or romantic relationship. ❑ *The couple have four children.* 3 N-COUNT A **couple** is two people that you see together on a particular occasion or that are associated in some way. ❑ *The four couples went out for dinner together.* 4 V-T If one thing produces a particular effect when it **is coupled with** another, the two things combine to produce that effect. ❑ *The country's economic problems are coupled with the worst political situation since 1945.*

coupon /ˈkuːpɒn/ (**coupons**) 1 N-COUNT A **coupon** is a piece of printed paper which is issued by the maker or supplier of a product and which allows you to pay less than usual for something. 2 N-COUNT A **coupon** is a small form which you fill in and send off to ask for information, to order something, or to enter a competition.

> **Word Link** *age ≈ state of, related to : camouflage, courage, marriage*

courage /ˈkʌrɪdʒ, AM ˈkɜːr-/ N-UNCOUNT **Courage** is the quality shown by someone who does something dangerous, even though they may be afraid. ❑ *The girl had the courage to tell the police.*

courageous /kəˈreɪdʒəs/ ADJ Someone who is **courageous** shows courage. ❑ *She had been very courageous during the war.* ● **courageously** ADV

courgette /kʊəˈʒet/ (**courgettes**) N-VAR In British English, **courgettes** are long thin green vegetables. The American word is **zucchini**.

courier /ˈkʊriə/ (**couriers, couriering, couriered**) 1 N-COUNT A **courier** is a person who is paid to take letters and parcels direct from one place to another. 2 N-COUNT A **courier** is a person employed by a travel company to look after people who are on holiday. 3 V-T If you **courier** something somewhere, you send it there by courier. ❑ *I couriered the report to Darren in New York.*

course /kɔːs/ (**courses, coursing, coursed**) 1 → see **of course** 2 N-UNCOUNT The **course** of a vehicle is the route along which it is travelling. ❑ *The pilot changed course and flew north.* 3 N-COUNT A **course** of action is an action or a series of actions that you can do in a particular situation. ❑ *Vietnam is trying to decide on its course for the future.* 4 N-SING You can refer to the way that events develop as **the course of** history, nature, or events. 5 N-COUNT A **course** is a series of lessons or lectures on a particular subject. ❑ *...a course in French literature.* 6 N-COUNT A **course of** medical treatment is a series of treatments that a doctor gives someone. ❑ *...a course of antibiotics.* 7 N-COUNT A **course** is one part of a meal. ❑ *...a three-course dinner.* 8 N-COUNT In sport, a **course** is an area of land where races are held or golf is played. 9 PHRASE If you are **on course for** something, you are likely to achieve it. 10 PHRASE If something **runs its course** or **takes its course**, it develops naturally and comes to a natural end. ❑ *Their relationship ran its course.* 11 **in due course** → see **due**

court /kɔːt/ (**courts, courting, courted**) 1 N-COUNT A **court** is a place where legal matters are decided by a judge and jury or by a magistrate. You can also refer to a judge, jury, or magistrates as a **court**. ❑ *She appeared in court as a witness.* ❑ *The court awarded the man one and a half million pounds.* 2 N-COUNT A **court** is an area for playing a game such as tennis or squash. 3 N-COUNT The **court** of a king or queen is the place where he or she lives and works. 4 PHRASE You can say someone **holds court** when they are surrounded by a lot of people who are paying them a lot of attention because they are interesting or famous; used showing disapproval. 5 V-T If you say that someone **is courting** disaster, you think they are acting in a way that makes it likely to happen. 6 V-T If you **court** something such as publicity or popularity, you try to obtain it for yourself.

courteous /ˈkɜːtiəs/ ADJ Someone who is **courteous** is polite, respectful, and considerate. ❑ *He is so courteous and helpful.* ● **courteously** ADV

courtesy /ˈkɜːtɪsi/ (**courtesies**) 1 N-UNCOUNT **Courtesy** is polite, respectful, and considerate behaviour. 2 N-COUNT **Courtesies** are polite and respectful things that you say or do. [FORMAL]

❑ *Hugh and John were exchanging courtesies.* **3** ADJ BEFORE N **Courtesy** is used to describe services that are provided free of charge by an organization to its customers. ❑ *A courtesy shuttle bus operates between the hotel and the town.*

C

courthouse /ˈkɔːthaʊs/ (**courthouses**) N-COUNT In American English, a **courthouse** is a building in which a law court meets. The usual British word is **court**.

courtier /ˈkɔːtiə/ (**courtiers**) N-COUNT **Courtiers** were members of the nobility at the court of a king or queen.

ˌcourt-ˈmartial (**court-martials, court-martialling, court-martialled**) **1** N-VAR A **court-martial** is a trial in a military court of a member of the armed forces. **2** V-T If a member of the armed forces **is court-martialled**, he or she is tried in a military court.

courtroom /ˈkɔːtruːm/ (**courtrooms**) N-COUNT A **courtroom** is a room in which a law court meets.

courtship /ˈkɔːtʃɪp/ N-UNCOUNT **Courtship** is the period during which a man and a woman spend a lot of time together, because they are intending to get married. [FORMAL]
→ see **love**

courtyard /ˈkɔːtjɑːd/ (**courtyards**) N-COUNT A **courtyard** is a flat open area of ground surrounded by buildings or walls.

cousin /ˈkʌzən/ (**cousins**) N-COUNT Your **cousin** is the child of your uncle or aunt.

cove /kəʊv/ (**coves**) N-COUNT A **cove** is a small bay on the coast.

covenant /ˈkʌvənənt/ (**covenants**) **1** N-COUNT A **covenant** is a formal written agreement between two or more people which is recognized in law. **2** N-COUNT A **covenant** is a formal written promise to pay a sum of money each year for a fixed period, especially to a charity.

cover /ˈkʌvə/ (**covers, covering, covered**) **1** V-T & PHR-VERB If you **cover** one thing **with** another, or if you **cover** it **up**, you place the second thing over the first in order to protect it, hide it, or close it. ❑ *Cover the biscuits with a cloth.* ❑ *A black patch covered his left eye.* **2** N-COUNT A **cover** is something which is put over an object, usually in order to protect it. The **cover** of a book or a magazine is the protective outside part of it. **3** N-PLURAL **Bed covers** are sheets, blankets, and quilts. **4** V-T If one thing **is covered with** or **in** another, the second forms a layer over its surface. ❑ *The desk was covered with papers.* **5** V-T If you **cover** a particular distance, you travel that distance. **6** V-T & N-UNCOUNT When an insurance policy **covers** a person or thing, or provides **cover**, it guarantees that money will be paid in relation to that person or thing. ❑ *This travel insurance covers you and your family.* ❑ *...insurance cover for flood damage.* **7** V-T If you **cover** a particular topic, you discuss it in a lecture, course, or book. ❑ *The course covers German history and politics.* **8** V-T If a journalist **covers** an event, he or she reports on it. **9** V-T If a sum of money **covers** something, it is enough to pay for it. ❑ *Please enclose £1.50 to cover postage.* **10** N-UNCOUNT & PHRASE You can refer to trees, rocks, or other places where you shelter from the weather or hide from someone as **cover**. If you **take cover**, you shelter from the weather or from an attack. ❑ *They ran for cover.* **11** PHRASE If you **cover** your **back** or **cover** your **rear**, you do something in order to protect yourself, for example against criticism or against accusations of doing something wrong. ❑ *He covered his back by recording their conversation.*

▶ **cover up** **1** PHR-VERB If you **cover up** something that you do not want people to know about, you conceal the truth about it. ❑ *How do I know you're not just covering up for your friend?* **2** → see also **cover** (meaning 1), **cover-up**

Thesaurus	*cover* Also look up:
V.	conceal, drape, hide, screen; *(ant.)* uncover **1**
	guard, insure, protect **6**

Word Partnership	Use *cover* with:
N.	cover ***your*** **face** **1**
	covered **in *something*** **4**
V.	**run for** cover, **take** cover **10**
PREP.	**under** cover **10**

coverage /ˈkʌvərɪdʒ/ N-UNCOUNT The **coverage** of something in the news is the reporting of it. ❑ *...TV coverage of football matches.*

covering /ˈkʌvərɪŋ/ (**coverings**) N-VAR A **covering** is a layer of something over something else. ❑ *Linoleum is a clean type of floor covering.*

covert /ˈkʌvət, ˈkəʊvɜːt/ ADJ **Covert** activities or situations are secret or hidden. [FORMAL] ❑ *Each show begins with the covert filming of their next victim.* ● **covertly** ADV ❑ *Joanna studied him covertly.*

ˈcover-up (**cover-ups**) N-COUNT A **cover-up** is an attempt to hide a crime or mistake.

covet /ˈkʌvɪt/ (**covets, coveting, coveted**) V-T If you **covet** something belonging to someone else, you want very much to have it for yourself. [FORMAL] ❑ *She openly coveted his job.*

coveted /ˈkʌvɪtɪd/ ADJ You use **coveted** to describe something that very many people would like to have. ❑ *...one of sport's most coveted trophies.*

cow /kaʊ/ (**cows, cowing, cowed**) **1** N-COUNT A **cow** is a large female animal kept on farms for its milk. **2** N-COUNT Some female animals, including elephants and whales, are called **cows**. **3** V-T If someone **is cowed**, they are frightened into behaving in a particular way. [FORMAL] ❑ *They had been cowed by the threat of violence.* ● **cowed** ADJ ❑ *She was so cowed by fear that she did what they said.*
→ see **dairy, meat**

coward /kaʊəd/ (**cowards**) N-COUNT A **coward** is someone who is easily frightened and avoids dangerous or difficult situations.

cowardice /ˈkaʊədɪs/ N-UNCOUNT **Cowardice** is cowardly behaviour.

cowardly /kaʊədli/ ADJ Someone who is **cowardly** is easily frightened and so avoids doing dangerous or difficult things. ❑ *I was too cowardly to complain.*

cowboy /ˈkaʊbɔɪ/ (**cowboys**) **1** N-COUNT A **cowboy** is a man employed to look after cattle in the United States of America. **2** N-COUNT You can refer to someone, especially a builder, as a **cowboy** if you think they are dishonest or do bad work. [BRIT]
→ see **hat**

coy /kɔɪ/ **1** ADJ If you describe someone as **coy**, you disapprove of them pretending to be shy and modest. ❑ *He is coy about his private life.* • **coyly** ADV ❑ *She smiled coyly.* • **coyness** N-UNCOUNT ❑ *...her coyness and flirting.* **2** ADJ If someone is being **coy**, they don't want to talk about something that they feel guilty or embarrassed about. ❑ *He is understandably coy about the incident.*

cozy /'kəʊzi/ → see **cosy**

CPR /ˌsi:pi:'ɑ:/ N-UNCOUNT **CPR** is a medical technique for reviving someone whose heart has stopped beating by pressing on their chest and breathing into their mouth. **CPR** is an abbreviation for **cardiopulmonary resuscitation**. [MEDICAL] ❑ *He began to administer CPR, hoping to get Mort breathing again.*

crab /kræb/ (**crabs**) N-COUNT A **crab** is a sea creature with a flat round body covered by a shell, and five pairs of legs with claws on the front pair. Crabs usually move sideways.
→ see **shellfish**

crack
❶ VERB USES
❷ NOUN AND ADJECTIVE USES

crack /kræk/ (**cracks, cracking, cracked**)
❶ **1** V-T/V-I If something **cracks**, or if you **crack** it, it becomes slightly damaged, with lines appearing on its surface. ❑ *A stone cracked the car window.* ❑ *...a cracked mirror.* **2** V-T If you **crack** something, you hit it and it breaks or is damaged. ❑ *Crack the eggs into a bowl.* **3** V-T If you **crack** a problem or a code, you solve it, especially after a lot of thought. ❑ *Francis Crick and James Watson cracked the code of DNA.* **4** V-I If someone **cracks**, they lose control of their emotions or actions because they are under a lot of pressure. ❑ *He is tough. I would have cracked under such pressure.* **5** V-T If you **crack** a joke, you tell it.
→ see **crash**

▶ **crack down** **1** PHR-VERB If people in authority **crack down on** a group of people, they become stricter in making them obey rules or laws. ❑ *The government is determined to crack down on vandals.* **2** → see also **crackdown**

▶ **crack up** PHR-VERB If someone **cracks up**, they are under such emotional strain that they become mentally ill. [INFORMAL]

crack /kræk/ (**cracks**)
❷ **1** N-COUNT A **crack** is a very narrow gap between two things. ❑ *Kate could see him through a crack in the curtains.* **2** N-COUNT A **crack** is a line that appears on the surface of something when it is slightly damaged. ❑ *The plate had a crack in it.* **3** N-COUNT A **crack** is a sharp sound, like the sound of a piece of wood breaking. ❑ *There was a loud crack and glass flew into the room.* **4** N-SING If you have a **crack at** something, you make an attempt to do or achieve something. [INFORMAL] ❑ *I'll have a crack at it.* **5** N-COUNT A **crack** is a slightly rude or cruel joke. **6** ADJ BEFORE N A **crack** soldier or sportsman is highly trained and very skilful. ❑ *...crack troops.*

Word Partnership	Use *crack* with:
ADJ.	crack **open** ① **1** **2**
N.	crack **a code**, crack **the system** ① **3**
	crack **jokes** ① **5**
V.	**have a** crack ② **1** **2**
ADJ.	**deep** crack ② **1** **2**

crackdown /'krækdaʊn/ (**crackdowns**) N-COUNT A **crackdown** is strong official action taken to punish people who break laws.

cracker /'krækə/ (**crackers**) **1** N-COUNT A **cracker** is a thin crisp savoury biscuit. **2** N-COUNT A **cracker** is a hollow cardboard tube covered with coloured paper. Crackers make a bang when they are pulled apart and usually contain a small toy, a joke, and a paper hat.

crackle /'krækəl/ (**crackles, crackling, crackled**) V-I & N-COUNT If something **crackles**, it makes a series of short harsh noises called **crackles**. ❑ *The radio crackled again.* ❑ *...the crackle of gunfire.*

cradle /'kreɪdəl/ (**cradles, cradling, cradled**)

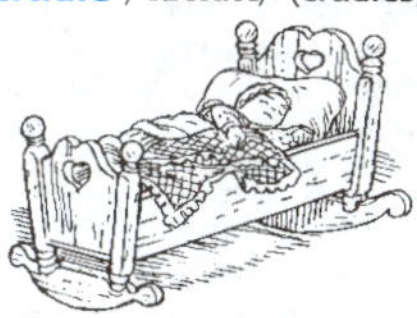
cradle

1 N-COUNT A **cradle** is a baby's bed with high sides. **2** N-SING A place that is referred to as **the cradle of** something is the place where it began. ❑ *...New York, the cradle of capitalism.* **3** V-T If you **cradle** someone or something in your arms, you hold them carefully. ❑ *I sat cradling the baby.*

craft /krɑ:ft, kræft/ (**crafts, crafting, crafted**)

In meaning 1, **craft** is both the singular and the plural form.

1 N-COUNT You can refer to a boat, a spacecraft, or an aircraft as a **craft**. ❑ *Hundreds of small craft sailed out to sea.* **2** N-COUNT A **craft** is an activity that involves doing something skilfully, especially an activity such as weaving, carving, or pottery that involves making things skilfully with your hands. ❑ *...the craft of writing.* ❑ *...traditional arts and crafts.* **3** V-T If something **is crafted**, it is made skilfully. ❑ *Pajo crafted some great songs.*
→ see **fly**, **ship**

craftsman /'krɑ:ftsmən, 'kræft-/ (**craftsmen**) N-COUNT A **craftsman** is a man who makes things skilfully with his hands.

craftsmanship /'krɑ:ftsmənʃɪp, 'kræft-/ **1** N-UNCOUNT **Craftsmanship** is the skill that someone uses when they make beautiful things with their hands. ❑ *...the craftsmanship of Fabergé.* **2** N-UNCOUNT **Craftsmanship** is the quality that something has when it is beautiful and has been carefully made. ❑ *This designer's clothes are known for their style and craftsmanship.*

crafty /'krɑ:fti, 'kræfti/ (**craftier, craftiest**) ADJ If you describe someone as **crafty**, you mean that they get what they want in a clever way, often by deceiving people. ❑ *...a crafty fellow.*

cram /kræm/ (**crams, cramming, crammed**) V-T/V-I If you **cram** things or people **into** a place, or if they **cram** it, there are so many of them in it at one time that it is completely full. ❑ *She crammed the books into the bookcase.* ❑ *Friends and family* *crammed the church for her wedding.*

crammed /kræmd/ ADJ If a place is **crammed with** things or people, it is very full of them. ❑ *The house is crammed with expensive furniture.*

cramp /kræmp/ (**cramps**) N-UNCOUNT & N-PLURAL **Cramp** is a sudden strong pain caused by a muscle suddenly contracting. ❑ *...stomach cramps.*

cramped /kræmpt/ ADJ A **cramped** room or building is not big enough for the people or things in it. ❑ *...a rather cramped little flat.*

crane

crane /kreɪn/ (**cranes, craning, craned**) **1** N-COUNT A **crane** is a large machine that moves heavy things by lifting them in the air. **2** N-COUNT A **crane** is a kind of large bird with a long neck and long legs. **3** V-T/V-I If you **crane**, or **crane** your neck, you stretch your neck in a particular direction in order to see or hear something better. ❑ *She craned forward to look at me.*

crank /kræŋk/ (**cranks, cranking, cranked**) **1** N-COUNT If you call someone a **crank**, you think they have peculiar ideas or behaviour. [INFORMAL] **2** V-T If you **crank** a device or machine, you make it move by turning a handle. ❑ *She cranked open the window and let the air inside.*

crash /kræʃ/ (**crashes, crashing, crashed**) **1** V-I/V-T & N-COUNT If a moving vehicle **crashes**, you **crash** it, or if it has a **crash**, it hits something and is damaged or destroyed. ❑ *His car crashed into the back of a van.* ❑ *His mother crashed her car into a tree.* ❑ *...a car crash.* **2** V-I & N-COUNT To **crash** means to move or fall violently, making a sudden loud noise, called a **crash**. ❑ *The walls above us crashed down.* ❑ *I remember hearing a loud crash in the middle of the night.* **3** V-I & N-COUNT If a business or financial system **crashes**, it fails suddenly, often with serious effects. Its sudden failure is called a **crash**. ❑ *His business crashed, with debts of £100,000.* ❑ *...a stock market crash.* **4** V-I If a computer or a computer program **crashes**, it fails suddenly. [COMPUTING]
→ see Word Web: **crash**

Thesaurus	*crash*	Also look up:
N.	collision, wreck **1**	
	bang **2**	
V.	collide, hit, smash **1** **2**	
	fail **3**	

crass /kræs/ ADJ **Crass** behaviour is stupid and insensitive.

crate /kreɪt/ (**crates**) N-COUNT A **crate** is a large box used for transporting or storing things.

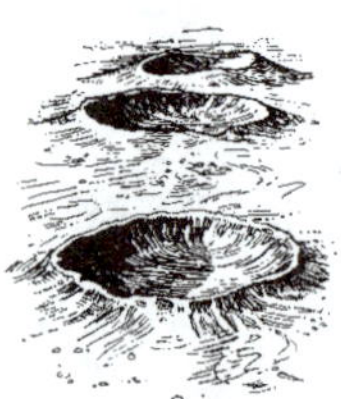
crater

crater /ˈkreɪtə/ (**craters**) N-COUNT A **crater** is a large hole in the ground, which has been caused by something hitting it or by an explosion.
→ see **astronomer, lake, meteor, moon, solar system**

crave /kreɪv/ (**craves, craving, craved**) V-T If you **crave** something, you want to have it very much. ❑ *She's an unhappy girl who craves affection.* ● **craving** (**cravings**) N-COUNT ❑ *...a craving for sugar.*

crawl /krɔːl/ (**crawls, crawling, crawled**) **1** V-I When you **crawl**, you move forward on your hands and knees. ❑ *Her baby has just learned to crawl.* **2** V-I & N-SING If someone or something **crawls** somewhere, or if they move there **at a crawl**, they move there slowly or with great difficulty. ❑ *He managed to crawl from the car after the accident.* ❑ *The traffic slowed to a crawl.* **3** V-I If you say that a place **is crawling with** people or things, you mean that it is full of them. [INFORMAL] ❑ *This place is crawling with police.* **4** N-UNCOUNT The **crawl** is a kind of swimming stroke which you do lying on your front, swinging one arm over your head and then the other arm, and kicking your legs.

crawl

crayon /ˈkreɪɒn/ (**crayons**) N-COUNT A **crayon** is a rod of coloured wax used for drawing.

craze /kreɪz/ (**crazes**) N-COUNT If there is a **craze** for something, it is very popular for a short time. ❑ *Walking is the latest fitness craze.*

crazed /kreɪzd/ ADJ **Crazed** people are wild and uncontrolled, and perhaps insane. ❑ *The singer was attacked by a crazed fan.*

crazy /ˈkreɪzi/ (**crazier, craziest**) **1** ADJ f you describe someone or something as **crazy**, you think they are very foolish or strange. [INFORMAL] ❑ *Some people think I was crazy to take this job.* ● **crazily** ADV ❑ *Suddenly I saw a man waving crazily at us.* **2** ADJ AFTER LINK-V If you are **crazy about** something, you are very enthusiastic about it. If you are **crazy about** someone, you are deeply in love with them. ❑ *He is crazy about gardening.* ❑ *We're crazy about each other.* **3** ADJ AFTER LINK-V If something **makes** or **drives** you **crazy**, it makes you extremely annoyed or upset. ❑ *Their endless arguing drove him crazy.*

creak /kriːk/ (**creaks, creaking, creaked**) V-I & N-COUNT If something **creaks**, it makes a short high-pitched sound, called a **creak**, when it moves. ❑ *The wooden steps creaked under his feet.* ❑ *The door opened with a creak.*

cream /kriːm/ (**creams, creaming, creamed**) **1** N-UNCOUNT **Cream** is a thick liquid that is produced from milk. You can use it in cooking or put it on fruit or puddings. ❑ *...strawberries and cream.* **2** N-VAR A **cream** is a substance that you rub into your skin, for example to keep it soft or to heal or protect it. ❑ *...sun protection creams.* **3** ADJ Something that is **cream** in colour is yellowish-white. **4** N-SING **The cream** is used to refer to the best people or things of a particular kind. ❑ *...the cream of society.*
▶ **cream off** PHR-VERB If you **cream off** part of a group of people, you separate them and treat them differently, because you think they are better than the rest. ❑ *The private schools cream off many of the best pupils.*

creamy /ˈkriːmi/ (**creamier, creamiest**) ADJ **Creamy** food or drink contains a lot of cream or milk or has a soft, smooth texture like cream.

Word Web crash

Every year the National Highway Traffic Safety Administration* does crash tests on new cars. They evaluate exactly what happens during an accident. How fast do you have to be going to **buckle** a bumper during a collision? Does the petrol tank **rupture**? Do the tyres **burst**? What happens when the windshield **breaks**? Does it **crack**, or does it **shatter** into a thousand pieces? Does the force of the **impact crush** the front of the car completely? This is actually a good thing. It means that the engine and bonnet would protect the passengers during the crash.

National Highway Traffic Safety Administration: a U.S. government agency that sets safety standards.

❑ *...rich, creamy coffee.* ❑ *...creamy mashed potato.*

crease /kri:s/ (**creases, creasing, creased**) **1** V-I/V-T & N-COUNT If cloth or paper **creases**, or if you **crease** it, lines called **creases** form in it because it has been crushed or folded. ❑ *Be careful not to crease the front of the shirt when ironing the back.* ❑ *Dad flattened the creases of the map.* ● **creased** ADJ ❑ *His clothes were creased, as if he had slept in them.* **2** V-I & N-COUNT If your face **creases**, lines called **creases** appear on it because you are frowning or smiling. ❑ *His face creased into a smile.* ❑ *...the tiny creases at the corners of his eyes.* ● **creased** ADJ ❑ *...Jock's creased face.*

Word Link *creat ≈ making : creation, creature, recreate*

Word Link *ator ≈ one who does : creator, decorator, narrator*

create /kri'eɪt/ (**creates, creating, created**) V-T To **create** something means to cause it to happen or exist. ❑ *The new factory will create 1,000 jobs.* ❑ *She could create a fight out of anything.* ● **creator** (**creators**) N-COUNT ❑ *...Ian Fleming, the creator of James Bond.*

Thesaurus *create* Also look up:

V. compose, craft, design, invent, make, produce; *(ant.)* destroy

creation /kri'eɪʃən/ (**creations**) **1** N-UNCOUNT The **creation of** something is the act of bringing it into existence. ❑ *The new businesses led to the creation of local jobs.* **2** N-UNCOUNT In many religions, **creation** is the making of the universe, earth, and creatures by God. ❑ *...the story of creation.* **3** N-COUNT You can refer to something that someone has made as a **creation**. ❑ *The story is purely of his own creation.*

creative /kri'eɪtɪv/ **1** ADJ A **creative** person has the ability to invent and develop original ideas, especially in art. **Creative** activities involve inventing and developing original ideas. ❑ *...creative writing.* ● **creativity** /ˌkri:eɪ'tɪvɪti/ N-UNCOUNT ❑ *...a period of creativity in the '50s and '60s.* **2** ADJ If you use something in a **creative** way, you use it in a new way that produces interesting and unusual results. ❑ *...his creative use of words.*

creature /'kri:tʃə/ (**creatures**) N-COUNT You can refer to any living thing that is not a plant as a **creature**. ❑ *Like all living creatures, birds need a good supply of water.*

crèche /kreʃ/ (**crèches**) N-COUNT A **crèche** is a place where small children are left and looked after while their parents are doing something else.

Word Link *cred ≈ to believe : credence, credentials, incredible*

credence /'kri:dəns/ N-UNCOUNT If something **gives** or **lends credence** to a theory or story, it makes it easier to believe.

credentials /krɪ'denʃəlz/ **1** N-PLURAL Your **credentials** are your previous achievements, training, and general background, which indicate that you are qualified to do something. ❑ *Her credentials are impressive.* **2** N-PLURAL Someone's **credentials** are a letter or certificate that proves their identity or qualifications. ❑ *Britain's new ambassador has presented his credentials to the President.*

credible /'kredɪbəl/ **1** ADJ **Credible** means able to be trusted or believed. ❑ *We have two very credible witnesses.* ● **credibility** N-UNCOUNT ❑ *Their managers have no credibility.* **2** ADJ A **credible** candidate, policy, or system is one that appears to have a chance of being successful. ❑ *...a credible opponent.*

credit /'kredɪt/ (**credits, crediting, credited**) **1** N-UNCOUNT **Credit** is a system where you pay for goods or services several weeks or months after you have received them. ❑ *You can pay for this sofa on credit.* **2** N-UNCOUNT If a person or their bank account is **in credit**, the bank account has money in it. ❑ *I made sure the account stayed in credit.* **3** N-UNCOUNT If you get **the credit for** something good, people praise you because you are thought to be responsible for it. ❑ *Some of the credit for her success must go to her very supportive husband.* **4** V-T If people **credit** someone **with** an achievement, people say or believe that they were responsible for it. ❑ *The family credit him with saving Helen's life.* **5** N-COUNT **The credits** refers to the list of people who helped to make a film, a record, or a television programme. **6** PHRASE If you say that, **to** someone's **credit**, they did something, you mean that they deserve praise for it. ❑ *To his credit, he has always disagreed with the use of violence.* **7** PHRASE If you have one or more achievements **to** your **credit**, you have achieved them. ❑ *I have got three titles to my credit, but you're only as good as your last tournament.*

C

Word Partnership Use *credit* with:

N.	credit **an account**, credit **history**, **letter of** credit 1
V.	**provide** credit 1
	deserve credit, **take** credit 3
ADJ.	**personal** credit 1

creditable /'kredɪtəbəl/ ADJ A **creditable** performance or achievement is of a reasonably high standard.

'credit card (**credit cards**) N-COUNT A **credit card** is a plastic card that you use to buy goods on credit.

creditor /'kredɪtə/ (**creditors**) N-COUNT Your **creditors** are the people whom you owe money to.

creed /kri:d/ (**creeds**) 1 N-COUNT A **creed** is a set of beliefs or principles that influence the way people live or work. ❑ *...their creed of self-help.* 2 N-COUNT A **creed** is a religion. [FORMAL] ❑ *...young people of every race and creed.*

creek /kri:k/ (**creeks**) 1 N-COUNT A **creek** is a narrow inlet where the sea comes a long way into the land. [BRIT] 2 N-COUNT A **creek** is a small stream or river. [AM]

creep /kri:p/ (**creeps, creeping, crept**) 1 V-I To **creep** somewhere means to move there quietly and slowly. ❑ *He crept up the stairs.* 2 V-I **Creep** can be used to indicate that something gradually reaches a particular level or that it is gradually introduced into a particular situation. ❑ *Prices have crept up by 9.5 per cent.* ❑ *A note of sadness crept into his voice.* 3 N-COUNT If you describe someone as a **creep**, you mean that you dislike them, because they flatter people but are not sincere. [INFORMAL]

Word Partnership Use *creep* with:

PREP.	creep **in**, creep **into**, creep **toward**, creep **up** 1

creepy /'kri:pi/ ADJ If you say that something or someone is **creepy**, you mean they make you feel very uneasy. [INFORMAL] ❑ *This place is really creepy at night.*

cremate /krɪ'meɪt, AM 'kri:meɪt/ (**cremates, cremating, cremated**) V-T When someone **is cremated**, their dead body is burned, usually as part of a funeral service. ● **cremation** (**cremations**) N-VAR ❑ *...the arrangements for her cremation.*

crept /krept/ **Crept** is the past tense and past participle of **creep**.

crescendo /krɪ'ʃendəʊ/ (**crescendos**) N-COUNT A **crescendo** is a noise that gets louder and louder. Some people use **crescendo** to refer to the point when a noise is at its loudest. ❑ *The applause after the finale rose to a crescendo.*

Word Link *cresc, creas ≈ growing : crescent, decrease, increase*

crescent /'kresənt, 'krez-/ (**crescents**) N-COUNT A **crescent** is a curved shape like the shape of the moon during its first and last quarters.

crest /krest/ (**crests**) 1 N-COUNT The **crest of** a hill or a wave is the highest part of it. 2 N-COUNT A **crest** is a design that is the symbol of a noble family, a town, or an organization.
→ see **sound**

crevice /'krevɪs/ (**crevices**) N-COUNT A **crevice** is a narrow crack in a rock.

crew /kru:/ (**crews**) 1 N-COUNT The **crew** of a ship, an aircraft, or a spacecraft consists of the people who work on it and operate it. **Crew** can take the singular or plural form of the verb. 2 N-COUNT A **crew** is a group of people with special technical skills who work together on a task or project. **Crew** can take the singular or plural form of the verb. ❑ *...a two-man film crew.*
→ see **theatre**

crib /krɪb/ (**cribs**) N-COUNT In American English, a **crib** is a bed for a baby, with bars or panels round it so that the baby cannot fall out. The British word is **cot**.

cricket /'krɪkɪt/ (**crickets**) 1 N-UNCOUNT **Cricket** is an outdoor game played by two teams who try to score points, called runs, by hitting a ball with a wooden bat. 2 N-COUNT A **cricket** is a small jumping insect that produces sharp sounds by rubbing its wings together.
→ see **insect**

cricketer /'krɪkɪtə/ (**cricketers**) N-COUNT A **cricketer** is a person who plays cricket.

crime /kraɪm/ (**crimes**) N-VAR A **crime** is an illegal action or activity for which a person can be punished by law. ❑ *...the scene of the crime.* ❑ *It's not a crime to be stupid.*
→ see Picture Dictionary: **crime**
→ see **city**

Word Partnership Use *crime* with:

N.	crime **prevention**, crime **scene**, crime **wave** 1
	partner in crime 1 2
V.	**commit a** crime, **fight against** crime 1
ADJ.	**organized** crime, **terrible** crime, **violent** crime 1

criminal /'krɪmɪnəl/ (**criminals**) 1 N-COUNT A **criminal** is a person who has committed a crime. 2 ADJ **Criminal** means connected with crime.

Picture Dictionary crime

graffiti mugging theft burglary shoplifting

❑ *He had a criminal record for petty theft.* ❑ *...criminal damage.* ● **criminally** ADV ❑ *...a hospital for the criminally insane.*

crimson /ˈkrɪmzən/ ADJ Something that is **crimson** is deep red in colour.

cringe /krɪndʒ/ (**cringes, cringing, cringed**) V-I If you **cringe at** something, you feel embarrassed or disgusted, and perhaps show this in your expression or by making a slight movement. ❑ *Chris cringed at the thought of what he had said.*

cripple /ˈkrɪpəl/ (**cripples, crippling, crippled**) **1** N-COUNT A person with a physical disability or a serious permanent injury is sometimes referred to as a **cripple**. Some people find this use offensive. **2** V-T If someone **is crippled** by an injury, they are so seriously affected by it that they can never move their body properly again. **3** V-T To **cripple** a machine, organization, or system means to damage it severely or prevent it from working properly. ❑ *The war threatened to cripple the US economy.*

crippling /ˈkrɪplɪŋ/ **1** ADJ BEFORE N A **crippling** illness or disability severely damages your health or body. ❑ *...crippling diseases such as arthritis.* **2** ADJ If you say that an action, policy, or situation has a **crippling** effect on something, you mean it has a very harmful effect.

crisis /ˈkraɪsɪs/ (**crises** /ˈkraɪsiːz/) N-VAR A **crisis** is a situation in which something or someone is affected by one or more very serious problems. ❑ *...the country's economic crisis.* ❑ *People don't always behave properly in times of crisis.*

crisp /krɪsp/ (**crisper, crispest, crisps**) **1** ADJ **Crisp** food is pleasantly hard and crunchy. ❑ *Grill the bacon until it is crisp.* ❑ *...crisp lettuce.* **2** N-COUNT In British English, **crisps** are very thin slices of potato that have been fried until they are hard and crunchy and that are eaten cold as a snack. The American word is **chips** or **potato chips**. **3** ADJ **Crisp** air is pleasantly fresh, cold, and dry. **4** ADJ A **crisp** remark or response is brief and perhaps unfriendly. ❑ *'Good.' His tone was crisp.*

criss-cross /ˈkrɪs krɒs, AM - krɔːs/ (**criss-crosses, criss-crossing, criss-crossed**) **1** V-T If a person or thing **criss-crosses** an area, they travel from one side to the other and back again many times. If a number of things **criss-cross** an area, they cross it, and cross over each other. ❑ *They criss-crossed the country by bus.* **2** ADJ BEFORE N A **criss-cross** pattern or design consists of lines crossing each other.

criterion /kraɪˈtɪəriən/ (**criteria** /kraɪˈtɪəriə/) N-COUNT A **criterion** is a factor on which you judge or decide something. ❑ *The bank is reviewing its criteria for lending money.*

critic /ˈkrɪtɪk/ (**critics**) **1** N-COUNT A **critic** is a person who writes reviews and expresses opinions about books, films, music, and art. ❑ *He was film critic for the Daily Telegraph.* **2** N-COUNT Someone who is a **critic** of a person or system disapproves of them and criticizes them publicly. ❑ *Her critics say she only cares about success.*

critical /ˈkrɪtɪkəl/ **1** ADJ A **critical** time or situation is extremely important. ❑ *He fell ill at a critical point in the campaign.* ● **critically** ADV ❑ *The phone company is having problems: most critically, it is finding it difficult to fix the technical problems.* **2** ADJ A **critical** situation is very serious and dangerous. ❑ *The situation has now become critical.* ● **critically** ADV ❑ *The country is running critically low on food.* **3** ADJ If you are **critical of** someone or something, you criticize them. ❑ *His report is highly critical of the judge.* ❑ *He apologised for the critical comments he made.* ● **critically** ADV ❑ *She spoke critically of Laura.* **4** ADJ BEFORE N A **critical** approach to something involves examining and judging it carefully. ❑ *...the critical analysis of political ideas.* ● **critically** ADV ❑ *William watched them critically.*

Word Partnership Use *critical* with:

N.	critical **issue**, critical **role** **1** critical **state** **1** **2**
V.	**become** critical **1**
PREP.	critical **of *someone***, critical **of *something*** **3**

criticism /ˈkrɪtɪsɪzəm/ (**criticisms**) **1** N-VAR **Criticism** is the action of expressing disapproval of something or someone. A **criticism** is a statement that expresses disapproval. ❑ *The criticism aimed at him has been unfair.* **2** N-UNCOUNT **Criticism** is a serious examination and judgement of something such as a book or play. ❑ *...literary criticism.*

Thesaurus *criticism* Also look up:

N.	disapproval, judgment, put-down; *(ant.)* approval, praise **1** commentary, critique, evaluation, review **2**

Word Partnership Use *criticism* with:

PREP.	criticism **against *something***, criticism **from *something***, criticism **of *something*** **1**
ADJ.	**constructive** criticism, **open to** criticism **1**
N.	**public** criticism **1** **literary** criticism **2**

criticize [BRIT also **criticise**] /ˈkrɪtɪsaɪz/ (**criticizes, criticizing, criticized**) V-T If you **criticize** someone or something, you express your disapproval of them by saying what you think is wrong with them. ❑ *The Moscow Police Force has been criticised for not taking racism seriously.*

critique /krɪˈtiːk/ (**critiques**) N-COUNT A **critique** is a written examination and judgement of a situation or of a person's work or ideas. [FORMAL] ❑ *...a critique of the power of newspapers.*

croak /krəʊk/ (**croaks, croaking, croaked**) **1** V-I When a frog or bird **croaks**, it makes a harsh low sound. **2** V-T When someone **croaks** something, they say it in a hoarse rough voice. ❑ *Tina croaked, 'Help me'.*

crockery /ˈkrɒkəri/ N-UNCOUNT **Crockery** consists of plates, cups, and saucers.

crocodile /ˈkrɒkədaɪl/ (**crocodiles**) N-COUNT A **crocodile** is a large reptile with a long body. Crocodiles live in rivers.

croissant /ˈkwæsɒn, AM kwɑːˈsɑːn/ (**croissants**) N-VAR **Croissants** are small crescent-shaped pieces of sweetened bread that are often eaten for breakfast.

→ see **bread**

crony /ˈkrəʊni/ (**cronies**) N-COUNT Your **cronies** are the friends who you spend a lot of time with; used showing disapproval. [INFORMAL] ❑ *...the boss and his cronies.*

crook /krʊk/ (**crooks**) **1** N-COUNT A **crook** is a criminal or a dishonest person. [INFORMAL] ❑ *The man is a crook and a liar.* **2** N-COUNT The **crook of** your arm or leg is the soft inside part where you bend it.

crooked /ˈkrʊkɪd/ **1** ADJ Something that is **crooked** is bent or twisted. ❑ *She has a crooked nose.* **2** ADJ If you describe a person or an activity as **crooked**, you mean that they are dishonest or criminal. ❑ *...crooked business deals.*

croon /kruːn/ (**croons, crooning, crooned**) V-T/V-I If you **croon**, or **croon** something, you sing or say something quietly and gently. ❑ *Lewis began to croon another Springsteen song.*

crop /krɒp/ (**crops, cropping, cropped**) **1** N-COUNT **Crops** are plants such as wheat and potatoes that are grown in large quantities for food. ❑ *Farmers here still plant their crops by hand.* **2** N-COUNT The plants or fruits that are collected at harvest time are referred to as a **crop**. ❑ *...this year's potato crop.* **3** N-SING You can refer to a group of people or things that have appeared together as a **crop of** them. ❑ *...the current crop of young British artists.* **4** V-T To **crop** someone's hair means to cut it short.
→ see **farm, grain, photography, plant**
▶ **crop up** PHR-VERB If something **crops up**, it happens or appears unexpectedly. ❑ *Problems always crop up where we least expect them.*

croquet /ˈkrəʊkeɪ, AM krəʊˈkeɪ/ N-UNCOUNT **Croquet** is a game in which the players use long-handled wooden mallets to hit balls through metal arches stuck in a lawn.

cross
❶ VERB AND NOUN USES
❷ ADJECTIVE USE

cross /krɒs, AM krɔːs/ (**crosses, crossing, crossed**)
❶ **1** V-T/V-I If you **cross** a room, road, or area of land, you move to the other side of it. If you **cross to** a place, you move over a room, road, or area in order to reach that place. ❑ *They crossed the border into Greece.* ❑ *She stood up and crossed to the door.* **2** V-T A road, railway, or bridge that **crosses** an area of land or water passes over it. ❑ *The main road crosses the river.* **3** V-T When lines or roads **cross**, they meet and go across each other. **4** V-T If you **cross** your arms, legs, or fingers, you put one of them on top of the other. ❑ *Paul crossed his arms over his chest.* **5** V-T If an expression **crosses** someone's **face**, it appears briefly on their face. [LITERARY] **6** V-T When a thought **crosses** your **mind**, you think of something or remember something. **7** N-COUNT A **cross** is a shape that consists of a vertical line with a shorter horizontal line across it. ❑ *...a cross on a silver chain.* **8** N-COUNT A **cross** is a written mark in the shape of an X. **9** N-COUNT Something that is a **cross between** two things is neither one thing nor the other, but a mixture of both. ❑ *The snowmobile is a cross between a sledge and a motorcycle.*
▶ **cross out** PHR-VERB If you **cross out** words, you draw a line through them.

cross /krɒs, AM krɔːs/ (**crosser, crossest**)
❷ ADJ Someone who is **cross** is angry or irritated. ❑ *I'm terribly cross with him.* • **crossly** ADV ❑ *'No, no, no,' Morris said crossly.*

ˌcross-ˈcountry **1** N-UNCOUNT **Cross-country** is the sport of running, riding, or skiing across open countryside. **2** ADJ BEFORE N & ADV A **cross-country** journey involves less important roads or railway lines, or takes you from one side of a country to the other. ❑ *...cross-country rail services.* ❑ *I drove cross-country in his van.*

ˌcross-exˈamine (**cross-examines, cross-examining, cross-examined**) V-T When a lawyer **cross-examines** someone during a trial or hearing, he or she questions them about the evidence that they have given. • **cross-examination** (**cross-examinations**) N-VAR ❑ *The cross-examination lasted for four hours.*
→ see **trial**

crossing /ˈkrɒsɪŋ, AM ˈkrɔːs-/ (**crossings**) **1** N-COUNT A **crossing** is a boat journey to the other side of a sea. **2** N-COUNT A **crossing** is a place where you can cross something such as a road or a border.

crossover /ˈkrɒsəʊvə, AM ˈkrɔːs-/ (**crossovers**) **1** N-VAR A **crossover of** one style and another is a combination of the two different styles. ❑ *...the crossover of pop, jazz and funk.* **2** N-SING A **crossover** is a change from one type of activity to another. ❑ *...the crossover from actress to singer.*

crossroads /ˈkrɒsrəʊdz, AM ˈkrɔːs-/

> **Crossroads** is both the singular and the plural form.

N-COUNT A **crossroads** is a place where two roads meet and cross.

ˈcross-section (**cross-sections**) **1** N-COUNT A **cross-section of** something such as a group of people is a typical or representative sample. ❑ *I was surprised at the cross-section of people there.* **2** N-COUNT A **cross-section of** an object is what you would see if you cut straight through the middle of it. ❑ *...the cross-section of an aeroplane.*

crossword /ˈkrɒswɜːd, AM ˈkrɔːs-/ (**crosswords**) N-COUNT A **crossword** or a **crossword puzzle** is a word game in which you work out answers to clues, and write the answers in the white squares of a pattern of black and white squares. ❑ *He enjoyed doing crossword puzzles.*

crossword puzzle

crotch /krɒtʃ/ (**crotches**) **1** N-COUNT Your **crotch** is the part of your body between the tops of your legs. **2** N-COUNT The **crotch** of a pair of trousers is the part that covers the area between the tops of your legs.

crouch /kraʊtʃ/ (**crouches, crouching, crouched**) **1** V-I & N-SING If you **are crouching**, or if you **crouch down**, your legs are bent under you so that you are close to the ground and leaning forward slightly. If you are **in a crouch**, your body is in this position. ❑ *We were crouching in the bushes.* ❑ *He crouched down beside him.* ❑ *They walked in a crouch.* **2** V-I If you **crouch over** something, you bend over it so that you are very near to it. ❑ *He crouched over the steering wheel.*

crow /krəʊ/ (**crows, crowing, crowed**) **1** N-COUNT A **crow** is a large black bird which makes a loud harsh noise. **2** V-I When a cock **crows**, it utters a loud sound, early in the morning. **3** V-I If you say that someone **is crowing about** something they have achieved, they keep talking about it proudly in a way that annoys you. [INFORMAL] ❑ *He wouldn't stop crowing about the money.*

crowd /kraʊd/ (**crowds, crowding, crowded**) **1** N-COUNT A **crowd** is a large group of people who have gathered together. ❑ *A huge crowd gathered in the square.* **2** N-COUNT A particular **crowd** is a group of friends, or people with the same interests or occupation. [INFORMAL] ❑ *All the old crowd are here at the party.* **3** V-I When people **crowd around** someone or something, they gather closely together around them. ❑ *The children crowded around him.* **4** V-T/V-I If people **crowd into** a place or **are crowded into** it, large numbers of them enter it so that it becomes very full. ❑ *One group of journalists were crowded into a minibus.*

crowded /'kraʊdɪd/ ADJ A **crowded** place is full of people or things. ❑ *The old town square was crowded with people.* ❑ *...a crowded city.*

crown /kraʊn/ (**crowns, crowning, crowned**) **1** N-COUNT A **crown** is a circular ornament, usually made of gold and jewels, which a king or queen wears on their head at official ceremonies. **2** V-T When a king or queen **is crowned**, a crown is placed on their head as part of a ceremony in which they are officially made king or queen. **3** V-T If one thing **crowns** another, it is on top of it. [LITERARY] ❑ *An ancient castle crowns the cliffs.* **4** N-COUNT Your **crown** is the top part of your head, at the back.
→ see **teeth**

crown

crucial /'kru:ʃəl/ ADJ Something that is **crucial** is extremely important. ❑ *An animal's sense of smell is crucial to its survival.* ❑ *...crucial decisions.* ● **crucially** ADV ❑ *Education is crucially important.*

crucify /'kru:sɪfaɪ/ (**crucifies, crucifying, crucified**) V-T In former times, if someone **was crucified**, they were killed by being tied or nailed to a cross and left to die. ● **crucifixion** /ˌkru:sɪ'fɪkʃən/ (**crucifixions**) N-VAR ❑ *...the crucifixion of Christians in Rome.*

crude /kru:d/ (**cruder, crudest**) **1** ADJ Something that is **crude** is simple and not sophisticated. ❑ *It's a crude way of dealing with the problem but it's the only way we know how.* ❑ *...crude wooden boxes.* ● **crudely** ADV ❑ *...a crudely carved statue.* **2** ADJ If you describe someone as **crude**, you disapprove of them because they speak or behave in a rude or offensive way. ❑ *...crude jokes.* ● **crudely** ADV ❑ *He hated it when she spoke so crudely.*

ˌcrude 'oil N-UNCOUNT **Crude oil** is oil in its natural state before it has been processed.
→ see **oil**

cruel /'kru:əl/ (**crueller, cruellest**) ADJ Someone who is **cruel** deliberately causes pain or distress. ❑ *Children can be so cruel.* ❑ *...her cruel and uncaring husband.* ● **cruelly** ADV ❑ *They treated her cruelly.* ● **cruelty** (**cruelties**) N-VAR ❑ *Britain has laws against cruelty to animals.*

Thesaurus	*cruel* Also look up:
ADJ.	harsh, mean, nasty, unkind; *(ant.)* gentle, kind

cruise /kru:z/ (**cruises, cruising, cruised**) **1** N-COUNT A **cruise** is a holiday spent on a ship or boat which visits a number of places. ❑ *He and his wife are planning to go on a world cruise.* **2** V-T/V-I If you **cruise** a sea, river, or canal, you travel around it or along it on a cruise. ❑ *You could cruise to Australia.* ❑ *She wants to cruise the canals of France.* **3** V-I If a car or a ship **cruises**, it moves at a constant moderate speed. ❑ *A police car cruised past.*
→ see **ship**

cruiser /'kru:zə/ (**cruisers**) **1** N-COUNT A **cruiser** is a motor boat with a cabin for people to sleep in. **2** N-COUNT A **cruiser** is a large fast warship.

crumb /krʌm/ (**crumbs**) N-COUNT **Crumbs** are tiny pieces that fall from bread, biscuits, or cake when you cut or eat them.

crumble /'krʌmbəl/ (**crumbles, crumbling, crumbled**) **1** V-T/V-I When something soft or brittle **crumbles**, or when you **crumble** it, it breaks into a lot of small pieces. ❑ *Crumble the cheese and stir into the mixture.* **2** V-I If an old building or piece of land **is crumbling**, or if it **is crumbling away**, parts of it keep breaking off. ❑ *The coastline is crumbling into the sea.* **3** V-I If something such as a system, relationship, or hope **crumbles**, it comes to an end. ❑ *His dreams of winning the championship crumbled.*

crumbly /'krʌmbli/ ADJ Something that is **crumbly** is easily broken into a lot of little pieces. ❑ *...crumbly cheese.*

crumple /'krʌmpəl/ (**crumples, crumpling, crumpled**) **1** V-T & PHR-VERB If you **crumple** something such as paper or cloth, or if you **crumple** it **up**, you squash it and it becomes full of creases and folds. ❑ *She crumpled the paper in her hand.* ❑ *Nancy looked at the note angrily, then crumpled it up.* ● **crumpled** ADJ ❑ *His uniform was crumpled.* **2** V-I If someone's face **crumples**, they suddenly look very disappointed or as if they want to cry.
▶ **crumple up** → see **crumple** (meaning 1)

crunch /krʌntʃ/ (**crunches, crunching, crunched**) **1** V-T If you **crunch** something hard, you crush it noisily between your teeth. ❑ *Richard crunched the apple.* **2** V-I & N-COUNT If something **crunches**, it makes a breaking or crushing noise, called a **crunch**. ❑ *...the crunch of tires on the gravel driveway.*

crunchy /'krʌntʃi/ ADJ **Crunchy** food is pleasantly hard or crisp, and makes a noise when you eat it.

crusade /kru:'seɪd/ (**crusades**) N-COUNT A **crusade** is a long and determined attempt to achieve something. ❑ *He made it his crusade to teach children to love books.* ● **crusader** (**crusaders**) N-COUNT ❑ *...a crusader for the rights of women.*

crush /krʌʃ/ (**crushes, crushing, crushed**) **1** V-T To **crush** something means to press it very hard so that its shape is destroyed or so that it breaks into pieces. ❑ *Andrew crushed his empty drinks can.*

❑ *...crushed ice.* **2** V-T If you **are crushed against** someone or something, you are pushed or pressed against them. ❑ *We were at the front of the hall, crushed against the stage.* **3** N-COUNT A **crush** is a dense crowd of people. ❑ *He got separated from us in the crush.* **4** V-T To **crush** a protest, army, or political organization means to defeat it completely. ● **crushing** N-UNCOUNT ❑ *...the violent crushing of the demonstration.* **5** N-COUNT If you **have a crush on** someone, you feel you are in love with them but you do not have a relationship with them. [INFORMAL]
→ see **crash**

crust /krʌst/ (**crusts**) **1** N-COUNT The **crust** on a loaf of bread is the outside part. **2** N-COUNT The earth's **crust** is its outer layer.
→ see **continent, core, earthquake**

crusty /ˈkrʌsti/ ADJ Something that is **crusty** has a hard, crisp, outer layer. ❑ *...crusty French bread.*

crutch /krʌtʃ/ (**crutches**) N-COUNT A **crutch** is a stick which someone with an injured foot or leg uses to support them when walking.

crux /krʌks/ N-SING **The crux of** a problem or argument is the most important or difficult part, which affects everything else. ❑ *The crux of their argument came down to two things: money and power.*

cry /kraɪ/ (**cries, crying, cried**) **1** V-I & N-SING When you **cry**, or when you have a **cry**, tears come from your eyes, usually because you are unhappy or hurt. ❑ *I hung up the phone and started to cry.* ❑ *I had a good cry.* ● **crying** N-UNCOUNT ❑ *...her baby son's crying.* **2** V-T & PHR-VERB To **cry** something, or to **cry** something **out**, means to shout or say something loudly. ❑ *'Nancy Drew,' she cried, 'stop it!'.* ❑ *'You're wrong, quite wrong!' Henry cried out.* **3** N-COUNT A **cry** is a loud high sound that you make when you feel a strong emotion such as fear, pain, or pleasure. ❑ *...a cry of horror.* **4** PHRASE If you say that something is **a far cry from** something else, you mean it is very different from it. ❑ *Their luxurious lifestyle is a far cry from his own poor childhood.*
→ see Word Web: **cry**

▶ **cry out** **1** PHR-VERB If you **cry out**, you call out loudly because you are frightened, unhappy or in pain. ❑ *He was crying out in pain when the ambulance arrived.* **2** → see **cry** (meaning 2)

▶ **cry out for** PHR-VERB If you say that something **cries out for** a particular thing, you mean that it needs that thing very much. ❑ *His body was crying out for some exercise.*

Thesaurus *cry* Also look up:

V.	sob, weep **1**
	call, shout, yell **2**
	howl, moan, shriek **3**

Word Partnership Use *cry* with:

V.	**begin to** cry, **start to** cry **1**
N.	cry **with anger**, cry **of pain** **2** **3**
	cry **for help**, cry **of horror**, cry **with joy**

cryptic /ˈkrɪptɪk/ ADJ A **cryptic** remark or message contains a hidden meaning. ❑ *His poems are described as cryptic.* ● **cryptically** ADV ❑ *'Perhaps,' she said cryptically.*

crystal /ˈkrɪstəl/ (**crystals**) **1** N-COUNT A **crystal** is a piece of a mineral that has formed naturally into a regular symmetrical shape. ❑ *...salt crystals.* **2** N-UNCOUNT **Crystal** is a transparent rock used in jewellery and ornaments. **3** N-UNCOUNT **Crystal** is very high quality glass, usually with its surface cut into patterns. ❑ *...crystal glasses.*
→ see Word Web: **crystal**
→ see **rock, sugar**

ˌcrystal ˈclear ADJ An explanation that is **crystal clear** is very easy to understand. ❑ *His message was crystal clear.*

crystallize [BRIT also **crystallise**] /ˈkrɪstəlaɪz/ (**crystallizes, crystallizing, crystallized**) **1** V-T/V-I If you **crystallize** an opinion or idea, or if it **crystallizes**, it becomes fixed and definite in your mind. ❑ *I hope our discussion has helped to crystallize your thoughts.* **2** V-I When a substance **crystallizes**, it turns into crystals. ❑ *Don't stir or the sugar will crystallise.*

cub /kʌb/ (**cubs**) N-COUNT A **cub** is a young wild animal such as a lion, wolf, or bear. ❑ *...five-week-old lion cubs.*

cube /kjuːb/ (**cubes**) N-COUNT A **cube** is a solid shape with six square surfaces which are all the same size.
→ see **solid, volume**

cubic /ˈkjuːbɪk/ ADJ BEFORE N **Cubic** is used to express units of volume. ❑ *...3 cubic metres of soil.*

Word Link *cle ≈ small : article, cubicle, particle*

cubicle /ˈkjuːbɪkəl/ (**cubicles**) N-COUNT A **cubicle** is a small enclosed area, for example one where you can have a shower or change your clothes.
→ see **office**

Word Web cry

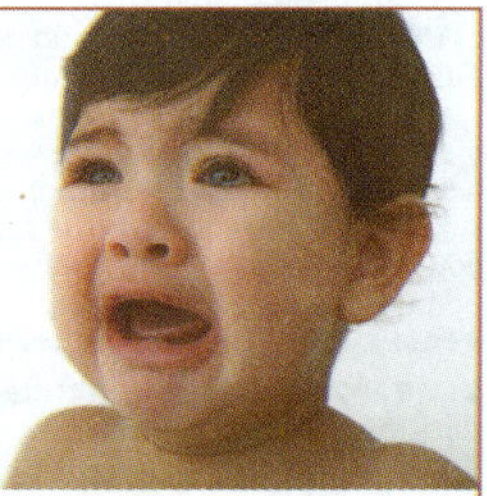

Have you ever seen someone **burst into tears** when something wonderful happened to them? We expect people to **cry** when they are **sad** or upset. But why do people sometimes **weep** when they are happy? Scientists have found that there are three different types of **tears**. Basal tears keep the **eyes** moist. Reflex tears clear the eyes of dirt or smoke. The third type, emotional tears occur when people experience strong feelings, either good or bad. These tears contain high levels of chemicals called manganese and prolactin. Decreasing the amount of these chemicals in the body helps us feel better. When people experience strong feelings, **shedding tears** may help restore emotional balance.

Word Web crystal

The outsides of **crystals** have smooth flat surfaces. These surfaces form because of the repeating patterns of atoms, molecules, or ions inside the crystal. Evaporation, temperature changes, and pressure can all help to form crystals. Crystals grow when sea water evaporates and leaves behind **salt**. When water freezes, **ice** crystals form. When melted rock cools, it becomes **rock** with a **crystalline** structure. Pressure can also create one of the hardest, most beautiful crystals—the **diamond**.

cuckoo /ˈkʊkuː/ (**cuckoos**) N-COUNT A **cuckoo** is a grey bird which makes an easily recognizable sound consisting of two quick notes.

cucumber /ˈkjuːkʌmbə/ (**cucumbers**) N-VAR A **cucumber** is a long dark green vegetable.
→ see **vegetable**

cuddle /ˈkʌdəl/ (**cuddles, cuddling, cuddled**) V-T & N-COUNT If you **cuddle** someone, or if you give them a **cuddle**, you put your arms round them and hold them close. ❏ *Steve cuddled his daughter.* ❏ *I wanted to give him a cuddle.*

cuddly /ˈkʌdəli/ (**cuddlier, cuddliest**) ADJ If you describe people or animals as **cuddly**, you find them attractive because they are plump or soft and look nice to cuddle.

cue /kjuː/ (**cues**) **1** N-COUNT A **cue** is something said or done by a performer that is a signal for another performer to begin speaking or to begin doing something. ❏ *He never missed a cue.* **2** N-COUNT A **cue** is a long, thin wooden stick that is used to hit the ball in games such as snooker, billiards, and pool. **3** PHRASE If you **take** your **cue from** someone, you use their behaviour as an indication of what you should do. ❏ *He took his cue from his friend, and apologized.* **4** PHRASE If you say that something happened **on cue**, you mean that it happened just when it was expected to happen, or just at the right time. ❏ *Kevin arrived right on cue.*

cuff /kʌf/ (**cuffs**) **1** N-COUNT The **cuffs** of a piece of clothing are the end parts of the sleeves. **2** N-PLURAL **Cuffs** are the same as **handcuffs**. **3** PHRASE An **off-the-cuff** remark is made without being prepared or thought about in advance. ❏ *Mr Baker was speaking off the cuff when he said those things.*

cuisine /kwɪˈziːn/ (**cuisines**) N-VAR The **cuisine** of a region is its characteristic style of cooking. ❏ *...traditional Russian cuisine.*

culinary /ˈkʌlɪnəri, AM ˈkjuːləneri/ ADJ BEFORE N **Culinary** means related to cooking. ❏ *...culinary delights.*

cull /kʌl/ (**culls, culling, culled**) **1** V-T If items or ideas **are culled from** a particular source or number of sources, they are taken and gathered together. ❏ *She culled her wonderful stories from the books in her grandmother's library.* **2** V-T & N-COUNT To **cull** animals means to kill some of them in order to reduce their numbers. You can also talk about a **cull**. ❏ *We need to cull the deer in the forest.* ❏ *...their annual seal cull.* • **culling** N-UNCOUNT ❏ *...the culling of pigs.*

culminate /ˈkʌlmɪneɪt/ (**culminates, culminating, culminated**) V-I If you say that an activity, process, or series of events **culminates in** or **with** a particular event, you mean that event happens at the end of it. ❏ *They had an argument, which culminated in Tom leaving home.* • **culmination** N-SING ❏ *The New Year's Eve party was the culmination of the city's Winter Festival.*

culprit /ˈkʌlprɪt/ (**culprits**) **1** N-COUNT The person who committed a crime or did something wrong can be referred to as the **culprit**. ❏ *We do not know who the culprits are.* **2** N-COUNT The cause of a problem or bad situation can be referred to as the **culprit**. ❏ *Carbon dioxide is the main culprit in climate change.*

cult /kʌlt/ (**cults**) **1** N-COUNT A **cult** is a fairly small religious group, especially one which is considered strange. ❏ *The teenager joined a religious cult.* **2** N-SING & ADJ When a person, object, or activity becomes a **cult**, they become very popular or fashionable. ❏ *The film is a cult classic.*

cultivate /ˈkʌltɪveɪt/ (**cultivates, cultivating, cultivated**) **1** V-T If you **cultivate** land, you prepare it and grow crops on it. ❏ *She cultivates a small garden of her own.* • **cultivation** N-UNCOUNT ❏ *...the cultivation of fruit and vegetables.* **2** V-T If you **cultivate** an attitude, image, or skill, you develop it and make it stronger. ❏ *Copernicus cultivated a powerful memory.* • **cultivation** N-UNCOUNT ❏ *...the cultivation of a positive approach to life.*
→ see **farm, grain**

cultivated /ˈkʌltɪveɪtɪd/ **1** ADJ If you describe someone as **cultivated**, you mean that they are well-educated and have good manners. ❏ *...an elegant, cultivated woman.* **2** ADJ BEFORE N **Cultivated** plants have been developed for growing on farms or in gardens. ❏ *...a mixture of wild and cultivated flowers.*

cultural /ˈkʌltʃərəl/ ADJ **Cultural** means relating to the arts generally, or to the arts and customs of a particular society. ❏ *...sports and cultural events.* ❏ *...cultural and educational exchanges between Britain and India.* • **culturally** ADV ❏ *Culturally, they have a lot in common with their neighbours across the border.*

culture /ˈkʌltʃə/ (**cultures**) **1** N-UNCOUNT **Culture** consists of activities such as the arts and philosophy, which are considered to be important for the development of civilization and of people's minds. ❏ *...the Department for Culture, Media and Sport.* **2** N-COUNT A **culture** is a particular society or civilization, especially considered in relation to its beliefs, way of life, or art. ❏ *It is very important to talk to people from different cultures.* **3** N-COUNT In science, a **culture** is a group of bacteria or cells grown in a laboratory as part of an experiment.
→ see Word Web: **culture**
→ see **myth**

C

Word Web culture

Each **society** has its own **culture** which influences how people live their lives. Culture includes **customs, language, art**, and other shared **traits** or characteristics. When people move from one culture to another, there is often cultural **diffusion**. For example, European artists first saw Japanese art about 150 years ago. This influenced and changed their painting style. The new style was called Impressionism. **Assimilation** happens when people enter a new culture. For instance, **immigrants** may start to follow American customs when they move to the U.S. People with different ideas from **mainstream** society may also form **subcultures** within the society.

Word Partnership Use *culture* with:

ADJ. **ancient** culture, **popular** culture 1 2
N. culture **and religion, society and** culture 1 2
culture **shock, richness of** culture 1 2

cultured /ˈkʌltʃəd/ ADJ If you describe someone as **cultured**, you mean that they are well educated and know a lot about the arts. ❑ *He is a cultured man with lots of friends.*

-cum- /-kʌm-/ You put **-cum-** between two words to form a compound noun referring to something or someone that is partly one thing and partly another. ❑ *...a dining-room-cum-study.*

cumbersome /ˈkʌmbəsəm/ 1 ADJ Something that is **cumbersome** is large and heavy and difficult to carry, wear, or handle. ❑ *Although the machine looks cumbersome, it is actually easy to use.* 2 ADJ A **cumbersome** system or process is complicated and inefficient. ❑ *The rules are confusing and cumbersome.*

cumulative /ˈkju:mjʊlətɪv/ ADJ If a series of events have a **cumulative effect**, each event makes the effect greater. ❑ *The benefits of regular exercise are cumulative.*

cunning /ˈkʌnɪŋ/ 1 ADJ A **cunning** person is clever and deceitful. • **cunningly** ADV ❑ *They were cunningly disguised as policemen.* 2 N-UNCOUNT **Cunning** is the ability to plan things cleverly, often by deceiving people. ❑ *Wahid used political cunning to win the election.*

cup /kʌp/ (**cups, cupping, cupped**) 1 N-COUNT A **cup** is a small round container with a handle, which you drink from. 2 N-COUNT A **cup** is something which is small, round, and hollow, like a cup. ❑ *Boil an egg for 4 minutes and serve in an egg cup.* 3 N-COUNT A **cup** is a large metal cup on a stem given as a prize to the winner of a game or competition. 4 V-T If you **cup** your **hands**, you make them into a curved dish-like shape. ❑ *He cupped his hands around his mouth and called out for his wife.* 5 V-T If you **cup** something **in** your hands, you make your hands into a curved dish-like shape and support it or hold it gently. ❑ *He cupped her chin in the palm of his hand.*
→ **dish, tea**

cupboard /ˈkʌbəd/ (**cupboards**) N-COUNT A **cupboard** is a piece of furniture with doors at the front and usually shelves inside.

curable /ˈkjʊərəbəl/ ADJ A **curable** disease or illness can be cured.

curate /ˈkjʊərət/ (**curates**) N-COUNT A **curate** is a clergyman who helps a vicar or priest.

Word Link *cur ≈ caring : curator, manicure, secure*

curator /kjʊˈreɪtə/ (**curators**) N-COUNT The **curator** of a museum or art gallery is the person in charge of the exhibits or works of art.

curb /kɜ:b/ (**curbs, curbing, curbed**) 1 V-T & N-COUNT If you **curb** something, you control it and keep it within limits. You can also talk about a **curb on** something. ❑ *We need to curb the amount of violence on TV.* ❑ *They are looking for curbs on fast-food advertising in schools.* 2 → see also **kerb**

curb

cure /kjʊə/ (**cures, curing, cured**) 1 V-T If a doctor or a medical treatment **cures** someone, or **cures** their illness, they make the person well again. ❑ *Doctors have cured him of the disease.* 2 N-COUNT A **cure for** an illness is a medicine or other treatment that cures the illness. 3 V-T If someone or something **cures** a problem, they bring it to an end. ❑ *We need to cure our environmental problems.* 4 N-COUNT A **cure for** a problem is something which brings it to an end. ❑ *There is no cure for the stress of moving house, but you can try to make it easier.* 5 V-T When food, tobacco, or animal skin **is cured**, it is dried, smoked, or salted so that it will last for a long time. ❑ *...sliced cured ham.*

curfew /ˈkɜ:fju:/ (**curfews**) N-COUNT A **curfew** is a law stating that people must stay inside their houses after a particular time at night. ❑ *The village was placed under curfew.*

curiosity /ˌkjʊəriˈɒsɪti/ (**curiosities**) 1 N-UNCOUNT **Curiosity** is a desire to know about things. ❑ *I came to New York out of curiosity, and I fell in love with the city.* 2 N-COUNT A **curiosity** is something which is interesting and fairly rare. ❑ *The house is full of curiosities, collected during their travels.*

curious /ˈkjʊəriəs/ 1 ADJ If you are **curious about** something, you are interested in it and want to learn more about it. ❑ *Steve was curious* about the city I came from. ❑ *...a group of curious women.* ● **curiously** ADV ❑ *The woman in the shop looked at them curiously.* 2 ADJ Something that is **curious** is unusual or difficult to understand. ❑ *There is a curious thing about her writings.* ● **curiously** ADV ❑ *Harry was curiously silent.*

curl /kɜːl/ (**curls, curling, curled**) 1 N-COUNT **Curls** are lengths of hair shaped in curves and circles. ❑ *...a little girl with blonde curls.* 2 V-T/V-I If your hair **curls**, or if you **curl** it, it is full of curls. ❑ *Maria had curled her hair for the party.* 3 N-COUNT A **curl of** something is a piece or quantity of it that is curved or spiral in shape. ❑ *...curls of lemon peel.* 4 V-T/V-I If something **curls** somewhere, or you **curl** it somewhere, it moves there in circles or spirals. ❑ *Smoke was curling up the chimney.* ❑ *He curled the ball into the net.*

▶ **curl up** 1 PHR-VERB When someone who is lying down **curls up**, they bring their arms, legs, and head in towards their stomach. ❑ *In cold weather, your cat will curl up into a ball to keep warm.* 2 PHR-VERB When something such as a leaf or a piece of paper **curls up**, its edges bend up or towards its centre. ❑ *The corners of the carpet were curling up.*

curly /ˈkɜːli/ (**curlier, curliest**) 1 ADJ **Curly** hair is full of curls. 2 ADJ **Curly** objects are curved or spiral-shaped. ❑ *Cauliflowers have long curly leaves.*

currency /ˈkʌrənsi, AM ˈkɜːr-/ (**currencies**) 1 N-VAR The money used in a country is referred to as its **currency**. ❑ *...Japanese currency.* 2 N-UNCOUNT If ideas, expressions, or customs have **currency**, they are generally used and accepted by people at that time. [FORMAL] ❑ *There were many years of silence before the term 'Holocaust' gained currency.*
→ see **money**

Word Link	*curr, curs ≈ running, flowing : concurrent, current, excursion*

current /ˈkʌrənt, AM ˈkɜːr-/ (**currents**) 1 N-COUNT A **current** is a steady, continuous, flowing movement of water or air. ❑ *He was carried away by the strong current of the river.* 2 N-COUNT An electric **current** is electricity flowing through a wire or circuit. 3 ADJ Something that is **current** is happening, being done, or being used at the present time. ❑ *The current situation is very different.* ❑ *...the current anti-racism movement in football.* ● **currently** ADV ❑ *He is currently single.*
→ see **beach, erosion, ocean, tide**

ˌcurrent acˈcount (**current accounts**) N-COUNT A **current account** is a bank account which you can take money out of at any time. [BRIT]

ˌcurrent afˈfairs N-PLURAL **Current affairs** are political events and problems which are discussed in the media. ❑ *...the BBC's current affairs programme 'Panorama'.*

curriculum /kəˈrɪkjʊləm/ (**curriculums** or **curricula** /kəˈrɪkjʊlə/) 1 N-COUNT A **curriculum** is all the different courses of study that are taught in a school, college, or university. ❑ *We must include Shakespeare in the school curriculum.* 2 N-COUNT A particular course of study can be referred to as a **curriculum**. ❑ *...the history curriculum.*

curry /ˈkʌri, AM ˈkɜːri/ (**curries**) N-VAR **Curry** is an Asian dish made with hot spices. ❑ *I had a curry last night.*

curse /kɜːs/ (**curses, cursing, cursed**) 1 V-I & N-COUNT If you **curse**, or if you utter a **curse**, you swear or say rude words because you are angry about something. [WRITTEN] ❑ *I tripped and cursed.* ❑ *Groans and curses filled the air.* 2 V-T If you **curse** someone or something, you say insulting things to them or complain strongly about them because you are angry with them. ❑ *We started driving again, cursing the delay.* ❑ *He cursed himself for not making a note of his address.* 3 N-COUNT If you say that there is a **curse on** someone, you mean that a supernatural power is causing unpleasant things to happen to them. 4 N-COUNT You can refer to something that causes a lot of trouble as a **curse**. ❑ *...the curse of high unemployment.*

cursor /ˈkɜːsə/ (**cursors**) N-COUNT On a computer screen, the **cursor** is a small, movable shape which indicates where anything typed by the user will appear. [COMPUTING]

curt /kɜːt/ ADJ If someone is **curt**, they speak in a brief and rather rude way. ❑ *'There is nothing more to say,' was the curt reply.* ● **curtly** ADV ❑ *'I'm leaving,' she said curtly.*

curtail /kɜːˈteɪl/ (**curtails, curtailing, curtailed**) V-T If you **curtail** something, you reduce or restrict it. [FORMAL] ❑ *Your spending is far too high, and must be curtailed.* ● **curtailment** N-UNCOUNT ❑ *...the curtailment of presidential power.*

curtain /ˈkɜːtən/ (**curtains**) 1 N-COUNT **Curtains** are hanging pieces of material which you can pull across a window to keep light out or prevent people from looking in. ❑ *She drew the curtains in her bedroom.* 2 N-SING In a theatre, the **curtain** is a large piece of material that hangs in front of the stage until a performance begins.

curve /kɜːv/ (**curves, curving, curved**) 1 N-COUNT A **curve** is a smooth, gradually bending line, for example part of the edge of a circle. ❑ *...a curve in the road.* 2 V-I If something **curves**, it is shaped like a curve, or moves in a curve. ❑ *A stone wall curved away to the left.* ❑ *The ball curved in the air.* ● **curved** ADJ ❑ *...a curved blade.* 3 N-COUNT You can refer to a change in something as a particular **curve**, especially when it is represented on a graph. ❑ *...the rising curve of youth unemployment.*

cushion /ˈkʊʃən/ (**cushions, cushioning, cushioned**) 1 N-COUNT A **cushion** is a fabric case filled with soft material, which you put on a seat to make it more comfortable. 2 V-T To **cushion** an impact means to reduce its effect. ❑ *They will use giant air bags to cushion their landing.*

custard /ˈkʌstəd/ N-UNCOUNT **Custard** is a sweet yellow sauce made from milk and eggs or from milk and a powder. It is eaten with puddings.
→ see **dessert**

custodial /kʌˈstəʊdiəl/ ADJ BEFORE N **Custodial** means relating to keeping people in prison. [FORMAL] ❑ *He was given a custodial sentence by the court.*

custodian /kʌˈstəʊdiən/ (**custodians**) N-COUNT The **custodian of** an official building, a companies' assets, or other valuable thing is the person in charge of it. ❑ *The government is the custodian of the interests of ordinary people.*

custody /ˈkʌstədi/ 1 N-UNCOUNT **Custody** is the legal right to look after a child, especially the right given to a child's father or mother when

Picture Dictionary **cut**

they get divorced. ❑ *I'm going to court to get custody of my children.* **2** PHRASE Someone who is **in custody** has been arrested and is being kept in prison until they can be tried.

custom /'kʌstəm/ (**customs**) **1** N-VAR A **custom** is an activity, a way of behaving, or an event which is usual or traditional in a particular society or in particular circumstances. ❑ *...an ancient Japanese custom.* ❑ *It is the custom to give presents at Christmas.* **2** → see also **customs**
→ see **culture**

customary /'kʌstəmri, AM -meri/ ADJ **Customary** means usual. ❑ *It is customary to offer a drink to guests.* ❑ *Yvonne took her customary seat in the classroom.*

customer /'kʌstəmə/ (**customers**) N-COUNT A **customer** is someone who buys goods or services, especially from a shop. ❑ *The shop was full of customers.*

Usage

When you buy goods from a particular shop or company, you are one of its **customers**. If you use the professional services of someone such as a lawyer or an accountant, you are one of their **clients**. Doctors and hospitals have **patients**, while hotels have **guests**. People who travel on public transport are referred to as **passengers**.

Word Partnership Use *customer* with:

N.	customer **account**, customer **loyalty**, customer **satisfaction**
V.	**greet** customers, **satisfy a** customer

ˌcustomer 'service N-UNCOUNT **Customer service** refers to the way that companies behave towards their customers, for example how well they treat them. ❑ *This mail-order business has very good customer service.*

customize [BRIT also **customise**] /'kʌstəmaɪz/ (**customizes, customizing, customized**) V-T If you **customize** something, you change its appearance or features to suit your tastes or needs. ❑ *Kids like to customise their bikes.*

customs /'kʌstəmz/ **1** N-PROPER **Customs** is the official organization responsible for collecting taxes on goods coming into a country and preventing illegal goods from being brought in. ❑ *Customs discovered the goods in his suitcase.* ❑ *...customs officers.* **2** N-UNCOUNT **Customs** is the place where people arriving from a foreign country have to declare goods that they bring with them. ❑ *He walked through customs.*

cut /kʌt/ (**cuts, cutting, cut**) **1** V-T & N-COUNT If you **cut** something, or if you make a **cut** in it, you push a knife or similar tool into it in order to remove a piece of it, or to mark or damage it. ❑ *Cut the tomatoes in half.* ❑ *The thieves cut a hole in the fence.* ❑ *You've had your hair cut, it looks great.* ❑ *The operation involves making several tiny cuts in the eye.* **2** V-T If you **cut yourself**, you accidentally injure yourself on a sharp object and you bleed. ❑ *Johnson cut himself shaving.* **3** N-COUNT A **cut** is an injury caused by touching or being touched by something sharp. ❑ *...a cut on his head.* **4** V-I If you **cut across** or **through** an area, you go through it because it is a short route to another place. ❑ *He decided to cut across the park.* **5** V-T & N-COUNT To **cut** something, or to make a **cut** in it, means to reduce it. ❑ *We must cut costs.* ❑ *The deal will cut 50 billion dollars from the final cost.* **6** V-T & N-COUNT When a part of a piece of writing or performance **is cut**, or when **cuts** have been made to it, parts of it are not printed, broadcast, or performed. ❑ *We've cut some scenes from the play.* ❑ *We had to make some cuts in the text.* **7** V-T & N-COUNT To **cut** a supply of something means to stop providing it or stop it being provided. A **cut** in the supply of something is the action of stopping it. ❑ *...cutting food and water supplies.* ❑ *...cuts in electricity supplies.* **8** PHRASE If something is **a cut above** other things of the same kind, it is better than them. **9** → see also **cutting**
→ see Picture Dictionary: **cut**

▸ **cut across** PHR-VERB If an issue or problem **cuts across** the division between two or more groups of people, it affects or matters to people in all the groups. ❑ *The problem of health-care cuts across all social groups.*

▸ **cut back** **1** PHR-VERB If you **cut back** some money that you are spending, or if you **cut back on** it, you reduce it. ❑ *The Government has cut back on spending.* **2** → see also **cutback**

▸ **cut down** **1** PHR-VERB If you **cut down on** something, you use or do less of it. ❑ *He cut down* on coffee. ❑ *Car owners were asked to cut down travel.* **2** PHR-VERB If you **cut down** a tree, you cut through its trunk so that it falls to the ground. **3** PHR-VERB If you **cut down** something, you reduce it. ❑ *Politicians must agree ways to cut down pollution.*

▶ **cut in** PHR-VERB If you **cut in on** someone, you interrupt them when they are speaking. ❑ *Daniel cut in on Joanne's conversation with her sister.*

▶ **cut off** **1** PHR-VERB If you **cut** something **off**, you remove it with a knife or a similar tool. ❑ *Mrs Brown cut off a large piece of meat.* ❑ *When I went home I cut all my hair off.* **2** PHR-VERB To **cut off** a place or a person means to separate them from things they are normally connected with. ❑ *The snow cut us off from the nearest village.* ❑ *We felt very cut off when we lived in the countryside without a car.* **3** PHR-VERB To **cut off** a supply of something means to stop providing it or stop it being provided. ❑ *The army has cut off electricity from the capital.* **4** PHR-VERB If you get **cut off** when you are talking on the telephone, the line is suddenly disconnected.

▶ **cut out** **1** PHR-VERB If you **cut** something **out**, you remove it from what surrounds it using scissors or a knife. ❑ *Cut out the photos from the magazine.* **2** PHR-VERB If you **cut out** a part of a text, you do not print, publish, or broadcast that part, in order to shorten the text or make it more acceptable. ❑ *They cut out all the interesting stuff from the interview with the prime minister.* **3** PHR-VERB To **cut out** something unnecessary means to remove it completely from a situation. ❑ *He has cut out sweets and chocolate from his diet.* **4** PHR-VERB If an object **cuts out** the light, it prevents light from reaching a place. ❑ *The curtains were drawn to cut out the sunlight.* **5** PHR-VERB If an engine **cuts out**, it suddenly stops working.

▶ **cut up** PHR-VERB If you **cut** something **up**, you cut it into several pieces. ❑ *Halve the tomatoes, then cut them up.*

Thesaurus *cut* Also look up:

V.	carve, slice, trim **1**
	graze, nick, stab **2**
	decrease, lower, reduce; *(ant.)* increase **5**
N.	gash, slit **1**
	gash, nick, wound **2**

cutback also **cut-back** /ˈkʌtbæk/ (**cutbacks**) N-COUNT A **cutback** is a reduction in something. ❑ *...cutbacks in spending on education.*

cute /kjuːt/ (**cuter, cutest**) ADJ **Cute** means pretty or attractive. ❑ *Oh, look at that dog! He's so cute.* ❑ *...a cute little house.*

Thesaurus *cute* Also look up:

ADJ.	adorable, charming, pretty; *(ant.)* homely, ugly

cutlery /ˈkʌtləri/ N-UNCOUNT The knives, forks, and spoons that you eat with are referred to as **cutlery**.

ˈcut-off also **cutoff** (**cut-offs**) N-COUNT A **cut-off** or a **cut-off** point is the level or limit at which you decide that something should stop happening. ❑ *The cut-off date for applications for the job is 16 July.*

cutter /ˈkʌtə/ (**cutters**) N-VAR A **cutter** is a tool that you use for cutting something. ❑ *...a pastry cutter.* ❑ *...a pair of wire cutters.*

cutting /ˈkʌtɪŋ/ (**cuttings**) **1** N-COUNT A **cutting** is a piece of writing cut from a newspaper or magazine. [BRIT] ❑ *...old newspaper cuttings.* **2** N-COUNT A **cutting** is a piece of stalk that you cut from a plant and use to grow a new plant. **3** ADJ A **cutting** remark is unkind and hurts people's feelings.

ˌcutting ˈedge N-SING If you are **at the cutting edge** of a field of activity, you are involved in its most important or exciting developments. ❑ *This company is at the cutting edge of mobile phone technology.*

→ see **technology**

CV /ˌsiː ˈviː/ (**CVs**) N-COUNT In British English, your **CV** is a brief written account of your personal details, your education, and jobs you have had, which you send when you are applying for a job. The American word is **resumé**.

cyanide /ˈsaɪənaɪd/ N-UNCOUNT **Cyanide** is a highly poisonous substance.

cybercafé /ˈsaɪbəkæfeɪ/ (**cybercafés**) N-COUNT A **cybercafé** is a café where people can pay to use the Internet.

cyberspace /ˈsaɪbəspeɪs/ N-UNCOUNT In computer technology, **cyberspace** refers to data banks and networks, considered as a space. [COMPUTING]

cycle /ˈsaɪkəl/ (**cycles, cycling, cycled**) **1** V-I If you **cycle**, you ride a bicycle. ❑ *I cycle to work at least twice a week.* ●**cycling** N-UNCOUNT ❑ *Quiet country roads are ideal for cycling.* **2** N-COUNT A **cycle** is a bicycle. **3** N-COUNT A **cycle** is a series of events or processes that is continually repeated, always in the same order. ❑ *...the cycles of nature.* ❑ *They must break out of the cycle of violence.*

→ see **hat, water**

cyclical /ˈsɪklɪkəl, ˈsaɪk-/ or **cyclic** /ˈsɪklɪk, ˈsaɪk-/ ADJ A **cyclical** process happens again and again in cycles. ❑ *The nature of life is cyclical.*

cyclist /ˈsaɪklɪst/ (**cyclists**) N-COUNT A **cyclist** is someone who rides a bicycle.

cyclone /ˈsaɪkləʊn/ (**cyclones**) N-COUNT A **cyclone** is a violent tropical storm.

→ see **hurricane**

cylinder /ˈsɪlɪndə/ (**cylinders**) N-COUNT A **cylinder** is a shape or container with flat circular ends and long straight sides. ❑ *...a cardboard cylinder.* ❑ *...a gas cylinder.*

→ see **engine, solid, volume**

cynic /ˈsɪnɪk/ (**cynics**) N-COUNT A **cynic** is someone who always thinks the worst of people or things.

cynical /ˈsɪnɪkəl/ ADJ If you describe someone as **cynical**, you think that they always think the worst of people or things. ❑ *...his cynical view of the world.* ❑ *My divorce has made me more cynical about relationships.* ●**cynically** ADV ❑ *If you go into business cynically to make money, you don't normally succeed.* ●**cynicism** /ˈsɪnɪsɪzəm/ N-UNCOUNT ❑ *...public cynicism about the war.*

cyst /sɪst/ (**cysts**) N-COUNT A **cyst** is a growth containing liquid that appears inside your body or under your skin.

C

Dd

dab /dæb/ (**dabs, dabbing, dabbed**) 1 V-T/V-I If you **dab** something or **dab at** something, you touch it several times using quick light movements. ❑ *He dabbed the stain with a handkerchief.* ❑ *He dabbed at his lips with the napkin.* 2 N-COUNT A **dab of** something is a small amount of it that is put onto a surface. [INFORMAL] ❑ *...a dab of glue.*

dabble /ˈdæbəl/ (**dabbles, dabbling, dabbled**) V-I If you **dabble in** something, you take part in it but not very seriously. ❑ *He dabbled in politics.*

dad /dæd/ (**dads**) N-COUNT & N-VOC Your **dad** is your father. [INFORMAL] ❑ *Help me Dad!* ❑ *He's living with his mum and dad.*

daddy /ˈdædi/ (**daddies**) N-COUNT & N-VOC Children often call their father **daddy**. [INFORMAL] ❑ *Little children like to watch their daddies shave.* ❑ *Look at me, Daddy!*

daffodil

daffodil /ˈdæfədɪl/ (**daffodils**) N-COUNT A **daffodil** is a yellow flower that blooms in the spring.

daft /dɑːft, dæft/ (**dafter, daftest**) ADJ **Daft** means stupid and not sensible. [BRIT, INFORMAL] ❑ *That's a daft question.*

dagger /ˈdægə/ (**daggers**) N-COUNT A **dagger** is a weapon like a knife with two sharp edges.

daily /ˈdeɪli/ (**dailies**) 1 ADV & ADJ BEFORE N If something happens **daily**, it happens every day. ❑ *The exhibition is open daily from 11am.* ❑ *I set out for my daily walk.* 2 ADJ BEFORE N **Daily** means relating to a single day or to one day at a time. ❑ *...their daily dose of vitamins.* 3 N-COUNT & ADJ BEFORE N A **daily** or a **daily** newspaper is a newspaper that is published every day except Sunday.

dainty /ˈdeɪnti/ ADJ A **dainty** movement, person, or object is small, delicate, or pretty. ❑ *...dainty feet.* ● **daintily** ADV ❑ *He noticed how daintily they all ate.*

dairy /ˈdeəri/ (**dairies**) 1 N-COUNT A **dairy** is a shop or company that sells milk, butter, and cheese. 2 N-COUNT A **dairy** on a farm is a building where milk is kept or where cream, butter, and cheese are made. 3 ADJ BEFORE N **Dairy** is used to refer to foods such as butter and chees e that are made from milk. ❑ *...dairy products.*
→ see Word Web: **dairy**

daisy /ˈdeɪzi/ (**daisies**) N-COUNT A **daisy** is a small wild flower with a yellow centre and white petals.
→ see **plant**

dam /dæm/ (**dams, damming, dammed**) 1 N-COUNT A **dam** is a wall built across a river to stop the flow of the water and make a lake. 2 V-T If you **dam** a river, you build a dam across it.
→ see Word Web: **dam**

dam

damage /ˈdæmɪdʒ/ (**damages, damaging, damaged**) 1 V-T If you **damage** something, you injure or harm it. ❑ *Halliday damaged his knee during training.* ❑ *They attempted to damage his reputation.* ● **damaging** ADJ ❑ *These are damaging short-term decisions.* 2 N-UNCOUNT **Damage** is injury or harm that is caused to something. ❑ *The bomb caused extensive damage to the restaurant.* ❑ *The damage to your professional reputation could be very serious.* 3 N-PLURAL When a court of law awards **damages** to someone, it orders money to be paid to them by a person who has harmed them.
→ see **disaster**

Thesaurus	*damage*	Also look up:
V.	break, harm, hurt 1	
N.	harm, loss 2	

dame /deɪm/ (**dames**) N-TITLE In Britain, **Dame** is a title given to a woman as a special honour. ❑ *...Dame Joan Sutherland.*

Word Web *dairy*

Farmers no longer **milk** one **cow** at a time. Today most dairy **farms** use machines instead. The **milk** is taken from the cow by a vacuum-powered **milking machine**. Then it goes through a pipeline to be stored in a **refrigerated** storage tank. From there it goes to a factory for pasteurization and packaging. The largest such dairy farm in the world is the Al Safi Dairy Farm in Saudi Arabia. It has 24,000 head of **cattle** and produces about 33 million gallons of milk each year.

Word Web dam

The Egyptians built the world's first **dam** in about 2900 BC. It directed water into a **reservoir** near the capital city of Memphis*. Later they built another dam to stop **flooding** just south of Cairo*. Today, dams are used with **irrigation** systems to prevent **droughts**. Modern hydroelectric dams use water to make more than 20% of the world's electricity. Brazil and Paraguay built the largest hydroelectric power station in the world—the Itaipu Dam. It took 18 years to build and cost 18 billion dollars! Hydroelectric power does not cause pollution. However, the dams can hurt fish and sometimes destroy valuable forests.

Memphis: an ancient city in Egypt.
Cairo: the capital of Egypt.

damn /dæm/ **1** EXCLAM & ADJ BEFORE N & ADV **Damn** is a mild swear word which people use to express anger or frustration or for emphasis. ❑ *Damn! she cried.* ❑ *I can't see a damn thing.* ❑ *She's damn lucky to be alive.* **2** PHRASE If you say that someone **does not give a damn** about something, you mean that they do not care about it at all. [INFORMAL]

damned /dæmd/ ADJ BEFORE N & ADV **Damned** is a mild swear word which people use to express anger or frustration or for emphasis. ❑ *It's a damned nuisance.* ❑ *We are making a damned good profit.*

damning /ˈdæmɪŋ/ ADJ Something that is **damning** suggests strongly that someone is guilty of a crime or error. ❑ *This was damning evidence.*

damp /dæmp/ (**damper, dampest, damps, damping, damped**) **1** ADJ **Damp** means slightly wet. ❑ *...a damp towel.* ● **dampness** N-UNCOUNT ❑ *...the dampness of the wall.* **2** N-UNCOUNT **Damp** is slight moisture in the air or on the walls of a house.
→ see **weather**

dampen /ˈdæmpən/ (**dampens, dampening, dampened**) **1** V-T To **dampen** something means to make it less lively or intense. ❑ *This did not dampen his enthusiasm.* **2** V-T If you **dampen** something, you make it slightly wet. ❑ *Dampen a sponge.*

dance /dɑːns, dæns/ (**dances, dancing, danced**) **1** V-I When you **dance**, you move around in time to music. ❑ *They could see a couple dancing together.* ❑ *We sang and we danced.* ● **dancing** N-UNCOUNT ❑ *Let's go dancing tonight.* **2** N-COUNT A **dance** is a series of steps and rhythmic movements which you do to music. It is also a piece of music which people can dance to. ❑ *The next dance was a waltz.* **3** N-COUNT A **dance** is a social event where people dance with each other. **4** N-UNCOUNT **Dance** is the activity of performing dances as a public entertainment or art form. ❑ *...an evening of dance.*
→ see Picture Dictionary: **dance**

Word Partnership Use *dance* with:

V.	**let's** dance **1**
	choreograph a dance, **learn to** dance **2**
N.	dance **class**, dance **moves**, dance **music**, dance **partner** **2**

Picture Dictionary dance

dancing

folk dancing

tap dancing

ballroom dancing

modern dance

ballet

D

'dance floor also **dancefloor** (**dance floors**) N-COUNT In a restaurant or night club, the **dance floor** is the area where people can dance.

dancer /'dɑːnsə, 'dæns-/ (**dancers**) N-COUNT A **dancer** is a person who is dancing, or who earns money by dancing.

dandelion /'dændɪlaɪən/ (**dandelions**) N-COUNT A **dandelion** is a wild plant which has yellow flowers first, then a fluffy ball of seeds.

danger /'deɪndʒə/ (**dangers**) **1** N-UNCOUNT **Danger** is the possibility that someone may be harmed or killed. ❑ *My friends risked tremendous danger in order to help me.* ❑ *Your life is in danger.* **2** N-COUNT A **danger** is something or someone that can hurt or harm you. ❑ *...the dangers of sunburn.* **3** N-SING If there is a **danger of** something unpleasant happening, it is possible that it will happen. ❑ *There is a danger of infection.*
→ see **hero**

Word Link	*ous ≈ having the qualities of: danger**ous**, fabul**ous**, nutriti**ous***

dangerous /'deɪndʒərəs/ ADJ If something is **dangerous**, it may hurt or harm you. ❑ *...dangerous chemicals.* ● **dangerously** ADV ❑ *He rushed downstairs dangerously fast.*

Thesaurus	*dangerous* Also look up:
ADJ.	risky, threatening, unsafe

Word Partnership	Use *dangerous* with:
N.	dangerous **area**, dangerous **criminal**, dangerous **driving**, dangerous **man**, dangerous **situation**
ADJ.	**potentially** dangerous

dangle /'dæŋgəl/ (**dangles, dangling, dangled**) V-I If something **dangles** from somewhere, it hangs or swings loosely. ❑ *A gold bracelet dangled from her wrist.*

dare /deə/ (**dares, daring, dared**) **1** V-T & MODAL If you **dare to** do something, you have enough courage to do it. ❑ *No one dared to complain.* ❑ *I didn't dare look at Ellen.* ❑ *They daren't leave him.*

Usage

You can leave out the word **to** after **dare**. ❑ *Nobody dared complain.* The form **dares** is never used in a question or in a negative statement. You use **dare** instead. ❑ *Dare she tell?...* ❑ *He dare not enter.*

2 V-T & N-COUNT If you **dare** someone **to** do something, or challenge them to do it **for a dare**, you challenge them to prove that they are not frightened of doing it. ❑ *I dared him to wear it to dinner.* ❑ *She swallowed a live worm for a dare.* **3** PHRASE You say **'how dare you'** when you are very shocked and angry about something that someone has done. ❑ *How dare you insult my singing!* **4** PHRASE You say **I dare say** or **I daresay** to show that you think something is probably true. [SPOKEN] ❑ *I dare say they're right.*

daren't /deənt/ 'Dare not' is usually written or said as **daren't.** [INFORMAL]

daring /'deərɪŋ/ **1** ADJ A **daring** person does things which might be dangerous or shocking. ❑ *He made a daring escape by helicopter.* **2** N-UNCOUNT **Daring** is the courage to do things which might be dangerous or shocking. ❑ *His dancing in the big love scenes is full of daring.*

dark /dɑːk/ (**darker, darkest**) **1** ADJ When it is **dark**, there is not enough light to see properly. ❑ *People usually switch on the lights once it gets dark.* ❑ *...a dark corridor.* ❑ *After dark, park your car in a well-lit, busy place.* ● **darkness** N-UNCOUNT ❑ *The whole city was thrown into darkness.* **2** N-SING **The dark** is the lack of light in a place. ❑ *I've always been afraid of the dark.* **3** ADJ Something that is **dark** or a **dark** colour is black or a shade close to black. ❑ *...a dark suit.* ❑ *...a dark blue dress.* **4** ADJ Someone who is **dark** has brown or black hair. **5** ADJ **Dark** looks or remarks suggest that something horrible is going to happen. ❑ *He's always been attracted to wild, really dark stories.* ● **darkly** ADV ❑ *They shook their heads and muttered darkly.* **6** PHRASE If you are **in the dark about** something, you do not know anything about it.

Word Partnership	Use *dark* with:
N.	dark **clouds**, dark **suit** **1** **3**
V.	**get** dark **1**; **afraid of the** dark, **scared of the** dark **1** **2**

darken /'dɑːkən/ (**darkens, darkening, darkened**) **1** V-T/V-I If something **darkens** or you **darken** it, it becomes darker. [WRITTEN] ❑ *The sky darkened abruptly.* ❑ *He has darkened his hair.* **2** V-I If someone's face **darkens**, they suddenly look angry. [WRITTEN]

darkroom /'dɑːkruːm/ (**darkrooms**) N-COUNT A **darkroom** is a room which is lit only by red light, so that photographs can be developed there.

darling /'dɑːlɪŋ/ (**darlings**) **1** N-VOC You call someone **darling** if you love them or like them very much. ❑ *Thank you, darling.* **2** ADJ BEFORE N & N-COUNT You can describe someone as **darling** or say that they are a **darling** when you love or like them very much. ❑ *...our darling child.* ❑ *She is a darling.*

darn /dɑːn/ (**darns, darning, darned**) V-T When you **darn** something made of cloth, you mend a hole in it by sewing stitches across the hole and then weaving stitches in and out of them.

dart /dɑːt/ (**darts, darting, darted**) **1** V-I If a person or animal **darts** somewhere, they move there suddenly and quickly. [WRITTEN] ❑ *Ingrid darted across the street.* **2** V-T/V-I If you **dart** a glance at someone or something, or if your eyes **dart** to them, you look at them very quickly. [WRITTEN] ❑ *Her eyes darted from one face to another.* **3** N-COUNT A **dart** is a small, narrow object with a sharp point which you can throw or shoot. **4** N-UNCOUNT **Darts** is a game in which you throw darts at a round board with numbers on it.

dash /dæʃ/ (**dashes, dashing, dashed**) **1** V-I & N-SING If you **dash** somewhere, or if you make a **dash** there, you go there quickly and suddenly. ❑ *He dashed upstairs.* ❑ *Frank considered making a dash for the door.* **2** N-COUNT A **dash of** something is a small quantity or amount of it. ❑ *Add a dash of lemon juice.* **3** V-T If an event or person **dashes** someone's hopes, it destroys them. ❑ *This injury dashed his hopes of an Olympic gold medal.* **4** N-COUNT A **dash** is a short horizontal line (—) used in writing.

▶ **dash off** 1 PHR-VERB If you **dash off** to a place, you go there very quickly. 2 PHR-VERB If you **dash off** a letter, you write it quickly without thinking much about it.

dashboard /ˈdæʃbɔːd/ (**dashboards**) N-COUNT The **dashboard** in a car is the panel facing the driver's seat where most of the instruments and switches are.

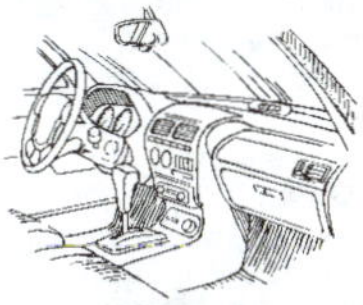
dashboard

dashing /ˈdæʃɪŋ/ ADJ A **dashing** person or thing is very stylish and attractive. [DATED] ❑ *...a dashing young officer.*

data /ˈdeɪtə/ 1 N-UNCOUNT & N-PLURAL **Data** is information, usually in the form of facts or statistics, that you can analyse. ❑ *The study was based on data from 2,100 women.* 2 N-UNCOUNT & N-PLURAL **Data** is information that can be stored and used by a computer program. ❑ *This CD-ROM holds huge amounts of data.*
→ see **forecast**

Thesaurus	*data* Also look up:
N.	facts, figures, information, results, statistics 1

database or **data base** /ˈdeɪtəbeɪs/ (**databases**) N-COUNT A **database** is a collection of data stored in a computer in a way that makes it easy to obtain. [COMPUTING] ❑ *It's a database of five-star hotels.*

date /deɪt/ (**dates, dating, dated**) 1 N-COUNT A **date** is a particular day or year, for example 7th June 2002, or 1066. ❑ *What's the date today?* ❑ *You will need to give the dates you wish to stay.* 2 V-T When you **date** something, you give the date when it began or was made. ❑ *Experts have dated the jug to the fifteenth century.* 3 V-T When you **date** a letter or a cheque, you write a particular day's date on it. 4 PHRASE **To date** means up until the present time. ❑ *This is his best novel to date.* 5 V-I If something **dates**, it goes out of fashion. ● **dated** ADJ ❑ *The decor looked dated.* 6 N-COUNT A **date** is an appointment to meet someone or go out with them, especially someone with whom you are having a romantic relationship. You can also refer to the person you go out with as your **date**. ❑ *I have a date with Bob.* ❑ *His date was one of the girls in the show.* 7 V-T If you **are dating** someone, you go out with them regularly because you are having a romantic relationship with them. ❑ *I dated his sister.* ❑ *They've been dating for three months.* 8 N-COUNT A **date** is a small, sticky, dark brown fruit with a stone inside. 9 → see also **out of date, up-to-date**
→ see **fossil**

▶ **date back** or **date from** PHR-VERB If something **dates back to** a particular time, or **dates from** that time, it started or was made at that time. ❑ *The treasure dates back to the sixth century BC.*

Word Partnership	Use *date* with:
N.	**birth** date, **cut-off** date, **due** date 1
V.	**set a** date 1
	date **and sign** 3

ˈdate rape N-UNCOUNT **Date rape** is when a man rapes a woman whom he has met socially.

daub /dɔːb/ (**daubs, daubing, daubed**) V-T When you **daub** a substance such as mud or paint on something, you spread it on that thing roughly or carelessly. ❑ *Some young men daubed their faces with blue, white and red paint.*

daughter /ˈdɔːtə/ (**daughters**) N-COUNT Your **daughter** is your female child.
→ see **child**

ˈdaughter-in-law (**daughters-in-law**) N-COUNT Your **daughter-in-law** is the wife of your son.

daunt /dɔːnt/ (**daunts, daunting, daunted**) V-T If something **daunts** you, it makes you feel afraid or worried about dealing with it. ❑ *The difficulty did not daunt her.* ● **daunted** ADJ AFTER LINK-V ❑ *I was daunted by the prospect of coping with teenagers.* ● **daunting** ADJ ❑ *He faces a daunting task.*

dawn /dɔːn/ (**dawns, dawning, dawned**) 1 N-VAR **Dawn** is the time of day when light first appears in the sky, before the sun rises. ❑ *Nancy woke at dawn.* 2 V-I When you say that a particular day **dawned**, you mean it began. [WRITTEN] ❑ *The next day dawned bright and fresh.* 3 N-SING **The dawn of** a period of time or a situation is the beginning of it. [LITERARY] ❑ *...the dawn of the radio age.* 4 V-I If something **is dawning**, it is beginning to develop or come into existence. [LITERARY] ❑ *Fowler became director in 1976, just as the age of the new electronic technology was dawning.* ● **dawning** N-COUNT ❑ *...the dawning of the space age.*

▶ **dawn on** or **dawn upon** PHR-VERB If a fact or idea **dawns on** you, or if it **dawns upon** you, you realize it. ❑ *It gradually dawned on me that I still had talent.*

day /deɪ/ (**days**) 1 N-COUNT A **day** is one of the seven twenty-four hour periods of time in a week. 2 N-VAR **Day** is the part of a day when it is light or the time when you are awake and doing things. ❑ *The snack bar is open during the day.* 3 N-COUNT You can refer to a period in history as a particular **day** or as particular **days**. ❑ *...the most celebrated artist of his day.* 4 PHRASE If you **call it a day**, you stop what you are doing and leave it to be finished later. ❑ *I'm tired, let's call it a day.* 5 PHRASE **One day, some day**, or **one of these days** means at some future time. ❑ *One day you'll find true love.* 6 **day and night** → see **night** 7 **night and day** → see **night**
→ see **year**

ˈday care N-UNCOUNT **Day care** is care that is provided during the day for people who cannot look after themselves, such as small children, old people, or people who are ill.

daydream /ˈdeɪdriːm/ (**daydreams, daydreaming, daydreamed**) V-I & N-COUNT When you **daydream**, or when you have a **daydream**, you think about pleasant things that you would like to happen. ❑ *He daydreams of being a famous journalist.* ❑ *She came out of her daydream.*

Word Link	***light** ≈ shining: daylight, enlighten, headlight*

daylight /ˈdeɪlaɪt/ N-UNCOUNT **Daylight** is the light that there is during the day, or the time of day when it is light. ❑ *It was still daylight.* ❑ *Quinn returned shortly after daylight.*

daytime /ˈdeɪtaɪm/ N-UNCOUNT **Daytime** is the part of a day when it is light. ❑ *In the daytime he*

D

tended to stay in his room.

ˌday-to-ˈday ADJ BEFORE N **Day-to-day** things or activities exist or happen every day as part of ordinary life. ❑ *...the day-to-day lives of students.*

dazed /deɪzd/ ADJ If someone is **dazed**, they are confused and unable to think clearly, often because of shock or a blow to the head.

dazzle /ˈdæzəl/ (**dazzles, dazzling, dazzled**) **1** V-T If someone or something **dazzles** you, you are extremely impressed by their skill or beauty. ❑ *George dazzled her with his knowledge of the world.* **2** N-UNCOUNT The **dazzle** of a light is its brightness, which makes it impossible for you to see properly for a short time. **3** V-T If a bright light **dazzles** you, you cannot see properly for a short time.

dazzling /ˈdæzlɪŋ/ **1** ADJ Something that is **dazzling** is very impressive or beautiful. ❑ *...a dazzling smile.* ● **dazzlingly** ADV ❑ *The view was dazzlingly beautiful.* **2** ADJ A **dazzling** light is very bright and makes you unable to see properly for a short time. ● **dazzlingly** ADV ❑ *The bay seemed dazzlingly bright.*

dead /ded/ **1** ADJ & N-PLURAL **Dead** people or **the dead** are no longer living. ❑ *My husband's been dead a year now.* **2** ADJ A telephone or piece of electrical equipment that is **dead** is not functioning. ❑ *David answered the phone and the line went dead.* **3** ADJ BEFORE N **Dead** is used to mean complete or absolute, especially with the words 'silence', 'centre', and 'stop'. ❑ *There was a dead silence.* **4** ADV **Dead** means precisely or exactly. ❑ *Mars was visible, dead in the centre of the telescope.* ❑ *A fishing boat came out of nowhere, dead ahead.* **5** ADV **Dead** is sometimes used to mean very. [INFORMAL] ❑ *His poems are dead boring.* **6** PHRASE To **stop dead** means to suddenly stop moving or doing something. ❑ *We all stopped dead and looked at it.*

Usage

Do not confuse **dead** with **died**. **Died** is the past tense and past participle of the verb **die**, and thus indicates the action of dying. ❑ *She died in 1934...* ❑ *Two men have died since the rioting started.* You do not use **died** as an adjective. You use **dead** instead. ❑ *More than 2,200 dead birds have been found.*

Thesaurus *dead* Also look up:

ADJ. deceased, lifeless; *(ant.)* alive, living **1**

ˌdead ˈend (**dead ends**) **1** N-COUNT If a street is a **dead end**, there is no way out at one end of it. **2** N-COUNT A job or course of action that is a **dead end** does not lead to further developments or progression. ❑ *Waitressing was a dead-end job.*

deadline /ˈdedlaɪn/ (**deadlines**) N-COUNT A **deadline** is a time or date before which a particular task must be finished or a particular thing must be done. ❑ *The last deadline for agreement is December 15th.*

deadlock /ˈdedlɒk/ N-UNCOUNT If a dispute or series of negotiations **reaches deadlock**, neither side is willing to give in, and so no agreement can be reached. ❑ *Peace talks between the two sides ended in deadlock.*

deadly /ˈdedli/ (**deadlier, deadliest**) **1** ADJ If something is **deadly**, it is likely or able to cause death. ❑ *...a deadly disease.* ❑ *They made deadly weapons.* **2** ADJ If you describe a person or their behaviour as **deadly**, you mean they are unpleasant or dangerous. A **deadly** situation has unpleasant or dangerous consequences. ❑ *...a deadly enemy.* ❑ *The agent's name was a deadly secret.*

deaf /def/ (**deafer, deafest**) **1** ADJ & N-PLURAL **Deaf** people or **the deaf** are unable to hear anything or unable to hear very well. ❑ *She is deaf.* ❑ *Many regular TV programmes are captioned for the deaf.* ● **deafness** N-UNCOUNT ❑ *...permanent deafness.* **2** ADJ AFTER LINK-V If you say that someone is **deaf to** people's pleas or criticisms, you disapprove of them because they refuse to pay attention to them. ❑ *She was deaf to what was happening around her.*

→ see **disability**

deafen /ˈdefən/ (**deafens, deafening, deafened**) V-T If a noise deafens you, or you **are deafened** by a noise, it is so loud that you cannot hear anything else. ❑ *The noise of the traffic deafened her.*

deafening /ˈdefənɪŋ/ ADJ A **deafening** noise is a very loud noise.

deal /diːl/ (**deals, dealing, dealt** /delt/) **1** QUANT **A good deal** or **a great deal of** something is a lot of it. ❑ *She knew a good deal more than she admitted.* ❑ *Lawrence Durrell wrote a great deal of poetry.* **2** N-COUNT A **deal** is an agreement or arrangement, especially in business. ❑ *Japan will have to do a deal with America on rice imports.* **3** V-I If a person, company, or shop **deals in** a particular type of goods, their business involves buying or selling those goods. ❑ *They deal in antiques.* ● **dealer** (**dealers**) N-COUNT ❑ *...an antique dealer.* **4** V-T & PHR-VERB When you **deal** cards, or when you **deal** them **out**, you give them out to the players in a game of cards. ❑ *He dealt each player a card.* ❑ *Dalton dealt out five cards to each player.*

▸ **deal out** **1** PHR-VERB If someone **deals out** a punishment or harmful action, they punish or harm someone. ❑ *The angry soldiers dealt out death in the village.* **2** → see also **deal** (meaning 4)

▸ **deal with** **1** PHR-VERB When you **deal with** a situation or problem, you do what is necessary to achieve the result you want. ❑ *How do you deal with an uninvited guest?* **2** PHR-VERB If a book, speech, or film **deals with** a subject, it is concerned with it. ❑ *These parts of his book deal with contemporary Paris.* **3** PHR-VERB If you **deal with** a particular person or organization, you have business relations with them. ❑ *When I worked there I dealt with British people all the time.*

dealings /ˈdiːlɪŋz/ N-PLURAL Someone's **dealings with** a person or organization are the relations that they have with them or the business that they do with them. ❑ *He has learnt little in his dealings with the international community.*

dean /diːn/ (**deans**) **1** N-COUNT A **dean** is an important administrator at a university or college. **2** N-COUNT A **dean** is a priest who is the main administrator of a large church.

dear /dɪə/ (**dearer, dearest, dears**) **1** ADJ BEFORE N You use **dear** to describe someone or something that you feel affection for. ❑ *Mrs Cavendish is a dear friend of mine.* **2** ADJ AFTER LINK-V If something is **dear to** you or **dear to** your **heart**, you care deeply about it. ❑ *His family life was very dear to him.*

3 N-VOC You can call someone **dear** as a sign of affection. ❑ *You're a lot like me, dear.* **4** ADJ BEFORE N **Dear** is written at the beginning of a letter, followed by the name or title of the person you are writing to. ❑ *He wrote: 'Dear Mr President.'* **5** ADJ Something that is **dear** costs a lot of money. ❑ *Taxis here are too dear.*

dearly /ˈdɪəli/ **1** ADV If you love someone **dearly**, you love them very much. **2** ADV If you would **dearly** like to do or have something, you would very much like to do it or have it. ❑ *I would dearly love to marry him.* **3** PHRASE If you **pay dearly for** doing something or it **costs** you **dearly**, you suffer a lot as a result. [FORMAL] ❑ *The victory cost him dearly.*

death /deθ/ (**deaths**) **1** N-VAR **Death** is the end of the life of a person or animal. ❑ *These people are in immediate danger of death from starvation.* ❑ *It's the thirtieth anniversary of her death.* **2** PHRASE If you say that something is a matter of **life and death**, you are emphasizing that it is extremely important, often because someone may die if people do not act immediately. ❑ *We're dealing with a life-and-death situation.* **3** PHRASE If someone **is put to death**, they are executed. **4** PHRASE You use **to death** to indicate that a particular action or process results in someone's death. ❑ *He was stabbed to death.* **5** PHRASE You use **to death** after an adjective or a verb to emphasize the action, state, or feeling mentioned. ❑ *The fans love him to death.* ❑ *I went out last night, but not for very long. I was bored to death.*

Word Partnership Use *death* with:

ADJ.	**accidental** death, **sudden** death, **violent** death
N.	**brush with** death, **cause of** death, ***someone's*** death, death **threat**

ˈdeath penalty N-SING **The death penalty** is the punishment of death, used in some countries for people who have committed very serious crimes. ❑ *They could face the death penalty.*

death row /ˌdeθˈrəʊ/ N-UNCOUNT If someone is **on death row**, they are in the part of a prison which contains the cells for criminals who have been sentenced to death.

ˈdeath toll also **death-toll** (**death tolls**) N-COUNT The **death toll** of an accident, disaster, or war is the number of people who die in it.

debacle also **débâcle** /deɪˈbɑːkəl, AM dɪˈb-/ (**debacles**) N-COUNT A **debacle** is an event or attempt that is a complete failure. ❑ *It will be hard to recover from this debacle.*

debatable /dɪˈbeɪtəbəl/ ADJ Something that is **debatable** is not definitely true or not certain. ❑ *Whether he would do any better is debatable.*

debate /dɪˈbeɪt/ (**debates, debating, debated**) **1** N-VAR A **debate** is a discussion about a subject on which people have different views. ❑ *There has been a lot of debate among scholars about this.* **2** V-T When people **debate** a topic, they discuss it fairly formally, putting forward different views. You can also say that one person **debates** a topic **with** another person. ❑ *The council will debate the issue today.* **3** N-COUNT A **debate** is a formal discussion, for example in a parliament, in which people express different opinions about a subject and then vote on it. ❑ *...a debate on defence spending.* **4** V-T If you **debate** what to do, you think about possible courses of action before deciding what to do. ❑ *We are debating what furniture to buy for the house.* ❑ *I debated going back inside.*

Word Partnership Use *debate* with:

V.	**open to** debate **1** **2**
ADJ.	**major** debate, **ongoing** debate, **political** debate, **presidential** debate, **televised** debate **1** **2**
N.	debate **over** ***something***, debate **the issue** **3** **4**

debit /ˈdebɪt/ (**debits, debiting, debited**) **1** V-T When your bank **debits** your account, money is taken from it and paid to someone else. **2** N-COUNT A **debit** is a record of the money taken from your bank account.

ˈdebit card (**debit cards**) N-COUNT A **debit card** is a bank card that you can use to pay for things. When you use it, the money is taken out of your bank account immediately.

debris /ˈdeɪbri, AM deɪˈbriː/ N-UNCOUNT **Debris** consists of pieces of things that have been destroyed, or rubbish that is lying around. ❑ *Five survivors were found in the debris.*

debt /det/ (**debts**) **1** N-VAR A **debt** is a sum of money that you owe someone. ❑ *He is still paying off his debts.* **2** N-UNCOUNT **Debt** is the state of owing money. ❑ *Debt can lead to stress.*

Word Partnership Use *debt* with:

V.	**incur** debt, **pay off a** debt, **reduce** debt, **repay a** debt **1**
ADV.	**deeply in** debt **2**

debtor /ˈdetə/ (**debtors**) N-COUNT A **debtor** is a country, organization, or person who owes money. ❑ *...improvements in the situation of debtor countries.*

debut /ˈdeɪbjuː, AM deɪˈbjuː/ (**debuts**) N-COUNT The **debut** of a performer or sports player is his or her first public performance or recording. ❑ *Her debut album is 'Sugar Time'.*

Dec. **Dec.** is a written abbreviation for **December**.

decade /ˈdekeɪd/ (**decades**) N-COUNT A **decade** is a period of ten years, especially one that begins with a year ending in 0, for example 1980 to 1989. ❑ *...the last decade of the nineteenth century.*

decadent /ˈdekədənt/ ADJ If you say that a person or society is **decadent**, you mean that they have low standards, especially low moral standards. ❑ *...decadent rock 'n' roll lifestyles.* • **decadence** N-UNCOUNT ❑ *...the decadence of Babylon and Rome.*

decay /dɪˈkeɪ/ (**decays, decaying, decayed**) **1** V-I & N-UNCOUNT When something **decays**, it becomes rotten. This process is called **decay**. ❑ *The smell of decaying bodies sits in the air.* ❑ *The tooth was in a state of decay.* • **decayed** ADJ ❑ *...decayed teeth.* **2** V-I & N-UNCOUNT If a society, system, or institution **decays**, it gradually becomes weaker or its condition gets worse. This process is called **decay**. ❑ *...decaying urban and rural areas.* ❑ *...inner city decay.*
→ see **teeth**

d

D

deceased /dɪ'si:st/

> **Deceased** is both the singular and the plural form.

1 N-COUNT **The deceased** is used to refer to a person or a group of people who have recently died. [FORMAL] ❑ *Do you know the last address of the deceased?* **2** ADJ A **deceased** person is one who has recently died. [FORMAL] ❑ *...his recently deceased mother.*

deceit /dɪ'si:t/ (**deceits**) N-VAR **Deceit** is behaviour that is intended to make people believe something which is not true. ❑ *...the deceit and lies of the past.*

deceitful /dɪ'si:tfʊl/ ADJ If you say that someone is **deceitful**, you mean that they behave in a dishonest way by making other people believe something that is not true. ❑ *I was frequently told as a child that I was very deceitful.*

deceive /dɪ'si:v/ (**deceives, deceiving, deceived**) V-T If you **deceive** someone, you make them believe something that is not true. ❑ *I am really hurt that he deceived me.* ❑ *He was accused of deceiving the public.*

December /dɪ'sembə/ (**Decembers**) N-VAR **December** is the twelfth and last month of the year in the Western calendar. ❑ *John and Sarah are planning to get married in December.*

decency /'di:sənsi/ N-UNCOUNT **Decency** is behaviour which follows accepted moral standards. ❑ *His sense of decency forced him to resign.* ❑ *No-one had the decency to tell me the truth.*

decent /'di:sənt/ **1** ADJ **Decent** means acceptable in standard or quality. ❑ *The lack of a decent education did not defeat Rey.* ● **decently** ADV ❑ *They say they will treat their prisoners decently.* **2** ADJ **Decent** is used to describe behaviour which is morally correct or acceptable. ❑ *After a decent interval, trade relations returned to normal.* ● **decently** ADV ❑ *I was wondering how soon I could decently leave.*

> **Word Link** *centr ≈ middle : centre, central, decentralized*

decentralized [BRIT also **decentralised**] /ˌdi:'sentrəlaɪzd/ ADJ In a **decentralized** political system, decisions are made by departments in local areas. ❑ *This decentralized structure made government difficult.* ● **decentralization** /ˌdi:ˌsentrəlaɪ'zeɪʃən/ N-UNCOUNT ❑ *He is against the idea of increased decentralization.*

deception /dɪ'sepʃən/ (**deceptions**) N-VAR **Deception** is the act of deceiving someone. ❑ *He admitted theft by deception.*

deceptive /dɪ'septɪv/ ADJ If something is **deceptive**, it encourages you to believe something which is not true. ❑ *First impressions were deceptive.* ● **deceptively** ADV ❑ *His poems are deceptively simple.*

decibel /'desɪbel/ (**decibels**) N-COUNT A **decibel** is a unit of measurement which is used to indicate how loud a sound is.

decide /dɪ'saɪd/ (**decides, deciding, decided**) **1** V-T If you **decide to** do something, you choose to do it. ❑ *She decided to do a secretarial course.* ❑ *He decided that he would drive back to town at once.* **2** V-T If a person or group of people **decides** something, they choose what something should be like or how a particular problem should be solved. ❑ *This will be taken into account when deciding her sentence.* **3** V-T If you **decide that** something is the case, you form that opinion after considering the facts. ❑ *He decided Franklin must be suffering from a bad cold.* ❑ *I couldn't decide whether they were insane or just stupid.* **4** V-T If an event or fact **decides** something, it makes a particular result definite or unavoidable. ❑ *His exam results will decide if he will win a place at a good university.* ❑ *Luck is not the only deciding factor.*

▶ **decide on** PHR-VERB If you **decide on** something or **decide upon** something, you choose it from two or more possibilities. ❑ *Therese decided on a career in publishing.*

> **Thesaurus** *decide* Also look up:
>
> V. choose, elect, pick, select **1**

> **Word Partnership** Use *decide* with:
>
> V. **try to** decide **1** **2**
> **help (to)** decide, **let** ***someone*** decide **1** **2** **3**
>
> ADJ. **unable to** decide **1** **2** **3**

decided /dɪ'saɪdɪd/ ADJ BEFORE N **Decided** means clear and definite. ❑ *He's a man of very decided opinions.*

decidedly /dɪ'saɪdɪdli/ ADV **Decidedly** means to a great extent and in a way that is obvious. ❑ *He was decidedly uncomfortable at what he saw.*

deciduous /dɪ'sɪdʒʊəs/ ADJ A **deciduous** tree loses its leaves in autumn every year.

→ see **tree**

decimal /'desɪməl/ (**decimals**) **1** ADJ A **decimal** system involves counting in units of ten. ❑ *...the decimal system of metric weights and measures.* **2** N-COUNT A **decimal** is a fraction written in the form of a dot followed by one or more numbers representing tenths, hundredths, and so on: for example .5, .51, .517.

→ see **fraction**

ˌdecimal 'point (**decimal points**) N-COUNT A **decimal point** is the dot in front of a decimal fraction.

decimate /'desɪmeɪt/ (**decimates, decimating, decimated**) V-T To **decimate** a group of people or animals means to destroy a very large number of them. ❑ *Pollution decimated the river's population of kingfishers.*

decipher /dɪ'saɪfə/ (**deciphers, deciphering, deciphered**) V-T If you **decipher** a piece of writing or a message, you work out what it says, even though it is difficult to read or understand. ❑ *I'm still no closer to deciphering the code.*

decision /dɪ'sɪʒən/ (**decisions**) **1** N-COUNT When you **make** a **decision**, you choose what should be done or which is the best of various alternatives. ❑ *I think I made the right decision.* ❑ *The decision was taken by the chairman.* **2** N-UNCOUNT **Decision** is the act of deciding something. ❑ *The moment of decision has arrived.*

Word Partnership Use *decision* with:

V. **arrive at a** decision, **make a** decision, **postpone a** decision, **reach a** decision 1
ADJ. **difficult** decision, **final** decision, **important** decision, **right** decision, **wise** decision, **wrong** decision 1

de'cision-making N-UNCOUNT **Decision-making** is the process of reaching decisions, especially in a large organization or in government. ❑ *She wants to see more women involved in decision-making.*

decisive /dɪ'saɪsɪv/ 1 ADJ If a fact, action, or event is **decisive**, it makes it certain that there will be a particular result. ❑ *The campaign entered its final, decisive phase.* ● **decisively** ADV ❑ *The plan was decisively rejected.* 2 ADJ If someone is **decisive**, they have the ability to make quick decisions. ❑ *He should give way to a younger, more decisive leader.* ● **decisively** ADV ❑ *'I'll call for you at half ten,' she said decisively.* ● **decisiveness** N-UNCOUNT ❑ *His supporters admire his decisiveness.*

deck /dek/ (**decks, decking, decked**) 1 N-COUNT A **deck** on a bus or ship is a downstairs or upstairs area. ❑ *...the top deck of the number 13 bus.* 2 N-SING The **deck** of a ship is a floor in the open air which you can walk on. 3 N-COUNT A tape **deck** or a record **deck** is a piece of equipment on which you play tapes or records. 4 N-COUNT In American English, a **deck of** cards is a complete set of playing cards. The usual British word is **pack**.
→ see **ship**
▶ **deck out** PHR-VERB If someone or something **is decked out with** or **in** something, they are decorated with it or wearing it. ❑ *She decked him out in expensive clothes.*

decking /'dekɪŋ/ N-UNCOUNT **Decking** is wooden boards that are fixed to the ground in a garden or other outdoor area for people to walk on. [mainly BRIT]

declaration /ˌdeklə'reɪʃən/ (**declarations**) 1 N-COUNT A **declaration** is an official announcement or statement. ❑ *..the country's declaration of independence.* 2 N-COUNT A **declaration** is a firm statement which shows that you have no doubts about what you are saying. ❑ *You must provide a full declaration of all your earnings.*

Word Link *clar ≈ clear : clarify, clarity, declare*

declare /dɪ'kleə/ (**declares, declaring, declared**) 1 V-T If you **declare that** something is the case, you say that it is true in a firm deliberate way. ❑ *He declared his intention to become the best golfer in the world.* 2 V-T If you **declare** something, you state it officially and formally. ❑ *The government is ready to declare a ceasefire.* ❑ *The judges will declare him innocent.* 3 V-T If you **declare** goods that you have bought abroad or money that you have earned, you say how much you have bought or earned so that you can pay tax on it.
→ see **war**

Word Link *clin ≈ leaning : decline, incline, recline*

decline /dɪ'klaɪn/ (**declines, declining, declined**) 1 V-I & N-VAR If something **declines**, or if there is a **decline in** something, it becomes smaller, weaker, or worse. ❑ *The number of staff has declined from 217 to 114.* ❑ *...declining standards of literacy.* ❑ *...a 14 per cent decline in sales.* 2 PHRASE If something is **in decline**, falling **into decline**, or **on the decline**, it is gradually growing smaller, weaker or worse. ❑ *Oil production is in decline.* ❑ *Local languages are on the decline.* 3 V-T If you **decline** something or **decline to** do something, you politely refuse to accept it or do it. [FORMAL] ❑ *I declined his offer of coffee.* ❑ *He declined to comment on the story.*

d

Word Link *cod ≈ writing : code, decode, encode*

decode /diː'kəʊd/ (**decodes, decoding, decoded**) V-T If you **decode** a message that has been written or spoken in a code, you change it into ordinary language. ❑ *The secret documents were decoded.*

decompose /ˌdiːkəm'pəʊz/ (**decomposes, decomposing, decomposed**) V-I When dead plants, humans or animals **decompose**, they change chemically and begin to rot. ❑ *The debris slowly decomposed into compost.* ❑ *The decomposed body was found in a wood.* ● **decomposition** /ˌdiːˌkɒmpə'zɪʃən/ N-UNCOUNT ❑ *The bodies were all in advanced stages of decomposition.*

decor /'deɪkɔː/ N-UNCOUNT The **decor** of a house or room is the style in which it is furnished and decorated.

Word Link *ator ≈ one who does : creator, decorator, narrator*

decorate /'dekəreɪt/ (**decorates, decorating, decorated**) 1 V-T If you **decorate** something, you make it more attractive by adding things to it. ❑ *He decorated his room with pictures.* 2 V-T/V-I If you **decorate** a building or room, you paint it or wallpaper it. ● **decorating** N-UNCOUNT ❑ *I did all the decorating myself.* ● **decorator** (**decorators**) N-COUNT ❑ *...a firm of painters and decorators.* 3 V-T If someone **is decorated**, they are given a medal or other honour as an official reward for something that they have done.

decoration /ˌdekə'reɪʃən/ (**decorations**) 1 N-VAR **Decorations** are features added to something to make it look more attractive. ❑ *...Christmas decorations.* ❑ *Whole currants look very pretty as decoration for cakes.* 2 N-UNCOUNT The **decoration** of a room or building is the furniture, wallpaper, and ornaments there. ❑ *Everybody has their own ideas on home decoration.* 3 N-COUNT A **decoration** is a medal or a title given to someone as an official honour.

decorative /'dekərətɪv/ ADJ Something that is **decorative** is intended to look attractive. ❑ *This is both functional and decorative.*

decoy /'diːkɔɪ/ (**decoys**) N-COUNT A **decoy** is a person or object that you use to lead someone away from where they intended to go, especially so that you can catch them.

Word Link *cresc, creas ≈ growing : crescent, decrease, increase*

decrease (**decreases, decreasing, decreased**) 1 V-T/V-I /dɪ'kriːs/ When something **decreases**, or when you **decrease** it, it becomes less in quantity, size, or intensity. ❑ *Population growth is decreasing by 1.4% each year.* ❑ *Exercise decreases* our risk of heart disease. ❑ *...decreasing interest rates.* **2** N-COUNT /ˈdiːkriːs/ A **decrease** is a reduction in the quantity or size of something. ❑ *...a decrease in the number of people without jobs.*

Thesaurus	*decrease* Also look up:
v.	decline, diminish, go down; *(ant.)* increase **1**

D

decree /dɪˈkriː/ (**decrees, decreeing, decreed**) **1** V-T If someone in authority **decrees that** something must happen, they order this officially. ❑ *They decreed that it should happen by 2010.* **2** N-COUNT A **decree** is an official order, especially one made by the ruler of a country. ❑ *...reform by presidential decree.*

dedicate /ˈdedɪkeɪt/ (**dedicates, dedicating, dedicated**) **1** V-T If you say that someone **has dedicated themselves to** something, you mean that they have given a lot of time and effort to it because they think that it is important. ❑ *He dedicated himself to politics.* ❑ *She dedicated her life to caring for others.* ● **dedicated** ADJ ❑ *...a dedicated doctor.* ● **dedication** N-UNCOUNT ❑ *...his obvious dedication to the job.* **2** V-T If you **dedicate** something such as a book or a piece of music **to** someone, you say that it is written for them, as a sign of affection or respect. ● **dedication** (**dedications**) N-COUNT ❑ *Such dedications are reserved for special concert guests.*

deduce /dɪˈdjuːs, AM -ˈduːs/ (**deduces, deducing, deduced**) V-T If you **deduce that** something is true, you reach that conclusion because of what you know to be true. ❑ *Galileo deduced that the planets were closer to Earth than the stars were.* ❑ *The date of the document can be deduced from references to the Civil War.*

deduct /dɪˈdʌkt/ (**deducts, deducting, deducted**) V-T When you **deduct** an amount **from** a total, you subtract it from the total. ❑ *The company deducted this payment from his compensation.* ❑ *He could deduct the fees he paid to the accountant.*

deduction /dɪˈdʌkʃən/ (**deductions**) **1** N-VAR A **deduction** is a conclusion that you reach because of what you know to be true. ❑ *He made sound deductions from the evidence.* **2** N-VAR A **deduction** is an amount subtracted from a total. ❑ *...tax deductions.*
→ see **science**

deed /diːd/ (**deeds**) **1** N-COUNT A **deed** is something that is done, especially something very good or very bad. [LITERARY] ❑ *One gets a warm feeling from doing a good deed.* **2** N-COUNT A **deed** is a legal document containing the terms of an agreement, especially an agreement concerning the ownership of land or a building. ❑ *Here is the deed of sale.*

deem /diːm/ (**deems, deeming, deemed**) V-T If something **is deemed to** have a quality or **to** do something, it is considered to have that quality or do that thing. [FORMAL] ❑ *Many people have ideas that their society deems to be outrageous.* ❑ *We regret that the strike was deemed necessary.*

deep /diːp/ (**deeper, deepest**) **1** ADJ & ADV If something is **deep**, it extends a long way down from the surface. ❑ *The water is very deep.* ❑ *...the deep cut on his left hand.* ❑ *She put her hand in deeper.* **2** ADJ You use **deep** to talk or ask about how much something measures from the surface to the bottom, or from front to back. ❑ *The water was only one metre deep.* **3** ADV **Deep** in an area means a long way inside it. ❑ *Oil and gas were trapped deep inside the earth when it was formed.* ❑ *They went deep into the jungle.* **4** ADJ You use **deep** to emphasize the seriousness, strength, importance, or degree of something. ❑ *...his deep love of Italy.* ● **deeply** ADV ❑ *Our conversations left me deeply depressed.* ❑ *She slept deeply but woke early.* **5** ADJ A **deep** breath uses the whole of your lungs. ● **deeply** ADV ❑ *She sighed deeply.* **6** ADJ A **deep** colour is strong and fairly dark. **7** ADJ A **deep** sound is a low one. ❑ *His voice was deep and mellow.* **8** PHRASE If you say that something **goes deep** or **runs deep**, you mean that it is very serious or strong and is hard to change. ❑ *His anger and anguish clearly went deep.*

deepen /ˈdiːpən/ (**deepens, deepening, deepened**) **1** V-T/V-I If a situation or emotion **deepens**, or if something **deepens** it, it becomes more intense. ❑ *As her feelings for Jay deepened, so did her desire for a permanent relationship.* **2** V-T/V-I When a sound **deepens** or **is deepened**, it becomes lower in tone. ❑ *Her voice has deepened with the years.* **3** V-T To **deepen** something means to make it deeper. ❑ *His intention was to deepen his understanding.* **4** V-I Where a river or a sea **deepens**, the water gets deeper.

ˌdeep-ˈseated ADJ A **deep-seated** problem, feeling, or belief is difficult to change because its causes have been there for a long time. ❑ *...deep-seated economic problems.*

deer /dɪə/

Deer is both the singular and the plural form.

N-COUNT A **deer** is a large wild animal. Male deer usually have large, branching horns.

deface /dɪˈfeɪs/ (**defaces, defacing, defaced**) V-T If someone **defaces** something such as a wall, they spoil it by writing or drawing things on it.

default /dɪˈfɔːlt/ (**defaults, defaulting, defaulted**) **1** V-I & N-UNCOUNT If someone **defaults on** something that they have legally agreed to do, or if they are **in default on** it, they fail to do it. ❑ *More borrowers are defaulting on loans.* **2** PHRASE If something happens **by default**, it happens only because something else has not happened. **3** N-UNCOUNT The **default** is a particular set of instructions which a computer always uses unless the person using the computer gives other instructions. [COMPUTING] ❑ *...default settings.*

defeat /dɪˈfiːt/ (**defeats, defeating, defeated**) **1** V-T If you **defeat** someone, you win a victory over them in a battle or contest. ❑ *His forces were defeated by government troops.* **2** V-T To **defeat** an action, plan, or proposal means to cause it to fail. ❑ *The motion was defeated by 88 votes to 489.* **3** V-T If a task or a problem **defeats** you, it is so difficult that you cannot do it or solve it. ❑ *The challenges of writing this novel almost defeated her.* **4** N-VAR **Defeat** is the state of being beaten in a battle, game, or contest, or of failing to achieve what you wanted to. ❑ *The most important thing is not to admit defeat.* ❑ *...the scale of the general election defeat.*

defect (**defects, defecting, defected**) **1** N-COUNT /ˈdiːfekt/ A **defect** is a fault or imperfection in a person or thing. ❑ *He was born with a hearing defect.* **2** V-I /dɪˈfekt/ If someone **defects**, they leave their own country, political party, or other group, and join an opposing one. ❑ *Many voters defected to the extreme right.* ● **defection** (**defections**) N-VAR ❑ *...his defection to their hated rivals...* ● **defector** (**defectors**) N-COUNT ❑ *The government attracted defectors from other parties.*

defective /dɪˈfektɪv/ ADJ If something is **defective**, there is something wrong with it. ❑ *...defective brakes.*

defence [AM **defense**] /dɪˈfens/ (**defences**) **1** N-UNCOUNT **Defence** is action taken to protect someone or something from attack. ❑ *The architecture was designed with defence in mind.* ❑ *Hagman spoke in defence of his friend.* **2** N-UNCOUNT **Defence** is the organization of a country's armies and weapons to protect the country or its interests. ❑ *Twenty eight percent of the budget is spent on defense.* **3** N-PLURAL The **defences** of a country or region are its armed forces and weapons. **4** N-COUNT A **defence** is something that people or animals can use or do to protect themselves. ❑ *The immune system is our main defence against disease.* **5** N-COUNT A **defence** is something that you say or write in support of ideas or actions that have been criticized. ❑ *He published a 10,000-word defence of his action.* **6** N-COUNT In a court of law, an accused person's **defence** is the process of presenting evidence in their favour. ❑ *He conducted his own defence.* **7** N-SING **The defence** is the case presented by a lawyer in a trial for the person who has been accused of a crime. You can also refer to the lawyers for this person as **the defence**. **8** N-COUNT In a sports team, **the defence** is the group of players who try to stop the opposing team scoring. For this meaning, **defence** can take the singular or plural form of the verb.

defenceless [AM **defenseless**] /dɪˈfensləs/ ADJ If someone is **defenceless**, they are weak and cannot defend themselves. ❑ *He was a totally defenceless baby.*

Word Link	*fend ≈ striking : defend, defender, offend*

defend /dɪˈfend/ (**defends, defending, defended**) **1** V-T If you **defend** someone or something, you take action to protect them. ❑ *He and his friends defended themselves against the attackers.* **2** V-T If you **defend** someone or something when they have been criticized, you argue in support of them. ❑ *Clarence's move was unpopular, but Matt defended it.* **3** V-T When a lawyer **defends** a person who has been accused of something, the lawyer argues on their behalf in a court of law that the charges are not true. ❑ *He is a lawyer who has defended all types of criminals.* **4** V-T If a sports champion **defends** his or her title, he or she is in a contest against someone who will become the new champion if they win.
→ see **hero**

Word Link	*ant ≈ one who does, has : defendant, dependant, occupant*

defendant /dɪˈfendənt/ (**defendants**) N-COUNT The **defendant** in a trial is the person accused of a crime.
→ see **trial**

defender /dɪˈfendə/ (**defenders**) **1** ADJ If you are a **defender of** a particular thing or person that has been criticized or attacked, you support that thing or person in public. ❑ *He was a strong defender of human rights.* **2** N-COUNT A **defender** in a game such as football is a player whose main task is to try and stop the other side scoring.

defense /dɪˈfens/ → see **defence**

defensive /dɪˈfensɪv/ **1** ADJ You use **defensive** to describe things that are intended to protect someone or something. ❑ *They were pushed into a more defensive position.* **2** ADJ & PHRASE If someone is **defensive**, or if they are **on the defensive**, they are behaving in a way that shows that they feel unsure or threatened. ❑ *She heard the defensive note in his voice.* ● **defensively** ADV ❑ *'It's nothing to be ashamed of', she replied defensively.*

defer /dɪˈfɜː/ (**defers, deferring, deferred**) **1** V-T If you **defer** an event or action, you arrange that it will take place at a later date than was planned. ❑ *Customers often defer payment for as long as possible.* **2** V-I If you **defer to** someone, you accept their opinion or do what they want because you respect them. ❑ *She defers to her husband on everything.*

deference /ˈdefrəns/ N-UNCOUNT **Deference** is polite and respectful behaviour to someone in a superior social position.

defiance /dɪˈfaɪəns/ N-UNCOUNT **Defiance** is behaviour or an attitude which shows that you are not willing to obey someone. ❑ *They took to the streets in defiance of the government.*

defiant /dɪˈfaɪənt/ ADJ If you are **defiant**, you refuse to obey someone or you ignore their disapproval of you. ❑ *The newspaper remained defiant over its latest confrontation with the royals.* ● **defiantly** ADV ❑ *They defiantly rejected any talk of a compromise.*

deficiency /dɪˈfɪʃənsi/ (**deficiencies**) **1** N-VAR **Deficiency** in something, especially something that your body needs, is a lack of it. [FORMAL] ❑ *...a vitamin deficiency.* **2** N-VAR A **deficiency** is a weakness or imperfection in someone or something. [FORMAL] ❑ *...the deficiencies of the British transport system.*

deficient /dɪˈfɪʃənt/ **1** ADJ If someone or something is **deficient in** a particular thing, they do not have as much of it as they need. [FORMAL] ❑ *...a diet deficient in vitamin B.* **2** ADJ Something that is **deficient** is not good enough. [FORMAL] ❑ *...deficient equipment.*

deficit /ˈdefəsɪt/ (**deficits**) N-COUNT A **deficit** is the amount by which the money received by a country or organization is less than the money it has spent. ❑ *...Britain's trade deficit.*

define /dɪˈfaɪn/ (**defines, defining, defined**) V-T If you **define** something, you say exactly what it is or exactly what it means. ❑ *Her speech defined America's role in Europe.* ❑ *My dictionary defines morning as 'the first part of the day, ending at or about noon'.*

definite /ˈdefɪnɪt/ **1** ADJ If something is **definite**, it is firm and clear, and unlikely to be changed. ❑ *It's too soon to give a definite answer.* **2** ADJ **Definite** means true rather than being someone's opinion or guess. ❑ *The police had nothing definite against her.*

Thesaurus	*definite* Also look up:
ADJ.	clear-cut, distinct, precise, specific; (*ant.*) ambiguous, vague **1**

ˌdefinite ˈarticle (**definite articles**) N-COUNT In

d

grammar, the word 'the' is sometimes called **the definite article**.

definitely /'defɪnɪtli/ ADV You use **definitely** to emphasize that something is the case and will not change. ❑ *I definitely agree with you.*

definition /ˌdefɪ'nɪʃən/ (**definitions**) **1** N-COUNT A **definition** of a word or term is a statement giving its meaning, especially in a dictionary. **2** PHRASE If you say that something has a particular quality **by definition**, you mean that it has this quality simply because of what it is. ❑ *A low-fat diet is not by definition a healthy diet.* **3** N-UNCOUNT **Definition** is the quality of being clear and distinct. ❑ *Their foreign policy lacks definition.*

D

definitive /dɪ'fɪnɪtɪv/ **1** ADJ Something that is **definitive** provides a firm, unquestionable conclusion. ❑ *No one has come up with a definitive answer.* ● **definitively** ADV ❑ *She never definitively told the children that their father had left.* **2** ADJ A **definitive** book or performance is thought to be the best of its kind ever.

Word Link	*de ≈ from, down, away : deflate, descend, detach*

deflate /dɪ'fleɪt/ (**deflates, deflating, deflated**) **1** V-T If you **deflate** a person, you cause them to lose confidence. ● **deflated** ADJ ❑ *When she refused, I felt deflated.* **2** V-T/V-I When a tyre or balloon **deflates**, or when you **deflate** it, all the air comes out of it.

deflect /dɪ'flekt/ (**deflects, deflecting, deflected**) **1** V-T If you **deflect** something such as someone's attention, you cause them to turn their attention to something else or to do something different. ❑ *It won't deflect us from what we are doing.* **2** V-T If you **deflect** something that is moving, you make it go in a slightly different direction, for example by hitting it or pushing it. ❑ *The goalkeeper deflected the ball to safety with his knees.* ● **deflection** (**deflections**) N-VAR ❑ *Rangers scored in the 21st minute with the help of a deflection.*

deforestation /di:'fɒrɪs'teɪʃən, AM -'fɔ:r-/ N-UNCOUNT **Deforestation** is the cutting down of trees over a large area. ❑ *...the deforestation of the Amazon.*
→ see **greenhouse effect**

deform /dɪ'fɔ:m/ (**deforms, deforming, deformed**) V-T If something **deforms** something such as a person's body, it causes it to have an unnatural shape. ❑ *...people deformed by scars.* ● **deformed** ADJ ❑ *He was born with a deformed right leg.*

deformity /dɪ'fɔ:mɪti/ (**deformities**) **1** N-COUNT A **deformity** is a part of someone's body which is not the normal shape because of injury or illness, or because they were born that way. **2** N-UNCOUNT **Deformity** is the condition of having a deformity. ❑ *They said Dylan could suffer long-term deformity to his bones.*

defraud /dɪ'frɔ:d/ (**defrauds, defrauding, defrauded**) V-T If someone **defrauds** you, they use tricks or lies to take something away from you or stop you from getting something that belongs to you. ❑ *One doctor had defrauded the system of more than $80,000.*

deft /deft/ ADJ A **deft** action is skilful and often quick. [WRITTEN] ● **deftly** ADV ❑ *They deftly caught him as he fell off the step.*

defunct /dɪ'fʌŋkt/ ADJ If something is **defunct**, it no longer exists or it is no longer functioning. ❑ *...the now defunct Social Democratic Party.*

defuse /ˌdi:'fju:z/ (**defuses, defusing, defused**) **1** V-T If you **defuse** a dangerous or tense situation, you calm it. ❑ *These measures defused the crisis.* **2** V-T If someone **defuses** a bomb, they remove the fuse from it so that it cannot explode.

defy /dɪ'faɪ/ (**defies, defying, defied**) **1** V-T If you **defy** people or laws, you refuse to obey them. ❑ *Many people defied the ban on street trading.* **2** V-T If you **defy** someone **to** do something which you think is impossible, you challenge them to do it. ❑ *I defy anyone to go to Dublin and not find good music.* **3** V-T If something **defies** description or understanding, it is so strange or surprising that it is almost impossible to describe it or understand it. ❑ *In his eyes you will see a joy that defies all description.*

degenerate (**degenerates, degenerating, degenerated**) **1** V-I /dɪ'dʒenəreɪt/ To **degenerate** means to become worse. ❑ *The present unrest could degenerate into violence.* ● **degeneration** N-UNCOUNT ❑ *...the degeneration of our political system.* **2** ADJ & N-COUNT /dɪ'dʒenərət/ If you say that someone is **degenerate**, or if you say they are a **degenerate**, you think they show very low standards of morality.

degrade /dɪ'greɪd/ (**degrades, degrading, degraded**) V-T Something that **degrades** someone humiliates them and makes them feel they are not respected. ❑ *A queen will degrade herself by such behaviour.* ● **degrading** ADJ ❑ *...degrading treatment.* ● **degradation** /ˌdegrə'deɪʃən/ (**degradations**) N-VAR ❑ *She described the degradations she had suffered.*

degree /dɪ'gri:/ (**degrees**) **1** N-COUNT You use **degree** to indicate the extent to which something happens or is the case. ❑ *These barriers ensure a very high degree of protection.* **2** N-COUNT A **degree** is a unit of measurement for temperatures, angles, and longitude and latitude; often written as °, for example 23°. **3** N-COUNT A **degree** is a university qualification gained after completing a course of study there. ❑ *She has a degree in English.*
→ see **graduation, thermometer**

Word Partnership	Use *degree* with:
N.	degree **of certainty**, degree **of difficulty** **1**
	45/90 degree **angle** **2**
	bachelor's/master's degree, degree **program**, **university** degree **3**
ADJ.	**high** degree **1**
	honorary degree **3**

Word Link	*hydr ≈ water : dehydrate, carbohydrate, hydraulic*

Word Link	*ation ≈ state of : dehydration, elevation, preservation*

dehydrate /ˌdi:haɪ'dreɪt, -'haɪdreɪt/ (**dehydrates, dehydrating, dehydrated**) **1** V-T When food **is dehydrated**, all the water is removed from it. ❑ *Vitamin C is added to most brands of dehydrated potato.* **2** V-I If you **are dehydrated**, you feel ill because you have lost too much water from your body. ● **dehydration** N-UNCOUNT ❑ *I drank three litres of water a day to prevent dehydration.*

Word Link *dei, div ≈ God, god : deity, divine, divinity*

deity /'deɪɪtɪ, AM 'diː-/ (**deities**) N-COUNT A **deity** is a god or goddess. [FORMAL]

delay /dɪ'leɪ/ (**delays, delaying, delayed**) 1 V-T If you **delay** doing something, you do not do it until a later time. ❑ *He intends to delay his departure until next Sunday.* 2 V-T To **delay** someone or something means to make them late or slow them down. ❑ *Various problems delayed production.* 3 N-VAR If there is a **delay**, something does not happen until later than planned or expected. ❑ *This caused delays and disruption to flights.*

Thesaurus *delay* Also look up:
V. hold up, postpone, stall; *(ant.)* hurry, rush 1
N. interruption, lag; *(ant.)* rush 3

delegate (**delegates, delegating, delegated**) 1 N-COUNT /'delɪgət/ A **delegate** is a person chosen to vote or make decisions on behalf of a group of people, especially at a conference or meeting. 2 V-T /'delɪgeɪt/ If you **delegate** duties, responsibilities, or power **to** someone, you give them those duties or responsibilities or that power, so that they can act on your behalf.

delegation /ˌdelɪ'geɪʃən/ (**delegations**) N-COUNT A **delegation** is a group of people chosen to represent a larger group of people.

delete /dɪ'liːt/ (**deletes, deleting, deleted**) V-T If you **delete** something that has been written down or stored in a computer, you cross it out or remove it.

Thesaurus *delete* Also look up:
V. cut out, erase, remove

deli /'deli/ (**delis**) N-COUNT A **deli** is a shop or part of a shop that sells unusual or foreign foods. **Deli** is an abbreviation for 'delicatessen'.

deliberate (**deliberates, deliberating, deliberated**) 1 ADJ /dɪ'lɪbərət/ If something that you do is **deliberate**, you intended to do it. ❑ *I have no doubt that it was a deliberate attack.* ● **deliberately** ADV ❑ *The blaze was started deliberately.* 2 ADJ A **deliberate** action or movement is slow and careful. ● **deliberately** ADV ❑ *He spoke slowly and deliberately.* 3 V-I /dɪ'lɪbəreɪt/ If you **deliberate**, you think about something carefully before making a decision. ❑ *The jury deliberated for five days before it reached a verdict.*
→ see **trial**

deliberation /dɪˌlɪbə'reɪʃən/ (**deliberations**) 1 N-UNCOUNT **Deliberation** is careful consideration of a subject. ❑ *After much deliberation, the winners have been chosen.* 2 N-PLURAL **Deliberations** are formal discussions.

delicacy /'delɪkəsi/ (**delicacies**) N-COUNT 1 A **delicacy** is a rare or expensive food that is considered especially nice to eat. ❑ *...delicacies such as smoked salmon.* 2 → see also **delicate**

delicate /'delɪkət/ 1 ADJ Something that is **delicate** is narrow and graceful or attractive. ❑ *...her long, delicate nose.* ● **delicately** ADV ❑ *...a small and delicately formed chin.* ● **delicacy** N-UNCOUNT ❑ *...the delicacy of his features.* 2 ADJ A **delicate** colour, taste, or smell is pleasant and not intense. ❑ *Smoked trout has a delicate flavour.* ● **delicately** ADV ❑ *...a soup delicately flavoured with nutmeg.* 3 ADJ A **delicate** object is fragile and needs to be handled carefully. 4 ADJ Someone who is **delicate** is not healthy and strong, and becomes ill easily. ❑ *He was a delicate child.* 5 ADJ A **delicate** situation or problem needs very careful and tactful treatment. ❑ *...the delicate issue of adoption.* ● **delicately** ADV ❑ *...a delicately-worded memo.* ● **delicacy** N-UNCOUNT ❑ *...a matter of some delicacy.*

d

delicatessen /ˌdelɪkə'tesən/ (**delicatessens**) N-COUNT A **delicatessen** is a shop that sells unusual or foreign foods.

delicious /dɪ'lɪʃəs/ ADJ **Delicious** food or drink has an extremely pleasant taste. ● **deliciously** ADV ❑ *This yoghurt is deliciously creamy.*

delight /dɪ'laɪt/ (**delights, delighting, delighted**) 1 N-UNCOUNT **Delight** is a feeling of very great pleasure. ❑ *The little girls giggled with delight.* ❑ *To my great delight, it worked.* 2 N-COUNT You can refer to someone or something that gives you great pleasure as a **delight**. ❑ *The aircraft was a delight to fly.* 3 V-T If something **delights** you, it gives you a lot of pleasure. ❑ *Their style of music delighted audiences all over the world.* 4 V-I & PHRASE If you **delight in** something, especially doing something, or if you **take delight in** it, you get a lot of pleasure from it. ❑ *Fred delighted in showing visitors around.* ❑ *He took delight in proving his critics wrong.*

delighted /dɪ'laɪtɪd/ ADJ If you are **delighted**, you are extremely pleased and excited about something. ❑ *He was delighted with the public response.* ● **delightedly** ADV ❑ *She smiled delightedly at him.*

delightful /dɪ'laɪtfʊl/ ADJ Someone or something that is **delightful** is very pleasant. ❑ *...a most delightful woman.* ● **delightfully** ADV ❑ *...a delightfully mellow flavour.*

delinquent /dɪ'lɪŋkwənt/ (**delinquents**) N-COUNT & ADJ A **delinquent** is a young person who repeatedly commits minor crimes. You can also describe their behaviour as **delinquent**. ● **delinquency** N-UNCOUNT ❑ *He had no history of delinquency.*

delirious /dɪ'lɪəriəs/ 1 ADJ Someone who is **delirious** is unable to think or speak in a rational way, usually because they have a fever. 2 ADJ Someone who is **delirious** is extremely excited and happy. ❑ *I was delirious with joy.* ● **deliriously** ADV ❑ *The football fans went home deliriously happy.*

deliver /dɪ'lɪvə/ (**delivers, delivering, delivered**) 1 V-T If you **deliver** something somewhere, you take it there. ❑ *The Canadians plan to deliver more food to southern Somalia.* ❑ *We were told the pizza would be delivered in 20 minutes.* 2 V-T If you **deliver** a lecture or speech, you give it. 3 V-T When someone **delivers** a baby, they help the woman who is giving birth. 4 V-T If someone **delivers** a blow to someone else, they hit them. ❑ *Who would deliver a blow like this to anyone?*

Word Partnership	Use *deliver* with:
N.	deliver **a letter**, deliver **mail**, deliver **a message**, deliver **news**, deliver **a package**, deliver **a service** 1
	deliver **a lecture**, deliver **a speech** 2
	deliver **a baby** 3
	deliver **a blow** 4

D

delivery /dɪ'lɪvəri/ (**deliveries**) 1 N-UNCOUNT **Delivery** is the act of bringing of letters, parcels, or goods to someone's house or office. ❑ *Please allow 28 days for delivery.* 2 N-COUNT A **delivery of** letters or goods is an occasion when they are delivered. ❑ *I got a delivery of fresh eggs this morning.* 3 N-UNCOUNT Someone's **delivery** of a speech is the way in which they give it. ❑ *His speeches were well written but his delivery was hopeless.* 4 N-VAR **Delivery** is the process of giving birth to a baby. ❑ *In the end, it was an easy delivery: a fine baby boy.*

delta /'deltə/ (**deltas**) N-COUNT A **delta** is a triangle-shaped area of flat land, where a river spreads out into several smaller rivers before entering the sea.
→ see **land, river**

delude /dɪ'lu:d/ (**deludes, deluding, deluded**) V-T If you **delude** someone, you make them believe something that is not true. ❑ *We delude ourselves that we are in control.*

deluge /'delju:dʒ/ (**deluges, deluging, deluged**) 1 V-T & N-COUNT If you **are deluged with** things, or if you receive a **deluge of** things, a very large number of them arrive or happen at the same time. ❑ *His office was deluged with complaints.* ❑ *A deluge of magazines began to arrive in the post.* 2 N-COUNT & V-T A **deluge** is a sudden heavy fall of rain. You can say that rain **deluges** a place when it falls very heavily there.

delusion /dɪ'lu:ʒən/ (**delusions**) N-VAR A **delusion** is a false belief. ❑ *I was under the delusion that he intended to marry me.*

deluxe or **de luxe** /dɪ'lʌks/ ADJ BEFORE N **Deluxe** goods or services are better and more expensive than ordinary ones. ❑ *...a five-star deluxe hotel.*

delve /delv/ (**delves, delving, delved**) 1 V-I If you **delve into** a subject, you try to discover more about it. ❑ *Jenny delved into her mother's past.* 2 V-I If you **delve** inside something such as a bag, you search inside it. ❑ *She delved into her rucksack and pulled out a folder.*

demand /dɪ'mɑ:nd, -'mænd/ (**demands, demanding, demanded**) 1 V-T & N-COUNT If you **demand** something, or if you make a **demand for** something, you ask for it forcefully. ❑ *They demanded an explanation.* ❑ *We demanded that a police officer arrest them.* ❑ *They rejected their demands.* 2 PHRASE If something is available **on demand**, you can have it whenever you ask for it. 3 V-T If one thing **demands** another, the first needs the second in order to happen or be dealt with successfully. ❑ *The task of rebuilding demanded much patience.* 4 N-UNCOUNT & PHRASE If there is **demand for** something, a lot of people want it. You can also say that something or someone is **in demand**. ❑ *Demand for coal is down.* ❑ *He was in demand as a lecturer.* 5 N-COUNT You talk about the **demands of** something or someone, or their **demands on** you when you mean the things they require or want from you, which will take a lot of effort on your part. ❑ *...the demands and challenges of a new job.* ❑ *I had no right to make demands on his time.*

Thesaurus	*demand* Also look up:
V.	command, insist on, order; *(ant.)* give, grant, offer 1
	necessitate, need, require; *(ant.)* give, supply 3

demanding /dɪ'mɑ:ndɪŋ, -'mænd-/ 1 ADJ A **demanding** job requires a lot of time, energy, or attention. 2 ADJ Someone who is **demanding** always wants something and is not easily satisfied. ❑ *...a very demanding child.*

demean /dɪ'mi:n/ (**demeans, demeaning, demeaned**) V-T To **demean** someone or something means to make people have less respect for them. ❑ *Racism demeans all humanity.* ● **demeaning** ADJ ❑ *Addressing women as 'girls' is demeaning.*

demeanour [AM **demeanor**] /dɪ'mi:nə/ N-UNCOUNT Your **demeanour** is the way you behave, which gives people an impression of your character and feelings. [FORMAL] ❑ *...a cheerful demeanour.*

Word Link	*ment ≈ mind : demented, mental, mentality*

demented /dɪ'mentɪd/ 1 ADJ Someone who is **demented** is mentally ill. 2 ADJ If you describe someone as **demented**, you think that their actions are strange, foolish, or uncontrolled.

dementia /dɪ'menʃə/ (**dementias**) N-VAR **Dementia** is a disease of the brain which leads to a progressive loss of intellectual power and memory. [TECHNICAL] ❑ *...senile dementia.*

Word Link	*milit ≈ soldier : demilitarize, military, militia*

demilitarize [BRIT also **demilitarise**] /ˌdi:'mɪlɪtəraɪz/ (**demilitarizes, demilitarizing, demilitarized**) V-T To **demilitarize** an area means to remove all military forces from it.

demise /dɪ'maɪz/ N-SING **The demise of** something or someone is their end or death. [FORMAL] ❑ *This marked the demise of the reform movement.*

demo /'deməʊ/ (**demos**) N-COUNT A **demo** is a demonstration by a group of people to show their opposition to something or their support for something. [BRIT] ❑ *...an anti-racist demo.*

demobilize [BRIT also **demobilise**] /ˌdi:'məʊbɪlaɪz/ (**demobilizes, demobilizing, demobilized**) V-T/V-I If a country **demobilizes** its troops, or if its troops **demobilize**, they are released from service and go home. ● **demobilization** N-UNCOUNT ❑ *...the demobilisation of the army.*

Word Link	*cracy ≈ rule by : aristocracy, bureaucracy, democracy*

Word Link	*demo ≈ people : democracy, democratically, undemocratic*

democracy /dɪ'mɒkrəsi/ (**democracies**) 1 N-UNCOUNT **Democracy** is a political system in which people choose their government by voting for them in elections. **2** N-COUNT A **democracy** is a country in which the people choose their government by voting for it.

Word Link ***crat ≈ power : aristocrat, bureaucrat, democrat***

democrat /'deməkræt/ (**democrats**) N-COUNT A **democrat** is a person who believes in the ideals of democracy, personal freedom, and equality.

Word Link ***demo ≈ people : democracy, democratically, undemocratic***

democratic /ˌdemə'krætɪk/ **1** ADJ A **democratic** country, organization, or system is governed by representatives who are elected by the people. ● **democratically** ADV ❑ *...the country's first democratically elected President.* **2** ADJ Something that is **democratic** is based on the idea that everyone should have equal rights and should be involved in making important decisions. ❑ *We work in a very democratic way.* ● **democratically** ADV ❑ *Decisions are made democratically among this group, who meet every month.*

demolish /dɪ'mɒlɪʃ/ (**demolishes, demolishing, demolished**) **1** V-T When a building **is demolished**, it is knocked down, often because it is old or dangerous. ❑ *The storm demolished many buildings.* ● **demolition** /ˌdemə'lɪʃən/ (**demolitions**) N-VAR ❑ *The project required the demolition of the bridge.* **2** V-T If you **demolish** someone's idea, argument, or belief, you prove that it is completely wrong.

demon /'diːmən/ (**demons**) N-COUNT A **demon** is an evil spirit. ● **demonic** /dɪ'mɒnɪk/ ADJ ❑ *...a demonic grin.*

demonstrate /'demənstreɪt/ (**demonstrates, demonstrating, demonstrated**) **1** V-T To **demonstrate** a fact or theory means to make it clear to people. ❑ *Women's groups said the case demonstrated the law's bias against women.* ❑ *They are anxious to demonstrate to the voters that they have practical policies.* ● **demonstration** (**demonstrations**) N-COUNT ❑ *We want a demonstration of his cooking skills.* **2** V-T If you **demonstrate** a skill, quality, or feeling, you show that you have it. ❑ *He demonstrated his courage in the war.* **3** V-T If you **demonstrate** something to someone, you show them how to do it or how it works. ❑ *The new CD-ROM system was being demonstrated in the middle of a large hall.* ● **demonstration** N-COUNT ❑ *...a cookery demonstration.* **4** V-I When people **demonstrate**, they take part in a march or a meeting to show that they oppose or support something. ❑ *More than 10,000 people demonstrated against racism yesterday.* ● **demonstration** N-COUNT ❑ *Riot police broke up a demonstration this afternoon.* ● **demonstrator** (**demonstrators**) N-COUNT ❑ *...a crowd of demonstrators.*
→ see **citizenship**

Thesaurus *demonstrate* Also look up:

v. describe, illustrate, prove, show **1**
march, picket, protest **3** **4**

demoralize [BRIT also **demoralise**] /dɪ'mɒrəlaɪz, AM -'mɔːr-/ (**demoralizes, demoralizing, demoralized**) V-T If something **demoralizes** you, it makes you lose confidence and feel depressed. ● **demoralized** ADJ ❑ *...a demoralized police force.* ● **demoralizing** ADJ ❑ *Current salaries are demoralizing.* ● **demoralization** N-UNCOUNT ❑ *...the demoralization that followed defeat.*

demote /dɪ'məʊt/ (**demotes, demoting, demoted**) V-T If someone in authority **demotes** you, they lower your rank, often as a punishment. ● **demotion** (**demotions**) N-VAR ❑ *He faces demotion or even losing his job.*

den /den/ (**dens**) **1** N-COUNT A **den** is the home of certain types of wild animals such as foxes. **2** N-COUNT A **den** is a secret place where people meet, usually for a dishonest purpose. ❑ *It was a den of thieves.*

denial /dɪ'naɪəl/ (**denials**) **1** N-VAR A **denial of** something such as an accusation is a statement that it is not true, does not exist, or did not happen.. ❑ *I am amazed at your denial of responsibility for what happened.* **2** N-UNCOUNT If there is **denial of** something to someone, they are not allowed to have it. ❑ *...their denial of human rights.*

denigrate /'denɪgreɪt/ (**denigrates, denigrating, denigrated**) V-T If you **denigrate** someone or something, you criticize or insult them, damaging their reputation. [FORMAL] ❑ *We must not denigrate the beliefs of others.* ● **denigration** N-UNCOUNT ❑ *He wrote about his wife's constant denigration.*

denim /'denɪm/ N-UNCOUNT **Denim** is a thick cotton cloth used to make clothes. Jeans are made from denim.

denomination /dɪˌnɒmɪ'neɪʃən/ (**denominations**) **1** N-COUNT A **denomination** is a religious group which has slightly different beliefs from other groups within the same faith. **2** N-COUNT The **denomination** of a banknote or coin is its official value. ❑ *Denominations ranged from ten cents to $5.*

denote /dɪ'nəʊt/ (**denotes, denoting, denoted**) V-T If one thing **denotes** another, it is a sign or indication of it. [FORMAL] ❑ *Red eyes denote tiredness.*

Word Link ***nounce ≈ reporting : announce, denounce, pronounce***

denounce /dɪ'naʊns/ (**denounces, denouncing, denounced**) **1** V-T If you **denounce** someone or something, you criticize them severely and publicly. ❑ *The demonstrators denounced him as a traitor.* **2** → see also **denunciation**

dense /dens/ (**denser, densest**) **1** ADJ Something that is **dense** contains a lot of things or people in relation to its size. ❑ *...a dense forest.* ● **densely** ADV ❑ *...a densely populated island.* **2** ADJ **Dense** fog or smoke is thick and difficult to see through.

density /'densɪti/ (**densities**) **1** N-VAR The **density of** something is the extent to which it fills a place. ❑ *This law restricts the density of housing.* **2** N-VAR The **density** of a substance or object is the relation of its mass or weight to its volume.

dent

dent /dent/ (**dents, denting, dented**) **1** V-T If something **dents** your ideas or your pride, it makes you believe that you or your ideas are not as good as you thought. **2** V-T & N-COUNT If you **dent** something, you damage it by hitting or pressing it, causing a hollow dip to form in it. The hollow is called a **dent**. ❑ *There was a dent in the bonnet of the car.*

> **Word Link** ***dent, dont ≈ tooth : dental, dentist, dentures***

D

dental /'dentəl/ ADJ BEFORE N **Dental** is used to describe things relating to teeth. ❑ *...free dental treatment.*

dentist /'dentɪst/ (**dentists**) N-COUNT A **dentist** is a person qualified to treat people's teeth.
→ see **teeth**

dentures /'dentʃəz/

> The form **denture** is used as a modifier.

N-PLURAL **Dentures** are artificial teeth.
→ see **teeth**

denunciation /dɪˌnʌnsi'eɪʃən/ (**denunciations**) N-VAR A **denunciation of** someone or something is a severe public criticism of them.

deny /dɪ'naɪ/ (**denies, denying, denied**) **1** V-T If you **deny** something, you say that it is not true. ❑ *She denied both accusations.* ❑ *The government denied that anybody died during the war.* **2** V-T If you **deny** someone something, you do not let them have it. ❑ *His ex-partner denies him access to his children.*

> **Word Partnership** Use *deny* with:
>
> N. deny **a charge, officials** deny **1**
> deny **access**, deny **entry**, deny **a request** **2**
> V. **confirm or** deny **1**

deodorant /di'əʊdərənt/ (**deodorants**) N-VAR **Deodorant** is a substance that you put on your body to reduce or hide the smell of perspiration.

depart /dɪ'pɑːt/ (**departs, departing, departed**) V-I To **depart from** a place means to leave it and start a journey to another place. [FORMAL] ❑ *Our flight departs from Heathrow airport.*

department /dɪ'pɑːtmənt/ (**departments**) N-COUNT A **department** is one of the sections of a large shop or organization such as a university. ❑ *...Bloomingdale's cosmetics department.* ❑ *...the geography department of Moscow University.* ● **departmental** /ˌdiːpɑːt'mentəl/ ADJ BEFORE N ❑ *...the departmental budget.*

de'partment store (**department stores**) N-COUNT A **department store** is a large shop which sells many different kinds of goods.

departure /dɪ'pɑːtʃə/ (**departures**) **1** N-VAR **Departure** is the act of leaving a place or a job. ❑ *...the President's departure for Helsinki.* ❑ *...his departure from the post of Prime Minister.* **2** N-COUNT If an action is a **departure from** what was planned or what is usually done, it is different from it. ❑ *That decision is a major departure from previous policy.*

de'parture lounge (**departure lounges**) N-COUNT In an airport, the **departure lounge** is the place where passengers wait before they get onto their plane.

> **Word Link** ***pend ≈ hanging : depend, pendant, pending,***

depend /dɪ'pend/ (**depends, depending, depended**) **1** V-I If you say that one thing **depends on** another, you mean that the first thing will be affected or decided by the second. ❑ *The cooking time depends on the size of the potato.* **2** V-I & PHRASE You use **depends** in expressions such as **it depends** or **depending on** to indicate that you cannot give a clear answer to a question because other factors will affect the answer. ❑ *'How long can you stay here?'—'I don't know. It depends.'* **3** V-I If you **depend on** someone or something, you need them in order to be able to survive. ❑ *Their survival depends on him.* **4** V-I If you can **depend on** someone or something, you know that they will help you or support you when you need them. ❑ *You can depend on me.*

dependable /dɪ'pendəbəl/ ADJ If someone or something is **dependable**, you know that they will always do what you need or expect them to do. ❑ *...a faithful and dependable friend.*

> **Word Link** ***ant ≈ one who does, has : defendant, dependant, occupant***

dependant also **dependent** /dɪ'pendənt/ (**dependants**) N-COUNT Your **dependants** are the people whom you support financially, such as your children. ❑ *...a single man with no dependants.*

> **Word Link** ***ent ≈ one who does, has : dependent, resident, superintendent***

> **Word Link** ***ence ≈ state, condition : dependence, excellence, independence***

dependent /dɪ'pendənt/ ADJ AFTER LINK-V To be **dependent on** someone or something means to need them in order to succeed or be able to survive. ❑ *Britain became increasingly dependent on American technology.* ● **dependence** N-UNCOUNT ❑ *...the country's total dependence on the oil industry.* ● **dependency** N-UNCOUNT ❑ *We need to understand the dependency that comes with old age.*

> **Word Link** ***pict ≈ painting : depict, picture, picturesque***

depict /dɪ'pɪkt/ (**depicts, depicting, depicted**) V-T To **depict** someone or something means to represent them in drawing, painting, or writing. ❑ *The pictures depict famous naval battles.* ● **depiction** (**depictions**) N-VAR ❑ *...their depiction in the book as thieves.*
→ see **art**

> **Word Link** ***ple ≈ filling : complement, complete, deplete***

deplete /dɪ'pliːt/ (**depletes, depleting, depleted**) V-T To **deplete** a stock or amount of something means to reduce it, usually to a very low level. ❑ *...substances that deplete the ozone layer.* ● **depleted** ADJ ❑ *...Robert E. Lee's worn and depleted army.* ● **depletion** N-UNCOUNT ❑ *...the depletion of water supplies.*

deplorable /dɪ'plɔːrəbəl/ ADJ If you say that something is **deplorable**, you mean that it is extremely bad or unpleasant. [FORMAL] ❑ *...deplorable living conditions.*

deplore /dɪ'plɔː/ (**deplores, deploring, deplored**) V-T If you **deplore** something, you think it is wrong or immoral. [FORMAL] ❑ *He deplores violence.*

deploy /dɪ'plɔɪ/ (**deploys, deploying, deployed**) V-T To **deploy** troops or resources means to organize or position them so that they are ready to be used. ● **deployment** N-UNCOUNT ❑ *...the deployment of extra forces in the area.*
→ see **army**

deport /dɪ'pɔːt/ (**deports, deporting, deported**) V-T If a government **deports** someone, it sends them out of the country. ❑ *These football fans are being deported from Italy.* ● **deportation** (**deportations**) N-VAR ❑ *They face deportation.*

depose /dɪ'pəʊz/ (**deposes, deposing, deposed**) V-T If a ruler or political leader **is deposed**, they are forced to give up their position. ● **deposition** /ˌdepə'zɪʃən/ N-UNCOUNT ❑ *...the deposition of the king.*

Word Link	***pos ≈ placing : deposit, preposition, repository***

deposit /dɪ'pɒzɪt/ (**deposits, depositing, deposited**) **1** N-COUNT A **deposit** is a sum of money given as part payment for something, or as security when you rent something. ❑ *A £50 deposit is required when ordering.* ❑ *She wanted the extra money as the deposit for a house.* **2** V-T & N-COUNT If you **deposit** a sum of money into your bank account, or if you put a **deposit** in your account, you pay a sum of money into a bank account or other savings account. ❑ *The customer has to deposit a minimum of £100 monthly.* **3** N-COUNT & V-T A **deposit** is an amount of a substance that has been left somewhere as a result of a natural or chemical process. You say the substance has been **deposited** there. ❑ *...underground deposits of gold and diamonds.*

depot /'depəʊ, AM 'diː-/ (**depots**) **1** N-COUNT A **depot** is a place where large amounts of raw materials, equipment, or other supplies are kept. ❑ *...a government arms depot.* **2** N-COUNT A **depot** is a large building or yard where buses or railway engines are kept when they are not being used. **3** N-COUNT A **depot** is a bus station or a railway station.

depreciate /dɪ'priːʃieɪt/ (**depreciates, depreciating, depreciated**) V-T/V-I If something such as currency **depreciates**, or if something **depreciates** it, it loses some of its original value. ❑ *The pound depreciated by 25 per cent.* ● **depreciation** (**depreciations**) N-VAR ❑ *Car depreciation is as high as 20% per annum.*

depress /dɪ'pres/ (**depresses, depressing, depressed**) **1** V-T If someone or something **depresses** you, they make you feel sad and disappointed. ❑ *The state of the country depresses me.* **2** V-T If something **depresses** prices, wages, or figures, it causes them to become less. ❑ *The stronger U.S. dollar depressed sales.*

depressed /dɪ'prest/ **1** ADJ If you are **depressed**, you are sad and feel you cannot enjoy anything, because your situation is difficult and unpleasant. ❑ *He seemed depressed when he heard the news.* **2** ADJ A **depressed** place or industry does not have enough business or employment to be prosperous. ❑ *The construction industry is depressed.*

depressing /dɪ'presɪŋ/ ADJ Something that is **depressing** makes you feel sad and disappointed. ❑ *The hospital was a very depressing place to be.* ● **depressingly** ADV ❑ *It all sounded depressingly familiar.*

depression /dɪ'preʃən/ (**depressions**) **1** N-VAR **Depression** is a mental state in which someone feels unhappy and has no energy or enthusiasm. ❑ *...suffering from depression.* ❑ *I fell into a depression.* **2** N-COUNT A **depression** is a time when there is very little economic activity, which results in a lot of unemployment and poverty. **3** N-COUNT A **depression** in a surface is an area which is lower than the parts surrounding it.

deprive /dɪ'praɪv/ (**deprives, depriving, deprived**) V-T If you **deprive** someone **of** something that they want or need, you take it away from them or prevent them from having it. ❑ *She was deprived of her passport.* ● **deprived** ADJ ❑ *...a deprived inner city area.* ● **deprivation** /ˌdeprɪ'veɪʃən/ (**deprivations**) N-VAR ❑ *Sleep deprivation is seriously affecting my work.*

dept **Dept** is a written abbreviation for 'department'.

depth /depθ/ (**depths**) **1** N-VAR The **depth** of something such as a hole is the distance between its top and bottom surfaces. ❑ *The water was 12 to 18 inches in depth.* **2** N-VAR The **depth** of a solid structure is the distance between its front surface and its back. **3** N-UNCOUNT If an emotion is very strongly felt, you can talk about its **depth**. ❑ *I am aware of the depth of your feelings on this subject.* **4** N-PLURAL **The depths of** an area are the parts of it which are very remote. ❑ *...somewhere in the depths of the forest.* **5** N-PLURAL **The depths of** something difficult or unpleasant are the middle and most severe or intense parts of it. ❑ *...the depths of a recession.* ❑ *...the depths of winter.* ❑ *I was in the depths of despair.* **6** PHRASE If you deal with a subject **in depth**, you consider all the aspects of it thoroughly. ❑ *...an in-depth investigation.* **7** PHRASE If you say that someone is **out of** their **depth**, you mean that they are in a situation that is much too difficult for them to be able to cope with it.

deputy /'depjʊti/ (**deputies**) N-COUNT A **deputy** is the second most important person in an organization or department. Someone's deputy often acts on their behalf when they are absent. ❑ *...the academy's deputy director.*

derail /ˌdiː'reɪl/ (**derails, derailing, derailed**) V-T/V-I If a train **is derailed**, or if it **derails**, it comes off the track on which it is running. ● **derailment** (**derailments**) N-VAR ❑ *Rail services have been suspended because of a derailment.*

deranged /dɪ'reɪndʒd/ ADJ Someone who is **deranged** behaves in a wild or strange way, often as a result of mental illness. ❑ *A deranged man shot 14 people.*

derelict /'derɪlɪkt/ ADJ A **derelict** place is empty and in a bad condition because it has not been used or lived in for a long time. ❑ *...a derelict warehouse.*

Word Link	***rid, ris ≈ laughing : deride, derision, ridicule***

deride /dɪ'raɪd/ (**derides, deriding, derided**) V-T If you **deride** someone or something, you say they are stupid or have no value. [FORMAL] ❑ *Other countries are derided for selling arms to the enemy.* ● **derision** /dɪ'rɪʒən/ N-UNCOUNT ❑ *He tried to calm*

d

them, but was greeted with shouts of derision.

derivative /dɪ'rɪvətɪv/ (**derivatives**) 1 N-COUNT A **derivative** is something which has been developed or obtained from something else. ❑ *...a derivative of sugar cane.* 2 ADJ If you say that something is **derivative**, you are criticizing it because it is not new or original but has been developed from something else. ❑ *Her style was derivative, though only of the best artists.*

D

derive /dɪ'raɪv/ (**derives, deriving, derived**) 1 V-T If you **derive** something such as pleasure or benefit **from** someone or something, you get it from them. ❑ *He derives pleasure from helping others.* 2 V-T/V-I If something **derives** or **is derived from** something else, it comes from that thing. ❑ *The word 'salad' is derived from the Roman word for salt.*

Word Link *de ≈ from, down, away : deflate, descend, detach*

Word Link *scend ≈ climbing : ascend, condescend, descend*

descend /dɪ'send/ (**descends, descending, descended**) 1 V-I/V-T If you **descend**, or if you **descend** something, you move downwards. [FORMAL] ❑ *We descended the stairs to the cellar.* 2 V-I If a mood **descends** somewhere, it starts to affect the people there. ❑ *An uneasy calm descended on the area.* 3 V-I If people **descend on** a place, a lot of them arrive there suddenly. ❑ *Reporters from around the globe descended on the villages.*

descendant /dɪ'sendənt/ (**descendants**) N-COUNT Someone's **descendants** are the people in later generations who are related to them.

descended /dɪ'sendɪd/ ADJ AFTER LINK-V A person who is **descended from** someone who lived a long time ago is directly related to them. ❑ *She was descended from a member of the royal family.*

descent /dɪ'sent/ (**descents**) 1 N-VAR A **descent** is a movement from a higher to a lower level. ❑ *The airliner began its descent.* 2 N-COUNT A **descent** is a surface that slopes downwards, for example the side of a steep hill. 3 N-UNCOUNT You use **descent** to talk about a person's family background, for example their nationality or social status. ❑ *All the contributors were of African descent.*

describe /dɪ'skraɪb/ (**describes, describing, described**) 1 V-T If you **describe** someone or something, you say what they are like. ❑ *We asked her to describe what she did in her spare time.* ❑ *This poem describes their life together.* 2 V-T If you **describe** someone or something **as** a particular thing, you say that they are like that thing. ❑ *They described themselves as liberals.*

Usage

When you use **describe** with an indirect object, you must put **to** in front of the indirect object. ❑ *He later described to me what he had found...* ❑ *Could you describe the man to the police?* You do not say, for example, 'He described me what he had found'.

description /dɪ'skrɪpʃən/ (**descriptions**) 1 N-VAR A **description of** someone or something is a statement which explains what they are or what they look like. ❑ *Each disc has a short description of the music on it.* 2 N-SING If someone or something is **of** a particular **description**, they are a particular type of person or thing. ❑ *He was an artist of some description.*

Thesaurus *description* Also look up:

N.	account, characterization, summary 1 category, class, kind, type 2

Word Partnership Use *description* with:

ADJ.	**accurate** description, **brief** description, **detailed** description, **physical** description, **vague** description 1
V.	**fit a** description, **give a** description, **match a** description 1

descriptive /dɪ'skrɪptɪv/ ADJ **Descriptive** language indicates what something is like. ❑ *The poem is very descriptive.*

desecrate /'desɪkreɪt/ (**desecrates, desecrating, desecrated**) V-T If someone **desecrates** something considered sacred or special, they deliberately damage or insult it. ● **desecration** N-UNCOUNT ❑ *...the desecration of the cemetery.*

desert (**deserts, deserting, deserted**) 1 N-VAR /'dezət/ A **desert** is a large area of land, usually in a hot region, which has almost no water, rain, trees, or plants. 2 V-T /dɪ'zɜːt/ If people **desert** a place, they leave it and it becomes empty. ❑ *A number of fishermen deserted the port of St Malo.* ● **deserted** ADJ ❑ *...a deserted side street.* 3 V-T If someone **deserts** you, they leave you and no longer help or support you. ❑ *Mrs Roding's husband deserted her years ago.* ● **desertion** (**desertions**) N-VAR ❑ *She felt alone after her father's desertion.* 4 V-I If someone **deserts** from the armed forces, they leave without permission. ● **desertion** N-VAR ❑ *Two soldiers face charges of desertion.* ● **deserter** (**deserters**) N-COUNT ❑ *...a young army deserter.*

→ see Picture Dictionary: **desert**
→ see **habitat**

deserve /dɪ'zɜːv/ (**deserves, deserving, deserved**) V-T If you say that someone **deserves** something, you mean that they should have it or do it because of their qualities or actions. ❑ *'He deserved to suffer,' said Penelope angrily.* ❑ *Every patient deserves better care.*

Word Partnership Use *deserve* with:

N.	deserve **a chance**, deserve **credit**, deserve **recognition**, deserve **respect**
V.	**don't** deserve, deserve **to know**
PRON.	deserve **nothing**

deserving /dɪ'zɜːvɪŋ/ ADJ If you describe a person or organization as **deserving**, you think they should be helped. [FORMAL] ❑ *This money could be used for more deserving causes.*

design /dɪ'zaɪn/ (**designs, designing, designed**) 1 V-T & N-UNCOUNT When you **design** something new, or when you are responsible for its **design**, you plan what it should be like. ❑ *He asked me to design the restaurant.* ❑ *The plan is designed to reduce the company's debt.* ❑ *...a new design of clock.* 2 N-UNCOUNT The **design of** something is the way in which it has been planned and made. ❑ *...a new design of clock.* 3 N-COUNT A **design** is a drawing

which someone produces to show how they would like something to be built or made. ❑ *...his design for a new office tower.* **4** N-COUNT A **design** is a decorative pattern of lines or shapes. ❑ *...swirling leaf designs.*
→ see **architecture, quilt**

designate /'dezɪgneɪt/ (**designates, designating, designated**) **1** V-T When you **designate** something or someone **as** a particular thing, you formally give them a description or name. ❑ *The area has been designated a national park.* ❑ *Designate someone as the spokesperson.* ● **designation** (**designations**) N-VAR ❑ *...the designation of Madrid as European City of Culture.* **2** V-T If something **is designated** for a particular purpose, it is set aside for that purpose. ❑ *Dogs are allowed only in designated areas.*

designer /dɪ'zaɪnə/ (**designers**) **1** N-COUNT A **designer** is a person whose job involves planning the form of a new object. ❑ *...a fashion designer.* **2** ADJ BEFORE N **Designer** clothes are expensive fashionable clothes created by a famous designer.

de,signer 'baby (**designer babies**) N-COUNT People use the term **designer baby** to refer to a baby that has developed from an embryo with certain desired characteristics.

desirable /dɪ'zaɪərəbəl/ **1** ADJ Something that is **desirable** is worth having or doing. ❑ *This home is in a very desirable area.* ● **desirability** N-UNCOUNT ❑ *The article is about the desirability of a new recycling program.* **2** ADJ Someone who is **desirable** is sexually attractive.

desire /dɪ'zaɪə/ (**desires, desiring, desired**) **1** V-T & N-COUNT If you **desire** something, or if you have a **desire for** it, you want it. [FORMAL] ❑ *I had a strong desire to help and care for people.* ❑ *They seem to have lost their desire for life.* ● **desired** ADJ ❑ *His warnings have provoked the desired response.* **2** V-T & N-UNCOUNT If you **desire** someone, or if you feel **desire** for them, you want to have sex with them.

Word Partnership Use *desire* with:

N.	**heart's** desire **1**
ADJ.	**strong** desire **1** **2**
	sexual desire **2**
V.	desire **to change** **1**
	have no desire, **satisfy a** desire **1** **2**
	express desire **2**

desk /desk/ (**desks**) N-COUNT A **desk** is a table which you sit at in order to write or work.
→ see **office**

desktop /'desktɒp/ (**desktops**) **1** N-COUNT The **desktop** of a computer is the display of icons that you see on the screen when the computer is ready to use. [COMPUTING] **2** N-COUNT A **desktop** or a **desktop computer** is a computer that is small enough to fit onto a desk but too big to carry around with you.

desolate /'desələt/ **1** ADJ A **desolate** place is empty and lacking in comfort. **2** ADJ If someone is **desolate**, they feel very lonely and depressed.

desolation /,desə'leɪʃən/ **1** N-UNCOUNT The **desolation** of a place is its depressing emptiness. ❑ *...a scene of desolation and ruin.* **2** ADJ **Desolation** is a feeling of great unhappiness. ❑ *...an overwhelming sense of desolation.*

despair /dɪ'speə/ (**despairs, despairing, despaired**) **1** V-I & N-UNCOUNT If you **despair**, or if you feel **despair**, you feel that everything is wrong and that nothing will improve. ❑ *She despaired at the thought of spending her life here.* ❑ *I looked at my wife in despair.* **2** V-I If you **despair of** something, you feel that there is no hope that it will happen or improve. ❑ *They despaired of ever having a family of their own.*

despatch /dɪ'spætʃ/ → see **dispatch**

D

Word Link *sper ≈ hope : desperate, exasperate, prosperity*

desperate /ˈdespərət/ **1** ADJ If you are **desperate**, you are in such a bad situation that you will try anything to change it. ❑ *...a desperate attempt to hijack a plane.* ❑ *Many refugees were desperate to leave.* ● **desperately** ADV ❑ *I tried desperately to help him.* **2** ADJ AFTER LINK-V If you are **desperate for** something or **desperate to** do something, you want to have it or do it very much. ❑ *People are desperate for him to do something.* ● **desperately** ADV ❑ *The boy desperately needed affection.*

Word Partnership Use *desperate* with:

N. desperate **act**, desperate **attempt**, desperate **measures**, desperate **need**, desperate **situation**, desperate **struggle** **1**
V. **sound** desperate **1**
grow desperate **2**

desperation /ˌdespəˈreɪʃən/ N-UNCOUNT **Desperation** is the feeling that you have when you are in such a bad situation that you will try anything to change it. ❑ *...acts of sheer desperation.*

despicable /dɪˈspɪkəbəl, AM ˈdespɪk-/ ADJ If you say that a person or action is **despicable**, you are emphasizing that they are extremely nasty or cruel. ❑ *...a despicable crime.*

despise /dɪˈspaɪz/ (**despises, despising, despised**) V-T If you **despise** someone or something, you hate them very much. ❑ *I despised myself for my cowardly behaviour.*

despite /dɪˈspaɪt/ PREP You use **despite** to introduce a fact which makes the other part of the sentence surprising. ❑ *Despite a bad choice of school, Elaine got enough qualifications to go to university.*

dessert /dɪˈzɜːt/ (**desserts**) N-VAR **Dessert** is something sweet, such as fruit or a pudding, that you eat at the end of a meal. ❑ *She had ice cream for dessert.*
→ see Picture Dictionary: **dessert**

Word Link *stab ≈ steady : destabilize, establish, instability*

destabilize [BRIT also **destabilise**] /diːˈsteɪbəlaɪz/ (**destabilizes, destabilizing, destabilized**) V-T To **destabilize** something such as a country or government means to create a situation which reduces its power or influence. ❑ *Their aim is to destabilize the government.*

destination /ˌdestɪˈneɪʃən/ (**destinations**) N-COUNT Your **destination** is the place you are going to. ❑ *His preferred holiday destination is Hawaii.*

destined /ˈdestɪnd/ ADJ AFTER LINK-V If something is **destined to** happen, or if someone is **destined to** do something, that thing will definitely happen. ❑ *He was destined to become a musician.* ❑ *Muriel was destined for great things.*

destiny /ˈdestɪni/ (**destinies**) **1** N-COUNT A person's **destiny** is everything that happens to them during their life, including what will happen in the future. **2** N-UNCOUNT **Destiny** is the force which some people believe controls the things that happen to you. ❑ *It is destiny that brings people together.*

destitute /ˈdestɪtjuːt, AM -tuːt/ ADJ Someone who is **destitute** has no money or possessions. [FORMAL] ❑ *...destitute people living on the streets.*

destroy /dɪˈstrɔɪ/ (**destroys, destroying, destroyed**) V-T To **destroy** something means to cause so much damage to it that it is completely ruined or does not exist any more. ❑ *The building was completely destroyed.* ❑ *He destroyed my confidence.* ● **destruction** /dɪˈstrʌkʃən/ N-UNCOUNT ❑ *...the destruction of the ozone layer.*

Thesaurus *destroy* Also look up:

V. annihilate, crush, demolish, eradicate, ruin, wipe out; *(ant.)* build, construct, create, repair

Word Link *struct ≈ building : construct, destructive, instruct*

destructive /dɪˈstrʌktɪv/ ADJ Something that is **destructive** causes or is capable of causing great damage, harm, or injury. ❑ *...the destructive power of nuclear weapons.* ❑ *Guilt can be very destructive.*

Word Link *de ≈ from, down, away : deflate, descend, detach*

detach /dɪˈtætʃ/ (**detaches, detaching, detached**) V-T/V-I If you **detach** one thing **from** another that it is fixed to, you remove it. If one thing **detaches from** another, it becomes separated from it. ❑ *Detach the grapes from the stalks.* ❑ *The white part of the application form had detached from the rest.*

Picture Dictionary **dessert**

detached /dɪˈtætʃt/ **1** ADJ Someone who is **detached** is not emotionally or personally involved in something. ❑ *He tries to remain emotionally detached from the prisoners.* **2** ADJ A **detached house** is not joined to any other house.

detachment /dɪˈtætʃmənt/ N-UNCOUNT **Detachment** is a feeling of not being emotionally or personally involved in something. ❑ *She has developed a sense of professional detachment.*

detail /ˈdiːteɪl/ (**details, detailing, detailed**) **1** N-VAR The **details of** something are its small, individual features or elements. If you examine or discuss something **in detail**, you examine all these features. ❑ *...the details of a peace agreement.* ❑ *I recall every detail of the party.* ❑ *...his attention to detail.* **2** N-PLURAL **Details** about something are items of information about it. ❑ *See below for details of how to apply.* **3** V-T If you **detail** things, you list them or give full information about them. [FORMAL] ❑ *The report detailed human rights abuses.*

Thesaurus	*detail* Also look up:
N.	component, element, feature, point **1** fact, information **3**
V.	depict, describe, specify; *(ant.)* approximate, generalize **3**

detailed /ˈdiːteɪld, AM dɪˈteɪld/ ADJ A **detailed** report or plan contains a lot of details. ❑ *...a detailed account of the decisions.*

Word Partnership	Use *detailed* with:
N.	detailed **account**, detailed **analysis**, detailed **description**, detailed **instructions**, detailed **plan**, detailed **record**

detain /dɪˈteɪn/ (**detains, detaining, detained**) **1** V-T When people such as the police **detain** someone, they keep them in a place under their control. ❑ *The police can detain a suspect for up to 48 hours.* **2** V-T To **detain** someone means to delay them, for example by talking to them. [FORMAL] ❑ *Thank you. We won't detain you any further.*

Word Link	***ee ≈ one who receives : detainee, nominee, refugee***

detainee /ˌdiːteɪˈniː/ (**detainees**) N-COUNT A **detainee** is someone who is being held prisoner by a government or being held by the police.

Word Link	***tect ≈ covering : detect, protect, protective***

detect /dɪˈtekt/ (**detects, detecting, detected**) V-T If you **detect** something, you find it or notice it. ❑ *...equipment used to detect radiation.* ❑ *Arnold detected sadness in the old man's face.* ● **detection** N-UNCOUNT ❑ *Early detection of breast cancer is vital.*

detective /dɪˈtektɪv/ (**detectives**) N-COUNT A **detective** is someone whose job is to discover the facts about a crime or other situation.

detector /dɪˈtektə/ (**detectors**) N-COUNT A **detector** is an instrument which is used to find or measure something. ❑ *...smoke detectors.*

detente also **détente** /deɪˈtɒnt/ N-UNCOUNT **Detente** is a state of friendly relations between two countries when previously there had been problems between them. [FORMAL] ❑ *...a policy of detente.*

detention /dɪˈtenʃən/ (**detentions**) N-VAR **Detention** is the arrest or imprisonment of someone, especially for political reasons. ❑ *After 17 months in detention, he was eventually put on trial.*

deter /dɪˈtɜː/ (**deters, deterring, deterred**) V-T To **deter** someone **from** doing something means to make them not want to do it. ❑ *This deterred criminals from carrying guns.* ❑ *Tougher sentences would do nothing to deter crime.*

detergent /dɪˈtɜːdʒənt/ (**detergents**) N-VAR **Detergent** is a chemical substance used for washing things such as clothes or dishes.
→ see **soap**

deteriorate /dɪˈtɪəriəreɪt/ (**deteriorates, deteriorating, deteriorated**) V-I If something **deteriorates**, it becomes worse. ❑ *Grant's health steadily deteriorated.* ● **deterioration** N-UNCOUNT ❑ *...a deterioration in working conditions.*

determination /dɪˌtɜːmɪˈneɪʃən/ N-UNCOUNT **Determination** is the quality that you show when you have decided to do something and you will not let anything stop you. ❑ *...the government's determination to beat inflation.*

Word Link	***term, termin ≈ limit, end : determine, terminal, terminate***

determine /dɪˈtɜːmɪn/ (**determines, determining, determined**) **1** V-T If something **determines** what will happen, it controls it. ❑ *The size of the chicken pieces will determine the cooking time.* ● **determination** N-UNCOUNT ❑ *Genes are important in the determination of body weight and size.* **2** V-T To **determine** something means to discover it or discover the facts about it. ❑ *The investigation will determine what really happened.* ❑ *I wanted to determine what to do next.* ● **determination** N-UNCOUNT ❑ *These facts were essential to the determination of guilt.*

determined /dɪˈtɜːmɪnd/ ADJ If you are **determined to** do something, you have made a firm decision to do it and will not let anything stop you. ❑ *His enemies are determined to ruin him.* ❑ *England made several determined efforts to score.* ● **determinedly** ADV ❑ *She shook her head, determinedly.*

determiner /dɪˈtɜːmɪnə/ (**determiners**) N-COUNT In grammar, a **determiner** is a word such as 'the' or 'my' that is used before a noun to indicate which particular thing or person you are referring to.

deterrent /dɪˈterənt, AM -ˈtɜːr-/ (**deterrents**) N-COUNT & ADJ BEFORE N A **deterrent**, or something that has a **deterrent** effect, is something that prevents people from doing something by making them afraid of what will happen to them if they do. ❑ *They believe that capital punishment is a deterrent.* ● **deterrence** N-UNCOUNT ❑ *...nuclear deterrence.*

detest /dɪˈtest/ (**detests, detesting, detested**) V-T If you **detest** someone or something, you dislike them very much. ❑ *Jean detested being photographed.*

detonate /ˈdetəneɪt/ (**detonates, detonating, detonated**) V-T/V-I If someone **detonates** a bomb, or if it **detonates**, it explodes. ● **detonation** (**detonations**) N-VAR ❑ *...accidental detonation of nuclear weapons.*

D

detour /'di:tʊə/ (**detours**) N-COUNT If you **make** a **detour** on a journey, you go by a route which is not the shortest way.

detract /dɪ'trækt/ (**detracts, detracting, detracted**) V-I If one thing **detracts from** another, it makes it seem less good or less impressive. ❑ *Even Sarah's rude comments could not detract from the excitement Meg felt.*

detriment /'detrɪmənt/ PHRASE If something happens **to the detriment of** something or someone, it causes them harm or damage. [FORMAL] ❑ *These tests give too much importance to written exams to the detriment of other skills.*

detrimental /ˌdetrɪ'mentəl/ ADJ Something that is **detrimental to** something else has a harmful or damaging effect on it. ❑ *Many foods are detrimental to health.* ❑ *The experts emphasized the detrimental effects of these drugs.*

devalue /ˌdi:'vælju:/ (**devalues, devaluing, devalued**) **1** V-T To **devalue** something means to cause it to be thought less important or less worthy of respect. ❑ *They spread tales about her in an attempt to devalue her work.* **2** V-T To **devalue** the currency of a country means to reduce its value in relation to other currencies. ● **devaluation** (**devaluations**) N-VAR ❑ *...the devaluation of the dollar.*

devastate /'devəsteɪt/ (**devastates, devastating, devastated**) V-T If something **devastates** a place, it damages it very badly or destroys it. ❑ *A fire devastated large parts of the building.* ● **devastation** N-UNCOUNT ❑ *A huge bomb blast brought chaos and devastation.*

devastated /'devəsteɪtɪd/ ADJ AFTER LINK-V If you are **devastated** by something, you are very shocked and upset by it.

devastating /'devəsteɪtɪŋ/ ADJ You describe something as **devastating** when it is very damaging or upsetting. ❑ *Affairs have a devastating effect on marriages.* ❑ *The diagnosis was devastating. She had cancer.*

develop /dɪ'veləp/ (**develops, developing, developed**) **1** V-I/V-T When someone or something **develops**, or when someone **develops** something, the person or thing grows or changes over a period of time and usually becomes more advanced or complete. ❑ *He has written extensively on how children develop, grow and learn.* ❑ *Most of these settlements developed from agricultural centres.* ❑ *These clashes could develop into open warfare.* ❑ *We must develop closer ties with Germany.* ● **development** N-UNCOUNT ❑ *...the development of the embryo.* **2** V-T If someone **develops** something such as a habit or illness, they begin to have it. ❑ *She developed a taste for expensive clothes.* ❑ *Four years ago she developed breast cancer.* **3** V-T If someone **develops** a new product, they design it and produce it. ❑ *He claims that several countries have secretly developed nuclear weapons.* ● **developer** (**developers**) N-COUNT ❑ *...a software developer.* ● **development** (**developments**) N-VAR ❑ *...investment in product development.* **4** V-I When a country **develops**, it changes from being a poor agricultural country to a rich industrial country. ● **developed** ADJ ❑ *...the developed nations.* **5** V-T To **develop** an area of land means to build houses or factories on it to make it more useful or profitable. ❑ *...the cost of acquiring or developing property.* ● **developer** N-COUNT ❑ *...property developers.* ● **development** N-UNCOUNT ❑ *...the fostering of development in the rural areas.* **6** V-T When a photographic film **is developed**, prints or negatives are made from it.
→ see **photography**

developing /dɪ'veləpɪŋ/ ADJ BEFORE N If you talk about **developing** countries or **the developing world**, you mean the countries or the parts of the world that are poor and have little industry.

development /dɪ'veləpmənt/ (**developments**) **1** N-COUNT A **development** is an event which is likely to have an effect on a situation. ❑ *...the latest developments in Moscow.* **2** N-COUNT A **development** is an area of houses or buildings which have been built by property developers.

deviant /'di:viənt/ (**deviants**) N-COUNT & ADJ A **deviant** or someone who shows **deviant** behaviour behaves in a way that is different from what is normally considered to be acceptable. ❑ *Today we find excuses for any kind of deviant behaviour – usually medical.* ● **deviance** N-UNCOUNT ❑ *...social deviance.*

deviate /'di:vieɪt/ (**deviates, deviating, deviated**) V-I To **deviate from** a plan or **from** a usual way of behaving means not to behave in the planned or usual way. ❑ *He planned his schedule far in advance, and he didn't deviate from it.* ● **deviation** (**deviations**) N-VAR ❑ *Deviation from the norm is not tolerated.*

device /dɪ'vaɪs/ (**devices**) **1** N-COUNT A **device** is an object that has been made for a particular purpose. ❑ *...a timer device for a bomb.* **2** N-COUNT A **device** is a method of achieving something. ❑ *...a device to force Mr Neill into negotiating.* **3** PHRASE If you **leave** someone **to** their **own devices**, you leave them alone to do as they wish.

devil /'devəl/ (**devils**) **1** N-PROPER In Christianity, Judaism, and Islam, **the Devil** is the most powerful evil spirit. **2** N-COUNT A **devil** is an evil spirit. **3** N-COUNT You can use **devil** when showing how you feel about someone. For example, you can call someone 'a poor devil' to show that you feel sorry for them. [INFORMAL]

devious /'di:viəs/ ADJ A **devious** person does dishonest things in a clever complicated way. ❑ *You have a very devious mind.*

devise /dɪ'vaɪz/ (**devises, devising, devised**) V-T If you **devise** something, you have the idea for it and design it. ❑ *We devised a plan.*

devoid /dɪ'vɔɪd/ ADJ AFTER LINK-V If you say that someone or something is **devoid of** a quality or thing, you are emphasizing that they have none of it. ❑ *...a face that was devoid of feeling.*

devolution /ˌdi:və'lu:ʃən, ˌdev-/ N-UNCOUNT **Devolution** is the transfer of some political power from central government to smaller government departments. ❑ *...the devolution of power to the regions.*

devote /dɪ'vəʊt/ (**devotes, devoting, devoted**) V-T If you **devote yourself**, your time, or your energy **to** something, you spend all or most of your time or energy on it. ❑ *He abandoned politics and devoted himself to business.*

devoted /dɪ'vəʊtɪd/ ADJ If you are **devoted to** someone or something, you care about them or love them very much. ❑ *...a loving and devoted husband.* ❑ *John is devoted to his garden.*

devotee /ˌdevəˈtiː/ (**devotees**) N-COUNT A **devotee of** a subject or activity is someone who is very enthusiastic about it.

devotion /dɪˈvəʊʃən/ N-UNCOUNT Your **devotion to** someone or something is your great love of them and commitment to them. ❑ *She was flattered by his devotion.* ❑ *...his devotion to his job.*

devour /dɪˈvaʊə/ (**devours, devouring, devoured**) V-T If a person or animal **devours** something, they eat it quickly and eagerly. ❑ *She devoured two bars of chocolate.*

devout /dɪˈvaʊt/ 1 ADJ A **devout** person has deep religious beliefs. ❑ *They were devout, serious girls.* 2 ADJ BEFORE N A **devout** believer in something supports it very strongly and enthusiastically. ❑ *...devout Marxists.*

dew /djuː/ N-UNCOUNT **Dew** is small drops of water that form on the ground and other surfaces outdoors during the night.

diabetes /ˌdaɪəˈbiːtiːz, AM -tɪs/ N-UNCOUNT **Diabetes** is a condition in which someone's body is unable to control the level of sugar in their blood.
→ see **sugar**

diabetic /ˌdaɪəˈbetɪk/ (**diabetics**) N-COUNT & ADJ A **diabetic** or a person who is **diabetic** suffers from diabetes.

Word Link *dia ≈ across, through : diagnose, diagonal, dialogue*

diagnose /ˈdaɪəgnəʊz, AM -nəʊs/ (**diagnoses, diagnosing, diagnosed**) V-T If someone or something **is diagnosed as** having a particular illness or problem, their illness or problem is identified. ❑ *They were diagnosed as having flu.* ❑ *He could diagnose an engine problem simply by listening.*
→ see **diagnosis, illness**

Word Link *osis ≈ state or condition : diagnosis, hypnosis, metamorphosis*

diagnosis /ˌdaɪəgˈnəʊsɪs/ (**diagnoses**) N-VAR **Diagnosis** is identifying what is wrong with someone who is ill or with something that is not working properly. ❑ *Dr Taylor made his diagnosis.*
→ see Word Web: **diagnosis**

diagnostic /ˌdaɪəgˈnɒstɪk/ ADJ BEFORE N **Diagnostic** devices or methods are used for discovering what is wrong with someone or something. ❑ *X-rays are important diagnostic tools.*

Word Link *gon ≈ angle : diagonal, octagon, pentagon*

diagonal /daɪˈægənəl/ ADJ A **diagonal** line or movement goes in a slanting direction. ● **diagonally** ADV ❑ *He ran diagonally across the pitch.*

Word Link *gram ≈ writing : diagram, program, telegram*

diagram /ˈdaɪəgræm/ (**diagrams**) N-COUNT A **diagram** is a drawing which is used to explain something.

Thesaurus *diagram* Also look up:
N. blueprint, chart, design, illustration, plan

dial

dial /daɪəl/ (**dials, dialling, dialled** or [AM] **dialing, dialed**) 1 N-COUNT The **dial** on a clock or meter is the part where the time or a measurement is indicated. 2 N-COUNT The **dial** on a radio is the control which you move in order to change the frequency. 3 N-COUNT The **dial** on some telephones is a circular disc that you rotate according to the number that you want to call. 4 V-T/V-I If you **dial**, or if you **dial** a number, you turn the dial or press the buttons on a telephone.

dialect /ˈdaɪəlekt/ (**dialects**) N-VAR A **dialect** is a form of a language spoken in a particular area. ❑ *They began to speak rapidly in dialect.*
→ see **English**

ˈdialog ˌbox (**dialog boxes**) N-COUNT A **dialog box** is a small area containing information or questions that appears on a computer screen when you are performing particular operations. [COMPUTING]

Word Link *di ≈ two : dialogue, dilemma, diverge*

Word Link *log ≈ reason, speech : apology, dialogue, logic*

dialogue [AM **dialog**] /ˈdaɪəlɒg, AM -lɔːg/ (**dialogues**) 1 N-VAR **Dialogue** is communication or discussion between people or groups. ❑ *...a dialogue between the two nations.* 2 N-VAR The **dialogue** in a book, film, or play consists of the things the characters in it say to each other. ❑ *He writes great dialogue.*

Word Link *meter ≈ measuring : barometer, diameter, perimeter*

diameter /daɪˈæmɪtə/ (**diameters**) N-COUNT

Word Web diagnosis

Many doctors suggest that their **patients** get a routine **physical examination** once a year—even if they're feeling healthy. This helps the **physician** to see any **symptoms** early and **diagnose** possible **diseases** at an early stage. The doctor may begin by using a **tongue depressor** to look down the patient's throat for possible **infections**. Then he or she may use a **stethoscope** to listen to subtle sounds in the heart, lungs, and stomach. A **blood pressure** reading is always part of the physical exam.

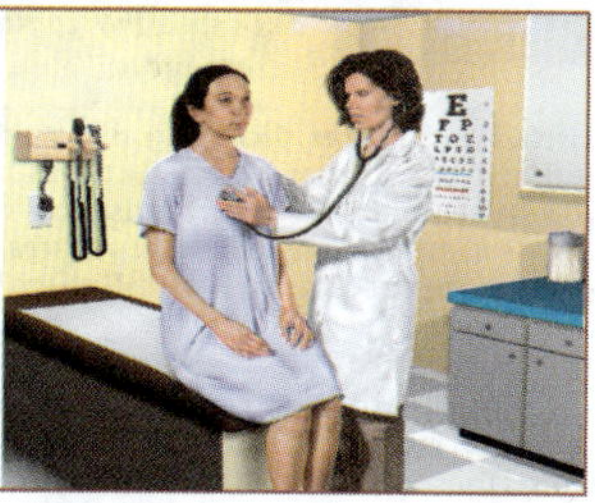

Word Web diary

Someone writes in a diary to tell about the things that happen in their daily life. Most diaries are private **documents** and are not shared with others. But sometimes an important diary is published as a book. One such example is *The Diary of a Young Girl*. In this **chronicle** Anne Frank writes of her family's experiences as they hid from the Nazis in World War II. They were found and arrested, and later Anne died in a concentration camp. This **primary source** document tells us Anne's story in her own words. It is full of rich details that are often missing from other historical **texts**. The book is now available in 60 different languages.

D

The **diameter** of a circle or sphere is the length of a straight line through the middle of it. ❑ *...thin pancakes 6 inches in diameter.*
→ see **area, circle**

diamond /'daɪəmənd/ (**diamonds**) 1 N-COUNT A **diamond** is a hard bright precious stone. ❑ *...diamond earrings.* 2 N-COUNT A **diamond** is a shape with four straight sides of equal length which are not at right angles to each other. 3 N-UNCOUNT **Diamonds** is one of the four suits in a pack of playing cards. Each card in the suit is called a **diamond** and is marked with one or more red symbols: ♦.
→ see **crystal**

diaper /'daɪəpə/ (**diapers**) N-COUNT In American English, a **diaper** is something which you put round a baby's bottom in order to soak up its waste. The British word is **nappy**.

diaphragm /'daɪəfræm/ (**diaphragms**) N-COUNT Your **diaphragm** is a muscle between your lungs and your stomach.
→ see **respiration**

diarrhoea [AM **diarrhea**] /ˌdaɪə'riːə/ N-UNCOUNT When someone **has diarrhoea**, a lot of liquid waste material comes out of their bowels because they are ill.

diary /'daɪəri/ (**diaries**) N-COUNT A **diary** is a notebook with a separate space for each day of the year.
→ see Word Web: **diary**
→ see **history**

dice /daɪs/ (**dices, dicing, diced**)

Dice is both the singular and the plural form of the noun.

1 N-COUNT A **dice** is a small cube with one to six spots on each face, used in games. ❑ *Roll the dice.* 2 V-T When you **dice** food, you cut it into small cubes.
→ see **cut**

Word Link *dict ≈ speaking : contradict, dictate, predict*

dictate (**dictates, dictating, dictated**) 1 V-T /dɪk'teɪt, AM 'dɪkteɪt/ If you **dictate** something, you say it aloud for someone else to write down. ❑ *Mr Phillips dictated a memo to his secretary.* 2 V-T If you **dictate to** someone, you tell them what they must do. ❑ *What gives them the right to dictate to us what we should eat?*

dictation /dɪk'teɪʃən/ (**dictations**) N-VAR **Dictation** is the speaking or reading aloud of words for someone else to write down.

dictator /dɪk'teɪtə, AM 'dɪkteɪt-/ (**dictators**) N-COUNT A **dictator** is a ruler who has complete power in a country; used showing disapproval.

dictatorial /ˌdɪktə'tɔːriəl/ ADJ If you describe someone's behaviour as **dictatorial**, you mean that they tell people what to do in a forceful and unfair way; used showing disapproval. ❑ *...his dictatorial management style.*

dictatorship /dɪk'teɪtəʃɪp/ (**dictatorships**) 1 N-VAR **Dictatorship** is a system in which a country is governed by a dictator. 2 N-COUNT A **dictatorship** is a country ruled by a dictator.

dictionary /'dɪkʃənri, AM -neri/ (**dictionaries**) N-COUNT A **dictionary** is a book in which the words and phrases of a language are listed, usually in alphabetical order, together with their meanings or their translations in another language.

did /dɪd/ **Did** is the past tense of **do**.

didn't /'dɪdənt/ **Didn't** is the usual spoken form of 'did not'.

die /daɪ/ (**dies, dying, died**) 1 V-I When people, animals, or plants **die**, they stop living. ❑ *My mother died of cancer.* ❑ *His friend died young.* 2 → See note at **dead** 3 V-I When something **dies**, or when it **dies away** or **dies down**, it becomes less intense, until it disappears. ❑ *My love for you will never die.* ❑ *The echoes of the thunder were dying away across the peaks.* ❑ *The wind died down.* 4 PHRASE If you say that old habits or attitudes **die hard**, you mean that they take a very long time to change, and may never disappear completely. 5 → see also **dying**

▶ **die out** PHR-VERB If something **dies out**, it becomes less and less common and eventually disappears. ❑ *How did the dinosaurs die out?*

Thesaurus *die* Also look up:

V. pass away; (*ant.*) live 1

Word Partnership Use *die* with:

V. **deserve to** die, **going to** die, **live or** die, **sentenced to** die, **want to** die 1
N. right **to die** 1

diesel /'diːzəl/ (**diesels**) 1 ADJ **Diesel** describes a type of engine in which oil is burnt by very hot air. It also describes a vehicle with this type of engine, or the heavy oil used as fuel in it. ❑ *The Intercity 125 is the world's fastest diesel train.* 2 N-VAR A **diesel** is a vehicle which has a diesel engine, or the heavy oil used as fuel in it.

diet /daɪət/ (**diets, dieting, dieted**) **1** N-VAR Your **diet** is the type and range of food that you regularly eat. ❑ *...a healthy diet.* **2** N-COUNT & V-I If you are **on a diet** or if you **are dieting**, you eat only certain foods because you are trying to lose weight. ● **dieter** (**dieters**) N-COUNT ❑ *Most dieters are miserable.*
→ see Word Web: **diet**
→ see **diet, vegetarian**

Word Partnership Use *diet* with:

ADJ.	**balanced** diet, **healthy** diet, **proper** diet, **vegetarian** diet **1** **strict** diet **2**
N.	diet **and exercise**, diet **pills**, diet **supplements** **2**
PREP.	**on a** diet **2**

dietary /ˈdaɪətri, AM -teri/ ADJ **Dietary** means relating to the kind of food you eat. ❑ *...dietary changes.*

differ /ˈdɪfə/ (**differs, differing, differed**) **1** V-I If two or more things **differ**, they are not like each other. ❑ *Their attitudes to promotion also differ from ours.* **2** V-I If people **differ**, they disagree with each other about something. ❑ *They differ on lots of issues.*

difference /ˈdɪfrəns/ (**differences**) **1** N-VAR The **difference** between things is the way in which they are different from each other. ❑ *...the great difference in size.* ❑ *The difference is that I expect so much of her, but not of him.* **2** N-SING The **difference between** two amounts is the amount by which one is less than the other. **3** N-COUNT If people **have their differences**, they disagree about things. **4** PHRASE If something **makes a difference**, it changes a situation. If it **makes no difference**, it does not change a situation. ❑ *We had terrible rows over his homework, but it made no difference.*

Word Partnership Use *difference* with:

ADJ.	**big/major** difference **1**
V.	**know the** difference, **notice a** difference, **tell the** difference **1** **pay the** difference **2** **settle a** difference **3** **make a** difference **4**
N.	difference **of opinion** **1** difference **in age**, difference **in price** **2**

different /ˈdɪfrənt/ **1** ADJ If one thing is **different from** another, it is not like the other thing. ❑ *London was different from most European capitals.* ❑ *We have totally different views.* ● **differently** ADV ❑ *Every individual learns differently.* **2** ADJ BEFORE N When you refer to two or more **different** things of a particular kind, you mean two or more separate things of that kind. ❑ *...different brands of drinks.* **3** ADJ AFTER LINK-V You can describe something as **different** when it is unusual and not like other things of the same kind. ❑ *The result is interesting and different.*

Usage

In British English, people sometimes say that one thing is **different to** another. ❑ *You're so different to what I imagined.* Some people consider this use to be incorrect, and insist that you should say **different from.** ❑ *We human beings are vastly different from all other species.* In American English, you can say that one thing is **different than** another. This use is often considered incorrect in British English, but it is sometimes the simplest possibility when the comparison involves a clause. ❑ *I am no different than I was 50 years ago.*

differential /ˌdɪfəˈrenʃəl/ (**differentials**) N-COUNT A **differential** is a difference between two values in a scale, for example a difference between rates of pay within a company. [TECHNICAL] ❑ *...the differential between their two currencies.* ❑ *...wage differentials.*

differentiate /ˌdɪfəˈrenʃieɪt/ (**differentiates, differentiating, differentiated**) V-T/V-I To **differentiate** things or **between** things means to show or recognize the difference between them. ❑ *A child may not differentiate between his imagination and the real world.* ❑ *At this age your baby cannot differentiate one person from another.* ● **differentiation** N-UNCOUNT ❑ *There was no differentiation in the levels of taxation.*

difficult /ˈdɪfɪkəlt/ **1** ADJ Something that is **difficult** is not easy to do, understand, or cope with. ❑ *I find it difficult to speak up for myself.* **2** ADJ If you say that someone is **difficult**, you think they are behaving in an unreasonable and unhelpful way. ❑ *I could be difficult about it, but why bother?*

Thesaurus *difficult* Also look up:

ADJ.	challenging, demanding, hard, tough; (*ant.*) easy, simple, uncomplicated **1** irritable; (*ant.*) accommodating **2**

difficulty /ˈdɪfɪkəlti/ (**difficulties**) **1** N-VAR A **difficulty** is a problem. If you are **in difficulty** or **in difficulties**, you are having a lot of problems. ❑ *We heard that the company was in difficulty.* ❑ *...economic*

Word Web diet

Recent U.S. government reports show that about 64% of American adults are **overweight** or **obese**. The number of people on **weight loss diets** is the highest ever. Many people are trying fad diets to lose weight. One diet tells people to eat mostly **protein**—meat, fish, and cheese—and very few **carbohydrates**. However, another diet tells people to eat at least 40% carbohydrates. A weight-loss diet works when you burn more **calories** than you eat. Most doctors agree that a balanced diet with plenty of exercise the best way to lose weight.

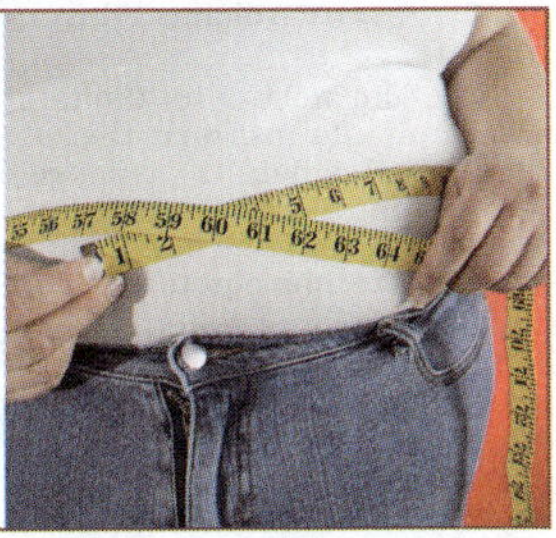

difficulties. **2** N-UNCOUNT If you **have difficulty** doing something, you are not able to do it easily. ❑ *Do you have difficulty getting up?*

diffident /ˈdɪfɪdənt/ ADJ Someone who is **diffident** is shy and lacks confidence. ● **diffidence** N-UNCOUNT ❑ *The trouble seems to be a kind of diffidence, a sense of embarrassment.*

diffuse (**diffuses, diffusing, diffused**) **1** V-T/V-I /dɪˈfjuːz/ If something such as knowledge or information **is diffused**, or if it **diffuses**, it is made available over a wide area or to a lot of people. [FORMAL] ❑ *Interest in books is more widely diffused than ever.* ● **diffusion** /dɪˈfjuːʒən/ N-UNCOUNT ❑ *...the diffusion of democracy.* **2** ADJ /dɪˈfjuːs/ Something that is **diffuse** is spread over a large area rather than concentrated in one place. [FORMAL] ❑ *Our search has been too diffuse.*
→ see **culture**

dig /dɪg/ (**digs, digging, dug** /dʌg/) **1** V-T/V-I When people or animals **dig**, they make a hole in the ground or in a pile of stones or debris. ❑ *He dug a hole in the lawn.* ❑ *Rescue workers are digging through the rubble.* **2** V-T/V-I If you **dig** one thing **into** another, or if one thing **digs into** another, the first thing is pushed hard into the second, or presses hard into it. ❑ *He felt the beads digging into his palm.*

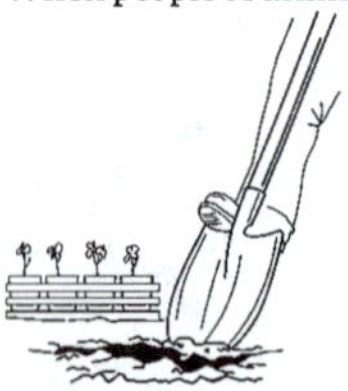

dig

3 N-COUNT A **dig** is a critical remark. ❑ *They have used the occasion to have a dig at the press.*
→ see **tunnel**

▶ **dig out** or **dig up** PHR-VERB If you **dig** something **out** or **dig** it **up**, you discover it after it has been stored, hidden, or forgotten for a long time.

digest /daɪˈdʒest/ (**digests, digesting, digested**) **1** V-T When you **digest** food, it passes through your body to your stomach, your stomach removes the substances that you need, and your body gets rid of the rest. ❑ *Fats are hard to digest.* ● **digestion** N-UNCOUNT ❑ *Peppermint aids digestion.* **2** V-T If you **digest** information, you think about it carefully so that you understand it or are capable of dealing with it. ❑ *She read everything, digesting every fragment of news.*
→ see **cook**

digestive /daɪˈdʒestɪv/ ADJ BEFORE N **Digestive** refers to the digestion of food. ❑ *...digestive disorders.*

digit /ˈdɪdʒɪt/ (**digits**) **1** N-COUNT A **digit** is a written symbol for any of the ten numbers from 0 to 9. **2** N-COUNT A **digit** is a finger, thumb, or toe. [FORMAL]

digital /ˈdɪdʒɪtəl/ **1** ADJ **Digital** systems record or transmit information in the form of thousands of very small signals. ❑ *...digital audio broadcasting.* **2** ADJ BEFORE N **Digital** watches or clocks show the time by displaying numbers.
→ see **DVD, technology, television, time**

ˌdigital ˈcamera (**digital cameras**) N-COUNT A **digital camera** is a camera that produces digital images that can be stored on a computer.

ˌdigital ˈradio N-UNCOUNT **Digital radio** is radio in which the signals are transmitted in digital form and decoded by the radio receiver.

ˌdigital ˈtelevision N-UNCOUNT **Digital television** is television in which the signals are transmitted in digital form and decoded by the television receiver.

Word Link	*dign ≈ proper, worthy : dignified, dignitary, indignant*

dignified /ˈdɪgnɪfaɪd/ ADJ If you say that someone or something is **dignified**, you mean they are calmly impressive and worthy of respect.

dignitary /ˈdɪgnɪtri, AM -teri/ (**dignitaries**) N-COUNT A **dignitary** is someone who has a high rank in government or in the Church.

dignity /ˈdɪgnɪti/ **1** N-UNCOUNT If someone behaves with **dignity**, they are serious, calm, and controlled. **2** N-UNCOUNT **Dignity** is the quality of being worthy of respect. ❑ *...respect for human dignity.*

dike

dike /daɪk/ → see **dyke**

dilapidated /dɪˈlæpɪdeɪtɪd/ ADJ A **dilapidated** building is old and in bad condition.

dilate /daɪˈleɪt/ (**dilates, dilating, dilated**) V-T/V-I When things such as blood vessels or the pupils of your eyes **dilate**, or when something **dilates** them, they become wider or bigger. ❑ *Exercise dilates blood vessels.* ● **dilated** ADJ ❑ *His eyes were dilated.*

Word Link	*di ≈ two : dialogue, dilemma, diverge*

dilemma /daɪˈlemə, AM dɪl-/ (**dilemmas**) N-COUNT A **dilemma** is a difficult situation in which you have to choose between two or more alternatives. ❑ *His dilemma is whether or not to return to his home country.*

diligent /ˈdɪlɪdʒənt/ ADJ **Diligent** people work hard and carefully. ❑ *...a diligent student.* ● **diligence** N-UNCOUNT ❑ *The police pursued their inquiries with great diligence.* ● **diligently** ADV ❑ *We worked diligently on our school assignments.*

dilute /daɪˈluːt/ (**dilutes, diluting, diluted**) V-T/V-I If a liquid **is diluted**, or if it **dilutes**, it is added to or mixes with water or another liquid, and becomes weaker. ❑ *Dilute it well with cooled, boiled water.*

dim /dɪm/ (**dimmer, dimmest, dims, dimming, dimmed**) **1** ADJ **Dim** light is not bright. You can also say that something is **dim** when the light is not bright enough to see very well. ❑ *Below decks, the lights were dim.* ❑ *He saw a dim outline of a small boat.* ● **dimly** ADV ❑ *...a dimly lit kitchen.* ❑ *The shoreline could be dimly seen.* **2** V-T/V-I If you **dim** a light, or if it **dims**, it becomes less bright.

dime /daɪm/ (**dimes**) N-COUNT A **dime** is an American coin worth ten cents.

dimension /daɪˈmenʃən, dɪm-/ (**dimensions**) **1** N-COUNT A particular **dimension** of something is a particular aspect of it. ❑ *Works of art have a spiritual dimension.* **2** N-PLURAL You can refer to the measurements of something as its **dimensions**. ❑ *...the dimensions of the new oilfield.*

Word Link *min ≈ small, lessen : diminish, minus, minute*

diminish /dɪ'mɪnɪʃ/ (**diminishes, diminishing, diminished**) V-T/V-I When something **diminishes**, or when it **is diminished**, its importance, size, or intensity is reduced. ❑ *The threat of nuclear war has diminished.*

diminutive /dɪ'mɪnjʊtɪv/ ADJ A **diminutive** person or object is very small. [FORMAL] ❑ *...the diminutive figure of Mr Nerette.*

din /dɪn/ N-SING A **din** is a very loud and unpleasant noise that lasts for some time. ❑ *...the din of the crowd.*

dine /daɪn/ (**dines, dining, dined**) V-I When you **dine**, you have dinner. [FORMAL] ❑ *The two men dined at the restaurant.*

diner /'daɪnə/ (**diners**) 1 N-COUNT In the United States, a **diner** is a small cheap restaurant that is open all day. 2 N-COUNT The **diners** in a restaurant are the people who are eating there.

dinghy /'dɪŋgi/ (**dinghies**) N-COUNT A **dinghy** is a small boat that you sail or row.

dingy /'dɪndʒi/ ADJ A **dingy** place is dark and depressing. ❑ *...his rather dingy office.*

'dining room (**dining rooms**) N-COUNT The **dining room** is the room in a house or hotel where people have their meals.
→ see **house**

dinner /'dɪnə/ (**dinners**) 1 N-VAR **Dinner** is the main meal of the day, eaten in the evening. ❑ *She invited us to her house for dinner.* 2 N-VAR Some people use **dinner** to refer to the meal you eat in the middle of the day. 3 N-COUNT A **dinner** is a formal social event in the evening at which a meal is served. ❑ *The Foundation is holding a dinner.* 4 → See note at **meal**
→ see **meal**

'dinner table (**dinner tables**) N-COUNT You refer to a table as the **dinner table** when it is being used for dinner. [BRIT] ❑ *Sam was left at the dinner table with Megan.*

dinosaur

dinosaur /'daɪnəsɔː/ (**dinosaurs**) N-COUNT **Dinosaurs** were large reptiles which lived in prehistoric times.

dip /dɪp/ (**dips, dipping, dipped**) 1 V-T If you **dip** something **into** a liquid, you put it in and then quickly take it out again. ❑ *They dipped the food into the sauce.* 2 V-I If something **dips**, it makes a downward movement. ❑ *The sun dipped below the horizon.* 3 N-COUNT A **dip** in a surface is a place that is lower than the rest of the surface. ❑ *The football pitch has a slight dip in the middle.*

diploma /dɪ'pləʊmə/ (**diplomas**) N-COUNT A **diploma** is a qualification which may be awarded to a student by a university or college, or by a high school in the United States.
→ see **graduation**

diplomacy /dɪ'pləʊməsi/ 1 N-UNCOUNT **Diplomacy** is the activity of managing relations between the governments of different countries. ❑ *The Foreign Secretary arrives in New York today for a busy week of diplomacy.* 2 N-UNCOUNT **Diplomacy** is the skill of saying or doing things without offending people. ❑ *He sometimes lacks diplomacy.*

diplomat /'dɪpləmæt/ (**diplomats**) N-COUNT A **diplomat** is a senior official, usually based at an embassy, who negotiates with another country on behalf of his or her own country.

diplomatic /ˌdɪplə'mætɪk/ 1 ADJ **Diplomatic** means relating to diplomacy and diplomats. ❑ *There was an attempt to resume diplomatic relations.* ● **diplomatically** ADV ❑ *The conflict can be resolved diplomatically.* 2 ADJ Someone who is **diplomatic** is able to say or do things without offending people. ● **diplomatically** ADV ❑ *She could have put it more diplomatically.*

dire /daɪə/ ADJ **Dire** is used to emphasize how serious or terrible a situation or event is. ❑ *He was in dire need of hospital treatment.*

direct /daɪ'rekt, dɪ-/ (**directs, directing, directed**) 1 ADJ & ADV **Direct** means going or aimed straight towards a place or object. ❑ *...a direct train service from Calais to Strasbourg.* ❑ *You can fly direct to Amsterdam from most British airports.* ● **directly** ADV ❑ *I flew directly from Istanbul to New York.* 2 → see also **directly** 3 ADJ & ADV You use **direct** to describe something such as contact or a relationship between two things or people which only involves the things or people that are mentioned, with nothing or nobody in between them. ❑ *He was in direct contact with his boss.* ❑ *Millions have died this century as a direct result of war.* ❑ *Grow the seeds in bright light but out of direct sunlight.* ❑ *I can deal direct with your Inspector.* ● **directly** ADV ❑ *People lost money directly because of this criminal action.* 4 ADJ If you describe a person or their behaviour as **direct**, you mean that they are honest and say exactly what they mean. ❑ *He always gives direct answers.* ● **directness** N-UNCOUNT ❑ *I like the openness and directness of northerners.* 5 V-T Something that **is directed at** a particular person or thing is aimed at them or is intended to affect them. ❑ *The demonstrators directed their rage at symbols of wealth.* 6 V-T If you **direct** someone somewhere, you tell them how to get there. ❑ *Could you direct them to Dr Lamont's office, please?* 7 V-T If someone **directs** a project or a group of people, they organize it and are in charge of it. ● **director** (**directors**) N-COUNT ❑ *He's the director of the intensive care unit.* 8 V-T If someone **directs** a film, play, or television programme, they decide how it should be made and performed. ❑ *Andrew both acted in and directed this film.* ● **director** N-COUNT ❑ *...the film director Franco Zeffirelli.* 9 → see also **director**

Thesaurus *direct* Also look up:

ADJ. nonstop, straight 1
candid, frank, plain 3

direction /daɪ'rekʃən, dɪr-/ (**directions**) 1 N-VAR A **direction** is the general line that someone or something is moving or pointing in. ❑ *St Andrews is ten miles in the opposite direction.* ❑ *Everyone started running in all directions.* 2 N-VAR **Directions** are instructions that tell you what to do or how to get to a place. ❑ *He gave give Dan directions to the computer room.* ❑ *The house was built under the direction of John's partner.*

Word Partnership Use *direction* with:

ADJ.	**general** direction, **opposite** direction, **right** direction, **wrong** direction 1
N.	**sense of** direction 1
V.	**change** direction, **move in a** direction 1 **lack** direction, **take** direction 2

D

directive /daɪ'rektɪv, dɪr-/ (**directives**) N-COUNT A **directive** is an official instruction that is given by someone in authority. ❑ *The government issued a directive to the armed forces.*

directly /daɪ'rektli, dɪr-/ 1 ADV If something is, for example, **directly** above something or in front of something, it is in exactly that position. ❑ *The road lay directly below us.* 2 ADV If you do one action **directly after** another, you do the second action as soon as the first one is finished. ❑ *Directly after lunch we were packed and ready to go.* 3 → see also **direct**

di,rect 'object (**direct objects**) N-COUNT The **direct object** of a transitive verb is the noun group which is used to refer to someone or something directly affected by or involved in the action performed by the subject. For example, in 'I saw him yesterday', 'him' is the direct object. Compare **indirect object**.

director /daɪ'rektə, dɪr-/ (**directors**) 1 N-COUNT The **directors** of a company are its most senior managers. ❑ *...the board of directors.* 2 → see also **direct**
→ see **theatre**

directorate /daɪ'rektərət, dɪr-/ (**directorates**) 1 N-COUNT A **directorate** is a board of directors in a company. 2 N-COUNT A **directorate** is a part of a government department which is responsible for one particular thing. ❑ *He works for the Health and Safety Directorate of the EU.*

di,rector 'general (**directors general**) N-COUNT The **director general** of a large organization is the person who is in charge of it.

directory /daɪ'rektəri, dɪr-/ (**directories**) 1 N-COUNT A **directory** is a book which gives lists of information such as people's names, addresses, and telephone numbers. ❑ *...a telephone directory.* 2 N-COUNT A **directory** is an area of a computer disk which contains one or more files or other directories. [COMPUTING]

dirt /dɜ:t/ 1 N-UNCOUNT If there is **dirt** on something, there is dust, mud, or a stain on it. 2 N-UNCOUNT You can refer to the earth on the ground as **dirt**.
→ see **erosion**

dirty /'dɜ:ti/ (**dirtier, dirtiest, dirties, dirtying, dirtied**) 1 ADJ & V-T If you **get** something **dirty**, or if you **dirty** it, it becomes marked or covered with stains, spots, or mud. ❑ *The kids have got their clothes dirty.* ❑ *The dog's hairs might dirty the seats.* 2 ADJ **Dirty** jokes, books, or language refer to sex in a way that many people find offensive.

disability /,dɪsə'bɪlɪti/ (**disabilities**) N-COUNT A **disability** is a physical or mental condition that restricts the way someone can live their life. ❑ *...facilities for people with disabilities.*
→ see Word Web: **disability**

disable /dɪ'seɪbəl/ (**disables, disabling, disabled**) 1 V-T If an injury or illness **disables** someone, it restricts the way they can live their life. 2 V-T To **disable** a system or mechanism means to stop it working. ❑ *He disabled the car alarm.*

disabled /dɪ'seɪbəld/ ADJ & N-PLURAL **Disabled** people or **the disabled** have an illness, injury, or condition that restricts the way they can live their lives.

disadvantage /,dɪsəd'vɑ:ntɪdʒ, -'væn-/ (**disadvantages**) 1 N-COUNT A **disadvantage** is a part of a situation which causes problems. ❑ *Every job has its disadvantages.* 2 PHRASE If you are **at a disadvantage**, you have a problem that other people do not have. ❑ *The children from poor families were at a disadvantage.*

disadvantaged /,dɪsəd'vɑ:ntɪdʒd, -'væn-/ ADJ & N-PLURAL **Disadvantaged** people or **the disadvantaged** live in bad economic or social conditions.

disaffected /,dɪsə'fektɪd/ ADJ **Disaffected** people no longer fully support something which they previously supported. ❑ *...people disaffected with the government.*

Word Link *dis ≈ negative, not : disagree, discomfort, disconnect*

disagree /,dɪsə'gri:/ (**disagrees, disagreeing, disagreed**) 1 V-I If you **disagree with** someone, you have a different opinion to them about something. ❑ *I respect him even though I often disagree with him.* ❑ *They can communicate even when they strongly disagree.* ❑ *Well, I disagree.* 2 V-I If you **disagree with** an action or suggestion, you disapprove of it. ❑ *I disagree with these laws in general.*

disagreement /,dɪsə'gri:mənt/ (**disagreements**) 1 N-UNCOUNT **Disagreement** means objecting to something. ❑ *They expressed some disagreement with the proposal.* 2 N-VAR When there is a **disagreement about** something, people

Word Web disability

Careful planning is making public places more **accessible** for people with **disabilities**. For hundreds of years **wheelchairs** have helped **paralysed** people move around their homes. Today, **ramps** help these people cross the street, enter buildings, and get to work. Extra-wide doorways allow them to use public toilets. **Blind** people are also more active and independent. **Seeing Eye dogs, canes**, and crosswalks that have sound signals all help them get around town safely. Some cinemas hire out headsets for the **hearing-impaired**. **Hearing dogs** help **deaf** people stay safe. And sign language allows people who are deaf or **dumb** to communicate using their hands.

Word Web **disaster**

We are learning more about nature's cycles. But natural **disasters** remain a big challenge. We can predict some disasters, such as **hurricanes** and **floods**. However, we still can't avoid the **damage** they do. Each year **monsoons** strike southern Asia. Monsoons are a combination of **typhoons**, **tropical storms**, and heavy **rains**. In addition to the damage caused by floods, **landslides** and **mudslides** add to the problem. In 2005 more than 90 million people suffered from disaster in China alone. Over 700 people died in that country and millions of acres of crops were destroyed. The **economic loss** totaled almost 6 billion dollars.

disagree or argue about what should be done. ❑ *We had a brief disagreement.*

disallow /ˌdɪsəˈlaʊ/ (**disallows, disallowing, disallowed**) V-T If something **is disallowed**, it is not allowed or accepted officially, because it has not been done correctly. ❑ *Antony was standing for President, but the election was disallowed.*

disappear /ˌdɪsəˈpɪə/ (**disappears, disappearing, disappeared**) **1** V-I If someone or something **disappears**, they go where they cannot be seen or found. ❑ *The plane disappeared off their radar.* ❑ *This woman disappeared thirteen years ago.* ● **disappearance** (**disappearances**) N-VAR ❑ *Her disappearance has baffled police.* **2** V-I To **disappear** means to stop existing or happening. ❑ *Year by year large areas of this small nation's countryside disappear.* ● **disappearance** N-UNCOUNT ❑ *...the disappearance of the dinosaurs.*

disappoint /ˌdɪsəˈpɔɪnt/ (**disappoints, disappointing, disappointed**) V-T If things or people **disappoint** you, they are not as good as you had hoped, or do not do what you hoped they would do. ❑ *I'm sorry if this reply will disappoint you.* ● **disappointing** ADJ ❑ *The meal was disappointing.* ● **disappointingly** ADV ❑ *Progress is disappointingly slow.*

disappointed /ˌdɪsəˈpɔɪntɪd/ ADJ If you are **disappointed**, you are sad because something has not happened or because something is not as good as you hoped it would be. ❑ *I was disappointed that he was not there.* ❑ *I'm surprised and disappointed in you.*

disappointment /ˌdɪsəˈpɔɪntmənt/ (**disappointments**) **1** N-UNCOUNT **Disappointment** is the state of feeling disappointed. ❑ *Book your ticket early to avoid disappointment.* **2** N-COUNT Someone or something that is a **disappointment** is not as good as you had hoped. ❑ *He was such a disappointment to his family.*

disapproval /ˌdɪsəˈpruːvəl/ N-UNCOUNT If you express **disapproval of** something, you indicate that you do not like it or that you think it is wrong. ❑ *His friends unite in their disapproval of Penny.* ❑ *His action was greeted with almost universal disapproval.*

disapprove /ˌdɪsəˈpruːv/ (**disapproves, disapproving, disapproved**) V-I If you **disapprove of** something, you do not like it or you think it is wrong. ❑ *Her mother disapproved of her working in a pub.* ❑ *No matter how much I disapprove, I still love her.* ● **disapproving** ADJ ❑ *Janet gave him a disapproving look.* ● **disapprovingly** ADV ❑ *Antonio looked at him disapprovingly.*

disarm /ˌdɪsˈɑːm/ (**disarms, disarming, disarmed**) **1** V-T To **disarm** a person or group means to take away their weapons. ❑ *We agreed to disarming troops.* **2** V-I If a country or group **disarms**, it gives up the use of its weapons. ❑ *We're not yet ready to disarm.* **3** V-T If a person or their behaviour **disarms** you, they cause you to feel less angry, hostile, or critical towards them. ❑ *She did her best to disarm her critics.* ● **disarming** ADJ ❑ *...a disarming smile.* ● **disarmingly** ADV ❑ *He is, as ever, disarmingly honest.*

disarmament /ˌdɪsˈɑːməmənt/ N-UNCOUNT **Disarmament** is the act of reducing the number of weapons that a country has.

disarray /ˌdɪsəˈreɪ/ N-UNCOUNT If people or things are **in disarray** they have become confused and disorganized. ❑ *The nation is in disarray following rioting.*

disaster /dɪˈzɑːstə, -ˈzæs-/ (**disasters**) **1** N-COUNT A **disaster** is a very bad accident such as an earthquake or a plane crash. ❑ *It was the second air disaster in the region.* **2** N-COUNT If you refer to something as a **disaster**, you are emphasizing that you think it is extremely bad. ❑ *It would be a disaster for them not to reach the semi-finals.* **3** N-UNCOUNT **Disaster** is something which has very bad consequences for you. ❑ *The potential for disaster is enormous.*
→ see Word Web: **disaster**

disastrous /dɪˈzɑːstrəs, -ˈzæs-/ ADJ Something that is **disastrous** has extremely bad consequences and effects or is very unsuccessful. ❑ *...the recent disastrous earthquake.* ❑ *England's cricketers had a disastrous day.* ● **disastrously** ADV ❑ *Their scheme went disastrously wrong.*

disband /ˌdɪsˈbænd/ (**disbands, disbanding, disbanded**) V-T/V-I If someone **disbands** or **disbands** a group of people, it stops operating as a single unit. ❑ *All the armed groups will be disbanded.* ❑ *The rebels are to disband by June.*

disbelief /ˌdɪsbɪˈliːf/ N-UNCOUNT **Disbelief** is not believing that something is true or real. ❑ *She looked at him in complete disbelief.*

disc [AM **disk**] /dɪsk/ (**discs**) **1** N-COUNT A **disc** is a flat, circular shape or object. **2** N-COUNT A **disc** is a piece of cartilage between the bones in your spine. **3** N-COUNT A **disc** is a music record. **4** → see also **disk**
→ see **DVD**

discard /dɪsˈkɑːd/ (**discards, discarding, discarded**) V-T If you **discard** something, you get rid of it because it is not wanted. ❑ *Read the instructions before discarding the box.* ❑ *...discarded clothes.*

discern /dɪˈsɜːn/ (**discerns, discerning,**

discerned) 1 V-T If you can **discern** something, you are aware of it and know what it is. [FORMAL] ❑ *It was hard to discern why this was happening.* 2 V-T If you can **discern** something, you can just see it, but not clearly. [FORMAL] ❑ *We could just discern a narrow road.* • **discernible** ADJ ❑ *Far away the outline of the island is just discernible.*

discerning /dɪ'sɜːnɪŋ/ ADJ A **discerning** person is good at judging the quality of something. ❑ *These holidays suit the discerning traveller.*

D

discharge (**discharges, discharging, discharged**)

verb /dɪs'tʃɑːdʒ/, noun /'dɪstʃɑːdʒ/.

1 V-T & N-UNCOUNT When someone **is discharged** from hospital, prison, or the armed forces, or when they are given a **discharge**, they are allowed to leave, or told that they must leave. ❑ *He has a broken nose but may be discharged today.* ❑ *He was given a conditional discharge.* 2 V-T If someone **discharges** their duties or responsibilities, they carry them out. [FORMAL] ❑ *He discharged his many duties with quiet competence.* 3 V-T If something **is discharged** from inside a place, it comes out. [FORMAL] ❑ *The salty water was discharged at sea.* 4 N-COUNT When there is a **discharge** of a substance, the substance comes out from inside somewhere. ❑ *...a watery discharge from their eyes.*

→ see **lightning**

disciple /dɪ'saɪpəl/ (**disciples**) N-COUNT If you are someone's **disciple**, you are influenced by their teachings and try to follow their example. ❑ *This major intellectual figure had disciples throughout Europe.*

disciplinary /'dɪsɪplɪnəri, AM -neri/ ADJ BEFORE N **Disciplinary** matters are concerned with rules, making sure that people obey them, and punishing people who do not. ❑ *No disciplinary action was taken.*

discipline /'dɪsɪplɪn/ (**disciplines, disciplining, disciplined**) 1 N-UNCOUNT **Discipline** is the practice of making people obey rules or standards of behaviour, and punishing them when they do not. ❑ *...discipline problems in the classroom.* 2 V-T If someone **is disciplined** for something that they have done wrong, they are punished for it. ❑ *The workman was disciplined by his company but not dismissed.* 3 N-UNCOUNT **Discipline** is the quality of being able to behave or work in a controlled way. ❑ *...calm, control and discipline.* 4 N-COUNT A **discipline** is an area of study, especially a subject of study in a college or university. [FORMAL] ❑ *...people from a wide range of disciplines.*

'disc jockey (**disc jockeys**) N-COUNT A **disc jockey** is the same as a **DJ**.

disclose /dɪs'kləʊz/ (**discloses, disclosing, disclosed**) V-T If you **disclose** new or secret information, you tell it to someone. ❑ *He will not disclose the names of his patients.* ❑ *The company disclosed that its chairman will step down in May.*

disclosure /dɪs'kləʊʒə/ (**disclosures**) N-VAR **Disclosure** is the act of revealing new or secret information. ❑ *...unauthorised newspaper disclosures.*

disco /'dɪskəʊ/ (**discos**) N-COUNT A **disco** is a place or event where people dance to pop music.

Word Link ***dis** ≈ negative, not : **dis**agree, **dis**comfort, **dis**connect*

discomfort /dɪs'kʌmfət/ (**discomforts**) 1 N-UNCOUNT **Discomfort** is an unpleasant or painful feeling in a part of your body. ❑ *Steve had some discomfort, but no real pain.* 2 N-UNCOUNT **Discomfort** is a feeling of worry or embarrassment. ❑ *He repeated his statement in discomfort and embarrassment.* 3 N-COUNT **Discomforts** are conditions which cause you to feel physically uncomfortable. ❑ *...the discomforts of camping.*

disconcerting /ˌdɪskən'sɜːtɪŋ/ ADJ If you say that something is **disconcerting**, you mean that it makes you feel uneasy, confused, or embarrassed. ❑ *He had a disconcerting habit of looking down at the ground as he spoke.* • **disconcertingly** ADV ❑ *She could be disconcertingly absent-minded.*

disconnect /ˌdɪskə'nekt/ (**disconnects, disconnecting, disconnected**) V-T To **disconnect** a piece of equipment means to detach it from its source of power.

disconnected /ˌdɪskə'nektɪd/ ADJ **Disconnected** things are not linked in any way. ❑ *...a series of disconnected dreams.*

discontent /ˌdɪskən'tent/ N-UNCOUNT **Discontent** is the feeling of not being satisfied with your situation.

discontinue /ˌdɪskən'tɪnjuː/ (**discontinues, discontinuing, discontinued**) 1 V-T If you **discontinue** something that you have been doing regularly, you stop doing it. [FORMAL] ❑ *Never discontinue treatment without consulting your doctor.* 2 V-T If a product **is discontinued**, the manufacturer stops making it.

discord /'dɪskɔːd/ (**discords**) N-UNCOUNT **Discord** is disagreement. [LITERARY] ❑ *Sadly this did not prevent discord and misunderstanding.*

discount (**discounts, discounting, discounted**) 1 N-COUNT /'dɪskaʊnt/ A **discount** is a reduction in the price of something. ❑ *All full-time staff get a 20% discount.* 2 V-T /dɪs'kaʊnt/ If you **discount** something, you reject or ignore it. ❑ *Traders discounted the rumor.*

discourage /dɪs'kʌrɪdʒ, AM -'kɜːr-/ (**discourages, discouraging, discouraged**) 1 V-T If someone or something **discourages** you, they cause you to lose your enthusiasm about doing something. ❑ *It may be difficult to do at first. Don't let this discourage you.* • **discouraged** ADJ ❑ *She was determined not to be discouraged.* • **discouraging** ADJ ❑ *Today's report is more discouraging for the economy.* 2 V-T To **discourage** an action, or to **discourage** someone **from** doing it, means to try and persuade them not to do it. ❑ *Milos tried to discourage her from being friendly with me.* • **discouragement** N-UNCOUNT ❑ *...active discouragement from teachers.*

discourse /'dɪskɔːs/ N-UNCOUNT **Discourse** is spoken or written communication between people. ❑ *...a tradition of political discourse.*

discover /dɪs'kʌvə/ (**discovers, discovering, discovered**) 1 V-T If you **discover** something that you did not know about before, you become aware of it or learn of it. ❑ *She discovered that they'd escaped.* ❑ *It was difficult to discover which documents were important.* 2 V-T If someone or something **is discovered**, someone finds them. ❑ *A few days later his body was discovered.* 3 V-T When you **discover** something new, you are the first person to find it or become aware of it. ❑ *...the first European to discover America.* ❑ *People discovered how to cultivate cereals thousands of years ago.*

Thesaurus *discover* Also look up:

V. come upon, detect, find out, learn, uncover; *(ant.)* ignore, miss, overlook 1

discovery /dɪs'kʌvəri/ (**discoveries**) 1 N-VAR If you make a **discovery**, you become aware of something or learn of something that you did not know about before. ❑ *I made an incredible discovery.* 2 N-COUNT If someone makes a **discovery**, they are the first person to find or become aware of something that no one knew about before. ❑ *...the discovery of the ozone hole over the South Pole.* 3 N-VAR When the **discovery** of people or objects happens, someone finds them.

discredit /dɪs'kredɪt/ (**discredits, discrediting, discredited**) 1 V-T To **discredit** someone or something means to cause other people to stop trusting or respecting them. ❑ *They tried to discredit government policies.* ● **discredited** ADJ ❑ *...discredited police evidence.* 2 V-T To **discredit** evidence or an idea means to make it appear false or doubtful.

discreet /dɪs'kri:t/ ADJ If you are **discreet**, you are careful to avoid attracting attention or revealing private information. ❑ *He followed at a discreet distance.* ❑ *...discreet jewellery.* ❑ *...discreet inquiries.* ● **discreetly** ADV ❑ *He looked discreetly around the room.*

discrepancy /dɪs'krepənsi/ (**discrepancies**) N-COUNT If there is a **discrepancy between** two things that ought to be the same, there is a difference between them. ❑ *There are major discrepancies in the accounts.*

discretion /dɪs'kreʃən/ 1 N-UNCOUNT **Discretion** is the quality of behaving in a quiet and controlled way without attracting attention or giving away private information. ❑ *Larsson sometimes joined in the fun, but with more discretion.* 2 N-UNCOUNT If someone in a position of authority has **the discretion to** do something in a situation, they have the freedom and authority to decide what to do. [FORMAL] ❑ *School governors have the discretion to allow parents to withdraw pupils.* ❑ *The rules are often bent at the organiser's discretion.*

discretionary /dɪs'kreʃənri, AM -neri/ ADJ **Discretionary** matters are not fixed by rules but are decided by the people in authority. ❑ *You are entitled to a discretionary grant for your course.*

discriminate /dɪs'krɪmɪneɪt/ (**discriminates, discriminating, discriminated**) 1 V-I If you can **discriminate between** two things, you can recognize the difference between them. ❑ *He is incapable of discriminating between a good idea and a terrible one.* 2 V-I To **discriminate against** a group of people or **in favour of** a group of people means to unfairly treat them worse or better than other groups. ❑ *This law discriminates against women.*

discrimination /dɪsˌkrɪmɪ'neɪʃən/ 1 N-UNCOUNT **Discrimination** is the practice of treating one person or group of people less fairly or less well than other people or groups. ❑ *...sex discrimination laws.* ❑ *...discrimination against old people.* 2 N-UNCOUNT **Discrimination** is awareness of what is good or of high quality. ❑ *They cooked without skill and ate without discrimination.*

discriminatory /dɪs'krɪmɪnətri, AM -tɔ:ri/ ADJ **Discriminatory** laws or practices are unfair because they treat one group of people less well than other groups. ❑ *...racially discriminatory laws.*

discuss /dɪs'kʌs/ (**discusses, discussing, discussed**) V-T If people **discuss** something, they talk about it, often in order to reach a decision. ❑ *I will discuss the situation with colleagues tomorrow.* ❑ *They discussed how to bring peace and unity to the country.*

Usage

Note that **discuss** is never used as an intransitive verb. You cannot say, for example, 'They discussed', 'I discussed with him', or 'They discussed about politics'. Instead, you can say that you **have a discussion** with someone about something. ❑ *I had a long discussion about all this with Stephen.* You can also add an object and say that you **discuss** something **with** someone. If the discussion is less formal, you can simply use the verb **talk**. ❑ *We talked all night long.*

Word Partnership Use *discuss* with:

V. **meet to** discuss, **refuse to** discuss
N. discuss **an issue**, discuss **a matter**, discuss **options**, discuss **plans**, discuss **problems** 1 2

discussion /dɪs'kʌʃən/ (**discussions**) N-VAR If there is **discussion** about something, people talk about it, often in order to reach a decision. ❑ *Council members held informal discussions yesterday.* ❑ *The proposals are still under discussion.*

Thesaurus *discussion* Also look up:

N. conference, conversation, debate, talk

disdain /dɪs'deɪn/ N-UNCOUNT If you feel **disdain for** someone or something, you dislike them because you think they are inferior or unimportant. ❑ *Janet looked at him with disdain.*

disease /dɪ'zi:z/ (**diseases**) N-VAR A **disease** is an illness which affects people, animals, or plants. ❑ *...the spread of disease in the area.* ❑ *...heart disease.*
→ see **diagnosis, illness, medicine**

diseased /dɪ'zi:zd/ ADJ Something that is **diseased** is affected by a disease. ❑ *Clear away dead or diseased plants.*

disenchanted /ˌdɪsɪn'tʃɑ:ntɪd, -'tʃænt-/ ADJ If you are **disenchanted with** something, you no longer think that it is good. ❑ *I'm disenchanted with the state of British theatre.* ● **disenchantment** /ˌdɪsɪn'tʃɑ:ntmənt, -'tʃænt-/ N-UNCOUNT ❑ *There's growing disenchantment with the Government.*

disengage /ˌdɪsɪn'geɪdʒ/ (**disengages, disengaging, disengaged**) 1 V-T/V-I If you **disengage** something, you separate it from the thing which it has become attached to. ❑ *John gently disengaged himself from his sister's embrace.* ❑ *His front brake cable disengaged.* 2 V-I If an army **disengages from** a conflict or an area, it withdraws from the fight or the area. ● **disengagement** N-UNCOUNT ❑ *...the policy of disengagement from the European war.*

disengaged /ˌdɪsɪn'geɪdʒd/ ADJ If someone is **disengaged from** something, they are not as involved with it as you would expect. ❑ *Both of the*

d

parents are emotionally disengaged from the child.

Word Link	*fig ≈ form, shape : configure, disfigure, figure*

disfigure /dɪs'fɪgə, AM -gjər/ (**disfigures, disfiguring, disfigured**) 1 V-T If someone **is disfigured**, their appearance is spoiled. ❑ *Many of the wounded were badly disfigured.* ● **disfigured** ADJ ❑ *...the scarred, disfigured face.* 2 V-T To **disfigure** an object or a place means to spoil its appearance. ❑ *Large blocks of flats disfigure our cities.*

D

Word Link	*grac ≈ pleasing : disgrace, grace, graceful*

disgrace /dɪs'greɪs/ (**disgraces, disgracing, disgraced**) 1 N-UNCOUNT & N-SING If you say that someone is **in disgrace**, you are emphasizing that other people disapprove of them and do not respect them because of something they have done. ❑ *The vice president resigned in disgrace.* ❑ *What went on was a scandal. It was a disgrace to Britain.* 2 N-SING If you say that something is **a disgrace**, you are emphasizing that it is very bad or wrong. ❑ *To withhold any information is an absolute disgrace.* 3 V-T If you say that someone **disgraces** someone else, you are emphasizing that their behaviour causes the other person to feel ashamed. ❑ *I have disgraced my family's name.*

disgraced /dɪs'greɪst/ ADJ You use **disgraced** to describe someone whose bad behaviour has caused them to lose the approval and respect of the public or of people in authority. ❑ *...the disgraced leader of the coup.*

disgraceful /dɪs'greɪsfʊl/ ADJ If you say that something is **disgraceful**, you disapprove of it strongly. ❑ *...his most disgraceful behaviour.* ● **disgracefully** ADV ❑ *His brother behaved disgracefully.*

disgruntled /dɪs'grʌntəld/ ADJ If you are **disgruntled**, you are angry and dissatisfied about something. ❑ *Disgruntled employees called for his resignation.*

disguise /dɪs'gaɪz/ (**disguises, disguising, disguised**) 1 V-T & N-VAR If you **disguise yourself**, or if you are **in disguise**, you alter your appearance so that people will not recognize you. ❑ *She disguised herself as a man.* ❑ *He was wearing that ridiculous disguise.* ● **disguised** ADJ ❑ *The extremists entered the building disguised as medical workers.* 2 V-T To **disguise** something means to hide it or change its appearance, so that people do not know about it or will not recognize it. ❑ *He made no attempt to disguise his agitation.* ● **disguised** ADJ ❑ *...a thinly disguised warning.*

disgust /dɪs'gʌst/ (**disgusts, disgusting, disgusted**) 1 N-UNCOUNT **Disgust** is a strong feeling of dislike or disapproval. ❑ *He spoke of his disgust at the incident.* 2 V-T To **disgust** someone means to make them feel a strong sense of dislike and disapproval. ❑ *He disgusted many people with his behaviour.*

disgusted /dɪs'gʌstɪd/ ADJ If you are **disgusted**, you have a strong feeling of dislike or disapproval. ❑ *I'm disgusted with the way that he was treated.* ● **disgustedly** ADV ❑ *Some of the soldiers disgustedly threw the medals into the water.*

disgusting /dɪs'gʌstɪŋ/ ADJ If you say that something is **disgusting**, you think it is extremely unpleasant or unacceptable. ❑ *...one of the most disgusting sights I ever saw.* ❑ *I think it's disgusting that people over 65 have to pay tax.*

dish /dɪʃ/ (**dishes, dishing, dished**) 1 N-COUNT A **dish** is a shallow container used for cooking or serving food. ❑ *...a dish of spaghetti.* 2 N-COUNT Food that is prepared in a particular style or combination can be referred to as a **dish**. ❑ *There are plenty of vegetarian dishes to choose from.* 3 N-COUNT You can use **dish** to refer to anything that is round and hollow in shape with a wide uncovered top. ❑ *...a satellite dish on the roof.*
→ see Picture Dictionary: **dish**
→ see **pottery**

▸ **dish out** 1 PHR-VERB If you **dish out** something, you distribute it among a number of people. [INFORMAL] ❑ *Our host dished out cucumber sandwiches to everyone.* 2 PHR-VERB If someone **dishes out** criticism or punishment, they give it to someone. 3 PHR-VERB If you **dish out** food, you serve it to people. ❑ *She dished him out a plate of stew.*

▸ **dish up** PHR-VERB If you **dish up** food, you serve it to people. ❑ *They dished up a superb meal.*

dishonest /dɪs'ɒnɪst/ ADJ If you say someone is **dishonest**, you mean that they are not honest and you cannot trust them. ❑ *It would be dishonest to mislead people.* ● **dishonestly** ADV ❑ *They acted dishonestly.*

dishonesty /dɪs'ɒnɪsti/ N-UNCOUNT **Dishonesty** is dishonest behaviour.

disillusion /ˌdɪsɪ'luːʒən/ (**disillusions, disillusioning, disillusioned**) 1 V-T If someone or something **disillusions** you, they make you realize that something is not as good as you thought. ❑ *He was disillusioned by his country's failure to change.* ● **disillusioned** ADJ ❑ *I've become very disillusioned with politics.* 2 N-UNCOUNT **Disillusion** is the same as **disillusionment**.

disillusionment /ˌdɪsɪ'luːʒənmənt/ N-UNCOUNT **Disillusionment** is the disappointment that you feel when you discover that someone or something is not as good as you had expected or thought. ❑ *...a sense of disillusionment with the government.*

disinfect /ˌdɪsɪn'fekt/ (**disinfects, disinfecting, disinfected**) V-T If you **disinfect** something, you clean it using a substance that kills germs. ❑ *Contact lenses should be disinfected daily.*

disinfectant /ˌdɪsɪn'fektənt/ (**disinfectants**) N-VAR **Disinfectant** is a substance that kills germs.

disintegrate /dɪs'ɪntɪgreɪt/ (**disintegrates, disintegrating, disintegrated**) 1 V-I If something **disintegrates**, it becomes seriously weakened and is divided or destroyed. ❑ *During October 1918 the Austro-Hungarian Empire began to disintegrate.* ● **disintegration** N-UNCOUNT ❑ *...the disintegration of a marriage.* 2 V-I If an object **disintegrates**, it breaks into many small pieces and is destroyed. ❑ *At 420 mph the windscreen disintegrated.*

disinterested /dɪs'ɪntrəstɪd/ 1 ADJ Someone who is **disinterested** is not involved in a situation or not likely to benefit from it and is therefore able to act in a fair and unselfish way. ❑ *Scientists can be expected to be impartial and disinterested.* 2 ADJ If you are **disinterested in** something, you are not interested in it. ❑ *Dan was disinterested in food.*

disk /dɪsk/ N-COUNT In a computer, the **disk** is the part where information is stored. [COMPUTING] ❑ *The program takes up 2.5 megabytes of disk space.*

'disk drive (**disk drives**) N-COUNT The **disk drive** on a computer is the part that contains the hard disk or into which a disk can be inserted. [COMPUTING]

dislike /ˌdɪs'laɪk/ (**dislikes, disliking, disliked**) 1 V-T & N-UNCOUNT If you **dislike** someone or something, or if you have a feeling of **dislike** towards them, you think they are unpleasant and you do not like them. ❑ *He disliked football.* ❑ *She looked at him with dislike.* 2 N-PLURAL Your **dislikes** are the things that you do not like. ❑ *Consider your likes and dislikes about your job.*

dislocate /'dɪsləkeɪt/ (**dislocates, dislocating, dislocated**) V-T If you **dislocate** a bone or a joint in your body, it moves out of its proper position. ❑ *Harrison dislocated a finger.* ❑ *...a dislocated shoulder.*

dislodge /ˌdɪs'lɒdʒ/ (**dislodges, dislodging, dislodged**) V-T To **dislodge** someone or something **from** a place or position means to make them move from that place or position. ❑ *Billy was trying to dislodge something from between his teeth.*

dismal /'dɪzməl/ 1 ADJ Something that is **dismal** is depressingly bad. ❑ *My prospects of a suitable job are dismal.* 2 ADJ Something that is **dismal** is bleak, sad, and depressing. ❑ *The main hospital is a bit dismal.* ❑ *...a dark dismal day.*

dismantle /ˌdɪs'mæntəl/ (**dismantles, dismantling, dismantled**) V-T If you **dismantle** a machine or structure, you take it apart carefully.

dismay /ˌdɪs'meɪ/ (**dismays, dismaying, dismayed**) N-UNCOUNT & V-T If you have a feeling of **dismay**, or if something **dismays** you, it makes you feel afraid, worried, or disappointed. [FORMAL] ❑ *Mr Reynolds expressed dismay at this idea.* ❑ *James realized she was crying and the thought dismayed him.* ● **dismayed** ADJ ❑ *He was dismayed to find that his hands were shaking.*

dismember /ˌdɪs'membə/ (**dismembers, dismembering, dismembered**) V-T To **dismember** the body of a dead person means to cut or pull it to pieces. ● **dismemberment** N-UNCOUNT ❑ *...torture or dismemberment.*

> **Word Link** *miss ≈ sending : dismiss, missile, missionary*

dismiss /ˌdɪs'mɪs/ (**dismisses, dismissing, dismissed**) 1 V-T If you **dismiss** something, you decide that it is not important enough for you to think about. ❑ *Mr Wakeham dismissed the reports as speculation.* 2 V-T When an employer **dismisses** an employee, they order the employee to leave his or her job. ❑ *He was dismissed for incompetence.* 3 V-T If you **are dismissed** by someone in authority, they tell you that you can go away from them. ❑ *Two more witnesses were called, heard and dismissed.*

> **Word Partnership** Use *dismiss* with:
>
> ADJ. **easy to** dismiss 1
> N. dismiss **an idea**, dismiss **a possibility** 1
> dismiss **an employee** 2
> dismiss **a case**, dismiss **charges** 3

dismissal /ˌdɪs'mɪsəl/ (**dismissals**) 1 N-VAR When an employee is dismissed from their job, you can refer to their **dismissal**. ❑ *They discussed Mr Low's dismissal from his post.* 2 N-UNCOUNT **Dismissal of** something means deciding or saying that it is not important. ❑ *...his arrogant dismissal of those who disagree.*

dismissive /ˌdɪs'mɪsɪv/ ADJ If you are **dismissive** of someone or something, you say or show that you think they are not important or have no value. ❑ *Mr Jones was dismissive of the report.* ❑ *This is the dismissive attitude scientists often take.* ● **dismissively** ADV ❑ *He describes Sally dismissively as 'that woman'.*

disobedience /ˌdɪsə'biːdiəns/ N-UNCOUNT **Disobedience** is deliberately refusing to do what someone in authority tells you to do, or to follow rules. ❑ *Will he be punished for his disobedience?*

disobey /ˌdɪsə'beɪ/ (**disobeys, disobeying, disobeyed**) V-T When someone **disobeys** a person or an order, they deliberately do not do what they have been told to do. ❑ *...a naughty boy who often disobeyed his mother and father.*

disorder /ˌdɪs'ɔːdə/ (**disorders**) 1 N-VAR A **disorder** is a problem or illness which affects a person's mind or body. ❑ *This nerve disorder causes paralysis of the arms.* 2 N-UNCOUNT **Disorder** is a state of being untidy, badly prepared, or badly organized. ❑ *The emergency room was in disorder.* 3 N-UNCOUNT **Disorder** is violence or rioting in public. ❑ *...forms of civil disorder – most notably, football hooliganism.*

D

disorderly /ˌdɪsˈɔːdəli/ ADJ If you describe something as **disorderly**, you mean that it is untidy, irregular, or disorganized. [FORMAL] ❑ *...the large and disorderly room.*

disorganized [BRIT also **disorganised**] /ˌdɪsˈɔːgənaɪzd/ ADJ **Disorganized** means badly organized, planned, or managed, often leading to a state of confusion. ❑ *The lectures are very disorganized.* ❑ *I'm completely disorganized.*

disorientated /ˌdɪsˈɔːrienteɪtɪd/ ADJ **Disorientated** means the same as **disoriented**.

disoriented [BRIT also **disorientated**] /ˌdɪsˈɔːrientid/ ADJ If you feel **disoriented**, you lose your sense of direction, or you feel generally lost and uncertain. ❑ *He is completely disoriented by what is going on.*

disown /dɪsˈəʊn/ (**disowns, disowning, disowned**) V-T If you **disown** someone or something, you no longer have any connection with them. ❑ *His wealthy parents disowned him.*

disparage /ˌdɪsˈpærɪdʒ/ (**disparages, disparaging, disparaged**) V-T If you **disparage** someone or something, you speak about them in a way which shows that you do not have a good opinion of them. ❑ *Larkin tended to disparage literature.* ● **disparagement** N-UNCOUNT ❑ *There was a certain tone of disparagement in his voice.* ● **disparaging** ADJ ❑ *A lot of very disparaging things have been said about Seattle.*

Word Link	***par** ≈ equal : compare, disparate, part*

disparate /ˈdɪspərət/ ADJ **Disparate** things are clearly different from each other in quality or type. [FORMAL] ❑ *Scientists are trying to pull together disparate ideas in astronomy.*

disparity /ˌdɪsˈpærɪti/ (**disparities**) N-VAR A **disparity between** two or more things is a noticeable difference between them. [FORMAL] ❑ *...disparities between poor and wealthy school districts.*

dispatch [BRIT also **despatch**] /dɪsˈpætʃ/ (**dispatches, dispatching, dispatched**) **1** V-T & N-UNCOUNT If you **dispatch** someone or something **to** a place, you send them there. You can also talk about **the dispatch of** people or things **to** a place. ❑ *The government dispatched soldiers to search the island.* **2** N-COUNT A **dispatch** is an official report sent to a person or organization by their representative in another place.

dispel /dɪsˈpel/ (**dispels, dispelling, dispelled**) V-T To **dispel** an idea or feeling means to stop people believing in it or feeling it. ❑ *The President dispelled the notion that he had neglected the economy.*

dispense /dɪsˈpens/ (**dispenses, dispensing, dispensed**) **1** V-T To **dispense** something means to give it to people. [FORMAL] ❑ *He is always happy to dispense advice.* **2** V-T When a chemist **dispenses** medicine, he or she prepares it and gives it to the patient.

▶ **dispense with** PHR-VERB If you **dispense with** something, you stop using it. ❑ *The princess dispensed with her bodyguards last year.*

dispenser /dɪsˈpensə/ (**dispensers**) N-COUNT A **dispenser** is a machine or container from which you can get things. ❑ *...cash dispensers.*

disperse /dɪsˈpɜːs/ (**disperses, dispersing, dispersed**) **1** V-T/V-I When a group of people **disperses**, or **is dispersed**, the group splits up and the people leave in different directions. ❑ *The crowd dispersed peacefully.* ❑ *Police eventually dispersed them with tear gas.* **2** V-T/V-I When things **disperse**, or when you **disperse** them, they spread over a wide area. ❑ *The leaflets were dispersed throughout the country.*

displace /dɪsˈpleɪs/ (**displaces, displacing, displaced**) **1** V-T If one thing **displaces** another, it forces the other thing out and occupies its position. ❑ *This story displaced the war news from the front page.* **2** V-T If someone **is displaced**, they are forced to move away from the area where they live. ❑ *...a camp housing more than 7,000 displaced people.* ● **displacement** N-UNCOUNT ❑ *...the gradual displacement of the Native American people.*

display /dɪsˈpleɪ/ (**displays, displaying, displayed**) **1** V-T & N-UNCOUNT If you **display** something, or if you put it **on display**, you put it in a place where people can see it. ❑ *War veterans proudly displayed their medals.* ❑ *These artists also have work on display.* **2** V-T & N-VAR If you **display** a quality or emotion, you behave in a way which shows that you have it. You can also talk about a **display of** a particular quality or emotion. ❑ *It was unlike Gordon to display his feelings.* ❑ *...his determined display of courage.* **3** N-COUNT A **display** is something which is intended to attract people's attention, for example an event or attractive arrangement of different things. ❑ *There is a permanent display of 300 of his paintings.* ❑ *...the firework display.*

displeasure /dɪsˈpleʒə/ N-UNCOUNT **Displeasure with** someone or something is a feeling of annoyance towards that person or about that thing. ❑ *He has voiced his displeasure over the results.*

disposable /dɪsˈpəʊzəbəl/ ADJ **Disposable** things are designed to be thrown away after use. ❑ *...disposable nappies.*

disposal /dɪsˈpəʊzəl/ **1** PHRASE If you have something **at** your **disposal**, you are able to use it whenever you want. If you are **at** someone's **disposal**, you are willing to help them in any way you can. ❑ *Do you have this information at your disposal?* **2** N-UNCOUNT The **disposal of** something is the act of getting rid of it. ❑ *...the disposal of radioactive waste.*

dispose /dɪsˈpəʊz/ (**disposes, disposing, disposed**)

▶ **dispose of** PHR-VERB If you **dispose of** something, you get rid of it, usually because you no longer want or need it. ❑ *Matthew disposed of the murder weapon.*

disposed /dɪsˈpəʊzd/ **1** ADJ AFTER LINK-V If you are **disposed to** do something, you are willing to do it. [FORMAL] ❑ *He was not disposed to discuss the matter.* **2** ADJ You can use **disposed** when you are talking about someone's general attitude or opinion. ❑ *Every government is ill-disposed to the press.*

disposition /ˌdɪspəˈzɪʃən/ (**dispositions**) N-COUNT Your **disposition** is the way that you tend to behave or feel. ❑ *...people of a nervous disposition.*

disprove /dɪsˈpruːv/ (**disproves, disproving, disproved**) V-T If you **disprove** an idea or belief, you show that it is not true.
→ see **science**

Word Link *put ≈ thinking : computer, dispute, undisputed*

dispute /dɪs'pjuːt/ (**disputes, disputing, disputed**) **1** N-VAR A **dispute** is a disagreement or quarrel between people. ❑ *...pay disputes with the government.* **2** V-T & PHRASE If you **dispute** a fact or opinion, you say that it is incorrect or untrue. If an issue is **in dispute**, people cannot agree about whether it is correct or true. ❑ *Nobody disputed that Davey was clever.* **3** V-T When people **dispute** something, they fight for control of it. ❑ *Fishermen from Bristol disputed fishing rights with the Danes.*

disqualify /dɪs'kwɒlɪfaɪ/ (**disqualifies, disqualifying, disqualified**) V-T When someone **is disqualified from** an event or an activity, they are officially stopped from taking part in it. ❑ *He was disqualified from driving for three years.* ● **disqualification** /ˌdɪsˌkwɒlɪfɪ'keɪʃən/ (**disqualifications**) N-VAR ❑ *...a four-year disqualification from athletics.*

disquiet /ˌdɪs'kwaɪət/ N-UNCOUNT **Disquiet** is a feeling of worry or anxiety. [FORMAL] ❑ *There is growing disquiet about the cost of police.*

disregard /ˌdɪsrɪ'gɑːd/ (**disregards, disregarding, disregarded**) V-T & N-UNCOUNT If you **disregard** something, or if you show **disregard for** it, you ignore it or do not take account of it. ❑ *He disregarded the advice of his executives.* ❑ *...a total disregard for the safety of the public.*

disrepute /ˌdɪsrɪ'pjuːt/ PHRASE If something is brought **into disrepute** or falls **into disrepute**, it loses its good reputation, because it is connected with activities that people do not approve of.

Word Link *rupt ≈ breaking : disrupt, erupt, interrupt*

disrupt /dɪs'rʌpt/ (**disrupts, disrupting, disrupted**) V-T If someone or something **disrupts** an event or process, they cause problems that prevent it from continuing normally. ❑ *Anti-war protesters disrupted the debate.* ● **disruption** (**disruptions**) N-VAR ❑ *The strike caused delays and disruption to flights.*

disruptive /dɪ'srʌptɪv/ ADJ If you say that someone is **disruptive**, you think they are preventing an activity or system from continuing normally. ❑ *He was a disruptive influence.*

diss /dɪs/ (**disses, dissing, dissed**) V-T If someone **disses** you, they criticize you unfairly or speak to you in a way that does not show respect. [mainly AM, INFORMAL] ❑ *Stella dissed her dad by leaving his wedding early.*

Word Link *sat, satis ≈ enough : dissatisfaction, insatiable, satisfy*

dissatisfaction /ˌdɪˌssætɪs'fækʃən/ N-UNCOUNT If you feel **dissatisfaction with** something, you are not satisfied with it. ❑ *She has already expressed her dissatisfaction with the policy.* ❑ *Low pay is a cause of job dissatisfaction among teachers.*

dissatisfied /ˌdɪ'ssætɪsfaɪd/ ADJ If you are **dissatisfied with** something, you are not contented or pleased with it. ❑ *82% of voters are dissatisfied with the way their country is being governed.*

Word Link *sect ≈ cutting : dissect, intersection, section*

dissect /daɪ'sekt, dɪ-/ (**dissects, dissecting, dissected**) V-T To **dissect** a dead body means to cut it up in order to examine it. ● **dissection** (**dissections**) N-VAR ❑ *...opposition to the dissection of animals in schools.*

disseminate /dɪ'semɪneɪt/ (**disseminates, disseminating, disseminated**) V-T To **disseminate** information means to distribute it, so that it reaches many people. [FORMAL] ❑ *Its aims are to collect and disseminate medical information.* ● **dissemination** N-UNCOUNT ❑ *...the dissemination of scientific ideas.*

dissent /dɪ'sent/ (**dissents, dissenting, dissented**) V-I & N-UNCOUNT If you **dissent**, or if you express **dissent**, you express disagreement with a decision or established opinion. [FORMAL] ❑ *One member dissented from the final vote.* ❑ *...voices of dissent.* ● **dissenting** ADJ ❑ *There were dissenting views among his colleagues.* ● **dissenter** (**dissenters**) N-COUNT ❑ *The Party does not tolerate dissenters.*

dissertation /ˌdɪsə'teɪʃən/ (**dissertations**) N-COUNT A **dissertation** is a long formal piece of writing, especially for a university degree.

dissident /'dɪsɪdənt/ (**dissidents**) N-COUNT **Dissidents** are people who criticize their repressive government. ❑ *...arrests of political dissidents.*

dissipate /'dɪsɪpeɪt/ (**dissipates, dissipating, dissipated**) V-T/V-I When something **dissipates**, or when you **dissipate** it, there is less of it or it becomes less strong, until it goes away completely. ❑ *The tension in the room dissipated.* ● **dissipation** N-UNCOUNT ❑ *...the dissipation of the ozone layer.*

dissociate /dɪ'səʊʃieɪt/ (**dissociates, dissociating, dissociated**) V-T If you **dissociate** yourself **from** someone or something, you say that you are not connected with them. ❑ *It seems harder and harder for the president to dissociate himself from the scandals.*

dissolve /dɪ'zɒlv/ (**dissolves, dissolving, dissolved**) **1** V-T/V-I If a substance **dissolves** in liquid, or if you **dissolve** a substance, it mixes with the liquid, becoming weaker until it finally disappears. ❑ *Heat until the sugar dissolves.* **2** V-T When something **is dissolved**, it is officially ended. [FORMAL] ❑ *The marriage was dissolved in 1976.* ● **dissolution** /ˌdɪsə'luːʃən/ N-UNCOUNT ❑ *...the dissolution of parliament.*

Word Link *suad, suas ≈ urging: dissuade, persuade, persuasive*

dissuade /dɪ'sweɪd/ (**dissuades, dissuading, dissuaded**) V-T If you **dissuade** someone **from** doing something, you persuade them not to do it. [FORMAL] ❑ *Do not let your anger dissuade you from being just.* ❑ *He considered emigrating, but his family managed to dissuade him.*

distance /'dɪstəns/ (**distances, distancing, distanced**) **1** N-VAR The **distance between** two places is the amount of space between them. ❑ *...the distance between the island and the nearby shore.* ❑ *...within walking distance.* **2** PHRASE If you are **at a distance from** something, or if you remember it **from a distance**, you are thinking about something which happened a long time ago. ❑ *Now I can look back on the whole tragedy from a*

d

distance of nearly forty years. **3** N-UNCOUNT **Distance** is detachment and remoteness in the way that someone behaves, so that they do not seem friendly. ❑ *There has been a sort of distance between us in the last few months.* **4** V-T If you **distance yourself from** someone or something, you become less involved with them. ❑ *The United States has distanced itself from the British plan.* ● **distanced** ADJ AFTER LINK-V ❑ *He'd become too distanced from his fans.*

D

Word Partnership Use *distance* with:

ADJ.	**safe** distance, **short** distance **1**
PREP.	distance **between, in the** distance, **within walking** distance **1** **at a** distance, **from a** distance **2**

distant /ˈdɪstənt/ **1** ADJ **Distant** means far away. [WRITTEN] ❑ *The mountains rolled away to a distant horizon.* ● **distantly** ADV ❑ *Rose heard a buzzer sound distantly.* **2** ADJ An event or time that is **distant** is far away in the past or future. ❑ *Things will improve in the not too distant future.* **3** ADJ A **distant** relative is one that you are not closely related to. ● **distantly** ADV ❑ *He's distantly related to the Royal family.* **4** ADJ AFTER LINK-V If you describe someone as **distant**, you find them emotionally detached and unfriendly. **5** ADJ If you describe someone as **distant**, you mean that they are not paying attention because they are thinking about something else. ❑ *He had a distant look on his face and seemed lost in thought.* ● **distantly** ADV ❑ *She nodded distantly and didn't seem to listen to his comments.*

Thesaurus *distant* Also look up:

ADJ.	faraway, remote; *(ant.)* close, near **1** aloof, cool, unfriendly **4**

distaste /ˌdɪsˈteɪst/ N-UNCOUNT If you feel **distaste for** someone or something, you dislike or disapprove of them. ❑ *She expressed her distaste for the idea.* ❑ *Roger looked at her with distaste.*

distasteful /ˌdɪsˈteɪstfʊl/ ADJ If something is **distasteful to** you, you dislike or disapprove of it. ❑ *Such ideas are distasteful to them.* ❑ *I find her gossip distasteful.*

distil [AM **distill**] /dɪsˈtɪl/ (**distils, distilling, distilled**) V-T If a liquid such as whisky **is distilled**, it is heated until it evaporates and then cooled until it becomes liquid again. ❑ *...a gallon of distilled water.* ● **distillation** N-UNCOUNT ❑ *...the distillation process.*

distinct /dɪˈstɪŋkt/ **1** ADJ If one thing is **distinct from** another, there is an important difference between them. ❑ *Engineering and technology are disciplines distinct from one another.* ● **distinctly** ADV ❑ *This industry has two distinctly different sectors.* **2** ADJ If something is **distinct**, you hear or see it clearly. ❑ *Mark still has a distinct Scottish accent.* ● **distinctly** ADV ❑ *I distinctly heard the loudspeaker.* **3** ADJ If an idea, thought, or intention is **distinct**, it is clear and definite. ❑ *There was a distinct change in her attitude.* ● **distinctly** ADV ❑ *I distinctly remember wishing I was not involved.*

distinction /dɪˈstɪŋkʃən/ (**distinctions**) **1** N-COUNT A **distinction** is a difference between similar things. If you **draw** or **make a distinction between** two things, you say that they are different. ❑ *There are obvious distinctions between the two areas.* ❑ *He draws a distinction between art and culture.* **2** N-UNCOUNT **Distinction** is the quality of being excellent. ❑ *...furniture of distinction.*

distinctive /dɪˈstɪŋktɪv/ ADJ Something that is **distinctive** has special qualities that make it easily recognizable. ❑ *His voice was very distinctive.* ● **distinctively** ADV ❑ *...a strong, distinctively tangy flavour.*

distinguish /dɪˈstɪŋgwɪʃ/ (**distinguishes, distinguishing, distinguished**) **1** V-T If you can **distinguish** one thing **from** another, you can see or understand the difference between them. ❑ *Could he distinguish right from wrong?* ❑ *...distinguishing between areas of light and dark.* **2** V-T A feature or quality that **distinguishes** one thing **from** another causes the two things to be regarded as different. ❑ *Something about music distinguishes it from all other art forms.* **3** V-T If you can **distinguish** something, you can see, hear, or taste it although it is very difficult to detect. [FORMAL] ❑ *He could distinguish voices.* **4** V-T If you **distinguish yourself**, you do something that makes you famous or important. ❑ *He distinguished himself as a long distance runner.*

distinguished /dɪˈstɪŋgwɪʃt/ ADJ A **distinguished** person is very successful, famous, or important. ❑ *...a distinguished academic family.*

distinguishing /dɪˈstɪŋgwɪʃɪŋ/ ADJ The **distinguishing features** of something are the features which make it different from other things of the same type. ❑ *Each of the islands has its own distinguishing features.*

distort /dɪˈstɔːt/ (**distorts, distorting, distorted**) **1** V-T If you **distort** a statement, fact, or idea, you report or represent it in an untrue way. ❑ *The media distorts reality.* ● **distorted** ADJ ❑ *This led some of us to a distorted view of the real crime.* ● **distortion** (**distortions**) N-VAR ❑ *It was a deliberate distortion of the facts.* **2** V-T If something you can see or hear **is distorted**, its appearance or sound is changed so that it seems strange. ❑ *A painter may exaggerate or distort shapes.* ● **distorted** ADJ ❑ *The slightly distorted image is caused by the projector.* ● **distortion** N-VAR ❑ *This technology removes distortion and echo from telephone calls.*

distract /dɪˈstrækt/ (**distracts, distracting, distracted**) V-T If something **distracts** you, or if it **distracts** your **attention**, it stops you concentrating. ❑ *Playing video games sometimes distracts him from his homework.* ● **distracting** ADJ ❑ *The barking of the little dog was very distracting.*

distracted /dɪˈstræktɪd/ ADJ If you are **distracted**, you are very worried or are not concentrating. ● **distractedly** ADV ❑ *He looked up distractedly. 'I'll be with you in a second'.*

distraction /dɪˈstrækʃən/ (**distractions**) **1** N-VAR A **distraction** is something that takes your attention away from what you are doing. ❑ *This is a distraction from what I really want to do.* **2** N-COUNT A **distraction** is an activity that is intended to entertain people. ❑ *Their national distraction is going to the disco.*

distraught /ˌdɪˈstrɔːt/ ADJ If someone is **distraught**, they are extremely upset or worried. ❑ *His distraught parents were comforted by relatives.*

distress /dɪˈstres/ (**distresses, distressing, distressed**) **1** N-UNCOUNT **Distress** is extreme unhappiness, suffering, or pain. ❑ *Jealousy causes distress and painful emotions.* **2** N-UNCOUNT

Distress is the state of being in extreme danger and needing urgent help. ❑ *The ship might be in distress.* **3** V-T If someone or something **distresses** you, they cause you to be upset or worried. ❑ *The idea of Toni being in danger distresses him enormously.* ● **distressed** ADJ ❑ *She was too exhausted and distressed to talk.* ● **distressing** ADJ ❑ *...distressing news.* ● **distressingly** ADV ❑ *Her face had grown distressingly old.*

Word Link	*tribute ≈ giving: attribute, contribute, distribute*

distribute /dɪ'strɪbju:t/ (**distributes, distributing, distributed**) **1** V-T If you **distribute** things, you hand them or deliver them to a number of people. ❑ *Soldiers are working to distribute food and blankets.* ● **distribution** N-UNCOUNT ❑ *...the distribution of leaflets and posters.* **2** V-T When a company **distributes** goods, it supplies them to the shops or businesses that sell them. ● **distribution** N-UNCOUNT ❑ *...the production and distribution of goods and services.* ● **distributor** (**distributors**) N-COUNT ❑ *...Spain's largest distributor of petroleum products.* **3** V-T If you **distribute** things **among** the members of a group, you share them among those members. ❑ *Distribute housework evenly among all family members.*

distribution /ˌdɪstrɪ'bju:ʃən/ (**distributions**) N-VAR The **distribution of** something is how much of it there is in each place or at each time. ❑ *...a more equitable distribution of wealth.*

district /'dɪstrɪkt/ (**districts**) **1** N-COUNT A **district** is an area of a town or country. ❑ *I drove around the business district.* **2** N-COUNT A **district** is an area of a town or country which has been given official boundaries for the purpose of administration. ❑ *...Glasgow District Council.*

ˌdistrict at'torney (**district attorneys**) N-COUNT In the United States, a **District Attorney** is a lawyer who works as the State prosecutor in a district. The abbreviation **D.A.** is also used.

distrust /ˌdɪs'trʌst/ (**distrusts, distrusting, distrusted**) V-T & N-UNCOUNT If you **distrust** someone or something, or if you feel **distrust** for them, you think that they are not honest, reliable, or safe. ❑ *I don't have any reason to distrust them.* ❑ *...a distrust of all political authority.*

disturb /dɪ'stɜ:b/ (**disturbs, disturbing, disturbed**) **1** V-T If you **disturb** someone, you interrupt what they are doing and cause them inconvenience. ❑ *She slept in a separate room in order not to disturb him.* **2** V-T If something **disturbs** you, it makes you feel upset or worried. ❑ *Her questions disturbed him.* **3** V-T If something **is disturbed**, its position or shape is changed. ❑ *Do not disturb the eggs as they cook.*

Word Partnership	Use *disturb* with:
N.	disturb **the neighbors**, disturb **the peace** 1
V.	**do not** disturb 1
	be careful not to disturb, **be sorry to** disturb 1 2

disturbance /dɪ'stɜ:bəns/ (**disturbances**) **1** N-COUNT A **disturbance** is an incident in which people behave violently in public. ❑ *During the disturbance, three men were hurt.* **2** N-UNCOUNT **Disturbance** means upsetting or disrupting something which was previously in a calm and orderly state. ❑ *The nursing home causes less disturbance to local residents than a school.*

disturbed /dɪ'stɜ:bd/ ADJ Someone who is **disturbed** is extremely worried, unhappy, or mentally ill. ❑ *...severely emotionally disturbed children.*

disturbing /dɪ'stɜ:bɪŋ/ ADJ Something that is **disturbing** makes you feel upset or worried. ❑ *There was something about him she found disturbing.* ● **disturbingly** ADV ❑ *...a disturbingly high number of injuries.*

disused /ˌdɪs'ju:zd/ ADJ A **disused** place or building is no longer used. ❑ *...a disused factory.*

ditch /dɪtʃ/ (**ditches, ditching, ditched**) **1** N-COUNT A **ditch** is a long narrow channel cut into the ground at the side of a road or field. **2** V-T If you **ditch** something, you get rid of it. [INFORMAL] ❑ *I decided to ditch the sofa bed.*

dither /'dɪðə/ (**dithers, dithering, dithered**) V-I If someone **dithers**, they hesitate because they are unable to make a quick decision about something. ❑ *After dithering for a fortnight I decided I had to see her again.*

dive /daɪv/ (**dives, diving, dived** or [AM also] **dove**) **1** V-I & N-COUNT If you **dive**, or if you **do** a **dive**, you jump head-first into water with your arms straight above your head. ❑ *She was standing by a pool, about to dive in.* ❑ *I performed the dive in front of 50 people.* **2** V-I & N-COUNT If you **dive**, or if you **do** a **dive**, you go under the surface of the sea or a lake, using special breathing equipment. ● **diver** (**divers**) N-COUNT ❑ *Divers have found the wreck.* ● **diving** N-UNCOUNT ❑ *This is diving at its most thrilling.* **3** V-I When birds and animals **dive**, they go quickly downwards, head-first, through the air or water. ❑ *The shark dived down and swam under the boat.* **4** V-I & N-COUNT If you **dive**, or if you make a **dive**, in a particular direction, you jump or rush in that direction. ❑ *They dived into a taxi.* ❑ *He made a sudden dive for Uncle Jim's legs.*

Word Link	*di ≈ two: dialogue, dilemma, diverge*

Word Link	*verg, vert ≈ turning: converge, diverge, subvert*

diverge /daɪ'vɜ:dʒ, AM dɪ-/ (**diverges, diverging, diverged**) **1** V-I When things **diverge**, they are different, or become different. ❑ *His interests increasingly diverged from those of his colleagues.* **2** V-I When roads or paths **diverge**, they begin leading in different directions. ❑ *This is where the railway lines for Florence and Ancona diverge.*

divergent /daɪ'vɜ:dʒənt, AM dɪ-/ ADJ Things that are **divergent** are different from each other. ❑ *Similar customs were known in widely divergent cultures.* ● **divergence** (**divergences**) N-VAR ❑ *There's a divergence of opinion within the party.*

diverse /daɪ'vɜ:s, AM dɪ-/ ADJ If a group or range is **diverse**, it is made up of a wide variety of things. ❑ *...shops selling a diverse range of gifts.*

Word Link	*ify ≈ making: clarify, diversify, intensify*

diversify /daɪ'vɜ:sɪfaɪ, AM dɪ-/ (**diversifies,**

diversifying, diversified) V-T/V-I When an organization or person **diversifies into** other things, or when they **diversify** their activities, they increase the variety of things that they do or make. ❑ *The company's troubles started when it diversified into new products.* ● **diversification** /daɪˌvɜːsɪfɪˈkeɪʃən, AM dɪ-/ (**diversifications**) N-VAR ❑ *There is not much diversification a hill farmer can attempt.*

D

diversion /daɪˈvɜːʃən, AM dɪˈvɜːrʒən/ (**diversions**) 1 N-COUNT A **diversion** is an action or event that attracts your attention away from what you are doing. ❑ *The robbers escaped after throwing smoke bombs to create a diversion.* ● **diversionary** ADJ ❑ *We fear there may be diversionary attacks elsewhere in the city.* 2 N-COUNT A **diversion** is a special route arranged for traffic when the normal route cannot be used. [BRIT] 3 → see also **divert**

diversity /daɪˈvɜːsɪti, AM dɪ-/ (**diversities**) 1 N-VAR The **diversity of** something is the fact that it contains many very different elements. ❑ *...to introduce more choice and diversity into the education system.* 2 N-SING A **diversity of** things is a range of things which are very different from each other. ❑ *...how to grow a diversity of vegetables .* → see **zoo**

divert /daɪˈvɜːt, AM dɪ-/ (**diverts, diverting, diverted**) 1 V-T To **divert** people or vehicles means to change their course. ❑ *Police diverted traffic away from the Square.* 2 V-T To **divert** money or resources means to cause them to be used for a different purpose. ❑ *The government diverted more public funds from west to east.* ● **diversion** N-UNCOUNT ❑ *...the illegal diversion of profits from secret arms sales.* 3 V-T If someone **diverts** your attention **from** something important or serious, they stop you thinking about it by making you think about something else. ❑ *They want to divert the attention of the people from the real issues.*

divide /dɪˈvaɪd/ (**divides, dividing, divided**) 1 V-T & PHR-VERB To **divide** something or to **divide** it **up**, means to separate it into two or more parts. ❑ *Divide the pastry in half.* ❑ *The idea is to divide up the country into four sectors.* ❑ *Paul divides most of his spare time between the study and his bedroom.* 2 V-T If you **divide** a larger number **by** a smaller number, you calculate how many times the smaller number can go exactly into the larger number. ❑ *Measure the floor area of the greenhouse and divide it by six.* 3 V-T If a border or line **divides** two areas, it keeps them separate from each other. ❑ *A long border divides Mexico from the United States.* 4 V-T If something **divides** people, it causes strong disagreement between them. ❑ *Enormous differences still divide the two sides.* ● **divided** ADJ ❑ *The democrats are divided over whether to admit him into their group.* 5 N-COUNT A **divide** is a significant difference between two groups. ❑ *This tends to widen the North-South divide.*
▸ **divide up** → see **divide** (meaning 1)

Thesaurus	*divide* Also look up:
V.	categorize, group, segregate, separate, split 1

dividend /ˈdɪvɪdend/ (**dividends**) 1 N-COUNT A **dividend** is the part of a company's profits which is paid to people who have shares in the company. 2 PHRASE If something **pays dividends**, it brings advantages at a later date. ❑ *A little planning now will pay dividends later.*

Word Link	***dei, div** ≈ God, god : **dei**ty, **div**ine, **div**inity*

divine /dɪˈvaɪn/ ADJ You use **divine** to describe something that is provided by or relates to a god or goddess. ❑ *He did not believe in divine retribution.* ● **divinely** ADV ❑ *The law was divinely ordained.* ● **divinity** /dɪˈvɪnɪti/ N-UNCOUNT ❑ *The emperor renounced his divinity.*

diving /ˈdaɪvɪŋ/ → see **dive**

division /dɪˈvɪʒən/ (**divisions**) 1 N-UNCOUNT The **division of** something is the act of separating it into two or more different parts. ❑ *...the re-unification of Germany, after its division into two states.* ❑ *...the division of labor between workers and management.* 2 N-COUNT A **division** is a significant distinction or difference of opinion between two groups. ❑ *...the division between rich and poor.* 3 N-UNCOUNT **Division** is the mathematical process of dividing one number by another. 4 N-COUNT A **division** is a department in a large organization. ❑ *...the bank's Latin American division.* ● **divisional** ADJ BEFORE N ❑ *...the divisional headquarters.*
→ see **mathematics**

divisive /dɪˈvaɪsɪv/ ADJ Something that is **divisive** causes hostility between people. [FORMAL] ❑ *Independence is a divisive issue.*

divorce /dɪˈvɔːs/ (**divorces, divorcing, divorced**) 1 V-T/V-I & N-VAR When someone **divorces** their husband or wife, or obtains a **divorce** from them, their marriage is legally ended. ❑ *Her parents divorced when she was nine.* ❑ *He divorced his wife in June after nine years of marriage.* ❑ *Numerous marriages now end in divorce.* ● **divorced** ADJ ❑ *Princess Margaret is divorced from Lord Snowdon.* 2 V-T If one thing **is divorced from** another, they become separate from each other. [FORMAL] ❑ *You can't divorce finance from manufacturing.*

divorcee /dɪvɔːˈsiː/ (**divorcees**) N-COUNT A **divorcee** is someone who is divorced.

divulge /daɪˈvʌldʒ, AM dɪ-/ (**divulges, divulging, divulged**) V-T If you **divulge** a piece of information, you tell someone about it. [FORMAL] ❑ *I do not want to divulge where the village is.*

DIY /ˌdiː aɪ ˈwaɪ/ N-UNCOUNT **DIY** is the activity of making or repairing things in your home. **DIY** is an abbreviation for 'do-it-yourself'.

dizzy /ˈdɪzi/ ADJ If you **feel dizzy**, you feel that you are losing your balance and are about to fall. ❑ *He kept feeling dizzy.* ● **dizziness** N-UNCOUNT ❑ *She suffered from dizziness.*

DJ also **dj** /ˌdiː ˈdʒeɪ/ (**DJs**) N-COUNT A **DJ** is someone who plays and introduces pop records on the radio or at a club. A **DJ** is the same as a **disc jockey**.

DNA /ˌdiː en ˈeɪ/ N-UNCOUNT **DNA** is an acid that is contained in the cells of living things. It determines the particular structure and functions of every cell. **DNA** is an abbreviation for 'deoxyribonucleic acid'.
→ see **clone**

do /də, STRONG duː/ (**does, doing, did, done**)

Two of the major uses of **do** are in forming negatives and questions.

1 V-T You use **do** to say that someone performs

an action, activity, or task. ❑ *...do the housework.* **2** V-T To **do** something about a problem means to try to solve it. ❑ *Though he didn't like it there wasn't much he could do about it.* **3** V-T You use **do** to say that something has a particular result or effect. ❑ *A few bombs can do a lot of damage.* ❑ *The publicity did her career no harm.* **4** V-T If you ask someone what they **do**, you are asking what their job is. **5** V-I If someone **does** well or badly, they are successful or unsuccessful. ❑ *Connie did well at school.* **6** V-T If you **do** a subject, you study it at school or college. ❑ *I'd like to do maths at university.* **7** V-T You use **do** when referring to the speed that something achieves or can achieve. ❑ *They were doing 70 miles an hour.* **8** V-I If you say that something will **do**, you mean that it is satisfactory. ❑ *Give them a prize. Anything will do.* **9** N-COUNT A **do** is a party, dinner party, or other social event. [BRIT, INFORMAL] ❑ *A friend of his is having a do in Stoke.* ❑ *They always have all-night dos there.* **10** → see also **done** **11** PHRASE If you say that you **could do with** something, you mean that you need it or would benefit from it. ❑ *I could do with a cup of tea.* **12** PHRASE If you ask **what** someone **is doing** in a particular place, you are expressing surprise that they are there. ❑ *What was he doing in Hyde Park at that time of the morning?* **13** PHRASE What something **has to do with** or **is to do with** is what it is connected or concerned with. ❑ *They were shouting at each other. It was something to do with money.*

▶ **do away with** PHR-VERB To **do away with** something means to get rid of it. ❑ *The long-range goal must be to do away with nuclear weapons.*

▶ **do out of** PHR-VERB If you **do** someone **out of** something, you unfairly cause them not to have it. [INFORMAL] ❑ *The others have done him out of his share.*

▶ **do up** **1** PHR-VERB If you **do** something **up**, you fasten it. ❑ *Mari did up the buttons.* ❑ *Do your coat up.* **2** PHR-VERB To **do up** an old building means to repair and decorate it. ❑ *Nicholas bought a barn in Provence and spent August doing it up.*

▶ **do without** PHR-VERB If you **do without** something, you manage or survive in spite of not having it. ❑ *I can do without your jokes, thank you very much.*

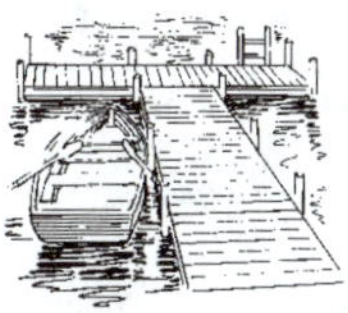
dock

dock /dɒk/ (**docks, docking, docked**) **1** N-COUNT A **dock** is an enclosed area of water where ships are loaded, unloaded, or repaired. **2** V-T/V-I When a ship **docks** or **is docked**, it is brought into a dock. ❑ *The vessel docked at Liverpool.* **3** V-T/V-I When one spacecraft **docks** or **is docked with** another, they join together in space. **4** N-SING In a law court, **the dock** is the place where the person accused of a crime sits. [BRIT] **5** V-T If you **dock** something such as someone's salary, you take some of it away as a punishment. ❑ *He was stripped of his rank and docked pay for one month.*

Word Link	*doct ≈ teaching : doctor, doctorate, doctrine*

doctor /'dɒktə/ (**doctors, doctoring, doctored**) **1** N-COUNT & N-TITLE & N-VOC A **doctor** is someone qualified in medicine who treats people who are ill. ❑ *Don't hesitate to call the doctor if you are at all uneasy.* ❑ *Doctor Paige will be here right after lunch.* **2** N-SING **The doctor's** is used to refer to the surgery or clinic where a doctor works. ❑ *I have an appointment at the doctor's.* **3** N-COUNT & N-TITLE **Doctor** is the title given to someone who has been awarded the highest academic degree by a university. ❑ *...a doctor of philosophy.* **4** V-T To **doctor** something means to deliberately change it in order to deceive people. ❑ *They doctored the photos, to make her look as bad as possible.*

doctorate /'dɒktərət/ (**doctorates**) N-COUNT A **doctorate** is the highest degree awarded by a university.

doctrine /'dɒktrɪn/ (**doctrines**) N-VAR A **doctrine** is a set of principles or beliefs. ❑ *...religious doctrine.* • **doctrinal** /dɒk'traɪnəl, AM 'dɑːktrɪnəl/ ADJ ❑ *...complex doctrinal questions.*

document (**documents, documenting, documented**) **1** N-COUNT /'dɒkjəmənt/ A **document** is an official piece of paper with writing on it. ❑ *...travel documents.* **2** V-T /'dɒkjəment/ If you **document** something, you make a detailed record of it on film, tape, or paper. ❑ *The book documents his prison experiences.*
→ see **diary, history, printing**

documentary /,dɒkjə'mentri/ (**documentaries**) **1** N-COUNT A **documentary** is a radio or television programme or a film which provides factual information about a particular subject. ❑ *...a TV documentary on homelessness.* **2** ADJ BEFORE N **Documentary** evidence consists of things that are written down.

documentation /,dɒkjəmen'teɪʃən/ N-UNCOUNT **Documentation** consists of documents which provide a record of something. ❑ *I had full documentation of our expenses.*

dodge /dɒdʒ/ (**dodges, dodging, dodged**) **1** V-I If you **dodge** somewhere, you move there suddenly to avoid being hit, caught, or seen. ❑ *We dodged behind a pillar out of sight of the tourists.* **2** V-T If you **dodge** a moving object, you avoid it by quickly moving aside. ❑ *He dodged the speeding car.* **3** V-T If you **dodge** something such as a problem, you avoid thinking about it or dealing with it. ❑ *I dodged military service by pretending to be ill.*

dodgy /'dɒdʒi/ (**dodgier, dodgiest**) **1** ADJ If you describe someone or something as **dodgy**, you disapprove of them because they seem rather dishonest and unreliable. **2** ADJ If you say that something is **dodgy**, you mean that it seems rather risky or unreliable. ❑ *...some pretty dodgy food.*

does /dəz, STRONG dʌz/ **Does** is the third person singular of the present tense of **do**.

doesn't /'dʌzənt/ **Doesn't** is the usual spoken form of 'does not'.

dog /dɒg, AM dɔːg/ (**dogs, dogging, dogged**) **1** N-COUNT A **dog** is an animal that is often kept as a pet or used to guard or hunt things. **2** V-T If problems or injuries **dog** you, they keep affecting you. ❑ *His retirement was dogged by illnesses.*
→ see **disability**

dogged /'dɒgɪd, AM 'dɔː-/ ADJ BEFORE N If you describe someone's actions as **dogged**, you mean that they are determined to continue with something, however difficult it becomes. ❑ *...one man's dogged determination to do something everyone*

d

else considered eccentric. • **doggedness** N-UNCOUNT ❑ *Most of my accomplishments came as the result of sheer doggedness.* • **doggedly** ADV ❑ *She fought doggedly for her rights.*

dogma /'dɒgmə, AM 'dɔːg-/ (**dogmas**) N-VAR If you refer to a belief or a system of beliefs as a **dogma**, you are criticizing it for expecting people to accept that it is true without questioning it. ❑ *The unions accuse the government of political dogma.*

D

dogmatic /dɒg'mætɪk, AM dɔːg-/ ADJ If you say that someone is **dogmatic**, you are criticizing them for following rules or principles rigidly without paying any attention to other factors. ❑ *...a dogmatic approach to solving political issues.* • **dogmatically** ADV ❑ *He would not dogmatically oppose government intervention.* • **dogmatism** /'dɒgmətɪzəm, AM 'dɔːg-/ N-UNCOUNT ❑ *Dogmatism cannot stand in the way of progress.*

,do-it-your'self N-UNCOUNT **Do-it-yourself** is the activity of making or repairing things in your home yourself, rather than employing other people. **Do-it-yourself** is the same as **DIY**.

doldrums /'dɒldrəmz/ PHRASE If an area of activity is **in the doldrums**, nothing new or exciting is happening.

dole /dəʊl/ (**doles, doling, doled**) **1** N-UNCOUNT In British English, **the dole** is money that is given regularly by the government to people who are unemployed. The usual American word is **welfare**. **2** PHRASE In British English, someone who is **on the dole** is registered as unemployed and receives money to live on from the government. The usual American expression is **on welfare**.
▶ **dole out** PHR-VERB If you **dole** something **out**, you give a certain amount of it to each member of a group.

doll /dɒl/ (**dolls**) N-COUNT A **doll** is a child's toy which looks like a small person or baby.

dolphin

dollar /'dɒlə/ (**dollars**) N-COUNT The **dollar** is a unit of money in the USA, Canada, and some other countries. It is represented by the symbol $.

dolphin /'dɒlfɪn/ (**dolphins**) N-COUNT A **dolphin** is a mammal with fins and a pointed nose which lives in the sea.
→ see **whale**

Word Link ***dom, domin ≈ rule, master : domain, dominate, predominant***

Word Link ***dom ≈ home : domain, dome, domestic***

dome

domain /də'meɪn/ (**domains**) **1** N-COUNT A **domain** is a particular area of activity or interest. [FORMAL] ❑ *...the domain of science.* **2** N-COUNT Someone's **domain** is the area where they have control or influence. [FORMAL] ❑ *Her office was her private, personal domain.*

dome /dəʊm/ (**domes**) N-COUNT A **dome** is a round roof. ❑ *...the dome of St Paul's cathedral.*

domestic /də'mestɪk/ **1** ADJ **Domestic** political activities and situations happen or exist within one particular country. ❑ *...a mixture of domestic and foreign news.* ❑ *...over 100 domestic flights a day to 15 UK destinations.* **2** ADJ BEFORE N **Domestic** means relating to or concerned with the home and family. ❑ *...his happy domestic life.* ❑ *...domestic appliances.* **3** ADJ BEFORE N **Domestic** animals are not wild, and are kept as pets or on farms.

dominant /'dɒmɪnənt/ ADJ Someone or something that is **dominant** is more powerful or noticeable than other people or things. ❑ *She was a dominant figure in the French film industry.* • **dominance** N-UNCOUNT ❑ *...the growing dominance of the English language.*

Thesaurus *dominance* Also look up:

N. authority, control, supremacy, upper hand

dominate /'dɒmɪneɪt/ (**dominates, dominating, dominated**) **1** V-T To **dominate** a situation means to be the most powerful or important person or thing in it. ❑ *The book is expected to dominate the best-seller lists.* ❑ *...countries where life is dominated by war.* • **domination** N-UNCOUNT ❑ *...the domination of the market by a small number of organizations.* **2** V-T If one person **dominates** another, they have power over them. ❑ *Women are no longer dominated by the men in their relationships.* • **dominating** ADJ ❑ *He had a very dominating personality.* • **domination** N-UNCOUNT ❑ *...five centuries of domination by the Romans.*

dominion /də'mɪnjən/ (**dominions**) **1** N-COUNT **Dominion** is control or authority. [FORMAL] ❑ *They truly believe they have dominion over us.* **2** N-COUNT A **dominion** is an area of land that is controlled by a ruler. ❑ *The Republic is a dominion of the Brazilian people.*

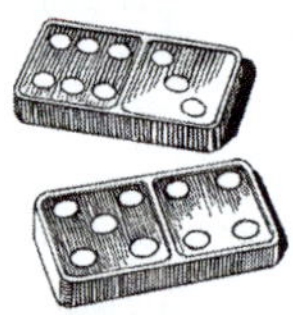

dominoes

domino /'dɒmɪnəʊ/ (**dominoes**) N-VAR **Dominoes** is a game played using small rectangular blocks, called **dominoes**, which are marked with two groups of spots on one side.

Word Link ***don ≈ giving : donate, donor, pardon***

donate /dəʊ'neɪt/ (**donates, donating, donated**) **1** V-T If you **donate** something **to** a charity or other organization, you give it to them. ❑ *They donated second-hand clothes.* • **donation** (**donations**) N-VAR ❑ *She made a £500,000 donation to the charity last year.* **2** V-T If you **donate** your blood or a part of your body, you allow doctors to use it to help somebody who is ill. • **donation** N-UNCOUNT ❑ *...kidney donation.*
→ see **donor**

Word Partnership Use *donation* with:

V. **accept a** donation, **make a** donation, **receive a** donation

ADJ. **charitable** donation, **generous** donation, **suggested** donation

done /dʌn/ **1** **Done** is the past participle of **do**. **2** ADJ AFTER LINK-V A task that is **done** has been completed. ❑ *The damage was done by the time Giggs came.* ❑ *As soon as the cake is done, remove it from the oven.*

donkey /ˈdɒŋki/ (**donkeys**) N-COUNT A **donkey** is an animal like a small horse with long ears.

Word Link	*don ≈ giving : donate, donor, pardon*

donor /ˈdəʊnə/ (**donors**) **1** N-COUNT A **donor** is someone who gives a part of their body or some of their blood to be used by doctors to help a person who is ill. **2** N-COUNT A **donor** is someone who gives something such as money to a charity or other organization.
→ see Word Web: **donor**

don't /dəʊnt/ **Don't** is the usual spoken form of **do not**.

donut /ˈdəʊnʌt/ (**donuts**) → see **doughnut**

doom /duːm/ N-UNCOUNT **Doom** is a terrible state or event in the future which you cannot prevent. ❑ *I awoke with a terrible sense of doom and fear.*

doomed /duːmd/ **1** ADJ Someone or something that is **doomed** is certain to fail. ❑ *...a doomed attempt to rescue the children.* **2** ADJ If someone is **doomed to** an unpleasant fate, they are certain to suffer it. ❑ *If he lived, he was doomed to spend the war as a prisoner.*

door /dɔː/ (**doors**) **1** N-COUNT A **door** is a swinging or sliding piece of wood, glass, or metal, which is used to open and close the entrance to a building, room, cupboard, or vehicle. ❑ *I knocked at the front door; there was no answer.* **2** N-COUNT A **door** is the space in a wall when a door is open. ❑ *She looked through the door.* **3** PHRASE When you **answer the door**, you go and open the door because a visitor has knocked on it or rung the bell. **4** PHRASE If someone goes **from door to door** or goes **door to door**, they go along a street calling at each house in turn, for example selling something. **5** PHRASE When you are **out of doors**, you are not inside a building, but in the open air. ❑ *The weather was fine enough for working out of doors.* **6** → see also **next door**

doorstep /ˈdɔːstep/ (**doorsteps**) **1** N-COUNT A **doorstep** is a step on the outside of a building, in front of a door. **2** PHRASE If a place is **on** your **doorstep**, it is very near to where you live. ❑ *...a giant oil refinery right on their doorstep.*

doorway /ˈdɔːweɪ/ (**doorways**) N-COUNT A **doorway** is the space in a wall where a door opens and closes. ❑ *He stood in the doorway, smiling.*

dope /dəʊp/ (**dopes, doping, doped**) **1** N-UNCOUNT **Dope** is an illegal drug, especially cannabis. [INFORMAL] **2** V-T If someone **dopes** a person or animal, they force them or trick them into taking drugs.

dormant /ˈdɔːmənt/ ADJ Something that is **dormant** has not been active or used for a long time, but is capable of becoming active. ❑ *...the long dormant volcano.* ❑ *The buds will remain dormant until spring.*
→ see **plant**

dormitory /ˈdɔːmɪtri, AM -tɔːri/ (**dormitories**) N-COUNT A **dormitory** is a large bedroom where several people sleep, for example in a boarding school.

dosage /ˈdəʊsɪdʒ/ (**dosages**) N-COUNT The **dosage** of a medicine or drug is the amount that should be taken. ❑ *...the correct dosage of insulin.*

dose /dəʊs/ (**doses, dosing, dosed**) **1** N-COUNT A **dose of** a medicine or drug is a measured amount of it. ❑ *One dose of penicillin can treat the infection.* **2** V-T To **dose** someone means to give them a medicine or drug. ❑ *He dosed himself with painkillers.*

dosh /dɒʃ/ N-UNCOUNT Dosh is money. [BRIT, INFORMAL]

dossier /ˈdɒsieɪ, -iə/ (**dossiers**) N-COUNT A **dossier** is a collection of papers containing information on a particular subject. ❑ *The government kept dossiers on thousands of its citizens.*

dot /dɒt/ (**dots**) N-COUNT A **dot** is a very small round mark. ❑ *...a black dot in the middle of the circle.*

ˌdot-ˈcom also **dot com** (**dot-coms**) N-COUNT A **dot-com** is a company that does all or most of its business on the Internet.

dote /dəʊt/ (**dotes, doting, doted**) V-I If you **dote on** someone, you love them very much and ignore their faults. ❑ *He dotes on his nine-year-old son.* • **doting** ADJ ❑ *...his doting parents.*

dotted /ˈdɒtɪd/ **1** ADJ **Dotted** lines are made of a row of dots. ❑ *Cut along the dotted line.* **2** ADJ AFTER LINK-V If an area is **dotted with** things, it has many of those things scattered over its surface. ❑ *The maps were dotted with the names of small towns.*

double /ˈdʌbəl/ (**doubles, doubling, doubled**) **1** ADJ BEFORE N You use **double** to describe a pair of similar things. ❑ *...a pair of double doors.* ❑ *Ring four two, double two, double two if you'd like to speak to our financial adviser.* ❑ *...a double murder.* **2** ADJ You

d

Word Web donor

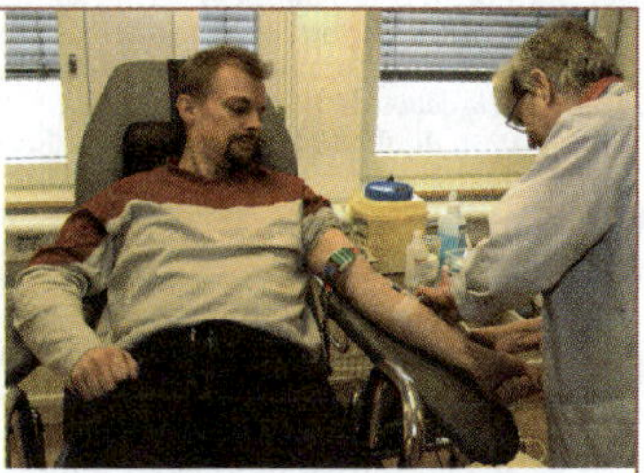

Many people **give donations** because they like to **help** others. They **donate money,** clothes, food, or volunteer their time. Some people even give parts of their bodies. Doctors performed the first successful human **organ transplants** in the 1950s. Today this type of operation is very common. The problem now is finding enough **donors** to meet the needs of potential **recipients**. Organs such as the **kidney** and the **liver** often come from a living donor. **Hearts, lungs,** and other vital organs come from donors who have died. Of course our health care system relies on **blood** donors. They help save lives every day.

use **double** to describe something which is twice the normal size or twice the normal capacity. ❑ *...a large double garage.* ❑ *Allow the loaves to rise until just about double in size.* **3** ADJ & N-COUNT A **double** room, or a **double**, is a room that is intended to be used by two people. ❑ *The Great Western Hotel is ideal, costing around £60 a night for a double.* **4** V-T/V-I If something **doubles**, or if you **double** it, it becomes twice as large. ❑ *The program will double the amount of money available.* **5** V-I If a person or thing **doubles as** someone or something else, they have a second job or purpose as well as their main one. ❑ *...a study which can double as a bedroom.* **6** N-UNCOUNT **Doubles** is a game of tennis or badminton in which two people play against two other people. **7** PHRASE If you **bend double**, you bend right over. If you **are bent double**, you are bending right over. **8** **in double figures** → see **figure**
→ see **hotel, tennis**
▶ **double up** or **double over** PHR-VERB If you **double up**, or if you **double over**, you bend your body quickly or violently. ❑ *She doubled up with laughter.* ❑ *I was doubled over in pain.*

double bass /ˌdʌbəl ˈbeɪs/ (**double basses**) N-VAR A **double bass** is the largest instrument in the violin family. You play it standing up.
→ see **string, orchestra**

ˈdouble-ˌclick (**double-clicks, double-clicking, double-clicked**) V-I If you **double-click on** an area of a computer screen, you point the mouse pointer at that area and press one of the buttons on the mouse twice quickly in order to make something happen. [COMPUTING] ❑ *Go to Control Panel and double-click on Sounds for a list of sounds.*

ˌdouble-ˈglaze (**double-glazes, double-glazing, double-glazed**) V-T If someone **double-glazes** a house or its windows, they fit the windows with a second layer of glass which keeps the inside of the house warmer and quieter. ● **double-glazing** N-UNCOUNT ❑ *Doreen had double-glazing put into their house.*

doubly /ˈdʌbli/ **1** ADV You use **doubly** to say that a situation has two aspects or features. ❑ *She now felt doubly guilty; she had embarrassed Franklin and she had cost her partner money.* **2** ADV You use **doubly** to say that something happens or is true to a greater degree than usual. ❑ *In pregnancy a high fibre diet is doubly important.*

doubt /daʊt/ (**doubts, doubting, doubted**) **1** N-VAR If you feel **doubt** or **doubts** about something, you feel uncertain about it. ❑ *This raises doubts about the point of advertising.* ❑ *There is little doubt that you try too hard.* **2** V-T If you **doubt** something, or if you **doubt** whether something is true or possible, you believe that it is probably not true, genuine, or possible. ❑ *No one doubted his ability.* ❑ *He doubted if he would learn anything new.* **3** V-T If you **doubt** someone, or if you **doubt** their **word**, you think they might not be telling the truth. ❑ *Don't think I doubt you.* **4** PHRASE If you are **in doubt** about something, of if it is **in doubt**, you are uncertain about it. ❑ *He is in no doubt as to what is needed.* ❑ *The outcome was still in doubt.* **5** PHRASE If something is **beyond doubt**, or if it is **beyond reasonable doubt**, you are certain that it is true. ❑ *She knew now beyond doubt that her husband loved her.* **6** PHRASE You use **no doubt** to emphasize that something seems very likely to you. ❑ *No doubt we will meet again.* **7** PHRASE You use **without doubt** or **without a doubt** to emphasize that something is true. ❑ *He is, without doubt, the best player in the world.* **8** to **give** someone **the benefit of the doubt** → see **benefit**

doubtful /ˈdaʊtfʊl/ **1** ADJ Something that is **doubtful** seems unlikely or uncertain. ❑ *It is doubtful whether he will appear again.* **2** ADJ If you are **doubtful about** something, you are uncertain about it. ❑ *I was still very doubtful about the chances for success.* ● **doubtfully** ADV ❑ *Keeton shook his head doubtfully.*

doubtless /ˈdaʊtləs/ ADV If you say that something is **doubtless** the case, you mean that you think it is probably or almost certainly the case. ❑ *They will doubtless get their land back.*

dough /dəʊ/ N-UNCOUNT **Dough** is a mixture of flour and water, and sometimes also sugar and fat, which can be cooked to make bread, pastry, and biscuits.

doughnut also **donut** /ˈdəʊnʌt/ (**doughnuts**) N-COUNT A **doughnut** is a lump or ring of sweet dough cooked in hot fat.

dour /dʊə, daʊə/ ADJ Someone who is **dour** has a severe and unfriendly manner.

douse also **dowse** /daʊs/ (**douses, dousing, doused**) **1** V-T If you **douse** a fire, you stop it burning by pouring a lot of water over it. **2** V-T If you **douse** someone or something **with** a liquid, you throw a lot of that liquid over them. ❑ *They doused their victim with petrol.*

dove

dove (**doves**) **1** N-COUNT /dʌv/ A **dove** is a white bird that looks like a pigeon. **2** /dəʊv/ **Dove** is a past tense of **dive**. [AM]

down
❶ PREPOSITION AND ADVERB USES
❷ ADJECTIVE USES
❸ NOUN USE

down /daʊn/
❶ **1** PREP & ADV **Down** means towards the ground or a lower level, or in a lower place. ❑ *A man came down the stairs.* ❑ *...a ledge 40ft down the mountain.* ❑ *She was still looking down at her papers.* **2** ADV If you put something **down**, you put it onto a surface. ❑ *Danny put down his glass.* **3** PREP If something is **down** a road or river, it is further along it. ❑ *...a few miles down the road at Burnham.* **4** ADV **Down** is often used to mean in the south or towards the south. ❑ *I went down to L.A. all the way from Seattle.* **5** ADV If the amount or level of something **goes down**, it decreases. ❑ *My weight went down by 15 pounds.* **6** PREP If someone or something is **down for** something, it has been arranged that they will do it or it will happen to them. ❑ *Mark told me that he was down for an interview.* **7** **up and down** → see **up** **8** **ups and downs** → see **up**

down /daʊn/
❷ **1** ADJ AFTER LINK-V If you are feeling **down**, you are feeling unhappy or depressed. [INFORMAL] **2** ADJ AFTER LINK-V If something is **down on** paper, it has been written on the paper. ❑ *That date wasn't down on our news sheet.* **3** ADJ AFTER LINK-V If a piece of equipment, especially a computer system, is **down**, it is temporarily not working

because of a fault. [COMPUTING]

down /daʊn/
❸ N-UNCOUNT **Down** consists of the small soft feathers on young birds.

Word Link *down ≈ below, lower : downfall, downhill, slowdown*

downfall /ˈdaʊnfɔːl/ **1** N-UNCOUNT The **downfall** of a successful or powerful person or institution is their failure. ❑ *His lack of experience led to his downfall.* **2** N-UNCOUNT Something that is someone's **downfall** is the thing that causes them to fail. ❑ *His honesty was his downfall.*

downgrade /ˌdaʊnˈgreɪd/ (**downgrades, downgrading, downgraded**) V-T If someone or something **is downgraded**, their situation is changed to a lower level of importance or value. ❑ *The boy's condition has been downgraded from critical to serious.* ❑ *I was downgraded to a clerical job.*

downhill /ˌdaʊnˈhɪl/ **1** ADV & ADJ BEFORE N If someone or something is moving **downhill**, they are moving down a slope. ❑ *He headed downhill towards the river.* ❑ *...downhill skiing.* **2** ADV You can say that something is going **downhill** when it is becoming worse.

Downing Street /ˈdaʊnɪŋstriːt/ N-PROPER **Downing Street** is the street in London in which the Prime Minister and the Chancellor of the Exchequer live. You can also use **Downing Street** to refer to the Prime Minister and his or her officials.

download /ˌdaʊnˈləʊd/ (**downloads, downloading, downloaded**) V-T To **download** data means to transfer it to or from a computer along a line such as a telephone line, a radio link, or a computer network. [COMPUTING] ❑ *Users can download the material to a desktop PC.*

downloadable /ˈdaʊnləʊdəbl/ ADJ If a computer file or program is **downloadable**, it can be downloaded to another computer. [COMPUTING] ❑ *...downloadable games.*

ˈdown payment (**down payments**) N-COUNT If you **make a down payment on** something, you pay a percentage of the total cost when you buy it. You pay the remaining amount later.

downpour /ˈdaʊnpɔː/ (**downpours**) N-COUNT A **downpour** is a heavy fall of rain.

downright /ˈdaʊnraɪt/ ADV & ADJ BEFORE N You use **downright** to emphasize unpleasant or bad qualities or behaviour. ❑ *His ideas were downright dangerous.* ❑ *...suspicion and downright hostility.*

downside /ˈdaʊnsaɪd/ N-SING **The downside of** a situation is the aspect of it which is less positive, pleasant, or useful than its other aspects. ❑ *The downside of this is a lack of clear leadership.*

downstairs /ˌdaʊnˈsteəz/ **1** ADV If you go **downstairs** in a building, you go down a staircase towards the ground floor. **2** ADV & ADJ BEFORE N If something or someone is **downstairs**, they are on the ground floor or on a lower floor than you. ❑ *...the flat downstairs.* ❑ *...the downstairs rooms.*

downstream /ˌdaʊnˈstriːm/ ADV & ADJ BEFORE N **Downstream** means towards the mouth of a river. ❑ *We drifted downstream.* ❑ *Breaking the dam could submerge downstream cities.*

ˌdown-to-ˈearth ADJ Someone who is **down-to-earth** is concerned with practical things, rather than with theories; used showing approval.

downtown /ˌdaʊnˈtaʊn/ ADV & ADJ BEFORE N **Downtown** means in or towards the centre of a city. ❑ *By day he worked downtown.* ❑ *...downtown Chicago.*

downturn /ˈdaʊntɜːn/ (**downturns**) N-COUNT If there is a **downturn in** the economy, it becomes worse or less successful.

downwards /ˈdaʊnwədz/

In usual British English, **downwards** is an adverb and **downward** is an adjective. In formal British English and in American English, **downward** is both an adjective and an adverb.

1 ADV & ADJ If you move or look **downwards**, you move or look towards the ground or a lower level. ❑ *Benedict pointed downwards.* ❑ *...a firm downward movement of the hands.* **2** ADV & ADJ If an amount or rate moves **downwards**, it decreases. ❑ *Interest rates are now heading downwards.*

dowse /daʊs/ → see **douse**

doze /dəʊz/ (**dozes, dozing, dozed**) V-I & N-SING When you **doze**, or when you **have a doze**, you sleep lightly or for a short period.
→ see **sleep**
▶ **doze off** PHR-VERB If you **doze off**, you fall into a light sleep. ❑ *Sarah dozed off for a few moments.*

dozen /ˈdʌzən/ (**dozens**) **1** NUM A **dozen** means twelve. ❑ *...a dozen eggs.* **2** QUANT If you refer to **dozens of** things or people, you are emphasizing that there are many of them. ❑ *...dozens of homes.*

Dr (**Drs**) **Dr** is a written abbreviation for **Doctor**.

drab /dræb/ ADJ Something that is **drab** is dull and not attractive or exciting. ● **drabness** N-UNCOUNT ❑ *...the drabness of the small room.*

draft /drɑːft, dræft/ (**drafts, drafting, drafted**) **1** V-T & N-COUNT When you **draft** a piece of writing, you write the first version of it, called a **draft**. ❑ *He drafted a standard letter to the editors.* **2** V-T If you **are drafted**, you are ordered to serve in the armed forces. **3** V-T If people **are drafted into** a place, they are moved there to do a particular job. ❑ *Extra police have been drafted into the town.* **4** → see also **draught**

Word Partnership Use *draft* with:

ADJ.	**final** draft, **rough** draft **1**
N.	**bank** draft, draft **a letter**, draft **a speech** **1**
V.	**revise a** draft, **write a** draft **1**
	dodge the draft **2**

drag /dræg/ (**drags, dragging, dragged**) **1** V-T If you **drag** something or someone somewhere, you pull them there with difficulty. ❑ *He got up and dragged his chair towards the table.* ❑ *He drags his leg, and he can hardly lift his arm.* **2** V-T To **drag** a computer image means to use the mouse to move the position of the image on the screen, or to change its size or shape. ❑ *Use the right mouse button to drag and drop a zip file to any directory.* **3** V-T If you **drag** someone somewhere, you make them go there, although they may be unwilling. ❑ *...when*

drag

d

you can drag him away from his work. ❑ *I find it really hard to drag myself out and exercise regularly.* **4** V-I If a period of time or an event **drags**, it is very boring and seems to last a long time. ❑ *The minutes dragged past.* **5** V-T If the police **drag** a river or lake, they pull nets or hooks across the bottom of it in order to look for something. **6** PHRASE If you **drag** your **feet**, or if you **drag** your **heels**, you delay doing something or do it very slowly because you do not want to do it. **7** PHRASE If a man is **in drag**, he is wearing women's clothes.

D

▶ **drag out** **1** PHR-VERB If you **drag** something **out**, you make it last for longer than is necessary. ❑ *The foreign ministry can drag out matters for several months.* **2** PHR-VERB If you **drag** something **out of** someone, you persuade them to tell you something that they do not want to tell you.

dragon /ˈdrægən/ (**dragons**) N-COUNT In stories and legends, a **dragon** is an animal like a big lizard. It has wings and claws, and breathes out fire.
→ see **fantasy**

dragonfly /ˈdrægənflaɪ/ (**dragonflies**) N-COUNT A **dragonfly** is a brightly coloured insect with a long thin body and two sets of wings.
→ see **insect**

drain /dreɪn/ (**drains, draining, drained**) **1** V-T/V-I If you **drain** a liquid from a place or object, you remove the liquid by causing it to flow somewhere else. If a liquid **drains** somewhere, it flows there. ❑ *Miners built the tunnel to drain water out of the mines.* ❑ *...springs and rivers that drain into lakes.* **2** N-COUNT A **drain** is a pipe that carries water or sewage away from a place, or an opening in a surface that leads to the pipe. **3** V-T If you **drain** a place or object, you remove the liquid that has been in it or surrounding it. ❑ *Drain the pasta well.* **4** V-T If something **drains** you, it exhausts you physically and emotionally. ● **drained** ADJ ❑ *She sighed and collapsed, completely drained.* ● **draining** ADJ ❑ *I've been through a very draining, demanding time.* **5** N-SING If something or someone is **a drain on** resources, they use them up. ❑ *...citizens who are a drain on public resources.* **6** PHRASE If you say that something is going **down the drain**, you mean that it is being destroyed or wasted. [INFORMAL]
→ see **bathroom**

drainage /ˈdreɪnɪdʒ/ N-UNCOUNT **Drainage** is the system or process by which water or other liquids are drained from a place.
→ see **farm**

drama /ˈdrɑːmə/ (**dramas**) **1** N-COUNT A **drama** is a serious play for the theatre, television, or radio. **2** N-UNCOUNT You refer to plays in general as **drama**. ❑ *He knew nothing of Greek drama.* **3** N-VAR You can refer to exciting or dangerous aspects of a real situation as its **drama**. ❑ *Here is their real story, filled with drama and passion.*
→ see Picture Dictionary: **drama**
→ see **genre**

dramatic /drəˈmætɪk/ (**dramatics**) **1** ADJ A **dramatic** change is sudden and noticeable. ❑ *Air safety has not improved since the dramatic advances of the 1970s.* ● **dramatically** ADV ❑ *The cost of living has increased dramatically.* **2** ADJ A **dramatic** action, event, or situation is exciting and impressive. ❑ *...a dramatic display of fireworks.*

dramatist /ˈdræmətɪst/ (**dramatists**) N-COUNT A **dramatist** is someone who writes plays.

dramatize [BRIT also **dramatise**] /ˈdræmətaɪz/ (**dramatizes, dramatizing, dramatized**) **1** V-T

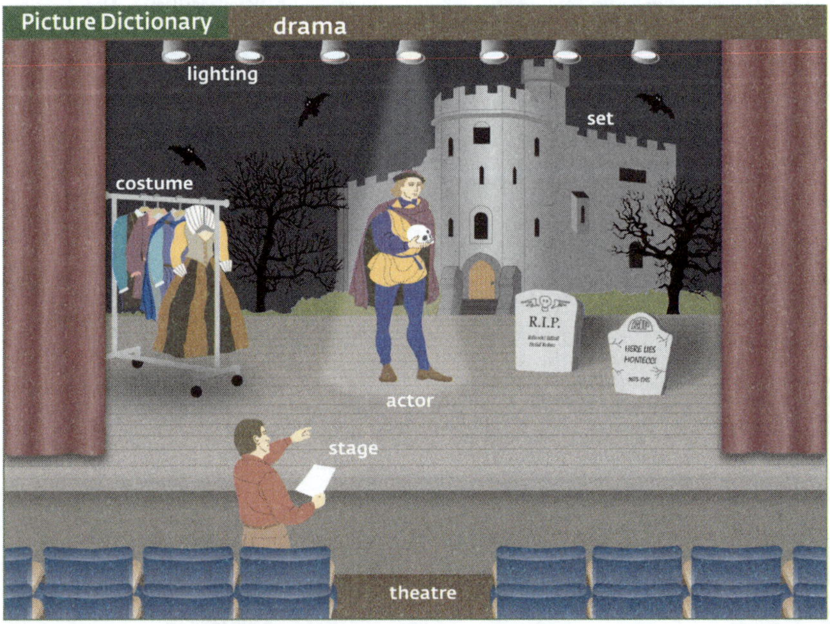

Picture Dictionary **draw**

draw

trace

sketch

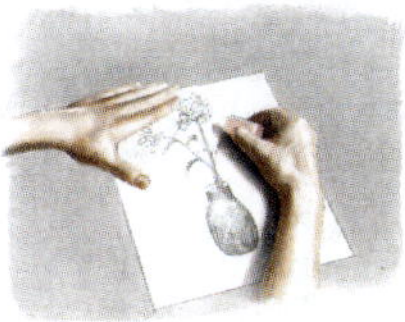
rub out

paint

copy

If a book or story **is dramatized**, it is written or presented as a play, a film, or a television drama. ● **dramatization** (**dramatizations**) N-COUNT ❑ *...a dramatization of Pride and Prejudice.* **2** V-T If someone **dramatizes** an event or situation, they try to make it seem more serious or exciting than it really is; used showing disapproval. ❑ *They have tried very hard to dramatize their own experience as victims.*

drank /dræŋk/ **Drank** is the past tense of **drink**.

drape /dreɪp/ (**drapes, draping, draped**) **1** V-T If you **drape** a piece of cloth somewhere, you place it there so that it hangs down. ❑ *Natasha took the coat and draped it over her shoulders.* ❑ *He draped himself in the Canadian flag.* **2** N-PLURAL In American English, **drapes** are pieces of heavy fabric you hang across a window and close to keep the light out or stop people looking in. The British word is **curtains**.

drastic /ˈdræstɪk/ **1** ADJ A **drastic** course of action is extreme and is usually taken urgently. ❑ *He's not going to do anything drastic about economic policy.* **2** ADJ A **drastic change** is a very great change. ● **drastically** ADV ❑ *Services have been drastically reduced.*

draught [AM **draft**] /drɑːft, dræft/ (**draughts**) N-COUNT A **draught** is an unwelcome current of air coming into a room or vehicle. ❑ *You need fresh air but obviously don't want to be in a draught.*

draw /drɔː/ (**draws, drawing, drew, drawn**) **1** V-T/V-I When you **draw**, or when you **draw** something, you use a pencil, pen, or crayon to produce a picture, pattern, or diagram. ❑ *He starts a painting by drawing shapes.* ● **drawing** N-UNCOUNT ❑ *I like dancing, singing and drawing.* **2** V-T/V-I You can use **draw** to indicate that someone or something moves somewhere or is moved there. ❑ *Claire saw the taxi drawing away.* ❑ *He drew her close to him.* ❑ *He drew his chair nearer the fire.* **3** V-T If you **draw** a curtain or blind, you pull it across a window to cover or uncover the window. **4** V-T If someone **draws** a gun, knife, or other weapon, they pull it out of its holder so that it is ready to use. **5** V-T If you **draw** a deep breath, you breathe in deeply once. **6** V-T If you **draw** something into or out of a particular place, you cause it to go into or come out of that place. ❑ *Villagers draw their water from wells.* **7** V-T If you **draw** money out of a bank or building society, you take it out so that you can use it. **8** V-T If you **draw** a comparison, conclusion, or distinction, you decide that it exists or is true. ❑ *Literary critics drew comparisons between George Sand and George Eliot.* **9** V-T If you **draw** someone's attention **to** something, you make them aware of it. ❑ *The exhibition will help draw attention to the museum.* **10** V-T If someone or something **draws** a particular reaction, people react to it in that way. ❑ *The policy drew fierce resistance from farmers.* **11** PHRASE When an event or period of time **draws to an end**, or when it **draws to a close**, it finishes. ❑ *The conflict is drawing to a close.* **12** → see also **drawing, drawn**
→ see Picture Dictionary: **draw**
→ see **animation, blog**

▶ **draw in** or **draw into** PHR-VERB If you **draw** someone **in**, or if you **draw** them **into** something you are involved with, you cause them to become involved with it. ❑ *She is the perfect hostess, drawing everyone into the conversation.*

▶ **draw on** **1** PHR-VERB If you **draw on** or **draw upon** something such as your skills or experience, you use them. ❑ *He drew on his experience as a yachtsman to make a documentary programme.* **2** PHR-VERB As a period of time **draws on**, it passes and the end of it gets closer. ❑ *...as the afternoon drew on.*

▶ **draw up** **1** PHR-VERB When you **draw up** a document, list, or plan, you prepare it and write it out. ❑ *The solicitors drew up a formal agreement.* **2** PHR-VERB If you **draw up** a chair, you move it nearer to a person or place.

▶ **draw upon** → see **draw on** (meaning 1)

Thesaurus *draw* Also look up:

v. illustrate, sketch, trace **1**
bring out, pull out, take out **4** **6**
inhale **5**
extract, take **6**

drawback /ˈdrɔːbæk/ (**drawbacks**) N-COUNT A **drawback** is an aspect of something that makes it less acceptable. ❑ *The apartment's only drawback was that it was too small.*

drawer /ˈdrɔːə/ (**drawers**) N-COUNT A **drawer** is

drawer

a part of a desk or other piece of furniture that is shaped like a rectangular box. You pull it towards you to open it.

drawing /ˈdrɔːɪŋ/ (**drawings**) 1 N-COUNT A **drawing** is a picture made with a pencil, pen, or crayon. ❑ *She did a drawing of me.* 2 → see also **draw**

D

ˈ**drawing room** (**drawing rooms**) N-COUNT A **drawing room** is a room, especially a large room in a large house, where people sit and relax. [DATED]

drawl /drɔːl/ (**drawls, drawling, drawled**) V-I/V-T & N-COUNT If someone **drawls**, or **drawls** something, or if they speak in a **drawl**, they speak slowly, with long vowel sounds. ❑ *'You guys don't mind if I smoke?' he drawled.* ❑ *...Jack's southern drawl.*

drawn /drɔːn/ 1 **Drawn** is the past participle of **draw**. 2 ADJ If someone looks **drawn**, they look very tired or ill.

ˌ**drawn-ˈout** ADJ You describe something as **drawn-out** when it lasts longer than you think it should. ❑ *...a long drawn-out war.*

dread /dred/ (**dreads, dreading, dreaded**) 1 V-T If you **dread** something unpleasant which may happen, you feel anxious about it. ❑ *I dreaded coming back.* ❑ *I'd been dreading that the birth would take a long time.* 2 N-UNCOUNT **Dread** is a feeling of great anxiety and fear about something that may happen.

dreaded /ˈdredɪd/ ADJ BEFORE N **Dreaded** means terrible and greatly feared. ❑ *...how to treat this dreaded disease.*

Word Link	*ful ≈ filled with : beautiful, careful, dreadful*

dreadful /ˈdredfʊl/ ADJ If you say that something is **dreadful**, you mean that it is very unpleasant or very poor in quality. ❑ *They told us the dreadful news.* ❑ *My financial situation is dreadful.* ● **dreadfully** ADV ❑ *There have been times when we've played dreadfully.*

dream /driːm/ (**dreams, dreaming, dreamed** or **dreamt** /dremt/) 1 V-I & N-COUNT When you **dream**, or when you **have** a **dream**, you experience imaginary events in your mind while you are asleep. ❑ *Ivor always dreamed very vividly.* ❑ *He had a dream about Claire.* 2 V-I If you often think about something that you would very much like to happen or have, you can say that you **dream of** it. ❑ *As a schoolgirl, she dreamed of becoming an actress.* 3 N-COUNT You can describe something that you would very much like to happen or have as your **dream**. ❑ *...his dream of becoming a pilot.* 4 V-I If you say you **would not dream of** doing something, you are emphasizing that you would not do it. ❑ *I wouldn't dream of making fun of you.*

▶ **dream up** PHR-VERB If you **dream up** a plan or idea, you work it out or create it in your mind. ❑ *I dreamed up a plan to solve both problems.*

Thesaurus	*dream* Also look up:
N.	nightmare, vision 1; ambition, aspiration, design, hope, wish 2
V.	hope, long for, wish 2

Word Partnership	Use *dream* with:
V.	**have a** dream 1; **fulfill a** dream, **pursue a** dream, **realize a** dream 2
N.	dream **interpretation** 1; dream **home**, dream **vacation** 3

dreamer /ˈdriːmə/ (**dreamers**) N-COUNT Someone who is a **dreamer** looks forward to pleasant things that may never happen, rather than being realistic and practical.

dreamy /ˈdriːmi/ (**dreamier, dreamiest**) ADJ If someone has a **dreamy** expression, they are not paying attention to things around them and look as if they are thinking about something pleasant. ❑ *He smiled his dreamy smile.*

dreary /ˈdrɪəri/ (**drearier, dreariest**) ADJ If something is **dreary**, it is so dull that it makes you feel bored or depressed. ❑ *...a dreary little town.*

dredge /dredʒ/ (**dredges, dredging, dredged**) V-T To **dredge** a river means to clear a channel by removing mud from the bottom.

▶ **dredge up** PHR-VERB If someone **dredges up** a piece of information they learnt a long time ago, or if they **dredge up** a distant memory, they manage to remember it. ❑ *He dredged up some of the French he had learned in high school.*

drench /drentʃ/ (**drenches, drenching, drenched**) V-T To **drench** something or someone means to make them completely wet. ❑ *...getting drenched by icy water.* ● **drenched** ADJ ❑ *We were completely drenched and cold.*

dress /dres/ (**dresses, dressing, dressed**) 1 N-COUNT A **dress** is a piece of clothing worn by a woman or girl which covers her body and extends down over her legs. 2 N-UNCOUNT You can refer to clothes worn by men or women as **dress**. ❑ *For major characters, consider details of dress, walk and habits of speech.* ❑ *...evening dress.* 3 V-T/V-I When you **dress**, or when you **dress yourself**, you put clothes on yourself. ❑ *He told Sarah to wait while he dressed.* 4 → See note at **wear**

▶ **dress up** PHR-VERB If you **dress up**, you put on different clothes, in order to look smarter or to disguise yourself. ❑ *You do not need to dress up for dinner.* ❑ *He was dressed up as Father Christmas.*

▶ **dress down** PHR-VERB If you **dress down**, you wear clothes that are less smart than usual.

Word Partnership	Use *dress* with:
ADJ.	**casual** dress, **formal** dress, **traditional** dress 2
V.	**put on a** dress, **wear a** dress 1
ADV.	dress **appropriately**, dress **casually**, dress **well** 3

dressed /dresd/ 1 ADJ AFTER LINK-V If you are **dressed**, you are wearing clothes rather than being naked. ❑ *He was fully dressed, including shoes.* 2 → See note at **wear** 3 ADJ AFTER LINK-V If you are **dressed** in a particular way, you are wearing clothes of a particular kind or colour. ❑ *He was dressed in a black suit.*

dresser /ˈdresə/ (**dressers**) 1 N-COUNT A **dresser** is a piece of furniture which is usually used for storing china. [BRIT] 2 N-COUNT a **dresser** is a chest of drawers, usually with a mirror on the top. [AM] 3 N-COUNT You use **dresser** to refer to the kind of clothes that a person wears. ❑ *...smart dressers.*

dressing /ˈdresɪŋ/ (**dressings**) 1 N-COUNT A **dressing** is a protective covering that is put on a wound. 2 N-VAR A salad **dressing** is a mixture of oil, vinegar, salt and pepper, which you pour over a salad.

'dressing gown (**dressing gowns**) N-COUNT A **dressing gown** is a loose-fitting coat worn over pyjamas or other night clothes.

'dressing room (**dressing rooms**) N-COUNT A **dressing room** is a room in a theatre or sports stadium where performers or players can change their clothes.

'dressing table (**dressing tables**) N-COUNT A **dressing table** is a small table in a bedroom with drawers and a mirror.

drew /druː/ **Drew** is the past tense of **draw**.

dribble /ˈdrɪbəl/ (**dribbles, dribbling, dribbled**) 1 V-T/V-I If a liquid **dribbles** somewhere, or if you **dribble** it, it drips down slowly or flows in a thin stream. ❑ *Sweat dribbled down Hart's face.* 2 V-I When a person **dribbles**, saliva comes from their mouth. 3 V-T/V-I When players **dribble** or **dribble** the ball in a game such as football, they give it several quick kicks or taps in order to keep it moving.

dried /draɪd/ **Dried** is the past tense and past participle of **dry**.

drier /ˈdraɪə/ → see **dry, dryer**

drift /drɪft/ (**drifts, drifting, drifted**) 1 V-I When something **drifts** somewhere, it is carried there by the wind or by water. ❑ *Mist drifted across the water.* 2 V-I & N-COUNT To **drift** somewhere, or to move there in a **drift**, means to move there slowly or gradually. ❑ *Half the crowd drifted outside before the end.* ❑ *...the drift towards the cities.* 3 V-I To **drift into** a situation means to get into it in a way that is not planned or controlled. ❑ *Many people drift into crime.* 4 N-COUNT A **drift** of snow is a deep pile formed by the wind.

→ see **continent, snow**

▶ **drift off** PHR-VERB If you **drift off** or **drift off to sleep**, you gradually fall asleep.

drill /drɪl/ (**drills, drilling, drilled**) 1 N-COUNT A **drill** is a tool for making holes. ❑ *...electric drills.* 2 V-T/V-I When you **drill into** something or **drill** a hole in it, you make a hole using a drill. 3 N-VAR A **drill** is a procedure which a group of people, especially soldiers, practise so that they can do something quickly and efficiently. ❑ *He concentrated on learning drill and parade routines.*

→ see **oil, tool**

drink /drɪŋk/ (**drinks, drinking, drank, drunk**) 1 V-T/V-I When you **drink**, or **drink** a liquid, you take it into your mouth and swallow it. ❑ *He drank some tea.* ● **drinker** (**drinkers**) N-COUNT ❑ *...a coffee drinker.* 2 N-COUNT A **drink** is an amount of a liquid which you drink. ❑ *I'll get you a drink of water.* 3 V-I To **drink** means to drink alcohol. ❑ *He drinks too much.* ● **drinking** N-UNCOUNT ❑ *She left him because of his drinking.* ● **drinker** N-COUNT ❑ *He was a heavy drinker.* 4 N-VAR **Drink** is alcohol, such as beer, wine, or whisky. A **drink** is an alcoholic drink. ❑ *Too much drink is bad for your health.* 5 → see also **drunk**

▶ **drink to** PHR-VERB If you **drink to** someone or something, you raise your glass before drinking, and say that you hope they will be happy or successful. ❑ *We drank to our success.*

,drink 'driver (**drink drivers**) N-COUNT In British English, a **drink driver** is someone who drives after drinking more than the amount of alcohol that is legally allowed. The American term is **drunk driver**. ● **drink driving** N-UNCOUNT ❑ *...a drink driving conviction.*

drip /drɪp/ (**drips, dripping, dripped**) 1 V-I When liquid **drips** somewhere, it falls in small drops. ❑ *Rain dripped from the brim of his cap.* 2 V-I When something **drips**, drops of liquid fall from it. ❑ *A tap in the kitchen was dripping.* 3 N-COUNT A **drip** is a small individual drop of a liquid. ❑ *...drips of water.* 4 N-COUNT A **drip** is a piece of medical equipment by which a liquid is slowly passed through a tube into a patient's bloodstream. ❑ *I was put on a drip.*

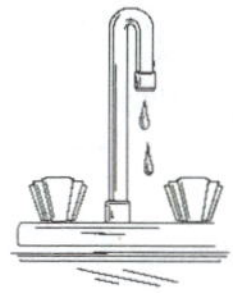

drip

drive /draɪv/ (**drives, driving, drove, driven** /ˈdrɪvən/) 1 V-I/V-T To **drive**, or **drive** a vehicle, means to control it so that it goes where you want it to go. ❑ *She never learned to drive.* ❑ *His daughter drove him to the train station.* ● **driving** N-UNCOUNT ❑ *...dangerous driving.* ● **driver** (**drivers**) N-COUNT ❑ *The driver got out of his van.* 2 N-COUNT A **drive** is a journey in a vehicle such as a car. ❑ *I thought we might go for a drive.* 3 N-COUNT A **drive** is a private road leading from a public road to a house. 4 V-T If something **drives** a machine, it supplies the power that makes it work. ❑ *Electric motors drive the wheels.* 5 N-COUNT You use **drive** to refer to the mechanical part of a computer which reads the data on disks and tapes, or writes data onto them. [COMPUTING] 6 V-T If you **drive** one thing **into** another, you push it in or hammer it in using a lot of effort. ❑ *Drive the pegs into the ground.* 7 V-T If you **drive** people or animals somewhere, you make them go to or from that place. ❑ *The last offensive drove thousands of people into Thailand.* 8 V-T The desire or feeling that **drives** someone **to** do something, especially something extreme, is what causes them to do it. ❑ *Jealousy drives people to murder.* 9 N-UNCOUNT **Drive** is energy and determination. ❑ *John will be remembered for his drive and enthusiasm.* 10 N-SING A **drive** is a special effort by a group of people to achieve something. ❑ *...a drive to end child poverty.* 11 → see also **driving, drove**

▶ **drive away** PHR-VERB To **drive** people **away** means to make them want to go away or stay away. ❑ *Increased crime is driving away customers.*

'drive-by ADJ BEFORE N A **drive-by** killing involves shooting someone from a moving car. ❑ *He was injured in a drive-by shooting.*

driver /ˈdraɪvə/ (**drivers**) 1 N-COUNT The **driver** of a vehicle is the person who is driving it. ❑ *The driver got out of his van.* 2 N-COUNT A **driver** is a computer program that controls a device such as a printer. [COMPUTING]

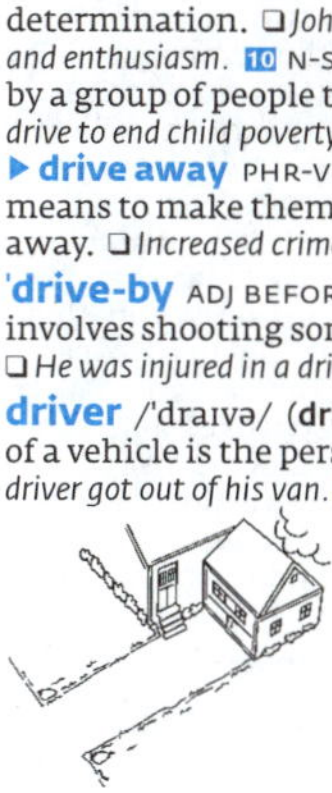

driveway

'drive-through ADJ BEFORE N A **drive-through** shop or restaurant is one where you can buy things without leaving your car. ❑ *...a drive-through burger bar.*

d

driveway /'draɪvweɪ/ (**driveways**) N-COUNT A **driveway** is a private road that leads from a public road to a house or garage.

driving /'draɪvɪŋ/ ADJ BEFORE N The **driving** force behind something is the person, group, or thing mainly responsible for it. ❑ *Consumer spending was the driving force behind the economic growth.*
→ see **car**

'driving licence (**driving licences**) N-COUNT In British English, a **driving licence** is a card showing that you are qualified to drive. The usual American term is **driver's license**.

drizzle /'drɪzəl/ (**drizzles, drizzling, drizzled**) **1** V-I If it **is drizzling**, light rain in falling in fine drops. **2** N-UNCOUNT **Drizzle** is light rain falling in fine drops.

drone /drəʊn/ (**drones, droning, droned**) V-I & N-SING If something **drones**, it makes a low continuous humming noise called a **drone**. ❑ *The plane droned overhead.* ❑ *...the constant drone of the motorways.*
▶ **drone on** PHR-VERB If someone **drones on about** something, they keep talking about it in a boring way.

drool /dru:l/ (**drools, drooling, drooled**) **1** V-I If someone **drools**, saliva falls from their mouth. **2** V-I If you **drool over** someone or something, you look at them with great pleasure. ❑ *Now you can have the chocolate cake you were drooling over this afternoon.*

droop /dru:p/ (**droops, drooping, drooped**) V-I If something **droops**, it hangs or leans downwards with no strength or firmness. ❑ *Pale roses drooped from a blue vase.*

drop /drɒp/ (**drops, dropping, dropped**) **1** V-I & N-COUNT If a level or amount **drops**, or if there is a **drop in** it, it quickly becomes less. ❑ *Temperatures can drop to freezing at night.* ❑ *The price of his London home dropped by £1.25m.* ❑ *She was prepared to take a drop in wages.* **2** V-T/V-I If you **drop** something, or if it **drops**, it falls straight down. ❑ *I dropped my glasses and broke them.* ❑ *My book dropped out of my bag.* ● **dropping** N-UNCOUNT ❑ *...the dropping of the first atomic bomb.* **3** N-COUNT You use **drop** to talk about vertical distances. ❑ *It's only a four-foot drop.* **4** V-T/V-I If a person or a part of their body **drops** to a lower position, or if they **drop** a part of their body to a lower position, they move to that position, often in a tired way. ❑ *Nancy dropped into a nearby chair.* ❑ *She let her head drop.* **5** V-T/V-I If your voice **drops**, or if you **drop** your voice, you speak more quietly. ❑ *He dropped his voice and looked at the door.* **6** V-T & PHR-VERB If the driver of a vehicle **drops** you somewhere, or if they **drop** you **off**, they stop the vehicle and you get out. ❑ *He dropped me outside the hotel.* ❑ *Just drop me off at the airport.* **7** V-T If you **drop** an idea, course of action, or habit, you decide not to continue with it. ❑ *He was told to drop the idea.* **8** PHRASE If you **drop a hint**, you give someone a hint in a casual way. **9** N-COUNT A **drop of** a liquid is a very small amount of it shaped like a little ball.
▶ **drop by** or **drop in** PHR-VERB If you **drop by**, or if you **drop in**, you visit someone informally. ❑ *He dropped by the office.* ❑ *Why not drop in for a chat?*
▶ **drop off** **1** → see **drop** (meaning 6) **2** PHR-VERB If you **drop off** or **drop off to sleep**, you go to sleep.
▶ **drop out** PHR-VERB If someone **drops out of** college or a race, for example, they leave it without finishing what they started.

Word Partnership	Use *drop* with:
N.	drop **in sales** 1 drop **a ball**, drop **a bomb** 2 drop **of blood**, **tear** drop, drop **of water** 9 drop **a hint** 8
ADJ.	**sudden** drop 1 **steep** drop 3

Word Link	*let ≈ little : booklet, droplet, leaflet*

droplet /'drɒplət/ (**droplets**) N-COUNT A **droplet** is a very small drop of liquid. ❑ *...droplets of water.*

drought /draʊt/ (**droughts**) N-VAR A **drought** is a long period of time during which no rain falls. ❑ *Drought and famines have killed up to two million people.*
→ see **dam**

drove /drəʊv/ (**droves**) **1** **Drove** is the past tense of **drive**. **2** N-COUNT **Droves** of people are very large numbers of them. ❑ *Droves of young men were strolling along the quays.* ❑ *They are leaving in droves.*

drown /draʊn/ (**drowns, drowning, drowned**) **1** V-T/V-I When someone **drowns**, or when they **are drowned**, they die because they have gone under water and cannot breathe. ❑ *Forty-eight people drowned after their boat capsized.* ❑ *She fell into the water and was nearly drowned.* **2** V-T & PHR-VERB If something **drowns** a sound, or if it **drowns** it **out**, it is louder than the sound and makes it impossible to hear it. ❑ *His speech was drowned by loud cries.* ❑ *Her voice was drowned out by a loud crash.*

drowsy /'draʊzi/ (**drowsier, drowsiest**) ADJ If you are **drowsy**, you feel sleepy and cannot think clearly. ❑ *He felt pleasantly drowsy.* ● **drowsiness** N-UNCOUNT ❑ *Big meals during the day cause drowsiness.*

drug /drʌg/ (**drugs, drugging, drugged**) **1** N-COUNT A **drug** is a chemical substance given to people to treat or prevent an illness or disease. **2** N-COUNT **Drugs** are substances that some people smoke or inject into their blood because of their stimulating effects. ❑ *She was sure Leo was taking drugs.* **3** V-T If you **drug** a person or animal, you give them a chemical substance in order to make them sleepy or unconscious. ❑ *They drugged the guard dog.*

'drug ˌaddict (**drug addicts**) N-COUNT A **drug addict** is someone who is addicted to illegal drugs.

drugstore /'drʌgstɔ:/ (**drugstores**) **1** N-COUNT In America, a **drugstore** is a shop where medicines, cosmetics, and some other goods are sold. **2** → See note at **pharmacy**

drum /drʌm/ (**drums, drumming, drummed**) **1** N-COUNT A **drum** is a musical instrument consisting of a skin stretched tightly over a round frame. ● **drummer** (**drummers**) N-COUNT ❑ *...a pop-group drummer.* **2** N-COUNT A **drum** is a large container in the shape of a cylinder which is used for storing fuel or other substances. ❑ *...an oil drum.* **3** V-T/V-I If something **drums on** a surface, or if you **drum** something **on** a surface, it hits it regularly, making a continuous beating sound. ❑ *He drummed his fingers on his desk.* → see **percussion**

▶ **drum into** PHR-VERB If you **drum** something **into** someone, you keep saying it to make them understand or remember it. ❑ *It was drummed into us that you need a degree to get a job.*

▶ **drum up** PHR-VERB If you **drum up** support or business, you try to get it. ❑ *The organisers failed to drum up much support.*

drunk /drʌŋk/ (**drunks**) **1** ADJ If someone is **drunk**, they have consumed too much alcohol. ❑ *I got drunk.* **2** N-COUNT A **drunk** is someone who is drunk or who often gets drunk. **3** **Drunk** is the past participle of **drink**.

ˌdrunk ˈdriver (**drunk drivers**) N-COUNT In American English, a **drunk driver** is someone who drives after drinking more than the amount of alcohol that is legally allowed. The usual British term is **drink driver**. ● **drunk driving** N-UNCOUNT ❑ *...his sixth drunk driving offense.*

drunken /ˈdrʌŋkən/ ADJ BEFORE N A **drunken** person is drunk or is frequently drunk; used showing disapproval. ❑ *...groups of drunken hooligans.* ● **drunkenly** ADV ❑ *Bob stormed drunkenly into her house.* ● **drunkenness** N-UNCOUNT ❑ *He was arrested for drunkenness.*

dry /draɪ/ (**drier** or **dryer, driest, dries, drying, dried**) **1** ADJ If something is **dry**, it has no water or other liquid on it or in it. ❑ *...a soft dry cloth.* ❑ *Pat it dry with a soft towel.* ● **dryness** N-UNCOUNT ❑ *Dryness around the roots can cause damage to the flowers.* **2** V-T/V-I When you **dry** something, or when it **dries**, it becomes dry. ❑ *Wash and dry the lettuce.* ❑ *Leave your hair to dry naturally.* **3** ADJ When the weather or a place is **dry**, there is no rain or much less rain than average. **4** ADJ If you say that your skin or hair is **dry**, you mean that it is less oily or soft than normal. ❑ *Dry hair is damaged by washing it too frequently.* ● **dryness** N-UNCOUNT ❑ *...dryness of the skin.* **5** ADJ **Dry** humour is amusing, mocking people in a subtle way. ● **dryly** ADV ❑ *'Never act with children,' he says dryly. 'Or fish.'* **6** ADJ If you describe something such as a book, play, or activity as **dry**, you mean that it is dull and uninteresting. ❑ *...dry, academic phrases.* **7** ADJ **Dry** sherry or wine does not taste sweet. **8** → see also **dried, dryer** → see **weather**

▶ **dry off** PHR-VERB If something **dries off**, or if you **dry** it **off**, the moisture on its surface disappears or is removed. ❑ *I dried myself off, and dressed.*

▶ **dry out** PHR-VERB If something **dries out**, it becomes completely dry. ❑ *If the soil is allowed to dry out the tree could die.*

▶ **dry up** **1** PHR-VERB If something **dries up**, it loses all its water or moisture. ❑ *The northern lakes dried up almost completely between sixty and seventy thousand years ago.* **2** PHR-VERB If a supply of something **dries up**, it stops. ❑ *Tourism is expected to dry up completely this summer.* **3** PHR-VERB If you **dry up** or **dry up the dishes**, you wipe the water off them with a cloth after they have been washed.

ˌdry-ˈclean (**dry-cleans, dry-cleaning, dry-cleaned**) V-T When clothes **are dry-cleaned**, they are cleaned with a liquid chemical rather than with water.

dryer also **drier** /draɪə/ (**dryers**) **1** N-COUNT A **dryer** is a machine for drying things, for example clothes or people's hair. ❑ *...hair dryers.* **2** → see also **dry**

ˌdry ˈrun (**dry runs**) N-COUNT If you have a **dry run**, you practise something to make sure that you are ready to do it properly. ❑ *The competition is planned as a dry run for the World Cup finals.*

Word Link	**du ≈ two : dual, duet, duplicate**

d

dual /ˈdjuːəl, AM ˈduː-/ ADJ BEFORE N **Dual** means having two parts, functions, or aspects. ❑ *...his dual role as head of the party and head of state.* ❑ *...dual British and French nationality.*

dub /dʌb/ (**dubs, dubbing, dubbed**) **1** V-T If someone or something **is dubbed** a particular thing, it is given that description or name. ❑ *Orson Welles dubbed her 'the most exciting woman in the world'.* **2** V-T If a film **is dubbed**, a different soundtrack is added with actors speaking in a different language. ❑ *It was dubbed into Spanish for Mexican audiences.*

dubious /ˈdjuːbiəs, AM ˈduː-/ **1** ADJ You describe something as **dubious** when you think it is not completely honest, safe, or reliable. ❑ *This claim seems rather dubious.* **2** ADJ AFTER LINK-V If you are **dubious about** something, you are unsure about it. ❑ *My parents were a bit dubious about it all at first.* ● **dubiously** ADV ❑ *He looked at Coyne dubiously.*

duchess /ˈdʌtʃɪs/ (**duchesses**) N-COUNT A **duchess** is a woman who has the same rank as a duke, or is a duke's wife or widow.

duck /dʌk/ (**ducks, ducking, ducked**) **1** N-COUNT A **duck** is a common water bird with short legs and a large flat beak. **2** N-UNCOUNT **Duck** is the meat of a duck eaten as food. **3** V-I If you **duck**, you move your head or body quickly downwards to avoid being seen or hit. ❑ *They ducked and when they looked again, the colonel lay flat.* ❑ *I wanted to duck down and slip past but they saw me.* **4** V-T You say that someone **ducks** a duty or responsibility when you disapprove of the fact that they avoid it. ❑ *He is an indecisive leader who ducks important decisions.*

▶ **duck out** PHR-VERB If you **duck out of** something that you are supposed to do, you avoid doing it. ❑ *George ducked out of football training.*

duct /dʌkt/ (**ducts**) N-COUNT A **duct** is a pipe or channel which carries a liquid or gas. ❑ *...an air duct in the ceiling.*

dud /dʌd/ (**duds**) ADJ & N-COUNT You say that something is **dud** or a **dud** when it does not work properly. [INFORMAL] ❑ *He replaced a dud valve.*

dude /duːd/ (**dudes**) N-COUNT A **dude** is a man. [mainly AM, INFORMAL] ❑ *My doctor is a real cool dude.*

due /djuː, AM duː/ (**dues**) **1** PREP If an event or situation is **due to** something else, it happens or exists as a result of it. ❑ *A lot of this is due to Mr Green's efforts.* **2** ADJ AFTER LINK-V If something is **due** at a particular time, it is expected to happen or to arrive at that time. ❑ *The results are due at the end of the month.* ❑ *Mr Carter is due in London on Monday.* **3** PHRASE If you say that something will happen **in due course**, you mean that it will happen eventually, when the time is right. ❑ *The arrangements will be published in due course.* **4** ADJ AFTER LINK-V If something is **due to** you, you have a right to it. ❑ *I've got some leave due to me.* ❑ *No further pension was due.* **5** ADJ AFTER LINK-V If someone is **due for** something, that thing is planned to happen or be given to them now, or very soon. ❑ *Miss Smith, you know you are due for a move?* **6** ADJ BEFORE N If you give something **due** consideration, you give it the consideration it deserves. ❑ *After due consideration it was decided to send him away.* **7** N-PLURAL **Dues** are sums of money that you pay regularly to an organization that you belong to. **8** PHRASE You can say **'with due respect'** when you are about to disagree politely with someone. ❑ *With all due respect, you're asking the wrong question.*

duel /'dju:əl, AM 'du:-/ (**duels**) N-COUNT A **duel** is a fight between two people in which they use guns or swords in order to decide an argument. [DATED]

Word Link *du ≈ two : dual, duet, duplicate*

duet /dju:'et, AM du:-/ (**duets**) N-COUNT A **duet** is a piece of music sung or played by two people.

dug /dʌg/ **Dug** is the past tense and past participle of **dig**.

duke /dju:k, AM du:k/ (**dukes**) N-COUNT A **duke** is a noble of high rank.

dull /dʌl/ (**duller, dullest, dulls, dulling, dulled**) **1** ADJ If you describe someone or something as **dull**, you mean that they are not interesting or exciting. ❑ *They are both nice people but can be rather dull.* ● **dullness** N-UNCOUNT ❑ *...the dullness of their routine life.* **2** ADJ A **dull** colour or light is not bright. ❑ *The stamp was a dark, dull blue colour.* ● **dully** ADV ❑ *The street lamps gleamed dully.* **3** ADJ A **dull** sound or feeling is weak and not intense. ❑ *...the dull boom of an explosion.* ❑ *...a dull ache.* ● **dully** ADV ❑ *His arm throbbed dully.* **4** V-T/V-I If something **dulls**, or if it **is dulled**, it becomes less intense, bright, or lively. ❑ *A cold can dull your sense of taste or smell.*

Thesaurus *dull* Also look up:
ADJ. dingy, drab, faded, plain **1** **2**

duly /'dju:li, AM 'du:-/ ADV **Duly** is used to say that something is done at the correct time or in the correct way. [FORMAL] ❑ *He is a duly elected president of the country.*

dumb /dʌm/ (**dumber, dumbest, dumbs, dumbing, dumbed**) **1** ADJ Someone who is **dumb** is completely unable to speak. ❑ *...a young deaf and dumb man.* **2** ADJ AFTER LINK-V If someone is **dumb** on a particular occasion, they cannot speak because they are angry or shocked. ❑ *We were all struck dumb for a minute.* **3** ADJ If you call a person **dumb**, you mean that they are stupid or foolish. ❑ *I've met a lot of dumb people.* **4** ADJ If you say that something is **dumb**, you think that it is silly and annoying. [AM, INFORMAL] ❑ *I came up with this dumb idea.*
→ see **disability**
▶ **dumb down** PHR-VERB If you **dumb down** something, you make it easier for people to understand, especially when this spoils it. ❑ *This sounded like a case for dumbing down the magazine, which no one favoured.* ● **dumbing down** N-UNCOUNT ❑ *...the dumbing down of the news.*

dummy /'dʌmi/ (**dummies**) **1** N-COUNT A **dummy** is a model of a person, often used to display clothes. ❑ *...a shop-window dummy.* **2** N-COUNT In British English, a **dummy** is a rubber or plastic object that you give to a baby to suck so that it feels comforted. The American word is **pacifier**. **3** ADJ You use **dummy** to describe objects that are not real, but have been made to look as if they are real. ❑ *...dummy weapons.*

dump /dʌmp/ (**dumps, dumping, dumped**) **1** V-T If something **is dumped** somewhere, it is put there because it is no longer wanted or needed. ❑ *The getaway car was dumped near a motorway tunnel.* ● **dumping** N-UNCOUNT ❑ *...the dumping of hazardous waste.* **2** V-T If you **dump** something somewhere, you put it there quickly and carelessly. [INFORMAL] ❑ *We dumped our bags at the nearby Grand Hotel and hurried towards the market.* **3** N-COUNT A **dump** is a site provided for people to leave their rubbish. **4** N-COUNT If you refer to a place as a **dump**, you mean it is unattractive and unpleasant to live in or visit. [INFORMAL]

dune /dju:n, AM du:n/ (**dunes**) N-COUNT A **dune** is a hill of sand near the sea or in a desert.
→ see **desert, beach**

dung /dʌŋ/ N-UNCOUNT **Dung** is faeces from large animals. ❑ *...little piles of cow dung.*

dungeon /'dʌndʒən/ (**dungeons**) N-COUNT A **dungeon** is a dark underground prison in a castle.

dunno /də'nəʊ/ **Dunno** is sometimes used in written English to represent an informal way of saying 'I don't know.' ❑ *'How did she get it?'—'I dunno.'*

duo /'dju:əʊ, AM 'du:-/ (**duos**) N-COUNT A **duo** consists of two people who do something together, especially perform together. ❑ *...a famous dancing and singing duo.*

dupe /dju:p, AM du:p/ (**dupes, duping, duped**) V-T If someone **dupes** you, they trick you. ❑ *...a plot to dupe collectors into buying fakes.*

Word Link *du ≈ two : dual, duet, duplicate*

duplicate (**duplicates, duplicating, duplicated**)
verb /'dju:plɪkeɪt, AM 'du:-/, noun /'dju:plɪkət, AM 'du:-/.

1 V-T If you **duplicate** something that has already been done, you repeat or copy it. ❑ *His task will be to duplicate his success overseas here at home.* ● **duplication** N-UNCOUNT ❑ *...unnecessary duplication of work.* **2** V-T If you **duplicate** something which has been written, drawn, or recorded onto tape, you make exact copies of it. ❑ *This business duplicates video and cinema tapes.* **3** N-COUNT A **duplicate** is an object which is a copy of something. ❑ *I've lost my card. I've got to get a duplicate.* ❑ *...a duplicate key*

durable /'djʊərəbəl, AM 'dʊr-/ ADJ **Durable** materials or products are strong and last a long time. ❑ *...hard, durable plastic.* ● **durability** N-UNCOUNT ❑ *Airlines recommend hard-sided cases for durability.*

duration /djʊ'reɪʃən, AM dʊr-/ N-UNCOUNT The **duration of** an event or state is the time that it lasts. ❑ *Courses are of two years' duration.*

during /'djʊərɪŋ, AM 'dʊrɪŋ/ **1** PREP If something happens **during** a period of time or **during** an event, it happens continuously, or happens several times between the beginning and end of that period or event. ❑ *Sandstorms are common during the Saudi Arabian winter.* **2** PREP An event that happens **during** a period of time happens at some point or moment in that period.

❑ *During the night the wind blew the pot over.*

Usage

You do not use **during** to say how long something lasts. You use **for**. You do not say, for example, 'I went to Wales during two weeks'. You say '**I went to Wales for two weeks**'.

dusk /dʌsk/ N-UNCOUNT **Dusk** is the time just before night when it is not yet completely dark.

dust /dʌst/ (**dusts, dusting, dusted**) **1** N-UNCOUNT **Dust** consists of very small dry particles of earth, sand, or dirt. ❑ *I could see a thick layer of dust on the stairs.* **2** V-T/V-I When you **dust** or **dust** furniture or other objects, you remove dust from them using a dry cloth. **3** PHRASE If you say that **the dust has settled**, you mean that a situation has become calmer after a series of confusing or chaotic events.

dustbin

dustbin /ˈdʌstbɪn/ (**dustbins**) N-COUNT In British English, a **dustbin** is a large container for rubbish. The usual American term is **garbage can**.

dusty /ˈdʌsti/ (**dustier, dustiest**) ADJ Something that is **dusty** is covered with dust.

dutiful /ˈdjuːtɪfʊl, AM ˈduː-/ ADJ If you are **dutiful**, you do everything that you are expected to do. ❑ *He was sitting beside her, the dutiful son, keeping her company.* ● **dutifully** ADV ❑ *The inspector dutifully recorded the date.*

duty /ˈdjuːti, AM ˈduːti/ (**duties**) **1** N-VAR **Duty** is the work that you have to do as your job. ❑ *Staff must report for duty at their normal place of work.* ❑ *I carried out my duties conscientiously.* **2** PHRASE If someone such as a policeman or a nurse is **off duty**, they are not working. If they are **on duty**, they are working. ❑ *Extra staff were on duty.* **3** N-SING If you say that something is **your duty**, you believe that you ought to do it because it is your responsibility. ❑ *I consider it my duty to write to you and thank you.* **4** N-VAR **Duties** are taxes which you pay to the government on goods that you buy. ❑ *...import duties.*

→ see **citizenship**

Thesaurus *duty* Also look up:

N. assignment, obligation, responsibility, task **1** **3**

Word Partnership Use *duty* with:

PREP. **off** duty, **on** duty **2**
N. **guard** duty, **jury** duty, **sense of** duty **3**
ADJ. **civic** duty, **military** duty, **patriotic** duty **3**

Word Link *free ≈ without : carefree, duty-free, hands-free*

ˌduty-ˈfree ADJ **Duty-free goods** are sold at airports or on planes or ships at a cheaper price than usual because they are not taxed.

duvet /ˈduːveɪ, AM duːˈveɪ/ (**duvets**) N-COUNT A **duvet** is a large cover filled with feathers or similar material, which you use to cover yourself in bed. [BRIT]

DVD /ˌdiː viː ˈdiː/ (**DVDs**) N-COUNT A **DVD** is a disc similar to a compact disc on which a film or music is recorded. **DVD** is an abbreviation for 'digital video disc' or 'digital versatile disc'. ❑ *...a DVD player.*

→ see **laser**

ˌDVˈD ˌburner (**DVD burners**) N-COUNT A **DVD burner** is a piece of computer equipment that you use for copying data from a computer onto a DVD. [COMPUTING]

ˌDVˈD ˌwriter (**DVD writers**) N-COUNT A **DVD writer** is the same as a **DVD burner**. [COMPUTING]

DVT /ˌdiː viː ˈtiː/ (**DVTs**) **DVT** is a serious medical condition caused by blood clots in the legs moving up to the lungs. **DVT** is an abbreviation for 'deep vein thrombosis'.

dwarf /dwɔːf/ (**dwarfs, dwarfing, dwarfed**) V-T If one person or thing **is dwarfed** by another, the second is so much bigger than the first that it makes them look very small. ❑ *The US air travel market dwarfs that of Britain.*

dwell /dwel/ (**dwells, dwelling, dwelled** or **dwelt**) **1** V-I If you **dwell on** something, especially something unpleasant, you think, speak, or write about it a lot or for quite a long time. ❑ *I'd rather not dwell on the past.* **2** V-I If you **dwell** somewhere, you live there. [FORMAL] ❑ *In 1961, Rushdie found a new place to dwell – in England.*

dweller /ˈdwelə/ (**dwellers**) N-COUNT A **dweller** is a person who lives in a particular kind of place. ❑ *...to encourage town dwellers to grow vegetables.*

dwelling /ˈdwelɪŋ/ (**dwellings**) N-COUNT A **dwelling** is a house or other place where someone lives. [FORMAL] ❑ *Some 3500 new dwellings are planned for the area.*

dwindle /ˈdwɪndəl/ (**dwindles, dwindling, dwindled**) V-I If something **dwindles**, it becomes smaller, weaker, or less in number. ❑ *The factory's workforce has dwindled in size.* ❑ *...his dwindling authority.*

dye /daɪ/ (**dyes, dyeing, dyed**) **1** V-T If you **dye** something, you change its colour by soaking it in a special liquid. ❑ *The women prepared, spun and dyed the wool.* **2** N-VAR **Dye** is a substance which is used to dye something.

dying /ˈdaɪɪŋ/ **1** **Dying** is the present participle of **die**. **2** ADJ BEFORE N & N-PLURAL **Dying** people or **the dying** are people who are very ill and likely to die soon. ❑ *...a dying man.* ❑ *The dead and the dying were everywhere.* **3** ADJ BEFORE N A **dying** tradition or industry is becoming less important and is likely to end altogether. **4** ADJ AFTER LINK-V You say that you **are dying for** something or **are dying to** do something to emphasize that you very much want to have it or do it. [INFORMAL] ❑ *I was dying for a drink of water.* ❑ *She was dying to talk to Frank.*

dyke also **dike** /daɪk/ (**dykes**) N-COUNT A **dyke** is a thick wall that prevents river or sea water flooding onto land.

Word Link *dyn ≈ power : dynamic, dynamite, dynamo*

dynamic /daɪˈnæmɪk/ (**dynamics**) **1** ADJ A **dynamic** person is full of energy; used showing approval. ❑ *...a dynamic and energetic* *leader.* • **dynamically** ADV ❑ *...one of the most dynamically imaginative jazz pianists.* • **dynamism** /ˈdaɪnəmɪzəm/ N-UNCOUNT ❑ *This situation calls for dynamism and new thinking.* **2** N-PLURAL The **dynamics** of a situation or group of people are the opposing forces within it that cause it to change. ❑ *...an understanding of family dynamics.*

Word Link	*ite ≈ mineral, rock : dynamite, granite, graphite*

D

dynamite /ˈdaɪnəmaɪt/ N-UNCOUNT **Dynamite** is a type of explosive.

Word Link	*dyn ≈ power : dynamic, dynamite, dynamo*

dynamo /ˈdaɪnəməʊ/ (**dynamos**) N-COUNT A **dynamo** is a device that uses the movement of a machine to produce electricity.

dynastic /dɪˈnæstɪk, AM ˈdaɪ-/ ADJ **Dynastic** means typical of or relating to a dynasty. ❑ *...dynastic rule.*

dynasty /ˈdɪnəsti, AM ˈdaɪn-/ (**dynasties**) N-COUNT A **dynasty** is a series of rulers of a country who all belong to the same family.

Ee

each /iːtʃ/ 1 QUANT If you refer to **each** thing or person in a group, or if you refer to **each one** of them, you are referring to every member as an individual. ❑ *Each book is beautifully illustrated.* ❑ *...two bedrooms, each with three beds.* ❑ *The tickets cost six pounds each.* ❑ *He gave each of them a photo.* ❑ *He read each one of the forty magazines.* 2 PRON You use **each other** when you are saying that each member of a group does something to the others. ❑ *We stared at each other.*

eager /ˈiːgə/ ADJ If you are **eager to** do or have something, you very much want to do it or have it. ❑ *Robert was eager to talk about his new job.* ❑ *She is a bright and eager student.* ● **eagerly** ADV ❑ *Scientists are eagerly awaiting the test results.* ● **eagerness** N-UNCOUNT ❑ *...an eagerness to learn.*

eagle

eagle /ˈiːgəl/ (**eagles**) N-COUNT An **eagle** is a large bird that hunts and kills small animals for food.

ear /ɪə/ (**ears**) 1 N-COUNT Your **ears** are the two parts of your body with which you hear sounds. 2 N-SING If you have **an ear for** music or language, you are able to hear its sounds accurately and to interpret them or reproduce them well. 3 N-COUNT The **ears** of a cereal plant such as wheat are the top parts containing the seeds.
→ see Word Web: **ear**
→ see **face**

earlier /ˈɜːliə/ 1 **Earlier** is the comparative of **early.** 2 ADJ & ADV **Earlier** means occurring at a point in time before the present or before the one you are talking about. ❑ *The president says that, despite earlier reports, he is not planning to resign.* ❑ *His father died earlier this year.*

earliest /ˈɜːliɪst/ 1 **Earliest** is the superlative of **early.** 2 PHRASE **At the earliest** means not before the date or time mentioned. ❑ *We won't finish the meeting until four o'clock at the earliest.*

earlobe /ˈɪələʊb/ (**earlobes**) N-COUNT Your **earlobes** are the soft parts at the bottom of your ears.
→ see **face**

early /ˈɜːli/ (**earlier, earliest**) 1 ADV & ADJ BEFORE N **Early** means before the usual time that something happens or before the time that was arranged or expected. ❑ *Why do we have to go to bed so early?.* ❑ *...early retirement.* 2 ADV & ADJ BEFORE N **Early** means near the beginning of an activity, process, or period of time. ❑ *...the early stages of pregnancy.* ❑ *It's too early to know who will win.* ❑ *The accident happened earlier in the game.* ❑ *...the early 1980s.*

earmark /ˈɪəmɑːk/ (**earmarks, earmarking, earmarked**) V-T If something **is earmarked for** a particular purpose, it is reserved for that purpose. ❑ *The education department has earmarked £6 million for the new school.*

earn /ɜːn/ (**earns, earning, earned**) 1 V-T If you **earn** money, you receive it in return for work that you do. ❑ *She earns £17,000 a year.* 2 V-T If something **earns** money, it produces money as profit. ❑ *Her bank account earns very little interest.* ❑ *...the money earned from tourists who visit the area.* 3 V-T If you **earn** something such as praise, you get it because you deserve it. ❑ *The company has earned a reputation for honesty.* ❑ *The way that he behaved earned him a great deal of respect.*

Thesaurus	*earn* Also look up:
v.	bring in, make, take in 1 2

Word Web ear

The **ear** collects **sound waves** and sends them to the brain. First the **external ear** picks up sound waves. Then these sound **vibrations** travel along the **ear canal** and strike the **eardrum**. The eardrum pushes against a series of tiny bones. These bones carry the vibrations into the **inner ear**. There they are picked up by the hair cells in the cochlea. At that point, the vibrations turn into electronic impulses. The cochlea is connected to the hearing **nerve**. It sends the electronic impulses to the brain.

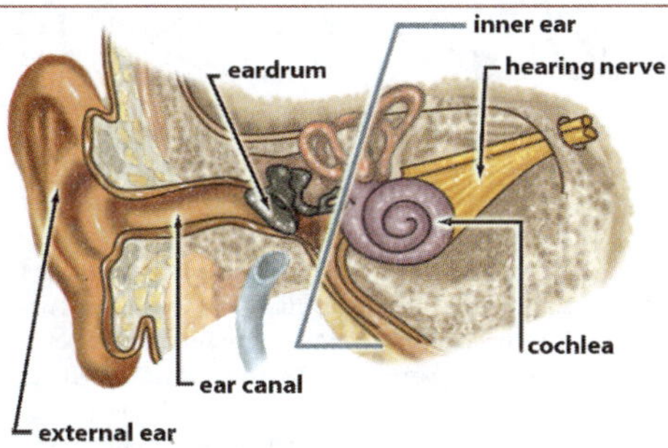

E

Word Web earth

The **earth** is made of material left over after the **sun** formed. In the beginning, about 4 billion years ago, the earth was made of liquid **rock**. During its first million years, it cooled into solid rock. **Life**, in the form of bacteria, began in the **oceans** about three and a half thousand million years ago. During the next billion years, the **continents** formed. At the same time, the level of **oxygen** in the **atmosphere** increased. **Life forms evolved**, and some of them began to breathe oxygen. **Evolution** allowed **plants** and **animals** to move from living in the oceans to living on the **land**.

earner /'ɜːnə/ (**earners**) N-COUNT An **earner** is someone or something that earns money or produces profit. ❑ *He is the biggest earner in British sport.* ❑ *This tax is a big revenue earner for the Government.*

earnest /'ɜːnɪst/ **1** PHRASE If something is done **in earnest**, it is done to a much greater extent and more seriously than before. ❑ *He'll start work on the project in earnest next week.* **2** ADJ **Earnest** people are very serious and sincere. ● **earnestly** ADV ❑ *I earnestly hope Mrs Smith will forgive me.*

earnings /'ɜːnɪŋz/ N-PLURAL Your **earnings** are the money that you earn by working. ❑ *Average weekly earnings in the north of England are £368.*

earring /'ɪərɪŋ/ (**earrings**) N-COUNT **Earrings** are pieces of jewellery which you attach to your ears.
→ see **jewellery**

earth /ɜːθ/ (**earths**) **1** N-PROPER **The Earth** is the planet on which we live. **2** N-SING **The earth** is the surface of the Earth. ❑ *As the bomb exploded, the earth shook.* **3** N-UNCOUNT **Earth** is the substance on the land surface of the earth in which plants grow. ❑ *Plants need earth, water and sun to grow.* **4** N-SING The **earth** in an electric plug or appliance is a wire through which electricity can pass into the ground, to make the equipment safe even if something goes wrong with it. **5** PHRASE You use **on earth** for emphasis in questions which begin with words such as 'how', 'why', 'what', or 'where'. ❑ *Why on earth would he want to go there?* **6** PHRASE If you come **down to earth**, you have to face the reality of everyday life after a period of great excitement. ❑ *He was brought down to earth by the death of his dog.* **7** → see also **down-to-earth**
→ see Word Web: **earth**
→ see **core, eclipse, erosion**

earthly /'ɜːθli/ **1** ADJ BEFORE N **Earthly** means happening in the material world of our life on earth and not in any spiritual life or life after death. Earthly is only used in front of a noun. ❑ *Many religions see food as a symbol of earthly life.* **2** PHRASE If you say that there is **no earthly reason** for something, you are emphasizing that there is no possible reason for it. ❑ *They see no earthly reason why they should have to do this.*

earthquake /'ɜːθkweɪk/ (**earthquakes**) N-COUNT An **earthquake** is a shaking of the ground caused by movement of the earth's crust.
→ see Word Web: **earthquake**

earthy /'ɜːθi/ (**earthier, earthiest**) **1** ADJ If you describe someone as **earthy**, you mean they are open and direct about subjects which other people avoid or feel ashamed about. ❑ *...his earthy humour.* **2** ADJ Something that is **earthy** looks, smells, or feels like earth. ❑ *...a strong, earthy smell.*

ease /iːz/ (**eases, easing, eased**) **1** PHRASE If you do something **with ease**, you do it without difficulty or effort. ❑ *Anne was intelligent and passed her exams with ease.* **2** N-UNCOUNT If you talk about the **ease of** a particular activity, you mean that it is easy to do or has been made easier to do. ❑ *The cricket team were surprised by the ease of their victory.* ❑ *The ease of flying from Britain to Pisa means people are visiting just for the weekend.* **3** PHRASE If you are **at ease**, you feel confident and comfortable. If you are **ill at ease**, you feel anxious or awkward. **4** V-T/V-I If something **eases**, or if it **eases off**, it is reduced in degree, speed, or intensity. ❑ *I gave him some paracetamol to ease the pain.* ❑ *The pressure has eased off.* ❑ *At last the rain eased up.* ● **easing** N-UNCOUNT ❑ *The treatment provides some easing of the*

Word Web earthquake

Earthquakes occur when two **tectonic plates** meet and start to move past each other. This meeting point is called the focus. It may be located anywhere from a few hundred meters to a few hundred kilometers below the surface of the earth. The resulting pressure causes a split in the earth's **crust** called a **fault**. Vibrations move out from the focus in all directions. These **seismic waves** cause little damage until they reach the surface. The **epicenter**, directly above the focus, receives the greatest damage. **Seismologists** use **seismographs** to measure the amount of ground movement during an earthquake.

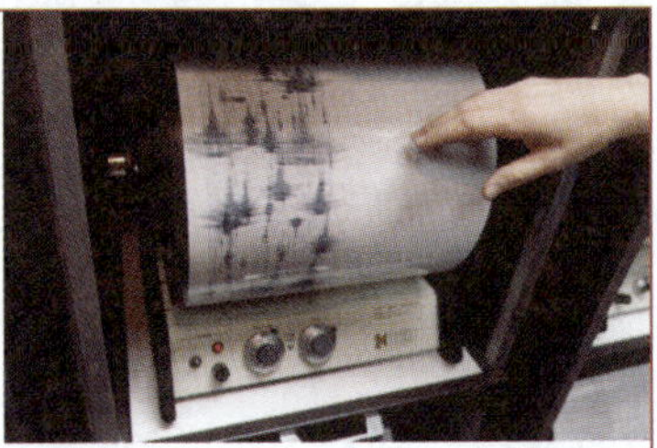

A seismograph recording a major earthquake.

pain. **5** V-T/V-I If you **ease** your way somewhere or **ease** somewhere, you move there slowly, carefully, and gently. If you **ease** something somewhere, you move it there slowly, carefully, and gently. ❑ *She eased back into the chair.* ❑ *Liz eased open the door and moved along the corridor.*

▶ **ease up** PHR-VERB If you **ease up**, you start to make less effort. ❑ *If your workout is still too hard, you need to ease up a little.*

easel

easel /ˈiːzəl/ (**easels**) N-COUNT An **easel** is a wooden frame that supports a picture which an artist is painting.
→ see **painting**

easily /ˈiːzɪli/ **1** ADV You use **easily** to emphasize that something is very likely to happen, or is certainly true. ❑ *The cost could easily be three times that amount.* ❑ *This second TV series is easily as good as the first.* **2** ADV You use **easily** to say that something happens more quickly than normal. ❑ *He always cried very easily.* **3** → see also **easy**

Thesaurus	*easily* Also look up:
ADV.	quickly, readily **1** **2**

east /iːst/ **1** N-SING The **east** is the direction in which you look to see the sun rise. **2** N-SING & ADJ The **east** of a place, or the **east** part of a place, is the part which is towards the east. ❑ *...a village in the east of the country.* ❑ *...the east coast.* **3** ADV **East** means towards the east, or positioned to the east of a place or thing. ❑ *She needed to go east, towards the sea.* ❑ *...just east of the town centre.* **4** ADJ An **east** wind blows from the east. **5** N-SING **The East** is used to refer either to the countries in the southern and eastern part of Asia, including India, China, and Japan, or to the former USSR and other countries in eastern Europe. **6** → see also **Far East, Middle East**

Easter /ˈiːstə/ N-UNCOUNT **Easter** is a Christian festival and holiday, when the resurrection of Jesus Christ is celebrated.

easterly /ˈiːstəli/ **1** ADJ An **easterly** point, area, or direction is to the east or towards the east. ❑ *Menorca is the most easterly of the Balearic Islands.* **2** ADJ An **easterly** wind blows from the east.

eastern /ˈiːstən/ **1** ADJ **Eastern** means in or from the east of a region or country. **2** ADJ **Eastern** means coming either from the people or countries of the East, such as India, China, and Japan, or from the countries in the East of Europe and the former USSR.

easterner /ˈiːstənə/ (**easterners**) N-COUNT An **easterner** is a person who was born in or who lives in the eastern part of a place or country.

eastward /ˈiːstwəd/ also **eastwards** ADV & ADJ **Eastward** or **eastwards** means towards the east. ❑ *A powerful storm is moving eastwards.* ❑ *Drive in an eastward direction.*

easy /ˈiːzi/ (**easier, easiest**) **1** ADJ If a job or action is **easy**, you can do it without difficulty. ❑ *Our maths homework was easy.* ❑ *She made easy conversation with her new neighbour.* ● **easily** ADV ❑ *These journeys are easily made by plane.* **2** ADJ An **easy** life or time is comfortable and without any problems. ❑ *Owning a car should make your life much easier.* **3** PHRASE If someone tells you to **take it easy**, they mean that you should relax and not do very much. [INFORMAL]

Thesaurus	*easy* Also look up:
ADJ.	basic, elementary, simple, uncomplicated; *(ant.)* complicated, difficult, hard **1**

ˌeasy-ˈgoing ADJ If you describe someone as **easy-going**, you mean that they are not easily worried or upset; used showing approval.

eat /iːt/ (**eats, eating, ate, eaten**) V-T/V-I When you **eat**, or **eat** something, you put it into your mouth, chew it, and swallow it. ❑ *I ate my chicken quickly.*
→ see **cook, food**

▶ **eat away** PHR-VERB If one thing **eats away** another or **eats away at** another, it gradually destroys it or uses it up. ❑ *The sea is eating away at the coastline.*

▶ **eat into** PHR-VERB If something **eats into** your time or resources, it uses them, when they should be used for other things. ❑ *Responsibilities at work eat into his spare time.*

Thesaurus	*eat* Also look up:
V.	chew, consume, dine, feast, munch, nibble, taste **1**

Word Partnership	Use *eat* with:
ADV.	eat **alone**, eat **too much**, eat **properly**, eat **together**, eat **well**
V.	eat **and drink**, eat **and sleep**, **want** ***something*** **to** eat

eater /ˈiːtə/ (**eaters**) N-COUNT You use **eater** to refer to someone who eats in a particular way or eats particular kinds of food. ❑ *...a healthy eater.* ❑ *...meat eaters.*

eavesdrop /ˈiːvzdrɒp/ (**eavesdrops, eavesdropping, eavesdropped**) V-I If you **eavesdrop on** someone, you listen secretly to what they are saying. ● **eavesdropper** (**eavesdroppers**) N-COUNT ❑ *His telephone call was recorded by an eavesdropper.*

ebb /eb/ (**ebbs, ebbing, ebbed**) **1** V-I When the tide or the sea **ebbs**, its level falls. **2** N-COUNT **The ebb** or **the ebb tide** is one of the regular periods when the sea gradually falls to a lower level. **3** V-I If a feeling or a person's strength **ebbs** or **ebbs away**, it weakens and gradually disappears. [FORMAL] ❑ *The government's popularity is ebbing away.* **4** PHRASE If someone or something is **at a low ebb**, they are not being very successful or profitable. ❑ *The club's fortunes were at a low ebb.* **5** PHRASE You can use **ebb and flow** to describe the way that something repeatedly increases and decreases. ❑ *...the ebb and flow of the fighting.*
→ see **ocean, tide**

Word Link	***ite*** **≈ mineral, rock : dynamite, granite, graphite**

eccentric /ɪkˈsentrɪk/ (**eccentrics**) ADJ & N-COUNT An **eccentric** person or an **eccentric** has habits or opinions that other people

E

Word Web echo

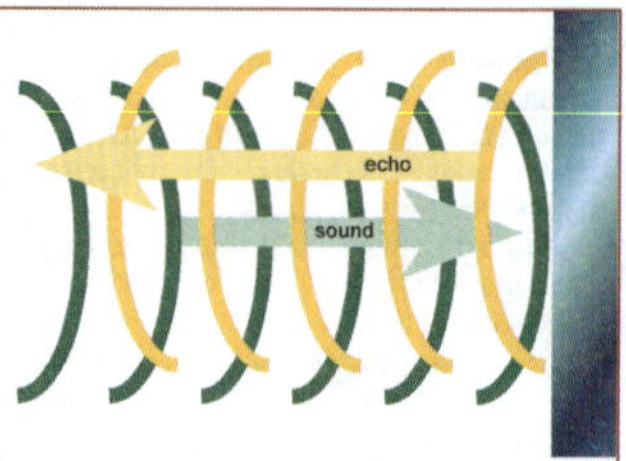

We can learn a lot from studying **echoes**. Geologists use **sound reflection** to predict how earthquake waves will travel hrough the earth. They also use **echolocation** to find underground oil reservoirs. Oceanographers use **sonar** to explore the ocean. Marine mammals, bats, and humans also use sonar for navigation. Architects study building materials and surfaces to understand how they absorb or **reflect** sound **waves**. They may use hard reflective surfaces to help create a noisy, exciting atmosphere in a restaurant. They may suggest curtains and carpeting to create a quiet, calm library.

think strange. • **eccentricity** /ˌeksen'trɪsɪti/ (**eccentricities**) N-VAR ❑ *He is famous for his eccentricity.*

ecclesiastical /ɪˌkli:zi'æstɪkəl/ ADJ **Ecclesiastical** means belonging to or connected with the Christian Church.

echelon /'eʃəlɒn/ (**echelons**) N-COUNT An **echelon** in an organization or society is a level or rank in it. [FORMAL] ❑ *...the lower echelons of society.*

echo /'ekəʊ/ (**echoes, echoing, echoed**) **1** N-COUNT An **echo** is a sound caused by a noise being reflected off a surface such as a wall. ❑ *He heard the echo of her footsteps along the hallway.* **2** V-I If sounds **echo**, or a place **echoes with** sounds, the sounds are reflected off a surface there and can be heard again. ❑ *The corridor echoed with the barking of dogs.* ❑ *...the echoing hall.* **3** V-T If you **echo** someone's words, you repeat them or express the same thing. ❑ *We all echoed Captain Ryan's opinion.* **4** N-COUNT An **echo** is an expression of an attitude, opinion, or statement which has already been expressed. ❑ *Her comments were an echo of remarks made by the Prime Minister earlier in the week.*
→ see Word Web: **echo**
→ see **sound**

Word Link *ec ≈ away, from, out : eccentric, eclectic, ecstatic*

eclectic /ɪ'klektɪk/ ADJ If you describe a collection of objects, ideas, or beliefs as **eclectic**, you mean that they are wide-ranging and come from many different sources. [FORMAL] ❑ *...an eclectic mix of people.*

eclipse /ɪ'klɪps/ (**eclipses, eclipsing, eclipsed**) **1** N-COUNT When there is an **eclipse** of the sun or **solar eclipse**, the moon is between the Earth and the sun, so that part or all of the sun is hidden. When there is an **eclipse** of the moon or **lunar eclipse**, the Earth is between the sun and the moon, so that part or all of the moon is hidden. **2** V-T If one thing **eclipses** another, the first thing becomes more important so that the second thing is no longer noticed. ❑ *Mozart has eclipsed nearly all other composers.*
→ see Word Web: **eclipse**

'eco-ˌfriendly ADJ **Eco-friendly** products or services are less harmful to the environment than other similar products or services. ❑ *...eco-friendly washing powder.*

ecology /ɪ'kɒlədʒi/ **1** N-UNCOUNT When you talk about **the ecology of** a place, you are referring to the relationships between living things and their environment. ❑ *The region has a unique ecology.* • **ecological** /ˌi:kə'lɒdʒɪkəl/ ADJ BEFORE N ❑ *...Siberia's ecological balance.* • **ecologically** ADV ❑ *Swedish people are very ecologically conscious.* **2** N-UNCOUNT **Ecology** is the study of the relationship between living things and their environment. • **ecologist** (**ecologists**) N-COUNT ❑ *The ecologists visited Sri Lanka to study its forests.*

economic /ˌi:kə'nɒmɪk, ˌek-/ **1** ADJ **Economic** means concerned with the organization of the money, industry, and trade of a country, region, or society. ❑ *...Poland's economic situation.* • **economically** ADV ❑ *...an economically strong area.* **2** ADJ If something is **economic**, it produces a profit. ❑ *The new system may be more economic.*
→ see **disaster**

economical /ˌi:kə'nɒmɪkəl, ˌek-/ **1** ADJ Something that is **economical** does not require a lot of money to operate. ❑ *...economical cars.* • **economically** ADV ❑ *We need to do this more efficiently and economically.* **2** ADJ If someone is **economical**, they spend money carefully and sensibly. • **economically** ADV ❑ *We live as economically as possible.*

Word Web eclipse

There is more than one kind of eclipse. When the **earth** passes between the **sun** and the **moon**, we see a **lunar eclipse**. When the moon passes between the sun and the earth, we see a **solar eclipse**. A total eclipse of the sun happens when the moon covers the sun completely. In the past, people were frightened of eclipses. Some civilizations understood eclipses. Their leaders pretended to control the sun in order to get the respect of their people. On July 22, 2009, a total eclipse of the sun will be visible in North America.

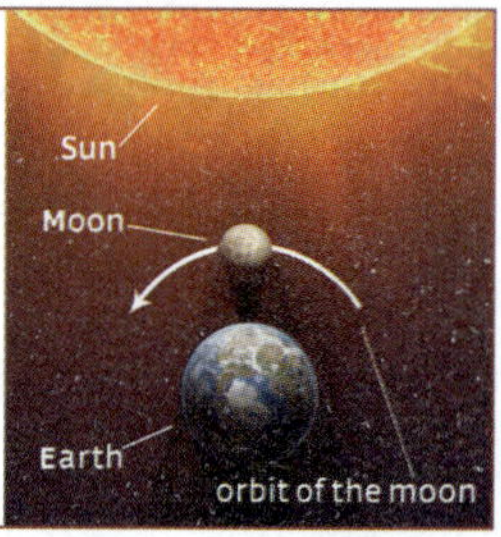

Thesaurus *economical* Also look up:

ADJ. cost-effective, inexpensive 1
careful, frugal, practical, 2

Word Link ***ics ≈ system, knowledge : economics, electronics, genetics***

economics /ˌiːkəˈnɒmɪks, ˌek-/ 1 N-UNCOUNT **Economics** is the study of the way in which money, industry, and trade are organized in a society. 2 N-UNCOUNT **The economics of** a society or industry is the system of organizing money and trade in it. ❑ *...the economics of the newspaper business.*

economist /ɪˈkɒnəmɪst/ (**economists**) N-COUNT An **economist** is a person who studies, teaches, or writes about economics.

economy /ɪˈkɒnəmi/ (**economies**) 1 N-COUNT The **economy** of a country or region is the system by which money, industry, and trade are organized. ❑ *He talked about the changes in the Indian economy.* 2 N-UNCOUNT **Economy** is careful spending or the careful use of things to save money or avoid waste. ❑ *There have been many improvements in the fuel economy of cars.*

ecosystem /ˈiːkəʊsɪstəm, AM ˈekə-/ (**ecosystems**) N-COUNT An **ecosystem** is all the plants and animals that live in a particular area together with the relationship that exists between them and their environment. [TECHNICAL] ❑ *...Antarctica's ecosystem.*

ecstasy /ˈekstəsi/ (**ecstasies**) 1 N-VAR **Ecstasy** is a feeling of great happiness. ❑ *I raised my arms in ecstasy when I won.* 2 N-UNCOUNT **Ecstasy** is an illegal drug which acts as a stimulant and can cause hallucinations.

Word Link ***ec ≈ away, from, out : eccentric, eclectic, ecstatic***

ecstatic /ekˈstætɪk/ ADJ If you are **ecstatic**, you feel very enthusiastic and happy. ❑ *The audience was ecstatic.* ❑ *The president was given an ecstatic welcome.* ● **ecstatically** ADV ❑ *...ecstatically happy.*

eczema /ˈeksmə, AM ɪgˈziːmə/ N-UNCOUNT **Eczema** is a skin condition which makes your skin itch and become sore and broken.

edge /edʒ/ (**edges, edging, edged**) 1 N-COUNT The **edge** of something is the place or line where it stops, or the part of it that is furthest from the middle. ❑ *We were on the edge of town.* ❑ *She was standing at the water's edge.*

edge

2 N-COUNT The **edge** of something sharp such as a knife is its sharp or narrow side. ❑ *...the sharp edge of the sword.* 3 V-I If you **edge** somewhere, you move there very slowly. ❑ *He edged closer to the door.* 4 N-SING If you have an **edge over** someone, you have an advantage over them. ❑ *The French team have extra time to prepare for the match and this could give them the edge over England.* 5 PHRASE If you are **on edge**, you are nervous and unable to relax.
▶ **edge out** PHR-VERB If someone **edges out** someone else, they just manage to beat them or get in front of them in a contest. ❑ *McGregor edged Johnson out of first place.*

Thesaurus *edge* Also look up:

N. border, boundary, rim; *(ant.)* center, middle 1
advantage 4

edgy /ˈedʒi/ ADJ If you feel **edgy**, you are nervous and anxious. [INFORMAL]

edible /ˈedɪbəl/ ADJ If something is **edible**, it is safe to eat. ❑ *...edible mushrooms.*

edict /ˈiːdɪkt/ (**edicts**) N-COUNT An **edict** is a command given by someone in authority. [FORMAL]

edifice /ˈedɪfɪs/ (**edifices**) N-COUNT An **edifice** is a large impressive building. [FORMAL] ❑ *The large stone edifice was built in 1900.*

edit /ˈedɪt/ (**edits, editing, edited**) 1 V-T If you **edit** a text, you correct it so that it is suitable for publication. ❑ *She helped him edit his report.* 2 V-T If you **edit** a book, you collect pieces of writing by different authors and prepare them for publication. ❑ *Toni Morrison edited the new collection of essays.* 3 V-T If you **edit** a film or a television or radio programme, you choose some of what has been filmed or recorded and arrange it in a particular order. ❑ *He taught me to edit film.* ❑ *He is editing together excerpts of some of his films.* 4 V-T Someone who **edits** a newspaper or magazine is in charge of it and makes decisions concerning the contents.
▶ **edit out** PHR-VERB If you **edit** something **out of** a book or film, you remove it. ❑ *His voice will be edited out of the final film.*

edition /ɪˈdɪʃən/ (**editions**) 1 N-COUNT An **edition** is a particular version of a book, magazine, or newspaper that is printed at one time. ❑ *This is the second edition of the book.* ❑ *...a paperback edition.* 2 N-COUNT An **edition** is a single television or radio programme that is one of a series. ❑ *This is the first edition of her new TV series.*

Word Partnership Use *edition* with:

N. **collector's** edition, **paperback** edition 1
ADJ. **limited** edition, **new** edition, **revised** edition, **special** edition 1

editor /ˈedɪtə/ (**editors**) 1 N-COUNT An **editor** is a person in charge of a newspaper or magazine, or a section of a newspaper or magazine, who makes decisions concerning the contents. 2 N-COUNT An **editor** is a person who checks and corrects texts before they are published. 3 N-COUNT An **editor** is a person who collects pieces of writing by different authors and prepares them for publication. ❑ *Michael Rosen is the editor of the collection of poems.* 4 N-COUNT An **editor** is a person who selects recorded material for a film or for a radio or television programme.

editorial /ˌedɪˈtɔːriəl/ (**editorials**) 1 ADJ BEFORE N **Editorial** means involved in preparing a newspaper, magazine, or book for publication. ❑ *...the editorial staff of the magazine 'Private Eye'.* 2 ADJ BEFORE N **Editorial** means involving the attitudes, opinions, and contents of a newspaper, magazine, or television programme. ❑ *We are not going to change our editorial policy.* 3 N-COUNT

An **editorial** is an article in a newspaper which gives the opinion of the editor or publisher on a particular topic.

educate /ˈedʒʊkeɪt/ (**educates, educating, educated**) 1 V-T When someone **is educated**, they are taught at a school or college. ❑ *He was educated at Fettes College in Edinburgh.* 2 V-T To **educate** people means to improve their understanding of a particular problem or issue. ❑ *This project will educate teenagers about healthy eating.*

E

Usage

Note that you do not use **educate** or **education** to talk about the way parents look after their children and gradually teach them about good behaviour and life in general. Instead, you should use the verb **bring up** or the noun **upbringing**, but not the verb **grow up**, which is always used without an object. ❑ *His parents brought him up to be polite.* ❑ *...the effect that a religious upbringing had on me.* ❑ *I grew up in a very rural area.*

Thesaurus *educate* Also look up:

V.	coach, instruct, teach, train 2

educated /ˈedʒʊkeɪtɪd/ ADJ **Educated** people have reached a high standard of learning.

education /ˌedʒʊˈkeɪʃən/ (**educations**) N-VAR **Education** means learning and teaching. ❑ *The prime minister has a passion for education.* ❑ *Parents are the most important people in a child's education.* ● **educational** ADJ ❑ *...high educational standards.*

Edwardian /edˈwɔːdiən/ (**Edwardians**) 1 ADJ **Edwardian** means connected with or typical of Britain in the first decade of the 20th century, when Edward VII was King. ❑ *...the Edwardian era.* 2 N-COUNT People associated with the Edwardian period are sometimes called **Edwardians**.

eel /iːl/ (**eels**) N-COUNT An **eel** is a fish with a long, thin body.

eerie /ˈɪəri/ ADJ Something that is **eerie** is strange and frightening. ❑ *...an eerie silence.* ● **eerily** ADV ❑ *The streets are eerily empty.*

effect /ɪˈfekt/ (**effects, effecting, effected**) 1 N-VAR An **effect** is a change, reaction, or impression that is caused by something or is the result of something. ❑ *...the effect of divorce on children.* ❑ *Head injuries can have lasting effects.* 2 V-T If you **effect** something, you succeed in causing it to happen. [FORMAL] ❑ *It is difficult to effect social change.* 3 → see also **side-effect** 4 PHRASE You add **in effect** to a statement which you feel is a reasonable description or summary of something. ❑ *The deal would create, in effect, the world's biggest airline.* 5 PHRASE You use **to this effect, to that effect**, or **to the effect that** when you are summarizing what someone has said, rather than repeating their actual words. ❑ *The teacher said something to the effect that I should pay attention and answer the question.* 6 PHRASE When something **takes effect, comes into effect**, or **is put into effect**, it begins to apply or starts to have results. 7 PHRASE You use **effect** in expressions such as **to good effect** and **to no effect** in order to indicate how successful or impressive an action is. ❑ *Mr Charles complained, to no effect.*

Word Partnership Use *effect* with:

ADJ.	**adverse** effect, **desired** effect, **immediate** effect, **lasting** effect, **negative/positive** effect 1
V.	**have an** effect, **produce an** effect 1 **take** effect 3
N.	effect **a change** 2

effective /ɪˈfektɪv/ 1 ADJ Something that is **effective** produces the intended results. ❑ *This is an effective way of teaching languages.* ❑ *This drug is effective against the most common form of the disease.* ● **effectively** ADV ❑ *I learned to work more effectively.* ● **effectiveness** N-UNCOUNT ❑ *...the effectiveness of marketing.* 2 ADJ BEFORE N **Effective** means having a particular role or result in practice, though not officially. ❑ *The army has been in effective control of the island since March.* 3 ADJ AFTER LINK-V When a law or an agreement becomes **effective**, it begins officially to apply.

Word Partnership Use *effective* with:

N.	effective **means**, effective **method**, effective **treatment**, effective **use** 1
ADV.	**highly** effective 1 effective **immediately** 3

effectively /ɪˈfektɪvli/ ADV You use **effectively** with a statement which you feel is a reasonable description or summary of a particular situation. ❑ *The President has effectively lost power.*

efficient /ɪˈfɪʃənt/ ADJ Something or someone that is **efficient** does a job successfully, without wasting time or energy. ❑ *Cycling is the most efficient form of transport.* ❑ *...energy-efficient lighting.* ● **efficiently** ADV ❑ *We all need to use energy more efficiently.* ● **efficiency** N-UNCOUNT ❑ *They were amazed at her efficiency.*

Word Partnership Use *efficient* with:

N.	**energy** efficient, **fuel** efficient, efficient **method**, efficient **system**, efficient **use of *something***
ADV.	**highly** efficient

effort /ˈefət/ (**efforts**) 1 N-VAR If you **make** an **effort** to do something, you try hard to do it. ❑ *He made no effort to hide his feelings.* ❑ *The man died despite the efforts of the doctors.* 2 N-VAR If you do something **with effort**, or if it is **an effort**, you can do it but you find it physically or mentally demanding. ❑ *She took a deep breath and sat up with great effort.* ❑ *Carrying the injured man took some effort.*

Thesaurus *effort* Also look up:

N.	attempt 1 exertion, labor, work 4

effortless /ˈefətləs/ ADJ If an action is **effortless**, it is achieved easily. ❑ *...effortless movement.* ● **effortlessly** ADV ❑ *The fish swam effortlessly, round and round, all at the same speed.*

EFL /ˌiː ef ˈel/ N-UNCOUNT **EFL** is used to describe things connected with the teaching of English to people whose first language is not English.

Picture Dictionary **egg**

EFL is an abbreviation for 'English as a Foreign Language'. ❑ *...an EFL teacher.*

e.g. /ˌiː ˈdʒiː/ **e.g.** is an abbreviation that means 'for example'. It is used before a noun, or to introduce another sentence. ❑ *...dairy products, e.g. cheese and butter.*

egg /eg/ (**eggs, egging, egged**) **1** N-COUNT An **egg** is the rounded object produced by a female bird from which a baby bird later emerges. Reptiles, fish, and insects also produce eggs. ❑ *A baby bird hatched from its egg.* **2** N-VAR An **egg** is a hen's egg considered as food. ❑ *Break the eggs into a large bowl.* ❑ *...bacon and egg.* **3** N-COUNT An **egg** is a cell in a female person or animal which can develop into a baby.
→ see Picture Dictionary: **egg**
→ see **bird, reproduction**
▶ **egg on** PHR-VERB If you **egg** someone **on**, you encourage them to do something daring or foolish.

ego /ˈiːgəʊ, ˈegəʊ/ (**egos**) N-VAR Someone's **ego** is their sense of their own importance and their opinion of their own worth. ❑ *He has a huge ego.*

eh /eɪ/ **Eh** is used to represent a noise that people make in conversation, for example to ask for or show agreement, or to ask something to be explained or repeated. ❑ *Let's talk all about it outside, eh?* ❑ *'He's ill in bed.'—'Eh?'—'He's ill in bed.'*

eight /eɪt/ (**eights**) NUM **Eight** is the number 8.

Word Link *teen ≈ plus ten, from 13-19 : eighteen, seventeen, teenager*

eighteen /ˌeɪˈtiːn/ NUM **Eighteen** is the number 18.

eighteenth /ˌeɪˈtiːnθ/ ORD The **eighteenth** item in a series is the one that you count as number eighteen.

eighth /eɪtθ/ (**eighths**) **1** ORD The **eighth** item in a series is the one that you count as number eight. ❑ *...the eighth century.* **2** N-COUNT An **eighth** is one of eight equal parts of something. ❑ *...an eighth of an inch.*

eightieth /ˈeɪtiəθ/ ORD The **eightieth** item in a series is the one that you count as number eighty.

eighty /ˈeɪti/ (**eighties**) **1** NUM **Eighty** is the number 80. **2** N-PLURAL When you talk about **the eighties**, you are talking about numbers between 80 and 89. For example, if you are **in your eighties**, you are aged between 80 and 89. If the temperature is **in the eighties**, the temperature is between 80 and 89 degrees. If something happened **in the eighties**, it happened between 1980 and 1989.

either /ˈaɪðə, ˈiːðə/ **1** CONJ You use **either** in front of the first of two or more alternatives, when you are stating the only possibilities or choices that there are. The other alternatives are introduced by 'or'. ❑ *Sightseeing is best done either by tour bus or by bicycle.* ❑ *People either love me or they hate me.* ❑ *Either she goes or I go.* **2** PRON & DET You can use **either** to refer to one of two things, people, or situations, when you want to say that they are both possible and it does not matter which one is chosen or considered. ❑ *The meeting could be held in either Manchester or Newcastle.* ❑ *She has never visited either country.* ❑ *Do either of you speak Russian?* **3** PRON & DET & CONJ You can use **either** in a negative statement to refer to each of two things, people, or situations to indicate that the negative statement includes both of them. ❑ *She thinks that I will never marry or have children. I don't want either.* ❑ *He couldn't remember either man's name.* **4** DET You use **either** to introduce a noun that refers to each of two things when you are talking about both of them. ❑ *There were basketball hoops at either end of the gymnasium.* **5** ADV You use **either** by itself in negative statements to indicate that there is a similarity or connection with a person or thing that you have just mentioned. ❑ *He did not say anything to her, and she did not speak to him either.*

Word Link *e ≈ away, out : eject, emigrate, emit*

eject /ɪˈdʒekt/ (**ejects, ejecting, ejected**) **1** V-T If someone **ejects** you **from** a place, they force you to leave. ❑ *The police used dogs to eject the protesters.* ● **ejection** (**ejections**) N-VAR ❑ *...the student's ejection from the classroom.* **2** V-T To **eject** something means to remove it or push it out forcefully. ❑ *She ejected the CD from the stereo.*

Word Link *labor ≈ working : collaborate, elaborate, laboratory*

elaborate (**elaborates, elaborating, elaborated**) **1** ADJ /ɪˈlæbərət/ You use **elaborate** to describe something that consists of many different parts, making it very detailed or complex. ❑ *The elaborate ceremony lasted for eight days.* ● **elaborately** ADV ❑ *...an elaborately carved wooden bed.* **2** V-T/V-I /ɪˈlæbəreɪt/ If you **elaborate on** a plan or a theory, or if you **elaborate** a plan or theory, you give more details about it. ❑ *The policeman did not elaborate on possible reasons for the killing.* ● **elaboration** N-UNCOUNT ❑ *...the elaboration of arguments.*

Word Link *lapse ≈ falling : collapse, elapse, lapse*

elapse /ɪˈlæps/ (**elapses, elapsing, elapsed**) V-I When time **elapses**, it passes. [FORMAL] ❑ *Forty-eight hours have elapsed since his arrest.*

elastic /ɪˈlæstɪk/ **1** N-UNCOUNT **Elastic** is a rubber material that stretches when you pull it and returns to its original size when you let it go. ❑ *She was wearing a bracelet of beads strung on a piece of elastic.* **2** ADJ Something that is **elastic** stretches easily. ❑ *It is made from an elastic material.*

elasticity /ˌiːlæsˈtɪsɪti, ɪˌlæst-/ N-UNCOUNT The

elasticity of a material or substance is its ability to return to its original shape, size, and condition after it has been stretched. ❑ *We all have different amounts of skin elasticity.*

elated /ɪ'leɪtɪd/ ADJ If you are **elated**, you are extremely happy and excited because of something that has happened. ❑ *'That was the best race of my life,' said an elated Clayton.* ● **elation** N-UNCOUNT ❑ *His supporters reacted to the news with elation.*
→ see **emotion**

E

elbow /'elbəʊ/ (**elbows, elbowing, elbowed**) **1** N-COUNT Your **elbow** is the joint where your arm bends in the middle. **2** V-T If you **elbow** someone away, you push them aside with your elbow. If you **elbow** your way somewhere, you move there by pushing other people out of the way, using your elbows. ❑ *The bodyguards elbowed away a fan.* ❑ *Her boyfriend elbowed the man off the pavement.* **3** V-T If someone **elbows** you, they intentionally hurt you by hitting you with their elbow. ❑ *He elbowed Harry right in the eye.*
→ see **body**

elder /'eldə/ (**elders**) **1** ADJ The **elder** of two people is the one who was born first. ❑ *...his elder brother.* **2** N-COUNT A person's **elder** is someone who is older than them. **3** N-COUNT In some societies, an **elder** is one of the respected older people who have influence and authority.

Usage

In British English, the adjective **elder** is usually only used to describe brothers and sisters. ❑ *...her elder sister.* You use **older** to talk about the age of other people or things. **Elder** cannot be followed by **than** but **older** can be followed by **than**. ❑ *I've got a sister who is older than me.*

elderly /'eldəli/ ADJ & N-PLURAL You use **elderly** as a polite way of saying that someone is old. **The elderly** are people who are old. ❑ *...an elderly couple.* ❑ *These diseases usually affect the elderly.*
→ see **age**

eldest /'eldɪst/ ADJ The **eldest** person in a group is the one who was born before all the others. ❑ *Lisa is her eldest daughter.*

elect /ɪ'lekt/ (**elects, electing, elected**) **1** V-T When people **elect** someone, they choose that person to represent them, by voting. ❑ *Manchester College elected him Principal in 1956.* ❑ *They elected a woman as their new president.* ❑ *...the newly elected prime minister.* **2** V-T If you **elect to** do something, you choose to do it. [FORMAL] ❑ *He elected to stay in India.*

election /ɪ'lekʃən/ (**elections**) **1** N-VAR An **election** is a process in which people vote to choose a person or group of people to hold an official position. ❑ *...Poland's first free elections for more than fifty years.* ❑ *...his election campaign.* **2** N-UNCOUNT The **election** of a person or a political party is their success in winning an election. ❑ *...the election of the Labour government in 1964.* ❑ *...Vaclav Havel's election as president.* **3** → see also **by-election, general election**
→ see **citizenship**

Word Partnership Use *election* with:

N.	election **campaign**, election **day**, election **official**, election **results** **1**
V.	**hold an** election, **lose an** election, **vote in an** election, **win an** election **1**

elector /ɪ'lektə/ (**electors**) N-COUNT An **elector** is a person who has the right to vote in an election.

electoral /ɪ'lektərəl/ ADJ BEFORE N **Electoral** means connected with an election. ❑ *...Italy's electoral system.*

electorate /ɪ'lektərət/ (**electorates**) N-COUNT The **electorate** of a country is the people there who have the right to vote in an election. **Electorate** can take the single or plural form of the verb. ❑ *Almost half of the electorate supports him.*

electric /ɪ'lektrɪk/ **1** ADJ BEFORE N An **electric** device works by means of electricity. **2** ADJ BEFORE N An **electric** current, voltage, or charge is one that is produced by electricity. **Electric** plugs, sockets, or power lines are designed to carry electricity. **3** ADJ If you describe the atmosphere of a place or event as **electric**, you mean that people are in a state of great excitement.

electrical /ɪ'lektrɪkəl/ **1** ADJ BEFORE N **Electrical** devices work by means of electricity. ❑ *...electrical equipment.* ● **electrically** ADV ❑ *...an electrically-powered car.* **2** ADJ BEFORE N **Electrical** engineers and industries are involved in the production or maintenance of electricity or electrical goods.
→ see **electricity, energy**

Word Link *ician ≈ person who works at : electrician, musician, physician*

electrician /ɪlek'trɪʃən, 'iːlek-/ (**electricians**) N-COUNT An **electrician** is a person whose job is to install and repair electrical equipment.

Word Link *electr ≈ electric : electrician, electricity, electron*

electricity /ɪlek'trɪsɪti, 'iːlek-/ N-UNCOUNT **Electricity** is a form of energy used for heating and lighting, and to provide power for machines.
→ see Word Web: **electricity**
→ see **energy, light bulb**

e͵lectric 'shock (**electric shocks**) → see **shock** (meaning 7)

electrify /ɪ'lektrɪfaɪ/ (**electrifies, electrifying, electrified**) **1** V-T If something **electrifies** you, it excites and surprises you a lot. ❑ *The world was electrified by his courage.* ● **electrifying** ADJ ❑ *...an electrifying performance.* **2** V-T When a railway system **is electrified**, it is connected by overhead wires or by a special rail to a supply of electricity. ● **electrification** /ɪ͵lektrɪfɪ'keɪʃən/ N-UNCOUNT ❑ *...the electrification of the London to Glasgow railway line.*

electrocute /ɪ'lektrəkjuːt/ (**electrocutes, electrocuting, electrocuted**) V-T If someone **is electrocuted**, they are accidentally killed or injured when they touch something connected to a source of electricity. ❑ *He accidentally electrocuted himself.* ● **electrocution** N-UNCOUNT ❑ *These animals were killed by electrocution.*

Word Link *electr ≈ electric : electrician, electricity, electron*

electron /ɪ'lektrɒn/ N-COUNT An **electron** is a tiny particle of matter that is smaller than an atom and has a negative electrical charge.
→ see **television**

electronic /ɪlek'trɒnɪk, 'iː-/ 1 ADJ BEFORE N An **electronic** device has transistors, silicon chips, or valves which control and change the electric current passing through it. 2 ADJ An **electronic** process involves the use of electronic devices. ❑ *...electronic communication.* ● **electronically** ADV ❑ *Data is sent electronically.*

Word Link *ics ≈ system, knowledge : economics, electronics, genetics*

electronics /ɪlek'trɒnɪks/ 1 N-UNCOUNT **Electronics** is the technology of using transistors and silicon chips, especially in devices such as radios, televisions, and computers. ❑ *...Europe's three largest electronics companies.* 2 N-PLURAL You can refer to electronic devices, or the part of a piece of equipment that consists of electronic devices, as **the electronics**. ❑ *A microchip contains all the electronics.*

elegant /'elɪgənt/ 1 ADJ If you describe a person or thing as **elegant**, you think they are pleasing and graceful in appearance or style. ❑ *...an elegant restaurant.* ● **elegance** N-UNCOUNT ❑ *...old-fashioned elegance.* ● **elegantly** ADV ❑ *...an elegantly dressed man.* 2 ADJ If you describe a piece of writing, an idea, or a plan as **elegant**, you mean that it is simple, clear, and clever. ● **elegance** N-UNCOUNT ❑ *...the simple elegance of his idea.* ● **elegantly** ADV ❑ *...her elegantly written diary.*

Thesaurus *elegant* Also look up:
ADJ. chic, exquisite, luxurious, stylish; *(ant.)* 1

element /'elɪmənt/ (**elements**) 1 N-COUNT An **element** of something is one of the parts which make up the whole thing. ❑ *It is one of the key elements of the peace plan.* ❑ *Fitness is an important element in our lives.* 2 N-COUNT When you talk about the particular **elements** within a society or organization, you are referring to groups of people who have similar aims, beliefs, or habits. ❑ *...criminal elements.* 3 N-COUNT If something has an **element of** a particular quality, it has a certain amount of it. ❑ *There is an element of truth in all of these claims.* 4 N-COUNT **The element** in an electrical appliance is the metal part which changes the electric current into heat. 5 N-PLURAL You can refer to the weather, especially wind and rain, as **the elements**. ❑ *All of us slept outside that night, exposed to the elements.* 6 PHRASE If someone is **in** their **element**, they are doing something that they enjoy and do well. ❑ *My mother was in her element, organizing everything.*
→ see Word Web: **element**

elementary /ˌelɪ'mentri/ ADJ **Elementary** things are very simple, straightforward, and basic. ❑ *...elementary computer skills.*

elephant

elephant /'elɪfənt/ (**elephants**) N-COUNT An **elephant** is a very large animal with a long trunk.

elevate /'elɪveɪt/ (**elevates, elevating, elevated**) 1 V-T When someone or something **is elevated to** a more important rank or status, they achieve it. [FORMAL] ❑ *She was elevated to the position of president of the council.* ● **elevation** N-UNCOUNT ❑ *...his elevation to chairman.* 2 V-T To **elevate** something means to increase it in amount or intensity. [FORMAL] ❑ *Stress can elevate blood pressure.* 3 V-T If you **elevate** something, you raise it above a horizontal level. [FORMAL]

Word Link *ation ≈ state of : dehydration, elevation, preservation*

elevation /ˌelɪ'veɪʃən/ (**elevations**) N-COUNT The **elevation** of a place is its height above sea level.

elevator /'elɪveɪtə/ (**elevators**) N-COUNT In American English, an **elevator** is a device that carries people up and down inside buildings. The usual British word is **lift**.

eleven /ɪ'levən/ NUM **Eleven** is the number 11.

eleventh /ɪ'levənθ/ ORD The **eleventh** item in a series is the one that you count as number eleven.

elicit /ɪ'lɪsɪt/ (**elicits, eliciting, elicited**) 1 V-T If you **elicit** a response or a reaction, you do or say something which makes other people respond or react. ❑ *His question elicited a positive answer.* 2 V-T

Word Web element

Elements—like copper, sodium, and oxygen—are made from only one type of **atom**. Each element has its own unique **properties**. For example, oxygen is a gas at room temperature and copper is a solid. Often elements come together with other types of elements to make **compounds**. When the atoms in a compound join together, they form a **molecule**. One of the best known molecules is H_2O. It is made up of two hydrogen atoms and one oxygen atom. This molecule is also known as water. The **periodic table** is a complete listing of all the elements we know.

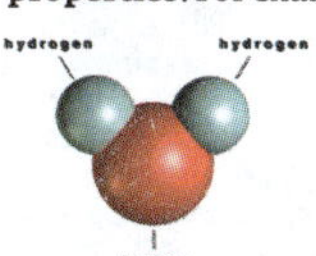

The Periodic Table of Elements

If you **elicit** a piece of information, you get it by asking the right questions. ❑ *My phone call elicited some interesting information.*

eligible /ˈelɪdʒɪbəl/ ADJ Someone who is **eligible for** something is entitled or able to have it. ❑ *You could be eligible for some money.* ❑ *Almost half the population are eligible to vote.* ● **eligibility** N-UNCOUNT ❑ *...rules on eligibility.*

eliminate /ɪˈlɪmɪneɪt/ (**eliminates, eliminating, eliminated**) **1** V-T To **eliminate** something means to remove it completely. [FORMAL] ❑ *If you are allergic to a food, eliminate it from your diet.* ● **elimination** N-UNCOUNT ❑ *...the complete elimination of nuclear weapons.* **2** V-T When a person or team **is eliminated from** a competition, they are defeated and so take no further part in it.

elite /ɪˈliːt, eɪ-/ (**elites**) N-COUNT & ADJ BEFORE N You can refer to the most powerful, rich, or talented people within a particular group or society as **the elite**. You can also talk about an **elite** group of people. ❑ *...Austria's intellectual elite.* ❑ *...elite troops.*

elitist /ɪˈliːtɪst, eɪ-/ (**elitists**) **1** ADJ If you describe an activity, a profession, or a system as **elitist**, you mean that it is practised only by a small group of powerful, rich, or talented people, or that it favours only this group of people; used showing disapproval. ❑ *The art world is totally elitist.* ● **elitism** N-UNCOUNT ❑ *...the elitism of certain universities.* **2** N-COUNT An **elitist** is someone who believes that they are part of an elite; used showing disapproval.

elm /elm/ (**elms**) N-VAR An **elm** is a tree with broad leaves which it loses in autumn.

eloquent /ˈeləkwənt/ ADJ A person who is **eloquent** is good at speaking and able to persuade people; used showing approval. ❑ *...an eloquent spokesman.* ❑ *...an eloquent speech.* ● **eloquence** N-UNCOUNT ❑ *He speaks with great eloquence.* ● **eloquently** ADV ❑ *Jan speaks eloquently about her art.*

else /els/ **1** ADV You use **else** after words such as 'anywhere', 'someone', 'what', 'everyone' and 'everything' to refer vaguely to another place, person, or thing, or to refer to all the other people, places, or things except the one you are talking about. ❑ *What else did you get for your birthday?* ❑ *I never wanted to live anywhere else.* ❑ *She is so much taller than everyone else.* **2** CONJ You use **or else** after stating a logical conclusion, to indicate that what you are about to say is evidence for that conclusion. ❑ *The government has obviously not learnt its lesson or else it would not be handling the problem so badly.* **3** CONJ You use **or else** to introduce a possibility or alternative. ❑ *Your book has to be funny or else people won't buy it.* ❑ *You are either a total genius or else you must be absolutely mad.* **4** PHRASE You can say **'if nothing else'** to indicate that what you are mentioning is, in your opinion, the only good thing in a particular situation. ❑ *If nothing else, at least we're sure to have some laughs this evening.*

elsewhere /ˌelˈsweə/ ADV **Elsewhere** means in other places or to another place. ❑ *Almost all of London's residents were born elsewhere.* ❑ *If you are not satisfied with the advice you receive, then go elsewhere.*

ELT /ˌiː el ˈtiː/ **ELT** is the teaching of English to people whose first language is not English. **ELT** is an abbreviation for 'English Language Teaching'.

elude /ɪˈluːd/ (**eludes, eluding, eluded**) **1** V-T If something that you want **eludes** you, you fail to obtain it. ❑ *Sleep eluded her.* ❑ *The right word eluded him.* **2** V-T If you **elude** someone or something, you avoid them or escape from them. ❑ *He eluded the police for 13 years.*

elusive /ɪˈluːsɪv/ ADJ Something or someone that is **elusive** is difficult to find, achieve, describe, or remember. ❑ *In London late-night taxis are elusive.*

e-mail also **E-mail** /ˈiːmeɪl/ (**e-mails, e-mailing, e-mailed**) **1** N-VAR **E-mail** is a system of sending written messages electronically from one computer to another. **E-mail** is an abbreviation for 'electronic mail'. [COMPUTING] ❑ *Do you want to send an e-mail?* **2** V-T If you **e-mail** someone, you send them an e-mail. ❑ *Jamie e-mailed me to say he couldn't come.*
→ see **Internet**

emanate /ˈemәneɪt/ (**emanates, emanating, emanated**) **1** V-T/V-I If a quality, idea, or feeling **emanates from** you, or if you **emanate** a quality or feeling, you give people a strong sense that you have that quality or feeling. [FORMAL] ❑ *He emanates sympathy.* **2** V-I If something **emanates from** somewhere, it comes from there. [FORMAL] ❑ *The reports emanated from America.*

Word Link	*man ≈ hand : emancipate, manicure, manual*

emancipate /ɪˈmænsɪpeɪt/ (**emancipates, emancipating, emancipated**) V-T If people **are emancipated**, they are freed from unpleasant or degrading social, political, or legal restrictions. [FORMAL] ❑ *The war emancipated the slaves.* ● **emancipation** N-UNCOUNT ❑ *...women's emancipation.*

embankment /ɪmˈbæŋkmənt/ (**embankments**) N-COUNT An **embankment** is a thick wall built of earth, often supporting a railway line or road.

Word Link	*em ≈ making, putting : embargo, embellish, empower*

embargo /ɪmˈbɑːgəʊ/ (**embargoes**) N-COUNT An **embargo** is an order made by a government to stop trade with another country.

embark /ɪmˈbɑːk/ (**embarks, embarking, embarked**) **1** V-I If you **embark on** something new, you start doing it. ❑ *He's embarking on a new career as a writer.* **2** V-I When you **embark** on a ship, you go on board before the start of a journey.

embarrass /ɪmˈbærəs/ (**embarrasses, embarrassing, embarrassed**) **1** V-T If something or someone **embarrasses** you, it makes you feel shy or ashamed. ❑ *It embarrassed him that he had no idea of how to do it.* ● **embarrassing** ADJ ❑ *It was an embarrassing situation for me.* ● **embarrassingly** ADV ❑ *Stephens won the race embarrassingly easily.* **2** V-T If something **embarrasses** a politician, it causes political problems for them. ❑ *The Government has been embarrassed by the affair.* ● **embarrassing** ADJ ❑ *He has put his family in an embarrassing position.*

embarrassed /ɪmˈbærəst/ ADJ A person who is **embarrassed** feels shy, ashamed, or guilty about something.

embarrassment /ɪmˈbærəsmənt/ (**embarrassments**) **1** N-UNCOUNT

Embarrassment is a feeling of shyness, shame, or guilt. ❑ *We apologise for any embarrassment this may have caused.* 2 N-SING If you refer to a person as **an embarrassment**, you mean that you disapprove of them but cannot avoid your connection with them. ❑ *His wife's family were an embarrassment to him.*

embassy /'embəsi/ (**embassies**) N-COUNT An **embassy** is a group of officials, headed by an ambassador, who represent their government in a foreign country. The building in which they work is also called an **embassy**.

embedded /ɪm'bedɪd/ 1 ADJ If an object is **embedded in** something, it is fixed there firmly and deeply. ❑ *There is glass embedded in the cut in his leg.* 2 ADJ If an attitude or feeling is **embedded in** a society or **in** someone's personality, it has become a permanent feature of it. ❑ *This belief was strongly embedded in nineteenth century society.*

Word Link	*em ≈ making, putting : embargo, embellish, empower*

embellish /ɪm'belɪʃ/ (**embellishes, embellishing, embellished**) 1 V-T If something **is embellished with** decorative features, they are added to make it more attractive. ❑ *The mirror was painted and embellished with stars.* ● **embellishment** (**embellishments**) N-VAR ❑ *The house was tiny with no ornaments or embellishment.* 2 V-T If you **embellish** a story, you make it more interesting by adding details which may be untrue.

embezzle /ɪm'bezəl/ (**embezzles, embezzling, embezzled**) V-T If someone **embezzles** money that their organization or company has placed in their care, they take it and use it illegally for their own purposes. ● **embezzlement** N-UNCOUNT ❑ *He was charged with embezzlement.*

emblem /'embləm/ (**emblems**) 1 N-COUNT An **emblem** is a design representing a country or organization. 2 N-COUNT An **emblem** is something symbolizing a quality or idea. ❑ *The eagle was an emblem of strength and courage.*

embodiment /ɪm'bɒdimənt/ N-SING If you describe someone or something as **the embodiment of** a quality or idea, you mean that it is their most noticeable characteristic or the basis of all they do. [FORMAL] ❑ *He is the embodiment of evil.*

embody /ɪm'bɒdi/ (**embodies, embodying, embodied**) 1 V-T If someone or something **embodies** an idea or quality, they are a symbol or expression of that idea or quality. ❑ *Jack Kennedy embodied the hopes of the 1960s.* 2 V-T If something **is embodied in** a particular thing, the second thing contains or consists of the first. ❑ *This ancient wisdom was embodied in every form of art.*

embrace /ɪm'breɪs/ (**embraces, embracing, embraced**) 1 V-T & N-COUNT When you **embrace** someone, you put your arms around them in order to show your affection for them. This action is called an **embrace**. ❑ *The couple embraced each other.* ❑ *A young couple were locked in an embrace.* 2 V-T If you **embrace** a change, political system, or idea, you start supporting it or believing in it completely. [FORMAL] ❑ *The new rules have been embraced by government organizations.* 3 V-T If something **embraces** a group of people, things, or ideas, it includes them. [FORMAL] ❑ *The Chelsea Flower Show embraces art, architecture and sculpture.*

embroider /ɪm'brɔɪdə/ (**embroiders, embroidering, embroidered**) V-T If cloth **is embroidered with** a design, the design is stitched into it. ❑ *The collar was embroidered with red roses.* ❑ *Matilda was embroidering a tablecloth.*

embroidery /ɪm'brɔɪdəri/ (**embroideries**) 1 N-VAR **Embroidery** consists of designs sewn onto cloth. 2 N-UNCOUNT **Embroidery** is the activity of sewing designs onto cloth.
→ see **quilt**

embroiled /ɪm'brɔɪld/ ADJ If you become **embroiled in** an argument or **with** a person, you become deeply involved in that argument or in a relationship with that person, often causing problems for yourself.

embryo /'embriəʊ/ (**embryos**) N-COUNT An **embryo** is an animal or human in the very early stages of development in the womb.
→ see **reproduction**

embryonic /ˌembri'ɒnɪk/ ADJ **Embryonic** means in a very early stage of development. [FORMAL] ❑ *...embryonic plans.*

emerald /'emərəld/ (**emeralds**) N-COUNT An **emerald** is a bright green precious stone.

Word Link	*merg ≈ sinking : emerge, merge, submerge*

emerge /ɪ'mɜːdʒ/ (**emerges, emerging, emerged**) 1 V-I When you **emerge**, you come out from a place where you could not be seen. ❑ *She emerged from the shadows.* 2 V-I If you **emerge from** a difficult or bad experience, you come to the end of it. ❑ *The nation is emerging from its economic problems.* 3 V-I When something such as a political movement **emerges**, it comes into existence. [JOURNALISM] ● **emergence** N-UNCOUNT ❑ *...the emergence of new political groups.*

emergency /ɪ'mɜːdʒənsi/ (**emergencies**) 1 N-COUNT An **emergency** is an unexpected and serious situation such as an accident, which must be dealt with quickly. ❑ *The hospital will only deal with emergencies.* 2 ADJ BEFORE N An **emergency** action is one that is done or arranged quickly, in response to an emergency. ❑ *...an emergency meeting of parliament.* 3 ADJ BEFORE N **Emergency** equipment or supplies are those intended for use in an emergency. ❑ *...an emergency exit.*
→ see **hospital**

Word Partnership	Use *emergency* with:
ADJ.	**major** emergency, **medical** emergency, **minor** emergency 1
N.	**state of** emergency 1
	emergency **care**, emergency **surgery** 2
	emergency **supplies**, emergency **vehicle** 3

Word Link	*e ≈ away, out : eject, emigrate, emit*

Word Link	*migr ≈ moving, changing : emigrate, immigrant, migrant*

emigrate /'emɪgreɪt/ (**emigrates, emigrating, emigrated**) V-I If you **emigrate**, you leave your own country to live in another. ❑ *He emigrated to Belgium.* ● **emigration** N-UNCOUNT ❑ *...the emigration of workers to the UK.*

Word Web emotion

Scientists believe that animals experience **emotions** such as **happiness** and **sadness** just like humans do. Research shows animals also feel **anger**, **fear**, **love**, and **hate**. Biochemical changes in mammals' brains cause these emotions. When an elephant gives birth, a **hormone** goes through her bloodstream. This causes feelings of **adoration** for her baby. The same thing happens to human mothers. When a dog chews on a bone, a chemical increases in its brain to produce feelings of **joy**. The same chemical produces **elation** in humans. Scientists aren't sure whether animals experience **shame**. However, they do know that animals experience **stress**.

eminent /ˈemɪnənt/ ADJ An **eminent** person is well-known and respected. ❑ *...an eminent scientist.* ● **eminence** N-UNCOUNT ❑ *He was a man of great eminence.*

eminently /ˈemɪnəntli/ ADV You use **eminently** in front of an adjective describing a positive quality in order to emphasize the quality expressed by that adjective. ❑ *His family was eminently respectable.*

emission /ɪˈmɪʃən/ (**emissions**) N-VAR An **emission of** light, heat, radiation, or a harmful gas is the release of it into the atmosphere. [FORMAL]
→ see **pollution**

Word Link *e ≈ away, out : eject, emigrate, emit*

emit /ɪˈmɪt/ (**emits, emitting, emitted**) V-T To **emit** a sound, smell or substance means to produce it or send it out. [FORMAL] ❑ *Polly emitted a low whistle.*

emotion /ɪˈməʊʃən/ (**emotions**) N-VAR Emotion is strong feeling such as joy or love. An **emotion** is one of these feelings. ❑ *Her voice trembled with emotion.* ❑ *Jealousy is a destructive emotion.*
→ see Word Web: **emotion**

emotional /ɪˈməʊʃənəl/ **1** ADJ **Emotional** means relating to emotions and feelings. ● **emotionally** ADV ❑ *It was a difficult situation for her, financially and emotionally.* **2** ADJ When someone is **emotional**, they show their feelings openly, especially because they are upset.

eˌmotional inˈtelligence N-UNCOUNT **Emotional intelligence** is used to refer to people's interpersonal and communication skills. ❑ *Without emotional intelligence, you'll never make a good leader.*

emotive /ɪˈməʊtɪv/ ADJ An **emotive** situation or issue is likely to make people feel strong emotions. ❑ *Research on human embryos is an emotive issue.*

Word Link *path ≈ feeling : apathy, empathy, sympathy*

empathy /ˈempəθi/ N-UNCOUNT **Empathy** is the ability to share another person's feelings as if they were your own. ❑ *He had a natural empathy with children.*

emperor /ˈempərə/ (**emperors**) N-COUNT An **emperor** is a man who rules an empire.
→ see **empire**

emphasis /ˈemfəsɪs/ (**emphases** /ˈemfəsiːz/) **1** N-VAR **Emphasis** is special importance that is given to one part or aspect of something. ❑ *At this hotel, the emphasis is firmly on comfort.* **2** N-VAR **Emphasis** is extra force that you put on a syllable, word, or phrase when you are speaking. ❑ *The emphasis is on the first syllable of the word.*

emphasize [BRIT also **emphasise**] /ˈemfəsaɪz/ (**emphasizes, emphasizing, emphasized**) V-T To **emphasize** something means to indicate that it is particularly important or true, or to draw special attention to it. ❑ *Your letter should emphasize your skills.*

emphatic /ɪmˈfætɪk/ **1** ADJ An **emphatic** statement is made forcefully. ● **emphatically** ADV ❑ *The president emphatically denied that he had done anything wrong.* **2** ADJ An **emphatic** victory is one where the winner wins easily.

empire /ˈempaɪə/ (**empires**) **1** N-COUNT An **empire** is a group of countries controlled by one powerful country. **2** N-COUNT A business **empire** is a group of companies controlled by one powerful person. ❑ *...the Mondadori publishing empire.*
→ see Word Web: **empire**
→ see **history**

empirical /ɪmˈpɪrɪkəl/ ADJ **Empirical** knowledge or evidence is based on observation, experiment, and experience rather than theories. ● **empirically** ADV ❑ *We can prove it empirically.*
→ see **science**

employ /ɪmˈplɔɪ/ (**employs, employing, employed**) **1** V-T If a person or company **employs** you, they pay you to work for them. ❑ *3,000 local workers are employed in the tourism industry.* **2** V-T If you **employ** methods, materials, or expressions, you use them. [FORMAL] ❑ *These cosmetics companies employ clever advertising methods.*

employee /ɪmˈplɔɪiː/ (**employees**) N-COUNT An **employee** is a person who is paid to work for a company or organization. ❑ *He is an employee of Fuji Bank.*
→ see **factory**

employer /ɪmˈplɔɪə/ (**employers**) N-COUNT Your **employer** is the organization or person that you work for.

employment /ɪmˈplɔɪmənt/ N-UNCOUNT If you are **in employment**, you have a paid job. ❑ *She was unable to find employment.*

Word Link *em ≈ making, putting : embargo, embellish, empower*

empower /ɪmˈpaʊə/ (**empowers, empowering,**

Word Web empire

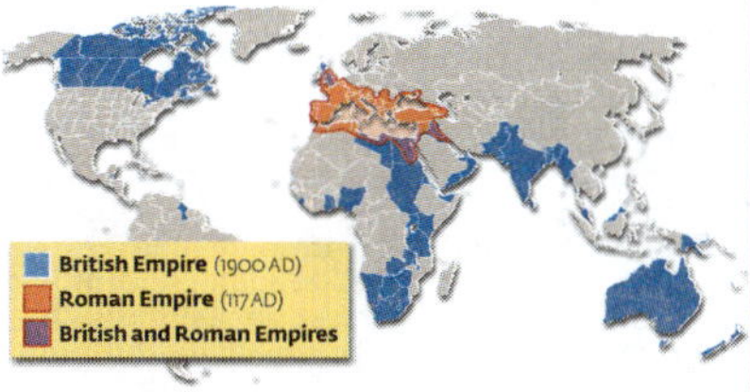

An **empire** is formed when a strong nation-state **conquers** other states and creates a larger **political union**. An early example is the Roman Empire which began in 31 BC. The Roman **emperor** Augustus Caesar* ruled a large area from the Mediterranean Sea* to Western Europe. Later, the British Empire ruled from about 1600 to 1900 AD. Queen Victoria's* empire spread across oceans and continents. One of her many titles was **Empress** of India. Both of these empires spread their political influence as well as their language and culture over large areas.

Augustus Caesar: the first emperor of Rome.
Mediterranean Sea: between Europe and Africa.
Queen Victoria (1819-1901): queen of Great Britain and Ireland.

empowered) V-T If someone or something **empowers** you, they give you the means to achieve something, for example to become more successful. ❑ *Health-awareness campaigns can empower people and save lives.* ● **empowerment** N-UNCOUNT ❑ *...the empowerment of women.*

Word Link *ess ≈ female : actress, empress, heiress*

empress /'emprɪs/ (**empresses**) N-COUNT An **empress** is a woman who rules an empire, or the wife of an emperor.
→ see **empire**

empty /'empti/ (**emptier, emptiest, empties, emptying, emptied**) **1** ADJ An **empty** place, vehicle, or container has no people or things in it. ❑ *The room was bare and empty.* ❑ *The roads were nearly empty of traffic.* ● **emptiness** N-UNCOUNT ❑ *...the emptiness of the desert.* **2** V-T If you **empty** a container, or if you **empty** something **out** of it, you remove its contents. ❑ *Empty the noodles into a bowl.* ❑ *He emptied the contents out into his hand.* **3** V-T/V-I If someone **empties** a room or place, or if it **empties**, everyone in that place leaves. ❑ *The stadium emptied at the end of the match.* **4** ADJ If you describe something as **empty**, you mean that it has no real value or meaning. ❑ *He accused the prime minister of making empty promises.* ● **emptiness** N-UNCOUNT ❑ *There was emptiness in my private life.*

Thesaurus *empty* Also look up:

ADJ.	vacant; (*ant.*) full, occupied **1**
	meaningless, without substance **2**
V.	drain out, pour out **3**
	evacuate, go out, leave **6** **4**

Word Partnership Use *empty* with:

N.	empty **bottle**, empty **box**, empty **building**, empty **room**, empty **seat**, empty **space**, empty **stomach** **1**
	empty **the rubbish** **2**
	empty **promise**, empty **threat** **4**
V.	**feel** empty **4**

ˌempty-'handed ADJ If you come back from somewhere **empty-handed**, you have failed to get what you intended to get.

emulate /'emjʊleɪt/ (**emulates, emulating, emulated**) V-T If you **emulate** someone or something, you copy them because you admire them. [FORMAL] ❑ *He knew that he wanted to emulate his parents and become a writer.*

Word Link *en ≈ making, putting : enable, enact, encode*

enable /ɪn'eɪbəl/ (**enables, enabling, enabled**) V-T If someone or something **enables** you **to** do something, they make it possible for you to do it. ❑ *This test will enable doctors to identify patients who need treatment.*

enact /ɪn'ækt/ (**enacts, enacting, enacted**) **1** V-T When a government **enacts** a proposal, they make it into a law. [TECHNICAL] ● **enactment** (**enactments**) N-VAR ❑ *...the enactment of the Human Rights Act 1998.* **2** V-T If people **enact** a story or play, they act it. [FORMAL]

enamel /ɪ'næməl/ N-UNCOUNT **Enamel** is a substance which can be heated and put onto metal in order to decorate or protect it.

encapsulate /ɪn'kæpsjʊleɪt/ (**encapsulates, encapsulating, encapsulated**) V-T If something **encapsulates** facts or ideas, it contains or represents them in a very small space or in a single object or event. ❑ *The article encapsulated the views of many people.*

Word Link *cas ≈ box, hold : case, encase, suitcase*

encase /ɪn'keɪs/ (**encases, encasing, encased**) V-T If something **is encased in** a container or material, it is completely enclosed within it or covered by it. ❑ *His injured ankle was encased in plaster.*

enchant /ɪn'tʃɑːnt, -'tʃænt/ (**enchants, enchanting, enchanted**) **1** V-T If you **are enchanted** by someone or something, you think they are very pleasing. ● **enchanting** ADJ ❑ *She's an enchanting child.* **2** V-T In fairy stories and legends, to **enchant** someone or something means to put a magic spell on them.

encircle /ɪn'sɜːkəl/ (**encircles, encircling, encircled**) V-T To **encircle** something or someone means to surround them completely. ❑ *A forty-foot-*

E

high wall encircles the prison.

enclave /ˈeŋkleɪv/ (**enclaves**) N-COUNT An **enclave** is a place that is different from the areas surrounding it, for example because the people there are from a different culture.

enclose /ɪnˈkləʊz/ (**encloses, enclosing, enclosed**) 1 V-T If a place or object **is enclosed** by something, the place or object is completely surrounded by that thing or is inside it. ❑ *The garden was enclosed by a hedge.* ❑ *Enclose the pot in a plastic bag.* 2 V-T If you **enclose** something with a letter, you put it in the same envelope. ❑ *Please remember to enclose a stamped addressed envelope.*

enclosure /ɪnˈkləʊʒə/ (**enclosures**) N-COUNT An **enclosure** is an area of land surrounded by a wall or fence and used for a special purpose. ❑ *...seats in the VIP enclosure.*

Word Link	***en** ≈ making, putting : **en**able, **en**act, **en**code*

Word Link	***cod** ≈ writing : **cod**e, de**cod**e, en**cod**e*

encode /ɪˈnkəʊd/ (**encodes, encoding, encoded**) V-T When information **is encoded**, it is put into a code. ❑ *During World War II, the code-breaking Enigma machine was used to crack German encoded messages.*

encompass /ɪnˈkʌmpəs/ (**encompasses, encompassing, encompassed**) V-T If something **encompasses** certain things, it includes all of them. ❑ *The map shows the western region, which encompasses nine states.*

encore /ˈɒŋkɔː, -ˈkɔː/ (**encores**) N-COUNT & CONVENTION An **encore** is a short extra performance at the end of a longer one, which an entertainer gives because the audience asks for it, often by shouting **'encore'**.

encounter /ɪnˈkaʊntə/ (**encounters, encountering, encountered**) 1 V-T If you **encounter** problems or difficulties, you experience them. ❑ *...problems encountered by disabled people.* 2 V-T & N-COUNT If you **encounter** someone, or if you **have** an **encounter with** them, you meet them. [FORMAL] ❑ *It was my first encounter with Daniel.*

Thesaurus	*encounter* Also look up:
V.	come across, run into; *(ant.)* avoid, miss 1 2

encourage /ɪnˈkʌrɪdʒ, AM -ˈkɜːr-/ (**encourages, encouraging, encouraged**) 1 V-T If you **encourage** someone, you give them confidence, for example by letting them know that what they are doing is good. ❑ *When things aren't going well, he encourages me, telling me not to give up.* 2 V-T If someone **is encouraged by** something, it gives them hope or confidence. ❑ *She has been encouraged by the loving support of her family.* ● **encouraged** ADJ ❑ *He was encouraged by their progress.* 3 V-T If you **encourage** someone **to** do something, you try to persuade them to do it, for example by trying to make it easier for them to do it. ❑ *We want to encourage people to go fishing, so we have arranged free transport to the river.* ❑ *Their task is to encourage more kids to eat healthy food.* 4 V-T If something **encourages** a particular activity or state, it causes it to happen or increase. ❑ *The articles are meant to encourage discussion on these topics.*

encouragement /ɪnˈkʌrɪdʒmənt, AM -ˈkɜːr-/ (**encouragements**) N-VAR **Encouragement** is the activity of encouraging someone, or something that is said or done in order to encourage them. ❑ *Thanks for your advice and encouragement.*

encouraging /ɪnˈkʌrɪdʒɪŋ, AM -ˈkɜːr-/ ADJ Something that is **encouraging** gives you hope or confidence. ❑ *It is encouraging that more pupils are taking maths and getting good grades.* ● **encouragingly** ADV ❑ *...encouragingly large audiences.*

encroach /ɪnˈkrəʊtʃ/ (**encroaches, encroaching, encroached**) 1 V-I If one thing **encroaches on** or **upon** another, it spreads or becomes stronger, and slowly begins to restrict the power, range, or effectiveness of the second thing; used showing disapproval. ❑ *He does not let his personal life encroach upon his professional life.* ● **encroachment** (**encroachments**) N-VAR ❑ *Many species face extinction as a result of man's encroachment on their habitat.* 2 V-I If something **encroaches on** a place, it spreads and takes over more and more of that place. [FORMAL] ❑ *The desert began encroaching on farmland.*

encyclopedia [BRIT also **encyclopaedia**] /ɪnˌsaɪkləˈpiːdiə/ (**encyclopedias**) N-COUNT An **encyclopedia** is a book, set of books, or CD-ROM in which many facts are arranged for reference.

end /end/ (**ends, ending, ended**) 1 N-SING **The end of** something such as a period of time or an activity is the last part of it or the final point in it. ❑ *...at the end of the 18th century.* ❑ *You can ask questions at the end.* 2 V-T/V-I & PHRASE When a situation, process, or activity **ends**, or when something or someone **ends** it, it reaches its final point and stops. You can also say that something has **come to an end** or is **at an end**. ❑ *The Vietnam War was just about to end.* ❑ *She began to cry. That ended our discussion.* ❑ *Her job contract came to an end.* ● **ending** N-SING ❑ *...the ending of a marriage.* 3 V-I A journey, road, or river that **ends** at a particular place stops there. ❑ *The road ended at a T-junction.* 4 N-COUNT The **end** of a long narrow object is the tip or smallest edge of it. ❑ *Make a little hole with the end of a pencil.* 5 N-COUNT An **end** is the purpose for doing something. ❑ *The church should not be used for political ends.* 6 → see also **ending, dead end** 7 PHRASE If you find it difficult to **make ends meet**, you do not have enough money. 8 PHRASE When something happens for days or weeks **on end**, it happens continuously during that time.
▸ **end up** PHR-VERB If you **end up** in a particular place or situation, you are in that place or situation after a series of events. ❑ *The painting ended up at the Tate Gallery.* ❑ *We ended up getting married.*

Thesaurus	*end* Also look up:
N.	close, conclusion, finale, finish, stop; *(ant.)* beginning 1 2

endanger /ɪnˈdeɪndʒə/ (**endangers, endangering, endangered**) V-T To **endanger** something or someone means to put them in a situation where they might be harmed or destroyed. ❑ *Fatty foods can endanger your future health.* ❑ *...endangered species.*

endear /ɪnˈdɪə/ (**endears, endearing, endeared**)

V-T If something **endears** you **to** someone, or if you **endear yourself to** them, you become well liked by them. ❑ *He endeared himself to everybody with his warm smile and enthusiasm.* • **endearing** ADJ ❑ *...an endearing personality.*

endeavour [AM **endeavor**] /ɪn'devə/ (**endeavours, endeavouring, endeavoured**) **1** V-T If you **endeavour to** do something, you try to do it. [FORMAL] ❑ *I will endeavour to arrange it.* **2** N-VAR An **endeavour** is an attempt to do something, especially if it is new and original. ❑ *...scientific endeavour.*

endemic /en'demɪk/ ADJ If a disease or illness is **endemic** in a place, it is frequently found among the people who live there. [FORMAL] ❑ *Polio was endemic when I was a child.*

ending /'endɪŋ/ (**endings**) **1** N-COUNT The **ending** of a book, play, or film is the last part of it. ❑ *The film has a happy ending.* **2** → see also **end**

Word Link	*less ≈ without : careless, endless, wireless*

endless /'endləs/ **1** ADJ If you describe something as **endless**, you mean that it lasts so long that it seems as if it will never end. ❑ *...an endless meeting.* • **endlessly** ADV ❑ *They talk about it endlessly.* **2** ADJ **Endless** means very large or long, with no variation. • **endlessly** ADV ❑ *Fields stretch endlessly to the horizon.*

endorse /ɪn'dɔːs/ (**endorses, endorsing, endorsed**) **1** V-T If you **endorse** someone or something, you say publicly that you support or approve of them. ❑ *I fully endorse their opinion.* • **endorsement** (**endorsements**) N-COUNT ❑ *...the committee's endorsement of the idea.* **2** V-T If you **endorse** a product or company, you appear in advertisements for it. ❑ *The twins endorsed a new perfume.* • **endorsement** N-COUNT ❑ *Her income from endorsements is around $7 million a year.*

endow /ɪn'daʊ/ (**endows, endowing, endowed**) **1** V-T If someone or something **is endowed with** a quality, they have it or are given it. [FORMAL] ❑ *Herbs endow food with subtle flavours.* **2** V-T If someone **endows** an institution, they provide it with a large amount of money which is invested to produce an annual income.

endowment /ɪn'daʊmənt/ (**endowments**) **1** N-COUNT An **endowment** is a gift of money that is made to an institution such as a school. **2** N-COUNT Someone's **endowments** are their natural qualities and abilities. [FORMAL] ❑ *...a biological endowment of a quick mind or a strong body.*

ˌend re'sult (**end results**) N-COUNT You can describe the result of a lengthy process or activity as its **end result**. ❑ *It was a long process, but the end result was worth it.*

endurance /ɪn'djʊərəns, AM -'dʊr-/ N-UNCOUNT **Endurance** is the ability to continue with a difficult experience or activity over a long period of time. ❑ *Tennis players are endurance athletes.*

endure /ɪn'djʊə, AM -'dʊr/ (**endures, enduring, endured**) **1** V-T If you **endure** a painful or difficult situation, you bear it calmly and patiently, usually because you have no other choice. ❑ *The company endured a difficult financial situation in the 1980s.* ❑ *He endured terrible pain in silence.* **2** V-I If something **endures**, it continues to exist. ❑ *Their marriage endured for forty years.* • **enduring** ADJ ❑ *...the start of an enduring friendship.*

'end ˌuser (**end users**) N-COUNT The **end user** of a product or service is the person that it has been designed for, not the person who installs or maintains it. ❑ *You have to describe things in a way that the end user can understand.*

enemy /'enəmi/ (**enemies**) **1** N-COUNT Your **enemy** is someone who intends to harm you. **2** N-SING In a war, **the enemy** is the army or country that you are fighting. **Enemy** can take the singular or plural form of the verb for this meaning. ❑ *The enemy attacked the city from all sides.* ❑ *The enemy are all around us.*

energetic /ˌenə'dʒetɪk/ ADJ An **energetic** person has a lot of energy. **Energetic** activities require a lot of energy. ❑ *We were very energetic when we were young.* ❑ *The energetic performance involved a lot of jumping about.* • **energetically** ADV ❑ *...dancing energetically.*

energy /'enədʒi/ (**energies**) **1** N-UNCOUNT **Energy** is the ability and strength to do active physical things. ❑ *He was saving his energy for the race.* **2** N-VAR If you put all your **energy** or **energies** into something, you put all your time and effort into it. ❑ *He put all of his energies into bringing up his son.* **3** N-UNCOUNT **Energy** is power obtained from electricity, coal, or water, that makes machines work or provides heat. ❑ *...nuclear energy.*
→ see Word Web: **energy**
→ see **calories, electricity, food, petroleum, solar**

Word Partnership Use *energy* with:

ADJ.	**physical** energy, **sexual** energy **1**
	full of energy **1** **2**
	atomic energy, **nuclear** energy, **solar** energy **3**
V.	**focus** energy **1** **2**
	conserve/save energy **3**

ˌenergy-ef'ficient ADJ A device or building that is **energy-efficient** uses relatively little energy to provide the power it needs. ❑ *...energy-efficient lights.*

enforce /ɪn'fɔːs/ (**enforces, enforcing, enforced**) **1** V-T If people in a position of authority **enforce** a law or rule, they make sure that it is obeyed. ❑ *The government enforced a ban on new refugees.* • **enforcement** N-UNCOUNT ❑ *The doctors want better enforcement of current laws.* **2** V-T If you **enforce** a particular condition, you force it to be done or to happen. ❑ *...his enforced absence through illness.*

engage /ɪn'geɪdʒ/ (**engages, engaging, engaged**) **1** V-T/V-I If you **engage in** or **are engaged in** an activity, you are doing it. [FORMAL] ❑ *Mickey was engaged in a telephone discussion with the manager.* **2** V-T If something **engages** you, it keeps you interested in it and thinking about it. [FORMAL] ❑ *The subject has engaged many researchers over the years.* **3** V-T If you **engage** someone **in** conversation, you have a conversation with them. [FORMAL] ❑ *We want to engage the leaders in conversation.* **4** V-T If you **engage** someone to do a particular job, you hire them to do it. [FORMAL]

engaged /ɪn'geɪdʒd/ **1** ADJ If two people are **engaged**, they have agreed to marry each other. **2** ADJ AFTER LINK-V Someone who is **engaged in** or

Word Web energy

Wood was the most important **energy** source for American settlers. Then, as industry developed, factories began to use **coal.** Coal was also used to **generate** most of the **electrical power** in the early 1900s. However, the popularity of automobile use soon made **petroleum** the most important **fuel. Natural gas** remains popular for home heating and industrial use. **Hydroelectric** power isn't a major source of energy in the U.S. It requires too much land and water to produce. Some companies built **nuclear** power plants to make **electricity** in the 1970s. Today **solar** panels convert sunlight and giant wind farms convert wind into electricity.

on a particular activity is doing it or involved with it. ❑ *Mike was engaged on the most exciting work of his career.* **3** ADJ AFTER LINK-V When a telephone line is **engaged**, it is already being used, so that you are unable to speak to the person you are phoning.

engagement /ɪnˈgeɪdʒmənt/ (**engagements**) **1** N-COUNT An **engagement** is an arrangement that you have made to do something at a particular time. [FORMAL] ❑ *He had an engagement at the restaurant at eight o'clock.* **2** N-COUNT An **engagement** is an agreement that two people have made to get married. You can also refer to the period of time during which they have this agreement as **their engagement**. **3** N-COUNT A military **engagement** is a battle.

engaging /ɪnˈgeɪdʒɪŋ/ ADJ An **engaging** person or thing is pleasant, interesting, or entertaining.

engender /ɪnˈdʒendə/ (**engenders, engendering, engendered**) V-T If someone or something **engenders** a particular feeling or situation, they cause it. [FORMAL] ❑ *They need someone who engenders trust.*

engine /ˈendʒɪn/ (**engines**) **1** N-COUNT A vehicle's **engine** is the part that produces the power to make it move. **2** N-COUNT An **engine** is the large vehicle that pulls a railway train.
→ see Word Web: **engine**
→ see **car**

Word Link *eer ≈ one who does : auctioneer, engineer, volunteer*

engineer /ˌendʒɪˈnɪə/ (**engineers, engineering, engineered**) **1** N-COUNT An **engineer** is a skilled person who uses scientific knowledge to design, construct, and maintain engines and machines or structures such as roads and bridges. **2** V-T When a vehicle, bridge, or building **is engineered**, it is planned and constructed using scientific methods. **3** N-COUNT An **engineer** is a person who repairs mechanical or electrical devices. ❑ *...an electrical engineer.* **4** V-T If you **engineer** an event or situation, you cause it to happen, in a clever or indirect way. ❑ *Robson finally engineered his first victory with the team.*

engineering /ˌendʒɪˈnɪərɪŋ/ N-UNCOUNT **Engineering** is the work involved in designing and constructing machinery, electrical devices, or roads and bridges.
→ see **clone**

English /ˈɪŋglɪʃ/ **1** ADJ **English** means belonging or relating to England. ❑ *...the English way of life.* **2** N-PLURAL **The English** are the people who come from England. **3** N-UNCOUNT **English** is the language spoken by people who live in Great Britain and Ireland, the United States, Canada, Australia, and many other countries.
→ see Word Web: **English**

engraved /ɪnˈgreɪvd/ ADJ If an object is **engraved**, a design or some writing has been cut into its surface. ❑ *...a stone engraved in the year 1861.* ❑ *...engraved glass.*

engrossed /ɪnˈgrəʊst/ ADJ If you are **engrossed in** something, it holds your attention completely. ❑ *Tony didn't see me because he was too engrossed in his work.*

engulf /ɪnˈgʌlf/ (**engulfs, engulfing, engulfed**) **1** V-T If one thing **engulfs** another, it spreads quickly through it or over it, covering it completely. [LITERARY] ❑ *Four people died when*

Word Web engine

In the **internal combustion engine** found in most cars, there are four, six, or eight **cylinders.** To start an engine, the **intake valve** opens and a small amount of **fuel** enters the **combustion** chamber of the cylinder. A **spark plug** ignites the fuel and air mixture, causing it to explode. This **combustion** moves the **cylinder head**, which causes the **crankshaft** to turn and the car to move. Next, the **exhaust valve** opens and the burned gases are drawn out. As the cylinder head returns to its original position, it compresses the new gas and air mixture and the process repeats itself.

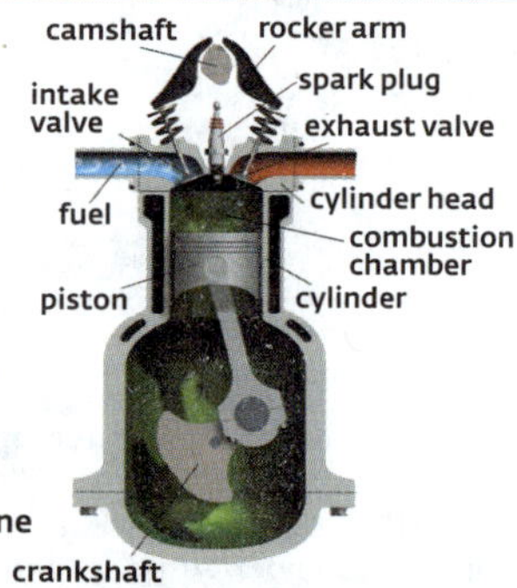

internal combustion engine

Word Web English

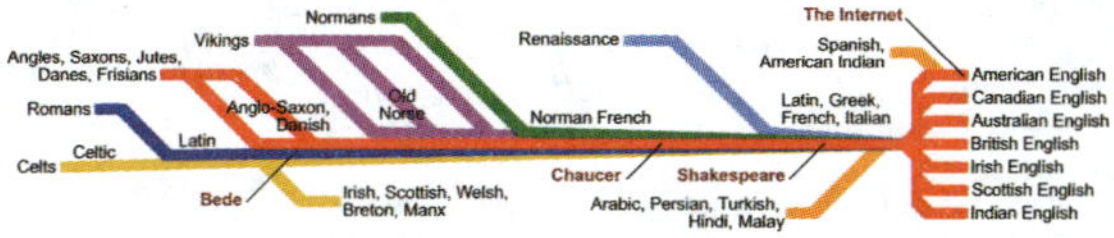

The **English language** has more **words** than any other language. Early English grew out of a **Germanic** language. Much of its **grammar** and basic **vocabulary** came from that language. But in 1066, England was conquered by the Normans. Norman French became the language of the rulers. Therefore many **French** and **Latin** words came into the English language. The playwright Shakespeare* **coined** over 1,600 new words in his plays. English has become an international language with many regional **dialects.**

William Shakespeare (1564-1616): an English playwright and poet.

fire engulfed a house in Durham yesterday. 2 V-T If something such as a conflict or hatred **engulfs** a place or a group of people, it spreads uncontrollably through that place or group, affecting everybody strongly. [LITERARY] ❑ *A row over tax has engulfed the government.*

enhance /ɪnˈhɑːns, -ˈhæns/ (**enhances, enhancing, enhanced**) V-T To **enhance** something means to improve its value, quality, or attractiveness. ❑ *They need training to enhance their teaching skills.* ● **enhancement** (**enhancements**) N-VAR ❑ *...the enhancement of our quality of life.*

enigma /ɪˈnɪgmə/ (**enigmas**) N-COUNT If you describe something or someone as an **enigma**, you mean they are mysterious or difficult to understand.

enigmatic /ˌenɪgˈmætɪk/ ADJ **Enigmatic** means mysterious and difficult to understand. ❑ *It is Orson Welles's most enigmatic film.* ● **enigmatically** ADV ❑ *He smiled enigmatically.*

Word Link *joy ≈ being glad : enjoy, joyful, joyous*

enjoy /ɪnˈdʒɔɪ/ (**enjoys, enjoying, enjoyed**) 1 V-T If you **enjoy** something, it gives you pleasure and satisfaction. ❑ *I enjoy playing cricket.* 2 V-T If you **enjoy yourself**, you do something you like doing. ❑ *Eleanor went to Baltimore, but did not enjoy herself.* 3 V-T If you **enjoy** something such as a privilege, you have it. ❑ *In Germany, people enjoy 40 days' paid holiday every year.*

enjoyable /ɪnˈdʒɔɪəbəl/ ADJ Something that is **enjoyable** gives you pleasure. ❑ *Shopping for clothes is an enjoyable experience.*

enjoyment /ɪnˈdʒɔɪmənt/ N-UNCOUNT **Your enjoyment of** something is the pleasure you get from having or experiencing it. ❑ *...the enjoyment of sharing a meal.*

enlarge /ɪnˈlɑːdʒ/ (**enlarges, enlarging, enlarged**) 1 V-T/V-I If you **enlarge** something, or if it **enlarges**, it becomes bigger. ❑ *They will either enlarge their kitchen or buy a new house.* ❑ *The European Union has enlarged.* ❑ *...enlarged photographs.* ● **enlargement** N-UNCOUNT ❑ *...the enlargement of the European Union.* 2 V-I If you **enlarge on** or **upon** something that has been mentioned, you give more details about it.
→ see **photography**

Word Link *light ≈ shining: daylight, enlighten, headlight*

enlighten /ɪnˈlaɪtən/ (**enlightens, enlightening, enlightened**) V-T To **enlighten** someone means to give them more knowledge and greater understanding about something. [FORMAL] ❑ *This book will enlighten the reader.* ● **enlightening** ADJ ❑ *...an enlightening talk on his work at the zoo.*

enlightened /ɪnˈlaɪtənd/ ADJ If you describe someone as **enlightened**, you admire them for having sensible modern attitudes. You can also talk about an **enlightened** place or period of history. ❑ *We live in enlightened times.*

enlist /ɪnˈlɪst/ (**enlists, enlisting, enlisted**) 1 V-I If someone **enlists**, he or she joins the army, navy, or air force. ❑ *He enlisted as a soldier in the Mexican War.* 2 V-T If you **enlist** someone's help, you persuade them to help you or support you.

enliven /ɪnˈlaɪvən/ (**enlivens, enlivening, enlivened**) V-T If something **enlivens** an event or situation, it makes it more lively or cheerful. ❑ *Nick's attempts to enliven boring lessons often had strange consequences.*

en masse /ˌɒn ˈmæs/ ADV If a group of people do something **en masse**, they all do it together. ❑ *They left their jobs en masse.*

enormous /ɪˈnɔːməs/ ADJ **Enormous** means extremely large in size, amount, or degree. ❑ *The main bedroom is enormous.* ❑ *It was an enormous disappointment.* ● **enormously** ADV ❑ *I admired him enormously.*

enough /ɪˈnʌf/ 1 QUANT **Enough** means as much as you need or as much as is necessary. ❑ *They had enough money for a one-way ticket.* ❑ *I was old enough to work.* ❑ *Although they are trying, they are not doing enough.* 2 QUANT If you say that something is **enough**, you mean that you do not want it to continue. ❑ *I think I have said enough.* ❑ *Ann had heard enough of this.* ❑ *Would you be quiet! I'm having enough trouble with these children!* 3 ADV You use **enough** to say that something is true to a moderate or fairly large degree. ❑ *Schmidt is a common enough German name.* ❑ *The evening was pleasant enough.* 4 ADV You use **enough** in expressions such as **strangely enough** and **interestingly enough** to indicate that you think a fact is strange or interesting. ❑ *He's Italian but, interestingly enough, doesn't speak a word of Italian.* 5 **sure enough** → see **sure**

Thesaurus *enough* Also look up:

QUANT. adequate, complete, satisfactory, sufficient; *(ant.)* deficient, inadequate, insufficient 1

enquire /ɪn'kwaɪə/ → see **inquire**
enquiry /ɪn'kwaɪəri/ → see **inquiry**
enrage /ɪn'reɪdʒ/ (**enrages, enraging, enraged**) V-T If you **are enraged** by something, it makes you extremely angry. ❑ *He enraged the government by saying no to the agreement.* • **enraged** ADJ ❑ *I became more and more enraged at my father.*
enrich /ɪn'rɪtʃ/ (**enriches, enriching, enriched**) V-T To **enrich** something means to improve its quality by adding something to it. ❑ *It is important to enrich the soil before planting.* • **enrichment** N-UNCOUNT ❑ *...cultural enrichment.*

E

enrol [AM **enroll**] /ɪn'rəʊl/ (**enrols, enrolling, enrolled**) V-T/V-I If you **enrol for** a course, or if you **are enrolled in** a college or university, you officially join it and pay a fee. ❑ *Chris enrolled at the university in 1995.* ❑ *I thought I'd enrol you with an art group.* • **enrolment** N-UNCOUNT ❑ *You must pay at the time of enrolment.*
en route /ˌɒn 'ruːt/ ADV If you are **en route to** a place, you are travelling there.
enshrined /ɪn'ʃraɪnd/ ADJ If something such as an idea or a right is **enshrined in** a society, constitution, or a law, it is protected by it. ❑ *Religious freedom is enshrined in European law.*
ensue /ɪn'sjuː, AM -'suː/ (**ensues, ensuing, ensued**) V-I If something **ensues**, it happens immediately after something else, usually as a result of it. ❑ *An embarrassing silence ensued.*
ensuing /ɪn'sjuːɪŋ/ ADJ BEFORE N **Ensuing** events happen immediately after other events. ❑ *The ensuing argument was bitter.*
ensure /ɪn'ʃʊə/ (**ensures, ensuring, ensured**) V-T To **ensure** that something happens means to make certain that it happens. [FORMAL] ❑ *Ensure that your address is correct.*
entail /ɪn'teɪl/ (**entails, entailing, entailed**) V-T If one thing **entails** another, it involves it or causes it. ❑ *The job entails speaking to the public.*

Word Link	tang ≈ touching : entangle, intangible, tangible

entangle /ɪn'tæŋgəl/ (**entangles, entangling, entangled**) **1** V-T If something **is entangled** in something such as a rope or net, it is caught in it very firmly. ❑ *Fishing nets entangle thousands of dolphins every year.* **2** V-T If something **entangles** you **in** problems or difficulties, it involves you in problems or difficulties from which it is hard to escape. ❑ *She entangled him in her schemes.* • **entangled** ADJ ❑ *The company became entangled in a legal battle.* • **entanglement** (**entanglements**) N-VAR ❑ *Somehow, his romantic entanglements always ended badly.*
enter /'entə/ (**enters, entering, entered**) **1** V-T/V-I When you **enter** a place, you come or go into it. [FORMAL] ❑ *He entered the room and stood near the door.* ❑ *As soon as I entered, they stopped talking.* **2** V-T If you **enter** an organization or institution, you start to work there or become a member of it. ❑ *She entered Parliament in 1959.* **3** V-T When something **enters** a new period in its development or history, it begins this period. ❑ *The war entered its second month in March.* **4** V-T If you **enter** a competition, race, or examination, you officially take part in it. ❑ *Jane has entered the London Marathon.* **5** V-T When you **enter** something in a book or computer, you write or type it in. ❑ *When a baby is born, they enter the baby's name into the computer.*
▶ **enter into** **1** PHR-VERB If you **enter into** something such as an agreement, discussion, or relationship with someone, you become involved in it. [FORMAL] ❑ *She wants to enter into talks with the leaders.* **2** PHR-VERB Something that **enters into** something else is a factor in it. ❑ *Self-interest didn't enter into it.*
enterprise /'entəpraɪz/ (**enterprises**) **1** N-COUNT An **enterprise** is a company or business. ❑ *...private enterprises.* **2** N-COUNT An **enterprise** is something new that you try to do, especially something difficult or involving a degree of risk. ❑ *Moving to a new country with no money is a risky enterprise.* **3** N-UNCOUNT If you say that someone shows **enterprise**, you approve of their willingness to try out new ways of doing something. ❑ *Sadly, his enterprise was not rewarded.* • **enterprising** ADJ ❑ *...an enterprising young man.*
entertain /ˌentə'teɪn/ (**entertains, entertaining, entertained**) **1** V-T/V-I If you **entertain**, or **entertain** people, you do something that amuses or interests them. ❑ *Children's television not only entertains but also educates.* • **entertaining** ADJ ❑ *...an entertaining movie.* **2** V-T/V-I If you **entertain**, or **entertain** guests, you give them food and hospitality. ❑ *She is a wonderful cook who loves to entertain.* • **entertaining** N-UNCOUNT ❑ *The magnificent hall is often used for entertaining.* **3** V-T If you **entertain** an idea or suggestion, you consider it. [FORMAL] ❑ *He began to entertain the idea of becoming an actor.*
entertainer /ˌentə'teɪnə/ (**entertainers**) N-COUNT An **entertainer** is a person whose job is to entertain audiences, for example by telling jokes, singing, or dancing.
entertainment /ˌentə'teɪnmənt/ (**entertainments**) N-VAR **Entertainment** consists of performances or activities that give people pleasure. ❑ *His new cookery programme is great entertainment.* ❑ *...discos and other entertainments.* → see **radio**
enthral [AM **enthrall**] /ɪn'θrɔːl/ (**enthrals, enthralling, enthralled**) V-T To **enthral** someone means to hold their attention and interest completely. ❑ *He enthralled audiences in Paris.* • **enthralling** ADJ ❑ *...an enthralling book.*
enthuse /ɪn'θjuːz, AM -'θuːz/ (**enthuses, enthusing, enthused**) **1** V-I If you **enthuse** about something, you talk about it in a way that shows how excited you are about it. ❑ *'I've found the most wonderful house to buy!' she enthused.* **2** V-T If you **are enthused by** something, it makes you feel enthusiastic. ❑ *Holst was enthused by his friend's ideas on art.*
enthusiasm /ɪn'θjuːziæzəm, AM -'θuː-/ (**enthusiasms**) N-UNCOUNT **Enthusiasm** is great eagerness to do something or to be involved in something. ❑ *If you show enough enthusiasm, maybe Warren will give you a job.*

Thesaurus	*enthusiasm*	Also look up:
N.	eagerness, energy, excitement, passion, zest; (*ant.*) apathy, indifference **1** **2**	

enthusiast /ɪn'θjuːziæst, AM -'θuː-/ (**enthusiasts**) N-COUNT An **enthusiast** is a person who is very interested in a particular activity or subject. ❑ *...keep-fit enthusiasts.*

enthusiastic /ɪnˌθjuːzi'æstɪk, AM -ˌθuː-/ ADJ If you are **enthusiastic about** something, you show how much you like or enjoy it by the way that you behave and talk. ❑ *He is enthusiastic about photography.* ● **enthusiastically** ADV ❑ *The young man told me enthusiastically about his family.*

entice /ɪn'taɪs/ (**entices, enticing, enticed**) V-T To **entice** someone means to try to persuade them to go somewhere or to do something. ❑ *They tried to entice her into politics.* ● **enticement** (**enticements**) N-VAR ❑ *There is a range of enticements to open an account with this bank.*

enticing /ɪn'taɪsɪŋ/ ADJ Something that is **enticing** is extremely attractive. ❑ *It was an enticing invitation.*

entire /ɪn'taɪə/ ADJ You use **entire** when you want to emphasize that you are referring to the whole of something. ❑ *He spent his entire life in China working as a doctor.* ❑ *The entire family was looking at him.*

Thesaurus	*entire* Also look up:
ADJ.	absolute, complete, total, whole; *(ant.)* incomplete, limited, partial

entirely /ɪn'taɪəli/ ADV **Entirely** means completely. ❑ *...an entirely new idea.* ❑ *Paul was not entirely happy with the plan.* ❑ *I agree entirely.*

entirety /ɪn'taɪərɪti/ PHRASE If you refer to something **in its entirety**, you mean all of it. ❑ *We plan to publish his diary in its entirety.*

entitle /ɪn'taɪtəl/ (**entitles, entitling, entitled**) **1** V-T If you **are entitled to** something, you have the right to have it or do it. ❑ *They are entitled to free school meals.* ● **entitlement** (**entitlements**) N-VAR ❑ *...the entitlement to vote.* **2** V-T You say that a book, film, or painting **is entitled** a particular thing when you are mentioning its title. ❑ *...a book entitled 'Grand Designs'.*

entity /'entɪti/ (**entities**) N-COUNT An **entity** is something that exists separately from other things and has a clear identity. [FORMAL] ❑ *The body and the spirit are separate entities.*

entourage /'ɒntʊrɑːʒ/ (**entourages**) N-COUNT The **entourage** of someone famous or important is the group of assistants or other people who travel with them. ❑ *Her entourage included her personal assistant, hairdresser, and bodyguard.*

entrance (**entrances, entrancing, entranced**) **1** N-COUNT /'entrəns/ An **entrance** is a way into a place, for example a door or gate. ❑ *She met him at the entrance of the church.* **2** N-COUNT Someone's **entrance** is their arrival in a room. ❑ *I told him the news soon after his entrance.* **3** N-UNCOUNT If you gain **entrance** to a place, profession or institution, you are able to go into it or are accepted as a member of it. ❑ *Gaining entrance to university was difficult when I was young.* **4** V-T /ɪn'trɑːns, -'træns/ If something **entrances** you, it makes you feel delight and wonder. ❑ *She entranced the audience with her singing.* ● **entranced** ADJ ❑ *For the next three hours we sat entranced.*

Thesaurus	*entrance* Also look up:
N.	doorway, entry; *(ant.)* exit ① **1** appearance, approach, debut ① **2**

entrant /'entrənt/ (**entrants**) N-COUNT An **entrant** is a person who officially enters a competition or institution. ❑ *...competition entrants.* ❑ *...a young school entrant.*

entrench /ɪn'trentʃ/ (**entrenches, entrenching, entrenched**) V-T If something such as power, a custom, or an idea is **entrenched**, it is firmly established and difficult to change. ● **entrenched** ADJ ❑ *Violence is entrenched in our society.*

Word Link	***eur** ≈ one who does : amateur, chauffeur, entrepreneur*

entrepreneur /ˌɒntrəprə'nɜː/ (**entrepreneurs**) N-COUNT An **entrepreneur** is a person who sets up businesses and business deals. ● **entrepreneurial** ADJ ❑ *...his entrepreneurial skills.*

entrust /ɪn'trʌst/ (**entrusts, entrusting, entrusted**) V-T If you **entrust** something important **to** someone, or if you **entrust** them **with** it, you make them responsible for it. ❑ *Miss Conway was entrusted with the children's education.*

entry /'entri/ (**entries**) **1** N-COUNT An **entry** is something that you complete in order to take part in a competition, for example the answers to a set of questions. ❑ *The closing date for entries is 31st December.* **2** N-COUNT An **entry** in a diary, computer file, or reference book is a single short item in it. ❑ *The meeting is recorded in Waite's diary, in the entry for 23 March 1936.* **3** N-COUNT A person's **entry** is their arrival in a room. ❑ *They hardly noticed Sue's entry into the room.* **4** N-UNCOUNT If you gain **entry** to a particular place, you are able to go in. ❑ *The teenagers were refused entry to the UK.* ❑ *No entry after 11pm.* **5** N-UNCOUNT Someone's **entry** into a society or group is their joining of it. ❑ *...his entry into the navy.* **6** N-COUNT The **entry** to a place is the way into it, for example a door or gate.
→ see **blog**

envelop /ɪn'veləp/ (**envelops, enveloping, enveloped**) V-T If one thing **envelops** another, it covers or surrounds it completely. ❑ *Fog enveloped the airport.*

envelope /'envələʊp, 'ɒn-/ (**envelopes**) N-COUNT An **envelope** is the rectangular paper cover in which you send a letter through the post.
→ see **office**

enviable /'enviəbəl/ ADJ An **enviable** quality is one that someone else has and that you wish you had too. ❑ *He has an enviable talent for making people laugh.*

envious /'enviəs/ ADJ If you are **envious of** someone else, you envy them. ● **enviously** ADV ❑ *Ferguson watched them enviously.*

environment /ɪn'vaɪərənmənt/ (**environments**) **1** N-VAR Someone's **environment** is their surroundings, especially the conditions in which they grow up, live, or work. ❑ *The twins were separated at birth and grew up in entirely different environments.* **2** N-SING **The environment** is the natural world of land, sea, air, plants, and animals. ❑ *People must respect the environment.* ● **environmental** /ɪnˌvaɪərən'mentəl/ ADJ BEFORE

e

N ❑ *'Greenpeace' is a well-known environmental group.*
→ see **habitat, pollution**

Word Partnership Use *environment* with:

ADJ.	**hostile** environment, **safe** environment, **supportive** environment, **unhealthy** environment 1
	natural environment 2
V.	**damage the** environment, **protect the** environment 2

E

environmentalist /ɪnˌvaɪərənˈmentəlɪst/ (**environmentalists**) N-COUNT An **environmentalist** is a person who wants to protect and preserve the natural environment.

envisage /ɪnˈvɪzɪdʒ/ (**envisages, envisaging, envisaged**) V-T If you **envisage** a situation or event, you imagine it, or think that it is likely to happen. ❑ *What sort of career do you envisage?*

envision /ɪnˈvɪʒən/ (**envisions, envisioning, envisioned**) V-T If you **envision** something, you envisage it. [AM]

envoy /ˈenvɔɪ/ (**envoys**) N-COUNT An **envoy** is a diplomat sent to a foreign country.

envy /ˈenvi/ (**envies, envying, envied**) V-T & N-UNCOUNT If you **envy** someone, you wish that you had the same things or qualities that they have. This feeling is called **envy**. ❑ *I envied her friendship with Sarah.* ❑ *Her sisters watched with envy.*

enzyme /ˈenzaɪm/ (**enzymes**) N-COUNT An **enzyme** is a chemical substance that is found in living creatures which produces changes in other substances without being changed itself. [TECHNICAL]

epic /ˈepɪk/ (**epics**) 1 N-COUNT An **epic** is a long book, poem, or film whose story extends over a long period of time or tells of great events. ❑ *The film 'Braveheart' is an historical epic, directed by Mel Gibson.* 2 ADJ Something that is described as **epic** is considered very impressive or ambitious. ❑ *...Columbus's epic voyage of discovery.*
→ see **hero**

epidemic /ˌepɪˈdemɪk/ (**epidemics**) N-COUNT If there is an **epidemic** of a particular disease somewhere, it spreads quickly to a very large number of people there. ❑ *...a flu epidemic.*
→ see **illness**

epilepsy /ˈepɪlepsi/ N-UNCOUNT **Epilepsy** is a brain condition which causes a person to suddenly lose consciousness and sometimes to have fits.

epileptic /ˌepɪˈleptɪk/ (**epileptics**) 1 N-COUNT An **epileptic** is a person who suffers from epilepsy. 2 ADJ **Epileptic** means suffering from or relating to epilepsy. ❑ *...an epileptic fit.*

episode /ˈepɪsəʊd/ (**episodes**) 1 N-COUNT You can refer to an event or a short period of time as an **episode** if you want to suggest that it is important or unusual, or has some particular quality. ❑ *It was an unhappy episode in our long (and usually friendly) relationship.* 2 N-COUNT An **episode** is one of the programmes in a serial on television or radio.
→ see **animation**

epitome /ɪˈpɪtəmi/ N-SING If you say that someone or something is **the epitome of** a particular thing, you mean that they are a perfect example of it. ❑ *...the epitome of Britishness.*

epitomize [BRIT also **epitomise**] /ɪˈpɪtəmaɪz/ (**epitomizes, epitomizing, epitomized**) V-T If you say that someone or something **epitomizes** a particular thing, you mean that they are a perfect example of it. ❑ *The film star Audrey Hepburn epitomized grace and elegance.*

epoch /ˈiːpɒk, AM ˈepək/ (**epochs**) N-COUNT If you refer to a long period of time as an **epoch**, you mean that important events or great changes took place during it. ❑ *The birth of Christ was the beginning of a major epoch of world history.*

equal /ˈiːkwəl/ (**equals, equalling, equalled** or [AM] **equaling, equaled**) 1 ADJ If two things are **equal**, or if one thing is **equal to** another, they are the same in size, number, or value. ❑ *...equal numbers of men and women.* ❑ *Research and teaching are of equal importance.* ❑ *...an amount equal to their monthly wages.* ● **equally** ADV ❑ *All these techniques are equally effective.* ❑ *The prize was divided equally between the six of us.* 2 ADJ If people are **equal**, they all have the same rights and are treated in the same way. ❑ *Men and women should be given equal opportunities.* ● **equally** ADV ❑ *The court system is supposed to treat everyone equally.* 3 N-COUNT If someone is **your equal**, they have the same ability or status that you have. ❑ *You should marry somebody who is your equal.* 4 V-T To **equal** something or someone means to be as good or as great as them. ❑ *Sampras has equalled Ivan Lendl's record of five championship titles in a season.* 5 ADJ AFTER LINK-V If someone is **equal to** a job or situation, they have the necessary abilities, strength, or courage to deal successfully with it. ❑ *He was sure that she would be equal to the difficult task ahead of her.*

Word Partnership Use *equal* with:

N.	equal **importance**, equal **number**, equal **parts**, equal **pay**, equal **share** 1
	equal **rights**, equal **treatment** 2

equality /ɪˈkwɒlɪti/ N-UNCOUNT **Equality** is a situation or state where all the members of a society or group have the same status, rights, and opportunities. ❑ *...racial equality.*

equalize [BRIT also **equalise**] /ˈiːkwəlaɪz/ (**equalizes, equalizing, equalized**) 1 V-I In sports such as football, if you **equalize**, you score a goal that makes the scores of the two teams equal. ❑ *Freddie Ljungberg equalised for Arsenal 10 minutes later.* 2 V-T To **equalize** a situation means to give everyone the same rights or opportunities. ❑ *Modern divorce laws equalize the rights of husbands and wives.* ● **equalization** N-UNCOUNT ❑ *...the equalization of parenting responsibilities between men and women.*

equally /ˈiːkwəli/ 1 ADV **Equally** is used to introduce a comment which balances or contrasts with another comment that has just been made. ❑ *When a child moves to a new country, it takes them about three months to understand the new language. Equally, the child will fit into the new culture and community very quickly.* 2 → see also **equal**

equate /ɪˈkweɪt/ (**equates, equating, equated**) V-T/V-I If you **equate** one thing **with** another, or if one thing **equates with** another, you believe that they are strongly connected. ❑ *I equate men wearing suits with power and authority.* ❑ *The British public* *equates leadership with strength.*

equation /ɪ'kweɪʒən/ (**equations**) N-COUNT An **equation** is a mathematical statement saying that two amounts or values are the same, for example 6x4=12x2.

equator /ɪ'kweɪtə/ N-SING **The equator** is an imaginary line round the middle of the earth, halfway between the North and South poles.
→ see **globe**

equestrian /ɪ'kwestriən/ ADJ **Equestrian** means connected with the activity of riding horses. ❑ *...equestrian skills.*

Word Link *equi ≈ equal : equilibrium, equitable, equivalent*

equilibrium /ˌiːkwɪ'lɪbriəm/ N-VAR **Equilibrium** is a state of balance or stability in a situation or in someone's mind. ❑ *He believed in keeping his diet and body in equilibrium.* ❑ *He had found his equilibrium and was in a good mood.*

equip /ɪ'kwɪp/ (**equips, equipping, equipped**) **1** V-T If you **equip** a person or thing **with** something such as a tool or a machine, you provide them with it. ❑ *They equipped their car with a new stereo.* ❑ *...well-equipped classrooms.* **2** V-T If something **equips** you **for** a particular task or experience, it gives you the knowledge, skills, and personal qualities you need for it. ❑ *These skills will equip you for the future.* ❑ *A basic first aid course will equip you to deal with any type of accident.*

equipment /ɪ'kwɪpmənt/ N-UNCOUNT **Equipment** consists of the things such as tools or machines which are used for a particular purpose.

Thesaurus *equipment* Also look up:
N. accessories, facilities, gear, machinery, supplies, tools, utensils

Word Link *equi ≈ equal : equilibrium, equitable, equivalent*

equitable /'ekwɪtəbəl/ ADJ Something that is **equitable** is fair and reasonable in a way that gives equal treatment to everyone. ❑ *...a fair and equitable system.*

equivalent /ɪ'kwɪvələnt/ (**equivalents**) **1** N-SING & ADJ If one amount or value is **the equivalent of** another, or if one is **equivalent to** the other, they are the same. ❑ *You need to pay the equivalent of one month's rent as a deposit.* ❑ *One kilogram is equivalent to 2.2 lb.* **2** N-COUNT & ADJ The **equivalent** of someone or something is a person or thing that has the same function in a different place, time, or system. ❑ *The equivalent of the Red Cross is called the 'Red Crescent' in Muslim countries.* ❑ *The equivalent Roman name for the Greek God 'Zeus' is 'Jupiter'.*

Thesaurus *equivalent* Also look up:
ADJ. equal, similar; *(ant.)* different **1**
N. counterpart, match, parallel, peer, substitute **2**

ER /ˌiː 'ɑː/ (**ERs**) N-COUNT In American English, the **ER** is the part of a hospital where people are taken for emergency treatment. **ER** is an abbreviation for 'emergency room'. The usual British words are **casualty** or **A&E**.

er /ɜː/ **Er** is used to represent the sound that people make when they hesitate, especially while they decide what to say next. ❑ *'Would anyone like tea or coffee?'—'Er, tea please.'*

era /'ɪərə/ (**eras**) N-COUNT An **era** is a period of time that is considered as a single unit because it has a particular feature.

eradicate /ɪ'rædɪkeɪt/ (**eradicates, eradicating, eradicated**) V-T To **eradicate** something means to get rid of it completely. [FORMAL] ❑ *Doctors are trying to eradicate illnesses such as malaria.* ● **eradication** N-UNCOUNT ❑ *...the eradication of homelessness.*

erase /ɪ'reɪz, AM ɪ'reɪs/ (**erases, erasing, erased**) **1** V-T If you **erase** a thought or feeling, you destroy it completely so that you can no longer remember it or feel it. ❑ *The team tried to erase the memory of their last defeat.* **2** V-T If you **erase** sound which has been recorded on a tape or information which has been stored in a computer, you completely remove or destroy it. ❑ *The files had been erased from the computer disks.* **3** V-T If you **erase** something such as writing or a mark, you remove it.
→ see **draw**

erect /ɪ'rekt/ (**erects, erecting, erected**) **1** V-T If people **erect** something such as a building or bridge, they build it. [FORMAL] ❑ *The Eiffel Tower was erected in 1889.* ● **erection** N-UNCOUNT ❑ *...the erection of a monument near the church.* **2** ADJ People or things that are **erect** are straight and upright. ❑ *Her head was erect and her back was straight.*

erection /ɪ'rekʃən/ (**erections**) N-COUNT If a man **has** an **erection**, his penis is stiff and sticking up because he is sexually aroused.

erode /ɪ'rəʊd/ (**erodes, eroding, eroded**) **1** V-T/V-I If rock or soil **erodes**, or if it **is eroded** by the weather or sea, it cracks and breaks so that it is gradually destroyed. ❑ *Soil is quickly eroded by wind and rain.* ● **erosion** N-UNCOUNT ❑ *...erosion*

Word Web erosion

There are two main causes of **soil erosion**—**water** and **wind**. **Rainfall**, especially heavy **thunderstorms**, breaks down **dirt**. Small particles of **earth**, **sand**, and **silt** are then carried away by the water. The runoff may form **gullies** on hillsides. Heavy rain sometimes even causes a large, flat soil surface to wash away all at once. This is called sheet erosion. When the soil contains too much water, **mudslides** occur. Strong **currents** of **air** cause wind erosion. There are two major ways to prevent this damage. Permanent **vegetation** anchors the soil and **windbreaks** reduce the force of the wind.

of the coastline. **2** V-T/V-I If something strong or something with a high value **erodes** or **is eroded**, it gradually weakens or decreases. [FORMAL] ❑ *Trust in the company has been eroded by scandals.* ● **erosion** N-UNCOUNT ❑ *...the erosion of power.*
→ see Word Web: **erosion**
→ see **beach, rock**

Word Link	*otic ≈ affecting, causing : chaotic, erotic, neurotic*

erotic /ɪˈrɒtɪk/ ADJ If you describe something as **erotic**, you mean that it involves or arouses sexual desire. ❑ *It wasn't an erotic experience at all.*

err /ɜː/ (**errs, erring, erred**) **1** V-I If you **err**, you do something wrong. [FORMAL] ❑ *When the goalkeeper erred, the other team scored a goal.* **2** PHRASE If you **err on the side of** a way of behaving, you tend to behave in that way. ❑ *They may want to err on the side of caution.*

errand /ˈerənd/ (**errands**) N-COUNT If you **go on** an **errand** for someone, you go a short distance in order to do something for them, for example to buy something from a shop.

erratic /ɪˈrætɪk/ ADJ Something that is **erratic** happens at unexpected times or moves in an irregular way. ❑ *The business is going reasonably well but my income is erratic.* ● **erratically** ADV ❑ *Police stopped him for driving erratically.*

erroneous /ɪˈrəʊniəs/ ADJ **Erroneous** beliefs or opinions are incorrect. ❑ *Many parents give their children crisps in the erroneous belief that they are 'healthier' than sweets.* ● **erroneously** ADV ❑ *It was erroneously reported that Mrs Robinson had died.*

error /ˈerə/ (**errors**) **1** N-VAR An **error** is a mistake. ❑ *NASA discovered an error in its calculations.* ❑ *The e-mail was sent in error.* **2** **trial and error** → see **trial**

Word Partnership	Use *error* with:
ADJ.	**clerical** error, **common** error, **fatal** error, **human** error **1**
V.	**commit an** error, **correct an** error, **make an** error **1**

Word Link	*rupt ≈ breaking : disrupt, erupt, interrupt*

erupt /ɪˈrʌpt/ (**erupts, erupting, erupted**) **1** V-I When a volcano **erupts**, it throws out a lot of hot lava, ash, and steam. ● **eruption** (**eruptions**) N-VAR ❑ *...the volcanic eruption of Tambora in 1815.* **2** V-I **Erupt** is used to indicate that something suddenly begins or intensifies. ❑ *Heavy fighting erupted there today.* ❑ *She suddenly erupted into laughter.* ● **eruption** N-COUNT ❑ *...this sudden eruption of violence.*
→ see **rock, volcano**

Word Link	*scal, scala ≈ ladder, stairs : escalate, escalator, scale*

escalator

escalate /ˈeskəleɪt/ (**escalates, escalating, escalated**) V-T/V-I If an unpleasant situation **escalates**, or if someone or something **escalates** it, it becomes worse. [JOURNALISM] ❑ *The conflict escalated beyond control.* ● **escalation** N-SING ❑ *...a sudden and alarming escalation of violence.*

escalator /ˈeskəleɪtə/ (**escalators**) N-COUNT An **escalator** is a moving staircase.

escape /ɪˈskeɪp/ (**escapes, escaping, escaped**) **1** V-I & N-COUNT If you **escape from** a place, or if you **make** your **escape from** a place, you succeed in getting away from it. ❑ *A prisoner has escaped from a prison in northern England.* **2** V-T/V-I & N-COUNT You **escape**, or **escape** something, when you survive something such as an accident. You can also talk about a particular kind of **escape**. ❑ *The two officers were lucky to escape serious injury.* ❑ *The man's girlfriend escaped unhurt.* ❑ *I hear you had a very narrow escape.* **3** N-COUNT If something is an **escape**, it makes people think about pleasant things instead of the boring or unpleasant aspects of their life. ❑ *For me, television is an escape.* **4** V-T If something **escapes** you, or if it **escapes** your **attention**, you forget it or are unaware of it. ❑ *The actor's name escapes me for the moment.*

Thesaurus	*escape* Also look up:
V.	break out, flee, run away **1**
N.	breakout, flight, getaway **1**

Word Partnership	Use *escape* with:
N.	**chance to** escape, escape **from prison** **1**
	escape **route** **2**
V.	**try to** escape **1**
	make an escape, **manage to** escape **1** **2**

escapism /ɪˈskeɪpɪzəm/ N-UNCOUNT If you describe an activity or type of entertainment as **escapism**, you mean that it makes people think about pleasant things instead of the boring or unpleasant aspects of their life. ● **escapist** ADJ ❑ *...an escapist film.*

escort (**escorts, escorting, escorted**) **1** N-COUNT & PHRASE /ˈeskɔːt/ An **escort** is a person or group of people travelling with someone in order to protect or guard them. If someone is taken somewhere **under escort**, they are accompanied by guards, either because they have been arrested or because they need to be protected. ❑ *He arrived with a police escort.* **2** N-COUNT An **escort** is a person who accompanies someone of the opposite sex to a social event. [FORMAL] **3** V-T /ɪsˈkɔːt/ If you **escort** someone somewhere, you go there with them to make sure that they go. ❑ *I escorted him to the door.*

Eskimo /ˈeskɪˌməʊ/ (**Eskimos**) N-COUNT An **Eskimo** is a member of the group of peoples who live in Alaska, Northern Canada, eastern Siberia, and other parts of the Arctic. These peoples now usually call themselves Inuits or Aleuts, and some people find the term Eskimo offensive.

esoteric /ˌiːsəʊˈterɪk, AM ˌesə-/ ADJ Something that is **esoteric** is understood by only a small number of people with special knowledge. [FORMAL] ❑ *Where did you find this esoteric piece of information?*

especially /ɪˈspeʃəli/ **1** ADV You use **especially** to emphasize that what you are saying applies more to one person or thing than to any others. ❑ *Apply sunscreen every two hours, especially if you have been swimming.* ❑ *He loves music, especially jazz.* **2** ADV You use **especially** to emphasize a characteristic or quality. ❑ *Peter was especially good at languages.*

Thesaurus *especially* Also look up:

ADV. exclusively, only, solely 1
extraordinarily, particularly 2

espionage /ˈespiənɑːʒ/ N-UNCOUNT **Espionage** is the activity of finding out the political, military, or industrial secrets of your enemies or rivals by using spies.

espouse /ɪˈspaʊz/ (**espouses, espousing, espoused**) V-T If you **espouse** a policy or plan, you support it. [FORMAL]

essay /ˈeseɪ/ (**essays**) N-COUNT An **essay** is a piece of writing on a particular subject. ❑ *...an essay on Van Gogh.*

essence /ˈesəns/ 1 N-UNCOUNT **The essence of** something is its basic and most important characteristic. ❑ *The essence of sport is fair competition.* 2 PHRASE You use **in essence** to indicate that you are talking about the basic and most important characteristics of something. [FORMAL] ❑ *The plan, in essence, is simple.* 3 PHRASE If you say that something **is of the essence**, you mean that it is absolutely necessary in a particular situation. ❑ *Time is of the essence – a matter of life or death in some cases.*

essential /ɪˈsenʃəl/ (**essentials**) 1 ADJ Something that is **essential** is absolutely necessary. ❑ *It is essential that you take my advice.* ❑ *Play is an essential part of a child's development.* 2 N-COUNT **The essentials** are things that are absolutely necessary in a situation. ❑ *The flat contained the basic essentials.*

Word Partnership Use *essential* with:

N. essential **element**, essential **function**, essential **information**, essential **ingredients**, essential **nutrients**, essential **oils**, essential **personnel**, essential **services** 1

essentially /ɪˈsenʃəli/ 1 ADV You use **essentially** to emphasize that you are talking about the most basic and important aspects of someone or something. ❑ *He was essentially a nice man.* 2 ADV You use **essentially** to indicate that what you are saying is basically or generally true, although it may not cover all the minor details. ❑ *He develops his opinions essentially by reading the newspapers.*

Word Link *stab ≈ steady : destabilize, establish, instability*

establish /ɪˈstæblɪʃ/ (**establishes, establishing, established**) 1 V-T If someone **establishes** an organization or a system, they create it. ❑ *She has established a successful marketing business.* • **establishment** N-SING ❑ *...the establishment of the Scottish parliament.* 2 V-T If you **establish** contact with a group of people, you start to have discussions with them. [FORMAL] • **establishment** N-SING ❑ *...the establishment of diplomatic relations.* 3 V-T If you **establish that** something is true, you discover facts that show that it is definitely true. [FORMAL] ❑ *A report has established that British children know nothing about the British Empire.* ❑ *Accident investigators have established the cause of the crash.* ❑ *...an established medical fact.*

Word Partnership Use *establish* with:

N. establish **control**, establish **independence**, establish **rules** 1
establish **contact**, establish **relations** 2
establish **credibility**, establish **identity**, establish **a reputation** 3

established /ɪˈstæblɪʃt/ ADJ An **established** person or organization has a good reputation or a secure position, usually because they have existed for a long time. ❑ *'Chanel' is an established name in the world of fashion.*

establishment /ɪˈstæblɪʃmənt/ (**establishments**) 1 N-COUNT An **establishment** is a shop, restaurant, or other business premises. [FORMAL] ❑ *...a scientific research establishment.* ❑ *...medical establishments.* 2 N-SING You refer to the people who have power and influence in the running of a country or organization as **the establishment**. ❑ *...Britain's art establishment.*

estate /ɪˈsteɪt/ (**estates**) 1 N-COUNT An **estate** is a large area of land in the country owned by one person or organization. 2 N-COUNT In Britain, people use **estate** to refer to a housing estate. 3 N-COUNT Someone's **estate** is the money and property they leave when they die. ❑ *His estate was worth £350,000.* 4 → see also **housing estate, real estate**

esˈtate agent (**estate agents**) N-COUNT In British English, an **estate agent** is someone who works for a company selling houses and land. The American word is **realtor**.

esteem /ɪˈstiːm/ N-UNCOUNT **Esteem** is admiration and respect. [FORMAL] ❑ *He is held in high esteem by colleagues.*

esthetic /iːsˈθetɪk, AM esˈθ-/ → see **aesthetic**

estimate (**estimates, estimating, estimated**)

verb /ˈestɪmeɪt/, noun /ˈestɪmət/.

1 V-T & N-COUNT If you **estimate** a quantity or value, or if you make an **estimate**, you make an approximate judgement or calculation of it. ❑ *It's difficult to estimate how much money she has.* ❑ *...an estimate of £1,000.* • **estimated** ADJ ❑ *An estimated 60,000 workers have lost their jobs.* 2 N-COUNT An **estimate** is a judgement about a person or situation which you make based on the available evidence. ❑ *My estimate of his ability as a footballer comes from watching him play.*

Thesaurus *estimate* Also look up:

V. appraise, gauge, guess, judge; *(ant.)* calculate 1
N. appraisal, valuation 1
evaluation 2

Word Partnership Use *estimate* with:

ADJ. **best** estimate, **conservative** estimate, **original** estimate, **rough** estimate 1
V. **make an** estimate 1

estranged /ɪˈstreɪndʒd/ ADJ You refer to someone as **estranged from** their family or friends when they are living separately from them and not communicating with them because they have argued. [FORMAL] ❑ *...his estranged wife.* ❑ *She was* *estranged from her father for ten years.* ● **estrangement** N-UNCOUNT ❑ *They want to end the estrangement between them.*

estuary /ˈestʃʊri, AM ˈestʃʊeri/ (**estuaries**) N-COUNT An **estuary** is the wide part of a river where it joins the sea.

etc **etc** is used at the end of a list to indicate that there are other items which you could mention if you had enough time or space. **etc** is a written abbreviation for **etcetera**. ❑ *We ate the sandwiches, cakes, etc that I had made.*

E

etcetera also **et cetera** /etˈsetrə/ → see **etc**

etch /etʃ/ (**etches, etching, etched**) **1** V-T If a line or pattern **is etched into** a surface, it is cut into the surface using acid or a sharp tool. ❑ *Patterns were etched into the walls.* **2** V-T If something **is etched on** your memory, you remember it very clearly because it made a strong impression on you. [LITERARY] ❑ *Their argument was still etched in her mind.*

etching /ˈetʃɪŋ/ (**etchings**) N-COUNT An **etching** is a picture printed from a metal plate that has had a design cut into it.

eternal /ɪˈtɜːnəl/ **1** ADJ Something that is **eternal** lasts for ever. ❑ *...eternal life.* ❑ *...eternal youth.* ● **eternally** ADV ❑ *She is eternally grateful to her family for their support.* **2** ADJ BEFORE N **Eternal** truths and values never change and are thought to be true in all situations. ❑ *...the eternal principles of right and wrong.*

eternity /ɪˈtɜːnɪti/ **1** N-UNCOUNT **Eternity** is time without an end, or a state of existence outside time, especially the state which some people believe they will pass into after they have died. ❑ *I have always been frightened by the idea of eternity.* **2** N-SING You can refer to a period of time as **an eternity** when it seems very long. [INFORMAL] ❑ *The war continued for an eternity.*

ethereal /ɪˈθɪəriəl/ ADJ If you describe someone or something as **ethereal**, you mean that they have a delicate beauty that seems almost supernatural. [FORMAL]

ethic /ˈeθɪk/ (**ethics**) **1** N-PLURAL **Ethics** are moral beliefs and rules about right and wrong. ❑ *She is an expert in medical ethics.* **2** N-SING An **ethic** of a particular kind is a moral belief that influences the behaviour and attitudes of a group of people. ❑ *He has a very strong work ethic.*

ethical /ˈeθɪkəl/ **1** ADJ **Ethical** means influenced by a system of moral beliefs about right and wrong. ❑ *...the ethical aspects of experimenting on animals.* ● **ethically** ADV ❑ *We can defend ethically everything we believe in.* **2** ADJ If you describe something you do as **ethical**, you mean that it is morally right or acceptable. ❑ *His behaviour was not ethical.* ● **ethically** ADV ❑ *The government wants businesses to behave ethically.*

ethnic /ˈeθnɪk/ ADJ **Ethnic** means relating to different racial or cultural groups of people. ❑ *...Britain's ethnic minorities.* ● **ethnically** ADV ❑ *...a young, ethnically mixed audience.*

ethos /ˈiːθɒs/ N-SING The **ethos** of a group of people is the set of ideas and attitudes associated with it. ❑ *The ethos of the hotel is excellent service.*

etiquette /ˈetɪket/ N-UNCOUNT **Etiquette** is a set of customs and rules for polite behaviour. ❑ *...business etiquette in Japan.*

EU /ˌiː ˈjuː/ N-PROPER **The EU** is an organization of European countries which have joint policies on matters such as trade, agriculture, and finance. **EU** is an abbreviation of 'European Union'.

euphemism /ˈjuːfəmɪzəm/ (**euphemisms**) N-COUNT A **euphemism** is a polite word or expression that people use to talk about something unpleasant or embarrassing, such as death or sex.

euphemistic /ˌjuːfəˈmɪstɪk/ ADJ **Euphemistic** language consists of polite words or expressions for unpleasant or embarrassing things. ● **euphemistically** ADV ❑ *Stealing things from a store is euphemistically called 'shoplifting'.*

euphoria /juːˈfɔːriə/ N-UNCOUNT **Euphoria** is a feeling of great happiness. ● **euphoric** /juːˈfɒrɪk/ ADJ ❑ *I was euphoric when I found a job as a music journalist.*

euro /ˈjʊərəʊ/ (**euros**) N-COUNT The **euro** is a unit of currency that is used by the member countries of the European Union which have joined the European Monetary union.

> **Word Link** *an, ian ≈ one of, relating to : Christian, European, pedestrian*

European /ˌjʊərəˈpiːən/ (**Europeans**) **1** ADJ **European** means coming from or relating to Europe. ❑ *...European countries.* **2** N-COUNT A **European** is a person who comes from Europe.

ˌEuropean ˈUnion N-PROPER **The European Union** is an organization of European countries which have joint policies on matters such as trade, agriculture, and finance.

Eurosceptic or **Euro-sceptic** or **eurosceptic** /ˈjʊərəʊˈskeptɪk/ (**Eurosceptics**) N-COUNT & ADJ A **Eurosceptic** is someone, especially a politician, who is opposed to closer links between Britain and the European Union. [BRIT] ❑ *...Eurosceptic MPs.*

euthanasia /ˌjuːθəˈneɪziə, AM -ʒə/ N-UNCOUNT **Euthanasia** is the practice of painlessly killing a dying person in order to stop their suffering.

> **Word Link** *vac ≈ empty : evacuate, vacant, vacate*

evacuate /ɪˈvækjʊeɪt/ (**evacuates, evacuating, evacuated**) V-T/V-I If people **are evacuated from** a place, or if they **evacuate** a place, they move out of it because it has become dangerous. ❑ *18,000 people have been evacuated from the area.* ❑ *The police ordered the residents to evacuate.* ● **evacuation** (**evacuations**) N-VAR ❑ *...the mass evacuation of the town.*

evacuee /ɪˌvækjʊˈiː/ (**evacuees**) N-COUNT An **evacuee** is someone who has been sent away from a dangerous place to somewhere safe.

evade /ɪˈveɪd/ (**evades, evading, evaded**) V-T If you **evade** something unpleasant or difficult, you avoid it. ❑ *He admitted that he had evaded paying tax.* ❑ *He evaded capture.*

evaluate /ɪˈvæljʊeɪt/ (**evaluates, evaluating, evaluated**) V-T If you **evaluate** something or someone, you consider them in order to make a judgement about them, for example about how good or bad they are. ❑ *We need to evaluate how it was done.* ● **evaluation** (**evaluations**) N-VAR ❑ *...the opinions and evaluations of our teachers.*

evaporate /ɪˈvæpəreɪt/ (**evaporates,**

evaporating, evaporated) V-I When a liquid **evaporates**, it changes into a gas, because its temperature has increased. • **evaporation** N-UNCOUNT ❑ *...the evaporation of water from the soil.*
→ see **matter, water**

evasion /ɪˈveɪʒən/ (**evasions**) N-VAR If you accuse someone of **evasion**, you mean that they are deliberately avoiding dealing with something unpleasant or difficult. ❑ *...the evasion of responsibility.*

evasive /ɪˈveɪsɪv/ ADJ If you describe someone as **evasive**, you mean that they deliberately avoid answering questions. • **evasively** ADV ❑ *'I can't give you an answer now,' Mark said evasively.*

eve /iːv/ (**eves**) N-COUNT **The eve of** an event is the day before it, or the period of time just before it. [JOURNALISM] ❑ *...on the eve of his 27th birthday.*

even
1 DISCOURSE USES
2 ADJECTIVE USES
3 PHRASAL VERB USES

even /ˈiːvən/
1 1 ADV You use **even** to suggest that what comes just after or just before it in the sentence is surprising. ❑ *Nobody trusted strangers, perhaps not even friends.* ❑ *Even people who are confident at other times can be nervous when being interviewed.* 2 PHRASE You use **even so** to introduce a surprising fact that relates to what you have just said. ❑ *The bus was only half full. Even so, a young man asked Nina if the seat next to her was free.* 3 ADV You use **even** with comparative adjectives and adverbs to emphasize a quality that someone or something has. ❑ *Stan was speaking even more slowly than usual.* 4 CONJ You use **even if** or **even though** to indicate that a particular fact does not make the rest of your statement untrue. ❑ *Even if you are on a strict diet, you can still go out for a meal.*

even /ˈiːvən/
2 1 ADJ An **even** measurement or rate stays at about the same level. ❑ *How important is it to have an even temperature?* • **evenly** ADV ❑ *He looked at Ellen, breathing evenly in her sleep.* 2 ADJ An **even** surface is smooth and flat. ❑ *The tables have smooth and even surfaces.* 3 ADJ If there is an **even** division of something, each person, group, or area involved has an equal amount. ❑ *Divide the class into even groups of three.* • **evenly** ADV ❑ *The island's population is 160,000, evenly divided between town and countryside.* 4 ADJ If a contest or competition is **even**, the people taking part are all equally skilful. • **evenly** ADV ❑ *...two evenly matched candidates.* 5 ADJ AFTER LINK-V If you are **even with** someone, you do not owe them anything, such as money or a favour. 6 PHRASE When a company or a person running a business **breaks even**, they make neither a profit nor a loss. 7 PHRASE If you say you will **get even with** someone, you mean that you intend to harm them because they have harmed you. [INFORMAL] 8 ADJ An **even** number can be divided exactly by the number two.

even /ˈiːvən/ (**evens, evening, evened**)
3 ▸ **even out** PHR-VERB When an amount of something **evens out**, or when you **even** it **out**, it becomes more evenly distributed or steadier. ❑ *House prices have evened out across the country.*

evening /ˈiːvnɪŋ/ (**evenings**) N-VAR The **evening** is the part of each day between the end of the afternoon and the time when you go to bed. ❑ *He doesn't do anything in the evenings.* ❑ *...6.00 in the evening.* ❑ *...her evening meal.*
→ see **time**

event /ɪˈvent/ (**events**) 1 N-COUNT An **event** is something that happens. ❑ *...recent events in Europe.* ❑ *The event was a great success.* 2 N-COUNT An **event** is an organized occasion. ❑ *...major sporting events.* 3 PHRASE You use **in the event of, in the event that**, and **in that event** when you are talking about a possible future situation, especially when you are planning what to do if it occurs. ❑ *In the event that they lose their jobs, the workers will get help and advice.*
→ see **history**

Thesaurus *event* Also look up:
N. happening, occasion, occurrence 1 2

eventual /ɪˈventʃʊəl/ ADJ BEFORE N The **eventual** result of something is what happens at the end of it. ❑ *...events leading to his eventual death.*

eventuality /ɪˌventʃʊˈælɪti/ (**eventualities**) N-COUNT An **eventuality** is a possible future event or result. [FORMAL] ❑ *We have planned for every eventuality, from running out of petrol to needing water.*

eventually /ɪˈventʃʊəli/ 1 ADV **Eventually** means in the end, especially after a lot of delays, problems, or arguments. ❑ *The flight eventually left six hours late.* 2 ADV **Eventually** means at the end of a situation or process or as the final result of it. ❑ *She eventually plans to run her own hotel.*

ever /ˈevə/ 1 ADV **Ever** means at any time. It is used in questions and negative statements. ❑ *Neither of us has ever skied.* ❑ *Have you ever been to France?* ❑ *You won't hear from Gaston ever again.* 2 ADV You use **ever** after comparatives and superlatives to emphasize the degree to which something is true. ❑ *She's got a great voice and is singing better than ever.* ❑ *This is the most awful evening I can ever remember.* 3 PHRASE You say **as ever** in order to indicate that something is not unusual. ❑ *He was alone as ever.* 4 PHRASE You use **ever since** to emphasize that something has been true since the time mentioned, and is still true now. ❑ *He's been here ever since you left!* 5 PHRASE You use **ever so** and **ever such** to emphasize that someone or something has a lot of a particular quality. [BRIT, INFORMAL] ❑ *He was ever such a good dancer.* ❑ *I like him ever so much.*

ever- /ˈevə-/ You use **ever-** in adjectives such as **ever-increasing** and **ever-present**, to show that something exists or continues all the time. ❑ *...an ever-changing world.*

evergreen /ˈevəgriːn/ (**evergreens**) N-COUNT An **evergreen** is a tree or bush which has green leaves all the year round.

every /ˈevri/ 1 DET & ADJ You use **every** to indicate that you are referring to all the members of a group or all the parts of something. ❑ *...recipes for every occasion.* ❑ *...every bus in London.* 2 DET You use **every** to say how often something happens or to indicate that something happens at regular intervals. ❑ *We had meetings every day.* ❑ *There is a burglary every three minutes in London.* 3 DET You use **every** before some nouns in order to emphasize what you are saying. ❑ *There is every chance that* *you will do well.* ❑ *I made every effort to be friendly.* **4** PHRASE You use the expressions **every now and then**, **every now and again**, **every once in a while**, and **every so often** to indicate that something happens occasionally. **5** PHRASE If something happens **every other** day or week, for example, or **every second** day or week, it happens on one day or week in each period of two days or weeks. ❑ *We go to London for meetings every other month.*

everybody /ˈevribɒdi/ → see **everyone**

E

everyday /ˈevrideɪ/ ADJ You use **everyday** to describe something which happens or is used every day, or forms a regular and basic part of your life. ❑ *...your everyday routine.* ❑ *He talked to us about everyday life in Rome.*

everyone /ˈevriwʌn/ also **everybody** PRON **Everyone** or **everybody** means all the people in a group or all people in general. ❑ *Everyone in the street was shocked.* ❑ *Everyone goes home at around 7 p.m.* ❑ *Everyone needs some free time for rest and relaxation.*

Usage

Be careful not to confuse **everyone** with **every one**. **Everyone** always refers to people. In the phrase **every one**, 'one' is a pronoun that can refer to any person or thing, depending on the context. It is often followed by the word **of**. ❑ *They have talked to every one of my classmates.* ❑ *Every one of them phoned me.* In these examples, **every one** is a more emphatic way of saying **all**.

everything /ˈevriθɪŋ/ **1** PRON You use **everything** to refer to all the objects, activities, or facts in a situation. ❑ *Everything else in his life had changed.* ❑ *He packed everything he would need into his new rucksack.* **2** PRON You use **everything** to refer to a whole situation or to life in general. ❑ *Is everything all right?*

everywhere /ˈevriweə/ **1** ADV You use **everywhere** to refer to a whole area or to all the places in a particular area. ❑ *Working people everywhere object to paying taxes.* ❑ *We went everywhere together.* **2** ADV You use **everywhere** to refer to all the places that someone goes to. ❑ *He made new friends everywhere he went.* **3** PRON If you say that someone or something is **everywhere**, you mean that they are present in a place in very large numbers. ❑ *There were empty boxes everywhere.*

evict /ɪˈvɪkt/ (**evicts, evicting, evicted**) V-T When people **are evicted**, they are officially forced to leave the house where they are living. ❑ *The police evicted ten families.* • **eviction** (**evictions**) N-VAR ❑ *He was facing eviction, along with his wife and family.*

evidence /ˈevɪdəns/ **1** N-UNCOUNT **Evidence** is anything that makes you believe that something is true or exists. ❑ *There is evidence that stress causes the disease.* ❑ *There is no evidence to support this.* **2** PHRASE If you **give evidence** in a court of law, you give a statement saying what you know about something. **3** PHRASE If someone or something is **in evidence**, they are present and can be clearly seen. ❑ *Several soldiers were in evidence at the border.*
→ see **experiment, trial**

Word Partnership Use *evidence* with:

V.	**find** evidence, **gather** evidence, **present** evidence, **produce** evidence, evidence **to support** ***something***
ADJ.	**new** evidence, **physical** evidence, **scientific** evidence

evident /ˈevɪdənt/ ADJ If something is **evident**, you notice it easily and clearly. ❑ *His footprints were clearly evident in the snow.* ❑ *It was evident that she had once been beautiful.*

evidently /ˈevɪdəntli/ ADV You use **evidently** to say that something is true, because you have seen evidence of it yourself or because someone has told you it is true. ❑ *The two Russians evidently knew each other.*

evil /ˈiːvəl/ (**evils**) **1** N-UNCOUNT **Evil** is used to refer to all the wicked and bad things that happen in the world. ❑ *...the battle between good and evil.* **2** N-COUNT An **evil** is a very unpleasant or harmful situation or activity. ❑ *...the evils of racism.* **3** ADJ If you describe someone or something as **evil**, you mean that they are wicked and cause harm to people. ❑ *...the country's most evil terrorists.* ❑ *This was a cowardly and evil act.*

evocative /ɪˈvɒkətɪv/ ADJ If something like a description is **evocative**, it strongly reminds you of something or gives you a powerful impression of what it is like. ❑ *Her story is evocative of Italian life.*

evoke /ɪˈvəʊk/ (**evokes, evoking, evoked**) V-T To **evoke** a particular memory, idea, emotion, or response means to cause it to happen or exist. ❑ *The scene evoked memories of those old movies.*

evolution /ˌiːvəˈluːʃən, ˌev-/ **1** N-UNCOUNT **Evolution** is a process of gradual change during which animals and plants change some of their

Word Web evolution

The **theory** of **human evolution** states that humans **evolved** from an ape-like ancestor. In 1856 the **fossils** of a **Neanderthal** were found. This was the first time that **scientists** realized that there were earlier forms of humans. **Anthropologists** have found other fossils that show how **hominids** changed over time. One of the earliest ancestors that has been found is called **Australopithecus**. This **species** lived about 4 million years ago in Africa. The most famous specimen of this species is named 'Lucy'. Scientists believe that she was among the first hominids to walk upright. The oldest fossils of **Homo sapiens** date back to approximately 130,000 years ago.

characteristics and sometimes develop into new species. **2** N-UNCOUNT You can use **evolution** to refer to any gradual process of change and development. ❑ *...the evolution of modern physics.*
→ see Word Web: **evolution**
→ see **earth**

evolutionary /ˌiːvəˈluːʃənri, AM -neri/ ADJ **Evolutionary** means relating to a process of gradual change and development. ❑ *...a period of evolutionary change.*

evolve /ɪˈvɒlv/ (**evolves, evolving, evolved**) **1** V-I When animals and plants **evolve**, they gradually change and develop into different forms. ❑ *Birds evolved from small dinosaurs called 'theropods'.* **2** V-T/V-I If something **evolves**, or if you **evolve** it, it gradually develops into something different and usually more advanced. ❑ *It was a tiny airline which eventually evolved into Pakistan International Airlines.*
→ see **earth**

ewe /juː/ (**ewes**) N-COUNT A **ewe** is an adult female sheep.

exacerbate /ɪgˈzæsəbeɪt/ (**exacerbates, exacerbating, exacerbated**) V-T If something **exacerbates** a bad situation, it makes it worse. [FORMAL] ● **exacerbation** N-UNCOUNT ❑ *...the exacerbation of global problems.*

exact /ɪgˈzækt/ (**exacts, exacting, exacted**) **1** ADJ Something that is **exact** is correct, accurate, and complete in every way. ❑ *I don't remember his exact words.* ❑ *We don't know the exact numbers.* ❑ *A small number – five, to be exact – have arrived.* ● **exactly** ADV ❑ *Where exactly is the smell coming from?* **2** ADJ BEFORE N You use **exact** before a noun to emphasize that you are referring to that particular thing and no other. ❑ *I can't find the exact thing I want.* **3** V-T When someone **exacts** something, they demand and obtain it from someone else. [FORMAL] ❑ *He has exacted a written apology from the chairman of the company.* **4** → see also **exactly**

Thesaurus *exact* Also look up:
ADJ. accurate, clear, precise, true; *(ant.)* wrong **1**

Word Partnership Use *exact* with:
N. exact **change**, exact **duplicate**, exact **number**, exact **opposite**, exact **replica**, exact **science**, exact **words** **1**
exact **cause**, exact **location**, exact **moment** **2**
exact **revenge** **3**

exacting /ɪgˈzæktɪŋ/ ADJ An **exacting** person or task requires you to work very hard. ❑ *They have the same exacting standards.*

exactly /ɪgˈzæktli/ **1** ADV **Exactly** means precisely, and not just approximately. ❑ *Andrew arrived home at exactly five o'clock.* ❑ *...exactly in the middle of the picture.* **2** ADV If you say **'Exactly'**, you are agreeing with someone or emphasizing the truth of what they say. If you say **'Not exactly'**, you are telling them politely that not everything they are saying is true or accurate. ❑ *'We don't know the answer to that.'—'Exactly, so let's try and find out.'* ❑ *'And you said no?'—'Well, not exactly.'* **3** ADV You use **not exactly** to indicate that a meaning or situation is slightly different from what people think or expect. ❑ *The two men are not exactly friends – they mistrust one another.*

exaggerate /ɪgˈzædʒəreɪt/ (**exaggerates, exaggerating, exaggerated**) V-T/V-I If you **exaggerate**, or **exaggerate** something, you make the thing that you are talking about seem bigger or more important than it actually is. ❑ *She exaggerated her qualifications in job applications.* ● **exaggeration** (**exaggerations**) N-VAR ❑ *It isn't an exaggeration to say that my mp3 player has changed my life.*

exaggerated /ɪgˈzædʒəreɪtɪd/ ADJ Something that is **exaggerated** is or seems larger, better, worse, or more important than it needs to be. ❑ *Politicians often make exaggerated claims about what they can do.*

exalted /ɪgˈzɔːltɪd/ ADJ An **exalted** person is very important. [LITERARY] ❑ *...the exalted members of the British government.*

exam /ɪgˈzæm/ (**exams**) N-COUNT An **exam** is a formal test taken to show your knowledge of a subject. ❑ *Did you pass your exams?* ❑ *I sat my exams in May.*

Usage
Note that to **pass** an exam always means to succeed in it. If you do not pass an exam, you **fail** it. If you simply do an exam or take part in it, you can say that you **take** the exam, or, in British English, that you **sit** the exam.

examination /ɪgˌzæmɪˈneɪʃən/ (**examinations**) N-COUNT An **examination** is an **exam**. [FORMAL]
→ see **diagnosis**

examine /ɪgˈzæmɪn/ (**examines, examining, examined**) **1** V-T If you **examine** something, you look at it or consider it carefully. ❑ *He examined her passport.* ❑ *The plans will be examined by the environment minister.* ● **examination** (**examinations**) N-VAR ❑ *Further examination is needed.* **2** V-T If you **are being examined**, you are given a formal test in order to show your knowledge of a subject.

Thesaurus *examine* Also look up:
V. analyze, go over, inspect, investigate, research, scrutinize **1**

examiner /ɪgˈzæmɪnə/ (**examiners**) N-COUNT An **examiner** is a person who sets or marks an exam.

example /ɪgˈzɑːmpəl, -ˈzæmp-/ (**examples**) **1** N-COUNT An **example** is something which represents or is typical of a particular group of things. ❑ *It's a great example of a small business that grew into a big one.* ❑ *Give me another example.* **2** PHRASE You use **for example** to show that you are giving an example of a particular kind of thing. ❑ *...professional people, for example, doctors.* **3** N-COUNT In a dictionary entry, an **example** is a phrase which shows how a word is used. **4** N-COUNT If you refer to a person as an **example to** other people, you mean that he or she behaves in a good way that other people should copy. ❑ *Tom has always been an example to the younger children.* **5** PHRASE If you **follow** someone's **example**, you copy their behaviour, especially because you admire them. **6** PHRASE If you **set an example**, you encourage people by your behaviour to behave in a similar way.

Thesaurus *example* Also look up:
N. model, representation, sample 1
ideal, role model, standard 2

Word Partnership Use *example* with:
ADJ. **classic** example, **good** example, **obvious** example, **perfect** example, **typical** example 1
V. **give an** example 1
follow an example 4

E

Word Link *sper ≈ hope : desperate, exasperate, prosperity*

exasperate /ɪɡ'zɑːspəreɪt, -'zæs-/ (**exasperates, exasperating, exasperated**) V-T If someone or something **exasperates** you, they annoy you, making you feel frustrated. ❑ *He hates school and exasperates his teachers.* ● **exasperated** ADJ ❑ *Sam was exasperated at the delay.* ● **exasperation** N-UNCOUNT ❑ *'Oh, not again!' Tamsin cried in exasperation.*

Word Link *cav ≈ hollow : cave, cavity, excavate*

excavate /'ekskəveɪt/ (**excavates, excavating, excavated**) V-T To **excavate** a piece of land means to remove earth carefully from it and look for the remains of objects or buildings, in order to find out about the past. ● **excavation** (**excavations**) N-VAR ❑ *...the excavation of Pompeii.*

Word Link *ex ≈ away, from, out : exceed, exit, explode*

exceed /ɪk'siːd/ (**exceeds, exceeding, exceeded**) 1 V-T If something **exceeds** a particular amount, it is greater than that amount. ❑ *Its research budget exceeds $700 million a year.* 2 V-T If you **exceed** a limit, you go beyond it. ❑ *I drive but I don't exceed the speed limit.*

exceedingly /ɪk'siːdɪŋli/ ADV **Exceedingly** means very much indeed. [DATED] ❑ *...an exceedingly good lunch.*

excel /ɪk'sel/ (**excels, excelling, excelled**) V-T/V-I If someone **excels in** or **at** something, they are very good at it. ❑ *She excelled at sports.* ❑ *He excels academically.*

Excellency /'eksələnsi/ (**Excellencies**) N-VOC People use expressions such as **Your Excellency** or **His Excellency** when they are addressing or referring to officials of very high rank, for example ambassadors or governors. ❑ *...His Excellency the Ambassador of the Republic of Poland.*

Word Link *ence ≈ state, condition : dependence, excellence, independence*

excellent /'eksələnt/ ADJ Something that is **excellent** is very good indeed. ❑ *Sue does an excellent job as Fred's personal assistant.* ● **excellence** N-UNCOUNT ❑ *...an award for excellence in journalism.* ● **excellently** ADV ❑ *They're both playing excellently.*

except /ɪk'sept/ PREP & CONJ You use **except** or **except for** to introduce the only thing or person that a statement does not apply to, or a fact that prevents a statement from being completely true. ❑ *I go running all year round, except in January.* ❑ *Everyone was late, except for Richard.*

exception /ɪk'sepʃən/ (**exceptions**) 1 N-VAR An **exception** is a situation, thing, or person that is not included in a general statement. ❑ *She never wears make-up, but this evening is obviously an exception.* ❑ *Everybody had the day off, with the exception of Lawrence.* 2 PHRASE If you **make an exception**, you consider or allow something that you would normally not consider or allow. ❑ *I don't like eating in hotels, but I made an exception for the restaurant in the Mandarin Hotel.* 3 PHRASE If you **take exception to** something, you feel offended or annoyed by it. ❑ *He took exception to my comments.*

exceptional /ɪk'sepʃənəl/ 1 ADJ You use **exceptional** to describe someone or something that has a particular quality to an unusually high degree. ❑ *...children with exceptional ability.* ● **exceptionally** ADV ❑ *...an exceptionally talented dancer.* 2 ADJ **Exceptional** situations are unusual or rare. ❑ *...exceptional circumstances, such as severe weather.*

excerpt /'eksɜːpt/ (**excerpts**) N-COUNT An **excerpt** is a short piece of writing, film or music taken from a larger piece. ❑ *...an excerpt from Tchaikovsky's Nutcracker Suite.*

excess (**excesses**)

noun /ɪk'ses/, adjective /'ekses/.

1 N-VAR & ADJ BEFORE N An **excess of** something or an **excess** amount of it is a larger amount than is needed or usual. ❑ *...the problems created by an excess of wealth.* ❑ *The major reason for excess weight is excess eating.* 2 PHRASE **In excess of** means more than a particular amount. ❑ *Last week, the film made in excess of £300,000 at the box office.* 3 N-VAR **Excess** is behaviour that is unacceptable because it is too extreme or immoral. ❑ *...the excesses of the regime.* 4 PHRASE If you do something **to excess**, you do it too much. ❑ *At Christmas, people tend to eat to excess.*

excessive /ɪk'sesɪv/ ADJ If something is **excessive**, it is too great in amount or degree. ❑ *...the use of excessive force by police.* ● **excessively** ADV ❑ *...excessively high wages.*

exchange /ɪks'tʃeɪndʒ/ (**exchanges, exchanging, exchanged**) 1 V-T & N-COUNT If two or more people **exchange** things, or if there is an **exchange of** them, they give them to each other at the same time. ❑ *We exchanged addresses.* ❑ *He exchanged a quick smile with her.* ❑ *...the exchange of prisoners of war.* 2 V-T If you **exchange** something, or if you **exchange** it **for** something else, you replace it with something. ❑ *We are happy to exchange your goods, or give you your money back.* 3 PHRASE If you give someone one thing **in exchange for** another, you give it to them because they are giving the other thing to you. If you do something for someone **in exchange for** another, you do it for someone because they did something for you. ❑ *I look after her garden in exchange for firewood.* 4 N-COUNT An **exchange** is a brief conversation. [FORMAL] ❑ *...angry exchanges between the player and England football fans.*

Word Partnership Use *exchange* with:

N. exchange **gifts**, exchange **greetings** 1
exchange **student** 3
ADJ. **cultural** exchange 3
brief exchange 4

ex'change rate (**exchange rates**) N-COUNT The **exchange rate** of a country's unit of currency is the amount of another country's currency that you get in exchange for it.

excise /'eksaɪz/ N-UNCOUNT **Excise** is a tax that the government of a country puts on goods produced for sale in that country.

excitable /ɪk'saɪtəbəl/ ADJ An **excitable** person becomes excited very easily.

excite /ɪk'saɪt/ (**excites, exciting, excited**) 1 V-T If something **excites** you, it makes you feel very happy or enthusiastic. ❑ *This new job really excites me.* 2 V-T If something **excites** a reaction or feeling, it causes it. ❑ *Motor racing excited his interest from an early age.*

excited /ɪk'saɪtɪd/ ADJ If you are **excited**, you are looking forward to something eagerly. ❑ *I'm very excited about playing for England.* ● **excitedly** ADV ❑ *He talked excitedly about going to the Olympic Games.*

excitement /ɪk'saɪtmənt/ (**excitements**) N-VAR You use **excitement** to refer to the state of being excited, or to something that excites you. ❑ *...in a state of great excitement.* ❑ *After the excitements of the day, we had a quiet evening.*

exciting /ɪk'saɪtɪŋ/ ADJ Something that is **exciting** makes you feel very happy or enthusiastic. ❑ *...the most exciting week of their lives.*

Word Link *claim, clam ≈ shouting : acclaim, exclaim, proclamation*

exclaim /ɪks'kleɪm/ (**exclaims, exclaiming, exclaimed**) V-T Writers sometimes use **exclaim** to show that someone is speaking suddenly, loudly, or emphatically. ❑ *'There!' Jack exclaimed.* ❑ *She exclaimed that she could never do something like that.*

excla'mation mark (**exclamation marks**) N-COUNT In British English, an **exclamation mark** is the punctuation mark (!). The American term is **exclamation point**.
→ see **punctuation**

exclude /ɪks'klu:d/ (**excludes, excluding, excluded**) 1 V-T If you **exclude** someone **from** a place or activity, you prevent them from entering it or taking part in it. ❑ *The university excluded women from its classes until 1968.* ● **exclusion** (**exclusions**) N-VAR ❑ *...his exclusion from the team.* 2 V-T If you **exclude** something that has some connection with what you are doing, you deliberately do not use it or consider it. ❑ *These prices exclude flights.* ● **exclusion** N-VAR ❑ *The exclusion of certain foods from your diet might help you.* 3 V-T To **exclude** a possibility means to decide or prove that it is wrong and not worth considering.

excluding /ɪk'sklu:dɪŋ/ PREP You use **excluding** before mentioning a person or thing to show that you are not including them in your statement. ❑ *The hotel is offering one night in a double room for £21, excluding breakfast.*

exclusive /ɪk'sklu:sɪv/ 1 ADJ Something that is **exclusive** is available only to people who are rich. ❑ *...Britain's most exclusive club.* 2 ADJ **Exclusive** means used or owned by only one person or group. ❑ *Our group will have exclusive use of a 60-foot boat.* 3 ADJ If two things are **mutually exclusive**, they cannot exist together. ❑ *Hard work and pleasure don't have to be mutually exclusive.*

exclusively /ɪk'sklu:sɪvli/ ADV **Exclusively** is used to refer to situations or activities that involve only the thing or things mentioned, and nothing else. ❑ *The hotel by the beach caters exclusively for surfers.*

excrete /ɪk'skri:t/ (**excretes, excreting, excreted**) V-T When you **excrete** waste matter from your body, you get rid of it. [FORMAL]

excruciating /ɪk'skru:ʃieɪtɪŋ/ ADJ **Excruciating** pain is extremely painful.

Word Link *curr, curs ≈ running, flowing : concurrent, current, excursion*

excursion /ɪk'skɜ:ʃən, AM -ʒən/ (**excursions**) N-COUNT An **excursion** is a short journey or visit. ❑ *...a coach excursion to Trondheim.*

excuse (**excuses, excusing, excused**) 1 N-COUNT /ɪk'skju:s/ An **excuse** is a reason which you give in order to explain why something has been done or has not been done, or to avoid doing something. ❑ *I made an excuse and ran towards the door.* ❑ *Having a baby is the perfect excuse to stay at home.* 2 V-T /ɪk'skju:z/ To **excuse** someone or to **excuse** their behaviour means to provide reasons for their actions, especially when other people disapprove of these actions. ❑ *That doesn't excuse my mother's behaviour.* 3 V-T If you **excuse** someone **for** something wrong that they have done, you forgive them. ❑ *I don't excuse them for what they've done.* 4 V-T If someone **is excused from** a duty or responsibility, they are told that they do not have to carry it out. ❑ *...a letter from his parents excusing him from school sports.* 5 V-T If you **excuse yourself**, you use a phrase such as **'Excuse me'** as a polite way of saying that you are about to leave. ❑ *He excused himself and went up to his room.* 6 PHRASE You say **'Excuse me'** when you want to politely get someone's attention. ❑ *Excuse me, but are you Mr Honig?* 7 PHRASE You use **'Excuse me'** to apologize for interrupting someone. ❑ *Excuse me interrupting, but I need to say something.*

Thesaurus *excuse* Also look up:

N. apology, explanation, reason 1
V. forgive, pardon, spare; *(ant.)* accuse, blame, punish 2

execute /'eksɪkju:t/ (**executes, executing, executed**) 1 V-T To **execute** someone means to kill them as a punishment. ❑ *The boy's father was executed for his crime.* ● **execution** (**executions**) N-VAR ❑ *...execution by hanging.* ● **executioner** (**executioners**) N-COUNT ❑ *...the executioner's axe.* 2 V-T If you **execute** a plan, you carry it out. [FORMAL] ● **execution** N-UNCOUNT ❑ *...day-to-day management and execution of public policy.* 3 V-T If you **execute** a difficult action or movement, you perform it. ❑ *The landing was skilfully executed by the pilot.*

executive /ɪg'zekjʊtɪv/ (**executives**) 1 N-COUNT An **executive** is someone employed by a company at a senior level. 2 N-SING The

executive of an organization is a committee which makes important decisions. ❑ *Some executive members want him to leave.*

exemplary /ɪgˈzempləri/ ADJ If you describe someone or something as **exemplary**, you consider them to be extremely good. ❑ *He showed exemplary courage.*

exemplify /ɪgˈzemplɪfaɪ/ (**exemplifies, exemplifying, exemplified**) V-T If something or someone **exemplifies** something, they are a typical example of it. ❑ *The style of this room exemplifies the idea of 'beauty and practicality'.*

E

exempt /ɪgˈzempt/ (**exempts, exempting, exempted**) **1** ADJ If you are **exempt from** a rule or duty, you do not have to obey it or perform it. ❑ *Men in college were exempt from military service.* **2** V-T To **exempt** a person **from** a rule or duty means to state officially that they do not have to obey it or perform it. ● **exemption** (**exemptions**) N-VAR ❑ *...new exemptions for students.*

exercise /ˈeksəsaɪz/ (**exercises, exercising, exercised**) **1** V-T/V-I & N-UNCOUNT When you **exercise**, you move your body energetically in order to get fit and remain healthy. The activity is referred to as **exercise**. ❑ *Exercising the body is good for your health.* ❑ *She exercises two or three times a week.* ❑ *Lack of exercise can lead to depression.* **2** V-T & N-SING If you **exercise** your authority, your rights, or a good quality such as mercy, you put it into use. **The exercise of** these things is the act of using them. [FORMAL] ❑ *They are simply exercising their right to free speech.* ❑ *...the exercise of political power.* **3** N-COUNT **Exercises** are a series of movements you do in order to get fit or remain healthy. **4** N-COUNT **Exercises** are activities which you do in order to maintain a skill or to train for a particular skill. ❑ *...creative writing exercises.*
→ see **muscle**

exert /ɪgˈzɜːt/ (**exerts, exerting, exerted**) **1** V-T If someone or something **exerts** influence or pressure **on** someone, they use their influence or put pressure on that person to do something. ❑ *The Catholic Church exerts a powerful influence over American politics.* **2** V-T If you **exert yourself**, you make a physical or mental effort to do something. ❑ *Do not exert yourself unnecessarily.* ● **exertion** (**exertions**) N-VAR ❑ *He clearly enjoyed the physical exertion.*
→ see **motion**

exhale /eksˈheɪl/ (**exhales, exhaling, exhaled**) V-T/V-I When you **exhale**, you breathe out. [FORMAL]
→ see **respiration**

exhale

exhaust /ɪgˈzɔːst/ (**exhausts, exhausting, exhausted**) **1** V-T If something **exhausts** you, it makes you very tired. ❑ *Walking in deep snow had exhausted him.* ● **exhausted** ADJ ❑ *She was too exhausted to talk.* ● **exhausting** ADJ ❑ *It's an exhausting job.* ● **exhaustion** N-UNCOUNT ❑ *They were taken to hospital, suffering from exhaustion.* **2** V-T If a supply of something such as money or food **is exhausted**, it has all been spent or eaten. ❑ *Their supplies of food and water were almost exhausted.* **3** V-T If you **have exhausted** a subject, you have talked about it so much that there is nothing more to say about it. **4** N-COUNT The **exhaust** on a motor vehicle is the series of pipes which carry waste gases from the engine. **5** N-UNCOUNT **Exhaust** is the waste gases produced by the engine of a motor vehicle.
→ see **pollution**

exhaustive /ɪgˈzɔːstɪv/ ADJ An **exhaustive** study or search is thorough and complete. ❑ *...exhaustive inquiries.* ● **exhaustively** ADV ❑ *Every issue has been exhaustively discussed.*

exhibit /ɪgˈzɪbɪt/ (**exhibits, exhibiting, exhibited**) **1** V-T To **exhibit** a particular quality, feeling, or type of behaviour means to show it. [FORMAL] ❑ *Seventy percent of the students exhibited signs of depression.* **2** V-T When an object of interest **is exhibited**, it is put in a public place for people to come and look at it. ❑ *...a massive elephant exhibited by London Zoo.* ● **exhibition** N-UNCOUNT ❑ *Five pieces of the Berlin Wall are currently on exhibition in London.* **3** N-COUNT An **exhibit** is an object of interest that is displayed in a museum or art gallery. **4** V-I When artists **exhibit**, they show their work in public. ❑ *She exhibited at the Royal Academy in 1936.* **5** N-COUNT An **exhibit** is an object that is shown in court as evidence in a legal case.

exhibition /ˌeksɪˈbɪʃən/ (**exhibitions**) **1** N-COUNT An **exhibition** is an event at which objects of interest are displayed in a public place. ❑ *...an important exhibition of paintings and drawings.* **2** N-SING If a player or team plays particularly well in a game, you can say that they give an **exhibition of** their skills. ❑ *The fans were treated to an exhibition of power and speed.* **3** → see also **exhibit**

exhibitor /ɪgˈzɪbɪtə/ (**exhibitors**) N-COUNT An **exhibitor** is a person whose work is being shown in an exhibition.

exhilarating /ɪgˈzɪləreɪtɪŋ/ ADJ If you describe an experience or feeling as **exhilarating**, you mean that it makes you feel very happy and excited. ❑ *It was an exhilarating journey.*

exile /ˈeksaɪl, ˈegz-/ (**exiles, exiling, exiled**) **1** V-T & N-UNCOUNT If someone **is exiled**, or if they are living **in exile**, they are living in a foreign country because they cannot live in their own country, usually for political reasons. ❑ *Napoleon was exiled to St Helena.* ❑ *He is now living in exile in Egypt.* **2** N-COUNT An **exile** is someone who lives in exile.

Word Partnership Use *exile* with:

V.	**force into** exile, **go into** exile, **live in** exile, **return from** exile, **send into** exile **1**
ADJ.	**self-imposed** exile **1** **political** exile **1** **2**

exist /ɪgˈzɪst/ (**exists, existing, existed**) **1** V-I If something **exists**, it is present in the world as a real thing. ❑ *He thought that if he couldn't see something, it didn't exist.* ❑ *She pretended that her problems didn't exist.* **2** → see also **existing**

existence /ɪgˈzɪstəns/ (**existences**) **1** N-UNCOUNT The **existence of** something is the fact that it is present in the world as a real thing. ❑ *...the existence of other planets.* **2** N-COUNT You can refer to someone's way of life as a particular **existence**. ❑ *Paula has a comfortable existence.*

Word Partnership Use *existence* with:

V. **come into** existence, **deny the** existence 1
ADJ. **continued** existence, **daily** existence, **everyday** existence 1 2

existing /ɪg'zɪstɪŋ/ ADJ BEFORE N **Existing** is used to describe something which is now present or available. ❑ *We need to make the existing products better.*

Word Link *ex ≈ away, from, out : exceed, exit, explode*

exit /'egzɪt, 'eksɪt/ (**exits, exiting, exited**) 1 N-COUNT An **exit** is a doorway through which you can leave a public building. ❑ *He walked towards the exit.* 2 N-COUNT An **exit** on a motorway is a place where traffic can leave it. ❑ *Take the A422 exit at Stratford.* 3 N-COUNT If you refer to someone's **exit**, you are referring to the fact that they left. ❑ *I made a quick exit.* 4 V-T/V-I If you **exit**, or **exit** a room or building, you leave it. [FORMAL] 5 V-T If you **exit** a computer program or system, you stop running it. ❑ *Do you want to exit this program?*

exodus /'eksədəs/ N-SING When there is an **exodus of** people from a place, a lot of people leave it at the same time. ❑ *...the exodus of refugees from a war zone.*

exotic /ɪg'zɒtɪk/ ADJ Something that is **exotic** is unusual and interesting, usually because it comes from a distant tropical country. ❑ *...brilliantly coloured, exotic flowers.* ● **exotically** ADV ❑ *...an exotically coloured bird.*

expand /ɪk'spænd/ (**expands, expanding, expanded**) V-T/V-I If something **expands**, or if you **expand** it, it becomes larger. ❑ *The old Greek city was expanded by the Romans.* ❑ *I own a bookshop and want to expand the business.* ● **expansion** (**expansions**) N-VAR ❑ *The company has plans for expansion.* ▶ **expand on** or **expand upon** PHR-VERB If you **expand on** something, you give more information about it. ❑ *In today's speech, the Prime Minister expanded on the comments he made last month.*

expanse /ɪk'spæns/ (**expanses**) N-COUNT An **expanse of** sea, sky, or land is a very large area of it.

expansion /ɪk'spænʃən/ → see **expand**

expansive /ɪk'spænsɪv/ 1 ADJ BEFORE N **Expansive** means covering or including a large area or many things. ❑ *...an expansive play area.* 2 ADJ If you are **expansive**, you talk a lot, or are friendly or generous, because you are happy and relaxed. ❑ *Fritz was a large and expansive man who loved to entertain.*

expatriate /ek'spætriət, -'peɪt-/ (**expatriates**) N-COUNT An **expatriate** is someone who is living in a country other than the one where they were born.

expect /ɪk'spekt/ (**expects, expecting, expected**) 1 V-T If you **expect** something **to** happen, you believe that it will happen. ❑ *He expects to lose his job soon.* ❑ *They no longer expect profits to improve.* 2 V-T If you **are expecting** something or someone, you believe that they will be delivered or arrive soon. ❑ *I am expecting several important letters.* ❑ *We were expecting him home.* 3 V-T If you **expect** something, or if you **expect** someone **to** do something, you believe that it is your right to have that thing, or it is that person's duty to do it for you. ❑ *I expect to have some time to myself.* ❑ *I wasn't expecting you to help.* 4 V-T/V-I If a woman **is expecting**, or **expecting** a baby, she is pregnant.

expectant /ɪk'spektənt/ 1 ADJ If you are **expectant**, you are excited because you think something interesting is about to happen. ● **expectantly** ADV ❑ *They waited, looking at him expectantly.* ● **expectancy** N-UNCOUNT ❑ *...an air of expectancy.* 2 → see also **life expectancy** 3 ADJ BEFORE N An **expectant** mother or father is someone whose baby is going to be born soon.

expectation /ˌekspek'teɪʃən/ (**expectations**) 1 N-VAR Your **expectations** are your beliefs that a particular thing will happen. ❑ *My expectation is that the price will rise.* ❑ *The air was tense with expectation.* 2 N-COUNT A person's **expectations** are beliefs which they have about the way someone should behave or something should happen. ❑ *She tried to live up to other people's expectations.*

expedient /ɪk'spiːdiənt/ (**expedients**) N-COUNT & ADJ An **expedient** is an action that achieves a particular purpose, but may not be morally right. You can also say that **it is expedient to** do something. ❑ *It was only by the expedient of complaining very loudly that Mr Stewart was finally let inside.* ❑ *It was expedient for us to be nice to him if we wanted to do well.* ● **expediency** N-UNCOUNT ❑ *Tony Blair's political expediency was obvious.*

expedition /ˌekspɪ'dɪʃən/ (**expeditions**) N-COUNT An **expedition** is a journey made for a particular purpose such as exploration.

Word Link *pel ≈ driving, forcing : compel, expel, propel*

Word Link *puls ≈ driving, pushing : compulsion, expulsion, impulse*

expel /ɪk'spel/ (**expels, expelling, expelled**) 1 V-T If someone **is expelled from** a school or organization, they are officially told to leave because they have behaved badly. ❑ *Darren was expelled from school for fighting.* ● **expulsion** /ɪk'spʌlʃən/ N-UNCOUNT ❑ *...her expulsion from secondary school.* 2 V-T If people **are expelled from** a place, they are made to leave it, usually by force. ❑ *Several patients were expelled from hospital.* ● **expulsion** N-UNCOUNT ❑ *...the expulsion of illegal workers.* 3 V-T To **expel** something such as a gas means to force it out. ❑ *He groaned, expelling the air from his lungs.*

expend /ɪk'spend/ (**expends, expending, expended**) V-T To **expend** energy, time, or money means to spend it or use it.

expenditure /ɪk'spendɪtʃə/ (**expenditures**) 1 N-VAR **Expenditure** is the spending of money on something, or the money that is spent on something. ❑ *...government expenditure on education.* 2 N-UNCOUNT **Expenditure of** energy or time is using it for a particular purpose.

expense /ɪk'spens/ (**expenses**) 1 N-VAR **Expense** is the money that something costs you or that you need to spend in order to do something. ❑ *Travel insurance may seem an unnecessary expense, but it is a must.* ❑ *...household expenses.* 2 N-PLURAL Your **expenses** are the money you spend while doing something in the course of your work,

E

Word Web experiment

Scientists learn much of what they know through **controlled experiments**. The **scientific method** provides a dependable way to understand natural **phenomena**. The first step in any experiment is **observation**. During this stage researchers examine the situation and ask a question about it. They may also read what others have discovered about it. Next, they state a **hypothesis**. Then they use the hypothesis to design an experiment and **predict** what will happen. Next comes the **testing** phase. Often researchers do several experiments using different **variables**. If all of the **evidence** supports the hypothesis, it becomes a new **theory**.

which will be paid back to you afterwards. ❑ *...travelling expenses.* 3 PHRASE If you do something **at** your **own expense**, you pay for it. ❑ *She travelled at her own expense to Russia.* 4 PHRASE If someone makes a joke **at** your **expense**, they do it to make you seem foolish.

expensive /ɪk'spensɪv/ ADJ If something is **expensive**, it costs a lot of money. ❑ *Cars are so expensive in this country.* ❑ *The most expensive houses are in the north of the city.* ● **expensively** ADV ❑ *She was expensively dressed.*

Thesaurus *expensive* Also look up:

ADJ. costly, pricey; *(ant.)* cheap, economical, inexpensive

experience /ɪk'spɪəriəns/ (**experiences, experiencing, experienced**) 1 N-UNCOUNT **Experience** is knowledge or skill in a particular job or activity, which you have gained from doing that job or activity. ❑ *She has experience of working with children.* ● **experienced** ADJ ❑ *...very experienced nurses.* 2 N-UNCOUNT **Experience** is used to refer to the past events, knowledge, and feelings that make up someone's life or character. ❑ *Experience has taught me to be careful.* 3 N-COUNT An **experience** is something that happens to you or something that you do. ❑ *Playing international rugby is a great experience.* 4 V-T If you **experience** a situation or feeling, it happens to you or you are affected by it. ❑ *Gordon says he experienced unhappiness throughout his time at school.*

Thesaurus *experience* Also look up:

N. know-how, knowledge, wisdom; *(ant.)* inexperience 1

Word Partnership Use *experience* with:

ADJ. **professional** experience 1
valuable experience 1 2 3
past experience, **shared** experience 2 3
learning experience, **religious** experience, **traumatic** experience 3
N. **work** experience 1
life experience 2
experience **a loss**, experience **symptoms** 4

experiment /ɪk'sperɪmənt/ (**experiments, experimenting, experimented**) 1 N-VAR An **experiment** is a scientific test which is done to discover what happens to something in particular conditions. ❑ *He carried out experiments with vaccines against typhoid fever.* 2 V-I If you **experiment with** something, or if you **experiment on** it, you do scientific tests to discover what happens to that thing in particular conditions. ❑ *The professor experimented on rabbits.* ● **experimentation** N-UNCOUNT ❑ *...animal experimentation.* 3 N-VAR An **experiment** is the trying out of a new idea or method in order to see what it is like and what effects it has. ❑ *...the country's five year experiment in democracy.* 4 V-I To **experiment** means to try out a new idea or method, in order to see what it is like and what effects it has. ❑ *Students should be allowed to experiment.* ● **experimentation** N-UNCOUNT ❑ *...musical experimentation.*
→ see Word Web: **experiment**
→ see **laboratory, science**

Word Partnership Use *experiment* with:

V. **conduct an** experiment 1
perform an experiment, **try an** experiment 1 2
ADJ. **scientific** experiment 1
simple experiment 1-3

experimental /ɪkˌsperɪ'mentəl/ 1 ADJ Something that is **experimental** is new or uses new ideas or methods. ❑ *...experimental pieces of music.* 2 ADJ BEFORE N **Experimental** means relating to scientific experiments. ❑ *...experimental research methods.* ● **experimentally** ADV ❑ *The sheep were experimentally given the disease.*

expert /'ekspɜːt/ (**experts**) 1 ADJ & N-COUNT If someone is **expert at** doing something, or if they are an **expert**, he or she is very skilled at doing something or knows a lot about a particular subject. ❑ *The doctors are expert at finding out what is wrong.* ❑ *They are experts on animal health.* ● **expertly** ADV ❑ *The writer is expertly played by the actor John Gordon-Sinclair.* 2 ADJ BEFORE N **Expert** advice or help is given by someone who has studied a subject thoroughly or who is very skilled at a particular job. ❑ *We'll need an expert opinion.*

Word Partnership Use *expert* with:

ADJ. **leading** expert 1
N. expert **advice**, expert **opinion**, expert **witness** 2

expertise /ˌekspɜː'tiːz/ N-UNCOUNT **Expertise** is special skill or knowledge. ❑ *...legal expertise.*

expire /ɪk'spaɪə/ (**expires, expiring, expired**) V-I When something such as a contract or a visa **expires**, it comes to an end or is no longer valid. ❑ *My passport has expired.*

explain /ɪk'spleɪn/ (**explains, explaining, explained**) **1** V-T If you **explain** something, you give details about it or describe it so that it can be understood. ❑ *I had a meeting with him and explained the situation.* ❑ *'They have a plan,' she explained.* **2** V-T If you **explain** something that has happened, you give reasons for it. ❑ *The receptionist apologized for the delay, explaining that it had been a busy day.* ❑ *Explain yourself to me.*

▶ **explain away** PHR-VERB If someone **explains away** a mistake or a bad situation that they are responsible for, they try to indicate that it is unimportant or that it is not really their fault. ❑ *I noticed blood on his clothing but he explained it away.*

Thesaurus *explain* Also look up:

V.	describe, tell **1**
	account for, justify **2**

explanation /ˌekspləˈneɪʃən/ (**explanations**) N-VAR If you give an **explanation**, you give reasons why something happened, or describe something in detail. ❑ *The parents want an honest explanation of what happened.*

Word Partnership Use *explanation* with:

ADJ.	**brief** explanation, **detailed** explanation, **logical** explanation, **only** explanation, **possible** explanation
V.	**give an** explanation, **offer an** explanation, **provide an** explanation

explanatory /ɪk'splænətəri, AM -tɔːri/ ADJ Something that is **explanatory** explains something by giving details about it. [FORMAL] ❑ *...explanatory notes.*

explicit /ɪk'splɪsɪt/ **1** ADJ Something that is **explicit** is shown or expressed clearly and openly, without hiding anything. ❑ *...explicit information about how to solve the problem.* ● **explicitly** ADV ❑ *...explicitly political activities.* **2** ADJ AFTER LINK-V If you are **explicit about** something, you express yourself clearly and openly. ❑ *Mr Blair needs to be more explicit about his plans.* ● **explicitly** ADV ❑ *She talked very explicitly about her illness.*

Word Link *ex ≈ away, from, out* : **ex**ceed, **ex**it, **ex**plode

explode /ɪk'spləʊd/ (**explodes, exploding, exploded**) **1** V-I If something such as a bomb **explodes**, it bursts with great force. ❑ *The bomb exploded, killing both men.* **2** V-I You can say that a person **explodes** when they express strong feelings suddenly and violently. ❑ *Simon exploded with anger.*

→ see **firework**

Thesaurus *explode* Also look up:

V.	blow up, erupt, go off **1**

exploit (**exploits, exploiting, exploited**) **1** V-T /ɪk'splɔɪt/ If someone **exploits** you, they unfairly use your work or ideas and give you little in return. ❑ *Some people say that he exploited his friends.* ● **exploitation** N-UNCOUNT ❑ *We must protect the staff and stop exploitation.* **2** V-T To **exploit** something means to use it to gain an advantage for yourself. ❑ *She has a talent for seeing and exploiting opportunities.* ● **exploitation** N-UNCOUNT ❑ *...their exploitation of the voting system.* **3** V-T To **exploit** resources or raw materials means to develop them and use them for industry or commercial activities. ● **exploitation** N-UNCOUNT ❑ *...the exploitation of oil.* **4** N-COUNT /'eksplɔɪt/ Someone's **exploits** are the brave or interesting things they have done. ❑ *...his exploits during the war.*

exploratory /ɪk'splɒrətri, AM -'plɔːrətɔːri/ ADJ **Exploratory** actions are done to discover or learn something. ❑ *...exploratory surgery.*

explore /ɪk'splɔː/ (**explores, exploring, explored**) **1** V-T/V-I If you **explore**, or **explore** a place, you travel around it to find out what it is like. ❑ *The best way to explore the area is in a boat.* ● **exploration** /ˌekspləˈreɪʃən/ (**explorations**) N-VAR ❑ *...space exploration.* ● **explorer** (**explorers**) N-COUNT ❑ *...Arctic explorers.* **2** V-T If you **explore** an idea, you think about it carefully to decide whether it is a good one. ❑ *The city is exploring the idea of building a youth hostel.* **3** V-I If people **explore for** a substance such as oil or minerals, they study an area and do tests on the land to see whether they can find it. ● **exploration** N-UNCOUNT ❑ *...oil exploration.*

explosion /ɪk'spləʊʒən/ (**explosions**) **1** N-COUNT An **explosion** is a sudden violent burst of energy, for example one caused by a bomb. ❑ *Six soldiers were injured in the explosion.* **2** N-COUNT An **explosion** of something is a large and rapid increase of it. ❑ *...the population explosion in North Africa.*

explosive /ɪk'spləʊsɪv/ (**explosives**) **1** N-VAR & ADJ An **explosive**, or an **explosive** substance or device, is a substance or device that can cause an explosion. **2** ADJ An **explosive** situation is likely to have serious or dangerous effects.

→ see **tunnel**

exponent /ɪk'spəʊnənt/ (**exponents**) **1** N-COUNT An **exponent of** an idea, theory, or plan is someone who speaks or writes in support of it. [FORMAL] ❑ *...an exponent of free speech.* **2** N-COUNT An **exponent of** a particular skill or activity is a person who is good at it. ❑ *...an exponent of classical Indian music.*

Word Link *port ≈ carrying* : ex**port**, im**port**, **port**able

export (**exports, exporting, exported**)

verb /ɪk'spɔːt/, noun /'ekspɔːt/.

1 V-T & N-UNCOUNT To **export** goods means to sell them to another country. Selling goods to another country is called **export**. ❑ *The cheese is exported worldwide.* ❑ *The company produces 200,000 cars a year, mostly for export.* ● **exporter** (**exporters**) N-COUNT ❑ *...banana exporters.* **2** N-COUNT **Exports** are goods which are sold to another country and sent there. ❑ *Ghana's main export is cocoa.*

expose /ɪk'spəʊz/ (**exposes, exposing, exposed**) **1** V-T To **expose** something means to uncover it and make it visible. ❑ *For a second his face was exposed.* **2** V-T If you **are exposed to** something dangerous, you are put in a situation in which it might harm you. ❑ *The workers were exposed to dangerous chemicals.* **3** V-T To **expose** a person or

e

situation means to reveal the truth about them. ❑ *A video exposed them as violent criminals.* **4** ADJ An **exposed** place has no natural protection against bad weather or enemies. ❑ *The camp was on an exposed hillside.*

exposition /ˌekspəˈzɪʃən/ (**expositions**) N-COUNT An **exposition of** an idea or theory is a detailed explanation of it. [FORMAL]

exposure /ɪkˈspəʊʒə/ (**exposures**) **1** N-UNCOUNT **Exposure to** something dangerous means being in a situation where it might affect you. ❑ *Too much exposure to the sun is bad for your skin.* **2** N-UNCOUNT **Exposure** is the harmful effect on your body caused by very cold weather. ❑ *Two people died of exposure.* **3** N-UNCOUNT **Exposure** is publicity. ❑ *He wants to get the artists more exposure.* **4** N-UNCOUNT The **exposure** of a well-known person is the revealing of the fact that they are bad or immoral in some way. ❑ *...the exposure of Anthony Blunt as a former spy.* **5** N-COUNT In photography, an **exposure** is a single photograph.

expound /ɪkˈspaʊnd/ (**expounds, expounding, expounded**) V-T If you **expound** an idea or opinion, you give a clear and detailed explanation of it. [FORMAL] ❑ *Schmidt liked to expound his views on economics.*

express /ɪkˈspres/ (**expresses, expressing, expressed**) **1** V-T When you **express** an idea or feeling, you show what you think or feel. ❑ *The president expressed the hope that 2007 would be a year for peace.* ❑ *I find it difficult to express myself.* **2** V-T If an idea or feeling **expresses itself** in some way, it can be clearly seen in someone's actions. ❑ *Frustration often expresses itself as anger.* **3** V-T If you **express** a quantity in a particular form, you write it down in that form. [TECHNICAL] ❑ *It is expressed as a percentage.* **4** ADJ BEFORE N An **express** command or order is stated clearly. [FORMAL] ❑ *The team's visit to the nightclub was against the express wishes of the coach.* ● **expressly** ADV ❑ *Suicide is expressly forbidden in Buddhism.* **5** ADJ BEFORE N An **express** intention or purpose is deliberate or specific. ❑ *I bought my first camera for the express purpose of taking photos of trains.* ● **expressly** ADV ❑ *...projects expressly designed to help farmers.* **6** ADJ BEFORE N An **express** service is one in which things are done faster than usual. ❑ *...an express delivery service.* **7** N-COUNT An **express** is a fast train or coach which stops at very few places.

Word Partnership Use *express* with:

N. express **appreciation**, express ***your* emotions**, express **gratitude**, express **sympathy**, **words to** express ***something*** **1**
express **purpose** **5**
express **mail**, express **service** **6**

expression /ɪkˈspreʃən/ (**expressions**) **1** N-COUNT An **expression** is a word or phrase. ❑ *'Craic' is an Irish expression for fun.* **2** N-VAR The **expression of** ideas or feelings is the showing of them through words, actions, or art. ❑ *...expressions of concern.* ❑ *...artistic expression.* **3** N-VAR Your **expression** is the way that your face shows what you are thinking or feeling.

expressive /ɪkˈspresɪv/ ADJ Something that is **expressive** indicates clearly a person's feelings or intentions. ❑ *...her wonderfully expressive face.* ❑ *...poems expressive of love for someone.* ● **expressively** ADV ❑ *He moved his hands expressively.*

expulsion /ɪkˈspʌlʃən/ → see **expel**

exquisite /ɪkˈskwɪzɪt, ˈekskwɪzɪt/ ADJ **Exquisite** means extremely beautiful. ❑ *His voice is exquisite.* ❑ *...her exquisite handwriting.* ● **exquisitely** ADV ❑ *...exquisitely made dolls' houses.*

extend /ɪkˈstend/ (**extends, extending, extended**) **1** V-I If something **extends for** a particular distance or time, it continues for that distance or time. ❑ *The caves extend for 18 kilometres.* ❑ *His career in cricket extended from 1894 to 1920.* **2** V-I If an object **extends from** a surface, it sticks out from it. ❑ *A six-foot roof extended from the garden's tall fence.* **3** V-I If something **extends to** a group of people, things, or activities, it includes or affects them. ❑ *The service extends to wrapping and delivering gifts.* **4** V-T If you **extend** something, you make it bigger, or make it last longer or include more. ❑ *We thought about extending the house.* ❑ *They have extended the deadline by twenty-four hours.* **5** V-T If you **extend** a part of your body, you straighten it or stretch it out. ❑ *Marshall extended his hand to Kelly.* **6** V-T To **extend** an offer or invitation to someone means to make it. [FORMAL]

extension /ɪkˈstenʃən/ (**extensions**) **1** N-COUNT An **extension** is a new room or building which is added to an existing building. ❑ *...the new extension to London's National Gallery.* **2** N-COUNT An **extension** is an extra period of time for which something continues to exist or be valid. ❑ *...an extension to their visas.* **3** N-COUNT Something that is an **extension of** something else is a development of it that includes or affects more people, things, or activities. ❑ *They objected to the extension of police powers.* **4** N-COUNT An **extension** is a telephone line that is connected to the switchboard of a company or institution, and that has its own number. ❑ *...extension 308.*

extensive /ɪkˈstensɪv/ **1** ADJ Something that is **extensive** covers a large area. ❑ *The hospital stands in extensive grounds.* ● **extensively** ADV ❑ *She has travelled extensively.* **2** ADJ If something is **extensive**, it is very great. ❑ *The fire caused extensive damage.* ● **extensively** ADV ❑ *This edition has been extensively re-written.* **3** ADJ **Extensive** means covering many details, ideas, or items. ❑ *The meeting is given extensive coverage in today's newspapers.* ● **extensively** ADV ❑ *All these issues have been extensively researched.*

extent /ɪkˈstent/ **1** N-SING **The extent of** something is its length, area, or size. ❑ *Global warming has reduced the extent of the rain forest.* **2** N-SING **The extent of** a situation is how great, important, or serious it is. ❑ *We don't know the extent of his injuries.* **3** N-UNCOUNT You use **extent** to say how true something is. ❑ *It was and, to a large extent, still is a good show.* ❑ *I got more nervous to the extent that I was almost physically sick.*

Word Partnership Use *extent* with:

N. extent **of the damage** **1**
V. **determine the** extent, **know the** extent **2**
ADJ. **full** extent, **lesser** extent **2**
a certain extent **3**

exterior /ɪkˈstɪəriə/ (**exteriors**) **1** N-COUNT

The **exterior** of something is its outside surface. ❑ *...the stone exterior of the building.* **2** N-COUNT You can refer to someone's outward appearance and behaviour as their **exterior**. ❑ *Beneath Pat's tough exterior is a shy and sensitive girl.* **3** ADJ BEFORE N You use **exterior** to refer to the outside parts of something, or to things that are outside something. ❑ *...exterior walls.*

Thesaurus	*exterior* Also look up:
N.	coating, cover, shell, skin **1**
ADJ.	external, outer, surface **3**

exterminate /ɪk'stɜːmɪneɪt/ (**exterminates, exterminating, exterminated**) V-T To **exterminate** a group of people or animals means to kill all of them. ❑ *We made a huge effort to exterminate the rats.* • **extermination** N-UNCOUNT ❑ *...the extermination of wild dogs.*

external /ɪk'stɜːnəl/ **1** ADJ BEFORE N **External** means happening, coming from, or existing outside a place, person, or area of activity. ❑ *...external influences.* ❑ *...the department for external affairs.* • **externally** ADV ❑ *Vitamins can be applied externally to the skin.* **2** ADJ BEFORE N **External** is used to describe people who come into an organization from outside to do a job there. ❑ *...external examiners.*
→ see **ear**

extinct /ɪk'stɪŋkt/ **1** ADJ If a species of animals is **extinct**, it no longer has any living members. ❑ *The wolf became extinct in Britain 250 years ago.* **2** ADJ An **extinct** volcano does not erupt or is unlikely to erupt.

extinction /ɪk'stɪŋkʃən/ N-UNCOUNT The **extinction** of a species of animal is the death of all its remaining members. ❑ *Tigers could face extinction within 10 years.*

extinguish /ɪk'stɪŋgwɪʃ/ (**extinguishes, extinguishing, extinguished**) V-T If you **extinguish** a fire or a light, you stop it burning or shining. ❑ *It took about an hour to extinguish the fire.*

extol /ɪk'stəʊl/ (**extols, extolling, extolled**) V-T If you **extol** something, you praise it enthusiastically. ❑ *He extols the virtues of family life.*

extra /'ekstrə/ (**extras**) **1** ADJ BEFORE N & ADV An **extra** thing, person, or amount is another one that is added to others of the same kind. ❑ *...extra blankets.* ❑ *...extra staff.* ❑ *The school will get £13,500 extra a year to spend on computers.* **2** N-COUNT **Extras** are things that are not necessary but make something more comfortable, useful, or enjoyable. ❑ *Extras on the DVD include an interview with JK Rowling.* **3** N-COUNT **Extras** are additional amounts of money added to the basic price of something. ❑ *There are no hidden extras.* **4** N-COUNT An **extra** is a person who plays an unimportant part in a film. **5** ADV You can use **extra** in front of adjectives and adverbs to emphasize the quality that they are describing. [INFORMAL] ❑ *You have to be extra careful.*

Word Link	*extra ≈ outside of* : **extract, extradite, extraordinary**

extract (**extracts, extracting, extracted**)

verb /ɪk'strækt/, noun /'ekstrækt/.

1 V-T & N-VAR To **extract** a substance means to obtain it from something else, for example by using industrial or chemical processes. An **extract** is a substance that has been obtained in this way. ❑ *You can extract citric acid from the juice of oranges.* ❑ *Some plant extracts are natural painkillers.* • **extraction** N-UNCOUNT ❑ *...the extraction of oil.* **2** V-T If you **extract** something **from** a place, you take it out or pull it out. [LITERARY] ❑ *He extracted a small notebook from his pocket.* **3** V-T If you **extract** information or a response **from** someone, you get it from them with difficulty. ❑ *He was not able to extract any information from the three men.* **4** V-T When a dentist **extracts** a tooth, he or she removes it from the patient's mouth. • **extraction** (**extractions**) N-VAR ❑ *The extraction was painless.* **5** N-COUNT An **extract from** a book or piece of writing is a small part of it that is printed or published separately.
→ see **industry, mineral**

extradite /'ekstrədaɪt/ (**extradites, extraditing, extradited**) V-T If someone **is extradited**, they are officially sent back to their own country to stand trial for a crime. [FORMAL] • **extradition** /ˌekstrə'dɪʃən/ (**extraditions**) N-VAR ❑ *The British government requested his extradition.*

extraordinary /ɪk'strɔːdənri, AM -neri/ **1** ADJ An **extraordinary** person or thing has some extremely good or special quality. ❑ *...an extraordinary musician.* • **extraordinarily** /ɪk'strɔːdənrɪli, AM -nerɪli/ ADV ❑ *She's extraordinarily talented.* **2** ADJ If you describe something as **extraordinary**, you mean that it is very unusual or surprising. ❑ *What an extraordinary thing to happen!* • **extraordinarily** ADV ❑ *Rainfall was extraordinarily high.*

extravagance /ɪk'strævəgəns/ (**extravagances**) N-COUNT An **extravagance** is something that you spend money on but cannot really afford. ❑ *Her only extravagance was books.*

extravagant /ɪk'strævəgənt/ **1** ADJ Someone who is **extravagant** spends more money than they can afford or uses more of something than is reasonable. ❑ *My mother thinks I am extravagant with money but it is my money and I will spend it on whatever I want.* • **extravagantly** ADV ❑ *Jeff shopped extravagantly for presents.* • **extravagance** N-UNCOUNT ❑ *...financial extravagance.* **2** ADJ Something that is **extravagant** costs more money than you can afford or uses more of something than is reasonable. ❑ *Her aunt gave her an unusually extravagant gift.* • **extravagantly** ADV ❑ *...an extravagantly expensive stereo.* **3** ADJ **Extravagant** behaviour is extreme behaviour that is often done for a particular effect. ❑ *...extravagant generosity.* • **extravagantly** ADV ❑ *She thanked her family extravagantly.* **4** ADJ **Extravagant** claims or ideas are unrealistic or impractical; used showing disapproval. ❑ *...extravagant claims for success.*

extravaganza /ɪkˌstrævə'gænzə/ (**extravaganzas**) N-COUNT An **extravaganza** is a very elaborate and expensive show or performance. ❑ *...a magnificent firework extravaganza.*

extreme /ɪk'striːm/ (**extremes**) **1** ADJ **Extreme** means very great in degree or intensity. ❑ *...people living in extreme poverty.* • **extremely** ADV ❑ *My mobile phone is extremely useful.* **2** ADJ You use **extreme** to describe situations and behaviour which are much more severe or unusual than you would expect. ❑ *'I would never do anything so*

e

E

extreme,' she said. 3 ADJ The **extreme** point or edge of something is its farthest point or edge. ❑ *...winds from the extreme north.* 4 N-COUNT You can use **extremes** to refer to situations or types of behaviour that have completely opposite qualities to each other. ❑ *...the extremes of success and failure.* 5 PHRASE You use **in the extreme** after an adjective to emphasize how bad or undesirable something is. ❑ *He has been stupid in the extreme.*

Word Partnership Use *extreme* with:

N.	extreme **caution**, extreme **difficulty** 1 extreme **case**, extreme **sports** 2 extreme **left**, extreme **right**, extreme **views** 3 4
ADJ.	**the opposite** extreme 4

extremist /ɪk'stri:mɪst/ (**extremists**) N-COUNT If you describe someone as an **extremist**, you disapprove of them because they try to bring about political change by using violent or extreme methods. ❑ *...members of the West German extremist group.* ● **extremism** N-UNCOUNT ❑ *...right-wing extremism.*

extrovert /'ekstrəvɜ:t/ (**extroverts**) N-COUNT & ADJ An **extrovert**, or someone who is **extrovert**, is very active, lively, and sociable. ❑ *His footballing skills and extrovert personality made him very popular with the public.*

exuberant /ɪg'zju:bərənt, AM -'zu:b-/ 1 ADJ Someone who is **exuberant** is full of energy, excitement, and cheerfulness. ❑ *She has a lively, exuberant personality.* ● **exuberance** N-UNCOUNT ❑ *Semionova has the confidence and exuberance of youth.* ● **exuberantly** ADV ❑ *They both laughed exuberantly.* 2 ADJ If you describe something as **exuberant**, you like it because it is lively, exciting, and full of energy and life. ❑ *His clothes had a kind of exuberant style.* ● **exuberance** N-UNCOUNT ❑ *They performed with exuberance and enthusiasm.* ● **exuberantly** ADV ❑ *They danced and sang exuberantly.*

exude /ɪg'zju:d, AM -'zu:d/ (**exudes, exuding, exuded**) 1 V-T/V-I If someone **exudes** a quality or feeling, or if it **exudes**, they show that they have it to a great extent. [FORMAL] ❑ *People from Barbados exude warmth and friendliness.* 2 V-T/V-I If something **exudes** a liquid or smell, or if a liquid or smell **exudes from** it, the liquid or smell comes out of it. [FORMAL] ❑ *The factory exuded a horrible smell.*

eye /aɪ/ (**eyes, eyeing** or **eying, eyed**) 1 N-COUNT Your **eyes** are the parts of your body with which you see. ● **-eyed** ❑ *...a blonde-haired, blue-eyed little girl.* ❑ *...wide-eyed with horror.* 2 N-COUNT You use **eye** when you are talking about a person's ability to judge things or about the way in which they are considering or dealing with things. ❑ *He has an eye for quality.* ❑ *The practice of religion in America sometimes seems strange to European eyes.* 3 V-T If you **eye** someone or something in a particular way, you look at them carefully in that way. ❑ *Sally eyed Claire with interest.* 4 N-COUNT An **eye** is a small metal loop which a hook fits into. 5 PHRASE If you say that something happens **before** your **eyes**, **in front of** your **eyes**, or **under** your **eyes**, you are emphasizing that it happens where you can see it clearly or while you are watching it. ❑ *He saw the plane crash before his eyes.* 6 PHRASE If something **catches** your **eye**, you suddenly notice it. ❑ *A quick movement across the room caught his eye.* 7 PHRASE If you **catch** someone's **eye**, you do something to attract their attention, so that you can speak to them. ❑ *He tried to catch her eye, but she did not see him.* 8 PHRASE To **clap eyes on** someone or something, or to **set** or **lay eyes on** them, means to see them. [INFORMAL] ❑ *It was the most evil human face I ever set eyes on.* 9 PHRASE If you **have** your **eye on** something, you want to have it. [INFORMAL] ❑ *I've had my eye on a new dress.* 10 PHRASE If you **keep an eye on** something or someone, you watch them carefully, for example to make sure that they are safe, or are not causing trouble. ❑ *He has been sent here to keep an eye on Benedict.* 11 PHRASE If you **keep** your **eyes open** or **keep an eye out for** someone or something, you watch for them carefully. [INFORMAL] ❑ *We kept our eyes open for any sign of the stolen car.* ❑ *Keep an eye out for the police.* 12 PHRASE If you **look** someone **in the eye** or **meet** their **eyes**, you look directly at them in a bold open way, for example in order to make them realize that you are not afraid of them or that you are telling the truth. ❑ *She felt so silly she could not look Robert in the eye.* ❑ *She met my eyes, but offered no explanation.* 13 PHRASE If someone sees or considers something **through** your **eyes**, they consider it in the way that you do, from your point of view.
→ see Word Web: **eye**
→ see **cry, face, hurricane**

eyeball /'aɪbɔ:l/ (**eyeballs**) N-COUNT Your **eyeballs** are the white balls that form your eyes.

eyebrow /'aɪbraʊ/ (**eyebrows**) 1 N-COUNT Your **eyebrows** are the lines of hair which grow above your eyes. 2 PHRASE If something causes you to **raise an eyebrow** or to **raise** your **eyebrows**, it causes you to feel surprised or disapproving. ❑ *He raised his eyebrows at some of the ideas.*
→ see **face**

'eye ˌcandy or **eye-candy** N-UNCOUNT **Eye candy** is used to refer to people or things that are attractive to look at but are not interesting

Word Web eye

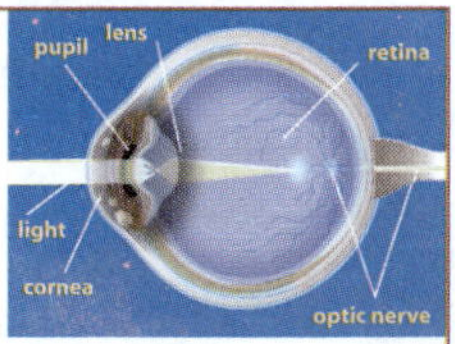

Light enters the **eye** through the **cornea**. The cornea bends the light and directs it through the **pupil**. The colored **iris** opens and closes the **lens**. This helps focus the **image** clearly on the **retina**. Nerve cells in the retina change the light into electrical signals. The **optic nerve** then carries these signals to the brain. In a **short-sighted** person the light rays focus in front of the lens. The image comes into focus in back of the lens in a **long-sighted** person. An irregularity in the cornea can cause **astigmatism**. Glasses or **contact lenses** can correct all three problems.

in other ways. [INFORMAL] ❑ *If you want to annoy contemporary artists, tell them that their work is 'eye-candy'.*

'eye-catching ADJ Something that is **eye-catching** is very noticeable. ❑ *...an eye-catching headline on the front page of the newspaper.*

eyelash /'aɪlæʃ/ (**eyelashes**) N-COUNT Your **eyelashes** are the hairs which grow on the edges of your eyelids.
→ see **face**

eyelid /'aɪlɪd/ (**eyelids**) N-COUNT Your **eyelids** are the two flaps of skin which cover your eyes when they are closed.
→ see **face**

eyesight /'aɪsaɪt/ N-UNCOUNT Your **eyesight** is your ability to see. ❑ *He has very poor eyesight.*

eyewitness /'aɪwɪtnəs/ (**eyewitnesses**) N-COUNT An **eyewitness** is a person who has seen an event and can therefore describe it, for example in a law court.

Ff

fable /ˈfeɪbəl/ (**fables**) N-VAR A **fable** is a traditional story which teaches a moral lesson.

F

fabric /ˈfæbrɪk/ (**fabrics**) **1** N-VAR **Fabric** is cloth. ❑ *...red cotton fabric.* ❑ *...silk and other delicate fabrics.* **2** N-SING **The fabric of** a society is its structure and customs. [FORMAL] ❑ *Years of civil war have ruined the country's social fabric.* **3** N-SING **The fabric of** a building is its walls, roof, and other parts. [FORMAL]
→ see **quilt**

fabricate /ˈfæbrɪkeɪt/ (**fabricates, fabricating, fabricated**) V-T If someone **fabricates** information, they invent it in order to deceive people. [FORMAL] ❑ *She fabricated the story about Clinton.* • **fabrication** (**fabrications**) N-VAR ❑ *The report in the newspapers was pure fabrication.*

Word Link	***ous* ≈ having the qualities of: dangerous, fabulous, nutritious**

fabulous /ˈfæbjʊləs/ ADJ You use **fabulous** to emphasize how wonderful or impressive you think something is. • **fabulously** ADV ❑ *She has fabulously rich parents.*

facade or **façade** /fəˈsɑːd/ (**facades**)
1 N-COUNT **The facade of** a large building is the outside of its front wall. ❑ *...the cathedral's facade.* **2** N-SING You say that something is a **facade** when its outward appearance deliberately gives a wrong impression. ❑ *Behind the confident facade is a sad and lonely man.*

face
❶ NOUN USES
❷ VERB USES

face /feɪs/ (**faces**)
❶ **1** N-COUNT Your **face** is the front of your head from your chin to your forehead. ❑ *She had a beautiful face.* ❑ *His face was covered with wrinkles.* **2** N-COUNT **The face of** a cliff, mountain, or building is a vertical surface or side of it. **3** N-COUNT The **face** of a clock is the surface which shows the time. **4** N-SING If you refer to a particular **face of** something, you mean one particular aspect of it. ❑ *...the unacceptable face of politics.* **5** N-UNCOUNT If you **lose face**, something that you do or something that happens makes people lose respect for you. If you are able to **save face**, you do something which restores your reputation. ❑ *If I cancel the wedding, I'll lose face with my family and friends.* **6** → see also **face value** **7** PHRASE If you take a particular action or attitude **in the face of** a problem or difficulty, you respond to that problem or difficulty in that way. ❑ *The women showed courage in the face of enormous difficulties.* **8** PHRASE If you **make** or **pull**

Picture Dictionary face

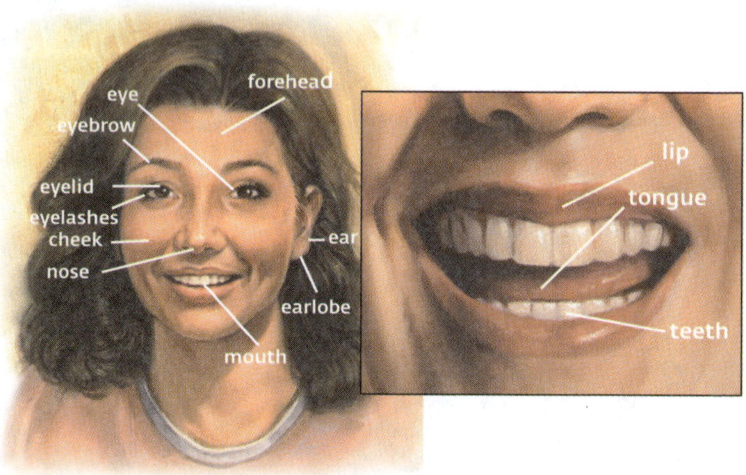

a face, you show your dislike for something by, for example, sticking out your tongue. **9** PHRASE If you manage to **keep a straight face**, you manage to look serious, although you want to laugh.
→ see Picture Dictionary: **face**

face /feɪs/ (**faces, facing, faced**)
2 **1** V-T To **face** a particular direction means to look in that direction from a position directly opposite it. ❑ *They stood facing each other.* ❑ *The garden faces south.* **2** V-T If you **are faced with** something difficult or unpleasant, you have to deal with it. ❑ *We are faced with a serious problem.* **3** V-T If you cannot **face** something, you do not feel able to deal with it because it seems so difficult or unpleasant. ❑ *She cannot face going out alone any more.* ❑ *I couldn't face seeing anyone.*
▶ **face up to** PHR-VERB If you **face up to** something difficult or unpleasant, you accept it and try to deal with it. ❑ *They are facing up to a future without their best teacher.*

faceless /ˈfeɪsləs/ ADJ If you describe someone or something as **faceless**, you dislike them because they have no character or individuality. ❑ *...faceless managers.*

facet /ˈfæsɪt, -set/ (**facets**) N-COUNT A **facet of** something is a single part or aspect of it. ❑ *The government is involved in every facet of people's lives.*

ˌface ˈvalue **1** N-SING The **face value** of things such as banknotes or tickets is the price stated on it. ❑ *He sold the ticket for twice its face value.* **2** PHRASE If you take something **at face value**, you accept it without thinking about it very much.

facial /ˈfeɪʃəl/ ADJ BEFORE N **Facial** is used to describe things that relate to your face. ❑ *...his facial expression.*

facilitate /fəˈsɪlɪteɪt/ (**facilitates, facilitating, facilitated**) V-T To **facilitate** a process means to make it easier. [FORMAL] ❑ *He was there to facilitate understanding between the two countries.*

facility /fəˈsɪlɪti/ (**facilities**) **1** N-COUNT **Facilities** are buildings, equipment, or services that are provided for a particular purpose. ❑ *...nursery facilities.* **2** N-COUNT A **facility** is a useful service or feature provided by an organization or machine. ❑ *...overdraft facilities.* ❑ *This system has an e-mail facility.*

fact /fækt/ (**facts**) **1** N-COUNT **Facts** are pieces of information which can be proved to be true. ❑ *...the facts about the robbery.* **2** N-UNCOUNT When you refer to something as **fact**, you mean that it is true or correct. ❑ *It is an historical fact.* **3** PHRASE You use **the fact that** after some verbs and prepositions, for example in expressions such as **despite the fact that** and **apart from the fact that**, to link the verb or preposition with a clause. ❑ *My family now accepts the fact that I don't eat sugar or bread.* **4** PHRASE You use **in fact, in actual fact, as a matter of fact**, or **in point of fact** to indicate that you are giving more detailed information about what you have just said. ❑ *We had a bad time while you were away. In fact, we nearly split up.*
→ see **history**

Word Partnership Use *fact* with:

V.	**accept a** fact, **check the** facts, **face a** fact **1** **know for a** fact **2**
N.	fact **and fiction** **1** **as a matter of** fact **2**
ADJ.	**hard** fact, **historical** fact, **important** fact, **obvious** fact, **random** fact, **simple** fact **1**

faction /ˈfækʃən/ (**factions**) N-COUNT A **faction** is an organized group of people within a larger group who oppose some of the ideas of the larger group. ❑ *...the leader of the rival faction.* ● **factional** ADJ ❑ *The factional fighting killed 4,000 people.*

Word Link *fact, fic ≈ making : artefact, artificial, factor*

factor /ˈfæktə/ (**factors**) N-COUNT A **factor** is one of the things that affects an event or situation. ❑ *...environmental factors, such as air pollution.*

Word Link *ory ≈ place where something happens: conservatory, factory, territory*

factory /ˈfæktri/ (**factories**) N-COUNT A **factory** is a large building where machines are used to make goods in large quantities.
→ see Word Web: **factory**
→ see **mass production**

factual /ˈfæktʃuəl/ ADJ Something that is **factual** contains or refers to facts rather than theories or opinions. ❑ *The report had several factual errors.*

faculty /ˈfækəlti/ (**faculties**) **1** N-COUNT Your **faculties** are your physical and mental abilities. ❑ *...faculties of memory and reason.* **2** N-COUNT In some universities, a **faculty** is a group of related departments. ❑ *...the Faculty of Social and Political Sciences.*

fad /fæd/ (**fads**) N-COUNT You can refer to an activity or topic of interest that is very popular for

Word Web factory

Life in a 19th century **factory** was very difficult. **Employees** often **worked** twelve hours a day, six days a week. **Wages** were low and **child labour** was common. Many **workers** were not allowed to take **breaks**. Some even had to eat while working. As early as 1832, doctors warned about the dangers of **air pollution**. The 20th century brought some big changes. Workers began to join **unions**. During World War I, **government regulations** set standards for **minimum wages** and better **working conditions**. In addition, **machines** took over some of the most difficult and dangerous jobs.

f

a short time as a **fad**.
→ see **diet**

fade /feɪd/ (**fades, fading, faded**) 1 V-T/V-I When something **fades**, or when something **fades** it, it slowly becomes less intense in brightness, colour, or sound. ❑ *They watched the star for 70 days before it faded from sight.* ❑ *Ultraviolet light will fade the colours.* ❑ *His voice faded away.* • **faded** ADJ ❑ *...faded blue jeans.* 2 V-I If memories, feelings, or possibilities **fade**, they slowly become less strong. ❑ *Hope started to fade.*
▶ **fade away** or **fade out** PHR-VERB When something **fades away** or **fades out**, it slowly becomes less noticeable or less important until it ends completely. ❑ *With time, your fears will fade away.*

F

Word Partnership Use *fade* with:

N.	**colours** fade, **images** fade 1
	memories fade 2
V.	**begin to** fade 1 2
ADV.	fade **quickly** 1 2

faeces [AM **feces**] /ˈfiːsiːz/ N-UNCOUNT **Faeces** is the solid waste substance that people and animals get rid of from their body through the anus. [FORMAL]

Fahrenheit /ˈfærənhaɪt/ 1 ADJ & N-UNCOUNT **Fahrenheit** is a scale for measuring temperature, in which water freezes at 32 degrees and boils at 212 degrees. It is represented by the symbol °F. ❑ *By mid-morning, the temperature was already above 100 degrees Fahrenheit.* 2 → See note at **temperature**
→ see **climate, thermometer**

fail /feɪl/ (**fails, failing, failed**) 1 V-T/V-I If you **fail** or **fail to** do something that you were trying to do, you do not succeed in doing it. ❑ *He failed to win enough votes.* ❑ *All our plans failed miserably.* 2 V-T If someone or something **fails to** do something that they should have done, they do not do it. ❑ *He failed to tell his bank manager that he was unemployed.* ❑ *The bomb failed to explode.* 3 V-T If someone **fails** you, they do not do what you expected or trusted them to do. ❑ *The political system has failed them.* 4 V-T If someone **fails** an examination, they do not reach the standard that is required. ❑ *I failed three of my final exams.* 5 → See note at **exam** 6 V-I If something **fails**, it stops working properly. ❑ *The lights mysteriously failed.*

failing /ˈfeɪlɪŋ/ (**failings**) 1 N-COUNT **The failings of** someone or something are their faults or unsatisfactory features. ❑ *The new law's failings could ruin many companies.* 2 PHRASE You say **failing that** to introduce an alternative, in case what you have just said is not possible. ❑ *Try talking to a friend about your problems, or failing that, write down your thoughts.*

failure /ˈfeɪljə/ (**failures**) 1 N-VAR **Failure** is a lack of success in doing or achieving something. ❑ *The marriage was a failure.* 2 N-UNCOUNT Your **failure to** do something you were expected to do is the fact that you do not do it. ❑ *...failure to help British citizens.* 3 N-VAR When there is a **failure** of something, it stops working properly. ❑ *There have been a series of engine failures.* ❑ *He was treated for kidney failure.*

Word Partnership Use *failure* with:

V.	failure **to communicate** 2
ADJ.	**afraid of** failure, **complete** failure, **dismal** failure, **doomed to** failure 1
N.	**feelings of** failure, **risk of** failure, **success or** failure 1
	business failure, **engine** failure, **heart** failure, **kidney** failure, **liver** failure 3

faint /feɪnt/ (**fainter, faintest, faints, fainting, fainted**) 1 ADJ Something that is **faint** is not strong or intense. ❑ *...the soft, faint sound of water.* ❑ *Their voices grew fainter.* • **faintly** ADV ❑ *She smiled faintly.* 2 V-I & N-COUNT If you **faint**, or if you fall into a **faint**, you lose consciousness for a short time. 3 ADJ AFTER LINK-V Someone who feels **faint** feels dizzy and unsteady.

fair /feə/ (**fairer, fairest, fairs**) 1 ADJ Something or someone that is **fair** is reasonable, right, and just. ❑ *It didn't seem fair to ignore her father.* ❑ *...a very fair man.* ❑ *Try to be fair and treat the children equally.* • **fairly** ADV ❑ *...solving problems quickly and fairly.* • **fairness** N-UNCOUNT ❑ *...the fairness of the election campaign.* 2 ADJ BEFORE N A **fair** amount, degree, size, or distance is quite large. ❑ *I spent a fair bit of time walking in the park.* 3 ADJ **Fair** hair or skin is light or pale in colour. 4 ADJ When the weather is **fair**, it is not cloudy or rainy. [FORMAL] 5 N-COUNT A **fair** is an event held in a field at which people pay to ride on machines for amusement or try to win prizes in games. [BRIT] 6 N-COUNT A **fair** is an event at which people display or sell goods. ❑ *...an antiques fair.* 7 → see also **fairly** 8 PHRASE You use **fair enough** when you want to say that a statement, decision, or action seems reasonable to a certain extent, but that perhaps someone has gone beyond what is reasonable. ❑ *If you don't like it, fair enough, but there's no need to attack the whole thing.* 9 PHRASE You say **fair enough** to acknowledge what someone has just said and to indicate that you think it is reasonable. ❑ *'The message was addressed to me and I don't see why I should show it to you.'—'Fair enough.'*

Word Partnership Use *fair* with:

ADJ.	fair **and balanced** 1
N.	fair **chance**, fare **deal**, fair **fight**, fair **game**, fair **play**, fair **price**, fair **share**, fair **trade**, fair **treatment**, fair **trial** 1
	fair **amount** 2
	fair **hair**, fair **skin** 3
	craft fair, **science** fair 6

fairground /ˈfeəgraʊnd/ (**fairgrounds**) N-COUNT A **fairground** is a part of a park or field where people pay to ride on various machines for amusement or try to win prizes in games.

fairly /ˈfeəli/ 1 ADV **Fairly** means to quite a large degree. ❑ *We did fairly well.* ❑ *Were you always fairly clever at school?* 2 → See note at **rather** 3 → see also **fair**

fairy /ˈfeəri/ (**fairies**) N-COUNT A **fairy** is an imaginary creature with magical powers.
→ see **fantasy**

ˈfairy ˌtale (**fairy tales**) N-COUNT A **fairy tale** is a story for children involving magical events and imaginary creatures.

faith /feɪθ/ (**faiths**) **1** N-UNCOUNT If you have **faith in** someone or something, you feel confident about their ability or goodness. ❑ *She had faith in Mr Penleigh.* ❑ *People have lost faith in Parliament.* **2** N-COUNT A **faith** is a particular religion, such as Christianity or Buddhism. ❑ *The College welcomes students of all races, faiths, and nationalities.* **3** N-UNCOUNT **Faith** is strong religious belief. ❑ *They respect his faith.* **4** PHRASE If you do something **in good faith**, you believe that it is the right thing to do in the circumstances.

faithful /ˈfeɪθfʊl/ **1** ADJ If you are **faithful to** a person, organization, or idea, you remain firm in your support for them. ❑ *The government stayed faithful to its peace plan.* ● **faithfully** ADV ❑ *She had served the police force faithfully for many years.* **2** ADJ Someone who is **faithful to** their husband, wife, or lover does not have a sexual relationship with anyone else. ❑ *She was faithful to her husband.* **3** ADJ A **faithful** account, version, or copy of something represents or reproduces the original accurately. ❑ *Welland's film is faithful to the novel.* ● **faithfully** ADV ❑ *I translated the meaning as faithfully as possible.*

faithfully /ˈfeɪθfʊli/ CONVENTION In British English, when you start a formal or business letter with 'Dear Sir' or 'Dear Madam', you write **Yours faithfully** before your signature at the end. The usual American expression is **Sincerely yours**.

fake /feɪk/ (**fakes, faking, faked**) **1** ADJ & N-COUNT **Fake** things or **fakes** have been made to look valuable or genuine, although they are not. ❑ *The bank manager discovered the fake money.* ❑ *He owns several famous works of art, and every one of them is a fake.* **2** V-T If someone **fakes** something, they try to make it look genuine, although it is not. ❑ *He faked his own death.* ❑ *I faked a yawn.*

Thesaurus	*fake* Also look up:
ADJ.	artificial, counterfeit, imitation **1**
V.	falsify, pretend **2**

fall /fɔːl/ (**falls, falling, fell, fallen**) **1** V-I If someone or something **falls**, they move quickly downwards. ❑ *Her sunglasses fell into the sea.* ❑ *Everything fell out of the bag.* ❑ *Bombs fell in the town.* **2** V-I & N-COUNT If a person or structure **falls**, **falls down**, or **falls over**, they move from an upright position, so that they are lying on the ground. You can also say that a person **has a fall**. ❑ *The woman gripped the man to stop herself from falling.* ❑ *I hit him so hard he fell down.* ❑ *Roads have been blocked by fallen trees.* ❑ *Roger had a fall and cut his head.* **3** V-I & N-COUNT When rain or snow **falls**, or when there is a **fall of** it, it comes down from the sky. **4** V-I & N-COUNT If something **falls**, or if there is a **fall in** it, it decreases in amount, value, or strength. ❑ *Her weight fell to forty-five kilos.* ❑ *There was a sharp fall in the value of the pound.* **5** V-I & N-SING If a powerful or successful person **falls**, they suddenly lose their power or position. You can also talk about that person's **fall**. ❑ *Mrs Thatcher fell from power.* ❑ *...the fall of the dictator.* **6** LINK-VERB You can use **fall** to show that someone or something passes into another state. For example, if someone **falls** ill, they become ill. ❑ *He undid his tie and collar and fell asleep.* **7** V-I If you say that something or someone **falls into** a particular category, you mean that they belong in that category. ❑ *This music doesn't fall into the category of jazz.* **8** V-I If silence or a feeling of sadness or tiredness **falls on** a group of people, they become silent, sad, or tired. [WRITTEN] ❑ *Silence fell on the passengers as the police checked identity cards.* **9** V-I When light or shadow **falls on** something, it covers it. ❑ *A shadow suddenly fell across the doorway.* **10** V-I When night or darkness **falls**, night begins and it becomes dark. **11** N-PLURAL You can refer to a waterfall as **the falls**. ❑ *...Niagara Falls.* **12** N-VAR In American English, **fall** is the season between summer and winter. The British word is **autumn**. ❑ *...in the fall of 1991.* **13** to **fall flat** → see **flat**

▸ **fall apart** **1** PHR-VERB If something **falls apart**, it breaks into pieces because it is old or badly made. ❑ *Bit by bit the building fell apart.* **2** PHR-VERB If an organization or system **falls apart**, it becomes disorganized and inefficient. ❑ *Employees say the company is falling apart.*

▸ **fall back on** PHR-VERB If you **fall back on** something, you do it or use it after other things have failed. ❑ *He fell back on his original training as a photographer when his new business failed.*

▸ **fall behind** PHR-VERB If you **fall behind**, you do not make progress or move forward as fast as other people. ❑ *He missed school and fell behind.* ❑ *Boris is falling behind all the top players.*

▸ **fall for** **1** PHR-VERB If you **fall for** someone, you are strongly attracted to them and start loving them. ❑ *I fell for him right away.* **2** PHR-VERB If you **fall for** a lie or trick, you believe it or are deceived by it. [INFORMAL] ❑ *It was all a lie, and you fell for it!*

▸ **fall off** PHR-VERB If something **falls off**, it separates from the thing to which it was attached. ❑ *...teapots, whose lids fall off when you pour tea.*

▸ **fall out** **1** PHR-VERB If a person's hair or a tooth **falls out**, it becomes loose and separates from their body. **2** PHR-VERB If you **fall out with** someone, you have an argument with them and stop being friendly. ❑ *She fell out with her husband.* ❑ *Mum and I used to fall out a lot.*

▸ **fall through** PHR-VERB If an arrangement **falls through**, it fails to happen. ❑ *My house sale fell through.*

Usage

You can use **fall down** to talk about people and objects, but not about things like **prices**. Instead you should use the verb **fall** by itself. ❑ *Jolil tripped and fell down.* ❑ *Share prices fell sharply.*

Thesaurus	*fall* Also look up:
V.	fall down, plunge, topple over **1** **2**
	come down **3**
	drop, plunge; *(ant.)* increase, rise **4**

fallacy /ˈfæləsi/ (**fallacies**) N-COUNT A **fallacy** is an idea which many people believe to be true, but which is false. ❑ *It is a fallacy that tourism has spoiled Mallorca.*

fallen /ˈfɔːlən/ **Fallen** is the past participle of **fall**.

fallout /ˈfɔːlaʊt/ N-UNCOUNT **Fallout** is the radiation that affects an area after a nuclear explosion.

f

F

false /fɔːls/ **1** ADJ If something is **false**, it is incorrect, untrue, or mistaken. ❑ *The President was given false information.* ❑ *He gave the hospital a false name.* ● **falsely** ADV ❑ *He was falsely accused of the crime.* **2** ADJ You use **false** to describe objects which are artificial but which are intended to look like the real thing or to be used instead of the real thing. ❑ *...false teeth.* **3** ADJ If you describe a person or their behaviour as **false**, you are criticizing them for not being sincere or for hiding their real feelings. ❑ *Her smile was false.* ● **falsely** ADV ❑ *He was falsely cheerful.*

ˌfalse aˈlarm (**false alarms**) N-COUNT When you think something dangerous is about to happen, but then discover that you were mistaken, you can say that it was a **false alarm**. ❑ *The bomb threat was just a false alarm.*

ˌfalse ˈstart (**false starts**) N-COUNT A **false start** is an attempt to start something, such as a speech, project, or plan, which fails because you were not properly prepared or ready to begin.

falsify /ˈfɔːlsɪfaɪ/ (**falsifies, falsifying, falsified**) V-T If someone **falsifies** a written record, they change it in a misleading way or add untrue details to it in order to deceive people. ❑ *Gibbs falsified the bank records.*

falter /ˈfɔːltə/ (**falters, faltering, faltered**) **1** V-I If something **falters**, it weakens and seems likely to collapse or to stop. ❑ *The economy is faltering.* ❑ *...the faltering peace process.* **2** V-I If you **falter**, you hesitate and become unsure or unsteady. ❑ *Her voice faltered.*

fame /feɪm/ N-UNCOUNT If you achieve **fame**, you become very well-known. ❑ *The film earned him international fame.*

Word Partnership Use *fame* with:

V.	**bring** fame, **gain** fame, **rise to** fame
N.	**claim to** fame, fame **and fortune**, **hall of** fame
ADJ.	**international** fame

famed /feɪmd/ ADJ If you are **famed for** something, you are very well-known because of it. ❑ *The city is famed for its restaurants.*

familiar /fəˈmɪliə/ **1** ADJ If someone or something is **familiar to** you, you recognize them or know them well. ❑ *French culture is quite familiar to him .* ❑ *They are familiar faces on TV.* ● **familiarity** /fəmɪliˈærɪti/ N-UNCOUNT ❑ *...the familiarity of her face.* **2** ADJ AFTER LINK-V If you are **familiar with** something, you know it or understand it well. ❑ *He was not very familiar with the area.* ● **familiarity** N-UNCOUNT ❑ *The enemy had the advantage of familiarity with the mountains.* **3** ADJ If you behave in a **familiar** way towards someone, you treat them very informally, so that you may offend them if you are not close friends. ❑ *John was being too familiar with the manager.* ● **familiarity** N-UNCOUNT ❑ *The waiter greeted her with warm familiarity.*

family /ˈfæmɪli/ (**families**)

Family can take the singular or plural form of the verb.

1 N-COUNT A **family** is a group of people who are related to each other, especially parents and their children. ❑ *...a family of five.* ❑ *They decided to start a family.* **2** N-COUNT When people talk about **their family**, they sometimes mean their ancestors. ❑ *Her family came to Los Angeles in 1901.*

→ see Picture Dictionary: **family**

Picture Dictionary family

ˌfamily ˈplanning N-UNCOUNT **Family planning** is the practice of using contraception to control the number of children you have.

famine /ˈfæmɪn/ (**famines**) N-VAR A **famine** is a serious shortage of food in a country, which may cause many deaths.

famous /ˈfeɪməs/ ADJ Someone or something that is **famous** is very well known. ❑ *...England's most famous artist.* ❑ *New Orleans is famous for its music.*

Usage

A **famous** person or thing is known to more people than a **well-known** one. A **notorious** person or thing is famous because they are connected with something bad or undesirable. **Infamous** is not the opposite of famous. It has a similar meaning to notorious, but is a stronger word. Someone or something that is **notable** is important or remarkable.

Thesaurus *famous* Also look up:

ADJ. acclaimed, celebrated, prominent, renowned; *(ant.)* anonymous, obscure, unknown

famously /ˈfeɪməsli/ ADV You use **famously** to refer to a fact that is well known, usually because it is remarkable. ❑ *Authors are famously ignorant about publishing.*

fan /fæn/ (**fans, fanning, fanned**) **1** N-COUNT If you are a **fan of** someone or something, you admire them and are very interested in them. ❑ *Billy Crystal fans will love this movie.* **2** N-COUNT A **fan** is an object that a person waves to keep cool or a device that keeps a room or machine cool. **3** V-T If you **fan yourself**, you wave a fan or other flat object in order to make yourself cooler. **4** V-T If you **fan** a fire, you wave something flat next to it in order to make it burn more strongly.
→ see **concert**

fan

▸ **fan out** PHR-VERB If a group of people or things **fan out**, they move forwards away from a particular point in different directions. ❑ *British, American, and French troops fanned out to the west.*

fanatic /fəˈnætɪk/ (**fanatics**) **1** N-COUNT If you describe someone as a **fanatic**, you disapprove of them because you consider their behaviour or opinions to be very extreme. ❑ *I am not a religious fanatic but I am a Christian.* ● **fanatical** ADJ ❑ *...a fanatical group calling for independence.* **2** N-COUNT If you say that someone is a **fanatic**, you mean that they are very enthusiastic about a particular activity, sport, or way of life. [INFORMAL] ❑ *Both Rod and Phil are football fanatics.*

ˈfan ˌbase or **fanbase** (**fan bases**) N-COUNT The **fan base** of someone such as a pop star or a pop group is their fans, considered as a whole. ❑ *His fan base is mostly middle-aged ladies.*

fanciful /ˈfænsɪfʊl/ ADJ If you describe an idea as **fanciful**, you disapprove of it because you think it comes from someone's imagination, and is therefore unrealistic or unlikely to be true. ❑ *...fanciful ideas about alien life.*

fancy

❶ WANTING, LIKING, OR THINKING
❷ ELABORATE OR EXPENSIVE

fancy /ˈfænsi/ (**fancies, fancying, fancied**)
❶ **1** V-T If you **fancy** something, you want to have it or do it. [BRIT, INFORMAL] ❑ *Do you fancy going to see a film sometime?* ❑ *I just fancied a drink.* **2** V-T If you **fancy** someone, you feel attracted to them, especially in a sexual way. [INFORMAL] ❑ *I didn't fancy him anyway.* **3** N-VAR A **fancy** is an idea that is unlikely, untrue, or imaginary. [LITERARY] ❑ *...a childhood fancy.* **4** EXCLAM You say **'fancy'** or **'fancy that'** when you want to express surprise or disapproval. ❑ *Fancy coming to a funeral in pink boots!* **5** PHRASE If something **takes** your **fancy** when you see or hear it, you like it. [INFORMAL] ❑ *Put any vegetable that takes your fancy into the stew.*

fancy /ˈfænsi/ (**fancier, fanciest**)
❷ **1** ADJ If you describe something as **fancy**, you mean that it is special, unusual, or elaborate. ❑ *...fancy jewellery.* **2** ADJ If you describe something as **fancy**, you mean that it is very expensive or of very high quality, and you often dislike it because of this. ❑ *They sent me to a fancy private school.*

fanfare /ˈfænfeə/ (**fanfares**) N-COUNT A **fanfare** is a short loud tune played on trumpets to announce a special event.

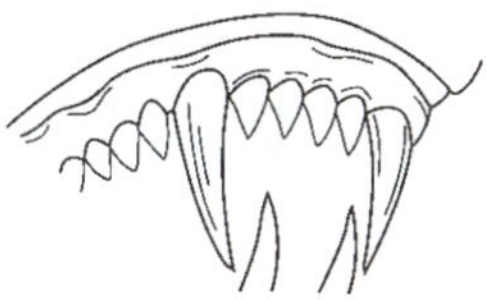

fangs

fang /fæŋ/ (**fangs**) N-COUNT **Fangs** are the two long, sharp, upper teeth that snakes and some other animals have.

fantasize [BRIT also **fantasise**] /ˈfæntəsaɪz/ (**fantasizes, fantasizing, fantasized**) V-T/V-I If you **fantasize**, or **fantasize about** something that you would like to happen, you think imaginatively about it. ❑ *I fantasised about writing music.* ❑ *She fantasised that he was still alive.*

fantastic /fænˈtæstɪk/ **1** ADJ If you say that something is **fantastic**, you are emphasizing that you think it is very good. [INFORMAL] ❑ *I have a fantastic social life.* **2** ADJ BEFORE N You use **fantastic** to emphasize the size, amount, or degree of something. [INFORMAL] ❑ *...fantastic amounts of money.* ● **fantastically** ADV ❑ *...a fantastically expensive restaurant.* **3** ADJ You describe something as **fantastic** when it seems strange and wonderful or unlikely. ❑ *...unlikely and fantastic legends from the fifteenth century.*

fantasy /ˈfæntəzi/ (**fantasies**) **1** N-COUNT A **fantasy** is a situation or event that you think about and that you want to happen, especially one that is unlikely to happen. ❑ *...fantasies of fame.* **2** N-VAR You can refer to a story or situation that someone creates from their imagination and that is not based on reality as **fantasy**. ❑ *...the words from a Disney fantasy.*
→ see Word Web: **fantasy**

ˌfantasy ˈfootball N-UNCOUNT **Fantasy football**

Word Web fantasy

All **fictional** writing involves the use of **imaginary** situations and characters. However, **fantasy** goes even further. This **genre** uses more **imagination** than **reality**. **Authors** create new creatures, **myths**, and **legends**. A **novelist** may use **realistic** people and settings. But a fantasy writer is free to create a whole different world where earthly laws no longer apply. Contemporary movies have found a rich source of stories in the fantasy genre. Today you can see many different films about **fairies**, **wizards**, and **dragons**.

is a game in which people choose real footballers to form an imaginary team, and win points based on the actual performances of the players.

FAQ /fæk/ (**FAQs**) **FAQ** is used especially on websites to refer to questions about a particular topic. **FAQ** is an abbreviation for 'frequently asked questions'.

far /fɑː/ (**farther** or **further**, **farthest** or **furthest**)

Far has two comparatives, **farther** and **further**, and two superlatives, **farthest** and **furthest**. **Farther** and **farthest** are used mainly in meaning 1, and are dealt with here. **Further** and **furthest** are dealt with in separate entries.

1 ADV If one place, thing, or person is **far** away **from** another, there is a great distance between them. ❑ *There's a nice little Italian restaurant not far from here.* ❑ *My sisters moved even farther away from home.* ❑ *...the far end of the room.* 2 ADV You use **far** in questions and statements about distances. ❑ *How far is it to Malcy?* ❑ *How far can you throw?* ❑ *She followed the tracks as far as the road.* 3 ADJ BEFORE N You use **far** to refer to the part of an area or object that is the greatest distance from the centre in a particular direction. ❑ *...at the far left of the blackboard.* 4 ADV A time or event that is **far** away in the future or the past is a long time from the present. ❑ *I asked him how far back in his life he could remember.* ❑ *I can't see any farther than the next six months.* ❑ *The first day of term seemed so far away.* 5 ADV You use **far** to indicate the extent to which something happens. ❑ *How far did the film tell the truth about Queen Victoria?* 6 ADV You can use **far** when talking about the progress that someone or something makes. ❑ *Discussions never progressed very far.* 7 ADV You can use **far** when talking about the degree to which someone's behaviour or actions are extreme. ❑ *This time he's gone too far.* 8 ADV You can use **far** to mean 'very much' when you are comparing two things and emphasizing the difference between them. ❑ *Women who eat plenty of fresh vegetables are far less likely to be stressed.* ❑ *The trial is taking far too long.* 9 PHRASE You can use **by far** or **far and away** in comparisons to emphasize that something is better or greater than anything else. ❑ *By far the most important issue for them is unemployment.* ❑ *Rangers are far and away the best team.* 10 PHRASE If you say that something is **far from** a particular thing or **far from** the truth, you are emphasizing that it is not that particular thing or not at all true. ❑ *She thought I disliked her, which was far from the truth.* 11 PHRASE If an answer or idea is **not far wrong**, **not far out**, or **not far off**, it is almost correct. ❑ *I wasn't far wrong.* 12 PHRASE **So far** means up until the present point in time or in a situation. ❑ *So far, they have not been successful.* 13 PHRASE If people come **from far and wide**, they come from a large number of places, some of them far away. If things spread **far and wide**, they spread over a very large area or distance. 14 **as far as** I am **concerned** → see **concern** 15 **a far cry from** → see **cry**

Usage

Far is used in negative sentences and questions about distance, but not usually in affirmative sentences. If you want to state the distance of a particular place from where you are, you can say that it is that distance **away**. ❑ *Durban is over 300 kilometres away.* If a place is very distant, you can say that it is **a long way away**, or that it is **a long way from** another place. ❑ *It is a long way from London.* ❑ *Anna was still a long way away.*

faraway /ˌfɑːrəˈweɪ/ 1 ADJ BEFORE N **Faraway** means a long distance from you or from a particular place. ❑ *...photographs of a faraway country.* 2 ADJ BEFORE N If you describe someone or their thoughts as **faraway**, you mean that they are thinking about something that is very different from the situation around them. ❑ *She had a faraway look in her eyes.*

farce /fɑːs/ (**farces**) 1 N-COUNT A **farce** is a humorous play in which the characters become involved in unlikely and complicated situations. 2 N-COUNT If you describe a situation or event as a **farce**, you mean that it is so disorganized or ridiculous that you cannot take it seriously. ❑ *Cycling is a complete farce because of the number of cars on our roads.* ● **farcical** ADJ ❑ *The whole idea is farcical.*

fare /feə/ (**fares**, **faring**, **fared**) 1 N-COUNT The **fare** is the money that you pay for a journey by bus, taxi, train, boat, or aeroplane. ❑ *He couldn't afford the train fare.* 2 V-I If you say that someone or something **fares** well or badly, you are referring to the degree of success they achieve in a particular situation or activity. ❑ *The honey industry fared well during the 1980s.*

ˌFar ˈEast N-PROPER **The Far East** consists of all the countries of Eastern Asia, including China and Japan.

farewell /ˌfeəˈwel/ (**farewells**) CONVENTION & N-COUNT **Farewell** means goodbye. [LITERARY] ❑ *'Farewell, my friend.'* ❑ *They said their farewells.*

Word Web farm

Farmers no longer simply plant a **crop** and **harvest** it. Today's **farmer** uses engineering and technology to make a living. Careful **irrigation** and **drainage** control the amount of water **plants** receive. **Insecticides** and fungicides protect plants from insects. **Fertilizers** make things grow. High-tech **agricultural** methods may increase the world's **food** supply. Using hydroponic methods, farmers use **chemical** solutions to **cultivate** plants. This has several advantages. **Soil** can contain **pests** and diseases not present in water alone. Growing plants hydroponically also requires less water and less labour than traditional growing methods.

ˌfar-ˈfetched ADJ If you describe a story or idea as **far-fetched**, you are criticizing it because you think it is unlikely to be true or practical. ❑ *The storyline was too far-fetched.*

farm /fɑːm/ (**farms, farming, farmed**) **1** N-COUNT A **farm** is an area of land consisting of fields and buildings, where crops are grown or animals are raised. ❑ *Both boys liked to work on the farm.* **2** V-T/V-I If you **farm**, or **farm** an area of land, you grow crops or raise animals on it. ❑ *He has lived and farmed here for 46 years.*
→ see Word Web: **farm**
→ see **dairy**

farmer /ˈfɑːmə/ (**farmers**) N-COUNT A **farmer** is a person who owns or manages a farm.
→ see **farm**

farmhouse /ˈfɑːmhaʊs/ (**farmhouses**) N-COUNT A **farmhouse** is the main house on a farm, usually where the farmer lives.

farming /ˈfɑːmɪŋ/ N-UNCOUNT **Farming** is the activity of growing crops or keeping animals on a farm.

farmland /ˈfɑːmlænd/ (**farmlands**) N-VAR **Farmland** is land which is farmed or which is suitable for farming.

farmyard /ˈfɑːmjɑːd/ (**farmyards**) N-COUNT On a farm, the **farmyard** is an area near the farmhouse which is enclosed by walls or buildings.

ˌfar ˈoff (**further off, furthest off**) **1** ADJ A **far off** time is a long time away in the future or past. ❑ *Their wedding day is not far off.* **2** ADJ & ADV A **far off** place is a long distance away. ❑ *...stars in far-off galaxies.* ❑ *The children who lived far off didn't go home.*

ˌfar-ˈreaching ADJ **Far-reaching** actions, events, or changes have a very great influence and affect a great number of things. ❑ *New technology can have far-reaching effects on society.*

farther /ˈfɑːðə/ **Farther** is a comparative of **far**.

farthest /ˈfɑːðɪst/ **Farthest** is a superlative of **far**.

fascia /ˈfeɪʃə/ (**fascias**) N-COUNT The **fascia** of a cellphone is its detachable cover.

fascinate /ˈfæsɪneɪt/ (**fascinates, fascinating, fascinated**) V-T If something or someone **fascinates** you, you find them extremely interesting. ❑ *Politics fascinated Franklin's father.*

fascinated /ˈfæsɪneɪtɪd/ ADJ If you are **fascinated**, you are extremely interested by something. ❑ *I sat on the stairs and watched, I was fascinated.*

fascinating /ˈfæsɪneɪtɪŋ/ ADJ If you find something **fascinating**, you find it extremely interesting. ❑ *Madagascar is a fascinating place.*

fascination /ˌfæsɪˈneɪʃən/ N-UNCOUNT **Fascination** is the state of being extremely interested in something. ❑ *I've had a lifelong fascination with the sea.*

fascist /ˈfæʃɪst/ (**fascists**) **1** N-COUNT & ADJ A **fascist** or a person with **fascist** views has a set of right-wing political beliefs that includes strong control by the state and a powerful role for the armed forces. ● **fascism** N-UNCOUNT ❑ *...the threat of fascism.* **2** N-COUNT If you refer to someone as a **fascist**, you disapprove of the fact that they have extreme views on something, and do not tolerate different views.

fashion /ˈfæʃən/ (**fashions, fashioning, fashioned**) **1** N-UNCOUNT **Fashion** is the area of activity that involves styles of clothing and appearance. **2** N-COUNT & PHRASE A **fashion** is a style of clothing or a way of behaving that is popular at a particular time. If something is **in fashion**, it is a fashion at a particular time, and if it is **out of fashion** it is not. **3** N-SING If you do something **in** a particular **fashion**, you do it in that way. [FORMAL] ❑ *This computer program works in a similar fashion.* **4** V-T If you **fashion** something, you make it. [FORMAL] **5** → see also **old-fashioned**

fashionable /ˈfæʃənəbəl/ ADJ Something that is **fashionable** is popular or approved of at a particular time. ❑ *It was fashionable to wear blue.* ● **fashionably** ADV ❑ *The women here are fashionably dressed.*

fast /fɑːst, fæst/ (**faster, fastest, fasts, fasting, fasted**) **1** ADJ & ADV **Fast** means moving, acting, or happening with great speed. ❑ *...fast cars.* ❑ *They work terrifically fast.* **2** ADV You use **fast** in questions or statements about speed. ❑ *How fast were you driving?* ❑ *We don't know how fast the process will be.* **3** ADV & ADJ **Fast** means happening without any delay. ❑ *We want you to leave as fast as possible.* ❑ *...a fast response from Congress.* **4** ADJ AFTER LINK-V If a watch or clock is **fast**, it is showing a time that is later than the real time. **5** ADV If something is held or fixed **fast**, it is held or fixed very firmly. ❑ *The ship is stuck fast on the rocks.* **6** ADV If you **hold fast to** a principle or idea, or if you **stand fast**, you do not change your mind about it. **7** V-I & N-COUNT If you **fast**, or if you go on a **fast**, you eat no food for a period of time, usually for religious reasons. ❑ *They fasted for three days.* ❑ *The fast ends at sunset.* **8** **fast asleep** → see **asleep**

f

Thesaurus *fast* Also look up:

ADJ. hasty, quick, rapid, speedy, swift; *(ant.)* leisurely, slow 1
ADV. quickly, rapidly, soon, swiftly; *(ant.)* leisurely, slowly 1
firmly, tightly; *(ant.)* loosely, unsteadily 6

F

fasten /ˈfɑːsən, ˈfæs-/ (**fastens, fastening, fastened**) 1 V-T/V-I When you **fasten** something, or when it **fastens**, you do it up or close it by means of buttons or a strap, buckle, or other device. ❑ *Fasten your seat belt.* ❑ *The dress fastens with a long zip.* 2 V-T If you **fasten** one thing **to** another, you attach the first thing to the second.

fastening /ˈfɑːsənɪŋ, ˈfæs-/ (**fastenings**) N-COUNT A **fastening** is something that you use to fasten something.

ˌfast ˈfood N-UNCOUNT **Fast food** is hot food such as hamburgers which is served quickly after you order it.
→ see **meal**

fastidious /fæˈstɪdiəs/ ADJ If you say that someone is **fastidious**, you mean that they pay great attention to detail because they like everything to be accurate and very orderly. ❑ *He was fastidious about his appearance.* ● **fastidiously** ADV ❑ *He fastidiously copied every word of his notes.*

ˈfast ˌlane (**fast lanes**) 1 N-COUNT On a motorway, the **fast lane** is the part of the road where the vehicles that are travelling fastest go. [BRIT] 2 N-SING If someone is living in the **fast lane**, they have a very busy, exciting life, although they sometimes seem to take a lot of risks.

fat /fæt/ (**fatter, fattest, fats**) 1 ADJ A **fat** person has a lot of flesh on their body and weighs too much. ❑ *I can eat what I like without getting fat.* ● **fatness** N-UNCOUNT ❑ *We visited his family and admired the fatness of their cattle.* 2 N-UNCOUNT **Fat** is the extra flesh that animals and humans have under their skin, which is used to store energy and to help keep them warm. 3 N-VAR **Fat** is a substance contained in many foods which your body uses to produce energy. ❑ *...low-fat yogurts.* 4 N-VAR **Fat** is a substance used in cooking which is obtained from vegetables or the flesh of animals. ❑ *Try not to eat dishes cooked in fat.* 5 ADJ A **fat** object, especially a book, is very thick or wide. ❑ *He took out his fat wallet.*
→ see **calories**

Usage

If you describe someone as **fat**, you are speaking in a very direct way, and this may be considered rude. If you want to say more politely that someone is rather fat, it is better to describe them as **plump**, or more informally, as **chubby**, but in general you should avoid using any of these words in the presence of the person you are describing. The same is true of **overweight** and **obese**, which are used to describe someone who may have health problems because of their size or weight. **Obese** is also a medical term used to describe someone who is extremely fat or overweight.

Thesaurus *fat* Also look up:

ADJ. big, chunky, heavy, obese, overweight, stout, thick; *(ant.)* lean, skinny, slim, thin 1

fatal /ˈfeɪtəl/ 1 ADJ A **fatal** action has undesirable results. ❑ *He made the fatal mistake of giving her some money.* ● **fatally** ADV ❑ *Failure could fatally damage his chances.* 2 ADJ A **fatal** accident or illness causes someone's death. ❑ *...a fatal stabbing.* ● **fatally** ADV ❑ *He was shot and fatally injured.*

fatality /fəˈtælɪti/ (**fatalities**) N-COUNT A **fatality** is a person's death, caused by an accident or violence. [FORMAL]

fate /feɪt/ (**fates**) 1 N-UNCOUNT **Fate** is a power that some people believe controls everything that happens. ❑ *Fate has brought them together.* 2 N-COUNT Someone's **fate** is what happens to them. ❑ *His fate is in the hands of his bankers.*

fateful /ˈfeɪtfʊl/ ADJ If you describe an action or event as **fateful**, you mean that it had important, and often bad, effects on later events. ❑ *It was a fateful decision, which would break the Government.*

father /ˈfɑːðə/ (**fathers, fathering, fathered**) 1 N-COUNT Your **father** is your male parent. 2 V-T When a man **fathers** a child, he makes a woman pregnant and their child is born. 3 N-COUNT **The father of** something is the man who invented or started it. ❑ *Max Dupain is the father of modern photography.* 4 N-VOC & N-TITLE In some Christian churches, priests are addressed or referred to as **Father**.
→ see **family**

fatherhood /ˈfɑːðəhʊd/ N-UNCOUNT **Fatherhood** is the state of being a father. ❑ *...the joys of fatherhood.*

ˈfather-in-law (**fathers-in-law**) N-COUNT Your **father-in-law** is the father of your husband or wife.
→ see **family**

fathom /ˈfæðəm/ (**fathoms, fathoming, fathomed**) 1 N-COUNT A **fathom** is a unit of length used for describing the depth of the sea. One fathom is equal to 6 feet or approximately 1.8 metres. 2 V-T & PHR-VERB If you cannot **fathom** something, or you cannot **fathom** it **out**, you cannot understand it, although you think carefully about it. ❑ *I really couldn't fathom what Steiner was talking about.*

fatigue /fəˈtiːg/ N-UNCOUNT **Fatigue** is a feeling of extreme physical or mental tiredness.

fatigues /fəˈtiːgz/ N-PLURAL **Fatigues** are clothes that soldiers wear when they are on the battlefield or when they are doing routine jobs.

fattening /ˈfætənɪŋ/ ADJ **Fattening** food is thought to make people fat.

fatty /ˈfæti/ 1 ADJ **Fatty** food contains a lot of fat. ❑ *...fatty meat such as sausages.* 2 ADJ BEFORE N **Fatty acids** or **fatty tissue** contain or consist of fat.

fault /fɔːlt/ (**faults, faulting, faulted**) 1 N-SING & PHRASE If a bad situation is **your fault**, or if you are **at fault**, you caused it or are responsible for it. ❑ *It was all his fault.* ❑ *He never accepted that he was at fault.* 2 N-COUNT A **fault** is a weakness or imperfection in a person or a piece of equipment. ❑ *Her worst*

fault as a TV reporter was that she didn't listen. ❑ *There is a fault in the computer program.* **3** V-T If you say that you **cannot fault** someone, you approve of the hard work they put into doing something or the efficient way that they do it. ❑ *It is hard to fault the way he runs his business.* **4** N-COUNT A **fault** is a large crack in the earth's surface. ❑ *...the San Andreas Fault.* **5** PHRASE If you **find fault with** something, you complain about it.
→ see **earthquake**

Thesaurus *fault* Also look up:
N. blunder, error, mistake, wrongdoing **1**
defect, flaw, imperfection, weakness **2**

faultless /ˈfɔːltləs/ ADJ Something that is **faultless** contains no mistakes. ❑ *Hans's English was faultless.*

faulty /fɔːlti/ ADJ A **faulty** machine or piece of equipment is not working properly. ❑ *His car has faulty brakes.*

fauna /ˈfɔːnə/ N-PLURAL Animals, especially those in a particular area, can be referred to as **fauna.** [TECHNICAL] ❑ *...the lake's remarkable flora and fauna.*

favour [AM **favor**] /ˈfeɪvə/ (**favours, favouring, favoured**) **1** N-UNCOUNT If you regard something or someone with **favour**, you like or support them. ❑ *The changes found favour with most people.* **2** N-COUNT If you ask someone to **do a favour** for you, you ask them to do something which will help you. ❑ *Can you do me a favour?* **3** V-T If you **favour** something, you prefer it to the other choices available. ❑ *We favour shopping centres in this country.* **4** V-T If you **favour** someone, you treat them better than you treat other people. ❑ *My brother felt that my mum favoured me.* **5** PHRASE If you are **in favour of** something, you think that it is a good thing. ❑ *I am in favour of tax cuts.* **6** PHRASE If one thing is rejected **in favour of** another, the second thing is done or chosen instead of the first. ❑ *Ordinary machines were scrapped in favour of computers.* **7** PHRASE If someone makes a judgement **in** your **favour**, they say that you are right. ❑ *The judge ruled in their favour.* **8** PHRASE If something is **in** your **favour**, it helps you or gives you an advantage. ❑ *The media were in favour of Mr Blair.* **9** PHRASE If someone or something is **in favour**, people like or support them. If they are **out of favour**, people no longer like or support them.

favourable [AM **favorable**] /ˈfeɪvərəbəl/ **1** ADJ If you are **favourable to** something, you agree with it or approve of it. ❑ *Many banks are favourable to the idea.* ❑ *We've had a lot of favourable comments from customers.* ● **favourably** ADV ❑ *He responded favourably to my suggestions.* **2** ADJ If something makes a **favourable impression** on you, or if it is **favourable to** you, you like it and approve of it. ❑ *He wanted to make a favourable impression on General MacArthur.* ❑ *These ideas were favourable to India.* **3** ADJ If you make a **favourable** comparison between two things, you say that the first is better than or as good as the second. ● **favourably** ADV ❑ *This compares favourably with the old method.* **4** ADJ **Favourable** conditions make something more likely to succeed. ❑ *The government made decisions which were favourable to industry.* ❑ *...favourable weather conditions.* ● **favourably** ADV ❑ *Japan is favourably placed to continue its success.*

favourite [AM **favorite**] /ˈfeɪvərɪt/ (**favourites**) **1** N-COUNT & ADJ BEFORE N Your **favourite**, or your **favourite** thing or person, is the one that you like most. ❑ *I love all sports but football is my favourite.* ❑ *Her favourite writer is Hans Christian Andersen.* **2** N-COUNT **The favourite** in a race or contest is the person or animal expected to win. ❑ *The Belgian Cup has been won by the favourites F.C. Liège.*

fawn /fɔːn/ (**fawns, fawning, fawned**) **1** ADJ & N-UNCOUNT Something that is **fawn** is pale yellowish-brown. **2** N-COUNT A **fawn** is a very young deer. **3** V-I If you say that someone **fawns over** a powerful or rich person, you disapprove of them because they flatter that person in order to get something for themselves. ❑ *People fawn over you when you're famous.* ❑ *...200 pages of fawning praise.*

fax /fæks/ (**faxes, faxing, faxed**) **1** N-COUNT A **fax** or a **fax machine** is a piece of equipment used to send and receive documents electronically along a telephone line. **2** V-T If you **fax** a document, you send a document from one fax machine to another. ❑ *Did you fax him a reply?* ❑ *Ask your secretary to fax it.* **3** N-COUNT You can refer to a copy of a document that is transmitted by a fax machine as a **fax.** ❑ *I sent him a fax.* ❑ *Did she get my fax yesterday?*

fear /fɪə/ (**fears, fearing, feared**) **1** N-VAR **Fear** is the unpleasant feeling of worry that you get when you think that you are in danger or that something horrible is going to happen. ❑ *I was shaking with fear.* ❑ *...his fears about his knee operation.* **2** PHRASE If you do not do something **for fear of** another thing happening, you do not do it because you do not wish that other thing to happen. ❑ *He did not move his feet for fear of making a noise.* **3** V-T If you **fear** something unpleasant, you are worried that it might happen, or might have happened. ❑ *She feared she had pneumonia.* ❑ *Two million refugees are fearing attack.* **4** V-I & N-VAR If you **fear for** someone or something, or if you have **fears for** them, you are worried that they might be in danger. ❑ *Carla fears for her son.* ❑ *There are fears for the safety of a 15-year-old girl.*
→ see **emotion**

Thesaurus *fear* Also look up:
N. alarm, dread, panic, terror **1**
concern, worry **3**

Word Partnership Use *fear* with:
ADJ. **constant** fear, **irrational** fear, **worst** fear **1**
V. **face** ***your*** fear, **hide** ***your*** fear, **live in** fear, **overcome** ***your*** fear **1 3**
N. fear **change**, fear **of failure**, **nothing to** fear, fear **of rejection**, fear **of the unknown**, fear **the worst** **1 3**

fearful /ˈfɪəfʊl/ **1** ADJ If you are **fearful of** something, you are afraid of it. ❑ *Bankers were fearful of a world banking crisis.* ● **fearfully** ADV ❑ *'What are you going to do?' Alex asked fearfully.* **2** ADJ BEFORE N You use **fearful** to emphasize how serious or bad something is. ❑ *...a fearful risk.* ● **fearfully** ADV ❑ *It's fearfully expensive!*

f

fearless /ˈfɪələs/ ADJ If you describe someone as **fearless**, you admire their courage. ❑ *They were young and fearless.* ● **fearlessly** ADV ❑ *...a fearlessly confident politician.*

Word Link	*some ≈ causing: awesome, fearsome, troublesome*

fearsome /ˈfɪəsəm/ ADJ If you describe something as **fearsome**, you are emphasizing the fact that it is terrible or frightening. ❑ *...fearsome weapons.*

feasible /ˈfiːzəbəl/ ADJ If something is **feasible**, it can be done, made, or achieved. ❑ *The committee will decide whether the idea is feasible.* ● **feasibility** N-UNCOUNT ❑ *Two companies are studying the feasibility of building a mill here.*

F

feast /fiːst/ (**feasts, feasting, feasted**) 1 N-COUNT A **feast** is a large and special meal. ❑ *...wedding feasts.* 2 V-I If you **feast**, you take part in a feast. [LITERARY] ● **feasting** N-UNCOUNT ❑ *The marriage is celebrated with dancing and feasting.* 3 V-I If you **feast on** a particular food, you eat a large amount of it with great enjoyment. ❑ *We feasted on cake.*

feat /fiːt/ (**feats**) N-COUNT A **feat** is an impressive and difficult act or achievement. ❑ *A racing car is an extraordinary feat of engineering.*

feather

feather /ˈfeðə/ (**feathers**) N-COUNT A bird's **feathers** are the light soft things covering its body. → see **bird**

feathered /ˈfeðəd/ ADJ **Feathered** is used to describe something covered in feathers or made from feathers. ❑ *...extravagant feathered hats.*

feature /ˈfiːtʃə/ (**features, featuring, featured**) 1 N-COUNT A particular **feature of** something is an interesting or important part or characteristic of it. ❑ *The garden is a special feature of their home.* ❑ *Games and celebrations were a feature of Roman life.* 2 N-PLURAL Your **features** are your eyes, nose, mouth, and other parts of your face. 3 V-T When a film or exhibition **features** someone or something, they are an important part of it. ❑ *The series featured top stars from cricket and rugby.* 4 V-I If someone or something **features in** something such as an exhibition or magazine, they are an important part of it. ❑ *Twelve superstars are featured in this show.* 5 N-COUNT A **feature** is a special article in a newspaper or magazine, or a special programme on radio or television. ❑ *...our special feature on cancer.* 6 N-COUNT A **feature** or a **feature film** is a full-length film about a fictional subject.

Word Partnership Use *feature* with:

ADJ. **key** feature 1
best feature, **striking** feature 1 2
special feature 1 5
facial feature 2
animated feature, **double** feature,
full-length feature 5

February /ˈfebjʊəri, AM -jʊeri/ (**Februaries**) N-VAR **February** is the second month of the year. ❑ *...one of the wettest Februaries this century.*

feces /ˈfiːsiːz/ → see **faeces**

fed /fed/ 1 **Fed** is the past tense and past participle of **feed**. 2 → see also **fed up**

federal /ˈfedərəl/ 1 ADJ BEFORE N In a **federal** country or system, a group of states is controlled by a central government. 2 ADJ BEFORE N **Federal** means belonging or relating to the national government of a federal country rather than to one of the states within it. ❑ *...a federal judge.* ● **federally** ADV ❑ *...federally funded apartments.*

federation /ˌfedəˈreɪʃən/ (**federations**) N-COUNT A **federation** is a group of organizations or states that have joined together for a common purpose. ❑ *...the British Athletic Federation.*

ˌfed ˈup ADJ AFTER LINK-V Someone who is **fed up** is bored or annoyed. [INFORMAL] ❑ *He had become fed up with city life.*

fee /fiː/ (**fees**) 1 N-COUNT A **fee** is a sum of money that you pay to be allowed to do something. ❑ *...the television licence fee.* 2 N-COUNT A **fee** is the money that someone is paid for a particular job or service. ❑ *...solicitors' fees.*

feeble /ˈfiːbəl/ (**feebler, feeblest**) 1 ADJ If you describe someone or something as **feeble**, you mean that they are physically weak. ❑ *He was old and feeble.* ● **feebly** ADV ❑ *His hand moved feebly.* 2 ADJ If you say that someone or something is **feeble**, you mean that they are not very good, convincing, or effective. ❑ *...a feeble argument.* ● **feebly** ADV ❑ *I said 'Sorry', very feebly.*

feed /fiːd/ (**feeds, feeding, fed**) 1 V-T If you **feed** a person or animal, you give them food. ❑ *She fed him a biscuit.* ❑ *He fed the ice cream to her.* ● **feeding** (**feedings**) N-VAR ❑ *...the feeding of farm animals.* 2 V-T To **feed** a family or a community means to supply food for them. ❑ *It can be expensive to feed a hungry family.* 3 V-I When an animal **feeds**, it eats something. ❑ *The insects feed on wood.* 4 V-I & N-COUNT When a baby **feeds**, or when it has a **feed**, it drinks breast milk or milk from its bottle. 5 V-T If you **feed** something somewhere, you put it in there at a steady rate. ❑ *She was feeding documents into a photocopier.* ❑ *Some blood vessels feed blood to the brain.*

Word Partnership Use *feed* with:

N. feed **the baby**, feed **the cat**, feed **the children**, feed ***your*** **family**, feed **the hungry** 1 2

feedback /ˈfiːdbæk/ N-UNCOUNT When you **get feedback** on your work or progress, someone tells you how well or badly you are doing.

feel /fiːl/ (**feels, feeling, felt**) 1 LINK-VERB If you **feel** an emotion or a physical sensation, you experience it. ❑ *I am feeling very depressed.* ❑ *I felt sick.* 2 LINK-VERB If you talk about how an experience or event **feels**, you are describing the emotions and sensations connected with it. ❑ *It feels good to finish a piece of work.* 3 N-SING & LINK-VERB The **feel** of an object, or the way it **feels**, is the physical quality that you notice when you touch it. ❑ *He remembered the feel of the grass.* ❑ *The metal felt smooth and cold.* 4 V-T If you **feel** an object, you touch it so that you can learn what it is like. ❑ *The doctor felt his head.* ❑ *Feel how soft this is.* 5 V-T If you **feel** something, you are aware that it is touching or happening to your body. ❑ *He felt a hand on his shoulder.* ❑ *I felt* *myself blush.* 6 V-T If you **feel** something, you become aware of it, even though you cannot see or hear it. ❑ *I could feel that the cat was watching me.* 7 V-T If you **feel** that something is true, you have a strong idea in your mind that it is the truth. ❑ *I feel certain that everything will be okay.* ❑ *She felt he was responsible.* 8 V-T If you **feel** that you should do something, you think that you should do it. ❑ *I feel that I should say sorry.* 9 V-I If you talk about how you **feel about** something, you talk about your opinion, attitude, or reaction to it. ❑ *How do you feel about spending less time with your kids?* 10 V-I If you **feel like** doing or having something, you want to do or have it. ❑ *She felt like going to sleep.* 11 N-SING The **feel** of something is the general impression that it gives you. ❑ *The room has a warm, cosy feel.* 12 → see also **feeling, felt**

▸ **feel for** 1 PHR-VERB If you **feel for** something, you try to find it using your hands rather than your eyes. ❑ *I felt for my wallet.* 2 PHR-VERB If you **feel for** someone, you have sympathy for them.

feelgood /ˈfiːlgʊd/ 1 ADJ BEFORE N A **feelgood** film presents people and life in a way which makes the people who watch it feel happy and optimistic. 2 PHRASE **The feelgood factor** is the fact that people are feeling hopeful and optimistic about the future. [JOURNALISM]

feeling /ˈfiːlɪŋ/ (**feelings**) 1 N-VAR A **feeling** is an emotion. ❑ *...a feeling of satisfaction.* 2 PHRASE **Bad feeling** or **ill feeling** is resentment or anger which exists between people, for example after an argument. ❑ *There is some bad feeling between the two families.* 3 N-COUNT If you have a **feeling** that something is true, you think that it is probably the truth. ❑ *I have a feeling that everything will be okay.* 4 N-SING If you have a **feeling of** being in a particular situation, you feel that you are in that situation. ❑ *I had the terrible feeling of being completely alone.* 5 N-PLURAL Your **feelings about** something are the things that you think and feel about it, or your attitude towards it. ❑ *...her strong feelings about the First World War.* 6 N-PLURAL When you refer to someone's **feelings**, you are talking about the things that might embarrass or upset them. If you **hurt** someone's **feelings**, you say or do something that upsets them. 7 N-UNCOUNT **Feeling** for someone is affection or sympathy for them. ❑ *Peter behaved with a stupid lack of feeling.* 8 N-COUNT A **feeling** is a physical sensation. ❑ *I had a strange feeling in my neck.* 9 N-UNCOUNT **Feeling** in part of your body is the ability to experience the sense of touch in this part of the body. ❑ *After the accident he had no feeling in his legs.*

feet /fiːt/ **Feet** is the plural of **foot**.

feign /feɪn/ (**feigns, feigning, feigned**) V-T If someone **feigns** a feeling or attitude, they pretend to have it. [FORMAL] ❑ *I didn't want to go to school, so I feigned illness.*

fell /fel/ (**fells, felling, felled**) 1 **Fell** is the past tense of **fall**. 2 V-T If trees are **felled**, they are cut down.

fella also **feller** /ˈfelə/ (**fellas**) N-COUNT You can refer to a man as a **fella**. [INFORMAL] ❑ *He's a nice fella.*

fellow /ˈfeləʊ/ (**fellows**) 1 ADJ BEFORE N You use **fellow** to describe people who are in the same situation as you, or people you feel you have something in common with. ❑ *He knew his fellow teachers were also frustrated.* 2 N-COUNT A **fellow** is a man or boy. [DATED, INFORMAL] ❑ *The fellow came to collect our drinks.* 3 N-COUNT A **fellow** of a society or academic institution is a member of it.

fellowship /ˈfeləʊʃɪp/ (**fellowships**) 1 N-COUNT A **fellowship** is a group of people that join together for a common purpose. ❑ *...the Fellowship of World Christians.* 2 N-UNCOUNT **Fellowship** is a feeling of friendship that people have when they are talking or doing something together. ❑ *...a sense of community and fellowship.* 3 N-COUNT A **fellowship** at a university is a post which involves research work.

felony /ˈfeləni/ (**felonies**) N-COUNT A **felony** is a very serious crime such as armed robbery. [AM, TECHNICAL]

felt /felt/ 1 **Felt** is the past tense and past participle of **feel**. 2 N-UNCOUNT **Felt** is a type of thick cloth made from wool or other fibres packed tightly together.

Word Link	*fem, femin ≈ woman : female, feminine, feminist*

female /ˈfiːmeɪl/ (**females**) 1 ADJ Someone who is **female** is a woman or a girl. ❑ *...a female singer.* 2 N-COUNT Women and girls are sometimes referred to as **females** when they are being considered as a type. ❑ *Hay fever affects males more than females.* 3 ADJ BEFORE N **Female** is used to describe things that relate to or affect women rather than men. ❑ *She set the female world record for diving last year.* 4 N-COUNT & ADJ You can refer to any creature that can lay eggs or produce babies from its body as a **female**, or as a **female** creature. ❑ *Each female lays just one egg.* ❑ *...the female blue whale.*
→ see **reproduction**

feminine /ˈfemɪnɪn/ ADJ **Feminine** means relating to women or considered typical of or suitable for them. ❑ *...traditional feminine roles.* • **femininity** /ˌfemɪˈnɪnɪti/ N-UNCOUNT ❑ *The women believe that small feet are a sign of femininity.*

feminism /ˈfemɪnɪzəm/ N-UNCOUNT **Feminism** is the belief that women should have the same rights and opportunities as men. • **feminist** (**feminists**) N-COUNT ❑ *...the feminist movement.*

fence /fens/ (**fences, fencing, fenced**) 1 N-COUNT A **fence** is a barrier made of wood or wire supported by posts. 2 V-T & PHR-VERB If you **fence** an area of land, if you **fence** it **off**, or if you **fence** it **in**, you surround it with a fence. ❑ *We could fence off the cliff top.* ❑ *He plans to fence in half his land.* 3 PHRASE You say that someone **is sitting on the fence** to express your disapproval of them because they refuse to state a definite opinion or to say who they support in a conflict. ❑ *They criticised the president for sitting on the fence.*

fencing /ˈfensɪŋ/ 1 N-UNCOUNT **Fencing** is a sport in which two competitors fight using very thin swords. 2 N-UNCOUNT **Fencing** consists of materials that are used to make fences.

fend /fend/ (**fends, fending, fended**) V-I If you have to **fend for yourself**, you have to look after yourself without relying on other people.

▸ **fend off** PHR-VERB If you **fend off** someone or something, you defend yourself against them, using either words or physical strength. ❑ *Marianne fended off questions about her marriage.* ❑ *I fended him off with my elbow.*

F

ferment (**ferments, fermenting, fermented**) **1** N-UNCOUNT /'fɜːment/ **Ferment** is excitement and trouble caused by change or uncertainty. ❑ *The country is in a state of political ferment.* **2** V-T/V-I /fə'ment/ If a food or drink **ferments**, or if it **is fermented**, a chemical change takes place in it so that alcohol is produced. ● **fermentation** N-UNCOUNT ❑ *The fermentation produces alcohol.*
→ see **fungus**

fern /fɜːn/ (**ferns**) N-COUNT A **fern** is a plant with long stems, thin leaves, and no flowers.

ferocious /fə'rəʊʃəs/ ADJ A **ferocious** animal, person, or action is fierce and violent. ❑ *...a pack of ferocious dogs.* ● **ferociously** ADV ❑ *She kicked out ferociously.*

ferocity /fə'rɒsɪti/ N-UNCOUNT When something is done with **ferocity**, it is done in a fierce and violent way.

ferry /'feri/ (**ferries, ferrying, ferried**) **1** N-COUNT A **ferry** is a boat that carries passengers or vehicles across a river or a narrow stretch of sea. **2** V-T To **ferry** people or goods means to transport them, usually by means of regular journeys between the same two places. ❑ *A plane arrived to ferry guests to the island.*
→ see **ship**

fertile /'fɜːtaɪl, AM -təl/ **1** ADJ Land or soil that is **fertile** is able to support a large number of strong healthy plants. ● **fertility** /fɜː'tɪlɪti/ N-UNCOUNT ❑ *...the fertility of the soil.* **2** ADJ BEFORE N You describe a place or situation as **fertile ground** when you think that something is likely to succeed or develop there. ❑ *For many years, the Caribbean has been fertile ground for literature.* **3** ADJ Someone who is **fertile** is able to reproduce and have babies. ● **fertility** N-UNCOUNT ❑ *Pregnancy is the only sure test for fertility.*
→ see **grassland**

fertilize [BRIT also **fertilise**] /'fɜːtɪlaɪz/ (**fertilizes, fertilizing, fertilized**) **1** V-T When an egg or plant **is fertilized**, the process of reproduction begins by sperm joining with the egg, or by pollen coming into contact with the reproductive part of a plant. ● **fertilization** N-UNCOUNT ❑ *...the length of time from fertilization until birth.* **2** V-T To **fertilize** land means to spread manure or chemicals on it to make plants grow well.
→ see **reproduction**

fertilizer [BRIT also **fertiliser**] /'fɜːtɪlaɪzə/ (**fertilizers**) N-VAR **Fertilizer** is a substance that you spread on the ground to make plants grow more successfully.
→ see **farm, pollution**

fervent /'fɜːvənt/ ADJ Someone who is **fervent about** something has strong and enthusiastic feelings about it. ❑ *...a fervent admirer of Morisot's work.* ● **fervently** ADV ❑ *The women fervently believe in equal opportunities.*

fervour [AM **fervor**] /'fɜːvə/ N-UNCOUNT **Fervour** is a very strong enthusiasm for something or belief in something. [FORMAL] ❑ *...religious fervour.*

fester /'festə/ (**festers, festering, festered**) **1** V-I If a situation or problem **is festering**, it is growing worse, because it is not being properly recognized or dealt with. ❑ *Bad feeling is starting to fester.* **2** V-I If a wound **festers**, it becomes infected.

festival /'festɪvəl/ (**festivals**) **1** N-COUNT A **festival** is an organized series of events and performances. ❑ *...summer festivals of music and dance.* **2** N-COUNT A **festival** is a day or period when people have a holiday and celebrate some special event, often a religious one.

festive /'festɪv/ **1** ADJ Something that is **festive** is special, colourful, or exciting, especially because of a holiday or celebration. ❑ *The town has a festive holiday atmosphere.* **2** ADJ BEFORE N **Festive** means relating to a holiday or celebration, especially Christmas. ❑ *...the festive period.*

Thesaurus	*festive* Also look up:
ADJ.	happy, joyous, merry; *(ant.)* gloomy, sombre **1**

festivity /fes'tɪvɪti/ (**festivities**) **1** N-UNCOUNT **Festivity** is the celebration of something in a happy way. ❑ *Shakespeare's play ends with a grand dance and much festivity.* **2** N-PLURAL **Festivities** are events organized to celebrate something.

fetch /fetʃ/ (**fetches, fetching, fetched**) **1** V-T If you **fetch** something or someone, you go and get them from where they are. ❑ *Sylvia fetched a towel from the bathroom.* ❑ *Fetch me a glass of water.* **2** V-T If something **fetches** a particular sum of money, it is sold for that amount. ❑ *The house should fetch around £400,000.* **3** → see also **far-fetched**

fete /feɪt/ (**fetes, feting, feted**) **1** N-COUNT A **fete** is an event held out of doors that includes competitions and the selling of home-made goods. **2** V-T If someone **is feted**, they are celebrated, welcomed, or admired by the public.

fetus /'fiːtəs/ → see **foetus**

feud /fjuːd/ (**feuds, feuding, feuded**) **1** N-COUNT A **feud** is a long-lasting and bitter dispute between two people or groups. **2** V-I If two people or groups **feud**, there is a feud between them. ❑ *He feuded with his ex-wife.*

feudal /'fjuːdəl/ ADJ BEFORE N **Feudal** means relating to the system in which people were given land and protection by people of higher rank, and worked and fought for them in return.

fever /'fiːvə/ (**fevers**) **1** N-VAR If you have a **fever**, your temperature is higher than usual because you are ill. **2** → see also **hay fever** **3** N-COUNT A **fever** is extreme excitement or agitation. ❑ *Angie waited in a fever of excitement.*
→ see **illness**

feverish /'fiːvərɪʃ/ **1** ADJ **Feverish** emotion or activity shows great excitement or agitation. ❑ *...feverish last-minute discussions.* ● **feverishly** ADV ❑ *Volunteers are working feverishly to move the heavy snow.* **2** ADJ If you are **feverish**, you are suffering from a fever.

few /fjuː/ (**fewer, fewest**) **1** QUANT **Few** is used to indicate a small number of things or people. ❑ *I gave a dinner party for a few close friends.* ❑ *A strict diet works for only a few.* ❑ *I'm giving a little tea-party for a few of the teachers.* **2** QUANT **Few** is used to indicate that a number of things or people is smaller than is desirable or than was expected. ❑ *She had few friends.* ❑ *The trouble is that few want to buy.* ❑ *Few of the beach houses had lights on.* **3** PHRASE You use **a good few** when you are referring to quite a lot of things or people. ❑ *He was a good few years older* than me. **4** PHRASE You use **as few as** before a number to suggest that it is surprisingly small. ❑ *The factory may make as few as 1,500 cars this year.* **5** PHRASE Things that are **few and far between** are very rare or uncommon. ❑ *Successful women politicians are few and far between.* **6** PHRASE You use **no fewer than** to suggest that a number is surprisingly large. ❑ *He invited no fewer than 4,000 people.*

Usage

Few and **a few** are both used in front of the plural of count nouns, but they do not have the same meaning. For example, if you say '**I have a few friends**', this is a positive statement and you are saying that you have some friends. However, if you say '**I have few friends**', this is a kind of negative statement and you are saying that you have almost no friends or that you do not have enough friends. You use **fewer** to talk about things that can be counted, for example ❑ *fewer than five visits*. When you are talking about amounts that cannot be counted, you should use **less**, for example ❑ *less money*.

fiancé /fiˈɒnseɪ, AM ˌfiːɑːnˈseɪ/ (**fiancés**) N-COUNT A woman's **fiancé** is the man she is engaged to and will marry.

fiancée /fiˈɒnseɪ, AM ˌfiːɑːˈnseɪ/ (**fiancées**) N-COUNT A man's **fiancée** is the woman he is engaged to and will marry.

fiasco /fiˈæskəʊ/ (**fiascos**) N-COUNT When something fails completely, you can describe it as a **fiasco**, especially if it seems ridiculous or disorganized. ❑ *The race was a complete fiasco.*

fibre [AM **fiber**] /ˈfaɪbə/ (**fibres**) **1** N-COUNT A **fibre** is a thin thread of a natural or artificial substance, especially one used to make cloth or rope. **2** N-COUNT A **fibre** is a thin piece of flesh like a thread which connects nerve cells in your body or which muscles are made of. ❑ *...the nerve fibres.* **3** N-UNCOUNT **Fibre** consists of the parts of plants or seeds that your body cannot digest, but which helps food pass quickly through your digestive system.
→ see **paper, vegetable**

fickle /ˈfɪkəl/ **1** ADJ A **fickle** person keeps changing their mind about what they like or want; used showing disapproval. ❑ *He is a handsome but fickle young actor.* **2** ADJ If you say that something is **fickle**, you mean that it often changes and is unreliable. ❑ *The weather near Lake Orta can be fickle.*

fiction /ˈfɪkʃən/ (**fictions**) **1** N-UNCOUNT **Fiction** is stories about imaginary people and events. ● **fictional** ADJ ❑ *Ulverton is a fictional village in Sussex.* **2** N-VAR A statement or report that is **fiction** is not true. ❑ *The report, showing £100 million in profits, was pure fiction.*
→ see **fantasy, genre, library**

fictitious /fɪkˈtɪʃəs/ ADJ Something that is **fictitious** is false or does not exist. ❑ *We're interested in who started these fictitious rumours.*

fiddle /ˈfɪdəl/ (**fiddles, fiddling, fiddled**) **1** V-I If you **fiddle with** an object, you keep moving it or touching it with your fingers. ❑ *She fiddled nervously with the buttons of her cardigan.* **2** V-T If someone **fiddles** financial documents, they alter them dishonestly to get money for themselves. [INFORMAL] ● **fiddling** N-UNCOUNT ❑ *There is evidence of fiddling in the firm's finance department.* **3** N-COUNT A **fiddle** is a dishonest action or scheme to get money. [BRIT, INFORMAL] ❑ *...a £10 million insurance fiddle.* **4** N-COUNT Some people call violins **fiddles**.

fiddly /ˈfɪdəli/ ADJ Something that is **fiddly** is difficult to do or use, because it involves small or complicated objects. [INFORMAL] ❑ *Fish can be fiddly to cook.*

fidelity /fɪˈdelɪti/ **1** N-UNCOUNT **Fidelity** is loyalty to a person, organization, or set of beliefs. [FORMAL] ❑ *I had to promise fidelity to the Queen.* **2** N-UNCOUNT The **fidelity** of something such as a report or translation is how true it is. [FORMAL]

f

fidget /ˈfɪdʒɪt/ (**fidgets, fidgeting, fidgeted**) V-I If you **fidget**, you keep moving your hands or feet or changing position slightly, because you are nervous or bored. ❑ *Brenda fidgeted in her seat.* ❑ *He fidgeted with his tie.*

field /fiːld/ (**fields, fielding, fielded**) **1** N-COUNT A **field** is an enclosed area of land where crops are grown or animals are kept. ❑ *...a field of wheat.* **2** N-COUNT A sports **field** is a grassy area where sports are played. **3** N-COUNT A **field** is an area of land or sea bed under which large amounts of a mineral have been found. ❑ *...a natural gas field.* **4** → see also **minefield, playing field** **5** PHRASE **Your field of vision** is the area that you can see without turning your head. ❑ *A big red ball bounced across his field of vision.* **6** N-COUNT A particular **field** is a subject or area of interest. ❑ *Each author is an expert in his field.* **7** ADJ **Field work** involves research that is done in a real, natural environment rather than in a theoretical way or in controlled conditions. ❑ *She did her field work in Somalia in the late 1980s.* **8** N-COUNT A **field** is an area of a computer's memory or a program where data can be entered, edited, or stored. **9** V-I The team that **is fielding** in a game of cricket or baseball is the team trying to catch the ball. ● **fielder** (**fielders**) N-COUNT ❑ *The fielder threw the ball back.* ● **fielding** N-UNCOUNT ❑ *Their fielding was very good.* **10** PHRASE If someone **is having a field day**, they are very busy doing something that they enjoy, even though it may hurt other people. ❑ *Crowds at the airport watched the stars arrive and photographers had a field day.*

Word Partnership Use *field* with:

ADJ.	**open** field **1**
N.	**ball** field, field **hockey**,
	track and field **2**
	oil field **3**
	field **of vision** **4**
	expert in a field, field **trip** **5**
V.	**work in a** field **5**

fierce /fɪəs/ (**fiercer, fiercest**) **1** ADJ A **fierce** animal or person is very aggressive or angry. ● **fiercely** ADV ❑ *'I don't know,' she said fiercely.* **2** ADJ **Fierce** feelings, actions, or conditions are very intense and strong. ❑ *...a fierce storm which went on for five days.* ● **fiercely** ADV ❑ *He has always been fiercely competitive.*

fiery /ˈfaɪəri/ **1** ADJ Something that is **fiery** is burning strongly or contains fire. [LITERARY] ❑ *A* *helicopter crashed in a fiery explosion.* 2 ADJ You can use **fiery** for emphasis when you are referring to bright colours such as red or orange. [LITERARY] ❑ *The sky is a fiery red.* 3 ADJ If you describe someone as **fiery**, you mean that they express very strong emotions, especially anger. ❑ *She had a fiery temper.*

fifteen /ˌfɪfˈtiːn/ NUM **Fifteen** is the number 15.

fifteenth /ˌfɪfˈtiːnθ/ ORD The **fifteenth** item in a series is the one that you count as number fifteen.

fifth /fɪfθ/ (**fifths**) 1 ORD The **fifth** item in a series is the one that you count as number five. 2 N-COUNT A **fifth** is one of five equal parts of something.

F

fiftieth /ˈfɪftiəθ/ ORD The **fiftieth** item in a series is the one that you count as number fifty.

fifty /ˈfɪfti/ (**fifties**) NUM **Fifty** is the number 50. For examples of how numbers such as fifty and eighty are used see **eighty**.

fig /fɪg/ (**figs**) N-COUNT A **fig** is a soft sweet fruit full of tiny seeds. Figs grow on trees in hot countries.
→ see **fruit**

fight /faɪt/ (**fights, fighting, fought** /fɔːt/) 1 V-T & N-COUNT If you **fight** something, or **fight** against something, you try in a determined way to prevent it or stop it happening. A **fight against** something is an attempt to stop it. ❑ *The police are working hard to fight crime.* ❑ *I've spent a lifetime fighting against racism.* ❑ *...the fight against cancer.* 2 V-T/V-I & N-COUNT If you **fight for** something, or **fight** to do something, you try in a determined way to get it or achieve it. A **fight for** something is an attempt to get it. ❑ *The vets fought to save the most popular horse after he fell during a race.* ❑ *...the fight for justice.* 3 V-I If a person or army **fights**, they oppose each other with weapons. ❑ *I will never fight for this country.* ❑ *The two countries have been fighting for more than two years.* • **fighting** N-UNCOUNT ❑ *More than nine hundred people have died in the fighting.* 4 V-T/V-I & N-COUNT If one person **fights with** another, if people **fight** or if they **have a fight**, they hit or kick each other because they want to hurt each other. ❑ *He fought him, kicking and punching.* ❑ *He had a fight with Smith.* 5 V-I & N-COUNT When people **fight about** something, or when they **have a fight**, they argue. ❑ *Mostly, they fight about paying bills.* ❑ *He had a big fight with his dad.* 6 V-T When politicians **fight** an election, they try to win it. 7 V-T If you **fight** your **way** to a place, you move towards it with great difficulty, usually because there are a lot of people in your way. ❑ *Female fans fought their way past bodyguards and tore at his clothes.* 8 V-T When you **fight** an emotion or desire, you try very hard not to feel it, show it, or act on it. ❑ *He fought the need to sleep.*
→ see **army**

▶ **fight back** 1 PHR-VERB If you **fight back** against someone who has attacked you or made difficulties for you, you defend yourself by taking action against them. ❑ *The teenage attackers ran away when the two men fought back.* 2 PHR-VERB When you **fight back** an emotion, you try very hard not to feel it, show it, or act on it. ❑ *She fought back the tears.*

▶ **fight off** 1 PHR-VERB If you **fight off** something such as an illness, a desire, or unpleasant feeling, you succeed in getting rid of it. ❑ *All day she had fought off the desire to telephone Harry.* 2 PHR-VERB If you **fight off** someone who has attacked you, you succeed in driving them away by fighting them. ❑ *The woman fought off her attacker.*

Thesaurus	*fight* Also look up:
N.	fist fight 4 argument, disagreement, squabble 5
V.	scuffle, squabble, tussle 4 argue, bicker, quarrel 5

Word Partnership	Use *fight* with:
N.	fight **crime**, fight **fire** 1 fight **a battle/ war**, fight **an enemy** 3
V.	**join a** fight 1 2 **win a** fight 1 2 **stay and** fight 1 3 **break up a** fight, **have a** fight, **pick a** fight, **start a** fight 4 5

fighter /ˈfaɪtə/ (**fighters**) 1 N-COUNT A **fighter** or a **fighter plane** is a fast military aircraft used for destroying other aircraft. 2 N-COUNT A **fighter** is someone who physically fights another person, especially a boxer.

figurative /ˈfɪgərətɪv, AM -gjər-/ ADJ If you use a word or expression in a **figurative** sense, you use it with a more abstract or imaginative meaning than its ordinary literal one. • **figuratively** ADV ❑ *The war will be horribly expensive - literally and figuratively.*

Word Link	***fig** ≈ form, shape : con**fig**ure, dis**fig**ure, **fig**ure*

figure /ˈfɪgə, AM -gjər/ (**figures, figuring, figured**) 1 N-COUNT A **figure** is a particular amount expressed as a number, especially a statistic. ❑ *Government figures show that one in two marriages end in divorce.* 2 N-COUNT A **figure** is any of the ten written symbols from 0 to 9 that are used to represent a number. 3 N-PLURAL An amount or number that is **in single figures** is between nought and nine. An amount or number that is **in double figures** is between ten and ninety-nine. 4 N-COUNT A **figure** is the shape of a person you cannot see clearly. ❑ *A figure appeared in the doorway.* 5 N-COUNT In art, a **figure** is a person in a drawing or a painting, or a statue of a person. 6 N-COUNT Your **figure** is the shape of your body. ❑ *Janet has a good figure.* 7 N-COUNT Someone who is referred to as a particular type of **figure** is well-known and important in some way. ❑ *...key figures in politics.* 8 N-COUNT If you say that someone is, for example, a mother **figure** or a hero **figure**, you mean that they have the qualities typical of mothers or heroes. ❑ *...authority figures such as parents and teachers.* 9 V-T If you **figure** that something is true, you think or guess that it is the truth. [INFORMAL] ❑ *I figured that's what she wanted.* 10 V-I A thing or person that **figures in** something appears in it or is included in it. ❑ *Human rights issues figured several times in the report.*

▶ **figure out** PHR-VERB If you **figure out** a solution to a problem or the reason for something, you succeed in solving it or understanding it. [INFORMAL] ❑ *His parents could not figure out how to* *start their new computer.*

figurehead /ˈfɪgəhed, AM -gjə-/ (**figureheads**) N-COUNT If you refer to someone as the **figurehead** of an organization or political movement, you mean that they are recognized as its leader, although they have no real power.

file /faɪl/ (**files, filing, filed**) 1 N-COUNT A **file** is a box or folder in which documents are kept. 2 N-COUNT A **file** is a set of related data that has its own name. [COMPUTING] 3 N-COUNT & PHRASE To keep a **file on** someone or something means to collect information about them. Information that is **on file** is recorded as part of a collection of information. ❑ *We already have files on people's tax details.* ❑ *We'll keep your details on file.* 4 V-T & PHR-VERB If you **file** a document, or if you **file** it **away**, you put it in the correct file. ❑ *I finished the notes of the meeting and filed them away.* 5 V-T/V-I When you **file** for something, or **file** an accusation, complaint, or request, you make it officially. ❑ *I filed for divorce.* 6 V-I & PHRASE When a group of people **files** somewhere, or when they walk somewhere **in single file**, they walk one behind the other in a line. ❑ *The children filed out of the house.* 7 N-COUNT A **file** is a tool with rough surfaces, used for smoothing and shaping hard materials. 8 V-T If you **file** an object, you smooth or shape it with a file.
→ see **tool**

ˈfile-ˌsharing or **file sharing** N-UNCOUNT **File-sharing** is a method of distributing computer files among a large number of users. [COMPUTING] ❑ *...file-sharing sites which offer music for free.*

fill /fɪl/ (**fills, filling, filled**) 1 V-T/V-I & PHR-VERB If you **fill** a container, or if you **fill** it **up**, you keep putting or pouring something into it until it is full. You can also say a container or something shaped like a container **fills with** something. ❑ *Fill a saucepan with water.* ❑ *The little boat filled with water quickly.* ❑ *Pass me your cup and I'll fill it up for you.* 2 V-T & PHR-VERB If something **fills** a space, or if it **fills up** a space, it is so large, or there are such large quantities of it, that there is very little room left. ❑ *The text fills 231 pages.* ❑ *Today's laboratories are filled up with complicated machines.* ● **filled** ADJ ❑ *...a flower-filled garden.* 3 V-T & PHR-VERB If you **fill** a crack or hole, or if you **fill** it **in**, you put a substance into it in order to make the surface smooth again. 4 V-T If something **fills** you **with** an emotion, you experience this emotion strongly. ❑ *He was filled with pride.* 5 V-T & PHR-VERB If you **fill** a period of time **with** a particular activity, or if you **fill** it **up with** that activity, you spend the time in this way. ❑ *To fill the evening, he arranged to have supper with one of his former students.* 6 V-T If something **fills** a need or gap, it means that the need or gap no longer exists. ❑ *Her sense of fun filled a gap in his life.* 7 V-T If someone or something **fills** a role or position, that is their role or position. ❑ *I was asked to fill the role of head teacher.* 8 PHRASE If you **have had** your **fill of** something, you do not want to experience it or do it any more.

▶ **fill in** 1 PHR-VERB When you **fill in** a form, you write information in the spaces on it. [BRIT] 2 PHR-VERB If you **fill** someone **in**, you give them detailed information about something. [INFORMAL] ❑ *He filled her in on Wilbur Kantor's visit.* 3 PHR-VERB If you **fill in for** someone else, you do their job for them in their absence. 4 → see also **fill** (meaning **3**)

▶ **fill out** PHR-VERB To **fill out** a form means the same as to **fill in** a form. [AM] ❑ *Fill out the application carefully.*

▶ **fill up** 1 PHR-VERB A type of food that **fills** you **up** makes you feel that you have eaten a lot, even though you have only eaten a small amount. 2 → see also **fill** (meanings **1, 2** and **5**)

Thesaurus	*fill* Also look up:
V.	inflate, load, pour into, put into; *(ant.)* empty, pour out 1
	crowd, take up 2
	block, close, plug, seal 3

fillet /ˈfɪlɪt, AM fɪˈleɪ/ (**fillets, filleting, filleted**) 1 N-VAR A **fillet** of fish or meat is a piece that has no bones in it. ❑ *...chicken fillets.* 2 V-T When you **fillet** fish or meat, you prepare it by taking the bones out.

filling /ˈfɪlɪŋ/ (**fillings**) 1 N-COUNT A **filling** is a small amount of metal or plastic that a dentist puts in a hole in a tooth. 2 N-VAR The **filling** in a pie, chocolate, sandwich or cake is the mixture inside it. 3 ADJ Food that is **filling** makes you feel full when you have eaten it. ❑ *...a filling meal.*
→ see **teeth**

film /fɪlm/ (**films, filming, filmed**) 1 N-VAR A **film** consists of moving pictures that have been recorded so that they can be shown in a cinema or on television. ❑ *We saw a film starring William Holden.* ❑ *The programme showed film of the four children laughing.* 2 V-T If you **film** someone or something, you use a camera to take moving pictures which can be shown in a cinema or on television. ❑ *A camera crew filmed her for French television.* ● **filming** N-UNCOUNT ❑ *Filming begins early next year.* 3 N-VAR A **film** is the roll of thin plastic that you use in a camera to take photographs. ❑ *...a roll of film.* 4 N-COUNT A **film of** powder, liquid, or grease is a very thin layer of it. ❑ *A film of dust covered every surface.*
→ see **genre, photography**

Word Partnership	Use *film* with:
N.	film **clip**, film **critic**, film **director**, film **festival**, film **producer**,
	film **studio** 1
	roll of film 4
V.	**direct a** film, **edit** film, **watch a** film 1
	develop film 3

filter /ˈfɪltə/ (**filters, filtering, filtered**) 1 V-T To **filter** a substance, or to **filter** particles **out** of a substance, means to pass it through a device which removes the particles from it. ❑ *You must boil or filter the water here to make it safe to drink.* 2 N-COUNT A **filter** is a device through which a substance is passed when it is being filtered. ❑ *...an oil filter.* 3 V-I When light or sound **filters into** a place, it comes in faintly. 4 N-COUNT A **filter** is a device through which sound or light is passed and which blocks or reduces particular frequencies. ❑ *He uses a camera fitted with a light filter for his experiments.* 5 V-I When news or information **filters through to** people, it gradually reaches them. ❑ *It was months before the results filtered through to the politicians.*

f

filth /fɪlθ/ 1 N-UNCOUNT **Filth** is a disgusting amount of dirt. ❑ *The floor and furniture are covered in filth.* 2 N-UNCOUNT People refer to words or pictures as **filth** when they think that they describe or represent something such as sex or nudity in a disgusting way.

filthy /ˈfɪlθi/ (**filthier, filthiest**) 1 ADJ Something that is **filthy** is very dirty indeed. ❑ *...a pair of filthy jeans.* 2 ADJ People describe things as **filthy** when they think that they are disgusting. ❑ *...a filthy habit.*

fin /fɪn/ (**fins**) 1 N-COUNT A fish's **fins** are the flat objects which stick out of its body and help it to swim. 2 N-COUNT A **fin** on something such as an aeroplane is a flat part which sticks out and helps to control its movement.
→ see **fish**

F

Word Link	*fin ≈ end : final, finale, finish*

final /ˈfaɪnəl/ (**finals**) 1 ADJ BEFORE N In a series of events, things, or people, the **final** one is the last one, or the one that happens at the end. ❑ *This is my final offer.* ❑ *Thousands of fans watched the final episode of the long-running American sitcom.* 2 ADJ If a decision is **final**, it cannot be changed or questioned. ❑ *I'm not going, and that's final.* 3 N-COUNT A **final** is the last game or contest in a series, which decides the overall winner. ❑ *...the Scottish Cup Final.* 4 → see also **quarter-final, semi-final** 5 N-PLURAL **Finals** are the last and most important examinations in a university course. ❑ *Anna sat her finals in the summer.*

Thesaurus	*final* Also look up:
ADJ.	last, ultimate 1
	absolute, decisive, definite, settled 2

finale /fɪˈnɑːli, -ˈnæli/ (**finales**) 1 N-COUNT The **finale** is the last section of a show or a piece of music. ❑ *...the finale of Shostakovich's Fifth Symphony.* 2 N-COUNT If you say that an event provides a particular kind of **finale to** something, you mean that it provides it with that kind of ending. ❑ *It was a sad finale to an otherwise spectacular career.*

finalist /ˈfaɪnəlɪst/ (**finalists**) N-COUNT A **finalist** is a person or team that takes part in the final of a competition. ❑ *...World Cup finalists.*

Word Link	*ize ≈ making : finalize, normalize, tranquillize*

finalize [BRIT also **finalise**] /ˈfaɪnəlaɪz/ (**finalizes, finalizing, finalized**) V-T If you **finalize** something that you are arranging, you complete the arrangements for it. ❑ *They have two days to finalise their orders.*

finally /ˈfaɪnəli/ 1 ADV If something **finally** happens, it happens after a long delay. ❑ *Finally, he answered the phone himself.* 2 ADV You use **finally** to indicate that something is the last in a series. ❑ *She moved from Germany to Russia and finally to America.* 3 ADV You use **finally** to introduce a final point or topic. ❑ *And finally, a word about the winner.*

finance /ˈfaɪnæns, fɪˈnæns/ (**finances, financing, financed**) 1 V-T & N-UNCOUNT To **finance** a project or purchase, or to provide **finance** for it, means to provide money to pay for it. ❑ *The cash is used to finance the purchase of equipment.* ❑ *He hoped an American would provide finance for the magazine.* 2 N-UNCOUNT **Finance** is the management of money, especially on a national level. ❑ *...the world of finance.* ❑ *...Canada's Minister of Finance.* 3 N-PLURAL Your **finances** are the amount of money that you have. ❑ *Here are some tips on how to manage your finances.*

financial /faɪˈnænʃəl, fɪ-/ ADJ **Financial** means relating to or involving money. ❑ *...financial difficulties.* • **financially** ADV ❑ *She would like to be more financially independent.*

fiˌnancial adˈviser N-COUNT (**financial advisers**) A **financial adviser** is someone whose job it is to advise people about financial products and services.

fiˌnancial ˈservices N-PLURAL A company or organization that provides **financial services** is able to help you do things such as make investments or buy a pension or mortgage.

fiˌnancial ˈyear (**financial years**) N-COUNT A **financial year** is a twelve month period beginning and ending in April, which governments and businesses use to plan their finances. [BRIT]

financier /faɪˈnænsiə, fɪ-/ (**financiers**) N-COUNT A **financier** is a person who provides money for projects or enterprises.

finch /fɪntʃ/ (**finches**) N-COUNT A **finch** is a small bird with a short strong beak.

find /faɪnd/ (**finds, finding, found**) 1 V-T If you **find** someone or something, you see them or learn where they are. ❑ *The police also found a gun.* ❑ *I can't find my shampoo.* 2 V-T If you **find** something that you need or want, you succeed in getting it. ❑ *We have to find him a job.* ❑ *My sister helped me find the money for a private operation.* 3 V-T PASSIVE If you say that something **is found in** a particular place, you mean that it is in that place. ❑ *Fibre is found in beans, fruit and vegetables.* 4 V-T If you **find yourself** doing something, you are doing it without intending to. ❑ *It's not the first time that you've found yourself in this situation.* 5 V-T If you **find that** something is the case, you become aware of it or realize it. ❑ *At my age I would find it hard to get another job.* ❑ *I've never found my diet a problem.* ❑ *She returned home and found her back door open.* 6 V-T When a court or jury **finds** a person guilty or not guilty, they decide if that person is guilty or innocent. ❑ *She was found guilty of murder.* 7 V-T You can use **find** to express your reaction to someone or something. ❑ *We're sure you'll find it exciting!* ❑ *I found that he was a good worker after I showed him what to do.* 8 N-COUNT If you describe something that has been discovered as a **find**, you mean that it is good or useful. ❑ *...the historical find of the century.* 9 PHRASE If you **find** your **way** somewhere, you get there by choosing the right way to go. ❑ *He was an expert at finding his way, even in strange cities.* 10 → see also **finding, found** 11 to **find fault with** → see **fault**

▸ **find out** 1 PHR-VERB If you **find** something **out**, you learn it, often by making an effort to do so. ❑ *They wanted to find out the truth.* 2 PHR-VERB If you **find** someone **out**, you discover they have been doing something dishonest.

finding /ˈfaɪndɪŋ/ (**findings**) N-COUNT Someone's **findings** are the information they get as the result of an investigation. ❑ *The committee reported its findings yesterday.*
→ see **laboratory, science**

fine
❶ ADJECTIVE USES
❷ PUNISHMENT

fine /faɪn/ (**finer, finest**)
❶ 1 ADJ You use **fine** to describe someone or something that is very good. ❑ *He is an excellent journalist and a very fine man.* ❑ *...London's finest cinema.* • **finely** ADV ❑ *They are finely engineered boats.* 2 ADJ AFTER LINK-V If you say that you are **fine**, you mean that you are feeling well and reasonably happy. 3 ADJ & ADV If you say that something is **fine**, you mean that it is satisfactory or acceptable. ❑ *All the instruments are working fine.* 4 ADJ When the weather is **fine**, it is sunny and not raining. 5 ADJ Something that is **fine** is very delicate, narrow, or small. ❑ *...the fine hairs on her arms.* • **finely** ADV ❑ *Chop the ingredients finely.* 6 ADJ A **fine** adjustment, detail, or distinction is very delicate, small, or exact.

fine /faɪn/ (**fines, fining, fined**)
❷ N-COUNT & V-T If you **get** a **fine**, or if you **are fined**, you are punished by being ordered to pay a sum of money. ❑ *You can be fined for driving without a seatbelt in Texas.*

ˌfine ˈart (**fine arts**) N-VAR Painting and sculpture can be referred to as **fine art** or as **the fine arts**. ❑ *He sells antiques and fine art.*

finesse /fɪˈnes/ N-UNCOUNT If you do something **with finesse**, you do it with great skill and elegance. ❑ *His boxing style lacks finesse.*

ˌfine-ˈtune (**fine-tunes, fine-tuning, fine-tuned**) V-T If you **fine-tune** something, you make very small and precise changes to it in order to make it work better. ❑ *We can fine-tune the plans quickly, if we need to.*

finger /ˈfɪŋgə/ (**fingers, fingering, fingered**) 1 N-COUNT Your **fingers** are the four long moveable parts at the end of your hands. ❑ *There was a ring on each of his fingers.* 2 V-T If you **finger** something, you touch or feel it with your fingers. ❑ *He fingered the coins in his pocket.* 3 PHRASE If you **cross** your **fingers**, you put one finger on top of another and hope for good luck. If someone **is keeping** their **fingers crossed**, they are hoping for good luck. 4 PHRASE If you **point the finger at** someone, you blame them or accuse them of something. ❑ *He wasn't pointing the finger at anyone in the government.* 5 PHRASE If you **put** your **finger on** something such as a problem or an idea, you see and identify exactly what it is. ❑ *He could never quite put his finger on who was responsible for all this.*
→ see **hand**

fingernail /ˈfɪŋgəneɪl/ (**fingernails**) N-COUNT Your **fingernails** are the hard areas on the ends of your fingers.
→ see **hand**

fingerprint /ˈfɪŋgəprɪnt/ (**fingerprints**) N-COUNT & PHRASE Your **fingerprints** are the unique marks made by the tip of your fingers when you touch something. If the police **take** someone's **fingerprints**, they make a record of that person's fingerprints.

fingertip /ˈfɪŋgətɪp/ (**fingertips**) 1 N-COUNT Your **fingertips** are the ends of your fingers. 2 PHRASE If something is **at** your **fingertips**, you can reach or get it easily. ❑ *I had the information at my fingertips.*

Word Link	*fin ≈ end : final, finale, finish*

finish /ˈfɪnɪʃ/ (**finishes, finishing, finished**) 1 V-T & PHR-VERB When you **finish** doing something, or when you **finish** it **off**, you do the last part of it, so that there is no more for you to do. In American English, you can also say **finish up**. ❑ *I've practically finished the ironing.* ❑ *She is busy finishing off a biography.* 2 PHRASE If you **put the finishing touches to** something, you do the last things that are necessary to complete it. 3 V-I When something **finishes**, it ends. ❑ *The teaching day finishes at around 4pm.* 4 N-SING **The finish** of something is the last part of it. ❑ *He wondered if his yacht would reach the finish.* 5 N-COUNT An object's **finish** is the appearance or texture of its surface. ❑ *...the finish of the woodwork.* 6 → see also **finished**

▸ **finish off** 1 PHR-VERB When you **finish off** something that you have been eating or drinking, you eat or drink the last part of it. 2 → see also **finish** (meaning 1)

▸ **finish up** 1 PHR-VERB If you **finish up** in a particular place or situation, you are in that place or situation after doing something. ❑ *He's probably going to finish up in jail.* 2 → see also **finish** (meaning 1)

▸ **finish with** PHR-VERB When you **finish with** someone or something, you stop being involved with them. ❑ *I finished with my boyfriend.*

Thesaurus	*finish* Also look up:
V.	conclude, end, wrap up; (*ant.*) begin, start 1 3

Word Partnership	Use *finish* with:
N.	finish **a conversation**, finish **a job**, finish **school**, **time to** finish, finish **work** 1, finish **line** 4
ADV.	finish **first**, finish **last** 1 3

finished /ˈfɪnɪʃt/ 1 ADJ AFTER LINK-V If you are **finished with** something, you are no longer doing it or interested in it. ❑ *I think he will be finished with boxing.* 2 ADJ AFTER LINK-V Someone or something that is **finished** is no longer important or effective. ❑ *Her power over me is finished.* ❑ *I thought I was finished.*

finite /ˈfaɪnaɪt/ ADJ Something that is **finite** has a limited size or extent. [FORMAL] ❑ *Coal and oil are finite resources.*

fir /fɜː/ (**firs**) N-COUNT A **fir** or a **fir tree** is a tall pointed evergreen tree.

fire
❶ BURNING, HEAT
❷ SHOOTING OR ATTACKING
❸ DISMISS

fire /faɪə/ (**fires**)
❶ 1 N-UNCOUNT **Fire** consists of the flames produced by things that are burning. ❑ *...a great orange ball of fire.* 2 N-VAR A **fire** is an occurrence of burning that you can't control. ❑ *Much of historic Rennes was destroyed by fire.* ❑ *...a forest fire.*

Word Web fire

A single **match**, a **camp fire**, or even a bolt of lightning can **spark** a **wild fire**. Wild fires spread across grasslands and **burn down** forests. Huge firestorms can **burn** out of control for days. They cause death and destruction. However, some ecosystems depend on fire. Once the fire passes, the **smoke** clears, the **smouldering** embers cool, and the **ash** settles. Then the cycle of life begins again. Humans have learned to use fire. The **heat** cooks our food. People build fires in **fireplaces** and **wood** stoves. The flames warm our hands. And before electricity, the **glow** of candlelight lit our homes.

3 N-COUNT A **fire** is a burning pile of coal, wood, or other fuel that you make. ❑ *I started to light the fire.* 4 N-COUNT A **fire** is a device that uses electricity or gas to heat a room. 5 PHRASE If something **catches fire**, it starts burning. 6 PHRASE If something is **on fire**, it is burning fiercely. 7 PHRASE If you **set fire to** something, or if you **set** it **on fire**, you start it burning.
→ see Word Web: **fire**
→ see **pottery**

fire /faɪə/ (**fires, firing, fired**)
❷ 1 V-T/V-I & N-UNCOUNT If someone **fires**, or **fires** a gun or a bullet, a bullet is sent from a gun that they are using. You can refer to the shots fired as **fire**. ❑ *...an exchange of fire during a police raid.* ● **firing** N-UNCOUNT ❑ *The firing continued.* 2 V-T If you **fire** questions **at** someone, you ask them a lot of questions very quickly, one after another.

fire /faɪə/ (**fires, firing, fired**)
❸ V-T If your employer **fires** you, he or she dismisses you from your job. ❑ *You're fired!*

firearm /ˈfaɪərɑːm/ (**firearms**) N-COUNT **Firearms** are guns. ❑ *Matthew finished his training and was allowed to carry a firearm.*
→ see **war**

ˈfire briˌgade (**fire brigades**) N-COUNT **The fire brigade** is an organization which has the job of putting out fires.

ˈfire ˌengine (**fire engines**) N-COUNT In British English, a **fire engine** is a large vehicle that carries firemen and equipment for putting out fires. The usual American term is **fire truck**.

fireman /ˈfaɪəmən/ (**firemen**) N-COUNT A **fireman** is a person whose job is to put out fires. The term **firefighter** is also used.

fireplace /ˈfaɪəpleɪs/ (**fireplaces**) N-COUNT In a room, the **fireplace** is the place where a fire can be lit.
→ see **fire**

firepower /ˈfaɪəpaʊə/ N-UNCOUNT The **firepower** of an army or military vehicle is the amount of ammunition it can fire.

firewood /ˈfaɪəwʊd/ N-UNCOUNT **Firewood** is wood that has been cut up for burning on a fire.

firework /ˈfaɪəwɜːk/ (**fireworks**) N-COUNT **Fireworks** are small objects that are lit to entertain people on special occasions. They burn in a bright, attractive, and often noisy way.
→ see Word Web: **fireworks**

firm /fɜːm/ (**firms, firmer, firmest**) 1 N-COUNT A **firm** is a business selling or producing something. ❑ *...a firm of heating engineers.* 2 ADJ Something that is **firm** is fairly hard and does not change much in shape when it is pressed. ❑ *Choose a soft, medium or firm mattress.* ● **firmness** N-UNCOUNT ❑ *Vegetables should retain some firmness.* 3 ADJ A **firm** grasp or push is one which is strong and controlled. ❑ *The quick handshake was firm and cool.* ● **firmly** ADV ❑ *She held me firmly by the elbow.* 4 ADJ A **firm** person behaves in a fairly strict way, and will not change their mind. ❑ *She was firm with him. 'I don't want to see you again'.* ● **firmly** ADV ❑ *'You need a good night's sleep,' he said firmly.* ● **firmness** N-UNCOUNT ❑ *His manner combines friendliness with firmness.* 5 PHRASE If someone **stands firm**, they refuse to surrender or change their mind about something. ❑ *The council is standing firm against the protests.* 6 ADJ A **firm** decision or piece of information is definite and unlikely to change. ❑ *We have no firm evidence.* ● **firmly** ADV ❑ *He is firmly convinced that this is the right decision.*

Thesaurus *firm* Also look up:

N.	business, company, enterprise, organization 1
ADJ.	dense, hard, sturdy; *(ant.)* yielding 2

first /fɜːst/ 1 ORD & PRON & ADV The **first** thing or person is the one that happens or comes before all the others of the same kind. ❑ *...the first month of her diet.* ❑ *Johnson came first in the one hundred metres.* ❑ *The second paragraph surprised me*

Word Web fireworks

Fireworks were created in China more than a thousand years ago. Historians believe that the discovery was made by alchemists.They heated **sulphur**, potassium **nitrate**, **charcoal**, and arsenic together and the mixture **exploded**. It made a very hot, bright fire. Later they mixed these **chemicals** in a hollow bamboo tube and threw it in the fire. Thus the firecracker was born. Marco Polo brought firecrackers to Europe from the Orient in 1292. Soon the Italians began experimenting with ways of producing colourful fireworks displays. This launched the era of modern pyrotechnics.

even more than the first. ❑ *They got married two years after they had first started going out.* **2** ADV If you do something **first**, you do it before anyone else does, or before you do anything else. ❑ *I do not remember who spoke first.* ❑ *First, tell me what you think of my products.* **3** N-SING An event that is described as **a first** has never happened before. ❑ *The meeting was a first for the company.* **4** PRON **The first** you hear of something or **the first** you know about it is the time when you first become aware of it. ❑ *That was the first we heard of it.* **5** ADV & ORD You use **first** when you are talking about what happens in the early part of an event or experience, in contrast to what happens later. ❑ *At first, he seemed surprised by my questions.* ❑ *Her first reaction was shock.* **6** ADV & PHRASE You use **first** or **first of all** to introduce the first of a number of things that you want to say. ❑ *First of all, we want to buy our own home.* **7** ADJ **First** refers to the best or most important thing or person of a particular kind. ❑ *The government's first duty is to protect its citizens.* **8** PHRASE If you **put** someone or something **first**, you treat them as more important than anything else.

ˌfirst ˈaid N-UNCOUNT **First aid** is medical treatment given as soon as possible to a sick or injured person. ❑ *The driver was giving first aid to the student, when the doctor arrived.*

ˌfirst ˈclass **1** ADJ Something or someone that is **first class**, is of the highest quality or standard. ❑ *The food was first class.* **2** N-UNCOUNT & ADJ & ADV **First class**, or **first-class** accommodation, is the best and most expensive accommodation on an aeroplane, ship, or train. ❑ *...a cabin in first class.* ❑ *...two first-class tickets to Dublin.* ❑ *She had never flown first class before.*

ˌfirst-ˈhand also **firsthand** ADJ **First-hand** information or experience is gained directly, rather than from other people. ❑ *She has no first-hand knowledge of Quebec.* ❑ *We've seen first-hand what's happening in Germany.*

firstly /ˈfɜːstli/ ADV You use **firstly** when you are about to mention the first in a series of items. ❑ *Noise affects us in two ways. Firstly, it can damage hearing.*

ˌfirst ˈname (**first names**) N-COUNT Your **first name** is the first of the names that you were given when you were born, as opposed to your surname. ❑ *Her first name is Mary. I don't know her surname.*

ˌfirst ˈrate ADJ If someone or something is **first rate**, they are of the highest quality. ❑ *...a first-rate scientist.*

fiscal /ˈfɪskəl/ ADJ BEFORE N **Fiscal** means related to government money or public money, especially taxes. ❑ *...fiscal policy.*

fish /fɪʃ/ (**fishes, fishing, fished**)

The plural is **fish** or **fishes**.

1 N-VAR A **fish** is a creature with a tail and fins that lives in water. **Fish** is the flesh of a fish eaten as food. **2** V-I If you **fish**, you try to catch fish. **3** V-T If you **fish** a particular area of water, you try to catch fish there. ❑ *On Saturday we fished the River Arno.*

→ see Picture Dictionary: **fish**
→ see **shark**

▶ **fish out** PHR-VERB If you **fish** something **out** from somewhere, you take or pull it out. ❑ *He fished out three old toys from the cupboard for his grandchildren.*

fisherman /ˈfɪʃəmən/ (**fishermen**) N-COUNT A **fisherman** is a person who catches fish as a job or for sport.

fishing /ˈfɪʃɪŋ/ N-UNCOUNT **Fishing** is the sport or business of catching fish.

fist /fɪst/ (**fists**) N-COUNT You refer to someone's hand as **their fist** when they have bent their fingers towards their palm. ❑ *He shook his fist angrily at me.*

fit
❶ BEING RIGHT OR GOING IN THE RIGHT PLACE
❷ HEALTHY
❸ UNCONTROLLABLE MOVEMENTS OR EMOTIONS

fit /fɪt/ (**fits, fitting, fitted** or [AM] **fit**)
❶ **1** V-T/V-I & N-SING If something **fits**, **fits** someone or something, or if it is a good **fit**, it is the right size and shape to go onto a person's body or into a particular position. ❑ *The clothes were made to fit a child.* ❑ *The pocket computer is small enough to fit into your pocket.* ❑ *The doors were quite a good fit.* **2** V-T If you **fit** something **into** a particular space or place, you put it there. ❑ *She fitted her key in the lock.* **3** V-T If you **fit** something somewhere, you attach it there securely. ❑ *Peter built the ladders, and the next day he fitted them to the wall.* **4** ADJ If someone or something is **fit for** a particular purpose, they are suitable or appropriate for it. ❑ *Only two of the bicycles were fit for the road.* ❑ *You're not fit to be a mother!* **5** PHRASE If someone **sees fit to** do

Picture Dictionary fish

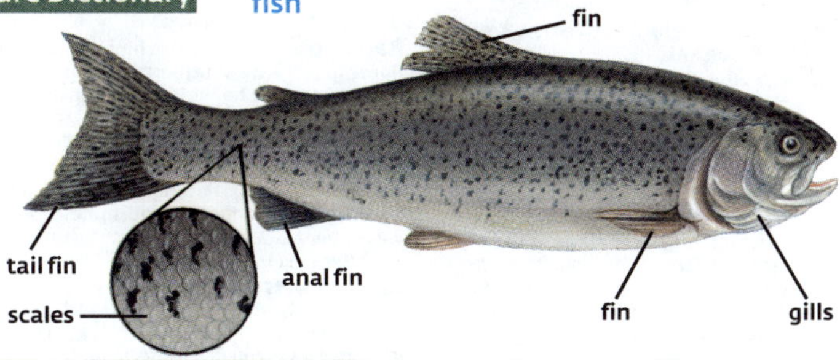

f

something, they decide that it is the right thing to do; used showing disapproval. ❑ *He's not a friend, but you saw fit to lend him money.*

▶ **fit in** **1** PHR-VERB If you manage to **fit** a person or task **in**, you manage to find time to deal with them. ❑ *I find that I just can't fit in the housework.* **2** PHR-VERB If you **fit into** a group, or if you **fit in**, you seem to belong in the group because you are similar to other people in it. ❑ *It's hard to see how he would fit into the team.*

▶ **fit out** or **fit up** PHR-VERB If you **fit** someone or something **out**, or if you **fit** them **up**, you provide them with equipment and other things that they need. ❑ *We helped to fit him out for a trip to the Baltic.*

F

fit /fɪt/ (**fitter, fittest**)
❷ **1** ADJ Someone who is **fit** is healthy and physically strong. **2** ADJ If you describe someone as **fit**, you mean that they are good-looking. [BRIT, INFORMAL] ❑ *A really fit guy came up to me on the dance floor.*

fit /fɪt/ (**fits**)
❸ **1** N-COUNT If someone has a **fit**, they suddenly lose consciousness and their body makes uncontrollable movements. ❑ *...epileptic fits.* **2** N-COUNT A **fit of** coughing, laughter, anger, or panic is a sudden uncontrolled outburst of it. ❑ *Pattie shot Tom in a fit of jealousy.*

fitness /ˈfɪtnəs/ **1** N-UNCOUNT **Fitness** is the state of being healthy and strong. ❑ *Many women regularly engage in sports and fitness activities.* **2** N-UNCOUNT Your **fitness** is your suitability **for** something or **to do** something. ❑ *You should talk to your doctor about your fitness to travel.* ❑ *They had to demonstrate their fitness for the job.*

fitted /ˈfɪtɪd/ **1** ADJ **Fitted** clothes or furnishings are designed to be exactly the right size for their purpose. ❑ *...a fitted jacket.* ❑ *...a fitted carpet.* **2** ADJ **Fitted furniture** is designed to fill a particular space and is fixed in place. ❑ *...fitted wardrobes.* **3** ADJ If a room is **fitted with** objects, those objects are in the room and are normally fixed in place. ❑ *An exercise room was fitted with an electronic bicycle.*

fitting /ˈfɪtɪŋ/ (**fittings**) **1** ADJ If something is **fitting**, it is right or suitable. ❑ *It was a fitting end to his career.* ● **fittingly** ADV ❑ *Fittingly, the talks on globalisation will take place in many different locations, Hong Kong, Delhi and Washington.* **2** N-COUNT A **fitting** is a small part on the outside of a piece of equipment or furniture, such as a handle or a tap. ❑ *...light fittings.* **3** N-PLURAL **Fittings** are things such as cookers or electric fires that are fixed inside a building but can be removed if necessary.

five /faɪv/ (**fives**) NUM **Five** is the number 5.

fiver /ˈfaɪvə/ (**fivers**) N-COUNT A **fiver** is a British five pound note. [INFORMAL]

fix /fɪks/ (**fixes, fixing, fixed**) **1** V-T If something **is fixed** somewhere, it is attached there securely. ❑ *It is fixed on the wall.* ❑ *He fixed a bayonet to the end of his rifle.* **2** V-T If you **fix** something, for example a date, price, or policy, you decide what it will be or you arrange it. ❑ *He's going to fix a time when I can see him.* ❑ *He vanished after you fixed him with a job.* **3** V-T To **fix** something means to repair it or to make it satisfactory. ❑ *If something is broken, we fix it.* ❑ *It's not too late to fix the problem.* **4** V-T/V-I If you **fix** your eyes or attention **on** something, you look at it or think about it with concentration. ❑ *Her brown eyes fixed on Kelly.* ❑ *The Olympic Games will fix the world's attention on Athens.* **5** V-T & N-COUNT If someone **fixes** a race, election, contest, or other event, they make unfair or illegal arrangements to affect the result. A **fix** is a situation where this happens. ❑ *They offered the players money to fix an important league match.* ❑ *The deal they've made is a fix.* **6** N-COUNT An injection of an addictive drug such as heroin can be referred to as a **fix**. [INFORMAL] **7** → see also **fixed**

▶ **fix up** **1** PHR-VERB If you **fix** someone **up with** something they need, you provide it. ❑ *He was fixed up with a job.* **2** PHR-VERB If you **fix** something **up**, you arrange it. ❑ *I fixed up an appointment to see her.*

Thesaurus *fix* Also look up:

v. fasten, nail, secure **1**
adjust, correct, repair, restore **3**

fixed /fɪkst/ ADJ You use **fixed** to describe something which stays the same and does not vary. ❑ *...fixed house prices.* ❑ *Some people have fixed ideas about things.* ❑ *...a fixed grin.*

Word Link ***fix ≈ fastening : fixture, prefix, suffix***

fixture /ˈfɪkstʃə/ (**fixtures**) **1** N-COUNT **Fixtures** are pieces of furniture or equipment, for example baths, which are permanently fixed inside a building. **2** N-COUNT If something or someone is a **fixture** in a particular place, they are always there. ❑ *She was a fixture in New York's nightclubs.* **3** N-COUNT In sport, a **fixture** is a competition arranged for a particular date. [BRIT] ❑ *Manchester United won this fixture 3-0.*

fizz /fɪz/ (**fizzes, fizzing, fizzed**) V-I & N-UNCOUNT If a drink **fizzes**, or if it has **fizz**, it produces lots of little bubbles of gas and makes a hissing sound. ❑ *What makes cola fizz?* ❑ *The champagne began to lose its fizz.*

fizzy /ˈfɪzi/ ADJ **Fizzy** drinks are full of little bubbles of gas.

flag /flæg/ (**flags, flagging, flagged**) **1** N-COUNT A **flag** is a piece of coloured cloth used as a sign for something or as a signal. ❑ *...the Spanish flag.* **2** PHRASE If you **fly the flag**, you show that you are proud of your country, or that you support a particular cause. ❑ *We are proud to be flying the flag for Britain.* **3** V-I If you **flag**, or if your spirits **flag**, you begin to lose enthusiasm or energy. ❑ *By 4,000m he was beginning to flag.*

flagrant /ˈfleɪgrənt/ ADJ BEFORE N You can use **flagrant** to describe an action or situation that is bad or shocking in an obvious or deliberate way. ❑ *...a flagrant act of aggression.*

flagship /ˈflægʃɪp/ (**flagships**) **1** N-COUNT A **flagship** is the most important ship in a fleet. **2** N-COUNT The **flagship** of a group of things that are owned or produced by a particular organization is the most important one. ❑ *The hospital has been the government's flagship.*

flail /fleɪl/ (**flails, flailing, flailed**) V-I If your arms or legs **flail**, **flail around**, or **flail about**, they wave about in an energetic but uncontrolled way. ❑ *His arms were flailing in all directions.*

flair /fleə/ **1** N-SING If you **have a flair for** a particular thing, you have a natural ability to do it well. ❑ *She has a flair for languages.* **2** N-UNCOUNT If you **have flair**, you do things in an interesting, and stylish way. ❑ *We played with flair and passion.*

flak /flæk/ N-UNCOUNT If you get a lot of **flak** from someone, they criticize you severely. If you take **the flak**, you get the blame for something. [INFORMAL]

flake /fleɪk/ (**flakes, flaking, flaked**) **1** N-COUNT A **flake** is a small thin piece of something that has broken off a larger piece. ❑ *A flake of plaster from the ceiling fell into his eye.* **2** V-I If paint **flakes**, or if it **flakes off**, small pieces of it come off.

flamboyant /flæmˈbɔɪənt/ ADJ If you say that someone or something is **flamboyant**, you mean that they are very noticeable and stylish. ❑ *Freddie Mercury was a flamboyant singer.* ● **flamboyance** N-UNCOUNT ❑ *...his usual mixture of flamboyance and flair.* ● **flamboyantly** ADV ❑ *She dressed flamboyantly.*

Word Link *flam ≈ burning : flame, flaming, inflame*

flame /fleɪm/ (**flames**) **1** N-VAR A **flame** is a hot bright stream of burning gas that comes from something that is burning. ❑ *The heat from the flames was so intense that roads melted.* **2** PHRASE If something is **in flames**, it is on fire. **3** PHRASE If something **bursts into flames**, it suddenly starts burning fiercely.
→ see **fire, laboratory**

flaming /ˈfleɪmɪŋ/ **1** ADJ **Flaming** is used to describe something that is burning and producing a lot of flames. ❑ *He flew the flaming aircraft back to Britain for a crash landing.* **2** ADJ BEFORE N Something that is **flaming red** or **flaming orange** is bright red or orange in colour.

flank /flæŋk/ (**flanks, flanking, flanked**) **1** N-COUNT An animal's **flanks** are the sides of its body. **2** N-COUNT A **flank** of an army or naval force is one side of it when it is organized for battle. **3** V-T If something **is flanked** by things, it has them at its side. ❑ *The bed is flanked by bookcases.*
→ see **horse**

flannel /ˈflænəl/ (**flannels**) **1** N-UNCOUNT **Flannel** is a lightweight cloth used for making clothes. ❑ *...a red flannel shirt.* **2** N-COUNT A **flannel** is a small cloth that you use for washing yourself. [BRIT]
→ see **bathroom**

flap /flæp/ (**flaps, flapping, flapped**) **1** V-T/V-I If something that is attached at one end **flaps**, or if you **flap** it, it moves quickly up and down or from side to side. ❑ *The bird flapped its wings.* **2** N-COUNT A **flap of** cloth or skin is a flat piece of it that moves freely because it is attached by only one edge. ❑ *...a loose flap of skin.* ❑ *...a small plastic flap.*

flare /fleə/ (**flares, flaring, flared**) **1** N-COUNT A **flare** is a small device that produces a bright flame. Flares are used as signals, for example on ships. **2** V-I If a fire **flares**, or if it **flares up**, the flames suddenly become larger. ❑ *Don't spill too much fat on the barbecue as it could flare up.* **3** V-I If something such as violence or anger **flares**, or if it **flares up**, it becomes worse. ❑ *Trouble flared in several American cities.* ❑ *Dozens of people were injured as fighting flared up.*

ˈflare-ˌup (**flare-ups**) N-COUNT If there is a **flare-up** of violence or of an illness, it suddenly starts or gets worse. ❑ *He had a flare-up of asthma.*

flash /flæʃ/ (**flashes, flashing, flashed**) **1** N-COUNT A **flash of** light is a sudden, short burst of it. ❑ *...a sudden flash of lightning.* **2** V-T/V-I If a light **flashes**, or if you **flash** a light, it shines brightly and suddenly. ❑ *Lightning flashed among the dark clouds.* ❑ *A driver flashed her headlights.* **3** V-I Something that **flashes past** moves or happens very quickly. ❑ *Cars flashed by every few minutes.* ❑ *A ridiculous thought flashed through Harry's mind.* **4** PHRASE If you say that something happens **in a flash**, you mean that it happens very quickly. ❑ *The answer came to him in a flash.*

flashback /ˈflæʃbæk/ (**flashbacks**) **1** N-COUNT In a film, novel, or play, a **flashback** is a scene that returns to events in the past. **2** N-COUNT If you have a **flashback to** a past experience, you have a sudden and vivid memory of it. ❑ *He had a flashback to the night his friend died.*

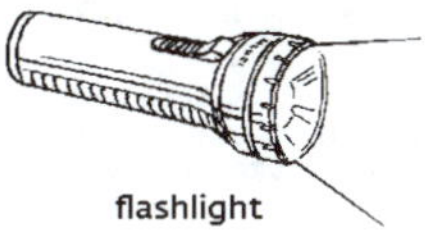
flashlight

flashlight /ˈflæʃlaɪt/ (**flashlights**) N-COUNT In American English, a **flashlight** is a small portable electric light which gets its power from batteries. The usual British word is **torch**.

flashy /ˈflæʃi/ (**flashier, flashiest**) ADJ If you describe a person or thing as **flashy**, you mean they are smart and noticeable, but in a rather vulgar way. [INFORMAL] ❑ *...a flashy sports car.*

flask /flɑːsk, flæsk/ (**flasks**) N-COUNT A **flask** is a bottle used for carrying alcoholic or hot drinks around with you. ❑ *...a flask of coffee.*
→ see **laboratory**

flat /flæt/ (**flats, flatter, flattest**) **1** N-COUNT In British English, a **flat** is a set of rooms for living in, that is part of a larger building. The usual American word is **apartment**. ❑ *...my two-bedroom flat.* **2** ADJ Something that is **flat** is level and smooth. ❑ *The sea was calm, perfectly flat.* **3** ADJ A **flat** object is not very tall or deep in relation to its length and width. ❑ *...a square flat box.* **4** ADJ A **flat** tyre or ball does not have enough air in it. **5** ADJ A **flat battery** has lost some or all of its electrical power. **6** ADJ BEFORE N A **flat** refusal or rejection is definite and firm. ❑ *The government issued a flat denial of Mr Prescott's claim.* ● **flatly** ADV ❑ *He flatly refused to discuss it.* **7** ADV If something is done in a particular amount of time **flat**, it is done in exactly that amount of time. ❑ *I explained it all in two minutes flat.* **8** ADJ You use **flat** to describe someone's voice when they are saying something without expressing any emotion. ❑ *'Whatever you want,' he said in a flat voice.* ● **flatly** ADV ❑ *'I know you,' he said flatly.* **9** ADJ BEFORE N A **flat** rate, price, or percentage is one that is fixed and which applies in every situation. ❑ *I was paid a flat fee of £7,000 for writing the play.* **10** ADJ **Flat** is used after a letter representing a musical note to show that the note should be played or sung half a tone lower than the note which otherwise corresponds to that letter. **Flat** is often represented by the symbol ♭ after the letter. **11** ADV & ADJ If a musical note is played or sung **flat**, it is slightly lower in pitch than it should be. **12** PHRASE If an event or attempt to do something **falls flat**, it fails. ❑ *It was a joke but it fell flat.* **13** PHRASE If you do something **flat out**, you do it as fast or as hard as you can. [BRIT] ❑ *Everyone is working flat out to finish by Monday.*

Thesaurus	*flat* Also look up:
ADJ.	even, horizontal, level, smooth 2

flatten /ˈflætən/ (**flattens, flattening, flattened**) 1 V-T/V-I & PHR-VERB If you **flatten** something, or if you **flatten** it **out**, you make it flat or flatter. You can also say that something **flattens** or **flattens out** . ❑ *Flatten the dough out and cut it into six pieces.* 2 V-T If you **flatten yourself against** something, you press yourself flat against it. ❑ *He flattened himself against a wall as I passed.*

F

flatter /ˈflætə/ (**flatters, flattering, flattered**) 1 V-T If someone **flatters** you, they praise you in an exaggerated way that is not sincere. ❑ *I knew she was just flattering me.* 2 V-T If you **flatter yourself** that something is the case, you believe, perhaps wrongly, something good about yourself. ❑ *He flatters himself that his work will be useful.*

flattered /ˈflætəd/ ADJ AFTER LINK-V If you are **flattered** by something that has happened, you are pleased about it because it makes you feel important. ❑ *I am flattered that they are being so helpful.*

flattering /ˈflætərɪŋ/ 1 ADJ If something is **flattering**, it makes you appear more attractive. ❑ *Her hair has been cut in a more flattering style.* 2 ADJ If someone's remarks or behaviour are **flattering**, they are pleasing because they show that the person has a high opinion of you. ❑ *It is always flattering when people copy you.*

flaunt /flɔːnt/ (**flaunts, flaunting, flaunted**) V-T If you say that someone **flaunts** their possessions or qualities, you mean that they display them in a very obvious way in. ❑ *They drove around in Rolls-Royces, openly flaunting their wealth.*

flavour [AM **flavor**] /ˈfleɪvə/ (**flavours, flavouring, flavoured**) 1 N-VAR The **flavour** of a food or drink is its taste. ❑ *This cheese has a strong flavour.* • **-flavoured** ❑ *...fruit-flavoured sparkling water.* 2 V-T If you **flavour** food or drink, you add something to give it a particular taste. ❑ *Flavour your favourite dishes with exotic herbs and spices.* 3 N-UNCOUNT The **flavour** of something is its distinctive characteristic or quality. ❑ *His paintings have a strong Italian flavour.*

flavouring [AM **flavoring**] /ˈfleɪvərɪŋ/ (**flavourings**) N-VAR **Flavourings** are substances that are added to food or drink to give it a particular taste.

flaw /flɔː/ (**flaws**) 1 N-COUNT A **flaw in** something such as a theory is a mistake in it. ❑ *There were a number of flaws in his theory.* ❑ *Almost all of these studies have serious flaws.* 2 N-COUNT A **flaw in** someone's character is an undesirable quality which they have. ❑ *The only flaw in his character is his short temper.*

flawed /flɔːd/ ADJ Something that is **flawed** has a mark or fault in it. ❑ *The research was seriously flawed.* ❑ *...a flawed genius.*

flawless /ˈflɔːləs/ ADJ If you say that something or someone is **flawless**, you mean that they have no faults or imperfections. ❑ *...her flawless complexion.* • **flawlessly** ADV ❑ *I wanted to do my job flawlessly.*

flea /fliː/ (**fleas**) N-COUNT A **flea** is a small jumping insect that sucks human or animal blood.

fleck /flek/ (**flecks**) N-COUNT **Flecks** are small marks on a surface, or objects that look like small marks. ❑ *Flecks of dark blue paint.*

fled /fled/ **Fled** is the past tense and past participle of **flee**.

fledgling /ˈfledʒlɪŋ/ (**fledglings**) 1 N-COUNT A **fledgling** is a young bird. 2 ADJ BEFORE N You use **fledgling** to describe an inexperienced person or a new organization. ❑ *...fledgling writers.*

flee /fliː/ (**flees, fleeing, fled**) V-T/V-I If you **flee from** something or someone, or if you **flee** them, you escape from them by running away. ❑ *In 1984 he fled to Costa Rica.* ❑ *...refugees fleeing persecution and torture.*

fleece /fliːs/ (**fleeces, fleecing, fleeced**) 1 N-COUNT A sheep's **fleece** is its coat of wool. 2 N-COUNT A **fleece** is the wool, in a single piece, that is cut off one sheep during shearing. 3 V-T If someone **fleeces** you, they get a lot of money from you by tricking you. [INFORMAL] ❑ *He fleeced her out of thousands of pounds.*

fleet /fliːt/ (**fleets**) 1 N-COUNT A **fleet** is an organized group of ships. ❑ *...local fishing fleets.* 2 N-COUNT You can refer to a group of vehicles as a **fleet**, especially when they all belong to a particular organization or when they are all going somewhere together. ❑ *The company has its own fleet of trucks.*

fleeting /ˈfliːtɪŋ/ ADJ **Fleeting** is used to describe something which lasts only for a very short time. ❑ *He made a fleeting visit to London.* • **fleetingly** ADV ❑ *He smiled fleetingly.*

flesh /fleʃ/ (**fleshes, fleshing, fleshed**) 1 N-UNCOUNT **Flesh** is the soft part of a person's or animal's body between the bones and the skin. ❑ *...the fish's pale pink flesh.* 2 N-UNCOUNT You can use **flesh** to refer to human skin and the human body, especially when you are considering it in a sexual way. ❑ *...the sins of the flesh.* 3 N-UNCOUNT The **flesh** of a fruit or vegetable is the soft inner part. 4 PHRASE If you meet or see someone **in the flesh**, you meet or see them in person. 5 PHRASE If you say that someone is your **own flesh and blood**, you are emphasizing that they are a member of your family.

▸ **flesh out** PHR-VERB If you **flesh out** something such as a story, you add more details to it. ❑ *He talked with him for an hour and a half, fleshing out the details of his plan.*

flew /fluː/ **Flew** is the past tense of **fly**.

Word Link	*flex ≈ bending : flex, flexible, reflex*

flex /fleks/ (**flexes, flexing, flexed**) 1 N-VAR A **flex** is an electric cable containing wires that is connected to an electrical appliance. 2 V-T If you **flex** your muscles or parts of your body, you bend, move, or stretch them to exercise them.

Word Link	*ible ≈ able to be : audible, flexible, possible*

flexible /ˈfleksɪbəl/ 1 ADJ A **flexible** object or material can be bent easily without breaking. ❑ *...flexible metal.* • **flexibility** N-UNCOUNT ❑ *The plastic's flexibility makes it possible to produce several different shapes.* 2 ADJ Something or someone that is **flexible** is able to change and adapt easily to new conditions and circumstances. ❑ *...flexible* working hours for employees. ●**flexibility** N-UNCOUNT ❑ *Manville has the financial flexibility to buy other companies at the best moment.*

flick /flɪk/ (**flicks, flicking, flicked**) 1 V-T/V-I & N-COUNT If something **flicks** in a particular direction, or if someone **flicks** it, it moves with a short, sudden movement. This action is called a **flick**. ❑ *His tongue flicked across his lips.* ❑ *She sighed and flicked a dishcloth at the counter.* ❑ *...a flick of the whip.* 2 V-T If you **flick a switch**, you press it quickly. ❑ *He flicked a light-switch.* 3 V-I If you **flick through** a book or magazine, you turn the pages quickly.

flicker /ˈflɪkə/ (**flickers, flickering, flickered**) 1 V-I & N-COUNT If a light or flame **flickers**, it shines unsteadily. You can also talk about a **flicker of** light. ❑ *A television flickered in the corner.* ❑ *I saw the flicker of flames.* 2 N-COUNT A **flicker of** feeling is one that is experienced or visible only faintly and briefly. ❑ *He felt a flicker of hope.* 3 V-I If an expression **flickers** across your face, it appears briefly. ❑ *A smile flickered across Vincent's face.*

flight /flaɪt/ (**flights**) 1 N-COUNT A **flight** is a journey made by flying, usually in an aeroplane. ❑ *The flight will take four hours.* 2 N-COUNT You can refer to an aeroplane carrying passengers on a particular journey as a particular **flight**. ❑ *I'll try to get on the flight to Karachi tonight.* ❑ *The flight was two hours late.* 3 N-UNCOUNT **Flight** is the action of flying, or the ability to fly. ❑ *...supersonic flight.* ❑ *These hawks are magnificent in flight.* 4 N-UNCOUNT **Flight** is the act of running away from something. ❑ *Frank was in full flight when he reached them.* ❑ *They came to this country in desperate flight from wars or famines.* 5 PHRASE If someone **takes flight**, they run away. 6 N-COUNT A **flight of** steps or stairs is a row of them leading from one level to another.
→ see **fly**

flimsy /ˈflɪmzi/ (**flimsier, flimsiest**) 1 ADJ Something that is **flimsy** is easily damaged because it is badly made or made of a weak material. ❑ *...a flimsy wooden door.* 2 ADJ **Flimsy** cloth or clothing is thin and does not give much protection. 3 ADJ If you describe something such as evidence or an excuse as **flimsy**, you mean that it is not very convincing.

flinch /flɪntʃ/ (**flinches, flinching, flinched**) 1 V-I If you **flinch**, you make a small, sudden movement without meaning to, usually because you are startled or frightened. ❑ *She flinched as he touched her shoulder.* 2 V-I If you do not **flinch from** something unpleasant, you do not attempt to avoid it. ❑ *He has never flinched from difficult decisions.*

fling /flɪŋ/ (**flings, flinging, flung** /flʌŋ/) 1 V-T If you **fling** something or someone somewhere, you throw them there suddenly, using a lot of force. ❑ *Peter flung his shoes into the corner.* ❑ *He flung himself to the floor.* 2 N-COUNT If two people have a **fling**, they have a brief sexual relationship. [INFORMAL] 3 N-SING You can refer to a short period of enjoyment as a **fling**, especially when it might be the last one that you will have. ❑ *This will be his last chance, his final fling before retiring.*

flip /flɪp/ (**flips, flipping, flipped**) 1 V-I If you **flip** or **flip through** a book, you turn the pages quickly. 2 V-T/V-I If something **flips over**, or if you **flip** it **over**, it suddenly turns over. ❑ *The plane flipped over and caught fire.* ❑ *He flipped it over neatly on to the plate.*

flirt /flɜːt/ (**flirts, flirting, flirted**) 1 V-I If you **flirt with** someone, you behave as if you are sexually attracted to them, in a playful or not very serious way. ❑ *Dad flirts with all the ladies.* ●**flirtation** (**flirtations**) N-VAR ❑ *Can flirtation over the Internet damage real-life relationships?* 2 N-COUNT A **flirt** is someone who flirts a lot. 3 V-I If you **flirt with** an idea or belief, you consider it or adopt it briefly, but do not become completely committed to it. ❑ *I was flirting with the idea of having my hair cut really short.*

flit /flɪt/ (**flits, flitting, flitted**) 1 V-I If someone **flits from** one place, thing or situation **to** another, they move or turn their attention from one to the other very quickly. ❑ *She is flitting between London and Glasgow.* ❑ *Nick flits from job to job.* 2 V-I If something such as a bird or a bat **flits** about, it flies quickly from one place to another. ❑ *A butterfly flits from flower to flower.*

f

float /fləʊt/ (**floats, floating, floated**) 1 V-I If something **is floating in** or **on** a liquid, it is lying or moving slowly on or just below the surface. ❑ *A tree branch was floating down the river.* 2 V-I Something that **floats** in the air hangs in it or moves slowly through it. ❑ *The white cloud of smoke floated away.* 3 N-COUNT A **float** is a light object that is used to help someone or something float in water. 4 V-T To **float** a new company means to make shares in it available for the public to buy. To **float** new shares means to make them available for the public to buy.

flock /flɒk/ (**flocks, flocking, flocked**) 1 N-COUNT A **flock of** birds, sheep, or goats is a group of them. **Flock** can take the singular or plural form of the verb. 2 N-COUNT You can refer to a group of people or things as a **flock of** them to emphasize that there are a lot of them. ❑ *...flocks of famous writers.* 3 V-I If people **flock to** a place or event, a lot of them go there. ❑ *The criticisms will not stop people flocking to see the film.*

flog /flɒg/ (**flogs, flogging, flogged**) 1 V-T If someone tries to **flog** something, they try to sell it. [BRIT, INFORMAL] 2 V-T If someone **is flogged**, they are hit very hard with a whip or stick as a punishment. ●**flogging** (**floggings**) N-VAR ❑ *He wanted to bring back hanging and flogging.*

flood /flʌd/ (**floods, flooding, flooded**) 1 N-VAR If there is a **flood**, a large amount of water covers an area which is usually dry. ❑ *70 people were killed in the floods.* 2 V-T/V-I If something such as a river or a burst pipe **floods** an area that is usually dry or if the area **floods**, it becomes covered with water. ❑ *The Chicago River flooded the city's underground tunnel system.* ❑ *The river flooded in February.* ●**flooding** N-UNCOUNT ❑ *The flooding is the worst this century.* 3 V-I & N-COUNT If you say that people or things **flood into** a place, or that there is a **flood of** them arriving somewhere, you are emphasizing that they arrive there in large numbers. ❑ *Large numbers of immigrants flooded into the area.* ❑ *He received a flood of letters.*
→ see **dam, disaster, storm**

floodlight /ˈflʌdlaɪt/ (**floodlights, floodlighting, floodlit**) 1 N-COUNT **Floodlights** are powerful lamps which are used to light sports grounds and the outsides of public buildings. 2 V-T If a building or place **is floodlit**, it is lit by floodlights. ❑ *A police helicopter hovered above, floodlighting the area.* ❑ *...a floodlit car park.*

floor /flɔː/ (**floors, flooring, floored**) **1** N-COUNT The **floor** of a room is the part that you walk on. ❑ *Jack sat on the floor watching TV.* **2** N-COUNT A **floor** of a building is all the rooms on a particular level. ❑ *It is on the fifth floor of the hospital.* **3** N-COUNT The ocean **floor** is the ground at the bottom of an ocean. The valley **floor** is the ground at the bottom of a valley. **4** V-T If you **are floored by** something, you are unable to respond to it because you are so surprised by it. ❑ *He was floored by the announcement.* **5** → see also **shop floor**

Usage

In British English, the **ground floor** of a building is the floor which is level with the ground. The floor on the next level is called the **first floor**. In American English, the **first floor** is the floor which is level with the ground and the next floor up is the **second floor**.

Word Partnership Use *floor* with:

V.	**fall on the** floor; **sit on the** floor; **sweep the** floor **1**
N.	floor **to ceiling**, floor **space** **1** **forest** floor, **ocean** floor **3**

floorboard /ˈflɔːbɔːd/ (**floorboards**) N-COUNT **Floorboards** are the long pieces of wood that some floors are made of.

flop /flɒp/ (**flops, flopping, flopped**) **1** V-I If someone or something **flops** somewhere, they fall there heavily or untidily. ❑ *His hair flopped over his left eye.* **2** V-I & N-COUNT If something **flops**, or if it is a **flop**, it is a total failure. ❑ *After college, he started his own gardening business, which flopped.* ❑ *The film is going to be another embarrassing flop.*

floppy /ˈflɒpi/ ADJ **Floppy** things are loose and tend to hang downwards. ❑ *...a floppy hat.*

ˌfloppy ˈdisk [BRIT also **floppy disc**] (**floppy disks**) N-COUNT A **floppy disk** is a small magnetic disk that used to be used for storing computer data and programs. [COMPUTING]

Word Link *flor ≈ flower : flora, floral, florist*

flora /ˈflɔːrə/ N-UNCOUNT You can refer to plants as **flora**, especially the plants growing in a particular area. **Flora** can take the singular or plural form of the verb. [TECHNICAL] ❑ *The forest has about 400 different types of flora.*

floral /ˈflɔːrəl/ **1** ADJ A **floral** fabric or design has a pattern of flowers on it. **2** ADJ BEFORE N You use **floral** to describe something that contains flowers or is made of flowers. ❑ *...pretty floral summer dresses.*

florist /ˈflɒrɪst, AM ˈflɔːr-/ (**florists**) **1** N-COUNT A **florist** is a shopkeeper who sells flowers and indoor plants. **2** N-COUNT A **florist** or a **florist's** is a shop where flowers and indoor plants are sold.

flounder /ˈflaʊndə/ (**flounders, floundering, floundered**) **1** V-I If something **is floundering**, it has many problems and may soon fail completely. ❑ *His career was left to flounder.* **2** V-I If someone **is floundering**, they do not know what to do or say. ❑ *I was floundering. I worked in a number of jobs. I had no direction in my life.*

flour /flaʊə/ (**flours**) N-VAR **Flour** is a white or brown powder that is made by grinding grain. It is used to make bread, cakes, and pastry.
→ see **grain**

flourish /ˈflʌrɪʃ, AM ˈflɜːr-/ (**flourishes, flourishing, flourished**) **1** V-I If something **flourishes**, it is successful or widespread, and developing quickly and strongly. ❑ *Business flourished and within six months they were earning 18,000 roubles a day.* ● **flourishing** ADJ ❑ *London quickly became a flourishing port.* **2** V-I If a plant or animal **flourishes**, it grows well or is healthy. ● **flourishing** ADJ ❑ *...the largest and most flourishing fox population in Europe.* **3** N-COUNT If you do something **with a flourish**, you do it with a bold confident movement, intended to make people notice it. ❑ *She finished dancing with a flourish.*

flout /flaʊt/ (**flouts, flouting, flouted**) V-T If you **flout** a law, order, or rule of behaviour, you deliberately and openly disobey it.

flow /fləʊ/ (**flows, flowing, flowed**) **1** V-I & N-COUNT If a liquid, gas, or electrical current **flows** somewhere, it moves there steadily and continuously. This movement is called a **flow**. ❑ *A stream flowed gently down into the valley.* ❑ *...increases in blood flow.* **2** V-I & N-SING If a number of people or things **flow** from one place to another, they move there steadily in large groups. This movement is called a **flow**. ❑ *Refugees continue to flow from Sudan.* ❑ *...the flow of cars and buses along the street.* **3** V-I & N-SING If information or money **flows** somewhere, it moves freely between people or organizations. This movement is called a **flow**. ❑ *A lot of this information flowed through other police departments.* ❑ *...a change to control the flow of information.* **4** V-I If someone's hair or clothing **flows**, it hangs freely and loosely. [LITERARY]
→ see **ocean, traffic**

flower /flaʊə/ (**flowers, flowering, flowered**) **1** N-COUNT A **flower** is the brightly coloured part of a plant which grows at the end of a stem. ❑ *...a bunch of flowers.* **2** V-I & PHRASE When a plant **flowers**, or when it is **in flower**, its flowers have appeared and opened. **3** V-I When something **flowers**, it gets stronger and more successful. ❑ *Their relationship flowered.* ● **flowering** N-UNCOUNT ❑ *...the flowering of new thinking.*
→ see Picture Dictionary: **flower**
→ see **plant**

Word Partnership Use *flower* with:

V.	**pick a** flower **1**
N.	flower **arrangement**, flower **garden**, flower **shop**, flower **show** **1**
ADJ.	**dried** flower, **fresh** flower **1**

ˈflower ˌbed (**flower beds**) N-COUNT A **flower bed** is an area of earth in which you grow plants.

flown /fləʊn/ **Flown** is the past participle of **fly**.

flu /fluː/ N-UNCOUNT **Flu** is an illness caused by a virus. The symptoms are like those of a bad cold, but more serious. ❑ *He had the flu.*

fluctuate /ˈflʌktʃʊeɪt/ (**fluctuates, fluctuating, fluctuated**) V-I If something **fluctuates**, it changes a lot in an irregular way. ❑ *Body temperature can fluctuate if you are ill.* ● **fluctuation** (**fluctuations**) N-VAR ❑ *Don't worry about tiny fluctuations in your weight.*

fluent /ˈfluːənt/ **1** ADJ Someone who is **fluent in** a particular language can speak it easily and

Picture Dictionary flowers

correctly. You can also say that someone speaks **fluent** French, Chinese, or other language. ● **fluently** ADV ❑ *He spoke three languages fluently.* ● **fluency** N-UNCOUNT ❑ *To work as a translator, you need fluency in at least one foreign language.* **2** ADJ If your speech, reading, or writing is **fluent**, you speak, read, or write easily, with no hesitation or mistakes. ● **fluently** ADV ❑ *Alex didn't read fluently till he was nearly seven.*

fluff /flʌf/ (**fluffs, fluffing, fluffed**) **1** N-UNCOUNT **Fluff** is the small masses of soft light thread that you find on clothes or in dusty corners of a room. ❑ *...some bits of fluff on her sweater.* **2** V-T & PHR-VERB If you **fluff** something, or if you **fluff** it **up**, you get a lot of air into it, for example by shaking or brushing it, in order to make it seem larger and lighter. ❑ *She stood up and fluffed her hair.*

fluffy /ˈflʌfi/ ADJ Something such as a towel or a toy animal that is **fluffy** is very soft and woolly.

fluid /ˈfluːɪd/ (**fluids**) **1** N-VAR A **fluid** is a liquid. [FORMAL] ❑ *Make sure that you drink plenty of fluids.* **2** ADJ **Fluid** movements, lines, or designs are smooth and graceful. ● **fluidity** /fluːˈɪdɪti/ N-UNCOUNT ❑ *...an exquisite fluidity of movement.* **3** ADJ A situation that is **fluid** is likely to change often.

fluke /fluːk/ (**flukes**) N-COUNT If you say that something good is a **fluke**, you mean that it happened accidentally rather than by being planned or arranged. [INFORMAL] ❑ *The discovery was a fluke.*

flung /flʌŋ/ **Flung** is the past tense and past participle of **fling**.

fluorescent /flʊəˈresənt/ **1** ADJ A **fluorescent** surface or colour has a very bright appearance when light is directed onto it. ❑ *...a piece of fluorescent tape.* **2** ADJ A **fluorescent** light shines with a very hard bright light and is usually in the form of a long strip.
→ see **light bulb**

flurry /ˈflʌri, AM ˈflɜːri/ (**flurries**) **1** N-COUNT A **flurry of** activity or speech is a short, energetic amount of it. ❑ *...a flurry of diplomatic activity to help end the war.* **2** N-COUNT A **flurry of** snow or wind is a small amount of it that moves suddenly.

flush /flʌʃ/ (**flushes, flushing, flushed**) **1** V-I & N-COUNT If you **flush**, or if there is a **flush** on your cheeks, your face goes red because you are embarrassed or hot. ❑ *There was a slight flush on his cheeks.* ● **flushed** ADJ ❑ *Her face was flushed with anger.* **2** V-T/V-I & N-COUNT When you **flush** a toilet, or when it **flushes**, you press a handle and water flows into the toilet bowl, cleaning it. This action is called a **flush**. **3** V-T If you **flush** people or animals **out** of a place, you force them to come out. ❑ *Help us to flush out the criminals.* **4** ADJ AFTER LINK-V If something is **flush with** a surface, it is level with it and does not stick up. ❑ *Make sure the tile is flush with the other tiles.*

fluster /ˈflʌstə/ (**flusters, flustering, flustered**) V-T If you **fluster** someone, you make them feel nervous and confused by rushing or interrupting them. ❑ *She is a very calm person. Nothing flusters her.* ● **flustered** ADJ ❑ *She was so flustered that she forgot her reply.*

flute /fluːt/ (**flutes**) N-COUNT A **flute** is a musical wind instrument consisting of a long tube with holes in it. You play it by blowing over a hole at one end while holding it sideways.
→ see **orchestra**

flutter /ˈflʌtə/ (**flutters, fluttering, fluttered**) **1** V-I/V-I If something light **flutters**, or if you **flutter** it, it moves through the air with small quick movements. ❑ *Her skirt was fluttering in the night breeze.* **2** V-I If your heart or stomach **flutters**, you experience a strong feeling of excitement or anxiety.

flux /flʌks/ N-UNCOUNT If something is in a **state of flux**, it is changing constantly. ❑ *...a period of economic flux.*

fly /flaɪ/ (**flies, flying, flew, flown**) **1** N-COUNT A **fly** is a small insect with two wings. **2** V-I When something such as a bird, insect, or aircraft **flies**, it moves through the air. ❑ *The planes flew through the clouds.* ❑ *The bird flew away.* ● **flying** ADJ BEFORE N ❑ *...species of flying insects.* **3** V-T If you **fly** somewhere, you travel there in an aircraft. If you **fly** something or someone somewhere, you send them there in an aircraft. ❑ *It may be possible to fly the women and children out on Thursday.* **4** V-T/V-I When a pilot **flies**, or **flies** an aircraft, he or she controls its movement. ❑ *He flew a small plane to Cuba.* ❑ *I also wanted to fly.* ● **flyer** (**flyers**) N-COUNT ❑ *...a highly experienced flyer.* **5** V-I If something **flies** or **is flying**, it moves about freely and loosely. ❑ *His long hair flew back in the wind.* ❑ *A red and black flag was flying from the balcony.* **6** V-I If you say

Word Web fly

About 500 years ago, Leonardo da Vinci* designed some simple flying machines. His sketches look a lot like modern **parachutes** and **helicopters**. About 300 years later, the Montgolfier brothers amazed the king of France with hot-air **balloon** flights. Soon inventors in many countries began experimenting with blimps, **hang gliders**, and human-powered **aircraft**. Most inventors tried to copy the **flight** of birds. Then in 1903, the Wright brothers invented the first true **airplane**. Their gasoline-powered **craft** carried one **passenger**. The trip lasted 59 seconds. Amazingly, 70 years later **jumbo jets** carrying 400 passengers happens every day.

Leonardo da Vinci (1452-1519): an Italian artist.

that someone or something **flies** in a particular direction, you are emphasizing that they move there with a lot of speed or force. ❑ *She flew to their bedsides when they were ill.* ❑ *The punch sent the young man flying.* 7 N-COUNT The front opening on a pair of trousers is referred to as **the fly** or **the flies**. 8 PHRASE If you **get off to a flying start**, you start something very well, for example a race or a new job.
→ see Word Web: **fly**
→ see **insect**

▶ **fly into** PHR-VERB If you **fly into** a rage or a panic, you suddenly become very angry or anxious and show this in your behaviour. ❑ *He would fly into a rage if he lost a game.*

flyer /flaɪə/ (**flyers**) 1 N-COUNT A **flyer** is a small printed notice which is used to advertise a particular company or event. 2 → see also **fly**

foal /fəʊl/ (**foals**) N-COUNT A **foal** is a very young horse.

foam /fəʊm/ (**foams, foaming, foamed**) 1 N-UNCOUNT **Foam** consists of a mass of small bubbles that are formed when air and a liquid are mixed together. ❑ *He licked the foam from his coffee from his lips.* 2 V-I If a liquid **foams**, it is full of small bubbles and keeps moving slightly. 3 N-UNCOUNT **Foam** or **foam rubber** is soft rubber full of small holes which is used, for example, to make mattresses and cushions.

ˈfocal ˌpoint /ˈfəʊkəl pɔɪnt/ (**focal points**) N-COUNT The **focal point of** something is the thing that people concentrate on or pay most attention to.

focus /ˈfəʊkəs/ (**focuses, focusing, focused** or **focusses, focussing, focussed**) 1 V-T/V-I If you **focus on** a particular topic, or if your attention **is focused on** it, you concentrate on it and deal with it. ❑ *Today he focussed on the economy.* 2 N-COUNT The **focus of** something is the main topic or main thing that it is concerned with. ❑ *The new system is the focus of much criticism.* 3 N-COUNT Your **focus on** something is the special attention that you pay it. ❑ *...his focus on foreign policy.* ❑ *IBM has shifted its focus to personal computers.* 4 V-T/V-I If you **focus** your eyes, or if your eyes **focus**, your eyes adjust so that you can see something clearly. If you **focus** a camera, telescope, or other instrument, you adjust it so that you can see clearly through it. 5 PHRASE If an image or a camera, telescope, or other instrument is **in focus**, the edges of what you see are clear and sharp. If it is **out of focus**, the edges of what you see are unclear. 6 V-T If you **focus** rays of light on a particular point, you pass them through a lens or reflect them from a mirror so that they meet at that point.
→ see **photography, telescope**

ˈfocus group (**focus groups**) N-COUNT A **focus group** is a group of people who are intended to represent the general public. Focus groups have discussions in which their opinions are recorded about particular subjects.

fodder /ˈfɒdə/ N-UNCOUNT **Fodder** is food that is given to animals such as cows or horses.

foe /fəʊ/ (**foes**) N-COUNT Your **foe** is your enemy. [LITERARY]

foetus also **fetus** /ˈfiːtəs/ (**foetuses**) N-COUNT A **foetus** is an unborn animal or human being in its later stages of development.
→ see **reproduction**

fog

fog /fɒg/ (**fogs**) N-VAR When there is **fog**, there are tiny drops of water in the air which form a thick cloud and make it difficult to see things. ❑ *The crash happened in thick fog.*

foggy /ˈfɒgi/ (**foggier, foggiest**) ADJ When it is **foggy**, there is fog.

foil /fɔɪl/ (**foils, foiling, foiled**) 1 N-UNCOUNT **Foil** is metal that is as thin as paper. It is used to wrap food in. 2 V-T If you **foil** someone's plan or attempt at something, you prevent it from being successful. [JOURNALISM] ❑ *He foiled an armed robbery.*

fold /fəʊld/ (**folds, folding, folded**) 1 V-T & PHR-VERB If you **fold** a piece of paper or cloth, or if you **fold** it **up**, you bend it so that one part covers another part. ❑ *He folded the paper carefully.* ❑ *Fold the omelette in half.* 2 N-COUNT A **fold** in a piece of paper or cloth is a bend that you make in it when you put one part of it over another part and press the edge.

fold

3 N-COUNT The **folds** in a piece of cloth are the curved shapes which are formed when it is not hanging or lying flat. 4 V-T/V-I & PHR-VERB If a piece of furniture or equipment **folds**, or if you **fold** it **up**, you make it smaller or flatter by bending or closing parts of it. ❑ *This seat folds flat and is easy to*

store. ❑ *Fold the ironing board up so that it is flat.* ❑ *...a folding beach chair.* **5** V-T If you **fold** your arms or hands, you bring them together and cross them or link them. **6** V-I If a business or organization **folds**, it is unsuccessful and has to close.

Word Partnership Use *fold* with:

ADV.	fold **carefully**, fold **gently**, fold **neatly** **1**
N.	fold **clothes**, fold **paper** **1**
	fold ***your* arms/hands** **5**

folder /ˈfəʊldə/ (**folders**) **1** N-COUNT A **folder** is a thin piece of cardboard in which you can keep loose papers. **2** N-COUNT A **folder** is a group of files that are stored together on a computer.
→ see **office**

foliage /ˈfəʊliɪdʒ/ N-UNCOUNT The **foliage** of a plant consists of its leaves.

folk /fəʊk/ (**folks**) **1** N-PLURAL & N-VOC You can refer to people as **folk** or **folks**. ❑ *...country folk.* ❑ *It's a question of money, folks.* **2** N-PLURAL You can refer to your close family, especially your mother and father, as your **folks**. [INFORMAL] ❑ *I haven't seen my folks for a month.* **3** ADJ BEFORE N **Folk** art and customs are traditional or typical of a particular community or nation. ❑ *...Irish folk music.*
→ see **dance**

folklore /ˈfəʊklɔː/ N-UNCOUNT **Folklore** consists of the traditional stories, customs, and habits of a particular community or nation. ❑ *According to folklore, sunshine on February 2nd means six more weeks of cold weather.*

follow /ˈfɒləʊ/ (**follows, following, followed**) **1** V-T/V-I If you **follow** someone who is going somewhere, you move along behind them. ❑ *We followed him up the steps.* ❑ *They took him into a small room and I followed.* **2** V-T If you **follow** someone to a place, you go to join them there at a later time. ❑ *He followed Janice to New York.* **3** V-T/V-I To **follow** an event, activity, or period of time means to happen or come after it, at a later time. ❑ *...the days following Daddy's death.* ❑ *He was arrested in the confusion which followed.* **4** V-T & PHR-VERB If you **follow** one thing **with** another, or if you **follow** it **up with** another, you do or say the second thing after you have done or said the first thing. ❑ *When playing sport, warm up first, then follow this with some simple stretching exercises.* **5** PHRASE You use **followed by** to say what comes after something else in a list or ordered set of things. ❑ *Potatoes are the most popular food, followed by white bread.* **6** V-T/V-I If **it follows** that a particular thing is true, that thing is a logical result of something else being true. ❑ *If a bird lays eggs one year, it follows that it will again next year.* **7** PHRASE You use **as follows** to introduce something such as a list, description, or explanation. ❑ *The winners are as follows: E. Walker; R. Foster; R. Gates.* **8** V-T If you **follow** a path or route, you go somewhere using the path or route to direct you. **9** V-T If you **follow** advice or instructions, you act or do something in the way that it indicates. **10** V-T If you **follow** something, you understand it. ❑ *Do you follow the plot so far?* **11** V-T If you **follow** something, you take an interest in it. ❑ *Do you follow the football at all?*
▶ **follow through** PHR-VERB If you **follow through** an action or plan, you continue doing or thinking about it until it is completed.

Word Partnership Use *follow* with:

ADV.	**closely** follow **1** **2** **4** **8**
	blindly follow **1** **2** **4** **8** **9**
N.	follow **advice**, follow **directions**, follow **instructions**, follow **a story** **1** **4** **9** **10**
	follow **a road**, follow **signs**, follow **a trail** **8**
	follow **a pattern**, follow **orders**, follow **rules** **9** **11**

follower /ˈfɒləʊə/ (**followers**) N-COUNT The **followers** of a person or belief are the people who support the person or accept the belief.

following /ˈfɒləʊɪŋ/ **1** PREP **Following** a particular event means after that event. ❑ *...the centuries following Christ's death.* **2** ADJ **The following** day, week, or year is the day, week, or year after the one you have just mentioned. ❑ *We went to dinner the following Monday evening.* **3** ADJ & PRON You use **the following** to refer to something that you are about to mention. ❑ *The method is explained in the following chapters.* ❑ *Add any of the following: salt, pepper, dried herbs.* **4** N-SING If you have a **following**, a group of people support or admire your beliefs or actions. ❑ *Australian rugby has a huge following in New Zealand.*

ˈfollow-ˌup (**follow-ups**) N-VAR A **follow-up** is something that is done as a continuation or second part of something done previously. ❑ *Students return for a one-day follow-up workshop.*

folly /ˈfɒli/ (**follies**) N-VAR If you say that an action or way of behaving is **folly** or is a **folly**, you mean that it is foolish. ❑ *...the follies of war.*

fond /fɒnd/ (**fonder, fondest**) **1** ADJ AFTER LINK-V If you are **fond of** someone or something, you like that person or thing. ❑ *I am very fond of Michael.* ● **fondness** N-UNCOUNT ❑ *I've always had a fondness for jewels.* **2** ADJ BEFORE N You use **fond** to describe people or their behaviour when they show affection. ❑ *He gave him a fond smile.* ● **fondly** ADV ❑ *Their eyes met fondly across the table.* **3** ADJ BEFORE N If you have **fond memories** of someone or something, you remember them with pleasure. ● **fondly** ADV ❑ *I remembered it fondly.*

food /fuːd/ (**foods**) **1** N-VAR **Food** is what people and animals eat. ❑ *Enjoy your food.* ❑ *...frozen foods.* **2** PHRASE If you give someone **food for thought**, you make them think carefully about something. ❑ *Lord Fraser's speech offers much food for thought.*
→ see Word Web: **food**
→ see **cook, farm, habitat, rice, sugar, vegetarian**

foodstuff /ˈfuːdstʌf/ (**foodstuffs**) N-COUNT **Foodstuffs** are substances which people eat. ❑ *...basic foodstuffs such as sugar, cooking oil and cheese.*

fool /fuːl/ (**fools, fooling, fooled**) **1** N-COUNT If you call someone a **fool**, you are indicating that you think they are not sensible and show a lack of good judgement. ❑ *'You fool!' she shouted.* ❑ *He'd been a fool to marry her.* **2** PHRASE If you **make a fool of** someone, you make people think they are silly. ❑ *He was making a fool of himself.* **3** V-T If someone **fools** you, they deceive or trick you. ❑ *They tried to fool you into coming after us.*
▶ **fool about** or **fool around** PHR-VERB If you

Word Web food

The **food chain** begins with sunlight. Green **plants** absorb and store **energy** from the sun through photosynthesis. This energy is passed on to an herbivore (such as a mouse) that **eats** these plants. The mouse is then eaten by a carnivore (such as a snake). The snake may be eaten by a **top predator** (such as a hawk). When the hawk dies, its body is broken down by bacteria. Soon the **nutrients** from the hawk's body become food for plants and the cycle begins again.

Food chain

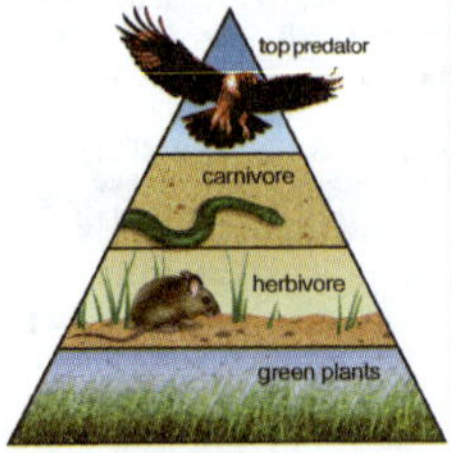

F

fool about, or if you **fool around**, you behave in a playful and silly way.

foolish /'fu:lɪʃ/ ADJ If you say that someone's behaviour is **foolish**, you mean that it is not sensible and shows a lack of good judgement. ❑ *It would be foolish to expect everything to remain the same.* ● **foolishly** ADV ❑ *He knows that he acted foolishly.* ● **foolishness** N-UNCOUNT ❑ *They don't accept any foolishness.*

foot /fʊt/ (**feet**)

> In meaning 3, the plural can be either **foot** or **feet**.

1 N-COUNT & PHRASE Your **feet** are the parts of your body that are at the ends of your legs and that you stand on. If you are **on** your **feet**, you are standing up. If you rise **to** your **feet**, you stand up. ❑ *Everyone was on their feet applauding.* 2 N-SING **The foot of** something is the part that is farthest from its top. ❑ *David called to the children from the foot of the stairs.* 3 N-COUNT A **foot** is a unit of length, equal to 12 inches or 30.48 centimetres. ❑ *The room was 6 foot wide and 10 foot high.* 4 PHRASE If you say that someone or something is **on** their **feet** again after a difficult period, you mean that they have recovered and are back to normal. 5 PHRASE If you go somewhere **on foot**, you walk, rather than use any form of transport. 6 PHRASE If someone **puts** their **foot down**, they use their authority in order to stop something happening. ❑ *He planned to go skiing on his own but his wife had decided to put her foot down.* 7 PHRASE If you **put** your **feet up**, you relax or have a rest, especially by sitting or lying with your feet supported off the ground. 8 PHRASE To **set foot** in a place means to go there. ❑ *I left and never set foot in Texas again.* 9 PHRASE If someone has to **stand on** their **own two feet**, they have to manage without help from other people.
→ see Picture Dictionary: **foot**
→ see **body, measurement**

footage /'fʊtɪdʒ/ N-UNCOUNT **Footage** of a particular event is a film, or the part of a film, showing this event. ❑ *...footage from this summer's festivals.*

football /'fʊtbɔ:l/ (**footballs**) 1 N-UNCOUNT In British English, **football** is a game played by

Picture Dictionary foot

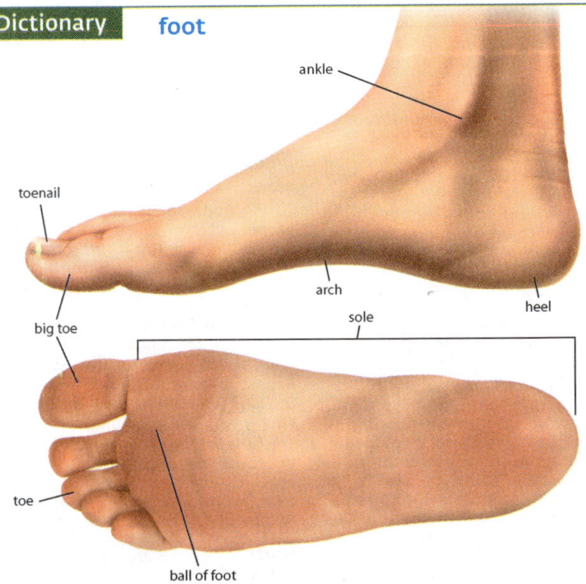

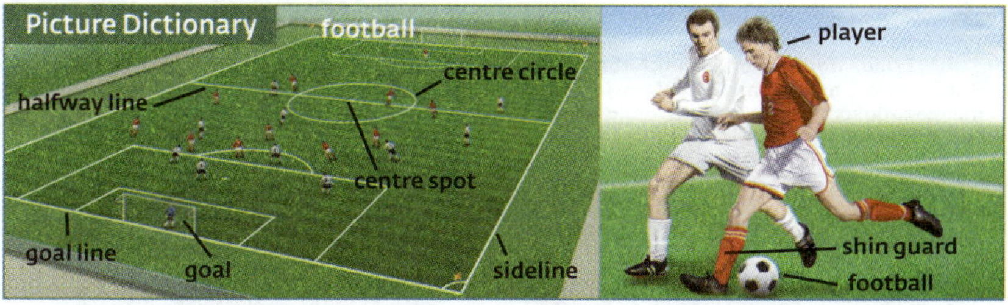

two teams of eleven players who try to score by kicking or heading a ball into their opponent's goal. The American word is **soccer**. ❑ *Several boys were playing football.* **2** N-UNCOUNT In American English, **football** is a game played by two teams of eleven players who try to score by taking the ball into their opponent's end. The British term is **American football**. **3** N-COUNT A **football** is a ball that is used for playing football.
→ see Picture Dictionary: **football**

footballer /ˈfʊtbɔːlə/ (**footballers**) N-COUNT In British English, a **footballer** is a person who plays football. The American term is **soccer player**.

foothills /ˈfʊthɪlz/ N-PLURAL The **foothills of** a mountain or a range of mountains are the lower hills or mountains around its base. ❑ *Pasadena is a town in the foothills of the San Gabriel mountains.*

foothold /ˈfʊthəʊld/ (**footholds**) **1** N-COUNT A **foothold** is a strong position from which further advances or progress may be made. ❑ *Companies must establish a firm foothold in Europe.* **2** N-COUNT A **foothold** is a ledge or hollow where you can safely put your foot when climbing.

footing /ˈfʊtɪŋ/ **1** N-UNCOUNT You use **footing** to describe the basis on which something is done or exists. ❑ *...research that places training on a more scientific footing.* **2** N-UNCOUNT You use **footing** to refer to your position and how securely your feet are placed on the ground. ❑ *He lost his footing and fell into the water.*

footnote /ˈfʊtnəʊt/ (**footnotes**) N-COUNT A **footnote** is a note at the bottom of a page which gives more information about something on the page.

footpath /ˈfʊtpɑːθ, -pæθ/ (**footpaths**) N-COUNT A **footpath** is a path for people to walk on.

footprint /ˈfʊtprɪnt/ (**footprints**) N-COUNT A **footprint** is the mark of a person's foot or shoe left on a surface.
→ see **fossil**

footstep /ˈfʊtstep/ (**footsteps**) **1** N-COUNT A **footstep** is the sound made by someone's feet touching the ground when they are walking or running. ❑ *They heard footsteps in the main room.* **2** PHRASE If you **follow in** someone's **footsteps**, you do the same things as they did earlier. ❑ *He followed in the footsteps of his father, a professional boxer.*

footwear /ˈfʊtweə/ N-UNCOUNT **Footwear** refers to things that people wear on their feet, for example shoes, boots, and sandals.

for /fə, STRONG fɔː/ **1** PREP If something is **for** someone, they are intended to have it or benefit from it. ❑ *I have some free advice for you.* ❑ *...a table for two.* **2** PREP If you work **for** someone, you are employed by them. ❑ *...a buyer for one of the largest chain stores.* **3** PREP & ADV If you are **for** something, you are in favour of it. ❑ *Are you for or against public transport?* **4** PHRASE If you are **all for** something, you are very much in favour of it. ❑ *I was all for it, but Wolfe said no.* **5** PREP You use **for** after words such as 'time', 'space', 'money', or 'energy' when you say how much there is or whether there is enough of it in order to be able to do or use a particular thing. ❑ *Many new trains have space for wheelchairs.* ❑ *It would take three to six hours for a round trip.* **6** PREP You use **for** when you are describing the purpose of something, the reason for something, or the cause of something. ❑ *...a room for rent.* ❑ *...a comfortable chair, for using in the living room.* ❑ *...a speech explaining his reasons for going.* **7** PREP A word or term **for** something is a way of referring to it. ❑ *The technical term for sunburn is 'erythema'.* **8** PREP You use **for** to say how long something lasts or continues. ❑ *She sat on her bed for a few minutes.* ❑ *They talked for a bit.* **9** PHRASE You use an expression such as **for the first time** when you are talking about how often something has happened. ❑ *He has married for the second time, this time to a Belgian.* **10** PREP You use **for** to say how far something extends. ❑ *We drove on for a few miles.* **11** PREP You use **for** with 'every' when you state the second part of a ratio. ❑ *There had been one divorce for every 100 marriages before the war.* **12** PREP You use **for** when you are talking about the cost of something. ❑ *The Martins sold their house for about 1.4 million pounds.* **13** PREP You use **for** when you are mentioning a person or thing that you have feelings about. ❑ *He began to feel sympathy for this unhappy man.* **14** PREP You use **for** when you are saying how something affects someone. ❑ *It would be excellent for him to travel a little.* **15** PREP You use **for** when you say that an aspect of something or someone is surprising in relation to other aspects of them. ❑ *He was tall for an eight-year-old.* **16** PREP If something is planned **for** a particular time or occasion, it is planned to happen then. ❑ *The party was scheduled for 7:00.* ❑ *I'll be home for Christmas.* **17** PREP If you leave **for** a place, or if you take a train, plane, or boat **for** a place, you are going there. **18** **as for** → see **as** **19** **but for** → see **but** **20** **for all** → see **all**

forage /ˈfɒrɪdʒ, AM ˈfɔːr-/ (**forages, foraging, foraged**) V-I To **forage for** something such as food means to search for it. ❑ *They were forced to forage for clothing and fuel.*

foray /ˈfɒreɪ, AM ˈfɔːreɪ/ (**forays**) **1** N-COUNT If you make a **foray into** a new or unfamiliar type of activity, you start to become involved in it. ❑ *...her first forays into politics.* **2** N-COUNT If a group of soldiers make a **foray into** an area, they make a quick attack there, usually in order to steal supplies.

forbid /fə'bɪd/ (**forbids, forbidding, forbade** /fə'bæd, -'beɪd/, **forbidden**) **1** V-T If you **forbid** someone **to** do something, or if you **forbid** an activity, you order that it must not be done. ❑ *They'll forbid you to marry.* ❑ *Saudi law forbids the use of right-hand drive vehicles.* **2** V-T If something **forbids** an event or course of action, it makes it impossible. ❑ *His own pride forbids him to ask Arthur's help.*

forbidden /fə'bɪdən/ ADJ If something is **forbidden**, you are not allowed to do it or have it. ❑ *Eating was forbidden.* ❑ *It is forbidden to drive faster than 20mph.*

force /fɔːs/ (**forces, forcing, forced**) **1** V-T If something or someone **forces** you **to** do something, they make you do it, even though you do not want to. ❑ *A back injury forced her to exit from the race.* ❑ *I cannot force you in this. You must decide.* ❑ *He tried to force her into a car.* ❑ *To force this agreement on the nation is wrong.* **2** V-T If you **force** something, you use a lot of strength to move it. ❑ *He forced the key into the lock.* ❑ *Police forced the door of the flat and arrested Mr Roberts.* **3** N-UNCOUNT **Force** is power or strength. ❑ *They tried to seize power by force.* ❑ *The garden catches the full force of the afternoon sun.* **4** N-COUNT Someone or something that is a **force** in a situation has a strong influence on it. ❑ *The FLN is still a big political force in the country.* **5** V-T If you **force a smile** or a **laugh**, you manage to smile or laugh even though you do not want to. ● **forced** ADJ ❑ *She called him darling. It sounded so forced.* **6** N-COUNT A **force** in physics is the pulling or pushing effect that one thing has on another. ❑ *...the earth's force of gravity.* **7** N-COUNT **Forces** are groups of soldiers or military vehicles that are organized for a particular purpose. ❑ *American forces have arrived in the region.* **8** PHRASE A law or system that is **in force** exists or is being used. ❑ *Martial law is in force.* **9** PHRASE If you **join forces with** someone, you work together to achieve a common aim or purpose. ❑ *He joined forces with his brother to start the business.* **10** to **force** someone's **hand** → see **hand**
→ see **motion**

Thesaurus *force* Also look up:

V.	coerce, make **1**
	push, thrust **2**
N.	energy, pressure, strength **3**

Word Partnership Use *force* with:

V.	force **to resign** **1**
N.	**use of** force **1 2 3**
	force **a smile** **5**
	force **of gravity** **6**
ADJ.	**driving** force, **excessive** force, **necessary** force, **powerful** force **3**
	full force **3 4**
	enemy forces, **military** forces **7**

forceful /'fɔːsfʊl/ **1** ADJ Someone who is **forceful** expresses their opinions in a strong and confident way. ❑ *He was so forceful that most people just agreed with him.* ● **forcefully** ADV ❑ *He argued forcefully.* **2** ADJ Something that is **forceful** causes you to think or feel something very strongly. ❑ *The bomb attack was a forceful reminder that we had to continue working for peace.*

forcible /'fɔːsɪbəl/ ADJ **Forcible** actions involve physical force or violence. ❑ *...the forcible removal of a leader from power.* ● **forcibly** ADV ❑ *Student leaders were forcibly removed from the university.*

ford /fɔːd/ (**fords**) N-COUNT A **ford** is a shallow place in a river where it is possible to cross safely without using a boat.

fore /fɔː/ PHRASE When something or someone **comes to the fore**, they suddenly become important or popular. ❑ *A number of short films brought new directors and actors to the fore.*

forearm /'fɔːrɑːm/ (**forearms**) N-COUNT Your **forearms** are the lower parts of your arms between your elbows and your wrists.

Word Link ***fore* ≈ *before* : *forecast, foresight, unforeseen***

forecast /'fɔːkɑːst, -kæst/ (**forecasts, forecasting, forecasted** or **forecast**) V-I & N-COUNT If you **forecast** future events, you say what you think is going to happen. A **forecast** is a prediction of future events. ❑ *They forecast that Rooney will score more than 200 goals during his career.* ❑ *The forecast is for wet weather.* ● **forecaster** (**forecasters**) N-COUNT ❑ *...our senior weather forecaster.*
→ see Word Web: **forecast**

forefinger /'fɔːfɪŋgə/ (**forefingers**) N-COUNT Your **forefinger** is the finger next to your thumb.

forefront /'fɔːfrʌnt/ N-SING If you are **at the forefront of** a campaign or other activity, you have a leading and influential position in it. ❑ *They have been at the forefront of political change.*

Word Web forecast

Meteorologists depend on good information. They make **observations**. They gather **data** about barometric **pressure**, **temperature**, and **humidity**. They track **storms** with **radar** and **satellites**. They track cold **fronts** and warm fronts. They put all of this information into their computers and **model** possible weather patterns. Today scientists are trying to make better **weather forecasts**. They are installing thousands of small, inexpensive **radar** units on rooftops and cell phone towers. They will gather information near the Earth's surface and high in the sky. This will give meteorologists more information to help them **predict** tomorrow's weather.

forego also **forgo** /fɔːˈgəʊ/ (**foregoes, foregoing, forewent, foregone**) V-T If you **forego** something, you decide not to have it or do it, although you would like to. [FORMAL] ❑ *Mary and Brian decided to forego their movie plans and watch television together at home.*

foreground /ˈfɔːgraʊnd/ **1** N-SING **The foreground** of a picture is the part that seems nearest to you. ❑ *...the woman in the foreground.* **2** N-SING If something or someone is **in the foreground**, they receive a lot of attention. ❑ *Important issues were placed in the foreground.*

forehead /ˈfɒrɪd, ˈfɔːhed/ (**foreheads**) N-COUNT Your **forehead** is the flat area at the front of your head above your eyebrows and below where your hair grows.
→ see **face**

foreign /ˈfɒrɪn, AM ˈfɔːr-/ **1** ADJ Something that is **foreign** comes from or relates to a country that is not your own. ❑ *She was on her first foreign holiday.* ❑ *...a foreign language.* **2** ADJ BEFORE N In politics and journalism, **foreign** is used to describe people and activities relating to countries that are not the country of the person or government concerned. ❑ *...the foreign minister.* ❑ *...the effects of US foreign policy.* **3** ADJ A **foreign body** is an object that has got into something, usually by accident, and should not be there. [FORMAL] ❑ *...a foreign body in the eye.* **4** ADJ Something that is **foreign to** a particular person or thing is not typical of them or is unknown to them. ❑ *The whole idea of being gentle with anyone is foreign to most men.*

Thesaurus *foreign* Also look up:

ADJ. alien, exotic, strange; *(ant.)* domestic, native **1** **2**

foreigner /ˈfɒrɪnə, AM ˈfɔːr-/ (**foreigners**) **1** N-COUNT A **foreigner** is someone who belongs to a country that is not your own. **2** → See note at **stranger**

ˌforeign exˈchange (**foreign exchanges**) **1** N-PLURAL **Foreign exchanges** are the institutions or systems involved with changing one currency into another. ❑ *The value of the euro has risen on the foreign exchanges.* **2** N-UNCOUNT **Foreign exchange** is foreign currency that is obtained through the foreign exchange system.

ˈForeign ˌOffice (**Foreign Offices**) N-COUNT **The Foreign Office** is the government department, especially in Britain, which is responsible for the government's relations with foreign governments.

foreman /ˈfɔːmən/ (**foremen**) N-COUNT A **foreman** is a person who is in charge of a group of workers.

Word Link ***most ≈ superlative degree : almost, foremost, utmost***

Word Link ***fore ≈ before : forecast, foremost, foresight***

foremost /ˈfɔːməʊst/ **1** ADJ **The foremost** thing or person in a group is the most important or best. ❑ *...the world's foremost scholar of Indian culture.* **2** PHRASE You use **first and foremost** to emphasize the most important quality of something or someone. ❑ *This book aims first and foremost to improve your painting.*

forename /ˈfɔːneɪm/ (**forenames**) N-COUNT Your **forenames** are your first names, as opposed to your surname. [FORMAL]

forensic /fəˈrensɪk/ ADJ BEFORE N When a **forensic** analysis is done, objects are examined scientifically in order to discover information about a crime. ❑ *Forensic experts searched the area for clues.*

forerunner /ˈfɔːrʌnə/ (**forerunners**) N-COUNT The **forerunner of** something is a similar thing that existed before it and influenced its development. ❑ *This machine was the forerunner of the modern helicopter.*

foresee /fɔːˈsiː/ (**foresees, foreseeing, foresaw, foreseen**) V-T If you **foresee** something, you expect and believe that it will happen. ❑ *He did not foresee any problems.* ❑ *...a dangerous situation which we could have foreseen.*

foreseeable /fɔːˈsiːəbəl/ PHRASE When you talk about **the foreseeable future**, you are referring to the period of time in the future during which it is possible to say what will happen. ❑ *She will not want to leave for the foreseeable future.*

Word Link ***fore ≈ before : forecast, foresight, unforeseen***

foresight /ˈfɔːsaɪt/ N-UNCOUNT **Foresight** is the ability to see what might happen in the future and to take appropriate action; used showing approval. ❑ *He had the foresight to remove his money from the bank before the war began.*

forest /ˈfɒrɪst, AM ˈfɔːr-/ (**forests**) N-VAR A **forest** is a large area where trees grow close together. ❑ *40% of the forest's 35 million trees are dead or dying.*
→ see Word Web: **forest**
→ see **habitat**

Word Web *forest*

Four hundred years ago, settlers in North America found endless **forests**. This large supply of **wood** helped them. They used **timber** to build homes and make furniture. They burned wood for cooking and heat. They cut down the **woods** to create farmland. By the late 1800s, most of the old growth forests on the East Coast had disappeared. The lumber industry has also destroyed millions of trees. Reforestation has replaced some of them. However, logging companies usually plant single species forests. Some people say these are not really forests at all—just **tree** farms.

f

forestall /fɔːˈstɔːl/ (**forestalls, forestalling, forestalled**) V-T If you **forestall** someone, you realize what they are likely to do and prevent them from doing it. ❑ *John went to open the door, but David forestalled him.*

forestry /ˈfɒrɪstri, AM ˈfɔːr-/ N-UNCOUNT **Forestry** is the science or skill of growing trees in forests.
→ see **industry**

forever /fəˈrevə/

> **Forever** is also spelled **for ever** for meanings 1 and 2.

F

1 ADV Something that will happen or continue **forever** will always happen or continue. ❑ *It was great fun but we knew it wouldn't go on for ever.* ❑ *I am forever grateful to the friend who helped us.* **2** ADV If something has gone or changed **forever**, it has gone and will never reappear. ❑ *I knew that my last chance had gone forever.* **3** ADV If you say that someone is **forever** doing something, you are emphasizing that they do it very often. ❑ *My girlfriend is forever telling me to calm down.*

Thesaurus *forever* Also look up:
ADV. always, endlessly, eternally **1**
permanently **2**

forewent /fɔːˈwent/ **Forewent** is the past tense of **forego**.

forfeit /ˈfɔːfɪt/ (**forfeits, forfeiting, forfeited**) **1** V-T If you **forfeit** a right, privilege, or possession, you have to give it up because you have done something wrong. ❑ *He believes that murderers forfeit their own right to life.* **2** N-COUNT A **forfeit** is something that you have to give up because you have done something wrong. ❑ *That is the forfeit he must pay.*

forgave /fəˈgeɪv/ **Forgave** is the past tense of **forgive**.

forge /fɔːdʒ/ (**forges, forging, forged**) **1** V-T If someone **forges** banknotes, documents, or paintings, they make false copies of them in order to deceive people. ❑ *Taylor forged her signature.* ● **forger** (**forgers**) N-COUNT ❑ *Han van Meergeren was a Dutch art forger.* **2** V-T If you **forge** an alliance or relationship, you succeed in creating it. ❑ *The programme aims to forge links between higher education and small businesses.* **3** N-COUNT A **forge** is a place where a blacksmith makes metal things such as horseshoes.
▶ **forge ahead** PHR-VERB If you **forge ahead with** something, you make a lot of progress with it. ❑ *George began to forge ahead with his studies.*

Word Partnership Use *forge* with:
N. forge **documents**, forge **an identity**, forge **a signature** **1**
forge **a bond**, forge **a friendship**, forge **links**, forge **a relationship**, forge **ties** **2**

forgery /ˈfɔːdʒəri/ (**forgeries**) **1** N-UNCOUNT **Forgery** is the crime of making fake banknotes, documents, or paintings. **2** N-COUNT You can refer to a forged banknote, document, or painting as a **forgery**.

forget /fəˈget/ (**forgets, forgetting, forgot, forgotten**) **1** V-T If you **forget** something, or if you **forget how to** do something, you cannot think of it or think of how to do it, although you knew in the past. ❑ *I forgot how to speak English, I could only speak Spanish.* ❑ *She forgot where she left the car.* **2** V-T If you **forget to** do something, you do not remember to do it. ❑ *She forgot to lock her door one day and two men got in.* ❑ *Don't forget that all dogs need fresh water.* **3** V-T If you **forget** something that you had intended to bring with you, you do not remember to bring it. ❑ *I forgot my passport when we were going to Paris.* **4** V-T/V-I If you **forget** something or someone, you deliberately do not think about them any more. ❑ *I can't forget what happened.* ❑ *I found it very easy to forget about Sam.* **5** PHRASE If someone **forgets himself** or **herself**, he or she behaves in an uncontrolled or unacceptable way.

Usage
Note that you cannot use the verb **forget** to say that you have put something somewhere and left it there. Instead you use the verb **leave.** ❑ *I left my bag on the bus.*

Thesaurus *forget* Also look up:
V. disregard, ignore, neglect, overlook **2**

Word Partnership Use *forget* with:
ADV. **never** forget, **quickly** forget, **soon** forget **1**
almost forget **1** **2** **3**
ADJ. **easy/hard to** forget **1**-**4**

forgetful /fəˈgetfʊl/ ADJ Someone who is **forgetful** often forgets things. ● **forgetfulness** N-UNCOUNT ❑ *Her forgetfulness is due to old age.*

forgive /fəˈgɪv/ (**forgives, forgiving, forgave, forgiven**) V-T If you **forgive** someone who has done something wrong, you stop being angry with them. ❑ *She forgave him for stealing her money.* ● **forgiving** ADJ ❑ *I don't think people are very forgiving.* ● **forgiveness** N-UNCOUNT ❑ *He fell to his knees and begged for forgiveness.*

forgo /fɔːˈgəʊ/ → see **forego**

forgot /fəˈgɒt/ **Forgot** is the past tense of **forget**.

forgotten /fəˈgɒtən/ **Forgotten** is the past participle of **forget**.

fork /fɔːk/ (**forks, forking, forked**) **1** N-COUNT A **fork** is an implement that you use when you are eating food. It consists of three or four long thin points on the end of a handle. **2** N-COUNT A **garden fork** is a tool that you use to dig your garden. It consists of three or four long thin points attached to a long handle. **3** N-COUNT & V-I If there is a **fork** in something such as a road or a river, or if it **forks**, it divides into two parts in the shape of a 'Y'. ❑ *You should take the right fork.* ❑ *The path forked in two directions.*
▶ **fork out** PHR-VERB If you **fork out for** something, you spend a lot of money on it. [INFORMAL] ❑ *He will have to fork out for private school fees.* ❑ *Britons fork out more than a billion pounds a year on toys.*

forlorn /fɔːˈlɔːn/ **1** ADJ If you are **forlorn**, you are lonely and unhappy. ● **forlornly** ADV ❑ *He* *waited forlornly in the rain.* **2** ADJ A **forlorn** hope or attempt has no chance of success. ❑ *...the forlorn hope of finding a better life in cities.*

form

❶ TYPE AND SHAPE
❷ MAKING THINGS
❸ DOCUMENT
❹ SOMEONE'S PHYSICAL CONDITION

form /fɔːm/ (**forms**)
❶ **1** N-COUNT A **form of** something is a type or kind of it. ❑ *He had a rare form of cancer.* ❑ *I am against hunting in any form.* **2** PHRASE If someone's behaviour is **true to form**, it is typical of them. ❑ *True to form, she was more than 90 minutes late.* **3** N-COUNT The **form** of something is its shape. ❑ *...the form of the body.* **4** N-COUNT You can refer to something that you can see as a **form**, especially if you cannot see it clearly. ❑ *She had never been so glad to see his large form.*

form /fɔːm/ (**forms, forming, formed**)
❷ **1** V-T/V-I When a particular shape **forms** or **is formed**, people or things move or are arranged so that this shape is made. ❑ *They formed a circle and sang.* ❑ *The captain told the soldiers to form into lines.* **2** V-T If something is arranged so that it has a particular shape or function, you can say that it **forms** something with that shape or function. ❑ *The buildings form a half circle.* **3** V-T If something consists of particular things or people, you can say that they **form** that thing. ❑ *Vegetables form part of his basic diet.* **4** V-T If you **form** an organization, group, or company, you start it. **5** V-T/V-I When something **forms**, it begins to exist. ❑ *The stars formed about 15,000 million years ago.* ❑ *Huge ice sheets were formed.*

form /fɔːm/ (**forms**)
❸ N-COUNT A **form** is a piece of paper with questions on it. You write the answers on the same piece of paper. ❑ *You need to fill in a form.*

form /fɔːm/
❹ N-UNCOUNT & PHRASE In sport, an athlete's **form** refers to their ability or success over a period of time. If they are **off form** they are performing badly; if they are **on form**, they are performing well. ❑ *His form this season has been brilliant.*

Thesaurus *form* Also look up:

N.	class, description, kind ① **1**
	body, figure, frame, shape ① **3**
	application, document, sheet ③
V.	construct, create, develop, establish ② **4** **5**

formal /ˈfɔːməl/ **1** ADJ **Formal** speech or behaviour is correct and serious, rather than relaxed and friendly, and is used especially in official situations. ❑ *...a formal letter of apology.* ● **formally** ADV ❑ *'Good afternoon, Mr Benjamin,' Schumacher said formally.* ● **formality** /fɔːˈmælɪti/ N-UNCOUNT ❑ *We wanted to avoid the formality of hotels, so we went camping.* **2** ADJ BEFORE N A **formal** statement, action, or event is an official one. ❑ *No formal announcement has been made.* ❑ *...a formal dinner.* ● **formally** ADV ❑ *They are now formally separated.* **3** ADJ BEFORE N **Formal** education or training is given in a school or college. ❑ *Even though his formal education stopped when he was 11, he was an excellent reader.*

formality /fɔːˈmælɪti/ (**formalities**) **1** N-COUNT **Formalities** are formal actions that are carried out on particular occasions. ❑ *...immigration formalities.* **2** → see also **formal**

formalize [BRIT also **formalise**] /ˈfɔːməlaɪz/ (**formalizes, formalizing, formalized**) V-T If you **formalize** a plan or arrangement, you make it official. ❑ *The arrangement should be formalized in court.*

format /ˈfɔːmæt/ (**formats, formatting, formatted**) **1** N-COUNT The **format of** something is the way it is arranged and presented. ❑ *I explained the format of the programme to him.* **2** V-T To **format** a computer disk means to run a program so that the disk can be written on. [COMPUTING]

formation /fɔːˈmeɪʃən/ (**formations**) **1** N-UNCOUNT The **formation of** something is its start or creation. ❑ *The name was changed two years after the club's formation.* ❑ *...the formation of a new government.* **2** N-COUNT A rock or cloud **formation** is rock or clouds of a particular shape. **3** N-UNCOUNT If things are **in formation**, they are arranged in a particular pattern. ❑ *He was flying in formation with seven other jets.*

formative /ˈfɔːmətɪv/ ADJ A **formative** period in your life or experience is one that has an important influence on your character and attitudes. ❑ *She spent her formative years growing up in east London.*

former /ˈfɔːmə/ **1** ADJ BEFORE N **Former** is used to indicate what someone or something used to be, but no longer is. ❑ *...former President Bill Clinton.* ❑ *...the former home of Sir Christopher Wren.* **2** ADJ BEFORE N **Former** is used to describe a situation or period of time which came before the present one. ❑ *She wants to remember him as he was in former years.* **3** PRON When two people, things, or groups have just been mentioned, you can refer to the first of them as **the former**. ❑ *Grogan could continue up the White Nile or go overland. He hoped the former would be possible.*

Thesaurus *former* Also look up:

ADJ.	prior **1**
	past, previous **1** **2**

formerly /ˈfɔːməli/ ADV If something happened or was **formerly** true, it happened or was true in the past. ❑ *He had formerly been in the Navy.*

formidable /ˈfɔːmɪdəbəl, fəˈmɪd-/ ADJ If you describe something or someone as **formidable**, you mean that you feel frightened by them because they are very impressive or considerable. ❑ *This is a formidable problem.*

formula /ˈfɔːmjʊlə/ (**formulas** or **formulae** /ˈfɔːmjʊli/) **1** N-COUNT A **formula** is a plan that is made as a way of dealing with a problem. ❑ *...this simple formula for a long and happy life.* **2** N-COUNT A **formula** is a group of letters, numbers, or other symbols which represents a scientific or mathematical rule. ❑ *...a mathematical formula.* **3** N-COUNT In science, the **formula** for a substance tells you what amounts of other substances are needed in order to make that substance. **4** N-UNCOUNT **Formula** is a powder which you mix with water to make artificial milk for babies.

formulate /ˈfɔːmjʊleɪt/ (**formulates, formulating, formulated**) **1** V-T If you **formulate** a plan or proposal, you develop it, thinking about the details carefully. ● **formulation** N-UNCOUNT ❑ *...the formulation of government plans.* **2** V-T If you **formulate** a thought or opinion, you express it in words.

forsake /fəˈseɪk/ (**forsakes, forsaking, forsook** /fəˈsʊk/, **forsaken**) **1** V-T If someone **forsakes** you, they leave you when they should have stayed, or stop helping you or looking after you. ❑ *The children have been forsaken by their teachers.* **2** V-T If you **forsake** something, you stop doing or having it. [LITERARY] ❑ *She forsook her notebook for new technology.*

fort /fɔːt/ (**forts**) N-COUNT A **fort** is a strong building that is used as a military base.

forth /fɔːθ/ **1** ADV To **go forth** from a place means to leave it. [LITERARY] ❑ *Go forth into the desert.* **2** ADV To **bring** something **forth** means to produce it or make it visible. [LITERARY] ❑ *...ways to bring forth new ideas.* **3** **and so forth** → see **so** **4** **back and forth** → see **back**

forthcoming /ˌfɔːθˈkʌmɪŋ/ **1** ADJ BEFORE N A **forthcoming** event is going to happen soon. ❑ *...the forthcoming election.* **2** ADJ AFTER LINK-V When something such as help or information is **forthcoming**, it is provided or made available. ❑ *They promised that the money would be forthcoming.* **3** ADJ If someone is **forthcoming**, they willingly give you information when you ask.

forthright /ˈfɔːθraɪt/ ADJ If you describe someone as **forthright**, you admire them because they say clearly and forcefully what they think and feel. ❑ *He was forthright about his ideas.*

fortieth /ˈfɔːtiəθ/ ORD The **fortieth** item in a series is the one that you count as number forty.

fortify /ˈfɔːtɪfaɪ/ (**fortifies, fortifying, fortified**) **1** V-T To **fortify** a place means to make it stronger and less easy to attack, often by building a wall or ditch round it. ❑ *The soldiers worked for a month to fortify the airbase.* **2** V-T If food or drink **is fortified**, another substance is added to it to make it healthier or stronger. ❑ *...food fortified with vitamins.*

fortnight /ˈfɔːtnaɪt/ (**fortnights**) N-COUNT A **fortnight** is a period of two weeks. ❑ *I hope to be back in a fortnight.*

fortress /ˈfɔːtrɪs/ (**fortresses**) N-COUNT A **fortress** is a castle or other strong, well-protected building, which is difficult for enemies to enter.

fortunate /ˈfɔːtʃʊnɪt/ ADJ If someone or something is **fortunate**, they are lucky. ❑ *He was fortunate to survive.* ● **fortunately** ADV ❑ *Fortunately, the weather was good.*

fortune /ˈfɔːtʃuːn/ (**fortunes**) **1** N-UNCOUNT **Fortune** or **good fortune** is good luck. **Ill fortune** is bad luck. **2** N-PLURAL The **fortunes** of someone or something are the extent to which they are doing well or being successful. ❑ *The film follows the fortunes of two women.* **3** N-COUNT A **fortune** is a very large amount of money.

forty /ˈfɔːti/ (**forties**) NUM **Forty** is the number 40. For examples of how numbers such as forty and eighty are used see **eighty**.

forum /ˈfɔːrəm/ (**forums**) N-COUNT A **forum** is a place, situation, or event in which people exchange ideas and discuss issues that are important to them. ❑ *The organisation provides a forum where problems can be discussed.*

> **Word Link** *ward ≈ in the direction of : backward, forward, inward*

forward /ˈfɔːwəd/ (**forwards, forwarding, forwarded**)

> **Forwards** is often used as an adverb instead of **forward** in meanings 1 and 4.

1 ADV If you move or look **forward** or **forwards**, you move or look in a direction that is in front of you. ❑ *She fell forwards on to her face.* ❑ *He didn't look at the car, but continued to walk forward.* **2** ADV & ADJ BEFORE N **Forward** means in a position near the front of something such as a building or vehicle. ❑ *The best seats are in the aisle and as far forward as possible.* ❑ *The troops moved to forward positions.* **3** ADV If something or someone is **put forward**, they are suggested or offered as suitable for a particular purpose. If someone **comes forward**, they present themselves as suitable for a particular purpose. ❑ *Next month, the organisation will put forward its new plans.* ❑ *A new witness has come forward.* **4** ADV **Forward** and **forwards** are used to indicate that someone is making progress. ❑ *That would be a great way forwards for the game.* **5** V-T If a letter or message **is forwarded to** someone, it is sent to the place where they are, after having been sent to a different place earlier. **6** ADJ If you describe someone as **forward**, you mean they speak very confidently and openly, sometimes offending people or not showing them enough respect. ● **forwardness** N-UNCOUNT ❑ *He shocked me with his forwardness.* **7** **backwards and forwards** → see **backward**

ˈforward ˌslash (**forward slashes**) N-COUNT A **forward slash** is the sloping line '/' that separates letters, words, or numbers.

fossil /ˈfɒsəl/ (**fossils**) N-COUNT A **fossil** is the hardened remains or impression of a prehistoric

Word Web fossil

There are two types of animal **fossils**—body fossils and **trace** fossils. Body fossils help us understand how the animal looked when it was alive. Trace fossils, such as **tracks** and **footprints**, show us how the animal moved. Since we don't find tracks of dinosaurs' tails, we know they lifted them up as they walked. Footprints tell us about the weight of the dinosaur and how fast it moved. Scientists use two methods to calculate the date of a fossil. They sometimes count the number of **rock** layers covering it. They also use **carbon** dating.

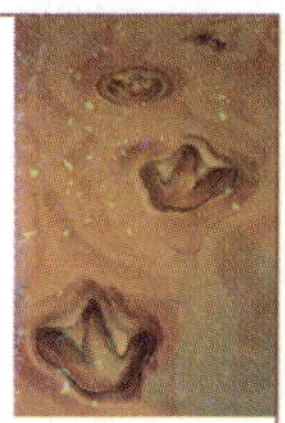

animal or plant inside a rock.
→ see Word Web: **fossil**
→ see **evolution**

ˌfossil ˈfuel (**fossil fuels**) N-VAR **Fossil fuels** are fuels such as coal, oil, and natural gas.
→ see **electricity, greenhouse effect, solar**

foster /ˈfɒstə, AM ˈfɔːst-/ (**fosters, fostering, fostered**) 1 ADJ BEFORE N **Foster parents** are people who officially take a child into their family for a period of time, without becoming the child's legal parents. The child is referred to as their **foster child**. 2 V-T If you **foster** a child, you take him or her into your family as a foster child. 3 V-T If you **foster** a feeling, activity, or idea, you help it to develop. ❑ *...the need to foster economic growth.*

fought /fɔːt/ **Fought** is the past tense and past participle of **fight**.

foul /faʊl/ (**fouler, foulest, fouls, fouling, fouled**) 1 ADJ If you describe something as **foul**, you mean it is dirty and smells or tastes unpleasant. 2 V-T If a place **is fouled** by someone or something, they make it dirty. ❑ *Two accidents near Los Angeles have fouled the ocean.* 3 ADJ **Foul language** is offensive and contains swear words or rude words. 4 ADJ If someone is in a **foul** temper or mood, they are very angry. 5 PHRASE If you **fall foul of** someone, you do something which gets you into trouble with them. 6 N-COUNT In sports such as football, a **foul** is an action that is against the rules.

found /faʊnd/ (**founds, founding, founded**) 1 **Found** is the past tense and past participle of **find**. 2 V-T When an organization, company, or city **is founded** by someone, they start it or create it. ❑ *He founded the Centre for Journalism Studies at University College Cardiff.* • **foundation** N-SING ❑ *...the foundation of Kew Gardens.* • **founder** (**founders**) N-COUNT ❑ *He was one of the founders of the university.*

Word Link	*found ≈ base : foundation, founded, founder*

foundation /faʊnˈdeɪʃən/ (**foundations**) 1 N-COUNT The **foundation of** something such as a belief or way of life is the idea or experience on which it is based. ❑ *The family is the foundation of society.* ❑ *Free speech is the foundation of democracy.* 2 N-PLURAL The **foundations** of a building or other structure are the layer of bricks or concrete below the ground that it is built on. 3 N-COUNT A **foundation** is an organization which provides money for a special purpose. ❑ *...the National Foundation for Youth Music.* 4 N-UNCOUNT If a story, idea, or argument has no **foundation**, there are no facts to prove that it is true. ❑ *The reports are without foundation.* 5 → see also **found**

founded /ˈfaʊndɪd/ ADJ AFTER LINK-V If something is **founded on** a particular thing, it is based on it. ❑ *Their friendship is founded on a love of cricket.*

founder /ˈfaʊndə/ (**founders, foundering, foundered**) 1 V-I If something such as a plan or a project **founders**, it fails. 2 V-I If a ship **founders**, it fills with water and sinks.

founding /ˈfaʊndɪŋ/ (**foundings**) N-COUNT & ADJ The **founding** of an organization, tradition, or club is the creation of it. You can also use **founding** to describe a person or thing relating to the founding of something. ❑ *I have been a member of this sports club since its founding in 1973.* ❑ *...a founding member of the Conservative Party.*

foundry /ˈfaʊndri/ (**foundries**) N-COUNT A **foundry** is a place where metal or glass is melted and made into particular objects.

fountain /ˈfaʊntɪn/ (**fountains**) 1 N-COUNT A **fountain** is an ornamental feature in a pool which consists of a jet of water that is forced up into the air by a pump. 2 N-COUNT A **fountain of** a liquid is an amount of it which is sent up into the air and falls back.

four /fɔː/ (**fours**) 1 NUM **Four** is the number 4. 2 PHRASE If you are **on all fours**, your knees, feet, and hands are on the ground. ❑ *She crawled on all fours over to the window.*

foursome /ˈfɔːsəm/ (**foursomes**) N-COUNT A **foursome** is a group of four people or things.

fourteen /ˌfɔːˈtiːn/ NUM **Fourteen** is the number 14.

fourteenth /ˌfɔːˈtiːnθ/ ORD The **fourteenth** item in a series is the one that you count as number fourteen.

fourth /fɔːθ/ (**fourths**) 1 ORD The **fourth** item in a series is the one that you count as number four. 2 N-COUNT In American English a **fourth** is one of four equal parts of something. The British word is **quarter**.

ˌfour-wheel ˈdrive (**four-wheel drives**) N-COUNT A **four-wheel drive** is a vehicle in which all four wheels receive power from the engine.

fowl /faʊl/

The plural is **fowl** or **fowls**.

N-COUNT A **fowl** is a bird, especially a duck, goose, or chicken.

fox

fox /fɒks/ (**foxes, foxing, foxed**) 1 N-COUNT A **fox** is a wild animal which looks like a dog and has reddish-brown fur and a thick tail. 2 V-T If you **are foxed** by something, you cannot understand it or solve it. [BRIT] ❑ *The question foxed one of the experts.*

foyer /ˈfɔɪə, ˈfwaɪeɪ/ (**foyers**) N-COUNT The **foyer** is the large area where people meet or wait just inside the doors of a theatre, cinema, or hotel.

Word Link	*fract, frag ≈ breaking : fraction, fracture, fragile*

fraction /ˈfrækʃən/ (**fractions**) 1 N-COUNT A **fraction** is a tiny amount or proportion of something. ❑ *I opened my eyes just a fraction.* 2 N-COUNT In arithmetic, a **fraction** is a part of a whole number. For example, ½ and ⅓ are fractions of 1.
→ see Picture Dictionary: **fraction**

fracture /ˈfræktʃə/ (**fractures, fracturing, fractured**) 1 V-T/V-I If something such as a bone **fractures**, or if it **is fractured**, it cracks or breaks. ❑ *He fractured his arm in the accident.* 2 N-COUNT A **fracture** is a crack or break in something. ❑ *...a hip fracture.*

fragile /ˈfrædʒaɪl, AM -dʒəl/ 1 ADJ If you

f

Picture Dictionary **fractions**

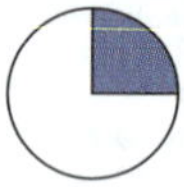

fraction	decimal	percentage
1/4	0.25	25%

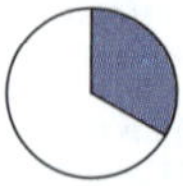

fraction	decimal	percentage
1/3	0.33	33%

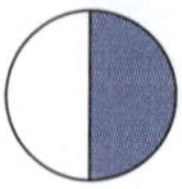

fraction	decimal	percentage
1/2	0.50	50%

adding fractions

problem:	solution:
1 1/4	1 1/4
+2 1/2	+2 2/4
?	3 3/4

subtracting fractions

problem:	solution:
5 2/3	5 4/6
- 1 1/6	- 1 1/6
?	4 3/6 = 4 1/2

describe a situation as **fragile**, you mean that it is weak or uncertain, and unlikely to be able to resist strong pressure or attack. ❑ *...the fragile peace agreed this month.* ● **fragility** /frəˈdʒɪlɪti/ N-UNCOUNT ❑ *...the fragility of the environment.* **2** ADJ Something that is **fragile** is easily broken or damaged. ❑ *He sat down on the fragile chair.* ● **fragility** N-UNCOUNT ❑ *...the fragility of their bones.* **3** ADJ Something that is **fragile** is very delicate in appearance. ❑ *...her fragile beauty.*

Thesaurus *fragile* Also look up:

ADJ. unstable, weak **1**
delicate; *(ant.)* sturdy **2**

fragment (**fragments, fragmenting, fragmented**) **1** N-COUNT /ˈfrægmənt/ A **fragment of** something is a small piece or part of it. ❑ *...fragments of glass.* ❑ *She read everything, every fragment of news.* **2** V-T/V-I /frægˈment/ If something **fragments**, or if another thing **fragments** it, it breaks or separates into small pieces. ❑ *Buddhism was in danger of fragmenting.* ● **fragmentation** N-UNCOUNT ❑ *...the fragmentation of the Soviet Union.* ● **fragmented** ADJ ❑ *The film is confusing and fragmented.*

fragrance /ˈfreɪgrəns/ (**fragrances**) N-VAR A **fragrance** is a pleasant or sweet smell.

fragrant /ˈfreɪgrənt/ ADJ Something that is **fragrant** has a sweet or pleasant smell. ❑ *Insects are attracted by fragrant flowers.*

frail /freɪl/ (**frailer, frailest**) **1** ADJ Someone who is **frail** is not very strong or healthy. **2** ADJ Something that is **frail** is easily broken or damaged.

frame /freɪm/ (**frames, framing, framed**) **1** N-COUNT The **frame** of a picture or mirror is the part around its edges. ❑ *...a photograph of her mother in a silver frame.* **2** V-T If a picture or photograph **is framed**, it is put in a frame. **3** N-COUNT A **frame** is a structure, for example of bars or posts, which gives an object its shape and strength. ❑ *We painted our table the same colour as the window frame.* **4** N-COUNT A **frame** of cinema film is one of the many separate photographs that it consists of. **5** N-COUNT You can refer to someone's body as **their frame**, especially when you are describing its general shape. ❑ *...her skinny frame.* **6** V-T If you **frame** something **in** a particular kind of language, you express it in that way. ❑ *Let me frame the question a little differently.* **7** V-T If someone **frames** an innocent person, they make other people think that person is guilty of a crime, by lying or inventing evidence. [INFORMAL]
→ see **animation, bed, painting**

ˌframe of ˈmind N-SING Your **frame of mind** is your mood or attitude at a particular time. ❑ *Lewis was not in the right frame of mind to continue.*

framework /ˈfreɪmwɜːk/ (**frameworks**) **1** N-COUNT A **framework** is a set of rules, ideas, or beliefs which you use in order to decide what to do. ❑ *...discussing issues within a Christian framework.* **2** N-COUNT A **framework** is a structure that forms a support or frame for something. ❑ *...wooden shelves on a steel framework.*

franchise /ˈfræntʃaɪz/ (**franchises**) **1** N-COUNT If a large company or organization grants a **franchise** to a smaller company, the smaller company is allowed to sell the products of the larger company or participate in an activity controlled by the larger company. ❑ *...the franchise to build and operate the tunnel.* **2** N-SING In politics, **the franchise** is the right to vote in an election, especially one to elect a parliament.

Word Link ***fract, frag** ≈ **breaking** : **fraction, fracture, fragile***

frank /fræŋk/ (**franker, frankest**) ADJ If someone is **frank**, they state things openly and honestly. ❑ *...a frank discussion.* ● **frankly** ADV ❑ *You can talk frankly to me.* ● **frankness** N-UNCOUNT ❑ *They were surprised by her frankness.*

frankly /ˈfræŋkli/ ADV You use **frankly** when you are expressing an opinion or feeling to emphasize that you mean what you are saying. ❑ *Frankly, Thomas, this is beginning to worry me.*

frantic /ˈfræntɪk/ ADJ If someone is **frantic**, they are behaving in a desperate, wild, and disorganized way, because they are frightened, worried, or in a hurry. ❑ *A bird had been locked in and was quite frantic.* ● **frantically** ADV ❑ *We have been frantically trying to save her life.*

fraternity /frəˈtɜːnɪti/ (**fraternities**) **1** N-UNCOUNT **Fraternity** is friendship between people who feel they are closely linked to each other. ❑ *Bob needs the fraternity of others who share his ideas.* **2** N-COUNT You can refer to a group of people with the same profession or interests as a particular **fraternity**. ❑ *...the sailing fraternity.* **3** N-COUNT In the United States, a **fraternity** is a society of male students at a university or college.

fraud /frɔːd/ (**frauds**) **1** N-VAR **Fraud** is the crime of gaining money by a trick or lying. ❑ *He was jailed for two years for fraud.* ❑ *...tax frauds.* **2** N-COUNT If you call someone or something a **fraud**, you are criticizing them because you think they are not genuine, or are less good than they claim or appear to be. ❑ *You're a fraud and a spy, Simons.*

Word Link *ulent ≈ full of : fraudulent, opulent, succulent*

fraudulent /ˈfrɔːdʒʊlənt/ ADJ A **fraudulent** activity is dishonest or untrue. ❑ *...fraudulent claims about being a nurse.* • **fraudulently** ADV ❑ *...fraudulently using a credit card.*

fraught /frɔːt/ **1** ADJ AFTER LINK-V If a situation or action is **fraught with** problems or difficulties, it is full of them. ❑ *This technique is fraught with dangers.* **2** ADJ If you say that a situation or action is **fraught**, you mean that it is worrying or stressful. ❑ *...a fraught day.*

fray /freɪ/ (**frays, fraying, frayed**) **1** V-I If something such as cloth or rope **frays**, its threads or fibres become worn and it is likely to tear or break. ❑ *The stitching began to fray at the edges.* **2** N-SING If you say that someone **joins the fray**, you mean that they become involved in an exciting or challenging activity or situation. ❑ *New candidates can enter the fray during the second round of voting.*

freak /friːk/ (**freaks**) **1** ADJ BEFORE N A **freak** event or action is very unusual or extreme. ❑ *...a freak accident.* **2** N-COUNT People are sometimes referred to as **freaks** when their behaviour or appearance is very different from that of most people; used showing disapproval. ❑ *Minorities are treated like freaks here.*

freckle /ˈfrekəl/ (**freckles**) N-COUNT If someone **has freckles**, they have small light brown spots on their skin.

free /friː/ (**freer, freest, frees, freeing, freed**) **1** ADJ If something is **free**, you can have it or use it without paying. ❑ *...a free brochure.* ❑ *The company said it would do the job for free.* **2** **free of charge** → see **charge** **3** ADJ Someone or something that is **free** is not controlled or limited by rules or custom or by other people. ❑ *Women should be free to dress as they please.* ❑ *...organising free and fair elections.* **4** PHRASE You say **'feel free'** to someone who has asked you if they can do something as a way of giving them permission. ❑ *Go ahead. Feel free.* ❑ *If you have any questions at all, please feel free to ask me.* **5** V-T If you **free** someone **of** something unpleasant or restricting, you remove it from them. ❑ *It will free us of debt.* **6** ADJ A person or thing that is **free of** something unpleasant does not have it or is not affected by it. ❑ *We want a future that is free of fear.* ❑ *The party was virtually trouble-free.* **7** ADJ Someone who is **free** is no longer a prisoner or a slave. ❑ *He left the court a free man.* ❑ *Ninety prisoners have been set free.* **8** V-T To **free** a prisoner or slave means to release them. **9** V-T If you **free** someone or something, you make them available for a task or purpose. ❑ *His contract with Disney will end shortly, freeing him to work on his own project.* **10** ADJ If you have a **free** period of time, or if you are **free** at a particular time, you are not working or occupied then. ❑ *She went shopping in her free time.* **11** ADJ If something such as a table or seat is **free**, it is not being used or occupied, or is not reserved for someone to use. ❑ *They took the only free table.* **12** ADJ AFTER LINK-V If something **gets free**, it is no longer trapped by something or attached to something. ❑ *He pulled his arm free.* **13** V-T If you **free** someone or something, you remove or loosen them from the place where they have been trapped or become fixed. ❑ *Firemen tried to free the injured.*

Thesaurus *free* Also look up:

ADJ.	complimentary **1**
	independent, unrestricted **2**
	available, vacant **10**
V.	emancipate, let go, liberate **7** **11**

Word Link *dom ≈ state of being : boredom, freedom, wisdom*

freedom /ˈfriːdəm/ (**freedoms**) **1** N-VAR **Freedom** is the state of being allowed to do what you want. ❑ *...freedom of speech.* ❑ *...individual freedoms and human rights.* **2** N-UNCOUNT When prisoners or slaves gain their **freedom**, they are set free or they escape. ❑ *He wanted to be released from prison, and freedom.* **3** N-UNCOUNT **Freedom from** something you do not want means not being affected by it. ❑ *Medicine can give you freedom from pain.*

Word Partnership Use *freedom* with:

ADJ.	**artistic** freedom, **political** freedom, **religious** freedom **1**
N.	freedom **of choice**, **feeling/sense of** freedom, freedom **of the press**, freedom **of speech** **1**
	struggle for freedom **1** **2**

free ˈenterprise N-UNCOUNT **Free enterprise** is an economic system in which businesses compete for profit without much government control.

freelance /ˈfriːlɑːns, -læns/ ADJ & ADV Someone who works **freelance** or who is, for example, a **freelance** journalist or photographer, organizes their own work, income, and taxes, rather than being employed by someone who pays them regularly. ❑ *She decided to go freelance.*

freely /ˈfriːli/ **1** ADV You use **freely** to indicate that something happens or is done many times or in large quantities, often without restraint. ❑ *We have used his ideas freely.* ❑ *Drinking water is freely available in schools.* **2** ADV If you can **talk freely**, you do not need to be careful about what you say. **3** ADV If someone gives or does something **freely**, they give or do it without being forced to do it. ❑ *Danny shared his knowledge freely.* **4** ADV If something or someone moves **freely**, they move easily and smoothly, without any obstacles or resistance. ❑ *The traffic flows freely in this city.*

freer /friːə/ **Freer** is the comparative of **free**.

freest /friːɪst/ **Freest** is the superlative of **free**.

freeway /ˈfriːweɪ/ (**freeways**) N-COUNT In American English, a **freeway** is a major road that has been specially built for fast travel over long distances. The usual British word is **motorway**.

ˌfree ˈwill PHRASE If you do something **of** your **own free will**, you do it because you want to and not because you are forced to. ❑ *If he does not leave of his own free will then we will have to force him out of the building.*

freeze /friːz/ (**freezes, freezing, froze, frozen**) **1** V-T/V-I If a liquid **freezes**, or if something **freezes** it, it becomes solid because of low temperatures. ❑ *Water freezes when the temperature drops below 0°C.* **2** V-T/V-I If you **freeze** something such as food, you preserve it by storing it at a temperature below 0° Celsius. You can also talk about how well food **freezes**. **3** V-I If you **freeze**, you feel very cold. ❑ *Your hands will freeze if you don't wear gloves.* **4** V-I If someone who is moving **freezes**, they suddenly stop and become completely still. ❑ *She froze when she saw the lion.* **5** V-T & N-COUNT If the government or a company **freeze** an activity, prices, or wages, or if it **puts** a **freeze** on them, it states officially that it will not allow them to increase for a fixed period of time. ❑ *OPEC has agreed to freeze its oil production.* ❑ *...a wage freeze.* **6** V-T If someone in authority **freezes** your bank accounts or other financial concerns, they obtain a legal order which stops you having access to them or using them. **7** → see also **freezing, frozen**

→ see **thermometer**

▶ **freeze out** PHR-VERB If you **freeze** someone **out of** an activity or situation, you prevent them from being involved in it by creating difficulties or by being unfriendly.

freezer /ˈfriːzə/ (**freezers**) N-COUNT A **freezer** is a fridge in which the temperature is kept below freezing point so that you can store food inside it for long periods.

freezing /ˈfriːzɪŋ/ **1** ADJ If you say that something or someone is **freezing** or **freezing cold**, you are emphasizing that they are very cold. ❑ *...a freezing January afternoon.* ❑ *You must be freezing.* **2** → See note at **cold**

freight /freɪt/ **1** N-UNCOUNT **Freight** is the movement of goods by lorries, trains, ships, or aeroplanes. ❑ *The whole thing will have to go by air freight.* **2** N-UNCOUNT **Freight** consists of the goods that are transported by lorries, trains, ships, or aeroplanes. ❑ *...26 tons of freight.*

→ see **train**

freighter /ˈfreɪtə/ (**freighters**) N-COUNT A **freighter** is a ship or aeroplane designed to carry goods.

frenetic /frɪˈnetɪk/ ADJ **Frenetic** activity is fast and energetic, but rather uncontrolled. ❑ *The pace of life in New York is frenetic.*

frenzied /ˈfrenzid/ ADJ **Frenzied** actions are carried out by someone who has lost control of their mind, senses, or feelings and is acting in a wild and violent way. ❑ *...a frenzied attack.*

frenzy /ˈfrenzi/ (**frenzies**) N-VAR **Frenzy** is great excitement or wild behaviour that often results from losing control of your feelings. ❑ *'Get out!' she ordered in a frenzy.*

frequency /ˈfriːkwənsi/ (**frequencies**) **1** N-UNCOUNT The **frequency** of an event is the number of times it happens. ❑ *The frequency of Kara's phone calls increased.* **2** N-VAR The **frequency** of a sound wave or radio wave is the rate at which it vibrates. [TECHNICAL]

→ see **sound, wave**

frequent (**frequents, frequenting, frequented**) **1** ADJ /ˈfriːkwənt/ If something is **frequent**, it happens often. ❑ *...frequent headaches.* ❑ *He is a frequent visitor to the house.* ● **frequently** ADV ❑ *He was frequently unhappy.* **2** V-T /frɪˈkwent/ If someone **frequents** a particular place, they regularly go there. [FORMAL] ❑ *I hear he frequents Kenny's, the restaurant on the High Street.*

Thesaurus	*frequent* Also look up:
ADJ.	common, everyday, habitual; *(ant.)* occasional, rare **1**

fresco /ˈfreskəʊ/ (**frescoes**) N-COUNT A **fresco** is a picture that is painted on a plastered wall when the plaster is still wet.

fresh /freʃ/ (**fresher, freshest**) **1** ADJ BEFORE N A **fresh** thing or amount replaces or is added to a previous one. ❑ *...fresh fears.* ❑ *I need a new challenge and a fresh start.* **2** ADJ Something that is **fresh** has been done, made, or experienced recently. ❑ *They found fresh footprints in the snow.* ❑ *The memory of the robbery was still fresh in her mind.* ● **freshly** ADV ❑ *...a freshly painted wall.* **3** ADJ **Fresh food** has been produced or picked recently, and has not been preserved. ❑ *...locally caught fresh fish.* ● **freshly** ADV ❑ *...freshly baked bread.* ● **freshness** N-UNCOUNT ❑ *I could taste the freshness of the food.* **4** ADJ If you describe something as **fresh**, you mean you like it because it is new and exciting. ❑ *These designers are full of fresh ideas.* ● **freshness** N-UNCOUNT ❑ *There was a freshness and enthusiasm about the new students.* **5** ADJ If something smells, tastes, or feels **fresh**, it is clean, cool, or refreshing. ❑ *The air was fresh.* **6** ADJ **Fresh water** is water that is not salty, for example the water in streams and lakes. **7** → see also **freshwater** **8** ADJ AFTER LINK-V If you **are fresh from** or **are fresh out of** a particular place or experience, you have just come from that place or you have just had that experience. ❑ *I returned to the office, fresh from Heathrow Airport.*

→ see **glacier, vegetable**

ˌfresh ˈair N-UNCOUNT You can describe the air outside as **fresh air**, especially when you mean that it is good for you. ❑ *Take exercise, preferably in the fresh air.*

fresher /ˈfreʃə/ (**freshers**) N-COUNT **Freshers** are students who are in their first year at a British university or college.

freshman /ˈfreʃmən/ (**freshmen**) N-COUNT **Freshmen** are students who are in their first year at an American university or college.

freshwater /ˈfreʃwɔːtə/ ADJ BEFORE N A **freshwater** lake or pool contains water that is not salty.

fret /fret/ (**frets, fretting, fretted**) V-I If you **fret about** something, you worry about it. ❑ *Vera is fretting about her sick children.*

friction /ˈfrɪkʃən/ (**frictions**) **1** N-VAR **Friction between** people is disagreement and quarrels between them. ❑ *The friction between us was* unpleasant. 2 N-UNCOUNT **Friction** is the force that makes it difficult for things to move freely when they are touching each other. 3 N-UNCOUNT **Friction** is the rubbing of one thing against another. ❑ *...the friction of his trousers against his leg.*

Friday /ˈfraɪdeɪ, -di/ (**Fridays**) N-VAR **Friday** is the day after Thursday and before Saturday.

fridge /frɪdʒ/ (**fridges**) N-COUNT In British English, a **fridge** is a large metal container for storing food at low temperatures to keep it fresh. The usual American word is **refrigerator**.

friend /frend/ (**friends**) 1 N-COUNT A **friend** is someone who you know well and like, but who is not related to you. ❑ *Joanne's my best friend.* 2 N-PLURAL If you are **friends with** someone, you are their friend and they are yours. ❑ *I still wanted to be friends with her.* ❑ *Sarah and Ella have been friends for seven years.* 3 PHRASE If you **make friends with** someone, you begin a friendship with them. ❑ *I soon made friends with some English speakers.* ❑ *I've never found it hard to make friends.* 4 N-PLURAL **The friends of** an organization, a country, or a cause are the people and organizations who help and support them. ❑ *...The Friends of Birmingham Royal Ballet.*

Word Partnership Use *friend* with:

ADJ. **best** friend, **close** friend, **dear** friend, **faithful** friend, **former** friend, **good** friend, **loyal** friend, **mutual** friend, **old** friend, **personal** friend, **trusted** friend 1
N. **childhood** friend, friend **of the family**, friend **or foe**, friend **or relative** 1
V. **tell a** friend 1
make a friend 1 3

friendly /ˈfrendli/ (**friendlier, friendliest, friendlies**) 1 ADJ A **friendly** person is kind and pleasant. ❑ *He had a pleasant, friendly face.* ● **friendliness** N-UNCOUNT ❑ *She loves the friendliness of the Irish people.* 2 ADJ AFTER LINK-V If you are **friendly with** someone, you like each other and enjoy spending time together. ❑ *I'm friendly with his mother.* 3 N-COUNT In sport, a **friendly** is a game which is not part of a competition, and is played for entertainment or practice.

Word Partnership Use *friendly* with:

N. friendly **atmosphere**, friendly **face**, friendly **neighbours**, friendly **service**, friendly **voice** 1
friendly **relationship** 2
friendly **game**, friendly **match** 3
V. **become** friendly 2

-friendly /-ˈfrendli/ **-friendly** combines with nouns to form adjectives which describe things that do not harm or that help the thing or person mentioned. ❑ *Palm oil is environment-friendly.* ❑ *...ozone-friendly fridges.*

Word Link *ship ≈ condition or state : censorship, citizenship, friendship*

friendship /ˈfrendʃɪp/ (**friendships**) N-VAR A **friendship** is a relationship or state of friendliness between two people who like each other. ❑ *This photograph tells the story of the incredible friendship between Brian and John.* ❑ *The two countries signed treaties of friendship and co-operation.*

frigate /ˈfrɪgət/ (**frigates**) N-COUNT A **frigate** is a small naval ship that can move at fast speeds.

fright /fraɪt/ (**frights**) 1 N-UNCOUNT **Fright** is a sudden feeling of fear. ❑ *Franklin jumped with fright.* 2 N-COUNT A **fright** is an experience which makes you suddenly afraid. ❑ *The last time you had a real fright, you nearly crashed the car.* 3 PHRASE If someone **takes fright**, they experience a sudden feeling of fear.

frighten /ˈfraɪtən/ (**frightens, frightening, frightened**) V-T If something or someone **frightens** you, they cause you to suddenly feel afraid or anxious. ❑ *He knew that Soli was trying to frighten him.*

▸ **frighten away** or **frighten off** 1 PHR-VERB If you **frighten away** a person or animal, or if you **frighten** them **off**, you make them afraid so that they run away or stay some distance away from you. ❑ *The boats were frightening away the fish.* 2 PHR-VERB To **frighten** someone **away** or **frighten** them **off** means to make them nervous so that they decide not to do something. ❑ *We don't want to frighten visitors off by making them feel that they're not welcome.*

▸ **frighten into** PHR-VERB If you **frighten** someone **into** doing something, you force them to do it by making them afraid.

▸ **frighten off** → see **frighten away**

frightened /ˈfraɪtənd/ ADJ If you are **frightened**, you feel anxious or afraid. ❑ *She was frightened of flying.*

frightening /ˈfraɪtənɪŋ/ ADJ If something is **frightening**, it makes you feel afraid or anxious. ❑ *It was a very frightening experience.* ● **frighteningly** ADV ❑ *She was frighteningly ill.*

frightful /ˈfraɪtfʊl/ 1 ADJ Something that is **frightful** is very bad or unpleasant. [DATED] ❑ *My father was not able to talk about the war, it was so frightful.* 2 ADJ BEFORE N **Frightful** is used to emphasize the extent or degree of something. [DATED] ❑ *It was a frightful shock for everyone.* ● **frightfully** ADV ❑ *I'm most frightfully sorry.*

frill /frɪl/ (**frills**) 1 N-COUNT A **frill** is a long, narrow, folded strip of cloth which is attached to something as a decoration. 2 N-PLURAL If something has **no frills**, it is simple and has no unnecessary or additional features. ❑ *...Ryanair, the no-frills airline.*

fringe /frɪndʒ/ (**fringes**) 1 N-COUNT In British English, a **fringe** is hair which is cut so that it hangs over your forehead. The usual American word is **bangs**. 2 N-COUNT A **fringe** is a decoration attached to clothes and other objects, consisting of a row of hanging threads. ❑ *...curtains with a white fringe.* 3 N-COUNT To be **on the fringe** or **on the fringes of** a place means to be on the outside edge of it. ❑ *...poor areas on the fringes of the city.* 4 N-COUNT The **fringe** or **fringes of** an activity or organization are its least typical or most extreme parts. ❑ *The Green Party remained on the fringe of the political scene.* ❑ *...fringe theatre style.* 5 N-COUNT **Fringe benefits** are extra things that some people get from their job in addition to their salary, for example a car.
→ see **hair**

f

fringed /frɪndʒd/ **1** ADJ BEFORE N **Fringed** clothes, curtains, or furnishings are decorated with fringes. **2** ADJ AFTER LINK-V If a place or object is **fringed with** things, they are situated along its edges. ❑ *...tiny islands fringed with golden sand.*

frivolous /ˈfrɪvələs/ **1** ADJ If you describe someone as **frivolous**, you mean they behave in a silly or light-hearted way, rather than being serious and sensible. ❑ *Isabelle was a frivolous little fool.* **2** ADJ If you describe an activity as **frivolous**, you disapprove of it because it is not useful and wastes time or money. ❑ *Fashion is a frivolous business.*

F

fro /frəʊ/ **to and fro** → see **to**

frog /frɒg, AM frɔːg/ (**frogs**) N-COUNT A **frog** is a small creature with smooth skin, big eyes, and long back legs which it uses for jumping.

frolic /ˈfrɒlɪk/ (**frolics, frolicking, frolicked**) V-I & N-VAR When people or animals **frolic**, they run around and play in a lively way. **Frolic** is this behaviour. ❑ *Tourists sunbathe and frolic in the ocean.* ❑ *...fun and frolic.*

from /frəm, STRONG frɒm, AM frʌm/ **1** PREP You use **from** to say what the source, origin, or starting point of something is. ❑ *It was a present from his wife.* ❑ *The results were taken from six surveys.* ❑ *...cheese from France.* **2** PREP If someone or something moves or is taken **from** a place, they leave it or are removed from it. ❑ *The guests watched as she ran from the room.* **3** PREP If you take something **from** an amount, you reduce the amount by that much. ❑ *£103 is taken from Mrs Adams' salary every month.* **4** PREP If you are away **from** a place, you are not there. ❑ *Her husband worked away from home a lot.* **5** PREP If you return **from** a place or activity, you return after being there or doing it. ❑ *My son Colin has just returned from Amsterdam.* **6** PREP If you see or hear something **from** a particular place, you are in that place when you see it or hear it. ❑ *Visitors can see the painting from behind a glass window.* **7** PREP Something that sticks out or hangs **from** an object is attached to it or touches it. ❑ *A gold bracelet is hanging from his wrist.* ❑ *...black flags hanging from the windows.* **8** PREP You can use **from** when giving distances. For example, if one place is fifty miles **from** another, the distance between them is fifty miles. ❑ *How far is it from here?* **9** PREP If a road goes **from** one place **to** another, you can travel along it between the two places. ❑ *...the road from St Petersburg to Tallinn.* **10** PREP **From** is used, especially in the expression **made from**, to say what substance has been used to make something. ❑ *Bread is made from flour.* **11** PREP If something happens **from** a particular time, it begins to happen then. ❑ *She studied painting from 1926.* **12** PREP You say **from** one thing **to** another when you are stating the range of things that are possible. ❑ *There are 94 countries represented at the Olympics, from Algeria to Zimbabwe.* **13** PREP If something changes **from** one thing **to** another, it stops being the first thing and becomes the second thing. ❑ *The expression on his face changed from sympathy to surprise.* **14** PREP You use **from** when mentioning the cause of something. ❑ *The problem simply resulted from a difference of opinion.* ❑ *He is suffering from headaches.* **15** PREP You use **from** to give the reason for an opinion. ❑ *I guessed from his name that Jose was Spanish.*

front /frʌnt/ (**fronts**) **1** N-COUNT & ADJ BEFORE N **The front of** something, or the **front** part of it, is the part of it that faces you or faces forward. ❑ *Stand at the front of the line.* ❑ *She was only six and still didn't have any front teeth.* **2** N-COUNT In a war, **the front** is the place where two armies are fighting. ❑ *Her husband is fighting at the front.* **3** N-COUNT If something happens on a particular **front**, it happens with regard to a particular situation or activity. ❑ *On the catering front, the new stadium has no restaurant facilities.* **4** N-SING If someone puts on a **front**, they pretend to have feelings which they do not have. ❑ *Michael put on a brave front.* **5** N-COUNT An organization or activity that is a **front for** another one that is illegal or secret is used to hide it. ❑ *The police knew that the firm was a front for organised crime.* **6** PHRASE If a person or thing is **in front**, they are ahead of others in a moving group. ❑ *He was driving too close to the car in front.* **7** PHRASE If you are **in front** in a competition or contest, you are winning. **8** PHRASE If someone or something is **in front of** a particular thing, they are facing it, ahead of it, or close to the front part of it. ❑ *She sat down in front of her mirror.* ❑ *Something ran out in front of my car.* **9** PHRASE If you do something **in front of** someone, you do it in their presence. ❑ *They never argued in front of their children.*
→ see **forecast**

frontal /ˈfrʌntəl/ **1** ADJ A **frontal** attack or challenge criticizes or threatens something in a very strong direct way. ❑ *...a frontal attack on science itself.* **2** ADJ **Frontal** means relating to or involving the front of something. ❑ *...the frontal region of the brain.*

frontier /ˈfrʌntɪə, -ˈtɪə/ (**frontiers**) **1** N-COUNT A **frontier** is a border between two countries. **2** N-COUNT The **frontiers of** a subject are the limits to which it can be known or done. ❑ *...pushing back the frontiers of science.*

ˌfront ˈline (**front lines**) N-COUNT **The front line** is the place where two armies are fighting each other.

ˌfront-ˈpage ADJ A **front-page** article or picture appears on the front page of a newspaper because it is very important or interesting.

ˌfront-ˈrunner (**front-runners**) N-COUNT In a competition or contest, the **front-runner** is the person who seems most likely to win it.

frost /frɒst, AM frɔːst/ (**frosts**) N-VAR When there is a **frost**, the outside temperature drops below freezing and the ground is covered with ice crystals.
→ see **snow**

frosty /ˈfrɒsti, AM ˈfrɔːsti/ **1** ADJ If the weather is **frosty**, the temperature is below freezing. ❑ *...sharp, frosty nights.* **2** ADJ You describe the ground or an object as **frosty** when it is covered with frost. ❑ *...the frosty pavement.* **3** ADJ If you describe someone's behaviour as **frosty**, you think it is unfriendly. ❑ *He gave Sam a frosty look.*

froth /frɒθ, AM frɔːθ/ (**froths, frothing, frothed**) **1** V-I If a liquid **froths**, small bubbles appear on the surface. ❑ *The sea froths over my feet.* **2** N-UNCOUNT **Froth** is a mass of small bubbles on the surface of a liquid. ❑ *...the froth of bubbles on the top of a glass of lemonade.*

frown /fraʊn/ (**frowns, frowning, frowned**) V-I

& N-COUNT If you **frown**, or if you have a **frown** on your face, you move your eyebrows close together because you are annoyed, worried, or thinking hard. ❑ *He frowned at her.* ❑ *There was a deep frown on the boy's face.*
▶ **frown on** or **frown upon** PHR-VERB If something **is frowned on**, or if it **is frowned upon**, people disapprove of it. ❑ *Back then it was frowned upon to work when you had children.*

froze /frəʊz/ **Froze** is the past tense of **freeze**.

frozen /ˈfrəʊzən/ **1** **Frozen** is the past participle of **freeze**. **2** ADJ If the ground is **frozen**, it has become very hard because the weather is very cold. ❑ *It was bitterly cold and the ground was frozen hard.* **3** ADJ **Frozen** food has been preserved by being kept at a very low temperature. ❑ *Frozen fish is a very healthy convenience food.* **4** ADJ If you say that you are **frozen**, you mean that you are very cold. ❑ *He touched his frozen face.*
→ see **glacier**

frugal /ˈfruːgəl/ **1** ADJ Someone who is **frugal** spends very little money on themselves. ❑ *She lives a frugal life.* ● **frugality** /fruːˈgælɪti/ N-UNCOUNT ❑ *His frugality allowed him to save $3,000.* **2** ADJ A **frugal** meal is small and inexpensive. ❑ *Polish nuns cooked frugal meals for the Pope.*

fruit /fruːt/

The plural is **fruit** or **fruits**.

1 N-VAR **Fruit** is something which grows on a tree or bush and which contains seeds or a stone covered by edible flesh. Apples, oranges, and bananas are all fruit. ❑ *Fresh fruit and vegetables provide vitamins.* **2** N-COUNT **The fruit** or **fruits of** someone's work or activity are the good things that result from it. ❑ *The book is the fruit of more than three years research.* **3** PHRASE If an action **bears fruit**, it produces good results. ❑ *The talks failed to bear fruit.*
→ see Picture Dictionary: **fruit**
→ see **dessert, grain**

fruitful /ˈfruːtfʊl/ ADJ Something that is **fruitful** produces good and useful results. ❑ *...a long, happy, fruitful relationship.*

fruition /frʊˈɪʃən/ N-UNCOUNT When something **comes to fruition**, it starts to produce the intended results. ❑ *These plans will take time to come to fruition.*

fruitless /ˈfruːtləs/ ADJ **Fruitless** actions, events, or efforts do not achieve anything at all. ❑ *It was a fruitless search.* ❑ *Talks have so far have been fruitless.*

fruity /ˈfruːti/ (**fruitier, fruitiest**) **1** ADJ Something that is **fruity** smells or tastes of fruit. ❑ *This shampoo smells fruity.* ❑ *...a lovely rich fruity cheese.* **2** ADJ A **fruity** laugh or voice is rich and deep.

frustrate /frʌˈstreɪt, AM ˈfrʌstreɪt/ (**frustrates, frustrating, frustrated**) **1** V-T If something **frustrates you**, it upsets or angers you because you are unable to do anything about the problems it creates. ❑ *These questions frustrated me.* ❑ *Drivers in Strasbourg are soon frustrated by the network of one-way streets.* ● **frustrated** ADJ ❑ *Roberta felt frustrated and angry.* ● **frustrating** ADJ ❑ *I found it very frustrating to teach Ted.* ● **frustration** (**frustrations**) N-VAR ❑ *...frustration among doctors.* **2** V-T To **frustrate** something such as a plan means to prevent it. ❑ *The government has deliberately frustrated his efforts to find work.*
→ see **anger**

fry /fraɪ/ (**fries, frying, fried**) **1** V-T When you **fry** food, you cook it in a pan containing hot fat. ❑ *Fry the breadcrumbs until golden brown.* ● **fried** ADJ ❑ *...fried fish.* **2** → See note at **cook** **3** N-PLURAL **Fry** are very small young fish. **4** N-PLURAL **Fries** are the same as **chips**.
→ see **cook, egg**

ˈfrying ˌpan (**frying pans**) N-COUNT A **frying pan** is a flat metal pan with a long handle, in which you fry food.
→ see **pan**

ft N-COUNT **ft** is a written abbreviation for **foot** or **feet**. ❑ *...flying at 1,000 ft.*

fudge /fʌdʒ/ (**fudges, fudging, fudged**) **1** N-UNCOUNT **Fudge** is a soft brown sweet made from butter, milk, and sugar. **2** V-T If you **fudge** something, you avoid making clear or definite decisions about it. ❑ *Both have fudged their calculations.*

fuel /ˈfjuːəl/ (**fuels, fuelling, fuelled** or [AM] **fueling, fueled**) **1** N-VAR **Fuel** is a substance such as coal, oil, or petrol that is burned to provide heat or power. ❑ *...the fuel necessary to heat their homes.* **2** → see also **fossil fuel** **3** V-T A machine or vehicle that **is fuelled** by a particular substance

f

works by burning that substance. ❑ *...power stations fuelled by oil.*

→ see **car, energy, engine, oil, petroleum**

Word Partnership Use *fuel* with:

N. **cost of** fuel, fuel **oil**, fuel **pump**, fuel **shortage**, fuel **supply**, fuel **tank** 1
ADJ. **unleaded** fuel 1

fugitive /'fju:dʒɪtɪv/ (**fugitives**) N-COUNT A **fugitive** is someone who is running away or hiding, usually in order to avoid being caught by the police.

F

fulfil also **fulfill** /fʊl'fɪl/ (**fulfils, fulfilling, fulfilled**) 1 V-T If you **fulfil** a promise, dream, or ambition, you do what you said or hoped you would do. ❑ *...to fulfil her ambitions and become an actress.* 2 V-T To **fulfil** a task, role, or function means to do what is required by it. 3 V-T If something **fulfils** you, you feel happy and satisfied with what you are doing. ❑ *...a hobby that fulfilled her.* ● **fulfilling** ADJ ❑ *...a fulfilling career.* ● **fulfilled** ADJ ❑ *I feel more fulfilled doing this than I've ever done before.* ● **fulfilment** N-UNCOUNT ❑ *...a great sense of fulfilment.*

full /fʊl/ (**fuller, fullest**) 1 ADJ Something that is **full** contains as much of a substance or as many objects as it can. ❑ *...a full tank of petrol.* ❑ *The car park was full.* 2 ADJ AFTER LINK-V If a place is **full of** things or people, it contains a large number of them. ❑ *His mouth was full of peas.* ❑ *The recipe book was full of useful ideas.* 3 ADJ AFTER LINK-V If someone or something is **full of** a feeling or quality, they have a lot of it. ❑ *I feel full of confidence.* 4 ADJ AFTER LINK-V If you feel **full**, you have eaten so much that you do not want anything else. ● **fullness** N-UNCOUNT ❑ *High fibre diets give the feeling of fullness.* 5 ADJ BEFORE N & ADV You can use **full** to indicate the greatest possible amount of something. ❑ *He liked playing his music at full volume.* ❑ *...in full daylight.* 6 ADJ BEFORE N You can use **full** to indicate that you are referring to the whole of something, or to emphasize the amount of a quality that it has. ❑ *Full details will be sent to you.* ❑ *May I have your full name?* ❑ *The farm was in full view of the house.* 7 ADJ If someone has a **full** life, they are always busy. 8 ADJ When there is a **full** moon, the moon appears as a bright, complete circle. 9 ADJ A **full** flavour is strong and rich. ❑ *...the full flavour of the coffee.* 10 PHRASE Something that has been done **in full** has been done or finished completely. ❑ *The medical experts reported on it in full.* 11 PHRASE Something that is done or experienced **to the full** is done to as great an extent as is possible. ❑ *You have a good mind which should be used to the full.*

Thesaurus *full* Also look up:

ADJ. brimming with; (*ant.*) empty 1
loaded, packed full of, packed with 1 2
bursting with 3
stuffed 4

,full-'blown ADJ BEFORE N **Full-blown** means having all the characteristics of a particular type of thing or person. ❑ *He worked as a film editor before becoming a full-blown director.*

,full-'length 1 ADJ BEFORE N A **full-length** book, record, or film is the normal length, rather than being shorter than normal. 2 ADJ BEFORE N A **full-length** coat or skirt is long enough to reach the lower part of a person's leg. 3 ADJ BEFORE N A **full-length** mirror or portrait shows the whole of a person. 4 ADV Someone who is lying **full-length** is lying down flat and stretched out. ❑ *She stretched herself out full-length.*

,full-'scale 1 ADJ BEFORE N **Full-scale** means as complete, intense, or great in extent as possible. ❑ *...a full-scale nuclear war.* 2 ADJ BEFORE N A **full-scale** drawing or model is the same size as the thing that it represents.

,full-'size or **full-sized** ADJ BEFORE N A **full-size** or **full-sized** model or picture is the same size as the thing or person that it represents.

,full 'stop (**full stops**) N-COUNT In British English, a **full stop** is the punctuation mark (.) which you use at the end of a sentence when it is not a question or exclamation. The American word is **period**.

→ see **punctuation**

,full-'time or **full time** ADJ & ADV **Full-time** work or study takes up the whole of each normal working week. ❑ *...a full-time job.* ❑ *Deirdre works full-time.*

fully /'fʊli/ 1 ADV **Fully** means to the greatest degree or extent possible. ❑ *She was fully aware of my thoughts.* ❑ *I don't fully agree.* 2 ADV If you describe, answer, or deal with something **fully**, you leave out nothing that should be said or dealt with. ❑ *These debates are discussed more fully later in this book.*

Word Partnership Use *fully* with:

ADJ. fully **adjustable**, fully **aware**, fully **clothed**, fully **functional**, fully **operational**, fully **prepared** 1
V. fully **agree**, fully **decide**, fully **develop**, fully **explain**, fully **extend**, fully **expect**, fully **formed**, fully **heal**, fully **realize**, fully **recover**, fully **understand** 1 2

fumble /'fʌmbəl/ (**fumbles, fumbling, fumbled**) V-I If you **fumble for** something, or if you **fumble with** it, you clumsily try and reach for it or hold it. ❑ *She got out of bed and fumbled for her dressing gown.*

fume /fju:m/ (**fumes, fuming, fumed**) 1 N-PLURAL **Fumes** are unpleasantly strong or harmful gases or smells. ❑ *...car exhaust fumes.* 2 V-T/V-I If you **are fuming** over something, you are very angry about it. ❑ *'It's monstrous!' Jackie fumed.* ❑ *Mrs. Vine was still fuming.*

fun /fʌn/ 1 N-UNCOUNT **Fun** is pleasant, enjoyable, and light-hearted activity or amusement. ❑ *We had so much fun doing it.* ❑ *You still have time to join in the fun.* 2 ADJ If someone is **fun**, you enjoy their company. If something is **fun**, you enjoy doing it. ❑ *Liz was wonderful fun to be with.* ❑ *It was a fun evening.* 3 PHRASE If you do something **in fun**, you do it as a joke or for amusement, without intending to cause any harm. ❑ *Don't say such things, even in fun.* 4 PHRASE If you **make fun of** someone or something, or if you **poke fun at** them, you tease them or make jokes about them. ❑ *They all made fun of my plan.*

Word Web fungus

Fungi can be both harmful and helpful. For example, **mold** and mildew destroy crops, ruin clothing, cause diseases, and can even lead to death. But many fungi are useful. For instance, a single-cell fungus called **yeast** makes bread rise. Another form of yeast makes wine **ferment**. It turns the sugar in grape juice into alcohol. And **mushrooms** are a part of the diet of people all over the world. Cheese makers use a specific fungus to produce the creamy white skin on brie. A different **microorganism** gives blue cheese its characteristic color. Truffles, the most expensive fungi, cost more than £100 an ounce.

f

Thesaurus *fun* Also look up:

N. amusement, enjoyment, play; *(ant.)* misery 1
ADJ. amusing, enjoyable, entertaining, happy, pleasant; *(ant.)* boring 2

function /ˈfʌŋkʃən/ (**functions, functioning, functioned**) 1 N-COUNT The **function of** something or someone is the useful thing that they do or are intended to do. ❑ *The main function of horror films is to scare us.* 2 V-I If a machine or system **is functioning**, it is working or operating. ❑ *Recycling programs cannot function without local help.* 3 V-I If someone or something **functions as** a particular thing, they do the work or fulfil the purpose of that thing. ❑ *This old farm now functions as a hotel.* 4 N-COUNT A **function** is a large formal dinner or party.

functional /ˈfʌŋkʃənəl/ 1 ADJ **Functional** things are useful rather than decorative. ❑ *...modern, functional furniture.* 2 ADJ **Functional** equipment works or operates in the way that it is supposed to. ❑ *We have fully functional smoke alarms.* 3 ADJ BEFORE N **Functional** means relating to the way something works or operates. ❑ *You already have the functional knowledge and skills that you need for the job.*

fund /fʌnd/ (**funds, funding, funded**) 1 N-PLURAL **Funds** are amounts of money that are available to be spent. ❑ *The concert will raise funds for Africa.* ❑ *...government funds.* 2 N-COUNT A **fund** is an amount of money that is collected for a particular purpose. ❑ *...a scholarship fund for engineering students.* 3 V-T To **fund** something means to provide money for it. ❑ *They will use the money to fund a new nurse.* ❑ *...government-funded institutions.* • **funding** N-UNCOUNT ❑ *They hope for government funding for the scheme.* 4 N-COUNT If you have a **fund of** something, you have a lot of it. ❑ *...an extraordinary fund of energy.*

fundamental /ˌfʌndəˈmentəl/ ADJ If something is **fundamental**, it is very important or basic. ❑ *If you want to make fundamental changes in your life, you need plenty of space and time.* ❑ *His family is fundamental to him – he's a wonderful husband and father.* • **fundamentally** ADV ❑ *He is fundamentally a good man.*

fundamentalism /ˌfʌndəˈmentəlɪzəm/ N-UNCOUNT **Fundamentalism** is belief in the original form of a religion or theory, without accepting any later ideas. ❑ *Religious fundamentalism was spreading in the region.* • **fundamentalist** (**fundamentalists**) N-COUNT ❑ *...fundamentalist Christians.*

fundamentals /fʌndəˈmentəlz/ N-PLURAL **The fundamentals of** something are its simplest, most important elements, ideas, or principles. ❑ *...the fundamentals of road safety.*

fundraiser /ˈfʌndreɪzə/ (**fundraisers**) 1 N-COUNT A **fundraiser** is an event which is intended to raise money for a particular purpose. ❑ *Organize a fundraiser for your church.* 2 N-COUNT A **fundraiser** is someone who works to raise money for a particular purpose.

ˈfund-ˌraising N-UNCOUNT **Fund-raising** is the activity of collecting money for a particular purpose.

funeral /ˈfjuːnərəl/ (**funerals**) N-COUNT A **funeral** is a ceremony for the burial or cremation of someone who has died. ❑ *His funeral will be on Thursday at Blackburn Cathedral.*

funfair /ˈfʌnfɛər/ (**funfairs**) N-COUNT A **funfair** is an event held in a park or field at which people pay to ride on various machines for amusement or try to win prizes in games.

fungus /ˈfʌŋgəs/ (**fungi** /ˈfʌŋgiː, ˈfʌndʒaɪ/) N-VAR A **fungus** is a plant that has no flowers, leaves, or green colouring, such as a mushroom or mould. • **fungal** ADJ ❑ *...fungal growth.*
→ see Word Web: **fungus**

funnel /ˈfʌnəl/ (**funnels, funnelling, funnelled** or [AM] **funneling, funneled**) 1 N-COUNT A **funnel** is an object with a wide top and a tube at the bottom, which is used to pour substances into a container. 2 N-COUNT A **funnel** is a chimney on a ship. 3 V-T/V-I If something **funnels** somewhere, or if it **is funnelled** there, it is directed through a narrow space. ❑ *The winds came from the north, funnelling down the valley.* 4 V-T If you **funnel** money or resources somewhere, you send them there from several sources. ❑ *...a plan to funnel financial aid through the World Bank.*

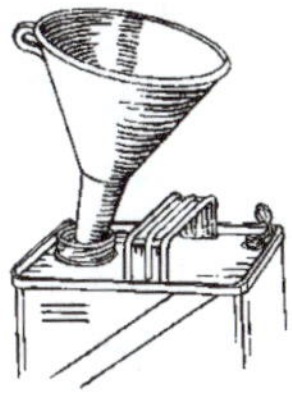

funnel

funny /ˈfʌni/ (**funnier, funniest**) 1 ADJ **Funny** things are amusing and make you smile or laugh. ❑ *...a funny story.* ❑ *What's so funny?* 2 ADJ You say that something is **funny** when it is strange, surprising, or puzzling. ❑ *It's funny how fast things change.* 3 ADJ If you feel **funny**, you feel slightly ill. [INFORMAL] ❑ *My head ached and my stomach felt funny.*

Thesaurus *funny* Also look up:

ADJ. amusing, comical, entertaining; *(ant.)* serious 1
bizarre, odd, peculiar 2

fur /fɜː/ (**furs**) 1 N-UNCOUNT **Fur** is the thick hair that grows on the bodies of many animals, such as rabbits and bears, and is sometimes used to make clothes or rugs. You can also refer to an artificial material that resembles this hair as **fur**. ❑ *...a black coat with a fur collar.* 2 N-COUNT A **fur** is a coat made from fur. ❑ *...women in furs.*

F

furious /ˈfjʊəriəs/ 1 ADJ If someone is **furious**, they are extremely angry. ❑ *He is furious at the way his wife has been treated.* • **furiously** ADV ❑ *'You clumsy idiot,' he said furiously.* 2 → See note at **angry** 3 ADJ You can use **furious** to indicate that something involves great energy, speed, or violence. ❑ *...months of furious debate.* • **furiously** ADV ❑ *I started writing furiously.*
→ see **anger**

furlong /ˈfɜːlɒŋ, AM -lɔːŋ/ (**furlongs**) N-COUNT A **furlong** is an imperial unit of length that is equal to 220 yards or 201.2 metres.

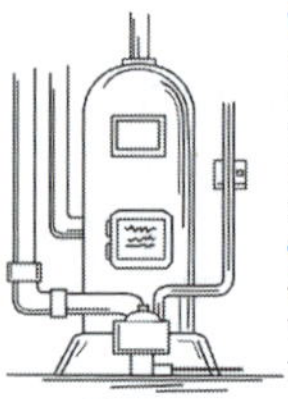
furnace

furnace /ˈfɜːnɪs/ (**furnaces**) N-COUNT A **furnace** is a container or enclosed space in which a very hot fire is made, for example to melt metal, burn rubbish, or produce steam.

furnish /ˈfɜːnɪʃ/ (**furnishes, furnishing, furnished**) 1 V-T When you **furnish** a room, you put furniture in it. ❑ *The room was tastefully furnished.* • **furnished** ADJ ❑ *...a furnished flat.* 2 V-T To **furnish** something means to provide it or supply it. [FORMAL] ❑ *They'll be able to furnish you with the details.*

furnishings /ˈfɜːnɪʃɪŋz/ N-PLURAL The **furnishings** of a room or house are the furniture, curtains, carpets, and decorations such as pictures.

furniture /ˈfɜːnɪtʃə/ N-UNCOUNT **Furniture** consists of large movable objects such as tables, chairs, or beds that are used in a room for sitting or lying on, or for putting things on or in. ❑ *...bedroom furniture.*

Usage

Note that **furniture** is only ever used as an uncount noun. You cannot say 'a furniture' or 'furnitures'. If you want to refer in general terms to something such as a table, a chair, or a bed, you can say a **piece of furniture** or an **item of furniture**.

furore [AM **furor**] /fjʊˈrɔːri, ˈfjʊərɔː/ N-SING A **furore** is a very angry or excited reaction by people to something. ❑ *...the furore over his comments about Northern Ireland.*

furrow /ˈfʌrəʊ, AM ˈfɜːr-/ (**furrows, furrowing, furrowed**) 1 N-COUNT A **furrow** is a long line in the earth made for planting seeds. 2 N-COUNT The **furrows** in someone's skin are deep folds or lines. ❑ *Deep furrows marked the corners of his mouth.* 3 V-T/V-I If someone **furrows** their brow or forehead, deep folds appear in it because they are frowning. [WRITTEN] ❑ *Her father furrowed his forehead.* ❑ *Occasionally her brow furrowed.*

furry /ˈfɜːri/ (**furrier, furriest**) 1 ADJ A **furry** animal is covered with thick soft hair. ❑ *...a long furry tail.* 2 ADJ Something that is **furry** resembles fur. ❑ *...a furry hat.*

further /ˈfɜːðə/ (**furthers, furthering, furthered**) 1 ADV **Further** means to a greater degree or extent. ❑ *As a result, living standards will fall further behind America, Britain and Japan.* 2 ADV If someone or something goes **further** or takes something **further**, they progress to a more advanced or detailed stage. ❑ *He did not develop that idea any further.* 3 ADJ BEFORE N A **further** thing or amount is an additional one. ❑ *Doctors are carrying out further tests.* 4 ADV **Further** means a greater distance than before or than something else. ❑ *Now we live further away from the city centre.* 5 ADV **Further** is used in expressions such as **'further back'** and **'further ahead'** to refer to a point in time that is earlier or later than the time you are talking about. ❑ *Ministers are looking further ahead, beyond the current situation.* 6 V-T If you **further** something, you help it to progress or to be successful. ❑ *Education is not only about furthering your career.*

ˌfurther eduˈcation N-UNCOUNT In Britain, **further education** is education after leaving school, at a college rather than a university. The usual American term is **continuing education**.

furthermore /ˌfɜːðəˈmɔː/ ADV **Furthermore** is used to introduce a statement adding to or supporting the previous one. ❑ *Let's go inside. It's nearly dark, and furthermore it's going to rain.*

furthest /ˈfɜːðɪst/ 1 ADV **Furthest** means to a greater extent or degree than ever before or than anything or anyone else. ❑ *Prices have fallen furthest in the south of England.* 2 ADJ & ADV The **furthest** one of a number of things is the one that is the greatest distance away. ❑ *...the furthest point from earth.* ❑ *...areas furthest from the coast.*

furtive /ˈfɜːtɪv/ ADJ If you describe someone's behaviour as **furtive**, you disapprove of them behaving as if they want to keep something secret or hidden. ❑ *...furtive meetings.* • **furtively** ADV ❑ *He glanced around furtively.*

fury /ˈfjʊəri/ N-UNCOUNT **Fury** is very strong anger. ❑ *He became red-faced with fury.*

fuse /fjuːz/ (**fuses, fusing, fused**) 1 N-COUNT In an electrical appliance, a **fuse** is a wire safety device which melts and stops the electric current if there is a fault. 2 V-T/V-I When an electric device **fuses**, or when you **fuse** it, it stops working because of a fault. ❑ *The light fused.* 3 N-COUNT A **fuse** is part of a bomb or firework which delays the explosion and gives people time to move away. 4 V-I When one thing **fuses with** another, they join together, usually to become one thing. ❑ *Manufactured glass is made by fusing various types of sand.* 5 V-T To **fuse** ideas, qualities, or things means to combine them. ❑ *It was the first time that black South African music was fused with jazz.*

fuselage /ˈfjuːzɪlɑːʒ/ (**fuselages**) N-COUNT The **fuselage** of an aeroplane or rocket is its main part.

fusion /ˈfjuːʒən/ (**fusions**) 1 N-VAR When two ideas, qualities, or things are combined, you can say that there is a **fusion of** them. ❑ *...a fusion of Eastern and Western cooking.* 2 N-UNCOUNT **Fusion**

is the process in which atomic particles combine and produce a large amount of nuclear energy. [TECHNICAL] ❑ *...research into nuclear fusion.*
→ see **sun**

fuss /fʌs/ (**fusses, fussing, fussed**) **1** N-SING & N-UNCOUNT **Fuss** is unnecessarily anxious or excited behaviour. ❑ *I don't know what all the fuss is about.* **2** V-I When people **fuss**, they behave in an unnecessarily anxious or excited way. ❑ *My mother is fussing about the journey.* **3** V-I If you **fuss over** someone or something, you pay them too much attention or worry about them too much. ❑ *All the Sisters fussed over her.* **4** PHRASE If you **make a fuss of** someone, you pay a lot of attention to them.

fussy /ˈfʌsi/ (**fussier, fussiest**) **1** ADJ Someone who is **fussy** is very concerned with unimportant details and is difficult to please. ❑ *She is very fussy about what she eats.* **2** ADJ If you describe things as **fussy**, you are criticizing them because they are too elaborate or detailed. ❑ *...fussy curtains.*

futile /ˈfjuːtaɪl, AM -təl/ ADJ If you say that something is **futile**, you mean there is no point in doing it, usually because it has no chance of succeeding. ❑ *...their futile attempts to avoid being seen.* ● **futility** /fjuːˈtɪlɪti/ N-UNCOUNT ❑ *...the futility of arguing with him.*

future /ˈfjuːtʃə/ (**futures**) **1** N-SING **The future** is the period of time after the present. ❑ *A decision is likely in the near future.* **2** ADJ BEFORE N **Future** things will happen or exist after the present time. ❑ *...the UK's future role in Europe.* **3** N-COUNT The **future** of someone or something is what will happen to them after the present time. ❑ *...his future as prime minister.* **4** N-COUNT Something that has a **future** is likely to be successful or to survive. ❑ *There's no future in this relationship.* **5** PHRASE You use **in future** when you are telling someone what you want or expect to happen from now on. ❑ *Be more careful in future.* **6** PHRASE If you say that something will happen **in the near future**, you mean that it will happen quite soon.

Word Partnership Use *future* with:

ADJ.	**bright** future, **distant** future, **immediate** future, **near** future, **uncertain** future **1**
V.	**discuss the** future, **have a** future, **plan for the** future, **predict/see the** future **1**
N.	future **date**, future **events**, future **generations**, future **plans**, **for** future **reference** **2**

ˌfuture ˈtense N-SING In grammar, the **future tense** is used to refer to things that will come after the present.

futuristic /ˌfjuːtʃəˈrɪstɪk/ ADJ Something that is **futuristic** looks or seems like something from the future. ❑ *...a futuristic building.*

fuzzy /ˈfʌzi/ (**fuzzier, fuzziest**) **1** ADJ **Fuzzy** hair sticks up in a soft curly mass. **2** ADJ A **fuzzy** picture or image is blurred and unclear. ❑ *...fuzzy photographs.* **3** ADJ BEFORE N **Fuzzy** logic is a type of computer logic that is supposed to imitate the way that humans think. [COMPUTING]

f

Gg

gadget /ˈgædʒɪt/ (**gadgets**) N-COUNT A **gadget** is a small machine or device which does a useful task. ❑ *...gadgets such as CD players.*
→ see **technology**

gag /gæg/ (**gags, gagging, gagged**) 1 N-COUNT A **gag** is a piece of cloth that is tied round or put inside someone's mouth to stop them from speaking. 2 V-T If someone **gags** you, they tie a piece of cloth around your mouth in order to stop you from speaking. ❑ *The men tied her to a chair and gagged her.* 3 V-T If a person **is gagged** by someone in authority, they are prevented from expressing their opinion or from publishing certain information; used showing disapproval. ❑ *The manager decided to fine the player and then gag him from telling his side of the story.* 4 N-COUNT A **gag** is a joke. [INFORMAL]

gain /geɪn/ (**gains, gaining, gained**) 1 V-T If you **gain** something, you acquire it gradually. ❑ *Students can gain experience by working on the college magazine.* ❑ *The helicopter gained speed as it flew towards land.* 2 V-I If you **gain from** something, you get some advantage from it. ❑ *Companies of all sizes should gain from the advice.* 3 N-COUNT A **gain** is an improvement or increase. ❑ *Figures for new home sales showed a gain of nearly 8%.* 4 PHRASE If you do something **for gain**, you do it in order to get some profit for yourself. [FORMAL] ❑ *...buying art for financial gain.* 5 V-T If you **gain** something, you obtain it, usually after a lot of effort. ❑ *Passing exams is not enough to gain a place at university.*

gait /geɪt/ (**gaits**) N-COUNT Someone's **gait** is their particular way of walking. [WRITTEN] ❑ *...a confident, easy gait.*

gala /ˈgɑːlə, AM ˈgeɪlə/ (**galas**) N-COUNT A **gala** is a special public celebration, performance, or festival. ❑ *...a gala evening at the Royal Opera House.*

galaxy /ˈgæləksi/ (**galaxies**) N-COUNT A **galaxy** is a huge group of stars and planets extending over millions of miles.
→ see Word Web: **galaxy**
→ see **star**

gale /geɪl/ (**gales**) N-COUNT A **gale** is a very strong wind. ❑ *...fierce winter gales.*
→ see **wind**

gall /gɔːl/ (**galls, galling, galled**) 1 N-SING If someone has **the gall to** do something dangerous or dishonest, they are brave enough to do it; used showing disapproval. ❑ *She had the gall to suggest that I might give her the information.* 2 V-T If someone's action **galls** you, it makes you angry because you cannot do anything about it. ❑ *It really galled Dana to think that Caroline knew all about it.*

gallant /ˈgælənt/

> The pronunciation /gəˈlænt/ is also used for meaning 2.

1 ADJ A **gallant** person behaves very bravely and honourably in a dangerous or difficult situation. ❑ *...gallant soldiers.* ● **gallantly** ADV ❑ *The town responded gallantly to the war.* 2 ADJ If you say that a man is **gallant**, you think he is polite and considerate towards other people, especially women. [DATED]

gallery /ˈgæləri/ (**galleries**) 1 N-COUNT A **gallery** is a place that has permanent exhibitions of works of art in it. ❑ *...an art gallery.* 2 N-COUNT **The gallery** in a theatre or concert hall is a raised area at the back like a large balcony.

galley /ˈgæli/ (**galleys**) N-COUNT On a ship or aircraft, **the galley** is the kitchen.

gallon /ˈgælən/ (**gallons**) N-COUNT A **gallon** is a unit of measurement for liquids that is equal to eight pints. In Britain, it is equal to 4.564 litres. In America, it is equal to 3.785 litres.
→ see **measurement**

gallop /ˈgæləp/ (**gallops, galloping, galloped**) 1 V-I & N-SING When a horse **gallops**, or when it runs at **a gallop**, it runs very fast, so that during each step all four legs are off the ground at the same time. ❑ *The horses galloped away.* ❑ *He heard voices again, followed by horses leaving at a gallop.* 2 V-I & N-COUNT If you **gallop**, you ride a horse that is galloping. A **gallop** is a ride on a galloping horse.

Word Web galaxy

The word **galaxy** with a small g refers to a very large group of **stars** and **planets**. It measures many millions of **light years** wide. There are about 100 billion galaxies in the **universe**. **Astronomers** classify galaxies into four different types. Irregular galaxies have no particular shape. Elliptical galaxies look like flattened spheres. Spiral galaxies have long curving arms. A barred spiral galaxy has straight lines of stars extending from its nucleus. Galaxy with a capital G refers to our own **solar system**. The name of our galaxy is the Milky Way. It is about 100,000 light years wide.

❑ *Major Winston galloped into the distance.* ❑ *...early morning gallops at his stables.*

galore /gəˈlɔː/ ADJ You use **galore** to emphasize that something you like exists in very large quantities. ❑ *There is singing and dancing galore in this year's movies.*

galvanize [BRIT also **galvanise**] /ˈgælvənaɪz/ (**galvanizes, galvanizing, galvanized**) V-T If you **are galvanized into** doing something, you are motivated by excitement, fear, or anger into doing it straight away. ❑ *'No, you will not,' said Sethos, galvanized into speech.*

gamble /ˈgæmbəl/ (**gambles, gambling, gambled**) 1 V-T/V-I & N-SING If you **gamble on** something, or if you take a **gamble**, you take a risky decision in the hope of gaining money, success, or an advantage. ❑ *Most firms are not willing to gamble on new products.* ❑ *They do not want to gamble their careers on this matter.* ❑ *It was a gamble to leave a 16-year-old in charge.* 2 V-T/V-I If you **gamble**, you bet money on the result of a game, a race, or competition. ❑ *John gambled heavily on the horses.* ❑ *He gambled away his family's money.* • **gambler** (**gamblers**) N-COUNT ❑ *I used to be a very heavy gambler.* • **gambling** N-UNCOUNT ❑ *The laws regulating gambling are quite tough.*

game /geɪm/ (**games**) 1 N-COUNT A **game** is an activity or sport usually involving skill, knowledge, or chance, in which you follow fixed rules and try to win against an opponent or to solve a puzzle. ❑ *...the wonderful game of football.* 2 N-COUNT In sport, a **game** is a match, or part of a match. ❑ *We won three games against Australia.* ❑ *...the last three points of the second game.* 3 N-PLURAL **Games** are organized events involving several different sports. ❑ *...the 1996 Olympic Games.* 4 N-COUNT You can describe a way of behaving as a **game** when it is used to try to gain advantage. ❑ *The minister has been playing a clever political game.* 5 N-UNCOUNT **Game** is wild animals or birds that are hunted for sport or food, for example deer and grouse. 6 ADJ AFTER LINK-V If you say that someone is **game** or **game for** something, you mean that they are willing to do something new, unusual, or risky. ❑ *He still had new ideas and was game to try them.* ❑ *He said he's game for a similar challenge next year.* 7 PHRASE If someone or something **gives the game away**, they reveal a secret or reveal their feelings. ❑ *The children's guilty faces gave the game away.* 8 PHRASE If you beat someone **at** their **own game**, you use the same methods that they have used, but more successfully, so that you gain an advantage over them. ❑ *To catch the killer, they had to play him at his own game.* 9 PHRASE If you say that something is **the name of the game**, you mean that it is the most important aspect of the activity you are talking about. ❑ *In politics, survival is the name of the game.*

→ see **chess, mammal**

gaming /ˈgeɪmɪŋ/ N-UNCOUNT **Gaming** means the same as **gambling**, especially at cards, roulette, and other games of chance.

gang /gæŋ/ (**gangs, ganging, ganged**) 1 N-COUNT A **gang** is a group of people who join together for some purpose, often criminal. ❑ *...members of a gang.* ❑ *The students were attacked by a gang of teenagers from another school.* 2 N-COUNT A **gang** is a group of manual workers who work together. ❑ *...a gang of labourers.*

▶ **gang up** PHR-VERB If people **gang up on** someone, they unite against them. [INFORMAL] ❑ *All the girls in my class ganged up on me.*

Thesaurus *gang* Also look up:

N. crowd, group, pack 1

Word Link *ster ≈ one who does : gangster, mobster, youngster*

gangster /ˈgæŋstə/ (**gangsters**) N-COUNT A **gangster** is a member of a group of violent criminals.

gaol /dʒeɪl/ → see **jail**

gap /gæp/ (**gaps**) 1 N-COUNT A **gap** is a space between two things or a hole in something solid. ❑ *The wind was blowing through the gaps in the wall.* 2 N-COUNT A **gap** is a period of time when you are not doing what you normally do. ❑ *During the four-year gap, William joined the Army.* 3 N-COUNT If there is something missing from a situation which prevents it from being complete, you can also say that there is a **gap**. ❑ *Tony saw a gap in the market for a cheese specialist.* 4 N-COUNT A **gap** is a great difference between two things, people, or ideas. ❑ *...the gap between rich and poor.* ❑ *America's trade gap is getting wider.*

gape /geɪp/ (**gapes, gaping, gaped**) 1 V-I If you **gape**, you look at someone or something in surprise, with your mouth open. ❑ *His secretary stopped taking notes and gaped at me.* 2 V-I If you say that something such as a hole or a wound **gapes**, you are emphasizing that it is deep or wide. ❑ *A hole gaped in the roof.* • **gaping** ADJ ❑ *...a gaping hole in the side of the ship.*

ˈgap year N-SING A **gap year** is a period of time during which a student takes a break from studying after they have finished school and before they start college or university. [BRIT]

garage /ˈgærɑːʒ, -rɪdʒ, AM gəˈrɑːʒ/ (**garages**) 1 N-COUNT A **garage** is a building in which you keep a car. 2 N-COUNT A **garage** is a place where you can get your car repaired, buy a car, or buy petrol.

garbage /ˈgɑːbɪdʒ/ N-UNCOUNT In American English, **garbage** is rubbish, especially waste from a kitchen. The usual British word is **rubbish**. ❑ *...garbage collection.*

→ see **pollution**

Usage

In American English, the words **garbage** and **trash** are most commonly used to refer to waste material that is thrown away. ❑ *...the smell of rotting garbage.* ❑ *She threw the bottle into the trash.* In British English, **rubbish** is the usual word. **Garbage** and **trash** are sometimes used in British English, but only informally and metaphorically. ❑ *I don't have to listen to this garbage.* ❑ *The book was trash.*

Thesaurus *garbage* Also look up:

N. junk, litter, rubbish, trash 1
foolishness, nonsense 2

garden /ˈgɑːdən/ (**gardens, gardening,**

g

G

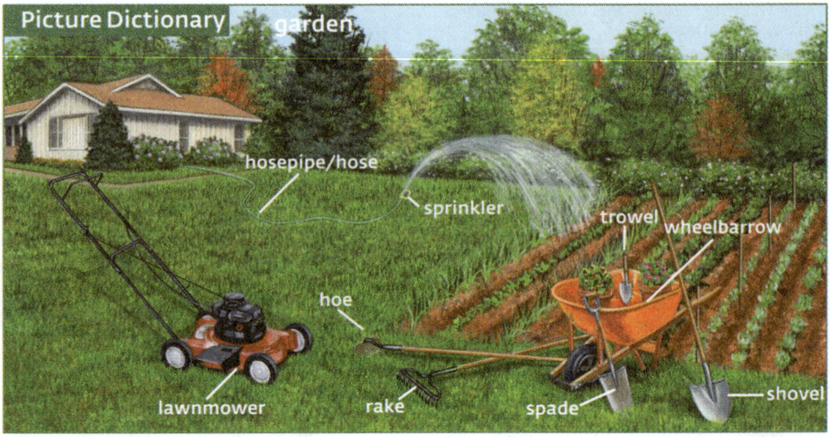

gardened) **1** N-COUNT In British English, a **garden** is an area of land next to a house, with plants, trees, and grass. The usual American word is **yard**. **2** V-I If you **are gardening**, you are doing work in your garden such as weeding or planting. • **gardener** **(gardeners)** N-COUNT ❑ *My father was a keen gardener.* • **gardening** N-UNCOUNT ❑ *I have started gardening again.* **3** N-COUNT **Gardens** are a park with plants, trees, and grass. ❑ *...the botanical gardens.*
→ see Picture Dictionary: **garden**

garish /ˈgeərɪʃ/ ADJ If you describe something as **garish**, you dislike it because it is very bright in an unattractive, showy way. ❑ *I had to wear some awful, garish clothes.*

garland /ˈgɑːlənd/ **(garlands)** N-COUNT A **garland** is a circular decoration made from flowers and leaves, worn round the neck or head.

garlic /ˈgɑːlɪk/ N-UNCOUNT **Garlic** is the small, white, round bulb of a plant related to the onion plant, which is used as a flavouring. ❑ *Add the garlic and fry everything for two minutes.*
→ see **spice**

garment /ˈgɑːmənt/ **(garments)** **1** N-COUNT A **garment** is a piece of clothing. [FORMAL] **2** → See note at **clothes**

garnish /ˈgɑːnɪʃ/ **(garnishes, garnishing, garnished)** **1** N-VAR A **garnish** is a small amount of herbs, salad, or other food that is used to decorate prepared food. **2** V-T To **garnish** food means to decorate it with a garnish.

garrison /ˈgærɪsən/ **(garrisons)** N-COUNT A **garrison** is a group of soldiers whose job is to guard the town or building where they live.

gas /gæs/ **(gases, gasses, gassing, gassed)**

> The form **gases** is the plural of the noun. The form **gasses** is the third person singular of the verb.

1 N-VAR A **gas** is any substance that is neither liquid nor solid, such as oxygen or hydrogen. Some gases burn easily and are used as a fuel for heating and cooking. ❑ *The house has gas heating, electricity and a water supply.* **2** → see also **tear gas** **3** N-VAR **Gas** is a poisonous gas that can be used as a weapon. ❑ *...mustard gas.* **4** V-T To **gas** a person or animal means to kill them by making them breathe poisonous gas. **5** N-UNCOUNT In American English, **gas** is the liquid used as a fuel for motor vehicles. The British word is **petrol**.
→ see **air, energy, greenhouse effect, matter, solar system**

gash /gæʃ/ **(gashes, gashing, gashed)** **1** N-COUNT A **gash** is a long deep cut. **2** V-T If you **gash** something, you accidentally make a long deep cut in it. ❑ *He gashed his leg while he was chopping wood.*

ˈgas mask **(gas masks)** N-COUNT A **gas mask** is a device worn over someone's face in order to protect them from poisonous gases.

gasoline /ˈgæsəliːn/ N-UNCOUNT In American English, **gasoline** is the liquid used as a fuel for motor vehicles. The British word is **petrol**.
→ see **oil**

gasp /gɑːsp, gæsp/ **(gasps, gasping, gasped)** V-I & N-COUNT If you **gasp**, or if you give a **gasp**, you take a short, quick breath through your mouth, especially when you are surprised or in pain. ❑ *She gasped for air.* ❑ *A gasp of horror was heard.*

gastric /ˈgæstrɪk/ ADJ BEFORE N **Gastric** is used to describe things which occur in the stomach. [TECHNICAL] ❑ *...gastric flu.*

gate /geɪt/ **(gates)** **1** N-COUNT A **gate** is a structure like a door which is used at the entrance to a field, a garden, or the grounds of a building. **2** N-COUNT In an airport, a **gate** is an exit through which passengers reach their aeroplane. ❑ *...the departure gate.*

gateway /ˈgeɪtweɪ/ **(gateways)** **1** N-COUNT A **gateway** is an entrance where there is a gate. ❑ *The castle has an attractive gateway.* **2** N-COUNT A **gateway to** something is a way of reaching, achieving, or discovering it. ❑ *New York is the great gateway to America.*
→ see **Internet**

gather /ˈgæðə/ **(gathers, gathering, gathered)** **1** V-T/V-I When people **gather** somewhere, or if someone **gathers** them there, they come together in a group. ❑ *We gathered around the fireplace.* ❑ *The man asked me to gather the children together.* **2** V-T &

PHR-VERB If you **gather** things, or if you **gather** them **up**, you collect them together. ❑ *Start gathering information several months before you need it.* ❑ *I needed a few minutes to gather my thoughts.* ❑ *When he had gathered up his papers, he went out.* **3** V-T If something **gathers** speed, momentum, or force, it gradually becomes faster or more powerful. ❑ *The train started off and quickly gathered speed.* **4** V-T You use **gather** in expressions such as '**I gather**' and '**as far as I can gather**' when you are introducing information that you have found out, especially when you have found it out in an indirect way. ❑ *I gather his report is critical of the judge.* ❑ *'He speaks English,' she said to Graham.—'I gathered that.'*
▶ **gather up** → see **gather** (meaning 2)

gathering /'gæðərɪŋ/ (**gatherings**) N-COUNT A **gathering** is a group of people meeting together. ❑ *...weekly social gatherings.*

gaudy /'gɔːdi/ (**gaudier, gaudiest**) ADJ If you describe something as **gaudy**, you mean it is very brightly coloured in an unattractive, showy way. ❑ *...gaudy jewellery.*

gauge /geɪdʒ/ (**gauges, gauging, gauged**) **1** V-T If you **gauge** something, you measure it or judge it. ❑ *He gauged the wind speed.* ❑ *To gauge reaction, we interviewed shoppers in London stores.* **2** N-COUNT A **gauge** is a device that measures the amount or quantity of something and shows the amount measured. ❑ *...temperature gauges.* **3** N-SING A **gauge of** a situation is a fact or event that can be used to judge it. ❑ *They see money as a gauge of success.*

gaunt /gɔːnt/ ADJ If someone looks **gaunt**, they look very thin, usually because of illness.

gauntlet /'gɔːntlɪt/ (**gauntlets**) **1** N-COUNT **Gauntlets** are long, thick, protective gloves. **2** PHRASE If you **run the gauntlet**, you are attacked or criticized by a lot of hostile people, especially because you have to pass through a group of them. ❑ *She was forced to run the gauntlet of about 300 journalists.* **3** PHRASE If you **throw down the gauntlet to** someone, you say or do something that challenges them to argue or compete with you. If someone **takes up the gauntlet**, they accept a challenge that has been offered.

gave /geɪv/ **Gave** is the past tense of **give**.

gay /geɪ/ (**gays, gayer, gayest**) **1** ADJ & N-PLURAL **Gay** people or **gays** are homosexuals. **2** ADJ **Gay** means lively and cheerful. [DATED] ❑ *The bag was small and light and made of gay blue canvas.*

gaze /geɪz/ (**gazes, gazing, gazed**) **1** V-I If you **gaze at** someone or something, you look steadily at them for a long time. ❑ *She lowered her head and gazed at the floor.* ❑ *The girls stood still, gazing around the building.* **2** N-COUNT You can talk about someone's **gaze** as a way of describing how they are looking at something, especially when they are looking steadily at it. ❑ *She felt uncomfortable under the woman's steady gaze.*

Usage

The verbs **gaze** and **stare** are both used to talk about looking at something for a long time. If you **gaze at** something, it is often because you think it is marvellous or impressive. ❑ *I gazed in wonder at the majestic Notre Dame.* If you **stare at** something or someone, it is often because you think they are strange or shocking. ❑ *Various families came out and stared at us.*

Word Link *ette ≈ small : cassette, cigarette, gazette*

gazette /gə'zet/ (**gazettes**) N-COUNT A **gazette** is a newspaper or journal. ❑ *...the Arkansas Gazette.*

GCE /ˌdʒiː siː 'iː/ (**GCEs**) **1** N-VAR A **GCE** is an examination taken by British school students at Advanced level, during their last year at school. **GCE** is an abbreviation for 'General Certificate of Education'. **2** → see also **A level**

GCSE /ˌdʒiː siː es 'iː/ (**GCSEs**) N-VAR A **GCSE** is an examination taken by British school students when they are fifteen or sixteen years old. **GCSE** is an abbreviation for 'General Certificate of Secondary Education'.

gear /gɪə/ (**gears, gearing, geared**) **1** N-COUNT A **gear** is a piece of machinery, for example in a car or on a bicycle, which helps to control its movement. When a vehicle's engine is operating at a particular rate, you can say it is **in** a particular **gear**. ❑ *The car was in fourth gear.* ❑ *He put the truck into first gear and drove off.* **2** N-UNCOUNT The **gear** for a particular activity is the equipment and special clothes that you use. ❑ *...fishing gear.* **3** ADJ If someone or something is **geared to** or **geared towards** a particular purpose, they are organized or designed in order to achieve that purpose. ❑ *My training was geared towards winning gold in Munich.*
▶ **gear up** PHR-VERB If someone **is gearing up for** a particular activity, they are preparing to do it. If they **are geared up for** it, they are prepared and able to do it. ❑ *All the parties will be gearing up for a general election.* ❑ *The factory was geared up to make 1,100 cars a day.*

gearbox /'gɪəbɒks/ (**gearboxes**) N-COUNT A **gearbox** is the system of gears in an engine or vehicle.

gee /dʒiː/ EXCLAM People sometimes say **gee** in order to express a strong reaction to something or to introduce a remark or response. [AM, INFORMAL] ❑ *Gee, it's hot.*

geese /giːs/ **Geese** is the plural of **goose**.

gel also **jell** /dʒel/ (**gels, gelling, gelled**) **1** V-I If people, things, or ideas **gel**, they or their different parts begin to work well together to form a successful whole. ❑ *They have gelled very well with the rest of the team.* ❑ *Then the business idea began to gel.* **2** N-VAR **Gel** is a smooth, soft, jelly-like substance, especially one used to keep your hair in a particular style.

gem /dʒem/ (**gems**) **1** N-COUNT A **gem** is a jewel. ❑ *...precious gems.* **2** N-COUNT If you describe something or someone as a **gem**, you mean that they are especially good or helpful. ❑ *...a gem of a hotel.*

gender /'dʒendə/ (**genders**) N-VAR A person's **gender** is the fact that they are male or female. You can refer to all male people or all female people as a particular **gender**. ❑ *Type in your height, weight, and gender.* ❑ *...the different abilities and skills of the two genders.*

gene /dʒiːn/ (**genes**) N-COUNT A **gene** is the part of a cell in a living thing which controls its physical characteristics, growth, and development.

genealogy /ˌdʒiːni'ælədʒi/ (**genealogies**) **1** N-UNCOUNT **Genealogy** is the study of the history of families. • **genealogical**

/ˌdʒiːniəˈlɒdʒɪkəl/ ADJ BEFORE N ❑ *...genealogical research on his family.* **2** N-COUNT A **genealogy** is the history of a family over several generations.

genera /ˈdʒenərə/ **Genera** is the plural of **genus**.

general /ˈdʒenrəl/ (**generals**) **1** N-COUNT & N-TITLE A **general** is an officer of a high rank in the armed forces. **2** ADJ BEFORE N If you talk about the **general** situation somewhere or if you talk about something in **general** terms, you are describing the situation as a whole rather than considering its details or exceptions. ❑ *The figures represent a general rise in unemployment.* ❑ *She recounted some of the recent events in very general terms.* **3** ADJ BEFORE N You use **general** to describe something that involves or affects most people, or most people in a group. ❑ *...general awareness of the problem.* **4** ADJ BEFORE N **General** is used to describe something that is not restricted to any one thing or area. ❑ *...a general store.* ❑ *...a general ache around the back of the neck.* ❑ *...a general sense of well-being.* **5** ADJ BEFORE N **General** is used to describe a person who has an average amount of knowledge or interest in a particular subject. ❑ *This book is intended for the general reader.* **6** ADJ BEFORE N **General** is used to describe someone's job, to indicate that they have responsibility for the whole of an organization. ❑ *He is the general manager of the museum.* **7** → see also **generally** **8** PHRASE You say **in general** when you are talking about the whole of a situation without going into details, or when you are referring to most people or things in a group. ❑ *We need to improve our educational system in general.* ❑ *People in general will support us.* **9** PHRASE **In general** is used to indicate that a statement is true in most cases. ❑ *In general, it was the better-educated voters who voted Yes.*

ˌgeneral eˈlection (**general elections**) N-COUNT A **general election** is an election for a new government, in which all the citizens of a country may vote.

generalize [BRIT also **generalise**] /ˈdʒenrəlaɪz/ (**generalizes, generalizing, generalized**) V-I If you **generalize**, you say something that is true in most cases. ❑ *It is impossible to generalize about the state of the country's health.* ● **generalization** (**generalizations**) N-VAR ❑ *You cannot make generalizations from a few cases.*

generalized [BRIT also **generalised**] /ˈdʒenrəlaɪzd/ ADJ **Generalized** means involving many different things, rather than one or two specific things. ❑ *The symptoms became more generalized.*

generally /ˈdʒenrəli/ **1** ADV You use **generally** to summarize a situation, activity, or idea without referring to the particular details of it. ❑ *Teachers generally have admitted a lack of enthusiasm.* **2** ADV You use **generally** to say that something happens or is used on most occasions but not on every occasion. ❑ *As women we generally feel too much.*

Thesaurus	*generally* Also look up:
ADV.	commonly, usually **1** **2**

ˌgeneral pracˈtitioner (**general practitioners**) N-COUNT A **general practitioner** is a doctor who treats all types of illnesses instead of specializing in one area of medicine. The abbreviation **GP** is also used.

ˌgeneral ˈpublic N-SING **The general public** is all the people in a society. ❑ *The general public knew very little about him.*

generate /ˈdʒenəreɪt/ (**generates, generating, generated**) **1** V-T To **generate** something means to cause it to begin and develop. ❑ *The reforms would generate new jobs.* **2** V-T To **generate** electricity or other forms of energy means to produce it. ❑ *...solar panels for generating power.* ● **generation** N-UNCOUNT ❑ *...the fuels used for electricity generation.* → see **energy**

generation /ˌdʒenəˈreɪʃən/ (**generations**) **1** N-COUNT A **generation** consists of all the people in a group or country who are of a similar age. ❑ *He's of a younger generation.* ❑ *...the leading American author of his generation.* **2** N-COUNT A **generation** is the period of time that it takes for children to grow up and become adults and have children of their own. ❑ *Its whole culture will be lost within a few generations.* **3** N-COUNT You can use **generation** to refer to a stage of development in the design and manufacture of machines or equipment. ❑ *...the next generation of Apple computers.* **4** → see also **generate**

generator /ˈdʒenəreɪtə/ (**generators**) N-COUNT A **generator** is a machine which produces electricity.
→ see **electricity**

generic /dʒɪˈnerɪk/ (**generics**) **1** ADJ BEFORE N **Generic** means applying to a whole group of similar things. [FORMAL] ❑ *Parmesan is a generic term used to describe a family of hard Italian cheeses.* **2** N-COUNT & ADJ A **generic** or a **generic** drug is a drug that does not have a trademark and is known by a general name. [TECHNICAL]

generous /ˈdʒenərəs/ **1** ADJ A **generous** person gives more of something, especially money, than is usual or expected. ❑ *German banks are generous in their lending.* ❑ *A generous gift of $140 will feed them for a month.* ● **generosity** /ˌdʒenəˈrɒsɪti/ N-UNCOUNT ❑ *She is well known for her generosity.* ● **generously** ADV ❑ *Please give generously.* **2** ADJ **Generous** means friendly, helpful, and willing to see the good qualities in people or things. ❑ *It's very generous of you to forgive me.* ● **generously** ADV ❑ *He said, very generously, that the project had been a huge success.* **3** ADJ Something that is **generous** is much larger than is usual or necessary. ❑ *...a generous portion of spaghetti.* ● **generously** ADV ❑ *Sprinkle generously with sugar.*

Thesaurus	*generous* Also look up:
ADJ.	charitable, kind; *(ant.)* mean, selfish **1** **2**
	abundant, overflowing; *(ant.)* meager **3**

geˌnetically ˈmodified ADJ **Genetically modified** plants and animals have had one or more genes changed. The abbreviation **GM** is often used. ❑ *...genetically modified foods.*

Word Link	*ics ≈ system, knowledge : economics, electronics, genetics*

genetics /dʒɪˈnetɪks/

The form **genetic** is used as a modifier.

1 N-UNCOUNT **Genetics** is the study of how characteristics are passed from one generation to

Word Web genre

Each of the arts includes several different types called **genre**. The four basic types of **literature** are **fiction**, nonfiction, **poetry**, and **drama**. In painting, some of the special areas are **realism**, expressionism, and Cubism. In music, they include **classical**, **jazz**, and **popular** forms. Each genre contains several parts. For example, popular music takes in country and western, **rap music**, and **rock**. Modern movie-making has produced a wide variety of genres. These include **horror films**, **comedies**, **action movies**, film noir, and **westerns**. Some artists don't like working within just one genre.

another by means of genes. 2 ADJ **Genetic** means concerned with genetics or genes. ❑ *...genetic scientists.* ● **genetically** ADV ❑ *...genetically engineered drugs.*
→ see **clone**

genial /ˈdʒiːniəl/ ADJ A **genial** person is kind and friendly. ● **genially** ADV ❑ *Liz laughed genially.* ● **geniality** N-UNCOUNT ❑ *...his habitual geniality.*

genitals /ˈdʒenɪtəlz/ N-PLURAL Your **genitals** are your external sexual organs.

genius /ˈdʒiːniəs/ (**geniuses**) 1 N-UNCOUNT **Genius** is very great ability or skill in something. ❑ *...his genius for chess.* 2 N-COUNT A **genius** is a highly intelligent, creative, or talented person.

Word Link *cide ≈ killing : genocide, pesticide, suicide*

genocide /ˈdʒenəsaɪd/ N-UNCOUNT **Genocide** is the murder of a whole community or race. [FORMAL]

genre /ˈʒɒnrə/ (**genres**) N-COUNT A **genre** is a particular style of literature, art, or music. [FORMAL] ❑ *...novels in the horror genre.*
→ see Word Web: **genre**
→ see **fantasy**

gent /dʒent/ (**gents**) 1 N-COUNT A **gent** is a gentleman. [DATED] 2 N-SING People sometimes refer to a men's public toilet as **the gents**. [BRIT, INFORMAL]

genteel /dʒenˈtiːl/ ADJ A **genteel** person is polite, respectable, and refined. ❑ *...a genteel middle-class family.*

gentle /ˈdʒentəl/ (**gentler, gentlest**) 1 ADJ A **gentle** person is kind, mild, and calm. ❑ *...a quiet and gentle man.* ❑ *...her gentle nature.* ● **gently** ADV ❑ *She smiled gently.* ● **gentleness** N-UNCOUNT ❑ *...his gentleness towards the children.* 2 ADJ If an action is **gentle**, it has little force. ❑ *...light, gentle strokes.* ❑ *...a gentle breeze.* ● **gently** ADV ❑ *Patrick took her gently by the arm.* 3 ADJ A **gentle** slope or curve is not steep or severe. ❑ *She was coming down the gentle slope towards the cottage.* ● **gently** ADV ❑ *...a gently sloping hill.*

gentleman /ˈdʒentəlmən/ (**gentlemen**) 1 N-COUNT A **gentleman** is a man from a family of high social standing. ❑ *...the traditional country gentleman.* 2 N-COUNT A **gentleman** is a man who is polite and well-educated. ❑ *He was always such a gentleman.* 3 N-COUNT You can refer politely to men as **gentlemen**. ❑ *This way, please, gentlemen.*

gentry /ˈdʒentri/ N-PLURAL The **gentry** are people of high social status. [BRIT, DATED]

genuine /ˈdʒenjuɪn/ 1 ADJ Something that is **genuine** is real and exactly what it appears to be. ❑ *...genuine leather.* ❑ *They're convinced the picture is genuine.* ● **genuinely** ADV ❑ *I was genuinely surprised.* 2 ADJ Someone who is **genuine** is honest and sincere. ❑ *She was a very genuine woman.*

Thesaurus *genuine* Also look up:
ADJ. actual, original, real, true; *(ant.)* bogus, fake 1
honest, open, sincere, true, valid; *(ant.)* dishonest 2

genus /ˈdʒenəs, AM ˈdʒiː-/ (**genera**) N-COUNT A **genus** is a class or group of similar animals or plants. [TECHNICAL]

geographical /ˌdʒiːəˈɡræfɪkəl/ or **geographic** /ˌdʒiːəˈɡræfɪk/ ADJ **Geographical** means relating to geography. ❑ *...a vast geographical area.* ● **geographically** ADV ❑ *Geographically, it's the highest point in London.*

Word Link *geo ≈ earth : geography, geology, geologist*

geography /dʒiˈɒɡrəfi/ 1 N-UNCOUNT **Geography** is the study of the countries of the world and of such things as land formations, seas, and climate. 2 N-UNCOUNT The **geography of** a place is the way that features such as rivers, mountains, and towns are arranged. ❑ *...policemen who knew the local geography.*

Word Link *logy, ology ≈ study of : anthropology, biology, geology*

geology /dʒiˈɒlədʒi/ 1 N-UNCOUNT **Geology** is the study of the earth's structure, surface, and origins. ● **geological** /ˌdʒiːəˈlɒdʒɪkəl/ ADJ ❑ *...a lengthy geological survey.* ● **geologist** (**geologists**) N-COUNT ❑ *...the latest discovery by geologists in Australia.* 2 N-UNCOUNT The **geology of** an area is the structure of its land.

geometric /ˌdʒiːəˈmetrɪk/ 1 ADJ **Geometric** means relating to geometry. ❑ *...geometric laws.* 2 ADJ **Geometric** patterns or shapes consist of regular shapes or lines. ❑ *...geometric designs.*

geometry /dʒiˈɒmɪtri/ 1 N-UNCOUNT **Geometry** is a mathematical science concerned with the measurement of lines, angles, curves, and shapes. 2 N-UNCOUNT The **geometry of** an object is its shape or the relationship of its parts to

each other. [FORMAL] ❑ *...the geometry of the building.*
→ see **mathematics**

Word Link	*iatr ≈ healing : geriatric, pediatrics, psychiatrist*

geriatric /ˌdʒeriˈætrɪk/ ADJ BEFORE N **Geriatric** is used to describe things relating to the illnesses and medical care of old people. [TECHNICAL] ❑ *...the future of geriatric care.*

germ /dʒɜːm/ (**germs**) 1 N-COUNT A **germ** is a very small organism that causes disease. ❑ *...cholera germs.* 2 N-COUNT The **germ of** something such as an idea is the beginning of it.
→ see **medicine, spice**

G

germinate /ˈdʒɜːmɪneɪt/ (**germinates, germinating, germinated**) V-T/V-I If a seed **germinates** or **is germinated**, it starts to grow. [TECHNICAL] ❑ *Heat will encourage seeds to germinate.* ● **germination** N-UNCOUNT ❑ *To speed up germination, it is worth soaking the seed in water.*
→ see **tree**

gesture /ˈdʒestʃə/ (**gestures, gesturing, gestured**) 1 V-I & N-COUNT If you **gesture**, you use movements of your hands or head called **gestures** to convey a message or feeling. ❑ *She gestured towards the front door.* ❑ *With a gesture of the hand, she beckoned him back.* 2 N-COUNT A **gesture** is something that you say or do in order to express your attitude or intentions. ❑ *He said he had made the offer as a gesture of goodwill.*

get

1 CHANGING, CAUSING, MOVING, OR REACHING
2 OBTAINING, RECEIVING, OR CATCHING
3 PHRASAL VERBS

get /get/ (**gets, getting, got** or [AM also] **gotten**)

In most of its uses **get** is a fairly informal word.

1 1 LINK-VERB **Get** often has the same meaning as 'become'. For example, if something **gets** cold, it becomes cold. ❑ *The boys were getting bored.* ❑ *From here on, it can only get better.* ❑ *It's getting late.* 2 **Get** is often used in place of 'be' as an auxiliary verb to form the passive. ❑ *Does she ever get asked for her autograph?* ❑ *A pane of glass got broken.* 3 V-T/V-I If someone or something **gets** into a particular state or situation, or if someone or something **gets** them into it, they start being in that state or situation. ❑ *Perhaps I shouldn't say that – I might get into trouble.* ❑ *How did we get into this mess?* ❑ *I don't know if I can get it clean.* 4 V-I To **get** somewhere means to move or arrive there. ❑ *I got off the bed and opened the door.* ❑ *Generally I get to work at 9.30am.* ❑ *It was dark by the time she got home.* 5 V-T If you **get** something or someone into a particular place or position, you move them there by means of a particular action or effort. ❑ *Mack got his wallet out.* ❑ *Go and get your coat on.* ❑ *The UN is getting aid to the affected countries.* 6 V-T If you **get** someone **to** do something, they do it because you asked, persuaded, or told them to do it. ❑ *Tom's on the phone. Can I get him to call you back?* 7 V-T If you **get** something done, you arrange for it to be done. ❑ *I have to get my car repaired.* 8 V-T If you **get to** do something, you manage to do it or have the opportunity to do it. ❑ *Do you get to see him often?* ❑ *They get to stay in nice hotels.* 9 V-T You can use **get** in expressions like **get moving, get going,** and **get working** when you want to tell people to begin moving, going, or working quickly. 10 V-I If you **get** to a particular stage in an activity, you reach that stage. ❑ *Patrick had got as far as finding some clients.* 11 V-T If something **gets** you, it annoys you. [INFORMAL] ❑ *What gets me is the attitude of so many of the people.*

get /get/ (**gets, getting, got** or [AM] **gotten**)
2 1 V-T If you **get** something that you want or need, you obtain it or receive it. ❑ *The problem was how to get enough food.* ❑ *I asked him to get me some information.* ❑ *Whenever I get the chance I go to Maxim's for dinner.* 2 V-T If you **get** someone or something, you go and bring them to a particular place. ❑ *Go and get your daddy for me.* ❑ *Get me a large whisky.* 3 V-T You can use **you get** instead of 'there is' or 'there are' to say that something exists, happens, or can be experienced. [SPOKEN] ❑ *You get a lot of Canadian tourists here.* 4 V-T If you **get** an illness or disease, you become ill with it. ❑ *When I was five I got measles.* 5 V-T If you **get** an idea, impression, or feeling, you have it or experience it. ❑ *I got a shock when I saw him.* ❑ *I get the feeling that you're an honest man.* 6 V-T If you **get** a joke or **get** the point of something, you understand it. 7 V-T When you **get** a train, bus, plane, or boat, you travel by that means of transport. 8 → see also **got** 9 to **give as good as** you **get** → see **give**

Thesaurus	*get* Also look up:
v.	become ① 1
	bring, collect, pick up ② 1
	know, sense ② 6

get /get/ (**gets, getting, got** or [AM] **gotten**)
3 ▶ **get about** 1 PHR-VERB If you **get about**, you move or travel from place to place. ❑ *Rail travel through France is the perfect way to get about.* 2 → see **get around**

▶ **get across** PHR-VERB If you **get** an idea or argument **across**, you succeed in making people understand it. ❑ *He got his message across very well.*

▶ **get along** PHR-VERB If you **get along with** someone, you have a friendly relationship with them. ❑ *It's impossible to get along with him.*

▶ **get around** 1 PHR-VERB If you **get around**, you go to a lot of different places as part of your way of life. 2 PHR-VERB If news **gets around, gets about,** or **gets round**, it is told to lots of people. ❑ *Word got around that he was taking drugs.* 3 PHR-VERB If you **get around** or **get round** a difficulty or restriction, you manage to avoid it or deal with it. ❑ *They got round the ban by setting up a new group with a new name.*

▶ **get around to** or **get round to** PHR-VERB When you **get around to** doing something that you have delayed or have been too busy to do, you finally do it. ❑ *I haven't got round to talking to him yet.*

▶ **get at** 1 PHR-VERB To **get at** something means to succeed in reaching it. ❑ *A goat was trying to get at the leaves.* 2 PHR-VERB If you **get at** someone, you keep criticizing or teasing them in an unkind way. [INFORMAL] ❑ *I'm just tired of you getting at me all the time.* 3 PHR-VERB If you ask someone what they **are getting at**, you ask them to explain what they mean. ❑ *What are you getting at now?*

▶ **get away** 1 PHR-VERB If you **get away**, you succeed in leaving a place or situation that you do not want to be in. ❑ *Dr Dunn was trying to get away when he was shot.* **2** PHR-VERB If you **get away**, you go away for a period of time in order to have a holiday.

▸ **get away with** PHR-VERB If you **get away with** doing something wrong or risky, you do not suffer any punishment or other bad consequences because of it. ❑ *I sometimes let him get away with not brushing his teeth.*

▸ **get back** PHR-VERB If you **get** something **back** after you have lost it or after it has been taken from you, you have it again. ❑ *You can cancel the contract and get your money back.*

▸ **get back to** **1** PHR-VERB If you **get back to** a previous activity or subject, you start doing the activity or talking about the subject again. ❑ *I couldn't get back to sleep.* ❑ *We got back to the subject of Tom Halliday.* **2** PHR-VERB To **get back to** a previous state or level means to return to it. ❑ *Life started to get back to normal.*

▸ **get by** PHR-VERB If you can **get by** with the few resources you have, you can manage to live or do things satisfactorily. ❑ *Jake managed to get by on a small amount of money.*

▸ **get down to** PHR-VERB When you **get down to** something, you start doing it. ❑ *With the election out of the way, the government can get down to business.*

▸ **get in** **1** PHR-VERB When a train, bus, or plane **gets in**, it arrives. ❑ *Her train gets in at about ten to two.* **2** PHR-VERB When a political party or a politician **gets in**, they are elected. **3** PHR-VERB If you **get** something you want to say **in**, you eventually manage to say it, usually in a situation where other people are talking a lot. ❑ *It was hard to get a word in.*

▸ **get in on** PHR-VERB If you **get in on** an activity, you start taking part in it, perhaps without being invited. [INFORMAL] ❑ *He had plans of his own to get in on the action.*

▸ **get into** **1** PHR-VERB If you **get into** an activity, you start doing it or being involved in it. ❑ *He was eager to get into politics.* **2** PHR-VERB If you **get into** a school, college, or university, you are accepted there as a student. **3** PHR-VERB If you ask what has **got into** someone, you mean that they are behaving in an unexpected way. [INFORMAL] ❑ *He didn't know what had got into him, to steal a watch.*

▸ **get off** **1** PHR-VERB If someone who has broken a law or rule **gets off**, they are not punished, or only slightly punished. ❑ *He is likely to get off with a small fine.* **2** PHR-VERB You can tell someone to **get off** when they are touching you and you do not want them to. ❑ *I kept telling him to get off.* ❑ *'Get off me!' I screamed.*

▸ **get on** **1** PHR-VERB If you **get on with** someone, you have a friendly relationship with them. ❑ *I get on very well with his wife.* **2** PHR-VERB If you **get on with** an activity, you continue doing it or start doing it. ❑ *Jane got on with her work.* **3** PHR-VERB If someone **is getting on** well or badly, they are making good or bad progress. ❑ *Livy's getting on very well in Russian.* **4** PHR-VERB If you try to **get on**, you try to be successful in your career. ❑ *She's keen. She's ambitious. She wants to get on.* **5** PHR-VERB If someone **is getting on**, they are getting old. [INFORMAL]

▸ **get on to** **1** PHR-VERB If you **get on to** a particular topic, you start talking about it. ❑ *We got on to the subject of relationships.* **2** PHR-VERB If you **get on to** someone, you contact them. ❑ *I got on to him and explained some of the things.*

▸ **get out** **1** PHR-VERB If you **get out** of a place or situation, you leave it. ❑ *I told him to leave and get out.* ❑ *Getting out of the contract would be no problem.* **2** PHR-VERB If you **get out**, you go to places and meet people. ❑ *Get out and enjoy yourself, make new friends.* **3** PHR-VERB If news or information **gets out**, it becomes known. ❑ *If word got out now, a scandal could be disastrous.*

▸ **get out of** PHR-VERB If you **get out of** doing something that you do not want to do, you avoid doing it. ❑ *It's amazing what people will do to get out of paying taxes.*

▸ **get over** **1** PHR-VERB If you **get over** an unpleasant experience or an illness, you recover from it. ❑ *It took me a very long time to get over the shock of her death.* **2** PHR-VERB If you **get over** a problem, you manage to deal with it.

▸ **get over with** PHR-VERB If you **get** something unpleasant **over with**, you do it or experience it quickly, since you cannot avoid it. ❑ *The sooner we start, the sooner we'll get it over with.*

▸ **get round** **1** → see **get around** **2** PHR-VERB If you **get round** someone, you persuade them to like you or do what you want, by pleasing or flattering them. ❑ *Max could always get round her.*

▸ **get round to** → see **get around to**

▸ **get through** **1** PHR-VERB If you **get through** a task, you complete it. ❑ *I think you can get through the first two chapters.* **2** PHR-VERB If you **get through** an unpleasant experience or time, you manage to live through it. ❑ *It is hard to see how people will get through the winter.* **3** PHR-VERB If you **get through** a large amount of something, you use it up. ❑ *You'll get through at least ten nappies a day.* **4** PHR-VERB If you **get through to** someone, you succeed in making them understand what you are trying to say. ❑ *A good friend might be able to get through to her and help her.* **5** PHR-VERB If you **get through to** someone, you succeed in contacting them on the telephone. ❑ *I can't get through to this number.*

▸ **get together** **1** PHR-VERB When people **get together**, they meet in order to discuss something or to spend time together. **2** PHR-VERB If you collect or assemble things or people for a particular purpose, you can say that you **get** them **together**. ❑ *We'll give you three days to get the money together.*

▸ **get up** **1** PHR-VERB If you are sitting or lying and then **get up**, you rise to a standing position. **2** PHR-VERB When you **get up**, you get out of bed. ❑ *They have to get up early in the morning.*

▸ **get up to** PHR-VERB If you say that someone **gets up to** something, you mean that they do it and you do not approve of it. [BRIT] ❑ *They get up to all sorts of things when you're not looking.*

getaway /'getəweɪ/ (**getaways**) N-COUNT When someone makes a **getaway**, they leave a place in a hurry, especially after committing a crime. ❑ *They made their getaway on a stolen motorcycle.*

ghastly /'gɑːstli, 'gæstli/ (**ghastlier, ghastliest**) ADJ If you describe someone or something as **ghastly**, you mean that they are very unpleasant. ❑ *A surprise party is almost always a ghastly shock.*

ghetto /'getəʊ/ (**ghettos** or **ghettoes**) N-COUNT A **ghetto** is a part of a town in which many poor people or many people of a particular race, religion, or nationality live. ❑ *She rose from the Los*

Angeles ghetto to become Wimbledon champion.

ghost /gəʊst/ (**ghosts**) N-COUNT A **ghost** is the spirit of a dead person that someone believes they can see or feel. ❑ *...the ghost of the drowned girl.*

ghostly /ˈgəʊstli/ (**ghostlier, ghostliest**) ADJ Something that is **ghostly** seems unreal or supernatural and may be frightening because of this. ❑ *The audience was shocked by the ghostly whiteness of the dancers.*

GI /ˌdʒiː ˈaɪ/ (**GIs**) N-COUNT A **GI** is a soldier in the United States army.

giant /dʒaɪənt/ (**giants**) 1 ADJ BEFORE N You use **giant** to describe something that is much larger or more important than most other things of its kind. ❑ *...a giant oak table.* 2 N-COUNT A large successful organization or country can be referred to as a **giant**. [JOURNALISM] ❑ *...Japanese electronics giant Sony.* 3 N-COUNT In children's stories, a **giant** is a person who is very big, tall and strong.

G

Thesaurus *giant* Also look up:

ADJ. colossal, enormous, gigantic, huge, immense, mammoth; *(ant.)* miniature 1

gibe /dʒaɪb/ → see **jibe**

giddy /ˈgɪdi/ (**giddier, giddiest**) ADJ If you feel **giddy**, you feel that you are about to fall over, usually because you are not well.

gift /gɪft/ (**gifts**) 1 N-COUNT A **gift** is something that you give someone as a present. ❑ *...suggestions for Christmas gifts.* 2 N-SING If someone has a **gift for** doing something, they have a natural ability for doing it. ❑ *He discovered a gift for teaching.*

gifted /ˈgɪftɪd/ ADJ A **gifted** person has a natural ability for doing most things or for doing a particular activity. ❑ *...a school for gifted children.*

gig /gɪg/ (**gigs**) N-COUNT A **gig** is a live performance by a pop or jazz musician, comedian, or disk jockey. [INFORMAL] ❑ *The Rolling Stones only do outdoor gigs.*

gigabyte /ˈgɪgəbaɪt/ (**gigabytes**) N-COUNT A **gigabyte** is one thousand and twenty-four megabytes. [COMPUTING]

gigantic /dʒaɪˈgæntɪk/ ADJ If you describe something as **gigantic**, you are emphasizing that it is extremely large in size, amount, or degree. ❑ *...a gigantic oak tree.* ❑ *It's come as a gigantic surprise.*

giggle /ˈgɪgəl/ (**giggles, giggling, giggled**) V-I & N-COUNT If you **giggle**, or if you let out a **giggle**, you laugh in a childlike, helpless way. ❑ *'I beg your pardon?' she giggled.* ❑ *She gave a little giggle.* → see **laugh**

gilded /gɪldɪd/ ADJ If something is **gilded**, it has been covered with a thin layer of gold or gold paint. ❑ *...gilded statues.*

gilt /gɪlt/ ADJ A **gilt** object is covered with a thin layer of gold or gold paint.

gimmick /ˈgɪmɪk/ (**gimmicks**) N-COUNT A **gimmick** is an unusual and unnecessary feature or action whose purpose is to attract attention or publicity; used showing disapproval. ❑ *It is just a public relations gimmick.*

gin /dʒɪn/ (**gins**) N-VAR **Gin** is a colourless alcoholic drink.

ginger /ˈdʒɪndʒə/ 1 N-UNCOUNT **Ginger** is the root of a plant that is used to flavour food. It has a sweet spicy flavour. 2 ADJ & N-UNCOUNT **Ginger** is used to describe something, usually a person's hair, that is orange-brown.

gingerly /ˈdʒɪndʒəli/ ADV If you do something **gingerly**, you do it in a careful, hesitant manner. [WRITTEN] ❑ *I drove gingerly past the security check points.*

gipsy /ˈdʒɪpsi/ (**gipsies**) → see **gypsy**

giraffe /dʒɪˈrɑːf, -ˈræf/ (**giraffes**) N-COUNT A **giraffe** is a large African animal with a very long neck, long legs, and dark patches on its body.

giraffe

girl /gɜːl/ (**girls**) 1 N-COUNT A **girl** is a female child. 2 N-COUNT Young women are often referred to as **girls**. Some people find this use offensive. ❑ *...a pretty twenty-year old girl.*

ˈgirl band (**girl bands**) N-COUNT A **girl band** is a band consisting of young women who sing popular music and dance.

girlfriend /ˈgɜːlfrend/ (**girlfriends**) 1 N-COUNT Someone's **girlfriend** is a girl or woman with whom they are having a romantic or sexual relationship. ❑ *He has been going out with his girlfriend for seven months.* 2 N-COUNT A **girlfriend** is a female friend. ❑ *I met a girlfriend for lunch.*

girth /gɜːθ/ (**girths**) N-VAR The **girth** of an object is its width or thickness. [FORMAL] ❑ *...a 43-inch long fish with a 9-inch girth.*

gist /dʒɪst/ N-SING **The gist of** a speech, conversation, or piece of writing is its general meaning. ❑ *I could not get the gist of their conversation.*

give

1 USED WITH NOUNS DESCRIBING ACTIONS
2 TRANSFERRING
3 OTHER USES, PHRASES, AND PHRASAL VERBS

give /gɪv/ (**gives, giving, gave, given**)
1 1 V-T You can use **give** with nouns that refer to physical actions. The whole expression refers to the performing of the action. ❑ *George gave a smile.* ❑ *She gave my hand a quick squeeze.* 2 V-T You use **give** to say that a person does a particular thing for someone else. ❑ *She gives piano lessons to some of the local children.* ❑ *They gave me dinner after the interview.* 3 V-T You use **give** with nouns that refer to information, opinions, or greetings to indicate that something is communicated. ❑ *He gave no details.* ❑ *He asked me to give you the news.* 4 V-T If someone or something **gives** you a particular idea, impression, or feeling, it causes you to have it. ❑ *They gave me the impression that they were doing exactly what they wanted.* ❑ *It will give great pleasure to the many thousands of children.* 5 V-T If you **give** something thought or attention, you think about it or deal with it. ❑ *I've been giving it some thought.* ❑ *We give priority to people who apply early.* 6 V-T If you **give** a speech or a performance, you speak or perform in public. ❑ *Mrs Butler gave us such an interesting talk last year.* 7 V-T If you **give** a party or

other social event, you organize it.
→ see **donor**

give /gɪv/ (**gives, giving, gave, given**)
❷ 1 V-T If you **give** someone something that you own or have bought, you provide them with it, so that they have it or can use it. ❑ *Many leading businessmen gave money to the Conservative Party.* ❑ *She gave me a doll for my birthday.* 2 V-T If you **give** someone something that you are holding or that is near you, you pass it to them, so that they are then holding it. ❑ *He took a handkerchief from his pocket and gave it to her.* 3 V-T To **give** someone or something a particular right or power means to allow them to have it. ❑ *The code gave rights to women as well as men.*

give /gɪv/ (**gives, giving, gave, given**)
❸ 1 V-I If something **gives**, it collapses or breaks under pressure. ❑ *My knees gave under me.* 2 V-T You use **give** in phrases such as **I'd give anything**, **I'd give my right arm**, and **what wouldn't I give** to emphasize that you are very keen to do or have something. ❑ *I'd give anything to be like you.* 3 PHRASE If someone **gives as good as** they **get**, they fight or argue as well or intensely as the person they are fighting or arguing with. 4 PHRASE If you say that something requires **give and take**, you mean that people must compromise for it to be successful. 5 PHRASE **Give or take** is used to indicate that an amount is approximate. ❑ *They grow to a height of 12 inches – give or take a couple of inches.* 6 to **give way** → see **way**

▶ **give away** 1 PHR-VERB If you **give away** something that you own, you give it to someone because you no longer want it. ❑ *He was giving his collection away for nothing.* 2 PHR-VERB If you **give away** information that should be kept secret, you reveal it to other people. ❑ *Her voice gave nothing away.*

▶ **give back** PHR-VERB If you **give** something **back**, you return it to the person who gave it to you. ❑ *I gave the textbook back to him.*

▶ **give in** 1 PHR-VERB If you **give in**, you admit that you are defeated or that you cannot do something. ❑ *All right. I give in. What did you do with it?* 2 PHR-VERB If you **give in**, you agree to do something that you do not want to do. ❑ *They won't give in to the workers' demands.*

▶ **give off** or **give out** PHR-VERB If something **gives off** or **gives out** a gas, heat, or a smell, it produces it and sends it out into the air. ❑ *Natural gas gives off less carbon dioxide than coal.*

▶ **give out** 1 PHR-VERB If you **give out** a number of things, you distribute them among a group of people. ❑ *They were giving out leaflets.* 2 → see also **give off**

▶ **give up** 1 PHR-VERB If you **give up** something, you stop doing it or having it. ❑ *I was trying to give up drugs.* ❑ *The doctors gave up hope as her condition became worse.* 2 PHR-VERB If you **give up**, you decide that you cannot do something and stop trying to do it. ❑ *After trying all morning, he gave up.* 3 PHR-VERB If you **give up** your job, you resign from it.

given /ˈgɪvən/ 1 **Given** is the past participle of **give**. 2 ADJ AFTER LINK-V If you are **given to** doing something, you often do it. [FORMAL] ❑ *I am not given to emotional displays.* 3 ADJ If something happens in a **given** situation, it happens in that particular situation. If something happens at a **given** time, it happens at that particular time. ❑ *Do you regularly work for more than 10 hours on any given day?* 4 PREP **Given** is used when indicating a possible situation in which someone has the opportunity or ability to do something. ❑ *Given the chance, I would go into space tomorrow.* 5 CONJ If you say **given that** something is the case, you mean 'taking that fact into account'. ❑ *Given that they failed last time, why should this attempt be any more successful?* 6 PREP If you say **given** a particular thing, you mean 'taking that thing into account'. ❑ *Given his problems, the decision has proved to be a wise one.*

g

glacial /ˈgleɪʃəl/ ADJ **Glacial** means relating to or produced by glaciers or ice. [TECHNICAL] ❑ *I am surrounded by fantastic lakes, waterfalls and glacial valleys.*
→ see **lake**

glacier /ˈglæsiə, AM ˈgleɪʃə/ (**glaciers**) N-COUNT A **glacier** is a huge mass of ice which moves very slowly, often down a mountain.
→ see Word Web: **glacier**
→ see **climate, mountain**

glad /glæd/ 1 ADJ AFTER LINK-V If you are **glad about** something, you are happy and pleased about it. Glad is never used in front of a noun for this meaning. ❑ *I'm glad I gave in in the end.* ❑ *The people seem really glad to see you.* ● **gladly** ADV ❑ *If this offer is genuine I will gladly accept it.* 2 ADJ If you say that you will be **glad to** do something, you mean that you are willing and eager to do it. ❑ *I'll be glad to show you everything.* ● **gladly** ADV ❑ *If you'd prefer something else I'll gladly change it for you.*

glamorous /ˈglæmərəs/ ADJ If you describe

Word Web **glacier**

Two-thirds of all **fresh water** in the world is **frozen**. The largest **glaciers** in the world are the **polar ice caps** of Antarctica and Greenland. They cover more than six million square miles. Their average depth is almost one mile. If all the glaciers **melted**, the average **sea level** would rise by over 250 feet. Glaciologists have noted that the Antarctic is about 1° C* warmer than it was 50 years ago. Some of them are worried. Continued warming might cause floating **ice** shelves there to begin to fall apart. This, in turn, could cause disastrous coastal flooding around the world.

1° Celsius = 33.8° Fahrenheit

someone or something as **glamorous**, you mean that they are more attractive, exciting, or interesting than ordinary people or things. ❑ *...the glamorous lifestyle of the rich and famous.*

glamour [AM **glamor**] /ˈglæmə/ N-UNCOUNT **Glamour** is the quality of being more attractive, exciting, or interesting than ordinary people or things. ❑ *He loved the glamour of show business.*

glance /glɑːns, glæns/ (**glances, glancing, glanced**) **1** V-I & N-COUNT If you **glance at** someone or something, or if you give them a **glance**, you look at them very quickly and then look away. ❑ *He glanced at his watch.* ❑ *The boys exchanged glances.* **2** V-I If you **glance through** or **at** a newspaper or book, you spend a short time looking at it without reading it carefully. ❑ *She glanced at her diary.* **3** PHRASE If you say that something seems to be true **at first glance**, you mean that it seems to be true when you first see it, but that your first impression may be wrong. ❑ *At first glance, everything appeared normal.*

G

gland /glænd/ (**glands**) N-COUNT **Glands** are organs in your body that produce chemical substances which your body needs in order to function. ❑ *...sweat glands.*

glare /gleə/ (**glares, glaring, glared**) **1** V-I & N-COUNT If you **glare at** someone, or if you give them a **glare**, you look at them angrily. ❑ *Joe glared at his brother.* ❑ *The waiter avoided Harold's furious glare.* **2** V-I & N-SING If the sun or a light **glares**, it shines with a very bright light which is difficult to look at, called a **glare**. ❑ *The sun glared down on the station platform.* ❑ *...the glare of the headlights.* **3** N-SING If you are in **the glare of** publicity or public attention, you are constantly being watched and talked about by the public. ❑ *The singer disliked the glare of publicity.*

glaring /ˈgleərɪŋ/ ADJ If you describe something bad as **glaring**, you mean that it is very obvious. ❑ *...glaring errors.* ● **glaringly** ADV ❑ *It was glaringly obvious.*

glass /glɑːs, glæs/ (**glasses**) **1** N-UNCOUNT **Glass** is the hard transparent substance that windows and bottles are made from. ❑ *...a pane of glass.* ❑ *...a sliding glass door.* **2** N-COUNT A **glass** is a container made of glass which you can drink from. ❑ *Jack held his glass out and Carl poured it full.* ❑ *I drank a glass of water.* **3** N-UNCOUNT Objects made of glass can be referred to as **glass**. ❑ *The exhibition includes a wide range of furniture, metalwork and glass.* **4** N-PLURAL **Glasses** are two lenses in a frame that some people wear in front of their eyes in order to see better. ❑ *He took off his glasses.*
→ see Word Web: **glass**
→ see **light bulb**

glaze /gleɪz/ (**glazes**) N-COUNT A **glaze** is a thin layer of a hard shiny substance on a piece of pottery.
→ see **pottery**

glazed /gleɪzd/ **1** ADJ If someone's eyes are **glazed**, their expression is dull or dreamy, because they are tired or are having difficulty concentrating. ❑ *There was a glazed look in her eyes.* **2** ADJ **Glazed** pottery is covered with a thin layer of a hard shiny substance. **3** ADJ A **glazed** window or door has glass in it.

gleam /gliːm/ (**gleams, gleaming, gleamed**) **1** V-I & N-SING If an object or the surface of something **gleams**, it shines because it is reflecting light. The light reflecting off something is called a **gleam**. ❑ *The cutlery gleamed.* ❑ *I could see the gleam of brass.* **2** N-COUNT A **gleam of** light is a faint light. [WRITTEN] ❑ *...the first gleam of dawn.* **3** V-I & N-SING If your eyes **gleam**, or if there is a **gleam** in your eyes, your eyes look bright and show that you are excited or happy. [WRITTEN]

glean /gliːn/ (**gleans, gleaning, gleaned**) V-T If you **glean** information, you obtain it slowly and with difficulty. ❑ *At present we're gleaning information from all sources.*

glee /gliː/ N-UNCOUNT **Glee** is a feeling of happiness and excitement, often caused by someone else's misfortune. ❑ *Investors have reacted with glee.*

gleeful /ˈgliːfəl/ ADJ Someone who is **gleeful** is happy or excited, often because of someone else's misfortune. ● **gleefully** ADV ❑ *The media gleefully reports the hatred between the two groups.*

glib /glɪb/ ADJ If you describe what someone says as **glib**, you disapprove of it because it suggests that something is simple or easy, when this is not the case. ● **glibly** ADV ❑ *We talk glibly of success.*

glide /glaɪd/ (**glides, gliding, glided**) **1** V-I If you **glide** somewhere, you move there smoothly and silently. ❑ *Waiters glide between tables carrying trays.* **2** V-I When birds or aeroplanes **glide**, they float on air currents. ❑ *Pelicans glide over the waves.*

glider /ˈglaɪdə/ (**gliders**) N-COUNT A **glider** is an aircraft without an engine which flies by floating on air currents.

glimmer /ˈglɪmə/ (**glimmers, glimmering, glimmered**) **1** V-I & N-COUNT If something **glimmers**, it produces a faint, often unsteady light called a **glimmer**. ❑ *...a few stars still glimmered.*

Word Web glass

The basic ingredients for **glass** are silica (found in **sand**) and **ash** (left over from burning wood). The earliest glass objects are glass **beads** made in Egypt around 3500 BC. By 14 AD, the Syrians had learned how to **blow** glass to form hollow containers. These included primitive **bottles** and **vases**. By 100 AD, the Romans were making clear glass windowpanes. Modern factories now produce **safety glass** which doesn't **shatter** when it breaks. It includes a layer of cellulose between two **sheets** of glass. **Bulletproof** glass consists of several layers of glass with a tough, **transparent** plastic between the layers.

❑ *...the glimmer of daylight.* **2** N-COUNT A **glimmer of** something is a faint sign of it. ❑ *...the first glimmer of hope.*

glimpse /glɪmps/ (**glimpses, glimpsing, glimpsed**) **1** V-T & N-COUNT If you **glimpse** someone or something, or if you get a **glimpse of** them, you see them very briefly and not very well. ❑ *She glimpsed a few of the soldiers through the window.* ❑ *I had a glimpse of a swimming pool through the trees.* **2** N-COUNT A **glimpse of** something is a brief experience of it or an idea about it that helps you understand it better. ❑ *The trip will give them a glimpse of a whole new world.*

glint /glɪnt/ (**glints, glinting, glinted**) **1** V-I & N-COUNT If something **glints**, or if there is a **glint of** light from it, it produces or reflects a quick flash of light. [WRITTEN] ❑ *The sea glinted in the sun.* ❑ *...the glint of gold.* **2** V-I & N-SING If someone's eyes **glint**, they shine and express a particular emotion. You can talk about a **glint** in someone's eyes. [WRITTEN] ❑ *Her eyes glinted with pride.* ❑ *There was a glint of mischief in his eyes.*

glisten /ˈglɪsən/ (**glistens, glistening, glistened**) V-I If something **glistens**, it shines, because it is smooth, wet, or oily. ❑ *Her eyes glistened with tears.* ❑ *...a man with glistening black hair.*

glitter /ˈglɪtə/ (**glitters, glittering, glittered**) **1** V-I If something **glitters**, it shines and sparkles. ❑ *The water glittered in the sunlight.* **2** N-UNCOUNT You can use **glitter** to refer to the superficial attractiveness or excitement connected with something. ❑ *...the glitter of the pop world.*

gloat /gləʊt/ (**gloats, gloating, gloated**) V-I When someone **gloats**, they show great pleasure at their own success or at other people's failure. ❑ *I expect a lot of people are gloating that we've lost three games now.*

Word Link *glob ≈ sphere : global, globally, globe*

global /ˈgləʊbəl/ ADJ **Global** means concerning or including the whole world. ❑ *...a global ban on nuclear testing.* ● **globally** ADV ❑ *...products sold globally.*

ˌglobal ˈvillage N-SING People sometimes use **global village** to refer to the world as a single community linked together by electronic communications.

ˌglobal ˈwarming N-UNCOUNT The problem of the gradual rise in the earth's temperature is referred to as **global warming**.
→ see **air, greenhouse effect, ozone**

globe /gləʊb/ (**globes**) **1** N-SING You can refer to the Earth as **the globe**. ❑ *...performers from around the globe.* **2** N-COUNT A **globe** is a ball-shaped object with a map of the world on it.
→ see Picture Dictionary: **globe**

gloom /gluːm/ **1** N-SING **Gloom** is a state of partial darkness. ❑ *My eyes were becoming accustomed to the gloom.* **2** N-UNCOUNT **Gloom** is a feeling of unhappiness or despair. ❑ *...the deepening gloom over the economy.*

gloomy /ˈgluːmi/ (**gloomier, gloomiest**) **1** ADJ Something that is **gloomy** is dark and rather depressing. ❑ *...the gloomy days of winter.* **2** ADJ If someone is **gloomy**, they are unhappy and have no hope. ❑ *They are gloomy about their chances of success.* ● **gloomily** ADV ❑ *Mark shook his head gloomily.* **3** ADJ If a situation is **gloomy**, it does not give you much hope of success or happiness.
→ see **weather**

glorify /ˈglɔːrɪfaɪ/ (**glorifies, glorifying, glorified**) V-T If you say that someone **glorifies** something, you mean that they praise it or make it seem good or special, usually when it is not. ❑ *Parents say that this computer game glorifies violence.* ● **glorification** /ˌglɔːrɪfɪˈkeɪʃən/ N-UNCOUNT ❑ *...the glorification of violence.*

glorious /ˈglɔːriəs/ **1** ADJ If you describe something as **glorious**, you are emphasizing

Picture Dictionary **globe**

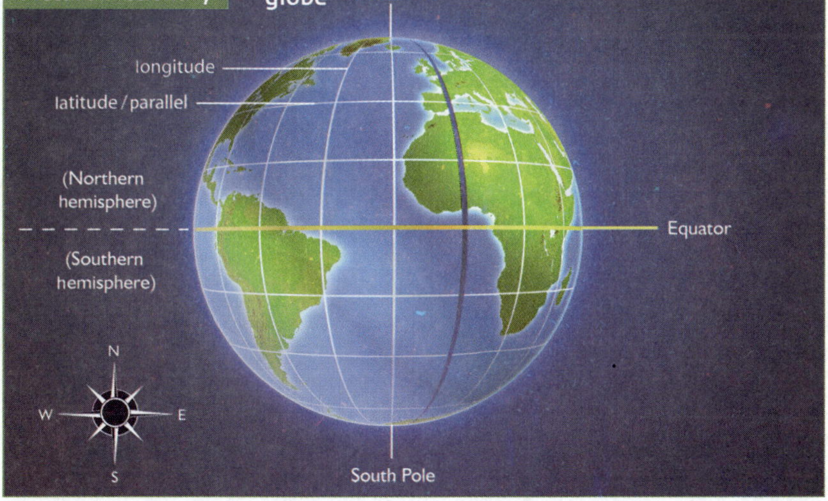

g

that it is very beautiful or wonderful. ❑ *...a glorious rainbow.* • **gloriously** ADV ❑ *...a gloriously sunny morning.* 2 ADJ A **glorious** career, victory, or occasion involves great fame or success.

glory /ˈglɔːri/ (**glories, glorying, gloried**) 1 N-UNCOUNT **Glory** is fame and admiration that you get for an achievement. ❑ *It was her moment of glory.* 2 N-UNCOUNT The **glory** of something is its great beauty or quality of being impressive. ❑ *For true orchestral glory, we had to wait for the second half of the concert.*

▶ **glory in** PHR-VERB If you **glory in** a situation or activity, you enjoy it very much. ❑ *The workers were glorying in their new-found freedom.*

Word Partnership Use *glory* with:

N.	**blaze of** glory, glory **days, hope and** glory, **moment of** glory 1
V.	**bask in the** glory 1

G

gloss /glɒs, AM glɔːs/ (**glosses, glossing, glossed**) 1 N-SING A **gloss** is a bright shine on a surface. ❑ *It gives hair a rich gloss.* 2 N-VAR **Gloss** or **gloss paint** is paint that forms a shiny surface when it dries.

▶ **gloss over** PHR-VERB If you **gloss over** a problem or mistake, you try to make it seem unimportant by ignoring it or by dealing with it very quickly. ❑ *Tell me the whole story, without glossing over the unpleasant bits.*

glossy /ˈglɒsi, AM ˈglɔːsi/ (**glossier, glossiest**) 1 ADJ Something that is **glossy** is smooth and shiny. ❑ *...glossy black hair.* 2 ADJ BEFORE N **Glossy** magazines, brochures, or photographs are produced on expensive shiny paper.

glove /glʌv/ (**gloves**) N-COUNT **Gloves** are pieces of clothing which cover your hand and wrist and have individual sections for each finger.

glow /gləʊ/ (**glows, glowing, glowed**) 1 V-I & N-COUNT If something **glows**, it produces a dull, steady light called a **glow**. ❑ *He blew on the charcoal until it glowed orange.* ❑ *...the glow of the fire.* 2 V-I If something **glows**, it looks bright because it is reflecting light. ❑ *The ship's sails glowed in the morning sun.* 3 V-I & N-SING If someone's skin **glows**, or if there is a **glow** to their skin, it looks healthy and pink, for example because they are excited or have been exercising. ❑ *Alison's skin glowed with health.* 4 V-I & N-SING If someone **glows with** an emotion such as pride or pleasure, the expression in their face shows they feel it. A **glow of** something like pride or pleasure is a strong feeling of it. ❑ *I felt a glow of achievement.*

→ see **fire, light bulb**

Thesaurus *glow* Also look up:

N.	beam, glimmer, light 1
	blush, flush, radiance 3 4
V.	gleam, radiate, shine 1-4

glowing /ˈgləʊɪŋ/ ADJ A **glowing** description of someone or something praises them highly. ❑ *...glowing school reports.*

glucose /ˈgluːkəʊz, -əʊs/ N-UNCOUNT **Glucose** is a type of sugar.

glue /gluː/ (**glues, glueing** or **gluing, glued**) 1 N-VAR **Glue** is a sticky substance used for joining things together. 2 V-T If you **glue** one object to another, you stick them together, using glue. ❑ *Glue the two halves together.* 3 V-T PASSIVE If you say that someone **is glued to** something, you mean that they are giving it all their attention. ❑ *She was glued to the television.*

glum /glʌm/ (**glummer, glummest**) ADJ Someone who is **glum** is sad and quiet, because they are disappointed or unhappy. • **glumly** ADV ❑ *Charles was sitting glumly in the front seat.*

glut /glʌt/ (**gluts**) N-COUNT If there is a **glut of** something such as goods or raw materials, there is so much of it that it cannot all be sold or used. ❑ *...a glut of summer fruit.*

gm **gm** is a written abbreviation for **gram**.

GM /ˌdʒiː ˈem/ 1 ADJ **GM** crops have had one or more genes changed, for example in order to make them resist pests better. **GM** is an abbreviation for 'genetically modified'. ❑ *...food containing GM ingredients.* 2 ADJ In Britain, **GM** schools receive money directly from the government rather than from a local authority. **GM** is an abbreviation for 'grant maintained'. ❑ *GM schools receive better funding than other state schools.*

ˈGM-free ADJ **GM-free** products or crops are products or crops that do not contain any genetically modified material. ❑ *...GM-free soya.*

GMO /ˌdʒiː em ˈəʊ/ (**GMOs**) N-COUNT A **GMO** is an animal, plant, or other organism whose genetic structure has been changed by genetic engineering. **GMO** is an abbreviation for 'genetically modified organism'.

GMT /ˌdʒiː em ˈtiː/ **GMT** is an abbreviation for 'Greenwich Mean Time', the standard time in Great Britain which is used to calculate the time in the rest of the world.

gnaw /nɔː/ (**gnaws, gnawing, gnawed**) 1 V-T/V-I If animals or people **gnaw** something, they bite it repeatedly. ❑ *The man sat down to gnaw at his bread and study the newspaper.* 2 V-I If a feeling or thought **gnaws at** you, it causes you to keep worrying. [LITERARY] ❑ *...a question gnawed at him.* ❑ *...gnawing doubts about the value of the whole affair.*

gnome /nəʊm/ (**gnomes**) N-COUNT In children's stories, a **gnome** is a tiny old man with a beard and pointed hat.

go

1 MOVING OR LEAVING
2 LINK-VERB USES
3 OTHER VERB USES, NOUN USES, AND PHRASES
4 PHRASAL VERBS

go /gəʊ/ (**goes, going, went, gone**)

In most cases the past participle of **go** is **gone**, but occasionally you use 'been': see **been**.

1 1 V-T/V-I When you **go** somewhere, you move or travel there. ❑ *We went to Rome.* ❑ *I went home at the weekend.* ❑ *It took us an hour to go three miles.* 2 V-I You use **go** to say that someone leaves the place where they are and does an activity, often a leisure activity. ❑ *We went swimming very early.* ❑ *He went for a walk.* 3 V-I When someone **goes to** do something, they move somewhere in order to do it, and they do it. In British English, someone can also **go and** do something. In American English,

someone can also **go do** something, but you say that someone **went and** did something. ❑ *Paddy had gone to live in Canada.* ❑ *I must go and see this film.* 4 V-I When you **go**, you leave the place where you are. ❑ *Let's go.* 5 V-I If you **go to** school, work, or church, you attend it regularly as part of your normal life. ❑ *His son went to a top university.* 6 V-I When you say where a road or path **goes**, you are saying where it begins or ends, or what places it is in. ❑ *...a mountain road that goes from Blairstown to Millbrook Village.* 7 V-I If you say where **money goes**, you are saying what it is spent on. ❑ *Most of my money goes on bills.* 8 V-I If you say that something **goes to** someone, you mean that it is given to them. ❑ *Our thanks go to the chairman.* ❑ *The job went to Yuri Skokov.* 9 V-I If something **goes**, someone gets rid of it. ❑ *100,000 jobs will go when the factory closes.* 10 V-I If something **goes into** something else, it fits into it or it is put into it. ❑ *He was trying to push it through the hole and it wouldn't go.* ❑ *The shoes go on the shoe shelf.* 11 V-I If something such as a piece of machinery **is going**, it is no longer working properly and may soon stop working altogether. You can also talk about someone's hearing, sight or mental powers **going**. ❑ *The battery was going.* ❑ *His eyes are going.* 12 → See note at **bring**

go /gəʊ/ (**goes, going, went, gone**)
❷ 1 LINK-VERB You can use **go** to say that someone or something changes to another state or condition. ❑ *Her face went red and tears came into her eyes.* 2 LINK-VERB You can use **go** when indicating whether or not someone wears or has something. For example, if someone **goes barefoot**, they do not wear any shoes.

go /gəʊ/ (**goes, going, went, gone**)
❸ 1 V-I You use **go** to talk about how successful an event or situation is. For example, if you say that an event **went well**, you mean that it was successful, and if you ask how something **is going**, you are asking how much success people are having with it. 2 V-I If something **goes with** something else, they look or taste nice together. ❑ *I need some grey gloves to go with my new scarf.* ❑ *Some colours go together and some don't.* 3 N-COUNT A **go** is an attempt at doing something. ❑ *I always wanted to have a go at football.* 4 N-COUNT If it is **your go** in a game, it is your turn to do something. 5 → see also **going, gone** 6 PHRASE If you **go all out to** do something or **go all out for** something, you make the greatest possible effort to do it or get it. [INFORMAL] 7 PHRASE If someone **has a go at** you, they criticize you, often unfairly. [INFORMAL] 8 PHRASE If someone is **making a go of** something such as a business or relationship, they are beginning to make it successful. 9 PHRASE If you **have** something **on the go**, you have started it and are busy doing it. ❑ *Do you have many projects on the go?* 10 PHRASE If someone is always **on the go**, they are busy and active. [INFORMAL] 11 PHRASE If you say that there is a certain amount of time **to go**, you mean that there is that amount of time left before something happens or ends. ❑ *There is a week to go until the first German elections.* 12 **to go without saying** → see **say** 13 **there you go** → see **there**

go /gəʊ/ (**goes, going, went, gone**)
❹ ▸ **go about** 1 PHR-VERB The way you **go about** a task or problem is the way you deal with it. 2 PHR-VERB When you **are going about** your normal activities, you are doing them. 3 PHR-VERB If you **go about** in a particular way, you behave or dress in that way. ❑ *He went about looking ill and unhappy.*

▸ **go after** PHR-VERB If you **go after** something, you try to get it, catch it, or hit it. ❑ *We're only going after military targets.*

▸ **go against** PHR-VERB If someone **goes against** your wishes, beliefs, or expectations, their behaviour is the opposite of what you want, believe in, or expect.

▸ **go ahead** 1 PHR-VERB If someone **goes ahead with** something, they begin to do it or make it. 2 PHR-VERB If a process or an organized event **goes ahead**, it takes place or is carried out.

▸ **go along with** 1 PHR-VERB If you **go along with** someone or something such as a rule or an idea, you agree with that person or you accept that idea. 2 PHR-VERB If you **go along with** a person or an idea, you agree with them.

▸ **go around** or **go round** 1 PHR-VERB If you **go around to** or **go round to** someone's house, you visit them at their house. [INFORMAL] 2 PHR-VERB If there is enough of something **to go around** or **to go round**, there is enough of it for people's needs.

▸ **go around with** or **go round with** PHR-VERB If you **go around with** or **go round with** a person or group of people, you are friends with them and go to places together. [BRIT]

▸ **go back on** PHR-VERB If you **go back on** a promise or agreement, you do not do what you promised or agreed to do.

▸ **go back to** PHR-VERB If you **go back to** a task or activity, you start doing it again after you have stopped for a period of time.

▸ **go before** PHR-VERB When someone or their case **goes before** a judge, they appear in court as part of a legal process.

▸ **go down** 1 PHR-VERB If a price, level, or amount **goes down**, it becomes lower than it was. ❑ *Crime has gone down 70%.* 2 PHR-VERB If you **go down on** your knees or **on** all fours, you lower your body until it is supported by your knees, or by your hands and knees. 3 PHR-VERB When the sun **goes down**, it drops below the horizon. 4 PHR-VERB If a ship **goes down**, it sinks. If a plane **goes down**, it crashes. 5 PHR-VERB If you say that a remark, idea, or type of behaviour **goes down** in a particular way, you mean that it gets that reaction. ❑ *His poems are a bit rude, which always goes down well with children.* 6 PHR-VERB Something that **is going down** is happening. [mainly AM, INFORMAL] ❑ *When Leo heard what was going down, he told Snoop he'd definitely be there.*

▸ **go down with** PHR-VERB If you **go down with** an illness or a disease, you catch it.

▸ **go for** 1 PHR-VERB If you **go for** a particular thing or way of doing something, you choose it. ❑ *I decided to go for the steak.* 2 PHR-VERB If you **go for** someone or something, you like them very much. [INFORMAL] ❑ *Girls like Rae don't usually go for men like Anthony.* 3 PHR-VERB If someone **goes for** you, they attack you. ❑ *David went for him, gripping him by the throat.*

▸ **go in** PHR-VERB If the sun **goes in**, it becomes covered by a cloud.

▸ **go in for** PHR-VERB If you **go in for** a particular activity, you start doing it.

▸ **go into** 1 PHR-VERB If you **go into** something, you describe it in detail. ❑ *I don't want to go into*

details about what she said. **2** PHR-VERB If you **go into** a particular occupation, you start doing that job. ❑ *Mr Pok has now gone into the tourism business.*
▶ **go off** **1** PHR-VERB If you **go off** something or someone, you stop liking them. [INFORMAL] **2** PHR-VERB If an explosive device or a gun **goes off**, it explodes or fires. **3** PHR-VERB If an alarm bell **goes off**, it makes a sudden loud noise. **4** PHR-VERB If an electrical device **goes off**, it stops operating. ❑ *All the lights went off.* **5** PHR-VERB Food or drink that has **gone off** is unfit to eat or drink. [BRIT]
▶ **go on** **1** PHR-VERB If you **go on** doing something, or **go on with** an activity, you continue to do it. ❑ *I'm all right here. Go on with your work.* **2** PHR-VERB If a process or institution **goes on**, it continues to happen or exist. ❑ *The war went on for nearly two years.* **3** PHR-VERB If something **is going on**, it is happening. ❑ *While this conversation was going on, I was listening.* **4** PHR-VERB If you **go on**, you continue saying something or talking about something. ❑ *Robert cleared his throat and went on.* **5** PHR-VERB The information you have **to go on** is the information you have available to base an opinion or judgement on. **6** PHR-VERB If an electrical device **goes on**, it begins operating.
▶ **go out** **1** PHR-VERB When you **go out**, you do something enjoyable away from your home, for example you go to a restaurant or the cinema. **2** PHR-VERB If you **go out with** someone, you have a romantic or sexual relationship with them. **3** PHR-VERB If a light **goes out**, it stops shining. **4** PHR-VERB If flames **go out**, they stop burning. **5** PHR-VERB When the tide **goes out**, the level of sea in a particular place gets lower.
▶ **go over** PHR-VERB If you **go over** a document, incident, or problem, you examine it very carefully and systematically. ❑ *An accountant has gone over the books.*
▶ **go over to** **1** PHR-VERB If someone or something **goes over to** a different way of doing things, they change to it. **2** PHR-VERB If you **go over to** a group or political party, you join them after previously belonging to an opposing group or party. ❑ *Only a small number of tanks and paratroops have gone over to his side.*
▶ **go round** PHR-VERB **Go round** means the same as **go around**.
▶ **go through** **1** PHR-VERB If you **go through** a difficult experience or period of time, you experience it. **2** PHR-VERB If you **go through** a lot of things such as papers or clothes, you look at them, usually in order to search for a particular item. ❑ *Someone had gone through my possessions.* **3** PHR-VERB When someone **goes through** a particular routine, they perform a task in a particular way. **4** PHR-VERB If a law, agreement, or official decision **goes through**, it is approved by a parliament or committee.
▶ **go through with** PHR-VERB If you **go through with** an action you have decided on, you do it, even though it may be very difficult for you.
▶ **go towards** PHR-VERB If an amount of money **goes towards** something, it is used to pay part of the cost of it.
▶ **go under** **1** PHR-VERB If a business **goes under**, it becomes bankrupt. **2** PHR-VERB If a boat or a person **goes under**, they sink below the surface of some water.
▶ **go up** **1** PHR-VERB If a price, amount, or level **goes up**, it becomes higher or greater than it was. **2** PHR-VERB If something **goes up**, it explodes or suddenly starts to burn. ❑ *The hotel went up in flames.*
▶ **go with** **1** PHR-VERB If one thing **goes with** another thing, the two things officially belong together, so that if you get one, you also get the other. ❑ *There's a £150,000 salary that goes with the job.* **2** PHR-VERB If one thing **goes with** another thing, they are usually found or experienced together. ❑ *...the responsibility that goes with being team captain.*
▶ **go without** PHR-VERB If you **go without** something that you need, you do not get it. ❑ *I have known what it is like to go without food for days.*

goad /gəʊd/ (**goads, goading, goaded**) V-T If you **goad** someone, you deliberately make them angry in order to get them to react in some way. ❑ *They were trying to goad him into an outburst of anger.*

'go-ahead **1** N-SING If you give someone **the go-ahead**, you give them permission to do something. ❑ *The government gave the go-ahead for five new road schemes.* **2** ADJ BEFORE N A **go-ahead** person or organization tries hard to succeed, often by using new methods.

goal /gəʊl/ (**goals**) **1** N-COUNT In games such as football or hockey, the **goal** is the space into which the players try to get the ball in order to score. **2** N-COUNT In games such as football or hockey, if a player scores a **goal**, they get the ball into the goal. **3** N-COUNT Your **goal** is something that you hope to achieve. ❑ *The goal is to raise as much money as possible.*
→ see **football**

Word Partnership	Use *goal* with:
V.	**shoot at a** goal **1**
	score a goal **2**
	accomplish a goal, **share a** goal **3**
ADJ.	**winning** goal **2**
	attainable goal, **main** goal **3**

goalie /ˈgəʊli/ (**goalies**) N-COUNT A **goalie** is a **goalkeeper**. [INFORMAL]

goalkeeper /ˈgəʊlki:pə/ (**goalkeepers**) N-COUNT A **goalkeeper** is the player in a sports team whose job is to guard the goal.

goalless /ˈgəʊllɪs/ ADJ In football, a **goalless** game is one which ends with neither team having scored a goal. ❑ *The fixture ended in a goalless draw.*

goalpost also **goal post** /ˈgəʊlpəʊst/ (**goalposts**) N-COUNT A **goalpost** is one of the two upright posts that are connected by a crossbar and form the goal in games such as football and hockey.

goat /gəʊt/ (**goats**) N-COUNT A **goat** is an animal which is a bit bigger than a sheep and has horns.

gobble /ˈgɒbəl/ (**gobbles, gobbling, gobbled**) V-T If you **gobble** food, you eat it quickly and greedily.

'go-between (**go-betweens**) N-COUNT If someone acts as a **go-between**, they take messages between people who are unable or unwilling to meet each other.

god /gɒd/ (**gods**) **1** N-PROPER The name **God** is given to the spirit or being who is worshipped as the creator and ruler of the world, especially by Christians, Jews, and Muslims. **2** CONVENTION

g

People sometimes use **God** in exclamations for emphasis, or to express surprise, fear, or excitement. Some people find this use offensive. ❑ *Oh my God, he's shot somebody.* **3** N-COUNT A **god** is one of the spirits or beings believed in many religions to have power over an aspect of the world. ❑ *...Pan, the God of nature.*

goddess /ˈgɒdes/ (**goddesses**) N-COUNT In many religions, a **goddess** is a female spirit or being that is believed to have power over a particular aspect of the world. ❑ *...Diana, the goddess of war.*

goggles

goggles /ˈgɒgəlz/ N-PLURAL **Goggles** are large glasses that fit closely to your face around your eyes to protect them, for example in a laboratory.

going /ˈgəʊɪŋ/ **1** PHRASE If you say that something **is going to** happen, you mean that it will happen in the future. ❑ *I think it's going to be successful.* ❑ *You're going to enjoy this.* ❑ *He's going to resign.* **2** N-UNCOUNT **The going** is the conditions that affect your ability to do something. ❑ *He has her support to fall back on when the going gets tough.* **3** ADJ BEFORE N The **going** rate for something is the usual amount of money that you expect to pay or receive for it. **4** → see also **go** **5** PHRASE When you **get going**, you start doing something or start a journey, especially after a delay. **6** PHRASE If you **keep going**, you continue doing something difficult or tiring. **7** PHRASE If someone or something **has** a lot **going for** them, they have a lot of advantages. ❑ *This area has a lot going for it.*

ˌgoings-ˈon N-PLURAL **Goings-on** are strange, amusing, or immoral activities.

gold /gəʊld/ **1** N-UNCOUNT **Gold** is a valuable yellow-coloured metal used for making jewellery, and as an international currency. ❑ *The price of gold was going up.* ❑ *...gold coins.* **2** N-UNCOUNT **Gold** is jewellery and other things that are made of gold. ❑ *We handed over all our gold and money.* **3** ADJ & N-VAR Something that is **gold** in colour is bright yellow. ❑ *...Michael's black and gold shirt.*
→ see **metal, mineral, money**

golden /ˈgəʊldən/ **1** ADJ Something that is **golden** is bright yellow. ❑ *...an endless golden beach.* **2** ADJ **Golden** things are made of gold. **3** ADJ BEFORE N If you describe something as **golden**, you mean it is wonderful because it is likely to be successful, or because it is the best of its kind. ❑ *This is a golden opportunity for peace.*

goldfish /ˈgəʊldfɪʃ/

Goldfish is both the singular and the plural form.

N-COUNT A **goldfish** is a small orange-coloured fish which is often kept as a pet in a bowl or a garden pond.

ˌgold ˈmedal (**gold medals**) N-COUNT A **gold medal** is a medal made of gold which is awarded as first prize in a contest or competition.

golf /gɒlf/ N-UNCOUNT **Golf** is a game in which you use long sticks called clubs to hit a ball into holes that are spread out over a large area of grassy land. ● **golfer** (**golfers**) N-COUNT ❑ *About 150 golfers arrived for the match.* ● **golfing** N-UNCOUNT ❑ *...a golfing holiday in Spain.*
→ see Picture Dictionary: **golf**

ˈgolf club (**golf clubs**) **1** N-COUNT A **golf club** is a long, thin, metal stick with a piece of wood or metal at one end that you use to hit the ball in golf. **2** N-COUNT A **golf club** is a social organization which provides a golf course and a clubhouse for its members.

ˈgolf course (**golf courses**) N-COUNT A **golf course** is an area of land where people play golf.

gone /gɒn, AM gɑːn/ **1** **Gone** is the past participle of **go**. **2** ADJ AFTER LINK-V Someone or something that is **gone** is no longer present or no longer exists. ❑ *While he was gone she had tea with the Colonel.* ❑ *By morning the smoke will be all gone.* **3** PREP If it is **gone** a particular time, it is later than that time. [BRIT, INFORMAL] ❑ *It was just gone 7 o'clock this evening when I finished.*

gong /gɒŋ, AM gɔːŋ/ (**gongs**) N-COUNT A **gong** is a flat, circular piece of metal that you hit with a hammer to make a loud sound.
→ see **percussion**

gonna /ˈgɒnə, AM ˈgɔːnə/ **Gonna** is used in written English to represent the words 'going to' when they are pronounced informally. ❑ *What am I gonna do?*

good /gʊd/ (**better, best**) **1** ADJ **Good** means pleasant or enjoyable. ❑ *We had a really good time together.* ❑ *There's nothing better than a cup of hot coffee.* ❑ *It's so good to hear your voice after all this time.* **2** ADJ **Good** means of a high quality, standard, or level. ❑ *Exercise is just as important to health as good food.* ❑ *He was very good at his work.* **3** ADJ A **good** idea, reason, method, or decision is a sensible or valid one. ❑ *It's a good idea to start by making a joke.* ❑ *Could you give me some advice on the best way to do this?* **4** ADJ Someone who is in a **good** mood is cheerful and pleasant to be with. **5** ADJ A **good** person is kind and thoughtful. ❑ *You are good to me.* **6** ADJ A child or animal that is **good** is well-behaved. **7** N-UNCOUNT **Good** is what is considered to be right according to moral standards or religious beliefs. ❑ *...good and evil.* **8** N-SING If something is done for **the good of** a person or organization, it is done in order to benefit them. ❑ *I'm only telling you this for your own good!* **9** N-UNCOUNT If you say that doing something is **no good** or does **not** do **any good**, you mean that doing it is not of any use or will not bring any success. ❑ *It's no good worrying about it now.* ❑ *We gave them water and kept them warm, but it didn't do any good.* **10** ADJ BEFORE N You use **good** to emphasize the great extent or degree of something. ❑ *We waited a good fifteen minutes.* **11** PHRASE **As good as** can be used to mean 'almost'. ❑ *His career is as good as over.* **12** PHRASE If something changes or disappears **for good**, it never changes back or reappears as it was before. ❑ *This drug cleared up the disease for good.* **13** PHRASE If you **make good** some damage or a loss, you repair the damage or replace what has been lost. **14** → see also **better, best, goods**

G

Thesaurus *good* Also look up:

ADJ. agreeable, enjoyable, nice, pleasant; *(ant.)* unpleasant **1**
able, capable, skilled; *(ant.)* unqualified, unskilled **2**

ˌgood afterˈnoon CONVENTION You say **'Good afternoon'** when you are greeting someone in the afternoon. [FORMAL]

goodbye also **good-bye** /ˌgʊdˈbaɪ/ (**goodbyes**) **1** CONVENTION You say **'Goodbye'** to someone when you or they are leaving, or at the end of a telephone conversation. **2** N-VAR When you say **goodbye** to someone or say your **goodbyes**, you say something such as 'goodbye' or 'bye' when you leave. ❑ *They came to the front door to say goodbye.*

ˌgood ˈevening CONVENTION You say **'Good evening'** when you are greeting someone in the evening. [FORMAL]

goodie /ˈgʊdi/ → see **goody**

ˌgood-ˈlooking (**better-looking, best-looking**) **1** ADJ A **good-looking** person has an attractive face. **2** → See note at **beautiful**

ˌgood ˈmorning CONVENTION You say **'Good morning'** when you are greeting someone in the morning. [FORMAL]

ˌgood-ˈnatured ADJ A **good-natured** person or animal is naturally friendly and does not get angry easily.

goodness /ˈgʊdnəs/ **1** CONVENTION People sometimes say **'goodness'** or **'my goodness'** to express surprise or for emphasis. ❑ *Goodness, I wonder if he knows.* ❑ *My goodness, he's earned millions in his career.* **2** **thank goodness** → see **thank** **3** N-UNCOUNT **Goodness** is the quality of being kind and honest. ❑ *He retains a faith in human goodness.*

goodnight also **good night** /ˌgʊdˈnaɪt/ CONVENTION You say **'Goodnight'** to someone late in the evening, before one of you goes home or goes to sleep.

goods /gʊdz/ N-PLURAL **Goods** are things that are made to be sold. ❑ *...consumer goods.*

Word Partnership Use *goods* with:

V. **buy** goods, **sell** goods, **transport** goods
N. **consumer** goods, **delivery of** goods, **exchange of** goods, **variety of** goods
ADJ. **sporting** goods, **stolen** goods

goodwill /ˌgʊdˈwɪl/ N-UNCOUNT **Goodwill** is a friendly or helpful attitude towards other people, countries, or organizations. ❑ *...a gesture of goodwill.*

goody also **goodie** /ˈgʊdi/ (**goodies**) **1** N-COUNT You can refer to pleasant, exciting, or attractive things as **goodies.** [INFORMAL] ❑ *...a little bag of goodies.* **2** N-COUNT You can refer to the heroes or the morally good characters in a story or situation as the **goodies.** [INFORMAL] ❑ *This Cup final is a clear case of goodies against baddies.*

goose /guːs/ (**geese**) N-VAR A **goose** is a large bird similar to a duck, with a long neck. The meat of this bird is also referred to as **goose.**

gore /gɔː/ (**gores, goring, gored**) **1** V-T If someone **is gored** by an animal, they are badly wounded by its horns or tusks. ❑ *Jake had been gored by a rhinoceros.* **2** N-UNCOUNT **Gore** is blood from a wound that has become thick. [LITERARY]

gorge /gɔːdʒ/ (**gorges, gorging, gorged**) **1** N-COUNT A **gorge** is a narrow steep-sided valley, usually where a river passes through mountains or an area of hard rock. **2** V-T/V-I If you **gorge** or **gorge yourself on** something, you eat lots of it in a very greedy way. ❑ *We gorged ourselves on delicious bread.*
→ see **river**

gorgeous /ˈgɔːdʒəs/ ADJ Someone or something that is **gorgeous** is extremely pleasant or attractive. [INFORMAL] ❑ *It's a gorgeous day.* ❑ *All the girls think Ryan is gorgeous.*

gorilla /gəˈrɪlə/ (**gorillas**) N-COUNT A **gorilla** is a very large ape.
→ see **primate**

gosh /gɒʃ/ CONVENTION Some people say **'Gosh'** to indicate surprise or shock. [INFORMAL] ❑ *Gosh, that was a heavy bag!*

gospel /ˈgɒspəl/ (**gospels**) **1** N-COUNT The **Gospels** are the four books of the Bible describing the life and teachings of Jesus Christ. **2** N-COUNT You can use **gospel** to refer humorously to a particular way of thinking that a person or group urges others to accept. ❑ *...the gospel according to my mum.* **3** ADJ If you take something **as gospel**, or **as the gospel truth**, you believe that it is completely true. **4** N-UNCOUNT **Gospel** or **gospel music** is a style of religious music that uses strong rhythms and vocal harmony.

gossip /ˈgɒsɪp/ (**gossips, gossiping, gossiped**) **1** N-UNCOUNT **Gossip** is informal conversation, often about other people's private affairs. ❑ *The conversation here is about politics, news and gossip about famous friends.* **2** V-I If you **gossip with** someone, you talk informally with them, especially about other people or local events. ❑ *Eva gossiped with Sarah.* ❑ *We spoke, debated, and gossiped through the night.* **3** N-COUNT If you describe someone as a

gossip, you disapprove of them because they often talk about other people's private affairs.

got /gɒt/ 1 **Got** is the past tense and past participle of **get**. 2 V-T You use **have got** in spoken English when you are saying that someone owns, possesses, or is holding a particular thing, or when you are mentioning a quality or characteristic that someone or something has. ❑ *I've got a coat just like this.* ❑ *Have you got any ideas?* 3 PHRASE You use **have got to** in spoken English when you are saying that something is necessary or must happen in the way stated. ❑ *I'm not happy with the situation, but I've just got to accept it.* ❑ *See, you've got to work very hard.* 4 PHRASE People sometimes use **have got to** in spoken English in order to emphasize that they are certain that something is true. In American English, the 'have' is sometimes omitted. ❑ *He's got to be happy with these results.*

Gothic /ˈgɒθɪk/ 1 ADJ **Gothic** is used to describe a style of architecture or church art, dating from the Middle Ages, that is distinguished by tall pillars, high curved ceilings, and pointed arches. 2 ADJ **Gothic** is used to describe stories in which strange, mysterious adventures happen in dark and lonely places such as the ruins of a castle.

gotta /ˈgɒtə/ **Gotta** is used in written English to represent the words 'got to' when they are pronounced informally, as a way of saying 'have to' or 'must'. ❑ *Prices are high and our kid's gotta eat.*

gotten /ˈgɒtən/ **Gotten** is the past participle of **get** in American English.

gouge /gaʊdʒ/ (**gouges, gouging, gouged**) V-T If you **gouge** something, you make a hole or a long cut in it, usually with a sharp object. ❑ *The bomb gouged a hole in a field next to the road.*

▶ **gouge out** PHR-VERB To **gouge out** a piece or part of something means to cut, dig, or force it from the surrounding surface. ❑ *...threatening to gouge his eyes out.*

gourmet /ˈgʊəmeɪ/ (**gourmets**) 1 ADJ BEFORE N **Gourmet** food is more unusual or sophisticated than ordinary food. 2 N-COUNT A **gourmet** is someone who enjoys good food, and who knows a lot about food and wine.

govern /ˈgʌvən/ (**governs, governing, governed**) 1 V-T To **govern** a country means to officially control and organize its economic, social, and legal systems. 2 V-T If a situation or activity **is governed** by a particular factor or rule, it is controlled by or depends on that factor or rule. ❑ *The industry is governed by strict rules and regulations.*

Thesaurus *govern* Also look up:

v. administer, command, control, direct, guide, head up, lead, manage, reign 1

government /ˈgʌvənmənt/ (**governments**) 1 N-COUNT The **government** of a country is the group of people who are responsible for governing it. When it is singular, **government** can take the singular or plural form of the verb. ❑ *The Government are forcing people out of jobs in this area.* ❑ *...fighting between government forces and left-wing rebels.* 2 N-UNCOUNT **Government** consists of the activities, methods, and principles involved in governing a country or other political unit. ❑ *...our system of government.* ● **governmental** /ˌgʌvənˈmentəl/ ADJ BEFORE N ❑ *...participation in the governmental process.*

→ see **country**

Usage

In Britain, the head of the government is the **Prime Minister**. The Prime Minister appoints the other **ministers**, who are responsible for particular areas of policy. The Prime Minister and other senior ministers together form the **Cabinet**. The policies of the government are debated and approved by **Parliament**, which consists of the **House of Commons** and the **House of Lords**. There are about 650 elected **Members of Parliament** (or **MPs**) in the House of Commons. In the United States, the head of the government is the **President**, who appoints the members of his **administration**. Policies are debated and approved by **Congress**, which consists of the **House of Representatives** and the **Senate**. Members of the House of Representatives are known as **congressmen** and **congresswomen**, and members of the **Senate** are called **senators**.

governor /ˈgʌvənə/ (**governors**) N-COUNT A **governor** is a person who is responsible for the political administration of a region, or for the administration of an institution. ❑ *The governor called for an inquiry.* ❑ *...the BBC board of governors.* ❑ *...the prison governor.*

gown

gown /gaʊn/ (**gowns**) 1 N-COUNT A **gown** is a long dress which women wear on formal occasions. 2 N-COUNT A **gown** is a loose black cloak worn on formal occasions by lawyers and academics.

GP /ˌdʒiː ˈpiː/ (**GPs**) N-COUNT A **GP** is a doctor who treats all types of illness, instead of specializing in one area of medicine. **GP** is an abbreviation for 'general practitioner'.

grab /græb/ (**grabs, grabbing, grabbed**) 1 V-T If you **grab** something, you take it or pick it up roughly. ❑ *I grabbed him by the neck.* 2 V-I & N-COUNT If you **grab at** something, or if you make a **grab for** it, you try to get hold of it. ❑ *I made a grab for the knife.* 3 V-T If you **grab** an opportunity, you take advantage of it eagerly. ❑ *She grabbed the chance of a job interview.* 4 PHRASE If something is **up for grabs**, it is available to anyone who is interested. [INFORMAL]

Thesaurus *grab* Also look up:

v. capture, catch, seize, snap up; *(ant.)* release 1

Word Link *grac ≈ pleasing : disgrace, grace, graceful*

grace /greɪs/ (**graces, gracing, graced**) 1 N-UNCOUNT If someone moves with **grace**, they move smoothly and elegantly. 2 N-UNCOUNT If someone behaves with **grace**, they behave in a polite and dignified way, even when they are upset. ❑ *He accepted defeat with grace.* 3 V-T If you say that something or someone **graces** a place,

Word Web graduation

University graduations are important events for students. This **ceremony** tells the world that the **student** is educated. At university, **graduates** receive different types of **degrees** depending on their subject and level of study. After three years of study, students earn a Bachelor of Arts or Bachelor of Science **degree**. A Master of Arts or Master of Science usually takes one or two more years. The PhD, or doctor of philosophy degree, may require several more years. In addition, a PhD student must write a **thesis** and defend it in front of a group of **professors**.

G

you mean that they make the place more pleasant or attractive. [FORMAL] ❑ *The garden is graced with palm trees and a pool.* ❑ *Her face has graced the cover of more than 500 magazines.* 4 N-UNCOUNT A period of **grace** is an extra period of time that you have been given to do something. ❑ *Businesses were given a year's grace, and payments will begin from March next year.* 5 PHRASE If you refer to someone's **fall from grace**, you are talking about the fact that they are suddenly no longer approved of or popular, often because they have done something unacceptable. You can also say that someone **has fallen from grace**.

Word Link *grac ≈ pleasing : disgrace, grace, graceful*

graceful /'greɪsfʊl/ 1 ADJ Someone or something that is **graceful** moves in a smooth and elegant way that is attractive to watch. ● **gracefully** ADV ❑ *She stepped gracefully onto the stage.* 2 ADJ Something that is **graceful** is attractive because it has a pleasing shape or style. ❑ *...a graceful medieval cathedral.* 3 ADJ **Graceful** behaviour is polite and pleasant. ● **gracefully** ADV ❑ *We managed to refuse gracefully.*

gracious /'greɪʃəs/ 1 ADJ If someone is **gracious**, they are considerate and pleasant. ❑ *...a gracious speech of thanks.* ● **graciously** ADV ❑ *The polite thing was to accept their offer graciously.* 2 ADJ You use **gracious** to describe the comfortable way of life of wealthy people. ❑ *...gracious suburbs with swimming pools and tennis courts.*

grade /greɪd/ (**grades, grading, graded**) 1 V-T If something **is graded**, its quality is judged or classified. ❑ *The oil is tasted and graded according to quality.* ❑ *South Point College does not grade the students' work.* 2 N-COUNT The **grade** of a product is its quality. ❑ *...a good grade of plywood.* 3 N-COUNT Your **grade** in an examination is the mark that you get. ❑ *Brad gained a grade B in maths and in science.* 4 N-COUNT Your **grade** in a company or organization is your level of importance or your rank. ❑ *...senior management grades.* 5 N-COUNT In schools in the United States, a **grade** is a group of classes in which all the children are of a similar age. 6 PHRASE If someone **makes the grade**, they succeed, especially by reaching the required standard. [INFORMAL]

gradient /'greɪdiənt/ (**gradients**) N-COUNT A **gradient** is a slope or the degree to which the ground slopes.

gradual /'grædʒʊəl/ ADJ A **gradual** change or process happens in small stages over a long period of time, rather than suddenly. ❑ *Her progress at school has been gradual.* ● **gradually** ADV ❑ *Gradually we learned to cope.*

graduate (**graduates, graduating, graduated**)

verb /'grædʒʊeɪt/, noun /'grædʒʊət/.

1 V-I & N-COUNT In Britain, when a student **graduates** from university, they have successfully completed a first degree course. A **graduate** is someone who has graduated from university. ❑ *She graduated in English and Drama from Manchester University.* ❑ *...graduates in engineering.* 2 V-I In the United States, when a student **graduates**, they have successfully completed their university, college, or school studies. 3 N-COUNT In the United States, a **graduate** is a student who has successfully completed high school. 4 V-I If you **graduate from** one thing **to** another, you go from a less important job or position to a more important one. ❑ *From commercials she quickly graduated to television shows.*
→ see **graduation**

graduation /ˌgrædʒʊ'eɪʃən/ (**graduations**) 1 N-UNCOUNT **Graduation** is the successful completion of a course of study at a university, college, or school, for which you receive a degree or diploma. ❑ *After graduation he joined a small law firm.* 2 N-COUNT A **graduation** is a special ceremony at which degrees or diplomas are given to students who have successfully completed their studies.
→ see Word Web: **graduation**

graffiti /grə'fiːti/ N-UNCOUNT **Graffiti** is words or pictures that are written or drawn in public places, for example on walls or trains.
→ see **crime**

graft /grɑːft, græft/ (**grafts, grafting, grafted**) 1 V-T If a piece of healthy skin or bone **is grafted on to** a damaged part of your body, it is attached to that part of your body by a medical operation. 2 N-COUNT A **graft** is skin or bone which is grafted onto your body. ❑ *I am having a skin graft on my arm soon.* 3 V-T If a part of one plant **is grafted onto** another plant, they are joined together so that they will become one plant. 4 N-UNCOUNT **Graft** means hard work. [BRIT] ❑ *The job involves a lot of hard graft and boring meetings.*

grain /greɪn/ (**grains**) 1 N-COUNT A **grain** of wheat, rice, or other cereal crop is a seed from it. 2 N-VAR **Grain** is a cereal crop, especially wheat or corn, that has been harvested for food. ❑ *...a bag of grain.* 3 N-COUNT A **grain of** something such as sand or salt is a tiny piece of it. 4 N-SING A **grain of** a quality is a very small amount of it. ❑ *There's a grain of truth in that.* 5 N-COUNT **The grain** of a piece of wood is the direction of its fibres. You can also refer to the pattern of lines on the surface of the wood as **the grain**. ❑ *Brush the paint over the wood in the direction of the grain.* 6 PHRASE If you say that an idea or action **goes against the grain**, you mean

Word Web grain

People first began **cultivating grain** about 10,000 years ago in Asia. Working in groups made growing and **harvesting** the **crop** easier. This probably led Stone Age people to live in communities. Today grain is still the principal food source for humans and domestic animals. Half of all the farmland in the world is used to produce grain. The most popular are **wheat, rice, corn**, and **oats**. An individual kernel of grain is actually a dry, one-seeded **fruit**. It combines the walls of the seed and the flesh of the fruit. Grain is often **ground** into **flour** or meal.

it is very difficult to accept it or do it, because it is different to your beliefs.
→ see Word Web: **grain**
→ see **rice**

gram [BRIT also **gramme**] /græm/ (**grams**) N-COUNT A **gram** is a unit of weight equal to one thousandth of a kilogram.

grammar /ˈgræmə/ (**grammars**) 1 N-UNCOUNT **Grammar** is the ways that words can be put together in order to make sentences. ❑ *He worked hard on his Latin grammar.* 2 N-UNCOUNT Someone's **grammar** is the way in which they obey or do not obey the rules of a language. ❑ *...a deterioration in spelling and grammar among teenagers.* 3 N-COUNT A **grammar** is a book that describes the rules of a language.
→ see **English**

ˈgrammar school (**grammar schools**) N-COUNT A **grammar school** is a school in Britain for children aged between eleven and eighteen with a high academic ability.

grammatical /grəˈmætɪkəl/ ADJ BEFORE N **Grammatical** is used to describe something relating to grammar.

gramme /græm/ → see **gram**

gran /græn/ (**grans**) N-COUNT & N-VOC Your **gran** is your grandmother. [INFORMAL]

grand /grænd/ (**grander, grandest**) 1 ADJ If you describe a building or landscape as **grand**, you mean that it is splendid or impressive. ❑ *...their rather grand house.* 2 ADJ **Grand** plans or actions are ambitious and intended to achieve important results. ❑ *The president announced yet another grand design for American education.* 3 ADJ If you describe people as **grand**, you mean they seem important or socially superior. 4 ADJ If you describe an activity or experience as **grand**, you think that it is pleasant and enjoyable. ❑ *He was having a grand time meeting new people.* 5 ADJ BEFORE N A **grand total** is a total obtained by adding a series of things together. 6 N-SING A **grand** is a thousand pounds or a thousand dollars. [INFORMAL]

grandad also **granddad** /ˈgrændæd/ (**grandads**) N-COUNT & N-VOC Your **grandad** is your grandfather. [INFORMAL]

grandchild /ˈgræntʃaɪld/ (**grandchildren**) N-COUNT Someone's **grandchild** is the child of their son or daughter.

granddaughter /ˈgrændɔːtə/ (**granddaughters**) N-COUNT Someone's **granddaughter** is the daughter of their son or daughter.

grandeur /ˈgrændʒə/ 1 N-UNCOUNT **Grandeur** is the quality in something which makes it seem impressive and elegant. ❑ *...the grandeur of the historic country house.* 2 N-UNCOUNT Someone's **grandeur** is the great importance and social status that they have, or think they have. ❑ *...mansions built by nineteenth-century men with delusions of grandeur.*

grandfather /ˈgrændfɑːðə/ (**grandfathers**) N-COUNT & N-VOC Your **grandfather** is the father of your father or mother.
→ see **family**

grandiose /ˈgrændiəʊs/ ADJ If you describe something as **grandiose**, you mean it is bigger or more elaborate than necessary; used showing disapproval. ❑ *He remained silent after hearing his leader's grandiose plan.*

ˌgrand ˈjury (**grand juries**) N-COUNT A **grand jury** is a jury, usually in the United States, which considers a criminal case in order to decide if someone should be tried in a court of law.

grandma /ˈgrænmɑː/ (**grandmas**) N-COUNT & N-VOC Your **grandma** is your grandmother. [INFORMAL]

grandmother /ˈgrænmʌðə/ (**grandmothers**) N-COUNT & N-VOC Your **grandmother** is the mother of your father or mother.
→ see **family**

grandpa /ˈgrænpɑː/ (**grandpas**) N-COUNT & N-VOC Your **grandpa** is your grandfather. [INFORMAL]

grandparent /ˈgrænpeərənt/ (**grandparents**) N-COUNT Your **grandparents** are the parents of your father or mother.

grandson /ˈgrænsʌn/ (**grandsons**) N-COUNT Someone's **grandson** is the son of their son or daughter.

grandstand /ˈgrændstænd/ (**grandstands**) N-COUNT A **grandstand** is a covered stand for spectators at sporting events.

Word Link *ite ≈ mineral, rock : dynamite, granite, graphite*

granite /ˈgrænɪt/ N-UNCOUNT **Granite** is a very hard rock used in building.

granny also **grannie** /ˈgræni/ (**grannies**) N-COUNT & N-VOC Your **granny** is your grandmother. [INFORMAL]

grant /grɑːnt, grænt/ (**grants, granting, granted**) 1 N-COUNT A **grant** is an amount of money that the government or other institution gives to a person or an organization for a particular purpose. ❑ *They got a special grant for research.* 2 V-T If someone in authority **grants** you something, they give it to you. ❑ *Permission was granted a few weeks ago.* 3 V-T If you **grant**

that something is true, you admit that it is true. [FORMAL] ❑ *Other architects granted that his work was remarkable.* **4** PHRASE If you say that someone **takes** you **for granted**, you are complaining that they benefit from your help, efforts, or presence without showing that they are grateful. **5** PHRASE If you **take it for granted** that something is the case, or if you **take** something **for granted**, you believe that it is true or you accept it as normal without thinking about it. ❑ *He seemed to take it for granted that he should represent us.* ❑ *All the things I took for granted at home just didn't happen in London.*

ˌgrant-mainˈtained ADJ A **grant-maintained** school is one which receives money directly from the national government rather than from a local authority. [BRIT]

G

grape /ɡreɪp/ (**grapes**) **1** N-COUNT **Grapes** are small green or purple fruit that can be eaten raw or used for making wine. **2** PHRASE If you describe someone's attitude as **sour grapes**, you mean that they criticize something because they want it but cannot have it themselves.
→ see **fruit**

grapefruit /ˈɡreɪpfruːt/

The plural is **grapefruit** or **grapefruits**.

N-VAR A **grapefruit** is a large, round, yellow fruit that has a sharp taste.

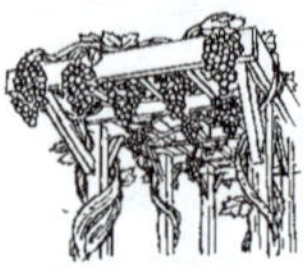

grapevines

grapevine /ˈɡreɪpvaɪn/ (**grapevines**) **1** PHRASE If you hear something **on the grapevine**, you hear it in casual conversation with other people. **2** N-COUNT A **grapevine** is a climbing plant on which grapes grow.

Word Link *graph ≈ writing : autograph, biography, graph*

graph /ɡrɑːf, ɡræf/ (**graphs**) N-COUNT A **graph** is a mathematical diagram which shows the relationship between two or more sets of numbers or measurements.
→ see Word Web: **graph**
→ see **chart**

graphic /ˈɡræfɪk/ (**graphics**) **1** ADJ A **graphic** description or account of something unpleasant is very clear and detailed. ❑ *This film contains graphic scenes which may offend.* ● **graphically** ADV ❑ *The author tells us graphically what the fighting was like.* **2** N-UNCOUNT **Graphics** is the activity of drawing or making pictures, especially in publishing, industry, or computing. **3** N-COUNT **Graphics** are drawings and pictures that are made using simple lines. ❑ *The company has released a new graphic to replace the old symbol.*

Word Link *ite ≈ mineral, rock : dynamite, granite, graphite*

graphite /ˈɡræfaɪt/ N-UNCOUNT **Graphite** is a hard black substance that is a form of carbon.

grapple /ˈɡræpəl/ (**grapples, grappling, grappled**) **1** V-I If you **grapple with** someone or something, you take hold of them and struggle with them. ❑ *He was grappling with an alligator.* ❑ *They grappled desperately for control of the weapon.* **2** V-I If you **grapple with** a problem, you try hard to solve it.

grasp /ɡrɑːsp, ɡræsp/ (**grasps, grasping, grasped**) **1** V-T & N-SING If you **grasp** something, you hold it firmly. A **grasp** is a firm hold or grip. ❑ *She was trying to grasp at something.* ❑ *His hand was taken in a warm, firm grasp.* **2** N-SING If something is **in** your **grasp**, you possess or control it. If something slips **from** your **grasp**, you lose it or lose control of it. ❑ *She allowed victory to slip from her grasp.* **3** V-T & N-SING If you **grasp** something that is complicated or difficult to understand, you understand it. A **grasp of** something is an understanding of it. ❑ *He instantly grasped that Stephen was talking about his wife.* ❑ *They have a good grasp of foreign languages.* **4** N-SING If you say that something is **within** someone's **grasp**, you mean that it is very likely that they will achieve it.

grass /ɡrɑːs, ɡræs/ (**grasses**) N-VAR **Grass** is a very common green plant with narrow leaves that forms a layer covering an area of ground.
→ see **grassland, habitat, plant**

grasshopper /ˈɡrɑːshɒpə, ˈɡræs-/ (**grasshoppers**) N-COUNT A **grasshopper** is an insect with long back legs that jumps high into

Word Web **graph**

There are three main elements in a **line** or **bar graph**:

- a **vertical axis** (the y-axis)
- a **horizontal axis** (the x-axis)
- at least one line or set of bars.

To understand a **graph**, do the following:

1. Read the **title** of the graph.
2. Read the **labels** and the **range** of numbers along the side (the **scale** or vertical axis).
3. Read the information along the bottom (horizontal axis) of the graph.
4. Determine what **units** the graph uses. This information can be found on the axis or in the **key**.
5. Look for patterns, groups, and differences.

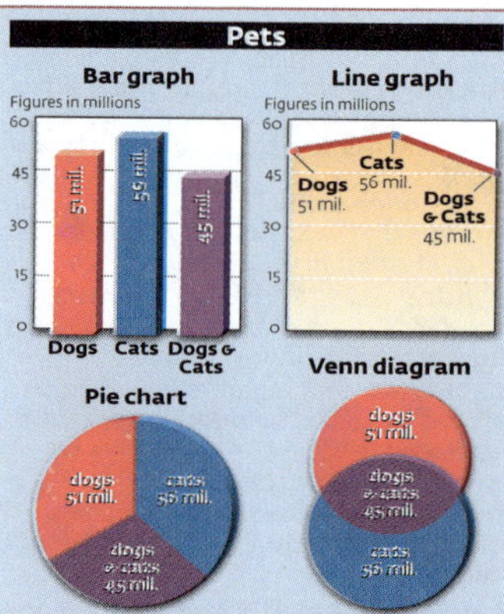

Word Web **grassland**

Grasslands are flat, open areas of land covered with **grass**. They get from 10 to 30 inches of rain per year. The **soil** there is deep and **fertile**. The **prairies** in the American Midwest used to be mostly grasslands. At that time, herds of bison, or **buffalo**, lived there along with antelopes. Because of the rich soil, almost all this prairie land has been converted to **agricultural** use. Very few buffalo or antelopes are still there. There are grasslands on every continent except Antarctica. In South America they are called pampas. In Europe they call them steppes and in Africa, savannas.

the air and makes a high, vibrating sound.

grassland /'grɑːslænd, 'græs-/ (**grasslands**) N-VAR **Grassland** is land covered with wild grass.
→ see Word Web: **grassland**
→ see **habitat**

ˌgrass 'roots or **grass-roots** or **grassroots** N-PLURAL The **grass roots** of an organization are the ordinary people in it, rather than its leaders. ❑ *You have to join the party at grass-roots level.*

grassy /'grɑːsi, 'græs-/ (**grassier, grassiest**) ADJ A **grassy** area of land is covered in grass.

grate /greɪt/ (**grates, grating, grated**) **1** N-COUNT A **grate** is a framework of bars in a fireplace, which holds the coal or wood. **2** V-T When you **grate** food, you shred it into very small pieces using a tool called a grater. **3** V-I When something **grates**, it rubs against something else, making a harsh unpleasant sound. ❑ *The metal grated against the floor.* **4** V-I If something such as someone's behaviour **grates on** you, it irritates you. ❑ *She grated on me – until we discovered we were both fans of Elvis.*
→ see **cut**

grateful /'greɪtfʊl/ ADJ If you are **grateful for** something that someone has given you or done for you, you are pleased and wish to thank them. ❑ *I am grateful to you for your help.* ● **gratefully** ADV ❑ *I gratefully accepted the offer.*

Word Link *grat ≈ pleasing : congratulate, gratify, gratitude*

gratify /'grætɪfaɪ/ (**gratifies, gratifying, gratified**) **1** V-T If you **are gratified** by something, it gives you pleasure or satisfaction. [FORMAL] ❑ *Sarah was gratified by their support.* ● **gratifying** ADJ ❑ *It is very gratifying to watch our business grow.* ● **gratification** /ˌgrætɪfɪ'keɪʃən/ N-UNCOUNT ❑ *Israelis reacted with gratification.* **2** V-T If you **gratify** a desire, you satisfy it. [FORMAL] ❑ *We gratified our friend's curiosity.* ● **gratification** N-UNCOUNT ❑ *...sexual gratification.*

gratitude /'grætɪtjuːd, AM -tuːd/ N-UNCOUNT **Gratitude** is the state of feeling grateful. ❑ *I wish to express my gratitude to Kathy Davis for her help.*

gratuitous /grə'tjuːɪtəs, AM -'tuː-/ ADJ If you describe something as **gratuitous**, you mean that it is unnecessary, and often harmful or upsetting. ❑ *...gratuitous violence.* ● **gratuitously** ADV ❑ *His remarks were gratuitously offensive.*

Word Link *grav ≈ heavy : grave, gravely, gravity*

grave /greɪv/ (**graves, graver, gravest**) **1** N-COUNT A **grave** is a place where a dead person is buried. **2** ADJ A **grave** situation is very serious. ❑ *...the grave crisis facing the country.* ● **gravely** ADV ❑ *...his gravely ill wife.* **3** ADJ A **grave** person is quiet and serious. ❑ *Mrs Williams was looking very grave.* ● **gravely** ADV ❑ *'I think you should see this', she said gravely.*

gravel /'grævəl/ N-UNCOUNT **Gravel** consists of very small stones. ❑ *...a gravel path.*

graveyard /'greɪvjɑːd/ (**graveyards**) N-COUNT A **graveyard** is an area of land where dead people are buried.

gravitational /ˌgrævɪ'teɪʃənəl/ ADJ BEFORE N **Gravitational** means relating to the force of gravity. ❑ *...the earth's gravitational pull.*
→ see **tide**

gravity /'grævɪti/ **1** N-UNCOUNT **Gravity** is the force which makes things fall when you drop them. **2** N-UNCOUNT **The gravity of** a situation is its importance and seriousness. ❑ *No one questioned the gravity of the crime itself.*
→ see **moon**

gravy /'greɪvi/ N-UNCOUNT **Gravy** is a sauce made from the juices that come from meat when it cooks.

gray /greɪ/ → see **grey**

graze /greɪz/ (**grazes, grazing, grazed**) **1** V-T/V-I When animals **graze**, or when they **are grazed**, they eat the grass or other plants that are growing in a particular place. ❑ *...a field where sheep were grazing.* **2** V-T If you **graze** a part of your body, you injure the skin by scraping against something. **3** N-COUNT A **graze** is a small wound caused by scraping against something. ❑ *...minor cuts and grazes.* **4** V-T If one thing **grazes** another thing, it touches that thing lightly as it passes by. ❑ *A bullet grazed my cheek.*

grease /griːs/ (**greases, greasing, greased**) **1** N-UNCOUNT **Grease** is a thick substance used to oil the moving parts of machines. **2** N-UNCOUNT **Grease** is an oily substance produced by your skin. **3** N-UNCOUNT **Grease** is animal fat produced by cooking meat. ❑ *...bacon grease.* **4** V-T If you **grease** something, you put grease or fat on it. ❑ *Lightly grease a baking tray.*

greasy /'griːsi, -zi/ (**greasier, greasiest**) ADJ Something that is **greasy** is covered with grease or contains a lot of grease. ❑ *...greasy hair.*

Word Web greenhouse effect

Over the past 100 years, the average **temperature** around the globe has risen dramatically. Researchers believe that this **global warming** comes from added **carbon dioxide** and other **gases** in the **atmosphere**. With **water vapour**, the gases form a layer that holds in heat. It acts like the glass in a greenhouse. Scientists call this the **greenhouse effect**. Some natural causes of this warming may include increased **solar radiation** and tiny changes in the earth's orbit. However, human activities, such as **deforestation**, and the use of **fossil fuels** seem to be an important cause.

Word Link *est ≈ most : greatest, kindest, latest*

great /greɪt/ (**greater, greatest**) 1 ADJ BEFORE N You use **great** to describe something that is very large. ❑ *...great columns of ice.* 2 ADJ **Great** is used to emphasize the large amount or degree of something. ❑ *She had great difficulty in keeping her eyes open.* ● **greatly** ADV ❑ *He will be greatly missed.* 3 ADJ You use **great** to describe someone or something that is important, famous, or exciting. ❑ *...the great novels of the 19th century.* ❑ *...the greatest scientist since Einstein.* ● **greatness** N-UNCOUNT ❑ *No-one doubted his claim to greatness.* 4 ADJ If something is **great**, it is very good. [INFORMAL] ❑ *I thought it was a great idea.* ❑ *It would make a great film.*

Usage

Great, **big** and **large** are all used to talk about size. In general, **large** is more formal than **big**, and **great** is more formal than **large**. **Big** and **large** are normally used to describe objects. If you use **great** to describe an object, you are suggesting that it is impressive because of its size. ❑ *The great bird of prey was a dark smudge against the sun*. You can use **large** or **great**, but not **big**, to describe amounts. ❑ *He noticed a large amount of blood on the floor*. ❑ *The coming of tourists in great numbers changes things*. **Great** is often used with nouns referring to things such as feelings or ideas. It is the only one of the three words that can be used in front of an uncount noun. ❑ *It gives me very great pleasure to welcome you to the town*. Remember that **great** has several other meanings, when it does not refer to size, but to something that is remarkable, very good, or enjoyable.

Thesaurus *great* Also look up:

ADJ. enormous, immense, vast; *(ant.)* small 1 2
distinguished, famous, important, remarkable 3

greed /gri:d/ N-UNCOUNT **Greed** is a desire for more of something than is necessary or fair.

greedy /gri:di/ (**greedier, greediest**) ADJ Someone who is **greedy** wants more of something than is necessary or fair. ❑ *...greedy bosses who award themselves huge pay rises.* ● **greedily** ADV ❑ *She ate the cakes greedily.*

green /gri:n/ (**greener, greenest, greens**) 1 ADJ & N-VAR Something that is **green** is the colour of grass or leaves. ❑ *...green olives.* ❑ *...a paler and softer shade of green.* 2 ADJ A place that is **green** is covered with grass, plants, and trees. ● **greenness** N-UNCOUNT ❑ *...the lush greenness of the river valleys.* 3 ADJ BEFORE N **Green** issues relate to the protection of the environment. ❑ *...the power of the Green movement in Germany.* 4 N-COUNT A **green** is a smooth, flat area of grass, for example the area around a hole on a golf course.
→ see **colour, golf, rainbow**

greenery /'gri:nəri/ N-UNCOUNT Plants that make a place look attractive are referred to as **greenery**.

greenhouse /'gri:nhaʊs/ (**greenhouses**) N-COUNT A **greenhouse** is a glass building in which you grow plants that need to be protected from bad weather.
→ see **barn**

'greenhouse effect N-SING **The greenhouse effect** is the rise in the earth's temperature caused by a build-up of gases around the earth.
→ see Word Web: **greenhouse effect**
→ see **ozone**

greet /gri:t/ (**greets, greeting, greeted**) 1 V-T When you **greet** someone, you say something friendly such as 'hello' when you meet them. 2 V-T If something **is greeted** in a particular way, people react to it in that way. ❑ *The move was greeted with disappointment by union leaders.* 3 V-T If you **are greeted** by something, it is the first thing you notice in a place. [LITERARY] ❑ *Customers are greeted by wonderful smells from the kitchen.*

greeting /'gri:tɪŋ/ (**greetings**) N-VAR A **greeting** is something friendly that you say or do when you meet someone. ❑ *He raised a hand in greeting.*

grenade /grɪ'neɪd/ (**grenades**) N-COUNT A **grenade** is a small bomb that can be thrown by hand.

grew /gru:/ **Grew** is the past tense of **grow**.

grey [AM **gray**] /greɪ/ (**greyer, greyest, greys**) ADJ & N-VAR **Grey** is the colour of ashes or of clouds on a rainy day. ❑ *...grey trousers.* ❑ *His hair is a dark shade of grey.*

Word Partnership Use *grey* with:

N. grey **eyes**, grey **hair**, **shades of** grey, grey **sky**, grey **suit**,
V. **go** grey, **turn** grey

greyhound /'greɪhaʊnd/ (**greyhounds**) N-COUNT A **greyhound** is a thin dog that can run very fast.

grid /grɪd/ (**grids**) 1 N-COUNT A **grid** is a pattern of straight lines that cross over each other to form squares. ❑ *...a grid of narrow streets.* 2 N-COUNT A **grid** is a network of wires and cables by which sources of power, such as electricity, are distributed throughout an area. ❑ *...the national electricity grid.*

gridlock /ˈgrɪdlɒk/ 1 N-UNCOUNT **Gridlock** is the situation that exists when all the roads in a particular place are so full of vehicles that none of them can move. 2 N-UNCOUNT You can use **gridlock** to refer to a situation in an argument or dispute when neither side is prepared to give in, so no agreement can be reached. ❑ *...political gridlock.* → see **traffic**

grief /griːf/ 1 N-UNCOUNT **Grief** is extreme sadness. ❑ *...her grief at her husband's suicide.* 2 PHRASE If someone or something **comes to grief**, they fail or are harmed. ❑ *So many marriages have come to grief over lack of money.*

Word Link	*griev ≈ heavy, serious : aggrieved, grievance, grieve*

grievance /ˈgriːvəns/ (**grievances**) N-VAR A **grievance** is a reason for complaining. ❑ *...an opportunity for them to discuss their grievances.*

grieve /griːv/ (**grieves, grieving, grieved**) 1 V-I If you **grieve** over something, especially someone's death, you feel very sad about it. ❑ *He still grieves for his wife, who died three years ago.* 2 V-T If something **grieves** you, it makes you feel unhappy or upset. ❑ *It grieved Elaine to be separated from her son.*

grievous /ˈgriːvəs/ ADJ Something that is **grievous** is extremely serious or worrying in its effects. [FORMAL] ❑ *...a very grievous mistake.* ● **grievously** ADV ❑ *Michael was grievously injured.*

grill /grɪl/ (**grills, grilling, grilled**) 1 V-T In British English, if you **grill** food, you cook it using strong heat directly above or below it. The American word is **broil**. ❑ *...grilled chicken.* 2 → See note at **cook** 3 N-COUNT A **grill** is a part of a cooker where food is grilled. 4 V-T If you **grill** someone, you ask them a lot of questions for a long period of time. [INFORMAL] ❑ *The police grilled him for hours.* → see **cook**

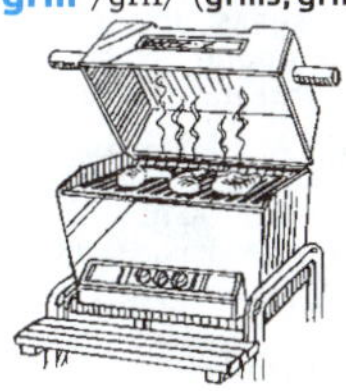
grill

grille /grɪl/ (**grilles**) N-COUNT A **grille** is a protective framework of bars or wire placed in front of a window or a piece of machinery.

grim /grɪm/ (**grimmer, grimmest**) 1 ADJ A situation or news that is **grim** is unpleasant. ❑ *There was more grim economic news yesterday.* 2 ADJ A **grim** place is unattractive and depressing. 3 ADJ If someone is **grim**, they are very serious or stern. [LITERARY] ❑ *Her face was grim.* ● **grimly** ADV ❑ *'That was no accident,' Frank said grimly.*

grimace /grɪˈmeɪs, ˈgrɪməs/ (**grimaces, grimacing, grimaced**) V-I & N-COUNT If you **grimace**, or if you make a **grimace**, you twist your face in an ugly way because you are unhappy, disgusted, or in pain. ❑ *He grimaced at his reflection.* ❑ *...a little grimace of pain.*

grin /grɪn/ (**grins, grinning, grinned**) V-I & N-COUNT If you **grin**, or if you give a **grin**, you smile broadly. ❑ *Nancy grinned at him.*

grind /graɪnd/ (**grinds, grinding, ground**) 1 V-T When something such as corn or coffee **is ground**, it is crushed until it becomes a fine powder. ❑ *...freshly ground coffee.* 2 V-T If you **grind** something into a surface, you press it hard into the surface. ❑ *She ground her heel into the sand.* 3 PHRASE If something **grinds to a halt**, it gradually slows down until it stops completely. ❑ *The industry would grind to a halt.* 4 N-SING You can refer to tiring, boring, and routine work as a **grind**. [INFORMAL] ❑ *...the daily grind of shaving.* 5 → see also **ground**

▸ **grind down** PHR-VERB If you **grind** someone **down**, you treat them very harshly, so that they do not have the will to resist you.

grinder /graɪndə/ (**grinders**) N-COUNT A **grinder** is a machine or device which crushes something into small pieces. ❑ *...coffee grinders.*

grip /grɪp/ (**grips, gripping, gripped**) 1 V-T & N-SING If you **grip** something, or if you take a **grip** on it, you hold it firmly. ❑ *She gripped the rope.* ❑ *His strong hand eased the bag from her grip.* 2 N-UNCOUNT If things such as shoes or car tyres have **grip**, they do not slip. 3 N-SING Someone's **grip on** a person or situation is the control they have over them. ❑ *The president maintains an iron grip on his country.* ❑ *He wondered if he was getting old and losing his grip.* 4 V-T If something **grips** you, it affects you strongly and your attention is concentrated on it. ❑ *The entire community has been gripped by fear.* ● **gripping** ADJ ❑ *The film turned out to be a gripping thriller.* 5 PHRASE If you **get to grips with** a problem, or if you **come to grips with** it, you consider it seriously, and start taking action to deal with it. ❑ *The government's first task is to get to grips with the economy.*

gripe /graɪp/ (**gripes, griping, griped**) V-I & N-COUNT If you say that someone **is griping about** something, you mean they are complaining about something in an annoying way. A **gripe** is a complaint. [INFORMAL] ❑ *I am tired of hearing motorists griping about the roads.* ● **griping** N-UNCOUNT ❑ *Still, the griping went on.*

grisly /ˈgrɪzli/ (**grislier, grisliest**) ADJ Something that is **grisly** is horrible and shocking. ❑ *...grisly murders.*

grit /grɪt/ (**grits, gritting, gritted**) 1 N-UNCOUNT **Grit** consists of tiny pieces of stone, often put on roads in winter to make them less slippery. 2 N-UNCOUNT If you say that someone has **grit**, you mean that they have determination and courage. ❑ *She has the grit to hang on when things go wrong.* 3 V-T If you **grit** your **teeth**, you decide to say nothing or to carry on, even though you are very angry or the situation is very difficult. ❑ *Ms Warner said she coped with such abuse 'through gritted teeth'.*

gritty /ˈgrɪti/ (**grittier, grittiest**) 1 ADJ Something that is **gritty** is covered with grit or has a texture like grit. ❑ *...coarse, gritty ash.* 2 ADJ Someone who is **gritty** is determined and courageous. ❑ *...gritty determination.*

groan /grəʊn/ (**groans, groaning, groaned**) V-I & N-COUNT If you **groan**, you make a long low sound of pain, unhappiness, or disapproval, called a **groan**. ❑ *He began to groan with pain.* ❑ *A groan of disappointment went round the group.*

G

grocer /ˈgrəʊsə/ (**grocers**) N-COUNT A **grocer** is a shopkeeper who sells foods such as flour, sugar, and tinned foods. You can refer to a shop where these goods are sold as a **grocer** or a **grocer's**.

grocery /ˈgrəʊsəri/ (**groceries**) **1** N-COUNT A **grocery** or a **grocery store** is a grocer's shop. [AM] **2** N-PLURAL **Groceries** are foods you buy at a grocer's or at a supermarket. ❑ *...two bags of groceries.*

groin /grɔɪn/ (**groins**) N-COUNT Your **groin** is the part of your body where your legs meet your abdomen.

groom /gruːm/ (**grooms, grooming, groomed**) **1** N-COUNT A **groom** is the same as a **bridegroom**. **2** N-COUNT A **groom** is someone whose job is to look after horses in a stable. **3** V-T If you **groom** an animal, you brush its fur. **4** V-T If you **are groomed for** a special job, someone prepares you for it. ❑ *George was being groomed for the top job.*

groomed /gruːmd/ ADJ You use **groomed** in expressions such as **well groomed** and **badly groomed** to say how neat, clean, and smart a person is. ❑ *...a well-groomed appearance.*

grooming /ˈgruːmɪŋ/ N-UNCOUNT **Grooming** refers to the things that people do to keep themselves clean and make their face, hair, and skin look nice. ❑ *...a concern for personal grooming.*

groove /gruːv/ (**grooves**) N-COUNT A **groove** is a deep line cut into a surface.

grope /grəʊp/ (**gropes, groping, groped**) **1** V-I If you **grope for** something that you cannot see, you search for it with your hands. ❑ *George groped in his pocket for his wallet.* ❑ *I didn't turn on the light, but groped my way across the room.* **2** V-I If you **grope for** something such as the solution to a problem, you try to think of it, when you have no real idea what it could be. ❑ *She groped for a simple word to express the idea.*

gross /grəʊs/ (**grosser, grossest**) **1** ADJ BEFORE N You use **gross** to emphasize the degree to which something is unacceptable or unpleasant. ❑ *The remark was a gross insult to workers.* ● **grossly** ADV ❑ *...grossly overpaid corporate lawyers.* **2** ADJ If you describe something or someone as **gross**, you think that they are very ugly, tasteless, or repulsive. [INFORMAL] ❑ *He wears really gross ties.* ❑ *Don't be so gross!* **3** ADJ BEFORE N & ADV A **gross** amount is the total amount after all the relevant amounts have been added together, and before any deductions are made. ❑ *Gross sales in June totalled £709 million.* ❑ *...a father earning £20,000 gross a year.* **4** ADJ BEFORE N The **gross weight** of something is its total weight, including its container or wrapping.

Word Partnership Use *gross* with:

N.	**act of** gross **injustice**, gross **mismanagement**, gross **negligence** **1** gross **income**, gross **margin** **3**
V.	**feel** gross **2**

grotesque /grəʊˈtesk/ **1** ADJ You say that something is **grotesque** when it is so unnatural, unpleasant, or exaggerated that it upsets or shocks you. ❑ *...a country where grotesque abuses are taking place.* ● **grotesquely** ADV ❑ *He says the law is grotesquely unfair.* **2** ADJ If something is **grotesque**, it is very ugly. ❑ *He painted and drew grotesque heads, especially skulls.* ● **grotesquely** ADV ❑ *...his grotesquely deformed legs.*

ground /graʊnd/ (**grounds, grounding, grounded**) **1** N-SING **The ground** is the surface of the earth or the floor of a room. ❑ *We slid down the roof and dropped to the ground.* ❑ *Avoid chairs with thin legs as they sink into soft ground.* **2** N-SING If you say that something takes place **on the ground**, you mean it takes place on the surface of the earth and not in the air. ❑ *The war was largely fought on the ground.* ❑ *...American naval, air and ground forces.* **3** N-COUNT A **ground** is an area which is used for a particular purpose. ❑ *...Indian hunting grounds.* ❑ *...the city's football ground.* **4** N-PLURAL The **grounds** of a large or important building are the garden or area of land which surrounds it. ❑ *...the palace grounds.* ❑ *...the grounds of the university.* **5** V-T If aircraft or pilots **are grounded**, they are not allowed to fly. **6** N-VAR You can use **ground** to refer to a place or situation in which particular methods or ideas can develop and be successful. ❑ *The company has maintained its reputation as the developing ground for new techniques.* **7** N-UNCOUNT **Ground** is used in expressions such as **gain ground** and **lose ground** in order to talk about the progress which someone or something makes in a situation or in a particular field. [JOURNALISM] ❑ *The election campaign gained ground during the last week.* ❑ *These novels are breaking new ground.* **8** N-VAR The **ground** or **grounds** for a particular feeling or course of action are the reason or justification for it. ❑ *Owen was against it, on the grounds of expense.* **9** V-T If an argument or opinion **is grounded in** or **on** something, it is based on that thing. ❑ *Her argument was grounded in fact.* **10** **Ground** is the past tense and past participle of **grind**. **11** PHRASE If something such as a project **gets off the ground**, it begins or starts functioning. ❑ *We help small companies to get off the ground.* **12** PHRASE If you **stand** your **ground** or **hold** your **ground**, you do not run away from a danger or threat, but face it bravely.
→ see **grain**

grounding /ˈgraʊndɪŋ/ N-SING If you have a **grounding in** a subject, you know the basic facts or principles of that subject. ❑ *The course provides a grounding in law.*

ˈground rule (**ground rules**) N-COUNT The **ground rules for** something are the basic principles on which future action will be based. ❑ *Rudy set ground rules for our meeting.*

Word Link ***ground ≈ bottom : background, groundwork, underground***

groundwork /ˈgraʊndwɜːk/ N-SING The **groundwork for** something is the early work on it which forms the basis for the rest. ❑ *Yesterday's meeting was to lay the groundwork for the task ahead.*

group /gruːp/ (**groups, grouping, grouped**) **1** N-COUNT A **group of** people or things is a number of them together in one place at one time. **Group** can take the singular or plural form of the verb. ❑ *The trouble involved a small group of football supporters.* ❑ *The students work in groups.* **2** N-COUNT A **group** is a set of people who have the same interests or objectives, and who organize themselves to work or act together. ❑ *...the Minority Rights Group.* ❑ *...members of an environmental group.* **3** N-COUNT A **group** is a set of people or things which have something in common. ❑ *...the most promising players in her age group.* **4** → see also **focus group, pressure group** **5** N-COUNT A **group** is a number of musicians who perform pop music together. **6** V-T If a number of things or people **are grouped together**, they are together in one place or within one organization or system. ❑ *The fact sheets are grouped into seven sections.* ❑ *...the Arab Maghreb Union, which groups together the five North African states.*

Thesaurus	*group* Also look up:
N.	collection, crowd, gang, organization, society **1** **2**
V.	arrange, categorize, class, order, rank, sort **5**

grouping /'gru:pɪŋ/ (**groupings**) N-COUNT A **grouping** is a set of people or things that have something in common. ❑ *There were two main political groupings.*

grouse /graʊs/ (**grouses, grousing, groused**)

In meaning 1, **grouse** is both the singular and the plural form.

1 N-COUNT **Grouse** are small fat birds which are often shot for sport and can be eaten. **2** V-I & N-COUNT If you **grouse**, you complain. A **grouse** is a complaint. ❑ *They groused about the parking regulations.*

grove /grəʊv/ (**groves**) N-COUNT A **grove** is a group of trees that are close together. ❑ *...an olive grove.*
→ see **tree**

grovel /'grɒvəl/ (**grovels, grovelling, grovelled** or [AM] **groveling, groveled**) **1** V-I If someone **grovels**, they behave very humbly towards another person, for example because they are frightened or because they want something; used showing disapproval. ❑ *I don't grovel to anybody.* ● **grovelling** ADJ ❑ *The Senator has been accused of grovelling.* **2** V-I If you **grovel**, you crawl on the ground, for example in order to find something. ❑ *We grovelled around the room on our knees.*

grow /grəʊ/ (**grows, growing, grew, grown**) **1** V-I When something or someone **grows**, they develop and increase in size or intensity. ❑ *All children grow at different rates.* ❑ *The economy continues to grow.* ❑ *Pressure for reform is likely to grow.* **2** V-I If a plant or tree **grows** in a particular place, it is alive there. ❑ *Trees and bushes grew down to the water's edge.* **3** V-T When you **grow** something, you cause it to develop or increase in size or length. ❑ *I always grow a few red onions.* ❑ *I'm growing my hair.* ● **grower** (**growers**) N-COUNT ❑ *...England's apple growers.* **4** LINK-VERB You use **grow** to say that someone or something gradually changes until they have a new quality, feeling, or attitude. ❑ *I grew a little afraid of the guy next door.* ❑ *He's growing old.* ❑ *He grew to love his work.* **5** → see also **grown**
→ see **plant**

▶ **grow apart** PHR-VERB If people who have a close relationship **grow apart**, they gradually start to have different interests and opinions, and their relationship starts to fail. ❑ *It sounds as if you have grown apart from Tom.*

▶ **grow into** PHR-VERB When a child **grows into** a piece of clothing that is too big for them, they get bigger so that it fits them properly.

▶ **grow on** PHR-VERB If someone or something **grows on** you, you start to like them more and more. ❑ *The place began to grow on me.*

▶ **grow out of** **1** PHR-VERB If you **grow out of** a type of behaviour, you stop behaving in that way as you develop or change. ❑ *Most children grow out of that sort of behaviour.* **2** PHR-VERB When a child **grows out of** a piece of clothing, they become so big that it no longer fits them.

▶ **grow up** **1** PHR-VERB When someone **grows up**, they gradually change from being a child into being an adult. **2** PHR-VERB If something **grows up**, it starts to exist and becomes larger or more important. ❑ *Several heavy industries grew up alongside the port.* **3** → see also **grown-up**

Word Partnership	Use *grow* with:
V.	**continue to** grow **1** **2** **4**
	try to grow **3**
ADJ.	grow **bored**, grow **closer**, grow **louder**, grow **silent** **1** **4**
	grow **older** **4**
N.	grow **food** **3**

growl /graʊl/ (**growls, growling, growled**) **1** V-I & N-COUNT When an animal **growls**, it makes a low rumbling noise, called a **growl**, usually because it is angry. ❑ *The dog growled at him.* **2** V-T & N-COUNT If someone **growls** something, they say it in a low rough voice, called a **growl**. [WRITTEN] ❑ *'What good is that?' I growled.*

grown /grəʊn/ **1** **Grown** is the past participle of **grow**. **2** ADJ A **grown** man or woman is one who is fully developed and mature. ❑ *Dad, I'm a grown woman. I know what I'm doing.*

,grown-'up (**grown-ups**) **1** N-COUNT Children, or people talking to children, often refer to adults as **grown-ups**. ❑ *Try to speak like a grown-up.* **2** ADJ Someone who is **grown-up** is mature and no longer dependent on their parents or another adult. ❑ *She was a widow with grown-up children.*

growth /grəʊθ/ (**growths**) **1** N-UNCOUNT The **growth of** something such as an industry, organization, or idea is its development in size, wealth, or importance. ❑ *...the growth of nationalism.* ❑ *...Japan's enormous economic growth.* **2** N-UNCOUNT **Growth** in a person, animal, or plant is the process of increasing in size and development. ❑ *...hormones which control fertility and body growth.* **3** N-COUNT A **growth** is an abnormal lump that grows inside or on a person, animal, or plant.

grub /grʌb/ (**grubs**) **1** N-COUNT A **grub** is an insect which has just hatched from its egg. **2** N-UNCOUNT **Grub** is food. [INFORMAL]

grubby /'grʌbi/ (**grubbier, grubbiest**) ADJ **Grubby** people or things are rather dirty. [INFORMAL] ❑ *...kids with grubby faces.*

grudge /grʌdʒ/ (**grudges**) N-COUNT If you have a **grudge against** someone, you have unfriendly feelings towards them because they have harmed you in the past.

grudging /'grʌdʒɪŋ/ ADJ A **grudging** feeling or action is one that you feel or do unwillingly. ❑ *They were forced to show a grudging respect.* ● **grudgingly** ADV ❑ *They grudgingly agreed to allow him to continue working.*

gruelling [AM **grueling**] /'gru:əlɪŋ/ ADJ A

gruelling activity is extremely difficult and tiring.

gruesome /'gru:səm/ ADJ Something that is **gruesome** is horrible and shocking. ❑ *...gruesome murders.*

grumble /'grʌmbəl/ (**grumbles, grumbling, grumbled**) V-I & N-COUNT If you **grumble about** something, you complain about it. You can refer to complaints like this as **grumbles**. ❑ *I shouldn't grumble about Mum.* ❑ *He grumbled that the law favoured the criminal.* ❑ *Everyone helped and there were no grumbles.*

grumpy /'grʌmpi/ (**grumpier, grumpiest**) ADJ If you say that someone is **grumpy**, you think they are bad-tempered and miserable. [INFORMAL] ● **grumpily** ADV ❑ *I rolled grumpily out of bed.*

G

grunt /grʌnt/ (**grunts, grunting, grunted**) **1** V-T/V-I & N-COUNT If someone **grunts**, they make a low rough noise called a **grunt**, often because they do not want to talk. ❑ *'Rubbish,' I grunted.* ❑ *He grunted his thanks.* ❑ *...grunts of approval.* **2** V-I When an animal, usually a pig, **grunts**, it makes a low rough noise.

guarantee /ˌgærən'ti:/ (**guarantees, guaranteeing, guaranteed**) **1** V-T & N-COUNT If one thing **guarantees** another, or if one thing is a **guarantee of** another, the first is certain to cause the second thing to happen. ❑ *Money does not guarantee happiness.* ❑ *Reports of this kind are guaranteed to cause anxiety.* ❑ *A famous old name on a firm is not always a guarantee of quality.* **2** V-T & N-COUNT If you **guarantee** something, you promise that it is definitely true, or that you will do or provide it for someone. You refer to a promise like this as your **guarantee**. ❑ *We guarantee to refund your money if you are not delighted.* ❑ *The government will guarantee your pension.* ❑ *He could give no guarantee that the move would be permanent.* **3** V-T & N-COUNT If a company **guarantees** its product or work it has carried out, it provides a written promise called a **guarantee** which states that if the product or work has any faults within a specified time, it will be repaired or replaced free of charge.

guard /gɑ:d/ (**guards, guarding, guarded**) **1** V-T If you **guard** a place, person, or object, you watch them carefully, either to protect them or to stop them from escaping. ❑ *A few men were left outside to guard her.* ❑ *...the heavily guarded border.* **2** N-COUNT & PHRASE A **guard** is someone such as a soldier or prison officer who is guarding a particular place or person. When a soldier or prison officer is guarding someone or something, you say that they are **on guard** or **standing guard**. **3** N-SING A **guard** is a specially organized group of people, such as soldiers or policemen, who protect or watch someone or something. ❑ *We have a security guard around the whole area.* **4** N-COUNT A **guard** is a person whose job is to check tickets on a train and ensure that the train travels safely and punctually. **5** V-T If you **guard** something important or secret, you protect or hide it. ❑ *He closely guarded her identity.* ● **guarded** ADJ ❑ *He was hoping to keep the visit a closely guarded secret.* **6** N-COUNT A **guard** is a protective device which covers a part of someone's body or a dangerous part of a piece of equipment. **7** PHRASE If someone **catches** you **off guard**, they surprise you by doing something when you are not expecting it. **8** PHRASE If you are **on** your **guard**, or if you are **on guard**, you are being very careful because you think a situation might become difficult or dangerous. ❑ *He was constantly on his guard, trusting no one.*

guard

▶ **guard against** PHR-VERB If you **guard against** something, you are careful to prevent it from happening, or you take action to avoid being affected by it. ❑ *To guard against mountain lion attacks, we advise people to keep pets inside at night.*

Word Partnership Use *guard* with:

N.	guard **a door/house/prisoner** 1 2
	prison guard, **security** guard 2

guardian /'gɑ:diən/ (**guardians**) **1** N-COUNT A **guardian** is someone who has been legally appointed to look after another person's affairs, for example those of a child or someone who is mentally ill. **2** N-COUNT If you consider someone a defender or protector of something, you can call them its **guardian**. ❑ *He became, at a very early age, a guardian of tradition.*

guerrilla also **guerilla** /gə'rɪlə/ (**guerrillas**) N-COUNT A **guerrilla** is a person who fights as part of an unofficial army, usually an army which is fighting against the existing government of a country.

guess /ges/ (**guesses, guessing, guessed**) **1** V-T & N-COUNT If you **guess** something, or if you make a **guess** about something, you form an idea or opinion about it, knowing that it may not be true or accurate because you do not have all the relevant facts. ❑ *Wood guessed that she was a very successful publisher or a banker.* ❑ *You can only guess at what suffering they endure.* ❑ *My guess is that the answer will be negative.* **2** V-T If you **guess that** something is the case, you correctly form the opinion that it is the case, although you do not have definite knowledge about it. ❑ *He should have guessed what would happen.* ❑ *Someone might have guessed our secret.* **3** PHRASE You say **I guess** to indicate slight uncertainty or reluctance about what you are saying. ❑ *I guess he's right.*

Thesaurus *guess* Also look up:

V.	estimate, predict, suspect 1
N.	assumption, prediction, theory 2

Word Partnership Use *guess* with:

N.	guess **a secret** 1 2
V.	**make a** guess 2 3
ADJ.	**educated** guess, **good** guess, **wild** guess 3

guest /gest/ (**guests**) **1** N-COUNT A **guest** is someone who has been invited to stay in your home, attend an event, or appear on a radio or television show. ❑ *She was a guest at the wedding.* ❑ *...a frequent chat show guest.* **2** N-COUNT A **guest** is someone who is staying in a hotel.
→ see **hotel**

Word Partnership Use *guest* with:

V.	**be *someone's*** guest, **entertain a** guest 1
	accommodate a guest 1 3
N.	guest **appearance**, guest **list**, guest **speaker** 1 2
	hotel guest 3
ADJ.	**unwelcome** guest 1 3

guidance /ˈgaɪdəns/ N-UNCOUNT **Guidance** is help and advice. ❑ *...the reports which were produced under his guidance.*

guide /gaɪd/ (**guides, guiding, guided**) 1 N-COUNT A **guide** is a person who shows tourists round places such as museums or cities, or shows people the way through difficult country. 2 V-T If you **guide** someone somewhere, you go there with them in order to show them the way, and perhaps to explain points of interest to them. ❑ *He took her by the arm and guided her out.* ❑ *...a guided tour of the eight-bedroom house.* 3 N-COUNT A **guide** or **guide book** is a book which gives information about a town, area, or country, or information to help you understand something. ❑ *...the Pocket Guide to Butterflies.* 4 N-COUNT A **guide** is something that can be used to help you plan your actions or to form an opinion about something. ❑ *As a rough guide, a horse needs 2.5 per cent of its body weight in food every day.* 5 V-T If you **guide** someone, you influence their actions or decisions. ❑ *Be guided by your body and try anything that seems to help the pain.*

Thesaurus *guide* Also look up:

V.	accompany, direct, instruct, lead, navigate; (*ant.*) follow 2
N.	directory, handbook, information 3

guideline /ˈgaɪdlaɪn/ (**guidelines**) N-COUNT A **guideline** is a rule or piece of advice about how to do something. ❑ *Are there strict guidelines for animal experimentation?*

guild /gɪld/ (**guilds**) N-COUNT A **guild** is an organization of people who do the same job or who share an interest. ❑ *...the Guild of Food Writers.*

guilt /gɪlt/ 1 N-UNCOUNT **Guilt** is an unhappy feeling that you have because you have done something bad. ❑ *...his feeling of guilt towards his son.* 2 N-UNCOUNT **Guilt** is the fact that you have done something bad or illegal. ❑ *There was some evidence of Mr Birrell's guilt.*

Word Partnership Use *guilt* with:

N.	**burden of** guilt, **feelings of** guilt, **sense of** guilt, guilt **trip** 1
V.	**admit** guilt 2

guilty /ˈgɪlti/ (**guiltier, guiltiest**) 1 ADJ If you **feel guilty**, you feel unhappy because you have done something bad or have failed to do something which you should have done. ● **guiltily** ADV ❑ *He glanced guiltily over his shoulder.* 2 ADJ BEFORE N You use **guilty** to describe an action or fact that you feel guilty about. ❑ *...a guilty secret.* 3 ADJ If someone is **guilty of** doing something bad or committing a crime, they have done a bad thing or committed a crime. ❑ *He was found guilty of causing death by dangerous driving.* ❑ *If someone is guilty, he should be punished.*
→ see **trial**

Word Partnership Use *guilty* with:

V.	**feel** guilty, **look** guilty 1
	find someone guilty, **plead (not)** guilty, **prove someone** guilty 3
N.	guilty **conscience**, guilty **secret** 2
	guilty **party**, guilty **plea**, guilty **verdict** 3
PREP.	guilty **of *something*** 3

ˈ**guinea pig** (**guinea pigs**) 1 N-COUNT If someone is used as a **guinea pig** in an experiment, a drug or other treatment is tested for the first time on them. ❑ *The doctor used himself as a guinea pig to perfect a treatment.* 2 N-COUNT A **guinea pig** is a small furry animal without a tail.

guise /gaɪz/ (**guises**) N-COUNT If something is done or appears **under the guise of** something else, the first thing looks like the second thing or is made to look like it, in order to hide its true appearance or nature. ❑ *The men committed this murder under the guise of a political act.* ❑ *The new leaders are merely the old guard in a different guise.*

guitar /gɪˈtɑː/ (**guitars**) N-COUNT A **guitar** is a wooden musical instrument with six strings which are plucked or strummed. ● **guitarist** (**guitarists**) N-COUNT ❑ *...the world's best jazz guitarists.*
→ see **string**

gulf /gʌlf/ (**gulfs**) 1 N-COUNT A **gulf** is an important or significant difference between two people, things, or groups. ❑ *There is a growing gulf between rich and poor.* 2 N-COUNT A **gulf** is a large area of sea which extends a long way into the surrounding land. ❑ *...the Gulf of Mexico.*

gullible /ˈgʌlɪbəl/ ADJ If you say that someone is **gullible**, you think they are easily lied to. ● **gullibility** N-UNCOUNT ❑ *When I think back, I am ashamed of my gullibility.*

gully /ˈgʌli/ (**gullies**) N-COUNT A **gully** is a long narrow valley with steep sides.
→ see **erosion**

gulp /gʌlp/ (**gulps, gulping, gulped**) 1 V-T & N-COUNT If you **gulp** food or drink, or if you take **gulps of** food or drink, you swallow large quantities of it. ❑ *She quickly gulped her tea.* ❑ *He'd gulped it down in one bite.* ❑ *...a large gulp of whisky.* ❑ *He took the burger and swallowed it in two gulps.* 2 V-I & N-COUNT If you **gulp**, you swallow air, making a noise in your throat called a **gulp** as you do so, usually because you are nervous. ❑ *I gulped, and then proceeded to tell her the whole story.* ❑ *I realised with a gulp why my doctor had given me that advice.*

gum /gʌm/ (**gums**) 1 N-UNCOUNT **Gum** is a substance, often mint-flavoured, which you chew for a long time but do not swallow. 2 N-UNCOUNT **Gum** is a type of glue that you use to stick paper together. 3 N-COUNT Your **gums** are the areas of firm pink flesh inside your mouth, which your teeth grow out of.
→ see **teeth**

gun /gʌn/ (**guns, gunning, gunned**) 1 N-COUNT A **gun** is a weapon from which bullets or pellets

g

are fired. 2 PHRASE If you **stick to** your **guns**, you continue to have your own opinion about something, even though other people disagree or try to make you change your mind. [INFORMAL]
▸ **gun down** PHR-VERB If someone **is gunned down**, they are shot and severely injured or killed.

gunfire /ˈɡʌnfaɪə/ N-UNCOUNT **Gunfire** is the repeated shooting of guns. ❑ *He died during an exchange of gunfire.*

gunman /ˈɡʌnmən/ (**gunmen**) N-COUNT A **gunman** is someone who uses a gun to commit a crime. [JOURNALISM]

gunpoint /ˈɡʌnpɔɪnt/ PHRASE If someone **holds** you **at gunpoint**, they threaten to shoot you if you do not obey them.

G

gunshot /ˈɡʌnʃɒt/ (**gunshots**) 1 N-COUNT A **gunshot** is the firing of a gun or the sound of a gun being fired. ❑ *He heard gunshots.* 2 N-UNCOUNT **Gunshot** is used to refer to bullets that are fired from a gun. ❑ *A policeman suffered gunshot wounds.*

gurgle /ˈɡɜːɡəl/ (**gurgles, gurgling, gurgled**) 1 V-I When water **gurgles**, it makes a bubbling sound. ❑ *...the sound of hot water gurgling through the van's engine.* 2 V-I When a baby **gurgles**, it makes bubbling sounds in its throat, usually because it is happy.

guru /ˈɡuːruː/ (**gurus**) 1 N-COUNT A **guru** is a spiritual leader and teacher, especially in Hinduism. 2 N-COUNT A **guru** is someone that many people regard as an expert or leader. ❑ *...fashion gurus.*

gush /ɡʌʃ/ (**gushes, gushing, gushed**) 1 V-I & N-SING When liquid **gushes** out of something, or if there is a **gush of** liquid from something, a large quantity of liquid flows out very quickly. ❑ *Piping-hot water gushed out.* ❑ *I heard a gush of water.* 2 V-I If you say that someone **gushes about** something, you mean that they express their admiration or pleasure in a way that seems exaggerated and false. ❑ *He gushed about his new-found happiness.*
• **gushing** ADJ ❑ *He wrote Jones a gushing fan letter a few years ago.*

gust /ɡʌst/ (**gusts, gusting, gusted**) 1 N-COUNT A **gust** is a short, strong, sudden rush of wind. 2 V-I When the wind **gusts**, it blows with short, strong, sudden rushes. ❑ *The wind gusted up to 164 miles an hour.*

gut /ɡʌt/ (**guts, gutting, gutted**) 1 N-PLURAL A person's or animal's **guts** are all their internal organs. [INFORMAL] 2 V-T If someone **guts** a fish or a dead animal, they remove its internal organs. 3 N-SING **The gut** is the tube inside your body through which food passes while it is being digested. 4 N-UNCOUNT **Guts** is courage. [INFORMAL] ❑ *The new Chancellor has the guts to push through unpopular tax increases.* 5 ADJ A **gut feeling** or **response** is based on instinct or emotion rather than on reason. ❑ *My gut reaction was very positive.* 6 V-T If a building **is gutted**, the inside is destroyed, leaving only the outside walls. ❑ *The fire gutted the building, where 60 people lived.*

gutter /ˈɡʌtə/ (**gutters**) 1 N-COUNT The **gutter** is the edge of a road next to the pavement, where rain collects and flows away. 2 N-COUNT A **gutter** is a channel fixed to the edge of a roof, which rain water drains into. 3 N-SING You can use **the gutter** to refer to a condition of life in which someone is poor and has no self-respect. ❑ *Instead of ending up in the gutter, he was remarkably successful.*

guy /ɡaɪ/ (**guys**) 1 N-COUNT A **guy** is a man. [INFORMAL] ❑ *I was working with a guy from Manchester.* 2 N-VOC & N-PLURAL Americans sometimes address a group of people, whether they are male or female, as **guys** or **you guys**.

gym /dʒɪm/ (**gyms**) 1 N-COUNT A **gym** is the same as a **gymnasium**. 2 N-UNCOUNT **Gym** means **gymnastics**.

gymnasium /dʒɪmˈneɪziəm/ (**gymnasiums**) N-COUNT A **gymnasium** is a club or room, usually containing special equipment, where people can exercise.

gymnastic /dʒɪmˈnæstɪk/ (**gymnastics**)

The form **gymnastic** is used as a modifier.

N-PLURAL **Gymnastics** consists of physical exercises that develop your strength, co-ordination, and agility. ❑ *...gymnastic exercises.*

gynaecology [AM **gynecology**] /ˌɡaɪnɪˈkɒlədʒi/ N-UNCOUNT **Gynaecology** is the branch of medical science which deals with women's diseases and medical conditions.

gypsy also **gipsy** /ˈdʒɪpsi/ (**gypsies**) N-COUNT A **gypsy** is a member of a race of people who travel from place to place in caravans, rather than living in one place.

Hh

habit /ˈhæbɪt/ (**habits**) 1 N-VAR A **habit** is something that you do often or regularly. ❑ *He has an awkward habit of smiling at the wrong moment.* ❑ *...a survey on eating habits in the UK.* 2 PHRASE If you **are in the habit of** doing something or **make a habit of** doing it, you do it regularly or often. If you **get into the habit of** doing something, you begin to do it regularly or often. ❑ *You can phone me at work as long as you don't make a habit of it.* 3 N-COUNT A **drug habit** is an addiction to a drug such as heroin.

habitat /ˈhæbɪtæt/ (**habitats**) N-COUNT The **habitat** of an animal or plant is its natural environment in which it normally lives or grows. → see Word Web: **habitat**

habitual /həˈbɪtʃuəl/ ADJ A **habitual** state or way of behaving is one that someone usually has or does, especially one that is considered to be typical or characteristic of them. ❑ *With her habitual honesty, she talked about being a mother.* ● **habitually** ADV ❑ *They habitually used bad language.*

hack /hæk/ (**hacks, hacking, hacked**) 1 V-T & PHR-VERB If you **hack** something, or if you **hack away at** it, you cut it with strong, rough strokes using a sharp tool such as an axe or knife. ❑ *Ten people were hacked to death.* ❑ *He started to hack away at the tree bark.* 2 N-COUNT If you refer to a professional writer such as a journalist as a **hack**, you disapprove of them because they write for money without worrying very much about the quality of their writing. 3 V-I When someone **hacks into** a computer system, they break into the system, especially in order to get secret information that is stored there. [COMPUTING] ● **hacker** (**hackers**) N-COUNT ❑ *Once inside their systems, the hackers stole information.* ● **hacking** N-UNCOUNT ❑ *...the illegal art of computer hacking.* → see **Internet**

▸ **hack away** → see **hack** (meaning 1)

▸ **hack off** PHR-VERB If you **hack** something **off**, you cut it off with strong, rough strokes using a sharp tool such as an axe or knife. ❑ *Kim even hacked off her long hair.*

had /hæd/ **Had** is the past tense and past participle of **have**.

haddock /ˈhædək/

The form **haddock** is also used as the plural.

N-VAR A **haddock** is a type of sea fish. **Haddock** is the flesh of this fish eaten as food.

hadn't /ˈhædənt/ **Hadn't** is the usual spoken form of 'had not'.

haemorrhage [AM **hemorrhage**] /ˈhemərɪdʒ/ (**haemorrhages, haemorrhaging, haemorrhaged**) V-I & N-VAR If someone **is haemorrhaging**, or if they have a **haemorrhage**, they are bleeding heavily because of broken blood vessels inside their body. ❑ *Paula became very ill and began to haemorrhage badly.* ● **haemorrhaging** N-UNCOUNT ❑ *The doctors said he died from shock and haemorrhaging.*

haggle /ˈhægəl/ (**haggles, haggling, haggled**) V-I If you **haggle**, you argue about something before reaching an agreement, especially about the cost of something. ❑ *Of course he'll still haggle over the price.* ● **haggling** N-UNCOUNT ❑ *How would you feel about haggling over the price of your next holiday?*

hail /heɪl/ (**hails, hailing, hailed**) 1 V-T If a person or event **is hailed as** important or successful, they are praised publicly. ❑ *US magazines hailed her as the greatest rock'n'roll singer in the world.* 2 N-UNCOUNT **Hail** consists of tiny balls of ice that fall like rain from the sky. 3 N-SING A **hail of** things, usually small objects, is a large number of them that hit you at the same time and with great force. ❑ *The leader and his assistant were*

Word Web: habitat

The **environment** where a plant or animal lives is its **habitat**. The habitat provides **food**, **water**, and **shelter**. Each habitat has different **temperatures**, **rainfall**, and amounts of **sunlight**. A **desert** is a sunny, dry habitat where few plants and animals can live. The **tropical rainforest** gets heavy rain every day and has many types of **vegetation** and animal life. **Grasslands** or **prairies** get little rain but are home to many **grass**-eating animals. The boreal **forest** is the largest **biome** in the world. Its winters are cold and snowy, and summers are warm, rainy, and humid.

desert

boreal forest

rainforest

grassland

h

Picture Dictionary hair

killed in a hail of bullets. **4** V-T If you **hail** a taxi, you wave at it in order to stop it and ask the driver to take you somewhere.
→ see **storm**

hair /heə/ (**hairs**) **1** N-VAR Your **hair** is the mass of fine thread-like strands that grow on your head. **2** N-VAR **Hair** is all the short, fine, thread-like material that grows on different parts of your body. ❑ *Most men have hair on their chest.* **3** N-VAR **Hair** is the rough, thread-like material that covers the body of an animal such as a dog, or makes up a horse's mane and tail. **4** N-COUNT **Hairs** are very fine thread-like strands that grow on some insects and plants.
→ see Picture Dictionary: **hair**
→ see Word Web: **hair**

Word Partnership Use *hair* with:

ADJ.	**black/blonde/brown/grey** hair, **curly/straight/wavy** hair **1**
V.	**bleach your** hair, **brush/comb your** hair, **colour your** hair, **cut your** hair, **do your** hair, **dry your** hair, **fix your** hair, **lose your** hair, **pull *someone's*** hair, **wash your** hair **1**
N.	**lock of** hair **1**

haircut /ˈheəkʌt/ (**haircuts**) **1** N-COUNT If you have a **haircut**, someone cuts your hair for you. **2** N-COUNT A **haircut** is the style in which your hair has been cut. ❑ *Who's that guy with the funny haircut?*

hairdresser /ˈheədresə/ (**hairdressers**) N-COUNT A **hairdresser** is a person who cuts, washes, and styles people's hair. You can refer to the shop where a hairdresser works as a **hairdresser** or a **hairdresser's**. ● **hairdressing** N-UNCOUNT ❑ *Michael started hairdressing when he was nine.*

hairstyle /ˈheəstaɪl/ (**hairstyles**) N-COUNT Your **hairstyle** is the style in which your hair has been cut or arranged. ❑ *I think her new short hairstyle looks great.*

hairy /ˈheəri/ (**hairier, hairiest**) **1** ADJ Someone or something that is **hairy** is covered with a lot of hair. **2** ADJ If you describe a situation as **hairy**, you mean that it is exciting but rather frightening. [INFORMAL] ❑ *His driving was a bit hairy.*

halal /həˈlɑːl/ N-UNCOUNT **Halal** is meat from animals that have been killed according to Muslim law. ❑ *...halal meat.*

half /hɑːf, AM hæf/ (**halves**) **1** N-COUNT & PREDET & ADJ **Half** of an amount or object is one of two equal parts that together make up the whole amount or object. ❑ *Cut the tomatoes in half.* ❑ *The bridge was re-built in two halves.* ❑ *She's half his age.* ❑ *...the first half hour.* **2** N-COUNT In games such as football and rugby, matches are divided into two equal periods of time which are called **halves**. ❑ *...early in the second half.* **3** ADV You use **half** to say that something is only partly the case or happens to only a limited extent. ❑ *His fridge is usually half empty.* ❑ *She'd half expected him to give up the course.* **4** ADV You can use **half** to say that someone has parents of different nationalities. For example, if you are **half** German, one of your parents is German. **5** PREP You use **half past** to refer to a time that is thirty minutes after a particular hour.

Word Web hair

Only about 90 percent of the **hair** on your **scalp** is alive. The other 10 percent is dead and getting ready to **fall out**. Each hair grows about a centimeter a month for two to six years. Then it falls out and the cycle starts all over again. It's normal to lose about 100 hairs a day from your scalp. To keep hair healthy, eat a healthy diet and use a good **shampoo** and conditioner. Gently **brush** and **comb** your hair. Avoid strong **dyes**. Using the "cool" setting on your hairdryer also helps.

❑ *...half past twelve.* 6 PHRASE If you increase something **by half**, half of the original amount is added to it. If you decrease it **by half**, half of the original amount is taken away from it. ❑ *The number of 7-year-olds who can't read has grown by half over the past 5 years.*

'half-ˌbrother (**half-brothers**) N-COUNT Someone's **half-brother** is a boy or man who has either the same mother or the same father as they have. ❑ *Peter, my half-brother, lives in Canada.*

ˌhalf-'hearted ADJ If someone does something in a **half-hearted** way, they do it without any real interest or effort. ❑ *...a half-hearted apology.* ❑ *Her job application was a bit half-hearted.* ● **half-heartedly** ADV ❑ *I can't do anything half-heartedly. I have to do everything 100 per cent.*

'half-ˌsister (**half-sisters**) N-COUNT Someone's **half-sister** is a girl or woman who has either the same mother or the same father as they have.

ˌhalf-'time N-UNCOUNT In sport, **half-time** is the short rest period between the two parts of a game.

halfway also **half-way** /ˌhɑːf'weɪ, AM ˌhæf-/ 1 ADV **Halfway** means in the middle of a place or in between two points, at an equal distance from each of them. ❑ *He was halfway up the ladder.* 2 ADV & ADJ BEFORE N **Halfway** means at the middle of a period of time or an event. ❑ *We were more than halfway through our tour.* ❑ *...the halfway point of the match.*

hall /hɔːl/ (**halls**) 1 N-COUNT In a house or flat, the **hall** is the area just inside the front door. 2 N-COUNT A **hall** is a large room or building which is used for public events such as concerts, exhibitions, and meetings. ❑ *...a dance in the village hall.* ❑ *...the Royal Albert Hall in London.*
→ see **house**

Word Partnership Use *hall* with:

PREP.	**across the** hall, **down the** hall, **in the** hall 1
N.	**concert** hall, **lecture** hall, **meeting** hall, **pool** hall 2

hallmark /'hɔːlmɑːk/ (**hallmarks**) 1 N-COUNT The **hallmark** of something or someone is their most typical quality or feature. ❑ *Good design is the hallmark of the company.* 2 N-COUNT A **hallmark** is an official mark that is put on objects made of gold, silver, or platinum that indicates the quality of the metal.

hallo /hæ'ləʊ/ → see **hello**

hallowed /'hæləʊd/ 1 ADJ **Hallowed** is used to describe something that is respected and admired, usually because it is old or important. ❑ *...the hallowed lawns of Wimbledon Tennis Club.* 2 ADJ **Hallowed** is used to describe something that is considered to be holy. ❑ *...hallowed ground.*

Halloween also **Hallowe'en** /ˌhæləʊw'iːn/ N-UNCOUNT **Halloween** is the night of the 31st of October and it is traditionally said to be the time when ghosts and witches can be seen.

h

Word Link *luc ≈ light : hallucination, lucid, translucent*

hallucination /həˌluːsɪ'neɪʃən/ (**hallucinations**) N-COUNT A **hallucination** is something that is not real that someone sees because they are ill or have taken a drug. ❑ *Geena has hallucinations about a house by the sea.*

hallway /'hɔːlweɪ/ (**hallways**) N-COUNT A **hallway** is the entrance hall of a house or other building.

halo /'heɪləʊ/ (**haloes** or **halos**) N-COUNT A **halo** is a circle of light that is drawn in pictures round the head of a holy figure such as a saint.

halt /hɔːlt/ (**halts, halting, halted**) 1 V-T/V-I & PHRASE When a vehicle or person **halts** or when something **halts** them, they stop moving along and stand still. You can also say that they **come to a halt**. ❑ *She held her hand out flat, to halt him.* ❑ *The lift came to a halt.* 2 V-T/V-I & PHRASE When something such as development or activity **halts**, or when you **halt** it, it stops completely. You can also say that these things **come to a halt**. ❑ *The government is trying to halt nearly two years of violence.*

halve /hɑːv, AM hæv/ (**halves, halving, halved**) 1 V-T/V-I When you **halve** something, or when it **halves**, it is reduced to half its previous size or amount. ❑ *Sales of their cars have halved in America in the past two weeks.* 2 V-T If you **halve** something, you divide it into two equal parts. ❑ *Halve the peppers and remove the seeds.* 3 **Halves** is the plural of **half**.

ham /hæm/ (**hams**) N-VAR **Ham** is meat from the top of the back leg of a pig, which has been cooked and is usually eaten cold. ❑ *...a huge baked ham.* ❑ *...ham sandwiches.*

hamburger /'hæmbɜːgə/ (**hamburgers**) N-COUNT A **hamburger** is a flat round mass of minced beef, fried and eaten in a bread roll.

hamlet /'hæmlɪt/ (**hamlets**) N-COUNT A **hamlet** is a small village.

hammer /'hæmə/ (**hammers, hammering, hammered**) 1 N-COUNT A **hammer** is a tool used for hitting things. It consists of a heavy piece of metal at the end of a handle. 2 V-T & PHR-VERB If you **hammer** something such as a nail, you hit it with a hammer. If you **hammer it in**, you hit

it into a surface, using a hammer. ❑ *Her mother hammered a nail into the window frame.* **3** V-T/V-I If you **hammer** a surface or **hammer on** it, you hit it several times. ❑ *He hammered his fists on the table.* **4** V-T If a person or organization **is being hammered**, they are being severely attacked, defeated, or harmed. [BRIT, INFORMAL] ❑ *Leverkusen have just been hammered 6-2 by Olympiakos in the first stage of the competition.*
→ see **tool**
▶ **hammer in** → see **hammer** (meaning **2**)
▶ **hammer out** PHR-VERB If you **hammer out** something such as a plan, you reach an agreement about it after a long or difficult discussion. ❑ *Diplomats met to hammer out a plan.*

hamper /ˈhæmpə/ (**hampers, hampering, hampered**) **1** V-T If someone or something **hampers** you, they make it difficult for you to do what you are trying to do. ❑ *Alderton's career as a professional footballer was hampered by a knee injury.* **2** N-COUNT A **picnic hamper** is a large basket with a lid, used for carrying food.

H

hamstring /ˈhæmstrɪŋ/ (**hamstrings, hamstringing, hamstrung**) **1** N-COUNT A **hamstring** is a tendon behind your knee joining the muscles of your thigh to the bones of your lower leg. **2** V-T If you **are hamstrung** by something, it makes it very difficult for you to take any action. [JOURNALISM] ❑ *These countries are often hamstrung by lack of money.*

hand

❶ NOUN AND PHRASE USES
❷ VERB USES

hand /hænd/ (**hands**)
❶ **1** N-COUNT Your **hands** are the parts of your body at the end of your arms, below the wrist. **2** N-COUNT The **hands of** a **clock** or **watch** are the thin pieces of metal or plastic that indicate what time it is. **3** N-SING If you ask someone for **a hand** with something, you are asking them to help you. ❑ *Come and give me a hand in the garden.* ❑ *I'd be glad to lend a hand.* **4** N-COUNT In a game of cards, your **hand** is the cards which are dealt to you. **5** PHRASE If something is **at hand, near at hand**, or **close at hand**, it is very near in place or time. ❑ *She lay in bed, with the phone close at hand.* **6** PHRASE If you do something **by hand**, you do it using your hands rather than a machine. ❑ *...a dress made entirely by hand.* **7** PHRASE When something **changes hands**, its ownership changes, usually because it is sold to someone else. **8** PHRASE If you **force** someone's **hand**, you force them to do something before they are ready to do it, or to do something they do not want to do. **9** PHRASE If someone gives you **a free hand**, they allow you to do what you want in a particular situation. **10** PHRASE If two things **go hand in hand**, they are closely connected and cannot be considered separately from each other. ❑ *Yvette's rise to fame went hand in hand with the growth of the club.* **11** PHRASE If you **have a hand in** something, you are one of the people involved in doing it or creating it. **12** PHRASE If a situation is **in hand**, it is under control. ❑ *The Olympic organisers say that matters are well in hand.* **13** PHRASE If someone **lives from hand to mouth**, they have hardly enough food or money to live on. **14** PHRASE If someone or something is **on hand**, they are near and able to be used if they are needed. ❑ *The footwear department has experts on hand to give you all the help and advice you need.* **15** PHRASE You use **on the other hand** to introduce the second of two contrasting points, facts, or ways of looking at something. You can use **on the one hand** in an earlier sentence to introduce the first part of the contrast. ❑ *On the one hand, if the body doesn't have enough cholesterol, we would not be able to survive. On the other hand, if the body has too much cholesterol, the excess begins to line the arteries.*

Usage

Be careful not to confuse **on the contrary** with **on the other hand**. **On the contrary** is used to contradict someone or something, to say that they are wrong. **On the other hand** is used to state a different, often contrasting aspect of the situation you are considering. ❑ *Prices of foods and consumer goods fell. Wages on the other hand increased.* ❑ *He had no wish to hurt her. On the contrary, he thought of her with warmth and affection.*

16 PHRASE If you reject an idea **out of hand**, you reject it without hesitating and without discussing it or considering it first. ❑ *I dismissed the idea out of hand.* **17** PHRASE If you have something **to hand** or **near to hand**, you have it with you or near you, ready to use when needed. ❑ *You may want to keep this brochure safe, so you have it to hand whenever you may need it.* **18** PHRASE If you **try** your **hand at** an activity, you attempt to do it, usually for the first time. **19** PHRASE If you **wash** your **hands of** someone or something, you refuse to be involved with them any more or to take responsibility for them.
→ see Picture Dictionary: **hand**
→ see **body, time**

hand /hænd/ (**hands, handing, handed**)
❷ V-T If you **hand** something to someone, you pass it to them. ❑ *He handed me a little bit of white paper.*
▶ **hand down** or **hand on** PHR-VERB If you **hand** something such as your knowledge or possessions **down**, or **hand** it **on**, you pass it on to other people, often people of a younger generation. ❑ *...a Ukrainian folk story handed down from their parents.*
▶ **hand in** PHR-VERB If you **hand** something **in**, you give it to someone in authority, so that they can deal with it. ❑ *If you find something on a bus, you must hand it in to the police.* ❑ *Messier finally handed in his resignation on Monday.*
▶ **hand on** → see **hand down**
▶ **hand out** **1** PHR-VERB If you **hand** something **out**, you give it to people. ❑ *One of my jobs was to hand out the prizes.* **2** → see also **handout**
▶ **hand over** PHR-VERB If you **hand** something **over** to someone, you give it to them. ❑ *He handed over a letter from the Prime Minister.*
▶ **hand over to** PHR-VERB If you **hand over to** someone, you give them the responsibility for dealing with a particular situation which was previously your responsibility. ❑ *The present leaders have decided to hand over to a younger generation.*

handbag /ˈhændbæg/ (**handbags**) N-COUNT In British English, a **handbag** is a small bag used by women to carry things such as money and keys. The usual American word is **purse**.

handbook /ˈhændbʊk/ (**handbooks**) N-COUNT

Picture Dictionary hand

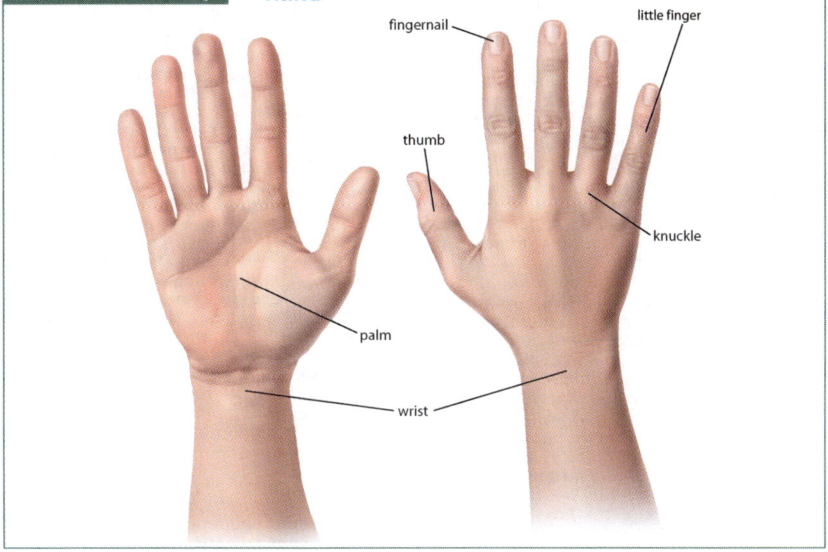

A **handbook** is a book giving advice or instructions on how to do a practical task.

handcuff /'hændkʌf/ (**handcuffs, handcuffing, handcuffed**) **1** N-PLURAL **Handcuffs** are two metal rings linked by a short chain which are locked round a prisoner's wrists. ❑ *He was led away to jail in handcuffs.* **2** V-T If the police **handcuff** someone, they put handcuffs around their wrists. ❑ *She was handcuffed to a police officer.*

Word Link *ful ≈ quantity that fills : handful, mouthful, plentiful*

handful /'hændfʊl/ (**handfuls**) **1** N-SING If there is only a **handful of** people or things, there are not very many of them. ❑ *...a handful of customers.* **2** N-COUNT A **handful of** something is the amount of it that you can hold in your hand. ❑ *...a handful of sand.* **3** N-COUNT If you describe someone, especially a child, as a **handful**, you mean that he or she is difficult to control. [INFORMAL]

handicap /'hændikæp/ (**handicaps, handicapping, handicapped**) **1** N-COUNT A **handicap** is a physical or mental disability. Many people find this term offensive. [DATED] ❑ *He lost his leg when he was ten, but learnt to live with his handicap.* **2** V-T & N-COUNT If an event or a situation **handicaps** someone or something, or if it is a **handicap to** them, it places them at a disadvantage. ❑ *High stress levels may handicap some students.* ❑ *The tax issue was undoubtedly a handicap to Labour.*

handicapped /'hændikæpt/ ADJ A **handicapped** person has a physical or mental disability. Many people find this term offensive. [DATED] ❑ *Alex was mentally handicapped.*

handkerchief /'hæŋkətʃɪf/ (**handkerchiefs**) N-COUNT A **handkerchief** is a small square of fabric which you use for blowing your nose.

handle

handle /'hændəl/ (**handles, handling, handled**) **1** N-COUNT A **handle** is the part of an object such as a tool, bag, or cup that you hold in order to be able to pick up and use the object. **2** N-COUNT A **handle** is a small round object or a lever that is attached to a door and is used for opening and closing it. ❑ *I turned the handle and went in.* **3** V-T/V-I When you **handle** something such as a weapon or car, you use or control it effectively. You can also say that a vehicle **handles well** or **badly**, depending on how easy it is to steer. ❑ *I want someone who can handle a gun.* ❑ *His ship handled well.* **4** V-T If you **handle** a problem or a particular area of work, you deal with it. ❑ *You must learn how to handle your feelings.* ❑ *She handled all the travel arrangements.* • **handling** N-UNCOUNT ❑ *He praised police for their calm handling of the situation.* **5** V-T When you **handle** an object or a person, you hold them or touch them with your hands. ❑ *I was really excited when I heard I might be handling a newborn baby.*

Word Partnership Use *handle* with:

N.	**ability to** handle ***something*** 3 4 handle **a job/problem/situation**, handle **pressure/responsibility** 4
ADJ.	**difficult/easy/hard to** handle 4

handler /'hændlə/ (**handlers**) N-COUNT A **handler** is someone whose job is to be in charge of a particular type of thing. ❑ *...baggage handlers at*

h

Gatwick airport. ❑ ...*dog handlers*.

handmade /ˌhænd'meɪd/ ADJ If something is **handmade**, it is made without using machines. ❑ ...*a pair of handmade shoes*.

handout /'hændaʊt/ (**handouts**) 1 N-COUNT A **handout** is money, clothing, or food which is given to people who are badly in need of it. ❑ *Every family should be given a monthly handout of £10 per person*. 2 N-COUNT A **handout** is a document which gives information about something.

Word Link	*free ≈ without : carefree, duty-free, hands-free*

'hands-ˌfree ADJ BEFORE N A **hands-free** phone or other device can be used without being held in your hand.

handshake /'hændʃeɪk/ (**handshakes**) N-COUNT If you give someone a **handshake**, you grasp their right hand with your right hand and move it up and down as a greeting, or to show that you have agreed about something.

H

handsome /'hænsəm/ 1 ADJ A **handsome** man has an attractive face. 2 ADJ A **handsome** woman has an attractive appearance with large regular features rather than small delicate ones. 3 ADJ BEFORE N A **handsome** sum of money is a large or generous amount. [FORMAL] ❑ *They will make a handsome profit*. 4 → See note at **beautiful**

ˌhands-'on ADJ **Hands-on** experience or work involves actually doing a particular thing, rather than just talking about it or getting someone else to do it. ❑ ...*hands-on experience of computers*.

handwriting /'hændraɪtɪŋ/ N-UNCOUNT Your **handwriting** is your style of writing with a pen or pencil.

handwritten /ˌhænd'rɪtən/ ADJ A **handwritten** piece of writing was written with a pen or pencil, rather than being typed.

handy /'hændi/ (**handier, handiest**) 1 ADJ Something that is **handy** is useful. ❑ ...*handy hints on looking after indoor plants*. 2 ADJ A thing or place that is **handy** is nearby and convenient. ❑ *Keep a pen and pad handy by the phone*. 3 ADJ AFTER LINK-V Someone who is **handy with** a particular tool or weapon is skilful at using it.

hang /hæŋ/ (**hangs, hanging, hung**)

The form **hanged** is used as the past tense and past participle in meaning 3.

1 V-T/V-I & PHR-VERB If something **hangs** in a high place or position, or if you **hang** it there, it is attached there so it does not touch the ground. **Hang up** means the same as **hang**. ❑ *A young woman was hanging clothes on a line*. ❑ *Some prisoners climbed onto the roof and hung up a banner*. ❑ *The walls are hung with old cinema posters*. 2 V-I If a piece of clothing or fabric **hangs** in a particular way or position, that is how it is worn or arranged. ❑ ...*the scarf hanging loose from her shoulders*. 3 V-T If someone **is hanged**, they are killed by having a rope tied around their neck and the support taken away from under their feet. ❑ *He was hanged last month for murder*. 4 V-I If a future event or a possibility **hangs over** you, it worries you. ❑ *The threat of war hangs over them*. 5 PHRASE If you **get the hang of** something, you begin to understand how to do it. [INFORMAL]

▶ **hang about** or **hang around** or **hang round** PHR-VERB If you **hang about, hang around**, or **hang round** somewhere, you stay or wait there. [INFORMAL] ❑ *He got sick of hanging around waiting for me*.

▶ **hang back** PHR-VERB If you **hang back**, you move or stay slightly behind a person or group, usually because you are nervous about something.

▶ **hang on** 1 PHR-VERB If you ask someone to **hang on**, you mean you want them to wait for a moment. [INFORMAL] ❑ *Hang on a second. I'll come with you*. 2 PHR-VERB If you **hang on**, you manage to survive until a situation improves. ❑ *Manchester United hung on to take the Cup*. 3 PHR-VERB If you **hang on to** or **hang onto** something that gives you an advantage, you succeed in keeping it for yourself. ❑ *The President has been trying hard to hang onto power*. 4 PHR-VERB If you **hang on to** or **hang onto** something, you hold it very tightly. 5 PHR-VERB If one thing **hangs on** another, it depends on it. ❑ *The survival of the sport hangs on this race*.

▶ **hang out** 1 PHR-VERB When you **hang out** washing, you hang it on a clothes line to dry. 2 PHR-VERB If you **hang out** in a particular place or area, you go and stay there for no particular reason, or spend a lot of time there. [INFORMAL] ❑ *We can just hang out and have a good time*.

▶ **hang round** → see **hang about**

▶ **hang up** 1 → see **hang** (meaning 1) 2 PHR-VERB If you **hang up** or you **hang up** the phone, you end a phone call. If you **hang up on** someone, you end the phone call suddenly and unexpectedly by putting back the receiver. ❑ *Don't hang up!* ❑ *He said he'd call again, and hung up on me*.

hangar /'hæŋə/ (**hangars**) N-COUNT A **hangar** is a large building in which aircraft are kept.

hanger /'hæŋə/ (**hangers**) N-COUNT A **hanger** is a curved piece of metal, plastic or wood used for hanging clothes on.

hangover /'hæŋəʊvə/ (**hangovers**) 1 N-COUNT A **hangover** is a headache and feeling of sickness that you have after drinking too much alcohol. 2 N-COUNT Something that is a **hangover from** the past is an idea or way of behaving which people used to have in the past but which people no longer generally have. ❑ *This idea is a hangover from 20th-century politics*.

haphazard /hæp'hæzəd/ ADJ If you describe something as **haphazard**, you are critical of it because it is not at all organized or is not arranged according to a plan. ❑ *Some students find the move from school to university haphazard and confusing*. ● **haphazardly** ADV ❑ *Books were arranged haphazardly on the shelves*.

hapless /'hæpləs/ ADJ BEFORE N A **hapless** person is unlucky. [FORMAL] ❑ ...*his hapless victim*.

happen /'hæpən/ (**happens, happening, happened**) 1 V-I When something **happens**, it occurs or is done without being planned. ❑ *Tell me what happened*. ❑ *The accident was similar to one that happened in 1973*. 2 V-I When something **happens to** you, it takes place and affects you. ❑ *It's the best thing that ever happened to me*. 3 V-T If you **happen to** do something, you do it by chance. If **it happens that** something is the case, it occurs by chance. ❑ *I looked in the nearest paper, which happened to be the Daily Mail*. 4 PHRASE You use **as it happens** in order to introduce a statement, especially one that is rather surprising. ❑ *As it happened, the demonstration was rather small*.

happening /ˈhæpənɪŋ/ (**happenings**) N-COUNT **Happenings** are things that happen, often in a way that is unexpected or hard to explain. ❑ *Their team of reporters will cover the latest happenings.*

happy /ˈhæpi/ (**happier, happiest**) **1** ADJ Someone who is **happy** has feelings of joy or contentment. ❑ *Marina was a confident, happy child.* ● **happily** ADV ❑ *Joe and Irene are still happily married.* ● **happiness** N-UNCOUNT ❑ *Money can't buy happiness.* **2** ADJ A time or place that is **happy** is full of pleasant feelings, or has an atmosphere in which people feel happy. ❑ *She had a very happy childhood.* **3** ADJ AFTER LINK-V If you are **happy with** a situation or arrangement, you are satisfied with it. ❑ *I'm not happy with what I've written.* **4** ADJ AFTER LINK-V If you are **happy to** do something, you are willing to do it. ❑ *I'm happy to help.* **5** ADJ BEFORE N You use **happy** in greetings to say that you hope someone will enjoy a special occasion. ❑ *Happy Birthday!* **6** **many happy returns** → see **return** **7** ADJ You use **happy** to describe something that is fortunate or lucky. ❑ *By happy coincidence, Robert met Richard and Julia in town.* ● **happily** ADV ❑ *Happily, his injuries were not serious.*
→ see **emotion**

Thesaurus *happy* Also look up:

ADJ. cheerful, content, delighted, glad, pleased, upbeat; *(ant.)* sad, unhappy **1**

Word Partnership Use *happy* with:

ADV. **extremely/perfectly/very** happy **1**
V. **feel** happy, **make *someone*** happy, **seem** happy **1**
N. happy **ending**, happy **family**, happy **marriage** **1** **2**

harass /ˈhærəs, həˈræs/ (**harasses, harassing, harassed**) V-T If you **harass** someone, you continually trouble them. ❑ *We are always being harassed by the police.* ● **harassment** N-UNCOUNT ❑ *...rules to prevent harassment.*

harassed /ˈhærəst, həˈræst/ ADJ If you are **harassed**, you are anxious and tense because you have too much to do or too many problems to cope with. ❑ *I grew more and more harassed over my lack of money and having too much to do.*

harbour [AM **harbor**] /ˈhɑːbə/ (**harbours, harbouring, harboured**) **1** N-COUNT A **harbour** is an area of deep water which is protected from the sea by land or walls, so that boats can be left there safely. **2** V-T If you **harbour** an emotion, you have it for a long period of time. ❑ *He had always harboured political ambitions.* **3** V-T If a person or country **harbours** someone who is wanted by the police, they let them stay in their house or country and offer them protection.

hard /hɑːd/ (**harder, hardest**) **1** ADJ Something that is **hard** is very firm to touch and is not easily bent, cut, or broken. ❑ *...the hard wooden floor.* ● **hardness** N-UNCOUNT ❑ *...the hardness of a cricket ball.* **2** ADJ Something that is **hard** is very difficult. ❑ *At my age I would find it hard to get another job.* ❑ *I have had a hard life.* **3** ADV & ADJ If you try **hard** or work **hard**, you make a great effort to achieve something. ❑ *Am I trying too hard?* ❑ *I admired him as a true scientist and hard worker.* ❑ *Their work is hard and unglamorous.* **4** ADV & ADJ **Hard** means with a lot of force. ❑ *He kicked the door as hard as he could.* ❑ *He gave her a hard push.* **5** ADJ & ADV Someone who is **hard** shows no kindness or pity. ❑ *His father was a hard man.* ❑ *Don't be so hard on him.* ❑ *The police cracked down hard on the protesters.* **6** ADJ A **hard** winter or a **hard** frost is very cold. **7** ADJ BEFORE N **Hard** evidence or facts are definitely true. ❑ *He wanted more hard facts.* **8** ADJ **Hard** drugs are strong illegal drugs such as heroin. **9** PHRASE If you say that something is **hard going**, you mean it is difficult and requires a lot of effort. ❑ *Learning Russian had been hard going at the start.* **10** PHRASE If someone is **hard put to** or **hard pushed to** do something, they have great difficulty doing it. ❑ *I'll be hard pushed to teach him anything.*

Thesaurus *hard* Also look up:

ADJ. firm, solid, tough; *(ant.)* gentle, soft **1**
complicated, difficult, tough; *(ant.)* easy **2**

hardback /ˈhɑːdbæk/ (**hardbacks**) N-VAR A **hardback** is a book which has a stiff cover. ❑ *'The Secret History' was published in hardback.*

ˈhard ˌcore N-SING You can refer to the members of a group who are most involved with its activities as the **hard core**. ❑ *...a hard-core group of right-wing politicians.*

ˌhard ˈcurrency (**hard currencies**) N-VAR A **hard currency** is one which is unlikely to lose its value and so is considered to be a good one to have or to invest in.

ˈhard ˌdisk (**hard disks**) N-COUNT A **hard disk** is a hard plastic disk inside a computer on which data and programs are stored. [COMPUTING]

harden /ˈhɑːdən/ (**hardens, hardening, hardened**) **1** V-T/V-I When something **hardens**, or when you **harden** it, it becomes stiff or firm. ❑ *Pour the mixture while hot, before it hardens.* **2** V-T When you **harden** your ideas or attitudes, they become fixed and you become determined that you will not change them. ● **hardening** N-UNCOUNT ❑ *...a hardening of the government's attitude.* **3** V-T/V-I When people **harden**, or when events **harden** them, they become less sympathetic and gentle. ❑ *Watching the horrors of the war hardened her.*

hardline also **hard-line** /ˌhɑːdˈlaɪn/ ADJ If you describe someone's policy or attitude as **hardline**, you mean that it is strict or extreme, and they refuse to change it. ❑ *He will continue with the same hardline policies towards crime.*

hardly /ˈhɑːdli/ **1** ADV You use **hardly** to say that something is only just true. ❑ *I hardly know you.* ❑ *Hardly anyone slept that night.* **2** ADV If you say **hardly** had one thing happened when something else happened, you mean that the first event was followed immediately by the second. ❑ *Harry had hardly taken his coat off when the phone rang.* **3** ADV You use **hardly** to mean 'not' when you want to suggest that you are expecting your listener or reader to agree with your comment. ❑ *It's hardly surprising his ideas didn't work.*

ˌhard-ˈpressed **1** ADJ If someone is **hard-pressed**, they are under a lot of strain and worry. ❑ *...hard-pressed, poorly paid professionals.* **2** ADJ If you will be **hard-pressed to** do something, you will have great difficulty doing it. ❑ *The airline will be hard-pressed to make a profit.*

hardship /ˈhɑːdʃɪp/ (**hardships**) N-VAR **Hardship** is a situation in which your life is difficult or unpleasant. ❑ *Many people suffer economic hardship.*

Word Link *ware ≈ merchandise : hardware, software, warehouse*

hardware /ˈhɑːdweə/ **1** N-UNCOUNT Computer **hardware** is computer equipment as opposed to the programs that are written for it. Printers and monitors are computer hardware. [COMPUTING] **2** N-UNCOUNT Military **hardware** is the equipment that is used by the armed forces, such as tanks and missiles. **3** N-UNCOUNT **Hardware** is equipment such as hammers and screws for use in the home and garden.

hardy /ˈhɑːdi/ (**hardier, hardiest**) ADJ People, animals, and plants that are **hardy** are strong and able to endure difficult conditions. ❑ *Ten hardy fans made the journey to Dublin.*

H

hare /heə/ (**hares**) N-COUNT A **hare** is an animal like a large rabbit, but with longer ears and legs.

hark /hɑːk/ (**harks, harking, harked**)

▸ **hark back to** **1** PHR-VERB If you say that one thing **harks back to** another thing in the past, you mean that it is similar to it or takes it as a model. ❑ *The shape of the roof harks back to the Victorian era.* **2** PHR-VERB When people **hark back to** something in the past, they remember it or tell someone about it. ❑ *Puttnam was harking back to a conflict that happened nearly fifty years ago.*

harm /hɑːm/ (**harms, harming, harmed**) **1** V-T & N-UNCOUNT To **harm** someone or something, or to cause them **harm**, means to injure or damage them. ❑ *The hijackers did not want to harm anyone.* ❑ *To cut taxes would probably do the economy more harm than good.* **2** PHRASE If you say that **there is no harm in** doing something, you mean that it might be worth doing, and you will not be blamed for doing it. ❑ *There's no harm in asking.*

Thesaurus *harm* Also look up:

V.	abuse, damage, hurt, injure, ruin, wreck; (*ant.*) benefit **1**
N.	abuse, damage, hurt, injury, ruin, violence **1**

Word Partnership Use *harm* with:

ADJ.	**bodily** harm **1**
V.	**cause** harm, **not mean any** harm **1**
N.	harm **the environment** **1**
ADV.	**more** harm **than good** **1**

harmful /ˈhɑːmfʊl/ ADJ Something that is **harmful** has a bad effect on someone or something else. ❑ *...the harmful effects of the sun.*

harmless /ˈhɑːmləs/ **1** ADJ Something that is **harmless** does not have any bad effects. ❑ *This experiment is harmless to the animals.* **2** ADJ If you describe someone or something as **harmless**, you mean that they are not important and therefore unlikely to annoy other people or cause trouble. ❑ *He seemed harmless enough.*

harmonic /hɑːˈmɒnɪk/ ADJ **Harmonic** means composed, played, or sung using two or more notes which sound right and pleasing together. ❑ *...harmonic structures.*

harmonious /hɑːˈməʊniəs/ **1** ADJ A **harmonious** relationship, agreement, or discussion is friendly and peaceful. ● **harmoniously** ADV ❑ *We must try to live harmoniously with our neighbours.* **2** ADJ Something that is **harmonious** has parts which go well together. ❑ *...a harmonious balance of mind, body, and spirit.*

harmonize [BRIT also **harmonise**] /ˈhɑːmənaɪz/ (**harmonizes, harmonizing, harmonized**) V-I If two or more things **harmonize with** each other, they fit in well with each other. ❑ *Her clothes harmonize well with each other.* ❑ *Their tastes don't harmonize.*

Word Link *mony ≈ resulting state : ceremony, harmony, testimony*

harmony /ˈhɑːməni/ (**harmonies**) **1** N-UNCOUNT If people are living **in harmony with** each other, they are in a state of peaceful agreement and co-operation. ❑ *...racial harmony.* ❑ *Man should live in harmony with nature.* **2** N-VAR **Harmony** is the pleasant combination of different notes of music played at the same time. ❑ *...complex harmonies.* ❑ *...singing in harmony.* **3** N-UNCOUNT The **harmony of** something is the way in which its parts are combined into a pleasant arrangement. ❑ *...the ordered harmony of the universe.*

harness /ˈhɑːnɪs/ (**harnesses, harnessing, harnessed**) **1** V-T To **harness** something means to control it and use it. ❑ *Turkey plans to harness the waters of the Tigris and Euphrates rivers.* **2** N-COUNT A **harness** is a set of straps which fits around a person or animal, for example to attach a piece of equipment to them. **3** V-T If a horse or other animal **is harnessed**, a harness is put on it. ❑ *The horses were harnessed to a heavy wagon.*

harp /hɑːp/ (**harps, harping, harped**) N-COUNT A **harp** is a large musical instrument consisting of a triangular frame with vertical strings which you pluck with your fingers.

→ see **string**

▸ **harp on** PHR-VERB If someone **harps on about** something, they keep talking about it; used showing disapproval. ❑ *She concentrated on the good parts of her trip and didn't harp on about the bad.*

harrowing /ˈhærəʊɪŋ/ ADJ A **harrowing** sight or experience is very upsetting or disturbing. ❑ *...harrowing pictures of the victims of the bombings.*

harsh /hɑːʃ/ (**harsher, harshest**) **1** ADJ **Harsh** climates or living conditions are very difficult for people, animals, and plants to exist in. ❑ *The weather grew harsh and chilly.* ● **harshness** N-UNCOUNT ❑ *...the harshness of their living conditions.* **2** ADJ **Harsh** actions or remarks are unkind and show no understanding or sympathy. ❑ *...the cold, harsh cruelty of her husband.* ● **harshly** ADV ❑ *Her husband is being harshly treated in prison.* ● **harshness** N-UNCOUNT ❑ *She apologized for the harshness of her words.* **3** ADJ Something that is **harsh** is so hard, bright, or rough that it seems unpleasant or harmful. ❑ *...harsh colours.*

harvest /ˈhɑːvɪst/ (**harvests, harvesting, harvested**) **1** V-T & N-SING When farmers **harvest** a crop, they gather it in. You can refer to this

activity as **the harvest**. ❑ *Students will visit the farms to see seeds being planted and harvested.* **2** N-COUNT A crop is called a **harvest** when it has been gathered. ❑ *...the wheat harvest.*
→ see **farm, grain**

has

> The auxiliary verb is pronounced /həz, STRONG hæz/. The main verb is usually pronounced /hæz/.

Has is the third person singular of the present tense of **have**.

hash /hæʃ/ (**hashes**) **1** N-COUNT A **hash** is the sign '#', found on telephone keypads and computer keyboards. [mainly BRIT, SPOKEN]

> In AM, usu use **pound sign**.

2 PHRASE If you **make a hash of** a job, you do it very badly. [INFORMAL] ❑ *Watson had made a thorough hash of it.*

hasn't /ˈhæzənt/ **Hasn't** is the usual spoken form of 'has not'.

hassle /ˈhæsəl/ (**hassles, hassling, hassled**) **1** N-VAR A **hassle** is a situation that is difficult and involves problems, effort, or arguments with people. ❑ *...all the usual hassles of travelling.* **2** V-T If someone **hassles** you, they irritate you by repeatedly telling you or asking you to do something that you do not want to do. [INFORMAL] ❑ *...if you are tired of being hassled by your parents.*

haste /heɪst/ N-UNCOUNT **Haste** is the quality of doing something too quickly, so that you are careless and make mistakes. ❑ *The translations show signs of haste.* ❑ *Loneliness can lead to people marrying in haste.*

hasten /ˈheɪsən/ (**hastens, hastening, hastened**) **1** V-T If you **hasten** an event or process, you make it happen faster or sooner. [WRITTEN] ❑ *It was part of a plan to hasten his departure.* **2** V-T If you **hasten to** do something, you are quick to do it. ❑ *'There's no point, Freddie,' Arnold hastened to say.*

hasty /ˈheɪsti/ (**hastier, hastiest**) **1** ADJ **Hasty** means done or arranged in a hurry, without planning or preparation. ❑ *The signs of their hasty departure could be seen everywhere.* ● **hastily** ADV ❑ *'No, I'm sure it's not,' said Virginia hastily.* **2** ADJ If you describe what someone does or says as **hasty**, you mean that they are acting too quickly, without thinking carefully; used showing disapproval. ❑ *The Government should not make hasty decisions.*

hat /hæt/ (**hats**) N-COUNT A **hat** is a covering that you wear on your head.
→ see Picture Dictionary: **hat**

hatch /hætʃ/ (**hatches, hatching, hatched**) **1** V-T/V-I When an egg **hatches**, or when it **is hatched**, a baby bird or animal comes out by breaking the shell. ❑ *The young birds disappeared soon after they were hatched.* **2** V-T If someone **hatches** a plot or a scheme, they think of it and work it out; used showing disapproval. ❑ *He hatched a plot to kidnap the Pope.* **3** N-COUNT A **hatch** is a small covered opening in a floor, wall, or ceiling.

hatchet /ˈhætʃɪt/ (**hatchets**) N-COUNT A **hatchet** is a small axe.

hate /heɪt/ (**hates, hating, hated**) **1** V-T & N-UNCOUNT If you **hate** someone or something, or if you have feelings of **hate** towards them, you have an extremely strong dislike for them. ❑ *Most people hate him, but they don't say so.* ❑ *...a violent man, full of hate.* **2** V-T You can use **hate** in expressions such as '**I hate to say it**' and '**I hate to tell you**' when you want to express regret about what you are about to say. ❑ *I hate to tell you this, but tomorrow's your last day working here.*
→ see **emotion**

Picture Dictionary

hats

hatred /ˈheɪtrɪd/ N-UNCOUNT **Hatred** is an extremely strong feeling of dislike for someone or something. ❑ *Their words were full of hatred for us.*

ˈhat-ˌtrick (**hat-tricks**) N-COUNT A **hat-trick** is a series of three achievements, for example three goals scored by the same person in a football match.

haul /hɔːl/ (**hauls, hauling, hauled**) 1 V-T If you **haul** a heavy object somewhere, you pull it there with a great effort. ❑ *A crane was used to haul the car out of the river.* 2 PHRASE If you say that a task or a journey is **a long haul**, you mean that it takes a long time and a lot of effort. ❑ *It had been a long haul since leaving Belfast at 7am and travelling via London to the Caribbean.*

haunt /hɔːnt/ (**haunts, haunting, haunted**) 1 V-T If something unpleasant **haunts** you, you keep thinking or worrying about it over a long period of time. ❑ *The decision to leave her children now haunts her.* 2 N-COUNT A place that is the **haunt** of a particular person is one which they often visit because they enjoy going there. ❑ *Morris came up to New York to visit his old haunts.* 3 V-T If people say that a ghost or spirit **haunts** a place or a person, they mean that a ghost or spirit regularly appears in that place or is seen by that person.

haunted /ˈhɔːntɪd/ 1 ADJ A **haunted** building or other place is one where a ghost regularly appears. 2 ADJ Someone who has a **haunted** expression looks very worried or troubled. ❑ *She looked so haunted, I almost didn't recognize her.*

haunting /ˈhɔːntɪŋ/ ADJ **Haunting** sounds, images, or words remain in your thoughts because they are very beautiful or sad. ❑ *...the haunting calls of wild birds.* ● **hauntingly** ADV ❑ *The ancient town is hauntingly beautiful.*

have /həv, STRONG hæv/ (**has, having, had**) 1 MODAL You use **have to** when you are saying that something is necessary, obligatory, or must happen. If you **do not have to** do something, it is not necessary or obligatory for you to do it. ❑ *He had to go to Germany.* ❑ *We'll have to find a taxi.* ❑ *They didn't have to pay tax.* 2 V-T You use **have** when you are saying that someone or something owns, possesses, or holds a particular thing, or when you are mentioning one of their qualities or characteristics. ❑ *Oscar has a new bicycle.* ❑ *You have beautiful eyes.* ❑ *Do you have any brothers and sisters?* 3 V-T If a woman **has** a baby, she gives birth to it. If she **is having** a baby, she is pregnant. 4 V-T If you **have** something **to** do, you are responsible for doing it or must do it. ❑ *He had plenty of work to do.* ❑ *I have some important calls to make.* 5 V-T If you **have** something such a part of your body in a particular position or state, it is in that position or state. ❑ *Mary had her eyes closed.* ❑ *They had the curtains open.* 6 V-T If someone **has** you **by** a part of your body, they are holding you there and they are trying to hurt you or force you to go somewhere. ❑ *Larry had him by the ear.* 7 V-T If you **have** something done, someone does it for you or you arrange for it to be done. ❑ *I had your room cleaned.* ❑ *You've had your hair cut.* 8 V-T If someone or something **has** something happen to them, usually something unpleasant, it happens to them. ❑ *We had our money stolen.* 9 PHRASE You can use **has it** in expressions like **'rumour has it that'** and **'as legend has it'** when you are quoting something that you have heard, but you do not necessarily think it is true. ❑ *Rumour has it that tickets were being sold for £300.*

haven /ˈheɪvən/ (**havens**) N-COUNT A **haven** is a place where people or animals feel safe, secure and happy. ❑ *Lake Baringo is a haven for a large number of birds.*

haven't /ˈhævənt/ **Haven't** is the usual spoken form of 'have not'.

havoc /ˈhævək/ 1 N-UNCOUNT **Havoc** is a state of chaos, confusion, and disorder. ❑ *The protestors caused havoc in the centre of the town.* 2 PHRASE If one thing **plays havoc with** another or **wreaks havoc on** it, it prevents it from continuing or functioning as normal, or damages it. ❑ *The weather played havoc with flights.*

hawk /hɔːk/ (**hawks**) N-COUNT A **hawk** is a large bird that hunts other animals.

hawk

hay /heɪ/ N-UNCOUNT **Hay** is grass which has been cut and dried so that it can be used to feed animals. ❑ *...bales of hay.* → see **barn**

ˈhay ˌfever N-UNCOUNT If someone suffers from **hay fever**, they have an allergy to pollen which makes their nose, throat, and eyes become red and swollen.

hazard /ˈhæzəd/ (**hazards, hazarding, hazarded**) 1 N-COUNT A **hazard** is something which could be dangerous to you. ❑ *Chewing gum may be a health hazard.* 2 V-T If you **hazard a guess** that something is the case, you make a guess about it which you know might be wrong. ❑ *It is possible only to hazard a guess at the reasons for this.*

hazardous /ˈhæzədəs/ ADJ **Hazardous** things are dangerous, especially to people's health or safety. ❑ *Some people think mobile phones are hazardous to health.*

haze /heɪz/ (**hazes**) 1 N-VAR **Haze** is a light mist caused by heat or dust in the air. ❑ *...the heat haze.* 2 N-SING If there is a **haze of** something such as smoke or steam, you cannot see clearly through it. [LITERARY] ❑ *...a haze of red dust.*

hazel /ˈheɪzəl/ (**hazels**) 1 N-VAR A **hazel** is a small tree which produces edible nuts. 2 ADJ **Hazel** eyes are greenish-brown.

hazy /ˈheɪzi/ (**hazier, haziest**) 1 ADJ When the sky or a view is **hazy**, you cannot see it clearly because there is a haze. ❑ *...a warm, hazy summer afternoon.* 2 ADJ If you are **hazy about** things, or if your thoughts are **hazy**, you are confused. ❑ *I'm a bit hazy about that.* ❑ *I have only a hazy memory of what he was really like.*

he /hi, STRONG hiː/ PRON You use **he** to refer to a man, boy, or male animal. **He** is used as the subject of a verb. ❑ *He lives in London.*

head

❶ NOUN USES
❷ VERB USES
❸ PHRASES

head /hed/ (**heads**)
❶ 1 N-COUNT Your **head** is the part of your body which has your eyes, mouth, nose, and brain in it. ❑ *She turned her head away.* 2 N-COUNT You can

use **head** to refer to your mind and your mental abilities. ❑ *I can't get that song out of my head.* ❑ *He could do complex maths in his head.* **3** N-COUNT The **head** of an organization, school, or department is the person in charge of it. ❑ *...heads of government.* ❑ *She became head of a girls' school.* **4** N-SING The **head** of something is the top, start, or most important end of it. ❑ *...the head of the stairs.* ❑ *A different name was placed at the head of the chart.*
→ see **body**

head /hed/ (**heads, heading, headed**)
2 **1** V-T If someone or something **heads** a line or procession, they are at the front of it. **2** V-T If something **heads** a list or group, it is at the top of it. ❑ *Running a business heads the list of their ambitions.* **3** V-T If a piece of writing **is headed** a particular title, it has that title written at the beginning of it. ❑ *Please read the section headed, 'General Information'.* **4** V-T/V-I If you **are heading for** a particular place or in a particular direction, you are going towards that place or in that direction. You can also say that you **are headed for** a particular place. ❑ *He headed for the bus stop.* ❑ *It is not clear how many of them will be heading back to Saudi Arabia.* **5** V-T/V-I If something or someone **is heading for** a particular result, the situation they are in is developing in a way that makes that result very likely. You can also say that something or someone **is headed** towards a particular result. ❑ *The old tradition seems headed for extinction.* **6** V-T When you **head** a ball, you hit it with your head. ❑ *He headed the ball into the goal.*
7 → see also **heading**

head /hed/ (**heads**)
3 **1** PHRASE The cost or amount **per head** or **a head** is the cost or amount for one person. ❑ *This chicken dish costs less than £1 a head.* **2** PHRASE If a problem or disagreement **comes to a head** or if you **bring** it **to a head**, it reaches a state where you have to do something about it urgently. ❑ *The bad times came to a head about a year ago when Colt and Ford left the band.* **3** PHRASE If you **get** something **into** your **head**, you suddenly decide that it is true and you will not change your mind about it. **4** PHRASE If you say that something such as praise or success **goes to** someone's **head**, you mean that they become arrogant as a result of it. **5** PHRASE If you **keep** your **head**, you remain calm in a difficult situation. If you **lose** your **head**, you panic or do not remain calm.

headache /ˈhedeɪk/ (**headaches**) **1** N-COUNT If you have a **headache**, you have a pain in your head. **2** N-COUNT If you say that something is a **headache**, you mean that it causes you difficulty or worry. ❑ *The biggest headache for mothers who want to return to work is childcare.*

header /ˈhedə/ (**headers**) N-COUNT A **header** is text such as a name or a page number that can be automatically displayed at the top of each page of a printed document.

heading /ˈhedɪŋ/ (**headings**) N-COUNT A **heading** is the title of a piece of writing, written or printed at the top of the page. ❑ *...chapter headings.*

Word Link	*light ≈ shining: daylight, enlighten, headlight*

headlight /ˈhedlaɪt/ (**headlights**) N-COUNT A vehicle's **headlights** are the large bright lights at the front.

headline /ˈhedlaɪn/ (**headlines**) **1** N-COUNT A **headline** is the title of a newspaper story, printed in large letters at the top of it. ❑ *The headline says 'New government plans'.* **2** N-PLURAL The **headlines** are the main points of a radio or television news broadcast. ❑ *Here are the headlines.* **3** PHRASE Someone or something that **hits the headlines** gets a lot of publicity from the media.

headlined /ˈhedlaɪnd/ ADJ AFTER LINK-V If a newspaper story is **headlined** something, that is its title. ❑ *...an article headlined 'Don't Panic'.*

headlong /ˈhedlɒŋ, AM -lɔːŋ/ **1** ADV If you move **headlong** in a particular direction, you move there very quickly. ❑ *He ran headlong for the open door.* **2** ADV & ADJ BEFORE N If you rush **headlong** into something, you do it quickly, without thinking carefully about it. ❑ *Do not leap headlong into decisions.* ❑ *...the headlong rush to independence.*

headmaster /ˌhedˈmɑːstə, -ˈmæst-/ (**headmasters**) N-COUNT A **headmaster** is a man who is the head teacher of a school. [BRIT]

headmistress /ˌhedˈmɪstrɪs/ (**headmistresses**) N-COUNT A **headmistress** is a woman who is the head teacher of a school. [BRIT]

ˌhead of ˈstate (**heads of state**) N-COUNT A **head of state** is the leader of a country, for example a president or queen.

ˌhead-ˈon **1** ADV & ADJ BEFORE N If two vehicles hit each other **head-on**, they hit each other with their front parts pointing towards each other. ❑ *The car collided head-on with a van.* ❑ *...a head-on collision.* **2** ADJ BEFORE N & ADV A **head-on** disagreement is firm and direct and has no compromises. ❑ *...a head-on clash between the president and the government.* ❑ *I chose to deal with the issue head-on.*

headphones

headphones /ˈhedfəʊnz/ N-PLURAL **Headphones** are small speakers which you wear over your ears in order to listen to music or other sounds without other people hearing.

headquarters /ˈhedkwɔːtəz/ N-COUNT The **headquarters** of an organization are its main offices. **Headquarters** can take the singular or plural form of the verb. ❑ *...the army's headquarters in Buenos Aires.*

ˌhead ˈstart N-SING If you have a **head start** on other people, you have an advantage over them in a competition or race. ❑ *A good education gives your child a head start in life.*

ˌhead ˈteacher also **headteacher** (**head teachers**) N-COUNT A **head teacher** is a teacher who is in charge of a school. [BRIT]

headway /ˈhedweɪ/ PHRASE If you **make headway**, you make progress towards achieving something. ❑ *You need a university degree to make real headway in industry.*

heady /ˈhedi/ (**headier, headiest**) ADJ A **heady** atmosphere or experience strongly affects your senses, for example by making you feel drunk or excited. ❑ *...the heady days just after their marriage.*

heal /hiːl/ (**heals, healing, healed**) **1** V-T/V-I When an injury such as a broken bone **heals**, or if someone or something **heals** it, it becomes healthy and normal again. ❑ *It will take three to four weeks before the fracture fully heals.* **2** V-T If you **heal** something such as a disagreement between people, you restore the situation to its former state. ❑ *She is no longer trying to heal the situation, but has accepted it now.*

healer /ˈhiːlə/ (**healers**) N-COUNT A **healer** is a person who treats sick people, especially one who believes that they are able to heal people through prayer or a supernatural power.

health /helθ/ **1** N-UNCOUNT Your **health** is the condition of your body. ❑ *Salty snacks are bad for your health.* **2** N-UNCOUNT **Health** is a state in which you are fit and well. ❑ *In the hospital they nursed me back to health.* **3** N-UNCOUNT The **health** of an organization or system is the success that it has and the fact that it is working well. ❑ *...the health of the economy.*

H

healthy /ˈhelθi/ (**healthier, healthiest**) **1** ADJ Someone who is **healthy** is well and is not suffering from any illness. Something that is **healthy** shows that a person is well. ❑ *She was a very healthy child.* ❑ *...healthy skin.* ● **healthily** ADV ❑ *I want to live healthily for as long as possible.* **2** ADJ Something that is **healthy** is good for you. ❑ *...a healthy diet.* **3** ADJ A **healthy** organization or system is successful. ❑ *...an economically healthy socialist state.* **4** ADJ A **healthy** amount of something is a large amount that shows success. ❑ *...healthy profits.*

Word Partnership Use *healthy* with:

N. healthy **baby** **1**
healthy **appetite**, healthy **diet/food**, healthy **glow**, healthy **lifestyle**, healthy **skin** **2**
healthy **attitude about *something*** **2**

heap /hiːp/ (**heaps, heaping, heaped**) **1** N-COUNT A **heap of** things is an untidy pile of them. ❑ *...a heap of clothes.* **2** V-T & PHR-VERB If you **heap** things, or if you **heap** them **up**, you arrange them in a pile. ❑ *Mrs. Madrigal heaped more carrots onto Michael's plate.* ❑ *The men were heaping up wood for a bonfire.* **3** V-T If you **heap** praise or criticism **on** someone or something, you give them a lot of praise or criticism. **4** QUANT **Heaps of** something or a **heap of** it is a large quantity of it. [INFORMAL] ❑ *You have heaps of time.* ❑ *I got in a heap of trouble.*

Usage

A **heap** of things is usually untidy, and often has the shape of a hill or mound. ❑ *Now, the house is a heap of rubble.* A **stack** is usually tidy, and often consists of flat objects placed directly on top of each other. ❑ *...a neat stack of dishes.* A **pile** of things can be tidy or untidy. ❑ *...a neat pile of clothes.*

hear /hɪə/ (**hears, hearing, heard** /hɜːd/) **1** V-T/V-I When you **hear** sounds, you are aware of them because they reach your ears. ❑ *I heard the sound of a car.* ❑ *He doesn't hear very well.* **2** V-T When a judge or a court **hears** a **case** or **hears evidence**, they listen to it officially in order to make a decision about it. [FORMAL] ❑ *The case will be heard next week.* **3** V-I If you **hear from** someone, you receive a letter or a telephone call from them. ❑ *The police want to hear from anyone who knows her.* **4** V-T/V-I If you **hear** some news or information, you learn it because someone tells it to you or it is mentioned on the radio or television. ❑ *My mother heard of this school through Leslie.* ❑ *I heard that he was forced to leave.* **5** PHRASE If you **have** never **heard of** someone or something, you do not know anything about them. **6** PHRASE If you **won't hear of** someone doing something, you refuse to let them do it.

Usage

Be careful not to confuse **hear** and **listen**. You use **hear** to talk about sounds that you are aware of because they reach your ears. You often use **can** with **hear**. ❑ *I can hear him shouting.* If you want to say that someone is paying attention to something they can hear, you say that they **are listening to** it. ❑ *He turned on the radio and listened to the news.* Note that **listen** is not followed directly by an object. You must always say that you listen **to** something. However, **listen** can also be used on its own without an object. ❑ *I was laughing too much to listen.*

Thesaurus *hear* Also look up:

V. detect, listen, pick up **1**

hearing /ˈhɪərɪŋ/ (**hearings**) **1** N-UNCOUNT **Hearing** is the sense which makes it possible for you to be aware of sounds. ❑ *My hearing has got better.* **2** N-COUNT A **hearing** is an official meeting held to collect facts about an incident or problem. **3** N-SING If someone gives you a **hearing** or a **fair hearing**, they listen to you when you give your opinion about something.
→ see **disability**

Word Partnership Use *hearing* with:

N. hearing **impairment/loss** **1**
court hearing **2**
V. **hold a** hearing, **testify at/before a** hearing **2**

heart /hɑːt/ (**hearts**) **1** N-COUNT Your **heart** is the organ in your chest that pumps the blood around your body. ❑ *...the beating of his heart.* **2** N-COUNT You can refer to someone's **heart** when you are talking about their deep feelings and beliefs. [LITERARY] ❑ *Alik's words filled her heart with joy.* **3** N-VAR You use **heart** when you are talking about someone's character and attitude towards other people. ❑ *She's got a good heart.* **4** N-SING If you refer to things **of the heart**, you mean love and romance. **5** N-SING **The heart of** something is the most important part of it. ❑ *Money is the heart of the problem.* **6** N-SING **The heart of** a place is its centre. ❑ *...the heart of London's West End.* **7** N-COUNT A **heart** is a shape that is sometimes used as a symbol of love. **8** N-VAR **Hearts** is one of the four suits in a pack of playing cards. Each card in the suit is called a **heart** and is marked with one or more symbols: ♥. **9** PHRASE If you feel or believe something **with all** your **heart**, you feel or believe it very strongly. ❑ *I love my family with all my heart.* **10** PHRASE If someone is a particular kind of person **at heart**, this is

what they are really like. **11** PHRASE If someone or something **breaks** your **heart**, or if they give you a **broken heart**, they make you very unhappy. **12** PHRASE If you know something such as a poem **by heart**, you have learnt all the words and can remember them. **13** PHRASE If you **have a change of heart**, your feelings about something change. **14** PHRASE If something is **close to** your **heart**, or if it is **dear to** your **heart**, you care deeply about it. **15** PHRASE If you say something **from the heart** or **from the bottom of your heart**, you sincerely mean what you say. ❑ *I don't want to leave without thanking you from the bottom of my heart.* **16** PHRASE If your **heart sinks**, you suddenly feel very disappointed or unhappy. ❑ *Our hearts sank when we saw this awful hotel.* **17** PHRASE If you **take heart from** something, you are made to feel encouraged and optimistic by it. **18** PHRASE If you **take** something **to heart**, you are deeply affected and upset by it.
→ see **donor**

heartache /ˈhɑːteɪk/ (**heartaches**) N-VAR **Heartache** is very great sadness and emotional suffering. [JOURNALISM] ❑ *...the heartache of her divorce.*

ˈheart ˌattack (**heart attacks**) N-COUNT If someone **has** a **heart attack**, their heart begins to beat irregularly or stops completely.

heartbeat /ˈhɑːtbiːt/ (**heartbeats**) **1** N-SING Your **heartbeat** is the regular movement of your heart as it pumps blood around your body. ❑ *Your baby's heartbeat will be monitored continuously.* **2** N-COUNT A **heartbeat** is one of the movements of your heart. ❑ *Count the number of heartbeats in 15 seconds.*

heartbreak /ˈhɑːtbreɪk/ (**heartbreaks**) N-VAR **Heartbreak** is very great sadness or unhappiness. ❑ *...the heartbreak of being told she couldn't have children.*

heartbreaking /ˈhɑːtbreɪkɪŋ/ ADJ Something that is **heartbreaking** makes you feel extremely sad and upset. ❑ *It was a heartbreaking decision for her.*

heartbroken /ˈhɑːtbrəʊkən/ ADJ Someone who is **heartbroken** is extremely sad and upset.

hearten /ˈhɑːtən/ (**heartens, heartening, heartened**) V-T If you **are heartened** by something, it encourages you and makes you cheerful. ❑ *The news heartened everybody.* ● **heartened** ADJ AFTER LINK-V ❑ *I feel heartened by her progress.* ● **heartening** ADJ ❑ *It is heartening to know he is alive.*

ˈheart ˌfailure N-UNCOUNT **Heart failure** is a serious medical condition in which someone's heart does not work as well as it should, sometimes stopping completely so that they die.

heartfelt /ˈhɑːtfelt/ ADJ **Heartfelt** is used to describe a deep or sincere feeling or wish. ❑ *My heartfelt sympathy goes out to all the relatives.*

hearth /hɑːθ/ (**hearths**) N-COUNT **The hearth** is the floor of a fireplace, which sometimes extends into the room.

heartland /ˈhɑːtlænd/ (**heartlands**) N-COUNT **Heartland** or **heartlands** is used to refer to the area or region where a particular set of activities or beliefs is most significant. ❑ *...the industrial heartland of America.*

hearty /ˈhɑːti/ (**heartier, heartiest**) **1** ADJ **Hearty** people or actions are loud, cheerful, and energetic. ● **heartily** ADV ❑ *He laughed heartily.* **2** ADJ **Hearty** feelings or opinions are strongly felt. ❑ *Arnold was in hearty agreement.* ● **heartily** ADV ❑ *I heartily agree with her comments.* **3** ADJ A **hearty** meal is large and very satisfying. ❑ *The boys ate a hearty breakfast.*

heat /hiːt/ (**heats, heating, heated**) **1** V-T & PHR-VERB When you **heat** something, or when you **heat** it **up**, you raise its temperature. ❑ *Heat the tomatoes and oil in a pan.* ❑ *Freda heated up a pie for me.* **2** N-UNCOUNT **Heat** is warmth or the quality of being hot. ❑ *...the fierce heat of the sun.* **3** N-UNCOUNT The **heat of** something is its temperature. ❑ *...the heat of the ovens in the factory.* **4** N-SING **The heat of** a particular activity is the point when there is the greatest activity or excitement. ❑ *...in the heat of the election campaign.* **5** N-COUNT A **heat** is one of a series of races or competitions. The winners of a heat take part in another race or competition, against the winners of other heats.
→ see **cook, fire, petroleum**

▶ **heat up** **1** PHR-VERB When something **heats up**, it gradually becomes hotter. ❑ *The big question is what will happen if the world heats up?* **2** → see also **heat** (meaning 1)
→ see **pan**

heated /ˈhiːtɪd/ ADJ If someone is **heated** about something, they get angry and excited about it. A **heated** discussion or quarrel is one where the people involved are angry and excited. ● **heatedly** ADV ❑ *The crowd argued heatedly about the best way to solve the problem.*

heater /ˈhiːtə/ (**heaters**) N-COUNT A **heater** is a piece of equipment which is used to warm a place or to heat water.

heather /ˈheðə/ N-UNCOUNT **Heather** is a low spreading plant with small purple, pink, or white flowers that grows wild on hills or moorland.

heating /ˈhiːtɪŋ/ **1** N-UNCOUNT **Heating** is the process or equipment involved in keeping a building warm. ❑ *...cottages for £150 a week, including heating.* **2** → see also **central heating**

heave /hiːv/ (**heaves, heaving, heaved**) **1** V-T & N-COUNT If you **heave** an object that is heavy or difficult to move, or if you move it with a **heave**, you push, pull, or lift it using a lot of effort. ❑ *Five strong men heaved it up the hill.* ❑ *It took only one heave to throw him into the river.* **2** V-I If something **heaves**, it moves up and down with large regular movements. ❑ *His chest heaved, and he took a deep breath.*

heaven /ˈhevən/ (**heavens**) **1** N-PROPER In some religions, **heaven** is said to be the place where God lives and where good people go when they die. **2** N-PLURAL **The heavens** are the sky. [DATED] ❑ *The stars shone brightly in the heavens.* **3** PHRASE You say **'good heavens'** to express surprise. ❑ *Good Heavens! That explains a lot!* **4** PHRASE You can say **'Heaven knows'** to emphasize that you do not know something, or that you find something very surprising. [BRIT, INFORMAL] ❑ *Heaven knows how it works.* **5** PHRASE You can say **'Heaven knows'** to emphasize something that you feel or believe very strongly. [BRIT, INFORMAL] ❑ *Heaven knows they have enough money already.* **6** **thank heavens** → see **thank**

heavenly /ˈhevənli/ **1** ADJ **Heavenly** describes

things relating to heaven. ❑ *...heavenly beings who serve God.* **2** ADJ If you describe something as **heavenly**, you mean that it is very pleasant and enjoyable. [INFORMAL] ❑ *The idea of spending two weeks with him is heavenly.*

heavily /ˈhevɪli/ ADV You can use **heavily** to indicate that something is great in amount, degree, or intensity. ❑ *He was bleeding heavily.* ❑ *The newspaper was heavily criticised.*

heavy /ˈhevi/ (**heavier, heaviest**) **1** ADJ Something that is **heavy** weighs a lot. ❑ *He opened the heavy Bible.* • **heaviness** N-UNCOUNT ❑ *I try to keep my weight below 13 stone; heaviness slows me down.* **2** ADJ You use **heavy** to ask or talk about how much someone or something weighs. ❑ *How heavy are you?* **3** ADJ Someone or something that is **heavy** is solid in appearance or structure. ❑ *...heavy old brown furniture.* ❑ *He was short and heavy.* • **heavily** ADV ❑ *...a big man of about forty, heavily built.* **4** ADJ **Heavy** means great in amount, degree, or intensity. ❑ *There has been heavy fighting.* ❑ *...the heavy responsibility that parents have.* • **heaviness** N-UNCOUNT ❑ *...the heaviness of the blood loss.* **5** ADJ If a person's breathing is **heavy**, it is very loud and deep. • **heavily** ADV ❑ *She closed her eyes, breathing heavily.* **6** ADJ BEFORE N A **heavy** movement or action is done with a lot of force or pressure. ❑ *You received a heavy blow on the back of the head.* • **heavily** ADV ❑ *I sat down heavily on the ground.* **7** ADJ If you describe a period of time or a schedule as **heavy**, you mean it involves a lot of work. ❑ *It's been a heavy day and I'm tired.* **8** ADJ **Heavy work** requires a lot of physical strength. **9** ADJ **Heavy** air or weather is unpleasantly still, hot, and damp. **10** ADJ A situation that is **heavy** is serious and difficult to cope with. [INFORMAL] ❑ *The film has some heavy themes but also plenty of laughs.*

Thesaurus	*heavy*	Also look up:
ADJ.	hefty, overweight; *(ant.)* light **1** **2** **3**	
	forceful, powerful **6**	
	complex, difficult, tough **10**	

ˌheavy-ˈduty ADJ A **heavy-duty** machine is strong and can be used a lot. ❑ *...heavy-duty equipment.*

ˌheavy-ˈhanded ADJ If you say that someone is **heavy-handed**, you mean that they are unnecessarily forceful and thoughtless. ❑ *Many people believe the soldiers are heavy-handed and are making the situation worse.*

heavyweight /ˈheviweɪt/ (**heavyweights**) **1** N-COUNT A **heavyweight** is a boxer or wrestler in the heaviest class. **2** N-COUNT If you refer to a person or organization as a **heavyweight**, you mean that they have a lot of influence, experience, and importance in a particular field. ❑ *...a political heavyweight.*

Hebrew /ˈhiːbruː/ N-UNCOUNT **Hebrew** is a language spoken by Jews.

heck /hek/ **1** EXCLAM You say **'heck!'** to express slight irritation or surprise. [INFORMAL] ❑ *Oh, heck. What can I write about?* ❑ *What the heck's that?* **2** PHRASE People use **a heck of** to emphasize how big something is or how much of it there is. [INFORMAL] ❑ *They're spending a heck of a lot of money.*

heckle /ˈhekəl/ (**heckles, heckling, heckled**) V-T & N-COUNT If people in an audience **heckle** public speakers, they interrupt them by making rude remarks, called **heckles**. ❑ *They heckled him and interrupted with angry questions.* ❑ *...a heckle from an audience member.* • **heckling** N-UNCOUNT ❑ *...the heckling of his audience.* • **heckler** (**hecklers**) N-COUNT ❑ *He was interrupted by hecklers.*

hectare /ˈhekteə/ (**hectares**) N-COUNT A **hectare** is a unit of area equal to 10,000 square metres.

hectic /ˈhektɪk/ ADJ A **hectic** situation involves a lot of rushed activity. ❑ *...his hectic work schedule.*

he'd /hɪd, hiːd/ **He'd** is the usual spoken form of 'he had', especially when 'had' is an auxiliary verb. **He'd** is also a spoken form of 'he would'.

hedge /hedʒ/ (**hedges, hedging, hedged**) **1** N-COUNT A **hedge** is a row of bushes along the edge of a garden, field, or road. **2** V-I If you **hedge**, you avoid answering a question or committing yourself to a particular action. ❑ *'I can't give you an answer now,' he hedged.* **3** PHRASE If you **hedge** your **bets**, you reduce the risk of losing a lot by supporting more than one person or thing.

hedgehog /ˈhedʒhɒg, AM -hɔːg/ (**hedgehogs**) N-COUNT A **hedgehog** is a small brown animal with sharp spikes covering its back.

hedgerow /ˈhedʒrəʊ/ (**hedgerows**) N-COUNT A **hedgerow** is a row of bushes, trees, and plants, usually growing along a country lane or between fields.

hedonist /ˈhiːdənɪst/ (**hedonists**) N-COUNT A **hedonist** is someone who believes that having pleasure is the most important thing in life. [FORMAL] • **hedonistic** /hiːdəˈnɪstɪk/ ADJ ❑ *...the hedonistic pleasures of partying.* • **hedonism** /ˈhiːdənɪzəm/ N-UNCOUNT ❑ *...a life of hedonism and glamour.*

heed /hiːd/ (**heeds, heeding, heeded**) **1** V-T If you **heed** someone's advice or warning, you pay attention to it and do what they suggest. [FORMAL] ❑ *Few people heeded his warning.* **2** PHRASE If you **take heed of** what someone says, or if you **pay heed to** them, you pay attention to them and consider carefully what they say.

heel /hiːl/ (**heels**) **1** N-COUNT Your **heel** is the back part of your foot, just below your ankle. **2** N-COUNT The **heel** of a shoe is the raised part on the bottom at the back.

→ see **foot**

hefty /ˈhefti/ (**heftier, heftiest**) ADJ **Hefty** means very large in size, weight, or amount. [INFORMAL] ❑ *He received a hefty fine.*

height /haɪt/ (**heights**) **1** N-VAR The **height** of a person or thing is their measurement from bottom to top. ❑ *Claire has long legs for her height.* **2** N-UNCOUNT **Height** is the quality of being tall. ❑ *Her height is intimidating for some men.* **3** N-VAR A particular **height** is the distance that something is above the ground. ❑ *The plane will fly at a height of about 300 metres.* **4** N-COUNT A **height** is a high position or place above the ground. ❑ *From a height, it looks like a desert.* **5** N-SING When an activity, situation, or organization is **at** its **height**, it is at its most successful, powerful, or intense. ❑ *Emigration from Britain to Brittany was at its height.* **6** N-SING If you say that something is **the height of** a quality,

you are emphasizing that it has that quality to the greatest degree possible. ❑ *I think it's the height of bad manners to wear a dirty shirt.*
→ see **area**

Word Partnership Use *height* with:

ADJ.	**average** height, **medium** height, **the right** height 1
V.	**reach a** height 1 4
N.	height **and weight**, height **and width** 1 **the** height **of *someone's*** **career** 5 **the** height **of fashion/popularity/ style** 6

heighten /ˈhaɪtən/ (**heightens, heightening, heightened**) V-T/V-I If something **heightens** a feeling, or a feeling **heightens**, the feeling increases in degree or intensity. ❑ *It has heightened awareness of racial differences.* ❑ *Anna's interest heightened.*

heir /eə/ (**heirs**) N-COUNT Someone's **heir** is the person who will inherit their money, property, or title when they die. ❑ *He was the only heir to his grandparents' fortune.*

Word Link *ess ≈ female : actress, empress, heiress*

heiress /ˈeərɪs/ (**heiresses**) N-COUNT An **heiress** is a woman who will inherit property, money, or a title.

held /held/ **Held** is the past tense and past participle of **hold**.

helicopter /ˈhelikɒptə/ (**helicopters**) N-COUNT A **helicopter** is an aircraft with no wings. It hovers or moves vertically and horizontally by means of large overhead blades which rotate.

helicopter

→ see **fly**

hell /hel/ (**hells**) 1 N-PROPER According to some religions, **Hell** is the place where the Devil lives, and where wicked people are sent to be punished when they die. 2 N-VAR If you say that a particular situation or place is **hell**, you are emphasizing that it is extremely unpleasant. [INFORMAL] ❑ *June says her life has been hell since her marriage ended nine months ago.* 3 PHRASE You can use **from hell** after a noun when you are emphasizing that something or someone is extremely unpleasant or evil. ❑ *...the holiday from hell.*

he'll /hɪl, hiːl/ **He'll** is the usual spoken form of 'he will'.

hello or **hallo** or **hullo** /heˈləʊ/ (**hellos**) CONVENTION & N-COUNT You say **'Hello'** when you are greeting someone or starting a telephone conversation. ❑ *'Hello, this is Susan. Could I speak to Nancy please?'* ❑ *He greeted me with a warm hello.*

helmet

helmet /ˈhelmɪt/ (**helmets**) N-COUNT A **helmet** is a hard hat which you wear to protect your head.
→ see **army, hat**

help /help/ (**helps, helping, helped**) 1 V-T/V-I If you **help** someone, you make something easier for them to do, for example by doing part of their work or by giving them advice or money. ❑ *He has helped to raise a lot of money.* ❑ *A neighbour helped me clean the house.* ❑ *He began to help with the housework.* 2 V-T/V-I & N-SING If something **helps**, or if someone or something is **a help**, they make something easier to do or get, or they improve a situation. ❑ *It will do very little to help our environment.* ❑ *I would be happy to help.* ❑ *The books were not much help.* 3 V-T If you **help yourself to** something, you serve yourself or you take it for yourself. ❑ *Help yourself to a Pepsi.* ❑ *There's bread on the table. Help yourself.* 4 N-UNCOUNT & EXCLAM **Help** is the assistance that someone gives when they go to rescue a person who is in danger. You shout **'help!'** when you are in danger in order to attract someone's attention so that they can come and rescue you. ❑ *He was screaming for help.* 5 PHRASE If you **can't help** the way you feel or behave, you cannot control it or stop it happening. You can also say that you **can't help yourself**. ❑ *'Please don't cry.'—'I can't help it.'* 6 → See note at **avoid** 7 PHRASE If something or someone **is of help**, they make things easier or better. ❑ *Can I be of help to you?*
→ see **donor**

▶ **help out** PHR-VERB If you **help** someone **out**, you help them by doing some work for them or by lending them some money.

Thesaurus *help* Also look up:

V.	aid, assist, support; (*ant.*) hinder 1
N.	aid, assistance, guidance, support 4

Word Partnership Use *help* with:

ADJ.	**financial** help, **professional** help 1
V.	**ask for** help, **get** help, **need** help, **want to** help 1 **try to** help 1 2 **cry/scream/shout for** help 5

helper /ˈhelpə/ (**helpers**) N-COUNT A **helper** is a person who helps another person or group with a job they are doing, usually an organized activity.

helpful /ˈhelpfʊl/ 1 ADJ If someone is **helpful**, they help you by doing work for you or by giving you advice or information. ❑ *The staff in the London office are helpful.* ● **helpfully** ADV ❑ *They had helpfully given us instructions.* 2 ADJ Something that is **helpful** makes a situation more pleasant or easier to tolerate. ❑ *Having the right equipment will be enormously helpful.*

helpless /ˈhelpləs/ ADJ If you are **helpless**, you do not have the strength or power to do anything useful or to protect yourself. ❑ *Your child will develop from a helpless baby to an independent toddler.* ● **helplessly** ADV ❑ *They watched helplessly as the house burnt to the ground.* ● **helplessness** N-UNCOUNT ❑ *...his sense of helplessness.*

hem /hem/ (**hems, hemming, hemmed**) 1 N-COUNT The **hem** of a piece of cloth is an edge which is folded over and sewn. The **hem** of a skirt or dress is the hem along its lower edge. 2 V-T If

you **hem** a piece of cloth, you fold the edge over and sew it to make it neat.
▸ **hem in** PHR-VERB If you are **hemmed in** by something, you are completely surrounded by it so that you cannot move. You can also say that a place is **hemmed in** when it is surrounded by something tall such as mountains or tall buildings. ❑ *You feel hemmed in. Find open spaces, get in touch with nature.* ❑ *...a small valley hemmed in by rocks.*

Word Link *sphere ≈ ball : atmosphere, hemisphere, sphere*

hemisphere /'hemɪsfɪə/ (**hemispheres**) N-COUNT A **hemisphere** is one half of the earth. ❑ *...the northern hemisphere.*
→ see **globe, solid**

hemorrhage /'hemərɪdʒ/ → see **haemorrhage**

hen /hen/ (**hens**) **1** N-COUNT A **hen** is a female chicken. **2** N-COUNT The female of any bird can be referred to as a **hen**. ❑ *...ostrich hens.*

H

hence /hens/ **1** ADV **Hence** means for the reason just mentioned. [FORMAL] ❑ *The Socialist Party was divided and hence very weak.* **2** ADV If something will happen a particular length of time **hence**, it will happen that length of time from now. ❑ *The election two years hence seems a long way off.*

henceforth /ˌhens'fɔːθ/ ADV **Henceforth** means from this time onwards. [FORMAL] ❑ *Henceforth, all churches and religious societies will be legally recognised.*

Word Link *itis ≈ inflammation : arthritis, hepatitis, meningitis*

hepatitis /ˌhepə'taɪtɪs/ N-UNCOUNT **Hepatitis** is a serious disease which affects the liver.

her /hə, STRONG hɜː/ **1** PRON & DET You use **her** to refer to a woman, girl, or female animal. ❑ *I really thought I'd lost her.* ❑ *Liz travelled round the world for a year with her boyfriend, James.* **2** PRON & DET **Her** is sometimes used to refer to a country or nation. ❑ *...Britain's friendship with her EU partner.* **3** PRON & DET People sometimes use **her** to refer informally to a car, ship, or machine. ❑ *Kemp got out of his car. 'Just fill her up, thanks.'*

herald /'herəld/ (**heralds, heralding, heralded**) **1** V-T & N-COUNT Something that **heralds** a future event or situation, or is a **herald of** it, is a sign that it is going to happen or appear. ❑ *Their discovery could herald a cure for cancer.* **2** V-T If an important event or action **is heralded** by people, announcements are made about it so that it is publicly known and expected. ❑ *Tonight's match between Real Madrid and Arsenal is being heralded as the match of the season.*

herb /hɜːb, AM ɜːb/ (**herbs**) N-COUNT A **herb** is a plant whose leaves are used in cookery to add flavour to food, or as a medicine. ● **herbal** ADJ ❑ *...herbal treatments for colds.*
→ see Picture Dictionary: **herb**

herd /hɜːd/ (**herds, herding, herded**) **1** N-COUNT A **herd** is a large group of animals of one kind that live together. ❑ *...a herd of cows.* **2** V-T If you **herd** people or animals somewhere, you make them move there in a group. ❑ *The group was herded into a bus.*

here /hɪə/ **1** ADV You use **here** when you are referring to the place where you are. ❑ *I'm here all by myself.* ❑ *Well, I can't stand here chatting all day.* ❑ *Sheila was in here a minute ago.* **2** ADV You use **here** when you are pointing towards a place that is near you, in order to draw someone else's attention to it. ❑ *Please just sign here.* ❑ *Come and sit here, Lauren.* **3** ADV You use **here** at the beginning of a sentence in order to draw attention to something or someone who has just arrived in the place where you are, or to draw attention to the place you have just arrived at. ❑ *'Here's the taxi,' she said politely.* ❑ *Here comes your husband.* **4** ADV You use **here** to refer to a particular point that you have reached in a discussion or process. ❑ *It's here that we come up against some problems.* **5** ADV You use **here** when you are offering or giving something to someone. ❑ *Here's my mother's number.* ❑ *Here's a letter I want you to sign.*

hereditary /hɪ'redɪtri/ **1** ADJ A **hereditary** characteristic or illness is passed on to a child from its parents before it is born. ❑ *'Hunter Syndrome' is a rare hereditary disease.* **2** ADJ A **hereditary** title or position in society is passed on as a right from parent to child.

Picture Dictionary herb

Word Web hero

Odysseus is a **hero** from Greek **mythology**. He is a warrior. He is brave in battle. He faces many **dangers**. However he knows he must return home after the Trojan War*. During his **epic** journey home, Odysseus faces many trials. He must survive wild storms at sea and fight a monster. He must also resist the temptations of sirens and outsmart the goddess Circe*. At home Penelope, Odysseus' wife, **defends** their home and **protects** their son. She remains **loyal** and **brave** through many trials. She is the **heroine** of the story.

Trojan War: a legendary war between Greece and Troy.
Circe: a Greek goddess.

Odysseus saves his men from the Cyclops.

h

heresy /ˈherɪsi/ (**heresies**) N-VAR **Heresy** is a belief or way of behaving that disagrees with generally accepted beliefs, especially religious ones. ❑ *Galileo was put on trial for heresy.*

heritage /ˈherɪtɪdʒ/ N-SING A country's **heritage** consists of all the qualities and traditions that have continued over many years, especially when they are considered to be of historical importance. ❑ *Bullfighting is part of Spain's heritage.*

hermit /ˈhɜːmɪt/ (**hermits**) N-COUNT A **hermit** is a person who deliberately lives alone, away from people and society.

hernia /ˈhɜːniə/ (**hernias**) N-COUNT A **hernia** is a medical condition in which one of your internal organs sticks through a weak point in the surrounding tissue.

hero /ˈhɪərəʊ/ (**heroes**) **1** N-COUNT The **hero** of a book, play, or film is the main male character, who usually has good qualities. **2** N-COUNT A **hero** is someone who has done something brave or good and is admired by a lot of people. ❑ *Nelson Mandela is a hero who has inspired millions of people.*
→ see Word Web: **hero**
→ see **myth**

heroic /hɪˈrəʊɪk/ (**heroics**) **1** ADJ **Heroic** people or actions are brave and determined. ❑ *A heroic six-year-old child saved his friend from being burned to death.* ❑ *...his heroic effort to negotiate the release of hostages.* ● **heroically** ADV ❑ *He had acted heroically aboard the Titanic.* **2** N-PLURAL You can describe actions involving bravery or determination as **heroics**. ❑ *...his wartime heroics as a fighter pilot.* **3** N-PLURAL If you describe someone's actions as **heroics**, you mean that they are foolish or dangerous because they are too difficult for the situation in which they occur. [SPOKEN] ❑ *His advice was: 'No heroics, stay within the law'.*

heroin /ˈherəʊɪn/ N-UNCOUNT **Heroin** is a powerful addictive drug used to prevent pain. Some people take it for pleasure and it is illegal in most countries.

heroine /ˈherəʊɪn/ (**heroines**) **1** N-COUNT The **heroine** of a book, play, or film is its main female character, who usually has good qualities. **2** N-COUNT A **heroine** is a woman who has done something brave or good and is admired by a lot of people. ❑ *Boadicea is our national heroine.*
→ see **hero**

heroism /ˈherəʊɪzəm/ N-UNCOUNT **Heroism** is great courage and bravery. ❑ *...acts of heroism.*

herpes /ˈhɜːpiːz/ N-UNCOUNT **Herpes** is the name used for several viruses which cause painful red spots to appear on the skin. [TECHNICAL]

herring /ˈherɪŋ/

The plural is **herring** or **herrings**.

N-VAR A **herring** is a long silver-coloured fish. **Herring** is the flesh of this fish eaten as food.

hers /hɜːz/ PRON You use **hers** to indicate that something belongs or relates to a woman, girl, or female animal that has already been mentioned, or whose identity is known. ❑ *His language was not so different from hers.* ❑ *...a great friend of hers.*

herself /həˈself/ **1** PRON You use **herself** to refer to the same woman, girl, or female animal that is mentioned as the subject of the clause, or as a previous object in the clause. ❑ *She let herself out of the room.* ❑ *Jane didn't feel good about herself.* **2** PRON You use **herself** to emphasize the female subject or object of a clause, and to make it clear who you are referring to. ❑ *Has anyone thought of asking Bethan herself?* **3** PRON If a girl or woman does something **herself**, she does it without any help or interference from anyone else. ❑ *The jam was marvellous. She had made it herself.*

he's /hɪz, hiːz/ **He's** is the usual spoken form of 'he is' or 'he has', especially when 'has' is an auxiliary verb.

hesitant /ˈhezɪtənt/ ADJ If you are **hesitant about** doing something, you do not do it quickly or immediately, usually because you are uncertain, embarrassed, or worried. ❑ *She was hesitant about telling her story.* ❑ *At first he was hesitant to accept the role.* ● **hesitancy** N-UNCOUNT ❑ *Why is there this hesitancy about saying whether you've made a decision?* ● **hesitantly** ADV ❑ *'Would you do me a favour?' she asked hesitantly.*

hesitate /ˈhezɪteɪt/ (**hesitates, hesitating, hesitated**) **1** V-I If you **hesitate**, you pause slightly while you are doing something or just before you do it, usually because you are uncertain, embarrassed, or worried. ❑ *She hesitated before replying.* ● **hesitation** (**hesitations**) N-VAR ❑ *After a moment's hesitation, the others followed him.* **2** V-T If you **hesitate to** do something, you are unwilling to do it because you are not certain whether it is the right thing to do. ❑ *Many women hesitate to discuss money.* ❑ *Don't hesitate to say no if you'd rather not.* • **hesitation** N-VAR ❑ *He promised there would be no more hesitations.*

Thesaurus	*hesitate* Also look up:
V.	falter, pause, wait 1 2

heterosexual /ˌhetərəʊ'sekʃʊəl/ (**heterosexuals**) ADJ & N-COUNT Someone who is **heterosexual** or a **heterosexual**, is sexually attracted to people of the opposite sex. • **heterosexuality** /ˌhetərəʊˌsekʃʊ'ælɪti/ N-UNCOUNT ❑ *...the notion that heterosexuality was 'normal'.*

hey /heɪ/ CONVENTION You say or shout **'hey'** to attract someone's attention or show surprise, interest, or annoyance. [INFORMAL] ❑ *Hey! You!*

H

heyday /'heɪdeɪ/ N-SING The **heyday** of someone or something is the time when they are most powerful, successful, or popular. ❑ *...the heyday of the railways.*

hi /haɪ/ CONVENTION You say **'hi'** when you are greeting someone. [INFORMAL] ❑ *'Hi, Darren.'*

hiccup also **hiccough** /'hɪkʌp/ (**hiccups, hiccuping, hiccuped**) 1 V-I & N-COUNT When you **hiccup**, or when you have **hiccups**, you make repeated sharp sounds in your throat, often because you have been eating or drinking too quickly. 2 N-COUNT You can refer to a minor problem as a **hiccup**. ❑ *There has only been one slight hiccup.*

hid /hɪd/ **Hid** is the past tense of **hide**.

hidden /'hɪdən/ 1 **Hidden** is the past participle of **hide**. 2 ADJ Something that is **hidden** is not easily noticed. ❑ *...hidden dangers.* 3 ADJ A place that is **hidden** is difficult to find. ❑ *...a hidden valley.*

hide /haɪd/ (**hides, hiding, hid, hidden**) 1 V-T To **hide** something means to cover it or put it somewhere so that it cannot be seen. ❑ *She hid her face in her hands.* ❑ *...a bomb hidden in a briefcase.* 2 V-T/V-I If you **hide**, or if you **hide yourself**, you go somewhere where you cannot easily be seen or found. ❑ *They hid themselves behind a tree.* 3 V-T If you **hide** what you feel or know, you keep it a secret. ❑ *Lee tried to hide his excitement.* 4 N-COUNT A **hide** is a place which is built to look like its surroundings, so that people can watch or photograph animals and birds without being seen by them. [BRIT] 5 N-VAR A **hide** is the skin of a large animal, used for making leather. ❑ *...cow hides.*

Thesaurus	*hide* Also look up:
V.	camouflage, cover, lock up 1

Word Partnership	Use *hide* with:
ADV.	**nowhere to** hide 1 2 3
V.	**attempt/try to** hide 1 2 3
	run and hide 2
N.	hide ***your*** **face** 1
	hide **a fact/secret**, hide ***your*** **disappointment/fear/feelings/tears** 3

hideous /'hɪdiəs/ ADJ If you say that someone or something is **hideous**, you mean that they are extremely unpleasant or ugly. ❑ *...a hideous crime.* ❑ *...his hideous face.* • **hideously** ADV ❑ *He is hideously disfigured.*

hiding /'haɪdɪŋ/ N-UNCOUNT If someone is **in hiding**, they have secretly gone somewhere where they cannot be found. ❑ *He is thought to be in hiding.* ❑ *He went into hiding 18 months ago.*

Word Link	
arch ≈ rule : anarchy, hierarchy, monarch	

hierarchy /'haɪərɑːki/ (**hierarchies**) 1 N-VAR A **hierarchy** is a system in which people have different ranks or positions depending on how important they are. ❑ *Our society is ordered by hierarchy.* • **hierarchical** /haɪə'rɑːkɪkəl/ ADJ ❑ *...a hierarchical society.* 2 N-COUNT The **hierarchy** of an organization such as the Church is the group of people who manage and control it.

hi-fi /'haɪ faɪ/ (**hi-fis**) N-COUNT A **hi-fi** is a set of stereo equipment which you use to play records, tapes, and compact discs.

Word Link	
est ≈ most : coldest, highest, largest	

high /haɪ/ (**higher, highest, highs**) 1 ADJ & ADV A **high** structure or mountain measures a great amount from the bottom to the top. ❑ *The house has a high wall around it.* ❑ *...the highest mountain in the world.* ❑ *...high-heeled shoes.* ❑ *The sofa was piled high with cushions.*

Usage

Be careful not to use **high** to describe people. The word you should use is **tall**. ❑ *She was rather tall for a woman.* **Tall** is also used to describe buildings such as skyscrapers, and other things whose height is much greater than their width. ❑ *...tall pine trees.* ❑ *...a tall glass vase.*

2 ADJ You use **high** to talk or ask about how much something upright measures from the bottom to the top. ❑ *The primrose is only six inches high with flat, pale yellow blossoms.* ❑ *How high is the door?* 3 ADJ & ADV If something is **high**, it is a long way above the ground, above sea level, or above a person or thing. ❑ *I looked down from the high window.* ❑ *The sun was high in the sky.* ❑ *...being able to run faster or jump higher than other people.* 4 ADJ & ADV **High** means great in amount, degree, or intensity. ❑ *Official reports said casualties were high.* ❑ *High winds have knocked down trees.* ❑ *Unemployment figures will rise even higher.* 5 ADJ If a number or level is in the **high** eighties, it is more than eighty-five, but not as much as ninety. 6 ADJ AFTER LINK-V If a food or other substance is **high in** a particular ingredient, it contains a large amount of that ingredient. ❑ *...high in calcium.* 7 N-COUNT If something reaches a **high** of a particular amount or degree, that is the greatest it has ever been. ❑ *Sales of German sausage have reached an all-time high.* 8 ADJ If you say that something is a **high priority** or is **high** on your list, you mean that you consider it to be one of the most important things you have to do. 9 ADJ **High** means advanced or complex. ❑ *...Japan's high-technology industries.* 10 ADJ Someone who is **high in** a particular profession or society, or who has a **high** position, has an important position and has great authority and influence. 11 ADJ If people have a **high** opinion

of you, they respect you very much. 12 ADJ If the quality or standard of something is **high**, it is very good indeed. 13 ADJ If someone has **high** principles or standards, they are morally good. 14 ADJ If your spirits are **high**, you feel happy and excited. 15 to **be high time** → see **time**

ˌhigh-ˈclass ADJ **High-class** is used to describe people and things which are the very best of their type. ❑ *...a high-class hotel.*

higher /haɪə/ **Higher** is the comparative form of **high**.

ˌhigher eduˈcation N-UNCOUNT **Higher education** is education at universities and colleges.

ˌhigh-ˈflying ADJ A **high-flying** person is very ambitious and is likely to be successful in their career. ❑ *...a high-flying executive.*

ˌhigh-ˈimpact ADJ **High-impact** exercise puts a lot of stress on your body. ❑ *...high-impact aerobics.*

highlands /ˈhaɪləndz/ N-PLURAL **Highlands** are mountainous areas. ❑ *...the highlands of Scotland.*

highlight /ˈhaɪlaɪt/ (**highlights, highlighting, highlighted**) 1 V-T If you **highlight** a point or problem, you draw attention to it. ❑ *The report highlights the need for a new airport.* 2 N-COUNT The **highlights** of an event, activity, or period of time are the most interesting or exciting parts of it.

highly /ˈhaɪli/ 1 ADV You use **highly** to emphasize that a particular quality exists to a great degree. ❑ *...highly confidential information.* ❑ *...highly skilled craftsmen.* 2 ADV You use **highly** to indicate that someone has an important position in an organization or set of people. ❑ *...a highly important government official.* 3 ADV If you **think highly** of something or someone, you think they are very good indeed.

Word Partnership Use *highly* with:

V. highly **recommended**, highly **respected** 1
ADJ. highly **addictive**, highly **competitive**, highly **contagious**, highly **controversial**, highly **critical**, highly **educated**, highly **intelligent**, highly **qualified**, highly **skilled**, highly **successful**, highly **technical**, highly **trained**, highly **unlikely**, highly **visible** 1
highly **paid** 1 2

Highness /ˈhaɪnɪs/ (**Highnesses**) N-VOC You use expressions such as **Your Highness** and **His Highness** to address or refer to a member of a royal family.

ˌhigh-ˈpitched ADJ A **high-pitched** sound is very high. ❑ *...a high-pitched scream.*

ˌhigh-ˈpowered ADJ **High-powered** professional people are in a job which carries a lot of responsibility or status. ❑ *...high-powered businessmen.*

ˌhigh-ˈprofile ADJ A **high-profile** person or event attracts a lot of attention or publicity. ❑ *...high-profile court cases.*

ˈhigh-rise (**high-rises**) N-COUNT & ADJ BEFORE N A **high-rise**, or a **high-rise** building, is a very tall modern building. ❑ *...high-rise flats.*

ˈhigh ˌschool (**high schools**) 1 N-VAR In Britain, a **high school** is a school for children aged between eleven and eighteen. 2 N-VAR In the United States, a **high school** is a school for children aged between fourteen and eighteen.
→ see **graduation**

ˈhigh ˌstreet (**high streets**) N-COUNT The **high street** of a town is the main street where most of the shops and banks are. [BRIT]

ˌhigh ˈtech also **hi tech** ADJ **High tech** activities or equipment involve or result from the use of high technology. ❑ *...such high-tech industries as computers.*

ˌhigh techˈnology N-UNCOUNT **High technology** is the development and use of advanced electronics and computers.

highway /ˈhaɪweɪ/ (**highways**) N-COUNT A **highway** is a main road, especially one that connects towns or cities. [AM]
→ see **traffic**

hijack /ˈhaɪdʒæk/ (**hijacks, hijacking, hijacked**) V-T & N-COUNT If someone **hijacks** a plane or other vehicle, they illegally take control of it by force while it is travelling from one place to another. An illegal action like this is called a **hijack**. ●**hijacker** (**hijackers**) N-COUNT ❑ *There was a struggle between the hijackers and the pilots.* ●**hijacking** (**hijackings**) N-COUNT ❑ *There are nearly 50 car hijackings every day.*

hike /haɪk/ (**hikes, hiking, hiked**) 1 V-I & N-COUNT If you **hike**, or if you go on a **hike**, you go for a long walk in the country. ❑ *You could hike through the Fish River Canyon.* ●**hiker** (**hikers**) N-COUNT ❑ *He was a keen hiker who enjoyed walking in Oxfordshire.* ●**hiking** N-UNCOUNT ❑ *...hiking on cliff paths.* 2 V-T & PHR-VERB To **hike** prices, rates, or taxes, or to **hike** them **up**, means to increase them suddenly or by a large amount. [JOURNALISM] ❑ *The government hiked the tax on air travel.*

hilarious /hɪˈleəriəs/ ADJ If something is **hilarious**, it is extremely funny. ●**hilariously** ADV ❑ *She found it hilariously funny.*

hill /hɪl/ (**hills**) N-COUNT A **hill** is an area of land that is higher than the land that surrounds it, but not as high as a mountain.

hilly /ˈhɪli/ (**hillier, hilliest**) ADJ A **hilly** area has a lot of hills.

him /hɪm/ 1 PRON You use **him** to refer to a man, boy, or male animal. ❑ *Elaine met him at the bus station.* 2 PRON **Him** can be used to refer to someone whose sex is not known or stated. Some people dislike this use and prefer to use 'him or her' or 'them'. [WRITTEN] ❑ *Spending time with the child during the day will make him feel more secure in the evening and at night.*

himself /hɪmˈself/ 1 PRON You use **himself** to refer to the same man, boy, or male animal that is mentioned as the subject of the clause, or as a previous object in the clause. ❑ *A driver blew up his car and himself.* ❑ *He poured himself a drink.* 2 PRON You use **himself** to emphasize the male subject or object of a clause, and to make it clear who you are referring to. ❑ *...a letter written by Pope John Paul II himself.* 3 PRON If a man or boy does something **himself**, he does it without any help. ❑ *George had written it himself.*

hind /haɪnd/ (**hinds**) 1 ADJ BEFORE N An animal's **hind legs** are at the back of its body. 2 N-COUNT A **hind** is a female deer.

hinder /ˈhɪndə/ (**hinders, hindering, hindered**) V-T If something **hinders** you, it makes it more difficult for you to do something. ❑ *A thigh injury hindered her ability to walk comfortably.*

hindrance /ˈhɪndrəns/ (**hindrances**) 1 N-COUNT A **hindrance** is someone or something that hinders you. 2 N-UNCOUNT **Hindrance** is the act of hindering someone or something. ❑ *They boarded their flight to Paris without hindrance.*

hindsight /ˈhaɪndsaɪt/ N-UNCOUNT **Hindsight** is the ability to understand something about an event after it has happened, although you did not understand or realize it at the time. ❑ *With hindsight, we would all do things differently.*

Hindu /ˈhɪnduː, hɪnˈduː/ (**Hindus**) 1 N-COUNT A **Hindu** is a person who believes in Hinduism. 2 ADJ **Hindu** is used to describe things that belong or relate to Hinduism. ❑ *...a Hindu temple.*

H

Hinduism /ˈhɪnduːɪzəm/ N-UNCOUNT **Hinduism** is an Indian religion, which has many gods and teaches that people have another life after they die.

hinge /hɪndʒ/ (**hinges, hinging, hinged**)

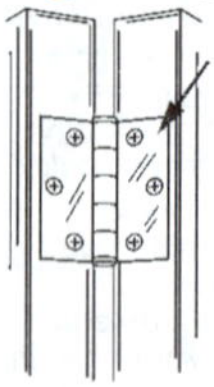

hinge

1 N-COUNT A **hinge** is a moveable joint made of metal, wood, or plastic that joins two things so that one of them can swing freely. 2 ADJ Something that is **hinged** is joined to another thing by means of a hinge. ❑ *The hinged seat lifts up to reveal a useful storage space.*
▸ **hinge on** PHR-VERB Something that **hinges on** one thing or event depends entirely on it. ❑ *The plan hinges on his agreement.*

hint /hɪnt/ (**hints, hinting, hinted**) 1 V-I/V-T & N-COUNT If you **hint at** something, or if you **drop a hint** about it, you suggest it in an indirect way. ❑ *She hinted at a trip to her favourite shop.* ❑ *The President hinted that he might make some changes.* 2 N-COUNT A **hint** is a helpful piece of advice. ❑ *The book gives handy hints on looking after indoor plants.* 3 N-SING A **hint of** something is a very small amount of it. ❑ *She added only a hint of chilli powder to the soup.*

Word Partnership Use *hint* with:

V.	**take a** hint 1
	drop a hint, **give a** hint 1 2
ADJ.	**broad** hint 1
	helpful hint 2

hip /hɪp/ (**hips**) 1 N-COUNT Your **hips** are the two areas or bones at the sides of your body between the tops of your legs and your waist. 2 ADJ If you say that someone is **hip**, you mean that they are fashionable. [INFORMAL] ❑ *...a hip young American writer.*

hippie also **hippy** /ˈhɪpi/ (**hippies**) N-COUNT In the 1960s and 1970s, **hippies** were people who rejected conventional society and tried to live a life based on peace and love.

hire /haɪə/ (**hires, hiring, hired**) 1 V-T & N-UNCOUNT If you **hire** something, or if you have it **on hire**, you pay money to use it for a period of time. [BRIT] ❑ *The bikes are on hire.* ❑ *We hired skis, boots and warm clothing.* 2 PHRASE If something is **for hire**, it is available for you to hire. [BRIT] 3 V-T/V-I If you **hire** someone, you pay them to work for you. ❑ *You will need to hire a lawyer.* ❑ *He will be in charge of all hiring and firing at PHA.*
▸ **hire out** PHR-VERB If you **hire out** something such as a car or a person's services, you allow them to be used in return for payment. ❑ *His agency hires out bodyguards.*

his /hɪz/ 1 DET & PRON You use **his** to indicate that something belongs or relates to a man, boy, or male animal. ❑ *He spent a large part of his career in Hollywood.* ❑ *My dinner jacket is as nice as his.* 2 DET **His** can be used to refer to someone whose sex is not known or stated. Some people dislike this use and prefer to use 'his or her' or 'their'. ❑ *...the relations between a teacher and his pupils.*

Hispanic /hɪˈspænɪk/ (**Hispanics**) ADJ & N-COUNT If you describe someone from the United States as **Hispanic**, or if you refer to them as a **Hispanic**, you mean that they or their family originally came from Latin America.

hiss /hɪs/ (**hisses, hissing, hissed**) 1 V-I & N-COUNT To **hiss** means to make a sound like a long 's', called a **hiss**. ❑ *The tires of Lenny's bike hissed over the wet pavement.* • **hissing** N-UNCOUNT ❑ *I could hear a steady hissing above my head.* 2 V-T If you **hiss** something, you say it in a strong angry whisper. ❑ *'Now, quiet,' my mother hissed.*

historian /hɪˈstɔːriən/ (**historians**) N-COUNT A **historian** is a person who specializes in the study of history and who writes about it.
→ see **history**

historic /hɪˈstɒrɪk, AM -ˈtɔːr-/ ADJ A **historic** event is important in history, or likely to be considered important at some time in the future. ❑ *...the historic changes in Eastern Europe.*

historical /hɪˈstɒrɪkəl, AM -tɔːr-/ 1 ADJ BEFORE N **Historical** people, situations, or things existed in the past and are considered to be a part of history. • **historically** ADV ❑ *Gibraltar has historically been very important to Britain.* 2 ADJ BEFORE N **Historical** books, works of art, or studies are concerned with people, situations, or things that existed in the past.

Word Partnership Use *historical* with:

N.	historical **events**, historical **figure**, historical **impact**, historical **significance** 1
	historical **detail/fact**, historical **records**, historical **research** 2

history /ˈhɪstəri/ (**histories**) 1 N-UNCOUNT You can refer to the events of the past as **history**. You can also refer to the past events which concern a particular topic or place as its **history**. ❑ *He later studied history at Indiana University.* ❑ *...great moments in football history.* 2 N-COUNT A **history** is an account of events that have happened in the past in a particular subject. ❑ *...an article on the history of broadcasting.* 3 N-COUNT Someone's **history** is the set of facts that are known about their past. ❑ *...the boy's medical history.* 4 N-COUNT If someone has a **history of** something bad, they keep doing that thing or it keeps happening to them. ❑ *...a man with a long history of violence.*
→ see Word Web: **history**

Word Web history

3800 BC The wheel is invented.

2600 BC The Pyramid of Giza is built.

31 BC Roman Empire founded.

700 AD The Great Wall of China is started.

1200 AD Incan empire is founded.

1492 Columbus sails for America.

1969 Humans land on the Moon.

Open any history textbook and you will find timelines. They show important dates for **ancient civilizations**—when **empires** appeared and disappeared, and when **wars** were fought. But, how much of what we read in **history** books is **fact**? **Accounts** of the **past** are often based on how archeologists interpret the **artefacts** they find. **Scholars** often rely on the **records** of the people who were in power. These **historians** included certain facts and left out others. Historians today look beyond official records. They research **documents** such as **diaries**, written by people who lived in the past. They describe **events** from different **points of view**.

h

Word Partnership Use *history* with:

V. **go down in** history, **make** history **teach** history 1
N. **the course of** history, **world** history 1 **family** history **life** history 2 3

hit /hɪt/ (**hits, hitting, hit**) 1 V-T If you **hit** someone or something, you deliberately strike or touch them forcefully, with your hand or with an object held in your hand. ❑ *Both men had been hit in the stomach with baseball bats.* 2 V-T & N-COUNT When a moving object **hits** another object, it strikes or touches it with a lot of force. This impact is called a **hit**. ❑ *The car hit a traffic sign.* ❑ *The house took a direct hit from a falling bomb.* 3 V-T If something **hits** a person, place, or thing, it affects them badly. ❑ *The earthquake hit northern Peru.* 4 V-T When a feeling or an idea **hits** you, it suddenly comes into your mind. ❑ *Then the answer hit me.* 5 N-COUNT If a record, play, or film is a **hit**, it is very popular and successful. 6 N-COUNT A **hit** is a single visit to a website. [COMPUTING] ❑ *Our company has had 78,000 hits on its website.* 7 PHRASE If two people **hit it off**, they become friendly as soon as they meet. [INFORMAL]
▶ **hit on** or **hit upon** PHR-VERB If you **hit on** an idea or a solution to a problem, or if you **hit upon** it, you think of it.

Thesaurus *hit* Also look up:

V. bang, beat, knock, pound, slap, smack, strike 1 2

Word Partnership Use *hit* with:

N. hit **a ball**, hit **the brakes**, hit **a button** 1 **earthquakes/famine/storms** hit ***someplace*** 3 a hit **movie/show/song** 5

ˌhit-and-ˈrun ADJ BEFORE N In a **hit-and-run accident**, the driver of a vehicle hits someone and then drives away without stopping. ❑ *...a hit-and-run driver in a stolen car.*

hitch /hɪtʃ/ (**hitches, hitching, hitched**) 1 N-COUNT A **hitch** is a slight problem. 2 V-T/V-I If you **hitch**, or if you **hitch** a lift, you hitchhike. ❑ *Philippe had hitched all over Europe.* 3 V-T If you **hitch** one thing **to** or **onto** something else, you fasten it there. ❑ *We hitched the horse to the cart.*

hitchhike also **hitch-hike** /ˈhɪtʃhaɪk/ (**hitchhikes, hitchhiking, hitchhiked**) V-I If you **hitchhike**, you travel by getting free lifts from passing vehicles. ❑ *Neff hitchhiked to London.*
● **hitchhiker** (**hitchhikers**) N-COUNT ❑ *On my way to Newcastle I picked up a hitchhiker.*

ˌhi ˈtech → see **high tech**

hitherto /ˌhɪðəˈtuː/ ADV You use **hitherto** to indicate that something was true up until the time you are talking about, although it may no longer be the case. [FORMAL] ❑ *A hitherto unknown poem has been found in the university archives.*

ˈhit list (**hit lists**) N-COUNT A terrorist's or gangster's **hit list** are the people they intend to kill.

HIV /ˌeɪtʃaɪ ˈviː/ 1 N-UNCOUNT **HIV** is a virus which reduces people's resistance to illness and can cause AIDS. **HIV** is an abbreviation for 'human immunodeficiency virus'. 2 PHRASE If someone is **HIV positive**, they are infected with the HIV virus, and may develop AIDS.

hive /haɪv/ (**hives**) 1 N-COUNT A **hive** is a structure in which bees are kept. 2 N-COUNT If you describe a place as a **hive of activity**, you approve of the fact that there is a lot of activity there or that people are busy working there.

hoard /hɔːd/ (**hoards, hoarding, hoarded**) 1 V-T If you **hoard** things such as food or money, you save or store them, often in secret, because they are valuable or important to you. ❑ *They began to hoard food and save money.* 2 N-SING A **hoard** is a store of things you have hoarded or secretly hidden.

hoarding /ˈhɔːdɪŋ/ (**hoardings**) N-COUNT In British English, a **hoarding** is a large board used for advertising which stands at the side of a road. The usual American word is **billboard**.

hoarse /hɔːs/ (**hoarser, hoarsest**) ADJ If you are **hoarse**, your voice sounds rough and unclear, for example because your throat is sore. ● **hoarsely** ADV ❑ *'Thank you,' Maria said hoarsely.*

hoax /həʊks/ (**hoaxes**) N-COUNT A **hoax** is a trick in which someone tells people something that is not true, for example that there is a bomb somewhere.

hob /hɒb/ (**hobs**) N-COUNT A **hob** is a surface on top of a cooker which can be heated in order to cook things.

hobble /ˈhɒbəl/ (**hobbles, hobbling, hobbled**) 1 V-I If you **hobble**, you walk with difficulty because you are in pain. ❑ *He got up slowly and hobbled over to the coffee table.* 2 V-T To **hobble** something or someone means to make it more difficult for them to be successful or to achieve what they want. ❑ *The poor transport system has hobbled the area.*

H

hobby /ˈhɒbi/ (**hobbies**) N-COUNT A **hobby** is something that you enjoy doing in your spare time, for example reading or playing tennis.

Thesaurus	*hobby* Also look up:
N.	activity, craft, interest, pastime

hockey /ˈhɒki/ 1 N-UNCOUNT **Hockey** is a sport played between two teams of 11 players who use long curved sticks to hit a small ball and try to score goals. 2 → see also **ice hockey**

hoe /həʊ/ (**hoes**) N-COUNT A **hoe** is a gardening tool with a long handle and a small square blade, which you use to remove small weeds and break up the surface of the soil.
→ see **garden**

hog /hɒg, AM hɔːg/ (**hogs, hogging, hogged**) 1 N-COUNT A **hog** is a pig. 2 V-T If you **hog** something, you use it or take all of it in a selfish or rude way. [INFORMAL] ❑ *Have you finished hogging the bathroom?*

hoist /hɔɪst/ (**hoists, hoisting, hoisted**) 1 V-T If you **hoist** a heavy object somewhere, you lift it or pull it up there, often using equipment or machinery of some kind. ❑ *Hoisting my suitcase on to my shoulder, I turned and headed towards my hotel.* ❑ *A twenty-foot steel pyramid is to be hoisted into position.* 2 N-COUNT A **hoist** is a machine for lifting heavy things. 3 V-T If you **hoist** a **flag** or a **sail**, you pull it up to its correct position using ropes.

hold
1 PHYSICALLY TOUCHING, SUPPORTING, OR CONTAINING
2 HAVING OR DOING
3 CONTROLLING OR REMAINING
4 PHRASES
5 PHRASAL VERBS

hold /həʊld/ (**holds, holding, held**)
1 1 V-T & N-COUNT When you **hold** something, you carry or support it, using your hands or your arms. Your **hold on** something is the fact that you are holding it. ❑ *Hold the baby while I load the car.* ❑ *I could feel him tighten his hold on the stick.* 2 N-UNCOUNT **Hold** is used in expressions such as **grab hold of, catch hold of,** and **get hold of,** to indicate that you close your hand tightly around something. ❑ *Mother took hold of the barking dogs by their collars.* 3 V-T If you **hold** your body or part of your body in a particular position, you keep it in that position. ❑ *Hold your hands in front of your face.* 4 V-T If one thing **holds** another in a particular position, it keeps it in that position. ❑ *The rock is holding the heavy door open.* 5 V-T If one thing is used to **hold** another, it is used to store it. ❑ *Two drawers hold her favourite T-shirts.* 6 V-T If something **holds** a particular amount of something, it can contain that amount. ❑ *The small bottles don't seem to hold much.* 7 N-COUNT The **hold** of a ship or aeroplane is the place where cargo is stored. 8 → see also **holding**

Thesaurus	*hold* Also look up:
V.	carry, cradle, embrace, hug, support ① 1

hold /həʊld/ (**holds, holding, held**)
2 1 V-T If you **hold** a particular opinion or belief, that is your opinion or belief. ❑ *He held firm opinions which I didn't agree with.* 2 V-T You can use **hold** to say that something has a particular quality or characteristic. ❑ *Death doesn't hold any fear for me.* 3 V-T **Hold** is used with nouns such as 'office', 'power', and 'responsibility' to indicate that someone has a particular position of power or authority. ❑ *He held the position of chairman for 11 years.* 4 V-T **Hold** is used with nouns such as 'permit', 'degree', or 'ticket' to indicate that someone has a particular document that allows them to do something. ❑ *He does not hold a driving licence.* ● **holder** (**holders**) N-COUNT ❑ *...season-ticket holders.* 5 V-T If you **hold** an event, you organize it and it takes place. ❑ *The German sports federation said it would hold an investigation.* 6 V-T If you **hold** a conversation with someone, you talk with them. ❑ *The Prime Minister is holding consultations with his colleagues.* 7 V-T If you **hold** someone's interest or attention, you keep them interested. ❑ *The book is sure to hold children's attention.* 8 → see also **holding**

hold /həʊld/ (**holds, holding, held**)
3 1 V-T If someone **holds** you in a place, they keep you there as a prisoner. ❑ *Somebody is holding your wife hostage.* 2 N-SING If you have a **hold over** or **on** someone, you have power or control over them. ❑ *Because he once loved her, she still has a hold on him.* 3 V-T/V-I You ask someone to **hold** when you are answering a telephone and you are asking them to wait for a short time. ❑ *Could you hold the line and I'll just get my pen.* 4 V-I If something **holds**, it remains the same. ❑ *Share prices held yesterday.* ❑ *Will the weather hold?* 5 CONVENTION If you say **'Hold it'**, you are telling someone to stop what they are doing and to wait. 6 CONVENTION If you say **'Hold on'**, you are telling someone to wait a short time. 7 → see also **holding**

hold /həʊld/ (**holds, holding, held**)
4 1 PHRASE If you **get hold of** something or someone, you manage to get them or find them. ❑ *It is hard to get hold of guns in this country.* 2 PHRASE If you **put** something **on hold**, you decide not to do it now, but to leave it till later. ❑ *He put his retirement on hold.* 3 PHRASE If you **hold** your **own**, you are not defeated by someone. ❑ *She can hold her own against almost any player.* 4 PHRASE If

something **takes hold**, it finally gains complete control or influence over something or someone. ❑ *She felt a strange excitement taking hold of her.*

hold /həʊld/ (**holds, holding, held**) ❻ ▶ **hold against** PHR-VERB If you **hold** something **against** someone, you resent or dislike them because of something which they did in the past.

▶ **hold back** 1 PHR-VERB If you **hold back**, you hesitate before doing something. ❑ *My fear of failure always held me back.* 2 PHR-VERB If you **hold** someone or something **back**, you prevent them from advancing or increasing. ❑ *Good weather in the UK is holding back sales of holidays to Spain.* 3 PHR-VERB If you **hold** something **back**, you do not tell someone the full details about it. ❑ *You seem to be holding something back.*

▶ **hold down** PHR-VERB If you **hold down** a **job**, you manage to keep it.

▶ **hold off** PHR-VERB If you **hold off** doing something, you delay doing it or delay making a decision about it. ❑ *He held off entering the family business until he was 36.*

▶ **hold on** or **hold onto** 1 PHR-VERB If you **hold on** or **hold onto** something, you keep your hand firmly round something. 2 PHR-VERB If you **hold onto** something that gives you an advantage, you succeed in keeping it for yourself, and prevent other people getting it. ❑ *He's a politician who knows how to hold onto power.* 3 PHR-VERB If you **hold onto** something, you keep it for a longer time than would normally be expected. ❑ *People hold onto letters for years and years.*

▶ **hold out** 1 PHR-VERB If you **hold out** your hand or something that is in your hand, you move it towards someone. ❑ *'I'm Nancy Drew,' she said, holding out her hand.* 2 PHR-VERB If you **hold out for** something, you refuse to accept something inferior or you refuse to surrender. ❑ *He can only hold out a few more weeks.*

▶ **hold up** 1 PHR-VERB If someone or something **holds** you **up**, they delay you. 2 PHR-VERB If someone **holds up** a place such as a bank, they rob it using a weapon. 3 → see also **hold-up**

▶ **hold with** PHR-VERB If you do not **hold with** something, you do not approve of it.

holder /həʊldə/ (**holders**) N-COUNT A **holder** is a device for storing a particular thing. ❑ *...a candle holder.* ❑ *...a toothbrush holder.*

holding /'həʊldɪŋ/ (**holdings**) 1 N-COUNT If you have a **holding in** a company, you own shares in it. ❑ *His biggest holding is in a company called 'Pixology'.* 2 N-COUNT A **holding** is an area of farm land rented or owned by the person who cultivates it. 3 N-PLURAL The **holdings** of a place such as a library or art gallery consists of the collection of items which are kept there.

'hold-up (**hold-ups**) 1 N-COUNT A **hold-up** is a situation in which someone is threatened with a weapon in order to make them hand over money or valuables. 2 N-COUNT A **hold-up** is something which causes a delay, for example traffic delays.

hole /həʊl/ (**holes, holing, holed**) N-COUNT A **hole** is an opening or hollow space in something. ❑ *The builders cut holes into the soft stone.* → see **golf**

▶ **hole up** PHR-VERB If you **hole up** somewhere, you hide or shut yourself away there. [INFORMAL] ❑ *She spent her free time holed up in her room with a book.*

Word Partnership Use *hole* with:

ADJ.	**big/huge/small** hole, **deep** hole **gaping** hole
V.	**cut/punch a** hole **in** ***something***, **dig a** hole, **drill/bore a** hole **in** ***something*** **fill/plug a** hole

holiday /'hɒlɪdei/ (**holidays, holidaying, holidayed**) 1 N-COUNT & PHRASE In British English, a **holiday** is a period of time when you are not working and are away from home for relaxation. You can also say that you are **on holiday** during this time. The American word is **vacation**. ❑ *We're going to Scotland for our holidays.* ❑ *I went on holiday to Ibiza.* 2 V-I If you **are holidaying** in a place, you are on holiday there. [BRIT] 3 N-COUNT A **holiday** is a day when people do not go to work or school because of a religious or national festival. ❑ *29 April is a national holiday in Japan.* 4 → see also **bank holiday** 5 N-PLURAL In British English, the **holidays** are the time when children do not have to go to school. The American word is **vacation**. ❑ *...the first day of the school holidays.*

holidaymaker also **holiday-maker** /'hɒlɪdeɪmeɪkə/ (**holidaymakers**) N-COUNT In British English, a **holidaymaker** is a person who is away from home on holiday. The American word is **vacationer**.

holiness /'həʊlinəs/ 1 N-UNCOUNT **Holiness** is the state or quality of being holy. 2 N-VOC People say **Your Holiness** or **His Holiness** when they address or refer respectfully to the Pope or to leaders of some other religions.

holistic /həʊ'lɪstɪk/ ADJ A **holistic approach** to something treats it as a whole, rather than as a number of different parts. [FORMAL]

holler /'hɒlə/ (**hollers, hollering, hollered**) V-T/V-I If you **holler**, you shout loudly. [AM, INFORMAL] ❑ *He'll be hollering at me for coming in late.*

hollow /'hɒləʊ/ (**hollows, hollowing, hollowed**) 1 ADJ Something that is **hollow** has a hole or space inside it. ❑ *...a hollow tree.* 2 ADJ A surface that is **hollow** curves inwards. ❑ *He had hollow cheeks, dark eyes and a long nose.* 3 N-COUNT A **hollow** is an area that is lower than the surrounding surface. ❑ *The water flows into a hollow and forms a pond.* 4 ADJ If you describe a statement, situation, or person as **hollow**, you mean they have no real value, worth, or effectiveness. • **hollowness** N-UNCOUNT ❑ *...the hollowness of these promises.* 5 ADJ BEFORE N A **hollow sound** is dull and echoing. ❑ *...the hollow sound of a gunshot.*

▶ **hollow out** PHR-VERB If you **hollow** something **out**, you remove the inside part of it. ❑ *Someone had hollowed out a large block of stone.*

holly /'hɒli/ (**hollies**) N-VAR **Hollies** are a group of evergreen trees and shrubs which have hard, shiny, prickly leaves, and also have bright red berries in winter.

holocaust /'hɒləkɔːst/ (**holocausts**) 1 N-VAR A **holocaust** is an event in which there is large-scale destruction and loss of life, especially in war. ❑ *...nuclear holocaust.* 2 N-PROPER **The Holocaust** was the killing by the Nazis of millions of Jews during the Second World War.

holy /'həʊli/ (**holier, holiest**) 1 ADJ Something that is **holy** is considered to be special because it relates to God or to a particular religion. ❑ *Jerusalem is a holy place.* 2 ADJ Someone who is **holy** leads a pure and good life which is dedicated to God or to a particular religion.

homage /'hɒmɪdʒ/ N-UNCOUNT **Homage** is respect shown towards someone or something you admire, or to someone who is in authority. ❑ *His house was a homage to the 18th century with huge oil paintings and gilt furniture.*

home /həʊm/ (**homes, homing, homed**) 1 N-COUNT Someone's **home** is the house or flat where they live. ❑ *They stayed at home and watched TV.* ❑ *She wanted to go home.* ❑ *Hi, Mum, I'm home!* 2 N-COUNT Your **home** is the place or country where you live or feel that you belong. ❑ *Ms Highsmith has made Switzerland her home.* 3 N-COUNT A **home** is a building where people who cannot care for themselves are looked after. ❑ *...a home for disabled children.* 4 N-SING The **home of** something is the place where it began or where it is most typically found. ❑ *This south-west region of France is the home of the famous cheese 'Roquefort'.* 5 ADV If you **press, drive**, or **hammer** a message or an opinion **home**, you emphasize it strongly. ❑ *We all need to discuss this issue and press home the argument.* 6 N-UNCOUNT & ADJ BEFORE N When a team plays **at home**, or when they play a **home** game, they play a game on their own ground, rather than on the opposing team's ground. 7 PHRASE If you feel **at home**, you feel comfortable and at ease in the place or situation that you are in.

▶ **home in** PHR-VERB If you **home in on** one particular aspect of something, you concentrate all your attention on it. ❑ *You must home in on what is important to your topic.*

Thesaurus *home* Also look up:

N. dwelling, house, residence 1
birthplace, home town 2

Word Partnership Use *home* with:

V. **bring/take *someone/something*** home, **build a** home, **buy a** home, **come** home, **drive** home, **feel at** home, **fly** home, **get** home, **go** home, **head for** home, **leave** home, **phone/ring** home, **return** home, **ride** home, **sit *at*** home, **stay *at*** home, **walk** home, **work at** home 1

ADJ. **close to** home, **new** home 1

homecoming /'həʊmkʌmɪŋ/ (**homecomings**) N-COUNT Your **homecoming** is your return to your home or country after you have been away for a long time.

ˌhome-'grown 1 ADJ **Home-grown** fruit and vegetables have been grown in your garden, rather than bought in a shop. 2 ADJ If you describe something as **home-grown**, you mean it develops in your own country or area rather than another country or area.

homeland /'həʊmlænd/ (**homelands**) N-COUNT Your **homeland** is your native country.

homeless /'həʊmləs/ ADJ & N-PLURAL You describe people who have nowhere to live as **homeless**. You can also refer to them as **the homeless**. ● **homelessness** N-UNCOUNT ❑ *...the only way to solve homelessness.*

homely /'həʊmli/ ADJ If you describe a room or house as **homely**, you like it because it makes you feel comfortable and at ease. ❑ *...a very homely atmosphere.*

ˌhome-'made or **homemade** ADJ **Home-made** things are made in someone's home, rather than in a shop or factory. ❑ *...a home-made cake.*

'Home ˌOffice N-PROPER **The Home Office** is the department of the British government which is responsible for domestic affairs, including the police, immigration, and broadcasting.

homeopathy [BRIT also **homoeopathy**] /ˌhəʊmi'ɒpəθi/ N-UNCOUNT **Homeopathy** is a way of treating illness in which the patient is given very small amounts of a drug which would produce symptoms of the illness if taken in large quantities. ● **homeopathic** /ˌhəʊmiəʊ'pæθɪk/ ADJ ❑ *...homeopathic medicine.*

homepage /'həʊmpeɪdʒ/ (**homepages**) N-COUNT On the Internet, a person's or organization's **homepage** is the main page of information about them. [COMPUTING]

ˌHome 'Secretary (**Home Secretaries**) N-COUNT The **Home Secretary** is the member of the British government who is in charge of the Home Office.

homesick /'həʊmsɪk/ ADJ If you are **homesick**, you feel unhappy because you are away from home and are missing your family and friends. ● **homesickness** N-UNCOUNT ❑ *Many students experience feelings of homesickness when they are living away from home for the first time.*

Word Link ***stead ≈ place, stand : homestead, instead, steady***

homestead /'həʊmsted/ (**homesteads**) N-COUNT A **homestead** is a farmhouse, together with the land around it.

ˌhome 'town or **hometown** (**home towns**) N-COUNT Someone's **home town** is the town where they live or the town that they come from.

homework /'həʊmwɜːk/ 1 N-UNCOUNT **Homework** is school work given to pupils to do at home. ❑ *Have you done your homework?* 2 N-UNCOUNT If you **do** your **homework**, you find out what you need to know in preparation for something. ❑ *Olga did her homework before applying for a loan.*

homicidal /ˌhɒmɪ'saɪdəl/ ADJ **Homicidal** is used to describe someone who is dangerous because they are likely to kill someone.

homicide /'hɒmɪsaɪd/ (**homicides**) N-VAR In American English, **homicide** is the deliberate and unlawful killing of a person. The usual British word is **murder**.

Word Link ***homo ≈ same : homogeneous, homophobia, homosexual***

homogeneous or **homogenous** /ˈhɒməˌdʒiːniəs, 'həʊ-/ ADJ **Homogeneous** is used to describe a group or thing which has members or parts that are all the same. ❑ *The unemployed are not a homogeneous group.*

homophobia /ˌhɒmə'fəʊbiə/ N-UNCOUNT **Homophobia** is a strong and unreasonable dislike of homosexual people. ● **homophobic** ADJ ❑ *...acts* *of homophobic violence.*

Word Link *homo ≈ same : homogeneous, homophobia, homosexual*

homosexual /ˈhɒməʊˌsekʃʊəl, ˈhəʊ-/ (**homosexuals**) ADJ & N-COUNT Someone who is **homosexual**, or who is a **homosexual**, is sexually attracted to people of the same sex. ❑ *...a homosexual relationship.* ● **homosexuality** /ˌhɒməˌsekʃʊˈælɪti/ N-UNCOUNT ❑ *It's a place where gays can openly discuss homosexuality.*

hone /həʊn/ (**hones, honing, honed**) V-T If you **hone** something, for example a skill or idea, you carefully develop it for a special purpose. ❑ *Jose Reyes hones his football skills by practising in his garden.*

honest /ˈɒnɪst/ 1 ADJ If you describe someone as **honest**, you mean that they always tell the truth, and do not try to deceive people or break the law. ❑ *He is a very honest, decent man.* ● **honestly** ADV ❑ *She fought honestly for freedom.* 2 ADJ If you are being **honest** in a particular situation, you are telling the complete truth or giving your sincere opinion, even if this is not very pleasant. ❑ *What do you think of the school, in your honest opinion?* ● **honestly** ADV ❑ *It came as a shock to hear an old friend speak so honestly about Ted.* 3 ADV You say **'honest'** before or after a statement to emphasize that you are telling the truth. [INFORMAL] ❑ *It wasn't me, honest.* ● **honestly** ADV ❑ *Honestly, I don't know anything about it.*

Thesaurus *honest* Also look up:

ADJ.	fair, genuine, sincere, true, truthful, upright 1
	candid, frank, straight, truthful 2

honestly /ˈɒnɪstli/ ADV 1 You use **honestly** to emphasize that you are annoyed or impatient. [SPOKEN] ❑ *Honestly, I'm sick of hearing about it.* 2 → see also **honest**

honesty /ˈɒnɪsti/ N-UNCOUNT **Honesty** is the quality of being honest. ❑ *I can answer you with complete honesty.*

honey /ˈhʌni/ (**honeys**) 1 N-VAR **Honey** is a sweet, sticky, edible substance made by bees. 2 N-VOC You call someone **honey** as a sign of affection. [mainly AM] ❑ *Honey, I don't really think that's a good idea.*

honeymoon /ˈhʌnimuːn/ (**honeymoons, honeymooning, honeymooned**) 1 N-COUNT A **honeymoon** is a holiday taken by a couple who have just married. 2 V-I When a couple who have just married **honeymoon** somewhere, they go there on their honeymoon. ❑ *They honeymooned in Venice.* 3 N-COUNT You can use **honeymoon** to refer to a period of time when someone has just started in a new job or role and everyone is pleased with them and does not criticize them. ❑ *The new Prime Minister will enjoy a honeymoon period.*
→ see **wedding**

honor /ˈɒnə/ → see **honour**

honorable /ˈɒnrəbəl/ → see **honourable**

honorary /ˈɒnərəri, AM -reri/ 1 ADJ BEFORE N An **honorary** title or membership is given as a mark of respect to someone who does not qualify for it in the normal way. ❑ *...an honorary member of the Golf Club.* 2 ADJ BEFORE N **Honorary** is used to describe an official job that is done without payment. ❑ *...the honorary secretary of the British Medical Association.*

honour [AM **honor**] /ˈɒnə/ (**honours, honouring, honoured**) 1 N-UNCOUNT **Honour** means doing what you believe to be right and being confident that you have done what is right. ❑ *I do not believe I can any longer serve with honour as a member of your government.* 2 N-COUNT An **honour** is a special award or job that is given to someone for something they have done. ❑ *He was showered with honours – among them an Oscar.* 3 V-T If someone **is honoured**, they are given public praise or an award for something they have done. ❑ *Two American surgeons were honoured with the 1990 Nobel Prize for Medicine.* 4 PHRASE If something is arranged **in honour of** a particular event, it is arranged in order to celebrate that event. 5 N-SING If you describe something that has happened to you as **an honour**, you mean that you are pleased and proud about it. ❑ *It's an honour to finally work with her.* 6 V-T PASSIVE If you say that you would **be honoured to** do something, you are saying very politely and formally that you would be pleased to do it. ❑ *I'd be honoured to accept.* 7 V-T If you **honour** an arrangement or promise, you keep to it. ❑ *They promised to honour the new agreement.* 8 N-VOC Judges are sometimes called **Your Honour** or referred to as **His Honour** or **Her Honour**.

Thesaurus *honour* Also look up:

N.	award, distinction, recognition 2
V.	commend, praise, recognize 3

Word Partnership Use *honour* with:

N.	**code of** honour, **sense of** honour 1
	honour **a ceasefire** 7
	honour **the memory of *someone/something*** 4
ADJ.	**great/highest** honour 2 5

honourable [AM **honorable**] /ˈɒnrəbəl/ ADJ If you describe people or actions as **honourable**, you mean that they are worthy of being respected or admired. ● **honourably** ADV ❑ *She had not behaved honourably during the election.*

hood /hʊd/ (**hoods**) 1 N-COUNT A **hood** is a part of some pieces of clothing which covers your head. 2 N-COUNT In American English the **hood** of a car is the cover over the engine at the front. The British word is **bonnet**.

hooded /ˈhʊdɪd/ 1 ADJ A **hooded** piece of clothing has a hood. ❑ *...a hooded sweatshirt.* 2 ADJ A **hooded** person is wearing a hood or a piece of clothing pulled down over their face, so they are difficult to recognize. ❑ *A group of hooded youths came towards me.*

hoof /huːf/ (**hoofs** or **hooves**) N-COUNT The **hooves** of an animal such as a horse are the hard parts of its feet.
→ see **horse**

hook /hʊk/ (**hooks, hooking, hooked**) 1 N-COUNT A **hook** is a bent piece of metal or plastic that is used for catching or holding things, or for hanging things up. ❑ *He felt a fish pull at his hook.* ❑ *...curtain hooks.* 2 V-T/V-I If you **hook** one

h

thing **onto** another, you attach it there using a hook. If something **hooks** somewhere, it can be hooked there. ❑ *We've got one of those gadgets that hooks onto the wall.* 3 N-COUNT A **hook** is a short sharp punch that you make with your elbow bent. 4 PHRASE If someone **gets off the hook**, they manage to get out of the awkward or unpleasant situation that they are in. ❑ *The government officials who were accused of stealing managed to get off the hook.* 5 PHRASE If you take a phone **off the hook**, you take the receiver off the part that it normally rests on, so that the phone will not ring.

▶ **hook up** PHR-VERB When someone **hooks up** a computer or other electronic machine, they connect it to other similar machines or to a central power supply. ❑ *...technicians who hook up computer systems and networks.*

hooked /hʊkt/ 1 ADJ **Hooked** objects are shaped like a hook. ❑ *...a hooked nose.* 2 ADJ AFTER LINK-V If you are **hooked on** something, you enjoy it so much that it takes up a lot of your interest and attention. ❑ *Many leaders have become hooked on power.* ❑ *Open this book and read a few pages and you will be hooked.* 3 ADJ AFTER LINK-V If someone is **hooked on** a drug, they are addicted to it.

H

hooker /ˈhʊkə/ (**hookers**) N-COUNT A **hooker** is a prostitute. [INFORMAL]

hooligan /ˈhuːlɪgən/ (**hooligans**) N-COUNT If you describe people, especially young people, as **hooligans**, you are critical of them because they behave in a noisy and violent way in a public place.

hooliganism /ˈhuːlɪgənɪzəm/ N-UNCOUNT **Hooliganism** is the behaviour and action of hooligans. ❑ *...football hooliganism.*

hoop /huːp/ (**hoops**) N-COUNT A **hoop** is a large ring made of wood, metal, or plastic.

hoot /huːt/ (**hoots, hooting, hooted**) 1 V-T/V-I & N-COUNT If you **hoot**, or **hoot** the horn on a vehicle, it makes a loud noise called a **hoot**. ❑ *I never hoot my horn when I pick a girl up for a date.* 2 V-I & N-COUNT If you **hoot**, you make a loud high-pitched noise, called a **hoot**, when you are laughing. ❑ *Bev hooted with laughter.* ❑ *There were hoots and cheers as the king appeared.* 3 V-I & N-COUNT When an owl **hoots**, it makes a sound like a long 'oo'. The sound is called a **hoot**.

hoover /ˈhuːvə/ (**hoovers, hoovering, hoovered**) 1 N-COUNT A **hoover** is an electric machine which sucks up dust and dirt from carpets. **Hoover** is a trademark. [BRIT] 2 V-T If you **hoover** a carpet, you clean it using a vacuum cleaner. [BRIT] • **hoovering** N-UNCOUNT ❑ *I finished off the hoovering.*

hooves /huːvz/ **Hooves** is a plural of **hoof**.

hop /hɒp/ (**hops, hopping, hopped**) 1 V-I & N-COUNT When you **hop**, you move along by jumping on one foot. A movement like this is called a **hop**. 2 V-I & N-COUNT When birds and some small animals **hop**, they move in small jumps, called **hops**, with two feet together. ❑ *A frog hopped across the road.* 3 V-I If you **hop** somewhere, you move there quickly or suddenly. [INFORMAL] ❑ *I hopped out of bed quickly.* 4 N-COUNT A **hop** is a short quick journey, usually by plane. ❑ *...a 20-minute hop in a private helicopter.*

hope /həʊp/ (**hopes, hoping, hoped**) 1 V-T/V-I If you **hope that** something is true, or if you **hope for** something, you want it to be true or to happen, and you usually believe that it is possible or likely. ❑ *Mabel's family had hoped for something better for their daughter.* ❑ *I hope to get a job within the next two weeks.* ❑ *'Will it happen again?'—'I hope not, but you never know.'* 2 N-UNCOUNT **Hope** is a feeling of desire and expectation that things will go well in the future. ❑ *Kevin hasn't given up hope of finding her.* 3 N-COUNT If someone wants something to happen, and considers it likely or possible, you can refer to their **hopes of** doing that thing, or to their **hope that** it will happen. ❑ *My hope is that I will marry her.* 4 PHRASE If you **hope for the best**, you hope that everything will happen in the way you want, although you know that it may not. ❑ *We are hoping for the best but preparing for the worst.* 5 PHRASE If you do one thing **in the hope of** another thing happening, you do it because you think it might cause or help the other thing to happen, which is what you want. ❑ *He was studying in the hope of being accepted by an engineering college.*

Thesaurus *hope* Also look up:

V.	aspire, desire, dream, wish 1
N.	ambition, aspiration, desire, dream, wish 2

Word Partnership Use *hope* with:

V.	**give** ***someone*** hope, **give up** ***all*** hope, **hold out** hope, **lose** ***all*** hope 2
ADJ.	**faint** hope, **false** hope, **little** hope 1 2
N.	**glimmer of** hope 2

hopeful /ˈhəʊpfʊl/ (**hopefuls**) 1 ADJ If you are **hopeful**, you are fairly confident that something that you want to happen will happen. ❑ *Surgeons were hopeful of saving Sara's left eye.* 2 ADJ If something such as a sign or event is **hopeful**, it makes you feel that what you want to happen will happen. ❑ *...hopeful forecasts that the economy will improve.* 3 N-COUNT If you refer to someone as a **hopeful**, you mean that they have a particular ambition and it is possible that they will achieve it. ❑ *...his job as football coach to young hopefuls.*

hopefully /ˈhəʊpfʊli/ ADV **Hopefully** is often used when mentioning something that you hope and are fairly confident will happen. ❑ *Hopefully, you won't have any problems after reading this.*

hopeless /ˈhəʊpləs/ 1 ADJ If you feel **hopeless**, you feel desperate because there seems to be no possibility of success. ❑ *Even able pupils feel hopeless about finding a job.* • **hopelessly** ADV ❑ *She was hopelessly in love with him.* • **hopelessness** N-UNCOUNT ❑ *She had a feeling of hopelessness about the future.* 2 ADJ Someone or something that is **hopeless** is certain to be unsuccessful. ❑ *I don't believe your situation is as hopeless as you think.* 3 ADJ You use **hopeless** to emphasize how bad an event or situation is. • **hopelessly** ADV ❑ *He was hopelessly in debt.*

horde /hɔːd/ (**hordes**) N-COUNT If you describe a large crowd of people as a **horde**, you mean that they are excited and, often, rather frightening or unpleasant. ❑ *A horde of people was screaming for tickets.*

horizon /həˈraɪzən/ (**horizons**) 1 N-SING **The horizon** is the distant line where the sky seems to touch the land or the sea. **2** N-COUNT Your **horizons** are the limits of what you want to do or of what you are interested or involved in. ❑ *Living in different countries broadens your horizons.* **3** PHRASE If something is **on the horizon**, it is going to happen or be done quite soon.

horizontal /ˈhɒrɪˌzɒntəl, AM ˈhɔːr-/ (**horizontals**) **1** ADJ Something that is **horizontal** is flat and parallel with the ground. ❑ *...vertical and horizontal lines.* ● **horizontally** ADV ❑ *...a horizontally striped tie.* **2** N-COUNT **The horizontal** is a line or structure that is horizontal. ❑ *Do not raise your left arm above the horizontal.*
→ see **graph**

hormone /ˈhɔːməʊn/ (**hormones**) N-COUNT A **hormone** is a chemical, usually occurring naturally in your body, that stimulates certain organs of your body. ● **hormonal** /hɔːˈməʊnəl/ ADJ ❑ *...hormonal balance.*
→ see **emotion**

horn /hɔːn/ (**horns**) **1** N-COUNT On a vehicle such as a car, the **horn** is the device that makes a loud noise as a signal or warning. **2** N-COUNT The **horns** of an animal such as a cow or deer are the hard pointed things that grow from its head. **3** N-UNCOUNT **Horn** is the hard substance that the horns of animals are made of. **4** N-COUNT A **horn** is a brass musical instrument, consisting of a pipe that is narrow at one end and wide at the other.

Word Link *scope ≈ looking : horoscope, microscope, telescope*

horoscope /ˈhɒrəskəʊp, AM ˈhɔːr-/ (**horoscopes**) N-COUNT Your **horoscope** is a forecast of events which some people believe will happen to you in the future, based on the position of the stars when you were born. ❑ *I always read my horoscope and follow the advice.*

horrendous /həˈrendəs, AM hɔːˈr-/ ADJ Something that is **horrendous** is very bad or unpleasant. ❑ *The violence was horrendous.* ● **horrendously** ADV ❑ *Our holiday was horrendously expensive.*

horrible /ˈhɒrɪbəl, AM ˈhɔːr-/ ADJ If you say that someone or something is **horrible**, you mean that they are very unpleasant. ❑ *...a horrible small boy.* ● **horribly** /ˈhɒrɪbli, AM ˈhɔːr-/ ADV ❑ *Everything's gone horribly wrong.*

horrid /ˈhɒrɪd, AM ˈhɔːr-/ ADJ If you describe someone or something as **horrid**, you mean they are very unpleasant. [INFORMAL] ❑ *What a horrid smell!* ❑ *I love both my parents, but they're horrid to each other.*

horrific /həˈrɪfɪk, AM hɔːˈr-/ ADJ If you describe something as **horrific**, you mean that it is so bad that people are horrified and shocked by it. ❑ *I have never seen such horrific injuries.* ● **horrifically** ADV ❑ *He had been horrifically burned.*

horrify /ˈhɒrɪfaɪ, AM ˈhɔːr-/ (**horrifies, horrifying, horrified**) V-T If someone **is horrified**, they feel shocked, disappointed, or disgusted. ❑ *This crime will horrify all parents.* ● **horrifying** ADJ ❑ *These were horrifying experiences.*

h

horror /ˈhɒrə, AM ˈhɔːr-/ (**horrors**) **1** N-UNCOUNT **Horror** is a strong feeling of alarm caused by something extremely unpleasant. ❑ *I felt numb with horror.* **2** N-SING If you have a **horror of** something, you are afraid of it or dislike it strongly. ❑ *...his horror of death.* **3** N-COUNT You can refer to extremely unpleasant or frightening experiences as **horrors**. ❑ *...the horrors of war.* **4** ADJ A **horror** film or story is intended to be very frightening.
→ see **genre**

horse /hɔːs/ (**horses**) N-COUNT A **horse** is a large animal which people can ride.
→ see Picture Dictionary: **horse**

horseback /ˈhɔːsbæk/ **1** N-UNCOUNT If you do something **on horseback**, you do it while riding a horse. **2** ADJ BEFORE N & ADV **Horseback** riding is the activity of riding a horse. ❑ *I like to go horseback riding and swimming.*

horseman /ˈhɔːsmən/ (**horsemen**) N-COUNT A **horseman** is a man who is riding a horse, or who rides horses well.

horsepower /ˈhɔːspaʊə/ N-UNCOUNT

Picture Dictionary **horse**

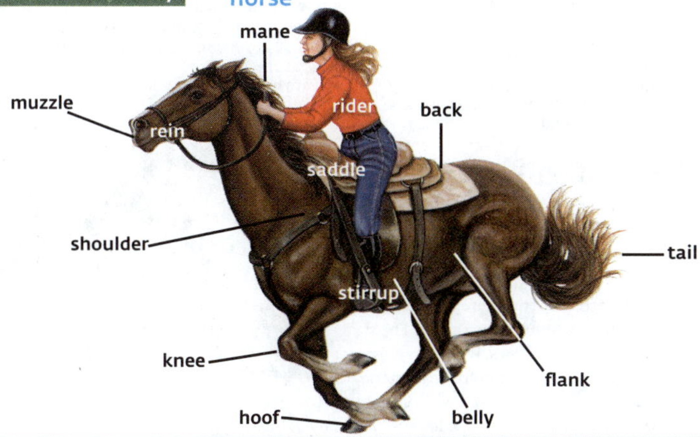

Horsepower is a unit of power used for measuring how powerful an engine is.

horseshoe /ˈhɔːsʃuː/ (**horseshoes**) N-COUNT A **horseshoe** is a piece of metal shaped like a U which is fixed to a horse's hoof.

horticulture /ˈhɔːtɪkʌltʃə/ N-UNCOUNT **Horticulture** is the study and practice of growing plants. • **horticultural** /ˌhɔːtɪˈkʌltʃərəl/ ADJ ❑ *...the horticultural show.*

hose /həʊz/ (**hoses, hosing, hosed**) 1 N-COUNT A **hose** is a long, flexible pipe through which water is carried in order to do things such as put out fires or water gardens. 2 V-T & PHR-VERB If you **hose** something, or if you **hose** it **down**, you wash it using a hose. ❑ *The truck was being hosed down by two firemen with water pumps.* ❑ *The crew hosed down the decks.*

hospice /ˈhɒspɪs/ (**hospices**) N-COUNT A **hospice** is a hospital for people who are dying. ❑ *... a hospice for cancer patients.*

hospitable /hɒˈspɪtəbəl, ˈhɒspɪt-/ ADJ A **hospitable** person is friendly, generous, and welcoming to guests or strangers. ❑ *He was very hospitable to me when I came to New York.*

Word Link	*hosp, host ≈ guest : hospital, hospitality, hostage*

hospital /ˈhɒspɪtəl/ (**hospitals**) N-VAR A **hospital** is a place where people who are ill are looked after by doctors and nurses. ❑ *My uncle went into hospital.*

→ see Word Web: **hospital**

Word Partnership	Use *hospital* with:
V.	**admit *someone* to a** hospital, **bring/rush/take *someone* to a** hospital, **end up in a** hospital, **go to a** hospital, **visit *someone* in a** hospital

hospitality /ˌhɒspɪˈtælɪti/ N-UNCOUNT **Hospitality** is friendly, welcoming behaviour towards guests or strangers.

hospitalize [BRIT also **hospitalise**] /ˈhɒspɪtəlaɪz/ (**hospitalizes, hospitalizing, hospitalized**) V-T If someone **is hospitalized**, they are sent or admitted to hospital. • **hospitalization** N-UNCOUNT ❑ *Occasionally hospitalization is required.*

host /həʊst/ (**hosts, hosting, hosted**) 1 N-COUNT & V-T The **host** at a party is the person who has invited the guests and who provides the food, drink, or entertainment. You can say they **host** the party. ❑ *The Prime Minister hosted a private lunch.* 2 N-COUNT & V-T A country, city, or organization that is the **host** of an event provides the facilities for that event to take place. You can say they **host** the event. ❑ *In March Luxembourg hosted a meeting of Olympic officials.* 3 N-COUNT & V-T The **host** of a radio or television show is the person who introduces it and talks to the people taking part. You can say they **host** the show. 4 QUANT A **host of** things is a lot of them. ❑ *...a whole host of electrical gadgets.*

hostage /ˈhɒstɪdʒ/ (**hostages**) N-COUNT & PHRASE A **hostage** is a person who is illegally held prisoner and threatened with injury or death unless certain demands are met by other people. If someone **is taken hostage** or **is held hostage**, they are captured and kept in this way.

hostel /ˈhɒstəl/ (**hostels**) N-COUNT A **hostel** is a large house where people can stay cheaply for a short time.

hostess /ˈhəʊstɪs/ (**hostesses**) N-COUNT The **hostess** at a party is the woman who has invited the guests and provides the food, drink, or entertainment.

hostile /ˈhɒstaɪl, AM -təl/ 1 ADJ If someone is **hostile** to another person or to an idea or suggestion, they show their dislike for them in an aggressive way. ❑ *The Governor faced hostile crowds.* • **hostility** /hɒˈstɪlɪti/ N-UNCOUNT ❑ *...hostility to British food in Paris.* 2 ADJ A **hostile** environment is one in which humans and animals find it difficult to live. ❑ *...some of the most hostile conditions in the world.* 3 ADJ A **hostile** takeover bid is one that is opposed by the company that is being bid for. [BUSINESS]

Word Partnership	Use *hostile* with:
ADV.	**increasingly** hostile 1-3
N.	hostile **attitude/feelings/intentions** 1 hostile **act/action**, hostile **environment** hostile **takeover** 2 3

hostilities /hɒˈstɪlɪtiz/ N-PLURAL You can refer to fighting between two countries or groups who are at war as **hostilities**.

hot /hɒt/ (**hotter, hottest, hots, hotting, hotted**) 1 ADJ If something is **hot**, it has a high temperature. ❑ *...hot water.* ❑ *...a hot meal.* 2 ADJ If you are **hot**, you feel uncomfortable because of the high temperature of your body or your surroundings. 3 ADJ You can say food is **hot**

Word Web **hospital**

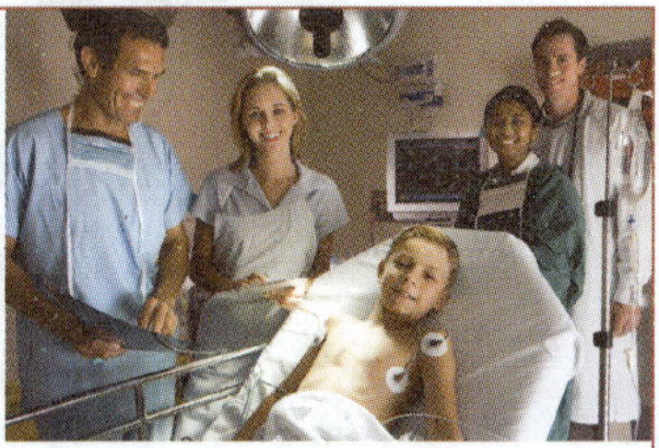

Children's **Hospital** in Boston has one of the best pediatric **wards** in the country. Its Advanced Fetal Care Center can even treat babies before they are born. The hospital has about 18,000 inpatient **admissions** every year. It also has over 150 outpatient programs and takes care of more than 300,000 **emergency cases**. The staff includes 700 **residents** and **fellows**, who are studying to become doctors. Many of the **physicians** teach at nearby Harvard University. The hospital also has excellent **researchers**. Their work helped find **vaccines** for **polio** and **measles**. The hospital has also led the way in liver, heart, and lung **transplants** in children.

when it has a burning taste caused by spices. ❑ *...a hot curry.* **4** ADJ You can use **hot** to describe an issue or event that is very important, exciting, or popular at the present time. [INFORMAL] ❑ *...the hottest movie of the summer.* ❑ *Ben is the hot favourite to win the award.*
→ see **weather**
▶ **hot up** PHR-VERB When something **hots up**, it becomes more active or exciting. [BRIT] ❑ *Poland's presidential campaign is hotting up.*

Usage

In informal English, if you want to emphasize how hot the weather is, you can say that it is **boiling** or **scorching**. In winter, if the temperature is above average, you can say that it is **mild**. In general, **hot** suggests a higher temperature than **warm**, and **warm** things are usually pleasant. ❑ *I imagined that I was back home in England, sitting in the garden on a warm evening.*

Thesaurus *hot* Also look up:

ADJ. sweltering; *(ant.)* chilly, cold **1**
spicy; *(ant.)* bland, mild **3**
cool, popular; *(ant.)* unpopular **4**

ˌhot ˈair balloon → see **balloon**
→ see **fly**
ˈhot ˌdog (**hot dogs**) N-COUNT A **hot dog** is a long bread roll with a sausage in it.
hotel /ˌhəʊˈtel/ (**hotels**) N-COUNT A **hotel** is a building where people stay, paying for their rooms and meals.
→ see Word Web: **hotel**

Word Partnership Use *hotel* with:

N. hotel **guest**, hotel **reservation**, hotel **room**
V. **check into a** hotel, **check out of a** hotel, **stay at a** hotel
ADJ. **luxury** hotel, **new** hotel

hotelier /ˌhəʊˈteliə, AM ˌəʊteˈljeɪ/ (**hoteliers**) N-COUNT A **hotelier** is a person who owns or manages a hotel or several hotels.
hotline /ˈhɒtlaɪn/ (**hotlines**) **1** N-COUNT A **hotline** is a telephone line that the public can use to contact an organization about a particular subject. **2** N-COUNT A **hotline** is a direct telephone line between heads of government for use in an emergency.

hotly /ˈhɒtli/ **1** ADV If you say something **hotly**, you say it angrily. ❑ *'That's not true,' Robyn said hotly.* ❑ *The bank hotly denies any wrongdoing.* **2** ADV If something is being **hotly** pursued or **hotly** contested, the people involved are very determined to catch it or to win it. ❑ *This year's final will be as hotly contested as ever.*
hound /haʊnd/ (**hounds, hounding, hounded**) **1** N-COUNT A **hound** is a type of dog, often used for hunting or racing. ❑ *The hounds ran after me.* **2** V-T If someone **hounds** you, they constantly disturb you or pester you. ❑ *I was constantly hounded by classmates.*
hour /aʊə/ (**hours**) **1** N-COUNT An **hour** is a period of sixty minutes. ❑ *The journey took three hours.* ❑ *They returned half an hour later.* **2** N-PLURAL You can refer to the period of time during which something happens or operates each day as the **hours** during which it happens or operates. ❑ *...the hours of darkness.* ❑ *Phone us during office hours.* ❑ *Peter came home in the early hours of the morning.* **3** N-SING **The hour** is used in expressions like **on the hour** to refer to times when it is exactly one o'clock, two o'clock, and so on. ❑ *Trains will leave St Albans at 36 minutes past the hour.* **4** → see also **rush hour**
→ see **time**
hourly /ˈaʊəli/ **1** ADJ BEFORE N & ADV An **hourly** event happens once every hour. ❑ *...hourly news bulletins.* ❑ *The hospital issued statements hourly.* **2** ADJ BEFORE N Your **hourly** earnings are the amount of money that you earn each hour. ❑ *...the decision to cut their hourly pay.*
house (**houses** /ˈhaʊzɪz/, **housing, housed**) **1** N-COUNT /haʊs/ A **house** is a building in which people live. You can also refer to all the people who live together in a house as **the house**. ❑ *He woke the whole house with his singing.* **2** PHRASE If someone **puts** their **house in order**, they arrange their affairs and solve their problems. **3** N-COUNT **House** is used in the names of some types of companies and establishments. ❑ *...a steak house.* ❑ *...a publishing house.* **4** N-COUNT You can refer to the two main bodies of Britain's and the United States of America's parliament as **the House** or a **House**. ❑ *Some members of the House worked all day yesterday.* **5** N-COUNT In a theatre or cinema, the **house** is the part where the audience sits. ❑ *...a full house at the Palace Theatre in London.* **6** V-T /haʊz/ To **house** someone means to provide a house or flat for them to live in. **7** V-T If a building **houses** something, that thing is kept or located in the building. ❑ *The gallery will house the*

h

Word Web hotel

When making **reservations** at a **hotel**, most people request a **single** or a **double** room. Sometimes the **clerk** invites the person to **upgrade** to a **suite**. When arriving at the hotel, the first person to greet the **guest** is the bellhop. He will put the person's suitcases on a **luggage cart** and later deliver them to their room. The guest then goes to the **front desk** and **checks in**. The clerk often describes **amenities** such as a **fitness club** or **spa**. Most hotels provide **room service** for late night snacks. There is often a concierge to help make reservations at restaurants and other entertainment outside of the hotel.

Picture Dictionary house

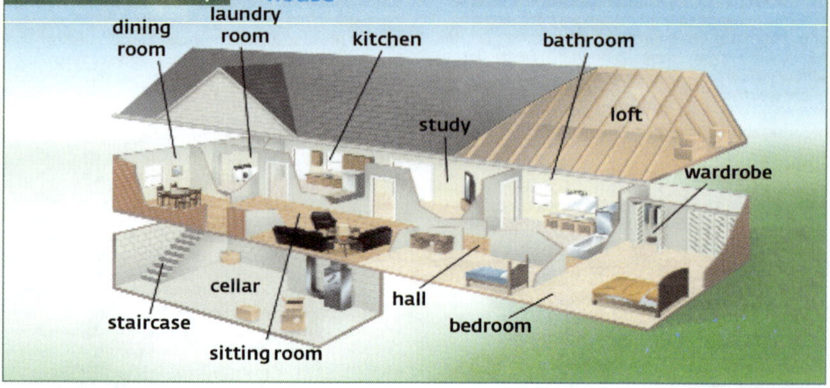

H

university's art collection.
→ see Picture Dictionary: **house**

Thesaurus *house* Also look up:

N. dwelling, home, place, residence [1]

Word Partnership Use *house* with:

ADJ. **empty** house, **expensive** house, **little** house, **new/old** house [1]
N. house **prices, a room in a** house [1]
V. **break into a** house, **build a** house, **buy a** house, **find a** house, **live in a** house, **own a** house, **rent a** house, **sell a** house [1]

ˌhouse arˈrest N-UNCOUNT If someone is **under house arrest**, they are officially ordered not to leave their home, because they are suspected of being involved in an illegal activity.

household /ˈhaʊshəʊld/ (**households**) [1] N-COUNT A **household** is all the people in a family or group who live together in a house. ❑ *...women-only households.* [2] N-SING The **household** is your home and everything connected with looking after it. ❑ *My husband gave me cash to manage the household.* ❑ *...the household chores.* [3] ADJ BEFORE N Someone or something that is a **household name** is very well known.

householder /ˈhaʊshəʊldə/ (**householders**) N-COUNT A **householder** is the owner or tenant of a house.

housekeeper /ˈhaʊskiːpə/ (**housekeepers**) N-COUNT A **housekeeper** is a person employed to do the cleaning and cooking in a house.

housekeeping /ˈhaʊskiːpɪŋ/ N-UNCOUNT **Housekeeping** is the work, organization, and financial planning involved in running a home.

ˌHouse of ˈCommons N-PROPER **The House of Commons** is the more powerful of the two parts of parliament in Britain and Canada. The building where the members meet is also called **the House of Commons**.

ˌHouse of ˈLords N-PROPER **The House of Lords** is the less powerful of the two parts of parliament in Britain and Canada. The building where the members meet is also called **the House of Lords**.

housewife /ˈhaʊswaɪf/ (**housewives**) N-COUNT A **housewife** is a married woman who does not have a paid job, but instead looks after her home and children.

housework /ˈhaʊswɜːk/ N-UNCOUNT **Housework** is the work such as cleaning and cooking that you do in your home.

housing /ˈhaʊzɪŋ/ N-COUNT **Housing** is the buildings that people live in. ❑ *...affordable housing.*

ˈhousing esˌtate (**housing estates**) N-COUNT A **housing estate** is a large number of houses or flats built close together. [BRIT]

hover /ˈhɒvə, AM ˈhʌv-/ (**hovers, hovering, hovered**) [1] V-I To **hover** means to stay in the same position in the air without moving forwards or backwards. ❑ *Butterflies hovered above the wild flowers.* ❑ *A police helicopter hovered overhead.* [2] V-I If someone **is hovering**, they are hesitating because they cannot decide what to do. ❑ *Judith was hovering in the doorway.*

how /haʊ/

How is mainly used in questions.

[1] ADV & CONJ You use **how** to ask about the way in which something happens or is done. ❑ *I want to know how he died.* ❑ *How do you manage to keep your house so tidy?* [2] ADV & CONJ You use **how** when you are asking for news about someone's health or life, or whether something was successful or enjoyable. ❑ *Hi! How are you?* ❑ *How's the job?* ❑ *How was your trip down to Orlando?* [3] ADV You use **how** in expressions such as **'how about...'** or **'how would you like...'** when you are making an offer or a suggestion. ❑ *How about a cup of coffee?* [4] ADV You use **how** to emphasize the degree to which something is true. ❑ *I didn't realize how heavy the shopping was.* [5] ADV You use **how** to ask questions about the quantity or degree of something. ❑ *How long will you be staying?* ❑ *How old is your son now?* [6] CONVENTION You can say **'How about you?'** when you are asking someone their opinion. ❑ *Well, I enjoyed that. How about you two?*

Usage

Be careful not to use **how** to ask questions about the appearance or character of someone or something. You use an expression with **what** and **like**. For example, if you ask '**How is Susan?**', you are asking about her health. If you want to know about her appearance, you ask '**What does Susan look like?**' If you want to know about her personality, you ask '**What is Susan like?**'

however /haʊ'evə/ **1** ADV You use **however** when you are adding a comment which contrasts with what has just been said. ❑ *Most of the class failed the exam. However, a couple of students did very well.* **2** CONJ & ADV You use **however** to say that it makes no difference how something is done or to what a degree or extent something is done. ❑ *Wear your hair however you want.* ❑ *However hard she tried, nothing seemed to work.* **3** ADV & CONJ You can use **however** in questions to express surprise at something. ❑ *However did you find this place?*

howl /haʊl/ (**howls, howling, howled**) **1** V-I & N-COUNT If a wolf or a dog **howls** or lets out a **howl**, it makes a long, loud, crying sound. **2** V-I & N-COUNT If a person **howls** or lets out a **howl**, they make a long, loud cry expressing pain, anger, or unhappiness. ❑ *Vincent let out a howl of pain.* **3** V-I & N-COUNT If people **are howling with** laughter, or if there are **howls of** laughter, people are laughing very loudly. **4** V-I When the wind **howls**, it blows hard, making a loud noise.
→ see **laugh**

HQ /ˌeɪtʃ'kjuː/ (**HQs**) N-VAR **HQ** is an abbreviation for 'headquarters'.

hr (**hrs**) **hr** is a written abbreviation for 'hour'. ❑ *...1 hr 15 mins.*

HTML /ˌeɪtʃtiː em 'el/ N-UNCOUNT **HTML** is a system of codes for producing documents for the Internet. **HTML** is an abbreviation for 'hypertext markup language'. [COMPUTING]

hub /hʌb/ (**hubs**) **1** N-COUNT The **hub** of a wheel is the part at the centre. **2** N-COUNT If you describe a place as a **hub of** an activity, you mean that it is a very important centre for that activity. ❑ *The area around Red Square was the hub of Moscow's business life.* **3** N-COUNT A **hub** or a **hub airport** is a large airport from which you can travel to many other airports. ❑ *Rome's international hub was named in honour of Leonardo Da Vinci.*

huddle /'hʌdəl/ (**huddles, huddling, huddled**) **1** V-I If you **huddle** somewhere, you sit, stand, or lie there holding your arms and legs close to your body, usually because you are cold or frightened. ❑ *She huddled inside the porch.* **2** V-I If people **huddle together** or **huddle round** something, they stand, sit, or lie close to each other, usually because they all feel cold or frightened. ❑ *We huddled round a small fire.* **3** N-COUNT A **huddle of** people or things is a small group standing or sitting close together. ❑ *...a huddle of stone buildings.*

hue /hjuː/ (**hues**) N-COUNT A **hue** is a colour. [LITERARY] ❑ *...a cloth of many hues.*

huff /hʌf/ (**huffs, huffing, huffed**) **1** V-T If you **huff**, you indicate that you are annoyed or offended, usually by the way that you say something. ❑ *'Well, I'm not going,' he huffed.* **2** PHRASE If someone is **in a huff**, they are behaving in a bad-tempered way because they are annoyed or offended.

hug /hʌg/ (**hugs, hugging, hugged**) **1** V-T & N-COUNT If you **hug** someone, or if you give them a **hug**, you put your arms around them and hold them tightly, as a sign of affection. ❑ *Lynn and I hugged each other.* ❑ *There were lots of hugs and kisses.* **2** V-T If you **hug** something, you hold it close to your body with your arms tightly round it. ❑ *She hugged her legs tight to her chest.* **3** V-T Something that **hugs** the ground or a stretch of land or water stays very close to it. [WRITTEN] ❑ *The road hugs the coast for hundreds of miles.*

huge /hjuːdʒ/ ADJ Something that is **huge** is extremely large in size, amount, or degree. ❑ *...a huge window.* ❑ *They have made huge profits.* ● **hugely** ADV ❑ *...a hugely successful career.*

hull /hʌl/ (**hulls**) N-COUNT The **hull** of a boat is the main part of its body.

hullo /hʌ'ləʊ/ → see **hello**

hum /hʌm/ (**hums, humming, hummed**) **1** V-I & N-SING If something **hums**, or if it makes a **hum**, it makes a low continuous noise. ❑ *The air conditioner hummed.* ❑ *...the hum of traffic.* **2** V-T/V-I When you **hum**, or **hum** a tune, you sing a tune with your lips closed. ❑ *She was humming to herself.*

Word Link — ***man** ≈ **human being** : **human**, **humanity**, **woman***

human /'hjuːmən/ (**humans**) **1** ADJ BEFORE N **Human** means relating to or concerning people. ❑ *...the human body.* ❑ *...human history.* ❑ *The crash was the result of human error.* **2** N-COUNT You can refer to people as **humans** when you are comparing them with animals or machines. ❑ *In humans, the same process takes about three months.*
→ see **evolution, primate**

Word Partnership — Use *human* with:

N. human **behavior**, human **body**, human **brain**, human **dignity**, human **error**, human **life**, human **weakness** **1**

ˌhuman 'being (**human beings**) N-COUNT A **human being** is a man, woman, or child.

humane /ˌhjuː'meɪn/ ADJ Someone who is **humane** is kind and compassionate. ❑ *...the desire for a more humane society.* ● **humanely** ADV ❑ *All prisoners are being humanely treated.*

humanism /'hjuːmənɪzəm/ N-UNCOUNT **Humanism** is the belief that people can achieve happiness and fulfilment without the need for religion. ● **humanist** (**humanists**) N-COUNT ❑ *...the country's leading humanists.*

Word Link — ***arian** ≈ **believing in, having** : **humanitarian**, **totalitarian**, **vegetarian***

humanitarian /hjuːˌmænɪ'teəriən/ (**humanitarians**) N-COUNT & ADJ If someone is a **humanitarian**, or if they hold **humanitarian** views, they try to avoid making people suffer or to help people who are suffering. ❑ *He says he acted on humanitarian grounds.*

humanity /hjuː'mænɪti/ (**humanities**) **1** N-UNCOUNT All the people in the world can be referred to as **humanity**. ❑ *They want to get as*

h

far away from humanity as possible. **2** N-UNCOUNT A person's **humanity** is their state of being a human being, rather than an animal or an object. [FORMAL] ❑ *The film deals with the pain Christoffer feels at losing his humanity.* **3** N-UNCOUNT **Humanity** is the quality of being kind, thoughtful, and sympathetic. ❑ *Her speech showed great maturity and humanity.* **4** N-PLURAL **The humanities** are subjects such as literature, philosophy, and history which are concerned with human ideas and behaviour.

ˌhuman ˈnature N-UNCOUNT **Human nature** is the natural qualities and behaviour that most people show. ❑ *It seems to be human nature to worry.*

ˌhuman ˈrace N-SING You can refer to all the people in the world as **the human race**.

ˌhuman ˈrights N-PLURAL **Human rights** are basic rights which many societies believe that all people should have.

humble /ˈhʌmbəl/ (**humbler, humblest, humbles, humbling, humbled**) **1** ADJ A **humble** person is not proud and does not believe that they are better than other people. ● **humbly** ADV ❑ *'I'm a very lucky man,' he said humbly.* **2** ADJ People and things that are considered very ordinary and unimportant can be described as **humble**. ❑ *...a humble fisherman.* ❑ *...the humble potato.* **3** V-T If something or someone **humbles** you, they make you realize that you are not as important or clever as you thought you were. ❑ *Ted's words humbled me.* ● **humbling** ADJ ❑ *...a very humbling experience.*

humid /ˈhjuːmɪd/ ADJ You use **humid** to describe an atmosphere or climate that is very damp, and usually very hot. ❑ *Visitors can expect hot and humid conditions.*
→ see **weather**

humidity /hjuːˈmɪdɪti/ N-UNCOUNT **Humidity** is dampness in the air. ❑ *The humidity is relatively low.*
→ see **forecast**

Word Link	*ate ≈ causing to be : complicate, humiliate, motivate*

humiliate /hjuːˈmɪlieɪt/ (**humiliates, humiliating, humiliated**) V-T To **humiliate** someone means to say or do something which makes them feel ashamed or stupid. ❑ *He enjoyed humiliating me.* ● **humiliated** ADJ ❑ *I have never felt so humiliated in my life.* ● **humiliating** ADJ ❑ *...a humiliating defeat.*

humiliation /hjuːˌmɪliˈeɪʃən/ (**humiliations**) N-VAR **Humiliation** is the embarrassment and shame you feel when someone makes you appear stupid, or when you make a mistake in public. A **humiliation** is an occasion or situation in which you feel this. ❑ *The election result is a humiliation for the prime minister.*

humility /hjuːˈmɪlɪti/ N-UNCOUNT Someone who has **humility** is not proud and does not believe that they are better than other people. ❑ *He should learn a little humility.*

humor /ˈhjuːmə/ → see **humour**

humorous /ˈhjuːmərəs/ ADJ If someone or something is **humorous**, they are amusing and witty. ❑ *...humorous stories.* ● **humorously** ADV ❑ *He regarded the whole thing humorously.*

humour [AM **humor**] /ˈhjuːmə/ (**humours, humouring, humoured**) **1** N-UNCOUNT You can refer to the amusing things that people say as their **humour**. ❑ *She is a fan of his outrageous humour.* **2** N-UNCOUNT If something has **humour**, it is funny and makes you want to laugh. ❑ *He tries to find the humour in most situations.* **3** N-UNCOUNT If you are in **good humour**, you feel happy. [WRITTEN] **4** V-T If you **humour** someone, you try to please them, so that they will not become upset. ❑ *I agreed, partly to humour him.*
→ see **laugh**

Word Partnership	Use *humour* with:
N.	**brand of** humour, **sense of** humour **1**
ADJ.	**good** humour **3**

hump /hʌmp/ (**humps, humping, humped**) **1** N-COUNT A **hump** is a small hill or raised piece of ground. ❑ *The path goes over a large hump.* **2** N-COUNT A camel's **hump** is the large lump on its back. **3** V-T If you **hump** a heavy object somewhere, you carry it there with difficulty. [BRIT, INFORMAL] ❑ *Charlie humped his rucksack up the stairs.*

hunch /hʌntʃ/ (**hunches, hunching, hunched**) **1** N-COUNT If you **have** a **hunch** that something is true, you think that it is likely to be true. [INFORMAL] ❑ *I had a hunch he had done it.* **2** V-T/V-I If you **hunch** your shoulders or **hunch** forward, you raise your shoulders, lower your head, and lean forward. ❑ *Pupils sat hunched over their books.*

hundred /ˈhʌndrəd/ (**hundreds**) **1** NUM **A hundred** or **one hundred** is the number 100. **2** N-PLURAL & PRON You can use **hundreds** to mean an extremely large number. ❑ *He received hundreds of letters.* **3** PHRASE You can use **a hundred per cent** or **one hundred per cent** to emphasize that something is definitely true. [INFORMAL] ❑ *I'm a hundred per cent certain that's what I saw.*

hundredth /ˈhʌndrədθ/ (**hundredths**) **1** ORD The **hundredth** item in a series is the one that you count as number one hundred. ❑ *...the hundredth anniversary of his birth.* **2** N-COUNT A **hundredth** is one of a hundred equal parts of something. ❑ *...one hundredth of a second.*

hung /hʌŋ/ **1** **Hung** is the past tense and past participle of most senses of **hang**. **2** ADJ A **hung parliament, council**, or **jury** consists of different groups of people who have different opinions, but no group forms a majority.

hunger /ˈhʌŋgə/ (**hungers, hungering, hungered**) **1** N-UNCOUNT **Hunger** is the feeling of weakness or discomfort that you get when you need something to eat. ❑ *Hunger is not as bad as thirst.* **2** N-UNCOUNT **Hunger** is a serious lack of food which causes suffering or death. ❑ *Thousands of people died of hunger.* **3** V-I & N-SING If you **hunger for** something, or if you have a **hunger for** it, you want it very much. [FORMAL] ❑ *Jules hungered for adventure.*

ˈhunger ˌstrike (**hunger strikes**) N-VAR If someone goes **on hunger strike**, they refuse to eat as a way of protesting about something. ❑ *The prisoners have been on hunger strike for 17 days.*

hungry /ˈhʌŋgri/ (**hungrier, hungriest**) **1** ADJ When you are **hungry**, you want food. ● **hungrily** ADV ❑ *James ate hungrily.* **2** PHRASE If people **go hungry**, they suffer from hunger, either for a long period because they are poor or for a short period because they miss a meal. **3** ADJ If you are **hungry**

for something, you want it very much. [LITERARY] ❑ *His players are hungry for success.*

Thesaurus	*hungry* Also look up:
ADJ.	starving; (*ant.*) full, stuffed 1

hunk /hʌŋk/ (**hunks**) N-COUNT A **hunk of** something is a large piece of it. ❑ *...a hunk of cheese.*

hunt /hʌnt/ (**hunts, hunting, hunted**) 1 V-T/V-I & N-COUNT When people or animals **hunt**, or **hunt** something, or when they go on a **hunt**, they chase and kill wild animals for food or as a sport. ❑ *He liked to hunt rabbits.* ❑ *...a bear hunt.* ● **hunting** N-UNCOUNT ❑ *...a ban on fox hunting.* 2 V-I & N-COUNT If you **hunt for** someone or something, or if you have a **hunt for** them, you search for them. ❑ *He hunted for an apartment.* ❑ *More than 70 police officers are involved in the hunt for her killer.* ● **hunting** N-UNCOUNT ❑ *...job hunting.*
▶ **hunt down** PHR-VERB If you **hunt** someone or something **down**, you succeed in finding them after searching for them. ❑ *It took her four months to hunt him down.*

hunter /ˈhʌntə/ (**hunters**) 1 N-COUNT A **hunter** is a person who hunts wild animals for food or as a sport. ❑ *...deer hunters.* 2 N-COUNT People who are searching for things of a particular kind can be referred to as **hunters.** ❑ *...bargain hunters.*

hurdle /ˈhɜːdəl/ (**hurdles**) 1 N-COUNT A **hurdle** is a difficulty that you must overcome in order to achieve something. ❑ *Preparing a CV is the first hurdle in a job search.* 2 N-COUNT **Hurdles** is a race in which people run and jump over a number of obstacles that are also called hurdles.

hurdler /ˈhɜːdlə/ (**hurdlers**) N-COUNT A **hurdler** is an athlete whose special event is the hurdles.

hurl /hɜːl/ (**hurls, hurling, hurled**) 1 V-T If you **hurl** an object, you throw it with a lot of force. ❑ *Groups of angry men hurled stones at police.* 2 V-T If you **hurl** abuse or insults **at** someone, you shout them aggressively.

hurricane /ˈhʌrɪkən, AM ˈhɜːrɪkeɪn/ (**hurricanes**) N-COUNT A **hurricane** is a very violent storm with strong winds.
→ see Word Web: **hurricane**
→ see **disaster**

hurried /ˈhʌrid, AM ˈhɜːr-/ ADJ A **hurried** action is done quickly. ❑ *...a hurried breakfast.* ● **hurriedly** ADV ❑ *She left the room hurriedly.*

hurry /ˈhʌri, AM ˈhɜːri/ (**hurries, hurrying, hurried**) 1 V-I If you **hurry** somewhere, you go there quickly. ❑ *Claire hurried along the road.* ❑ *She had to hurry home and look after her son.* 2 V-T If you **hurry to** do something, you start doing it as soon as you can, or you try to get it done quickly. ❑ *Shoppers hurried to buy food before the shop closed.* 3 V-T & PHR-VERB If you **hurry** someone or something, **hurry** them **up**, or **hurry** them **along**, you try to make something happen more quickly. ❑ *Sorry to hurry you, John.* ❑ *Can you advise me how I can hurry up the process?* ❑ *Petter saw no reason to hurry the divorce along.* 4 PHRASE If you are **in a hurry to** do something, you need or want to do something quickly. If you do something **in a hurry**, you do it quickly. ❑ *My colleague was in a hurry to get back to work.*
▶ **hurry up** 1 PHR-VERB If you tell someone to **hurry up**, you are telling them to do something more quickly. ❑ *Hurry up with that coffee, will you.* 2 → see **hurry** (meaning **3**)

Thesaurus	*hurry* Also look up:
V.	run, rush; (*ant.*) relax, slow down 1

h

hurt /hɜːt/ (**hurts, hurting, hurt**) 1 V-T & ADJ If you **hurt yourself**, or **hurt** a part of your body, or if you are **hurt**, you are injured. ❑ *He fell and hurt his back.* ❑ *His friends asked him if he was hurt.* 2 V-T/V-I If you **hurt** someone, you cause them to feel pain. ❑ *I didn't mean to hurt her.* ❑ *Ouch. That hurt.* 3 V-I If a part of your body **hurts**, you feel pain there. ❑ *My leg hurts and it's been hurting for three days.* 4 V-T & ADJ If someone **hurts** you, or if you are **hurt**, you are upset because someone has said or done something rude or inconsiderate. ❑ *He is afraid of hurting Bessy's feelings.* ❑ *He gave me a slightly hurt look.* 5 V-T You can say that something **hurts** someone or something when it damages them. ❑ *These injuries could hurt his skiing career.*

Thesaurus	*hurt* Also look up:
ADJ.	injured, wounded 1
	saddened, upset 4
V.	harm, injure, wound 2
	ache, smart, sting 3

Word Partnership	Use *hurt* with:
ADV.	**badly/seriously** hurt 1 3
V.	**get** hurt 1
	feel hurt 2
N.	hurt ***someone's* chances**, hurt **the economy**, hurt ***someone's* feelings**, hurt **sales** 4 5

Word Web *hurricane*

A **hurricane** is a violent **storm** or a tropical **cyclone** that develops in the Atlantic Ocean or Caribbean Sea. When a hurricane develops in the Pacific it is known as a **typhoon**. A hurricane begins as a **tropical depression**. It becomes a **tropical storm** when its **winds** reach 39 miles per hour (mph). When wind speeds reach 74 mph, a distinct **eye** forms in the center. Then the storm is officially a hurricane. It has heavy **rains** and very high winds. When a hurricane makes landfall or moves over cool water, it loses some of its power.

hurtle /'hɜːtəl/ (**hurtles, hurtling, hurtled**) V-I If someone or something **hurtles** somewhere, they move there very quickly, often in a rough or violent way. ❑ *I hurtled down the stairs.*

husband /'hʌzbənd/ (**husbands**) N-COUNT A woman's **husband** is the man she is married to.
→ see **family, love**

hush /hʌʃ/ (**hushes, hushing, hushed**) **1** CONVENTION You say **'Hush!'** to someone when you are asking or telling them to be quiet. **2** N-SING You say that there is a **hush** in a place when it is quiet and peaceful, or when it suddenly becomes quiet. ❑ *A hush fell over the crowd.*
▶ **hush up** PHR-VERB If someone in authority **hushes up** something bad or wrong, they prevent other people from finding out about it. ❑ *The government chose to hush up the scandal.*

hushed /hʌʃt/ ADJ **Hushed** means quiet and calm. ❑ *...a hushed atmosphere.*

H

hustle /'hʌsəl/ (**hustles, hustling, hustled**) **1** V-T If you **hustle** someone, you make them move quickly, usually by pulling or pushing them. ❑ *The guards hustled Harry out of the car.* **2** V-I If you **hustle**, you go somewhere or do something hurriedly. ❑ *He hustled straight up the steps to the plane.*

hut /hʌt/ (**huts**) N-COUNT A **hut** is a small, simple building, often made of wood, mud, or grass.

hybrid /'haɪbrɪd/ (**hybrids**) **1** N-COUNT A **hybrid** is an animal or plant that has been bred from two different types of animal or plant. [TECHNICAL] **2** N-COUNT You can use **hybrid** to refer to something that is a mixture of other things. ❑ *The building is a hybrid of old and new.*
→ see **car**

Word Link	*hydr ≈ water : dehydrate, carbohydrate, hydraulic*

hydraulic /haɪ'drɒlɪk, AM -'drɔːl-/ ADJ BEFORE N **Hydraulic** means involving a fluid that is under pressure, such as water or oil. ❑ *...hydraulic pumps.*

hydrogen /'haɪdrədʒən/ N-UNCOUNT **Hydrogen** is a colourless gas that is the lightest and most common element in the universe.
→ see **sun**

hygiene /'haɪdʒiːn/ N-UNCOUNT **Hygiene** is the practice of keeping yourself and your surroundings clean, especially in order to prevent the spread of disease. ● **hygienic** /haɪ'dʒiːnɪk, AM ˌhaɪ'dʒienɪk/ ADJ ❑ *...extremely hygienic conditions.*

hymn /hɪm/ (**hymns**) N-COUNT A **hymn** is a song sung by Christians to praise God.

hype /haɪp/ N-UNCOUNT If you describe the publicity for something such as a new film as **hype**, you disapprove of it because it is very intensive and exaggerated. ❑ *There has been so much hype and I don't want it to become more important than the actual game.*

hyperlink /'haɪpəlɪŋk/ (**hyperlinks**) N-COUNT In an HTML document, a **hyperlink** is a link to another part of the document or to another document. Hyperlinks are shown as words with a line under them. [COMPUTING]

hyphen /'haɪfən/ (**hyphens**) N-COUNT A **hyphen** is the punctuation sign (-) used to join words together to make a compound.
→ see **punctuation**

Word Link	*osis ≈ state or condition : diagnosis, hypnosis, metamorphosis*

hypnosis /hɪp'nəʊsɪs/ **1** N-UNCOUNT **Hypnosis** is a state of unconsciousness produced when someone has been hypnotized. **2** N-UNCOUNT **Hypnosis** is the art or practice of hypnotizing someone.

hypnotic /hɪp'nɒtɪk/ **1** ADJ Something that is **hypnotic** makes you feel as if you have been hypnotized. ❑ *...the TV screen's hypnotic power.* **2** ADJ If someone is in a **hypnotic** state, they have been hypnotized.

hypnotize [BRIT also **hypnotise**] /'hɪpnətaɪz/ (**hypnotizes, hypnotizing, hypnotized**) **1** V-T If someone **hypnotizes** you, they put you into a state of unconsciousness in which you seem to be asleep but can respond to certain things you see or hear. ● **hypnotism** N-UNCOUNT ❑ *She has an extraordinary talent for hypnotism.* ● **hypnotist** (**hypnotists**) N-COUNT ❑ *...regular visits to a hypnotist.* **2** V-T If you **are hypnotized** by someone or something, you are so fascinated by them that you cannot think of anything else. ❑ *I was hypnotized by her great black eyes.*

hypocrisy /hɪ'pɒkrɪsi/ (**hypocrisies**) N-VAR If you accuse someone of **hypocrisy**, you disapprove of them because they act in a way which goes against the beliefs or qualities they say they have. ❑ *He accused newspapers of hypocrisy in their treatment of the story.*

Word Link	*hypo ≈ below, under : hypocrite, hypothesis, hypothetical*

hypocrite /'hɪpəkrɪt/ (**hypocrites**) N-COUNT If you accuse someone of being a **hypocrite**, you disapprove of them because they act in a way which goes against the beliefs or qualities they say they have.

hypocritical /ˌhɪpə'krɪtɪkəl/ ADJ If you accuse someone of being **hypocritical**, you disapprove of them because they act in a way which goes against the beliefs or qualities they say they have. ❑ *If someone is being hypocritical then it is fair to tell people.*

hypothesis /haɪ'pɒθɪsɪs/ (**hypotheses**) N-COUNT A **hypothesis** is an explanation or theory which has not yet been proved to be correct. [FORMAL]
→ see **experiment, science**

hypothetical /ˌhaɪpə'θetɪkəl/ ADJ If something is **hypothetical**, it is based on possible situations, not actual ones. ❑ *...a purely hypothetical question.* ● **hypothetically** ADV ❑ *We're talking hypothetically.*

hysterectomy /ˌhɪstə'rektəmi/ (**hysterectomies**) N-COUNT A **hysterectomy** is a surgical operation to remove a woman's womb.

hysteria /hɪ'stɪəriə, AM -'ster-/ **1** N-UNCOUNT **Hysteria** among a group of people is a state of uncontrolled excitement or panic. ❑ *Everyone got carried away by the hysteria.* **2** N-UNCOUNT A person who is suffering from **hysteria** is mentally disturbed, often as a result of shock. [TECHNICAL]

hysterical /hɪ'sterɪkəl/ **1** ADJ Someone who is **hysterical** is in a state of uncontrolled excitement or panic. ❑ *Calm down. Don't get hysterical.* ● **hysterically** ADV ❑ *Everyone was laughing hysterically.* **2** ADJ If you describe someone or something as **hysterical**, you mean that you think they are very funny. [INFORMAL] ● **hysterically** ADV ❑ *It wasn't supposed to be a comedy but I found it hysterically funny.* **3** ADJ A **hysterical** illness is caused by mental disturbance that is often the result of shock. [TECHNICAL] ❑ *Her hysterical symptoms included paralysis.*

hysterics /hɪ'sterɪks/ **1** N-PLURAL If someone is **in hysterics** or **is having hysterics**, they are in a state of uncontrolled excitement or panic. **2** N-PLURAL You can say that someone is **in hysterics** or **is having hysterics** when they are laughing uncontrollably. [INFORMAL]

Ii

I /aɪ/ PRON **I** is used as the subject of a verb. A speaker or writer uses **I** to refer to himself or herself. ❑ *She liked me, I think.* ❑ *Jim and I are getting married.*

ice /aɪs/ (**ices, icing, iced**) 1 N-UNCOUNT **Ice** is frozen water. ❑ *When you go skating, remember to bend forward as you place one foot on the ice.* ❑ *...orange juice with ice.* 2 V-T If you **ice** a cake, you cover it with icing. ❑ *We were all given little iced cakes.* 3 N-COUNT An **ice** is an ice cream. 4 PHRASE If you **break the ice** at a party or meeting, or in a new situation, you do something to make people feel relaxed. ❑ *At parties, I tell jokes to break the ice.* 5 PHRASE If you say that something **cuts no ice** with you, you mean that you are not impressed or influenced by it. ❑ *Your apologies will cut no ice with them.* 6 PHRASE If you put a plan or project **on ice**, you delay doing it. 7 → see also **iced, icing**
→ see **crystal, glacier, snow**

iceberg /ˈaɪsbɜːg/ (**icebergs**) 1 N-COUNT An **iceberg** is a large, tall piece of ice floating in the sea. 2 **tip of the iceberg** → see **tip**

ˌice ˈcream (**ice creams**) 1 N-UNCOUNT **Ice cream** is a very cold sweet food made from frozen milk, fats, and sugar. 2 N-COUNT An **ice cream** is a portion of ice cream.
→ see **dessert**

iced /aɪst/ 1 ADJ BEFORE N An **iced** drink has been made very cold, often by putting ice in it. ❑ *...iced tea.* 2 → see also **ice**

ˈice hockey N-UNCOUNT **Ice hockey** is a game like hockey played on ice.

ˈice-skate (**ice-skates**) N-COUNT **Ice-skates** are boots with a thin metal bar underneath that people wear to move about on ice.

ice skates

ˈice-skater (**ice-skaters**) N-COUNT An **ice-skater** is someone who moves about on ice wearing ice-skates.

ˈice-skating N-UNCOUNT **Ice-skating** is a sport or leisure activity which involves people moving about on ice wearing ice-skates.

icicle /ˈaɪsɪkəl/ (**icicles**) N-COUNT An **icicle** is a long pointed piece of ice hanging from a surface.

icing /ˈaɪsɪŋ/ N-UNCOUNT **Icing** is a sweet substance made from powdered sugar that is used to cover and decorate cakes.

icon also **ikon** /ˈaɪkɒn/ (**icons**) 1 N-COUNT If you describe something or someone as an **icon**, you mean that they are important as a symbol of something. ❑ *She has been described as 'an icon of style'.* ❑ *...Picasso and the other icons of modernism.* 2 N-COUNT An **icon** is a picture of Christ or a saint painted on a wooden panel. Icons are regarded as holy by some Christians. 3 N-COUNT An **icon** is a picture on a computer screen representing a particular computer function. If you want to use it, you move the cursor onto the icon using a mouse. [COMPUTING]

icy /ˈaɪsi/ (**icier, iciest**) 1 ADJ **Icy** air or water is extremely cold. ❑ *...an icy wind.* ❑ *His shoes and clothing were wet and icy cold.* 2 ADJ An **icy** road has ice on it.

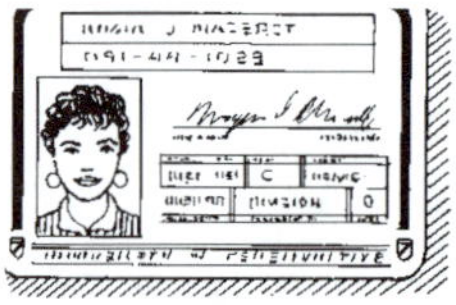

ID card

ID /ˌaɪ ˈdiː/ (**IDs**) N-VAR If you have **ID**, you are carrying a document such as an identity card or driving licence which proves that you are a particular person. ❑ *I had no ID on me so I couldn't prove I was the owner of the car.*

I'd /aɪd/ **I'd** is the usual spoken form of 'I had', especially when 'had' is an auxiliary verb. **I'd** is also a spoken form of 'I would'. ❑ *I felt absolutely certain that I'd seen her before.* ❑ *There's a question I'd like to ask.*

idea /aɪˈdiːə/ (**ideas**) 1 N-COUNT An **idea** is a plan or suggestion. ❑ *It's a good idea to avoid salty food.* ❑ *I really like the idea of helping people.* ❑ *She told me she'd had a brilliant idea.* 2 N-COUNT Your **idea of** something is your belief about what it is like or what it should be like. ❑ *This was his idea of a good present.* ❑ *Everyone has their own ideas about how to bring up children.* ❑ *The theory supports the idea that there are many other solar systems.* 3 N-SING If you have an **idea of** something, you have some general understanding or knowledge of it, although you may not know many details about it. ❑ *Could you give us an idea of the type of letters you've received?* ❑ *I had an idea that he joined the army later, after university.* ❑ *We haven't the faintest idea where he is.* 4 N-SING The **idea** of an action or activity is its aim or purpose. ❑ *The idea is to give children freedom to explore.* 5 PHRASE If you **get the idea**, you understand how to do something or understand what you are being told. ❑ *When you get the idea, you'll be able to do it very quickly.*

Word Partnership Use *idea* with:

ADJ.	**bad** idea, **bright** idea, **brilliant** idea, **great** idea, **crazy** idea, **different** idea, **dumb** idea, **interesting** idea, **new** idea, **original** idea 1 2
	the main idea, **the whole** idea 1 4
V.	**get an** idea, **have an** idea 1 3 5

Word Link *ide, ideo ≈ idea : ideal, idealise, ideology*

ideal /aɪˈdiːəl/ (**ideals**) **1** N-COUNT An **ideal** is a principle, idea, or standard that you believe is right and worth trying to achieve. ❑ *The trouble is, these young people have no ideals.* **2** N-SING Your **ideal** of something is the person or thing that seems to you to be the best possible example of it. ❑ *The ideal is a long, active, busy life.* **3** ADJ The **ideal** person or thing for a particular purpose is the best one for it. ❑ *He is the ideal person for the job.* ❑ *The conditions were ideal for racing.* ● **ideally** ADV ❑ *The hotel is ideally situated for country walks.* **4** ADJ BEFORE N An **ideal** society or world is the best possible one that you can imagine. **5** → see also **ideally**

idealise /aɪˈdiːəlaɪz/ → see **idealize**

idealism /aɪˈdiːəlɪzəm/ N-UNCOUNT **Idealism** is the behaviour and beliefs of someone who has ideals and tries to follow them, even though this may not be practical. ● **idealist** (**idealists**) N-COUNT ❑ *He is such an idealist that he cannot see the problems.*

idealistic /ˌaɪdiəˈlɪstɪk/ ADJ **Idealistic** people base their behaviour on ideals, even though this may not be practical.

idealize [BRIT also **idealise**] /aɪˈdiːəlaɪz/ (**idealizes, idealizing, idealized**) V-T If you **idealize** someone or something, you think of them as perfect or much better than they really are. ❑ *People idealize the past.*

ideally /aɪˈdiːəli/ **1** ADV If you say that **ideally** something should happen, you mean that you would like it to happen, although it may not be possible. ❑ *Ideally, you should drink every 10-15 minutes during exercise.* **2** → see also **ideal**

Word Link *ident ≈ same : identical, identification, unidentified*

identical /aɪˈdentɪkəl/ ADJ Things that are **identical** are exactly the same. ❑ *Nearly all the houses were identical.* ● **identically** ADV ❑ *...nine identically dressed dancers.*
→ see **clone**

identifiable /aɪˌdentɪˈfaɪəbəl/ ADJ Something or someone that is **identifiable** can be recognized. ❑ *The building is easily identifiable as a Catholic church.*

identification /aɪˌdentɪfɪˈkeɪʃən/ N-UNCOUNT When someone asks you for **identification**, they are asking to see something such as a passport which proves who you are.

identify /aɪˈdentɪfaɪ/ (**identifies, identifying, identified**) **1** V-T If you can **identify** someone or something, you can recognize them and say who or what they are. ❑ *Police have identified about 10 murder suspects.* ❑ *Now we have identified the problem, we must decide how to overcome it.* ● **identification** /aɪˌdentɪfɪˈkeɪʃən/ (**identifications**) N-VAR ❑ *He made a formal identification of the body.* **2** V-T If something **identifies** you, it makes it possible for people to recognize you. ❑ *She wore a little red hat to identify her.* **3** V-I If you **identify with** someone or something, you feel that you understand them. ❑ *As an actress, she only plays a role if she can identify with the character.* ● **identification** N-VAR ❑ *Marilyn had an intense identification with animals.* **4** V-T If you **identify** one thing **with** another, you consider them to be closely associated. ❑ *Many women cannot identify themselves with the term 'feminist'.* ● **identification** N-VAR ❑ *...the identification of Spain with Catholicism.*

identity /aɪˈdentɪti/ (**identities**) **1** N-COUNT Your **identity** is who you are. ❑ *The police soon established his true identity.* **2** N-VAR The **identity** of a person or place is the characteristics that they have that make them different from others. ❑ *I wanted a sense of my own identity.*

Word Partnership Use *identity* with:

N.	identity **theft** 1
	identity **crisis, sense of** identity 2
ADJ.	**ethnic** identity, **national** identity, **personal** identity 2

iˈdentity card (**identity cards**) N-COUNT An **identity card** is a card with a person's name, photograph, date of birth, and other information about them on it.

iˈdentity ˌtheft N-UNCOUNT **Identity theft** is the crime of getting personal information about another person without their knowledge, for example in order to gain access to their bank account. ❑ *Identity theft is one of the fastest-growing areas of crime in the UK.*

ideology /ˌaɪdiˈɒlədʒi/ (**ideologies**) N-VAR An **ideology** is a set of beliefs, especially the political beliefs on which people, parties, or countries base their actions. ❑ *...capitalist ideology.* ● **ideological** /ˌaɪdiəˈlɒdʒɪkəl/ ADJ ❑ *...the ideological divisions between the parties.* ● **ideologically** ADV ❑ *The new government is ideologically in favour of higher taxation.*

idiom /ˈɪdiəm/ (**idioms**) N-COUNT An **idiom** is a group of words which have a different meaning when used together from the one they would have if you took the meaning of each word individually. For example, 'to live from hand to mouth' is an idiom meaning to have very little food or money to live on.

idiot /ˈɪdiət/ (**idiots**) N-COUNT If you call someone an **idiot**, you mean that they are very stupid. ❑ *I was an idiot to stay there.*

idle /ˈaɪdəl/ (**idler, idlest**) **1** ADJ If you describe someone as **idle** you disapprove of them not doing anything when they should be doing something. ❑ *The shops are full of idle staff.* ● **idly** ADV ❑ *We were not idly sitting around.* **2** ADJ AFTER LINK-V Machines or factories that are **idle** are not being used. ❑ *The machine is lying idle.* **3** ADJ BEFORE N **Idle** is used to describe something that is done for no particular reason, or does not achieve anything useful. ❑ *...idle chatter.* ● **idly** ADV ❑ *We talked idly about magazines.*

idol /ˈaɪdəl/ (**idols**) N-COUNT An **idol** is someone such as a film star or pop star, who is greatly admired or loved by their fans. ❑ *...a teen idol.*

idolize [BRIT also **idolise**] /ˈaɪdəlaɪz/ (**idolizes, idolizing, idolized**) V-T If you **idolize** someone, you admire them very much. ❑ *Naomi idolised her father.*

idyllic /ɪˈdɪlɪk, AM aɪd-/ ADJ Something that is **idyllic** is extremely pleasant and peaceful without any difficulties. ❑ *...an idyllic setting for a honeymoon.* ❑ *He found that married life was not idyllic.*

i.e. /ˌaɪ ˈiː/ You use **i.e.** to introduce a word or sentence expressing what you have just said in a different and clearer way. ❑ *The Uzbeks speak a Turkic language (i.e. one related to Turkish).*

if /ɪf/ **1** CONJ You use **if** in conditional sentences to introduce the circumstances in which an event or situation might happen or might have happened. ❑ *She gets very upset if I don't include her in everything.* ❑ *Are you a student with great ideas? If so, we would love to hear from you.* **2** CONJ You use **if** in indirect questions when the answer is either 'yes' or 'no'. ❑ *I wonder if you would give us some information, please?* **3** CONJ You use **if** to suggest that something might be slightly different from what you are stating in the main part of the sentence, for example that there might be slightly more or less of a particular quality. ❑ *That standard is quite difficult, if not impossible, to achieve.* ❑ *What one quality, if any, do you dislike about your partner?* **4** PHRASE You use **'if anything'** when you are saying something which confirms a negative statement that you have just made. ❑ *There has yet to be an improvement. If anything, the situation has got worse.* **5** PHRASE You use **as if** to describe something or someone by comparing them with another thing or person. ❑ *He pointed two fingers at his head, as if he were holding a gun.* **6** PHRASE You use **if only** when you are mentioning a reason for doing something. ❑ *She always writes to me once a month, if only to remind me that I haven't answered her last letter.* **7** PHRASE You use **if only** to express a wish, especially one that is impossible. ❑ *If only you had told me that last week.* ❑ *If only it were that simple!*

I

iffy /'ɪfi/ **1** ADJ If something is **iffy**, it is uncertain. [INFORMAL] ❑ *His political future has looked iffy for most of the year.* **2** ADJ If you say that something is **iffy**, you mean that it is not very good in some way. [INFORMAL] ❑ *If your next record's a bit iffy, you're forgotten.*

igloo /'ɪglu/ (**igloos**) N-COUNT **Igloos** are dome-shaped houses built from blocks of ice by the Inuit people.

ignite /ɪg'naɪt/ (**ignites, igniting, ignited**) V-T/V-I When you **ignite** something, or when it **ignites**, it starts burning. ❑ *The bombs ignited a fire which destroyed some houses.* ❑ *I was afraid the petrol tank was going to ignite.*

ignition /ɪg'nɪʃən/ N-SING In a car, the **ignition** is the mechanism which ignites the fuel and starts the engine, usually operated by turning a key. ❑ *Uncle Jim put the key in the ignition.*

ignorant /'ɪgnərənt/ **1** ADJ If you refer to someone as **ignorant**, you mean that they do not know much because they are not well educated. If someone is **ignorant** of a fact, they do not know it. ❑ *Often people don't ask questions because they don't want to seem ignorant.* ❑ *Many people are ignorant of the facts about global warming.* ● **ignorance** N-UNCOUNT ❑ *I am embarrassed by my ignorance of European history.* **2** ADJ People are sometimes described as **ignorant** when they behave in a rude or inconsiderate way. Some people think this use is not correct.

ignore /ɪg'nɔː/ (**ignores, ignoring, ignored**) V-T If you **ignore** someone or something, you deliberately take no notice of them. ❑ *Her husband ignored her.* ❑ *They had ignored the warning signs.*

ikon /'aɪkɒn/ → see **icon**

ill /ɪl/ (**ills**) **1** ADJ & N-PLURAL If you are **ill**, you are suffering from a health problem. People who are ill in some way can be referred to as, for example, **the** mentally **ill**. ❑ *I was feeling ill.* ❑ *She visits the seriously ill.* **2** N-PLURAL Difficulties or problems can be referred to as **ills**. [FORMAL] ❑ *One woman blamed the ills of society on bad housing.* **3** ADJ BEFORE N **Ill** can be used in front of some nouns to mean 'bad'. [FORMAL] ❑ *She brought ill luck into her family.* **4** N-UNCOUNT **Ill** is evil or harm. [LITERARY] ❑ *They say they mean no ill.* **5** **ill at ease** → see **ease**

Usage

The words **ill** and **sick** are very similar in meaning but are used in slightly different ways. **Ill** is generally not used before a noun, and can be used in verbal expressions such as **fall ill** and **be taken ill**. ❑ *He fell ill shortly before Christmas.* ❑ *The trial was delayed after one of the jury members was taken ill.* **Sick** is often used before a noun. ❑ *...sick children.* In British English, **ill** is a slightly more polite, less direct word than **sick**. **Sick** often suggests the actual physical feeling of being ill, for example nausea or vomiting. ❑ *I spent the next 24 hours in bed, being sick.* In American English, **sick** is often used where British people would say **ill**. ❑ *Some people get hurt in accidents or get sick.*

Word Partnership

Use *ill* with:

ADV.	**critically** ill, **mentally** ill, **physically** ill, **seriously** ill, **terminally** ill, **very** ill **1**
V.	**become** ill, **feel** ill, **look** ill **1**

I'll /aɪl/ **I'll** is the usual spoken form of 'I will' or 'I shall'. ❑ *I'll drive you to your hotel.*

Word Link

***il** ≈ not : **il**legal, **il**literate, **il**logical*

illegal /ɪ'li:gəl/ ADJ If something is **illegal**, the law says that it is not allowed. ❑ *It is illegal to bring animals into Britain without a licence.* ❑ *...illegal trade.* ● **illegally** ADV ❑ *The previous government acted illegally.* ❑ *Illegally parked cars will be removed.*

illegitimate /ˌɪlɪ'dʒɪtɪmət/ **1** ADJ A person who is **illegitimate** was born of parents who were not legally married to each other. **2** ADJ Something that is **illegitimate** is not right, according to the law or to accepted standards. ❑ *Most of the world declared the elections illegitimate.*

ˌill-'fated ADJ If you describe something as **ill-fated**, you mean that it ended or will end in an unsuccessful or unfortunate way. ❑ *...Scott's ill-fated expedition to the South Pole.*

ˌill 'health N-UNCOUNT Someone who suffers from **ill health** has an illness or is often ill.

illicit /ɪ'lɪsɪt/ ADJ An **illicit** activity or substance is not allowed according to the law or to social customs. ❑ *...the illicit trade in weapons.*

Word Link

***liter** ≈ letter : il**liter**ate, **liter**al, **liter**ature*

illiterate /ɪ'lɪtərət/ ADJ Someone who is **illiterate** cannot read or write.

illness /'ɪlnəs/ (**illnesses**) **1** N-UNCOUNT **Illness** is the fact or experience of being ill. ❑ *Her father suffers from mental illness.* ❑ *He is taking a day off work due to illness.* **2** N-COUNT An **illness** is a particular disease such as a cold, measles, or pneumonia. → see Word Web: **illness**

Word Web illness

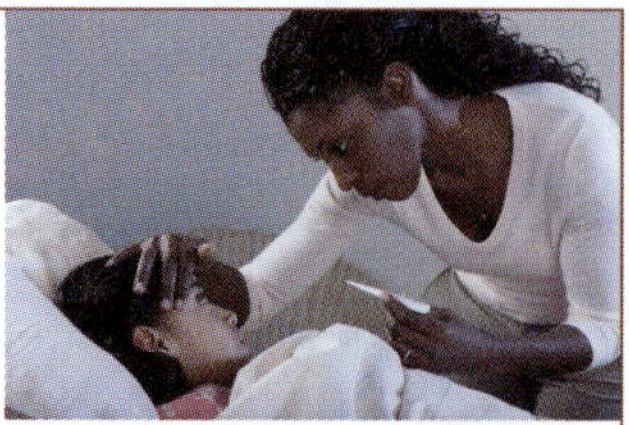

Most **infectious diseases** pass from person to person. However, some people have caught **viruses** from animals. During the 2002 SARS **epidemic**, doctors discovered that the disease came from birds. SARS caused over 800 deaths in 32 countries. The disease had to be stopped quickly. Hospitals **quarantined** SARS patients so that they would not make other people sick. Medical workers used **symptoms** such as **fever**, **chills**, and a **cough** to help **diagnose** the disease. **Treatment** was not easy. By the time the symptoms appeared, the disease had already caused a lot of damage. **Patients** were given oxygen and **physiotherapy** to help clear the lungs.

Thesaurus *illness* Also look up:

N. ailment, disease, sickness; *(ant.)* health, wellness 1 2

Word Partnership Use *illness* with:

N. **signs/symptoms of *an*** illness 1 2
ADJ. **mental** illness, **serious** illness, **terminal** illness 1 2
long/short illness, **mysterious** illness, **sudden** illness 2
V. **suffer from *an*** illness, **treat *an*** illness 1 2
diagnose an illness, **have an** illness 2

Word Link *il ≈ not : illegal, illiterate, illogical*

illogical /ɪˈlɒdʒɪkəl/ ADJ An **illogical** feeling or action is not reasonable and does not result from ordered thinking. ❑ *His behaviour was illogical.*

illuminate /ɪˈluːmɪneɪt/ (**illuminates, illuminating, illuminated**) 1 V-T To **illuminate** something means to shine light on it and make it brighter. [WRITTEN] ❑ *The walls were illuminated by moonlight.* ● **illumination** N-UNCOUNT ❑ *...the days before illumination by electricity.* 2 V-T If you **illuminate** something that is difficult to understand, you make it clearer by explaining it or giving examples. [FORMAL] ❑ *The instructors use games to illuminate their subject.* ● **illuminating** ADJ ❑ *This is a most illuminating book.*

illusion /ɪˈluːʒən/ (**illusions**) 1 N-COUNT An **illusion** is something that appears to exist or to be a particular thing but in reality does not exist or is something else. ❑ *The bright paint gave the illusion of sunlight.* 2 N-VAR An **illusion** is a false idea or belief. ❑ *He's under the illusion that money automatically makes people happy.*

Word Partnership Use *illusion* with:

PREP. **be under an** illusion 2
V. **create an** illusion, **give an** illusion **about/of/that *something*** 1 2

illustrate /ˈɪləstreɪt/ (**illustrates, illustrating, illustrated**) 1 V-T If something **illustrates** a situation, it shows that the situation exists. ❑ *This story illustrates how violence has become part of everyday life.* ❑ *Our discovery illustrates that we don't know everything about the Earth.* ● **illustration** (**illustrations**) N-VAR ❑ *Mr Clinton said the incident was an illustration of terrorism.* 2 V-T If you use an example, story, or diagram to **illustrate** a point, you use it to show that what you are saying is true or to make your meaning clearer. ❑ *She illustrates her lecture with real examples.* ● **illustration** N-VAR ❑ *Here, by way of illustration, are some extracts from our new catalogue.* 3 V-T If you **illustrate** a book, you put pictures or diagrams into it. ● **illustration** N-VAR ❑ *The book is full of colourful illustrations.*
→ see **animation**

illustrious /ɪˈlʌstriəs/ ADJ An **illustrious** person is famous and distinguished.

I'm /aɪm/ **I'm** is the usual spoken form of 'I am'. ❑ *I'm having a bath and then I'm going to bed.*

image /ˈɪmɪdʒ/ (**images**) 1 N-COUNT If you have an **image** of someone or something, you have a picture or idea of them in your mind. ❑ *These terrible images stick in the mind.* 2 N-COUNT The **image** of a person or organization is the way that they appear to other people. ❑ *I don't think she should change her image at all.* ❑ *They have damaged the image of the Scottish Parliament.* 3 N-COUNT An **image** is a picture or reflection of someone or something. ❑ *We have the technology to send video images over mobile phones.* 4 N-COUNT An **image** is a description or symbolic representation of something in a poem or other work of art. ❑ *...the image of 'star-filled seas' in the first verse.*
→ see **eye, photography, telescope, television**

Word Partnership Use *image* with:

ADJ. **corporate** image, **negative/positive** image, **public** image 2
N. image **on a screen** 3
V. **display an** image, **project an** image 3

imagery /ˈɪmɪdʒri/ N-UNCOUNT You can talk about, for example, a poem's or film's **imagery** when you are referring to the symbols or descriptions in it which create a strong picture in your mind. ❑ *...the nature imagery in the poem.*

imaginable /ɪˈmædʒɪnəbəl/ ADJ You use **imaginable** in expressions like 'the worst thing imaginable' or 'every imaginable thing' to emphasize that it is the most extreme example of something, or all the possible examples of something. ❑ *...some of the most horrible circumstances imaginable.* ❑ *He had the worst imaginable day.*

imaginary /ɪˈmædʒɪnəri, AM -neri/ ADJ An **imaginary** person, place, or thing exists only in

i

your mind or in a story, and not in real life. ❑ *Lots of children have imaginary friends.*
→ see **fantasy**

imagination /ɪˌmædʒɪˈneɪʃən/ (**imaginations**) N-VAR Your **imagination** is your ability to form pictures or ideas in your mind of new, exciting, or imaginary things. ❑ *Antonia has a vivid imagination.* ❑ *Africa was alive in my imagination long before I ever went there.* ❑ *Buying your wife flowers or perfume shows no imagination.*
→ see **fantasy**

Word Partnership Use *imagination* with:

ADJ.	**active** imagination, **lively** imagination, **vivid** imagination
PREP.	**beyond *(someone's)*** imagination
N.	**lack of** imagination

imaginative /ɪˈmædʒɪnətɪv/ ADJ If you are **imaginative** or you have **imaginative** ideas, you are easily able to think of or create new or exciting things. ❑ *...hundreds of cooking ideas and imaginative recipes.* ● **imaginatively** ADV ❑ *The hotel is decorated imaginatively and attractively.*

I

imagine /ɪˈmædʒɪn/ (**imagines, imagining, imagined**) **1** V-T If you **imagine** a situation, your mind forms a picture or idea of it. ❑ *He could not imagine a more peaceful scene.* ❑ *Can you imagine how she felt?* ❑ *Imagine you're lying on a beach.* **2** V-T If you **imagine that** something is true, you think that it is true. ❑ *He imagined that he heard a strange noise in the house.* ❑ *'Was he meeting someone?'—'I imagine so.'* **3** V-T If you **imagine** something, you think that you have seen, heard, or experienced something, although actually you have not. ❑ *I must have imagined the whole thing.*

Thesaurus *imagine* Also look up:

V.	picture, see, visualize **1**
	believe, guess, think **2**

Word Partnership Use *imagine* with:

V.	**can/can't/could/couldn't** imagine ***something***, **try to** imagine **1-3**
ADJ.	**difficult/easy/hard/impossible to** imagine **1-3**

Word Link *im ≈ not : imbalance, immature, impossible*

imbalance /ɪmˈbæləns/ (**imbalances**) N-VAR If there is an **imbalance** in a situation, the things involved are not the same size, or are not the right size in relation to each other. ❑ *...the imbalance between the two sides in this war.*

imbue /ɪmˈbjuː/ (**imbues, imbuing, imbued**) V-T If you **imbue** something **with** a quality, you fill it with the quality. [FORMAL] ❑ *His time in India imbued him with a deep love of the country.*

imitate /ˈɪmɪteɪt/ (**imitates, imitating, imitated**) **1** V-T If you **imitate** someone, you copy what they do or produce. ❑ *Birds are starting to imitate the ring tones of mobile phones.* ● **imitator** (**imitators**) N-COUNT ❑ *He has had many imitators but no equals.* **2** V-T If you **imitate** someone or something, you copy the way they speak or behave, often as a joke.

imitation /ˌɪmɪˈteɪʃən/ (**imitations**) **1** N-COUNT An **imitation** of something is a copy of it. ❑ *...an accurate imitation of Chinese architecture.* **2** N-UNCOUNT **Imitation** means copying someone else's actions. ❑ *Molly learned golf by imitation.* **3** ADJ BEFORE N **Imitation** things are not genuine but are made to look as if they are. ❑ *...imitation leather.* **4** N-COUNT If you **do** an **imitation of** another person, you copy the way they speak or behave, often as a joke.

immaculate /ɪˈmækjʊlət/ **1** ADJ If something is **immaculate**, it is extremely clean, tidy, or neat. ❑ *Her front room was immaculate.* ● **immaculately** ADV ❑ *He was immaculately dressed.* **2** ADJ If something is **immaculate**, it is perfect, without any faults. ❑ *Moreno produced an immaculate performance.*

immaterial /ˌɪməˈtɪəriəl/ ADJ AFTER LINK-V If something is **immaterial**, it is not important or not relevant. ❑ *It is immaterial whether we like him or not.*

immature /ˌɪməˈtjʊə, AM -ˈtʊr/ **1** ADJ Something that is **immature** is not yet fully developed. ❑ *...babies with immature lungs.* **2** ADJ If you describe someone as **immature**, you mean that they do not behave in a sensible and adult way. ❑ *...immature drivers who disobey the rules of the road.* ❑ *She's just being childish and immature.*

Thesaurus *immature* Also look up:

ADJ.	underdeveloped **1**
	childish, foolish, juvenile **2**

immediate /ɪˈmiːdiət/ **1** ADJ An **immediate** result, action, or reaction happens or is done without any delay. ❑ *These events had an immediate effect.* ❑ *My immediate reaction was to laugh.* ● **immediately** ADV ❑ *He immediately ran for help.* ❑ *Ingrid answered Peter's letter immediately.* **2** ADJ **Immediate** needs and concerns must be dealt with quickly. ❑ *The immediate problem is lack of food.* **3** ADJ BEFORE N **Immediate** means very close to something or someone else in a sequence. ❑ *...the house of their immediate neighbours.* ❑ *...his immediate boss.* ● **immediately** ADV ❑ *She always sits immediately behind the driver.* **4** ADJ BEFORE N Your **immediate family** are your parents, brothers, and sisters.

Word Partnership Use *immediate* with:

N.	immediate **action**, immediate **plans**, immediate **reaction**, immediate **response**, immediate **results** **1**
	immediate **future**, immediate **surroundings** **3**
	immediate **family** **4**

immediately /ɪˈmiːdiətli/ **1** ADV If something is **immediately** obvious, it can be seen or understood without any delay. ❑ *The reasons for this may not be immediately clear.* **2** CONJ If one thing happens **immediately** after something else happens, it happens after that event, without any delay. ❑ *Immediately after you have finished, re-start your computer and check the hard disk.* **3** → see also **immediate**

Thesaurus	*immediately*	Also look up:
ADV.	at once, now, right away; *(ant.)* later 2	

immense /ɪ'mens/ ADJ **Immense** means extremely large or great. ❑ *I watched her go with immense sadness.* ❑ *The job ahead is immense and will take time.*

immensely /ɪ'mensli/ ADV **Immensely** means to a very great extent or degree. ❑ *Chess is immensely popular in Russia.* ❑ *I enjoyed this movie immensely.*

immerse /ɪ'mɜːs/ (**immerses, immersing, immersed**) 1 V-T If you **immerse yourself in** something that you are doing, you become completely involved in it. ❑ *I immersed myself in the new job.* ● **immersed** ADJ AFTER LINK-V ❑ *He's really becoming immersed in his work.* 2 V-T If you **immerse** something **in** a liquid, you put it into the liquid so that it is completely covered.

Word Link	***migr ≈ moving, changing : emigrate, immigrant, migrant***

immigrant /'ɪmɪgrənt/ (**immigrants**) N-COUNT An **immigrant** is a person who has come to live in a country from another country.
→ see **culture**

immigration /ˌɪmɪ'greɪʃən/ 1 N-UNCOUNT **Immigration** is the fact or process of people coming into a country in order to live and work there. ❑ *The government has decided to tighten immigration laws.* 2 N-UNCOUNT **Immigration** or **immigration control** is the place at a port, airport, or international border where officials check the passports of people who wish to come into the country.

imminent /'ɪmɪnənt/ ADJ Something that is **imminent** will happen very soon. ❑ *There was no imminent danger.*

immoral /ɪ'mɒrəl, AM -'mɔːr-/ ADJ If you describe someone or their behaviour as **immoral**, you mean that their behaviour is morally wrong. ❑ *Terrorism is illegal and immoral.*

Word Link	***mort ≈ death : immortal, mortal, mortuary***

immortal /ɪ'mɔːtəl/ (**immortals**) 1 ADJ & N-COUNT Someone or something that is **immortal** or an **immortal** is famous and likely to be remembered for a long time. ❑ *This company thought up the immortal line 'A Diamond is Forever.'* ❑ *He called Moore 'one of the immortals of soccer'.* ● **immortality** /ˌɪmɔː'tælɪti/ N-UNCOUNT ❑ *Some people want to achieve immortality through their works.* 2 ADJ In stories, someone who is **immortal** lives for ever. ● **immortality** N-UNCOUNT ❑ *The ancient Greeks believed in the immortality of the soul.*

immortalize [BRIT also **immortalise**] /ɪ'mɔːtəlaɪz/ (**immortalizes, immortalizing, immortalized**) V-T If someone or something **is immortalized** in something such as a film or a book, they are made famous and will be remembered for a very long time because of it.

immune /ɪ'mjuːn/ 1 ADJ AFTER LINK-V If you are **immune to** a disease, you cannot be affected by it. ❑ *She is immune to measles.* ● **immunity** N-UNCOUNT ❑ *Birds in outside cages develop immunity to these bacteria.* 2 ADJ AFTER LINK-V If you are **immune to** something that happens or is done, you are not affected by it. ❑ *He did not become immune to the sight of death.* 3 ADJ AFTER LINK-V Someone or something that is **immune from** a particular process or situation is able to escape it. ❑ *Nobody's life is immune from pain.* ● **immunity** N-UNCOUNT ❑ *The police are offering immunity from prosecution to witnesses who help identify the murderers.*

im'mune system (**immune systems**) N-COUNT Your **immune system** consists of all the cells and processes in your body which protect you from illness and infection.

immunize [BRIT also **immunise**] /'ɪmjʊnaɪz/ (**immunizes, immunizing, immunized**) V-T If you **are immunized against** a disease, you are given a drug which prevents you from being affected by it. ❑ *Every student is immunized against hepatitis B.* ❑ *He proposed a national programme to immunize children.* ● **immunization** (**immunizations**) N-VAR ❑ *...immunization against childhood diseases.*

impact (**impacts, impacting, impacted**)

noun /'ɪmpækt/, verb /ɪm'pækt/

1 N-COUNT & V-T If something makes an **impact on** a situation or person, or if something **impacts on** a situation or person, it has a strong effect on them. ❑ *The meeting will have a real impact on the future of the country.* ❑ *All this will impact on the company's finances.* 2 N-UNCOUNT The **impact** of one object on another is the force with which it hits it. ❑ *The windscreen of the car was smashed by the impact with the bicyclist.*
→ see **crash**

Word Partnership	Use *impact* with:
ADJ.	**historical** impact, **important** impact 1
V.	**have an** impact, **make an** impact 1
	die on impact 2
PREP.	**on** impact 2

impair /ɪm'peə/ (**impairs, impairing, impaired**) V-T To **impair** something such as an ability or the way that something functions means to damage it, preventing it from working properly. [FORMAL] ❑ *Lack of sleep impairs your ability to think and make decisions.* ● **impaired** ADJ ❑ *...permanently impaired hearing.*

impairment /ɪm'peəmənt/ (**impairments**) N-COUNT If someone has an **impairment**, they have a medical condition which prevents their eyes, ears, or brain from working properly.

impart /ɪm'pɑːt/ (**imparts, imparting, imparted**) 1 V-T If you **impart** information **to** someone, you tell it to them. [FORMAL] 2 V-T If something **imparts** a particular quality **to** something, it gives it that quality. [FORMAL] ❑ *Peanut oil imparts a unique flavour to food.*

impartial /ɪm'pɑːʃəl/ ADJ If you are **impartial**, you are able to act fairly because you are not personally involved in a situation. ❑ *...impartial advice on which products best suit the customer's needs.* ● **impartially** ADV ❑ *We promise to impartially investigate the matter.* ● **impartiality** /ˌɪmpɑːʃi'ælɪti/ N-UNCOUNT ❑ *...a justice system that lacks impartiality.*

impasse /'æmpæs, 'ɪm-/ N-SING An **impasse** is a situation in which it is impossible to make any progress. ❑ *The company has reached an impasse in negotiations with the union.*

impassioned /ɪm'pæʃənd/ ADJ If you make an **impassioned** speech, you express strong personal feelings about an issue. [WRITTEN]

impassive /ɪm'pæsɪv/ ADJ An **impassive** person does not show any emotion. ● **impassively** ADV ❑ *At his trial, he listened impassively to the sentence.*

impatient /ɪm'peɪʃənt/ **1** ADJ If you are **impatient**, you are annoyed because you have had to wait too long for something. ❑ *I was growing impatient with my slow progress.* ● **impatiently** ADV ❑ *Frank waited impatiently for the lift to arrive.* ● **impatience** N-UNCOUNT ❑ *I remember his impatience with long speeches.* **2** ADJ AFTER LINK-V If you are **impatient to** do something or **impatient for** something to happen, you are eager to do it or eager for it to happen and do not want to wait. ❑ *He was impatient to get home.*

impeccable /ɪm'pekəbəl/ ADJ If you describe something such as someone's behaviour or appearance as **impeccable**, you are emphasizing that it is excellent and has no faults. ❑ *She had impeccable taste in clothes.* ● **impeccably** ADV ❑ *The children behaved impeccably.*

I

impede /ɪm'piːd/ (**impedes, impeding, impeded**) V-T To **impede** someone or something means to make their movement, development, or progress difficult. [FORMAL] ❑ *Injuries, including a broken leg, impeded his progress as a football player.*

impediment /ɪm'pedɪmənt/ (**impediments**) **1** N-COUNT An **impediment to** something prevents it from happening, or from progressing or developing easily. [FORMAL] ❑ *This latest development is a major impediment to peace.* **2** N-COUNT A **speech impediment** is a disability which makes speaking difficult.

impending /ɪm'pendɪŋ/ ADJ BEFORE N An **impending** event is one that is going to happen very soon. [FORMAL] ❑ *...a feeling of impending disaster.*

impenetrable /ɪm'penɪtrəbəl/ **1** ADJ An **impenetrable** wall or barrier is impossible to get through. **2** ADJ If you describe something such as a book as **impenetrable**, you are emphasizing that it is impossible to understand.

imperative /ɪm'perətɪv/ **1** ADJ You can say that it is **imperative that** something is done when you want to emphasize that it must be done. ❑ *It is imperative that the two countries do not go to war.* **2** N-SING In grammar, a clause that is in **the imperative** contains the base form of a verb and usually has no subject. Imperative clauses are used to tell someone to do something. Examples are 'Go away' and 'Please be careful'.

Word Partnership	Use *imperative* with:
ADV.	**absolutely** imperative **1**
N.	imperative **need** **1**

imperfect /ɪm'pɜːfɪkt/ **1** ADJ Something that is **imperfect** has faults. ❑ *...an imperfect world.* **2** N-SING In grammar, **the imperfect** or **the imperfect tense** of a verb is used in describing continuous situations or repeated actions in the past.

imperfection /ˌɪmpə'fekʃən/ (**imperfections**) N-VAR An **imperfection** is a fault or weakness.

imperial /ɪm'pɪəriəl/ **1** ADJ BEFORE N **Imperial** means belonging or relating to an empire, emperor, or empress. ❑ *...the Imperial Palace in Tokyo.* **2** ADJ BEFORE N The **imperial** system of measurement uses miles, yards, feet, and inches to measure length, ounces and pounds to measure weight, and pints and gallons to measure volume.

imperialism /ɪm'pɪəriəlɪzəm/ N-UNCOUNT **Imperialism** is a system in which a rich and powerful country controls other countries. ● **imperialist** (**imperialists**) N-COUNT ❑ *...an imperialist power that interferes in the affairs of weaker countries.*

impersonal /ɪm'pɜːsənəl/ **1** ADJ If you describe a place, organization, or activity as **impersonal**, you feel that the people there see you as unimportant or unwanted. ❑ *...expensive, but rather impersonal hotels.* **2** ADJ **Impersonal** means not concerned with any particular person. ❑ *Textbooks are usually impersonal in tone.*

impersonate /ɪm'pɜːsəneɪt/ (**impersonates, impersonating, impersonated**) V-T If you **impersonate** someone, you pretend to be that person, either to deceive people or to entertain them. ❑ *He was arrested for impersonating a doctor.* ● **impersonation** (**impersonations**) N-COUNT ❑ *Michael does a wonderful impersonation of an old woman's voice.*

impetus /'ɪmpɪtəs/ N-UNCOUNT Something that gives a process **impetus** or gives it an **impetus** makes it happen or progress more quickly. ❑ *The bank loan gave me the impetus to set up my business.*

implacable /ɪm'plækəbəl/ ADJ If you describe someone as **implacable**, you mean that their attitude or feelings about something are firm and will not be changed by other people's opinions. ❑ *He now had three implacable enemies against him.* ● **implacably** ADV ❑ *I was implacably against the war.*

implant (**implants, implanting, implanted**) **1** V-T /ɪm'plɑːnt, -'plænt/ If something such as a heart **is implanted into** a person's body, it is put there by means of a medical operation. ❑ *Their dog has an identifying microchip implanted under his skin.* **2** N-COUNT /'ɪmplɑːnt, -plænt/ An **implant** is something implanted into a person's body. ❑ *...artificial bone implants.*

implement (**implements, implementing, implemented**) **1** V-T /'ɪmplɪment/ If you **implement** a plan, system, or law, you carry it out. ● **implementation** N-UNCOUNT ❑ *...the implementation of the peace agreement.* **2** N-COUNT /'ɪmplɪmənt/ An **implement** is a tool or other piece of equipment.

implicate /'ɪmplɪkeɪt/ (**implicates, implicating, implicated**) V-T If you **implicate** someone **in** a crime or something bad, you show that they were involved in it. ❑ *A newspaper article implicated the army in the killings.*

implication /ˌɪmplɪ'keɪʃən/ (**implications**) N-COUNT The **implications of** something are the things that are likely to happen as a result of it. ❑ *...the political implications of his decision.*

Word Partnership	Use *implication* with:
ADJ.	**clear** implication, **important** implication, **obvious** implication

implicit /ɪm'plɪsɪt/ **1** ADJ Something that is **implicit** is expressed in an indirect way.

• **implicitly** ADV ❑ *Mr Jones was implicitly criticised in the report.* **2** ADJ If you have an **implicit** belief or faith **in** something, you believe it completely and have no doubts about it. ❑ *Her father had implicit faith in his daughter's honesty.* • **implicitly** ADV ❑ *I trust him implicitly.*

implore /ɪm'plɔː/ (**implores, imploring, implored**) V-T If you **implore** someone **to** do something, you beg them to do it. [FORMAL] ❑ *I implored Michael not to say anything.*

imply /ɪm'plaɪ/ (**implies, implying, implied**) V-T To **imply that** something is the case means to say or do something to make it appear that it is the case. ❑ *The article implied that the attack was racist.* ❑ *Saying 'no' implies a lack of interest.*

Thesaurus *imply* Also look up:
V. hint, point to, suggest

Word Link *port ≈ carrying : export, import, portable*

import (**imports, importing, imported**) **1** V-T /ɪm'pɔːt/ When a country or organization **imports** a product, they buy it from another country for use in their own country. ❑ *The US imports over half of its oil.* ❑ *...the price of imported sugar.* • **importation** N-UNCOUNT ❑ *...restrictions concerning the importation of birds.* • **importer** (**importers**) N-COUNT ❑ *...oil importers.* **2** N-COUNT /'ɪmpɔːt/ **Imports** are products or raw materials bought from another country for use in your own country.

important /ɪm'pɔːtənt/ **1** ADJ Something that is **important** is very significant, valuable, or necessary. ❑ *Her sons are the most important thing in her life.* • **importantly** ADV ❑ *I was hungry, and, more importantly, my children were hungry.* • **importance** N-UNCOUNT ❑ *The price is of no importance.* **2** ADJ An **important** person has influence or power. ❑ *...a very important lawyer.* • **importance** N-UNCOUNT ❑ *Johnson photographed just about everyone of importance in the arts.*

Usage
You do not use **important** to say that an amount or quantity is very large. You do not talk, for example, about 'an important sum of money'. Instead, you use words such as **large**, **considerable**, or **substantial**. ❑ *...a large sum of money.* ❑ *...a man with considerable influence.* ❑ *...substantial savings when buying several products.*

Thesaurus *important* Also look up:
ADJ. critical, essential, principal, significant; *(ant.)* unimportant **1** distinguished **2**

impose /ɪm'pəʊz/ (**imposes, imposing, imposed**) **1** V-T If you **impose** something **on** people, you force them to accept it. ❑ *Don't impose your own tastes on your children.* • **imposition** /ˌɪmpə'zɪʃən/ N-UNCOUNT ❑ *...the imposition of higher taxes.* **2** V-I If someone **imposes on** you, they expect you to do something for them which you do not want to do. ❑ *I hope you don't feel we are imposing on you.* ❑ *I didn't want to impose on my married friends.* • **imposition** (**impositions**) N-COUNT ❑ *I know this is an imposition. But please listen to me.*

imposing /ɪm'pəʊzɪŋ/ ADJ If you describe someone or something as **imposing**, you think their appearance or manner is very impressive. ❑ *...the imposing gates at the entrance.*

Word Link *im ≈ not : imbalance, immature, impossible*

impossible /ɪm'pɒsɪbəl/ **1** ADJ Something that is **impossible** cannot be done or cannot happen. ❑ *It was impossible to deny the story.* • **impossibly** ADV ❑ *Mathematical physics is an almost impossibly difficult subject.* • **impossibility** (**impossibilities**) N-VAR ❑ *Why did he not see the impossibility of his idea?* **2** ADJ You can say that a situation or person is **impossible** when they are very difficult to deal with. ❑ *The Government was now in an impossible position.* ❑ *You are an impossible man!*

Word Partnership Use *impossible* with:
V. impossible **to describe**, impossible **to find**, impossible **to ignore**, impossible **to prove**, impossible **to say/tell**, **seem** impossible **1**
N. **an** impossible **task** **1**
ADV. **absolutely** impossible, **almost** impossible, **nearly** impossible **1**

impotent /'ɪmpətənt/ **1** ADJ If you feel **impotent**, you feel that you have no power to influence people or events. ❑ *As no one listened to them, they felt impotent.* • **impotence** N-UNCOUNT ❑ *Many refugees feel a sense of impotence.* **2** ADJ If a man is **impotent**, he is unable to have sex normally. • **impotence** N-UNCOUNT ❑ *...men who suffer from impotence.*

impound /ɪm'paʊnd/ (**impounds, impounding, impounded**) V-T If policemen or other officials **impound** something that you own, they legally take it from you. [FORMAL] ❑ *The police impound cars driven by drivers without car insurance.*

impoverish /ɪm'pɒvərɪʃ/ (**impoverishes, impoverishing, impoverished**) V-T To **impoverish** someone or something means to make them poor. ❑ *This policy enriches the rich and impoverishes the poor.* • **impoverished** ADJ ❑ *...one of the most impoverished suburbs of Rio de Janeiro.*

impractical /ɪm'præktɪkəl/ ADJ If an idea or course of action is **impractical**, it is not sensible or practical. ❑ *This small car would be totally impractical for my lifestyle: I've got four kids.*

impress /ɪm'pres/ (**impresses, impressing, impressed**) **1** V-T/V-I If someone or something **impresses** you, you feel great admiration for them. ❑ *The students were trying to impress their girlfriends.* ❑ *They are really desperate to impress.* • **impressed** ADJ AFTER LINK-V ❑ *I'm very impressed with the new airport.* **2** V-T If you **impress** something **on** or **upon** someone, you make them understand its importance. ❑ *I always impressed upon the children that if they worked hard they would succeed.*

impression /ɪm'preʃən/ (**impressions**) **1** N-COUNT Your **impression** of someone or something is what you think they are like. Your **impression** of a situation is what you think is going on. ❑ *What were your first impressions of college?* ❑ *My impression is that they are totally out*

i

of control. **2** N-SING If someone or something **gives** a particular **impression**, they cause you to believe that something is the case, often when it is not actually the case. ❑ *They certainly gave the impression of a couple who enjoyed each other's company.* **3** N-COUNT If you **do** an **impression** of someone, you imitate their voice or manner in an amusing way. **4** N-COUNT An **impression** of an object is the mark that it has left after being pressed hard onto a surface. **5** PHRASE If you are **under the impression** that something is the case, you believe it to be the case. ❑ *His family was under the impression that he had died.* **6** PHRASE If someone or something **makes an impression**, they have a strong effect on people or a situation. ❑ *He has already made a good impression on me.*

impressive /ɪm'presɪv/ ADJ **Impressive** is used to describe people or things which impress you. ❑ *The film's special effects are particularly impressive.* ● **impressively** ADV ❑ *...an impressively energetic woman.*

imprint (**imprints, imprinting, imprinted**)

noun /'ɪmprɪnt/, verb /ɪm'prɪnt/

1 N-COUNT & V-T If something leaves an **imprint on** your mind, or if it **is imprinted on** your mind, you cannot forget it because it has had a strong effect on you. ❑ *Experiences during childhood leave a deep imprint on the memory.* ❑ *The event was imprinted on their minds.* **2** N-COUNT An **imprint** is a mark made by the pressure of an object on a surface. **3** V-T If a surface **is imprinted with** a mark or design, that mark or design is printed on the surface or pressed into it.

imprison /ɪm'prɪzən/ (**imprisons, imprisoning, imprisoned**) V-T If you **are imprisoned**, you are locked up or kept somewhere. ● **imprisonment** N-UNCOUNT ❑ *She was sentenced to seven years' imprisonment.*

improbable /ɪm'prɒbəbəl/ ADJ Something that is **improbable** is unlikely to be true or to happen. ❑ *It is improbable that I will ever work again.* ● **improbability** (**improbabilities**) N-VAR ❑ *...the improbability of arresting those who were responsible.*

impromptu /ɪm'prɒmptju:, AM -tu:/ ADJ An **impromptu** action is one that you do without planning it in advance. ❑ *The children gave the visitors an impromptu concert.*

improper /ˌɪm'prɒpə/ **1** ADJ **Improper** activities are illegal or dishonest. [FORMAL] ❑ *Mr Matthews maintained that he had done nothing improper.* ● **improperly** ADV ❑ *I did not act improperly.* **2** ADJ BEFORE N **Improper** conditions or methods of treatment are not suitable or adequate for a particular purpose. ❑ *Improper use of this medicine could lead to a dangerous reaction.* ● **improperly** ADV ❑ *Doctors were improperly trained.* **3** ADJ If you describe someone's behaviour as **improper**, you mean that it is rude or shocking. [DATED] ● **improperly** ADV ❑ *...improperly dressed.*

improve /ɪm'pru:v/ (**improves, improving, improved**) **1** V-T/V-I If something **improves**, or if you **improve** it, it gets better. ❑ *The weather is improving.* ❑ *He improved their house.* ● **improvement** (**improvements**) N-VAR ❑ *80% of people with back pain reported an improvement after this treatment.* **2** V-I If you **improve on** a previous achievement, you achieve a better standard or result. ❑ *Can annual profits improve on last year's £65.8 million?* ● **improvement** N-VAR ❑ *We expect some improvement in the number of tourists next year.*

Word Partnership Use *improve* with:

ADV.	**significantly** improve, improve **slightly** 1 2
V.	**continue to** improve, **expected to** improve, **need to** improve, **try to** improve 1 2

improvise /'ɪmprəvaɪz/ (**improvises, improvising, improvised**) **1** V-T/V-I If you **improvise**, you make or do something using whatever you have or without having planned it in advance. ❑ *We improvised tents from sheets of plastic.* ❑ *We didn't make a plan, so we had to improvise.* **2** V-T/V-I When actors or musicians **improvise**, they make up the words or music while they are performing. ❑ *The actors improvised the scene in rehearsal.* ❑ *Richard and Lenny improvised on piano and guitar.*

Word Link ***puls** ≈ **driving, pushing** : **compulsion, expulsion, impulse***

impulse /'ɪmpʌls/ (**impulses**) **1** N-COUNT An **impulse** is a sudden desire to do something. ❑ *All day she had resisted the impulse to telephone Harry.* **2** PHRASE If you do something **on impulse**, you suddenly decide to do it, without planning it. ❑ *After lunch she decided on impulse to take a bath.* **3** N-COUNT An **impulse** is a short electrical signal sent along a wire or nerve or through the air.

Word Partnership Use *impulse* with:

ADJ.	**first** impulse, **strong** impulse, **sudden** impulse 1
V.	**control an** impulse, **resist an** impulse 1 **act on** impulse 2

impulsive /ɪm'pʌlsɪv/ ADJ Someone who is **impulsive** does things suddenly without thinking about them carefully first. ❑ *Don't make an impulsive decision.* ● **impulsively** ADV ❑ *Impulsively, she touched his arm.*

impure /ɪm'pjʊə/ ADJ An **impure** substance is not of good quality because it has other substances mixed with it.

impurity /ɪm'pjʊərɪti/ (**impurities**) N-COUNT **Impurities** are substances that are present in small quantities in another substance and make it dirty or of an unacceptable quality.

in

1. POSITION OR MOVEMENT
2. INCLUSION OR MOVEMENT
3. TIME AND NUMBERS
4. STATES AND QUALITIES
5. OTHER USES AND PHRASES

in /ɪn/

❶ 1 PREP Something that is **in** something else is enclosed by it or surrounded by it. ❑ *He was in his car.* ❑ *Put the knives in the kitchen drawer.* ❑ *Mix the sugar and water in a cup.* **2** PREP If something happens **in** a place, it happens there. ❑ *The rockets landed in the desert.* **3** ADV If you are **in**, you are at home or your place of work. ❑ *My flatmate was in* at the time. **4** ADV When you come **in**, you enter a room or building. ❑ *They shook hands and went in.* **5** ADV If a train, boat, or plane is **in** or has come **in**, it has arrived. ❑ *Look. The train's in.* **6** ADV When the sea or tide **comes in**, the sea moves towards the shore rather than away from it. **7** PREP Something that is **in** a window, especially a shop window, is just behind the window so that you can see it from outside. ❑ *There was a camera for sale in the window.* **8** PREP When you see something **in** a mirror, you see its reflection. **9** PREP If you are dressed **in** a piece of clothing, you are wearing it. ❑ *They were still in their pyjamas.* ❑ *...three women in black.*

→ see **location**

in /ɪn/

2 **1** PREP If something is **in** a book, film, play, or picture, you can read it or see it there. ❑ *...one of the funniest scenes in the film.* **2** PREP If you are **in** something such as a play or a race, you are one of the people taking part. ❑ *Alf offered her a part in the play he was directing.* **3** PREP Something that is **in** a group or collection is a member of it or part of it. ❑ *There were 12 students in my class.* **4** PREP You use **in** to specify a general subject or field of activity. ❑ *...future developments in medicine.*

in /ɪn/

3 **1** PREP If something happens **in** a particular year, month, or other period of time, it happens during that time. ❑ *In the evening, the people go to the mosques.* ❑ *He believes food prices will go up in the future.* **2** PREP If you do something **in** a particular period of time, that is how long it takes you to do it. ❑ *He completed the book in two years.* **3** PREP If something will happen **in** a particular length of time, it will happen after that length of time. ❑ *They'll be back in a few months.* **4** PREP You use **in** to indicate roughly how old someone is. For example, if someone is **in** their fifties, they are between 50 and 59 years old. **5** PREP You use **in** to indicate roughly how many people or things do something. ❑ *The jugs were produced in their millions.* **6** PREP You use **in** to express a ratio, proportion, or probability. ❑ *The doctors said that he had a one in 500 chance of surviving.*

in /ɪn/

4 **1** PREP If something or someone is **in** a particular state or situation, that is their present state or situation. ❑ *Their equipment was in poor condition.* ❑ *Dave was in a hurry.* **2** PREP You use **in** to indicate the feeling or desire which someone has when they do something, or which causes them to do it. ❑ *Simpson looked at them in surprise.* ❑ *They have been living in fear for months now.* **3** PREP You use **in** to indicate how someone is expressing something. ❑ *'Good evening,' Frank said in Russian.* ❑ *All requests must be made in writing.* **4** PREP You use **in** to describe the arrangement or shape of something. ❑ *The people danced in a circle, holding hands.* **5** PREP You use **in** to specify which feature or aspect of something you are talking about. ❑ *The movie is two hours in length.* ❑ *...an increase in the standard of living.*

in /ɪn/

5 **1** ADJ Something that is **in** is fashionable or popular. [INFORMAL] ❑ *The miniskirt was in then.* **2** PHRASE If you say that someone **is in for** a shock or a surprise, you mean they are going to experience it. **3** PHRASE If someone **has it in for** you, they dislike you and try to cause problems for you. [INFORMAL] **4** PHRASE If you are **in on** something, you are involved in it or know about it. ❑ *I'm going to let you in on a little secret.* **5** PHRASE You use **in that** to explain a statement you have just made. ❑ *I'm lucky in that I've got four sisters.*

in.

The plural can be **in.** or **ins.**

In. is a written abbreviation for **inch**.

Word Link *in ≈ not : inability, inaccurate, incorrect*

inability /ˌɪnəˈbɪlɪti/ N-UNCOUNT Your **inability to** do something is the fact that you are unable to do it. ❑ *...her inability to concentrate.*

inaccessible /ˌɪnəkˈsesɪbəl/ ADJ An **inaccessible** place is impossible or very difficult to reach. ❑ *It is a wild, inaccessible part of the island.*

inaccurate /ɪnˈækjʊrət/ ADJ If a statement or measurement is **inaccurate**, it is not accurate or correct. ● **inaccuracy** (**inaccuracies**) N-VAR ❑ *There are many inaccuracies in her article.*

inaction /ɪnˈækʃən/ N-UNCOUNT If you refer to someone's **inaction**, you think they should be taking action, rather than doing nothing. ❑ *They complained about police inaction on violence and crime in the area.*

inactive /ɪnˈæktɪv/ ADJ Someone or something that is **inactive** is not doing anything or is not working. ❑ *Most volcanoes are inactive most of the time.* ● **inactivity** /ˌɪnækˈtɪvɪti/ N-UNCOUNT ❑ *After years of inactivity I took up running.*

inadequate /ɪnˈædɪkwət/ **1** ADJ If something is **inadequate**, there is not enough of it or it is not good enough. ❑ *The firm has employed staff with inadequate training.* ● **inadequacy** (**inadequacies**) N-VAR ❑ *...the inadequacy of the water supply.* ● **inadequately** ADV ❑ *Many people are inadequately prepared for retirement.* **2** ADJ If you feel **inadequate**, you feel that you do not have the qualities necessary to do something or to cope with life. ● **inadequacy** N-UNCOUNT ❑ *...her sense of inadequacy.*

inadvertent /ˌɪnədˈvɜːtənt/ ADJ An **inadvertent** action is one that you do without realizing what you are doing. ❑ *He said he was guilty of an 'inadvertent mistake'.* ● **inadvertently** ADV ❑ *Perhaps you inadvertently pressed the wrong button.*

inappropriate /ˌɪnəˈprəʊpriət/ ADJ Something that is **inappropriate** is not suitable for a particular situation or purpose. ❑ *His behaviour was inappropriate.*

inasmuch as also **in as much as** /ˌɪnəzˈmʌtʃæz/ CONJ You use **inasmuch as** to introduce a statement which explains something you have just said, and adds to it. [FORMAL] ❑ *I am extremely lucky inasmuch as I have a very loving wife.*

inaugural /ɪnˈɔːgjʊrəl/ ADJ BEFORE N An **inaugural** meeting or speech is the first one of a new organization or leader.

inaugurate /ɪnˈɔːgjʊreɪt/ (**inaugurates, inaugurating, inaugurated**) **1** V-T When a new leader **is inaugurated**, they are formally given their new position at an official ceremony. ● **inauguration** (**inaugurations**) N-VAR ❑ *...the inauguration of the new Governor.* **2** V-T If you **inaugurate** a new system or organization, you start it. [FORMAL]

incapable /ɪn'keɪpəbəl/ ADJ Someone who is **incapable of** doing something is unable to do it. ❑ *He was a man incapable of violence.*

'in-car ADJ **In-car** devices are ones that are designed to be used in a car. ❑ *...a range of in-car entertainment systems.*

incarcerate /ɪn'kɑːsəreɪt/ (**incarcerates, incarcerating, incarcerated**) V-T If someone **is incarcerated**, they are imprisoned. [FORMAL] ● **incarceration** N-UNCOUNT ❑ *...incarceration in prison.*

Word Link *carn ≈ flesh : carnage, incarnation, reincarnation*

incarnation /ˌɪnkɑː'neɪʃən/ (**incarnations**) **1** N-COUNT If you say that someone is the **incarnation of** a particular quality, you mean that they represent that quality or are typical of it in an extreme form. ❑ *She is the incarnation of courage.* **2** N-COUNT An **incarnation** is one of the lives that a person has, according to some religions.

incendiary /ɪn'sendiəri, AM -eri/ ADJ BEFORE N **Incendiary** attacks or weapons cause large fires. ❑ *More than 10,000 incendiary bombs were dropped.*

incense (**incenses, incensing, incensed**) **1** N-UNCOUNT /'ɪnsens/ **Incense** is a substance that is burned for its sweet smell, often during a religious ceremony. **2** V-T /ɪn'sens/ Something that **incenses** you makes you extremely angry. ● **incensed** ADJ ❑ *Mr McMahon was so incensed by his behaviour that he punched him.*

incentive /ɪn'sentɪv/ (**incentives**) N-VAR An **incentive** is something that encourages you to do something. ❑ *...tax incentives for companies that create jobs.*

incessant /ɪn'sesənt/ ADJ An **incessant** process or activity never stops. ❑ *...incessant rain.* ● **incessantly** ADV ❑ *Dee talked incessantly.*

incest /'ɪnsest/ N-UNCOUNT **Incest** is the crime of two members of the same family having sexual intercourse.

inch /ɪntʃ/ (**inches, inching, inched**) **1** N-COUNT An **inch** is a unit of length, equal to 2.54 centimetres. **2** V-T/V-I If you **inch** somewhere, you move there very slowly and carefully. If you **inch** something somewhere, you move it there in this way. ❑ *A climber was inching up the wall of rock.* ❑ *He inched the van forward.*
→ see **measurement**

incidence /'ɪnsɪdəns/ (**incidences**) N-VAR The **incidence** of something (usually something bad) is the frequency with which it occurs, or the occasions when it occurs. ❑ *We are seeing a fall in the incidence of crime.*

incident /'ɪnsɪdənt/ (**incidents**) N-COUNT An **incident** is an event, especially one involving something unpleasant. [FORMAL] ❑ *Police were still investigating the incident yesterday.*

Thesaurus *incident* Also look up:
N. episode, event, fact, happening, occasion, occurrence

incidental /ˌɪnsɪ'dentəl/ ADJ If one thing is **incidental to** another, it is less important than the other thing or is not a major part of it. ❑ *The music proved to be incidental to the main business of the evening.* ❑ *At the bottom of the bill, you will notice various incidental expenses.*

incidentally /ˌɪnsɪ'dentli/ ADV You use **incidentally** to introduce a point which is not directly relevant to what you are saying. ❑ *A South African named Retief Goosen won the competition. Incidentally, his name is pronounced Hoosen.*

incinerate /ɪn'sɪnəreɪt/ (**incinerates, incinerating, incinerated**) V-T When authorities **incinerate** rubbish or waste material, they burn it. ● **incineration** N-UNCOUNT

incinerator /ɪn'sɪnəreɪtə/ (**incinerators**) N-COUNT An **incinerator** is a machine for burning rubbish.

incisive /ɪn'saɪsɪv/ ADJ **Incisive** speech or writing is clear and strong.

incite /ɪn'saɪt/ (**incites, inciting, incited**) V-T If someone **incites** people **to** behave in a violent or unlawful way, they encourage them to behave in that way. ❑ *The goal of this movie is to incite the audience to scream.* ❑ *...material that may incite racial hatred.* ● **incitement** (**incitements**) N-VAR

inclination /ˌɪnklɪ'neɪʃən/ (**inclinations**) N-VAR An **inclination** is a feeling that makes you want to act in a particular way. ❑ *She showed no inclination to go.* ❑ *...his artistic inclinations.*

Word Link *clin ≈ leaning : decline, incline, recline*

incline /'ɪnklaɪn/ (**inclines**) N-COUNT An **incline** is a slope. [FORMAL]

inclined /ɪn'klaɪnd/ **1** ADJ AFTER LINK-V If you say that you are **inclined to** have a particular opinion, you mean that you hold this opinion but you are not expressing it strongly. ❑ *I am inclined to agree with Alan.* **2** ADJ Someone who is, for example, mathematically or artistically **inclined** has a natural talent for mathematics or art.

include /ɪn'kluːd/ (**includes, including, included**) V-T If something **includes** something else, it has it as one of its parts. If you **include** one thing **in** another, you make it part of it. ❑ *The programme includes swimming, fishing and canoeing.* ❑ *Food is included in the price.*

including /ɪn'kluːdɪŋ/ PREP You use **including** to introduce examples of people or things that are part of the group of people or things that you are talking about. ❑ *Twelve people, including six police officers, were taken to hospital.*

inclusion /ɪn'kluːʒən/ (**inclusions**) N-VAR The **inclusion** of one thing **in** another is the act of making it a part of the second thing. ❑ *...his inclusion in the team.*

inclusive /ɪn'kluːsɪv/ **1** ADJ & ADV If a price is **inclusive**, it includes all the charges connected with the goods or services offered. ❑ *The price of the trip was £824 (inclusive of flights).* ❑ *...a special introductory offer of £5,995 fully inclusive.* **2** ADJ You use **inclusive** to indicate that the first and last things mentioned are included in a series. ❑ *Children aged 6 to 15 inclusive get in free.*

incoherent /ˌɪnkəʊ'hɪərənt/ ADJ If someone is **incoherent**, they are talking in a confused and unclear way. ❑ *The man was almost incoherent with fear.*

income /'ɪnkʌm/ (**incomes**) **1** N-COUNT The

income of a person or organization is the money that they earn or receive. ❑ *...families on low incomes.* **2** → See note at **pay**

Word Partnership Use *income* with:

ADJ.	**average** income, **fixed** income, **large/small** income, **a second** income, **steady** income, **taxable** income
N.	**loss of** income, **source of** income
V.	**earn *an*** income, **supplement *your*** income

'income tax (**income taxes**) N-VAR **Income tax** is a part of your income that you have to pay regularly to the government.

incoming /'ɪnkʌmɪŋ/ **1** ADJ BEFORE N An **incoming** message or phone call is one that you receive. ❑ *We keep a tape of incoming calls.* **2** ADJ BEFORE N An **incoming** plane or passenger is one that is arriving at a place. ❑ *...a passenger off the incoming flight.*

incompatible /ˌɪnkəm'pætɪbəl/ ADJ If one thing or person is **incompatible with** another, they are very different from each other and therefore cannot exist or work together. ❑ *His behaviour has been incompatible with his role as head of state.* ● **incompatibility** N-UNCOUNT ❑ *He sees no incompatibility between poetry and science.*

incompetent /ɪn'kɒmpɪtənt/ ADJ If you describe someone as **incompetent**, you are criticizing them because they cannot do their job or a task properly. ● **incompetence** N-UNCOUNT ❑ *She was sacked for incompetence.*

incomplete /ˌɪnkəm'pliːt/ ADJ Something that is **incomplete** is not yet finished, or does not have all the parts or details that it needs. ❑ *The clearing of rubbish is still incomplete.*

incomprehensible /ˌɪnkɒmprɪ'hensɪbəl/ ADJ Something that is **incomprehensible** is impossible to understand.

inconceivable /ˌɪnkən'siːvəbəl/ ADJ If something is **inconceivable**, it is very unlikely to happen or be true. ❑ *It was inconceivable that he was a criminal.*

inconclusive /ˌɪnkən'kluːsɪv/ ADJ If something is **inconclusive**, it does not provide any clear answer or result. ❑ *Our research has proved inconclusive.*

incongruous /ɪn'kɒŋgruəs/ ADJ Something that is **incongruous** seems strange because it does not fit in with the rest of a situation. [FORMAL] ❑ *She was small and looked incongruous in an army uniform.* ● **incongruously** ADV ❑ *The glass building towers incongruously over the mud huts and low buildings of the small town.*

inconsiderate /ˌɪnkən'sɪdərət/ ADJ If you describe someone as **inconsiderate**, you are criticizing them for not taking enough care over how their behaviour affects other people.

inconsistent /ˌɪnkən'sɪstənt/ **1** ADJ If you describe someone as **inconsistent**, you are criticizing them for not behaving in the same way every time a similar situation occurs. ❑ *His inconsistent approach to tackling problems cost him his job.* ● **inconsistency** (**inconsistencies**) N-VAR ❑ *His worst fault was his inconsistency.* **2** ADJ AFTER LINK-V Something that is **inconsistent with** a particular set of ideas or values is not in accordance with them. ❑ *They say her new songs are inconsistent with her style.*

incontinent /ɪn'kɒntɪnənt/ ADJ Someone who is **incontinent** is unable to control their bladder or bowels. ● **incontinence** N-UNCOUNT ❑ *Incontinence is not just a condition of old age.*

inconvenience /ˌɪnkən'viːniəns/ (**inconveniences, inconveniencing, inconvenienced**) **1** N-VAR If someone or something causes **inconvenience**, they cause problems or difficulties. ❑ *We apologize for any inconvenience caused during the repairs.* **2** V-T If someone **inconveniences** you, they cause problems or difficulties for you. ❑ *He promised to try not to inconvenience them any further.*

inconvenient /ˌɪnkən'viːniənt/ ADJ Something that is **inconvenient** causes problems or difficulties for someone. ❑ *She arrived at an extremely inconvenient moment.*

Word Link *corp ≈ body : corporal, corpse, incorporate*

incorporate /ɪn'kɔːpəreɪt/ (**incorporates, incorporating, incorporated**) V-T If something such as a group or device **incorporates** a particular thing, the group or device has that thing in it as one of its parts. [FORMAL] ❑ *The new cars will incorporate several major improvements.*

Word Link *in ≈ not : inability, inaccurate, incorrect*

incorrect /ˌɪnkə'rekt/ ADJ Something that is **incorrect** is wrong or untrue. ❑ *The findings were based on incorrect data.* ● **incorrectly** ADV ❑ *The doors were fitted incorrectly.*

Word Link *cresc, creas ≈ growing : crescent, decrease, increase*

increase (**increases, increasing, increased**)

verb /ɪn'kriːs/, noun /'ɪnkriːs/

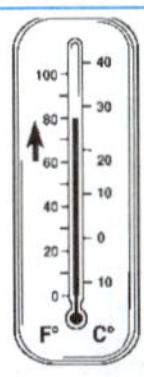

increase

1 V-T/V-I & N-COUNT If something **increases** or **is increased**, or if there is an **increase in** it, it becomes larger in number, level, or amount. ❑ *Japan's industrial output increased by 2%.* ❑ *We are having an increasing number of problems.* ❑ *...a huge increase in average salaries.* **2** PHRASE If something is **on the increase**, it is becoming more frequent. ❑ *Violent crime is on the increase.*

Word Partnership Use *increase* with:

ADV.	increase **dramatically**, increase **rapidly** **1**
N.	increase **in crime**, increase **in demand**, **population** increase, **price** increase, **salary** increase, increase **in size**, increase **in spending**, increase **in temperature**, increase **in value** **1**
ADJ.	**big** increase, **marked** increase, **sharp** increase **1**

increasingly /ɪn'kriːsɪŋli/ ADV You use **increasingly** to indicate that a situation or quality is becoming greater, stronger, or more common. ❑ *He found it increasingly difficult to make decisions.* ❑ *Increasingly, African wild areas have become less wild.*

Word Link	*cred ≈ to believe : credence, credentials, incredible*

incredible /ɪn'kredɪbəl/ 1 ADJ If you describe someone or something as **incredible**, you like them very much or are impressed by them, because they are extremely or unusually good. ❑ *The wildflowers will be incredible after this rain.* 2 ADJ Something that is **incredible** is amazing or very difficult to believe. ❑ *...the incredible stories that children may tell us.* ● **incredibly** ADV ❑ *Incredibly, some people don't like chocolate.* 3 ADJ You use **incredible** to emphasize the amount or intensity of something. ❑ *We import an incredible amount of cheese from abroad.* ● **incredibly** ADV ❑ *It was incredibly hard work.*

Word Partnership	Use *incredible* with:
N.	incredible **discovery**, incredible **prices** 1 incredible **experience** 1 2
ADV.	**absolutely** incredible 1 2

I

incredulous /ɪn'kredʒʊləs/ ADJ If you are **incredulous**, you cannot believe something because it is very surprising or shocking. ❑ *There was a brief, incredulous silence.* ● **incredulously** ADV ❑ *'You told Pete?' Rachel said incredulously.*

incriminate /ɪn'krɪmɪneɪt/ (**incriminates, incriminating, incriminated**) V-T If something **incriminates** you, it suggests that you are the person responsible for something bad, especially a crime. ❑ *They are afraid of incriminating themselves and say no more than is necessary.* ● **incriminating** ADJ ❑ *...incriminating evidence.*

incumbent /ɪn'kʌmbənt/ (**incumbents**) N-COUNT An **incumbent** is the person who is holding an official post at a particular time. [FORMAL] ❑ *In general, incumbents have a 94% chance of being re-elected.*

incur /ɪn'kɜː/ (**incurs, incurring, incurred**) V-T If you **incur** something unpleasant, it happens to you because of something you have done. [FORMAL] ❑ *The government has incurred huge debts.*

Word Link	*able ≈ able to be : affordable, incurable, portable*

incurable /ɪn'kjʊərəbəl/ 1 ADJ An **incurable** disease cannot be cured. ● **incurably** ADV ❑ *...patients who are incurably ill.* 2 ADJ You can use **incurable** to indicate that someone has a particular quality or attitude and will not change. ❑ *To be a successful politician, you must be an incurable optimist.* ● **incurably** ADV ❑ *We decided our boyfriends are incurably unromantic.*

indebted /ɪn'detɪd/ ADJ AFTER LINK-V If you say that you are **indebted to** someone, you mean that you are very grateful to them for something. ❑ *I am deeply indebted to him for his help.*

indecent /ɪn'diːsənt/ ADJ Something that is **indecent** is shocking, usually because it relates to sex or nakedness. ❑ *Three arrests were made for indecent behaviour.* ● **indecency** N-UNCOUNT ❑ *...the indecency of their language.* ● **indecently** ADV ❑ *...an indecently short skirt.*

indecision /ˌɪndɪ'sɪʒən/ N-UNCOUNT **Indecision** is uncertainty about what you should do. ❑ *After months of indecision, the government finally agreed on a plan.*

indecisive /ˌɪndɪ'saɪsɪv/ ADJ If you are **indecisive**, you find it difficult to make decisions.

indeed /ɪn'diːd/ 1 ADV You use **indeed** to agree in a very positive way with something that has just been said. ❑ *The payments had indeed been made.* ❑ *'Did you know him?'—'I did indeed.'* ❑ *'Know what I mean?'—'Indeed I do.'* 2 ADV You use **indeed** to introduce a further comment or statement which strengthens the point you have already made. ❑ *We have nothing against him; indeed, we like him.* 3 ADV You use **indeed** at the end of a clause to give extra force to the word 'very', or to emphasize a particular word. ❑ *The show was very good indeed.*

indefinite /ɪn'defɪnɪt/ 1 ADJ If something is **indefinite**, people have not decided when it will end. ❑ *He is now on an 'indefinite break' from his £200,000 a year job.* ● **indefinitely** ADV ❑ *The visit has been postponed indefinitely.* 2 ADJ If something such as a plan is **indefinite**, it is not exact or clear. ❑ *...an indefinite situation of neither peace nor war.*

inˌdefinite 'article (**indefinite articles**) N-COUNT In grammar, the words 'a' and 'an' are sometimes called **indefinite articles**. ❑ *He was a sculptor and an artist.*

inˌdefinite 'pronoun (**indefinite pronouns**) N-COUNT An **indefinite pronoun** is a pronoun such as 'someone', 'anything', or 'nobody', which you use to refer in a general way to a person or thing without saying who or what they are, or what kind of person or thing you mean. ❑ *I did ask around but nobody knew anything.*

Word Link	*ence ≈ state, condition : dependence, excellence, independence*

independent /ˌɪndɪ'pendənt/ 1 ADJ Someone who is **independent** does not rely on other people. ❑ *She would like to be financially independent.* ● **independently** ADV ❑ *We help disabled students to live and study as independently as possible.* ● **independence** N-UNCOUNT ❑ *He was afraid of losing his independence.* 2 ADJ If one thing or person is **independent of** another, they are separate and not connected, so the first one is not affected or influenced by the second. ❑ *Your questions should be independent of each other.* ● **independently** ADV ❑ *...several people working independently in different places.* ● **independence** N-UNCOUNT 3 ADJ **Independent** countries and states are not ruled by other countries but have their own government. ● **independence** N-UNCOUNT ❑ *In 1816, Argentina declared its independence from Spain.*

index /'ɪndeks/ (**indices, indexes, indexing, indexed**)

> **Indexes** is the usual plural, but the form **indices** /'ɪndɪsiːz/ can be used for meaning 1.

1 N-COUNT An **index** is an alphabetical list at the back of a book saying where particular things are mentioned in the book. 2 V-T If a book or collection of books **has been indexed**, someone has made an alphabetical list of the items in it. ❑ *The documents are alphabetically indexed.* 3 N-COUNT An **index** is a system by which changes in the value of something can be compared or measured.

❑ *...America's Dow Jones shares index.* **4** V-T If a quantity or value **is indexed to** another, a system is arranged so that it increases or decreases whenever the other one increases or decreases. ❑ *Their wages are indexed to price increases.*

indicate /ˈɪndɪkeɪt/ (**indicates, indicating, indicated**) **1** V-T If one thing **indicates** another, the first thing shows that the second is true or exists. ❑ *A survey has indicated that most retired people are independent and enjoying life.* **2** V-T If you **indicate** an opinion, an intention, or a fact, you mention it in a rather indirect way. ❑ *Mr Rivers has indicated that he may resign.* **3** V-T If you **indicate** something to someone, you point to it. ❑ *He indicated a chair.* **4** V-T/V-I When the driver of a car **indicates**, they operate flashing lights on one side of their vehicle which show the direction they are going to turn.

Thesaurus	*indicate* Also look up:
V.	demonstrate, hint, mean, reveal, show **1** **2**

indication /ˌɪndɪˈkeɪʃən/ (**indications**) N-VAR An **indication** is a sign which gives you an idea of what someone feels, what is happening, or what is likely to happen. ❑ *I cannot decide now or even give any indication of my own views.* ❑ *He gave no indication that he was unhappy.*

indicative /ɪnˈdɪkətɪv/ **1** ADJ If something is **indicative of** the existence or nature of something, it is a sign of it. ❑ *Often physical appearance is indicative of how a person feels.* **2** N-SING In grammar, a clause that is in **the indicative**, or in **the indicative mood**, has a subject followed by a verb group. Examples are 'I'm hungry' and 'She was followed'.

indicator /ˈɪndɪkeɪtə/ (**indicators**) **1** N-COUNT An **indicator** is a measurement or value which gives you an idea of what something is like. ❑ *The phone has a low battery indicator.* **2** N-COUNT A car's **indicators** are the flashing lights that tell you that it is going to turn left or right.

indices /ˈɪndɪsiːz/ **Indices** is one of the plurals of **index**.

indict /ɪnˈdaɪt/ (**indicts, indicting, indicted**) V-T When someone **is indicted for** a crime, they are officially charged with it. ❑ *We are determined to arrest people indicted for war crimes.* ❑ *Jones was later indicted on criminal charges.* ● **indictment** (**indictments**) N-VAR ❑ *He is currently under indictment in Switzerland.*

indictment /ɪnˈdaɪtmənt/ (**indictments**) N-COUNT If you say that a fact or situation is an **indictment of** something, you mean that it shows how bad that thing is. ❑ *This is a terrible indictment of the way we live now.*

indifferent /ɪnˈdɪfərənt/ **1** ADJ If you are **indifferent to** something, you have no interest in it. ❑ *Few people remain indifferent to this issue.* ● **indifferently** ADV ❑ *'Not that it matters,' said Tim indifferently.* ● **indifference** N-UNCOUNT ❑ *She soon discovered his complete indifference to money.* **2** ADJ If you describe something or someone as **indifferent**, you mean that it is of a rather low standard. ❑ *She had starred in several very indifferent movies.*

indigenous /ɪnˈdɪdʒɪnəs/ ADJ **Indigenous** people or things belong to the country in which they are found, rather than coming there or being brought there from another country. ❑ *The Chumash were a tribe indigenous to California.*

indigestion /ˌɪndɪˈdʒestʃən/ N-UNCOUNT If you have **indigestion**, you have pains in your stomach that are caused by difficulties in digesting food.

Word Link	**dign** ≈ **proper, worthy**: **dignified, dignitary, indignant**

indignant /ɪnˈdɪgnənt/ ADJ If you are **indignant**, you are shocked and angry, because you think that something is not fair. ● **indignantly** ADV ❑ *'That is not true,' Erica said indignantly.*

indignation /ˌɪndɪgˈneɪʃən/ N-UNCOUNT **Indignation** is a feeling of shock and anger which you have when you think that something is unfair. ❑ *The story filled me with indignation.*

indignity /ɪnˈdɪgnɪti/ (**indignities**) N-VAR If you talk about the **indignity of** doing something, you mean that doing it is humiliating or embarrassing. ❑ *...the indignity of prison life.*

indirect /ˌɪndaɪˈrekt, -dɪr-/ **1** ADJ An **indirect** result or effect is not caused immediately and obviously by a thing or person, but happens because of something else that they have done. ❑ *Millions could die of hunger as an indirect result of the war.* ● **indirectly** ADV ❑ *I realised I had indirectly caused their unhappiness.* **2** ADJ An **indirect route** or **journey** does not use the shortest way between two places. **3** ADJ An **indirect answer** or **reference** does not directly mention the thing that is actually being talked about. ❑ *'She wants me to come with her' was her indirect answer.*

ˌindirect ˈobject (**indirect objects**) N-COUNT An **indirect object** is an object which is used with a transitive verb to indicate who benefits from an action or gets something as a result. For example, in 'She gave him her address', 'him' is the indirect object. Compare **direct object**.

ˌindirect ˈspeech **Indirect speech** is the same as **reported speech**.

indiscriminate /ˌɪndɪˈskrɪmɪnət/ ADJ If you describe an action as **indiscriminate**, you are critical of it because it does not involve any careful thought or choice. ❑ *...the indiscriminate killing of refugees.* ● **indiscriminately** ADV ❑ *It is worth being selective rather than buying indiscriminately.*

indispensable /ˌɪndɪˈspensəbəl/ ADJ If someone or something is **indispensable**, they are absolutely essential and other people or things cannot function without them. ❑ *She was becoming indispensable to him.*

indisputable /ˌɪndɪˈspjuːtəbəl/ ADJ If a fact is **indisputable**, it is obviously and definitely true. ❑ *This CD is an indisputable masterpiece.* ● **indisputably** ADV ❑ *She has an indisputably lovely voice.*

indistinguishable /ˌɪndɪˈstɪŋgwɪʃəbəl/ ADJ If one thing is **indistinguishable from** another, the two things are so similar that it is difficult to know which is which. ❑ *In most cases the copies were indistinguishable from the originals.*

individual /ˌɪndɪˈvɪdʒuəl/ (**individuals**) **1** ADJ BEFORE N **Individual** means relating to one person or thing, rather than to a large group. ❑ *The charges are £25 for an individual membership and £44 for a family membership.* ● **individually** ADV ❑ *Individually, many of these pictures are superb.* **2** N-COUNT An **individual** is a person.

i

Thesaurus *individual* Also look up:

ADJ. distinctive, original, unique 1
N. human being, person 2

individuality /ˌɪndɪvɪdʒuˈælɪti/ N-UNCOUNT The **individuality** of a person or thing consists of the qualities that make them different from other people or things. ❑ *People should be free to express their individuality.*

indoor /ˈɪndɔː/ ADJ BEFORE N **Indoor** activities or things are ones that happen or are used inside a building, rather than outside. ❑ *...an indoor market.*

indoors /ˌɪnˈdɔːz/ ADV If something happens **indoors**, it happens inside a building. ❑ *Perhaps we should go indoors.*

induce /ɪnˈdjuːs, AM -ˈduːs-/ (**induces, inducing, induced**) 1 V-T To **induce** a particular state or condition means to cause it. ❑ *Surgery could induce a heart attack.* 2 V-T If you **induce** someone **to** do something, you persuade or influence them to do it. ❑ *I would do anything to induce them to stay.*

inducement /ɪnˈdjuːsmənt, AM -ˈduːs-/ (**inducements**) N-COUNT An **inducement** is something which might persuade someone to do a particular thing. ❑ *We were offered financial inducements to tell our story to the newspapers.*

induction /ɪnˈdʌkʃən/ (**inductions**) N-VAR **Induction** is a procedure or ceremony for introducing someone to a new job or way of life. ❑ *...the induction of the girls into the sport.*

indulge /ɪnˈdʌldʒ/ (**indulges, indulging, indulged**) 1 V-T/V-I If you **indulge in** something, you allow yourself to have or do something that you know you will enjoy. ❑ *A friend advised me to indulge in some beauty treatments.* ❑ *You can indulge yourself without spending a fortune.* 2 V-T If you **indulge** someone, you let them have or do whatever they want. ❑ *He did not agree with indulging children.*

indulgent /ɪnˈdʌldʒənt/ ADJ If you are **indulgent**, you treat a person with special kindness. ❑ *His indulgent mother let him do anything he wanted.* ● **indulgently** ADV ❑ *Ned smiled at him indulgently.* ● **indulgence** (**indulgences**) N-VAR ❑ *...the king's indulgence towards his sons.*

industrial /ɪnˈdʌstriəl/ 1 ADJ **Industrial** means relating to industry. ❑ *...industrial machinery and equipment.* 2 ADJ An **industrial city** or **country** is one in which industry is important or highly developed.

Word Partnership Use *industrial* with:

N. industrial **machinery**, industrial **production**, industrial **products** 1
industrial **area**, industrial **city**, industrial **country** 2

inˌdustrial ˈaction N-UNCOUNT If a group of workers **take industrial action**, they stop working or take other action to protest about their pay or working conditions.

inˈdustrial estate (**industrial estates**) N-COUNT An **industrial estate** is an area which has been specially planned for a lot of factories. [BRIT]

industrialist /ɪnˈdʌstriəlɪst/ (**industrialists**) N-COUNT An **industrialist** is a person who owns or controls large industrial companies or factories.

industrialize [BRIT also **industrialise**] /ɪnˈdʌstriəlaɪz/ (**industrializes, industrializing, industrialized**) V-T/V-I When a country **industrializes**, or when it **is industrialized**, it develops a lot of industries. ❑ *Germany began to industrialise in the 19th century.* ❑ *These methods industrialized the Russian economy.* ● **industrialization** N-UNCOUNT ❑ *Industrialization began early in Spain.*

inˌdustrial reˈlations N-PLURAL **Industrial relations** refers to the relationship between employers and workers.

industry /ˈɪndəstri/ (**industries**) 1 N-UNCOUNT **Industry** is the work and processes involved in making things in factories. 2 N-COUNT A particular **industry** consists of all the people and activities involved in making a particular product or providing a particular service. ❑ *...the motor vehicle industry.*
→ see Word Web: **industry**

inedible /ɪnˈedɪbəl/ ADJ Something that is **inedible** is poisonous or tastes too bad to eat.
→ see **cook**

ineffective /ˌɪnɪˈfektɪv/ ADJ If you say that something is **ineffective**, you mean that it has no effect on a process or situation. ❑ *...an ineffective method of controlling your dog.*

ineffectual /ˌɪnɪˈfektʃuəl/ ADJ If someone or something is **ineffectual**, they fail to do what

Word Web industry

There are three general categories of **industry**. Primary industry means **extracting raw materials** from the environment. Examples include **agriculture, forestry,** and **mining**. In secondary industry people **refine** raw materials to make new **products**. It also includes **assembling** parts created by other **manufacturers**. There are two types of secondary industry—**light industry** (such as **textile weaving**) and **heavy industry** (such as shipbuilding). The third industry, tertiary industry, is **services** that do not produce a product. Some examples are **banking, tourism,** and **education**. Recently, computers have created millions of jobs in the **information technology** field. Some researchers describe this as a fourth type of industry.

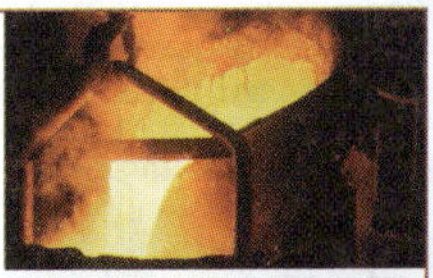

they are expected to do or are trying to do. ❑ *The government appears to be both ineffectual and indecisive.* • **ineffectually** ADV ❑ *I tried, ineffectually, to comfort her.*

inefficient /ˌɪnɪˈfɪʃənt/ ADJ A person, organization, system, or machine that is **inefficient** does not work in the most economical way. ❑ *...the closure of inefficient factories.* • **inefficiency** N-UNCOUNT ❑ *...the inefficiency of this system.* • **inefficiently** ADV ❑ *We still use power very inefficiently.*

inept /ɪnˈept/ ADJ Someone who is **inept** does something with a complete lack of skill. ❑ *You are completely inept at writing.* ❑ *...his inept effort to find a girlfriend.*

inequality /ˌɪnɪˈkwɒlɪti/ (**inequalities**) N-VAR **Inequality** is a difference in social status, wealth, or opportunity between people or groups. ❑ *...the inequality between rich and poor.*

Word Partnership Use *inequality* with:

ADJ.	**economic** inequality, **growing/increasing** inequality, **racial** inequality, **social** inequality
N.	**gender** inequality, **income** inequality

inert /ɪnˈɜːt/ ADJ Someone or something that is **inert** does not move at all and appears to be lifeless. ❑ *The body was cold and inert.*

inertia /ɪnˈɜːʃə/ N-UNCOUNT If you have a feeling of **inertia**, you feel very lazy and don't want to do anything.

inescapable /ˌɪnɪˈskeɪpəbəl/ ADJ If something is **inescapable**, it is impossible not to notice it or be affected by it. ❑ *That is the inescapable conclusion of the report.*

inevitable /ɪnˈevɪtəbəl/ ADJ & N-SING If something is **inevitable**, it is certain to happen and cannot be prevented or avoided. You can refer to something inevitable as **the inevitable**. ❑ *If this case succeeds, it is inevitable that other trials will follow.* ❑ *Be realistic and prepare yourself for the inevitable.* • **inevitability** N-UNCOUNT ❑ *We must all face the inevitability of death.* • **inevitably** ADV ❑ *Technological changes will inevitably lead to unemployment.*

inexpensive /ˌɪnɪkˈspensɪv/ ADJ Something that is **inexpensive** does not cost much. ❑ *...a large variety of inexpensive restaurants.*

inexperience /ˌɪnɪkˈspɪəriəns/ N-UNCOUNT If you refer to someone's **inexperience**, you mean that they have little knowledge or experience of a particular situation or activity. ❑ *Critics attacked the inexperience of his staff.*

inexperienced /ˌɪnɪkˈspɪəriənst/ ADJ If you are **inexperienced**, you have little or no experience of a particular activity. ❑ *...an easy-to-use program for inexperienced computer users.*

inexplicable /ˌɪnɪkˈsplɪkəbəl/ ADJ If something is **inexplicable**, you cannot explain it. • **inexplicably** ADV ❑ *She suddenly and inexplicably announced her resignation.*

inextricably /ˌɪnekˈstrɪkəbəli/ ADV If two or more things are **inextricably** linked, they cannot be separated. ❑ *Our survival is inextricably linked to the survival of the rainforest.*

infamous /ˈɪnfəməs/ 1 ADJ **Infamous** people or things are well known because of something bad. ❑ *He founded the infamous secret police of the USSR.* 2 → See note at **famous**

infancy /ˈɪnfənsi/ 1 N-UNCOUNT **Infancy** is the period in your life when you are a very young child. ❑ *Fewer children die at birth or in infancy than ever before.* 2 N-UNCOUNT If something is **in** its **infancy**, it is new and has not developed very much. ❑ *Computer science was still in its infancy then.*

infant /ˈɪnfənt/ (**infants**) N-COUNT An **infant** is a very young child or baby. [FORMAL]
→ see **age, child**

infantry /ˈɪnfəntri/ N-UNCOUNT The **infantry** are the soldiers in an army who fight on foot.

infect /ɪnˈfekt/ (**infects, infecting, infected**) 1 V-T To **infect** people, animals, plants, or food means to cause them to suffer from germs or to carry germs. ❑ *...people infected with TB.* ❑ *He infected her with HIV.* • **infection** N-UNCOUNT ❑ *...trying to lessen the risk of infection.* 2 V-T If a virus **infects** a computer, it affects the computer by damaging or destroying programs. [COMPUTING] ❑ *This virus infected thousands of computers.*

Word Partnership Use *infect* with:

N.	**bacteria** infect, infect **cells**, infect **people** 1
	viruses infect, infect **with a virus** 1 2
PRON.	infect **others** 1

infection /ɪnˈfekʃən/ (**infections**) N-COUNT An **infection** is a disease caused by germs. ❑ *I had an ear infection.*
→ see **diagnosis**

Word Partnership Use *infection* with:

N.	**cases of** infection, **rates of** infection, **risk of** infection, **symptoms of** infection
V.	**cause an** infection, **have an** infection, **prevent** infection, **spread an** infection

infectious /ɪnˈfekʃəs/ 1 ADJ If you have an **infectious** disease, people near you can catch it from you. 2 ADJ If a feeling is **infectious**, it spreads to other people. ❑ *Her laughter was infectious.*
→ see **illness**

infer /ɪnˈfɜː/ (**infers, inferring, inferred**) V-T If you **infer** that something is true, you decide that it is true on the basis of information you have. ❑ *He is a manager and I infer that you are not.*

inference /ˈɪnfərəns/ (**inferences**) N-COUNT An **inference** is a conclusion that you draw about something. ❑ *There were two inferences to be drawn from her letter.*

inferior /ɪnˈfɪəriə/ (**inferiors**) 1 ADJ Something that is **inferior** is not as good as something else. ❑ *The cassettes were of inferior quality.* ❑ *There is no reason to consider women as inferior.* 2 ADJ & N-COUNT If one person is regarded as **inferior to** another or as that person's **inferior**, they are considered to have less ability, status, or importance. ❑ *He preferred people who were intellectually inferior to himself.* ❑ *Most career women make me feel inferior.* ❑ *It was a gentleman's duty to be polite, even to his inferiors.* • **inferiority** /ɪnfɪəriˈɒrɪti, AM -ˈɔːr-/ N-UNCOUNT ❑ *...feelings of inferiority that come from childhood.*

infertile /ɪn'fɜːtaɪl, AM -təl/ **1** ADJ Someone who is **infertile** is unable to produce babies. ● **infertility** /ˌɪnfɜː'tɪlɪti/ N-UNCOUNT ❑ *Male infertility is becoming more common.* **2** ADJ **Infertile** land has poor quality soil, so plants cannot grow well there.

infested /ɪn'festɪd/ ADJ If a place is **infested with** something undesirable such as insects or other pests, there are lots of them in it. ❑ *The prison is infested with rats.* ❑ *...shark-infested waters.*

infidelity /ˌɪnfɪ'delɪti/ (**infidelities**) N-VAR **Infidelity** occurs when a person who is married or in a steady relationship has sex with another person. ❑ *Andrew learned of his wife's infidelity.*

infiltrate /'ɪnfɪltreɪt/ (**infiltrates, infiltrating, infiltrated**) V-T If people **infiltrate** an organization, they join it secretly in order to spy on it or influence it. ❑ *More criminals are infiltrating the fine art world.* ● **infiltration** (**infiltrations**) N-VAR ❑ *...the problem of Communist infiltration of the armed forces.*

I

infinite /'ɪnfɪnɪt/ ADJ Something that is **infinite** is extremely large in amount or degree, or has no limit. ❑ *I don't have an infinite amount of time, you know.* ● **infinitely** ADV ❑ *His design was infinitely better than anything I had done.*

infinitive /ɪn'fɪnɪtɪv/ (**infinitives**) N-COUNT The **infinitive** of a verb is its base form or simplest form, such as 'do', 'take', and 'eat'. The infinitive is often used with 'to' in front of it.

infinity /ɪn'fɪnɪti/ **1** N-UNCOUNT **Infinity** is a number that is larger than any other number and so can never be given an exact value. **2** N-UNCOUNT **Infinity** is a point that is further away than any other point and so can never be reached. ❑ *...a starless night sky stretching to infinity.*

infirmary /ɪn'fɜːməri/ (**infirmaries**) N-COUNT Some hospitals are called **infirmaries**. ❑ *...the Radcliffe Infirmary in Oxford.*

Word Link	***flam ≈ burning : flame, flaming, inflame***

inflame /ɪn'fleɪm/ (**inflames, inflaming, inflamed**) V-T If something **inflames** a situation, or if it **inflames** people's feelings, it makes people more angry or feel more strongly. [JOURNALISM] ❑ *Political passions have been inflamed by the scandal.*

inflamed /ɪn'fleɪmd/ ADJ If part of your body is **inflamed**, it is red or swollen because of an infection or injury. [FORMAL]

inflammation /ˌɪnflə'meɪʃən/ (**inflammations**) N-VAR An **inflammation** is a swelling in your body that results from an infection or injury. [FORMAL] ❑ *...inflammation of the liver.*

inflammatory /ɪn'flæmətəri, AM -tɔːri/ ADJ An **inflammatory** action or remark is likely to make people react very angrily. ❑ *Someone made an inflammatory racist remark.*

inflate

inflatable /ɪn'fleɪtəbəl/ ADJ An **inflatable** object is one that you fill with air when you want to use it. ❑ *...an inflatable boat.*

inflate /ɪn'fleɪt/ (**inflates, inflating, inflated**) V-T/V-I If you **inflate** something such as a balloon or tyre, or if it **inflates**, it becomes bigger as it is filled with air or another gas. ❑ *Don's lifejacket failed to inflate.*

inflated /ɪn'fleɪtɪd/ **1** ADJ If you describe a price or salary as **inflated**, you mean that it is higher than is reasonable. **2** ADJ If you say that someone has an **inflated** opinion of themselves, you mean that they think that they are better or more important than they really are.

inflation /ɪn'fleɪʃən/ N-UNCOUNT **Inflation** is a general increase in the prices of goods and services in a country. ❑ *...an inflation rate of only 2.2%.*

Word Partnership	Use *inflation* with:
ADJ.	**high/low** inflation
N.	inflation **fears, increase in** inflation, inflation **rate**
V.	**control** inflation, **reduce** inflation

inflationary /ɪn'fleɪʃənri, AM -neri/ ADJ **Inflationary** means connected with inflation or causing inflation. ❑ *...inflationary wage claims.*

inflect /ɪn'flekt/ (**inflects, inflecting, inflected**) V-I If a word **inflects**, its ending or form changes in order to show its grammatical function or number. If a language **inflects**, it has words in it that inflect. ● **inflection** (**inflections**) N-VAR ❑ *...a full set of inflections.*

inflexible /ɪn'fleksɪbəl/ ADJ Something or someone that is **inflexible** cannot or will not change or be altered, even if the situation changes. ❑ *Workers insisted the new system was too inflexible.* ● **inflexibility** N-UNCOUNT ❑ *Joyce was irritated by the inflexibility of her colleagues.*

Word Link	***flict ≈ striking : affliction, conflict, inflict***

inflict /ɪn'flɪkt/ (**inflicts, inflicting, inflicted**) V-T To **inflict** something unpleasant **on** someone or something means to make them suffer it. ❑ *...sports that inflict cruelty on animals.*

influence /'ɪnflʊəns/ (**influences, influencing, influenced**) **1** N-UNCOUNT **Influence** is the power to make other people agree with your opinions or make them do what you want. ❑ *Did Eva Braun have any influence on Hitler?* ❑ *The government should continue to use its influence for the release of all hostages.* **2** V-T If you **influence** someone, you use your power to make them agree with you or do what you want. ❑ *My dad influenced me to do electronics.* **3** N-COUNT & V-T If someone or something has an **influence on** people or events, or if they **influence** people or events, they affect the way people think or act, or what happens. ❑ *The Beatles had a huge influence on my life.* ❑ *What you eat may influence your risk of getting cancer.* **4** N-COUNT Someone or something that is a good or bad **influence** has a good or bad effect on someone. ❑ *TV is a bad influence on people.*

influential /ˌɪnflʊ'enʃəl/ ADJ Someone who is **influential** has a lot of influence over people or events. ❑ *It helps to have influential friends.* ❑ *Many members of their family had been influential in Italy's history.*

influx /'ɪnflʌks/ N-SING An **influx of** people or things into a place is their steady arrival there in large numbers. ❑ *...an influx of refugees.*

info /'ɪnfəʊ/ N-UNCOUNT **Info** is information. [INFORMAL] ❑ *For more info phone 0800 100 8000.*

inform /ɪn'fɔːm/ (**informs, informing, informed**) **1** V-T If you **inform** someone **of** something, you tell them about it. ❑ *They informed him of any progress they had made.* ❑ *...efforts to inform people about the dangers of AIDS.* **2** → see also **informed**

informal /ɪn'fɔːməl/ ADJ You use **informal** to describe behaviour, speech, or situations that are relaxed and casual rather than correct and serious. ❑ *This door leads to the informal living area.* ● **informally** ADV ❑ *They frequently chat informally over coffee.*

Thesaurus	*informal* Also look up:
ADJ.	casual, natural, relaxed, unofficial

informant /ɪn'fɔːmənt/ (**informants**) N-COUNT An **informant** is someone who gives another person information, especially someone who gives information to the police.

information /ˌɪnfə'meɪʃən/ N-UNCOUNT If you have **information** about a particular thing, you know something about it. ❑ *We look at every piece of information we receive.* ❑ *For further information contact the number below.*

Usage

Note that **information** is only ever used as an uncount noun. You cannot say 'an information' or 'informations'. However, you can say a **piece of information** or an **item of information** when you are referring to a particular fact that someone has informed you of.

Word Partnership	Use *information* with:
ADJ.	**additional** information, **background** information, **classified** information, **important** information, **new** information, **personal** information
V.	**find** information, **get** information, **have** information, **need** information, **provide** information, **retrieve** information, **store** information, **want** information

infor,mation tech'nology N-UNCOUNT **Information technology** is the theory and practice of using computers to store and analyse information. [COMPUTING] → see **industry**

informative /ɪn'fɔːmətɪv/ ADJ Something that is **informative** gives you useful information. ❑ *It is a really informative book.*

informed /ɪn'fɔːmd/ ADJ Someone who is **informed** knows about a subject. An **informed** guess or decision is based on knowledge about a subject. ❑ *We can now make a more informed choice about what we buy.*

informer /ɪn'fɔːmə/ (**informers**) N-COUNT An **informer** is someone who tells the police that another person has done something wrong.

infra-red /ˌɪnfrə'red/ ADJ BEFORE N **Infra-red** radiation has a longer wavelength than light, so you cannot see it without special equipment. → see **sun**

infrastructure /'ɪnfrəstrʌktʃə/ (**infrastructures**) N-VAR The **infrastructure** of a country or society consists of the basic facilities such as transport, communications, power supplies, and buildings, which enable it to function properly.

infringe /ɪn'frɪndʒ/ (**infringes, infringing, infringed**) **1** V-T If someone **infringes** a law or an agreement, they break it. ❑ *There is a fine of up to £5,000 for infringing this law.* ● **infringement** (**infringements**) N-VAR ❑ *The match officials blow whistles to indicate an infringement of the rules.* **2** V-T If something **infringes** people's rights or freedoms, or if it **infringes on** them, it prevents them from having the rights or freedoms they are entitled to. ● **infringement** N-VAR ❑ *The women claim that the law is an infringement of their human rights.*

infuriate /ɪn'fjʊərieɪt/ (**infuriates, infuriating, infuriated**) V-T If something or someone **infuriates** you, they make you extremely angry. ❑ *Here's a list of things that infuriate passengers.* ● **infuriating** ADJ ❑ *Modern life can be so infuriating.*

i

infuse /ɪn'fjuːz/ (**infuses, infusing, infused**) V-T To **infuse** a quality **into** someone or something, or to **infuse** them **with** a quality, means to fill them with it. [FORMAL] ❑ *The students were infused with a sense of excitement and discovery.*

ingenious /ɪn'dʒiːniəs/ ADJ Something that is **ingenious** is very clever and involves new ideas or equipment. ❑ *...a truly ingenious invention.*

ingenuity /ˌɪndʒə'njuːɪti, AM -'nuː-/ N-UNCOUNT **Ingenuity** is skill at inventing things or at working out how to achieve things.

ingrained /ˌɪn'greɪnd/ ADJ **Ingrained** habits and beliefs are difficult to change or remove. ❑ *...deeply ingrained family loyalty.*

ingredient /ɪn'griːdiənt/ (**ingredients**) **1** N-COUNT **Ingredients** are the things that are used to make something, especially all the different foods you use when you are cooking a particular dish. **2** N-COUNT An **ingredient** of a situation is one of the parts of it which give it character or make it successful.

Word Partnership	Use *ingredient* with:
ADJ.	**active** ingredient, **a common** ingredient, **secret** ingredient **1** **important** ingredient, **key** ingredient, **main** ingredient **1** **2**

inhabit /ɪn'hæbɪt/ (**inhabits, inhabiting, inhabited**) V-T If a place **is inhabited** by a group of people or a species of animal, those people or animals live there. ❑ *...the people who inhabit these beautiful islands.*

inhabitant /ɪn'hæbɪtənt/ (**inhabitants**) N-COUNT The **inhabitants** of a place are the people who live there.

inhale

inhale /ɪn'heɪl/ (**inhales, inhaling, inhaled**) V-T/V-I When you **inhale**, you breathe in. When you **inhale** something such as smoke, you take it into your lungs when you breathe in. ❑ *He was treated for the effects of inhaling smoke.* → see **respiration**

inherent /ɪn'herənt, -'hɪər-/ ADJ The **inherent** qualities of something are the necessary and natural parts of it. ❑ *...the inherent dangers of war.* • **inherently** ADV ❑ *Aeroplanes are not inherently dangerous.*

inherit /ɪn'herɪt/ (**inherits, inheriting, inherited**) **1** V-T If you **inherit** money or property, you receive it from someone who has died. ❑ *He inherited these paintings from his father.* **2** V-T If you **inherit** something such as a situation or attitude, you take it over from people who came before you. ❑ *Australia has inherited much of the UK's approach to town planning.* **3** V-T If you **inherit** a characteristic, you are born with it, because your parents or ancestors had it. ❑ *Her children have inherited her love of sport.*

inheritance /ɪn'herɪtəns/ (**inheritances**) N-VAR An **inheritance** is money or property which you receive from someone who is dead. ❑ *...families fighting over their inheritance.*

inhibit /ɪn'hɪbɪt/ (**inhibits, inhibiting, inhibited**) V-T If something **inhibits** an event or process, it prevents it or slows it down. ❑ *Sugary drinks inhibit digestion.*

I

inhibited /ɪn'hɪbɪtɪd/ ADJ If you say that someone is **inhibited**, you mean they find it difficult to behave naturally and show their feelings, and that you think this is a bad thing. ❑ *Inhibited children are shy and timid.*

inhibition /ˌɪnɪ'bɪʃən/ (**inhibitions**) N-VAR **Inhibitions** are feelings of embarrassment that make it difficult for you to behave naturally. ❑ *They behave with a total lack of inhibition.*

inhuman /ˌɪn'hjuːmən/ **1** ADJ If you describe something as **inhuman**, you mean that it is extremely cruel. ❑ *Killing whales is unnecessary and inhuman.* **2** ADJ Something that is **inhuman** is not human or does not seem human, and is strange or frightening. ❑ *...inhuman screams.*

initial /ɪ'nɪʃəl/ (**initials, initialling, initialled** or [AM] **initialing, initialed**) **1** ADJ BEFORE N You use **initial** to describe something that happens at the beginning of a process. ❑ *The initial reaction has been excellent.* **2** N-COUNT & V-T **Initials** are the capital letters which begin each word of a name. When you write your initials on a document, to show for example, that you have seen it, you **initial** it. ❑ *I initialled the pages and signed at the bottom.*

initially /ɪ'nɪʃəli/ ADV **Initially** means in the early stages of a process or situation. ❑ *Initially, I wanted to be a ballet dancer.*

initiate /ɪ'nɪʃieɪt/ (**initiates, initiating, initiated**) **1** V-T If you **initiate** something, you start it or cause it to happen. ❑ *They initiated a discussion on economics.* • **initiation** N-UNCOUNT ❑ *There was a year between initiation and completion.* **2** V-T If someone **is initiated into** a particular group or society, they become a member of it by taking part in ceremonies at which they learn its special knowledge or customs. ❑ *He wants to be initiated into their religion.* • **initiation** (**initiations**) N-VAR ❑ *...an initiation ceremony.*

initiative /ɪ'nɪʃətɪv/ (**initiatives**) **1** N-COUNT An **initiative** is an important act intended to solve a problem. ❑ *There's talk of a new peace initiative.* **2** N-SING In a fight or contest, if you **have the initiative**, you are in a stronger position than your opponents. **3** N-UNCOUNT If you have **initiative**, you are able to take action without needing other people to tell you what to do. ❑ *She was disappointed that he had no initiative.* **4** PHRASE If you **take the initiative** in a situation, you are the first person to act, and are therefore able to control the situation.

inject /ɪn'dʒekt/ (**injects, injecting, injected**) **1** V-T To **inject** someone **with** a substance such as a medicine, or to **inject** it **into** them, means to use a needle and a syringe to put it into their body. ❑ *She was injected with painkillers.* ❑ *They injected healthy cells into the weakened muscles.* **2** V-T If you **inject** a new, exciting, or interesting quality **into** a situation, you add it. ❑ *She kept trying to inject a little fun into their relationship.* **3** V-T If you **inject** money or resources **into** a business or organization, you provide more money or resources for it.

injection /ɪn'dʒekʃən/ (**injections**) **1** N-COUNT If you have an **injection**, someone puts a medicine into your body using a needle and a syringe. ❑ *It must be given by injection, usually twice daily.* **2** N-COUNT An **injection of** money or resources into a business or organization is the act of providing more money or resources for it.

injunction /ɪn'dʒʌŋkʃən/ (**injunctions**) N-COUNT An **injunction** is an order from a court, usually telling someone not to do something. [LEGAL] ❑ *An injunction banned her from his home.*

injure /'ɪndʒə/ (**injures, injuring, injured**) **1** V-T If you **injure** a person or animal, you damage some part of their body. ❑ *He would not injure any living thing.* **2** → See note at **wound**
→ see **war**

Word Partnership	Use *injure* with:
ADV.	**seriously** injure
PRON.	injure ***someone***, injure ***yourself***
V.	**kill or** injure

injured /'ɪndʒəd/ **1** ADJ & N-PLURAL An **injured** person has physical damage to part of their body, usually as a result of an accident or fighting. **The injured** are people who are injured. ❑ *Many of them died because they were so badly injured.* **2** → See note at **wound** **3** ADJ If you feel **injured**, or if your feelings are **injured**, you feel upset because you believe something unfair has been done to you. ❑ *...a look of injured pride.*

Word Partnership	Use *injured* with:
ADJ.	**dead/killed and** injured **1**
ADV.	**badly** injured, **critically** injured, **seriously** injured **1**
N.	injured **in an accident/attack**, injured **people** **1**
V.	**get** injured, **rescue the** injured **1**

injury /'ɪndʒəri/ (**injuries**) **1** N-VAR An **injury** is damage done to a person's body. ❑ *The passengers escaped serious injury.* **2** → See note at **wound**

Word Partnership	Use *injury* with:
ADJ.	**bodily** injury, **internal** injury, **minor** injury, **personal** injury, **serious** injury, **severe** injury
V.	**escape** injury, **suffer an** injury

injustice /ɪn'dʒʌstɪs/ (**injustices**) N-VAR **Injustice** is unfairness in a situation. ❑ *People could see that we were fighting against injustice.*

ink /ɪŋk/ (**inks**) N-VAR **Ink** is the coloured liquid used for writing or printing. ❑ *The letter was handwritten in black ink.*
→ see **blog**

inland **1** ADV /ɪn'lænd/ If something is situated **inland**, it is away from the coast, towards or near the middle of a country. ❑ *The majority live further inland.* **2** ADJ BEFORE N /'ɪnlænd/ **Inland** lakes and places are not on the coast, but in or near the middle of a country.

'in-laws N-PLURAL Your **in-laws** are the parents and close relatives of your husband or wife.

inlet /'ɪnlet/ (**inlets**) N-COUNT An **inlet** is a narrow strip of water which goes from a sea or lake into the land.

inmate /'ɪnmeɪt/ (**inmates**) N-COUNT The **inmates** of a prison or a psychiatric hospital are the prisoners or patients who are living there.

inn /ɪn/ (**inns**) N-COUNT An **inn** is a small hotel or a pub, usually an old one. [DATED]

Word Link	*nat ≈ being born : innate, native, prenatal*

innate /ɪ'neɪt/ ADJ An **innate** quality or ability is one which a person is born with. ❑ *Americans have an innate sense of fairness.* • **innately** ADV ❑ *...her innately feminine qualities.*

inner /'ɪnə/ **1** ADJ BEFORE N The **inner** parts of something are the parts which are contained or enclosed inside the other parts, and which are closest to the centre. ❑ *She went into an inner office.* **2** ADJ BEFORE N Your **inner** feelings are feelings which you have but do not show to other people.

,inner 'circle (**inner circles**) N-COUNT An **inner circle** is a group of people who have a lot of power or control in a group or organization, and who work together in secretive ways. ❑ *...the inner circle of scientists who produced the atomic bomb.*

,inner 'city (**inner cities**) N-COUNT You use **inner city** to refer to areas near the centre of a city where people live and where there are often social and economic problems. ❑ *...the fear of living in the inner city.* ❑ *...inner-city areas.*
→ see **city**

innings /'ɪnɪŋz/

Innings is both the singular and the plural form.

N-COUNT An **innings** is a period in a game of cricket during which a particular player or team is batting.

innocence /'ɪnəsəns/ **1** N-UNCOUNT **Innocence** is the quality of having no experience or knowledge of the more complex or unpleasant aspects of life. ❑ *...childhood innocence.* **2** N-UNCOUNT If someone proves their **innocence**, they prove that they are not guilty of a crime.

innocent /'ɪnəsənt/ **1** ADJ If someone is **innocent**, they did not commit a crime which they have been accused of. ❑ *He was sure that the man was innocent of murder.* **2** ADJ If someone is **innocent**, they have no experience or knowledge of the more complex or unpleasant aspects of life. ❑ *They seemed so young and innocent.* • **innocently** ADV ❑ *The baby smiled innocently.* **3** ADJ **Innocent** people are those who are not involved in a crime, conflict, or other situation, but who nevertheless get injured or killed. ❑ *All those wounded were innocent victims.* **4** ADJ An **innocent** remark or action is not meant to offend people, although it may do so. ❑ *It was probably an innocent question.*

Word Partnership	Use *innocent* with:
V.	**plead** innocent, **presumed** innocent, **proven** innocent **1**
N.	innocent **man/woman** **1**
	innocent **children** **2**
	innocent **bystander**, innocent **civilians**, innocent **people**, innocent **victim** **3**
ADV.	**perfectly** innocent **4**

innocuous /ɪ'nɒkjʊəs/ ADJ Something that is **innocuous** is not at all harmful. [FORMAL] ❑ *Both mushrooms look innocuous but are in fact deadly.*

Word Link	*nov ≈ new : innovation, novel, renovate*

innovation /,ɪnə'veɪʃən/ (**innovations**) **1** N-COUNT An **innovation** is a new thing or new method of doing something. **2** N-UNCOUNT **Innovation** is the introduction of new things or new methods. ❑ *These areas may be the focus of future innovation.*

innovative /'ɪnəveɪtɪv/ **1** ADJ Something that is **innovative** is new and original. **2** ADJ An **innovative** person introduces changes and new ideas.
→ see **technology**

innovator /'ɪnəveɪtə/ (**innovators**) N-COUNT An **innovator** is someone who introduces changes and new ideas.

innuendo /,ɪnjʊ'endəʊ/ (**innuendoes** or **innuendos**) N-VAR **Innuendo** is indirect reference to something rude or unpleasant. ❑ *...the innuendo in that article.*

Word Link	*numer ≈ number : innumerable, numerical, numerous*

innumerable /ɪ'nju:mərəbəl, AM -'nu:-/ ADJ **Innumerable** means very many, or too many to be counted. ❑ *He has invented innumerable excuses, told endless lies.*

inordinate /ɪn'ɔ:dɪnɪt/ ADJ If you describe something as **inordinate**, you are emphasizing that it is much greater than expected. [FORMAL] ❑ *...their inordinate number of pets.* • **inordinately** ADV ❑ *He is inordinately proud of his wife.*

input /'ɪnpʊt/ (**inputs, inputting, input**) **1** N-VAR **Input** consists of information or resources that a group or project receives. ❑ *We need your input and welcome it.* **2** V-T If you **input** information into a computer, you feed it in, for example by typing it on a keyboard. [COMPUTING] **3** N-UNCOUNT **Input** is information that is fed into a computer. [COMPUTING]

inquest /'ɪnkwest/ (**inquests**) N-COUNT An **inquest** is an official inquiry into the cause of someone's death.

inquire also **enquire** /ɪn'kwaɪə/ (**inquires, inquiring, inquired**) **1** V-T/V-I If you **inquire about** something, you ask for information about it. [FORMAL] ❑ *'Is something wrong?' he enquired.* ❑ *He inquired whether there were any messages for him.* 2 V-I If you **inquire into** something, you investigate it carefully. ❑ *Inspectors were inquiring into the affairs of the company.*

▶ **inquire after** PHR-VERB If you **inquire after** someone, you ask how they are. ❑ *Ellie called to inquire after my health.*

Thesaurus	*inquire* Also look up:
V.	ask, question, quiz

inquiring also **enquiring** /ɪn'kwaɪərɪŋ/ 1 ADJ BEFORE N If you have an **inquiring mind**, you have a great interest in learning new things. 2 ADJ BEFORE N If you have an **inquiring** expression on your face, you are showing that you want to know something. [WRITTEN]

inquiry also **enquiry** /ɪn'kwaɪəri/ (**inquiries**) 1 N-COUNT An **inquiry** is a question which you ask in order to get information. ❑ *He made some inquiries and discovered she had gone abroad.* 2 N-COUNT An **inquiry** is an official investigation. 3 N-UNCOUNT **Inquiry** is the process of investigating something to get information about it. ❑ *...a new line of inquiry.*

inquisitive /ɪn'kwɪzɪtɪv/ ADJ An **inquisitive** person likes finding out about things, especially secret things. ❑ *Brian had an inquisitive nature.*

Word Link	*san ≈ health : insane, sane, sanitation*

insane /ɪn'seɪn/ 1 ADJ & N-PLURAL Someone who is **insane** has a mind that does not work in a normal way, with the result that their behaviour is very strange. **The insane** are people who are insane. ❑ *His first wife went insane.* ● **insanity** /ɪn'sænɪti/ N-UNCOUNT ❑ *I knew I was sinking into insanity.* 2 ADJ If you describe a decision or action as **insane**, you think it is very foolish. ● **insanely** ADV ❑ *I would be insanely jealous if Bill left me for another woman.* ● **insanity** N-UNCOUNT ❑ *...the financial insanity of the 1980s.*

Word Link	*sat, satis ≈ enough : dissatisfaction, insatiable, satisfy*

insatiable /ɪn'seɪʃəbəl/ ADJ If someone has an **insatiable** desire for something, they want as much of it as they can possibly get. ❑ *He had an insatiable appetite for publicity.*

Word Link	*scrib ≈ writing : inscribe, scribble, transcribe*

inscribe /ɪn'skraɪb/ (**inscribes, inscribing, inscribed**) V-T If you **inscribe** words on an object, you write or carve the words on it. ❑ *...pieces of stone inscribed with Buddhist texts.*

inscription /ɪn'skrɪpʃən/ (**inscriptions**) N-COUNT An **inscription** is a piece of writing carved into a surface, or written on a book or photograph.

insect /'ɪnsekt/ (**insects**) N-COUNT An **insect** is a small creature with six legs. Most insects have wings.

→ see Picture Dictionary: **insects**

insecticide /ɪn'sektɪsaɪd/ (**insecticides**) N-VAR **Insecticide** is a chemical used to kill insects.

→ see **farm**

insecure /ˌɪnsɪ'kjʊə/ 1 ADJ If you **feel insecure**, you feel that you are not good enough or are not loved. ❑ *Most mothers are insecure about their skills as mothers.* ● **insecurity** (**insecurities**) N-VAR ❑ *I*

Picture Dictionary **insects**

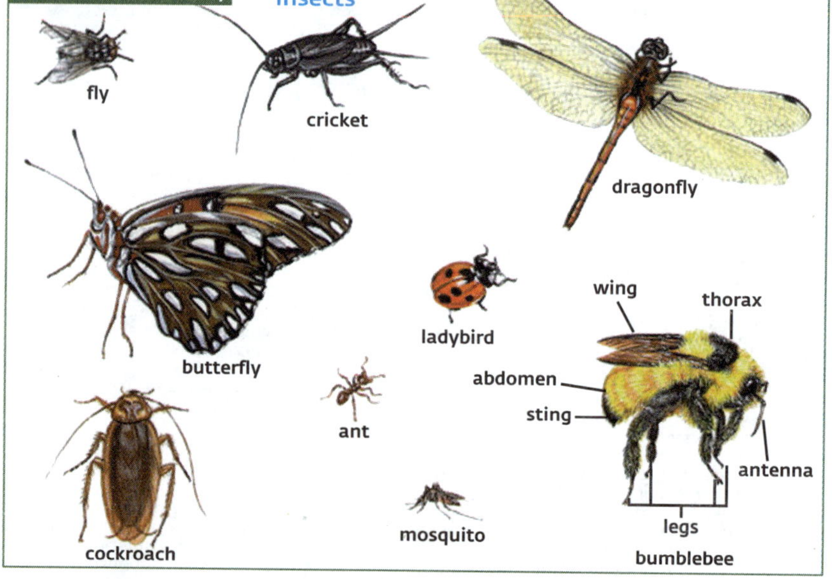

believe that his childhood insecurity went very deep. **2** ADJ Something that is **insecure** is not safe or protected. ❑ *...low-paid, insecure jobs.* ● **insecurity** N-UNCOUNT ❑ *...the insecurity of modern life.*

insensitive /ɪn'sensɪtɪv/ ADJ If you describe someone as **insensitive**, you mean that they are not aware of other people's feelings or problems. ❑ *These were very insensitive remarks.* ● **insensitivity** /ɪnˌsensɪ'tɪvɪti/ N-UNCOUNT ❑ *...my insensitivity towards her.*

inseparable /ɪn'seprəbəl/ **1** ADJ If two things are **inseparable**, they cannot be considered separately. ❑ *Freedom is inseparable from social justice.* **2** ADJ Friends who are **inseparable** spend a lot of time together.

insert /ɪn'sɜːt/ (**inserts, inserting, inserted**) **1** V-T If you **insert** an object **into** something, you put the object inside it. ❑ *He slowly inserted the key into the lock.* ● **insertion** (**insertions**) N-VAR ❑ *This treatment involves the insertion of needles at precise points on the body.* **2** V-T If you **insert** a comment or detail in a piece of writing or a speech, you include it.

inside /ˌɪn'saɪd/ (**insides**) **1** PREP & ADV Something or someone that is **inside** a place, container, or object is in it or surrounded by it. ❑ *There were several letters inside the box.* ❑ *There is a telephone inside the entrance hall.* ❑ *He ripped open the envelope and read what was inside.* **2** N-COUNT The **inside of** something is the part or area that its sides surround or contain. ❑ *I painted the inside of the house.* **3** ADJ BEFORE N On a wide road, the **inside** lanes are the ones closest to the edge of the road. **4** N-PLURAL Your **insides** are your internal organs, especially your stomach. [INFORMAL] **5** ADJ BEFORE N **Inside knowledge** is obtained from someone who is involved in a situation and therefore knows a lot about it. ❑ *It is likely that he has inside information about what is really taking place.* **6** PHRASE If something such as a piece of clothing is **inside out**, the inside part has been turned so that it faces outwards.

Thesaurus	*inside* Also look up:
PREP.	in; (*ant.*) outside **1**
N.	interior, middle **2**

insider /ˌɪn'saɪdə/ (**insiders**) N-COUNT An **insider** is someone who is involved in a situation and who knows more about it than other people. ❑ *Insiders estimated that the loss could approach $10 million.* ❑ *...insider knowledge.*

insidious /ɪn'sɪdiəs/ ADJ Something that is **insidious** is unpleasant and develops gradually without being noticed. ❑ *The changes are insidious, and will not produce a noticeable effect for 15 to 20 years.*

insight /'ɪnsaɪt/ (**insights**) N-VAR If you gain **insight into** a complex situation or problem, you learn something useful or valuable about it. ❑ *...an insight into the practical problems of disabled people.*

insignificant /ˌɪnsɪg'nɪfɪkənt/ ADJ Something that is **insignificant** is unimportant, especially because it is very small. ❑ *In 1949 Bonn was a small, insignificant city.* ● **insignificance** N-UNCOUNT ❑ *...the sense of insignificance that everybody felt.*

insist /ɪn'sɪst/ (**insists, insisting, insisted**) **1** V-T/V-I If you **insist** that something should be done, you say very firmly that it must be done. ❑ *She insisted on being present.* ❑ *I didn't want to join in, but Kenneth insisted.* ● **insistence** N-UNCOUNT ❑ *She had come to the party at her boyfriend's insistence.* **2** V-T If you **insist** that something is true, you say it very firmly and refuse to change your mind. ❑ *US officials insisted there was no special treatment for the American prisoner.*

insistent /ɪn'sɪstənt/ **1** ADJ Someone who is **insistent** keeps insisting that a particular thing should be done or is the case. ❑ *Abramov was insistent that the matter should be resolved quickly.* ● **insistently** ADV ❑ *'What is it?' his wife asked again, gently but insistently.* **2** ADJ An **insistent** noise or rhythm continues for a long time and holds your attention.

insomnia /ɪn'sɒmniə/ N-UNCOUNT Someone who **suffers from insomnia** finds it difficult to sleep. → see **sleep**

inspect /ɪn'spekt/ (**inspects, inspecting, inspected**) V-T If you **inspect** something, you examine it or check it carefully. ❑ *The nurse inspected his wound.* ● **inspection** (**inspections**) N-VAR ❑ *A thorough engineer's inspection is advisable.*

inspector /ɪn'spektə/ (**inspectors**) **1** N-COUNT An **inspector** is someone whose job is to inspect things. ❑ *The factory was finally shut down by safety inspectors.* **2** N-COUNT & N-TITLE In Britain, an **inspector** is a police officer who is higher in rank than a sergeant and lower in rank than a superintendent. ❑ *...Inspector Joplin.*

inspiration /ˌɪnspɪ'reɪʃən/ **1** N-UNCOUNT **Inspiration** is a feeling of excitement and enthusiasm gained from new ideas. ❑ *Diana played extremely well giving a lot of inspiration to other women.* **2** N-SING The **inspiration for** something such as a piece of work or a theory is the person or thing that provides the basic idea or example for it. ❑ *India's myths and songs are the inspiration for her book.* ❑ *My inspiration comes from poets like Baudelaire.*

Word Link	***spir* ≈ breath : *aspire, inspire, respiratory***

inspire /ɪn'spaɪə/ (**inspires, inspiring, inspired**) **1** V-T If a work of art or an action **is inspired** by something, that thing is the idea or the motivation for it. ❑ *The book was inspired by a real person.* ❑ *What inspired you to change your name?* ● **-inspired** ❑ *...Mediterranean-inspired cookery.* **2** V-T If someone or something **inspires** you, they give you new ideas and a strong feeling of enthusiasm. ❑ *It's a story that should inspire people.* ● **inspiring** ADJ ❑ *...a brilliant and inspiring teacher.* **3** V-T Someone or something that **inspires** a particular emotion or reaction in people makes them feel it. ❑ *He inspires strong loyalty in his friends.*

Word Link	***stab* ≈ steady : *destabilize, establish, instability***

instability /ˌɪnstə'bɪlɪti/ (**instabilities**) N-VAR **Instability** is a lack of stability in a place, situation, or person. ❑ *...political instability.*

install /ɪn'stɔːl/ (**installs, installing, installed**) **1** V-T If you **install** a piece of equipment, you fit it or put it somewhere so that it is ready to be used. ❑ *They installed a new phone line.* ● **installation** /ˌɪnstə'leɪʃən/ N-UNCOUNT ❑ *...the installation of fire alarms.* **2** V-T If someone **is installed** in a new job or important position, they are officially given the job or position. ❑ *The army has promised to install a new government.*

Word Partnership Use *install* with:

ADJ. **easy** to install 1
N. install **equipment**, install **machines**, install **software** 1

instalment [AM **installment**] /ɪn'stɔ:lmənt/ (**instalments**) 1 N-COUNT If you pay for something **in instalments**, you pay small sums of money at regular intervals over a period of time. ❑ *The final instalment of the debt will be repaid next year.* 2 N-COUNT An **instalment** of a story is one of its separate parts that are published or broadcast one after the other. ❑ *...the latest instalment in J.K.Rowling's 'Harry Potter' series.*

instance /'ɪnstəns/ (**instances**) 1 PHRASE You use **for instance** when you are mentioning something or someone that is an example of what you are talking about. ❑ *They want to do the right thing – to dress properly, for instance.* 2 N-COUNT An **instance** is a particular example or occurrence of something. ❑ *...another instance of robbery.* 3 PHRASE You say **in the first instance** to mention the first of a series of actions or possibilities. [FORMAL] ❑ *In the first instance, please write to us with your full details.*

instant /'ɪnstənt/ (**instants**) 1 N-COUNT An **instant** is an extremely short period of time or a point in time. ❑ *The pain disappeared in an instant.* ❑ *At that instant, the lights went out.* 2 CONJ If you say that someone does something **the instant** something else happens, you are emphasizing that they do the first thing immediately after the second thing happens. ❑ *She knew the instant he walked in that it was true.* 3 ADJ You use **instant** to describe something that happens immediately. ❑ *He took an instant dislike to Michael.* ● **instantly** ADV ❑ *The man was killed instantly.* 4 ADJ BEFORE N **Instant food** can be prepared very quickly, for example by just adding water. ❑ *...instant coffee.*

Thesaurus *instant* Also look up:

N. minute, second, split second 1

Word Partnership Use *instant* with:

PREP. **for an** instant, **in an** instant 1
ADJ. **the next** instant 1 2
N. instant **access**, instant **success** 3

instantaneous /ˌɪnstən'teɪniəs/ ADJ Something that is **instantaneous** happens immediately and very quickly. ❑ *They said that his death had been instantaneous.* ● **instantaneously** ADV ❑ *The police responded almost instantaneously.*

Word Link *stead ≈ place, stand : homestead, instead, steady*

instead /ɪn'sted/ PREP & ADV If you do one thing **instead of** another, you do the first thing and not the second thing, especially as the result of a choice or a change of behaviour. ❑ *She spent nearly four months away that summer, instead of the usual two.* ❑ *His right eye was damaged so he relies on his left eye instead.*

instigate /'ɪnstɪgeɪt/ (**instigates, instigating, instigated**) V-T To **instigate** an event or situation means to cause it to happen. ❑ *They are instigating the violence.* ● **instigation** N-UNCOUNT ❑ *The talks are taking place at Germany's instigation.* ● **instigator** (**instigators**) N-COUNT ❑ *Turkey was not only the host, but also the instigator of the conference.*

instil [AM **instill**] /ɪn'stɪl/ (**instils, instilling, instilled**) V-T If you **instil** an idea or feeling **in** or **into** someone, you make them think it or feel it. ❑ *He's trying to instil more discipline in his team.*

instinct /'ɪnstɪŋkt/ (**instincts**) 1 N-VAR An **instinct** is the natural tendency that a person has to behave or react in a particular way. ❑ *...a basic instinct for survival.* ❑ *...the dog's natural instinct to hunt.* 2 N-COUNT An **instinct** is a feeling that you have about a particular situation, rather than an opinion based on facts. ❑ *I should have followed my first instinct, which was not to do the interview.*

instinctive /ɪn'stɪŋktɪv/ ADJ An **instinctive** feeling, idea, or action is one that you have or do without thinking. ❑ *It's an instinctive reaction – if a child falls you pick it up.* ● **instinctively** ADV ❑ *He knew instinctively that here was more bad news.*

institute /'ɪnstɪtju:t, AM -tu:t/ (**institutes, instituting, instituted**) 1 N-COUNT An **institute** is an organization or building where a particular type of work is done, especially research or teaching. ❑ *...the Royal National Institute of the Blind.* 2 V-T If you **institute** a system, rule, or plan, you start it. [FORMAL] ❑ *JPL created a development office to institute these changes.*

institution /ˌɪnstɪ'tju:ʃən, AM -'tu:-/ (**institutions**) 1 N-COUNT An **institution** is an official organization which is important in society. Parliament, the Church, and large banks are all institutions. ● **institutional** ADJ BEFORE N 2 N-COUNT An **institution** is a place such as a mental hospital, children's home, or prison, where people are kept and looked after. ❑ *Larry has been in an institution since he was four.* 3 N-COUNT An **institution** is a custom that is considered an important feature of society, because it has existed for a long time. ❑ *...the institution of marriage.*

ˌin-'store ADJ & ADV **In-store** facilities are facilities that are available within a department store, supermarket or other large shop. ❑ *...an in-store bakery.* ❑ *Ask in-store for details.*

Word Link *struct ≈ building : construct, destructive, instruct*

instruct /ɪn'strʌkt/ (**instructs, instructing, instructed**) 1 V-T Someone who **instructs** people **in** a subject or skill teaches it to them. ❑ *He instructed family members in nursing techniques.* 2 V-T If you **instruct** someone **to** do something, you formally tell them to do it. ❑ *Robertson was instructed to send a message to the General immediately.*

instruction /ɪn'strʌkʃən/ (**instructions**) 1 N-PLURAL **Instructions** are clear and detailed information on how to do something. ❑ *...some basic instructions on how to cook a turkey.* 2 N-COUNT An **instruction** is something that someone tells you to do. ❑ *He had instructions to keep this guest happy.* 3 N-UNCOUNT **Instruction** in a subject or skill is teaching that someone gives you about it. ❑ *...religious instruction.*

Thesaurus *instruction* Also look up:

N. direction, order 1
education, learning 3

Word Partnership Use *instruction* with:

ADJ. **explicit** instruction 1 2
N. **classroom** instruction, instruction **manual** 3
V. **give** instruction, **provide** instruction, **receive** instruction 3

instructive /ɪn'strʌktɪv/ ADJ Something that is **instructive** gives useful information. ❑ *...an instructive documentary.*

instructor /ɪn'strʌktə/ (**instructors**) N-COUNT An **instructor** is a teacher, especially of driving, skiing, or swimming. ❑ *...his karate instructor.*

Thesaurus *instructor* Also look up:

N. leader, professor, teacher

instrument /'ɪnstrəmənt/ (**instruments**) 1 N-COUNT An **instrument** is a tool or device that is used to do a particular task. ❑ *...navigation instruments.* ❑ *...instruments for cleaning and polishing teeth.* 2 N-COUNT A **musical instrument** is an object such as a piano, guitar, or flute which you play in order to produce music. 3 N-COUNT Something that is an **instrument** for achieving a particular aim is used by people to achieve that aim. ❑ *The law should be an instrument of change.* → see **concert, orchestra**

instrumental /ˌɪnstrə'mentəl/ (**instrumentals**) 1 ADJ & N-COUNT **Instrumental** music is performed using musical instruments and not voices. An **instrumental** is a piece of instrumental music. 2 ADJ Someone or something that is **instrumental** in a process or event helps to make it happen. ❑ *He was instrumental in the team's victory over Sweden.*

insufficient /ˌɪnsə'fɪʃənt/ ADJ Something that is **insufficient** is not enough for a particular purpose. [FORMAL] ❑ *There are insufficient funds to pay the debt.* ● **insufficiently** ADV ❑ *They do work that is insufficiently interesting.*

Word Link *insula ≈ island : insular, insulate, insulation*

insular /'ɪnsjʊlə, AM -sə-/ ADJ **Insular** people don't want to meet new people or to consider new ideas.

insulate /'ɪnsjʊleɪt, AM -sə-/ (**insulates, insulating, insulated**) 1 V-T If you **insulate** something, you cover it or surround it in a thick layer, in order to prevent heat or sound from passing through it. ❑ *Can we insulate our home from the noise?* 2 V-T If a piece of equipment **is insulated**, it is covered with rubber or plastic to prevent electricity passing through it and giving the person using it an electric shock. 3 V-T If a person or group **is insulated from** harmful things, they are protected from them. ❑ *The countryside was insulated from the worst effects of the war.*

insulation /ˌɪnsjʊ'leɪʃən, AM -sə-/ N-UNCOUNT **Insulation** is a thick layer of material used to insulate something.

insulin /'ɪnsjʊlɪn, AM -sə-/ N-UNCOUNT **Insulin** is a substance that most people produce naturally in their body and which controls the level of sugar in their blood. If your body does not produce enough insulin, then it develops a disease called diabetes.

insult (**insults, insulting, insulted**) 1 V-T /ɪn'sʌlt/ If you **insult** someone, you offend them by being rude to them. ❑ *I did not mean to insult you.* ● **insulted** ADJ ❑ *I was deeply insulted.* ● **insulting** ADJ ❑ *...an insulting remark.* 2 N-COUNT /'ɪnsʌlt/ An **insult** is a rude remark or action which offends someone. ❑ *They shouted insults at each other.* 3 PHRASE If an action or event **adds insult to injury**, it makes an unfair or unacceptable situation even worse.

insurance /ɪn'ʃʊərəns/ 1 N-UNCOUNT **Insurance** is an arrangement in which you pay money regularly to a company, and they pay money to you if something unpleasant happens to you, for example if your property is stolen. ❑ *...health insurance.* 2 N-SING If you do something as an **insurance against** something unpleasant, you do it in order to protect yourself in case the unpleasant thing happens. ❑ *Farmers grow a mixture of crops as an insurance against the failure of one particular crop.*

Word Partnership Use *insurance* with:

N. insurance **claim**, insurance **company**, insurance **coverage**, insurance **payments**, insurance **policy** 1
V. **buy/purchase** insurance, **carry** insurance, **sell** insurance 1

insure /ɪn'ʃʊə/ (**insures, insuring, insured**) 1 V-T If you **insure yourself** or your property, you pay money to an insurance company so that if you become ill or if your property is stolen, the company will pay you a sum of money. ❑ *In some U.S. states, people can't insure themselves against hurricanes.* 2 → see also **ensure**

Word Partnership Use *insure* with:

N. insure ***your*** **car/health/house/property**, insure ***your*** **safety**
ADJ. **difficult to** insure, **necessary to** insure

insurer /ɪn'ʃʊərər/ (**insurers**) N-COUNT An **insurer** is a company that sells insurance.

insurrection /ˌɪnsə'rekʃən/ (**insurrections**) N-VAR An **insurrection** is violent action taken by a group of people against the rulers of their country. ❑ *...an armed insurrection.*

Word Link *tact ≈ touching : contact, intact, tactic*

intact /ɪn'tækt/ ADJ Something that is **intact** is complete and has not been damaged or spoilt. ❑ *The roof was still intact.* ❑ *His reputation remained intact.*

intake /'ɪnteɪk/ (**intakes**) 1 N-COUNT Your **intake** of food, drink, or air is the amount that you eat, drink, or breathe in, or the process of taking it into your body. ❑ *Cut down your salt intake.* 2 N-COUNT The people who are accepted into an institution or organization at a particular time

i

are referred to as a particular **intake**. ❑ *...one of this year's intake of students.*
→ see **engine**

Word Link *tang ≈ touching : entangle, intangible, tangible*

intangible /ɪnˈtændʒɪbəl/ ADJ A quality or idea that is **intangible** is hard to define or explain. ❑ *I feel that something intangible but truly terrible has happened.*

integral /ˈɪntɪgrəl/ ADJ If something is an **integral** part of another thing, it is an essential part of it. ❑ *Dreams are an integral part of our life.*

integrate /ˈɪntɪgreɪt/ (**integrates, integrating, integrated**) **1** V-T/V-I If people **integrate into** a social group, or if they **are integrated into** it, they join it and become a part of it. ❑ *Many ex-prisoners become truly integrated into our communities.* ❑ *I really made an effort to integrate with the locals.* ● **integrated** ADJ ❑ *...integrated schooling.* ● **integration** N-UNCOUNT ❑ *...the integration of disabled people into mainstream society.* **2** V-T If you **integrate** things, you combine them so that they are closely linked or so that they form one thing. ❑ *The two airlines will integrate their services.* ● **integrated** ADJ ❑ *...integrated computer systems.*

I

Thesaurus *integrate* Also look up:
V. assimilate, combine, consolidate, incorporate, synthesize, unite; (*ant.*) separate **1** **2**

integrity /ɪnˈtegrɪti/ N-UNCOUNT **Integrity** is the quality of being honest in your moral principles. ❑ *...a man of integrity.*

intellect /ˈɪntɪlekt/ N-UNCOUNT **Intellect** is the ability to think and to understand ideas and information. ❑ *...a woman of powerful intellect.*

intellectual /ˌɪntɪˈlektʃuəl/ (**intellectuals**) **1** ADJ BEFORE N **Intellectual** means involving a person's ability to think and to understand ideas and information. ❑ *...the intellectual development of children.* ● **intellectually** ADV ❑ *...intellectually demanding work.* **2** N-COUNT & ADJ An **intellectual** is someone who spends a lot of time studying and thinking about complicated ideas. You can say that someone like this is **intellectual**. ❑ *They were very intellectual and she found it difficult, I think, to fit in.*

intelligence /ɪnˈtelɪdʒəns/ **1** N-UNCOUNT Your **intelligence** is your ability to understand and learn things. ❑ *...a man of exceptional intelligence.* **2** N-UNCOUNT **Intelligence** is the ability to think and understand instead of doing things by instinct. ❑ *Whales have intelligence and are capable of making choices.* **3** N-UNCOUNT **Intelligence** is information gathered by the government about their country's enemies. ❑ *...the intelligence services.*

Word Partnership Use *intelligence* with:
ADJ. **human** intelligence **2**
secret intelligence **3**
N. intelligence **agent**, intelligence **expert**, **military** intelligence **3**

intelligent /ɪnˈtelɪdʒənt/ **1** ADJ An **intelligent** person has the ability to think, understand, and learn things quickly and well. ❑ *...the most intelligent man I have ever met.* ● **intelligently** ADV ❑ *They are incapable of thinking intelligently about politics.* **2** ADJ Something that is **intelligent** has the ability to think and understand instead of doing things by instinct. ❑ *...the search for intelligent life elsewhere in the universe.*

Thesaurus *intelligent* Also look up:
ADJ. bright, clever, sharp, smart; (*ant.*) dumb, stupid **1** **2**

intelligible /ɪnˈtelɪdʒəbəl/ ADJ Something that is **intelligible** can be understood. ❑ *Not a single word was intelligible.*

intend /ɪnˈtend/ (**intends, intending, intended**) **1** V-T If you **intend to** do something, you have decided or planned to do it. ❑ *I intend to go to university.* ❑ *...the hotel in which they intended staying.* **2** V-T Something that **is intended for** a particular person or purpose, or **is intended to** have a particular effect, has been planned for that person or purpose, or planned to have that effect. ❑ *The money is intended for food and medical supplies.* ❑ *The violence was intended to prevent new peace talks.* ❑ *Today's announcement was intended as a warning.*

intense /ɪnˈtens/ **1** ADJ Something that is **intense** is very great in strength or degree. ❑ *The pain was intense.* ❑ *...intense heat.* ● **intensely** ADV ❑ *She is intensely irritating.* ● **intensity** N-UNCOUNT ❑ *...the intensity of the poetry.* **2** ADJ An **intense** person is very serious. ❑ *...an intense young man.*

Word Link *ify ≈ making : clarify, diversify, intensify*

intensify /ɪnˈtensɪfaɪ/ (**intensifies, intensifying, intensified**) V-T/V-I If you **intensify** something, or if it **intensifies**, it becomes greater in strength or degree. ❑ *They discussed intensifying the anti-terror efforts of the police.*

intensive /ɪnˈtensɪv/ **1** ADJ An **intensive** activity involves the concentration of energy or people on one particular task. ❑ *...four weeks of intensive study.* ● **intensively** ADV ❑ *Wilson has worked intensively on his speed and strength.* **2** ADJ **Intensive** farming involves producing as many crops or animals as possible from your land, usually with the aid of chemicals.

inˌtensive ˈcare N-UNCOUNT If someone is **in intensive care**, they are in hospital being cared for and watched very closely because they are seriously ill.

intent /ɪnˈtent/ (**intents**) **1** N-UNCOUNT Your **intent** is your intention to do something. [FORMAL] ❑ *Mr Spencer has announced his intent to resign.* **2** ADJ If someone is **intent**, they appear to be concentrating very seriously on what they are doing or feeling. [WRITTEN] ❑ *Amy watched the child's intent face.* ● **intently** ADV ❑ *She stared intently at the TV screen.* **3** ADJ AFTER LINK-V If you are **intent on** doing something, you are determined to do it. ❑ *He is intent on repeating his victory.* **4** PHRASE You say **to all intents and purposes** to suggest that a situation is not exactly as you describe it but the effect is the same as if it were. ❑ *To all intents and purposes he was my father.*

intention /ɪnˈtenʃən/ (**intentions**) N-VAR An **intention** is an idea or plan of what you are going to do. ❑ *His intention is to return to Berlin.* ❑ *I have* *absolutely no intention of resigning.*

intentional /ɪn'tenʃənəl/ ADJ Something that is **intentional** is deliberate. ❑ *The kick was intentional.* ● **intentionally** ADV ❑ *I've never intentionally hurt anyone.*

interact /ˌɪntə'rækt/ (**interacts, interacting, interacted**) V-I The way that two people or things **interact** is the way that they communicate or work in relation to each other. ❑ *At birth, you become a social being, interacting with others.* ● **interaction** (**interactions**) N-VAR ❑ *...studies on parent-child interaction.*

interactive /ˌɪntə'ræktɪv/ ADJ An **interactive** computer program or television system is one which allows direct communication between the user and the machine.

intercept /ˌɪntə'sept/ (**intercepts, intercepting, intercepted**) V-T If you **intercept** someone or something that is travelling from one place to another, you stop them. ❑ *The bombers were intercepted by army patrols.* ● **interception** (**interceptions**) N-VAR ❑ *...the interception of a ship off the west coast of Scotland.*

Word Link	*inter ≈ between : interchange, interconnect, internal*

interchange (**interchanges**)

verb /ˌɪntə'tʃeɪndʒ/, noun /'ɪntətʃeɪndʒ/

V-T & N-VAR If you **interchange** things, or if there is an **interchange of** things, you exchange one thing for the other. ❑ *Your task is to interchange words so that the sentence makes sense.*

interchangeable /ˌɪntə'tʃeɪndʒəbəl/ ADJ Things that are **interchangeable** can be exchanged with each other without making any difference. ● **interchangeably** ADV ❑ *...two different words used interchangeably to describe one action.*

interconnect /ˌɪntəkə'nekt/ (**interconnects, interconnecting, interconnected**) V-T/V-I Things that **interconnect** or that **are interconnected** are connected to or with each other. ❑ *As more and more machines are interconnected, the problem is much more complex.* ❑ *...interconnecting rooms.* ● **interconnection** (**interconnections**) N-VAR ❑ *...the variety of interconnections between music and other arts.*

intercontinental /ˌɪntəkɒntɪ'nentəl/ ADJ BEFORE N **Intercontinental** is used to describe something that exists or happens between continents. ❑ *...intercontinental flights.*

intercourse /'ɪntəkɔːs/ N-UNCOUNT If people have **intercourse**, they have sex. [FORMAL]

interdependent /ˌɪntədɪ'pendənt/ ADJ People or things that are **interdependent** all depend on each other. ❑ *Most economies today are highly interdependent.* ● **interdependence** N-UNCOUNT ❑ *...the interdependence of the world's economies.*

interest /'ɪntrəst, -tərest/ (**interests, interesting, interested**) **1** V-T If something **interests** you, you want to learn more about it or to continue doing it. ❑ *These are the stories that interest me.* **2** N-COUNT Your **interests** are the things that you enjoy doing. ❑ *His interests include cooking and photography.* **3** N-SING & N-UNCOUNT If you have an **interest in** something, you like it and want to learn or hear more about it. ❑ *He showed a great interest in animals.* ❑ *She liked him at first, but soon lost interest.* **4** N-COUNT If you have an **interest in** something being done, you want it to be done because you will benefit from it. ❑ *The US clearly has an interest in developing free trade.* **5** N-UNCOUNT **Interest** is extra money that you receive if you have invested a sum of money, or extra money that you pay if you have borrowed money. ❑ *Does your current account pay interest?* **6** → see also **self-interest, vested interest** **7** PHRASE Something that is **in the interests of** a person or group will benefit them in some way. ❑ *An agreement would be in the interests of the British fishing industry.* **8** PHRASE If you do something **in the interests of** a particular result or situation, you do it in order to achieve that result or maintain that situation. ❑ *In the interests of road safety, traffic should slow down.*

Word Partnership	Use *interest* with:
N.	**level of** interest, **places of** interest, **self-**interest **1** **3** **conflict of** interest **4** interest **charges**, interest **expenses**, interest **payments** **5**
ADJ.	**great** interest, **little** interest, **strong** interest **1** **2**
V.	**attract** interest, **express** interest, **lose** interest **3** **earn** interest, **pay** interest **5**

interested /'ɪntrestɪd/ **1** ADJ AFTER LINK-V If you are **interested in** something, you think it is important and you are keen to learn more about it or spend time doing it. ❑ *I wasn't particularly interested in physics.* ❑ *I'm interested to know what people's views are.* **2** ADJ BEFORE N An **interested** party or group of people is affected by or involved in a particular event or situation.

Word Partnership	Use *interested* with:
ADV.	**really** interested, **very** interested **1**
V.	**become** interested, interested **in buying, get** interested, interested **in getting**, interested **in helping**, interested **in learning**, interested **in making, seem** interested **1**

interesting /'ɪntrestɪŋ/ ADJ If you find something **interesting**, it attracts you or holds your attention. ❑ *It was interesting to be in a different environment.* ❑ *...a very interesting book.* ● **interestingly** ADV ❑ *Interestingly enough, a few weeks later, Benjamin remarried.*

Word Partnership	Use *interesting* with:
ADV.	**especially** interesting, **really** interesting, **very** interesting
N.	interesting **idea**, interesting **people**, interesting **point**, interesting **question**, interesting **story**, interesting **things**

interface /'ɪntəfeɪs/ (**interfaces**) N-COUNT The **interface** of a piece of computer software is the way it appears on screen and how easy it is to operate. [COMPUTING] ❑ *...the development of better user interfaces.*

interfere /ˌɪntə'fɪə/ (**interferes, interfering, interfered**) **1** V-I If someone **interferes in** a situation, they get involved in it although it does not concern them and their involvement is not wanted. ❑ *I wish everyone would stop interfering.* ❑ *...interfering neighbours.* **2** V-I If something **interferes with** a situation, process, or activity, it has a damaging effect on it. ❑ *Bad weather is interfering with flights to the capital.*

interference /ˌɪntəˈfɪərəns/ **1** N-UNCOUNT **Interference** is the act of interfering in something. ❑ *...interference in the republic's internal affairs.* **2** N-UNCOUNT When there is **interference**, a radio signal is affected by other radio waves so that it cannot be received properly.

interim /ˈɪntərɪm/ **1** ADJ BEFORE N **Interim** describes things that are intended to be used until something permanent is arranged. ❑ *...an interim government.* ❑ *...an interim report.* **2** PHRASE **In the interim** means until a particular thing happens.

interior /ɪnˈtɪəriə/ (**interiors**) **1** N-COUNT **The interior of** something is the inside or central part of it. ❑ *...the boat's interior.* ❑ *...the interior walls.* **2** N-SING **The interior** of a country or continent is the central area of it. ❑ *...a 5-day trip into the interior.*

Thesaurus *interior* Also look up:
N. inside; *(ant.)* exterior, outside **1**

interlude /ˈɪntəluːd/ (**interludes**) N-COUNT An **interlude** is a short period of time during which an activity or event stops. ❑ *...a happy interlude in the Kents' life.*

Word Link ***med ≈ middle : intermediary, media, medium***

intermediary /ˌɪntəˈmiːdiəri/ (**intermediaries**) N-COUNT An **intermediary** is a person who passes messages between two people or groups.

intermediate /ˌɪntəˈmiːdiət/ **1** ADJ An **intermediate** stage or level is one that occurs between two other stages or levels. **2** ADJ **Intermediate students** are no longer beginners, but are not yet advanced.

interminable /ɪnˈtɜːmɪnəbəl/ ADJ If you describe something as **interminable**, you think it lasts too long and wish it would stop. ❑ *...an interminable wait of six hours.* • **interminably** ADV ❑ *The game went on, interminably it seemed.*

intermittent /ˌɪntəˈmɪtənt/ ADJ Something that is **intermittent** happens occasionally rather than continuously. ❑ *...three hours of intermittent rain.* • **intermittently** ADV ❑ *The talks went on intermittently for years.*

intern /ɪnˈtɜːn/ (**interns, interning, interned**) V-T If someone **is interned**, they are put in prison for political reasons. ❑ *He was interned as an enemy agent.*

Word Link ***inter ≈ between : interchange, interconnect, internal***

internal /ɪnˈtɜːnəl/ **1** ADJ BEFORE N You use **internal** to describe things that exist or happen inside a place or organization. ❑ *The country increased internal security.* ❑ *...the internal mailbox.* **2** ADJ BEFORE N **Internal** is used to describe things that exist or happen inside a particular person, object, or place. ❑ *The internal bleeding was severe.* • **internally** ADV ❑ *Internally, the army was out of control.*
→ see **engine**

international /ˌɪntəˈnæʃənəl/ ADJ **International** means between or involving different countries. ❑ *Let's look now at the international sports scene.* • **internationally** ADV ❑ *She's internationally famous.*

Internet /ˈɪntənet/ N-PROPER **The Internet** is the worldwide network of computer links which allows computer users to connect with computers all over the world. [COMPUTING]
→ see Word Web: **Internet**

ˈInternet ˌcafé (**Internet cafés**) N-COUNT An **Internet café** is a café with computers where people can pay to use the Internet. [COMPUTING]

interpersonal /ˌɪntəˈpɜːsənəl/ ADJ BEFORE N **Interpersonal** means relating to relationships between people. ❑ *...interpersonal skills.*

interpret /ɪnˈtɜːprɪt/ (**interprets, interpreting, interpreted**) **1** V-T/V-I If you **interpret** what someone is saying, you translate it immediately into another language. ❑ *I hired a local journalist to interpret for me.* **2** V-T If you **interpret** something in a particular way, you decide that this is its meaning. ❑ *The judge has to interpret the law for the court.* • **interpreter** (**interpreters**) N-COUNT ❑ *Interpreters and translators are employed by local authorities.*
→ see **dream**

interpretation /ɪnˌtɜːprɪˈteɪʃən/ (**interpretations**) **1** N-VAR An **interpretation** of

Word Web **Internet**

The **Internet** allows information to be shared by users around the world. The **World-Wide Web** allows users to access **servers** anywhere. **User names** and **passwords** give access and protect information. **E-mail** travels through **networks**. **Websites** are created by companies and individuals to share information. **Web pages** can include images, words, sound, and video. Some organizations built private **intranets**. These groups have to guard the **gateway** between their system and the larger Internet. **Hackers** can break into computer networks. They sometimes steal information or damage the system. **Webmasters** usually build firewalls for protection.

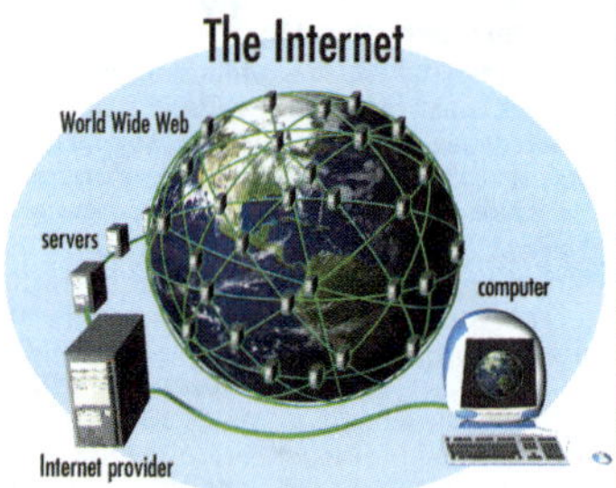

something is an opinion of what it means. ❑ *The Finance Minister put a different interpretation on the figures.* **2** N-VAR A performer's **interpretation of** a piece of music or a dance is the particular way in which they choose to perform it.
→ see **art**

interrogate /ɪn'terəgeɪt/ (**interrogates, interrogating, interrogated**) V-T If someone, especially a police officer, **interrogates** someone, they question him or her for a long time, in order to get information from you. • **interrogation** (**interrogations**) N-VAR ❑ *He confessed under interrogation.*

interrogative /ˌɪntə'rɒgətɪv/ N-SING A clause that is in **the interrogative** is in the form of a question.

Word Link	*rupt ≈ breaking : disrupt, erupt, interrupt*

interrupt /ˌɪntə'rʌpt/ (**interrupts, interrupting, interrupted**) **1** V-T/V-I If you **interrupt** someone who is speaking, you say or do something that causes them to stop. ❑ *They interrupted me every time I tried to say something.* ❑ *Turkin tapped him on the shoulder. 'Sorry to interrupt, Colonel.'* • **interruption** (**interruptions**) N-VAR ❑ *The sudden interruption stopped Linda in mid-sentence.* ❑ *...the constant telephone interruptions.* **2** V-T If someone or something **interrupts** a process or activity, they stop it for a period of time. ❑ *He has interrupted his holiday in Spain.* • **interruption** N-VAR ❑ *...interruptions in the supply of food.*

Word Link	*sect ≈ cutting : dissect, intersection, section*

intersection /ˌɪntə'sekʃən/ (**intersections**) N-COUNT An **intersection** is a place where roads cross each other. ❑ *...a busy motorway intersection.*

interspersed /ˌɪntə'spɜːst/ ADJ If one group of things are **interspersed with** or **among** another, the second things occur between or among the first things. ❑ *The bursts of gunfire were interspersed with single shots.*

interstate /'ɪntəsteɪt/ (**interstates**) **1** ADJ BEFORE N **Interstate** means between states, especially the states of the United States. ❑ *Her job involves a lot of interstate travel.* **2** N-COUNT In the US, an **interstate** is a major road linking states.

interval /'ɪntəvəl/ (**intervals**) **1** N-COUNT The **interval between** two events or dates is the period of time between them. ❑ *There was a long interval of silence.* **2** N-COUNT An **interval** during a play, concert, or game is a short break between two of the parts. **3** PHRASE If something happens **at intervals**, it happens several times with pauses in between. **4** PHRASE If things are placed **at** particular **intervals**, there are spaces of a particular size between them. ❑ *Red and white barriers marked the road at intervals of about a mile.*

intervene /ˌɪntə'viːn/ (**intervenes, intervening, intervened**) V-I If you **intervene in** a situation, you become involved in it and try to change it. ❑ *The Government is doing nothing to intervene in the crisis.* ❑ *The situation calmed down when police intervened.* • **intervention** /ˌɪntə'venʃən/ (**interventions**) N-VAR ❑ *...its intervention in the internal affairs of many countries.*

intervening /ˌɪntə'viːnɪŋ/ **1** ADJ BEFORE N An **intervening** period of time is one which separates two events or points in time. ❑ *I spent the intervening time in London.* **2** ADJ BEFORE N An **intervening** object or area comes between two other objects or areas.

interview /'ɪntəvjuː/ (**interviews, interviewing, interviewed**) **1** V-T & N-COUNT When an employer **interviews** you, or when you go for an **interview**, he or she asks you questions in order to find out whether you are suitable for a job. ❑ *He was interviewed for a management job.* ❑ *I had an interview for a job as a TV researcher.* **2** V-T & N-COUNT When a journalist **interviews** someone such as a famous person, they ask them a series of questions. This type of discussion is also called an **interview**. ❑ *...an interview with the American Vogue fashion editor.* • **interviewer** (**interviewers**) N-COUNT

Word Partnership	Use *interview* with:
N.	**job** interview **1** **magazine/newspaper/radio television** interview, **(tele)phone** interview **1** **2**
V.	**conduct an** interview, **give an** interview, **request an** interview **1** **2**

interviewee /ˌɪntəvjʊ'iː/ (**interviewees**) N-COUNT An **interviewee** is a person who is being interviewed.

intestine /ɪn'testɪn/ (**intestines**) N-COUNT Your **intestines** are the tubes in your body through which food from your stomach passes. • **intestinal** /ɪn'testɪnəl/ ADJ BEFORE N ❑ *...the intestinal wall.*

intimacy /'ɪntɪməsi/ N-UNCOUNT When there is **intimacy between** people, they have a close relationship. ❑ *They shared a few precious moments of intimacy.*

intimate (**intimates, intimating, intimated**)

adjective and noun /'ɪntɪmət/, verb /'ɪntɪmeɪt/

1 ADJ If two people have an **intimate** friendship, they are very good friends. • **intimately** ADV ❑ *He did not feel he knew them intimately.* **2** ADJ You use **intimate** to describe an occasion or the atmosphere of a place that you like because it is quiet and pleasant, and seems suitable for close conversations between friends. ❑ *...an intimate candlelit dinner for two.* **3** ADJ To be **intimate with** someone means to have a sexual relationship with them. • **intimately** ADV **4** ADJ If you have an **intimate knowledge of** something, you know it in great detail. ❑ *...their intimate knowledge of the motor industry.* • **intimately** ADV ❑ *...musicians whose work she knew intimately.* **5** V-T If you **intimate that** something is the case, you say it in an indirect way. [FORMAL] ❑ *He went on to intimate that he was thinking of selling the company.*

intimidate /ɪn'tɪmɪdeɪt/ (**intimidates, intimidating, intimidated**) V-T To **intimidate** someone means to frighten them, sometimes as a deliberate way of making them do something. ❑ *Attempts were made to intimidate people into voting for the governing party.* • **intimidated** ADJ ❑ *Women can come in here and not feel intimidated.* • **intimidating** ADJ ❑ *An intimidating atmosphere met them as they walked out into the stadium.* • **intimidation** N-UNCOUNT ❑ *...a campaign of intimidation against supporters of the prime minister.*

i

into /ɪntuː/

> In addition to the uses shown below, **into** is used with verbs of movement, such as 'walk into', and in phrasal verbs such as 'enter into'.

1 PREP If you go **into** a place or object, you go inside it. ❑ *I have no idea how he got into Iraq.* ❑ *She got into bed.* ❑ *Put them into a dish.* ❑ *The olives are packed into jars by hand.* **2** PREP If you **bump** or **crash into** something, you hit it accidentally. ❑ *The car hit the kerb and smashed into the barriers.* **3** PREP If you get **into** a piece of clothing, you put it on. ❑ *She changed into a different outfit.* **4** PREP If you get **into** a particular state, you start being in that state. ❑ *That got him into trouble.* ❑ *I slid into a depression.* **5** PREP If something changes **into** something else, it then has a new form, shape, or nature. ❑ *I turned a nasty moment into a bit of a joke.* **6** PREP An investigation **into** a subject or event is concerned with that subject or event. ❑ *...research into AIDS.* **7** PREP You use **into** with many verbs to do with persuading someone to do something. ❑ *Gerry tried to talk her into renting a flat in Paris.* **8** PREP If something is cut or split **into** a number of pieces or sections, it is divided so that it becomes several smaller pieces or sections. ❑ *Sixteen teams are taking part, divided into four groups.*

I

intolerable /ɪn'tɒlərəbəl/ ADJ If something is **intolerable**, it is so bad that no one can accept it. ❑ *This put intolerable pressure on them.* ● **intolerably** ADV ❑ *...intolerably hot conditions.*

intolerant /ɪn'tɒlərənt/ ADJ If you describe someone as **intolerant**, you mean that they do not accept behaviour and opinions that are different from their own; used showing disapproval. ❑ *He was intolerant of both suggestions and criticisms.* ● **intolerance** N-UNCOUNT ❑ *...his intolerance of anybody else's opinion.*

intoxicated /ɪn'tɒksɪkeɪtɪd/ **1** ADJ Someone who is **intoxicated** is drunk. [FORMAL] **2** ADJ If you are **intoxicated** by something, you are so excited that you find it hard to think clearly and sensibly. ❑ *They seem to be intoxicated by their success.*

intractable /ɪn'træktəbəl/ **1** ADJ **Intractable** people are very difficult to influence or control. [FORMAL] ❑ *He protested, but Jon was intractable.* **2** ADJ **Intractable** problems are very difficult to deal with. [FORMAL] ❑ *The situation has become intractable.*

intranet /'ɪntrənet/ (**intranets**) N-COUNT An **intranet** is a network of computers, similar to the Internet, within a company or organization. [COMPUTING]
→ see **Internet**

intransigent /ɪn'trænsɪdʒənt/ ADJ If you describe someone as **intransigent**, you mean that they refuse to change their behaviour or opinions; used showing disapproval. [FORMAL] ❑ *They put pressure on the Government to change its intransigent position.* ● **intransigence** N-UNCOUNT ❑ *He often appeared angry and frustrated by the intransigence of both sides.*

intransitive /ɪn'trænsɪtɪv/ ADJ An **intransitive** verb does not have an object.

intravenous /ˌɪntrə'viːnəs/ ADJ **Intravenous** foods or drugs are given to sick people through their veins, rather than their mouths. ❑ *...an intravenous drip.* ● **intravenously** ADV ❑ *Premature babies have to be fed intravenously.*

intrepid /ɪn'trepɪd/ ADJ An **intrepid** person acts bravely, ignoring difficulties and danger. ❑ *...an intrepid traveller.*

intricate /'ɪntrɪkət/ ADJ Something that is **intricate** has many small parts or details. ❑ *The cloth has an intricate pattern.* ● **intricately** ADV ❑ *...intricately carved sculptures.* ● **intricacy** N-UNCOUNT ❑ *...the richness and intricacy of medieval art.*

intrigue (**intrigues, intriguing, intrigued**) **1** N-VAR /'ɪntriːg/ **Intrigue** is the making of secret plans that are intended to harm or deceive other people. ❑ *...the plots and intrigues in the novel.* **2** V-T /ɪn'triːg/ If something **intrigues** you, you are fascinated by it and curious about it. ❑ *The job intrigued her greatly.* ● **intrigued** ADJ ❑ *I would be intrigued to hear others' views.*

intriguing /ɪn'triːgɪŋ/ ADJ If you describe someone or something as **intriguing**, you mean that they interest you and you are curious about them. ❑ *This intriguing book is both thoughtful and informative.* ● **intriguingly** ADV ❑ *The results are intriguingly different each time.*

intrinsic /ɪn'trɪnsɪk/ ADJ If something has **intrinsic** value or **intrinsic** interest, it is valuable or interesting because of its basic nature or character, and not because of its connection with other things. [FORMAL] ❑ *Diamonds have little intrinsic value.* ● **intrinsically** ADV ❑ *Sometimes I wonder if people are intrinsically evil.*

introduce /ˌɪntrə'djuːs, AM -'duːs/ (**introduces, introducing, introduced**) **1** V-T If you **introduce** one person **to** another, or if you **introduce** two people, you tell them each other's names, so that they can get to know each other. ❑ *Tim, may I introduce you to my uncle?* ❑ *Let me introduce myself.* **2** V-T To **introduce** something means to cause it to enter a place or exist in a system for the first time. ❑ *The word 'Pagoda' was introduced to Europe by the Portuguese.* **3** V-T If you **introduce** someone **to** something, you cause them to learn about it or to have their first experience of it. ❑ *He introduced her to literature.* **4** V-T The person who **introduces** a television or radio programme speaks at the beginning of it, and often between the different items in it, in order to explain what the programme or the items are about. ❑ *'Health Matters' is introduced by Dick Oliver.*

> **Word Partnership** Use *introduce* with:
>
> V. **allow me to** introduce, **let me** introduce, **want to** introduce **1**
>
> N. introduce **a bill**, introduce **changes**, introduce **legislation**, introduce **reform** **2**

introduction /ˌɪntrə'dʌkʃən/ (**introductions**) **1** N-VAR When you make an **introduction**, you tell two people each other's names so that they can get to know each other. **2** N-UNCOUNT The **introduction** of something into a place or system is the occasion when it enters the place or exists in the system for the first time. ❑ *...the introduction of student loans.* **3** N-SING Someone's **introduction to** something is the occasion when they experience it for the first time. ❑ *And that was my introduction to the oil fields.* **4** N-COUNT The **introduction** to a book or talk comes at the beginning and tells you what the rest of the book or talk is about. **5** N-COUNT If you refer to a book as an **introduction to** a particular subject, you mean that it explains the basic facts about it.

introductory /ˌɪntrəˈdʌktəri/ **1** ADJ An **introductory** remark, book, or course is intended to give you a general idea of a particular subject, often before more detailed information is given. **2** ADJ An **introductory offer** or **price** on a new product is something such as a free gift or a low price that is meant to attract new customers.

Word Link	*trude ≈ pushing : intrude, intruder, protrude*

intrude /ɪnˈtruːd/ (**intrudes, intruding, intruded**) V-I If you say that someone or something **is intruding into** a particular place or situation, you mean that they are not wanted or welcome there. ❑ *The press have been blamed for intruding into people's personal lives.* ❑ *I hope I'm not intruding.* ❑ *Personal feelings must not be allowed to intrude.*

intruder /ɪnˈtruːdə/ (**intruders**) N-COUNT An **intruder** is a person who enters a place without permission.

intrusion /ɪnˈtruːʒən/ (**intrusions**) N-VAR If you describe something as an **intrusion**, you mean that it disturbs you when you are in a private place or in a private situation. ❑ *I hope you don't mind this intrusion.* ❑ *He objects to the intrusion into his private life.*

intrusive /ɪnˈtruːsɪv/ ADJ Something that is **intrusive** disturbs your mood or your life. ❑ *He became violent towards intrusive photographers.*

intuition /ˌɪntjʊˈɪʃən, AM -tʊ-/ (**intuitions**) N-VAR Your **intuitions** are feelings you have that something is true even when you have no evidence or proof of it. ❑ *Her intuition told her that something was wrong.*

intuitive /ɪnˈtjuːətɪv, AM -ˈtuː-/ ADJ If you have an **intuitive** idea or feeling about something, you feel that it is true although you have no evidence or proof of it. ● **intuitively** ADV ❑ *He seemed to know intuitively that I was missing my mother.*

Inuit /ɪnjuɪt/ (**Inuit** or **Inuits**) N-COUNT The **Inuit** are a group of people whose ancestors were the original people of Eastern Canada and Greenland.

inundate /ˈɪnʌndeɪt/ (**inundates, inundating, inundated**) V-T If you **are inundated with** letters or demands, you receive so many that you cannot deal with them all. ❑ *They inundated me with fan letters.*

invade /ɪnˈveɪd/ (**invades, invading, invaded**) **1** V-T/V-I To **invade** a country means to enter it by force with an army. ● **invader** (**invaders**) N-COUNT ❑ *...action against a foreign invader.* **2** V-T If you say that people or animals **invade** a place, you mean that they enter it in large numbers, often in a way that is unpleasant or difficult to deal with. ❑ *Now and again the kitchen is invaded by ants.*

invalid (**invalids**) **1** N-COUNT /ˈɪnvəlɪd/ An **invalid** is someone who is very ill or disabled and needs to be cared for by someone else. **2** ADJ /ɪnˈvælɪd/ If an action, procedure, or document is **invalid**, it cannot be accepted, because it breaks the law or some official rule. ❑ *The results of the experiment were declared invalid.* **3** ADJ An **invalid** argument or conclusion is wrong because it is based on a mistake.

invaluable /ɪnˈvæljəbəl/ ADJ If you describe something as **invaluable**, you mean that it is extremely useful. ❑ *I was able to gain invaluable experience that year.*

invariably /ɪnˈveəriəbli/ ADV If something **invariably** happens or is **invariably** true, it always happens or is always true. ❑ *They almost invariably get it wrong.*

invasion /ɪnˈveɪʒən/ (**invasions**) **1** N-VAR If there is an **invasion** of a country, a foreign army enters it by force. ❑ *...the Roman invasion of Britain.* **2** N-UNCOUNT If you refer to the arrival of a large number of people or things as an **invasion**, you are emphasizing that they are unpleasant or difficult to deal with. ❑ *...the annual invasion of the house by flies.* **3** N-VAR If you describe an action as an **invasion**, you disapprove of it because it affects someone or something in a way that is not desirable. ❑ *Is reading a child's diary always an invasion of privacy?*

invent /ɪnˈvent/ (**invents, inventing, invented**) **1** V-T If you **invent** something, you are the first person to think of it or make it. ❑ *He invented the first electric clock.* ● **inventor** (**inventors**) N-COUNT ❑ *...Alexander Graham Bell, the inventor of the telephone.* **2** V-T If you **invent** a story or excuse, you try to persuade people that it is true when it is not. ❑ *I must invent something to tell my mother.*

invention /ɪnˈvenʃən/ (**inventions**) **1** N-COUNT An **invention** is a machine or system that has been invented by someone. ❑ *The spinning wheel was a Chinese invention.* **2** N-VAR If you refer to someone's account of something as an **invention**, you mean that it is not true and that they have made it up. ❑ *The story was pure invention.* **3** N-UNCOUNT **Invention** is the act of inventing something that has never been made or used before. ❑ *...the invention of the wheel.*

inventive /ɪnˈventɪv/ ADJ An **inventive** person is good at inventing things or has clever and original ideas. ❑ *She taught me to be more inventive with my cooking.* ● **inventiveness** N-UNCOUNT ❑ *He surprised us with his inventiveness.*

inventory /ˈɪnvəntri, AM -tɔːri/ (**inventories**) **1** N-COUNT An **inventory** is a written list of all the objects in a place. **2** N-COUNT An **inventory** is a supply or stock of something. [AM]

Word Link	*vert ≈ turning : convert, invert, revert*

invert /ɪnˈvɜːt/ (**inverts, inverting, inverted**) V-T If you **invert** something, you turn it upside down or back to front. [FORMAL] ❑ *Invert the cake onto a cooling rack.* ❑ *...an inverted triangle.*

inˌverted ˈcommas N-PLURAL In British English, **inverted commas** are the punctuation marks (' ') or (" ") which are used in writing to show where speech or a quotation begins and ends. The usual American term is **quotation marks**.

invest /ɪnˈvest/ (**invests, investing, invested**) **1** V-T/V-I If you **invest in** something, or if you **invest** a sum of money, you use your money in a way that you hope will increase its value, for example by buying shares or property. ❑ *They intend to invest directly in shares.* ❑ *He wants advice on how to invest the money.* ● **investor** (**investors**)

N-COUNT ❑ *It is likely that investors will face losses.* **2** V-I If you **invest in** something useful, you buy it because it will help you to do something more efficiently or more cheaply. ❑ *The company has invested in an electronic order-control system.* **3** V-T If you **invest** time or energy **in** something, you spend a lot of time or energy on something that you consider to be useful or likely to be successful. ❑ *She has invested all her energies in raising her children.*

investigate /ɪn'vestɪgeɪt/ (**investigates, investigating, investigated**) V-T/V-I If someone, especially an official, **investigates** an event or allegation, they try to find out what happened or what is the truth. ❑ *Police are still investigating how the accident happened.* ● **investigation** (**investigations**) N-VAR ❑ *He faces an investigation for failing to pay taxes.*

investigative /ɪn'vestɪgətɪv, AM -geɪt-/ ADJ **Investigative** work, especially journalism, involves investigating things. ❑ *...an investigative reporter.*

I

investigator /ɪn'vestɪgeɪtə/ (**investigators**) N-COUNT An **investigator** is someone who investigates things, especially as part of their job.

investment /ɪn'vesmənt/ (**investments**) **1** N-UNCOUNT **Investment** is the activity of investing money. ❑ *They are looking for pension and investment advice.* **2** N-COUNT An **investment** is an amount of money that you invest, or the thing that you invest it in. ❑ *This makes it easier to help you manage your investments.* ❑ *People buy houses as investments.* **3** N-COUNT If you describe something you buy as an **investment**, you mean that it will be useful, especially because it will help you to do a task more cheaply or efficiently. ❑ *A laptop can be a good investment.*

Word Link	*vig ≈ awake, strong : invigorating, vigil, vigilant*

invigorating /ɪn'vɪgəreɪtɪŋ/ ADJ Something that is **invigorating** makes you feel refreshed and more energetic. ❑ *...the invigorating northern air.*

Word Link	*vict, vinc ≈ conquering : convince, invincible, victorious*

invincible /ɪn'vɪnsɪbəl/ ADJ If you describe an army or a sports team as **invincible**, you believe that they cannot be defeated. ❑ *He knocked out the seemingly invincible Mike Tyson.*

invisible /ɪn'vɪzɪbəl/ **1** ADJ If something is **invisible**, you cannot see it, because it is hidden or because it is very small or faint. ❑ *The scar was almost invisible.* ● **invisibly** ADV ❑ *A thin line of smoke rose almost invisibly.* **2** ADJ If you say that a particular problem or situation is **invisible**, you are complaining that it is being ignored. ❑ *The problems of the poor are largely invisible.* ● **invisibility** N-UNCOUNT ❑ *...the invisibility of women in that society.*
→ see **sun**

invitation /ˌɪnvɪ'teɪʃən/ (**invitations**) **1** N-COUNT An **invitation** is a written or spoken request to come to an event such as a party or a meeting. ❑ *The Syrians have not yet accepted an invitation to attend.* **2** N-COUNT An **invitation** is the card or paper on which an invitation is written or printed. **3** N-SING If you believe that someone's action is likely to have a particular result, especially a bad one, you can refer to the action as an **invitation to** that result. ❑ *Don't leave your shopping on the back seat of your car – it's an open invitation to a thief.*

Word Partnership	Use *invitation* with:
V.	**accept an** invitation, **decline an** invitation, **extend an** invitation **1** **get/receive an** invitation **1** **2**

invite (**invites, inviting, invited**) **1** V-T /ɪn'vaɪt/ If you **invite** someone **to** something such as a party or a meal, you ask them to come to it. ❑ *She invited him to her birthday party.* ❑ *I invited her in for a coffee.* ❑ *Bob invited her to join him at the races.* **2** V-T If you **are invited to** do something, you are formally asked to do it. ❑ *The officials will be invited to explain their reasoning.* **3** V-T If something you say or do **invites trouble** or **criticism**, it makes trouble or criticism more likely. ❑ *Their refusal to compromise will invite more criticism from the UN.* **4** N-COUNT /'ɪnvaɪt/ An **invite** is an invitation to something such as a party or a meal. [INFORMAL]

Word Partnership	Use *invite* with:
N.	invite ***someone* to dinner**, invite **friends**, invite **people** **1** invite **criticism**, invite **questions** **3**

inviting /ɪn'vaɪtɪŋ/ ADJ If you say that something is **inviting**, you mean it has qualities that attract you. ❑ *The February air was cool and inviting.* ● **invitingly** ADV ❑ *The waters of the tropics are invitingly clear.*

invoice /'ɪnvɔɪs/ (**invoices, invoicing, invoiced**) **1** N-COUNT An **invoice** is an official document that lists goods or services that you have received and says how much money you owe for them. **2** V-T If you **invoice** someone, you send them an invoice.

invoke /ɪn'vəʊk/ (**invokes, invoking, invoked**) **1** V-T If you **invoke** a law, you state that you are taking a particular action because that law allows you to. ❑ *The judge invoked an international law that protects refugees.* **2** V-T If you **invoke** something such as a saying or a famous person, you refer to them in order to support your argument. ❑ *Adam Smith's name is frequently invoked by economists.*

Word Link	*vol ≈ will : benevolent, involuntary, volunteer*

involuntary /ɪn'vɒləntri, AM -teri/ ADJ If you make an **involuntary** movement or sound, you make it suddenly and without intending to. ❑ *The involuntary shaking is caused by his illness.* ● **involuntarily** /ɪn'vɒləntrəli, AM -'terɪli/ ADV ❑ *I smiled involuntarily.*
→ see **muscle**

involve /ɪn'vɒlv/ (**involves, involving, involved**) **1** V-T If an activity **involves** something, that thing is a necessary part of it. ❑ *Nicky's job involves spending a lot of time with other people.* **2** V-T If a situation or activity **involves** someone, they are taking part in it. ❑ *The riot involved a hundred prisoners.* **3** V-T If you **involve** someone **in** something, you get them to take part in it. ❑ *Before long he started involving me in other aspects of the job.*

involved /ɪn'vɒlvd/ **1** ADJ AFTER LINK-V If

you are **involved in** a situation or activity, you are taking part in it or have a strong connection with it. ❑ *...an organisation for people involved in agriculture.* 2 ADJ AFTER LINK-V The things **involved** in something such as a job or system are the necessary parts of it. ❑ *Let's take a look at some of the figures involved.* 3 ADJ If a situation or activity is **involved**, it is very complicated. 4 ADJ AFTER LINK-V If one person is **involved with** another, especially someone they are not married to, they are having a close relationship. ❑ *He became romantically involved with a married woman.*

involvement /ɪn'vɒlvmənt/ N-UNCOUNT Your **involvement in** something is the fact that you are taking part in it. ❑ *You have no proof of my involvement in anything.* ❑ *She disliked his involvement with the group.*

Word Link	*ward ≈ in the direction of* : **backward, forward, inward**

inward /'ɪnwəd/ 1 ADJ BEFORE N Your **inward** thoughts or feelings are the ones that you do not express or show to other people. ❑ *I sighed with inward relief.* ● **inwardly** ADV ❑ *I stayed polite, but inwardly I was furious.* 2 ADJ BEFORE N An **inward** movement is one towards the inside or centre of something. ❑ *...a sharp, inward breath.*

inwards /'ɪnwədz/

The form **inward** is also used. In American English, **inward** is more usual.

ADV If something moves or faces **inwards**, it moves or faces towards the inside or centre of something. ❑ *She pressed back against the door until it swung inwards.*

iodine /'aɪədi:n, AM -daɪn/ N-UNCOUNT **Iodine** is a dark-coloured substance used in medicine to clean wounds and in photography.

IP address /aɪ 'pi: əˌdres, AM ˌædres/ (**IP addresses**) N-COUNT An **IP address** is a series of numbers that identifies which particular computer or network is connected to the Internet. **IP** is an abbreviation for 'Internet Protocol'. [COMPUTING]

iPod /'aɪpɒd/ (**iPods**) N-COUNT An **iPod** is a portable MP3 player that can play music downloaded from the Internet. IPod is a trademark. [COMPUTING]

IQ /ˌaɪ 'kju:/ (**IQs**) N-VAR Your **IQ** is your level of intelligence, as indicated by a special test. **IQ** is an abbreviation for 'Intelligence Quotient'. ❑ *His IQ is above average.*

irate /aɪ'reɪt/ ADJ If someone is **irate**, they are very angry about something. ❑ *Bob was irate, shouting and swearing about the flight delay.*

iris /'aɪərɪs/ (**irises**) 1 N-COUNT The **iris** is the round coloured part of a person's eye. 2 N-COUNT An **iris** is a tall plant with long leaves and large purple, yellow, or white flowers.
→ see **eye, muscle**

iron /aɪən/ (**irons, ironing, ironed**) 1 N-UNCOUNT **Iron** is an element which usually takes the form of a hard, dark-grey metal. ❑ *...the huge, iron gate.* 2 ADJ BEFORE N You can use **iron** to describe the character or behaviour of someone who is very firm in their decisions and actions. ❑ *...a man of iron will.* 3 N-COUNT An **iron** is an electrical device with a flat metal base. You heat

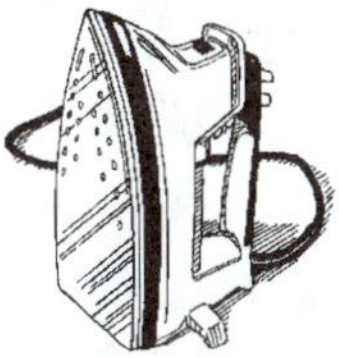

iron

it until the base is hot, then rub it over clothes to remove creases. 4 V-T If you **iron** clothes, you remove the creases from them using an iron. ❑ *...a freshly ironed shirt.* ● **ironing** N-UNCOUNT ❑ *I managed to get all the ironing done.* 5 → see also **cast-iron** ▸ **iron out** PHR-VERB If you **iron out** difficulties, you deal with them and bring them to an end.

Word Partnership	Use *iron* with:
N.	iron **bar**, iron **gate** 1
	an iron **fist/hand** 2
	iron **a shirt** 4
ADJ.	**cast** iron, **wrought** iron 1
	a hot iron 3

ironic /aɪ'rɒnɪk/ 1 ADJ When you make an **ironic** remark, you say something that you do not mean, as a joke. ❑ *People used to call me Mr Popularity at secondary school, but they were being ironic.* ● **ironically** ADV ❑ *'A very good year for women!' she said ironically.* 2 ADJ An **ironic** situation is strange or amusing because it is the opposite of what you expect. ❑ *I always wanted to be a dancer, which is ironic, because I can't dance at all!* ● **ironically** ADV ❑ *Ironically, for a man who hated war, he made a great war photographer.*

irony /'aɪrəni/ (**ironies**) 1 N-UNCOUNT **Irony** is a form of humour which involves saying things that you do not mean. ❑ *There was no irony in his voice.* 2 N-VAR The **irony** of a situation is an aspect of it which is strange or amusing, because it is the opposite of what you expect. ❑ *The irony is this document may become more available in the US than in Britain where it was published.*

Word Link	*ir ≈ not* : **irrational, irregular, irrelevant**

Word Link	*ratio ≈ reasoning* : **irrational, rational, rationale**

irrational /ɪ'ræʃənəl/ ADJ **Irrational** feelings or behaviour are not based on logical reasons or thinking. ❑ *An irrational fear is called a phobia.* ● **irrationally** ADV ❑ *He is in a disturbed state of mind and could act irrationally.* ● **irrationality** N-UNCOUNT

irreconcilable /ɪˌrekən'saɪləbəl/ 1 ADJ If two things such as opinions or proposals are **irreconcilable**, they are so different from each other that it is not possible to have them both. [FORMAL] ❑ *These old concepts are irreconcilable with modern life.* 2 ADJ An **irreconcilable** disagreement is so serious that it cannot be settled. [FORMAL] ❑ *...an irreconcilable clash of personalities.*

irregular /ɪ'regjʊlə/ 1 ADJ If events or actions occur at **irregular** intervals, the periods of time between them are of different lengths. ❑ *She was taken to hospital suffering from an irregular heartbeat.* ❑ *He works irregular hours.* ● **irregularly** ADV ❑ *The headaches occur irregularly and without warning.* ● **irregularity** /ɪˌregjʊ'lærɪti/ (**irregularities**) N-VAR ❑ *...a dangerous irregularity in her heartbeat.* 2 ADJ Something that is **irregular** is not smooth or straight, or does not form a regular pattern. ❑ *The paint dried in irregular patches.* ● **irregularly** ADV ❑ *...the irregularly shaped lake.* **3** ADJ **Irregular** behaviour is unusual and often dishonest. ❑ *The minister is accused of irregular business practices.* ● **irregularity** N-VAR ❑ *They received reports of voting irregularities.*

Word Link *ir ≈ not : irrational, irregular, irrelevant*

irrelevant /ɪ'relɪvənt/ ADJ If you say that something is **irrelevant**, you mean that it is not important to or not connected with the present situation or discussion. ❑ *He either ignored questions or gave irrelevant answers.* ❑ *He said politics has become increasingly irrelevant to most Americans.* ● **irrelevance** N-SING

irresistible /ˌɪrɪ'zɪstɪbəl/ **1** ADJ If your wish to do something is **irresistible**, it is so powerful that you cannot prevent yourself doing it. ❑ *He experienced an irresistible need to yawn.* ● **irresistibly** ADV ❑ *He found himself being irresistibly drawn to Gail's home.* **2** ADJ If you describe something or someone as **irresistible**, you mean that they are so good or attractive that you cannot stop yourself from liking them or wanting them. ❑ *What is it about Tim that you find so irresistible?* ● **irresistibly** ADV ❑ *She had a charm which men found irresistibly attractive.*

irrespective /ˌɪrɪ'spektɪv/ PREP If something is true or happens **irrespective of** other things, those things do not affect it. [FORMAL] ❑ *This service should be available to everybody, irrespective of whether they can afford it.*

irresponsible /ˌɪrɪ'spɒnsɪbəl/ ADJ If you describe someone as **irresponsible**, you are criticizing them because they do things without properly considering their possible consequences. ❑ *Many people have an irresponsible attitude towards marriage.* ● **irresponsibly** ADV ❑ *They have behaved irresponsibly.* ● **irresponsibility** N-UNCOUNT ❑ *She was embarrassed by her son's irresponsibility.*

Word Link *vere ≈ fear, awe : irreverent, revere, reverence*

irreverent /ɪ'revərənt/ ADJ If you describe someone as **irreverent**, you mean that they do not show respect for people or things that are generally respected. ● **irreverence** N-UNCOUNT ❑ *...his irreverence for authority.*

irreversible /ˌɪrɪ'vɜːsɪbəl/ ADJ If a change is **irreversible**, things cannot be changed back to the way they were before. ❑ *She suffered irreversible brain damage.*

irrevocable /ɪ'revəkəbəl/ ADJ Actions or decisions that are **irrevocable** cannot be stopped or changed. [FORMAL] ❑ *His mother's death was an irrevocable loss.* ● **irrevocably** ADV ❑ *My relationships with friends have been irrevocably altered.*

irrigate /'ɪrɪgeɪt/ (**irrigates, irrigating, irrigated**) V-T To **irrigate** land means to supply it with water in order to help crops to grow. ❑ *The water from the lake is used to irrigate the area.* ● **irrigation** N-UNCOUNT ❑ *...a sophisticated irrigation system.*
→ see **dam**

irritable /'ɪrɪtəbəl/ ADJ If you are **irritable**, you are easily annoyed. ❑ *He had missed his dinner, and grew irritable.* ● **irritably** ADV ❑ *'Why are you whispering?' he asked irritably.* ● **irritability** N-UNCOUNT ❑ *She showed no sign of irritability.*

irritant /'ɪrɪtənt/ (**irritants**) **1** N-COUNT If you describe something as an **irritant**, you mean that it keeps annoying you. [FORMAL] ❑ *He said the issue was a major irritant.* **2** N-COUNT An **irritant** is a substance which causes a part of your body to become painful or itchy. [FORMAL]

irritate /'ɪrɪteɪt/ (**irritates, irritating, irritated**) **1** V-T If something **irritates** you, it keeps annoying you. ❑ *Her high voice really irritated Maria.* ● **irritated** ADJ ❑ *Her teacher is getting irritated with her.* **2** → See note at **angry** ● **irritating** ADJ ❑ *...his irritating habit of interrupting.* ● **irritatingly** ADV ❑ *The question stays irritatingly unanswered.* **3** V-T If something **irritates** a part of your body, it causes it to itch or be painful. ❑ *Skin is easily irritated.*

irritation /ˌɪrɪ'teɪʃən/ (**irritations**) **1** N-UNCOUNT **Irritation** is a feeling of annoyance. ❑ *He tried not to let his irritation show.* **2** N-COUNT An **irritation** is something that keeps annoying you. ❑ *He describes the tourists as an irritation.* **3** N-UNCOUNT **Irritation** in your skin or eyes is a feeling of soreness or itching there.

is /ɪz/ **Is** is the third person singular of the present tense of **be**.

Islam /'ɪzlɑːm, AM ɪs'lɑːm/ N-UNCOUNT **Islam** is the religion of the Muslims, which teaches that there is only one God and that Mohammed is His prophet. ● **Islamic** /ɪz'læmɪk/ ADJ ❑ *...Islamic law.*

island /'aɪlənd/ (**islands**) N-COUNT An **island** is a piece of land that is completely surrounded by water. ❑ *...the beautiful island of Gozo.* ❑ *We spent a day on Caldey Island.*
→ see **land**

islander /'aɪləndə/ (**islanders**) N-COUNT **Islanders** are people who live on an island.

isle /aɪl/ (**isles**) N-COUNT **Isle** is used in the names of some islands. ❑ *...the Isle of Man.*

isn't /'ɪzənt/ **Isn't** is the usual spoken form of 'is not'.

isolate /'aɪsəleɪt/ (**isolates, isolating, isolated**) V-T To **isolate** someone or something means to make them become separate from other people or things of the same kind, either physically or socially. ❑ *We can use genetic engineering techniques to isolate the gene.* ● **isolated** ADJ ❑ *They are finding themselves increasingly isolated within the teaching profession.* ● **isolation** N-UNCOUNT ❑ *...the public isolation of the Prime Minister.*

isolated /'aɪsəleɪtɪd/ **1** ADJ An **isolated** place is a long way away from large towns and is difficult to reach. ❑ *Aubrey's family's farm is very isolated.* **2** ADJ BEFORE N An **isolated example** is an example of something that is not very common. ❑ *...an isolated case of cheating.*

isolation /ˌaɪsə'leɪʃən/ **1** PHRASE If you do something **in isolation**, you do it without other people being present or without their help.
2 → see also **isolate**

ISP /ˌaɪ es 'piː/ (**ISPs**) N-COUNT An **ISP** is a company that provides Internet and e-mail services. **ISP** is an abbreviation for 'Internet service provider'. [COMPUTING]

issue /'ɪsjuː, 'ɪʃuː/ (**issues, issuing, issued**) **1** N-COUNT An **issue** is an important subject that people are arguing about or discussing. ❑ *...the issue of human rights.* ❑ *Is it right for the Church to* *express a view on political issues?* 2 N-COUNT An **issue** of a magazine or newspaper is a particular edition of it. ❑ *...the latest issue of the 'Lancet'.* 3 N-SING If something is **the issue**, it is the thing you consider to be the most important part of a situation or discussion. ❑ *Although we were arguing about money, that was not the real issue.* ❑ *She avoided the issue.* 4 V-T If someone **issues** a statement, they make it formally or publicly. ❑ *His kidnappers issued a second threat to kill him.* 5 V-T If you **are issued with** something, it is officially given to you. ❑ *Staff will be issued with new uniforms.* 6 PHRASE If you **have issues** with a particular aspect of your life, you have problems connected with it. ❑ *The group talked through their issues with food.* 7 PHRASE The question or point **at issue** is the question or point that is being argued about or discussed. ❑ *The point at issue is who controls the company.* 8 PHRASE If you **make an issue of** something, you try to make other people think about it or discuss it, because you are concerned or annoyed about it. ❑ *It seemed the Colonel had no desire to make an issue of the affair.*

→ see **philosophy**

it /ɪt/

> **It** is used as the subject of a verb or as the object of a verb or preposition.

1 PRON You use **it** to refer to an object, animal, or other thing that has already been mentioned, or to a situation that you have just described. ❑ *He saw the silver car down the road. It was more than a hundred yards from him.* ❑ *Antonia will not be jealous, or if she is, she will not show it.* 2 PRON You use **it** before certain nouns, adjectives, and verbs to introduce your feelings or point of view about a situation. ❑ *It was nice to see Steve again.* ❑ *It's a pity you never got married, Sarah.* 3 PRON You use **it** in passive clauses which report a situation or event. ❑ *It has been said that life begins at 40.* 4 PRON You use **it** to say what the time, day, or date is. ❑ *It's three o'clock in the morning.* ❑ *It was a Monday.* 5 PREP You use **it** to describe the weather, the light, or the temperature. ❑ *It was very wet and windy.* ❑ *It's getting dark. Let's go inside.* 6 PRON You use **it** when you are telling someone who you are, or asking them who they are. ❑ *'Who is it?' he called.* ❑ *Hello Freddy, it's only me, Maxine.* 7 PREP When you are emphasizing or drawing attention to something, you can put that thing immediately after **it** and a form of the verb 'be'. ❑ *It's my father they want.*

italic /ɪˈtælɪk/ (**italics**) N-PLURAL & ADJ **Italics** or **italic** letters are letters which slope to the right. They can be used to emphasize particular words. The examples in this dictionary are printed in italics.

itch /ɪtʃ/ (**itches, itching, itched**) 1 V-I & N-COUNT If you **itch**, or if a part of your body **itches**, you have an unpleasant feeling on your skin, called an **itch**, that makes you want to scratch. ❑ *His body itched from head to toe.* ❑ *Scratch my back – I've got an itch.* ● **itching** N-UNCOUNT ❑ *The itching is caused by contact with certain plants.* ● **itchy** ADJ ❑ *...itchy, sore eyes.* 2 V-T & N-SING If you are **itching to** do something, or if you have an **itch to** do something, you are very eager or impatient to do it. [INFORMAL] ❑ *I was itching to get involved.* ❑ *...those with an itch to be rich.*

it'd /ɪtəd/ **It'd** is a spoken form of 'it had', especially when 'had' is an auxiliary. **It'd** is also a spoken form of 'it would'. ❑ *It'd just started.* ❑ *It'd be fun to have a party.*

item /ˈaɪtəm/ (**items**) 1 N-COUNT An **item** is one of a collection or list of objects. ❑ *The most valuable item on show will be a Picasso drawing.* 2 N-COUNT An **item** is one of a list of things for someone to do, deal with, or talk about. ❑ *The other item on the agenda is the concert.*

Thesaurus	*item* Also look up:
N.	issue, subject, task 2

itinerary /aɪˈtɪnərəri, AM -eri/ (**itineraries**) N-COUNT An **itinerary** is a plan of a journey, including the route and the places that will be visited. ❑ *The next place on our itinerary was Silistra.*

it'll /ɪtəl/ **It'll** is a spoken form of 'it will'. ❑ *It'll be nice to meet her.*

its /ɪts/ DET You use **its** to indicate that something belongs or relates to a thing, place, or animal that has just been mentioned or whose identity is known. ❑ *The British Labour Party concludes its annual conference today.*

> **Usage**
>
> Do not confuse **its** and **it's**. **Its** means 'belonging to it'. **It's** is short for 'it is' or 'it has'. ❑ *The horse raised its head.* ❑ *It's hot in here.* ❑ *It's stopped raining.*

it's /ɪts/ **It's** is a spoken form of 'it is' or 'it has', especially when 'has' is an auxiliary verb.

itself /ɪtˈself/ 1 PRON You use **itself** as the object of a verb or preposition when it refers to something that is the same thing as the subject of the verb. ❑ *The body rebuilds itself while we sleep.* ❑ *The back part of the chair bends double and folds into itself.* 2 PRON You use **itself** to emphasize the thing you are referring to. ❑ *I think life itself is a learning process.* 3 PRON If you say that someone is, for example, politeness **itself** or kindness **itself**, you are emphasizing they are extremely polite or extremely kind.

I've /aɪv/ **I've** is the usual spoken form of 'I have', especially when 'have' is an auxiliary verb. ❑ *I think I've got something in my eye.*

IVF /ˌaɪ viː ˈef/ N-UNCOUNT **IVF** is a method of helping a woman to have a baby by fertilizing an egg outside her body. **IVF** is an abbreviation for 'in vitro fertilization'.

ivory /ˈaɪvəri/ N-UNCOUNT **Ivory** is a valuable type of bone, which forms the tusks of an elephant. ❑ *...ivory carvings.*

ivy /ˈaɪvi/ N-UNCOUNT **Ivy** is an evergreen plant that grows up walls or along the ground.

i

Jj

jab /dʒæb/ (**jabs, jabbing, jabbed**) **1** V-T/V-I If you **jab** something, you push it with a quick sudden movement. ❑ *The doctor jabbed a needle into the baby's arm.* ❑ *He jabbed at me with his finger.* **2** N-COUNT A **jab** is an injection to prevent illness. [BRIT, INFORMAL]

jack

jack /dʒæk/ (**jacks, jacking, jacked**) **1** N-COUNT A **jack** is a device for lifting a heavy object such as a car off the ground. **2** N-COUNT A **jack** is a playing card whose value is between a ten and a queen.
▶ **jack up** PHR-VERB If you say that someone or something **jacks up** a price or amount, you mean it rises to an unreasonable level. [INFORMAL] ❑ *Six Arab nations jacked up ticket prices nearly 100%.*

jacket /ˈdʒækɪt/ (**jackets**) **1** N-COUNT A **jacket** is a short coat. **2** → see also **lifejacket** **3** N-COUNT The **jacket** of a book is the paper cover that protects it.
→ see **clothing**

jackpot /ˈdʒækpɒt/ (**jackpots**) N-COUNT A **jackpot** is a large sum of money which is the most valuable prize in a game or lottery.

Jacuzzi /dʒəˈkuːzi/ (**Jacuzzis**) N-COUNT A **Jacuzzi** is a large round bath which is fitted with a device that makes the water bubble. **Jacuzzi** is a trademark.

jade /dʒeɪd/ N-UNCOUNT **Jade** is a hard green type of stone used for making jewellery and ornaments.

jaded /ˈdʒeɪdɪd/ ADJ If you are **jaded**, you have no enthusiasm because you are tired and bored.

jagged /ˈdʒægɪd/ ADJ Something that is **jagged** has a rough uneven shape or edge with lots of sharp points. ❑ *...a piece of metal with jagged edges.*

jail /dʒeɪl/ (**jails, jailing, jailed**) **1** N-VAR A **jail** is a building where criminals are kept in order to punish them. ❑ *He spent six months in jail.* **2** V-T If someone **is jailed**, they are put in jail.

jam /dʒæm/ (**jams, jamming, jammed**) **1** N-VAR **Jam** is a food that you spread on bread, made by cooking fruit with a large amount of sugar. The usual American word is **jelly**. **2** V-T If you **jam** something somewhere, you push it there roughly. ❑ *Pete jammed his hands into his pockets.* **3** V-T/V-I If something **jams**, or if you **jam** it, it becomes fixed in one position and cannot move freely or work properly. ❑ *His gun jammed the second time he fired.* ❑ *Gently remove the jammed paper from the printer.* **4** V-T To **jam** a radio or electronic signal means to interfere with it and prevent it from being received or heard clearly. ● **jamming** N-UNCOUNT ❑ *The plane is used for electronic jamming.* **5** V-T/V-I If a lot of people **jam** a place, or if they **jam into** it, they are packed tightly together and can hardly move. ❑ *Thousands of people jammed the streets.* ❑ *They jammed into buses provided by the Red Cross.* ● **jammed** ADJ ❑ *The stadium was jammed.* **6** N-COUNT If there is a **jam** on a road, there are so many vehicles that they cannot move. **7** N-SING If you are **in a jam**, you are in a very difficult situation. [INFORMAL]
→ see **traffic**

Word Partnership	Use *jam* with:
N.	jam **jar**, **strawberry** jam **1** **traffic** jam **6**

jangle /ˈdʒæŋgəl/ (**jangles, jangling, jangled**) V-T/V-I & N-COUNT If metal objects **jangle**, or if they **are jangled**, they hit each other and make an unpleasant ringing noise, called a **jangle**. ❑ *I jangled the keys in my pocket.*

janitor /ˈdʒænɪtə/ (**janitors**) N-COUNT A **janitor** is a person whose job is to look after a building. The British term is **caretaker**. [AM]

January /ˈdʒænjəri, AM -jʊeri/ (**Januaries**) N-VAR **January** is the first month of the year. ❑ *They got married last January.*

jar

jar /dʒɑː/ (**jars, jarring, jarred**) **1** N-COUNT A **jar** is a glass container with a lid, used for storing food. ❑ *...two jars of coffee.* **2** V-I If something **jars on** you, you find it unpleasant or shocking. ❑ *Sometimes a light remark jarred on her father.* ● **jarring** ADJ ❑ *...jarring, over-the-top behaviour.* **3** V-T/V-I If an object **jars**, or if something **jars** it, the object moves with a fairly hard shaking movement. ❑ *Tony jarred his knee while he was playing football.*
→ see **container**

jargon /ˈdʒɑːgən/ N-UNCOUNT **Jargon** consists of words and expressions that are used in special or technical ways by particular groups of people, often making the language difficult to understand. ❑ *...the latest business jargon.*

jaunty /ˈdʒɔːnti/ (**jauntier, jauntiest**) ADJ If you describe someone or something as **jaunty**, you mean that they are full of confidence and energy. ❑ *...a jaunty novel about a trip to the seaside.* ● **jauntily** ADV ❑ *He walked jauntily into the café.*

javelin /ˈdʒævlɪn/ (**javelins**) **1** N-COUNT A **javelin** is a long spear that is thrown in sports competitions. **2** N-SING You can refer to the competition in which the javelin is thrown as **the javelin**.

jaw /dʒɔː/ (**jaws**) **1** N-COUNT Your **jaw** is the part of your face below your mouth and cheeks. **2** N-COUNT A person's or animal's **jaws** or **jawbones** are the two bones in their head which their teeth are attached to.

jazz /dʒæz/ N-UNCOUNT **Jazz** is a style of music invented by black American musicians in the early part of the twentieth century. It has very strong rhythms and the musicians often improvise.
→ see **genre**

jealous /ˈdʒeləs/ **1** ADJ If someone is **jealous**, they feel angry or bitter because they think that another person is trying to take a lover, friend, or possession, away from them. ❑ *She was jealous of her husband's friendship with their son.* ● **jealously** ADV ❑ *It is a jealously guarded secret.* **2** ADJ If you are **jealous of** another person's possessions or qualities, you feel angry or bitter because you do not have them. ❑ *You're jealous because they didn't like your idea.* ❑ *She was jealous of his well-paid job.* ● **jealously** ADV ❑ *Gloria watched them jealously.*

jealousy /ˈdʒeləsi/ (**jealousies**) N-VAR **Jealousy** is the feeling of anger or bitterness which someone has when they think that another person is trying to take a lover, friend, or possession, away from them, or when they wish that they could have the qualities or possessions that another person has. ❑ *He could not control his jealousy when he saw her new husband.* ❑ *Her beauty causes envy and jealousy.*

jeans /dʒiːnz/ N-PLURAL **Jeans** are casual trousers that are usually made of strong blue denim. You can also say **a pair of jeans**.
→ see **clothing**

Jeep /dʒiːp/ (**Jeeps**) N-COUNT A **Jeep** is a small four-wheeled vehicle that can travel over rough ground. **Jeep** is a trademark.

jeer /dʒɪə/ (**jeers, jeering, jeered**) **1** V-T/V-I If people **jeer at** someone or **jeer** someone, they show that they do not respect them by saying rude and insulting things to them. ❑ *The angry crowds jeered him.* ❑ *Protestors jeered at the passers-by.* ● **jeering** N-UNCOUNT ❑ *There was constant jeering during the football match.* **2** N-COUNT **Jeers** are the rude and insulting things which people shout in order to show that they do not respect someone.

jell /dʒel/ → see **gel**

jelly /ˈdʒeli/ (**jellies**) **1** N-VAR **Jelly** is a transparent food made from gelatine, fruit juice, and sugar, which is eaten as a dessert. [BRIT] **2** N-VAR **Jelly** is a food that you spread on bread, made by cooking fruit with a large amount of sugar. The British word is **jam**.
→ see **dessert**

jeopardize [BRIT also **jeopardise**] /ˈdʒepədaɪz/ (**jeopardizes, jeopardizing, jeopardized**) V-T If someone or something **jeopardizes** a situation or activity, they do something that may destroy it or cause it to fail. ❑ *The bad weather could jeopardize the race.*

jeopardy /ˈdʒepədi/ PHRASE If someone or something is **in jeopardy**, they are in a dangerous situation. ❑ *A series of setbacks have put the whole project in jeopardy.*

jerk /dʒɜːk/ (**jerks, jerking, jerked**) V-T/V-I & N-COUNT If you **jerk** something or someone, or if they **jerk** in a particular direction, they move a short distance very suddenly and quickly. A **jerk** is a short sudden movement. ❑ *He jerked his head in my direction.* ❑ *The car jerked to a halt.* ❑ *He showed me the bathroom with a jerk of his head.*

jerky /ˈdʒɜːki/ (**jerkier, jerkiest**) ADJ **Jerky** movements are very sudden and abrupt and do not flow smoothly. ❑ *Do not make any jerky movements near wild animals.* ● **jerkily** ADV ❑ *He moved jerkily towards the car.*

jersey /ˈdʒɜːzi/ (**jerseys**) **1** N-COUNT A **jersey** is a knitted piece of clothing that covers the upper part of your body and your arms. [DATED] **2** N-UNCOUNT **Jersey** is a knitted fabric used especially to make women's clothing. ❑ *...a black jersey top.*

Jesus /ˈdʒiːzəs/ N-PROPER **Jesus** or **Jesus Christ** is the name of the man who Christians believe was the son of God, and whose teachings are the basis of Christianity.

jet /dʒet/ (**jets, jetting, jetted**) **1** N-COUNT A **jet** is an aeroplane that is powered by jet engines. **2** V-I If you **jet** somewhere, you travel there in a fast aeroplane. ❑ *Val is jetting off to Jamaica tomorrow.* **3** N-COUNT A **jet of** liquid or gas is a strong, fast, thin stream of it. ❑ *...a jet of water.*
→ see **fly**

ˌjet ˈengine (**jet engines**) N-COUNT A **jet engine** works by pushing hot air and gases out at the back.

ˈjet ˌlag or **jetlag** N-UNCOUNT If you are suffering from **jet lag**, you feel tired and slightly confused after a long journey by aeroplane.

ˈjet ˌski or **jet-ski** (**jet skis**) N-COUNT A **jet ski** is a small machine like a motorcycle that is powered by a jet engine and can travel on the surface of water. **Jet ski** is a trademark.

jettison /ˈdʒetɪsən/ (**jettisons, jettisoning, jettisoned**) V-T If someone **jettisons** something that is not needed, they throw it away or get rid of it. ❑ *The pilot jettisoned the extra fuel.* ❑ *The Government has jettisoned the plan.*

jetty /ˈdʒeti/ (**jetties**) N-COUNT A **jetty** is a wide stone wall or wooden platform where boats stop to let people get on and off, or to load or unload goods.

Jew /dʒuː/ (**Jews**) N-COUNT A **Jew** is a person who believes in and practises the religion of Judaism.

jewel /ˈdʒuːəl/ (**jewels**) N-COUNT A **jewel** is a precious stone used to decorate valuable things such as rings or necklaces. ❑ *The jewels in the collection include sapphires and a huge diamond.*

jeweller [AM **jeweler**] /ˈdʒuːələ/ (**jewellers**) **1** N-COUNT A **jeweller** is a person who makes, sells, and repairs jewellery and watches. **2** N-COUNT A **jeweller** or a **jeweller's** is a shop where jewellery and watches are made, sold, and repaired.

jewellery [AM **jewelry**] /ˈdʒuːəlri/ N-UNCOUNT **Jewellery** consists of ornaments that people wear such as rings and bracelets.
→ see Picture Dictionary: **jewellery**

Jewish /dʒuːɪʃ/ ADJ **Jewish** means belonging or relating to the religion of Judaism or to Jews. ❑ *...the Jewish festival of the Passover.*

jibe or **gibe** /dʒaɪb/ (**jibes, jibing, jibed**) V-I & N-COUNT If someone **jibes**, they say something rude and insulting, called a **jibe**, which is

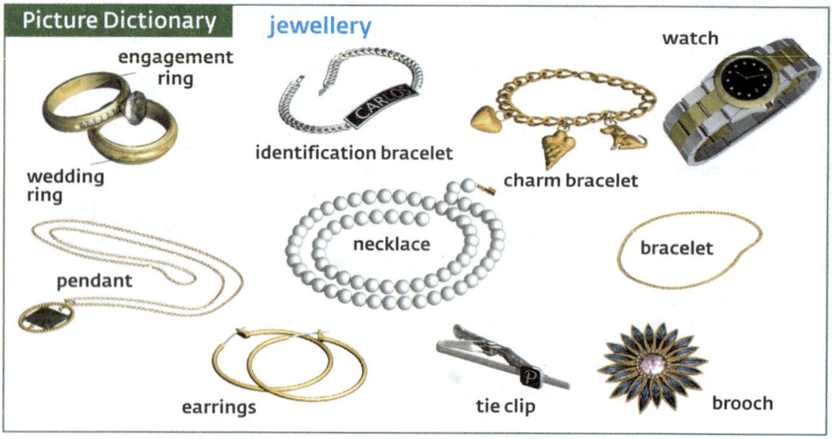

intended to make another person look foolish. [WRITTEN] ❑ *'No doubt he'll give me the chance to fight him again,' he jibed.* ❑ *...a cheap jibe about his loss of hair.*

J

jig /dʒɪɡ/ (**jigs, jigging, jigged**) **1** N-COUNT A **jig** is a lively folk dance. **2** V-I To **jig** means to dance or move energetically, especially bouncing up and down. ❑ *His son, Christopher, laughed and jigged around to the music.*

jigsaw /ˈdʒɪɡsɔː/ (**jigsaws**) N-COUNT A **jigsaw** or **jigsaw puzzle** is a picture on cardboard or wood that has been cut up into odd shapes and which has to be put back together again.

jigsaw puzzle

jingle /ˈdʒɪŋɡəl/ (**jingles, jingling, jingled**) **1** V-T/V-I When something **jingles**, or when you **jingle** it, it makes a gentle ringing noise, like small bells. ❑ *Brian put his hands in his pockets and jingled some change.* **2** N-COUNT A **jingle** is a short and simple tune, often with words, used to advertise a product on radio or television.

jitters /ˈdʒɪtəz/ N-PLURAL If someone has **the jitters**, they are very nervous or uncertain about something. [INFORMAL] ❑ *She had the jitters on the first day of her new job.*

jittery /ˈdʒɪtəri/ ADJ If someone is **jittery**, they are very nervous or uncertain about something. [INFORMAL] ❑ *Investors are jittery about the country's economy.*

job /dʒɒb/ (**jobs**) **1** N-COUNT A **job** is the work that someone does to earn money. ❑ *After I finish school, I will get a job.* ❑ *Thousands of people have lost their jobs.* **2** N-COUNT A **job** is a particular task. ❑ *He was given the job of washing the car.* **3** N-COUNT The **job** of a particular person or thing is their duty or function. ❑ *Their main job is to deliver letters on time.* **4** N-SING If you say, for example, that someone has done a **good job** or an **excellent job of** something, you mean that they have done it well. ❑ *He did a very good job of explaining what happened.*

Thesaurus *job* Also look up:

N. employment, occupation, profession, vocation, work **1**
assignment, duty, obligation, task **2** **3**

jobless /ˈdʒɒbləs/ ADJ Someone who is **jobless** does not have a job, but would like one. ❑ *...jobless people.*

ˈjob satisˌfaction N-UNCOUNT **Job satisfaction** is the pleasure that you get from doing your job.

ˈjob ˌshare (**job shares, job sharing, job shared**) V-I & N-COUNT If two people **job share**, or if they do a **job share**, they share the same job by working part-time, for example one person in the mornings and the other in the afternoons. ❑ *They both want to job share.* ❑ *She works in a bank job share.*

jockey /ˈdʒɒki/ (**jockeys**) N-COUNT A **jockey** is someone who rides a horse in a race.

jog /dʒɒɡ/ (**jogs, jogging, jogged**) **1** V-I & N-COUNT If you **jog**, or if you go for a **jog**, you run slowly, often as a form of exercise. ❑ *I got up early the next morning to jog.* ● **jogger** (**joggers**) N-COUNT ❑ *The park was full of joggers.* ● **jogging** N-UNCOUNT ❑ *Many students keep fit through jogging.* **2** V-T If you **jog** something, you push or bump it slightly so that it moves. ❑ *Don't jog the camera.*

join /dʒɔɪn/ (**joins, joining, joined**) **1** V-T If someone or something **joins** another, they move or go to the same place. ❑ *His wife and children moved to join him in their new home.* **2** V-T If you **join** an organization, you become a member of it. ❑ *He joined the Army five years ago.* **3** V-T & PHR-VERB If you **join** an activity, or if you **join in** an activity, you become involved in it. ❑ *The Prime Minister joined the debate.* ❑ *Thousands of people will join in the celebrations.* **4** V-T If you **join** a queue, you go and stand at the end of it. **5** V-T/V-I If two roads or rivers **join**, or if one **joins** the other, they meet or come together at a particular point. ❑ *The road joins the High Street, next to MacDonald's.* **6** V-T & N-COUNT To **join** two things means to fasten, fix, or connect them together. A **join** is a place where two things are fastened or fixed together. ❑ *'And' is often used to join two sentences.* ❑ *The car parks are joined by a* footpath. ❑ *Don't worry – you can't see the join.* **7** to **join forces** → see **force** **8** to **join the ranks** → see **rank**

▸ **join in** → see **join** (meaning 3)

▸ **join up** **1** PHR-VERB If someone **joins up**, they become a member of the armed forces. [BRIT] **2** PHR-VERB If a person or thing **joins up with** another, or if the two of them **join up**, they move or go to the same place. ❑ *Hawkins joined up with Mick in Malaga, and they went travelling.*

joint /dʒɔɪnt/ (**joints**) **1** ADJ BEFORE N **Joint** means shared by or belonging to two or more people. ❑ *...a joint bank account.* • **jointly** ADV ❑ *The project is jointly run by the BBC and the British Film Institute.* **2** N-COUNT A **joint** is a part of your body such as your elbow or knee where two bones meet and are able to move together. ❑ *Her joints ache if she exercises.* **3** N-COUNT A **joint** is a place where two things meet or are fixed together. ❑ *Some plants grow in joints between paving blocks.*

joint 'venture (**joint ventures**) N-COUNT A **joint venture** is a business or project in which two or more companies or individuals have invested, with the intention of working together.

joke /dʒəʊk/ (**jokes, joking, joked**) **1** V-I & N-COUNT If you **joke**, or if you **make a joke**, you say something amusing or tell a funny story to make people laugh. ❑ *She joked about her appearance.* ❑ *I was only joking, Charlie.* ❑ *He made a joke about a lawyer.* • **joker** (**jokers**) N-COUNT ❑ *He is a bit of a joker.* **2** N-SING If you say that someone or something is **a joke**, you mean that they are ridiculous and not worthy of respect. [INFORMAL] ❑ *The decision was a joke.* **3** PHRASE You say **you're joking** or **you must be joking** to someone when they have just told you something very surprising or difficult to believe. [SPOKEN] ❑ *I've retired from work.—You're joking. You don't look old enough.* **4** PHRASE If you describe a situation as **no joke**, you are emphasizing that it is very difficult or unpleasant. [INFORMAL] ❑ *Two hours on a bus is no joke.*

joker /'dʒəʊkə/ (**jokers**) N-COUNT The **joker** in a pack of cards is the card which does not belong to any of the four suits.

jolly /'dʒɒli/ (**jollier, jolliest**) **1** ADJ A **jolly** person is happy and cheerful. **2** ADJ A **jolly** event is lively and enjoyable. ❑ *I was looking forward to a jolly party.* **3** ADV You can use **jolly** to emphasize something. [BRIT, DATED] ❑ *It was jolly hard work.*

jolt /dʒəʊlt/ (**jolts, jolting, jolted**) **1** V-T/V-I & N-COUNT If something **jolts**, or if something else **jolts** it, it moves suddenly and violently. A **jolt** is a sudden violent movement. ❑ *The train jolted into motion.* ❑ *He fell into the river when his boat was jolted.* ❑ *One tiny jolt could worsen her injuries.* **2** V-T & N-COUNT If you **are jolted** by something, it gives you an unpleasant surprise or shock. A **jolt** is a surprise or shock like this. ❑ *Scandals jolted the Royal family last year.* ❑ *A loud noise in the hall jolted her awake.* ❑ *His death has given us all a jolt.*

jostle /'dʒɒsəl/ (**jostles, jostling, jostled**) **1** V-T/V-I If people **jostle** you, they bump against you or push you in a crowd. ❑ *I was jostled by a group of fans.* ❑ *Journalists and photographers jostled for space.* ❑ *Brian jostled his way through the crowd.* **2** V-I If people or things **are jostling for** something such as attention or a reward, they are competing with each other for it. ❑ *The two managers are jostling for the top job.*

jot /dʒɒt/ (**jots, jotting, jotted**)

▸ **jot down** PHR-VERB If you **jot** something **down**, you write it down in the form of a short informal note. ❑ *Keep a notebook nearby to jot down queries.*

journal /'dʒɜːnəl/ (**journals**) **1** N-COUNT A **journal** is a magazine or newspaper, especially one that deals with a specialized subject. ❑ *...scientific journals.* **2** N-COUNT A **journal** is an account which you write of your daily activities. ❑ *He wrote in his journal.*

Word Link	*ist ≈ one who practices : biologist, journalist, pharmacist*

journalist /'dʒɜːnəlɪst/ (**journalists**) N-COUNT A **journalist** is a person whose job is to collect news, and write about it in newspapers or magazines or talk about it on television or radio. ❑ *...a journalist with the Financial Times.* • **journalism** N-UNCOUNT ❑ *He had a career in journalism.*

journey /'dʒɜːni/ (**journeys, journeying, journeyed**) V-I & N-COUNT If you **journey** somewhere, or if you make a **journey** there, you travel there. ❑ *Naomi journeyed to the United States.* ❑ *During the journey to the airport he was followed by photographers.*

Thesaurus	*journey* Also look up:
N.	adventure, trip, visit, voyage

Word Partnership	Use *journey* with:
V.	**begin a** journey, **complete a** journey, **make a** journey
N.	journey **of discovery**, **end of a** journey, **first/last leg of a** journey

joy /dʒɔɪ/ (**joys**) **1** N-UNCOUNT **Joy** is a feeling of great happiness. ❑ *Richard shouted with joy.* ❑ *...tears of joy.* **2** N-COUNT Something that is a **joy** makes you feel happy or gives you great pleasure. ❑ *That is one of the joys of being a chef.*
→ see **emotion**

Word Partnership	Use *joy* with:
ADJ.	**filled with** joy, **great** joy, **pure** joy, **sheer** joy **1**
N.	**tears of** joy **1**
V.	**bring** ***someone*** joy, **cry/weep for** joy, **feel** joy **1**

Word Link	*joy ≈ being glad : enjoy, joyful, joyous*

joyful /'dʒɔɪfʊl/ **1** ADJ Something that is **joyful** causes happiness and pleasure. ❑ *A wedding is a joyful celebration of love.* **2** ADJ A **joyful** person is extremely happy. ❑ *...crowds of joyful students.* • **joyfully** ADV ❑ *They greeted him joyfully.*

joyous /'dʒɔɪəs/ ADJ **Joyous** means extremely happy. [LITERARY] ❑ *...a joyous celebration of life.* • **joyously** ADV ❑ *Sarah accepted joyously.*

joyrider /'dʒɔɪraɪdə/ (**joyriders**) N-COUNT A **joyrider** is someone who steals a car and drives it around at high speed for fun.

jubilant /'dʒuːbɪlənt/ ADJ If you are **jubilant**, you feel extremely happy because of a success. ❑ *I was* *jubilant after Mr Ferris's victory.*

jubilee /'dʒu:bɪli:/ (**jubilees**) N-COUNT A **jubilee** is a special anniversary of an event, especially the 25th or 50th anniversary. ❑ *...Queen Victoria's jubilee.*

Judaism /'dʒu:deɪɪzəm/ N-UNCOUNT **Judaism** is the religion of the Jewish people, which is based on the Old Testament of the Bible and the laws written in the Talmud.

judge /dʒʌdʒ/ (**judges, judging, judged**) 1 N-COUNT A **judge** is the person in a court of law who decides how the law should be applied, for example how criminals should be punished. ❑ *The judge found her not guilty of murder.* ❑ *...Judge Mr Justice Schiemann.* 2 V-T If you **judge** someone or something, you form an opinion about them based on the evidence or information that you have. ❑ *She judged me by the colour of my skin.* ❑ *He judged that this was the moment to speak.* ❑ *Judging by the opinion polls, he seems to be winning.* 3 N-COUNT If someone is a good **judge of** something, they can understand it and make decisions about it. ❑ *I am an excellent judge of character.* 4 N-COUNT A **judge** is a person who chooses the winner of a competition. ❑ *The judges will choose the winner after lunch.* 5 V-T If you **judge** a competition, you decide who the winner is. ❑ *Entrants will be judged according to age.*
→ see **trial**

judgment [BRIT also **judgement**] /'dʒʌdʒmənt/ (**judgments**) 1 N-COUNT A **judgment** is an opinion that you have or express after thinking carefully about something. ❑ *In your judgment, what has changed over the last year?* ❑ *I don't really want to make any judgments on their decisions.* 2 N-UNCOUNT **Judgment** is the ability to make sensible guesses about a situation or sensible decisions about what to do. ❑ *I think you have made a bad judgement.* ❑ *Nobody questions my judgement.* 3 N-VAR A **judgment** is a decision made by a judge or by a court of law. ❑ *The industry was waiting for a judgment from the European Court.* ❑ *The Court will give its judgement within the next ten days.*

judicial /dʒu:'dɪʃəl/ ADJ BEFORE N **Judicial** means relating to the legal system and to judgments made in a court of law. ❑ *...an independent judicial system.*

judiciary /dʒu:'dɪʃəri, AM -ʃieri/ N-SING **The judiciary** is the branch of authority in a country which is concerned with justice and the legal system. [FORMAL]

judicious /dʒu:'dɪʃəs/ ADJ An action or decision that is **judicious** shows good judgment and sense. [FORMAL] ❑ *The Prime Minister allows the judicious use of the police force to protect our citizens.* • **judiciously** ADV ❑ *They spend their money judiciously.*

judo /'dʒu:dəʊ/ N-UNCOUNT **Judo** is a sport or martial art in which two people wrestle and try to throw each other to the ground.

jug

jug /dʒʌg/ (**jugs**) N-COUNT A **jug** is a container which is used for holding and pouring liquids.
→ see **kitchen**

juggle /'dʒʌgəl/ (**juggles, juggling, juggled**) 1 V-T If you have to **juggle** lots of different things, you have difficulty fitting them all in so that you have enough time for all of them. ❑ *Mike juggled a family of 11 with a career as a journalist.* 2 V-T/V-I If you **juggle** or **juggle** something, you entertain people by throwing things into the air, catching each one and throwing it up again so that there are several of them in the air at the same time. ❑ *She juggled five eggs.* • **juggling** N-UNCOUNT ❑ *...a workshop in juggling.* • **juggler** (**jugglers**) N-COUNT ❑ *...a professional juggler.*

juice /dʒu:s/ (**juices**) 1 N-VAR **Juice** is the liquid that can be obtained from a fruit. ❑ *...a glass of fresh orange juice.* 2 N-PLURAL The **juices** of a joint of meat are the liquid that comes out of it when you cook it. 3 N-PLURAL The **juices** in your stomach are the fluids that help you to digest food.

Word Partnership Use *juice* with:

ADJ.	**fresh-squeezed** juice 1
N.	**bottle of** juice, **fruit** juice, **glass of** juice 1

juicy /'dʒu:si/ (**juicier, juiciest**) 1 ADJ If food is **juicy**, it has a lot of juice in it and is very enjoyable to eat. ❑ *...a juicy steak.* 2 ADJ You can describe information as **juicy** if it is exciting or scandalous. [INFORMAL]

July /dʒʊ'laɪ/ (**Julys**) N-VAR **July** is the seventh month of the year. ❑ *...one of the hottest Julys on record.*

jumble /'dʒʌmbəl/ (**jumbles, jumbling, jumbled**) 1 N-COUNT A **jumble of** things is a lot of different things that are all mixed together in a disorganized or confused way. ❑ *...a jumble of words.* 2 V-T/V-I & PHR-VERB If you **jumble** things, or if they **jumble**, they become mixed together so that they are untidy or not in the correct order. To **jumble up** means the same as to **jumble**. ❑ *They jumble together shampoos, toys, chocolate and clothes.* ❑ *The wires are all jumbled up.* 3 N-UNCOUNT **Jumble** is old or unwanted things that people give away to charity. [BRIT]

'jumble ˌsale (**jumble sales**) N-COUNT A **jumble sale** is a sale of unwanted goods, usually held to raise money for charity. [BRIT] ❑ *We are having a jumble sale at our school.*

jumbo /'dʒʌmbəʊ/ (**jumbos**) 1 ADJ BEFORE N **Jumbo** is used to describe things which are very large. ❑ *...a jumbo box of tissues.* 2 N-COUNT A **jumbo** or a **jumbo jet** is a very large jet aeroplane.

jump /dʒʌmp/ (**jumps, jumping, jumped**) 1 V-I & N-COUNT When you **jump**, you bend your knees, push against the ground with your feet, and move quickly upwards into the air. This action is called a **jump**. ❑ *He jumped from the window of his flat to avoid the man.* ❑ *...the longest jump by a man.* 2 V-T If you **jump** something such as a fence, you move quickly up and through the air over or across it. 3 V-I If you **jump** somewhere, you move there quickly and suddenly. ❑ *She jumped to her feet and ran downstairs.* 4 V-I If something makes you **jump**, it makes you make a sudden movement because you are frightened or surprised. 5 V-I & N-COUNT If an amount or level **jumps**, or if there is a **jump in** an amount or level, it suddenly increases by a large amount in a short time. ❑ *Sales jumped from $94 million to over $101 million.* ❑ *...a big jump in profits.*

6 V-I If you **jump at** an offer or opportunity, you accept it quickly and eagerly. ❑ *He would jump at the chance to play for England.* 7 V-T If someone **jumps** you, they attack you suddenly or unexpectedly. [mainly AM, INFORMAL] ❑ *Half a dozen sailors jumped him.*

Thesaurus	*jump* Also look up:
V.	bound, hop, leap, lunge 1
	hurdle 2
	increase, rise, shoot up 5

Word Partnership	Use *jump* with:
N.	jump **to *your* feet** 3
	jump **in prices**, jump **in sales** 5
ADJ.	**big** jump 1 5

jumper /ˈdʒʌmpə/ (**jumpers**) N-COUNT In British English, a **jumper** is a knitted piece of clothing which covers the upper part of your body and your arms. The American word is **sweater**.

junction /ˈdʒʌŋkʃən/ (**junctions**) N-COUNT A **junction** is a place where roads or railway lines join. The usual American word is **intersection**. ❑ *Turn left at the junction.*

June /dʒuːn/ (**Junes**) N-VAR **June** is the sixth month of the year. ❑ *We went on holiday in June.*

jungle /ˈdʒʌŋgəl/ (**jungles**) 1 N-VAR A **jungle** is a forest in a tropical country where tall trees and other plants grow very closely together. 2 N-SING If you describe a situation as a **jungle**, you dislike it because it is complicated and difficult to get what you want from it. ❑ *...a jungle of complex rules.*

junior /ˈdʒuːniə/ (**juniors**) 1 N-COUNT & ADJ A **junior**, or a **junior** official or employee, holds a lower-ranking position in an organization or profession. ❑ *...a junior minister in the prime minister's office.* 2 N-SING If you are someone's **junior**, you are younger than they are. ❑ *...a woman 12 years his junior.*

ˌjunior ˈhigh (**junior highs**) N-VAR In the United States, **junior high** is the school that young people attend between the ages of 11 or 12 and 14 or 15.

junk /dʒʌŋk/ 1 N-UNCOUNT **Junk** is an amount of old or useless things. [INFORMAL] ❑ *What shall we do with all this junk?* 2 N-UNCOUNT You can use **junk** to refer to old and second-hand goods that people buy and collect.

junkie /ˈdʒʌŋki/ (**junkies**) N-COUNT A **junkie** is a drug addict. [INFORMAL]

junta /ˈdʒʌntə, ˈhʊntə/ (**juntas**) N-COUNT If you refer to a government as a **junta**, you mean that it is a military dictatorship that has taken power by force.

jurisdiction /ˌdʒʊərɪsˈdɪkʃən/ N-UNCOUNT **Jurisdiction** is the power that a court of law or an official has to carry out legal judgments or enforce laws. ❑ *The British police have no jurisdiction over foreign bank accounts.*

juror /ˈdʒʊərə/ (**jurors**) N-COUNT A **juror** is a member of a jury.
→ see **citizenship**

jury /ˈdʒʊəri/ (**juries**)

> When it is in the singular, **jury** can take the singular or plural form of the verb.

1 N-COUNT In a court of law, the **jury** is the group of people who have been chosen from the general public to listen to the facts about a crime and to decide whether the person accused is guilty or not. 2 N-COUNT A **jury** is a group of people who choose the winner of a competition.
→ see **trial**

Word Partnership	Use *jury* with:
N.	jury **duty**, **trial by** jury 1
V.	jury **convicts** 1
	jury **announces** 1 2
ADJ.	**hung** jury 1

> **just**
> ❶ ADVERB USES AND PHRASES
> ❷ ADJECTIVE USE

just /dʒʌst/
❶ 1 ADV If you say that something has **just** happened, you mean that it happened a very short time ago. ❑ *I've just bought a new house.* 2 ADV If you say that you are **just** doing something, you mean that you will finish doing it very soon. If you say that you are **just** going to do something, you mean that you will do it very soon. ❑ *I'm just making the sauce for the lamb.* ❑ *I'm just going to walk down the lane now and post some letters.* 3 ADV You use **just** to indicate that something is no more important, interesting, or difficult than you say it is. ❑ *It's just a suggestion.* 4 ADV You use **just** to indicate that what you are saying is the case, but only by a very small degree or amount. ❑ *I could just see her hand.* 5 ADV You use **just** to emphasize the word or phrase following it, in order to express feelings such as annoyance, admiration, or certainty. ❑ *She just won't relax.* ❑ *It's just stupid.* 6 ADV You use **just** with instructions, polite requests, or statements of intention, to make your request or statement seem less difficult than someone might think. ❑ *I'm just going to ask you a bit more about your father's business.* 7 ADV You use **just** to mean exactly, when you are specifying something precisely or asking for precise information. ❑ *We have no idea just how many people voted.* ❑ *My arm hurts too, just here.* 8 PHRASE You use **just about** to indicate that what you are talking about is so close to the truth that it can be regarded as being true. ❑ *She reads just about everything.* 9 PHRASE You use **it's just that** when you are making a complaint, suggestion, or excuse, so that the person you are talking to will not get annoyed with you. ❑ *Your hair is all right; it's just that you need a haircut.* 10 **just now** → see **now** 11 **only just** → see **only**

just /dʒʌst/
❷ ADJ If you describe a situation, action, or idea as **just**, you mean that it is right or acceptable according to particular moral principles. [FORMAL] ❑ *...a just cause.* ● **justly** ADV ❑ *They were not treated justly in the past.*

justice /ˈdʒʌstɪs/ (**justices**) 1 N-UNCOUNT **Justice** is fairness in the way that people are treated. ❑ *He only wants freedom, justice and equality.* 2 N-UNCOUNT The **justice of** a claim, argument, or cause is its quality of being reasonable and right. ❑ *People need to understand the justice of our cause.* 3 N-UNCOUNT **Justice** is the system that a country uses in order to deal with people who break the law. ❑ *A lawyer is part of the machinery of justice.* **4** N-COUNT In American English, a **justice** is a judge. **5** N-TITLE **Justice** is used before the names of judges. ❑ *...Mr Justice Hutchison.* **6** PHRASE If a criminal **is brought to justice**, he or she is tried in a court of law and punished. ❑ *He demanded that they were brought to justice.* **7** PHRASE If you **do justice to** someone or something, you deal with them properly and completely. ❑ *Does Hollywood do justice to the life of Iris Murdoch?*

Word Partnership Use *justice* with:

ADJ.	**racial** justice, **social** justice **1**
	criminal justice, **equal** justice **3**
V.	**seek** justice **1**
N.	**obstruction of** justice, justice **system** **3**

justifiable /ˌdʒʌstɪˈfaɪəbəl/ ADJ An opinion, action, or fact that is **justifiable** is acceptable or correct because there is a good reason for it. ❑ *Secretly listening to people's phone calls is justifiable in the fight against crime.* ● **justifiably** ADV ❑ *He was justifiably proud of his work.*

J

justification /ˌdʒʌstɪfɪˈkeɪʃən/ (**justifications**) N-VAR A **justification for** something is an acceptable reason or explanation for it. ❑ *The only justification for a zoo is educational.*

justified /ˈdʒʌstɪfaɪd/ ADJ AFTER LINK-V An action that is **justified** is reasonable and acceptable. ❑ *In my opinion, the decision was justified.*

justify /ˈdʒʌstɪfaɪ/ (**justifies, justifying, justified**) V-T If someone or something **justifies** a particular decision, action, or idea, they show or prove that it is reasonable or necessary. ❑ *Religion must never be used to justify violence.*

jut /dʒʌt/ (**juts, jutting, jutted**) V-I If something **juts out**, it sticks out above or beyond a surface. ❑ *The northern end of the island juts out like a finger into the sea.*

juvenile /ˈdʒuːvənaɪl/ (**juveniles**) **1** N-COUNT A **juvenile** is a child or young person who is not yet old enough to be regarded as an adult. [FORMAL] **2** ADJ If you describe someone's behaviour as **juvenile**, you are critical of it because you think that it is silly or immature.

juxtapose /ˌdʒʌkstəˈpəʊz/ (**juxtaposes, juxtaposing, juxtaposed**) V-T If you **juxtapose** two contrasting objects, images, or ideas, you put them together, so that the differences between them are strongly emphasized. [FORMAL] ❑ *Interviews with politicians were juxtaposed with trivial news items.* ● **juxtaposition** (**juxtapositions**) N-VAR ❑ *...the juxtaposition of sound and picture.*

Kk

k /keɪ/ **K** or **k** is used to represent the number 1000, especially when referring to sums of money. For example, £10k means £10,000.

kangaroo

kangaroo /ˌkæŋgəˈruː/ (**kangaroos**) N-COUNT A **kangaroo** is a large Australian animal. Female kangaroos carry their babies in a pocket on their stomachs.

karate /kəˈrɑːti/ N-UNCOUNT **Karate** is a martial art in which people fight using their hands, elbows, feet, and legs.

keel /kiːl/ (**keels, keeling, keeled**) PHRASE If something is **on an even keel**, it is working or progressing smoothly and steadily, without any sudden changes. ❑ *There is enough income to keep the family on an even keel.*
▶ **keel over** PHR-VERB If something or someone **keels over**, they fall over sideways. ❑ *She had a heart attack and keeled over.*

keen /kiːn/ (**keener, keenest**) **1** ADJ AFTER LINK-V If you are **keen on** doing something, you very much want to do it. If you are **keen that** something should happen, you very much want it to happen. ❑ *He was never keen on moving to England.* ❑ *She's still keen to keep in touch.* ● **keenness** N-UNCOUNT ❑ *...the country's keenness for better relationships with its neighbours.* **2** ADJ AFTER LINK-V If you are **keen on** something or someone, you like them a lot. ● **keenness** N-UNCOUNT ❑ *...his keenness for the arts.* **3** ADJ If someone is **keen**, they have a lot of enthusiasm for a particular activity or for things in general. ❑ *I've interviewed him and he seems very keen.* ❑ *She was a keen photographer.* ● **keenness** N-UNCOUNT ❑ *...the keenness of the students.* **4** ADJ A **keen** sense or emotion is very strong and intense. ❑ *...his keen sense of loyalty.* ● **keenly** ADV ❑ *Charles listened keenly.* ❑ *The contest was very keenly fought.*

keep /kiːp/ (**keeps, keeping, kept**) **1** LINK-VERB If someone **is kept** in a particular state, they remain in it. ❑ *The noise kept him awake.* ❑ *They huddled together to keep warm.* ❑ *Their main aim is to help keep youngsters out of trouble.* **2** V-T/V-I If you **keep** in a particular position or place, or if someone **keeps** you in it, you remain in it. ❑ *Keep away from the doors while the train is moving.* ❑ *He kept his head down.* ❑ *Doctors will keep her in hospital for at least another week.* **3** V-T & PHR-VERB If you **keep** doing something, or if you **keep on** doing it, you do it repeatedly or continue to do it. You can also say that someone or something **keeps** you doing something. ❑ *I keep forgetting it's December.* ❑ *Did he give up or keep on trying?* ❑ *I have a job that keeps me busy.* **4** V-T **Keep** is used with some nouns to indicate that someone does something for a period of time or continues to do it. For example, if you **keep a grip on** something, you continue to hold or control it. ❑ *He kept a look-out on the road.* **5** V-T If you **keep** something that you possess, you continue to have it. If you **keep** it somewhere, you store it there. ❑ *The city of Leningrad was deciding whether to keep its name.* ❑ *To make it easier to contact us, keep this card handy.* ❑ *She kept her money under the mattress.* **6** V-T When you **keep** something such as a promise or an appointment, you do what you said you would do. **7** V-T If you **keep** a record of a series of events, you make a written record of it. ❑ *Eleanor began to keep a diary.* **8** V-T If someone or something **keeps** you **from** doing something, they prevent you from doing it. ❑ *What can you do to keep it from happening again?* **9** V-T If someone or something **keeps** you, they delay you and make you arrive somewhere later than expected. ❑ *'What kept you?'—'I went in the wrong direction.'* **10** V-T If you **keep** something **from** someone, you do not tell them about it. ❑ *He had to keep the truth from his children.* **11** N-SING **Your keep** is the cost of food and other things that you need every day. ❑ *Ray will earn his keep on local farms while studying.* **12** PHRASE If you **keep yourself to yourself**, or if you **keep to yourself**, you stay on your own most of the time and do not mix with other people. **13** PHRASE If something is **in keeping with** something else, it is appropriate or suitable according to that thing. ❑ *In keeping with tradition, the Emperor did not attend the ceremony.* **14** to **keep** your **head** → see **head**
▶ **keep down** PHR-VERB If you **keep** the amount of something **down**, you do not let it increase. ❑ *Administration costs were kept down to just £460.*
▶ **keep on** **1** → see **keep** (meaning 3) **2** PHR-VERB If you **keep** someone **on**, you continue to employ them, for example after other employees have lost their jobs. ❑ *20 members of staff are being kept on.*
▶ **keep to** **1** PHR-VERB If you **keep to** a rule, plan, or agreement, you do exactly what you are expected or supposed to do. ❑ *You've got to keep to the speed limit.* **2** PHR-VERB If you **keep** something **to** a particular number or quantity, you limit it to that number or quantity. ❑ *Keep costs to a minimum.*
▶ **keep up** **1** PHR-VERB If someone or something **keeps up with** another person or thing, the first one moves or progresses as fast as the second. ❑ *She shook her head and started to walk on. He kept up with her.* ❑ *Things are changing so fast, it's hard to keep up.* **2** PHR-VERB If you **keep** something **up**, you continue to do it or provide it. ❑ *They can no longer keep up the payments.*

keeper /ˈkiːpə/ (**keepers**) **1** N-COUNT In football, the **keeper** is the same as the **goalkeeper**. [BRIT, INFORMAL] **2** N-COUNT A **keeper** at a zoo is a person who takes care of the animals.

Picture Dictionary **keyboard**

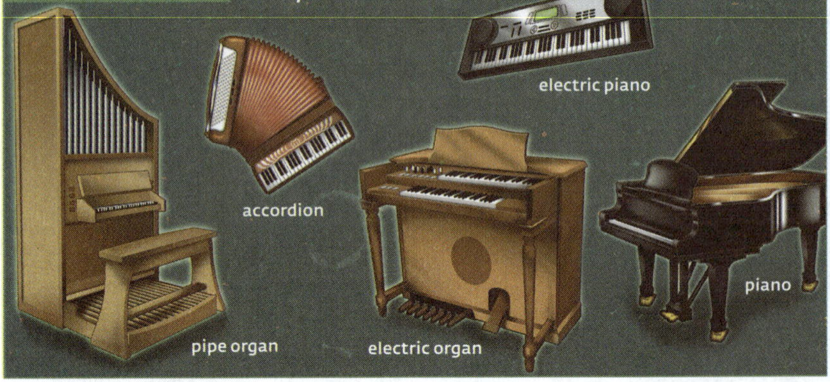

kennel /ˈkenəl/ (**kennels**) 1 N-COUNT A **kennel** is a small hut made for a dog to sleep in. 2 N-COUNT **Kennels** or **a kennels** or **a kennel** is a place where dogs are bred and trained, or looked after when their owners are away.

K

kept /kept/ **Kept** is the past tense and past participle of **keep**.

kerb [AM **curb**] /kɜːb/ (**kerbs**) N-COUNT The **kerb** is the raised edge of a pavement which separates it from the road.

kerosene /ˈkerəsiːn/ N-UNCOUNT In American English, **kerosene** is a strong-smelling liquid which is used as a fuel in heaters, lamps, and engines. The usual British word is **paraffin**.

kettle /ˈketəl/ (**kettles**) N-COUNT A **kettle** is a covered container that you use for boiling water.
→ see **tea**

key /kiː/ (**keys**) 1 N-COUNT A **key** is a specially shaped piece of metal which fits in a lock and is turned in order to open it. 2 N-COUNT The **keys** of a computer keyboard are the buttons that you press in order to operate it. 3 N-COUNT The **keys** of a piano or organ are the black and white bars that you press in order to play it. 4 N-COUNT In music, a **key** is a scale of musical notes that starts at one particular note. ❑ *...the key of A minor.* 5 ADJ BEFORE N The **key** person or thing in a group is the most important one. ❑ *Education is likely to be a key issue in the next election.* 6 N-COUNT The **key to** a desirable situation or result is the way in which it can be achieved. ❑ *Diet and relaxation are the keys to good health.*
→ see **graph**

Thesaurus *key* Also look up:

ADJ. critical, important, major, vital 5

Word Partnership Use *key* with:

V. **turn a** key 1
ADJ. key **component**, key **decision**, key **factor**, key **figure**, key **ingredient**, key **issue**, key **official**, key **player**, key **point**, key **question**, key **role**, key **word** 5
key **to success** 6

keyboard /ˈkiːbɔːd/ (**keyboards**) 1 N-COUNT The **keyboard** of a computer is the set of keys that you press in order to operate it. 2 N-COUNT The **keyboard** of a piano or organ is the set of black and white keys that you press in order to play it.
→ see Picture Dictionary: **keyboard**
→ see **computer**

ˈkey ˌcard (**key cards**) N-COUNT A **key card** is a small plastic card which you can use instead of a key to open a door or barrier, for example in some hotels and car parks.

kg **kg** is the written abbreviation for **kilogram**.

khaki /ˈkɑːki, AM ˈkæki/ ADJ Something that is **khaki** is greenish brown in colour.

kick /kɪk/ (**kicks, kicking, kicked**) 1 V-T & N-COUNT If you **kick** someone or something, or if you give them a **kick**, you hit them with your foot. ❑ *She kicked him in the leg.* ❑ *The police kicked down the door.* ❑ *He suffered a kick to the knee.* 2 V-T/V-I If you **kick**, you move your legs with very quick, small, and forceful movements, once or repeatedly. ❑ *They were dragged away struggling and kicking.* ❑ *The baby smiled and kicked her legs.* 3 PHRASE If someone **gets a kick from** something, they get pleasure or excitement from it. [INFORMAL] 4 V-T If you **kick** a bad habit, you stop having that habit. [INFORMAL] ❑ *I've kicked the habit; it was bad for my health.*

kick

▶ **kick off** PHR-VERB If an event, game, series, or discussion **kicks off**, or if someone **kicks** it **off**, it begins. [INFORMAL] ❑ *The Mayor kicked off the party.*

▶ **kick out** PHR-VERB To **kick** someone **out of** a place means to force them to leave it. [INFORMAL] ❑ *Her family kicked her out of the house.*

Thesaurus *kick* Also look up:

N. enjoyment, excitement, fun, thrill 3
V. abandon, give up, quit, stop; *(ant.)* start, take up 4

Word Partnership Use *kick* with:

N. kick **a door** 1
kick **a ball, penalty** kick 2
kick **a habit,** kick **smoking** 4

'kick-,off (**kick-offs**) N-VAR In football or rugby, **kick-off** is the time at which a particular match starts.

'kick-,start (**kick-starts, kick-starting, kick-started**) V-T To **kick-start** a process that has stopped working or progressing is to do something that will quickly start it going again. ❑ *He moved to New York to kick-start his career.*

kid /kɪd/ (**kids, kidding, kidded**) 1 N-COUNT You can refer to a child as a **kid.** [INFORMAL] ❑ *They've got three kids.* 2 N-COUNT Young people who are no longer children are sometimes referred to as **kids.** [INFORMAL] ❑ *...gangs of kids on motorbikes.* 3 V-I If you **are kidding,** you are saying something that is not really true, as a joke. [INFORMAL] ❑ *Oh come on, I was just kidding.* ❑ *I need to use your phone. I'm not kidding. This really is an emergency.* 4 V-T If people **kid themselves,** they allow themselves to believe something that is not true. [INFORMAL] ❑ *He is kidding himself if he thinks that anyone is going to buy his book.* 5 N-COUNT A **kid** is a young goat.

Word Partnership Use *kid* with:

ADJ. **fat** kid, **friendly** kid, **good** kid, **little** kid, **new** kid, **nice** kid, **poor** kid, **skinny** kid, **smart** kid, **tough** kid, **young** kid 1
N. kid **brother/sister, school** kid, kid **stuff** 1
V. **raise a** kid 1

kidnap /'kɪdnæp/ (**kidnaps, kidnapping, kidnapped** or [AM] **kidnaping, kidnaped**) 1 V-T To **kidnap** someone is to take them away illegally and by force, and usually to hold them prisoner in order to demand something from their family, employer, or government. ❑ *Police in Brazil uncovered a plot to kidnap him.* ● **kidnapper** (**kidnappers**) N-COUNT ❑ *The kidnappers set him free last week.* ● **kidnapping** (**kidnappings**) N-VAR ❑ *He was shot during the kidnapping.* 2 N-VAR **Kidnap** or a **kidnap** is the crime of kidnapping someone. ❑ *He went to prison for the kidnap of a 25-year-old woman.*

kidney /'kɪdni/ (**kidneys**) N-COUNT Your **kidneys** are the two organs in your body that filter waste matter from your blood and send it out of your body in your urine. ❑ *...kidney disease.*
→ see **donor**

kill /kɪl/ (**kills, killing, killed**) 1 V-T/V-I If a person, animal, or other living thing **is killed,** something or someone causes them to die. ❑ *Six people have been killed in a road crash.* ❑ *The earthquake killed 62 people.* ❑ *Knives can kill.* ● **killing** (**killings**) N-VAR ❑ *...a brutal killing.* 2 V-T & PHR-VERB If something **kills** an activity, process, or feeling or **kills** it **off,** it prevents it from continuing. ❑ *It was their final chance to kill off the project.* ❑ *A boring election like that kills off your interest in politics for ever.* 3 V-T If you **are killing time,** you are doing something because you have some time available, not because you really want to do it. ❑ *To kill the hours while she waited, Anna worked in the garden.*
→ see **war**
▶ **kill off** 1 → see **kill** (meaning 2) 2 PHR-VERB If you **kill** things **off,** you destroy or kill all of them. ❑ *The bears in this area have been killed off.* ❑ *You must boil it to kill off any infection.*

Usage

There are several words which mean similar things to **kill.** To **murder** someone means to kill them deliberately. **Assassinate** is used to talk about the murder of an important person, often for political reasons. If a large number of people are murdered, the words **slaughter** or **massacre** are sometimes used. **Slaughter** can also be used to talk about killing animals for their meat.

Thesaurus *kill* Also look up:

V. execute, murder, put down, slay, wipe out 1

killer /'kɪlə/ (**killers**) 1 N-COUNT A **killer** is a person who has killed someone. ❑ *The police are searching for his killers.* 2 N-COUNT You can refer to anything that causes death as a **killer.** ❑ *Heart disease is the biggest killer of men in most countries.*

kilo /'kiːləʊ/ (**kilos**) N-COUNT A **kilo** is the same as a **kilogram.**

Word Link *kilo ≈ thousand : kilobyte, kilogram, kilometre*

kilogram also **kilogramme** /'kɪləgræm/ (**kilograms**) N-COUNT A **kilogram** is a metric unit of weight. One kilogram is a thousand grams, and is equal to 2.2 pounds.

kilometre [AM **kilometer**] /'kɪləmiːtə, kɪ'lɒmɪtə/ (**kilometres**) N-COUNT A **kilometre** is a metric unit of distance or length. One kilometre is a thousand metres, and is equal to 0.62 miles.
→ see **measurement**

kin /kɪn/ PHRASE Your **next of kin** is your closest relative, especially in official or legal documents. [FORMAL] ❑ *We have notified the next of kin.*

Word Link *est ≈ most : greatest, kindest, latest*

Word Link *ness ≈ state, condition : awareness, consciousness, kindness*

kind /kaɪnd/ (**kinds, kinder, kindest**) 1 N-VAR If you talk about a particular **kind of** thing, you are talking about one of the classes or sorts of that thing. ❑ *Has Jamie ever been in any kind of trouble?* ❑ *I'm not the kind of person to get married.* ❑ *This book prize is the biggest of its kind in the world.* ❑ *Donations came from all kinds of people.* 2 ADJ Someone who is **kind** behaves in a gentle, caring, and helpful way towards other people. ❑ *She is warm-hearted and kind to everyone.* ❑ *It was very kind of you to come.* ● **kindly** ADV ❑ *He very kindly asked me to the party.* ● **kindness** N-UNCOUNT ❑ *We have been treated with such kindness by everybody.* 3 ADJ AFTER LINK-V You can use **kind** in expressions such as **please be so kind as to** in order to ask someone to do something in a firm but polite way. ❑ *I wonder if you'd be kind enough to call him.* 4 PHRASE You use **kind of** when you want to say that something or someone can be roughly described in a particular way. [SPOKEN] ❑ *She wasn't beautiful. But she was kind of cute.* ❑ *It kind of gives us an idea of what's happening.* 5 PHRASE Payment **in kind**

is payment in the form of goods or services, rather than money. ❑ *You can pay in kind rather than in cash, for instance, by babysitting or cooking meals.* 6 → see also **kindly**

Thesaurus *kind* Also look up:
N. sort, type 1
ADJ. affectionate, considerate, gentle 2

kindergarten /'kɪndəgɑːtən/ (**kindergartens**) 1 N-VAR A **kindergarten** is a school for young children who are not old enough to go to a primary school. ❑ *She's in kindergarten now.* 2 → see also **nursery**

kindly /'kaɪndli/ (**kindlier, kindliest**) 1 ADJ A **kindly** person is kind, caring, and sympathetic. 2 ADV If someone asks you to **kindly** do something, they are asking you in a way which shows that they have authority over you, or that they are angry with you. ❑ *Will you kindly do as you're told?* 3 PHRASE If someone **does not take kindly to** something, they do not like it. ❑ *She did not take kindly to being offered advice by her younger sister.* 4 → see also **kind**

king /kɪŋ/ (**kings**) 1 N-COUNT A **king** is a man who is a member of the royal family of his country, and who is the head of state of that country. ❑ *...the king and queen of Spain.* 2 N-COUNT In chess, the **king** is the piece which each player must try to capture. 3 N-COUNT A **king** is a playing card with a picture of a king on it.
→ see **chess**

K

kingdom /'kɪŋdəm/ (**kingdoms**) 1 N-COUNT A **kingdom** is a country or region that is ruled by a king or queen. 2 N-SING All the animals, birds, and insects in the world can be referred to together as the **animal kingdom**. All the plants can be referred to as the **plant kingdom**.
→ see **plant**

kiosk /'kiːɒsk/ (**kiosks**) N-COUNT A **kiosk** is a small shop in a public place such as a street or station. It sells things such as snacks or newspapers which you buy through a window.

kiss /kɪs/ (**kisses, kissing, kissed**) V-T/V-I & N-COUNT If you **kiss** someone, or if you give them a **kiss**, you touch them with your lips to show affection or to greet them. ❑ *She kissed him on the cheek.* ❑ *They kissed for almost half-a-minute.* ❑ *Give me a kiss.*
→ see Word Web: **kiss**

kit /kɪt/ (**kits, kitting, kitted**) 1 N-COUNT A **kit** is a group of items that are kept together because they are used for similar purposes. ❑ *...a first aid kit.* 2 N-UNCOUNT Your **kit** is the special clothing you use for a particular activity or sport. [BRIT] ❑ *I forgot my football kit.* 3 N-COUNT A **kit** is a set of parts that can be put together in order to make something. ❑ *...model aeroplane kits.*
▶ **kit out** PHR-VERB If someone or something **is kitted out**, they have all the clothing or equipment they need at a particular time. [BRIT, INFORMAL] ❑ *Kit yourself out in warm boots and a hat.*

kitchen /'kɪtʃɪn/ (**kitchens**) N-COUNT A **kitchen** is a room used for cooking and related jobs such as washing dishes.
→ see **house**

kite /kaɪt/ (**kites**) N-COUNT A **kite** is an object consisting of a light frame covered with paper or cloth, which you fly in the air at the end of a long string.

kitsch /kɪtʃ/ N-UNCOUNT & ADJ You can refer to a work of art or an object as **kitsch** if it is showy and in bad taste, for example because it is designed to appeal to people's sentimentality. ❑ *...collectors of Fifties kitsch.* ❑ *Green eye shadow has long been considered kitsch.*

kitten /'kɪtən/ (**kittens**) N-COUNT A **kitten** is a very young cat.

kitty /'kɪti/ (**kitties**) N-COUNT A **kitty** is an amount of money collected from several people, which is used to buy things that they will share or use together. ❑ *You haven't put any money in the kitty.*

'kiwi ˌfruit (**kiwi fruits**)

Kiwi fruit can also be used as the plural form.

N-VAR A **kiwi fruit** is a fruit with a brown hairy skin and green flesh.
→ see **fruit**

km **km** is a written abbreviation for **kilometre**.

knack /næk/ N-SING If you have the **knack of** doing something difficult or skilful, you are able to do it easily. ❑ *He's got the knack of getting people to listen.*

knead /niːd/ (**kneads, kneading, kneaded**) V-T When you **knead** dough, you press and squeeze it with your hands to make it smooth.

knee /niː/ (**knees**) 1 N-COUNT Your **knee** is the place where your leg bends. ❑ *The snow was up to his knees.* ❑ *...a knee injury.* 2 N-COUNT If something or someone is **on** your **knee**, they are resting or sitting on the upper part of your legs when you are sitting down. ❑ *I sat in the back of the taxi with my son on my knee.* 3 N-PLURAL If you are **on** your **knees**, you are kneeling. ❑ *She fell to the ground on her knees*

Word Web **kiss**

Some anthropologists believe mothers invented the **kiss**. They chewed a bit of food and then used their lips to place it in their child's mouth. Others believe that kissing started with primates. There are many types of kisses. Kisses express affection or accompany a greeting or a goodbye. Friends and family members exchange **social kisses** on the **lips** or sometimes on the **cheek**. When people are about to kiss they pucker their lips. In European countries, friends kiss each other lightly on both cheeks. And in the Middle East, a kiss between two leaders shows support for each other.

and prayed. **4** PHRASE If a country or organization **is brought to its knees**, it is almost completely destroyed by someone or something.
→ see **body, horse**

Word Partnership	Use *knee* with:
N.	knee **injury** **1**
V.	**bend your** knees, knees **buckle** **1**
	fall on your knees **3**
ADJ.	**left/right** knee, **weak**-kneed **1**

kneel /niːl/ (**kneels, kneeling, knelt** /nelt/ or **kneeled**) V-I & PHR-VERB When you **kneel** or **kneel down**, you move your body into a position with your knees on the ground and your lower legs stretched out behind them. If you **are kneeling**, you are in this position. ❑ *She kneeled down beside him.* ❑ *She was kneeling in prayer.*

knew /njuː, AM nuː/ **Knew** is the past tense of **know**.

knickers /ˈnɪkəz/ N-PLURAL **Knickers** are a piece of underwear worn by women and girls which have holes for the legs and elastic around the top. [BRIT] ❑ *...six pairs of knickers.*

knife /naɪf/ (**knives, knifes, knifing, knifed**)

> **Knives** is the plural form of the noun and **knifes** is the third person singular of the present tense of the verb.

1 N-COUNT A **knife** is a tool consisting of a sharp flat piece of metal attached to a handle, used to cut things or as a weapon. ❑ *...a knife and fork.* **2** V-T To **knife** someone means to attack and injure them with a knife. ❑ *She was knifed in the back.*
→ see **tool**

knight /naɪt/ (**knights, knighting, knighted**) **1** N-COUNT In medieval times, a **knight** was a man of noble birth, who served his king or lord in battle. **2** V-T If someone **is knighted**, they are given a knighthood. **3** N-COUNT In chess, a **knight** is a piece shaped like a horse's head.
→ see **chess**

knighthood /ˈnaɪthʊd/ (**knighthoods**) N-COUNT A **knighthood** is a title given to a man in Britain or the Commonwealth for outstanding achievements or for service to his country. A man with a knighthood puts 'Sir' in front of his name.

knit /nɪt/ (**knits, knitting, knitted**) V-T When someone **knits** something, they make it from wool or a similar thread using knitting needles or a machine. ❑ *She knitted him 10 pairs of socks.* ❑ *...her grey knitted cardigan.* ● **knitting** N-UNCOUNT ❑ *...a relaxing hobby, such as knitting.*

knitting /ˈnɪtɪŋ/ N-UNCOUNT **Knitting** is something, such as a piece of clothing, that is being knitted. ❑ *Miss Marple sits in the corner with her knitting.*

knives /naɪvz/ **Knives** is the plural of **knife**.

knob /nɒb/ (**knobs**) **1** N-COUNT A **knob** is a round handle or switch. ❑ *She reached for the door knob.* ❑ *He turned a knob on the radio.* **2** N-COUNT A **knob of** butter is a small amount of it. [BRIT]

knock /nɒk/ (**knocks, knocking, knocked**) **1** V-I & N-COUNT If you **knock on** something such as a door or window, you hit it, usually several times, to attract someone's attention. A **knock** is the action or sound of knocking. ❑ *She went directly to Simon's apartment and knocked on the door.* ❑ *They heard a knock.* ● **knocking** N-SING ❑ *...a loud knocking at the door.* **2** V-T & N-COUNT If you **knock** something, or if you give it a **knock**, you touch it or hit it roughly and it moves or falls over. ❑ *She accidentally knocked the book off the shelf.* ❑ *Alex King took a knock to his knee.* **3** V-T To **knock** someone into a particular place or condition means to hit them very hard so that they fall over or become unconscious. ❑ *Someone had knocked him unconscious.* **4** V-I If something **knocks**, it makes a repeated banging noise. ❑ *The walls squeaked and the pipes knocked.* **5** V-T If you **knock** something or someone, you criticize them. [INFORMAL]

knock

▶ **knock about** or **knock around** **1** PHR-VERB If someone **knocks** you **around** or **knocks** you **about**, they hit or kick you several times. [BRIT, INFORMAL] ❑ *He started knocking her about.* **2** PHR-VERB If someone **knocks around** or **knocks about** somewhere, they spend time there. [BRIT, INFORMAL] ❑ *Do you have a big group of friends that you knock around with?*

▶ **knock down** **1** PHR-VERB If someone **is knocked down**, they are hit by a vehicle and are injured or killed. **2** PHR-VERB To **knock down** a building means to demolish it.

▶ **knock off** PHR-VERB To **knock off** an amount from a price, time, or level means to reduce it by that amount. ❑ *He has knocked 10 seconds off the world record.*

▶ **knock out** **1** PHR-VERB To **knock** someone **out** means to cause them to become unconscious. ❑ *I nearly knocked him out.* **2** PHR-VERB If a person or team **is knocked out of** a competition, they are defeated in a game, so that they take no more part in the competition. **3** → see also **knockout**

Word Partnership	Use *knock* with:
ADJ.	**loud** knock **1**
	knock ***someone*** **out cold**, knock ***someone*** **unconscious** **3**
V.	**answer a** knock, **hear a** knock **1**
N.	knock **on/at a door** **1**

ˈknock-ˌon ADJ BEFORE N If something has a **knock-on** effect, it causes a series of events to happen, one after another. [BRIT] ❑ *Their problems could have a knock-on effect on their children.*

knockout also **knock-out** /ˈnɒkaʊt/ (**knockouts**) **1** N-COUNT If a boxer wins a fight by a **knockout**, his opponent falls to the ground and is unable to stand up before the referee has counted to ten. **2** ADJ BEFORE N A **knockout** blow is an action or event that completely destroys an opponent. **3** ADJ BEFORE N In a **knockout** competition, the loser of each game leaves the competition, until one competitor is left as the winner. [BRIT]

knot /nɒt/ (**knots, knotting, knotted**) **1** V-T & N-COUNT If you **knot** something such as a piece of string, or if you tie a **knot** in it, you pass one end of it through a loop and pull it tight. ❑ *He put on his shirt and knotted his tie carefully.* **2** PHRASE If you say that two people **tie the knot**, you mean that they

k

knot

get married. [INFORMAL] **3** N-SING A **knot of** people is a group of them standing very close together. ❑ *...a little knot of children.* **4** V-I & N-COUNT If your stomach **knots**, or if there is a **knot** in your stomach, it feels tight because you are afraid or excited. ❑ *I felt my stomach knot with excitement.* **5** N-COUNT A **knot** is a unit used for measuring the speed of ships and aircraft, equal to approximately 1.85 kilometres per hour. ❑ *...speeds of up to 30 knots.*

know /nəʊ/ (**knows, knowing, knew, known**) **1** V-T/V-I If you **know** something, you have it correctly in your mind. ❑ *Everyone knows his name.* ❑ *We know what happened there.* ❑ *'How did he meet your mother?'—'I don't know.'* **2** V-T/V-I If you **know about** something or **know how to** do something, you understand part or all of it, or have the necessary skills and understanding to do it. ❑ *She doesn't know about it yet.* ❑ *Do you know any English?* ❑ *The hospitals know how to deal with the disease.* **3** V-I If you **know of** something, you have heard about it but you do not necessarily have a lot of information about it. ❑ *We know of the problem but have no further details.* **4** V-T If you **know** a person, place, or thing, you are familiar with them. ❑ *I've known him for nine years.* ❑ *I know Birmingham quite well.* **5** V-T If someone or something **is known as** a particular name, they are called by that name. ❑ *The disease is more commonly known as Mad Cow Disease.* ❑ *Everyone knew him as Grundy.* **6** → see also **known** **7** PHRASE If you **get to know** someone, you find out what they are like by spending time with them. **8** PHRASE You say **'I know'** to indicate that you agree with what has just been said, or to indicate that you realize something is true. ❑ *'This weather is so awful.'—'I know, I know.'* **9** PHRASE Someone who is **in the know** has information about something that only a few people have any knowledge of. **10** PHRASE You say **'you know'** to emphasize something or to make your statement clearer. ❑ *The conditions in there are awful, you know.* **11** PHRASE You say **'You never know'** or **'One never knows'** to indicate that something is possible, although it is unlikely. ❑ *I imagine he'll stay here but you never know.*

Thesaurus *know* Also look up:

V.	comprehend, recognize, understand **1**
	be acquainted, be familiar with **4**

'know-,how also **knowhow** N-UNCOUNT **Know-how** is knowledge of the methods or techniques of doing something. [INFORMAL] ❑ *...technical know-how.*

knowingly /ˈnəʊɪŋli/ **1** ADV If you **knowingly** do something wrong, you are aware that it is wrong when you do it. ❑ *She never knowingly put herself in dangerous situations.* **2** ADV If you look or gesture **knowingly**, you show that you understand something, even though it has not been mentioned directly. ❑ *The officers nodded knowingly to each other.*

knowledge /ˈnɒlɪdʒ/ **1** N-UNCOUNT **Knowledge** is information and understanding about a subject, which someone has in their mind. ❑ *He says he had no knowledge of the payments.* ❑ *...the latest advances in scientific knowledge.* **2** PHRASE If you say that something is true **to the best of** your **knowledge**, you mean that you think that it is true, although you are not completely sure. **3** PHRASE If you do something **safe in the knowledge** that something else is true, you do the first thing confidently because you are sure of the second thing. [WRITTEN] ❑ *I arrived late, safe in the knowledge that she never arrives on time.*

Word Partnership Use *knowledge* with:

V.	**acquire** knowledge, **gain** knowledge, **have** knowledge, **lack** knowledge, **require** knowledge, **test** ***your*** knowledge, **use** ***your*** knowledge
ADJ.	**background** knowledge, **common** knowledge, **general** knowledge, **prior** knowledge, **scientific** knowledge, **useful** knowledge, **vast** knowledge
N.	knowledge **base**

knowledgeable /ˈnɒlɪdʒəbəl/ ADJ A **knowledgeable** person knows a lot about many different things or a lot about a particular subject. ❑ *He's a nice man and very knowledgeable about paintings.*

known /nəʊn/ **1** **Known** is the past participle of **know**. **2** ADJ You use **known** to describe someone or something that is clearly recognized by or familiar to all people, or to a particular group of people. ❑ *...a known criminal.* **3** PHRASE If you **let it be known** that something is true, you make sure that people know it, without telling them directly. ❑ *The prime minister had let it be known that he likes the idea.* **4** → see also **well-known**

knuckle /ˈnʌkəl/ (**knuckles**) N-COUNT Your **knuckles** are the rounded pieces of bone where your fingers join your hands, and where your fingers bend.
→ see **hand**

Koran /kɔːˈrɑːn/ N-PROPER **The Koran** is the sacred book on which the religion of Islam is based.

Ll

l l is a written abbreviation for 'litre'.

lab /læb/ (**labs**) N-COUNT A **lab** is the same as a **laboratory**. [INFORMAL]

label /ˈleɪbəl/ (**labels, labelling, labelled** or [AM] **labeling, labeled**) 1 N-COUNT & V-T A **label** is a piece of paper or plastic that is attached to an object, giving information about it. An object with a label on it **is labelled**. ❑ *All the products are labelled with full instructions.* 2 N-COUNT If you say that someone gets a particular **label**, you mean that people describe them with a particular word or phrase. ❑ *She has earned the label of the most hated woman in America.* 3 V-T If you say that someone or something **is labelled as** a particular thing, you mean that people generally describe them that way and you think that this is unfair. ❑ *They don't want to be labelled as a problem family.*
→ see **graph**

Thesaurus *label* Also look up:

N.	sticker, tag, ticket 1
V.	brand, characterize, classify 3

labor /ˈleɪbə/ → see **labour**
→ see **factory**

Word Link *labor ≈ working : collaborate, elaborate, laboratory*

laboratory /ləˈbɒrətri, AM ˈlæbrətɔːri/ (**laboratories**) N-COUNT A **laboratory** is a building or room where scientific experiments and research are performed.
→ see Picture Dictionary: **laboratory equipment**
→ see Word Web: **laboratory**

Word Partnership Use *laboratory* with:

N. laboratory **conditions**, laboratory **equipment**, laboratory **experiment**, **research** laboratory, laboratory **technician**, laboratory **test**

laborer → see **labourer**

laborious /ləˈbɔːriəs/ ADJ A **laborious task** or **process** takes a lot of effort. • **laboriously** ADV ❑ *He sat behind a desk laboriously writing.*

labour [AM **labor**] /ˈleɪbə/ (**labours, labouring, laboured**) 1 ADJ A **Labour** politician or voter is a member of the Labour Party or votes for the Labour Party. 2 N-VAR **Labour** is very hard work. ❑ *The prison was built by the labour of prisoners in the 1920s.* ❑ *The chef looked up from his labours.* 3 V-T/V-I If you **labour to** do something, you do it with difficulty. ❑ *For 25 years he laboured to build a religious community.* ❑ *Everyone laboured in the garden.* 4 N-UNCOUNT **Labour** is used to refer to the people who work in a country or industry. ❑ *...skilled labour.* 5 V-T If you **labour** a **point** or an **argument**, you keep making the same point or saying the same thing, although it is unnecessary. 6 N-UNCOUNT **Labour** is the last stage of pregnancy, in which a woman gives birth to a baby. ❑ *She was in labour.*

labourer /ˈleɪbərə/ (**labourers**) N-COUNT A **labourer** is a person who does a job which involves a lot of hard physical work. ❑ *He's a farm labourer.*

labyrinth /ˈlæbɪrɪnθ/ (**labyrinths**) 1 N-COUNT A **labyrinth** is a complicated series of paths or passages, through which it is difficult to find your way. 2 N-COUNT If you describe a situation, process, or area of knowledge as a **labyrinth**, you mean that it is very complicated. ❑ *The mind is a labyrinth.*

lace

lace /leɪs/ (**laces, lacing, laced**) 1 N-UNCOUNT **Lace** is very delicate cloth which is made by twisting together fine threads, creating holes in between. 2 N-COUNT **Laces** are thin pieces of material that are used to fasten some types of

Word Web laboratory

The discovery of the life-saving drug penicillin was a lucky accident. While cleaning up his **laboratory**, a **researcher** named Alexander Fleming* noticed that the bacteria in one petri **dish** had been killed by some kind of **mold**. He took a **sample** and found that it was a form of penicillin. Fleming and others did further **research** and **published** their **findings** in 1928, but few people took notice. However, ten years later a team at Oxford University, in England, read Fleming's **study** and began animal and human **experiments**. Within ten years, drug companies were manufacturing 650 billion units of penicillin a month!

Alexander Fleming (1881-1955): a Scottish biologist and pharmacologist.

Picture Dictionary — laboratory equipment

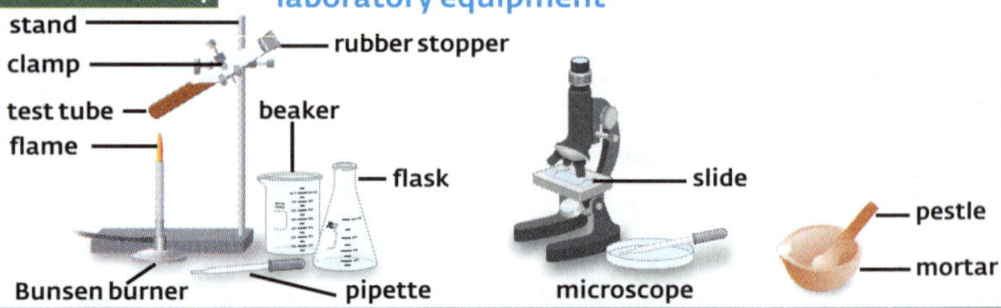

clothing, especially shoes. ❑ *He put on his shoes and tied the laces.* **3** V-T & PHR-VERB If you **lace** something such as a pair of shoes, or if you **lace** them **up**, you tighten them by pulling the laces through the holes, and tying them together. **4** V-T To **lace** food or drink **with** a substance such as alcohol or a drug means to put a small amount of the substance into the food or drink. ❑ *She laced his food with sleeping pills.*

lack /læk/ (**lacks, lacking, lacked**) **1** N-UNCOUNT If there is a **lack of** something, there is not enough of it, or there is none at all. ❑ *Despite his lack of experience, he got the job.* ❑ *The criminal charges were dropped for lack of evidence.* **2** V-T/V-I If you say that someone or something **lacks** something, or that something **is lacking in** them, you mean they do not have any or enough of that thing. ❑ *It lacked the power of the Italian cars.* ❑ *Certain vital information is lacking in the report.* ● **lacking** ADJ AFTER LINK-V ❑ *She felt nervous and lacking in confidence.*

L

Word Partnership Use *lack* with:

N. lack ***of*** **confidence**, lack ***of*** **control**, lack ***of*** **enthusiasm**, lack ***of*** **evidence**, lack ***of*** **exercise**, lack ***of*** **experience**, lack ***of*** **food**, lack ***of*** **information**, lack ***of*** **knowledge**, lack ***of*** **money**, lack ***of*** **progress**, lack ***of*** **resources**, lack ***of*** **skills**, lack ***of*** **sleep**, lack ***of*** **support**, lack ***of*** **trust**, lack ***of*** **understanding** **1**

lacklustre [AM **lackluster**] /ˈlæklʌstə/ ADJ If you describe something or someone as **lacklustre**, you mean that they are not very impressive or lively. ❑ *His party gave a lacklustre performance during the election campaign.*

lacquer /ˈlækə/ (**lacquers**) N-VAR **Lacquer** is a special type of liquid which is put on wood or metal to protect it and make it shiny.

lacy /ˈleɪsi/ (**lacier, laciest**) ADJ **Lacy** things are made from lace or have pieces of lace attached to them. ❑ *...lacy tablecloths.*

ladder

lad /læd/ (**lads**) N-COUNT A **lad** is a boy or young man. [BRIT, INFORMAL] ❑ *He's always been a big lad for his age.*

ladder /ˈlædə/ (**ladders**) N-COUNT A **ladder** is a piece of equipment used for climbing up something such as a wall. It consists of two long pieces of wood or metal with steps fixed between them.

laden /ˈleɪdən/ **1** ADJ If someone or something is **laden with** a lot of heavy things, they are holding or carrying them. [LITERARY] ❑ *The tables were laden with exotic fruit.* ❑ *The car is heavily laden with skis.* **2** ADJ If you describe a person or thing as **laden with** something, particularly something bad, you mean that they have a lot of it or are full of it. ❑ *We're so laden with guilt.*

lady /ˈleɪdi/ (**ladies**) **1** N-COUNT & N-VOC You can use the word **lady** when you are referring to a woman, especially when you are showing politeness or respect. ❑ *Shall we join the ladies?* ❑ *Your table is ready, ladies.* **2** N-TITLE **Lady** is a title used in front of the names of some women from the upper classes. ❑ *...Lady Diana Spencer.* **3** N-SING People sometimes refer to a public toilet for women as **the ladies**.

lag /læg/ (**lags, lagging, lagged**) **1** V-I If you **lag behind** someone or something, you make slower progress than them. ❑ *He now lags 10 points behind the champion.* **2** N-COUNT A **time lag** is a period of time between two related events. ❑ *There's a time lag between becoming infected and developing the disease.*
→ see **insect**

lager /ˈlɑːgə/ (**lagers**) N-VAR **Lager** is a kind of pale beer.

lagoon /ləˈguːn/ (**lagoons**) N-COUNT A **lagoon** is an area of calm sea water that is separated from the ocean by sand or rock.

laid /leɪd/ **Laid** is the past tense and past participle of **lay**.

ˌlaid-ˈback ADJ If you describe someone as **laid-back**, you mean that they behave in a relaxed way as if nothing ever worries them.

lain /leɪn/ **Lain** is the past participle of some meanings of **lie**.

lake /leɪk/ (**lakes**) N-COUNT A **lake** is a large area of fresh water, surrounded by land.
→ see Word Web: **lake**
→ see **land, river**

lamb /læm/ (**lambs**) **1** N-COUNT A **lamb** is a young sheep. **2** N-UNCOUNT **Lamb** is the flesh of a lamb eaten as food. ❑ *...leg of lamb.*

lame /leɪm/ **1** ADJ A **lame** person or animal cannot walk properly because an injury or illness has damaged one or both of their legs. ❑ *She was lame in one leg.* ❑ *His horse went lame.* **2** ADJ If you describe an excuse or effort as **lame**, you mean that it is weak. ❑ *He made some lame excuse about feeling sick.* ● **lamely** ADV ❑ *Mauresmo hit the*

Word Web lake

Several forces create **lakes**. The movement of a glacier can carve out a deep **basin** in the soil. The Great Lakes between the U.S. and Canada are **glacial** lakes. Very deep lakes appear when large pieces of the earth's crust suddenly shift. Lake Baikal in Russia is more than a mile deep. When a volcano erupts, it creates a **crater**. Crater Lake in Oregon is the perfectly round remains of a volcanic cone. The **water** comes from melted snow and rain. Erosion also creates lakes. When the wind blows away sand, the hole left behind forms a natural lake **bed**.

ball lamely into the net.

lament /lə'ment/ (**laments, lamenting, lamented**) 1 V-T If you **lament** something, you express your regret about it. [LITERARY] ❑ *He laments that people are afraid of the police.* ❑ *'Profits are down 40 per cent,' he lamented.* 2 N-COUNT Someone's **lament** is something that they say that expresses their disappointment about something. ❑ *The lament that he lost his wife runs through his autobiography.*

lamp /læmp/ (**lamps**) N-COUNT A **lamp** is a light that works by using electricity or by burning oil or gas. ❑ *She switched on the bedside lamp.*

land /lænd/ (**lands, landing, landed**) 1 N-UNCOUNT **Land** is an area of ground. ❑ *...agricultural land.* ❑ *The couple have not been found despite an air, land and sea search.* 2 N-COUNT A particular **land** is a particular country. [LITERARY] ❑ *...2,000 miles away in a strange land.* 3 → See note at **country** 4 V-I When someone or something **lands**, they come down to the ground after moving through the air or falling. ❑ *He was lifted into the air and landed 20ft away.* 5 V-T/V-I When a plane or spacecraft **lands**, or when someone **lands** it, it arrives somewhere after a journey. ❑ *The jet landed after a three-hour flight.* ● **landing** (**landings**) N-COUNT ❑ *I made a controlled landing into the sea.* 6 V-T To **land** goods somewhere means to successfully unload them there at the end of a journey, especially by ship. ❑ *The boats will land their fish at these ports.* 7 V-T If something **lands** you **in** an unpleasant situation, or if it **lands** you **with** it, it causes you to have to deal with it. [BRIT, INFORMAL] ❑ *His big ideas have landed him in trouble again.* ❑ *The other options could land us with more expense.*
→ see **continent, earth**

Thesaurus *land* Also look up:

N. area, country, real estate 1
V. arrive, touch down; *(ant.)* take off 3 4

Word Partnership Use *land* with:

ADJ. **agricultural** land, **fertile** land, **flat** land, **grazing** land, **private** land, **public** land, **vacant** land, **vast** land 1
N. **acres of** land, **area of** land, **desert** land, land **development**, land **management**, land **ownership**, **parcel of** land, **piece of** land, **plot of** land, **strip of** land, land **use** 1
V. **buy** land, **own** land, **sell** land 1

landfill /'lændfɪl/ (**landfills**) N-VAR **Landfill** is a method of disposing of very large amounts of rubbish by burying it in a large deep hole. A **landfill** is a large deep hole that rubbish is buried in. ❑ *...the environmental costs of landfill.*

landing /'lændɪŋ/ (**landings**) N-COUNT In a building, a **landing** is a flat area at the top of a staircase.

landlady /'lændleɪdi/ (**landladies**) N-COUNT Someone's **landlady** is the woman who allows them to live or work in a building which she owns, in return for rent.

landlord /'lændlɔːd/ (**landlords**) N-COUNT Someone's **landlord** is the man who allows them to live or work in a building which he owns, in return for rent.

Word Link *mark ≈ boundary, sign : bookmark, landmark, unmarked*

landmark /'lændmɑːk/ (**landmarks**) 1 N-COUNT A **landmark** is a building or feature which is easily noticed and can be used to judge your position or the position of other buildings or features. ❑ *The Eiffel Tower is a landmark in Paris.* 2 N-COUNT You can refer to an important stage in the development of something as a **landmark**. ❑ *The baby was a landmark in our relationship.*

landscape /'lændskeɪp/ (**landscapes, landscaping, landscaped**) 1 N-VAR The **landscape** is everything that you can see when you look across an area of land, including hills, rivers, buildings, and trees. ❑ *...Arizona's desert landscape.* 2 N-COUNT A **landscape** is a painting of the countryside. ❑ *Constable's series of landscapes is on show at the National Gallery.* 3 V-T If an area of land **is landscaped**, it is altered to create a pleasing artistic effect. ● **landscaping** N-UNCOUNT ❑ *The car-parking areas will be surrounded by landscaping.*
→ see **art, painting**

Usage

Do not confuse **landscape, scenery, countryside**, and **nature**. With **landscape**, the emphasis is on the physical features of the land, while **scenery** includes everything you can see when you look out over an area of land usually in the country. ❑ *...the landscape of woods and distant mountains.* ❑ *...unattractive urban scenery.* **Countryside** is land which is away from towns and cities. ❑ *...3,500 acres of flat countryside.* **Nature** includes the landscape, the weather, animals, and plants. ❑ *These creatures were the finest and rarest works of nature.*

l

landslide /ˈlændslaɪd/ (**landslides**) 1 N-COUNT If an election is won **by a landslide**, it is won by a large number of votes. 2 N-COUNT A **landslide** is a large amount of earth and rocks falling down a cliff or the side of a mountain.
→ see **disaster**

lane /leɪn/ (**lanes**) 1 N-COUNT A **lane** is a type of road, especially in the country. 2 N-COUNT Roads, race courses, and swimming pools are divided into parallel strips called **lanes**. ❑ *...the slow lane.* 3 N-COUNT A **lane** is a route that is frequently used by aircraft or ships. ❑ *...a busy shipping lane.*
→ see **traffic**

language /ˈlæŋgwɪdʒ/ (**languages**) 1 N-COUNT A **language** is a system of sounds and written symbols used by the people of a particular country, area, or tribe to communicate with each other. ❑ *...the English language.* ❑ *We expect students to learn a second language.* 2 N-UNCOUNT **Language** is the ability to use words in order to communicate. ❑ *...how children acquire language.* 3 N-UNCOUNT You can refer to the words used in connection with a particular subject as the **language** of that subject. ❑ *...the language of business.* 4 N-UNCOUNT The **language** of a piece of writing or a speech is the style in which it is written or spoken. ❑ *The booklet summarises it in plain language.*
→ see **culture, English**

Thesaurus *language* Also look up:

N. communication, dialect 1 2
jargon, slang, terminology 3

Word Partnership Use *language* with:

V. **know a** language, **learn a** language, **speak a** language, **study a** language, **teach a** language, **understand a** language, **use a** language 1
N. language **acquisition**, language **barrier**, **child** language, language **of children**, language **classes**, language **comprehension**, language **development**, **proficiency in a** language, language **skills** 1 2
ADJ. **a different** language, **foreign** language, **native** language, **official** language, **second** language, **universal** language 1
bad language, **foul** language, **plain** language, **simple** language, **technical** language, **vulgar** language 4

ˈlanguage ˌschool (**language schools**) N-COUNT A **language school** is a private school where a foreign language is taught.

languid /ˈlæŋgwɪd/ ADJ If you are **languid**, you show little energy or interest and are very slow and casual in your movements. [LITERARY] • **languidly** ADV ❑ *We sat about languidly.*

languish /ˈlæŋgwɪʃ/ (**languishes, languishing, languished**) V-I If you **languish** somewhere, you are forced to remain and suffer in an unpleasant situation. ❑ *Pollard continues to languish in prison.*

lantern /ˈlæntən/ (**lanterns**) N-COUNT A **lantern** is a lamp in a metal frame with glass sides.

lantern

lap /læp/ (**laps, lapping, lapped**) 1 N-COUNT **Your lap** is the flat area formed by your thighs when you are sitting down. ❑ *She waited quietly with her hands in her lap.* 2 N-COUNT In a race, you say that a competitor has completed a **lap** when he or she has gone round the course once. 3 V-T If you **lap** another competitor in a race, you pass them while they are still on the previous lap. 4 V-T/V-I When water **laps** against something such as the shore or the side of a boat, it touches it gently and makes a soft sound. [WRITTEN] ❑ *Water lapped the walls.* • **lapping** N-UNCOUNT ❑ *The only sound was the lapping of the waves.* 5 V-T & PHR-VERB When an animal **laps** a drink, or when it **laps** it **up**, it uses its tongue to flick the liquid into its mouth.
▶ **lap up** 1 PHR-VERB If you **lap up** information or attention, you accept it eagerly. ❑ *Their fans will lap this up.* 2 → see **lap** (meaning **5**)

lapel

lapel /ləˈpel/ (**lapels**) N-COUNT The **lapels** of a jacket or coat are the two flaps at the front that are folded back on each side.

Word Link *lapse ≈ falling : collapse, elapse, lapse*

lapse /læps/ (**lapses, lapsing, lapsed**) 1 N-COUNT A **lapse of** something such as concentration or judgement is a temporary lack of it, which can cause you to make a mistake. 2 V-I & N-COUNT If you **lapse into** a particular kind of behaviour, or have a **lapse into** that behaviour, you start behaving that way. ❑ *He lapsed into long silences.* ❑ *Her lapse into German wasn't unusual.* 3 N-SING A **lapse of** time is a period that is long enough for a situation to change. ❑ *They renewed diplomatic relations today after a lapse of 24 years.* 4 V-I If a period of time **lapses**, it passes. ❑ *A few days had lapsed since Grace's death.*

laptop /ˈlæptɒp/ (**laptops**) N-COUNT A **laptop** or a **laptop computer** is a small computer that you can carry around with you. [COMPUTING]
→ see **computer**

large /lɑːdʒ/ (**larger, largest**) 1 ADJ A **large** thing or person is greater in size than usual or average. ❑ *The fish lives mainly in large rivers and lakes.* ❑ *He was a large man with a thick square head.* 2 ADJ A **large** amount or number of people or things is more than the average amount or number. ❑ *A large number of centres offer full-time courses.* 3 ADJ **Large** is used to indicate that a problem or issue which is being discussed is very important or serious. ❑ *There is no doubt that we have a really large problem here.* 4 PHRASE You use **at large** to indicate that you are talking about most of the people mentioned. ❑ *This matter concerns the family, but also the public at large.* 5 PHRASE If you say that a dangerous person, thing, or animal is **at large**, you mean that they have not been captured or made safe. ❑ *The man who tried to kill her is still at large.* 6 PHRASE You use **by and large** to indicate that a statement is mostly but not completely true. ❑ *By and large, he does not watch many movies.*

Usage

Large, big, and **great** are all used to talk about size. In general, **large** is more formal than **big**, and **great** is more formal than **large**. **Big** and **large** are normally used to describe objects. If you use **great** to describe an object, you are suggesting that it is impressive because of its size. ❑ *The great bird was a dark shape against the sun.* You can use **large** or **great**, but not **big**, to describe amounts. ❑ *He noticed a large amount of blood on the floor.* ❑ *Tourists coming in great numbers changes things.* **Great** is often used with nouns referring to things such as feelings or ideas. It is the only one of the three words that can be used in front of an uncount noun. ❑ *It gives me very great pleasure to welcome you to Kings Norton.* Remember that **great** has several other meanings, when it does not refer to size, but to something that is remarkable, very good, or enjoyable.

Thesaurus *large* Also look up:

ADJ. big, sizeable, spacious, substantial; *(ant.)* small **1**

largely /ˈlɑːdʒli/ **1** ADV You use **largely** to say that a statement is mostly but not completely true. ❑ *The early studies were done largely by male researchers.* **2** ADV You use **largely** to introduce the main reason for an event or situation. ❑ *Today, largely because of their diets, over 50 percent of Americans are at risk of heart disease.*

ˌlarge-ˈscale also **large scale** **1** ADJ BEFORE N A **large-scale** action or event happens over a wide area or involves a lot of people or things. ❑ *...a large-scale military operation.* **2** ADJ BEFORE N A **large-scale** map or diagram represents a small area of land or a building or machine in a way that shows small details of it.

lark /lɑːk/ (**larks**) N-COUNT A **lark** is a small brown bird that has a pleasant song.

larva /ˈlɑːvə/ (**larvae** /ˈlɑːviː/) N-COUNT A **larva** is an insect at the stage before it becomes an adult.

laser /ˈleɪzə/ (**lasers**) N-COUNT A **laser** is a narrow beam of concentrated light produced by a special machine, which is also called a **laser**. → see Word Web: **laser**

lash /læʃ/ (**lashes, lashing, lashed**) **1** N-COUNT Your **lashes** are the hairs that grow on the edge of your eyelids. **2** V-T If you **lash** something somewhere, you tie it firmly to something. ❑ *Secure the anchor by lashing it to the rail.* ❑ *All the equipment has to be lashed down.* **3** V-T/V-I If wind, rain, or water **lashes** someone or something, it hits them violently. [WRITTEN] ❑ *Suddenly rain lashed against the windows.* **4** V-T & N-COUNT If someone **lashes** another person, they hit that person with a whip. This action is called a **lash**. ❑ *One man was sentenced to five lashes.*

▶ **lash out** **1** PHR-VERB If you **lash out**, you try to hit someone with your hands or feet or with a weapon. **2** PHR-VERB If you **lash out at** someone or something, you speak to them very angrily or cruelly.

lass /læs/ (**lasses**) N-COUNT A **lass** is a young woman or girl. [BRIT, INFORMAL]

last /lɑːst, læst/ (**lasts, lasting, lasted**) **1** ADJ & PRON You use **last** to describe the most recent period of time, event, or thing. ❑ *I got married last July.* ❑ *Much has changed since my last visit.* ❑ *We do not want another year like the last.* **2** ORD & PRON The **last** thing, person, event, or period of time is the one that happens or comes after all the others of the same kind. ❑ *...the last three pages of the chapter.* ❑ *My aunt and uncle were the last ones to leave.* **3** DET & N-SING **Last** is used to refer to the only thing, person, or part of something that remains. ❑ *...the last piece of pizza.* ❑ *He finished the last of the wine.* **4** ADJ & PRON You can use **last** to emphasize that you do not want to do something or that something is unlikely to happen. ❑ *The last thing I want to do is teach.* ❑ *I would be the last to say that science has explained everything.* **5** ADV If something **last** happened on a particular occasion, it has not happened since then. ❑ *When were you there last?* ❑ *The house seemed smaller than when I last saw it.* **6** ADV If something happens **last**, it happens after everything else. ❑ *I was always chosen last for the football team.* **7** PRON If you are **the last to** do or know something, everyone else does or knows it before you. **8** V-T/V-I If something **lasts**, it continues to exist or happen. ❑ *The games lasted only half the normal time.* ❑ *Enjoy it because it won't last.* **9** V-T/V-I If something **lasts** for a particular length of time, it continues to be able to be used for that time. ❑ *This battery lasts twice as long as the smaller size.* **10** → see also **lasting** **11** PHRASE If something has happened **at last** or **at long last**, it has happened after you have been hoping for it for a long time. ❑ *I'm so glad that we've found you at last!* **12** PHRASE You use expressions such as **the night before last, the election before last**, and **the leader before last**, to refer to the period

Word Web laser

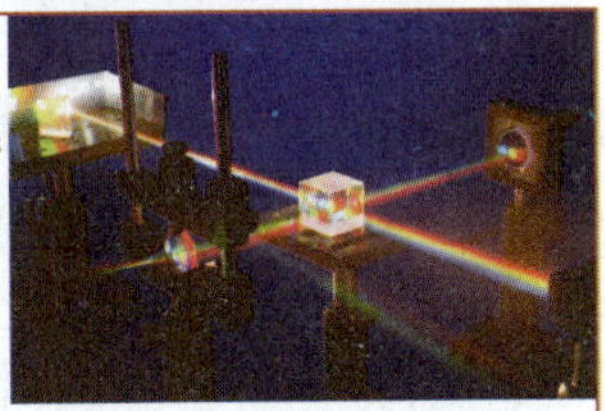

Lasers are an amazing form of technology. Laser **beams** read **CDs** and **DVDs**. They can create three-dimensional holograms. Laser **light shows** add excitement at concerts. **Fibre optic cables** carry strong flashes of laser light. This allows a single cable to transmit thousands of email and phone messages at the same time. Laser **scanners** read prices from bar codes. Lasers are also used as medical tools, such as the scalpels in **surgery**. They are also used to remove hair, birthmarks and tattoos. Dentists use lasers to remove cavities in teeth. Laser eye surgery has become very popular. In manufacturing, lasers make precise cuts in everything from fabric to steel.

of time, event, or person that happened or came immediately before the most recent one in a series. **13** PHRASE You can use expressions such as **the last I heard** and **the last she heard** to introduce a piece of information that is the most recent that you have on a particular subject. ❑ *The last I heard, Joe and Irene were still happily married.* **14** PHRASE You use expressions such as **to the last detail** and **to the last man** to indicate that a plan, situation, or activity includes every single person, thing, or part involved. **15** to **have the last laugh** → see **laugh** **16** **the last straw** → see **straw**

ˌlast-ˈditch ADJ BEFORE N A **last-ditch** action is done only because there are no other ways left to try to achieve something or to prevent something happening. ❑ *...a last-ditch attempt to prevent civil war.*

lasting /ˈlɑːstɪŋ, ˈlæst-/ ADJ Something that is **lasting** continues to exist or to be effective for a very long time. ❑ *She left a lasting impression on him.*

lastly /ˈlɑːstli, ˈlæst-/ **1** ADV You use **lastly** when you want to make a final point that is connected with the ones you have already mentioned. ❑ *Lastly, can I ask about your future plans?* **2** ADV You use **lastly** when you are saying what happens after everything else in a series of actions or events. ❑ *Stir in the cream and lemon juice. Lastly add the walnuts.*

ˌlast-ˈminute → see **minute**

L

latch /lætʃ/ (**latches, latching, latched**) **1** N-COUNT A **latch** is a fastening on a door or gate. It consists of a metal bar which you lower to lock the door and raise to open it. **2** N-COUNT A **latch** is a lock on a door which locks automatically when you shut the door.

▶ **latch onto** or **latch on** **1** PHR-VERB If you **latch onto** a person or an idea, or if you **latch on**, you become very interested in the person or idea, often because you find them useful. ❑ *Other companies were quick to latch on.* **2** PHR-VERB If one thing **latches onto** another, or if it **latches on**, it attaches itself to it. ❑ *Antibodies in their blood latch onto the virus and kill it.*

late /leɪt/ (**later, latest**) **1** ADV & ADJ **Late** means near the end of a period of time. ❑ *It was late in the afternoon.* ❑ *...the late 1960s.* **2** ADV & ADJ **Late** means after the time that was arranged or expected. ❑ *Steve arrived late.* ❑ *His career lasted, despite a late start, for over 30 years.* **3** ADJ AFTER LINK-V If it is **late**, it is near the end of the day or it is past the time that you feel something should have been done. ❑ *We've got to go now. It's getting late.* **4** ADV & ADJ **Late** means after the usual time that a particular event or activity happens. ❑ *We went to bed very late.* ❑ *They had a late lunch.* ● **lateness** N-UNCOUNT ❑ *He apologised for his lateness.* **5** ADJ BEFORE N You use **late** when you are talking about someone who is dead. ❑ *...the late Mr Parkin.* **6** → see also **later, latest** **7** PHRASE If you say that someone is doing something **late in the day**, you mean that it may fail because they have waited too long before doing it. ❑ *The politicians were accused of acting too late in the day.* **8** PHRASE You use **of late** to refer to an event or state of affairs that happened or began to exist a short time ago. [FORMAL] ❑ *Neither player has been performing well of late.*

lately /ˈleɪtli/ ADV **Lately** means recently. ❑ *Dad's health hasn't been too good lately.*

latent /ˈleɪtənt/ ADJ **Latent** is used to describe something which is hidden and not obvious at the moment, but which may develop further in the future. ❑ *Most of us have the latent talent to produce this kind of art.*

later /ˈleɪtə/ **1** **Later** is the comparative of **late**. **2** ADV & ADJ You use **later** or **later on** to refer to a time or situation that is after the one that you have been talking about or after the present one. ❑ *Later on I'll be speaking to Patty Davis.* ❑ *The competition was then re-scheduled for a later date.* **3** ADJ You use **later** to refer to the last part of someone's life or career or of a period in history. ❑ *He found happiness in later life.*

lateral /ˈlætərəl/ ADJ **Lateral** means relating to the sides of something, or moving in a sideways direction. ❑ *...the lateral movement of the bridge.*

> **Word Link** *est ≈ most : greatest, kindest, latest*

latest /ˈleɪtɪst/ **1** **Latest** is the superlative of **late**. **2** ADJ You use **latest** to describe something that is the most recent thing of its kind. ❑ *...her latest book.* **3** ADJ You can use **latest** to describe something that is extremely modern and up-to-date, and is therefore better than the other things of its type. ❑ *Computers have always represented the latest in technology.* **4** PHRASE You use **at the latest** to emphasize that something must happen at or before a particular time. ❑ *She'll be back by ten o'clock at the latest.*

ˌLatin Aˈmerican (**Latin Americans**) ADJ & N-COUNT **Latin American** means belonging or relating to the countries of South America, Central America, and Mexico. A **Latin American** is someone who lives in or comes from Latin America. ❑ *...Latin American art.*

latitude /ˈlætɪtjuːd, AM -tuːd/ (**latitudes**) N-VAR The **latitude** of a place is its distance from the Equator. Compare **longitude**. ❑ *All three cities lie on the same latitude, 43 degrees north.*
→ see **globe**

latter /ˈlætə/ **1** PRON & ADJ BEFORE N When two people, things, or groups have just been mentioned, you can refer to the second one as **the latter** or describe them as **the latter** person, thing, or group. ❑ *He found his cousin and uncle. The latter was sick.* **2** ADJ BEFORE N You use **latter** to describe the later part of a period of time or an event. ❑ *The Vanderbilts went to Paris in the latter part of the century.*

> **Usage**
>
> **The latter** should only be used to refer to the second of two items which have already been mentioned: ❑ *We have an apartment in the city and a house in the country, the latter being our favourite holiday spot.* The last of three or more items can be referred to as **the last-named.** Compare this with **the former** which is used to talk about the first of two things already mentioned.

ˈlatter-day ADJ BEFORE N **Latter-day** is used to describe a person or thing that is a modern equivalent of someone or something in the past. ❑ *He said that the latter-day hippies could stop on his land.*

lattice /ˈlætɪs/ (**lattices**) N-COUNT A **lattice** is a pattern or structure made of strips which cross over each other diagonally leaving holes in between. ❑ *He was crawling along the narrow steel lattice of the bridge.*

laugh /lɑːf, læf/ (**laughs, laughing, laughed**) **1** V-I & N-COUNT When you **laugh**, or when you give a **laugh**, you make a sound with your throat while smiling. ❑ *The British don't laugh at the same jokes as the French.* ❑ *He gave a deep laugh.* **2** V-I If people **laugh at** someone or something, they make jokes about them. ❑ *I thought they were laughing at me because I was ugly.* **3** PHRASE If you say that you **have the last laugh**, you mean that you make your critics look foolish or wrong, by being right or successful when you were not expected to be.
→ see Word Web: **laugh**

▶ **laugh off** PHR-VERB If you **laugh off** a difficult or serious situation, you try to suggest that it is amusing and unimportant. ❑ *I told her to laugh it off, but she couldn't.*

Thesaurus *laugh* Also look up:

V.	chuckle, crack up, giggle, howl; *(ant.)* cry **1**

Word Partnership Use *laugh* with:

ADJ.	**big** laugh, **good** laugh, **hearty** laugh, **little** laugh **1**
V.	**begin/start to** laugh, **hear *someone*** laugh, **make *someone*** laugh, **try to** laugh **1**

laughter /ˈlɑːftə, ˈlæf-/ N-UNCOUNT **Laughter** consists of people laughing. ❑ *Everybody roared with laughter.*
→ see **laugh**

Word Partnership Use *laughter* with:

ADJ.	**hysterical** laughter, **loud** laughter, **nervous** laughter
N.	**burst of** laughter, **sound of** laughter
V.	**burst into** laughter, **hear** laughter, **roar with** laughter

launch /lɔːntʃ/ (**launches, launching, launched**) **1** V-T & N-COUNT To **launch** a ship or a lifeboat means to put it into water, often for the first time. The occasion when this happens is called its **launch**. ❑ *Coastguards launched three lifeboats.* ❑ *The launch of a ship was a big occasion.* **2** V-T & N-VAR To **launch** a rocket, missile, or satellite means to send it into the air or into space. You can also refer to its **launch**. ❑ *A Delta II rocket was launched from Cape Canaveral.* ❑ *This morning's launch of the space shuttle Columbia has been delayed.* **3** V-T & N-COUNT To **launch** a large and important activity, for example a military attack, means to start it. The start of something like this is its **launch**. ❑ *The President was on holiday when the coup was launched.* ❑ *...the launch of a nationwide advertising campaign.* **4** V-T & N-COUNT If a company **launches** a new product, it starts to make it available to the public. You say this is the **launch** of the product. ❑ *Crabtree & Evelyn has just launched a new jam.* ❑ *The company's spending has risen following the launch of a new magazine.*
→ see **satellite**

▶ **launch into** PHR-VERB If you **launch into** something such as a speech, task, or fight, you start it enthusiastically. ❑ *Geoff has launched himself into fatherhood with great enthusiasm.*

launder /ˈlɔːndə/ (**launders, laundering, laundered**) **1** V-T When you **launder** clothes, bed linen, or towels, you wash and iron them. ❑ *...a freshly laundered white shirt.* **2** V-T To **launder** money means to process money that has been obtained illegally through a legitimate business or to send it abroad to a foreign bank, so that nobody knows that it was illegally obtained. ● **launderer** (**launderers**) N-COUNT

laundry /ˈlɔːndri/ (**laundries**) **1** N-UNCOUNT **Laundry** is used to refer to clothes, sheets, and towels that are about to be washed, are being washed, or have just been washed. ❑ *I'll do your laundry.* ❑ *...dirty laundry.* **2** N-COUNT A **laundry** is a place where clothes, sheets, and towels are washed and dried.
→ see **house, soap**

lava /ˈlɑːvə/ N-UNCOUNT **Lava** is the very hot liquid rock that comes out of a volcano.
→ see **rock, volcano**

lavatory /ˈlævətri, AM -tɔːri/ (**lavatories**) N-COUNT A **lavatory** is a toilet. [BRIT]

lavender /ˈlævɪndə/ N-UNCOUNT **Lavender** is a garden plant with sweet-smelling purple flowers.

lavish /ˈlævɪʃ/ (**lavishes, lavishing, lavished**) **1** ADJ If you describe something as **lavish**, you mean that a lot of time, effort, or money has been spent on it to make it as impressive as possible. ❑ *...a lavish party.* ● **lavishly** ADV ❑ *IBM spent lavishly on their workers' education.* **2** ADJ If you say that something is **lavish**, you mean it is extravagant and wasteful. ❑ *He stole jewellery and paintings to pay for a lavish lifestyle.* **3** V-T If you **lavish** something such as money, affection, or time **on** someone or something, you spend a lot of money on them or give them a lot of affection or attention. ❑ *Prince Sadruddin lavished praise on Britain's contribution.* ❑ *The emperor promoted the general and lavished him with gifts.*

l

Word Web laugh

There is an old saying, "**Laughter** is the best medicine." New scientific research supports the idea that **humour** really is good for your health. For example, laughing 100 times provides the same exercise benefits as a 15-minute bike ride. When a person **bursts out laughing**, levels of stress hormones in the bloodstream immediately drop. And laughter is more than just a sound. **Howling with laughter** gives face, stomach, leg, and back muscles a good workout. From polite **giggles** to noisy guffaws, laughter allows the release of anger, sadness, and fear. And that has to be good for you.

law /lɔː/ (**laws**) **1** N-SING **The law** is a system of rules that a society or government develops in order to deal with crime, business agreements, and social relationships. ❑ *It is against the law to cycle on pavements.* **2** N-PLURAL The **laws** of an organization or activity are its rules, which are used to organize and control it. **3** N-COUNT A **law** is a rule or set of rules for good behaviour which is considered right and important by the majority of people for moral, religious, or emotional reasons. ❑ *A new law means all black cabs must have wheelchair access.* **4** N-COUNT A **law** is a natural process in which a particular event or thing always leads to a particular result, or a scientific rule that someone has invented to explain such a process. ❑ *...the law of gravity.* **5** N-UNCOUNT **Law** or **the law** is all the professions which deal with advising people about the law, representing people in court, or giving decisions and punishments. **Law** is also the study of systems of law and how laws work. ❑ *...a career in law.* ❑ *...a law degree.* **6** PHRASE If someone **takes the law into** their **own hands**, they punish someone according to their own ideas of justice, often when this involves breaking the law.

'law-abiding ADJ A **law-abiding** person always obeys the law. ❑ *This was a peaceful law-abiding community.*

ˌlaw and 'order N-UNCOUNT When there is **law and order** in a country, the laws are generally accepted and obeyed there. ❑ *The minister praised the army for maintaining law and order in the country.*

L

lawful /ˈlɔːfʊl/ ADJ If an activity, organization, or product is **lawful**, it is allowed by law. [FORMAL] ● **lawfully** ADV ❑ *Did the police act lawfully in shooting him?*

lawless /ˈlɔːləs/ ADJ **Lawless** actions break the law, especially in a wild and violent way. ❑ *The president is trying to maintain authority over his lawless state.* ● **lawlessness** N-UNCOUNT ❑ *...acts of lawlessness.*

lawn /lɔːn/ (**lawns**) N-VAR A **lawn** is an area of grass that is kept cut short and is usually part of a garden or park.

lawnmower also **lawn mower** /ˈlɔːnməʊə/ (**lawnmowers**) N-COUNT A **lawnmower** is a machine for cutting grass on lawns.
→ see **hose**

lawsuit /ˈlɔːsuːt/ (**lawsuits**) N-COUNT A **lawsuit** is a case in a court of law which concerns a dispute between two people or organizations. [FORMAL]

lawyer /ˈlɔɪə/ (**lawyers**) N-COUNT A **lawyer** is a person who is qualified to advise people about the law and represent them in court.
→ see **trial**

Word Link *lax ≈ allowing, loosening : lax, laxative, relax*

lax /læks/ ADJ If you say that a person's behaviour or a system is **lax**, you mean they are not careful or strict in making or obeying rules or maintaining high standards. ❑ *One of the problems is lax security.* ● **laxity** N-UNCOUNT ❑ *The lawyer suggested there had been police laxity in the murder enquiry.*

laxative /ˈlæksətɪv/ (**laxatives**) N-VAR & ADJ A **laxative**, or a **laxative** substance, is something which you eat or drink which helps you to pass faeces through your body.

lay
1 PLACING AND PUTTING
2 NON-PROFESSIONAL

lay /leɪ/ (**lays, laying, laid**)
1 **1** **Lay** is the past tense of some meanings of **lie**. **2** V-T If you **lay** something somewhere, you put it there in a careful or neat way. ❑ *Mothers often lay babies on their backs to sleep.* **3** V-T If you **lay** something such as carpets, cables, or foundations, you put them into their permanent position. ❑ *Public services have to dig up roads to lay pipes.* **4** V-T When someone **lays** a trap, they prepare it to catch someone or something. ❑ *They were laying a trap for the kidnapper.* **5** V-T/V-I When a female bird **lays**, or **lays** an egg, an egg comes out of its body. **6** V-T **Lay** is used with some nouns to talk about making preparations for something. For example, if you **lay the basis for** something or **lay plans for** it, you prepare it carefully so that you can continue with it, develop it, or benefit from it later. ❑ *His work laid the foundations of modern psychology.* **7** V-T **Lay** is used with some nouns in expressions about accusing or blaming someone. For example, if you **lay the blame** for a mistake on someone, you say it is their fault. ❑ *John refused to lay the blame on his boss.*

Usage

Do not confuse the verb **lay** with the verb **lie**. The past tense and past participle of **lay** are **laid** and it is usually a transitive verb. ❑ *They laid him on the floor.* However, **lie** is an intransitive verb with the past tense **lay** and the past participle **lain**. ❑ *I lay on the floor with my legs in the air.* ❑ *He had lain in great pain in a darkened room.* Because **lay** is used to talk about putting something in a particular place or position, it is related to the verb **lie**. If someone **lays** something somewhere, it **lies** there. Because of their related meanings, people sometimes confuse the two verbs.

▶ **lay aside** PHR-VERB If you **lay aside** a feeling or belief, you reject it or give it up in order to progress with something. ❑ *To make a success of future talks, both sides will have to lay aside their long-term differences.*

▶ **lay down** PHR-VERB If rules or people in authority **lay down** what people must do, they tell people what they must do. ❑ *The Companies Act lays down a set of minimum requirements.*

▶ **lay into** PHR-VERB If you **lay into** someone, you start attacking them physically or criticizing them. [INFORMAL] ❑ *The women laid into him with handbags.*

▶ **lay off** **1** PHR-VERB If workers **are laid off** by their employers, they are told to leave their jobs, usually because there is no more work for them to do. ❑ *They did not sell a single car for a month and had to lay off workers.* **2** PHR-VERB If you tell someone to **lay off**, you mean that they should leave you or someone else alone. [INFORMAL]

▶ **lay on** PHR-VERB If you **lay on** food, entertainment, or a service, you provide it or supply it, especially in a generous or grand way. ❑ *They laid on a superb evening.*

▶ **lay out** **1** PHR-VERB If you **lay out** ideas or plans, you explain or present them clearly, for example in a document or a meeting. ❑ *Maxwell listened closely as Johnson laid out his plan.* **2** PHR-VERB To **lay out** an area of land or a building means to plan and design how its different parts should be arranged. **3** → see also **layout**

lay /leɪ/
2 **1** ADJ BEFORE N You use **lay** to describe people who are involved with a Christian church but are not monks, nuns, or members of the clergy. ❑ *He served as a lay reader in the Church of England.* **2** ADJ BEFORE N You use **lay** to describe someone who is not an expert or professional in a particular subject or activity. ❑ *Even a lay person can see that this new research is a step forward.*

layer /'leɪə/ (**layers, layering, layered**)
1 N-COUNT A **layer** of a material or substance is a quantity or flat piece of it that covers a surface or that is between two other things. ❑ *A fresh layer of snow covered the street.* ❑ *Cover the cheese with another layer of pastry.* **2** N-COUNT If something such as a system or an idea has many **layers**, it has many different levels or parts. ❑ *He is not concerned with deeper layers of meaning.* **3** V-T If you **layer** something, you arrange it in layers. ❑ *Try layering the fish with seaweed.* ❑ *...a layered haircut.*
→ see **ozone**

Word Partnership	Use *layer* with:
ADJ.	**bottom/top** layer, **lower/upper** layer, **outer** layer, **protective** layer, **single** layer, **thick/thin** layer **1**
N.	layer **cake**, layer **of dust**, layer **of fat**, **ozone** layer, layer **of skin**, **surface** layer **1**

layman /'leɪmən/ (**laymen**) N-COUNT A **layman** is a person who is not an expert or a professional in a particular subject or activity. ❑ *To the layman, this may not seem to matter.*

layout /'leɪaʊt/ (**layouts**) N-COUNT The **layout** of a garden, building, or piece of writing is the way in which the parts of it are arranged.

lazy /'leɪzi/ (**lazier, laziest**) **1** ADJ If someone is **lazy**, they do not want to work or make an effort. ❑ *I was too lazy to learn how to read music.* • **laziness** N-UNCOUNT ❑ *It was really laziness that stopped me.* **2** ADJ BEFORE N **Lazy** actions or activities are done in a slow and relaxed way, without making much effort. ❑ *We had a lazy lunch, then lay on the beach.* • **lazily** ADV ❑ *She smiled lazily.*

lb

The plural is **lbs** or **lb**.

lb is a written abbreviation for **pound**, when 'pound' refers to weight.

lead
1 BEING AHEAD OR TAKING SOMEONE SOMEWHERE
2 SUBSTANCES

lead /li:d/ (**leads, leading, led**)
1 **1** V-T/V-I If you **lead** a group of moving people, you walk or ride in front of them. ❑ *Bierhoff led the team on to the pitch.* ❑ *Tom was leading, his bag on his back.* **2** V-T If you **lead** someone to a particular place or thing, you take them there. ❑ *The nurse led me to a large room.* **3** V-I If something such as a road or door **leads** to a place, you can get to that place by following the road or going through the door. ❑ *...a main road leading north.* **4** V-T/V-I If you **are leading** in a race or competition, you are winning. ❑ *So far Fischer leads by five wins to two.* **5** N-SING If you have **the lead** or are **in the lead** in a race or competition, you are winning. The amount by which someone is winning can also be referred to as their **lead**. ❑ *England took the lead after 31 minutes.* ❑ *Sainz now has a lead of 28 points.* **6** V-T If you **lead** a group, an organization, or an activity, you are in charge of it. ❑ *He led the country between 1949 and 1984.* **7** N-COUNT If you give a **lead**, you do something which is considered a good example to follow. ❑ *Many others followed his lead.* **8** V-T You can use **lead** when you are saying what kind of life someone has. For example, if you **lead** a busy **life**, your life is busy. **9** V-I If something **leads to** a situation or event, it causes that situation or event to happen. ❑ *Disagreements between the republics could lead to civil war.* ❑ *What led you to do this work?* **10** V-T If someone or something **leads** you **to** think or expect something, they cause you to think or expect it, although it is not true or does not happen. ❑ *It was not as easy as we were led to believe.* **11** V-T If you **lead** a discussion or person onto a particular subject, you cause the discussion to develop in such a way that the subject is introduced. ❑ *After a while I led the conversation around to her job.* **12** N-COUNT A **lead** is a piece of information or an idea which may help people to discover the facts in a situation. ❑ *Police say they have no leads so far on the murder.* **13** N-SING **The lead** in a play, film, or show is the most important role in it. The person who plays this part can also be called **the lead**. ❑ *She has recently played the lead in Pearl Harbor.* **14** N-COUNT A dog's **lead** is a long chain or piece of leather attached to the dog's collar so that you can control the dog. **15** N-COUNT A **lead** in a piece of electrical equipment is a piece of wire which supplies electricity to the equipment. **16** → see also **leading** **17** to **lead** someone **astray** → see **astray**
→ see **mineral**

▸ **lead on to** PHR-VERB If one event or action **leads on to** another, it causes it or makes it possible. [BRIT] ❑ *Dancing led on to singing, acting and modelling.*

▸ **lead up to** **1** PHR-VERB Events that **lead up to** a situation happen one after the other until that situation is reached. ❑ *What events led up to these deaths?* **2** PHR-VERB The period of time **leading up to** an event is the period of time immediately before it happens. ❑ *...the weeks leading up to Christmas.*

lead /led/ (**leads**)
2 **1** N-UNCOUNT **Lead** is a soft, grey, heavy metal. **2** N-COUNT The **lead** in a pencil is the central part of it which makes a mark on paper.

Thesaurus	*lead* Also look up:
V.	escort, guide, precede; (*ant.*) follow ① **1** **2**
	govern, head, manage ① **6**

leader /'li:də/ (**leaders**) **1** N-COUNT The **leader** of an organization or a group of people is the person who is in charge of it. ❑ *...the Liberal Party leader.* **2** N-COUNT The **leader** in a race or

l

competition is the person who is winning at a particular time.

leadership /ˈliːdəʃɪp/ **1** N-SING You can refer to the people who are in charge of a group or organization as **the leadership**. ❑ *...the leadership of the local council.* **2** N-UNCOUNT Someone's **leadership** is their position or state of being in control of a group of people. ❑ *The agency doubled in size under her leadership.* **3** N-UNCOUNT **Leadership** refers to the qualities or methods that make someone a good leader. ❑ *There are times when firm leadership is required.*

leading /ˈliːdɪŋ/ **1** ADJ BEFORE N The **leading** people or things in a group are the most important or successful. ❑ *...a leading industrial nation.* **2** ADJ BEFORE N The **leading** role in a play or film is the main one. A **leading** lady or man is an actor who plays this role.

leaf /liːf/ (**leaves, leafs, leafing, leafed**)

The plural of the noun is **leaves**; the third person singular, present tense of the phrasal verb is **leafs**.

N-COUNT A **leaf** is one of the parts of a tree or plant that is flat, thin, and usually green.

leaf

→ see **flower, tea**

▶ **leaf through** PHR-VERB If you **leaf through** a book or magazine, you turn the pages quickly without looking at them carefully.

Word Link *let ≈ little : booklet, droplet, leaflet*

leaflet /ˈliːflət/ (**leaflets**) N-COUNT A **leaflet** is a little book or a piece of paper containing information about a particular subject. ❑ *...a leaflet called 'Sexual Harassment at Work'.*

leafy /ˈliːfi/ (**leafier, leafiest**) **1** ADJ **Leafy** trees and plants have a lot of leaves. ❑ *...green leafy vegetables.* **2** ADJ You say that a place is **leafy** when there are a lot of trees and plants there. ❑ *...London's leafy suburbs.*
→ see **vegetable**

league /liːg/ (**leagues**) **1** N-COUNT A **league** is a group of people, clubs, or countries that have joined together for a particular purpose or because they share a common interest. ❑ *...the League of Nations.* **2** N-COUNT You use **league** to make comparisons between different people or things, especially in terms of their quality. ❑ *These sales figures put them in the same league as The Rolling Stones.* **3** PHRASE If you say that someone is **in league with** someone else to do something bad, they are working together to do that thing. ❑ *I felt they were in league with each other against me.*

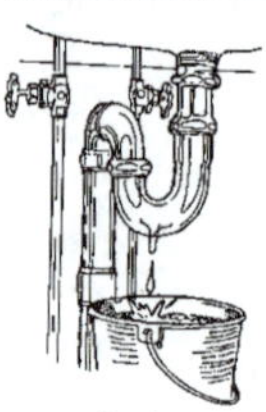

leak

leak /liːk/ (**leaks, leaking, leaked**) **1** V-I & N-COUNT If a container or other object **leaks**, or if it has a **leak**, there is a hole or crack in it which lets liquid or gas escape. You can also say the liquid or gas **leaks** from its container. ❑ *The roof leaked.* ❑ *The tanker is still leaking oil.* ❑ *...a gas leak.* **2** V-T & N-COUNT If a secret document or piece of information **is leaked** or if there is a **leak** involving it, someone lets the public know about it. ❑ *A civil servant was imprisoned for leaking a document to the press.* ❑ *They'll find out who was responsible for these leaks.*

Thesaurus *leak* Also look up:

N.	crack, hole, opening **1**
V.	discharge, drip, ooze, seep, trickle **1**
	come out, divulge, pass on **2**

Word Partnership Use *leak* with:

V.	**cause a** leak, **spring a** leak **1**
N.	**fuel** leak, **gas** leak, **oil** leak, leak **in the roof**, **water** leak **1**
	leak **information**, leak **news**, leak **a story** **2**

leakage /ˈliːkɪdʒ/ (**leakages**) N-VAR **Leakage** is the escape of liquid or gas from a container through a crack or hole.

lean /liːn/ (**leans, leaning, leaned** or [BRIT also] **leant** /lent/, **leaner, leanest**) **1** V-I When you **lean** in a particular direction, you bend your body in that direction. ❑ *They stopped to lean over a gate.* **2** V-T/V-I If you **lean on** something, you rest against it so that it partly supports you. If you **lean** an object somewhere, you place the object so that its weight is partly supported. ❑ *Lou was at the bus stop, leaning on her stick.* ❑ *Lean the plants against a wall.*

lean

3 V-I If you **lean** towards an idea or a way of behaving, you tend to think or act in that way. ❑ *The chairman was leaning in favour of appointing a new manager.* **4** ADJ A **lean** person is thin but looks strong and fit. **5** ADJ **Lean** meat has very little fat. **6** ADJ A **lean** period of time is one in which people have little money or success. ❑ *It is a lean time for the oil business.*

▶ **lean on** PHR-VERB If you **lean on** someone, you depend on them for support and help. ❑ *You can lean on me.*

Thesaurus *lean* Also look up:

V.	bend, incline, prop, tilt **1**
	recline, rest **2**
ADJ.	angular, slender, slim, wiry **4**

Word Partnership Use *lean* with:

ADV.	lean **heavily** **2**
ADJ.	**long and** lean, **tall and** lean **4**
N.	lean **body** **4**
	lean **beef**, lean **meat** **5**

leap /liːp/ (**leaps, leaping, leaped** or **leapt** /lept/)

In British English, the form **leapt** is usually used in the past tense and past participle. American English usually uses **leaped**.

1 V-I & N-COUNT If you **leap**, or if you take a **leap**, you jump high in the air or jump a long distance.

❑ *He had leapt from a window and escaped.* **2** V-I If you **leap** somewhere, you move there suddenly and quickly. ❑ *The two men leaped into the jeep.* ❑ *The car leapt forward.* **3** V-I & N-COUNT You can say that things **leap** or take a **leap** when they suddenly advance or increase by a large amount. ❑ *Their share will leap to about 15 per cent.* ❑ *...a giant leap in productivity.* **4** V-I If you **leap at** a chance or opportunity, you accept it quickly and eagerly.

learn /lɜːn/ (**learns, learning, learned** or [BRIT also] **learnt** /lɜːnt/) **1** V-T/V-I When you **learn**, you obtain knowledge or a skill through studying or training. ❑ *Their children are going to learn English.* ❑ *He is learning to play the piano.* ❑ *You need to learn how to use a computer.* • **learner** (**learners**) N-COUNT ❑ *...help for slow learners.* • **learning** N-UNCOUNT ❑ *...a bilingual approach to the learning of English.* **2** V-T If you **learn** something such as a poem or the script of a play, you study or repeat the words so that you can remember them. **3** V-T If people **learn to** behave or react in a particular way, their attitudes gradually change and they start behaving in that way. ❑ *He learned to hide his views.* ❑ *It took years to learn how to do it.* **4** V-T/V-I If you **learn from** an experience, you change the way you behave so that it does not happen again, or so that you can deal with it if it happens again. ❑ *He has learned a lot from his mistakes.* **5** V-T/V-I If you **learn of** something, you find out about it. ❑ *We first learned of her plans in a newspaper report.* ❑ *She wasn't surprised to learn that he was involved.*
→ see **brain**

Thesaurus	*learn* Also look up:
V.	master, pick up, study **1**
	discover, find out, understand **5**

learned /ˈlɜːnɪd/ ADJ A **learned** person has gained a lot of knowledge by studying. **Learned** books have been written by a learned person. ❑ *...a genuinely learned man.*

lease /liːs/ (**leases, leasing, leased**) **1** N-COUNT A **lease** is a legal agreement under which someone pays money to another person in exchange for the use of a building or piece of land for a specified period of time. ❑ *He took a 10-year lease on the house.* **2** V-T If you **lease** property or something such as a car, or if someone **leases** it **to** you, they allow you to use it in return for regular payments of money. ❑ *He leased an apartment.* ❑ *She hopes to lease the building to students.* **3** PHRASE If you say that someone or something has been given **a new lease of life**, you are emphasizing that they are much more lively or successful than they have been in the past.

least /liːst/

Least is often considered to be the superlative form of **little**.

1 ADJ & ADV & PRON You use **the least** to mean a smaller amount or extent than anyone or anything else, or the smallest amount or extent possible. ❑ *If you like cheese, buy the ones with the least fat.* ❑ *I'm the least experienced person.* ❑ *We might get caught when we least expect it.* ❑ *...the gap between the people earning the most and the people earning the least money.* **2** ADJ You use **least** in structures where you are emphasizing that a particular situation or event is much less important or serious than other possible or actual ones. ❑ *Feeling sick is the least of her worries.* **3** PHRASE You use **at least** to say that a number, amount, or action is the minimum possible or likely, and that more may be possible. The forms **at the least** and **at the very least** are also used. ❑ *The menu features at least 15 different sorts of fish.* ❑ *She could take a nice holiday at least.* **4** PHRASE You use **at least** when you are mentioning an advantage that still exists in a bad situation. ❑ *At least we know he is still alive.* **5** PHRASE You can use **in the least** and **the least bit** to emphasize a negative. ❑ *I'm not like that at all. Not in the least.* ❑ *Alice wasn't the least bit frightened.* **6** PHRASE You can use **not least** to emphasize an important example or reason. ❑ *Dieting can be bad for you, not least because it is a cause of stress.* **7** PHRASE You can use **to say the least** to suggest that a situation is actually much more extreme or serious than you say it is. ❑ *The food was basic to say the least.*

Thesaurus	*least* Also look up:
ADJ.	fewest, lowest, minimum, smallest **1**

leather /ˈleðə/ (**leathers**) N-VAR **Leather** is treated animal skin which is used for making shoes, clothes, bags, and furniture. ❑ *...a leather jacket.*

leave /liːv/ (**leaves, leaving, left** /left/) **1** V-T/V-I If you **leave** a place or person, you go away from that place or person. ❑ *I simply couldn't leave my little girl.* ❑ *My flight leaves in an hour.* ❑ *The older children had left for school.* **2** V-T/V-I If you **leave** an institution, group, or job, you stop attending that institution, being a member of that group, or doing that job. ❑ *He left school with no qualifications.* ❑ *...a leaving present.* **3** V-T If someone **leaves** their husband, wife, or partner, they end the relationship and stop living with him or her. ❑ *I'm afraid Bill has left me.* **4** V-T If you **leave** something somewhere, you put it there and it remains there when you go away. ❑ *I left my bags in the car.* ❑ *Leave your key with a neighbour.* ❑ *He left me a nice little note.* **5** V-T If someone or something **leaves** an amount of something, that amount remains available after the rest has been used or has gone. ❑ *He always left a little food for the next day.* ❑ *It doesn't leave me much time.* **6** V-T If something **leaves** a mark, effect, or sign, it causes that mark, effect, or sign to remain as a result. ❑ *He wiped his hand across his face, leaving a streak like paint.* ❑ *She left a lasting impression on him.* **7** V-T If an event **leaves** people or things in a particular state, they are in that state when the event has finished. ❑ *Street fights have left at least ten people dead.* **8** V-T If you **leave** someone **to** do something, you go away from them so that they do it on their own, or you give them the responsibility for dealing with it. ❑ *I'd better leave you to get on with it.* **9** PHRASE If you **leave** someone or something **alone**, you do not bother them or try to do anything with them. ❑ *He followed me everywhere and just would not leave me alone.* ❑ *Pets are being left alone for longer.* **10** V-T If you **leave** something until a particular time, you delay dealing with it. ❑ *Don't leave it all until the last minute.* **11** V-T If you **leave** property or money **to** someone, you arrange for it to be given to them after you have died. **12** V-T If you say that someone **leaves** a wife, husband, or a particular number of children, you mean that the wife, husband, or children remain alive after that person has died. **13** N-UNCOUNT & PHRASE **Leave** is a period of time when you are not working at your job. If you are **on leave**, you are not at your job. ❑ *Why don't you take a few days' leave?*

▶ **leave behind** **1** PHR-VERB If you **leave** someone or something **behind**, you go away permanently from them. ❑ *When he went, he left behind a wife and two young children.* **2** PHR-VERB If someone or something **leaves behind** an object or a situation, that object or situation remains after they have gone. ❑ *Beethoven left behind an enormous number of notebooks.* **3** PHR-VERB If a person, country, or organization **is left behind**, they do not achieve as much as others or they do not progress as quickly, so they are at a disadvantage.

▶ **leave off** PHR-VERB If someone or something **is left off** a list, they are not included on that list.

▶ **leave out** PHR-VERB If you **leave** someone or something **out of** something such as an activity or a collection, you do not include them in it. ❑ *I never left him out of my team.*

Thesaurus *leave* Also look up:

v. abandon, depart, go away; *(ant.)* arrive, come, stay **1**
give up, quit, resign; *(ant.)* remain, stay **2**
abandon, desert, ditch, take off **3**

L

leaves /liːvz/ **Leaves** is the plural form of **leaf**.

lecture /ˈlektʃə/ (**lectures, lecturing, lectured**) **1** N-COUNT A **lecture** is a talk that someone gives in order to teach people about a particular subject, usually at a university. **2** V-I If you **lecture on** a particular subject, you give a lecture or a series of lectures about it. ❑ *He was then invited to lecture on the history of art.* **3** V-T & N-COUNT If someone **lectures** you **about** something, or if they **give** you a **lecture**, they criticize you or tell you how they think you should behave. ❑ *Dad would lecture me about getting a haircut.* ❑ *Our captain gave us a lecture on safety.*

lecturer /ˈlektʃərə/ (**lecturers**) N-COUNT A **lecturer** is a teacher at university or college.

led /led/ **Led** is the past tense and past participle of **lead**.

ledge /ledʒ/ (**ledges**) **1** N-COUNT A **ledge** is a narrow shelf along the bottom edge of a window. **2** N-COUNT A **ledge** is a piece of rock shaped like a narrow shelf on the side of a cliff or mountain.

ledger /ˈledʒə/ (**ledgers**) N-COUNT A **ledger** is a book in which a company or other organization writes down the amounts of money it spends and receives.

leek /liːk/ (**leeks**) N-VAR **Leeks** are long green and white vegetables which smell similar to onions.

leer /lɪə/ (**leers, leering, leered**) V-I & N-COUNT If someone **leers at** you, or if they look at you with a **leer**, they smile in an unpleasant way; used showing disapproval. ❑ *The soldier leered at Sarah.* ❑ *The clerk gave me my key with a leer.*

left /left/ **1** **Left** is the past tense and past participle of **leave**. **2** ADJ & PHRASE If there is a certain amount of something **left**, or if you have a certain amount of it **left over**, it remains when the rest has gone or been used. ❑ *Is there any milk left?* ❑ *They still have six games left to play.* **3** N-SING & ADV & ADJ BEFORE N **The left** is one of two opposite directions, sides, or positions. In the word 'to', the 't' is to the left of the 'o'. If you are facing north and you turn **left**, you will be facing west. **Left** is used to describe the one of two things that someone has, for example their arm or leg, that is on the left. ❑ *In Britain cars drive on the left.* ❑ *To my left, I noticed a light.* ❑ *Go left at the traffic lights.* ❑ *Derek had the stick in his left hand.* **4** N-SING You can refer to political ideas which are closer to socialism than to capitalism, or to people who support these ideas, as **the left**. ❑ *The change has been bitterly opposed by the left.*

ˈleft-click (**left-clicks, left-clicking, left-clicked**) V-I To **left-click** or to **left-click on** something means to press the left-hand button on a computer mouse. [COMPUTING] ❑ *Left-click on one of the choices to operate it.*

ˈleft-hand ADJ BEFORE N **Left-hand** describes the position of something when it is on the left side. ❑ *...the back left-hand corner of the drawer.*

ˌleft-ˈhanded ADJ Someone who is **left-handed** finds it easier to use their left hand rather than their right hand for activities such as writing and throwing a ball.

leftist /ˈleftɪst/ (**leftists**) N-COUNT & ADJ BEFORE N Socialists and communists are sometimes referred to as **leftists**. ❑ *she became involved in leftist policies.*

leftover /ˈleftəʊvə/ (**leftovers**) ADJ BEFORE N & N-PLURAL **Leftover** things or **leftovers** are things which remain after the other similar things have been used, especially food which remains after a meal.

ˌleft-ˈwing also **left wing** **1** ADJ **Left-wing** people have political ideas that are based on socialism. ❑ *They will not be voting for him because he is too left-wing.* **2** N-SING The **left wing** of a political group consists of the members of it whose beliefs are closer to socialism than are those of its other members.

leg /leg/ (**legs**) **1** N-COUNT A person or animal's **legs** are the long parts of their body that they use to stand on and walk with. **2** N-COUNT The **legs of** a pair of trousers are the parts that cover your legs. **3** N-COUNT A **leg** of lamb or pork is a piece of meat from the thigh of a sheep, lamb, or pig. **4** N-COUNT The **legs** of a table, chair, or other piece of furniture are the parts that rest on the floor, supporting the furniture's weight. **5** N-COUNT A **leg** of a long journey is one part of it. ❑ *The first leg of the journey was by boat to Lake Naivasha.*

→ see **body**

legacy /ˈlegəsi/ (**legacies**) **1** N-COUNT A **legacy** is money or property which someone leaves to you in their will when they die. **2** N-COUNT The **legacy of** an event or period of history is something which is a direct result of it and which continues to exist after it is over. ❑ *Seafood pies are a legacy of the Middle Ages.*

legal /ˈliːgəl/ **1** ADJ BEFORE N **Legal** is used to describe things that relate to the law. ❑ *He found he had a legal problem.* ❑ *...the British legal system.* ● **legally** ADV ❑ *Mr. Scott is, legally speaking, responsible for this.* **2** ADJ An action or situation that is **legal** is allowed by law. ❑ *This driver had more* than the legal limit of alcohol. • **legally** ADV ❑ *We accept that the sculptures were legally acquired.* • **legality** /li'gælɪti/ N-UNCOUNT ❑ *We are questioning the legality of the deal.*

Word Partnership	Use *legal* with:
N.	legal **action**, legal **advice**, legal **battle**, legal **bills**, legal **costs/expenses**, legal **department**, legal **documents**, legal **expert**, legal **fees**, legal **guardian**, legal **issue**, legal **liability**, legal **matters**, legal **obligation**, legal **opinion**, legal **problems/troubles**, legal **procedures/proceedings**, legal **profession**, legal **responsibility**, legal **rights**, legal **services**, legal **status**, legal **system** 1
ADV.	**perfectly** legal 2

legalize [BRIT also **legalise**] /'li:gəlaɪz/ (**legalizes, legalizing, legalized**) V-T If something **is legalized**, the law is changed so that it is allowed. ❑ *The letting of private homes was legalized in 1990.*

legend /'ledʒənd/ (**legends**) 1 N-VAR A **legend** is a very old and popular story that may be based on real events. ❑ *...the legends of ancient Greece.* 2 N-COUNT If you refer to someone as a **legend**, you mean that they are very famous and admired. ❑ *...Hollywood legend Audrey Hepburn.*
→ see **fantasy**

legendary /'ledʒəndri, AM -deri/ 1 ADJ If you describe someone or something as **legendary**, you mean that they are very famous and that many stories are told about them. ❑ *...the legendary jazz singer Adelaide Hall.* 2 ADJ A **legendary** person, place, or event is described in a legend.

leggings /'legɪŋz/ N-PLURAL **Leggings** are tight trousers that are made out of a fabric which stretches easily.

legion /'li:dʒən/ (**legions**) 1 N-COUNT A **legion** is a large group of soldiers who form one section of an army. 2 N-COUNT A **legion of** people or things is a large number of them. ❑ *...legions of stories about noisy neighbours.*

legislate /'ledʒɪsleɪt/ (**legislates, legislating, legislated**) V-T/V-I When a government **legislates**, it passes a new law. ❑ *You can't legislate against prejudice.* ❑ *You cannot legislate to change attitudes.*

legislation /ˌledʒɪ'sleɪʃən/ N-UNCOUNT **Legislation** consists of a law or laws passed by a government. ❑ *The new legislation protects women's rights.*

Word Partnership	Use *legislation* with:
ADJ.	**federal** legislation, **new** legislation, **proposed** legislation
V.	**draft** legislation, **enact** legislation, **introduce** legislation, **oppose** legislation, **pass** legislation, **support** legislation, **veto** legislation

legislative /'ledʒɪslətɪv, AM -leɪ-/ ADJ BEFORE N **Legislative** means involving or relating to the process of making and passing laws.

legislator /'ledʒɪsleɪtə/ (**legislators**) N-COUNT A **legislator** is someone involved in making or passing laws.

legislature /'ledʒɪslətʃə, AM -leɪ-/ (**legislatures**) N-COUNT The **legislature** of a state or country is the group of people within it who have the power to make and pass laws. [FORMAL]

legitimate /lɪ'dʒɪtɪmət/ 1 ADJ Something that is **legitimate** is acceptable according to the law. ❑ *They claimed the perfectly legitimate banknotes were fakes.* • **legitimacy** N-UNCOUNT ❑ *The company is challenging the legitimacy of the deal.* • **legitimately** ADV ❑ *He still claims to be the legitimately elected president.* 2 ADJ If you say that something such as a feeling or opinion is **legitimate**, you think that it is reasonable and acceptable. ❑ *That's a perfectly legitimate fear.* • **legitimately** ADV ❑ *You can legitimately claim to feel angry and disappointed.*

leisure /'leʒə, AM 'li:ʒ-/ 1 N-UNCOUNT **Leisure** is the time when you do not have to work and can do things that you enjoy. ❑ *It was a relaxing way to fill my leisure time.* 2 PHRASE If someone does something **at leisure** or **at** their **leisure**, they do it when they want to, without hurrying. ❑ *Stroll at leisure through the gardens.*

leisurely /'leʒəli, AM 'li:ʒ-/ ADJ & ADV A **leisurely** action is done in a relaxed and unhurried way. ❑ *Tweedy walked at a leisurely pace.*

lemon /'lemən/ (**lemons**) N-VAR A **lemon** is a sour yellow citrus fruit. ❑ *...a slice of lemon.*
→ see **fruit**

lemonade /ˌlemə'neɪd/ N-UNCOUNT **Lemonade** is a clear, sweet, fizzy drink, or a drink that is made from lemons, sugar, and water.

lend /lend/ (**lends, lending, lent**) 1 V-T When people or organizations such as banks **lend** you money, they give it to you and you agree to pay it back at a future date, often with an extra amount as interest. ❑ *I lent him ten pounds to take his children to the cinema.* ❑ *The White House said that America would lend another $1.5 billion.* • **lender** (**lenders**) N-COUNT ❑ *...the six leading money lenders.* • **lending** N-UNCOUNT ❑ *...a fall in bank lending.* 2 V-T If you **lend** something that you own, you allow someone to have or to use it for a period of time. ❑ *Will you lend me your jacket?* 3 V-T To **lend** something such as a particular quality **to** something means to give it that quality. ❑ *He lent his support to the plan.* 4 V-T If something **lends itself to** a particular activity, it is very suitable for it. ❑ *Piano lends itself to all styles of music.*

length /leŋθ/ (**lengths**) 1 N-VAR The **length** of something is the amount that it measures from one end to the other. ❑ *It is about a metre in length.* ❑ *...the length of the fish.* 2 N-UNCOUNT The **length** of something is its quality of being long. ❑ *I noticed, too, the length of her fingers.* 3 N-VAR The **length** of something such as a piece of writing is the amount of writing that is contained in it. 4 N-VAR The **length** of an event, activity, or situation is the time it lasts. ❑ *The film is over two hours in length.* 5 N-COUNT A

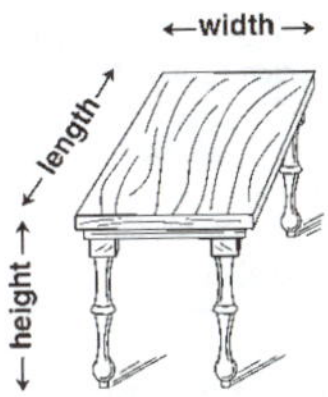

length

l

length of wood, string, cloth, or other material is a piece of it. ❑ *Hang lengths of fabric behind the glass.* 6 N-COUNT If you swim a **length** in a swimming pool, you swim from one end to the other. 7 N-SING If something happens or exists along **the length of** something, it happens or exists for the whole way along it. ❑ *I looked along the length of the building.* 8 PHRASE If you do something **at length**, you do it for a long time and in great detail. ❑ *They spoke at length.* 9 PHRASE If you **go to great lengths to** achieve something, you try very hard and may do extreme things in order to achieve it. ❑ *Greta went to great lengths to hide from reporters.*

Word Partnership Use *length* with:

N. length **and width** 1
length **of** ***your*** **stay**, length **of time**, length **of treatment** 4
ADJ. **average** length, **entire** length 1 3 4

lengthen /ˈleŋθən/ (**lengthens, lengthening, lengthened**) V-T/V-I When something **lengthens**, or when you **lengthen** it, it becomes longer. ❑ *Holidays have lengthened.*

lengthy /ˈleŋθi/ (**lengthier, lengthiest**) 1 ADJ Something that is **lengthy** lasts for a long time. ❑ *We will have lengthy dry and sunny spells.* 2 ADJ A **lengthy** report, book, or document contains a lot of speech or writing.

Word Partnership Use *lengthy* with:

N. lengthy **period** 1
lengthy **description**, lengthy **discourse**, lengthy **discussion**, lengthy **report** 2

lenient /ˈliːniənt/ ADJ When someone in authority is **lenient**, they are not as strict or as severe as expected. ❑ *He received an unexpectedly lenient sentence.* ● **leniently** ADV ❑ *He will be treated more leniently if he keeps quiet.*

lens /lenz/ (**lenses**) N-COUNT A **lens** is a thin, curved piece of glass or plastic in something such as a camera or pair of glasses which makes things appear larger or clearer.
→ see **eye**

lent /lent/ **Lent** is the past tense and past participle of **lend**.

Lent N-UNCOUNT **Lent** is the period of forty days before Easter, during which some Christians give up something that they enjoy. ❑ *It was a favourite meal on Fridays and fast days, particularly during Lent.*

lentil /ˈlentɪl/ (**lentils**) N-COUNT **Lentils** are a type of dried seed used in cooking.

leopard /ˈlepəd/ (**leopards**) N-COUNT A **leopard** is a type of large wild cat from Africa or Asia. Leopards have yellow fur and black spots.

lesbian /ˈlezbiən/ (**lesbians**) N-COUNT & ADJ A **lesbian** or a **lesbian** woman is a woman who is sexually attracted to women.

less /les/ 1 QUANT & ADV You use **less** to indicate that there is a smaller number of things or a smaller amount of something than before or than average, or than something else. ❑ *People should eat less fat.* ❑ *Over here, things have been a bit less dramatic.* ❑ *He still eats cheese, but less often.* ❑ *...spending less and saving more.* ❑ *Last year less of the money went into high-technology companies.* 2 PREP You use **less than** before a number or amount to say that the actual number or amount is smaller than this. ❑ *Motorways actually cover less than 0.1 percent of the countryside.* 3 PREP When you are referring to amounts, you use **less** in front of a number or quantity to indicate that it is to be subtracted from another number or quantity already mentioned. ❑ *...Fees: £750, less £400.* 4 PHRASE You use **less and less** to say that something is becoming smaller all the time in degree or amount. ❑ *The couple seem to spend less and less time together.* 5 PHRASE You can use **no less** to emphasize your surprise or admiration at the amount or importance of someone or something. ❑ *He had returned to England in an aircraft carrier no less.* 6 PHRASE You use **no less than** before an amount to indicate that you think the amount is larger than you expected. ❑ *He is booked for no less than four US television interviews.* 7 PHRASE You use **less than** to say that something does not have a particular quality. For example, something that is **less than** perfect is not perfect. 8 **more or less** → see **more**

Usage

You use **less** to talk about amounts that cannot be counted, except in the phrase **no less than.** ❑ *...less money.* ❑ *...no less than nine goals.* When you are talking about things that can be counted, you should use **fewer**, for example ❑ *fewer than five visits.*

lessen /ˈlesən/ (**lessens, lessening, lessened**) V-T/V-I If something **lessens**, or if you **lessen** it, it becomes smaller in amount, degree, or importance. ❑ *Changes to their diet would lessen the risk of heart disease.* ● **lessening** N-UNCOUNT ❑ *...a lessening of violence.*

lesser /ˈlesə/ ADJ & ADV You use **lesser** in order to indicate that something is smaller in extent or amount than another thing that has been mentioned. ❑ *The responsibility lies with Harris and, to a lesser extent, Clarke.* ❑ *...lesser known works by famous artists.*

lesson /ˈlesən/ (**lessons**) 1 N-COUNT A **lesson** is a fixed period of time during which people are taught something. ❑ *Johanna took piano lessons.* 2 N-COUNT If an experience teaches you a **lesson**, it makes you realize the truth or realize what should be done. ❑ *There's still one lesson to be learned from the crisis.* 3 PHRASE If you say that you are going to **teach** someone **a lesson**, you mean that you are going to punish them for something that they have done so that they do not do it again.

Thesaurus *lesson* Also look up:

N. class, course, instruction, session 1

Word Partnership Use *lesson* with:

ADJ. **private** lesson 1
hard lesson, **important** lesson, **painful** lesson, **valuable** lesson 2
V. **get a** lesson, **give a** lesson 1 2
learn a lesson, **teach** ***someone*** **a** lesson 2 3

lest /lest/ CONJ If you do something **lest** something unpleasant should happen, you do it to try to prevent the unpleasant thing from happening. [FORMAL] ❑ *I was afraid to open the door lest he should follow me.*

let /let/ (**lets, letting, let**) **1** V-T If you **let** something happen, you allow it to happen. ❑ *Thorne let him talk.* ❑ *Mum doesn't let me have many sweets.* ❑ *I can't let myself be distracted.* **2** V-T If you **let** someone into, out of, or through a place, you allow them to enter, leave, or go through it. ❑ *I let myself into the flat.* ❑ *I'd better go and let the dog out.* **3** V-T You use **let me** when you are introducing something you want to do, or something you are offering to do. ❑ *Let me explain.* ❑ *Let me get you something to drink.* **4** V-T You use **let's** or **let us** when you are making a suggestion. ❑ *I'm bored. Let's go home.* ❑ *'Shall we go in?'—'Yes, let's.'* **5** V-T & PHR-VERB If you **let** your house or land to someone, or if you **let** it **out**, you allow them to use it in exchange for regular payments. ❑ *I couldn't sell the flat, so I let it out.* **6** PHRASE **Let alone** is used after a statement, usually a negative one, to indicate that the statement is even more true of the person or situation that you are going to mention next. ❑ *It is incredible that the 12-year-old managed to reach the pedals, let alone drive the car.* **7** PHRASE If you **let go of** someone or something, you stop holding them. ❑ *She let go of Mona's hand.* **8** PHRASE If you **let** someone **know** something, you make sure that they know about it. ❑ *If you do want to go, please let me know.*

▸ **let down** **1** PHR-VERB If you **let** someone **down**, you disappoint them, usually by not doing something that you said you would do. ❑ *Don't worry, Robert, I won't let you down.* **2** PHR-VERB If you **let down** something filled with air, such as a tyre, you allow air to escape from it. ❑ *After the party was over, they let down the balloons.*

▸ **let in** PHR-VERB If an object **lets in** something such as air or water, it allows air or water to get into it or pass through it. ❑ *There is no glass in the front door to let in light.*

▸ **let in on** PHR-VERB If you **let** someone **in on** something that is a secret from most people, you allow them to know about it.

▸ **let off** **1** PHR-VERB If someone in authority **lets** you **off** a task or duty, they give you permission not to do it. [BRIT] ❑ *They let me off a couple of performances to go to Yorkshire.* **2** PHR-VERB If you **let** someone **off**, you give them a lighter punishment than they expect or no punishment at all. ❑ *Because he was seriously ill, the judge let him off.* **3** PHR-VERB If you **let off** an explosive or a gun, you explode or fire it. ❑ *They let off fireworks to celebrate the Revolution.*

▸ **let on** PHR-VERB If you do not **let on** that something is true, you do not tell anyone that it is true. [BRIT] ❑ *I'd be in trouble if I let on.*

▸ **let out** **1** PHR-VERB If something or someone **lets** water, air, or breath **out**, they allow it to flow out or escape. ❑ *It lets sunlight in but doesn't let heat out.* **2** → see also **let** (meaning 5)

▸ **let up** PHR-VERB If an unpleasant, continuous process **lets up**, it stops or reduces. ❑ *The traffic in the city never lets up, even at night.*

Thesaurus	*let* Also look up:
v.	allow, approve, permit; *(ant.)* prevent, stop **1** **2**

lethal /ˈliːθəl/ ADJ Something that is **lethal** can kill you. ❑ *...a lethal dose of sleeping pills.*

lethargic /lɪˈθɑːdʒɪk/ ADJ If you are **lethargic**, you have no energy or enthusiasm. ❑ *He felt too miserable and lethargic to get dressed.*

lethargy /ˈleθədʒi/ N-UNCOUNT **Lethargy** is a condition in which you have no energy or enthusiasm.

let's /lets/ **Let's** is the usual spoken and written form of **let us**.

letter /ˈletə/ (**letters**) **1** N-COUNT When you write a **letter**, you write a message on paper and send it to someone. ❑ *I had received a letter from a friend.* ❑ *...a letter of resignation.* **2** N-COUNT **Letters** are written symbols which represent the sounds of a language. ❑ *...the letter E.*

letterbox also **letter box** /ˈletəbɒks/ (**letterboxes**) N-COUNT A **letterbox** is a rectangular hole in a door through which letters are delivered.

lettering /ˈletərɪŋ/ N-UNCOUNT You can use **lettering** to refer to writing, especially when you are describing the type of letters used. ❑ *...a blue sign with white lettering.*

lettuce /ˈletɪs/ (**lettuces**) N-VAR A **lettuce** is a plant with large green leaves that you eat in salads.

leukaemia [AM **leukemia**] /luˈkiːmiə/ N-UNCOUNT **Leukaemia** is a serious disease of the blood.

level /ˈlevəl/ (**levels, levelling, levelled** or [AM] **leveling, leveled**) **1** N-COUNT A **level** is a point on a scale, for example a scale of amount, importance, or difficulty. ❑ *...the lowest level of inflation for some years.* ❑ *On a personal level, Michael is very warm and likeable.* **2** N-SING The **level** of something is its height or the height of its surface. ❑ *He held the gun at waist level.* ❑ *The water level of the Mississippi River is already 6.5 feet below normal.* **3** ADJ AFTER LINK-V If one thing is **level with** another thing, it is at the same height. ❑ *He leaned over the counter so he was almost level with the boy's face.* **4** ADJ Something that is **level** is completely flat. ❑ *I was unable to walk, except on level ground.* **5** V-T If someone or something such as a violent storm **levels** a building or area of land, they flatten or destroy it completely. ❑ *Further tremors could level more buildings.* **6** ADV & ADJ AFTER LINK-V If you **draw level with** someone or something, you get closer to them until you are by their side. ❑ *Everyone waited till she drew level with them on the platform.* ❑ *He waited until they were level with the door.* **7** V-T If an accusation or criticism **is levelled at** someone, they are criticized for something they have done or are accused of doing something wrong. ❑ *His main criticism was levelled at the singing, rather than the dancing.* **8** **a level playing field** → see **playing field**

▸ **level off** or **level out** PHR-VERB If an amount or something that is changing **levels off** or **levels out**, it stops changing so quickly. ❑ *Inflation is finally levelling out at around 11% a month.*

l

Word Partnership Use *level* with:

ADJ. **basic** level, **increased** level, **intermediate** level, **top** level, **upper** level 1
high/low level 1 2
N. level **of activity**, level **of awareness**, **cholesterol** level, **college** level, **comfort** level, level **of difficulty**, **energy** level, **noise** level, **reading** level, **skill** level, **stress** level, level **of violence** 1
eye level, **ground** level, **street** level 3

lever /'li:və, AM 'lev-/ (**levers**) 1 N-COUNT A **lever** is a handle or bar that you pull or push to operate a piece of machinery. ❑ *Pull the gear lever.* 2 N-COUNT A **lever** is a long bar, one end of which is placed under a heavy object so that when you press down on the other end you can move the object.

leverage /'li:vərɪdʒ, AM 'lev-/ 1 N-UNCOUNT **Leverage** is the ability to influence and control situations or people. ❑ *Being Mayor gives him the leverage to get things done.* 2 N-UNCOUNT **Leverage** is the force that is applied to an object when something such as a lever is used.

levy /'levi/ (**levies, levying, levied**) V-T & N-COUNT If a government or organization **levies** a tax or other sum of money, it demands it. The money itself is called a **levy**.

liability /ˌlaɪə'bɪlɪti/ (**liabilities**) 1 N-COUNT If you say that someone or something is a **liability**, you mean that they cause a lot of problems or embarrassment. ❑ *If he becomes a liability, he will be of no use to us at all.* 2 N-COUNT An organization's **liabilities** are the sums of money which it owes.

liable /'laɪəbəl/ 1 ADJ AFTER LINK-V If people or things are **liable to** do something or **liable to** something, they have a tendency to do it or to experience it. [FORMAL] ❑ *...equipment that is liable to break.* ❑ *...a woman particularly liable to depression.* 2 ADJ AFTER LINK-V If you are **liable for** something, you are legally responsible for it. ❑ *The directors cannot be held personally liable for business debts.* ● **liability** N-UNCOUNT ❑ *The Government will not admit liability for his injuries.*

liaise /li'eɪz/ (**liaises, liaising, liaised**) V-I When organizations or people **liaise**, or when one organization **liaises with** another, they co-operate and inform each other about their work. [BRIT] ❑ *Social services and health workers liaise closely.*

liaison /li'eɪzɒn, AM 'li:eɪz-/ (**liaisons**) 1 N-UNCOUNT **Liaison** is co-operation and the exchange of information between different organizations or people. ❑ *The police are working in close liaison with our own organization.* 2 N-COUNT You can refer to a romantic relationship between two people as a **liaison**.

Word Link *ar, er ≈ one who acts as : buyer, liar, seller*

liar /laɪə/ (**liars**) N-COUNT A **liar** is someone who tells lies.

libel /'laɪbəl/ (**libels, libelling, libelled**) 1 N-VAR **Libel** is something in writing which wrongly accuses someone of something, and which is therefore against the law. [LEGAL] ❑ *Warren sued him for libel over the remarks.* 2 V-T If someone **libels** you, they write something in a newspaper or book which wrongly damages your reputation and is therefore against the law.

Word Link *liber ≈ free : liberal, liberate, liberty*

liberal /'lɪbərəl/ (**liberals**) 1 ADJ & N-COUNT If someone has **liberal views**, or if they are a **liberal**, they are tolerant and believe in people's right to behave differently or hold their own opinions. ❑ *She is known to have liberal views on divorce.* 2 ADJ BEFORE N & N-COUNT A **Liberal** politician or voter or a **Liberal** is a member of a Liberal Party or votes for a Liberal Party. 3 ADJ **Liberal** means giving, using, or taking a lot of something. ❑ *The authors have made liberal use of capital letters.* ● **liberally** ADV ❑ *Brush the top liberally with olive oil.*

ˌLiberal 'Democrat Party N-PROPER **The Liberal Democrat Party** is the third largest political party in Britain and the main centre party.

liberalize [BRIT also **liberalise**] /'lɪbrəlaɪz/ (**liberalizes, liberalizing, liberalized**) V-T/V-I When a country or government **liberalizes**, or **liberalizes** its laws or its attitudes, it allows people more freedom in their actions. ❑ *...the decision to liberalize travel restrictions.* ● **liberalization** N-UNCOUNT ❑ *One answer is greater openness and political liberalization.*

liberate /'lɪbəreɪt/ (**liberates, liberating, liberated**) 1 V-T To **liberate** a place or the people in it means to free them from the political or military control of another country, area, or group of people. ❑ *They planned to march on and liberate the city.* ● **liberation** N-UNCOUNT ❑ *...the liberation of the Channel Islands.* 2 V-T To **liberate** someone **from** something means to help them escape from it or overcome it, and lead a better way of life. ❑ *He asked if the leadership was committed to liberating its people from poverty.* ● **liberating** ADJ ❑ *It can be a very liberating experience.* ● **liberation** N-UNCOUNT ❑ *...the women's liberation movement.*

Thesaurus *liberate* Also look up:

V. emancipate, free, let out, release; *(ant.)* confine, enslave 1 2

liberated /'lɪbəreɪtɪd/ ADJ If you describe someone as **liberated**, you mean that they do not accept their society's traditional values or restrictions on behaviour. ❑ *She was determined that she would become a liberated businesswoman.*

liberty /'lɪbəti/ (**liberties**) 1 N-VAR **Liberty** is the freedom to live your life in the way that you want and go where you want to go. ❑ *...the rights and liberties of the English people.* 2 PHRASE If you are **at liberty to** do something, you have been given permission to do it. ❑ *We are not at liberty to give you that information.*

Thesaurus *liberty* Also look up:

N. freedom, independence, privilege 1

Word Web library

Public libraries are changing. Many new **services** are now available. Websites often allow you to search the library's **catalogue** of books and **periodicals** from your own computer. Many libraries have computers with Internet access for the public. Some offer literacy classes, tutoring, and homework assistance. Of course, you can still **borrow** and **return books**, **magazines**, DVDs, CDs, and other **media** free of charge. You can still go to the **fiction** section to find a good **novel**. You can still go to the nonfiction bookshelves for an interesting **biography**. And if you need help, the **librarian** is still there to answer your questions.

Word Partnership Use *liberty* with:

ADJ. **human** liberty, **individual** liberty, **personal** liberty, **religious** liberty [1]

librarian /laɪ'breəriən/ (**librarians**) N-COUNT A **librarian** is a person who works in, or is in charge of a library.
→ see **library**

library /'laɪbrəri, AM -breri/ (**libraries**) N-COUNT A **public library** is a building where things such as books, newspapers, videos, and music are kept for people to read, use, or borrow.
→ see Word Web: **library**

lice /laɪs/ **Lice** is the plural of **louse**.

licence [AM **license**] /'laɪsəns/ (**licences**) N-COUNT A **licence** is an official document which gives you permission to do, use, or own something. ❑ *...his pilot's licence.*

Word Partnership Use *licence* with:

ADJ. **suspended** licence, **valid** licence [1]
N. **driver's** licence, licence **fees**, **hunting** licence, **liquor** licence, **marriage** licence, **pilot's** licence, **software** licence [1]
V. **get/obtain a** licence, **renew a** licence, **revoke a** licence [1]

license /'laɪsəns/ (**licenses, licensing, licensed**) V-T If a government or other authority **licenses** a person, organization, or activity, they officially give permission for the person or organization to do something, or for the activity to take place. ❑ *The authorities are licensing businesses to stop environmental damage.*

licensed /'laɪsənst/ [1] ADJ If you are **licensed to** do something, you are given the official authority to do it. ❑ *The club was licensed to hold parties.* [2] ADJ If something that you own or use is **licensed**, you have official permission to own it or use it. ❑ *...a licensed rifle.*

'license plate (**license plates**) N-COUNT In American English, a **license plate** is a sign on the front and back of a vehicle that shows its registration number. The British term is **number plate**.

lick /lɪk/ (**licks, licking, licked**) V-T & N-COUNT When you **lick** something, or when you give it a **lick**, you move your tongue across its surface. ❑ *She folded up her letter, licking the envelope.* ❑ *...taking tiny licks at a huge ice-cream.*

lid /lɪd/ (**lids**) [1] N-COUNT A **lid of** a container is the top which you open to reach inside. [2] N-COUNT Your **lids** are the pieces of skin which cover your eyes when you close them.

lie
❶ POSITION OR SITUATION
❷ THINGS THAT ARE NOT TRUE

lie /laɪ/ (**lies, lying, lay, lain**)
❶ [1] V-I If you **are lying** somewhere, you are in a horizontal position and are not standing or sitting. ❑ *There was a child lying on the ground.* ❑ *He lay awake, thinking.* [2] V-I If an object **lies** in a particular place, it is in a flat position in that place. ❑ *Broken glass lay all over the carpet.* [3] V-I If a place **lies** in a particular position, it is situated there. ❑ *The Virgin Islands lie between the Caribbean Sea and Atlantic Ocean.* [4] LINK-VERB You can use **lie** to say that something is or remains in a particular state or condition. ❑ *His country's economy lies in ruins.* [5] V-T/V-I You can use **lie** to say what position someone is in during a competition. [BRIT] ❑ *Blyth Tait is lying in second place.* ❑ *She was lying first.* [6] V-I You can talk about where something such as a problem, solution, or fault **lies** to say what you think it involves or is caused by. ❑ *The problem lay in the large amounts spent on defence.* [7] V-I If something **lies ahead**, it is going to happen in the future.

Usage

Do not confuse the verb **lie** with the verb **lay**. The past tense of **lie** is **lay** and the past participle is **lain**. It is an intransitive verb. ❑ *I lay on the floor with my legs in the air.* ❑ *He had lain in great pain in a darkened room.* However, **lay**, whose past tense and past participle are **laid**, is usually a transitive verb. ❑ *They laid him on the floor.* Because **lay** is used to talk about putting something in a particular place or position, it is related to the verb **lie**. If someone **lays** something somewhere, it **lies** there. Because of their related meanings, people sometimes confuse the two verbs.

▶ **lie around** PHR-VERB If things are left **lying around** or **lying about**, they are not tidied away. ❑ *My dad had some old books lying around the house.*
▶ **lie behind** PHR-VERB If you refer to what **lies behind** a situation or event, you are referring to the reason the situation exists or the event happened. ❑ *Who can tell what lies behind this apparently generous offer?*

lie /laɪ/ (**lies, lying, lied**)
❷ [1] V-I & N-COUNT If someone **is lying**, or if they are telling a **lie**, they are saying something which they know is untrue. ❑ *He lies about his*

age. ❑ *The minister has admitted that he lied to the public.* ❑ *All the boys told lies about their adventures.* • **lying** N-UNCOUNT ❑ *He's not very good at lying, is he?* 2 PHRASE If you say that someone **is living a lie**, you mean that in every part of their life they are hiding the truth about themselves from other people.

Thesaurus	*lie* Also look up:
v.	recline, rest; *(ant.)* stand ① 1 2 deceive, distort, fake, falsify, mislead ② 1

lieutenant /lefˈtenənt, AM luː-/ (**lieutenants**) N-COUNT A **lieutenant** is a junior officer in the army, navy, or air force.

life /laɪf/ (**lives**) 1 N-UNCOUNT **Life** is the quality which people, animals, and plants have when they are not dead. ❑ *...a baby's first minutes of life.* 2 N-UNCOUNT You can use **life** to refer to things or groups of things which are alive. ❑ *...some facts about animal and plant life.* 3 N-COUNT Someone's **life** is their state of being alive, or the period of time during which they are alive. ❑ *Your life is in danger.* ❑ *She lived here for the final years of her life.* 4 N-UNCOUNT **Life** is the events and experiences that happen to people. ❑ *It was the sort of life that she had dreamed about at school.* 5 N-COUNT You can use **life** to refer to particular activities which people regularly do during their lives. ❑ *My personal life had to take second place to my career.* 6 N-UNCOUNT A person or place that is **full of life** is full of activity and excitement. ❑ *The town itself was full of life and character.* 7 N-SING The **life** of something such as a machine or organization is the period of time that it lasts for. ❑ *This treatment could extend the life of the roof for another five years.* 8 N-UNCOUNT If someone is sentenced to **life**, they are sent to prison for the rest of their life, or for a very long time. 9 PHRASE If someone **is fighting for** their **life**, they are very seriously ill or injured and may die. [JOURNALISM] 10 **a new lease of life** → see **lease**
→ see **earth**

L

lifeboat /ˈlaɪfbəʊt/ (**lifeboats**) N-COUNT A **lifeboat** is a boat used to rescue people who are in danger at sea.

ˈlife-cycle (**life-cycles**) N-COUNT The **life-cycle** of an animal or plant is the series of changes it passes through from the beginning of its life until its death.
→ see **plant**

ˌlife exˈpectancy (**life expectancies**) N-VAR The **life expectancy** of a person, animal, or plant is the length of time that they are normally likely to live. ❑ *In Russia today, life expectancy is 12 years shorter than in Western Europe.*

lifeguard /ˈlaɪfgɑːd/ (**lifeguards**) N-COUNT A **lifeguard** is a person who works at a beach or swimming pool and rescues people when they are in danger of drowning.

life jacket

lifejacket also **life jacket** /lˈaɪfdʒækɪt/ (**lifejackets**) N-COUNT A **lifejacket** is a sleeveless jacket which keeps you floating in water. [BRIT]

lifeless /ˈlaɪfləs/ 1 ADJ A person or animal that is **lifeless** is dead, or so still that they appear to be dead. 2 ADJ A **lifeless** place or area does not have anything living or growing there at all. 3 ADJ If you describe a person, or something such as an artistic performance or a town as **lifeless**, you mean they lack any lively or exciting qualities. ❑ *His novels are dull, lifeless things.*

lifeline /ˈlaɪflaɪn/ (**lifelines**) N-COUNT A **lifeline** is something that enables an organization or group to survive or to continue with an activity. ❑ *These orders will be a lifeline for Britain's shipyards.*

lifelong /ˈlaɪflɒŋ, AM -lɔːŋ/ ADJ BEFORE N **Lifelong** means existing or happening for the whole of a person's life. ❑ *...her lifelong friendship with Naomi.*

lifespan /ˈlaɪfspæn/ (**lifespans**) N-COUNT The **lifespan** of a person, animal, or plant is the period of time for which they live or are normally expected to live. ❑ *A 15-year lifespan is common for a dog.*

lifestyle also **life-style** /ˈlaɪfstaɪl/ (**lifestyles**) 1 N-COUNT Your **lifestyle** is the way you live, for example the things you normally do. ❑ *They enjoyed a lifestyle that many people would envy.* 2 ADJ **Lifestyle** magazines, television programmes, and products are aimed at people who wish to be associated with glamorous and successful lifestyles.

ˈlife-threatening ADJ A **life-threatening** situation or illness is one in which there is a strong possibility that someone will die.

lifetime /ˈlaɪftaɪm/ (**lifetimes**) 1 N-COUNT A **lifetime** is the length of time that someone is alive. ❑ *I haven't done much travelling during my lifetime.* 2 N-SING The **lifetime of** something is the period of time that it lasts. ❑ *...the lifetime of a parliament.* 3 PHRASE If you describe something, for example an opportunity, as the opportunity **of a lifetime**, you are emphasizing that you are not likely to have that opportunity again.

lift /lɪft/ (**lifts, lifting, lifted**) 1 V-T & PHR-VERB If you **lift** something, or if you **lift** it **up**, you move it to a higher position. ❑ *She lifted her drink to her lips.* ❑ *Amy lifted her arm to wave.* ❑ *She put her arms around him and lifted him up.* 2 V-I If fog, cloud, or mist **lifts**, it reduces, making the weather clearer and brighter. 3 N-COUNT In British English, a **lift** is a device that carries people or goods up and down inside tall buildings. The American word is **elevator**. 4 N-COUNT If you **give** someone a **lift**, you drive them from one place to another. 5 V-T If people in authority **lift** a law or rule, they end it. ❑ *France finally lifted its ban on imports of British beef.*

Thesaurus	*lift* Also look up:
v.	boost, hoist, pick up; *(ant.)* drop, lower, put down 1 cancel, repeal, terminate 5

ligament /ˈlɪgəmənt/ (**ligaments**) N-COUNT A **ligament** is a band of strong tissue in your body, which connects bones.

light
❶ BRIGHTNESS OR ILLUMINATION
❷ NOT GREAT IN WEIGHT, AMOUNT, OR INTENSITY
❸ UNIMPORTANT OR NOT SERIOUS

light /laɪt/ (**lights, lighting, lit, lighted, lighter, lightest**)

The form **lit** is the usual past tense and past participle, but the form **lighted** is also used.

❶ 1 N-UNCOUNT **Light** is the brightness that lets you see things. Light comes from the sun, moon, lamps, and fire. ❑ *It was difficult to see in the dim light.* 2 N-COUNT A **light** is anything that produces light, especially an electric bulb. ❑ *Don't forget to turn the lights out.* ❑ *...street lights.* 3 V-T A place or object that **is lit** by something has light shining in it or on it. ❑ *The room was lit by one light only.* 4 ADJ If it is **light**, there is enough natural daylight to see by. ❑ *It was still light when we arrived.* 5 ADJ If a building or room is **light**, it has a lot of natural light in it. 6 V-T If you **light** something, you make it start burning. ❑ *She lit the fire as soon as I arrived.* 7 N-SING If someone asks for a **light**, they want a match or a cigarette lighter so they can start smoking. [INFORMAL] 8 N-COUNT If something is presented **in** a particular **light**, it is presented so that you think about it in a particular way. ❑ *He has worked hard to show New York in a better light.* 9 PHRASE If you **set light to** something, you make it start burning. 10 PHRASE If someone or something **sheds light on, throws light on,** or **casts light on** something, they add to the information people have about it, helping them to understand it more. ❑ *His lecture is supposed to shed light on the secrets of the animal kingdom.* 11 PHRASE If something **comes to light** or **is brought to light**, it becomes known. ❑ *The film brought to light his talent as a violinist.* 12 PHRASE If something is possible **in the light of** particular information or knowledge, it becomes possible because you have this information or knowledge. ❑ *They are going to reopen the case in the light of new evidence.* 13 → see also **lighter, lighting**

→ see **colour, eye, laser, light bulb, ozone**

▶ **light up** 1 PHR-VERB If you **light** something **up**, or if it **lights up**, it becomes bright. ❑ *The keypad lights up when you pick up the handset.* 2 PHR-VERB If your face or eyes **light up**, you suddenly look very surprised or happy.

Thesaurus	*light*	Also look up:
N.	brightness, gleam, glow, radiance, shine ① 1	
ADJ.	bright, sunny ① 4	

light /laɪt/ (**lighter, lightest**)

❷ 1 ADJ Something that is **light** does not weigh very much. ❑ *Try to wear light, loose clothes.* ● **lightness** N-UNCOUNT ❑ *It is made of steel for lightness and strength.* 2 ADJ Something that is **light** is not very great in amount, degree, or intensity. ❑ *...the usual light traffic in the city.* ❑ *There was a light knock at the door.* ● **lightly** ADV ❑ *Cook the onions until they are lightly browned.* ❑ *He kissed her lightly on the cheek.* 3 ADJ Something that is **light** is very pale in colour. ❑ *He has light hair and grey eyes.* ❑ *He has a light green van.* 4 ADJ **Light** work does not involve much physical effort.

light /laɪt/ (**lighter, lightest**)

❸ 1 ADJ You can describe things such as books or music as **light** when they are entertaining without making you think very deeply. 2 ADJ If you say something in a **light** way, you sound as if you think that it is not important or serious. ❑ *Talk to him in a friendly, light way about the relationship.* ❑ *I'll finish on a lighter note.* ● **lightly** ADV ❑ *'Once a detective, always a detective,' he said lightly.*

ˈlight bulb (**light bulbs**) N-COUNT A **light bulb** is the round glass part of an electric light or lamp which light shines from.

→ see Word Web: **light bulb**

Word Link	***light** ≈ not heavy : **light**en, **light**-hearted, **light**weight*

lighten /ˈlaɪtən/ (**lightens, lightening, lightened**) 1 V-T/V-I When something **lightens**, or when you **lighten** it, it becomes less dark. ❑ *She was asked to lighten her hair for a TV series.* 2 V-T/V-I If your attitude or mood **lightens**, you feel more cheerful, happy, and relaxed. ❑ *The sun was shining, yet it did nothing to lighten his mood.* 3 V-T If you **lighten** something, you make it less heavy.

lighter /ˈlaɪtə/ (**lighters**) N-COUNT A **lighter** is a small device that produces a flame that is used to light cigarettes.

ˌlight-ˈhearted 1 ADJ **Light-hearted** things are intended to be entertaining or amusing, and not at all serious. ❑ *The opera is simply light-hearted fantasy.* 2 ADJ Someone who is **light-hearted** is cheerful and happy. ❑ *They were light-hearted and prepared to enjoy life.*

lighthouse

lighthouse /ˈlaɪthaʊs/ (**lighthouses**) N-COUNT A **lighthouse** is a tower near or in the sea which contains a powerful flashing lamp to guide ships or to warn them of danger.

lighting /ˈlaɪtɪŋ/ N-UNCOUNT The **lighting** in a place is the way that it is lit, or the quality of the light in it. ❑ *You can easily install additional lighting.* ❑ *...street lighting.*

→ see **concert, drama, photography, theatre**

Word Web light bulb

The incandescent **light bulb** has changed little since the 1870s. It consists of a **glass** globe with an inert gas, such as argon, some wires, and a filament. **Electricity** flows through the wires and the tungsten filament. The filament then heats up and **glows**. Light bulbs aren't very efficient. They give off more heat than **light**. **Fluorescent** lights are much more efficient. They contain liquid mercury and argon gas. A layer of phosphor, a chemical that glows, covers the inside of the tube. When electricity begins to flow, the mercury becomes a gas and **emits** ultraviolet light. This causes the phosphor coating to **shine**.

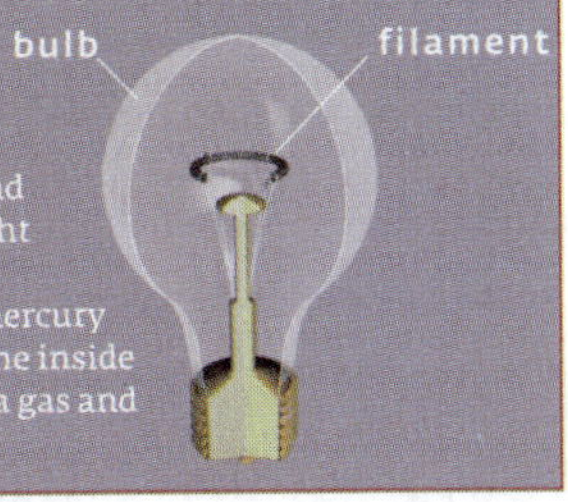

Word Web **lightning**

Lightning forms in storm clouds. Strong winds cause tiny **particles** within the clouds to rub together violently. This creates **positive charges** on some particles and **negative charges** on others. The negatively charged particles sink to the bottom of the cloud. There they are attracted by the positively charged surface of the earth. Gradually a large negative charge forms in a cloud. When it is large enough, a **bolt** of lightning strikes the earth. When a bolt branches out in several directions, the result is called forked **lightning**. Sheet lightning occurs when the bolt **discharges** within a cloud, instead of on the earth.

lightning /ˈlaɪtnɪŋ/ 1 N-UNCOUNT **Lightning** is the bright flashes of light in the sky that you see during a thunderstorm. 2 ADJ BEFORE N **Lightning** describes things that happen very quickly or last for only a short time. ❑ *He returned home from a lightning trip to Europe yesterday.*
→ see Word Web: **lightning**
→ see **storm, telescope, wave**

Word Link *light ≈ not heavy : lighten, light-hearted, lightweight*

lightweight /ˈlaɪtweɪt/ (**lightweights**) 1 ADJ Something that is **lightweight** weighs less than most other things of the same type. ❑ *The company produces a range of lightweight cycles.* 2 N-COUNT A **lightweight** is a boxer or wrestler in one of the lightest classes. 3 ADJ & N-COUNT If you describe someone as **lightweight**, or as a **lightweight**, you are criticizing them for not being important or skilful in a particular area of activity. ❑ *Some of the discussion in the book is lightweight and unconvincing.*

ˈlight year (**light years**) 1 N-COUNT A **light year** is the distance that light travels in a year. 2 N-COUNT You can say that two things are **light years apart** to emphasize a very great difference between them. [INFORMAL] ❑ *She says the French education system is light years ahead of the English one.*
→ see **galaxy**

likable /ˈlaɪkəbəl/ → see **likeable**

L

like
❶ EXPRESSING SIMILARITY
❷ EXPRESSING PREFERENCES AND WISHES

like /laɪk/
❶ 1 PREP If one person or thing is **like** another, they have similar characteristics or behave in similar ways. ❑ *Kathy is a great mate, we are like sisters.* ❑ *It's a bit like going to the dentist; it's never as bad as you fear.* ● **-like** ❑ *...flu-like illnesses.* 2 PREP If you ask or talk about what someone or something is **like**, you are asking or talking about their qualities, features, or characteristics. ❑ *What was Bulgaria like?* 3 PREP You use **like** to introduce an example of the thing that you have just mentioned. ❑ *It is major cities like London that are having the most trouble.* 4 PREP If you say that someone is behaving **like** something or someone else, you mean that they are behaving in a way that is typical of that kind of thing or person. ❑ *Mike was behaving like an idiot.* 5 PREP **Like** is sometimes used in order to say that something appears to be the case when it is not. Some people consider this use to be incorrect and prefer to use 'as if'. ❑ *I felt like I was going on an adventure.* 6 PREP You can use **like** in expressions such as **nothing like** to make an emphatic negative statement. ❑ *Three million dollars will be nothing like enough.* 7 PHRASE You say **'and the like'** to indicate that there are other similar things or people that can be included in what you are saying. ❑ *Keep fit through jogging, aerobics, weight training, and the like.* 8 PHRASE You say **'like this'**, **'like that'**, or **'like so'** when you are showing someone how something is done. ❑ *It opens and closes, like this.* 9 PHRASE You use the expression **something like** with an amount, number, or description to indicate that it is approximately accurate. ❑ *They get something like £3,000 a year.*

like /laɪk/ (**likes, liking, liked**)
❷ 1 V-T If you **like** something or someone, you think they are interesting, enjoyable, or attractive. ❑ *I can't think why Grace doesn't like me.* ❑ *Do you like to go swimming?* ❑ *That's one of the things I like about you.* 2 N-PLURAL Someone's **likes** are the things that they enjoy or find pleasant. ❑ *I knew everything about Jemma: her likes and dislikes.* 3 V-T If you **like** something such as a particular course of action or way of behaving, you approve of it. ❑ *Jan, his wife, didn't like him working so much.* 4 V-T If you say that you **would like** something or **would like to** do something, you are expressing a wish or desire. ❑ *I'd like a bubble bath.* ❑ *Would you like to come back for coffee?* 5 PHRASE You say **if you like** when you are expressing something in a different way, or in a way that you think some people might disagree with or find strange. ❑ *The hotel is very friendly and it's like a big house party, if you like.* 6 → see also **liking**

Thesaurus *like* Also look up:

PREP.	alike, comparable, similar ① 1
V.	admire, appreciate, enjoy; (*ant.*) dislike ② 1

likeable also **likable** /ˈlaɪkəbəl/ ADJ Someone or something that is **likeable** is pleasant and easy to like. ❑ *He was a very likeable man.*

likelihood /ˈlaɪklihʊd/ N-UNCOUNT The **likelihood of** something happening is how likely it is to happen. ❑ *The likelihood of infection is very small.*

likely /ˈlaɪkli/ (**likelier, likeliest**) 1 ADJ If something is **likely to** happen, it probably will happen. ❑ *When people see that something actually works, they are much more likely to accept change.* 2 ADJ If something is **likely**, it is probably true. ❑ *It* *appeared most likely that a new engine would be required.* **3** ADJ BEFORE N A **likely** person, place, or thing is one that will probably be suitable for a particular purpose. ❑ *He seemed a likely candidate to become Prime Minister.*

ˈlike-minded ADJ **Like-minded** people have similar opinions, ideas, or interests.

liken /ˈlaɪkən/ (**likens, likening, likened**) V-T If you **liken** one thing or person **to** another, you say that they are similar. ❑ *They liken themselves to the couple in the film "My Big Fat Greek Wedding".*

Word Link	*like ≈ similar : alike, likeness, likewise*

likeness /ˈlaɪknəs/ (**likenesses**) **1** N-SING If one thing has a **likeness to** another, it is similar to it. ❑ *He was called Stan because of his likeness to the comedian, Stanley Laurel.* ❑ *There's a likeness between their features, but their eyes aren't similar.* **2** N-COUNT If a picture is **a good likeness of** someone, it looks very much like them.

likewise /ˈlaɪkwaɪz/ **1** ADV You use **likewise** when you are comparing two things and saying that they are similar. ❑ *Her mother, Gerda, likewise now lives in Los Angeles.* **2** ADV If you do one thing, and someone else does **likewise**, they do the same thing. ❑ *He lent money, made donations and encouraged others to do likewise.*

liking /ˈlaɪkɪŋ/ **1** N-SING If you have a **liking for** something or someone, you like them. ❑ *The US-born singer also has a liking for basketball and baseball.* **2** PHRASE If something is, for example, too fast **for** your **liking**, you would prefer it to be slower. ❑ *He had become too powerful for their liking.* **3** PHRASE If something is **to** your **liking**, it suits your interests, tastes, or wishes. ❑ *London was more to his liking than Rome.*

lilac /ˈlaɪlək/

The plural is **lilac** or **lilacs**.

1 N-VAR A **lilac** is a small tree with pleasant-smelling purple, pink, or white flowers. **2** ADJ & N-COUNT Something that is **lilac** is pale pinkish-purple in colour.

lily /ˈlɪli/ (**lilies**) N-COUNT A **lily** is a plant with large sweet-smelling flowers.

limb /lɪm/ (**limbs**) **1** N-COUNT Your **limbs** are your arms and legs. ❑ *Get a free massage to ease your tired limbs.* **2** PHRASE If someone **has gone out on a limb**, they have done or said something that is risky or extreme.
→ see **mammal**

limbo /ˈlɪmbəʊ/ N-UNCOUNT If you are **in limbo**, you are in a situation where you seem to be caught between two stages and it is unclear what will happen next. ❑ *I've made no firm decisions yet - I'm in limbo.*

lime /laɪm/ (**limes**) **1** N-COUNT A **lime** is a small, round citrus fruit with green skin. **2** N-UNCOUNT **Lime** is a substance containing calcium. It is found in soil and water.

limelight /ˈlaɪmlaɪt/ N-UNCOUNT If someone is **in the limelight**, they are getting a lot of attention, because they are famous or because they have done something very unusual or exciting.

limestone /ˈlaɪmstəʊn/ (**limestones**) N-VAR **Limestone** is a white rock which is used for building and making cement.

limit /ˈlɪmɪt/ (**limits, limiting, limited**) **1** N-COUNT A **limit** is the greatest amount, extent, or degree of something that is possible. ❑ *Employees must remain within the city limits.* ❑ *There is no limit to how much fresh fruit you can eat in a day.* **2** N-COUNT A **limit** is the largest or smallest amount of something such as time or money that is allowed because of a rule, law, or decision. ❑ *The three-month time limit ends in mid-June.* **3** V-T If you **limit** something, you prevent it from becoming greater than a particular amount or degree. ❑ *This would limit unemployment to around 2.5 million.* ● **limitation** N-UNCOUNT ❑ *...the limitation of nuclear weapons.* **4** V-T If you **limit yourself to** something, or if someone or something **limits** you, the number of things that you have or do is reduced. ❑ *Travellers should limit themselves to one item of hand luggage.* ● **limiting** ADJ ❑ *This may seem limiting, but for a writer it is full of possibilities.* **5** V-T If something **is limited to** a particular place or group of people, it exists only in that place, or is had or done only by that group. ❑ *Entry to this competition is limited to UK residents only.* **6** PHRASE If a place is **off limits**, you are not allowed to go there. ❑ *Parts of the church are off limits to visitors.* **7** PHRASE If someone **is over the limit**, they have drunk more alcohol than they are legally allowed to when driving a vehicle. [BRIT]

limitation /ˌlɪmɪˈteɪʃən/ (**limitations**) **1** N-VAR A **limitation on** something is a rule or decision which prevents that thing from growing or extending beyond certain limits. ❑ *In essence we are suffering a limitation on our religious freedom.* **2** N-PLURAL The **limitations** of someone or something are the things that they cannot do, or the things that they do badly. ❑ *Parents often blame schools for the educational limitations of their children.* **3** N-VAR A **limitation** is a fact or situation that allows only some actions and makes others impossible. ❑ *Many adults experience stiffness and limitation in the movement of their neck and shoulders.* **4** → see also **limit**

limited /ˈlɪmɪtɪd/ **1** ADJ Something that is **limited** is not very great in amount, range, or degree. ❑ *They may only have a limited amount of time.* **2** ADJ BEFORE N A **limited** company is one in which the shareholders are legally responsible for only a part of any money that it may owe if it goes bankrupt. [BRIT]

ˌlimited eˈdition (**limited editions**) N-COUNT A **limited edition** is something such as a book which has been produced in very small numbers, so that each one will be valuable in the future.

limitless /ˈlɪmɪtləs/ ADJ If you describe something as **limitless**, you mean that there is or appears to be so much of it that it will never be used up. ❑ *...a limitless supply of energy.*

limousine /ˌlɪməˈziːn/ (**limousines**) N-COUNT A **limousine** is a large and very comfortable car. Limousines are usually driven by a chauffeur and are used by very rich or important people.

limp /lɪmp/ (**limps, limping, limped, limper, limpest**) **1** V-I & N-COUNT If you **limp**, or if you walk with a **limp**, you walk in an uneven way because one of your legs or feet is hurt. ❑ *He limped off with a leg injury.* ❑ *Seven years later, he still walks with a limp.* **2** ADJ If something is **limp**, it is soft or weak when it should be firm or strong. ❑ *She pushed her limp hair back from her face.* ● **limply** ADV ❑ *The newspaper hung limply from his fingers.*

line
1 NOUN USES
2 VERB USES
3 PHRASES

line /laɪn/ (**lines**)
1 1 N-COUNT A **line** is a long thin mark on a surface. ❑ *Draw a line down the centre of the page.* 2 N-COUNT The **lines** on someone's face are the wrinkles that appear there as they grow older. 3 N-COUNT A **line of** people or things is a number of them that are arranged in a row. ❑ *...a line of women queueing for bread.* 4 N-COUNT You can refer to a long piece of string or wire as a **line** when it is being used for a particular purpose. ❑ *She put her washing on the line.* ❑ *...a piece of fishing-line.* 5 N-COUNT **Line** is used to refer to a route along which people or things move or are sent. ❑ *The telephone lines went dead.* ❑ *They've got to ride right to the end of the line.* 6 N-COUNT You can use **line** to refer to the edge, outline, or shape of something. 7 N-COUNT **Line** refers to the boundary between certain areas, things, or types of people. ❑ *...just over the California state line in Nevada.* ❑ *Thirteen per cent of the population live below the poverty line.* 8 N-COUNT An actor's **lines** are the words they speak in a play or film. 9 N-COUNT The **line** that someone takes on a problem or topic is their attitude or policy towards it. ❑ *...countries which take a hard line on terrorism.* 10 N-COUNT Your **line of work** is the kind of work that you do. 11 N-COUNT A **line** is a type of product that a company makes or sells. ❑ *This is our best-selling line, so why not order two?* 12 → see also **lining, bottom line, front line, production line**
→ see **football, graph, mathematics, train**

line /laɪn/ (**lines, lining, lined**)
2 1 V-T If people or things **line** a place such as a road, large numbers of them are present along its edges or sides. ❑ *Thousands of local people lined the streets.* ❑ *...a long tree-lined drive.* 2 V-T If you **line** something such as a container, you put a layer of something on the inside surface of it. ❑ *Bears line their dens with leaves or grass.* 3 V-T If something **lines** a container or area, it forms a layer on the inside surface. ❑ *...the muscles that line the intestines.*
▶ **line up** 1 PHR-VERB If people or things **are lined up**, they move so that they stand in a row or form a queue. ❑ *The boy lined up his toys on the windowsill.* ❑ *The senior leaders lined up behind him in neat rows.* 2 PHR-VERB If you **line up** an event or activity, you arrange for it to happen. If you **line** someone **up** for an event or activity, you arrange for them to be available for that event or activity. ❑ *Bob Dylan was lining up a two-week UK tour.*

line /laɪn/ (**lines**)
3 1 PHRASE If something happens somewhere **along the line** or somewhere **down the line**, it happens during the course of a situation or activity. ❑ *Somewhere along the line he got an engineering degree.* 2 PHRASE If you **draw the line at** a particular activity, you refuse to do it, usually because you disapprove of it. ❑ *She draws the line at telling other people how to lead their lives.* 3 PHRASE If you are **in line for** something, you are likely to get it. ❑ *I hoped to be in line for a place in a French team.* 4 PHRASE If one thing is **in line with** another, or is brought **into line with** it, the first thing is, or becomes, similar to the second, especially in a way that has been agreed, planned, or expected. ❑ *Prices will go up in line with people's incomes.* 5 PHRASE If you do something **on line**, you do it using a computer or a computer network. [COMPUTING] 6 PHRASE If something such as your job, career, or reputation is **on the line**, you may lose or harm it as a result of the situation you are in. ❑ *He wouldn't put his career on the line to help a friend.* 7 PHRASE If someone steps **out of line**, they disobey someone or behave in an unacceptable way. 8 PHRASE If you **read between the lines**, you understand what someone really means, or what is really happening in a situation, even though it is not said openly. 9 to **toe the line** → see **toe**

linear /ˈlɪniə/ 1 ADJ A **linear** process is one in which something progresses straight from one stage to another. ❑ *Life is a series of events, progressing in a linear way from beginning to end.* 2 ADJ A **linear** shape consists of straight lines.

linen /ˈlɪnɪn/ N-UNCOUNT **Linen** is a kind of cloth that is made from a plant called flax.

liner /ˈlaɪnə/ (**liners**) N-COUNT A **liner** is a large passenger ship.
→ see **ship**

linesman /ˈlaɪnzmən/ (**linesmen**) N-COUNT A **linesman** is an official in games such as football and tennis who indicates when the ball goes outside the boundary lines.

ˈline-up (**line-ups**) N-COUNT A **line-up** is a group of people or a series of things that are assembled to take part in a particular activity or event. ❑ *...a new series with a great line-up of musicians.*

linger /ˈlɪŋgə/ (**lingers, lingering, lingered**) 1 V-I If something **lingers**, it continues to exist for a long time. ❑ *The smell of her perfume lingered on in the room.* ❑ *...the lingering effects of radiation.* 2 V-I If you **linger** somewhere, you stay there for a longer time than is necessary. ❑ *Customers are welcome to linger here over coffee.*

lingerie /ˈlænʒəri, AM -ˈreɪ/ N-UNCOUNT You can refer to women's underwear and night clothes as **lingerie**.

Word Link *lingu ≈ language : bilingual, linguist, linguistics*

linguist /ˈlɪŋgwɪst/ (**linguists**) 1 N-COUNT A **linguist** is someone who is good at speaking or learning foreign languages. 2 N-COUNT A **linguist** is someone who studies or teaches linguistics.

linguistics /lɪŋˈgwɪstɪks/

The form **linguistic** is used as a modifier.

1 N-UNCOUNT **Linguistics** is the study of the way in which language works. 2 ADJ **Linguistic** abilities or ideas relate to language or linguistics. ❑ *...linguistic theory.*

lining /ˈlaɪnɪŋ/ (**linings**) 1 N-COUNT The **lining** of a piece of clothing or a curtain is a material attached to the inside of it in order to make it thicker or warmer. ❑ *...a black jacket with a red lining.* 2 N-COUNT The **lining** of your stomach or other organ is a layer of tissue on the inside of it.

link /lɪŋk/ (**links, linking, linked**) 1 V-T & N-COUNT If something **links** two things, or if there is a **link between** them, there is a logical relationship between them. ❑ *Liver cancer is linked to the hepatitis B virus.* ❑ *The link between crime and poverty has long been established.* 2 V-T & N-COUNT If something **links** two places or objects, or if there is a **link between** them, there is a physical connection between them. ❑ *The Rama Road links the capital, Managua, with the Caribbean coast.* ❑ *...the high-speed rail link between London and the Channel Tunnel.* 3 V-T If you **link** one person or thing **to** another, you claim that there is a relationship or connection between them. ❑ *Jones has linked the crime to social circumstances.* 4 V-T If you **link** one thing with another, you join them by putting one thing through the other. ❑ *She linked her arm through his.* 5 N-COUNT A **link** of a chain is one of the rings in it.

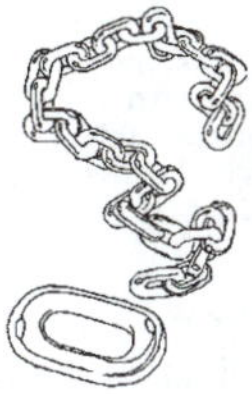
link

▶ **link up** 1 PHR-VERB If you **link up with** someone, you join them for a particular purpose. ❑ *They linked up with another anti-nuclear group.* ❑ *The Russian and American armies linked up for the first time.* 2 PHR-VERB If one thing **is linked up to** another, the two things are connected to each other. ❑ *One day everyone will be linked up to broadband.*

Word Partnership Use *link* with:

ADJ. **direct** link, **establish a** link, **find a** link, **possible** link, **strong/weak** link, **vital** link 1 2 3 4
V. **attempt to** link 3 4

'link-up (**link-ups**) N-COUNT A **link-up** is a relationship or partnership between two organizations. ❑ *The US airline has just announced a link-up with British Airways.*

lion /laɪən/ (**lions**) N-COUNT A **lion** is a large wild member of the cat family that is found in Africa. Lions have yellowish fur, and male lions have long hair on their head and neck.

'lion's share N-SING If a person, group, or project gets **the lion's share of** something, they get the largest part of it. ❑ *The lion's share of the work will go to American companies.*

lip /lɪp/ (**lips**) 1 N-COUNT Your **lips** are the two outer parts of the edge of your mouth. 2 PHRASE If you say that someone **keeps a stiff upper lip**, you mean that they do not show any emotion even though it is difficult for them not to. 3 **to bite your lip** → see **bite**
→ see **face, kiss**

'lip-service N-UNCOUNT If you say that someone **pays lip-service to** an idea, you are criticizing them because they say they are in favour of it, but do nothing to support it. ❑ *He did no more than pay lip-service to their views.*

lipstick /'lɪpstɪk/ (**lipsticks**) N-VAR **Lipstick** is a coloured substance which women put on their lips.

liqueur /lɪ'kjʊə, AM -'kɜːr/ (**liqueurs**) N-VAR A **liqueur** is a strong sweet alcoholic drink.

liquid /'lɪkwɪd/ (**liquids**) N-VAR A **liquid** is a substance such as water which is not solid and which can be poured. ❑ *Solids turn to liquids at certain temperatures.* ❑ *...liquid fuel.*
→ see **matter**

liquidate /'lɪkwɪdeɪt/ (**liquidates, liquidating, liquidated**) V-T To **liquidate** a company means to close it down and sell all its assets, usually because it is in debt. ● **liquidation** (**liquidations**) N-VAR ❑ *The company went into liquidation.* ● **liquidator** (**liquidators**) N-COUNT ❑ *The firm has gone into the hands of liquidators.*

liquor /'lɪkə/ (**liquors**) N-VAR In American English, alcoholic drink such as whisky and vodka is sometimes referred to as **liquor**. The British word is **spirits**.

list /lɪst/ (**lists, listing, listed**) 1 N-COUNT A **list** is a set of things which all belong to a particular category, written down one below the other. ❑ *On the shopping list are chicken, lamb, and fish.* 2 V-T To **list** a set of things means to write them or say them one after another, usually in a particular order. ❑ *Concerts are listed by date, then by city.*

Word Partnership Use *list* with:

ADJ. **disabled** list, **injured** list 1
complete list, **long** list, **short** list 1 2
V. **add** ***someone/something*** **to a** list, list **includes, make a** list 1 2
N. list **of candidates**, list **of demands**, **guest** list, list **of ingredients**, list **of items**, list **of names**, **price** list, list **of questions**, **reading** list, list **of things**, **wine** list, **wish** list, list **of words** 1 2

listen /'lɪsən/ (**listens, listening, listened**) 1 V-I If you **listen to** someone who is talking or **to** a sound, you give your attention to them. ❑ *Sonia was not listening.* ❑ *He spent his time listening to the radio.* 2 V-I If you **listen for** a sound, you keep alert, ready to hear it if it occurs. ❑ *They spend the flight listening for any noise that may seem odd.* 3 V-I If you **listen to** someone, you do what they advise you to do, or you believe them. ❑ *When I asked him to stop, he would not listen.* ❑ *Anne, you need to listen to me this time.* 4 CONVENTION You say **listen** when you want someone to pay attention to you because you are going to say something. ❑ *Listen, I finish at one.*

▶ **listen in** PHR-VERB If you **listen in to** or **on** a private conversation, you secretly listen to it. ❑ *They can now listen in on mobile phone conversations.*

Usage

Do not confuse **listen** and **hear**. If you want to say that someone is paying attention to something they can hear, you say that they **are listening** to it. ❑ *He turned on the radio and listened to the news.* Note that **listen** is not followed directly by an object. You must always say that you listen **to** something. However, **listen** can also be used on its own without an object. ❑ *I was laughing too much to listen.* You use **hear** to talk about sounds that you are aware of because they reach your ears. You often use **can** with **hear**. ❑ *I can hear him shouting.*

Thesaurus *listen* Also look up:

V. catch, pick up, tune in; *(ant.)* ignore 1
heed, mind 3

l

Word Partnership Use *listen* with:

V.	listen **to *someone's* voice** 1
	sit *up* and listen, **willing to** listen 1-3
ADV.	listen **carefully**, listen **closely** 1 2

listener /ˈlɪsnə/ (**listeners**) N-COUNT People who listen to the radio are often referred to as **listeners**. ❑ *I'm a regular listener to her show.*
→ see **radio**

listless /ˈlɪstləs/ ADJ Someone who is **listless**, has no energy or enthusiasm. ● **listlessly** ADV ❑ *Usually, you just sit listlessly, too hot to do anything.*

lit /lɪt/ **Lit** is a past tense and past participle of **light**.

liter /ˈliːtə/ → see **litre**

literacy /ˈlɪtərəsi/ N-UNCOUNT **Literacy** is the ability to read and write. ❑ *Many adults have some problems with literacy.*

Word Link *liter ≈ letter : illiterate, literal, literature*

literal /ˈlɪtərəl/ 1 ADJ The **literal** meaning of a word is its most basic meaning. ❑ *In its literal sense, democracy means 'government by and for the people'.* 2 ADJ A **literal translation** is one in which you translate each word separately, rather than expressing the meaning in a more natural way. ❑ *A literal translation of the German word 'Kindergarten' is 'garden of children'.* ● **literally** ADV ❑ *The word 'volk' translates literally as 'folk'.*

literally /ˈlɪtərəli/ ADV You can use **literally** to emphasize a word or expression which is being used in a creative way to exaggerate a situation. Some careful speakers of English think that this use is incorrect. ❑ *The views are literally breath-taking.*

literary /ˈlɪtərəri, AM -reri/ 1 ADJ **Literary** means connected with literature. ❑ *...a literary masterpiece.* 2 ADJ **Literary** words are often unusual in some way and are used to create a special effect in a poem, speech, or novel.

literate /ˈlɪtərət/ 1 ADJ Someone who is **literate** is able to read and write. ❑ *Over one quarter of the adult population are not fully literate.* 2 ADJ If you describe someone as **literate**, you mean that they are intelligent and well-educated, especially about literature and the arts. ❑ *Scientists should be literate as well as able to handle figures.*

literature /ˈlɪtrətʃə, AM -tərətʃʊr/ 1 N-UNCOUNT Novels, plays, and poetry are referred to as **literature**. ❑ *I teach literature to groups of young people.* 2 N-UNCOUNT **Literature** is printed information about something. ❑ *Full literature on these products is available.*
→ see **genre**

litigation /ˌlɪtɪˈgeɪʃən/ N-UNCOUNT **Litigation** is the process of taking legal action. [TECHNICAL] ❑ *The company remains in litigation with one of the directors.*

litre [AM **liter**] /ˈliːtə/ (**litres**) N-COUNT A **litre** is a metric unit of volume. It is equal to approximately 1.76 British pints or 2.11 American pints. ❑ *...15 litres of water.*
→ see **measurement**

litter /ˈlɪtə/ (**litters, littering, littered**) 1 N-UNCOUNT **Litter** is rubbish which is left lying around outside.

litter

2 V-T If a number of things **litter** a place, they are scattered around in it. ❑ *Glass from broken bottles litters the pavement.* ● **littered** ADJ ❑ *There was a desk littered with papers, and a few books.* 3 ADJ AFTER LINK-V If you say that something such as history or someone's speech is **littered with** something, you mean that there are many examples of the second thing in the first. ❑ *The document is littered with spelling, punctuation and grammar errors.*

Thesaurus *litter* Also look up:

N.	clutter, debris, garbage, refuse, waste 1
V.	clutter, scatter 2

little /ˈlɪtəl/ 1 QUANT You use **little** to emphasize that there is only a small amount of something. ❑ *I need very little sleep these days.* ❑ *Little is known about his childhood.* 2 QUANT **A little of** something is a small amount of it. ❑ *A little food would do us all good.* ❑ *Pour a little of the sauce over the chicken.* 3 ADV **Little** means not very often or to only a small extent. ❑ *On their way back to Marseille they spoke very little.* 4 ADJ **Little** things are small in size. **Little** is slightly more informal than **small**. ❑ *We sat around a little table, eating and drinking.* ❑ *...the little group of students.* 5 ADJ BEFORE N A **little** distance, period of time, or event is short in length. ❑ *Go down the road a little way.* ❑ *Let's just wait a little while and see what happens.* 6 ADJ BEFORE N You use **little** to indicate that something is not serious or important. ❑ *... irritating little habits.* ❑ *Harry got angry over little things.* 7 PHRASE **A little** or **a little bit** means to a small extent or degree or for a short period. ❑ *He was a little bit afraid of his father.* ❑ *He walked a little by himself.* 8 PHRASE If something happens **little by little**, it happens very gradually. ❑ *Little by little he was becoming weaker.*

Usage

You can use the adjective **little** to talk about things that are small, for example ❑ *...a little house* and ❑ *...little children*, but it is not normally used to emphasize or draw attention to the fact that something is small. For instance, you cannot say 'The town is little' or 'I have a very little car', but you can say '**The town is small**' or '**I have a very small car**'. **Little** is a less precise word than **small** and may be used to suggest the speaker's feelings or attitude towards the person or thing being described. For that reason, **little** is often used after another adjective. ❑ *What a nice little house you've got here!* ❑ *It's a dull little town.* **Little** and **a little** are both used as determiners in front of uncount nouns, but they do not have the same meaning. For example, if you say '**I have a little money**', this is a positive statement and you are saying that you have some money. However, if you say '**I have little money**', this is a kind of negative statement and you are saying that you have almost no money or that you do not have enough money.

Thesaurus *little* Also look up:

ADJ. miniature, petite, slight, small, young; *(ant.)* big 4
casual, insignificant, minor, small, unimportant; *(ant.)* important 6

live
❶ VERB USES
❷ ADJECTIVE AND ADVERB USES

live /lɪv/ (**lives, living, lived**)
❶ 1 V-I If someone **lives in** a particular place, their home is there. ❑ *She has lived here for 10 years.* ❑ *We used to live in the same road.* ❑ *He still lives with his parents.* 2 V-T/V-I The way someone **lives** is the kind of life they have or the circumstances they are in. ❑ *We lived very simply.* ❑ *We can start living a normal life again now.* 3 V-T/V-I To **live** means to be alive. If you say that someone **lived to** a particular age, you mean that they stayed alive until that age. ❑ *He's got a terrible disease and will not live long.* ❑ *He lived to be 103.* ❑ *Ian was her only living relative.* 4 V-I If people **live by** doing a particular activity, they get the money, food, or clothing they need by doing that activity. ❑ *The people here lived by hunting.* 5 V-I If you say that someone **lives for** a particular thing, you are emphasizing that it is the most important thing in their life. ❑ *Laura lived for those kids.* 6 PHRASE If you **live it up**, you have a very enjoyable and exciting time. [INFORMAL] 7 to **live from hand to mouth** → see **hand** 8 to **live a lie** → see **lie**
▶ **live down** PHR-VERB If you are unable to **live down** a mistake, failure, or bad reputation, you are unable to make people forget about it. ❑ *I thought I'd never live it down.*
▶ **live off** 1 PHR-VERB If you **live off** another person, you rely on them to provide you with money. ❑ *He had lived off his father all his life.* 2 → see **live on** (meaning 1)
▶ **live on** 1 PHR-VERB If you **live on** a particular amount of money, or if you **live off** it, you have that amount of money to buy things. ❑ *Most students are unable to live on £4000 per year.* 2 PHR-VERB If someone **lives on** a particular kind of food, it is, or seems to be, the only thing that they eat. ❑ *The children live on chips.* 3 PHR-VERB If a person or occasion **lives on in** someone's mind or in history, they are remembered because they are significant or important.
▶ **live up to** PHR-VERB If someone or something **lives up to** what they were expected to be or do, they achieve what was expected of them.

Usage

When you are talking about someone's home, the verb **live** has a different meaning in the continuous tenses than it does in the simple tenses. For example, if you say **'I'm living in London'**, this suggests that the situation is temporary and you may soon move to a different place. If you say 'I live in London', this suggests that London is your permanent home. The verb **work** behaves in a similar way. You use the continuous tenses, with the '-ing' form, to talk about a temporary job, but the simple tenses to talk about a permanent job.

live /laɪv/
❷ 1 ADJ BEFORE N **Live** animals or plants are alive, rather than being dead or artificial. 2 ADJ & ADV A **live** television or radio programme is one in which an event is broadcast at the time that it happens. ❑ *...live pictures of the weather.* ❑ *It was broadcast live in 50 countries.* 3 ADJ & ADV A **live performance** is given in front of an audience, rather than being recorded. ❑ *She's much happier performing live.* 4 ADJ A **live** wire or piece of electrical equipment is directly connected to a source of electricity.

Thesaurus *live* Also look up:

V. dwell, inhabit, occupy, reside ① 1
manage, subsist, survive ① 2
exist ① 3
ADJ. active, alive, living, vigorous ② 1

livelihood /ˈlaɪvlihʊd/ (**livelihoods**) N-VAR Your **livelihood** is your job or the source of your income. ❑ *Fishermen depend on the sea for their livelihood.*

lively /ˈlaɪvli/ (**livelier, liveliest**) 1 ADJ You can describe someone as **lively** when they behave in an enthusiastic and cheerful way. ● **liveliness** N-UNCOUNT ❑ *Amy could sense his liveliness.* 2 ADJ A **lively** event or a **lively** discussion, for example, has lots of interesting and exciting things happening or being said in it. ❑ *...a lively debate.* 3 ADJ BEFORE N You use **lively** to describe a feeling which is strong and enthusiastic. ❑ *He had a lively interest in Buddhism.*

Word Partnership Use *lively* with:

ADV. **very** lively 1-3
N. lively **atmosphere**, lively **conversation**, lively **debate**, lively **discussion**, lively **music**, lively **performance** 2
lively **imagination**, lively **interest**, lively **sense of humor** 3

liven /ˈlaɪvən/ (**livens, livening, livened**)
▶ **liven up** 1 PHR-VERB If a place or event **livens up**, or if you **liven** it **up**, it becomes more interesting and exciting. ❑ *How could we decorate the room to liven it up?* 2 PHR-VERB If people **liven up**, or if something **livens** them **up**, they become more cheerful and energetic. ❑ *Talking about her daughters livens her up.*

liver /ˈlɪvə/ (**livers**) 1 N-COUNT Your **liver** is a large organ in your body which cleans your blood. 2 N-UNCOUNT **Liver** is the liver of some animals, which is cooked and eaten.
→ see **donor**

lives 1 /laɪvz/ **Lives** is the plural of **life**. 2 /lɪvz/ **Lives** is the third person singular form of **live**.

livestock /ˈlaɪvstɒk/ N-UNCOUNT Animals such as cattle and sheep which are kept on a farm are referred to as **livestock**.
→ see **barn**

livid /ˈlɪvɪd/ ADJ Someone who is **livid** is extremely angry. [INFORMAL] ❑ *I am absolutely livid about it.*

living /ˈlɪvɪŋ/ 1 N-SING The work that you do **for a living** is the work that you do to earn the money that you need. ❑ *He earns his living doing a variety of things.* 2 N-UNCOUNT You use **living** when talking about the quality of people's daily lives. ❑ *...the stresses of city living.* 3 N-PLURAL **The living**

are people who are alive, rather than people who have died.

'living-room (**living-rooms**) N-COUNT The **living-room** in a house is the room where people sit and relax.

→ see **house**

lizard /ˈlɪzəd/ (**lizards**) N-COUNT A **lizard** is a reptile with short legs and a long tail.

→ see **desert**

load /ləʊd/ (**loads, loading, loaded**) 1 V-T & PHR-VERB If you **load** a vehicle or container, or if you **load** it **up**, you put a large quantity of things or heavy things into it. ❑ *The three men soon finished loading the truck.* ❑ *Mr Dambar loaded his plate with lasagne.* 2 N-COUNT A **load** is something large or heavy which is being carried. ❑ *This car is easy to drive and takes a big load.* 3 V-T To **load** a gun, camera, or other piece of equipment means to put something such as a bullet or film in it so that it is ready to use. ❑ *He carried a loaded gun.* 4 QUANT **A load of** something or **loads of** it is a large amount of it. **A load of** people or things or **loads of** them is a large number of them. [INFORMAL] ❑ *I've got loads of money.*

→ see **photography**

Thesaurus *load* Also look up:

V.	arrange, fill, pack, pile up, stack 1
N.	bundle, cargo, freight, haul, shipment 2

L

Word Partnership Use *load* with:

N.	load **a truck** 1
V.	**carry a** load, **handle a** load, **lighten a** load, **take on a** load 2 6
ADJ.	**big** load, **full** load, **heavy** load 2 6

loaded /ˈləʊdɪd/ 1 ADJ A **loaded remark** or **question** has more meaning or purpose than it appears to have, because the person who makes or asks it hopes it will cause people to respond in a particular way. ❑ *That's a very loaded question.* 2 ADJ If something is **loaded with** things, it has a large number of them in it or on it. ❑ *...a fully loaded jet airliner.* ❑ *The lorry is loaded with fruit.* 3 ADJ If you say that something is **loaded in favour of** someone or something, you mean it works unfairly to their advantage. If you say it is **loaded against** them, you mean it works unfairly to their disadvantage. ❑ *The press is loaded in favour of the present government.*

loaf /ləʊf/ (**loaves** /ləʊvz/) N-COUNT A **loaf of bread** is bread in a shape that can be cut into slices.

→ see **bread**

loan /ləʊn/ (**loans, loaning, loaned**) 1 N-COUNT A **loan** is a sum of money that you borrow. ❑ *The president made it easier for small businesses to get bank loans.* 2 V-T & N-SING If someone **loans** something **to** you, or if they **give** you **a loan of** it, they lend it to you. ❑ *He offered to loan us all the plants required for the exhibit.* ❑ *I am in need of a loan of a bike for five weeks.* 3 PHRASE If something or someone is **on loan to** a person or organization, that person or organization is borrowing them. ❑ *...paintings on loan from the National Gallery.*

Word Partnership Use *loan* with:

V.	**apply for a** loan, **get/receive a** loan, **make a** loan, **pay** *off* **a** loan, **repay a** loan 1
N.	loan **agreement**, loan **application**, **bank** loan, **home** loan, **interest on a** loan, **mortgage** loan, loan **payment/repayment**, **savings and** loan, **student** loan 1

loath or **loth** /ləʊθ/ ADJ AFTER LINK-V If you are **loath to** do something, you do not want to do it.

loathe /ləʊð/ (**loathes, loathing, loathed**) V-T If you **loathe** something or someone, you dislike them very much. ❑ *The critics loathed this play.* ● **loathing** N-UNCOUNT ❑ *She looked at him with loathing.*

loaves /ləʊvz/ **Loaves** is the plural of **loaf**.

lob /lɒb/ (**lobs, lobbing, lobbed**) V-T & N-COUNT If you **lob** something such as a ball, you throw or hit it high in the air. A **lob** is a throw or hit like this. ❑ *Croyden lobbed a rock over the wall.*

lobby /ˈlɒbi/ (**lobbies, lobbying, lobbied**) 1 N-COUNT The **lobby** of a building is the main entrance area with corridors and staircases leading off it. 2 V-T/V-I To **lobby** a member of a government means to try to persuade them that a particular thing should be done. ❑ *The firm had been lobbying for a change in the law since 1995.* 3 N-COUNT A **lobby** is a group of people who represent a particular organization or campaign, and who try to persuade the government to do something. ❑ *...the anti-nuclear lobby.*

lobe /ləʊb/ (**lobes**) N-COUNT The **lobe** of your ear is the soft part at the bottom.

lobster /ˈlɒbstə/ (**lobsters**) N-COUNT A **lobster** is a sea creature with a hard shell, two large claws, and eight legs.

→ see **shellfish**

lobster

local /ˈləʊkəl/ (**locals**) 1 ADJ **Local** means existing in or belonging to the area where you live, or to the area that you are talking about. ❑ *...the local newspaper.* ❑ *Some local residents joined the students' protest.* ● **locally** ADV ❑ *Her clothes were bought locally.* 2 N-COUNT You can refer to the people who live in a particular district as **the locals**. [INFORMAL]

Word Partnership Use *local* with:

N.	local **area**, local **artist**, local **business**, local **community**, local **customs**, local **group**, local **hospital**, local **library**, local **news**, local **office**, local **newspaper**, local **people**, local ***phone* call**, local **residents**, local **restaurant**, local **store** 1
	local **government**, local **officials**, local **police**, local **politicians**, local **politics** 2

locality /ləʊˈkælɪti/ (**localities**) N-COUNT A **locality** is a small area of a country or city. ❑ *Find*

Picture Dictionary location

out what is available in your locality.

locate /ləʊˈkeɪt, AM ˈləʊkeɪt/ (**locates, locating, located**) **1** V-T If you **locate** something or someone, you find them. [FORMAL] **2** V-T If you **locate** something in a particular place, you put, build, or set it there. [FORMAL] ● **located** ADJ ❑ *The restaurant is located near the cathedral.*

location /ləʊˈkeɪʃən/ (**locations**) **1** N-COUNT A **location** is a place, especially the place where something happens or is situated. ❑ *Macau's newest hotel has a beautiful location.* **2** PHRASE If a film is made **on location**, it is made away from a studio. → see Picture Dictionary: **location**

Word Partnership Use *location* with:

ADJ. **central** location, **convenient** location, **secret** location **1**
exact location, **geographic** location, **present** location, **specific** location **2**
V. **pinpoint a** location **1** **2**

loch /lɒx, lɒk/ (**lochs**) N-COUNT A **loch** is a large Scottish lake.

lock /lɒk/ (**locks, locking, locked**) **1** V-T When you **lock** something, you fasten it by means of a key. ❑ *She locked the door.* **2** N-COUNT The **lock** on something such as a door is the device which fastens it when you turn a key in it. ❑ *He heard a key turning in the lock.* **3** V-T If you **lock** something or someone in a place, room, or container, you put them there and fasten the lock. ❑ *They locked them in a dark cell.* **4** V-T/V-I When you **lock** something in a particular position or place, or when it **locks** there, it is held or fitted firmly in that position or place. ❑ *He locked his fingers behind his head.* ❑ *The wheels came down and locked into position.* **5** N-COUNT A **lock** is a place on a canal or river which can be closed at each end by gates, so boats can move to a higher or lower section by changing the water level inside the gates. **6** N-COUNT A **lock of** hair is a small bunch of hairs on your head that grow together in the same direction.

▶ **lock away** **1** PHR-VERB If you **lock** something **away** in a place or container, you put or hide it there and fasten the lock. ❑ *He had even locked away all the videos.* **2** PHR-VERB To **lock** someone **away** or to **lock** them **up** means to put them in prison or in a secure psychiatric hospital. ❑ *Locking them away is not enough, you have to give them treatment.*

▶ **lock up** **1** PHR-VERB When you **lock up** a building or car, or when you **lock up**, you make sure that all the doors and windows are locked so that nobody can get in. **2** → see **lock away** (meaning **2**)

Word Partnership Use *lock* with:

N. lock **a car**, lock **a door**, lock **a room** **1**
combination lock, **door** lock, lock **and key**, **key in a** lock **2**
V. **change a** lock, **open a** lock, **pick a** lock **2**

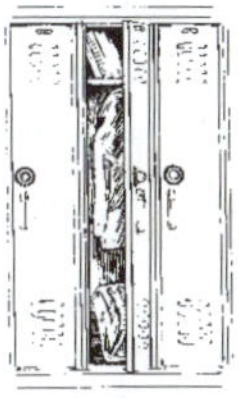
locker

locker /ˈlɒkə/ (**lockers**) N-COUNT A **locker** is a small cupboard for someone's personal belongings, for example in a changing room.

locomotive /ˈləʊkəməʊtɪv/ (**locomotives**) N-COUNT A **locomotive** is a railway engine. [FORMAL]

locust /ˈləʊkəst/ (**locusts**) N-COUNT **Locusts** are insects that live in hot countries. They fly in large groups and eat crops.

lodge /lɒdʒ/ (**lodges, lodging, lodged**) **1** N-COUNT A **lodge** is a house or hut in the country or the mountains where people stay on holiday. ❑ *It was intended to be used as a lodge rather than a main family house.* **2** V-I If you **lodge** in someone else's house, you live there paying rent.

● **lodger** (**lodgers**) N-COUNT ❑ *Jennie took a lodger to help pay the bills.* 3 V-T/V-I If something **lodges** somewhere, it becomes stuck there. ❑ *The bullet lodged in the policeman's leg.* ❑ *His car has a bullet lodged in the door.* 4 V-T If you **lodge** a **complaint**, you formally make it.

lodging /ˈlɒdʒɪŋ/ (**lodgings**) N-VAR You can refer to a room that is rented in someone's house as a person's **lodging** or **lodgings**. ❑ *He was given free lodging.*

Word Link	*loft ≈ air : aloft, loft, lofty*

loft /lɒft, AM lɔːft/ (**lofts**) N-COUNT A **loft** is the space inside the sloping roof of a building.

lofty /ˈlɒfti, AM ˈlɔːf-/ (**loftier, loftiest**) 1 ADJ A **lofty** idea or aim is noble, important, and admirable. ❑ *The writer has lofty ideals: to learn about justice and about truth.* 2 ADJ A **lofty** building or room is very high. [FORMAL]

log /lɒg, AM lɔːg/ (**logs, logging, logged**) 1 N-COUNT A **log** is a thick piece of wood cut from a branch or trunk of a tree.

log

2 N-COUNT A **log** is an official written account of what happens each day, for example on a ship. ❑ *He wrote about his experience in his ship's log.* 3 V-T If you **log** an event or fact, you record it officially in writing. ❑ *Details of the crime are then logged in the computer.*

→ see **blog, forest**

▶ **log in** or **log on** PHR-VERB When someone **logs in** or **logs on**, or when they **log into** a computer system, they gain access to the system, usually by typing their name and a password. [COMPUTING]

▶ **log out** or **log off** PHR-VERB When someone who is using a computer system **logs out** or **logs off**, they finish using the system by typing a particular command. [COMPUTING]

Word Link	*log ≈ reason, speech : apology, dialogue, logic*

logic /ˈlɒdʒɪk/ N-UNCOUNT **Logic** is a way of reasoning that involves a series of statements, each of which must be true if the statement before it is true.

→ see **philosophy**

logical /ˈlɒdʒɪkəl/ 1 ADJ In a **logical** argument, each step or point must be true if the step before it is true. ❑ *Each logical step has been checked by other mathematicians.* ● **logically** ADV ❑ *My professional training has taught me to look at things logically.* 2 ADJ A **logical** conclusion or result is the only reasonable one. ❑ *If the climate gets drier, then the logical conclusion is that more drought will occur.* ● **logically** ADV ❑ *Logically, the universe cannot be younger than any of the stars it contains.* 3 ADJ A **logical** course of action seems reasonable or sensible in the circumstances. ❑ *It seemed a logical choice.*

logistics /ləˈdʒɪstɪks/

The form **logistic** is used as a modifier.

1 N-PLURAL If you refer to **the logistics of** doing a complicated task, you are referring to the skilful organization of people and equipment, so that it can be done. ❑ *...the logistics of getting such a big show on the road.* 2 ADJ **Logistic** or **logistical** means relating to the organization of something complicated. ❑ *Producing a musical so far from home involved a variety of logistical problems.*

logo /ˈləʊgəʊ/ (**logos**) N-COUNT The **logo** of an organization is the special design that it puts on all its products. ❑ *...the famous MGM logo of the roaring lion.*

loiter /ˈlɔɪtə/ (**loiters, loitering, loitered**) V-I If you **loiter** somewhere, you stay there or walk about there without any real purpose. ❑ *Men loiter at the entrance of the factory.*

lone /ləʊn/ ADJ BEFORE N A **lone** person or thing is alone or is the only one in a particular place. ❑ *He was shot by a lone gunman.*

lonely /ˈləʊnli/ (**lonelier, loneliest**) 1 ADJ A **lonely** person is unhappy because they are alone, or because they do not have any friends. You can also use **lonely** to describe a situation or period of time in which someone feels lonely. ❑ *...lonely people who just want to talk.* ❑ *...those long, lonely nights.* ● **loneliness** N-UNCOUNT ❑ *He felt a sudden loneliness.* 2 ADJ A **lonely** place is one where very few people come. ❑ *...dark, lonely streets.*

loner /ˈləʊnə/ (**loners**) N-COUNT A **loner** is a person who likes being alone. ❑ *I'm very much a loner – I never go out.*

long
1 TIME
2 DISTANCE AND SIZE
3 VERB USES

long /lɒŋ, AM lɔːŋ/ (**longer, longest**) 1 1 ADV & ADJ & PHRASE **Long** means a great amount of time or for a great amount of time. ❑ *The repairs did not take too long.* ❑ *I learned long ago to avoid these invitations.* ❑ *The railway had obviously been built long after the house.* ❑ *We sat down and had a long talk.* 2 ADV & ADJ You use **long** to ask or talk about amounts of time. ❑ *How long can you stay?* ❑ *The average journey there is five hours long.* 3 PHRASE If you say that something is true **as long as** or **so long as** something else is true, you mean that it is true only if the second thing is true. ❑ *Tiles can be fixed to any surface as long as it's flat.* 4 PHRASE The expression **for long** is used to mean 'for a great amount of time'. ❑ *'Did you live there?'—'Not for long'.* 5 PHRASE Something that is **no longer** true, or that is not true **any longer**, used to be true but is not true now. ❑ *Food shortages are no longer a problem.* ❑ *He wasn't sitting by the door any longer.* 6 PHRASE If you say that someone **won't be long**, you think that they will arrive or return soon. ❑ *'Where is she?'—'I'm sure she won't be long.'*

long /lɒŋ, AM lɔːŋ/ (**longer, longest**) 2 1 ADJ You use **long** to talk or ask about the distance from one end of something to the other. ❑ *...a long table.* ❑ *How long is the tunnel?* ❑ *It's quite a long way from here.* 2 ADJ A **long** book or other piece of writing contains a lot of words. ❑ *He was making quite a long speech.*

long /lɒŋ, AM lɔːŋ/ (**longs, longing, longed**) 3 V-T/V-I If you **long for** something, you want it very much. ❑ *He longed for the winter to finish.* ❑ *I'm* *longing to meet her.* • **longing** (**longings**) N-VAR ❑ *...her longing to return home.*

ˌlong-ˈdistance ADJ BEFORE N & ADV **Long-distance** travel or communication involves places that are far apart. ❑ *...long-distance journeys.* ❑ *I phoned Nicola long-distance.*

longevity /lɒnˈdʒevɪti/ N-UNCOUNT **Longevity** is living for a long time or lasting for a long time. [FORMAL] ❑ *These women enjoy greater longevity than ever before.*

longitude /ˈlɒndʒɪtjuːd, AM -tuːd/ (**longitudes**) N-VAR The **longitude** of a place is its distance to the west or east of a line passing through Greenwich in England. Compare **latitude**. → see **globe**

ˌlong-ˈlost ADJ BEFORE N You use **long-lost** to describe someone or something that you have not seen for a long time. ❑ *...the arrival of their long-lost cousins.*

ˌlong-ˈrange ADJ A **long-range** plan or prediction relates to a period extending a long time into the future. ❑ *He used that to establish a long-range plan.*

ˌlong-ˈstanding ADJ A **long-standing** situation has existed for a long time. ❑ *I have a long-standing relationship with him.*

ˌlong-ˈsuffering ADJ Someone who is **long-suffering** patiently bears continual trouble or bad treatment. ❑ *He went back to his loyal, long-suffering wife.*

ˌlong-ˈterm 1 ADJ Something that is **long-term** has continued for a long time or will continue for a long time in the future. ❑ *...the long-term unemployed.* ❑ *We need to take more exercise for our long-term health.* 2 N-SING When you talk about what happens **in the long term**, you are talking about what happens over a long period of time. ❑ *In the long term the company hopes to open in Moscow.*

ˈlong-time ADJ You use **long-time** to describe something that has existed or been a particular thing for a long time. ❑ *She lives with her long-time boyfriend.*

loo /luː/ (**loos**) N-COUNT A **loo** is a toilet. [BRIT, INFORMAL]

look

1 USING YOUR EYES OR YOUR MIND
2 APPEARANCE

look /lʊk/ (**looks, looking, looked**)
1 1 V-I & N-SING If you **look**, or if you have a **look**, in a particular direction, you direct your eyes there in order to see what is there. ❑ *I looked down the hallway.* ❑ *Look, right there!* ❑ *Lucille took a last look in the mirror.* ❑ *Assisi has a couple of churches that are worth a look.* 2 → See note at **see** 3 N-COUNT A **look** is an expression on someone's face, showing what they are feeling or thinking. ❑ *He gave her a blank look.* ❑ *A look of disgust came over his face.* 4 V-I & N-COUNT If you **look for** something or someone, or if you have a **look for** them, you try to find them. ❑ *I'm looking for my friend.* ❑ *Have you looked on the piano?* ❑ *Go and have another look.* 5 V-I & N-COUNT If you **look at** a subject or situation, or have a **look at** it, you examine it, consider it, or judge it. ❑ *My eye hurts; can you look at it?* ❑ *Next term we'll look at the Second World War period.* ❑ *...a quick look at the morning newspapers.* ❑ *Brian looked at her with new respect.* 6 V-T/V-I You can use **look** to draw attention to something or someone, for example because you find them very significant or annoying. ❑ *Look what a mess you've made of your life.* 7 CONVENTION You say **look** when you want someone to pay attention to what you are going to say. ❑ *Look, I'm sorry. I didn't mean it.* 8 V-I If a building or part of a building **looks out** onto something, it has a view of it. ❑ *The terrace looks out on the sea.* 9 to **look** someone **in the eye** → see **eye**

▶ **look after** 1 PHR-VERB If you **look after** someone or something, you keep them healthy, safe, or in good condition. ❑ *I love looking after the children.* 2 PHR-VERB If you **look after** something, it is your responsibility to deal with it. ❑ *We'll help you look after your money.*

▶ **look around** → see **look round**

▶ **look back** PHR-VERB If you **look back**, you think about things that happened in the past. ❑ *Looking back, I was rather stupid.*

▶ **look down on** PHR-VERB If you say that someone **looks down on** someone or something, you mean that they consider that person or thing to be inferior, usually when this is not the case. ❑ *I wasn't successful, so they looked down on me.*

▶ **look forward to** PHR-VERB If you **are looking forward to** something, you want it to happen because you think you will enjoy it. ❑ *I'm really looking forward to meeting him.*

▶ **look into** PHR-VERB If you **look into** something, you find out about it. ❑ *He had once looked into buying his own island.*

▶ **look on** 1 PHR-VERB If you **look on** while something happens, you watch it happening without taking part yourself. ❑ *Local people looked on in silence as the two coffins passed.* 2 PHR-VERB If you **look on** someone or something in a particular way, you think of them in that way. ❑ *Employers look kindly on their permanent staff.*

▶ **look out** 1 PHR-VERB You say **'look out'** to warn someone of danger. 2 → see also **lookout**

▶ **look out for** PHR-VERB If you **look out for** something, you stay alert so that you will notice it if or when it happens. ❑ *Look out for special deals.*

▶ **look round** PHR-VERB If you **look round** a place, or if you **look around** it, you walk round it and look at the different parts of it. ❑ *We went to look round the show homes.* ❑ *I'm going to look around and see what I can find.*

▶ **look through** PHR-VERB If you **look through** a book, a magazine, or a group of things, you get an idea of what is in it by examining a lot of the items in it. ❑ *Peter started looking through the mail.*

▶ **look to** PHR-VERB If you **look to** someone or something **for** a particular thing, you expect or hope that they will provide it. ❑ *The nation looks to them for help.*

▶ **look up** 1 PHR-VERB If you **look up** a piece of information, you find it out by looking in a book or list. ❑ *I looked your address up in your file.* 2 PHR-VERB If you **look** someone **up**, you visit them after you have not seen them for a long time. ❑ *I'll look him up when I'm in town.* 3 PHR-VERB If a situation **is looking up**, it is improving. [INFORMAL]

▶ **look up to** PHR-VERB If you **look up to** someone, you respect and admire them. ❑ *A lot of the younger girls look up to her.*

Usage

If you want to say that someone is paying attention to something they can see, you say that they **are looking at** it or **watching** it. In general, you **look at** something that is not moving, while you **watch** something that is moving or changing. ❑ *I asked him to look at the picture above his bed.* ❑ *He watched Blake run down the stairs.* **Look** is never followed by an object. You must always use **at** or some other preposition. ❑ *I looked towards the plane.* You use **see** to talk about things that you are aware of because a visual impression reaches your eyes. You often use **can** in this case. ❑ *I can see the fax here on the desk.*

look /lʊk/ (**looks, looking, looked**) ❷ 1 LINK-VERB & N-SING You use **look** when describing the appearance of a person or thing or the impression that they give. ❑ *I shall use the money to make my home look lovely.* ❑ *They look just like stars.* ❑ *He looked as if he was going to smile.* ❑ *He has the look of a man who hasn't slept well.* 2 N-PLURAL When you refer to someone's **looks**, you are referring to how physically attractive they are. ❑ *Personality is just as important as good looks.* 3 LINK-VERB You use **look** when indicating what you think will happen in the future or how a situation seems to you. ❑ *He had lots of time to think, and the future didn't look good.* ❑ *It looks likely that the deal will go through.* 4 PHRASE You use expressions such as **by the look of him** and **by the looks of it** when you want to give an opinion based on the appearance of someone or something. ❑ *He was quite ill by the look of him.* 5 PHRASE If you **don't like the look of** something or someone, their appearance suggests that they might be the cause of something unpleasant. ❑ *I don't like the look of those clouds.* ❑ *I didn't like the look of him at all.*

lookout /ˈlʊkaʊt/ (**lookouts**) 1 N-COUNT A **lookout** is a place from which you can see clearly in all directions. ❑ *A tower serves as a lookout for children who like to watch storms over Lake Michigan.* 2 N-COUNT A **lookout** is someone who is watching for danger. 3 PHRASE If you are **on the lookout for** something, you are watching out for it. ❑ *He was always on the lookout for good new music.*

loom /luːm/ (**looms, looming, loomed**) 1 V-I If something **looms** over you, or if it **looms up**, it appears as a large or unclear shape, often in a frightening way. ❑ *The mountains loomed out of the blackness.* 2 V-I If a worrying or threatening event or situation **is looming**, it seems likely to happen soon. ❑ *The possibility of civil war looms ahead.* 3 N-COUNT A **loom** is a device that is used for weaving cloth.

loom

loony /ˈluːni/ (**loonies**) ADJ & N-COUNT If you describe someone's behaviour as **loony**, or if you refer to someone as a **loony**, you mean that they behave in a way that seems mad or strange. [INFORMAL] ❑ *I've done a lot of loony things, but this is the worst.* ❑ *They all thought I was a loony.*

loop /luːp/ (**loops, looping, looped**) 1 N-COUNT A **loop** is a curved or circular shape in something long, such as a piece of string. 2 V-T If you **loop** something such as a piece of rope around an object, you tie a length of it in a loop around the object. ❑ *He looped the rope over the wood.* 3 V-I If something **loops** somewhere, it goes there in a circular direction. ❑ *The road looped through the hills.*

loophole /ˈluːphəʊl/ (**loopholes**) N-COUNT A **loophole in the law** is a small mistake or omission which some people use to avoid doing something that the law intends them to do. ❑ *They've found a legal loophole which will allow them to stay as they are.*

loose /luːs/ (**looser, loosest**) 1 ADJ Something that is **loose** is not firmly held or fixed in place. ❑ *Two wooden beams came loose from the ceiling.* ❑ *...a loose thread.* ● **loosely** ADV ❑ *...a shirt tied loosely at the waist.* 2 ADJ If people or animals **break loose** or are **set loose**, they are freed after they have been restrained. ❑ *The soldiers tried to stop her but she broke loose.* 3 PHRASE If a person or animal is **on the loose**, they are free because they have escaped from a person or place. 4 ADJ **Loose** clothes do not fit closely. ● **loosely** ADV ❑ *His shirt hung loosely over his shoulders.* 5 ADJ A **loose** grouping or arrangement is flexible rather than strictly controlled or organized. ❑ *...a loose association of independent states.* ● **loosely** ADV ❑ *...a loosely organised studio band.*

Thesaurus *loose* Also look up:

ADJ. slack, wobbly 1
free 2 3
baggy 4

ˌloose ˈend (**loose ends**) N-COUNT A **loose end** is part of a story or situation that has not yet been explained. ❑ *There are some annoying loose ends in the plot.*

loosen /ˈluːsən/ (**loosens, loosening, loosened**) 1 V-T If someone in authority **loosens** restrictions or laws, they make them less severe. 2 V-T/V-I If something that is tied or fastened **loosens** or **is loosened**, it becomes or you make it less tight or less firmly held in place.

▸ **loosen up** 1 PHR-VERB If a person or situation **loosens up**, they become more relaxed. 2 PHR-VERB If you **loosen up**, you do simple exercises to get your muscles ready for a physical activity.

loot /luːt/ (**loots, looting, looted**) 1 V-T If people **loot** a building, or if they **loot** things from it, they steal things from it during a battle or a riot. ❑ *The museum was bombed and looted.* ● **looting** N-UNCOUNT ❑ *There has been rioting and looting.* ● **looter** (**looters**) N-COUNT ❑ *Hundreds of looters attacked shops during the march.* 2 N-UNCOUNT **Loot** is stolen money and goods. [INFORMAL]

lopsided also **lop-sided** /ˌlɒpˈsaɪdɪd/ ADJ Something that is **lopsided** is uneven because one side is, for example, higher or much greater than the other. ❑ *...a friendly, lopsided grin.*

lord /lɔːd/ (**lords**) 1 N-COUNT In Britain, a **lord** is a man who has a high rank in the nobility. ❑ *She married a lord.* 2 N-TITLE **Lord** is a title used in front of the names of some male members of the nobility, and of judges, bishops, and some high ranking officials. [BRIT] ❑ *He was Lord Chancellor from 1970 until 1974.* 3 N-PROPER In the Christian church, people refer to God and to Jesus Christ as **the Lord**.

lore /lɔː/ 1 N-UNCOUNT The **lore** of a particular country or culture is its traditional stories and history. ❑ *...ancient Catalan lore.* 2 → see also **folklore**

lorry /ˈlɒri, AM ˈlɔːri/ (**lorries**) N-COUNT In British English, a **lorry** is a large vehicle used to transport goods by road. The American word is **truck**.

lose /luːz/ (**loses, losing, lost**) 1 V-T/V-I If you **lose** a fight or an argument, someone else defeats you. ❑ *A C Milan lost the Italian Cup Final.* ❑ *No one likes to lose.* 2 V-T If you **lose** something, you cannot find it, or you no longer have it because it has been taken away from you. ❑ *I lost my keys.* ❑ *He lost his place in the team.* 3 V-T If someone **loses** a quality or belief, they no longer have it. ❑ *He lost all sense of reason.* 4 V-T You say you **lose** something when you have less of it. ❑ *She lost a lot of blood.* ❑ *The best way to lose weight is to exercise.* ❑ *The company was losing money.* 5 V-T If you **lose** a relative or friend, they die. 6 V-T If you **lose** an opportunity or **lose** time, you waste it. ❑ *'We can't afford to lose time,' she insists.* 7 → see also **lost**
→ see **diet**

▶ **lose out** PHR-VERB If you **lose out**, you suffer a loss or disadvantage. ❑ *Women have lost out in this new pay deal.*

loser /ˈluːzə/ (**losers**) N-COUNT The **losers** of a contest or struggle are the people who are defeated. If you say someone is a **good loser** you mean that they accept that they have lost a contest without complaining. If you say that someone is a **bad loser**, you mean that they hate losing and complain a lot about it.

loss /lɒs, AM lɔːs/ (**losses**) 1 N-UNCOUNT **Loss** is the fact of no longer having something or of having less of it than before. ❑ *...loss of sight.* ❑ *The loss of income for the government is significant.* 2 N-COUNT A **loss** is the disadvantage you suffer when a valuable and useful person or thing leaves or is taken away. ❑ *His death was a great loss to her.* ❑ *...a terrible loss of human life.* ❑ *They hope that job losses will be kept to a minimum.* 3 N-UNCOUNT **Loss** is the feeling of sadness you experience when someone you like is taken away from you. ❑ *...your feelings of loss and grief.* 4 N-VAR If a business makes a **loss**, it earns less than it spends. 5 PHRASE If you are **at a loss**, you do not know what to do in a particular situation. 6 PHRASE If you **cut** your **losses**, you stop what you are doing because it is making a bad situation become worse.
→ see **disaster**

Word Partnership Use *loss* with:

N. loss **of appetite**, loss **of control**, loss **of income**, loss **of a job** 1
blood loss, **hair** loss, **hearing** loss, **memory** loss, **weight** loss 1 6
ADJ. **great/huge/substantial** loss 1-7
tragic loss 2 3
net loss 7

lost /lɒst, AM lɔːst/ 1 **Lost** is the past tense and past participle of **lose**. 2 ADJ If you are **lost**, you do not know where you are or you are unable to find your way. ❑ *I realised I was lost.* 3 ADJ If something gets **lost**, you cannot find it. 4 ADJ If you **feel lost**, you feel uncomfortable because you are in an unfamiliar situation. 5 PHRASE If advice or a comment **is lost on** someone, they do not understand it, or they pay no attention to it.

Thesaurus *lost* Also look up:

ADJ. adrift 2
missing 3

lot /lɒt/ (**lots**) 1 QUANT **A lot of** something or **lots of** it is a large amount of it. ❑ *A lot of our land is used for farming.* ❑ *He drank lots of milk.* ❑ *I learned a lot from him.* 2 ADV **A lot** means to a great extent or degree. ❑ *They went out a lot.* 3 N-COUNT You can use **lot** to refer to a set or group of things or people. ❑ *We've just sacked one lot of builders.* 4 N-SING You can refer to a specific group of people as a particular **lot**. [INFORMAL] ❑ *They're a boring lot.*

loth /ləʊθ/ → see **loath**

lotion /ˈləʊʃən/ (**lotions**) N-VAR A **lotion** is a liquid that you use to clean, improve, or protect your skin or hair. ❑ *...suntan lotion.*

lottery /ˈlɒtəri/ (**lotteries**) 1 N-COUNT A **lottery** is a type of gambling in which people bet on a number or a series of numbers being chosen as the winner. Lotteries usually offer large cash prizes and are often organized so that a percentage of the profits is donated to good causes. 2 N-SING If you describe something as a **lottery**, you mean that what happens depends entirely on luck or chance. ❑ *He depended on life being more than a lottery.*

Word Link *er ≈ more : bigger, louder, taller*

loud /laʊd/ (**louder, loudest**) 1 ADJ & ADV If a noise is **loud**, the level of sound is very high and it can easily be heard. Someone or something that is **loud** produces a lot of noise. ❑ *There was a loud bang.* ❑ *He turns the television up very loud.* ● **loudly** ADV ❑ *His footsteps echoed loudly in the hall.* 2 PHRASE If you say something **out loud**, you say it so that it can be heard, rather than just thinking it. ❑ *I laughed out loud.* 3 ADJ If you describe a piece of clothing as **loud**, you dislike it because it is too bright and tasteless.

Word Partnership Use *loud* with:

N. loud **bang**, loud **crash**, loud **explosion**, loud **music**, loud **noise**, loud **voice** 1
ADJ. loud **and clear** 1
V. **laugh out** loud, **read out** loud, **say *something* out** loud, **think out** loud 2

loudspeaker /ˌlaʊdˈspiːkə/ (**loudspeakers**) N-COUNT A **loudspeaker** is a piece of equipment, for example part of a radio, through which sound comes out.

lounge /laʊndʒ/ (**lounges, lounging, lounged**) 1 N-COUNT A **lounge** is a room in a house, or in a hotel, where people sit and relax. 2 N-COUNT At an airport, the **departure lounge** is a large room where passengers go before boarding their plane. 3 V-I If you **lounge** somewhere, you lean against something or lie somewhere in a relaxed way. ❑ *They ate and drank and lounged in the shade.*

▶ **lounge about** or **lounge around** PHR-VERB If you **lounge about** or **lounge around**, you spend your time in a relaxed and lazy way. ❑ *He remembered lounging around the swimming pool.*

louse /laʊs/ (**lice**) N-COUNT **Lice** are small

insects that live on the bodies of people or animals.

lousy /ˈlaʊzi/ (**lousier, lousiest**) **1** ADJ If you describe something as **lousy**, you mean that it is of very bad quality. [INFORMAL] ❑ *The food was lousy.* **2** ADJ If you **feel lousy**, you feel very ill. [INFORMAL]

lout /laʊt/ (**louts**) N-COUNT If you describe a young man as a **lout**, you are critical of him because he behaves in a rude or aggressive way. ❑ *A dozen louts shouted at the visiting players.*

lovable /ˈlʌvəbəl/ ADJ If you describe someone as **lovable**, you mean they have attractive qualities and are easy to like.

love /lʌv/ (**loves, loving, loved**) **1** V-T & N-UNCOUNT If you **love** someone, or if you feel **love for** them, you feel romantically or sexually attracted to them, and they are very important to you. ❑ *Oh, Amy, I love you.* ❑ *We often communicate our love by letter.* **2** V-T & N-UNCOUNT If you **love** someone, or if you have **love for** them, you care for them very much. ❑ *You love your parents, don't you?* ❑ *A second baby doesn't change our love for the first.* **3** V-T & N-UNCOUNT If you **love** something, or if you have a **love of** it, you like it very much. ❑ *I love taking photographs.* ❑ *I'm a person that loves to be in the outdoors.* ❑ *...a love of literature.* **4** V-T You can say that you **love** something when you consider that it is important and want to protect or support it. ❑ *I love my country as you love yours.* **5** V-T If you **would love to** have or do something, you very much want to have or do it. ❑ *I would love a hot bath and clean clothes.* ❑ *His wife would love him to give up his job.* **6** CONVENTION You can write **love** or **love from**, followed by your name, when you end an informal letter. ❑ *...with love from Grandma.* **7** N-VOC Some people use **love** as an affectionate way of addressing someone. [INFORMAL] ❑ *Well, I'll see you then, love.* **8** NUM In tennis, **love** is a score of zero. **9** → See note at **zero** **10** PHRASE If you **fall in love with** someone, you start to feel romantically attracted to them, and they are very important to you. ❑ *I fell in love with him.* ❑ *We fell madly in love.* **11** PHRASE When two people **make love**, they have sex. **12** → see also **loving**

→ see Word Web: **love**

→ see **emotion**

Thesaurus *love* Also look up:

N. adoration, devotion, tenderness; *(ant.)* hate **1**-**3**

V. adore, cherish, treasure; *(ant.)* dislike, hate **1**-**4**

ˈlove affair (**love affairs**) N-COUNT A **love affair** is a romantic relationship between two people.

ˈlove life (**love lives**) N-COUNT Someone's **love life** is the part of their life that consists of their romantic relationships.

lovely /ˈlʌvli/ (**lovelier, loveliest**) ADJ If you describe someone or something as **lovely**, you mean that they are very beautiful or that you like them very much. ❑ *You look lovely, Marcia.* ❑ *He had a lovely voice.* ● **loveliness** N-UNCOUNT ❑ *She had a loveliness that made people stare.*

ˈlove-making N-UNCOUNT **Love-making** refers to sexual activities that take place between two people who love each other.

lover /ˈlʌvə/ (**lovers**) **1** N-COUNT Someone's **lover** is someone who they are having a sexual relationship with but are not married to. **2** N-COUNT If you are a **lover of** something such as animals or the arts, you enjoy them very much and take great pleasure in them. ❑ *She is a great lover of horses.* ❑ *...art lovers.*

loving /ˈlʌvɪŋ/ **1** ADJ Someone who is **loving** feels or shows love to other people. ❑ *...a most loving husband.* ● **lovingly** ADV ❑ *Brian looked lovingly at Mary Ann.* **2** ADJ **Loving** actions are done with great enjoyment and care. ❑ *The house has been restored with loving care.* ● **lovingly** ADV ❑ *...lovingly prepared food.*

low /ləʊ/ (**lower, lowest, lows**) **1** ADJ Something that is **low** measures a short distance from the bottom to the top. ❑ *She put it down on the low table.* ❑ *...low, green hills.* **2** ADJ If something is **low**, it is close to the ground, to sea level, or to the bottom of something. ❑ *He hit his head on the low doorway.* ❑ *Late in the afternoon the sun was low in the sky.* **3** ADJ **Low** means small in amount or degree, or at the bottom of a particular scale or system. ❑ *...low incomes.* ❑ *...temperatures in the low 80s.* ❑ *Food supplies were getting very low.* ❑ *These hotels are at the lower end of the price range.* **4** N-COUNT A **low** is a level or amount that is less than it was before. ❑ *The prime minister's popularity is at an all-time low.* **5** ADJ If the quality or standard of something is **low**, it is poor. ❑ *...work of very low quality.* **6** ADJ If someone is **low**, or if their **spirits** are **low**, they are feeling depressed. ❑ *We are all very tired and a bit low.* **7** ADJ If you have a **low opinion** of someone, you disapprove of them or dislike them. **8** ADJ A **low** sound is deep and quiet. ❑ *Father whistled a few low notes.* ❑ *She spoke in a low voice.* **9** ADJ If something such as a radio or a light is **low**, it is only producing a small amount of sound, heat, or light. ❑ *The heater is on low.* **10** PHRASE If you **are lying low**, you are avoiding being seen or drawing

Word Web love

Until the Middle Ages, **romance** was not an important part of **marriage**. Parents decided who their children would marry. The social class and political connections of a future spouse were very important. No one expected a couple to fall in love. However, during the Middle Ages, poets and musicians began to write about love in a new way. These **romantic** poems and songs describe a new type of **courtship**. In them, the man **woos** a woman for her **affection**. This is the basis for the modern idea of a romantic **bond** between **husband** and **wife**.

attention to yourself. [INFORMAL] ❑ *It is safer to lie low till the men are gone.* **11** **at a low ebb** → see **ebb** **12** **a low profile** → see **profile**

lower /ˈləʊə/ (**lowers, lowering, lowered**) **1** **Lower** is the comparative of **low**. **2** ADJ You can use **lower** to refer to the bottom one of a pair of things. ❑ *She bit her lower lip.* **3** V-T If you **lower** something, you move it slowly downwards. ❑ *Gracefully she lowered herself into a chair.* **4** V-T To **lower** an amount, value, or quality means to make it less. ❑ *The Central Bank has lowered interest rates.* ● **lowering** N-SING ❑ *...the lowering of the voting age to 18.*

ˌlower ˈclass also **lower-class** (**lower classes**) N-COUNT & ADJ Some people use **the lower class** or **the lower classes** to refer to the division of society that they consider to have the lowest social status. **The lower class** can take the singular or plural form of the verb. ❑ *Most of the victims come from the lower classes.* ❑ *...students from lower-class families.*

ˌlow-ˈimpact ADJ **Low-impact** exercise does not put a lot of stress on your body.

ˌlow-ˈkey ADJ Something that is **low-key** is restrained rather than noticeable or intense. ❑ *The wedding will be very low-key.*

lowly /ˈləʊli/ (**lowlier, lowliest**) ADJ Something that is **lowly** is low in position or status. ❑ *Her first job was as a lowly secretary.*

loyal /ˈlɔɪəl/ ADJ If you describe someone as **loyal**, you mean they remain firm in their friendship or support for someone or something. ❑ *They remained loyal to the president.* ● **loyally** ADV ❑ *They have loyally supported their party.* → see **hero**

loyalty /ˈlɔɪəlti/ (**loyalties**) **1** N-UNCOUNT **Loyalty** is behaviour in which you stay firm in your friendship or support for someone or something. ❑ *I'm a believer in family loyalty against the world.* **2** N-COUNT **Loyalties** are feelings of friendship, support, or duty. ❑ *Mr Armstrong has divided loyalties when England play Scotland at rugby.*

LP /ˌel ˈpiː/ (**LPs**) N-COUNT An **LP** is a record which usually has about 25 minutes of music or speech on each side.

Ltd In Britain, **Ltd** is a written abbreviation for **limited**, used after the name of a company.

lubricate /ˈluːbrɪkeɪt/ (**lubricates, lubricating, lubricated**) V-T If you **lubricate** something such as a part of a machine, you put oil onto it to make it move smoothly. ❑ *Lubricate all the moving parts.* ● **lubrication** N-UNCOUNT ❑ *Use some oil for lubrication.*

Word Link *luc ≈ light : hallucination, lucid, translucent*

lucid /ˈluːsɪd/ **1** ADJ **Lucid** writing or speech is clear and easy to understand. ❑ *...his lucid explanation of the work.* ● **lucidly** ADV ❑ *...presenting complex matters lucidly.* ● **lucidity** /luːˈsɪdɪti/ N-UNCOUNT ❑ *...the lucidity of his arguments.* **2** ADJ When someone is **lucid**, they are able to think clearly again after a period of illness or confusion. ● **lucidity** N-UNCOUNT ❑ *Gran had occasional moments of lucidity.*

luck /lʌk/ **1** N-UNCOUNT **Luck** is success or good things that happen to you, which do not come from your own abilities or efforts. ❑ *He does deserve some good luck.* ❑ *We have had no luck finding accommodation.* **2** PHRASE You can say **'Bad luck'**, **'Hard luck'**, or **'Tough luck'** to someone when you want to express your sympathy to them. **3** PHRASE You say **'Good luck'** or **'Best of luck'** to someone when you are wishing them success in something they are trying to do. **4** PHRASE When someone **tries** their **luck at** something, they try to succeed at it. ❑ *She went back to try her luck at modelling.* **5** PHRASE You can add **with luck** or **with any luck** to a statement to indicate that you hope that a particular thing will happen. ❑ *With any luck, the money will turn up somewhere.*

Word Partnership Use *luck* with:

V. **bring *someone*** luck, **need a little** luck, **need some** luck, **push *your*** luck, **try *your*** luck, **wish *someone*** luck **1** **have any/bad/better/good/no** luck **1** **2**

ADJ. **dumb** luck, **good** luck, **just** luck, **pure** luck, **sheer** luck **1**

luckily /ˈlʌkɪli/ ADV You add **luckily** to your statement to indicate that you are glad that something happened or is the case. ❑ *Luckily, we both love football.*

lucky /ˈlʌki/ (**luckier, luckiest**) **1** ADJ If someone is **lucky**, they are in a very desirable situation. ❑ *I am luckier than most. I have a job.* **2** ADJ A **lucky** person always has good luck. ❑ *He had always been lucky at cards.* **3** ADJ If an event or situation is **lucky**, it has good effects or consequences, which happen by chance. ❑ *It's lucky that no lives were lost.* **4** ADJ A **lucky** object is something that someone believes helps them to be successful. ❑ *Seven is my lucky number.* **5** PHRASE If you say that someone **will be lucky to** do or get something, you mean that they are very unlikely to be able to do or get it. ❑ *You'll be lucky to get change out of £750.*

Word Partnership Use *lucky* with:

ADV. lucky **enough**, **pretty** lucky, **really** lucky, **so** lucky, **very** lucky **1**

V. **be** lucky, **feel** lucky, **get** lucky, lucky **to get *something***, lucky **to have *something*** **1**

N. lucky **break**, lucky **guess** **3**

lucrative /ˈluːkrətɪv/ ADJ A **lucrative** business or activity earns you a lot of money.

ludicrous /ˈluːdɪkrəs/ ADJ If you describe something as **ludicrous**, you mean that it is very foolish or unreasonable. ❑ *It was ludicrous to suggest that the visit could be kept secret.* ● **ludicrously** ADV ❑ *The prices are ludicrously low.*

luggage

lug /lʌg/ (**lugs, lugging, lugged**) V-T If you **lug** a heavy object somewhere, you carry it there with difficulty. [INFORMAL] ❑ *Nobody wants to lug around huge suitcases.*

luggage /ˈlʌgɪdʒ/ N-UNCOUNT **Luggage** consists of the suitcases and bags that you take when you travel. → see **hotel**

Usage

Luggage is an uncount noun. You can have **a piece of luggage** or **some luggage** but you cannot have 'a luggage' or 'some luggages'.

lukewarm /ˌlu:kˈwɔ:m/ **1** ADJ **Lukewarm water** is only slightly warm. ❑ *Wash your face with lukewarm water.* **2** ADJ If you describe a person or their attitude as **lukewarm towards** someone or something, you mean they do not show much enthusiasm or interest towards them. ❑ *The new design received the same lukewarm response as his first idea.*

lull /lʌl/ (**lulls, lulling, lulled**) **1** N-COUNT A **lull** is a period of quiet or of little activity. ❑ *There was a brief lull in the conversation.* **2** V-T If you **are lulled into** feeling good or safe, someone or something causes you to feel that way. ❑ *The massage lulled me into a deep sleep.*

lumber /ˈlʌmbə/ (**lumbers, lumbering, lumbered**) **1** N-UNCOUNT In American English, **lumber** consists of wood that has been roughly cut up. The British word is **timber**. **2** V-I If someone **lumbers** around, they move slowly and clumsily. ❑ *He lumbered back to his chair.*
→ see **forest**

▶ **lumber with** PHR-VERB If you **are lumbered with** someone or something, you have to take responsibility for them, although you do not want to. [BRIT, INFORMAL] ❑ *I was lumbered with the job of looking after the money.*

L

luminous /ˈlu:mɪnəs/ ADJ Something that is **luminous** shines or glows in the dark. ❑ *...the luminous dial on the clock.*

lump /lʌmp/ (**lumps, lumping, lumped**) **1** N-COUNT A **lump** is a solid piece of something. ❑ *...a lump of coal.* **2** N-COUNT A **lump** on someone's body is a small, hard piece of flesh caused by an injury or an illness. ❑ *I've got a lump on my neck.*

▶ **lump together** PHR-VERB If a number of different people or things **are lumped together**, they are considered as a group rather than separately. [INFORMAL] ❑ *To lump together all African nations is not fair.*

ˈlump sum (**lump sums**) N-COUNT A **lump sum** is a large amount of money that is given or received all at once. ❑ *He received a tax-free lump sum of £50,000.*

lumpy /ˈlʌmpi/ (**lumpier, lumpiest**) ADJ Something that is **lumpy** contains lumps or is covered in lumps. ❑ *She stretched out on the lumpy bed.*

lunar /ˈlu:nə/ ADJ BEFORE N **Lunar** means relating to the moon. ❑ *...man's first lunar landing.*
→ see **eclipse**

lunatic /ˈlu:nətɪk/ (**lunatics**) N-COUNT & ADJ If you describe someone as a **lunatic**, or if you say that their behaviour is **lunatic**, you mean that they behave in a stupid and possibly dangerous way.

lunch /lʌntʃ/ (**lunches, lunching, lunched**) **1** N-VAR **Lunch** is a meal that you have in the middle of the day. ❑ *We all went out for lunch.* **2** → See note at **meal** **3** V-I When you **lunch** somewhere, you eat lunch there. [FORMAL]
→ see **meal**

Word Partnership Use *lunch* with:

ADJ.	**free** lunch, **good** lunch, **hot** lunch, **late** lunch **1**
V.	**bring *your*** lunch, **break for** lunch, **buy *someone*** lunch, **eat** lunch, **go *somewhere* for** lunch, **go to** lunch, **have** lunch, **pack a** lunch, **serve** lunch **1**

luncheon /ˈlʌntʃən/ (**luncheons**) N-VAR **Luncheon** is a formal meal in the middle of the day.

lunchtime or **lunch time** /ˈlʌntʃtaɪm/ (**lunchtimes**) N-VAR **Lunchtime** is the period of the day when people have their lunch. ❑ *Could we meet at lunchtime?*

lung /lʌŋ/ (**lungs**) N-COUNT Your **lungs** are the two organs inside your chest which you use for breathing.
→ see **donor, respiration**

lunge /lʌndʒ/ (**lunges, lunging, lunged**) V-I & N-COUNT If you **lunge**, or if you make a **lunge**, in a particular direction, you move there suddenly and clumsily. ❑ *He lunged at me, grabbing me violently.*

lurch /lɜ:tʃ/ (**lurches, lurching, lurched**) V-I & N-COUNT If you **lurch**, or give a **lurch**, you make a sudden, jerky movement, especially forwards. ❑ *Henry looked, stared, and lurched to his feet.* ❑ *The car took a lurch forward.*

lure /ljʊə, AM lʊr/ (**lures, luring, lured**) **1** V-T To **lure** someone means to trick them into a particular place or to trick them into doing something that they should not do. ❑ *They were being lured into a trap.* **2** N-COUNT A **lure** is an attractive quality that something has. ❑ *The lure of rural life is as strong as ever.*

lurid /ˈljʊərɪd, AM ˈlʊrɪd/ **1** ADJ If you say that something is **lurid**, you disapprove of it because it involves a lot of violence, sex, or shocking detail. ❑ *It is the lurid headlines that are most entertaining.* **2** ADJ If you describe something as **lurid**, you do not like it because it is very brightly coloured. ❑ *...a lurid red.*

lurk /lɜ:k/ (**lurks, lurking, lurked**) **1** V-I If someone **lurks** somewhere, they hide there, usually because they intend to do something bad. ❑ *...the trees where Harper lurked with his gun.* **2** V-I If something such as a memory, suspicion, or danger **lurks**, it exists, but you are only slightly aware of it. ❑ *Around every corner lurked doubt and uncertainty.*

luscious /ˈlʌʃəs/ ADJ **Luscious** food is juicy and delicious.

lush /lʌʃ/ (**lusher, lushest**) ADJ **Lush** fields or gardens have a lot of very healthy grass or plants.

lust /lʌst/ (**lusts, lusting, lusted**) **1** V-I & N-UNCOUNT If you **lust after** someone or **lust for** them, you feel a very strong sexual desire for them. **Lust** is this feeling. **2** V-I & N-UNCOUNT If you **lust for** something or **lust after** it, you have a very strong and eager desire to have it. A **lust for** something is this desire. ❑ *They all lusted after the top job.*

luxurious /lʌgˈʒʊəriəs/ **1** ADJ Something that is **luxurious** is very comfortable and expensive. ❑ *...Roberto's luxurious life-style.* ● **luxuriously** ADV ❑ *The dining-room is luxuriously furnished.* **2** ADJ **Luxurious** actions express great pleasure and comfort. • **luxuriously** ADV ❑ *Liz laughed, stretching luxuriously.*

luxury /ˈlʌkʃəri/ (**luxuries**) 1 N-UNCOUNT **Luxury** is very great comfort, especially among beautiful and expensive surroundings. ❑ *He leads a life of luxury.* 2 N-COUNT & ADJ BEFORE N A **luxury** is something expensive which you do not really need but which you enjoy. ❑ *I do like the luxuries of life – good wine, clothes, holidays.* ❑ *...luxury food.* 3 N-SING A **luxury** is a pleasure which you do not often experience. ❑ *Hot baths are my favourite luxury.*

Thesaurus *luxury* Also look up:

N. comfort, richness, splendour 1
extra, extravagance, treat 2 3

lying /ˈlaɪɪŋ/ **Lying** is the present participle of **lie**.

lynch /lɪntʃ/ (**lynchs, lynching, lynched**) V-T If an angry crowd of people **lynch** someone they believe is guilty of committing a crime, they kill that person by hanging them, without letting them have a trial.

lyric /ˈlɪrɪk/ (**lyrics**) 1 ADJ BEFORE N **Lyric** poetry is written in a simple and direct style. ❑ *... Lawrence's short stories and lyric poetry.* 2 N-PLURAL The **lyrics** of a song are its words. ❑ *... Kurt Weill's opera with lyrics by Langston Hughes.*

lyrical /ˈlɪrɪkəl/ ADJ Something that is **lyrical** is poetic and romantic. ❑ *His paintings became more lyrical.*

lyricist /ˈlɪrɪsɪst/ (**lyricists**) N-COUNT A **lyricist** is someone who writes the words for modern songs or for musicals.

Mm

m **1** **m** is a written abbreviation for **metres** or **metre**. ❑ *The boat is 12.5m long and 3.6m wide.* **2** **m** is a written abbreviation for the number **million**. ❑ *The company's profit is expected to rise to £8m.*

ma'am /mæm, mɑːm/ N-VOC People sometimes say **ma'am** as a formal and polite way of addressing a woman whose name they do not know, or a woman of superior rank.

macabre /məˈkɑːbrə/ ADJ You describe something such as an event or story as **macabre** when it is strange and horrible, usually because it involves death or injury.

machete /məˈʃeti/ (**machetes**) N-COUNT A **machete** is a large knife with a broad blade used for cutting and as a weapon.

machine /məˈʃiːn/ (**machines**) **1** N-COUNT A **machine** is a piece of equipment which uses electricity or an engine in order to do a particular kind of work. ❑ *Weston instructed him on how to operate the machine.* **2** N-COUNT You use **machine** to refer to a large, well-controlled organization. ❑ *Anna Wintour has made 'Vogue' into a money-making machine.*

M

Thesaurus *machine* Also look up:

N. appliance, computer, gadget, mechanism **1**
organization, structure, system **2**

Word Partnership Use *machine* with:

V. **design a** machine, **invent a** machine, **use a** machine **1**
ADJ. **heavy** machine, **new** machine, machine **washable** **1**
N. machine **oil**, machine **parts**, machine **shop**, **Xerox** machine **1**

ma'chine ˌgun (**machine guns**) N-COUNT A **machine gun** is a gun which fires a lot of bullets very quickly one after the other. ❑ *He took a machine gun from another soldier and shot us all.*

machinery /məˈʃiːnəri/ **1** N-UNCOUNT **Machinery** is machines in general, or machines that are used in a factory. **2** N-UNCOUNT The **machinery** of a government or organization is the system that it uses to deal with things. ❑ *This strengthened the machinery of the United Nations.*

macho /ˈmætʃəʊ, AM ˈmɑː-/ ADJ You use **macho** to describe men who behave in an aggressively masculine way. [INFORMAL] ❑ *Arnold Schwarzenegger was the biggest macho movie star on Earth.*

mad /mæd/ (**madder, maddest**) **1** ADJ Someone who is **mad** has a mental illness which makes them behave in strange ways. ❑ *She was afraid of going mad.* ● **madness** N-UNCOUNT ❑ *...the classic symptoms of madness.* **2** ADJ You describe someone as **mad** when they do or say things that you think are very foolish. ❑ *It would be mad to waste such a good opportunity.* ● **madness** N-UNCOUNT ❑ *I decided it would be madness to give up now.* **3** ADJ You use **mad** to describe wild uncontrolled behaviour. ❑ *There was a mad rush for the doors.* ❑ *The crowd went mad.* **4** ADJ You can say that someone is **mad** when they are very angry. [INFORMAL] ❑ *They both got mad at me for interfering.* **5** ADJ AFTER LINK-V If you are **mad about** something or someone, you like them very much indeed. [INFORMAL] ❑ *He was mad about golf.* **6** PHRASE If you say that someone or something **drives** you **mad**, you mean that you find them extremely annoying. [INFORMAL] ❑ *His messiness drives me mad.* **7** PHRASE If you do something **like mad**, you do it very energetically or enthusiastically. [INFORMAL] ❑ *He was trying like mad, but he just couldn't do it.*

Thesaurus *mad* Also look up:

ADJ. deranged, insane **1**
angry, furious **4**
crazy, foolish, senseless **2**

madam /ˈmædəm/ N-VOC **Madam** is a formal and polite way of addressing a woman. ❑ *Thank you, madam.*

madden /ˈmædən/ (**maddens, maddening, maddened**) V-T If something **maddens** you, it makes you feel very angry or annoyed. ❑ *The noise maddened him.* ● **maddening** ADJ ❑ *...his maddening habits.* ● **maddeningly** ADV ❑ *The service in this restaurant is maddeningly slow.*

made /meɪd/ **1** **Made** is the past tense and past participle of **make**. **2** ADJ AFTER LINK-V If something is **made of** or **made out of** a particular substance or material, that substance or material was used to build or construct it. ❑ *...a ring made of silver.*

madly /ˈmædli/ **1** ADV If you do something **madly**, you do it in a fast, excited, or eager way. ❑ *We waved madly at the plane, but the pilot didn't see us.* **2** ADV If you are **madly** in love with someone, you love them very much.

mag /mæg/ (**mags**) N-COUNT A **mag** is the same as a **magazine**. [INFORMAL] ❑ *...sports mags.*

magazine /ˌmægəˈziːn, AM ˈmægəziːn/ (**magazines**) N-COUNT A **magazine** is a weekly or monthly publication which contains articles, stories, photographs and advertisements. ❑ *...a women's magazine.*
→ see **library**

maggot /ˈmægət/ (**maggots**) N-COUNT **Maggots** are tiny creatures that look like very small worms and turn into flies.

magic /ˈmædʒɪk/ **1** N-UNCOUNT & ADJ **Magic**

is a special power that occurs in stories and that some people believe in, that can make apparently impossible things happen. ❑ *They all disappeared as if by magic into the darkness of the night.* **2** N-UNCOUNT **Magic** is the art of performing tricks to entertain people, for example by seeming to make things appear and disappear. ❑ *He used to perform magic at my parties.* **3** N-UNCOUNT & ADJ The **magic of** something is a special quality that makes it seem wonderful and exciting. ❑ *...the magic of movies.* ❑ *...those magic moments.*

Thesaurus *magic* Also look up:
N. illusion, witchcraft **1**
appeal, beauty, charm **3**

magical /'mædʒɪkəl/ **1** ADJ Something that is **magical** seems to use magic or to be able to produce magic. ❑ *...the magical powers of Harry Potter.* ● **magically** ADV ❑ *This problem isn't going to magically disappear.* **2** ADJ You can say that something is **magical** when it has a special mysterious quality that makes it seem wonderful and exciting. ❑ *Paris is a magical city.*

Word Link *ician ≈ person who works at : magician, musician, physician*

magician /mə'dʒɪʃən/ (**magicians**) **1** N-COUNT A **magician** is a person who entertains people by doing magic tricks. **2** N-COUNT In fairy stories, a **magician** is a man who has magic powers.

magistrate /'mædʒɪstreɪt/ (**magistrates**) N-COUNT A **magistrate** is a person who is appointed to act as a judge in law courts which deal with minor crimes or disputes.

Word Link *magn ≈ great : magnate, magnificent, magnify*

magnate /'mægneɪt/ (**magnates**) N-COUNT A **magnate** is someone who has earned a lot of money from a particular business or industry. ❑ *...a shipping magnate.*

magnet /'mægnɪt/ (**magnets**) N-COUNT A **magnet** is a piece of iron which attracts iron or steel towards it.
→ see Word Web: **magnet**

magnetic /mæg'netɪk/ **1** ADJ If something is **magnetic**, it has the power of a magnet or functions like a magnet. ❑ *The region around the magnet, in which there is a magnetic force, is called a magnetic field.* **2** ADJ **Magnetic** tapes or objects are coated in a magnetic substance which contains coded information that can be read or written on by computers. ❑ *...a magnetic strip.* [COMPUTING] **3** ADJ If you describe something or someone as **magnetic**, you mean that they have qualities which people find very attractive. ❑ *...her magnetic personality.*

magnetism /'mægnɪtɪzəm/ **1** N-UNCOUNT **Magnetism** is a power that attracts some substances towards others. **2** N-UNCOUNT Someone with **magnetism** has unusual and exciting qualities which people find very attractive. ❑ *President Kennedy had a personal magnetism that made him very popular.*

magnificent /mæg'nɪfɪsənt/ ADJ Something or someone that is **magnificent** is extremely good, beautiful, or impressive. ❑ *...a magnificent achievement.* ● **magnificence** N-UNCOUNT ❑ *...the magnificence of the sunset.* ● **magnificently** ADV ❑ *The team played magnificently.*

magnify /'mægnɪfaɪ/ (**magnifies, magnifying, magnified**) **1** V-T To **magnify** an object means to make it appear larger than it really is, by means of a special lens or mirror. ❑ *This microscope can magnify objects up to 200 times.* ● **magnification** /ˌmægnɪfɪ'keɪʃən/ N-UNCOUNT ❑ *The bigger the magnification you require, the larger the lens you need.* **2** V-T To **magnify** something means to increase its effect, size, or intensity. ❑ *Problems, fears and worries seem greatly magnified at night.*

magnitude /'mægnɪtjuːd, AM -tuːd/ N-UNCOUNT The **magnitude** of something is its great size or importance. ❑ *They underestimated the magnitude of the task.*

magpie /'mægpaɪ/ (**magpies**) N-COUNT A **magpie** is a black and white bird with a long tail.

mahogany /mə'hɒgəni/ N-UNCOUNT **Mahogany** is a dark reddish-brown wood that is used to make furniture.

maid /meɪd/ (**maids**) N-COUNT A **maid** is a female servant.

maiden /'meɪdən/ (**maidens**) **1** N-COUNT A **maiden** is a young girl or woman. [LITERARY] **2** ADJ BEFORE N **Maiden** is used to describe some activities and events when they are the first of that kind that a particular person or thing has done. ❑ *...the ship's maiden voyage.*

mail /meɪl/ (**mails, mailing, mailed**) **1** N-UNCOUNT **Mail** is the letters and parcels that are delivered to you. ❑ *Nora looked through the mail.* **2** N-SING **The mail** is the system used for collecting and delivering letters and parcels. ❑ *The cheque is in the mail.* ❑ *The company will contact owners by mail.* **3** V-T If you **mail** something, you post it. ❑ *I mailed a letter to you yesterday.* ❑ *They mailed me the cheque.* **4** → see also **e-mail**

mailbox /'meɪlbɒks/ (**mailboxes**) **1** N-COUNT In the United States, a **mailbox** is a box outside your

m

Word Web magnet

Magnets have a north **pole** and a south pole. One side has a **negative charge** and the other side has a **positive** charge. The negative side of a magnet **attracts** the positive side of another magnet. Two sides that have the same charge will **repel** each other. The earth itself is a huge magnet, with a North Pole and a South Pole. A **compass** uses a magnetized needle to show direction. The "north" end of the needle always points toward the earth's North Pole.

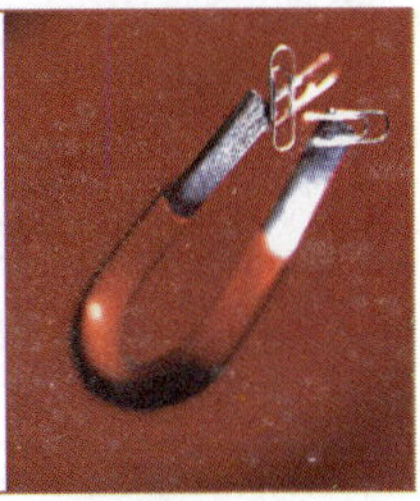

house where letters are delivered. **2** N-COUNT In American English, a **mailbox** is a metal box with a hole in it where you put letters that you want to send. The British term is **post box**.

ˌmail ˈorder N-UNCOUNT If you buy things by **mail order**, you choose them from a catalogue and they are sent to you by post.

maim /meɪm/ (**maims, maiming, maimed**) V-T To **maim** someone means to injure them so badly that part of their body is permanently damaged. ❑ *The children had been maimed by landmines.*

main /meɪn/ (**mains**) **1** ADJ The **main** thing is the most important one. ❑ *...one of the main tourist areas of Amsterdam.* ❑ *My main concern is to protect the children.* **2** PHRASE If something is true **in the main**, it is generally true, although there may be exceptions. ❑ *They are, in the main, fine folk.* **3** N-COUNT The **mains** are the pipes which supply gas or water to buildings, or which take sewage away from them. ❑ *A water mains pipe in the kitchen had burst.* **4** N-PLURAL **The mains** are the wires which supply electricity to buildings, or the place where the wires end inside the building. [BRIT] ❑ *You must switch off the electricity at the mains.*

Thesaurus	*main* Also look up:
ADJ.	chief, major, primary, principal **1**

ˌmain ˈclause (**main clauses**) N-COUNT In grammar, a **main clause** is a clause that can stand alone as a complete sentence.

M

mainframe /ˈmeɪnfreɪm/ (**mainframes**) N-COUNT A **mainframe** or a **mainframe computer** is a large computer which can be used by many people at the same time. [COMPUTING]

mainland /ˈmeɪnlænd/ N-SING **The mainland** is the large main part of a country, in contrast to the islands around it. ❑ *...the coast of mainland Britain.* ❑ *...the ferry to the mainland.*

mainly /ˈmeɪnli/ ADV You use **mainly** to say that a statement is true in most cases or to a large extent. ❑ *The staff were mainly Russian.*

ˌmain ˈroad (**main roads**) N-COUNT A **main road** is an important road that leads from one town or city to another.

mainstay /ˈmeɪnsteɪ/ (**mainstays**) N-COUNT The **mainstay** of something is the most important part of it. ❑ *Fish and rice were the mainstays of the country's diet.*

mainstream /ˈmeɪnstriːm/ N-SING People or ideas that are part of **the mainstream** are regarded as normal and conventional. ❑ *...those outside the mainstream of society.* ❑ *...mainstream opinion.*
→ see **culture**

maintain /meɪnˈteɪn/ (**maintains, maintaining, maintained**) **1** V-T If you **maintain** something, you continue to have it, and do not let it stop or grow weaker. ❑ *I maintained contact with the children.* **2** V-T If you **maintain** something **at** a particular rate or level, you keep it at that rate or level. ❑ *They want to maintain tourism at the current level in the Mediterranean.* **3** V-T To **maintain** someone means to provide them with money and the things that they need. ❑ *...the basic costs of maintaining a child.* **4** V-T If you **maintain** a building, vehicle, road, or machine, you keep it in good condition. **5** V-T If you **maintain that** something is true, you state your opinion very strongly. ❑ *He had always maintained his innocence.*

Thesaurus	*maintain* Also look up:
V.	keep up, look after, protect, repair **4**

maintenance /ˈmeɪntɪnəns/ **1** N-UNCOUNT The **maintenance of** a building, road, vehicle, or machine is the process of keeping it in good condition. ❑ *They can no longer afford the car's high maintenance costs.* **2** N-UNCOUNT **Maintenance** is money that someone gives regularly to another person to pay for the things that they need. ❑ *Should fathers be jailed for refusing to pay child maintenance?* **3** N-UNCOUNT If you ensure the maintenance of a state or process, you make sure that it continues. ❑ *...the maintenance of peace in Asia.*

maize /meɪz/ N-UNCOUNT **Maize** is a tall plant which produces corn.

majestic /məˈdʒestɪk/ ADJ If you describe something or someone as **majestic**, you think they are very beautiful, dignified, and impressive. ❑ *...a majestic country home.* ● **majestically** ADV ❑ *She rose majestically to her feet.*

majesty /ˈmædʒɪsti/ (**majesties**) **1** N-VOC & N-COUNT **Your Majesty, His Majesty, Her Majesty**, or **Their Majesties** are used to address or refer to kings or queens. **2** N-UNCOUNT The **majesty of** a place or thing is its quality of being beautiful, dignified, and impressive. ❑ *...the breathtaking majesty of the view.*

Word Link	***major ≈ larger*** : *major, majority, sergeant major*

major /ˈmeɪdʒə/ (**majors**) **1** ADJ BEFORE N You use **major** to describe something that is more important, serious, or significant than other things. ❑ *Lack of drinking water was a major problem.* **2** N-COUNT & N-TITLE A **major** is an army officer of medium rank.

Thesaurus	*major* Also look up:
ADJ.	chief, critical, crucial, key, main, principal; *(ant.)* little, minor, unimportant **1**

majority /məˈdʒɒrɪti, AM -ˈdʒɔːr-/ (**majorities**) **1** N-SING & PHRASE The **majority of** people or things in a group is more than half of them. When there is more of one group than another, you can say that they are **in a majority** or **in the majority**. ❑ *The majority of people only get two weeks' holiday a year.* ❑ *Supporters of the treaty are still in the majority.* **2** N-COUNT In an election or vote, a **majority** is the difference between the number of votes gained by the winner and the number gained by the person or party that comes second. ❑ *The decision was passed by a majority of eight to two.*

Word Partnership	Use *majority* with:
ADJ.	**overwhelming** majority, **vast** majority **1**
N.	majority **opinion**, majority **of people**, majority **of the population**, majority **rule**, majority **vote** **1**

Word Web make-up

The women of ancient Egypt were among the first to **wear make-up**. They **applied foundation** to lighten their skin and used kohl as eye shadow to darken their eyelids. Greek women used charcoal as an eyeliner and rouge on their cheeks. In 14th century Europe, the most popular **cosmetic** was a **powder** made from wheat flour. Women whitened their faces to show their high social class. A light **complexion** indicated the woman didn't have to work outdoors. **Cosmetics** containing poisons, such as lead and arsenic, sometimes caused illness and death. Make-up use grew in the early 1900s. For the first time many women could afford to buy mass-produced **lipstick**, **mascara**, and **face powder**.

make /meɪk/ (**makes, making, made**)

> **Make** is used with many nouns to talk about performing actions, and creating, constructing, or preparing something.

1 V-T If someone or something **makes** you do something, they cause or force you to do it. ❑ *He made me do all the work.* ❑ *The perfume irritated Maggie's nose and made her sneeze.* **2** V-T You use **make** to talk about causing someone or something to be a particular thing or to have a particular quality. ❑ *...James Bond, the role that made him a star.* ❑ *She made life very difficult for me.* **3** V-T If you **make yourself** understood, heard, or known, you succeed in getting people to understand you, hear you, or know that you are there. ❑ *He shouted to make himself heard above the music.* **4** V-T If you **make** something **into** something else, you change it in some way so that it becomes that other thing. ❑ *The play was made into a film in 1982.* **5** V-T If you **make** money, you get it by working, by selling something, or by winning it. **6** V-T If you **make friends** or **enemies**, someone becomes your friend or enemy, often because of a particular thing you have done. **7** V-T If something **makes** something else, it is responsible for the success of that thing. ❑ *The hotel made the holiday.* **8** V-T You can use **make** to say that someone or something has the right qualities for a particular task or role. ❑ *She'll make a good actress, if she gets the right training.* **9** V-T If someone **makes** a particular team or **makes** a particular high position, they do so well that they are put in that team or get that position. ❑ *The athletes are happy to make the British team.* **10** V-T You can use **make** to say what two numbers add up to. ❑ *Four twos make eight.* **11** N-COUNT The **make of** a product such as a car or radio is the name of the company that made it. ❑ *...a certain make of watch.* **12** PHRASE If you **make do with** something, you use or have it instead of something else that you do not have, although it is not as good. ❑ *Why make do with a copy if you can afford the genuine article?* **13** PHRASE If you **make it** somewhere, you succeed in getting there, especially in time to do something. ❑ *She made it to America, after all.* **14** PHRASE If you **make it**, you are successful in achieving something difficult, or in surviving through a very difficult period. ❑ *You're brave and courageous. You can make it.*

▸ **make for** PHR-VERB If you **make for** a place, you move towards it. ❑ *He stood up and made for the door.*

▸ **make of** PHR-VERB If you ask someone what they **make of** something, you want to know what their impression or opinion of it is. ❑ *Nancy didn't know what to make of Mick's apology.*

▸ **make off** PHR-VERB If you **make off**, you leave somewhere as quickly as possible. ❑ *The robbers made off in a stolen car.*

▸ **make out** **1** PHR-VERB If you can **make** something **out**, you can see, hear, or understand it. ❑ *I made out a tall, pale, shadowy figure.* ❑ *He couldn't make out what she was saying.* **2** PHR-VERB If you **make out that** something is the case, you try to get people to believe it. ❑ *They tried to make out that I had done it.*

▸ **make up** **1** PHR-VERB The people or things that **make up** something are the members or parts that form that thing. ❑ *Women officers make up 13 per cent of the police force.* **2** PHR-VERB If you **make up** a **story** or **excuse**, you invent it. ❑ *She made up excuses to avoid him.* **3** PHR-VERB If two people **make up** after a quarrel or disagreement, or if they **make it up**, they become friends again. ❑ *They had an argument, but they made it up very soon.* **4** PHR-VERB To **make up for** something that is lost or missing means to replace it or compensate for it. ❑ *The work is not great but the money you earn makes up for this.* **5** PHR-VERB If you **make it up to** someone for disappointing them, you do something for them to show how sorry you are. ❑ *I feel really guilty about it. How can I make it up to my friend?*

> **Thesaurus** *make* Also look up:
> V. build, compose, create, fabricate, produce; *(ant.)* destroy **4**

maker /ˈmeɪkə/ (**makers**) N-COUNT The **maker of** something is the person or company that makes it. ❑ *...Japan's two largest car makers.*

makeshift /ˈmeɪkʃɪft/ ADJ **Makeshift** things are temporary and of poor quality, and are used because there is nothing better available. ❑ *20,000 people were living there in makeshift shelters.*

ˈmake-ˌup **1** N-UNCOUNT **Make-up** consists of things such as lipstick or eye shadow which you can put on your face to make yourself look more attractive. **2** N-UNCOUNT The **make-up of** something is the different parts that it consists of, and the way these parts are arranged. ❑ *They reached agreement on the make-up of the country's future government.*
→ see Word Web: **make-up**
→ see **theatre**

making /ˈmeɪkɪŋ/ (**makings**) **1** N-UNCOUNT The **making** of something is the act of producing, constructing, or creating it. ❑ *...the making of this movie.* **2** PHRASE If you describe a person or thing as something **in the making**, you mean that they are going to become known or recognized as that

m

thing. ❑ *Her drama teacher is confident Julie is a star in the making.* 3 PHRASE If something **is the making of** a person or thing, it is the reason that they become successful or become very much better than they used to be. 4 PHRASE If someone or something has **the makings of** something, it seems possible or likely that they will become that thing, as they have the necessary qualities. ❑ *Godfrey has the makings of a successful journalist.* 5 PHRASE If something, such as a problem you have, is **of** your **own making**, you have caused or created it yourself. ❑ *The university's financial troubles are of its own making.*

Word Link *mal ≈ bad : malaria, malfunction, malicious*

malaria /mə'leəriə/ N-UNCOUNT **Malaria** is a serious disease caught from mosquitoes.

male /meɪl/ (**males**) 1 N-COUNT & ADJ A **male** person or animal belongs to the sex that cannot have babies or lay eggs. ❑ *Researchers studied 2,000 male students over three years.* 2 ADJ A **male** flower or plant fertilizes the part that will become the fruit.
→ see **reproduction**

malfunction /ˌmæl'fʌŋkʃən/ (**malfunctions, malfunctioning, malfunctioned**) V-I & N-COUNT If a machine or computer **malfunctions**, it fails to work properly. If this happens, you say there is a **malfunction**. ❑ *...malfunctioning equipment.* ❑ *...a technical malfunction.*

malice /'mælɪs/ N-UNCOUNT **Malice** is a deliberate desire to harm people. ❑ *There was no malice on his part.*

M

malicious /mə'lɪʃəs/ ADJ **Malicious** talk or behaviour is intended to harm people or their reputation, or to embarrass or upset them. ❑ *...malicious gossip.* • **maliciously** ADV ❑ *Sue grinned maliciously.*

malignant /mə'lɪgnənt/ ADJ A **malignant tumour** or **disease** is serious, spreads rapidly to other parts of the body, and may cause death. ❑ *...a malignant brain tumour.*

maligned /mə'laɪnd/ ADJ If you describe someone or something as **maligned**, you mean that people often criticize them and say unpleasant things about them, and that this is unfair. ❑ *The secretarial route is much maligned but can provide a way into many careers.*

mall /mɔːl, mæl/ (**malls**) N-COUNT A **mall** is a large enclosed shopping area.

mallet /'mælɪt/ (**mallets**) N-COUNT A **mallet** is a wooden hammer with a square head.

malnutrition /ˌmælnjuː'trɪʃən, AM -nuːt-/ N-UNCOUNT If someone is suffering from **malnutrition**, they are physically weak and extremely thin because they have not eaten enough food or had a balanced diet.

malpractice /ˌmæl'præktɪs/ (**malpractices**) N-VAR If you accuse someone of **malpractice**, you are accusing them of breaking the law or the rules of their profession in order to gain some advantage for themselves. [FORMAL]

malt /mɔːlt/ N-UNCOUNT **Malt** is a substance made from grain that is used to make some alcoholic drinks.

mammal /'mæməl/ (**mammals**) N-COUNT **Mammals** are animals such as dogs and humans that give birth to babies rather than laying eggs, and feed their young with milk.
→ see Word Web: **mammal**
→ see **bat, whale**

mammoth /'mæməθ/ (**mammoths**) 1 ADJ You can use **mammoth** to emphasize that a task is very great and needs a lot of effort to achieve. ❑ *Making the film 'The Incredibles' was a mammoth task.* 2 N-COUNT A **mammoth** was a prehistoric animal like a large elephant with long curling tusks.

man /mæn/ (**men, mans, manning, manned**) 1 N-COUNT A **man** is an adult male human. 2 N-VAR **Man** and **men** are sometimes used to refer to all humans, including women and girls (though some people find this use offensive). ❑ *I believe in the philosophy: 'Give a man a fish and he eats for a day; teach a man how to fish and he eats forever.'* 3 N-PLURAL In the armed forces, the **men** are the ordinary soldiers, sailors, or airmen, but not the officers. 4 V-T If you **man** something such as a place, vehicle or machine, you operate it or are in charge of it. ❑ *The station is seldom manned in the evening.* 5 **the man in the street** → see **street**

manage /'mænɪdʒ/ (**manages, managing, managed**) 1 V-T If you **manage to** do something, especially something difficult, you succeed in doing it. ❑ *The company managed to stay in business.* ❑ *I couldn't manage to get to sleep.* 2 V-T If someone **manages** an organization, business, or system, they are responsible for controlling it. ❑ *Within two years he was managing the store.* ❑ *They doubted the government's ability to manage the economy.* 3 V-T If you **manage** time, money, or other resources, you deal with them carefully and do not waste them. ❑ *In a busy world, managing your time is increasingly important.* 4 V-I If you **manage**, you succeed in

Word Web **mammal**

Elephants, dogs, mice, and humans all belong to the class of animals called **mammals**. Mammals give birth to live babies rather than laying eggs. The females also suckle their **young** with milk from their bodies. Mammals are warm-blooded and usually have hair on their bodies. Some mammals, such as the brown bear and the raccoon, are omnivorous—they eat meat and plants. Deer and zebras are herbivorous, living mostly on grass and leaves. Lions and tigers are carnivorous—they eat meat. They must have a supply of large **game** to survive. Mammals have a variety of different types of **limbs**. Monkeys have long arms for climbing. Seals have flippers for swimming.

coping with a difficult situation. ❑ *How did your mother manage when your father left?*

manageable /ˈmænɪdʒəbəl/ ADJ Something that is **manageable** is of a size, quantity, or level of difficulty that people are able to deal with. ❑ *Cut down the task to a manageable size.*

Word Link *ment ≈ state, condition : agreement, management, movement*

management /ˈmænɪdʒmənt/ (**managements**) **1** N-UNCOUNT **Management** is the control and organizing of something. ❑ *The zoo needs better management.* ❑ *...time management.* **2** N-VAR You can refer to the people who control and organize a business or other organization as **the management**. **Management** can take the singular or plural form of the verb. ❑ *The management is doing its best.*

Word Partnership Use *management* with:

ADJ. **new** management, **senior** management **2**
N. **anger** management, **business** management, **crisis** management, **money** management, management **skills**, **stress** management **1** management **style**, **waste** management **1** management **team**, management **training** **2**

ˌmanagement conˈsultant (**management consultants**) N-COUNT A **management consultant** is someone whose job is to advise companies on the most efficient ways to run their business.

manager /ˈmænɪdʒə/ (**managers**) N-COUNT A **manager** is the person responsible for running part of or the whole of a business organization. → see **concert**

manageress /ˌmænɪdʒəˈres/ (**manageresses**) N-COUNT The **manageress** of a shop, restaurant, or other small business is the woman who is responsible for running it.

managerial /ˌmænɪˈdʒɪəriəl/ ADJ **Managerial** means relating to the work of a manager. ❑ *...managerial skills.*

ˌmanaging diˈrector (**managing directors**) N-COUNT The **managing director** of a company is the senior working director, and is in charge of the way the company is managed.

mandate /ˈmændeɪt/ (**mandates, mandating, mandated**) **1** N-COUNT A government's **mandate** is the authority it has to carry out particular policies or tasks as a result of winning an election or vote. ❑ *...a mandate for continued economic reform.* **2** V-T & N-COUNT When someone **is mandated to** do something, or when they are given a **mandate to** do it, they are given the authority to do it, or are instructed to do it. ❑ *He had been mandated to resolve the situation.*

mandatory /ˈmændətri, AM -tɔːri/ ADJ If an action or procedure is **mandatory**, people have to do it, because it is a rule or it is fixed by law. [FORMAL] ❑ *...the mandatory life sentence for murder.*

mane /meɪn/ (**manes**) N-COUNT The **mane** on a horse or lion is the long thick hair that grows from its neck.

maneuver /məˈnuːvə/ → see **manoeuvre**

mangle /ˈmæŋgəl/ (**mangles, mangling, mangled**) V-T If something **is mangled**, it is very forcefully crushed and twisted out of shape. ❑ *...the mangled wreckage.*

mango /ˈmæŋgəʊ/ (**mangoes** or **mangos**) N-COUNT A **mango** is a large, sweet yellowish fruit which grows in hot countries.

Word Link *hood ≈ state, condition : adulthood, childhood, manhood*

manhood /ˈmænhʊd/ N-UNCOUNT **Manhood** is the state of being a man rather than a boy, or the period of a man's adult life. ❑ *They failed to help their sons grow from boyhood to manhood.*

mania /ˈmeɪniə/ (**manias**) N-COUNT If you say that a person or group has a **mania for** something, you mean that they enjoy it very much or devote a lot of time to it. ❑ *He described himself as having a mania for privacy.* ❑ *There has been no escaping football mania during the World Cup.*

maniac /ˈmeɪniæk/ (**maniacs**) N-COUNT A **maniac** is a mad person who is violent and dangerous.

manic /ˈmænɪk/ ADJ If you describe someone as **manic**, you mean that they do things extremely quickly or energetically, often because they are very excited or anxious. ● **manically** ADV ❑ *We cleaned the house manically.*

Word Link *man ≈ hand : emancipate, manicure, manual*

Word Link *cur ≈ caring : curator, manicure, secure*

manicure /ˈmænɪkjʊə/ (**manicures, manicuring, manicured**) V-T & N-COUNT If you **manicure** your hands or nails, or if you have a **manicure**, you care for them by softening your skin and cutting and painting your nails.

manifest /ˈmænɪfest/ (**manifests, manifesting, manifested**) **1** ADJ If you say that something is **manifest**, you mean it is clearly true and that nobody would disagree with it if they saw it or considered it. [FORMAL] ❑ *...the manifest failure of the policies.* ● **manifestly** ADV ❑ *He has manifestly failed in his job.* **2** V-T & ADJ If you **manifest** a particular quality, feeling, or illness, or if it becomes **manifest**, it becomes visible or obvious. [FORMAL] ❑ *The virus needs two weeks to manifest itself.* ❑ *The same alarm is manifest everywhere.*

manifestation /ˌmænɪfeˈsteɪʃən/ (**manifestations**) N-COUNT A **manifestation** of something is one of the different ways in which it can appear. [FORMAL] ❑ *...different manifestations of the disease.*

manifesto /ˌmænɪˈfestəʊ/ (**manifestos** or **manifestoes**) N-COUNT A **manifesto** is a statement published by a person or group of people, especially a political party, in which they say what their aims and policies are. ❑ *...their election manifesto.*

manipulate /məˈnɪpjʊleɪt/ (**manipulates, manipulating, manipulated**) **1** V-T If you say that someone **manipulates** people or events,

m

you disapprove of them because they control or influence them to produce a particular result. ❑ *She manipulated Terry into giving her a job.* ● **manipulation** (**manipulations**) N-VAR ❑ *A serious problem with Internet voting is that it is open to manipulation.* **2** V-T If you **manipulate** something that requires skill, such as a complicated piece of equipment or a difficult idea, you operate it or process it. ❑ *The technology uses a pen to manipulate a computer.* ● **manipulation** N-VAR ❑ *...the manipulation of laboratory tools.*

manipulative /mə'nɪpjʊlətɪv/ ADJ If you describe someone as **manipulative**, you disapprove of them because they manipulate people. ❑ *...aggressive and manipulative behaviour.*

mankind /ˌmæn'kaɪnd/ N-UNCOUNT You can refer to all human beings as **mankind** when you are considering them as a group. ❑ *...the evolution of mankind.*

manly /'mænli/ ADJ If you describe a man's behaviour as **manly**, you approve of it because it shows qualities that are considered ideal in a man. ● **manliness** N-UNCOUNT ❑ *He praised competitive sports as tests of manliness.*

ˌman-'made ADJ **Man-made** things are created or caused by people, rather than occurring naturally. ❑ *...man-made lakes.*

manned /mænd/ → see **man**

manner /'mænə/ (**manners**) **1** N-SING The **manner** in which you do something is the way that you do it. ❑ *She smiled in a friendly manner.* **2** N-SING Someone's **manner** is the way in which they behave and talk when they are with other people. ❑ *His manner was cold and reserved.* ● **-mannered** ❑ *He was a quiet, mild-mannered man.* **3** N-PLURAL If someone has **good manners**, they are polite and observe social customs. If someone has **bad manners**, they are not polite and do not observe these customs. **4** PHRASE If you refer to **all manner of** objects or people, you are talking about objects or people of many different kinds. ❑ *...all manner of wildlife.*

M

Word Partnership Use *manner* with:

ADJ. **effective** manner, **efficient** manner **1**
abrasive manner, **abrupt** manner, **appropriate** manner, **businesslike** manner, **different** manner, **friendly** manner, **usual** manner **1** **2**

manoeuvre [AM **maneuver**] /mə'nuːvə/ (**manoeuvres, manoeuvring, manoeuvred**) **1** V-T & N-VAR If you **manoeuvre** something into or out of an awkward position, you skilfully move it there. A **manoeuvre** is a movement like this. ❑ *I manoeuvred my way among the tables.* ❑ *...a ship capable of high speed and rapid manoeuvre.* **2** N-COUNT A **manoeuvre** is something clever which you do to change a situation to your advantage. ❑ *...manoeuvres to avoid war.* **3** N-PLURAL Military **manoeuvres** are training exercises which involve the movement of soldiers and equipment over a large area.

manor /'mænə/ (**manors**) N-COUNT A **manor** is a large country house with land.

manpower /'mænpaʊə/ N-UNCOUNT Workers are sometimes referred to as **manpower** when they are being considered as a part of the process of producing goods or providing services.

mansion /'mænʃən/ (**mansions**) N-COUNT A **mansion** is a very large house.

manslaughter /'mænslɔːtə/ N-UNCOUNT **Manslaughter** is the unlawful killing of a person by someone who did not intend to kill them. [TECHNICAL] ❑ *She was guilty of manslaughter, not murder.*

mantelpiece also **mantlepiece** /'mæntəlpiːs/ (**mantelpieces**) N-COUNT A **mantelpiece** is a shelf over a fireplace.

mantra /'mæntrə/ (**mantras**) N-COUNT A **mantra** is a chant used by Buddhists and Hindus when they meditate.

Word Link *man ≈ hand : emancipate, manicure, manual*

manual /'mænjʊəl/ (**manuals**) **1** ADJ **Manual** work is unskilled work using your hands or your physical strength. ❑ *...manual workers.* **2** ADJ BEFORE N **Manual** equipment is operated by hand, rather than by electricity or by a motor. ● **manually** ADV ❑ *The device is manually operated.* **3** N-COUNT A **manual** is a book which tells you how to do something or how a piece of machinery works. ❑ *...the instruction manual.*

manufacture /ˌmænjʊ'fæktʃə/ (**manufactures, manufacturing, manufactured**) **1** V-T & N-UNCOUNT To **manufacture** things means to make them in a factory. The **manufacture** of things is the process of making them in a factory. ❑ *The company manufactures cosmetics products.* ● **manufacturing** N-UNCOUNT ❑ *The manufacturing of computers is a specialised business.* **2** V-T If you say that someone **manufactures** information, you are criticizing them because the information is not true. ❑ *They manufactured an elaborate story.* → see **mass production**

manufacturer /ˌmænjʊ'fæktʃərə/ (**manufacturers**) N-COUNT A **manufacturer** is a business that makes goods in large quantities. → see **industry**

manure /mə'njʊə, AM -'nʊr/ N-UNCOUNT **Manure** is animal faeces that is spread on the ground in order to improve the growth of plants.

Word Link *script ≈ writing : manuscript, scripture, transcript*

manuscript /'mænjʊskrɪpt/ (**manuscripts**) **1** N-COUNT A **manuscript** is a handwritten or typed document, especially a writer's first version of a book before it is published. **2** N-COUNT A **manuscript** is an old document that was written by hand before printing was invented. ❑ *...early printed books and rare manuscripts.*

many /'meni/ **1** QUANT **Many** is used to indicate a large number of people or things. ❑ *I don't think many people would argue with that.* ❑ *In many of these neighbourhoods a lot of people don't have telephones.* **2** QUANT **Many** is used to talk and ask questions about numbers or quantities. ❑ *No-one knows how many people died.* ❑ *How many miles do you run a week?* **3** PHRASE You use **as many as** before a number to suggest that it is surprisingly large. ❑ *As many as four and a half million people watched today's parade.* **4** PHRASE You use **a good many** or **a**

great many to emphasize that you are referring to a large number of things or people. ❑ *We had a great many presents.* **5** **in so many words** → see **word**

Usage

You only use **many** to talk about things that can be counted. You use **much** if you want to talk about a large amount of something. ❑ *...too much money.* ❑ *There are many books on the subject.*

map /mæp/ (**maps, mapping, mapped**) N-COUNT A **map** is a drawing of a particular area, showing its main features as they appear if you looked at them from above. ❑ *Have you got a map of the city centre?*

▶ **map out** PHR-VERB If you **map out** a plan or task, you work out how you will do it. ❑ *We mapped out our future.*

Word Partnership Use *map* with:

ADJ.	**detailed** map
V.	**draw a** map, **look at a** map, **open a** map, **read a** map

maple /ˈmeɪpəl/ (**maples**) N-VAR A **maple** is a tree with large leaves with five points. **Maple** is the wood of this tree.

mar /mɑː/ (**mars, marring, marred**) V-T To **mar** something means to spoil or damage it. [WRITTEN] ❑ *The election was marred by cheating.*

marathon /ˈmærəθən, AM -θɒn/ (**marathons**) **1** N-COUNT A **marathon** is a race in which people run a distance of 26 miles (about 42 km). **2** ADJ BEFORE N A **marathon** task takes a long time to do and is very tiring. ❑ *...a marathon session of talks.*

marble /ˈmɑːbəl/ (**marbles**) **1** N-UNCOUNT **Marble** is a very hard rock used, for example, to make statues and fireplaces. ❑ *...classical marble statues of Caesar.* **2** N-VAR **Marbles** are small coloured glass balls used by children to play a game called **marbles**.

march /mɑːtʃ/ (**marches, marching, marched**) **1** V-T/V-I & N-COUNT When soldiers **march** somewhere, or when a commanding officer **marches** them somewhere, they walk there with very regular steps, as a group. You can also say they go on a **march**. ❑ *We marched fifteen miles to the river.* **2** V-I & N-COUNT When a large group of people **march**, or when they hold a **march**, they walk somewhere together in order to protest about something. ❑ *The demonstrators marched through the capital.* ❑ *...a march for peace.* ● **marcher** (**marchers**) N-COUNT ❑ *Police stopped the marchers.* **3** V-I If you **march** somewhere, you walk there quickly, for example because you are angry. ❑ *He marched into the kitchen without knocking.* **4** V-T If you **march** someone somewhere, you force them to walk there with you by holding their arm. ❑ *I marched him across the room and out of the house.* **5** N-SING **The march of** something is its steady progress. ❑ *...the incredible march of technology.*

March /mɑːtʃ/ (**Marches**) N-VAR **March** is the third month of the year. ❑ *She died in March 2001.*

mare /meə/ (**mares**) N-COUNT A **mare** is an adult female horse.

margarine /ˌmɑːdʒəˈriːn, AM ˈmɑːrdʒərɪn/ N-UNCOUNT **Margarine** is a substance similar to butter, made from vegetable oil and sometimes animal fats.

margin /ˈmɑːdʒɪn/ (**margins**) **1** N-COUNT A **margin** is the difference between two amounts, especially the difference in the number of votes or points between the winner and the loser in a contest. ❑ *They ended up with a 50-point winning margin.* **2** N-COUNT If there is a **margin for** something in a situation, there is some freedom to choose what to do or decide how to do it. ❑ *He knew he had to be very fast; there was no margin for error.* **3** N-COUNT The **margins** on a page are the blank spaces at each side.

Word Partnership Use *margin* with:

ADJ.	**comfortable** margin, **large** margin, **narrow** margin, **slim** margin, **wide** margin **2**
N.	margin **for error** **2**

marginal /ˈmɑːdʒɪnəl/ ADJ Something that is **marginal** is small and not very important. ❑ *...a marginal increase in cost.* ● **marginally** ADV ❑ *Sales last year were marginally higher than in 2005.*

marijuana /ˌmærɪˈwɑːnə/ N-UNCOUNT **Marijuana** is an illegal drug which is usually smoked.

marina /məˈriːnə/ (**marinas**) N-COUNT A **marina** is a small harbour for pleasure boats.

marinade /ˌmærɪˈneɪd/ (**marinades, marinading, marinaded**) **1** N-COUNT A **marinade** is a sauce of oil, vinegar, and spices, which you soak meat or fish in before cooking it, in order to flavour it. **2** V-T/V-I To **marinade** means the same as to **marinate**.

marinate /ˈmærɪneɪt/ (**marinates, marinating, marinated**) V-T/V-I If you **marinate** meat or fish or if it **marinates**, you soak it in oil, vinegar, and spices before cooking it, in order to flavour it.

Word Link *mar ≈ sea : marine, maritime, submarine*

marine /məˈriːn/ (**marines**) **1** N-COUNT A **marine** is a soldier who is trained for duties at sea and on land. **2** ADJ BEFORE N **Marine** is used to describe things relating to the sea. ❑ *...marine life.* ❑ *...a solicitor specialising in marine law.* → see **ship**

marital /ˈmærɪtəl/ ADJ BEFORE N **Marital** means relating to marriage. ❑ *...their marital problems.*

maritime /ˈmærɪtaɪm/ ADJ BEFORE N **Maritime** means relating to the sea and to ships. ❑ *...the National Maritime Museum.*

mark /mɑːk/ (**marks, marking, marked**) **1** V-T & N-COUNT If something **marks** a surface, or if it makes a **mark** on it, a small area of the surface is stained or damaged. ❑ *Wood marks easily.* ❑ *The dogs are always rubbing against the wall and making dirty marks.* **2** V-T & N-COUNT If you **mark** something with a particular word or symbol, you write that word or symbol on it. This word or symbol is called a **mark**. ❑ *The bank marked the cheque 'certified'.* ❑ *He made marks with a pencil.* **3** V-T & N-COUNT When a teacher **marks** a student's work, he or she decides how good it is and writes comments or a score on it. This score is called a **mark**. ❑ *He marked essays in his study.* ❑ *He did well to get such a good mark.*

m

4 N-COUNT When something reaches a particular **mark**, it reaches that particular number, point, or stage. ❑ *We have had temperatures reaching the 30° mark in the last week.* 5 N-COUNT The **mark of** a particular thing, feeling, or quality is something which enables you to recognize it or which shows that it exists. ❑ *The mark of a civilized society is that it looks after its oldest members.* 6 V-T If something **marks** a place or position, it shows where a particular thing is or was. ❑ *This river marks the border with Thailand.* ● **marker** (**markers**) N-COUNT ❑ *...stone markers.* 7 V-T An event that **marks** a particular stage or point is a sign that something different is about to happen. ❑ *The announcement marks the end of an extraordinary period in European history.* 8 → see also **marked, marking** 9 PHRASE If something or someone **leaves** their **mark** or **leaves a mark**, they have a lasting effect. ❑ *His experiences in Spain left their mark on him.* 10 PHRASE If you **make** your **mark** or **make a mark**, you become noticed or famous by doing something impressive or unusual. ❑ *She made her mark in the film industry in the 1960s.* 11 PHRASE If something is **off the mark** or **wide of the mark**, it is inaccurate or incorrect. If it is **on the mark**, it is accurate or correct. ❑ *He wasn't far off the mark in his comments.*

▶ **mark down** 1 PHR-VERB If you **mark** something **down**, you write it down. ❑ *I marked the date down in my diary.* 2 PHR-VERB To **mark** an item **down** or **mark** its price **down** means to reduce its price. ❑ *Clothes are the best bargain, with many items marked down.*

▶ **mark off** PHR-VERB If you **mark off** an item on a list, you put a mark on it, for example to indicate that it has been dealt with. ❑ *She called out names and marked them off her list.*

M

marked /mɑːkt/ ADJ Something that is **marked** is very obvious and easily noticed. ❑ *The charity sees a marked increase in offers of help at Christmas.* ● **markedly** /ˈmɑːkɪdli/ ADV ❑ *Technology has markedly improved our lives.*

market /ˈmɑːkɪt/ (**markets, marketing, marketed**) 1 N-COUNT A **market** is a place where goods are bought and sold, usually in the open air. ❑ *He sold boots on a market stall.* 2 N-COUNT The **market** for a commodity or product is the total number of people who want to buy it. ❑ *China is the world's biggest market for mobile phones.* 3 V-T To **market** a product means to organize its sale, by deciding on its price, where it should be sold, and how it should be advertised. ❑ *The film has been marketed as a comedy.* ● **marketing** N-UNCOUNT ❑ *...Renault's marketing department.* 4 PHRASE If something is **on the market** or comes **onto the market**, it is available for people to buy.

Thesaurus *market* Also look up:

N. farmers' market, grocery store, supermarket 1

marketplace also **market place** /ˈmɑːkɪtpleɪs/ (**marketplaces**) 1 N-COUNT In business, **the marketplace** refers to the activity of buying and selling products. ❑ *Is there enough demand in the marketplace for a product at this price?* 2 N-COUNT A **marketplace** is a small area in a town where goods are bought and sold, often in the open air.

marking /ˈmɑːkɪŋ/ (**markings**) N-COUNT **Markings** are lines or patterns on an animal or object which help to identify it. ❑ *...the black markings on their tails.*

marmalade /ˈmɑːməleɪd/ (**marmalades**) N-VAR **Marmalade** is a food like jam made from oranges or lemons.

maroon /məˈruːn/ (**maroons, marooning, marooned**) 1 ADJ & N-UNCOUNT Something that is **maroon** is a dark reddish-purple. ❑ *...maroon velvet curtains.* 2 V-T If someone **is marooned** somewhere, they are left in a place that is difficult for them to escape from. ❑ *He was marooned on a desert island for five years.*

marquis also **marquess** /ˈmɑːkwɪs/ (**marquises**) N-COUNT A **marquis** is a male member of the nobility.

Word Link *age ≈ state of, related to : camouflage, courage, marriage*

marriage /ˈmærɪdʒ/ (**marriages**) 1 N-VAR A **marriage** is the relationship between a husband and wife, or the state of being married. ❑ *...a good marriage.* ❑ *...six years of marriage.* 2 N-VAR A **marriage** is the act of marrying someone, or the ceremony at which this is done. ❑ *I opposed her marriage to Darryl.*
→ see **love, wedding**

married /ˈmærid/ 1 ADJ If you are **married**, you have a husband or wife. ❑ *She is married to an Englishman.* ❑ *...a married man.* 2 ADJ BEFORE N **Married** means relating to marriage. ❑ *...the first ten years of our married life.*

marry /ˈmæri/ (**marries, marrying, married**) 1 V-T/V-I When two people **get married** or **marry**, they become each other's husband and wife during a special ceremony. ❑ *Laura just got married to Jake.* ❑ *They married a month after they met.* ❑ *He wants to marry her.* 2 V-T When a clergyman or registrar **marries** two people, he or she is in charge of their marriage ceremony.

marsh /mɑːʃ/ (**marshes**) N-VAR A **marsh** is a wet muddy area of land.

marshal /ˈmɑːʃəl/ (**marshals, marshalling, marshalled** or [AM] **marshaling, marshaled**) 1 V-T If you **marshal** people or things, you gather them together and organize them. ❑ *Richard was marshalling the doctors and nurses.* 2 N-COUNT A **marshal** is an official who helps to organize a public event. ❑ *The race is controlled by well-trained marshals.* 3 N-COUNT In the United States and some other countries, a **marshal** is a police officer, often one who is responsible for a particular area.

martial /ˈmɑːʃəl/ 1 ADJ **Martial** is used to describe things that relate to soldiers or war. [FORMAL] ❑ *The election on Sunday was held under martial law with 17,000 troops on the streets.* 2 → see also **court-martial**

ˌmartial ˈart (**martial arts**) N-COUNT A **martial art** is one of the techniques of self-defence that come from the Far East, for example karate and judo.

martyr /ˈmɑːtə/ (**martyrs, martyred**) 1 N-COUNT A **martyr** is someone who is killed or made to suffer greatly because of their religious or political beliefs. ❑ *He said that he was willing to die as a martyr.* 2 V-T If someone **is martyred**, they are killed or made to suffer greatly because of their religious or political beliefs.

marvel /ˈmɑːvəl/ (**marvels, marvelling, marvelled** or [AM] **marveling, marveled**) 1 V-T/V-I If you **marvel at** something, you express your great surprise or admiration. ❑ *They marvelled at her great energy.* 2 N-COUNT A **marvel** is something that makes you feel great surprise or admiration. ❑ *...the marvels of nature.*

marvellous [AM **marvelous**] /ˈmɑːvələs/ ADJ If you describe someone or something as **marvellous**, you are emphasizing that they are very good. ❑ *...a marvellous actor.* ❑ *He looked marvellous.* ● **marvellously** ADV ❑ *He paints marvellously.*

Marxism /ˈmɑːksɪzəm/ N-UNCOUNT **Marxism** is a political philosophy based on the writings of Karl Marx which stresses the importance of the struggle between different social classes.

Marxist /ˈmɑːksɪst/ (**Marxists**) ADJ & N-COUNT **Marxist** means based on Marxism or relating to Marxism. A **Marxist** is a person who believes in Marxism or who is a member of a Marxist party. ❑ *...Marxist politics.*

mascara /mæˈskɑːrə, AM -ˈskær-/ N-UNCOUNT **Mascara** is a substance used to colour eyelashes.

mascot /ˈmæskɒt/ (**mascots**) N-COUNT A **mascot** is an animal, toy, or symbol which is associated with a particular organization or event, and which is thought to bring good luck. ❑ *...the official mascot of the Olympic Games.*

masculine /ˈmæskjʊlɪn/ ADJ **Masculine** characteristics or things relate to or are considered typical of men, rather than women. ❑ *...masculine characteristics like a deep voice and facial hair.* ● **masculinity** /ˌmæskjʊˈlɪnɪti/ N-UNCOUNT ❑ *Why do men seem to need to prove their masculinity?*

mash /mæʃ/ (**mashes, mashing, mashed**) V-T If you **mash** food that is solid but soft, you crush it so that it forms a soft mass. ❑ *Mash the bananas with a fork.*

mask /mɑːsk, mæsk/ (**masks, masking, masked**) 1 N-COUNT A **mask** is something which you wear over your face for protection or to disguise yourself. ❑ *...actors wearing masks.* 2 V-T & N-COUNT If you **mask** your feelings, you deliberately do not show them. This type of behaviour can be referred to as a **mask**. ❑ *They hid their real feelings under the mask of a smile.* 3 V-T If one thing **masks** another, the first thing prevents people from noticing or recognizing the second thing. ❑ *A thick grey cloud masked the sun.*

mask

masked /mɑːskt/ ADJ Someone who is **masked** is wearing a mask.

masochism /ˈmæsəkɪzəm/ N-UNCOUNT **Masochism** is behaviour in which someone gets pleasure (especially sexual pleasure) from their own pain or suffering. ● **masochist** (**masochists**) N-COUNT ❑ *No one liked losing a fight, he said, unless he was a masochist.* ● **masochistic** /ˌmæsəˈkɪstɪk/ ADJ ❑ *...masochistic tendencies.*

mason /ˈmeɪsən/ (**masons**) N-COUNT A **mason** is a person who makes things out of stone.

masonry /ˈmeɪsənri/ N-UNCOUNT **Masonry** consists of the parts of a building which are built from brick or stone.

masquerade /ˌmæskəˈreɪd/ (**masquerades, masquerading, masqueraded**) V-I To **masquerade as** someone or something means to pretend to be that person or thing. ❑ *He masqueraded as a doctor and fooled everyone.*

mass /mæs/ (**masses, massing, massed**) 1 N-SING A **mass of** something is a large amount of it. ❑ *She had a mass of red hair.* 2 QUANT **Masses of** something means a large amount of it. [INFORMAL] ❑ *There's masses of work for her to do.* 3 ADJ BEFORE N **Mass** is used to describe something which involves or affects a very large number of people. ❑ *The singer doesn't have mass appeal.* 4 N-PLURAL **The masses** are the ordinary people in society. ❑ *His music is commercial. It is aimed at the masses.* 5 V-T/V-I When people or things **mass** somewhere, or **are massed**, large numbers of them gather there. ❑ *The General was massing his troops for the attack.* ● **massed** ADJ BEFORE N ❑ *...massed ranks of football fans.* 6 N-VAR The **mass** of an object is the amount of physical matter that it has. [TECHNICAL] 7 N-VAR **Mass** is a Christian church ceremony during which people eat bread and drink wine in order to remember the last meal of Jesus Christ.
→ see **transportation**

massacre /ˈmæsəkə/ (**massacres, massacring, massacred**) 1 N-VAR A **massacre** is the killing of many people in a violent and cruel way. 2 V-T If people **are massacred**, a large number of them are killed in a violent and cruel way. ❑ *300 men were massacred by the army.* 3 → See note at **kill**

massage /ˈmæsɑːʒ, AM məˈsɑːʒ/ (**massages, massaging, massaged**) V-T & N-VAR If you **massage** someone, or if you give them a **massage**, you rub their body to make them relax or to stop their muscles from hurting. ❑ *She massaged her sister's hands and feet.* ❑ *The main benefits of massage are relaxation and stress relief.*

masse → see **en masse**

massive /ˈmæsɪv/ ADJ Something that is **massive** is very large in size. ❑ *A massive fire destroyed their home.* ● **massively** ADV ❑ *The film is based on the massively successful JK Rowling book.*

ˌmass ˈmedia N-SING **The mass media** are television, radio, newspapers, and the Internet.

ˌmass-proˈduce (**mass-produces, mass-producing, mass-produced**) V-T To **mass-produce** something means to manufacture it in large quantities, using machinery. ❑ *...machinery to mass-produce clothing.* ● **mass-produced** ADJ BEFORE N ❑ *...the first mass-produced bike.*
→ see Word Web: **mass production**

mast /mɑːst, mæst/ (**masts**) 1 N-COUNT The **masts** of a boat are the tall upright poles that support its sails. 2 N-COUNT A **radio, television** or **mobile phone mast** is a very tall pole that is used as an aerial.

master /ˈmɑːstə, ˈmæs-/ (**masters, mastering, mastered**) 1 N-COUNT A servant's **master** is the man that he or she works for. [DATED] 2 V-T If you **master** something, you manage to learn how to do it properly or understand it completely. ❑ *Students are expected to master a second language.* 3 ADJ BEFORE N You use **master** to describe someone's job when they are very skilled at it.

Word Web mass production

Before 1913, the automobile was an expensive, custom-made product. But that year Henry Ford* created the first moving **assembly line** in his car **factory**. This changed the **manufacturing** process forever. It also introduced the world to **mass production**. For the first time, workers stayed in one place in the factory. Their work came to them on a conveyor belt. And Ford's cars used only **standardized** parts. These things helped **streamline** the process, and produce more cars. Today's assembly lines look quite different. The **components** still move along on a conveyor belt. However, machines and **robots** do most of the work.

Henry Ford (1863-1947): an American automobile manufacturer.

❑ *...a master chef.* 4 N-UNCOUNT If you are **master of** a situation, you have control over it. ❑ *He was certain that he was master of his own fate.* 5 N-COUNT A **master** is a male schoolteacher. [BRIT] 6 → see also **headmaster**

Thesaurus *master* Also look up:

N. owner; *(ant.)* servant, slave 1
V. learn, study, understand 2

mastermind /ˈmɑːstəmaɪnd, ˈmæs-/ (**masterminds, masterminding, masterminded**) 1 V-T If you **mastermind** a complicated activity, you plan and organize it. ❑ *He masterminded the sale of the company.* 2 N-COUNT The **mastermind behind** a complicated plan, often a criminal one, is the person who plans and organizes it.

M

masterpiece /ˈmɑːstəpiːs, ˈmæs-/ (**masterpieces**) N-COUNT A **masterpiece** is an extremely good painting, novel, film, or other work of art.

mastery /ˈmɑːstəri, ˈmæs-/ 1 N-UNCOUNT If you show **mastery of** a particular skill or language, you show you have learnt or understood it completely and have no difficulty using it. ❑ *He doesn't have mastery of the basic rules of grammar.* 2 N-UNCOUNT **Mastery** is power or control over something. ❑ *...his mastery over his emotions.*

mat /mæt/ (**mats**) 1 N-COUNT A **mat** is a small piece of material which you put on a table to protect it from a hot plate or cup. 2 N-COUNT A **mat** is a small piece of carpet or other thick material that you put on the floor.

match /mætʃ/ (**matches, matching, matched**) 1 N-COUNT A **match** is an organized game of football, cricket, or other sport. 2 N-COUNT A **match** is a small wooden stick with a substance on one end that produces a flame when you strike it against a rough surface.

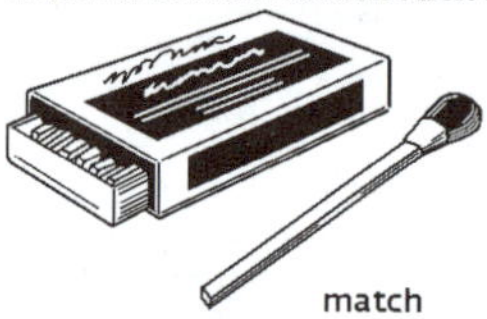

match

3 V-T/V-I If one thing **matches** another, or if the two things **match**, they look good together, usually because they have similar colours or designs. ❑ *You don't have to match your lipstick exactly to your outfit.* ● **matching** ADJ BEFORE N ❑ *...a matching handbag.* 4 V-I If something such as an amount or a quality **matches with** another, or if the two things **match**, they are both the same or equal. ❑ *Our results do not match with their results.* 5 V-T To **match** something means to be equal to it in speed, size, or quality. ❑ *They played some good football, but I think we easily matched them.* 6 PHRASE If one person or thing is **no match for** another, they are unable to compete successfully with the other person or thing. ❑ *Safin was no match for Federer in the tennis final.* → see **fire**

Word Partnership Use *match* with:

N. **boxing** match, **chess** match, **tennis** match, **wrestling** match 1
ADJ. **bad** match, **good** match, **perfect** match 6
V. **strike a** match 2

matched /mætʃt/ 1 ADJ If two people are well **matched**, they are suited to one another and are likely to have a successful relationship. ❑ *My parents were not very well matched.* 2 ADJ In competitive situations, if opponents are well **matched**, they are both of the same standard in strength or ability.

mate /meɪt/ (**mates, mating, mated**) 1 N-COUNT You can refer to someone's friends as their **mates**. [BRIT, INFORMAL] 2 N-COUNT An animal's **mate** is its sexual partner. 3 V-I When animals **mate**, they have sex in order to produce young. ❑ *They want the males to mate with wild females.*

material /məˈtɪəriəl/ (**materials**) 1 N-VAR A **material** is a solid substance. ❑ *...a building material such as stone.* 2 N-VAR **Material** is cloth. ❑ *...the thick material of her skirt.* 3 N-PLURAL **Materials** are the things that you need for a particular activity. ❑ *...sewing materials.* 4 ADJ **Material** things are possessions or money, rather than abstract things. ❑ *She enjoys the material comforts of her married life.* ● **materially** ADV ❑ *He tried to help this child materially and spiritually.* → see **industry**

materialism /məˈtɪəriəlɪzəm/ N-UNCOUNT **Materialism** is the attitude of someone who attaches a lot of importance to money and possessions.

materialize [BRIT also **materialise**] /məˈtɪəriəlaɪz/ (**materializes, materializing,**

Word Web mathematics

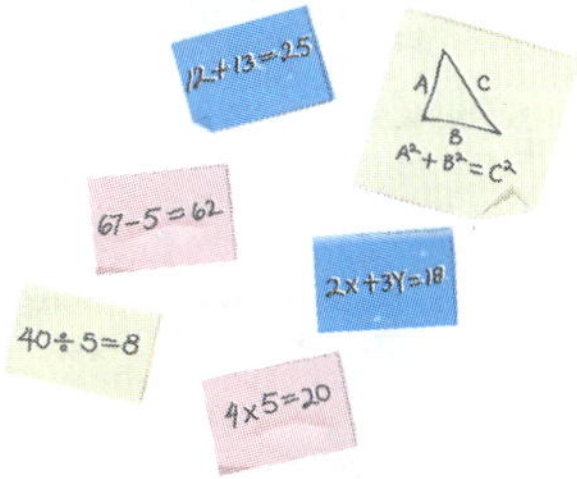

During prehistoric times people **counted** things they could see—for example, four sheep. Later they began to use **numbers** with abstract **quantities** like time—for example, two days. This led to the development of basic **arithmetic**—**addition**, **subtraction**, **multiplication**, and **division**. When people discovered how to write numerals, they could do difficult **mathematical calculations** with larger numbers. **Mathematicians** developed new types of **maths** to **measure** land and keep financial records. **Algebra** and **geometry** developed in the Middle East between 2,000 and 3,000 years ago. Algebra uses letters to represent some numbers. Geometry is about the relationships among **lines**, **angles**, and **shapes**.

materialized) V-I If an event **does not materialize**, it does not happen. ❑ *The rebellion failed to materialize.*

maternal /məˈtɜːnəl/ ADJ **Maternal** feelings or actions are typical of those of a mother towards her child. ❑ *Carol had no maternal feelings.*

maternity /məˈtɜːnɪti/ ADJ BEFORE N **Maternity** is used to describe things relating to pregnancy and birth. ❑ *...the city's maternity hospital.*

math /mæθ/ → see **maths**
→ see **mathematics**

mathematical /ˌmæθəˈmætɪkəl/ ADJ BEFORE N Something that is **mathematical** involves numbers and calculations. • **mathematically** ADV ❑ *...mathematically proven facts.*
→ see **mathematics**

mathematician /ˌmæθəməˈtɪʃən/ (**mathematicians**) N-COUNT A **mathematician** is a person who is trained in the study of numbers and calculations.
→ see **mathematics**

mathematics /ˌmæθəˈmætɪks/ N-UNCOUNT **Mathematics** is the study of numbers, quantities, or shapes.
→ see Word Web: **mathematics**

maths /mæθs/ N-UNCOUNT In British English, mathematics is usually referred to as **maths**. The American word is **math**.

matinee also **matinée** /ˈmætɪneɪ, AM -ˈneɪ/ (**matinees**) N-COUNT A **matinee** is a performance of a play or a showing of a film in the afternoon.

matt /mæt/ ADJ A **matt** colour, paint, or surface is dull rather than shiny.

matter /ˈmætə/ (**matters, mattering, mattered**) **1** N-COUNT A **matter** is a task, situation, or event which you have to deal with or think about. ❑ *...business matters.* ❑ *She wanted to discuss some private matter.* **2** N-SING You use **matter** in expressions such as **'What's the matter?'** or **'Is anything the matter?'** when you think that someone has a problem and you want to know what it is. **3** N-PLURAL You use **matters** to refer to the situation you are talking about. ❑ *It is hard to see how this would improve matters.* **4** N-UNCOUNT You can refer to books, newspapers, and other texts as printed **matter** or reading **matter**. **5** N-UNCOUNT **Matter** is the physical part of the universe consisting of solids, liquids, and gases. **6** N-SING You can use matter in expressions such as **'a matter of weeks'** when you are emphasizing that it is a short period of time. **7** V-I If something **matters**, it is important because it has an effect on a situation. ❑ *Most young people take their music seriously; it matters to them.* **8** PHRASE If you say that something is **another matter** or **a different matter**, you mean that it is very different from the situation that you have just discussed or is an exception to a rule or general statement that you have just made. ❑ *Being responsible for one's own health is one thing, but being responsible for another person's health is quite a different matter.* **9** PHRASE You say **'it doesn't matter'** to tell someone who is apologizing to you that you are not angry or upset, and that they should not worry.

Word Web matter

Matter exists in three states—**solid**, **liquid**, and **gas**. Changes in the state of matter happen frequently. For example, when a solid becomes hot enough, it **melts** and becomes a liquid. When a liquid is hot enough, it **evaporates** into a gas. The process also works the other way around. A gas which becomes very cool will **condense** into a liquid. And a liquid that is cooled enough will freeze and become a solid. Other changes in **state** are possible. Sublimation describes what happens when a solid, such as dry ice, turns directly into a gas, carbon dioxide. And did you know that glass is actually a liquid, not a solid?

10 PHRASE You use **no matter** in expressions such as **no matter how** and **no matter what** to indicate that something is true or happens in all circumstances. ❑ *Any dog bite, no matter how small, needs immediate medical attention.* **11** PHRASE If you are going to do something **as a matter of** urgency or priority, you are going to do it as soon as possible, because it is important. **12** PHRASE If you say that something is **just a matter of time**, you mean that it is certain to happen at some time in the future. ❑ *It was just a matter of time before I won again.* **13** **as a matter of fact** → see **fact**
→ see Word Web: **matter**

ˌmatter-of-ˈfact ADJ If you say someone is being **matter-of-fact**, you mean that they are being unemotional in a tense or difficult situation. ❑ *John gave Francis the news in a matter-of-fact way.* ● **matter-of-factly** ADV ❑ *'She thinks you're a spy,' Scott said matter-of-factly.*

mattress /ˈmætrəs/ (**mattresses**) N-COUNT A **mattress** is a large flat pad which is put on a bed to make it comfortable to sleep on.
→ see **bed**

mature /məˈtjʊə/ (**matures, maturing, matured**) **1** V-I When a child or young animal **matures**, it becomes an adult. **2** ADJ A **mature** person or animal is fully grown. ● **maturity** N-UNCOUNT ❑ *We stop growing at maturity.* **3** ADJ If you describe someone as **mature**, you think that their behaviour is responsible and sensible. ● **maturity** N-UNCOUNT ❑ *Her speech showed great maturity.* **4** V-I When something **matures**, it reaches a state of complete development. ❑ *When the trees matured they were cut.*

M

maul /mɔːl/ (**mauls, mauling, mauled**) V-T If someone **is mauled** by an animal, they are attacked and badly injured by it. ❑ *The dog mauled one of the girls.*

maverick /ˈmævərɪk/ (**mavericks**) N-COUNT If you describe someone as a **maverick**, you mean that they do not think or behave in the same way as other people.

Word Link	*maxim ≈ greatest : maxim, maximize, maximum*

maxim /ˈmæksɪm/ (**maxims**) N-COUNT A **maxim** is a rule for good or sensible behaviour, especially one in the form of a saying. ❑ *I believe in the maxim 'Live simply that others may simply live.'*

maximize [BRIT also **maximise**] /ˈmæksɪmaɪz/ (**maximizes, maximizing, maximized**) V-T To **maximize** something means to make it as large or important as you can. ❑ *In order to maximize profit, the firm maximized output.*

maximum /ˈmæksɪməm/ **1** ADJ BEFORE N & N-SING The **maximum** amount or the **maximum** is the amount which is the largest that is possible, allowed, or required. ❑ *The maximum height for a fence or hedge is 2 metres.* ❑ *...a maximum of two years in prison.* **2** ADJ BEFORE N You use **maximum** to emphasize how great an amount is. ❑ *...the maximum amount of information.* ❑ *It was achieved with minimum fuss and maximum efficiency.* **3** ADV If you say that something is a particular amount **maximum**, you mean that this is the greatest amount it should be or could possibly be, although a smaller amount is acceptable or very possible. ❑ *We need an extra 6g a day maximum.*

Thesaurus	*maximum* Also look up:
ADJ.	biggest, greatest, highest, most; (*ant.*) minimum, lowest **1** **2**

Word Partnership	Use *maximum* with:
N.	maximum **benefit**, maximum **charge**, maximum **efficiency**, maximum **fine**, maximum **flexibility**, maximum **height**, maximum **penalty**, maximum **rate**, maximum **sentence**, maximum **speed** **1** **2**

may /meɪ/ **1** MODAL If you say that something **may** happen or be true, you mean that it is possible. ❑ *We may have some rain today.* ❑ *I don't know if they'll publish it or not. They may.* ❑ *This opportunity may not come again.* **2** MODAL If someone **may** do something, they are allowed to do it. ❑ *May we come in?* ❑ *You may leave.* ❑ *Adolescents under the age of 18 may not work in jobs that require them to drive.* **3** MODAL You use **may** in statements where you are accepting the truth of a situation, but contrasting it with something that is more important. ❑ *I may be poor, but I'm not stupid.*

May /meɪ/ (**Mays**) N-VAR **May** is the fifth month of the year. ❑ *I went to Portugal in May with my friends.*

maybe /ˈmeɪbi/ **1** ADV You use **maybe** to express uncertainty, for example when you do not know that something is definitely true. ❑ *Maybe she is in love.* ❑ *I do think about having children, maybe when I'm 40.* ❑ *'Is she coming back?'—'Maybe.'* **2** ADV You use **maybe** when you are making a rough guess at a number, quantity, or value, rather than stating it exactly. ❑ *The men were maybe a hundred metres away.*

mayhem /ˈmeɪhem/ N-UNCOUNT **Mayhem** is a situation that is not controlled or ordered, when people are behaving in a disorganized, confused, and often violent way. ❑ *Their arrival caused mayhem as crowds rushed towards them.*

mayonnaise /ˌmeɪəˈneɪz/ N-UNCOUNT **Mayonnaise** is a sauce made from egg yolks, oil, and vinegar, eaten cold.

mayor /meə, ˈmeɪə/ (**mayors**) N-COUNT The **mayor** of a town or city is the person who has been elected to represent it for a fixed period of time.

maze /meɪz/ (**mazes**) N-COUNT A **maze** is a complex system of passages or paths separated by walls or hedges.

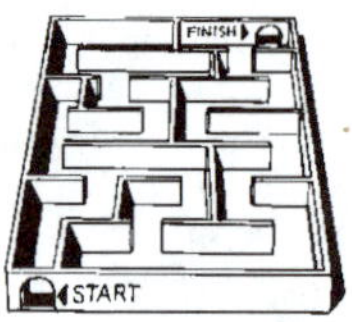

maze

me /mi, STRONG miː/ PRON A speaker or writer uses **me** to refer to himself or herself. **Me** is a first person singular pronoun. **Me** is used as the object of a verb or a preposition. ❑ *This decision affected me for the rest of my life.* ❑ *She looked up at me.*

meadow /ˈmedəʊ/ (**meadows**) N-COUNT A **meadow** is a field with grass and flowers growing in it.

Word Web meal

Customs for eating meals are very different around the world. In the Middle East, popular **breakfast** foods include pita bread, olives and white cheese. In China, favourite **fast food** breakfast items are steamed buns and fried breadsticks. The **continental breakfast** in Europe is bread, butter, jam, and a hot drink. In many places **lunch** is a light **meal**, such as a **sandwich**. But in Germany, lunch is the main meal of the day. In most places, **dinner** is the name of the meal eaten in the evening. However, some people say they eat dinner at noon and supper at night.

meagre [AM **meager**] /ˈmiːgə/ ADJ Something that is **meagre** is very small in amount. ❑ *...a meagre 3.1% pay rise.* ❑ *Their food supply is meagre.*

meal /miːl/ (**meals**) N-COUNT A **meal** is an occasion when people eat. You can refer to the food that they eat at that time as a **meal**. ❑ *She drank water with her meal.*
→ see Word Web: **meal**

Usage

The first meal of the day is called **breakfast**. The most common word for the midday meal is **lunch**, but in some parts of Britain, and in some contexts, **dinner** is used as well. ❑ *...school dinners.* ❑ *...Christmas dinner.* However, **dinner** is used mainly to refer to a meal in the evening. In British English, it may also suggest a formal or special meal. **Supper** and **tea** are sometimes also used to refer to this meal, though for some people, **supper** is a snack in the late evening and **tea** is a light meal in the afternoon.

Thesaurus *meal* Also look up:

N.	breakfast, dinner, lunch, supper

Word Partnership Use *meal* with:

V.	**cook a** meal, **eat a** meal, **enjoy a** meal, **have a** meal, **miss a** meal, **order a** meal, **prepare a** meal, **serve a** meal, **skip a** meal
ADJ.	**big** meal, **delicious** meal, **good** meal, **hot** meal, **large** meal, **simple** meal, **well-balanced** meal

mean

❶ SIGNIFY
❷ UNKIND
❸ AVERAGE

mean /miːn/ (**means, meaning, meant**)
❶ 1 V-T If you want to know what something or someone **means**, you want to know what they are referring to, or what message they are conveying. ❑ *What does 'evidence' mean?* ❑ *What do you think he means by that?* ❑ *In modern Welsh, 'glas' means 'blue'.* ❑ *The red signal means you have to stop.* 2 V-T If something **means** a lot to you, it is important to you. ❑ *It meant a lot to them to win.* 3 V-T If one thing **means** another, it shows that the second thing is true or makes it certain to happen. ❑ *Becoming rich didn't mean an end to money worries.* 4 V-T If you **mean** what you say, you are serious and you are not joking, exaggerating, or just being polite. ❑ *He could see I meant what I said.* ❑ *Does he really mean it when he says he is sorry?* 5 V-T If you **mean to** do something, you intend to do it. ❑ *I have been meaning to write this letter for some time now.* ❑ *I didn't mean to hurt you.* 6 PHRASE You say **'I mean'** when you are explaining, justifying, or correcting what you have just said. ❑ *It was his idea. Gordon's, I mean.* ❑ *I'm sure he wouldn't mind. I mean, I was the one who asked him.* ❑ *It was law or classics – I mean English or classics.* 7 to **mean business** → see **business**

mean /miːn/ (**meaner, meanest**)
❷ 1 ADJ If you say that someone is **mean**, you disapprove of them because they are unwilling to spend much money or to use very much of a particular thing. ❑ *He's mean with money.* ❑ *...a rather mean portion of apple tart.* ● **meanness** N-UNCOUNT ❑ *...the meanness of some employers.* 2 ADJ If you are **mean** to someone, you are unkind to them. ● **meanness** N-UNCOUNT ❑ *You upset him out of meanness.* 3 PHRASE You use **no mean** to emphasize that someone or something is good or remarkable. ❑ *She was no mean actress.*

Thesaurus *mean* Also look up:

V.	aim, intend, plan ① 5
ADJ.	nasty, unfriendly, unkind; *(ant.)* kind ② 2

mean /miːn/
❸ 1 N-SING **The mean** is a number that is the average of a set of numbers. ❑ *The mean age of the sample was 35.* 2 → see also **means**

meander /miˈændə/ (**meanders, meandering, meandered**) 1 V-I If a river or road **meanders**, it has a lot of bends in it. ❑ *A railway track meanders through the valley.* 2 V-I If you **meander** through a place, you move slowly through it for pleasure. ❑ *It's so restful to meander along Irish country roads.*

meaning /ˈmiːnɪŋ/ (**meanings**) 1 N-VAR The **meaning** of something such as a word, symbol, or gesture is the thing that it refers to or the message that it conveys. ❑ *...two words with similar meanings.* ❑ *I have been trying hard to interpret the meaning of this dream.* 2 N-UNCOUNT If an activity or action has **meaning**, it has a purpose and is worthwhile. ❑ *...a challenge that gives meaning to life.*

m

Word Partnership Use *meaning* with:

N. meaning **of a term**, meaning **of a word** 1
ADJ. **deeper** meaning, **literal** meaning, **new** meaning, **real** meaning, **true** meaning 1
V. **explain the** meaning **of *something***, **understand the** meaning **of *something*** 1

meaningful /ˈmiːnɪŋfʊl/ 1 ADJ If you describe something as **meaningful**, you mean that it is serious, important, or useful in some way. ❑ *...satisfying, meaningful work.* ● **meaningfully** ADV ❑ *By joining voluntary organisations they can participate actively and meaningfully.* 2 ADJ BEFORE N A **meaningful** look, gesture, or remark is intended to express something which is not obvious, but which is understood. ● **meaningfully** ADV ❑ *She rolled her eyes meaningfully.*

meaningless /ˈmiːnɪŋləs/ ADJ Something that is **meaningless** has no meaning or purpose. ❑ *The sentence 'kicked the ball the man' is meaningless.* ❑ *Many staff found their day-to-day work meaningless.*

means /miːnz/

In meaning 1, **means** is both the singular and the plural form.

1 N-COUNT A **means of** doing something is a method or instrument which can be used to do it. ❑ *They didn't provide me with any means of transport.* ❑ *The move is a means to fight crime.* 2 N-PLURAL You can refer to the money that someone has as their **means.** [FORMAL] ❑ *...a health service that's available to all, regardless of means.* ❑ *As a student you're always living beyond your means.* 3 PHRASE You can say **'by all means'** to tell someone that you are willing to allow them to do something. ❑ *'Can I come and have a look at your house?'—'Yes, by all means.'* 4 PHRASE If you do something **by means of** a particular method or instrument, you do it using that method or instrument. ❑ *This is a two-year course taught by means of lectures and seminars.* 5 PHRASE You use expressions such as **'by no means'** and **'not by any means'** to emphasize that something is not true. ❑ *This is by no means out of the ordinary.*

meant /ment/ 1 **Meant** is the past tense and past participle of **mean.** 2 ADJ AFTER LINK-V If something or someone is **meant to** do a particular thing or is **meant for** a particular purpose, that is what was intended or planned. ❑ *The stories were never meant for publication.* ❑ *I'm meant to be on holiday.* 3 ADJ AFTER LINK-V If you say that something is **meant to** have a particular quality or characteristic, you mean it has a reputation for being like that. ❑ *Juventus are meant to be one of the top teams in the world.*

meantime /ˈmiːntaɪm/ N-UNCOUNT **In the meantime** means in the period of time between two events, or while an event is happening. ❑ *Reduce the heat and simmer for 30 minutes. In the meantime, fry the spicy sausage.*

meanwhile /ˈmiːnwaɪl/ ADV **Meanwhile** means in the period of time between two events, or while an event is happening. ❑ *Take the dish out of the oven and leave to cool. Meanwhile, whip the cream lightly.*

measles /ˈmiːzəlz/ N-UNCOUNT **Measles** is an infectious illness that gives you a high temperature and red spots.
→ see **hospital**

measurable /ˈmeʒərəbəl/ ADJ If something is **measurable**, it is large enough to be noticed or to be significant. [FORMAL] ❑ *Both leaders expected measurable progress.*

measure /ˈmeʒə/ (**measures, measuring, measured**) 1 V-T If you **measure** the quality, quantity, or value of something, you decide how great it is, by using particular procedures or instruments. ❑ *He measured the child's ability to imitate rhythms and sounds.* ❑ *The rate of human heartbeat is measured by counting the pulse rate.* 2 V-T If something **measures** a particular length, width, or amount, that is its size or intensity, expressed in numbers. ❑ *This plate measures 30cm across.* 3 N-SING A **measure of** a particular quality, feeling, or activity is a fairly large amount of it. [FORMAL] ❑ *Each of them attained a measure of success.* 4 N-SING If something is a **measure of** a particular situation, it shows that the situation is very serious or has developed to a very great extent. ❑ *That is a measure of how bad things have become.* 5 N-COUNT When someone takes **measures** to do something, they carry out particular actions in order to achieve a particular result. ❑ *...new government measures to fight crime.* 6 PHRASE If something is done **for good measure**, it is done in addition to a number of other things. ❑ *I repeated my question for good measure.*
→ see **mathematics, thermometer**
▶ **measure up** PHR-VERB If you do not **measure up to** a standard or **to** someone's expectations, you are not good enough to achieve the standard or fulfil the person's expectations. ❑ *Nobody can measure up to his high standards.*

Word Partnership Use *measure* with:

N. measure **intelligence**, measure **performance**, measure **progress**, **tests** measure 1
emergency measure, **safety** measure, **security** measure 5
V. **adopt a** measure, **approve a** measure, **support a** measure, **veto a** measure 5
ADJ. **drastic** measure, **economic** measure 5

measurement /ˈmeʒəmənt/ (**measurements**) 1 N-COUNT A **measurement** is a result that you obtain by measuring something. ❑ *We took lots of measurements.* 2 N-VAR **Measurement** of something is the process or activity of measuring it. 3 N-PLURAL Your **measurements** are the size of your chest, waist, hips, and other parts of your body.
→ see Picture Dictionary: **measurements**

meat /miːt/ (**meats**) N-VAR **Meat** is the flesh of a dead animal that people cook and eat. ❑ *...cold meats and salads.*
→ see Word Web: **meat**
→ see **vegetarian**

mechanic /mɪˈkænɪk/ (**mechanics**) 1 N-COUNT A **mechanic** is someone whose job is to repair and maintain machines and engines, especially car engines. 2 N-PLURAL **The mechanics of** a system or activity are the way in which it works or the way in which it is done. ❑ *What are the mechanics of this new process?*

Picture Dictionary measurements

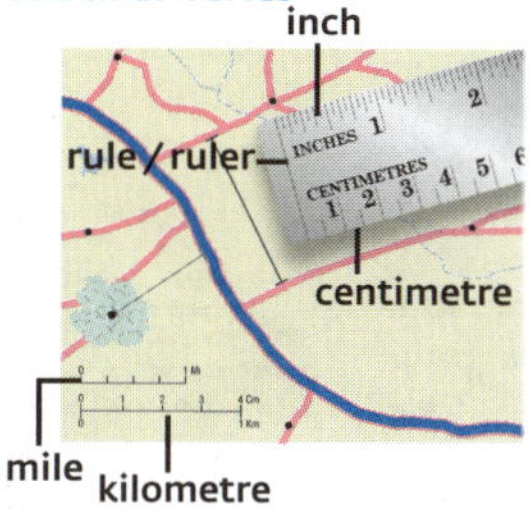

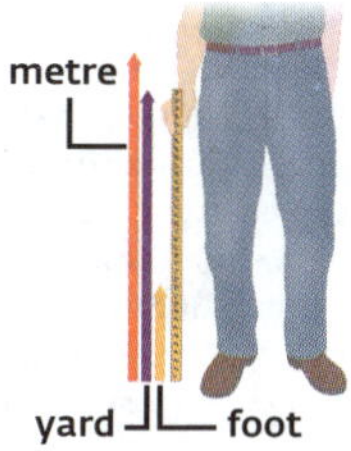

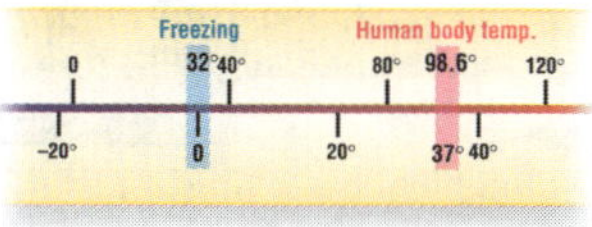

To convert Fahrenheit to Celsius
Tc = 5/9(Tf - 32)

To convert Celsius to Fahrenheit:
Tf = 32 + (9/5 x Tc)

mechanical /mɪˈkænɪkəl/ **1** ADJ A **mechanical** device has moving parts and uses power in order to do a particular task. ● **mechanically** ADV ❑ *The locks are mechanically operated.* **2** ADJ A **mechanical** action is done automatically, without thinking about it. ● **mechanically** ADV ❑ *He nodded mechanically, his eyes fixed on the girl.*

mechanism /ˈmekənɪzəm/ (**mechanisms**) **1** N-COUNT A **mechanism** is a part of a machine that does a particular task. ❑ *...the locking mechanism.* **2** N-COUNT A **mechanism** is a way of getting something done within a particular system. ❑ *...a mechanism for protecting human rights.*

medal

mechanize [BRIT also **mechanise**] /ˈmekənaɪz/ (**mechanizes, mechanizing, mechanized**) V-T If a type of work **is mechanized**, it is done by machines. ● **mechanization** N-UNCOUNT ❑ *...the mechanisation of agriculture.*

medal /ˈmedəl/ (**medals**) N-COUNT A **medal** is a small metal disc, given as an award for bravery or as a prize in a sporting event.

medallist /ˈmedəlɪst/ (**medallists**) N-COUNT A **medallist** is a person who has won a medal in sport.

meddle /ˈmedəl/ (**meddles, meddling, meddled**) V-I If you say that someone **meddles in** something, you are criticizing the fact that they try to influence or change it without being asked. ❑ *She told me not to meddle in things that don't concern me.*

Word Link *med ≈ middle : intermediary, media, medium*

media /ˈmiːdiə/ **1** N-SING You can refer to television, radio, and newspapers as **the media**. **Media** can take the singular or plural form of the verb. ❑ *The media has brought too much attention to the Royal Family.* **2** **Media** is a plural of **medium**.
→ see **library**

mediaeval → see **medieval**

mediate /ˈmiːdieɪt/ (**mediates, mediating, mediated**) V-T/V-I If someone **mediates** between two groups, or **mediates** an agreement

Word Web meat

The English language has different words for animals and the **meat** that comes from those animals. This is because of influences from other languages. In the

year 1066 AD the Anglo-Saxons of England lost a major battle to the French-speaking Normans. As a result, the Normans became the ruling class and the Anglo-Saxons worked on farms. The Anglo-Saxons tended the

animals. They tended **sheep**, **cows**, **chickens**, and **pigs** in the fields. The wealthier Normans, who purchased and ate the meat from these animals, used French words. They bought "mouton," which became the word **mutton**, "bouef," which became **beef**, "poulet," which became **poultry**, and "porc," which became **pork**.

Word Web medicine

Medicine began in the Western Hemisphere in ancient Greece. The Greek philosopher Hippocrates separated medicine from religion and **disease** from supernatural explanations. He created the Hippocratic **oath** which describes a **physician's** duties. During the Middle Ages, Andreas Vesalius helped to advance medicine through his **research** on **anatomy**. Another major step forward was Friedrich Henle's development of **germ** theory. An understanding of germs led to Joseph Lister's demonstrations of the use of **antiseptics**, and Alexander Fleming's discovery of the **antibiotic** penicillin.

Important Medical Advances

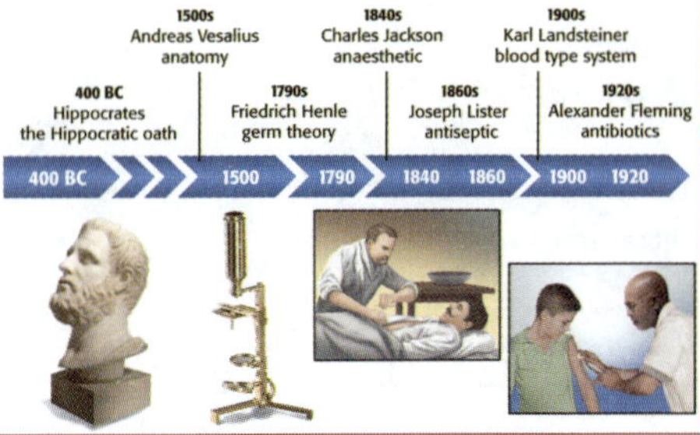

between them, they try to settle a dispute between them. ❑ *He tried to mediate between the two sides.* ● **mediation** N-UNCOUNT ❑ *...United Nations mediation between the two sides.* ● **mediator** (**mediators**) N-COUNT ❑ *Turkey acted as a mediator between the two countries.*

medical /ˈmedɪkəl/ (**medicals**) **1** ADJ BEFORE N **Medical** means relating to illness and injuries and to their treatment or prevention. ❑ *Four of our men needed medical treatment.* ● **medically** ADV ❑ *I am not medically qualified.* **2** N-COUNT A **medical** is a thorough examination of your body by a doctor.

Word Partnership Use *medical* with:

N. medical **advice**, medical **attention**, medical **bills**, medical **care**, medical **centre**, medical **doctor**, medical **emergency**, medical **practise**, medical **problems**, medical **research**, medical **science**, medical **supplies**, medical **tests**, medical **treatment** **1**

medication /ˌmedɪˈkeɪʃən/ (**medications**) N-VAR **Medication** is medicine that is used to cure an illness. ❑ *She is not on any medication.*

medicinal /meˈdɪsənəl/ ADJ **Medicinal** substances are used to treat and cure illness. ❑ *...medicinal plants.*

medicine /ˈmedsən, AM ˈmedɪsɪn/ (**medicines**) **1** N-UNCOUNT **Medicine** is the treatment of illness and injuries by doctors and nurses. ❑ *He pursued a career in medicine.* **2** N-VAR A **medicine** is a substance that you swallow in order to cure an illness.
→ see Word Web: **medicine**

Word Partnership Use *medicine* with:

V. **practice** medicine, **study** medicine **1** **give *someone*** medicine, **take** medicine, **use** medicine **2**

medieval also **mediaeval** /ˌmediˈiːvəl, AM ˌmiːd-/ ADJ **Medieval** things relate to or date from the period in European history between about 500 AD and about 1500 AD. ❑ *...a medieval castle.*

mediocre /ˌmiːdiˈəʊkə/ ADJ If you describe something as **mediocre**, you mean that it is of rather poor quality. ❑ *The food was mediocre.* ● **mediocrity** /ˌmiːdiˈɒkrɪti, ˌmed-/ N-UNCOUNT ❑ *...the mediocrity of most contemporary literature.*

meditate /ˈmedɪteɪt/ (**meditates, meditating, meditated**) **1** V-I If you **meditate on** something, you think about it carefully and deeply for a long time. **2** V-I If you **meditate**, you remain in a calm, silent state for a period of time, often as part of a religious training. ● **meditation** N-UNCOUNT ❑ *Many busy executives have begun to practise meditation.*

Word Link ***med ≈ middle : intermediary, media, medium***

medium /ˈmiːdiəm/

The plural of the noun is **mediums** or **media**.

1 ADJ You use **medium** to describe something which is average in size, degree or amount, or approximately half way along a scale between two extremes. ❑ *He was of medium height.* ❑ *Only a low or medium heat is necessary.* ❑ *...medium brown hair.* **2** N-COUNT A **medium** is the means that you use to communicate or express something. ❑ *In Sierra Leone, English is used as the medium of instruction.* **3** → see also **media**

meek /miːk/ ADJ & N-PLURAL A **meek** person is quiet and timid and does what other people say. **The meek** are people who are meek. ● **meekly** ADV ❑ *'Thank you, Peter,' Amy said meekly.*

meet /miːt/ (**meets, meeting, met**) **1** V-T & PHR-VERB If you **meet** someone, or if you **meet up with** them, you happen to be in the same place as them and have a conversation with them. ❑ *He's the kindest person I've ever met.* ❑ *Hey, Terry, come and meet my Dad.* ❑ *We met by chance.* ❑ *By chance, he met up with Elia Kazan, the photographer.* **2** V-I If two or more people **meet**, or if they **meet up**, they go to the same place, which they have earlier arranged to do, so that they can talk or do something together. ❑ *Let's meet at the beach tomorrow.* ❑ *We tend to meet up for lunch once a week.* ❑ *The committee met last week to discuss the company's problems.* **3** V-T If you **meet** someone who is travelling, or if you **meet** their train, plane, or bus, you go to the station, airport, or bus stop in order to be there when they arrive. ❑ *Lili and* *my father met me off the boat.* **4** V-T If something **meets** a need, requirement, or condition, it is satisfactory or sufficiently large to fulfil it. ❑ *Many developing countries do not meet the conditions for World Bank loans.* **5** V-T If you **meet** something such as a problem or challenge, you deal satisfactorily with it. ❑ *They had worked hard to meet the deadline.* **6** V-T If you **meet** the cost of something, you provide the money for it. ❑ *The government met some of the cost of the damage.* **7** V-T If someone or something **meets** an attitude or reaction, or if they **meet with** it, they experience that attitude or get that reaction from people. ❑ *They met opposition from trade unions.* ❑ *The idea met with a cool response.* **8** V-I The place where two areas or lines **meet** is the place where they are next to one another or join. ❑ *The track widened as it met the road.* **9** to **make ends meet** → see **end** **10** to **meet** someone's **eyes** → see **eye**

▶ **meet up** → see **meet** (meaning **2**)

Thesaurus *meet* Also look up:

V. bump into, encounter, run into **1**
gather, get together **2**
comply with, follow, fulfill **4**
accomplish, achieve, complete, make **5**

meeting /ˈmiːtɪŋ/ (**meetings**) **1** N-COUNT A **meeting** is an event at which a group of people come together to discuss things or make decisions. You can also refer to the people at a meeting as **the meeting**. ❑ *He travels to London regularly for business meetings.* ❑ *The meeting decided that further efforts were needed.* **2** N-COUNT A **meeting** is an occasion when you meet someone. ❑ *...a chance meeting.*

Word Partnership Use *meeting* with:

N. meeting **agenda**, **board** meeting, **business** meeting **1**
V. **attend a** meeting, **call a** meeting, **go to a** meeting, **have a** meeting, **hold a** meeting, **plan a** meeting, **schedule a** meeting **1**

megabyte /ˈmegəbaɪt/ (**megabytes**) N-COUNT In computing, a **megabyte** is one million bytes of data.

melancholy /ˈmelənkɒli/ ADJ & N-UNCOUNT Someone who is **melancholy** or who has **melancholy** feelings has an intense feeling of sadness. This feeling can be called **melancholy**. [LITERARY]

mellow /ˈmeləʊ/ (**mellower, mellowest, mellows, mellowing, mellowed**) **1** ADJ **Mellow** is used to describe things that have a pleasant, soft, rich colour, usually red, yellow, or brown. ❑ *...the soft, mellow light of evening.* **2** ADJ A **mellow** flavour or sound is pleasant, smooth, and rich. **3** V-I & ADJ If someone **mellows**, or if they become **mellow**, they become kinder or less extreme in their behaviour. ❑ *I think he has mellowed over the years.* ❑ *Is she more mellow and tolerant?*

melodrama /ˈmelədrɑːmə/ (**melodramas**) N-VAR A **melodrama** is a story or play in which there are a lot of exciting or sad events and in which people's emotions are very exaggerated.

melodramatic /ˌmelədrəˈmætɪk/ ADJ If you are being **melodramatic**, you treat a situation as much more serious than it really is.

melody /ˈmelədi/ (**melodies**) N-COUNT A **melody** is a tune. [LITERARY]

melon /ˈmelən/ (**melons**) N-VAR A **melon** is a large, sweet, juicy fruit with a thick green or yellow skin.

melt /melt/ (**melts, melting, melted**) **1** V-T/V-I When a solid substance **melts**, or when it **is melted**, it changes to a liquid because of being heated. ❑ *The snow melted.* ❑ *Break up the chocolate and melt it.* **2** V-I & PHR-VERB If something **melts**, or if it **melts away**, it gradually disappears. ❑ *The youths ran away and melted into the darkness.* ❑ *His anger melted away.*
→ see **glacier, matter**

▶ **melt down** PHR-VERB If an object **is melted down**, it is heated until it melts. ❑ *Their equipment was melted down as scrap metal.*

member /ˈmembə/ (**members**) N-COUNT A **member of** a group or organization is one of the people, animals, or things belonging to it. ❑ *Their behaviour put members of the public at risk.* ❑ *The sunflower is a member of the daisy family.* ❑ *Britain is a full member of NATO.*

ˌMember of ˈParliament (**Members of Parliament**) **1** N-COUNT A **Member of Parliament** is a person who has been elected to represent people in a country's parliament. It is usually abbreviated to **MP**. **2** → See note at **government**

membership /ˈmembəʃɪp/ (**memberships**) **1** N-UNCOUNT **Membership** is the fact or state of being a member of an organization. ❑ *...his membership of the Communist Party.* **2** N-VAR The **membership** of an organization is the people who belong to it. ❑ *The party membership reached 97,000.*

membrane /ˈmembreɪn/ (**membranes**) N-COUNT A **membrane** is a thin skin which connects or covers parts of a person's or animal's body.

memo /ˈmeməʊ/ (**memos**) N-COUNT A **memo** is an official note from one person to another within the same organization.

memoirs /ˈmemwɑːz/ N-PLURAL If someone writes their **memoirs**, they write a book about their life.

memorabilia /ˌmemərəˈbɪliə/ N-PLURAL **Memorabilia** consists of things that you collect because they are connected with a person or an organization in which you are interested. ❑ *...rock and pop memorabilia.*

memorable /ˈmemərəbəl/ ADJ Something that is **memorable** is likely to be remembered, because it is special or unique. ❑ *It had been a memorable day.*

memorandum /ˌseməˈrændəm/

The plural is **memoranda** or **memorandums**.

N-COUNT A **memorandum** is a **memo**. [FORMAL]

Word Link *memor ≈ memory : commemorate, memorial, memory*

memorial /mɪˈmɔːriəl/ (**memorials**) **1** N-COUNT A **memorial** is a structure built in order to remind people of a famous person or event. ❑ *...a memorial to Columbus.* ❑ *Every village had a war memorial.* **2** ADJ BEFORE N A **memorial**

m

memorial

event or prize is in honour of someone who has died, so that they will be remembered. ❑ *A memorial service was held for her at St Paul's Church.*

memorize [BRIT also **memorise**] /ˈmeməraɪz/ (**memorizes, memorizing, memorized**) V-T If you **memorize** something, you learn it so that you can remember it exactly.

Word Link *memor ≈ memory : commemorate, memorial, memory*

memory /ˈmeməri/ (**memories**) **1** N-COUNT Your **memory** is your ability to remember things. ❑ *All the details of the meeting are fresh in my memory.* ❑ *He had a good memory for faces.* ❑ *He claims to have lost his memory.* **2** N-COUNT A **memory** is something that you remember about the past. ❑ *He had happy memories of his father.* **3** N-SING If you talk about the **memory** of someone who has died, especially someone who was loved or respected, you are referring to the ways in which they are remembered. ❑ *The meeting opened with a minute's silence in memory of those who had died.* **4** N-COUNT A computer's **memory** is the capacity of the computer to store information. **5** PHRASE If you do something **from memory**, you do it without looking at anything written or printed. ❑ *She could recite long passages of the book from memory.*

M

Word Partnership Use *memory* with:

ADJ. **collective** memory, **conscious** memory, **failing** memory, **fresh in *your*** memory, **long-/short-term** memory, **poor** memory, **in recent** memory **1** **bad** memory, **good** memory **1** **2** **happy** memory, **painful** memory, **sad** memory, **vivid** memory **2**

N. **computer** memory, **random access** memory, memory **storage** **4**

men /men/ **Men** is the plural of **man**.

menace /ˈmenɪs/ (**menaces, menacing, menaced**) **1** N-COUNT Something or someone that is a **menace** is likely to cause serious harm. ❑ *In my view he is a menace to the public.* ❑ *...the menace of terrorism.* **2** N-UNCOUNT **Menace** is a quality or atmosphere of danger or threat. ❑ *...a vague feeling of menace.* **3** V-T If someone or something **menaces** you, they threaten to harm you or are likely to do so. ❑ *They lived in an area menaced by storms.* ● **menacing** ADJ ❑ *Mary Ann gave her a menacing look.* ● **menacingly** ADV ❑ *James moved menacingly towards him.*

mend /mend/ (**mends, mending, mended**) **1** V-T If you **mend** something that is damaged or broken, you repair it so that it works properly or can be used. ❑ *They mended the leaking roof.* ❑ *William took his watch to be mended.* **2** PHRASE If you are **on the mend**, you are recovering after an illness or injury.

Word Link *itis ≈ inflammation : arthritis, hepatitis, meningitis*

meningitis /ˌmenɪnˈdʒaɪtɪs/ N-UNCOUNT **Meningitis** is a serious infectious illness which affects your brain and spinal cord.

menopause /ˈmenəpɔːz/ N-SING **The menopause** is the time during which a woman stops menstruating, usually when she is about fifty. ● **menopausal** ADJ ❑ *...a menopausal woman.*

menstrual /ˈmenstruəl/ ADJ BEFORE N **Menstrual** means relating to menstruation. ❑ *...the menstrual cycle.*

menstruate /ˈmenstrueɪt/ (**menstruates, menstruating, menstruated**) V-I When a woman **menstruates**, a flow of blood comes from her womb. Women menstruate once a month. [FORMAL] ● **menstruation** N-UNCOUNT ❑ *...the cycles of menstruation and fertility.*

menswear /ˈmenzweə/ N-UNCOUNT **Menswear** is clothing for men.

Word Link *ment ≈ mind : demented, mental, mentality*

mental /ˈmentəl/ **1** ADJ BEFORE N **Mental** means relating to the mind and the process of thinking. ❑ *...the mental development of children.* ● **mentally** ADV ❑ *He became mentally ill.* **2** ADJ BEFORE N A **mental** act is one that involves only thinking and not physical action. ❑ *...mental arithmetic.* ● **mentally** ADV ❑ *I mentally rehearsed what I would do.*

mentality /menˈtælɪti/ (**mentalities**) N-COUNT Your **mentality** is your attitudes or ways of thinking. ❑ *...the criminal mentality.*

mention /ˈmenʃən/ (**mentions, mentioning, mentioned**) **1** V-T & N-VAR If you **mention** something, or if you give a **mention** to it, you say something about it, usually briefly. ❑ *I did not mention it to her.* ❑ *She mentioned that it was her husband's birthday.* ❑ *There was no mention of elections.* **2** PHRASE You use **not to mention** when you want to add extra information which emphasizes the point that you are making. ❑ *The audience, not to mention the actors, were not amused.*

Word Partnership Use *mention* with:

V. **fail to** mention, **forget to** mention, **make *no*** mention **of *someone/something***, **neglect to** mention **1**

mentor /ˈmentɔː/ (**mentors**) N-COUNT Someone's **mentor** is a person who teaches them and gives them a lot of advice over a period of time. [FORMAL] ❑ *...his political mentor.*

menu /ˈmenjuː/ (**menus**) **1** N-COUNT In a restaurant or café, the **menu** is a list of the available meals and drinks. ❑ *They ordered everything on the menu.* **2** N-COUNT On a computer, a **menu** is a list of choices of things you can do using the computer. [COMPUTING]

MEP /ˌem iː ˈpiː/ (**MEPs**) N-COUNT An **MEP** is a person who has been elected to the European Parliament. **MEP** is an abbreviation for 'Member of the European Parliament'.

mercenary /ˈmɜːsənri, AM -neri/ (**mercenaries**) **1** N-COUNT A **mercenary** is a soldier who is paid to fight by a country or group that he or she does not belong to. **2** ADJ If you describe someone as **mercenary**, you mean that they are only interested in the money that they can get from a particular person or situation.

Word Link ***merc ≈ trading : commerce, merchandise, merchant***

merchandise /ˈmɜːtʃəndaɪz, -daɪs/ N-UNCOUNT **Merchandise** is goods that are bought or sold. [FORMAL] ❑ *The merchandise is reasonably priced.*

merchandising /ˈmɜːtʃəndaɪzɪŋ/ N-UNCOUNT **Merchandising** is used to refer to the way shops and businesses organize the sale of their products, for example the way they are displayed and the prices that are chosen.

merchant /ˈmɜːtʃənt/ (**merchants**) 1 N-COUNT A **merchant** is a person whose business is buying or selling goods in large quantities. ❑ *...a carpet merchant.* 2 ADJ BEFORE N **Merchant** seamen or ships are involved in carrying goods for trade.

mercifully /ˈmɜːsɪfʊli/ ADV You can use **mercifully** to show that you are glad about something, because it avoids a dangerous or unpleasant situation. ❑ *Mercifully, a friend came to the rescue.* ❑ *Crime is mercifully rare here.*

merciless /ˈmɜːsɪləs/ ADJ If you describe someone as **merciless**, you mean that they are very cruel or determined and do not show any concern for the effect their actions have on other people. ● **mercilessly** ADV ❑ *We teased him mercilessly.*

mercury /ˈmɜːkjʊri/ N-UNCOUNT **Mercury** is a silver-coloured liquid metal, used in thermometers.

mercy /ˈmɜːsi/ 1 N-UNCOUNT If someone in authority shows **mercy**, they choose not to harm or punish someone they have power over. ❑ *They cried for mercy.* 2 PHRASE If you are **at the mercy of** something or someone, you cannot prevent yourself being affected or harmed by them. ❑ *The islands of the Caribbean are always at the mercy of the weather.*

mere /mɪə/ (**merest**) ADJ BEFORE N You use **mere** to emphasize how unimportant, insufficient, or small something is. **Mere** does not have a comparative form. The superlative form **merest** is used for emphasis, rather than in comparisons. ❑ *Tickets are a mere £7.50.* ❑ *She avoided even the merest touch of his hand.* ● **merely** ADV ❑ *The brain accounts for merely three per cent of body weight.*

merely /ˈmɪəli/ 1 ADV You use **merely** to emphasize that something is only what you say and not better, more important, or more exciting. ❑ *She knows when he is merely being polite.* 2 ADV You use **not merely** before the less important of two statements, as a way of emphasizing the more important statement. ❑ *These were not merely crimes of theft but of violence.*

Word Link ***merg ≈ sinking : emerge, merge, submerge***

merge /mɜːdʒ/ (**merges, merging, merged**) V-T/V-I If one thing **merges with** another, or if one thing **is merged with** another, they combine or come together to make one whole thing. ❑ *The two countries merged into one.* ❑ *We've merged the old with the new.*

merger /ˈmɜːdʒə/ (**mergers**) N-COUNT A **merger** is the joining together of two separate companies or organizations so that they become one. ❑ *...the merger of two Japanese banks.*

merit /ˈmerɪt/ (**merits, meriting, merited**) 1 N-VAR If you refer to the **merit** or **merits** of something, you mean that it has good or useful qualities. ❑ *Their best work has great artistic merit.* ❑ *Both projects have their merits.* 2 V-T If someone or something **merits** a particular action or treatment, they are good, important, or serious enough for someone to treat them in this way. [FORMAL] ❑ *Such ideas merit careful consideration.* 3 PHRASE If you judge something or someone **on merit** or **on** their **merits**, your judgement is based on their actual qualities, rather than on particular rules, traditions, or prejudices. ❑ *Everybody is selected on merit.* ❑ *Each case is judged on its merits.*

mermaid /ˈmɜːmeɪd/ (**mermaids**) N-COUNT In fairy stories and legends, a **mermaid** is a woman with a fish's tail instead of legs, who lives in the sea.

merry /ˈmeri/ ADJ **Merry** means happy and cheerful. ❑ *...a merry little tune.* ❑ *We wished them a Merry Christmas.* ● **merrily** ADV ❑ *Chris laughed merrily.*

mesh /meʃ/ (**meshes, meshing, meshed**) 1 N-VAR **Mesh** is material like a net made from wire, thread, or plastic. ❑ *...wire mesh.* 2 V-T/V-I If two things or ideas **mesh**, or if they **are meshed**, they go together well. ❑ *This story never quite meshed with the facts.*

mesmerize [BRIT also **mesmerise**] /ˈmezməraɪz/ (**mesmerizes, mesmerizing, mesmerized**) V-T If you **are mesmerized** by something, you are so fascinated by it that you cannot think about anything else. ❑ *I was mesmerized by his performance.*

mess /mes/ (**messes, messing, messed**) 1 N-SING If something is a **mess** or **in a mess**, it is dirty or untidy. ❑ *I'll clear up the mess later.* ❑ *The wrong shampoo can leave curly hair in a tangled mess.* 2 N-COUNT If you say that a situation is a **mess**, you mean that it is full of trouble or problems. You can also say that something is **in a mess.** ❑ *I've made such a mess of my life.* ❑ *This is why the economy is in such a mess.*

▶ **mess around** or **mess about** 1 PHR-VERB If you **mess around**, you spend time doing silly or casual things without any particular purpose or result. ❑ *Boys and girls enjoy messing about with machines.* 2 PHR-VERB If you say that someone **is messing around with** something, you mean that they are interfering with it in a harmful way. ❑ *Accidents can happen when people mess around with guns.*

▶ **mess up** 1 PHR-VERB If someone **messes** something **up**, or if they **mess up**, they cause something to fail or be spoiled. [INFORMAL] ❑ *He had messed up his career.* ❑ *If I messed up, I would probably be fired.* 2 PHR-VERB If you **mess up** a place or a thing, you make it untidy or dirty. ❑ *The builders messed up her flat.*

Word Partnership Use *mess* with:

V.	**clean up a** mess, **leave a** mess, **make a** mess 1 **get into a** mess 2

message /ˈmesɪdʒ/ (**messages**) 1 N-COUNT A **message** is a piece of information or a request that you send to someone or leave for them when you

m

Word Web metal

copper

aluminium

gold

In their natural state, most **metals** are not pure. They are usually combined with other materials in mixtures known as **ores**. Almost all metals are **shiny**. Many metals share these special properties. They are ductile, meaning that they can be made into **wire**. They are malleable and can be formed into thin, flat sheets. They are also good **conductors** of heat and electricity. Except for **copper** and **gold**, most metals are grey or silver in colour.

cannot speak to them directly. ❑ *I got a message you were trying to reach me.* **2** N-COUNT The **message** that someone is trying to communicate is the idea, argument, or opinion that they are trying to communicate. ❑ *I think they got the message that this is wrong.*

Word Partnership Use *message* with:

ADJ. **clear** message, **important** message, **urgent** message **1** **2**
powerful message, **simple** message, **strong** message, **wrong** message **2**

V. **give** ***someone*** **a** message, **leave a** message, **read a** message, **take a** message **1**
deliver a message, **get a** message, **hear a** message, **send a** message **1** **2**
get a message **across**, **spread a** message **2**

messenger /ˈmesɪndʒə/ (**messengers**) N-COUNT A **messenger** takes a message to someone, or takes messages regularly as their job. ❑ *The document was sent by messenger.*

Messiah /mɪˈsaɪə/ N-PROPER For Jews, **the Messiah** is a king or leader who will be sent to them by God. For Christians, **the Messiah** is Jesus Christ.

Messrs /ˈmesəz/ **Messrs** is used as the plural of **Mr** in front of the names of two or more men. [FORMAL] ❑ *Perhaps Messrs Bush and Blair should make this the next big issue.*

messy /ˈmesi/ **1** ADJ A **messy** person or activity makes things dirty or untidy. ❑ *She was a terribly messy cook.* ❑ *The work tends to be a bit messy.* **2** ADJ Something that is **messy** is dirty or untidy. ❑ *This first coat of paint looks messy.* **3** ADJ If you describe a situation as **messy**, you dislike it because it is confused or complicated. ❑ *Negotiations were messy and time-consuming.*

met /met/ **Met** is the past tense and past participle of **meet**.

metabolic /ˌmetəˈbɒlɪk/ ADJ BEFORE N **Metabolic** means relating to a person's or animal's metabolism. [TECHNICAL] ❑ *People who have a low metabolic rate will gain weight easily.*

Word Link ***meta ≈ beyond, change : metabolism, metamorphosis, metaphor***

metabolism /mɪˈtæbəlɪzəm/ (**metabolisms**) N-VAR Your **metabolism** is the way that chemical processes in your body cause food to be used in an efficient way, for example to give you energy. [TECHNICAL]

metal /ˈmetəl/ (**metals**) N-VAR **Metal** is a hard substance such as iron, steel, copper, or lead. ❑ *...furniture in wood, metal and glass.* ❑ *...a metal bar.*
→ see Word Web: **metal**
→ see **mineral**

metallic /məˈtælɪk/ ADJ **Metallic** things consist of metal or sound or look like they consist of metal. ❑ *...a metallic dish.* ❑ *There was a loud metallic sound.*

Word Link ***osis ≈ state or condition : diagnosis, hypnosis, metamorphosis***

metamorphosis /ˌmetəˈmɔːfəsɪs/ (**metamorphoses**) N-VAR When a **metamorphosis** occurs, a person or thing develops and changes into something completely different. [FORMAL] ❑ *...his metamorphosis from a Republican to a Democrat.*

metaphor /ˈmetəfɔːr/ (**metaphors**) N-VAR A **metaphor** is an imaginative way of describing something by referring to something else which has the qualities that you want to express. ❑ *She sees chess as a metaphor for life.*

metaphorical /ˌmetəˈfɒrɪkəl, AM -ˈfɔːr-/ ADJ You use **metaphorical** to indicate that you are not using words with their ordinary meaning, but are describing something by means of an image or symbol. ❑ *Salt is a metaphorical symbol in all religions.* ● **metaphorically** ADV ❑ *You're speaking metaphorically, I hope.*

mete /miːt/ (**metes, meting, meted**)
▸ **mete out** PHR-VERB To **mete out** a punishment means to punish someone. [FORMAL] ❑ *A two-year sentence was meted out to the convicted man.*

meteor /ˈmiːtiə/ (**meteors**) N-COUNT A **meteor** is a piece of rock flying through space, especially one that is shining or burning brightly.
→ see Word Web: **meteor**

meteorite /ˈmiːtiəraɪt/ (**meteorites**) N-COUNT A **meteorite** is a large piece of rock or metal from space that has landed on Earth.

meteorological /ˌmiːtiərəˈlɒdʒɪkəl/ ADJ BEFORE N **Meteorological** means relating to the weather or to weather forecasting. [TECHNICAL] ❑ *NASA publishes detailed maps and meteorological forecasts.*

meter /ˈmiːtə/ (**meters**) **1** N-COUNT A **meter** is a device that measures and records something such as the amount of gas or electricity that you have used. ❑ *...the electricity meter.* ❑ *...a parking meter.* **2** → see also **metre**

methane /ˈmiːθeɪn, AM ˈmeθ-/ N-UNCOUNT **Methane** is a colourless gas that has no smell.

method /ˈmeθəd/ (**methods**) N-VAR A **method**

Word Web meteor

As an asteroid flies through **space**, small pieces called meteoroids sometimes break off. When a meteoroid enters the earth's **atmosphere**, we call it a **meteor**. As the earth passes through asteroid belts we see spectacular **meteor showers**. Meteors that reach the earth are called meteorites. Scientists believe a huge meteorite struck the earth about 65 million years ago. It left a large hole in Mexico called the Chicxulub **Crater**. It's about 150 miles wide. The crash caused earthquakes and huge tidal waves called tsunamis. It may also have produced a change in the earth's environment. Some scientists believe this event caused the dinosaurs to die out.

is a particular way of doing something. ❑ *E-mail is an informal method of communication.* ❑ *...new teaching methods.*
→ see **experiment, science**

Thesaurus *method* Also look up:
N. manner, procedure, process, system, technique

Word Partnership Use *method* with:
ADJ. **alternative/traditional** method, **best** method, **effective** method, **new** method, **preferred** method, **scientific** method
N. method **of payment**, **teaching** method
V. **develop a** method, **use a** method

methodical /mə'θɒdɪkəl/ ADJ If you describe someone as **methodical**, you mean that they do things carefully, thoroughly, and in order. ❑ *Da Vinci was methodical in his research.* • **methodically** ADV ❑ *She methodically put the things into her suitcase.*

methodology /ˌmeθə'dɒlədʒi/ (**methodologies**) N-VAR A **methodology** is a system of methods and principles for doing something. [FORMAL] ❑ *Teaching methodologies vary according to the topic.* • **methodological** ADJ ❑ *...methodological disagreements.*

meticulous /mə'tɪkjʊləs/ ADJ If someone is **meticulous**, they do things very carefully and with great attention to detail. • **meticulously** ADV ❑ *The flat has been meticulously cleaned.*

metre [AM **meter**] /'miːtə/ (**metres**) N-COUNT A **metre** is a unit of length equal to 100 centimetres. ❑ *The scarf is 2.3 metres long.*
→ see **measurement**

metric /'metrɪk/ ADJ The **metric** system of measurement uses metres, grammes, and litres.

metro /'metrəʊ/ (**metros**) N-COUNT **The metro** is the underground railway system in some cities, for example in Paris.
→ see **transportation**

Word Link *poli ≈ city : cosmopolitan, metropolis, politics*

metropolis /mə'trɒpəlɪs/ (**metropolises**) N-COUNT You can refer to a large, important, busy city as a **metropolis**. ❑ *New York remains my favourite metropolis.*

metropolitan /ˌmetrə'pɒlɪtən/ ADJ BEFORE N **Metropolitan** means belonging to or typical of a large busy city. ❑ *...major metropolitan hospitals.*

mg **mg** is a written abbreviation for **milligram** or **milligrams**. ❑ *...300 mg of calcium.*

mice /maɪs/ **Mice** is the plural of **mouse**.

microbe /'maɪkrəʊb/ (**microbes**) N-COUNT A **microbe** is a very small living thing, which you can only see with a microscope.

Word Link *micro ≈ small : microchip, microeconomics, microscope*

microchip /'maɪkrəʊtʃɪp/ (**microchips**) N-COUNT A **microchip** is a small piece of silicon inside a computer, on which electronic circuits are printed. [COMPUTING]

microcosm /'maɪkrəʊkɒzəm/ (**microcosms**) N-COUNT A place or event that is a **microcosm of** a larger one has all the main features of the larger one and seems like a smaller version of it. [FORMAL] ❑ *In many ways, Pennsylvania is a microcosm of the United States.*

ˌmicro-'organism (**micro-organisms**) N-COUNT A **micro-organism** is a very small living thing which you can only see with a microscope. [TECHNICAL]
→ see **fungus**

Word Link *phon ≈ sound : microphone, symphony, telephone*

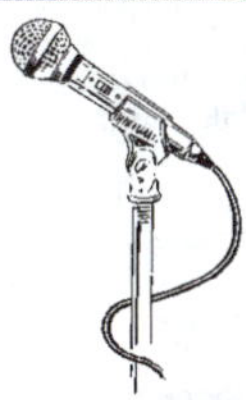

microphone

microphone /'maɪkrəfəʊn/ (**microphones**) N-COUNT A **microphone** is a device used to record sounds or make them louder.
→ see **concert**

microprocessor /ˌmaɪkrəʊ'prəʊsesə/ (**microprocessors**) N-COUNT A **microprocessor** is a microchip which can be programmed to do a large number of tasks or calculations.

Word Link *scope ≈ looking : horoscope, microscope, telescope*

microscope /'maɪkrəskəʊp/ (**microscopes**) N-COUNT A **microscope** is an instrument which magnifies very small objects so that you can study them.

microscopic /ˌmaɪkrə'skɒpɪk/ ADJ **Microscopic** objects are extremely small, and usually can be seen only through a microscope. ❑ *...microscopic plants and animals.*

microwave /ˈmaɪkrəʊweɪv/ (**microwaves, microwaving, microwaved**) **1** N-COUNT A **microwave** or a **microwave oven** is an oven which cooks food very quickly by a kind of radiation rather than by heat. **2** V-T To **microwave** food or drink means to cook or heat it in a microwave oven.
→ see **cook**

ˌmid-ˈair also **midair** N-UNCOUNT If something happens **in mid-air**, it happens in the air rather than on the ground. ❑ *The aircraft exploded in mid-air.* ❑ *...a mid-air collision.*

midday /ˌmɪdˈdeɪ/ N-UNCOUNT **Midday** is twelve o'clock in the middle of the day.

middle /ˈmɪdəl/ (**middles**) **1** N-COUNT The **middle** of something is the part that is farthest from its edges, ends, or outside surface. ❑ *Howard stood in the middle of the room.* ❑ *She made sure that the roast potatoes weren't raw in the middle.* **2** ADJ BEFORE N The **middle** thing or person in a row or series is the one with an equal number of things or people on each side, or before it and after it. ❑ *The middle drawer contained socks.* ❑ *...the middle child in a family of seven children.* **3** N-SING & ADJ BEFORE N The **middle** of an event or period of time, or the **middle** part of it, is the part that comes after the first part and before the last part. ❑ *I woke up in the middle of the night.* ❑ *...the middle years of the twentieth century.* **4** ADJ BEFORE N The **middle** course or way is a moderate course of action that lies between two opposite and extreme courses. ❑ *It was an attempt to find a middle way between doing nothing and doing everything.* **5** PHRASE If you are **in the middle of** doing something, you are busy doing it. ❑ *I'm in the middle of writing a book.* **6** **the middle of nowhere** → see **nowhere**

M

ˌmiddle ˈage N-UNCOUNT **Middle age** is the period in your life when you are between about 40 and 60 years old.

ˌmiddle-ˈaged ADJ **Middle-aged** people are between the ages of about 40 and 60.
→ see **age**

ˌmiddle ˈclass (**middle classes**) N-COUNT & ADJ **The middle class** or **middle classes** are the people in a society who are not working class or upper class, for example managers, doctors, and lawyers. You can say people like this are **middle class**. ❑ *...middle-class voters.*

ˌMiddle ˈEast N-PROPER **The Middle East** is the area around the eastern Mediterranean that includes Iran and all the countries in Asia that are to the west and south-west of Iran. ❑ *...the two great rivers of the Middle East.*

middleman /ˈmɪdəlmæn/ (**middlemen**) **1** N-COUNT A **middleman** is a person or company that buys things from the people who produce them and sells them to other people at a profit. **2** N-COUNT A **middleman** is a person who helps in negotiations between people who are unwilling to meet each other directly. ❑ *The two sides would only meet indirectly, through middlemen.*

Word Link	***mid* ≈ *middle* : *midland, midnight, midweek***

Midlands /ˈmɪdləndz/ N-PROPER **The Midlands** is the region in the central part of a country, in particular the central part of England.

midnight /ˈmɪdnaɪt/ N-UNCOUNT **Midnight** is twelve o'clock in the middle of the night.
→ see **time**

midst /mɪdst/ **1** PHRASE If you are **in the midst of** doing something, you are doing it at present. ❑ *Susan's students are in the midst of their first research project.* **2** PHRASE If something happens **in the midst of** a situation or an event, it happens during that situation or event. ❑ *Eleanor arrived in the midst of a storm.* **3** PHRASE If someone or something is **in the midst of** a group of people or things, they are among them or surrounded by them. ❑ *...a house in the midst of huge trees.*

midway /ˌmɪdˈweɪ/ **1** ADV & ADJ BEFORE N If something is **midway between** two places, it is between them and the same distance from each of them. ❑ *...a cottage midway between London and Oxford.* ❑ *...the midway point between Gloucester, Hereford and Worcester.* **2** ADV & ADJ BEFORE N If something happens **midway through** a period of time, it happens during the middle part of it. ❑ *He returned midway through the afternoon.* ❑ *...the midway point in the season.*

midweek /ˌmɪdˈwiːk/ ADJ BEFORE N & ADV **Midweek** describes something that happens in the middle of the week. ❑ *...midweek flights from Gatwick.* ❑ *They'll be able to go up to London midweek.*

midwife /ˈmɪdwaɪf/ (**midwives**) N-COUNT A **midwife** is a nurse who advises pregnant women and helps them to give birth.

might /maɪt/ **1** MODAL You use **might** to indicate that something will possibly happen or be true in the future. ❑ *I might regret it later.* ❑ *He might not be back until tonight.* **2** MODAL You use **might** to indicate that there is a possibility that something is true. ❑ *You might be right.* ❑ *He might not be interested in her any more.* ❑ *I heard what might have been an explosion.* **3** MODAL You use **might** to make a suggestion or to give advice in a very polite way. ❑ *'You might sound slightly more enthusiastic!' he said.* ❑ *I thought we might go for a drive on Sunday.* **4** MODAL You use **might** as a polite way of interrupting someone, asking a question, making a request, or introducing what you are going to say next. [FORMAL, SPOKEN] ❑ *Might I make a suggestion?* ❑ *Might I trouble you for some more tea?* **5** N-UNCOUNT **Might** is power or strength. [FORMAL] ❑ *The might of the army was a decisive factor.*

mightn't /ˈmaɪtənt/ **Mightn't** is a spoken form of 'might not'.

might've /ˈmaɪtəv/ **Might've** is the usual spoken form of 'might have', especially when 'have' is an auxiliary verb.

mighty /ˈmaɪti/ (**mightier, mightiest**) **1** ADJ **Mighty** means very large or powerful. [LITERARY] ❑ *...a mighty explosion.* ❑ *...one of the mightiest armies in history.* **2** ADV **Mighty** means very. [AM, INFORMAL] ❑ *You look mighty pretty tonight.*

migraine /ˈmiːgreɪn, AM ˈmaɪ-/ (**migraines**) N-VAR A **migraine** is a very severe headache.

Word Link	***migr* ≈ *moving, changing* : *emigrate, immigrant, migrant***

migrant /ˈmaɪgrənt/ (**migrants**) N-COUNT A **migrant** is a person who moves from one place to another, especially in order to find work. ❑ *...migrant workers.*

migrate /maɪ'greɪt, AM 'maɪgreɪt/ (**migrates, migrating, migrated**) **1** V-I If people **migrate**, they move from one place to another, especially in order to find work. ❑ *Peasants have migrated from the countryside to the cities.* ● **migration** (**migrations**) N-VAR ❑ *...the migration of Soviet Jews to Israel.* **2** V-I When birds, fish, or animals **migrate**, they go and live in a different area for part of the year, in order to breed or to find food. ● **migration** N-VAR ❑ *...the migration of birds.*

mike /maɪk/ (**mikes**) N-COUNT A **mike** is a microphone. [INFORMAL]

mild /maɪld/ (**milder, mildest**) **1** ADJ Something that is **mild** is not very strong or severe. ❑ *...a mild onion flavour.* ❑ *...a mild headache.* ● **mildly** ADV ❑ *...mildly spiced rice.* ❑ *She looked mildly amused.* **2** ADJ **Mild** weather is less cold than usual. **3** → See note at **hot**

mile /maɪl/ (**miles**) **1** N-COUNT A **mile** is a unit of distance equal to approximately 1.6 kilometres. ❑ *These animals usually swim no faster than five miles per hour.* **2** N-PLURAL **Miles** is used to refer to a long distance. ❑ *The nearest doctor is miles away.* ❑ *'Shall I come to see you?'—'Are you kidding? It's miles.'*
→ see **measurement**

Word Partnership	Use *mile* with:
ADJ.	mile **high**, mile **long**, **nautical** mile, **square** mile, mile **wide** **1**

mileage /'maɪlɪdʒ/ (**mileages**) **1** N-VAR **Mileage** refers to a distance that is travelled, measured in miles. ❑ *They kept track of their mileage.* **2** N-UNCOUNT The **mileage** in a particular course of action is its usefulness in getting you what you want. ❑ *They hope to get political mileage out of such stories.*

milestone /'maɪlstəʊn/ (**milestones**) N-COUNT A **milestone** is an important event in the history or development of something. ❑ *The decision is a milestone in relations between the two countries.*

milieu /'mi:ljɜ:, AM mɪ'lju:/ (**milieux** or **milieus**) N-COUNT The **milieu** in which you live or work is the group of people that you live or work among. [FORMAL] ❑ *...a very different cultural milieu.*

militant /'mɪlɪtənt/ (**militants**) ADJ & N-COUNT Someone who is **militant**, or who is a **militant**, is active in trying to bring about political change. ❑ *...one of the most militant unions.* ❑ *...an attack by militants.* ● **militancy** N-UNCOUNT ❑ *...the growing militancy of university students.*

Word Link	*milit ≈ soldier : demilitarize, military, militia*

military /'mɪlɪtri, AM -teri/ **1** ADJ **Military** means relating to a country's armed forces. ❑ *Military action became necessary.* ● **militarily** /ˌmɪlɪ'teərɪli/ ADV ❑ *US troops won militarily in Saigon but lost politically in Washington.* **2** N-SING **The military** are the armed forces of a country. **Military** can take the singular or plural form of the verb. ❑ *Did you serve in the military?*
→ see **army**

militia /mɪ'lɪʃə/ (**militias**) N-COUNT A **militia** is an organization that operates like an army but whose members are not professional soldiers.
→ see **army**

milk /mɪlk/ (**milks, milking, milked**) **1** N-UNCOUNT **Milk** is the white liquid produced by cows and goats, which people drink and make into butter, cheese, and yoghurt. **2** V-T When someone **milks** a cow or goat, they get milk from it from an organ called the udder, which hangs beneath its body. ● **milking** N-UNCOUNT ❑ *He helped to bring in the cows for milking.* **3** N-UNCOUNT **Milk** is the white liquid produced by women to feed their babies. **4** V-T If you say that someone **milks** something, you mean that they get as much benefit or profit as they can from it, without caring about other people; used showing disapproval. ❑ *The couple milked money from a hospital charity for themselves.*
→ see **dairy**

milky /'mɪlki/ **1** ADJ Something that is **milky** in colour is pale white. ❑ *A milky mist filled the valley.* **2** ADJ **Milky** food or drink contains a lot of milk. ❑ *...milky coffee.*

mill /mɪl/ (**mills, milling, milled**) **1** N-COUNT A **mill** is a building where grain is crushed to make flour. **2** N-COUNT A **mill** is a small device used for grinding something such as coffee or pepper. ❑ *...a pepper mill.* **3** N-COUNT A **mill** is a factory used for making and processing materials such as steel, wool, or cotton.
▶ **mill around** or **mill about** PHR-VERB When a crowd of people **are milling around**, they are moving around in a disorganized way. ❑ *A lot of people were milling around outside.*

Word Link	*mill ≈ thousand : millennium, millilitre, million*

millennium /mɪ'leniəm/ (**millennia** or **millenniums**) N-COUNT A **millennium** is a thousand years.

Word Link	*milli ≈ thousandth : milligram, millilitre, millimetre*

milligram also **milligramme** /'mɪlɪgræm/ (**milligrams**) N-COUNT A **milligram** is a metric unit of weight equal to one thousandth of a gram. ❑ *...0.5 milligrams of mercury.*

millilitre [AM **milliliter**] /'mɪlɪli:tə/ (**millilitres**) N-COUNT A **millilitre** is a metric unit of volume for liquids and gases that is equal to a thousandth of a litre. ❑ *...100 millilitres of blood.*

millimetre [AM **millimeter**] /'mɪlɪmi:tə/ (**millimetres**) N-COUNT A **millimetre** is a metric unit of length equal to one tenth of a centimetre. ❑ *The dots are only a quarter of a millimetre across.*

million /'mɪliən/ (**millions**) **1** NUM **A million** or **one million** is the number 1,000,000. **2** QUANT People say that there are **millions of** people or things when they are emphasizing that there is a very large number of them. ❑ *The programme was viewed on television in millions of homes.* ❑ *This war has brought misery to millions.*

millionaire /ˌmɪliə'neə/ (**millionaires**) N-COUNT A **millionaire** is someone who has money or property worth at least a million pounds or dollars.

millionth /'mɪliənθ/ (**millionths**) ORD The **millionth** item in a series is the one you count as number one million.

Word Link *mim ≈ copying : mime, mimic, pantomime*

mime /maɪm/ (**mimes, miming, mimed**) 1 N-VAR **Mime** is the use of movements and gestures to express something or tell a story without using speech. ❑ *...a mime artist.* 2 V-T If you **mime** something, you describe or express it using mime rather than speech. ❑ *I remember asking her to mime getting up in the morning.*

mimic /ˈmɪmɪk/ (**mimics, mimicking, mimicked**) 1 V-T If you **mimic** someone's actions or voice, you imitate them in an amusing or entertaining way. ❑ *He could mimic anybody.* 2 N-COUNT A **mimic** is a person who is able to mimic people.

min. **Min.** is a written abbreviation for **minimum**, or for **minutes** or **minute**.

mince /mɪns/ (**minces, mincing, minced**) 1 N-UNCOUNT In British English, **mince** is meat cut into very small pieces. The usual American word is **hamburger meat.** 2 V-T If you **mince** food such as meat, you cut it into very small pieces. 3 PHRASE If you say someone does not **mince** their **words** or does not **mince words,** you mean they speak in a forceful direct way, especially when saying something unpleasant to someone.
→ see **cut**

mind
❶ THINKING
❷ EXPRESSING OPINION
❸ CARE

mind /maɪnd/ (**minds**)
❶ 1 N-COUNT Your **mind** is your ability to think and reason. You also talk about someone having a particular type of **mind** when it is part of their character, or a result of their education or professional training. ❑ *She has a very good analytical mind.* ❑ *Andrew, you have a very suspicious mind.* 2 PHRASE If you say that an idea or possibility never **crossed** your **mind**, you mean that you did not think of it. 3 PHRASE If you see something **in** your **mind's eye**, you are able to imagine it clearly in your mind. ❑ *In his mind's eye, he could see the headlines in the newspapers.* 4 PHRASE If you tell someone to **bear** something **in mind** or to **keep** something **in mind**, you are reminding or warning them about something important which they should think about and remember. 5 PHRASE If you **make up** your **mind** or **make** your **mind up**, you decide which of a number of possible things you will have or do. 6 PHRASE If something is **on** your **mind**, you are worried or concerned about it and think about it a lot. ❑ *This game has been on my mind all week.* 7 PHRASE If your **mind is on** something or you **have** your **mind on** something, you are thinking about that thing rather than something else. ❑ *He tried to read but his mind was on other things.* 8 PHRASE If you **have** or **keep an open mind**, you avoid forming an opinion or making a decision until you know all the facts. ❑ *Police kept an open mind about the death.* 9 PHRASE If you say that someone is **out of** their **mind**, you mean that they are mad or very foolish. 10 PHRASE Your **state of mind** is your mental state at a particular time. ❑ *Over time the patient's state of mind gradually improved.* 11 PHRASE If something **takes** your **mind off** a problem or unpleasant situation, it helps you to forget about it for a while.

mind /maɪnd/ (**minds, minding, minded**)
❷ 1 V-T/V-I If you **do not mind** something, you are not annoyed or bothered by it. ❑ *Do you mind being alone?* ❑ *I hope you don't mind me calling in like this, without an appointment.* ❑ *It involved a little extra work, but nobody seemed to mind.* 2 V-T If someone **does not mind what** happens or **what** something is like, they do not have a strong preference for any particular thing. ❑ *I don't mind what we play, really.* 3 PHRASE If you **change** your **mind**, or if someone or something **changes** your **mind**, you change a decision you have made or an opinion that you had. 4 PHRASE You use **never mind** to tell someone that you do not think that they need to do something or worry about something. ❑ *'I'll go up in one second, I promise.'—'Never mind,' I said with a sigh. 'I'll do it.'* ❑ *'Was his name David?'—'No I don't think it was, but never mind, go on.'* 5 PHRASE You use **to my mind** to indicate that the statement you are making is your own opinion. ❑ *There are scenes in this play which to my mind are incredibly violent.* 6 PHRASE If you say that you **wouldn't mind** something, you mean that you would quite like it. ❑ *I wouldn't mind a coffee.* ❑ *Anne wouldn't mind going to Italy to live.*

mind /maɪnd/ (**minds, minding, minded**)
❸ 1 V-T If you tell someone to **mind** something or to **mind** that they do something, you are warning them to be careful so that they do not hurt themselves or other people, or damage something. ❑ *Mind that bike!* ❑ *Mind you don't burn those sausages.* 2 V-T If you **mind** a child or something such as a shop or luggage, you look after it, usually while the person who owns it or is usually responsible for it is elsewhere. ❑ *Jim will mind the store while I'm away.*

minder /ˈmaɪndə/ (**minders**) N-COUNT A **minder** is a person whose job is to protect someone such as a celebrity or businessman.

mindful /ˈmaɪndfʊl/ ADJ AFTER LINK-V If you are **mindful of** something, you think about it and consider it when taking action. [FORMAL] ❑ *Always be mindful of safety.*

mindless /ˈmaɪndləs/ 1 ADJ If you describe a destructive action as **mindless**, you mean that it is not at all sensible and is done for no good reason. ❑ *...mindless violence.* 2 ADJ If you describe an activity as **mindless**, you mean that it is so dull that people do it without thinking. ❑ *...the mindless repetitiveness of some tasks.* • **mindlessly** ADV ❑ *...mindlessly banging a tennis ball against the wall.*

mine /maɪn/ (**mines, mining, mined**) 1 PRON **Mine** is the first person singular possessive pronoun. A speaker or writer uses **mine** to indicate that something belongs or relates to himself or herself. ❑ *She was seated at the table next to mine.* ❑ *That wasn't his fault; it was mine.* 2 N-COUNT A **mine** is a place where deep holes or tunnels are dug under the ground in order to extract minerals. ❑ *...a coal mine.* 3 V-T When a mineral **is mined**, it is obtained from the ground by digging deep holes and tunnels. ❑ *He started mining coal at the age of ten.* • **miner** (**miners**) N-COUNT ❑ *My father was a miner.* • **mining** N-UNCOUNT ❑ *...traditional industries such as coal mining.* 4 N-COUNT A **mine** is a bomb hidden in the ground or in water which explodes when something touches it.

Word Web mineral

The **extraction** of **minerals** from ore is an ancient process. Neolithic man discovered **copper** around 8000 BC. Using fire and charcoal, they **reduced** the ore to its pure **metal** form. About 4,000 years later, Egyptians learned to pour hot, melted copper into moulds. **Silver** ore often contains large amounts of copper and **lead**. Silver **refineries** often use the **smelting** process to remove these other metals from the silver. Most **gold** does not exist as an ore. Instead, veins of gold run through the earth. Refiners use chemicals such as cyanide to get pure gold.

minefield /'maɪnfi:ld/ (**minefields**) N-COUNT A **minefield** is an area of land or water where explosive mines have been hidden.

mineral /'mɪnərəl/ (**minerals**) N-COUNT A **mineral** is a substance such as tin, salt, or coal that is formed naturally in rocks and in the earth.
→ see Word Web: **mineral**
→ see **rock**

'mineral ˌwater (**mineral waters**) N-VAR **Mineral water** is water that comes out of the ground naturally and is considered healthy to drink.

mingle /'mɪŋgəl/ (**mingles, mingling, mingled**) **1** V-I If things such as sounds, smells, or feelings **mingle**, they become mixed together but are usually still recognizable. ❑ *Relief mingled with anxiety.* ❑ *I breathed in the mingled smells of earth and smoke.* **2** V-I If you **mingle**, you move among a group of people, chatting to different people. ❑ *Guests ate and mingled.* ❑ *Reporters mingled freely with the crowd.*

mingle

Word Link *mini ≈ very small : mini**ature**, mini**bus**, mini**disc***

miniature /'mɪnɪtʃə, AM 'mɪniətʃʊr/ (**miniatures**) **1** ADJ BEFORE N **Miniature** things are much smaller than other things of the same kind. ❑ *...miniature roses.* **2** PHRASE If you describe one thing as another thing **in miniature**, you mean that it is much smaller than the other thing, but is otherwise exactly the same. ❑ *Ecuador provides a perfect introduction to South America; it's a continent in miniature.* **3** N-COUNT A **miniature** is a very small detailed painting, often of a person.

minibus /'mɪnibʌs/ (**minibuses**) N-COUNT A **minibus** is a large van which has seats in the back and windows along its sides. ❑ *He was taken by minibus to the swimming pool.*

minidisc /'mɪnidɪsk/ (**minidiscs**) N-COUNT A **minidisc** is a small compact disc which you can record music or data on. Minidisc is a trademark.

Word Link *minim ≈ smallest : minim**al**, minim**ize**, minim**um***

minimal /'mɪnɪməl/ ADJ Something that is **minimal** is very small in quantity or degree. ❑ *The co-operation between the two is minimal.* ● **minimally** ADV ❑ *He was paid, but only minimally.*

minimalist /'mɪnɪməlɪst/ (**minimalists**) ADJ & N-COUNT **Minimalist** ideas, artists, or designers are influenced by a style in which a small number of very simple things are used to create a particular effect. Artists and designers like this are called **minimalists.** ❑ *The two designers settled upon a minimalist approach.* ● **minimalism** N-UNCOUNT ❑ *...chic minimalism.*

minimize [BRIT also **minimise**] /'mɪnɪmaɪz/ (**minimizes, minimizing, minimized**) **1** V-T If you **minimize** a risk or problem, you reduce it to the lowest possible level. ❑ *It's worth trying to minimize the risk of accidents.* **2** V-T If you **minimize** something, you make it seem smaller or less important than it really is. ❑ *At his trial, he tried to minimize his behaviour.* **3** V-T If you **minimize** a window on a computer screen, you make it very small, because you do not want to use it.

minimum /'mɪnɪməm/ **1** ADJ BEFORE N & N-SING A **minimum** amount of something, or a **minimum**, is the smallest amount that is possible, allowed, or required. ❑ *...five feet nine, the minimum height for a policeman.* ❑ *This will take a minimum of one hour.* **2** ADJ BEFORE N & N-SING You use **minimum**, or a **minimum**, to state how small an amount is. ❑ *He does his job with a minimum of complaining.*

Word Partnership Use *minimum* with:

ADJ.	**absolute** minimum, **bare** minimum **1** **2**
N.	minimum **age**, minimum **balance**, minimum **payment**, minimum **purchase**, minimum **requirement**, minimum **salary** **1**

mining /'maɪnɪŋ/ → see **mine**
→ see **industry, tunnel**

minister /'mɪnɪstə/ (**ministers, ministering, ministered**) **1** N-COUNT A **minister** is a person who is in charge of a government department. ❑ *...the new Defence Minister.* **2** → See note at **government** **3** N-COUNT A **minister** is a member of the clergy, especially in a Protestant church. **4** V-I If you **minister to** people or **to** their needs, you serve them or help them, for example by making sure that they have everything they need or want. ❑ *For 44 years he ministered to the poor.*

ministerial /ˌmɪnɪ'stɪəriəl/ ADJ BEFORE N **Ministerial** means relating to government ministers. ❑ *A ministerial meeting was held today.*

ministry /'mɪnɪstri/ (**ministries**) **1** N-COUNT A **ministry** is a government department. ❑ *...the Ministry of Justice.* **2** N-COUNT The **ministry** of a

m

religious person is the work that they do that is inspired by their religious beliefs. ❑ *His ministry is among the poor.* 3 N-SING Members of the clergy belonging to some branches of the Christian church are referred to as **the ministry**. ❑ *So what prompted him to enter the ministry?*

mink /mɪŋk/

The plural is **mink** or **minks**.

1 N-COUNT A **mink** is a small furry animal with highly valued fur. 2 N-UNCOUNT **Mink** is the fur of a mink. 3 N-COUNT A **mink** is a coat or other garment made from the fur of a mink.

minor /ˈmaɪnə/ (**minors**) 1 ADJ You use **minor** to describe something that is less important, serious, or significant than other things in a group or situation. ❑ *He had a minor role in the film.* ❑ *The problem is minor, and should be quickly overcome.* 2 N-COUNT A **minor** is a person who is still legally a child. In Britain, people are minors until they reach the age of eighteen.

Thesaurus *minor* Also look up:

ADJ. insignificant, lesser, small, unimportant; *(ant.)* important, major, significant 1

Word Partnership Use *minor* with:

N. minor **adjustment**, minor **damage**, minor **detail**, minor **illness**, minor **injury**, minor **operation**, minor **problem**, minor **surgery** 1

ADV. **relatively** minor 1

minority /mɪˈnɒrɪti, AM -ˈnɔːr-/ (**minorities**) 1 N-SING If you talk about a **minority of** people or things in a larger group, you are referring to a number of them that forms less than half of the larger group. ❑ *In a tiny minority of cases mistakes were made.* ❑ *...a minority opinion.* 2 PHRASE If people are **in a minority** or **in the minority**, they belong to a group of people or things that form less than half of a larger group. 3 N-COUNT A **minority** is a group of people of the same race, culture, or religion who live in a place where most of the people around them are of a different race, culture, or religion. ❑ *...the region's ethnic minorities.*

Word Partnership Use *minority* with:

N. minority **leader**, minority **party** 1 minority **applicants**, minority **community**, minority **group**, minority **population**, minority **students**, minority **voters**, minority **women** 3

mint /mɪnt/ (**mints, minting, minted**) 1 N-UNCOUNT **Mint** is a fresh-tasting herb. 2 N-COUNT A **mint** is a sweet with a peppermint flavour. 3 N-SING **The mint** is the place where the official coins of a country are made. 4 V-T To **mint** coins or medals means to make them in a mint. ● **minting** N-UNCOUNT ❑ *...the minting of new gold coins.*

→ see **money**

Word Link *min* ≈ *small, less : diminish, minus, minute*

minus /ˈmaɪnəs/ (**minuses**) 1 CONJ You use **minus** to show that one number or quantity is being subtracted from another. ❑ *One minus one is zero.* ❑ *The winner gets $25, minus a 15% fee.* 2 ADJ **Minus** before a number or quantity means that the number or quantity is less than zero. ❑ *...temperatures of minus 65 degrees.* 3 PREP If someone or something is **minus** something, they do not have that thing. ❑ *He reappeared ten minutes later minus his tie.* 4 N-COUNT A **minus** is a disadvantage. ❑ *The minuses far outweigh that possible gain.*

Thesaurus *minus* Also look up:

PREP. without 3

N. deficiency, disadvantage, drawback 4

Word Link *cule* ≈ *small : minuscule, molecule, ridicule*

minuscule /ˈmɪnɪskjuːl/ ADJ If you describe something as **minuscule**, you mean it is very small. ❑ *The disease only affects a minuscule percentage of people.*

minute (**minutes**) 1 N-COUNT /ˈmɪnɪt/ A **minute** is one of the sixty equal parts of an hour. People often say **'a minute'** or **'minutes'** when they mean a short length of time. ❑ *The pizza will take about twenty minutes to cook.* ❑ *See you in a minute.* 2 CONVENTION People often use expressions such as **'wait a minute'** or **'just a minute'** when they want to stop you doing or saying something. ❑ *Wait a minute, everyone, something is wrong here.* 3 N-PLURAL The **minutes** of a meeting are the written records of the things that are discussed or decided at it. 4 ADJ /maɪˈnjuːt, AM -ˈnuːt/ If you say that something is **minute**, you mean that it is very small. ❑ *You only need a minute amount.* ● **minutely** ADV ❑ *...a minutely detailed description.* 5 PHRASE If you say that something will or may happen **at any minute** or **any minute now**, you are emphasizing that it is likely to happen very soon. 6 PHRASE A **last-minute** action is done at the latest time possible. ❑ *He will probably wait until the last minute.* 7 PHRASE You use **the next minute** or expressions such as '**one minute** he was there, **the next** he was gone' to emphasize that something happens suddenly. ❑ *The next minute my father came in.* 8 PHRASE If you say that something happens **the minute** something else happens, you are emphasizing that it happens immediately after the other thing. ❑ *The minute you do this, you'll lose control.* 9 PHRASE If you say that something must be done **this minute**, you mean that it must be done immediately. ❑ *Sit down this minute.*

→ see **time**

Word Partnership Use *minute* with:

DET. **a** minute **or two**, **another** minute, **each** minute, **every** minute, **half a** minute 1 **any** minute **now**, **at any** minute 2

V. **take a** minute, **wait a** minute 1 2

N. minute **detail**, minute **quantity of** ***something*** 4

miracle /ˈmɪrəkəl/ (**miracles**) **1** N-COUNT If you say that an event or invention is a **miracle**, you mean that it is very surprising and fortunate. ❑ *It is a miracle no one was killed.* **2** N-COUNT A **miracle** is a wonderful and surprising event that is believed to be caused by God.

miraculous /mɪˈrækjʊləs/ **1** ADJ If you describe something as **miraculous**, you mean that it is very surprising and fortunate. ❑ *The horse made a miraculous recovery.* ● **miraculously** ADV ❑ *Miraculously, the guards escaped death.* **2** ADJ If someone describes a wonderful event as **miraculous**, they believe the event has been caused by God. ● **miraculously** ADV ❑ *He was miraculously healed of a severe fever.*

mirror /ˈmɪrə/ (**mirrors, mirroring, mirrored**) **1** N-COUNT A **mirror** is an object made of glass in which you can see your reflection. **2** V-T If you see something reflected in water, you can say that the water **mirrors** it. [LITERARY] **3** V-T If something **mirrors** something else, it has similar features to it, and therefore seems like a copy or representation of it. ❑ *The book mirrors my own interests and experiences.*
→ see **telescope**

Word Partnership	Use *mirror* with:
N.	**reflection in a** mirror **1**
PREP.	**in front of a** mirror **1**
V.	**glance in a** mirror, **look in a** mirror, **reflect in a** mirror, **see in a** mirror **1**

miscalculate /ˌmɪsˈkælkjʊleɪt/ (**miscalculates, miscalculating, miscalculated**) V-T/V-I If you **miscalculate**, you make a mistake in judging a situation or in making a calculation. ❑ *He has badly miscalculated the mood of the people.* ● **miscalculation** (**miscalculations**) N-VAR ❑ *It is the single greatest miscalculation of his political career.*

miscarriage /ˌmɪsˈkærɪdʒ/ (**miscarriages**) N-COUNT If a woman has a **miscarriage**, she gives birth to a foetus before it is properly formed and it dies.

miscellaneous /ˌmɪsəˈleɪniəs/ ADJ BEFORE N A **miscellaneous** group consists of many different kinds of things or people that are difficult to put into a particular category. ❑ *...miscellaneous stories from around the world.*

mischief /ˈmɪstʃɪf/ **1** N-UNCOUNT **Mischief** is eagerness to have fun, especially by embarrassing people or by playing harmless tricks. ❑ *He was always up to mischief.* **2** N-UNCOUNT **Mischief** is trouble or harm that is caused by something. ❑ *People can get up to mischief when they're not employed.* ❑ *These old attitudes and prejudices have done so much mischief.*

mischievous /ˈmɪstʃɪvəs/ **1** ADJ A **mischievous** person is eager to have fun by embarrassing people or by playing harmless tricks. ● **mischievously** ADV ❑ *Kathryn winked mischievously.* **2** ADJ A **mischievous** act or suggestion is intended to cause trouble. ❑ *She dismissed the story as mischievous and false.*

misconception /ˌmɪskənˈsepʃən/ (**misconceptions**) N-COUNT A **misconception** is an idea that is not correct or which has been misunderstood. ❑ *These discussions bring to light misconceptions.*

misconduct /ˌmɪsˈkɒndʌkt/ N-UNCOUNT **Misconduct** is bad or unacceptable behaviour, especially by a professional person or someone who is normally respected by people. ❑ *She was found guilty of professional misconduct.*

misdemeanour [AM **misdemeanor**] /ˌmɪsdɪˈmiːnə/ (**misdemeanours**) N-COUNT A **misdemeanour** is an act that some people consider to be wrong or unacceptable. [FORMAL] ❑ *Emily knew nothing about her husband's misdemeanours.*

Word Link	***miser ≈ wretched : miserable, miserably, misery***

miserable /ˈmɪzərəbəl/ **1** ADJ If you are **miserable**, you are very unhappy. ● **miserably** ADV ❑ *He looked miserably down at his plate.* **2** ADJ A **miserable** place or **miserable** weather makes you feel depressed, for example because it is very dull. ❑ *It was a grey, wet, miserable day.*

Thesaurus	*miserable* Also look up:
ADJ.	unhappy **1**
	unfortunate, wretched **2**

misery /ˈmɪzəri/ (**miseries**) **1** N-VAR **Misery** is great unhappiness. ❑ *All their money brought nothing but sadness and misery.* **2** N-UNCOUNT **Misery** is the way of life and unpleasant living conditions of people who are very poor. ❑ *For years he lived in misery in a dirty apartment.*

misfit /ˈmɪsfɪt/ (**misfits**) N-COUNT A **misfit** is a person who is not easily accepted by other people, often because their behaviour is very different from that of everyone else.

misfortune /ˌmɪsˈfɔːtʃuːn/ (**misfortunes**) N-VAR A **misfortune** is something unpleasant or unlucky that happens to someone. ❑ *She seemed to enjoy the misfortunes of others.*

misgiving /ˌmɪsˈgɪvɪŋ/ (**misgivings**) N-VAR If you have **misgivings** about something that is being proposed or done, you feel that it is not quite right, and are worried that it may have undesirable consequences. ❑ *I had serious misgivings about the plan.*

misguided /ˌmɪsˈgaɪdɪd/ ADJ If you describe an opinion or plan as **misguided**, you are critical of it because you think it is based on a mistake or misunderstanding. ❑ *He is misguided in expecting honesty from her.*

mishap /ˈmɪshæp/ (**mishaps**) N-VAR A **mishap** is an unfortunate but not very serious event that happens to you. ❑ *After a number of mishaps she managed to get back to Germany.*

Word Link	***mis ≈ bad : misinterpret, misleading, mismanage***

misinterpret /ˌmɪsɪnˈtɜːprɪt/ (**misinterprets, misinterpreting, misinterpreted**) V-T If you **misinterpret** something, you understand it wrongly. ❑ *It was clear that he had misinterpreted the situation completely.* ● **misinterpretation** N-UNCOUNT ❑ *The message left no room for misinterpretation.*

misjudge /ˌmɪsˈdʒʌdʒ/ (**misjudges, misjudging, misjudged**) V-T If you say that someone **has misjudged** a person or situation, you mean that they have formed an incorrect idea or opinion about them, and often that they have made a wrong decision as a result of this. ❑ *Perhaps I had misjudged him, and he was not so selfish after all.*

mislead /ˌmɪsˈliːd/ (**misleads, misleading, misled**) V-T If you say that someone **has misled** you, you mean that they have made you believe something which is not true, either by telling you a lie or by giving you a wrong idea or impression.

Word Link	*mis ≈ bad : misinterpret, misleading, mismanage*

misleading /ˌmɪsˈliːdɪŋ/ ADJ If you describe something as **misleading**, you mean that it gives you a wrong idea or impression. ❑ *It would be misleading to say that we are friends.* ● **misleadingly** ADV ❑ *The data was presented misleadingly.*

misled /ˌmɪsˈled/ **Misled** is the past tense and past participle of **mislead**.

mismanage /ˌmɪsˈmænɪdʒ/ (**mismanages, mismanaging, mismanaged**) V-T To **mismanage** something means to manage it badly. ❑ *75% of voters think the President has mismanaged the economy.* ● **mismanagement** N-UNCOUNT ❑ *This is further proof of the mismanagement of the project.*

misplaced /ˌmɪsˈpleɪst/ ADJ If you describe a feeling or action as **misplaced**, you are critical of it because you think it is inappropriate, or directed towards the wrong thing or person. ❑ *Many fears turn out to be misplaced or inaccurate.*

misread (**misreads, misreading, misread**)

present tense /ˌmɪsˈriːd/, past tense and past participle /ˌmɪsˈred/.

M

1 V-T If you **misread** a situation or someone's behaviour, you do not understand it properly. ❑ *The government misread the mood of the voters.* ● **misreading** (**misreadings**) N-COUNT ❑ *...a misreading of opinion in France.* **2** V-T If you **misread** something that has been written or printed, you look at it and think that it says something that it does not say. ❑ *I misread the map.*

misrepresent /ˌmɪsreprɪˈzent/ (**misrepresents, misrepresenting, misrepresented**) V-T If someone **misrepresents** a person or situation, they give a wrong or inaccurate account of what the person or situation is like. ❑ *The press misrepresented him as arrogant and bullying.* ● **misrepresentation** N-UNCOUNT ❑ *The programme's researchers are guilty of misrepresentation.*

miss /mɪs/ (**misses, missing, missed**) **1** N-TITLE You use **Miss** in front of the name of a girl or unmarried woman. ❑ *The shop was run by Miss Ivy Streeter.* **2** V-T/V-I & N-COUNT If you **miss** when you are trying to hit something, you fail to hit it. A **miss** is an occasion when you miss something. ❑ *She threw the book across the room, narrowly missing my head.* ❑ *He threw the paper towards the bin, but missed.* ❑ *Striker Alan Smith was guilty of two misses.* **3** V-T If you **miss** something, you fail to notice it. ❑ *It's the first house on the right. You can't miss it.* **4** V-T If you **miss** the point or **miss** the joke, you fail to understand or appreciate a particular point or joke that someone is making. **5** V-T If you **miss** someone or something, you feel sad because the person is no longer with you, or because you no longer have the thing. ❑ *Your mother and I are going to miss you at Christmas.* ❑ *He missed having good friends.* **6** V-T If you **miss** something such as a plane or train, you arrive too late to catch it. ❑ *He missed the last bus home.* **7** V-T If you **miss** an event or activity, you do not go to it or take part in it, because you are unable to or have forgotten to. ❑ *Makku and I missed our lesson.* ❑ *He missed the first game because of an injury.* **8** → see also **missing**

▶ **miss out** **1** PHR-VERB If you **miss out on** something that would be beneficial or interesting to you, you are not involved in it or do not take part in it. ❑ *We're missing out on a great opportunity.* **2** PHR-VERB If you **miss out** something or someone, you do not include them. [BRIT] ❑ *What about Sally? You've missed her out.*

Word Link	*miss ≈ sending : dismiss, missile, missionary*

missile /ˈmɪsaɪl, AM -səl/ (**missiles**) **1** N-COUNT A **missile** is a tube-shaped weapon that moves long distances through the air and explodes when it reaches its target. **2** N-COUNT Anything that is thrown as a weapon can be called a **missile**. [FORMAL] ❑ *Supporters hurled missiles at rival fans.*

missing /ˈmɪsɪŋ/ **1** ADJ If someone or something is **missing** or has **gone missing**, they are not where you expect them to be, and you cannot find them. ❑ *His wallet was missing.* ❑ *She reported him to the police as a missing person.* **2** ADJ If a part of something is **missing**, it has been removed or has come off and has not been replaced. ❑ *Three buttons were missing from his shirt.*

Word Partnership	Use *missing* with:
ADV.	**still** missing **1**
N.	missing **piece** **1** **2** missing **children**, missing **girl**, missing **people**, missing **soldiers** **1**

mission /ˈmɪʃən/ (**missions**) **1** N-COUNT A **mission** is an important task that you are given to do, especially one that involves travelling to another country. ❑ *In 1987, he went missing on a mission to Beirut.* **2** N-COUNT A **mission** is a group of people who have been sent to a foreign country to carry out an official task. ❑ *...the head of South Africa's trade mission to Zimbabwe.* **3** N-COUNT A **mission** is a special journey made by a military aeroplane or space rocket. ❑ *The plane was on a bombing mission.* **4** N-COUNT If you have a **mission**, there is something that you believe it is your duty to try to achieve. ❑ *Her mission in life is to show that being disabled doesn't mean being helpless.*

Word Partnership	Use *mission* with:
ADJ.	**dangerous** mission, **secret** mission, **successful** mission **1**
N.	**combat** mission, **rescue** mission, **suicide** mission, **training** mission **1** **3**
V.	**accomplish a** mission, **carry out a** mission **1** **2** **3** **4**

missionary /ˈmɪʃənri, -neri/ (**missionaries**) N-COUNT A **missionary** is a Christian who has been sent to a foreign country to teach people about Christianity.

mist /mɪst/ (**mists, misting, misted**) N-VAR **Mist** consists of many tiny drops of water in the air, which make it difficult to see very far. ❑ *I couldn't see anything through the mist.*

▶ **mist over** or **mist up** PHR-VERB When a piece

of glass **mists over** or **mists up**, it becomes covered with tiny drops of water, so that you cannot see through it easily. ❑ *The windows misted up.*

mistake /mɪ'steɪk/ (**mistakes, mistaking, mistook, mistaken**) **1** N-COUNT & PHRASE If you **make a mistake**, or if you do something **by mistake**, you do something wrong, for example because you do not know what is right or because you are not thinking clearly. ❑ *...spelling mistakes.* ❑ *The official who ignored the warning made a mistake.* ❑ *Someone must have sold it by mistake.* **2** V-T If you **mistake** one person or thing **for** another, you wrongly think that they are the other person or thing. ❑ *I mistook you for Carlos.* **3** PHRASE You can say **there is no mistaking** something when you are emphasizing that you cannot fail to recognize or understand it. ❑ *There's no mistaking his voice.*

Word Partnership	Use *mistake* with:
ADJ.	**big** mistake, **common** mistake, **costly** mistake, **fatal** mistake, **honest** mistake, **huge** mistake, **serious** mistake, **terrible** mistake, **tragic** mistake **1**
V.	**admit a** mistake, **correct a** mistake, **fix a** mistake, **make a** mistake, **realize a** mistake **1**

mistaken /mɪ'steɪkən/ ADJ If you are **mistaken**, or if you have a **mistaken** belief, you are wrong about something. ❑ *You couldn't be more mistaken, Alex.* ❑ *...a victim of mistaken identity.* ● **mistakenly** ADV ❑ *Some of the crew mistakenly believed the ship was under attack.*

mister /'mɪstə/ → see **Mr**

mistook /mɪ'stʊk/ **Mistook** is the past tense of **mistake**.

mistress /'mɪstrəs/ (**mistresses**) N-COUNT A married man's **mistress** is a woman he is having a sexual relationship with, but who is not his wife.

mistrust /ˌmɪs'trʌst/ (**mistrusts, mistrusting, mistrusted**) V-T & N-UNCOUNT If you **mistrust** someone or something, you do not trust them. **Mistrust** is the feeling that you have towards someone who you do not trust. ❑ *There was mutual mistrust between the two men.*

misty /'mɪsti/ ADJ If it is **misty**, there is a lot of mist in the air.

misunderstand /ˌmɪsʌndə'stænd/ (**misunderstands, misunderstanding, misunderstood**) V-T If you **misunderstand** someone or something, you do not understand them properly. ❑ *He misunderstood the rules.*

misunderstanding /ˌmɪsʌndə'stændɪŋ/ (**misunderstandings**) **1** N-VAR A **misunderstanding** is a failure to understand something such as a situation or a person's remarks. ❑ *It is a simple misunderstanding.* **2** N-COUNT You can refer to a disagreement or slight argument as a **misunderstanding**. ❑ *We had a misunderstanding.*

misunderstood /ˌmɪsʌndə'stʊd/ **1** **Misunderstood** is the past tense and past participle of **misunderstand**. **2** ADJ If you describe someone as **misunderstood**, you mean that people have wrong ideas about them, and do not recognize their qualities or achievements. ❑ *...a misunderstood genius.*

misuse (**misuses, misusing, misused**) **1** V-T /ˌmɪs'juːz/ If you **misuse** something, you use it incorrectly, carelessly, or dishonestly. ❑ *Mr Chung was accused of misusing company money.* **2** N-VAR /ˌmɪs'juːs/ The **misuse** of something is incorrect, careless, or dishonest use of it. ❑ *...the misuse of language.*

mite /maɪt/ (**mites**) **1** PHRASE **A mite** means to a small extent or degree. ❑ *I can't help feeling just a mite uneasy about it.* **2** N-COUNT **Mites** are very tiny creatures that live, for example, on plants or in animals' fur.

mitigate /'mɪtɪgeɪt/ (**mitigates, mitigating, mitigated**) V-T To **mitigate** something means to make it less unpleasant, serious, or painful. [FORMAL] ❑ *Supportive friends and family mitigate stress.*

mitigating /'mɪtɪgeɪtɪŋ/ ADJ BEFORE N **Mitigating** circumstances are facts which make a crime less serious or more justifiable. [FORMAL]

mix /mɪks/ (**mixes, mixing, mixed**) **1** V-T/V-I If two substances **mix**, or if you **mix** one substance **with** another, they combine to form a single substance. ❑ *Oil and water don't mix.* ❑ *Mix the spices with the sugar.* **2** V-T If you **mix** something, you prepare it by mixing two or more things together. ❑ *He mixed the cement himself.* **3** N-VAR A **mix** is a powder containing all the substances that you need in order to make something, to which you add liquid. ❑ *...cake mix.* **4** N-COUNT A **mix** is two or more things combined together. ❑ *The story is a magical mix of fantasy and reality.* **5** V-I If you **mix with** other people, you meet them and talk to them. ❑ *He loved to mix with the rich and famous.* ❑ *The meeting gave both younger and older students the opportunity to mix.* **6** → see also **mixed up**

▶ **mix up** PHR-VERB If you **mix up** two things or people, you confuse them, so that you think that one of them is the other one. ❑ *I mixed Jane up with someone else.*

Word Partnership	Use *mix* with:
N.	mix **ingredients**, mix **with water** **1** **2**
ADV.	mix **thoroughly**, mix **together** **1** **2**

mixed /mɪkst/ **1** ADJ You use **mixed** to describe something which consists of different people or things of the same general kind. ❑ *His clubs attract a mixed crowd.* ❑ *I had mixed feelings about this news.* **2** ADJ **Mixed** means involving people from two or more different races. ❑ *...a woman of mixed race.* ❑ *...mixed marriages.* **3** ADJ **Mixed** education or accommodation is intended for both males and females. ❑ *...a mixed secondary school.*

ˌmixed 'up **1** ADJ If you are **mixed up**, you are confused. ❑ *I get mixed up about times and places.* ❑ *Elena is a very mixed-up child.* **2** ADJ AFTER LINK-V If you say that someone is **mixed up with** a person or **in** an activity that you disapprove of, you mean they are involved with that person or activity. ❑ *She got herself mixed up in terrorism.*

mixer /'mɪksə/ (**mixers**) N-COUNT A **mixer** is a machine used for mixing things together. ❑ *...a food mixer.*
→ see **kitchen**

mixture /'mɪkstʃə/ (**mixtures**) **1** N-SING A **mixture of** things consists of several different things together. ❑ *The weather will be a mixture of*

m

rain, light winds, cloud and sunshine. **2** N-COUNT A **mixture** is a substance that consists of other substances which have been stirred or shaken together. ❑ *...a sticky mixture of flour and water.*

Thesaurus	*mixture* Also look up:
N.	blend, compound, fusion **2**

ml **ml** is a written abbreviation for **millilitre** or **millilitres.** ❑ *...300ml water.*

mm **mm** is a written abbreviation for **millimetre** or **millimetres.** ❑ *45mm of rain fell.*

moan /məʊn/ (**moans, moaning, moaned**) **1** V-I & N-COUNT If you **moan**, you make a low, miserable cry called a **moan**, because you are unhappy or in pain. ❑ *Lauren moaned in her sleep.* ❑ *She let out a faint moan.* **2** V-T/V-I To **moan** means to speak in a way which shows that you are very unhappy. ❑ *'Look what he did,' she moaned.* ❑ *He is always moaning about the price of petrol.*

mob /mɒb/ (**mobs, mobbing, mobbed**) **1** N-COUNT A **mob** is a large disorganized crowd of people. ❑ *The mob then set fire to the police station.* **2** V-T If someone **is mobbed**, a disorderly crowd of people gathers very closely around them. ❑ *They are mobbed by fans wherever they go.*

Word Link	***mobil ≈ moving : automobile, mobile, mobilize***

mobile /ˈməʊbaɪl, AM -bəl/ **1** ADJ Something or someone that is **mobile** is able to move or be moved easily. ❑ *He is now mobile thanks to an electric wheelchair.* ❑ *...a mobile library.* ● **mobility** /məʊˈbɪlɪti/ N-UNCOUNT ❑ *These wheelchairs will give patients greater mobility.* **2** ADJ If you are socially **mobile**, you are able to move to a different social class. ● **mobility** N-UNCOUNT ❑ *...class barriers which prevented social mobility.*
→ see **cellphone**

Word Partnership	Use *mobile* with:
N.	mobile **communications**, mobile **device**, mobile **service** **1**

ˌmobile ˈphone (**mobile phones**) N-COUNT In British English, a **mobile phone** is a telephone that you can carry with you and use to make or receive calls wherever you are. The usual American word is **cellphone**.

Word Link	***mobil ≈ moving : automobile, mobile, mobilize***

mobilize [BRIT also **mobilise**] /ˈməʊbɪlaɪz/ (**mobilizes, mobilizing, mobilized**) **1** V-T If you **mobilize** a group of people, or if you **mobilize** support, you get people to support something in an active way. ❑ *The king had wanted to mobilise popular support.* ● **mobilization** N-UNCOUNT ❑ *We need a general mobilization of public opinion to fight unemployment.* **2** V-T/V-I If a country **mobilizes** its armed forces, or if it **mobilizes**, it prepares for war. [FORMAL] ❑ *The French mobilized 160,000 troops.* ● **mobilization** N-UNCOUNT ❑ *There was a demand for full-scale mobilisation to defend the republic.*

mock /mɒk/ (**mocks, mocking, mocked**) **1** V-T If you **mock** someone, you laugh at them, tease them, or try to make them look foolish. ● **mocking** ADJ ❑ *...his deliberately mocking tone.* **2** ADJ BEFORE N You use **mock** to describe something which is not genuine, but which is intended to be very similar to the real thing. ❑ *Tex's voice was raised in mock horror.* ❑ *...mock exams.*

mockery /ˈmɒkəri/ **1** N-UNCOUNT **Mockery** is words, behaviour, or opinions that are unkind and scornful. ❑ *There was a hint of mockery in his voice.* **2** N-SING If something **makes a mockery of** something, it makes it appear worthless and foolish. ❑ *Allowing her to avoid prison would make a mockery of the law.*

modal /ˈməʊdəl/ (**modals**) N-COUNT In grammar, a **modal** or a **modal verb** is a word such as 'can' or 'would' which is used in a verbal group and which expresses ideas such as possibility, intention, and necessity.

Word Link	***mod ≈ measure, manner : mode, model, modern***

mode /məʊd/ (**modes**) N-COUNT A **mode of** something is one of the different forms it can take. [FORMAL] ❑ *...road, rail and other modes of transport.*

model /ˈmɒdəl/ (**models, modelling, modelled** or [AM] **modeling, modeled**) **1** N-COUNT A **model** of an object is a smaller copy of it that shows what it looks like or how it works. ❑ *...an architect's model of a wooden house.* ❑ *...a model aeroplane.* **2** N-COUNT A **model** is a system that is being used and that people might want to copy in order to achieve similar results. ❑ *The southern Italian diet is held up as a model of healthy eating.* **3** N-COUNT If you say that someone or something is a **model of** a particular quality, you approve of them because they have that quality to a large degree. ❑ *Until this moment she had always considered Suzy to be a model of sanity.* **4** ADJ BEFORE N A **model** wife or a **model** teacher, for example, is an excellent wife or an excellent teacher. ❑ *She is a model pupil.* **5** V-T If one thing **is modelled on** another, the first thing is made so that it is like the second thing in some way. ❑ *She asked the author if she had modelled her hero on anybody in particular.* **6** N-COUNT A particular **model** of a machine is a version of it. ❑ *There is a basic model for students and a more powerful one for teachers.* **7** N-COUNT An artist's **model** is a person who is painted, drawn, or sculpted by them. **8** N-COUNT A fashion **model** is a person whose job is to display clothes by wearing them. **9** V-T/V-I If someone **models** or **models** clothes, they display them by wearing them. ● **modelling** N-UNCOUNT ❑ *She was offered a modelling contract.*
→ see **forecast**

Word Partnership	Use *model* with:
V.	**build a** model, **make a** model **1** **base** *something* **on a** model, **follow a** model, **serve as a** model **1**-**3**
N.	**business** model **2**
ADJ.	**basic** model, **current** model, **latest** model, **new** model, **standard** model **6**

moderate (**moderates, moderating, moderated**) **1** ADJ & N-COUNT /ˈmɒdərət/ **Moderate** political opinions or policies are not extreme. A person who has these opinions can be referred to as a **moderate**. ❑ *...an easy-going man of very moderate views.* 2 ADJ A **moderate** amount is neither large nor small. ❑ *...moderate exercise.* ● **moderately** ADV ❑ *...a moderately attractive woman.* 3 V-T/V-I /ˈmɒdəreɪt/ If you **moderate** something, or if it **moderates**, it becomes less extreme or violent. ❑ *He has moderated his brash style.*

Word Partnership Use *moderate* with:

N. moderate **approach**, moderate **position**, moderate **view** 1
moderate **amount**, moderate **exercise**, moderate **growth**, moderate **heat**, moderate **improvement**, moderate **prices**, moderate **speed** 2

moderation /ˌmɒdəˈreɪʃən/ 1 N-UNCOUNT If someone's behaviour shows **moderation**, they act in a way that is reasonable and not extreme. ❑ *He urged the party to show moderation.* 2 PHRASE If you do something **in moderation**, you do not do it too much. ❑ *Do everything in moderation.*

Word Link *mod ≈ measure, manner : mode, model, modern*

modern /ˈmɒdən/ 1 ADJ BEFORE N **Modern** means relating to the present time. ❑ *...the challenges facing every modern marriage.* 2 ADJ Something that is **modern** is new and involves the latest ideas or equipment. ❑ *...modern technology.*

Thesaurus *modern* Also look up:

ADJ. contemporary, current, present 1
state-of-the-art, up-to-date 2

Word Partnership Use *modern* with:

N. modern **art**, modern **civilization**, modern **culture**, modern **dance**, modern **era**, modern **life**, modern **literature**, modern **music**, modern **science**, modern **society**, modern **times**, modern **warfare** 1
modern **conveniences**, modern **equipment**, modern **methods**, modern **techniques**, modern **technology** 2

modernize [BRIT also **modernise**] /ˈmɒdənaɪz/ (**modernizes, modernizing, modernized**) V-T To **modernize** a system means to replace old equipment or methods with new ones. ❑ *...plans to modernize the factory.* ● **modernization** N-UNCOUNT ❑ *...a five-year modernization programme.*

modest /ˈmɒdɪst/ 1 ADJ A **modest** house or other building is not large or expensive. ❑ *She lives in a modest apartment in Santa Monica.* 2 ADJ Something that is **modest** is quite small in amount. ❑ *...a modest improvement.* ● **modestly** ADV ❑ *Sales are expected to drop only modestly this year.* 3 ADJ If you say that someone is **modest**, you approve of them because they do not talk much about their abilities, achievements, or possessions. ● **modestly** ADV ❑ *Hubbard modestly describes himself as an average runner.*

modesty /ˈmɒdɪsti/ N-UNCOUNT Someone who shows **modesty** does not talk much about their abilities, achievements, or possessions; used showing approval.

modifier /ˈmɒdɪfaɪə/ (**modifiers**) N-COUNT A **modifier** is a word which comes in front of a noun in a noun group.

modify /ˈmɒdɪfaɪ/ (**modifies, modifying, modified**) V-T If you **modify** something, you change it slightly in order to improve it. ❑ *He modified the recipe and it became one of the restaurant's most popular dishes.* ● **modification** /ˌmɒdɪfɪˈkeɪʃən/ (**modifications**) N-COUNT ❑ *Relatively minor modifications were required.*

module /ˈmɒdʒuːl/ (**modules**) 1 N-COUNT A **module** is one of the units that some university or college courses are divided into. [BRIT] 2 N-COUNT A **module** is part of a spacecraft which can operate independently of the main part, often at a distance from it.

moist /mɔɪst/ (**moister, moistest**) ADJ Something that is **moist** is slightly wet.

moisture /ˈmɔɪstʃə/ N-UNCOUNT **Moisture** is tiny drops of water in the air or on a surface.

mold /məʊld/ → see **mould**
→ see **fungus, laboratory**

mole /məʊl/ (**moles**) 1 N-COUNT A **mole** is a natural dark spot on someone's skin. 2 N-COUNT A **mole** is a small animal with black fur that lives underground. 3 N-COUNT A **mole** is a member of a government or organization who secretly reveals confidential information to the press or to a rival organization.

molecular /məˈlekjʊlə/ ADJ BEFORE N **Molecular** means relating to molecules. ❑ *...molecular genetics.*

Word Link *cule ≈ small : minuscule, molecule, ridicule*

molecule /ˈmɒlɪkjuːl/ (**molecules**) N-COUNT A **molecule** is the smallest amount of a chemical substance which can exist. ❑ *...water molecules.*
→ see **element**

molest /məˈlest/ (**molests, molesting, molested**) V-T A person who **molests** someone touches them sexually against their will.

molten /ˈməʊltən/ ADJ **Molten rock, metal** or **glass** has been heated to a very high temperature and has become a hot thick liquid.
→ see **volcano**

mom /mɒm/ (**moms**) N-COUNT & N-VOC Your **mom** is your mother. [AM, INFORMAL]

moment /ˈməʊmənt/ (**moments**) 1 N-COUNT A **moment** is a very short period of time. ❑ *She stared at him a moment, then turned away.* ❑ *In moments, I was asleep.* 2 N-COUNT A particular **moment** is the point in time at which something happens. ❑ *Many people still remember the moment when they heard that President Kennedy had been assassinated.* 3 PHRASE You use **at the moment** to indicate that a particular situation exists at the time when you are speaking. ❑ *He has a knee injury at the moment.* 4 PHRASE If someone does something **at the last moment**, they do it at the latest possible time. ❑ *They changed their minds at the last moment and refused to go.* 5 PHRASE You use **for the moment** to indicate that something is true now, even if it will not be true later or in the future. ❑ *For the moment, however, he has other things*

m

Word Web money

Early traders used a system of **barter** which didn't involve **money**. For example, a farmer might trade a cow for a wooden cart. In China, India, and Africa, cowrie shells* became a form of **currency**. The first **coins** were crude lumps of metal. Uniform circular coins appeared in China around 1500 BC. In 1150 AD, the Chinese started using paper bills for money. In 560 BC, the Lydians (living in what is now Turkey) **minted** three types of coins—a **gold** coin, a **silver** coin, and a mixed metal coin. Their use quickly spread through Asia Minor and Greece.

cowrie shell: a small, shiny, oval shell.

on his mind. 6 PHRASE If you say that something happens **the moment** something else happens, you are emphasizing that it happens immediately after the other thing. ❑ *The moment I closed my eyes, I fell asleep.*

Word Partnership Use *moment* with:

ADV.	a moment **ago, just a** moment 1
N.	moment **of silence,** moment **of thought** 1
V.	**stop for a** moment, **take a** moment, **think for a** moment, **wait a** moment 1
ADJ.	**an awkward** moment, **a critical** moment, **the right** moment 2

momentary /ˈməʊməntəri, AM -teri/ ADJ Something that is **momentary** lasts for only a very short time. • **momentarily** /ˌməʊmənˈteərɪli/ ADV ❑ *She paused momentarily.*

momentous /məʊˈmentəs/ ADJ A **momentous** event is very important.

momentum /məʊˈmentəm/ 1 N-UNCOUNT If a process or movement **gains momentum**, it develops or progresses increasingly quickly, and becomes increasingly less likely to stop. ❑ *The campaign against him gathered momentum.* 2 N-UNCOUNT **Momentum** is the force that causes an object to continue moving, because of its mass and speed. [TECHNICAL]
→ see **motion**

Word Partnership Use *momentum* with:

V.	**build** momentum, **gain** momentum, **gather** momentum, **have** momentum, **lose** momentum, **maintain** momentum 1 2

Word Link *arch ≈ rule : anarchy, hierarchy, monarch*

monarch /ˈmɒnək/ (**monarchs**) N-COUNT A **monarch** is a king or queen.

monarchist /ˈmɒnəkɪst/ (**monarchists**) ADJ & N-COUNT If someone has **monarchist** opinions or if they are a **monarchist**, they believe that their country should have a monarch.

monarchy /ˈmɒnəki/ (**monarchies**) N-COUNT A **monarchy** is a system in which a monarch rules over a country. ❑ *...a debate on the future of the monarchy.*

monastery /ˈmɒnəstri, AM -teri/ (**monasteries**) N-COUNT A **monastery** is a building in which monks live.

monastic /mɒˈnæstɪk/ ADJ **Monastic** means relating to monks or to a monastery. ❑ *He was drawn to the monastic life.*

Monday /ˈmʌndeɪ, -di/ (**Mondays**) N-VAR **Monday** is the day after Sunday and before Tuesday.

monetary /ˈmʌnɪtri, AM ˈmɑːnɪteri/ ADJ BEFORE N **Monetary** means relating to money, or to the money supply. [FORMAL] ❑ *...monetary policy.*

money /ˈmʌni/ 1 N-UNCOUNT **Money** consists of the coins or banknotes that you can spend, or a sum that can be represented by these. ❑ *They spent all their money on clothes.* ❑ *I needed to earn some money.* 2 PHRASE If you **get** your **money's worth,** you are satisfied with it because you think it is worth the amount of money you have spent on it. ❑ *The band's fans got their money's worth at the concert.*
→ see Word Web: **money**
→ see **donor**

Thesaurus *money* Also look up:

N.	capital, cash, currency, funds, wealth 1

ˈmoney ˌlaundering N-UNCOUNT **Money laundering** is the crime of processing stolen money through a legitimate business or sending it abroad to a foreign bank, to hide the fact that the money was illegally obtained. ❑ *...the largest money-laundering scandal in history.*

monitor /ˈmɒnɪtə/ (**monitors, monitoring, monitored**) 1 V-T If you **monitor** something, you regularly check its development or progress. ❑ *Officials were not allowed to monitor the voting.* 2 N-COUNT A **monitor** is a machine used to check or record things. ❑ *...a heart monitor.* 3 N-COUNT A **monitor** is a machine similar to a television that shows information on a screen.
→ see **computer**

Word Partnership Use *monitor* with:

N.	monitor **activity**, monitor **elections**, monitor **performance**, monitor **progress**, monitor **a situation** 1 **colour** monitor, **computer** monitor, **video** monitor 3
ADV.	**carefully** monitor, **closely** monitor 1

monk /mʌŋk/ (**monks**) N-COUNT A **monk** is a member of a male religious community.

monkey /ˈmʌŋki/ (**monkeys**) N-COUNT A **monkey** is an animal that lives in hot countries that has a long tail and climbs trees.
→ see **primate**

Word Link *mono* ≈ *one* : *monogamous, monologue, monopoly*

monogamy /məˈnɒgəmi/ N-UNCOUNT **Monogamy** is the state or custom of having a sexual relationship with only one partner or of being married to only one person. • **monogamous** ADJ ❑ *...a monogamous relationship.*

monolithic /ˌmɒnəˈlɪθɪk/ ADJ If you describe an organization or system as **monolithic**, you are critical of it because it is very large and very slow to change. ❑ *...a monolithic bureaucracy.*

monologue /ˈmɒnəlɒg, AM -lɔːg/ (**monologues**) N-COUNT If you refer to a long speech by one person during a conversation as a **monologue**, you mean it prevents other people from talking or expressing their opinions. ❑ *Morris ignored the question and continued his monologue.*

monopolize [BRIT also **monopolise**] /məˈnɒpəlaɪz/ (**monopolizes, monopolizing, monopolized**) V-T If someone **monopolizes** something, they have a very large share of it and prevent other people from having a share. ❑ *Johnson, as usual, monopolized the conversation.*

monopoly /məˈnɒpəli/ (**monopolies**) 1 N-VAR If a company, person, or state has a **monopoly on** something such as an industry, they have complete control over it. ❑ *The East India Company had a monopoly on all trade to Britain from the East.* 2 N-COUNT A **monopoly** is a company which is the only one that makes a particular product or offers a particular service and which therefore completely controls an industry.

monotonous /məˈnɒtənəs/ ADJ Something that is **monotonous** is very boring because it has a regular repeated pattern which never changes. ❑ *It's monotonous work, like most factory jobs.*

monsoon /mɒnˈsuːn/ (**monsoons**) N-COUNT **The monsoon** is the season of very heavy rain in Southern Asia.
→ see **disaster**

monster /ˈmɒnstə/ (**monsters**) 1 N-COUNT A **monster** is a large imaginary creature that is very frightening. 2 ADJ BEFORE N **Monster** means extremely large. [INFORMAL] ❑ *The film will be a monster hit.*

monstrous /ˈmɒnstrəs/ 1 ADJ If you describe a situation or someone's actions as **monstrous**, you mean that it is very shocking or unfair. • **monstrously** ADV ❑ *His family has behaved monstrously.* 2 ADJ If you describe something, especially an unpleasant thing, as **monstrous**, you mean that it is extremely large. ❑ *...monstrous waves and severe winds.*

month /mʌnθ/ (**months**) N-COUNT A **month** is one of the twelve periods of time that a year is divided into, for example January or February.
→ see **year**

monthly /ˈmʌnθli/ ADJ BEFORE N & ADV A **monthly** publication or event appears or happens every month. ❑ *...a monthly newsletter.* ❑ *I get paid monthly.*

monument /ˈmɒnjʊmənt/ (**monuments**) N-COUNT A **monument** is a large structure, usually made of stone, which is built to remind people of an event in history or of a famous person.

monumental /ˌmɒnjʊˈmentəl/ ADJ You can use **monumental** to emphasize the size or extent of something. ❑ *It had been a monumental mistake.* ❑ *...his monumental work on Chinese astronomy.*

mood /muːd/ (**moods**) 1 N-COUNT Your **mood** is the way you are feeling at a particular time. ❑ *Lily was in one of her aggressive moods.* 2 N-SING The **mood** of a group of people is the way that they think and feel about an idea, event, or question at a particular time. ❑ *They misread the mood of the crowd.* 3 N-COUNT If someone is **in a mood**, their behaviour shows that they are feeling angry and impatient.

Word Partnership Use *mood* with:

ADJ.	**bad/good** mood, **depressed** mood, **foul** mood, **positive** mood, **tense** mood 1
N.	mood **change**, mood **disorder**, mood **swings** 1
V.	**create a** mood, **set a** mood 2

moody /ˈmuːdi/ ADJ A **moody** person often becomes depressed or angry without any warning. • **moodily** ADV ❑ *He sat and stared moodily out of the window.* • **moodiness** N-UNCOUNT ❑ *His moodiness was caused by his poor health.*

moon /muːn/ (**moons**) 1 N-SING **The moon** is the object in the sky that goes round the Earth once every four weeks and that you can often see at night as a circle or part of a circle. ❑ *...the light of a full moon.* 2 N-COUNT A **moon** is an object like a small planet that travels around a planet. ❑ *...Neptune's large moon.* 3 PHRASE If you say that you are **over the moon**, you mean that you are very pleased about something. [BRIT, INFORMAL] ❑ *I am over the moon about it.*
→ see Word Web: **moon**
→ see **astronomer, eclipse, satellite, solar system, tide**

moonlight /ˈmuːnlaɪt/ (**moonlights, moonlighting, moonlighted**) 1 N-UNCOUNT **Moonlight** is the light that comes from the moon at night. ❑ *They walked along the road in the moonlight.* 2 V-I If someone **moonlights**, they have a second job in addition to their main job, often without informing their main employers or the tax office. ❑ *He moonlights as a taxi driver.*

moor /mʊə/ (**moors, mooring, moored**) 1 N-VAR A **moor** is an area of high open ground covered mainly with rough grass and heather. [BRIT] 2 V-T/V-I If you **moor** or **moor** a boat, you attach it to the land with a rope or cable so that it cannot drift away. ❑ *I decided to moor near some tourist boats.*

Word Web moon

Scientists believe the **moon** is many millions of years old. They think a large asteroid hit the earth. A big piece of the earth broke off. It went flying into **space**. However, Earth's **gravity** caught it. It began to circle the earth. This piece became our moon. The moon orbits the earth once a month. It also **rotates** on its **axis** every 30 days. The moon has no **atmosphere**, so meteoroids crash into it. When a meteoroid hits the moon, it makes a **crater**. Craters cover the surface of the moon.

mooring /'mʊərɪŋ/ (**moorings**) N-COUNT A **mooring** is a place or object on land to which a boat is tied so that it cannot drift away.

moorland /'mʊələnd/ (**moorlands**) N-VAR **Moorland** is land which consists of moors.

moose /mu:s/

Moose is both the singular and the plural form.

N-COUNT A **moose** is a large North American deer.

mop /mɒp/ (**mops, mopping, mopped**) **1** N-COUNT A **mop** consists of a sponge or many pieces of string attached to a long handle and is used for washing floors. **2** V-T If you **mop** a floor, you clean it with a mop. **3** V-T If you **mop** sweat from your forehead, you wipe the sweat away with a handkerchief. ❑ *The Inspector took out a handkerchief and mopped his brow.*

▸ **mop up** PHR-VERB If you **mop up** a liquid, you clean it with a cloth so that the liquid is absorbed. ❑ *A waiter mopped up the mess.*

M

mope /məʊp/ (**mopes, moping, moped**) V-I If you **mope**, or if you **mope around** or **mope about**, you feel miserable and are not interested in anything. ❑ *Get on with life and don't sit back and mope!* ❑ *He moped around the office, feeling bored.*

moped /'məʊped/ (**mopeds**) N-COUNT A **moped** is a kind of motorcycle with a very small engine.

moral /'mɒrəl, AM 'mɔ:r-/ (**morals**) **1** N-PLURAL **Morals** are principles and beliefs concerning right and wrong behaviour. ❑ *They have no morals.* **2** ADJ BEFORE N **Moral** means relating to beliefs about what is right or wrong. ● **morally** ADV ❑ *Is it ever morally justifiable to allow a patient to die?.* **3** ADJ A **moral** person behaves in a way that is believed by most people to be good and right. ● **morally** ADV ❑ *The Left regarded the war as morally wrong.* **4** ADJ BEFORE N If you give someone **moral** support, you encourage them in what they are doing by expressing approval. **5** N-SING The **moral of** a story or event is what you learn from it about how you should or should not behave.

→ see **philosophy**

morale /mə'rɑ:l, -'ræl/ N-UNCOUNT **Morale** is the amount of confidence and optimism that people have. ❑ *Many teachers are suffering from low morale.*

morality /mə'rælɪti/ (**moralities**) **1** N-UNCOUNT **Morality** is the belief that some behaviour is right and acceptable and that other behaviour is wrong. ❑ *...standards of morality and justice.* **2** N-UNCOUNT **The morality of** something is how right or acceptable it is. ❑ *They debated the morality of the death penalty.*

moratorium /ˌmɒrə'tɔ:riəm, AM ˌmɔ:r-/ (**moratoriums** or **moratoria**) N-COUNT If there is a **moratorium on** a particular activity, it is officially stopped for a period of time. [FORMAL] ❑ *Spain imposed a moratorium on the building of nuclear power stations.*

morbid /'mɔ:bɪd/ ADJ If someone has a **morbid** interest in a particular subject, especially a strange or unpleasant subject, they are fascinated by it. ❑ *...a morbid fear of cancer.* ● **morbidly** ADV ❑ *I became depressed and morbidly fascinated with death.*

more /mɔ:/

More is often considered to be the comparative form of **much** and **many**.

1 QUANT You use **more** to say that there is a greater number of things or a greater amount of something than before or than average, or than something else. ❑ *We need to teach more children foreign languages.* ❑ *Prison conditions have become more brutal.* ❑ *We can satisfy our basic wants more easily than in the past.* ❑ *He had four hundred dollars in his pocket. Billy had more.* **2** PREP You use **more than** before a number or amount to say that the actual number or amount is even greater. ❑ *...a survey of more than 1,500 schools.* **3** ADV You can use **more** or **some more** to indicate that something continues to happen for a further period of time. ❑ *We can talk more about Leo on Thursday.* ❑ *Would you mind if I just stayed in my room and read some more?* **4** ADV You use **more** to indicate that something is repeated. ❑ *Aubrey sighed once more.* ❑ *These exercises should be repeated several times more.* **5** DET & PRON You use **more** to refer to an additional thing or amount. ❑ *Are you sure you wouldn't like some more water?* ❑ *They should do more to help themselves.* **6** PHRASE You can use **more and more** to indicate that something is becoming greater in amount, extent, or degree all the time. ❑ *Bob became more and more furious.* ❑ *More and more women are playing sport.* **7** PHRASE You use **more than** to say that something is true to a greater degree than is necessary or than average. ❑ *This country produces more than enough food to feed itself.* **8** PHRASE You use **no more than** or **not more than** when you want to emphasize how small a number or amount is. ❑ *Each meal requires no more than thirty minutes to prepare.* **9** PHRASE If something is **more or less** true, it is true in a general way, but is not completely true. ❑ *The discussion is more or less over.* **10** PHRASE You can use **what is more** or **what's more** to introduce an extra piece of information which supports or emphasizes the point you are making. ❑ *You'll find good sales staff there. And, what's more, you'll find extremely low prices.* **11** **all the more** → see **all** **12** **any more** → see **any**

moreover /mɔ:'rəʊvə/ ADV You use **moreover** to introduce a piece of information that adds to or supports the previous statement. [FORMAL] ❑ *There was indeed a man standing behind her. Moreover, he was observing her strangely.*

morgue /mɔːɡ/ (**morgues**) N-COUNT A **morgue** is a building or room where dead bodies are kept before being cremated or buried.

morning /ˈmɔːnɪŋ/ (**mornings**) 1 N-VAR The **morning** is the part of a day between the time that people wake up and noon. ❑ *On Sunday morning Bill was woken by the telephone.* 2 N-COUNT If you refer to a particular time **in the morning**, you mean a time during the part of a day between midnight and noon. ❑ *I often stay up until two or three in the morning.* 3 PHRASE If you say that something will happen **in the morning**, you mean that it will happen during the morning of the following day.
→ see **time**

Thesaurus *morning* Also look up:
N. dawn, light, sunrise 1

morose /məˈrəʊs/ ADJ Someone who is **morose** is miserable, bad-tempered, and not willing to talk very much to other people.. • **morosely** ADV ❑ *One elderly man sat morosely by the window.*

morphine /ˈmɔːfiːn/ N-UNCOUNT **Morphine** is a drug used to relieve pain.

morsel /ˈmɔːsəl/ (**morsels**) N-COUNT A **morsel** is a very small amount of something, especially a very small piece of food. ❑ *...a delicious morsel of meat.*

Word Link ***mort ≈ death : immortal, mortal, mortuary***

mortal /ˈmɔːtəl/ (**mortals**) 1 ADJ If you refer to the fact that people are **mortal**, you mean that they have to die and cannot live forever. • **mortality** N-UNCOUNT ❑ *She has suddenly come face to face with her own mortality.* 2 N-COUNT You can describe someone as a **mortal** when you want to say that they are an ordinary person, rather than someone who has power or has achieved something. ❑ *Musicians, like the rest of us, are mere mortals.* 3 ADJ BEFORE N You can use **mortal** to show that something is very serious or may cause death. ❑ *Our citizens' lives were in mortal danger.* • **mortally** ADV ❑ *...a mortally wounded soldier.*

mortality /mɔːˈtælɪti/ N-UNCOUNT The **mortality** in a particular place or situation is the number of people who die. ❑ *...the infant mortality rate in Britain.*

mortar /ˈmɔːtə/ (**mortars**) 1 N-COUNT A **mortar** is a short cannon which fires shells high into the air for a short distance. 2 N-UNCOUNT **Mortar** is a mixture of sand, water, and cement, which is put between bricks to make them stay firmly together.

mortgage /ˈmɔːɡɪdʒ/ (**mortgages, mortgaging, mortgaged**) 1 N-COUNT A **mortgage** is a loan of money which you get from a bank or building society in order to buy a house. 2 V-T If you **mortgage** your house or land, you use it as a guarantee to a company in order to borrow money from them.

mortician /mɔːˈtɪʃən/ (**morticians**) N-COUNT In American English, a **mortician** is a person whose job is to deal with the bodies of people who have died and to arrange funerals. The British word is **undertaker**.

mortuary /ˈmɔːtʃʊəri, AM -eri/ (**mortuaries**) N-COUNT A **mortuary** is a building or a room in a hospital where dead bodies are kept before they are buried or cremated.

mosaic /məʊˈzeɪɪk/ (**mosaics**) N-VAR A **mosaic** is a design made of small pieces of coloured stone or glass set in concrete or plaster.

Moslem /ˈmɒzləm, ˈmʊzlɪm/ → see **Muslim**

mosque /mɒsk/ (**mosques**) N-COUNT A **mosque** is a building where Muslims go to worship.

mosquito /mɒˈskiːtəʊ/ (**mosquitoes** or **mosquitos**) N-COUNT **Mosquitoes** are small flying insects which bite people in order to suck their blood.
→ see **insect**

moss /mɒs, AM mɔːs/ (**mosses**) N-VAR **Moss** is a very small soft green plant which grows on damp soil, or on wood or stone.

most /məʊst/

Most is often considered to be the superlative form of **much** and **many**.

1 QUANT You use **most** to refer to the majority of a group of people or things or the largest part of something. ❑ *Most people think the Queen has done a good job.* ❑ *Most of the book is completely true.* ❑ *All of the rooms have private baths, and most have radios and TV.* 2 ADJ & PRON You use **the most** to mean a larger amount than anyone or anything else, or the largest amount possible. ❑ *The President himself won the most votes.* ❑ *The most they earn in a day is ten roubles.* 3 ADV & PHRASE You use **most** or **most of all** to indicate that something is true or happens to a greater degree or extent than anything else. ❑ *What she feared most was becoming like her mother.* ❑ *Professor Morris was the person he most disliked.* ❑ *She said she wanted most of all to be fair.* 4 ADV You use **most** to say that someone or something has a greater amount of a particular quality than other things of its kind. ❑ *He was one of the world's most influential modern jazz performers.* 5 ADV If you do something **the most**, you do it to the greatest extent possible or with the greatest frequency. ❑ *What question are you asked the most?* 6 ADV You use **most** to emphasize an adjective or adverb. [FORMAL] ❑ *I believe he is most seriously ill.* 7 PHRASE You use **at most** or **at the most** to say that a number or amount is the maximum that is possible or likely. ❑ *I was twelve or thirteen years old at most when this happened.* 8 PHRASE If you **make the most of** something, you get the maximum use or advantage from it. ❑ *Make the most of every opportunity.*

Usage

Note that you can say '**Most of the children love sweets**', but you cannot say 'Most of children love sweets'. However, when a pronoun is used, you can say '**Most of them love sweets**'.

mostly /ˈməʊstli/ ADV You use **mostly** to indicate that a statement is true about the majority of a group of things or people, true most of the time, or true in most respects. ❑ *I work with mostly highly motivated people.* ❑ *Cars are mostly metal.*

motel /məʊˈtel/ (**motels**) N-COUNT A **motel** is a hotel intended for people who are travelling by car.

moth /mɒθ, AM mɔːθ/ (**moths**) N-COUNT A **moth** is an insect like a butterfly, which usually flies about at night.

mother /ˈmʌðə/ (**mothers, mothering, mothered**) **1** N-COUNT & N-VOC Your **mother** is the woman who gave birth to you. ❑ *She's an English teacher and a mother of two children.* **2** V-T If you **mother** someone, you treat them with great care and affection, as if they were a small child. ❑ *Stop mothering me.*
→ see **family**

motherhood /ˈmʌðəhʊd/ N-UNCOUNT **Motherhood** is the state of being a mother.

ˈmother-in-ˌlaw (**mothers-in-law**) N-COUNT Someone's **mother-in-law** is the mother of their husband or wife.
→ see **family**

motherland /ˈmʌðəlænd/ N-SING The **motherland** is the country in which you were born and to which you still feel emotionally linked. ❑ *...love for the motherland.*

motherly /ˈmʌðəli/ ADJ **Motherly** feelings or actions are like those of a mother. ❑ *It was a moving display of motherly love and forgiveness.*

motif /məʊˈtiːf/ (**motifs**) N-COUNT A **motif** is a design used as a decoration or as part of an artistic pattern. ❑ *...a rose motif.*

Word Link *mot ≈ moving : **motion, motivate, promote***

motion /ˈməʊʃən/ (**motions, motioning, motioned**) **1** N-UNCOUNT **Motion** is continual movement. ❑ *The wind from the car's motion whipped her hat off her head.* **2** N-COUNT A **motion** is an action, gesture, or movement. ❑ *He made a neat chopping motion with his hand.* **3** V-T/V-I If you **motion** to someone, you move your hand or head as a way of telling them to do something or where to go. ❑ *She motioned for the doors to be opened.* ❑ *I motioned him to join us.* **4** N-COUNT A **motion** in a meeting or debate is a proposal which is discussed and voted on. **5** → see also **slow motion** **6** PHRASE If you say that someone **is going through the motions**, you think they are only saying or doing something because it is expected of them and not because they are interested in it, enthusiastic about it, or sympathetic to it. **7** PHRASE If a process or event is **set in motion**, something causes it to happen or begin to happen. ❑ *This set in motion events that brought about the end of the Soviet Union.*
→ see Word Web: **motion**

Word Partnership Use *motion* with:

ADJ.	**constant** motion, **full** motion, **perpetual** motion **1** **circular** motion, **smooth** motion **1** **2** **quick** motion **2**

motionless /ˈməʊʃənləs/ ADJ Someone or something that is **motionless** is not moving at all. ❑ *He remained quite motionless behind his desk.*

ˈmotion ˌpicture (**motion pictures**) N-COUNT A **motion picture** is a film made for cinema. [AM]

Word Link *ate ≈ causing to be : **complicate, humiliate, motivate***

motivate /ˈməʊtɪveɪt/ (**motivates, motivating, motivated**) **1** V-T If you **are motivated** by something, especially an emotion, it causes you to behave in a particular way. ❑ *The crime was not politically motivated.* ❑ *What motivates people to steal?* **2** V-T If someone **motivates** you **to** do something, they make you feel determined to do it. ❑ *This teacher motivates her students to do their best.* ● **motivated** ADJ ❑ *...highly-motivated employees.*

motivation /ˌməʊtɪˈveɪʃən/ (**motivations**) **1** N-COUNT Your **motivation** for doing something is what causes you to want to do it. ❑ *His prime motivation is usually money.* **2** N-UNCOUNT If you have the **motivation** to do something, you feel determined to do it. ❑ *The players were tired and lacked motivation.*

motive /ˈməʊtɪv/ (**motives**) N-COUNT Your **motive for** doing something is your reason for doing it. ❑ *Police have ruled out robbery as a motive for the killing.*

motor /ˈməʊtə/ (**motors**) **1** N-COUNT A **motor** in a machine, vehicle, or boat is the part that uses electricity or fuel to produce movement, so that the machine, vehicle, or boat can work. **2** ADJ BEFORE N **Motor** vehicles and boats have a petrol or diesel engine. **3** ADJ BEFORE N **Motor** is used to describe activities relating to motor vehicles. ❑ *...the future of the British motor industry.* **4** → see also **motoring**

motorcycle

motorbike /ˈməʊtəbaɪk/ (**motorbikes**) N-COUNT A **motorbike** is the same as a **motorcycle**.

ˈmotor ˌcar (**motor cars**) N-COUNT A **motor car** is the same as a **car**. [DATED]

motorcycle /ˈməʊtəsaɪkəl/

Word Web motion

Newton's three laws of **motion** describe how **forces** affect the movement of objects. This is the first law: an object at **rest** won't move unless a force makes it move. Also, a moving object keeps its **momentum** unless something stops it. The second law is about **acceleration**. The **rate** of acceleration depends on two things: how strong the push on the object is, and how much the object weighs. The third law says that for every **action** there is an equal and opposite **reaction**. When one object **exerts** a force on another, the second object pushes back with an equal force.

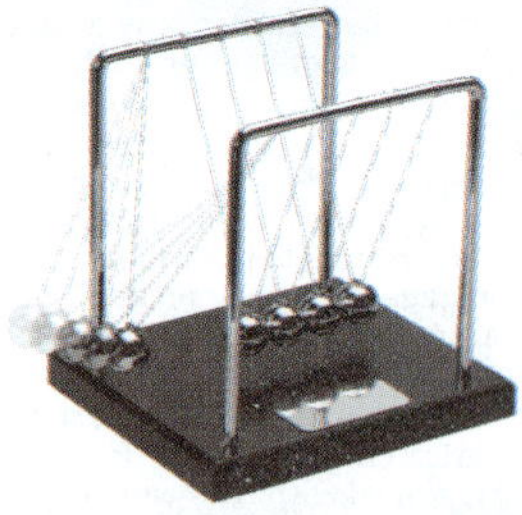

(**motorcycles**) N-COUNT A **motorcycle** is a two-wheeled vehicle with an engine.

motorcyclist /ˈməʊtəsaɪklɪst/ (**motorcyclists**) N-COUNT A **motorcyclist** is someone who rides a motorcycle.

motoring /ˈməʊtərɪŋ/ ADJ BEFORE N **Motoring** means relating to cars and to driving. ❑ *...one of Britain's largest motoring organisations.*

motorist /ˈməʊtərɪst/ (**motorists**) N-COUNT A **motorist** is someone who drives a car.

motorized [BRIT also **motorised**] /ˈməʊtəraɪzd/ ADJ A **motorized** vehicle has an engine. ❑ *It was the first time motorized vehicles were used in a war.*

motorway /ˈməʊtəweɪ/ (**motorways**) N-VAR In British English, a **motorway** is a wide road specially built for fast travel over long distances. The usual American word is **freeway**.

motto /ˈmɒtəʊ/ (**mottoes** or **mottos**) N-COUNT A **motto** is a short sentence or phrase that expresses the attitude to life of a particular person or group. ❑ *The motto of the club is: THINK QUICK!*

mould [AM **mold**] /məʊld/ (**moulds, moulding, moulded**) 1 N-COUNT A **mould** is a container used to make something into a particular shape. 2 V-T If you **mould** plastic or clay, you make it into a particular shape. ❑ *Mould the cheese mixture into small balls.* 3 V-T To **mould** someone or something means to change or influence them over a period of time so that they develop in a particular way. ❑ *We should not try to mould our children into something they do not wish to be.* 4 N-VAR **Mould** is a soft grey, green, or blue substance that sometimes forms on old food or on damp walls or clothes.

mound /maʊnd/ (**mounds**) N-COUNT A **mound of** things is a large heap or pile of them. ❑ *The men helped each other move mounds of snow from pavements and driveways.*

mount /maʊnt/ (**mounts, mounting, mounted**) 1 V-T To **mount** a campaign or event means to organize it and make it take place. ❑ *The police have mounted a campaign to discourage the use of guns.* 2 V-I If something **mounts**, or if it **mounts up**, it increases. ❑ *For several hours, tension mounted.* ❑ *Her medical bills mounted up.* 3 V-T If you **mount** the stairs or a platform, you go up the stairs or go up onto the platform. [FORMAL] ❑ *The car mounted the pavement.* 4 V-T/V-I If you **mount**, or **mount** a horse or cycle, you climb on to it so that you can ride it. ❑ *They all mounted and rode off.* 5 V-T If you **mount** an object **on** something, you fix it there firmly. ❑ *Her husband mounts the work on velour paper.* ● **-mounted** ❑ *...a wall-mounted electric fan.* 6 **Mount** is used as part of the name of some mountains. ❑ *...Mount Everest.* 7 → see also **mounted**

mountain /ˈmaʊntɪn, AM -tən/ (**mountains**) 1 N-COUNT A **mountain** is a very high area of land with steep sides. ❑ *...the north side of the mountain.* ❑ *...a lovely little mountain village.* 2 N-COUNT A **mountain of** something is a very large amount of it. [INFORMAL] ❑ *They have mountains of coffee to sell.*
→ see Picture Dictionary: **mountain**
→ see **land**

ˈmountain ˌbike (**mountain bikes**) N-COUNT A **mountain bike** is a type of bicycle with a strong frame and thick tyres.

mountaineer /ˌmaʊntɪˈnɪə/ (**mountaineers**) N-COUNT A **mountaineer** is someone who climbs mountains as a hobby or sport.

mountainous /ˈmaʊntɪnəs/ ADJ A **mountainous** place has a lot of mountains. ❑ *...the mountainous region of Campania.*

mountainside /ˈmaʊntɪnsaɪd/ (**mountainsides**) N-COUNT A **mountainside** is one of the steep sides of a mountain.

mounted /ˈmaʊntɪd/ 1 ADJ BEFORE N **Mounted** police or soldiers ride horses when they are on duty. 2 → see also **mount**

mourn /mɔːn/ (**mourns, mourning, mourned**) 1 V-T/V-I If you **mourn**, or **mourn** someone who has died, you are very sad that they have died and

Picture Dictionary mountain

m

show your sorrow in the way that you behave. ❑ *The whole nation mourned the death of their leader.* **2** V-T If you **mourn** something, you regret that you no longer have it and show your regret in the way that you behave. ❑ *We mourned the loss of our cities.*

mourner /ˈmɔːnə/ (**mourners**) N-COUNT You can refer to the people at a funeral as the **mourners**.

mournful /ˈmɔːnfʊl/ ADJ If you are **mournful**, you are very sad. ❑ *He looked mournful, and near to tears.* ● **mournfully** ADV ❑ *He stood mournfully at the gate, waving goodbye.*

mouse /maʊs/ (**mice** /maɪs/) **1** N-COUNT A **mouse** is a small furry animal with a long tail. **2** N-COUNT A **mouse** is a device that you use to perform operations on a computer without using the keyboard. [COMPUTING]
→ see **computer**

mousse /muːs/ (**mousses**) **1** N-VAR **Mousse** is a sweet light food made from eggs and cream. **2** N-UNCOUNT **Mousse** is a soft substance which you can put in your hair to make it easier to shape into a particular style.
→ see **dessert**

moustache [AM **mustache**] /məˈstɑːʃ, AM ˈmʌstæʃ/ (**moustaches**) N-COUNT A man's **moustache** is the hair that grows on his upper lip.

mouth (**mouths, mouthing, mouthed**)

noun /maʊθ/ in the singular, /maʊðz/ in the plural.

1 N-COUNT Your **mouth** is your lips, or the space behind your lips where your teeth and tongue are. ❑ *He covered his mouth with his hand.* ❑ *I nodded because my mouth was full of cake.* ● **-mouthed** ❑ *They listened in open-mouthed horror.* **2** N-COUNT The **mouth** of a cave, hole, or bottle is its entrance or opening. **3** N-COUNT The **mouth** of a river is the place where it flows into the sea. **4** V-T /maʊð/ If you **mouth** something, you form words with your lips without making any sound. ❑ *I mouthed a goodbye and hurried away.* ❑ *'It's for you,' he mouthed.* **5** to **live from hand to mouth** → see **hand**
→ see **face, respiration**

Word Link	*ful ≈ quantity that fills : handful, mouthful, plentiful*

mouthful /ˈmaʊθfʊl/ (**mouthfuls**) N-COUNT A **mouthful of** food or drink is an amount that you put or have in your mouth. ❑ *She gulped down a mouthful of coffee.*

mouthpiece /ˈmaʊθpiːs/ (**mouthpieces**) **1** N-COUNT The **mouthpiece** of a telephone is the part that you speak into. **2** N-COUNT The **mouthpiece** of a musical instrument is the part that you blow into. **3** N-COUNT The **mouthpiece** of an official person or organization is someone who informs other people of the opinions and policies of that organization or person. ❑ *Their mouthpiece is the vice-president.*

Word Link	*mov ≈ moving : movable, movement, movie*

movable also **moveable** /ˈmuːvəbəl/ ADJ Something that is **movable** can be moved from one place or position to another. ❑ *...movable goods.*
→ see **printing**

move /muːv/ (**moves, moving, moved**) **1** V-T/V-I When you **move** something, or when it **moves**, its position changes. ❑ *He moved the fridge into the kitchen.* ❑ *The train began to move.* **2** V-I & N-COUNT When you **move**, or when you make a **move**, you change your position or go to a different place. ❑ *She moved away from the window.* ❑ *Daniel's eyes followed her every move.* **3** V-I & N-COUNT If a person or company **moves**, they leave the building where they have been living or working, and go to live or work in a different place. A **move** is an act of moving. ❑ *She decided to move to London.* ❑ *The move to Prague was a daunting prospect.* **4** V-T/V-I & N-COUNT If you **move** job or **move from** one job or interest to another, you change to it. A **move** is an act of moving. ❑ *Christina moved jobs to get experience.* ❑ *During 39 years with the company, he moved from graduate trainee to chairman.* ❑ *...his move to AC Milan from Barcelona.* **5** V-I & N-COUNT If you **move** towards a particular state, activity, or opinion, you start to be in that state, do that activity, or have that opinion. A **move** is an act of moving in this way. ❑ *It was important to find a way to move towards peace in the region.* ❑ *Nobody made a move to stop them.* **6** V-I If a situation **is moving**, it is developing or progressing. ❑ *Events are moving fast.* **7** V-T If something **moves** you **to** do something, it causes you to do it. ❑ *The tears in her eyes moved him to say he loved her.* **8** V-T If something **moves** you, it causes you to feel a deep emotion, usually sadness or sympathy. ❑ *His prayer moved me to tears.* ● **moved** ADJ AFTER LINK-V ❑ *Those who listened to him were deeply moved.* **9** N-COUNT A **move** is an action that you take in order to achieve something. ❑ *It may also be a good move to suggest she talks things over with a friend.* **10** PHRASE If you are **on the move**, you are going from one place to another. **11** → see also **moving**

▶ **move about** or **move around** PHR-VERB If you **move about** or **move around**, you keep changing your job or keep changing the place where you live. ❑ *He moved around the country working on farms.*

▶ **move in** **1** PHR-VERB If you **move in** somewhere, or if you **move into** a new house or place, you begin to live in a different house or place. ❑ *A friend has moved in with me to rent my spare room.* ❑ *My parents are about to move into a new house.* **2** PHR-VERB If soldiers or police **move in**, they go towards a place or person in order to attack them or deal with them. ❑ *Forces moved in on the town of Knin.*

▶ **move off** PHR-VERB When vehicles or people **move off**, they start moving away from a place. ❑ *Gil waved his hand and the car moved off.*

▶ **move on** PHR-VERB When you **move on** somewhere, you leave the place where you have been staying or waiting and go or travel somewhere else. ❑ *He wants to sell his land and move on.* ❑ *Mr Brooke moved on from Paris to Belgrade.*

▶ **move out** PHR-VERB If you **move out**, you leave the house or place where you have been living, and go and live somewhere else. ❑ *He decided to move out and buy another house.*

▶ **move up** PHR-VERB If you **move up**, you change your position, especially in order to be nearer someone or to make room for someone else. ❑ *Move up, John, and let the lady sit down.*

moveable /ˈmuːvəbəl/ → see **movable**

Word Link	ment ≈ state, condition : agreement, management, movement

Word Link	mov ≈ moving : movable, movement, movie

movement /'mu:vmənt/ (**movements**) **1** N-VAR **Movement** involves changing position or going from one place to another. ❑ *There was a constant movement of people in and out of the lounge at the party.* ❑ *Her hand movements became more animated.* **2** N-VAR **Movement** is a gradual development or change of an attitude, opinion, or policy. ❑ *...the movement towards democracy in Latin America.* **3** N-PLURAL Your **movements** are everything which you do or plan to do during a period of time. ❑ *I want a full account of your movements the night Mr Gower was killed.* **4** N-COUNT A **movement** is a group of people who share the same beliefs, ideas, or aims. ❑ *...the women's movement.*
→ see **brain**

movie /'mu:vi/ (**movies**) **1** N-COUNT In American English, a **movie** is a motion picture. The British word is **film**. ❑ *...a horror movie.* **2** N-PLURAL In American English, when people **go to the movies**, they see a movie in a movie theater. The British term is **the cinema**.
→ see **DVD, genre**

moving /'mu:vɪŋ/ **1** ADJ If something is **moving**, it makes you feel a strong emotion such as pity. ❑ *It was a moving moment.* • **movingly** ADV ❑ *You wrote very movingly of your sister's illness.* **2** ADJ BEFORE N A **moving** model or part of a machine moves or is able to move. **3** → see also **move**

mow /məʊ/ (**mows, mowing, mowed, mown** or **mowed**) V-T/V-I If you **mow** or **mow** an area of grass, you cut it using a lawnmower or a mower.
▶ **mow down** PHR-VERB If a large number of people **are mown down**, they are killed violently by a vehicle or gunfire.

mower /'məʊə/ (**mowers**) N-COUNT A **mower** is a machine for cutting grass, corn, or wheat.

MP /ˌem 'pi:/ (**MPs**) N-COUNT In Britain, an **MP** is a person who has been elected to represent the people from a particular area in the House of Commons. **MP** is an abbreviation for 'Member of Parliament'.

MP3 /ˌem pi: 'θri:/ N-UNCOUNT **MP3** is a kind of technology that enables you to record and play music from the Internet. [COMPUTING] ❑ *...MP3 files.*

ˌMP'3 ˌplayer (**MP3 players**) N-COUNT An **MP3 player** is a machine on which you can play music downloaded from the Internet.

mph **mph** is written after a number to indicate the speed of something such as a vehicle. **mph** is an abbreviation for 'miles per hour'.

Mr /'mɪstə/ N-TITLE **Mr** is used before a man's name when you are speaking or referring to him. ❑ *Hello, Mr Simpson.* ❑ *...Mr Bob Price.*

Mrs /'mɪsɪz/ N-TITLE **Mrs** is used before the name of a married woman when you are speaking or referring to her. ❑ *Hello, Mrs Miles.* ❑ *...Mrs Anne Pritchard.*

Ms /məz, mɪz/ N-TITLE **Ms** is used before a woman's name when you are speaking to her or referring to her. If you use **Ms**, you are not specifying if the woman is married or not. ❑ *...Ms Elizabeth Harman.*

MSP /ˌem es 'pi:/ (**MSPs**) N-COUNT An **MSP** is someone who has been elected as a member of the Scottish Parliament. **MSP** is an abbreviation for 'Member of the Scottish Parliament'.

much /mʌtʃ/ **1** ADV You use **much** to indicate the great intensity, extent, or degree of something such as an action, feeling, or change. **Much** is usually used with 'so', 'too', and 'very', and in negative clauses for this meaning. ❑ *She shouts too much.* ❑ *Thank you very much.* ❑ *My hairstyle hasn't changed much since I was five.* **2** ADV You use **much** in order to emphasize that there is a large amount of a particular quality. ❑ *He is much too nice to tell me it's none of my business.* ❑ *We were so much happier before we were rich.* **3** ADV If one thing is **much** the same as another thing, it is very similar to it. ❑ *Sheep's milk is produced in much the same way as goat's milk.* ❑ *It looks pretty much like Michael's signature.* **4** QUANT You use **much** to indicate that you are referring to a large amount of something. ❑ *This approach has been used in the past, though without much success.* ❑ *There was so much to talk about.* ❑ *She does much of her work abroad.* **5** QUANT You use **much** to ask questions or make statements about the amount or degree of something. ❑ *How much do you earn?* ❑ *She knows how much this upsets me.* **6** ADV If something does not happen **much**, it does not happen very often. ❑ *His father never talked much about the war.* **7** PHRASE If you describe something as **not much of** a particular type of thing, you mean that it is small or of poor quality. ❑ *It hasn't been much of a holiday.* **8** PHRASE If something is **not so much** one thing **as** another, it is more like the second thing than the first. ❑ *I don't really think of her as a daughter so much as a very good friend.* **9** PHRASE You say **nothing much** to refer to something that is not very interesting or important. ❑ *'What was stolen?'—'Oh, nothing much.'* **10** PHRASE You use **much less** after a statement to indicate that the statement is even more true of the person, thing, or situation that you are going to mention next. ❑ *They are always short of water to drink, much less to wash in.* **11** PHRASE If you say **so much for** a particular thing, you mean that it has not been successful or helpful. [INFORMAL] ❑ *So much for all his clever theories!* **12** PHRASE If a situation or action is **too much for** you, you cannot cope with it. ❑ *The pain was too much for her to bear.* **13** **a bit much** → see **bit**

Usage

You should use **much** if you want to talk about a large amount of something. ❑ *...too much money*. You only use **many** to talk about things that can be counted. ❑ *There are many books on the subject.*

muck /mʌk/ (**mucks, mucking, mucked**) N-UNCOUNT **Muck** is dirt or some other unpleasant substance. [INFORMAL]
▶ **muck about** or **muck around** PHR-VERB If you **muck about** or **muck around**, you behave in a stupid way and waste time. [BRIT, INFORMAL] ❑ *He spent his summers mucking about in boats.*

mucus /'mju:kəs/ N-UNCOUNT **Mucus** is a liquid that is produced in some parts of your body, for example the inside of your nose. [FORMAL]

m

mud /mʌd/ N-UNCOUNT **Mud** is a sticky mixture of earth and water.

muddle /ˈmʌdəl/ (**muddles, muddling, muddled**) **1** N-VAR A **muddle** is a confused state or situation. ❑ *My thoughts are all in a muddle.* **2** V-T & PHR-VERB If you **muddle** things or people, or if you **muddle** them **up**, you get them mixed up, so that you do not know which is which. ❑ *One or two critics have muddled the two names.* ❑ *He sometimes muddles me up with other patients.* ● **muddled up** ADJ ❑ *I am getting my words muddled up.*

▶ **muddle through** PHR-VERB If you **muddle through**, you manage to do something even though you do not really know how to do it properly.

▶ **muddle up** → see **muddle** (meaning **2**)

muddled /ˈmʌdəld/ ADJ If someone is **muddled**, they are confused about something.

muddy /ˈmʌdi/ (**muddier, muddiest, muddies, muddying, muddied**) **1** ADJ Something that is **muddy** contains, or is covered in, mud. ❑ *...his muddy boots.* **2** ADJ BEFORE N A **muddy** colour is dull and brownish. ❑ *...a muddy green-brown.* **3** V-T If you **muddy** something, you cause it to be muddy. ❑ *They muddied their shoes.* **4** V-T If someone or something **muddies** a situation or issue, they cause it to seem less clear and less easy to understand. ❑ *Their relationship has sometimes been muddied by politics.*

muffle /ˈmʌfəl/ (**muffles, muffling, muffled**) V-T If something **muffles** a sound, it makes it quieter and more difficult to hear. ❑ *Blake held his hand over his mouth to muffle his voice.*

M

mug /mʌg/ (**mugs, mugging, mugged**) **1** N-COUNT A **mug** is a large deep cup with straight sides. ❑ *She sipped from her coffee mug.* ❑ *...a mug of sweet tea.* **2** V-T If someone **mugs** you, they attack you in order to steal your money. ● **mugging** (**muggings**) N-VAR ❑ *...a victim of mugging.* ● **mugger** (**muggers**) N-COUNT ❑ *If you come face to face with a mugger, what do you do?*
→ see **crime**

mule /mjuːl/ (**mules**) N-COUNT A **mule** is an animal whose parents are a horse and a donkey.

mull /mʌl/ (**mulls, mulling, mulled**)
▶ **mull over** PHR-VERB If you **mull** something **over**, you think about it for a long time before deciding what to do.

Word Link	*multi ≈ many : multilateral, multimedia, multinational*

multilateral /ˌmʌltiˈlætərəl/ ADJ **Multilateral** means involving at least three different groups of people or nations. ❑ *...multilateral trade talks in Geneva.*

multimedia /ˌmʌltiˈmiːdiə/ **1** N-UNCOUNT In computing, you use **multimedia** to refer to programs and products which involve the use of sound, pictures, and film, as well as ordinary text. **2** N-UNCOUNT In education, **multimedia** is the use of television and other different media in a lesson, instead of only textbooks.

multinational also **multi-national** /ˌmʌltiˈnæʃənəl/ (**multinationals**) **1** ADJ & N-COUNT A **multinational** company or a **multinational** has branches in many different countries. ❑ *...multinationals such as Ford and IBM.* **2** ADJ **Multinational** is used to describe something that involves several different countries. ❑ *The US troops were part of a multinational force.*

multiple /ˈmʌltɪpəl/ (**multiples**) **1** ADJ You use **multiple** to describe things that consist of many parts, involve many people, or have many uses. ❑ *He received multiple injuries.* ❑ *The most common multiple births are twins.* **2** N-COUNT If one number is a **multiple of** a smaller number, it can be exactly divided by that smaller number. ❑ *We count seconds, minutes and hours in multiples of six and ten.*

multiple sclerosis /ˌmʌltɪpəl skləˈrəʊsɪs/ N-UNCOUNT **Multiple sclerosis** is a serious disease of the nervous system. The abbreviation **MS** is also used.

multiplicity /ˌmʌltɪˈplɪsɪti/ QUANT A **multiplicity of** things is a large number or large variety of them. [FORMAL] ❑ *...a writer who uses a multiplicity of styles.*

multiply /ˈmʌltɪplaɪ/ (**multiplies, multiplying, multiplied**) **1** V-T/V-I When something **multiplies**, or when you **multiply** it, it increases greatly in number or amount. ❑ *Her husband multiplied his demands on her time.* ● **multiplication** /ˌmʌltɪplɪˈkeɪʃən/ N-UNCOUNT ❑ *...the multiplication of bacteria.* **2** V-T If you **multiply** one number **by** another, you calculate the total which you get when you add the number to itself as many times as is indicated by the second number. ❑ *Seven multiplied by three is twenty-one.* ❑ *...the remarkable ability to multiply huge numbers.* ● **multiplication** N-UNCOUNT ❑ *...subtraction, multiplication and division.*
→ see **mathematics**

multitude /ˈmʌltɪtjuːd, AM -tuːd/ (**multitudes**) QUANT A **multitude of** things or people is a very large number of them. ❑ *There's a multitude of reasons why I became an actor.*

mum /mʌm/ (**mums**) N-COUNT & N-VOC Your **mum** is your mother. [BRIT, INFORMAL] ❑ *He misses his mum.*

mumble /ˈmʌmbəl/ (**mumbles, mumbling, mumbled**) V-T & N-COUNT If you **mumble** something, or if you speak in a **mumble**, you speak very quietly and not clearly so that the words are difficult to understand. ❑ *He mumbled a few words.*

mummy /ˈmʌmi/ (**mummies**) **1** N-COUNT & N-VOC Some people, especially children, call their mother **mummy**. [BRIT, INFORMAL] **2** N-COUNT A **mummy** is a dead body which was preserved long ago by being rubbed with oils and wrapped in cloth.

munch /mʌntʃ/ (**munches, munching, munched**) V-T To **munch** food means to chew it in a noisy way. ❑ *They munched apples.*

mundane /ˌmʌnˈdeɪn/ ADJ Something that is **mundane** is ordinary and not interesting. ❑ *...the mundane realities of life.*

municipal /mjuːˈnɪsɪpəl/ ADJ BEFORE N **Municipal** means associated with the local government of a city or town.

municipality /mjuːˌnɪsɪˈpælɪti/ (**municipalities**) N-COUNT A **municipality** is a city or town with its own local council and officials. You can also refer to that city or town's local government as **the municipality**. ❑ *These public woodlands belong to the municipality.*

munitions /mjuːˈnɪʃənz/ N-PLURAL **Munitions** are bombs, guns, and other military supplies.

mural /ˈmjʊərəl/ (**murals**) N-COUNT A **mural** is a picture which is painted on a wall.

murder /ˈmɜːdə/ (**murders, murdering, murdered**) **1** N-VAR **Murder** is the crime of deliberately killing a person. ❑ *He was jailed for life after being found guilty of murder.* ❑ *She was convicted of three murders.* **2** V-T To **murder** someone means to commit the crime of killing them deliberately. ● **murderer** (**murderers**) N-COUNT ❑ *...a notorious mass murderer.* **3** → See note at **kill**

murderous /ˈmɜːdərəs/ ADJ If you describe a person or their actions as **murderous**, you mean that they intend to kill someone or are likely to kill someone. ❑ *This murderous lunatic could kill them both.*

murky /ˈmɜːki/ (**murkier, murkiest**) **1** ADJ A **murky** place or time of day is dark and rather unpleasant. ❑ *...one murky November afternoon.* **2** ADJ **Murky** water is dark and dirty. **3** ADJ If you describe an activity or situation as **murky**, you suspect that it is dishonest. [BRIT] ❑ *...his murky past life.* **4** ADJ If you describe something as **murky**, you mean that it is difficult to understand. ❑ *The law here is a little bit murky.*

murmur /ˈmɜːmə/ (**murmurs, murmuring, murmured**) **1** V-T & N-COUNT If you **murmur** something, or if you speak in a **murmur**, you speak very quietly, so that not many people can hear what you are saying. ❑ *He turned and murmured something to the professor.* ❑ *They spoke in low murmurs.* **2** N-SING A **murmur** is a continuous low sound, like the noise of a river or of distant voices. ❑ *I could hear the murmur of the sea.*

muscle /ˈmʌsəl/ (**muscles, muscling, muscled**) **1** N-VAR Your **muscles** are the internal pieces of body tissue which connect your bones together, and which you expand and contract when you make a movement. ❑ *Exercise will tone up your stomach muscles.* **2** N-UNCOUNT If you say that someone has **muscle**, you mean that they have power and influence. ❑ *Eisenhower used his muscle to change the law.* **3** PHRASE If a group, organization, or country **flexes** its **muscles**, it behaves in a way designed to show people that it has power and is considering using it.
→ see Word Web: **muscle**
→ see **nervous system**
▶ **muscle in** PHR-VERB If someone **muscles in on** something, they force their way into a situation where they have no right to be and where they are not welcome; used showing disapproval. ❑ *Cohen complained that Kravis was muscling in on his deal.*

Word Partnership Use *muscle* with:

N.	muscle **aches**, muscle **mass**, muscle **pain**, muscle **tone** **1**
V.	**contract a** muscle, **flex a** muscle, **pull a** muscle **1**

muscular /ˈmʌskjʊlə/ **1** ADJ BEFORE N **Muscular** means involving or affecting your muscles. ❑ *...muscular effort.* **2** ADJ A **muscular** person has strong, firm muscles. ❑ *...his tanned muscular legs.*

muse /mjuːz/ (**muses, musing, mused**) V-T/V-I If you **muse on** something, you think about it, usually saying or writing what you are thinking at the same time. [WRITTEN] ❑ *Many of the papers muse on the fate of the President.* ❑ *General George Patton once mused that Americans love a winner.* ● **musing** (**musings**) N-COUNT ❑ *His musings were interrupted by Montagu.*

museum /mjuːˈziːəm/ (**museums**) N-COUNT A **museum** is a public building where interesting and valuable objects are kept and displayed.

mushroom /ˈmʌʃruːm/ (**mushrooms, mushrooming, mushroomed**) **1** N-VAR **Mushrooms** are fungi with short stems and round tops. You can eat some kinds of mushrooms. ❑ *...mushroom omelette.* **2** V-I If something **mushrooms**, it grows or appears very quickly. ❑ *A capital of a few hundred thousand people has mushroomed to a crowded city of 2 million.*
→ see **fungus**

music /ˈmjuːzɪk/ **1** N-UNCOUNT **Music** is the pattern of sounds produced by people singing or playing instruments. ❑ *...classical music.* **2** N-UNCOUNT **Music** is the symbols written on paper that represent musical sounds. ❑ *He cannot read music.*
→ see Word Web: **music**
→ see **concert, genre**

Word Partnership Use *music* with:

ADJ.	**live** music, **loud** music, **new** music, **pop(ular)** music **1**
N.	**background** music, music **critic**, music **festival** **1**
	music **business**, music **industry**, music **lesson** **2**
V.	**download** music, **hear** music, **listen to** music, **play** music **1**
	compose music, **study** music, **write** music **2**

m

Word Web muscle

There are three types of **muscles** in the body. **Voluntary** or **skeletal** muscles make external movements. **Involuntary** or **smooth** muscles move within the body. For example, the smooth muscles in the **iris** of the eye adjust the size of the pupil. This controls how much light enters the eye. **Cardiac** muscles are only in the heart. They work constantly but they never get tired. When we **exercise**, voluntary muscles **contract** and then **relax**. Repeated **workouts** can **build** these muscles and increase their **strength**. If we don't exercise, these muscles can atrophy and become **weak**.

Word Web music

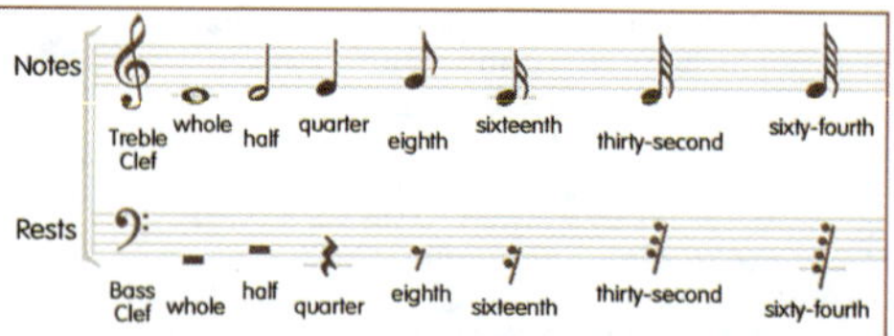

Wolfgang Amadeus Mozart lived only 35 years (1756-1791). However, he is one of the most important **musicians** in history. Mozart began playing the **piano** when he was four years old. A year later he **composed** his first **song**. He hadn't learned musical notation yet, so his father wrote the score for him. Mozart played for royalty across Europe. Soon Mozart became known as a gifted **composer**. He wrote more than 50 **symphonies**. He also composed numerous **operas**, **concertos**, arias, and other musical works.

musical /ˈmjuːzɪkəl/ (**musicals**) 1 ADJ BEFORE N **Musical** describes things that are concerned with playing or studying music. ❑ *...Stan Getz's musical career.* • **musically** ADV ❑ *Musically there is a lot to enjoy.* 2 N-COUNT A **musical** is a play or film that uses singing and dancing in the story. 3 ADJ Someone who is **musical** has a natural ability and interest in music. ❑ *My father was very musical.*
→ see **theatre**

ˌmusical ˈinstrument (**musical instruments**) N-COUNT A **musical instrument** is an object such as a piano, guitar, or violin which you play in order to produce music.

Word Link *ician ≈ person who works at : electrician, musician, physician*

musician /mjuːˈzɪʃən/ (**musicians**) N-COUNT A **musician** is a person who plays a musical instrument as their job or hobby.
→ see **concert, DVD, music, orchestra**

Muslim /ˈmʊzlɪm, ˈmuːs-, AM ˈmʌz-/ (**Muslims**) N-COUNT & ADJ A **Muslim** or a person who is **Muslim** is someone who believes in Islam and lives according to its rules.

muslin /ˈmʌzlɪn/ N-UNCOUNT **Muslin** is a very thin cotton cloth.

mussel /ˈmʌsəl/ (**mussels**) N-COUNT A **mussel** is a kind of shellfish.
→ see **shellfish**

must /məst, STRONG mʌst/ 1 MODAL You use **must** to indicate that you think it is very important or necessary for something to happen. ❑ *What you wear should be stylish and clean, and must definitely fit well.* ❑ *The doctor must not allow the patient to be put at risk.* 2 MODAL You use **must** to express your firm intention to do something. ❑ *I must be leaving.* 3 MODAL You use **must** to make forceful suggestions or invitations. ❑ *You must see a doctor, Frederick.* ❑ *You must see the painting Paul has given me.* 4 MODAL You use **must** in questions to express your anger or irritation about something that someone has done. ❑ *Why must you do everything as if you have to win?* 5 PHRASE You say **'if you must'** when you know that you cannot stop someone doing something that you think is wrong, stupid, or annoying. ❑ *'Could I have a word?'—'Oh dear, if you must.'* 6 N-COUNT If something is a **must**, it is absolutely necessary. [INFORMAL] ❑ *A trip to this important religious monument is a must for all visitors.* 7 MODAL You use **must** to indicate that you are fairly sure that something is the case, often because of the available evidence. ❑ *This must be the loveliest place in the world.* ❑ *He must have decided not to come.*

mustache /məˈstɑːʃ, AM ˈmʊstæʃ/ → see **moustache**

mustard /ˈmʌstəd/ N-UNCOUNT **Mustard** is a yellow or brown paste made from seeds, which tastes spicy.

muster /ˈmʌstə/ (**musters, mustering, mustered**) 1 V-T If you **muster support, strength**, or **energy**, you gather as much as you can in order to do something. ❑ *He travelled around West Africa trying to muster support for his movement.* 2 V-T/V-I When soldiers **muster** or **are mustered**, they gather in one place in order to take part in military action.

mustn't /ˈmʌsənt/ **Mustn't** is the usual spoken form of 'must not'.

must've /ˈmʌstəv/ **Must've** is a spoken form of 'must have', especially when 'have' is an auxiliary verb.

Word Link *mut ≈ changing : commute, mutant, mutate*

mutant /ˈmjuːtənt/ (**mutants**) N-COUNT A **mutant** is an animal or plant that is physically different from others of the same species as the result of a change in its genetic structure.

mutate /mjuːˈteɪt, AM ˈmjuːteɪt/ (**mutates, mutating, mutated**) V-T/V-I If an animal or plant **mutates**, or if something **mutates** it, it develops different characteristics as a result of a change in its genes. ❑ *HIV may have mutated into a new, as yet undetected, virus.* • **mutation** (**mutations**) N-VAR ❑ *...accidental mutations of the genes.*

mute /mjuːt/ (**mutes, muting, muted**) 1 ADJ Someone who is **mute** does not speak. ❑ *He was mute, distant, and indifferent.* 2 V-T If you **mute** a noise or sound, you make it quieter. • **muted** ADJ ❑ *'Yes,' he muttered, his voice so muted I hardly heard his reply.* 3 V-T If someone **mutes** something such as their feelings or their activities, they reduce the strength or intensity of them. ❑ *They have now muted their objections to the plan.* • **muted** ADJ ❑ *Reaction to the news was muted.*

mutilate /ˈmjuːtɪleɪt/ (**mutilates, mutilating, mutilated**) V-T If a person or animal **is mutilated**, their body is damaged very severely, usually by someone who physically attacks them. • **mutilation** (**mutilations**) N-VAR ❑ *...cases of torture and mutilation.*

mutiny /ˈmjuːtɪni/ (**mutinies**) N-VAR A **mutiny** is a rebellion by a group of people, usually soldiers or sailors, against a person in authority.

mutter /ˈmʌtə/ (**mutters, muttering, muttered**) V-T/V-I & N-COUNT If you **mutter** or **mutter** something, or if you speak in a **mutter**, you speak very quietly so that you cannot easily be heard, often because you are complaining about something. ❑ *She heard the old woman muttering about something.* ❑ *...a mutter of protest.* ● **muttering** (**mutterings**) N-VAR ❑ *He heard muttering from the front of the crowd.*

mutton /ˈmʌtən/ N-UNCOUNT **Mutton** is meat from an adult sheep.
→ see **meat**

mutual /ˈmjuːtʃuəl/ ADJ You use **mutual** to describe a situation, feeling, or action that is experienced, felt, or done by both of two people mentioned. ❑ *The East and the West can work together for their mutual benefit.* ❑ *It's plain that he adores his daughter, and the feeling is mutual.* ● **mutually** ADV ❑ *...a mutually convenient time.*

muzzle /ˈmʌzəl/ (**muzzles, muzzling, muzzled**) **1** N-COUNT The **muzzle** of a gun is the end where the bullets come out when it is fired. **2** N-COUNT A **muzzle** is a device that is put over a dog's nose and mouth so that it cannot bite people or bark. **3** V-T If you **muzzle** a dog, you put a muzzle over its nose and mouth.
→ see **horse**

my /maɪ/ DET A speaker or writer uses **my** to indicate that something belongs or relates to himself or herself. ❑ *I invited him back to my flat.* ❑ *John's my best friend.*

myriad /ˈmɪriəd/ (**myriads**) QUANT You can use **myriad** to refer to a very large number or great variety of people or things. ❑ *They face a myriad of problems with their children.* ❑ *...the myriad other tasks we are trying to perform in the world.* ❑ *...these myriads of fish.*

myself /maɪˈself/ **1** PRON A speaker or writer uses **myself** to refer to himself or herself. **Myself** is used as the object of a verb or preposition when the subject refers to the same person. ❑ *I asked myself what I should do.* ❑ *I looked at myself in the mirror.* **2** PRON You use **myself** to emphasize a first person singular subject. Some speakers use **myself** instead of 'me' as the object of a verb or preposition. ❑ *I myself enjoy cinema.* ❑ *...a complete beginner like myself.* **3** PRON If you say something such as 'I did it **myself**', you are emphasizing that you did it, rather than anyone else.

mysterious /mɪˈstɪəriəs/ **1** ADJ Someone or something that is **mysterious** is strange, not known about, or not understood. ❑ *He died in mysterious circumstances.* ❑ *...a mysterious illness.* ● **mysteriously** ADV ❑ *A couple of messages had mysteriously disappeared.* **2** ADJ AFTER LINK-V If someone is **mysterious about** something, they deliberately do not talk about it, often because they want people to be curious about it. ❑ *As for his job – well, he is very mysterious about it.* ● **mysteriously** ADV ❑ *Asked what she meant, she said mysteriously: 'Work it out for yourself.'*

mystery /ˈmɪstəri/ (**mysteries**) **1** N-COUNT A **mystery** is something that is not understood or known about. ❑ *The source of the gunshots still remains a mystery.* **2** N-UNCOUNT If you talk about the **mystery** of someone or something, you are talking about how difficult they are to understand or to know about. ❑ *She's a lady of mystery.* ❑ *...the mystery of the human mind.* **3** ADJ BEFORE N A **mystery** person or thing is one whose identity or nature is not known. ❑ *A mystery buyer purchased 1.5 million MGN shares.* **4** N-COUNT A **mystery** is a story in which strange things happen that are not explained until the end.

Word Partnership Use *mystery* with:

V.	**remain a** mystery, **unravel a** mystery **1** **solve a** mystery **1** **4**
N.	**murder** mystery, mystery **novel**, mystery **readers** **4**

mystic /ˈmɪstɪk/ (**mystics**) **1** N-COUNT A **mystic** is a person who believes in religious practices in which people search for truth, knowledge, and unity with God through meditation and prayer. ● **mysticism** N-UNCOUNT ❑ *...a mixture of mysticism and Roman Catholicism.* **2** ADJ BEFORE N **Mystic** means the same as **mystical**. ❑ *...mystic union with God.*

mystical /ˈmɪstɪkəl/ ADJ Something that is **mystical** involves spiritual powers and influences that most people do not understand. ❑ *That was clearly a deep mystical experience.*

mystify /ˈmɪstɪfaɪ/ (**mystifies, mystifying, mystified**) V-T If you **are mystified** by something, you find it impossible to explain or understand. ❑ *There was something strange in her attitude which mystified me.* ● **mystifying** ADJ ❑ *I find your attitude mystifying.*

mystique /mɪˈstiːk/ N-UNCOUNT **Mystique** is an atmosphere of mystery and secrecy which is associated with a particular person or thing. ❑ *...the mystique that surrounds fine art.*

myth /mɪθ/ (**myths**) **1** N-VAR A **myth** is a well-known story which was made up in the past to explain natural events or to justify religious beliefs or social customs. ❑ *...a famous Greek myth.* ● **mythical** ADJ ❑ *The Hydra is a mythical beast that had seven or more heads.* **2** N-VAR If you describe a belief or explanation as a **myth**, you mean that many people believe it but it is actually untrue. ❑ *It is a myth that youngsters no longer want to read.*
→ see Word Web: **myth**
→ see **fantasy**

Word Partnership Use *myth* with:

ADJ.	**ancient** myth **1** **popular** myth **2**

mythic /ˈmɪθɪk/ **1** ADJ Someone or something that is **mythic** exists only in myths. ❑ *...the mythic figure of King Arthur.* **2** ADJ If you describe someone or something as **mythic**, you mean that they have become very famous. ❑ *He has become a star of mythic proportions.*

mythical /ˈmɪθɪkəl/ ADJ If you describe something as **mythical**, you think it is untrue or does not exist. ❑ *...the mythical underwater city of Atlantis.*

mythology /mɪˈθɒlədʒi/ N-UNCOUNT **Mythology** is a group of myths, especially those from a particular country, religion, or culture. ❑ *...Greek mythology.* ● **mythological** ADJ ❑ *This mythological beast was part lion and part goat.*
→ see **hero, myth**

m

Word Web myth

The scholar Joseph Campbell* believed that **mythologies** explain how a **culture** understands their world. **Stories, symbols, rituals**, and **myths** explain the **psychological**, **social,** cosmological, and **spiritual** parts of life. Campbell also believed that artists and thinkers are mythmakers. He explored **archetypal themes** in myths. He showed that these themes appear in many different cultures. For example, the **hero's** journey appear in a poem called *The Odyssey**. This poem is from ancient Greece. The hero's journey also appeared later in England in a story about King Arthur's* search for the Holy Grail*. The film *Star Wars* is a 20th century version of the hero's journey.

Joseph Campbell (1904–1987): an American professor and author.
The Odyssey: an epic poem from ancient Greece.
King Arthur: a legendary king of Great Britain.
Holy Grail: a cup that legends say Jesus used.

M

Nn

nag /næg/ (**nags, nagging, nagged**) **1** V-T If you say that someone **is nagging** you, you are annoyed with them because they are continuously asking you to do something. ❑ *My girlfriend nagged me to cut my hair.* • **nagging** N-UNCOUNT ❑ *Her endless nagging made him leave home.* **2** V-T/V-I If something such as a doubt or worry **nags at** you, or **nags** you, it keeps worrying you. ❑ *The problem nagged Amy all through lunch.*

nail /neɪl/ (**nails, nailing, nailed**) **1** N-COUNT A **nail** is a thin piece of metal with one pointed end and one flat end. You hit the flat end with a hammer in order to push the nail into something such as a wall. **2** V-T If you **nail** something somewhere, you fix it there using one or more nails. ❑ *The windows were all nailed shut.* **3** N-COUNT Your **nails** are the thin hard parts that grow at the ends of your fingers and toes.

nails

▸ **nail down** **1** PHR-VERB If you **nail down** something unknown or uncertain, you find out exactly what it is. ❑ *I want our investigation to nail down some answers.* **2** PHR-VERB If you **nail down** an agreement, you manage to reach a firm agreement with a definite result.

naive or **naïve** /naɪˈiːv, AM nɑː-/ ADJ If you describe someone as **naive**, you think they lack experience, causing them to expect things to be uncomplicated or easy, or people to be honest or kind when they are not. ❑ *I was naive to think they would agree.* • **naively** ADV ❑ *I naively thought that everything would be fine once we were married.* • **naivety** N-UNCOUNT ❑ *I was worried by his naivety.*

naked /ˈneɪkɪd/ **1** ADJ Someone who is **naked** is not wearing any clothes. ❑ *He stood naked in front of me.* • **nakedness** N-UNCOUNT ❑ *He pulled the blanket over his body to hide his nakedness.* **2** ADJ You can describe an object as **naked** when it does not have its normal covering. ❑ *...a naked light bulb.* **3** ADJ BEFORE N **Naked** emotions are easily recognized because they are very strongly felt. [WRITTEN] ❑ *I could see the naked hatred in her face.* • **nakedly** ADV ❑ *He nakedly desired success.* **4** PHRASE If you say that something cannot be seen by **the naked eye**, you mean that it cannot be seen without the help of equipment such as a telescope or microscope.

name /neɪm/ (**names, naming, named**) **1** N-COUNT The **name** of a person, thing, or place is the word or words that you use to identify them. ❑ *His name is Michael.* ❑ *They changed the name of the street.* **2** V-T When you **name** someone or something, you give them a name. If you **name** someone or something **after** a person or thing, you give them the same name as that person or thing. ❑ *My mother insisted on naming me Horace.* ❑ *He named his first child after his brother.* **3** V-T If you **name** someone, you identify them by stating their name. ❑ *The victim has been named as twenty-year-old John Barr.* **4** N-COUNT You can refer to the reputation of a person or thing as their **name**. ❑ *The Queen gives royalty a good name.* **5** → see also **brand name, Christian name** **6** PHRASE You can use **by name**, or **by the name of**, when you are saying what someone is called. ❑ *...a banker by the name of Kathryn Brown.* **7** PHRASE If someone **calls** you **names**, they insult you by saying unpleasant things to you or about you. ❑ *They called her rude names.* **8** PHRASE If something is **in** your **name**, it officially belongs to you or has been reserved for you. ❑ *They reserved a double room in the name of Muller.* **9** PHRASE If you do something **in the name of** an ideal or a person, you do it because you believe in or represent that ideal or person. ❑ *He destroyed everything he owned in the name of art.* **10** PHRASE If you **make a name for** yourself or **make** your **name as** something, you become well-known for that thing. ❑ *She made a name for herself as a photographer.* **11** PHRASE If you say that something is **the name of the game**, you mean that it is the most important aspect of a situation. [INFORMAL] ❑ *Family values are the name of the game.*
→ see **Internet**

Word Partnership	Use *name* with:
N.	name **and address**, **company** name, name **and number** **1**
ADJ.	**common** name, **familiar** name, **famous** name **full** name, **real** name, **well-known** name **1**

namely /ˈneɪmli/ ADV You use **namely** to introduce more detailed information about what you have just said. ❑ *One group has been forgotten, namely pensioners.*

nanny /ˈnæni/ (**nannies**) N-COUNT A **nanny** is a person who is paid by parents to look after their children.

nap /næp/ (**naps, napping, napped**) V-I & N-COUNT If you **nap**, or if you have a **nap**, you sleep for a short period of time, usually during the day.
→ see **sleep**

napkin /ˈnæpkɪn/ (**napkins**) N-COUNT A **napkin** is a small piece of cloth or paper used to protect your clothes when you are eating.

nappy /ˈnæpi/ (**nappies**) N-COUNT In British English, a **nappy** is a piece of thick cloth or paper which is fastened round a baby's bottom in order to absorb its waste. The usual American word is **diaper**.

narcotic /nɑːˈkɒtɪk/ (**narcotics**) N-COUNT & ADJ **Narcotics**, or **narcotic** drugs, are drugs such as opium or heroin which make you sleepy and stop you feeling pain, but are also addictive.

Word Link	*ator ≈ one who does : creator, decorator, narrator*

narrate /nəˈreɪt, AM ˈnæreɪt/ (**narrates, narrating, narrated**) V-T If you **narrate** a story, you tell it. [FORMAL] ❑ *The book is narrated by Richard Papen.* ● **narration** N-UNCOUNT ❑ *The narration by Janet Suzman is exciting.* ● **narrator** (**narrators**) N-COUNT ❑ *The story's narrator is a famous actress.*

narrative /ˈnærətɪv/ (**narratives**) N-COUNT A **narrative** is a story or an account of events.

narrow /ˈnærəʊ/ (**narrower, narrowest, narrows, narrowing, narrowed**) 1 ADJ Something that is **narrow** measures a very small distance from one side to the other, especially compared to its length or height. ❑ *Her bed was too narrow and too firm.* ❑ *She had long, narrow feet.* ● **narrowness** N-UNCOUNT ❑ *...the narrowness of the river mouth.* 2 V-I If something **narrows**, it becomes less wide. ❑ *The wide path narrows before crossing a stream.* 3 ADJ If you describe someone's ideas, attitudes, or beliefs as **narrow**, you disapprove of them because they are not imaginative but are old-fashioned or very strict, and often ignore the more important aspects of a situation. ❑ *It was a narrow and old-fashioned view of family life.* ● **narrowness** N-UNCOUNT ❑ *...the narrowness of their opinions.* 4 V-T/V-I If something **narrows**, or if you **narrow** it, its extent, range, or scope becomes smaller. ❑ *The EU and America narrowed their political differences.* ● **narrowing** N-UNCOUNT ❑ *...a narrowing of the gap between rich and poor.* 5 ADJ If you have a **narrow** victory, you succeed in winning but only by a small amount. ❑ *Mr Kerry won the debate by a narrow margin.* ● **narrowly** ADV ❑ *She narrowly failed to win enough votes.* 6 ADJ BEFORE N If you have a **narrow** escape, something unpleasant nearly happens to you. ● **narrowly** ADV ❑ *Five firemen narrowly escaped death.*

▶ **narrow down** PHR-VERB If you **narrow down** a range of things, you reduce the number of things included in it. ❑ *I've narrowed the list down to twenty-three.*

Thesaurus	*narrow*	Also look up:
ADJ.	close, cramped, restricted, tight; *(ant.)* broad, wide 1	

Word Partnership	Use *narrow* with:
ADV.	**relatively** narrow, **too** narrow 1
N.	narrow **band**, narrow **hallway**, narrow **opening**, narrow **path** 1
	narrow **definition**, narrow **focus**, narrow **mind**, narrow **view** 3

nasal /ˈneɪzəl/ 1 ADJ If someone's voice is **nasal**, it sounds as if air is passing through their nose as well as their mouth while they are speaking. ❑ *He had a high-pitched nasal voice.* 2 ADJ BEFORE N **Nasal** is used to describe things relating to the nose. ❑ *Nasal sprays are sometimes used to treat asthma.*
→ see **smell**

nasty /ˈnɑːsti, ˈnæsti/ (**nastier, nastiest**) 1 ADJ Something that is **nasty** is very unpleasant or unattractive. ❑ *This divorce could become nasty.* ● **nastiness** N-UNCOUNT ❑ *...the nastiness of modern politics.* 2 ADJ If you describe a disease or injury as **nasty**, you mean that it is serious or looks very unpleasant. ❑ *Lili had a nasty chest infection.* 3 ADJ If you describe a person or their behaviour as **nasty**, you mean that they behave in an unkind and unpleasant way. ❑ *The guards looked really nasty.* ❑ *She is so nasty to me.* ● **nastily** ADV ❑ *'Thank you,' Mr Saunders said nastily.*

nation /ˈneɪʃən/ (**nations**) 1 N-COUNT A **nation** is an individual country, especially when it is considered from the point of view of its cultural or ethnic identity. ❑ *...the Arab nations.* 2 → See note at **country**
→ see **country**

Thesaurus	*nation*	Also look up:
N.	country, democracy, population, republic, society	

national /ˈnæʃənəl/ (**nationals**) 1 ADJ **National** means relating to the whole of a country, rather than to part of it or to other nations. ❑ *...national and local news.* ❑ *...major national and international issues.* ● **nationally** ADV ❑ *...a nationally televised speech.* 2 ADJ BEFORE N **National** means typical of the people or customs of a particular country or nation. ❑ *Baseball is America's national sport.* 3 N-COUNT A **national** of a country is a citizen of that country who is staying in a different country. ❑ *He was a British national, living in Trinidad.*

ˌnational ˈanthem (**national anthems**) N-COUNT A **national anthem** is a nation's official song.

nationalise /ˈnæʃənəlaɪz/ → see **nationalize**

nationalist /ˈnæʃənəlɪst/ (**nationalists**) 1 ADJ BEFORE N & N-COUNT **Nationalist** ideas or movements are connected with attempts to obtain political independence for a particular group of people. A **nationalist** is a person with nationalist beliefs. ❑ *...Welsh and Scottish nationalist politicians.* ● **nationalism** N-UNCOUNT ❑ *...the rise of nationalism.* 2 ADJ BEFORE N & N-COUNT **Nationalist** is used when describing people who believe that their nation is better than others. A **nationalist** is someone with nationalist views. ❑ *My more nationalist friends think the South is the greatest place on earth.* ● **nationalistic** ADJ ❑ *The challenge is to be proud of your culture without becoming nationalistic or racist.* ● **nationalism** N-UNCOUNT ❑ *...cultural nationalism.*

nationality /ˌnæʃəˈnælɪti/ (**nationalities**) N-VAR If you have the **nationality** of a particular country, you have the legal right to be a citizen of it. ❑ *He has British nationality.*

nationalize [BRIT also **nationalise**] /ˈnæʃənəlaɪz/ (**nationalizes, nationalizing, nationalized**) V-T If a government **nationalizes** a private industry, that industry becomes owned by the state and controlled by the government. ❑ *The coffee industry was nationalised after independence.* ● **nationalization** N-UNCOUNT ❑ *...the nationalization of the coal mines.*

ˌnational ˈpark (**national parks**) N-COUNT A **national park** is a large area of natural land protected by the government because of its natural beauty, plants, or animals.

Word Link *wide ≈ extending throughout : nationwide, widespread, worldwide*

nationwide /ˌneɪʃən'waɪd/ ADJ & ADV **Nationwide** activities or situations happen or exist in all parts of a country. You can say they happen or exist **nationwide.** ❑ *Car crime is a nationwide problem.* ❑ *...available from shops nationwide.*

Word Link *nat ≈ being born : innate, native, prenatal*

native /'neɪtɪv/ (**natives**) 1 ADJ BEFORE N Your **native** country or area is the country or area where you were born and brought up. ❑ *Teresa visited her native Albania.* 2 N-COUNT & ADJ A **native** of a particular country or region, or a person who is **native to** that country or region, is a person who was born there. ❑ *Dr Aubin is a native of St Blaise.* ❑ *...men and women native to Japan.* 3 ADJ BEFORE N Your **native language** or **tongue** is the first language that you learned to speak when you were a child. 4 N-COUNT & ADJ Animals or plants that are **natives** of a region, or are **native to** it, grow there naturally and have not been brought there. ❑ *The coconut palm is a native of Malaysia.* ❑ *Many of the plants are native to Brazil.*

Word Partnership Use *native* with:

N. native **country**, native **land** 1
native **language**, native **tongue** 3

natural /'nætʃərəl/ (**naturals**) 1 ADJ If you say that it is **natural** for someone to act in a particular way, you mean that it is reasonable in the circumstances. ❑ *It is only natural for young people to want excitement.* ❑ *Grief is a perfectly natural response.* 2 ADJ If someone's behaviour is **natural**, they are relaxed and do not appear to be hiding anything or pretending to be something they are not. ● **naturally** ADV ❑ *You can talk quite naturally to her.* ● **naturalness** N-UNCOUNT ❑ *...the naturalness of the acting.* 3 ADJ **Natural** behaviour or ability is instinctive and has not been learned. ❑ *The insect's natural instinct is to eat.* ❑ *Martin was a natural swimmer.* ● **naturally** ADV ❑ *Some children are naturally quieter than others.* 4 N-COUNT If you describe someone as a **natural**, you mean that they do something very well and very easily. ❑ *He's a natural with children.* 5 ADJ BEFORE N **Natural** things exist in nature and were not created by people. ❑ *...a natural disaster like an earthquake.* ● **naturally** ADV ❑ *Some chemicals are found naturally in water.*

Thesaurus *natural* Also look up:

ADJ. normal 1 2
genuine, sincere, unaffected 2
innate, instinctive 3
wild; *(ant.)* artificial 5

Word Partnership Use *natural* with:

ADV. **perfectly** natural 1 2
N. natural **reaction**, natural **tendency** 3
natural **beauty**, natural **disaster**, natural **food** 5

naturalist /'nætʃərəlɪst/ (**naturalists**) N-COUNT A **naturalist** is a person who studies plants, animals, and other living things.

naturally /'nætʃərəli/ 1 ADV You use **naturally** to indicate that something is obvious and not surprising. ❑ *He will never play football again. Naturally he is very upset.* 2 ADV If one thing develops **naturally** from another, it develops as a normal result of it. ❑ *When fathers are involved in child-care, it leads naturally to better father-son relationships.* 3 PHRASE If a skill or quality **comes naturally to** you, you have it instinctively, without having to work very hard to get it. ❑ *Self-confidence came naturally to Sergei.*

ˌnatural re'sources N-PLURAL The **natural resources** of a place are all its land, forests, energy sources, and minerals which exist naturally there and can be used by people. ❑ *Nigeria is a nation rich in natural resources.*

nature /'neɪtʃə/ (**natures**) 1 N-UNCOUNT **Nature** refers to all the animals, plants, and other things in the world that are not made by people, and all the events and processes that are not caused by people. ❑ *These grasses grow wild in nature.* ❑ *...the balance of nature.* 2 N-VAR The **nature** of something is its basic quality or character. Someone's **nature** is their character, which they show by their behaviour. ❑ *...the ambitious nature of the project.* ❑ *He was by nature friendly.* 3 PHRASE If a way of behaving is **second nature to** you, you do it almost without thinking because it is easy or obvious to you. ❑ *Secrecy is second nature to these people.*

Usage

Do not confuse **nature**, **landscape**, **scenery**, and **countryside**. Nature includes the landscape, the weather, animals, and plants. ❑ *These creatures roamed the Earth as the finest and rarest wonders of nature.* With **landscape**, the emphasis is on the physical features of the land, while **scenery** includes everything you can see when you look out over an area of land, usually in the country. ❑ *...the landscape of steep woods and distant mountains.* ❑ *...unattractive urban scenery.* **Countryside** is land which is away from towns and cities. ❑ *...3,500 acres of mostly flat countryside.*

Word Partnership Use *nature* with:

V. **love** nature, **preserve** nature 1
N. **love of** nature, **wonders of** nature 1
nature **of life**, nature **and nurture**
nature **of society**, nature **of work** 2

naughty /'nɔːti/ ADJ You say that small children are **naughty** when they behave badly. ❑ *You're being very naughty.*

nausea /'nɔːziə/ N-UNCOUNT **Nausea** is a feeling of sickness and dizziness. ❑ *I had a strong feeling of nausea.*

nautical /'nɔːtɪkəl/ ADJ **Nautical** things and people are involved with ships. ❑ *...a nautical chart.*

Word Link *nav ≈ ship : naval, navigate, navy*

naval /'neɪvəl/ ADJ BEFORE N **Naval** people and things belong to a country's navy. ❑ *Polyarny is a naval base in Russia.*

navel /'neɪvəl/ (**navels**) N-COUNT Your **navel** is

Word Web navigation

Early explorers used the **sun** and **stars** to navigate the seas. The sextant helped later navigators use stars to figure out their **position**. By measuring their position at noon, sailors could determine their latitude. The **compass** helped sailors figure out their position at any time of night or day. It also worked in any weather. Today all sorts of travelers use the global positioning system (GPS) as a guide. A GPS **receiver** is connected to a system of 24 **satellites** that can establish a location within a few feet.

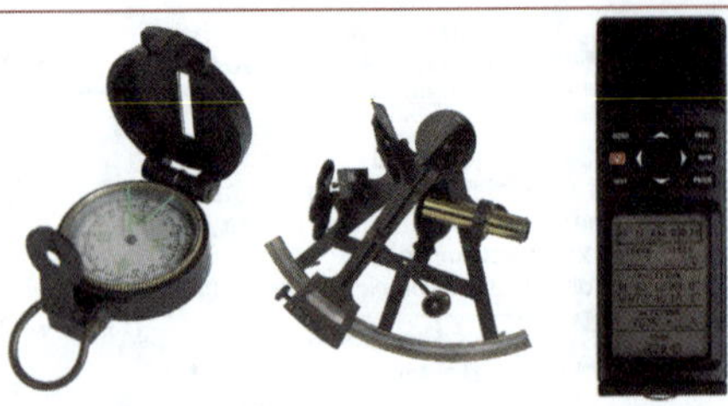

compass sextant GPS

the small hollow just below your waist at the front of your body.

Word Link *nav* ≈ *ship* : *naval, navigate, navy*

navigate /'nævɪgeɪt/ (**navigates, navigating, navigated**) **1** V-T/V-I When someone **navigates** an area, or when they **navigate**, they steer a ship or plane through the area towards a particular destination. ❑ *Every year they navigate the Greek islands in a boat.* ● **navigation** N-UNCOUNT ❑ *The expedition was ruined by poor navigation.* ● **navigator** (**navigators**) N-COUNT ❑ *He was a navigator in the air force during the war.* **2** V-I If a passenger in a car **navigates**, he or she tells the driver, often using a road map, what roads the car should be driven along in order to get somewhere. ❑ *You drive. I'll navigate.* **3** V-T If you **navigate** your way somewhere, you go there with difficulty, because the route is complicated or there are obstacles. ❑ *He tried to navigate his way through the crowds.*
→ see Word Web: **navigation**
→ see **star**

navy /'neɪvi/ (**navies**) **1** N-COUNT A country's **navy** is the part of its armed forces that fights at sea. ❑ *Her son was a captain in the Navy.* **2** ADJ & N-UNCOUNT **Navy** or **navy blue** is very dark blue.

NB /ˌen 'biː/ You write **NB** to draw someone's attention to what you are going to write next. ❑ *NB: This service costs extra.*

near /nɪə/ (**nearer, nearest, nears, nearing, neared**) **1** PREP & ADV & ADJ If something is **near** a place or thing or **near to** it, it is a short distance from it. ❑ *The farmhouse is near the cottage.* ❑ *He sat as near to the door as he could.* ❑ *He walked to the nearest shop.* **2** ADV & PREP & ADJ If you are **near to** a particular state or **near** it, you have almost reached it. ❑ *The repairs to the machine were near to completion.* ❑ *He was near tears.* **3** ADV & PREP If two things are similar, you can say that they are **near to** each other or **near** each other. ❑ *She was the nearest thing he had to a mother.* ❑ *Her feelings were nearer hatred than love.* **4** PREP & ADV If something happens **near** a particular time or **near to** it, it happens just before or just after that time. ❑ *I'll tell you nearer the day.* ❑ *The announcement was made near to Christmas.* **5** ADV If a time or event is **near**, it will happen very soon. ❑ *The time for my departure was getting nearer.* **6** V-T If someone or something **is nearing** a particular place, stage, or point in time, they will soon reach it. ❑ *He slowed the car as he neared the house.* ❑ *His age is hard to guess – he must be nearing fifty.* **7** PREP & ADJ You use **near** to say that something is a little more or less than an amount or number stated. ❑ *Temperatures dropped to near zero last December.* **8** PHRASE If something is **near enough** a quantity or **near enough** true, it is almost that quantity or almost true. ❑ *I've been working at it for near enough an hour.* **9** PHRASE You use **nowhere near** and **not anywhere near** to emphasize that something is not the case. ❑ *They are nowhere near good enough.* **10** **in the near future** → see **future**

nearby /ˌnɪə'baɪ/ ADV & ADJ If something is **nearby**, it is only a short distance away. ❑ *He lives nearby.* ❑ *People started shouting at a nearby table.*

nearly /'nɪəli/ **1** ADV If something is **nearly** a quantity, it is very close to that quantity but slightly less than it. If something is **nearly** a certain state, it is very close to that state but has not quite reached it. ❑ *Goldsworth stared at me in silence for nearly twenty seconds.* ❑ *It was already nearly eight o'clock.* ❑ *I've nearly finished.* **2** PHRASE You use **not nearly** to emphasize that something is not the case. For example, if something is **not nearly** big enough, it is much too small. ❑ *Father's flat in Paris wasn't nearly as expensive as this.*

Thesaurus *nearly* Also look up:
ADV. almost, approximately **1**

neat /niːt/ (**neater, neatest**) **1** ADJ A **neat** place, thing, or person is tidy, smart, and orderly. ❑ *She put her clothes in a neat pile.* ● **neatly** ADV ❑ *He folded his paper neatly.* ● **neatness** N-UNCOUNT ❑ *...the neatness of her appearance.* **2** ADJ A **neat** explanation or method is clever and convenient. ❑ *It was a neat, clever plan.* ● **neatly** ADV ❑ *Real people do not fit neatly into these categories.* ● **neatness** N-UNCOUNT ❑ *...the neatness of his conclusions.* **3** ADJ If you drink an alcoholic drink **neat**, you drink it without anything added. ❑ *...neat whisky.*

Thesaurus *neat* Also look up:
ADJ. orderly, tidy, uncluttered **1**

necessarily /ˌnesɪ'serɪli, -srɪli/ **1** ADV If you say that something is **not necessarily** true, you mean that it may not be true or is not always true. ❑ *Women do not necessarily have to act like men to be successful.* ❑ *'He was lying, of course.'—'Not necessarily.'*

2 ADV If you say that something **necessarily** happens, you mean that it has to happen and cannot be any different. ❑ *Business relationships are necessarily a bit more formal.*

necessary /ˈnesɪsəri/ ADJ Something that is **necessary** is needed to get a particular result or effect. ❑ *We will do whatever is necessary.* ❑ *We use this room as an extra bedroom, when necessary.*

Thesaurus	*necessary* Also look up:
ADJ.	essential, mandatory, obligatory, required; *(ant.)* unnecessary

necessitate /nɪˈsesɪteɪt/ (**necessitates, necessitating, necessitated**) V-T If something **necessitates** a particular course of action, it makes it necessary. [FORMAL] ❑ *A letter to the Pope necessitates careful thought.*

necessity /nɪˈsesɪti/ (**necessities**) **1** N-UNCOUNT **Necessity** is the need to do something. ❑ *He'd learned the necessity of hiding his feelings.* ❑ *Most people work from economic necessity.* **2** PHRASE If something is **of necessity** true, it is true because nothing else is possible or imaginable in the circumstances. **3** N-COUNT **Necessities** are things that you must have to live. ❑ *Water is a basic necessity of life.*

neck /nek/ (**necks**) **1** N-COUNT Your **neck** is the part of your body which joins your head to the rest of your body. ❑ *She threw her arms round his neck and hugged him.* **2** N-COUNT The **neck** of a dress or shirt is the part which is round your neck or just below it. **3** N-COUNT The **neck** of something such as a bottle or a guitar is the long narrow part at one end of it. **4** PHRASE If two or more competitors are **neck and neck**, they are level with each other and have an equal chance of winning. **5** **a pain in the neck** → see **pain**
→ see **body**

Word Partnership	Use *neck* with:
N.	**back of the** neck, **head and** neck, neck **injury** **1**
ADJ.	**broken** neck, **long** neck, **stiff** neck, **thick** neck **1** **3**

necklace /ˈneklɪs/ (**necklaces**) N-COUNT A **necklace** is a piece of jewellery such as a chain or string of beads, which someone wears round their neck.
→ see **jewellery**

nectarine /ˈnektəriːn, -rɪn/ (**nectarines**) N-COUNT A **nectarine** is a fruit similar to a peach with a smooth skin.

née /neɪ/ **née** is used before a name to indicate that it was a woman's surname before she got married. [FORMAL] ❑ *...Nicola Lewis (née May).*

need /niːd/ (**needs, needing, needed**) **1** V-T If you **need** something, or **need to** do something, you cannot successfully achieve what you want or live properly without it. ❑ *He needed money.* ❑ *I need to make a phone call.* ❑ *I need you to do something for me.* **2** N-COUNT If you have a **need to** do or have something, you cannot successfully achieve what you want without it. ❑ *Charles has never felt the need to compete.* ❑ *...his need for attention.* **3** V-T If an object or place **needs** something doing to it, that action must or should be done to improve the object or place. If a task **needs** doing, it must or should be done to improve a situation. ❑ *The building needs a lot of repairs.* **4** N-SING If there is a **need for** something, that thing would improve a situation. ❑ *There is a need for better schools.* **5** MODAL & V-T If you say that someone **needn't** do something, or that they **don't need to** do it, you are telling them not to do it, or advising or suggesting that they should not do it. ❑ *Look, you needn't shout.* ❑ *She need not know I'm here.* ❑ *We don't need to spend any more time on it.* **6** MODAL & V-T If someone **needn't** have done something, or if they **didn't need to** do it, it was not necessary or useful for them to do it, although they did it. ❑ *I was a little nervous, but I needn't have worried.* ❑ *You didn't need to give me any more money.* **7** PHRASE If you say that you will do something, especially an extreme action, **if need be**, or **if needs be**, you mean that you will do it if it is necessary. ❑ *We can survive in the forest for three months, if need be.* **8** PHRASE People **in need** do not have enough of essential things such as money, food, or good health. ❑ *When you were in need, I gave you money.* **9** PHRASE If someone or something is **in need of** something, they need it or ought to have it. ❑ *I was all right but in need of rest.*

Thesaurus	*need* Also look up:
V.	demand, require **1**

needle /ˈniːdəl/ (**needles, needling, needled**) **1** N-COUNT A **needle** is a small very thin piece of metal with a hole at one end and a sharp point at the other, which is used for sewing. **2** N-COUNT Knitting **needles** are thin metal or plastic sticks that are used for knitting. **3** N-COUNT The **needle** on a record player is the small pointed instrument that touches the record and picks up the sound signals. **4** N-COUNT A **needle** is a thin hollow metal rod with a sharp point, which forms part of a syringe. It is used to give injections or to take blood from someone's body. **5** N-COUNT On an instrument measuring speed, weight, or electricity, the **needle** is the thin piece of metal or plastic which moves backwards and forwards and shows the measurement. **6** N-COUNT The **needles** of a fir or pine tree are its thin pointed leaves. **7** V-T If someone **needles** you, they annoy you by criticizing you repeatedly. ❑ *He had needled Jerrold, which might be unwise.*

needle

needless /ˈniːdləs/ **1** ADJ Something that is **needless** is completely unnecessary. ❑ *His death was so needless.* • **needlessly** ADV ❑ *A lot of women suffer needlessly.* **2** PHRASE You say **needless to say** to emphasize that what you are saying is obvious. ❑ *Needless to say, I am very happy.*

needn't /ˈniːdənt/ **Needn't** is the usual spoken form of 'need not'.

needy /ˈniːdi/ (**needier, neediest**) ADJ & N-PLURAL **Needy** people do not have enough food, medicine, or clothing or an adequate house to live in. **The needy** are people who are needy. ❑ *...housing for needy families.* ❑ *...money for the needy.*

negate /nɪˈgeɪt/ (**negates, negating, negated**)

V-T If one thing **negates** another, it causes that other thing to lose the effect or value that it had. [FORMAL] ❑ *A bad diet may negate the effects of training.*

negative /'negətɪv/ (**negatives**) 1 ADJ A fact, situation, or experience that is **negative** is unpleasant, depressing, or harmful. ❑ *The news is not all negative.* ❑ *...the negative effect of unemployment.* 2 ADJ A **negative** reply or decision indicates the answer 'no'. ❑ *The question invites a negative response.* ● **negatively** ADV ❑ *60 percent of people answered negatively.* 3 ADJ If someone is **negative**, they consider only the bad aspects of a situation, rather than the good ones. ❑ *The public has a negative view of the Government's economic policies.* ● **negatively** ADV ❑ *Why do so many people think negatively?* ● **negativity** N-UNCOUNT ❑ *She has been accused of negativity.* 4 N-COUNT A **negative** is a word, expression, or gesture that means 'no' or 'not'. ❑ *He uses five negatives in fifty-three words.* 5 ADJ If a medical test or scientific test is **negative**, it shows that something has not happened or is not present. ❑ *The results were negative.* 6 N-COUNT A **negative** is the image that is first produced when you take a photograph. 7 ADJ A **negative** number is less than zero.

Word Partnership Use *negative* with:

N. negative **effect**, negative **experience**, negative **image**, negative **publicity** 1
negative **attitude**, negative **thoughts** 2
negative **comment**, negative **reaction**, negative **response** 3

neglect /nɪ'glekt/ (**neglects, neglecting, neglected**) 1 V-T & N-UNCOUNT If you **neglect** someone or something, you do not look after them properly. **Neglect** is failure to look after someone or something properly. ❑ *Don't neglect your health.* ❑ *The house has suffered years of neglect.* ● **neglected** ADJ ❑ *...neglected children.* 2 V-T If you **neglect to** do something, you fail to do it. ❑ *He neglected to give her his telephone number.* ❑ *They never neglect their duties.*

N

negligent /'neglɪdʒənt/ ADJ When you are **negligent**, you fail to do something that you should do. ❑ *The doctors have denied they were negligent.* ● **negligently** ADV ❑ *They have acted negligently.* ● **negligence** N-UNCOUNT ❑ *They accuse the airline of negligence.*

negligible /'neglɪdʒɪbəl/ ADJ Something that is **negligible** is so small or unimportant that it is not worth considering. ❑ *The risks are negligible.*

negotiable /nɪ'gəʊʃəbəl/ ADJ Something that is **negotiable** can be changed or agreed by means of discussion. ❑ *The fee is negotiable.*

negotiate /nɪ'gəʊʃieɪt/ (**negotiates, negotiating, negotiated**) 1 V-T/V-I If one person or group **negotiates with** another, they talk about a problem or a situation in order to solve the problem or complete the arrangement. You can also say that two people or groups **negotiate** or **negotiate** something. ❑ *The government would not negotiate with the rebels.* ❑ *Berger wants to negotiate a deal with Everton football club.* ● **negotiator** (**negotiators**) N-COUNT ❑ *...Japanese trade negotiators.* 2 V-T If you **negotiate** a place or an obstacle, you successfully travel across it or around it. ❑ *I negotiated my way out of the airport.*

ne'gotiating table N-SING If you say that people are **at the negotiating table**, you mean that they are having discussions in order to settle a dispute or reach an agreement.

negotiation /nɪˌgəʊʃi'eɪʃən/ (**negotiations**) N-VAR **Negotiations** are discussions that take place between people with different interests, in which they try to reach an agreement. ❑ *Four years of negotiation ended in failure.*

neighbour [AM **neighbor**] /'neɪbə/ (**neighbours**) 1 N-COUNT Your **neighbours** are the people who live near you, especially the people who live in the house or flat which is next to yours. 2 N-COUNT Your **neighbour** is the person who is standing or sitting next to you. ❑ *The woman spoke to her neighbour.* 3 N-COUNT You can refer to something which is near or next to something else of the same kind as its **neighbour**. ❑ *Raspberries and blackberries are not good neighbours.*

neighbourhood [AM **neighborhood**] /'neɪbəhʊd/ (**neighbourhoods**) N-COUNT A **neighbourhood** is one of the parts of a town where people live. ❑ *Margaret no longer goes for evening walks around her neighbourhood.*

Word Partnership Use *neighbourhood* with:

ADJ. **poor** neighbourhood, **residential** neighbourhood, **run down** neighbourhood

neighbouring [AM **neighboring**] /'neɪbərɪŋ/ ADJ BEFORE N **Neighbouring** describes the places and things that are near to the place or thing that you are talking about. ❑ *...Thailand and its neighbouring countries.*

neither /'naɪðə, 'niːðə/ 1 CONJ You use **neither** in front of the first of two or more words or expressions when you are linking two or more things which are not true or do not happen. The other thing, or the last of the other things, is introduced by 'nor'. ❑ *Professor Hisamatsu spoke neither English nor German.* ❑ *The play was neither as funny nor as disturbing as she said it was.* 2 DET & PRON You use **neither** to refer to each of two things or people, when you are making a negative statement that includes both of them. ❑ *At first, neither man could speak.* ❑ *Neither of us felt like going out.* 3 CONJ If you say that one person or thing does not do something and **neither** does another, what you say is true of all the people or things that you are mentioning. ❑ *I never learned to swim and neither did they.*

neon /'niːɒn/ 1 N-UNCOUNT **Neon** is a gas which exists in very small amounts in the atmosphere. 2 ADJ **Neon** lights or signs are made from glass tubes filled with neon gas which produce a bright electric light.

nephew /'nefjuː, 'nev-/ (**nephews**) N-COUNT Your **nephew** is the son of your sister or brother.

nerve /nɜːv/ (**nerves**) 1 N-COUNT **Nerves** are long thin fibres that transmit messages between your brain and other parts of your body. 2 N-PLURAL If you talk about someone's **nerves**, you mean their ability to remain calm and not become worried in a stressful situation. ❑ *A cup of tea calmed my nerves.* 3 N-PLURAL You can refer to someone's feelings of anxiety or tension as **nerves**. ❑ *I don't suffer from nerves.* 4 N-UNCOUNT

Word Web nervous system

The body's **nervous system** is a two-way road which carries electrochemical messages to and from different parts of the body. **Sensory** neurons carry information from both inside and outside the body to the **central nervous system** (CNS). The CNS is made of both the **brain** and the **spinal cord**. Motor neurons carry impulses from the CNS to **organs** and to **muscles** such as the muscles in the hand, telling them how to move. **Nerves** are made of sensory and motor neurons. Nerves run through the whole body.

Nerve is the courage you need to do something difficult or dangerous. ❑ *I don't have the nerve to talk to him.* **5** PHRASE If someone or something **gets on** your **nerves**, they annoy or irritate you. [INFORMAL] **6** PHRASE If you say that someone **had a nerve** or **had the nerve to** do something, you mean that they made you angry by doing something rude or lacking in respect. [INFORMAL] ❑ *He had the nerve to ask me who I was.*
→ see **ear, eye, nervous system, smell**

nervous /ˈnɜːvəs/ **1** ADJ If you are **nervous**, you are worried and frightened, and show this in your behaviour. ❑ *It has made me nervous about going out.* ● **nervously** ADV ❑ *Joe giggled nervously.* ● **nervousness** N-UNCOUNT ❑ *I smiled warmly so he wouldn't see my nervousness.* **2** ADJ A **nervous** person is very tense and easily upset. **3** ADJ BEFORE N A **nervous** illness or condition is one that affects your mental state.

Word Partnership Use *nervous* with:

PREP.	nervous **about** ***something*** **1**
V.	**become** nervous, **feel** nervous, **get** nervous, **look** nervous, **make** ***someone*** nervous **1**
ADV.	**increasingly** nervous, **a little** nervous, **too** nervous, **very** nervous **1** **2**

ˌnervous ˈbreakdown (**nervous breakdowns**) N-COUNT If someone has a **nervous breakdown**, they become extremely depressed and anxious, and have to be treated by a psychiatrist.

ˈnervous system (**nervous systems**) N-COUNT Your **nervous system** is all the nerves in your body together with your brain and spinal cord, which control your movements and feelings.
→ see Word Web: **nervous system**

nest

nest /nest/ (**nests, nesting, nested**) **1** N-COUNT A **nest** is a place that birds, insects and other animals make to lay eggs in or give birth to their young in. ❑ *...a wasps' nest.* **2** V-I When a bird **nests** somewhere, it builds a nest and settles there to lay its eggs. ❑ *Owls nested in the trees.*
→ see **bird**

nestle /ˈnesəl/ (**nestles, nestling, nestled**) **1** V-I If you **nestle** somewhere, you move into a comfortable position, often by pressing against someone or something soft. ❑ *The two little girls nestled against their mother.* **2** V-I If a building, place, or thing **nestles** somewhere, it is in that place or position and seems safe or sheltered. ❑ *The town nestles in the valley, surrounded by hills.*

net /net/ (**nets, netting, netted**)

> Net is also spelled **nett** in British English for meanings 5 and 6.

1 N-UNCOUNT **Net** is a kind of material made of threads, strings, or wires woven together so that there are small equal spaces between them. ❑ *...net curtains.* **2** N-COUNT A **net** is a piece of net which you use, for example, to protect something or to catch fish. ❑ *A fisherman sat mending his nets.* **3** N-COUNT The **net** is the piece of netting used to divide the two halves of a tennis court, or to form the back of a goal in football. ❑ *He kicked the ball into the back of the net.* **4** V-T If you **net** something, you manage to get it, often by using skill. ❑ *The sale will net $1.5 million.* **5** ADJ BEFORE N & ADV A **net** amount or result is the final amount or result, when everything necessary has been considered or included. ❑ *...a rise in sales and net profit.* ❑ *...net salary after tax.* **6** ADJ BEFORE N The **net weight** of something is its weight without its container or wrapping.
→ see **tennis**

Word Partnership Use *net* with:

N.	**fishing** net **1** **2**
	net **earnings**, net **gain**, net **income/loss**, net **increase**, net **proceeds**, net **profit**, net **result** net **revenue** **5**

netball /ˈnetbɔːl/ N-UNCOUNT **Netball** is a game played by two teams of seven players, usually women. Each team tries to score goals by throwing a ball through a net which is at the top of a pole at each end of the court.

nett → see **net**

nettle /ˈnetəl/ (**nettles**) N-COUNT A **nettle** is a wild plant with leaves that sting when you touch them.

network /ˈnetwɜːk/ (**networks**) **1** N-COUNT A **network** of lines, roads, veins, or other long thin things is a large number of them which cross each other or meet at many points. ❑ *The park is surrounded by a network of streets.* ❑ *Butterfly wings are covered with a network of veins.* **2** N-COUNT A **network** of people or organizations is a large number of them that have a connection with each other and work together as a system. ❑ *...their network of offices.* **3** N-COUNT A radio or television **network** is a company or group of companies that broadcasts the same radio or television programmes throughout an area.
→ see **Internet**

Word Partnership Use *network* with:

ADJ. **extensive** network, **nationwide** network, **vast** network, **wireless** network, **worldwide** network 1 2
N. network **administrator**, **computer** network, network **coverage**, network **support** 2
broadcast network, **cable** network, **radio** network, **television/TV** network 3

'network card (**network cards**) N-COUNT A **network card** is a card that connects a computer to a network. [COMPUTING]

networking /'netwɜːkɪŋ/ N-UNCOUNT **Networking** is the process of establishing business contacts, often through social activities. ❑ *Quite a bit of networking happens at conferences.*

Word Link *otic ≈ affecting, causing : chaotic, erotic, neurotic*

neurotic /njʊə'rɒtɪk, AM nʊr-/ (**neurotics**) ADJ & N-COUNT If someone is **neurotic**, or if they are a **neurotic**, they continually show a lot of unreasonable fears and worry. ❑ *They were neurotic about their health.*

neutral /'njuːtrəl, AM 'nuːt-/ 1 ADJ A **neutral** person or country does not support anyone in a disagreement, war, or contest. ❑ *It is morally impossible to remain neutral in this conflict.* ● **neutrality** /njuː'trælɪti, AM 'nuːt-/ N-UNCOUNT ❑ *...political neutrality.* 2 ADJ If your facial expression or language is **neutral**, you do not show what you are thinking or feeling. ❑ *After a pause I said in my most neutral voice: 'Really'.* 3 N-UNCOUNT **Neutral** is the position between the gears of a vehicle, in which the gears are not connected to the engine. ❑ *Graham put the van in neutral and jumped out.* 4 ADJ In an electrical device or system, the **neutral wire** is one of the three wires needed to complete the circuit so that the current can flow.
→ see **war**

N

neutralize [BRIT also **neutralise**] /'njuːtrəlaɪz, AM 'nuːt-/ (**neutralizes, neutralizing, neutralized**) V-T To **neutralize** something means to prevent it from having any effect or from working properly. ❑ *Fruit and vegetables help to neutralize chemical poisons in the body.*

never /'nevə/ 1 ADV **Never** means at no time in the past or future. ❑ *I have never lost the weight I gained in my teens.* ❑ *Never say that.* ❑ *This must never happen again.* 2 ADV **Never** means not in any circumstances. ❑ *Divorce is never easy for children.* 3 PHRASE **Never ever** is an emphatic expression for 'never'. [SPOKEN] ❑ *He's vowed never ever to talk about it.* 4 ADV **Never** is used to refer to the past and to say that something did not happen. ❑ *He never achieved anything.* ❑ *I planned to meet Nick in London, but he never came.* 5 **never mind** → see **mind**

,never-'ending ADJ If you describe something bad or unpleasant as **never-ending**, you are emphasizing that it seems to last a very long time. ❑ *...a never-ending series of problems.*

nevertheless /,nevəðə'les/ ADV You use **nevertheless** when saying something that contrasts with what has just been said. [FORMAL] ❑ *He was injured during the World Cup but, nevertheless, travelled to Sydney with the team.*

new /njuː, AM nuː/ (**newer, newest**) 1 ADJ Something that is **new** has been recently created or invented. ❑ *They've just opened a new hotel.* ❑ *Their story is the subject of a new film.* ❑ *These ideas are nothing new in America.* 2 ADJ Something that is **new** has not been used or owned by anyone. ❑ *There are many boats, new and used, for sale.* 3 ADJ You use **new** to describe something which has replaced another thing because someone no longer has it, or because it is no longer useful. ❑ *I had to find somewhere new to live.* ❑ *My mobile phone needs a new battery.* 4 ADJ **New** is used to describe something that has only recently been discovered or noticed. ❑ *The new planet is about ten times the size of the earth.* 5 ADJ BEFORE N **New** is used to describe someone or something that has recently changed state. ❑ *...a new mother.* 6 ADJ AFTER LINK-V If you are **new to** a situation or place, or if the situation or place is **new to** you, you have not previously seen it or had any experience of it. ❑ *She wasn't new to the company.* ❑ *His name was new to me.* ❑ *I'm new here.*

Thesaurus *new* Also look up:

ADJ. contemporary, current, latest, modern, novel; *(ant.)* existing, old, past 1

newborn also **new-born** /'njuːbɔːn, AM 'nuː-/ (**newborns**) ADJ & N-COUNT A **newborn** baby or animal or a **newborn** is a baby or animal that has just been born. ❑ *...his newborn child.*

newcomer /'njuːkʌmə, AM 'nuː-/ (**newcomers**) N-COUNT A **newcomer** is a person who has recently started a new activity, arrived in a place, or joined an organization. ❑ *The actress is a relative newcomer to television.*

,new-'found also **newfound** ADJ BEFORE N A **new-found** quality or ability is one that you have discovered recently. ❑ *...his new-found confidence.*

newly /'njuːli, AM 'nuːli/ ADV **Newly** is used before past participles or adjectives to indicate that an action or a situation is very recent. ❑ *...a newly married man.* ❑ *...the newly independent countries of Africa.*

news /njuːz, AM nuːz/ 1 N-UNCOUNT **News** is information about a recently changed situation or a recent event. ❑ *We waited for news of him.* ❑ *I wish I had better news for you.* ❑ *Mr Forsberg welcomed the news.* 2 N-UNCOUNT **News** is information that is published in newspapers and broadcast on radio and television. ❑ *This is the top story in the news.* 3 N-SING **The news** is a television or radio broadcast which consists of information about recent events. ❑ *...the six o'clock news.*

Usage

Note that, although **news** looks like a plural, it is in fact an uncount noun in meanings 1 and 2. ❑ *Good news is always worth waiting for.* You cannot say 'a news', but you can say a **piece of news** when you are referring to a particular fact or message. ❑ *One of my Dutch colleagues told me a very exciting piece of news.* When you are talking about television and radio news, or newspapers, you can refer to an individual story or report as a **news item**.

'news agency (**news agencies**) N-COUNT A

news agency is an organization which collects news stories from all over the world and sells them to journalists.

newsagent /ˈnjuːzeɪdʒənt, AM ˈnuːz-/ (**newsagents**) N-COUNT In Britain, a **newsagent** or a **newsagent's** is a shop where newspapers, sweets, soft drinks, and stationery are sold. You can also refer to the shopkeeper as a **newsagent**.

newscaster /ˈnjuːzkɑːstə, AM ˈnuːzkæstə/ (**newscasters**) N-COUNT A **newscaster** is a person who reads the news on television or radio.

ˈnews conference (**news conferences**) N-COUNT A **news conference** is a meeting held by a famous or important person in which they answer journalists' questions.

newsgroup /ˈnjuːzgruːp, AM ˈnuːz-/ (**newsgroups**) N-COUNT A **newsgroup** is an Internet site where people can put information and opinions about a particular subject. [COMPUTING]

newsletter /ˈnjuːzletə, AM ˈnuːz-/ (**newsletters**) N-COUNT A **newsletter** is one or more printed sheets of paper containing information about an organization that is sent regularly to its members.

newspaper /ˈnjuːspeɪpə, AM ˈnuːz-/ (**newspapers**) 1 N-VAR A **newspaper** is a publication consisting of large sheets of folded paper, on which news is printed. ❑ *They read the story in the newspaper.* ❑ *Each mango is wrapped in newspaper.* 2 N-COUNT A **newspaper** is an organization that produces a newspaper. ❑ *He worked for a small newspaper in Queensland.*

newsprint /ˈnjuːzprɪnt, AM ˈnuːz-/ N-UNCOUNT **Newsprint** is the cheap paper on which newspapers are printed.

ˌnew ˈwave (**new waves**) N-COUNT In the arts or in politics, a **new wave** is a group or movement that deliberately introduces new or unconventional ideas. ❑ *...the new wave of Irish crime writers.*

ˌNew ˈYear 1 N-UNCOUNT **New Year** or **the New Year** is the time when people celebrate the start of a year. ❑ *Happy New Year, everyone.* ❑ *The restaurant was closed over the New Year.* 2 N-SING **The New Year** is the first few weeks of a year. ❑ *Isabel was expecting their baby in the New Year.*

next /nekst/ 1 ORD The **next** period of time, event, person, or thing is the one that comes immediately after the present one or after the previous one. ❑ *I got up early the next morning.* ❑ *...the next available flight.* ❑ *Who will be our next teacher?* ❑ *I don't want to be the next to die.* 2 DET & PRON You use **next** in expressions such as **next Friday** and **next year** to refer, for example, to the Friday or year which follows immediately after the present one or after the previous one. ❑ *Let's plan a big party next week.* ❑ *John is coming the weekend after next.* 3 ADJ The **next** place or person is the one nearest to you or the first one that you come to. ❑ *...in the next room.* ❑ *Stop at the next corner.* 4 ADV The thing that happens **next** is the thing that happens immediately after something else. ❑ *Allow the sauce to cool. Next, add the cheese.* ❑ *The news is next.* 5 ADV When you **next** do something, you do it for the first time since you last did it. ❑ *I next saw him at his house.* 6 ADV You use **next** to say that something has more of a quality than all other things except one. ❑ *If you can't be with your family, the next best thing is to talk to them.* 7 PHRASE You can say **the next thing I knew** to suggest that a new situation was surprising because it happened very suddenly. [INFORMAL, SPOKEN] ❑ *The next thing I knew, the house was on fire.* 8 PREP If one thing is **next to** another, it is at the side of it. ❑ *She sat down next to him on the sofa.* 9 PHRASE You use **next to** before a negative, or a word that suggests something negative, to mean almost. ❑ *Most weight loss products are next to useless.*

Word Partnership Use *next* with:

N.	next **election**, next **generation**, next **level**, next **meeting**, next **move**, next **question**, next **step**, next **stop**, next **time**, next **train** 1
	next **day/hour/month/week/year** 1 2
V.	**come** next, **go** next, **happen** next 3 4

ˌnext ˈdoor 1 ADV & ADJ BEFORE N If a room or building is **next door**, it is the next one to the right or left. ❑ *He lived in the house next door to me.* ❑ *...the old lady who lived next door.* ❑ *Juan came out of the next-door room.* 2 ADV & ADJ The people **next door** are the people who live in the house to the right or left of yours. ❑ *...our next door neighbour.*

nibble /ˈnɪbəl/ (**nibbles, nibbling, nibbled**) 1 V-T & N-COUNT If you **nibble** food, or if you eat it in **nibbles**, you eat it by biting very small pieces off it. ❑ *She nibbled a piece of dry toast.* 2 V-I When animals **nibble at** something, or when they **nibble away at** it, they take small bites of it quickly and repeatedly.

nice /naɪs/ (**nicer, nicest**) 1 ADJ If you say that something is **nice**, you mean that it is pleasant, enjoyable, or attractive. ❑ *It's nice to be here together again.* ❑ *We had a nice meal.* ● **nicely** ADV ❑ *He's just written a book, which is nicely illustrated.* 2 ADJ If you say that it is **nice of** someone **to** say or do something, you are saying that they are being kind and thoughtful. This is often used as a way of thanking someone. ❑ *'How are your boys?'—'How nice of you to ask.'* 3 ADJ If someone is **nice**, they are friendly and pleasant. ❑ *He was a nice man, very quiet and polite.* ❑ *They were extremely nice to me.* ● **nicely** ADV ❑ *He treated you very nicely.*

Thesaurus *nice* Also look up:

ADJ.	friendly, kind, likeable, pleasant, polite; (*ant.*) mean, unpleasant 3

Word Partnership Use *nice* with:

ADJ.	nice **and clean** 1
V.	**look** nice, nice **to see** ***someone/something*** 1
N.	nice **clothes**, nice **day**, nice **guy**, nice **people**, nice **place**, nice **smile**, nice **weather** 1

nicely /ˈnaɪsli/ ADV Something that is happening or working **nicely** is happening or working in a satisfactory way. ❑ *The girls play nicely together.*

niche /niːʃ, AM nɪtʃ/ (**niches**) 1 N-COUNT A **niche** is a hollow area in a wall or a natural hollow part in a cliff. ❑ *...a niche in the rock where the path ended.* 2 N-COUNT Your **niche** is the job or activity

n

which is exactly suitable for you. ❑ *Simon Jones quickly found his niche as a teacher.*

nick /nɪk/ (**nicks, nicking, nicked**) **1** V-T If someone **nicks** something, they steal or take it. [BRIT, INFORMAL] ❑ *He's nicked all your ideas.* ❑ *Michelle had her purse nicked.* **2** V-T If you **nick** something, you accidentally make a small cut or scratch into the surface of it. ❑ *He nicked himself on the chin with his razor.* **3** N-COUNT A **nick** is a small cut or scratch in the surface of something. ❑ *There was a bad nick on his neck.* **4** PHRASE If something is achieved **in the nick of time**, it is achieved successfully, at the last possible moment. [INFORMAL] ❑ *It seems we got here just in the nick of time.*

nickel /ˈnɪkəl/ (**nickels**) **1** N-UNCOUNT **Nickel** is a silver-coloured metal that is used in making steel. **2** N-COUNT In the United States and Canada, a **nickel** is a coin worth five cents.

nickname /ˈnɪkneɪm/ (**nicknames, nicknaming, nicknamed**) **1** N-COUNT A **nickname** is an informal name for someone or something. ❑ *Red got his nickname for his red hair.* **2** V-T If someone or something **is nicknamed** a particular name, they are given that name as a nickname. ❑ *Richard has been nicknamed 'Mr Bean' by friends.*

nicotine /ˈnɪkɪtiːn/ N-UNCOUNT **Nicotine** is an addictive substance in tobacco.

niece /niːs/ (**nieces**) N-COUNT Your **niece** is the daughter of your sister or brother.

niggle /ˈnɪgəl/ (**niggles, niggling, niggled**) V-T & N-COUNT If something **niggles** you, it makes you worry slightly over a long time. You can call a worry like this a **niggle**. ❑ *The truth might niggle him for ever.* ❑ *Why is there a little niggle at the back of my mind?*

N

night /naɪt/ (**nights**) **1** N-VAR The **night** is the part of each period of twenty-four hours when it is dark outside, especially the time when most people are sleeping. ❑ *He didn't leave the house all night.* ❑ *Finally night fell.* **2** N-COUNT The **night** is the period of time between the end of the afternoon and the time that you go to bed. ❑ *So whose party was it last night?* ❑ *I really enjoy going out on Friday night.* **3** N-UNCOUNT If you refer to a particular time **at night**, you mean a time during the part of a day after it gets dark and before midnight. ❑ *We got back about eleven o'clock at night.* **4** PHRASE If something happens **day and night** or **night and day**, it happens all the time without stopping. ❑ *His team is working day and night to finish.* **5** PHRASE If you have **an early night**, you go to bed early. If you have **a late night**, you go to bed late.
→ see **star, time**

Word Partnership Use *night* with:

V.	**sleep at** night, **spend a/the** night, **stay out at** night, **stay the** night, **work at** night **1**
ADJ.	**cold** night, **cool** night, **dark** night, **rainy** night, **warm** night **1**
N.	**election** night, **wedding** night **2**

nightclub /ˈnaɪtklʌb/ (**nightclubs**) N-COUNT A **nightclub** is a place where people go late in the evening to drink and dance.

nightlife /ˈnaɪtlaɪf/ N-UNCOUNT The **nightlife** in a place is the entertainment and social activities that are available at night. ❑ *It's a university town, with lots of nightlife.*

nightly /ˈnaɪtli/ ADJ BEFORE N & ADV A **nightly** event happens every night. ❑ *...secret nightly meetings.* ❑ *Dinner is served nightly.*

nightmare /ˈnaɪtmeə/ (**nightmares**) **1** N-COUNT A **nightmare** is a very frightening dream. ❑ *All the victims still suffered nightmares.* **2** N-COUNT If you say that an experience is a **nightmare**, you mean that it is very unpleasant. [INFORMAL] ❑ *The bus journey was a nightmare.*

ˈnight time N-UNCOUNT **Night time** is the period of time between when it gets dark and when the sun rises. ❑ *He likes to have his bath at night time.*

nil /nɪl/ **1** NUM **Nil** means the same as zero. It is often used in scores of sports games. ❑ *They lost two nil to Italy.* **2** N-UNCOUNT If you say that something is **nil**, you mean that it does not exist at all. ❑ *Their legal rights are virtually nil.*

nimble /ˈnɪmbəl/ (**nimbler, nimblest**) **1** ADJ Someone who is **nimble** is able to move their fingers, hands, or legs quickly and easily. ❑ *Both the piano and the violin require nimble fingers to play.* **2** ADJ Someone who has a **nimble** mind is clever and can think quickly.

nine /naɪn/ (**nines**) NUM **Nine** is the number 9.

nineteen /ˌnaɪnˈtiːn/ (**nineteens**) NUM **Nineteen** is the number 19.

nineteenth /ˌnaɪnˈtiːnθ/ ORD The **nineteenth** item in a series is the one that you count as number nineteen.

ninetieth /ˈnaɪntiəθ/ ORD The **ninetieth** item in a series is the one that you count as number ninety.

ninety /ˈnaɪnti/ (**nineties**) NUM **Ninety** is the number 90. For examples of how numbers such as ninety and eighty are used see **eighty**.

ninth /naɪnθ/ ORD The **ninth** item in a series is the one that you count as number nine.

nip /nɪp/ (**nips, nipping, nipped**) **1** V-I If you **nip** somewhere, usually somewhere nearby, you go there quickly or for a short time. [BRIT, INFORMAL] ❑ *Should I nip out and get some coffee?* **2** V-T If a person or an animal **nips** you, they pinch or bite you lightly. ❑ *He was nipped by a rat.* **3** to **nip** something **in the bud** → see **bud**

nipple /ˈnɪpəl/ (**nipples**) N-COUNT The **nipples** on someone's body are the two small pieces of slightly hard flesh on their chest. Babies suck milk through their mothers' nipples.

nitrate /ˈnaɪtreɪt/ (**nitrates**) N-VAR A **nitrate** is a chemical compound that includes nitrogen and oxygen. Nitrates are used as fertilizers.
→ see **firework**

nitrogen /ˈnaɪtrədʒən/ N-UNCOUNT **Nitrogen** is a colourless element that has no smell and is usually found as a gas.
→ see **air**

no /nəʊ/

The plural of the noun can be **noes** or **no's**.

1 CONVENTION You use **no** to give a negative answer to a question, to say that something is not true, to refuse an offer, or to refuse permission. ❑ *'Any problems?'—'No, I'm O.K.'* ❑ *'You're getting worse than me.'—'No I'm not.'* ❑ *'Here, have mine.'—'No, this is fine.'* ❑ *No. I forbid it.* **2** CONVENTION You use **no** to say that you agree with or understand a negative statement that someone else has made. ❑ *'I don't know him, do I?'—'No, you don't.'* **3** CONVENTION You use **no** to express shock or disappointment at something. ❑ *Oh no, not another day of this.* **4** CONVENTION You use **no** as a way of introducing a correction to what you have just said. ❑ *It means the whole group, no, more than that, it means the entire species.* **5** DET You use **no** to mean not any or not one person or thing. ❑ *He had no intention of paying the cash.* ❑ *No letters survive from this early period.* **6** DET You use **no** to emphasize that someone or something is not a particular thing or does not have a particular quality. ❑ *He is no singer.* ❑ *Today's elections are of no great importance.* **7** ADV You use **no** when emphasizing that something does not exceed a particular amount or number, or does not have more of a particular quality than something else. ❑ *...no later than the end of 1994.* ❑ *No fewer than thirty climbers reached the summit.* ❑ *He will be no more helpful than his brother.* **8** DET **No** is used in notices or instructions to say that a particular thing is forbidden. ❑ *...'no smoking' signs.* ❑ *No talking in class.* **9** N-COUNT A **no** is the answer 'no' or a vote against something. ❑ *Is that a yes or a no?* **10** PHRASE If you say **there is no** doing a particular thing, you mean that it is impossible to do that thing. ❑ *There is no going back to the life she had.*

No. (**Nos**) **No.** is a written abbreviation for **number.** ❑ *...No. 10 Downing Street.*

nobility /nəʊ'bɪlɪti/ **1** N-UNCOUNT **Nobility** is the quality of being noble. [FORMAL] ❑ *...instincts of nobility and generosity.* **2** N-SING **The nobility** of a society are all the people who have titles and high social rank. ❑ *They married into the nobility.*

noble /'nəʊbəl/ (**nobler, noblest, nobles**) **1** ADJ If you say that someone is a **noble** person, you admire and respect them because they are honest, brave, and not selfish. ❑ *He was a noble man who was always willing to help.* ● **nobly** ADV ❑ *They have supported us nobly in this war.* **2** ADJ & N-COUNT If someone is **noble** or a **noble**, they belong to a high social class and have a title. ❑ *...rich and noble families.*

nobody /'nəʊbɒdi/ (**nobodies**) **1** PRON **Nobody** means not a single person. ❑ *Nobody realizes how bad things are.* ❑ *For a long time, nobody spoke.* **2** N-COUNT If someone says that a person is a **nobody**, they are saying in an unkind way that the person is not at all important. ❑ *I have nothing to fear from a nobody like you.*

Usage

You do not use **nobody** or **no one** in front of **of** to talk about a particular group of people. The word you need is **none.** ❑ *None of the men has been injured.* ❑ *None of the victims has been identified.*

nocturnal /nɒk'tɜːnəl/ **1** ADJ **Nocturnal** means happening at night. ❑ *...teenagers' nocturnal activities.* **2** ADJ **Nocturnal** creatures are active mostly at night.
→ see **bat**

nod /nɒd/ (**nods, nodding, nodded**) **1** V-I & N-COUNT If you **nod**, or if you give a **nod**, you move your head down and up to show agreement, understanding, or approval. ❑ *'Are you okay?' I asked. She nodded.* ❑ *Todd agreed with a nod of his head.* **2** V-I & N-COUNT If you **nod**, or if you give a **nod** in a particular direction, you move your head once in that direction in order to indicate something. ❑ *'Does it work?' he asked, nodding at the piano.* ❑ *'It was on the news earlier,' said Leo, with a nod towards the television.* **3** V-I & N-COUNT If you **nod**, or if you give a **nod**, you bend your head once, as a way of saying hello or goodbye. ❑ *All the girls nodded and said 'Hi'.* ❑ *He gave Sabrina a quick nod of acknowledgement.*
▶ **nod off** PHR-VERB If you **nod off**, you fall asleep, especially when you had not intended to. [INFORMAL] ❑ *I almost nodded off listening to the lecture.*

noise /nɔɪz/ (**noises**) **1** N-UNCOUNT **Noise** is a loud or unpleasant sound. ❑ *There was too much noise in the room.* **2** N-COUNT A **noise** is a sound that someone or something makes. ❑ *...animal noises.* ❑ *He heard a noise somewhere under his window.*

Word Partnership Use *noise* with:

N.	**background** noise, noise **level**, noise **pollution, traffic** noise **1**
ADJ.	**loud** noise **1 2**
V.	**hear a** noise, **make** noise **2**

noisy /'nɔɪzi/ (**noisier, noisiest**) **1** ADJ Someone or something that is **noisy** makes a lot of loud or unpleasant noise. ❑ *...my noisy old car.* ● **noisily** ADV ❑ *He slammed the car door noisily.* **2** ADJ A place that is **noisy** is full of loud or unpleasant noise. ❑ *...the crowded and noisy café.*

nomadic /nəʊ'mædɪk/ ADJ **Nomadic** people travel from place to place rather than living in one place all the time. ❑ *...gypsies who have given up their nomadic way of life.*

'no-man's land N-UNCOUNT **No-man's land** is an area of land that is not owned or controlled by anyone. ❑ *...the no-man's land between the two countries.*

Word Link ***nom ≈ name : nominal, nominate, nominee***

nominal /'nɒmɪnəl/ **1** ADJ You use **nominal** to indicate that someone or something is supposed to have a particular identity or status, but in reality does not have it. ❑ *As he was still not allowed to run a company, his wife became its nominal head.* ● **nominally** ADV ❑ *Nominally she is the king's prisoner.* **2** ADJ A **nominal** price or sum of money is very small in comparison with the real cost or value of the thing that is being bought or sold. ❑ *All the ferries carry bicycles for a nominal charge.*

nominate /'nɒmɪneɪt/ (**nominates, nominating, nominated**) V-T If someone **is nominated for** a job, position, or prize, their name is formally suggested as a candidate for it. ❑ *He was nominated for a best actor Oscar.* ❑ *The university asks staff to nominate people for honorary degrees.*

nomination /'nɒmɪneɪʃən/ (**nominations**) N-COUNT A **nomination** is an official suggestion of someone for a job, position, or prize. ❑ *...a list of nominations for senior positions.*

Word Link ***ee ≈ one who receives : detainee, nominee, refugee***

nominee /ˌnɒmɪ'niː/ (**nominees**) N-COUNT A **nominee** is someone who is nominated for something. ❑ *...nominees for the Nobel Peace Prize.*

n

nonchalant /ˈnɒnʃələnt, AM -ˈlɑːnt/ ADJ Someone who is **nonchalant** appears not to worry or care about things. ❑ *Denis tried to look nonchalant and uninterested.* ● **nonchalance** /ˈnɒnʃələns, AM -ˈlɑːns/ N-UNCOUNT ❑ *The man's attitude was one of casual nonchalance.* ● **nonchalantly** ADV ❑ *'Does Steve intend to return with us?' Joanna asked as nonchalantly as she could.*

none /nʌn/ 1 QUANT **None of** something means not even a small amount of it. **None of** a group of people or things means not even one of them. ❑ *She did none of the work on the car.* ❑ *None of us knew how to treat her.* ❑ *They asked me for fresh ideas, but I had none.* 2 PHRASE You use **none the** to say that someone or something does not have any more of a particular quality than they did before. ❑ *Having talked to him, I was none the wiser.* 3 PHRASE You use **none too** in front of an adjective or adverb in order to emphasize that the quality mentioned is not present. ❑ *He was none too thrilled to hear from me at that hour.*

nonetheless /ˌnʌnðəˈles/ ADV You use **nonetheless** when saying something that contrasts with what has just been said. [FORMAL] ❑ *His face is serious but nonetheless very friendly.*

ˌnon-exˈistent ADJ If you say that something is **non-existent**, you mean that it does not exist when you feel that it should. ❑ *Hygiene was non-existent: no running water, no bathroom.*

ˌno-ˈnonsense ADJ If you describe someone as a **no-nonsense** person or something as a **no-nonsense** thing, you approve of the fact that they are efficient and concentrate on important matters rather than trivial things. ❑ *The furniture is plain and no-nonsense.*

N

Word Link	*non ≈ not : nonsense, non-smoker, non-violence*

nonsense /ˈnɒnsəns/ 1 N-UNCOUNT If you say that something spoken or written is **nonsense**, you mean that you consider it to be untrue or silly. ❑ *...all that poetic nonsense about love.* ❑ *'I'm putting on weight.'—'Nonsense my dear.'* 2 N-UNCOUNT You can use **nonsense** to refer to something that you think is foolish or that you disapprove of. ❑ *There is a limit to how much of this nonsense people will put up with.* 3 PHRASE To **make a nonsense of** something or to **make nonsense of** it means to make it seem ridiculous or pointless. ❑ *The fighting made a nonsense of promises made in London last week.*

ˌnon-ˈsmoker (**non-smokers**) N-COUNT A **non-smoker** is someone who does not smoke.

ˌnon-ˈstick ADJ **Non-stick** cooking equipment such as pans or baking tins has a special coating, which prevents food from sticking to it.

ˌnon-ˈstop also **nonstop** ADJ Something that is **non-stop** continues without any pauses or breaks. ❑ *...80 minutes of non-stop music.*

Thesaurus	*non-stop* Also look up:
ADJ.	continuous, direct, uninterrupted

ˌnon-ˈviolent 1 ADJ **Non-violent** methods of bringing about change do not involve hurting people or causing damage. ● **non-violence** N-UNCOUNT ❑ *...a firm public commitment to non-violence.* 2 ADJ You can refer to someone or to something such as a crime as **non-violent** when that person or thing does not hurt or injure people. ❑ *...non-violent offenders.*

noodle /ˈnuːdəl/ (**noodles**) N-COUNT **Noodles** are long, thin pieces of pasta.

noon /nuːn/ N-UNCOUNT **Noon** is twelve o'clock in the middle of the day. ❑ *The long day of meetings started at noon.*
→ see **time**

ˈno one also **no-one** 1 PRON **No one** means not a single person, or not a single member of a particular group or set. ❑ *No one can predict what will happen in the months ahead.* 2 → See note at **nobody**

noose /nuːs/ (**nooses**) N-COUNT A **noose** is a loop at the end of a piece of rope or wire that is used to trap animals or hang people.

nope /nəʊp/ CONVENTION **Nope** is sometimes used instead of 'no' as a response. [INFORMAL, SPOKEN] ❑ *'Has the prisoner next door talked to you?'—'Nope,' the man answered.*

nor /nɔː/ 1 CONJ You use **nor** after 'neither' to introduce the second thing that a negative statement applies to. ❑ *Neither Mr Robertson nor Mr Woodhead was available.* ❑ *I can give you neither an opinion nor any advice.* 2 CONJ You use **nor** after a negative statement in order to indicate that the negative statement also applies to you or to someone or something else. ❑ *'If my husband has no future,' she said, 'then nor do my children.'*

norm /nɔːm/ (**norms**) 1 N-COUNT **Norms** are ways of behaving that are considered normal in a particular society. ❑ *...the norms of democracy.* ❑ *...a social norm that says swearing is inappropriate behaviour.* 2 N-SING If you say that a situation is **the norm**, you mean that it is usual and expected. ❑ *Families of six or seven are the norm in Borough Park.*

normal /ˈnɔːməl/ ADJ Something that is **normal** is usual and ordinary, and in accordance with what people expect. ❑ *Her teeth were smaller than a normal woman's.* ❑ *The two countries resumed normal diplomatic relations.*

Thesaurus	*normal* Also look up:
ADJ.	ordinary, regular, typical, usual

Word Partnership	Use *normal* with:
N.	normal **conditions**, normal **development**, normal **routine**
V.	**return to** normal
ADV.	**back to** normal, **completely** normal, **perfectly** normal

normality /nɔːˈmælɪti/ N-UNCOUNT **Normality** is a situation in which everything is normal. ❑ *Gradually we tried to return to some kind of normality.*

Word Link	*ize ≈ making : finalize, normalize, tranquillize*

normalize [BRIT also **normalise**] /ˈnɔːməlaɪz/ (**normalizes, normalizing, normalized**) V-T/V-I When you **normalize** a situation, or when it **normalizes**, it becomes normal or returns to normal. ❑ *The two governments were close to normalizing relations.* ❑ *His weight began to normalize after his illness.* ● **normalization** N-UNCOUNT ❑ *...the normalization of diplomatic relations.*

normally /'nɔːməli/ **1** ADV If you say that something **normally** happens or that you **normally** do a particular thing, you mean that it is what usually happens or what you usually do. ❑ *We don't normally travel on the day of a game.* ❑ *Normally, the transport system in Paris carries 950,000 passengers a day.* **2** ADV If you do something **normally**, you do it in the usual or conventional way. ❑ *The pressure made it hard to perform normally.*

north /nɔːθ/ **1** N-SING The **north** is the direction on your left when you are looking towards the direction where the sun rises. ❑ *Birds usually migrate from north to south.* **2** N-SING & ADJ The **north** of a place or the **north** part of it is the part which is towards the north. ❑ *...people in the North and Midlands.* ❑ *...the north coast of Crete.* **3** ADV **North** means towards the north, or positioned to the north of a place. ❑ *Anita drove north up Pacific Highway.* ❑ *...a little village a few miles north of Portsmouth.* **4** ADJ A **north** wind blows from the north.

ˌnorth-ˈeast **1** N-SING The **north-east** is the direction halfway between north and east. ❑ *...a small town a short distance to the north-east.* **2** N-SING & ADJ The **north-east** of a place or the north-east part of it is the part which is towards the north-east. ❑ *...in the north-east of England.* ❑ *...the north-east outskirts of London.* **3** ADV **North-east** means towards the north-east, or positioned to the north-east of a place or thing. ❑ *...army cars moving north-east.* ❑ *...Careysburg, twenty miles north-east of the capital, Monrovia.* **4** ADJ A **north-east** wind blows from the north-east.

ˌnorth-ˈeastern also **north eastern** ADJ **North-eastern** means in or from the north-east of a region or country. ❑ *...the north-eastern coast of the United States.*

northerly /'nɔːðəli/ **1** ADJ **Northerly** means towards the north. ❑ *...the most northerly island in the British Isles.* ❑ *I wanted to go a more northerly route across Montana.* **2** ADJ A **northerly** wind blows from the north.

northern /'nɔːðən/ ADJ **Northern** means in or from the north of a region or country. ❑ *...Northern Ireland.* ❑ *Prices at three-star hotels fell in several northern cities.*

northward /'nɔːθwəd/ also **northwards** /'nɔːθwədz/ ADV & ADJ **Northward** or **northwards** means towards the north. ❑ *The storm is continuing to move northward.* ❑ *The northward journey was no more than 120 miles.*

ˌnorth-ˈwest **1** N-SING The **north-west** is the direction halfway between north and west. ❑ *...Ushant, five miles to the north-west.* **2** N-SING & ADJ The **north-west** of a place is the north-west part of it is the part which is towards the north-west. ❑ *...the extreme north-west of South America.* ❑ *...the North-West Regional Health Authority.* **3** ADV **North-west** means towards the north-west, or positioned to the north-west of a place or thing. ❑ *Take the narrow lane going north-west.* **4** ADJ A **north-west** wind blows from the north-west.

ˌnorth-ˈwestern ADJ **North-western** means in or from the north-west of a region or country. ❑ *He was from north-western Russia.*

nose /nəʊz/ (**noses**) **1** N-COUNT Your **nose** is the part of your face which sticks out above your mouth. You use it for smelling and breathing. **2** N-COUNT The **nose** of a car or plane is its front part. **3** PHRASE If you do something **under** someone's **nose**, you do it in front of them, so that they could easily see you doing it. ❑ *She stole items from right under the noses of other shoppers.*
→ see **face, respiration, smell**

Word Partnership	Use *nose* with:
ADJ.	**big** nose, **bloody** nose, **broken** nose, **long** nose, **red** nose, **runny** nose, **straight** nose **1**

nostalgia /nɒ'stældʒə/ N-UNCOUNT **Nostalgia** is an affectionate feeling for things you have experienced in the past.

nostalgic /nɒs'tældʒɪk/ ADJ If you feel **nostalgic**, you think affectionately about experiences you have had in the past. ❑ *Many people were nostalgic for the good old days.*
• **nostalgically** ADV ❑ *People look back nostalgically on the period.*

nostril /'nɒstrɪl/ (**nostrils**) N-COUNT Your **nostrils** are the two openings at the end of your nose.

not /nɒt/ **1** You use **not**, usually in the form **n't**, to form questions to which you expect the answer 'yes'. ❑ *Haven't they got enough problems?* **2** You use **not**, usually in the form **n't**, in questions which imply that someone should have done something, or to express surprise that something is not the case. ❑ *Why didn't you do it months ago?* ❑ *Hasn't anyone ever kissed you before?* **3** You use **not**, usually in the form **n't**, in question tags after a positive statement. ❑ *You will take me tomorrow, won't you?* **4** You use **not**, usually in the form **n't**, in polite suggestions. ❑ *Why don't you fill out our application form?* **5** You use **not** to represent the negative of a word, group, or clause that has just been used. ❑ *'Have you found Paula?'—'I'm afraid not.'* ❑ *I really didn't care if he came or not.* **6** You use **not** before 'all', 'every', or 'always' to say that there are exceptions to something that is generally true. You also use **not** before words like 'only' and 'just' to say that something is true, but it is not the whole truth. ❑ *Not every applicant had a degree.* ❑ *Brendel is not only a great pianist, but a great musician.* **7** You can use **not** or **not even** in front of 'a' or 'one' to emphasize that there is none at all of what is being mentioned. ❑ *I sent report after report. But not one word was published.* **8** You use **not** when you are contrasting something that is true with something that people might wrongly believe to be true. ❑ *Training is an investment not a cost.* **9** CONJ You use **not that** to introduce a negative clause that contradicts or modifies what the previous statement implies. ❑ *The leading actor gets about four hours' sleep a night. Not that he's complaining.* **10** CONVENTION **Not at all** is an emphatic way of saying 'No' or of agreeing that the answer to a question is 'No'. ❑ *'Sorry. I sound like Abby, don't I?'—'No. Not at all.'* **11** **not least** → see **least** **12** **not to mention** → see **mention** **13** **nothing if not** → see **nothing** **14** **more often than not** → see **often**

notable /'nəʊtəbəl/ **1** ADJ Something or someone that is **notable** is important or interesting. ❑ *...a fishing town notable for its church.* **2** → See note at **famous**

notably /'nəʊtəbli/ ADV You use **notably** before mentioning the most important example of the

n

thing you are talking about. ❑ *...more important problems, notably the fate of the children.*

notch /nɒtʃ/ (**notches, notching, notched**) **1** N-COUNT A **notch** is a small V-shaped or circular cut in the surface or edge of something. **2** N-COUNT You can refer to a step on a scale of measurement or achievement as a **notch**. [JOURNALISM] ❑ *Average earnings increased another notch in August.*
▶ **notch up** PHR-VERB If you **notch up** something such as a score or total, you achieve it. [JOURNALISM] ❑ *The shop notched up sales worth £1 million.*

note /nəʊt/ (**notes, noting, noted**) **1** N-COUNT A **note** is a short letter. ❑ *I'll have to leave a note for Karen.* **2** N-COUNT A **note** is something that you write down to remind you about something. ❑ *Take notes during the meeting.* **3** V-T & PHR-VERB When you **note** something, or when you **note** it **down**, you write it down so that you have a record of it. You can also say that a piece of writing **notes** something when it is recorded there. ❑ *She was, she noted in her diary, 'very angry with him'.* ❑ *He noted down the address.* ❑ *The report notes a drop in spending.* **4** V-T If you **note** a fact, you become aware of it. ❑ *We noted his absence about an hour ago.* ❑ *Please note that there are a limited number of tickets.* **5** N-COUNT In a book or article, a **note** is a short piece of additional information. ❑ *See Note 16 on page p. 223.* **6** N-COUNT In music, a **note** is a sound of a particular pitch, or a written symbol representing this sound. **7** N-COUNT In British English, a **note** is a piece of paper money. The usual American word is **bill**. ❑ *...a five pound note.* **8** N-SING You can use **note** to refer to a quality or feeling that something has, or the impression that it gives you. You can say that someone or something **strikes** or **sounds** a particular **note**. ❑ *He could hear the note of urgency in their voices.* ❑ *The film ends on a positive note.* ❑ *He welcomed the news but sounded a note of caution.* **9** PHRASE If you **compare notes with** someone or if the two of you **compare notes**, you talk to them and find out whether they have the same opinion, information, or experiences as yourself. ❑ *...the chance to compare notes with other mothers.* **10** PHRASE Someone or something that is **of note** is important, worth mentioning, or well-known. ❑ *He has written nothing of note recently.* **11** PHRASE If you **take note of** something, you pay attention to it because you think that it is important. ❑ *He advises you to take note of where the exits are.* **12** → see also **noted**
▶ **note down** PHR-VERB → see **note** (meaning 3)

Word Partnership	Use *note* with:
V.	**leave a** note, **send a** note **1** **find a** note, **read a** note, **scribble a** note, **write a** note **1** **2** **make a** note **2** **take** note **of** ***something*** **4** **sound a** note, **strike a** note **6**

notebook

notebook /ˈnəʊtbʊk/ (**notebooks**) N-COUNT A **notebook** is a small book for writing notes in.

noted /ˈnəʊtɪd/ ADJ Someone who is **noted for** something is well-known and admired for it. ❑ *...the scientist, noted for his work on infectious diseases.*

nothing /ˈnʌθɪŋ/ **1** PRON **Nothing** means not a single thing, or not a single part of something. ❑ *He said nothing to reporters.* ❑ *There is nothing wrong with the car.* **2** PRON You use **nothing** to indicate that something or someone is not important or significant. ❑ *Because he always had money it meant nothing to him.* ❑ *She kept crying over nothing.* **3** PHRASE **Nothing but** a particular thing means only that thing. ❑ *All that money brought nothing but sadness.* ❑ *She did nothing but complain about him.* **4** PHRASE You use **nothing if not** to indicate that someone or something clearly has a lot of a particular quality. ❑ *She has been nothing if not professional.* **5** PHRASE You can use **nothing less than** to emphasize your next words, often indicating that something seems very surprising or important. ❑ *He's nothing less than a liar!* **6** PHRASE You say **nothing of the sort** to emphasize a refusal or a negative statement. ❑ *It was supposed to be a success. It was nothing of the sort.* **7** **to say nothing of** → see **say** **8** **to think nothing of** → see **think**

notice /ˈnəʊtɪs/ (**notices, noticing, noticed**) **1** V-T/V-I If you **notice** something, you become aware of it. ❑ *You didn't notice anything special about him?* ❑ *Mrs Shedden noticed a bird sitting on the garage.* ❑ *Do they think we won't notice?* **2** PHRASE If something **comes to** your **notice** or **is brought to** your **notice**, you become aware of it. If it **escapes** your **notice**, you are not aware of it. ❑ *He brought the matter to their notice.* **3** PHRASE If you **take notice of** something, you pay attention to it. ❑ *Noel was someone people took notice of.* ❑ *I always knew something was wrong, but no one would take any notice.* **4** N-COUNT A **notice** is a written announcement in a place where everyone can read it. ❑ *A few hotels had 'No Vacancies' notices in their windows.* **5** N-UNCOUNT **Notice** is advance warning about something. ❑ *I was given four days' notice to prepare for the wedding.* ❑ *She was transferred to a new office without notice.* ❑ *Thank you all for coming along at such short notice.* **6** PHRASE If a situation will exist **until further notice**, it will continue until someone changes it. **7** PHRASE If your employer **gives** you **notice**, he or she tells you that you must leave within a set period of time. If you **give notice** or **hand in** your **notice**, you tell your employer that you intend to leave within a set period of time.

Thesaurus	*notice* Also look up:
V.	note, observe, perceive, see **1**
N.	advertisement, announcement **2** **4**

Word Partnership	Use *notice* with:
N.	notice **a change**, notice **a difference** **1**
V.	**begin to** notice, **fail to** notice, **pretend not to** notice **1** **give** notice, **receive** notice, **serve** notice **5**

noticeable /ˈnəʊtɪsəbəl/ ADJ Something that is **noticeable** is very obvious, so that it is easy to see or recognize. ❑ *It was noticeable that his face was red.* • **noticeably** ADV ❑ *The baby became noticeably more upset.*

notify /ˈnəʊtɪfaɪ/ (**notifies, notifying, notified**)

V-T If you **notify** someone **of** something, you officially inform them of it. ❑ *The captain notified the coastguard of the tragedy.* ❑ *We have notified the police.* • **notification** /ˌnəʊtɪfɪˈkeɪʃən/ (**notifications**) N-VAR ❑ *Everyone should have received notification by now.*

notion /ˈnəʊʃən/ (**notions**) N-COUNT A **notion** is a belief or idea. ❑ *...the notion that life might exist on other planets.*

Thesaurus *notion* Also look up:

N. belief, concept, idea, opinion, thought

notoriety /ˌnəʊtəˈraɪɪti/ N-UNCOUNT If someone or something achieves **notoriety**, they become well-known for something bad.

notorious /nəʊˈtɔːriəs/ **1** ADJ Someone or something that is **notorious** is famous for something bad. ❑ *The area is notorious for crime.* • **notoriously** ADV ❑ *Doctors notoriously neglect their own health.* **2** → See note at **famous**

notwithstanding /ˌnɒtwɪðˈstændɪŋ/ PREP & ADV If something is true **notwithstanding** something else, it is true in spite of that other thing. [FORMAL] ❑ *He hated the man, notwithstanding the similar views they both held.* ❑ *Bad weather notwithstanding, the summer holiday was a great success.*

nought /nɔːt/ (**noughts**) NUM **Nought** is the number 0.

Usage

In spoken British English, **nought** is much more common than **zero**. ❑ *The acceleration is so extreme, from nought to 60 in a second.* As a number, **zero** is used mainly in scientific contexts, or when you want to be precise. However, when you are stating a telephone number, you say **o** (/əʊ/). In some sports contexts, especially football scores, **nil** is used. ❑ *England beat Poland two-nil at Wembley.* In tennis, **love** is the usual word. ❑ *He won the first set and took a two-games-to-love lead in the second.*

noun /naʊn/ (**nouns**) N-COUNT A **noun** is a word such as 'woman', 'guilt', or 'John' which is used to refer to a person or thing.

nourish /ˈnʌrɪʃ, AM ˈnɜːrɪʃ/ (**nourishes, nourishing, nourished**) V-T To **nourish** a person, animal, or plant means to provide them with the food that is necessary for growth and health. ❑ *We should nourish the body with good wholesome food.* • **nourishing** ADJ ❑ *...sensible, nourishing food.* • **nourishment** N-UNCOUNT ❑ *Breast milk is your baby's best source of nourishment.*

Word Link *nov ≈ new : innovation, novel, renovate*

novel /ˈnɒvəl/ (**novels**) **1** N-COUNT A **novel** is a book containing a long story about imaginary people and events. **2** ADJ **Novel** things are unlike anything that has been done, experienced, or created before. ❑ *...taking pieces of past music and making them into something novel.*
→ see **library**

novelist /ˈnɒvəlɪst/ (**novelists**) N-COUNT A **novelist** is a person who writes novels.
→ see **fantasy**

novelty /ˈnɒvəlti/ (**novelties**) **1** N-UNCOUNT **Novelty** is the quality of being different, new, and unusual. ❑ *The novelty of the situation excited him.* **2** N-COUNT A **novelty** is something that is new and therefore interesting. ❑ *...the days when a motor car was a novelty.* **3** N-COUNT **Novelties** are cheap unusual objects sold as gifts or souvenirs.

November /nəʊˈvembə/ (**Novembers**) N-VAR **November** is the eleventh month of the year. ❑ *It was one of the coldest Novembers of the past century.*

novice /ˈnɒvɪs/ (**novices**) N-COUNT A **novice** is someone who has been doing something for only a short time and so is not experienced at it. ❑ *Most of us are novices on the computer.* ❑ *...a novice writer.*

now /naʊ/ **1** ADV & PRON You use **now** to refer to the present time, often in contrast to the past or the future. ❑ *Beef steak now costs well over £3 a kilo.* ❑ *I must go now.* ❑ *She should know that by now.* ❑ *Now is your chance to talk to him.* **2** CONJ You use **now** or **now that** to indicate that an event has occurred and as a result something else may or will happen. ❑ *Now you're settled, why don't you take up some serious study?* **3** ADV You use **now** in statements which specify the length of time up to the present that something has lasted. ❑ *They've been married now for 30 years.* **4** ADV You can say **'Now'** to introduce new information into a story or account. ❑ *Now, I hadn't told him that, so he must have found out on his own.* **5** PHRASE If you say that something will happen **any day now, any moment now,** or **any time now,** you mean that it will happen very soon. ❑ *We expect him home again any day now.* **6** PHRASE **Just now** means a very short time ago. ❑ *You looked upset just now.* **7** PHRASE If you say that something happens **now and then** or **every now and again,** you mean that it happens sometimes but not very often or regularly. ❑ *Now and then they heard the noise of a heavy truck.*

nowadays /ˈnaʊədeɪz/ ADV **Nowadays** means at the present time, in contrast with the past. ❑ *I don't see much of Tony nowadays.*

nowhere /ˈnəʊweə/ **1** ADV You use **nowhere** to emphasize that a place has more of a particular quality than any other places, or that it is the only place where something happens or exists. ❑ *This kind of forest exists nowhere else in the world.* **2** ADV You use **nowhere** when making negative statements to say that a suitable place of the specified kind does not exist. ❑ *There was nowhere to hide.* ❑ *I have nowhere else to go.* **3** PHRASE If you say that something or someone appears **from nowhere** or **out of nowhere,** you mean that they appear suddenly and unexpectedly. ❑ *A car came from nowhere, and I had to jump back.* **4** PHRASE If you say that you **are getting nowhere** or that something **is getting** you **nowhere**, you mean that you are not achieving anything or having any success. ❑ *Oh, stop it! This argument is getting us nowhere.* **5** PHRASE If you say that a place is **in the middle of nowhere,** you mean it is a long way from other places. **6** **nowhere near** → see **near**

Word Partnership Use *nowhere* with:

V. nowhere **to be found**, nowhere **to be seen**, **go** nowhere, ***have*** nowhere **to go**, ***have*** nowhere **to hide**, ***have*** nowhere **to run** **2**

nuance /ˈnjuːɑːns, AM ˈnuː-/ (**nuances**) N-VAR A **nuance** is a small and subtle difference in sound,

n

feeling, appearance, or meaning. ❑ *...every subtle nuance of colour in the painting.*

nuclear /ˈnjuːkliə, AM ˈnuːk-/ ADJ BEFORE N **Nuclear** means relating to the nuclei of atoms, or to the energy produced when these nuclei are split or combined. ❑ *...a nuclear power station.* ❑ *...nuclear weapons.*
→ see **energy**

ˌnuclear reˈactor (**nuclear reactors**) N-COUNT A **nuclear reactor** is a machine which produces nuclear energy.

nucleus /ˈnjuːkliəs, AM ˈnuː-/ (**nuclei**) **1** N-COUNT The **nucleus** of an atom or cell is the central part of it. **2** N-COUNT The **nucleus of** a group of people is the small number of members which form the most important part of the group. ❑ *...the nucleus of people who started the magazine.*

nude /njuːd, AM nuːd/ (**nudes**) **1** ADJ & PHRASE Someone who is **nude** or who is **in the nude** is not wearing any clothes. ● **nudity** /ˈnjuːdɪti, AM ˈnuː-/ N-UNCOUNT ❑ *...nudity and bad language on TV.* **2** N-COUNT A **nude** is a picture or statue of a nude person.

nudge /nʌdʒ/ (**nudges, nudging, nudged**) V-T & N-COUNT If you **nudge** someone, or if you **give** them a **nudge**, you push them gently with your elbow.

nuisance /ˈnjuːsəns, AM ˈnuː-/ (**nuisances**) N-COUNT If you say that someone or something is a **nuisance**, you mean that they annoy you or cause you problems. If you say that someone **makes a nuisance of** themselves, you mean that they are a nuisance. ❑ *He could be a bit of a nuisance.*

N

numb /nʌm/ (**numbs, numbing, numbed**) **1** ADJ If a part of your body is **numb**, you cannot feel anything there. ❑ *He could feel his fingers growing numb.* ● **numbness** N-UNCOUNT ❑ *Nerve injury can cause numbness in the thigh.* **2** V-T If a blow or cold weather **numbs** a part of your body, you can no longer feel anything in it. ❑ *The cold numbed my fingers.* **3** ADJ If you are **numb with** shock or fear, you are so shocked or frightened that you cannot think clearly or feel any emotion. **4** V-T If an event or experience **numbs** you, you can no longer think clearly or feel any emotion. ● **numbed** ADJ ❑ *I'm so numbed with shock that I can hardly think.*

number /ˈnʌmbə/ (**numbers, numbering, numbered**) **1** N-COUNT A **number** is a word such as 'two', 'nine', or 'twelve', or a symbol such as 1, 3, or 47, which is used in counting something. ❑ *I don't know the room number.* ❑ *...number 3, Argyll Street.* **2** N-COUNT Someone's **number** is the series of digits that you dial when you telephone them. ❑ *Sarah dialled my number.* ❑ *'You must have a wrong number,' she said.* **3** V-T If you **number** something, you give it a number in a series and write the number on it. ❑ *He cut his paper up into tiny squares, and he numbered each one.* **4** N-COUNT You use **number** with words such as 'large' or 'small' to say approximately how many things or people there are. ❑ *I have had an enormous number of letters.* **5** N-SING If there are **a number of** things or people, there are several of them. If there are **any number of** things or people, there is a large quantity of them. ❑ *Sam told a number of lies.* ❑ *There must be any number of people in my position.* **6** V-T If a group of people or things **numbers** a particular total, that is how many there are. ❑ *...a small army which numbered 100,000 men.*
→ see **mathematics, zero**

ˌnumber ˈone ADJ **Number one** means better, more important, or more popular than anything else of its kind. ❑ *Clean water is the number one issue by far.*

ˈnumber plate (**number plates**) N-COUNT In British English, a **number plate** is a sign on the front and back of a vehicle that shows its registration number. The American term is **license plate**.

Word Link	*numer* ≈ *number* : *innumerable, numerical, numerous*

numerical /njuːˈmerɪkəl, AM ˈnuː-/ ADJ **Numerical** means expressed in numbers or relating to numbers. ❑ *Put them in numerical order.* ● **numerically** ADV ❑ *...a numerically small nation.*

numerous /ˈnjuːmərəs, AM ˈnuːm-/ ADJ If people or things are **numerous**, they exist or are present in large numbers. ❑ *Crimes were just as numerous then as they are today.*

nun /nʌn/ (**nuns**) N-COUNT A **nun** is a member of a female religious community.

nurse /nɜːs/ (**nurses, nursing, nursed**) **1** N-COUNT A **nurse** is a person whose job is to care for people who are ill. **2** V-T If you **nurse** someone, you care for them while they are ill. ❑ *In hospital they nursed me back to health.* ● **nursing** N-UNCOUNT ❑ *I wanted to go into something like nursing.*

Word Partnership	Use *nurse* with:
ADJ.	nurse's **aide**, **visiting** nurse **1**

nursery /ˈnɜːsəri/ (**nurseries**) **1** N-COUNT A **nursery** is a place where children who are not old enough to go to school are looked after. ❑ *Her company ran its own nursery.* **2** N-COUNT A **nursery** is a place where plants are grown in order to be sold.

ˈnursery rhyme (**nursery rhymes**) N-COUNT A **nursery rhyme** is a traditional poem or song for young children.

ˈnursing home (**nursing homes**) N-COUNT A **nursing home** is a private hospital for old people.

nurture /ˈnɜːtʃə/ (**nurtures, nurturing, nurtured**) **1** V-T If you **nurture** a young child or a young plant, you care for it while it is growing and developing. [FORMAL] ❑ *Parents want to know the best way to nurture and raise their child.* **2** V-T If you **nurture** plans, ideas, or people, you encourage their development and success. [FORMAL] ❑ *She has always nurtured the talent of others.*

nut /nʌt/ (**nuts**) **1** N-COUNT The firm shelled fruit of some trees and bushes are called **nuts**. **2** N-COUNT A **nut** is a small piece of metal with a hole through which you put a bolt. Nuts and bolts are used to hold things together such as pieces of machinery.
→ see **food, peanut**

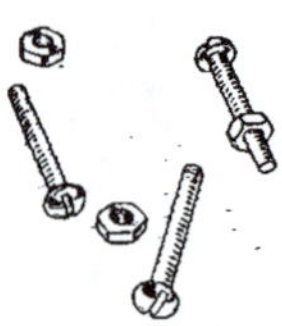
nuts and bolts

nutrient /ˈnjuːtriənt, AM ˈnuː-/ (**nutrients**) N-COUNT **Nutrients** are chemical substances that people and animals need from food and plants need from soil. ❑ *...essential nutrients.*
→ see **food**

nutrition /njuːˈtrɪʃən, AM ˈnuː-/ N-UNCOUNT **Nutrition** is the process of taking and absorbing nutrients from food. ❑ *There are alternative sources of nutrition to animal meat.*

nutritional /njuːˈtrɪʃənəl, AM ˈnuː-/ ADJ The **nutritional content** of food is all the proteins, vitamins, and minerals that are in it which help you to remain healthy. ❑ *It sometimes helps to know the nutritional content of foods.* ● **nutritionally** ADV ❑ *...a nutritionally balanced diet.*

Word Link	***ous ≈ having the qualities of:*** ***dangerous, fabulous, nutritious***

nutritious /njuːˈtrɪʃəs, AM nuː-/ ADJ **Nutritious food** contains the proteins, vitamins, and minerals which help your body to be healthy. ❑ *...a hot, nutritious meal.*

nylon /ˈnaɪlɒn/ N-UNCOUNT **Nylon** is a strong, flexible, artificial material. ❑ *Green nylon nets were piled up on the beach.*

Oo

oak /əʊk/ (**oaks**) N-VAR An **oak** or an **oak tree** is a type of large tree. **Oak** is the wood of this tree. ❑ *...a strong oak door.*
→ see **plant**

oar

oar /ɔː/ (**oars**) N-COUNT **Oars** are long poles with flat ends which are used for rowing a boat.
→ see **boat**

oasis /əʊ'eɪsɪs/ (**oases** /əʊ'eɪsiːz/) 1 N-COUNT An **oasis** is a small area in a desert where water and plants are found. 2 N-COUNT You can refer to any pleasant place or situation as an **oasis** when it is surrounded by unpleasant ones. ❑ *The hotel is an oasis of calm in this busy city.*
→ see **desert**

oath /əʊθ/ (**oaths**) 1 N-COUNT An **oath** is a formal promise. ❑ *The soldier took an oath to defend his country.* 2 N-SING In a court of law, if someone **takes the oath**, they formally promise to tell the truth. You can say that someone is **on oath** or **under oath** when they have made this promise.

O

oats /əʊts/ N-PLURAL **Oats** are a cereal crop or its grains, used for making porridge or feeding animals.
→ see **grain**

obedient /əʊ'biːdiənt/ ADJ An **obedient** person or animal does what they are told to do. ❑ *He was always a very obedient boy.* • **obedience** N-UNCOUNT ❑ *Next, I took our dog to obedience classes.* • **obediently** ADV ❑ *I obediently followed his instructions.*

obese /əʊ'biːs/ 1 ADJ Someone who is **obese** is extremely fat. ❑ *By the age of four, eight per cent of children are obese.* • **obesity** N-UNCOUNT ❑ *There is a link between diet, obesity, and disease.* 2 → See note at **fat**
→ see **diet, sugar**

obey /əʊ'beɪ/ (**obeys, obeying, obeyed**) V-T/V-I If you **obey** a rule, instruction, or person, you do what you are told to do. ❑ *Most people obey the law.* ❑ *There are a lot of rules that children have to obey.*

Word Partnership Use *obey* with:

N.	obey **a command**, obey **the law**, obey **orders**, obey **the rules**
V.	**refuse to** obey

obituary /əʊ'bɪtʃʊəri, AM -ʃʊeri/ (**obituaries**) N-COUNT Someone's **obituary** is an account of their character and achievements which is published shortly after they have died. ❑ *I read your brother's obituary in the newspaper.*

object (**objects, objecting, objected**) 1 N-COUNT /'ɒbdʒɪkt/ An **object** is anything that has a fixed shape or form and that is not alive. ❑ *...an object the shape of a coconut.* ❑ *...everyday objects such as wooden spoons.* 2 N-COUNT The **object of** what someone is doing is their aim or purpose. ❑ *The object of the game is to answer the questions on the card.* 3 N-COUNT The **object of** a particular feeling or reaction is the person or thing it is directed towards, or the person or thing that causes it. ❑ *The object of her desire was 24-year-old Ross Ferguson.* 4 N-COUNT In grammar, the **object** of a clause is a noun group which refers to a person or thing that is affected by the action of the verb. In the sentence 'She married a young engineer', 'a young engineer' is the object. 5 → see also **direct object, indirect object** 6 PHRASE If you say, for example, that **money is no object**, you are emphasizing that you are willing or able to spend as much money as necessary. 7 V-I /əb'dʒekt/ If you **object to** something, you express your dislike or disapproval of it. ❑ *Working people everywhere object to paying taxes.*

Thesaurus *object* Also look up:

N.	item, thing 1
	aim, goal, intent 2
V.	argue, disagree, oppose, protest against 5

Word Partnership Use *object* with:

ADJ.	**foreign** object, **moving** object, **solid** object 1
V.	object **to *someone/something*** 6

objection /əb'dʒekʃən/ (**objections**) N-VAR If you **make** an **objection to** something, you say that you do not like it or agree with it. ❑ *Two main objections to the proposal have been raised.* ❑ *I have no objection to banks making money.*

objective /əb'dʒektɪv/ (**objectives**) 1 N-COUNT Your **objective** is what you are trying to achieve. ❑ *His objective was to win.* 2 ADJ BEFORE N **Objective** means based on facts and not influenced by personal feelings. ❑ *There wasn't enough objective evidence in this case to satisty Dr Stevenson.* ❑ *A journalist should be completely objective.* • **objectively** ADV ❑ *Stand back and look objectively at the problem.* • **objectivity** /ˌɒbdʒek'tɪvɪti/ N-UNCOUNT ❑ *...the objectivity of science.*

obligation /ˌɒblɪ'geɪʃən/ (**obligations**) N-VAR If you **have** an **obligation to** do something, it is your duty to do it. If you have an **obligation to** a person, it is your duty to look after them. ❑ *He felt an obligation to save the man.* ❑ *We have an obligation to the children.*

Thesaurus *obligation* Also look up:

N. duty, responsibility

Word Partnership Use *obligation* with:

ADJ. **legal** obligation, **moral** obligation
N. **sense of** obligation
V. **feel an** obligation, **fulfill an** obligation, **meet an** obligation, obligation **to pay**

obligatory /ə'blɪgətri, AM -tɔːri/ ADJ If something is **obligatory**, you must do it, because there is a rule or law about it. ❑ *It is obligatory to use the child safety equipment provided.* ❑ *...an obligatory AIDS test.*

oblige /ə'blaɪdʒ/ (**obliges, obliging, obliged**) **1** V-T/V-I If you **oblige** someone, you help them by doing what they have asked you to do. ❑ *If you ever need help with the babysitting, I'd be glad to oblige.* ❑ *Mary had already obliged him with introductions to some singers.* **2** V-T If a situation or law **obliges** you **to** do something, it makes it necessary for you to do it. [FORMAL] ❑ *The law obliges you to obtain a work permit.*

obliged /ə'blaɪdʒd/ ADJ If you **feel obliged to** do something, you feel that you should do it, or a rule insists that you do it.

obliging /ə'blaɪdʒɪŋ/ ADJ If you describe someone as **obliging**, you think that they are willing and eager to be helpful. ❑ *...an extremely pleasant and obliging man.* ● **obligingly** ADV ❑ *Benedict obligingly held the door open.*

oblique /əʊ'bliːk/ ADJ An **oblique** statement is not expressed directly or openly, making it difficult to understand. ❑ *Mr Golding delivered an oblique warning.* ● **obliquely** ADV ❑ *He obliquely referred to the US.*

obliterate /ə'blɪtəreɪt/ (**obliterates, obliterating, obliterated**) **1** V-T If something **obliterates** an object or place, it destroys it completely. ❑ *Whole villages were obliterated by fire.* ● **obliteration** N-UNCOUNT ❑ *...the obliteration of three rainforests.* **2** V-T If you **obliterate** something such as a memory or emotion, you remove it completely from your mind. [LITERARY] ❑ *With time, he managed to obliterate memories of the past.*

oblivion /ə'blɪviən/ **1** N-UNCOUNT **Oblivion** is the state of not being aware of what is happening around you, for example because you are asleep or unconscious. ❑ *Rachael tried to wish herself into oblivion.* **2** N-UNCOUNT **Oblivion** is the state of having been forgotten. ❑ *His football career was facing oblivion.*

oblivious /ə'blɪviəs/ ADJ If you are **oblivious to** something, you are not aware of it. ❑ *She lay where she was, oblivious to pain.*

obnoxious /ɒb'nɒkʃəs/ ADJ If you describe someone as **obnoxious**, you think that they are very unpleasant. ❑ *He was a most obnoxious man. No-one liked him.*

obscene /ɒb'siːn/ ADJ If you describe something as **obscene**, you mean it offends you because it relates to sex or violence in an unpleasant and shocking way. ❑ *I think these photographs are obscene.*

obscenity /ɒb'senɪti/ (**obscenities**) **1** N-UNCOUNT **Obscenity** is behaviour that offends people because it relates to sex in an unpleasant or indecent way. ❑ *The photographs were not art but obscenity.* **2** N-COUNT An **obscenity** is a very rude word or expression. ❑ *They shouted obscenities at us.*

obscure /ɒb'skjʊə/ (**obscurer, obscurest, obscures, obscuring, obscured**) **1** ADJ If something or someone is **obscure**, they are unknown, or are known by only a few people. ❑ *The origin of the custom is obscure.* ❑ *...an obscure Greek composer.* ● **obscurity** N-UNCOUNT ❑ *The latter half of his life was spent in obscurity.* **2** V-T If one thing **obscures** another, it prevents it from being seen or heard properly. ❑ *Trees obscured his view; he couldn't see much of the beach.* **3** ADJ If you describe something as **obscure**, you find it is difficult to understand or deal with, usually because it involves so many parts or details. ❑ *The contracts are written in obscure language.* ● **obscurity** N-UNCOUNT ❑ *Harris was annoyed by the obscurity of Henry's reply.*

observation /ˌɒbzə'veɪʃən/ (**observations**) **1** N-UNCOUNT **Observation** is the action or process of carefully watching someone or something. ❑ *...careful observation of the movement of the planets.* ❑ *In hospital she'll be under observation all the time.* ● **observational** ADJ ❑ *...observational studies of young children.* **2** N-COUNT An **observation** is something that you have learned by seeing or watching something and thinking about it. ❑ *This book contains observations about the causes of the disease.* **3** N-COUNT If a person **makes** an **observation**, they make a comment about something or someone, usually as a result of watching how they behave. ❑ *He made the oservation at dinner among friends.* **4** N-UNCOUNT **Observation** is the ability to notice things that are not usually noticed. ❑ *My powers of observation and memory have improved.*
→ see **forecast, science**

Word Partnership Use *observation* with:

PREP. **by** observation, **through** observation, **under** observation **1**
ADJ. **careful** observation **1**
direct observation **1**-**3**
V. **make an** observation **3**

observatory /əb'zɜːvətri, AM -tɔːri/ (**observatories**) N-COUNT An **observatory** is a building with a large telescope from which scientists study the stars and planets.

Word Link *serv* ≈ *keeping* : *conserve, observe, preserve*

observe /əb'zɜːv/ (**observes, observing, observed**) **1** V-T If you **observe** someone or something, you watch them carefully. ❑ *Professor Simms observes the behaviour of babies.* **2** V-T If you **observe** someone or something, you see or notice them. [FORMAL] ❑ *He observed a reddish spot on the surface of the planet.* **3** V-T If you **observe** something such as a law or custom, you obey it or follow it. ❑ *The cameras force drivers to observe speed restrictions.* ● **observance** N-UNCOUNT ❑ *...the observance of religious rules.*

O

Thesaurus *observe* Also look up:

V. study, watch 1
detect, notice, spot 2

observer /əb'zɜːvə/ (**observers**) 1 N-COUNT An **observer** is someone who sees or notices something. ❑ *'Tom lost his temper completely,' said an observer.* 2 N-COUNT An **observer** is someone who studies current events and situations. ❑ *...an independent political observer.*

obsess /əb'ses/ (**obsesses, obsessing, obsessed**) V-T/V-I If something **obsesses** you, you keep thinking about it and find it difficult to think about anything else. ❑ *The idea of space travel has obsessed me since I was about six.* ❑ *She began obsessing about her weight.* ● **obsessed** ADJ ❑ *He was obsessed with American gangster movies.*

obsession /əb'seʃən/ (**obsessions**) N-VAR If you say that someone has an **obsession with** someone or something, you feel they are spending too much of their time thinking about that person or thing. ❑ *She would try to forget her obsession with Christopher.*

obsessive /əb'sesɪv/ ADJ If someone's behaviour is **obsessive**, they cannot stop doing something or thinking about something. ❑ *Williams is obsessive about motor racing.* ● **obsessively** ADV ❑ *He couldn't help worrying obsessively about what would happen.*

obsolete /ˌɒbsə'liːt/ ADJ Something that is **obsolete** is no longer needed because a better thing now exists. ❑ *The equipment became obsolete almost as soon as it was made.*

obstacle /'ɒbstəkəl/ (**obstacles**) N-COUNT An **obstacle** is something which makes it difficult for you to go forward or do something. ❑ *A rabbit can jump obstacles up to three feet high.* ❑ *The most difficult obstacle to overcome was the heavy rain.*

Word Partnership Use *obstacle* with:

N. obstacle **course**, obstacle **to peace**
V. **be an** obstacle, **hit an** obstacle, **overcome an** obstacle
ADJ. **big/biggest** obstacle, **main** obstacle, **major** obstacle, **serious** obstacle

obstetrician /ˌɒbstə'trɪʃən/ (**obstetricians**) N-COUNT An **obstetrician** is a doctor who is trained to deal with childbirth and the care of pregnant women.

obstinate /'ɒbstɪnət/ ADJ If you describe someone as **obstinate**, you are critical of them because they are very determined to do what they want, and refuse to be persuaded to do something else. ❑ *He is obstinate and will not give up.* ● **obstinately** ADV ❑ *Smith obstinately refused to carry out the order.* ● **obstinacy** N-UNCOUNT ❑ *She was capable of great obstinacy.*

obstruct /ɒb'strʌkt/ (**obstructs, obstructing, obstructed**) 1 V-T To **obstruct** someone or something means to block their path, making it difficult for them to move forward. ❑ *Lorries have completely obstructed the road.* 2 V-T To **obstruct** something such as justice or progress means to prevent it from happening properly or from developing. ❑ *The authorities are obstructing a United Nations investigation.*

obstruction /ɒb'strʌkʃən/ (**obstructions**) 1 N-VAR An **obstruction** is something that blocks a road or path. ❑ *Drivers parking near his house are causing an obstruction.* 2 N-UNCOUNT **Obstruction** is the act of deliberately preventing something from happening. ❑ *Obstruction of justice is an offence.*

obtain /ɒb'teɪn/ (**obtains, obtaining, obtained**) V-T To **obtain** something means to get it or achieve it. [FORMAL] ❑ *Evans was trying to obtain a false passport.*

Word Partnership Use *obtain* with:

ADJ. **able to** obtain, **difficult to** obtain, **easy to** obtain, **unable to** obtain
N. obtain **approval**, obtain **a copy**, obtain **financing**, obtain **help**, obtain **information**, obtain **insurance**, obtain **permission**, obtain **weapons**

obvious /'ɒbviəs/ ADJ If something is **obvious**, it is easy to see or understand. ❑ *It's obvious he's worried about us.* ❑ *...her obvious creative talents.*

Thesaurus *obvious* Also look up:

ADJ. noticeable, plain, unmistakeable

Word Partnership Use *obvious* with:

ADV. **fairly** obvious, **immediately** obvious, **less** obvious, **most** obvious, **painfully** obvious, **quite** obvious, **so** obvious
N. obvious **answer**, obvious **choice**, obvious **differences**, obvious **example**, obvious **question**, obvious **reasons**, obvious **solution**

obviously /'ɒbviəsli/ 1 ADV You use **obviously** when you are stating something that you expect your listener to know already. ❑ *Obviously I'll be disappointed if I don't get the job.* 2 ADV You use **obviously** to indicate that something is easily noticed, seen, or recognized. ❑ *They obviously appreciate you very much.*

occasion /ə'keɪʒən/ (**occasions**) 1 N-COUNT An **occasion** is a time when something happens. ❑ *On one occasion, the car almost hit a truck.* 2 N-COUNT An **occasion** is an important event, ceremony, or celebration. ❑ *The launch of a ship was a big occasion.* 3 N-COUNT An **occasion for** doing something is an opportunity for doing it. [FORMAL] ❑ *It is an occasion for all the family to celebrate.* 4 PHRASE If something happens **on occasion** or **on occasions**, it happens sometimes, but not very often. ❑ *Some of the players may, on occasion, break the rules.*

Word Partnership Use *occasion* with:

ADJ. **festive** occasion, **historic** occasion, **rare** occasion, **solemn** occasion, **special** occasion 1 2
V. **mark an** occasion 2

occasional /ə'keɪʒənəl/ ADJ **Occasional** means happening sometimes, but not regularly or often. ❑ *I've had occasional mild headaches.* ● **occasionally** ADV ❑ *He still misbehaves occasionally.*

occult /ɒ'kʌlt, 'ɒkʌlt/ N-SING **The occult** is the

O

Word Web ocean

Oceans cover more than 75% of the earth. These huge bodies of saltwater are always moving. On the surface, the wind pushes the water into **waves**. At the same time, **currents** under the surface flow like rivers through the oceans. These currents are affected by the earth's rotation. It shifts them to the right in the northern hemisphere and to the left in the southern hemisphere. Other forces affect the oceans as well. For example, the gravitational pull of the moon and sun cause the **ebb** and **flow** of ocean **tides**.

knowledge and study of supernatural or magical forces.

occupancy /ˈɒkjʊpənsi/ N-UNCOUNT **Occupancy** is the act of using a room, building, or area of land for a fixed period of time. ❑ *Hotel occupancy has been as low as 40%.*

Word Link *ant ≈ one who does, has : defendant, dependant, occupant*

occupant /ˈɒkjʊpənt/ (**occupants**) N-COUNT The **occupants** of a building or room are the people who live or work there. ❑ *Most of the occupants had left before the fire started.*

occupation /ˌɒkjʊˈpeɪʃən/ (**occupations**) **1** N-COUNT Your **occupation** is your job or profession. ● **occupational** ADJ ❑ *...the occupational hazards of mining.* **2** N-COUNT An **occupation** is something that you do for pleasure or as part of your daily life. ❑ *Skiing is a dangerous occupation.* **3** N-UNCOUNT The **occupation** of a country is its invasion and control by a foreign army. ❑ *...life in Paris during the German occupation.*

occupy /ˈɒkjʊpaɪ/ (**occupies, occupying, occupied**) **1** V-T The people who **occupy** a building or place are the people who live or work there. ❑ *The contract allows the buyer to work on the property, but not to occupy it.* ● **occupier** (**occupiers**) N-COUNT ❑ *...junk mail addressed to 'the occupier'.* **2** V-T PASSIVE If something such as a seat **is occupied**, someone is using it, so that it is not available for anyone else. ❑ *Two of the beds were occupied.* **3** V-T If something **occupies** you, or if you **occupy yourself with** it, you are busy doing it or thinking about it. ❑ *Her political career has occupied all of her time.* ❑ *He occupied himself with packing the car.* ● **occupied** ADJ ❑ *I had been so occupied with other things.* **4** V-T If soldiers **occupy** a place or country, they move into it, using force in order to gain control of it. ❑ *U.S. forces now occupy a part of the country.* **5** V-T If someone or something **occupies** a particular place in a system, process, or plan, they have that place. ❑ *Hussein occupied the post of Secretary General until 1963.*

Word Partnership Use *occupy* with:

N. occupy **a house**, occupy **land** **1**
occupy **a place** **1** **2**
occupy **an area**, **forces** occupy ***someplace***, occupy **space**, **troops** occupy ***someplace*** **4**
occupy **a position** **5**

occur /əˈkɜː/ (**occurs, occurring, occurred**) **1** V-I When an event **occurs**, it happens. ❑ *The crash occurred on a bend in the road.* ❑ *Events like this occur daily.* **2** V-I When something **occurs** in a particular place, it exists or is present there. ❑ *These chemicals occur naturally in water.* **3** V-I If a thought or idea **occurs to** you, you suddenly think of it or realize it. ❑ *It did not occur to me to check my insurance policy.*

Thesaurus *occur* Also look up:

V. come about, develop, happen **1**
dawn on, strike **3**

Word Partnership Use *occur* with:

N. **accidents** occur, **changes** occur, **deaths** occur, **diseases** occur, **events** occur, **injuries** occur, **problems** occur **1**
ADV. **frequently** occur, **naturally** occur, **normally** occur, **often** occur, **usually** occur **1** **2**

occurrence /əˈkʌrəns, AM -ˈkɜːr-/ (**occurrences**) N-COUNT An **occurrence** is something that happens. [FORMAL] ❑ *Complaints seemed to be an everyday occurrence.*

ocean /ˈəʊʃən/ (**oceans**) N-COUNT **The ocean** is the sea. ❑ *There were few sights as beautiful as the calm ocean.* ❑ *...the Indian Ocean.*
→ see Word Web: **ocean**
→ see **beach, earth, river, ship, tide, whale**

o'clock /əˈklɒk/ ADV You use **o'clock** after numbers from one to twelve to say what time it is. ❑ *It's almost eight o'clock.* ❑ *...at ten o'clock last night.*

October /ɒkˈtəʊbə/ (**Octobers**) N-VAR **October** is the tenth month of the year. ❑ *I moved to England last October.*

octopus

octopus /ˈɒktəpəs/ (**octopuses**) N-VAR An **octopus** is a sea creature with eight tentacles.

odd /ɒd/ (**odder, oddest**) **1** ADJ If you say that someone or something is **odd**, you mean that they are strange or unusual. ❑ *He'd always been odd.* ❑ *He used to wear rather odd clothes.* ● **oddly** ADV ❑ *...an oddly shaped hill.* ❑ *He was behaving extremely oddly.* **2** ADJ You use **odd** before a noun to indicate that the type or size of something is not important. ❑ *...moving from place to place where she could find the odd bit of work.* ❑ *He likes the odd drink.* **3** ADJ You say that two things are **odd** when they do not belong to the same set or pair. ❑ *...odd socks.* **4** ADJ **Odd** numbers cannot be divided exactly by the number two. **5** ADV You use **odd** after a number to indicate that it is approximate. [INFORMAL] ❑ *I've lived here for forty odd years.* **6** PHRASE In a group of people or things, **the odd one out** is the one that is different from all the others.

Thesaurus	*odd* Also look up:
ADJ.	bizarre, different, eccentric, peculiar, strange, unusual, weird; *(ant.)* normal, regular **1**

Word Partnership	Use *odd* with:
V.	**feel** odd, **look** odd, **seem** odd, **sound** odd, **strike *someone* as** odd, **think *something*** odd **1**
N.	odd **combination**, odd **thing** **1** odd **job** **2**
ADJ.	odd **numbered** **4**

oddity /ˈɒdɪti/ (**oddities**) **1** N-COUNT An **oddity** is someone or something that is strange or unusual. ❑ *Tourists are still something of an oddity here.* **2** N-COUNT **The oddity of** something is the fact that it is strange. ❑ *...one of the oddities of the legal system.*

odds /ɒdz/ **1** N-PLURAL You refer to the probability of something happening as **the odds** that it will happen. ❑ *What are the odds of winning a prize?* **2** PHRASE If something happens **against all odds**, it happens or succeeds although it seemed impossible or very unlikely. ❑ *Some people do manage to achieve great things against all odds.* **3** PHRASE If you are **at odds with** someone, you are disagreeing or quarrelling with them.

Word Partnership	Use *odds* with:
PREP.	**against all** odds, odds **against *something***, **the** odds **of *something***
N.	odds **in *someone's/something's* favour**, odds **of winning**
V.	**beat the** odds

odour [AM **odor**] /ˈəʊdə/ (**odours**) N-COUNT An **odour** is a smell, especially one that is unpleasant. ❑ *...the odour of smoke.*

→ see **smell, taste**

odyssey /ˈɒdɪsi/ (**odysseys**) N-COUNT An **odyssey** is a long exciting journey on which a lot of things happen. [LITERARY]

of /əv, STRONG ɒv, AM ʌv/ **1** PREP You use **of** to say who or what someone or something belongs to, or is connected with. ❑ *...the holiday homes of the rich.* ❑ *...the new mayor of Los Angeles.* **2** PREP You use **of** to say what something relates to or concerns. ❑ *...her feelings of jealousy.* ❑ *...cancer of the throat.* **3** PREP You use **of** to say who or what a feeling or quality relates to. ❑ *I have grown very fond of Alec.* ❑ *She would be guilty of betraying her mother.* **4** PREP You use **of** to talk about someone or something else who is also involved in an action. ❑ *He'd been dreaming of her.* ❑ *They cannot accuse him of ignoring the problem.* **5** PREP You use **of** to show that someone or something is part of a larger group. ❑ *She is the youngest child of three.* ❑ *...a blade of grass.* **6** PREP You use **of** to talk about amounts. ❑ *...a rise of 13.8%.* ❑ *...a glass of water.* ❑ *...eight years of war.* **7** PREP You use **of** to say how old someone or something is. ❑ *She is a young woman of twenty-six.* ❑ *She felt as if she were a girl of 18 again.* **8** PREP You use **of** to say the date when talking about what day of the month it is. ❑ *...the 4th of July.* **9** PREP You use **of** to say when something happened. ❑ *...the economic mistakes of the past.* ❑ *Rene announced his retirement at the end of the month.* **10** PREP You use **of** to say what substance or materials something is formed from. ❑ *...a mixture of paint-thinner and petrol.* ❑ *The traditional thermometer is made of brass.* **11** PREP You use **of** to say what caused or is causing a person's or animal's death. ❑ *Her husband is dying of cancer.* **12** PREP You use **of** to talk about someone's qualities or characteristics. ❑ *Andrew is a man of honour.* ❑ *She's a woman of few words.* **13** PREP You use **of** to describe someone's behaviour. ❑ *That's very kind of you.*

ˌof ˈcourse **1** ADV You say **of course** to say that something is not surprising because it is normal, obvious, or well-known. ❑ *Of course there were lots of other interesting things at the exhibition.* **2** ADV You use **of course** in order to emphasize a statement that you are making. ❑ *Of course I'm not afraid!* **3** CONVENTION You say **of course** as a polite way of giving permission. [SPOKEN] ❑ *'Could I see these documents?'—'Of course.'* **4** CONVENTION **Of course not** is an emphatic way of saying no. [SPOKEN] ❑ *'You won't tell him, will you?'—'Of course not.'*

off /ɒf, AM ɔːf/ **1** PREP & ADV When something is **taken off** something else or **moves off** it, it is no longer touching that thing. ❑ *He took his feet off the desk.* ❑ *Lee broke off a small piece of chocolate.* **2** PREP & ADV When you **get off** a bus, train, or plane, you get out of it. ❑ *As he stepped off the aeroplane, he was shot dead.* ❑ *At the next stop the man got off.* **3** ADV When you **go off**, you leave the place where you were. ❑ *He was just about to drive off.* **4** PREP & ADV If you **keep off** a street or piece of land, you do not go onto it. ❑ *The police had warned visitors to keep off the beach.* ❑ *...a sign saying 'Keep Off'.* **5** PREP & ADV If something is situated **off** a place such as a room or road, it is near to it, but not exactly in it. ❑ *The boat was sailing off the northern coast.* ❑ *...an apartment just off Park Avenue.* **6** ADV If you **fight** something **off** or **keep** it **off**, you make it go away or prevent it. ❑ *...the body's ability to fight off the common cold.* **7** ADV & PREP If you have **time off**, you do not go to work for a period of time. ❑ *The rest of the men had the day off.* ❑ *He could not get time off work.* **8** ADJ & ADV If something such as a machine or an electric light is **off**, it is not in use. ❑ *He saw her bedroom light was off.* ❑ *The microphones had been switched off.* **9** ADJ If an agreement or an arranged event is **off**, it has been cancelled. ❑ *The meeting is off.* **10** ADJ AFTER LINK-V If food has **gone off**, it tastes and smells unpleasant because it is going bad. **11** PREP If you are **off** something, you have stopped using it or liking it. [INFORMAL] ❑ *I'm off coffee at the moment.* ❑ *The doctor took her off the drugs.* **12** ADV If something is a long time **off**, it will not happen for a long time. ❑ *The cure is probably still two years off.* **13** PHRASE If something happens **on and off** or **off and on**, it happens occasionally, or only for part of a period of time, not in a regular or continuous

O

way. ❑ *I was still working on and off as a waitress.*

offal /ˈɒfəl, AM ˈɔːfəl/ N-UNCOUNT **Offal** is the liver, kidneys, and other internal organs of an animal, when they are used for food.

ˌoff-ˈbalance also **off balance** ADJ AFTER LINK-V If someone or something is **off-balance**, they can easily fall or be knocked over because they are not standing firmly. ❑ *She was thrown off-balance.*

ˌoff ˈduty also **off-duty** ADJ When someone such as a soldier or policeman is **off duty**, they are not working. ❑ *...an off-duty policeman.*

offence [AM **offense**] /əˈfens/ (**offences**) 1 N-COUNT An **offence** is a crime. [FORMAL] ❑ *He has committed hundreds of offences.* 2 N-UNCOUNT If you give **offence**, you upset or embarrass someone. ❑ *We did not mean to cause any offence.* 3 PHRASE If you **take offence**, you are upset by something that someone says or does. ❑ *She never takes offence at anything.*

Thesaurus *offence* Also look up:

N. crime, violation, wrongdoing 1
assault, attack, insult, snub 2

Word Partnership Use *offence* with:

V. **commit an** offence 1 2
take offence 5
ADJ. **criminal** offence 1
serious offence 3

Word Link *fend ≈ striking : defend, defender, offend*

offend /əˈfend/ (**offends, offending, offended**) 1 V-T If you **offend** someone, you upset or embarrass them. ● **offended** ADJ ❑ *She is terribly offended and hurt.* 2 V-I If someone **offends**, they commit a crime. ❑ *Some will continue to offend, again and again.* ● **offender** (**offenders**) N-COUNT ❑ *...a prison for young offenders.*

offense /əˈfens, ˈɒfens/ → see **offence**

offensive /əˈfensɪv/ (**offensives**) 1 ADJ Something that is **offensive** upsets or embarrasses people because it is rude or insulting. ❑ *...an offensive remark.* 2 N-COUNT An **offensive** is a strong attack. ❑ *...a military offensive on a training camp.* 3 PHRASE If you **go on the offensive, go over to the offensive**, or **take the offensive**, you begin to take strong action against people who have been attacking you.

Word Partnership Use *offensive* with:

N. offensive **language** 1
offensive **capability**, **ground** offensive, offensive **operations**, offensive **weapons** 2
V. **launch an** offensive, **mount an** offensive 2 3
take the offensive 3

offer /ˈɒfə, AM ˈɔːfər/ (**offers, offering, offered**) 1 V-T If you **offer** something **to** someone, you ask them if they would like to have it or to use it. ❑ *I offered my seat to a lady on the bus.* ❑ *She offered him a cup of tea.* 2 V-T If you **offer to** do something, you say that you are willing to do it. ❑ *Greg offered to teach him to ski.* ❑ *'Can I get you a drink?' she offered.* 3 V-T If you **offer** a particular amount of money **for** something, you say that you will pay that much for it. ❑ *He offered £250,000 for the house.* 4 N-COUNT An **offer** is something that someone says they will give you or do for you. ❑ *It was an offer he could not refuse.* ❑ *Ingrid did not accept Steele's offer to drive her to her car.* 5 N-COUNT An **offer** in a shop is a specially low price for a product, or something extra that you get by buying the product. ❑ *...special offers on holiday cottages.* 6 PHRASE If something is **on offer**, it is available to be used or bought. ❑ *...some of the excellent books on offer.*

offering /ˈɒfərɪŋ, AM ˈɔːf-/ (**offerings**) N-COUNT An **offering** is something that is specially produced to be sold.

office /ˈɒfɪs, AM ˈɔːf-/ (**offices**) 1 N-COUNT An **office** is a room or a part of a building where people work sitting at desks. ❑ *I arrived at the office early.* 2 N-COUNT An **office** is a department of an organization, especially the government, where people deal with a particular kind of administrative work. ❑ *Contact your local tax office.* 3 N-COUNT An **office** is a small building or room where people can go for information, tickets, or a service of some kind. ❑ *...the tourist office.* 4 N-UNCOUNT Someone who holds **office** has an important job or a position of authority in government or in an organization. ❑ *...the President's ten years in office.*
→ see Picture Dictionary: **office**

officer /ˈɒfɪsə, AM ˈɔːf-/ (**officers**) 1 N-COUNT In the armed forces, an **officer** is a person in a position of authority. ❑ *...army officers.* 2 N-COUNT An **officer** is a person who has a responsible position in an organization, especially a

Picture Dictionary *office*

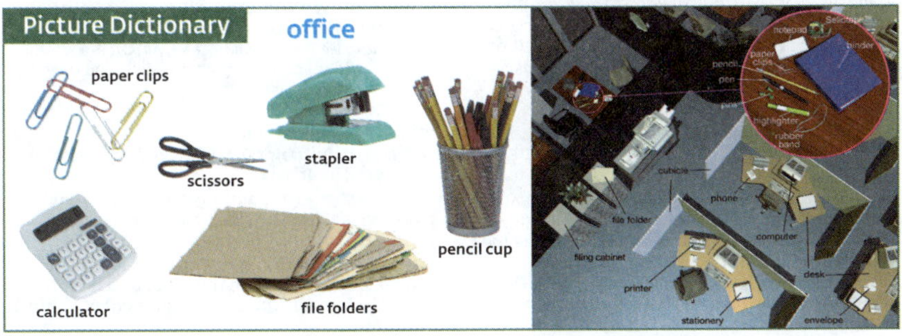

government organization. ❑ *...a local authority education officer.* **3** N-COUNT & N-VOC Members of the police force can be referred to or addressed as **officers**. ❑ *...senior police officers.* ❑ *Thank you, Officer.*

official /əˈfɪʃəl/ (**officials**) **1** ADJ Something that is **official** is approved by the government or by someone else in authority. ❑ *...the official unemployment figures.* ● **officially** ADV ❑ *The election results have still not been officially announced.* **2** ADJ BEFORE N **Official** is used to describe things which are done or used by people in authority as part of their job or position. ❑ *Mr Ridley is currently on an official visit to Hungary.* ❑ *...the Irish President's official residence.* **3** N-COUNT An **official** is a person who holds a position of authority in an organization. ❑ *...a senior UN official.*

Thesaurus *official* Also look up:

ADJ. authentic, formal, legitimate, valid; *(ant.)* unauthorized, unofficial **1**
N. administrator, director, executive, manager **3**

Word Partnership Use *official* with:

N. official **documents**, official **language**, official **report**, official **sources**, official **statement** **1**
official **duties**, official **visit** **2**
ADJ. **administration** official, **city** official, **elected** official, **government** official, **local** official, **military** official, **senior** official, **top** official **3**

ˈoff-ˌlicence (**off-licences**) N-COUNT In Britain, an **off-licence** is a shop which sells alcoholic drinks. The usual American expression is **liquor store**.

O

offline or **off-line** /ˌɒfˈlaɪn, AM ˌɔːf-/ ADJ & ADV If a computer is **offline**, it is not connected to the Internet. [COMPUTING] ❑ *Most software programs allow you to write e-mails offline.*

ˌoff-ˈpeak ADJ BEFORE N & ADV **Off-peak** things are available at a time when there is less demand for them, so that they are cheaper than usual. ❑ *...off-peak electricity.* ❑ *Calls cost 39p a minute off-peak.*

offset /ˌɒfˈset, AM ˌɔːf-/ (**offsets, offsetting, offset**) V-T If one thing **is offset** by another, the effect of the first thing is reduced by the second. ❑ *Gains of 225 seats were offset by losses of 183.*

offshoot /ˈɒfʃuːt, AM ˈɔːf-/ (**offshoots**) N-COUNT If one thing is an **offshoot** of another thing, it has developed from the other thing. ❑ *The technology we use is an offshoot of the motor industry.*

offshore also **off-shore** /ˌɒfˈʃɔː, AM ˌɔːf-/ ADJ & ADV **Offshore** means situated or happening in the sea, near to the coast. ❑ *...an offshore island.* ❑ *One day a larger ship anchored offshore.*

offside also **off-side** /ˌɒfˈsaɪd, AM ˌɔːf-/ **1** ADJ & ADV If a player in a game of football or hockey is **offside**, they have broken the rules by moving too far forward. ❑ *Russell was clearly offside.* ❑ *Williams was standing at least ten yards offside.* **2** N-SING The **offside of** a vehicle is the side farthest from the pavement when you are driving. [BRIT]

offspring /ˈɒfsprɪŋ, AM ˈɔːf-/

Offspring is both the singular and the plural form.

N-COUNT You can refer to a person's children or to an animal's young as their **offspring**. [FORMAL]

often /ˈɒfən, AM ˈɔːf-/ **1** ADV If something happens **often**, it happens many times or much of the time. ❑ *They often spent Christmas with his family.* ❑ *They used these words freely, often in front of their parents too.* ❑ *That doesn't happen very often.* **2** ADV You use **often** after 'how' to ask questions about frequency. You also use **often** in statements to give information about the frequency of something. ❑ *How often do you brush your teeth?* ❑ *They exercise twice as often as the general population.* **3** PHRASE If something happens **every so often**, it happens regularly, but with fairly long intervals between each occasion. ❑ *Every so often he turned and looked at her.* **4** PHRASE If you say that something happens **more often than not** or **as often as not**, you mean that it happens fairly frequently, and that this can be considered as typical of the kind of situation you are talking about. ❑ *More often than not you'll find us in the kitchen in the evenings.*

Usage

You do not use **often** to talk about something that happens several times within a short period of time. You say '**I phoned her several times yesterday**' or '**I kept phoning her yesterday**'.

Thesaurus *often* Also look up:

ADV. regularly, repeatedly, usually; *(ant.)* never, rarely, seldom **1**

oh /əʊ/ **1** CONVENTION You use **oh** to introduce a response or a comment on something that has just been said. [SPOKEN] ❑ *'Would you like me to phone and explain the situation?'—'Oh, would you?'* **2** EXCLAM You use **oh** to express a feeling such as surprise, pain, annoyance, or joy. [SPOKEN] ❑ *'Oh!' Kenny said. 'Has everyone gone?'* ❑ *'Oh no,' Smith complained.* **3** CONVENTION You use **oh** when you are hesitating while speaking. ❑ *I've been here, oh, since the end of June.*

oil /ɔɪl/ (**oils, oiling, oiled**) **1** N-VAR **Oil** is a smooth thick liquid used as a fuel and for lubricating machines. Oil is found underground. ❑ *The company buys and sells about 600,000 barrels of oil a day.* ❑ *Check your engine oil regularly.* **2** V-T If you **oil** something, you put oil onto it or into it in order to make it work smoothly or to protect it. ❑ *A team of assistants oiled the machine.* **3** N-VAR **Oil** is a smooth thick liquid made from plants or fish and used in cookery. ❑ *...olive oil.*
→ see Word Web: **oil**
→ see **petroleum, ship**

ˈoil ˌpaint (**oil paints**) N-VAR **Oil paint** is a thick paint used by artists.

ˈoil ˌpainting (**oil paintings**) N-COUNT An **oil painting** is a picture which has been painted using oil paints.

ˈoil ˌslick (**oil slicks**) N-COUNT An **oil slick** is a layer of oil that floats on the sea or on a lake. It is formed when oil accidentally spills out of a ship or container.

Word Web oil

There is a great demand for **petroleum** in the world today. Companies are always **drilling oil wells** in oilfields on land and on the ocean floor. In the ocean, drilling **rigs** or **oil platforms** sit on concrete or metal man-made islands. Others float on ships. The **crude oil** from these wells goes to **refineries** through **pipelines** or in huge **tanker** ships. At the refinery, the crude oil is processed into a variety of products including **petrol, aviation fuel,** and **plastics.**

oily /ˈɔɪli/ (**oilier, oiliest**) ADJ Something that is **oily** is covered with oil, contains oil, or looks, feels, or tastes like oil. ❑ *...an oily rag.* ❑ *Paul found the sauce too oily.* ❑ *...a tonic for oily skin.*

ointment /ˈɔɪntmənt/ (**ointments**) N-VAR An **ointment** is a smooth thick substance that is put on sore skin or a wound to help it heal. ❑ *A range of ointments and creams is available for the treatment of eczema.*

okay also **OK** /ˌəʊˈkeɪ/ **1** ADJ & ADV If you say that something is **okay**, you mean that it is good enough. [INFORMAL] ❑ *Is it okay if I come by myself?* ❑ *We seemed to manage okay for the first year.* **2** ADJ AFTER LINK-V If you say that someone is **okay**, you mean that they are safe and well. ❑ *Check that the baby's okay.* **3** CONVENTION You can say **okay** to show that you agree to something. ❑ *'Shall I give you a ring on Friday?'—'Yeah, okay.'* **4** CONVENTION You can say **'Okay?'** to check whether the person you are talking to understands what you have said and accepts it. ❑ *We'll get together next week, OK?*

old /əʊld/ (**older, oldest**) **1** ADJ & N-PLURAL Someone who is **old** has lived for many years and is no longer young. You can refer to old people as **the old**. ❑ *...a white-haired old man.* **2** ADJ Something that is **old** has existed for a long time. ❑ *These books must be very old.* ❑ *...an old Arab proverb.* **3** ADJ Something that is **old** is no longer in good condition because of its age or because it has been used a lot. ❑ *...an old toothbrush.* **4** ADJ You use **old** to talk or ask about the age of someone or something. ❑ *The paintings were a thousand years old.* ❑ *How old are you now?* **5** → See note at **elder** **6** ADJ BEFORE N You use **old** to refer to something that is no longer used, that no longer exists, or that has been replaced by something else. ❑ *The old road had disappeared under grass.* **7** ADJ BEFORE N You use **old** to refer to something that used to belong to you, or to a person or thing that used to have a particular role in your life. ❑ *I'll make up the bed in your old room.* ❑ *Jane returned to her old boyfriend.* **8** ADJ BEFORE N An **old** friend or enemy is someone who has been your friend or enemy for a long time. **9** PHRASE You use **any old** to emphasize that the quality or type of something is not important. If you say that a particular thing is not **any old** thing, you are emphasizing how special it is. ❑ *Any old paper will do.* ❑ *This is not just any old front room.*

Thesaurus *old* Also look up:

ADJ. elderly, mature, senior; *(ant.)* young **1**
ancient, antique, archaic, dated, old-fashioned, outdated, traditional; *(ant.)* new **2**

ˌold ˈage **1** N-UNCOUNT Your **old age** is the period of years towards the end of your life. ❑ *They worry about how they will support themselves in their old age.* **2** N-UNCOUNT **Old age** is the quality or state of being old and near the end of one's life. ❑ *The last lion in the zoo died from old age.*

ˌold-ˈfashioned ADJ Something that is **old-fashioned** is no longer used, done, or believed by most people, because it has been replaced by something that is more modern. ❑ *The house was old-fashioned and in bad condition.* ❑ *They still make cheese the old-fashioned way.*

olive /ˈɒlɪv/ (**olives**) **1** N-VAR **Olives** are small green or black fruit with a bitter taste. The tree on which olives grow is called an **olive tree** or an **olive**. **2** ADJ & N-VAR Something that is **olive** is yellowish-green in colour.

ˈolive ˌoil N-UNCOUNT **Olive oil** is edible oil obtained by pressing olives.

Olympic /əˈlɪmpɪk/ (**Olympics**) **1** ADJ BEFORE N **Olympic** means relating to the Olympic Games. ❑ *...the reigning Olympic champion.* **2** N-PROPER **The Olympics** are the **Olympic Games**.

OˌlympicˈGames N-PROPER **The Olympic Games** are a set of international sports competitions which take place every four years, each time in a different country. **Olympic Games** can take the singular or plural form of the verb.

omelette [AM **omelet**] /ˈɒmlət/ (**omelettes**) N-COUNT An **omelette** is a food made by beating eggs and cooking them in a flat pan.
→ see **egg**

omen /ˈəʊmen/ (**omens**) N-COUNT If you say that something is an **omen**, you think it indicates what is likely to happen in the future and whether it will be good or bad. ❑ *She is hoping that her success is an omen for the future.*

ominous /ˈɒmɪnəs/ ADJ If you describe something as **ominous**, you mean that it worries you because it makes you think that something unpleasant is going to happen. ❑ *The clouds were growing more ominous.* ● **ominously** ADV ❑ *The bar seemed ominously quiet.*

omission /əʊˈmɪʃən/ (**omissions**) N-VAR An **omission** is the act of not including something or not doing something. ❑ *There was one embarrassing omission from his new book.*

omit /əʊˈmɪt/ (**omits, omitting, omitted**) **1** V-T If you **omit** something, you do not include it in an activity or piece of work. ❑ *Omit the salt in this recipe.* **2** V-T If you **omit to** do something, you do not do it. [FORMAL] ❑ *His new girlfriend had omitted to tell him she was married.*

O

Thesaurus	*omit* Also look up:
v.	forget, leave out, miss; *(ant.)* add, include 1

on /ɒn/ 1 PREP If someone or something is **on** a surface or object, the surface or object is underneath them and is supporting their weight. ❑ *He is sitting beside her on the sofa.* ❑ *There was a little house on the top of the mountain.* ❑ *...the Chinese rug on the floor.* 2 PREP If something is **on** a surface or object, it is stuck to it or attached to it. ❑ *...the peeling paint on the ceiling.* ❑ *There was butter on his chin.* 3 PREP If you get **on** a bus, train, or plane, you go in it in order to travel somewhere. You say you are **on** the bus, train, or plane when you are travelling in it. ❑ *I never go on the bus into the town.* 4 PREP If there is something **on** a piece of paper, it has been written or printed there. ❑ *...the writing on the back of the card.* ❑ *...the numbers she put on the chart.* 5 ADV When you **put** a piece of clothing **on**, you place it over a part of your body in order to wear it. If you **have** it **on**, you are wearing it. ❑ *He put his coat on.* ❑ *I had a hat on.* 6 PREP You can say that you have something **on** you if you are carrying it in your pocket or in a bag. ❑ *I didn't have any money on me.* 7 PREP If something happens **on** a particular day or date, that is when it happens. ❑ *This year's event will take place on June 19th.* ❑ *She travels to Korea on Monday.* 8 PREP You use **on** when mentioning an event that was followed by another one. ❑ *She waited in her hotel to welcome her children on their arrival from London.* 9 PREP If something is done **on** an instrument, machine, or system, it is done using that instrument, machine, or system. ❑ *I do all my work on the computer.* 10 ADJ & ADV If something such as a machine or an electric light is **on**, it is functioning or in use. ❑ *The light was on and the door was open.* ❑ *I've turned the central heating on again.* 11 PREP Books, discussions, or ideas **on** a particular subject are concerned with that subject. ❑ *...a book on baby care.* ❑ *...a service which gives advice on legal matters.* 12 PREP If something affects you, you can say that it has an effect **on** you. 13 PREP When you buy something or pay for something, you spend money **on** it. ❑ *I didn't want to waste money on a hotel.* 14 PREP When you spend time or energy **on** a particular activity, you spend time or energy doing it. ❑ *Children spend so much time on computer games.* 15 ADV You use **on** to say that someone is continuing to do something. ❑ *They walked on in silence.* 16 PREP If you are **on** a council or committee, you are a member of it. ❑ *Claire and Beryl were on the organizing committee.* 17 PREP If someone is **on** a medicine or drug, they are taking it regularly. If someone lives **on** a particular kind of food, they eat it. ❑ *She was on antibiotics for an eye infection.* ❑ *We lived on bread and cheese, apples and water.* 18 ADV When an activity is taking place, you can say that it is **on**. ❑ *It tells you what's on at the cinema.* 19 PREP If something is being broadcast, you can say that it is **on** the radio or television. ❑ *He watched every sporting event on television.* 20 ADV If you say that someone goes **on at** you, you mean that they continually criticize you, complain to you, or ask you to do something. [SPOKEN] ❑ *She's been on at me for weeks to show her round the house.* ❑ *He used to keep on at me about the need to win.* 21 PHRASE If you **have a lot on**, you are very busy. If you **do not have much on**, you are not busy. [SPOKEN] ❑ *I have a lot on in the next week.* 22 **and so on** → see **so**
→ see **location**

once /wʌns, wɒns/ 1 ADV If something happens **once**, it happens one time only, or one time within a particular period of time. ❑ *Mary had only been to Manchester once before.* 2 ADV If something was **once** true, it was true at some time in the past, but is no longer true. ❑ *The house where she lives was once the village post office.* 3 CONJ If something happens **once** another thing has happened, it happens immediately afterwards. ❑ *Once customers start to use these systems they almost never take their business elsewhere.* 4 PHRASE If something happens **once and for all**, it happens completely or finally. ❑ *We have to resolve this matter once and for all.* 5 PHRASE If you do something **at once**, you do it immediately. ❑ *I have to go, I really must, at once.* 6 PHRASE If several things happen **at once** or **all at once**, they all happen at the same time. ❑ *You can't be doing two things at once.* 7 PHRASE **For once** is used to emphasize that something happens on this particular occasion, especially if it has never happened before, and may never happen again. ❑ *For once, dad is not complaining.* 8 **once upon a time** → see **time** 9 **once in a while** → see **while**

one /wʌn, wɒn/ (**ones**) 1 NUM **One** is the number 1. ❑ *They had three sons and one daughter.* ❑ *...one thousand years ago.* ❑ *...one of the children killed in the crash.* 2 DET & PRON You can use **one** to refer to the first of two or more things that you are comparing. ❑ *Prices vary from one shop to another.* ❑ *The twins were dressed differently and one was thinner than the other.* 3 PRON You can use **one** or **ones** when it is clear what type of thing or person you are referring to and you are describing them or giving more information about them. ❑ *They are selling their house to move to a smaller one.* ❑ *We test each one to see that it flies well.* 4 DET You can use **one** when referring to a time in the past or in the future. ❑ *How would you like to have dinner one night?* 5 PRON Speakers and writers sometimes use **one** to make statements about people in general which also apply to themselves. **One** can be used as the subject or object of a sentence. [FORMAL] ❑ *Where does one go from there?* ❑ *Shares and bonds can bring one quite a considerable additional income.* 6 PHRASE **One or two** means a few. ❑ *We may make one or two changes.* 7 **one another** → see **another**

ˌone-ˈoff (**one-offs**) 1 N-COUNT A **one-off** is something that is made or happens only once. [mainly BRIT] 2 ADJ BEFORE N A **one-off** thing is made or happens only once. [mainly BRIT] ❑ *...one-off cash benefits.*

onerous /ˈəʊnərəs, AM ˈɑːn-/ ADJ If you describe a task as **onerous**, you dislike having to do it because you find it difficult or unpleasant. [FORMAL] ❑ *The responsibilities of a huge home can be onerous.*

one's /wʌnz/ 1 DET Speakers and writers use **one's** to indicate that something belongs or relates to people in general, or to themselves in particular. [FORMAL] ❑ *It is natural to care for one's family and one's children.* 2 **One's** can be used as a spoken form of 'one is' or 'one has', especially when 'has' is an auxiliary verb. ❑ *No one's going to hurt you.* ❑ *No-one's got respect for him any more.*

O

oneself /wʌn'self/ **1** PRON A speaker or writer uses **oneself** to refer to themselves or to any person in general. ❑ *...a way of making oneself feel sophisticated.* ❑ *To work one must have time to oneself.* **2** PRON To do something **oneself** means to do it without any help or interference from anyone else. [FORMAL] ❑ *Some things one must do oneself.* **3** PRON You use **oneself** to emphasize that something happens to you rather than to people in general. ❑ *It is better to die oneself than to kill.*

ˌone-'sided **1** ADJ In a **one-sided** activity or relationship, one of the people or groups involved does much more than the other or is much stronger than the other. ❑ *The negotiating was completely one-sided.* ❑ *...a very one-sided match.* **2** ADJ If you describe someone as **one-sided**, you are critical of them because they have considered only one side of an issue or event. ❑ *Don't be one-sided in your reporting.*

'one-ˌtime or **onetime** ADJ BEFORE N **One-time** can be used to describe something such as a job or role which someone used to have, or something which happened or existed in the past. ❑ *...a one-time rock star.*

ˌone-to-'one ADJ BEFORE N & ADV In a **one-to-one** relationship, you deal with only one other person. ❑ *One-to-one lessons cost 80 euros an hour.* ❑ *She likes to talk to people one to one.*

ˌone-'way **1** ADJ In **one-way** streets or traffic systems, vehicles can only travel in one direction. **2** ADJ A **one-way** ticket enables you to travel to a place, but not to come back again.

ongoing /ˌɒn'gəʊɪŋ/ ADJ An **ongoing** situation is continuing to happen. ❑ *There is an ongoing debate on the issue.*

onion /'ʌnjən/ (**onions**) N-VAR An **onion** is a small round vegetable. It is white with a brown skin, and has a strong smell and taste.
→ see **spice, vegetable**

online also **on-line** /ˌɒn'laɪn/ ADJ & ADV **Online** means available on or connected to the Internet. [COMPUTING] ❑ *...an online catalogue.* ❑ *You can chat to other people online.*

onlooker /'ɒnlʊkə/ (**onlookers**) N-COUNT An **onlooker** is someone who watches an event take place but does not take part in it. ❑ *A small crowd of onlookers were there to watch.*

only /'əʊnli/ **1** ADV You use **only** to indicate the one thing that is true, appropriate, or necessary in a particular situation. ❑ *Only the President could authorize the use of the atomic bomb.* ❑ *A business can only be built on a sound financial base.* **2** ADV You use **only** to introduce the thing which must happen before the thing mentioned in the main part of the sentence can happen. ❑ *The lawyer is paid only if he wins.* **3** ADJ BEFORE N If you talk about the **only** person or thing involved in a particular situation, you mean there are no others involved in it. ❑ *She was the only woman in the legal department.* **4** ADJ BEFORE N An **only** child is a child who has no brothers or sisters. **5** ADV You use **only** to emphasize that something is unimportant or small. ❑ *I was only joking.* ❑ *Child car seats only cost about £10 a week to hire.* ❑ *Teenagers typically earn only half the adult wage.* **6** CONJ **Only** can be used to add a comment which slightly changes or corrects what you have just said. [INFORMAL] ❑ *It's a bit like my house, only nicer.* ❑ *Come and see me when you're ready. Only don't take too long about it.* **7** PHRASE You can say that something has **only just** happened when you want to emphasize that it happened a very short time ago. ❑ *I've only just arrived.* **8** PHRASE You use **only just** to emphasize that something is true, but by such a small degree that it is almost not true at all. ❑ *For centuries farmers there have only just managed to survive.* **9** **if only** → see **if**

Usage

When **only** is used as an adverb, its position in the sentence depends on the word or phrase it applies to. If **only** applies to the subject of a clause, you put it in front of the subject. ❑ *Only strong characters can make such decisions.* Otherwise, you normally put it in front of the verb, or after the first auxiliary, or after the verb **be.** ❑ *I only want my son back, that is all.* ❑ *He had only agreed to see me because we had met before.* ❑ *I was only able to wash four times in 66 days.* However, some people think it is more correct to put **only** directly in front of the word or phrase it applies to. This is the best position if you want to be quite clear or emphatic. ❑ *It applies only to passengers carrying British passports.* ❑ *She'd done it only because it was necessary.* For extra emphasis, you can put **only** after the word or phrase it applies to. ❑ *The event will be for women only.* ❑ *I'll say this once and once only.*

Thesaurus *only* Also look up:

ADJ. alone, individual, single, solitary, unique **3**

ˌon-'screen also **onscreen** **1** ADJ BEFORE N **On-screen** means appearing on the screen of a television, cinema, or computer. ❑ *...an easy-to-follow on-screen display.* **2** ADJ BEFORE N & ADV **On-screen** means relating to the roles being played by film or television actors, in contrast with their real life. ❑ *...her on-screen romance with Pierce Lawton.* ❑ *He was immensely attractive to women, onscreen and offscreen.*

onset /'ɒnset/ N-SING The **onset** of something unpleasant is the beginning of it. ❑ *...the onset of the disease.*

onslaught /'ɒnslɔːt/ (**onslaughts**) **1** N-COUNT An **onslaught on** someone or something is a very violent attack against them. ❑ *A terrorist onslaught on central London caused many deaths.* **2** N-COUNT If you refer to an **onslaught of** something, you mean that there is a large amount of it, often so that it is very difficult to deal with. ❑ *Drivers face a new onslaught of road bumps and speed cameras.*

onto also **on to** /'ɒntuː/ **1** PREP If someone or something moves **onto** an object, or if they are put **onto** it, they are then on that object or surface. ❑ *I lowered myself onto the bed.* ❑ *Rub cream on to your baby's skin.* **2** PREP When you get **onto** a bus, train, or plane, you enter it. **3** PREP **Onto** is used after verbs such as 'hold', 'hang', and 'cling' to indicate what someone is holding firmly or where something is being held firmly. ❑ *She had to hold onto the door handle until the pain passed.* **4** PREP If people who are talking get **onto** a different subject, they begin talking about it. ❑ *Let's get on to more important matters.* **5** PREP If someone is **onto**

something, they are about to make a discovery. [INFORMAL] ❑ *They knew they were onto something big when they started digging.* **6** PREP If someone is **onto** you, they have discovered that you are doing something illegal or wrong. [INFORMAL] ❑ *The police were onto him.*

onus /ˈəʊnəs/ N-SING If you say that the **onus** is **on** someone **to** do something, you mean it is their duty or responsibility to do it. ❑ *The onus is on the shopkeeper to provide quality goods.*

onward /ˈɒnwəd/ or **onwards** /ˈɒnwədz/ **1** ADJ & ADV **Onward** means moving forward or continuing a journey. ❑ *The onward journey by train or car takes about four hours.* ❑ *He led us onwards through the forest.* ❑ *The bus continued onward.* **2** ADJ & ADV **Onward** means developing, progressing, or becoming more important over a period of time. ❑ *...the onward march of progress in the British aircraft industry.* ❑ *The White House feels no need to rush onwards to a new agreement.* **3** ADV If something happens from a particular time **onwards** or **onward**, it begins to happen at that time and continues to happen afterwards. ❑ *...from the turn of the century onward.*

ooze /uːz/ (**oozes, oozing, oozed**) **1** V-T/V-I When a thick or sticky liquid **oozes** from something, the liquid flows slowly and in small quantities. ❑ *The wounds were still oozing blood.* ❑ *He could see the cut now, still oozing slightly.* **2** V-T If you say that someone or something **oozes** a quality or characteristic, you mean that they show it very strongly. ❑ *The Elizabethan house oozes charm.*

opaque /əʊˈpeɪk/ **1** ADJ If an object or substance is **opaque**, you cannot see through it. ❑ *...opaque glass windows.* **2** ADJ If you say that something is **opaque**, you meant that it is difficult to understand. ❑ *...the opaque language of the inspector's reports.*

O

open

1. UNCOVERING
2. BUILDINGS, PLACES, AND EVENTS
3. OTHER MEANINGS
4. PHRASES AND PHRASAL VERBS

open /ˈəʊpən/ (**opens, opening, opened**) **1** **1** V-T/V-I When you **open** something such as a door or the lid of a box, or when it **opens**, you move it so that it no longer covers a hole or gap. ❑ *He opened the window.* ❑ *The church doors opened and the crowd came out.* **2** V-T If you **open** something such as a container or a letter, you move, remove, or cut part of it so that you can take out what is inside. ❑ *The Inspector opened the packet of cigarettes.* **3** V-T/V-I If you **open** something such as a book, an umbrella, or your hand, or if it **opens**, the different parts of it move away from each other so that the inside of it can be seen. ❑ *He opened the book.* ❑ *The officer's mouth opened.* **4** V-T/V-I When you **open** your eyes, or when they **open**, you move your eyelids upwards so that you can see. **5** V-T/V-I If people **open** something such as a blocked road or a border, or if it **opens**, people can then pass along it or through it. ❑ *The rebels have opened the road from Monrovia to the Ivory Coast.* **6** ADJ You use **open** to describe something which has been opened. ❑ *...an open window.* ❑ *I tore the letter open.* ❑ *Her eyes were open.* **7** ADJ If an item of clothing is **open**, it is not fastened. ❑ *His open shirt revealed a gold chain.* **8** V-I When flowers **open**, their petals spread out.

Usage

You do not use **open** as a verb or adjective to talk about electrical devices. If someone causes an electrical device to work by pressing a switch or turning a knob, you say that they **put it on**, **switch it on**, or **turn it on**. If the device is already working, you say that it is **on**. ❑ *The answering machine is on.* ❑ *He cannot sleep with the light on.*

open /ˈəʊpən/ (**opens, opening, opened**) **2** **1** V-T/V-I When a shop, office, or public building **opens**, or when it **is opened**, its doors are unlocked and the people in it start working. ❑ *Banks closed on Friday afternoon and did not open again until Monday morning.* **2** ADJ AFTER LINK-V When a shop, office, or public building is **open**, its doors are unlocked and the people in it are working. ❑ *His shop is open Monday through Friday.* **3** V-T/V-I When a public building, factory, or company **opens** or when someone **opens** it, it starts operating for the first time. ❑ *The original station opened in 1754.* • **opening** (**openings**) N-COUNT ❑ *He was there for the official opening.* **4** V-I When an event such as a conference or a play **opens**, it begins to take place or to be performed. ❑ *An emergency session of Parliament will open later this morning.* • **opening** N-SING ❑ *...the opening of the talks.* **5** V-I If a place **opens into** another, larger place, you can move from one directly into the other. ❑ *The corridor opened into a small smoky room.* **6** ADJ An **open** area is a large area that does not have many structures or obstructions in it. ❑ *Officers will continue their search of nearby open ground.* **7** ADJ BEFORE N An **open** structure or object is not covered or enclosed. ❑ *...a room with an open fire.*

open /ˈəʊpən/ (**opens, opening, opened**) **3** **1** ADJ If you describe a person or their character as **open**, you mean they are honest and do not want or try to hide anything or to deceive anyone. ❑ *He had always been open with her.* • **openness** N-UNCOUNT ❑ *I was impressed by his openness.* **2** ADJ AFTER LINK-V If you are **open to** suggestions or ideas, you are ready and willing to consider or accept them. ❑ *They are open to suggestions on how things might be improved.* **3** ADJ AFTER LINK-V If you say that a system, person, or idea is **open to** something such as abuse or criticism, you mean they might receive abuse and criticism because of the qualities they possess or the effects they have had. ❑ *All the group members know that the leader is open to criticism.* **4** V-T If you **open** an account with a bank or a commercial organization, you begin to use their services. **5** → see also **opening, openly**

open /ˈəʊpən/ (**opens, opening, opened**) **4** **1** PHRASE If you do something **in the open**, you do it out of doors. **2** PHRASE If a situation is brought out **into the open**, people are told about it and it is no longer a secret.

▶ **open up** **1** PHR-VERB If something **opens up** opportunities or possibilities, or if opportunities or possibilities **open up**, they are able to arise or develop. ❑ *New opportunities are opening up for investors.* **2** PHR-VERB If a place, economy, or area of interest **opens up**, or if someone **opens it up**, it becomes accessible to more people. ❑ *The Internet definitely opens up new markets.* **3** PHR-VERB When you **open up** a building, you unlock and open the door so that people can get in. ❑ *The postmaster and his wife arrived to open up the shop.*

ˌopen-ˈair also **open air** 1 ADJ An **open-air** place or event is outside rather than in a building. ❑ *...the Open Air Theatre in Regents Park.* 2 N-SING If you are **in the open air**, you are outside rather than in a building.

ˌopen-ˈended ADJ When people begin an **open-ended** discussion or activity, they do not start with any intention of achieving a particular decision or result. ❑ *...open-ended questions about passengers' expectations.*

opener /ˈəʊpənə/ (**openers**) N-COUNT An **opener** is a tool which is used to open containers such as bottles and cans.
→ see **kitchen**

opening /ˈəʊpənɪŋ/ (**openings**) 1 ADJ BEFORE N The **opening** event, item, day, or week in a series is the first one. ❑ *...the season's opening game.* 2 N-SING The **opening** of something such as a book or concert is the first part of it. ❑ *...the opening of the film.* 3 N-COUNT An **opening** is a hole or empty space through which things can pass. ❑ *...a narrow opening in the fence.* 4 N-COUNT An **opening** is a good opportunity to do something. ❑ *All she needed was an opening to show her abilities.* 5 N-COUNT An **opening** is a job that is available. ❑ *We don't have any openings now.* 6 → see also **open**

Thesaurus *opening* Also look up:

N. cut, door, gap, slot, space, window 3
job, position 5

openly /ˈəʊpənli/ ADV If you do something **openly**, you do it without trying to hide anything. ❑ *We can now talk openly about cancer.*

ˌopen-ˈminded ADJ If you describe someone as **open-minded**, you approve of them because they are willing to listen to and consider other people's ideas. ● **open-mindedness** N-UNCOUNT ❑ *...honesty, open-mindedness and willingness to learn.*

Word Link *oper ≈ work : co-operate, opera, operation*

opera /ˈɒpərə/ (**operas**) N-VAR An **opera** is a musical entertainment. It is like a play, but most of the words are sung. ● **operatic** /ˌɒpəˈrætɪk/ ADJ ❑ *...the local amateur operatic society.*
→ see **music**

operate /ˈɒpəreɪt/ (**operates, operating, operated**) 1 V-T/V-I If you **operate** a business or organization, you work to keep it running properly. If a business or organization **operates**, it carries out its work. ❑ *The family owned and operated the factory.* ❑ *...allowing foreign banks to operate in Australia.* ● **operation** N-UNCOUNT ❑ *...funds for the everyday operation of the business.* 2 V-I The way that something **operates** is the way that it works or has an effect. ❑ *Ceiling and wall lights operate independently.* ● **operation** N-UNCOUNT ❑ *We need someone with experience of the operation of national exam systems.* 3 V-T When you **operate** a machine or device, you make it work. ● **operation** N-UNCOUNT ❑ *...the operation of the aeroplane.* 4 V-I When surgeons **operate on** a patient, they cut open the patient's body in order to remove, replace, or repair a diseased or damaged part.

Word Partnership Use *operate* with:

N. operate **a business/company**, **schools** operate 1
forces operate 1 2
V. ***be* allowed to** operate, **continue to** operate 1 2 3
ADV. operate **efficiently** 1 2
operate **independently** 2

ˈoperating ˌtheatre (**operating theatres**) N-COUNT In British English, an **operating theatre** is a room in a hospital where surgeons carry out operations. The usual American term is **operating room**.

operation /ˌɒpəˈreɪʃən/ (**operations**) 1 N-COUNT An **operation** is a highly organized activity that involves many people doing different things. ❑ *The rescue operation began on Friday afternoon.* ❑ *...a military operation.* 2 N-COUNT A business or company can be referred to as an **operation**. ❑ *...Phillips' electronics operation.* 3 N-COUNT If a patient has an **operation**, a surgeon cuts open their body in order to remove, replace, or repair a diseased or damaged part. 4 N-UNCOUNT If a system is **in operation**, it is being used. ❑ *Until the rail links are in operation, passengers can only travel through the tunnel by coach.* 5 N-UNCOUNT If a machine or device is **in operation**, it is working. ❑ *There are three ski lifts in operation.* 6 → see also **operate**

Word Partnership Use *operation* with:

N. **relief** operation, **rescue** operation 1
ADJ. **covert** operation, **massive** operation, **military** operation, **undercover** operation 1
major operation, **successful** operation 1-3
emergency operation 1 3
V. **carry out an** operation, **plan an** operation 1
perform an operation 1 3

operational /ˌɒpəˈreɪʃənəl/ 1 ADJ A machine or piece of equipment that is **operational** is in use or is ready to be used. ❑ *The whole system will be fully operational by the end of December.* 2 ADJ **Operational** factors or problems relate to the working of a system, device, or plan. ❑ *He completely modernisesd the service's operational methods.* ● **operationally** ADV ❑ *The aircraft is not yet operationally effective.*

operative /ˈɒpərətɪv/ ADJ Something that is **operative** is working or having an effect. ❑ *The plan was operative by the end of the year.*

operator /ˈɒpəreɪtə/ (**operators**) 1 N-COUNT An **operator** is a person who works at a telephone exchange or on the switchboard of an office or hotel. ❑ *He dialled the operator.* 2 N-COUNT An **operator** is someone who is employed to operate or control a machine. 3 N-COUNT An **operator** is a person or a company that runs a business. ❑ *...the nation's largest cable TV operator.*

opinion /əˈpɪnjən/ (**opinions**) 1 N-COUNT Your **opinion** about something is what you think or believe about it. ❑ *I wasn't asking for your opinion.*

O

2 N-SING Your **opinion of** someone is your judgment of their character or ability. ❑ *The writer holds a good opinion of himself.* **3** N-UNCOUNT You can refer to the beliefs or views that people have as **opinion.** ❑ *Scientific opinion is divided over the health risks.*

Thesaurus *opinion* Also look up:

N. feeling, judgment, thought, viewpoint **1**-**3**

Word Partnership Use *opinion* with:

V. **express an** opinion, **give an** opinion, **share an** opinion **1** **2**
ask for an opinion **1** **2** **3**
ADJ. **favourable** opinion **1** **2**
expert opinion, **legal** opinion, **majority** opinion, **medical** opinion **3**

o'pinion ˌpoll (**opinion polls**) N-COUNT An **opinion poll** involves asking people for their opinion on a particular subject, especially one concerning politics.

opium /ˈəʊpiəm/ N-UNCOUNT **Opium** is a powerful drug made from the seeds of a type of poppy.

opponent /əˈpəʊnənt/ (**opponents**) **1** N-COUNT A politician's **opponents** are other politicians who belong to a different party or have different aims or policies. **2** N-COUNT In a sporting contest, your **opponent** is the person who is playing against you. **3** N-COUNT The **opponents** of an idea or policy do not agree with it. ❑ *...opponents of the spread of nuclear weapons.*
→ see **chess**

opportunist /ˌɒpəˈtjuːnɪst, AM -ˈtuːn-/ (**opportunists**) **1** ADJ & N-COUNT If you describe someone as **opportunist**, or if you call them an **opportunist**, you are critical of them because they take advantage of situations in order to gain money or power. ❑ *...corrupt and opportunist politicians.*
• **opportunism** N-UNCOUNT ❑ *...political opportunism.*

opportunistic /ˌɒpətjuːˈnɪstɪk, AM -tuːn-/ ADJ If you describe someone's behaviour as **opportunistic**, you are critical of them because they take advantage of situations in order to gain money or power. ❑ *Many of the party's members joined only for opportunistic reasons.*

opportunity /ˌɒpəˈtjuːnɪti, AM -ˈtuːn-/ (**opportunities**) N-VAR An **opportunity** is a situation in which it is possible for you to do something that you want to do. ❑ *I had an opportunity to go to New York.* ❑ *A trip to London provides a super opportunity for shopping.*

Word Partnership Use *opportunity* with:

ADJ. **economic** opportunity, **educational** opportunity, **equal** opportunity, **golden** opportunity, **great** opportunity, **lost** opportunity, **rare** opportunity, **unique** opportunity
N. **business** opportunity, **employment** opportunity, **investment** opportunity
V. **have an** opportunity, **miss an** opportunity, **see an** opportunity, **seize an** opportunity, opportunity **to speak**, **take advantage of an** opportunity

oppose /əˈpəʊz/ (**opposes, opposing, opposed**) V-T If you **oppose** someone or their plans or ideas, you disagree with what they want to do and try to prevent them from doing it. ❑ *...protesters opposing nuclear tests.*

opposed /əˈpəʊzd/ **1** ADJ AFTER LINK-V If you are **opposed to** something, you disagree with it or disapprove of it. ❑ *I am opposed to any form of terrorism.* **2** ADJ You say that two ideas or systems are **opposed** when they are opposite to each other or very different from each other. ❑ *...two opposed ideologies.* **3** PHRASE You use **as opposed to** when you want to make it clear that you are talking about a particular thing and not something else. ❑ *We ate in the restaurant, as opposed to the café.*

opposing /əˈpəʊzɪŋ/ **1** ADJ BEFORE N **Opposing** ideas or tendencies are totally different from each other. ❑ *I have a friend who has the opposing view.* **2** ADJ BEFORE N **Opposing** groups of people disagree about something or are in competition with one another.

opposite /ˈɒpəzɪt/ (**opposites**) **1** PREP & ADV If one thing is **opposite** another, it is facing it. ❑ *Two young people sat opposite me.* ❑ *I glanced up at the building opposite.* **2** ADJ BEFORE N The **opposite** side or part of something is the one that is farthest away from you. ❑ *...the opposite corner of the room.* **3** ADJ **Opposite** is used to describe things of the same kind which are as different as possible in a particular way. ❑ *...a word with the opposite meaning.* ❑ *...a car going in the opposite direction.* **4** N-COUNT **The opposite of** someone or something is the person or thing that is most different from them. ❑ *He was the complete opposite of Raymond.*

Word Partnership Use *opposite* with:

ADJ. **directly** opposite **1**
exactly (the) opposite, **precisely (the)** opposite, **quite the** opposite **1** **3** **4**
complete opposite, **exact** opposite **3** **4**
N. opposite **corner**, opposite **end**, opposite **side** **2**
opposite **direction**, opposite **effect** **3**
PREP. **the** opposite **of** ***someone/something*** **4**

ˌopposite ˈsex N-SING If you are talking about men and refer to **the opposite sex**, you mean women. If you are talking about women and refer to **the opposite sex**, you mean men.

opposition /ˌɒpəˈzɪʃən/ **1** N-UNCOUNT **Opposition** is strong, angry, or violent disagreement and disapproval. ❑ *The government is facing a new wave of opposition.* **2** N-SING **The opposition** refers to the politicians or political parties that form part of a country's parliament but are not in the government.

oppress /əˈpres/ (**oppresses, oppressing, oppressed**) **1** V-T To **oppress** people means to treat them cruelly, or to prevent them from having the same opportunities or freedom as others. ❑ *These people often are oppressed by their governments.*
• **oppressed** ADJ ❑ *...oppressed minorities.*
• **oppression** N-UNCOUNT ❑ *...the oppression of black people throughout history.* • **oppressor** (**oppressors**) N-COUNT ❑ *Will the oppressors always win because there are simply more of them than us?* **2** V-T If something **oppresses** you, it makes you feel depressed and

uncomfortable. [LITERARY] ❑ *It was not just the weather which oppressed her.*

oppressive /ə'presɪv/ **1** ADJ **Oppressive** laws, societies, and customs treat people cruelly and unfairly. ❑ *The new laws will be just as oppressive as those they replace.* **2** ADJ You say that the weather is **oppressive** when it is hot and humid. ❑ *The oppressive afternoon heat made him tired.* **3** ADJ An **oppressive** situation makes you feel depressed or uncomfortable. ❑ *...the oppressive sadness that he felt.*

Word Link	***opt ≈ choosing : adopt, opt, optional***

opt /ɒpt/ (**opts, opting, opted**) V-I/V-T If you **opt for** something, you choose it or decide to do it in preference to anything else. ❑ *You may wish to opt for one method or the other.* ❑ *She opted to spend Christmas with her younger brother.*

▶ **opt out** PHR-VERB If you **opt out of** something, you choose not to be involved in it. ❑ *...powers for hospitals to opt out of health authority control.* ❑ *Under the agreement the Vietnamese can opt out at any time.*

optic /'ɒptɪk/ ADJ BEFORE N **Optic** means relating to the eyes or to sight. ❑ *The optic nerve is a part of the brain.*

→ see **eye**

Word Link	***op ≈ eye : optical, optician, optometrist***

optical /'ɒptɪkəl/ **1** ADJ **Optical** instruments, devices, or processes involve or relate to vision or light. ❑ *...optical telescopes.* **2** ADJ BEFORE N **Optical** means relating to the way that things appear to people. ❑ *...an optical illusion.*

optician /ɒp'tɪʃən/ (**opticians**) N-COUNT An **optician** is someone whose job involves testing people's eyesight and making and selling glasses and contact lenses.

Word Link	***optim ≈ the best : optimism, optimist, optimum***

Word Link	***ism ≈ action or state : communism, optimism, patriotism***

optimism /'ɒptɪmɪzəm/ N-UNCOUNT **Optimism** is the feeling of being hopeful about the future or about the success of something. ❑ *The president expressed optimism about reaching a peaceful settlement.* ● **optimist** (**optimists**) N-COUNT ❑ *Susan remains an optimist.*

optimistic /ˌɒptɪ'mɪstɪk/ ADJ Someone who is **optimistic** is hopeful about the future or about the success of something. ❑ *She is optimistic that an agreement can be worked out soon.* ● **optimistically** ADV ❑ *He talked optimistically about the future.*

optimum /'ɒptɪməm/ ADJ The **optimum** level or state of something is the best level or state that it could achieve. [FORMAL] ❑ *These are the basic requirements for optimum health.*

option /'ɒpʃən/ (**options**) **1** N-COUNT An **option** is one of two or more things that you can choose between. ❑ *He became a lawyer because it seemed a safe option.* ❑ *What other options do you have?* **2** N-SING If you have **the option of** doing something, you can choose whether to do it or not. ❑ *Women should be given the option of having the treatment.* **3** PHRASE If you **keep** your **options open** or **leave** your **options open**, you avoid making an immediate decision about something. ❑ *I am keeping my options open; I can decide in a few months.*

Thesaurus	*option*	Also look up:
N.	alternative, choice, opportunity, preference, selection **1** **2**	

optional /'ɒpʃənəl/ ADJ If something is **optional**, you can choose whether or not you do it or have it. ❑ *Optional fees include cooking tuition.*

optometrist /ɒp'tɒmətrɪst/ (**optometrists**) N-COUNT An **optometrist** is the same as an **optician**.

Word Link	***ulent ≈ full of : fraudulent, opulent, succulent***

opulent /'ɒpjʊlənt/ ADJ **Opulent** things look grand and expensive. [FORMAL] ❑ *...his opulent new office.* ● **opulence** N-UNCOUNT ❑ *In contrast to the opulence of the bedroom, the bathroom is simple and practical.*

or /ə, STRONG ɔː/ **1** CONJ You use **or** to link alternatives. ❑ *Would you like tea or coffee?* ❑ *He said he would try to write or call.* ❑ *I don't know whether people will buy it or not.* **2** CONJ **Or** is used between two numbers to indicate that you are giving an approximate amount. ❑ *Drink two or three glasses of water after exercising.* **3** CONJ You use **or** to introduce a comment which corrects or modifies what you have just said. ❑ *The man was a fool, or at least incompetent.* **4** CONJ You can use **or** to introduce an explanation or justification for what you have just said. ❑ *She had to have the operation, or she would die.* **5** **or else** → see **else** **6** **or so** → see **so**

Usage
You do not use **or** after **neither**. You use **nor** instead. ❑ *He speaks neither English nor German.*

O

oral /'ɔːrəl/ (**orals**) **1** ADJ **Oral** is used to describe things that involve speaking rather than writing. ❑ *...an oral exam in the form of an interview.* ● **orally** ADV ❑ *...the tradition that is passed down orally.* **2** N-COUNT An **oral** is an examination, especially in a foreign language, that is spoken rather than written. **3** ADJ BEFORE N **Oral** medicines are ones that you swallow. ❑ *...an oral vaccine.* ● **orally** ADV ❑ *...tablets taken orally.*

orange /'ɒrɪndʒ, AM 'ɔːr-/ (**oranges**) **1** ADJ & N-VAR Something that is **orange** is of a colour between red and yellow. ❑ *...men in bright orange shirts.* **2** N-COUNT An **orange** is a round orange fruit that is juicy and sweet. **3** N-UNCOUNT **Orange** is a drink that is made from or tastes of oranges.

→ see **colour, fruit, rainbow**

oration /ɒr'eɪʃən/ (**orations**) N-COUNT An **oration** is a formal speech made in public. [FORMAL] ❑ *...a brief funeral oration.*

oratory /'ɒrətəri, AM 'ɔːrətɔːri/ N-UNCOUNT **Oratory** is the art of making formal speeches. [FORMAL] ❑ *...American political oratory.*

orbit /'ɔːbɪt/ (**orbits, orbiting, orbited**) **1** N-VAR An **orbit** is the curved path followed by an object going round a planet, a moon, or the sun. ❑ *Mars and Earth have orbits which change with time.* **2** V-T If

Word Web orchestra

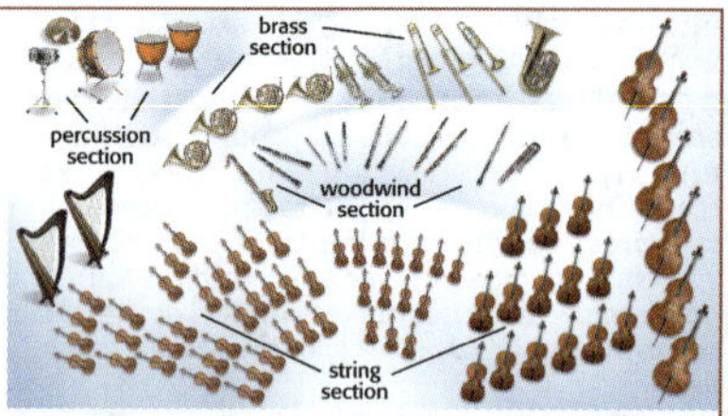

The modern **symphony orchestra** usually has between 60 and 100 **musicians.** The largest group of musicians are in the **string** section. It gives the orchestra its rich, flowing sound. String **instruments** include **violins, violas, cellos,** and usually **double basses. Flutes,** oboes, **clarinets,** and bassoons make up the **woodwind** section. The **brass** section is usually quite small. Too much of this sound could overwhelm the quieter strings. Brass **instruments** include the French horn, **trumpet, trombone** and tuba. The size of the **percussion** section depends on the **composition** being performed. However, there is almost always a timpani player.

orbit

something such as a satellite **orbits** a planet, a moon, or the sun, it goes round and round it.
→ see **satellite, solar system**

orbital /ˈɔːbɪtəl/ 1 ADJ BEFORE N An **orbital** road goes all the way round a large city. [BRIT] 2 ADJ BEFORE N **Orbital** describes things relating to the orbit of an object in space. ❑ *...the Earth's orbital path.*

orchard /ˈɔːtʃəd/ (**orchards**) N-COUNT An **orchard** is an area of land on which fruit trees are grown.
→ see **barn**

orchestra /ˈɔːkɪstrə/ (**orchestras**) N-COUNT An **orchestra** is a large group of musicians who play a variety of different instruments together. ● **orchestral** /ɔːˈkestrəl/ ADJ BEFORE N ❑ *...orchestral music.*
→ see Word Web: **orchestra**
→ see **theatre**

O

orchestrate /ˈɔːkɪstreɪt/ (**orchestrates, orchestrating, orchestrated**) 1 V-T If you **orchestrate** something, you organize it very carefully in order to produce a particular result or situation. ❑ *He orchestrated a campaign to stop the destruction of villages.* 2 V-T When someone **orchestrates** a piece of music, they rewrite it so that it can be played by an orchestra. ● **orchestration** N-UNCOUNT ❑ *...his orchestration of Bach's piano work.*

orchid /ˈɔːkɪd/ (**orchids**) N-COUNT An **orchid** is a plant with brightly coloured, unusually shaped flowers.

ordain /ɔːˈdeɪn/ (**ordains, ordaining, ordained**) V-T When someone **is ordained**, they are made a member of the clergy in a religious ceremony.

ordeal /ɔːˈdiːl/ (**ordeals**) N-COUNT An **ordeal** is an extremely unpleasant and difficult experience. ❑ *She described her agonising ordeal.*

order
❶ CONJUNCTION USES
❷ COMMANDS AND REQUESTS
❸ ARRANGEMENTS, SITUATIONS, AND GROUPINGS

order /ˈɔːdə/
❶ 1 CONJ If you do something **in order to** achieve a particular thing, you do it because you want to achieve that thing. ❑ *People bought computers in order to work at home.* ❑ *We teach algebra in order that all children learn to think.* 2 CONJ If something must happen **in order for** something else to happen, the second thing cannot happen if the first thing does not happen. ❑ *In order for him to win, he has to get at least nine Democratic votes.*

order /ˈɔːdə/ (**orders, ordering, ordered**)
❷ 1 V-T & N-COUNT If someone in authority **orders** something, **orders** you **to** do something, or gives you an **order**, they tell you to do something. ❑ *The President has ordered a full investigation.* ❑ *He ordered his men to stop shooting.* ❑ *She was fined £1,200 for disobeying orders.* 2 N-COUNT An **order** is something that you ask to be brought or sent to you, and that you are going to pay for. ❑ *The waiter returned with their order.* 3 V-T When you **order** something that you are going to pay for, you ask for it to be brought or sent to you. ❑ *Iris ordered coffees for herself and Tania.* 4 PHRASE If you are **under orders to** do something, you have been told to do it by someone in authority. ❑ *I am under orders not to discuss the subject.* 5 → see also **mail order**
6 **a tall order** → see **tall**
▶ **order around** or **order about** PHR-VERB If someone **is ordering** you **around**, they are telling you what to do as if they have authority over you.

order /ˈɔːdə/ (**orders**)
❸ 1 N-UNCOUNT If things are arranged or done **in** a particular **order**, one thing is put first or done first, another thing second, another thing third, and so on. ❑ *Arrange the entries in numerical order.* 2 N-UNCOUNT **Order** is the situation that exists when everything is in the correct place or is done at the correct time. ❑ *She longed for some order in her life.* 3 N-UNCOUNT **Order** is the situation that exists when people live together peacefully rather than fighting or causing trouble. ❑ *Troops were sent to the islands to restore order.* 4 N-SING When people talk about a particular **order**, they mean the way society is organized at a particular time. ❑ *...questioning the existing social order.* 5 N-COUNT A religious **order** is a group of monks or nuns who live according to certain rules. 6 N-COUNT If you refer to something **of** a particular **order**, you mean something of a particular quality, amount, or degree. [FORMAL] ❑ *...a poet of the highest order.* 7 → see also **law and order** 8 PHRASE A machine or device that is **in working order** is functioning properly and is not broken. ❑ *...a ten-year-old car that is in perfect working order.* 9 PHRASE A machine or device that is **out of order** is broken and does not work.

Thesaurus	*order* Also look up:
N.	command, direction, instruction ② 1
V.	charge, command, direct, tell ② 1 buy, request ② 3

orderly /ˈɔːdəli/ (**orderlies**) 1 ADJ Something that is **orderly** is well organized or well arranged. ❑ *...a beautiful, clean and orderly city.* ● **orderliness** N-UNCOUNT ❑ *...parents' concerns with neatness and orderliness.* 2 N-COUNT An **orderly** is an untrained hospital attendant.

ordinal /ˌɔːdɪnəl/ (**ordinals**) N-COUNT An **ordinal** or an **ordinal number** is a number such as 'first', 'third', or 'tenth', which tells you what position something has in an ordered group of things.

ordinarily /ˈɔːdɪnərəli, AM -ˈnerɪli/ ADV If something is **ordinarily** the case, it is usually the case. ❑ *The streets would ordinarily have been full of people.*

ordinary /ˈɔːdɪnri, AM -neri/ 1 ADJ **Ordinary** people or things are not special or different in any way. ❑ *Most ordinary people would agree with me.* ❑ *It was just an ordinary weekend.* 2 PHRASE Something that is **out of the ordinary** is unusual or different. ❑ *The boy's knowledge was out of the ordinary.*

Thesaurus	*ordinary* Also look up:
ADJ.	common, everyday, normal, regular, standard, typical, usual; *(ant.)* abnormal, unusual 1

Word Partnership	Use *ordinary* with:
N.	ordinary **citizens**, ordinary **circumstances**, ordinary **day**, ordinary **expenses**, ordinary **folk**, ordinary **life**, ordinary **people**, ordinary **person** 1
PREP.	**out of the** ordinary 2

ordination /ˌɔːdɪˈneɪʃən/ (**ordinations**) N-VAR When someone's **ordination** takes place, they are made a member of the Christian clergy in a special ceremony.

ore /ɔː/ (**ores**) N-VAR **Ore** is rock or earth from which metal can be obtained.
→ see **metal**

organ /ˈɔːgən/ (**organs**) 1 N-COUNT An **organ** is a part of your body that has a particular purpose or function, for example your heart or your lungs. ❑ *...the liver and other organs.* 2 N-COUNT An **organ** is a large musical instrument with pipes of different lengths through which air is forced. It has keys and pedals rather like a piano, and is often found in a church. ● **organist** (**organists**) N-COUNT ❑ *...the acclaimed organist John Scott.*
→ see **donor, keyboard, nervous system**

organic /ɔːˈgænɪk/ 1 ADJ **Organic** gardening or farming uses only natural animal and plant products and does not use artificial fertilizers or pesticides. ● **organically** ADV ❑ *...organically-grown vegetables.* 2 ADJ Something that is **organic** is produced by or found in living things. ❑ *25% of their weekly rubbish was organic waste from kitchens and gardens.*

organisation /ˌɔːgənaɪˈzeɪʃən/ → see **organization**

organisational /ˌɔːgənaɪˈzeɪʃənəl/ → see **organizational**

organise /ˈɔːgənaɪz/ → see **organize**

organism /ˈɔːgənɪzəm/ (**organisms**) N-COUNT An **organism** is an animal or plant, especially one that is so small that you cannot see it without using a microscope.

organization [BRIT also **organisation**] /ˌɔːgənaɪˈzeɪʃən/ (**organizations**) 1 N-COUNT An **organization** is an official group of people, for example a political party, a business, a charity, or a club. ❑ *...charitable organizations.* ❑ *...the International Labour Organisation.* ● **organizational** ADJ BEFORE N ❑ *Deal with the problem at an organizational level.* 2 N-UNCOUNT The **organization** of something is the way in which its different parts are arranged or relate to each other. ❑ *...the proposed changes in the organization of the Health Service.* ● **organizational** ADJ BEFORE N ❑ *Big organisational changes are needed.* 3 N-UNCOUNT The **organization** of an activity or public event involves making all the arrangements for it. ❑ *He was involved in the organization of conferences and seminars.* ● **organizational** ADJ BEFORE N ❑ *...Evelyn's excellent organisational skills.*

organize [BRIT also **organise**] /ˈɔːgənaɪz/ (**organizes, organizing, organized**) 1 V-T If you **organize** an activity or event, you make all the arrangements for it. ❑ *Maggie organized the trip to the railway museum.* ● **organizer** (**organizers**) N-COUNT ❑ *Organizers in London say they are planning a large-scale event like the 1985 Live Aid concert.* 2 V-T If you **organize** something that someone wants or needs, you make sure that it is provided. ❑ *He asked her to organize coffee and sandwiches.* 3 V-T If you **organize** things, you put them into order. ❑ *He began to organize his materials.*

Thesaurus	*organize* Also look up:
V.	co-ordinate, plan, set up 1 arrange, line up, straighten out 3

organized [BRIT also **organised**] /ˈɔːgənaɪzd/ 1 ADJ BEFORE N An **organized** activity or group involves a number of people doing something together in a structured way, rather than doing it by themselves. ❑ *...organised groups of art thieves.* ❑ *...organised religion.* 2 ADJ People who are **organized** work in an efficient and effective way.

orgasm /ˈɔːgæzəm/ (**orgasms**) N-COUNT An **orgasm** is the moment of greatest pleasure and excitement during sexual activity.

orgy /ˈɔːdʒi/ (**orgies**) 1 N-COUNT An **orgy** is a party in which people behave in a very uncontrolled way, especially one involving sexual activity. 2 N-COUNT You can refer to an activity as an **orgy** to emphasize that it is done to an excessive extent. ❑ *...an orgy of destruction.*

orient /ˈɔːriənt/ (**orients, orienting, oriented**)

The form **orientate** is also used.

1 V-T When you **orient yourself to** a new situation, you become familiar with it. [FORMAL] ❑ *You will need to orient yourself to your new job.* 2 V-T When you **orient yourself**, you find out exactly where you are and in which direction you are

facing. ❑ *She lay still for a few seconds, trying to orient herself.*

oriental /ˌɔːri'entəl/ ADJ **Oriental** means coming from or associated with eastern Asia, especially China and Japan. ❑ *...oriental carpets.*

orientated /'ɔːrianteɪtɪd/ ADJ **Orientated** means the same as oriented. ❑ *...modern child-orientated hotels.*

orientation /ˌɔːrian'teɪʃən/ N-UNCOUNT Someone's **orientation** is their basic beliefs or preferences. ❑ *...sexual orientation.*

oriented /'ɔːrientɪd/ ADJ AFTER LINK-V You use **oriented** to indicate what someone or something is interested in or concerned with. ❑ *The town has lots of family-oriented things to do.*

origin /'ɒrɪdʒɪn, AM 'ɔːr-/ (**origins**) **1** N-VAR You can refer to the beginning, cause, or source of something as its **origin** or its **origins**. ❑ *...theories about the origin of life.* ❑ *Many drugs have their origins in herbs.* **2** N-VAR Your **origin** or **origins** is the country, race, or social class of your parents or ancestors. ❑ *...people of Asian origin.* ❑ *...their country of origin.*

Word Partnership	Use *origin* with:
N.	origin **of life**, **point of** origin, origin **of the universe** **1**
	country of origin, **family of** origin **2**
ADJ.	**unknown** origin **1** **2**
	ethnic origin, **national** origin **2**

original /ə'rɪdʒɪnəl/ (**originals**) **1** ADJ You use **original** to refer to something that existed at the beginning of a process or activity, or the characteristics that something had when it first existed. ❑ *...Strathclyde police, who carried out the original investigation.* • **originally** ADV ❑ *France originally refused to sign the treaty.* **2** N-COUNT If something such as a document or work of art is an **original**, it is not a copy or a later version. ❑ *Copy the questionnaire and send the original to your employer.* **3** ADJ An **original** piece of writing or music was written recently and has not been published or performed before. ❑ *We always commission original work.* **4** ADJ If you describe someone or their work as **original**, you mean that they are very imaginative and have new ideas. ❑ *The critic has to find something original and entertaining to say.* • **originality** /əˌrɪdʒɪ'nælɪti/ N-UNCOUNT ❑ *He was capable of writing things of great originality.*

Thesaurus	*original* Also look up:
ADJ.	early, first, initial **1**
	authentic, genuine **2**
	creative, unique **4**
N.	master; *(ant.)* copy **2**

Word Partnership	Use *original* with:
N.	original **name**, original **owner**, original **plan** **1**
	original **version** **1** **2** **3**
	original **work** **1**-**4**
	original **idea** **1** **4**
	original **music**, original **songs**, original **story** **3** **4**

originate /ə'rɪdʒɪneɪt/ (**originates, originating, originated**) V-I If something **originated** at a particular time or in a particular place, it began to happen or exist at that time or in that place. ❑ *The disease originated in Africa.*

ornament /'ɔːnəmənt/ (**ornaments**) **1** N-COUNT An **ornament** is an attractive object that you display in your home or garden. **2** N-UNCOUNT **Ornament** refers to decorations and patterns on a building or piece of furniture.

ornamental /ˌɔːnə'mentəl/ ADJ Something that is **ornamental** is intended to be attractive rather than useful. ❑ *...an ornamental pond.*

ornate /ɔː'neɪt/ ADJ Something that is **ornate** has a lot of decoration on it. ❑ *...an ornate iron staircase.*

orphan /'ɔːfən/ (**orphans, orphaned**) **1** N-COUNT An **orphan** is a child whose parents are dead. **2** V-T PASSIVE If a child **is orphaned**, his or her parents die. ❑ *Jones was orphaned at the age of ten.*

orphanage /'ɔːfənɪdʒ/ (**orphanages**) N-COUNT An **orphanage** is a place where orphans are looked after.

Word Link	***dox** ≈ opinion : ortho**dox**, para**dox**, unortho**dox***

orthodox /'ɔːθədɒks/ **1** ADJ **Orthodox** beliefs, methods, or systems are the ones that are accepted or used by most people. ❑ *Many of these ideas are now accepted as part of orthodox medicine.* **2** ADJ If you describe someone as **orthodox**, you mean that they hold the older and more traditional ideas of their religion or party. ❑ *...Orthodox Jews.*

orthodoxy /'ɔːθədɒksi/ (**orthodoxies**) **1** N-COUNT An **orthodoxy** is an accepted view about something. ❑ *These ideas rapidly became the new orthodoxy in linguistics.* **2** N-VAR The old traditional beliefs of a religion, political party, or philosophy can be referred to as **orthodoxy**. ❑ *...a return to political orthodoxy.*

ostensibly /ɒ'stensɪbli/ ADV If something is **ostensibly** true, it seems or is officially stated to be true, but you or other people have doubts about whether it is. ❑ *...ostensibly independent organizations.*

ostentatious /ˌɒsten'teɪʃəs/ **1** ADJ If you describe something or someone as **ostentatious**, you disapprove of them because their content, appearance, or behaviour is intended to impress people with its wealth and importance. ❑ *...an ostentatious wedding reception.* • **ostentatiously** ADV ❑ *They lived comfortably, but not ostentatiously.* **2** ADJ An **ostentatious** action is done in an exaggerated way in order to attract people's attention. • **ostentatiously** ADV ❑ *He yawned ostentatiously.*

ostrich

ostrich /'ɒstrɪtʃ, AM 'ɔːst-/ (**ostriches**) N-COUNT An **ostrich** is a very large African bird with a long neck that cannot fly.

other /'ʌðə/ (**others**)

> When **other** follows the determiner 'an', it is written as one word: see **another**.

1 ADJ BEFORE N & PRON You use **other** to refer to

an additional thing or person of the same type as one that has been mentioned or is known about. ❑ *They were just like any other young couple.* ❑ *Four men were killed; one other was injured.* **2** ADJ BEFORE N & PRON You use **other** to indicate that something is not the thing already mentioned, but something else. ❑ *Calls cost 36p per minute at weekends, and 48p per minute at all other times.* ❑ *Some of these methods will work. Others will not.* **3** ADJ BEFORE N & PRON You use **other** to refer to the second of two things or people when the identity of the first is already known or understood, or has already been mentioned. ❑ *The Captain was at the other end of the room.* ❑ *She had the telephone in one hand and a calculator in the other.* **4** ADJ BEFORE N & PRON You use **other** to refer to the rest of the people or things in a group, or to people or things like the ones just mentioned. ❑ *When the other pupils were taken to an exhibition, he was left behind.* ❑ *...the new physics and astronomy of Copernicus, Galileo, and others.* **5** ADJ BEFORE N & PRON **Other** people are people in general, excluding yourself or the particular person you have mentioned. ❑ *She likes to be with other people.* ❑ *...a brave man who died helping others.* **6** ADJ BEFORE N You use **other** in expressions of time such as **the other day** or **the other week** to refer to a day or week in the recent past. [INFORMAL] ❑ *The other evening we had a party.* **7** PHRASE You use **none other than** and **no other than** to emphasize the name of a person or thing when something about that person or thing is surprising. ❑ *The manager was none other than his son.* **8** PHRASE You use **other than** after a negative in order to introduce an exception to what you have said. ❑ *Geoffrey was left no choice other than to resign.* **9** **each other** → see **each** **10** **every other** → see **every** **11** **one or other** → see **one** **12** **in other words** → see **word**

Word Link	***wise*** ≈ *in the direction or manner of*: ***clockwise, likewise, otherwise***

otherwise /ˈʌðəwaɪz/ **1** ADV You use **otherwise** after stating a situation or fact, to say what the result or consequence would be if this situation or fact was not the case. ❑ *I'm lucky that I'm interested in school work; otherwise I'd go mad.* **2** ADV You use **otherwise** when stating the general condition or quality of something, when you are also mentioning an exception to this. ❑ *He woke at about 7 am, very hungry but otherwise happy.* **3** ADV You use **otherwise** to refer to actions or ways of doing something that are different from the one mentioned in your main statement. ❑ *Take approximately 60mg up to four times a day, unless advised otherwise by a doctor.*

ought /ɔːt/ **1** MODAL If you say that someone **ought to** do something, you mean that it is the right or sensible thing to do. If you say that someone **ought to have** done something, you mean that it would have been the right or sensible thing to do, but they did not do it. ❑ *People ought to say what they really think.* ❑ *You ought to ask a lawyer's advice.* ❑ *Perhaps I ought not to interfere.* ❑ *The Prime Minister ought to have acted earlier.* **2** MODAL If you say that something **ought to** be true, you mean that you expect it to be true. If you say that something **ought to have** happened, you mean that you expect it to have happened. ❑ *'This ought to be fun,' he told Alex.* ❑ *He ought to have reached the house some time ago.*

oughtn't /ˈɔːtənt/ **Oughtn't** is a spoken form of 'ought not'.

ounce /aʊns/ (**ounces**) **1** N-COUNT An **ounce** is a unit of weight used in Britain and the USA. There are sixteen ounces in a pound and one ounce is equal to 28.35 grams. **2** N-SING You can refer to a very small amount of something, such as a quality or characteristic, as an **ounce of** that thing. ❑ *I used every ounce of energy trying to hide.*

our /aʊə/ **1** DET A speaker or writer uses **our** to indicate that something belongs or relates both to himself or herself and to one or more other people. ❑ *We're expecting our first baby.* ❑ *I locked myself out of our apartment.* **2** DET A speaker or writer sometimes uses **our** to indicate that something belongs or relates to people in general. ❑ *The quality of our life depends on keeping well.*

ours /aʊəz/ PRON A speaker or writer uses **ours** to refer to something that belongs or relates to a group of people which includes himself or herself. ❑ *There are few strangers in a town like ours.*

ourselves /aʊəˈselvz/ **1** PRON A speaker or writer uses **ourselves** to refer to himself or herself and one or more other people as a group. ❑ *We sat round the fire to keep ourselves warm.* ❑ *We admitted to ourselves that we were tired.* **2** PRON A speaker or writer sometimes uses **ourselves** to refer to people in general. ❑ *When we exert ourselves our heart rate increases.*

oust /aʊst/ (**ousts, ousting, ousted**) V-T If someone **is ousted from** a position of power or **from** a job or place, they are forced to leave it. ❑ *The leaders have been ousted from power by nationalists.* ❑ *They tried to oust him in a parliamentary vote.* ● **ousting** N-UNCOUNT ❑ *...the ousting of the radicals.*

out /aʊt/ **1** ADV When you go **out of** a place or get **out of** something such as a vehicle, you leave it, so that you are no longer inside it. If you keep **out of** a place, you do not go into it. ❑ *The waitress came out of the kitchen.* ❑ *She got out of bed and put on her robe.* ❑ *Nurses and doctors rushed out.* ❑ *Electric fences keep out animals.*

out

2 ADV If you are **out**, you are not at home or not at your usual place of work. ❑ *She left the house while you were out.* ❑ *I went out looking for the kids.* **3** ADV If you take something **out of** a place or container, you remove it from there. ❑ *Carefully pull out the centre pages.* ❑ *He took out his notebook.* ❑ *I always took my key out of my bag and put it in my pocket.* **4** ADV If you look or shout **out of** a window, you look or shout through it at someone or something that is outside. ❑ *I looked out of the window and watched the beautiful sunset.* ❑ *I called out of the window but there was no one there.* **5** PREP If you get **out of** a situation or **out of** something such as the rain or wind, you are no longer in it. ❑ *Children may lie to get out of trouble.* ❑ *Stay out of politics.* ❑ *Keep your child out of the sun.* **6** ADJ AFTER LINK-V & ADV If a light or fire is **out**, it is no longer shining or burning. If it goes **out**, it stops burning or shining. ❑ *The candle went out.* **7** ADJ AFTER LINK-V & ADV If flowers are **out**, their petals have opened. If they come **out**, their petals open. **8** ADJ AFTER LINK-V & ADV If something such as a book or record is **out** or comes **out**, it is available for people to buy. ❑ *Our new spring catalogue is out now.* 9 ADJ AFTER LINK-V In a game or sport, if someone is **out**, they can no longer take part either because the rules say so or because they are unable to. 10 ADJ AFTER LINK-V If you say that a proposal or suggestion is **out**, you mean that it is unacceptable or impossible. 11 ADJ AFTER LINK-V If you say that a calculation or measurement is **out**, you mean that it is incorrect. ❑ *They were only a few inches out.* 12 ADJ AFTER LINK-V If you say that someone is **out to** do something, usually something that you disapprove of, you mean they intend to do it. [INFORMAL] ❑ *Most companies these days are just out to make a quick profit.* 13 PREP You use **out of** to say what causes someone to do something. ❑ *He took the job out of a sense of duty.* 14 PREP If you get something such as pleasure, an advantage, or information **out of** something or someone, they give it to you or cause you to have it. ❑ *To get the most out of your money, you have to invest it.* ❑ *Employers are looking to get more work out of fewer people.* 15 PREP If you are **out of** something, you no longer have any of it. ❑ *We're out of milk.* 16 PREP If something is made **out of** a particular material, it is formed or constructed using it. 17 PREP You use **out of** to indicate what proportion of a group of things something is true of. ❑ *One out of every two households owns a microwave.*

outback /ˈaʊtbæk/ N-SING The parts of Australia where very few people live are referred to as **the outback.**

outbreak /ˈaʊtbreɪk/ (**outbreaks**) N-COUNT An **outbreak of** something unpleasant is a sudden occurrence of it. ❑ *...the outbreak of war.*

outburst /ˈaʊtbɜːst/ (**outbursts**) 1 N-COUNT An **outburst of** an emotion, especially anger, is a sudden strong expression of that emotion. ❑ *...a spontaneous outburst of cheers and applause.* 2 N-COUNT An **outburst of** violent activity is a sudden period of this activity. ❑ *Five people were killed today in a fresh outburst of violence.*

O

outcast /ˈaʊtkɑːst, -kæst/ (**outcasts**) N-COUNT An **outcast** is someone who is rejected by a group of people. ❑ *All of us felt like social outcasts.*

outcome /ˈaʊtkʌm/ (**outcomes**) N-COUNT The **outcome of** an action or process is the result of it. ❑ *What is the most likely outcome of today's meeting?*

outcry /ˈaʊtkraɪ/ (**outcries**) N-COUNT An **outcry** is a reaction of strong disapproval and anger shown by the public or media about a recent event. ❑ *The killing caused an international outcry.*

outdated /ˌaʊtˈdeɪtɪd/ ADJ Something that is **outdated** is old-fashioned and no longer useful. ❑ *...outdated and inefficient factories.*

outdo /ˌaʊtˈduː/ (**outdoes, outdoing, outdid, outdone**) V-T If you **outdo** someone, you are more successful than they are at a particular activity. ❑ *Each man tried to outdo the other.*

outdoor /ˌaʊtˈdɔː/ ADJ BEFORE N **Outdoor activities** or things take place or are used outside, rather than in a building. ❑ *She excelled at outdoor sports.* ❑ *...outdoor furniture.*

outdoors /ˌaʊtˈdɔːz/ ADV & N-SING If something happens **outdoors**, or if it happens **in the outdoors**, it happens outside in the fresh air rather than in a building. ❑ *It was warm enough to be outdoors all afternoon.*

outer /ˈaʊtə/ ADJ BEFORE N The **outer** parts of something are the parts which enclose the other parts, and which are farthest from the centre. ❑ *The burn damaged only the outer layer of skin.* ❑ *...the outer suburbs of the city.*

ˌouter ˈspace N-UNCOUNT **Outer space** refers to the area outside the Earth's atmosphere where planets and stars are.
→ see **satellite**

outfit /ˈaʊtfɪt/ (**outfits, outfitting, outfitted**) 1 N-COUNT An **outfit** is a set of clothes. ❑ *...smart new outfits for work.* ❑ *...a nurse's outfit.* 2 N-COUNT You can refer to a group of people or an organization as an **outfit.** [INFORMAL] ❑ *We are a professional outfit.* 3 V-T To **outfit** someone or something means to provide them with equipment for a particular purpose. [AM] ❑ *I outfitted an attic bedroom as a studio.*

outgoing /ˌaʊtˈgəʊɪŋ/ 1 ADJ BEFORE N An **outgoing president, chairman,** or **minister** is one who is going to leave. 2 ADJ An **outgoing** person is very friendly and likes meeting people. 3 ADJ BEFORE N **Outgoing** things such as **planes, mail,** and **passengers** are leaving or being sent somewhere.

outgoings /ˈaʊtgəʊɪŋz/ N-PLURAL Your **outgoings** are the regular amounts of money which you have to spend every week or every month, for example in order to pay your rent or bills. [BRIT]

outgrow /ˌaʊtˈgrəʊ/ (**outgrows, outgrowing, outgrew, outgrown**) 1 V-T If a child **outgrows** a piece of clothing, they get bigger and can no longer wear it. 2 V-T If you **outgrow** a particular way of thinking or behaving, you change so that you no longer think or behave in that way.

outing /ˈaʊtɪŋ/ (**outings**) N-COUNT An **outing** is a short enjoyable trip, usually with a group of people, away from your home, school, or place of work. ❑ *...a family outing to London.*

outlaw /ˈaʊtlɔː/ (**outlaws, outlawing, outlawed**) V-T When something **is outlawed**, it is made illegal. ❑ *In 1975, gambling was outlawed.*

outlay /ˈaʊtleɪ/ (**outlays**) N-COUNT An **outlay** is an amount of money that is invested in a piece of equipment, project, or business. [FORMAL]

outlet /ˈaʊtlet/ (**outlets**) 1 N-COUNT If someone has an **outlet for** their feelings or ideas, they have a means of expressing and releasing them. ❑ *Boxing is the main outlet for his energy.* 2 N-COUNT An **outlet** is a shop or organization which sells the goods made by a particular manufacturer. ❑ *...the largest retail outlet in the city.* 3 N-COUNT An **outlet** is a hole or pipe through which water or air can flow away. ❑ *...the sewage outlet.* 4 N-COUNT In American English, an **outlet** is a device in a wall where you can connect electrical equipment to the electricity supply. The British word is **socket.**

outline /ˈaʊtlaɪn/ (**outlines, outlining, outlined**) 1 V-T & N-COUNT If you **outline** an idea or a plan, or if you present an **outline of** it, you explain it in a general way. ❑ *The mayor outlined his plan to clean up the town.* ❑ *...an outline of the survey findings.* 2 N-COUNT The **outline of** an object is the general shape of it that you can see, for example when there is a light behind it. ❑ *...the outline of the goalposts.* 3 V-T PASSIVE When an object **is**

outlined, you can see its general shape because there is a light behind it. ❑ *The hotel was outlined against the lights.*

Word Partnership Use *outline* with:

V. **write an** outline 1
N. **chapter** outline, outline **a paper**, outline **a plan** 1
ADJ. **broad** outline, **detailed** outline, **general** outline 1

outlive /ˌaʊtˈlɪv/ (**outlives, outliving, outlived**) V-T If one person **outlives** another, they are still alive after the other person has died. If one thing **outlives** another thing, the first thing continues to exist after the second has disappeared or been replaced. ❑ *I'm sure Rose will outlive many of us.* ❑ *This is a style that will outlive passing fashions.*

outlook /ˈaʊtlʊk/ (**outlooks**) 1 N-COUNT Your **outlook** is your general attitude towards life. ❑ *The experience improved my outlook on life.* 2 N-SING The **outlook for** something is whether or not it is going to be prosperous, successful, or safe. ❑ *He said the economic outlook remained good.*

outlying /ˈaʊtlaɪɪŋ/ ADJ BEFORE N **Outlying** places are far away from the main cities of a country. ❑ *Tourists can visit outlying areas like the Napa Valley.*

outnumber /ˌaʊtˈnʌmbə/ (**outnumbers, outnumbering, outnumbered**) V-T If one group of people or things **outnumbers** another, the first group has more people or things in it than the second group. ❑ *...a town where men outnumber women.*

ˌout of ˈdate ADJ Something that is **out of date** is old-fashioned and no longer useful. ❑ *His medical knowledge had quickly gone out of date.* ❑ *He is completely out of date with the modern view of things.*

ˌout of ˈwork ADJ Someone who is **out of work** does not have a job.

outpost /ˈaʊtpəʊst/ (**outposts**) N-COUNT An **outpost** is a small settlement in a foreign country or in a distant area. ❑ *...a remote mountain outpost.*

output /ˈaʊtpʊt/ (**outputs**) 1 N-VAR You use **output** to refer to the amount of something that a person or thing produces. ❑ *This is the largest drop in industrial output for ten years.* 2 N-VAR The **output** from a computer is the information that it displays on a screen or prints on paper as a result of a particular program. [COMPUTING]

outrage (**outrages, outraging, outraged**)

verb /ˌaʊtˈreɪdʒ/, noun /ˈaʊtreɪdʒ/.

1 V-T If something **outrages** you, it makes you shocked and angry. ❑ *The union is outraged by the court's decision.* ● **outraged** ADJ ❑ *Outraged readers said the story was extremely offensive.* 2 N-UNCOUNT **Outrage** is a feeling of shock and anger about something. ❑ *The decision provoked outrage from women.* 3 N-COUNT You can refer to an act or event which you find very shocking as an **outrage**. ❑ *It was an outrage that we were arrested.*

outrageous /aʊtˈreɪdʒəs/ ADJ If you describe something as **outrageous**, you are emphasizing that it is unacceptable or very shocking. ❑ *...his outrageous drunken behaviour.* ● **outrageously** ADV ❑ *...outrageously expensive clothes.*

outright

adjective /ˈaʊtraɪt/, adverb /ˌaʊtˈraɪt/.

1 ADJ BEFORE N & ADV You use **outright** to describe actions and behaviour that are open and direct, rather than indirect. ❑ *...an outright lie.* ❑ *Why don't you tell me outright?* 2 ADJ BEFORE N & ADV **Outright** means complete and total. ❑ *She had failed to win an outright victory.* ❑ *The peace plan wasn't rejected outright.* 3 PHRASE If someone **is killed outright**, they die immediately, for example in an accident.

outset /ˈaʊtset/ PHRASE If something happens **at the outset** of an event, process, or period of time, it happens at the beginning of it. If something happens **from the outset**, it happens from the beginning and continues to happen. ❑ *Decide at the outset what you want.* ❑ *It was clear from the outset that the project would fail.*

outside /ˌaʊtˈsaɪd/ (**outsides**) 1 N-COUNT & ADJ BEFORE N The **outside** of something such as a building or a container is the part which surrounds or encloses the rest of it. ❑ *The moth was on the outside of the glass.* ❑ *...the outside wall.* 2 ADV & PREP & ADJ BEFORE N If you are **outside** a building, place, or country, you are not in it. ❑ *They heard voices coming from outside.* ❑ *The victim was outside a shop when he was attacked.* ❑ *...an outside toilet.* 3 ADJ BEFORE N When you talk about the **outside** world, you are referring to things that happen or exist in places other than your own home or community. ❑ *She hid her true character from the outside world.* 4 ADJ BEFORE N On a road with two or more lanes, the **outside lane** is the one for overtaking or for travelling at high speed. 5 ADJ BEFORE N & PREP **Outside** people or organizations are not part of a particular organization or group. ❑ *...outside consultants.* ❑ *He is hoping to recruit a chairman from outside the company.* 6 PREP You use **outside** to refer to a particular thing or range of things which are not part of something or not included within it. ❑ *It's a beautiful boat, but it's outside my price range.* 7 PREP Something that happens **outside** a particular period of time does not happen during that time. ❑ *They are open outside normal daily banking hours.*

Thesaurus *outside* Also look up:

ADJ. exterior, outdoor; *(ant.)* inside, interior 1
PREP. beyond; *(ant.)* near 3

Word Partnership Use *outside* with:

N. **the** outside **of a building** 1
outside **a building**, outside **a car**, outside **a city/town**, outside **a country**, outside **a room**, outside **a store** 2
outside **interests, the** outside **world** 3
outside **sources** 5
ADJ. **cold** outside, **dark** outside 2
V. **gather** outside, **go** outside, **park** outside, **sit** outside, **stand** outside, **step** outside, **wait** outside 2

outsider /ˌaʊtˈsaɪdə/ (**outsiders**) 1 N-COUNT An **outsider** is someone who does not belong to a particular group or organization, or is not accepted by them. ❑ *Malone felt as much an outsider as any of them.* 2 N-COUNT In a competition, an

O

outsider is a competitor who is unlikely to win.

outskirts /'aʊtskɜːts/ N-PLURAL **The outskirts of** a city or town are the parts that are farthest from its centre. ❑ *...the outskirts of New York.*

outspoken /ˌaʊt'spəʊkən/ ADJ If you are **outspoken**, you give your opinions about things openly, even if they shock people. ❑ *...his outspoken criticism of the prime minister.* ● **outspokenness** N-UNCOUNT ❑ *Her outspokenness had annoyed many voters.*

outstanding /ˌaʊt'stændɪŋ/ **1** ADJ If you describe a person or their work as **outstanding**, you think that they are remarkable and impressive. ❑ *...an outstanding athlete.* ● **outstandingly** ADV ❑ *...outstandingly successful schools.* **2** ADJ **Outstanding** means very obvious or important. ❑ *...an outstanding example of a small business that grew into a big one.* **3** ADJ Money that is **outstanding** has not yet been paid and is still owed to someone. ❑ *The total debt outstanding is $70 billion.* **4** ADJ **Outstanding issues** or **problems** have not yet been resolved.

outstretched /ˌaʊt'stretʃt/ ADJ If your **arms**, **fingers**, **legs**, or **feet** are **outstretched**, they are stretched as far as they can go. ❑ *He held his arms outstretched.*

outstrip /ˌaʊt'strɪp/ (**outstrips, outstripping, outstripped**) V-T If one thing **outstrips** another, the first thing becomes larger in amount, or more successful or important, than the second thing. ❑ *...wage rises that far outstripped productivity.*

outward /'aʊtwəd/ **1** ADJ BEFORE N An **outward journey** is a journey that you make away from a place that you are intending to return to later. ❑ *Tickets must be bought in advance, with outward and return dates specified.* **2** ADJ BEFORE N The **outward** feelings, qualities, or attitudes of someone or something are the ones they appear to have rather than the ones that they actually have. ❑ *He gave no outward sign of what he felt.* ● **outwardly** ADV ❑ *People were outwardly hostile.* **3** ADJ BEFORE N The **outward** features of something are the ones that you can see from the outside. ❑ *Mark was lying unconscious but with no outward sign of injury.*

O

outwards /'aʊtwədz/

> The form **outward** is also used. In American English, **outward** is more usual.

ADV If something **moves** or **faces outwards**, it moves or faces away from the place you are in or the place you are talking about. ❑ *The top door opened outwards.*

outweigh /ˌaʊt'weɪ/ (**outweighs, outweighing, outweighed**) V-T If, for example, the **benefits** of something **outweigh** the disadvantages, it has some disadvantages but is more beneficial than harmful. [FORMAL] ❑ *The medical benefits of x-rays far outweigh the risk of having them.*

outwit /ˌaʊt'wɪt/ (**outwits, outwitting, outwitted**) V-T If you **outwit** someone, you use your intelligence or a clever trick to defeat them or to gain an advantage over them. ❑ *To win the presidency he had to outwit his rivals.*

oval /'əʊvəl/ (**ovals**) N-COUNT & ADJ An **oval** or an **oval** shape is a round shape which is similar to a circle, but is wider in one direction than the other, like the shape of an egg. ❑ *...a pale oval face.*
→ see **circle, shape**

ovary /'əʊvəri/ (**ovaries**) N-COUNT A woman's **ovaries** are the two organs in her body that produce eggs.

ovation /əʊ'veɪʃən/ (**ovations**) N-COUNT An **ovation** is a long burst of applause from an audience for a particular performer.

oven /'ʌvən/ (**ovens**) N-COUNT An **oven** is a cooker or part of a cooker that is like a box with a door. You cook food inside an oven.

> **over**
> 1 POSITION AND MOVEMENT
> 2 AMOUNTS AND TIME
> 3 CAUSE AND INFLUENCE

over /'əʊvə/
1 **1** PREP & ADV If one thing is **over** another thing or is moving **over** it, the first thing is directly above the second, either resting on it, or with a space between them. ❑ *He looked at himself in the mirror over the table.* ❑ *There's a small bridge over the stream.* ❑ *...planes flying over every 10 or 15 minutes.* **2** PREP & ADV If one thing is **over** another thing, it covers part or all of it. ❑ *He was wearing a light-grey suit over a shirt.* ❑ *They covered the room over with a glass roof.* **3** PREP & ADV If you lean **over** an object, you bend your body so that the top part of it is above the object. ❑ *She bent over the table, frowning.* ❑ *Sam leant over to open the door of the car.* **4** PREP If you **look over** or **talk over** an object, you look or talk across the top of it. ❑ *I went and stood beside him, looking over his shoulder.* **5** PREP If a window has a **view over** an area of land or water, you can see the land or water through the window. **6** PREP & ADV If someone or something goes **over** a barrier or boundary, they get to the other side of it by going across it, or across the top of it. ❑ *Two policemen jumped over the wall in pursuit.* ❑ *I climbed over into the back seat.* **7** PREP If something is on the opposite side of a road or river, you can say that it is **over** the road or **over** the river. ❑ *Richard Garrick lived in the house over the road.* **8** ADV You use **over** to indicate a particular position or place away from you. ❑ *He noticed Rolfe standing silently over by the window.* **9** PHRASE **Over here** means near you, or in the country you are in. **Over there** means in a place a short distance away from you, or in another country. ❑ *Why don't you come over here tomorrow evening.* ❑ *She'd married an American and settled down over there.* **10** ADV If something **rolls over** or is **turned over**, its position changes so that the part that was facing upwards is now facing downwards. ❑ *His car rolled over after a tyre was punctured.*
→ see **location**

over /'əʊvə/
2 **1** PREP & ADV If something is **over** a particular amount, measurement, or age, it is more than that amount, measurement, or age. ❑ *Cigarettes kill over a hundred thousand Britons every year.* ❑ *...people aged 65 and over.* **2** PHRASE **Over and above** an amount, especially a normal amount, means more than that amount or in addition to it. ❑ *Why should you be paid extra, over and above your salary, to do that job?* **3** ADJ AFTER LINK-V If an activity is **over** or **all over**, it is completely finished. ❑ *The bad times were over.* ❑ *I am glad it's all over.* **4** PREP If something happens **over** a period of time, it

happens during that time. ❑ *Many strikes over the last few years have not ended successfully.* 5 PREP If you are **over** an illness or an experience, it has finished and you have recovered from its effects. ❑ *I'm glad that you're over the flu.*

over /ˈəʊvə/

3 1 PREP You use **over** to indicate what a disagreement or feeling relates to or is caused by. ❑ *...concern over recent events in Burma.* 2 PREP If you have **control** or **influence over** someone or something, you are able to control them or influence them. ❑ *The oil companies have lost their power over oil prices.*

overall (**overalls**)

adjective and adverb /ˌəʊvərˈɔːl/, noun /ˈəʊvərɔːl/.

1 ADJ BEFORE N & ADV You use **overall** to indicate that you are talking about a situation in general or about the whole of something. ❑ *Cut down your overall amount of physical activity.* ❑ *...the quality of education overall.* 2 N-PLURAL **Overalls** are a piece of clothing that combine trousers and a shirt which you wear over your clothes to protect them while you are working. 3 N-COUNT An **overall** is a type of coat that you wear over your clothes to protect them while you are working.

overboard /ˈəʊvəbɔːd/ ADV If you **fall overboard**, you fall over the side of a ship into the water.

overcame /ˌəʊvəˈkeɪm/ **Overcame** is the past tense of **overcome**.

overcharge /ˌəʊvəˈtʃɑːdʒ/ (**overcharges, overcharging, overcharged**) V-T If someone **overcharges** you, they charge you too much for their goods or services.

overcoat /ˈəʊvəkəʊt/ (**overcoats**) N-COUNT An **overcoat** is a thick warm coat.

overcome /ˌəʊvəˈkʌm/ (**overcomes, overcoming, overcame, overcome**) 1 V-T If you **overcome** a problem or a feeling, you successfully deal with it and control it. ❑ *Molly had overcome her fear of flying.* 2 V-T If you **are overcome by** a feeling, you feel it very strongly. ❑ *The night before the test I was overcome by fear.* 3 V-T If you **are overcome by** smoke or a poisonous gas, you become very ill or die from breathing it in.

Word Partnership Use *overcome* with:

ADJ.	**difficult to** overcome, **hard to** overcome 1
N.	overcome **difficulties**, overcome **a fear**, overcome **an obstacle/problem**, overcome **opposition** 1 overcome **by emotion**, overcome **by fear** 2

overcrowded /ˌəʊvəˈkraʊdɪd/ ADJ An **overcrowded** place has too many things or people in it. ❑ *It's one of the most overcrowded prisons in the country.*

overcrowding /ˌəʊvəˈkraʊdɪŋ/ N-UNCOUNT If there is **overcrowding** in a place, there are more people living there than it was designed for. ❑ *...overcrowding and lack of facilities for patients.*

overdo /ˌəʊvəˈduː/ (**overdoes, overdoing, overdid, overdone**) 1 V-T If someone **overdoes** something, they behave in an exaggerated or extreme way. ❑ *When you have five or six different medicines – that's overdoing it.* 2 V-T If you **overdo** an activity, you try to do more than you can physically manage. ❑ *Don't overdo it when your body is already stressed after travelling.*

overdose /ˈəʊvədəʊs/ (**overdoses, overdosing, overdosed**) N-COUNT & V-I If someone **takes** an **overdose** of a drug, or if they **overdose on** it, they take more of it than is safe. ❑ *Guitarist Jimi Hendrix died of a drug overdose.* ❑ *She overdosed on heroin.*

overdraft /ˈəʊvədrɑːft, -dræft/ (**overdrafts**) N-COUNT If you **have** an **overdraft**, you have spent more money than you have in your bank account.

overdue /ˌəʊvəˈdjuː, AM -ˈduː/ 1 ADJ If you say that a change or an event is **overdue**, you mean that it should have happened before now. ❑ *This debate is long overdue.* 2 ADJ **Overdue** sums of money have not been paid, even though it is later than the date on which they should have been paid.

overeat /ˌəʊvəˈiːt/ (**overeats, overeating, overate, overeaten**) V-I If you **overeat**, you eat more than you should.

overestimate /ˌəʊvərˈestɪmeɪt/ (**overestimates, overestimating, overestimated**) V-T If you **overestimate** someone or something, you think that they are better, bigger, or more important than they really are. ❑ *I think you overestimate me, Fred.*

overflow (**overflows, overflowing, overflowed**) 1 V-I /ˌəʊvəˈfləʊ/ If a liquid or a river **overflows**, it comes over the edges of the container or the place it is in. ❑ *The sewers were overflowing and the river was bursting its banks.* 2 V-I If a place or container **is overflowing with** people or things, there are too many of them in it. ❑ *The great hall was overflowing with people.*

overgrown /ˌəʊvəˈgrəʊn/ ADJ If a place is **overgrown**, it is thickly covered with plants because it has not been looked after. ❑ *The courtyard was overgrown with weeds.*

overhang /ˌəʊvəˈhæŋ/ (**overhangs, overhanging, overhung**) V-T If one thing **overhangs** another, it sticks out over and above it. ❑ *Part of the rock wall overhung the path.*

overhaul (**overhauls, overhauling, overhauled**)

verb /ˌəʊvəˈhɔːl/, noun /ˈəʊvəhɔːl/.

1 V-T & N-COUNT If a piece of equipment **is overhauled**, or if you give it an **overhaul**, it is cleaned, checked thoroughly, and repaired if necessary. ❑ *He had had his car overhauled three times.* 2 V-T & N-COUNT If you **overhaul** a system or method, or if you give it an **overhaul**, you examine it carefully and change it in order to improve it. ❑ *...a complete overhaul of air traffic control systems.*

overhead

adjective /ˈəʊvəhed/, adverb /ˌəʊvəˈhed/.

ADJ BEFORE N & ADV You use **overhead** to indicate that something is above you or above the place you are talking about. ❑ *...the overhead light.* ❑ *Helicopters have been flying overhead.*

overheads /ˈəʊvəhedz/ N-PLURAL The **overheads** of a business are its regular and essential expenses.

overhear /ˌəʊvəˈhɪə/ (**overhears, overhearing,**

O

overheard) V-T If you **overhear** someone, you hear what they are saying when they are not talking to you and do not know that you are listening. ❑ *I overheard two doctors discussing my case.*

overheat /ˌəʊvəˈhiːt/ (**overheats, overheating, overheated**) V-T/V-I If a machine **overheats**, or if you **overheat** it, it becomes hotter than is necessary or desirable. ❑ *The engine was overheating and the car was not handling well.* • **overheated** ADJ ❑ *...that stuffy, overheated apartment.*

overhung /ˌəʊvəˈhʌŋ/ **Overhung** is the past tense and past participle of **overhang**.

overjoyed /ˌoʊvərˈdʒɔɪd/ ADJ If you are **overjoyed**, you are extremely pleased about something. ❑ *Shelley was overjoyed to see me.*

overland /ˈəʊvəlænd/ ADJ BEFORE N & ADV An **overland** journey is made across land rather than by ship or aeroplane. ❑ *...the overland route.* ❑ *They're travelling to Baghdad overland.*

overlap (**overlaps, overlapping, overlapped**)

verb /ˌəʊvəˈlæp/, noun /ˈəʊvəlæp/.

1 V-T/V-I If one thing **overlaps** another, one part of the first thing covers a part of the other. You can also say that two things **overlap**. ❑ *Overlap the slices carefully so there are no gaps.* ❑ *The edges must overlap.* **2** V-T/V-I & N-COUNT If one idea or activity **overlaps** another, they involve some of the same subjects, people, or periods of time. You can also say that two ideas or activities **overlap**, or that there is an **overlap between** them. ❑ *...the overlap between civil and military technology.*

overleaf /ˌəʊvəˈliːf/ ADV **Overleaf** is used in books and magazines to say that something is on the other side of the page you are reading. ❑ *Answer the questionnaire overleaf.*

O

overload /ˌəʊvəˈləʊd/ (**overloads, overloading, overloaded**) **1** V-T If you **overload** a vehicle, you put more things or people in it than it was designed to carry. ❑ *Don't overload the boat or it will sink.* • **overloaded** ADJ ❑ *Some trains were so overloaded that their suspension collapsed.* **2** V-T & N-COUNT To **overload** someone **with** work or problems means to give them more work or problems than they can manage. This can also be called an **overload**. ❑ *...an effective method that will not overload staff with yet more paperwork.* ❑ *57 per cent complained of work overload.* • **overloaded** ADJ ❑ *The bar waiter was already overloaded with orders.*

overlook /ˌəʊvəˈlʊk/ (**overlooks, overlooking, overlooked**) **1** V-T If a building or window **overlooks** a place, you can see the place from the building or window. ❑ *Comfortable rooms overlook a flower-filled garden.* **2** V-T If you **overlook** a fact or problem, you do not notice it, or do not realize how important it is. ❑ *We often overlook warning signals about our own health.* **3** V-T If you **overlook** someone's faults or bad behaviour, you forgive them and take no action. ❑ *A satisfying relationship enables you to overlook each other's faults.*

overly /ˈəʊvəli/ ADV **Overly** means more than is normal, necessary, or reasonable. ❑ *Employers may become overly cautious about taking on new staff.*

overnight /ˌəʊvəˈnaɪt/ **1** ADV & ADJ BEFORE N **Overnight** means during the night or at some point during the night. ❑ *The weather remained calm overnight.* ❑ *...overnight accommodation.* **2** ADV & ADJ BEFORE N You can say that something happens **overnight** when it happens quickly and unexpectedly. ❑ *The rules are not going to change overnight.* ❑ *He became an overnight success.*

overpower /ˌəʊvəˈpaʊə/ (**overpowers, overpowering, overpowered**) **1** V-T If you **overpower** someone, you defeat them because you are stronger than they are. ❑ *It took ten men to overpower him.* **2** V-T If a feeling **overpowers** you, it suddenly affects you very strongly. ❑ *A sudden dizziness overpowered him.* • **overpowering** ADJ ❑ *The desire for revenge can be overpowering.*

overpowering /ˌəʊvəˈpaʊərɪŋ/ ADJ An **overpowering** person makes other people feel uncomfortable because they have such a strong personality.

overran also **over-ran** /ˌəʊvəˈræn/ **Overran** is the past tense of **overrun**.

overrate also **over-rate** /ˌəʊvəˈreɪt/ (**overrates, overrating, overrated**) V-T If you say that something or someone **is overrated**, you mean that people have a higher opinion of them than they deserve. ❑ *This movie is greatly overrated.* • **overrated** ADJ ❑ *He is simply an overrated composer.*

override also **over-ride** /ˌəʊvəˈraɪd/ (**overrides, overriding, overrode, overridden**) **1** V-T If one thing in a situation **overrides** other things, it is more important than them. ❑ *The welfare of a child should always override the wishes of its parents.* • **overriding** ADJ ❑ *...the overriding need to cut the budget.* **2** V-T If someone in authority **overrides** a person or their decisions, they cancel their decisions. ❑ *You do not have the authority to override him.*

overrule also **over-rule** /ˌəʊvəˈruːl/ (**overrules, overruling, overruled**) V-T If someone in authority **overrules** a person or their decision, they officially decide that the decision is incorrect or not valid. ❑ *The Court of Appeal overruled their decision.*

overrun also **over-run** /ˌəʊvəˈrʌn/ (**overruns, overrunning, overran**) **1** V-T If an army **overruns** a country, it succeeds in occupying it quickly. **2** V-T If you say that a place **is overrun with** things that you consider undesirable, you mean that there are a large number of them there. ❑ *The flower beds were overrun with weeds.* **3** V-I If an event or meeting **overruns**, it continues for a longer time than it should have. ❑ *Tuesday's lunch overran by three-quarters of an hour.*

overseas /ˌəʊvəˈsiːz/ **1** ADJ BEFORE N & ADV You use **overseas** to describe things that happen or exist abroad. ❑ *...his long overseas trip.* ❑ *...if you're staying for more than three months or working overseas.* **2** ADJ BEFORE N An **overseas** student or visitor comes from abroad.

oversee /ˌəʊvəˈsiː/ (**oversees, overseeing, oversaw, overseen**) V-T If someone in authority **oversees** a job or an activity, they make sure that it is done properly. ❑ *An architect or surveyor will oversee the work.*

overshadow /ˌəʊvəˈʃædəʊ/ (**overshadows, overshadowing, overshadowed**) **1** V-T If an unpleasant event or feeling **overshadows** something, it makes it less happy or enjoyable. ❑ *His behaviour will possibly overshadow his daughter's success.* **2** V-T If someone or something **is overshadowed by** another person or thing, they are less successful, important, or impressive than the other person or thing. ❑ *Hester is overshadowed* *by her younger and more attractive sister.*

oversight /ˈəʊvəsaɪt/ (**oversights**) N-COUNT If there has been an **oversight**, someone has forgotten to do something which they should have done. ❑ *By an unfortunate oversight, full instructions do not come with the product.*

oversized /ˈəʊvəsaɪzd/ ADJ **Oversized** things are bigger than usual. ❑ *...an oversized bed.*

overstate /ˌəʊvəˈsteɪt/ (**overstates, overstating, overstated**) V-T If you say that someone is **overstating** something, you mean they are describing it in a way that makes it seem more important or serious than it really is. ❑ *Many scientists think that the report overstates the dangers.*

overt /ˌəʊˈvɜːt/ ADJ An **overt** action or attitude is done or shown in an open and obvious way. ❑ *No one spoke a word of overt cricism about her decision.* ● **overtly** ADV ❑ *The family was not overtly religious.*

overtake /ˌəʊvəˈteɪk/ (**overtakes, overtaking, overtook, overtaken**) 1 V-T/V-I If you **overtake** or **overtake** a moving vehicle or person, you pass them because you are moving faster than they are. 2 V-T If an event **overtakes** you, it happens unexpectedly or suddenly. ❑ *His career has been somewhat overtaken by events.*

overthrow (**overthrows, overthrowing, overthrew, overthrown**)

verb /ˌəʊvəˈθrəʊ/, noun /ˈəʊvəθrəʊ/.

V-T & N-SING When a government or a leader **is overthrown**, they are removed from power by force. You can also talk about the **overthrow of** a government or leader. ❑ *That government was overthrown in a military coup.* ❑ *...the overthrow of the government.*

overtime /ˈəʊvətaɪm/ N-UNCOUNT **Overtime** is time that you spend doing your job in addition to your normal working hours. ❑ *He used to work overtime to finish a job.*

overtone /ˈəʊvətəʊn/ (**overtones**) N-COUNT If something has **overtones of** a particular thing or quality, it has a small amount of that thing or quality but does not openly express it. ❑ *His speech had overtones of a sermon.*

overtook /ˌəʊvəˈtʊk/ **Overtook** is the past tense of **overtake.**

overture /ˈəʊvətʃʊə/ (**overtures**) N-COUNT An **overture** is a piece of music, often one that is used as the introduction to an opera or play.

overturn /ˌəʊvəˈtɜːn/ (**overturns, overturning, overturned**) 1 V-T/V-I If something **overturns**, or if you **overturn** it, it turns upside down or on its side. ❑ *Alex jumped up so violently that he overturned his glass.* 2 V-T If someone in authority **overturns** a legal decision, they officially decide that that decision is incorrect or not valid. 3 V-T To **overturn** a government or system means to remove it or destroy it.

overview /ˈəʊvəvjuː/ (**overviews**) N-COUNT An **overview of** a situation is a general understanding or description of it as a whole. ❑ *...a historical overview of the Sikh religion.*

overweight /ˌəʊvəˈweɪt/ 1 ADJ Someone who is **overweight** weighs more than is considered healthy or attractive. 2 → See note at **fat** → see **diet**

overwhelm /ˌəʊvəˈwelm/ (**overwhelms, overwhelming, overwhelmed**) 1 V-T If you **are overwhelmed** by a feeling or event, it affects you very strongly and you do not know how to deal with it. ❑ *Despair overwhelmed me.* ● **overwhelmed** ADJ ❑ *...overwhelmed by the crowds and noise.* 2 V-T If a group of people **overwhelm** a place or another group, they gain control over them. ❑ *The attack would overwhelm the weakened enemy.*

overwhelming /ˌəʊvəˈwelmɪŋ/ 1 ADJ If something is **overwhelming**, it affects you very strongly, and you do not know how to deal with it. ❑ *...an overwhelming desire to have another child.* ● **overwhelmingly** ADV ❑ *Women found him overwhelmingly attractive.* 2 ADJ You can use **overwhelming** to emphasize that an amount or quantity is much greater than other amounts or quantities. ❑ *The overwhelming majority of small businesses fail within the first 24 months.* ● **overwhelmingly** ADJ ❑ *The House of Commons has overwhelmingly rejected calls to bring back the death penalty.*

overwork /ˌəʊvəˈwɜːk/ (**overworks, overworking, overworked**) V-I & N-UNCOUNT If you **overwork**, or if you suffer from **overwork**, you work too hard, and are likely to become very tired or ill. ❑ *He overworks the poor clerk he employs.* ❑ *...a heart attack brought on by overwork.* ● **overworked** ADJ ❑ *...an overworked doctor.*

ovulate /ˈɒvjʊleɪt/ (**ovulates, ovulating, ovulated**) V-I When a woman **ovulates**, she produces an egg from her ovary. [FORMAL] ● **ovulation** N-UNCOUNT ❑ *The woman can tell when ovulation is about to occur.*

owe /əʊ/ (**owes, owing, owed**) 1 V-T If you **owe** money to someone, they have lent it to you and you have not yet paid it back. ❑ *The company owes money to more than 60 banks.* ❑ *Blake already owed him nearly £50.* 2 V-T If someone or something **owes** a particular quality, their success, or their existence **to** a person or thing, they only have it because of that person or thing. ❑ *I owe him my life.* 3 V-T If you say that you **owe** someone gratitude, respect, or loyalty, you mean that they deserve it from you. [FORMAL] ❑ *I owe you an apology.* ❑ *I owe a big debt of gratitude to her.* 4 V-T If you say that you **owe it to** someone **to** do something, you mean that you should do that thing because they deserve it. ❑ *I can't go. I owe it to him to stay.* 5 PREP You use **owing to** to introduce the reason for something. ❑ *He was out of work owing to a physical injury.*

Word Partnership Use *owe* with:

N.	owe **a debt**, owe **money**, owe **taxes** 1 owe **a great deal to *someone*** 2 owe ***someone* an apology** 3

owl /aʊl/ (**owls**) N-COUNT An **owl** is a bird with large eyes which hunts small animals at night.

own /əʊn/ (**owns, owning, owned**) 1 ADJ & PRON You use **own** to indicate that something belongs to or is typical of a particular person or thing. ❑ *My wife decided I should have my own shop.* ❑ *I let her tell me about it in her own way.* ❑ *...a sense of style that is very much her own.* 2 ADJ & PRON You use **own** to emphasize that someone does something without any help from other people. ❑ *He'll have to make his own arrangements.* ❑ *There's no career*

O

Word Web ozone

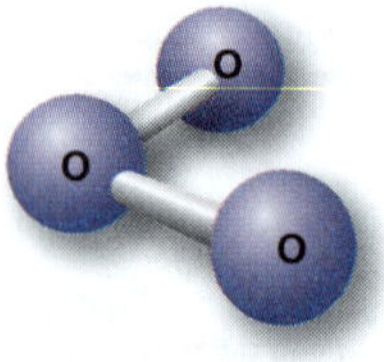

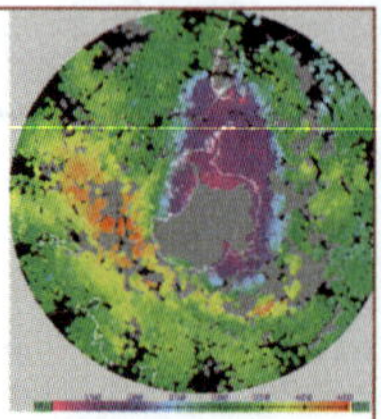

In the Earth's **atmosphere** there are small amounts of **ozone**. Ozone is a molecule that is made up of three **oxygen** atoms. Too much ozone can cause problems. Near the ground, it can be a **pollutant**.Cars and factories produce **carbon monoxide** and **carbon dioxide**. These gases mix with ozone and make **smog**. Too little ozone can also cause problems. The **ozone layer** in the upper **atmosphere** stops harmful **ultraviolet light** from reaching the Earth. Some scientists say a large hole is opening in the ozone layer. This may add to the **greenhouse effect** and **global warming**.

structure, you have to create your own. **3** V-T If you **own** something, it is your property. ❑ *He owns a house in the South of France.* **4** PHRASE When you are **on** your **own**, you are alone. **5** PHRASE If you do something **on** your **own**, you do it without any help from other people. ❑ *I work best on my own.* **6** PHRASE If someone or something **comes into** their **own**, they become very successful or start to perform very well because the circumstances are right. ❑ *The goalkeeper came into his own with a series of brilliant saves.*

▶ **own up** PHR-VERB If you **own up to** something wrong that you have done, you admit that you did it. ❑ *None of the passengers owned up to breaking the no-smoking ban.*

owner /ˈəʊnə/ (**owners**) N-COUNT The **owner** of something is the person to whom it belongs. ❑ *...the owner of the store.* ❑ *Every pet owner knows their animal's personality.*

ownership /ˈəʊnəʃɪp/ N-UNCOUNT **Ownership** of something is the state of owning it. ❑ *...the growth of home ownership in Britain.*

ox /ɒks/ (**oxen**) N-COUNT An **ox** is a castrated bull.

oxygen /ˈɒksɪdʒən/ N-UNCOUNT **Oxygen** is a colourless gas in the air which is needed by all plants and animals.
→ see **air, earth, ozone, respiration**

oyster /ˈɔɪstə/ (**oysters**) N-COUNT An **oyster** is a large flat shellfish which produces pearls.
→ see **shellfish**

oz **oz** is a written abbreviation for **ounce**.

ozone /ˈəʊzəʊn/ N-UNCOUNT **Ozone** is a form of oxygen. There is a layer of ozone high above the earth's surface.
→ see Word Web: **ozone**

ˌozone-ˈfriendly ADJ **Ozone-friendly** chemicals, products, or technology do not cause harm to the ozone layer.

ˈozone ˌlayer N-SING **The ozone layer** is the part of the Earth's atmosphere that has the highest number of ozone molecules.
→ see **air**

Pp

p /piː/ **p** is an abbreviation for **pence** or **page**. ❑ *They cost 5p each.* ❑ *See Note 16 on p. 223.*

pace /peɪs/ (**paces, pacing, paced**) **1** N-UNCOUNT The **pace of** something is the speed at which it happens or is done. ❑ *Many people were not satisfied with the pace of change.* ❑ *...the gentle pace of life on the island.* **2** N-SING Your **pace** is the speed at which you walk. ❑ *He moved at a faster pace.* **3** N-COUNT A **pace** is the distance you move when you take one step. ❑ *I took a pace backwards.* **4** V-T/V-I If you **pace** a small area, you keep walking up and down it, because you are anxious or impatient. ❑ *Kravis paced the room nervously.* ❑ *He found John pacing around the flat.* **5** PHRASE To **keep pace with** something that is changing means to change quickly in response to it. ❑ *Their wages did not keep pace with inflation.* **6** PHRASE If you do something **at** your **own pace**, you do it at a speed that is comfortable for you.

Word Partnership Use *pace* with:

N.	pace **of change** 1
ADJ.	**brisk** pace, **fast** pace, **record** pace, **slow** pace 1 2
V.	**pick up the** pace, **set a** pace 1 2

pacifier /ˈpæsɪfaɪər/ (**pacifiers**) N-COUNT In American English, a **pacifier** is a rubber or plastic object that you give to a baby to suck so that it feels comforted. The British word is **dummy**.

pacifist /ˈpæsɪfɪst/ (**pacifists**) N-COUNT & ADJ A **pacifist** or someone with **pacifist** views believes that war and violence are always wrong. • **pacifism** N-UNCOUNT ❑ *He didn't hide his pacifism.*

pack /pæk/ (**packs, packing, packed**) **1** V-T/V-I & PHR-VERB When you **pack**, or when you **pack up**, you put your belongings into a bag, because you are leaving. ❑ *I packed my bags and left home.* ❑ *He began packing up his things.* ❑ *I packed and left.*

pack

• **packing** N-UNCOUNT ❑ *She left Frances to finish her packing.* **2** V-T To **pack** things, for example in a factory, means to put them into containers or parcels so that they can be transported and sold. ❑ *Machines pack the olives in jars.* **3** V-T/V-I If people or things **pack into** a place, or if they **pack** a place, there are so many of them that the place is full. ❑ *A thousand supporters packed into the stadium.* ❑ *Thousands of people packed the square.* • **packed** ADJ ❑ *The stores were packed with shoppers.* **4** N-COUNT A **pack of** things is a collection of them in one packet. ❑ *...a free information pack.* ❑ *...a pack of sandwiches.* **5** N-COUNT A **pack** is a bag containing your belongings that you carry on your back when you are travelling. ❑ *I hid the money in my pack.* **6** N-COUNT A **pack of** wolves or dogs is a group of them hunting together. **7** N-COUNT In British English, a **pack of** cards is a complete set of playing cards. The usual American word is **deck**.

▸ **pack off** PHR-VERB If you **pack** someone **off** somewhere, you send them there. [INFORMAL] ❑ *At the age of nine she was packed off to boarding school.*

package /ˈpækɪdʒ/ (**packages, packaging, packaged**) **1** N-COUNT A **package** is a small parcel. ❑ *The package was addressed to Yusuf.* **2** N-COUNT A **package** is a set of proposals that are made by a government or organization. ❑ *...an economic aid package.* **3** V-T When something **is packaged**, it is put into packets to be sold.

Thesaurus *package* Also look up:

N.	batch, bundle, container, pack, parcel 1

packaging /ˈpækɪdʒɪŋ/ N-UNCOUNT **Packaging** is the container or wrappings that something is sold in. ❑ *...layers of expensive packaging.*

packet /ˈpækɪt/ (**packets**) N-COUNT A **packet** is a small box, bag, or envelope in which a quantity of something is sold. ❑ *The packet says the product contains cream.* ❑ *Tom gave them each a packet of crisps.* → see **container**

pact /pækt/ (**pacts**) N-COUNT A **pact** is a formal agreement between two or more people, organizations, or governments. ❑ *Four days later the Atlantic Pact was signed and NATO was created.*

pad /pæd/ (**pads, padding, padded**) **1** N-COUNT A **pad** is a thick flat piece of a material such as cloth or foam rubber. Pads are used, for example, to clean things or for protection. ❑ *...a pad of cotton-wool.* **2** N-COUNT A **pad** of paper is a number of pieces of paper which are fixed together along the top or the side, so that each piece can be torn off when it has been used. ❑ *Keep a pad handy to makes notes on.* **3** V-T/V-I When someone **pads** somewhere, they walk there with steps that are fairly quick, light, and quiet. ❑ *Freddy speaks very quietly and pads around in slippers.* ❑ *I often bumped into him as he padded the corridors.* **4** V-T If you **pad** something, you put something soft in it or over it in order to make it less hard or to protect it. ❑ *Pad the back of a car seat with a pillow.*

padded /pædɪd/ ADJ Something that is **padded** has soft material on it or inside it which makes it less hard, protects it, or gives it a different shape. ❑ *...a man in a padded jacket.*

padding /ˈpædɪŋ/ N-UNCOUNT **Padding** is soft material on the outside or inside of something which makes it less hard, protects it, or gives it a different shape. ❑ *Football players must wear padding* to protect them.

paddle /'pædəl/ (**paddles, paddling, paddled**) **1** N-COUNT A **paddle** is a short pole with a wide flat part at one end or at both ends, used to move a small boat through water. **2** V-I & N-COUNT If you **paddle**, or if you go for a **paddle**, you walk or stand in shallow water for pleasure. ❑ *They paddled in the stream.*
→ see **boat**

paddock /'pædək/ (**paddocks**) **1** N-COUNT A **paddock** is a small field where horses are kept. **2** N-COUNT In horse racing, the **paddock** is the place where the horses walk about before a race.

paddy /'pædi/ (**paddies**) N-COUNT A **paddy** or a **paddy field** is a flooded field that is used for growing rice.

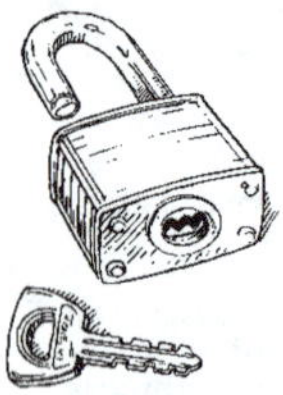
padlock

padlock /'pædlɒk/ (**padlocks, padlocking, padlocked**) N-COUNT & V-T A **padlock** is a lock used for fastening two things or two parts of something together. When you **padlock** something, you lock it or fasten it using a padlock. ❑ *Eddie parked his bike and padlocked it.*

paediatrician [AM **pediatrician**] /ˌpiːdiə'trɪʃən/ (**paediatricians**) N-COUNT A **paediatrician** is a doctor who specializes in treating sick children.

paediatrics [AM **pediatrics**] /ˌpiːdi'ætrɪks/ (**paediatric**)

The form **paediatric** is used as a modifier.

N-UNCOUNT **Paediatrics** is the area of medicine that is concerned with the treatment of children's illnesses. ❑ *...a paediatric surgeon.*

pagan /'peɪgən/ ADJ **Pagan** beliefs and activities do not belong to any of the main religions of the world and take nature and a belief in many gods as a basis. They are older than other religions.

page /peɪdʒ/ (**pages**) **1** N-COUNT A **page** is a side of one of the pieces of paper in a book, magazine, or newspaper. ❑ *Turn to page 4.* **2** N-COUNT The **pages** of a book, magazine, or newspaper are the pieces of paper it consists of. ❑ *He turned the pages of his notebook.*
→ see **printing**

pageant /'pædʒənt/ (**pageants**) N-COUNT A **pageant** is a colourful public parade, show, or ceremony, often organized to celebrate a historic event.

paid /peɪd/ **1** **Paid** is the past tense and past participle of **pay**. **2** ADJ **Paid** means to do with the money a worker receives from his or her employer. You can say, for example, that someone is **well paid** when they receive a lot of money for the work that they do. ❑ *...a legal right to paid holiday leave.*

pain /peɪn/ (**pains, paining, pained**) **1** N-VAR If you feel **pain**, or if you are **in pain**, you feel great discomfort in a part of your body, because of illness or an injury. ❑ *...a bone disease that caused a lot of pain.* ❑ *I felt a sharp pain in my back.* **2** N-UNCOUNT **Pain** is the unhappiness that you feel when something upsetting happens. ❑ *His eyes were filled with pain.* **3** V-T If something **pains** you, it makes you feel upset or unhappy. ❑ *It pains me to think of you struggling all alone.* • **pained** ADJ ❑ *A pained expression came over her face.* **4** PHRASE If you say that something or someone is **a pain** or **a pain in the neck**, you mean they are very annoying or irritating. [INFORMAL] ❑ *You can be a real pain in the neck sometimes.* **5** PHRASE If you **take pains to** do something, you try hard to do it successfully. ❑ *He took great pains to entertain me.*

Thesaurus *pain* Also look up:

N.	ache, agony, discomfort **1** anguish, distress, heartache, suffering **2**
V.	bother, distress, grieve, hurt, upset, wound **3**

painful /'peɪnfʊl/ **1** ADJ If a part of your body is **painful**, it hurts. ❑ *Her knee was still very painful.* • **painfully** ADV ❑ *He covered his mouth and coughed painfully.* **2** ADJ If something such as an illness, injury, or operation is **painful**, it causes you a lot of physical pain. ❑ *...a painful back injury.* • **painfully** ADV ❑ *He hit his head painfully against the floor.* **3** ADJ Situations, memories, or experiences that are **painful** are difficult and unpleasant to deal with, and often make you feel sad and upset. ❑ *She finds it too painful to return there without him.*

Word Partnership Use *painful* with:

ADV.	**extremely** painful, **more/less** painful, **often** painful, **sometimes** painful, **too** painful, **very** painful **1-3**
N.	painful **death**, painful **experience**, painful **feelings**, painful **lesson**, painful **memory**, painful **process** **1-3**

painfully /'peɪnfʊli/ ADV You use **painfully** to emphasize a quality or situation that is undesirable. ❑ *Things are moving painfully slowly.* ❑ *He was painfully aware of the gaps in his education.*

painkiller /'peɪnkɪlə/ (**painkillers**) N-COUNT A **painkiller** is a drug which reduces or stops physical pain.

painless /'peɪnləs/ **1** ADJ Something such as a treatment that is **painless** causes no physical pain. ❑ *The operation itself is painless.* • **painlessly** ADV ❑ *She died peacefully and painlessly.* **2** ADJ If a process or activity is **painless**, you do not have to make a great effort or suffer in any way. ❑ *The resort makes things as painless for the tourist as possible.* • **painlessly** ADV ❑ *This game for children painlessly teaches pre-reading skills.*

painstaking /'peɪnsteɪkɪŋ/ ADJ A **painstaking** search, examination, or investigation is done extremely carefully and thoroughly. • **painstakingly** ADV ❑ *They carried out their duties painstakingly.*

paint /peɪnt/ (**paints, painting, painted**) **1** N-VAR **Paint** is a coloured liquid that you put on a wall or other surface with a brush in order to protect the surface or to make it look nice, or that you use to produce a picture. ❑ *They saw some large letters in white paint.* ❑ *You could use the same colour of paint throughout the house.* **2** V-T/V-I If you **paint** a wall or an object, you cover it with paint. ❑ *I painted the walls white.* ❑ *I spent all weekend painting and decorating.* **3** V-T/V-I If you **paint** something, or if you **paint** a picture of it, you produce a picture of it using paint. ❑ *He is painting the volcano.* ❑ *Her*

Word Web painting

Oil **painting** uses special tools and techniques. First, artists stretch a piece of **canvas** over a wooden **frame**. Then they cover the canvas with a **coat** of white **paint**. When it dries, they put it on an **easel**. Most painters use a **palette** knife on a **palette** to mix **colours** together. They paint the canvas with soft bristle **paintbrushes**. When they are finished, they use turpentine to clean the brushes and the palette. Three common oil painting styles are the **still life**, the **landscape**, and the **portrait**.

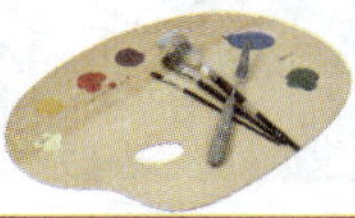

ambition is to paint and make money from it.
→ see **draw, painting, petroleum**

Word Partnership Use *paint* with:

ADJ. **blue/green/red/white/yellow** paint 1
fresh paint, **peeling** paint 2
N. **can of** paint 1
coat of paint 2
paint **a picture**, paint **a portrait** 4

paintbrush /'peɪntbrʌʃ/ (**paintbrushes**) N-COUNT A **paintbrush** is a brush which you use for painting.
→ see **painting**

painter /'peɪntə/ (**painters**) 1 N-COUNT A **painter** is an artist who paints pictures. ❑ *...England's greatest modern painter.* 2 N-COUNT A **painter** is someone who paints walls, doors, and some other parts of buildings as their job.

painting /'peɪntɪŋ/ (**paintings**) 1 N-COUNT A **painting** is a picture which someone has painted. 2 N-UNCOUNT **Painting** is the activity of painting pictures. ❑ *She really enjoyed painting.*
→ see Word Web: **painting**
→ see **art**

pair /peə/ (**pairs**) 1 N-COUNT A **pair of** things are two things of the same size and shape that are intended to be used together. ❑ *...a pair of socks.* ❑ *...a pair of earrings.* 2 N-COUNT Some objects that have two main parts of the same size and shape are referred to as a **pair**. ❑ *...a pair of jeans.* ❑ *...a pair of binoculars.* 3 N-SING You can refer to two people as a **pair** when they are standing or walking together. ❑ *A pair of teenagers were arrested by police on Friday.* 4 → see also **au pair**

Usage

The noun **pair** can take either a singular verb or a plural verb, depending on whether it refers to one thing seen as a unit or a collection of two things or people. ❑ *A good pair of trainers is essential.* ❑ *The pair are still friends.*

Thesaurus *pair* Also look up:

N. combination, couple, duo, match, two 2

pajamas /pə'dʒɑːməz/ → see **pyjamas**

pal /pæl/ (**pals**) N-COUNT Your **pals** are your friends. [INFORMAL] ❑ *The two women became close pals.*

palace /'pælɪs/ (**palaces**) N-COUNT A **palace** is a very large splendid house, especially the home of a king, queen, or president.

palate /'pælɪt/ (**palates**) 1 N-COUNT Your **palate** is the top part of the inside of your mouth. 2 N-COUNT You can refer to someone's ability to judge good food and wine as their **palate**. ❑ *The pudding was too sugary for our palates.*

pale /peɪl/ (**paler, palest**) 1 ADJ Something that is **pale** is not strong or bright in colour. ❑ *...pale blue.* 2 ADJ If someone looks **pale**, their face is a lighter colour than usual, because they are ill, frightened, or shocked.

palette /'pælɪt/ (**palettes**) N-COUNT A **palette** is a flat piece of wood or plastic on which an artist mixes paints.
→ see **painting**

pall /pɔːl/ (**palls, palling, palled**) 1 V-I If something **palls**, it becomes less interesting or less enjoyable. ❑ *The job was beginning to pall.* 2 N-COUNT A **pall of** smoke is a thick cloud of it. [LITERARY]

palm /pɑːm/ (**palms**) 1 N-COUNT A **palm** or **palm tree** is a tree that grows in hot countries. It has long leaves at the top and no branches. 2 N-COUNT The **palm of** your hand is the flat surface which your fingers can bend towards.
→ see **desert, hand**

palpable /'pælpəbəl/ ADJ Something that is **palpable** is very obvious. ❑ *The tension was palpable.* ● **palpably** ADV ❑ *He was palpably nervous.*

paltry /'pɔːltri/ ADJ A **paltry** amount of money or something else is very small. ❑ *...a paltry 0.2% rise in profits.*

pamper /'pæmpə/ (**pampers, pampering, pampered**) V-T If you **pamper** someone, you do everything for them, and give them everything they want. ● **pampered** ADJ ❑ *I was a very pampered child.*

pamphlet /'pæmflət/ (**pamphlets**) N-COUNT A **pamphlet** is a very thin book with a paper cover, which gives information about something.

pan /pæn/ (**pans**) N-COUNT A **pan** is a round metal container with a handle, which is used for cooking things, usually on top of a cooker.
→ see Word Web: **pan**

panacea /ˌpænə'siːə/ (**panaceas**) N-COUNT If you say that something is not a **panacea** for a particular set of problems, you mean that it will not solve all those problems. [JOURNALISM] ❑ *Western aid may help but will not be a panacea.*

panache /pə'næʃ/ N-UNCOUNT If you do something **with panache**, you do it in a confident and stylish way. ❑ *The orchestra performed with great panache.*

pancake /'pænkeɪk/ (**pancakes**) N-COUNT

P

Word Web pan

No **saucepan** or **frying pan** is perfect. **Copper pans** conduct heat well. This makes them good for cooking on the stove. However, copper reacts with the acid in some foods and wines. For this reason, the best pans have a thin layer of **tin** covering the copper. **Cast iron** pans are very heavy and **heat up** slowly. But they stay hot for a long time. Some people like **stainless steel** pans because they heat up quickly and don't react with chemicals in food. However, a stainless pan may not heat up evenly.

pancakes

A **pancake** is a thin, flat, circular piece of cooked batter that is eaten hot, often with a sweet or savoury filling.

panda /'pændə/ (**pandas**) N-COUNT A **panda** is a large animal with black and white fur which lives in China.
→ see **zoo**

pander /'pændə/ (**panders, pandering, pandered**) V-I If you **pander to** someone, you do everything they want, often to get some advantage for yourself; used showing disapproval. ❑ *...politicians who pander to millionaires.*

pane /peɪn/ (**panes**) N-COUNT A **pane of** glass is a flat sheet of glass in a window or door.

panel /'pænəl/ (**panels**) **1** N-COUNT A **panel** is a small group of people who are chosen to do something, for example to discuss something in public or to make a decision. ❑ *Our panel of experts answer your questions.* **2** N-COUNT A **panel** is a flat rectangular piece of wood or other material that forms part of a larger object such as a door. **3** N-COUNT A control **panel** or instrument **panel** is a board containing switches and controls.

panelled [AM **paneled**] /'pænəld/ ADJ If something such as a room or door is **panelled**, its walls or surface are covered in decorative wooden panels. ❑ *...panelled walls.*

P

pang /pæŋ/ (**pangs**) N-COUNT A **pang** is a sudden strong feeling, for example of sadness or pain. ❑ *Ruth felt a pang of guilt.*

panic /'pænɪk/ (**panics, panicking, panicked**) **1** N-VAR **Panic** is a strong feeling of anxiety or fear that makes you act without thinking carefully. ❑ *A look of panic crossed the man's face.* ❑ *In a panic, I rushed to the kitchen.* **2** V-T/V-I If you **panic**, or if someone or something **panics** you, you become anxious or afraid, and act without thinking carefully. ❑ *Jason panicked when the spider fell onto his knee.*

Thesaurus *panic* Also look up:

N.	agitation, alarm, dread, fear, fright; *(ant.)* calm **1**

panorama /ˌpænə'rɑːmə, -'ræmə/ (**panoramas**) N-COUNT A **panorama** is a view in which you can see a long way over a wide area of land. ❑ *You look out on a panorama of London.* • **panoramic** ADJ ❑ *We had a panoramic view of the beach.*

pant /pænt/ (**pants, panting, panted**) V-I If you **pant**, you breathe quickly and loudly, because you have been doing something energetic.

Word Link *mim ≈ copying : mime, mimic, pantomime*

pantomime /'pæntəmaɪm/ (**pantomimes**) N-VAR A **pantomime** is a funny musical play for children, usually performed at Christmas. ❑ *She regularly appeared in pantomime.*

pants /pænts/ **1** N-PLURAL In British English, **pants** are a piece of underwear with two holes to put your legs through and elastic around the top. The usual American word is **underpants**. **2** N-PLURAL In American English, **pants** are a piece of clothing that you wear over your body from the waist downwards, and that cover each leg separately. The usual British word is **trousers**.

papa /pə'pɑː, AM 'pɑːpə/ (**papas**) N-COUNT & N-VOC Some people refer to or address their father as **papa**. [DATED]

papal /'peɪpəl/ ADJ BEFORE N **Papal** is used to describe things relating to the Pope. ❑ *...a papal visit to Japan.*

paper /'peɪpə/ (**papers, papering, papered**) **1** N-UNCOUNT **Paper** is a material that you write on or wrap things with. ❑ *...a piece of paper.* ❑ *...a paper bag.* **2** PHRASE If you put your thoughts down **on paper**, you write them down. **3** N-COUNT A **paper** is a newspaper. ❑ *...the daily papers.* **4** N-PLURAL **Papers** are sheets of paper with information on them. ❑ *...a briefcase carrying personal papers.* **5** N-PLURAL Your **papers** are your official documents, for example your passport or identity card. ❑ *The officer asked him for his papers.* **6** N-COUNT A **paper** is a long essay on an academic subject. **7** N-COUNT A **paper** prepared by a government or a committee is a report on a question they have been considering or a set of proposals for changes in the law. ❑ *...a new government paper on European policy.* **8** V-T If you **paper** a wall, you put wallpaper on it. ❑ *We papered all four bedrooms.*
→ see Word Web: **paper**

Word Partnership Use *paper* with:

ADJ.	**blank** paper, **brown** paper, **coloured** paper, **recycled** paper **1**
	daily paper **3**
V.	**fold** paper **1**
	read the paper **3**
	present a paper, **publish a** paper **6**
	draft a paper, **write a** paper **6 7**
N.	**morning** paper **3**
	research paper **6 7**

paperback /'peɪpəbæk/ (**paperbacks**) N-VAR A

Word Web paper

Around 3000 BC, the Egyptians began to make **paper** from the papyrus plant. They cut the stems of the plant into thin slices and pressed them into **sheets**. A very different process developed in China about the same time. It was more like today's paper-making process. Chinese paper makers cooked **fibre** made of tree bark. Then they pressed it into moulds and let it dry. Around 200 BC, a third paper-making process began in the Middle East. Craftsmen started using animal skins to make parchment. Today, paper manufacturing destroys millions of trees every year. This has led to **recycling** programs and paperless offices.

paperback is a book with a paper cover. ❑ *...a cheap paperback.* ❑ *The book is now out in paperback.*

paperwork /ˈpeɪpəwɜːk/ N-UNCOUNT **Paperwork** consists of the letters, reports, and records which have to be dealt with as the routine part of a job. ❑ *He does his paperwork here.*

par /pɑː/ **1** PHRASE If you say that someone or something is **below par**, you mean that they are below the standard you expected. ❑ *Duffy's playing is well below par.* **2** PHRASE If one thing is **on a par with** another, the two things are equally good or bad. ❑ *This match was on a par with the German Cup Final.*

Word Link *para ≈ guarding against : parable, parachute, paramilitary*

parable /ˈpærəbəl/ (**parables**) N-COUNT A **parable** is a short story which makes a moral or religious point.

parachute /ˈpærəʃuːt/ (**parachutes, parachuting, parachuted**) **1** N-COUNT A **parachute** is a device which enables a person to jump from an aircraft and float safely to the ground. It consists of a large piece of thin cloth attached to your body by strings. **2** V-T/V-I If a person **parachutes**, or if someone **parachutes** them somewhere, they jump from an aircraft using a parachute. ❑ *They were parachuted into the country at night.*

parachute

→ see **fly**

parade /pəˈreɪd/ (**parades, parading, paraded**) **1** N-COUNT A **parade** is a line of people or vehicles moving together through a public place in order to celebrate an important day or event. **2** V-I When people **parade**, they walk together in a formal group or in a line, usually in front of spectators. ❑ *Soldiers paraded down the Champs Elysées.* **3** V-T If someone **parades** something, they show it in public in order to impress people. ❑ *I paraded all the paintings in front of them.*

parade

paradise /ˈpærədaɪs/ (**paradises**) **1** N-PROPER According to some religions, **paradise** is a wonderful place where people go after they die, if they have led good lives. **2** N-VAR You can refer to a place or situation that seems perfect as **paradise** or a **paradise**.

Word Link *para ≈ beside : paradox, parallel, paramilitary*

Word Link *dox ≈ opinion : orthodox, paradox, unorthodox*

paradox /ˈpærədɒks/ (**paradoxes**) **1** N-COUNT You describe a situation as a **paradox** when it involves two or more facts or qualities which seem to contradict each other. • **paradoxical** ADJ ❑ *It may seem paradoxical, but a slight warming in the polar regions will actually mean more arctic ice, not less.* • **paradoxically** ADV ❑ *Paradoxically, the less you have to do the more tired you feel.* **2** N-VAR A **paradox** is a statement in which it seems that if one part of it is true, the other part of it cannot be true.

paraffin /ˈpærəfɪn/ N-UNCOUNT **Paraffin** is a strong-smelling liquid which is used as a fuel in heaters, lamps, and engines. The usual American word is **kerosene**.

paragon /ˈpærəgɒn/ (**paragons**) N-COUNT If you say that someone is a **paragon of** virtue, or some other good quality, you mean that they have a lot of that quality. ❑ *...a paragon of neatness and efficiency.*

paragraph /ˈpærəgrɑːf, -græf/ (**paragraphs**) N-COUNT A **paragraph** is a section of a piece of writing. A paragraph always begins on a new line and contains at least one sentence.

parallel /ˈpærəlel/ (**parallels, parallelling, parallelled** or [AM] **paralleling, paralleled**) **1** N-COUNT If something has a **parallel**, or if there are **parallels** between two or more things, they are similar to each other in some way. ❑ *It's an ecological disaster with no parallel anywhere else in the world.* ❑ *He drew parallels between the UK election last year and the US election of 1996.* **2** V-T & ADJ If one thing **parallels** another, or if two things are **parallel**, they happen at the same time or are similar, and often seem to be connected. ❑ *His remarks parallelled those of the president.* ❑ *...parallel talks between the two countries' Foreign Ministers.* **3** ADJ If two lines or two objects are **parallel**, they are the same distance apart along their whole length.

paralyse [AM **paralyze**] /ˈpærəlaɪz/ (**paralyses, paralysing, paralysed**) **1** V-T If someone **is paralysed** by an accident or illness, they have no feeling in their body, or in part of their body, and are unable to move. • **paralysed** ADJ ❑ *...a paralysed*

right arm. **2** V-T If a person, place, or organization **is paralysed** by something, they are unable to act or function properly. ❑ *The city was paralysed by the bombing.*
→ see **disability**

paralysis /pəˈræləsɪs/ N-UNCOUNT **Paralysis** is the loss of feeling in all or part of your body and the inability to move. ❑ *...paralysis of the leg.*

paramedic /ˈpærəˈmedɪk, AM -medɪk/ (**paramedics**) N-COUNT A **paramedic** is a person whose training is similar to that of a nurse and who helps to do medical work. ❑ *We intend to have a paramedic on every ambulance within the next three years.*

Word Link *para ≈ beside : paradox, parallel, paramilitary*

Word Link *para ≈ guarding against : parable, parachute, paramilitary*

paramilitary /ˌpærəˈmɪlɪtri, AM -teri/ (**paramilitaries**) ADJ BEFORE N & N-COUNT **Paramilitary** organizations are groups who are organized like an army but do not belong to any official army. **Paramilitaries** are members of a paramilitary organization.

paramount /ˈpærəmaʊnt/ ADJ Something that is **paramount** or of **paramount** importance is more important than anything else. ❑ *The child's welfare must be paramount.*

paranoia /ˌpærəˈnɔɪə/ **1** N-UNCOUNT If you say that someone suffers from **paranoia**, you think that they are too suspicious and afraid of other people. ❑ *He viewed the world with paranoia.* **2** N-UNCOUNT If someone suffers from **paranoia**, they are suffering from a mental illness which makes them wrongly believe that other people are trying to harm them. [TECHNICAL]

paranoid /ˈpærənɔɪd/ **1** ADJ If you say that someone is **paranoid**, you mean that they are extremely suspicious and afraid of other people. ❑ *I'm not going to get paranoid about it.* **2** ADJ Someone who is **paranoid** suffers from the mental illness of paranoia. [TECHNICAL]

P

paraphernalia /ˌpærəfəˈneɪliə/ N-UNCOUNT You can refer to a large number of objects that someone has with them or that are connected with a particular activity as **paraphernalia**. ❑ *The bag was full of the paraphernalia cyclists carry around.*

paraphrase /ˈpærəfreɪz/ (**paraphrases, paraphrasing, paraphrased**) V-T/V-I & N-COUNT If you **paraphrase** someone, or if you **paraphrase** something that they have said or written, you express what they have said or written in a different way. A **paraphrase** is something that has been paraphrased. ❑ *I'm paraphrasing, but this is what he said.* ❑ *The writer has attempted to paraphrase Mabry's words.* ❑ *This was an exact quote rather than a paraphrase.*

parasite /ˈpærəsaɪt/ (**parasites**) **1** N-COUNT A **parasite** is a small animal or plant that lives on or inside a larger animal or plant. ● **parasitic** /ˌpærəˈsɪtɪk/ ADJ ❑ *...parasitic worms.* **2** N-COUNT If you call someone a **parasite**, you disapprove of them because you think that they get money or other things from people without doing anything in return.

paratrooper /ˈpærətruːpə/ (**paratroopers**) N-COUNT **Paratroopers** are soldiers who are trained to be dropped by parachute into battle or into enemy territory.

parcel /ˈpɑːsəl/ (**parcels**) **1** N-COUNT A **parcel** is something wrapped in paper, usually so that it can be sent to someone by post. The more usual American word is **package**. **2** **part and parcel** → see **part**

parched /pɑːtʃt/ **1** ADJ If the ground is **parched**, it is very dry, because there has been no rain. ❑ *...a hill of parched brown grass.* **2** ADJ If your mouth, throat, or lips are **parched**, they are unpleasantly dry. **3** ADJ AFTER LINK-V If you say you are **parched**, you mean that you are very thirsty.

Word Link *don ≈ giving : donate, donor, pardon*

pardon /ˈpɑːdən/ (**pardons, pardoning, pardoned**) **1** CONVENTION You say **'Pardon?'**, or **'I beg your pardon?'** or, in American English, **'Pardon me?'** when you want someone to repeat what they have just said, either because you have not heard or understood it or because you are surprised by it. ❑ *'Will you let me open it?'—'Pardon?'—'Can I open it?'* **2** CONVENTION You say **'I beg your pardon'** or **'I do beg your pardon'** as a way of apologizing for accidentally doing something wrong, such as disturbing someone or making a mistake. ❑ *I'm sorry I've interrupted you. I beg your pardon.* **3** V-T & N-COUNT If someone who has been found guilty of a crime **is pardoned** or is given a **pardon**, they are officially allowed to go free and are not punished.

pare /peə/ (**pares, paring, pared**) **1** V-T When you **pare** something, or **pare** part of it **off** or **away**, you cut off its skin or its outer layer. ❑ *Place the apple juice, pared lemon rind and sugar into a saucepan.* **2** V-T & PHR-VERB If you **pare** something **down** or **back**, or if you **pare** it, you reduce it. ❑ *Management costs have been pared down.*

parent /ˈpeərənt/ (**parents**) N-COUNT Your **parents** are your father and mother. ● **parental** /pəˈrentəl/ ADJ ❑ *He was always careful to ask for parental permission.*
→ see **child**

parenthood /ˈpeərənthʊd/ N-UNCOUNT **Parenthood** is the state of being a parent.

parenting /ˈpeərəntɪŋ/ N-UNCOUNT **Parenting** is the activity of bringing up and looking after your child.

parish /ˈpærɪʃ/ (**parishes**) **1** N-COUNT A **parish** is a village or part of a town which has its own church and clergyman. **2** N-COUNT A **parish** is a small country area in England with its own elected council.

parishioner /pəˈrɪʃənə/ (**parishioners**) N-COUNT A clergyman's **parishioners** are the people in his parish.

park /pɑːk/ (**parks, parking, parked**) **1** N-COUNT A **park** is a public area of land with grass and trees, usually in a town, where people go to relax and enjoy themselves. **2** N-VAR In Britain, a private area of grass and trees around a large country house is referred to as a **park**. **3** V-T/V-I When you **park** a vehicle, or when you **park** somewhere, you drive the vehicle into a position where it can stay for a period of time and leave it. ❑ *Could you park over there?* ● **parked** ADJ ❑ *...rows of parked cars.*

• **parking** N-UNCOUNT ❑ *Parking is allowed only on one side of the street.* **4** → see also **car park, national park**

Usage

Note that you do not use the word **parking** to refer to a place where cars are parked. Instead, you refer to a **car park** in British English, and a **parking lot** in American English. **Parking** is used only to refer to the action of parking your car, or the state of being parked. ❑ *...a 'No Parking' sign.*

'parking lot (**parking lots**) N-COUNT In American English, a **parking lot** is an area of ground where people can leave their cars. The British term is **car park**.

parliament /ˈpɑːləmənt/ (**parliaments**) **1** N-VAR The **parliament** of a country is the group of people who make or change its laws. **2** → See note at **government** **3** → see also **Member of Parliament**

parliamentary /ˌpɑːləˈmentəri/ ADJ BEFORE N **Parliamentary** is used to describe things that are connected with a parliament. ❑ *...a parliamentary debate.*

parlour [AM **parlor**] /ˈpɑːlə/ (**parlours**) N-COUNT **Parlour** is used in the names of some types of shops which provide a service. ❑ *...a pizza parlour.*

parody /ˈpærədi/ (**parodies, parodying, parodied**) V-T & N-VAR When someone **parodies** a particular work, thing, or person, they imitate them in an amusing or exaggerated way. You call an imitation like this a **parody**. ❑ *Timothy parodied perfectly his father and other gentlemen at the club.* ❑ *...a parody of middle-class life.*

parole /pəˈrəʊl/ (**paroles, paroling, paroled**) **1** N-UNCOUNT & PASSIVE-VERB When prisoners are given **parole**, or when they **are paroled**, they are released before their sentence is due to end, on condition that they behave well. **2** PHRASE If someone is **on parole**, they will stay out of prison if they behave well.

parrot /ˈpærət/ (**parrots, parroting, parroted**) **1** N-COUNT A **parrot** is a tropical bird with a curved beak and brightly-coloured or grey feathers. Parrots can be kept as pets. **2** V-T If you **parrot** what someone else has said, you repeat it without really understanding what it means. ❑ *She was only parroting back what she'd heard.*

parsley /ˈpɑːsli, AM -zli/ N-UNCOUNT **Parsley** is a small plant with curly leaves used for flavouring or decorating savoury food.

parsnip /ˈpɑːsnɪp/ (**parsnips**) N-COUNT A **parsnip** is a root vegetable similar in shape to a carrot.

Word Link *par ≈ equal : compare, disparate, part*

part

❶ PIECE, SECTION
❷ ROLE
❸ SEPARATE

part /pɑːt/ (**parts**)
❶ **1** N-VAR If one thing is a **part of** another thing or **part of** it, the first thing is one of the pieces, sections, or elements that the second thing consists of. ❑ *I like that part of Cape Town.* ❑ *Respect is a very important part of a relationship.* ❑ *Switzerland is not part of the EC.* **2** N-COUNT A **part** for a machine or vehicle is one of the smaller pieces that is used to make it. ❑ *...spare parts for military equipment.* **3** PHRASE **The best part of** or **the better part of** a period of time or an amount means most of that time or that amount. ❑ *We spent the better part of an hour searching, but eventually found her.* **4** PHRASE You use **in part** to indicate that something exists or happens to some extent but not completely. ❑ *The design is based in part on the paintings of Gustav Klimt.* **5** PHRASE **For the most part** means mostly or usually. ❑ *For the most part, I did not complain.* **6** PHRASE If you say that something is **part and parcel of** something else, you mean that it is involved or included in it. ❑ *Violence is part and parcel of everyday life round here.*

part /pɑːt/ (**parts**)
❷ **1** N-COUNT A **part in** a play or film is one of the roles in it. ❑ *I got a part in a romantic comedy.* **2** N-SING Your **part in** something that happens is your involvement in it. ❑ *He was jailed for his part in a robbery.* **3** PHRASE You can say, for example, that **for** your **part** you thought or did something, to introduce what you thought or did. ❑ *The Russians for their part gave exactly the same advice.* **4** PHRASE If someone **looks the part**, they dress or behave in the way that is characteristic of a particular kind of person. ❑ *She began to look the part of a would-be MP. She was always perfectly groomed and well-dressed.* **5** PHRASE If you talk about a feeling or action **on** someone's **part**, you are referring to something that they feel or do. ❑ *That was actually an error on my part.* **6** PHRASE You can say that someone or something **plays a part in** something to talk about the fact that they are involved in it and the effect they have on it. ❑ *Work plays an important part in a single woman's life.* **7** PHRASE If you **take part in** an activity, you are involved in it with other people. ❑ *He did not take part in the meeting.*

part /pɑːt/ (**parts, parting, parted**)
❸ **1** V-T/V-I If things which are touching **part**, or if they **are parted**, they move away from each other. ❑ *Her lips parted and she smiled.* ❑ *Livy parted the curtains.* **2** V-T If your hair **is parted**, it is combed in two different directions so that there is a straight line from the front of your head to the back. **3** V-I When two people **part**, they leave each other or separate. [FORMAL] ❑ *He is parting from his wife.* • **parting** (**partings**) N-VAR ❑ *After her parting with Jackson she lived in Provence.*
▶ **part with** PHR-VERB If you **part with** something that you would prefer to keep, you give it or sell it to someone else. ❑ *Think carefully before parting with money.*

Thesaurus *part* Also look up:

N.	component, fraction, half, ingredient, piece, portion, section; *(ant.)* entirety, whole ① **1**
	role, share ② **2**
V.	break up, separate, split, tear ③ **3**

partial /ˈpɑːʃəl/ **1** ADJ You use **partial** to refer to something that is true or exists to some extent, but is not complete or total. ❑ *The event was only a partial success.* • **partially** ADV ❑ *I am partially*

P

deaf. **2** ADJ AFTER LINK-V If you are **partial to** something, you like it. ❑ *Loyd is very partial to burger and chips.*

participant /pɑːˈtɪsɪpənt/ (**participants**) N-COUNT The **participants** in an activity are the people who take part in it.

participate /pɑːˈtɪsɪpeɪt/ (**participates, participating, participated**) V-I If you **participate in** an activity, you are involved in it with other people. ❑ *Both boys and girls can enjoy and participate in football.* ● **participation** N-UNCOUNT ❑ *...participation in religious activities.*

participle /ˈpɑːtɪsɪpəl/ (**participles**) N-COUNT In grammar, a **participle** is a form of a verb that can be used in compound tenses of the verb. English verbs have a past participle, which usually ends in '-ed', and a present participle, which ends in '-ing'.

Word Link	*cle ≈ small : article, cubicle, particle*

particle /ˈpɑːtɪkəl/ (**particles**) N-COUNT A **particle of** something is a very small piece or amount of it. ❑ *...food particles.* ❑ *...a particle of hot metal.*

→ see **lightning**

particular /pəˈtɪkjʊlə/ **1** ADJ BEFORE N You use **particular** to emphasize that you are talking about one thing or one kind of thing rather than other similar ones. ❑ *One particular memory still upsets me.* **2** PHRASE You use **in particular** to indicate that what you are saying applies especially to one thing or person. ❑ *Why did he notice her car in particular?* **3** ADJ BEFORE N If a person or thing has a **particular** quality or possession, it belongs only to them. ❑ *Mr. Clifford has particular responsibility for the company's business in Chile.* **4** ADJ BEFORE N You can use **particular** to emphasize that something is greater or more intense than usual. ❑ *We have always paid particular attention to the needs of our older customers.* **5** ADJ Someone who is **particular** chooses or does things very carefully and is not easily satisfied. ❑ *He was very particular about his appearance.*

P

particularly /pəˈtɪkjʊləli/ ADV You use **particularly** to indicate that what you are saying applies especially to one thing or situation. ❑ *Keep your office tidy, particularly your desk.* ❑ *I would particularly like to go to Rio.*

particulars /pəˈtɪkjʊləz/ N-PLURAL The **particulars** of something or someone are facts or details about them which are kept as a record. ❑ *Two officers arrived to take down my particulars.*

partisan /ˌpɑːtɪˈzæn, AM -zən/ (**partisans**) **1** ADJ & N-COUNT Someone who is **partisan** or a **partisan** strongly supports a particular person or cause, often without thinking carefully about what they represent. **2** N-COUNT **Partisans** are people who get together to fight enemy soldiers who are occupying their country.

partition /pɑːˈtɪʃən/ (**partitions, partitioning, partitioned**) **1** V-T & N-COUNT If you **partition** a room, you separate one part of it from another by means of a wall that is referred to as a **partition**. **2** V-T & N-UNCOUNT To **partition** a country means to divide it into two or more independent countries. The **partition** of a country is the act of dividing it like this.

partly /ˈpɑːtli/ ADV You use **partly** to indicate that something is true or exists to some extent, but not completely. ❑ *It's partly my fault.* ❑ *The employee works partly in the office and partly at home.*

partner /ˈpɑːtnə/ (**partners, partnering, partnered**) **1** N-COUNT Your **partner** is the person you are married to or are having a long-term sexual relationship with. **2** V-T & N-COUNT If you **partner** someone in an activity such as a game or dance, you play or dance with them, which means that you are each other's **partner**. **3** N-COUNT The **partners** in a firm or business are the people who share the ownership of it. ❑ *He's a partner in a law firm.* **4** N-COUNT The **partner** of a country or organization is another country or organization with which they have an alliance or agreement. ❑ *...Britain's trading partners.*

partnership /ˈpɑːtnəʃɪp/ (**partnerships**) N-VAR A **partnership** is a relationship in which two or more people or organizations work together as partners. ❑ *Managers must work in partnership with the workers.*

ˌpart-ˈtime ADJ & ADV If someone is a **part-time** worker or has a **part-time** job, they work for only part of each day or week. You can also say that they work **part-time**.

party /ˈpɑːti/ (**parties, partying, partied**) **1** N-COUNT A **party** is a social event at which people enjoy themselves doing things such as eating, drinking, or dancing. ❑ *We threw a huge birthday party.* **2** N-COUNT A political **party** is an organization whose members have similar aims and beliefs, and that tries to get its members elected to government. ❑ *...the Labour party.* **3** N-COUNT A **party of** people is a group of them doing something together, for example travelling. ❑ *...a party of sightseers.* **4** V-I If you **party**, you enjoy yourself doing things with other people such as eating, drinking and dancing. ❑ *They partied all night.* **5** N-COUNT One of the people involved in a legal agreement or dispute can be referred to as a particular **party**. [TECHNICAL] ❑ *Who is the guilty party?* **6** PHRASE If you **are party to** an action or agreement, or **are a party to** it, you are involved in it, and are therefore partly responsible for it. ❑ *They refused to be party to the agreement.*

pass /pɑːs, pæs/ (**passes, passing, passed**) **1** V-T/V-I To **pass** someone or something means to go past them. ❑ *We passed the mountains of Torres Vedras.* ❑ *I stood aside to let her pass.* **2** V-I To **pass** in a particular direction means to move or go in that direction. ❑ *He passed through the doorway.* ❑ *The route passes through St-Paul-sur-Ubaye.* **3** V-T If you **pass** something **through**, **over**, or **round** something else, you move or push it through, over, or round that thing. ❑ *She passed the needle through the cloth.* ❑ *He passed a hand over his eyes.* **4** V-T If you **pass** an object to someone, you pick it up and give it to them. If you **pass** a ball to someone, you hit, kick, or throw it to them. ❑ *Pass the salt, please.* **5** V-T/V-I & PHR-VERB If something **passes from** one person to another, or if it **is passed to** them or **is passed on to** them, the second person is given it. ❑ *His mother's house passed to him after her death.* ❑ *He has asked me to pass on his thanks.* **6** V-I When a period of time **passes**, it happens and ends. ❑ *Minutes passed before we were noticed.* ● **passing** N-SING ❑ *...the passing of time.* **7** V-T If you **pass** time in a particular way, you spend it in that way.

❑ *The children passed the time playing in the streets.* **8** V-T If an amount **passes** a particular total or level, it becomes greater than that total or level. ❑ *The population of the earth has passed five billion.* **9** V-T & N-COUNT If someone or something **passes** a test, they are considered to be of an acceptable standard. To get a **pass** in a test means to pass it. ❑ *Kevin has just passed his driving test.* ❑ *94.3% of candidates obtained a pass.* **10** → See note at **exam** **11** N-COUNT A **pass** is a document that allows you to do something. ❑ *Only cars with a pass may enter this parking lot.* **12** V-T When people in authority **pass** a new law or a proposal, they formally agree to it or approve it. ❑ *They passed a law that will force soccer fans to carry identity cards.* **13** V-I If something **passes** without comment or **passes** unnoticed, nobody comments on it or notices it. ❑ *I cannot allow this nonsense to pass without comment.* **14** N-COUNT A **pass** is a narrow way between two mountains. **15** → see also **passing** **16** to **pass the buck** → see **buck** **17** to **pass sentence** → see **sentence**

▶ **pass around** or **pass round** PHR-VERB If a group of people **pass** something **around**, or **pass** it **round**, they each take it and then give it to the next person. ❑ *The biscuits were passed around.*

▶ **pass away** PHR-VERB You can say that someone **passed away** to mean that they died, if you want to avoid using the word 'die'.

▶ **pass for** PHR-VERB If someone **passes for** or **passes as** a particular person or thing, it means that they are accepted as that person or thing, in spite of not having all the right qualities. ❑ *...a woman passing as a man.* ❑ *I look exactly like that girl. I could pass for her twin.*

▶ **pass off** PHR-VERB If an event **passes off** without any trouble, it ends without any trouble. [BRIT] ❑ *The main demonstration passed off peacefully.*

▶ **pass off as** PHR-VERB If someone **passes** something **off as** another thing, they dishonestly convince people that it is that other thing. ❑ *She passed herself off as a Canadian.*

▶ **pass on** → see **pass** (meaning 5)

▶ **pass out** PHR-VERB If you **pass out**, you faint or collapse.

▶ **pass over** PHR-VERB If someone **is passed over for** a job, they do not get the job and someone younger or less experienced is chosen instead. ❑ *She was repeatedly passed over for promotion.*

▶ **pass round** → see **pass around**

▶ **pass up** PHR-VERB If you **pass up** an opportunity, you do not take advantage of it. ❑ *We can't pass up a chance like this.*

passage /ˈpæsɪdʒ/ (**passages**) **1** N-COUNT A **passage** is a long, narrow space between walls or fences connecting one room or place with another. **2** N-COUNT A **passage** in a book, speech, or piece of music is a section of it. ❑ *He read a passage from Shakespeare.* **3** N-UNCOUNT The **passage** of someone or something is their movement or progress from one place or stage to another. ❑ *...the passage of food through the body.* ❑ *The soldiers were friendly and offered us safe passage in their vehicle.* **4** N-SING **The passage of** time is the fact of it passing.

passageway /ˈpæsɪdʒweɪ/ (**passageways**) N-COUNT A **passageway** is a long, narrow space between walls or fences connecting one room or place with another.

passenger /ˈpæsɪndʒə/ (**passengers**) N-COUNT A **passenger** in a bus, boat, or plane is a person who is travelling in it, but who is not driving it or working on it.
→ see **fly, train**

passing /ˈpɑːsɪŋ, ˈpæs-/ **1** ADJ BEFORE N A **passing** feeling or action does not last long and is not very serious or important. ❑ *He only took a passing interest in the girl.* ❑ *It was just a passing comment.* **2** PHRASE If you mention something **in passing**, you mention it briefly while you are talking or writing about something else. **3** N-SING You can talk about **the passing of** a person or thing to mean the fact of their dying or coming to an end, especially when you are sad about this. ❑ *I was lucky to meet him and am sad at his passing.* ❑ *So we celebrated the passing of a century.* **4** → see also **pass**

passion /ˈpæʃən/ (**passions**) **1** N-UNCOUNT **Passion** is a very strong feeling of sexual attraction for someone. ❑ *I had a passion for a dark-haired boy named James.* **2** N-UNCOUNT **Passion** is a very strong belief in something, to the point where you become excited or emotional about it. ❑ *He spoke with great passion.* **3** N-COUNT If you have a **passion for** something, you like it very much. ❑ *...my passion for buying books.*

Thesaurus	*passion*	Also look up:
N.	affection, desire, love, lust **1**	
	enthusiasm, fondness, interest **3**	

passionate /ˈpæʃənət/ **1** ADJ A **passionate** person has very strong feelings about something. ❑ *I'm a passionate believer in public art.* ❑ *He made a passionate 16-minute speech.* ● **passionately** ADV ❑ *I am passionately opposed to the idea.* **2** ADJ A **passionate** person has strong romantic or sexual feelings and expresses them in their behaviour. ● **passionately** ADV ❑ *He was passionately in love with her.*

passive /ˈpæsɪv/ **1** ADJ If you describe someone as **passive**, you mean they do not take action but instead let things happen to them; used showing disapproval. ● **passively** ADV ❑ *He sits passively in front of the TV.* **2** N-SING In grammar, **the passive** is formed using 'be' and the past participle of a verb. The subject of a passive clause does not perform the action expressed by the verb but is affected by it. For example, in 'He's been murdered', the verb is in the passive.

Passover /ˈpɑːsəʊvə, ˈpæs-/ N-UNCOUNT **Passover** is a Jewish festival beginning in March or April and lasting for seven or eight days.

passport /ˈpɑːspɔːt, ˈpæs-/ (**passports**) **1** N-COUNT Your **passport** is an official document which you need to show when you enter or leave a country. **2** N-SING If you say that something is a **passport to** something such as success, you mean that it makes that thing possible. ❑ *They say that this qualification is a passport to a higher salary and a wider choice of jobs.*

password /ˈpɑːswɜːd, ˈpæs-/ (**passwords**) N-COUNT A **password** is a secret word or phrase that enables you to enter a place or use a computer system.
→ see **mountain, Internet**

past /pɑːst, pæst/ (**pasts**) **1** N-SING **The past**

is the period of time before the present, and the things that happened in that period. ❑ *This is what has happened in the past.* **2** ADJ BEFORE N **Past** events and things happened or existed before the present time. ❑ *...details of his past activities.* **3** N-COUNT **Your past** consists of all the things that you have done or that have happened to you. ❑ *Harry then finds out about her past.* ❑ *...Germany's recent past.* **4** ADJ BEFORE N You use **past** to talk about a period of time that has just finished. ❑ *...the events of the past few days.* ❑ *I have been homeless for the past year.* **5** ADJ BEFORE N The **past tense** of a verb is used to refer to things that happened or existed before the time when you are speaking or writing. For regular verbs, the past tense is the '-ed' form, for example 'They walked back to the car'. **6** PREP & ADV You use **past** when you are stating the time, when it is thirty minutes or less after a particular hour. ❑ *It's ten past eleven.* ❑ *At a quarter past seven, we left the hotel.* ❑ *I have my lunch at half past.* **7** PREP & ADV If you **go past** someone or something, you go near them and keep moving, so that they are then behind you. ❑ *I ran past him.* ❑ *An ambulance drove past.* **8** PREP If something is **past** a place, it is on the other side of it. ❑ *The farm was just past the next village.*
→ see **history**

pasta

pasta /ˈpæstə, AM ˈpɑːstə/ N-UNCOUNT **Pasta** is a type of food made from a mixture of flour, eggs, and water that is formed into different shapes. Spaghetti and macaroni are types of pasta.

paste /peɪst/ (**pastes, pasting, pasted**) **1** N-VAR **Paste** is a soft, wet, sticky mixture of a substance, which can be spread easily. ❑ *...wallpaper paste.* ❑ *...tomato paste.* **2** V-T If you **paste** something on a surface, you stick it to the surface with glue or adhesive paste. ❑ *The children were pasting gold stars on a chart.*

P

pastel /ˈpæstəl, AM pæˈstel/ (**pastels**) ADJ & N-COUNT **Pastel** colours are pale rather than dark or bright. ❑ *...delicate pastel shades.* ❑ *The room is decorated in pastels.*
→ see **blog**

pastime /ˈpɑːstaɪm, ˈpæs-/ (**pastimes**) N-COUNT A **pastime** is something that you enjoy doing in your spare time. ❑ *His favourite pastime is golf.*

pastoral /ˈpɑːstərəl, ˈpæst-/ **1** ADJ BEFORE N The **pastoral** activities of a religious leader relate to the general needs of people, rather than just their religious needs. ❑ *...the pastoral care of the sick.* **2** ADJ BEFORE N **Pastoral** means characteristic of peaceful country life. ❑ *...the pastoral beauty of a park.*

pastry /ˈpeɪstri/ (**pastries**) **1** N-UNCOUNT **Pastry** is a food made of flour, fat, and water that is used for making pies and flans. **2** N-COUNT A **pastry** is a small cake made with pastry.

pasture /ˈpɑːstʃə, ˈpæs-/ (**pastures**) N-VAR **Pasture** is land that has grass growing on it and that is used for farm animals to graze on.
→ see **barn**

pat /pæt/ (**pats, patting, patted**) V-T & N-COUNT If you **pat** something or someone, or if you **give** them a **pat**, you tap them lightly with your hand held flat, usually as a sign of encouragement, affection, or friendship. ❑ *'Don't you worry,' she said, patting me on the knee.* ❑ *He gave her a pat on the shoulder.*

patch /pætʃ/ (**patches, patching, patched**) **1** N-COUNT A **patch** on a surface is a part of it which is different in appearance from the area around it. ❑ *...the bald patch on the top of his head.* ❑ *...two damp patches on the carpet.* **2** N-COUNT A **patch of** land is a small area of land, often one used for growing a particular crop. ❑ *...a patch of wild cornflowers.* ❑ *...a vegetable patch.* **3** N-COUNT A **patch** is a piece of material used to cover a hole in something. **4** V-T If you **patch** something that has a hole in it, you mend it by fixing something over the hole. ❑ *Walker patched the barn roof.* **5** PHRASE If you go through **a bad patch** or **a rough patch**, you have a lot of problems for a time.
▶ **patch up** **1** PHR-VERB If you **patch up** an argument or relationship, you try to be friendly again and not to argue any more. ❑ *They have gone on holiday to try to patch up their marriage.* **2** PHR-VERB If you **patch up** something which is damaged, you mend it.

patchwork /ˈpætʃwɜːk/ ADJ BEFORE N A **patchwork** quilt has been made by sewing small pieces of material together.

patchy /ˈpætʃi/ (**patchier, patchiest**) **1** ADJ A **patchy** substance or colour is not spread evenly, but is scattered around in small quantities. ❑ *...patchy fog.* **2** ADJ If something is **patchy**, it is not completely reliable or satisfactory because it is not always good. ❑ *The evidence is patchy.*

pâté /ˈpæteɪ, AM pɑːˈteɪ/ (**pâtés**) N-VAR **Pâté** is a mixture of meat, fish, or vegetables with various flavourings, which is mixed into a paste and eaten cold.

patent /ˈpeɪtənt, AM ˈpæt-/ (**patents, patenting, patented**)

The pronunciation /ˈpætənt/ is also used for meanings 1 and 2 in British English.

1 N-COUNT A **patent** is an official right to be the only person or company to make and sell a new product. ❑ *P&G applied for a patent on its cookies.* **2** V-T If you **patent** something, you obtain a patent for it. ❑ *The invention has been patented by the university.* **3** ADJ You use **patent** to emphasize that the nature or existence of something, especially something bad, is obvious. ❑ *This was patent nonsense.* ● **patently** ADV ❑ *He made his anger patently obvious.*

paternal /pəˈtɜːnəl/ ADJ BEFORE N **Paternal** is used to describe feelings or actions which are typical of those of a father towards his child. ❑ *...selfless paternal love.*

path /pɑːθ, pæθ/ (**paths**) **1** N-COUNT A **path** is a strip of ground that people walk along. ❑ *...the garden path.* **2** N-COUNT Your **path** is the space ahead of you as you move along. ❑ *The reporters blocked his path.* **3** N-COUNT The **path of** something is the line which it moves along in a particular direction. ❑ *Without looking, he stepped into the path of the car.* **4** N-COUNT A **path** that you take is a particular course of action or way of doing something. ❑ *...a step on the path of peace.*
→ see **golf**

pathetic /pəˈθetɪk/ **1** ADJ If you describe a person or animal as **pathetic**, you mean that they are sad and weak or helpless, and they make you feel very sorry for them. ❑ *...a pathetic little three-legged dog.* ● **pathetically** ADV ❑ *She was pathetically thin.* **2** ADJ If you describe someone or something as **pathetic**, you mean that they make you feel impatient or angry, often because they are very bad or weak. ❑ *What pathetic excuses!* ● **pathetically** ADV ❑ *There's a pathetically low fine of 25 euros for dropping litter.*

pathological /ˌpæθəˈlɒdʒɪkəl/ **1** ADJ You describe a person as **pathological** when they behave in an extreme and unacceptable way, and have very powerful feelings which they cannot control. ❑ *He experiences almost pathological jealousy.* **2** ADJ **Pathological** means relating to pathology. ❑ *Students are trained to use pathological tests.* [TECHNICAL]

pathology /pəˈθɒlədʒi/ N-UNCOUNT **Pathology** is the study of the way diseases and illnesses develop, and examining dead bodies in order to find out the cause of death. [TECHNICAL] ● **pathologist** (**pathologists**) N-COUNT ❑ *The pathologist admitted having made a mistake.*

pathos /ˈpeɪθɒs/ N-UNCOUNT **Pathos** is a quality in a situation that makes people feel sadness and pity. ❑ *The show has a sense of wonder and a degree of pathos.*

pathway /ˈpɑːθweɪ, ˈpæθ-/ (**pathways**) N-COUNT A **pathway** is the same as a **path**.

patience /ˈpeɪʃəns/ N-UNCOUNT If you **have patience**, you are able to stay calm and not get annoyed, for example when something takes a long time. ❑ *He doesn't have the patience to wait.*

patient /ˈpeɪʃənt/ (**patients**) **1** N-COUNT A **patient** is a person who is receiving treatment from a doctor or who is registered with a doctor. ❑ *I was her last patient that day.* **2** ADJ If you are **patient**, you stay calm and do not get annoyed, for example when something takes a long time. ❑ *I must be patient and wait.* ● **patiently** ADV ❑ *She waited patiently for Frances to finish talking.*
→ see **diagnosis, illness**

patio /ˈpætiəʊ/ (**patios**) N-COUNT A **patio** is a paved area in a garden, where people can sit to eat or relax. ❑ *We had lunch on the patio.*

patriot /ˈpætriət, ˈpeɪt-/ (**patriots**) N-COUNT A **patriot** is someone who loves their country.

Word Link	***ism** ≈ action or state : communism, optimism, patriotism*

patriotic /ˌpætriˈɒtɪk, ˌpeɪt-/ ADJ Someone who is **patriotic** loves their country and feels very loyal towards it. ● **patriotism** /ˈpætriətɪzəm, ˈpeɪt-/ N-UNCOUNT ❑ *He had joined the army out of a sense of patriotism.*

patrol /pəˈtrəʊl/ (**patrols, patrolling, patrolled**) **1** V-T & N-VAR When soldiers, police, or guards **patrol** an area or building, or when they are doing a **patrol** of it or **are on patrol**, they move around it in order to make sure that there is no trouble. ❑ *100 police were on patrol.* **2** N-COUNT A **patrol** is a group of soldiers or vehicles that are patrolling an area. ❑ *A nail bomb was thrown at an army patrol.*

patron /ˈpeɪtrən/ (**patrons**) **1** N-COUNT A **patron** is a person who supports and gives money to artists, writers, or musicians. ❑ *...a patron of modern art.* **2** N-COUNT The **patron of** a charity, group, or campaign is an important person who allows his or her name to be connected with it for publicity. ❑ *The duchess is a patron of the charity.* **3** N-COUNT The **patrons of** a place such as a pub or a hotel are its customers. ❑ *There is free parking for patrons.*

patronage /ˈpætrənɪdʒ, ˈpeɪt-/ N-UNCOUNT **Patronage** is the support and money given by someone to a person or a group such as a charity. ❑ *...government patronage of the arts.*

patronize [BRIT also **patronise**] /ˈpætrənaɪz, AM ˈpeɪt-/ (**patronizes, patronizing, patronized**) V-T If someone **patronizes** you, they speak or behave towards you in a way which seems friendly, but which shows that they think they are superior to you. ❑ *Don't you patronize me!* ● **patronizing** ADJ ❑ *He has a patronising attitude to the homeless.*

patter /ˈpætə/ (**patters, pattering, pattered**) V-I & N-SING If something **patters** on a surface, it hits it quickly several times, making quiet tapping sounds. You can refer to these sounds as a **patter**. ❑ *Rain pattered gently outside.* ❑ *Hyde could hear the patter of snow against his sleeve.*

pattern /ˈpætən/ (**patterns**) **1** N-COUNT A **pattern** is a particular way in which something is usually or repeatedly done. ❑ *His sleeping pattern was bad.* **2** N-COUNT A **pattern** is a design of lines or shapes repeated at regular intervals. ❑ *...a three-dimensional pattern of coloured dots.* **3** N-COUNT A **pattern** is a diagram or shape that you can use as a guide when you are making something such as a model or a piece of clothing.
→ see Picture Dictionary: **pattern**
→ see **quilt**

Word Partnership	Use *pattern* with:
ADJ.	**familiar** pattern, **normal** pattern, **typical** pattern **1** **different** pattern, **same** pattern, **similar** pattern **1** **2**
V.	**change a** pattern, **fit a** pattern, **see a** pattern **1** **follow a** pattern **1**-**3**

patterned /ˈpætənd/ ADJ Something that is **patterned** is covered with a pattern or design. ❑ *...a patterned sweater.*

pause /pɔːz/ (**pauses, pausing, paused**) **1** V-I If you **pause** while you are speaking or doing something, you stop for a short time and then continue. ❑ *The crowd paused, wondering what to do next.* **2** N-COUNT A **pause** is a short period when something stops before it continues again. ❑ *There was a pause while she set down the plates.*

Word Partnership	Use *pause* with:
ADJ.	**awkward** pause, **brief** pause, **long** pause, **short** pause, **slight** pause **2**

pave /peɪv/ (**paves, paving, paved**) **1** V-T When an area of ground **has been paved**, it has been covered with blocks of stone or concrete. **2** PHRASE If one thing **paves the way for** another, it creates a situation in which the other thing is able to happen. ❑ *A peace agreement last year paved the way for this week's elections.*

pavement /ˈpeɪvmənt/ (**pavements**)

P

Picture Dictionary **patterns**

1 N-COUNT In British English, a **pavement** is a path with a hard surface by the side of a road. The usual American word is **sidewalk**. 2 N-COUNT The **pavement** is the hard surface of a road. [AM] ❑ *The car spun on the icy pavement.*

pavilion /pəˈvɪliən/ (**pavilions**) 1 N-COUNT A **pavilion** is a building on the edge of a sports field where players can change their clothes and wash. [BRIT] 2 N-COUNT A **pavilion** is a large temporary structure such as a tent, which is used at outdoor public events.

paw /pɔː/ (**paws, pawing, pawed**) 1 N-COUNT The **paws** of an animal such as a cat, dog, or bear are its feet. 2 V-T If an animal **paws** something, it draws its paw or hoof over it.

pawn /pɔːn/ (**pawns, pawning, pawned**) 1 V-T If you **pawn** something that you own, you leave it with a pawnbroker, who gives you money for it and who can sell it if you do not pay back the money before a certain time. 2 N-COUNT In chess, a **pawn** is the smallest and least valuable playing piece. 3 N-COUNT If you say that someone is using you as a **pawn**, you mean that they are using you for their own advantage. ❑ *It is easy for children to become pawns in the battle between parents.*
→ see **chess**

pawnbroker /ˈpɔːnbrəʊkə/ (**pawnbrokers**) N-COUNT A **pawnbroker** is a person who will lend you money if you give them something that you own. The pawnbroker can sell that thing if you do not pay back the money before a certain time.

pay /peɪ/ (**pays, paying, paid**) 1 V-T/V-I When you **pay** an amount of money **to** someone, you give it to them because you are buying something from them or because you owe it to them. When you **pay** something such as a bill or a debt, you pay the amount that you owe. ❑ *Richer people may have to pay more in taxes.* ❑ *All you pay for is breakfast and dinner.* ❑ *We paid £35 for each ticket.* ❑ *You can pay by credit card.* 2 V-T & N-UNCOUNT When you are **paid**, or when you receive your **pay**, you get your wages or salary from your employer. ❑ *I get paid monthly.* ❑ *They have not had a pay rise for two years.*

Usage

When used as a noun, **pay** is a general word which you can use to refer to the money you get from your employer for doing your job. Professional people and office workers receive a **salary**, which is paid monthly. However, when talking about someone's salary, you usually give the annual figure. ❑ *I'm paid a salary of £15,000 a year.* Manual workers are paid **wages**, or **a wage**. The plural is more common than the singular, especially when you are talking about the actual cash that someone receives. ❑ *Every week he handed all his wages to his wife.* Wages are usually paid, and quoted, as an hourly or a weekly sum. ❑ *...a starting wage of five dollars an hour.* Your **income** consists of all the money you receive from all sources, including your pay.

3 V-T/V-I If a course of action **pays**, or **pays** you, it results in some advantage or benefit for you. ❑ *It pays to keep your body and mind in good shape.* 4 V-I If you **pay for** something that you do or have, you suffer as a result. ❑ *You will pay for this. Murder for murder, blood for blood.* 5 V-T You use **pay** with some nouns, for example in the expressions **pay a visit** and **pay attention**, to indicate that something is given or done. ❑ *He felt a bump, but paid no attention to it.* 6 PHRASE If you **pay** your **way**, you have or earn enough money to pay for what you need, without needing other people to give or lend you money. ❑ *I went to college anyway, paying my own way.* 7 → see also **paid**

▶ **pay back** PHR-VERB If you **pay back** money that you have borrowed from someone, you give them an equal amount at a later time.

▶ **pay off** 1 PHR-VERB If you **pay off** a debt, you give someone all the money that you owe them. 2 PHR-VERB If an action **pays off**, it is successful. ❑ *All their hard work has finally paid off.* 3 → see also **payoff**

▶ **pay out** PHR-VERB If you **pay out** money, usually a large amount, you spend it on something. ❑ *Football clubs can pay out millions of pounds for players.*

P

▶ **pay up** PHR-VERB If you **pay up**, you give someone the money that you owe them.

payable /ˈpeɪəbəl/ **1** ADJ If an amount of money is **payable**, it has to be paid or it can be paid. ❑ *Tax was not payable on goods for export.* **2** ADJ If a cheque is made **payable to** you, it has your name written on it to indicate that you are the person who will receive the money.

payee /ˌpeɪˈiː/ (**payees**) N-COUNT The **payee** of a cheque or similar document is the person who should receive the money. [FORMAL]

payer /ˈpeɪə/ (**payers**) N-COUNT You can refer to someone as a **payer** if they pay a particular kind of bill or fee. For example, a tax **payer** is someone who pays taxes.

payment /ˈpeɪmənt/ (**payments**) **1** N-UNCOUNT **Payment** is the act of paying money to someone or of being paid. ❑ *Players now expect payment for interviews.* **2** N-COUNT A **payment** is an amount of money that is paid to someone. ❑ *We agreed to make 12 monthly payments.*

Word Partnership Use *payment* with:

V.	**accept** payment, **make a** payment, **receive** payment **1**
ADJ.	**late** payment, **minimum** payment, **monthly** payment **1**
N.	payment **in cash**, payment **by cheque**, **mortgage** payment **1** payment **date** **1** **2** payment **method**, payment **plan** **2**

payoff /ˈpeɪɒf/ (**payoffs**) **1** N-COUNT A **payoff** is a payment which is made to someone, often secretly or illegally, so that they will not cause trouble. **2** N-COUNT A **payoff** is an advantage or benefit that results from an action.

payroll /ˈpeɪrəʊl/ (**payrolls**) N-COUNT The people on the **payroll** of a company or an organization are the people who work for it and are paid by it.

PC /ˌpiː ˈsiː/ (**PCs**) **1** N-COUNT & N-TITLE In Britain, a **PC** is a male police officer of the lowest rank. **PC** is an abbreviation for 'police constable'. **2** N-COUNT A **PC** is a computer that is used by one person in a small business, at school, or at home. **PC** is an abbreviation for 'personal computer'. [COMPUTING] **3** ADJ If you say that someone is **PC**, you mean that they are extremely careful not to offend or upset any group of people in society. **PC** is an abbreviation for 'politically correct'.

PDA /ˌpiː diː ˈeɪ/ (**PDAs**) N-COUNT A **PDA** is a hand-held computer, used mainly for storing and accessing personal information such as addresses, telephone numbers, and memos. PDA is an abbreviation for 'personal digital assistant'.

pea /piː/ (**peas**) N-COUNT **Peas** are small, round, green seeds eaten as a vegetable.

peace /piːs/ **1** N-UNCOUNT **Peace** is a state of undisturbed quiet and calm. ❑ *I'll leave you in peace now.* **2** N-UNCOUNT When there is **peace** in a country, it is not involved in a war. ❑ *Then they made a wish for world peace.* **3** N-UNCOUNT & PHRASE If there is **peace** among a group of people, or if they live or work **in peace with** each other, they live or work together without fighting or quarrelling. ❑ *We want our children to live happily together in peace and harmony.*

peaceful /ˈpiːsfʊl/ **1** ADJ A **peaceful** place or time is quiet, calm, and undisturbed. ❑ *Mornings are usually quiet and peaceful in Hueytown.* ● **peacefully** ADV ❑ *The night passed peacefully.* **2** ADJ Someone who **feels** or **looks peaceful** feels or looks calm and free from worry. ● **peacefully** ADV ❑ *Gaston was sleeping peacefully.* **3** ADJ **Peaceful** means not involving violence or conflict. ❑ *...a peaceful demonstration.* ● **peacefully** ADV ❑ *The protest passed off peacefully.*

peach /piːtʃ/ (**peaches**) **1** N-COUNT A **peach** is a soft, round, juicy fruit with sweet yellow flesh and pinky-yellow skin. **2** ADJ & N-VAR Something that is **peach** is pale pinky-orange in colour. ❑ *...a peach silk blouse.* ❑ *The bedroom is peach and green.*

peak /piːk/ (**peaks, peaking, peaked**) **1** N-COUNT The **peak** of a process or activity is the point at which it is at its strongest, most successful, or most fully developed. ❑ *...the peak of the morning rush hour.* **2** ADJ BEFORE N The **peak** level or value of something is its highest level or value. ❑ *...the traffic at peak times.* **3** V-I When someone or something **peaks**, they reach their highest value or highest level of success. ❑ *Temperatures peaked at over thirty degrees Celsius.* **4** N-COUNT A **peak** is a mountain, or the top of a mountain. ❑ *...snow-covered peaks.* **5** N-COUNT The **peak** of a cap is the part at the front that sticks out above your eyes.
→ see **mountain**

peal /piːl/ (**peals, pealing, pealed**) **1** V-I & N-COUNT When bells **peal**, or when there is a **peal of** bells, they ring one after the other, making a musical sound. ❑ *Church bells pealed at midnight.* **2** N-COUNT A **peal of** laughter or thunder consists of a long loud series of sounds. [LITERARY]

peanut /ˈpiːnʌt/ (**peanuts**) N-COUNT **Peanuts** are small nuts often eaten as a snack.
→ see Word Web: **peanut**

pear /peə/ (**pears**) N-COUNT A **pear** is a juicy fruit which is narrow at the top and wider at the bottom. It has white flesh and green or yellow skin.
→ see **fruit**

pearl /pɜːl/ (**pearls**) N-COUNT A **pearl** is a hard, shiny, white ball-shaped object which grows inside the shell of an oyster. Pearls are used for making jewellery. ❑ *...a string of pearls.* ❑ *...pearl earrings.*

peasant /ˈpezənt/ (**peasants**) N-COUNT People refer to the small farmers or farm labourers in a poor country as **peasants**.

peat /piːt/ N-UNCOUNT **Peat** is dark decaying plant material which is found in some cool wet regions. It can be burned as a fuel or used as compost.

pebble /ˈpebəl/ (**pebbles**) N-COUNT A **pebble** is a small stone.
→ see **beach**

peck /pek/ (**pecks, pecking, pecked**) **1** V-T/V-I If a bird **pecks** something, it moves its beak forward quickly and bites at it. ❑ *A swan was pecking at a piece of bread.* ❑ *Chickens pecked in the dust.* **2** V-T & N-COUNT If you **peck** someone **on** the cheek, or if you give them a **peck on** the cheek, you give them a quick light kiss.

peculiar /pɪˈkjuːliə/ **1** ADJ If you describe

P

Word Web peanut

The **peanut** is not really a **nut**. It is a legume and grows under the ground. Peanuts originated in South America about 3,500 years ago. Explorers took them to Africa. Later, African slaves introduced the peanut into North America. Only poor people ate them at first. But they were a popular **snack** by 1900. You could buy **roasted** peanuts on city streets and at baseball games and circuses. Some scientists believe that roasted peanuts cause more **allergic** reactions than boiled peanuts. George Washington Carver, an African-American scientist, found 325 different uses for peanuts—including peanut butter.

someone or something as **peculiar**, you think that they are strange or unusual, often in an unpleasant way. ❑ *Rachel thought it tasted peculiar.* ● **peculiarly** ADV ❑ *His face had become peculiarly grey.* **2** ADJ AFTER LINK-V If something is **peculiar to** a particular thing, person, or situation, it belongs or relates only to that thing, person, or situation. ❑ *The violence is not peculiar to certain cities. And no city is immune.* ● **peculiarly** ADV ❑ *Motor racing is a peculiarly British skill.*

peculiarity /pɪˌkjuːliˈærɪti/ (**peculiarities**) **1** N-COUNT A **peculiarity** is a characteristic or quality which belongs or relates only to one person or thing. ❑ *The peculiarity of these gardens is that only evergreen trees have been used.* **2** N-COUNT A **peculiarity** that someone or something has is something strange or unusual. ❑ *Did his mother notice any peculiarity in his behaviour?*

Word Link *ped ≈ foot : pedal, pedestal, pedestrian*

pedal /ˈpedəl/ (**pedals, pedalling, pedalled** or [AM] **pedaling, pedaled**) **1** N-COUNT The **pedals** on a bicycle are the two parts that you push with your feet in order to make the bicycle move. **2** V-T/V-I When you **pedal** a bicycle, you push the pedals around with your feet to make it move. ❑ *I pedalled to school.* **3** N-COUNT A **pedal** in a car or on a machine is a lever that you press with your foot in order to control the car or machine. ❑ *...the brake pedal.*
→ see **bicycle**

P

peddle /ˈpedəl/ (**peddles, peddling, peddled**) **1** V-T Someone who **peddles** things goes from place to place trying to sell them. [DATED] **2** V-T Someone who **peddles** drugs sells them illegally. ● **peddling** N-UNCOUNT ❑ *...the war against drug peddling.* **3** V-T If someone **peddles** an idea or piece of information, they try to get people to accept it; used showing disapproval. ❑ *They both continue to peddle different stories about the negotiations.*

pedestal /ˈpedɪstəl/ (**pedestals**) N-COUNT A **pedestal** is the base on which a statue or a column stands.

Word Link *an, ian ≈ one of, relating to : Christian, European, pedestrian*

pedestrian /pɪˈdestriən/ (**pedestrians**) N-COUNT A **pedestrian** is a person who is walking, especially in a town. ❑ *...streets crowded with pedestrians.*

pediatrician → see **paediatrician**

Word Link *iatr ≈ healing : geriatric, pediatrics, psychiatrist*

pediatrics → see **paediatrics**

pedigree /ˈpedɪgriː/ (**pedigrees**) **1** N-COUNT If a dog, cat, or other animal has a **pedigree**, its ancestors are known and recorded. **2** ADJ A **pedigree** animal is descended from animals which have all been of a particular breed, and is therefore considered to be of good quality. **3** N-COUNT Someone's **pedigree** is their background or ancestry. ❑ *She's certainly got the pedigree and the brains.*

peek

peek /piːk/ (**peeks, peeking, peeked**) V-I & N-COUNT If you **peek at** something or someone, or if you have a **peek at** them, you have a quick look at them, often secretly. [INFORMAL] ❑ *She had twice peeked at him through the fence.*

peel /piːl/ (**peels, peeling, peeled**) **1** N-VAR The **peel** of a fruit such as a lemon or apple is its skin. In American English, you can also refer to a **peel**. ❑ *...grated lemon peel.* ❑ *...a banana peel.* **2** V-T When you **peel** fruit or vegetables, you remove their skins. **3** V-T/V-I & PHR-VERB If you **peel** something **off** a surface, or if it **peels** or **peels off**, it comes away from the surface. ❑ *It took two days to peel off the labels.* ❑ *Paint was peeling off the walls.* ❑ *The acid makes the skin peel slightly.*
→ see **cut**

peep /piːp/ (**peeps, peeping, peeped**) **1** V-I & N-SING If you **peep at** something, or if you take a **peep at** it, you have a quick look at it, often secretly. ❑ *She peeped to see if he had noticed her.* ❑ *'Fourteen minutes,' Chris said, taking a peep at his watch.* **2** V-I If something **peeps out** from somewhere, a small part of it is visible. ❑ *Here and there a face peeped out from a doorway.*

peer /pɪə/ (**peers, peering, peered**) **1** V-I If you **peer at** something, you look at it very hard, usually because it is difficult to see clearly. ❑ *I was peering at a computer print-out.* ❑ *The customs official peered into the driver's window.* **2** N-COUNT A **peer** is a member of the group of people in society who have titles and high social rank. **3** N-PLURAL Your **peers** are people of the same age or status as you. ❑ *Children need to be with their peers.*

peerage /ˈpɪərɪdʒ/ (**peerages**) **1** N-COUNT If someone has a **peerage**, they have the rank of a peer. **2** N-SING The peers of a country are referred to as **the peerage**.

'peer ˌpressure N-UNCOUNT If someone does something because of **peer pressure**, they do it because other people in their social group do it. ❑ *Andy says he felt a sort of peer pressure to find a wife and settle down.*

peg /peg/ (**pegs, pegging, pegged**) 1 N-COUNT A **peg** is a small hook or knob on a wall or door which is used for hanging things on. 2 N-COUNT A **peg** is a small device which you use to fasten clothes to a washing line. [BRIT] 3 N-COUNT A tent **peg** is a small piece of wood or metal that is hammered into the ground, keeping a section of the tent in place. 4 V-T If the price of something **is pegged at** a particular level, it is fixed at that level. You can also say that one country's currency **is pegged to** another country's when the value of the first currency is fixed in relation to the second. [JOURNALISM] ❑ *The peso was then strictly pegged to the dollar.*

pellet /'pelɪt/ (**pellets**) N-COUNT A **pellet** is a small ball of paper, mud, lead, or other material.

pelt /pelt/ (**pelts, pelting, pelted**) 1 N-COUNT The **pelt** of an animal is its skin which can be used to make clothing or rugs. 2 V-T If you **pelt** someone **with** things, you throw things at them. ❑ *Crowds pelted police cars with stones.* 3 V-I If the rain **is pelting down**, it is raining very hard. [INFORMAL] ❑ *It absolutely pelted down all day.* ❑ *We drove through pelting rain.*

pelvic /'pelvɪk/ ADJ BEFORE N **Pelvic** means near or relating to your pelvis.

pelvis /'pelvɪs/ (**pelvises**) N-COUNT Your **pelvis** is the wide curved group of bones at the level of your hips.

pen /pen/ (**pens, penning, penned**) 1 N-COUNT A **pen** is a writing instrument, which you use to write in ink. 2 V-T If someone **pens** a letter, article, or book, they write it. ❑ *She penned a memo to his secretary.* 3 N-COUNT A **pen** is a small fenced area in which farm animals are kept for a short time. 4 V-T If people or animals **are penned** somewhere, they have to remain in a very small area. ❑ *I stayed in my room, penned up like a prisoner.*
→ see **office**

penal /'piːnəl/ ADJ BEFORE N **Penal** means relating to the punishment of criminals. ❑ *...the British penal system.*

penalize [BRIT also **penalise**] /'piːnəlaɪz/ (**penalizes, penalizing, penalized**) V-T If someone **is penalized** for something, they are made to suffer some disadvantage because of it. ❑ *Some of the players may break the rules and be penalized.*

penalty /'penəlti/ (**penalties**) 1 N-COUNT A **penalty** is a punishment for doing something which is against a law or rule. ❑ *The death penalty for murder was abolished here in 1969.* 2 N-COUNT In sports such as football and hockey, a **penalty** is a free kick or hit at a goal, which is given to the attacking team if the defending team commit a foul near their own goal.

pence /pens/ → see **penny**

penchant /'pɒnʃɒn, 'pentʃənt/ N-SING If someone has a **penchant for** something, they have a special liking for it or a tendency to do it. [FORMAL] ❑ *I have developed a penchant for designer clothes.*

pencil /'pensəl/ (**pencils, pencilling, pencilled**) 1 N-COUNT A **pencil** is a thin wooden rod with graphite down the centre which is used for writing or drawing. 2 V-T If you **pencil** a letter or a note, you write it using a pencil. ❑ *He pencilled a note to Joseph Daniels.*
→ see **blog, office**

Word Link	*pend ≈ hanging : depend, pendant, pending*

pendant /'pendənt/ (**pendants**) N-COUNT A **pendant** is an ornament on a chain that you wear round your neck.
→ see **jewellery**

pending /'pendɪŋ/ 1 ADJ If something such as a legal procedure is **pending**, it is waiting to be dealt with or settled. [FORMAL] ❑ *As the court cases are pending we cannot say any more.* 2 PREP If something is done **pending** a future event, it is done until that event happens. ❑ *He was later released pending further enquiries.*

pendulum /'pendʒʊləm/ (**pendulums**) 1 N-COUNT The **pendulum** of a clock is a rod with a weight at the end which swings from side to side in order to make the clock keep regular time. 2 N-SING People use the word **pendulum** as a way of talking about regular changes in a situation or in people's opinions. ❑ *The political pendulum is starting to swing away from the Labour Party.*

penetrate /'penɪtreɪt/ (**penetrates, penetrating, penetrated**) 1 V-T If someone or something **penetrates** a physical object or an area, they succeed in getting into it or passing through it. ❑ *His men were ordered to shoot anyone trying to penetrate the area.* ● **penetration** N-UNCOUNT ❑ *This toothbrush allows greater penetration into the gaps between your teeth.* 2 V-T If someone **penetrates** an organization or a profession, they succeed in entering it although it is difficult to do so. ❑ *Smaller Scottish companies are not managing to penetrate the US business world.* 3 V-T If someone **penetrates** an enemy group, they succeed in joining it in order to get information or cause trouble. ● **penetration** N-UNCOUNT ❑ *...the successful penetration by the KGB of the French intelligence service.*

penetrating /'penɪtreɪtɪŋ/ 1 ADJ A **penetrating** sound is loud and clear. 2 ADJ If someone gives you a **penetrating** look, you feel that they know what you are thinking. 3 ADJ Someone who has a **penetrating** mind understands and recognizes things quickly and thoroughly. ❑ *He never stops asking penetrating questions.*

penguin

penguin /'peŋgwɪn/ (**penguins**) N-COUNT A **penguin** is a black and white sea bird found mainly in the South Pole. Penguins cannot fly.

peninsula /pə'nɪnsjʊlə/ (**peninsulas**) N-COUNT A **peninsula** is a long narrow piece of land that is joined at one part to the mainland and is almost completely surrounded by water.
→ see **land**

penis /'piːnɪs/ (**penises**) N-COUNT A man's **penis** is the part of his body that he uses when urinating

P

and when having sex.

penniless /ˈpeniləs/ ADJ Someone who is **penniless** has not got any money.

penny /ˈpeni/ (**pennies, pence**)

The form **pence** is used for the plural of meaning 1.

1 N-COUNT In Britain, a **penny** is a coin or an amount which is worth one hundredth of a pound. 2 N-COUNT In America, a **penny** is a coin or an amount that is worth one cent. [INFORMAL]

Usage

Pennies usually refers to a number of individual coins. ❑ *He took two pennies out of his pocket.* You use **pence** or **p** when you are talking about a sum of money. ❑ *It only cost fifty pence.* ❑ *Admission for children is 50p.*

pension /ˈpenʃən/ (**pensions**) N-COUNT A **pension** is a sum of money which a retired, widowed, or disabled person regularly receives from the state or from a former employer.

pensioner /ˈpenʃənə/ (**pensioners**) N-COUNT A **pensioner** is a person who receives a pension.

Pentagon /ˈpentəgən, AM -gɑːn/ N-PROPER **The Pentagon** is the main building of the US Defense Department in Washington.

penthouse /ˈpenthaʊs/ (**penthouses**) N-COUNT A **penthouse** is a luxurious flat or set of rooms at the top of a tall building.

pent-up /ˌpent ˈʌp/ ADJ **Pent-up** emotions have been held back and not expressed. ❑ *He still felt a lot of pent-up anger.*

Word Link *ultim ≈ end, last : penultimate, ultimate, ultimatum*

penultimate /peˈnʌltɪmət/ ADJ The **penultimate** thing in a series is the one before the last.

P

people /ˈpiːpəl/ (**peoples, peopled**)

In meaning 1, **people** is normally used as the plural of **person**, instead of 'persons'.

1 N-PLURAL **People** are men, women, and children. ❑ *Millions of people lost their homes.* ❑ *...the people of Angola.* 2 N-PLURAL **The people** is sometimes used to refer to ordinary men and women, in contrast to the upper classes or the government. ❑ *...a lack of understanding between the people and their leadership.* 3 N-COUNT A **people** consists of all the men, women, and children of a particular country or race. ❑ *...the native peoples of Central and South America.* 4 V-T PASSIVE If a place **is peopled by** a particular group of people, those people live there.

ˈpeople ˌsmuggling or **people trafficking** N-UNCOUNT **People smuggling** or **people trafficking** is the practice of bringing immigrants into a country illegally. ❑ *...the fight against people smuggling.*

pepper /ˈpepə/ (**peppers, peppering, peppered**) 1 N-UNCOUNT **Pepper** is a hot-tasting spice which is used to flavour food. ❑ *...freshly ground black pepper.* 2 N-COUNT A **pepper** is a hollow green, red or yellow vegetable. 3 V-T If something **is peppered with** things, they are scattered over it. ❑ *Like his son, he peppers his conversation with jokes.*
→ see **spice, vegetable**

peppermint /ˈpepəmɪnt/ (**peppermints**) 1 N-UNCOUNT **Peppermint** is a strong fresh-tasting flavouring that is obtained from the peppermint plant or made artificially. 2 N-COUNT A **peppermint** is a peppermint-flavoured sweet.

ˈpepper ˌspray (**pepper sprays**) N-VAR **Pepper spray** is a device that causes tears and sickness and is sometimes used against rioters and attackers. ❑ *The officers blasted him with pepper spray.*

per /pɜː/ PREP You use **per** to express rates and ratios. For example, if a vehicle is travelling at 40 miles per hour, it will travel 40 miles in an hour.

per annum /pər ˈænəm/ ADV A particular amount **per annum** means that amount each year. ❑ *...a fee of £35 per annum.*

per capita /pəˈkæpɪtə/ ADJ BEFORE N & ADV The **per capita** amount of something is the average amount of it for each person in a particular area or country. [TECHNICAL] ❑ *They have the world's largest per capita income.* ❑ *It's the highest murder rate per capita in the western world.*

Word Link *per ≈ through, thoroughly : perceive, perfect, permit*

perceive /pəˈsiːv/ (**perceives, perceiving, perceived**) 1 V-T/V-I If you **perceive** something, especially something that is not obvious, you see, notice, or realize it. ❑ *A blind person can perceive with other senses.* 2 V-T If you **perceive** someone or something **as** doing or being a particular thing, it is your opinion that they do this thing or that they are that thing. ❑ *The problem should be perceived as an opportunity.*

per cent also **percent** /pəˈsent/

Per cent is both the singular and the plural form.

N-COUNT & ADJ BEFORE N You use **per cent** to talk about amounts. For example, if an amount is 10 per cent (10%) of a larger amount, it is equal to 10 hundredths of the larger amount.

Word Link *cent ≈ hundred : centigrade, centimetre, percentage*

percentage /pəˈsentɪdʒ/ (**percentages**) N-COUNT A **percentage** is a fraction of an amount expressed as a particular number of hundredths.
→ see **fraction**

perception /pəˈsepʃən/ (**perceptions**) 1 N-COUNT Your **perception of** something is the way that you think about it or the impression you have of it. ❑ *Our perceptions of death affect the way we live.* 2 N-UNCOUNT Someone who has **perception** realizes or notices things that are not obvious. 3 N-UNCOUNT **Perception** is the recognition of things by using your senses, especially the sense of sight.

perceptive /pəˈseptɪv/ ADJ A **perceptive** person realizes or notices things that are not obvious.

perch /pɜːtʃ/ (**perches, perching, perched**) 1 V-I & N-COUNT When a bird **perches on** a branch or a wall, it lands on it and stays there. The branch or place that the bird sits on is called a **perch**. 2 V-I If you **perch on** something, you sit down lightly on the very edge of it. ❑ *Vicki shut the door and perched on Stella's desk.* 3 V-I/V-T If something **perches on** something or **is perched on** something, it is on the top or edge of something. ❑ *...a simple white house perched on a rocky cliff.* 4 V-T If you **perch** one thing **on** another, you put it on the top or edge, so that it looks as if it might fall off. ❑ *He picked up a baseball cap and perched it on his head.*

Word Link *cuss ≈ striking : concussion, percussion, repercussions*

percussion /pə'kʌʃən/ N-UNCOUNT **Percussion** instruments are musical instruments that you hit, such as drums.
→ see **orchestra**

perennial /pə'reniəl/ ADJ You use **perennial** to describe problems or situations that keep occurring or which seem to exist all the time. ❑ *...the perennial problem of homelessness.*
→ see **plant**

Word Link *per ≈ through, thoroughly : perceive, perfect, permit*

perfect (**perfects, perfecting, perfected**) 1 ADJ /'pɜːfɪkt/ Something that is **perfect** is as good as it can possibly be. ❑ *He spoke perfect English.* ❑ *It's not a perfect solution, but it's the best we can do.* ● **perfectly** ADV ❑ *The system worked perfectly.* 2 ADJ If you say that something is **perfect for** a particular person, thing, or activity, you are emphasizing that it is very suitable for them or for that activity. ❑ *Tiles are perfect for kitchens because they're easy to clean.* 3 ADJ BEFORE N You can use **perfect** to add emphasis. ❑ *What he said made perfect sense.* ● **perfectly** ADV ❑ *They made everything perfectly clear for us.* 4 ADJ BEFORE N The **perfect** tenses of a verb are the ones used to talk about things that happened or began before a particular time, as in 'He's already left' (present perfect) and 'They had always liked her' (past perfect). The present perfect tense is sometimes called the **perfect tense**. 5 V-T /pə'fekt/ If you **perfect** something, you improve it so that it becomes as good as it can possibly be. ❑ *The animated cartoon was perfected by Walt Disney in the 1930s.*

Thesaurus *perfect* Also look up:
ADJ. flawless, ideal; (*ant.*) defective, faulty 1

perfection /pə'fekʃən/ N-UNCOUNT **Perfection** is the quality of being perfect. ❑ *...fresh fish, cooked to perfection.*

perfectionist /pə'fekʃənɪst/ (**perfectionists**) N-COUNT Someone who is a **perfectionist** refuses to do or accept anything that is not perfect.

perform /pə'fɔːm/ (**performs, performing, performed**) 1 V-T When you **perform** a task or action, you complete it. ❑ *We need someone to perform her duties while she's away.* 2 V-I The way that someone or something **performs** is how well they work or achieve good results. ❑ *Parents have a right to know how well schools are performing.* ● **performer** (**performers**) N-COUNT ❑ *The company has been a strong performer for several years now.* 3 V-T/V-I To **perform** a play, a piece of music, or a dance means to do it in front of an audience. ❑ *He began performing in the early fifties.* ● **performer** N-COUNT ❑ *...a solo performer.*

Word Partnership Use *perform* with:
N. perform **miracles**, perform **tasks** 1
ADJ. **able to** perform 1 2 3
V. **continue to** perform 1 2 3
ADV. perform **well** 2

Word Link *ance ≈ quality, state : performance, resistance, trance*

performance /pə'fɔːməns/ (**performances**) 1 N-COUNT A **performance** involves entertaining an audience by singing, dancing, or acting. ❑ *...a performance of Bizet's Carmen.* 2 N-VAR Someone's or something's **performance** is how well they do something. ❑ *That study looked at the performance of 18 surgeons.*
→ see **concert**

perfume /'pɜːfjuːm, pə'fjuːm/ (**perfumes**) 1 N-VAR **Perfume** is a pleasant-smelling liquid which women put on their necks and wrists to make themselves smell nice. 2 N-COUNT A **perfume** is a pleasant smell. [LITERARY] ❑ *...the perfume of roses.*

perhaps /pə'hæps, præps/ ADV You use **perhaps** to indicate that you are not sure whether something is true, possible, or likely. ❑ *In the end they lost millions, perhaps billions.* ❑ *It was big, perhaps three feet long and almost as high.* ❑ *Perhaps the message will get through.*

peril /'perɪl/ (**perils**) N-VAR & PHRASE **Perils** are great dangers. If someone or something is **in peril**, they are in great danger. [FORMAL] ❑ *...the perils of the sea.*

perilous /'perɪləs/ ADJ Something that is **perilous** is very dangerous. ❑ *...a perilous journey across the war-zone.* ● **perilously** ADV ❑ *The track climbed perilously upwards.*

Word Link *meter ≈ measuring : barometer, diameter, perimeter*

Word Link *peri ≈ around : perimeter, periodic, periphery*

perimeter /pə'rɪmɪtə/ (**perimeters**) N-COUNT The **perimeter** of an area of land is the whole of its outer edge or boundary.
→ see **area**

period /'pɪəriəd/ (**periods**) 1 N-COUNT A particular **period** is a particular length of time. ❑ *...a period of a few months.* ❑ *...a period of economic good health.* ❑ *...the Roman period.* 2 ADJ **Period** costumes, furniture and instruments were made at an earlier time in history, or look as if they were made then. 3 N-COUNT When a woman has a **period**, she bleeds from her womb. This usually happens once a month, unless she is pregnant. 4 N-COUNT In American English, a **period** is the punctuation mark (.) which you use at the end of a sentence when it is not a question or an exclamation. The British term is **full stop**.

periodic /ˌpɪəri'ɒdɪk/ ADJ A **periodic** event or situation happens occasionally, at fairly regular intervals. ❑ *Cecil carried out periodic engine checks.*

periodical /ˌpɪəri'ɒdɪkəl/ (**periodicals**) 1 N-COUNT A **periodical** is a magazine. 2 ADJ **Periodical** means the same as **periodic**.

P

• **periodically** ADV ❑ *They hold these meetings periodically.*
→ see **library**

peripheral /pəˈrɪfərəl/ **1** ADJ **Peripheral** areas are ones which are on the edge of larger ones. ❑ *It's a rare illness that affects the peripheral nervous system.* **2** ADJ A **peripheral** activity or issue is not very important compared with other activities or issues.

Word Link	*peri ≈ around : perimeter, periodic, periphery*

periphery /pəˈrɪfəri/ (**peripheries**) **1** N-COUNT If something is on the **periphery** of an area, place, or thing, it is on the edge of it. [FORMAL] ❑ *Ireland is located on the periphery of Europe.* **2** N-COUNT The **periphery** of a subject is the part of it that is not considered to be as central and important as the main part. ❑ *He brought the centre and the periphery of American politics together.*

perish /ˈperɪʃ/ (**perishes, perishing, perished**) **1** V-I To **perish** means to die or be destroyed. [WRITTEN] ❑ *193 passengers perished in the ferry disaster.* **2** V-I If a substance or material, such as rubber, **perishes**, it starts to fall to pieces. ❑ *The car tyre had perished.*

perjury /ˈpɜːdʒəri/ N-UNCOUNT If someone who is giving evidence in a court of law commits **perjury**, they lie. [TECHNICAL]

perk /pɜːk/ (**perks, perking, perked**) N-COUNT **Perks** are benefits that are given to people who have a particular job or belong to a particular group. ❑ *Cheap travel is one of the perks of being a student.*

▸ **perk up** PHR-VERB If something **perks** you **up**, or if you **perk up**, you become cheerful, after feeling tired, bored, or depressed. ❑ *...suggestions to make you smile and perk you up.*

perm /pɜːm/ (**perms, perming, permed**) V-T & N-COUNT When a hair stylist **perms** someone's hair, or when they **give** someone a **perm**, they curl their hair and treat it with chemicals so that it stays curly for several months. [BRIT] ❑ *She had her hair permed.*

P

permanent /ˈpɜːmənənt/ ADJ **Permanent** means lasting for ever or occurring all the time. ❑ *...permanent damage to the brain.* ❑ *The change is likely to be permanent.* ❑ *You can't live in a permanent state of fear.* • **permanently** ADV ❑ *She now lives permanently in Australia.* ❑ *...the only way to lose weight permanently.* • **permanence** N-UNCOUNT ❑ *One should really consider the permanence of a tattoo.*

Thesaurus	*permanent* Also look up:
ADJ.	constant, continual; (*ant.*) fleeting, temporary

permeate /ˈpɜːmieɪt/ (**permeates, permeating, permeated**) **1** V-T If an idea, feeling, or attitude **permeates** society or a system, it affects every part of it. ❑ *His sense of humour permeated his work.* **2** V-T If a liquid, smell, or flavour **permeates** something, it spreads through it. ❑ *Let the pepper flavour permeate the vinegar.*

permissible /pəˈmɪsəbəl/ ADJ Something that is **permissible** is allowed because it does not break any laws or rules. ❑ *Violent acts should not be permissible in sport.*

permission /pəˈmɪʃən/ N-UNCOUNT If you **give** someone **permission to** do something, you tell them that they can do it. ❑ *He asked permission to leave the room.* ❑ *They cannot leave the country without permission.* ❑ *He got permission from his commanding officer.*

Word Partnership	Use *permission* with:
V.	**ask (for)** permission, **get** permission, permission **to leave**, **need** permission, **obtain** permission, **receive** permission, **request** permission, **seek** permission
ADJ.	**special** permission, **written** permission

permissive /pəˈmɪsɪv/ ADJ A **permissive** person allows or tolerates things which other people disapprove of. • **permissiveness** N-UNCOUNT ❑ *He is strongly troubled by the permissiveness of our society.*

Word Link	*per ≈ through, thoroughly : perceive, perfect, permit*

permit (**permits, permitting, permitted**) **1** V-T /pəˈmɪt/ If someone **permits** you **to** do something, they allow you to do it. [FORMAL] ❑ *The guards permitted me to bring my camera.* **2** V-T/V-I If a situation **permits** something, it makes it possible for that thing to exist, happen, or be done. [FORMAL] ❑ *They are planting flowers wherever space permits.* **3** N-COUNT /ˈpɜːmɪt/ A **permit** is an official document allowing you to do something. ❑ *...a work permit.*

pernicious /pəˈnɪʃəs/ ADJ If you describe something as **pernicious**, you mean that it is very harmful. [FORMAL] ❑ *Where does this pernicious idea come from?*

perpetrate /ˈpɜːpɪtreɪt/ (**perpetrates, perpetrating, perpetrated**) V-T If someone **perpetrates** an immoral or harmful act, they commit it. [FORMAL] ❑ *42 per cent of theft is perpetrated by customers.* • **perpetrator** (**perpetrators**) N-COUNT ❑ *...perpetrators of terrorist acts.*

perpetual /pəˈpetʃʊəl/ ADJ A **perpetual** feeling, state, or quality never ends or changes. [FORMAL] ❑ *...his perpetual enthusiasm.* • **perpetually** ADV ❑ *They were all perpetually starving.*

perpetuate /pəˈpetʃʊeɪt/ (**perpetuates, perpetuating, perpetuated**) V-T To **perpetuate** a situation, system, or belief, especially one that is bad or wrong, means to cause it to continue. ❑ *We must not perpetuate the religious divisions of the past.*

perplexed /pəˈplekst/ ADJ If you are **perplexed**, you are puzzled or do not know what to do. ❑ *He was perplexed by the question.*

persecute /ˈpɜːsɪkjuːt/ (**persecutes, persecuting, persecuted**) V-T If someone is **persecuted**, they are treated cruelly and unfairly, often because of their race or beliefs. ❑ *In the Middle Ages, the Church persecuted scientists like Copernicus.* • **persecution** N-UNCOUNT ❑ *...victims of political persecution.* • **persecutor** (**persecutors**) N-COUNT ❑ *Could he forgive his persecutors?*

persevere /ˌpɜːsɪˈvɪə/ (**perseveres, persevering, persevered**) V-I If you **persevere with** something difficult, you continue doing it and do not give up. ❑ *Working out with someone else can be the key to persevering with a new exercise routine.* • **perseverance**

N-UNCOUNT ❑ *We will now see the result of patience and perseverance.*

persist /pə'sɪst/ (**persists, persisting, persisted**) **1** V-I If something that is not wanted **persists**, it continues to exist. ❑ *Contact your doctor if the cough persists.* **2** V-I If you **persist in** doing something, you continue to do it, even though other people oppose you or it is difficult. ❑ *This small boy persists in stealing apples from our trees.*

persistent /pə'sɪstənt/ **1** ADJ If something bad is **persistent**, it continues to exist or happen for a long time. ❑ *His cough grew more persistent.* ● **persistently** ADV ❑ *The younger members were persistently late.* ● **persistence** N-UNCOUNT ❑ *...the persistence of this problem.* **2** ADJ **Persistent** people continue trying to do something, even though other people oppose them or it is difficult. ❑ *He phoned again this morning. He's very persistent.* ● **persistently** ADV ❑ *If Brian persistently misbehaved, his Dad punished him.* ● **persistence** N-UNCOUNT ❑ *Finding the correct answer requires some persistence.*

person /'pɜːsən/ (**persons**)

> The usual plural of person is **people**. The form **persons** is used as the plural in formal language.

1 N-COUNT A **person** is a man, woman, or child. ❑ *The amount of sleep we need varies from person to person.* ❑ *At least fifty people have been killed.* **2** PHRASE If you do something **in person**, you do it yourself rather than letting someone else do it for you. ❑ *You must collect the mail in person.* **3** PHRASE If you meet, hear, or see someone **in person**, you are in the same place as them, rather than speaking to them on the telephone or writing to them. **4** N-COUNT In grammar, the term **first person** is used when referring to 'I' and 'we', **second person** when referring to 'you', and **third person** when referring to 'he', 'she', 'it', 'they', and all other noun groups. **Person** is also used like this when referring to the verb forms that go with these pronouns and noun groups.

persona /pə'səʊnə/ (**personas** or **personae**) N-COUNT Someone's **persona** is the aspect of their character or nature that they present to other people. [FORMAL] ❑ *We have all noticed our manager's calm persona.*

personal /'pɜːsənəl/ **1** ADJ BEFORE N A **personal** opinion, quality, or thing belongs or relates to a particular person. ❑ *That's my personal opinion.* ❑ *...books and other personal belongings.* **2** ADJ BEFORE N If you give something your **personal** attention, you deal with it yourself rather than letting someone else deal with it. ❑ *...a personal letter from the President.* **3** ADJ **Personal** matters relate to your feelings, relationships, and health. ❑ *He resigned for personal reasons.* **4** ADJ **Personal** comments are critical of someone's appearance or character in an offensive way. ❑ *Employers should avoid personal remarks in interviews.*

,personal com'puter (**personal computers**) N-COUNT A **personal computer** is a computer which is used by one person, normally independently. The abbreviation **PC** is also used. [COMPUTING]

personality /,pɜːsə'nælɪti/ (**personalities**) **1** N-VAR Your **personality** is your whole character and nature. ❑ *He has a friendly personality.* ❑ *It's your personality that counts in this business.* **2** N-COUNT You can refer to a famous person, especially in entertainment, broadcasting, or sport, as a **personality**. ❑ *...television personalities.*

Word Partnership Use *personality* with:

ADJ.	**strong** personality, **unique** personality **1**
N.	personality **trait** **1** **radio** personality, **television/TV** personality **2**

personalized [BRIT also **personalised**] /'pɜːsənəlaɪzd/ ADJ **Personalized** objects are marked with the name or initials of their owner. ❑ *...personalised stationery.*

personally /'pɜːsənəli/ **1** ADV You use **personally** to emphasize that you are giving your own opinion. ❑ *Personally I think it's a waste of time.* **2** ADV If you do something **personally**, you do it yourself rather than letting someone else do it. ❑ *The Queen greets each head of government personally.* **3** ADV If you meet or know someone **personally**, you have met them or you know them, rather than knowing about them or knowing their work. ❑ *He didn't know them personally, but he knew their reputation.*

,personal 'pronoun (**personal pronouns**) N-COUNT A **personal pronoun** is a pronoun such as 'I', 'you', 'she', or 'they' which is used to refer to the speaker or the person listening to them, or to a person or thing whose identity is clear.

personify /pə'sɒnɪfaɪ/ (**personifies, personifying, personified**) V-T If you say that someone **personifies** a particular thing or quality, you mean that they are a perfect example of that thing, or they have a lot of that quality. ❑ *She seemed to personify goodness.* ● **personification** /pə,sɒnɪfɪ'keɪʃən/ N-SING ❑ *Joplin was the personification of the '60s female rock singer.*

personnel /,pɜːsə'nel/ N-PLURAL The **personnel** of an organization are the people who work for it.

perspective /pə'spektɪv/ (**perspectives**) **1** N-COUNT A **perspective** is a particular way of thinking about something. ❑ *His father's death gave him a new perspective on life.* **2** PHRASE If you get something **in perspective** or **into perspective**, you judge its real importance by considering it in relation to everything else. If you get something **out of perspective**, you fail to do this.

Thesaurus *perspective* Also look up:

N.	attitude, outlook, viewpoint **1**

perspiration /,pɜːspɪ'reɪʃən/ N-UNCOUNT **Perspiration** is the liquid that appears on your skin when you are hot or frightened. [FORMAL]

Word Link ***suad, suas ≈ urging: dissuade, persuade, persuasive***

persuade /pə'sweɪd/ (**persuades, persuading, persuaded**) **1** V-T If you **persuade** someone **to** do a particular thing, you get them to do it, usually by convincing them that it is a good idea. ❑ *My husband persuaded me to come.* **2** V-T If you **persuade** someone that something is true, you say things that eventually make them believe that it is true. ❑ *I managed to persuade Steve that it was a good idea.*

P

Thesaurus *persuade* Also look up:

v. cajole, convince, influence, sway, talk into, win over; *(ant.)* discourage, dissuade 1 2

Word Partnership Use *persuade* with:

v. **attempt to** persuade, **be able to** persuade, **fail to** persuade, **try to** persuade 1 2

persuasion /pəˈsweɪʒən/ (**persuasions**) 1 N-UNCOUNT **Persuasion** is the act of persuading someone to do something or to believe that something is true. ❑ *She will change things by persuasion if possible.* 2 N-COUNT If you are **of** a particular political or religious **persuasion**, you have that political or religious belief. [FORMAL]

Word Link *suad, suas ≈ urging: dissuade, persuade, persuasive*

persuasive /pəˈsweɪsɪv/ ADJ Someone or something that is **persuasive** is likely to persuade you to do or believe a particular thing. ❑ *This is not persuasive evidence.* ● **persuasively** ADV ❑ *When he rang and talked persuasively to me, how could I resist?*

pertain /pəˈteɪn/ (**pertains, pertaining, pertained**) V-I Something that **pertains to** something else belongs or relates to it. [FORMAL] ❑ *...information pertaining to terrorist activities.*

pertinent /ˈpɜːtɪnənt/ ADJ Something that is **pertinent** is relevant to a particular subject. [FORMAL] ❑ *She asked some pertinent questions.*

pervade /pəˈveɪd/ (**pervades, pervading, pervaded**) V-T Something that **pervades** a place or thing is present or noticed throughout it. [FORMAL] ❑ *The smell of glue pervaded the factory.*

pervasive /pəˈveɪsɪv/ ADJ Something that is **pervasive** is present or felt throughout a place or thing. [FORMAL] ❑ *This shows how pervasive the Internet is.*

perverse /pəˈvɜːs/ ADJ Someone who is **perverse** deliberately does things that are unreasonable. ● **perversely** ADV ❑ *She was perversely pleased to be causing trouble.* ● **perversity** N-UNCOUNT

perversion /pəˈvɜːʃən, -ʒən/ (**perversions**) 1 N-VAR The **perversion of** something is the changing of it so that it is no longer what it should be. ❑ *That is a perversion of the truth.* 2 N-VAR A **perversion** is a sexual desire or action that is considered abnormal and unacceptable.

pervert (**perverts, perverting, perverted**) 1 V-T /pəˈvɜːt/ If you **pervert** something, you interfere with it so that it is not what it used to be or should be. [FORMAL] ❑ *He attempted to pervert the course of justice.* 2 N-COUNT /ˈpɜːvɜːt/ People with abnormal or unacceptable sexual desires are called **perverts**.

perverted /pəˈvɜːtɪd/ ADJ Someone who is **perverted** has abnormal behaviour or ideas, especially sexual ones.

pessimism /ˈpesɪmɪzəm/ N-UNCOUNT **Pessimism** is the belief that bad things are going to happen. ● **pessimist** (**pessimists**) N-COUNT ❑ *I don't consider myself a pessimist.* ● **pessimistic** /ˌpesɪˈmɪstɪk/ ADJ ❑ *People are now more pessimistic about the future.*

pest /pest/ (**pests**) 1 N-COUNT A **pest** is an insect or small animal which damages crops or food supplies. 2 N-COUNT You can describe someone, especially a child, as a **pest** if they keep bothering you. [INFORMAL]
→ see **farm**

pester /ˈpestə/ (**pesters, pestering, pestered**) V-T If you say that someone **is pestering** you, you mean that they keep asking you to do something, or keep talking to you, and you find this annoying. ❑ *He is fed up with people pestering him for money.*

Word Link *cide ≈ killing : genocide, pesticide, suicide*

pesticide /ˈpestɪsaɪd/ (**pesticides**) N-VAR **Pesticides** are chemicals which farmers put on their crops to kill harmful insects.
→ see **pollution**

pet /pet/ (**pets, petting, petted**) 1 N-COUNT A **pet** is an animal that you keep in your home to give you company and pleasure. ❑ *...dogs and other pets.* 2 ADJ BEFORE N Someone's **pet** subject is one that they particularly like. Someone's **pet** hate is something that they particularly dislike. 3 V-T If you **pet** an animal, you pat or stroke it affectionately.

petal /ˈpetəl/ (**petals**) N-COUNT The **petals** of a flower are the thin coloured outer parts which together form the flower.
→ see **flower**

peter /ˈpiːtə/ (**peters, petering, petered**)
▸ **peter out** PHR-VERB If something **peters out**, it gradually comes to an end. ❑ *The track then petered out altogether.*

petite /pəˈtiːt/ ADJ A **petite** woman is small and slim.

petition /pəˈtɪʃən/ (**petitions, petitioning, petitioned**) 1 N-COUNT A **petition** is a document signed by a lot of people which asks for some official action to be taken. ❑ *The petition calls for a halt to nuclear tests.* 2 V-T If you **petition** someone in authority, you make a formal request to them. ❑ *Her followers petitioned the Vatican to make her a saint.*

petrified /ˈpetrɪfaɪd/ ADJ If you are **petrified**, you are extremely frightened. ❑ *I've always been petrified of being alone.*

petrol /ˈpetrəl/ N-UNCOUNT In British English, **petrol** is a liquid used as a fuel for motor vehicles. The usual American word is **gas** or **gasoline**.

petroleum /pəˈtrəʊliəm/ N-UNCOUNT **Petroleum** is oil which is found underground or under the sea bed. Petrol and other fuels are obtained from petroleum.
→ see Word Web: **petroleum**
→ see **energy, oil**

petty /ˈpeti/ (**pettier, pettiest**) 1 ADJ You can use **petty** to describe things such as rules, problems, or arguments which you think are trivial or unimportant. ❑ *...endless rules and petty regulations.* 2 ADJ If you describe someone's behaviour as **petty**, you disapprove of it because you think it shows that they care too much about small, unimportant things. ● **pettiness** N-UNCOUNT ❑ *Never had she met such pettiness.* 3 ADJ BEFORE N **Petty** is used to describe minor crimes or criminals. ❑ *...petty crime, such as handbag-theft.*

P

Word Web **petroleum**

Most **petroleum** is used as **fuel**. We use **petrol** to power our cars and **heating oil** to warm our homes. About 20% of **crude oil** becomes **gas** and 10% becomes heating oil. Today 90% of the **energy** used in transportation comes from petroleum. Other petroleum products include household items such as **paint**, **deodorant**, and **shampoo**. Some of our clothes are also made using petroleum. These include **shoes**, **jumpers**, and **polyester shirts** and **dresses**. Petroleum products are also important for building new houses. They are used to make water **pipes**, **shower** doors, and even **toilet** seats.

pew /pjuː/ (**pews**) N-COUNT A **pew** is a long wooden seat for people in church.

pewter /ˈpjuːtə/ N-UNCOUNT **Pewter** is a grey metal made by mixing tin and lead.

phantom /ˈfæntəm/ (**phantoms**) **1** N-COUNT A **phantom** is a ghost. **2** ADJ BEFORE N You use **phantom** to describe something which does not really exist, but which someone believes or pretends does exist. ❑ *He invented a phantom life.*

Word Link *pharma ≈ drug : pharmaceutical, pharmacist, pharmacy*

pharmaceutical /ˌfɑːməˈsuːtɪkəl/ (**pharmaceuticals**) **1** ADJ BEFORE N **Pharmaceutical** means connected with the industrial production of medicines. ❑ *...pharmaceutical companies.* **2** N-PLURAL **Pharmaceuticals** are medicines.

Word Link *ist ≈ one who practices : biologist, journalist, pharmacist*

pharmacist /ˈfɑːməsɪst/ (**pharmacists**) N-COUNT A **pharmacist** is a person who is qualified to prepare and sell medicines.

pharmacy /ˈfɑːməsi/ (**pharmacies**) **1** N-COUNT A **pharmacy** is a place where medicines are sold or given out. **2** N-UNCOUNT **Pharmacy** is the job or the science of preparing medicines.

Usage

In British English, **pharmacy** is not the usual way of referring to a shop where medicines are sold or given out. The usual term is **chemist** or **chemist's**. ❑ *She went into a chemist's and bought some aspirin.* In American English, the word **drugstore** is used, but this usually refers to a shop where you can buy drinks, snacks, and other small items, as well as medicines. ❑ *I bought the local paper at the drugstore.*

phase /feɪz/ (**phases, phasing, phased**) **1** N-COUNT A **phase** is a particular stage in a process or in the development of something. ❑ *This first phase of economic reform was very popular.* **2** V-T If an action or change **is phased** over a period of time, it is done in stages. ❑ *The job cuts will be phased over two years.*

▶ **phase in** PHR-VERB If a new way of doing something **is phased in**, it is introduced gradually. ❑ *The pay rise will be phased in over two years.*

▶ **phase out** PHR-VERB If something **is phased out**, people gradually stop using it or doing it. ❑ *The analogue phone system is being phased out.*

PhD /ˌpiː eɪtʃˈdiː/ (**PhDs**) N-COUNT A **PhD** is a degree awarded to people who have done advanced research. **PhD** is an abbreviation for 'Doctor of Philosophy'.
→ see **graduation**

pheasant /ˈfezənt/

The plural is **pheasant** or **pheasants**.

N-COUNT A **pheasant** is a bird with a long tail, sometimes shot for sport and then eaten.

phenomenal /fɪˈnɒmɪnəl/ ADJ Something that is **phenomenal** is extraordinarily great or good. ● **phenomenally** ADV ❑ *...her phenomenally successful singing career.*

phenomenon /fɪˈnɒmɪnən, AM -nɑːn/ (**phenomena** /fɪˈnɒmɪnə/) N-COUNT A **phenomenon** is something that is observed to happen or exist. [FORMAL] ❑ *Lightning is a natural phenomenon.*
→ see **science**

Word Link *soph ≈ wise : philosopher, philosophy, sophisticated*

philosopher /fɪˈlɒsəfə/ (**philosophers**) N-COUNT A **philosopher** is a person who studies or writes about philosophy.
→ see **philosophy**

philosophic /ˌfɪləˈsɒfɪk/ ADJ **Philosophic** means the same as **philosophical**.

philosophical /ˌfɪləˈsɒfɪkəl/ **1** ADJ **Philosophical** means concerned with or relating to philosophy. ❑ *...philosophical discussions.* **2** ADJ Someone who is **philosophical** does not get upset when disappointing or disturbing things happen. ❑ *He was philosophical about his defeat.* ● **philosophically** ADV ❑ *She says philosophically: 'It could have been worse.'*

philosophy /fɪˈlɒsəfi/ (**philosophies**) **1** N-UNCOUNT **Philosophy** is the study or creation of theories about basic things such as the nature of existence or how people should live. ❑ *...traditional Chinese philosophy.* **2** N-COUNT A **philosophy** is a particular set of theories or beliefs. ❑ *The Republicans and Democrats have different political philosophies.*
→ see Word Web: **philosophy**

Word Link *phob ≈ fear : agoraphobia, claustrophobia, phobia*

phobia /ˈfəʊbiə/ (**phobias**) N-COUNT A **phobia** is an unreasonably strong fear of something. ❑ *He had a phobia about flying.*

P

Word Web philosophy

Plato

Aristotle

Confucius

Philosophy helps us **understand** ourselves and the purpose of our lives. **Philosophers** have studied the same **issues** for thousands of years. The Chinese philosopher Confucius* wrote about personal and **political morals**. He taught that people should love others and honour their parents. They should do what is right, not what is best for themselves. He thought that a ruler who used force had failed. The Greek philosopher Plato* wrote about politics and science. Later, Aristotle* created a system of **logic** and **reasoning**. He wanted to be absolutely sure of what is true and what isn't.

Confucius (551-479 BC)
Plato (427-347 BC)
Aristotle (384-322 BC)

phone /fəʊn/ (**phones, phoning, phoned**) **1** N-UNCOUNT The **phone** is an electrical system used to talk to someone in another place by dialling a number on a piece of equipment and speaking into it. ❑ *We never discuss any matters over the phone.* ❑ *Do you have his address and phone number?* **2** N-COUNT A **phone** is the piece of equipment that is used to talk to someone by phone. ❑ *Jamie answered the phone.* **3** V-T/V-I & PHR-VERB When you **phone** someone, or when you **phone** them **up**, you dial their phone number and speak to them by phone. ❑ *He phoned me to say he was visiting Manchester.* ❑ *I waited for her to phone.* ❑ *I'll phone up and ask them.* **4** PHRASE If you are **on the phone**, you are speaking to someone by telephone. ❑ *He's on the phone to his girlfriend.* **5** PHRASE If someone is **on the phone**, they have a telephone in their house or office which is connected to the rest of the telephone system. ❑ *The Frosts were not on the phone.*
→ see **office**

P

'phone booth (**phone booths**) N-COUNT In American English, a **phone booth** is a small shelter in the street in which there is a public telephone. The British term is **telephone box** or **phone box**.

'phone box (**phone boxes**) N-COUNT In British English, a **phone box** is a small shelter in the street in which there is a public telephone. The usual American term is **phone booth**.

'phone call (**phone calls**) N-COUNT If you make a **phone call**, you speak to someone by phone.

phonecard /fəʊnkɑːd/ (**phonecards**) N-COUNT A **phonecard** is a plastic card that you can use instead of money in some public telephones.

'phone-in (**phone-ins**) N-COUNT A **phone-in** is a radio or television programme in which people telephone with questions or opinions and their calls are broadcast.

phoney also **phony** /'fəʊni/ (**phonier, phoniest, phoneys** or **phonies**) **1** ADJ If you describe something as **phoney**, you disapprove of it because it is not genuine. [INFORMAL] ❑ *He telephoned with some phoney excuse.* **2** ADJ & N-COUNT If you say that someone is **phoney**, or if you say they are a **phoney**, you disapprove of them because they are pretending to be someone that they are not.

phonics /'fɒnɪks/ N-UNCOUNT **Phonics** is a method of teaching people to read by training them to associate written letters with their sounds.

phosphate /'fɒsfeɪt/ (**phosphates**) N-VAR A **phosphate** is a chemical compound that is used in fertilizers.

photo /'fəʊtəʊ/ (**photos**) N-COUNT A **photo** is the same as a **photograph**. [INFORMAL]
→ see **photography**

Word Link *photo ≈ light : photocopier, photograph, photography*

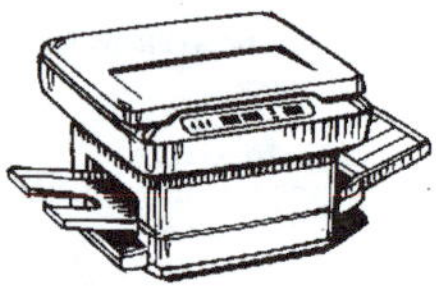
photocopier

photocopier /'fəʊtəʊkɒpiə/ (**photocopiers**) N-COUNT A **photocopier** is a machine which quickly copies documents by photographing them.

photocopy /'fəʊtəʊkɒpi/ (**photocopies, photocopying, photocopied**) **1** V-T If you **photocopy** a document, you make a copy of it with a photocopier. **2** N-COUNT A **photocopy** is a document made by a photocopier.

photograph /'fəʊtəgrɑːf, -græf/ (**photographs, photographing, photographed**) **1** N-COUNT A **photograph** is a picture that is made using a camera. ❑ *Her photograph was on the front page.* **2** V-T When you **photograph** someone or something, you use a camera to obtain a picture of them. ❑ *He hates being photographed.*

photographer /fə'tɒgrəfə/ (**photographers**) N-COUNT A **photographer** is someone who takes photographs, especially as their job.
→ see **photography**

photographic /ˌfəʊtə'græfɪk/ ADJ **Photographic** means connected with photographs or photography. ❑ *...photographic equipment.*

photography /fə'tɒgrəfi/ N-UNCOUNT **Photography** is the skill, job, or process of producing photographs. ❑ *...fashion photography.*
→ see Word Web: **photography**

'photo shoot (**photo shoots**) N-COUNT A **photo**

Word Web photography

It's easy to **take** a **picture** with a digital **camera**. You just look through the viewfinder and push the **shutter button**. But professional **photographers** need to produce high quality **photos**. So their job is harder. First they choose the right **film** and **load** the camera. Then they check the **lighting** and carefully **focus** the camera. They usually take several **shots**, one after another. Then it's time to **develop** the film and make **prints**. Sometimes a photographer will **crop** a photo or **enlarge** it to create a more striking **image**.

shoot is an occasion when a photographer takes pictures, especially of models or famous people, to be used in a newspaper or magazine.

phrasal verb /ˌfreɪzəl 'vɜːb/ (**phrasal verbs**) N-COUNT A **phrasal verb** is a combination of a verb and an adverb or preposition, for example 'shut up' or 'look after', which together have a particular meaning.

phrase /freɪz/ (**phrases, phrasing, phrased**) **1** N-COUNT A **phrase** is a short group of words that are used as a unit and whose meaning is not always obvious from the words contained in it. **2** V-T If you **phrase** something in a particular way, you say or write it in that way. ❑ *Try to phrase the question differently.* **3** PHRASE If someone has a particular **turn of phrase**, they have a particular way of saying or writing something. ❑ *Rita's stories were good; she had a nice turn of phrase.*

Word Link *physi ≈ of nature : physical, physician, physics*

physical /'fɪzɪkəl/ **1** ADJ **Physical** means connected with a person's body, rather than with their mind. ❑ *Physical activity promotes good health.* ❑ *The attraction between them is physical.* • **physically** ADV ❑ *She is now physically disabled.* **2** ADJ BEFORE N **Physical** things are real things that can be touched or seen. ❑ *These people admire physical size in a leader.* **3** ADJ BEFORE N **Physical** means connected with physics. ❑ *...physical laws.*
→ see **diagnosis**

Word Link *ician ≈ person who works at : electrician, musician, physician*

physician /fɪ'zɪʃən/ (**physicians**) N-COUNT A **physician** is a doctor. [AM]
→ see **diagnosis, hospital, medicine**

physicist /'fɪzɪsɪst/ (**physicists**) N-COUNT A **physicist** is a person who studies physics.

physics /'fɪzɪks/ N-UNCOUNT **Physics** is the scientific study of forces such as heat, light, sound, pressure, gravity, and electricity.

physiology /ˌfɪzi'ɒlədʒi/ **1** N-UNCOUNT **Physiology** is the scientific study of how people, animals, and plants grow and function. **2** N-SING The **physiology of** an animal or plant is the way that it functions. ❑ *...the physiology of the brain.* • **physiological** /ˌfɪziə'lɒdʒɪkəl/ ADJ ❑ *...the physiological effects of stress.*

physiotherapist /ˌfɪziəʊ'θerəpɪst/ (**physiotherapists**) N-COUNT A **physiotherapist** is a person whose job is using physiotherapy to treat people.

physiotherapy /ˌfɪziəʊ'θerəpi/ N-UNCOUNT **Physiotherapy** is medical treatment given to people who cannot move a part of their body and involves exercise, massage, or heat treatment.
→ see **illness**

physique /fɪ'ziːk/ (**physiques**) N-VAR Your **physique** is the shape and size of your body. ❑ *He was small, but with a powerful physique.*

piano /pi'ænəʊ/ (**pianos**) N-COUNT A **piano** is a large musical instrument with a row of black and white keys, which you strike with your fingers. • **pianist** /'piːənɪst, AM pi'æn-/ (**pianists**) N-COUNT ❑ *Howard is a talented pianist.*
→ see **keyboard, music**

pick /pɪk/ (**picks, picking, picked**) **1** V-T If you **pick** a particular person or thing, you choose that one. ❑ *His job is to pick the team and I had to respect his decision not to pick me.* **2** N-SING You can refer to the best things or people in a particular group as **the pick of** that group. ❑ *This shop carries the pick of the best designer labels.* **3** V-T When you **pick** flowers, fruit, or leaves, you break them off the plant and collect them. **4** V-T If you **pick** something **from** a place, you take it from that place, using your fingers. ❑ *He picked the telephone off the shelf.* **5** V-T If you **pick** an **argument** or a **fight** with someone, you deliberately cause one. **6** V-T If someone **picks** a **lock**, they open it without using a key, for example by using a piece of wire. **7** PHRASE If you **pick** your **way** across an area, you walk across it very carefully in order to avoid obstacles or dangerous objects. ❑ *Rescue workers are still picking their way through the ruins.*

▸ **pick at** PHR-VERB If you **pick at** the **food** you are eating, you eat only very small amounts of it.

▸ **pick on** PHR-VERB If someone **picks on** you, they repeatedly criticize or attack you unfairly. ❑ *They were always picking on her.*

▸ **pick out** PHR-VERB If you can **pick out** something or someone, you recognize them when it is difficult to see them. ❑ *With my binoculars, I pick out a figure a mile or so away.*

▸ **pick up** **1** PHR-VERB If you **pick** something **up**, you lift it upwards from a surface using your fingers. ❑ *Ridley picked up the pencil.* **2** PHR-VERB When you **pick up** something or someone, you collect them from somewhere, usually in a car. ❑ *We drove to the airport to pick up Susan.* **3** PHR-VERB If you **pick up** a skill or an idea, you acquire it without effort. [INFORMAL] ❑ *Where did you pick up your English?* **4** PHR-VERB If a piece of equipment **picks up** a signal or sound, it receives it or detects it. ❑ *We can pick up Italian television.* **5** PHR-VERB If trade or the economy of a country **picks up**, it improves. **6** PHR-VERB If you **pick up** an illness, you get it from somewhere or something. ❑ *Some passengers had picked up food poisoning.*

Thesaurus *pick* Also look up:

V. choose, decide on, elect, select 1
collect, gather, harvest, pull 3

pickaxe [AM **pickax**] /'pɪkæks/ (**pickaxes**) N-COUNT A **pickaxe** is a large tool consisting of a curved, pointed piece of metal with a long handle joined to the middle. Pickaxes are used for breaking up rocks or the ground.

picket /'pɪkɪt/ (**pickets, picketing, picketed**) 1 V-T/V-I If people who are demonstrating or on strike **picket** a place, they stand outside it in order to make a protest or to prevent people from going in. ❑ *Protesters picketed the Australian Embassy.* 2 N-COUNT A **picket** is a group of people who are picketing a place. ❑ *...a twenty-four hour picket.*

pickle /'pɪkəl/ (**pickles**) 1 N-PLURAL **Pickles** are vegetables or fruit which have been kept in vinegar or salt water for a long time to give them a strong sharp taste. 2 N-VAR **Pickle** is a cold, spicy sauce that is made by boiling chopped vegetables and fruit with spices.

pickled /'pɪkəld/ ADJ **Pickled** food has been kept in vinegar and salt water so that it develops a strong sharp taste and does not go bad. ❑ *...a jar of pickled cabbage.*

picnic /'pɪknɪk/ (**picnics, picnicking, picnicked**) N-COUNT & V-I When people have a **picnic**, or when they **picnic** somewhere, they eat a meal in the open air. ❑ *I took the kids for a picnic.* ❑ *We picnicked on the riverbank.*

pictorial /pɪk'tɔ:riəl/ ADJ **Pictorial** means relating to or using pictures. ❑ *...a pictorial history of the aircraft of the RAF.*

Word Link *pict ≈ painting : depict, picture, picturesque*

picture /'pɪktʃə/ (**pictures, picturing, pictured**) 1 N-COUNT A **picture** consists of lines and shapes which are drawn, painted, or printed on a surface and show a person, thing, or scene. 2 N-COUNT A **picture** is a photograph. ❑ *I've got a picture of her that I always keep with me.* 3 V-T If someone or something **is pictured in** a newspaper or magazine, they appear in a photograph in it. ❑ *Cruz was pictured arriving at the airport.* 4 N-COUNT You can refer to the image you see on a television screen as a **picture**. 5 N-COUNT You can refer to a film as a **picture**. ❑ *...a director of successful action pictures.* 6 N-PLURAL In British English, if you go to **the pictures**, you go to a cinema to see a film. The American word is **movies**. 7 V-T & N-COUNT If you **picture** something, or if you have a **picture of** something in your mind, you have a clear idea or memory of it in your mind. ❑ *He pictured her with long black hair.* ❑ *We have a picture of how we'd like things to be.* 8 N-COUNT If you give a **picture of** what someone or something is like, you describe them. ❑ *The book paints a picture of a man who is sad and confused.* 9 N-SING When you refer to **the picture** in a particular place, you are referring to the situation there. ❑ *It's a similar picture in Africa.* 10 PHRASE If you **get the picture**, you understand a particular situation, especially one which someone is describing to you. [INFORMAL] 11 PHRASE If you **put** someone **in the picture**, you tell them about a situation which they need to know about.
→ see **photography**

Thesaurus *picture* Also look up:

N. drawing, illustration, image, painting 1
photograph 2
V. envision, imagine, visualize 7

Word Partnership Use *picture* with:

ADJ. **pretty as a** picture 1
mental picture 7
clear picture 7 9
accurate picture, **complete** picture, **different** picture, **larger** picture, **overall** picture, **vivid** picture, **whole** picture 7-9

'**picture ˌmessaging** N-UNCOUNT **Picture messaging** is the sending of photographs or pictures from one mobile phone to another. ❑ *...picture messaging on camera phones.* ❑ *...a picture messaging service.*

picturesque /ˌpɪktʃə'resk/ ADJ A **picturesque** place is attractive, interesting, and unspoiled. ❑ *...a picturesque village in Cornwall.*

pie /paɪ/ (**pies**) N-VAR A **pie** consists of meat, vegetables, or fruit, baked in pastry. ❑ *...a slice of apple pie.*
→ see **chart, dessert**

piece /pi:s/ (**pieces, piecing, pieced**) 1 N-COUNT A **piece of** something is a portion, part, or section of it that has been removed, broken off, or cut off. ❑ *...a piece of paper.* ❑ *Cut the ham into pieces.* ❑ *The vehicle was blown to pieces by the explosion.* 2 N-COUNT A **piece of** something of a particular kind is an individual thing of that kind. ❑ *Let me give you one piece of advice.* ❑ *...a beautiful piece of furniture.* 3 N-COUNT A **piece** is something that is written or created, such as an article, work of art, or musical composition. ❑ *There was a piece about him on television.* ❑ *He replaced the stolen paintings with less valuable pieces.* 4 PHRASE If someone or something is still **in one piece** after a dangerous journey or experience, they are safe and not damaged or hurt. 5 PHRASE If you have to **pick up the pieces** after a disaster, you have to try to get the situation back to normal again. 6 PHRASE If you **go to pieces**, you are so upset or nervous that you lose control of yourself and cannot do what you should do. [INFORMAL]
→ see **chess**

▶ **piece together** 1 PHR-VERB If you **piece together** the truth about something, you gradually discover it. ❑ *Francis was able to piece together what had happened.* 2 PHR-VERB If you **piece** something **together**, you gradually make it complete by joining its parts together. ❑ *Doctors carefully pieced together the broken bones.*

piecemeal /'pi:smi:l/ ADJ & ADV A **piecemeal** process happens gradually and in irregular or unconnected stages. ❑ *The report criticizes this piecemeal approach to the problem.* ❑ *It was built piecemeal over some 130 years.*

pier /pɪə/ (**piers**) N-COUNT A **pier** is a large

platform which sticks out into the sea and which people can walk along.

pierce /pɪəs/ (**pierces, piercing, pierced**) V-T If a sharp object **pierces** something, or if you **pierce** something **with** a sharp object, the object goes into it and makes a hole in it. ❑ *Pierce the skin of the potato with a fork.* ❑ *I'm having my ears pierced.*

piercing /ˈpɪəsɪŋ/ (**piercings**) **1** ADJ A **piercing** sound is high-pitched and sharp in an unpleasant way. ❑ *Suddenly there was a piercing scream.* **2** ADJ Someone with **piercing** eyes has bright eyes which seem to look at you very intensely. **3** N-COUNT A **piercing** is a hole that has been made in part of someone's body that they can put jewellery in. ❑ *Kids experiment with their looks – clothes, piercings and hair styles.*

piety /ˈpaɪəti/ N-UNCOUNT **Piety** is strong religious belief or behaviour.

pig /pɪɡ/ (**pigs**) **1** N-COUNT A **pig** is a farm animal with a pink, white, or black skin. Pigs are kept for their meat, which is called pork, ham, or bacon. **2** N-COUNT If you call someone a **pig**, you are insulting them, usually because you think that they are greedy or unkind.
→ see **meat**

pigeon /ˈpɪdʒɪn/ (**pigeons**) N-COUNT A **pigeon** is a grey bird which is often seen in towns.

pigment /ˈpɪɡmənt/ (**pigments**) N-VAR A **pigment** is a substance that gives something a particular colour. [FORMAL] ❑ *Melanin is the pigment that gives skin its colour.*

pike /paɪk/

The plural is **pike** or **pikes**.

N-VAR A **pike** is a large river fish that eats other fish.

pile /paɪl/ (**piles, piling, piled**) **1** N-COUNT A **pile** of things is a quantity of them lying on top of one another. ❑ *The leaves had been swept into piles.* ❑ *...a pile of boxes.* **2** V-T If you **pile** a quantity of things somewhere, you put them there so that they form a pile. You can also say a surface **is piled with** things. ❑ *He was piling clothes into the suitcase.* **3** QUANT A **pile of** something or **piles of** it is a large amount of it. [INFORMAL] ❑ *He had piles of money.* **4** V-I If people **pile into** or **out of** a place, they all get into it or out of it in a disorganized way. ❑ *Everyone piled out of the car.* **5** N-UNCOUNT The **pile** of a carpet is its soft surface, which consists of lots of little threads standing on end.

▸ **pile up** **1** PHR-VERB If you **pile up** a quantity of things, or if they **pile up**, they gradually form a pile. ❑ *Mail was still piling up at the office.* **2** PHR-VERB If problems or losses **pile up**, or if you **pile** them **up**, you get more and more of them. ❑ *Problems were piling up at work.* ❑ *He piled up huge debts.*

Usage

A **pile** of things can be tidy or untidy. ❑ *...a neat pile of clothes.* A **heap** is usually untidy, and often has the shape of a hill or mound. ❑ *Now, the house is a heap of rubble.* A **stack** is usually tidy, and often consists of flat objects placed directly on top of each other. ❑ *...a neat stack of dishes.*

pilgrim /ˈpɪlɡrɪm/ (**pilgrims**) N-COUNT A **pilgrim** is a person who makes a journey to a holy place.

pilgrimage /ˈpɪlɡrɪmɪdʒ/ (**pilgrimages**) N-VAR If someone makes a **pilgrimage** to a place, they make a journey there because the place is holy according to their religion, or very important to them personally. ❑ *...a private pilgrimage to family graves.*

pill /pɪl/ (**pills**) **1** N-COUNT **Pills** are small solid round masses of medicine or vitamins that you swallow. **2** N-SING If a woman is **on the pill**, she takes a special pill that prevents her from becoming pregnant. ❑ *She had been on the pill for three years.* ❑ *...the contraceptive pill.*

pillar /ˈpɪlə/ (**pillars**) **1** N-COUNT A **pillar** is a tall solid structure which is usually used to support part of a building. **2** N-COUNT If you describe someone as a **pillar of the community**, you approve of them because they play an important and active part in the community.

pillow /ˈpɪləʊ/ (**pillows**) N-COUNT A **pillow** is a rectangular cushion which you rest your head on when you are in bed.
→ see **bed, sleep**

pilot /ˈpaɪlət/ (**pilots, piloting, piloted**) **1** N-COUNT A **pilot** is a person who is trained to fly an aircraft. **2** V-T When someone **pilots** an aircraft, they act as its pilot. **3** ADJ A **pilot scheme** or **project** is one which is used to test an idea before deciding whether to introduce it on a larger scale. **4** V-T If an organization or government **pilots** a new scheme, they test it before deciding whether to introduce it on a larger scale. ❑ *The Government piloted a scheme allowing people to vote by text message.*

pimp /pɪmp/ (**pimps**) N-COUNT A **pimp** is a man who finds clients for a prostitute and takes a large part of the prostitute's earnings.

pin /pɪn/ (**pins, pinning, pinned**) **1** N-COUNT **Pins** are very small thin pieces of metal with points at one end, which are used to fasten things together. **2** V-T If you **pin** something somewhere, you fasten it there with a pin. ❑ *They pinned a notice to the door.* ❑ *General Carl Vuono pinned on the medals.* **3** N-COUNT You can refer to any long narrow piece of metal or wood with a blunt end, especially one that is used to fasten two things together, as a **pin**. ❑ *Surgeons will insert a 12-inch pin in his broken leg.* **4** V-T If someone **pins** you in a particular position, they press you firmly against something so that you cannot move. ❑ *I pinned him against the wall.* **5** V-T If someone tries to **pin** something bad **on** you, they say that you were responsible for it. ❑ *They couldn't pin the killing on anyone.* **6** V-T If you **pin** your hopes **on** something or someone, your future success or happiness depends on them. ❑ *Are we right to pin our hopes on our young people?*
→ see **jewellery**

▸ **pin down** **1** PHR-VERB If you try to **pin** something **down**, you try to discover exactly what, where, or when it is. ❑ *It has taken a long time to pin down its exact location.* **2** PHR-VERB If you **pin** someone **down**, you force them to make a definite statement. ❑ *She couldn't pin him down to a date.*

PIN /pɪn/ N-SING Someone's **PIN** or **PIN number** is a secret number which they can use, for example, with a bank card to withdraw money from a cash machine.

pincer /ˈpɪnsə/ (**pincers**) **1** N-PLURAL **Pincers** consist of two pieces of metal that are joined in

P

the middle. They are used as a tool for gripping things or for pulling things out. **2** N-COUNT The **pincers** of an animal such as a crab or a lobster are its front claws.

pinch /pɪntʃ/ (**pinches, pinching, pinched**) **1** V-T & N-COUNT If you **pinch** someone, or if you give them a **pinch**, you squeeze a part of their body between your thumb and first finger. ❑ *She pinched his cheek.* **2** N-SING A **pinch of** an ingredient such as salt is the amount of it that you can hold between your thumb and your first finger. ❑ *...a pinch of sugar.* **3** V-T If someone **pinches** something, especially something of little value, they steal it. [INFORMAL] **4** PHRASE If a person or company **is feeling the pinch**, they do not have as much money as they used to, and cannot buy the things that they want.

pine /paɪn/ (**pines, pining, pined**) **1** N-VAR A **pine** or a **pine tree** is a tall tree with long thin leaves which it keeps all year round. **Pine** is the wood of this tree. **2** V-I If you **are pining for** something or someone, you feel sad because you cannot have them or cannot be with them. ❑ *I pine for the countryside.* ❑ *Make sure your pet won't pine while you're away.*

pineapple /ˈpaɪnæpəl/ (**pineapples**) N-VAR A **pineapple** is a large oval fruit with sweet, juicy, yellow flesh and thick, brown, skin.
→ see **fruit**

pink /pɪŋk/ (**pinker, pinkest, pinks**) ADJ & N-VAR **Pink** is the colour between red and white. ❑ *...a soft pink.*

pinnacle /ˈpɪnɪkəl/ (**pinnacles**) **1** N-COUNT A **pinnacle** is a tall pointed piece of a building or a rock. **2** N-COUNT The **pinnacle of** something is the best or highest level of it. ❑ *Do you regard your selection as Captain as the pinnacle of your career?*

pinpoint /ˈpɪnpɔɪnt/ (**pinpoints, pinpointing, pinpointed**) V-T If you **pinpoint** something, you discover or describe exactly what or where it is. ❑ *We cannot pinpoint the exact time of death.* ❑ *The control room can pinpoint the location of the car.*

pint /paɪnt/ (**pints**) N-COUNT A **pint** is a unit of measurement for liquids. In Britain, it is equal to 568 cubic centimetres or one eighth of an imperial gallon. In America, it is equal to 473 cubic centimetres or one eighth of an American gallon. ❑ *...a pint of milk.* ❑ *These glasses hold a full pint.*
→ see **measurement**

ˈpin-up (**pin-ups**) N-COUNT A **pin-up** is a picture of an attractive woman or man who appears on posters, often wearing very few clothes. A **pin-up** is also the woman or man who appears on posters in this way. ❑ *She was already a famous model and pin-up.*

pioneer /ˌpaɪəˈnɪə/ (**pioneers, pioneering, pioneered**) **1** V-T & N-COUNT Someone who **pioneers** a new activity, invention, or process is one of the first people to do it. You can also refer to them as a **pioneer of** it. ❑ *Professor Alec Jeffreys invented and pioneered DNA tests.* ❑ *...one of the leading pioneers of British photo journalism.* ● **pioneering** ADJ ❑ *The school has won awards for its pioneering work with the community.* **2** N-COUNT **Pioneers** are people who leave their own country to go and settle in a part of another country that has not been settled in before.

pious /paɪəs/ ADJ Someone who is **pious** is very religious and moral. ❑ *He was brought up by pious female relatives.* ● **piously** ADV ❑ *Conti kneeled and crossed himself piously.*

pip /pɪp/ (**pips, pipping, pipped**) **1** N-COUNT **Pips** are the small hard seeds in a fruit such as an apple or orange. **2** V-T & PHRASE In British English, if someone **is pipped to the post**, or **pipped to** or **for** a prize or an award, they are narrowly defeated. ❑ *The film was pipped to the post only by Harry Potter.* ❑ *Lewis was pipped for the gold medal by Evans.*

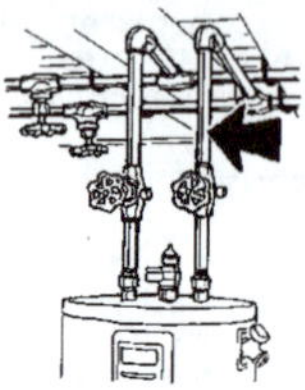
pipe

pipe /paɪp/ (**pipes, piping, piped**) **1** N-COUNT A **pipe** is a long, round, hollow object through which a liquid or gas can flow. ❑ *...water pipes.* **2** V-T If liquid or gas **is piped** somewhere, it is transferred from one place to another through a pipe. ❑ *Clean water is piped into our own homes.* **3** N-COUNT A **pipe** is an object which is used for smoking tobacco. **4** N-COUNT A **pipe** is a simple musical instrument, shaped like a tube with holes in it.
→ see **keyboard**

pipeline /ˈpaɪplaɪn/ (**pipelines**) **1** N-COUNT A **pipeline** is a large pipe used for carrying oil or gas over a long distance. **2** PHRASE If something is **in the pipeline**, it has already been planned or begun. ❑ *There are still four movies in the pipeline.*
→ see **oil**

piping /ˈpaɪpɪŋ/ N-UNCOUNT **Piping** is lengths of pipe or tube made from metal or plastic. ❑ *...rolls of bright yellow plastic piping.*

piracy /ˈpaɪrəsi/ **1** N-UNCOUNT **Piracy** is robbery at sea carried out by pirates. **2** N-UNCOUNT You can refer to the illegal copying of things such as CDs, DVDs and computer programs as **piracy**.

pirate /ˈpaɪrət/ (**pirates, pirating, pirated**) **1** N-COUNT **Pirates** are sailors who attack other ships and steal property from them. **2** V-T Someone who **pirates** CDs, DVDs, books, or computer programs copies and sells them when they have no right to do so. ❑ *...a pirated edition of the book.*

piste /piːst/ (**pistes**) N-COUNT A **piste** is a track of firm snow for skiing on.

pistol /ˈpɪstəl/ (**pistols**) N-COUNT A **pistol** is a small handgun.

piston /ˈpɪstən/ (**pistons**) N-COUNT A **piston** is a cylinder or metal disc that is part of an engine.

pit /pɪt/ (**pits, pitting, pitted**) **1** N-COUNT A **pit** is a large hole that is dug in the ground. **2** N-COUNT A **pit** is a coal mine. **3** N-PLURAL In motor racing, **the pits** are the areas where drivers stop for fuel and repairs during races. **4** V-T If two opposing things or people **are pitted against** one another, they are in conflict. ❑ *These two strong men pitted their skills against each other.* **5** → see also **pitted**
→ see **fruit**

pitch /pɪtʃ/ (**pitches, pitching, pitched**) **1** N-COUNT In British English, a **pitch** is an area of ground that is marked out and used for playing a game such as football, cricket, or hockey. The more usual American word is **field**. ❑ *...cricket pitches.* **2** V-T If you **pitch** something somewhere,

you throw it forcefully while aiming carefully. ❑ *Simon pitched the empty bottle into the lake.* 3 V-T/V-I If someone or something **pitches** somewhere, or if they **are pitched** somewhere, they fall forwards suddenly and with a lot of force. ❑ *I was pitched into the water and swam to the edge.* 4 N-UNCOUNT The **pitch** of a sound is how high or low it is. ❑ *He raised his voice to an even higher pitch.* 5 V-T If something **is pitched at** a particular level, it is set at that level. ❑ *Prices at the hotel are pitched at just over £40 a night.* 6 N-SING If something such as a feeling or a situation rises to a high **pitch** or **fever pitch**, it rises to a high level. ❑ *The competitors have all worked themselves up to a very high pitch.* ❑ *Excitement was at fever pitch.* 7 V-T To **pitch** a tent means to put it up in a place where you are going to stay.
▶ **pitch in** PHR-VERB If you **pitch in**, you join in and help with an activity. [INFORMAL] ❑ *The entire company pitched in to help.*

pitcher

pitcher /ˈpɪtʃə/ (**pitchers**) 1 N-COUNT A **pitcher** is a jug. 2 N-COUNT In baseball, the **pitcher** is the person who throws the ball to the person who is batting.

pitfall /ˈpɪtfɔːl/ (**pitfalls**) N-COUNT The **pitfalls** involved in a particular activity or situation are the things that may go wrong or may cause problems. ❑ *What are the pitfalls of working abroad?*

pitiful /ˈpɪtɪfʊl/ 1 ADJ Someone or something that is **pitiful** is so sad, weak, or small that you feel pity for them. ❑ *It was the most pitiful sight I had ever seen.* ● **pitifully** ADV ❑ *His legs were pitifully thin.* 2 ADJ If you describe something as **pitiful**, you mean that it does not deserve respect or consideration. ❑ *...the team's pitiful performance against Belgium last night.*

pitted /ˈpɪtɪd/ ADJ If the surface of something is **pitted**, it is covered with a lot of small shallow holes. ❑ *...the pitted surface of the moon.*

pity /ˈpɪti/ (**pities, pitying, pitied**) 1 N-UNCOUNT & V-T If you feel **pity for** someone, or if you **pity** them, you feel very sorry for them. ❑ *He felt a sudden pity for her.* ❑ *I don't know whether to hate or pity him.* 2 PHRASE If you **take pity on** someone, you feel sorry for them and help them. ❑ *No woman had ever taken pity on him.* 3 N-SING If you say that it is **a pity** that something is the case, you mean that you feel disappointment or regret about it. ❑ *It is a great pity that all children cannot have the same chances.*

pivot /ˈpɪvət/ (**pivots, pivoting, pivoted**) 1 N-COUNT The **pivot** in a situation is the most important thing which everything else is based on or arranged around. ❑ *Johnny was the pivot of her life.* 2 V-I If something or someone **pivots**, they balance or turn on a central point. ❑ *He pivoted around and punched Graham.* 3 N-COUNT A **pivot** is the pin or central point on which something balances or turns.

pivotal /ˈpɪvətəl/ ADJ A **pivotal** role, point, or figure in something is one that is very important and affects the success of that thing. ❑ *Parents play a pivotal role in the choices students make.*

pizza /ˈpiːtsə/ (**pizzas**) N-VAR A **pizza** is a flat piece of dough covered with tomatoes, cheese, and other savoury food, which is baked in an oven.

placard /ˈplækɑːd/ (**placards**) N-COUNT A **placard** is a large notice that is carried in a march or demonstration. ❑ *The protesters sang songs and carried placards.*

Word Link	***plac ≈ pleasing : complacent, placate, placid***

placate /pləˈkeɪt, AM ˈpleɪkeɪt/ (**placates, placating, placated**) V-T If you **placate** someone, you stop them feeling angry or resentful by doing or saying things that will please them. ❑ *...an attempt to placate his critics.*

placatory /pləˈkeɪtəri/ ADJ A **placatory** remark or action is intended to make someone stop feeling angry. [FORMAL] ❑ *When next to speak he was more placatory.* ❑ *He raised a placatory hand. 'All right, we'll see what we can do.'*

place /pleɪs/ (**places, placing, placed**) 1 N-COUNT A **place** is any point, building, area, town, or country. ❑ *...Stratford, the place where she met her husband, Jack.* ❑ *The snow was two metres deep in places.* 2 N-SING **Place** can be used after 'any', 'no', 'some', or 'every' to mean 'anywhere', 'nowhere', 'somewhere', or 'everywhere'. [AM, INFORMAL] ❑ *The poor guy didn't have any place to go.* ❑ *Why not go out and see if there's some place we can dance?* 3 N-COUNT Your **place** is the house or flat where you live. [INFORMAL] ❑ *Let's all go back to my place!* 4 N-COUNT & PHRASE You can refer to the position where something belongs, or where it is supposed to be, as its **place**. If something is **in place**, it is in its correct or usual position. If it is **out of place**, it is not in its correct or usual position. ❑ *He returned the book to its place on the shelf.* 5 N-COUNT A **place** is a position that is available for someone to occupy. ❑ *I found a place to park.* 6 N-COUNT The **place** of someone or something in a society, system, or situation is their position or role in relation to it. ❑ *They want to see more women take their place in management roles.* 7 N-COUNT & V-T Your **place** in a race or competition is your position in relation to the other competitors. If, for example, a competitor **is placed** first, second, or last, that is their position at the end of a race or competition. 8 N-COUNT If you **get** a **place** in a team, on a committee, or on a course, you are accepted for a place on it. ❑ *I got a place at York University.* 9 V-T If you **place** something somewhere, you put it in a particular position. ❑ *Brett placed the note in the inside pocket of his jacket.* 10 V-T If you **place** a person or thing in a particular state, you cause them to be in it. ❑ *These practices place infants in danger.* ❑ *Police placed the girls under arrest.* 11 V-T If you **place** someone or something in a particular class or group, you classify them in that way. ❑ *What elements, do you think, place music in the 'classical' category?* 12 V-T If you **place** an **order** for some goods or for a meal, you ask a company to send you the goods or a waiter to bring you the meal. 13 V-T If you **place** an **advertisement** in a newspaper, you arrange for the advertisement to appear in the newspaper. ❑ *They placed an advertisement in the local paper.* 14 V-T If you say that you cannot **place** someone, you mean that you recognize them but cannot remember exactly who they are or where you have met them before. ❑ *She felt she should know him, but could not quite place him.* 15 PHRASE If you have been trying to understand something puzzling

P

and then everything **falls into place**, you suddenly understand how different pieces of information are connected and everything becomes clearer. **16** PHRASE If things **fall into place**, events happen naturally to produce a situation you want. ❑ *Once the decision was made, things quickly fell into place.* **17** PHRASE If something such as a law, a policy, or an administrative structure is **in place**, it is working or able to be used. ❑ *Similar laws are already in place in Wales.* **18** PHRASE If one thing or person is used or appears **in place of** another or **in** another's **place**, they replace the other thing or person. ❑ *If you wish, use olive oil in place of butter.* **19** PHRASE You say **in the first place** when you are talking about the beginning of a situation or about the situation as it was before a series of events. ❑ *Why did you come to Washington in the first place?* **20** PHRASE If you **put** someone **in** their **place**, you show them that they are less important or clever than they think they are. **21** PHRASE When something **takes place**, it happens, especially in a controlled or organized way. ❑ *The discussion took place in a famous hotel.*
→ see **zero**

Usage

You do not normally use **place** on its own to refer to somewhere where someone can sit. The word you need is **seat.** ❑ *There was only one seat free on the train.* More generally, you can refer to a **space** which someone or something can occupy. ❑ *He was clearing a space for her to lie down.* You do not use **place** as an uncount noun to refer to an open or empty area. You should use **room** or **space** instead. **Room** is more likely to be used when you are talking about space inside an enclosed area. ❑ *There's not enough room in the bathroom for both of us.* ❑ *Leave plenty of space between you and the car in front.*

placement /ˈpleɪsmənt/ (**placements**) **1** N-UNCOUNT The **placement of** something is the act of putting it in a particular place. ❑ *He organized the placement of furniture and the hanging of pictures.* **2** N-COUNT If someone who is training gets a **placement**, they get a job for a period of time which is intended to give them experience in the work they are training for. **3** N-UNCOUNT The **placement** of someone in a job, home, or school is the act or process of finding them a job, home, or school. ❑ *...placement in a care home.*

Word Link *plac ≈ pleasing : complacent, placate, placid*

placid /ˈplæsɪd/ ADJ If you describe a person or animal as **placid**, you mean they are calm and do not become excited, angry, or upset very easily.

plague /pleɪɡ/ (**plagues, plaguing, plagued**) **1** N-COUNT A **plague** is an infectious disease that spreads quickly and kills large numbers of people. ❑ *A cholera plague killed many prisoners of war.* **2** N-COUNT A **plague of** unpleasant things is a large number of them that arrive or happen at the same time. ❑ *...a plague of rats.* **3** V-T If you **are plagued** by unpleasant things, they continually cause you a lot of trouble or suffering. ❑ *Fears about job security plague the workforce.* **4** V-T If someone **plagues** you, they keep bothering you or asking you for something. ❑ *I'm not going to plague you with a lot more questions.*

plaice /pleɪs/

Plaice is both the singular and the plural form.

N-VAR A **plaice** is a flat sea fish. **Plaice** is the flesh of this fish eaten as food.

plain /pleɪn/ (**plains, plainer, plainest**) **1** ADJ A **plain** object, surface, or fabric is entirely in one colour and has no pattern, design, or writing on it. ❑ *A plain carpet makes a room look bigger.* **2** ADJ **Plain** things are very simple in style. ❑ *...plain food, freshly made from good quality ingredients.* • **plainly** ADV ❑ *...plainly dressed.* **3** ADJ If a fact, situation, or statement is **plain**, it is easy to recognize or understand. ❑ *It was plain to him that I was unhappy.* **4** ADJ If you describe someone, especially a woman or girl, as **plain**, you think they look ordinary and are not at all beautiful. **5** N-COUNT A **plain** is a large, flat area of land with very few trees on it.

Thesaurus *plain* Also look up:

ADJ. bare, modest, simple; *(ant.)* elaborate, fancy **1**
common, everyday, modest, ordinary, simple, usual; *(ant.)* elaborate, fancy **2**
clear, distinct, evident, transparent **3**

Word Partnership Use *plain* with:

N. plain **style** **2**
plain **English**, plain **language**, plain **speech**, plain **truth** **3**

plainly /ˈpleɪnli/ **1** ADV If something is **plainly** the case, it is obviously the case. ❑ *The judge's conclusion was plainly wrong.* **2** ADV You use **plainly** to indicate that something is easily seen, noticed, or recognized. ❑ *Through the cracks we could plainly see inside.* **3** ADV If you say something **plainly**, it is easy to understand and cannot be mistaken. ❑ *'You're a coward,' Mark said very plainly.*

plaintiff /ˈpleɪntɪf/ (**plaintiffs**) N-COUNT A **plaintiff** is a person who brings a legal case against someone in a court of law.
→ see **trial**

plaintive /ˈpleɪntɪv/ ADJ A **plaintive** sound or voice is sad and high-pitched. [LITERARY] ❑ *...the plaintive cry of the sea birds.*

plait /plæt, AM pleɪt/ (**plaits, plaiting, plaited**) **1** V-T If you **plait** three or more lengths of hair or rope together, you twist them over and under each other to make one thick length. **2** N-COUNT In British English, a **plait** is a length of hair that has been plaited. The American word is **braid**.
→ see **hair**

plan /plæn/ (**plans, planning, planned**) **1** N-COUNT & PHRASE A **plan** is a method of achieving something that you have worked out carefully in advance. When things are going **according to plan**, they are working out in the way that you had planned. ❑ *...a peace plan.* ❑ *Everything was going to plan until the last minute.* **2** V-T/V-I If you **plan** what you are going to do, you decide in detail what you are going to do. ❑ *He planned to leave Baghdad on Monday.* ❑ *Plan for the future.* ❑ *We meet once a week to plan lessons.* **3** N-PLURAL If you have **plans**, you are intending to do a particular thing. ❑ *'I'm sorry,' she said. 'I have plans for tonight.'*

Picture Dictionary plants

4 N-COUNT A **plan of** something that is going to be built or made is a detailed diagram or drawing of it. 5 → see also **planning**

▶ **plan on** PHR-VERB If you **plan on** doing something, you intend to do it. ❑ *They were planning on getting married.*

plane /pleɪn/ (**planes, planing, planed**) 1 N-COUNT A **plane** is a vehicle with wings and one or more engines which can fly. ❑ *He had plenty of time to catch his plane.* 2 N-COUNT A **plane** is a flat level surface which may be sloping at a particular angle. ❑ *...a building with angled planes.* 3 N-COUNT If you say that something is **on a higher plane**, you mean that it is more spiritual or less concerned with worldly things. ❑ *The music and the poetry take you to a higher plane.* 4 N-COUNT A **plane** is a tool that has a flat bottom with a sharp blade in it, used for shaping wood. 5 V-T If you **plane** a piece of wood, you make it smaller or smoother by using a plane.

Thesaurus	*plane* Also look up:
N.	aircraft, airplane, craft, jet 1
	horizontal, level, surface 2

planet /ˈplænɪt/ (**planets**) N-COUNT A **planet** is a large, round object in space that moves around a star. The Earth is a planet. ❑ *...the nine planets in the solar system.*

→ see **astronomer, galaxy, satellite, solar system**

planetary /ˈplænɪtri, AM -teri/ ADJ BEFORE N **Planetary** means relating to or belonging to planets. ❑ *...planetary systems.*

plank /plæŋk/ (**planks**) N-COUNT A **plank** is a long rectangular piece of wood.

planner /ˈplænə/ (**planners**) N-COUNT **Planners** are people whose job is to make decisions about what is going to be done in the future. ❑ *...James, a 29-year-old town planner.*

planning /ˈplænɪŋ/ 1 N-UNCOUNT **Planning** is the process of deciding in detail how to do something before you actually start to do it. ❑ *The trip needs careful planning in advance.* 2 N-UNCOUNT **Planning** is control by the local government of the way that land is used and of what new buildings are built.

plant /plɑːnt, plænt/ (**plants, planting, planted**) 1 N-COUNT A **plant** is a living thing that grows in earth and has a stem, leaves, and roots. ❑ *Water each plant as often as required.* 2 V-T When you **plant** a seed, plant, or young tree, you put it into earth so that it will grow. ● **planting** N-UNCOUNT ❑ *Flooding in the country has delayed planting.* 3 V-T When someone **plants** land, they put plants or seeds into the land to grow. ❑ *They have been planting a large vegetable garden.* 4 N-COUNT A **plant** is a factory, or a place where power is generated. ❑ *...car assembly plants.* 5 N-UNCOUNT **Plant** is large machinery used in industrial processes. [TECHNICAL] 6 V-T If you **plant** something somewhere, you put it there firmly. ❑ *She crossed the room and planted herself in front of him.* 7 V-T If someone **plants** a **bomb** somewhere, they hide it in the place where they want it to explode. 8 V-T If something such as a weapon or drug **is planted on** someone, it is put amongst their belongings or in their house so that they will be wrongly accused of a crime.

→ see Picture Dictionary: **plants**

→ see **earth, farm, food, tree**

plantation /plɑːnˈteɪʃən, plæn-/ (**plantations**) 1 N-COUNT A **plantation** is a large piece of land, where crops such as cotton, tea, or sugar are grown. 2 N-COUNT A **plantation** is a large number of trees planted together.

plaque /plæk, plɑːk/ (**plaques**) 1 N-COUNT A **plaque** is a flat piece of metal or wood, which is fixed to a wall or monument in memory of a person or event. 2 N-UNCOUNT **Plaque** is a harmful substance that forms on the surface of your teeth.

→ see **teeth**

plasma /ˈplæzmə/ N-UNCOUNT **Plasma** is the clear fluid part of blood which contains the red and white cells.

ˈplasma ˌscreen (**plasma screens**) N-COUNT A **plasma screen** is a type of thin television screen or computer screen that produces high-quality images.

plaster /ˈplɑːstə, ˈplæs-/ (**plasters, plastering, plastered**) 1 N-UNCOUNT **Plaster** is a smooth paste made of sand, lime, and water which dries and forms a hard layer. Plaster is used to cover

P

walls and ceilings. **2** V-T If you **plaster** a wall or ceiling, you cover it with a layer of plaster. **3** N-COUNT A **plaster** is a strip of sticky material with a small pad, used for covering small cuts or sores on your body. [BRIT] **4** PHRASE If a broken leg or arm is **in plaster**, it is covered in a hard case made from a special type of plaster to protect the broken bones.

plastered /ˈplɑːstəd, ˈplæs-/ **1** ADJ AFTER LINK-V If something is **plastered to** a surface, it is sticking to the surface. ❑ *His hair was plastered to his head.* **2** ADJ AFTER LINK-V If a surface is **plastered with** something, it is covered with it. ❑ *My hands, boots and trousers were plastered with mud.*

plastic /ˈplæstɪk/ (**plastics**) N-VAR **Plastic** is a light but strong material produced by a chemical process. ❑ *...a black plastic bag.*
→ see **oil**

ˌplastic ˈsurgery N-UNCOUNT **Plastic surgery** is the practice of performing operations to repair or replace skin which has been damaged, or to improve people's appearance.

plate /pleɪt/ (**plates**) **1** N-COUNT A **plate** is a round or oval flat dish used to hold food. A **plate of** food is the amount of food on the plate. ❑ *...a huge plate of bacon and eggs.* **2** N-COUNT A **plate** is a flat piece of metal, for example on part of a machine. **3** N-UNCOUNT **Plate** is dishes, bowls, and cups that are made of precious metal. **4** N-COUNT A **plate** in a book is a picture or photograph which takes up a whole page. **5** N-COUNT A dental **plate** is a piece of shaped plastic which a set of false teeth is attached to. **6** → see also **number plate**
→ see **continent, dish, earthquake, rock**

plateau /ˈplætəʊ, AM plæˈtəʊ/ (**plateaus** or **plateaux**) **1** N-COUNT A **plateau** is a large area of high fairly flat land. **2** N-COUNT If an activity or process has reached a **plateau**, it is going through a stage where there is no change or development.
→ see **land**

plated /ˈpleɪtɪd/ ADJ AFTER LINK-V If something made of metal is **plated with** a thin layer of another type of metal, it is covered with it. ❑ *...jewellery plated with 24-carat gold.*

platform /ˈplætfɔːm/ (**platforms**) **1** N-COUNT A **platform** is a flat raised structure or area on which someone or something can stand. ❑ *He walked to the platform to begin his speech.* ❑ *...a viewing platform overlooking Mont Blanc.* **2** N-COUNT A **platform** in a railway station is the area beside the rails where you wait for or get off a train. **3** N-COUNT The **platform** of a political party is what they say they will do if they are elected. ❑ *He was elected on a nationalist platform last May.*
→ see **oil**

platinum /ˈplætɪnəm/ N-UNCOUNT **Platinum** is a very valuable silvery-grey metal.

platitude /ˈplætɪtjuːd, AM -tuːd/ (**platitudes**) N-COUNT A **platitude** is a statement considered to be meaningless because it has been made many times before in similar situations. ❑ *They don't want platitudes; they want the truth.*

platonic /pləˈtɒnɪk/ ADJ A **platonic** relationship is one of friendship and does not involve sexual attraction.

platter /ˈplætə/ (**platters**) N-COUNT A **platter** is a large flat plate used for serving food.
→ see **dish**

P

plausible /ˈplɔːzɪbəl/ ADJ A **plausible** explanation or statement seems likely to be true or valid. ❑ *Is it plausible that the President did not know what was going on?* • **plausibly** ADV ❑ *He could plausibly have been in contact with all these people.* • **plausibility** N-UNCOUNT ❑ *...the plausibility of the theory.*

play /pleɪ/ (**plays, playing, played**) **1** V-I & N-UNCOUNT When children or animals **play**, or when they spend time in **play**, they spend time doing enjoyable things, such as using toys and taking part in games. ❑ *Polly was playing with her teddy bear.* ❑ *...a few hours of play before bed.* **2** V-T/V-I & N-UNCOUNT When you **play** a sport, game, or match, you take part in it. **Play** is the activity of playing sport or the time during which a game or match is played. ❑ *Alain was playing cards with his friends.* ❑ *I want to play for my country.* ❑ *Play was halted because of rain.* **3** V-T/V-I When one person or team **plays** another, or **plays against** them, they compete against them in a sport or game. ❑ *Northern Ireland will play Latvia.* **4** N-COUNT A **play** is a piece of writing performed in a theatre, on the radio, or on television. ❑ *It's my favourite Shakespeare play.* **5** V-T If an actor **plays** a character in a play or film, he or she performs as that character. ❑ *His ambition is to play the part of Dracula.* **6** V-T/V-I If you **play** a musical instrument, or if you **play** a tune on it, you produce music from it. ❑ *The orchestra played beautifully.* **7** V-T/V-I If you **play** a record, CD, or tape, you put it onto a record player or into a CD-player or tape recorder and sound is produced. ❑ *There is classical music playing in the background.* **8** V-T If you **play** a joke or a trick **on** someone, you deceive them or give them a surprise in a way that you think is funny, but may cause them problems or annoy them. ❑ *Someone had played a trick on her; they had stretched a piece of string across the top of the steps.* **9** PHRASE If you ask **what** someone **is playing at**, you are angry because you think they are doing something stupid or wrong. [INFORMAL] **10** PHRASE If something or someone **plays a part** or **plays a role** in a situation, they are involved in it and have an effect on it. ❑ *Miller played a major role in the country's development.*
→ see **DVD, theatre**

▸ **play along** PHR-VERB If you **play along with** a person, you appear to agree with them and do what they want, even though you are not sure whether they are right. ❑ *I had to play along with her and pretend that we really were in love.*

▸ **play around** **1** PHR-VERB If you **play around**, you behave in a silly way to amuse yourself or other people. [INFORMAL] ❑ *Stop playing around and eat!* **2** PHR-VERB If you **play around with** a problem or an arrangement of objects, you try different ways of organizing it in order to find the best solution or arrangement. [INFORMAL]

▸ **play at** PHR-VERB If you say that someone is **playing at** an activity, you disapprove of the fact that they are doing it casually and not very seriously. ❑ *She was playing at being the good little wife.*

▸ **play back** PHR-VERB When you **play back** a tape or film, you listen to the sounds or watch the pictures after recording them.

▸ **play down** PHR-VERB If you **play down** something, you try to make people think that it is less important than it really is. ❑ *Managers played down reports that 10,000 jobs could be lost.*

▸ **play off against** PHR-VERB If you **play** people

off against each other, you make them compete or argue, so that you gain some advantage. ❑ *Eleanor began to play her parents off against each other.*

▶ **play on** PHR-VERB If you **play on** someone's fears, you deliberately use them in order to achieve what you want. ❑ *The new laws play on the population's fear of change.*

▶ **play up** PHR-VERB If something such as a machine or a part of your body **is playing up**, or if it **is playing** you **up**, it is not working properly. [BRIT, INFORMAL] ❑ *The engine had been playing up.* ❑ *His back is playing him up again.*

player /ˈpleɪə/ (**players**) **1** N-COUNT A **player** in a sport or game is a person who takes part. **2** N-COUNT You can use **player** to refer to a musician. ❑ *...a professional trumpet player.* **3** N-COUNT A **player** is an actor. ❑ *Oscar nominations went to all five leading players.* **4** → see also **record player**
→ see **chess, football**

playful /ˈpleɪfʊl/ ADJ A **playful** gesture is friendly and cheerful. ❑ *...a playful kiss.* ● **playfully** ADV ❑ *She pushed him away playfully.* ● **playfulness** N-UNCOUNT ❑ *...the child's natural playfulness.*

playground /ˈpleɪgraʊnd/ (**playgrounds**) N-COUNT A **playground** is a piece of land where children can play.

playgroup /ˈpleɪgruːp/ (**playgroups**) N-VAR A **playgroup** is an informal kind of school for very young children where they learn by playing.

playing card

ˈplaying card (**playing cards**) N-COUNT **Playing cards** are thin pieces of card with numbers and pictures on them, which are used to play games.

ˈplaying field (**playing fields**) **1** N-COUNT A **playing field** is a large area of grass where people play sports. **2** PHRASE You talk about a **level playing field** to mean a situation that is fair, because no competitor or opponent has an advantage over another.

ˈplay-off also **playoff** (**playoffs**) N-COUNT A **play-off** is an extra game played to decide the winner of a sports competition when two or more people have got the same score.

playwright /ˈpleɪraɪt/ (**playwrights**) N-COUNT A **playwright** is a person who writes plays.
→ see **theatre**

plaza /ˈplɑːzə, AM ˈplæzə/ (**plazas**) N-COUNT A **plaza** is an open square in a city.

plc also **PLC** /ˌpiː el ˈsiː/ (**plcs**) In Britain, **plc** is an abbreviation for 'public limited company'. It is used after the name of a company whose shares can be bought by the public. ❑ *...British Telecommunications plc.*

plea /pliː/ (**pleas**) **1** N-COUNT A **plea** is a request for something made in an intense or emotional way. [JOURNALISM] ❑ *...his emotional plea for the public's help.* **2** N-COUNT In a court of law, a person's **plea** is the answer that they give when they have been charged with a crime. ❑ *...a plea of not guilty.*

plead /pliːd/ (**pleads, pleading, pleaded**) **1** V-I If you **plead with** someone **to** do something, you ask them in an intense, emotional way to do it. ❑ *He was kneeling on the floor pleading for mercy.* ❑ *The lady pleaded with her daughter to come back home.* **2** V-I When someone charged with a crime **pleads guilty** or **not guilty** in a court of law, they officially state that they are guilty or not guilty of the crime. **3** V-T If someone **pleads the case** or **cause** of someone or something, they speak out in their support or defence. ❑ *He continued to plead the cause of freedom.* **4** V-T If you **plead** a particular thing as a reason for doing or not doing something, you give it as your excuse. ❑ *Mr Giles pleads ignorance as his excuse.*
→ see **trial**

pleading /ˈpliːdɪŋ/ (**pleadings**) **1** ADJ A **pleading** expression or gesture shows that you want something very much. ❑ *...his pleading eyes.* **2** N-VAR **Pleading** is asking someone for something you want very much, in an intense or emotional way. ❑ *He simply ignored Sid's pleading.*

pleasant /ˈplezənt/ (**pleasanter, pleasantest**) **1** ADJ Something that is **pleasant** is enjoyable or attractive. ❑ *It's always pleasant to do what you enjoy.* ● **pleasantly** ADV ❑ *The room was pleasantly warm.* **2** ADJ Someone who is **pleasant** is friendly and likeable.

Thesaurus *pleasant* Also look up:

ADJ. agreeable, cheerful, delightful, friendly, likeable, nice; *(ant.)* unpleasant **2**

please /pliːz/ (**pleases, pleasing, pleased**) **1** CONVENTION You say **please** when you are politely asking or inviting someone to do something, or when you are asking someone for something. ❑ *Can you help us please?* ❑ *Please come in.* **2** CONVENTION You say **please** when you are accepting something politely. ❑ *'Tea?'—'Yes, please.'* **3** V-T If someone or something **pleases** you, they make you feel happy and satisfied. ❑ *I was tidying my bedroom to please mum.* ❑ *Nothing pleased him.* **4** PHRASE You use **please** in expressions such as **as she pleases, whatever you please**, and **anything he pleases** to indicate that someone can do or have whatever they want. ❑ *Women should be free to dress as they please.* **5** CONVENTION You say **'please yourself'** to indicate in a rather rude way that you do not mind or care whether the person you are talking to does a particular thing or not. [INFORMAL]

pleased /pliːzd/ **1** ADJ AFTER LINK-V If you are **pleased**, you are happy about something or satisfied with it. ❑ *I think he's going to be pleased that we identified the real problems.* ❑ *I'm pleased with the way things have been going.* ❑ *They're pleased to be going home.* **2** CONVENTION You say **'Pleased to meet you'** as a polite way of greeting someone you are meeting for the first time.

pleasing /ˈpliːzɪŋ/ ADJ Something that is **pleasing** gives you pleasure and satisfaction. ❑ *...a pleasing climate.* ● **pleasingly** ADV ❑ *The design is pleasingly simple.*

pleasurable /ˈpleʒərəbəl/ ADJ **Pleasurable** experiences or sensations are pleasant and enjoyable. ❑ *He found sailing more pleasurable than skiing.*

pleasure /ˈpleʒə/ (**pleasures**) **1** N-UNCOUNT If something gives you **pleasure**, you get a feeling of happiness, satisfaction, or enjoyment from it. ❑ *Everybody takes pleasure in eating.* **2** N-UNCOUNT **Pleasure** is the activity of enjoying yourself rather than working. ❑ *He mixed business and pleasure.* **3** N-COUNT A **pleasure** is an activity or experience that you find very enjoyable and satisfying. ❑ *Watching TV is our only pleasure.* **4** CONVENTION You can say '**It's a pleasure**' or '**My pleasure**' as a polite way of replying to someone who has just thanked you for doing something. ❑ *'Thanks very much anyhow.'—'It's a pleasure.'*

pleat /pliːt/ (**pleats**) N-COUNT A **pleat** in a piece of clothing is a permanent fold made in the cloth.

pleated /ˈpliːtɪd/ ADJ A **pleated** piece of clothing has pleats in it.

pledge /pledʒ/ (**pledges, pledging, pledged**) V-T & N-COUNT When someone **pledges to** do something, or when they make a **pledge to** do it, they promise solemnly that they will do it or provide it. ❑ *Britain pledged $36 million to the victims.* ❑ *He pledged that the company would do 'what is right'.* ❑ *...a pledge to cut unemployment.*

Word Link	*plen ≈ full : plentiful, plenty, replenish*

Word Link	*ful ≈ quantity that fills : handful, mouthful, plentiful*

plentiful /ˈplentɪfʊl/ ADJ Things that are **plentiful** exist in such large amounts or numbers that there is enough for people's wants or needs. ❑ *...a plentiful supply of vegetables.*

plenty /ˈplenti/ QUANT If there is **plenty of** something, there is a large amount of it, often more than is needed. ❑ *There was still plenty of time to eat.* ❑ *I don't like long interviews. Fifteen minutes is plenty.*

Thesaurus	*plenty* Also look up:
QUANT.	abundance, capacity, quantity; *(ant.)* scarcity

pliers /plaɪəz/ N-PLURAL **Pliers** are a tool with two handles at one end and two hard, flat, metal parts at the other. **Pliers** are used to hold or pull out things such as nails, or to bend or cut wire. → see **tool**

plight /plaɪt/ N-SING If you talk about someone's **plight**, you mean the difficult or dangerous situation they are in. [FORMAL] ❑ *...the plight of Third World countries.*

plod /plɒd/ (**plods, plodding, plodded**) **1** V-I If someone **plods** somewhere, they walk there slowly and heavily. ❑ *The horse plodded along, half asleep.* **2** V-I If you **plod on with** a job, you keep on doing it, without worrying about how fast you are progressing. ❑ *I am happy, plodding on with my life.* ❑ *Production continued to plod along at a painfully slow pace.*

plot /plɒt/ (**plots, plotting, plotted**) **1** N-COUNT & V-T/V-I If there is a **plot to** do something illegal or wrong, or if people **plot to** do something like this, they plan secretly to do it. ❑ *...a plot to bomb the airport.* ❑ *By the time they were married, she was already plotting against him.* ● **plotter** (**plotters**) N-COUNT ❑ *Plotters tried to gain power in Moscow.* **2** N-VAR The **plot** of a film, novel, or play is the story and the way in which it develops. **3** N-COUNT A **plot** is a small piece of land, especially one that is intended for a purpose such as building houses or growing vegetables. **4** V-T When people **plot** a strategy or a course of action, they carefully plan each step of it. **5** V-T When someone **plots** something on a graph, they mark certain points on it and then join the points up. **6** V-T To **plot** the position or progress of something means to follow its position or progress and show it on a map or diagram.

plough [AM **plow**] /plaʊ/ (**ploughs, ploughing, ploughed**) **1** N-COUNT A **plough** is a large farming tool with sharp blades, which is attached to a tractor or an animal and used to turn over the soil before planting. **2** V-T When a farmer **ploughs** an area of land, they turn over the soil using a plough.

plough

▶ **plough into** **1** PHR-VERB If something, for example a car, **ploughs into** something else, it crashes violently into it. **2** PHR-VERB If you say that money **is ploughed into** something such as a business, you are emphasizing that a large amount of money is being invested in it. ❑ *...the need to plough money into education and training.* → see **barn**

▶ **plough on** PHR-VERB If you **plough on**, you continue moving or trying to complete something, even though it takes a lot of effort. ❑ *The Government ploughed on with the sale.*

▶ **plough through** **1** PHR-VERB If you **plough through** something such as a large meal or a long piece of work, you finally finish it, although it takes a lot of effort. **2** PHR-VERB If a person or vehicle **ploughs through** a place or substance, they move through it with great force or effort. ❑ *The boat ploughed through the water.*

plow /plaʊ/ → see **plough**

ploy /plɔɪ/ (**ploys**) N-COUNT If you describe something someone does as a **ploy**, you mean that they have planned it carefully and are doing it in order to gain an advantage for themselves. ❑ *That's only a ploy to get more customers.*

pluck /plʌk/ (**plucks, plucking, plucked**) **1** V-T If you **pluck** a fruit, flower, or leaf, you take it between your fingers and pull it from its stalk. [WRITTEN] ❑ *I plucked a lemon from the tree.* **2** V-T If you **pluck** something from somewhere, you take it in your fingers or hands and pull it sharply from where it is. ❑ *He plucked the note from her hand.* **3** V-T If you **pluck** the strings of a musical instrument such as a guitar, you pull them with your fingers and let them go, so that they make a sound. **4** V-T If you **pluck** a bird that has been killed to be eaten, you pull its feathers out to prepare it for cooking. **5** V-T If you **pluck** your **eyebrows**, you shape them by pulling out some of the hairs, using a device called tweezers. **6** V-T If someone is rescued from a dangerous or bad situation, you can say that they **are plucked from** it or **are plucked to safety**. [JOURNALISM] ❑ *They were plucked from the river when people heard their cries for help.* **7** PHRASE If you **pluck up the courage to** do something frightening, you make an effort to be brave enough to do it. ❑ *I finally plucked up the courage to go home.*

▶ **pluck at** PHR-VERB If you **pluck at** something, you take it between your fingertips and pull it sharply but gently. ❑ *The boy plucked at Adam's sleeve.*

plug /plʌg/ (**plugs, plugging, plugged**) **1** N-COUNT A **plug** on a piece of electrical equipment is a small plastic object with two or three metal pins which fit into the holes of an electric socket.

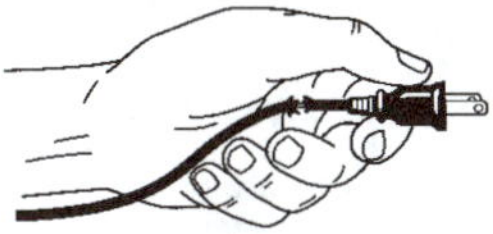
plugs

2 N-COUNT A **plug** is a thick circular piece of rubber or plastic that you use to block the hole in a bath or sink. when it is filled with water.

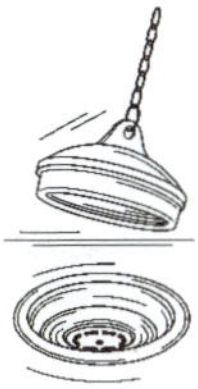

3 V-T If you **plug** a hole, a gap, or a leak, you block it with something. ❑ *Chet used his shirt to plug the hole in the boat.* **4** V-T & N-COUNT If someone **plugs** something such as a book or a film, or if they give it a **plug**, they talk about it in order to encourage people to buy it or see it. [INFORMAL] ❑ *...another actor plugging his latest book.* **5** PHRASE If someone in a position of power **pulls the plug on** a project or on someone's activities, they use their power to stop them continuing.

▶ **plug in** or **plug into** PHR-VERB If you **plug** a piece of electrical equipment **into** an electricity supply, or if you **plug** it **in**, you push its plug into an electric socket so that it can work. ❑ *I filled the kettle and plugged it in.*

plum /plʌm/ (**plums**) **1** N-COUNT A **plum** is a small sweet fruit with a smooth red or yellow skin and a stone in the middle. **2** ADJ BEFORE N A **plum job** is a very good job that a lot of people would like.

plumber /ˈplʌmə/ (**plumbers**) N-COUNT A **plumber** is a person whose job is to connect and repair things such as water and drainage pipes, baths, and toilets.

plumbing /ˈplʌmɪŋ/ **1** N-UNCOUNT **The plumbing** in a building consists of the water and drainage pipes, baths, and toilets in it. **2** N-UNCOUNT **Plumbing** is the work of connecting and repairing water and drainage pipes, baths, and toilets.

plume /pluːm/ (**plumes**) N-COUNT A **plume of** smoke, dust, fire, or water is a large quantity of it that rises into the air in a column.

plummet /ˈplʌmɪt/ (**plummets, plummeting, plummeted**) V-I If an amount, rate, or price **plummets**, it decreases quickly by a large amount. [JOURNALISM] ❑ *Prices have plummeted over the past month.*

plump /plʌmp/ (**plumper, plumpest, plumps, plumping, plumped**) **1** ADJ A **plump** person is rather fat. **2** → See note at **fat**

▶ **plump for** PHR-VERB If you **plump for** someone or something, you choose them after hesitating and thinking. ❑ *Did you plump for the salmon or the roast beef?*

plunder /ˈplʌndə/ (**plunders, plundering, plundered**) V-T & N-UNCOUNT If someone **plunders** a place, or if they are involved in the **plunder** of a place, they steal things from it. [WRITTEN] ❑ *They have plundered £4 billion from the Government reserves.* ❑ *This money was obtained as a result of robbery and plunder.*

plunge /plʌndʒ/ (**plunges, plunging, plunged**) **1** V-I If something or someone **plunges** in a particular direction, especially into water, they fall, rush, or throw themselves in that direction. ❑ *At least 50 people died when a bus plunged into a river.* **2** V-T If you **plunge** an object **into** something, you push it quickly or violently into it. ❑ *She plunged her hands into the water.* **3** V-T/V-I If something **plunges** someone or something **into** a particular state or situation, or if they **plunge into** it, they are suddenly in that state or situation. ❑ *Homes were plunged into darkness as electricity cables crashed down.* ❑ *The economy is plunging into recession.* **4** V-T/V-I If you **plunge into** an activity or **are plunged into** it, you become very involved in it. ❑ *He plunged himself into work.* **5** V-I & N-COUNT If an amount or rate **plunges**, or if there is a **plunge** in an amount or rate, it decreases quickly and suddenly. ❑ *His weight began to plunge.* **6** PHRASE If you **take the plunge**, you decide to do something that you consider difficult or risky. ❑ *I took the plunge and left my job.*

plural /ˈplʊərəl/ (**plurals**) N-COUNT & ADJ BEFORE N The **plural** of a word or its **plural** form is the form that is used when referring to more than one person or thing. ❑ *What is the plural of 'person'?* ❑ *...the plural pronoun 'we'.*

pluralism /ˈplʊərəlɪzəm/ N-UNCOUNT If there is **pluralism** within a society, it has many different groups and political parties. [FORMAL]

plus /plʌs/ (**pluses** or **plusses**) **1** CONJ You use **plus** to show that one number or quantity is being added to another. ❑ *Two plus two equals four.* ❑ *Send a cheque for £18.99 plus £2 for postage and packing.* **2** ADJ **Plus** before a number or quantity means that the number or quantity is greater than zero. ❑ *Temperatures range from minus 20 degrees at night to plus 20 degrees in the day.* **3** CONJ You can use **plus** when mentioning an additional item or fact. ❑ *The car has enough room for two adults and three children, plus a dog in the boot.* **4** ADJ You use **plus** after a number or quantity to indicate that the actual number or quantity is greater than the one mentioned. ❑ *There are only 35 staff to serve 30,000-plus customers.* **5** N-COUNT A **plus** is an advantage or benefit. [INFORMAL] ❑ *Experience in sales is a big plus.*

plush /plʌʃ/ (**plusher, plushest**) ADJ If you describe something as **plush**, you mean that it is very smart, comfortable, or expensive. ❑ *...a plush hotel.*

plutonium /pluːˈtəʊniəm/ N-UNCOUNT **Plutonium** is a radioactive element used especially in nuclear weapons and as a fuel in nuclear power stations.

ply /plaɪ/ (**plies, plying, plied**) **1** V-T If someone **plies** you **with** food or drink, they keep giving it to you in an insistent way. ❑ *When we arrived they plied us with cups of tea.* **2** V-T If a ship, aircraft, or vehicle **plies** a route, it makes regular journeys along that route.

plywood /ˈplaɪwʊd/ N-UNCOUNT **Plywood** is wood that consists of thin layers of wood stuck together.

p.m. /ˌpiː ˈem/ ADV **p.m.** is used after a number to show that you are referring to a particular time between noon and midnight. ❑ *The library is open from 7:00 a.m. to 9:00 p.m. every day.*

PM /ˌpiː ˈem/ (**PMs**) N-COUNT **The PM** is an abbreviation for the **Prime Minister**. [INFORMAL]

pneumonia /njuːˈməʊniə/ N-UNCOUNT **Pneumonia** is a serious disease which affects your lungs and makes breathing difficult.

poach /pəʊtʃ/ (**poaches, poaching, poached**) **1** V-T If someone **poaches** animals, fish, or birds, they illegally catch them on someone else's property. • **poacher** (**poachers**) N-COUNT ❑ *More than half of Africa's elephants have been killed by poachers.* • **poaching** N-UNCOUNT ❑ *...a man accused of salmon poaching.* **2** V-T If an organization **poaches** members or customers **from** another organization, they secretly or dishonestly persuade them to join them or become their customers. ❑ *He has poached staff from the company.* • **poaching** N-UNCOUNT ❑ *Measures were introduced to keep members and prevent poaching.* **3** V-T If you **poach** food such as fish or eggs, you cook it gently in boiling water or milk. ❑ *...a poached egg.*

pocket /ˈpɒkɪt/ (**pockets, pocketing, pocketed**) **1** N-COUNT A **pocket** is a small bag or pouch that forms part of a piece of clothing. ❑ *...his jacket pocket.* **2** N-COUNT You can use **pocket** in expressions that refer to money that people have, get, or spend. ❑ *Tax cuts will put money in taxpayers' pockets.* **3** ADJ BEFORE N You use **pocket** to describe something that is small enough to fit into a pocket. ❑ *...a pocket calculator.* **4** V-T If someone **pockets** something, usually something that does not belong to them, they keep it or steal it. [INFORMAL] ❑ *O'Connor pocketed the money.* **5** PHRASE If you are **out of pocket**, you have less money than you should have or than you intended. ❑ *He says that the deal would leave him £4,500 out of pocket.*

P

ˈpocket money N-UNCOUNT In British English, **pocket money** is a small amount of money given regularly to children by their parents. The usual American word is **allowance**.

pod /pɒd/ (**pods**) N-COUNT A **pod** is a seed container that grows on some plants such as peas.

podcast /ˈpɒdkɑːst/ (**podcasts**) N-COUNT A **podcast** is an audio file that can be downloaded and listened to on a computer or iPod. ❑ *Now there are thousands of podcasts available daily.*

podium /ˈpəʊdiəm/ (**podiums**) N-COUNT A **podium** is a small platform on which someone stands in order to give a lecture or conduct an orchestra.

poem /ˈpəʊɪm/ (**poems**) N-COUNT A **poem** is a piece of writing in which the words are chosen for their beauty and sound and are carefully arranged, often in short lines.

poet /ˈpəʊɪt/ (**poets**) N-COUNT A **poet** is a person who writes poems.

poetic /pəʊˈetɪk/ **1** ADJ Something that is **poetic** is very beautiful, expressive, and sensitive. ❑ *...an amusing and poetic description of modern Dublin.* **2** ADJ **Poetic** means relating to poetry. ❑ *There's a very rich poetic tradition in Gaelic.*

poetry /ˈpəʊɪtri/ N-UNCOUNT Poems, considered as a form of literature, are referred to as **poetry**. ❑ *Lawrence Durrell wrote a great deal of poetry.* ❑ *...a poetry book.*
→ see **genre**

poignant /ˈpɔɪnjənt/ ADJ Something that is **poignant** makes you feel very sad or full of pity. ❑ *A poignant moment in the movie comes when he remembers his childhood days.*

point /pɔɪnt/ (**points, pointing, pointed**) **1** N-COUNT A **point** is an opinion or fact expressed by someone. ❑ *The research made some useful points.* ❑ *He illustrates his point with a story.* **2** N-COUNT If you say that someone **has a point**, or if you **take their point** or **see their point**, you mean that you accept that what they have said is worth considering. ❑ *'If he'd already killed once, surely he'd have killed Sarah?' She had a point there.* **3** N-SING **The point of** what you are saying or discussing is the most important part. If you say that something is **beside the point**, you mean it is not relevant to what you are saying or discussing. ❑ *My point is that I'm not going to change.* ❑ *He has completely missed the point of recent discussions.* ❑ *He came straight to the point. 'It's bad news,' he said.* **4** N-SING If you ask what **the point of** something is, or say that there is **no point in** it, you are indicating that a particular action has no purpose or would not be useful. ❑ *Many do not even turn up to classes. They cannot see the point.* ❑ *There is no point in staying any longer.* **5** N-COUNT A **point** is an aspect or quality of something or someone. ❑ *Science was never my strong point at school.* **6** N-COUNT A **point** is a particular position or time. ❑ *The pain was coming from a point in his right leg.* ❑ *At this point Diana arrived.* **7** N-COUNT The **point** of something such as a needle or knife is the thin, sharp end of it. **8** N-COUNT In some sports and games, a **point** is one of the single marks that are added together to give the total score. ❑ *New Zealand beat Scotland by 21 points to 18.* **9** N-COUNT You use **point** to refer to the dot or mark in a decimal number that separates the whole numbers from the fractions. [SPOKEN] ❑ *...7.8 per cent.* **10** N-COUNT The **points** of a compass are the marks on it that show the directions, especially north, south, east, and west. **11** V-I If you **point at** or **to** a thing or person, you hold out your finger or an object such as a stick to show someone where the thing or person is. ❑ *He pointed to a chair, and she sat down.* **12** V-T If you **point** something **at** someone, you aim the tip or end of it towards them. ❑ *A man pointed a gun at them.* **13** V-I If something **points to** a place or **points** in a particular direction, it shows where that place is or faces in that direction. ❑ *An arrow pointed to the toilets.* **14** V-I If something **points to** a particular situation, it suggests that the situation exists or is likely to occur. ❑ *The report points to increased confidence in the industry.* **15** PHRASE If you **make a point of** doing something, you do it in a deliberate or obvious way. ❑ *He had made a point of never talking about the event.* **16** PHRASE If you are **on the point of** doing something, you are about to do it. ❑ *He was on the point of saying something when the phone rang.* **17** PHRASE If you say that something is true **up to a point**, you mean that it is partly but not completely true. ❑ *The system worked up to a point.* **18** → see also **pointed** **19** **in point of fact** → see **fact** **20** to **point the finger at** someone → see **finger**

▶ **point out** **1** PHR-VERB If you **point out** an

object or place to someone, you direct their attention to it. ❑ *Now and then they would stop to point things out to each other.* **2** PHR-VERB If you **point out** a fact or mistake, you tell someone about it. ❑ *Critics point out that the prince should be paying tax.*

Thesaurus	*point* Also look up:
N.	argument, gist, topic **3**
	location, place, position, spot **6**

ˌpoint-ˈblank **1** ADV & ADJ BEFORE N If you say something **point-blank**, you say it very directly, without explaining or apologizing. ❑ *I asked him point-blank why he was doing it.* ❑ *...their point-blank refusal.* **2** ADV & ADJ BEFORE N If someone or something is shot **point-blank** or **at point-blank range**, they are shot by a gun which is held extremely close to them.

pointed /ˈpɔɪntɪd/ **1** ADJ An object that is **pointed** has a narrow end or tip. ❑ *...pointed shoes.* ❑ *...pointed roofs.* **2** ADJ **Pointed** comments or behaviour express criticism in a clear and direct way. ❑ *They asked Klein some rather pointed questions.* ● **pointedly** ADV ❑ *They were pointedly absent from the news conference.*

pointer /ˈpɔɪntə/ (**pointers**) N-COUNT A **pointer** is a piece of advice or information which helps you to understand a situation or solve a problem. ❑ *Here are a few pointers to help you make a choice.*

pointless /ˈpɔɪntləs/ ADJ Something that is **pointless** has no purpose. ❑ *Violence is always pointless.* ● **pointlessly** ADV ❑ *Four years of my life had been ruined, pointlessly.*

ˌpoint of ˈview (**points of view**) **1** N-COUNT You can refer to the opinions that you have about something as your **point of view**. **2** PHRASE If you consider something **from** a particular **point of view**, you are using one aspect of a situation to judge it. ❑ *From the point of view of food safety, we are not concerned.*
→ see **history**

poise /pɔɪz/ N-UNCOUNT If someone has **poise**, they are calm, dignified, and self-controlled. ❑ *It took a moment for Mark to recover his poise.*

poised /pɔɪzd/ **1** ADJ If a part of your body is **poised**, it is completely still but ready to move at any moment. ❑ *He studied the keyboard carefully, one finger poised.* **2** ADJ AFTER LINK-V If someone is **poised to** do something, they are ready to take action at any moment. ❑ *Britain was poised to send medical staff to the country.* ❑ *Foster looked poised for a comfortable win when he won the point.* **3** ADJ If you are **poised**, you are calm, dignified, and in control of your emotions.

poison /ˈpɔɪzən/ (**poisons, poisoning, poisoned**) **1** N-VAR **Poison** is a substance that harms or kills people or animals if they swallow or absorb it. ❑ *Mercury is a known poison.* **2** V-T To **poison** someone or something means to give poison to them or to add poison to them, causing them harm. ❑ *There were rumours that she had poisoned him.* ❑ *The land has been completely poisoned by chemicals.* ● **poisoning** (**poisonings**) N-VAR ❑ *She was sent to prison for poisoning.* **3** V-T Something that **poisons** a good situation or relationship spoils it or destroys it. ❑ *The letter poisoned her relationship with her family for ever.*

poisonous /ˈpɔɪzənəs/ **1** ADJ Something that is **poisonous** will kill you or harm you if you swallow or absorb it. ❑ *Ten workmen breathed in poisonous gas.* **2** ADJ A **poisonous** animal produces a poison that will kill you or make you ill if the animal bites you.

poke /pəʊk/ (**pokes, poking, poked**) **1** V-T & N-COUNT If you **poke** someone or something, or if you give them a **poke**, you quickly push them with your finger or a sharp object. You can also say that you **poke** your finger or an object **into** someone or something. ❑ *Her mother opened the oven door and poked a fork into the turkey skin.* ❑ *John smiled at them and gave Richard a playful poke.* **2** V-T/V-I If something **pokes from** behind or under something, or if someone **pokes** it there, you can see part of it appearing from behind or under that thing. ❑ *His tiny head poked from the covers.* ❑ *Julie tapped on my door and poked her head in.* **3** to **poke fun at** → see **fun**

▶ **poke around** PHR-VERB If you **poke around** for something, you search for it, usually by moving lots of objects around. [INFORMAL] ❑ *He opened up the car bonnet and started poking around in the engine.*

▶ **poke at** PHR-VERB If you **poke at** something, you make lots of little pushing movements at it with a sharp object.

poker /ˈpəʊkə/ N-UNCOUNT **Poker** is a card game that people usually play in order to win money.

polar /ˈpəʊlə/ ADJ BEFORE N **Polar** refers to the area around the North and South Poles. ❑ *...studying life in the polar regions.*
→ see **glacier**

ˈpolar bear (**polar bears**) N-COUNT A **polar bear** is a large white bear which is found near the North Pole.

polarize [BRIT also **polarise**] /ˈpəʊləraɪz/ (**polarizes, polarizing, polarized**) V-T/V-I If something **polarizes** people, it causes them to become two separate groups with opposite opinions or positions. ❑ *The issue of immigration was polarizing the country.* ❑ *Opinion polarised along familiar left/right lines.* ● **polarization** N-UNCOUNT ❑ *...polarization between the blacks and whites in the US.*

pole /pəʊl/ (**poles**) **1** N-COUNT A **pole** is a long, thin piece of wood or metal, used especially for supporting things. ❑ *...a 40-foot telephone pole.* **2** N-COUNT The earth's **poles** are the two opposite ends of its axis.
→ see **globe, magnet**

polemic /pəˈlemɪk/ (**polemics**) N-VAR A **polemic** is a fierce written or spoken attack on, or defence of, a particular belief or opinion. ❑ *...Edmund Burke's polemic against the French Revolution.*

police /pəˈliːs/ (**polices, policing, policed**) **1** N-SING & N-PLURAL The **police** are the official organization that is responsible for making sure that people obey the law. The men and women who belong to this organization are referred to as **police**. ❑ *Police say they have arrested twenty people.* ❑ *More than one hundred police have arrived at the area.* **2** V-T To **police** a place, an event, or an activity means to preserve law and order within it or to ensure that what is done is fair and legal. ❑ *It is difficult to police the border effectively.* ❑ *The FSA polices the financial services industry.*

poˈlice force (**police forces**) N-COUNT A **police force** is the police organization in a particular country or area.

P

policeman /pə'li:smən/ (**policemen**) N-COUNT A **policeman** is a man who is a member of the police force.

po'lice officer (**police officers**) N-COUNT A **police officer** is a member of the police force.

po'lice station (**police stations**) N-COUNT A **police station** is the local office of a police force in a particular area.

policewoman /pə'li:swʊmən/ (**policewomen**) N-COUNT A **policewoman** is a woman who is a member of the police force.

policy /'pɒlɪsi/ (**policies**) **1** N-VAR A **policy** is a set of plans or principles that is used as a basis for making decisions, especially in politics, economics, or business. ❑ *What is their policy on nuclear weapons development?* **2** N-COUNT An insurance **policy** is a document which shows the agreement that you have made with an insurance company.

polio /'pəʊliəʊ/ N-UNCOUNT **Polio** is a serious infectious disease which can cause paralysis.
→ see **hospital**

polish /'pɒlɪʃ/ (**polishes, polishing, polished**) **1** N-UNCOUNT **Polish** is a substance that you put on the surface of an object in order to clean it, protect it, and make it shine. ❑ *...furniture polish.* **2** V-T If you **polish** something, you put polish on it or rub it with a cloth to make it shine. ● **polished** ADJ ❑ *...a highly polished floor.* **3** N-UNCOUNT If you say that a person, performance, or piece of work has **polish**, you mean that they show confidence and sophistication. ● **polished** ADJ ❑ *He is polished, charming, and a gentleman.* **4** V-T & PHR-VERB If you **polish** your technique, performance, or skill at doing something, or if you **polish** it **up**, you work on improving it. ❑ *Polish up your writing skills.*
▶ **polish off** PHR-VERB If you **polish off** food or drink, you finish it. [INFORMAL]

polish

polite /pə'laɪt/ (**politer, politest**) ADJ A **polite** person has good manners and is not rude to other people. ❑ *...polite conversation.* ● **politely** ADV ❑ *'Your home is beautiful,' I said politely.* ● **politeness** N-UNCOUNT ❑ *She listened to him, but only out of politeness.*

Thesaurus *polite* Also look up:
ADJ. considerate, courteous, gracious, respectful; *(ant.)* brash, rude

political /pə'lɪtɪkəl/ **1** ADJ **Political** means relating to the way power is achieved and used in a country or society. ❑ *All other political activity has been completely banned.* ● **politically** ADV ❑ *The killings were politically motivated.* **2** ADJ If you are **political**, you are interested in politics and hold strong beliefs about it.
→ see **empire, philosophy**

politician /ˌpɒlɪ'tɪʃən/ (**politicians**) N-COUNT A **politician** is a person whose job is in politics, especially a member of parliament.

Word Link *poli ≈ city : cosmopolitan, metropolis, politics*

politics /'pɒlɪtɪks/ **1** N-UNCOUNT **Politics** is the actions or activities which people use to achieve power in a country or organization. **Politics** can take the singular or plural form of the verb. ❑ *He appealed for more women to take part in politics.* **2** N-PLURAL Your **politics** are your beliefs about how a country ought to be governed. ❑ *His politics are conservative.*

poll /pəʊl/ (**polls**) **1** N-COUNT A **poll** is a survey in which people are asked their opinions about something. **2** → see also **opinion poll** **3** N-PLURAL **The polls** means an election for a country's government, or the place where people go to vote in an election. ❑ *Voters will go to the polls on Sunday.*

pollen /'pɒlən/ N-UNCOUNT **Pollen** is a powder produced by flowers in order to fertilize other flowers.

polling /'pəʊlɪŋ/ N-UNCOUNT **Polling** is the act of voting in an election.

pollutant /pə'lu:tənt/ (**pollutants**) N-VAR **Pollutants** are substances that pollute the environment, especially poisonous chemicals that are produced as waste by vehicles and by industry.
→ see **ozone**

pollute /pə'lu:t/ (**pollutes, polluting, polluted**) V-T To **pollute** water, air, or land means to make it dirty and dangerous to live in or to use, especially with poisonous chemicals or sewage. ● **polluted** ADJ ❑ *...foul polluted water.*

pollution /pə'lu:ʃən/ **1** N-UNCOUNT **Pollution** is poisonous substances that are polluting water, air, or land. ❑ *The level of pollution in the river was falling.* **2** N-UNCOUNT **Pollution** is the process of polluting the water, air, or land.
→ see Word Web: **pollution**
→ see **air, factory, solar**

polo /'pəʊləʊ/ N-UNCOUNT **Polo** is a ball game played between two teams of players riding on horses.

polyester /ˌpɒli'estə, AM 'pɒliestə/ (**polyesters**)

Word Web pollution

Pollution affects the whole **environment**. **Airborne emissions** from factories and car **exhaust** cause air pollution. These smoky **emissions** combine with fog and make the **smog**. Pollutants in the air can travel long distances. **Acid rain** caused by factories in the Midwest falls on states in the east. There it damages trees and kills fish in lakes. Chemicals from factories, **sewage**, and **garbage** pollute the water and land in many areas. Too many **pesticides** and **fertilizers** make the problem worse. These chemicals build up in the soil and poison the earth.

P

N-VAR **Polyester** is a type of cloth made from artificial fibres, and used especially to make clothes.
→ see **petroleum**

polythene /ˈpɒlɪθiːn/ N-UNCOUNT **Polythene** is a type of plastic made into thin sheets or bags.

pomp /pɒmp/ N-UNCOUNT **Pomp** is the use of a lot of fine clothes, and decorations, and formal words or actions. ❑ *...the pomp and ceremony of the Pope's visit.*

pompous /ˈpɒmpəs/ ADJ If you describe someone as **pompous**, you mean that they behave or speak in a very serious way because they think they are more important than they really are; used showing disapproval. ● **pomposity** /pɒmˈpɒsɪti/ N-UNCOUNT ❑ *...a scientist who hated pomposity.* ● **pompously** ADV ❑ *'This is clearly a very important project,' I said pompously.*

pond /pɒnd/ (**ponds**) N-COUNT A **pond** is a small, usually man-made, area of water. ❑ *...a garden pond.*

ponder /ˈpɒndə/ (**ponders, pondering, pondered**) V-T/V-I If you **ponder** a question, you think about it carefully. ❑ *I'm continually pondering how to improve the team.* ❑ *He sat and pondered.*

ponderous /ˈpɒndərəs/ **1** ADJ **Ponderous** speech or writing is dull and serious. ● **ponderously** ADV ❑ *...the ponderously named Association of Residential Letting Agents.* **2** ADJ A movement or action that is **ponderous** is very slow or clumsy. [WRITTEN] ● **ponderously** ADV ❑ *Wilson shifted ponderously in his chair.*

pony /ˈpəʊni/ (**ponies**) N-COUNT A **pony** is a type of small horse.

ponytail /ˈpəʊniteɪl/ (**ponytails**) N-COUNT If someone has their hair in a **ponytail**, it is tied up at the back so that it hangs down like a tail.
→ see **hair**

poodle /puːdəl/ (**poodles**) N-COUNT A **poodle** is a type of dog with thick curly hair.

pool /puːl/ (**pools, pooling, pooled**) **1** N-COUNT A **pool** is the same as a **swimming pool**. **2** N-COUNT A **pool** is a small area of still water. ❑ *I loved the Japanese water gardens with the little bridges and pools.* **3** N-COUNT A **pool of** liquid or light is a small area of it. ❑ *She was found lying in a pool of blood.* **4** N-COUNT A **pool of** people, money, or things is a number or quantity of them that is available for use. ❑ *...a reserve pool of cash.* **5** V-T If people **pool** their money, knowledge, or equipment, they share it or put it together so that it can be used for a particular purpose. ❑ *Philip and I pooled our savings to start up my business.* **6** N-UNCOUNT **Pool** is a game played on a special table. Players use a long stick called a cue to hit a white ball so that it knocks coloured balls into six holes around the edge of the table. **7** N-PLURAL If you do **the pools**, you take part in a gambling competition in which people try to guess the results of football matches. [BRIT]

poor /pʊə, pɔː/ (**poorer, poorest**) **1** ADJ & N-PLURAL Someone who is **poor** has very little money and few possessions. **The poor** are people who are poor. ❑ *He was one of thirteen children from a poor family.* ❑ *He often talked about helping the poor.* **2** ADJ A **poor** country or area is inhabited by people who are poor. ❑ *...children in a poor neighbourhood.* **3** ADJ BEFORE N You use **poor** to express sympathy for someone. ❑ *Poor Gordon!* **4** ADJ If you describe something as **poor**, you mean that it is of a low quality or standard. ❑ *The flat was in a poor state of repair.* ● **poorly** ADV ❑ *...poorly built blocks of flats.* **5** ADJ If you describe an amount, rate, or number as **poor**, you mean that it is less than expected or less than is considered reasonable. ❑ *...poor wages and working conditions.* ● **poorly** ADV ❑ *The evening meetings were poorly attended.* **6** ADJ You use **poor** to describe someone who is not very skilful in a particular activity. ❑ *He was a poor actor.* ● **poorly** ADV ❑ *Italy performed poorly in the match.* **7** ADJ AFTER LINK-V If something is **poor in** a particular quality or substance, it contains very little of the quality or substance. ❑ *Some foods are very rich in energy but poor in vitamins.*

Thesaurus	*poor* Also look up:
ADJ.	impoverished, penniless; (*ant.*) rich, wealthy **1** **2** inferior **4**

poorly /ˈpʊəli, ˈpɔː-/ (**poorlier, poorliest**) ADJ If someone is **poorly**, they are ill. [BRIT, INFORMAL] ❑ *Miss Cartwright looks very poorly.*

pop /pɒp/ (**pops, popping, popped**) **1** N-UNCOUNT **Pop** is modern music that usually has a strong rhythm and uses electronic equipment. ❑ *...a life-size poster of a pop star.* **2** V-I & N-COUNT If something **pops**, it makes a short sharp sound, called a **pop**. ❑ *The cork popped and shot to the ceiling.* ❑ *His back tyre just went pop on a motorway.* **3** V-I & PHR-VERB If your eyes **pop**, or if they **pop out**, you look very surprised or excited. [INFORMAL] ❑ *My eyes popped at the sight of the food.* **4** V-T If you **pop** something somewhere, you put it there. [BRIT, INFORMAL] ❑ *He popped a chocolate into his mouth.* **5** V-I If you **pop** somewhere, you go there for a short time. [BRIT, INFORMAL] ❑ *He's just popped out to the shops. He won't be a minute.*
▶ **pop up** PHR-VERB If someone or something **pops up**, they appear in a place or situation unexpectedly. ❑ *You solve one problem and another immediately pops up.*

popcorn /ˈpɒpkɔːn/ N-UNCOUNT **Popcorn** is a snack which consists of grains of maize that have been heated until they have burst and become large and light.

Pope /pəʊp/ (**Popes**) N-COUNT & N-TITLE **The Pope** is the head of the Roman Catholic Church. ❑ *...Pope John Paul II.*

poppy /ˈpɒpi/ (**poppies**) N-COUNT A **poppy** is a plant with large, delicate, red flowers.

Word Link	***popul*** ≈ ***people*** : ***popul**ace*, ***popul**ar*, ***popul**ation*

populace /ˈpɒpjʊləs/ N-SING The **populace** of a country is its people. [FORMAL] ❑ *...a large section of Pakistan's populace.*

popular /ˈpɒpjʊlə/ **1** ADJ Someone or something that is **popular** is liked by a lot of people. ❑ *...the most popular politician in France.* ❑ *These delicious pastries will be very popular.* ● **popularity** /ˌpɒpjʊˈlærɪti/ N-UNCOUNT ❑ *...his popularity with ordinary people.* ❑ *Golf increased in popularity during the 1980s.* **2** ADJ **Popular** ideas or attitudes are approved of or held by most people.

❑ *The military government has been unable to win popular support.* ● **popularity** N-UNCOUNT ❑ *Watson's views gained in popularity.* **3** ADJ BEFORE N **Popular** newspapers, television programmes, or forms of art are aimed at ordinary people and not at experts or intellectuals. ❑ *...one of the classics of modern popular music.* **4** ADJ BEFORE N **Popular** is used to describe political activities which involve the ordinary people of a country. ❑ *...the Popular Front for the Liberation of Palestine.*
→ see **genre**

Word Partnership Use *popular* with:

N. popular **culture**, popular **film**, popular **magazine**, popular **movie**, popular **novel**, popular **restaurant**, popular **show**, popular **song** **1** **3**

ADV. **extremely** popular, **increasingly** popular, **more** popular, **most** popular, **wildly** popular **1** **2**

popularize [BRIT also **popularise**] /ˈpɒpjʊləraɪz/ (**popularizes, popularizing, popularized**) V-T To **popularize** something means to make a lot of people interested in it and able to enjoy or understand it. ● **popularization** N-UNCOUNT ❑ *...the popularisation of sport through television.*

popularly /ˈpɒpjʊləli/ **1** ADV If something or someone is **popularly** known as something, most people call them that, although it is not their official name or title. ❑ *...an infection popularly called mad cow disease.* **2** ADV If something is **popularly** believed or supposed to be the case, most people believe or suppose it to be the case, although it may not be true. ❑ *His mother was popularly believed to be a witch.*

populate /ˈpɒpjʊleɪt/ (**populates, populating, populated**) V-T If an area **is populated by** people or animals, those people or animals live there. ❑ *The forests here are populated by bears and wolves.* ● **populated** ADJ ❑ *The southeast is the most densely populated area.*

P

Word Link *popul ≈ people : populace, popular, population*

population /ˌpɒpjʊˈleɪʃən/ (**populations**) **1** N-VAR The **population** of a place is the people who live there, or the number of people living there. ❑ *Bangladesh now has a population of about 110 million.* ❑ *...a massive increase in population.* **2** N-COUNT If you refer to a particular type of **population** in a place, you are referring to all the people or animals of that type there. [FORMAL] ❑ *This affects 75.6 per cent of the male population over sixteen.*
→ see **country**

ˈpop-up ADJ On a computer screen, a **pop-up** menu or advertisement is a small window that appears on the screen when you perform particular operations. [COMPUTING] ❑ *...a program for stopping pop-up ads.*

porcelain /ˈpɔːsəlɪn/ N-UNCOUNT **Porcelain** is a hard, shiny substance made by heating clay. It is used to make cups, plates, and ornaments.
→ see **pottery**

porch /pɔːtʃ/ (**porches**) **1** N-COUNT A **porch** is a sheltered area at the entrance to a building. It has a roof and sometimes walls. **2** N-COUNT In American English, a **porch** is a raised platform built along the outside wall of a house and often covered with a roof. The British word is **veranda**.

porch

pore /pɔː/ (**pores, poring, pored**) **1** N-COUNT Your **pores** are the tiny holes in your skin. **2** N-COUNT The **pores** of a plant are the tiny holes on its surface.
▶ **pore over** PHR-VERB If you **pore over** or **through** information, you look at it, studying it very carefully. ❑ *We spent hours poring over travel brochures.*

pork /pɔːk/ N-UNCOUNT **Pork** is meat from a pig, usually fresh and not smoked or salted.
→ see **meat**

porn /pɔːn/ N-UNCOUNT **Porn** is the same as **pornography**. [INFORMAL]

pornography /pɔːˈnɒgrəfi/ N-UNCOUNT **Pornography** refers to books, magazines, and films that are designed to cause sexual excitement; used showing disapproval. ● **pornographic** /ˌpɔːnəˈgræfɪk/ ADJ ❑ *...pornographic videos.*

porous /ˈpɔːrəs/ ADJ Something that is **porous** has many small holes in it, allowing water and air to pass through. ❑ *...a porous material like sand or charcoal.*
→ see **pottery**

porridge /ˈpɒrɪdʒ, AM ˈpɔːr-/ N-UNCOUNT **Porridge** is a thick sticky food made from oats cooked in water or milk and eaten hot, especially for breakfast.

port /pɔːt/ (**ports**) **1** N-COUNT A **port** is a town or a harbour area with docks and warehouses, where ships load or unload goods or passengers. ❑ *...the Mediterranean port of Marseilles.* **2** ADJ & N-UNCOUNT The **port** side of a ship is the left side when you are on it and facing towards the front. ❑ *The boat began a slow turn to port.* **3** N-VAR **Port** is a type of strong, sweet red wine.
→ see **ship**

Word Link *port ≈ carrying : export, import, portable*

Word Link *able ≈ able to be : affordable, incurable, portable*

portable /ˈpɔːtəbəl/ (**portables**) ADJ & N-COUNT A **portable** machine or device is designed to be easily carried or moved. The machine or device can be called a **portable**. ❑ *...a portable computer.* ❑ *We bought a portable for the bedroom.*

porter /ˈpɔːtə/ (**porters**) **1** N-COUNT A **porter** is a person whose job is to be in charge of the entrance of a building such as a hotel. [BRIT] **2** N-COUNT A **porter** is a person whose job is to carry things, for example people's luggage at a railway station.

portfolio /pɔːtˈfəʊliəʊ/ (**portfolios**) N-COUNT A **portfolio** is a set of pictures or photographs of someone's work, which they show to potential employers. ❑ *Edith showed them a portfolio of her cartoons.*

portion /ˈpɔːʃən/ (**portions**) **1** N-COUNT A

portion of something is a part of it. ❑ *A small portion of the castle was damaged.* ❑ *I have spent a considerable portion of my life here.* **2** N-COUNT A **portion** is the amount of food that is given to one person at a meal. ❑ *Would you prefer a dessert or a portion of fresh fruit?*

portrait /ˈpɔːtreɪt/ (**portraits**) N-COUNT A **portrait** is a painting, drawing, or photograph of a person. ❑ *...a portrait of the Queen.*
→ see **painting**

portray /pɔːˈtreɪ/ (**portrays, portraying, portrayed**) **1** V-T When an actor or actress **portrays** someone, he or she plays that person in a play or film. ❑ *He portrayed the king in 'Camelot'.* **2** V-T To **portray** someone or something in a particular way means to represent them in that way, for example in a book or film. ❑ *This novelist accurately portrays modern domestic life.*

portrayal /pɔːˈtreɪəl/ (**portrayals**) N-COUNT A **portrayal of** someone or something is a representation of them in a book, film, or play. ❑ *...a sensitive portrayal of a friendship between two 11-year-old boys.*

pose /pəʊz/ (**poses, posing, posed**) **1** V-T If something **poses** a problem or danger, it is the cause of that problem or danger. ❑ *His ill health poses serious problems for the future.* **2** V-T If you **pose** a question, you ask it. [FORMAL] **3** V-I If you **pose as** someone, you pretend to be that person in order to deceive people. ❑ *He posed as a wealthy businessman.* **4** V-I & N-COUNT If you **pose for** a photograph or painting, you stay in a particular position so that someone can photograph or paint you. This position is called a **pose**. ❑ *How did you get him to pose for this picture?*

posh /pɒʃ/ (**posher, poshest**) **1** ADJ If you describe something as **posh**, you mean that it is smart, fashionable, and expensive. [INFORMAL] ❑ *...a posh hotel.* **2** ADJ If you describe a person as **posh**, you mean that they belong to or behave as if they belong to a high social class. ❑ *He sounded so posh on the phone.*

position /pəˈzɪʃən/ (**positions, positioning, positioned**) **1** N-COUNT The **position** of someone or something is the place where they are. ❑ *The captain reported the ship's name and position.* **2** N-COUNT When someone or something is in a particular **position**, they are sitting, lying, or arranged in that way. ❑ *She pulled herself up into a sitting position.* **3** V-T & PHRASE If you **position** someone or something somewhere, or if you place them **in position**, you put them exactly where you want them to be. ❑ *The cameras were positioned so it was difficult for people to hide their faces.* ❑ *Gently lower the plants into position in their pots.* **4** N-COUNT Your **position** in society is the role and the importance that you have in it. ❑ *...their changing role and position in society.* **5** N-COUNT A **position** in a company or organization is a job. [FORMAL] ❑ *He left a career in teaching to take up a position with the Arts Council.* **6** N-COUNT Your **position** in a race or competition is how well you did in relation to the other competitors or how well you are doing. ❑ *Our car was in eighth position.* **7** N-COUNT You can describe your situation at a particular time by saying that you are in a particular **position**. ❑ *He's going to be in a very difficult position.* **8** PHRASE If you are **in a position to** do something, you are able to do it. ❑ *I am not in a position to comment.* **9** N-COUNT Your **position on** a particular matter is your attitude towards it. [FORMAL] ❑ *What's your position on the use of calculators in the classroom?*
→ see **navigation**

Word Partnership Use *position* with:

ADJ.	**better** position **1**-**7**
	(un)comfortable position **2** **7**
	difficult position, **financial** position **7**
	official position **9**

positive /ˈpɒzɪtɪv/ **1** ADJ If you are **positive**, you are hopeful and confident, and think of the good aspects of a situation rather than the bad ones. ❑ *Be positive about your future.* ● **positively** ADV ❑ *Try thinking positively about yourself.* **2** ADJ A **positive** situation or experience is pleasant and helpful to you in some way. ❑ *Working abroad should be an exciting and positive experience.* **3** ADJ If you make a **positive** decision or take **positive** action, you do something definite in order to deal with a task or problem. ❑ *I made a positive decision to do something about my shyness.* **4** ADJ A **positive response** shows agreement, approval, or encouragement. ● **positively** ADV ❑ *We expect both men to respond positively to the challenge.* **5** ADJ AFTER LINK-V If you are **positive about** something, you are completely sure about it. ❑ *I'm as positive as I can be about it.* **6** ADJ BEFORE N **Positive evidence** gives definite proof of something. ❑ *We have positive proof that he was the thief.* ● **positively** ADV ❑ *He has positively identified the body.* **7** ADJ AFTER LINK-V If a medical or scientific test is **positive**, it shows that something has happened or is present. ❑ *If the test is positive, a course of antibiotics may be prescribed.* **8** ADJ BEFORE N A **positive** number is greater than zero.

positively /ˈpɒzɪtɪvli/ ADV You use **positively** to emphasize that something is the case. ❑ *This is positively the worst thing that I could have imagined.*

possess /pəˈzes/ (**possesses, possessing, possessed**) **1** V-T If you **possess** something, you have it or own it. ❑ *He is said to possess a fortune.* **2** V-T To **possess** a quality, ability, or feature means to have it. ❑ *...the practical skills that some people possess.*

possession /pəˈzeʃən/ (**possessions**) **1** N-UNCOUNT If you are **in possession of** something, you have it, because you have obtained it or because it belongs to you. [FORMAL] ❑ *Those documents are now in the possession of the Guardian newspaper.* ❑ *...illegal possession of weapons.* **2** N-COUNT **Your possessions** are the things that you own or have with you at a particular time. ❑ *People had lost their homes and all their possessions.*

Word Partnership Use *possession* with:

N.	**cocaine** possession, **drug** possession, possession **of a firearm**, possession **of illegal drugs**, **marijuana** possession, possession **of property**, **weapons** possession **1**

possessive /pəˈzesɪv/ (**possessives**) **1** ADJ If someone is **possessive**, they want all their partner's love and attention. ❑ *She became increasingly possessive and jealous.* ● **possessiveness** N-UNCOUNT ❑ *I've ruined every relationship with*

P

my possessiveness. **2** N-COUNT In grammar, **the possessive** is the form of a noun or pronoun used to indicate possession, for example 'George's' and 'his'.

possibility /ˌpɒsɪ'bɪlɪti/ (**possibilities**) **1** N-COUNT If you say there is a **possibility** that something is the case or that something will happen, you mean that it might be the case or it might happen. ❑ *Tax on food has become a very real possibility.* **2** N-COUNT A **possibility** is one of several things that could be done. ❑ *There were several possibilities open to each of us.*

Usage

Note that you do not use **possibility** in sentences like 'I had the possibility to do it'. The words you need are **opportunity** or **chance**. ❑ *Later Donald had the opportunity of driving the car.* ❑ *The people of Northern Ireland would have the chance to shape their own future.*

Word Link ***ible ≈ able to be : audible, flexible, possible***

possible /'pɒsɪbəl/ **1** ADJ If it is **possible to** do something, it can be done. ❑ *If it is possible to find out where your brother is, we shall.* ❑ *I need to see you, right away if possible.* **2** ADJ If you do something **as** soon **as possible**, you do it as soon as you can. If you get **as** much **as possible** of something, you get as much of it as you can. ❑ *She decided to learn as much as possible about the subject.* **3** ADJ A **possible** event is one that might happen. ❑ *Her family is discussing a possible move to America.* **4** ADJ If you say that it is **possible that** something is true or correct, you mean that you do not know whether it is true or correct, but you accept that it might be. ❑ *It is possible that there's an explanation for all this.* **5** ADJ You use **possible** with superlative adjectives to emphasize that something has more of a quality than anything else of its kind. ❑ *They have joined the company at the worst possible time.* ❑ *He is doing the best job possible.* **6** N-SING **The possible** is everything that can be done in a situation. ❑ *He has the courage to push the limits of the possible.*

P

Thesaurus *possible* Also look up:

ADJ. feasible, likely; *(ant.)* impossible, unlikely **1**

possibly /'pɒsɪbli/ **1** ADV You use **possibly** to indicate that you are not sure whether something is true or will happen. ❑ *'What do you estimate they're worth?'—'Possibly two hundred thousand dollars.'* **2** ADV You use **possibly** to emphasize that you are surprised or puzzled. ❑ *How could they possibly eat that stuff?* ❑ *What could this possibly mean?* **3** ADV You use **possibly** with a negative modal to emphasize that something cannot happen or cannot be done. ❑ *No, I can't possibly answer that!* ❑ *There's nothing more they can possibly do.*

post

❶ LETTERS, PARCELS, AND INFORMATION
❷ JOBS AND PLACES
❸ POLES

post /pəʊst/ (**posts, posting, posted**)
❶ **1** N-SING In British English, **the post** is the public service by which letters and parcels are collected and delivered. The American word is **mail**. ❑ *The winner will be informed by post.* ❑ *The cheque is in the post.* ● **postal** ADJ BEFORE N ❑ *...the American postal service.* **2** N-UNCOUNT In British English, you can use **post** to refer to letters and parcels that are delivered to you. The American word is **mail**. ❑ *He looked through the post without opening any of it.* **3** V-T In British English, if you **post** a letter or parcel, you send it to someone by putting it in a letterbox or taking it to a post office. The American word is **mail**. ❑ *I'm posting you a cheque tonight.*

post /pəʊst/ (**posts, posting, posted**)
❷ **1** N-COUNT A **post** in a company or organization is a job or official position in it. [FORMAL] ❑ *He accepted the post of deputy prime minister.* **2** V-T If you **are posted** somewhere, you are sent there by your employers to work. ❑ *Eric was posted to Japan for a year.* **3** → see also **posting**

post /pəʊst/ (**posts**)
❸ N-COUNT A **post** is an upright pole fixed into the ground. ❑ *The device is fixed to a post.*

postage /'pəʊstɪdʒ/ N-UNCOUNT **Postage** is the money that you pay for sending letters and parcels by post. ❑ *Send a cheque for £18.99 plus £2 for postage and packing.*

'post box (**post boxes**) N-COUNT In British English, a **post box** is a metal box with a hole in it where you put letters that you want to send. The American word is **mailbox**.

postcard /'pəʊstkɑːd/ (**postcards**) N-COUNT A **postcard** is a piece of card, often with a picture on one side, which you can write on and post to someone without using an envelope.

postcode /'pəʊstkəʊd/ (**postcodes**) N-COUNT In British English, your **postcode** is a short sequence of numbers and letters at the end of your address. The American term is **zip code**.

poster /'pəʊstə/ (**posters**) N-COUNT A **poster** is a large notice, advertisement, or picture that you stick on a wall.

Word Link ***post ≈ after : postgraduate, postpone, posterity***

posterity /pɒ'sterɪti/ N-UNCOUNT You can refer to everyone who will be alive in the future as **posterity**. [FORMAL] ❑ *A photographer recorded the scene on video for posterity.*

postgraduate /ˌpəʊst'grædʒʊət/ (**postgraduates**) N-COUNT A **postgraduate** is a student with a first degree from a university who is studying or doing research at a more advanced level. [BRIT]

posting /'pəʊstɪŋ/ (**postings**) **1** N-COUNT A **posting** is a job which involves going to a different town or country. ❑ *Sales experience is required for overseas postings.* **2** → see also **post** **3** N-COUNT A **posting** is a message that is placed on the Internet, for example on a bulletin board or website, for everyone to read. [COMPUTING]

postman /'pəʊstmən/ (**postmen**) N-COUNT In British English, a **postman** is a man whose job is to collect and deliver letters and parcels that are sent by post. The usual American word is **mailman**.

Word Web pottery

There are three basic types of **pottery**. Earthenware **dishes** are made from **clay** and **fired** at a relatively low temperature. Earthenware is **porous** and must be **glazed** in order to hold water. Potters first created earthenware objects about 15,000 years ago. Stoneware pieces are heavier and are fired at a higher temperature. They are impermeable even without a glaze. **Porcelain ceramics** are fragile. They have thin walls and are **translucent.** Stoneware and porcelain are not as old as earthenware. They appeared about 2,000 years ago when the Chinese started building high-temperature kilns. Another name for porcelain is **china**.

post-mortem /ˌpəʊst ˈmɔːtəm/ (**post-mortems**) 1 N-COUNT A **post-mortem** is a medical examination of a dead person's body to find out how they died. 2 N-COUNT A **post-mortem** is an examination of something that has recently happened, especially something that has failed or gone wrong. ❑ *...the election post-mortem.*

ˈpost office (**post offices**) N-COUNT A **post office** is a building where you can buy stamps, post letters, and parcels, and use other services provided by the national postal service.

Word Link *post ≈ after : postgraduate, postpone, posterity*

postpone /pəʊsˈpəʊn/ (**postpones, postponing, postponed**) V-T If you **postpone** an event, you arrange for it to take place at a later time than was originally planned. ❑ *The visit has been postponed until next month.* ● **postponement** (**postponements**) N-VAR ❑ *There were several postponements of flights.*

postulate /ˈpɒstʃʊleɪt/ (**postulates, postulating, postulated**) V-T If you **postulate** something, you suggest it as the basis for a theory, argument, or calculation. [FORMAL] ❑ *Scientists postulated that modern birds were linked to dinosaurs.*

posture /ˈpɒstʃə/ (**postures**) 1 N-VAR Your **posture** is the position or manner in which you stand or sit. ❑ *You can make your stomach look flatter by improving your posture.* 2 N-COUNT A **posture** is an attitude that you have towards something. [FORMAL] ❑ *None of the banks changed their posture on the deal.*
→ see **brain**

ˌpost-ˈwar also **postwar** ADJ **Post-war** is used to describe things that happened, existed, or were made in the period immediately after a war, especially the Second World War (1939-45). ❑ *...postwar architecture.*

pot /pɒt/ (**pots, potting, potted**) 1 N-COUNT A **pot** is a deep round container for cooking food. ❑ *...metal cooking pots.* 2 N-COUNT A **pot** is a teapot or coffee pot. ❑ *There's tea in the pot.* 3 V-T If you **pot** a plant, you put it into a flowerpot.
→ see **container**

potato /pəˈteɪtəʊ/ (**potatoes**) N-VAR **Potatoes** are vegetables with brown or red skins and white insides.
→ see **vegetable**

potent /ˈpəʊtənt/ ADJ Something that is **potent** is effective and powerful. ❑ *The drug is extremely potent.* ● **potency** N-UNCOUNT ❑ *Sunscreen can lose its potency if it is left over winter in the bathroom cabinet.*

potential /pəˈtenʃəl/ 1 ADJ BEFORE N You use **potential** to say that someone or something is capable of developing into the particular kind of person or thing. ❑ *The firm has identified 60 potential customers.* ● **potentially** ADV ❑ *This is a potentially dangerous situation.* 2 N-UNCOUNT If something **has potential**, it is capable of being useful or successful in the future. ❑ *The boy has great potential.* 3 N-UNCOUNT If you say that someone or something has **potential for** doing something, you mean that it is possible that they may do it. If there is **the potential for** something, it may happen. ❑ *We have always been concerned about his potential for violence.*

potion /ˈpəʊʃən/ (**potions**) N-COUNT A **potion** is a drink that contains medicine, poison, or something that is supposed to have magic powers. ❑ *...a magic potion to get him better.*

potter /ˈpɒtə/ (**potters, pottering, pottered**) N-COUNT A **potter** is someone who makes pottery.
→ see **container, wheel**
▶ **potter about** or **potter around** PHR-VERB If you **potter about** or **potter around**, you spend your time slowly doing a few pleasant or unimportant tasks. [BRIT]

pottery /ˈpɒtəri/ 1 N-UNCOUNT **Pottery** is objects made from clay. 2 N-UNCOUNT **Pottery** is the craft or activity of making objects out of clay. ❑ *...pottery classes.*
→ see Word Web: **pottery**

potty /ˈpɒti/ (**potties, pottier, pottiest**) 1 N-COUNT A **potty** is a deep bowl which a small child uses as a toilet. 2 ADJ If you say that someone is **potty**, you think that they are crazy or foolish. [BRIT, INFORMAL] ❑ *I have to get out of here. I'll go potty if I stay.*

pouch /paʊtʃ/ (**pouches**) 1 N-COUNT A **pouch** is a flexible container like a small bag. ❑ *On my belt in its little leather pouch was my Swiss knife.* 2 N-COUNT The **pouch** of an animal such as a kangaroo is the pocket of skin on its stomach in which its baby grows.

poultry /ˈpəʊltri/ N-UNCOUNT You can refer to chickens, ducks, and other birds that are kept for their eggs and meat as **poultry**. Meat from these birds is also referred to as **poultry**. ❑ *...traditional methods of farming poultry.* ❑ *The menu features roast meats and poultry.*
→ see **meat**

pounce /paʊns/ (**pounces, pouncing, pounced**) 1 V-I If a person or animal **pounces on** another person or animal, they leap towards them and try to take hold of them or attack them. ❑ *He pounced on the photographer and smashed his camera.* ❑ *Before I could save the bird, the cat pounced.* **2** V-I If someone **pounces on** something such as a mistake, they draw attention to it, usually in order to gain an advantage for themselves. ❑ *The press were ready to pounce on any mistakes.*

pound /paʊnd/ (**pounds, pounding, pounded**) **1** N-COUNT The **pound** is the unit of money which is used in Britain. It is represented by the symbol £. Some other countries, for example Egypt, also have a unit of money called a **pound**. ❑ *My mum and dad gave me five pounds.* **2** N-COUNT A **pound** is a unit of weight used mainly in Britain, America, and other countries where English is spoken. One pound is equal to 0.454 kilograms. ❑ *Her weight was under ninety pounds.* ❑ *...a pound of cheese.* **3** → See note at **weight** **4** V-T/V-I If you **pound** something, or if you **pound on** it, you hit it loudly and repeatedly with your fists. ❑ *He pounded the table with his fist.* ❑ *Somebody began pounding on the front door.* **5** V-I If your heart **is pounding**, it is beating with a strong fast rhythm, usually because you are afraid or excited. ❑ *I'm sweating, my heart is pounding. I can't breathe.* ● **pounding** N-UNCOUNT ❑ *...the fast pounding of her heart.*

pour /pɔː/ (**pours, pouring, poured**) **1** V-T If you **pour** a liquid, you make it flow steadily out of a container by holding the container at an angle. ❑ *She poured some water into a plastic bowl.* **2** V-T If you **pour** someone a drink, you fill a cup or glass with it so that they can drink it. ❑ *He poured himself a glass of milk.* **3** V-I When a liquid or other substance **pours** somewhere, it flows there quickly and in large quantities. ❑ *There was smoke pouring from all four engines.* ❑ *Tears poured down both our faces.* **4** V-I When it rains very heavily, you can say that **it is pouring**. ❑ *The rain was pouring down.* ● **pouring** ADJ ❑ *They left the school in pouring rain.* **5** V-I If people **pour into** or **out of** a place, they go there quickly and in large numbers. ❑ *At six p.m. people poured out of the offices.* **6** V-I If something **pours into** a place, a lot of it is obtained or given. ❑ *Letters and cards of support have been pouring in.*

pour

▶ **pour out** PHR-VERB If you **pour out** a drink, you fill a cup or glass with it. ❑ *Carefully and slowly he poured the water out.*

Word Partnership Use *pour* with:

N. pour **a liquid**, pour **a mixture**, pour **water** **1**
pour **coffee**, pour **a drink** **2**

pout /paʊt/ (**pouts, pouting, pouted**) V-I & N-COUNT If you **pout**, or if you give a **pout**, you stick out your lips, usually as a way of showing that you are annoyed. ❑ *He complained and pouted when he did not get what he wanted.*

poverty /ˈpɒvəti/ N-UNCOUNT **Poverty** is the state of being very poor. ❑ *...people living in poverty.*

powder /ˈpaʊdə/ (**powders**) N-VAR **Powder** consists of many tiny particles of a solid substance. ❑ *Her face was covered with white powder.*

powdered /ˈpaʊdəd/ ADJ A **powdered** substance is one which is in the form of a powder. ❑ *...powdered milk.*

power /paʊə/ (**powers, powering, powered**) **1** N-UNCOUNT If someone has **power**, they have a lot of control over people and activities. ❑ *These women have reached positions of great power and influence.* **2** N-UNCOUNT Your **power to** do something is your ability to do it. ❑ *He thinks that sport has the power to change the world.* ❑ *He was so shocked that he lost the power of speech.* **3** N-UNCOUNT If it is **in** your **power to** do something, you are able to do it or you have the resources to deal with it. ❑ *We must do everything in our power to ensure success.* **4** N-VAR If someone in authority has the **power to** do something, they have the legal right to do it. ❑ *The Prime Minister has the power to appoint senior ministers.* ❑ *...the legal powers of British Customs officers.* **5** N-UNCOUNT If people take **power** or come to **power**, they take charge of a country's affairs. People who are **in power** are in charge of a country's affairs. **6** N-UNCOUNT The **power** of something is its physical strength or other capability. ❑ *This car has better power, better tyres, and better brakes.* ❑ *...massive computing power.* **7** N-UNCOUNT **Power** is energy, especially electricity, that is obtained in large quantities from a fuel source. ❑ *Power has been restored to most places now.* **8** V-T The device or fuel that **powers** a machine provides the energy that makes the machine work.
→ see **electricity, energy, solar**

powerful /ˈpaʊəfʊl/ **1** ADJ A **powerful** person or organization is able to control or influence people and events. ❑ *...Russia and India, two large, powerful countries.* **2** ADJ You say that someone's body is **powerful** when it is physically strong. ❑ *...his powerful muscles.* ● **powerfully** ADV ❑ *...a strong, powerfully-built man.* **3** ADJ A **powerful** machine or substance is effective because it is very strong. ❑ *...powerful computer systems.* ● **powerfully** ADV ❑ *...the plant's powerfully calming effect on the nervous system.* **4** ADJ A **powerful** smell is very strong. **5** ADJ A **powerful** voice is loud and can be heard from a long way away. **6** ADJ You describe a piece of writing, speech, or work of art as **powerful** when it has a strong effect on people's feelings or beliefs. ● **powerfully** ADV ❑ *...a powerfully acted play.*

powerless /ˈpaʊələs/ **1** ADJ Someone who is **powerless** is unable to control or influence events. ● **powerlessness** N-UNCOUNT ❑ *...childhood feelings of powerlessness.* **2** ADJ AFTER LINK-V If you are **powerless to** do something, you are unable to do it. ❑ *He was sympathetic, but powerless to help.*

ˈpower line (**power lines**) N-COUNT A **power line** is a cable, especially above ground, along which electricity passes to an area or building.

ˈpower plant (**power plants**) N-COUNT A **power plant** is a place where electricity is generated.

ˈpower station (**power stations**) N-COUNT A **power station** is a place where electricity is generated.
→ see **electricity**

pp. **pp.** is the plural of 'p' and means 'pages'. ❑ *See chapter 6, pp. 137–41.*

practicable /ˈpræktɪkəbəl/ ADJ If a task, plan, or idea is **practicable**, people are able to do it or carry it out. ❑ *Teachers can only do what is*

P

reasonable and practicable.

practical /'præktɪkəl/ (**practicals**) 1 ADJ **Practical** means involving real situations, rather than ideas and theories. ❑ *They offer practical suggestions for healthy eating.* 2 ADJ You describe people as **practical** when they make sensible decisions and deal effectively with problems. ❑ *We are practical people who judge by results.* 3 ADJ **Practical** ideas and methods are likely to be effective or successful in a real situation. ❑ *Our system is the most practical way of preventing crime.* 4 ADJ You can describe clothes and things in your house as **practical** when they are useful rather than just being fashionable or attractive. ❑ *Our clothes are lightweight, fashionable, and practical for holidays.* 5 N-COUNT A **practical** is an examination or lesson in which you make things or do experiments rather than simply write answers to questions.

Thesaurus *practical* Also look up:
ADJ. businesslike, pragmatic, reasonable, sensible, systematic; (*ant.*) impractical 2 3

practicality /ˌpræktɪ'kælɪti/ (**practicalities**) N-COUNT The **practicalities of** a situation are the aspects of it which are concerned with real events rather than with ideas or theories. ❑ *...the practicalities of running a home.*

practically /'præktɪkəli/ 1 ADV **Practically** means almost. ❑ *He'd known the old man practically all his life.* 2 ADV You use **practically** to describe something which involves real actions or events rather than ideas or theories. ❑ *The course is more practically based than the Masters degree.*

practice /'præktɪs/ (**practices**) 1 N-COUNT You can refer to something that people do regularly as a **practice**. ❑ *...the practice of using chemicals to colour the hair.* 2 N-VAR **Practice** means doing something regularly in order to do it better. A **practice** is a session of this. ❑ *...basketball practice.* ❑ *He recorded the fastest time in a final practice today.* 3 N-UNCOUNT The work done by doctors and lawyers is referred to as the **practice** of medicine and law. People's religious activities are referred to as the **practice** of a religion. ❑ *I had to change my attitude towards medical practice.* ❑ *...rules regarding appearance, dress, and religious practice.* 4 N-COUNT A doctor's or lawyer's **practice** is his or her business, often shared with other doctors or lawyers. 5 → see also **practice** 6 PHRASE What happens **in practice** is what actually happens, in contrast to what is supposed to happen. ❑ *In practice, however, he is unlikely to be able to do this.* 7 PHRASE If you are **out of practice** at doing something, you have not had much experience of it recently, although you used to do it a lot or be quite good at it. 8 PHRASE If you **put** an idea or method **into practice**, you make use of it. ❑ *The Prime Minister has a chance to put his new ideas into practice.*

Thesaurus *practice* Also look up:
N. exercise, rehearsal, training, workout 1
custom, habit, method, procedure, system, way 2

practise [AM **practice**] /'præktɪs/ (**practises, practising, practised**) 1 V-T If you **practise** something, you keep doing it regularly in order to do it better. ❑ *Lauren practises the piano every day.* 2 V-T When people **practise** something such as a custom, craft, or religion, they take part in the activities associated with it. ❑ *Their family practises traditional Judaism.* ❑ *The art of folding paper has been practised in Japan since the 6th century.* • **practising** ADJ BEFORE N ❑ *All employees must be practising Christians.* 3 V-T/V-I Someone who **practises** medicine or law works as a doctor or lawyer. ❑ *He practised as a lawyer until his retirement.*

practised [AM **practiced**] /'præktɪst/ ADJ Someone who is **practised at** something is good at it because they have had a lot of experience of it. ❑ *...once you are practised at this sort of relaxation.* ❑ *...a practised and experienced surgeon.*

practitioner /præk'tɪʃənə/ (**practitioners**) N-COUNT Doctors are sometimes referred to as **practitioners**. [FORMAL]

pragmatic /præg'mætɪk/ ADJ A **pragmatic** way of dealing with something is based on practical considerations, rather than theoretical ones. A **pragmatic** person deals with things in a practical way. • **pragmatically** ADV ❑ *These firms respond pragmatically to local conditions.*

pragmatism /'prægmətɪzəm/ N-UNCOUNT **Pragmatism** means thinking or dealing with problems in a practical way, rather than by using theory or abstract principles. [FORMAL] • **pragmatist** (**pragmatists**) N-UNCOUNT ❑ *He is a political pragmatist, not an idealist.*

prairie /'preəri/ (**prairies**) N-VAR A **prairie** is a large area of flat grassy land in North America. → see **grassland, habitat**

praise /preɪz/ (**praises, praising, praised**) 1 V-T & N-UNCOUNT If you **praise** someone or something, or if you express your **praise for** them, you express approval for their achievements or qualities. ❑ *He praised the fans for their continued support.* ❑ *She is full of praise for the excellent services available.* 2 V-T & N-UNCOUNT If you **praise** God, or if you offer him your **praise**, you express your respect, honour, and thanks to God. ❑ *Hindus were singing hymns in praise of the god Rama.* 3 PHRASE If you **sing** someone's **praises**, you praise them in an enthusiastic way.

pram /præm/ (**prams**) N-COUNT A **pram** is like a baby's cot on wheels, which you can push along when you want to take the baby somewhere.

prank /præŋk/ (**pranks**) N-COUNT A **prank** is a childish trick. [DATED]

prawn /prɔːn/ (**prawns**) N-COUNT In British English, a **prawn** is a small edible shellfish, similar to a shrimp. The usual American word is **shrimp**. → see **shellfish**

pray /preɪ/ (**prays, praying, prayed**) V-T/V-I When people **pray**, they speak to God in order to give thanks or to ask for help. ❑ *Kelly prayed that God would judge her kindly.*

prayer /preə/ (**prayers**) 1 N-UNCOUNT **Prayer** is the activity of speaking to God. ❑ *The night was spent in prayer.* 2 N-COUNT A **prayer** is the words that someone says when they speak to God. 3 N-COUNT You can refer to a strong hope that you have as your **prayer**. ❑ *This drug could be the answer to our prayers.* 4 N-PLURAL A short religious service at which people gather to pray can be referred to as

P

prayers. ❑ ...*Muslims attending prayers.*

preach /pri:tʃ/ (**preaches, preaching, preached**) **1** V-T/V-I When someone, especially a member of the clergy, **preaches**, or **preaches** a **sermon**, he or she gives a talk on a religious or moral subject as part of a church service. ❑ *The bishop preached to a crowd of several hundred local people.* ● **preacher** (**preachers**) N-COUNT ❑ ...*acceptance of women preachers.* **2** V-T/V-I When people **preach** a belief or a course of action, they try to persuade other people to accept the belief or take the course of action. ❑ *For many years I have preached against war.*

precarious /prɪˈkeəriəs/ **1** ADJ If your situation is **precarious**, you are not in complete control of events and might fail in what you are doing at any moment. ● **precariously** ADV ❑ *He felt as if he was holding on precariously to his job.* **2** ADJ Something that is **precarious**, is not securely held in place and is likely to fall at any moment. ❑ ...*a very precarious ladder.* ● **precariously** ADV ❑ *One of my bags was precariously balanced on the wall.*

Word Link	pre ≈ before : precaution, precede, prediction

Word Link	caut ≈ taking care : caution, cautious, precaution

precaution /prɪˈkɔːʃən/ (**precautions**) N-COUNT A **precaution** is an action that is intended to prevent something dangerous or unpleasant from happening. ❑ *They took the precaution of getting legal advice.* ❑ ...*safety precautions.*

precede /prɪˈsiːd/ (**precedes, preceding, preceded**) V-T If one event or period of time **precedes** another, it happens before it. [FORMAL] ❑ *The wedding was preceded by a party in a night club.* ● **preceding** ADJ BEFORE N ❑ ...*friends I had already met during the preceding months.*

precedence /ˈpresɪdəns/ PHRASE If one thing **takes precedence over** another, the first thing is regarded as more important than the second one. ❑ *He took precedence over everyone else.*

P

precedent /ˈpresɪdənt/ (**precedents**) N-VAR If there is a **precedent for** an action or event, it has happened before, and this can be regarded as an argument for doing it again. [FORMAL] ❑ *The decision could set a precedent for other public institutions.*

precinct /ˈpriːsɪŋkt/ (**precincts**) **1** N-COUNT A shopping **precinct** is an area in the centre of a town in which cars are not allowed. [BRIT] **2** N-COUNT In the United States, a **precinct** is a part of a city which has its own police force and fire service. **3** N-PLURAL The **precincts** of an institution are its buildings and land. [FORMAL]

precious /ˈpreʃəs/ **1** ADJ If you say that something such as a resource is **precious**, you mean that it is valuable and should not be wasted or used badly. ❑ *A family holiday allows you to spend precious time together.* **2** ADJ **Precious** objects and materials are worth a lot of money because they are rare. **3** ADJ If something is **precious to** you, you regard it as important and do not want to lose it. ❑ *Her family's support is particularly precious to Josie.* **4** PHRASE If you say that there is **precious little** of something, you are emphasizing that there is very little of it, and that it would be better if there were more. ❑ *They have had precious little to celebrate.* ❑ *The Government has precious few options left.*

precipitate (**precipitates, precipitating, precipitated**) **1** V-T /prɪˈsɪpəteɪt/ If something **precipitates** an event or situation, usually a bad one, it causes it to happen suddenly or sooner than normal. [FORMAL] ❑ *A slight mistake could precipitate a disaster.* **2** ADJ /prɪˈsɪpɪtət/ A **precipitate** action or decision happens or is made more quickly or suddenly than most people think is sensible. [FORMAL] ● **precipitately** ADV ❑ *I fled precipitately in the opposite direction.*

precise /prɪˈsaɪs/ **1** ADJ You use **precise** to emphasize that you are referring to an exact thing, rather than something vague. ❑ ...*the precise location of the ship.* **2** ADJ Something that is **precise** is exact and accurate in all its details. ❑ *They speak very precise English.*

precisely /prɪˈsaɪsli/ **1** ADV **Precisely** means accurately and exactly. ❑ *The meeting began at precisely 4.00 p.m.* **2** ADV You use **precisely** to emphasize that a reason or fact is the only important one there is, or that it is obvious. ❑ *That is precisely the result that we wanted.*

precision /prɪˈsɪʒən/ N-UNCOUNT If you do something with **precision**, you do it exactly as it should be done. ❑ *The choir sang with precision.*

preclude /prɪˈkluːd/ (**precludes, precluding, precluded**) V-T If something **precludes** you **from** doing something or going somewhere, it prevents you from doing it or going there. ❑ *Poor English precluded them from ever finding a job.*

precocious /prɪˈkəʊʃəs/ ADJ **Precocious** children do or say things that seem very advanced for their age.

preconception /ˌpriːkənˈsepʃən/ (**preconceptions**) N-COUNT Your **preconceptions** about something are the beliefs you form about it before you have enough information or experience. ❑ ...*preconceptions about the sort of people who do computing.*

precondition /ˌpriːkənˈdɪʃən/ (**preconditions**) N-COUNT If one thing is a **precondition for** another, it must happen or be done before the second thing can happen or exist. [FORMAL] ❑ *We're open to dialogue any time, anywhere, without preconditions.*

precursor /priːˈkɜːsə/ (**precursors**) N-COUNT A **precursor of** something is a similar thing that happened or existed before it. ❑ ...*the European Monetary Institute, the precursor of a European central bank.*

predator /ˈpredətə/ (**predators**) N-COUNT A **predator** is an animal that kills and eats other animals.
→ see **food, shark**

predatory /ˈpredətri, AM -tɔːri/ ADJ **Predatory** animals or birds kill and eat other animals. ❑ ...*predatory birds like the eagle.*

predecessor /ˈpriːdɪsesə, AM ˈpred-/ (**predecessors**) **1** N-COUNT **Your predecessor** is the person who had your job before you. ❑ *He learned everything he knew from his predecessor.* **2** N-COUNT The **predecessor** of an object or machine is the object or machine that came before it in a sequence or process of development. ❑ *The car is 40mm shorter than its predecessor.*

predicament /prɪˈdɪkəmənt/ (**predicaments**) N-COUNT If you are **in a predicament**, you are in a difficult situation. ❑ *The news left her in a peculiar predicament.*

Word Link *dict ≈ speaking : contradict, dictate, predict*

predict /prɪˈdɪkt/ (**predicts, predicting, predicted**) V-T If you **predict** an event, you say that it will happen. ❑ *He predicted that my hair would grow back quickly.*
→ see **experiment, forecast**

predictable /prɪˈdɪktəbəl/ ADJ Something that is **predictable** is obvious in advance and will happen. ❑ *The result was entirely predictable.* ● **predictably** ADV ❑ *His article is, predictably, a fierce attack on capitalism.* ● **predictability** N-UNCOUNT ❑ *...the predictability of their relationship.*

Word Link *pre ≈ before : precaution, precede, prediction*

prediction /prɪˈdɪkʃən/ (**predictions**) N-VAR If you **make a prediction**, you say what you think will happen. ❑ *...their prediction that he would change her life.*
→ see **science**

predispose /ˌpriːdɪˈspəʊz/ (**predisposes, predisposing, predisposed**) **1** V-T If something **predisposes** you **to** think or behave in a particular way, it makes it likely that you will think or behave in that way. [FORMAL] ❑ *He argued that his genes had predisposed him to a life of crime.* ● **predisposed** ADJ AFTER LINK-V ❑ *Franklin was predisposed to believe him.* **2** V-T If something **predisposes** you **to** a disease or condition, it makes it likely that you will suffer from that disease or condition. ● **predisposed** ADJ AFTER LINK-V ❑ *Some people are genetically predisposed to diabetes.*

predisposition /ˌpriːdɪspəˈzɪʃən/ (**predispositions**) N-COUNT If you have a **predisposition to** a particular disease, condition, or way of behaving, something in your nature makes it likely that you will suffer from that disease or condition, or that you will behave in that way. ❑ *...a predisposition to mental illness.* ❑ *...a woman's predisposition to use the right side of her brain.*

Word Link *dom, domin ≈ rule, master : domain, dominate, predominant*

predominant /prɪˈdɒmɪnənt/ ADJ If something is **predominant**, it is more important or noticeable than anything else in a set of people or things. ❑ *Amanda's predominant emotion was one of confusion.* ● **predominantly** ADV ❑ *Business is conducted predominantly by phone.* ● **predominance** N-UNCOUNT ❑ *...the predominance of men in entertainment TV.*

predominate /prɪˈdɒmɪneɪt/ (**predominates, predominating, predominated**) V-I If one type of person or thing **predominates** in a group, there are more of that type than any other. [FORMAL] ❑ *In older age groups women predominate because men tend to die younger.*

pre-ˈeminent ADJ The **pre-eminent** person in a group is the most important or powerful one. [FORMAL] ❑ *...the pre-eminent political figure in the country.* ● **pre-eminence** N-UNCOUNT ❑ *...the pre-eminence of post-war US literature.*

pre-empt /priː ˈempt/ (**pre-empts, pre-empting, pre-empted**) V-T If you **pre-empt** an action, you prevent it from happening by doing something before it can happen. ❑ *You can pre-empt pain by taking a painkiller at the first warning sign.*

pre-emptive /priː ˈemptɪv/ ADJ A **pre-emptive** attack or strike is intended to weaken or damage an enemy or opponent, for example by destroying their weapons before they can do any harm.

preface /ˈprefɪs/ (**prefaces, prefacing, prefaced**) **1** N-COUNT A **preface** is an introduction at the beginning of a book. **2** V-T If you **preface** an action or speech **with** something else, you do or say this other thing first. ❑ *She prefaced everything with, 'The problem is…'*

prefer /prɪˈfɜː/ (**prefers, preferring, preferred**) V-T If you **prefer** someone or something, you like that person or thing better than another. ❑ *Does he prefer a particular sort of music?* ❑ *I preferred books and people to politics.*

Usage

Note that **prefer** can often sound rather formal in ordinary conversation. Verbal expressions such as **like...better** and **would rather** are used more frequently. For example, instead of saying **'I prefer football to tennis'**, you can say **'I like football better than tennis'**, instead of **'I'd prefer an apple'**, you can say **'I'd rather have an apple'**, and instead of **'I'd prefer to walk'**, you can say **'I'd rather walk'**.

preferable /ˈprefrəbəl/ ADJ If one thing is **preferable to** another, it is more desirable or suitable. ❑ *Grilling foods is preferable to frying.* ❑ *It is preferable to use only vegetable oil for cooking.* ● **preferably** ADV ❑ *Take exercise, preferably in the fresh air.*

preference /ˈprefərəns/ (**preferences**) **1** N-VAR If you have a **preference for** something, you would like to have or do that thing rather than something else. ❑ *His designs show a preference for natural materials.* **2** N-UNCOUNT If you **give preference to** someone, you choose them rather than someone else. ❑ *The company gave preference to local workers.*

preferential /ˌprefəˈrenʃəl/ ADJ If you get **preferential treatment**, you are treated better than other people.

Word Link *fix ≈ fastening : fixture, prefix, suffix*

prefix /ˈpriːfɪks/ (**prefixes**) N-COUNT A **prefix** is a letter or group of letters which is added to the beginning of a word in order to form a different word. For example, the prefix 'un-' is added to 'happy' to form 'unhappy'.

pregnant /ˈpregnənt/ ADJ If a woman or female animal is **pregnant**, she has a baby or babies developing in her body. ❑ *Lena got pregnant.* ❑ *Tina was pregnant with their first daughter.* ● **pregnancy** N-UNCOUNT ❑ *Is it safe to drink coffee during pregnancy?*
→ see **reproduction**

Word Partnership Use *pregnant* with:

N. pregnant **with a baby/child**, pregnant **mother**, pregnant **wife**, pregnant **woman**
V. **be** pregnant, **become** pregnant, **get** pregnant

P

preheat /ˌpriːˈhiːt/ (**preheats, preheating, preheated**) V-T If you **preheat** an oven, you switch it on and allow it to reach a certain temperature before you put food inside it.

prehistoric /ˌpriːhɪˈstɒrɪk, AM -ˈtɔːr-/ ADJ **Prehistoric** people and things existed at a time before information was written down. ❑ *...the famous prehistoric cave paintings of Lascaux.*

prejudice /ˈpredʒʊdɪs/ (**prejudices, prejudicing, prejudiced**) 1 N-VAR **Prejudice** is an unreasonable dislike of someone or something, or an unreasonable preference for one group over another. ❑ *...racial prejudice.* ❑ *The survey found that there is prejudice against working mothers.* 2 V-T To **prejudice** someone or something means to influence them in such a way that they are no longer fair and objective. ❑ *Dawson prejudiced the jury against him by using bad language during his trial.* 3 V-T If someone **prejudices** another person's situation, they do something which makes it worse than it should be. ❑ *Having children is going to prejudice your chances of getting a job overseas.*

Thesaurus	*prejudice* Also look up:
N.	bias, bigotry, disapproval, intolerance; (*ant.*) tolerance 1

prejudiced /ˈpredʒʊdɪsd/ ADJ If someone is **prejudiced** against a particular group, they have an unreasonable dislike of them. ❑ *She was prejudiced against men in general.*

preliminary /prɪˈlɪmɪnri, AM -neri/ (**preliminaries**) N-COUNT & ADJ **Preliminaries**, or **preliminary** activities or discussions, take place in preparation for an event before it starts. ❑ *All the preliminaries are in place and we will start building the stadium soon.* ❑ *...preliminary tests.*

prelude /ˈpreljuːd, AM ˈpreɪluːd/ (**preludes**) N-COUNT You describe an event as a **prelude to** a more important event when it happens before it and acts as an introduction to it. ❑ *For him, reading was a necessary prelude to sleep.*

P

premature /ˌpreməˈtʃʊə, AM ˌpriː-/ 1 ADJ Something that is **premature** happens too early or earlier than expected. ❑ *His career as a footballer was brought to a premature end by injury.* • **prematurely** ADV ❑ *The woman looked as if she was in her thirties, and had prematurely grey hair.* 2 ADJ A **premature** baby is born before the date when it was due to be born.

premier /ˈpremiə, AM prɪˈmɪr/ (**premiers**) 1 N-COUNT The leader of a government can be referred to as the **premier**. ❑ *...the Australian premier.* 2 ADJ BEFORE N **Premier** is used to describe something that is considered to be the best or most important thing of its kind. ❑ *...the country's premier opera company.*

premiere /ˈpremieə, AM prɪˈmjer/ (**premieres**) N-COUNT The **premiere** of a new play or film is the first public performance of it.

premiership /ˈpremiəʃɪp, AM prɪˈmɪr-/ N-SING **Premiership** is the position of being the leader of a government. ❑ *...the final years of Margaret Thatcher's premiership.*

premise /ˈpremɪs/ (**premises**)

Premiss is also used in British English for sense 2.

1 N-PLURAL The **premises** of a business are all the buildings and land that it occupies. ❑ *There is a kitchen on the premises.* ❑ *The company moved to premises in the city centre.* 2 N-COUNT A **premise** is something that you suppose is true and that you use as a basis for developing an idea. [FORMAL] ❑ *The premise is that schools will work harder to improve if they must compete.*

premium /ˈpriːmiəm/ (**premiums**) 1 N-COUNT A **premium** is money that you pay regularly to an insurance company for an insurance policy. 2 N-COUNT A **premium** is a sum of money that you have to pay for something in addition to the normal cost. ❑ *People will normally pay a premium for a good house in a nice area.* 3 PHRASE If something is **at a premium**, it is wanted or needed, but is difficult to get or achieve. ❑ *Space is at a premium, so houses are built close together and gardens are small.*

premonition /ˌpreməˈnɪʃən, AM ˌpriː-/ (**premonitions**) N-COUNT If you have a **premonition**, you have a feeling that something is going to happen, often something unpleasant. ❑ *That morning I had a terrible premonition about my daughter and asked her not to go out.*

Word Link	***nat** ≈ being born : innate, native, prenatal*

prenatal /ˌpriːˈneɪtəl/ ADJ **Prenatal** things relate to the medical care of pregnant women.

preoccupy /priˈɒkjʊpaɪ/ (**preoccupies, preoccupying, preoccupied**) V-T If something **is preoccupying** you, you are thinking about it a lot. ❑ *Thoughts of money preoccupy many of us.* • **preoccupied** ADJ ❑ *Try not to become so preoccupied with work that you forget about your family and friends.* • **preoccupation** (**preoccupations**) N-VAR ❑ *My girlfriend's preoccupation with her weight is really boring.*

preparation /ˌprepəˈreɪʃən/ (**preparations**) 1 N-UNCOUNT **Preparation** is the process of getting something ready for use or for a particular purpose. ❑ *Mental preparation is an important area of sport.* ❑ *...food preparation.* 2 N-PLURAL **Preparations** are the arrangements that are made for a future event. ❑ *...preparations for the wedding.*

preparatory /prɪˈpærətri, AM -tɔːri/ ADJ **Preparatory** actions are done as a preparation for something else. [FORMAL] ❑ *A year's preparatory work will be necessary before building can start.*

prepare /prɪˈpeə/ (**prepares, preparing, prepared**) 1 V-T If you **prepare** something, you make it ready for something that is going to happen. ❑ *Before painting, you must prepare the walls by washing them.* 2 V-T/V-I If you **prepare for** an event or action that will happen soon, you get yourself ready for it or make the necessary arrangements. ❑ *The Prime Minister has told Members of Parliament to start preparing for the next election.* ❑ *He went back to his hotel and prepared to catch a train for New York.* 3 V-T When you **prepare** food, you get it ready to be eaten.

Word Partnership	Use *prepare* with:
N.	prepare **a list**, prepare **a plan**, prepare **a report** 1 prepare **for battle/war**, prepare **for the future**, prepare **for the worst** 2 prepare **dinner**, prepare **food**, prepare **a meal** 3

prepared /prɪˈpeəd/ 1 ADJ AFTER LINK-V If you

are **prepared to** do something, you are willing to do it. ❑ *I'm prepared to take your advice.* **2** ADJ AFTER LINK-V If you are **prepared for** something that you think is going to happen, you are ready for it. ❑ *Be prepared for both warm and cool weather.* ● **preparedness** N-UNCOUNT ❑ *...the country's preparedness for war.* **3** ADJ Something that is **prepared** has been done or made beforehand, so that it is ready when it is needed. ❑ *He started reading his prepared speech.*

Word Link *pos ≈ placing : deposit, preposition, repository*

preposition /ˌprepəˈzɪʃən/ (**prepositions**) N-COUNT A **preposition** is a word such as 'by', 'for', 'into', or 'with', which usually has a noun group as its object.

preposterous /prɪˈpɒstərəs/ ADJ If you describe something as **preposterous**, you mean that it is extremely unreasonable and foolish. ● **preposterously** ADV ❑ *These prices are preposterously high.*

prerequisite /ˌpriːˈrekwɪzɪt/ (**prerequisites**) N-COUNT If one thing is a **prerequisite for** another, it must happen or exist before the second thing is possible. ❑ *A positive attitude is a prerequisite for a happy life.*

prerogative /prɪˈrɒgətɪv/ (**prerogatives**) N-COUNT Something that is the **prerogative of** a particular person or group is a privilege or a power that only they have. [FORMAL] ❑ *It is the Government's prerogative to choose the president of the commission.*

prescribe /prɪˈskraɪb/ (**prescribes, prescribing, prescribed**) **1** V-T If a doctor **prescribes** treatment, he or she states what medicine or treatment a patient should have. **2** V-T If a person or set of laws or rules **prescribes** an action or duty, they state that it must be carried out. [FORMAL] ❑ *This law prescribes the method of electing a president.*

prescription /prɪˈskrɪpʃən/ (**prescriptions**) **1** N-COUNT A **prescription** is a medicine which a doctor has told you to take, or the form on which the doctor has written the details of that medicine. **2** PHRASE If a medicine is available **on prescription**, you can get it from a chemist if a doctor gives you a prescription for it.

presence /ˈprezəns/ **1** N-SING Someone's **presence** in a place is the fact that they are there. ❑ *His presence in the village led to trouble.* **2** N-UNCOUNT If you say that someone has **presence**, you mean that they impress people by their appearance and manner. ❑ *He has great presence and dignity.* **3** PHRASE If someone or something **makes** their **presence felt**, they do something which forces people to pay attention to them. **4** PHRASE If you are **in** someone's **presence**, you are in the same place as they are, and are close enough to them to be seen or heard.

present
❶ EXISTING OR HAPPENING NOW
❷ BEING SOMEWHERE
❸ GIFT
❹ VERB USES

present /ˈprezənt/
❶ **1** ADJ BEFORE N You use **present** to describe people and things that exist now, rather than in the past or the future. ❑ *...the country's present leader.* ❑ *We can't say anything at the present time.* **2** N-SING **The present** is the period of time that we are in now and the things that are happening now. ❑ *It is natural to worry about the future, but it is important to live in the present.* **3** ADJ BEFORE N The **present** tenses of a verb are the ones used to talk about things that happen regularly or situations that exist at this time. **4** PHRASE A situation that exists **at present** exists now, although it may change. **5** PHRASE **The present day** is the period of history that we are in now. ❑ *...Western European art from 1800 to the present day.*

present /ˈprezənt/
❷ **1** ADJ If someone is **present** at an event, they are there. ❑ *The whole family was present.* **2** ADJ If something, especially a substance or disease, is **present in** something else, it exists within that thing. ❑ *Vitamin P is present in fresh fruits.*

present /ˈprezənt/ (**presents**)
❸ N-COUNT A **present** is something that you give to someone, for example for their birthday or for Christmas. ❑ *This book would make a great Christmas present.*

present /prɪˈzent/ (**presents, presenting, presented**)
❹ **1** V-T If you **present** someone **with** a prize or **with** information, or if you **present** it **to** them, you formally give it to them. ❑ *The prime minister presented the prizes.* ❑ *We presented three options for discussion.* ● **presentation** /ˌprezənˈteɪʃən, AM ˌpriːzen-/ (**presentations**) N-VAR ❑ *...the presentation of the awards.* **2** V-T Something that **presents** a difficulty or a challenge causes or provides it. ❑ *This presents us with a huge problem.* **3** V-T If you **present** someone or something in a particular way, you describe them in that way. ❑ *The British like to present themselves as a nation of dog-lovers.* **4** V-T If someone **presents** a programme on television or radio, they introduce each item in it. ● **presenter** (**presenters**) N-COUNT ❑ *...a TV presenter.*

presentation /ˌprezənˈteɪʃən, AM ˌpriːzen-/ (**presentations**) **1** N-UNCOUNT **Presentation** is the appearance of something, which someone has worked to create. ❑ *Presentation of food is important - it's worth making the effort so that even simple dishes look special.* **2** N-COUNT A **presentation** is a formal event at which someone is given a prize or award. **3** N-COUNT When someone gives a **presentation**, they give a formal talk. ❑ *John gave an excellent presentation.* **4** N-COUNT A **presentation** is something that is performed before an audience. ❑ *...the Royal Opera's presentation of Julius Caesar.*

ˌpresent-ˈday also **present day** ADJ BEFORE N **Present-day** things, situations, and people exist at the time in history we are now in. ❑ *Alfred Brendel was born in Moravia, which is in the present-day Czech Republic.*

presently /ˈprezəntli/ **1** ADV If you say that something is **presently** happening, you mean that it is happening now. ❑ *She is presently working on a number of projects.* ❑ *There is presently nobody living on the island.* **2** ADV You use **presently** to indicate that something happened quite a short time after something you have just mentioned. [WRITTEN] ❑ *He was taken to a small office. Presently, a young woman came in.* **3** ADV If you say that something will happen **presently**, you mean that it will happen quite soon. ❑ *'Who's Agnes?'—'You'll be meeting her presently.'*

preservative /prɪ'zɜːvətɪv/ (**preservatives**) N-VAR A **preservative** is a chemical that is added to substances to prevent them from decaying. ❑ *Nitrates are used as food preservatives.*

Word Link	*ation ≈ state of : dehydration, elevation, preservation*

Word Link	*serv ≈ keeping : conserve, observe, preserve*

preserve /prɪ'zɜːv/ (**preserves, preserving, preserved**) 1 V-T If you **preserve** a situation or condition, you make sure that it stays as it is, and does not change or end. ❑ *We will do everything to preserve peace.* ● **preservation** /ˌprezə'veɪʃən/ N-UNCOUNT ❑ *...the preservation of human life.* 2 V-T If you **preserve** something, you take action to save it or protect it. ❑ *We need to preserve the rainforest.* ● **preservation** N-UNCOUNT ❑ *...the preservation of ancient buildings.* 3 V-T If you **preserve** food, you treat it in order to prevent it from decaying.

Word Link	*sid ≈ sitting : preside, president, reside*

preside /prɪ'zaɪd/ (**presides, presiding, presided**) V-I If you **preside over** a meeting or event, you are in charge or act as the chairperson.

presidency /'prezɪdənsi/ (**presidencies**) N-COUNT The **presidency** of a country or organization is the position of being the president or the period of time during which someone is president. ❑ *D'Estaing lost the French presidency to Mitterand in 1981.*

president /'prezɪdənt/ (**presidents**) 1 N-COUNT & N-TITLE The **president** of a country that has no king or queen is the person who has the highest political position and is the leader of the country. ❑ *...the first president, George Washington.* 2 → See note at **government** 3 N-COUNT The **president** of an organization is the person with the highest position in it. ❑ *...the president of the Art Academy.*

P

presidential /ˌprezɪ'denʃəl/ ADJ BEFORE N **Presidential** activities or things relate or belong to a president. ❑ *...the presidential election.*

press /pres/ (**presses, pressing, pressed**) 1 V-T If you **press** something somewhere, you push it firmly against something else. ❑ *He pressed his back against the door.* ❑ *He pressed his toes into the sand.* 2 V-T & N-COUNT If you **press** a button or switch, or if you give it a **press**, you push it with your finger in order to make a machine or device work. ❑ *David pressed a button and the door closed.* ❑ *E-mail allows students on opposite sides of the world to communicate at the press of a button.* 3 V-T/V-I If you **press** something, or if you **press down on** it, you push against it with your hand or foot. ❑ *I pressed the brake but nothing happened.* ❑ *She leaned forward with her hands pressing down on the desk.* 4 V-T If you **press** clothes, you iron them. 5 V-I If you **press for** something, you try hard to persuade someone to give it to you or agree to it. ❑ *The police have pressed for changes in the law.* 6 V-T If you **press** someone, you try hard to persuade them to do or say something. ❑ *They pressed him for more information.* 7 V-T If you **press charges** against someone, you make an official accusation which has to be decided in a court of law. ❑ *Police said they will press charges.* 8 N-SING **The press** refers to newspapers and the journalists who write them. **The press** can take the singular or plural form of the verb. ❑ *They held a meeting, but did not let the Press attend.* 9 N-COUNT A **press** or a **printing press** is a machine used for printing books, newspapers, and leaflets. 10 → see also **pressing**
→ see **printing**

▶ **press on** or **press ahead** PHR-VERB If you **press on**, you continue doing something in a determined way, and do not allow difficulties to delay you. ❑ *The Dutch government pressed on with their plans.*

Word Partnership	Use *press* with:
N.	press **a button, at the** press **of a button** 2
	press **charges** 7
	press **accounts,** press **coverage, freedom of the** press, press **reports** 8

'press conference (**press conferences**) N-COUNT A **press conference** is a meeting held by a famous or important person in which they answer journalists' questions.

pressing /'presɪŋ/ ADJ A **pressing** problem, need, or issue has to be dealt with immediately.

'press release (**press releases**) N-COUNT A **press release** is a written statement about a matter of public interest which is given to the press by an organization involved in the matter. ❑ *The government put out a press release about the incident.*

'press-up (**press-ups**) N-COUNT In British English, **press-ups** are exercises that you do by lying with your face towards the floor and pushing with your hands to raise your body until your arms are straight. The usual American term is **push-up**. ❑ *He did 30 press-ups.*

pressure /'preʃə/ (**pressures, pressuring, pressured**) 1 N-UNCOUNT **Pressure** is the force produced when you press hard on something. ❑ *Put pressure on the cut to stop the bleeding.* 2 N-UNCOUNT The **pressure** in a place or container is the force produced by the quantity of gas or liquid in that place or container. ❑ *High pressure over Scotland will produce dry, warm weather.* 3 → see also **blood pressure** 4 N-UNCOUNT If there is **pressure on** someone **to** do something, someone is trying to persuade or force them to do it. ❑ *He put pressure on her to agree.* 5 N-VAR If you feel **pressure**, you feel that you have too much to do and not enough time to do it, or that people expect a lot from you. ❑ *Do you work well under pressure?* ❑ *...the pressures of modern life.* 6 V-T If you **pressure** someone **to** do something, you try forcefully to persuade them to do it. ❑ *He is pressuring her to get married.* ❑ *Don't pressure me.* ● **pressured** ADJ ❑ *You're obviously feeling tired and pressured.*
→ see **forecast, weather**

'pressure group (**pressure groups**) N-COUNT A **pressure group** is an organization that campaigns to try to persuade a government to do something. ❑ *...the environmental pressure group Greenpeace.*

pressurize [BRIT also **pressurise**] /'preʃəraɪz/ (**pressurizes, pressurizing, pressurized**) V-T If you are **pressurized into** doing something, you are forcefully persuaded to do it. ❑ *They pressurized him into making the decision immediately.*

pressurized [BRIT also **pressurised**] /'preʃəraɪzd/ ADJ In a **pressurized** container or area, the pressure inside is different from the pressure outside. ❑ *Auguste Piccard invented the pressurised aircraft cabin.*

prestige /pre'stiːʒ/ N-UNCOUNT If a person, a country, or an organization has **prestige**, they are admired and respected because they are important or successful. ❑ *...the prestige of the United Nations.* ❑ *...high prestige jobs.*

prestigious /pre'stɪdʒəs/ ADJ A **prestigious** institution or activity is respected and admired by people. ❑ *...the largest and most prestigious businesses in America.*

presumably /prɪ'zjuːməbli, AM -'zuːm-/ ADV If you say that something is **presumably** the case, you mean that you think it is true, although you are not certain. ❑ *Presumably the front door was locked?* ❑ *He went to the hotel reception desk, presumably to check out.*

Word Link *sume ≈ taking : assume, consume, presume*

presume /prɪ'zjuːm, AM -'zuːm/ (**presumes, presuming, presumed**) 1 V-T If you **presume** that something is the case, you think that it is true, although you are not certain. ❑ *I presume you're here on business.* ❑ *The missing person is presumed dead.* 2 V-T If you say that someone **presumes to** do something, you mean that they do it even though they have no right to do it. [FORMAL] ❑ *They presumed to question his judgement.*

Word Link *sumpt ≈ taking : assumption, consumption, presumption*

presumption /prɪ'zʌmpʃən/ (**presumptions**) N-COUNT A **presumption** is something that is accepted as true but is not certain to be true. ❑ *...the presumption that you are innocent until proved guilty.*

presumptuous /prɪ'zʌmptʃuəs/ ADJ If you describe someone as **presumptuous**, you disapprove of them because they do things that they have no right to do. ❑ *It would be presumptuous for us to go there – we weren't invited.*

pretence [AM **pretense**] /prɪ'tens, AM 'priːtens/ (**pretences**) 1 N-VAR A **pretence** is a way of behaving that is intended to make people believe something that is not true. ❑ *William made a pretence of writing a note in his book.* 2 PHRASE If you do something **under false pretences**, you do it when people do not know the truth about you and your intentions. ❑ *He married her under false pretences. He wanted her money.*

pretend /prɪ'tend/ (**pretends, pretending, pretended**) 1 V-T If you **pretend** that something is true, you try to make people believe that it is true, although it is not. ❑ *The boy pretended to be asleep.* 2 V-T If you **pretend** that you are doing something, you imagine that you are doing it. ❑ *When I was a child, I used to pretend that I was a fairy princess.*

pretense → see **pretence**

pretension /prɪ'tenʃən/ (**pretensions**) N-VAR Someone with **pretensions** pretends that they are more important than they really are. ❑ *We like him for his honesty and his lack of pretension.*

pretentious /prɪ'tenʃəs/ ADJ Someone or something that is **pretentious** tries to appear more important or significant than they really are. ❑ *The film was boring and pretentious.*

pretext /'priːtekst/ (**pretexts**) N-COUNT A **pretext** is a reason which you pretend has caused you to do something. ❑ *I went into his bedroom on the pretext of looking for a book.*

pretty /'prɪti/ (**prettier, prettiest**) 1 ADJ If you describe someone, especially a girl, as **pretty**, you mean that they look nice and are attractive in a delicate way. ❑ *She is a shy, pretty girl with enormous blue eyes.* 2 ADJ A place or a thing that is **pretty** is attractive and pleasant. ❑ *...a pretty flowered cotton dress.* • **prettily** ADV ❑ *The living-room was prettily decorated.* 3 ADV You can use **pretty** before an adjective or adverb to mean 'quite' or 'rather'. [INFORMAL] ❑ *I'm pretty good at swimming.* 4 PHRASE **Pretty much** or **pretty well** means 'almost'. [INFORMAL] ❑ *I travel pretty much every week.*

Usage

When you are describing someone's appearance, you usually use **pretty** and **beautiful** to describe women, girls, and babies. **Beautiful** is a much stronger word than **pretty**. The equivalent word for a man is **handsome**. **Good-looking** and **attractive** can be used to describe people of either sex. **Pretty** can also be used to modify adjectives and adverbs but is less strong than **very**. In this sense, **pretty** is informal. Therefore, if you said to someone, '**Your work is rather good**' or '**Your work is pretty good**', they would be more likely to be pleased than if you said '**Your work is quite good**' or '**Your work is fairly good**'.

Thesaurus *pretty* Also look up:

ADJ. beautiful, cute, lovely 1
beautiful, charming, pleasant 2

prevail /prɪ'veɪl/ (**prevails, prevailing, prevailed**) 1 V-I If a proposal, principle, or opinion **prevails**, it gains influence or is accepted. ❑ *We hope that common sense will prevail.* 2 V-I If a situation or attitude **prevails** in a particular place at a particular time, it is normal or most common at that place and time. ❑ *Confusion prevailed at the time of the revolution.* 3 V-I If you **prevail upon** someone **to** do something, you succeed in persuading them to do it. ❑ *He prevailed upon her to lie about their relationship.*

prevalent /'prevələnt/ ADJ A condition or belief that is **prevalent** is very common. ❑ *I think this attitude is prevalent now.* • **prevalence** N-UNCOUNT ❑ *...the prevalence of asthma in Britain.*

prevaricate /prɪ'værɪkeɪt/ (**prevaricates, prevaricating, prevaricated**) V-I If you **prevaricate**, you avoid giving a direct answer or making a decision. ❑ *She saw no reason to prevaricate.*

prevent /prɪ'vent/ (**prevents, preventing, prevented**) V-T If you **prevent** something, you stop it happening or being done. ❑ *This new system will prevent water being wasted.* ❑ *The French president hopes to prevent the Socialists from winning.* • **prevention** N-UNCOUNT ❑ *...crime prevention.*

P

Word Partnership Use *prevent* with:

N. prevent **attacks**, prevent **cancer**, prevent **damage**, prevent **disease**, prevent **infection**, prevent **injuries**, prevent **loss**, prevent **pregnancy**, prevent **problems**, prevent **violence**, prevent **war**

preventative /prɪˈventətɪv/ ADJ BEFORE N **Preventative** means the same as **preventive**.

preventive /prɪˈventɪv/ ADJ BEFORE N **Preventive** actions are intended to help prevent things such as disease or crime. ❑ *Not enough money is spent on preventive medicine.*

preview /ˈpriːvjuː/ (**previews**) N-COUNT A **preview** is an opportunity to see something such as a film or invention before it is open or available to the public.

previous /ˈpriːviəs/ ADJ BEFORE N A **previous** event or thing is one that occurred before the one you are talking about. ❑ *She has a child from a previous marriage.*

previously /ˈpriːviəsli/ 1 ADV **Previously** means at some time before the period that you are talking about. ❑ *He now works in a bank, but previously he was a teacher.* 2 ADV You can use **previously** to say how much earlier one event was than another. ❑ *Ingrid had moved to San Diego two weeks previously*

ˌpre-ˈwar ADJ **Pre-war** is used to describe things that happened, existed, or were made in the period immediately before a war, especially the Second World War (1939-45). ❑ *...pre-war British movies.*

prey /preɪ/ (**preys, preying, preyed**) 1 N-UNCOUNT A creature's **prey** are the creatures that it hunts and eats in order to live. 2 V-I A creature that **preys on** other creatures lives by catching and eating them. ❑ *Mountain bears prey on sheep.* 3 N-UNCOUNT If someone or something is **prey to** something bad, they have a tendency to let themselves be affected by it. ❑ *He was prey to depression.* 4 PHRASE To **fall prey to** something bad means to be affected by it. ❑ *The children are falling prey to disease.*
→ see **shark**

price /praɪs/ (**prices, pricing, priced**) 1 N-VAR The **price** of something is the amount of money that you must pay to buy it. ❑ *House prices have risen in this area.* ❑ *Mobile phones have come down in price recently.*

Usage

The **price** of goods is the amount of money that the seller is asking people to pay in order to buy them. ❑ *The price marked on the box was five pounds.* When you are referring to services, or to things that you pay to use, you usually talk about a **charge** or a **fee**, rather than a **price**. ❑ *There is a 50p charge for postal bookings.* ❑ *...£400 in unpaid parking fees.* The **cost** of something is the amount of money that you actually pay, or would pay, for it. ❑ *The total cost of decorating the room came to £800.* The **cost** of goods is usually the same as their **price**.

2 V-T If something **is priced at** a particular amount, the price is set at that amount. ❑ *The book is priced at £8.99.* ● **pricing** N-UNCOUNT ❑ *Pricing is very important. If you get it wrong, you end up with no profit.* 3 N-SING The **price** that you pay **for** something is an unpleasant thing you have to do in order to get it. ❑ *He made a mistake and has paid a very high price for it.* 4 PHRASE If you want something **at any price**, you are determined to get it, even if unpleasant things happen as a result.

priceless /ˈpraɪsləs/ 1 ADJ Something that is **priceless** is worth a very large amount of money. ❑ *...his priceless collection of Chinese art.* 2 ADJ If you say that something is **priceless**, you mean that it is extremely useful. ❑ *The website provides priceless information.*

pricey /ˈpraɪsi/ (**pricier, priciest**) ADJ If something is **pricey**, it is expensive. [INFORMAL]

prick /prɪk/ (**pricks, pricking, pricked**) 1 V-T If you **prick** something, you make small holes in it with a sharp object such as a pin. ❑ *Prick the potatoes and rub them with salt.* 2 V-T & N-COUNT If something sharp **pricks** you, or if you feel a **prick**, something sticks into you and causes you pain. ❑ *She pricked her finger with the needle.* ❑ *She felt a prick on her neck.*

prickly /ˈprɪkəli/ (**pricklier, prickliest**) 1 ADJ Something that is **prickly** feels rough and uncomfortable, as if it has a lot of sharp points. 2 ADJ Someone who is **prickly** loses their temper or gets upset very easily. ❑ *You know how prickly she is.*

pride /praɪd/ (**prides, priding, prided**) 1 N-UNCOUNT **Pride** is a feeling of satisfaction which you have because you or people close to you have done something good or possess something good. ❑ *He felt a sense of pride after he had finished the job.* ❑ *Take pride in your work.* 2 V-T If you **pride yourself on** a quality or skill that you have, you are very proud of it. ❑ *He prides himself on his honesty.* 3 N-UNCOUNT **Pride** is also a sense of dignity and self-respect. ❑ *His pride stops him from asking other people for help.* 4 N-UNCOUNT Someone's **pride** is the feeling that they have that they are better or more important than other people; used showing disapproval. ❑ *His pride was his downfall.* 5 PHRASE Someone or something that is **your pride and joy** is very important to you and makes you feel very happy. ❑ *The car is his pride and joy.* 6 PHRASE If something takes **pride of place**, it is treated as the most important thing in a group of things.

priest /priːst/ (**priests**) 1 N-COUNT A **priest** is a member of the Christian clergy in the Catholic, Anglican, or Orthodox church. 2 N-COUNT In many non-Christian religions a **priest** is a man who has particular duties and responsibilities in a place where people worship.

priestess /ˈpriːstes/ (**priestesses**) N-COUNT A **priestess** is a woman in a non-Christian religion who has particular duties and responsibilities in a place where people worship.

priesthood /ˈpriːsthʊd/ 1 N-UNCOUNT **Priesthood** is the position of being a priest or the period of time during which someone is a priest. ❑ *At the beginning of his priesthood, he was a priest in Wales.* 2 N-SING **The priesthood** consists of all the members of the Christian clergy.

prim /prɪm/ (**primmer, primmest**) ADJ If you describe someone as **prim**, you mean that they behave too correctly and are too easily shocked by anything rude or improper. • **primly** ADV ❑ *The girls were seated primly, with their backs straight and feet together.*

primal /'praɪməl/ ADJ **Primal** is used to describe something that relates to the origins of things or that is very basic. [FORMAL] ❑ *Jealousy is a primal emotion.*

primarily /'praɪmərɪli, AM praɪ'meərɪli/ ADV You use **primarily** to say what is mainly true in a particular situation. ❑ *The body is made up primarily of bone and muscle.*

Word Link *prim ≈ first : primary, primate, prime*

primary /'praɪməri, AM -meri/ **1** ADJ BEFORE N You use **primary** to describe something that is extremely important or most important for someone or something. [FORMAL] ❑ *The primary source of water in the region is the river.* **2** ADJ BEFORE N In Britain, **primary** education is given to pupils between the ages of 5 and 11. The American equivalent is **elementary** education.
→ see **colour**

primate /'praɪmət/ (**primates**) N-COUNT A **primate** is a member of the group of mammals which includes humans, monkeys, and apes.
→ see Word Web: **primate**

prime /praɪm/ (**primes, priming, primed**) **1** ADJ BEFORE N You use **prime** to describe something that is most important in a situation. ❑ *The police see him as the prime suspect.* ❑ *The movie industry's prime audience lies in the 17 to 24 age group.* **2** ADJ BEFORE N You use **prime** to describe something that is of the best possible quality. ❑ *He keeps his car in prime condition.* **3** ADJ BEFORE N A **prime** example of something is a very typical example of it. ❑ *Jodie Foster is seen as the prime example of the child actor who became a respected adult star.* **4** N-SING **Your prime** is the stage in your life when you are most active or most successful. ❑ *She was in her intellectual prime.* **5** V-T If you **prime** someone **to** do something, you prepare them to do it, for example by giving them information about it beforehand. ❑ *Claire wished she'd primed Sarah before the meeting.*

Prime Minister (**Prime Ministers**) N-COUNT The leader of the government in some countries is called the **Prime Minister**.

primitive /'prɪmɪtɪv/ **1** ADJ **Primitive** means belonging to a society in which people live in a very simple way, usually without industries or a writing system. ❑ *...primitive tribes.* **2** ADJ **Primitive** means belonging to a very early period in the development of an animal or plant. ❑ *It is a primitive instinct to run away from danger.* **3** ADJ If you describe something as **primitive**, you mean that it is very simple in style or very old-fashioned. ❑ *This is rather primitive technology.*

primrose /'prɪmrəʊz/ (**primroses**) N-COUNT A **primrose** is a wild plant with pale yellow flowers.

prince /prɪns/ (**princes**) N-COUNT & N-TITLE A **prince** is a male member of a royal family, especially the son of a king or queen.

princess /ˌprɪn'ses, AM -'səs/ (**princesses**) N-COUNT & N-TITLE A **princess** is a female member of a royal family, especially the daughter of a king or queen or the wife of a prince.

Word Link *prin ≈ first, beginning : principal, principally, principle*

principal /'prɪnsɪpəl/ (**principals**) **1** ADJ BEFORE N **Principal** means first in order of importance. ❑ *Salt is the principal source of sodium in our diets.* **2** N-COUNT The **principal** of a school or college is the person in charge of it.

principally /'prɪnsɪpəli/ ADV **Principally** means more than anything else. ❑ *The advertising campaign is principally aimed at women.*

principle /'prɪnsɪpəl/ (**principles**) **1** N-VAR A **principle** is a belief that you have about the way you should behave. ❑ *...moral principles.* ❑ *...a man of principle.* **2** N-COUNT The **principles** of a particular theory or philosophy are its basic rules or laws. ❑ *...the principles of Buddhism.* **3** PHRASE If you refuse to do something **on principle**, you refuse to do it because of your beliefs. ❑ *He would vote against it on principle.* **4** PHRASE If you agree with something **in principle**, you agree in general terms to the idea of it, although you do not know the details or know if it will be possible. ❑ *I agree with it in principle but I don't think it will happen in practice.*

principled /'prɪnsɪpəld/ ADJ If you describe someone as **principled**, you approve of them because they have strong moral principles.

print /prɪnt/ (**prints, printing, printed**) **1** V-T If someone **prints** a book, newspaper, or leaflet, they produce it in large quantities by a mechanical process. • **printing** N-UNCOUNT ❑ *...a printing and publishing company.* **2** V-T If a newspaper or magazine **prints** a piece of writing, it includes it or publishes it. **3** V-T If numbers or letters **are printed** on an object, they appear on it. ❑ *The company prints its address and phone number on its products.* **4** V-T If a text or a picture **is printed**, a copy of it is produced by means of a computer printer or some other type of equipment. ❑ *This book was printed in Germany.* **5** V-T If you **print**, you write in letters that are not joined together. **6** N-UNCOUNT **Print** is used to refer to letters and numbers as they appear on the pages of a printed document. ❑ *...columns of tiny print.* **7** PHRASE If you or your words appear **in print**, or get **into print**, what you say or write is published in a book or newspaper. **8** PHRASE If a book is **in print**, it is available from a publisher. If it is **out of print**, it is no longer available.
→ see Word Web: **printing**
→ see **photography**

▶ **print out** **1** PHR-VERB If you **print out** a document or some information, you produce a copy of it on paper using a computer. You can also say that a computer **prints** something **out**. ❑ *I shall print it out and put it in the post.* **2** → see also **printout**

printer /'prɪntə/ (**printers**) **1** N-COUNT A **printer** is a machine that can be connected to a computer in order to make copies on paper of information held by the computer. [COMPUTING] **2** N-COUNT A **printer** is a person or firm whose job is printing books, leaflets, or similar material.
→ see **computer, office, printing**

printout also **print-out** /'prɪntaʊt/ (**printouts**) N-VAR A **printout** is a piece of paper on which information from a computer has been printed.

P

Word Web printing

Before **printing** was invented scribes wrote **documents** by hand. The first **printers** were the Chinese. They used pieces of wood with rows of **characters** carved into them. Later, they started using **movable type** made of baked clay. They created full **pages** by lining up rows of type. A German named Gutenberg made the first metal type. He also invented the **printing press**. The idea came from the wine press, which was hundreds of years old. In the 1500s, printed advertisements were handbills. The earliest newspapers were **published** in the 1600s.

[COMPUTING] ❑ *...a computer printout of various financial projections.*

prior /praɪə/ **1** ADJ BEFORE N You use **prior** to indicate that something has already happened, or must happen, before another event takes place. [FORMAL] ❑ *The course requires prior knowledge of German.* **2** PREP If something happens **prior to** a particular time or event, it happens before it. [FORMAL] ❑ *A man was seen hanging around the area prior to the murder.*

priority /praɪˈɒrɪti, AM -ˈɔːr-/ (**priorities**) **1** N-COUNT If something is a **priority**, it is the most important thing you have to achieve or deal with before everything else. ❑ *Quality is our number one priority.* ❑ *Their first priority is to stop the violence.* **2** PHRASE If you **give priority to** something or someone, you treat them as more important than anything or anyone else. ❑ *The school gives priority to maths teaching.* **3** PHRASE If something **takes priority over** other things or **has priority over** them, it is regarded as being more important than them and is dealt with first. ❑ *Academic work takes priority over socializing for most students.*

priory /ˈpraɪəri/ (**priories**) N-COUNT A **priory** is a place where a small number of monks live and work together.

P

prise /praɪz/ (**prises, prising, prised**) **1** V-T If you **prise** something open, or if you **prise** it away from a surface, you force it to open or force it to come away from the surface. ❑ *She prised open the window.* ❑ *We managed to prise the lid off the jar.* **2** V-T If you **prise** information **out of** someone, you persuade them to tell you although they may not want to.

prison /ˈprɪzən/ (**prisons**) N-VAR A **prison** is a building where criminals are kept.

Word Partnership Use *prison* with:

N. **life in** prison, prison **officials**, prison **population**, prison **reform**, prison **sentence**, prison **time**

V. **die in** prison, **escape from** prison, **face** prison, **go to** prison, **release** *someone* **from** prison, **send** *someone* **to** prison, **serve/spend time in** prison

prisoner /ˈprɪzənə/ (**prisoners**) **1** N-COUNT A **prisoner** is a person who is kept in a prison as a punishment or because they have been captured by an enemy. **2** PHRASE If someone **is taken prisoner**, they are captured. If someone **is held prisoner**, they are guarded so that they cannot escape. → see **war**

pristine /ˈprɪstiːn/ ADJ **Pristine** things are extremely clean or new. ❑ *The house is in pristine condition.*

privacy /ˈprɪvəsi, AM ˈpraɪ-/ N-UNCOUNT **Privacy** is the fact of being alone so that you can do things without being seen or disturbed. ❑ *You can do these exercises in the privacy of your own home.* ❑ *I enjoy my privacy.*

private /ˈpraɪvɪt/ (**privates**) **1** ADJ **Private** industries and services are owned and controlled by an individual person or group, rather than by the state. ❑ *...private education.* ● **privately** ADV ❑ *...privately owned businesses.* **2** ADJ If something is **private**, it is for the use of one person or group, rather than for the general public. ❑ *His father has a private plane.* ❑ *...a private golf club.* **3** ADJ **Private** activities involve only a small number of people, and very little information about them is given to other people. ● **privately** ADV ❑ *I have not talked to William privately for weeks.* **4** PHRASE If you do something **in private**, you do it without other people being present, often because it is something that you want to keep secret. **5** ADJ Your **private life** is that part of your life that is concerned with your personal relationships and activities, rather than with your work or business. **6** ADJ Your **private** thoughts or feelings are ones that you do not talk about to other people. ❑ *People were left to their private sorrow.* ● **privately** ADV ❑ *Privately, he is very disappointed.* **7** ADJ If you describe a place as **private**, you mean that it is a quiet place and you can be alone there without being disturbed. ❑ *Can we go somewhere private to discuss this?* **8** N-COUNT & N-TITLE A **private** is a soldier of the lowest rank.

ˌprivate ˈschool (**private schools**) N-COUNT A **private school** is a school which is not supported financially by the government and which parents have to pay for their children to go to.

privatize [BRIT also **privatise**] /ˈpraɪvətaɪz/ (**privatizes, privatizing, privatized**) V-T If an organization that is owned by the state **is privatized**, the government sells it to one or more private companies. ● **privatization** (**privatizations**) N-VAR ❑ *...the privatisation of the rail industry.*

privilege /ˈprɪvɪlɪdʒ/ (**privileges**) **1** N-COUNT A **privilege** is a special right or advantage that only one person or group has. ❑ *...special privileges for government officials.* **2** N-UNCOUNT **Privilege** is the power and advantages that belong to a small group of people, usually because of their wealth or their high social class. ❑ *...a life of privilege.*

Word Partnership	Use *privilege* with:
ADJ.	**executive** privilege, **special** privilege 1
N.	**power and** privilege 2

privileged /ˈprɪvɪlɪdʒd/ ADJ Someone who is **privileged** has an advantage or opportunity that most other people do not have, often because of their wealth or high social class. ❑ *...a very wealthy, privileged elite.*

prize /praɪz/ (**prizes, prizing, prized**) 1 N-COUNT A **prize** is something valuable, such as money or a trophy, that is given to the winner of a game or competition. ❑ *He won first prize.* ❑ *The winner won £300 in prize money.* 2 ADJ BEFORE N You use **prize** to describe things that are of such good quality that they win prizes or deserve to win prizes. ❑ *...a prize bull.* 3 V-T Something that **is prized** is wanted and admired because it is considered to be very valuable or very good quality. ❑ *Model boats are prized by collectors.*

Word Partnership	Use *prize* with:
ORD.	**first** prize 1
ADJ.	**grand** prize, **top** prize 1
V.	**award a** prize, **claim a** prize, **receive a** prize, **share a** prize, **win a** prize 1

pro /prəʊ/ (**pros**) 1 N-COUNT A **pro** is a professional, especially a professional sportsman or sportswoman. 2 PHRASE The **pros and cons** of something are its advantages and disadvantages.

Word Link	*prob ≈ testing : probability, probation, probe*

probability /ˌprɒbəˈbɪlɪti/ (**probabilities**) 1 N-VAR The **probability of** something happening is how likely it is to happen, sometimes expressed as a fraction or a percentage. ❑ *The victim's probability of dying was 80%.* 2 N-VAR You say that there is a **probability** that something will happen when it is likely to happen. ❑ *The probability is that he will return to Britain.* 3 PHRASE You use **in all probability** when you are confident that something is true or correct, or is likely to happen. ❑ *In all probability, we shall never know the truth.*

probable /ˈprɒbəbəl/ ADJ Something that is **probable** is likely to be true or likely to happen. ❑ *It is probable that the volcano will erupt again.*

probably /ˈprɒbəbli/ ADV If you say that something is **probably** true, you think that it is likely to be true, although you are not sure. ❑ *You probably won't understand this word.* ❑ *Van Gogh is probably the best-known painter in the world.*

probation /prəˈbeɪʃən, AM ˈprəʊ-/ N-UNCOUNT **Probation** is a period of time during which a person who has committed a crime is supervised to ensure that they do not break the law again, rather than being put in prison. ❑ *The woman was put on probation for two years.*

proˈbation officer (**probation officers**) N-COUNT A **probation officer** is a person whose job is to supervise and help people who have been put on probation.

probe /prəʊb/ (**probes, probing, probed**) 1 V-I & N-COUNT If you **probe into** something, you ask questions or make enquiries in order to discover facts about it. This questioning or enquiring is called a **probe.** ❑ *The police probed into his background and became suspicious.* ❑ *...a new probe into a shooting in Queensland.* 2 V-T/V-I If you **probe** or **probe** a place, you search it in order to find someone or something that you looking for. ❑ *For centuries scientists have probed the mysteries of the human mind.* ❑ *I probed around in the bushes.*

problem /ˈprɒbləm/ (**problems**) 1 N-COUNT A **problem** is an unsatisfactory situation that causes difficulties for people. ❑ *He left home at the age of 16 because of family problems.* 2 N-COUNT A **problem** is a puzzle that requires logical thought or mathematics to solve it.
→ see **fraction**

Thesaurus	*problem* Also look up:
N.	complication, difficulty, hitch 1 puzzle, question, riddle 2

problematic /ˌprɒbləˈmætɪk/ ADJ Something that is **problematic** involves problems and difficulties. ❑ *Some places are problematic for women travelling alone.*

procedural /prəˈsiːdʒərəl/ ADJ **Procedural** means involving a formal procedure. [FORMAL] ❑ *The discussions will focus on procedural issues.*

procedure /prəˈsiːdʒə/ (**procedures**) N-VAR A **procedure** is a way of doing something, especially the usual or correct way. ❑ *The procedure is long and complicated.* ❑ *...safety procedures.*

Word Partnership	Use *procedure* with:
ADJ.	**simple** procedure, **standard (operating)** procedure, **surgical** procedure
V.	**follow a** procedure, **perform a** procedure, **use a** procedure

Word Link	*pro ≈ in front, before : proceed, produce, prologue*

proceed (**proceeds, proceeding, proceeded**) 1 V-T /prəˈsiːd/ If you **proceed to** do something, you do it after doing something else. ❑ *He then proceeded to tell us everything.* 2 V-I To **proceed** means to continue as planned. [FORMAL] ❑ *I believe this is the sensible way to proceed.* 3 V-I If you **proceed** in a particular direction, you go in that direction. [FORMAL] ❑ *He proceeded down the street.* 4 N-PLURAL /ˈprəʊsiːdz/ The **proceeds** of an event or activity are the money that has been obtained from it. ❑ *The proceeds from the concert will go to charity.*

proceedings /prəˈsiːdɪŋz/ 1 N-PLURAL Legal **proceedings** are legal action taken against someone. [FORMAL] ❑ *The man faces criminal proceedings for stealing her car.* 2 N-PLURAL You can refer to an organized series of events that happen in a place as **the proceedings.** [FORMAL] ❑ *The proceedings began at 8 o'clock.*

process /ˈprəʊses, AM ˈprɑːses/ (**processes, processing, processed**) 1 N-COUNT A **process** is a series of actions or events which have a particular result. ❑ *...the 12-week training process.* ❑ *Too much sun can speed up the ageing process.* 2 V-T When raw materials or foods **are processed**, they are treated by a chemical or industrial process before they are used or sold. ❑ *...diets high in processed*

P

foods. • **processing** N-UNCOUNT ❑ *...a nuclear fuel processing plant.* **3** V-T When a person or computer **processes** information, they deal with the information by putting it through a system or into a computer. • **processing** N-UNCOUNT ❑ *...data processing.* **4** → see also **word processing** **5** PHRASE If you **are in the process of** doing something, you have started to do it and are still doing it. **6** PHRASE If you are doing something and you do something else **in the process**, you do the second thing as a result of doing the first thing. ❑ *Frodo is determined to complete the task even if he is killed in the process.*

procession /prəˈseʃən/ (**processions**) N-COUNT A **procession** is a group of people who are walking, riding, or driving in a line as part of a public event. ❑ *...religious processions.*

processor /ˈprəʊsesə, AM ˈprɑːs-/ (**processors**) N-COUNT A **processor** is the part of a computer that interprets commands and performs the processes the user has asked the computer to do. [COMPUTING]

proclaim /prəʊˈkleɪm/ (**proclaims, proclaiming, proclaimed**) V-T If people **proclaim** something, they formally announce it or make it known. ❑ *He proclaimed himself President in 1983 and was formally elected in 1986.*

Word Link	*claim, clam ≈ shouting : acclaim, exclaim, proclamation*

proclamation /ˌprɒkləˈmeɪʃən/ (**proclamations**) N-COUNT A **proclamation** is a public announcement about something important.

procure /prəˈkjʊə/ (**procures, procuring, procured**) V-T If you **procure** something, especially something that is difficult to get, you obtain it. [FORMAL] ❑ *It was very difficult to procure food.* • **procurement** N-UNCOUNT ❑ *...procurement of milk.*

P

prod /prɒd/ (**prods, prodding, prodded**) **1** V-T & N-COUNT If you **prod** someone or something, or if you **give** them a **prod**, you give them a quick push with your finger or with a pointed object. ❑ *I prodded her shoulder gently.* **2** V-T If you **prod** someone **into** doing something, you remind them or persuade them to do it. ❑ *You need to talk to someone who will prod you to think deeper about your problems.* • **prodding** N-UNCOUNT ❑ *After some prodding, Maureen, reluctantly, sang for me.*

prodigious /prəˈdɪdʒəs/ ADJ Something that is **prodigious** is very large or impressive. [LITERARY] ❑ *...prodigious amounts of work.* • **prodigiously** ADV ❑ *She ate prodigiously.*

prodigy /ˈprɒdɪdʒi/ (**prodigies**) N-COUNT A **prodigy** is someone who has a great natural talent for something which shows itself at an early age.

Word Link	*pro ≈ in front, before : proceed, produce, prologue*

produce (**produces, producing, produced**) **1** V-T /prəˈdjuːs, AM -ˈduːs/ To **produce** something means to cause it to happen. ❑ *These drugs are known to produce side-effects.* **2** V-T If you **produce** something, you make or create it. ❑ *We produce quality furniture.* • **producer** (**producers**) N-COUNT ❑ *...the world's biggest producer of metals.* **3** V-T If you **produce** evidence or an argument, you show it or explain it to people. ❑ *He produced evidence to support his theory.* **4** V-T If you **produce** an object from somewhere, you show it or bring it out so that it can be seen. ❑ *When you hire a car you must produce a passport.* **5** V-T If someone **produces** a play, film, programme, or record, they organize it and decide how it should be made. • **producer** N-COUNT ❑ *...a film producer.* **6** N-UNCOUNT /ˈprɒdjuːs, AM -duːs/ **Produce** is food such as fruit and vegetables that are grown in large quantities to be sold.
→ see **theatre**

product /ˈprɒdʌkt/ (**products**) **1** N-COUNT A **product** is something that is produced and sold in large quantities. **2** N-COUNT If you say that someone or something is a **product of** a particular situation or process, you mean that the situation or process made that person or thing what they are. ❑ *The book is the product of many years of study.*
→ see **industry**

production /prəˈdʌkʃən/ (**productions**) **1** N-UNCOUNT **Production** is the process of manufacturing or growing something in large quantities, or the amount of goods manufactured or grown. ❑ *This model of car won't go into production before 2005.* ❑ *We need to increase production.* **2** N-UNCOUNT The **production of** something is its creation as the result of a natural process. ❑ *The drug helps the production of blood cells.* **3** N-UNCOUNT **Production** is the process of organizing and preparing a play, film, programme, or record. **4** N-COUNT A **production** is a play, opera, or other show that is performed in a theatre. ❑ *...a recent production of Hamlet.*
→ see **theatre**

proˈduction line (**production lines**) N-COUNT A **production line** is an arrangement of machines in a factory where the products pass from one machine to another until they are finished.

productive /prəˈdʌktɪv/ **1** ADJ Something or someone that is **productive** is very efficient at producing something. ❑ *Good training helps workers to become more productive.* **2** ADJ If you say that a relationship is **productive**, you mean that good or useful things happen as a result of it. ❑ *Our discussions were highly productive.*

productivity /ˌprɒdʊkˈtɪvɪti/ N-UNCOUNT **Productivity** is the rate at which goods are produced. ❑ *Productivity continues to grow.*

Prof /prɒf/ N-TITLE **Prof.** is a written abbreviation for **professor**. ❑ *...Prof. Richard Joyner.*

profess /prəˈfes/ (**professes, professing, professed**) **1** V-T If you **profess to** do or have something, you claim that you do it or have it, often when you do not. [FORMAL] ❑ *She professed to hate her name.* **2** V-T If you **profess** a feeling, opinion, or belief, you express it. [FORMAL] ❑ *He professed to be happy.* ❑ *He professed himself 'thrilled' at the results.*

profession /prəˈfeʃən/ (**professions**) **1** N-COUNT A **profession** is a type of job that requires advanced education or training. **2** N-COUNT You use **profession** to refer to all the people who have the same profession. ❑ *...the medical profession.*

professional /prəˈfeʃənəl/ (**professionals**) **1** ADJ BEFORE N **Professional** means relating to a person's work, especially work that requires special training. ❑ *His professional career started* at Liverpool University. ● **professionally** ADV ❑ *...a professionally-qualified architect.* **2** N-COUNT & ADJ BEFORE N A **professional**, or a **professional** person, has a job that requires advanced education or training. ❑ *My father wanted me to become a professional.* **3** ADJ BEFORE N & N-COUNT You use **professional** to describe people who do a particular thing to earn money rather than as a hobby. You call these people **professionals**. ❑ *...a professional footballer.* ❑ *He has been a professional since March 1985.* ● **professionally** ADV ❑ *By the age of 16 he was playing the drums professionally.* **4** ADJ If you say that something that someone does or produces is **professional**, you approve of it because you think it shows skill and high standards. ❑ *He worked hard and did everything in a professional manner.* ● **professionalism** N-UNCOUNT ❑ *The company is proud of its professionalism.* ● **professionally** ADV ❑ *I believe that I acted professionally and responsibly.*

professor /prəˈfesə/ (**professors**) **1** N-COUNT & N-TITLE A **professor** in a British university is the most senior teacher in a department. ❑ *In 1979, only 2% of British professors were female.* **2** N-COUNT & N-TITLE A **professor** in an American or Canadian university or college is a teacher there.
→ see **graduation**

proffer /ˈprɒfə/ (**proffers, proffering, proffered**) V-T If you **proffer** something to someone, you offer it to them. [FORMAL] ❑ *The army has not yet proffered an explanation.*

proficient /prəˈfɪʃənt/ ADJ If you are **proficient in** something, you can do it well. ❑ *They are both proficient in Polish.* ● **proficiency** N-UNCOUNT ❑ *...basic proficiency in English.*

profile

profile /ˈprəʊfaɪl/ (**profiles**) **1** N-COUNT Your **profile** is the outline of your face seen from the side. **2** PHRASE If someone has a **high profile**, people notice them and what they do. **3** PHRASE If you **keep a low profile**, you avoid doing things that will make people notice you.

profit /ˈprɒfɪt/ (**profits, profiting, profited**) **1** N-VAR A **profit** is an amount of money that you gain when you are paid more for something than it cost you. ❑ *The bank made profits of £3.5 million.* **2** V-I If you **profit** or **profit from** something, you earn a profit from it or gain some advantage or benefit from it. ❑ *Jennifer knew she would profit from a more relaxed lifestyle.* ❑ *Powerful people often profit at the expense of the poor.*

profitable /ˈprɒfɪtəbəl/ **1** ADJ A **profitable** activity or organization makes a profit. ❑ *...a profitable business.* ● **profitably** ADV ❑ *These French stores are trading profitably.* ● **profitability** N-UNCOUNT ❑ *...a plan to increase profitability.* **2** ADJ Something that is **profitable** results in some benefit for you. ❑ *...a profitable exchange of ideas.* ● **profitably** ADV ❑ *He spent his time profitably.*

profound /prəˈfaʊnd/ **1** ADJ You use **profound** to emphasize that something is very great or intense. ❑ *These changes had a profound effect.* ● **profoundly** ADV ❑ *This event profoundly affected my life.* **2** ADJ A **profound** idea or work shows great intellectual depth and understanding. ❑ *...profound concepts like the origins of the Universe.*

profuse /prəˈfjuːs/ ADJ **Profuse** means doing something or happening a lot. ❑ *They offered their profuse apologies.* ● **profusely** ADV ❑ *He was bleeding profusely.*

profusion /prəˈfjuːʒən/ N-SING & N-UNCOUNT If there is a **profusion of** something or if it occurs **in profusion**, there is a very large quantity or variety of it. [FORMAL] ❑ *Wild flowers grew there in profusion.*

prognosis /prɒgˈnəʊsɪs/ (**prognoses** /prɒgˈnəʊsiːz/) N-COUNT A **prognosis** is an estimate about the future of someone or something. [FORMAL] ❑ *Heart failure has a poor prognosis: nearly 40 per cent of people with the condition die within a year.*

Word Link	*gram ≈ writing : diagram, program, telegram*

program /ˈprəʊgræm/ (**programs, programming, programmed**) V-T & N-COUNT When you **program** a computer, you give it a set of instructions called a **program**, to make it able to perform a particular task. [COMPUTING] ● **programming** N-UNCOUNT ❑ *...programming skills.* ● **programmer** (**programmers**) N-COUNT ❑ *...a computer programmer.*
→ see **radio**

Word Partnership	Use *program* with:
N.	**computer** program, **software** program
V.	**create a** program, **expand a** program, **implement a** program, **launch a** program, **run a** program program **a computer**

programme [AM **program**] /ˈprəʊgræm/ (**programmes, programming, programmed**) **1** N-COUNT A **programme** of actions or events is a series of actions or events that are planned to be done. ❑ *...a full programme of family activities.* **2** N-COUNT A television or radio **programme** is something that is broadcast on television or radio. ❑ *...local news programmes.* **3** N-COUNT A theatre or concert **programme** is a booklet giving information about the play or concert. **4** V-T When you **programme** a machine or system, you set its controls so that it will work in a particular way. ❑ *A computer is only as clever as the person who programmed it.*

progress (**progresses, progressing, progressed**) **1** N-UNCOUNT /ˈprəʊgres, AM ˈprɑː-/ **Progress** is the process of gradually improving or getting nearer to achieving or completing something. ❑ *There are signs of progress in Tom's reading.* **2** N-SING **The progress of** a situation or action is the way in which it develops. ❑ *He did not comment on the progress of his work.* **3** PHRASE If something is **in progress**, it has started and is still continuing. **4** V-I /prəˈgres/ To **progress** means to improve or to become more advanced or higher in rank. ❑ *He has definitely progressed as a cricketer.* **5** V-I If events **progress**, they continue to happen gradually over a period of time. ❑ *The players improved as the tournament progressed.*

progression /prəˈgreʃən/ (**progressions**) N-COUNT A **progression** is a gradual development from one state to another. ❑ *There are three stages in* *the progression of the disease.*

progressive /prəˈgresɪv/ (**progressives**) **1** ADJ & N-COUNT Someone who is **progressive** has modern ideas about how things should be done, rather than traditional ones. You can call someone like this a **progressive**. ❑ *It is the country's most progressive theatre company.* ❑ *The Republicans were split between progressives and conservatives.* **2** ADJ A **progressive** change happens gradually over a period of time. ❑ *...progressive loss of memory.* • **progressively** ADV ❑ *Her cold became progressively worse.*

prohibit /prəˈhɪbɪt, AM prəʊ-/ (**prohibits, prohibiting, prohibited**) V-T If someone **prohibits** something, they forbid it or make it illegal. [FORMAL] ❑ *The laws prohibit foreign journalists from working in Zimbabwe.* • **prohibition** N-UNCOUNT ❑ *...the prohibition of advertising.*

prohibitive /prəˈhɪbɪtɪv, AM prəʊ-/ ADJ If something's cost is **prohibitive**, it is so high that many people cannot afford it. ❑ *...the prohibitive cost of childcare.* • **prohibitively** ADV ❑ *Meat was prohibitively expensive.*

project (**projects, projecting, projected**) **1** N-COUNT /ˈprɒdʒekt/ A **project** is a carefully planned task that requires a lot of time and effort. ❑ *...local development projects such as hospitals and schools.* **2** N-COUNT A **project** is a detailed study of a subject by a pupil or student. **3** V-T /prəˈdʒekt/ If something **is projected**, it is planned or expected. ❑ *Profits are projected at 84 million pounds.* **4** V-T If you **project** a film or picture onto a screen or wall, you make it appear there. ❑ *The pictures were projected onto a huge back wall.* **5** V-T If you **project** a particular feeling or quality, you show it in your behaviour. If you **project** someone or something in a particular way, you try to make people see them in that way. ❑ *He wasn't able to project himself as a strong leader.* ❑ *Many people project her as an intellectual.* **6** V-I If something **projects**, it sticks out beyond a surface or edge. [FORMAL] ❑ *Large rocks projected above the water.*

P

Word Partnership Use *project* with:

V.	**approve a** project, **launch a** project **1** **complete a** project, **start a** project **1** **2**
N.	**construction** project, **development** project, project **director/manager** **1** **research** project, **writing** project **1** **2** **science** project **1** **2**
ADJ.	**involved in a** project, **latest** project, **new** project, **special** project **1** **2**

projection /prəˈdʒekʃən/ (**projections**) **1** N-COUNT A **projection** is an estimate of a future amount. ❑ *...sales projections.* **2** N-UNCOUNT The **projection** of a film or picture is the act of projecting it onto a screen or wall. ❑ *...the most up-to-date projection facilities in the world.*

projector /prəˈdʒektə/ (**projectors**) N-COUNT A **projector** is a machine that projects films or slides onto a screen or wall.

proliferate /prəˈlɪfəreɪt/ (**proliferates, proliferating, proliferated**) V-I If things **proliferate**, they increase in number very quickly. [FORMAL] ❑ *Errors began to proliferate.* • **proliferation** N-UNCOUNT ❑ *...the proliferation of TV channels.*

prolific /prəˈlɪfɪk/ ADJ A **prolific** writer, artist, or composer produces a large number of works.

Word Link ***pro** ≈ in front, before : **pro**ceed, **pro**duce, **pro**logue*

prologue /ˈprəʊlɒg, AM -lɔːg/ (**prologues**) N-COUNT A **prologue** is a speech or section of text that introduces a play or book.

prolong /prəˈlɒŋ, AM -lɔːŋ/ (**prolongs, prolonging, prolonged**) V-T To **prolong** something means to make it last longer. ❑ *The war prolonged his stay in the city.*

prolonged /prəˈlɒŋd, AM -lɔːŋd/ ADJ A **prolonged** event or situation continues for a long time. ❑ *...a prolonged period of peace.*

prominent /ˈprɒmɪnənt/ **1** ADJ Someone or something that is **prominent** is well-known and important or respected. ❑ *...a prominent London lawyer.* ❑ *...Romania's most prominent independent newspaper.* • **prominence** N-UNCOUNT ❑ *Crime prevention must be given more prominence.* **2** ADJ Something that is **prominent** is very noticeable. ❑ *...his prominent nose.* • **prominently** ADV ❑ *The music of The Beatles figured prominently in the concert.*

promiscuous /prəˈmɪskjʊəs/ ADJ Someone who is **promiscuous** has sex with many different people; used showing disapproval. • **promiscuity** /ˌprɒmɪˈskjuːɪti/ N-UNCOUNT ❑ *...the promiscuity of the 1960s.*

promise /ˈprɒmɪs/ (**promises, promising, promised**) **1** V-T & N-COUNT If you **promise** that you will do something, or if you make a **promise** that you will do it, you say that you will definitely do it. ❑ *He promised to wait.* ❑ *Promise me you will not waste your time.* **2** V-T & N-COUNT If you **promise** someone something, or if you make them a **promise** about it, you tell them that you will definitely give it to them or make sure that they have it. ❑ *We promise you an exciting trip.* **3** V-T If a situation or event **promises to** have a particular quality, it shows signs that it will have that quality. ❑ *Next year promises to be difficult for many businesses.* **4** N-UNCOUNT If someone or something shows **promise**, they seem likely to be very good or successful.

Word Partnership Use *promise* with:

N.	**campaign** promise **1** **2**
V.	**break a** promise, **deliver on a** promise, **keep a** promise, **make a** promise **1** **2** **hold** promise, **show** promise **4**
ADJ.	**broken** promise, **empty** promise, **false** promise **1** **2** **enormous** promise, **great** promise, **real** promise **4**

promising /ˈprɒmɪsɪŋ/ ADJ Someone or something that is **promising** seems likely to be very good or successful. ❑ *He's one of the country's most promising poets.*

Word Link ***mot** ≈ moving : **mot**ion, **mot**ivate, pro**mot**e*

promote /prəˈməʊt/ (**promotes, promoting, promoted**) **1** V-T If people **promote** something, they help to make it happen, increase, or become more popular. ❑ *She came to London to promote her*

latest book. ● **promotion** (**promotions**) N-VAR ❑ *...TV commercials and other promotions.* **2** V-T If someone **is promoted**, they are given a more important job in the organization they work for. ❑ *I was promoted to editor.* ● **promotion** N-VAR ❑ *After six months I was offered promotion to manager.*
→ see **concert**

promoter /prəˈməʊtə/ (**promoters**) **1** N-COUNT A **promoter** is a person who helps organize and finance an event, especially a sports event. **2** N-COUNT The **promoter of** a cause or idea tries to make it become popular. ❑ *...a promoter of African music.*

promotional /prəˈməʊʃənəl/ ADJ **Promotional** material, events, or ideas are designed to advertise a product or service and increase its sales.

prompt /prɒmpt/ (**prompts, prompting, prompted**) **1** V-T If something **prompts** someone **to** do something, it makes them decide to do it. ❑ *The experience prompted him to start his own business.* **2** V-T If you **prompt** someone, you encourage or remind them to do something or to continue doing something. ❑ *'Well, Daniel?' William prompted.* ● **prompting** (**promptings**) N-VAR ❑ *She telephoned the police at my prompting.* **3** ADJ A **prompt** action is done without any delay. ❑ *Prompt action is needed.*

promptly /ˈprɒmptli/ **1** ADV If you do something **promptly**, you do it immediately. ❑ *I set my alarm clock for seven-thirty and promptly fell asleep.* **2** ADV If you do something **promptly at** a particular time, you do it at exactly that time. ❑ *We left the hotel promptly at nine o'clock.*

prone /prəʊn/ ADJ AFTER LINK-V If someone or something is **prone to** something, usually something bad, they have a tendency to be affected by it or to do it. ❑ *Queensland is prone to storms at this time of year.* ● **-prone** ❑ *...a clumsy, accident-prone person.*

pronoun /ˈprəʊnaʊn/ (**pronouns**) N-COUNT A **pronoun** is a word which is used instead of a noun group to refer to someone or something. 'He', 'she', 'them', and 'something' are pronouns.

> **Word Link** — *nounce ≈ reporting : announce, denounce, pronounce*

pronounce /prəˈnaʊns/ (**pronounces, pronouncing, pronounced**) **1** V-T To **pronounce** a word means to say it. ❑ *He pronounced the word 'facts' as if it were 'fax'.* **2** V-T If you **pronounce** something, you state it formally or publicly. [FORMAL] ❑ *The government pronounced its decision.*
→ see **trial**

pronounced /prəˈnaʊnst/ ADJ Something that is **pronounced** is very noticeable. ❑ *He walks with a pronounced limp.*

pronouncement /prəˈnaʊnsmənt/ (**pronouncements**) N-COUNT **Pronouncements** are public or official statements on an important subject.

pronunciation /prəˌnʌnsiˈeɪʃən/ (**pronunciations**) N-VAR The **pronunciation** of words is the way they are pronounced. ❑ *Use a dictionary when you need to check the spelling and pronunciation of a word.*

proof /pruːf/ (**proofs**) N-UNCOUNT **Proof** is a fact or a piece of evidence which shows that something is true or exists. ❑ *This is proof that he is wrong.*

> **Word Partnership** — Use *proof* with:
> ADJ. **convincing** proof, **final** proof, **living** proof, proof **positive**
> V. **have** proof, **need** proof, **offer** proof, **provide** proof, **require** proof, **show** proof

-proof /-pruːf/ (**-proofs, -proofing, -proofed**) **1** **-proof** combines with nouns and verbs to form adjectives which indicate that something cannot be damaged or badly affected by a particular thing or person. ❑ *...a microwave-proof dish.* **2** **-proof** combines with nouns to form verbs which refer to protecting something against being damaged or badly affected by the thing mentioned. ❑ *She spent £900 on sound-proofing the connecting wall to her neighbour's house.*

prop /prɒp/ (**props, propping, propped**) **1** V-T & PHR-VERB If you **prop** an object **on** or **against** something, or if you **prop** it **up**, you support it by putting something underneath it or by resting it against something. ❑ *He propped the books on the desk.* ❑ *Prop up your back against a wall.* **2** N-COUNT A **prop** is a stick or other object used to support something. **3** N-COUNT The **props** in a play or film are the objects and furniture used in it.
→ see **theatre**

▶ **prop up** **1** PHR-VERB To **prop up** something means to support it or help it to survive. ❑ *The Government should not be propping up bad businesses.* **2** → see **prop** (meaning 1)

propaganda /ˌprɒpəˈgændə/ N-UNCOUNT **Propaganda** is information, often inaccurate information, which an organization publishes or broadcasts in order to influence people; used showing disapproval. ❑ *...anti-European propaganda.*

propagate /ˈprɒpəgeɪt/ (**propagates, propagating, propagated**) V-T If people **propagate** an idea or a piece of information, they spread it and try to make people believe it or support it. [FORMAL] ● **propagation** N-UNCOUNT ❑ *...the propagation of Buddhism.*

> **Word Link** — *pel ≈ driving, forcing : compel, expel, propel*

propel /prəˈpel/ (**propels, propelling, propelled**) **1** V-T To **propel** someone or something in a certain direction means to cause them or it to move in that direction. ❑ *Rebecca took Steve's elbow and propelled him towards the door.* **2** V-T If something **propels** you into a particular activity, it causes you to be involved in it. ❑ *It was this event which propelled her into politics.*

propeller /prəˈpelə/ (**propellers**) N-COUNT A **propeller** on a boat or aircraft is a device with blades which is turned by the engine, causing the boat or aircraft to move.

propensity /prəˈpensɪti/ (**propensities**) N-COUNT If someone has a **propensity to** do something or a **propensity for** something, they tend to behave in a particular way. [FORMAL] ❑ *He has a propensity to get very angry when people do not agree with him.*

proper /ˈprɒpə/ **1** ADJ BEFORE N You use **proper** to describe things that you consider to be real or satisfactory. ❑ *I've just started a proper job with security, a pension and good prospects.* ● **properly** ADV

❑ *You're too thin. You're not eating properly.* **2** ADJ BEFORE N The **proper** thing is the one that is correct or most suitable. ❑ *We followed the proper procedures.* **3** ADJ If you say that a way of behaving is **proper**, you mean that it is considered socially acceptable and right. ❑ *...the rules of proper behaviour.* ● **properly** ADV ❑ *He's a spoilt child and it's time he learnt to behave properly.*

ˌproper ˈnoun (**proper nouns**) N-COUNT In grammar, a **proper noun** is a noun which refers to a particular person, place, or institution. Proper nouns begin with a capital letter, for example George Clooney; London; University of Glasgow.

property /ˈprɒpəti/ (**properties**) **1** N-UNCOUNT Someone's **property** consists of all the things that belong to them, or something that belongs to them. [FORMAL] ❑ *...stolen property.* **2** N-COUNT A **property** is a building and the land belonging to it. [FORMAL] **3** N-COUNT The **properties** of a substance or object are the ways in which it behaves in particular conditions. [TECHNICAL] ❑ *...the healing properties of plants.*
→ see **element**

prophecy /ˈprɒfɪsi/ (**prophecies**) N-VAR A **prophecy** is a statement in which someone says they strongly believe that something will happen.

prophesy /ˈprɒfɪsaɪ/ (**prophesies, prophesying, prophesied**) V-T If you **prophesy** something, you say that you strongly believe that it will happen. ❑ *There are so many different factors that it would be stupid to prophesy the future.*

prophet /ˈprɒfɪt/ (**prophets**) N-COUNT A **prophet** is a person believed to be chosen by God to say the things that God wants to tell people.

prophetic /prəˈfetɪk/ ADJ If something was **prophetic**, it described or suggested something that did actually happen later. ❑ *At the time, no one knew that the play was a prophetic vision of everyday life in the twenty-first century.*

P

proponent /prəˈpəʊnənt/ (**proponents**) N-COUNT A **proponent of** a particular idea or course of action actively supports it. [FORMAL] ❑ *Fanny Wright was a well-known proponent of women's rights.*

proportion /prəˈpɔːʃən/ (**proportions**) **1** N-COUNT A **proportion of** an amount or group is a part of it. [FORMAL] ❑ *South Africa will receive the largest proportion of the aid money.* **2** N-COUNT The **proportion of** one kind of person or thing in a group is the number of people or things of that kind compared to the total number in the group. ❑ *The proportion of women who work in law has risen to 39%.* **3** N-PLURAL If you refer to the **proportions** of something, you are referring to its size, usually when this is extremely large. [WRITTEN] ❑ *Plants grow to huge proportions in hot countries.* **4** PHRASE If one thing increases or decreases **in proportion to** another thing, it increases or decreases to the same degree as that thing. ❑ *Its price goes up in proportion to how much people want it.* **5** PHRASE If something is small or large **in proportion to** something else, it is small or large when you compare it with that thing. ❑ *His head was large in proportion to the rest of his body.* **6** PHRASE If you get something **out of proportion**, you think it is more important or worrying than it really is. If you keep something **in proportion**, you have a realistic view of how important it is.

proportional /prəˈpɔːʃənəl/ ADJ If one amount is **proportional to** another, the two amounts increase and decrease at the same rate so there is always the same relationship between them. ❑ *Your weight is proportional to how much you eat.*

proportionate /prəˈpɔːʃənət/ ADJ **Proportionate** means the same as **proportional**. ● **proportionately** ADV ❑ *Proportionately more Americans get married nowadays than before.*

proposal /prəˈpəʊzəl/ (**proposals**) **1** N-COUNT A **proposal** is a suggestion or plan, often a formal or written one. ❑ *...the government's proposal to stop free health care.* **2** N-COUNT A **proposal** is the act of asking someone to marry you.

Word Partnership Use *proposal* with:

ADJ.	**new** proposal, **original** proposal **1**
V.	**adopt a** proposal, **approve a** proposal, **support a** proposal, **vote on a** proposal **1**
	accept a proposal, **make a** proposal, **reject a** proposal **1** **2**
N.	**budget** proposal, **peace** proposal **1**
	marriage proposal **2**

propose /prəˈpəʊz/ (**proposes, proposing, proposed**) **1** V-T If you **propose** a plan or idea, you suggest it. ❑ *They proposed a peace plan.* **2** V-T If you **propose to** do something, you intend to do it. ❑ *We don't know what they propose to do.* **3** V-I If you **propose to** someone, you ask them to marry you.

Word Partnership Use *propose* with:

N.	propose **changes**, propose **legislation**, propose **a plan**, propose **a solution**, propose **a tax**, propose **a theory**, propose **a toast** **1** **2**
	propose **marriage** **3**

proposition /ˌprɒpəˈzɪʃən/ (**propositions**) **1** N-COUNT If you describe something such as a task or an activity as, for example, a difficult **proposition** or an attractive **proposition**, you mean that it is difficult or pleasant to do. ❑ *Making lots of money quickly is an attractive proposition.* **2** N-COUNT A **proposition** is a statement or an idea which people can consider or discuss to decide whether it is true. [FORMAL] **3** N-COUNT A **proposition** is an offer or suggestion. ❑ *He came to see me with a business proposition.*

Word Link *propr ≈ owning : appropriate, proprietary, proprietor*

proprietary /prəˈpraɪətri, AM -teri/ ADJ BEFORE N **Proprietary** substances are ones sold under a trade name. [FORMAL] ❑ *...proprietary technology.*

proprietor /prəˈpraɪətə/ (**proprietors**) N-COUNT The **proprietor** of a hotel, shop, newspaper, or other business is the person who owns it.

prosaic /prəʊˈzeɪɪk/ ADJ Something that is **prosaic** is dull and lacks interest. ❑ *The truth is quite prosaic.*

prose /prəʊz/ N-UNCOUNT **Prose** is ordinary written language, in contrast to poetry. ❑ *He no longer writes poems, only prose.*

prosecute /ˈprɒsɪkjuːt/ (**prosecutes,**

prosecuting, prosecuted) V-T/V-I If the authorities **prosecute**, or **prosecute** someone, they charge them with a crime and put them on trial. ❑ *The police decided not to prosecute.* ● **prosecution** (**prosecutions**) N-VAR ❑ *People will face prosecution if they threaten staff.*

prosecution /ˌprɒsɪˈkjuːʃən/ N-SING The lawyers who try to prove that a person on trial is guilty are called **the prosecution**. ❑ *The prosecution argued that Tully stole the car.*

prosecutor /ˈprɒsɪkjuːtə/ (**prosecutors**) N-COUNT In some countries, a **prosecutor** is a lawyer or official who brings charges against alleged criminals or tries to prove in a trial that they are guilty.

prospect (**prospects, prospecting, prospected**) **1** N-VAR /ˈprɒspekt/ A **prospect** is a possibility or a possible event. ❑ *There is no prospect of these questions being answered.* **2** N-PLURAL Someone's **prospects** are their chances of being successful. ❑ *I worked abroad to improve my career prospects.* **3** V-I /prəˈspekt, AM ˈprɑːspekt/ To **prospect for** a substance such as oil or gold means to look for it in the ground or under the sea. ❑ *He prospected for gold in Rhodesia.*

prospective /prəˈspektɪv, AM prɑː-/ ADJ BEFORE N You use **prospective** to describe a person who wants to be the thing mentioned or is likely to be the thing mentioned. ❑ *...prospective buyers.*

prospectus /prəˈspektəs, AM prɑː-/ (**prospectuses**) N-COUNT A **prospectus** is a document produced by a college, school, or company which gives details about it and the courses it runs.

prosper /ˈprɒspə/ (**prospers, prospering, prospered**) V-I If people or businesses **prosper**, they are financially successful.

Word Link *sper ≈ hope : desperate, exasperate, prosperity*

prosperity /prɒˈsperɪti/ N-UNCOUNT **Prosperity** is a condition in which a person or community is being financially successful. ❑ *...a new era of peace and prosperity.*

prosperous /ˈprɒspərəs/ ADJ **Prosperous** people or places are rich and successful.

prostitute /ˈprɒstɪtjuːt, AM -tuːt/ (**prostitutes**) N-COUNT A **prostitute** is a person who has sex with people in exchange for money.

prostitution /ˌprɒstɪˈtjuːʃən, AM -ˈtuː-/ N-UNCOUNT **Prostitution** involves having sex in exchange for money.

Word Link *agon ≈ struggling : agony, agonize, protagonist*

protagonist /prəˈtæɡənɪst, AM prəʊ-/ (**protagonists**) **1** N-COUNT A **protagonist** in a play, novel, or real event is one of the main people in it. [FORMAL] ❑ *In Dickens's book 'Great Expectations', the protagonist is called Pip.* **2** N-COUNT A **protagonist of** an idea or movement is a supporter of it.

Word Link *tect ≈ covering : detect, protect, protective*

protect /prəˈtekt/ (**protects, protecting, protected**) V-T To **protect** someone or something means to prevent them from being harmed or damaged. ❑ *What can women do to protect themselves?* ❑ *...a plan for protecting the rights of children.* ● **protector** (**protectors**) N-COUNT ❑ *Traditionally, men are seen as the protectors of women.*
→ see **hero**

Word Partnership Use *protect* with:

N. protect **against attacks**, protect **children**, protect **citizens**, **duty to** protect, **efforts to** protect, protect **the environment**, **laws** protect, protect **people**, protect **privacy**, protect **property**, protect **women**, protect **workers**

ADJ. **designed to** protect, **necessary to** protect, **supposed to** protect

protection /prəˈtekʃən/ N-UNCOUNT If something gives **protection against** something unpleasant, it prevents people or things from being harmed or damaged by it. ❑ *Self confidence is the best protection against bullying.*

protective /prəˈtektɪv/ **1** ADJ **Protective** means designed or intended to protect something or someone from harm. ❑ *...protective gloves.* **2** ADJ If someone is **protective** towards you, they show a strong desire to keep you safe. ❑ *It is natural that parents feel very protective towards their children.*

protégé /ˈprɒtɪʒeɪ, AM ˈprəʊt-/ (**protégés**)

The spelling **protégée** is also used when referring to a woman.

N-COUNT A **protégé** is a young person who is helped and guided by an older and more experienced person over a period of time.

protein /ˈprəʊtiːn/ (**proteins**) N-VAR **Protein** is a substance which the body needs and which is found in meat, eggs, and milk. ❑ *...a high-protein diet.*
→ see **calories, diet**

protest (**protests, protesting, protested**) **1** V-T/V-I /prəˈtest/ To **protest** means to say or show publicly that you do not agree with something. In British English, you **protest about** something or **against** something. In American English, you **protest** something. ❑ *Groups of women protested against the arrests.* ❑ *They protested high prices.* ● **protester** (**protesters**) N-COUNT ❑ *...anti-war protesters.* **2** V-T If you **protest** that something is the truth, you insist that it is true, when other people think that it may not be. ❑ *She protested that she was not a liar.* ❑ *'I never said that to her,' he protested.* ❑ *He always protested his innocence.* **3** N-VAR /ˈprəʊtest/ A **protest** is the act of saying or showing publicly that you do not approve of something. ❑ *...a protest against the new law.* ❑ *People walked out of the meeting in protest.*

Word Partnership Use *protest* with:

N. protest **demonstrations**, protest **groups**, protest **march**, protest **rally**, **workers** protest **1**

ADJ. **anti-war** protest, **anti-government** protest, **organized** protest, **peaceful** protest, **political** protest **3**

Protestant /ˈprɒtɪstənt/ (**Protestants**) N-COUNT A **Protestant** is someone who belongs

P

to the branch of the Christian church which separated from the Catholic church in the sixteenth century.

protocol /'prəʊtəkɒl, AM -kɔːl/ (**protocols**) N-VAR **Protocol** is a system of rules or agreements about the correct way to act in formal situations. ❑ *It will take many years to change the protocol.*

prototype /'prəʊtətaɪp/ (**prototypes**) N-COUNT A **prototype** is the first model or example of a new type of thing. ❑ *Dave built a prototype of his invention.*

protracted /prə'træktɪd, AM prəʊ-/ ADJ Something that is **protracted** lasts longer than usual or longer than you had hoped. ❑ *The two sides held protracted talks.*

Word Link *trude ≈ pushing : intrude, intruder, protrude*

protrude /prə'truːd, AM prəʊ-/ (**protrudes, protruding, protruded**) V-I If something **protrudes from** somewhere, it sticks out. [FORMAL] ❑ *Huge rocks protruded from the water.*

proud /praʊd/ (**prouder, proudest**) 1 ADJ If you feel **proud**, you feel pleasure and satisfaction at something that you own, have done, or are connected with. ❑ *I felt proud of his efforts.* ❑ *They are proud that she is doing well at school.* ❑ *...the proud father of a 5-month-old baby son.* ● **proudly** ADV ❑ *'That's the job finished,' he said proudly.* 2 ADJ Someone who is **proud** has a lot of dignity and self-respect. ❑ *He was too proud to ask his family for help.* 3 ADJ Someone who is **proud** feels that they are better or more important than other people.

proud

prove /pruːv/ (**proves, proving, proved** or **proven**) 1 LINK-VERB If something **proves to** be true or to have a particular quality, it becomes clear after a period of time that it is true or has that quality. ❑ *The reports proved to be true.* ❑ *This method has proven difficult.* 2 V-T If you **prove** that something is true, you show by means of argument or evidence that it is definitely true. ❑ *Professor Cantor has proved his theory.* ❑ *This proves how much we love each other.* ❑ *It has made me determined to prove him wrong.* 3 V-T If you **prove yourself**, you show by your actions that you have a certain good quality. ❑ *I had to prove myself before I could be promoted.*
→ see **science**

Word Partnership Use *prove* with:

ADJ.	prove **(to be) difficult**, prove **helpful**, prove **useful**, prove **worthy** 1 **difficult to** prove, **hard to** prove 2
V.	**have to** prove, **try to** prove 2 **able to** prove 2 3 **have *something* to** prove 3

Word Link *verb ≈ word : adverb, proverb, verbal*

proverb /'prɒvɜːb/ (**proverbs**) N-COUNT A **proverb** is a short sentence that people often quote, which gives advice or tells you something about life. For example, 'A bird in the hand is worth two in the bush.'

proverbial /prə'vɜːbiəl/ ADJ BEFORE N You use **proverbial** to show that you know the way you are describing something is one that is often used or is part of a popular saying. ❑ *It's the proverbial 'chicken and egg' situation - we don't know what happened first.*

provide /prə'vaɪd/ (**provides, providing, provided**) 1 V-T If you **provide** something that someone needs or wants, you give it to them or make it available to them. ❑ *They provided lots of information.* ❑ *The government was unable to provide them with help.* 2 V-T If a law or agreement **provides** that something will happen, it states that it will happen. [FORMAL] ❑ *The law provides that, by the end of the year, they must leave the country.*
▶ **provide for** 1 PHR-VERB If you **provide for** someone, you support them financially and make sure that they have the things that they need. ❑ *Elaine won't let him provide for her.* ❑ *Her father always made sure that she was well provided for.* 2 PHR-VERB If you **provide for** something that might happen or that might need to be done, you make arrangements to deal with it. [FORMAL] ❑ *James had provided for this sort of emergency.*

provided /prə'vaɪdɪd/ CONJ If something will happen **provided** or **providing** that something else happens, the first thing will happen only if the second thing also happens. ❑ *Anyone can stay at the Hotel Bora Bora, provided they can afford $4,800 a night.*

providence /'prɒvɪdəns/ N-UNCOUNT **Providence** is God, or a force which is believed to arrange the things that happen to us. [LITERARY]

providing /prə'vaɪdɪŋ/ → see **provided**

province /'prɒvɪns/ (**provinces**) 1 N-COUNT A **province** is a large section of a country which has its own administration. 2 N-PLURAL **The provinces** are all the parts of a country except the part where the capital is situated. ❑ *The French government transferred 30,000 jobs from Paris to the provinces.*

provincial /prə'vɪnʃəl/ 1 ADJ BEFORE N **Provincial** means connected with the parts of a country outside the capital. ❑ *...provincial towns.* 2 ADJ If you describe someone or something as **provincial**, you disapprove of them because you think that they are not sophisticated. ❑ *The audience was dull and very provincial.*

provision /prə'vɪʒən/ (**provisions**) 1 N-UNCOUNT The **provision of** something is the act of giving it or making it available to people who need or want it. ❑ *The government is responsible for the provision of health and education services.* 2 N-UNCOUNT If you make **provision for** a future need, you make arrangements to ensure that it is dealt with. ❑ *It is the duty of the state to make provision for the education of all children.* 3 N-COUNT A **provision** in an agreement or law is an arrangement included in it. 4 N-PLURAL **Provisions** are supplies of food.

provisional /prə'vɪʒənəl/ ADJ You use **provisional** to describe something that has been arranged or appointed for the present, but may be changed soon. ❑ *A provisional date for the meeting has been set for June the fifteenth.* ● **provisionally** ADV ❑ *A deal has been provisionally agreed.*

provocation /ˌprɒvə'keɪʃən/ (**provocations**) N-VAR **Provocation** is a deliberate attempt to make someone react angrily. ❑ *She attacked me without provocation.*

provocative /prəˈvɒkətɪv/ **1** ADJ Something that is **provocative** is intended to make people react angrily. ❑ *...a provocative speech.* **2** ADJ **Provocative** behaviour or dress is intended to make someone feel sexual desire.

provoke /prəˈvəʊk/ (**provokes, provoking, provoked**) **1** V-T If you **provoke** someone, you deliberately annoy them and try to make them behave aggressively. ❑ *They are trying to provoke him into doing something stupid.* **2** V-T If something **provokes** a violent or unpleasant reaction, it causes it. ❑ *The article in the newspaper provoked anger.*

prowess /ˈpraʊɪs/ N-UNCOUNT Someone's **prowess** is their great ability at doing a particular thing. [FORMAL] ❑ *...his prowess as a rugby player.*

prowl /praʊl/ (**prowls, prowling, prowled**) V-I When animals or people **prowl around**, they move around quietly, for example when they are hunting. ❑ *She prowled around the apartment, unable to sleep.*

Word Link	***proxim** ≈ near : approximate, approximation, proximity*

proximity /prɒkˈsɪmɪti/ N-UNCOUNT **Proximity to** a place or person is the fact of being near to them. [FORMAL] ❑ *The town's proximity to London means the houses there are quite expensive.*

proxy /ˈprɒksi/ (**proxies**) N-VAR A **proxy** is a person or thing that is acting or being used in the place of someone or something else. If you do something **by proxy**, you arrange for someone else to do it for you. ❑ *If you cannot come to the meeting, you may vote by proxy.*

prude /pruːd/ (**prudes**) N-COUNT If you call someone a **prude**, you disapprove of them because you think that they are too easily shocked and embarrassed by nudity or sex.

prudent /ˈpruːdənt/ ADJ Someone who is **prudent** is sensible and careful. ❑ *It is always prudent to start a fitness programme slowly.* • **prudently** ADV ❑ *Prudently, Joanna said nothing.* • **prudence** N-UNCOUNT ❑ *A lack of prudence may lead to money problems.*

prune /pruːn/ (**prunes, pruning, pruned**) **1** N-COUNT A **prune** is a dried plum. **2** V-T When you **prune** a tree or bush, you cut off some of the branches so that it will grow better the next year.

pry /praɪ/ (**pries, prying, pried**) **1** V-I If you say that someone is **prying**, you disapprove of them because they are trying to find out about someone else's private affairs. ❑ *We do not like people prying into our private life.* **2** V-T If you **pry** something **open** or **pry** it away from a surface, you force it open or away from a surface. ❑ *She pried open the cat's jaws to give it its medicine.* ❑ *I pried the top off a can of chilli.*

PS /ˌpiː ˈes/ You write **PS** before a comment you add at the end of a letter, after you have signed it. ❑ *PS Please show your friends this letter.*

pseudonym /ˈsjuːdənɪm, AM ˈsuː-/ (**pseudonyms**) N-COUNT A **pseudonym** is a name which someone, usually a writer, uses instead of his or her real name.

Word Link	***psych** ≈ mind : psyche, psychiatrist, psychic*

psyche /ˈsaɪki/ (**psyches**) N-COUNT Your **psyche** is your mind and your deepest feelings and attitudes. ❑ *...the mysteries of the human psyche.*

psychedelic /ˌsaɪkəˈdelɪk/ ADJ **Psychedelic** art has bright colours and strange patterns.

Word Link	***iatr** ≈ healing : geriatric, pediatrics, psychiatrist*

psychiatry /saɪˈkaɪətri, AM sɪ-/ N-UNCOUNT **Psychiatry** is the branch of medicine concerned with the treatment of mental illness. • **psychiatric** /ˌsaɪkiˈætrɪk/ ADJ ❑ *...psychiatric illnesses.* • **psychiatrist** /saɪˈkaɪətrɪst, AM sɪ-/ (**psychiatrists**) N-COUNT ❑ *His family told him to see a psychiatrist.*

psychic /ˈsaɪkɪk/ **1** N-COUNT & ADJ If you believe that someone is a **psychic**, or is **psychic**, you believe that they have strange mental powers, such as being able to read the minds of other people or to see into the future. **2** ADJ **Psychic** means relating to the mind rather than the body. [FORMAL] ❑ *...psychic powers.*

psychoanalysis /ˌsaɪkəʊəˈnælɪsɪs/ N-UNCOUNT **Psychoanalysis** is the treatment of someone who has mental problems by asking them about their feelings and their past in order to discover what may be causing their condition. • **psychoanalyst** /ˌsaɪkəʊˈænəlɪst/ (**psychoanalysts**) N-COUNT ❑ *Jane is seeing a psychoanalyst.*

psychological /ˌsaɪkəˈlɒdʒɪkəl/ ADJ **Psychological** means concerned with a person's mind and thoughts. ❑ *Robyn's loss of memory is a psychological problem.* • **psychologically** ADV ❑ *It was very important psychologically for us to win.* → see **myth**

psychology /saɪˈkɒlədʒi/ **1** N-UNCOUNT **Psychology** is the scientific study of the human mind and the reasons for people's behaviour. • **psychological** /ˌsaɪkəˈlɒdʒɪkəl/ ADJ ❑ *...psychological problems.* • **psychologist** (**psychologists**) N-COUNT ❑ *She trained as a psychologist.* **2** N-UNCOUNT The **psychology of** a person is the kind of mind that they have, which makes them think or behave in the way that they do. ❑ *...the psychology of teachers.*

psychopath /ˈsaɪkəʊpæθ/ (**psychopaths**) N-COUNT A **psychopath** is someone who has serious mental problems and who may act in a violent way without feeling sorry for what they have done.

psychosis /saɪˈkəʊsɪs/ (**psychoses**) N-VAR **Psychosis** is severe mental illness which can make people lose contact with reality. [MEDICAL]

psychotherapy /ˌsaɪkəʊˈθerəpi/ N-UNCOUNT **Psychotherapy** is the use of psychological methods to treat people who are mentally ill. • **psychotherapist** (**psychotherapists**) N-COUNT ❑ *He went to see a psychotherapist.*

psychotic /saɪˈkɒtɪk/ (**psychotics**) N-COUNT & ADJ A **psychotic** or someone who is **psychotic** has a severe mental illness which has made them lose contact with reality. [MEDICAL]

pub /pʌb/ (**pubs**) **1** N-COUNT In Britain, a **pub** is a building where people can buy and drink alcoholic drinks. 2 → See note at **café**

puberty /ˈpjuːbəti/ N-UNCOUNT **Puberty** is the stage in someone's life when their body starts to become physically mature.

public /ˈpʌblɪk/

> In meaning 1, **public** can take the singular or plural form of the verb.

1 N-SING You can refer to people in general as **the public**. ❑ *The public is tired of hearing about this.* ❑ *The public need to know.* 2 ADJ BEFORE N **Public** means relating to all the people in a country or community. ❑ *The government is under pressure from public opinion.* 3 ADJ BEFORE N **Public** statements, actions, and events are made or done in such a way that everyone can see them or be aware of them. ❑ *This is the ministry's first public statement on the subject.* ❑ *This was the actress's last public appearance.* • **publicly** ADV ❑ *He never spoke publicly about his wife.* 4 ADJ BEFORE N A **public figure** or a person in **public life** is known about by many people because they serve the public in their job. ❑ *He is the most popular public figure in South Africa.* 5 ADJ AFTER LINK-V If a fact is **made public** or **becomes public**, it becomes known to everyone rather than being kept secret. 6 ADJ BEFORE N **Public** means relating to the government or state, or things that are done by the state for the people. ❑ *I think this is a waste of public money.* 7 ADJ BEFORE N **Public** things and places are provided for everyone to use, or are open to anyone. ❑ *...the New York Public Library.* ❑ *...public transport.* ❑ *...public areas.* 8 PHRASE If someone is in **the public eye**, many people know who they are, because they are famous or because they are often mentioned on television or in the newspapers. ❑ *His family is always in the public eye.* 9 PHRASE If you say or do something **in public**, you say or do it when a group of other people are present. ❑ *He made his statement in public.*
→ see **library**

P

publication /ˌpʌblɪˈkeɪʃən/ (**publications**) 1 N-UNCOUNT The **publication** of a book or magazine is the act of printing it and making it available. ❑ *Her novel is due for publication in October.* 2 N-COUNT A **publication** is a book, magazine, or article that has been published.

publicist /ˈpʌblɪsɪst/ (**publicists**) N-COUNT A **publicist** is a person who publicizes things, especially as part of a job in advertising or journalism.

publicity /pʌˈblɪsɪti/ 1 N-UNCOUNT **Publicity** is advertising, information, or actions intended to attract the public's attention to someone or something. ❑ *...a £20m publicity campaign.* 2 N-UNCOUNT When newspapers and television pay a lot of attention to something, you can say that it is receiving **publicity**. ❑ *Rock stars get a lot of publicity.*

Word Partnership	Use *publicity* with:
V.	**generate** publicity 1 2 **get** publicity, **receive** publicity, publicity **surrounding** ***someone/something*** 2
ADJ.	**bad** publicity, **negative** publicity 2

publicize [BRIT also **publicise**] /ˈpʌblɪsaɪz/ (**publicizes, publicizing, publicized**) V-T If you **publicize** a fact or event, you make it widely known to the public. ❑ *The author appeared on television to publicize her new book.*

ˌpublic reˈlations 1 N-UNCOUNT **Public relations** is the part of an organization's work that is concerned with obtaining the public's approval for what it does. The abbreviation **PR** is also used. ❑ *The chairman's statement is just a public relations exercise. It doesn't really mean anything.* 2 N-PLURAL **Public relations** are the state of the relationship between an organization and the public. ❑ *His behaviour was not good for public relations.*

ˌpublic ˈschool (**public schools**) 1 N-VAR In Britain, a **public school** is a private school that provides secondary education which parents have to pay for. 2 N-VAR In the USA, Australia, and some other countries, a **public school** is a school that is supported financially by the government and usually provides free education.

ˌpublic ˈsector N-SING **The public sector** is the part of a country's economy which is controlled or supported financially by the government.

publish /ˈpʌblɪʃ/ (**publishes, publishing, published**) 1 V-T When a company **publishes** a book or magazine, it prints copies of it, which are sent to shops and sold. 2 V-T When the people in charge of a newspaper or magazine **publish** a piece of writing or a photograph, they print it in their newspaper or magazine. ❑ *The magazine published an article which made fun of the prime minister.* 3 V-T If someone **publishes** a book or an article that they have written, they arrange to have it published. ❑ *He has published two books of poetry.*
→ see **laboratory, printing**

publisher /ˈpʌblɪʃə/ (**publishers**) N-COUNT A **publisher** is a person or company that publishes books, newspapers, or magazines.

publishing /ˈpʌblɪʃɪŋ/ N-UNCOUNT **Publishing** is the business of publishing books.

ˈpublishing house (**publishing houses**) N-COUNT A **publishing house** is a company which publishes books.

pudding /ˈpʊdɪŋ/ (**puddings**) 1 N-VAR A **pudding** is a cooked sweet food made with flour, fat, and eggs, and usually served hot. 2 N-UNCOUNT Some people refer to the sweet course of a meal as the **pudding**. [BRIT] ❑ *What's for pudding?*
→ see **dessert**

puddle /ˈpʌdəl/ (**puddles**) N-COUNT A **puddle** is a small shallow pool of rain or other liquid on the ground.

puff /pʌf/ (**puffs, puffing, puffed**) 1 V-I & N-COUNT If someone **puffs on** or **at** a cigarette, cigar, or pipe, or if they take a **puff** of it, they smoke it. ❑ *He puffed on a pipe as he listened.* ❑ *She took quick puffs at her cigarette.* 2 V-I If you **are puffing**, you are breathing loudly and quickly with your mouth open because you are out of breath after a lot of physical effort. 3 N-COUNT A **puff of** air or smoke is a small amount of it that is blown out from somewhere.

pull

pull /pʊl/ (**pulls, pulling, pulled**) 1 V-T & N-COUNT When you **pull** something, you hold it firmly and move it towards you or away from its previous position. A **pull** is an instance of pulling. ❑ *I helped pull him out of the water.* ❑ *She gave the carpet a firm pull to straighten it.* 2 V-T When a vehicle, animal, or person **pulls** a cart or piece of machinery, they are attached to it or hold it, so that it moves along behind them when they move forward. ❑ *...a train pulling wagons.* 3 V-T If you **pull** a part of your body in a particular direction, you move it with effort or force in that direction. ❑ *She pulled her hand from her pocket.* 4 V-T If you **pull** a muscle, you injure it by straining it. 5 N-COUNT A **pull** is a strong physical force which causes things to move in a particular direction. ❑ *...the pull of gravity.*

▶ **pull away** 1 PHR-VERB When a vehicle or driver **pulls away**, the vehicle starts moving forward. 2 PHR-VERB If you **pull away from** someone that you have had close links with, you deliberately become less close to them. ❑ *Kevin began to pull away from his parents.*

▶ **pull back** PHR-VERB If someone **pulls back from** an action, they decide not to continue or persist with it, because it could have bad consequences. ❑ *He asked both countries to pull back from violence.*

▶ **pull down** PHR-VERB To **pull down** a building or statue means to deliberately destroy it.

▶ **pull in** PHR-VERB When a vehicle or driver **pulls in** somewhere, the vehicle stops there. ❑ *He pulled in at the side of the road.*

▶ **pull into** PHR-VERB When a vehicle or driver **pulls into** a road or driveway, the vehicle makes a turn into the road or driveway and stops there.

▶ **pull off** PHR-VERB If you **pull off** something very difficult, you manage to achieve it successfully. ❑ *It will be amazing if they pull it off.*

▶ **pull out** 1 PHR-VERB When a vehicle or driver **pulls out**, the vehicle moves out into the road or nearer the centre of the road. ❑ *She pulled out into the street.* 2 PHR-VERB If you **pull out of** an agreement, a contest, or an organization, you withdraw from it. 3 PHR-VERB If troops **pull out of** a place, they leave it.

▶ **pull over** PHR-VERB When a vehicle or driver **pulls over**, the vehicle moves closer to the side of the road and stops there.

▶ **pull through** PHR-VERB If someone with a serious illness or in a very difficult situation **pulls through**, they recover.

▶ **pull together** 1 PHR-VERB If people **pull together**, they co-operate with each other. ❑ *If we all pull together, I'm sure we will be able to win.* 2 PHR-VERB If you are upset or depressed and someone tells you to **pull yourself together**, they are telling you in a rather unsympathetic way to control your feelings and behave calmly.

▶ **pull up** PHR-VERB When a vehicle or driver **pulls up**, the vehicle slows down and stops.

pullover /ˈpʊləʊvə/ (**pullovers**) N-COUNT A **pullover** is a woollen piece of clothing that covers the upper part of your body and your arms. [BRIT]

pulp /pʌlp/ 1 N-SING If an object is pressed into a **pulp**, it is crushed or beaten until it is soft, smooth, and wet. 2 N-SING In fruit and vegetables, **the pulp** is the soft inner part.

pulpit /ˈpʊlpɪt/ (**pulpits**) N-COUNT A **pulpit** is a small raised platform in a church with a rail around it, where a member of the clergy stands to preach.

pulsate /pʌlˈseɪt, AM ˈpʌlseɪt/ (**pulsates, pulsating, pulsated**) V-I If something **pulsates**, it moves in and out or shakes with strong regular movements. ❑ *...a star that pulsates.*

pulse /pʌls/ (**pulses**) 1 N-COUNT Your **pulse** is the regular beating of blood through your body, which you can feel, for example, at your wrist or neck. ❑ *Martin's pulse raced, and he felt scared.* 2 PHRASE When someone **takes** your **pulse** or **feels** your **pulse**, they find out the speed of your heartbeat by feeling the pulse in your wrist. 3 N-COUNT A **pulse of** electrical current, light, or sound is a sharp temporary increase in its level. 4 N-PLURAL Some large dried seeds which can be cooked and eaten are called **pulses**, for example the seeds of peas, beans, and lentils.

pump /pʌmp/ (**pumps, pumping, pumped**) 1 N-COUNT A **pump** is a machine that is used to force a liquid or gas to flow in strong regular movements in a particular direction. ❑ *...a petrol pump.* 2 V-T To **pump** a liquid or gas in a certain direction means to force it to flow in that direction, using a pump. ❑ *Workers pumped water from the building's basement.* 3 N-COUNT A **pump** is a device for bringing water to the surface from below the ground. 4 V-T To **pump** water, oil, or gas means to get a supply of it from below the surface of the ground, using a pump. ❑ *The Russians have pumped huge amounts of oil.* ❑ *The water is pumped up from beneath the ground.* 5 N-COUNT A **pump** is a device that you use to force air into something, for example a tyre. ❑ *...a bicycle pump.* 6 V-T If someone has their stomach **pumped**, doctors remove the contents of their stomach. 7 V-T If you **pump** money **into** a project or an industry, you invest a lot of money in it. [INFORMAL] 8 N-COUNT **Pumps** are canvas shoes with flat rubber soles which people wear for sports and leisure.

▶ **pump out** PHR-VERB To **pump out** something means to produce or supply it continually and in large amounts. ❑ *The television pumps out hours of cookery programmes each day.*

▶ **pump up** PHR-VERB If you **pump up** something such as a tyre, you fill it with air, using a pump.

pumpkin /ˈpʌmpkɪn/ (**pumpkins**) N-VAR A **pumpkin** is a large, round, orange-coloured vegetable with a thick skin.

pun /pʌn/ (**puns**) N-COUNT A **pun** is a clever and amusing use of a word with more than one meaning, or a word that sounds like another word, so that what you say has two different meanings. ❑ *The Germans have called the euro 'teuro', a pun on the German word 'teuer', which means expensive.*

punch /pʌntʃ/ (**punches, punching, punched**) 1 V-T & N-COUNT If you **punch** someone or something, or if you throw a **punch** at them, you hit them hard with your fist. ❑ *I was so angry that I almost punched him.* 2 V-T If you **punch** something such as the buttons on a keyboard, you touch them in order to store information on a machine such as a computer or to give the machine a command to do something. 3 V-T If you **punch holes** in something, you make holes in it by pushing or pressing it with something sharp. 4 N-COUNT A **punch** is a tool used for

punch

P

making holes in something. **5** PHRASE If you say that someone does not **pull** their **punches** when they are criticizing someone or something, you mean that they say exactly what they think and do not moderate their criticism. **6** N-VAR **Punch** is a drink usually made from wine or spirits mixed with sugar, fruit, and spices.

▶ **punch in** PHR-VERB If you **punch in** a number on a machine or **punch** numbers **into** it, you push the machine's numerical keys in order to give it a command to do something. ❑ *All you need to do is punch in four numbers.*

punctual /ˈpʌŋktʃʊəl/ ADJ Someone who is **punctual** arrives somewhere or does something at the right time and is not late. ❑ *He's always very punctual.* ● **punctually** ADV ❑ *My guests arrived punctually.*

punctuate /ˈpʌŋktʃʊeɪt/ (**punctuates, punctuating, punctuated**) V-T If an activity or situation **is punctuated** by particular things, it is interrupted by them at intervals. [FORMAL] ❑ *The silence was punctuated by the sound of traffic.*

punctuation /ˌpʌŋktʃʊˈeɪʃən/ N-UNCOUNT **Punctuation** is the system of signs such as full stops, commas, and question marks that you use in writing to divide words into sentences and clauses.
→ see Picture Dictionary: **punctuation**

ˌpunctuˈation mark (**punctuation marks**) N-COUNT A **punctuation mark** is a sign such as a full stop, comma, or question mark.

puncture /ˈpʌŋktʃə/ (**punctures, puncturing, punctured**) **1** N-COUNT A **puncture** is a small hole in a car or bicycle tyre that has been made by a sharp object. **2** V-T If a sharp object **punctures** something, it makes a hole in it. ❑ *A nail punctured one of the front tyres.*

pundit /ˈpʌndɪt/ (**pundits**) N-COUNT A **pundit** is a person who knows a lot about a subject and is often asked to give information or their opinion about it to the public.

P

pungent /ˈpʌndʒənt/ ADJ Something that is **pungent** has a strong bitter smell or taste. ❑ *...the pungent smell of onions and garlic.*

Word Link	*pun ≈ punishing : punish, punishment, punitive*

punish /ˈpʌnɪʃ/ (**punishes, punishing, punished**) **1** V-T To **punish** someone means to make them suffer in some way because they have done something wrong. ❑ *George never needed to punish his children.* **2** V-T To **punish** a crime means to punish anyone who commits that crime. ❑ *Federal laws punish crimes such as murder.*

punishing /ˈpʌnɪʃɪŋ/ ADJ A **punishing** schedule, activity, or experience requires a lot of physical effort and makes you very tired or weak.

punishment /ˈpʌnɪʃmənt/ (**punishments**) **1** N-UNCOUNT **Punishment** is the act of punishing someone or being punished. ❑ *The man is guilty and deserves punishment.* **2** N-VAR A **punishment** is a particular way of punishing someone. ❑ *The usual punishment is a fine of £100.* **3** → see also **capital punishment, corporal punishment**

punitive /ˈpjuːnɪtɪv/ ADJ **Punitive** actions are intended to punish people. [FORMAL] ❑ *...punitive measures such as fines.*

punk /pʌŋk/ (**punks**) **1** N-UNCOUNT **Punk** or **punk rock** is rock music that is played in a fast, loud, and aggressive way. Punk rock was particularly popular in the late 1970s. **2** N-COUNT A **punk** or a **punk rocker** is a person who likes punk music and dresses in a very noticeable and unconventional way. **3** N-COUNT A **punk** is a young person who behaves in an unruly, aggressive, or anti-social manner. [AM, INFORMAL]

punter /ˈpʌntə/ (**punters**) **1** N-COUNT A **punter** is a person who bets money, especially on horse races. [BRIT, INFORMAL] **2** N-COUNT People sometimes refer to their customers or clients as **punters**. [BRIT, INFORMAL]

pup /pʌp/ (**pups**) N-COUNT A **pup** is a young dog. The young of some other animals, for example seals, are called **pups**.

pupil /ˈpjuːpɪl/ (**pupils**) **1** N-COUNT The **pupils** of a school are the children who go to it. **2** N-COUNT A **pupil** of a painter, musician, or other expert is someone who studies with that expert, learning his or her skills. **3** N-COUNT The **pupils** of your eyes are the small, round, black holes in the centre of them.
→ see **eye**

puppet /ˈpʌpɪt/ (**puppets**) **1** N-COUNT A **puppet** is a doll that you can move, either by pulling strings which are attached to it, or by putting your hand inside its body and moving your fingers. **2** N-COUNT You can refer to a person or country as a **puppet** when you mean their actions are controlled by a more powerful person or government, even though they may appear to be independent. ❑ *...a puppet government.*

puppy /ˈpʌpi/ (**puppies**) N-COUNT A **puppy** is a young dog.

Picture Dictionary — **punctuation**

A: I want to learn to drive; however, cars scare me.
semi-colon — full stop

B: Why not take a driver-training course?
hyphen — question mark

A: I'm not ready.
apostrophe

B: I know! If you want, I'll teach you to drive.
exclamation mark — comma

A: OK, but remember this: it was your idea, not mine.
colon

purchase /'pɜːtʃɪs/ (**purchases, purchasing, purchased**) **1** V-T When you **purchase** something, you buy it. [FORMAL] ● **purchaser** (**purchasers**) N-COUNT ❑ *The company is the largest purchaser of fresh fruit in the US.* **2** N-UNCOUNT The **purchase of** something is the act of buying it. [FORMAL] ❑ *The purchase of a holiday home in Spain is very popular.* **3** N-COUNT A **purchase** is something that you buy. [FORMAL] ❑ *The woman paid for her purchases and left the shop.*

pure /pjʊə/ (**purer, purest**) **1** ADJ **Pure** means not mixed with anything else. ❑ *This dress is pure silk.* ❑ *His hair was pure white.* ● **purity** N-UNCOUNT ❑ *In Hindu culture, water is a symbol of purity.* **2** ADJ Something that is **pure** is clean and does not contain any harmful substances. ❑ *The water is pure enough to drink.* ● **purity** N-UNCOUNT ❑ *They were worried about the purity of the tap water.* **3** ADJ If you describe someone as **pure**, you mean that they are free from things that are considered to be sinful or bad, especially sex. [LITERARY] ● **purity** N-UNCOUNT ❑ *...physical purity.* **4** ADJ BEFORE N **Pure** science or **pure** research is concerned only with theory and not with how this theory can be used in practical ways. ❑ *...pure maths.* **5** ADJ BEFORE N **Pure** means complete and total. ❑ *I met him by pure chance.* ❑ *...a look of pure surprise.*
→ see **science**

puree /'pjʊəreɪ, AM pjʊ'reɪ/ (**purees**) N-VAR **Puree** is food which has been mashed, sieved, or blended so that it forms a thick, smooth sauce. ❑ *...a tin of tomato puree.*

purely /'pjʊəli/ ADV You use **purely** to emphasize that the thing you are mentioning is the most important feature or that it is the only thing which should be considered. ❑ *He admitted that he bought the car purely for its looks.*

purge /pɜːdʒ/ (**purges, purging, purged**) **1** V-T & N-COUNT To **purge** an organization **of** its unacceptable members, or to make a **purge of** an organization, means to remove its unacceptable members from it. You can also talk about **purging** people **from** an organization. ❑ *They want to purge the country of corruption.* ❑ *Purges began soon after the election.* **2** V-T If you **purge** something **of** undesirable things, you get rid of them. ❑ *He tried to purge his mind of these terrible thoughts.*

purify /'pjʊərɪfaɪ/ (**purifies, purifying, purified**) V-T To **purify** a substance means to make it pure by removing any harmful, dirty, or inferior substances from it. ● **purification** N-UNCOUNT ❑ *...a water purification plant.*

purist /'pjʊərɪst/ (**purists**) N-COUNT A **purist** is someone who believes in absolute correctness, especially concerning a particular subject which they know a lot about.

puritan /'pjʊərɪtən/ (**puritans**) N-COUNT & ADJ You describe someone as a **puritan**, or you describe their behaviour as **puritan**, when they live according to very strict moral or religious principles, especially by avoiding physical pleasures; used showing disapproval.

puritanical /ˌpjʊərɪ'tænɪkəl/ ADJ If you describe someone as **puritanical**, you mean that they disapprove of pleasure, for example because they are strictly religious; used showing disapproval. ❑ *...puritanical attitudes.*

purity → see **pure**

purple /'pɜːpəl/ ADJ Something that is **purple** is reddish-blue in colour.

purport /pə'pɔːt/ (**purports, purporting, purported**) V-T If someone or something **purports to** do or be a particular thing, they claim to do or be that thing. [FORMAL] ❑ *This book purports to tell the truth.*

purpose /'pɜːpəs/ (**purposes**) **1** N-COUNT The **purpose** of something is the reason for which it is made or done. ❑ *What is the purpose of your visit?* ❑ *Nuclear energy is used for military purposes.* **2** N-COUNT Your **purpose** is the thing that you want to achieve. ❑ *I don't know exactly what their purpose is.* **3** N-UNCOUNT **Purpose** is the feeling of having a definite aim and of being determined to achieve it. ❑ *The teachers are enthusiastic and have a sense of purpose.* **4** PHRASE You use **for all practical purposes** or **to all intents and purposes** to suggest that a situation is not exactly as you describe it, but the effect is the same as if it were. ❑ *He treated me like a son; to all intents and purposes he was my father.* **5** PHRASE If you do something **on purpose**, you do it deliberately. ❑ *Was it an accident or did David do it on purpose?*

Word Partnership Use *purpose* with:

V.	**serve a** purpose **1**
	accomplish a purpose, **achieve a** purpose **2**
ADJ.	**main** purpose, **original** purpose, **primary** purpose, **real** purpose, **sole** purpose **1-3**

ˌpurpose-'built ADJ A **purpose-built** building has been specially designed and built for a particular use.

purposeful /'pɜːpəsfʊl/ ADJ If someone is **purposeful**, they show that they have a definite aim and a strong desire to achieve it. ❑ *She had a purposeful air.* ● **purposefully** ADV ❑ *He walked purposefully towards the house.*

purr /pɜː/ (**purrs, purring, purred**) **1** V-I When a cat **purrs**, it makes a low vibrating sound with its throat. **2** V-I & N-COUNT When an engine or machine **purrs**, it makes a quiet, continuous, vibrating sound, called a **purr**. ❑ *The boats purred out of the harbour.*

purse /pɜːs/ (**purses, pursing, pursed**) **1** N-COUNT In British English, a **purse** is a very small bag that people, especially women, keep their money in. The usual American term is **change purse**. **2** N-COUNT In American English, a **purse** is a small bag that women carry. The usual British word is **handbag**. **3** V-T If you **purse** your **lips**, you move them into a small rounded shape.

pursue /pə'sjuː, -'suː/ (**pursues, pursuing, pursued**) **1** V-T If you **pursue** a particular aim or result, you make efforts to achieve it or to progress in it. [FORMAL] ❑ *She came to England to pursue an acting career.* **2** V-T If you **pursue** a particular topic, you try to find out more about it by asking questions. [FORMAL] ❑ *If they say no to your request, don't be afraid to pursue the matter.* **3** V-T If you **pursue** a person, vehicle, or animal, you follow them, usually in order to catch them. [FORMAL] ● **pursuer** (**pursuers**) N-COUNT ❑ *He could hear his pursuers getting closer.*

pursuit /pə'sjuːt, AM -'suːt/ (**pursuits**)

1 N-UNCOUNT Your **pursuit of** something that you want consists of your attempts at achieving it. ❑ *...the pursuit of happiness.* ❑ *We must work together in pursuit of peace and justice.* **2** N-UNCOUNT If you are **in pursuit of** a person, vehicle, or animal you are chasing them. [FORMAL] **3** N-COUNT Your **pursuits** are your activities, usually activities that you enjoy when you are not working. ❑ *They both love outdoor pursuits.*

purveyor /pə'veɪər/ (**purveyors**) N-COUNT The **purveyors of** information, goods, or services are the people who provide them. [FORMAL] ❑ *...purveyors of luxury goods.*

push /pʊʃ/ (**pushes, pushing, pushed**) **1** V-T/V-I When you **push** something, you use force to make it move away from you or away from its previous position. You can also say that you give it a **push**. ❑ *The woman pushed back her chair and stood up.* ❑ *He pushed the door open.* ❑ *He gave me a sharp push.* ❑ *The men pushed and the horses pulled, and together they dragged the tree to the side of the road.* **2** V-T/V-I If you **push** through things that are blocking your way or **push** your **way** through them, you use force in order to move past them. ❑ *Dix pushed forward carrying a glass.* ❑ *He pushed his way towards her, laughing.* **3** V-T To **push** a value or amount **up** or **down** means to cause it to increase or decrease. ❑ *The 1980s boom pushed house prices up in many areas.* **4** V-T & N-COUNT If you **push** someone to do something or **push** them **into** doing it, you urge, encourage, or force them to do it. A **push** is the action of pushing someone to do something. ❑ *James pushed her into stealing the money.* ❑ *She bought a dog because she needed a push to go walking.* **5** V-I & N-COUNT If you **push for** something, or if you make a **push for** it, you try very hard to achieve it. ❑ *Keep pushing for everything that you want.* ❑ *There was a final push to arrive at an agreement.* **6** V-T If someone **pushes** an idea, a point, or a product, they try in a forceful way to convince people to accept it or buy it. ❑ *Salespeople always try to push their products.* **7** V-T When someone **pushes** drugs, they sell them illegally. [INFORMAL] ● **pusher** (**pushers**) N-COUNT ❑ *...drug pushers.*

▶ **push ahead** or **push forward** PHR-VERB If you **push ahead with** something or **push forward with** it, you make progress with it. ❑ *The government pushed ahead with building the airport.*

▶ **push around** PHR-VERB If someone **pushes** you **around**, they give you orders in a rude and insulting way.

▶ **push aside** PHR-VERB If you **push** something **aside**, you ignore it or refuse to think about it. ❑ *He pushed aside unpleasant thoughts.*

▶ **push forward** → see **push ahead**

▶ **push in** PHR-VERB When someone **pushes in**, they come into a queue in front of other people; used showing disapproval.

▶ **push on** PHR-VERB When you **push on**, you continue with a journey or task. ❑ *Searching for treasure, Columbus pushed on to Cuba.*

▶ **push over** PHR-VERB If you **push** someone or something **over**, you push them so that they fall onto the ground. ❑ *The man pushed her over before taking her handbag.*

▶ **push through** PHR-VERB If someone **pushes through** a law, reform, or policy, they succeed in getting it accepted, often despite opposition. ❑ *He tried to push the reform through Parliament.*

Thesaurus *push* Also look up:

V. drive, force, move, pressure, propel, shove, thrust; *(ant.)* pull **1** **2**
encourage, urge **4**

Word Partnership Use *push* with:

N. push **a button, at the** push **of a button,** push **a door** **1**
push **prices**, push **rates** **3**
push **an agenda**, push **legislation** **6**
push **drugs** **7**

pushchair /'pʊʃtʃeə/ (**pushchairs**) N-COUNT In British English, a **pushchair** is a small chair on wheels, in which a small child can sit and be wheeled around. The usual American word is **stroller**.

pushover or **push-over** /'pʊʃoʊvər/ (**pushovers**) N-COUNT You say that someone is a **pushover** when you find it easy to persuade them to do what you want. [INFORMAL] ❑ *We did not expect to find him a pushover and he has not been one.*

put /pʊt/ (**puts, putting, put**) **1** V-T When you **put** something in a particular place or position, you move it into that place or position. ❑ *Lisa put the photograph on the desk.* **2** V-T If you **put** someone somewhere, you cause them to go there and to stay there. ❑ *I've put the children to bed.* **3** V-T To **put** someone or something in a particular state or situation means to cause them to be in that state or situation. ❑ *This is going to put the company out of business.* ❑ *He put himself at risk.* **4** V-T If you **put** your trust, faith, or confidence **in** someone or something, you trust them or have faith or confidence in them. ❑ *Are we right to put our confidence in computers?* **5** V-T If you **put** time, strength, or energy **into** an activity, you use it in doing that activity. ❑ *Eleanor did not put much energy into the discussion.* **6** V-T When you **put** an idea or remark in a particular way, you express it in that way. ❑ *The police might have 'made some mistakes', as he put it.* ❑ *You can't put that sort of fear into words.* **7** V-T When you **put** a question to someone, you ask them the question. ❑ *We put this question to Professor Goodwin.* **8** V-T If you **put** something **at** a particular value or **in** a particular category, or **put** a particular value **on** it, you estimate it to have that value or to be in that category. ❑ *I would put her age at about 50.* **9** V-T If you **put** written information somewhere, you write, type, or print it there. ❑ *They put an announcement in the local paper.*

▶ **put across** or **put over** PHR-VERB When you **put** something **across** or **put** it **over**, you succeed in describing or explaining it to someone. ❑ *I put across my point of view and he put across his.*

▶ **put aside** PHR-VERB If you **put** something **aside**, you keep it to be dealt with or used at a later time. ❑ *I put money aside each month because I'm saving for a holiday.*

▶ **put away** **1** PHR-VERB If you **put** something **away**, you put it into the place where it is normally kept when it is not being used. ❑ *Put your maths books away, it's time for your history lesson.* **2** PHR-VERB If someone **is put away**, they are sent to prison or to a mental hospital for a long time. [INFORMAL]

▶ **put back** PHR-VERB To **put** something **back**

P

means to delay it or postpone it. ❑ *The trip has been put back to Easter.*

▶ **put by** PHR-VERB If you **put** money **by**, you save it so that you can use it at a later time. ❑ *There was enough money put by for her train ticket.*

▶ **put down** 1 PHR-VERB If you **put** something **down** somewhere, you write or type it there. ❑ *Mr Allen put down his thoughts on paper.* 2 PHR-VERB If you **put down** some money, you pay part of the price of something as a deposit. ❑ *He bought a property for £100,000 and put down £20,000.* 3 PHR-VERB When soldiers, police, or the government **put down** a riot or rebellion, they stop it by using force. 4 PHR-VERB If someone **puts** you **down**, they treat you in an unpleasant way by criticizing you in front of other people or making you appear foolish. [INFORMAL] 5 PHR-VERB When an animal **is put down**, it is killed because it is dangerous or very ill.

▶ **put down to** PHR-VERB If you **put** something **down to** a particular thing, you believe that it is caused by that thing. ❑ *We have sold a lot this year. I put it down to having good staff.*

▶ **put forward** PHR-VERB If you **put forward** a plan, proposal, or name, you suggest that it should be considered for a particular purpose or job. ❑ *I asked my boss to put my name forward for the job in Zurich.*

▶ **put in** 1 PHR-VERB If you **put in** an amount of time or effort doing something, you spend that time or effort doing it. ❑ *We put in three hours' work every evening.* 2 PHR-VERB If you **put in** a request or **put in for** something, you make a formal request or application. ❑ *I put in for a job as a secretary.*

▶ **put off** 1 PHR-VERB If you **put** something **off**, you delay doing it. ❑ *She put off telling him until the last moment.* 2 PHR-VERB If you **put** someone **off**, you make them wait for something that they want. ❑ *'He wants to come over,' Sarah said. 'I put him off until later tonight.'* 3 PHR-VERB To **put** someone **off** something means to cause them to dislike it. ❑ *Her parents' divorce has not put Diana off marriage.* 4 PHR-VERB If someone or something **puts** you **off**, they distract you from what you are trying to do and make it more difficult for you to do it. [BRIT] ❑ *The noise put her off revising for her exams.*

▶ **put on** 1 PHR-VERB When you **put on** clothing or make-up, you place it on your body in order to wear it. ❑ *I got up and put my clothes on.* 2 → See note at **wear** 3 PHR-VERB If you **put on** a way of behaving, you behave in a way that is not natural to you or that does not express your real feelings. ❑ *It was hard to believe she was sorry: she was just putting it on.* 4 PHR-VERB When people **put on** a show, exhibition, or service, they perform it or organize it. ❑ *We decided that we would put on a play.* 5 PHR-VERB If someone **puts on** weight, they become heavier. ❑ *Leo has put on three stone.* 6 PHR-VERB If you **put on** a piece of equipment or a device, you make it start working. ❑ *I put the radio on.* 7 PHR-VERB If you **put on** a record, tape, or CD, you place it on a record, tape, or CD player and listen to it. 8 PHR-VERB If you **put** something **on**, you begin to cook or heat it. ❑ *Put on a pan of water to simmer.*

▶ **put out** 1 PHR-VERB If you **put out** an announcement or story, you make it known to a lot of people. ❑ *The news agency put out a statement from the Prime Minister.* 2 PHR-VERB If you **put out** a fire, candle, or cigarette, you make it stop burning. ❑ *I tried to put out the fire.* 3 PHR-VERB If you **put out** an electric light, you make it stop shining by pressing a switch. 4 PHR-VERB If you **put out** things that will be needed, you place them somewhere ready to be used. ❑ *I put the teapot out on the table.* 5 PHR-VERB If you **put out** your **hand**, you move it forward, away from your body. ❑ *She put her hand out and touched her mother's arm.* 6 PHR-VERB If you **put** someone **out**, you cause them trouble or inconvenience because they have to do something for you. ❑ *I've always put myself out for others.* ❑ *Margaret hasn't exactly put herself out to welcome him.*

▶ **put over** → see **put across**

▶ **put through** 1 PHR-VERB When someone **puts through** a telephone call or a caller, they make the connection that allows the caller to speak to the person they are phoning. ❑ *The operator put me through to her.* 2 PHR-VERB If someone **puts** you **through** an unpleasant experience, they make you experience it. ❑ *He put them through a really tough week of training.*

▶ **put together** 1 PHR-VERB If you **put** something **together**, you join its different parts to each other so that it can be used. ❑ *He took the watch to pieces, cleaned it and put it together again.* 2 PHR-VERB If you **put together** a group of people or things, you form them into a team or collection. ❑ *He is putting a team together for next season.* 3 PHR-VERB If you **put together** an agreement, plan, or product, you design and create it. ❑ *We set to work putting the plan together.*

▶ **put up** 1 PHR-VERB If people **put up** a wall, building, tent, or other structure, they construct it. ❑ *They put up their tents and settled down for the night.* 2 PHR-VERB If you **put up** a poster or notice, you fix it to a wall or board. ❑ *They're putting new street signs up.* 3 PHR-VERB To **put up** resistance to something means to resist it. ❑ *He was old and very weak. He couldn't put up a fight.* 4 PHR-VERB If you **put up** money for something, you provide the money that is needed to pay for it. ❑ *People put up various amounts of money between £50,000 and £250,000.* 5 PHR-VERB To **put up** the price of something means to cause it to increase. ❑ *The new tax will put up the cost of petrol.* 6 PHR-VERB If a person or hotel **puts** you **up**, you stay at the person's home or at the hotel for one or more nights. ❑ *They put him up when he was homeless.*

▶ **put up with** PHR-VERB If you **put up with** something, you tolerate or accept it, even though you find it unpleasant or unsatisfactory. ❑ *I won't put up with that sort of behaviour.*

putt /pʌt/ (**putts, putting, putted**) V-T/V-I In golf, when you **putt** the ball, or **putt**, you hit the ball a short distance.

puzzle /ˈpʌzəl/ (**puzzles, puzzling, puzzled**) 1 V-T If something or someone **puzzles** you, you do not understand them and find them confusing. ❑ *This question has puzzled me for years.* ❑ *My sister puzzles me.* ● **puzzled** ADJ ❑ *He had a puzzled look on his face.* ● **puzzling** ADJ ❑ *Some of this book is rather puzzling.* 2 V-I If you **puzzle over** something, you try hard to think of the answer or the explanation for it.

puzzle

❑ *She puzzled over his behaviour all day.* **3** N-COUNT A **puzzle** is a question, game, or toy which you have to think about carefully in order to answer it correctly or put it together properly. **4** N-SING You can describe a person or thing that is hard to understand as **a puzzle.** ❑ *'Women are a puzzle,' he said.*

pyjamas [AM **pajamas**] /pɪ'dʒɑːməz/ N-PLURAL A pair of **pyjamas** consists of loose trousers and a loose jacket that are worn in bed.

pyramid /'pɪrəmɪd/ (**pyramids**) N-COUNT A **pyramid** is a three-dimensional shape with a flat base and flat triangular sides which slope upwards to a point.

→ see **solid, volume**

python /'paɪθən/ (**pythons**) N-COUNT A **python** is a type of large snake.

Qq

quadruple /ˌkwɒˈdruːpəl/ (**quadruples, quadrupling, quadrupled**) 1 V-T/V-I If someone **quadruples** an amount, or if it **quadruples**, it becomes four times bigger. ❑ *The price has quadrupled in the last few years.* 2 PREDET If one amount is **quadruple** another amount, it is four times bigger. 3 ADJ You use **quadruple** to indicate that something happens four times or has four parts. ❑ *Toby Keith was a quadruple winner at the annual awards.*

quail /kweɪl/

The plural is **quails** or **quail**.

quail

N-COUNT A **quail** is a small bird which is often shot and eaten.

quaint /kweɪnt/ (**quainter, quaintest**) ADJ Something that is **quaint** is attractive because it is unusual and rather old-fashioned. ❑ *...a quaint little cottage.*

quake /kweɪk/ (**quakes, quaking, quaked**) 1 N-COUNT A **quake** is the same as an **earthquake**. [INFORMAL] 2 V-I If you **quake**, you tremble or shake, usually because you are afraid. ❑ *I just stood there quaking with fear.*

qualification /ˌkwɒlɪfɪˈkeɪʃən/ (**qualifications**) 1 N-COUNT Your **qualifications** are the examinations that you have passed. ❑ *...people with good academic qualifications.* 2 N-COUNT The **qualifications** needed for a particular activity or task are the qualities and skills that you need in order to do it. ❑ *He had all the qualifications to become a good prime minister.* 3 N-VAR A **qualification** is something that you add to a statement to make it less strong or less generalized. ❑ *This statement requires qualification and clarification.* 4 → see also **qualify**

Word Partnership Use *qualification* with:

N. qualification **for a job**, **standards for** qualification 2
ADJ. **necessary** qualification 2
PREP. **without** qualification 3

qualified /ˈkwɒlɪfaɪd/ ADJ BEFORE N If you give someone or something **qualified** support or approval, you give support or approval that is not total and suggests that you have some doubts. ❑ *Williams answered both questions with a qualified yes.*

qualifier /ˈkwɒlɪfaɪə/ (**qualifiers**) N-COUNT A **qualifier** is an early game or round in a competition. ❑ *Wales lost 5-1 to Romania in a World Cup qualifier.*

qualify /ˈkwɒlɪfaɪ/ (**qualifies, qualifying, qualified**) 1 V-I When someone **qualifies**, they pass the examinations that they need to pass in order to work in a particular profession. ❑ *I qualified as a doctor.* ❑ *...qualified teachers.* ● **qualification** /ˌkwɒlɪfɪˈkeɪʃən/ N-UNCOUNT ❑ *Following qualification, he worked as a laywer.* 2 V-T/V-I If someone **qualifies for** something, or if something **qualifies** them **for** it, they have the right to do it or to have it. ❑ *What qualifies me for this job? Experience, for one thing.* 3 V-I If you **qualify** in a competition, you are successful in one part of it and go on to the next stage. ❑ *Manchester United qualified for the final by beating Chelsea.* ● **qualifier** (**qualifiers**) N-COUNT ❑ *Robert Kibe was the fastest qualifier for the 800 metres final.* 4 V-T If you **qualify** a statement, you add a detail or explanation to it to make it less strong or less generalized. ❑ *'I'd be a great leader,' he adds, and then qualifies this. 'But I don't think I'd know enough.'* 5 → see also **qualification**

Word Partnership Use *qualify* with:

PREP. qualify **as** ***something*** 1
qualify **for** ***something*** 2
V. **chance to** qualify, **fail to** qualify 1 2 3

qualitative /ˈkwɒlɪtətɪv, AM -teɪt-/ ADJ **Qualitative** means relating to the quality of something, rather than to things that can be measured. [FORMAL] ❑ *Do you think there is a qualitative difference between them?*

quality /ˈkwɒlɪti/ (**qualities**) 1 N-UNCOUNT The **quality** of something is how good or bad it is. ❑ *...high-quality paper.* 2 N-UNCOUNT Something of **quality** is of a high standard. ❑ *...a sign of quality.* ❑ *We are offering a quality service.* 3 N-COUNT Someone's **qualities** are their good characteristics. ❑ *...mature people with leadership qualities.* 4 N-COUNT You can describe a particular characteristic of a person or thing as a **quality**. ❑ *I have always believed in the sea's healing qualities.*

Word Partnership Use *quality* with:

N. **air** quality, quality **of life**, quality **of service**, **water** quality, quality **of work** 1
ADJ. **best/better/good** quality, **high/higher/highest** quality, **low** quality, **poor** quality, **top** quality 1 2

qualm /kwɑːm/ (**qualms**) N-COUNT If you **have no qualms about** what you are doing, you are not worried that it may be wrong. ❑ *I have no qualms about recommending the same approach to other doctors.*

Word Link *quant ≈ how much : quantifier, quantitative, quantity*

quantifier /'kwɒntɪfaɪə/ (**quantifiers**) N-COUNT In grammar, a **quantifier** is a word or phrase like 'plenty' or 'a lot', which allows you to refer to the quantity of something without being absolutely precise. It is often followed by 'of', as in 'a lot of money'.

quantitative /'kwɒntɪtətɪv, AM -teɪt-/ ADJ **Quantitative** means relating to things that can be measured, rather than to the quality of things. ❑ *...quantitative data such as surveys, tests, and experiments.*

quantity /'kwɒntɪti/ (**quantities**) **1** N-VAR A **quantity** is an amount that you can measure or count. ❑ *...a small quantity of water.* ❑ *The trees produce large quantities of fruit every year.* **2** N-UNCOUNT Things that are produced or available **in quantity** are produced or available in large amounts. ❑ *They can afford to import bananas in quantity.*
→ see **mathematics**

quantum /'kwɒntəm/ **1** ADJ BEFORE N In physics, **quantum theory** and **quantum mechanics** are concerned with the behaviour of atomic particles. **2** ADJ BEFORE N You can use **quantum** in the expressions **quantum leap** and **quantum jump**, which mean a very great and sudden increase in size, amount, or quality. ❑ *There was a quantum leap forward in 1998, when new trains were introduced.*

quarantine /'kwɒrənti:n, AM 'kwɔ:r-/ N-UNCOUNT If a person or animal is **in quarantine**, they are kept separate from other people or animals in case they have an infectious disease.
→ see **illness**

quarrel /'kwɒrəl, AM 'kwɔ:r-/ (**quarrels, quarrelling, quarrelled** or [AM] **quarreling, quarreled**) **1** N-COUNT & V-I If you have a **quarrel with** a friend or family member, or if you **quarrel with** them, you have an angry argument with them. ❑ *I had a terrible quarrel with my other brothers.* ❑ *My brother quarrelled with my father.* **2** N-SING If you say that you have **no quarrel with** someone, you mean that you have no reason to argue with them.

Q

quarry /'kwɒri, AM 'kwɔ:ri/ (**quarries, quarrying, quarried**) **1** N-COUNT A **quarry** is an area that is dug out from a piece of land or mountainside in order to extract stone, slate, or minerals. **2** V-T When stone or minerals **are quarried**, or when an area **is quarried** for them, they are removed from the area by digging, drilling, or using explosives.

Word Link *quart ≈ four : quart, quarter, quarterback*

quart /kwɔ:t/ (**quarts**) N-COUNT A **quart** is a unit of volume that is equal to two pints.

quarter /'kwɔ:tə/ (**quarters**) **1** N-COUNT & PREDET & ADJ BEFORE N A **quarter** is one of four equal parts of something. ❑ *Cut the peppers into quarters.* ❑ *Portugal is less than one quarter the size of Spain.* ❑ *...the past quarter century.* **2** N-COUNT A **quarter** is a fixed period of three months. ❑ *We update that database once a quarter.* **3** N-UNCOUNT When you are telling the time, you use **quarter** to talk about the fifteen minutes before or after the hour. For example, 8.15 is **quarter past** eight, and 8.45 is **quarter to** nine. In American English you can also say that 8.15 is a **quarter after** eight and 8.45 is a **quarter of** nine. **4** N-COUNT You can refer to the area in a town where a particular group of people live or work as a particular **quarter**. ❑ *...the Chinese quarter.* **5** N-COUNT If you talk about feelings or reactions from a certain **quarter**, you mean the feelings or reactions of a group of people, but you do not want to mention the names of the people. ❑ *Violence from this quarter has increased sharply.* **6** N-PLURAL You can refer to the room or rooms provided for a person such as a soldier to live in as that person's **quarters**. ❑ *...the officers' quarters.* **7** PHRASE If you do something **at close quarters**, you do it from a place that is very near to someone or something. ❑ *You can watch aircraft take off or land at close quarters.*

Word Partnership Use *quarter* with:

N.	quarter **(of a) century**, quarter **(of a) pound** **1**
ADJ.	**first/fourth/second/third** quarter **2**
PREP.	**for the** quarter, **in the** quarter **2** quarter **after**, quarter **of**, quarter **past**, quarter **to** **3**

quarterback /'kwɔ:təbæk/ (**quarterbacks**) N-COUNT In American football, a **quarterback** is the player on the attacking team who begins each play and decides which play to use.

,quarter-'final also **quarterfinal** (**quarter-finals**) N-COUNT A **quarter-final** is one of the four matches in a competition which decides which four players or teams will compete in the semi-final.

quarterly /'kwɔ:təli/ ADJ & ADV A **quarterly** event happens four times a year, at intervals of three months. ❑ *...the bank's latest quarterly report.* ❑ *Customers pay their bills on a quarterly basis.*

,quarter 'pounder (**quarter pounders**) N-COUNT A **quarter pounder** is a hamburger that weighs four ounces before it is cooked. Four ounces is a quarter of a pound.

quartet /kwɔ:'tet/ (**quartets**) **1** N-COUNT A **quartet** is a group of four people who play musical instruments or sing together. **2** N-COUNT A **quartet** is a piece of music for four instruments or four singers.

quartz /kwɔ:ts/ N-UNCOUNT **Quartz** is a kind of hard shiny crystal, used in making electronic equipment and very accurate watches and clocks.

quash /kwɒʃ/ (**quashes, quashing, quashed**) V-T If someone in authority **quashes** a decision or judgment, they officially reject it and it becomes no longer legally valid. ❑ *The band wanted to play in Russia in the 1980s, but their plans were quashed by the authorities.*

quay /ki:/ (**quays**) N-COUNT A **quay** is a long platform beside the sea or a river where boats can be tied.

queen /kwi:n/ (**queens**) **1** N-COUNT & N-TITLE A **queen** is a woman who rules a country as its monarch, or a woman who is married to a king. ❑ *...Queen Victoria.* ❑ *The king and queen left the country.* **2** N-COUNT In chess, the **queen** is the most powerful piece, which can be moved in any

direction. **3** N-COUNT A **queen** is a playing card with a picture of a queen on it. ❑ *...the queen of spades.*
→ see **chess**

queer /kwɪə/ (**queerer, queerest**) ADJ **Queer** means strange. [DATED] ❑ *There's something a bit queer going on.*

quell /kwel/ (**quells, quelling, quelled**) **1** V-T To **quell** opposition or violence means to stop it by using persuasion or force. ❑ *Troops eventually quelled the unrest.* **2** V-T If you **quell** unpleasant feelings, you stop yourself or other people from having these feelings. ❑ *The minister is trying to quell fears of an oil crisis.*

quench /kwentʃ/ (**quenches, quenching, quenched**) V-T When you are thirsty, you can **quench** your **thirst** by having a drink. ❑ *He stopped to quench his thirst at a stream.*

querulous /ˈkwerələs/ ADJ Someone who is **querulous** often complains about things. [FORMAL] ❑ *A querulous voice said, 'Are you going to order, or what?'*

query /ˈkwɪəri/ (**queries, querying, queried**) **1** N-VAR A **query** is a question about a particular point. ❑ *He is unable to answer queries personally.* **2** V-T If you **query** something, you check it by asking about it because you are not sure if it is correct. ❑ *No one queried my decision.* **3** V-T To **query** means to ask a question. ❑ *Reporters queried why he had two wives at the same time.*

quest /kwest/ (**quests**) N-COUNT A **quest** is a long and difficult search for something. ❑ *My quest for a better bank continues.*

question /ˈkwestʃən/ (**questions, questioning, questioned**) **1** N-COUNT A **question** is something which you say or write in order to ask about a particular matter. ❑ *He refused to answer further questions.* ❑ *They asked a lot of questions about China.* **2** V-T If you **question** someone, you ask them questions about something. ❑ *I questioned him on his adventures.* ● **questioner** (**questioners**) N-COUNT ❑ *He always looked questioners in the eye.* ● **questioning** N-UNCOUNT ❑ *The police have held thirty-two people for questioning.* **3** V-T If you **question** something, you express doubts about it. ❑ *They never question the doctor's decisions.* **4** N-UNCOUNT If there is some **question** about something, there is doubt about it. If something is **in question** or has been called **into question**, doubt has been expressed about it. ❑ *The club's spending policy is in question.* **5** N-COUNT A **question** is a problem or point which needs to be discussed. ❑ *The whole question of aid is a difficult one.* **6** N-COUNT The **questions** in an examination are the problems or topics which are set in order to test your knowledge or ability. ❑ *That question did come up on the test.* **7** PHRASE The time, place, person, or thing **in question** is the one you have just been talking about. ❑ *The player in question is Mark Williams.* **8** PHRASE If something is **out of the question**, it is impossible. ❑ *When I discovered that the dress cost six hundred pounds it was out of the question.* **9** PHRASE If you say **there is no question of** something happening, you are emphasizing that it is not going to happen. ❑ *There was no question of starting again.* **10** PHRASE If you do something **without question**, you do it without arguing or asking why it is necessary. ❑ *It was without question the best holiday we've ever had.*

Word Partnership Use *question* with:

V.	**answer a** question, **ask a** question, **beg the** question, **pose a** question, **raise a** question **1**
N.	**answer/response to a** question **1**
ADJ.	**difficult** question, **good** question, **important** question **1**

questionable /ˈkwestʃənəbəl/ ADJ If you say that something is **questionable**, you do not consider it to be completely honest or reasonable. ❑ *It was a questionable decision.*

ˈquestion ˌmark (**question marks**) N-COUNT A **question mark** is the punctuation mark (?) which is used in writing at the end of a question.
→ see **punctuation**

questionnaire /ˌkwestʃəˈneə, ˌkes-/ (**questionnaires**) N-COUNT A **questionnaire** is a written list of questions which are answered by a number of people in order to provide information for a report or survey. ❑ *Please fill in the questionnaire.*

queue /kjuː/ (**queues, queueing** or **queuing, queued**) **1** N-COUNT In British English, a **queue** is a line of people or vehicles that are waiting for something. The American word is **line**. ❑ *He got a tray and joined the queue.* **2** V-I & PHR-VERB In British English, when people **queue**, or when they **queue up**, they stand in a line waiting for something. The American term is **line up**.

quibble /ˈkwɪbəl/ (**quibbles, quibbling, quibbled**) **1** V-I When people **quibble**, they argue about a small matter which is not important. ❑ *It seems silly to quibble over such minor details.* **2** N-COUNT A **quibble** is a minor objection to something.

quick /kwɪk/ (**quicker, quickest**) **1** ADJ Someone or something that is **quick** moves or does things with great speed. ❑ *You'll have to be quick.* ❑ *He was a very quick learner.* ● **quickly** ADV ❑ *Stop me if I'm speaking too quickly.* ● **quickness** N-UNCOUNT ❑ *...the natural quickness of his mind.* **2** ADJ Something that is **quick** takes or lasts only a short time. ❑ *He took one last quick look about the room.* ● **quickly** ADV ❑ *You can become fitter than you are quite quickly.* **3** ADJ **Quick** means happening with very little delay. ❑ *They were quick to dismiss the rumours.* ❑ *...a quick end to the war.* ● **quickly** ADV ❑ *We need to get it back as quickly as possible.*

Thesaurus *quick* Also look up:

ADJ.	brisk, fast, rapid, speedy, swift; *(ant.)* slow **1**

Word Partnership Use *quick* with:

N.	quick **learner** **1**
	quick **glance**, quick **kiss**, quick **look**, quick **question**, quick **smile** **2**
	quick **action**, quick **profit**, quick **response**, quick **start**, quick **thinking** **3**
V.	**think** quick **3**

quicken /ˈkwɪkən/ (**quickens, quickening, quickened**) V-T/V-I If something **quickens**, or if you **quicken** it, it becomes faster or moves at a greater speed. ❑ *He quickened his pace a little.*

q

quid /kwɪd/

Quid is both the singular and the plural form.

N-COUNT A **quid** is a pound in money. [BRIT, INFORMAL] ❑ *It cost him five hundred quid.*

quiet /ˈkwaɪət/ (**quieter, quietest**) **1** ADJ Something or someone that is **quiet** makes only a small amount of noise. ❑ *Tania kept the children reasonably quiet.* ❑ *The street was unnaturally quiet.* ● **quietly** ADV ❑ *Two students whisper quietly to each other.* ● **quietness** N-UNCOUNT ❑ *...the smoothness and quietness of the flight.* **2** ADJ If a place, situation, or time is **quiet**, there is no excitement, activity, or trouble. ❑ *She wanted a quiet life.* ● **quietly** ADV ❑ *He lives quietly in the country.* ● **quietness** N-UNCOUNT ❑ *I appreciate the quietness and privacy here.* **3** ADJ AFTER LINK-V & N-UNCOUNT If you are **quiet**, you are not saying anything. You say there is **quiet** when no one is talking. ❑ *I told them to be quiet and go to sleep.* ❑ *He called for quiet.* ● **quietly** ADV ❑ *Amy stood quietly in the doorway watching him.* **4** PHRASE If you **keep quiet about** something, or if you **keep** something **quiet**, you do not say anything about it. ❑ *He denied the department had tried to keep the plan quiet.*

Word Partnership Use *quiet* with:

ADV.	**really** quiet, **relatively** quiet, **too** quiet, **very** quiet **1**–**3**
V.	**be** quiet, **keep** quiet **1** **4**
N.	**peace and** quiet, quiet **neighbourhood/street**, quiet **place/spot** **1** **2**
	quiet **day/evening/night**, quiet **life** **2**

quieten /ˈkwaɪətən/ (**quietens, quietening, quietened**) V-T/V-I If you **quieten** someone or something, or if they **quieten**, they become less noisy or less active. ❑ *A man shouted and the dogs suddenly quietened.*

quilt /kwɪlt/ (**quilts**) **1** N-COUNT A **quilt** is a bed-cover filled with warm soft material, which is often decorated with lines of stitching. **2** N-COUNT A **quilt** is the same as a **duvet**. [BRIT] → see Word Web: **quilt**

Q

quip /kwɪp/ (**quips, quipping, quipped**) V-I & N-COUNT To **quip** or to make a **quip** means to say something that is intended to be amusing or clever. [WRITTEN] ❑ *'He'll have to go on a diet,' Ballard quipped.*

quirk /kwɜːk/ (**quirks**) **1** N-COUNT A **quirk** is a habit or aspect of a person's character which is odd or unusual. **2** N-COUNT A **quirk** is a strange occurrence that is difficult to explain.

quirky /ˈkwɜːki/ (**quirkier, quirkiest**) ADJ Someone or something that is **quirky** is rather odd or unpredictable in their appearance, character, or behaviour. ❑ *...her quirky and original style.* ● **quirkiness** N-UNCOUNT ❑ *You will probably notice an element of quirkiness in his behaviour.*

quit /kwɪt/ (**quits, quitting, quit**) **1** V-T If you **quit** something, you leave it or you stop doing it. ❑ *She quit her job as a nurse eight years ago.* **2** PHRASE If you say you are going to **call it quits**, you mean that you have decided to stop doing something or being involved in something.

quite /kwaɪt/ **1** ADV You use **quite** to indicate that something is the case to a fairly great extent. **Quite** is less emphatic than 'very' and 'extremely'. ❑ *I felt quite bitter about it at the time.* ❑ *I was quite a long way away.* ❑ *I quite enjoy living here.* **2** ADV You use **quite** to indicate certainty or to emphasize that something is definitely the case. ❑ *It is quite clear that we were acting in self defence.* ❑ *I quite agree with you.* **3** ADV You use **quite** after a negative to weaken the force of your statement. ❑ *Something here is not quite right.* ❑ *I didn't quite understand what all this was about.* **4** PREDET You use **quite** in front of a noun group to emphasize that a person or thing is very impressive or unusual. ❑ *He's quite a character.* **5** ADV You can say **'quite'** to express your agreement with someone. [SPOKEN] ❑ *'And if you buy the book it's your choice isn't it?'—'Quite.'*

Usage

You can use **quite** in front of **a** or **an** when it is followed by an adjective plus noun. For example, you can say **'It's quite an old car'** as well as **'The car is quite old'**, and **'It was quite a warm day'** as well as **'The day was quite warm'**. Note that, in sentences like these, **quite** comes in front of the indefinite article. You cannot say, for example, **'It's a quite old car'**. **Quite** can be used to modify adjectives and adverbs, and is slightly stronger than **fairly** but less strong than **very**. **Quite** may suggest that something has more of a quality than expected. ❑ *Nobody here's ever heard of it but it is actually quite common.*

quiver /ˈkwɪvə/ (**quivers, quivering, quivered**) **1** V-I If something **quivers**, it shakes with very small movements. ❑ *Her bottom lip quivered.* **2** V-I & N-COUNT If you say that someone **is quivering with** an emotion such as rage or happiness, or if they feel a **quiver of** emotion, you mean that their appearance or voice clearly shows this emotion. ❑ *I recognized it instantly and felt a quiver of panic.*

quiz /kwɪz/ (**quizzes, quizzing, quizzed**) **1** N-COUNT A **quiz** is a game or competition in which someone tests your knowledge by asking you questions. **2** V-T If you **are quizzed** by someone about something, they ask you questions because they want to get information from you. ❑ *Four men were being quizzed by police.*

quota /ˈkwəʊtə/ (**quotas**) **1** N-COUNT A **quota** is the limited number or quantity which is officially allowed. ❑ *There is a quota of four tickets per person.* **2** N-COUNT Someone's **quota of** something is their expected or deserved share of it. ❑ *He eats the recommended quota of fruit and vegetables a day.*

quotation /kwəʊˈteɪʃən/ (**quotations**) **1** N-COUNT A **quotation** is a sentence or phrase taken from a book, poem, or play. **2** N-COUNT When someone gives you a **quotation**, they tell you how much they will charge to do a particular piece of work. [BRIT]

quoˈtation ˌmark (**quotation marks**) N-COUNT **Quotation marks** are punctuation marks used in writing to show where speech or a quotation begins and ends. They are usually written or printed as ('') and ("").

quote /kwəʊt/ (**quotes, quoting, quoted**) **1** V-T If you **quote** something, you repeat what someone has written or said. If you **quote** someone as saying something, you repeat what they have

Word Web quilt

The Hmong* tribes are famous for their colourful **quilts**. Many people think of a quilt as a bed covering. But these **textiles** feature pictures that tell stories about the people who made them. A favourite story shows how the Hmong fled from China to southeast Asia in the early 1800s. The story sometimes shows the quiltmaker arriving in a new country. The seamstress **sews** small pieces of colourful **fabric** together to make the **design**. The needlework is very complicated. It includes cross-stitching, **embroidery,** and appliqué. A common border **pattern** is a design that stands for mountains—the Hmong's original home.

Hmong: a group of people who live in the mountains of China, Vietnam, Laos, and Thailand.

written or said. ❑ *She quoted a line from a book by Romain Gary.* 2 V-T If you **quote** something such as a law or a fact, you state it because it supports what you are saying. ❑ *She quoted statistics to show how well the economy was doing.* 3 N-COUNT A **quote** from a book, poem, or play is a sentence or phrase from it. 4 V-T & N-COUNT If someone **quotes** you a price **for** doing something, or if they give you a **quote for** doing it, they say how much money they would charge you to do it. ❑ *He quoted a price for the repairs.* 5 N-PLURAL **Quotes** are the same as **quotation marks**. ❑ *The word 'remember' is in quotes.*

Thesaurus *quote* Also look up:

V. cite, recite, repeat 1 2
N. estimate, price 3

Rr

rabbi /'ræbaɪ/ (**rabbis**) N-COUNT & N-TITLE A **rabbi** is a Jewish religious leader.

rabbit

rabbit /'ræbɪt/ (**rabbits**) 1 N-COUNT A **rabbit** is a small furry animal with long ears which is often kept as a pet. 2 N-UNCOUNT **Rabbit** is the flesh of this animal eaten as food.

rabble /'ræbəl/ N-SING A **rabble** is a crowd of noisy disorganized people; used showing disapproval.

rabies /'reɪbiːz/ N-UNCOUNT **Rabies** is a serious infectious disease which humans can get from the bite of an animal such as a dog which has the disease.

race /reɪs/ (**races, racing, raced**) 1 N-COUNT A **race** is a competition to see who is the fastest, for example in running or driving. 2 V-T/V-I If you **race**, you take part in a race. ❑ *'I'll race you to the beach!' Chip called.* ❑ *I haven't raced against her this year.* 3 N-COUNT A **race** is a situation in which people or organizations compete with each other for power or control. ❑ *The race for the White House begins today.* 4 V-I If you **race** somewhere, you go there as quickly as possible. ❑ *He raced across town to the railway station.* 5 V-I If something **races**, it moves at a very fast rate. ❑ *Her heart raced.* 6 N-VAR A **race** is one of the major groups which human beings can be divided into according to their physical features, such as their skin colour. ❑ *...problems resulting from differences in race and religion.* 7 PHRASE You describe a situation as a **race against time** when you have to work very fast in order to do something before a particular time. 8 → see also **human race**

racecourse also **race course** /'reɪskɔːs/ (**racecourses**) N-COUNT In British English, a **racecourse** is a track on which horses race. The American word is **racetrack**.

racehorse also **race horse** /'reɪshɔːs/ (**racehorses**) N-COUNT A **racehorse** is a horse that is trained to run in races.

racer /'reɪsə/ (**racers**) 1 N-COUNT A **racer** is a person or animal that takes part in races. ❑ *He used to be a ski racer.* 2 N-COUNT A **racer** is a vehicle such as a car or bicycle that is designed to be used in races and therefore travels fast.

ˌrace re'lations N-PLURAL **Race relations** are the ways in which people of different races living together in the same community behave towards each other.

racetrack also **race track** /'reɪstræk/ (**racetracks**) N-COUNT A **racetrack** is a track for races.

racial /'reɪʃəl/ ADJ **Racial** describes things relating to people's race. ❑ *...the politics of racial minorities.* • **racially** ADV ❑ *The attack was not racially motivated.*

Word Partnership Use *racial* with:

N. racial **differences**, racial **discrimination**, racial **diversity**, racial **equality**, racial **groups**, racial **minorities**, racial **prejudice**, racial **tensions**

racing /'reɪsɪŋ/ N-UNCOUNT **Racing** refers to races between animals, especially horses, or between vehicles.
→ see **bicycle**

racist /'reɪsɪst/ (**racists**) N-COUNT & ADJ A **racist**, or a person with **racist** views, believes that people of some races are inferior to others. ❑ *...a gang of white racists.* ❑ *...dealing with a racist society.* • **racism** N-UNCOUNT ❑ *...the fight against racism.*

rack /ræk/ (**racks, racking, racked**)

The verb is also spelled **wrack** in American English.

1 N-COUNT A **rack** is a piece of equipment used for holding things or for hanging things on. ❑ *...a luggage rack.* ❑ *...racks of clothes.* 2 V-T If someone **is racked by** or **with** something, it causes them great suffering or pain. ❑ *His mother is racked with guilt.*

racket /'rækɪt/ (**rackets**)

The spelling **racquet** is also used in meaning 3.

racket

1 N-SING A **racket** is a loud unpleasant noise. ❑ *He makes such a racket.* 2 N-COUNT You can refer to an illegal activity used to make money as a **racket**. [INFORMAL] ❑ *...a drugs racket.* 3 N-COUNT A **racket** is an oval-shaped bat with strings across it which is used in games such as tennis.

racy /'reɪsi/ (**racier, raciest**) ADJ **Racy** writing or behaviour is lively and slightly shocking.

Word Link *rad ≈ ray : radar, radiant, radiation*

radar /'reɪdɑː/ N-UNCOUNT **Radar** is a way of discovering the position or speed of objects such as aircraft or ships by using radio signals.
→ see **bat, forecast**

radiant /'reɪdiənt/ 1 ADJ Someone who is **radiant** is so happy that their joy shows in their face. ❑ *The bride looked truly radiant.* • **radiance** N-UNCOUNT ❑ *There is a radiance to her smile.* 2 ADJ Something that is **radiant** glows brightly. ❑ *Out on the bay the morning is radiant.* • **radiance** N-UNCOUNT

❑ *...the radiance of early morning.*

radiate /'reɪdieɪt/ (**radiates, radiating, radiated**) **1** V-I If things **radiate from** a place, they form a pattern that spreads out like lines drawn from the centre of a circle to its edge. ❑ *...paths radiating from the centre.* **2** V-T/V-I If you **radiate** an emotion or quality or if it **radiates from** you, people can see it very clearly in your face and in your behaviour. ❑ *She radiates happiness.*

radiation /ˌreɪdi'eɪʃən/ **1** N-UNCOUNT **Radiation** is very small particles of a radioactive substance. Large amounts of radiation can cause illness and death. **2** N-UNCOUNT **Radiation** is energy, often in waves of heat or light, that comes from a particular source.
→ see **cancer, greenhouse effect, wave**

Word Partnership Use *radiation* with:

ADJ. **nuclear** radiation **1**
N. radiation **levels**, radiation **therapy/treatment** **1**
radiation **damage**, **effects of** radiation, **exposure to** radiation **1** **2**

radiator

radiator /'reɪdieɪtə/ (**radiators**) **1** N-COUNT A **radiator** is a hollow metal device which is connected to a central heating system and used to heat a room. **2** N-COUNT A car **radiator** is the part of the engine which is used to cool the engine.

radical /'rædɪkəl/ (**radicals**) **1** ADJ **Radical** changes and differences are very important and great in degree. ❑ *...radical economic reforms.* ● **radically** ADV ❑ *...radically different beliefs.* **2** N-COUNT & ADJ A **radical** or a person who has **radical** views believes that there should be great changes in society and tries to bring about these changes. ❑ *...radical politicians.*

radii /'reɪdiaɪ/ **Radii** is the plural of **radius**.

radio /'reɪdiəʊ/ (**radios, radioing, radioed**) **1** N-UNCOUNT **Radio** is the broadcasting of programmes for the public to listen to. You can refer to the programmes broadcast in this way as **the radio**. ❑ *He started his career working for local radio.* ❑ *She's been on the radio a lot recently.* **2** N-COUNT A **radio** is the piece of equipment used to listen to radio programmes. **3** N-UNCOUNT **Radio** is a system of sending sound over a distance using electrical signals. ❑ *They lost radio contact with the aircraft soon after take-off.* **4** N-COUNT A **radio** is a piece of equipment that is used for sending and receiving messages. **5** V-T/V-I If you **radio**, or **radio** someone, you send a message to them by radio. ❑ *The officer radioed for advice.*
→ see Word Web: **radio**
→ see **telescope, wave**

radioactive /ˌreɪdiəʊ'æktɪv/ ADJ Something that is **radioactive** contains a substance that produces energy in the form of powerful rays which are harmful in large doses. ❑ *...radioactive waste.* ● **radioactivity** /ˌreɪdiəʊæk'tɪvɪti/ N-UNCOUNT ❑ *...low levels of radioactivity.*

radius /'reɪdiəs/ (**radii** /'reɪdiaɪ/) **1** N-SING The **radius** around a point is the distance from it in any direction. ❑ *Nigel is looking for work in a ten-mile radius around his home.* **2** N-COUNT The **radius** of a circle is the distance from its centre to its outside edge.
→ see **area**

RAF /ˌɑːr eɪ 'ef, ræf/ N-PROPER **The RAF** is the air force of the United Kingdom. **RAF** is an abbreviation for 'Royal Air Force'.

raffle /'ræfəl/ (**raffles**) N-COUNT A **raffle** is a competition in which you buy numbered tickets. Afterwards some numbers are chosen and if your ticket has one of these numbers on it, you win a prize.

raft /rɑːft, ræft/ (**rafts**) **1** N-COUNT A **raft** is a floating platform made from large pieces of wood tied together. **2** N-COUNT A **raft** is a small inflatable rubber or plastic boat. **3** N-COUNT A **raft of** people or things is a lot of them. ❑ *He has a raft of advisers around him.*

rafter /'rɑːftə, 'ræf-/ (**rafters**) N-COUNT **Rafters** are the sloping pieces of wood that support a roof.

rag /ræg/ (**rags**) **1** N-VAR A **rag** is a piece of old cloth which you can use to clean or wipe things. ❑ *...dry it with a rag.* **2** N-PLURAL **Rags** are old torn clothes. ❑ *...small children, some dressed in rags.* **3** N-COUNT People refer to a newspaper as a **rag** when they have a low opinion of it. [INFORMAL] ❑ *I've read all about it in the local rag.*

rage /reɪdʒ/ (**rages, raging, raged**) **1** N-VAR **Rage** is strong, uncontrollable anger. ❑ *I flew into a rage.* ❑ *...a fit of rage.* **2** V-I You say that something powerful or unpleasant **rages** when it continues with great force or violence. ❑ *The fire raged for more than four hours.* ● **raging** ADJ BEFORE N ❑ *...a raging river.* **3** V-I If you **rage** about something, you speak or think very angrily about it. ❑ *He began to rage against his bad luck.*
→ see **anger**

r

Word Web radio

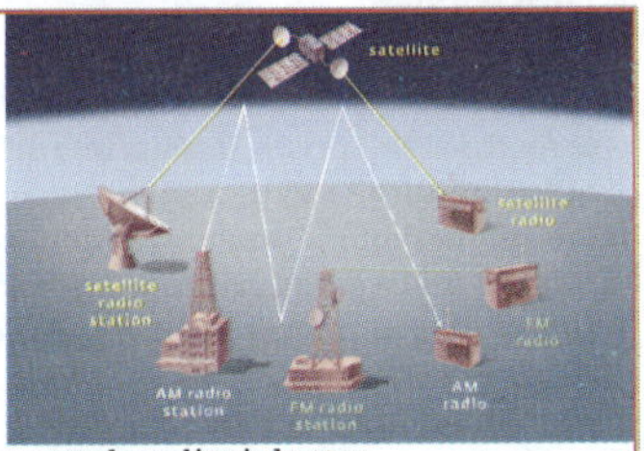

Radio's first use was for **communication** between ships. Ships also radioed **stations** on land. In 1912, the *Titanic* sank in the North Atlantic with over 2,000 people on board. A radio call to a nearby ship helped save a third of the passengers. What we call a radio is actually a **receiver**. The **waves** it receives come from a **transmitter**. Radio is an important source of **entertainment**. AM radio has many kinds of radio **programmes**. **Listeners** often prefer musical programs on the FM waveband or from **satellites** because the sound quality is better.

Thesaurus *rage* Also look up:
N. anger, frenzy, madness, tantrum 1
V. fume, scream, yell 3

ragged /ˈrægɪd/ 1 ADJ **Ragged** clothes are old and torn. If someone is **ragged**, they are wearing old torn clothing. ❑ *Ragged children played in the streets.* 2 ADJ You can say that something is **ragged** when it is uneven or untidy. ❑ *The men formed a ragged line.*

raid /reɪd/ (**raids, raiding, raided**) 1 V-T & N-COUNT When soldiers or the police **raid** a place, they enter it by force to attack it, or to look for someone or something. This action is called a **raid**. ❑ *Thirty policemen raided a house in East London.* ● **raider** (**raiders**) N-COUNT ❑ *The raiders continued to destroy American air and sea forces.* 2 V-T & N-COUNT If someone **raids** a building or place, they enter it by force in order to steal something. This action is called a **raid**. [BRIT] ❑ *A 19-year-old man has been found guilty of raiding a bank.* ● **raider** N-COUNT ❑ *The raiders escaped with cash and mobile phones.*

rail /reɪl/ (**rails**) 1 N-COUNT A **rail** is a horizontal bar which is fixed to something and used as a fence or a support, or to hang things on. ❑ *She held on to the hand rail in the lift.* ❑ *...curtain rail.* 2 N-COUNT **Rails** are the steel bars which trains run on. 3 N-UNCOUNT If you travel or send something **by rail**, you travel or send it on a train. ❑ *The president travelled by rail to his home town.* ❑ *...the electric rail link between Manchester and Sheffield.*
→ see **train, transportation**

railing /ˈreɪlɪŋ/ (**railings**) N-COUNT A fence made from metal bars is called a **railing** or **railings**.

railroad /ˈreɪlrəʊd/ (**railroads**) N-COUNT In American English, a **railroad** is the same as a **railway**.

railway /ˈreɪlweɪ/ (**railways**) 1 N-COUNT A **railway** is a route between two places along which trains travel on steel rails. [BRIT] 2 N-COUNT A **railway** is a company or organization that operates railway routes. [BRIT] ❑ *The French national railway is called the SNCF.*
→ see **train**

R

rain /reɪn/ (**rains, raining, rained**) 1 N-UNCOUNT **Rain** is water that falls from the clouds in small drops. ❑ *I hope you didn't get too wet standing out in the rain.* 2 V-I When rain falls, you can say that **it is raining**. ❑ *It rained all weekend.* 3 V-T/V-I & PHR-VERB If things **rain on** a person or place, or if they **rain down**, they fall on that person or place in large quantities. ❑ *In Calcutta yesterday plastic bottles rained on to the pitch from the crowd.* ❑ *Pieces of the plane rained down on the crowd.*
→ see **disaster, storm, water**
▶ **rain off** PHR-VERB If a sports match **is rained off**, it cannot take place because of the rain.

Thesaurus *rain* Also look up:
N. drizzle, shower, sleet 1

rainbow /ˈreɪnbəʊ/ (**rainbows**) N-COUNT A **rainbow** is the arch of different colours that you sometimes see in the sky when it is raining.
→ see Word Web: **rainbow**

raincoat /ˈreɪnkəʊt/ (**raincoats**) N-COUNT A **raincoat** is a waterproof coat.
→ see **clothing**

raindrop /ˈreɪndrɒp/ (**raindrops**) N-COUNT A **raindrop** is a single drop of rain.

rainfall /ˈreɪnfɔːl/ N-UNCOUNT **Rainfall** is the amount of rain that falls in a place during a particular period of time. ❑ *People are worried by the low level of rainfall this year.*
→ see **erosion, habitat, storm**

rainforest /ˈreɪnfɒrɪst, AM -fɔːr-/ (**rainforests**) N-VAR A **rainforest** is a thick forest of tall trees found in tropical areas where there is a lot of rain.
→ see **habitat**

rainy /ˈreɪni/ (**rainier, rainiest**) ADJ If it is **rainy**, it is raining a lot. ❑ *...one rainy night in Seattle.*

raise /reɪz/ (**raises, raising, raised**) 1 V-T If you **raise** something, you move it to a higher position. ❑ *She went to the window and raised the blinds.* ❑ *He raised his hand.* ❑ *...a small raised platform.* 2 V-T If you **raise** the rate or level of something, you increase it. ❑ *The Republic of Ireland is expected to raise interest rates.* 3 V-T To **raise** the standard of something means to improve it. ❑ *We must raise the standard of teaching in England and Wales.* 4 V-T If you **raise** your voice, you speak more loudly. 5 V-T If an event **raises** a particular emotion or question, it makes people feel the emotion or consider the question. ❑ *The news has raised hopes that the war may end soon.* 6 V-T If you **raise** a subject, objection, or question, you mention it or bring it to someone's attention. ❑ *He never raised the idea of marriage with me.* 7 N-COUNT In American English, a **raise** is an increase in your wages or salary. The British word is **rise**. 8 V-T To **raise** money **for** a particular cause means to get people to donate money towards it. 9 V-T To **raise** a child means to look after it until it is grown up. 10 V-T To **raise** a particular type of animal or crop means to breed the animal or grow

Word Web rainbow

Sunlight contains all colours. When a **ray** of sunlight passes through a **prism**, it splits into different colours. This is also what happens when light passes through the drops of water in the air. The light is refracted, and we see a **rainbow**. The colours of the rainbow are **red, orange, yellow, green, blue, indigo**, and **violet**. One tradition says that there is a pot of gold at the end of the rainbow. Other myths say that the rainbow is a bridge between Earth and the land of the gods.

the crop. ❑ *They raise sheep for meat, skins, and wool.*

Usage

You should be careful not to confuse the verbs **raise** and **rise**. **Raise** is a transitive verb and means 'to put or push something up', whereas **rise** is an intransitive verb and means 'to go up by itself'. **Rise** can also not be used in the passive. ❑ *...the government's decision to raise prices.* ❑ *The number of dead is likely to rise.*

raisin /ˈreɪzən/ (**raisins**) N-COUNT **Raisins** are dried grapes.

rake /reɪk/ (**rakes, raking, raked**) **1** N-COUNT A **rake** is a garden tool consisting of a row of metal teeth attached to a long handle. **2** V-T To **rake** leaves or soil means to use a rake to gather the leaves or to make the soil smooth.
→ see **hose**

rake

▶ **rake in** PHR-VERB If someone **is raking in** money, they are earning a lot of it fairly easily. [INFORMAL] ❑ *He raked in £33,000 profit from his shares.*

rally /ˈræli/ (**rallies, rallying, rallied**) **1** N-COUNT A **rally** is a large public meeting held in support of something such as a political party. ❑ *...an election rally.* **2** N-COUNT A **rally** is a competition in which vehicles are driven over public roads. ❑ *...a successful rally driver.* **3** V-T/V-I When people **rally to** something or when something **rallies** them, they unite to support it. ❑ *He tried to rally his supporters.* **4** V-I When someone or something **rallies**, they begin to recover or improve after having been weak. ❑ *Over the next week, Brian began to rally, improving each day.*

▶ **rally around** or **rally round** PHR-VERB When people **rally around** or **rally round**, they work as a group in order to support someone at a difficult time. ❑ *Connie's friends rallied round her.*

Word Partnership Use *rally* with:

ADJ.	**political** rally **1**
N.	**campaign** rally, **protest** rally, rally **in support of** ***someone/something*** **1**
	prices/stocks rally **4**
PREP.	rally **behind** ***someone/something*** **3**

ram /ræm/ (**rams, ramming, rammed**) **1** V-T If one vehicle **rams** another, it crashes into it with a lot of force. **2** V-T If you **ram** something somewhere, you push it there with great force. ❑ *He rammed the key into the lock.* **3** N-COUNT A **ram** is an adult male sheep.

ramble /ˈræmbəl/ (**rambles, rambling, rambled**) **1** V-I & N-COUNT If you **ramble**, or if you go on a **ramble**, you go on a long walk in the countryside. ❑ *...an hour's ramble through the woods.* ● **rambler** (**ramblers**) N-COUNT ❑ *...a popular route for ramblers.* **2** V-I & PHR-VERB If someone **rambles**, or if they **ramble on**, they talk for a long time in a confused way. ❑ *She began rambling on about her childhood.*

ramification /ˌræmɪfɪˈkeɪʃən/ (**ramifications**) N-COUNT The **ramifications of** a decision or event are all its consequences and effects, especially ones which were not obvious at first. ❑ *...the political ramifications of the riots.*

ramp /ræmp/ (**ramps**) N-COUNT A **ramp** is a sloping surface between two places that are at different levels. ❑ *I pushed her wheelchair up the ramp.*
→ see **traffic**

rampage (**rampages, rampaging, rampaged**)

verb /ræmˈpeɪdʒ/; phrase /ˈræmpeɪdʒ/.

V-I & PHRASE If people or animals **rampage** through a place, or if they **go on the rampage** through a place, they rush about in a wild or violent way, causing damage or destruction. ❑ *Hundreds of fans went on the rampage after the match.*

rampant /ˈræmpənt/ ADJ If a situation or activity that people do not want or like is **rampant**, it is growing or spreading in an uncontrolled way. ❑ *...rampant corruption.*

ramshackle /ˈræmʃækəl/ ADJ A **ramshackle** building is badly made or in a very bad condition.

ran /ræn/ **Ran** is the past tense of **run**.

ranch /rɑːntʃ, ræntʃ/ (**ranches**) N-COUNT A **ranch** is a large farm used for raising animals.

random /ˈrændəm/ ADJ & PHRASE Something that is done or chosen in a **random** way, or **at random**, is done or chosen without a definite plan or pattern. ❑ *...a random sample of 930 women.* ❑ *Names were selected at random by computer.* ● **randomly** ADV ❑ *The two runners were randomly chosen for testing.*

R&R N-UNCOUNT **R&R** refers to time that you spend relaxing, when you are not working. **R&R** is an abbreviation for 'rest and recreation'. ❑ *Our holiday homes are just the thing for serious R&R.*

rang /ræŋ/ **Rang** is the past tense of some meanings of **ring**.

range /reɪndʒ/ (**ranges, ranging, ranged**) **1** N-COUNT A **range of** things is a number of different things of the same general kind. ❑ *...a wide range of furniture including dining chairs and tables.* ❑ *...worries over a range of environmental issues.* **2** N-COUNT A **range** is the complete group that is included between two points on a scale of measurement or quality. ❑ *The age range is from eighteen to forty.* ❑ *There are not many houses available in that price range.* **3** N-COUNT The **range of** something is the maximum area within which it can reach things or detect things. ❑ *...a radio with a range of 2 miles.* ❑ *...sounds that are within the human range of hearing.* **4** V-I If things **range between** two points or **range from** one point **to** another, they vary within these points on a scale of measurement or quality. ❑ *They range in price from $3 to $15.* **5** V-T If people or things **are ranged** somewhere, they are arranged in a row or in lines. [FORMAL] ❑ *Wooden chairs were ranged against one wall.* **6** N-COUNT A **range of** mountains or hills is a line of them. **7** N-COUNT A rifle **range** or a firing **range** is a place where people can shoot at targets. **8** PHRASE If something is **in range** or **within range**, it is near enough to be reached or detected. If it is **out of range**, it is too far away to be reached or detected. ❑ *...within range of their aircraft.* ❑ *The fish stayed 50 yards offshore, well out of range.* **9** PHRASE If you see or hit something **at close range**, or **from close range**, you are very close to it when you see it or hit it. ❑ *...photographing wild animals from close range.*
→ see **graph**

r

Word Partnership Use *range* with:

ADJ. **broad** range, **limited** range, **narrow** range, **wide** range 1
full range, **normal** range, **whole** range 2
N. range **of emotions**, range **of possibilities** 1
age range, **price** range, **temperature** range 2

ranger /ˈreɪndʒə/ (**rangers**) N-COUNT A **ranger** is a person whose job is to look after a forest or park.

rank /ræŋk/ (**ranks, ranking, ranked**) 1 N-VAR Someone's **rank** is their position in an organization, or in society. ❑ *...the rank of captain.* ❑ *...a person of high rank.* 2 V-T/V-I When someone or something **is ranked** a particular position, they are at that position on a scale. ❑ *The British player ranks 20th in the world.* ❑ *...a scientist whose work ranked with that of Einstein.* 3 N-PLURAL **The ranks** are the ordinary members of an organization, especially of the armed forces. ❑ *...an army general who has risen from the ranks.* 4 N-PLURAL When you become a member of a large group of people, you can say that you are joining its **ranks**. ❑ *He soon joined the ranks of the unemployed.* 5 ADJ You can describe something as **rank** when it has a strong and unpleasant smell. [LITERARY] ❑ *...the rank smell of unwashed skin.* 6 N-COUNT A taxi **rank** is a place where taxis park and wait to be hired. 7 PHRASE If a member of a group or organization **breaks ranks**, they disobey the instructions of their group or organization. 8 PHRASE If the members of a group **close ranks**, they support each other in a united way to oppose any attack or criticism.

Word Partnership Use *rank* with:

PREP. rank **above**, rank **below** 1
ADJ. **high** rank, **top** rank 1 2
ADV. rank **high** 2

ˌrank and ˈfile N-SING **The rank and file of** an organization are the ordinary members of an organization, rather than the leaders. ❑ *They did not ask the rank and file of the organization whether they agreed.*

R

ransack /ˈrænsæk/ (**ransacks, ransacking, ransacked**) V-T If people **ransack** a building or a room, they disturb everything in it and leave it in a mess, often because they are looking for something. ❑ *The thieves ransacked the house.*

ransom /ˈrænsəm/ (**ransoms**) 1 N-VAR A **ransom** is money that is demanded as payment for the return of someone who has been kidnapped. ❑ *The kidnappers are demanding a ransom of five million dollars.* 2 PHRASE If a kidnapper **holds** someone **to ransom**, they keep that person prisoner until they are given what they want.

rant /rænt/ (**rants, ranting, ranted**) V-I & N-COUNT If someone **rants**, or if they have a **rant**, they talk in a loud, excited, and angry way. ❑ *...a rant against the meat industry.* ● **ranting** (**rantings**) N-VAR ❑ *He had been listening to the man's rantings all night.*

rap /ræp/ (**raps, rapping, rapped**) 1 N-VAR & V-I **Rap** is a type of music in which the words are not sung but are spoken in a rapid, rhythmic way. Someone who **raps** performs rap. ● **rapper** (**rappers**) N-COUNT ❑ *...the French rapper MC Solaar.* 2 V-T/V-I & N-COUNT If you **rap on** something or **rap** it, you hit it with a series of quick blows. A **rap** is a quick hit or knock on something. ❑ *Mike rapped the table.* ❑ *There was a rap on the door.*

rape /reɪp/ (**rapes, raping, raped**) V-T & N-VAR If someone **is raped**, they are forced to have sex against their will. **Rape** is the crime of forcing someone to have sex. ❑ *She hated the man who had raped her.* ● **rapist** (**rapists**) N-COUNT ❑ *The judge gave the rapist five years in prison.*

rapid /ˈræpɪd/ ADJ If something is **rapid**, it happens or moves very quickly. ❑ *His heart rate was unusually rapid.* ● **rapidly** ADV ❑ *...Queensland's rapidly increasing population.* ● **rapidity** /rəˈpɪdɪti/ N-UNCOUNT ❑ *The rapidity with which the weather can change is amazing.*

Thesaurus *rapid* Also look up:

ADJ. fast, speedy, swift; (*ant.*) slow

Word Partnership Use *rapid* with:

N. rapid **change**, rapid **decline**, rapid **development**, rapid **expansion**, rapid **growth**, rapid **increase**, rapid **pace**, rapid **progress**, rapid **pulse**

rapids /ˈræpɪdz/ N-PLURAL **Rapids** are parts of a river where the water moves very fast.

rapport /ræˈpɔː/ N-UNCOUNT **Rapport** is a feeling of understanding and sympathy between two or more people. ❑ *...the extraordinary rapport between the two leaders.*

rapture /ˈræptʃə/ (**raptures**) N-VAR **Rapture** is a feeling of extreme joy or pleasure. [LITERARY] ❑ *They were in raptures over the French countryside.*

rapturous /ˈræptʃərəs/ ADJ A **rapturous** feeling or reaction is one of great happiness or enthusiasm. ● **rapturously** ADV ❑ *The performance was received rapturously by the audience.*

rare /reə/ (**rarer, rarest**) 1 ADJ If something is **rare**, it is not common, and is therefore interesting, valuable, or unusual. ❑ *...rare trees and plants.* ❑ *It was rare for him to eat alone.* 2 ADJ Meat that is **rare** is cooked very lightly so that the inside is still red.

rarely /ˈreəli/ ADV **Rarely** means not very often. ❑ *I very rarely wear a raincoat.*

rarity /ˈreərɪti/ (**rarities**) 1 N-COUNT If someone or something is a **rarity**, they are interesting or valuable because they are so unusual. ❑ *Cars are a rarity here.* 2 N-UNCOUNT The **rarity** of something is the fact that it is very uncommon. ❑ *The book was expensive due to its rarity and good condition.*

rash /ræʃ/ (**rasher, rashest, rashes**) 1 ADJ If someone is **rash** or does **rash** things, they act without thinking carefully first. ❑ *I don't want to make any rash decisions.* ● **rashly** ADV ❑ *I made some money, but I rashly gave it away.* 2 N-COUNT A **rash** is an area of red spots on your skin which appear when you are ill or have an allergy. 3 N-SING A **rash of** events or things is a large number of them that all happen or appear within a short period of time. ❑ *...a rash of violent attacks.*

rasp /rɑːsp, ræsp/ (**rasps, rasping, rasped**) 1 V-T/V-I & N-SING If someone **rasps**, their voice or breathing is harsh and unpleasant to listen to. A **rasp** is this sound. ❑ *'Where did you put it?' he rasped.* ❑ *...the rasp of Rennie's voice.* 2 V-I & N-SING If something **rasps**, it makes a harsh, unpleasant sound as it rubs against something hard or rough. A **rasp** is this sound. ❑ *The key rasped in the lock and the door swung open.* ❑ *...the rasp of the animal's claws on wood.*

raspberry /ˈrɑːzbri, AM ˈræzberi/ (**raspberries**) N-COUNT A **raspberry** is a small, soft, red fruit that grows on bushes.

rat /ræt/ (**rats**) N-COUNT A **rat** is an animal which has a long tail and looks like a large mouse. ❑ *...a laboratory experiment with rats.*

rate /reɪt/ (**rates, rating, rated**) 1 N-COUNT The **rate** at which something happens is the speed or frequency with which it happens. ❑ *...the rate at which hair grows.* ❑ *New diet books appear at a rate of nearly one a week.* 2 N-COUNT A **rate** is the amount of money that is charged for goods or services. ❑ *...cheap rates for travellers using Gatwick Airport.* 3 N-COUNT The **rate** of taxation or interest is its level, expressed as a percentage. ❑ *The richest Americans pay taxes at a rate of 28%.* 4 V-T If you **rate** someone or something as good or bad, you consider them to be good or bad. ❑ *The film was rated excellent.* 5 → see also **rating** 6 PHRASE You use **at any rate** to indicate that the important thing is what you are going to say now, and not what was said before. ❑ *Well, at any rate, let me thank you for all you did.* 7 PHRASE If you say that **at this rate** something bad or extreme will happen, you mean that it will happen if things continue to develop as they have been doing. ❑ *At this rate they wouldn't get home before eight.*
→ see **motion**

Word Partnership Use *rate* with:

N.	**birth** rate, rate **of change**, **crime** rate, **heart** rate, **pulse** rate, **survival** rate, **unemployment** rate 1
	interest rate 3
ADJ.	**average** rate, **faster** rate, **slow** rate, **steady** rate 1
	high rate, **low** rate 1–3

rather /ˈrɑːðə, ˈræð-/ 1 PREP & CONJ You use **rather than** when you are contrasting two things or situations. **Rather than** introduces the thing or situation that is not the case or that you do not want or approve of. ❑ *I tend to use the bike rather than the car.* ❑ *She made students think for themselves, rather than telling them everything.* 2 ADV You use **rather** to introduce a correction or contrast to what you have just said. ❑ *Twenty million years ago, Colorado was not a dry place. Rather, it was warm and damp.* 3 PHRASE If you **would rather** do something, you would prefer to do it. ❑ *Kids would rather play than study.* 4 → See note at **prefer** 5 ADV You use **rather** to indicate that something is true to a fairly great extent. ❑ *...a rather unusual situation.* 6 ADV You use **rather** before verbs that introduce your thoughts and feelings, in order to express your opinion politely, especially when a different opinion has been expressed. [BRIT] ❑ *I rather think he was telling the truth.*

Usage

Rather, pretty, quite, and **fairly** can all be used to modify adjectives and adverbs, but are all less strong than **very. Rather** and **pretty** are the strongest of these words and are the closest to **very. Pretty**, in this sense, is informal. Therefore, if you said to someone, '**Your work is rather good**' or '**Your work is pretty good**', they would be more likely to be pleased than if you said '**Your work is quite good**' or '**Your work is fairly good**'. However, **rather** is commonly used with words indicating negative qualities. ❑ *I was feeling rather sad.* It is the only one of these words that can be used with comparatives, and with **too**. ❑ *Global warming could be rather worse than we think it will be.* ❑ *He was becoming rather too friendly with my ex-boyfriend.* **Quite** is slightly stronger than **fairly**, and may suggest that something has more of a quality than expected. ❑ *Nobody here's ever heard of it but it is actually quite common.*

ratify /ˈrætɪfaɪ/ (**ratifies, ratifying, ratified**) V-T When national leaders or organizations **ratify** a treaty or written agreement, they make it official by giving their formal approval to it, usually by signing it or voting for it. ● **ratification** /ˌrætɪfɪˈkeɪʃən/ (**ratifications**) N-COUNT ❑ *...the ratification of the treaty.*

rating /ˈreɪtɪŋ/ (**ratings**) N-COUNT A **rating** of something is a score or assessment of how good or popular it is. ❑ *A student with 95% in the examination scored a rating of five.*

Word Partnership Use *rating* with:

N.	**approval** rating
ADJ.	**high** rating, **low** rating, **poor** rating, **top** rating

ratio /ˈreɪʃiəʊ, AM -ʃəʊ/ (**ratios**) N-COUNT The **ratio** of something is the relationship between two things expressed in numbers or amounts, to show how much greater one is than the other. ❑ *The adult to child ratio is 1 to 6.*

ration /ˈræʃən/ (**rations, rationing, rationed**) 1 N-COUNT When there is a shortage of something, your **ration** of it is the amount that you are allowed to have. ❑ *Families get a ration of tea, oil, sugar and rice.* 2 V-T When something **is rationed**, you are only allowed to have a limited amount of it. ❑ *Motorists will be rationed to thirty litres of petrol a month.* ● **rationing** N-UNCOUNT ❑ *Tea rationing ended in Britain in 1952.* 3 N-PLURAL **Rations** are the food which is given to people who do not have enough food or to soldiers.

Word Link *ratio ≈ reasoning : irrational, rational, rationale*

rational /ˈræʃənəl/ 1 ADJ **Rational** decisions and thoughts are based on reason rather than on emotion. ❑ *He is incapable of making a rational decision.* ● **rationally** ADV ❑ *We discussed it rationally.* 2 ADJ A **rational** person is someone who thinks clearly and is not emotionally or mentally unbalanced. ❑ *Rachel looked calmer and more rational now.*

r

Word Partnership Use *rational* with:

N. rational **approach**, rational **choice**, rational **decision**, rational **explanation** 1
rational **human being**, rational **person** 2

Word Link *ratio ≈ reasoning : irrational, rational, rationale*

rationale /ˌræʃəˈnɑːl, -ˈnæl/ (**rationales**) N-COUNT The **rationale for** a course of action or a belief is the set of reasons on which it is based. ❑ *Their rationale was 'where learning is fun, it is done better'.*

rationalist /ˈræʃənəlɪst/ (**rationalists**) N-COUNT & ADJ A **Rationalist**, or a person with **rationalist** views, believes that their life should be based on reason and logic, rather than emotions or religious beliefs. ● **rationalism** N-UNCOUNT ❑ *...the rationalism of Western culture.*

rationalize [BRIT also **rationalise**] /ˈræʃənəlaɪz/ (**rationalizes, rationalizing, rationalized**) 1 V-T If you try to **rationalize** attitudes or actions that are difficult to accept, you think of reasons to justify or explain them. ❑ *I tried to rationalize my feelings.* ● **rationalization** /ˌræʃənəlaɪˈzeɪʃən/ (**rationalizations**) N-VAR ❑ *...the rationalization of middle-class values.* 2 V-T When a company, system, or industry **is rationalized**, it is made more efficient, usually by getting rid of staff and equipment. ● **rationalization** N-UNCOUNT ❑ *...the rationalization of the textile industry.*

rationing /ˈræʃənɪŋ/ → see **ration**

rattle /ˈrætəl/ (**rattles, rattling, rattled**) 1 V-T/V-I & N-COUNT When something **rattles**, or when you **rattle** it, it makes short sharp knocking sounds because it is being shaken or it keeps hitting against something hard. A **rattle** is this noise. ❑ *A train rattled by.* ❑ *...the rattle of gunfire.* 2 N-COUNT A **rattle** is a baby's toy with loose bits inside which make a noise when the baby shakes it. 3 V-T If something or someone **rattles** you, they make you nervous. ❑ *The question really rattled her.* ● **rattled** ADJ ❑ *His supporters seem a bit rattled.* ▸ **rattle off** PHR-VERB If you **rattle off** something, you say it or do it very quickly and without much effort. ❑ *He rattled off the names.*

R

raucous /ˈrɔːkəs/ ADJ A **raucous** sound is loud, harsh, and rather unpleasant. ❑ *...the raucous cries of the sea-birds.* ● **raucously** ADV ❑ *They laughed together raucously.*

ravage /ˈrævɪdʒ/ (**ravages, ravaging, ravaged**) V-T A town, country, or economy that **has been ravaged** has been damaged so much that it is almost completely destroyed. ❑ *The country has been ravaged by civil war.*

ravages /ˈrævɪdʒiz/ N-PLURAL **The ravages of** time, war, or the weather are the damaging effects that they have. ❑ *...the ravages of winter.*

rave /reɪv/ (**raves, raving, raved**) 1 V-T/V-I If someone **raves**, they talk in an excited and uncontrolled way. ❑ *What is wrong with you, acting like that?' she raved.* ❑ *I saw a picture of him raving at a referee.* 2 V-I If you **rave about** something, you speak or write about it with great enthusiasm. ❑ *Rachel raved about Japanese food after her holiday to Japan.* 3 N-COUNT A **rave** or a **rave review** is a very enthusiastic review. ❑ *The new restaurant had rave reviews.* 4 N-COUNT A **rave** is a large musical event in a club or in the open air which attracts people who like dancing to modern, electronic, dance music. 5 → see also **raving**

raven /ˈreɪvən/ (**ravens**) 1 N-COUNT A **raven** is a large bird with shiny black feathers and a deep harsh call. 2 ADJ **Raven** hair is shiny, black, and smooth. [WRITTEN]

ravine /rəˈviːn/ (**ravines**) N-COUNT A **ravine** is a very deep narrow valley with steep sides.

raving /ˈreɪvɪŋ/ ADJ & ADV You use **raving** to describe someone who you think is completely mad. [INFORMAL] ❑ *Malcolm looked at her as if she was a raving lunatic.* ❑ *Jean-Paul has gone raving mad.*

raw /rɔː/ 1 ADJ A **raw** substance is in its natural state before being processed. ❑ *The ships were carrying raw sugar from Cuba.* 2 ADJ **Raw** food has not been cooked or has not been cooked enough. ❑ *...a popular dish made of raw fish.* 3 ADJ If a part of your body is **raw**, it is red and painful because the skin has been damaged. 4 ADJ If you describe someone in a new job as **raw**, or as a **raw** recruit, you mean that they lack experience in that job. ❑ *Davies is still raw but looks as if he will do well in the future.* 5 PHRASE If you say that you are getting **a raw deal**, you mean that you are being treated unfairly. [INFORMAL]

Thesaurus *raw* Also look up:

ADJ. natural 1
fresh; (*ant.*) cooked 2
scraped, skinned 3

ray /reɪ/ (**rays**) 1 N-COUNT **Rays** of light are narrow beams of light. 2 N-SING A **ray of** hope, comfort, or other positive quality is a small amount that makes a bad situation seem less bad. ❑ *The drug is a ray of hope for the 500,000 victims of Alzheimer's disease in Britain today.*
→ see **rainbow, telescope**

razor /ˈreɪzə/ (**razors**) N-COUNT A **razor** is a tool that people use for shaving.

Rd **Rd** is a written abbreviation for 'road'. ❑ *...100 Euston Rd, London, NW1 2AJ.*

-'re **-'re** is a shortened form of 'are' that is used in spoken English and in informal written English. ❑ *We're not, are we?* ❑ *What're you going to do?* ❑ *People're working on that now.*

reach /riːtʃ/ (**reaches, reaching, reached**) 1 V-T When someone or something **reaches** a place, they arrive there. ❑ *He did not stop running until he reached the door.* 2 V-I If you **reach** somewhere, you move your arm and hand to take or touch something. ❑ *Judy reached into her handbag.* 3 V-T If you can **reach** something, you are able to touch it by stretching out your arm or leg. ❑ *Can you reach your toes with your fingertips?* 4 V-T If you try to **reach** someone, you try to contact them, usually by telephone. ❑ *Has the doctor told you how to reach him in emergencies?* 5 V-T If someone or something **has reached** a certain stage or amount, they are at that stage or amount. ❑ *The figure could reach 100,000 next year.* 6 V-T/V-I If something **reaches** a place or level, it extends as far as that place or level. ❑ *...a nightshirt which reached to his knees.* ❑ *She has blonde hair that reaches her waist.* 7 V-T When people **reach** an agreement or compromise, they succeed in achieving it. ❑ *They are meeting in Lusaka in an attempt to reach an agreement.*

Word Partnership Use *reach* with:

N. reach **a destination** 1
reach **a goal**, reach ***one's* potential** 5
reach **(an) agreement**, reach **a compromise**, reach **a conclusion**, reach **a consensus**, reach **a decision** 7

react /ri'ækt/ (**reacts, reacting, reacted**) 1 V-I When you **react to** something that has happened to you, you behave in a particular way because of it. ❑ *They reacted violently to the news.* ❑ *The victims' families reacted with anger and disbelief.* 2 V-I If you **react against** someone's way of behaving, you deliberately behave in a different way. ❑ *My father never saved money and perhaps I reacted against that. I save as much as I can.* 3 V-I If you **react to** a treatment or substance, you are affected unpleasantly or made ill by it. ❑ *He reacted very badly to the radiation treatment.* 4 V-I When one chemical substance **reacts with** another, they combine chemically to form another substance. ❑ *Calcium reacts with water.* ❑ *The two gases react to produce carbon dioxide and water.*

Word Partnership Use *react* with:

ADJ. **slow** to react 1
N. react **to news**, react **to a situation** 1
ADV. react **differently**, react **emotionally**, **how to** react, react **negatively**, react **positively**, react **quickly** 1
react **strongly**, react **violently** 1 3 4

reaction /ri'ækʃən/ (**reactions**) 1 N-VAR Your **reaction to** something that has happened or something that you have experienced is what you feel, say, or do because of it. ❑ *Reaction to the President's visit has been mixed.* ❑ *His answer caused a strong reaction.* 2 N-COUNT A **reaction against** something is a way of behaving or doing something that is deliberately different from what has been done before. ❑ *The colours I used were a reaction against the dull surroundings.* ❑ *...a strong reaction against the reform.* 3 N-COUNT If you **have a reaction to** a treatment or substance, you are affected unpleasantly or made ill by it. ❑ *He suffered his first reaction to nuts when he was three.* 4 N-PLURAL Your **reactions** are your ability to move quickly in response to something. ❑ *The sport requires very fast reactions.* 5 N-COUNT The **reaction between** two chemical substances is what happens when they combine to form another substance. ❑ *Ozone is produced by the reaction between oxygen and ultra-violet light.* ❑ *...chemical reactions.*
→ see **motion**

Word Partnership Use *reaction* with:

ADJ. **emotional** reaction, **initial** reaction, **mixed** reaction, **negative** reaction, **positive** reaction 1
allergic reaction 3
chemical reaction 5

reactionary /ri'ækʃənri, AM -neri/ (**reactionaries**) N-COUNT & ADJ A **reactionary** or a **reactionary** person or group tries to prevent changes in the political or social system of their country; used showing disapproval. ❑ *Reactionary politicians spread fear amongst the population.*

reactor /ri'æktə/ (**reactors**) N-COUNT A **reactor** is a device which produces nuclear energy.

read (**reads, reading, read**)

When it is the present tense, **read** is pronounced /ri:d/; **read** is also the past tense and past participle, when it is pronounced /red/.

1 V-T/V-I & N-COUNT When you **read** something such as a book or article, you look at and understand or say aloud the words that are written there. You can also say you have a **read**. ❑ *He read through the pages slowly.* ❑ *I read the children a story before bedtime.* ❑ *I got into bed to have a good read.* 2 V-T If you can **read** music, you have the ability to look at and understand the written symbols that are used to represent musical sounds. 3 V-T You can use **read** when saying what is written somewhere. For example, if a notice **reads** 'Exit', the word 'Exit' is written on it. 4 V-I If you refer to how a piece of writing **reads**, you are referring to its style. ❑ *The translation reads very well.* 5 N-COUNT If you say that a book is a **good read**, you mean that it is very enjoyable to read. 6 V-T If you **read** someone's mind or their mood, you know what they are thinking or feeling without them telling you. 7 V-T When you **read** a measuring device, you look at it to see what the measurement on it is. ❑ *You need to be able to read a thermometer.* 8 → see also **reading** 9 **to read between the lines** → see **line**

▸ **read into** PHR-VERB If you **read** a meaning **into** something, you think it is there although it may not be. ❑ *Don't try to read too much into children's drawings.*

▸ **read out** PHR-VERB If you **read** something **out**, you say the words aloud, especially in a loud, clear voice. ❑ *We read plays out in class.*

▸ **read up on** PHR-VERB If you **read up on** a subject, you read a lot about it so that you become informed on it.

Thesaurus *read* Also look up:

V. scan, skim, study 1

Word Partnership Use *read* with:

ADV. read **carefully**, read **silently** 1
V. **learn (how)** to read, **like to** read, **listen to *someone*** read, **want to** read 1
N. **ability to** read, read **a book/magazine/(news)paper**, read **a sentence**, read **a sign**, read **a statement**, read **a verdict** 1

readable /'ri:dəbəl/ ADJ If a book or article is **readable**, it is enjoyable and easy to read.

reader /'ri:də/ (**readers**) N-COUNT The **readers** of a book, newspaper, or magazine are the people who read it.

readership /'ri:dəʃɪp/ N-SING The **readership** of a book, newspaper, or magazine is the number or type of people who read it. ❑ *...an international readership.*

r

readily /'redɪli/ **1** ADV If you do something **readily**, you do it willingly. ❑ *When I was invited to the party, I readily accepted.* **2** ADV You use **readily** to say that something can be done or obtained quickly and easily. ❑ *I don't readily make friends.*

Word Partnership	Use *readily* with:
V.	readily **accept**, readily **admit**, readily **agree** **1**
ADV.	readily **apparent** **1**
ADJ.	***be*** readily **available**, **make** readily **available** **2**

reading /'ri:dɪŋ/ (**readings**) **1** N-UNCOUNT **Reading** is the activity of reading books. ❑ *I have always loved reading.* **2** N-COUNT A **reading** is an event at which extracts from books are read to an audience. **3** N-COUNT The **reading** on a measuring device is the measurement that it shows.

readjust /ˌri:ə'dʒʌst/ (**readjusts, readjusting, readjusted**) **1** V-I When you **readjust to** a new situation, you adapt to it. ❑ *Astronauts find it difficult to readjust to life on earth.* ● **readjustment** (**readjustments**) N-VAR ❑ *...a period of readjustment.* **2** V-T If you **readjust** something, you change it so that it is more effective or appropriate. ❑ *She reached up and readjusted his tie.* ● **readjustment** N-VAR ❑ *...readjustment of state borders.*

ready /'redi/ (**readying, readied**) **1** ADJ AFTER LINK-V If someone or something is **ready**, they have reached the required stage for something or they are properly prepared for action or use. ❑ *It took her a long time to get ready for church.* ❑ *Your breakfast's ready.* ● **readiness** N-UNCOUNT ❑ *...a week's training in readiness for Saturday's match.* **2** ADJ AFTER LINK-V If you are **ready to** do something, you want to do it. ❑ *She was always ready to give interviews.* ● **readiness** N-UNCOUNT ❑ *...his readiness to listen to criticism.* **3** ADJ AFTER LINK-V If someone or something is **ready to** do something, they are about to do it or likely to do it. ❑ *He looked ready to fall asleep.* **4** ADJ AFTER LINK-V If you are **ready for** something, you need it or want it. ❑ *After five days in the heat of Bangkok, we were ready for the beach.* **5** ADJ BEFORE N You use **ready** to describe things that are able to be used quickly and easily. ❑ *...a ready supply of well-trained workers.* **6** V-T When you **ready** something, you prepare it for a particular purpose. [FORMAL] ❑ *Soldiers were readying themselves for the final battle.* **7** **Ready** combines with past participles to indicate that something has already been done, and that therefore you do not have to do it yourself. ❑ *...ready-printed forms.* **8** PHRASE If you have something **at the ready**, you have it in a position where it can be quickly and easily used. ❑ *...photographers with cameras at the ready.*

Word Partnership	Use *ready* with:
N.	ready **for bed**, ready **for dinner** **1**
V.	**get** ready **1**
	ready **to burst** **1** **2**
	ready **to begin**, ready **to fight**, ready **to go/leave**, ready **to play**, ready **to start** **1**–**4**
ADV.	**always** ready, **not quite** ready, **not** ready **yet** **1**–**4**

R

ˌ**ready-'made** **1** ADJ If something that you buy is **ready-made**, you can use it immediately. ❑ *...ready-made meals.* **2** ADJ **Ready-made** means extremely convenient or useful for a particular purpose. ❑ *...a ready-made topic of conversation.*

Word Link	***firm*** ≈ ***making strong*** : ***affirm, confirm, reaffirm***

reaffirm /ˌri:ə'fɜ:m/ (**reaffirms, reaffirming, reaffirmed**) V-T If you **reaffirm** something, you state it again clearly and firmly. [FORMAL] ❑ *The government has reaffirmed that it will do anything to keep people safe.*

real /ri:l/ **1** ADJ Something that is **real** actually exists and is not imagined or theoretical. ❑ *No, it wasn't a dream. It was real.* **2** ADJ A material or object that is **real** is genuine and not artificial or an imitation. ❑ *...real leather.* ❑ *Is this a real gun or not?* **3** ADJ BEFORE N You can use **real** to say that someone or something has all the characteristics or qualities that such a person or thing typically has. ❑ *...his first real girlfriend.* **4** ADJ BEFORE N You can use **real** to describe something that is the true or original thing of its kind. ❑ *Her real name was Miriam Pinckus.* **5** ADV You can use **real** to emphasize an adjective or adverb. [AM, INFORMAL] ❑ *He is finding prison life real tough.* **6** PHRASE If someone does something **for real**, they actually do it and do not just pretend to do it. ❑ *He thought it was all a big joke; he had no idea it was for real.* **7** PHRASE You use **in real terms** to refer to the actual value or cost of something. For example, if your salary rises by 5% but prices rise by 10%, in real terms you get less salary. **8** PHRASE If you say that a thing or event is **the real thing**, you mean that it is the actual thing or event, and not an imitation or rehearsal. ❑ *We had lessons on how to tell the copies from the real thing.*

'**real esˌtate** N-UNCOUNT **Real estate** is property in the form of buildings and land. [AM]

realise /'ri:əlaɪz/ → see **realize**

realism /'ri:əlɪzəm/ **1** N-UNCOUNT When people show **realism** in their behaviour, they recognize and accept the true nature of a situation and try to deal with it in a practical way. ● **realist** (**realists**) N-COUNT ❑ *I would love to play for England but as a realist, I understand that I am not good enough.* **2** N-UNCOUNT If things and people are presented with **realism** in painting, novels, or films, they are presented in a way that is like real life; used showing approval. ● **realist** ADJ BEFORE N ❑ *He is the most popular realist painter for years.*
→ see **genre**

realistic /ˌri:ə'lɪstɪk/ **1** ADJ If you are **realistic** about a situation, you recognize and accept its true nature and try to deal with it practically. ❑ *It's realistic to expect things to go wrong sometimes.* ● **realistically** ADV ❑ *As an adult, you can look at the situation realistically.* **2** ADJ You say that a painting, story, or film is **realistic** when the people and things in it are like people and things in real life. ● **realistically** ADV ❑ *The film starts off realistically and then turns into a fantasy.*
→ see **art, fantasy**

Word Partnership Use *realistic* with:

V.	**be** realistic 1
ADV.	**more** realistic, **very** realistic 1 2
N.	realistic **assessment**, realistic **expectations**, realistic **goals**, realistic **view** 1

Word Link *real ≈ actual : reality, realize, really*

reality /ri'ælɪti/ (**realities**) 1 N-UNCOUNT You use **reality** to refer to real things or the real nature of things rather than imagined, invented, or theoretical ideas. ❑ *He was confusing fiction and reality.* 2 N-COUNT The **reality of** a situation is the truth about it, especially when it is unpleasant. ❑ *...the harsh reality of show business.* 3 N-VAR If something becomes a **reality**, it actually exists or is actually happening. ❑ *The reality is that they are poor.* 4 PHRASE You can use **in reality** to introduce a statement about the real nature of something, when it contrasts with something incorrect that has just been described. ❑ *He seemed happy, but in reality he was not.*
→ see **fantasy**

Word Partnership Use *reality* with:

ADJ.	**virtual** reality 1
V.	**distort** reality 1
	become a reality 3
N.	reality **of life**, reality **of war** 2
PREP.	**in** reality 4

re'ality ˌcheck (**reality checks**) N-COUNT If you say that something is a **reality check** for someone, you mean that it makes them recognize the truth about a situation, especially about the difficulties involved in something they want to achieve. ❑ *Oprah called her experience of being a juror a 'huge reality check'.*

re'ality TˌV N-UNCOUNT **Reality TV** is a type of television which aims to show how ordinary people behave in everyday life, or in situations, often created by the programme makers, which are intended to represent everyday life.

realize [BRIT also **realise**] /'ri:əlaɪz/ (**realizes, realizing, realized**) 1 V-T/V-I If you **realize** that something is true, you become aware of that fact or understand it. ❑ *People don't realize how serious this is.* ❑ *They slowly realized that there were going to be big changes.* • **realization** (**realizations**) N-COUNT ❑ *There is a growing realisation that things cannot continue like this.* 2 V-T If your hopes, desires, or fears **are realized**, the things that you hope for, desire, or fear actually happen. [FORMAL] • **realization** N-UNCOUNT ❑ *...the realization of his worst fears.*

Word Partnership Use *realize* with:

ADV.	**suddenly** realize 1
	finally realize, **fully** realize 1 3
V.	**begin to** realize, **come to** realize, **fail to** realize, **make *someone*** realize 1
N.	realize **a dream**, realize **your potential** 3

really /'ri:əli/ 1 ADV You can use **really** to emphasize a statement. [SPOKEN] ❑ *I'm very sorry. I really am.* ❑ *I really do feel that you are being unfair.* 2 ADV You use **really** when you are discussing the real facts about something, in contrast to the ones someone wants you to believe. ❑ *My father didn't really love her.* ❑ *What was really going on?* 3 ADV People sometimes use **really** to slightly reduce the force of a negative statement. ❑ *I'm not really surprised.* ❑ *'Did they hurt you?'—'Not really.'* 4 CONVENTION You can say **'Really?'** to express surprise or disbelief. ❑ *'We saw a very bright shooting star.'—'Did you really?'*

Usage

When **really** is used in a negative sentence, its position in relation to the verb affects the meaning. For instance, if you say **'I really don't like Richard'**, with **really** in front of the verb, you are emphasizing how much you dislike Richard. However, if you say **'I don't really like Richard'**, with **really** coming after the negative, you are still saying that you dislike Richard, but the feeling is not particularly strong.

realm /relm/ (**realms**) N-COUNT You can use **realm** to refer to any area of activity, interest, or thought. [FORMAL] ❑ *...the realm of politics.*

ˌreal 'world N-SING If you talk about **the real world**, you are referring to the world and life in general, in contrast to a particular person's own life, experience, and ideas. ❑ *Many students cannot cope with the real world when they leave university.*

reap /ri:p/ (**reaps, reaping, reaped**) V-T If you **reap** the benefits or the rewards of something, you enjoy the good things that happen as a result of it.

reappear /ˌri:ə'pɪə/ (**reappears, reappearing, reappeared**) V-I When people or things **reappear**, they return after they have been away or out of sight for some time. • **reappearance** (**reappearances**) N-COUNT ❑ *The reappearance of her mother seemed to be a terrible shock to her.*

rear /rɪə/ (**rears, rearing, reared**) 1 N-SING **The rear of** something is the back part of it. ❑ *...the rear of the building.* 2 V-T If you **rear** children or young animals, you look after them until they are old enough to look after themselves. ❑ *I was reared in east Texas.* 3 V-I & PHR-VERB If a horse **rears** or **rears up**, it moves the front part of its body upwards, so that its front legs are high in the air and it is standing on its back legs.

rearrange /ˌri:ə'reɪndʒ/ (**rearranges, rearranging, rearranged**) V-T If you **rearrange** things, you change the way they are organized or ordered. ❑ *She rearranged the furniture.* • **rearrangement** (**rearrangements**) N-VAR ❑ *...a rearrangement of the university's departments.*

reason /'ri:zən/ (**reasons, reasoning, reasoned**) 1 N-COUNT The **reason for** something is a fact or situation which explains why it happens. ❑ *There is a reason for everything that happens.* ❑ *Who would have a reason to want to kill her?* ❑ *...the reason why Italian tomatoes have so much flavour.* 2 N-UNCOUNT If you say that you have **reason to** believe something or **to** have a particular emotion, you mean that you have evidence for your belief or there is a definite cause of your feeling. ❑ *He had reason to be upset.* 3 N-UNCOUNT The ability that people have to think and to make sensible judgments can be referred to as **reason**. ❑ *...a conflict between emotion and reason.* 4 V-T If you

r

reason that something is true, you decide that it is true after thinking carefully about all the facts. ❑ *I reasoned that if he could do it, so could I.* ❑ *'Motherhood would be a full-time job,' she reasoned.* **5** PHRASE If one thing happens **by reason of** another, it happens because of it. [FORMAL] **6** → see also **reasoned, reasoning**

▶ **reason with** PHR-VERB If you try to **reason with** someone, you try to persuade them to do something or to accept something by using sensible arguments.

Word Partnership Use *reason* with:

ADJ. **main** reason, **major** reason, **obvious** reason, **only** reason, **primary** reason, **real** reason, **same** reason, **simple** reason **1**
compelling reason, **good** reason, **sufficient** reason **1** **2**

reasonable /ˈriːzənəbəl/ **1** ADJ If you think that someone is fair and sensible you can say they are **reasonable**. ❑ *He's a reasonable man.* ❑ *...a perfectly reasonable decision.* ● **reasonably** ADV ❑ *'I'm sorry, Andrew,' she said reasonably.* ● **reasonableness** N-UNCOUNT ❑ *Bertha spoke with calm reasonableness.* **2** ADJ If you say that an expectation or explanation is **reasonable**, you mean that there are good reasons why it may be correct. ❑ *It seems reasonable to expect things to change.* ● **reasonably** ADV ❑ *Today's young adults can reasonably expect to live well into their 70s.* **3** ADJ If you say that the price of something is **reasonable**, you mean that it is fair and not too high. ● **reasonably** ADV ❑ *...reasonably-priced accommodation.* **4** ADJ You can use **reasonable** to describe something that is fairly good, but not very good. ● **reasonably** ADV ❑ *I can dance reasonably well.* **5** ADJ A **reasonable** amount of something is a fairly large amount of it. ❑ *...a good diet and a reasonable amount of exercise.* ● **reasonably** ADV ❑ *She fixed the car reasonably quickly.*

Thesaurus *reasonable* Also look up:

ADJ. rational **1**
likely, probable, right **2**
acceptable, fair, sensible; *(ant.)* unreasonable **3**

Word Partnership Use *reasonable* with:

N. reasonable **person** **1**
beyond a reasonable **doubt**, reasonable **expectation**, reasonable **explanation** **2**
reasonable **cost**, reasonable **price**, reasonable **rates** **3**
reasonable **amount** **3** **5**
reasonable **chance**, reasonable **time** **4**

reasoned /ˈriːzənd/ ADJ A **reasoned** discussion or argument is based on sensible reasons, rather than on feelings.

reasoning /ˈriːzənɪŋ/ N-UNCOUNT **Reasoning** is the process by which you reach a conclusion after considering all the facts. ❑ *...the reasoning behind the decision.*
→ see **philosophy**

R

reassert /ˌriːəˈsɜːt/ (**reasserts, reasserting, reasserted**) **1** V-T If you **reassert** your control or authority, you make it clear that you are still in a position of power, or you strengthen the power that you had. **2** V-T If something such as an idea or habit **reasserts itself**, it becomes noticeable again.

reassess /ˌriːəˈses/ (**reassesses, reassessing, reassessed**) V-T If you **reassess** a situation, you think about it and decide whether you need to change your opinion about it. ● **reassessment** (**reassessments**) N-VAR ❑ *We need an urgent reassessment of the entire programme.*

reassure /ˌriːəˈʃʊə/ (**reassures, reassuring, reassured**) V-T If you **reassure** someone, you say or do things to make them stop worrying about something. ● **reassurance** (**reassurances**) N-VAR ❑ *She needed reassurance that she was good enough.*

Word Partnership Use *reassure* with:

N. reassure **citizens**, reassure **customers**, reassure **investors**, reassure **the public**
V. **seek to** reassure, **try to** reassure

reassured /ˌriːəˈʃʊəd/ ADJ If you **feel reassured**, you feel less worried about something. ❑ *We both felt reassured after a talk with the doctor.*

reassuring /ˌriːəˈʃʊərɪŋ/ ADJ If you find someone's words or actions **reassuring**, they make you feel less worried. ● **reassuringly** ADV ❑ *'It's okay now,' he said reassuringly.*

rebate /ˈriːbeɪt/ (**rebates**) N-COUNT A **rebate** is an amount of money which is paid to you when you have paid more tax, rent, or rates than you needed to.

rebel (**rebels, rebelling, rebelled**)

verb /rɪˈbel/, noun /ˈrebəl/.

1 N-COUNT **Rebels** are people who are fighting against their own country's army in order to change the political system there. ❑ *...fighting between rebels and government forces.* **2** V-I & N-COUNT If politicians **rebel against** one of their own party's policies, they show that they oppose it. Politicians who do this are sometimes referred to as **rebels**. **3** V-I When someone **rebels**, they start to behave differently from other people and reject the values of society or of their parents. **4** N-COUNT If you say that someone is a **rebel**, you mean that they behave differently from other people and reject the values of society or of their parents.

rebellion /rɪˈbeliən/ (**rebellions**) **1** N-VAR A **rebellion** is a violent organized action by a large group of people who are trying to change their country's political system. **2** N-VAR A **rebellion** is a situation in which politicians show their opposition to their own party's policies.

rebellious /rɪˈbeliəs/ ADJ A **rebellious** person behaves in an unacceptable way and does not do what they are told. ● **rebelliousness** N-UNCOUNT ❑ *His rebelliousness increased when he became a teenager.*

rebirth /ˌriːˈbɜːθ/ N-SING You can refer to a change that leads to a new period of growth and improvement in something as its **rebirth**. ❑ *...the rebirth of democracy in Latin America.*

rebound /rɪˈbaʊnd/ (**rebounds, rebounding, rebounded**) **1** V-I If something **rebounds** from a solid surface, it bounces or springs back from it.

❑ *The ball rebounded off the wall.* 2 V-I If an action or situation **rebounds on** you, it has an unpleasant effect on you, especially when this effect was intended for someone else. ❑ *Mia realised her trick had rebounded on her.*

rebuff /rɪˈbʌf/ (**rebuffs, rebuffing, rebuffed**) V-T & N-VAR If someone **rebuffs** your suggestion or advice, or if they treat it with a **rebuff**, they respond in an unfriendly way and refuse to accept it.

rebuild /ˌriːˈbɪld/ (**rebuilds, rebuilding, rebuilt**) 1 V-T When people **rebuild** something such as a building, they build it again after it has been damaged or destroyed. 2 V-T When people **rebuild** something such as an institution, a system, or an aspect of their lives, they take action to restore it to its previous state.

rebuke /rɪˈbjuːk/ (**rebukes, rebuking, rebuked**) V-T & N-VAR If you **rebuke** someone, or if you give them a **rebuke**, you speak severely to them because they have said or done something that you do not approve of. [FORMAL]

recall /rɪˈkɔːl/ (**recalls, recalling, recalled**) 1 V-T When you **recall** something, you remember it. ❑ *I recalled everything that Ray had told me.* ❑ *She could not recall ever seeing him before.* 2 V-T When you **recall** something, you remember it and tell others about it. ❑ *Henderson recalled that he first met Pollard during a business trip.* ❑ *'That evening, he was friendly,' she recalled.* 3 V-T If you **are recalled** to your home, country, or the place where you work, you are ordered to return there. ❑ *Spain has recalled its ambassador for discussion.*

recapture /ˌriːˈkæptʃə/ (**recaptures, recapturing, recaptured**) 1 V-T & N-SING When soldiers **recapture** a place, they win control of it again from an opposing army who had taken it from them. You can also refer to the **recapture** of a place. 2 V-T & N-SING To **recapture** a person or animal which has escaped from somewhere means to catch them again. You can also refer to the **recapture** of a person or animal. 3 V-T When you **recapture** something such as an experience, emotion, or a quality you had in the past, or when something **recaptures** it for you, you experience it again. ❑ *Many men reach a certain age and then try to recapture their youth.*

recede /rɪˈsiːd/ (**recedes, receding, receded**) 1 V-I If something **recedes** from you, it moves away into the distance. ❑ *Luke's footsteps receded into the night.* 2 V-I When something such as a quality, problem, or illness **recedes**, it becomes weaker, smaller, or less intense. 3 V-I If a man's hair starts to **recede**, it no longer grows on the front of his head.

receipt /rɪˈsiːt/ (**receipts**) 1 N-COUNT A **receipt** is a piece of paper that you get from someone as confirmation that they have received money or goods from you. ❑ *I wrote her a receipt for the money.* 2 N-PLURAL **Receipts** are the amount of money received during a particular period, for example by a shop or theatre. ❑ *On Saturdays, the shopkeeper takes the week's receipts to the bank.* 3 N-UNCOUNT The **receipt of** something is the act of receiving it. [FORMAL] ❑ *We cannot confirm receipt of letters.*

receive /rɪˈsiːv/ (**receives, receiving, received**) 1 V-T When you **receive** something, you get it after someone gives it to you or sends it to you. ❑ *They will receive their awards at a ceremony in Stockholm.* 2 V-T You can use **receive** to say that certain kinds of thing happen to someone. For example if they are injured, you can say that they received an injury. ❑ *Mr Byers has unfairly received the blame.* 3 V-T If you say that something **is received** in a particular way, you mean that people react to it in that way. ❑ *The book has been well received.*

receiver /rɪˈsiːvə/ (**receivers**) 1 N-COUNT A telephone **receiver** is the part that you hold near to your ear and speak into. 2 N-COUNT A **receiver** is the part of a radio or television that picks up incoming signals and converts them into sound or pictures. 3 N-COUNT A **receiver** is someone who is officially appointed to manage the affairs of a business, usually when it is facing financial failure.
→ see **navigation, radio, television, tennis**

recent /ˈriːsənt/ ADJ A **recent** event or period of time happened only a short while ago. ❑ *...her recent trip to Argentina.* ❑ *The situation has got better in recent years.*

recently /ˈriːsəntli/ ADV If you have done something **recently** or if something happened **recently**, it happened only a short time ago. ❑ *Mr Stevens recently celebrated his eightieth birthday.* ❑ *Until recently she was renting a house.*

reception /rɪˈsepʃən/ (**receptions**) 1 N-UNCOUNT In a hotel, office, or hospital, **reception** is the place where people are received and their reservations, appointments and inquiries are dealt with. ❑ *'Here's a message for you,' the young lady at reception said.* ❑ *...the hotel reception desk.* 2 N-COUNT A **reception** is a formal party which is given to celebrate a special event or to welcome someone. ❑ *The wedding and the reception will be held on Saturday.* 3 N-COUNT If something or someone has a particular kind of **reception**, that is the way people react to them. ❑ *His book received a cool reception from the public.* 4 N-UNCOUNT If you get good **reception** from your radio or television, the sound or picture is clear because the signal is strong.
→ see **wedding**

receptionist /rɪˈsepʃənɪst/ (**receptionists**) N-COUNT In a hotel, office, or hospital, the **receptionist** is the person whose job is to answer the telephone, arrange reservations or appointments, and deal with people when they first arrive.

receptive /rɪˈseptɪv/ ADJ Someone who is **receptive to** new ideas or suggestions is prepared to consider them or accept them.

recess /rɪˈses, ˈriːses/ (**recesses, recessing, recessed**) 1 N-VAR A **recess** is a break between the sessions of work of an official body such as a committee, a court of law, or a government. ❑ *The conference broke for a recess.* 2 V-I When formal proceedings **recess**, they stop temporarily. ❑ *The court has recessed for lunch.* 3 N-COUNT In a room, a **recess** is part of a wall which is built further back than the rest of the wall. 4 N-PLURAL **The recesses of** something are its deep or hidden parts. ❑ *He came out from the dark recesses of the garage.*

recession /rɪˈseʃən/ (**recessions**) N-VAR A **recession** is a period when the economy of a country is not very successful. ❑ *The high price of oil sent Europe into deep recession.*

recipe /ˈresɪpi/ (**recipes**) 1 N-COUNT A **recipe** is a list of ingredients and a set of instructions that tell you how to cook something. 2 N-SING If you say that something is **a recipe for** a particular situation, you mean that it is likely to result in that situation. ❑ *Two women in the same kitchen is often a recipe for disaster.*

recipient /rɪˈsɪpiənt/ (**recipients**) N-COUNT The **recipient of** something is the person who receives it. [FORMAL] ❑ *...recipients of government money.*
→ see **donor**

reciprocal /rɪˈsɪprəkəl/ ADJ A **reciprocal** action or agreement involves two people or groups who do the same thing to each other or agree to help each another in a similar way. [FORMAL] ❑ *...the reciprocal relationship between workers and employers.*

reciprocate /rɪˈsɪprəkeɪt/ (**reciprocates, reciprocating, reciprocated**) V-T/V-I If your feelings or actions towards someone **are reciprocated**, the other person feels or behaves in the same way towards you as you have felt or behaved towards them. ❑ *I hope they reciprocate by coming to support us.* ❑ *Tell her you like her and see if your feelings are reciprocated.*

recital /rɪˈsaɪtəl/ (**recitals**) N-COUNT A **recital** is a performance of music or poetry, usually given by one person.

recite /rɪˈsaɪt/ (**recites, reciting, recited**) 1 V-T When someone **recites** a poem or other piece of writing, they say it aloud after they have learned it. 2 V-T If you **recite** something such as a list, you say it aloud. ❑ *All he could do was recite a list of my faults.*

reckless /ˈrekləs/ ADJ A **reckless** person shows a lack of care about danger or about the results of their actions. ❑ *She was reckless and totally without fear.* ❑ *...reckless driving.* • **recklessly** ADV ❑ *She spent money recklessly.* • **recklessness** N-UNCOUNT ❑ *...the recklessness of youth.*

reckon /ˈrekən/ (**reckons, reckoning, reckoned**) 1 V-T If you **reckon** that something is true, you think that it is true. [INFORMAL] ❑ *Toni reckoned that it must be about three o'clock.* 2 V-T If something **is reckoned to** be a particular figure, it is calculated to be roughly that amount. ❑ *The figure is now reckoned to be 22,000.*

R

▶ **reckon with** 1 PHR-VERB If you had not **reckoned with** something, you had not expected it and so were not ready for it. ❑ *Giles had not reckoned with the strength of Sally's feelings for him.* 2 PHRASE If you refer to a person or force as someone or something **to be reckoned with**, you mean they will be difficult to deal with because they are quite powerful or skilful. ❑ *Women have become a force to be reckoned with.*

reckoning /ˈrekənɪŋ/ (**reckonings**) N-VAR Someone's **reckoning** is a calculation they make about something. ❑ *By my reckoning, 50% of the people in our team will be able to come.*

reclaim /rɪˈkleɪm/ (**reclaims, reclaiming, reclaimed**) 1 V-T If you **reclaim** something that you have lost or had taken away from you, you succeed in getting it back. ❑ *You can reclaim the tax that you have paid.* 2 V-T When people **reclaim** land, they make it suitable for use. ❑ *...1,100 acres of reclaimed land in Tokyo Bay.*

Word Link	*clin ≈ leaning : decline, incline, recline*

recline /rɪˈklaɪn/ (**reclines, reclining, reclined**) 1 V-I If you **recline** on something, you sit or lie on it with the upper part of your body supported at an angle. ❑ *The guests were reclining in lounge chairs.* 2 V-T/V-I If a seat **reclines**, or if you can **recline** it, you can lower the back so that it is more comfortable to sit in. ❑ *First-class seats in planes recline almost like beds.*

recluse /rɪˈkluːs, AM ˈrekluːs/ (**recluses**) N-COUNT A **recluse** is a person who lives alone and deliberately avoids other people.

reclusive /rɪˈkluːsɪv/ ADJ If someone is **reclusive**, they prefer to live on their own and deliberately avoid other people.

Word Link	*cogn ≈ knowing : cognitive, recognition, recognize*

recognition /ˌrekəgˈnɪʃən/ 1 N-UNCOUNT **Recognition** is the act of recognizing someone or identifying something when you see it. ❑ *He searched for a sign of recognition on her face.* 2 N-UNCOUNT **Recognition** of something is an understanding and acceptance of it. ❑ *...their recognition of workers' rights.* 3 N-UNCOUNT When a person receives **recognition** for the things that they have done, people acknowledge the value or skill of their work. ❑ *Her father's work has received popular recognition.* 4 PHRASE If something is done **in recognition of** someone's achievements, it is done as a way of showing official appreciation of them. ❑ *They gave him a bottle of champagne in recognition of his achievements in Australian soccer.*

recognizable [BRIT also **recognisable**] /ˌrekəgˈnaɪzəbəl/ ADJ Something that is **recognizable** is easy to recognize or identify. ❑ *This tree is recognizable by its beautiful silver leaves.*

recognize [BRIT also **recognise**] /ˈrekəgnaɪz/ (**recognizes, recognizing, recognized**) 1 V-T If you **recognize** someone or something, you know who or what they are, because you have seen or heard them before or because they have been described to you. ❑ *The receptionist recognized him at once.* ❑ *...a man I easily recognized as Luke's father.* 2 V-T You say that you **recognize** something when you realize or accept that it exists or that it is true. ❑ *They have been slow to recognize AIDS as a problem.* 3 V-T If people or organizations **recognize** something as valid, they officially accept it or approve of it. ❑ *Russia has recognized Ukraine's independence.* 4 V-T When people **recognize** the work someone has done, they show their appreciation of it, often by giving that person an award.

recoil /rɪˈkɔɪl/ (**recoils, recoiling, recoiled**) 1 V-I If something makes you **recoil**, you move your body quickly away from it because it frightens, offends, or hurts you. ❑ *I thought he was going to kiss me. I recoiled in horror.* 2 V-I If you say that someone **recoils from** doing something or **recoils at** the idea of something, you mean that they are reluctant to do it because they dislike it so much. ❑ *People used to recoil from the idea of being in debt, but now being in debt is normal.*

recollection /ˌrekəˈlekʃən/ (**recollections**) N-VAR If you have a **recollection of** something, you remember it. ❑ *...a book of childhood recollections.*

❑ *He had no recollection of the accident.*

recommend /ˌrekəˈmend/ (**recommends, recommending, recommended**) 1 V-T If someone **recommends** something or someone **to** you, they suggest that you would find them good or useful. ❑ *I have just spent a holiday there and would recommend it to anyone.* ❑ *I'll recommend you for a promotion.* ● **recommended** ADJ ❑ *This book is highly recommended.* ● **recommendation** (**recommendations**) N-COUNT ❑ *Most people choose a product on the recommendation of others.* 2 V-T If you **recommend** that something is done, you advise that it should be done. ❑ *It is recommended that you should go and see your doctor.* ● **recommendation** N-COUNT ❑ *The committee's recommendations will not be made public.* 3 V-T If something or someone has a particular quality **to recommend** it, that quality makes it attractive or gives it an advantage over similar things. ❑ *With so many qualities to recommend it, the price of Scottish salmon is good value.*

Word Partnership Use *recommend* with:

ADV. **highly** recommend, **strongly** recommend 1 2
N. **doctors** recommend, **experts** recommend 1 2
recommend **changes** 2

reconcile /ˈrekənsaɪl/ (**reconciles, reconciling, reconciled**) 1 V-T If you **reconcile** two beliefs, facts, or demands that seem to be opposed or completely different, you find a way in which they can both be true or both be fulfilled. ❑ *It's difficult to reconcile the demands of my job and the desire to be a good father.* ● **reconciliation** /ˌrekənsɪliˈeɪʃən/ N-SING ❑ *...a reconciliation of fact and fantasy.* 2 V-T If you **are reconciled with** someone, you become friendly with them again after a disagreement. ❑ *...my attempt to reconcile him with Toby.* ● **reconciliation** (**reconciliations**) N-VAR ❑ *The couple have separated but he wants a reconciliation.* 3 V-T If you **reconcile yourself to** an unpleasant situation, you accept it. ❑ *She had reconciled herself to never seeing him again.* ● **reconciled** ADJ AFTER LINK-V ❑ *He seemed reconciled to defeat.*

reconnaissance /rɪˈkɒnɪsəns/ N-UNCOUNT **Reconnaissance** is the process of obtaining military information about a place using soldiers, planes, or satellites.

reconsider /ˌriːkənˈsɪdə/ (**reconsiders, reconsidering, reconsidered**) V-T/V-I If you **reconsider** or if you **reconsider** a decision or method, you think about it and try to decide whether it should be changed. ❑ *The United States must reconsider its decision.*

reconstruct /ˌriːkənˈstrʌkt/ (**reconstructs, reconstructing, reconstructed**) 1 V-T If you **reconstruct** something that has been destroyed or badly damaged, you build it and make it work again. ❑ *He had surgery to reconstruct his face, which had been badly damaged in an accident.* ● **reconstruction** N-UNCOUNT ❑ *...the post-war reconstruction of Germany.* 2 V-T To **reconstruct** something such as a system means to change its construction so that it works in a different way. ❑ *Why not reconstruct the competition so that it includes South Africa, Australia and New Zealand?* 3 V-T If you **reconstruct** a past event, you obtain a complete description of it by combining a lot of small pieces of information. ● **reconstruction** (**reconstructions**) N-COUNT ❑ *Mrs Kerr took part in a reconstruction of the crime.*

record (**records, recording, recorded**)

noun /ˈrekɔːd, AM -kərd/, verb /rɪˈkɔːd/.

1 N-COUNT If you keep a **record** of something, or if you keep something **on record**, you keep an account of it in writing, photographs, or on a computer so that it can be referred to later. ❑ *The result will go on your medical records.* ❑ *A photograph of each customer will be kept on record.* 2 N-COUNT Someone's **record** is the facts that are known about their achievements or character. ❑ *Professor Blainey has an excellent record as a researcher.* 3 V-T If you **record** a piece of information or an event, you write it down, photograph it, or put it into a computer so that in the future people can refer to it. ❑ *The letters record the details of her life.* 4 V-T When music or speech **is recorded**, it is put onto a CD, a tape, or a record, so that it can be heard again later. 5 N-COUNT A **record** is a round flat piece of black plastic on which music is stored. You listen to the sound by playing the record on a record player. 6 N-COUNT A **record** is the best result that has ever been achieved in a particular sport or activity, for example the fastest time or the furthest distance. ❑ *She holds the record for the 800 metres.* 7 → see also **recording, track record** 8 PHRASE If you say something **off the record**, you do not intend what you say to be taken as official, or published with your name attached to it. 9 PHRASE If you **set the record straight** or **put the record straight**, you show that something which has been regarded as true is in fact not true.
→ see **diary, history**

Word Partnership Use *record* with:

N. **criminal** record 2
record **earnings**, record **numbers** 3
record **a song** 4
record **album**, record **club**, record **company**, **hit** record, record **industry**, record **label**, record **producer**, record **store** 5
record **high**, record **low**, record **temperatures**, record **time**, **world** record 6
V. **break a** record, **set a** record 6

recorder /rɪˈkɔːdə/ (**recorders**) N-COUNT A **recorder** is a hollow musical instrument that you play by blowing down one end and covering a series of holes with your fingers.

recording /rɪˈkɔːdɪŋ/ (**recordings**) 1 N-COUNT A **recording of** something is a record, tape, CD, or video of it. 2 N-UNCOUNT **Recording** is the process of making CDs, records, tapes, or videos. ❑ *...the recording industry.*

ˈrecord ˌplayer (**record players**) N-COUNT A **record player** is a machine on which you play records.

recount (**recounts, recounting, recounted**) 1 V-T /rɪˈkaʊnt/ If you **recount** a story or event, you tell or describe it to people. [FORMAL] ❑ *He recounted how Williams had visited him.* 2 N-COUNT /ˈriːkaʊnt/ A **recount** is a second count of votes in an election when the result is very close.

r

recoup /rɪ'ku:p/ (**recoups, recouping, recouped**) V-T If you **recoup** a sum of money that you have spent or lost, you get it back. ❑ *We will try to recoup the money by selling our best players.*

recourse /rɪ'kɔ:s/ N-UNCOUNT If you have **recourse to** something, you use it to help you in a difficult situation. ❑ *They were able to come to an agreement without recourse to war.*

recover /rɪ'kʌvə/ (**recovers, recovering, recovered**) **1** V-I When you **recover from** an illness or an injury, you become well again. ❑ *He is recovering from a knee injury.* **2** V-I If you **recover from** an unhappy or unpleasant experience, you stop being upset by it. ❑ *It was a tragedy from which he never fully recovered.* **3** V-T If you **recover** something that has been lost or stolen, you find it or get it back. ❑ *Police recovered stolen laptops from five houses in south-east London yesterday.* **4** V-T If you **recover** your former mental or physical state, it comes back again. ❑ *She never recovered consciousness.*

Usage

Recover is a fairly formal word. In conversation, you usually say that someone **gets better.** ❑ *Qualified nurses help patients get better more quickly.*

recovery /rɪ'kʌvəri/ (**recoveries**) **1** N-VAR If a sick person makes a **recovery**, he or she becomes well again. ❑ *He made a complete recovery.* **2** N-VAR When there is a **recovery** in a country's economy, it improves. **3** N-UNCOUNT You talk about the **recovery of** something when you get it back after it has been lost or stolen. ❑ *...a reward for the recovery of a painting by Picasso.* **4** N-UNCOUNT You talk about the **recovery of** someone's physical or mental state when they return to this state. ❑ *...the sudden loss and recovery of consciousness.*

Word Link — ***creat ≈ making : creation, creature, recreate***

recreate /ˌri:kri'eɪt/ (**recreates, recreating, recreated**) V-T If you **recreate** something, you succeed in making it happen or exist again. ❑ *I am trying to recreate family life far from home.* ● **recreation** (**recreations**) N-COUNT ❑ *...a recreation of the Battle of Hastings.*

R

recreation /ˌrekri'eɪʃən/ (**recreations**) N-VAR **Recreation** consists of things that you do in your spare time to relax. ❑ *All family members should have their own interests and recreations.* ● **recreational** ADJ ❑ *...parks and other recreational areas.*

recrimination /rɪˌkrɪmɪ'neɪʃən/ (**recriminations**) N-VAR **Recriminations** are accusations that two people or groups make about each other. ❑ *Their relationship ended in recrimination and divorce.*

recruit /rɪ'kru:t/ (**recruits, recruiting, recruited**) **1** V-T If you **recruit** people for an organization, you get them to join it or work for it. ❑ *The police are trying to recruit more black and Asian officers.* ● **recruiting** N-UNCOUNT ❑ *...an army recruiting office.* ● **recruitment** N-UNCOUNT ❑ *...a crisis in teacher recruitment.* **2** N-COUNT A **recruit** is a person who has recently joined an organization or army.

reˌcruitment conˈsultant (**recruitment consultants**) N-COUNT A **recruitment consultant** is a person who helps professional people to find work by introducing them to potential employers.

Word Link — ***rect ≈ right, straight : correct, rectangle, rectify***

rectangle /'rektæŋgəl/ (**rectangles**) N-COUNT A **rectangle** is a shape with four sides whose angles are all right angles. Each side of a rectangle is the same length as the one opposite to it.
→ see **shape, volume**

rectangular /rek'tæŋgjʊlə/ ADJ Something that is **rectangular** is shaped like a rectangle. ❑ *...a rectangular table.*

rectify /'rektɪfaɪ/ (**rectifies, rectifying, rectified**) V-T If you **rectify** something that is wrong, you change it so that it becomes correct or satisfactory. ❑ *We are trying hard to rectify the situation.*

recuperate /rɪ'ku:pəreɪt/ (**recuperates, recuperating, recuperated**) V-I When you **recuperate**, you recover your health or strength after you have been ill or injured. ❑ *He is recuperating from a serious back injury.* ● **recuperation** N-UNCOUNT ❑ *Sleep is necessary for recuperation.*

recur /rɪ'kɜ:/ (**recurs, recurring, recurred**) V-I If something **recurs**, it happens more than once. ❑ *...a recurring dream she has had since childhood.* ● **recurrence** /rɪ'kʌrəns, AM -'kɜ:r-/ (**recurrences**) N-VAR ❑ *Police want to prevent a recurrence of the violence.*

recurrent /rɪ'kʌrənt, AM -'kɜ:r-/ ADJ A **recurrent** event or feeling happens or is experienced more than once. ❑ *...buildings in which staff suffer recurrent illness.*

recycle /ˌri:'saɪkəl/ (**recycles, recycling, recycled**) V-T If you **recycle** things that have already been used, such as bottles or sheets of paper, you process them so that they can be used again.
→ see **paper**

red /red/ (**redder, reddest, reds**) **1** ADJ & N-VAR Something that is **red** is the colour of blood or of a ripe tomato. **2** ADJ You describe someone's hair as **red** when it is between red and brown in colour. **3** PHRASE If a person or company is **in the red** or if their bank account is **in the red**, they have spent more money than they have in their account and therefore they owe money to the bank. **4** PHRASE If you **see red**, you become very angry.
→ see **colour, rainbow**

ˌred ˈcard (**red cards**) N-COUNT In football or rugby, the **red card** is a card that the referee shows to a player who has to leave the pitch for breaking the rules.

reddish /'redɪʃ/ ADJ **Reddish** means slightly red in colour.

redeem /rɪ'di:m/ (**redeems, redeeming, redeemed**) **1** V-T If you **redeem yourself**, you do something that gives people a good opinion of you again after you have behaved or performed badly. ❑ *He realized the mistake he had made and wanted to redeem himself.* **2** V-T When something **redeems** an unpleasant thing or situation, it prevents it from being completely bad. ❑ *I wanted to redeem my mistakes by being a better husband.* **3** V-T If you **redeem** a debt or an obligation, you pay money that you owe or that you promised to pay.

redemption /rɪ'dempʃən/ N-UNCOUNT **Redemption** is the act of redeeming something or of being redeemed by something. ❑ *There* *can be no redemption for these men and their crimes.* ❑ *...redemption of the loan.*

redevelopment /ˌriːdɪˈveləpmənt/ N-UNCOUNT When **redevelopment** takes place, old buildings in a part of a town are knocked down and new ones are built in their place.

ˌred-ˈhot ADJ Something that is **red-hot** is extremely hot.

redirect /ˌriːdɪˈrekt, -daɪ-/ (**redirects, redirecting, redirected**) **1** V-T If you **redirect** your energy, resources, or ability, you begin doing something different or trying to achieve something different. ❑ *He redirected his attention quickly.* **2** V-T If you **redirect** someone or something, you change their course. ❑ *She redirected them to the men's department.*

redistribute /ˌriːdɪˈstrɪbjuːt/ (**redistributes, redistributing, redistributed**) V-T If money or goods **are redistributed**, they are shared among people or organizations in a different way from the way that they were previously shared. ❑ *...the President's plan to redistribute 5,000 farms to 30,000 black Zimababweans.* ● **redistribution** N-UNCOUNT ❑ *...a redistribution of wealth.*

redress /rɪˈdres/ (**redresses, redressing, redressed**) **1** V-T If you **redress** something such as a wrong or a grievance, you do something to correct it or to improve things for the person who has been badly treated. [FORMAL] ❑ *This is an opportunity for us to redress the mistakes made by the international community.* **2** V-T If you **redress** the **balance** or the **imbalance** between two things that have become unequal, you make them equal again. ❑ *We must redress the balance between the rich and the poor.* **3** N-UNCOUNT **Redress** is compensation for something wrong that has been done. [FORMAL] ❑ *...their legal battle to seek redress.*

ˌred ˈtape N-UNCOUNT You refer to official rules and procedures as **red tape** when they seem unnecessary and cause delay.

reduce /rɪˈdjuːs, AM -ˈduːs/ (**reduces, reducing, reduced**) **1** V-T If you **reduce** something, you make it smaller. ❑ *It reduces the risks of heart disease.* **2** V-T If someone **is reduced to** a weaker or inferior state, they become weaker or inferior as a result of something that happens to them. ❑ *They were reduced to poverty.* **3** V-T If something is changed to a different or less complicated form, you can say that it **is reduced to** that form. ❑ *The portrait has been reduced to an outline and a pair of eyes.* **4** V-T If you say that someone **is reduced to** doing something, you mean that they have to do it, although it is unpleasant or humiliating. ❑ *He was reduced to begging for food.*
→ see **mineral**

Word Partnership Use *reduce* with:

N.	reduce **anxiety**, reduce **costs**, reduce **crime**, reduce **debt**, reduce **pain**, reduce **spending**, reduce **stress**, reduce **taxes**, reduce **violence**, reduce **waste** **1**
ADV.	**dramatically** reduce, **greatly** reduce, **significantly** reduce, **substantially** reduce **1**
V.	**help** reduce, **plan to** reduce, **try to** reduce **1**

reduction /rɪˈdʌkʃən/ (**reductions**) N-VAR When there is a **reduction in** something, it is made smaller. ❑ *The sale starts on 4 January with reductions of 40% on all flights.*

redundancy /rɪˈdʌndənsi/ (**redundancies**) N-VAR If there are **redundancies** within an organization, some of its employees are dismissed because their jobs are no longer necessary or because the organization can no longer afford to pay them. [BRIT] ❑ *Thousands of workers are facing redundancy.*

redundant /rɪˈdʌndənt/ **1** ADJ If you are **made redundant**, you lose your job because it is no longer necessary or because your employer cannot afford to keep paying you. [BRIT] ❑ *Her teacher was made redundant when the school was closed down.* **2** ADJ Something that is **redundant** is no longer needed because it has been replaced by something else. ❑ *Changes in technology mean that many skills are now redundant.*

reed /riːd/ (**reeds**) N-VAR **Reeds** are tall plants that grow in shallow water or wet ground.

reef /riːf/ (**reefs**) N-COUNT A **reef** is a long line of rocks or sand, the top of which is just above or just below the surface of the sea. ❑ *A coral reef encloses the bay.*

reek /riːk/ (**reeks, reeking, reeked**) **1** V-I & N-SING If something **reeks of** something else, usually something unpleasant, it smells very strongly of it. You can also talk about the **reek of** something. ❑ *The air reeked of burning oil.* ❑ *The whole house reeked.* ❑ *...the cold, the rain, the reek of dead fish.* **2** V-I If you say that something **reeks of** unpleasant ideas, feelings, or practices, you disapprove of it because it gives a firm impression that it involves those ideas, feelings, or practices. ❑ *The whole thing reeks of dishonesty.*

reel /riːl/ (**reels, reeling, reeled**) **1** N-COUNT A **reel** is a cylinder-shaped object around which you wrap something such as thread or cinema film. **2** V-I When someone **reels**, they move about unsteadily as if they were going to fall. ❑ *He lost his balance and reeled back.* **3** V-I If you are **reeling from** a shock, you are feeling extremely surprised or upset because of it. ❑ *I'm still reeling from the shock of hearing it.* **4** V-I If you say that your brain or your mind **is reeling**, you mean that you are very confused because you have too much to think about.

▸ **reel off** PHR-VERB If you **reel off** information, you repeat it from memory quickly and easily. ❑ *She reeled off the titles of several of his books.*

ˌre-eˈlect (**re-elects, re-electing, re-elected**) V-T When someone such as a politician **is re-elected**, they win a new election and are therefore able to continue in their position as, for example, a member of parliament. ❑ *The president will promote the new idea if he is re-elected.* ● **re-election** N-UNCOUNT ❑ *I would like to see him stand for re-election.*

ˌre-exˈamine (**re-examines, re-examining, re-examined**) V-T If a person or group of people **re-examine** their ideas or beliefs, they think about them carefully because they are no longer sure if they are correct. ❑ *France and Germany re-examined their foreign policies at the end of the Cold War.* ● **re-examination** (**re-examinations**) N-VAR ❑ *It was time for a re-examination of the situation.*

refer /rɪ'fɜː/ (**refers, referring, referred**) 1 V-I If you **refer to** a particular subject or person, you mention them. ❑ *In his speech, he referred to a recent trip to Canada.* ● **reference** /'refərəns/ (**references**) N-VAR ❑ *He made no reference to any agreement.* 2 V-I If you **refer to** someone or something by a particular name, you call them this name. ❑ *He always referred to his friend as Mr Lowry.* 3 V-I If a word or expression **refers to** something, it describes them or is connected with them. ❑ *The expression 'touch wood' refers to the wooden cross of Jesus.* 4 V-I If you **refer to** a book or other source of information, you look at it in order to find something out. ❑ *He kept referring to the dictionary.* ● **reference** N-UNCOUNT ❑ *Keep this sheet for future reference.* 5 V-T If a person or problem **is referred to** another person or to an organization, that person or organization is asked to deal with them. ❑ *I was referred to an ear specialist.*

referee

referee /ˌrefə'riː/ (**referees, refereeing, refereed**) 1 N-COUNT The **referee** is the official who controls a sports match. 2 V-I If you **referee** a sports match, you act as referee.
→ see **tennis**

reference /'refərəns/ (**references**) 1 N-COUNT A **reference** is something such as a number or a name that tells you where you can obtain information. ❑ *...a map reference.* 2 ADJ BEFORE N **Reference** books are ones you look at when you need specific information about a subject. 3 PHRASE You use **with reference to** or **in reference to** to indicate who or what you are referring to. ❑ *I am writing with reference to your recent article on Spain.* 4 N-COUNT A **reference** is a letter written by someone who knows you which describes your character and abilities. 5 → see also **refer**

Word Partnership	Use *reference* with:
ADJ.	**clear** reference, **specific** reference 1
	quick reference 2
N.	reference **number** 1
	reference **books**, reference **materials** 2

R

referendum /ˌrefə'rendəm/ (**referendums** or **referenda** /ˌrefə'rendə/) N-COUNT A **referendum** is a vote in which all the people in a country are asked whether they agree or disagree with a particular policy. ❑ *The government is going to hold a referendum.*

referral /rɪ'fɜːrəl/ (**referrals**) N-VAR **Referral** is the act of officially sending someone to a person or authority that is authorized or better qualified to deal with them. A **referral** is an instance of this. ❑ *...a referral to an eye specialist.*

refill (**refills, refilling, refilled**)

verb /ˌriː'fɪl/, noun /'riːfɪl/.

V-T & N-COUNT If you **refill** something, or if you give it a **refill**, you fill it again after it has been emptied. ❑ *Max asked for a refill and held out his cup.*

refine /rɪ'faɪn/ (**refines, refining, refined**) 1 V-T When a substance **is refined**, it is made pure by the removal of other substances from it. ❑ *...refined sugar.* ● **refining** N-UNCOUNT ❑ *...oil refining.* 2 V-T If something such as a process, a theory, or a machine **is refined**, it is improved by being changed in small ways. ❑ *Techniques are constantly being refined.* ● **refinement** (**refinements**) N-VAR ❑ *Further refinements are needed.*
→ see **industry, sugar**

refined /rɪ'faɪnd/ ADJ **Refined** people are polite and well-mannered.

Word Link	*ery ≈ place where something happens : bakery, brewery, refinery*

refinery /rɪ'faɪnəri/ (**refineries**) N-COUNT A **refinery** is a factory which refines a substance such as oil or sugar.
→ see **mineral, oil**

refit (**refits, refitting, refitted**)

verb /ˌriː'fɪt/, noun /'riːfɪt/.

V-T & N-COUNT When a ship **is refitted**, or when it is given a **refit**, it is repaired or is given new parts, equipment, or furniture.

Word Link	*re ≈ back, again : reflect, refuel, restate*

reflect /rɪ'flekt/ (**reflects, reflecting, reflected**) 1 V-T If something **reflects** an attitude or situation, it shows that the attitude or situation exists. ❑ *His confidence was reflected in his great performance.* 2 V-T/V-I When light or heat **is reflected** off a surface, it is sent back from the surface rather than passing through it. ❑ *The light reflects off the window.* ❑ *The roof is white to reflect heat in the summer.* 3 V-T When something **is reflected** in a mirror or in water, you can see its image there. 4 V-I When you **reflect on** something, you think deeply about it. ❑ *I reflected on the child's future.* 5 V-I If an action or situation **reflects** in a particular way **on** someone or something, it gives people a good or bad impression of them. ❑ *The secret messages do not reflect well on her.*
→ see **echo, telescope**

reflection /rɪ'flekʃən/ (**reflections**) 1 N-COUNT A **reflection** is an image that you can see in a mirror or in water. 2 N-COUNT A **reflection of** a person's attitude or a situation indicates that the attitude or situation exists. ❑ *His drawings are a reflection of his own unhappiness.* 3 N-SING If you say that something is a **reflection on** someone or a **sad reflection on** someone, you mean that it gives a bad impression of them. ❑ *It's a reflection on your ability as a teacher.* 4 N-UNCOUNT **Reflection** is careful thought about a particular topic. ❑ *After a moment's reflection, he decided to tell them the truth.* 5 N-PLURAL Your **reflections** are your thoughts about a particular topic. ❑ *...his reflections on the meaning of life.*
→ see **echo**

reflection

reflective /rɪ'flektɪv/ 1 ADJ If you are **reflective**, you think deeply about things. [WRITTEN] ● **reflectively** ADV ❑ *He sipped his drink reflectively.* 2 ADJ AFTER LINK-V If something is **reflective of** a particular situation or attitude, it shows that situation or attitude exists. ❑ *Their* views are reflective of what's really happening. **3** ADJ A **reflective** surface or material sends back light or heat. [FORMAL] ❑ *...new reflective paint.*

Word Link *flex ≈ bending : flex, flexible, reflex*

reflex /ˈriːfleks/ (**reflexes**) **1** N-COUNT A **reflex** or a **reflex action** is a normal uncontrollable reaction of your body to something that you feel, see, or experience. ❑ *Sneezing is a reflex action.* **2** N-PLURAL Your **reflexes** refer to your body's ability to react quickly when something unexpected happens. ❑ *...the reflexes of an athlete.*

reflexive pronoun /rɪˈfleksɪv ˈprəʊnaʊn/ (**reflexive pronouns**) N-COUNT A **reflexive pronoun** is a pronoun such as 'myself' which refers back to the subject of a sentence or clause.

reflexive verb /rɪˈfleksɪv vɜːb/ (**reflexive verbs**) N-COUNT A **reflexive verb** is a transitive verb whose subject and object always refer to the same person or thing, so the object is always a reflexive pronoun. An example is 'to enjoy yourself'.

reform /rɪˈfɔːm/ (**reforms, reforming, reformed**) **1** N-VAR **Reform** consists of changes and improvements to a law, social system, or institution. These changes can be called **reforms**. ❑ *He wants reform of the health service.* **2** V-T To **reform** something such as a law, a social system, or an institution means to improve it by making changes. ❑ *He believes we need to reform the legal system.* ● **reformer** (**reformers**) N-COUNT ❑ *...prison reformers.* **3** V-I When someone **reforms**, they stop doing something that society does not approve of. ● **reformed** ADJ ❑ *...a reformed criminal.*

Word Partnership Use *reform* with:

ADJ.	**economic** reform, **political** reform **1**
N.	**education** reform, **election** reform, **health care** reform, reform **movement**, **party** reform, **prison** reform, **tax** reform **1**

refrain /rɪˈfreɪn/ (**refrains, refraining, refrained**) **1** V-I If you **refrain from** doing something, you deliberately do not do it. [FORMAL] ❑ *He asked them to refrain from asking questions.* **2** N-COUNT A **refrain** is a short simple part of a song which you repeat several times.

refresh /rɪˈfreʃ/ (**refreshes, refreshing, refreshed**) **1** V-T If something **refreshes** you when you are hot, tired, or thirsty, it makes you feel cooler or more energetic. ● **refreshed** ADJ ❑ *He awoke feeling completely refreshed.* ● **refreshing** ADJ ❑ *...refreshing drinks.* **2** PHRASE If someone **refreshes** your **memory**, they tell you something you have forgotten.

refreshing /rɪˈfreʃɪŋ/ **1** ADJ If something is **refreshing**, it is pleasantly different from what you are used to. ❑ *It's refreshing to hear somebody telling the truth.* ● **refreshingly** ADV ❑ *He was refreshingly honest.* **2** → see also **refresh**

refreshment /rɪˈfreʃmənt/ (**refreshments**) **1** N-PLURAL **Refreshments** are drinks and small amounts of food that are provided, for example, during a meeting or journey. **2** N-UNCOUNT You can refer to food and drink as **refreshment**. [FORMAL] ❑ *May I offer you some refreshment?*

refrigerate /rɪˈfrɪdʒəreɪt/ (**refrigerates, refrigerating, refrigerated**) V-T If you **refrigerate** food, you make it cold, for example by putting it in a refrigerator. ● **refrigeration** N-UNCOUNT ❑ *Refrigeration slows down the growth of bacteria.* → see **dairy**

refrigerator /rɪˈfrɪdʒəreɪtə/ (**refrigerators**) N-COUNT A **refrigerator** is a large container which is kept cool inside, usually by electricity, so that the food and drink in it stays fresh.

Word Link *re ≈ back, again : reflect, refuel, restate*

refuel /ˌriːˈfjuːəl/ (**refuels, refuelling, refuelled** or [AM] **refueling, refueled**) V-T/V-I When an aircraft or other vehicle **refuels**, or when someone **refuels** it, it is filled with more fuel so that it can continue its journey. ● **refuelling** N-UNCOUNT ❑ *It will make two stops for refuelling.*

refuge /ˈrefjuːdʒ/ (**refuges**) **1** N-UNCOUNT If you take **refuge** somewhere, you try to protect yourself from physical harm by going there. ❑ *Many Cubans took refuge in the United States.* **2** N-COUNT A **refuge** is a place where you go for safety and protection. ❑ *...a refuge for the homeless.*

Word Link *ee ≈ one who receives : detainee, nominee, refugee*

refugee /ˌrefjuːˈdʒiː/ (**refugees**) N-COUNT **Refugees** are people who have been forced to leave their country because there is a war there or because of their political or religious beliefs.

refund (**refunds, refunding, refunded**) **1** N-COUNT /ˈriːfʌnd/ A **refund** is a sum of money which is returned to you, for example because you have returned goods to a shop. ❑ *If you are not satisfied, you can return the product for a full refund.* **2** V-T /rɪˈfʌnd/ If someone **refunds** your money, they return it to you.

Thesaurus *refund* Also look up:

N.	payment, reimbursement **1**
V.	give back, pay back, reimburse **2**

refurbish /riːˈfɜːbɪʃ/ (**refurbishes, refurbishing, refurbished**) V-T To **refurbish** a building or room means to clean and decorate it, and make it more attractive or better equipped. ● **refurbishment** (**refurbishments**) N-VAR ❑ *The museum is closed for refurbishment.*

refusal /rɪˈfjuːzəl/ (**refusals**) N-VAR A **refusal** is the fact of firmly saying or showing that you will not do, allow, or accept something. ❑ *...the Prince's refusal to go to the concert.*

refuse (**refuses, refusing, refused**) **1** V-T/V-I /rɪˈfjuːz/ If you **refuse to** do something, you deliberately do not do it, or say firmly that you will not do it. ❑ *He refused to talk to the newspapers after the trial.* ❑ *He expects me to stay here and I can't really refuse.* **2** V-T If someone **refuses** you something, they do not allow you to have it. ❑ *The government has refused permission for the demonstration.* **3** V-T If you **refuse** something that is offered to you, you do not accept it. ❑ *The patient is allowed to refuse treatment.* **4** N-UNCOUNT /ˈrefjuːs/ **Refuse** consists of the rubbish and unwanted things in a house, shop, or factory that are regularly thrown away. [FORMAL]

r

Thesaurus *refuse* Also look up:

V. decline, reject, turn down; (*ant.*) accept 1 3
N. garbage, rubbish, waste 4

Word Partnership Use *refuse* with:

V. refuse **to answer**, refuse **to co-operate**, refuse **to go**, refuse **to participate**, refuse **to pay** 1
refuse **to allow**, refuse **to give** 1 2
refuse **to accept** 1 3

refute /rɪ'fju:t/ (**refutes, refuting, refuted**) 1 V-T If you **refute** something such as a theory or argument, you prove that it is wrong. [FORMAL] ❑ *It is impossible to refute that kind of rumour.* 2 V-T If you **refute** an allegation or accusation, you say that it is not true. [FORMAL] ❑ *He angrily refutes it.*

regain /rɪ'geɪn/ (**regains, regaining, regained**) V-T If you **regain** something that you have lost, you get it back again. ❑ *The army has regained control of the city.*

Word Link *reg ≈ rule : regal, regime, regimental*

regal /'ri:gəl/ ADJ If you describe something as **regal**, you mean that it is suitable for a king or queen, because it is very splendid or dignified. ❑ *...his regal manner.*

regard /rɪ'gɑ:d/ (**regards, regarding, regarded**) 1 V-T If you **regard** someone or something in a particular way, you think of them in that way, or have that opinion of them. ❑ *He regarded him as stupid.* ❑ *He was regarded as the most successful prime minister of modern times.* 2 N-UNCOUNT If you have a high **regard for** someone, you have a lot of respect for them. ❑ *She was pleased by Harry's regard for her parents.* 3 N-PLURAL **Regards** is used in expressions like '**kind regards**' and '**with warm regards**' as a way of expressing friendly feelings towards someone. ❑ *Give my regards to your husband.* 4 PHRASE You can use **as regards, with regard to**, or **in regard to** to indicate what you are referring to. ❑ *As regards the war, Haig always believed we would win.* 5 PHRASE You can use **in this regard** or **in that regard** to refer back to something you have just said. ❑ *In this regard nothing has changed.*

R

regarding /rɪ'gɑ:dɪŋ/ PREP You can use **regarding** to indicate what you are referring to. ❑ *He would not give us any information regarding the project.*

regardless /rɪ'gɑ:dləs/ 1 PHRASE If something happens **regardless of** something else, it is not affected or influenced at all by that other thing. ❑ *Regardless of the fact that he is wrong, we have to do as he says.* 2 ADV If you say someone did something **regardless**, you mean they did it even though there were problems that could have stopped them. ❑ *The company is continuing with the work regardless.*

regatta /rɪ'gætə/ (**regattas**) N-COUNT A **regatta** is a sports event consisting of races between yachts or rowing boats.

regenerate /rɪ'dʒenəreɪt/ (**regenerates, regenerating, regenerated**) V-T To **regenerate** something that has been declining means to develop and improve it to make it more active or successful. ❑ *The government will try to regenerate poor areas of the city.* ● **regeneration** N-UNCOUNT ❑ *...plans for the regeneration of the area.*

reggae /'regeɪ/ N-UNCOUNT **Reggae** is a kind of West Indian popular music with a very strong beat.

regime /reɪ'ʒi:m/ (**regimes**) N-COUNT If you refer to a government as a **regime**, you are critical of it because you think it is not democratic and uses unacceptable methods. ❑ *...a military regime.*

regiment /'redʒɪmənt/ (**regiments**) N-COUNT A **regiment** is a large group of soldiers commanded by a colonel. ● **regimental** /ˌredʒɪ'mentəl/ ADJ BEFORE N ❑ *...the regimental headquarters.*

region /'ri:dʒən/ (**regions**) 1 N-COUNT A **region** is an area of a country or of the world. ❑ *...one of the most popular regions in France.* ● **regional** ADJ ❑ *...regional differences.* 2 PHRASE You say **in the region of** to indicate that you are mentioning an approximate amount. ❑ *The new stadium will cost in the region of six million pounds.*

register /'redʒɪstə/ (**registers, registering, registered**) 1 N-COUNT A **register** is an official list or record. ❑ *...the register of voters.* 2 V-I If you **register for** something, you put your name on an official list. ❑ *He registered for a German class.* 3 V-T If you **register** something, you have it recorded on an official list. ❑ *The boy's mother never registered his birth.* 4 V-T/V-I When something **registers** on a scale or measuring instrument, it shows a particular value. ❑ *The earthquake registered 5.3 points on the Richter scale.* ❑ *The tremors registered on the Richter scale.* 5 V-T If you **register** a feeling or opinion that you have, you make it clear to other people. ❑ *Her face registered her surprise.*

Word Partnership Use *register* with:

N. **voters** register 1
V. register **to vote** 2

registrar /ˌredʒɪ'strɑ:, AM -'strɑ:r/ (**registrars**) 1 N-COUNT A **registrar** is a person whose job is to keep official records, especially of births, marriages, and deaths. 2 N-COUNT A **registrar** is a senior administrative official in a college or university.

registration /ˌredʒɪ'streɪʃən/ N-UNCOUNT The **registration** of something is the recording of it in an official list.

registry /'redʒɪstri/ (**registries**) N-COUNT A **registry** is a place where official records are kept.

regress /rɪ'gres/ (**regresses, regressing, regressed**) V-I When people or things **regress**, they return to an earlier and less advanced stage of development. [FORMAL] ❑ *...if your child regresses to babyish behaviour.* ● **regression** N-UNCOUNT ❑ *...regression in a student's learning process.*

regret /rɪ'gret/ (**regrets, regretting, regretted**) 1 V-T If you **regret** something that you have done, you wish that you had not done it. ❑ *I gave him exactly what he wanted, and I've regretted it ever since.* 2 N-VAR **Regret** is a feeling of sadness or disappointment. ❑ *He feels deep regret about his friend's death.* 3 N-UNCOUNT & V-T If someone expresses **regret** about something, or if they **regret** something, they are saying in a polite way that they are sorry about it. [FORMAL] ❑ *The decision to sack her was taken with regret because she was a very hard worker.* ❑ *I regret to say that Mr Brand is very ill.*

Word Partnership	Use *regret* with:
N.	regret **a decision** 1
	regret **a loss** 2
V.	**come to** regret 1 2
	express regret 3

regrettable /rɪ'gretəbəl/ ADJ You describe something as **regrettable** when you think that it is bad and that it should not happen or have happened. ❑ *Obviously, it is regrettable that we made the mistake.* ● **regrettably** ADV ❑ *Regrettably we could not find him.*

regroup /ˌriː'gruːp/ (**regroups, regrouping, regrouped**) V-I If a group of people who work as a team **regroup**, they reorganize themselves because their previous attempt to do something has failed.

regular /'regjʊlə/ (**regulars**) 1 ADJ **Regular** things happen at equal intervals, or involve things happening at equal intervals. ❑ *Close your eyes and let your breathing become regular.* ❑ *...a regular pattern of sleeping and waking.* ● **regularly** ADV ❑ *He also writes regularly for 'International Management' magazine.* ● **regularity** /ˌregjʊ'lærɪti/ N-UNCOUNT ❑ *...the regularity of the tides.* 2 ADJ **Regular** events happen often. ❑ *They agreed to meet on a regular basis.* ● **regularly** ADV ❑ *You must eat regularly to stay healthy.* ● **regularity** N-UNCOUNT ❑ *Books about Russia's past appear with increasing regularity.* 3 N-COUNT & ADJ BEFORE N If you are a **regular** at a place, or a **regular** visitor there, you go there often. ❑ *...regulars at his local pub.* ❑ *...regular churchgoers.* 4 ADJ BEFORE N **Regular** means 'normal'. ❑ *We were told to treat him like a regular student.* 5 ADJ If something has a **regular** shape, both halves are the same and it has straight edges or a smooth outline. ❑ *...a tall man with regular features.* 6 ADJ A **regular** verb, noun, or adjective inflects in the same way as most other verbs, nouns, or adjectives in the same language. An example of a regular noun is 'cat' whose plural form is 'cats'.

Word Partnership	Use *regular* with:
N.	regular **basis**, regular **checkup**, regular **exercise**, regular **meetings**, regular **schedule**, regular **visits** 1 2
	regular **customer**, regular **visitor** 3
	regular **coffee**, regular **guy**, regular **hours**, regular **post**, regular **season** 4
	regular **verbs** 6

regulate /'regjʊleɪt/ (**regulates, regulating, regulated**) V-T To **regulate** an activity or process means to control it, especially by means of rules. ❑ *...plans to regulate animal testing.* ● **regulation** N-UNCOUNT ❑ *...the regulation of nurseries.*

regulation /ˌregjʊ'leɪʃən/ (**regulations**) 1 N-COUNT **Regulations** are rules made by a government or other authority in order to control the way something is done or the way people behave. ❑ *...new safety regulations.* 2 → see also **regulate**
→ see **factory**

regulator /'regjʊleɪtə/ (**regulators**) N-COUNT A **regulator** is a person or organization appointed by a government to regulate the activities of private companies who provide a service to the public. ● **regulatory** ADJ BEFORE N ❑ *...the UK's financial regulatory system.*

rehabilitate /ˌriːhə'bɪlɪteɪt/ (**rehabilitates, rehabilitating, rehabilitated**) V-T To **rehabilitate** someone who has been ill or in prison means to help them to live a normal life again. ● **rehabilitation** N-UNCOUNT ❑ *...a rehabilitation centre for athletes recovering from injury.*

rehearsal /rɪ'hɜːsəl/ (**rehearsals**) N-VAR A **rehearsal** of a play, dance, or piece of music is the time when those taking part practise it. ❑ *...rehearsals for the school play.*
→ see **theatre**

rehearse /rɪ'hɜːs/ (**rehearses, rehearsing, rehearsed**) V-T/V-I When people **rehearse**, or **rehearse** a play, dance, or piece of music, they practise it. ❑ *Thousands of people have been rehearsing for the opening ceremony.*

reign /reɪn/ (**reigns, reigning, reigned**) 1 V-I If you say, for example, that silence **reigns** in a place, you mean that the place is silent. ❑ *Calm reigned over the city.* 2 V-I & N-COUNT When a king or queen **reigns**, he or she is the leader of the country. The **reign** of a king or queen is the period when they reign.

reimburse /ˌriːɪm'bɜːs/ (**reimburses, reimbursing, reimbursed**) V-T If you **reimburse** someone **for** something, you pay them back the money that they have spent or lost because of it. [FORMAL] ❑ *I'll be happy to reimburse you for extra costs.* ● **reimbursement** (**reimbursements**) N-VAR ❑ *She is demanding reimbursement for medical expenses.*

rein /reɪn/ (**reins, reining, reined**) 1 N-PLURAL **Reins** are the long leather straps attached to a horse's head which are used to make it go faster or stop. 2 PHRASE If you **give free rein to** someone, you give them a lot of freedom to do what they want.
→ see **horse**
▶ **rein in** PHR-VERB To **rein in** something means to control it. ❑ *He has to rein in his enthusiasm.*

Word Link	*carn* ≈ *flesh* : *carnage, incarnation, reincarnation*

reincarnation /ˌriːɪŋkɑː'neɪʃən/ (**reincarnations**) 1 N-UNCOUNT If you believe in **reincarnation**, you believe that people are born again as other people or animals after they die. 2 N-COUNT A **reincarnation** is a person or animal who is believed to contain the spirit of a dead person.

reindeer /'reɪndɪə/

> **Reindeer** is both the singular and the plural form.

N-COUNT A **reindeer** is a type of deer that lives in northern areas of Europe, Asia, and America.

reinforce /ˌriːɪn'fɔːs/ (**reinforces, reinforcing, reinforced**) 1 V-T If something **reinforces** something such as a feeling, process, or belief, it makes it stronger. ❑ *They want to reinforce the message that everyone will know someone with the disease at some point.* ● **reinforcement** (**reinforcements**) N-VAR ❑ *...the reinforcement of important values.* 2 V-T

r

To **reinforce** an object means to make it stronger or harder. ❑ *They reinforced the walls with sheets of metal.* ❑ *...reinforced glass.*

reinforcements /ˌriːɪn'fɔːsmənts/ N-PLURAL **Reinforcements** are soldiers who are sent to join an army in order to make it stronger.

reinstate /ˌriːɪn'steɪt/ (**reinstates, reinstating, reinstated**) V-T If you **reinstate** someone, you give them back a job which had been taken from them. ❑ *They reinstated him as manager.* ● **reinstatement** N-UNCOUNT ❑ *Parents campaigned for her reinstatement.*

reiterate /riː'ɪtəreɪt/ (**reiterates, reiterating, reiterated**) V-T If you **reiterate** something, you say it again or emphasize it. [FORMAL] ❑ *Let me reiterate that I knew this about him.*

reject (**rejects, rejecting, rejected**) **1** V-T /rɪ'dʒekt/ If you **reject** something such as a proposal or request, you do not accept it or agree to it. ❑ *The president was right to reject the offer.* ● **rejection** (**rejections**) N-VAR ❑ *...his rejection of our ideas.* **2** V-T If someone **is rejected** for a job or course of study, it is not offered to them. ● **rejection** N-COUNT ❑ *Be prepared for lots of rejections before you get a job.* **3** V-T If you **reject** someone who feels affection for you, you show them that you do not feel affection for them. ● **rejection** N-VAR ❑ *...feelings of rejection.* **4** N-COUNT /'riːdʒekt/ A **reject** is a product that has not been accepted for use or sale, because there is something wrong with it.

Word Partnership	Use *reject* with:
V.	**vote to** reject **1**
N.	reject **an offer**, reject **a plan**, reject **a proposal**, **voters** reject **1** reject **an application**, reject **an idea** **1** **2**

rejoice /rɪ'dʒɔɪs/ (**rejoices, rejoicing, rejoiced**) V-I If you **rejoice**, you are very pleased about something and you show it in your behaviour. [LITERARY] ● **rejoicing** N-UNCOUNT ❑ *There was general rejoicing at the news.*

rejuvenate /rɪ'dʒuːvəneɪt/ (**rejuvenates, rejuvenating, rejuvenated**) V-T If something **rejuvenates** you, it makes you feel or look young again. ❑ *The Italian climate rejuvenated him.* ● **rejuvenating** ADJ ❑ *...rejuvenating face-cream.*

R

rekindle /ˌriː'kɪndəl/ (**rekindles, rekindling, rekindled**) V-T If something **rekindles** an interest, feeling, or thought that you used to have, it makes you think about it or feel it again. ❑ *The tragedy rekindled old memories.*

relapse (**relapses, relapsing, relapsed**)

verb /rɪ'læps/, noun /rɪ'læps/ or /'riːlæps/.

1 V-I & N-COUNT If someone **relapses into** a way of behaving, or if they have a **relapse**, they start to behave in that way again. ❑ *After hearing this, the policeman relapsed into silence.* ❑ *We hope that there will not be a relapse into war.* **2** V-I & N-COUNT If a sick person **relapses**, or if they have a **relapse**, their health suddenly gets worse after it had been improving.

relate /rɪ'leɪt/ (**relates, relating, related**) **1** V-I If something **relates to** a particular subject, it concerns that subject. ❑ *The complaint relates to the quality of the food.* ● **-related** ❑ *...work-related illness.* **2** V-I The way that two things **relate** is the connection between them. ❑ *How do maths and physics relate to each other?* ● **related** ADJ ❑ *Crime and poverty are closely related.* ❑ *...diving and related activities.* **3** V-I The way that people **relate** is the way that they communicate with each other and behave towards each other. ❑ *They didn't know how to relate to my sister.* **4** V-T If you **relate** a story, you tell it. [FORMAL]

related /rɪ'leɪtɪd/ **1** ADJ AFTER LINK-V People who are **related** belong to the same family. ❑ *We look alike, but we're not related.* **2** → see also **relate**

relation /rɪ'leɪʃən/ (**relations**) **1** N-PLURAL **Relations** between people, groups, or countries are contacts between them and the way they behave towards each other. ❑ *Relations between the two countries are much better now.* **2** N-UNCOUNT The **relation of** one thing **to** another is the connection between them. ❑ *...the relation of crime to prison numbers.* **3** PHRASE You can talk about something **in relation to** something else when you want to compare the size, condition, or position of the two things. ❑ *The amount he had to pay was small in relation to his salary.* **4** N-COUNT Your **relations** are the members of your family.

relationship /rɪ'leɪʃənʃɪp/ (**relationships**) **1** N-COUNT The **relationship** between two people or groups is the way they feel and behave towards each other. ❑ *...close family relationships.* **2** N-COUNT A **relationship** is also a close friendship between two people, especially one involving romantic or sexual feelings. ❑ *...two people in a loving relationship.* **3** N-COUNT The **relationship** between two things is the way in which they are connected. ❑ *...a relationship between diet and cancer.*

relative /'relətɪv/ (**relatives**) **1** N-COUNT Your **relatives** are the members of your family. ❑ *Ask a relative to look after the children.* **2** ADJ You use **relative** when you are comparing two or more things, particularly their size or quality. ❑ *The fighting began again after a period of relative calm.* ❑ *If you drive at 50mph on a motorway, it seems very slow. It's all relative.* ● **relatively** ADV ❑ *The amounts needed are relatively small.* **3** PHRASE **Relative to** something means with reference to it or in comparison with it. ❑ *The price of gold rose relative to that of silver.*

Word Partnership	Use *relative* with:
ADJ.	**close** relative, **distant** relative **1**
N.	**friend and** relative **1** relative **calm**, relative **ease**, relative **safety**, relative **stability** **2**

ˌrelative 'clause (**relative clauses**) N-COUNT A **relative clause** is a subordinate clause which specifies or gives information about a person or thing. Relative clauses come after a noun or pronoun and, in English, often begin with a relative pronoun such as 'who', 'which', or 'that'.

ˌrelative 'pronoun (**relative pronouns**) N-COUNT A **relative pronoun** is a word such as 'who', 'that', or 'which' that is used to introduce a relative clause.

Word Link	*lax ≈ allowing, loosening : lax, laxative, relax*

relax /rɪ'læks/ (**relaxes, relaxing, relaxed**)

1 V-T/V-I If you **relax**, or if something **relaxes** you, you feel calmer and less worried or tense. ❑ *I ought to relax and stop worrying about it.* ❑ *Do something that relaxes you.* ● **relaxation** N-UNCOUNT ❑ *...relaxation techniques.* ● **relaxed** ADJ ❑ *The atmosphere at lunch was relaxed.* ● **relaxing** ADJ ❑ *...a quiet, relaxing holiday.* 2 V-T/V-I When part of your body **relaxes**, or when you **relax** it, it becomes less stiff, firm, or tense. ❑ *Massage is used to relax muscles.* 3 V-T If you **relax** your grip on something, you hold it less tightly than before. 4 V-T/V-I If you **relax** a rule, or if it **relaxes**, you make it less strict. ❑ *Rules over student behaviour have relaxed recently.*
→ see **muscle**

Thesaurus *relax* Also look up:

V. calm down, rest, unwind 1
ease off, loosen 3 4

Word Partnership Use *relax* with:

V. **sit back and** relax 1
begin to relax, **try to** relax 1 2
N. **time to** relax 1
relax ***your*** **body, muscles** relax 2

relay (**relays, relaying, relayed**) 1 N-COUNT /ˈriːleɪ/ A **relay** or a **relay race** is a race between two or more teams in which each member of the team runs or swims one section of the race. 2 V-T /rɪˈleɪ/ To **relay** television or radio signals means to send them on or broadcast them.

release /rɪˈliːs/ (**releases, releasing, released**) 1 V-T & N-COUNT If a prisoner or animal **is released**, they are set free. You can also talk about someone's **release**. ❑ *He demanded the release of all political prisoners.* 2 V-T & N-UNCOUNT To **release** someone **from** an obligation, task, or feeling, or to give them **release from** it means to free them from it. [FORMAL] ❑ *She felt he had released her from the promise she made all those years ago.* 3 V-T & N-UNCOUNT If someone in authority **releases** information, they make it available. You can also talk about the **release** of information. 4 V-T If you **release** someone or something, you stop holding them. [FORMAL] ❑ *He stopped and turned, releasing her arm.* 5 V-T & N-COUNT When a form of energy or a substance such as a gas **is released** from something, it escapes from it. You can also talk about the **release** of energy or a substance. ❑ *...the release of gases into the environment.* 6 V-T & N-COUNT When a new CD, video, or film **is released**, it becomes available so that people can buy it or see it. You refer to this new CD, video or film as a **new release**. 7 → see also **press release**

relegate /ˈrelɪgeɪt/ (**relegates, relegating, relegated**) 1 V-T If a team that competes in a league **is relegated**, it is moved to a lower division because it finished at or near the bottom of its division at the end of a season. ● **relegation** N-UNCOUNT ❑ *Relegation to the Third Division would be a disaster.* 2 V-T If someone or something **is relegated to** a less important position or role, they are moved to that position or role.

relent /rɪˈlent/ (**relents, relenting, relented**) V-I If you **relent**, you allow someone to do something that you had previously refused to allow them to do. ❑ *Finally she relented and let her daughter marry him.*

relentless /rɪˈlentləs/ ADJ If something is **relentless**, it never stops or becomes less intense. ❑ *The pressure was relentless.* ❑ *She moves with relentless energy from one project to another.* ● **relentlessly** ADV ❑ *The sun is beating down relentlessly.*

relevant /ˈreləvənt/ ADJ If something is **relevant to** a situation or person, it is important or significant in that situation or to that person. ❑ *Don't worry about last year. It's what happens today that is really relevant.* ❑ *Dr Venter said that he would ask the relevant people.* ● **relevance** N-UNCOUNT ❑ *Many of the experiments performed on animals had little relevance to humans.*

reliable /rɪˈlaɪəbəl/ 1 ADJ **Reliable** people or things can be trusted to work well or to behave in the way that you want them to. ● **reliably** ADV ❑ *It's been working reliably for years.* ● **reliability** N-UNCOUNT ❑ *He's worried about his car's reliability.* 2 ADJ **Reliable** information is very likely to be correct, because it comes from a trustworthy or accurate source. ● **reliably** ADV ❑ *Sonia, we are reliably informed, loves her family very much.* ● **reliability** N-UNCOUNT ❑ *They questioned the reliability of the report.*

Word Partnership Use *reliable* with:

N. reliable **service** 1
reliable **data,** reliable **information,**
reliable **source** 2
ADV. **highly** reliable, **less/more/most**
reliable, **usually** reliable, **very**
reliable 1 2

reliant /rɪˈlaɪənt/ ADJ AFTER LINK-V A person or thing that is **reliant on** something needs it and often cannot live or work without it. ● **reliance** N-UNCOUNT ❑ *...the country's reliance on foreign help.*

relic /ˈrelɪk/ (**relics**) 1 N-COUNT If you describe something or someone as a **relic of** or **from** an earlier period, you dislike them and think that they should not have survived into the present. ❑ *The wide tie was a relic from the 1970s.* 2 N-COUNT A **relic** is something which was made or used a long time ago and which is kept for its historical significance. ❑ *...a museum of war relics.*

relief /rɪˈliːf/ 1 N-UNCOUNT If you feel a sense of **relief**, you feel glad because something unpleasant has not happened or is no longer happening. ❑ *I breathed a sigh of relief.* ❑ *It's a great relief to be back.* 2 N-UNCOUNT If something provides **relief from** pain or distress, it stops the pain or distress, or it makes it less intense. 3 N-UNCOUNT **Relief** is money, food, or clothing that is provided for people who are very poor or hungry, or who have been affected by war or a natural disaster.

Word Partnership Use *relief* with:

V. **express** relief 1
feel relief, **seek** relief 1 2
bring relief, **get** relief, **provide**
relief 1-3
supply relief 2 3
N. **sense of** relief, **sigh of** relief 1
pain relief, relief **from symptoms,**
relief **from tension** 2
disaster relief, **emergency** relief 3

r

relieve /rɪ'li:v/ (**relieves, relieving, relieved**) 1 V-T If something **relieves** an unpleasant feeling or situation, it makes it less unpleasant or causes it to disappear completely. ❑ *Drugs can relieve much of the pain.* 2 V-T If someone **relieves** you **of** something, they take it away from you. ❑ *A porter relieved her of the three large suitcases.* 3 V-T If you **relieve** someone, you take their place and do the job or task being done previously by that person.

relieved /rɪ'li:vd/ ADJ If you are **relieved**, you feel glad because something unpleasant has not happened or is no longer happening.

religion /rɪ'lɪdʒən/ (**religions**) 1 N-UNCOUNT **Religion** is belief in a god or gods. ❑ *...Indian philosophy and religion.* 2 N-COUNT A **religion** is a particular set of beliefs in a god or gods and the activities connected with these beliefs. ❑ *...the Christian religion.*

religious /rɪ'lɪdʒəs/ 1 ADJ BEFORE N **Religious** means connected with religion or with one particular religion. ❑ *...different religious beliefs.* 2 ADJ A **religious** person has a strong belief in a god or gods.

relinquish /rɪ'lɪŋkwɪʃ/ (**relinquishes, relinquishing, relinquished**) V-T If you **relinquish** something such as power or control, you give it up. [FORMAL]

relish /'relɪʃ/ (**relishes, relishing, relished**) V-T & N-UNCOUNT If you **relish** something, or if you do something **with relish**, you get a lot of enjoyment from it. ❑ *I relish the challenge of doing jobs that others don't want to do.*

relive /ˌri:'lɪv/ (**relives, reliving, relived**) V-T If you **relive** something that has happened to you in the past, you remember it and imagine that you are experiencing it again.

relocate /ˌri:ləʊ'keɪt, AM -'ləʊkeɪt/ (**relocates, relocating, relocated**) V-T/V-I If people or businesses **relocate**, or if they **are relocated**, they move to a different place. ❑ *The firm wants to relocate its head office from London to Glasgow.* • **relocation** N-UNCOUNT ❑ *...the company's relocation out of town.*

reluctant /rɪ'lʌktənt/ ADJ If you are **reluctant to** do something, you do not really want to do it. • **reluctantly** ADV ❑ *We have reluctantly agreed to let him go.* • **reluctance** N-UNCOUNT ❑ *Frank got on the train with great reluctance.*

R

rely /rɪ'laɪ/ (**relies, relying, relied**) 1 V-I If you **rely on** someone or something, you need them in order to live or work properly. ❑ *He relies on his wife for most of his money.* 2 V-I If you can **rely on** someone to work well or behave as you want them to, you can trust them to do this.

remain /rɪ'meɪn/ (**remains, remaining, remained**) 1 LINK-VERB To **remain** in a particular state means to stay in that state and not change. ❑ *The three men remained silent.* ❑ *He remained a world-class athlete.* 2 V-I If you **remain** in a place, you do not move away from it. ❑ *She remained at home, waiting for the phone to ring.* 3 V-I You can say that something **remains** when it still exists. ❑ *Other dangers still remain.* 4 LINK-VERB If something **remains** to be done, it still needs to be done. 5 N-PLURAL **The remains of** something are the parts of it that are left after most of it has been taken away or destroyed. ❑ *...the burnt-out remains of a car.* 6 N-PLURAL The **remains** of a person or animal are the parts of their body that are left after they have died. ❑ *...human remains.* 7 N-PLURAL **Remains** are objects and parts of buildings from an earlier period of history. ❑ *...Roman remains.* 8 → see also **remaining**

remainder /rɪ'meɪndə/ N-SING **The remainder of** something is the part of it that remains after the other parts have gone or been dealt with. ❑ *He drank the remainder of his coffee.*

remaining /rɪ'meɪnɪŋ/ 1 ADJ BEFORE N The **remaining** things or people out of a group are the things or people that still exist, are still present, or have not yet been dealt with. ❑ *Pour the remaining ingredients into a bowl.* 2 → see also **remain**

remake (**remakes, remaking, remade**)

verb /ˌri:'meɪk/, noun /'ri:meɪk/.

V-T & N-COUNT If a film **is remade**, or if there is a **remake of** it, a new film is made that has the same story, and often the same title, as the original film.

remand /rɪ'mɑ:nd, -'mænd/ (**remands, remanding, remanded**) V-T & N-UNCOUNT If a person who is accused of a crime **is remanded in custody**, or if they are **on remand**, they are kept in prison until their trial. If they **are remanded on bail**, they are released and told to return to the court at a later date, when their trial will take place. ❑ *She has already spent a year in prison on remand.*

remark /rɪ'mɑ:k/ (**remarks, remarking, remarked**) 1 V-T/V-I If you **remark that** something is the case, you say that it is the case. ❑ *'Some people have too much money,' Winston remarked.* ❑ *She remarked on the boy's progress.* 2 N-COUNT If you make a **remark** about something, you say something about it.

Word Partnership	Use *remark* with:
ADJ.	**casual** remark 2
V.	**hear a** remark, **make a** remark 2

remarkable /rɪ'mɑ:kəbəl/ ADJ Someone or something that is **remarkable** is very impressive or unusual. • **remarkably** ADV ❑ *The book is remarkably accurate.*

remedial /rɪ'mi:diəl/ ADJ **Remedial** activities are intended to improve something. [FORMAL] ❑ *What kind of remedial action do we need?*

remedy /'remədi/ (**remedies, remedying, remedied**) 1 V-T & N-COUNT If you **remedy** something that is wrong or harmful, or if you find a **remedy for** it, you correct or improve it. ❑ *They took action to remedy the situation.* ❑ *...a remedy for unemployment.* 2 N-COUNT A **remedy** is something that is intended to stop illness or pain. ❑ *...Chinese herbal remedies.*

remember /rɪ'membə/ (**remembers, remembering, remembered**) 1 V-T/V-I If you **remember** people or events from the past, you still have an idea of them in your mind and you are able to think about them. ❑ *I remember her perfectly.* ❑ *I can't remember.* ❑ *I remember that it snowed quite a lot.* 2 V-T If you **remember that** something is the case, you suddenly become aware of it again after a time when you did not think about it. ❑ *She remembered that she was going to the cinema that evening.* ❑ *Then I remembered the party, which cheered me up.* 3 V-T If you **remember to** do something, you do it when you intend to. ❑ *Please remember to send a cheque for £29.99.*

Thesaurus *remember* Also look up:
V. look back, recall, think back; (*ant.*) forget 1

Word Partnership Use *remember* with:
ADJ. **easy to** remember, **important to** remember 1 2 3
ADV. **always** remember, remember **clearly**, remember **correctly**, remember **exactly**, **still** remember remember **vividly** 1
CONJ. remember **what**, remember **when**, remember **where**, remember **why** 1

remembrance /rɪ'membrəns/ N-UNCOUNT If you do something **in remembrance of** a dead person, you do it as a way of showing that you remember them and respect them. [FORMAL]

remind /rɪ'maɪnd/ (**reminds, reminding, reminded**) 1 V-T If someone **reminds** you **of** a fact or event that you already know about, they say something which makes you think about it. ❑ *They reminded him of the risks.* 2 V-T If someone **reminds** you **to** do something, they say something which makes you remember to do it. ❑ *The teacher reminded them to bring in their homework on Monday.* 3 V-T If someone or something **reminds** you **of** another person or thing, they are similar to the other person or thing and they make you think about them. ❑ *The president reminds me of a manager I once knew.*

Word Partnership Use *remind* with:
PREP. remind ***someone*** **of** ***something*** 1
remind ***you*** **of** ***someone/something*** 3
V. **let me** remind **you**, **may I** remind **you** 2

reminder /rɪ'maɪndə/ (**reminders**) 1 N-COUNT If one thing is a **reminder of** another, the first thing makes you think about the second. ❑ *The accident was a harsh reminder that doors and windows should be locked.* 2 N-COUNT A **reminder** is a letter that is sent to tell you that you have not done something such as pay a bill.

reminisce /ˌremɪ'nɪs/ (**reminisces, reminiscing, reminisced**) V-I If you **reminisce about** something from your past, you write or talk about it with pleasure. [FORMAL]

reminiscence /ˌremɪ'nɪsəns/ (**reminiscences**) N-COUNT Someone's **reminiscences** are things which they remember from the past, and which they talk or write about. [FORMAL]

reminiscent /ˌremɪ'nɪsənt/ ADJ AFTER LINK-V If one thing is **reminiscent of** another, the first thing reminds you of the second. [FORMAL] ❑ *...red-roofed houses reminiscent of the houses found in France.*

remission /rɪ'mɪʃən/ (**remissions**) 1 N-VAR If someone who has had a serious disease is **in remission** or if the disease is **in remission**, the disease has been controlled so that they are not as ill as they were. 2 N-UNCOUNT If someone in prison gets **remission**, their prison sentence is reduced, usually because they have behaved well. [BRIT]

remit /'riːmɪt/ (**remits**) N-COUNT Someone's **remit** is the area of activity which they are expected to deal with, or which they have authority to deal with. ❑ *The centre has a remit to advise new businesses.*

remnant /'remnənt/ (**remnants**) N-COUNT A **remnant of** something is a small part of it that is left when the main part has disappeared or been destroyed. ❑ *Beneath the present church were remnants of Roman mosaics.*

remorse /rɪ'mɔːs/ N-UNCOUNT **Remorse** is a strong feeling of guilt and regret about something wrong that you have done. [FORMAL]

remote /rɪ'məʊt/ (**remoter, remotest**) 1 ADJ **Remote** areas are far away from places where most people live. • **remoteness** N-UNCOUNT ❑ *...the remoteness of the island.* 2 ADJ If something is **remote from** what people want or need, it is not relevant to it because it is so different from it or has no connection with it. ❑ *Teenagers are forced to study subjects that seem remote from their daily lives.* 3 ADJ If you describe someone as **remote**, you mean that they are not friendly and do not get closely involved with other people. 4 ADJ If there is a **remote possibility** that something will happen, there is only a very small possibility that it will happen.

reˌmote conˈtrol (**remote controls**) 1 N-UNCOUNT **Remote control** is a system of controlling a machine or vehicle from a distance by using radio or electronic signals. 2 N-COUNT The **remote control** for a television, video recorder, or music system is the device that you use to control it from a distance.

remotely /rɪ'məʊtli/ ADV You use **remotely** to emphasize a negative statement. ❑ *Nobody was remotely interested.*

removal /rɪ'muːvəl/ (**removals**) 1 N-UNCOUNT The **removal** of something is the act of removing it. ❑ *...the removal of the tumour during the operation.* 2 N-VAR **Removal** is the process of transporting furniture from one building to another. [BRIT] ❑ *...a lorry suitable for house removals.* ❑ *...a removal van.*

remove /rɪ'muːv/ (**removes, removing, removed**) 1 V-T If you **remove** something **from** a place, you take it away. ❑ *He went to the refrigerator and removed a bottle of milk.* ❑ *Three bullets were removed from his leg.* 2 V-T When you **remove** clothing, you take it off. 3 V-T If you **remove** an obstacle or a problem, you get rid of it. ❑ *Her fears had been removed after their conversation.*

Thesaurus *remove* Also look up:
V. take away, take out 1
take off, undress 2

removed /rɪ'muːvd/ ADJ If an idea or situation is **far removed from** something, it is very different from it. ❑ *Her dream home is far removed from reality.*

renaissance /rɪ'neɪsɒns, AM ˌrenɪ'sɑːns/ N-SING If something experiences a **renaissance**, it becomes popular or successful again after a time when people were not interested in it.

render /'rendə/ (**renders, rendering, rendered**) 1 V-T You can use **render** to say that something is changed into a different state. ❑ *The report had so many mistakes it was rendered useless.* 2 V-T If you **render** someone help or assistance, you help them. [FORMAL] ❑ *We would be very grateful for any help you can render him.* **3** V-T To **render** something in a particular language or in a particular way means to express it in that language or in that way. ❑ *All the signs were rendered in English and Spanish.* • **rendering** (**renderings**) N-COUNT ❑ *...a rendering of Verdi's Requiem by the BBC Symphony Orchestra.*

rendezvous /'rɒndeɪvuː/ (**rendezvous, rendezvousing** /'rɒndeɪvuːɪŋ/, **rendezvoused** /'rɒndeɪvuːd/)

> The form **rendezvous** is pronounced /'rɒndeɪvuːz/ when it is the plural of the noun or the third person singular of the verb.

V-I & N-COUNT If you **rendezvous with** someone or if the two of you **rendezvous**, you meet at a particular time and place, often secretly. Your meeting is called a **rendezvous**. ❑ *The restaurant is an ideal place for a romantic rendezvous.*

renegade /'renɪgeɪd/ (**renegades**) N-COUNT & ADJ BEFORE N A **renegade** is a person who abandons their former group and joins an opposing or different group. You use **renegade** to describe a person who does this. ❑ *Three men were shot dead by a renegade policeman.*

renew /rɪ'njuː, AM -'nuː/ (**renews, renewing, renewed**) **1** V-T If you **renew** an activity or a relationship, you begin it again. ❑ *When the two men met again after the war they renewed their friendship.* ❑ *...renewed fighting.* **2** V-T When you **renew** something such as a licence or a contract, you extend the period of time for which it is valid. ❑ *The club is going to renew his licence this year.* **3** V-T You can say that something **is renewed** when it grows or succeeds again after a time when it was destroyed, lost, or failing. ❑ *...a renewed interest in Italian cinema.*

> **Thesaurus** *renew* Also look up:
> V. continue, resume, revive **1**

renewable /rɪ'njuːəbəl, AM -'nuː-/ **1** ADJ **Renewable** resources are ones such as wind, water, and sunlight, which are constantly replacing themselves and therefore do not become used up. **2** ADJ If a contract or agreement is **renewable**, it can be extended when it reaches the end of a fixed period of time.

R

renewal /rɪ'njuːəl, -'nuː-/ (**renewals**) **1** N-SING If there is a **renewal of** an activity or situation, it starts again. **2** N-VAR The **renewal** of a document such as a licence or a contract is an official extension of the time for which it remains valid. ❑ *His contract is up for renewal.*

renounce /rɪ'naʊns/ (**renounces, renouncing, renounced**) V-T If you **renounce** something, you reject it or give it up. ❑ *She has renounced marriage and motherhood.*

> **Word Link** *nov ≈ new : innovation, novel, renovate*

renovate /'renəveɪt/ (**renovates, renovating, renovated**) V-T If someone **renovates** an old building or machine, they repair it and get it back into good condition. • **renovation** (**renovations**) N-VAR ❑ *The building will need extensive renovation.*

renown /rɪ'naʊn/ N-UNCOUNT A person **of renown** is well-known, usually because they do or have done something good. ❑ *...a celebrity of world renown.*

renowned /rɪ'naʊnd/ ADJ A person or place that is **renowned for** something, usually something good, is well known because of it. ❑ *The hotel is renowned for its friendliness.*

rent /rent/ (**rents, renting, rented**) **1** V-T If you **rent** something, you regularly pay its owner in order to have it and use it yourself. ❑ *...a rented car.* **2** V-T & PHR-VERB If you **rent** something **to** someone, or if you **rent** it **out to** them, you let them have it and use it in exchange for a sum of money which they pay you regularly. ❑ *She rented rooms to university students.* **3** N-VAR **Rent** is the amount of money that you pay regularly for the use of a house, flat, or piece of land. ❑ *They recently increased my rent.*

rental /'rentəl/ (**rentals**) **1** N-VAR The **rental** of something such as a car or television is the fact of paying an amount of money in order to have and use it. ❑ *...Scotland's largest car rental company.* **2** N-COUNT The **rental** is the amount of money that you have to pay to use something such as a television, telephone, car, or property. [BRIT] **3** ADJ BEFORE N You use **rental** to describe things that are connected with the renting out of goods, properties, and services. ❑ *She picked up a rental car.*

reorganize [BRIT also **reorganise**] /riˈɔːgənaɪz/ (**reorganizes, reorganizing, reorganized**) V-T To **reorganize** something means to change the way in which it is organized or done. • **reorganization** (**reorganizations**) N-VAR ❑ *...the reorganization of the education system.*

rep /rep/ (**reps**) **1** N-COUNT A **rep** is a person who travels round selling their company's products or services to other companies. **2** N-COUNT A **rep** is a person who acts as a representative for a group of people. ❑ *The class rep must go to the student-teacher meetings.* **3** N-UNCOUNT In the theatre, **rep** is the same as **repertory**.

repaid /rɪ'peɪd/ **Repaid** is the past tense and past participle of **repay**.

repair /rɪ'peə/ (**repairs, repairing, repaired**) **1** V-T If you **repair** something that has been damaged or is not working properly, you mend it. ❑ *We had three weeks to repair it.* • **repairer** (**repairers**) N-COUNT ❑ *...builders, plumbers and TV repairers.* **2** N-VAR A **repair** is something that you do to mend something that has been damaged. ❑ *Do you know how to carry out repairs on your car?* ❑ *Her marriage is beyond repair.* **3** PHRASE If something such as a building is **in good repair**, it is in good condition. If it is **in bad repair**, it is in bad condition.

> **Word Partnership** Use *repair* with:
> N. **auto** repair, **car** repair, repair **a chimney**, repair **equipment**, **home** repair, repair **parts**, **road** repair, repair **a roof** repair **service**, repair **shop** **1**
> repair **damage** **1** **2**
> repair **a relationship** **2**

repatriate /ˌriː'pætrieɪt, AM -'peɪt-/ (**repatriates, repatriating, repatriated**) V-T If a country **repatriates** someone, it sends them back to their home country. • **repatriation** (**repatriations**) N-VAR ❑ *...the repatriation of Albanian refugees.*

repay /rɪ'peɪ/ (**repays, repaying, repaid**) 1 V-T If you **repay** a debt, you pay back the money you owe to somebody. 2 V-T If you **repay** a favour that someone did for you, you do something or give them something in return. ❑ *It was very kind. I don't know how I can ever repay you.*

repayment /rɪ'peɪmənt/ (**repayments**) 1 N-COUNT A **repayment** is an amount of money paid at regular intervals in order to repay a debt. 2 N-UNCOUNT The **repayment** of money is the act or process of paying it back to the person you borrowed it from.

repeal /rɪ'piːl/ (**repeals, repealing, repealed**) V-T & N-COUNT If the government **repeals** a law, it officially ends it so that it is no longer valid. You call this the **repeal** of a law.

repeat /rɪ'piːt/ (**repeats, repeating, repeated**) 1 V-T If you **repeat** something, you say or write it again. ❑ *She repeated what she had said before.* 2 V-T If you **repeat** something that someone else has said or written, you say or write the same thing. ❑ *She had an irritating habit of repeating everything I said to her.* 3 V-T If you **repeat** an action, you do it again. 4 V-T & N-COUNT If an event or series of events **repeats itself**, or if there is a **repeat of** an event, it happens again. ❑ *The government is determined not to let history repeat itself.* 5 N-COUNT A **repeat** is a television or radio programme that has been broadcast before.

Thesaurus *repeat* Also look up:

V.	reiterate, restate 1 2
N.	encore 5

repeated /rɪ'piːtɪd/ ADJ BEFORE N **Repeated** actions or events are ones which happen many times. ● **repeatedly** ADV ❑ *John has said repeatedly that this is true.*

repel /rɪ'pel/ (**repels, repelling, repelled**) 1 V-T When an army **repels** an attack or an invasion, they successfully fight and drive back soldiers from another army. [FORMAL] 2 V-T If something **repels** you, you find it horrible and disgusting. ● **repelled** ADJ ❑ *You may feel repelled at the idea of reading this book.*
→ see **magnet**

repellent /rɪ'pelənt/ (**repellents**)

The spelling **repellant** is also used for meaning 2.

1 ADJ If you think that something is horrible and disgusting, you can say it is **repellent.** [FORMAL] ❑ *...a very large, very repellent toad.* 2 N-VAR **Insect repellents** are chemical substances that you use to keep insects away.

repent /rɪ'pent/ (**repents, repenting, repented**) V-I If you **repent**, you say or show you feel sorry for something wrong you have done. ● **repentance** N-UNCOUNT ❑ *They showed no repentance during their trial.* ● **repentant** ADJ ❑ *...a repentant criminal.*

Word Link *cuss ≈ striking : concussion, percussion, repercussions*

repercussions /ˌriːpə'kʌʃənz/ N-PLURAL If an action or event has **repercussions**, it causes unpleasant things to happen some time after the original action or event. ❑ *This action could have serious repercussions.*

repertoire /'repətwɑː/ N-SING A performer's **repertoire** is all the pieces of music or parts in plays that he or she has learned and can perform. ❑ *...a wide repertoire of songs.*

repetition /ˌrepɪ'tɪʃən/ (**repetitions**) N-VAR If there is a **repetition of** an event, it happens again. ❑ *...a repetition of last month's violence.*

repetitive /rɪ'petɪtɪv/ ADJ **Repetitive** actions are repeated many times and are therefore boring. ❑ *Factory workers often do repetitive jobs.*

replace /rɪ'pleɪs/ (**replaces, replacing, replaced**) 1 V-T To **replace** a person or thing means to put another person or thing in their place. ❑ *A lawyer replaced Bob as chairman of the company.* ❑ *They were planning to pull down the building and replace it with shops and offices.* ● **replacement** N-UNCOUNT ❑ *He described the replacement of Mr Gorbachev as president of the Soviet Union as a tremendous surprise.* 2 V-T If you **replace** something that is damaged or lost, you get a new one. ● **replacement** N-UNCOUNT ❑ *...the replacement of damaged or lost books.* 3 V-T If you **replace** something, you put it back where it was before. ❑ *Replace the caps on the bottles.*

replacement /rɪ'pleɪsmənt/ (**replacements**) N-COUNT One thing or person that replaces another can be referred to as their **replacement.** ❑ *Taylor has nominated Adams as his replacement.*

replay (**replays, replaying, replayed**)

verb /ˌriː'pleɪ/, noun /'riːpleɪ/.

1 V-T & N-COUNT In sport, if a match **is replayed**, it is played again, usually because there is no winner from the first match. The second match is called a **replay.** 2 N-COUNT A **replay** of something which has been recorded digitally or on a video tape is another showing of it. ❑ *...a slow-motion replay.*

Word Link *plen ≈ full : plentiful, plenty, replenish*

replenish /rɪ'plenɪʃ/ (**replenishes, replenishing, replenished**) V-T If you **replenish** something, you make it full or complete again. [FORMAL] ❑ *They replenished their food and water supplies.* ● **replenishment** N-UNCOUNT ❑ *...the replenishment of fuel supplies.*

replica /'replɪkə/ (**replicas**) N-COUNT A **replica of** something such as a statue, machine, or weapon is an accurate copy of it.

reply /rɪ'plaɪ/ (**replies, replying, replied**) 1 V-I & N-COUNT When you **reply to** something that someone has said or written to you, you say or write something, called a **reply**, as an answer. ❑ *I've not replied to Lee's letter yet.* ❑ *David has had 12 replies to his ad.* 2 V-I If you **reply** to something such as an attack **with** a particular action, you do something in response. ❑ *The demonstrators threw rocks and the police replied with tear gas.*

Thesaurus *reply* Also look up:

V.	acknowledge, answer, respond, return 1
N.	acknowledgement, answer, response 1

Word Partnership Use *reply* with:

N.	reply **card**, reply **envelope**, reply **form** 1
V.	**receive a** reply 1
	make a reply 1 2

report /rɪ'pɔːt/ (**reports, reporting, reported**) **1** V-T If you **report** something that has happened, you tell people about it. ❑ *I reported the theft to the police.* ❑ *Hotels report that business is booming.* ❑ *The prime minister is reported as saying that force will have to be used.* ❑ *She reported him missing the next day.* **2** V-I & N-COUNT If you **report on** an event or subject, or if you give someone a **report on** it, you tell people about it, because it is your job or duty to do so. ❑ *I'll report back to you every night.* ❑ *...a progress report on how the project is going.* **3** N-COUNT A **report** is a news article or broadcast which gives information about something that has just happened. **4** N-COUNT A school **report** is a written account of a pupil's work and behaviour for the previous term or year. **5** V-T If someone **reports** you **to** a person in authority, they tell the person about something wrong that you have done. ❑ *His wife reported him to the police.* ❑ *She was reported for speeding.* **6** V-I If you **report to** a person or place, you go to them and say that you are ready to start work. ❑ *Who do you report to?* ❑ *None of the men reported for duty.*

reportedly /rɪ'pɔːtɪdli/ ADV If you say that something is **reportedly** the case, you mean that someone has said that it is the case, but you have no evidence of it. [FORMAL] ❑ *More than two hundred people have reportedly been injured.*

re,ported 'speech N-UNCOUNT **Reported speech** gives an account of something that someone has said, but without quoting their actual words. **Reported speech** is usually introduced by a verb such as 'say' or 'tell' followed by 'that', as in 'He said that he was tired.'

reporter /rɪ'pɔːtə/ (**reporters**) N-COUNT A **reporter** is someone who writes news articles or broadcasts news reports. ❑ *...a TV reporter.*

reporting /rɪ'pɔːtɪŋ/ N-UNCOUNT **Reporting** is the presenting of news in newspapers, on radio, and on television. ❑ *...political reporting.*

repossess /,riːpə'zes/ (**repossesses, repossessing, repossessed**) V-T If a person's house or car **is repossessed**, it is taken from them because the loan payments have not been paid.

repossession /,riːpə'zeʃən/ (**repossessions**) **1** N-VAR The **repossession** of someone's house is the act of repossessing it. **2** N-COUNT You can refer to a house or car that has been repossessed as a **repossession**. ❑ *Many of the cars you will see at auction are repossessions.*

R

represent /,reprɪ'zent/ (**represents, representing, represented**) **1** V-T If someone **represents** you, they act on your behalf. ❑ *We elect politicians to represent us.* **2** V-T If you say that something **represents** a change, achievement, or victory, you mean that it is a change, achievement, or victory. ❑ *The president said the proposals did not represent a change in policy.* **3** V-T If a sign or symbol **represents** something, it is accepted as meaning that thing. ❑ *In Chinese philosophy, water represents wealth.* **4** V-T If you **represent** a person or thing **as** a particular thing, you describe them as being that thing. ❑ *He complained that the press had represented him as a fool.*

representation /,reprɪzen'teɪʃən/ (**representations**) **1** N-UNCOUNT If a group or person has **representation** in a parliament or on a committee, someone in parliament or on the committee will vote or make decisions on their behalf. ❑ *Puerto Ricans are U.S. citizens but they have no representation in Congress.* **2** N-COUNT You can describe a picture or statue of someone as a **representation of** them. [FORMAL] ❑ *...a representation of Christ.*

representative /,reprɪ'zentətɪv/ (**representatives**) **1** N-COUNT A **representative** is a person who acts for another person or group of people. ❑ *...trade union representatives.* **2** ADJ BEFORE N A **representative** group acts on behalf of a larger group. **3** ADJ If something is **representative of** a group, it is typical of that group. ❑ *He felt that their views were not representative of Britain as a whole.*

repress /rɪ'pres/ (**represses, repressing, repressed**) **1** V-T If you **repress** a feeling, you make a deliberate effort not to show or have this feeling; used showing disapproval. ❑ *She repressed her anger about her problems.* • **repression** N-UNCOUNT ❑ *...repression of our emotions.* **2** V-T If a section of society **is repressed**, their freedom is restricted by the people who have authority over them; used showing disapproval. ❑ *He warned that the new government will repress and rob the people.* • **repression** (**repressions**) N-VAR ❑ *...a society torn apart by violence and repression.*

repressed /rɪ'prest/ ADJ **Repressed** people try to stop themselves having natural feelings and desires, especially sexual ones; used showing disapproval.

repressive /rɪ'presɪv/ ADJ A **repressive** government is one which uses force to control people and to restrict their freedom.

reprieve /rɪ'priːv/ (**reprieves, reprieving, reprieved**) **1** V-T If someone who has been sentenced in court **is reprieved**, their punishment is officially postponed or cancelled. **2** N-COUNT A **reprieve** is a delay before a very unpleasant or difficult situation which may or may not take place. ❑ *A South African family have just won a reprieve in their fight to stay in Canada.*

reprimand /'reprɪmɑːnd, -'mænd/ (**reprimands, reprimanding, reprimanded**) V-T & N-COUNT If someone in authority **reprimands** you, or if they give you a **reprimand**, they speak to you angrily or seriously for doing something wrong. ❑ *He was reprimanded by a teacher for running in the corridor.* ❑ *He was fined five thousand pounds and given a severe reprimand.*

reprint (**reprints, reprinting, reprinted**) **1** V-T /,riː'prɪnt/ When a book **is reprinted**, further copies of it are printed after all the other ones have been sold. **2** N-COUNT /'riːprɪnt/ A **reprint** is a new copy of a book or article, printed because all the other ones have been sold or because minor changes have been made to the original.

reprisal /rɪ'praɪzəl/ (**reprisals**) N-VAR If you do something to someone in **reprisal**, you do something violent or unpleasant to them because they have done something similar to you. ❑ *...the fear of reprisals.*

reproach /rɪ'prəʊtʃ/ (**reproaches, reproaching, reproached**) **1** V-T If you **reproach** someone, you say or show that you are disappointed, upset, or angry because they have done something wrong. ❑ *She reproached him for breaking his promise.* **2** N-VAR If you look at or speak to someone with **reproach**, you indicate to someone that you are sad and

Word Web reproduction

Human **reproduction** requires a **sperm** from the **male** and an **egg** from the **female.** These two cells come together to begin the new life. This process is called **fertilization.** It is the beginning of the woman's **pregnancy.** From fertilization to eight weeks of development, we call the fertilized egg a **zygote.** From eight to twelve weeks, it is called an **embryo.** After three months of development, we call it a **fetus. Birth** usually takes place after nine months of pregnancy.

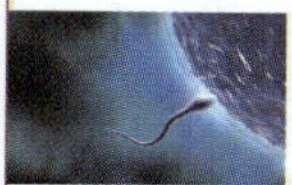
egg and sperm

zygote

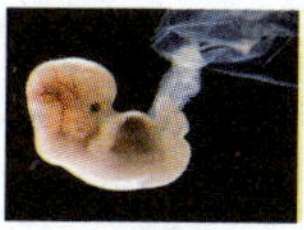
embryo

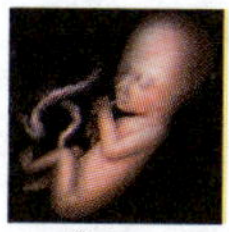
fetus

mother, father, and baby

disappointed, or angry because they have done something wrong. ❑ *His behaviour is beyond reproach.*

reproduce /ˌriːprəˈdjuːs, AM -ˈduːs/ (**reproduces, reproducing, reproduced**) **1** V-T If you **reproduce** something, you copy it. ❑ *The Scream by Edvard Munch has become the most reproduced picture in the world.* **2** V-T/V-I When people, animals, or plants **reproduce**, they produce more of their own species. ❑ *The desire to reproduce is a strong need with many couples.*

reproduction /ˌriːprəˈdʌkʃən/ (**reproductions**) **1** N-COUNT A **reproduction** is a copy of something such as an antique or a painting. **2** N-UNCOUNT **Reproduction** is the process by which living things produce more of their own species.
→ see Word Web: **reproduction**

reproductive /ˌriːprəˈdʌktɪv/ ADJ **Reproductive** processes and organs are concerned with the reproduction of living things.

reptile /ˈreptaɪl, AM -tɪl/ (**reptiles**) N-COUNT **Reptiles** are a group of animals which have scales on their skin and lay eggs. Snakes and crocodiles are reptiles.

republic /rɪˈpʌblɪk/ (**republics**) N-COUNT A **republic** is a country that has a president or whose system of government is based on the idea that every citizen has equal status. ❑ *In 1918 Austria became a republic.* ❑ *...the Republic of Ireland.*

republican /rɪˈpʌblɪkən/ (**republicans**) **1** ADJ & N-COUNT A **republican** government has a president or is based on the idea that every citizen has equal status. You can also talk about someone who has **republican** views, or who is a **republican**. ❑ *He was born into a republican family.* **2** N-COUNT & ADJ In Northern Ireland, if someone is a **Republican** or if they have **republican** views, they believe that Northern Ireland should not be ruled by Britain but should become part of the Republic of Ireland.

repudiate /rɪˈpjuːdieɪt/ (**repudiates, repudiating, repudiated**) V-T If you **repudiate** something or someone, you show that you strongly disagree with them and do not want to be connected with them. ❑ *Leaders urged people to repudiate the violence.* ● **repudiation** N-UNCOUNT ❑ *...his public repudiation of the decision.*

repulsive /rɪˈpʌlsɪv/ ADJ **Repulsive** means horrible and disgusting. ❑ *...a repulsive thought.*

reputable /ˈrepjʊtəbəl/ ADJ A **reputable** company or person is reliable and trustworthy.

reputation /ˌrepjʊˈteɪʃən/ (**reputations**) **1** N-COUNT To have a **reputation for** something means to be known or remembered for it. ❑ *...his reputation for honesty.* **2** N-COUNT Your **reputation** is the opinion that people have of you. ❑ *The stories ruined his reputation.*

Word Partnership Use *reputation* with:

ADJ.	**bad** reputation, **good** reputation **1** **2**
V.	**acquire a** reputation, **build a** reputation, **damage** ***someone's*** reputation, **earn a** reputation, **establish a** reputation, **gain a** reputation, **have a** reputation, **ruin** ***someone's*** reputation, **tarnish** ***someone's*** reputation **1** **2**

reputed /rɪˈpjuːtɪd/ ADJ If something is **reputed to** be true or **to** exist, some people say that it is true or that it exists. ❑ *He is reputed to earn ten million pounds a year.* ● **reputedly** ADV ❑ *The beaches there are reputedly beautiful.*

request /rɪˈkwest/ (**requests, requesting, requested**) **1** V-T If you **request** something, you ask for it politely or formally. ❑ *They requested a meeting with the prime minister.* **2** N-COUNT If you make a **request**, you politely ask for something or ask someone to do something. ❑ *He made an official request to postpone the meeting.* **3** PHRASE If something is done **on request**, it is given or done when you ask for it. ❑ *More information is available on request.* **4** PHRASE If you do something **at** someone's **request**, you do it because they ask you to.

require /rɪˈkwaɪə/ (**requires, requiring, required**) **1** V-T To **require** something means to need it. ❑ *The crisis requires immediate action.* **2** V-T If a law or rule **requires** you **to** do something, you have to do it. [FORMAL] ❑ *The rules require employers to provide safety training.* ❑ *He knows exactly what's required of him.*

requirement /rɪˈkwaɪəmənt/ (**requirements**) **1** N-COUNT A **requirement** is a quality or qualification that you must have in order to be allowed to do something or to be suitable for something. ❑ *These products meet all legal* *requirements.* **2** N-COUNT Your **requirements** are the things that you need. ❑ *This hotel will suit your requirements.*

Word Partnership Use *requirement* with:

ADJ. **legal** requirement, **minimum** requirement **1**
V. **meet a** requirement **1**

requisite /'rekwɪzɪt/ ADJ **Requisite** means necessary for a particular purpose. [FORMAL] ❑ *He doesn't have the requisite training and skills for this job.*

rescue /'reskjuː/ (**rescues, rescuing, rescued**) **1** V-T & N-VAR If you **rescue** someone, you get them out of a dangerous or unpleasant situation. A **rescue** is an attempt to save someone from a situation like this. ❑ *He rescued her from a horrible situation.* ❑ *...a major air-sea rescue.* ❑ *There was little hope of rescue.* ● **rescuer** (**rescuers**) N-COUNT ❑ *Rescuers eventually reached the trapped men.* **2** PHRASE If you **go to** someone's **rescue** or **come to** their **rescue**, you help them when they are in danger or difficulty.

Word Partnership Use *rescue* with:

N. **firemen** rescue, rescue **a hostage**, rescue **miners**, rescue **people**, **police** rescue, **volunteers** rescue, rescue **wildlife** **1**
rescue **attempt**, rescue **crews**, rescue **effort**, rescue **mission**, rescue **operation**, rescue **teams**, rescue **workers** **2**

research /rɪ'sɜːtʃ/ (**researches, researching, researched**) V-T & N-VAR If you **research** something or if you do **research into** it, you try to discover facts about it. ❑ *She spent two years researching and filming her documentary.* ❑ *...medical research.* ● **researcher** (**researchers**) N-COUNT ❑ *...a scientific researcher.*
→ see **hospital, laboratory, medicine, science, zoo**

Word Partnership Use *research* with:

ADJ. **biological** research, **clinical** research, **current** research, **experimental** research, **medical** research, **recent** research, **scientific** research
N. **animal** research, **cancer** research, research **and development**, research **facility**, research **findings**, **laboratory** research, research **methods**, research **paper**, research **project**, research **report**, research **results**, research **scientist**

resemblance /rɪ'zembləns/ (**resemblances**) N-VAR If there is a **resemblance between** two people or things, they are similar to each other. ❑ *There was a clear resemblance between him and Peter.*

resemble /rɪ'zembəl/ (**resembles, resembling, resembled**) V-T If one thing or person **resembles** another, they are similar to each other. ❑ *She resembles her mother.*

resent /rɪ'zent/ (**resents, resenting, resented**) V-T If you **resent** someone or something, you feel bitter and angry about them. ❑ *He resented his wife's lack of interest in his hobbies.*

resentful /rɪ'zentfʊl/ ADJ If you are **resentful**, you feel resentment. ❑ *I felt very resentful and angry about losing my job.*

resentment /rɪ'zentmənt/ (**resentments**) N-VAR **Resentment** is a feeling of bitterness and anger. ❑ *Unemployment can cause a lot of resentment.*

reservation /ˌrezə'veɪʃən/ (**reservations**) **1** N-VAR If you have **reservations about** something, you are not sure that it is entirely good or right. **2** N-COUNT If you **make** a **reservation**, you arrange for something such as a table in a restaurant to be kept for you. ❑ *I've made a dinner reservation for Friday night.*
→ see **hotel**

reserve /rɪ'zɜːv/ (**reserves, reserving, reserved**) **1** V-T If something **is reserved for** a particular person or purpose, it is kept specially for that person or purpose. ❑ *A double room has been reserved for him.* ❑ *They reserved two seats on a flight to London.* **2** N-COUNT A **reserve** is a supply of something that is available for use when needed. ❑ *...the world's oil reserves.* **3** PHRASE If you have something **in reserve**, you have it available for use when it is needed. ❑ *He keeps some cash in reserve for emergencies.* **4** N-COUNT In sport, a **reserve** is someone who is available to play in a team if one of the members cannot play. [BRIT] **5** N-COUNT A nature **reserve** is an area of land where animals, birds, and plants are officially protected. **6** N-UNCOUNT If someone shows **reserve**, they keep their feelings hidden. ❑ *The British are known for their reserve.*

reserved /rɪ'zɜːvd/ ADJ Someone who is **reserved** keeps their feelings hidden. ❑ *Even though I'm quite a reserved person, I like meeting people.*

reservoir /'rezəvwɑː/ (**reservoirs**) **1** N-COUNT A **reservoir** is a lake used for storing water before it is supplied to people. **2** N-COUNT A **reservoir of** something is a large quantity of it that is available for use when needed. ❑ *He has a reservoir of knowledge to draw on.*
→ see **dam**

Word Link ***sid ≈ sitting : preside, president, reside***

reside /rɪ'zaɪd/ (**resides, residing, resided**) V-I If someone **resides** somewhere, they live there or are staying there. [FORMAL] ❑ *Margaret resides with her elderly mother.*

residence /'rezɪdəns/ (**residences**) **1** N-COUNT A **residence** is a house where people live. [FORMAL] ❑ *The hotel was previously a private residence.* **2** N-UNCOUNT Your place of **residence** is the place where you live. [FORMAL] **3** PHRASE If someone is **in residence** in a place, they are living there. **4** PHRASE If you **take up residence** somewhere, you start living there.

Word Link ***ent ≈ one who does, has : dependent, resident, superintendent***

resident /'rezɪdənt/ (**residents**) **1** N-COUNT The **residents** of a house or area are the people who live there. **2** ADJ AFTER LINK-V Someone who is **resident** in a country or town lives there. ❑ *He has been resident in Paris since 1997.*
→ see **country**

residential /ˌrezɪˈdenʃəl/ **1** ADJ A **residential** area contains houses rather than offices or factories. **2** ADJ A **residential** institution is one where you can live while you are studying there or being cared for there. ❑ *...a residential home for children with disabilities.*

residual /rɪˈzɪdʒuəl/ ADJ **Residual** is used to describe what remains of something when most of it has gone. ❑ *The next morning she still had a slight residual headache.*

residue /ˈrezɪdjuː, AM -duː/ (**residues**) N-COUNT A **residue** of something is a small amount that remains after most of it has gone. ❑ *Always rinse shampoo thoroughly – any residue will leave hair dull and sticky.*

resign /rɪˈzaɪn/ (**resigns, resigning, resigned**) **1** V-I If you **resign from** a job or position, you formally announce that you are leaving it. ❑ *He resigned as chairman of the council.* **2** V-T If you **resign yourself to** an unpleasant situation or fact, you accept it because you do not think that you can change it. ❑ *He resigned himself to selling his home to pay off his debts.* **3** → see also **resigned**

Thesaurus	*resign* Also look up:
v.	leave, quit, step down **1**

resignation /ˌrezɪɡˈneɪʃən/ (**resignations**) **1** N-VAR Your **resignation** is a formal statement of your intention to leave a job or position. ❑ *He wrote his letter of resignation.* **2** N-UNCOUNT **Resignation** is the acceptance of an unpleasant situation or fact because you do not think that you can change it. ❑ *His voice was heavy with resignation.*

resigned /rɪˈzaɪnd/ ADJ If you are **resigned to** an unpleasant situation or fact, you accept it because you cannot change it. ❑ *They are resigned to defeat.*

resilient /rɪˈzɪliənt/ ADJ **Resilient** people are able to recover easily and quickly from unpleasant or damaging events. ● **resilience** N-UNCOUNT ❑ *John's resilience helped him through the difficult times.*

resin /ˈrezɪn/ (**resins**) **1** N-VAR **Resin** is a sticky substance produced by some trees. **2** N-VAR **Resin** is a chemically produced substance used to make plastics.

resist /rɪˈzɪst/ (**resists, resisting, resisted**) **1** V-T If you **resist** a change, you refuse to accept it and try to prevent it. ❑ *The prime minister resisted demands for his resignation.* **2** V-T To **resist** someone or to **resist** an attack by them means to fight back. ❑ *The man resisted the robbers' demands to hand over his money.* **3** V-T If you **resist** the temptation to do something, you stop yourself from doing it although you would like to do it. ❑ *She cannot resist giving him advice.* **4** V-T If someone or something **resists** damage of some kind, they are not harmed or damaged by it. ❑ *This material resists stains.*

Word Link	***ance ≈ quality, state : performance, resistance, trance***

resistance /rɪˈzɪstəns/ **1** N-UNCOUNT **Resistance to** a change or a new idea is a refusal to accept it. ❑ *...his stubborn resistance to anything new.* **2** N-UNCOUNT When there is **resistance** to an attack, people fight back. ❑ *The troops encountered fierce resistance.* **3** N-UNCOUNT The **resistance** of your body **to** germs or diseases is its power to remain unharmed or unaffected by them. → see **bicycle**

resistant /rɪˈzɪstənt/ **1** ADJ People who are **resistant to** something are opposed to it and want to prevent it. ❑ *Humans are basically resistant to change.* **2** ADJ If something is **resistant to** something else, it is not harmed by it. ❑ *...how to improve plants to make them more resistant to disease.*

resolute /ˈrezəluːt/ ADJ Someone who is **resolute** refuses to change their mind or to give up a course of action. [FORMAL] ● **resolutely** ADV ❑ *He resolutely refused to speak English.*

resolution /ˌrezəˈluːʃən/ (**resolutions**) **1** N-COUNT A **resolution** is a formal decision taken at a meeting by means of a vote. ❑ *The resolution declared the republic independent.* **2** N-COUNT If you make a **resolution**, you decide to try very hard to do something. ❑ *She made a resolution to take more exercise.* **3** N-UNCOUNT **Resolution** is determination to do something. ❑ *She acted with resolution, courage, and intelligence.* **4** N-UNCOUNT The **resolution of** a problem or difficulty is the solving of it. [FORMAL] ❑ *...the successful resolution of the argument.* ❑ *...a peaceful resolution to the crisis.*

resolve /rɪˈzɒlv/ (**resolves, resolving, resolved**) **1** V-T To **resolve** a problem or argument, means to find a solution to it. [FORMAL] ❑ *We must find a way to resolve these problems.* **2** V-T If you **resolve to** do something, you make a firm decision to do it. [FORMAL] ❑ *She resolved to become an architect.* ❑ *She resolved that she would get in touch with him.* **3** N-UNCOUNT **Resolve** is determination to do something. [FORMAL] ❑ *We share the prime minister's resolve to destroy terrorism.*

resolved /rɪˈzɒlvd/ ADJ If you are **resolved to** do something, you are determined to do it. [FORMAL] ❑ *He was resolved to marry her.*

resonant /ˈrezənənt/ ADJ If a sound is **resonant**, it is deep, clear, and echoing. ● **resonance** N-UNCOUNT ❑ *His voice had lost its resonance; it was tense and strained.*

Word Link	***son ≈ sound : resonate, sonic, unison***

resonate /ˈrezəneɪt/ (**resonates, resonating, resonated**) V-I If something **resonates**, it vibrates and produces a deep strong sound. ❑ *The music was so loud that it resonated in my head.*

resort /rɪˈzɔːt/ (**resorts, resorting, resorted**) **1** V-I If you **resort to** a course of action that you disapprove of, you adopt it because you cannot see any other way of achieving what you want. ❑ *I begged them not to resort to violence.* **2** PHRASE If you do something **as a last resort**, you do it because you can find no other way of getting out of a difficult situation or of solving a problem. ❑ *War should only be used as a last resort.* **3** N-COUNT A holiday **resort** is a place where people can spend their holidays.

resounding /rɪˈzaʊndɪŋ/ **1** ADJ **Resounding** means very successful. ❑ *The party was a resounding success.* **2** ADJ A **resounding** sound is loud and echoing. ❑ *...a resounding slap on the face.*

resource /rɪˈzɔːs, AM ˈriːsɔːrs/ (**resources**) N-COUNT The **resources** of a country, organization, or person are the materials, money, and other things they have and can use. ❑ *...scarce water resources.* ❑ *Her family do not have the financial resources*

r

to deal with the crisis they face.

resourceful /rɪ'zɔːsfʊl/ ADJ Someone who is **resourceful** is good at finding ways of dealing with problems. ● **resourcefulness** N-UNCOUNT ❑ *Tom has great energy and resourcefulness.*

respect /rɪ'spekt/ (**respects, respecting, respected**) **1** V-T & N-UNCOUNT If you **respect** someone, or if you have **respect for** them, you have a good opinion of their character or ideas. ❑ *I want him to respect me as a career woman.* **2** V-T & N-UNCOUNT If you **respect** someone's wishes, rights, or customs, or if you show **respect for** them, you avoid doing things that they would dislike or regard as wrong. ❑ *I respected her wishes and left.* **3** → see also **respected** **4** PHRASE You use expressions like **in this respect** and **in many respects** to indicate that what you are saying applies to the feature you have just mentioned or to many features of something. ❑ *In many respects, he was a lucky man.* **5** PHRASE You use **with respect to**, or in British English **in respect of**, to say what something relates to. [FORMAL] ❑ *We are not pleased with the situation there with respect to human rights.* **6** PHRASE If you **pay** your **respects** or your **last respects to** someone who has died, you go to their funeral or memorial service. ❑ *Friends and family paid their last respects to the star at a ceremony in New Jersey.*

Thesaurus *respect* Also look up:

V.	admire, esteem **1**
N.	consideration, courtesy, esteem **2**

respectable /rɪ'spektəbəl/ **1** ADJ Someone or something that is **respectable** is approved of by society and considered to be morally correct. ❑ *He seemed like a very respectable person.* ● **respectability** N-UNCOUNT ❑ *...his desire for respectability.* **2** ADJ **Respectable** means adequate or acceptable. ❑ *At last I have something respectable to wear!*

respected /rɪ'spektɪd/ ADJ Someone or something that is **respected** is admired and considered important by many people. ❑ *She is a respected member of the community.*

respectful /rɪ'spektfʊl/ ADJ If you are **respectful**, you show respect for someone. ❑ *Your children are very well-behaved and respectful.* ● **respectfully** ADV ❑ *The two leaders treated one another warmly and respectfully.*

respective /rɪ'spektɪv/ ADJ BEFORE N **Respective** means relating separately to the people you have just mentioned. ❑ *Kate and Sarah went off to their respective bedrooms.*

R

respectively /rɪ'spektɪvli/ ADV **Respectively** means in the same order as the items you have just mentioned. ❑ *Their sons, Ben and Jonathan, were three and six respectively.*

Word Link *spir ≈ breath : aspire, inspire, respiratory*

respiratory /'respərətri, AM -tɔːri/ ADJ **Respiratory** means relating to breathing. [MEDICAL] ❑ *...respiratory disease.*
→ see Word Web: **respiratory system**

respite /'respaɪt, -pɪt/ N-SING A **respite** is a short period of rest from something unpleasant. [FORMAL] ❑ *The heat can be intense: the only respite comes with cooler evenings.*

'respite ˌcare N-UNCOUNT **Respite care** is short-term care that is provided for very old or very sick people so that the person who usually cares for them can have a break.

respond /rɪ'spɒnd/ (**responds, responding, responded**) V-I When you **respond to** something that is done or said, you react by doing or saying something. ❑ *She did not respond to the questions.* ❑ *He responded with a smile.*

response /rɪ'spɒns/ (**responses**) N-COUNT Your **response to** an event or **to** something that is said is your reply or reaction to it. ❑ *In response to my question, he lifted his head and thought for a moment.*

Word Partnership Use *response* with:

ADJ.	**correct** response, **enthusiastic** response, **immediate** response, **military** response, **negative/positive** response, **overwhelming** response, **quick** response, **written** response

responsibility /rɪˌspɒnsɪ'bɪlɪti/ (**responsibilities**) **1** N-UNCOUNT If you have **responsibility for** something or someone, it is your job or duty to deal with them. ❑ *He has responsibility for five employees.* **2** N-PLURAL Your **responsibilities** are the duties that you have because of your job or position. ❑ *...work and family responsibilities.* **3** N-SING If you think that you have a **responsibility to** do something, you feel that you ought to do it because it is morally right or your duty to do it. ❑ *We have a responsibility to respect other people's rights.* **4** N-UNCOUNT If you accept **responsibility for** something that has happened, you agree that you were to blame for it. ❑ *Michael has admitted responsibility for the accident.*
→ see **citizenship**

Word Web respiratory system

Respiration moves **air** into and out of the **lungs**. Air enters through the **nose** or **mouth**. It travels down the windpipe and into the **lungs**. In the lungs **oxygen** absorbs into the bloodstream. Blood carries oxygen to the heart and other organs. The lungs also remove **carbon dioxide** from the blood. This gas is then **exhaled** through the mouth. During inhalation the **diaphragm** moves downward and the lungs fill with air. During exhalation the diaphragm relaxes and air flows out. Adult humans **breathe** about six litres of air each minute.

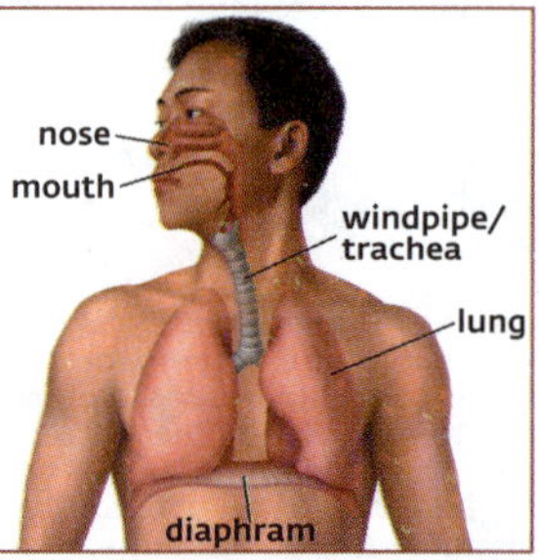

Word Partnership Use *responsibility* with:

V. **be given** responsibility 1 2
assume responsibility, **bear** responsibility, **share** responsibility, **take** responsibility 1-4
have (a) responsibility 1 3
accept responsibility, **claim** responsibility 4
ADJ. **financial** responsibility, **personal** responsibility 1-4
moral responsibility 3

responsible /rɪˈspɒnsɪbəl/ 1 ADJ AFTER LINK-V If you are **responsible for** something bad that has happened, it is your fault. ❑ *He felt responsible for her death.* 2 ADJ AFTER LINK-V If you are **responsible for** something, it is your job or duty to deal with it. ❑ *...the minister responsible for the environment.* 3 ADJ AFTER LINK-V If you are **responsible to** a person or group, you are controlled by them and have to report to them about what you have done. ❑ *I'm responsible to my board of directors.* 4 ADJ **Responsible** people behave properly, without needing to be supervised. ● **responsibly** ADV ❑ *He urged everyone to act responsibly.*

responsive /rɪˈspɒnsɪv/ ADJ A **responsive** person is quick to react to people or events and to show emotions such as pleasure and affection. ❑ *These children are responsive and loving.* ● **responsiveness** N-UNCOUNT ❑ *The company's success is based on its responsiveness to its customers.*

rest
❶ QUANTIFIER USES
❷ VERB AND NOUN USE

rest /rest/
❶ 1 QUANT **The rest of** something is all that remains of it. ❑ *He was unable to travel to Barcelona with the rest of the team.* ❑ *I worked in the morning, then took the rest of the day off.*

Usage
If you are talking about something that cannot be counted, the verb following **rest** is singular. ❑ *The rest of the food was delicious.* If you are talking about several people or things, the verb is plural. ❑ *The rest of the boys were delighted.*

2 PHRASE You can add **and the rest** or **all the rest of it** to the end of a statement or list when you want to refer vaguely to other similar things. ❑ *Even though he talks about being friendly and all the rest of it, he doesn't behave that way.*

rest /rest/ (**rests, resting, rested**)
❷ 1 V-I/V-T & N-VAR If you **rest**, or **rest** a part of your body, or if you **have a rest**, you do not do anything active for a period of time. ❑ *Try to rest your mind as well as your body.* ❑ *I've worked hard for 47 years so I think I'm due for a rest by now.* ● **rested** ADJ AFTER LINK-V ❑ *He looked relaxed and well rested after his vacation.* 2 V-I If something such as an idea **rests on** a particular thing, it depends on that thing. [FORMAL] ❑ *His theory rests on the view that human beings are motivated by fear or greed, or both.* 3 V-T/V-I If something **rests** somewhere, or if you **rest** it there, its weight is supported there. ❑ *His head was resting on her shoulder.* ❑ *He rested his arms on the table.* ❑ *He rested on his walking stick for a while.* 4 PHRASE When an object that has been moving **comes to rest**, it stops.
→ see **motion, sleep**

Thesaurus *rest* Also look up:
V. lie down, relax ② 1

Word Link *re ≈ back, again : reflect, refuel, restate*

restate /ˌriːˈsteɪt/ (**restates, restating, restated**) V-T If you **restate** something, you say or write it again, expressing the same message in a slightly different way. [FORMAL]

restaurant /ˈrestərɒnt, AM -rənt/ (**restaurants**) 1 N-COUNT A **restaurant** is a place where you can buy and eat a meal. 2 → See note at **café**
→ see **city**

restless /ˈrestləs/ 1 ADJ If you are **restless**, you are bored or dissatisfied, and want to do something else. ● **restlessness** N-UNCOUNT ❑ *Many fears and anxieties cause a feeling of restlessness.* 2 ADJ You say that someone is **restless** when they keep moving around, because they find it difficult to stay still. ● **restlessly** ADV ❑ *He paced up and down restlessly.*

restore /rɪˈstɔː/ (**restores, restoring, restored**) 1 V-T To **restore** something means to cause it to exist again. ❑ *The army was brought in to restore order.* ● **restoration** /ˌrestəˈreɪʃən/ N-UNCOUNT ❑ *...the restoration of democracy.* 2 V-T To **restore** someone or something **to** a previous state or condition means to cause them to be in that state or condition again. ❑ *We will restore her to health.* ❑ *His country desperately needs Western aid to restore its weak economy.* 3 V-T To **restore** an old building, painting, or piece of furniture means to repair and clean it, so that it looks like it did when it was new. ● **restoration** N-UNCOUNT ❑ *...the restoration of the ancient castle.*

restrain /rɪˈstreɪn/ (**restrains, restraining, restrained**) 1 V-T If someone **restrains** you, they stop you from doing what you intended or wanted to do, usually by using physical strength. 2 V-T If you **restrain** an emotion or **restrain yourself from** doing something, you prevent yourself from showing that emotion or performing that action. ❑ *He could not restrain his tears.* ● **restrained** ADJ ❑ *He said that, during these difficult times, we must be calm, balanced and restrained.* 3 V-T To **restrain** something that is growing or increasing means to prevent it from getting too large. ❑ *...efforts to restrain inflation.*

restraint /rɪˈstreɪnt/ (**restraints**) 1 N-VAR **Restraints** are rules or conditions that limit or restrict someone or something. ❑ *The Prime Minister called for new restraints on trade unions.* 2 N-UNCOUNT **Restraint** is calm, controlled, and unemotional behaviour. ❑ *They behaved with great restraint.*

restrict /rɪˈstrɪkt/ (**restricts, restricting, restricted**) 1 V-T If you **restrict** something, you put a limit on it to stop it becoming too large. ❑ *Laws were passed to restrict foreign imports.* ● **restricted** ADJ ❑ *The college gardens have restricted public opening times.* ● **restriction** (**restrictions**) N-VAR ❑ *...restrictions on the use of mobile phones while*

r

driving. **2** V-T To **restrict** the movement or actions of someone or something means to prevent them from moving or acting freely. ❑ *These dams have restricted the flow of the river downstream.* ● **restricted** ADJ ❑ *The pilot was flying his aircraft in restricted airspace.* ● **restriction** N-VAR ❑ *...the relaxation of travel restrictions.* **3** V-T If you **restrict** someone else's activities **to** one thing, they can only do or deal with that thing. ❑ *As a journalist, she doesn't intend to restrict herself to writing about politics.* **4** V-T If something **is restricted to** a particular group, only that group can have it or do it. ❑ *Access is restricted to staff.*

restrictive /rɪˈstrɪktɪv/ ADJ **Restrictive** things make it difficult for you to do what you want to. ❑ *...restrictive immigration laws.*

restructure /ˌriːˈstrʌktʃə/ (**restructures, restructuring, restructured**) V-T To **restructure** an organization or system means to change the way it is organized, usually in order to make it work more effectively. ❑ *...his plans to restructure Russia's local government.* ● **restructuring** (**restructurings**) N-VAR ❑ *The company is working on an emergency restructuring plan.*

result /rɪˈzʌlt/ (**results, resulting, resulted**) **1** N-COUNT A **result** is something that happens or exists because of something else that has happened. ❑ *She says her music is changing as a result of being a mother.* ❑ *It's worth spending more to get better results.* **2** V-I If something **results in** a particular situation or event, it causes that situation or event to happen. ❑ *A good 10 hours' sleep will result in your feeling refreshed.* **3** V-I If something **results from** a particular event or action, it is caused by that event or action. ❑ *Between 5 and 10 per cent of reported food poisoning may have resulted from holidays abroad.* ❑ *The company restructuring will result in job losses.* **4** N-COUNT A **result** is the situation that exists at the end of a contest. ❑ *...election results.* **5** N-COUNT A **result** is the number that you get when you do a calculation. ❑ *The laboratory, which calculated the results, had made an error.* **6** N-COUNT Your **results** are the marks or grades that you get for examinations. ❑ *Kate's exam results were excellent.*

resume /rɪˈzjuːm, AM -ˈzuːm/ (**resumes, resuming, resumed**) V-T/V-I If you **resume** an activity, or if it **resumes**, it begins again. [FORMAL] ❑ *The search for the missing people resumed early today.*

résumé also **resumé** /ˈrezjʊmeɪ, AM -zʊm-/ (**résumés**) **1** N-COUNT A **résumé** is a short account of something that has happened or that someone has said or written. ❑ *Here is a resumé of his most recent speech.* **2** N-COUNT In American English, your **résumé** is a brief account of your personal details, your education, and the jobs you have had. The usual British word is **CV**.

resumption /rɪˈzʌmpʃən/ N-UNCOUNT When there is a **resumption** in an activity, it begins again. ❑ *...the resumption of peace talks.*

resurgence /rɪˈsɜːdʒəns/ N-UNCOUNT If there is a **resurgence of** an attitude or activity, it reappears and grows. [FORMAL] ❑ *...the resurgence of nationalism in Europe.*

resurrect /ˌrezəˈrekt/ (**resurrects, resurrecting, resurrected**) V-T When you **resurrect** something that has ended, you cause it to exist again. ❑ *He tried to resurrect his political career.*

resurrection /ˌrezəˈrekʃən/ N-UNCOUNT The **resurrection of** something that had ended is the act of making it exist again. ❑ *...the resurrection of democracy.*

resuscitate /rɪˈsʌsɪteɪt/ (**resuscitates, resuscitating, resuscitated**) V-T If you **resuscitate** someone who has stopped breathing, you cause them to start breathing again. [FORMAL] ● **resuscitation** N-UNCOUNT ❑ *Despite attempts at resuscitation, Mr Hunt died.*

retail /ˈriːteɪl/ (**retails, retailing, retailed**) **1** N-UNCOUNT **Retail** is the activity of selling goods direct to the public. ❑ *Retail sales grew just 3.8 percent last year.* **2** V-I If an item in a shop **retails at** or **for** a particular price, it is for sale at that price.

retailer /ˈriːteɪlə/ (**retailers**) N-COUNT A **retailer** is a person or business that sells goods to the public.

retailing /ˈriːteɪlɪŋ/ N-UNCOUNT **Retailing** is the activity of selling goods direct to the public.

ˈretail ˌpark (**retail parks**) N-COUNT A **retail park** is a large, specially built area usually at the edge of a town or city where there are a lot of large shops.

retain /rɪˈteɪn/ (**retains, retaining, retained**) V-T To **retain** something means to continue to have that thing. [FORMAL] ❑ *The president is battling to retain power.*

Thesaurus	*retain* Also look up:
V.	hold, keep, maintain, remember, save; *(ant.)* give up, lose

retaliate /rɪˈtælieɪt/ (**retaliates, retaliating, retaliated**) V-I If you **retaliate** when someone harms you, you harm them in return. ❑ *The army said it would retaliate against any attacks.* ● **retaliation** N-UNCOUNT ❑ *The attack was in retaliation for the death of the soldiers.*

retarded /rɪˈtɑːdɪd/ ADJ **Retarded** people are less advanced mentally than most people of their age. Some people find this word offensive. [DATED] ❑ *Doctors said that the baby would probably be mentally retarded.*

retention /rɪˈtenʃən/ N-UNCOUNT The **retention of** something is the keeping of it. [FORMAL] ❑ *...the recruitment and retention of staff.*

rethink /ˌriːˈθɪŋk/ (**rethinks, rethinking, rethought**) V-T & N-SING If you **rethink** something such as a plan, or if you have a **rethink** about it, you think about it again and change it. ❑ *We need to rethink our attitudes toward health and sickness.* ❑ *The Labour Party called for a rethink of Britain's foreign aid policy.*

reticent /ˈretɪsənt/ ADJ If you are **reticent about** something, you do not talk about it. ❑ *She is very reticent about her achievements.* ● **reticence** N-UNCOUNT ❑ *She responded without reticence or hesitation.*

retina /ˈretɪnə/ (**retinas**) N-COUNT Your **retina** is the part of your eye at the back of your eyeball. → see **eye**

retire /rɪˈtaɪə/ (**retires, retiring, retired**) **1** V-I When older people **retire**, they leave their job and stop working. ❑ *He retired last year at the age of 70.* ❑ *He has decided to retire from grand prix racing at the end of the season.* ● **retired** ADJ ❑ *...a retired policeman.* **2** V-I If you **retire to** another room or place, you go there. [FORMAL]

retirement /rɪ'taɪəmənt/ **1** N-UNCOUNT **Retirement** is the time when a worker retires. ❑ *The Governor is going to take early retirement.* **2** N-UNCOUNT A person's **retirement** is the period in their life after they have retired. ❑ *In his retirement, he is looking forward to playing more golf.*

retort /rɪ'tɔːt/ (**retorts, retorting, retorted**) V-T & N-COUNT To **retort** something, or to answer with a **retort**, means to reply angrily. ❑ *He was asked if he was afraid. 'Afraid of what?' he retorted.* ❑ *He retorted that he knew nothing about the matter.*

retrace /rɪ'treɪs/ (**retraces, retracing, retraced**) V-T If you **retrace** your **steps**, you return to where you started from, using the same route. ❑ *He retraced his steps to the place where he had left the bag.*

retract /rɪ'trækt/ (**retracts, retracting, retracted**) V-T If you **retract** something that you have said or written, you say publicly that you did not mean it. [FORMAL] ❑ *He later retracted his statement.* ● **retraction** (**retractions**) N-COUNT ❑ *He issued a retraction of the claim against her.*

retreat /rɪ'triːt/ (**retreats, retreating, retreated**) **1** V-I If you **retreat** from someone or something, you move away from them. ❑ *He retreated to his bedroom to think things over.* **2** V-I & N-VAR If an army **retreats**, or if it is **in retreat**, it moves away from an enemy in order to avoid fighting. ❑ *The soldiers were forced to retreat.* ❑ *...Napoleon's retreat from Moscow.* **3** N-COUNT A **retreat** is a quiet secluded place where you go to rest or to do something in private.

retribution /ˌretrɪ'bjuːʃən/ N-UNCOUNT **Retribution** is punishment for a crime. [FORMAL] ❑ *It is important to remember that retribution is not the same as justice.*

retrieval /rɪ'triːvəl/ N-UNCOUNT The **retrieval** of something is the process of getting it back. ❑ *Data is stored in a computer so that retrieval can be done very easily.*

retrieve /rɪ'triːv/ (**retrieves, retrieving, retrieved**) V-T If you **retrieve** something, you get it back from the place where you left it. ❑ *He retrieved his jacket from the back seat of the car.*

retro /'retrəʊ/ ADJ **Retro** clothes, music, and objects are based on the styles of the past. ❑ *...beautiful retro clothing.*

retrospect /'retrəspekt/ PHRASE The way that things seem **in retrospect** is the way they seem after an event, when you are able to consider them from a more experienced point of view. ❑ *In retrospect, I wish I hadn't done it.*

retrospective /ˌretrə'spektɪv/ (**retrospectives**) **1** N-COUNT A **retrospective** is an exhibition or showing of work done by an artist over many years, rather than his or her most recent work. **2** ADJ **Retrospective** laws or legal actions take effect from a date before the date when they are officially approved. ● **retrospectively** ADV ❑ *The government imposed the tax retrospectively.*

return /rɪ'tɜːn/ (**returns, returning, returned**) **1** V-I & N-SING When you **return to** a place, you go back there. Your **return** is your arrival back at a place. ❑ *Three days after returning to Britain he was arrested.* ❑ *She returned home to Birmingham.* ❑ *He has not worked since his return from Berlin.* **2** V-T & N-SING If you **return** something that you have borrowed or taken, you give it back or put it back. The **return of** something is the act of giving or putting it back. ❑ *He returned her passport.* ❑ *She demanded the return of her money.* **3** V-T If you **return** someone's action, you do the same thing to them as they have just done to you. If you **return** someone's feeling, you feel the same way towards them as they feel towards you. ❑ *I returned his smile.* ❑ *She was devoted to her daughter who clearly returned her love and affection.* **4** V-I & N-SING If you **return to** a subject or an activity, you start talking about that subject or doing that activity again. A **return to** an activity is the starting of it again. ❑ *He called for an end to the strike and a return to work.* **5** V-I & N-SING If you **return to** a state you were in before, you go back to that state again. You can refer to a change back to a former state as a **return to** that state. ❑ *Life has not yet returned to normal.* ❑ *These conditions will allow a lasting peace and a return to normality.* **6** V-T When a judge or jury **returns** a verdict, they announce whether a person is guilty or not. **7** N-COUNT A **return** or a **return ticket** is a ticket that allows you to travel to a place and then back again. **8** N-VAR The **return on** an investment is the profit you get from it. ❑ *Investors require higher returns on riskier investments.* **9** PHRASE If you do something **in return for** what someone has done for you, you do it because of what they did. ❑ *There's little I can do for him in return.* **10** PHRASE You say **'many happy returns'** to wish someone a happy birthday.
→ see **library**

Thesaurus *return* Also look up:

N.	arrival, homecoming; *(ant.)* departure **1**
V.	come again, come back, go back, reappear **1**
	give back, hand back, pay back; *(ant.)* keep **2**

Word Partnership Use *return* with:

V.	**decide to** return, **plan to** return, **want to** return **1** **2** **3**
N.	return **a (phone) call** **3**
	return **to work** **4**
	return **trip** **5**
	return **on an investment**, **rate of** return **8**

reunification /ˌriːjuːnɪfɪ'keɪʃən/ N-UNCOUNT The **reunification** of a country or city that has been divided into two or more parts for some time is the joining of it together again.

reunion /riː'juːniən/ (**reunions**) N-VAR A **reunion** is a party or occasion when people who have not seen each other for a long time meet again. ❑ *...a family reunion.* ❑ *It was a very emotional reunion.*

reunite /ˌriːjuː'naɪt/ (**reunites, reuniting, reunited**) **1** V-T/V-I If you **are reunited with** your family or friends, you meet them again after being separated from them. ❑ *At last Mary was reunited with her sister.* ❑ *They were reunited a month later.* ❑ *The tragedy has reunited the family.* **2** V-T To **reunite** a divided organization or country means to cause it to be united again. ❑ *His first job will be to reunite the army.*

rev /rev/ (**revs, revving, revved**) **1** V-T & PHR-VERB To **rev** the engine of a vehicle, or **rev**

r

up the engine of a vehicle, means to increase the engine speed by pressing the accelerator. ❑ *The old bus was revving its engine.* ❑ *Mark revved up his motorbike.* **2** N-PLURAL An engine's **revs** are its speed, measured in revolutions per minute.

revamp /riːˈvæmp/ (**revamps, revamping, revamped**) V-T & N-COUNT If someone **revamps** something, they change things about it in order to try and improve it. **Revamps** are changes to something. ❑ *She has completely revamped her image.* ❑ *...major organizational revamps.*

reveal /rɪˈviːl/ (**reveals, revealing, revealed**) **1** V-T To **reveal** something means to make people aware of it. ❑ *Only future research can reveal the answer to this mystery.* **2** V-T If you **reveal** something that has been out of sight, you uncover it so that people can see it. ❑ *A carpet was removed to reveal the original pine floor.*

revealing /rɪˈviːlɪŋ/ **1** ADJ A **revealing** action or statement tells you something that you were not aware of. ❑ *...a revealing comment.* **2** ADJ **Revealing** clothes show a lot of your body.

revel /ˈrevəl/ (**revels, revelling, revelled** or [AM] **reveling, reveled**) V-I If you **revel in** a situation or experience, you enjoy it very much. ❑ *He revelled in his victory.*

revelation /ˌrevəˈleɪʃən/ (**revelations**) **1** N-VAR The **revelation of** something is the act of making it known. A **revelation** is an interesting fact that is made known to people. ❑ *...the revelation of his crimes.* ❑ *...revelations about his private life.* **2** N-SING If something is a **revelation to** you, it makes you aware of something that you did not know before. ❑ *The whole experience was a revelation.*

revenge /rɪˈvendʒ/ N-UNCOUNT **Revenge** involves hurting someone who has hurt you. ❑ *...acts of revenge.* ❑ *The other children took revenge on the boy, claiming he was a school bully.* ❑ *They said that the attack was in revenge for the killing of their leader.*

revenue /ˈrevənjuː/ (**revenues**) N-UNCOUNT & N-PLURAL **Revenue** or **revenues** is used to refer to the money that a government or organization receives from people. ❑ *The airline expects its revenue from China to double within the next five years.* ❑ *...a 40% increase in revenues.*

R

reverberate /rɪˈvɜːbəreɪt/ (**reverberates, reverberating, reverberated**) V-I When a loud sound **reverberates**, it echoes through a place. ❑ *The noise reverberated through the house.*

Word Link	***vere** ≈ fear, awe : **irreverent**, **revere**, **reverence***

revere /rɪˈvɪə/ (**reveres, revering, revered**) V-T If you **revere** someone, you respect and admire them greatly. [FORMAL] ❑ *He revered his father.* ● **revered** ADJ ❑ *...some of the country's most revered institutions.* ● **reverence** /ˈrevərəns/ N-UNCOUNT ❑ *They shared a reverence for women.*

Reverend /ˈrevərənd/ N-TITLE **Reverend** is a title used before the name of a member of the clergy. ❑ *...the Reverend Jim Simons.*

Word Link	***vers** ≈ turning : **reversal**, **versatile**, **version***

reversal /rɪˈvɜːsəl/ (**reversals**) N-COUNT When there is a **reversal of** a process or policy, it is changed to the opposite process or policy. ❑ *The move represents a complete reversal of previous US policy.*

reverse /rɪˈvɜːs/ (**reverses, reversing, reversed**) **1** V-T To **reverse** a process, decision, or policy means to change it to its opposite. ❑ *The Government has had to reverse its policy.* **2** V-T If you **reverse** the order of a set of things, you arrange them in the opposite order, so that the first thing comes last. **3** V-T & N-UNCOUNT When a car **is being reversed**, or when it is being driven **in reverse**, it is being driven backwards. **4** ADJ & N-SING **Reverse** or **the reverse** means opposite to what has just been described or mentioned. ❑ *Instead of bringing about peace the meeting may well have the reverse effect.* ❑ *It's not difficult, quite the reverse.* **5** PHRASE If something happens **in reverse** or goes **into reverse**, it happens in the opposite way to usual or to what has been happening. ❑ *The process also works in reverse.*

Word Link	***vert** ≈ turning : **convert**, **invert**, **revert***

revert /rɪˈvɜːt/ (**reverts, reverting, reverted**) V-I When people or things **revert to** a former state, system, or type of behaviour, they go back to it. ❑ *She reverted to her old ways.*

review /rɪˈvjuː/ (**reviews, reviewing, reviewed**) **1** V-T & N-COUNT When someone **reviews** something such as a new book or play, they write a report or give a talk on television or radio in which they express their opinion of it. This report is called a **review**. ● **reviewer** (**reviewers**) N-COUNT ❑ *...a film reviewer.* **2** V-T & N-VAR If you **review** a situation or system, you examine it in order to decide whether changes are needed. This process is called a **review**. ❑ *He said the Government would review the situation in June.* ❑ *This policy is due for review this year.* **3** PHRASE If something is **under review**, it is being examined in order to decide whether changes are needed.

Word Partnership	Use *review* with:
N.	**book** review, **film/movie** review, **restaurant** review **1** review **a case**, review **evidence**, **performance** review **2**

revise /rɪˈvaɪz/ (**revises, revising, revised**) **1** V-T If you **revise** something, you alter it in order to make it better or more accurate. ❑ *I have revised my opinion of him.* ❑ *Experts are starting to revise their estimates of how serious the problem may be.* ● **revision** /rɪˈvɪʒən/ (**revisions**) N-VAR ❑ *The book is badly in need of revision.* **2** V-I When you **revise** for an examination, you read things again in order to learn them thoroughly. [BRIT] ❑ *She got up early to revise.* ● **revision** N-UNCOUNT ❑ *...exam revision.*

revisit /ˌriːˈvɪzɪt/ (**revisits, revisiting, revisited**) V-T If you **revisit** a place, you return there for a visit after you have been away for a long time.

Word Link	***vita** ≈ life : **revitalize**, **vital**, **vitality***

revitalize [BRIT also **revitalise**] /ˌriːˈvaɪtəlaɪz/ (**revitalizes, revitalizing, revitalized**) V-T To **revitalize** something means to make it more active or lively. ❑ *...Government plans for revitalising the economy of South Wales.*

Word Link *viv ≈ living : revival, survive, vivid*

revival /rɪ'vaɪvəl/ (**revivals**) 1 N-VAR When there is a **revival of** something, it becomes active or popular again. ❑ *...signs of economic revival.* ❑ *...a revival of interest in his work.* 2 N-COUNT A **revival** is a new production of a play, an opera, or a ballet. ❑ *...John Clement's revival of Chekhov's 'The Seagull'.*

revive /rɪ'vaɪv/ (**revives, reviving, revived**) 1 V-T/V-I When something such as a feeling or a practice **revives** or **is revived**, it becomes active or successful again. ❑ *...an attempt to revive the British economy.* 2 V-T When someone **revives** a play, opera, or ballet, they present a new production of it. 3 V-T/V-I If you **revive** someone who has fainted, or if they **revive**, they become conscious again. ❑ *He called an ambulance and tried to revive her.*

revoke /rɪ'vəʊk/ (**revokes, revoking, revoked**) V-T When someone in authority **revokes** something such as an order, they cancel it. [FORMAL] ❑ *The council revoked its decision and the library remained open.*

revolt /rɪ'vəʊlt/ (**revolts, revolting, revolted**) 1 N-VAR A **revolt** is a violent attempt by a group of people to change their country's political system. 2 V-I When people **revolt**, they use violence to try to change a country's political system. ❑ *In 1848 the Hungarians revolted against Austrian rule.* 3 N-VAR A **revolt** by a person or group against someone or something is a rejection of the authority of that person or thing. ❑ *The Prime Minister is facing a revolt by some of his MPs.* 4 V-I When people **revolt**, they reject the authority of someone or something. ❑ *She revolted against her family and moved to France.*

revolting /rɪ'vəʊltɪŋ/ ADJ **Revolting** means horrible and disgusting. ❑ *The smell was revolting.*

revolution /ˌrevə'luːʃən/ (**revolutions**) 1 N-VAR A **revolution** is a successful attempt by a large group of people to change their country's political system, using force. ❑ *Since the revolution there has been political turmoil.* ❑ *...the Russian Revolution.* 2 N-COUNT A **revolution** is an important change in a particular area of human activity. ❑ *...the industrial revolution.*

revolutionary /ˌrevə'luːʃənri, AM -neri/ (**revolutionaries**) 1 ADJ **Revolutionary** activities, organizations, or people have the aim of causing a political revolution. ❑ *...the Cuban revolutionary leader, Jose Marti.* 2 N-COUNT A **revolutionary** is a person who tries to cause a revolution or who takes part in one. 3 ADJ **Revolutionary** ideas and developments involve great changes in the way something is done or made. ❑ *...a revolutionary concept in aviation.*

revolutionize [BRIT also **revolutionise**] /ˌrevə'luːʃənaɪz/ (**revolutionizes, revolutionizing, revolutionized**) V-T When something **revolutionizes** an activity, it causes great changes in the way it is done. ❑ *These ideas will revolutionize the way people use computers.*

revolve /rɪ'vɒlv/ (**revolves, revolving, revolved**) 1 V-I If one thing **revolves around** another thing, the second thing is the main feature or focus of the first thing. ❑ *Since childhood, her life has revolved around tennis.* ❑ *The conversation revolved around Daniel's trip to New York.* 2 V-I When something **revolves**, it moves or turns in a circle around a central point or line. ❑ *The satellite revolves around the Earth once every hundred minutes.*

revolver /rɪ'vɒlvə/ (**revolvers**) N-COUNT A **revolver** is a kind of hand gun.

revue /rɪ'vjuː/ (**revues**) N-COUNT A **revue** is a light theatrical entertainment consisting of songs, dances, and jokes about recent events.

revulsion /rɪ'vʌlʃən/ N-UNCOUNT **Revulsion** is a strong feeling of disgust or disapproval. ❑ *They expressed their shock and revulsion at his violent death.*

reward /rɪ'wɔːd/ (**rewards, rewarding, rewarded**) 1 N-COUNT A **reward** is something that you are given because you have behaved well, worked hard, or provided a service to the community. ❑ *As a reward for good behaviour, give your child a new toy.* 2 N-COUNT A **reward** is a sum of money offered to anyone who can give information about lost or stolen property or about someone who is wanted by the police. 3 V-T If you do something and **are rewarded with** a particular benefit, you receive that benefit as a result of doing it. ❑ *He was rewarded with prizes for both Best Director and Best Film.*

Thesaurus *reward* Also look up:
N. bonus, prize; *(ant.)* punishment 1

rewarding /rɪ'wɔːdɪŋ/ ADJ Something that is **rewarding** gives you satisfaction or brings you benefits. ❑ *...a rewarding and full career.*

rewritable /ˌriː'raɪtəbəl/ ADJ A **rewritable** CD or DVD is a CD or DVD that you can record onto more than once. ❑ *...rewritable discs.*

rewrite /ˌriː'raɪt/ (**rewrites, rewriting, rewrote, rewritten**) V-T If someone **rewrites** a piece of writing such as a book, a script, or a law, they write it in a different way in order to improve it. ❑ *The students rewrote their papers and submitted them to their teacher.*

rhetoric /'retərɪk/ N-UNCOUNT **Rhetoric** is speech or writing that is meant to convince and impress people but may not be sincere or honest. ❑ *My speech contained facts, not just rhetoric.*

rhetorical /rɪ'tɒrɪkəl, AM -'tɔːr-/ 1 ADJ A **rhetorical question** is used in order to make a statement rather than to get an answer. • **rhetorically** ADV ❑ *'Do these kids know how lucky they are?' Jackson asked rhetorically.* 2 ADJ **Rhetorical** language is intended to be grand and impressive. [FORMAL]

rhino /'raɪnəʊ/ (**rhinos**) N-COUNT A **rhino** is the same as a **rhinoceros**.

rhinoceros /raɪ'nɒsərəs/ (**rhinoceroses**) N-COUNT A **rhinoceros** is a large African or Asian animal with thick grey skin and one or two horns on its nose.

rhyme /raɪm/ (**rhymes, rhyming, rhymed**) 1 V-I If one word **rhymes with** another, they have a very similar sound. ❑ *Love rhymes with dove.* ❑ *...names that rhyme: Donnie, Ronnie, Connie.* 2 N-COUNT A **rhyme** is a short poem with rhyming words at the ends of its lines. 3 → see also **nursery rhyme** 4 N-UNCOUNT **Rhyme** is the use of rhyming words as a technique in poetry.

rhythm /'rɪðəm/ (**rhythms**) N-VAR A **rhythm** is a regular series of sounds, movements, or actions.

r

Word Web rice

An old Chinese myth says that an animal gave **rice** to humans. A large flood destroyed all the crops. When the people returned from the hills, they saw a dog. It had rice **seeds** in its tail. They planted this new **grain** and were never hungry again. In many Asian countries the words for rice and **food** are the same. Rice has many other uses. It is the main ingredient in some kinds of laundry **starch**. The Japanese make a liquor called saké from it. And in Thailand, rice **straw** is made into hats and shoes.

❑ *Their bodies moved together to the rhythm of the music.* ❑ *Sleeping during the day spoils the normal rhythm of the body.*

rhythmic /ˈrɪðmɪk/ or **rhythmical** /ˈrɪðmɪkəl/ ADJ A **rhythmic** movement or sound is repeated at regular intervals. ❑ *...the rhythmic crash of the waves.* ● **rhythmically** ADV ❑ *She moved rhythmically to the music.*

rib /rɪb/ (**ribs**) N-COUNT Your **ribs** are the curved bones that go from your backbone around your chest.

ribbon /ˈrɪbən/ (**ribbons**) N-VAR A **ribbon** is a long narrow piece of cloth used as a fastening or decoration, for example on a birthday present.

rice /raɪs/ N-UNCOUNT **Rice** consists of white or brown grains taken from a cereal plant.
→ see Word Web: **rice**
→ see **grain**

rich /rɪtʃ/ (**richer, richest, riches**) 1 ADJ & N-PLURAL A **rich** person has a lot of money or valuable possessions. **The rich** are rich people. ❑ *Their one aim in life is to get rich.* ❑ *...the rich and famous.* 2 N-PLURAL **Riches** are valuable possessions or large amounts of money. ❑ *Some people want fame or riches.* 3 ADJ If something is **rich in** a useful or valuable substance, it has a lot of that substance. ❑ *Bananas are rich in vitamin A.* ❑ *...Angola's northern oil-rich coastline.* 4 ADJ A **rich** life is one that is interesting because it is full of different events and activities. ❑ *...the rich history of the island.* ● **richness** N-UNCOUNT ❑ *...the richness of human life.* 5 ADJ **Rich** food contains a lot of fat or oil.

Thesaurus *rich* Also look up:

ADJ. affluent, wealthy; *(ant.)* poor 1

Word Partnership Use *rich* with:

ADJ. rich **and beautiful**, rich **and famous**, rich **and powerful** 1
V. **become** rich, **get** rich **(quick)** 1
N. rich **kids**, rich **man/people**, rich **and poor** 1
rich **country/nation**, rich **in natural resources** 3
rich **culture**, rich **heritage**, rich **history**, rich **tradition** 4
rich **diet**, rich **food** 5

richly /ˈrɪtʃli/ 1 ADV If something is **richly** coloured, flavoured, or scented, it has a pleasantly strong colour, flavour, or scent. ❑ *...richly-coloured fabrics.* 2 ADV You use **richly** to say that a place or thing has a large amount of elaborate or valuable things. ❑ *...the richly-decorated silver pot.* 3 ADV If you say that someone **richly** deserves an award, success, or victory, you feel very strongly that they deserve it. ❑ *He achieved the success he so richly deserved.*

rickety /ˈrɪkɪti/ ADJ A **rickety** building or piece of furniture seems likely to collapse or break. ❑ *Mona climbed the rickety wooden stairway.*

rid /rɪd/ (**rids, ridding, rid**) 1 PHRASE When you **get rid of** something that you do not want or like, you take action so that you no longer have it. ❑ *He needs to get rid of the car for financial reasons.* 2 PHRASE If you **get rid of** someone who is causing problems for you, you make them leave. ❑ *His boss wants to get rid of him.* 3 V-T If you **rid** a place or person **of** something undesirable or unwanted, you succeed in removing it completely. ❑ *He tried to rid himself of these unpleasant thoughts.* 4 ADJ AFTER LINK-V If you **are rid of** someone or something unpleasant or annoying, they are no longer with you or causing problems for you. ❑ *He longed to be rid of his problems.*

ridden /ˈrɪdən/ **Ridden** is the past participle of **ride**.

riddle /ˈrɪdəl/ (**riddles**) 1 N-COUNT A **riddle** is a puzzle in which you ask a question that seems to be nonsense but which has a clever or amusing answer. 2 N-COUNT You can describe something that is puzzling as a **riddle**. ❑ *Scientists have solved a riddle that has puzzled researchers for years.*

riddled /ˈrɪdəld/ 1 ADJ AFTER LINK-V If something is **riddled with** bullets or bullet holes, it is full of them. 2 ADJ If something is **riddled with** undesirable qualities or features, it is full of them. ❑ *The report was riddled with errors.* ❑ *...a dangerous, crime-riddled city.*

ride /raɪd/ (**rides, riding, rode, ridden**) 1 V-T/V-I If you **ride** a horse, you sit on it and control its movements. ❑ *Can you ride?* ❑ *As a child he learned to ride a horse.* 2 V-T If you **ride** a bicycle or a motorcycle you sit on it, control it, and travel along on it. ❑ *He likes to play golf, fish, ski and ride his bicycle.* 3 V-I When you **ride** in a vehicle such as a car, you travel in it. 4 N-COUNT A **ride** is a journey on a horse or bicycle, or in a vehicle. 5 PHRASE If you say that someone or something **is riding high**, you mean that they are popular or successful at the present time. 6 PHRASE If you say that someone faces **a rough ride**, you think that things are going to be difficult for them. [INFORMAL] 7 → see also **riding**

R

Usage

When you want to mention that someone is controlling a horse, bicycle, or motorbike, you can use **ride** as a transitive verb, with the object coming immediately after it. ❑ *Whether you ride a motorbike, scooter or moped, get yourself properly trained.* However, if you want to mention that someone is a passenger in a vehicle, **ride** must be followed by a preposition. ❑ *I was riding on the back of a friend's bicycle.* ❑ *We never let our children ride in the front seat of our car.* If **ride** is used without an object, a preposition, or any other phrase that specifies the context, it usually refers to the activity of riding a horse. ❑ *'Do you ride?'—'No, I've never been on a horse.'*

Word Partnership Use *ride* with:

V.	**give *someone* a** ride, **go for a** ride, **offer *someone* a** ride 3
ADV.	ride **home** 3
N.	**bus/car/subway/train** ride 3
ADJ.	**long** ride, **scenic** ride, **short** ride, **smooth** ride 4

rider /'raɪdə/ (**riders**) N-COUNT A **rider** is someone who rides a horse, bicycle, or motorcycle.
→ see **horse**

ridge /rɪdʒ/ (**ridges**) 1 N-COUNT A **ridge** is a long narrow piece of raised land. ❑ *...a narrow mountain ridge.* 2 N-COUNT A **ridge** is a raised line on a flat surface. ❑ *...the bony ridge of the eye socket.*
→ see **mountain**

Word Link *cule ≈ small : minuscule, molecule, ridicule*

Word Link *rid, ris ≈ laughing : deride, derision, ridicule*

ridicule /'rɪdɪkjuːl/ (**ridicules, ridiculing, ridiculed**) V-T & N-UNCOUNT If you **ridicule** someone or something, or if you consider them with **ridicule**, you make fun of them in an unkind way. ❑ *He ridiculed my suggestion.* ❑ *The press has held the government up to ridicule.*

ridiculous /rɪ'dɪkjʊləs/ ADJ If you say that something or someone is **ridiculous**, you mean that they are very foolish. ❑ *The idea is completely ridiculous.*

ridiculously /rɪ'dɪkjʊləsli/ ADV You use **ridiculously** to emphasize the fact that you think something is unreasonable or very surprising. ❑ *She looked ridiculously young to be a mother.*

riding /'raɪdɪŋ/ N-UNCOUNT **Riding** is the activity or sport of riding horses. ❑ *I went riding.*

rife /raɪf/ ADJ AFTER LINK-V If something bad or unpleasant is **rife**, it is very common. ❑ *Food and water are running out and disease is rife.*

rifle /'raɪfəl/ (**rifles, rifling, rifled**) 1 N-COUNT A **rifle** is a gun with a long barrel. 2 V-T/V-I If you **rifle through** things, or if you **rifle** them, you make a quick search among them in order to find something or steal something. ❑ *The thief rifled through her handbag.*

rift /rɪft/ (**rifts**) 1 N-COUNT A **rift** between people is a serious quarrel that stops them having a co-operative relationship. ❑ *The serious rifts within the country could lead to civil war.* 2 N-COUNT A **rift** is a large split that appears in the ground.

rig /rɪg/ (**rigs, rigging, rigged**) 1 V-T If someone **rigs** a contest, they dishonestly arrange it to get the result they want or to give someone an unfair advantage. ❑ *She accused her opponents of rigging the vote.* • **rigging** N-UNCOUNT ❑ *There were reports of election rigging.* 2 N-COUNT A **rig** is a large structure that is used for extracting oil or gas from the ground or the sea bed. ❑ *...gas rigs in the North Sea.*
→ see **oil**

▶ **rig up** PHR-VERB If you **rig up** a device or structure, you make it or fix it in place using any materials that are available. ❑ *I'll rig up a curtain.*

right
1 CORRECTNESS AND MORALITY
2 DIRECTION AND POLITICAL GROUPS
3 USED FOR EMPHASIS OR IN SPEECH

right /raɪt/ (**rights, righting, righted**)
1 1 ADJ & ADV If something is **right**, it is correct according to the facts or plans. If someone is **right** about something, they are correct about it. ❑ *This clock never tells the right time.* ❑ *...delivery of the right pizza to the right place.* ❑ *Am I right or am I wrong?* ❑ *He guessed right.* 2 ADJ & N-UNCOUNT **Right** is used to refer to activities or actions that are considered to be morally or legally good and acceptable. If someone has behaved in a way which is right, you can say that they are **in the right**. ❑ *It was right and proper not to show the film.* ❑ *I was right to issue that order.* ❑ *At least he knew right from wrong.* ❑ *Legally, you are in the right.* • **rightness** N-UNCOUNT ❑ *We had no doubts about the rightness of our cause.* 3 N-COUNT If you have a **right to** do or **to** have something, you are morally or legally entitled to do it or to have it. Your **rights** are the things you are entitled to do or have. ❑ *We have the right to protest.* ❑ *...voting rights.* 4 ADJ If something such as an action or decision is the **right** one, it is the best or most suitable one. ❑ *They decided the time was right for their escape.* ❑ *She's the right person for the job.* 5 ADJ AFTER LINK-V If a situation or thing is **right**, it is satisfactory and as you would like it to be. If something is not **right** about a situation or thing, there is something unsatisfactory or odd about it. ❑ *I was pleased with my performance on Saturday – everything went right.* ❑ *The boyfriends she had before she met Andy never seemed quite right.* 6 ADJ If you say that someone is seen in all the **right** places or knows all the **right** people, you mean that they go to places which are socially acceptable or know people who are socially acceptable. 7 V-T If you **right** a wrong, you do something to make up for a mistake or something bad you did in the past. 8 V-T If you **right** something that has fallen or rolled over, it returns to its normal upright position. ❑ *The boat righted itself.* 9 ADJ BEFORE N The **right** side of a material is the side that is intended to be seen. 10 PHRASE If something is not the case but you think that it should be, you can say that **by rights** it should be the case. ❑ *She does work which by rights should be done by her boss.* 11 PHRASE If someone is a successful or respected person **in their own right**, they are successful or respected because of

r

their own efforts and talents rather than those of the people they are connected with. 12 **it serves you right** → see **serve** 13 **on the right side of someone** → see **side**
→ see **citizenship**

right /raɪt/

The spelling **Right** is also used for meaning 2.

❷ 1 N-SING & ADV & ADJ BEFORE N **The right** is one of two opposite directions, sides, or positions. If you are facing north and you turn to the right, you will be facing east. **Right** is used to describe things which are on the right side of your body. ❑ *The car park is on the right.* ❑ *To her right was a large wall.* ❑ *Turn right into the street.* ❑ *Her right arm is broken.* 2 N-SING You can refer to political ideas based on capitalist or conservative ideas, or to the people who support these ideas, as **the right**. ❑ *...his supporters on the Right of the party.*

right /raɪt/

❸ 1 ADV You can use **right** to emphasize the exact position or time of something. ❑ *A car appeared right in front of him.* ❑ *I had to decide right then.* 2 ADJ You can use **right** to emphasize a noun, usually referring to something bad. [BRIT, INFORMAL] ❑ *He made a right mess.* 3 PHRASE If you do something **right away** or **right off**, you do it immediately. [SPOKEN] ❑ *Right off I want to confess that I was wrong.* 4 ADV You use **right** in order to attract someone's attention or to indicate that you have dealt with one thing so you can go on to another. ❑ *Right, let's get ready to leave!* 5 → see also **all right**

ˈright ˌangle (**right angles**) 1 N-COUNT A **right angle** is an angle of 90°. 2 PHRASE If two things are **at right angles**, they form an angle of 90° where they touch each other. You can also say that one thing is **at right angles to** another.

ˈright-ˌclick (**right-clicks, right-clicking, right-clicked**) V-I/V-T To **right-click** or to **right-click on** something means to press the right-hand button on a computer mouse. [COMPUTING] ❑ *Right-click on the desktop and select New Folder.* ❑ *Right-click the picture and left-click 'Edit Picture' from the menu.*

righteous /ˈraɪtʃəs/ 1 ADJ Someone who is **righteous** is morally good, especially according to the rules of a religion. ❑ *He was full of righteous indignation.* 2 → see also **self-righteous**
• **righteousness** N-UNCOUNT ❑ *...God's message of righteousness.*

rightful /ˈraɪtfʊl/ ADJ BEFORE N If you say that someone or something has returned to its **rightful** place or position, they have returned to the place or position that you think they should have. ❑ *The car must be returned to its rightful owner.* • **rightfully** ADV ❑ *She's inherited the money which is rightfully hers.*

ˈright-ˌhand ADJ BEFORE N If something is on the **right-hand** side of something, it is positioned on the right of it. ❑ *...the upper right-hand corner of the picture.*

ˌright-ˈhanded ADJ & ADV Someone who is **right-handed**, or who does things **right-handed**, uses their right hand rather than their left hand for activities such as writing or picking things up.

ˌright-ˈwing

The spelling **right wing** is also used for meaning 2.

1 ADJ A **right-wing** person or group has conservative or capitalist views. • **right-winger** (**right-wingers**) N-COUNT ❑ *Right-wingers demanded tax cuts.* 2 N-SING **The right wing** of a political party consists of the members of it who have the most conservative or the most capitalist views.

rigid /ˈrɪdʒɪd/ 1 ADJ If you describe laws, systems, or attitudes as **rigid**, you disapprove of them because they cannot be changed or because someone refuses to change them. ❑ *This approach indicates a rigid view of education.* • **rigidity** /rɪˈdʒɪdɪti/ N-UNCOUNT ❑ *...the rigidity of government policy.* • **rigidly** ADV ❑ *These rules are rigidly enforced.* 2 ADJ A **rigid** substance or object is stiff and does not bend or stretch easily. • **rigidity** N-UNCOUNT ❑ *...the strength and rigidity of glass.*

rigor → see **rigour**

rigorous /ˈrɪɡərəs/ ADJ If you describe something as **rigorous**, you approve of the fact that it is done carefully and strictly. ❑ *...rigorous military training.* • **rigorously** ADV ❑ *...rigorously-conducted research.*

rigour [AM **rigor**] /ˈrɪɡə/ (**rigours**) 1 N-PLURAL If you refer to **the rigours of** something, you mean the difficult or unpleasant things that are associated with it. ❑ *...the rigours of the Canadian winter.* 2 N-UNCOUNT If something is done with **rigour**, it is done in a strict, thorough way.

rim /rɪm/ (**rims**) N-COUNT The **rim** of a container or a circular object is the edge which goes all the way round the top or round the outside. ❑ *...a round mirror with a white metal rim.*

rind

rind /raɪnd/ (**rinds**) 1 N-VAR The **rind** of a fruit such as a lemon is its thick outer skin. 2 N-VAR The **rind** of cheese or bacon is the hard outer edge which you do not usually eat.

ring
❶ TELEPHONING OR MAKING A SOUND
❷ SHAPES AND GROUPS

ring /rɪŋ/ (**rings, ringing, rang, rung**)
❶ 1 V-T & PHR-VERB & N-COUNT In British English, if you **ring** someone, or if you **ring** them **up**, or if you give them a **ring**, you phone them. The usual American word is **call**. ❑ *She rang home today.* ❑ *He rang up the hospital to make another appointment.* 2 V-I & N-COUNT When a telephone **rings**, it makes a sound called a **ring**, to let you know that someone is phoning you. 3 V-T/V-I & N-COUNT When you **ring** a bell or when a bell **rings**, it makes a metallic sound called a **ring**. ❑ *He heard the school bell ring.* ❑ *He went to the front door and rang the bell.* • **ringing** N-UNCOUNT ❑ *...the ringing of church bells.* 4 N-SING You can use **ring** to describe a quality that something such as a statement or argument seems to have. For example, if an argument has **a plausible ring**, it seems quite believable. 5 PHRASE If a statement **rings true**, it seems to be true or genuine. If it **rings hollow**, it does not seem to be true or genuine.
→ see **jewellery, circle**
▸ **ring back** PHR VERB In British English, if

you **ring** someone **back**, you phone them, either because they phoned you earlier and you were out or because you did not finish an earlier conversation. The American term is **call back.**

▶ **ring off** PHR-VERB In British English, when you **ring off** you put down the receiver at the end of a telephone call. The American term is **hang up.**

ring /rɪŋ/ (**rings, ringed**)
❷ 1 N-COUNT A **ring** is a small circle of metal that you wear on your finger. ❑ *...a gold wedding ring.* 2 N-COUNT An object or substance that is in the shape of a circle can be described as a **ring.** ❑ *...a ring of blue smoke.* 3 N-COUNT At a boxing match or circus, the **ring** is the place where the contest or performance takes place. ❑ *He is not allowed inside a boxing ring.* 4 V-T PASSIVE If a place **is ringed with** or **by** something, it is surrounded by that thing. ❑ *The city is ringed by mountains.* 5 N-COUNT You can refer to an organized group of people who are involved in an illegal activity as a **ring.** ❑ *...an international spy ring.*

ringing /ˈrɪŋɪŋ/ ADJ BEFORE N A **ringing** sound can be heard very clearly. ❑ *The metal bowl fell onto the stone floor with a clear, ringing sound.*

ˈring ˌtone (**ring tones**) N-COUNT The **ring tone** is the sound made by a telephone, especially a mobile phone, when it rings.

rink /rɪŋk/ (**rinks**) N-COUNT A **rink** is a large area where people go to skate.

rinse /rɪns/ (**rinses, rinsing, rinsed**) 1 V-T & N-COUNT When you **rinse** something, or when you give it a **rinse**, you wash it in clean water in order to remove dirt or soap from it. ❑ *Shampoo and rinse your hair.* 2 N-COUNT A hair **rinse** is a hair dye which is not permanent but gradually fades over time.

riot /raɪət/ (**riots, rioting, rioted**) 1 V-I & N-COUNT When people **riot**, or when there is a **riot**, a crowd of people behave violently in a public place. ❑ *They rioted in protest against the Government.* ● **rioter** (**rioters**) N-COUNT ❑ *The rioters began throwing stones.* ● **rioting** N-UNCOUNT ❑ *...three days of rioting.* 2 PHRASE If people **run riot**, they behave in a wild and uncontrolled manner. ❑ *Parents use discipline to stop their children running riot.*

rip /rɪp/ (**rips, ripping, ripped**) 1 V-T/V-I If you **rip** something, you tear it forcefully with your hands or with a tool such as a knife. If something **rips**, it is torn forcefully. ❑ *I tried not to rip the paper as I unwrapped the present.* 2 N-COUNT A **rip** is a long cut or split in something made of cloth or paper. 3 V-T If you **rip** something away, you remove it quickly and forcefully. ❑ *Her earring was ripped off in the fight.*
→ see **cut**

rip

▶ **rip off** PHR-VERB If someone **rips** you **off**, they cheat you by charging too much for goods or services. [INFORMAL] ❑ *People are buying these products and getting ripped off.*

▶ **rip up** PHR-VERB If you **rip** something **up**, you tear it into small pieces.

ripe /raɪp/ (**riper, ripest**) 1 ADJ **Ripe** fruit or grain is fully grown and ready to be harvested or eaten. 2 ADJ AFTER LINK-V If something is **ripe for** a change, that change is likely to happen soon. ❑ *The nation was ripe for revolution.* 3 PHRASE If you say **the time is ripe** for something, you mean that a suitable time has arrived for doing it. ❑ *The time is ripe for a different leader.*

ripen /ˈraɪpən/ (**ripens, ripening, ripened**) V-T/V-I When crops **ripen**, or when something **ripens** them, they become ripe. ❑ *You can ripen the tomatoes on a sunny windowsill.*

ripple /ˈrɪpəl/ (**ripples, rippling, rippled**)
1 N-COUNT & V-I **Ripples** are little waves on the surface of water caused by the wind or by something moving. When water **ripples**, a number of little waves appear on its surface. 2 V-I If something such as a feeling **ripples** through a person or group, it gradually spreads across them. ❑ *A faint smile rippled across her face.*

ripple

rise /raɪz/ (**rises, rising, rose, risen** /ˈrɪzən/)
1 V-I If something **rises** or **rises up**, it moves upwards. ❑ *Black smoke rose from one building.* 2 V-I When you **rise**, you stand up. [FORMAL] ❑ *Luther rose slowly from the chair.* 3 V-I When you **rise**, you get out of bed. [WRITTEN] ❑ *Tony had risen early.* 4 V-I When the sun or moon **rises**, it appears from below the horizon. 5 V-I If land **rises**, it slopes upwards. ❑ *On the right, the land rose sharply.* 6 V-I & N-COUNT If an amount **rises**, or if there is a **rise in** an amount, the amount increases. ❑ *Profits rose from £842,000 to £1.82m.* ❑ *He has got a pay rise of nearly £4,000.* 7 V-I & N-SING If someone **rises to** a higher position or status, they become more powerful or successful. You can also talk about someone's **rise.** ❑ *He has risen rapidly through the ranks of government.* ❑ *...the rise of Martin Luther King.* 8 V-I If a sound **rises**, it becomes louder or higher. ❑ *His voice rose to a scream.* 9 PHRASE If something **gives rise to** an event or situation, it causes that event or situation to happen. 10 to **rise to the challenge** → see **challenge**

▶ **rise above** PHR-VERB If you **rise above** a problem, you do not allow it to affect you. ❑ *We must rise above our circumstances.*

▶ **rise up** PHR-VERB When the people in a country **rise up**, they rebel against the people in authority and start fighting them. ❑ *The people rose up against their rulers.*

Usage

You should be careful not to confuse the verbs **rise** and **raise. Rise** is an intransitive verb and means 'to go up by itself', whereas **raise** is a transitive verb and means 'to put or push something up'. **Rise** cannot be used in the passive. ❑ *The number of dead is likely to rise.* ❑ *...the government's decision to raise prices.*

risk /rɪsk/ (**risks, risking, risked**) 1 N-VAR If there is a **risk of** something unpleasant, there is a possibility that it will happen. ❑ *There is a risk that this project will fail.* ❑ *There was no risk of being overheard.* 2 N-COUNT If you say that something or someone is a **risk**, you mean they are likely to cause harm. ❑ *Pollution has become a health risk in a hundred American cities.* ❑ *He is a risk to national security.* 3 N-COUNT If something that you do is

r

a **risk**, it might have unpleasant or undesirable results. ❑ *You're taking a big risk telling him this.* **4** V-T If you **risk** something unpleasant, you do something knowing that the unpleasant thing might happen as a result. ❑ *He's willing to risk making a fool of himself.* **5** V-T If you **risk** doing something, you do it, even though you know that it might have undesirable consequences. ❑ *Daniel risked a look over his shoulder.* **6** V-T If you **risk** your **life** or something that is worth having, you do something which might result in it being lost or harmed. ❑ *You shouldn't have risked your job for me.* **7** PHRASE If someone or something is **at risk**, they are in a situation where something unpleasant might happen to them. ❑ *People are at risk of starvation.* **8** PHRASE If you tell someone that they are doing something **at** their **own risk**, you are warning them that, if they are harmed, it will be their own responsibility. **9** PHRASE If you **run** the **risk of** doing or experiencing something undesirable, you do something knowing that the undesirable thing might happen as a result. ❑ *The officers ran the risk of being dismissed.*

Thesaurus *risk* Also look up:

N.	accident, danger, gamble, hazard; *(ant.)* safety **1** **3**
V.	chance, endanger, gamble, jeopardize **1** **4** **5**

risky /ˈrɪski/ (**riskier, riskiest**) ADJ If an activity or action is **risky**, it is dangerous or could fail. ❑ *This strategy is risky.*

rite /raɪt/ (**rites**) N-COUNT A **rite** is a traditional ceremony that is carried out in a particular group or society. ❑ *...a religious rite.*
→ see **graduation**

ritual /ˈrɪtʃʊəl/ (**rituals**) **1** N-VAR & ADJ BEFORE N A **ritual** is a religious service or other ceremony which involves a series of actions performed in a fixed order. **Ritual** activities happen as part of a ritual. ❑ *...ritual dances.* **2** N-COUNT A **ritual** is a way of behaving or a series of actions which people regularly carry out in a particular situation. ❑ *It was a ritual that Lisa and Sarah had lunch together once a week.*
→ see **myth**

rival /ˈraɪvəl/ (**rivals, rivalling, rivalled** or [AM] **rivaling, rivaled**) **1** N-COUNT & ADJ If people or groups are **rivals**, they are competing against each other. You can also talk about **rival** groups. ❑ *He is well ahead of his nearest rival.* ❑ *...a dispute between rival teenage gangs.* **2** V-T If you say that one thing **rivals** another, you mean that they are both of the same standard or quality. ❑ *In my opinion, French cooking is rivalled only by the cuisine of China.*

rivalry /ˈraɪvəlri/ (**rivalries**) N-VAR **Rivalry** is competition or conflict between people or groups. ❑ *What causes rivalry between brothers?*

river /ˈrɪvə/ (**rivers**) N-COUNT A **river** is a large amount of fresh water flowing continuously in a long line across land, such as the Amazon or the Nile.
→ see Picture Dictionary: **river**
→ see **landform**

riverside /ˈrɪvəsaɪd/ N-SING **The riverside** is the area of land by the banks of a river. ❑ *...a riverside path.*

rivet /ˈrɪvɪt/ (**rivets, riveting, riveted**) **1** V-T If you **are riveted** by something, it fascinates you and holds your interest completely. • **riveting** ADJ ❑ *...the most riveting TV show of the year.* **2** N-COUNT A **rivet** is a type of bolt used for fastening pieces of metal together.

roach /rəʊtʃ/ (**roaches**) N-COUNT A **roach** is the same as a **cockroach**. [AM]

road /rəʊd/ (**roads**) N-COUNT A **road** is a long piece of hard ground built between two places so that people can drive or ride easily from one to the other. ❑ *There was very little traffic on the roads.* ❑ *They will travel by road to Jordan.*
→ see **traffic**

ˈroad ˌrage N-UNCOUNT **Road rage** is an angry or violent reaction by a driver towards another road user. ❑ *He was a victim of road rage.*

roadside /ˈrəʊdsaɪd/ (**roadsides**) N-COUNT **The roadside** is the area at the edge of a road. ❑ *...roadside restaurants.*

roadworks /ˈrəʊdwɜːks/ N-PLURAL **Roadworks**

Picture Dictionary river

Word Web rock

igneous sedimentary metamorphic

Rocks are made of **minerals**. Sometime they may contain only one **element**. Usually they contain **compounds** of several elements. Each type of rock also has its own **crystal** structure. Rock is always changing. When **lava erupts** from a **volcano**, it forms **igneous** rock. Wind, water, and ice **erode** this type of rock, and the **sediment** collects in rivers. Layers of sediment builds up and forms **sedimentary** rock. When **tectonic plates** move, they create heat and pressure. This melting and crushing changes sedimentary rock into **metamorphic** rock.

are repairs or other work being done on a road.

roam /rəʊm/ (**roams, roaming, roamed**) V-T/V-I If you **roam** an area or **roam** around it, you wander around it without having a particular purpose. ❑ *Rival gangs roamed the city.*

roar /rɔː/ (**roars, roaring, roared**) 1 V-I & N-COUNT If something **roars**, it makes a very loud noise. This noise is called a **roar**. ❑ *Her heart was pounding and the blood roared in her ears.* ❑ *A police car roared past.* ❑ *...the roar of traffic.* 2 V-I If someone **roars**, they shout very loudly. If they **roar with** laughter, they laugh very loudly. ❑ *The crowd roared with laughter.* 3 V-I & N-COUNT When a lion **roars**, or when it gives a **roar**, it makes the loud sound typical of a lion.

roaring /'rɔːrɪŋ/ 1 ADJ BEFORE N A **roaring fire** has large flames and is sending out a lot of heat. 2 ADJ BEFORE N If something is a **roaring success**, it is very successful indeed.

roast /rəʊst/ (**roasts, roasting, roasted**) 1 V-T When you **roast** meat or other food, you cook it by dry heat in an oven or over a fire. 2 → See note at **cook** 3 ADJ BEFORE N **Roast** meat has been roasted. ❑ *I love roast chicken.*
→ see **cook, peanut**

rob /rɒb/ (**robs, robbing, robbed**) 1 V-T If a person or place **is robbed**, money or property is stolen from them, often using force. ❑ *He was arrested after robbing a bank.* ● **robber** (**robbers**) N-COUNT ❑ *Armed robbers broke into a jeweller's shop.* 2 V-T If someone **is robbed of** something that they should have, it is taken away from them. ❑ *A knee injury robbed him of his place in the football team.*

robbery /'rɒbəri/ (**robberies**) N-VAR **Robbery** is the crime of stealing money or property, often using force. ❑ *The gang committed dozens of armed robberies.*

robe /rəʊb/ (**robes**) 1 N-COUNT A **robe** is a long, loose piece of clothing, usually worn in religious or official ceremonies. 2 N-COUNT A **bath robe** is a piece of clothing, similar to a coat, which people wear at home before or after bathing or showering.

robin /'rɒbɪn/ (**robins**) N-COUNT A **robin** is a small brown bird with a red breast.

robot /'rəʊbɒt, AM -bət/ (**robots**) N-COUNT A **robot** is a machine which moves and performs certain tasks automatically. ❑ *...robot vacuum cleaners.*
→ see **mass production**

robust /rəʊ'bʌst, 'rəʊbʌst/ ADJ Someone or something that is **robust** is very strong or healthy.

rock /rɒk/ (**rocks, rocking, rocked**) 1 N-UNCOUNT **Rock** is the hard substance which the Earth is made of. ❑ *The hills above the valley are bare rock.* 2 N-COUNT A **rock** is a large piece of rock that sticks up out of the ground or the sea, or that has broken away from a mountain or a cliff. 3 N-COUNT A **rock** is a piece of rock that is small enough for you to pick up. 4 V-T/V-I When something **rocks**, or when you **rock** it, it moves slowly and regularly backwards and forwards or from side to side. ❑ *His body rocked from side to side with the movement of the train.* ❑ *She sat rocking her baby.* 5 V-T If an event or a piece of news **rocks** people, it shocks and horrifies them. [JOURNALISM] ❑ *The scandal has rocked the country.* 6 N-UNCOUNT **Rock** or **rock music** is loud music with a strong beat that is played using instruments including electric guitars and drums. 7 PHRASE If you say that something such as a marriage or a business is **on the rocks**, you mean that it is having severe difficulties and looks likely to end soon. 8 PHRASE If you say that something has **reached** or **hit rock bottom**, you mean that it is at such a low level that it cannot go any lower. ❑ *Morale in the army was at rock bottom.* 9 to **rock the boat** → see **boat**
→ see Word Web: **rock**
→ see **crystal, earth, fossil, genre**

,rock and 'roll N-UNCOUNT **Rock and roll** is a kind of pop music developed in the 1950s which has a strong beat for dancing.

rocket /'rɒkɪt/ (**rockets, rocketing, rocketed**) 1 N-COUNT A **rocket** is a space vehicle shaped like a long tube. 2 N-COUNT A **rocket** is a missile containing explosive and powered by gas. ❑ *...an anti-tank rocket.* 3 V-I If prices or profits **rocket**, they suddenly increase very quickly. [JOURNALISM] ❑ *The crisis sent oil prices rocketing.*

rocky /'rɒki/ (**rockier, rockiest**) ADJ A **rocky** place is covered with rocks or consists of large areas of bare rock. ❑ *We made our way down the rocky path.*

rod /rɒd/ (**rods**) N-COUNT A **rod** is a long thin bar made of metal or wood.

rode /rəʊd/ **Rode** is the past tense of **ride**.

rodent /'rəʊdənt/ (**rodents**) N-COUNT **Rodents** are small mammals, for example rats and squirrels, with sharp front teeth.

rodeo /'rəʊdiəʊ, rəʊ'deɪəʊ/ (**rodeos**) N-COUNT In the United States, a **rodeo** is a public entertainment in which cowboys show skills such as riding wild horses.

rogue /rəʊg/ (**rogues**) N-COUNT A **rogue** is a man who behaves in a dishonest way. [DATED]

role /rəʊl/ (**roles**) 1 N-COUNT The **role** of someone or something in a situation is their

function or position in it. ❑ *Parents need to be clear about their role in raising their children.* ❑ *Music plays a major role in his life.* **2** N-COUNT A **role** is one of the characters that an actor or singer plays in a film, play, or opera. ❑ *He gave her a leading role in his film.*
→ see **theatre**

Word Partnership Use *role* with:

N.	**leadership** role, role **reversal** **1** **lead** role **2**
V.	**play a** role, **take on a** role **2**
ADJ.	**active** role, **key** role, **parental** role, **positive** role, **significant** role, **traditional** role, **vital** role **1** **bigger/larger** role, **leading** role, **major** role, **starring** role **2**

'role ˌmodel (**role models**) N-COUNT A **role model** is someone you admire and try to imitate.

roll /rəʊl/ (**rolls, rolling, rolled**) **1** V-T/V-I If something **rolls** or if you **roll** it, it moves along a surface, turning over many times. ❑ *The ball rolled into the net.* ❑ *Roll the meatballs in flour.* **2** V-I When vehicles **roll** somewhere, they move there slowly. ❑ *Tanks rolled into the heart of the city.* **3** V-I If drops of liquid **roll down** a surface, they move quickly down it. ❑ *Tears rolled down her cheeks.* **4** V-T & PHR-VERB If you **roll** something flexible **into** a cylinder or a ball, or if you **roll** it **up**, you form it into a cylinder or a ball by wrapping it around itself or by shaping it between your hands. ❑ *They rolled up the carpet as neatly as possible.* **5** N-COUNT A **roll of** paper, cloth, or plastic is a cylinder of it that has been wrapped around itself or around a tube. ❑ *...a dozen rolls of film.* **6** N-COUNT A **roll** is a very small circular loaf of bread. **7** N-COUNT A **roll** is an official list of people's names. ❑ *His name is on the electoral roll.* **8** → see also **rolling** **9** PHRASE If someone is **on a roll**, they are having great success which seems likely to continue. [INFORMAL] **10** PHRASE If something is several things **rolled into one**, it combines the main features or qualities of those things. ❑ *The flat is tiny and this room is our kitchen, sitting and dining room all rolled into one.* **11** to **start the ball rolling** → see **ball**
→ see **bread**

▸ **roll in** PHR-VERB If money or profits **are rolling in**, they are being received in large quantities. [INFORMAL]

▸ **roll up** **1** PHR-VERB If you **roll up** your sleeves or trouser legs, you fold the ends back several times, making them shorter. **2** → see also **roll** (meaning **4**)

roller /ˈrəʊlə/ (**rollers**) N-COUNT A **roller** is a cylinder that turns round in a machine or device.

Rollerblade /ˈrəʊləbleɪd/ (**Rollerblades**) N-COUNT **Rollerblades** are a type of roller skates with a single line of wheels along the bottom. **Rollerblade** is a trademark. ● **rollerblader** (**rollerbladers**) N-COUNT ❑ *The rollerblader crashed into a cyclist.* ● **rollerblading** N-UNCOUNT ❑ *At the weekend I like to go rollerblading.*

'roller-ˌcoaster also **roller coaster** (**roller-coasters**) **1** N-COUNT A **roller-coaster** is a ride at a fairground consisting of a small railway that goes up and down steep slopes fast. **2** N-COUNT If you say that someone or something is **on a roller-coaster**, you mean that they go through many dramatic changes in a short time. [JOURNALISM] ❑ *I've been on an emotional roller coaster since I've been here.*

roller coaster

'roller-ˌskate (**roller-skates**) N-COUNT **Roller-skates** are shoes with four small wheels on the bottom.

rolling /ˈrəʊlɪŋ/ ADJ BEFORE N **Rolling** hills have gentle slopes that extend into the distance.

'roll-ˌneck (**roll-necks**) ADJ & N-COUNT A **roll-neck** sweater or a **roll-neck** is a sweater with a high neck that can be rolled over. [mainly BRIT]

ROM /rɒm/ **1** N-UNCOUNT **ROM** is the permanent part of a computer's memory. The information stored there can be used but not changed. **ROM** is an abbreviation for 'read-only memory'. [COMPUTING] **2** → see also **CD-ROM**

Roman /ˈrəʊmən/ (**Romans**) **1** ADJ & N-COUNT **Roman** means related to or connected with ancient Rome and its empire. A **Roman** was a citizen of ancient Rome or its empire. **2** ADJ & N-COUNT **Roman** means related to or connected with modern Rome. A **Roman** is someone who lives in or comes from Rome.

ˌRoman 'Catholic (**Roman Catholics**) N-COUNT & ADJ **Roman Catholic** means the same as **Catholic**.

romance /rəˈmæns, ˈrəʊmæns/ (**romances**) **1** N-COUNT A **romance** is a relationship between two people who are in love with each other. ❑ *...a holiday romance.* **2** N-UNCOUNT **Romance** refers to the actions and feelings of people who are in love. ❑ *He makes time for romance by cooking candlelit dinners for his girlfriend.* **3** N-UNCOUNT You can refer to the pleasure and excitement of doing something as **romance**. ❑ *...the romance of travel.* **4** N-COUNT A **romance** is a novel about a love affair.
→ see **love**

romantic /rəʊˈmæntɪk/ (**romantics**) **1** ADJ Someone who is **romantic** or does **romantic** things says and does things that make their partner feel special and loved. ❑ *...a romantic dinner for two.* **2** ADJ BEFORE N **Romantic** means connected with love. ❑ *He was not interested in a romantic relationship with Ingrid.* ● **romantically** ADV ❑ *We are not romantically involved.* **3** ADJ BEFORE N A **romantic** play, film, or story describes or represents a love affair. **4** ADJ & N-COUNT If you say that someone has a **romantic** view or idea of things, or that they are a **romantic**, you are criticizing them because their view of things is unrealistic. ❑ *He has a romantic view of life in the countryside.*
→ see **love**

romp /rɒmp/ (**romps, romping, romped**) V-I When children **romp**, they play and move around in a noisy happy way. ❑ *Dogs and little children romped happily in the garden.*

roof /ruːf/ (**roofs**)

The plural can be pronounced /ruːfs/ or /ruːvz/.

1 N-COUNT The **roof** of a building or car is the covering on top of it. ❑ *...a white cottage with a red slate roof.* **2** N-COUNT **The roof of** your mouth is the top part of the inside of it. **3** N-COUNT The **roof** of an underground space such as a cave or mine is the highest part of it. **4** PHRASE If the

roof

level or price of something **goes through the roof**, it increases very suddenly and rapidly. [INFORMAL] ❑ *Prices for Korean art have gone through the roof.* **5** PHRASE If someone **hits the roof** or **goes through the roof**, they are very angry indeed. [INFORMAL]

Word Partnership Use *roof* with:

N.	roof **of a building/house, metal** roof, **rain on a** roof, **slate** roof, **tin** roof **1**
V.	roof **collapses**, roof **leaks, repair a** roof **1**

rooftop also **roof-top** /'ru:ftɒp/ (**rooftops**) N-COUNT A **rooftop** is the outside part of the roof of a building. ❑ *...an attic with views over the rooftops.*

rookie /'rʊki/ (**rookies**) N-COUNT A **rookie** is a person who does not have much experience because they are new to a job. [AM, INFORMAL] ❑ *I don't want another rookie to train.*

room /ru:m, rʊm/ (**rooms**) **1** N-COUNT & N-SING A **room** is one of the separate sections in a building. You can refer to all the people in a room as **the room**. ❑ *The largest conference room seats 5,000 people.* ❑ *The whole room roared with laughter.* **2** N-COUNT If you talk about your **room**, you are referring to a room that you alone use, especially your bedroom or your office. ❑ *Go to my room and bring down my handbag, please.* **3** N-UNCOUNT If there is **room for** something, there is enough space for it. ❑ *The car has enough room for seven passengers.* **4** N-UNCOUNT If there is **room for** a particular kind of behaviour, people are able to behave in that way. ❑ *Mr Harris left no room for doubt that he was in charge.*

Usage

You should use **room** or **space** to refer to an open or empty area. You do not use **place** as an uncount noun in this sense. **Room** is more likely to be used when you are talking about space inside an enclosed area. ❑ *There's not enough room in the kitchen for all of us.* ❑ *Leave plenty of space between you and the car in front.*

roommate also **room-mate** /'ru:mmeɪt, 'rʊm-/ (**roommates**) **1** N-COUNT Your **roommate** is the person you share an apartment or house with. [AM] **2** N-COUNT Your **roommate** is the person you share a rented room with. [BRIT]

roomy /'ru:mi/ (**roomier, roomiest**) ADJ Something that is **roomy** has plenty of space. ❑ *...a roomy kitchen.*

roost /ru:st/ (**roosts, roosting, roosted**) **1** N-COUNT A **roost** is a place where birds or bats rest. **2** V-I When birds or bats **roost** somewhere, they rest there.
→ see **bat**

root /ru:t/ (**roots, rooting, rooted**) **1** N-COUNT The **roots** of a plant are the parts that grow underground. **2** N-COUNT The **root** of a hair or tooth is the part beneath the skin. **3** N-PLURAL You can refer to the place or culture that a person or their family comes from as their **roots**. ❑ *I am proud of my Brazilian roots.* **4** N-COUNT You can refer to the cause of a problem or of an unpleasant situation as the **root of** it or the **roots of** it. ❑ *We got to the root of the problem.* ❑ *They were treating the symptoms and not the root cause of the illness.* **5** V-I If you **root** through things, you search through them thoroughly. ❑ *Dogs rooted in the rubbish at the roadside.* **6** PHRASE If an idea, belief, or custom **takes root**, it becomes established among a group of people. ❑ *Time is needed for democracy to take root.* **7** → see also **grass roots**
→ see **flower**

▶ **root out** **1** PHR-VERB If you **root out** a person, you find them and force them from the place they are in, usually in order to punish them. ❑ *It didn't take long to root him out.* **2** PHR-VERB If you **root out** a problem or an unpleasant situation, you find out the cause of it and put an end to it. ❑ *He says he doesn't care how long it takes to root out terrorism.*

Word Partnership Use *root* with:

N.	**tree** root **1**
	root **canal** **2**
	root **cause of *something***, root **of a problem** **4**
V.	**take** root **6**

rooted /'ru:tɪd/ **1** ADJ AFTER LINK-V If one thing is **rooted in** another, it is strongly influenced by it or has developed from it. ❑ *The crisis is rooted in deep rivalries between the two groups.* **2** ADJ A deeply **rooted** opinion is a firm one that is unlikely to change. ❑ *Sadly, racism is a deeply-rooted prejudice.*

rope /rəʊp/ (**ropes, roping, roped**) **1** N-VAR A **rope** is a very thick cord, made by twisting together several thinner cords. ❑ *He tied the rope around his waist.* **2** V-T If you **rope** one thing **to** another, you tie them together with a rope. ❑ *I roped myself to the chimney for safety when I was repairing the roof.*

rope

▶ **rope in** PHR-VERB If you say that you **were roped in** to do a particular task, you mean that someone persuaded you to help them do that task. [INFORMAL]

rose /rəʊz/ (**roses**) **1** N-COUNT A **rose** is a flower which has a pleasant smell and grows on a bush with thorns. ❑ *She bent to pick a rose.* **2** **Rose** is the past tense of **rise**.

rosé /'rəʊzeɪ, AM rəʊ'zeɪ/ N-UNCOUNT **Rosé** is wine which is pink in colour.

rosette /rəʊ'zet/ (**rosettes**) N-COUNT A **rosette** is a large circular badge made from coloured ribbons which is worn as a prize or to show support for a sports team or political party.

roster /'rɒstə/ (**rosters**) N-COUNT A **roster** is a list of people, especially one giving details about who is employed to do a particular job or the order in which people do that job.

rosy /'rəʊzi/ (**rosier, rosiest**) **1** ADJ **Rosy** means pink in colour. ❑ *She has rosy cheeks.* **2** ADJ If you say that a situation **looks rosy**, you mean that it is likely to be good or successful.

rot /rɒt/ (**rots, rotting, rotted**) **1** V-I/V-T When food, wood, or other substances **rot**, or when something **rots** them, they decay and fall apart. ❑ *...rotting vegetation.* ❑ *Sugary drinks rot your teeth.* **2** N-UNCOUNT If there is **rot** in something made of wood, parts of it have decayed and fallen apart. ❑ *There was rot in the roof beams.* **3** N-SING You can use **the rot** to refer to a gradual worsening of something. ❑ *The rot set in long before these crazy decisions were taken.*

▸ **rot away** PHR-VERB When something **rots away**, it decays. ❑ *The pillars rotted away and were replaced.*

rota /ˈrəʊtə/ (**rotas**) N-COUNT A **rota** is a list which gives details of the order in which different people have to do a particular job. [BRIT] ❑ *They organised a rota for the housework.*

Word Link	***rot** ≈ turning : **rot**ary, **rot**ate, **rot**ation*

rotary /ˈrəʊtəri/ ADJ BEFORE N **Rotary** means turning or able to turn in a circular movement round a fixed point.

rotate /rəʊˈteɪt, AM ˈrəʊteɪt/ (**rotates, rotating, rotated**) **1** V-T/V-I When something **rotates**, or when you **rotate** it, it turns with a circular movement. ❑ *Move your toes and rotate your ankles.* ● **rotation** (**rotations**) N-VAR ❑ *...the daily rotation of the earth.* **2** V-T/V-I If people or things **rotate**, or if someone **rotates** them, they take it in turns to do something. ● **rotation** N-VAR ❑ *...crop rotation.* → see **moon**

rotten /ˈrɒtən/ **1** ADJ If food, wood, or another substance is **rotten**, it has decayed and can no longer be used. ❑ *...rotten fruit.* **2** ADJ If you say that something is **rotten**, you think it is bad, unpleasant, or unfair. [INFORMAL] ❑ *It's a rotten idea.*

rotund /rəʊˈtʌnd/ ADJ If someone is **rotund**, they are round and plump. [FORMAL] ❑ *A rotund smiling gentleman appeared.*

rouble /ˈruːbəl/ (**roubles**) N-COUNT The **rouble** is the unit of currency used in Russia.

R

rough /rʌf/ (**rougher, roughest, roughs, roughing, roughed**) **1** ADJ If a surface is **rough**, it is uneven and not smooth. ❑ *...the rough road.* ● **roughness** N-UNCOUNT ❑ *...the roughness of his jacket.* **2** ADJ You say that people are **rough** when they use too much force. ● **roughly** ADV ❑ *They pushed him roughly aside.* **3** ADJ A **rough** place is unpleasant and dangerous because there is a lot of violence or crime there. ❑ *...a rough part of town.* **4** ADJ A **rough** calculation or guess is approximate rather than exact or detailed. ● **roughly** ADV ❑ *Roughly half a million protesters gathered in Washington.* **5** ADJ If someone is having a **rough** time, they are experiencing something difficult or unpleasant. ❑ *Tomorrow, he knew, would be a rough day.* **6** ADV You say that someone is **sleeping rough** or **living rough** when they have nowhere to live.

roulette /ruːˈlet/ N-UNCOUNT **Roulette** is a gambling game in which a ball is dropped onto a revolving wheel with numbered holes in it. The players bet on which hole the ball will end up in. ❑ *I played some roulette at the casino.*

round

❶ PREPOSITION AND ADVERB USES
❷ NOUN USES
❸ ADJECTIVE USE
❹ VERB USES

round /raʊnd/
❶ **1** PREP & ADV To be positioned **round** a place or object means to surround it or be on all sides of it. ❑ *They were sitting round the kitchen table.* ❑ *Visibility was good all round.* **2** PREP If you move **round** a corner or obstacle, you move to the other side of it. If you look **round** a corner or obstacle, you look to see what is on the other side. ❑ *Suddenly a car came round the corner.* ❑ *One of the men knocked and looked round the door.* **3** PREP & ADV You use **round** to say that something happens in or is near different parts of a place or area. ❑ *He owns all the land round here.* ❑ *Shirley showed them round.* **4** ADV If you move things **round**, you move them so they are in different places. ❑ *He has refurnished his house, changed things round and redecorated.* **5** ADV & PREP If you **go round to** someone's house, you visit them. ❑ *He came round with a cake.* ❑ *I went round to my sister's house.* **6** PREP If you **get round** a problem or difficulty, you find a way of dealing with it. **7** **round the corner** → see **corner** **8** **all year round** → see **year**

Usage

Round and **around** are used in various ways as prepositions and adverbs, often as part of phrasal verbs. In most cases, you can use either word without any difference of meaning. In American English, **around** is more common than **round**. When you are talking about movement in no particular direction, you can use **about** as well as **around** and **round**. ❑ *It's such fun up there, flying around in a small plane.* ❑ *I spent a couple of hours driving round town.* ❑ *People walked about eating ice cream.* When you are talking about something being generally present or available, you can use **around** or **about**, but not **round**, as adverbs. ❑ *I am the happiest man around at the moment.* ❑ *There are not that many jobs about.*

round /raʊnd/ (**rounds**)
❷ **1** N-COUNT A **round of** events is a series of related events, especially one which comes after or before a similar series of events. ❑ *Another round of talks will be held next week.* **2** N-COUNT In a sporting competition, a **round** is a series of games in which the winner goes on to play in the next round. **3** N-COUNT In a boxing or wrestling match, a **round** is one of the periods during which the participants fight. **4** N-COUNT A **round of** golf is one game, usually including 18 holes. **5** N-COUNT A doctor's **rounds** are a series of visits they make as part of their job. **6** N-COUNT If you buy a **round of** drinks, you buy a drink for each member of the group of people that you are with. **7** N-COUNT A **round of** ammunition is a bullet.

round /raʊnd/ (**rounder, roundest**)
❸ ADJ If something has a **round** shape, it has a curved shape, like a circle or ball. ❑ *She has a round face.*

round /raʊnd/ (**rounds, rounding, rounded**) ❹ **1** V-T If you **round** a place or obstacle, you move in a curve past the edge or corner of it. ❑ *The house disappeared from sight as we rounded a corner.* **2** V-T If you **round** an amount **up** or **down**, or if you **round** it **off**, you change it to the nearest whole number or nearest multiple of a number. **3** → see also **rounded**

▶ **round on** PHR-VERB In British English, if someone **rounds on** you, they criticize you fiercely. The usual American expression is **turn on**. ❑ *Bob rounded angrily on his friend.*

▶ **round up** PHR-VERB If people or animals **are rounded up**, someone gathers them together.

roundabout /'raʊndəbaʊt/ (**roundabouts**) **1** N-COUNT In British English, a **roundabout** is a circle at a place where several roads meet. The American term is **traffic circle**. **2** N-COUNT In a fair or playground, a **roundabout** is a large circular platform with seats which goes round and round. [BRIT] **3** ADJ If you do something in a **roundabout** way, you deliberately avoid doing or saying it in a simple, clear, and direct way.

rounded /'raʊndɪd/ ADJ Something that is **rounded** is curved rather than pointed or sharp.

ˌround 'trip (**round trips**) N-COUNT If you make a **round trip**, you travel to a place and then back again.

rouse /raʊz/ (**rouses, rousing, roused**) **1** V-T/V-I If someone **rouses** you when you are sleeping, or if you **rouse**, you wake up. [FORMAL] ❑ *The sound of the telephone ringing roused him from sleep.* **2** V-T If you **rouse yourself to** do something, you make yourself do it. ❑ *He roused himself to be cheerful.* **3** V-T If something **rouses** you, it makes you very emotional or excited. ❑ *...a man not quickly roused to anger.* ● **rousing** ADJ ❑ *...a rousing speech.* → see **dream**

rout /raʊt/ (**routs, routing, routed**) V-T & N-COUNT If an army or a sports team **routs** its opponents, it defeats them completely and easily. You can refer to a defeat like this as a **rout**. ❑ *The football match became a rout.*

route /ru:t, AM raʊt/ (**routes, routing, routed**) **1** N-COUNT A **route** is a way from one place to another. ❑ *...the most direct route to the town centre.* **2** V-T If vehicles, goods, or passengers **are routed** in a particular direction, they are made to travel in that direction. **3** PHRASE **En route to** a place means on the way to it. ❑ *The ship is en route from Spain to the Molucca Islands.* ❑ *...holiday makers en route for the US.* **4** N-COUNT You can refer to a way of achieving something as a **route**. ❑ *Keynes arrived at the same conclusions following a very different route.*

Word Partnership Use *route* with:

N.	**escape** route, **parade** route **1**
ADJ.	**alternative** route, **different** route, **direct** route, **main** route, **scenic** route, **shortest** route **1**

routine /ru:'ti:n/ (**routines**) **1** ADJ **Routine** activities are done regularly as a normal part of a job or process. ❑ *...routine medical tests.* ● **routinely** ADV ❑ *Doctors routinely wash their hands before examining a new patient.* **2** N-VAR A **routine** is the usual series of things that you do at a particular time in a particular order. ❑ *...their daily routine.* ❑ *The fire alarm went off and the building was cleared as a matter of routine.*

Word Partnership Use *routine* with:

N.	routine **day**, **exercise** routine, routine **maintenance**, routine **tests**, **work** routine **1**
	morning routine **2**
ADJ.	**daily** routine, **normal** routine, **regular** routine, **usual** routine **1** **2**

roving /rəʊvɪŋ/ ADJ BEFORE N You use **roving** to describe a person who travels around, rather than staying in a fixed place. ❑ *...a roving reporter.*

row (**rows, rowing, rowed**) **1** N-COUNT /rəʊ/ A **row of** things or people is a number of them arranged in a line. ❑ *...a row of cottages.* **2** PHRASE If something happens several times **in a row**, it happens that number of times without a break. ❑ *They have won five championships in a row.* **3** V-T/V-I When you **row**, or when you **row** a boat, you make it move through the water by using oars. ❑ *Jim rowed across the Atlantic in 1997.* ● **rowing** N-UNCOUNT ❑ *...competitions in rowing, swimming and water skiing.* **4** N-COUNT /raʊ/ A **row** is a serious disagreement between people or organizations, often one involving a noisy argument. ❑ *The incident provoked a diplomatic row between the two countries.* ❑ *Maxine and I had a terrible row about how I spent my money.* **5** V-I If two people **row**, or if one person **rows with** another, they have a noisy argument. ❑ *They row all the time.* ❑ *He has been rowing with his girlfriend.* **6** N-COUNT If you say that someone is making a **row**, you mean that they are making a loud unpleasant noise. [BRIT, INFORMAL] ❑ *What a row you two were making last night!* **7** → see also **death row**

rowdy /'raʊdi/ (**rowdier, rowdiest**) ADJ If people are **rowdy**, they are noisy, rough, and likely to cause trouble. ❑ *He has complained to the police about his rowdy neighbours.*

Word Link *roy* ≈ *king* : *royal, royalist, royalty*

royal /'rɔɪəl/ ADJ **Royal** means related or belonging to a king, queen, or emperor, or to a member of their family. ❑ *...the Japanese royal couple.*

royalist /'rɔɪəlɪst/ (**royalists**) N-COUNT A **royalist** is someone who thinks it is right that their country should have a royal family.

royalty /'rɔɪəlti/ (**royalties**) **1** N-UNCOUNT The members of a royal family can be referred to as **royalty**. ❑ *...a ceremony attended by royalty.* **2** N-PLURAL **Royalties** are payments made to authors and musicians when their work is sold or performed.

rub /rʌb/ (**rubs, rubbing, rubbed**) **1** V-T If you **rub** something, you move your hand or a cloth backwards and forwards over it while pressing firmly. ❑ *She took off her glasses and rubbed them hard.* **2** V-T/V-I If you **rub** a part of your body **against** a surface, you move it backwards and forwards while pressing it against the surface. ❑ *The cat rubbed against my legs.* ❑ *He rubbed his hand over his eyes.* **3** V-T If you **rub** a substance onto a surface, you spread it over the surface using your hand. ❑ *She rubbed cream onto the cut on her knee.* **4** V-T/V-I If two things **rub together**, or if you **rub** them

together, they move backwards and forwards, pressing against each other. ❑ *He rubbed his hands together.* **5** to **rub shoulders** → see **shoulder**
▶ **rub off on** PHR-VERB If someone's habits or characteristics **rub off on** you, you start developing the same habits or characteristics after spending time with them. [INFORMAL] ❑ *He was a very enthusiastic teacher and that rubbed off on his students.*
▶ **rub out** PHR-VERB If you **rub out** something written on paper or on a blackboard, you remove it by rubbing it with a rubber or a cloth.

Word Partnership Use *rub* with:

PREP.	rub **against** 2
ADV.	rub **together** 4

rubber /ˈrʌbə/ (**rubbers**) **1** N-UNCOUNT **Rubber** is a strong, waterproof, elastic substance used for making tyres, boots, and other products. **2** N-COUNT A **rubber** is a small piece of rubber used to rub out mistakes that you have made while writing or drawing. [BRIT]

ˌrubber ˈstamp also **rubber-stamp** (**rubber stamps, rubber stamping, rubber stamped**) V-T When someone in authority **rubber stamps** a decision, plan, or law, they agree to it. ❑ *Union leaders rubber stamped the deal.*

rubbish /ˈrʌbɪʃ/ (**rubbishes, rubbishing, rubbished**) **1** N-UNCOUNT **Rubbish** consists of unwanted things or waste material such as old food. **2** N-UNCOUNT If you think that something is foolish or of very poor quality you can say that it is **rubbish**. [INFORMAL] ❑ *These reports are total and utter rubbish.* ❑ *He described her book as absolute rubbish.* **3** V-T If you **rubbish** a person, their ideas, or their work, you say they are of little value. ❑ *In the letter she rubbished her political opponents.*

Usage

In British English, **rubbish** is the word most commonly used to refer to waste material that is thrown away. In American English, the words **garbage** and **trash** are more usual. ❑ *...the smell of rotting garbage.* ❑ *She threw the bottle into the trash.* **Garbage** and **trash** are sometimes used in British English, but only informally and metaphorically. ❑ *I don't have to listen to this garbage.* ❑ *The book was trash.*

R

rubble /ˈrʌbəl/ N-UNCOUNT **Rubble** consists of the pieces of brick, stone, or other materials that remain when a building is destroyed.

ruby /ˈruːbi/ (**rubies**) N-COUNT A **ruby** is a dark red precious stone.

rucksack /ˈrʌksæk/ (**rucksacks**) N-COUNT A **rucksack** is a bag, often on a frame, used for carrying things on your back.

rucksack

rudder /ˈrʌdə/ (**rudders**) N-COUNT A **rudder** is a device for steering a boat or aeroplane.

ruddy /ˈrʌdi/ (**ruddier, ruddiest**) ADJ If someone has a **ruddy** complexion, their face is a reddish colour. ❑ *He has a round ruddy face and short hair.*

rude /ruːd/ (**ruder, rudest**) **1** ADJ If someone is **rude**, they behave in a way that is not polite. ❑ *He's rude to her friends.* • **rudely** ADV ❑ *She behaved very rudely.* • **rudeness** N-UNCOUNT ❑ *Sam ignored Mary's rudeness.* **2** ADJ **Rude** words and behaviour are likely to embarrass or offend people, because they relate to sex or other bodily functions. ❑ *...a rude joke.* **3** ADJ BEFORE N **Rude** is used to describe events that are unexpected and unpleasant. ❑ *The changes came as a rude shock.* • **rudely** ADV ❑ *People were awakened rudely by a siren.*

Thesaurus *rude* Also look up:

ADJ.	impolite, vulgar; *(ant.)* polite 1

rudimentary /ˌruːdɪˈmentri/ ADJ **Rudimentary** means very basic or not developed to a satisfactory degree. ❑ *He has only a rudimentary knowledge of French.* ❑ *...rudimentary equipment.*

rueful /ˈruːfʊl/ ADJ If someone is **rueful**, they feel or express regret or sorrow in a quiet and gentle way. [LITERARY] ❑ *He shook his head and gave me a rueful smile.* • **ruefully** ADV ❑ *'My wife wouldn't let me,' he says ruefully.*

ruffle /ˈrʌfəl/ (**ruffles, ruffling, ruffled**) **1** V-T If you **ruffle** someone's hair, you move your hand backwards and forwards through it as a way of showing your affection towards them. **2** V-T/V-I If a bird **ruffles** its **feathers**, or if its **feathers ruffle**, they stand out on its body, for example when it is cleaning itself. **3** N-COUNT **Ruffles** are folds of cloth at the neck or cuffs of a piece of clothing.

ruffled /ˈrʌfəld/ **1** ADJ Something that is **ruffled** is no longer smooth or neat. ❑ *Her hair was ruffled.* **2** ADJ BEFORE N **Ruffled** clothes are decorated with small folds of material.

rug /rʌg/ (**rugs**) **1** N-COUNT A **rug** is a piece of thick material that you put on the floor and use like a carpet. ❑ *...a Persian rug.* **2** N-COUNT A **rug** is a small blanket which you use to cover your shoulders or your knees.

rugby /ˈrʌgbi/ N-UNCOUNT **Rugby** is a game played by two teams, who try to get an oval ball past a line at their opponents' end of the pitch.

rugged /ˈrʌgɪd/ **1** ADJ A **rugged** area of land is rocky and uneven. [LITERARY] ❑ *...a rugged mountainous area.* **2** ADJ If you describe a man as **rugged**, you mean that he has strong masculine features; used showing approval. **3** ADJ A **rugged** piece of equipment is made of strong long-lasting material. ❑ *...rugged footwear.*

ruin /ˈruːɪn/ (**ruins, ruining, ruined**) **1** V-T To **ruin** something means to severely harm, damage, or spoil it. ❑ *My wife is ruining her health through worry.* **2** PHRASE If something is **in ruins**, it has gone completely wrong, and there is no chance of putting it right. ❑ *His travel plans lay in ruins.* **3** N-COUNT & PHRASE A **ruin** is a building that has been partly destroyed. You can say that a building like this is **in ruins**. ❑ *Part of the roof had fallen in; the building was a ruin.* ❑ *The town was in ruins.* **4** N-PLURAL **The ruins of** something are the parts of it that remain after it has been severely damaged or weakened. ❑ *...the ruins of Machu Picchu.* **5** V-T & N-UNCOUNT If someone or something **ruins** you, or if you face financial **ruin**, someone or something causes you to no longer have any money.

ruined /ˈruːɪnd/ ADJ BEFORE N A **ruined** building

has been badly damaged or has fallen apart. ❑ *...a ruined church.*

rule /ruːl/ (**rules, ruling, ruled**) 1 N-COUNT **Rules** are specific, often written, instructions telling you what you can and cannot do. ❑ *...a booklet explaining the rules of basketball.* ❑ *You know that's against the rules.* 2 N-COUNT The **rules of** something such as a language or a science are statements that describe the way that things usually happen in a particular situation. ❑ *...the rules of physics.* 3 N-SING If something is **the rule,** it is the normal state of affairs. ❑ *For most people, seven hours' sleep a night is the rule.* 4 V-T The person or group that **rules** a country controls its affairs. ❑ *Emperor Hirohito ruled Japan for 62 years until his death in 1989.* 5 V-I When someone in authority **rules on** a particular matter, they give an official decision about it. [FORMAL] ❑ *The court has not yet ruled on the case.* 6 → see also **ruling; ground rule** 7 PHRASE If you say that something happens **as a rule,** you mean that it usually happens. ❑ *As a rule she eats dinner with us.* 8 PHRASE If someone in authority **bends the rules,** they allow you to do something, even though it is against the rules.
→ see **measurement**

▶ **rule out** 1 PHR-VERB If you **rule out** an idea or course of action, you reject it because it is impossible or unsuitable. 2 PHR-VERB If something **rules out** a situation, it prevents it from happening or from being possible. ❑ *A knee injury ruled the player out of the World Cup.*

Thesaurus *rule* Also look up:

N.	guideline, law, standard 1 2 authority, leadership 5
V.	command, dictate, govern 4 5

Word Partnership Use *rule* with:

V.	**break a** rule, **change a** rule, **follow a** rule 1
N.	**gag** rule 1 **exception to a** rule 1 3 **majority** rule, **minority** rule 5 **courts** rule, **judges** rule 5
PREP.	**against a** rule, **under a** rule 1 rule **over** ***something*** 4

ruler /ˈruːlə/ (**rulers**) 1 N-COUNT A **ruler** is a person who rules a country. ❑ *...a wise ruler.* 2 N-COUNT A **ruler** is a long flat object with straight edges used for measuring things or drawing straight lines.

ruler

ruling /ˈruːlɪŋ/ (**rulings**) 1 ADJ BEFORE N The **ruling** group of people in an organization or country is the group that controls its affairs. ❑ *Japan's ruling political party has selected its leader.* 2 N-COUNT A **ruling** is an official decision made by a judge or court. ❑ *We wish to challenge the ruling in a higher court.*

rum /rʌm/ N-UNCOUNT **Rum** is an alcoholic drink made from sugar cane juice.

rumble /ˈrʌmbəl/ (**rumbles, rumbling, rumbled**) V-I & N-COUNT If something **rumbles,** or if it makes a **rumble,** it makes a low continuous noise, often while moving slowly. ❑ *...the distant rumble of traffic.*

rumbling /ˈrʌmblɪŋ/ (**rumblings**) 1 N-PLURAL A **rumbling** is a low continuous noise. ❑ *...the rumbling of an empty stomach.* 2 N-COUNT **Rumblings** are signs that a bad situation is developing or that people are becoming dissatisfied. ❑ *There were rumblings of discontent among the staff.*

rummage /ˈrʌmɪdʒ/ (**rummages, rummaging, rummaged**) V-I & N-COUNT If you **rummage through** something, or if you have a **rummage through** it, you search for something you want by moving things around in a careless or hurried way. ❑ *He rummaged through boxes and drawers.* ❑ *I like a rummage in second-hand shops.*

rumour [AM **rumor**] /ˈruːmə/ (**rumours**) N-COUNT A **rumour** is a piece of information that may or may not be true, but that people are talking about.

Word Partnership Use *rumour* with:

ADJ.	**false** rumour
V.	**hear a** rumour, **spread a** rumour, **start a** rumour

rumoured [AM **rumored**] /ˈruːməd/ V-T PASSIVE If something **is rumoured to** be the case, people are suggesting that it is the case, but they do not know for certain. ❑ *Her parents are rumoured to be divorcing.*

rump /rʌmp/ (**rumps**) N-COUNT An animal's **rump** is its rear end.

run /rʌn/ (**runs, running, ran, run**) 1 V-I & N-COUNT When you **run,** or when you have a **run,** you move quickly, leaving the ground during each stride. ❑ *I ran back to the house.* ❑ *Antonia ran to meet them.* ❑ *After a six-mile run, Jackie returned home.* ● **running** N-UNCOUNT ❑ *...cross-country running.* ❑ *...running shoes.* 2 V-I You say that something long, such as a road, **runs** in a particular direction when you are describing its course or position. ❑ *The path runs through the woods.* ❑ *The hallway ran the length of the house.* 3 V-T If you **run** an object or your hand **over** or **through** something, you move the object or your hand over it or through it. ❑ *He ran his hands through his hair.* ❑ *He ran his belt through the loops on his jeans.* 4 V-I In American English, if someone **runs** in an election, they take part as a candidate. The usual British word is **stand.** ❑ *He announced he would run for president.* 5 V-T If you **run** an organization or an activity, you are in charge of it or you organize it. ❑ *Is this any way to run a country?* ❑ *...a well-run, profitable organisation.* ● **running** N-SING ❑ *...the day-to-day running of the business.* 6 V-I If you talk about how a system, an organization, or someone's life **is running,** you are saying how well it is operating or progressing. ❑ *The business is running well again.* 7 V-T/V-I If you **run** an experiment, computer program, or other process, you start it and let it continue. ❑ *He ran a lot of tests.* ❑ *This program runs on a standard personal computer.* 8 V-T/V-I When a machine **is running,** or when you **are running** it, it is switched on and operating. ❑ *Joyce's camera was still running.* 9 V-I A machine that **runs on** or **off** a particular source of energy functions using that source of energy.

r

❑ *All military vehicles run on diesel fuel.* 10 V-I If a train or bus **runs** somewhere, it travels on a regular route at set times. ❑ *A shuttle bus runs frequently between the city centre and the airport.* 11 V-T If you **run** someone somewhere in a car, you drive them there. [INFORMAL] ❑ *Could you run me into the city centre?* 12 V-I If a liquid **runs** in a particular direction, it flows in that direction. ❑ *Tears were running down her cheeks.* 13 V-T If you **run** water, you cause it to flow from a tap. ❑ *They heard him running the kitchen tap.* ❑ *I ran a warm bath.* ● **running** ADJ BEFORE N ❑ *...cold running water.* 14 V-I If the dye in some cloth or the ink on some paper **runs**, it comes off or spreads when the cloth or paper gets wet. 15 V-I If a play, event, or legal contract **runs** for a particular period of time, it lasts for that period of time. ❑ *The play ran for three years in the West End.* ❑ *The contract will run from 2000 to 2020.* 16 N-COUNT In the theatre, a **run** is the period of time during which performances of a play are given. 17 V-I **Run** is used in combination with other words and phrases, where the meaning of the combination depends mostly on the other word or phrase. ❑ *Time is running short.* ❑ *I'm running late again.* ❑ *Unemployment is still running at 25 per cent.* 18 → see also **running** 19 PHRASE If you talk about what will happen **in the long run**, you are saying what you think will happen over a long period of time in the future. If you talk about what will happen **in the short run**, you are saying what you think will happen in the near future. 20 PHRASE If someone is **on the run**, they are trying to escape or hide from someone such as the police or an enemy.

▶ **run across** PHR-VERB If you **run across** someone or something, you meet them or find them unexpectedly. ❑ *We ran across some old friends.*

▶ **run away** PHR-VERB If you **run away from** a place, you secretly leave it. ❑ *I ran away from home when I was sixteen.*

▶ **run away with** PHR-VERB If you let your emotions **run away with** you, you fail to control them.

▶ **run down** 1 PHR-VERB If you **run down** people or things, you criticize them strongly. ❑ *The British have a tendency to run themselves down.* 2 PHR-VERB If a vehicle or its driver **runs** someone **down**, the vehicle hits them and injures them. 3 → see also **run-down**

R

▶ **run into** 1 PHR-VERB If you **run into** problems or difficulties, you unexpectedly begin to experience them. ❑ *His company has run into trouble.* 2 PHR-VERB If you **run into** someone, you meet them unexpectedly. ❑ *He ran into his friends in the corridor.* 3 PHR-VERB If a vehicle **runs into** something, it accidentally hits it. 4 PHR-VERB You use **run into** when indicating that the cost or amount of something is very great. ❑ *The cost could run into thousands of pounds.*

▶ **run off** 1 PHR-VERB If you **run off with** someone, you secretly go away with them in order to live with them or marry them. ❑ *She would never run off with another woman's husband.* 2 PHR-VERB If you **run off** copies of a piece of writing, you produce them using a machine.

▶ **run out** 1 PHR-VERB If you **run out of** something, or if it **runs out**, you have no more of it left. ❑ *They have run out of ideas.* ❑ *Time is running out.* 2 PHR-VERB When a legal document **runs out**, it stops being valid. 3 to **run out of steam** → see **steam**

▶ **run over** PHR-VERB If a vehicle **runs over** someone or something, it knocks them down. ❑ *He ran over an elderly man.*

▶ **run through** 1 PHR-VERB If you **run through** a performance or a series of actions, you rehearse it or practise it. 2 PHR-VERB If you **run through** a list of items, you read or mention all the items quickly. ❑ *I ran through the options with him.*

▶ **run up** 1 PHR-VERB If someone **runs up** bills or debts, they acquire them by buying a lot of things or borrowing money. ❑ *He ran up a £1,400 bill at the hotel.* 2 → see also **run-up**

▶ **run up against** PHR-VERB If you **run up against** problems, you suddenly begin to experience them.

Thesaurus *run* Also look up:

V.	dash, jog, sprint 1
	follow, go 2
	administer, conduct, manage 5

runaway /ˈrʌnəweɪ/ (**runaways**) 1 ADJ You use **runaway** to describe a situation in which something increases or develops very quickly and cannot be controlled. ❑ *The shop's sale was a runaway success.* 2 N-COUNT A **runaway** is someone, especially a child, who leaves home without telling anyone or without permission. 3 ADJ A **runaway** vehicle is moving and its driver has lost control of it. ❑ *The runaway car crashed into a tree.*

ˌrun-ˈdown 1 ADJ /ˌrʌn ˈdaʊn/ If someone is **run-down**, they are tired or slightly ill. [INFORMAL] 2 ADJ A **run-down** building or organization is in very poor condition. ❑ *...a run-down block of flats.* 3 N-SING If you give someone a **run-down of** a group of things or a **run-down on** something, you give them details of it. [INFORMAL] ❑ *Here's a run-down of the options.*

rung

rung /rʌŋ/ (**rungs**) 1 **Rung** is the past participle of **ring**. 2 N-COUNT The **rungs** of a ladder are the wooden or metal bars that form the steps. 3 N-COUNT If you reach a particular **rung** in an organization or in a process, you reach that level in it. ❑ *...the first rung of the property ladder.*

ˈrun-ˌin (**run-ins**) N-COUNT If you have a **run-in with** someone, you have an argument or quarrel with them. [INFORMAL]

runner /ˈrʌnə/ (**runners**) 1 N-COUNT A **runner** is a person who runs, especially for sport or pleasure. ❑ *...a marathon runner.* ❑ *I am a very keen runner.* 2 N-COUNT A **drugs runner** or **gun runner** is someone who illegally takes drugs or guns into a country. 3 N-COUNT **Runners** are thin strips of wood or metal underneath something which help it to move smoothly. ❑ *...plastic drawer runners.*

ˈrunner ˌbean (**runner beans**) N-COUNT **Runner beans** are long green beans that are eaten as a vegetable.

ˌrunner-ˈup (**runners-up**) N-COUNT A **runner-up** is someone who finishes in second place in a race or competition.

running /ˈrʌnɪŋ/ 1 ADJ BEFORE N You use

running to describe things that continue or keep occurring over a period of time. ❑ *The song turned into a running joke.* **2** ADJ BEFORE N You use **running** to describe something that keeps being changed or added to as something progresses. ❑ *As we sat watching the video, Ann did a running commentary.* **3** ADJ You can use **running** when indicating that something keeps happening. ❑ *She wore the same clothes two days running.* ❑ *Spain won the Cup for the third year running.* **4** → see also **run** **5** PHRASE If someone is **in the running for** something, they have a good chance of winning or obtaining it. If they are **out of the running**, they have no chance of winning or obtaining it.

ˈrunning ˌmate (**running mates**) N-COUNT In an American election campaign, a candidate's **running mate** is the person that they have chosen to be their deputy if they win.

runny /ˈrʌni/ (**runnier, runniest**) **1** ADJ Something that is **runny** is more liquid than usual or than was intended. ❑ *Warm the honey until it becomes runny.* **2** ADJ If someone's nose or eyes are **runny**, liquid is flowing from them.

ˈrun-ˌup N-SING **The run-up to** an event is the period of time just before it. ❑ *...the run-up to the elections.*

runway /ˈrʌnweɪ/ (**runways**) N-COUNT At an airport, the **runway** is the long strip of ground with a hard surface which an aeroplane takes off from or lands on.

rupture /ˈrʌptʃə/ (**ruptures, rupturing, ruptured**) **1** V-T/V-I & N-COUNT If you **rupture** a part of your body, if a part of your body **ruptures** or if you have a **rupture**, a part of your body tears or bursts open. ❑ *The footballer ruptured his spleen in an accident.* ❑ *...a ruptured appendix.*
→ see **crash**

rural /ˈrʊərəl/ ADJ **Rural** means relating to country areas as opposed to large towns. ❑ *...the closure of rural schools.* ❑ *He spoke with a heavy rural accent.*

ruse /ruːz, AM ruːs/ (**ruses**) N-COUNT A **ruse** is an action or plan which is intended to deceive someone. [FORMAL] ❑ *The whole thing may be a ruse.*

rush /rʌʃ/ (**rushes, rushing, rushed**) **1** V-I If you **rush** somewhere, you go there quickly. ❑ *I've got to rush. Got a meeting in a few minutes.* ❑ *Shoppers rushed to the door.* **2** V-T If people **rush to** do something, they do it as soon as they can, because they are very eager to do it. ❑ *The banks rushed to buy as many dollars as they could.* **3** N-SING A **rush** is a situation in which you need to go somewhere or do something very quickly. ❑ *The men left in a rush.* ❑ *...the rush not to be late for school.* **4** N-SING If there is a **rush for** something, many people suddenly try to get it or do it. ❑ *...the rush for tickets.* **5** V-T If you **rush** something, you do it in a hurry. ❑ *Chew your food well and do not rush meals.* ● **rushed** ADJ ❑ *...a rushed job.* **6** V-T If you **rush** someone or something to a place, you take them there quickly. ❑ *We got an ambulance and rushed her to hospital.* **7** V-T/V-I If you **rush into** something, or if you **are rushed into** it, you do it without thinking about it for long enough. ❑ *He will not rush into any decisions.* ❑ *Don't be rushed into committing yourself.* ● **rushed** ADJ ❑ *I felt rushed and under pressure to accept their offer.* **8** N-SING If you experience a **rush of** a feeling, you suddenly experience it very strongly. ❑ *A rush of love swept over him.* **9** N-COUNT **Rushes** are plants with long thin stems that grow near water.

Word Partnership Use *rush* with:

ADJ.	**mad** rush **2** **3**
	sudden rush **2** **3** **4**
N.	rush **to judgment** **5**
	rush **of adrenaline** **8**

ˈrush ˌhour (**rush hours**) N-COUNT **The rush hour** is one of the periods of the day when most people are travelling to or from work. ❑ *Try to avoid rush-hour traffic.*

rust /rʌst/ (**rusts, rusting, rusted**) **1** N-UNCOUNT **Rust** is a brown substance that forms on iron or steel when it comes into contact with water. **2** V-I When a metal object **rusts**, it becomes covered in rust.

rustic /ˈrʌstɪk/ ADJ You can use **rustic** to describe things or people that are simple or unsophisticated in a way that is typical of the countryside; used showing approval. ❑ *...the rustic charm of a country lifestyle.*

rustle /ˈrʌsəl/ (**rustles, rustling, rustled**) V-I/V-T & N-COUNT When something thin and dry **rustles**, or when you **rustle** it, it makes soft sounds as it moves, called **rustles**. ❑ *The leaves rustled in the wind.* ❑ *She rustled her papers impatiently.* ❑ *...the rustle of her silk skirt.* ● **rustling** (**rustlings**) N-VAR ❑ *There was a rustling of paper.*

rusty /ˈrʌsti/ (**rustier, rustiest**) **1** ADJ A **rusty** metal object has a lot of rust on it. ❑ *...a rusty old van.* **2** ADJ If a skill that you have or your knowledge of something is **rusty**, it is not as good as it used to be, because you have not used it for a long time. ❑ *Jane's typing skills are rather rusty.*

rut /rʌt/ (**ruts**) **1** N-COUNT If someone is **in a rut**, they have become fixed in their way of thinking and doing things, and find it difficult to change. ❑ *I don't like being in a rut - I like to keep moving on.* **2** N-COUNT A **rut** is a deep narrow mark made in the ground by the wheels of a vehicle.

ruthless /ˈruːθləs/ ADJ Someone who is **ruthless** is very harsh or determined, and will do anything that is necessary to achieve their aim. ❑ *...his ruthless treatment of employees.* ● **ruthlessly** ADV ❑ *She is ruthlessly efficient.* ● **ruthlessness** N-UNCOUNT ❑ *...a mixture of ambition and ruthlessness.*

rye /raɪ/ N-UNCOUNT **Rye** is a cereal grown in cold countries. Its grains can be used to make flour, bread, or other foods.
→ see **bread**

Ss

Sabbath /ˈsæbəθ/ N-PROPER **The Sabbath** is the day of worship and rest for the members of some religious groups, especially Jews and Christians. For Jews, it is Saturday; for Christians, it is Sunday.

sabotage /ˈsæbətɑːʒ/ (**sabotages, sabotaging, sabotaged**) 1 V-T & N-UNCOUNT If a machine, railway line, or bridge **is sabotaged**, it is deliberately damaged or destroyed, for example in a war. **Sabotage** is the act of sabotaging something. ❑ *The train crash was caused by an act of sabotage.* 2 V-T If someone **sabotages** a plan or a meeting, they deliberately prevent it from being successful. ❑ *They tried to sabotage the peace talks.*

sack /sæk/ (**sacks, sacking, sacked**) 1 N-COUNT A **sack** is a large bag made of rough woven material. 2 V-T & N-SING If your employers **sack** you from your job, or if they give you **the sack**, they tell you that you can no longer work for them. ❑ *One girl got the sack for telling lies.* ● **sacking** (**sackings**) N-COUNT ❑ *...the sacking of twenty-three workers.*

sacred /ˈseɪkrɪd/ 1 ADJ Something that is **sacred** is believed to be holy. ● **sacredness** N-UNCOUNT ❑ *...the sacredness of the site.* 2 ADJ BEFORE N Something connected with religion or used in religious ceremonies is described as **sacred**. ❑ *...sacred songs or music.* 3 ADJ You can describe something as **sacred** when you regard it as too important to be changed or interfered with. ● **sacredness** N-UNCOUNT ❑ *...the sacredness of life.*

sacrifice /ˈsækrɪfaɪs/ (**sacrifices, sacrificing, sacrificed**) 1 V-T & N-COUNT To **sacrifice** an animal, or to offer it as a **sacrifice**, means to kill it in a special religious ceremony. ● **sacrificial** /ˌsækrɪˈfɪʃəl/ ADJ BEFORE N ❑ *...the sacrificial lamb.* 2 V-T & N-VAR If you **sacrifice** something valuable or important, you give it up, usually to obtain something else. You call the thing you give up a **sacrifice**. ❑ *He sacrificed his own career to promote his wife's.*

S

sad /sæd/ (**sadder, saddest**) 1 ADJ If you are **sad**, you feel unhappy. **Sad** stories, situations, or events make you feel unhappy. ❑ *I'm sad that Julie's marriage has split up.* ❑ *...a grim, sad story of loss and failure.* ● **sadly** ADV ❑ *He will be sadly missed by all who knew him.* ● **sadness** N-UNCOUNT ❑ *We face this difficult decision with great sadness.* 2 ADJ **Sad** means unfortunate or undesirable. ● **sadly** ADV ❑ *I returned from my holiday safely but sadly, my luggage didn't.*

→ see **cry, emotion**

Thesaurus *sad* Also look up:

ADJ. depressed, down, gloomy, unhappy; (*ant.*) cheerful, happy 1
miserable, tragic, unhappy 2

Word Partnership Use *sad* with:

V.	**feel** sad, **look** sad, **seem** sad 1
ADV.	**kind of** sad, **a little** sad, **really** sad, **so** sad, **too** sad, **very** sad 1
N.	sad **news**, sad **story** 2 sad **day**, sad **eyes**, sad **face**, sad **fact**, sad **truth** 1

sadden /ˈsædən/ (**saddens, saddening, saddened**) V-T If something **saddens** you, it makes you feel sad. ● **saddened** ADJ AFTER LINK-V ❑ *He is saddened that they did not win anything.*

saddle /ˈsædəl/ (**saddles, saddling, saddled**) 1 N-COUNT A **saddle** is a leather seat that you put on the back of an animal so that you can ride the animal. 2 N-COUNT A **saddle** is a seat on a bicycle or motorcycle. 3 V-T & PHR-VERB If you **saddle** an animal, or if you **saddle** it **up**, you put a saddle on it. 4 V-T If you **saddle** someone **with** a problem or **with** a responsibility, you put them in a position where they have to deal with it. ❑ *An extravagant lifestyle left him saddled with debts.*

→ see **horse**

▸ **saddle up** → see **saddle** (meaning 3)

sadism /ˈseɪdɪzəm/ N-UNCOUNT **Sadism** is behaviour in which a person gets pleasure from hurting other people. ● **sadist** (**sadists**) N-COUNT ❑ *He was not simply a bully, but a sadist.* ● **sadistic** ADJ ❑ *Sadistic guards punched the prisoners.*

sae or **SAE** or **s.a.e.** /ˌes eɪ ˈiː/ (**saes**) N-COUNT An **sae** is an envelope on which you put your name and address, and a stamp. You send it to someone in order to save them the cost of posting you something. **sae** is an abbreviation for **stamped addressed envelope.** [BRIT]

safari /səˈfɑːri/ (**safaris**) N-COUNT A **safari** is an expedition for hunting or observing wild animals, especially in East Africa.

safe /seɪf/ (**safer, safest, safes**) 1 ADJ Something that is **safe** does not cause physical harm or danger. ❑ *Should we trust our government to decide which foods are safe?* ❑ *The beaches are excellent and safe for swimming.* ● **safely** ADV ❑ *The dog was safely locked up.* ❑ *I told him to drive safely.* 2 ADJ AFTER LINK-V If someone or something is **safe**, they are not in danger of being harmed or damaged. ❑ *Crime Prevention Officers can visit your home and suggest ways to make it safer.* ❑ *Where is Sophy? Is she safe?* ● **safely** ADV ❑ *Guests were brought out of the building safely by firemen.* 3 ADJ BEFORE N If people or things have a **safe** journey, they reach their destination without being harmed. ❑ *...the safe delivery of food and other supplies.* ● **safely** ADV ❑ *Once Mrs Armsby was safely home, she called the police.* 4 ADJ A **safe** place is one where it is unlikely that any harm will happen to the people or things that are there. • **safely** ADV ❑ *The radio can be placed safely in a pocket for the bike ride.* **5** ADJ If it is **safe to** say or assume something, you can say it with little risk of being wrong. • **safely** ADV ❑ *If I go to a grocer I know and trust, I can safely assume the eggs will be fresh.* **6** N-COUNT A **safe** is a strong metal cupboard with special locks, in which you keep money, jewellery, or other valuable things. **7** PHRASE If you say that someone or something is **in safe hands**, you mean that they are being looked after by a reliable person and will not be harmed or damaged. **8** PHRASE If you say you are doing something **to be on the safe side**, you mean that you are doing it as a precaution, in case something unexpected or unpleasant happens.

Word Partnership Use *safe* with:

N.	safe **drinking water**, safe **operation** **1**
	children/kids are safe, safe **at home** **2**
	safe **environment**, safe **neighbourhood**, safe **place**, safe **streets** **4**
	safe **bet**, safe **investment** **5**
ADV.	**completely** safe, **perfectly** safe, **reasonably** safe, **relatively** safe **1** **2**

safeguard /ˈseɪfgɑːd/ (**safeguards, safeguarding, safeguarded**) **1** V-T To **safeguard** something or someone means to protect them from being harmed or lost. [FORMAL] ❑ *It is estimated that the project will safeguard about 1,000 jobs in the area.* **2** N-COUNT A **safeguard** is a law or rule that is intended to prevent someone or something from being harmed. ❑ *If you arrange to meet anyone for the first time, make sure a friend knows exactly where you are going, as a safeguard.*

ˌsafe ˈsex also **safer sex** N-UNCOUNT **Safe sex** is sexual activity in which people protect themselves against the risk of AIDS and other sexually transmitted diseases, usually by using condoms.

safety /ˈseɪfti/ **1** N-UNCOUNT **Safety** is the state of being safe from harm or danger. ❑ *...a number of recommendations to improve safety on aircraft.* ❑ *...the safety of one's own home.* **2** N-SING If you are concerned about the **safety of** something, you are concerned that it might be harmful or dangerous. If you are concerned for someone's **safety**, you are concerned that they might be in danger. ❑ *...public fears about the safety of nuclear power.* ❑ *There is grave concern for the safety of witnesses.* **3** ADJ BEFORE N **Safety** features or measures are intended to make something less dangerous. ❑ *Smoke alarms are an invaluable safety measure but cannot always prevent tragedy.* ❑ *It's wise to wear safety goggles.*
→ see **glass**

Word Partnership Use *safety* with:

V.	**improve** safety, **provide** safety **1**
	ensure safety **1** **3** **4**
	fear for ***someone's*** safety **4**
N.	**child** safety, **fire** safety, **health and** safety, **highway/traffic** safety, safety **measures**, **public** safety, safety **regulations**, safety **standards**, **workplace** safety **1**
	safety **concerns**, **food** safety **2**
	safety **device**, safety **equipment** **3**

ˈsafety ˌbelt (**safety belts**) N-COUNT A **safety belt** is a strap that you fasten across your body for safety when travelling in a car or aeroplane.

ˈsafety ˌnet (**safety nets**) N-COUNT A **safety net** is something that you can rely on to help you if you get into a difficult situation. ❑ *I have savings because I like to have a safety net.*

sag /sæg/ (**sags, sagging, sagged**) **1** V-I When something **sags**, it hangs down loosely or sinks downwards in the middle. ❑ *...a sagging armchair.* **2** V-I To **sag** means to become weaker. ❑ *Her energy seemed to sag.* ❑ *...their sagging popularity.*

saga /ˈsɑːgə/ (**sagas**) N-COUNT A **saga** is a long story, account, or sequence of events.

sage /seɪdʒ/ (**sages**) **1** ADJ & N-COUNT **Sage** means wise and knowledgeable. A **sage** is a person who is regarded as being very wise. • **sagely** ADV ❑ *We all nodded sagely and pretended we understood.* **2** N-UNCOUNT **Sage** is a herb.

said /sed/ **Said** is the past tense and past participle of **say**.

sail /seɪl/ (**sails, sailing, sailed**) **1** N-COUNT **Sails** are large pieces of material attached to the mast of a boat.

sail

2 V-T/V-I If you **sail** a boat, or if a boat **sails**, it moves across water using its sails. ❑ *I shall get myself a little boat and sail her around the world.* **3** V-I You say a ship **sails** when it moves over the sea. ❑ *The trawler had sailed from the port of Zeebrugge.* **4** PHRASE When a ship **sets sail**, it leaves a port. **5** V-I If someone or something **sails** somewhere, they move there steadily and fairly quickly. ❑ *She rose from the table and sailed towards the kitchen.*
▶ **sail through** PHR-VERB If someone or something **sails through** a difficult situation or experience, they deal with it easily and successfully. ❑ *She sailed through her maths exams.*

sailing /ˈseɪlɪŋ/ (**sailings**) **1** N-COUNT A **sailing** is a voyage made by a ship carrying passengers. ❑ *We'll get the next sailing.* **2** N-UNCOUNT **Sailing** is the activity or sport of sailing boats. **3** PHRASE In British English, if you say that a task was not all **plain sailing**, you mean that it was not very easy. The American term is **clear sailing**. ❑ *It hasn't all been plain sailing: I have had one or two minor problems.*
→ see **boat**

sailor /ˈseɪlə/ (**sailors**) N-COUNT A **sailor** is a person who works on a ship as a member of its crew.

saint /seɪnt/ (**saints**) **1** N-COUNT & N-TITLE A **saint** is a dead person who is officially recognized and honoured by the Christian church because his or her life was a perfect example of the way Christians should live. **2** N-COUNT If you refer to a living person as a **saint**, you mean that they are extremely kind and patient. • **saintly** ADJ ❑ *...his saintly wife.*

sake /seɪk/ **1** PHRASE If you do something **for the sake of** a particular thing, you do it for that purpose or in order to achieve that result. ❑ *For the sake of argument, let's assume that you're right.* **2** PHRASE If you do something **for its own sake**, you do it because you enjoy it, and not for any other reason. ❑ *...the pursuit of power for its own sake.* **3** PHRASE When you do something **for** someone's **sake**, you do it in order to help them or make them happy. ❑ *She wanted to get well for the sake of her husband.*

salad /'sæləd/ (**salads**) N-VAR A **salad** is a mixture of uncooked vegetables, eaten as part of a meal.

salary /'sæləri/ (**salaries**) N-VAR Your **salary** is the money that you are paid each month by your employer.

> **Usage**
>
> Professional people and office workers receive a **salary**, which is paid monthly. However, when talking about someone's salary, you usually give the annual figure. ❑ *I'm paid a salary of £15,000 a year.* **Pay** is a general noun which you can use to refer to the money you get from your employer for doing your job. Manual workers are paid **wages**, or **a wage**. The plural is more common than the singular, especially when you are talking about the actual cash that someone receives. ❑ *Every week he handed all his wages in cash to his wife.* Wages are usually paid, and quoted, as an hourly or a weekly sum. ❑ *...a starting wage of five dollars an hour.* Your **income** consists of all the money you receive from all sources, including your pay.

sale /seɪl/ (**sales**) **1** N-SING The **sale** of goods is the selling of them for money. ❑ *Shops reported an increase in the sale of snacks and soft drinks.* **2** N-PLURAL The **sales** of a product are the quantity that is sold. ❑ *This newspaper has sales of 1.72 million.* **3** N-PLURAL You refer to the part of a company that deals with selling as **sales**. ❑ *Sonia and Sue work in sales.* ❑ *...the sales department.* **4** N-COUNT A **sale** is an occasion when a shop sells things at less than their normal price. ❑ *These jeans were half-price in a sale.* **5** PHRASE If something is **for sale** or **up for sale**, it is available to buy. ❑ *The company is up for sale.* **6** PHRASE Products that are **on sale** can be bought in shops. [BRIT] ❑ *Tickets go on sale this Friday.*

'sales ˌclerk (**sales clerks**) N-COUNT In American English, a **sales clerk** is a person who works in a shop, selling things to customers. The British word is **shop assistant.**

S

salesman /'seɪlzmən/ (**salesmen**) N-COUNT A **salesman** is a man whose job is selling things to people.

salesperson /'seɪlzpɜːsən/ (**salespeople** or **salespersons**) N-COUNT A **salesperson** is a person whose job is selling things to people.

saliva /sə'laɪvə/ N-UNCOUNT **Saliva** is the watery liquid that forms in your mouth.

salmon /'sæmən/

> **Salmon** is both the singular and the plural form.

N-VAR A **salmon** is a large edible silver-coloured fish with pink flesh. **Salmon** is the flesh of this fish eaten as food.

salon /'sælɒn, AM sə'lɑːn/ (**salons**) N-COUNT A **salon** is a place where people such as hairdressers work. ❑ *...a new hair salon.*

saloon /sə'luːn/ (**saloons**) **1** N-COUNT In British English, a **saloon** or a **saloon car** is a car with seats for four or more people, a fixed roof, and a boot that is separated from the rear seats. **2** N-COUNT A **saloon** is a place where alcoholic drinks are sold and drunk. [AM]

salt /sɔːlt/ (**salts, salting, salted**) **1** N-UNCOUNT **Salt** is a substance in the form of white powder or crystals, used to improve the flavour of food or to preserve it. Salt occurs naturally in sea water. **2** V-T When you **salt** food, you add salt to it. • **salted** ADJ ❑ *...lightly salted butter.*
→ see **crystal**

salty /'sɔːlti/ (**saltier, saltiest**) ADJ **Salty** things contain salt or taste of salt. ❑ *Salty snacks are bad for your health.*
→ see **taste**

salute /sə'luːt/ (**salutes, saluting, saluted**) **1** V-T/V-I & N-COUNT If you **salute** or **salute** someone, you greet them or show your respect with a formal sign. Soldiers salute officers by raising their right hand so that their fingers touch their forehead. A **salute** is a formal sign of greeting or respect. ❑ *I stood to attention and saluted.* ❑ *The soldier gave a salute and moved off.* ❑ *He raised his arm in salute.* **2** V-T & N-COUNT To **salute** a person or an achievement means to publicly show or state your admiration for them. A public show of admiration for someone or something is called a **salute.** ❑ *I salute him for the courage he has shown.*

salvage /'sælvɪdʒ/ (**salvages, salvaging, salvaged**) **1** V-T & N-UNCOUNT If something **is salvaged**, someone manages to save it, for example from a ship that has sunk or a building that has been destroyed. **Salvage** is the act of salvaging things from somewhere. ❑ *The treasures were salvaged from a ship that sank in 1648.* ❑ *...a huge salvage operation.* **2** N-UNCOUNT The **salvage** from wrecked ships or destroyed buildings consists of the things that are saved from them. ❑ *...the value of the salvage.* **3** V-T If you **salvage** something **from** a difficult situation, you manage to get something useful from it so that it is not a complete failure. ❑ *Diplomats still hope to salvage something from the meeting.*

salvation /sæl'veɪʃən/ **1** N-UNCOUNT In Christianity, **salvation** is being saved from sin. **2** N-UNCOUNT The **salvation** of someone or something is the act of saving them from harm. ❑ *His marriage is beyond salvation.*

same /seɪm/ **1** ADJ If two or more things, actions, or qualities are **the same**, or if one is **the same as** another, the two are very similar or exactly like each other in some way. ❑ *The houses were all the same.* ❑ *Driving a boat is not the same as driving a car.* ❑ *Cut up the potatoes so that the pieces are all the same size.* **2** ADJ You use **same** to indicate that you are referring to only one place, time, or thing, and not to different ones. ❑ *Your birthday is on the same day as mine.* **3** ADJ Something that is still **the same** has not changed in any way. ❑ *Only 17% said the economy would improve, but 25% believed it would stay the same.* **4** ADJ & PRON You use **same** to refer to something that has already been mentioned. ❑ *I had the same experience when I became a teacher.* ❑ *We made the decision which was right for us. Other parents must do the same.* **5** **at the same time** → see **time** **6** PHRASE You say **all the same** or **just the same** to indicate that a situation or your opinion has not changed, in spite of what has happened or been said. ❑ *I had a lot of support, but it was hard all the same.* **7** PHRASE If you say that two or more people or things which are thought to be different are **one and the same**, you mean that they are in fact the same person or thing, or they are very similar and should be considered as one thing. ❑ *Nancy's father and her attorney are one and the same person.*

Thesaurus	*same* Also look up:
ADJ.	alike, equal, identical; *(ant.)* different 1 constant, unchanged; *(ant.)* different 3

sample /ˈsɑːmpəl, ˈsæm-/ (**samples, sampling, sampled**) 1 N-COUNT A **sample of** a substance or product is a small quantity of it, showing you what it is like. ❑ *The designer will send you a folder containing samples of fabric, wallpaper and paint.* ❑ *They gave away 2000 free samples of the product.* 2 N-COUNT A **sample of** a substance is a small amount of it that is examined and analyzed scientifically. ❑ *They took samples of my blood.* 3 N-COUNT A **sample of** people or things is a number of them chosen from a larger group and then used in tests or used to provide information about the whole group. ❑ *...a random sample of more than 200 males.* 4 V-T If you **sample** food or drink, you taste a small amount of it in order to find out if you like it. 5 V-T If you **sample** a place or situation, you experience it for a short time in order to find out about it. ❑ *...the chance to sample a different way of life.*
→ see **laboratory**

Thesaurus	*sample* Also look up:
N.	bit, piece, portion, specimen 1 2
V.	experience, taste, try 4 5

sanction /ˈsæŋkʃən/ (**sanctions, sanctioning, sanctioned**) 1 V-T & N-UNCOUNT If someone in authority **sanctions** an action or practice, they officially approve of it and allow it to be done. The **sanction** of someone in authority is their official approval. ❑ *He is now ready to sanction the use of force.* ❑ *The king could not enact laws without the sanction of Parliament.* 2 N-PLURAL **Sanctions** are measures taken by countries to restrict trade and official contact with a country that has broken international law. ❑ *He was against the lifting of sanctions.* 3 N-COUNT A **sanction** is a severe course of action which is intended to make people obey the law. ❑ *The ultimate sanction of most employers is to fire an employee.*

Word Partnership	Use *sanction* with:
ADJ.	**legal** sanction, **official** sanction, **proposed** sanction 2 3
PREP.	sanction **against**, **without** sanction 1
V.	**impose a** sanction, **lift a** sanction 2 3

sanctity /ˈsæŋktɪti/ N-UNCOUNT If you talk about **the sanctity of** something, you mean that it is very important and should be treated with respect. ❑ *...the sanctity of marriage.*

sanctuary /ˈsæŋktʃʊəri, AM -tʃʊeri/ (**sanctuaries**) 1 N-VAR A **sanctuary** is a place of safety for people who are being persecuted. ❑ *His church became a sanctuary for thousands of people.* ❑ *They sought sanctuary in the French embassy.* 2 N-COUNT A wildlife **sanctuary** is a place where birds or animals are protected and allowed to live freely.

sand /sænd/ (**sands, sanding, sanded**) 1 N-UNCOUNT **Sand** is a powder that consists of extremely small pieces of stone. ❑ *They walked barefoot across the sand to the water's edge.* ❑ *...grains of sand.* 2 N-PLURAL **Sands** are a large area of sand, for example a beach. ❑ *...miles of golden sands.* 3 V-T If you **sand** an object, you rub it with an abrasive paper called sandpaper in order to make it smooth or to get rid of paint or rust. ❑ *Sand the surface carefully.*
→ see **beach, desert, erosion, glass**

sandal /ˈsændəl/ (**sandals**) N-COUNT **Sandals** are light shoes that have straps instead of a solid part over the top of your foot.
→ see **shoe**

sandstone /ˈsændstəʊn/ N-UNCOUNT **Sandstone** is a type of rock which contains a lot of sand.

sandwich /ˈsænwɪdʒ, -wɪtʃ/ (**sandwiches, sandwiched**) 1 N-COUNT A **sandwich** consists of two slices of bread with a layer of food between them. ❑ *...a cheese sandwich.* 2 V-T PASSIVE When something **is sandwiched between** two other things, it is in a narrow space between them. ❑ *...a small shop sandwiched between a bar and a laundrette.*
→ see **meal**

sandy /ˈsændi/ (**sandier, sandiest**) ADJ A **sandy** area is covered with sand. ❑ *...sandy beaches.*

Word Link	*san ≈ health : insane, sane, sanitation*

sane /seɪn/ (**saner, sanest**) 1 ADJ Someone who is **sane** is able to think and behave normally and reasonably, and is not mentally ill. ❑ *He appears to be quite sane.* 2 ADJ If you describe an action or idea as **sane**, you mean that it is reasonable and sensible. ❑ *...extremely sane advice.*

sang /sæŋ/ **Sang** is the past tense of **sing**.

sanitary /ˈsænɪtri, AM -teri/ ADJ **Sanitary** means concerned with keeping things clean and hygienic. ❑ *There have been warnings of danger from aftershocks, fires, and poor sanitary conditions.*

sanitation /ˌsænɪˈteɪʃən/ N-UNCOUNT **Sanitation** is the process of keeping places clean and hygienic, especially by providing a sewage system and a clean water supply. ❑ *...the dangers of poor sanitation.*

S

sanity /ˈsænɪti/ 1 N-UNCOUNT A person's **sanity** is their ability to think and behave normally and reasonably. ❑ *The incident made us question our sanity.* 2 N-UNCOUNT If there is **sanity** in a situation or activity, there is a purpose and a regular pattern, rather than confusion and worry. ❑ *She did what she could to restore sanity to the situation.*

sank /sæŋk/ **Sank** is the past tense of **sink**.

sap /sæp/ (**saps, sapping, sapped**) 1 V-T If something **saps** your strength or confidence, it gradually weakens or destroys it. ❑ *The illness sapped his strength.* 2 N-UNCOUNT **Sap** is the watery liquid in plants and trees.

sarcasm /ˈsɑːkæzəm/ N-UNCOUNT **Sarcasm** refers to speech or writing which actually means the opposite of what it seems to say. Sarcasm is usually intended to ridicule or insult someone. ❑ *His tone was not unkind but it had an edge of sarcasm on it.*

Word Web satellite

The **moon** is the earth's best-known **satellite**. In 1957 humans began **launching** objects into **space**. That's when the first man-made satellite, Sputnik, began to **orbit** the earth. Today, hundreds of satellites circle the **planet**. The largest satellite is the International **Space Station**. It completes an orbit about every 90 minutes and sometimes can be seen from the earth. Others, such as the Hubbel Telescope, help us learn more about **outer space**. The NOAA 12 measures the earth's climate. TV weather forecasts often use pictures taken from satellites. Many TV programmes are also broadcast by satellite.

sarcastic /sɑːˈkæstɪk/ ADJ Someone who is **sarcastic** says the opposite of what they really mean in order to mock or insult someone. ❑ *...sarcastic remarks.* ● **sarcastically** ADV ❑ *'What a surprise!' Caroline murmured sarcastically.*

sardine /sɑːˈdiːn/ (**sardines**) N-COUNT **Sardines** are a kind of small sea fish, often eaten as food.

sardonic /sɑːˈdɒnɪk/ ADJ If you describe someone as **sardonic**, you mean that they are mocking or scornful, often in a rather calm, quiet way. ❑ *...a sardonic sense of humour.* ● **sardonically** ADV ❑ *He grinned sardonically.*

sat /sæt/ **Sat** is the past tense and past participle of **sit**.

Satan /ˈseɪtən/ N-PROPER **Satan** is a name sometimes given to the Devil. ● **satanic** ADJ ❑ *...satanic rituals.*

satellite /ˈsætəlaɪt/ (**satellites**) **1** N-COUNT A **satellite** is an object which has been sent into space in order to collect information or to be part of a communications system. ❑ *The signals are sent by satellite link.* **2** N-COUNT A **satellite** is a natural object in space that moves round a planet or star.
→ see Word Web: **satellite**
→ see **astronomer, forecast, navigation, radio, television**

ˈsatellite ˌdish (**satellite dishes**) N-COUNT A **satellite dish** is a piece of equipment which receives satellite television signals.

S

satin /ˈsætɪn, AM -tən/ N-UNCOUNT **Satin** is a smooth and shiny type of cloth.

satire /ˈsætaɪə/ (**satires**) **1** N-UNCOUNT **Satire** is the use of humour to mock or criticize political ideas or the way that people behave. ❑ *Politicians are usually an easy target for satire.* **2** N-COUNT A **satire** is a play or piece of writing that uses satire. ❑ *...a sharp satire on the political process.*

satirical /səˈtɪrɪkəl/ ADJ A **satirical** drawing, piece of writing, or comedy show uses satire to criticize something. ❑ *...a satirical novel about London life.*

satisfaction /ˌsætɪsˈfækʃən/ **1** N-UNCOUNT **Satisfaction** is the pleasure you feel when you do something you wanted or needed to do. ❑ *Both sides expressed satisfaction with the progress made.* ❑ *...job satisfaction.* **2** N-UNCOUNT If you get **satisfaction** from someone, you get money or an apology from them because of some harm or injustice which has been done to you. ❑ *If you can't get any satisfaction, complain to the manager.*

satisfactory /ˌsætɪsˈfæktəri/ ADJ If something is **satisfactory**, it is acceptable to you or fulfils a particular need or purpose. ❑ *I never got a satisfactory answer.* ● **satisfactorily** ADV ❑ *Their motives have never been satisfactorily explained.*

satisfied /ˈsætɪsfaɪd/ ADJ If you are **satisfied with** something, you are pleased because you have got what you wanted. ❑ *We are not satisfied with these results.* ❑ *...satisfied customers.*

Word Link *sat, satis ≈ enough : dissatisfaction, insatiable, satisfy*

satisfy /ˈsætɪsfaɪ/ (**satisfies, satisfying, satisfied**) **1** V-T If someone or something **satisfies** you, they give you enough of what you want to make you pleased or contented. ❑ *The pace of change has not been quick enough to satisfy everyone.* **2** V-T If someone **satisfies** you **that** something is true or has been done properly, they convince you by giving you more information or by showing you what has been done. ❑ *He satisfied himself that his companions were acting in good faith.* **3** V-T If you **satisfy** the requirements for something, you are good enough or suitable to fulfil these requirements. ❑ *Candidates must satisfy the general conditions for admission.*

Word Partnership Use *satisfy* with:

N. satisfy **an appetite**, satisfy **demands**, satisfy **a desire**, satisfy **a need** **1**
satisfy **critics**, satisfy ***someone's*** **curiosity** **2**

satisfying /ˈsætɪsfaɪɪŋ/ ADJ Something that is **satisfying** gives you a feeling of pleasure and fulfilment. ❑ *...intellectually satisfying work.*

saturate /ˈsætʃʊreɪt/ (**saturates, saturating, saturated**) **1** V-T If people or things **saturate** a place or object, they fill it completely so that no more can be added. ❑ *No one wants to saturate the city with car parks.* ● **saturation** N-UNCOUNT ❑ *...the saturation of the market with various kinds of goods.* **2** V-T If someone or something **is saturated**, they become extremely wet. ❑ *His work clothes were saturated with oil and had to be cleaned.*

Saturday /ˈsætədeɪ, -di/ (**Saturdays**) N-VAR **Saturday** is the day after Friday and before Sunday.

sauce /sɔːs/ (**sauces**) N-VAR A **sauce** is a thick liquid which is served with other food. ❑ *...a sauce of garlic, tomatoes, and cheese.*

saucepan /ˈsɔːspən, AM -pæn/ (**saucepans**) N-COUNT A **saucepan** is a deep metal cooking pot, usually with a long handle and a lid.
→ see **pan**

saucer /ˈsɔːsə/ (**saucers**) N-COUNT A **saucer** is a small curved plate on which you stand a cup.
→ see **dish**

saucy /ˈsɔːsi/ (**saucier, sauciest**) ADJ Someone or something that is **saucy** refers to sex in a light-hearted, amusing way. ❑ *...a saucy joke.*

sauna /ˈsɔːnə/ (**saunas**) **1** N-COUNT A **sauna** is a hot steam bath. **2** N-COUNT A **sauna** is a room or building where you can have a sauna.

saunter /ˈsɔːntə/ (**saunters, sauntering, sauntered**) V-I If you **saunter** somewhere, you walk there in a slow casual way. ❑ *He sauntered beside the river.*

sausage /ˈsɒsɪdʒ, AM ˈsɔːs-/ (**sausages**) N-VAR A **sausage** consists of minced meat, mixed with other ingredients, inside a long thin skin.

sauté /ˈsəʊteɪ, AM sɔːˈteɪ/ (**sautés, sautéing, sautéed**) V-T When you **sauté** food, you fry it quickly in hot oil or butter.

savage /ˈsævɪdʒ/ (**savages, savaging, savaged**) **1** ADJ If someone or something is **savage**, they are extremely cruel, violent, and uncontrolled. ❑ *...a savage attack.* ●**savagely** ADV ❑ *He was savagely beaten.* **2** N-COUNT If you refer to people as **savages**, you dislike them because you think that they are cruel, violent, or uncivilized. **3** V-T If someone **is savaged** by a dog or other animal, the animal attacks them violently. **4** V-T If someone or something that they have done **is savaged** by another person, that person criticizes them severely. ❑ *The film was savaged by critics.*

savagery /ˈsævɪdʒri/ N-UNCOUNT **Savagery** is extremely cruel and violent behaviour. ❑ *...the sheer savagery of war.*

save /seɪv/ (**saves, saving, saved**) **1** V-T If you **save** someone or something, you help them to avoid harm or to escape from a dangerous or unpleasant situation. ❑ *...a campaign to save kids from drowning.* ❑ *The government attempted to save 40,000 jobs in the industry.* **2** V-T & N-COUNT If a goalkeeper **saves** a shot, or if they make a **save**, they prevent the ball from going into the goal. **3** V-T If you **save** something, you keep it because it will be needed later. ❑ *She decided to save half the cake for Penelope.* **4** V-I & PHR-VERB If you **save**, or if you **save up**, you gradually collect money by spending less than you get, usually in order to buy something that you want. ❑ *Tim and Barbara are now saving for a house.* ❑ *Put money aside in order to save up enough to buy a new car.* ●**saver** (**savers**) N-COUNT ❑ *Low interest rates are bad news for savers.* **5** V-T If you **save** something such as time or money, you prevent the loss or waste of it. ❑ *It saves time in the kitchen to have things you use a lot within reach.* ❑ *...money-saving special offers.* **6** V-T If you **save** someone an unpleasant task or experience, you do something which helps or enables them to avoid it. ❑ *If you had said that earlier, it would have saved me a lot of trouble.*
▶ **save up** → see **save** (meaning **4**)

savings /ˈseɪvɪŋz/ N-PLURAL Your **savings** are the money that you have saved, especially in a bank or a building society. ❑ *Her savings were in the Post Office Savings Bank.*

saviour [AM **savior**] /ˈseɪvjə/ (**saviours**) **1** N-COUNT A **saviour** is a person who saves someone or something from danger, ruin, or defeat. ❑ *...the saviour of English football.* ❑ *She regarded him as her saviour.* **2** N-PROPER In the Christian religion, **the Saviour** is Jesus Christ.

savour [AM **savor**] /ˈseɪvə/ (**savours, savouring, savoured**) V-T If you **savour** something pleasant, you enjoy it as much as you can or for as long as possible. ❑ *Savour the flavour of each mouthful.* ❑ *We both want to savour every moment of being together.*

savoury [AM **savory**] /ˈseɪvəri/ (**savouries**) **1** ADJ **Savoury** food has a salty or spicy flavour rather than a sweet one. ❑ *...savoury dishes.* **2** N-COUNT **Savouries** are small portions of savoury food, usually eaten as a snack. [BRIT]

saw /sɔː/ (**saws, sawing, sawed, sawn**) **1** **Saw** is the past tense of **see**. **2** N-COUNT A **saw** is a tool for cutting wood, which has a blade with sharp teeth along one edge. **3** V-T If you **saw** something, you cut it with a saw.
→ see **cut, tool**

sawdust /ˈsɔːdʌst/ N-UNCOUNT **Sawdust** is the very fine fragments of wood which are produced when you saw wood.

sawn /sɔːn/ **Sawn** is the past participle of **saw**.

sax /sæks/ (**saxes**) N-COUNT A **sax** is the same as a **saxophone**. [INFORMAL]

saxophone /ˈsæksəfəʊn/ (**saxophones**) N-COUNT A **saxophone** is a musical wind instrument in the shape of a curved metal tube with keys and a curved mouthpiece. ●**saxophonist** /sækˈsɒfənɪst, AM ˈsæksəfəʊn-/ (**saxophonists**) N-COUNT ❑ *Sonny Rollins is a famous jazz saxophonist.*

say /seɪ/ (**says** /sez/, **saying, said**) **1** V-T When you **say** something, you speak words. You can also use **say** to signal that you are stating a fact or your opinion. ❑ *'I'm sorry,' he said.* ❑ *I packed and said goodbye to Charlie.* ❑ *Did he say where he was going?* ❑ *I would say that Susan will learn a lot from what she did.* **2** V-T You can mention the contents of a piece of writing by mentioning what it **says** or what someone **says** in it. ❑ *Auntie Winnie wrote back saying Mary wasn't well.* **3** V-T If you **say** something **to yourself**, you think it. ❑ *Perhaps I'm still dreaming, I said to myself.* **4** V-T You indicate the information given by something such as a clock, dial, or map by mentioning what it **says**. ❑ *The clock said four minutes past eleven.* **5** V-T If something **says** something **about** a person, situation, or thing, it reveals something about them. ❑ *'We regard good quality health care as a human right; it says something about the decency and fairness of our society,' he said.* **6** CONVENTION You can use **say** when you mention something as an example or when you mention an approximate amount or time. ❑ *Several mini-workouts throughout the day - of between, say, five or 10 minutes each - can be as effective as one continuous 30-minute session in the gym.* **7** N-SING If you **have a say in** something, you have the right to give your opinion and influence decisions. When you **have your say**, you use this right or give your opinion. ❑ *The public should have a say in this matter.* **8** PHRASE You can use **'You can say**

that again' to express strong agreement with what someone has just said. [INFORMAL] ❑ *'Must have been a difficult job.'—'You can say that again.'* **9** PHRASE If something **goes without saying**, it is obvious or definitely true. ❑ *It goes without saying that most gardeners love the outdoor life.* **10** PHRASE If you say that something **says it all**, you mean that it shows you very clearly the truth about a situation or someone's feelings. ❑ *This is my third visit in a week, which says it all.* **11** PHRASE You use **to say nothing of** when you add something which gives even more strength to the point you are making. ❑ *Setting the time on the VCR is apparently too tricky for most people, to say nothing of actually recording something.* **12** PHRASE You use **that is to say** to indicate that you are about to express the same idea more clearly. [FORMAL] ❑ *Good writers are those who keep the language efficient. That is to say, keep it accurate, keep it clear.* **13** PHRASE If you say there is a lot **to be said for** something, you think it has a lot of good qualities or aspects. ❑ *There's a lot to be said for living in the countryside.*

Usage

Note that, with the verb **say**, if you want to mention the person who is being addressed, you should use the preposition **to**. 'What did she say you?' is wrong. '**What did she say to you?**' is correct. The verb **tell**, however, is usually followed by a direct object indicating the person who is being addressed. ❑ *He told Alison he was ill.* ❑ *What did she tell you?* 'What did she tell to you?' is wrong. **Say** is the most general verb for reporting the words that someone speaks. **Tell** is used to report information that is given to someone. ❑ *The manufacturer told me that the product did not contain peanuts.* **Tell** can also be used with a 'to' infinitive to report an order or instruction. ❑ *My mother told me to be quiet and eat my dinner.*

saying /ˈseɪɪŋ/ (**sayings**) N-COUNT A **saying** is a traditional sentence that people often say and that gives advice or information about life. ❑ *We now realize the truth of that old saying: Charity begins at home.*

scaffold

scaffolding /ˈskæfəldɪŋ/ N-UNCOUNT **Scaffolding** is a temporary framework of poles and boards that is used by workmen to stand on while they are working on the outside structure of a building.

scald /skɔːld/ (**scalds, scalding, scalded**) **1** V-T If you **scald yourself**, you burn yourself with very hot liquid or steam. ❑ *She scalded herself with coffee.* ❑ *...scalding hot water.* **2** N-COUNT A **scald** is a burn caused by very hot liquid or steam.

Word Link *scal, scala ≈ ladder, stairs : escalate, escalator, scale*

scale /skeɪl/ (**scales, scaling, scaled**) **1** N-SING If you refer to the **scale** of something, you are referring to its size or extent, especially when it is very big. ❑ *...poverty on a massive scale.* ❑ *The British aid programme is small in scale.* **2** N-COUNT A **scale** is a set of levels or numbers which are used in a particular system of measuring things or comparing things. ❑ *...an earthquake measuring five-point-five on the Richter scale.* ❑ *...those on the high end of the pay scale.* **3** N-COUNT In music, a **scale** is a fixed sequence of musical notes, each one higher than the next, which begins at a particular note. ❑ *...the scale of C major.* **4** N-VAR The **scale** of a map, plan, or model is the relationship between the size of something in the map, plan, or model and its size in the real world. ❑ *The map has a scale of 1:10,000.* **5** ADJ A **scale model** of something is smaller than the original, but the sizes of all the parts are in the same, exact relation to each other. ❑ *...a detailed scale model of the house.* **6** PHRASE If the different parts of a map, drawing, or model are **to scale**, they are the right size in relation to each other. **7** N-PLURAL **Scales** are a piece of equipment for weighing things or people. ❑ *...kitchen scales.* ❑ *I step on the scales practically every morning.* **8** N-COUNT The **scales** of a fish or reptile are the small flat pieces of hard skin that cover its body. **9** V-T If you **scale** something such as a mountain or a wall, you climb up it or over it. ❑ *She was the first woman to scale Everest.*
→ see **graph, kitchen, thermometer**
▶ **scale down** PHR-VERB If you **scale down** something, you make it smaller in size, amount, or extent than it used to be. ❑ *This factory has scaled down its workforce from six hundred to only six.*

scalp /skælp/ (**scalps**) N-COUNT Your **scalp** is the skin under the hair on your head.

scamper /ˈskæmpə/ (**scampers, scampering, scampered**) V-I When people or small animals **scamper** somewhere, they move there quickly with small light steps. ❑ *The child scampered off without waiting for her mother.*

scan /skæn/ (**scans, scanning, scanned**) **1** V-T When you **scan** an area, a group of things, or a piece of writing, you look at it carefully, usually because you are looking for something in particular. ❑ *Joss scanned the crowd for the child's mother.* ❑ *She scanned the advertisements in the newspapers.* **2** V-T If a machine **scans** luggage or other items, it examines it quickly, for example by moving a beam of light or X-rays over it. **3** N-COUNT A **scan** is a medical test in which a machine sends a beam of X-rays over a part of your body in order to check whether your organs are healthy. ❑ *...a brain scan.* **4** N-COUNT If a pregnant woman has a **scan**, a machine using sound waves produces an image of her womb on a screen so that a doctor can see if her baby is developing normally.

scandal /ˈskændəl/ (**scandals**) **1** N-COUNT A **scandal** is a situation, event, or someone's behaviour that shocks a lot of people because they think it is immoral. ❑ *...a financial scandal.* **2** N-SING If you say that something is a **scandal**, you are angry about it and think that the people responsible for it should be ashamed. ❑ *It is a scandal that a person can be stopped for no reason by the police.*

scandalous /ˈskændələs/ **1** ADJ You can describe something as **scandalous** if it makes you very angry and you think the people responsible for it should be ashamed. ❑ *...a scandalous waste of money.* • **scandalously** ADV ❑ *Many workers were being paid scandalously low wages.* **2** ADJ **Scandalous**

S

behaviour or activity is considered immoral and shocking.

scanner /ˈskænə/ (**scanners**) N-COUNT A **scanner** is a machine which is used to examine, identify, or record things, for example by moving a beam of light, sound, or X-rays over them.
→ see **laser**

scant /skænt/ ADJ You use **scant** to indicate that there is very little of something or not as much of something as there should be. ❑ *She criticised the police for paying scant attention to the crime.*

scapegoat /ˈskeɪpgəʊt/ (**scapegoats**) N-COUNT If someone is made a **scapegoat for** something bad that has happened, people blame them or punish them for it, although it may not be their fault. ❑ *People always look for a scapegoat when something goes wrong.*

scar /skɑː/ (**scars, scarring, scarred**) **1** N-COUNT A **scar** is a mark on the skin which is left after a wound has healed. **2** V-T If your skin **is scarred**, it is badly marked as a result of a wound. ❑ *He was scarred for life during a fight.* **3** N-COUNT & V-T If an unpleasant physical or emotional experience leaves a **scar** on someone, or if it **scars** them, it has a permanent effect on their mind. ❑ *His emotional scars will never disappear.*

scarce /skeəs/ (**scarcer, scarcest**) ADJ If something is **scarce**, there is not enough of it. ❑ *Jobs are becoming increasingly scarce here.*

scarcely /ˈskeəsli/ **1** ADV You use **scarcely** to emphasize that something is only just true or only just the case. ❑ *He could scarcely breathe.* ❑ *I scarcely knew him.* **2** ADV You can use **scarcely** to say that something is certainly not true or is certainly not the case. ❑ *It was scarcely in the government's interest to let the public know.* **3** ADV If you say **scarcely** had one thing happened when something else happened, you mean that the first event was followed immediately by the second. ❑ *Bruce had scarcely shaken our hands when the phone rang.*

scarcity /ˈskeəsɪti/ (**scarcities**) N-VAR If there is a **scarcity of** something, there is not enough of it. [FORMAL] ❑ *Conditions have got worse with the scarcity of good drinking water.*

scare /skeə/ (**scares, scaring, scared**) **1** V-T & N-COUNT If someone or something **scares** you, or if they give you a **scare**, they frighten you. ❑ *I didn't mean to scare you.* ❑ *It scared him to realise how close he had come to losing everything.* ❑ *Don't you realize what a scare you gave us all?* **2** N-COUNT A **scare** is a situation in which many people are afraid or worried because they think something dangerous is happening which will affect them all. ❑ *...a public health scare.* **3** N-COUNT A **bomb scare** or a **security scare** is a situation in which there is believed to be a bomb in a place.
▸ **scare off** or **scare away** PHR-VERB If you **scare off** a person or animal, or if you **scare** them **away**, you frighten them so that they go away. ❑ *The alarm scared off his attacker.*

scared /skeəd/ **1** ADJ If you are **scared of** someone or something, you are frightened of them. ❑ *I'm certainly not scared of him.* ❑ *I was too scared to move.* **2** ADJ If you are **scared that** something unpleasant might happen, you are nervous and worried because you think that it might happen. ❑ *I was scared that I might be sick.* ❑ *He was scared of letting us down.*

scarf /skɑːf/ (**scarfs** or **scarves**) N-COUNT A **scarf** is a piece of cloth that you wear round your neck or head, usually to keep yourself warm.

scarlet /ˈskɑːlət/ ADJ & N-UNCOUNT Something that is **scarlet** is bright red.

scary /ˈskeəri/ (**scarier, scariest**) ADJ Something that is **scary** is rather frightening. [INFORMAL] ❑ *There's something very scary about him.* ❑ *...scary movies.*

scathing /ˈskeɪðɪŋ/ ADJ If you say that someone is being **scathing about** something, you mean that they are being very critical of it. ❑ *He made some scathing comments about her clothes.* • **scathingly** ADV ❑ *He said scathingly, 'Your cooking grows worse by the minute!'*

scatter /ˈskætə/ (**scatters, scattering, scattered**) **1** V-T If you **scatter** things over an area, you throw or drop them so that they spread all over the area. ❑ *She scattered food for the chickens.* **2** V-T/V-I If a group of people **scatter**, they suddenly separate and move in different directions. ❑ *They stared for a second, then scattered in panic.*

scattered /ˈskætəd/ **1** ADJ **Scattered** things are spread over an area in an untidy or irregular way. ❑ *He picked up the scattered toys.* ❑ *Clothes were scattered across the floor.* **2** ADJ AFTER LINK-V If something is **scattered with** a lot of small things, they are spread all over it. ❑ *Every surface is scattered with photographs.*

scattering /ˈskætərɪŋ/ N-SING A **scattering of** things is a small number of them spread over an area. ❑ *...a road with an inn, a few shops and a scattering of houses.*

scavenge /ˈskævɪndʒ/ (**scavenges, scavenging, scavenged**) V-I If people or animals **scavenge for** food or other things, they collect them by searching among waste or unwanted objects. ❑ *Children scavenged for food to survive.* • **scavenger** (**scavengers**) N-COUNT ❑ *...scavengers such as rats.*

scenario /sɪˈnɑːriəʊ, AM -ˈner-/ (**scenarios**) N-COUNT If you talk about a likely or possible **scenario**, you are talking about the way in which a situation may develop. ❑ *What does he see as the most likely scenario in the coming months?*

scene /siːn/ (**scenes**) **1** N-COUNT A **scene** in a play, film, or book is part of it in which a series of events happen in the same place. ❑ *...the opening scene of 'A Christmas Carol'.* **2** N-COUNT You refer to a place as a **scene** when you are describing its appearance and indicating what impression it makes on you. ❑ *It's a scene of complete devastation.* **3** N-COUNT **The scene of** an event is the place where it happened. ❑ *This area has been the scene of fierce fighting.* **4** N-SING You can refer to an area of activity as a particular type of **scene**. ❑ *...the alternative music scene.* **5** N-COUNT If you **make a scene**, you embarrass people by publicly showing your anger about something. **6** PHRASE If something is done **behind the scenes**, it is done secretly rather than in public. ❑ *Mr Cain worked quietly behind the scenes to make this deal.* **7** PHRASE Something that **sets the scene for** a particular event creates the conditions in which the event is likely to happen. ❑ *Community leaders have set the scene for a change in policy.*
→ see **animation, blog**

scenery /ˈsiːnəri/ **1** N-UNCOUNT The **scenery**

in a country area is the land, water, or plants that you can see around you. ❑ *...the island's spectacular scenery.* **2** N-UNCOUNT In a theatre, the **scenery** is the painted cloth and boards at the back of the stage which represent where the action is taking place.

Usage

Be careful not to confuse **scenery**, **landscape**, **countryside** and **nature**. With **landscape**, the emphasis is on the physical features of the land, while **scenery** includes everything you can see when you look out over an area of land, usually in the country. ❑ *...the landscape of steep woods and distant mountains.* ❑ *...unattractive urban scenery.* **Countryside** is land which is away from towns and cities. ❑ *...3,500 acres of mostly flat countryside.* **Nature** includes the landscape, the weather, animals, and plants. ❑ *These creatures roamed the Earth as the finest and rarest wonders of nature.*

scenic /'si:nɪk/ ADJ **Scenic** places have attractive scenery. ❑ *...a well-known scenic spot.*

scent /sent/ (**scents, scenting, scented**) **1** N-COUNT The **scent** of something is the pleasant smell that it has. ❑ *...bushes with white flowers and a wonderful scent.* **2** N-VAR **Scent** is a pleasant-smelling liquid which women put on their necks and wrists to make themselves smell nice. **3** N-VAR The **scent** of a person or animal is the smell that they give off. ❑ *It didn't take long for the dogs to pick up our scent.* **4** V-T When an animal **scents** something, it becomes aware of it by smelling it. ❑ *The herd of antelope scented the lion.*

scented /'sentɪd/ ADJ **Scented** things have a pleasant smell, either naturally or because perfume has been added to them. ❑ *...scented candles.*

sceptic [AM **skeptic**] /'skeptɪk/ (**sceptics**) N-COUNT A **sceptic** is a person who has doubts and asks questions about things that other people believe. ❑ *He now has to convince sceptics that he has a serious plan.*

sceptical [AM **skeptical**] /'skeptɪkəl/ ADJ If you are **sceptical** about something, you have doubts about it. ❑ *He took a sceptical view of the Government's intentions.*

S

scepticism [AM **skepticism**] /'skeptɪsɪzəm/ N-UNCOUNT **Scepticism** is great doubt about whether something is true or useful. ❑ *The report was inevitably greeted with scepticism.*

schedule /'ʃedju:l, AM 'skedʒu:l/ (**schedules, scheduling, scheduled**) **1** N-COUNT A **schedule** is a plan that gives a list of events or tasks and the times at which each one should happen or be done. ❑ *He has been forced to adjust his schedule.* **2** N-UNCOUNT You can use **schedule** to refer to the time or way something is planned to be done. For example, if something is completed **on schedule**, it is completed at the time planned. ❑ *The jet arrived in Johannesburg two minutes ahead of schedule.* **3** V-T If something **is scheduled to** happen at a particular time, arrangements are made for it to happen at that time. ❑ *The space shuttle was scheduled to blast off at 04:38.* ❑ *The meeting with Mr Bush is scheduled for tomorrow morning.* **4** N-COUNT A **schedule** is a written list of things, for example a list of prices, details, or conditions.

Word Partnership Use *schedule* with:

ADJ. **busy** schedule, **hectic** schedule **1**
regular schedule **1** **4**
N. **change of** schedule, schedule **of events**, **payment** schedule, **play-off** schedule, **work** schedule **1** **4**
bus schedule, **train** schedule **4**
PREP. **according to** schedule, **ahead of** schedule, **behind** schedule, **on** schedule **2**

scheme /ski:m/ (**schemes, scheming, schemed**) **1** N-COUNT A **scheme** is a plan or arrangement, especially one produced by a government or other organization. ❑ *...schemes to help fight unemployment.* ❑ *...a private pension scheme.* **2** V-I If you say that people **are scheming**, you mean that they make secret plans in order to gain something for themselves; used showing disapproval. ❑ *She was shocked to find that her own son was scheming against her.* ❑ *...a scheming career woman.* **3** PHRASE **The scheme of things** is the way that everything in the world or in a particular situation seems to be organized. ❑ *Looking out over the sea, you realise just how small you are in the scheme of things.*

Thesaurus *scheme* Also look up:

N. design, plan, strategy **1**

schizophrenia /ˌskɪtsə'fri:niə/ N-UNCOUNT **Schizophrenia** is a serious mental illness that prevents people from relating their thoughts and feelings to what is happening around them.

schizophrenic /ˌskɪtsə'frenɪk/ (**schizophrenics**) ADJ & N-COUNT Someone who is **schizophrenic** or who is a **schizophrenic** is suffering from schizophrenia. ❑ *Mrs Browning thought he might be schizophrenic.*

Word Link *schol ≈ school : scholar, scholarly, scholarship*

scholar /'skɒlə/ (**scholars**) N-COUNT A **scholar** is a person who studies an academic subject and knows a lot about it. ❑ *...a leading religious scholar.*
→ see **history**

scholarly /'skɒləli/ **1** ADJ A **scholarly** person spends a lot of time studying and knows a lot about academic subjects. **2** ADJ A **scholarly** book or article contains a lot of academic information and is intended for academic readers.

scholarship /'skɒləʃɪp/ (**scholarships**) **1** N-COUNT If you get a **scholarship** to a school or university, your studies are paid for by the school or university, or by some other organization. **2** N-UNCOUNT **Scholarship** is serious academic study and the knowledge that is obtained from it. ❑ *He is known for his scholarship and intelligence.*

school /sku:l/ (**schools**) **1** N-VAR A **school** is a place where children are educated. You usually refer to this place as **school** when you are talking about the time that children spend there. ❑ *...a school built in the Sixties.* ❑ *...two boys wearing school uniform.* ❑ *...a boy who was in my class at school.* **2** N-COUNT A **school** is the pupils or staff at a school. **School** can take the singular or plural form of the verb. ❑ *The whole school's talking about* *the news.* **3** N-COUNT A place where a particular skill or subject is taught can be referred to as a **school**. ❑ *...a riding school.* **4** N-VAR A university, college, or university department specializing in a particular type of subject can be referred to as a **school**. ❑ *...the school of veterinary medicine at the University of Pennsylvania.* **5** N-VAR **School** is used to refer to university or college. [AM, INFORMAL] ❑ *Wayne went back to school for his MBA after becoming a father.* **6** PHRASE A **school of thought** is a theory or opinion shared by a group of people. ❑ *There are three main schools of thought on how the money should be spent.* **7** N-COUNT A **school of** fish or dolphins is a large group of them.

schoolboy /'sku:lbɔɪ/ (**schoolboys**) N-COUNT A **schoolboy** is a boy who goes to school.

schoolchild /'sku:ltʃaɪld/ (**schoolchildren**) N-COUNT **Schoolchildren** are children who go to school.

schooldays also **school days** /'sku:ldeɪz/ N-PLURAL Your **schooldays** are the period of your life when you are at school. ❑ *He has known her since his schooldays.*

schoolgirl /'sku:lgɜ:l/ (**schoolgirls**) N-COUNT A **schoolgirl** is a girl who goes to school.

schooling /'sku:lɪŋ/ N-UNCOUNT **Schooling** is education that children receive at school. ❑ *Their schooling was disrupted by illness.*

'school ˌrun (**school runs**) N-COUNT The **school run** is the journey that parents make each day when they take their children to school and bring them home from school. [BRIT] ❑ *The government is trying to encourage parents to leave their cars at home for the school run.*

schoolteacher /'sku:lti:tʃə/ (**schoolteachers**) N-COUNT A **schoolteacher** is a teacher in a school.

Word Link	*sci ≈ knowing : conscience, conscious, science*

science /saɪəns/ (**sciences**) **1** N-UNCOUNT **Science** is the study of the nature and behaviour of natural things and the knowledge that we obtain about them. ❑ *They discussed the relationship between science and religion.* **2** N-COUNT A **science** is a particular branch of science, for example physics or biology. **3** N-COUNT A **science** is the study of some aspect of human behaviour, for example sociology or anthropology. **4** → see also **social science**

→ see Word Web: **science**

ˌscience 'fiction N-UNCOUNT **Science fiction** consists of stories and films about events that take place in the future or in other parts of the universe.

scientific /ˌsaɪən'tɪfɪk/ **1** ADJ **Scientific** is used to describe things that relate to science or to a particular science. ❑ *...scientific research.* • **scientifically** ADV ❑ *...scientifically advanced countries.* **2** ADJ If you do something in a **scientific** way, you do it carefully and thoroughly, using experiments or tests. ❑ *This is not a scientific way to test opinion.* • **scientifically** ADV ❑ *Psychology can be seen as an effort to study human behaviour scientifically.*

→ see **experiment, science**

scientist /'saɪəntɪst/ (**scientists**) N-COUNT A **scientist** is someone who has studied science and whose job is to teach or do research in science.

→ see **evolution, experiment**

sci-fi /'saɪ faɪ/ N-UNCOUNT **Sci-fi** is **science fiction**. ❑ *...low-budget sci-fi films.*

scissors /'sɪzəz/ N-PLURAL **Scissors** are a small tool with two sharp blades which are screwed together. You use scissors for cutting things such as paper and cloth. ❑ *She picked up a pair of scissors.*

→ see **office**

scoff /skɒf/ (**scoffs, scoffing, scoffed**) V-I If you **scoff**, you speak in a ridiculing way about something. ❑ *Some people scoff at the idea that animals communicate.*

scold /skəʊld/ (**scolds, scolding, scolded**) V-T If you **scold** someone, you speak angrily to them because they have done something wrong. [FORMAL] ❑ *'You should be at school,' he scolded.*

scoop /sku:p/ (**scoops, scooping, scooped**) **1** V-T If you **scoop** someone or something somewhere, you put your hands or arms under or round them and quickly move them there. ❑ *Michael knelt next to her and scooped her into his arms.* **2** V-T To **scoop** something from a container means to remove it with something such as a spoon. ❑ *He was standing in the kitchen scooping ice cream into a bowl.* **3** N-COUNT A **scoop** is an object like a spoon which is used for picking up a quantity of a food such as ice cream or flour. ❑ *She gave him an extra scoop of whipped cream.* **4** N-COUNT A **scoop** is an exciting news story which is reported in one newspaper before it appears anywhere else.

S

Word Web science

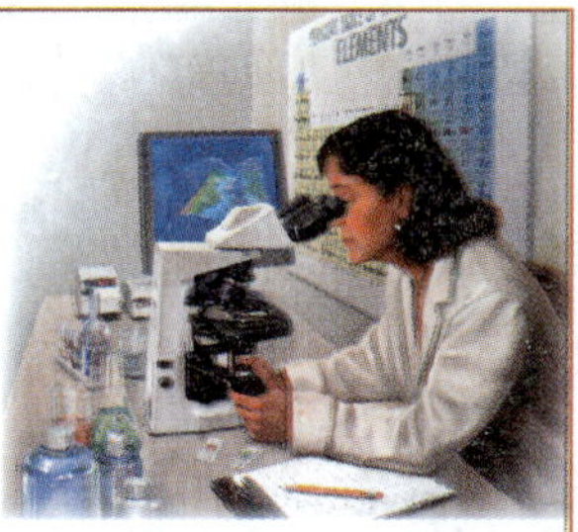

Science is the study of physical laws. These laws govern the natural world. Science uses **research** and **experiments** to explain various **phenomena**. Scientists follow the **scientific method** which begins with **observation** and measurement. Then they state a **hypothesis**, which is a possible explanation for the observations and measurements. Next, scientists make a **prediction**, which is a logical **deduction** based on the hypothesis. The last step is to conduct experiments which **prove** or **disprove** the hypothesis. Scientists construct and modify **theories** based on **empirical findings. Pure** science deals with theories only. When people use science to do something, that is applied science.

▶ **scoop out** PHR-VERB If you **scoop out** part of something, you remove it using a spoon or other tool. ❑ *Cut a marrow in half and scoop out the seeds.*
▶ **scoop up** PHR-VERB If you **scoop** something **up**, you put your hands or arms under it and lift it in a quick movement. ❑ *Use both hands to scoop up the leaves.*

scooter /'sku:tə/ (**scooters**) **1** N-COUNT A **scooter** is a small lightweight motorcycle. **2** N-COUNT A **scooter** is a child's toy which has two wheels joined by a board and a handle on a long pole attached to the front wheel.

scope /skəʊp/ **1** N-UNCOUNT If there is **scope for** a particular kind of behaviour, you have the opportunity to act in this way. ❑ *He believed in giving his staff scope for initiative.* ❑ *We believe that there is great scope for improved performance.* **2** N-UNCOUNT The **scope** of an activity, topic, or piece of work is the area which it deals with or includes. ❑ *...the huge scope of his novel.* ❑ *She is confident her job will grow in scope.*

scorch /skɔ:tʃ/ (**scorches, scorching, scorched**) V-T To **scorch** something means to burn it slightly or damage it with heat. ❑ *The bomb scorched the side of the building.* ● **scorched** ADJ ❑ *...scorched black earth.*

scorching /'skɔ:tʃɪŋ/ **1** ADJ **Scorching** or **scorching hot** weather or temperatures are very hot indeed. ❑ *It was a scorching hot day.* **2** → See note at **hot**

score /skɔ:/ (**scores, scoring, scored**) **1** V-T/V-I In a sport or game, if a player **scores** or **scores** a goal or a point, they gain a goal or point. ❑ *Gascoigne scored in the first minute of the match.* ● **scorer** (**scorers**) N-COUNT ❑ *Who is the club's leading scorer?* **2** N-COUNT The **score** in a game is the number of goals, runs, or points obtained by the teams or players. ❑ *4-1 was the final score.* **3** V-T If you **score** a success, a victory, or a hit, you are successful in what you are doing. ❑ *The missile scored a direct hit on the building.* **4** N-COUNT The **score** of a piece of music is the written version of it. **5** QUANT **Scores of** things or people means a large number of them. ❑ *Campaigners lit scores of bonfires.* ❑ *Two people were killed and scores were injured.* **6** V-T If you **score** a surface with something sharp, you cut or scratch a line in it. **7** PHRASE You can use **on that score** or **on this score** to refer to something that has just been mentioned, especially an area of difficulty or concern. ❑ *Lucy didn't want to come and Sandra didn't want her to, so they were in agreement on that score.* **8** PHRASE If you **settle a score** or **settle an old score** with someone, you take revenge on them for something they have done in the past.
→ see **music**

scorn /skɔ:n/ (**scorns, scorning, scorned**) **1** N-UNCOUNT If you treat someone or something with **scorn**, you show that you do not respect them. ❑ *Their words were met by a look of scorn from the king.* **2** V-T If you **scorn** someone or something, you show that you do not respect them. ❑ *His daughters scorned him, claiming he was boring.* **3** V-T If you **scorn** something, you refuse to accept it because you think it is not good enough or suitable for you. ❑ *They all scorned traditional family values.*

scornful /'skɔ:nfəl/ ADJ If you are **scornful of** someone or something, you show contempt for them. ❑ *He is deeply scornful of politicians.* ● **scornfully** ADV ❑ *They laughed scornfully.*

Scotch /skɒtʃ/ (**Scotches**) N-VAR **Scotch** or **Scotch whisky** is whisky made in Scotland. ❑ *...a bottle of Scotch.* ❑ *He ordered a scotch.*

scour /skaʊə/ (**scours, scouring, scoured**) **1** V-T If you **scour** a place **for** someone or something, you make a thorough search there for them. ❑ *They scoured antiques shops for furniture for their new home.* **2** V-T If you **scour** something such as a sink, floor, or pan, you clean its surface by rubbing it hard with something rough.

scourge /skɜ:dʒ/ (**scourges**) N-COUNT A **scourge** is something that causes a lot of trouble to a group of people. ❑ *...the scourge of terrorism.*

scout /skaʊt/ (**scouts, scouting, scouted**) **1** N-COUNT A **scout** is someone who is sent to an area of countryside to find out the position of an enemy army. **2** V-I If you **scout for** something, you go searching for it. ❑ *They scouted around for more fuel.*

scowl /skaʊl/ (**scowls, scowling, scowled**) V-I & N-COUNT When someone **scowls**, they frown to show that they are angry. A **scowl** is the expression on someone's face when they scowl. ❑ *She scowled at her friends.* ❑ *Chris met the remark with a scowl.*

scramble /'skræmbəl/ (**scrambles, scrambling, scrambled**) **1** V-I If you **scramble** over rough or difficult ground, you move quickly over it using your hands to help you. ❑ *She scrambled down rocks to reach him.* **2** V-I To **scramble** means to move somewhere in a hurried and awkward way. ❑ *She scrambled out of the car just before it burst into flames.* **3** V-I & N-COUNT If a number of people **scramble for** something, or if there is a **scramble for** it, they compete with each other for it, in a rough way. ❑ *I had to scramble for tickets to the show.* ❑ *...the scramble for jobs.* **4** V-T If you **scramble** eggs, you mix the whites and yolks of the eggs, then cook the mixture by stirring and heating it in a pan. ● **scrambled** ADJ ❑ *...scrambled eggs and bacon.*
→ see **egg**

scrap /skræp/ (**scraps, scrapping, scrapped**) **1** N-COUNT A **scrap of** something is a very small piece or amount of it. ❑ *...a fire fuelled by scraps of wood.* ❑ *They need every scrap of information they can get.* **2** V-T If you **scrap** something, you get rid of it or cancel it. ❑ *These plans were scrapped late last night.* **3** N-UNCOUNT **Scrap** is metal from old or damaged machinery or cars. ❑ *...a lorry piled with scrap metal.* **4** N-COUNT You can refer to a fight or a argument as a **scrap**. [INFORMAL]

scrape /skreɪp/ (**scrapes, scraping, scraped**) **1** V-T If you **scrape** something from a surface, you remove it, especially by pulling a sharp object over the surface. ❑ *She went round the car scraping the frost off the windows.* **2** V-I & N-SING If something **scrapes** against something else it rubs against it, making a noise, called a **scrape**. ❑ *The cab driver struggled with her luggage, scraping a bag against the door.* ❑ *...the scrape of our boots.* ● **scraping** N-SING ❑ *...the scraping of a chair across the floor.* **3** V-T If you **scrape** a part of your body, you accidentally rub it against something hard and rough, and damage it slightly.
▶ **scrape through** PHR-VERB If you **scrape through** an examination, you succeed in passing it but with a score that is so low that you almost

S

failed. ❑ *...the minimum amount of work necessary to scrape through.*
▶ **scrape together** PHR-VERB If you **scrape together** an amount of money or a number of things, you succeed in obtaining it with difficulty. ❑ *They only just managed to scrape the money together.*

scratch /skrætʃ/ (**scratches, scratching, scratched**) **1** V-T If you **scratch yourself**, you rub your fingernails against your skin because it is itching. ❑ *He scratched himself under his arm.* ❑ *The old man scratched his side.* **2** V-T If a sharp object **scratches** something or someone, it makes small shallow cuts on their surface or skin. ❑ *Be careful: knives will scratch the table.* **3** N-COUNT **Scratches** on someone or something are small shallow cuts. **4** PHRASE If you do something **from scratch**, you do it without making use of anything that has been done before. ❑ *...building a house from scratch.* **5** PHRASE If something is not **up to scratch**, it is not good enough. ❑ *If the facilities are not up to scratch, he has a right to complain.*

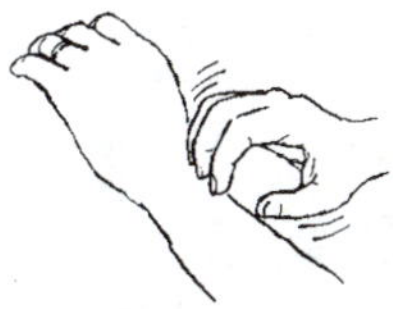
scratch

ˈscratch ˌcard (**scratch cards**) N-COUNT A **scratch card** is a card with hidden words or symbols on it. You scratch the surface off to see the words or symbols and find out if you have won a prize.

scrawl /skrɔːl/ (**scrawls, scrawling, scrawled**) **1** V-T If you **scrawl** something, you write it in a careless and untidy way. ❑ *He scrawled a hasty note to his wife.* **2** N-VAR You can refer to writing that looks careless and untidy as **scrawl**.

scream /skriːm/ (**screams, screaming, screamed**) **1** V-I & N-COUNT When someone **screams**, they make a loud high-pitched cry, called a **scream**, usually because they are in pain or frightened. ❑ *He staggered around the room, screaming in agony.* ❑ *...screams of terror.* **2** V-T If you **scream** something, you shout it in a loud high-pitched voice. ❑ *He grabbed Anthea and screamed abuse at her.*

screech /skriːtʃ/ (**screeches, screeching, screeched**) **1** V-I & N-COUNT If a vehicle **screeches**, its tyres make an unpleasant high-pitched noise, called a **screech**, on the road. ❑ *A black Mercedes screeched to a halt beside the helicopter.* ❑ *He slowed the car with a screech of tyres.* **2** V-I & N-COUNT If you **screech**, or if you give a **screech**, you shout something in a loud, unpleasant, high-pitched voice. ❑ *The parrot opened its beak and screeched.* ❑ *...her voice rising to a screech.*

screen /skriːn/ (**screens, screening, screened**) **1** N-COUNT A **screen** is the flat vertical surface on which pictures or words are shown on a television, on a computer, or in a cinema. **2** V-T When a film or a television programme **is screened**, it is shown in the cinema or broadcast on television. ❑ *Channel Nine is screening the West Indies cricket tour.* • **screening** (**screenings**) N-VAR ❑ *The film-makers will be present at the screenings.* **3** N-COUNT A **screen** is a vertical panel that is used to separate different parts of a room. ❑ *They put a screen in front of me so I couldn't see what was going on.* **4** V-T If something **is screened** by another thing, it is behind it and hidden by it. ❑ *The road behind the hotel was screened by a block of flats.* **5** V-T/V-I To **screen** people **for** a disease means to examine them to make sure that they do not have it. ❑ *This test screens for people at risk of tooth decay.* • **screening** N-VAR ❑ *...screening for deafness at birth.*
→ see **television**

screenplay /ˈskriːnpleɪ/ (**screenplays**) N-COUNT A **screenplay** is a script for a film including instructions for the cameras.

ˈscreen ˌsaver (**screen savers**) N-COUNT A **screen saver** is a moving picture which appears on a computer screen when the computer is not being used. [COMPUTING]

screenwriter /ˈskriːnraɪtə/ (**screenwriters**) N-COUNT A **screenwriter** is a person who writes screenplays.

screw /skruː/ (**screws, screwing, screwed**) **1** N-COUNT A **screw** is a small metal device for fixing things together. It has a wide top, a pointed end, and a groove along its length. **2** V-T If you **screw** something somewhere, you fix it there by means of a screw or screws. ❑ *I screwed the shelf to the wall.* ❑ *Screw down any loose floorboards.* **3** V-T To **screw** something somewhere means to fasten or fix it in place by twisting it round and round. ❑ *He screwed the cap back on the bottle.* **4** V-T If you **screw** your **face** or your **eyes into** an expression of pain or discomfort, you tighten the muscles of your face showing that you are in pain or uncomfortable. ❑ *He screwed his face into an expression of pain.* **5** V-T If someone **screws** something, especially money, **out of** you, they get it from you by putting strong pressure on you. [INFORMAL] ❑ *He's always trying to screw cheaper prices out of his suppliers.*
▶ **screw up** PHR-VERB If someone **screws** something **up**, or if they **screw up**, they cause something to fail or be spoiled. [INFORMAL] ❑ *You can't open the window because it screws up the air conditioning.*

screwdriver /ˈskruːdraɪvə/ (**screwdrivers**) N-COUNT A **screwdriver** is a tool for fixing screws into place.
→ see **tool**

Word Link	*scrib ≈ writing : inscribe, scribble, transcribe*

scribble /ˈskrɪbəl/ (**scribbles, scribbling, scribbled**) **1** V-T/V-I If you **scribble** or **scribble** something, you write it quickly and untidily. ❑ *John scribbled his calculation on a scrap of paper.* ❑ *As I scribbled in my diary, the lights went out.* **2** V-I To **scribble** means to make meaningless marks or rough drawings using a pencil or pen. ❑ *When Caroline was five she scribbled all over the kitchen walls.* **3** N-VAR **Scribble** is something that has been written or drawn quickly and roughly.

script /skrɪpt/ (**scripts**) **1** N-COUNT The **script** of a play, film, or television programme is the written version of it. **2** N-VAR A **script** is a particular system of writing. ❑ *...written in Arabic script.*
→ see **animation**

Word Link	*script ≈ writing : manuscript, scripture, transcript*

scripture /ˈskrɪptʃə/ (**scriptures**) N-VAR **Scripture** or **the scriptures** refers to writings that are regarded as sacred in a particular religion, for example the Bible in Christianity.

scroll /skrəʊl/ (**scrolls, scrolling, scrolled**) **1** N-COUNT A **scroll** is a long roll of paper or other material with writing on it. ❑ *...ancient scrolls.* **2** V-I If you **scroll** through text on a computer screen, you move the text up or down to find the information that you need. [COMPUTING] ❑ *I scrolled down to find 'United States of America'.*

'scroll ˌbar (**scroll bars**) N-COUNT On a computer screen, a **scroll bar** is a long thin box along one edge of a window, which you click on with the mouse to move the text up, down, or across the window. [COMPUTING]

scrub /skrʌb/ (**scrubs, scrubbing, scrubbed**) **1** V-T & N-SING If you **scrub** something, or if you give it **a scrub**, you rub it hard in order to clean it, using a stiff brush and water. ❑ *The corridors are scrubbed clean.* ❑ *I scrubbed off the dirt.* ❑ *That floor needs a good scrub.* **2** N-UNCOUNT **Scrub** is land consisting of low trees and bushes in an area which gets very little rain.

scruffy /'skrʌfi/ (**scruffier, scruffiest**) ADJ **Scruffy** things or people are dirty and untidy. ❑ *...a scruffy T-shirt.*

scrupulous /'skru:pjʊləs/ **1** ADJ A **scrupulous** person or organization takes great care to do what is fair, honest, or morally right. ❑ *He behaved with scrupulous fairness according to the rules.* ● **scrupulously** ADV ❑ *He is scrupulously fair.* **2** ADJ **Scrupulous** means thorough, exact, and careful about details. ❑ *They have acted with scrupulous attention to the law.* ● **scrupulously** ADV ❑ *The streets and parks were scrupulously clean.*

scrutinize [BRIT also **scrutinise**] /'skru:tɪnaɪz/ (**scrutinizes, scrutinizing, scrutinized**) V-T If you **scrutinize** something, you examine it very carefully. ❑ *The insurance industry will continue to be closely scrutinized by the government.*

scrutiny /'skru:tɪni/ N-UNCOUNT If something is **under scrutiny**, it is being studied or observed very carefully. ❑ *His private life came under scrutiny.*

scuffle /'skʌfəl/ (**scuffles, scuffling, scuffled**) V-I & N-COUNT If people **are scuffling**, or if they are involved in a **scuffle**, they are fighting for a short time in a disorganized way. ❑ *Police scuffled with some of the protesters.* ❑ *Violent scuffles broke out between rival groups.*

S

sculpt /skʌlpt/ (**sculpts, sculpting, sculpted**) V-T/V-I When an artist **sculpts** or **sculpts** something, they carve it or shape it out of a hard material such as stone. ❑ *...figures sculpted in stone.* ● **sculptor** (**sculptors**) N-COUNT ❑ *This sculptor takes his inspiration from nature.*

sculpture /'skʌlptʃə/ (**sculptures**) **1** N-VAR A **sculpture** is a work of art that is produced by carving or shaping materials such as stone or clay. **2** N-UNCOUNT **Sculpture** is the art of making sculptures.

scum /skʌm/ N-UNCOUNT **Scum** is a layer of a substance on the surface of a liquid which looks unpleasant. ❑ *In this area, the water is hard and tends to form scum.*

scupper /'skʌpə/ (**scuppers, scuppering, scuppered**) V-T To **scupper** a plan or attempt means to spoil it completely. [BRIT] ❑ *This is a deliberate attempt to scupper the peace talks.*

scurry /'skʌri, AM 'skɜ:ri/ (**scurries, scurrying, scurried**) **1** V-I When people or small animals **scurry** somewhere, they move quickly and hurriedly, especially because they are frightened. ❑ *The attack began, sending people scurrying for cover.* **2** V-I If people **scurry to** do something, they do it as quickly as they can. ❑ *Reporters scurried to find telephones.*

scuttle /'skʌtəl/ (**scuttles, scuttling, scuttled**) V-I When people or small animals **scuttle** somewhere, they run there with short quick steps. ❑ *Two small children scuttled away in front of them.*

sea /si:/ (**seas**) **1** N-SING **The sea** is the salty water that covers much of the earth's surface. ❑ *Many of these kids have never seen the sea.* **2** N-COUNT A **sea** is a large area of salty water that is part of an ocean or is surrounded by land. You use **seas** when you are describing the sea at a particular time or in a particular area. ❑ *...the North Sea.* ❑ *The seas are warm further south.* **3** N-SING A **sea of** people or things is a very large number of them. ❑ *...the sea of bottles and glasses on the table.* **4** PHRASE **At sea** means on or under the sea, far away from land. ❑ *The boats remain at sea for an average of ten days.* **5** PHRASE If someone is **all at sea**, they are in a state of confusion.

Word Partnership Use *sea* with:

ADJ.	**calm** sea, **deep** sea **1**
N.	sea **air**, sea **coast**, **land and** sea, sea **voyage** **1**
PREP.	**above the** sea, **across the** sea, **below the** sea, **beneath the** sea, **by** sea, **from the** sea, **into the** sea, **near the** sea, **over the** sea **1**

seafood /'si:fu:d/ N-UNCOUNT **Seafood** refers to shellfish and other sea creatures that you can eat.

seagull /'si:gʌl/ (**seagulls**) N-COUNT A **seagull** is a type of bird that lives near the sea.

seal /si:l/ (**seals, sealing, sealed**) **1** N-COUNT A **seal** is an animal which eats fish and lives partly on land and partly in the sea. It has short fur and uses short limbs, called flippers, to enable it to swim. **2** V-T When you **seal** an envelope, you close it by sticking down the flap. ❑ *He sealed the envelope and put on a stamp.* **3** V-T & N-COUNT If you **seal** a container or an opening, or if you form a **seal**, you cover it with something in order to prevent air, liquid, or other material getting in or out. ❑ *Lids seal in heat and keep food moist.* ❑ *Wet the edges of the pie and join them to form a seal.* **4** N-COUNT A **seal** is a device, used for example in a machine, which closes an opening tightly so that air, liquid, or other substances cannot get in or out. ❑ *Check door seals on fridges and freezers regularly.* **5** N-COUNT A **seal** is an official mark on a document which shows that it is genuine. **6** V-T & PHR-VERB If someone in authority **seals** an area, or if they **seal** it **off**, they stop people entering or passing through it, for example by placing barriers in the way. ❑ *The army has sealed the border.* ❑ *Police and troops sealed off the area.*

'sea ˌlevel N-UNCOUNT If you are at **sea level**, you are at the same level as the surface of the sea. ❑ *The stadium is 2275 metres above sea level.*
→ see **glacier**

seam /si:m/ (**seams**) **1** N-COUNT A **seam** is a line of stitches joining two pieces of cloth together. **2** N-COUNT A **seam of coal** is a long narrow layer of it beneath the ground. 3 PHRASE If a place is very full, you can say that it is **bursting at the seams**.

seaman /'si:mən/ (**seamen**) N-COUNT A **seaman** is a sailor.

seamless /'si:mləs/ ADJ You use **seamless** to describe something that has no breaks or gaps in it or which continues smoothly, without stopping. ❑ *The links between the songs turn the record into a single, seamless whole.* ● **seamlessly** ADV ❑ *...allowing new and old to blend seamlessly.*

search /sɜ:tʃ/ (**searches, searching, searched**) 1 V-T/V-I If you **search for** something or someone, you look carefully for them. If you **search** a place, you look carefully for something there. ❑ *The police have started searching for the missing men.* ❑ *Airline staff searched the bag at O'Hare airport.* 2 N-COUNT A **search** is an attempt to find something by looking for it carefully. ❑ *After an hour-long search, she finally found her ring.* 3 V-T If the police **search** you, they examine your clothing for hidden objects. 4 V-I If you **search for** information on a computer, you give the computer an instruction to find that information. [COMPUTING] ❑ *I searched for my name on the Internet.* 5 PHRASE If you go **in search of** something, you try to find it. ❑ *They left the country in search of jobs.*

Word Partnership Use *search* with:

N.	search **for a job, talent** search, search **for the truth** 1
	search **an area**, search **for clues** 1 2
	investigators search, **police** search, search **suspects** 3
	computer search, search **criteria**, search **for information**, search **the Internet, online** search 4
V.	**conduct a** search 2 4

'search ˌengine (**search engines**) N-COUNT A **search engine** is a computer program that searches for documents on the Internet. [COMPUTING]

searching /'sɜ:tʃɪŋ/ ADJ A **searching question** is intended to discover the truth about something.

searing /'sɪərɪŋ/ 1 ADJ BEFORE N **Searing** is used to indicate that something such as pain or heat is very intense. ❑ *...the searing heat of the desert.* 2 ADJ BEFORE N A **searing** speech or piece of writing is very critical. ❑ *...a searing interview with the prime minister.*

seaside /'si:saɪd/ N-SING You can refer to an area that is close to the sea, especially where people go for their holidays, as **the seaside.** [BRIT]

season /'si:zən/ (**seasons, seasoning, seasoned**) 1 N-COUNT The **seasons** are the periods into which a year is divided and which each have their own typical weather conditions. ❑ *Autumn's my favourite season.* ❑ *...the rainy season.* 2 N-COUNT A **season** is the period during each year when something usually happens. ❑ *...the start of the football season.* 3 V-T If you **season** food, you add salt, pepper, or spices to it. ❑ *Season the meat with salt and pepper.* 4 PHRASE If fruit or vegetables are **in season**, it is the time of year when they are ready for eating and are widely available. 5 PHRASE If a female animal is **in season**, she is in a state where she is ready for mating.
→ see Word Web: **seasons**
→ see **plant**

seasonal /'si:zənəl/ ADJ **Seasonal** means happening during one particular time of the year. ❑ *...seasonal variations in temperature.*

seasoned /'si:zənd/ ADJ **Seasoned** is used to describe people who have a lot of experience of something. ❑ *...seasoned travellers.*

seasoning /'si:zənɪŋ/ N-UNCOUNT **Seasoning** is salt, pepper, or spices that are added to food to improve its flavour.

'season ˌticket (**season tickets**) N-COUNT A **season ticket** is a ticket for a series of events, such as football matches, or a number of journeys, that you usually buy at a reduced rate.

seat /si:t/ (**seats, seating, seated**) 1 N-COUNT A **seat** is an object that you can sit on, for example a chair. ❑ *...the back seat of their car.* ❑ *All seats for the show are priced at £12.00.* 2 → See note at **place**

Word Web seasons

The ancient Mayans* built a pyramid at Chichen Itzá*. One use of this pyramid was to predict the **seasons** of the **year**. The pyramid cast shadows, and the shadows moved during the year. Trained leaders observed these changing patterns of **light** throughout the year. The shadows fell in specific places at the time of the solstices and equinoxes. They showed the leaders the best times to plant and harvest crops. The shadows also told them when to hold special religious ceremonies. Thousands of tourists visit Chichen Itzá each spring to observe the arrival of the vernal* equinox.

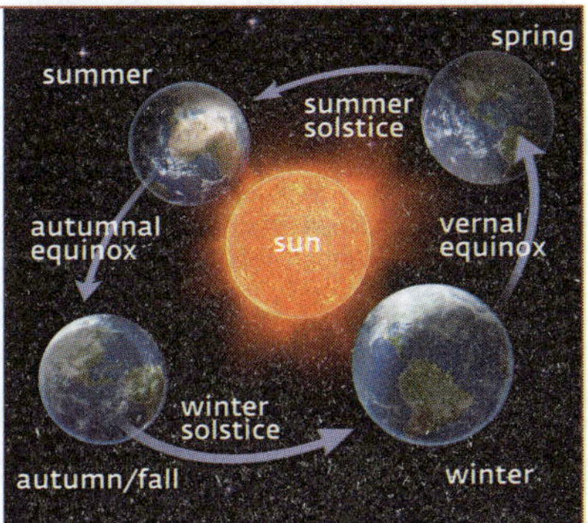

Mayans (250-900 AD): Indians who lived in Mexico and Central America.
Chichen Itzá (700-900 AD): a Mayan city in Mexico.
vernal: spring

S

3 N-COUNT The **seat** of a chair is the part that you sit on. 4 V-T If you **seat yourself** somewhere, you sit down. ❑ *I seated myself by the door.* ❑ *The room was empty apart from one man seated beside the fire.* 5 V-T A building or vehicle that **seats** a particular number of people has enough seats for that number. ❑ *The theatre seats 570.* 6 N-COUNT When someone is elected to parliament, you can say that they or their party have won a **seat**. 7 N-COUNT If someone has a **seat** on the board of a company or on a committee, they are a member of it. 8 PHRASE If you **take a back seat**, you allow other people to have all the power and to make all the decisions. 9 PHRASE If you say that someone is **in the driving seat** or **in the driver's seat**, you mean that they are in control in a situation. ❑ *An improved, different service is needed - one where users are in the driving seat.* 10 PHRASE If you **take a seat**, you sit down. ❑ *Take a seat. What can I do for you?*

Word Partnership Use *seat* with:

ADJ. **back** seat, **empty** seat, **front** seat, **vacant** seat, **vacated** seat 1
congressional seat 5
N. **car** seat, **child** seat, **driver's** seat, **passenger** seat, seat **at a table**, **theater** seat, **toilet** seat 1
seat **on the board** 6

ˈseat-ˌbelt also **seatbelt** (**seat-belts**) N-COUNT A **seat-belt** is a strap that you fasten across your body for safety when travelling in a car or aeroplane.

seat belt

seating /ˈsiːtɪŋ/ N-UNCOUNT The **seating** in a place consists of the seats there. ❑ *The cafeteria has seating for up to 200.*

seaweed /ˈsiːwiːd/ (**seaweeds**) N-VAR **Seaweed** is a plant that grows in the sea.

secluded /sɪˈkluːdɪd/ ADJ A **secluded** place is quiet, private, and undisturbed. ❑ *...a secluded corner of the restaurant.*

seclusion /sɪˈkluːʒən/ N-UNCOUNT If you are **in seclusion**, you are in a quiet place away from other people. ❑ *They lived in seclusion on their farm.* ❑ *They love the seclusion of their garden.*

S

second
1 PART OF A MINUTE
2 COMING AFTER SOMETHING ELSE
3 SENDING SOMEONE TO DO A JOB

second /ˈsekənd/ (**seconds**)
1 N-COUNT A **second** is one of the sixty parts that a minute is divided into. People often say **'a second'** or **'seconds'** when they simply mean a very short length of time. ❑ *It only takes forty seconds.* ❑ *Seconds later, firemen reached his door.*
→ see **time**

second /ˈsekənd/ (**seconds, seconding, seconded**)
2 1 ORD The **second** item in a series is the one that you count as number two. ❑ *It is the second time I have met him.* ❑ *...Cambodia's second biggest city.* ❑ *Why is walking so great? First, it does you good all over. Second, walking doesn't exhaust your body.* 2 PHRASE If you say that something is **second to none**, you are emphasizing that it is very good indeed or very large indeed. 3 PHRASE If you say that something is **second only to** something else, you mean that it is the best or biggest that exists, except for that thing. ❑ *Venus is second only to the moon in brightness in the night sky.* 4 N-COUNT **Seconds** are goods that are sold cheaply because they are slightly faulty. 5 V-T If you **second** a proposal in a meeting or debate, you formally agree with it so that it can then be discussed or voted on. ❑ *These members proposed and seconded his nomination.* 6 V-T If you **second** what someone has said, you say that you agree with them or say the same thing yourself. ❑ *She seconded the nomination of the new leader.* 7 **second nature** → see **nature**

second /sɪˈkɒnd/ (**seconds, seconding, seconded**)
3 V-T If you **are seconded** somewhere, you are moved there temporarily by the organization you work for in order to do special duties. ❑ *Several hundred soldiers were seconded to help farmers.*

secondary /ˈsekəndri, AM -deri/ 1 ADJ If you describe something as **secondary**, you mean that it is less important than something else. ❑ *Money is considered to be of secondary importance in this scheme of things.* 2 ADJ In Britain, **secondary** education is for pupils between the ages of 11 and 18.
→ see **colour**

ˌsecond ˈbest ADJ & N-SING Something that is **second best** or **a second best** is not as good as the best thing of its kind but is better than all the other things. ❑ *...his second-best suit.* ❑ *He refused to settle for anything that was second best.*

ˌsecond-ˈclass ADJ BEFORE N **Second-class** things are regarded as less valuable or less important than others of the same kind. ❑ *He was not prepared to see his country become a second-class republic.*

ˌsecond-ˈhand 1 ADJ & ADV **Second-hand** things are not new and have been owned by someone else. ❑ *Far more boats are bought second-hand than are bought brand new.* 2 ADJ BEFORE N A **second-hand** shop sells second-hand goods. 3 ADJ & ADV **Second-hand** information or opinions are those you learn about from other people rather than directly or from your own experience. ❑ *I heard stories second-hand that they were having a fantastic time.*

secondly /ˈsekəndli/ ADV You say **secondly** when you want to make a second point or give a second reason for something. ❑ *Firstly, I don't know exactly when I am going to America; secondly, who is going to look after Doran?*

ˌsecond-ˈrate ADJ If you describe something as **second-rate**, you mean that it is of poor quality.

ˌsecond ˈthoughts 1 N-PLURAL If you have **second thoughts about** a decision, you have doubts and begin to wonder if it was wise. 2 PHRASE In British English, you can say **on second thoughts** when you suddenly change your mind about something that you are saying or something that you have decided to do. In American English, you say **on second thought**. ❑ *'On second thoughts,' he said, 'I'll come with you.'*

secrecy /'si:krəsi/ N-UNCOUNT **Secrecy** is the act of keeping something secret, or the state of being kept secret. ❑ *He signed a pledge of secrecy.*

secret /'si:krɪt/ (**secrets**) **1** ADJ If something is **secret**, it is known about by only a small number of people, and is not told or shown to anyone else. ❑ *The police tried to keep the documents secret.* ● **secretly** ADV ❑ *The meeting was secretly recorded.* **2** N-COUNT A **secret** is a fact that is known by only a small number of people, and is not told to anyone else. ❑ *He wanted to keep our love a secret.* **3** N-SING If a way of behaving is **the secret of** achieving something, it is the best way or the only way to achieve it. ❑ *The secret of success is honesty.* **4** PHRASE If you do something **in secret**, you do it without anyone else knowing.

Thesaurus *secret* Also look up:

ADJ. hidden, private, unknown; (*ant.*) known **1**

secretarial /ˌsekrə'teəriəl/ ADJ **Secretarial** work or training involves the work of a secretary.

secretary /'sekrətri, AM -teri/ (**secretaries**) **1** N-COUNT A **secretary** is a person who is employed to do office work, such as typing letters or answering phone calls. **2** N-COUNT The **secretary** of an organization such as a trade union or a club is its official manager. **3** N-COUNT The **secretary** of a company is the person who has the legal duty of keeping the company's records. **4** N-COUNT **Secretary** is used in the titles of ministers and officials who are in charge of main government departments. ❑ *...the British Foreign Secretary.*

ˌSecretary of 'State (**Secretaries of State**) **1** N-COUNT In the United States, **the Secretary of State** is the head of the government department which deals with foreign affairs. **2** N-COUNT In Britain, **the Secretary of State** for a particular government department is the head of that department.

secrete /sɪ'kri:t/ (**secretes, secreting, secreted**) V-T If part of a plant or animal **secretes** a liquid, it produces it. [FORMAL] ● **secretion** N-UNCOUNT ❑ *...insulin secretion.*

secretion /sɪ'kri:ʃən/ (**secretions**) **1** N-COUNT A **secretion** is a liquid that is produced by a plant or animal. [FORMAL] **2** → see also **secrete**

secretive /'si:krətɪv, sɪ'kri:t-/ ADJ If you are **secretive**, you like to keep your knowledge, feelings, or intentions hidden.

ˌsecret po'lice N-UNCOUNT The **secret police** is a police force, especially in a non-democratic country, that works secretly and is concerned with political crimes.

ˌsecret 'service (**secret services**) N-COUNT A country's **secret service** is a government department whose job is to find out enemy secrets and to prevent its own government's secrets from being discovered.

sect /sekt/ (**sects**) N-COUNT A **sect** is a group of people that has separated from a larger group and has a particular set of religious or political beliefs.

sectarian /sek'teəriən/ ADJ **Sectarian** means resulting from the differences between different religious sects. ❑ *The attack was sectarian.*

Word Link *sect ≈ cutting : dissect, intersection, section*

section /'sekʃən/ (**sections**) **1** N-COUNT A **section of** something is one of the parts that it is divided into. ❑ *A section of the Bay Bridge collapsed.* ❑ *This paragraph is the longest section of the document.* **2** → see also **cross-section**

Word Partnership Use *section* with:

ADJ. **main** section, **new** section, **special** section, **thin** section

N. section **of a city**, section **of a coast**, **rhythm** section, **sports** section

sector /'sektə/ (**sectors**) N-COUNT A **sector** of something, especially a country's economy, is a particular part of it. ❑ *...the nation's manufacturing sector.* ❑ *...the poorest sectors of Pakistani society.*

Word Partnership Use *sector* with:

N. **banking** sector, **business** sector, **government** sector, **growth in a** sector, **job in a** sector, **manufacturing** sector, **technology** sector, **telecommunications** sector

secular /'sekjʊlə/ ADJ You use **secular** to describe things that have no connection with religion. ❑ *...a secular state.*

Word Link *cur ≈ caring : curator, manicure, secure*

secure /sɪ'kjʊə/ (**secures, securing, secured**) **1** ADJ If something such as a job or institution is **secure**, it is safe and reliable, and unlikely to be lost or fail. ❑ *The industry has a strong and secure future.* **2** ADJ A **secure** place is tightly locked or well protected, so that people cannot enter it or leave it. ● **securely** ADV ❑ *Medicines should always be securely locked away.* **3** V-T If you **secure** a place, you make it safe from harm or attack. [FORMAL] ❑ *Troops secured the airport.* **4** ADJ If an object is **secure**, it is fixed firmly in position. ● **securely** ADV ❑ *They tied the ends of the bags securely.* **5** V-T If you **secure** an object, you fasten it firmly to another object. ❑ *Rugs are secured to the floor with tacks.* **6** ADJ If you feel **secure**, you feel safe and happy and are not worried about your life. **7** V-T If you **secure** something, you get it after a lot of effort. [FORMAL] ❑ *He failed to secure enough votes for outright victory.*

Thesaurus *secure* Also look up:

ADJ. safe, sheltered **1**

V. attach, fasten **5**

catch, get, obtain; (*ant.*) lose **7**

security /sɪ'kjʊərɪti/ (**securities**) **1** N-UNCOUNT **Security** refers to all the precautions that are taken to protect a place. ❑ *Airport security was tightened.* ❑ *...security guards.* **2** N-UNCOUNT A feeling of **security** is a feeling of being safe and free from worry. ❑ *He loves the security of a happy home life.* **3** N-UNCOUNT The **security** of something such as a job is the fact that it is safe or reliable, and unlikely to be lost or to fail.

❑ *The entire workforce have fears about job security.* **4** N-UNCOUNT If you pledge something as **security** for a loan, you promise to give it to the person who lends you money, if you fail to pay the money back. **5** → see also **social security**

se'curity ˌcamera (**security cameras**) N-COUNT A **security camera** is a video camera that records people's activities in order to detect and prevent crime.

sedate /sɪ'deɪt/ (**sedates, sedating, sedated**) **1** ADJ If you describe someone as **sedate**, you mean that they are quiet and calm, though perhaps rather dull. **2** V-T If someone **is sedated**, they are given a drug to calm them or to make them sleep.

sedation /sɪ'deɪʃən/ N-UNCOUNT If someone is **under sedation**, they have been given medicine or drugs in order to calm them or make them sleep.

sedative /'sedətɪv/ (**sedatives**) N-COUNT A **sedative** is a drug that calms you or makes you sleep.

sedentary /'sedəntəri, AM -teri/ ADJ Someone who has a **sedentary** lifestyle or job sits down a lot of the time and does not take much exercise.

sediment /'sedɪmənt/ (**sediments**) N-VAR **Sediment** is solid material that settles at the bottom of a liquid.
→ see **rock**

seduce /sɪ'dju:s, AM -'du:s/ (**seduces, seducing, seduced**) **1** V-T If something **seduces** you, it is so attractive that it tempts you to do something that you would not normally approve of. ❑ *We are seduced into buying all these brilliantly packaged items.* • **seduction** /sɪ'dʌkʃən/ (**seductions**) N-VAR ❑ *This country has resisted the seductions of mass tourism.* **2** V-T If someone **seduces** another person, they use their charm to persuade that person to have sex with them. • **seduction** N-VAR ❑ *Her methods of seduction are subtle.*

seductive /sɪ'dʌktɪv/ **1** ADJ Something that is **seductive** is very attractive or tempting. ❑ *It's a seductive argument.* **2** ADJ A **seductive** person is sexually attractive. • **seductively** ADV ❑ *She danced seductively.*

S

see /si:/ (**sees, seeing, saw, seen**) **1** V-T/V-I When you **see** someone or something, you notice them using your eyes. ❑ *Did you see that policeman?* ❑ *I saw a man making his way towards me.* ❑ *I saw her get out of the car.* ❑ *It's dark and I can't see.* **2** V-T If you go to **see** someone, you visit them or meet them. ❑ *You need to see a doctor.* **3** V-T If you go to **see** an entertainment such as a film or sports game, you go to watch it. ❑ *It was one of the most amazing films I've ever seen.* **4** V-T If you **see** what something is or what it means, you realize or understand what it is or what it means. ❑ *Amy saw that he was laughing at her.* ❑ *We don't see any reason to change the law.* ❑ *'He came home in my car.'—'I see.'* **5** V-T If you **see** someone or something **as** a certain thing or **see** a particular quality in them, you have the opinion that they are that thing or have that quality. ❑ *He saw her as a rival.* ❑ *I don't see it as my duty to take sides.* **6** V-T If you **see** something happening in the future, you imagine it, or predict that it will happen. ❑ *I can see them doing really well.* **7** V-T If a period of time or a person **sees** a particular change or event, you mean that the change or event takes place in that period of time or while that person is alive. ❑ *Yesterday saw two serious accidents.* ❑ *He worked with me for three years and I was sorry to see him resign.* **8** V-T If you say that you will **see** what is happening, you mean that you will try to find out what is happening. If you say that you will **see** if you can do something, you mean that you will try to do it. ❑ *Let me just see what's on TV next.* ❑ *We'll see what we can do, miss.* **9** V-T & PHRASE If you **see** that something is done, or if you **see to it** that it is done, you make sure that it is done. ❑ *See that you take care of him.* ❑ *Catherine saw to it that the information went directly to Walter.* **10** V-T If you **see** someone to a particular place, you accompany them to make sure that they get there safely, or to show politeness. ❑ *'Goodnight.'—'I'll see you to your taxi.'* **11** V-T **See** is used in books to indicate to readers where they should look for more information. ❑ *See Chapter 7 below for further comments on the textile industry.* **12** PHRASE People say '**let me see**' or '**let's see**' when they are trying to remember or calculate something, or are trying to find something. ❑ *Let's see: what else have I to tell you?* **13** PHRASE People say '**I'll see**' or '**We'll see**' to indicate that they do not intend to make a decision immediately, and will decide later. **14** PHRASE You can use **seeing that** or **seeing as** to introduce a reason for what you are saying or a reason why you think something is the case. ❑ *I was more nervous than normal, seeing as I was the team captain.* **15** PHRASE '**See you**', '**be seeing you**', and '**see you later**' are ways of saying goodbye to someone when you expect to meet them again soon.

▶ **see about** PHR-VERB When you **see about** something, you arrange for it to be done or provided. ❑ *I must see about buying a new car.*

▶ **see off** **1** PHR-VERB If you **see off** an opponent, you defeat them. ❑ *He saw off a strong challenge from two other candidates.* **2** PHR-VERB When you **see** someone **off**, you go with them to the place that they are leaving from, and say goodbye to them there.

▶ **see through** **1** PHR-VERB If you **see through** someone or their behaviour, you realize what their intentions are, even though they are trying to hide them. ❑ *I saw through your plan from the start.* **2** → see also **see-through**

▶ **see to** **1** PHR-VERB If you **see to** something that needs attention, you deal with it. ❑ *Franklin saw to the luggage.* **2** → see also **see** (meaning **9**)

Usage

You use **see** to talk about things that you are aware of because a visual impression reaches your eyes. You often use **can** in this case. ❑ *I can see the fax here on the desk.* If you want to say that someone is paying attention to something they can see, you say that they **are looking at** it or **watching** it. In general, you **look at** something that is not moving, while you **watch** something that is moving or changing. ❑ *I asked him to look at the picture.* ❑ *He watched Blake run down the stairs.*

Thesaurus *see* Also look up:

v. glimpse, look, observe, watch **1**
grasp, observe, understand **4**

seed /siːd/ (**seeds**) **1** N-VAR A **seed** is one of the small hard parts of a plant from which a new plant grows. **2** N-PLURAL You can refer to the beginning of a feeling or process that gradually develops as the **seeds of** that feeling or process. ❑ *His questions planted the seeds of doubt in my mind.*
→ see **fruit, plant, rice**

seedling /ˈsiːdlɪŋ/ (**seedlings**) N-COUNT A **seedling** is a young plant grown from a seed.

seedy /ˈsiːdi/ (**seedier, seediest**) ADJ If you describe a person or place as **seedy**, you disapprove of them because they look dirty and not respectable. ❑ *...a seedy hotel.*

seek /siːk/ (**seeks, seeking, sought**) **1** V-T If you **seek** something, you try to find it or obtain it. [FORMAL] ❑ *Pat decided she would seek work.* ● **seeker** (**seekers**) N-COUNT ❑ *The beaches draw sun-seekers from all over Europe.* **2** V-T If you **seek to** do something, you try to do it. ❑ *They never sought to impose their views on us.*
▸ **seek out** PHR-VERB If you **seek out** someone or something, you keep looking for them until you find them. ❑ *The press tried to seek him out.*

Word Partnership Use *seek* with:

N. seek **advice**, seek **approval**, seek **assistance/help**, seek **asylum**, seek **election**, seek **employment**, seek **justice**, seek **permission**, seek **protection**, seek **revenge**, seek **shelter** seek **support**

seem /siːm/ (**seems, seeming, seemed**) **1** LINK-VERB You use **seem** to say that someone or something gives the impression of having a particular quality, or that something gives the impression of happening in the way you describe. ❑ *Everyone seems busy.* ❑ *They seemed an ideal couple.* ❑ *Audiences seem to love it.* ❑ *It seemed as if she'd been gone forever.* **2** V-T You use **seem** when you are describing your own feelings or thoughts, in order to make your statement less forceful. ❑ *I seem to have lost all my self-confidence.* ❑ *I seem to remember giving you very precise instructions.* **3** V-T If you say that you **cannot seem to** or **could not seem to** do something, you mean that you have tried to do it and were unable to. ❑ *Kim's mother couldn't seem to stop crying.*

seeming /ˈsiːmɪŋ/ ADJ BEFORE N **Seeming** means appearing to be the case, but not necessarily the case. [FORMAL] ❑ *...the company's seeming inability to control costs.* ● **seemingly** ADV ❑ *He has moved to Spain, seemingly to enjoy a slower style of life.*

seen /siːn/ **Seen** is the past participle of **see**.

seep /siːp/ (**seeps, seeping, seeped**) V-I If liquid or gas **seeps** into a place, it slowly leaks into it. ❑ *The gas is seeping out of the rocks.*

seethe /siːð/ (**seethes, seething, seethed**) **1** V-I If you **are seething**, you are very angry about something but do not express your feelings about it. ❑ *I seethed with rage.* **2** V-I If you say that a place **is seething**, you are emphasizing that it is very full of people or things and that they are all moving about. ❑ *The restaurants were seething with customers.* ● **seething** ADJ ❑ *...a seething mass of people.*

ˈsee-ˌthrough ADJ **See-through** clothes are made of thin cloth, so that you can see a person's body or underwear through them. ❑ *...a see-through veil.*

segment /ˈsegmənt/ (**segments**) N-COUNT A **segment of** something is one part of it. ❑ *...the poorer segments of society.*
→ see **fruit**

segregate /ˈsegrɪgeɪt/ (**segregates, segregating, segregated**) V-T To **segregate** two groups or types of people or things means to keep them apart. ❑ *They were segregated from the rest of the community.* ● **segregated** ADJ ❑ *...racially-segregated schools.* ● **segregation** N-UNCOUNT ❑ *...the sex segregation of the work-force.*

seize /siːz/ (**seizes, seizing, seized**) **1** V-T If you **seize** something, you take hold of it quickly and firmly. ❑ *He seized my arm.* **2** V-T When a group of people **seize** a place or **seize** control of it, they take control of it quickly and suddenly, using force. ❑ *Troops seized the airport.* **3** V-T When someone **is seized**, they are arrested or captured. ❑ *Men carrying guns seized the five soldiers.* **4** V-T If you **seize** an opportunity, you take advantage of it and do something that you want to do. ❑ *I seized the chance to interview Chris.*
▸ **seize on** PHR-VERB If you **seize on** something, or if you **seize upon** it, you show great interest in it, often because it is useful to you. ❑ *When describing nature, a writer should seize upon small details.*
▸ **seize up** PHR-VERB If an engine or part of your body **seizes up**, it stops working.
▸ **seize upon** → see **seize on**

seizure /ˈsiːʒə/ (**seizures**) **1** N-COUNT If someone **has** a **seizure**, they have a heart attack or an epileptic fit. ❑ *...a mild cardiac seizure.* **2** N-COUNT If there is a **seizure of** power in a place, a group of people suddenly take control of it, using force. ❑ *...the seizure of territory through force.*

seldom /ˈseldəm/ ADV If something **seldom** happens, it does not happen often. ❑ *They seldom speak.* ❑ *We are seldom at home.*

select /sɪˈlekt/ (**selects, selecting, selected**) **1** V-T If you **select** something, you choose it from a number of things of the same kind. ❑ *A panel of judges selected the finalists.* ● **selection** N-UNCOUNT ❑ *The selection of jurors was at random.* **2** ADJ You use **select** to describe things that are considered to be among the best of their kind. ❑ *...a meeting of a very select club.*

Thesaurus *select* Also look up:

V. choose, pick out, take **1**
ADJ. best, exclusive **2**

selection /sɪˈlekʃən/ (**selections**) **1** N-COUNT A **selection of** people or things is a set of them chosen from a larger group. ❑ *...this selection of popular songs.* **2** N-SING The **selection of** goods in a shop is the range of goods available. ❑ *There is a wide selection of silk ties at £10.* **3** → see also **select**

selective /sɪˈlektɪv/ **1** ADJ BEFORE N A **selective** process applies only to a few things or people. ❑ *...selective education.* ● **selectively** ADV ❑ *They fund research selectively, giving most money to those with the best grades.* **2** ADJ When someone is **selective**, they choose things carefully, for example the things that they buy or do. ❑ *Sales still happen, but buyers are more selective.* ● **selectively** ADV ❑ *People on small incomes need to shop selectively.*

S

self /self/ (**selves**) N-COUNT Your **self** is your basic personality or nature. ❑ *You're looking more like your usual self.*

ˌself-ˈconfident ADJ Someone who is **self-confident** behaves confidently because they feel sure of their abilities or value. ❑ *...a self-confident young woman.* ● **self-confidence** N-UNCOUNT ❑ *I've developed a lot of self-confidence.*

ˌself-ˈconscious ADJ Someone who is **self-conscious** is easily embarrassed and nervous about the way they look or appear. ❑ *I felt a bit self-conscious in my bathing suit.*

ˌself-conˈtained 1 ADJ You can describe someone as **self-contained** when they do not need help or resources from other people. ❑ *She's very self-contained.* 2 ADJ A **self-contained** flat has all its own facilities including a kitchen and bathroom.

ˌself-conˈtrol N-UNCOUNT Your **self-control** is your ability to control your feelings and appear calm. ❑ *I wish I had shown more self-control.*

ˌself-deˈfence [AM **self-defense**] N-UNCOUNT **Self-defence** is the use of force to protect yourself against someone who is attacking you. ❑ *He acted in self-defence.*

ˌself-determiˈnation N-UNCOUNT **Self-determination** is the right of a country to be independent, instead of being controlled by a foreign country, and to choose its own form of government.

ˌself-emˈployed ADJ & N-PLURAL **Self-employed** people or **the self-employed** are people who organize their own work and taxes and are paid by people for a service they provide, rather than being paid a regular salary by a company.

ˌself-esˈteem N-UNCOUNT Your **self-esteem** is how you feel about yourself and whether you have a good opinion of yourself. ❑ *Losing my job was terrible for my self-esteem.*

ˌself-ˈevident ADJ A fact or situation that is **self-evident** is so obvious that there is no need for proof or explanation. ❑ *It's self-evident that this man's unreliable.*

ˌself-ˈhelp N-UNCOUNT **Self-help** consists of people providing support and help for each other in an informal way, rather than relying on official organizations. ❑ *...a self-help group for depressed people.*

S

ˌself-ˈimage N-COUNT Your **self-image** is your opinion of yourself. ❑ *You must strive to improve your self-image.*

ˌself-imˈposed ADJ A **self-imposed** situation, restriction, or task is one that you have created or accepted for yourself. ❑ *All my problems were self-imposed.* ❑ *The self-imposed deadline for talks is Sunday.*

ˌself-inˈdulgent ADJ If you are **self-indulgent**, you allow yourself to have things that you enjoy but do not need. ❑ *To buy flowers for myself seems self-indulgent.* ● **self-indulgence** (**self-indulgences**) N-VAR ❑ *Those days of carefree self-indulgence are over.*

ˌself-ˈinterest N-UNCOUNT If you accuse someone of **self-interest**, you disapprove of them because they always want to do what is best for themselves rather than for anyone else. ❑ *Their protests are motivated purely by self-interest.*

selfish /ˈselfɪʃ/ ADJ If you say that someone is **selfish**, you disapprove of them because they care only about themselves, and not about other people. ❑ *...the selfish interests of a few people.* ● **selfishly** ADV ❑ *39% of women complain that their partners act selfishly.* ● **selfishness** N-UNCOUNT ❑ *...a world where everyone leads lives of utter selfishness.*

selfless /ˈselfləs/ ADJ If you say that someone is **selfless**, you approve of them because they care about other people more than themselves. ❑ *Her generosity to me was entirely selfless.*

ˌself-ˈpity N-UNCOUNT **Self-pity** is a feeling of unhappiness and depression that you have about your problems, especially when this is unnecessary or greatly exaggerated. ❑ *I never felt self-pity because I always had faith.*

ˌself-reˈspect N-UNCOUNT **Self-respect** is a feeling of confidence and pride in your own ability and worth. ❑ *I lost all my self-respect.*

ˌself-ˈrighteous ADJ If you describe someone as **self-righteous**, you disapprove of them because they are convinced that they are morally right and that other people are wrong. ❑ *...self-righteous reformers.* ● **self-righteousness** N-UNCOUNT ❑ *Heather's voice was filled with self-righteousness.*

ˌself-ˈstudy N-UNCOUNT **Self-study** is study that you do on your own, without a teacher. ❑ *...self-study courses.*

ˌself-ˈstyled ADJ BEFORE N If you describe someone as a **self-styled** leader or expert, you disapprove of them because they claim to be a leader or expert but they do not have the right to call themselves this. ❑ *...a self-styled expert on women.*

ˌself-sufˈficient ADJ If a country or group is **self-sufficient**, it is able to produce or make everything that it needs. ❑ *Rural areas tend to be more self-sufficient.* ● **self-sufficiency** N-UNCOUNT ❑ *...Japan's self-sufficiency in rice.*

sell /sel/ (**sells, selling, sold**) 1 V-T If you **sell** something that you own, you let someone have it in return for money. ❑ *The directors sold the business for £14.8 million.* 2 V-T If a shop **sells** a product, people can buy it from that shop. ❑ *We sell cosmetics.* 3 V-I If something **sells for** a particular price, or if it **sells at** that price, that is what it costs. 4 V-I If something **sells**, it is bought in fairly large quantities. ❑ *The products will sell well in the run-up to Christmas.*

▶ **sell out** 1 PHR-VERB If a shop **sells out of** something, it sells all its stocks of it. 2 PHR-VERB If a performance of a play, film, or other entertainment **is sold out**, all the tickets have been sold. 3 PHR-VERB If you accuse someone of **selling out**, you disapprove of the fact that they do something which used to be against their principles. [INFORMAL] ❑ *Still radical after all these years, he has never sold out.* 4 → see also **sell-out**

Word Link	ar, er ≈ one who acts as : buyer, liar, seller

seller /ˈselə/ (**sellers**) 1 N-COUNT A **seller** is a person or business that sells something. ❑ *Enron was once the world's top buyer and seller of natural gas.* 2 N-COUNT If you describe a product as, for example, a **big seller**, you mean that large numbers of it are being sold. 3 → see also **best-seller**

ˈsell-ˌoff (**sell-offs**) N-COUNT The **sell-off** of something, for example an industry that is owned by the state, is the act of selling it.

ˈsell-ˌout (**sell-outs**) **1** N-COUNT If a play, sports event, or other entertainment is a **sell-out**, all the tickets for it are sold. **2** N-COUNT If you describe someone's behaviour as a **sell-out**, you disapprove of them doing something which used to be against their principles. ❑ *He dismissed the agreement as a sell-out.* **3** → see also **sell out**

selves /selvz/ **Selves** is the plural of **self**.

semblance /ˈsembləns/ N-SING If there is a **semblance of** a particular condition or quality, it appears to exist, though in fact it may not. [FORMAL] ❑ *A semblance of normality has been restored.*

semen /ˈsiːmen/ N-UNCOUNT **Semen** is the liquid containing sperm that is produced by the male sex organs.

semester /səˈmestə/ (**semesters**) N-COUNT In colleges and universities in the United States and some other countries, a **semester** is one of two periods into which the year is divided.

Word Link	*semi ≈ half : semi-colon, semiconductor, semi-final*

ˌsemi-ˈcolon (**semi-colons**) N-COUNT A **semi-colon** is the punctuation mark (;).
→ see **punctuation**

semiconductor /ˌsemikənˈdʌktə/ (**semiconductors**) N-COUNT A **semiconductor** is a substance used in electronics whose ability to conduct electricity increases with greater heat.
→ see **solar**

ˌsemi-deˈtached ADJ A **semi-detached** house is a house that is joined to another house on one side by a shared wall.

ˈsemi-ˌfinal (**semi-finals**) N-COUNT A **semi-final** is one of the two matches or races in a competition that are held to decide who will compete in the final.

seminal /ˈsemɪnəl/ ADJ **Seminal** is used to describe things such as books or events that have a great influence in a particular field. [FORMAL] ❑ *He wrote a seminal book on the subject.*

seminar /ˈsemɪnɑː/ (**seminars**) N-COUNT A **seminar** is a class at a university in which the teacher and a small group of students discuss a topic.

semitic /sɪˈmɪtɪk/ **1** ADJ **Semitic** is sometimes used to mean Jewish. ❑ *His anti-Semitic beliefs were well-known.* **2** ADJ **Semitic** is used to describe a group of languages that includes Arabic and Hebrew, or the people who speak these languages.

Senate /ˈsenɪt/

Senate can take the singular or plural form of the verb.

1 N-PROPER **The Senate** is the smaller and more important of the two councils in the government of some countries, such as the United States of America. **2** → See note at **government**

Word Link	*sen ≈ old : senator, senile, senior*

senator /ˈsenɪtə/ (**senators**) **1** N-COUNT A **senator** is a member of a law-making Senate. **2** → See note at **government**

send /send/ (**sends, sending, sent**) **1** V-T When you **send** someone something, you arrange for them to receive it, for example by post. ❑ *Myra sent me a note thanking me for dinner.* ❑ *I sent a letter to the Prime Minister.* ❑ *He worked abroad and sent money home to his mother.* • **sender** (**senders**) N-COUNT ❑ *£200 will go to the sender of the first correct answer to the competition.* **2** V-T If you **send** someone somewhere, you arrange for them to go there or stay there. ❑ *Tom came up to see her, but she sent him away.* ❑ *The government sent troops to the region.* ❑ *I was sent for blood tests.* **3** V-T If you **send** a signal or message, you cause it to go to a place by means of radio waves. ❑ *The space probe Voyager sent back pictures of Neptune.* **4** V-T If something **sends** things or people in a particular direction, it causes them to move in that direction. ❑ *The force of the blast sent him flying.* **5** V-T If something **sends** someone or something into a particular state, it causes them to be in that state. ❑ *This comedy series has sent audiences into fits of laughter.*

▶ **send for** **1** PHR-VERB If you **send for** someone, you send them a message asking them to come and see you. ❑ *I've sent for the doctor.* **2** PHR-VERB If you **send for** something, or if you **send off for** it, you write and ask for it to be sent to you.

▶ **send off** **1** PHR-VERB If you **send off** a letter or parcel, you send it somewhere by post. **2** PHR-VERB If a footballer **is sent off**, the referee makes him or her leave the field during a game, as a punishment for seriously breaking the rules.

▶ **send off for** → see **send for** (meaning **2**)

▶ **send out** **1** PHR-VERB If you **send out** things such as leaflets or bills, you send them to a large number of people at the same time. ❑ *She sent out four hundred invitations to the party.* **2** PHR-VERB To **send out** a signal, sound, light, or heat means to produce it.

▶ **send out for** PHR-VERB If you **send out for** food, you phone and ask for it to be delivered to you. ❑ *Let's send out for a pizza.*

senile /ˈsiːnaɪl/ ADJ If old people become **senile**, they become confused and are unable to look after themselves. • **senility** /sɪˈnɪlɪti/ N-UNCOUNT ❑ *Alzheimer's disease causes premature senility.*

senior /ˈsiːnjə/ (**seniors**) **1** ADJ BEFORE N The **senior** people in an organization have the highest and most important jobs in it. ❑ *...senior officials in the government.* **2** ADJ & N-COUNT If someone is **senior to** you, or if they are your **senior**, they have a more important job or position than you. **3** N-SING **Senior** is used when indicating how much older one person is than another. ❑ *Her best friend is many years her senior.*

ˌsenior ˈcitizen (**senior citizens**) N-COUNT A **senior citizen** is a person who is old enough to receive an old-age pension.
→ see **age**

Word Link	*sens ≈ feeling : sensation, senseless, sensitive*

sensation /senˈseɪʃən/ (**sensations**) **1** N-VAR **Sensation** is the ability to feel things physically. A **sensation** is a particular physical feeling. ❑ *She lost all sensation in her left leg.* ❑ *...a tingling sensation.* **2** N-COUNT A **sensation** is the general feeling caused by a particular experience. ❑ *It's a funny sensation to know someone's talking about you.* **3** N-COUNT If a person or event is a **sensation**, they cause great excitement and interest. ❑ *The film turned her into an overnight sensation.*
→ see **taste**

S

sensational /sen'seɪʃənəl/ **1** ADJ A **sensational** event or situation is so remarkable that it causes great excitement and interest. ❑ *The world champions suffered a sensational defeat.* ● **sensationally** ADV ❑ *He sensationally announced that he is to quit.* **2** ADJ You can describe something as **sensational** when you think that it is extremely good. ● **sensationally** ADV ❑ *...sensationally good food.*

sense /sens/ (**senses, sensing, sensed**) **1** N-COUNT Your **senses** are the physical abilities of sight, smell, hearing, touch, and taste. ❑ *...a keen sense of smell.* **2** V-T If you **sense** something, you become aware of it, although it is not very obvious. ❑ *I sensed that he wasn't telling me the whole story.* **3** N-SING If you have a **sense of** guilt or shame, for example, you feel guilty or ashamed. ❑ *Redundancy often brings a sense of failure.* **4** N-UNCOUNT **Sense** is the ability to make good judgements and to behave sensibly. ❑ *They had the sense to seek help.* **5** N-COUNT A **sense** of a word or expression is one of its possible meanings. **6** → see also **common sense, sense of humour** **7** PHRASE If something **makes sense**, or if you **make sense of** it, you understand it or find it sensible. ❑ *From an early age we try to make sense of the world.* ❑ *It makes sense to have a healthy lifestyle.* **8** PHRASE If you say that someone **has come to** their **senses** or **has been brought to** their **senses**, you mean that they have stopped being foolish and are being sensible again.
→ see **smell**

Word Link *sens ≈ feeling : sensation, senseless, sensitive*

senseless /'sensləs/ **1** ADJ A **senseless** action seems to have no meaning or purpose. ❑ *...senseless violence.* **2** ADJ AFTER LINK-V If someone is **senseless**, they are unconscious. ❑ *I was beaten senseless.*

ˌsense of 'humour N-UNCOUNT Someone's **sense of humour** is the fact that they find certain things amusing. ❑ *We share the same sense of humour.* ❑ *He's got no sense of humour.*

sensibility /ˌsensɪ'bɪlɪti/ (**sensibilities**) N-VAR Someone's **sensibility** is their ability to experience deep feelings. [FORMAL]

S

sensible /'sensɪbəl/ ADJ A **sensible** person is able to make good decisions and judgements based on reason. ❑ *It would be sensible to get a solicitor.* ● **sensibly** ADV ❑ *We need to make sure that the money is being spent sensibly.*

Usage

Be careful not to use **sensible** to describe someone whose feelings or emotions are strongly affected by their experiences. The word you need is **sensitive.** ❑ *...a highly sensitive artist.*

sensitive /'sensɪtɪv/ **1** ADJ If you are **sensitive to** other people's problems and feelings, you understand and are aware of them. ❑ *Teachers must be sensitive to children's needs.* ❑ *He was always so sensitive and caring.* ● **sensitively** ADV ❑ *Domestic violence needs to be treated seriously and sensitively.* ● **sensitivity** /ˌsensɪ'tɪvɪti/ N-UNCOUNT ❑ *...sensitivity for each other's feelings.* **2** ADJ If you are **sensitive about** something, it worries or upsets you. ❑ *Young people are very sensitive about their appearance.* ● **sensitivity** (**sensitivities**) N-VAR ❑ *Do not offend the sensitivities of religious groups.* **3** ADJ A **sensitive** subject or issue needs to be dealt with carefully because it is likely to cause disagreement or make people upset. ❑ *Job losses remain a politically sensitive issue.* **4** ADJ Something that is **sensitive to** a physical force or substance can be affected by it. ❑ *This chemical is sensitive to light.* ● **sensitivity** N-UNCOUNT ❑ *Her headache was accompanied by intense sensitivity to light and noise.* **5** ADJ A **sensitive** piece of scientific equipment is capable of measuring or recording very small changes. ❑ *...an extremely sensitive microscope.*

Word Partnership Use *sensitive* with:

N.	sensitive **areas**, sensitive **issue** **3**
	heat sensitive, sensitive **information**,
	light sensitive, sensitive **material**,
	sensitive **skin** **4**
	sensitive **equipment** **5**
ADV.	**overly** sensitive, **so** sensitive, **too** sensitive **1** **2**
	highly sensitive, **very** sensitive **1**-**5**
	politically sensitive **3**

sensor /'sensə/ (**sensors**) N-COUNT A **sensor** is an instrument which reacts to certain physical conditions such as heat or light.

Word Link *ory ≈ relating to : advisory, contradictory, sensory*

sensory /'sensəri/ ADJ BEFORE N **Sensory** means relating to the physical senses. ❑ *...sensory awareness.*
→ see **nervous system, smell**

sensual /'senʃʊəl/ **1** ADJ A **sensual** person has a great liking for physical pleasures, especially sexual pleasures. ● **sensuality** /ˌsenʃʊ'ælɪti/ N-UNCOUNT ❑ *Dionysus was the god of sensuality.* **2** ADJ Something that is **sensual** gives pleasure to your physical senses rather than to your mind. ❑ *...sensual dance rhythms.* ● **sensuality** N-UNCOUNT ❑ *...the sensuality of silk.*

sensuous /'senʃʊəs/ **1** ADJ **Sensuous** things give pleasure to the mind or body through the senses. ❑ *...sensuous, atmospheric camerawork.* ● **sensuously** ADV ❑ *...sensuously shaped glass vases.* **2** ADJ **Sensuous** means showing or suggesting a great liking for sexual pleasure. ● **sensuously** ADV ❑ *The nose was straight, the mouth sensuously wide and full.*

sent /sent/ **Sent** is the past tense and past participle of **send**.

sentence /'sentəns/ (**sentences, sentencing, sentenced**) **1** N-COUNT A **sentence** is a group of words which, when they are written down, begin with a capital letter and end with a full stop, question mark, or exclamation mark. Most sentences contain a subject and a verb. **2** N-VAR In a law court, a **sentence** is the punishment that a person receives after they have been found guilty of a crime. ❑ *He served a prison sentence for bank robbery.* **3** V-T & PHRASE When judges **sentence** someone, or when they **pass sentence on** someone, they state in court what the person's punishment will be. ❑ *The court sentenced him to five*

years' imprisonment.
→ see **trial**

sentiment /'sentɪmənt/ (**sentiments**) 1 N-VAR A **sentiment** is an attitude, feeling, or opinion. ❑ *...nationalist sentiments.* 2 N-UNCOUNT **Sentiment** is an emotion such as tenderness, affection, or sadness, which influences a person's behaviour. ❑ *Laura kept the letter out of sentiment.*

sentimental /ˌsentɪ'mentəl/ 1 ADJ A **sentimental** person or thing feels or makes you feel emotions such as tenderness, affection, or sadness, sometimes in a way that is exaggerated or foolish. ❑ *...sentimental love songs.* ❑ *I'm trying not to be sentimental about the past.* ● **sentimentality** N-UNCOUNT ❑ *In this book there is no sentimentality.* ● **sentimentally** ADV ❑ *We look back sentimentally to a 'golden era'.* 2 ADJ **Sentimental** means relating to a person's emotions. ❑ *...objects of sentimental value.*

sentry /'sentri/ (**sentries**) N-COUNT A **sentry** is a soldier who guards a camp or a building.

separate (**separates, separating, separated**) 1 ADJ /'sepərət/ If one thing is **separate from** another, the two things are apart and are not connected. ❑ *Business bank accounts were kept separate from personal ones.* ❑ *I've always kept my private and professional life separate.* ❑ *The word 'quarter' has two completely separate meanings.* ● **separately** ADV ❑ *Each case is dealt with separately.* 2 PHRASE When two or more people who have been together for some time **go** their **separate ways**, they go to different places or end their relationship. 3 V-T/V-I /'sepəreɪt/ If you **separate** people or things that are together, or if they **separate**, they move apart. ❑ *Stir the rice with a fork to separate the grains.* ❑ *They separated. Stephen returned to the square.* ● **separation** (**separations**) N-VAR ❑ *Mrs Holland can't cope with separation from her family.* 4 V-T & PHR-VERB If you **separate** one idea or fact **from** another, or if you **separate** it **out**, you consider them individually and see or show that they are distinct and different things. ❑ *It is difficult to separate the two aims.* ❑ *Most people can separate out their emotions from their rational thoughts.* ● **separation** N-VAR ❑ *...the separation of church and state.* 5 V-T A quality or factor that **separates** one thing **from** another is the reason why the two things are different from each other. ❑ *What separates man from machine is the ability to think.* 6 V-T If an object, distance, or period of time **separates** two people or things, it exists between them. ❑ *This fence separates the yard from the road.* ❑ *Just four miles separate the two communities.* 7 V-T & PHR-VERB If you **separate** a group of people or things, or if you **separate** them **out**, you divide them into smaller groups or elements. ❑ *The police separated the men into three groups.* ● **separation** N-VAR ❑ *...the separation of the country into separate and independent states.* 8 V-I If a couple who are married or living together **separate**, they decide to live apart. ● **separated** ADJ AFTER LINK-V ❑ *Her parents are separated.* ● **separation** N-VAR ❑ *They agreed to a trial separation.*

▸ **separate out** → see **separate** (meanings **4, 7**)

Thesaurus	*separate* Also look up:
ADJ.	disconnected, divided 1
V.	divide, remove, split 3 4 5

separatist /'sepərətɪst/ (**separatists**) N-COUNT **Separatists** are people of an ethnic or cultural group within a country who want to establish their own separate government. ● **separatism** N-UNCOUNT ❑ *In 1964, Malcolm X was calling for black separatism.*

September /sep'tembə/ (**Septembers**) N-VAR **September** is the ninth month of the year. ❑ *He plans to visit Britain in early September.*

sequel /'siːkwəl/ (**sequels**) 1 N-COUNT The **sequel to** a book or film is another book or film which continues the story. 2 N-COUNT The **sequel to** an event is something that happened after it or because of it. ❑ *The immediate sequel to the Congress in 1980 was the visit of Pope John Paul II to Britain in 1982.*

sequence /'siːkwəns/ (**sequences**) 1 N-COUNT A **sequence of** things is a number of them that come one after another in a particular order. ❑ *This sequence of events led to the accident.* 2 N-COUNT A particular **sequence** is a particular order in which things happen or are arranged. ❑ *What number comes next in the sequence: 2, 4, 6, 8, 10?* 3 N-COUNT A film **sequence** is a short part of a film. ❑ *...the film's opening sequence.*

sequin /'siːkwɪn/ (**sequins**) N-COUNT **Sequins** are small, shiny discs that are sewn on clothes to decorate them.

serene /sɪ'riːn/ ADJ **Serene** means calm and quiet. ● **serenely** ADV ❑ *She carried on serenely sipping her water.* ● **serenity** /sɪ'renɪti/ N-UNCOUNT ❑ *...the serenity of the mountains.*

sergeant /'sɑːdʒənt/ (**sergeants**) 1 N-VOC & N-TITLE A **sergeant** is an officer of middle rank in the army or air force. 2 N-VOC & N-TITLE A **sergeant** is an officer in the police force.

Word Link	*major ≈ larger : major, majority, sergeant major*

ˌsergeant 'major (**sergeant majors**) N-VOC & N-TITLE A **sergeant major** is an army officer of high rank.

serial /'sɪəriəl/ (**serials**) 1 N-COUNT A **serial** is a story which is broadcast or published in a number of parts over a period of time. ❑ *...a popular radio serial.* 2 ADJ BEFORE N **Serial** killings or attacks are a series of killings or attacks committed by the same person. This person is known as a **serial** killer or attacker. ❑ *...a serial offender.*

series /'sɪəriːz/

> **Series** is both the singular and the plural form.

1 N-COUNT A **series of** things or events is a number of them that come one after the other. ❑ *...a series of explosions.* 2 N-COUNT A radio or television **series** is a set of related programmes with the same title. ❑ *...a new drama series called 'Under The Hammer'.*

serious /'sɪəriəs/ 1 ADJ **Serious** problems or situations are very bad and cause people to be worried or afraid. ❑ *Crime is an increasingly serious problem in this area.* ❑ *...a serious accident.* ● **seriously** ADV ❑ *His wife was seriously injured in the attack.* ● **seriousness** N-UNCOUNT ❑ *...the seriousness of the crisis.* 2 ADJ **Serious** matters are important and deserve careful thought. ❑ *This incident raised serious questions about the security precautions taken for such events.* ❑ *This question deserves serious consideration.* ● **seriously** ADV ❑ *The management* *should think seriously about their positions.* 3 ADJ If you are **serious about** something, you are sincere about it, and not joking. ❑ *You really are serious about this, aren't you?* ● **seriously** ADV ❑ *I seriously hope it will never come to that.* ● **seriousness** N-UNCOUNT ❑ *In all seriousness, there is nothing else I can do.* 4 ADJ **Serious** people are thoughtful, quiet, and do not laugh very often. ● **seriously** ADV ❑ *They spoke to me very seriously but politely.*

seriously /'sɪəriəsli/ 1 ADV You say **seriously** to indicate that you really mean what you say, or to ask someone else if they really mean what they have said. ❑ *Seriously, I shall miss you.* ❑ *'Let's get married.'—'Seriously?'* 2 PHRASE If you **take** someone or something **seriously**, you believe that they are important and deserve attention. ❑ *The phrase was not meant to be taken seriously.*

sermon /'sɜːmən/ (**sermons**) N-COUNT A **sermon** is a talk on a religious or moral subject given during a church service.

serpent /'sɜːpənt/ (**serpents**) N-COUNT A **serpent** is a snake. [LITERARY]

serum /'sɪərəm/ (**serums**) N-VAR A **serum** is a liquid that is injected into someone's blood to protect them against a poison or disease.

servant /'sɜːvənt/ (**servants**) 1 N-COUNT A **servant** is someone who is employed to work in another person's house, for example to cook or clean. 2 → see also **civil servant**

serve /sɜːv/ (**serves, serving, served**) 1 V-T If you **serve** your country, an organization, or a person, you do useful work for them. ❑ *He served the government loyally for 30 years.* 2 V-T/V-I If something **serves as** a particular thing or **serves** a particular purpose, that is its use or function. ❑ *The small building served as a school.* ❑ *I really do not think that an inquiry would serve any useful purpose.* 3 V-T If something **serves** people or an area, it provides them with something that they need. ❑ *This hospital serves about 250,000 people.* ❑ *These small businesses serve the community well.* 4 V-T If you **serve** people or if you **serve** food and drink, you give people food and drink. ❑ *Our waiter served us quickly.* ❑ *We served lunch to the children.* 5 V-T Someone who **serves** customers in a shop or a bar helps them and provides them with what they want to buy. ❑ *The waitress served me coffee and croissants.* 6 V-T If you **serve** a prison sentence, you spend a period of time in jail. ❑ *He is serving a five-year sentence for robbery.* 7 V-I & N-COUNT When you **serve** in a game like tennis, you start play by hitting the ball. A **serve** is the act of doing this. ❑ *He threw the ball up to serve.* ❑ *His second serve hit the net.* 8 PHRASE If you say it **serves** someone **right** when something unpleasant happens to them, you mean that it is their own fault and you have no sympathy for them. ❑ *It serves her right for being so stubborn.* 9 → see also **serving**

▶ **serve up** PHR-VERB If you **serve up** food, you give it to people. ❑ *He served the meal up on delicate white plates.*

S

Word Partnership Use *serve* with:

N. serve **a community**, serve **the public** 1 4
serve **a purpose** 2
serve ***someone's* needs** 3
serve **cake**, serve **food** 4

server /'sɜːvə/ (**servers**) N-COUNT A **server** is part of a computer network which does a particular task, for example storing or processing information, for all or part of the network. [COMPUTING]
→ see **Internet, tennis**

service /'sɜːvɪs/ (**services, servicing, serviced**)

In meaning 10, **services** is both the singular and the plural form.

1 N-COUNT A **service** is an organization or system that provides something for the public. ❑ *...the social services.* ❑ *...the postal service.* ❑ *...service industries, such as banks and airlines.* 2 N-COUNT A **service** is a job that an organization or business can do for you. ❑ *...a one hour dry-cleaning service.* 3 N-PLURAL **The services** are the army, navy, and air force. 4 N-UNCOUNT **Service** is the state or activity of working for a particular person or organization. ❑ *Pat is leaving the company after 12 years' service.* 5 N-UNCOUNT The level or standard of **service** provided by an organization or company is the amount or quality of the work it can do for you. ❑ *How do you think we could improve customer service?* 6 N-UNCOUNT When you receive **service** in a restaurant, hotel, or shop, an employee asks you what you want or gives you what you have ordered. ❑ *Restaurants usually charge between 10 and 12.5 per cent for service.* 7 PHRASE If a machine or vehicle is **in service**, it is being used or is able to be used. If it is **out of service**, it cannot be used. 8 V-T & N-COUNT If you **service** a machine or vehicle, or if it has a **service**, it is examined, adjusted, and cleaned so that it will keep working efficiently and safely. ❑ *All gas fires should be serviced annually.* ❑ *The car is due for a service.* 9 N-COUNT A **service** is a religious ceremony. ❑ *The wedding service was held in this church.* 10 N-COUNT A **services** is a place on a motorway where there is a petrol station, restaurant, shop, and toilets. [BRIT] ❑ *...a motorway services.* 11 → see also **Civil Service**
→ see **industry, library**

serviceman /'sɜːvɪsmən/ (**servicemen**) N-COUNT A **serviceman** is a man who is in the army, navy, or air force.

'service pro,vider (**service providers**) N-COUNT A **service provider** is a company that provides a service, especially an Internet service.

serving /'sɜːvɪŋ/ (**servings**) N-COUNT A **serving** is an amount of food given to one person at a meal. ❑ *Each serving contains 240 calories.*

session /'seʃən/ (**sessions**) 1 N-COUNT A **session** is a meeting or series of meetings of a court, parliament, or other official group. ❑ *...an emergency session of the UN Security Council.* ❑ *The next parliamentary session starts in November.* 2 N-COUNT A **session** of a particular activity is a period of that activity. ❑ *...a photo session.*

set
❶ NOUN USES
❷ VERB AND ADJECTIVE USES

set /set/ (**sets**)
❶ 1 N-COUNT A **set of** things is a number of things that are thought of as a group. ❑ *They have a spare set of keys for their house.* ❑ *...a chess set.* 2 N-COUNT In tennis, a **set** is one of the groups of six or more games that form part of a match.

3 N-COUNT The **set** for a play or film scene is the scenery and furniture that is used on the stage or in the studio. ❑ *Stars sometimes behave badly on set.* **4** N-COUNT A **television set** is a television.
→ see **drama, theatre**

set /set/ (**sets, setting, set**)
❷ **1** V-T If you **set** something somewhere, you put it there, especially in a careful or deliberate way. ❑ *He set the glass on the counter.* **2** ADJ AFTER LINK-V If something is **set in** a particular place or position, it is in that place or position. ❑ *The castle is set in 25 acres of beautiful gardens.* **3** V-T You can use **set** to say that a person or thing causes something to be in a particular condition or situation. For example, if something **sets** someone free, it causes them to be free. ❑ *This idea set her imagination free.* ❑ *Dozens of people were injured and many vehicles set on fire.* **4** V-T When you **set** a clock or control, you adjust it to a particular point or level. ❑ *Set the volume as high as possible.* **5** V-T If you **set** a date, price, goal, or level, you decide what it will be. ❑ *They haven't yet set a date for the wedding.* **6** V-T To **set** an examination or a question paper means to decide what questions will be asked in it. **7** V-T If you **set** something such as a record, an example, or a precedent, you create it for people to copy or to try to achieve. ❑ *If you swear in front of children, then you set a bad example.* **8** V-T If someone **sets** you a task or a target, you have to do that task or achieve that target. ❑ *The secret to happiness is to keep setting yourself new challenges.* **9** ADJ AFTER LINK-V If a play, film, or story is **set in** a particular place or period of time, the events in it happen in that place or period. **10** PHRASE Something that **sets the scene for** a particular event, or **sets the stage for** a particular event, creates the conditions in which the event is likely to happen. ❑ *This incident set the stage for the 1986 revolution.* **11** ADJ You use **set** to describe something which is fixed and cannot be changed. ❑ *...a set price.* ❑ *...a set menu.* **12** ADJ AFTER LINK-V If you are **set to** do something, you are ready to do it or are likely to do it. If something is **set to** happen, it is about to happen or likely to happen. ❑ *This novel is set to become a classic.* **13** ADJ AFTER LINK-V If you are **set on** something, you are strongly determined to do or have it. ❑ *She was set on going to an all-girls school.* **14** V-I When something such as jelly, glue, or cement **sets**, it becomes firm or hard. **15** V-I When the sun **sets**, it goes below the horizon. **16** → see also **setting** **17** to **set eyes on** something → see **eye** **18** to **set fire to** something → see **fire** **19** to **set foot** somewhere → see **foot** **20** to **set sail** → see **sail**

▶ **set apart** PHR-VERB If a characteristic **sets** you **apart** from other people, it makes you different from them in a noticeable way. ❑ *Even as a child, his natural ability set him apart.*

▶ **set aside** **1** PHR-VERB If you **set** something **aside** for a special use or purpose, you keep it available for that use or purpose. ❑ *Try to set aside time each day to relax.* **2** PHR-VERB If you **set aside** a belief, principle, or feeling, you decide that you will not be influenced by it. ❑ *Players said they will set aside personal feelings for the good of the club.*

▶ **set back** **1** PHR-VERB If something **sets** you **back** or **sets back** a project or scheme, it causes a delay. **2** PHR-VERB If something **sets** you **back** a certain amount of money, it costs you that much money. [INFORMAL] **3** → see also **setback**

▶ **set down** PHR-VERB If a committee or organization **sets down** rules or guidelines for doing something, they decide what they should be and officially record them. ❑ *The rules are set down by the Personal Investment Authority.*

▶ **set in** PHR-VERB If something unpleasant **sets in**, it begins and seems likely to continue or develop. ❑ *Panic was setting in.*

▶ **set off** **1** PHR-VERB When you **set off**, you start a journey. ❑ *He set off for the station.* **2** PHR-VERB If something **sets off** something such as an alarm or a bomb, it activates it so that the alarm rings or the bomb explodes.

▶ **set out** **1** PHR-VERB When you **set out**, you start a journey. ❑ *I set out for the cottage.* **2** PHR-VERB If you **set out to** do something, you start trying to do it. ❑ *We set out to find the truth behind the mystery.* **3** PHR-VERB If you **set** things **out**, you arrange or display them. ❑ *She set out the cups and saucers.* **4** PHR-VERB If you **set out** facts or opinions, you explain them in writing or speech in a clear, organized way. ❑ *The agreement sets out how the two countries will co-operate.*

▶ **set up** **1** PHR-VERB If you **set** something **up**, you make the preparations that are necessary for it to start. ❑ *She wants to set up children's ski schools.* ● **setting up** N-UNCOUNT ❑ *The government announced the setting up of a special fund.* **2** PHR-VERB If you **set up** a temporary structure, you place it or build it somewhere. ❑ *Brian set up a large, white tent on the lawn.* **3** PHR-VERB If you **set up** somewhere or **set yourself up** somewhere, you establish yourself in a new business or area. ❑ *He used to be an accountant, but has now set himself up as a fashion designer.* **4** → see also **set-up**

setback /ˈsetbæk/ (**setbacks**) **1** N-COUNT A **setback** is an event that delays your progress or reverses some of the progress that you have made. ❑ *He suffered a serious setback in his political career.* **2** → see also **set back**

settee /seˈtiː/ (**settees**) N-COUNT A **settee** is a long comfortable seat with a back and arms, for two or three people.

setting /ˈsetɪŋ/ (**settings**) **1** N-COUNT The **setting** for something is the particular place or the type of surroundings in which it is located or where it happens. ❑ *The hotel is in a beautiful setting by a river.* **2** N-COUNT A **setting** is one of the positions to which the controls of a device such as a cooker or heater can be adjusted. ❑ *Fry the vegetables on a high setting.*

settle /ˈsetəl/ (**settles, settling, settled**) **1** V-T If two people **settle** an argument or problem, or if someone or something **settles** it, they solve it by making a decision about who is right or about what to do. ❑ *They are both looking for ways to settle their differences.* **2** V-T If you **settle** a bill or debt, you pay the amount that you owe. **3** V-T If something **is settled**, it has all been decided and arranged. ❑ *That's settled then. We'll leave tonight.* **4** V-I When people **settle** in a place, they start living there permanently. ❑ *He visited Paris and eventually settled there.* **5** V-T/V-I If you **settle yourself** somewhere or **settle** somewhere, you sit down or make yourself comfortable. ❑ *He settled into a chair.* ❑ *Molly settled herself on a bench.* **6** V-I If something **settles**, it sinks slowly and becomes still. ❑ *Dust had settled on the furniture.* **7** **when the dust settles** → see **dust** **8** to **settle a score** → see **score**

S

▶ **settle down** 1 PHR-VERB When someone **settles down**, they start living a quiet life in one place, especially when they get married or buy a house. 2 PHR-VERB If a situation or a person that has been going through a lot of problems or changes **settles down**, they become calm. ❑ *We had a few problems, but things have settled down now.* 3 PHR-VERB If you **settle down to** do something, or if you **settle down to** something, you prepare to do it and concentrate on it. ❑ *Daniel settled down to work.*

▶ **settle for** PHR-VERB If you **settle for** something, you choose or accept it, especially when it is not what you really want but there is nothing else available. ❑ *The team will have to settle for third or fourth place.*

▶ **settle into** PHR-VERB If you **settle into** a new place, job, or routine, or **settle in**, you become used to it. ❑ *I'm sure they will settle in very quickly.*

▶ **settle on** PHR-VERB If you **settle on** a particular thing, you choose it after considering other possible choices.

▶ **settle up** PHR-VERB When you **settle up**, you pay a bill or a debt.

Word Partnership Use *settle* with:

N.	settle **a case**, settle **a claim**, settle **differences**, settle **a dispute**, settle **a matter**, settle **a lawsuit/suit**, settle **things**
V.	**agree to** settle, **decide to** settle 1-4

settled /ˈsetəld/ 1 ADJ A **settled** situation or system stays the same all the time. ❑ *...a period of settled weather.* 2 ADJ AFTER LINK-V If you feel **settled**, you have been living or working in a place long enough to feel comfortable.

settlement /ˈsetəlmənt/ (**settlements**) 1 N-COUNT A **settlement** is an official agreement between two sides who were involved in a conflict. ❑ *...a peace settlement.* ❑ *...pay settlements.* 2 N-COUNT A **settlement** is a place where people have come to live and have built homes. ❑ *...the oldest settlement in New Brunswick.*

settler /ˈsetələ/ (**settlers**) N-COUNT **Settlers** are people who go to live in a new country. ❑ *...the early settlers in North America.*

S

ˌset-top ˈbox (**set-top boxes**) N-COUNT A **set-top box** is a piece of equipment that rests on top of your television and receives digital television signals.

ˈset-ˌup (**set-ups**) 1 N-COUNT A particular **set-up** is a particular system or way of organizing something. [INFORMAL] ❑ *He discussed how we could change our family set-up to improve our parenting.* 2 → see also **set up**

seven /ˈsevən/ (**sevens**) NUM **Seven** is the number 7.

Word Link *teen ≈ plus ten, from 13-19 : eighteen, seventeen, teenager*

seventeen /ˌsevənˈtiːn/ NUM **Seventeen** is the number 17.

seventeenth /ˌsevənˈtiːnθ/ ORD The **seventeenth** item in a series is the one that you count as number seventeen.

seventh /ˈsevənθ/ (**sevenths**) 1 ORD The **seventh** item in a series is the one that you count as number seven. 2 N-COUNT A **seventh** is one of seven equal parts of something.

seventieth /ˈsevəntiəθ/ ORD The **seventieth** item in a series is the one that you count as number seventy.

seventy /ˈsevənti/ (**seventies**) NUM **Seventy** is the number 70. For examples of how numbers such as seventy and eighty are used see **eighty**.

sever /ˈsevə/ (**severs, severing, severed**) 1 V-T To **sever** something means to cut right through it or cut it off. ❑ *He was hit by a car and his left arm was almost severed.* ❑ *...a severed fuel line.* 2 V-T If you **sever** a relationship or connection with someone, you end it suddenly and completely. ❑ *She severed her ties with England.*

several /ˈsevrəl/ QUANT **Several** is used to refer to a number of people or things that is not large but is greater than two. ❑ *Several hundred students gathered on campus.* ❑ *Several of my friends are doctors.*

severe /sɪˈvɪə/ (**severer, severest**) 1 ADJ You use **severe** to emphasize how bad or serious something is. ❑ *The bomb caused severe damage.* ❑ *...a severe shortage of drinking water.* ● **severely** ADV ❑ *He was severely injured in a fire.* ● **severity** /sɪverɪti/ N-UNCOUNT ❑ *Several methods are used to lessen the severity of the symptoms.* 2 ADJ **Severe** punishments or actions are very extreme. ❑ *He got a severe telling-off from his parents.* ● **severely** ADV ❑ *This campaign aims to change the law to punish dangerous drivers more severely.* ● **severity** N-UNCOUNT ❑ *Everyone was shocked by the severity of the sentence.*

Thesaurus *severe* Also look up:

ADJ.	critical, extreme, intense, tough 1 2

Word Partnership Use *severe* with:

N.	severe **consequences**, severe **depression**, severe **disease/illness**, severe **drought**, severe **flooding**, severe **injuries**, severe **pain**, severe **problem**, severe **symptoms**, severe **weather** 1
	severe **penalty**, severe **punishment** 2
ADV.	**less/more/most** severe, **very** severe 1 2

sew /səʊ/ (**sews, sewing, sewed, sewn**) V-T/V-I When you **sew**, you use a needle and thread to make or mend something such as clothes. ❑ *Anyone can sew on a button.* ❑ *She taught her daughter to sew.* ❑ *She mended socks and sewed clothes at night.* ● **sewing** N-UNCOUNT ❑ *I was very good at sewing.* → see **quilt**

sewage /ˈsuːɪdʒ/ N-UNCOUNT **Sewage** is waste matter such as faeces or dirty water from homes and factories, which flows away through sewers. → see **pollution**

sewer /ˈsuːə/ (**sewers**) N-COUNT A **sewer** is a large underground channel that carries waste matter and rainwater away.

sewing /ˈsəʊɪŋ/ 1 N-UNCOUNT **Sewing** is clothes or other things that are being sewn. ❑ *She took out her sewing.* 2 → see also **sew**

sewn /səʊn/ **Sewn** is the past participle of **sew**.

sex /seks/ (**sexes, sexing, sexed**) 1 N-COUNT The **sexes** are the two groups, male and female, into which people and animals are divided. 2 N-COUNT The **sex** of a person or animal is their characteristic of being either male or female. ❑ *We don't want to know the sex of our baby before its birth.* ❑ *...victims of sex discrimination.* 3 N-UNCOUNT **Sex** is the physical activity by which people can produce children. If two people **have sex**, they perform the physical act of sex.
▶ **sex up** PHR-VERB To **sex** something **up** means to make it more interesting and exciting. [INFORMAL] ❑ *They wanted to modernise the programme, sex it up.*

sexist /ˈseksɪst/ (**sexists**) ADJ & N-COUNT If you describe someone as **sexist** or as a **sexist**, you mean that they show prejudice and discrimination against the members of one sex, usually women. ❑ *Old-fashioned sexist attitudes are still common.* ● **sexism** N-UNCOUNT ❑ *...their battle against sexism.*

sexual /ˈsekʃʊəl/ 1 ADJ **Sexual** feelings or activities are connected with the act of sex or with desire for sex. ❑ *This was the first sexual relationship I had.* ● **sexually** ADV ❑ *...sexually transmitted diseases.* 2 ADJ **Sexual** means relating to the differences between men and women. ❑ *...sexual discrimination.* 3 ADJ **Sexual** means relating to the biological process by which people and animals produce young. ❑ *...sexual maturity.* ● **sexually** ADV ❑ *...organisms which reproduce sexually.*

ˌsexual ˈintercourse N-UNCOUNT **Sexual intercourse** is the physical act of sex between two people. [FORMAL]

sexuality /ˌsekʃʊˈælɪti/ 1 N-UNCOUNT A person's **sexuality** is their sexual feelings. ❑ *...a discussion of women's sexuality.* 2 N-UNCOUNT You can refer to a person's **sexuality** when you are talking about whether they are heterosexual, homosexual, or bisexual.

sexy /ˈseksi/ (**sexier, sexiest**) ADJ You can describe people and things as **sexy** if you think they are sexually exciting or sexually attractive.

sh /ʃ/ CONVENTION You can say **'Sh!'** to tell someone to be quiet. ❑ *Sh! I have only a moment to talk, and you must listen carefully!*

shabby /ˈʃæbi/ (**shabbier, shabbiest**) 1 ADJ **Shabby** things or places look old and in bad condition. 2 ADJ A **shabby** person is wearing old, worn clothes.

shack /ʃæk/ (**shacks**) N-COUNT A **shack** is a small hut built from bits of wood or metal.

shade /ʃeɪd/ (**shades, shading, shaded**) 1 N-UNCOUNT **Shade** is a cool area of darkness where the sun does not reach. ❑ *These plants need some shade, humidity and fresh air.* 2 V-T If a place **is shaded** by something, that thing prevents light from falling on it. ❑ *Most plants prefer to be lightly shaded from direct sunlight.* ❑ *...a shaded spot.* 3 N-UNCOUNT **Shade** is darkness or shadows as they are shown in a picture. ❑ *...Rembrandt's skilful use of light and shade.* 4 N-COUNT The **shades of** a particular colour are its different forms. ❑ *The flowers were a lovely shade of pink.* 5 N-COUNT The **shades of** something abstract are its many, slightly different forms. ❑ *...newspapers of every shade of opinion.* 6 N-COUNT A **shade** is a decorative covering that is fitted round or over an electric light bulb. 7 N-COUNT In American English, a **shade** is a piece of stiff cloth or heavy paper that you can pull down over a window in order to prevent sunlight from coming in. The British word is **blind**.

shadow /ˈʃædəʊ/ (**shadows, shadowing, shadowed**) 1 N-COUNT A **shadow** is a dark shape on a surface that is made when something stands between a light and the surface. ❑ *An oak tree cast its shadow over a tiny round pool.* 2 N-UNCOUNT **Shadow** is darkness caused by light not reaching a place. ❑ *Most of the lake was in shadow.* 3 V-T If someone **shadows** you, they follow you very closely wherever you go. ❑ *I noticed a police car shadowing us.* 4 ADJ BEFORE N In Britain, **the Shadow Cabinet** consists of the leaders of the main opposition party.

shadowy /ˈʃædəʊi/ 1 ADJ A **shadowy** place is dark and full of shadows. 2 ADJ **Shadowy** activities or people are mysterious and secretive. ❑ *...the shadowy world of spies.*

shady /ˈʃeɪdi/ (**shadier, shadiest**) 1 ADJ A **shady** place is pleasant because it is sheltered from bright sunlight. 2 ADJ **Shady** activities or people seem to be dishonest or illegal. ❑ *John was a bit of a shady character.*

shaft /ʃɑːft, ʃæft/ (**shafts**) 1 N-COUNT A **shaft** is a long narrow passage made so that people or things can travel up and down it. ❑ *...a disused mine shaft.* 2 N-COUNT A **shaft** in a machine is a rod that turns round and round to transfer movement in the machine. ❑ *...the drive shaft.* 3 N-COUNT A **shaft of** light is a beam of light.

shaggy /ˈʃægi/ (**shaggier, shaggiest**) ADJ **Shaggy** hair or fur is long and untidy. ❑ *...a dark shaggy beard.*

shake /ʃeɪk/ (**shakes, shaking, shook, shaken** /ʃeɪkən/) 1 V-T & N-COUNT If you **shake** someone or something, or if you give them a **shake**, you move them quickly backwards and forwards or up and down. ❑ *Shake the rugs well.* ❑ *As soon as he got inside, the dog shook himself.* ❑ *She gave me a little shake.* 2 V-T/V-I If something **shakes**, or if a force **shakes** it, it moves from side to side or up and down with quick small movements. ❑ *The explosion shook buildings several kilometres away.* 3 V-T If an event or a piece of news **shakes** you, it makes you feel shocked or upset. ❑ *Well it shook me quite a bit, but I was feeling very emotional.* 4 PHRASE If you **shake** someone **'s hand**, you hold their right hand in your own when you are meeting them, saying goodbye, congratulating them, or showing friendship. 5 PHRASE If you **shake** your **head**, you move it from side to side in order to say 'no'.
▶ **shake off** PHR-VERB If you **shake off** someone or something that you do not want, you manage to get away from them or get rid of them.

ˈshake-ˌup also **shakeup** (**shake-ups**) N-COUNT A **shake-up** is a major set of changes in an organization or system. ❑ *The RAC plans to set up its own law firm after a shake-up of the legal profession.*

shaky /ˈʃeɪki/ (**shakier, shakiest**) 1 ADJ If your body or your voice is **shaky**, you cannot control it properly and it trembles, for example because you are ill or nervous. ❑ *Even minor operations can leave you feeling a bit shaky.* ● **shakily** ADV ❑ *'I'm okay,' she said shakily.* 2 ADJ If you describe a situation as **shaky**, you mean that it is weak or unstable, and seems likely to end soon. ❑ *The Prime Minister's political position became increasingly shaky.*

shall /ʃəl, STRONG ʃæl/

Shall is a modal verb. It is used with the base form of a verb.

1 MODAL You use **shall** with 'I' and 'we' in questions in order to make offers or suggestions, or to ask for advice. ❑ *Shall I get the keys?* ❑ *Let's have a walk, shall we?* ❑ *What shall I do?* 2 MODAL You use **shall**, usually with 'I' and 'we', when you are referring to something that you intend to do, or when you are referring to something that you are sure will happen to you in the future. ❑ *We shall be landing in Paris in sixteen minutes.* ❑ *I shall miss him terribly.* 3 MODAL If you say that something **shall** happen, you are saying that it must happen, usually because of a rule or law. [FORMAL] ❑ *The president shall hold office for five years.*

shallow /ˈʃæləʊ/ (**shallower, shallowest**) 1 ADJ A **shallow** hole, container, or layer of water measures only a short distance from the top to the bottom. ❑ *The water is quite shallow.* 2 ADJ If you describe a person, piece of work, or idea as **shallow**, you disapprove of them because they lack any serious or careful thought. 3 ADJ If your breathing is **shallow**, you take only a small amount of air into your lungs at each breath.

shallows /ˈʃæləʊz/ N-PLURAL **The shallows** are the shallow part of an area of water.

sham /ʃæm/ (**shams**) N-COUNT If you describe something as a **sham**, you disapprove of it because it is not what it seems to be. ❑ *The government's promises were exposed as a hollow sham.*

shambles /ˈʃæmbəlz/ N-SING If a place, event, or situation is **a shambles**, everything is in disorder. ❑ *The sitting-room was a total shambles.*

shame /ʃeɪm/ (**shames, shaming, shamed**) 1 N-UNCOUNT **Shame** is an uncomfortable feeling that you have when you know that you have done something wrong or embarrassing, or when someone close to you has. ❑ *She felt a deep sense of shame.* ❑ *I was, to my shame, a coward.* 2 N-UNCOUNT If someone brings **shame on** you, they make other people lose their respect for you. ❑ *I don't want to bring shame on the family name.* 3 V-T If something **shames** you, it causes you to feel shame. ❑ *Her son's bad behaviour humiliated and shamed her.* 4 V-T If you **shame** someone **into** doing something, you force them to do it by making them feel ashamed not to. 5 N-SING If you say that something is **a shame**, you are expressing your regret about it and indicating that you wish it had happened differently. ❑ *What a shame the weather is so poor.* ❑ *It was a shame to waste this opportunity.*
→ see **emotion**

Word Partnership Use *shame* with:

N.	**feelings of** shame, **sense of** shame 1
V.	**experience** shame, **feel** shame 1

shameful /ˈʃeɪmfʊl/ ADJ You can describe someone's actions or attitude as **shameful** when they act or think in a way that you find unacceptable, and for which you think they should feel ashamed. ❑ *...the most shameful episode in US naval history.* • **shamefully** ADV ❑ *They have been shamefully treated.*

shameless /ˈʃeɪmləs/ ADJ If you describe someone or their behaviour as **shameless**, you mean that their behaviour is extremely bad and they ought to be ashamed of it. ❑ *...a shameless attempt to get votes under false pretences.* • **shamelessly** ADV ❑ *He admitted to lying to his family and manipulating them shamelessly.*

shampoo /ʃæmˈpuː/ (**shampoos, shampooing, shampooed**) 1 N-VAR **Shampoo** is a liquid that you use for washing your hair. 2 V-T When you **shampoo** your hair, you wash it using shampoo.

shan't /ʃɑːnt, ʃænt/ **Shan't** is the usual spoken form of 'shall not'.

shape /ʃeɪp/ (**shapes, shaping, shaped**) 1 N-VAR The **shape of** an object, a person, or an area is the form or pattern of its outline. ❑ *...a keyring in the shape of a fish.* ❑ *The room was square in shape.* 2 N-COUNT A **shape** is something which has a definite form, for example a circle or triangle. ❑ *...a diamond shape.* 3 V-T If you **shape** an object, you cause it to have a particular shape. ❑ *Cut the dough in half and shape each half into a loaf.* 4 N-SING The **shape of** something such as a plan or organization is its structure and size. ❑ *...the future shape of Western Europe.* 5 V-T To **shape** a situation or an activity means to strongly influence the way it develops. ❑ *Our families shape our lives and make us what we are.* 6 PHRASE If someone or something is **in** good **shape**, they are healthy and fit. If they are **out of shape**, they are unhealthy and unfit.
→ see Picture Dictionary: **shapes**
→ see **circle, mathematics**
▶ **shape up** PHR-VERB The way that someone or something **is shaping up** is the way that they are developing. ❑ *This is shaping up to be the closest election in recent history.*

Word Partnership Use *shape* with:

V.	**change** shape 1
	change the shape **of** *something* 4
	get in shape 6
ADJ.	**dark** shape 1
	(pretty) bad/good/great shape, **better/worse** shape, **physical** shape, **terrible** shape 6

shaped /ʃeɪpt/ ADJ AFTER LINK-V Something that is **shaped** in a particular way has the shape indicated. ❑ *...a bar of soap shaped like a lemon.* ❑ *...large, heart-shaped leaves.*

share /ʃeə/ (**shares, sharing, shared**) 1 V-T If you **share** something **with** another person, you both have it, use it, do it, or experience it. ❑ *The local tribe is friendly and they share their water supply with you.* ❑ *We share similar opinions about music.* ❑ *He shared a huge house with his sisters.* ❑ *Two Americans shared this year's Nobel Prize for Medicine.* ❑ *Yes, I want to share my life with you.* 2 N-COUNT If you have or do your **share of** something, you have or do the amount that is reasonable or fair. ❑ *Women often complain that men do not do their fair share of the housework.* 3 N-COUNT The **shares** of a company are the equal parts into which its ownership is divided. People can buy shares in a company as an investment.
▶ **share out** PHR-VERB If you **share** something **out**, you give each person in a group an equal or fair part of it. ❑ *The funding will be shared out between universities, hospitals and research bodies.*

shareholder /ˈʃeəhəʊldə/ (**shareholders**)

S

Picture Dictionary shapes

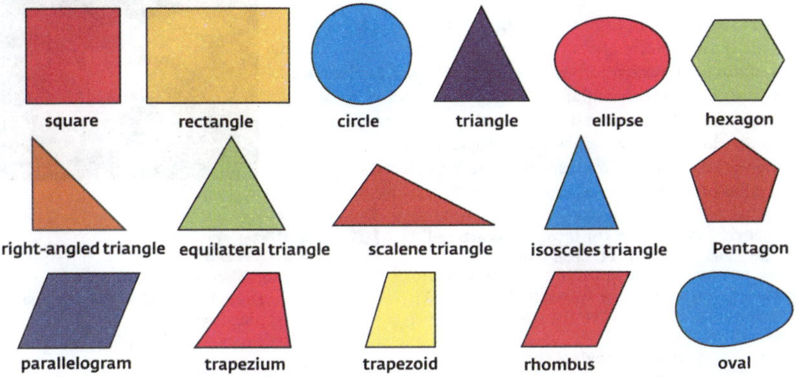

N-COUNT In British English, a **shareholder** is a person who owns shares in a company. The usual American word is **stockholder**.

shark

shark /ʃɑːk/ (**sharks**) N-COUNT **Sharks** are very large fish with sharp teeth.
→ see Word Web: **shark**

sharp /ʃɑːp/ (**sharper, sharpest**) **1** ADJ A **sharp** point or edge is very small or thin and can cut through things very easily. ❑ *One end of the stick was sharpened into a sharp point.* **2** ADJ & ADV A **sharp** bend or turn is one that changes direction suddenly. ❑ *The crash occurred on a sharp bend in the road.* ❑ *Do not cross the bridge but turn sharp left.* • **sharply** ADV ❑ *The canyon bent sharply to the north.* **3** ADJ If you describe someone as **sharp**, you are praising them because they are quick to notice or understand things or to react to them. ❑ *He is very sharp, a quick thinker.* • **sharpness** N-UNCOUNT ❑ *I liked their sharpness of mind.* **4** ADJ If someone says something in a **sharp** way, they say it suddenly and rather firmly or angrily. ❑ *His sharp reply clearly made an impact.* • **sharply** ADV ❑ *Environmentalists were sharply critical of the policy.* • **sharpness** N-UNCOUNT ❑ *Malone was surprised at the sharpness in his voice.* **5** ADJ A **sharp** change, movement, or feeling occurs suddenly, and is great in amount, force, or degree. ❑ *There's been a sharp rise in the rate of inflation.* ❑ *...a sharp pain.* • **sharply** ADV ❑ *Theft from farms has risen sharply this year.* **6** ADJ A **sharp** difference, image, or sound is very easy to see, hear, or distinguish. ❑ *All the footprints are quite sharp and clear.* • **sharply** ADV ❑ *Opinions on this are sharply divided.* • **sharpness** N-UNCOUNT ❑ *They were amazed at the sharpness of the photograph.* **7** ADJ A **sharp** taste or smell is rather strong or bitter, but is often also clear and fresh. • **sharpness** N-UNCOUNT ❑ *The onion added a sharpness to the dish.* **8** ADV **Sharp** is used after stating a particular time to show that something happens at exactly that time. ❑ *She opened the store at 8.00 sharp.* **9** ADJ **Sharp** is used after a letter representing a musical note to show that the note should be played or sung half a tone higher than the note which otherwise corresponds to that letter. **Sharp** is often represented by the symbol ♯.

sharp

Word Partnership Use *sharp* with:

ADV.	**very** sharp **1**-**8**
N.	sharp **edge**, sharp **point**, sharp **teeth** **1**
	sharp **eyes**, sharp **mind** **3**
	sharp **criticism** **4**
	sharp **decline**, sharp **increase**, sharp **pain** **5**
	sharp **contrast** **6**

sharpen /ˈʃɑːpən/ (**sharpens, sharpening, sharpened**) **1** V-T If you **sharpen** an object, you make its edge very thin or you make its end pointed. **2** V-T If something **sharpens** your skills, senses, or understanding, it makes you better at noticing things, thinking, or doing something. ❑ *You can sharpen your skills with rehearsal.*
▸ **sharpen up** PHR-VERB If you **sharpen** something **up**, or if it **sharpens up**, it becomes smarter or better than it was. [INFORMAL] ❑ *He made 15 suggestions to Mr Scarlett for sharpening up the text.*

shatter /ˈʃætə/ (**shatters, shattering, shattered**) **1** V-T/V-I If something **shatters**, or if someone or something **shatters** it, it breaks into a lot of small pieces. ❑ *The force of the explosion shattered the windows.* • **shattering** N-UNCOUNT ❑ *...the shattering of glass.* **2** V-T If something **shatters** your beliefs or hopes, it destroys them. **3** V-T If someone **is shattered** by an event, it shocks and upsets them. ❑ *The tragedy shattered his life.* • **shattering** ADJ ❑ *Yesterday's decision was a shattering blow.*
→ see **crash, glass**

S

Word Web shark

Sharks are different from other **fish**. The **skeleton** of a shark is made of **cartilage**, not bone. The flexibility of cartilage allows this **predator** to manoeuvre around its **prey** easily. Sharks also have several gill **slits** with no flap covering them. Its scales are also much smaller and harder than fish scales. And its teeth are special too. Sharks grow new teeth when they lose old ones. It's almost impossible to escape from a shark. Some of them can swim up to 44 miles per hour. But sharks only kill 50 to 75 people worldwide each year.

shattered /ˈʃætəd/ 1 ADJ If you are **shattered**, you are shocked and upset. ❑ *His death was so sudden. I am shattered.* 2 ADJ If you say that you are **shattered**, you mean you are extremely tired and have no energy left. [BRIT] ❑ *He was shattered and too tired to concentrate on schoolwork.*

shave /ʃeɪv/ (**shaves, shaving, shaved**) 1 V-T/V-I & N-COUNT To **shave**, or to have a **shave**, means to cut hair from your face or body using a razor or shaver. ❑ *Many women shave their legs.* ❑ *He shaved, showered, dressed and went downstairs.* ● **shaving** N-UNCOUNT ❑ *...a range of shaving products.* 2 V-T If you **shave off** part of a piece of wood or other material, you cut very thin pieces from it. ❑ *She was shaving off thin slices of courgette.*

shaver /ˈʃeɪvə/ (**shavers**) N-COUNT A **shaver** is an electric device used for shaving hair from the face and body.

shaving /ˈʃeɪvɪŋ/ (**shavings**) N-COUNT **Shavings** are small, very thin pieces or wood or other material which have been cut from a larger piece. ❑ *...metal shavings.*

shawl /ʃɔːl/ (**shawls**) N-COUNT A **shawl** is a large piece of woollen cloth worn over a woman's shoulders or head, or wrapped around a baby to keep it warm.
→ see **clothing**

she /ʃi, STRONG ʃiː/ PRON You use **she** to refer to a woman, girl, or female animal. **She** is used as the subject of a verb. ❑ *She was seventeen.*

shear /ʃɪə/ (**shears, shearing, sheared, shorn**)

The past participle can be **sheared** or **shorn**.

1 V-T To **shear** a sheep means to clip all its wool off. ● **shearing** N-UNCOUNT ❑ *...a display of sheep shearing.* 2 N-PLURAL A pair of **shears** is a garden tool like a large pair of scissors.

sheath /ʃiːθ/ (**sheaths**) N-COUNT A **sheath** is a covering for the blade of a knife.

shed /ʃed/ (**sheds, shedding, shed**) 1 N-COUNT A **shed** is a small building used for storing things such as garden tools. 2 V-T When a tree **sheds** its leaves, its leaves fall off, usually in the autumn. When an animal **sheds** hair or skin, some of its hair or skin drops off. 3 V-T To **shed** something means to get rid of it. [JOURNALISM] ❑ *The firm is to shed 700 jobs.* 4 V-T If you **shed** tears, you cry. ❑ *They will shed a few tears at their daughter's wedding.* 5 V-T To **shed** blood means to kill people in a violent way. ❑ *My family have fought in wars and shed blood for this country.* 6 to **shed light on** → see **light**
→ see **cry, garden**

Word Partnership Use *shed* with:

N. storage **shed** 1
shed ***your* clothes**, shed ***your* image**,
shed **pounds** 3
shed **a tear**, shed **tears** 4
shed **blood** 5

she'd /ʃiːd, ʃɪd/ **She'd** is the usual spoken form of 'she had', especially when 'had' is an auxiliary verb. **She'd** is also a spoken form of 'she would'. ❑ *She'd found a job.* ❑ *She'd do anything to help her family.*

sheen /ʃiːn/ N-SING If something has a **sheen**, it has a smooth and gentle brightness.

sheep /ʃiːp/

Sheep is both the singular and the plural form.

N-COUNT A **sheep** is a farm animal with a thick woolly coat.
→ see **meat**

sheepish /ˈʃiːpɪʃ/ ADJ If you look **sheepish**, you look slightly embarrassed because you feel foolish. ● **sheepishly** ADV ❑ *He grinned sheepishly.*

sheer /ʃɪə/ 1 ADJ BEFORE N You can use **sheer** to emphasize that a state or situation is complete and does not involve anything else. ❑ *...acts of sheer desperation.* 2 ADJ BEFORE N A **sheer** cliff or drop is extremely steep or completely vertical. 3 ADJ BEFORE N **Sheer** material is very thin, light, and delicate. ❑ *...sheer black tights.*

Word Partnership Use *sheer* with:

N. sheer **delight**, sheer **force**, sheer **luck**, sheer **number**, sheer **pleasure**, sheer **power**, sheer **size**, sheer **strength**, sheer **terror**, sheer **volume** 1

sheet /ʃiːt/ (**sheets**) 1 N-COUNT A **sheet** is a large rectangular piece of cloth that you sleep on or cover yourself with in a bed. ❑ *Once a week, my mother changes the sheets.* 2 N-COUNT A **sheet of** paper is a rectangular piece of paper. 3 N-COUNT A **sheet of** glass, metal, or wood is a large, flat, thin piece of it.
→ see **bed, glass, paper**

sheikh or **sheik** /ʃeɪk, AM ʃiːk/ (**sheikhs**) N-COUNT A **sheikh** is a male Arab chief or ruler.

shelf /ʃelf/ (**shelves**) N-COUNT A **shelf** is a flat piece of wood, metal, or glass which is attached to a wall or to the sides of a cupboard. ❑ *He took a book from the shelf.*
→ see **library**

shell /ʃel/ (**shells, shelling, shelled**) 1 N-VAR The **shell** of an egg or nut is the hard covering which surrounds it. The substance that a shell is made of is called **shell**. ❑ *An egg shell may be very thin but its shape gives it great strength.* 2 N-COUNT The **shell** of a tortoise, snail, or crab is the hard protective covering on its back. 3 N-COUNT **Shells** are the coverings which surround, or used to surround, small sea creatures. ❑ *The sand was pure white, scattered with sea shells.* 4 V-T If you **shell** nuts, peas, prawns, or other food, you remove their natural outer covering. 5 N-COUNT A **shell** is a weapon consisting of a metal container filled with explosives that can be fired from a large gun over long distances. 6 V-T To **shell** a place means to fire explosive shells at it. • **shelling** (**shellings**) N-VAR ❑ *Out on the streets, the shelling continued.*
▶ **shell out** PHR-VERB If you **shell out for** something, you spend a lot of money on it. [INFORMAL] ❑ *We didn't even have to shell out for taxis because we had our own driver.*

she'll /ʃiːl, ʃɪl/ **She'll** is the usual spoken form of 'she will'.

shellfish /ˈʃelfɪʃ/

Shellfish is both the singular and the plural form.

N-COUNT A **shellfish** is a small creature with a shell that lives in the sea.
→ see Picture Dictionary: **shellfish**

shelter /ˈʃeltə/ (**shelters, sheltering, sheltered**) 1 N-COUNT A **shelter** is a small building or covered place which is made to protect people from bad weather or danger. 2 N-UNCOUNT If a place provides **shelter**, it provides protection from bad weather or danger. ❑ *The number of families seeking shelter rose by 17 percent.* 3 V-I If you **shelter** in a place, you stay there and are protected from bad weather or danger. ❑ *…a man sheltering in a doorway.* 4 V-T If a place or thing **is sheltered** by something, it is protected by it from wind and rain. 5 V-T If a person **shelters** someone, usually someone who is being hunted by police or other people, they provide them with a place to stay or live. ❑ *A neighbour sheltered the boy for seven days.*
→ see **habitat**

Word Partnership Use *shelter* with:

N.	**bomb** shelter 1 shelter **and clothing**, **emergency** shelter, **food and** shelter, **homeless** shelter 2
ADJ.	**temporary** shelter 1 2
V.	**find** shelter, **provide** shelter, **seek** shelter 2

sheltered /ˈʃeltəd/ 1 ADJ A **sheltered** place is protected from wind and rain. ❑ *…a sandy beach next to a sheltered bay.* 2 ADJ If you say someone has had a **sheltered life**, you mean that they have not experienced things that most people of their age have experienced, and that as a result they are rather naive.

shelve /ʃelv/ (**shelves, shelving, shelved**) 1 V-T If someone **shelves** a plan, they decide not to continue with it at that time. ❑ *The project has now been shelved.* 2 **Shelves** is the plural of **shelf**.

shepherd /ˈʃepəd/ (**shepherds, shepherding, shepherded**) 1 N-COUNT A **shepherd** is a person whose job is to look after sheep. 2 V-T If you **are shepherded** somewhere, someone takes you there to make sure you arrive at the right place safely. ❑ *The tourists were then shepherded on to buses.*

sheriff /ˈʃerɪf/ (**sheriffs**) N-COUNT & N-TITLE In the United States, a **sheriff** is a person who is elected to make sure that the law is obeyed in a particular county.

sherry /ˈʃeri/ (**sherries**) N-VAR **Sherry** is a type of strong wine that is made in south-western Spain.

she's /ʃiːz, ʃɪz/ **She's** is the usual spoken form of 'she is' or 'she has', especially when 'has' is an auxiliary verb. ❑ *She's going to have a baby.* ❑ *She's been married for seven years.*

shield /ʃiːld/ (**shields, shielding, shielded**) 1 V-T If something or someone **shields** you **from** a danger or risk, they protect you from it. ❑ *He shielded his head from the sun with a newspaper.* 2 N-COUNT A **shield** is a large piece of metal or leather which soldiers used to carry to protect their bodies while they were fighting.
→ see **army**

Picture Dictionary shellfish

S

shift /ʃɪft/ (**shifts, shifting, shifted**) 1 V-T/V-I If you **shift** something, or if it **shifts**, it moves slightly. ❑ *He shifted from foot to foot.* 2 V-I & N-COUNT If someone's opinion, a situation, or a policy **shifts**, it changes slightly. You call a change like this a **shift**. ❑ *Public opinion on this issue has shifted over time.* 3 N-COUNT A **shift** is a set period of work in a place like a factory or hospital. ❑ *His father worked shifts in a steel mill.* ❑ *...the afternoon shift.*

Word Partnership Use *shift* with:

N. shift *your* **weight** 1
shift *your* **position** 1 2
shift *your* **attention**, shift **in focus**, **policy** shift, shift **in/of power**, shift **in priorities** 2
shift **change**, **night** shift 3

ADJ. **dramatic** shift, **major** shift, **significant** shift 2

shimmer /ˈʃɪmə/ (**shimmers, shimmering, shimmered**) V-I & N-COUNT If something **shimmers**, it shines with a faint unsteady light called a **shimmer**. ❑ *The lights shimmered on the water.*

shin /ʃɪn/ (**shins**) N-COUNT Your **shin** is the front part of your leg between your knee and ankle.

shine /ʃaɪn/ (**shines, shining, shined, shone**)

The past tense and past participle of the verb is **shone**, except for meaning 4 when it is **shined**.

1 V-I When the sun or a light **shines**, it gives out bright light. 2 V-T If you **shine** a torch or lamp somewhere, you point its light there. ❑ *One of the men shone a torch in her face.* 3 V-I & N-SING Something that **shines**, or that has a **shine**, is very bright because it is reflecting light. ❑ *This gel gives a beautiful shine to the hair.* 4 V-I Someone who **shines** at a skill or activity does it very well. ❑ *He failed to shine academically.*
→ see **light bulb**

Thesaurus *shine* Also look up:

V. glare, gleam, illuminate, shimmer 1 2
N. light, radiance, sheen 3

S

shingle /ˈʃɪŋgəl/ N-UNCOUNT **Shingle** is a mass of small stones on the shore of a sea or river.

shining /ˈʃaɪnɪŋ/ ADJ A **shining** achievement or quality is a very good one which should be admired. ❑ *She is a shining example to us all.*

shiny /ˈʃaɪni/ (**shinier, shiniest**) ADJ **Shiny** things are bright and reflect light. ❑ *...a shiny new sports car.*
→ see **metal**

ship /ʃɪp/ (**ships, shipping, shipped**) 1 N-COUNT A **ship** is a large boat which carries passengers or cargo. ❑ *He went by ship to England.* 2 V-T If people or things **are shipped** somewhere, they are sent there by ship. ● **shipment** N-UNCOUNT ❑ *The furniture was ready for shipment.*
→ see Word Web: **ship**

Word Partnership Use *ship* with:

N. **bow of a** ship, **captain of a** ship, **cargo** ship, ship's **crew** 1

V. **board a** ship, **build a** ship, ship **docks**, **jump** ship, **sink a** ship 1

shipment /ˈʃɪpmənt/ (**shipments**) N-COUNT A **shipment** is an amount of a particular kind of cargo that is sent to another country on a ship.

shipping /ˈʃɪpɪŋ/ N-UNCOUNT **Shipping** is the transport of cargo as a business, especially on ships.

shipwreck /ˈʃɪprek/ (**shipwrecks, shipwrecked**) 1 N-VAR When there is a **shipwreck**, a ship is destroyed in an accident at sea. ❑ *...the dangers of storm and shipwreck.* 2 N-COUNT A **shipwreck** is a ship which has been destroyed in an accident at sea. 3 V-T PASSIVE If someone **is shipwrecked**, their ship is destroyed in an accident at sea but they survive and reach land.

shipyard /ˈʃɪpjɑːd/ (**shipyards**) N-COUNT A **shipyard** is a place where ships are built and repaired.

shirt /ʃɜːt/ (**shirts**) N-COUNT A **shirt** is a piece of clothing worn on the upper part of your body with a collar, sleeves, and buttons down the front.
→ see **clothing**

shiver /ˈʃɪvə/ (**shivers, shivering, shivered**) V-I & N-COUNT When you **shiver**, or when you feel a **shiver**, your body shakes slightly because you are cold or frightened. ❑ *Her scream sent shivers down my spine.*

Word Web ship

Large **ocean-going vessels** are an important way of carrying people and **cargo**. **Oil tankers** and **container ships** are common in many **ports**. **Ocean liners** carry tourists and give them a place to stay. Some of these **ships** are several stories tall. The **captain** steers a **cruise ship** from the **bridge**, while passengers enjoy themselves on the promenade **deck**. Huge **warships** carry thousands of soldiers to battlefields around the world. **Aircraft carriers** have a **flight deck** where planes can take off and land. **Ferries**, **barges**, fishing **craft**, and research **boats** are also an important part of the **marine** industry.

Word Partnership Use *shiver* with:

V. **feel a** shiver, shiver **goes/runs down** ***your*** spine, ***something*** **makes** ***you*** shiver, ***something*** **sends a** shiver **down** ***your*** **spine**

shoal /ʃəʊl/ (**shoals**) N-COUNT A **shoal of** fish is a large group of them swimming together.

shock /ʃɒk/ (**shocks, shocking, shocked**) **1** N-COUNT If you have a **shock**, you suddenly have an unpleasant or surprising experience. ❑ *It took me a very long time to get over the shock of her death.* **2** N-UNCOUNT **Shock** is a person's emotional and physical condition when something frightening or upsetting has happened to them. ❑ *She's still in a state of shock.* **3** N-UNCOUNT If someone is **in shock**, they are suffering from a serious physical condition in which their blood cannot circulate properly, for example because they have had a bad injury. **4** V-T If something **shocks** you, it makes you feel very upset. ❑ *Her behaviour at her husband's funeral shocked her friends.* ● **shocked** ADJ ❑ *This was a nasty attack and the victim is still very shocked.* **5** V-T If someone or something **shocks** you, it upsets or offends you because you think it is rude or morally wrong. ❑ *Pictures of the starving prisoners shocked the world.* ● **shocked** ADJ ❑ *I am very sad and very shocked by this terrible crime.* **6** N-VAR A **shock** is a slight movement in something when it is hit by something else. ❑ *A clump of trees absorbed the shock of the explosion.* **7** N-COUNT If you get a **shock** or an **electric shock**, you get a sudden painful feeling when you touch something which is connected to a supply of electricity.

Word Partnership Use *shock* with:

V. **come as a** shock **1**
send a shock **1** **7**
express shock, **feel** shock **2**
N. **in a state of** shock, shock **value** **2**

shocking /ˈʃɒkɪŋ/ ADJ You can say that something is **shocking** if you think that it is very bad. [INFORMAL] ● **shockingly** ADV ❑ *His memory was becoming shockingly bad.*

ˈshock ˌwave (**shock waves**) **1** N-COUNT A **shock wave** is an area of intense pressure moving through the air caused by an explosion or an earthquake, or by an object travelling faster than the speed of sound. **2** N-COUNT If the effect of something unpleasant or surprising sends **shock waves** through a place, more and more people are offended, shocked, or surprised as they find out about it. ❑ *The crime sent shock waves throughout the country.*
→ see **sound**

shod /ʃɒd/ **1** ADJ You can use **shod** when you are describing the kind of shoes that a person is wearing. [FORMAL] ❑ *Mr Forth rested his expensively-shod feet on the table.* **2** **Shod** is the past tense and past participle of **shoe**.

shoddy /ˈʃɒdi/ ADJ If you describe a product or someone's work as **shoddy**, you think that it has been made or done carelessly or badly. ● **shoddily** ADV ❑ *...shoddily-built cars.*

shoe /ʃuː/ (**shoes, shoeing, shod**) **1** N-COUNT **Shoes** are objects worn on your feet. Shoes cover most of your foot but not your ankle. ❑ *I need a new pair of shoes.* **2** PHRASE If you talk about being **in** someone's **shoes**, you talk about what you would do or how you would feel if you were in their situation. ❑ *I wouldn't want to be in his shoes.* **3** V-T To **shoe** a horse means to fix horseshoes onto its hooves.
→ see Picture Dictionary: **shoe**
→ see **clothing**

shone /ʃɒn, AM ʃəʊn/ **Shone** is the past tense and past participle of **shine**.

shook /ʃʊk/ **Shook** is the past tense of **shake**.

shoot /ʃuːt/ (**shoots, shooting, shot**) **1** V-T To **shoot** a person or animal means to kill or injure them by firing a gun at them. ❑ *The gamekeepers here shoot 100 foxes a year.* ● **shooting** (**shootings**) N-COUNT ❑ *Two people were found injured after the shooting.* **2** V-I To **shoot** means to fire a bullet from a weapon such as a gun. ❑ *They started shooting at us.* **3** V-I If someone or something **shoots** in a particular direction, they move in that direction quickly and suddenly. ❑ *A van*

Picture Dictionary shoe

S

shot out of a junction and crashed into the back of their car. **4** V-T & N-COUNT When people **shoot** a film or **shoot** photographs, they make a film or take photographs using a camera. A **shoot** is an instance of shooting a film or photograph. ❑ *The castle is being used for a video shoot.* **5** V-I In sports such as football or basketball, when someone **shoots**, they try to score by kicking, throwing, or hitting the ball towards the goal. **6** N-COUNT **Shoots** are plants that are beginning to grow, or new parts growing from a plant or tree. **7** → see also **shot**

▶ **shoot down** **1** PHR-VERB If someone **shoots down** an aeroplane or helicopter, they make it fall to the ground by hitting it with a bullet or missile. **2** PHR-VERB If you **shoot** someone **down** or **shoot down** their ideas, you ridicule that person or their ideas.

▶ **shoot up** PHR-VERB If something **shoots up**, it grows or increases very quickly. ❑ *Sales shot up by 9%.*

shop /ʃɒp/ (**shops, shopping, shopped**) **1** N-COUNT In British English, a **shop** is a building or part of a building where things are sold. The usual American word is **store**. ❑ *She runs her own antiques shop.* **2** V-I When you **shop**, you go to shops and buy things. ❑ *He always shops at the local supermarket.* ● **shopper** (**shoppers**) N-COUNT ❑ *...crowds of Christmas shoppers.* **3** → see also **shopping, coffee shop**

▶ **shop around** PHR-VERB If you **shop around**, you go to different shops or companies and compare prices and quality before buying something.

Usage

When you want to refer to a particular type of shop, you can often simply use the word for the person who owns or manages the shop. ❑ *Down the road there is another greengrocer.* ❑ *Bring me back a paper from the newsagent.* Alternatively, you can use the possessive form with **'s**, without a following noun. ❑ *Fruit can be purchased at the greengrocer's.* ❑ *She works at a local newsagent's.* You can also use the same pattern with other words that refer to a person or business that provides a service, such as **hairdresser** or **dentist**. ❑ *She goes to the hairdresser every six weeks or so.* ❑ *I don't like going to the dentist's.*

S

Word Partnership Use *shop* with:

N. **antique** shop, **barber** shop, **beauty** shop, shop **owner**, **pet** shop, **repair** shop, **souvenir** shop **1**

'shop ˌassistant (**shop assistants**) N-COUNT In British English, a **shop assistant** is a person who works in a shop selling things to customers. The usual American word is **sales clerk**.

ˌshop 'floor N-SING **The shop floor** refers to all the workers in a factory or the area where they work, especially in contrast to the management. ❑ *A sign at the entrance to the shop floor says 'Employees only'.*

shopkeeper /'ʃɒpki:pə/ (**shopkeepers**) N-COUNT A **shopkeeper** is a person who owns a small shop. [BRIT]

shoplift /'ʃɒplɪft/ (**shoplifts, shoplifting, shoplifted**) V-I If someone **shoplifts**, they steal goods from a shop during the time that the shop is open. ● **shoplifter** (**shoplifters**) N-COUNT ❑ *The police arrested the shoplifters.* ● **shoplifting** N-UNCOUNT ❑ *The grocer accused her of shoplifting.* → see **crime**

shopping /'ʃɒpɪŋ/ **1** N-UNCOUNT When you **do the shopping**, you go to shops and buy things. **2** N-UNCOUNT Your **shopping** consists of things that you have just bought from shops, especially food.

Word Partnership Use *shopping* with:

N. shopping **bag, Christmas** shopping, shopping **district, food** shopping, **grocery** shopping, **holiday** shopping, **online** shopping, shopping **spree** **1**

'shopping ˌcentre [AM **shopping center**] (**shopping centres**) N-COUNT A **shopping centre** is an area in a town where a lot of shops have been built close together.

'shopping ˌmall (**shopping malls**) N-COUNT A **shopping mall** is a covered area where many shops have been built and where cars are not allowed.

shore /ʃɔ:/ (**shores, shoring, shored**) N-COUNT & PHRASE The **shore** of a sea, lake, or wide river is the land along the edge of it. Someone who is **on shore** is on the land rather than on a ship.

▶ **shore up** PHR-VERB If you **shore up** something which is becoming weak, you do something in order to strengthen it. ❑ *These factors all helped to shore up the UK economy.*

shoreline /'ʃɔ:laɪn/ (**shorelines**) N-COUNT The **shoreline** is the edge of a sea, lake, or wide river.

shorn /ʃɔ:n/ **1** ADJ If hair is **shorn**, it has been cut very short. [LITERARY] **2** **Shorn** is the past participle of **shear**.

short

❶ ADJECTIVE AND ADVERB USES
❷ NOUN USES

short /ʃɔ:t/ (**shorter, shortest**) ❶ **1** ADJ If something is **short** or lasts for a **short** time, it is not very long or does not last very long. ❑ *The announcement was made a short time ago.* ❑ *I recently returned from a short break in Nice.* **2** ADV If something is cut **short** or stops **short**, it is stopped before people expect it to or before it has finished. ❑ *Jackson cut short his trip to Africa.* **3** ADJ Someone who is **short** is not as tall as most people are. **4** ADJ Something that is **short** measures only a small amount from one end to the other. ❑ *The city centre and shops are only a short distance away.* **5** ADJ AFTER LINK-V If a name or abbreviation is **short for** another name, it is the short version of that name. ❑ *My name's Kes - it's short for Kesewa.* **6** ADJ AFTER LINK-V If you are **short of** something or if it is **short**, you do not have enough of it. ❑ *Her father's illness left the family short of money.* **7** ADJ If you have a **short** temper, you get angry easily. **8** PHRASE If something is **short of** a place or amount, it has not quite reached it. ❑ *They were still $91 short of their target.* **9** PHRASE If someone **stops short of** doing something, they nearly do it but do not actually do it. ❑ *He stopped short of explicitly criticizing the government.* **10** PHRASE You use the expression **in short** when you have been giving a lot of details

and you want to give a conclusion or summary. ❑ *Try tennis, badminton or windsurfing. In short, anything challenging.*
→ see **hair**

short /ʃɔːt/ (**shorts**)
❷ 1 N-PLURAL **Shorts** are trousers with short legs. ❑ *I decided to put on a pair of shorts.* 2 N-PLURAL **Shorts** are men's underpants with short legs. 3 N-COUNT A **short** is a small, strong alcoholic drink of a spirit such as whisky or gin. [BRIT]

Thesaurus	*short* Also look up:
ADJ.	brief, quick; *(ant.)* long ① 1
	petite, slight, small; *(ant.)* tall ① 3

shortage /ˈʃɔːtɪdʒ/ (**shortages**) N-VAR If there is a **shortage of** something, there is not enough of it. ❑ *...a shortage of funds.* ❑ *Their country is suffering from food shortages.*

shortcoming /ˈʃɔːtkʌmɪŋ/ (**shortcomings**) N-COUNT The **shortcomings** of a person or thing are their faults or weaknesses. ❑ *I am aware of my own shortcomings.*

ˌshort ˈcut (**short cuts**) 1 N-COUNT A **short cut** is a quicker route than the one that you usually take. ❑ *I tried to take a short cut and got lost.* 2 N-COUNT A **short cut** is a method of achieving something more quickly or more easily than if you use the usual methods. ❑ *There is no shortcut to losing weight.*

shorten /ˈʃɔːtən/ (**shortens, shortening, shortened**) 1 V-T/V-I If you **shorten** an event or the length of time that something lasts, or if it **shortens**, it does not last as long as it would otherwise do or as it used to do. ❑ *Smoking can shorten your life.* ❑ *The days shorten in winter.* 2 V-T/V-I If you **shorten** an object, or if it **shortens**, it becomes smaller in length. ❑ *She's having an operation to shorten her nose.*

shortfall /ˈʃɔːtfɔːl/ (**shortfalls**) N-COUNT If there is a **shortfall** in something, there is not enough of it. ❑ *The government refused to make up a £30,000 shortfall in funding.*

shorthand /ˈʃɔːthænd/ N-UNCOUNT **Shorthand** is a quick way of writing which uses signs to represent words or syllables.

shortlist /ˈʃɔːtlɪst/ (**shortlists, shortlisting, shortlisted**) 1 N-COUNT A **shortlist** is a list of people or things which have been chosen from a larger group, for example for a job or a prize. The successful person or thing is then chosen from the small group. [BRIT] ❑ *These six books are on the shortlist for the Booker Prize.* 2 V-T If someone or something **is shortlisted**, they are put on a shortlist. [BRIT]

ˌshort-ˈlived ADJ Something that is **short-lived** does not last very long. ❑ *Our excitement was short-lived.*

shortly /ˈʃɔːtli/ 1 ADV If something happens **shortly** after or before something else, it happens a short amount of time after or before it. ❑ *The telephone call came shortly before dinnertime.* 2 ADV If something is going to happen **shortly**, it is going to happen soon. ❑ *Their trial will begin shortly.*

ˌshort-ˈsighted 1 ADJ In British English, if you are **short-sighted**, you cannot see things properly when they are far away, because there is something wrong with your eyes. The American term is **near-sighted.** 2 ADJ If you say that someone's actions or decisions are **short-sighted**, you mean they fail to take account of things that will probably happen in the future. ❑ *This is a short-sighted approach to the problem of global warming.*

ˈshort-ˌterm ADJ **Short-term** is used to describe things that will last for a short time, or things that will have an effect soon rather than in the distant future. ❑ *They have a short-term vacancy for a secretary.* ❑ *We all need to keep some of our savings in cash for short-term needs.*

shot /ʃɒt/ (**shots**) 1 **Shot** is the past tense and past participle of **shoot.** 2 N-COUNT If you **fire a shot**, you fire a gun once. ❑ *My first two shots missed the target.* 3 N-COUNT Someone who is a **good shot** can shoot well. Someone who is a **bad shot** cannot shoot well. 4 N-COUNT In sport, a **shot** is the act of kicking or hitting a ball, especially in an attempt to score. ❑ *He had only one shot at goal.* 5 N-COUNT A **shot** is a photograph or a particular sequence of pictures in a film. ❑ *A video crew was taking shots of the street.* 6 N-COUNT If you **have a shot at** something, or if you **give it a shot**, you attempt to do it. [INFORMAL] 7 N-COUNT A **shot of** a drug is an injection of it. ❑ *The doctor gave me a shot of painkiller.* 8 PHRASE If you **give** something your **best shot**, you do it as well as you possibly can. [INFORMAL] 9 PHRASE The person who **calls the shots** is in a position to tell others what to do. ❑ *There is no mistaking who calls the shots.* 10 PHRASE If you describe something as a **long shot**, you mean that it is unlikely to succeed, but is worth trying. ❑ *The deal was a long shot, but Bagley had little to lose.* 11 **a shot in the arm** → see **arm**
→ see **photography**

Word Partnership	Use *shot* with:
V.	**fire a** shot, **hear a** shot 2
	miss a shot, **take a** shot 2 4
	block a shot, **hit a** shot 4
	get a shot, **give *someone* a** shot 7
ADJ.	**single** shot, **warning** shot 2
	good shot 2 3
	winning shot 4

shotgun /ˈʃɒtgʌn/ (**shotguns**) N-COUNT A **shotgun** is a gun which fires a lot of small metal balls at one time.

should /ʃəd, STRONG ʃʊd/

Should is a modal verb. It is used with the base form of a verb.

1 MODAL You use **should** when you are giving advice or recommendations or when you are mentioning things that are not the case but that you think ought to be. ❑ *I should exercise more.* ❑ *Should our children be taught to swim at school?* 2 MODAL You use **should** to tell someone what to do or to report a rule or law which tells someone what to do. ❑ *A judge has ruled that the two men should stand trial.* 3 MODAL You use **should** in questions when you are asking someone for advice, permission, or information. ❑ *Should I or shouldn't I go to university?* 4 MODAL If you say that something **should have** happened, you mean that it did not happen, but that you wish it had happened or that you expected it to happen. ❑ *I should have studied this morning but I was feeling a bit*

S

ill. ❑ *I shouldn't have said what I did.* 5 MODAL You use **should** when you are saying that something is probably the case or will probably happen in the way you are describing. If you say that something **should have** happened by a particular time, you mean that it will probably have happened by that time. ❑ *You should have no problem passing the exam.* ❑ *We should have finished by a quarter past two.* 6 MODAL You use **should** in 'that' clauses after some verbs and adjectives when you are talking about a future event or situation. ❑ *He stood up and indicated that I should do the same.* 7 MODAL You use **should** in expressions such as **I should imagine** to indicate that you think something is true but you are not sure. ❑ *I should think it's going to rain soon.*

shoulder /ˈʃəʊldə/ (**shoulders, shouldering, shouldered**) 1 N-COUNT Your **shoulders** are the parts of your body between your neck and the tops of your arms. ❑ *He glanced over his shoulder.* 2 V-T If you **shoulder** something heavy, you put it across one of your shoulders so that you can carry it more easily. ❑ *He shouldered his bike and walked across the finish line.* 3 N-PLURAL When you talk about someone's problems or responsibilities, you can say that they carry them **on** their **shoulders**. ❑ *He has a huge burden on his shoulders.* 4 V-T If you **shoulder** the responsibility or blame for something, you accept it. ❑ *He shouldered the responsibility for his father's mistakes.* 5 PHRASE If you **rub shoulders with** famous people, you meet them and talk to them. 6 **a chip on** someone's **shoulder** → see **chip**
→ see **body, horse**

Word Partnership	Use *shoulder* with:
ADJ.	**bare** shoulder, **broken** shoulder, **dislocated** shoulder, **left/right** shoulder 1
N.	**head on** ***someone's*** shoulder 1 shoulder **a burden** 3
V.	**look over** ***your*** shoulder, **tap** ***someone*** **on the** shoulder 1

shouldn't /ˈʃʊdənt/ **Shouldn't** is the usual spoken form of 'should not'.

should've /ʃʊdəv/ **Should've** is the usual spoken form of 'should have', especially when 'have' is an auxiliary verb.

S

shout /ʃaʊt/ (**shouts, shouting, shouted**) 1 V-I/V-T & PHR-VERB If you **shout**, or **shout** something **out**, you say it very loudly. ❑ *'She's alive!' he shouted triumphantly.* ❑ *Andrew rushed out of the house, shouting for help.* ❑ *Suddenly I heard a voice shout out my name.* ● **shouting** N-UNCOUNT ❑ *My children heard the shouting first.* 2 N-COUNT A **shout** is the noise made when someone speaks very loudly. ❑ *I heard a distant shout.*

▸ **shout down** PHR-VERB If people **shout down** someone who is trying to speak, they prevent them from being heard by shouting at them. ❑ *Some people at the meeting weren't allowed to speak because they were shouted down.*

▸ **shout out** → see **shout** (meaning 1)

shove /ʃʌv/ (**shoves, shoving, shoved**) V-T & N-COUNT If you **shove** someone or something, or if you **give** them a **shove**, you give them a hard push. ❑ *He shoved her out of the way.* ❑ *She gave Gracie a shove towards the house.*

shovel /ˈʃʌvəl/ (**shovels, shovelling, shovelled** or [AM] **shoveling, shoveled**) 1 N-COUNT A **shovel** is a tool like a spade, used for lifting and moving earth, coal, or snow. 2 V-T If you **shovel** earth, coal, or snow, you lift and move it with a shovel. 3 V-T If you **shovel** something somewhere, you push a lot of it there quickly. ❑ *Randall shovelled food into his mouth.*
→ see **garden, hose**

show /ʃəʊ/ (**shows, showing, showed, shown**) 1 V-T If something **shows that** a state of affairs exists, it gives information that proves it or makes it clear to people. ❑ *Research shows that women do upwards of 70% of housework.* ❑ *These numbers show an increase of over one million in unemployment.* ❑ *The blood tests will show whether you have been infected.* 2 V-T If a picture, chart, film, or piece of writing **shows** something, it represents it or gives information about it. ❑ *The film shows a boy's struggle to fulfil his dreams to become a ballet dancer.* 3 V-T If you **show** someone something, you give it to them, take them to it, or point to it, so that they can see it or know what you are referring to. ❑ *Sophie showed me the letter from her brother.* ❑ *I showed them where the money was.* 4 V-T If you **show** someone **to** a room or seat, you lead them to it. ❑ *Your office is ready for you. I'll show you the way.* 5 V-T If you **show** someone **how** to do something, you do it yourself so that they can watch and learn how to do it. ❑ *Claire showed the children how to make a chocolate cake.* ❑ *He has shown us a new way to look at these problems.* 6 V-T/V-I If something **shows**, or if you **show** it, it is visible or noticeable. ❑ *There was a light showing beneath the curtain.* ❑ *Ferguson was unhappy and it showed.* ❑ *When he smiled, he showed a row of strong white teeth.* 7 V-T If something **shows** a quality or characteristic, or if that quality or characteristic **shows itself**, the quality or characteristic can be noticed or observed. ❑ *The peace talks showed signs of progress.* 8 N-COUNT A **show of** a feeling or quality is an attempt by someone to make it clear that they have that feeling or quality. ❑ *Workers gathered in the city centre in a show of support for the government.* 9 PHRASE If you **have** something **to show for** your efforts, you have achieved something as a result of what you have done. ❑ *He has had several job interviews but has nothing to show for them.* 10 N-COUNT A television or radio **show** is a programme on television or radio. 11 N-COUNT A **show** in a theatre is an entertainment or concert, especially one that includes different items such as music, dancing, and comedy. 12 V-T When a film or television programme **is shown**, it appears in a cinema or is broadcast on television. ❑ *This website offers a round-up of which films are showing.* 13 N-COUNT A **show** is a public exhibition. ❑ *...the Chelsea Flower Show.* 14 PHRASE If you say that something is **for show**, you mean that it has no real purpose and is done just to give a good impression. ❑ *With him, it was all an act. It was just for show.* 15 PHRASE If something is **on show**, it has been put in a place where it can be seen by the public. ❑ *...the most valuable item on show.*
→ see **concert, laser**

▸ **show around** PHR-VERB If you **show** someone **around** a place, you go round it with them, pointing out its interesting features. ❑ *She showed him around the flat.*

▸ **show off** 1 PHR-VERB If you say that someone

is showing off, you are criticizing them for trying to impress people by showing in a very obvious way what they can do or what they own. ❑ *All right, there's no need to show off.* **2** PHR-VERB If you **show off** something that you have or own, you show it to a lot of people because you are proud of it. ❑ *She showed off her huge diamond engagement ring.* **3** → see also **show-off**

'show ˌbusiness N-UNCOUNT **Show business** is the entertainment industry. ❑ *He started his career in show business by playing the saxophone.*

showdown /ˈʃəʊdaʊn/ (**showdowns**) N-COUNT A **showdown** is a big argument or conflict which is intended to settle a dispute. ❑ *This pushed the Prime Minister towards a final showdown with his party.*

shower /ʃaʊə/ (**showers, showering, showered**) **1** N-COUNT A **shower** is a device which sprays you with water so that you can wash yourself. ❑ *She heard him turn on the shower.* **2** N-COUNT & V-I If you **have** a **shower**, or if you **shower**, you wash yourself by standing under a shower. ❑ *She takes two showers a day.* ❑ *There wasn't time to shower.* **3** N-COUNT A **shower** is a short period of light rain. ❑ *The weather forecast was for scattered showers.* **4** N-COUNT You can refer to a lot of things that are falling as a **shower of** them. ❑ *Showers of sparks flew in all directions.* **5** V-T If you **are showered with** a lot of small objects or pieces, they are scattered over you. ❑ *The bride and groom were showered with flower petals.* **6** V-T If you **shower** someone **with** presents or kisses, you give them a lot of them.
→ see **bathroom, soap, wedding**

'shower gel (**shower gels**) N-VAR **Shower gel** is liquid soap you use in the shower.

shown /ʃəʊn/ **Shown** is the past participle of **show**.

'show-ˌoff (**show-offs**) **1** N-COUNT If you say that someone is a **show-off**, you are criticizing them for trying to impress people by showing in a very obvious way what they can do or what they own. [INFORMAL] ❑ *I was an awful show-off as a child.* **2** → see also **show off**

showpiece /ˈʃəʊpiːs/ (**showpieces**) N-COUNT A **showpiece** is something that is admired as a fine example of its type, especially something which is intended to make people admire its owner or creator. ❑ *I don't want my home to be a showpiece. I want it to be comfortable.*

showroom /ˈʃəʊruːm/ (**showrooms**) N-COUNT A **showroom** is a shop in which goods such as cars, furniture, or electrical appliances are displayed for sale.

shrank /ʃræŋk/ **Shrank** is the past tense of **shrink**.

shrapnel /ˈʃræpnəl/ N-UNCOUNT **Shrapnel** consists of small pieces of metal scattered from exploding bombs and shells.

shred /ʃred/ (**shreds, shredding, shredded**) V-T & N-COUNT If you **shred** something such as food or paper, or if you cut it into **shreds**, you cut or tear it into very small pieces. ❑ *Finely shred the carrots.*

shrewd /ʃruːd/ (**shrewder, shrewdest**) ADJ A **shrewd** person is able to understand and judge situations quickly and to use this understanding to their own advantage. ● **shrewdly** ADV ❑ *She looked at him shrewdly.* ● **shrewdness** N-UNCOUNT ❑ *His natural shrewdness tells him what is needed to succeed.*

shriek /ʃriːk/ (**shrieks, shrieking, shrieked**) V-T/V-I & N-COUNT If you **shriek**, you give a sudden loud scream, called a **shriek**. ❑ *She shrieked and jumped from the bed.* ❑ *'Stop it! Stop it!' shrieked Jane.* ❑ *Sue let out a terrific shriek.*

shrill /ʃrɪl/ (**shriller, shrillest**) ADJ A **shrill** sound is high-pitched, piercing, and unpleasant to listen to. ❑ *...the shrill whistle of the engine.*

shrimp /ʃrɪmp/

The plural is **shrimps** or **shrimp**.

N-COUNT **Shrimps** are small shellfish with long tails and many legs.

shrine /ʃraɪn/ (**shrines**) N-COUNT A **shrine** is a holy place associated with a sacred person or object. ❑ *...the holy shrine of Mecca.*

shrink /ʃrɪŋk/ (**shrinks, shrinking, shrank, shrunk**) **1** V-T/V-I If something **shrinks** or you **shrink** it, it becomes smaller. ❑ *The vast forests of West Africa have shrunk.* **2** V-I If you **shrink away** from someone or something, you move away because you are frightened or horrified by them. ❑ *He reached for Benjy, who shrank back in fear.* ❑ *They didn't shrink from danger.* **3** N-COUNT A **shrink** is a psychiatrist. [INFORMAL]

shrivel /ˈʃrɪvəl/ (**shrivels, shrivelling, shrivelled** or [AM] **shriveling, shriveled**) V-I & PHR-VERB When something **shrivels** or **shrivels up**, it becomes dry and wrinkled. ❑ *Within three to four days the flowers shrivel and turn black.* ❑ *The leaves started to shrivel up.* ● **shrivelled** ADJ ❑ *It looked old and shrivelled.*

shroud /ʃraʊd/ (**shrouds, shrouding, shrouded**) **1** N-COUNT A **shroud** is a cloth used for wrapping a dead body. **2** PHRASE If something has been **shrouded in mystery** or **shrouded in secrecy**, very little information about it has been made available. ❑ *The fate of the emperor had been shrouded in mystery for two decades.*

shrub /ʃrʌb/ (**shrubs**) N-COUNT **Shrubs** are low plants like small trees with several stems instead of a trunk.
→ see **plant**

shrug /ʃrʌg/ (**shrugs, shrugging, shrugged**) V-I & N-COUNT If you **shrug**, you raise your shoulders to show that you are not interested in something or that you do not know or care about something. This movement is called a **shrug**. ❑ *Anne shrugged, as if she didn't know.* ❑ *'I suppose so,' said Mark with a shrug.*

▶ **shrug off** PHR-VERB If you **shrug** something **off**, you treat it as not important or serious. ❑ *He shrugged off the criticism.*

shrunk /ʃrʌŋk/ **Shrunk** is the past participle of **shrink**.

shudder /ˈʃʌdə/ (**shudders, shuddering, shuddered**) **1** V-I & N-COUNT If you **shudder**, you tremble with fear or disgust. This movement is called a **shudder**. ❑ *She had shuddered at the thought.* ❑ *She gave a violent shudder.* **2** V-I If something such as a machine **shudders**, it shakes suddenly and violently. ❑ *The whole ship shuddered and trembled.*

shuffle /ˈʃʌfəl/ (**shuffles, shuffling, shuffled**) **1** V-I & N-SING If you **shuffle**, or if you walk with a **shuffle**, you walk without lifting your feet properly. ❑ *An old man shuffled out of a doorway.* ❑ *She is quite weak and walks with a shuffle.* **2** V-T/V-I If

S

you **shuffle** when you are sitting or standing, you move your bottom or your feet about, because you feel uncomfortable or embarrassed. ❑ *He grinned and shuffled his feet.* **3** V-T If you **shuffle** things such as pieces of paper, you move them around so that they are in a different order.

shun /ʃʌn/ (**shuns, shunning, shunned**) V-T If you **shun** someone or something, you deliberately avoid them. ❑ *Everybody shunned him.*

shunt /ʃʌnt/ (**shunts, shunting, shunted**) V-T If someone or something **is shunted** somewhere, they are moved or sent there, usually because someone finds them inconvenient. ❑ *He spent eight years being shunted between prisons.*

shut /ʃʌt/ (**shuts, shutting, shut**) **1** V-T/V-I & ADJ AFTER LINK-V If you **shut** something such as a door, you move it so that it covers a hole or a space. If it **shuts** or is **shut**, it covers a hole or space. ❑ *The screen door shut gently.* ❑ *The windows were fastened tight shut.* **2** V-T & ADJ AFTER LINK-V If you **shut** your eyes or your mouth, or if they are **shut**, your eyelids are closed or your lips are placed together. **3** V-I & ADJ AFTER LINK-V When a shop or restaurant **shuts**, or if it is **shut**, it is closed and you cannot go into it until it opens again. ❑ *What time does the café shut?* ❑ *The local shop may be shut.*

▶ **shut away** PHR-VERB If you **shut yourself away**, you avoid going out and seeing other people. ❑ *She was desperately upset and shut herself away for the whole day.*

▶ **shut down** **1** PHR-VERB If a factory or business **is shut down**, it is closed permanently. ❑ *Smaller contractors were forced to shut down.* **2** → see also **shutdown**

▶ **shut in** PHR-VERB If you **shut** someone or something **in** a room, you close the door so that they cannot leave it.

▶ **shut off** PHR-VERB If you **shut off** something such as an engine or a power supply, you turn it off to stop it working. ❑ *The water was shut off.*

▶ **shut out** **1** PHR-VERB If you **shut** someone or something **out**, you prevent them from getting into a place. ❑ *'I shut him out of the house,' said Maureen.* **2** PHR-VERB If you **shut out** a thought or a feeling, you stop yourself thinking about it or feeling it. ❑ *I shut out the memory.*

▶ **shut up** PHR-VERB If you **shut up**, you stop talking. If you say **'shut up'** to someone, you are rudely telling them to stop talking. ❑ *He wished she would shut up.*

S

Word Partnership Use *shut* with:

N.	shut **a door**, shut **a gate**, shut **a window** **1**
V.	**force** ***something*** shut, **pull** ***something*** shut, **push** ***something*** shut, **slam** ***something*** shut **1**
ADV.	shut **tight/tightly** **1** **2**
	shut **temporarily** **3**

shutdown /ˈʃʌtdaʊn/ (**shutdowns**) **1** N-COUNT A **shutdown** is the closing of a factory or other business. **2** → see also **shut down**

shutter /ˈʃʌtə/ (**shutters**) **1** N-COUNT The **shutter** in a camera is the part which opens to allow light through the lens when a photograph is taken. **2** N-COUNT **Shutters** are wooden or metal covers fitted to a window.
→ see **photography**

shuttle /ˈʃʌtəl/ (**shuttles, shuttling, shuttled**) **1** N-COUNT A **shuttle** is the same as a **space shuttle**. **2** ADJ A **shuttle** is a plane, bus, or train which makes frequent journeys between two places. **3** V-T If someone or something **is shuttled from** one place **to** another, they are frequently sent from one place to the other. ❑ *Refugees are often shuttled from one country to another.*

shuttlecock /ˈʃʌtəlkɒk/ (**shuttlecocks**) N-COUNT A **shuttlecock** is the small object that you hit over the net in a game of badminton.

shy /ʃaɪ/ (**shyer, shyest, shies, shying, shied**) **1** ADJ A **shy** person is nervous and uncomfortable in the company of other people. ❑ *He is a painfully shy person.* ● **shyly** ADV ❑ *The children smiled shyly.* ● **shyness** N-UNCOUNT ❑ *He overcame his shyness.* **2** ADJ & V-I If you are **shy of** doing something, or if you **shy away from** doing it, you are unwilling to do it, often because you are afraid or not confident enough. ❑ *You should not be shy of saying what you feel about this.* ❑ *We shied away from making a decision.* **3** V-I When a horse **shies**, it moves away suddenly because something has frightened it.

Thesaurus *shy* Also look up:

ADJ.	nervous, quiet, sheepish, uncomfortable; *(ant.)* confident **1**

sibling /ˈsɪblɪŋ/ (**siblings**) **1** N-COUNT Your **siblings** are your brothers and sisters. [FORMAL] **2** → See note at **brother**

sick /sɪk/ (**sicker, sickest**) **1** ADJ & N-PLURAL If you are **sick**, you are ill. **The sick** are people who are sick. ❑ *He's very sick. He needs medication.* ❑ *There were no doctors to treat the sick.* **2** ADJ AFTER LINK-V If you are being **sick**, the food that you have eaten comes up from your stomach and out of your mouth. If you feel **sick**, you feel as if you are going to be sick. ❑ *She got up and was sick in the bathroom.* **3** N-UNCOUNT **Sick** is vomit. [BRIT] **4** ADJ If you are **sick of** something, you are annoyed or bored by it and want it to stop. ❑ *I am sick and tired of hearing all these people moaning.* **5** ADJ If you describe something such as a joke or story as **sick**, you mean that it deals with death or suffering in an unpleasantly frivolous way. **6** PHRASE If someone or something **makes** you **sick**, they make you feel angry or disgusted. ❑ *The pictures made me sick.*

Usage

The words **sick** and **ill** are very similar in meaning but are used in slightly different ways. **Ill** is generally not used before a noun, and can be used in verbal expressions such as **fall ill** and **be taken ill**. ❑ *He fell ill shortly before Christmas.* ❑ *The trial was delayed after one of the jurors was taken ill.* **Sick** is often used before a noun. ❑ *...sick children.* In British English, **ill** is a slightly more polite, less direct word than **sick**. **Sick** often suggests the actual physical feeling of being ill, for example nausea or vomiting. ❑ *I spent the next 24 hours in bed, groaning and being sick.* In American English, **sick** is often used where British people would say **ill**. ❑ *Some people get hurt in accidents or get sick.*

Word Partnership Use *sick* with:

N. sick **children**, sick **mother**, sick **patients**, sick **people**, sick **person** 1
ADV. **really** sick, **very** sick 1
V. **care for the** sick 1
become sick, **feel** sick, **get** sick 1 2

sicken /ˈsɪkən/ (**sickens, sickening, sickened**) V-T If something **sickens** you, it makes you feel disgusted. ● **sickening** ADJ ❑ *It was a sickening attack on a defenceless person.*

sickly /ˈsɪkli/ (**sicklier, sickliest**) 1 ADJ A **sickly** person is weak and unhealthy. ❑ *He had been a sickly child.* 2 ADJ A **sickly** smell or taste is unpleasant and makes you feel slightly sick. ❑ *...a sweet, sickly smell.*

sickness /ˈsɪknəs/ (**sicknesses**) 1 N-UNCOUNT **Sickness** is the state of being ill or unhealthy. ❑ *In fifty-two years of working he had only one week of sickness.* 2 N-UNCOUNT **Sickness** is the uncomfortable feeling that you are going to vomit. 3 N-COUNT A **sickness** is a particular illness. ❑ *...radiation sickness.*

side /saɪd/ (**sides, siding, sided**) 1 N-COUNT The **side of** something is a position to the left or right of it, rather than in front of it, behind it, or on it. ❑ *...the nations on either side of the Pacific.* ❑ *...both sides of the border.* ❑ *Park on the side of the road.* 2 N-COUNT The **sides** of an object are the outside surfaces that are not the top or the bottom. ❑ *We put a label on the side of the box.* ❑ *A carton of milk lay on its side.* 3 N-COUNT The **sides** of a hollow or a container are its inside vertical surfaces. ❑ *...narrow valleys with steep sides.* 4 N-COUNT The two **sides of** an area, surface, or object are its two halves or surfaces. ❑ *...the right side of your face.* ❑ *Write on one side of the page only.* 5 N-COUNT Your **sides** are the parts of your body from your armpits down to your hips. 6 ADJ BEFORE N **Side** is used to describe things that are not the main or most important ones of their kind. ❑ *...a side door.* 7 N-COUNT You can call the two groups of people involved in an argument, war, or game the two **sides** of that argument, war, or game. 8 N-COUNT The two **sides of** an argument are the opposing points of view. ❑ *...sharp reactions from people on both sides of the issue.* 9 V-I If you **side with** someone, you support them in an argument. 10 N-COUNT A particular **side** of something is one aspect of it. ❑ *Anxiety has both a mental and a physical side.* 11 PHRASE If someone stays **at** your **side** or **by** your **side**, they stay near you and support or comfort you. ❑ *He was constantly at his wife's side.* 12 PHRASE If two people or things are **side by side**, they are next to each other. ❑ *We sat side by side.* 13 PHRASE If something moves **from side to side**, it moves repeatedly to the left and to the right. ❑ *She shook her head from side to side.* 14 PHRASE If you are **on** someone's **side**, you are supporting them in an argument or a war. 15 PHRASE If you do something **on the side**, you do it in addition to your main work. ❑ *...ways of making a little bit of money on the side.* 16 PHRASE If you **put** something **to one side**, you temporarily ignore it in order to concentrate on something else. ❑ *Health and safety regulations are often put to one side.* 17 PHRASE If you get **on the wrong side of** someone, you do something to annoy them and make them dislike you. If you stay **on the right side of** someone, you try to please them and avoid annoying them. 18 to **err on the side of** something → see **err** 19 **to be on the safe side** → see **safe**

ˈside-ˌeffect (**side-effects**) N-COUNT The **side-effects** of a drug are the effects it has on you in addition to its function of curing illness or pain. ❑ *...unpleasant side-effects, such as nausea, vomiting and sweating.*

sideline /ˈsaɪdlaɪn/ (**sidelines**) 1 N-COUNT A **sideline** is something that you do in addition to your main job in order to earn extra money. ❑ *Mr Brown sells computer disks as a sideline.* 2 N-COUNT The **sidelines** of a playing area such as a tennis court or football pitch are the lines marking the long sides. 3 N-PLURAL If you are **on the sidelines** in a situation, you are not involved in it. ❑ *We do not want to be left on the sidelines when critical decisions are taken.*
→ see **football, tennis**

ˈside ˌroad (**side roads**) N-COUNT A **side road** is a road which leads off a busier, more important road.

ˈside ˌsalad (**side salads**) N-COUNT A **side salad** is a bowl of salad which is served with a main meal.

sidestep also **side-step** /ˈsaɪdstep/ (**sidesteps, sidestepping, sidestepped**) V-T If you **sidestep** a problem, you avoid dealing with it. ❑ *He never sidesteps a question.*

ˈside ˌstreet (**side streets**) N-COUNT A **side street** is a quiet, often narrow street which leads off a busier street.

sidewalk /ˈsaɪdwɔːk/ (**sidewalks**) N-COUNT In American English, a **sidewalk** is a path with a hard surface by the side of a road. The British word is **pavement**.

sideways /ˈsaɪdweɪz/ ADV & ADJ BEFORE N **Sideways** means from or to the side of something or someone. ❑ *I took a step sideways.* ❑ *...a sideways glance.*

siege /siːdʒ/ (**sieges**) N-VAR A **siege** is a military operation in which an army or police force surrounds a place in order to force the people to surrender and come out. ❑ *We must do everything possible to lift the siege.* ❑ *Supplies are on their way to the city which is under siege.*

Word Partnership Use *siege* with:

PREP. **after a** siege, **during a** siege, **under** siege
V. **end a** siege, **lift a** siege

sieve /sɪv/ (**sieves, sieving, sieved**) 1 N-COUNT A **sieve** is a tool consisting of a metal or plastic ring with a fine wire net attached. It is used for separating liquids from solids or larger pieces of something from smaller pieces. 2 V-T When you **sieve** a liquid or a powder, you put it through a sieve. ❑ *Sieve the flour into a mixing bowl.*

sift /sɪft/ (**sifts, sifting, sifted**) 1 V-T If you **sift** a substance such as flour or sand, you put it through a sieve to remove large lumps. 2 V-I If you **sift through** something such as evidence, you examine it thoroughly. ❑ *Experts spent all day sifting through the wreckage.*

sigh /saɪ/ (**sighs, sighing, sighed**) V-I & N-COUNT When you **sigh**, or when you let out a **sigh**, you let out a deep breath. ❑ *She sighed deeply.* ❑ *She kicked off* her shoes with a sigh.

Word Partnership Use *sigh* with:

ADJ. **collective** sigh, **deep** sigh, **long** sigh
V. **breathe a** sigh, **give a** sigh, **hear a** sigh, **heave a** sigh, **let out a** sigh

sight /saɪt/ (**sights, sighting, sighted**)
1 N-UNCOUNT Your **sight** is your ability to see. ❑ *My sight is failing, and I can't see to read any more.* 2 V-T If someone **is sighted** somewhere, they are seen there briefly or suddenly. ❑ *A woman like her was sighted near Enmore.* 3 N-SING **The sight of** something is the act of seeing it or an occasion on which you see it. ❑ *I faint at the sight of blood.* 4 N-PLURAL **The sights** are interesting places often visited by tourists. ❑ *We toured the sights of Paris.* 5 N-PLURAL The **sights** of a weapon such as a rifle are the part which help you aim it accurately. 6 PHRASE If one thing is **a sight better** or **a sight worse** than a similar thing, it is very much better or very much worse; informal. ❑ *He's a good swimmer but he could be a darned sight better.* 7 PHRASE If you **know** someone **by sight**, you can recognize them when you see them, but you have never spoken to them. 8 PHRASE If you **catch sight of** someone, you see them suddenly or briefly. ❑ *He caught sight of her black hat in the crowd.* 9 PHRASE If something is **in sight**, you can see it. If it is **out of sight**, you cannot see it. 10 PHRASE If a result or a decision is **in sight** or **within sight**, it is likely to happen within a short time. ❑ *An agreement on trade policy was in sight.* 11 PHRASE If you **lose sight of** an important feature or detail, you no longer pay attention to it because you are worrying about less important things. 12 PHRASE If members of a police force or an army have been ordered to **arrest** or **shoot** someone **on sight**, they have been told to arrest or shoot someone as soon as they see them. ❑ *Troops shot anyone suspicious on sight.* 13 PHRASE If you **set** your **sights on** something, you are determined to have it. ❑ *They set their sights on the world record.*

Word Partnership Use *sight* with:

V. **catch** sight **of** ***someone/something*** 8
ADJ. **common** sight, **familiar** sight, **welcome** sight 3

S

sighting /ˈsaɪtɪŋ/ (**sightings**) N-COUNT A **sighting of** something is an occasion on which it is seen. ❑ *...the sighting of a rare sea bird.*

sightseeing /ˈsaɪtsiːɪŋ/ N-UNCOUNT **Sightseeing** is the activity of visiting the interesting places that tourists usually visit.
→ see **city**

sign
❶ INDICATORS
❷ WRITING YOUR NAME

sign /saɪn/ (**signs**)
❶ 1 N-COUNT A **sign** is a mark or shape with a particular meaning, for example in mathematics or music. ❑ *...an equals sign.* 2 N-COUNT A **sign** is a movement of your arms, hands, or head which is intended to have a particular meaning. ❑ *Their leader was pictured giving the V-for-victory sign.* 3 N-COUNT A **sign** is a piece of wood, metal, or plastic with words or pictures on it, giving information or instructions. ❑ *Follow the road signs on to the motorway.* 4 N-COUNT If there is a **sign of** something, there is evidence that it exists. ❑ *The enemy handed back a hundred prisoners of war as a sign of good will.* ❑ *The sky is clear and there's no sign of rain or snow.* 5 N-COUNT In astrology, a **zodiac sign** is one of the twelve areas into which the heavens are divided.

sign /saɪn/ (**signs, signing, signed**)
❷ 1 V-T When you **sign** a document, you put your signature on it. ❑ *Before his operation the patient was asked to sign a consent form.* ● **signing** N-UNCOUNT ❑ *Spain's top priority is the signing of the treaty.*
2 V-T/V-I If an organization **signs** someone, or if someone **signs for** an organization, they sign a contract agreeing to work for that organization for a specified period of time. ❑ *He has signed to play football with a new team.*
▶ **sign away** PHR-VERB If you **sign** something **away**, you sign official documents to say that you no longer have a right to it. ❑ *The Duke signed away his inheritance.*
▶ **sign for** PHR-VERB If you **sign for** something, you officially state that you have received it, by signing a form or book.
▶ **sign in** PHR-VERB If you **sign in**, you officially indicate that you have arrived at a hotel or club by signing a book or form.
▶ **sign on** 1 PHR-VERB When an unemployed person **signs on**, they officially inform the authorities that they are unemployed, so that they can receive money from the government in order to live. [BRIT] 2 PHR-VERB If you **sign on for** something, or if you **sign up for** it, you officially agree to work for an organization or do a course of study by signing a contract or form. ❑ *He signed up for a driving course.*
▶ **sign out** PHR-VERB If you **sign out**, you indicate that you have left a hotel or club by signing a book or form.
▶ **sign up** → see **sign on** (meaning **2**)

Thesaurus *sign* Also look up:

N. nod, signal, wave ① 2
V. authorize, autograph, endorse ② 1

signage /ˈsaɪnɪdʒ/ N-UNCOUNT **Signage** is signs, especially road signs and advertising signs, considered collectively. ❑ *They don't allow signage around the stadium.*

signal /ˈsɪgnəl/ (**signals, signalling, signalled** or [AM] **signaling, signaled**) 1 N-COUNT A **signal** is a sound or action which is intended to send a particular message. ❑ *The king sends a clear signal of friendship to other nations.* ❑ *Don't shoot without my signal.* 2 V-T/V-I If you **signal** something, or if you **signal to** someone, you make a gesture or sound in order to give someone a particular message. ❑ *She signalled a passing taxi.* 3 V-T & N-COUNT If something **signals** a situation, or if it is a **signal of** it, it suggests that the situation is happening or likely to happen. ❑ *The lifting of sanctions signalled the end of an era.* ❑ *Local leaders saw the visit as an important signal of support.* 4 N-COUNT A **signal** is a piece of equipment beside a railway, which tells train drivers when to stop. 5 N-COUNT A **signal** is a series of sound or light waves which carry

Picture Dictionary **sign language**

The Manual Alphabet

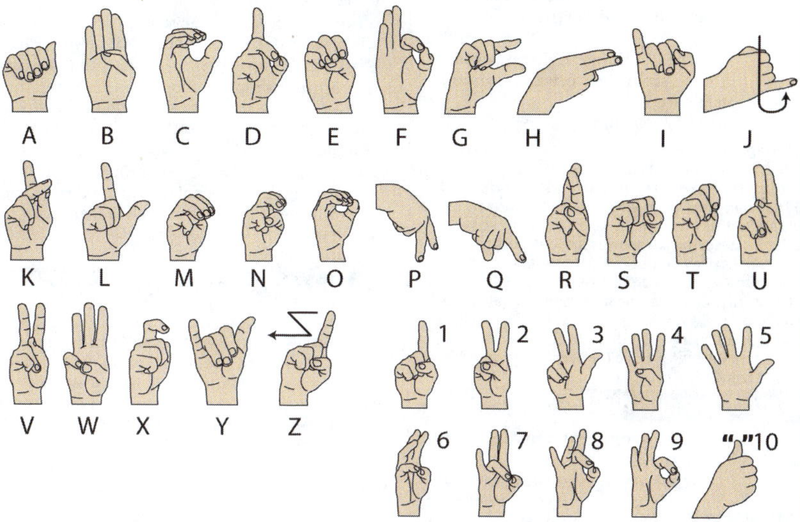

information. ❑ *...high-frequency radio signals.*
→ see **cellphone, television**

Word Partnership Use *signal* with:

- V. **give a** signal, **send a** signal 1 5
- ADJ. **clear** signal, **strong** signal, **wrong** signal 1 3
- **important** signal 3

signatory /ˈsɪɡnətri, AM -tɔːri/ (**signatories**) N-COUNT The **signatories to** an official document are the people who sign it. ❑ *Australia was a signatory to the International Convention on Civil and Political Rights.*

signature /ˈsɪɡnətʃə/ (**signatures**) N-COUNT Your **signature** is your name, written in your own characteristic way.

significance /sɪɡˈnɪfɪkəns/ N-UNCOUNT The **significance of** something is its importance. ❑ *The President's visit has great symbolic significance.*

Word Partnership Use *significance* with:

- ADJ. **cultural** significance, **great** significance, **historic/historical** significance, **political** significance, **religious** significance
- V. **explain the** significance **of** *something*, **understand the** significance **of** *something*

significant /sɪɡˈnɪfɪkənt/ 1 ADJ A **significant** amount of something is large enough to be important or noticeable. ● **significantly** ADV ❑ *Cars can be made significantly more fuel-efficient.* 2 ADJ A **significant** action or gesture is intended to have a special meaning. ❑ *Mrs Brown gave Rosie a significant glance.*

Thesaurus *significant* Also look up:

- ADJ. big, important, large; *(ant.)* insignificant, minor, small 1

signify /ˈsɪɡnɪfaɪ/ (**signifies, signifying, signified**) V-T An event or a sign or gesture that **signifies** something has a particular meaning. ❑ *Red signifies good fortune in China.*

ˈsign ˌlanguage (**sign languages**) N-VAR **Sign language** is movements of your hands and arms used to communicate. There are several official systems of sign language, used, for example, by deaf people. ❑ *Her son used sign language to tell her what happened.*
→ see Picture Dictionary: **sign language**

Sikh /siːk/ (**Sikhs**) N-COUNT A **Sikh** is a member of an Indian religion which separated from Hinduism in the sixteenth century and which teaches that there is only one God.

silence /ˈsaɪləns/ (**silences, silencing, silenced**) 1 N-VAR If there is **silence**, it is completely quiet. ❑ *They stood in silence.* 2 N-UNCOUNT Someone's **silence** about something is their refusal to tell people anything about it. ❑ *Lewis maintained his silence yesterday.* 3 V-T To **silence** someone or something means to stop them speaking or making a noise. ❑ *Eleanor screamed and he silenced her by clapping a hand over her mouth.* 4 V-T If someone **silences** you, they stop you expressing opinions

S

that they do not agree with. ❑ *He tried to silence anyone who spoke out against him.*

Word Partnership Use *silence* with:

ADJ. **awkward** silence, **complete** silence, **long** silence, **sudden** silence, **total** silence 1
V. silence **falls, listen in** silence, **observe a** silence, **sit in** silence, **watch** *something* **in** silence 1
break a/*your* silence 2

silent /'saɪlənt/ 1 ADJ AFTER LINK-V Someone or something that is **silent** is making no sound. ❑ *The heavy guns again fell silent.* ● **silently** ADV ❑ *She and Ned sat silently for a moment.* 2 ADJ BEFORE N If you describe someone as **silent** person, you mean that they do not talk to people very much, sometimes giving the impression of being unfriendly. ❑ *He was the silent type who sat in a corner, painfully shy.* 3 ADJ AFTER LINK-V If you are **silent about** something, you do not tell people about it. ❑ *The government have told the scientists to remain silent about their work.*

Word Partnership Use *silent* with:

V. **go** silent, **keep** silent, **remain** silent, **sit** silent 1
N. silent **prayer**, silent **reading** 1

silhouette /ˌsɪlʊ'et/ (**silhouettes**) N-COUNT A **silhouette** is the outline of a dark shape against a bright light or pale background. ❑ *She looked at the dark silhouette of the man sitting a few yards away.*

silicon /'sɪlɪkən/ N-UNCOUNT **Silicon** is a non-metallic element that is found combined with oxygen in sand and in minerals such as quartz and granite. Silicon is used to make parts of computers and other electronic equipment.

silicone /'sɪlɪkəʊn/ N-UNCOUNT **Silicone** is a substance made from silicon, which is used to make things such as oils and polishes.

silk /sɪlk/ (**silks**) N-VAR **Silk** is a very smooth, fine cloth made from a substance produced by a kind of moth.

silky /'sɪlki/ (**silkier, silkiest**) ADJ Something that is **silky** is smooth and soft. ❑ *...silky fabrics.*

S

sill /sɪl/ (**sills**) N-COUNT A **sill** is a ledge at the bottom of a window.

silly /'sɪli/ (**sillier, silliest**) ADJ Someone who is being **silly** is behaving in a foolish or childish way. ● **silliness** N-UNCOUNT ❑ *Let's not have any more silliness.*

silt /sɪlt/ N-UNCOUNT **Silt** is fine sand, soil, or mud which is carried along by a river.
→ see **erosion**

silver /'sɪlvə/ 1 N-UNCOUNT **Silver** is a valuable greyish-white metal used for making jewellery and ornaments. ❑ *...a brooch made from silver.* 2 N-UNCOUNT **Silver** consists of coins that look like silver. ❑ *...£150,000 in silver.* 3 N-UNCOUNT You can use **silver** to refer to all the things in a house that are made of silver, especially the cutlery and dishes. ❑ *He polished the silver and dusted all the books.* 4 ADJ & N-COUNT **Silver** is used to describe things that are shiny greyish-white in colour. ❑ *He had thick silver hair.*
→ see **mineral, money**

ˌsilver 'medal (**silver medals**) N-COUNT A **silver medal** is a medal made of silver which is awarded as second prize in a contest.

silvery /'sɪlvəri/ ADJ **Silvery** things look like silver or are the colour of silver. ❑ *...silvery hair.*

'SIM ˌcard (**SIM cards**) N-COUNT A **SIM card** is a microchip in a mobile phone that identifies the user and allows them to use the phone network. **SIM** is an abbreviation for 'Subscriber Identity Module'.

similar /'sɪmɪlə/ ADJ If one thing is **similar to** another, or if a number of things are **similar**, they have features that are the same. ❑ *The accident is similar to one that happened in 1973.* ❑ *...a collection of similar pictures.*

Word Link *simil* ≈ *similar* : *assimilate, similarity, similarly*

similarity /ˌsɪmɪ'lærɪti/ (**similarities**) N-VAR If there is a **similarity between** two or more things, they share some features that are the same. ❑ *...the astonishing similarity between my brother and my son.* ❑ *She is also 25 and comes from Birmingham, but the similarity between them ends there.*

similarly /'sɪmɪləli/ 1 ADV You use **similarly** to say that something is similar to something else. ❑ *People who develop Type 2 diabetes often have a similarly affected relative.* 2 ADV You use **similarly** to say that there is a correspondence or similarity between the way two things happen or are done. ❑ *He learned his English mainly from comic books. Similarly, I learned most of my French from Tintin and Asterix.*

simmer /'sɪmə/ (**simmers, simmering, simmered**) V-T/V-I When you **simmer** food, or when it **simmers**, you cook it gently at just below boiling point. ❑ *Turn the heat down so the sauce simmers gently.*

simple /'sɪmpəl/ (**simpler, simplest**) 1 ADJ If something is **simple**, it is not complicated, and is therefore easy to understand or do. ❑ *...simple pictures and diagrams.* ❑ *...simple maths.* ● **simply** ADV ❑ *State simply and clearly the reasons why you are applying for this job.* 2 ADJ **Simple** means containing all the basic or necessary things, but nothing extra. ❑ *...a simple dinner of rice and beans.* ● **simply** ADV ❑ *He dressed simply and led a quiet family life.* 3 ADJ BEFORE N You use **simple** to emphasize that the thing you are referring to is the only important or relevant reason for something. ❑ *His refusal to talk was simple stubbornness.* 4 ADJ In English grammar, **simple tenses** are ones which are not formed using the auxiliary verb 'be', as in 'I dressed and went for a walk' and 'This food tastes awful'. Compare **continuous**. 5 → see also **simply**

Thesaurus *simple* Also look up:

ADJ. clear, easy, understandable; (*ant.*) complicated 1
plain 2

Word Partnership Use *simple* with:

N. simple **concept**, simple **explanation**, simple **instructions**, simple **language**, simple **message**, simple **procedure**, simple **steps** 1
simple **life**, simple **pleasure** 2
ADV. simple **enough**, **fairly** simple, **pretty** simple, **quite** simple, **rather** simple, **really** simple, **relatively** simple, **very** simple 1 2

simplicity /sɪm'plɪsɪti/ 1 N-UNCOUNT The **simplicity** of something is the fact that it is uncomplicated and can be understood or done easily. ❑ *Because of its simplicity, this test could be carried out easily by a family doctor.* 2 N-UNCOUNT When you talk about something's **simplicity**, you approve of it because it is natural and simple rather than elaborate or ornate. ❑ *...the simplicity of the design.*

simplify /'sɪmplɪfaɪ/ (**simplifies, simplifying, simplified**) V-T If you **simplify** something, you make it easier to understand. ❑ *He simplified complex ideas and presented them along with simple diagrams.* ● **simplified** ADJ ❑ *...a shorter, simplified version of his speech.* ● **simplification** /ˌsɪmplɪfɪ'keɪʃən/ (**simplifications**) N-VAR ❑ *...the simplification of court procedures.*

simplistic /sɪm'plɪstɪk/ ADJ A **simplistic** view or interpretation of something makes it seem much simpler than it really is. ❑ *Many people have a simplistic view of crime and its causes.*

simply /'sɪmpli/ 1 ADV You use **simply** to emphasize that something consists of only one thing, happens for only one reason, or is done in only one way. ❑ *Lam will be under pressure, simply because of his lack of experience.* 2 ADV You use **simply** to emphasize what you are saying. ❑ *The concert was simply marvellous.* 3 → see also **simple**

simulate /'sɪmjʊleɪt/ (**simulates, simulating, simulated**) V-T To **simulate** something means to pretend to do it or to produce something like it. ❑ *We used this trick in the Army to simulate illness.* ❑ *The wood was painted to simulate stone.* ● **simulation** (**simulations**) N-VAR ❑ *With each new edition, the game gets closer to being an accurate simulation of reality.*

simultaneous /ˌsɪməl'teɪniəs, AM ˌsaɪm-/ ADJ Things which are **simultaneous** happen or exist at the same time. ❑ *...the simultaneous release of the book and the film.* ● **simultaneously** ADV ❑ *The two guns fired almost simultaneously.*

sin /sɪn/ (**sins, sinning, sinned**) N-VAR & V-I If someone **commits** a **sin**, or if they **sin**, they do something which is believed to break the laws of God. ❑ *The Spanish Inquisition charged him with sinning against God and man.* ● **sinner** (**sinners**) N-COUNT ❑ *I do not believe that you are sinners.*

since /sɪns/ 1 PREP & ADV & CONJ You use **since** when you are mentioning a time or event in the past and indicating that a situation has continued from then until now. ❑ *This research has been in progress since 1961.* ❑ *I simply gave in to him, and I've regretted it ever since.* ❑ *I've been bored to death since I left my job.* 2 ADV & CONJ You use **since** to mention a time or event in the past when you are describing an event or situation that has happened after that time. ❑ *I haven't seen him since the war.* ❑ *So much has changed in this country since I was a teenager.* 3 ADV When you are talking about an event or situation in the past, you use **since** to indicate that another event happened at some point later in time. ❑ *Six thousand people were arrested, but have since been released.* 4 PHRASE If you say that something has **long since** happened, you mean that it happened a long time ago. ❑ *Her parents have long since died.* 5 CONJ You use **since** to introduce a reason. ❑ *I'm forever on a diet, since I put on weight easily.*

sincere /sɪn'sɪə/ ADJ If you say that someone is **sincere**, you approve of them because they really mean the things they say. ● **sincerity** /sɪn'serɪti/ N-UNCOUNT ❑ *I was impressed with his deep sincerity.*

sincerely /sɪn'sɪəli/ 1 ADV If you say or feel something **sincerely**, you really mean it or feel it. ❑ *...sincerely held religious beliefs.* 2 CONVENTION In British English, people write **Yours sincerely** before their signature at the end of a formal letter when they have addressed it to someone by name. The usual American term is **Sincerely yours**.

sinful /'sɪnfʊl/ ADJ If you describe something or someone as **sinful**, you think that they are wicked or immoral. ❑ *...sinful thoughts.*

sing /sɪŋ/ (**sings, singing, sang, sung**) 1 V-T/V-I If you **sing**, you make musical sounds with your voice, usually producing words that fit a tune. ❑ *Ms Turner sang the theme tune from Goldeneye.* ❑ *Sing us a song!* ● **singing** N-UNCOUNT ❑ *The dancing and singing ended at midnight.* 2 V-I When birds or insects **sing**, they make pleasant high-pitched sounds. ❑ *The bird was singing a beautiful song.* ● **singing** N-UNCOUNT ❑ *The singing of birds is drowned out by motorway traffic.* 3 to **sing** someone's **praises** → see **praise**

▶ **sing along** PHR-VERB If you **sing along with** a piece of music, you sing it while you are listening to someone else perform it. ❑ *Fifteen hundred people all sang along.*

Word Partnership Use *sing* with:

V. **begin to** sing, **can/can't** sing, **dance and** sing, **hear** ***someone*** sing, **like to** sing 1
N. sing **a song** 1
birds sing 2
sing ***someone's*** **praises** 3

singer /'sɪŋə/ (**singers**) N-COUNT A **singer** is a person who sings, especially as a job.
→ see **concert**

single /'sɪŋgəl/ (**singles, singling, singled**) 1 ADJ BEFORE N You use **single** to emphasize that you are referring to one thing, and no more than one thing. ❑ *She hasn't said a single word.* 2 ADJ BEFORE N You use **single** to indicate that you are considering something on its own and separately from other things like it. ❑ *Every single house in town had been damaged.* ❑ *...the world's single most important source of oil.* 3 ADJ Someone who is **single** is not married. ❑ *When I was single I never worried about money.* 4 ADJ A **single** bed or room is intended for one person. 5 ADJ & N-COUNT In British English, a **single ticket** or a **single** is a ticket for a journey from one place to another but not back again. The usual American term is **one-way** ticket. ❑ *...a Club Class single to Los Angeles.* 6 N-COUNT A **single**

is a CD which has one main song on it. ❑ *...the band's British and American hit singles.* **7** N-UNCOUNT **Singles** is a game of tennis or badminton in which one player plays another.
→ see **hotel, tennis**

▶ **single out** PHR-VERB If you **single** someone **out**, you choose them and give them special attention or treatment. ❑ *His boss singled him out for a special mention.*

single- **Single-** is used to form words which describe something that has one part or feature, rather than having two or more of them. ❑ *...a single-sex school.* ❑ *...a single-track road.*

ˌsingle-ˈhanded ADV If you do something **single-handed**, you do it without help from anyone else. ❑ *I brought up my seven children single-handed.* ● **single-handedly** ADV ❑ *Olga Korbut single-handedly turned gymnastics into a major event.*

ˌsingle-ˈminded ADJ A **single-minded** person has only one aim and is determined to achieve it. ❑ *...a single-minded determination to win.* ● **single-mindedness** N-UNCOUNT ❑ *Athletes must have single-mindedness as they train.*

ˌsingle ˈparent (**single parents**) N-COUNT A **single parent** is someone who is bringing up a child or children on their own, because the other parent is not living with them.

singular /ˈsɪŋgjʊlə/ **1** ADJ BEFORE N & N-SING The **singular form** of a word or **the singular** is the form that is used when referring to one person or thing. ❑ *The word 'you' can be singular or plural.* ❑ *The inhabitants of the Arctic are known as the Inuit. The singular is Inuk.* **2** ADJ **Singular** means very great and remarkable. [FORMAL] ● **singularly** ADV ❑ *He is singularly unsuited for this job.*

sinister /ˈsɪnɪstə/ ADJ Someone or something that is **sinister** seems evil or harmful. ❑ *There was something sinister about him that she found disturbing.*

sink /sɪŋk/ (**sinks, sinking, sank, sunk**) **1** N-COUNT A **sink** is a basin with taps that supply water. ❑ *There were dirty dishes in the sink.* **2** V-T/V-I If a boat **sinks**, or if something **sinks** it, it disappears below the surface of a mass of water. ❑ *In a naval battle your aim is to sink the enemy's ship.* **3** V-I If something **sinks**, it disappears below the surface of a mass of water. ❑ *A fresh egg will sink and an old egg will float.* **4** V-I If you **sink**, you move into a lower position, for example by sitting down in a chair or kneeling. [WRITTEN] ❑ *She sank into an armchair.* **5** V-I If something **sinks** to a lower level or standard, it falls to that level or standard. ❑ *Pay increases have sunk to around seven per cent.* **6** V-I If your voice **sinks**, it becomes quieter. [WRITTEN] ❑ *She heard their voices sink into a confidential whisper.* **7** V-I To **sink into** an unpleasant or undesirable situation or state means to pass gradually into it. ❑ *The country's economy has sunk into chaos.* **8** PHRASE If your **heart sinks**, you become depressed. ❑ *My heart sank because I thought he was going to leave me for another girl.* **9** V-T/V-I If something sharp **sinks** or **is sunk into** something solid, it goes deeply into it. ❑ *The dog sank its teeth into my leg.* **10** → see also **sunken**

▶ **sink in** PHR-VERB When a statement or fact **sinks in**, you finally understand or realize it fully. ❑ *The news took a while to sink in.*

S

Word Partnership Use *sink* with:

N. **bathroom** sink, **dishes in a** sink, **kitchen** sink **1**
sink **a ship** **2**

sip /sɪp/ (**sips, sipping, sipped**) V-T/V-I & N-COUNT If you **sip** a drink, **sip at** a drink, or if you drink it in **sips**, you drink a small amount at a time. ❑ *She sipped her coffee.* ❑ *I sipped at my water.*

siphon also **syphon** /ˈsaɪfən/ (**siphons, siphoning, siphoned**) **1** V-T If you **siphon** a liquid, you draw it from somewhere through a tube by using atmospheric pressure. ❑ *The firefighters siphoned water out of the river.* **2** N-COUNT A **siphon** is a tube used for siphoning liquid.

sir /sɜː/ **1** N-VOC People sometimes say **sir** as a polite way of addressing a man whose name they do not know or a man of superior rank. 'Dear Sir' is used at the beginning of official letters addressed to men. ❑ *Good afternoon, sir, and welcome to The New World Diner.* **2** N-TITLE **Sir** is the title used in front of the name of a knight or baronet. ❑ *...Sir Geoffrey Howe.*

siren /ˈsaɪərən/ (**sirens**) N-COUNT A **siren** is a warning device which makes a long, loud, wailing noise. Most fire engines, ambulances, and police cars have sirens.

sister /ˈsɪstə/ (**sisters**) **1** N-COUNT Your **sister** is a girl or woman who has the same parents as you. **2** N-COUNT & N-TITLE **Sister** is a title given to a woman who belongs to a religious community such as a convent. ❑ *I'm Sister Agnes.* **3** N-COUNT & N-TITLE In Britain, a **sister** is a senior female nurse who supervises a hospital ward. ❑ *Sister Middleton tended the seriously hurt policeman.* **4** N-COUNT You might use **sister** to describe a woman who belongs to the same race, religion, country, or organization as you, or who has ideas that are similar to yours. ❑ *...our Jewish brothers and sisters.*
→ see **family**

Usage

Note that there is no common English word that can refer to both a brother and a sister. You simply have to use both words. ❑ *He has 13 brothers and sisters.* The word **sibling** exists, but it is rare and formal.

ˈsister-in-ˌlaw (**sisters-in-law**) N-COUNT Your **sister-in-law** is the sister of your husband or wife, or the woman who is married to your brother.
→ see **family**

sit /sɪt/ (**sits, sitting, sat**) **1** V-I If you **are sitting** somewhere, for example in a chair, your weight is supported by your buttocks rather than your feet. ❑ *Joshua was sitting on the floor.* **2** V-I When you **sit** somewhere, you lower your body until you are sitting on something. ❑ *He set the cases against a wall and sat on them.* **3** V-T If you **sit** someone somewhere, you tell them to sit there or put them in a sitting position. ❑ *When I was three, he'd sit me on his knee.* **4** V-I If you **sit on** a committee, you are a member of it. **5** V-T In British English, if you **sit** an examination, you do it. In American English, you **take** an examination. **6** → See note at **exam** **7** V-I When a parliament, law court, or other official body **is sitting**, it is officially doing its work. [FORMAL] **8** PHRASE If you **sit tight**, you remain where you are and do not take any action. ❑ *Sit tight. I'll be right back.* **9** to **sit on the fence** → see **fence**

▶ **sit around** [BRIT also **sit about**] PHR-VERB If you **sit around** or **sit about**, you spend time doing nothing useful. [INFORMAL] ❑ *Eve isn't the type to sit around doing nothing.*

▶ **sit back** PHR-VERB If you **sit back** while something is happening, you relax and do not become involved in it. ❑ *Get everyone talking and then sit back and enjoy the conversation.*

▶ **sit in on** PHR-VERB If you **sit in on** a meeting or lesson, you are present while it is taking place but do not take part in it. ❑ *Will they permit you to sit in on a few classes?*

▶ **sit on** PHR-VERB If you say that someone **is sitting on** something, you mean that they are deliberately not dealing with it or not revealing it to others. ❑ *The police sat on vital information for years.*

▶ **sit out** PHR-VERB If you **sit** something **out**, you wait for it to finish, without taking any action. ❑ *The German player had to sit out the match because of a knee injury.*

▶ **sit through** PHR-VERB If you **sit through** something such as a film or lecture, you stay until it is finished, although you are not enjoying it. ❑ *He sat through the press conference with a resigned expression.*

▶ **sit up** **1** PHR-VERB If you **sit up**, you move into a sitting position when you have been leaning back or lying down. **2** PHR-VERB If you **sit up**, you do not go to bed although it is very late. ❑ *We sat up, drinking coffee and talking.*

Word Partnership Use *sit* with:

V.	sit **and eat**, sit **and enjoy**, sit **and listen**, sit **and talk**, sit **and wait**, sit **and watch (or** sit **watching)** **1**
	sit **down to dinner/eat**, sit **down and relax** **1** **2**
PREP.	sit **in a circle**, sit **on the porch**, sit **on the sidelines** **1**
	sit **around/at a table**, sit **on a bench**, sit **in a chair**, sit **on the floor**, sit **on *someone's* lap** **1** **2**
ADV.	sit **alone**, sit **back**, sit **comfortably**, sit **quietly**, sit **still** **1**

site /saɪt/ (**sites, siting, sited**) **1** N-COUNT A **site** is a piece of ground that is used for a particular purpose or where a particular thing happens or is situated. ❑ *...a building site.* ❑ *...the site of the worst ecological disaster on earth.* ❑ *...the site of Moses' tomb.* **2** V-T If something **is sited** in a particular place or position, it is placed there. ❑ *He said such weapons had never been sited in Germany.* ● **siting** N-SING ❑ *The siting of mobile phone masts has provoked protests across Britain.*

'sitting-ˌroom (**sitting-rooms**) N-COUNT A **sitting-room** is a room in a house where people sit and relax. [BRIT]

situated /'sɪtʃʊeɪtɪd/ ADJ If something is **situated** somewhere, it is in a particular place or position. ❑ *His hotel is situated near the Loire.*

Word Link ***site, situ** ≈ **position, location** :* ***campsite, situation, website***

situation /ˌsɪtʃʊ'eɪʃən/ (**situations**) **1** N-COUNT You use **situation** to refer generally to what is happening at a particular place and time, or to refer to what is happening to you. ❑ *Army officers said the situation was under control.* ❑ *Some men are not used to coping with women as equals in a work situation.* ❑ *I did what any person would do in my situation.* **2** N-COUNT The **situation** of a building or town is its surroundings. [FORMAL] ❑ *They loved the hotel's situation on an island.*

Word Partnership Use *situation* with:

ADJ.	**bad** situation, **complicated** situation, **current** situation, **dangerous** situation, **difficult** situation, **economic** situation, **financial** situation, **political** situation, **present** situation, **same** situation, **tense** situation, **terrible** situation, **unique** situation, **unusual** situation, **whole** situation **1**
V.	**describe a** situation, **discuss a** situation, **handle a** situation, **improve a** situation, **understand a** situation **1**

'sit-ˌup (**sit-ups**) N-COUNT **Sit-ups** are exercises that you do by sitting up from a lying position, keeping your feet on the floor, and without using your hands.

six /sɪks/ (**sixes**) NUM **Six** is the number 6.

sixteen /ˌsɪks'tiːn/ (**sixteens**) NUM **Sixteen** is the number 16.

sixteenth /ˌsɪks'tiːnθ/ (**sixteenths**) **1** ORD The **sixteenth** item in a series is the one that you count as number sixteen. **2** N-COUNT A **sixteenth** is one of sixteen equal parts of something.

sixth /sɪksθ/ (**sixths**) **1** ADJ The **sixth** item in a series is the one that you count as number six. **2** N-COUNT A **sixth** is one of six equal parts of something.

'sixth ˌform (**sixth forms**) N-COUNT The **sixth form** in a British school consists of the classes that pupils go into at the age of sixteen to study for 'A' Levels and other exams.

sixtieth /'sɪkstiəθ/ ADJ The **sixtieth** item in a series is the one that you count as number sixty.

sixty /'sɪksti/ (**sixties**) NUM **Sixty** is the number 60. For examples of how numbers such as sixty and eighty are used, see **eighty**.

ˌsix-yard 'box N-SING On a football pitch, **the six-yard box** is the rectangular area marked in front of each goal.

sizable /'saɪzəbəl/ → see **sizeable**

size /saɪz/ (**sizes, sizing, sized**) **1** N-UNCOUNT The **size** of something is how big or small it is. ❑ *The company has more than doubled in size.* ❑ *...an area five times the size of Britain.* ❑ *Cut the chicken into bite-size pieces.* ● **-sized** ❑ *...a medium-sized college.* **2** N-UNCOUNT The **size** of something is the fact that it is very large. ❑ *Jack walked around the hotel and was fascinated by its sheer size.* **3** N-COUNT A **size** is one of a series of graded measurements, especially for things such as clothes or shoes. ❑ *My sister is the same height but only a size 12.*

▶ **size up** PHR-VERB If you **size up** a person or situation, you carefully look at the person or think about the situation, so that you can decide how to act. [INFORMAL] ❑ *He spent the evening sizing me up intellectually.*

S

Word Partnership Use *size* with:

ADJ.	**average** size, **full** size 1 **sheer** size 2 **right** size, size **large/medium/small** 3
N.	**bite** size, **class** size, **family** size, **life** size, **pocket** size 1 size **chart**, **king/queen** size 3
V.	**double in** size, **increase in** size, **vary in** size 1 **a** size **fits** 3

sizeable also **sizable** /ˈsaɪzəbəl/ ADJ **Sizeable** means fairly large. ❑ *...a sizeable chunk of land.*

sizzle /ˈsɪzəl/ (**sizzles, sizzling, sizzled**) V-I If something **sizzles**, it makes a hissing sound like the sound made by frying food. ❑ *The sausages and burgers sizzled.*

skate /skeɪt/ (**skates, skating, skated**) 1 N-COUNT **Skates** are **ice-skates** or **roller-skates**. 2 V-I If you **skate**, you move about wearing ice-skates or roller-skates. ❑ *Dan skated up to him.* ● **skater** (**skaters**) N-COUNT ❑ *His dream was to become a professional skater.* ● **skating** N-UNCOUNT ❑ *They all went skating together.*

skateboard /ˈskeɪtbɔːd/ (**skateboards**) N-COUNT A **skateboard** is a narrow board with wheels at each end, which people stand on and ride for pleasure.
→ see Picture Dictionary: **skateboarding**

skeletal /ˈskelɪtəl/ ADJ BEFORE N **Skeletal** means relating to skeletons. ❑ *...the skeletal remains of seven adults.*
→ see **muscle**

skeleton /ˈskelɪtən/ (**skeletons**) 1 N-COUNT Your **skeleton** is the framework of bones in your body. 2 ADJ BEFORE N A **skeleton** staff is the smallest number of staff necessary to run an organization.
→ see **shark**

skeptic /ˈskeptɪk/ → see **sceptic**

skeptical /ˈskeptɪkəl/ → see **sceptical**

skepticism /ˈskeptɪsɪzəm/ → see **scepticism**

sketch /sketʃ/ (**sketches, sketching, sketched**) 1 N-COUNT A **sketch** is a drawing that is done quickly without a lot of details. ❑ *Make a rough sketch showing where the vehicles were.* 2 V-T/V-I If you **sketch** something, you make a quick rough drawing of it. ❑ *He sketched a map on the back of a menu.* ❑ *My wife sat and sketched.* 3 N-COUNT A **sketch of** an incident or person is a brief description of them without many details. ❑ *Leonard gave a brief sketch of his childhood.* 4 V-T & PHR-VERB If you **sketch** or **sketch out** a plan or incident, you briefly describe or state its main points. ❑ *I visited him in Johannesburg and sketched what I was trying to do.* 5 N-COUNT A **sketch** is a short humorous piece of acting, usually forming part of a comedy show.
→ see **animation, blog, draw**

sketchy /ˈsketʃi/ (**sketchier, sketchiest**) ADJ Something that is **sketchy** is incomplete and does not have many details. ❑ *Details are sketchy, but first reports say at least two people were injured.*

skewer /ˈskjuːə/ (**skewers, skewering, skewered**) 1 N-COUNT A **skewer** is a long metal pin which is used to hold pieces of food together during cooking. 2 V-T If you **skewer** something, you push a long, thin, pointed object through it.

Picture Dictionary **skateboarding**

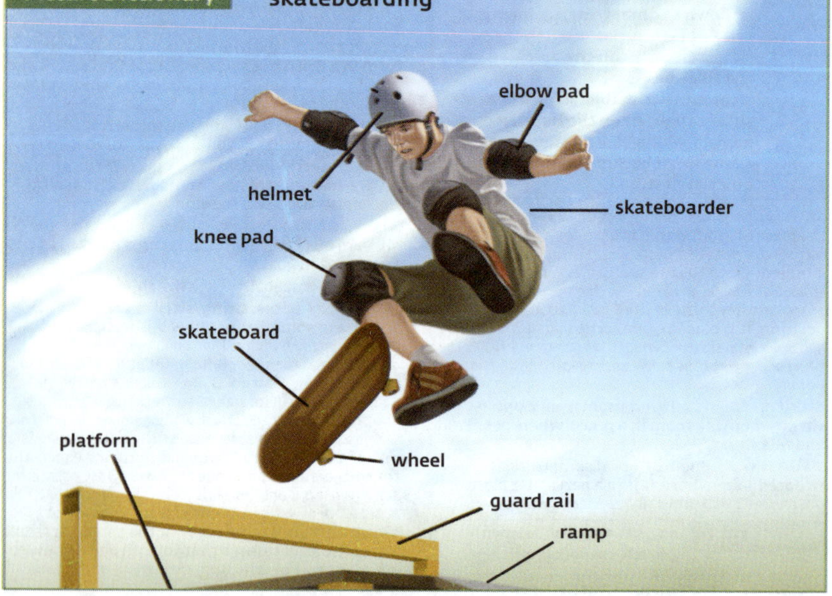

S

❑ *He skewered one of the sausages.*

ski /ski:/ (**skis, skiing, skied**) 1 N-COUNT **Skis** are long, flat, narrow pieces of wood, metal, or plastic that are fastened to boots so that you can move easily over snow. 2 V-I When people **ski**, they move over snow on skis. ● **skier** (**skiers**) N-COUNT ❑ *He is an enthusiastic skier.* ● **skiing** N-UNCOUNT ❑ *...a skiing holiday.* 3 ADJ BEFORE N **Ski** is used to refer to things that are concerned with skiing. ❑ *...a Swiss ski resort.* ❑ *...ski boots.*

skid /skɪd/ (**skids, skidding, skidded**) V-I & N-COUNT If a vehicle **skids**, or if it goes into a **skid**, it slides sideways or forwards in an uncontrolled way. ❑ *There was heavy snow and the plane skidded on landing.*

skilful [AM **skillful**] /ˈskɪlfʊl/ ADJ Someone who is **skilful** at something does it very well. ❑ *He is a particularly skilful artist.* ● **skilfully** ADV ❑ *The story is skilfully written from a child's point of view.*

skill /skɪl/ (**skills**) 1 N-COUNT A **skill** is a type of activity or work which requires special training or knowledge. ❑ *We focus on the basic skills of reading and arithmetic.* 2 N-UNCOUNT **Skill** is the knowledge and ability that enables you to do something well. ❑ *I tried fishing but had no skill and no luck.*

Thesaurus *skill* Also look up:

N. ability, proficiency, talent 1 2

skilled /skɪld/ 1 ADJ Someone who is **skilled** has the knowledge and ability to do something well. ❑ *A train driver is a highly skilled professional.* 2 ADJ **Skilled** work can only be done by people who have had some training.

skillful /ˈskɪlfʊl/ → see **skilful**

skim /skɪm/ (**skims, skimming, skimmed**) 1 V-T If you **skim** something from the surface of a liquid, you remove it. ❑ *Skim the fat off the gravy.* 2 V-T/V-I If something **skims** a surface or **skims over** it, it moves quickly along just above it. ❑ *We watched the flying fishes skimming across the water.* 3 V-T/V-I If you **skim** a piece of writing or **skim through** it, you read through it quickly. ❑ *He skimmed the pages, then read them again more carefully.*

skimpy /ˈskɪmpi/ (**skimpier, skimpiest**) ADJ **Skimpy** means too small in size or quantity. **Skimpy** clothes show a lot of someone's body. ❑ *...a skimpy skirt.*

skin /skɪn/ (**skins, skinning, skinned**) 1 N-VAR Your **skin** is the natural covering of your body. ❑ *His skin is clear and smooth.* 2 N-VAR An animal **skin** is skin which has been removed from a dead animal. ❑ *He held a bag made of crocodile skin.* 3 N-VAR The **skin** of a fruit or vegetable is its outer layer or covering. ❑ *...banana skins.* 4 N-VAR If a **skin** forms on the surface of a liquid, a thin solid layer forms on it. ❑ *Stir the sauce occasionally to prevent a skin forming.* 5 V-T & N-VAR If you **skin** a dead animal, you remove its skin, which is then referred to as an animal **skin**. ❑ *...the cruelty involved in breeding and skinning animals such as mink.*
→ see Word Web: **skin**

Word Partnership Use *skin* with:

N. skin **and bones**, skin **cancer**, skin **cells**, skin **colour (or colour of *someone's* skin)**, skin **cream**, skin **problems**, skin **type** 1
leopard skin 2

ADJ. **dark** skin, **dry** skin, **fair** skin, **oily** skin, **pale** skin, **sensitive** skin, **smooth** skin, **soft** skin 1

skinny /ˈskɪni/ (**skinnier, skinniest**) ADJ If you say that someone is **skinny**, you mean that they are very thin in a way you find unattractive. [INFORMAL] ❑ *She had thin hair and skinny legs.*

skip /skɪp/ (**skips, skipping, skipped**) 1 V-I & N-COUNT If you **skip** along, you move along with a series of little jumps from one foot to the other, called **skips**. ❑ *They skipped down the street.* ❑ *Anna gave a little skip of joy.* 2 V-I When someone **skips**, they jump up and down over a rope which they or other people are holding at each end and turning round and round. ● **skipping** N-UNCOUNT ❑ *I enjoy skipping, walking, and playing games.* 3 V-T If you **skip** something that you usually do or that most people do, you decide not to do it. ❑ *It is important not to skip meals.* 4 V-T/V-I If you **skip** a part of something you are reading or a story you are telling, you miss that part out. ❑ *She retold her own life story, skipping over the war years.* 5 N-COUNT A **skip** is a large, open, metal container used to hold and take away rubbish. [BRIT]

skipper /ˈskɪpə/ (**skippers**) N-COUNT The **skipper** of a boat or of a sports team is its captain. [INFORMAL]

skirmish /ˈskɜ:mɪʃ/ (**skirmishes**) N-COUNT A **skirmish** is a short unexpected fight or battle. ❑ *One soldier was killed in the skirmish.*

skirt /skɜ:t/ (**skirts, skirting, skirted**) 1 N-COUNT A **skirt** is a piece of clothing worn

Word Web skin

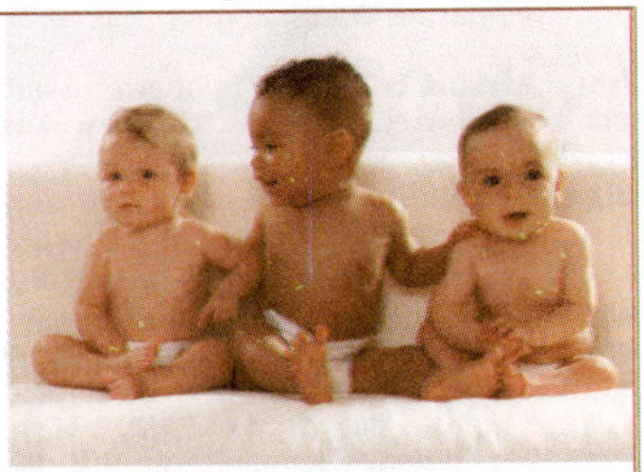

What is the best thing you can do for your **skin**? Stay out of the sun. When skin **cells** grow normally, the skin remains smooth and firm. However, the sun's **ultraviolet** rays sometimes cause damage. This can lead to **sunburn**, **wrinkles**, and skin cancer. The damage may not be apparent for several years. However, doctors have discovered that even a light **suntan** can be dangerous. **Sunlight** makes the melanin in skin turn dark. This is the body's attempt to protect itself from the ultraviolet radiation. Dermatologists recommend limiting exposure to the sun and always using a **sunscreen**.

S

by women and girls. It fastens at the waist and hangs down around the legs. **2** V-T Something that **skirts** an area is situated around the edge of it. ❑ *The path skirted the main lawn.* **3** V-T If you **skirt** something, you go around the edge of it. ❑ *She skirted round the room to the door.* **4** V-T/V-I If you **skirt** or **skirt round** a problem or question, you avoid dealing with it. ❑ *They skirted round issues that they felt were too painful to confront.*
→ see **clothing**

skull /skʌl/ (**skulls**) N-COUNT Your **skull** is the bony part of your head which holds your brain. ❑ *The headache started at the base of his skull.*

sky /skaɪ/ (**skies**) N-VAR The **sky** is the space around the earth which you can see when you stand outside and look upwards. ❑ *...warm sunshine and clear blue skies.*
→ see **star**

Word Partnership Use *sky* with:

ADV.	sky **above, the** sky **overhead, up in the** sky
ADJ.	**black** sky, **blue** sky, **bright** sky, **clear** sky, **cloudless** sky, **dark** sky, **empty** sky, **high in the** sky

skyline /ˈskaɪlaɪn/ (**skylines**) N-COUNT The **skyline** is the line or shape that is formed where the sky meets buildings or the land. ❑ *The village church is clear on the skyline.*

ˈsky ˌmarshal (**sky marshals**) N-COUNT A **sky marshal** is an armed security guard who travels on passenger flights. [mainly AM]

skyscraper /ˈskaɪskreɪpə/ (**skyscrapers**) N-COUNT A **skyscraper** is a very tall building in a city.
→ see **city**

slab /slæb/ (**slabs**) N-COUNT A **slab of** something is a thick flat piece of it. ❑ *...enormous slabs of meat.* ❑ *...huge concrete slabs.*

slack /slæk/ (**slacker, slackest**) **1** ADJ Something that is **slack** is loose and not tightly stretched. ❑ *...her dull, slack skin.* **2** ADJ A **slack** period is a time when there is not much activity. ❑ *Business has been a bit slack.* **3** ADJ If someone is **slack** in their work, they do not do it properly.

slacken /ˈslækən/ (**slackens, slackening, slackened**) **1** V-T/V-I If something **slackens**, or if you **slacken** it, it becomes slower, less active, or weaker. ❑ *The wind slackened.* ❑ *He slackened his pace for me.* **2** V-T/V-I If your **grip** or a part of your body **slackens**, or if you **slacken** it, it becomes looser or more relaxed. ❑ *Muscles stretch, slacken and relax during childbirth.*
▶ **slacken off** PHR-VERB If something **slackens off**, it becomes slower, less active, or weaker. ❑ *At about five o'clock, business slackened off.*

S

slacks /slæks/ N-PLURAL **Slacks** are casual trousers. [DATED] ❑ *She was wearing black slacks.*

slain /sleɪn/ **Slain** is the past participle of **slay**.

slam /slæm/ (**slams, slamming, slammed**) **1** V-T/V-I If you **slam** a door or window, or if it **slams**, it shuts noisily and with great force. ❑ *He slammed the gate shut behind him.* **2** V-T If you **slam** something **down**, you put it there quickly and with great force. ❑ *She slammed down the phone.* **3** V-T/V-I If one thing **slams into** another, or if it **slams against** another, it crashes into it with great force. ❑ *He was killed when his car slammed into a truck.* ❑ *He slammed his fist against the wall.*

Word Partnership Use *slam* with:

N.	slam **a door** **1**
V.	**hear *something*** slam **1**
ADJ.	slam **(*something*) shut** **1**

slander /ˈslɑːndə, ˈslæn-/ (**slanders, slandering, slandered**) **1** N-VAR **Slander** is an untrue spoken statement about someone which is intended to damage their reputation. ❑ *He has accused his former wife of slander.* **2** V-T If someone **slanders** you, they make untrue spoken statements about you in order to damage your reputation.

slang /slæŋ/ N-UNCOUNT **Slang** is words, expressions, and meanings that are informal and are used by people who know each other very well or who have the same interests. ❑ *...US Army slang.*

slant /slɑːnt, slænt/ (**slants, slanting, slanted**) **1** V-I Something that **slants** is sloping, rather than horizontal or vertical. ❑ *The morning sun slanted through the glass roof.* **2** N-SING If something is **on a slant**, it is in a sloping position. **3** V-T If information or a system **is slanted**, it is made to show favour towards a particular group or opinion. ❑ *The programme was slanted to make the home team look good.* **4** N-SING A particular **slant** on a subject is a particular way of thinking about it, especially one that is unfair. ❑ *They give a slant to every news item.*

slap /slæp/ (**slaps, slapping, slapped**) **1** V-T & N-COUNT If you **slap** someone, or if you **give** them a **slap**, you hit them with the palm of your hand. ❑ *I slapped him hard across the face.* **2** PHRASE If you describe something that someone does as **a slap in the face**, you mean that it shocks or upsets you because it shows that they do not support you or respect you. **3** V-T If you **slap** someone **on the back**, you hit them in a friendly way on their back. **4** V-T If you **slap** something onto a surface, you put it there quickly and carelessly, often with a lot of force. ❑ *I slapped the sweets down on the table.* ❑ *They slapped paint on to the wall.*

Word Partnership Use *slap* with:

N.	**a** slap **on the back, a** slap **in the face, a** slap **on the wrist** **1**

slash /slæʃ/ (**slashes, slashing, slashed**) **1** V-T If you **slash** something, you make a long deep cut in it. ❑ *Four cars had their tyres slashed.* **2** V-I If you **slash at** something, you quickly hit at it with something. ❑ *She slashed at me with a large kitchen knife.* **3** V-T To **slash** something such as costs or jobs means to reduce them by a large amount. [INFORMAL] **4** N-COUNT You say **slash** to refer to a sloping line that separates letters, words, or numbers. For example, if you are giving the number 340/2/K you say 'Three four zero, slash two, slash K.'

slate /sleɪt/ (**slates**) **1** N-UNCOUNT **Slate** is a dark grey rock that can be easily split into thin layers. **2** N-COUNT A **slate** is one of the small flat pieces of slate that are used for covering roofs.

slaughter /ˈslɔːtə/ (**slaughters, slaughtering, slaughtered**) **1** V-T & N-UNCOUNT If large numbers of people or animals **are slaughtered**,

Word Web sleep

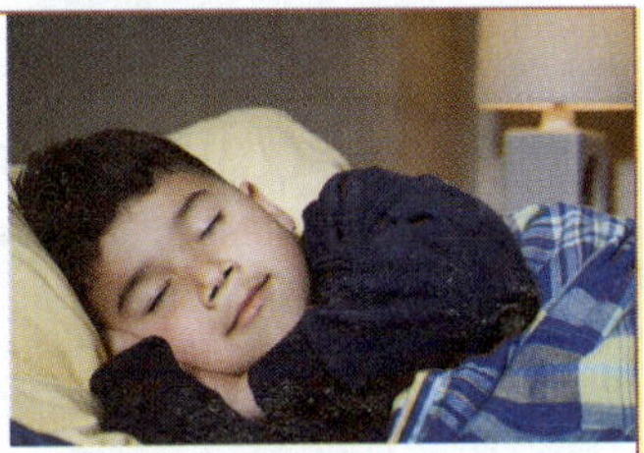

Do you ever go to **bed** and then discover you can't **fall asleep**? You **yawn**. You feel **tired**. But your body isn't ready for **rest**. You **toss** and **turn** and pound the **pillow** for hours. After a while you may **doze**, but then five minutes later you're **wide awake**. The scientific name for this condition is **insomnia**. There are many causes for **sleeplessness**. If you **nap** too late in the day it may change your normal sleep cycle. Worrying can also affect sleep patterns.

they are killed in a way that is cruel, unjust, or unnecessary. **Slaughter** is the cruel, unjust, or unnecessary killing of large numbers of people or animals. ❑ *He was responsible for the slaughter of many families.* 2 V-T & N-UNCOUNT To **slaughter** animals such as cows and sheep means to kill them for their meat. **Slaughter** is the killing of animals for their meat. ❑ *The pigs are ready for slaughter at four to six months.* 3 → See note at **kill**

slave /sleɪv/ (**slaves**) 1 N-COUNT A **slave** is a person who is owned by another person and has to work for that person without pay. 2 V-I If you say that a person **is slaving over** something or **is slaving for** something, you mean that they are working very hard. ❑ *He slaved over his poem for three evenings.*

slavery /ˈsleɪvəri/ N-UNCOUNT **Slavery** is the system by which people are owned by other people as slaves. ❑ *After years of slavery he escaped from his master.*

slay /sleɪ/ (**slays, slaying, slew, slain**) V-T To **slay** a person or animal means to kill them. [LITERARY] ❑ *Saint George is supposed to have slain a dragon.*

sleazy /ˈsliːzi/ (**sleazier, sleaziest**) 1 ADJ If you describe a place as **sleazy**, you dislike it because it looks dirty and not respectable. [INFORMAL] ❑ *...sleazy nightclubs.* 2 ADJ If you describe something or someone as **sleazy**, you disapprove of them because you think they are not respectable. [INFORMAL] ❑ *...sleazy magazines.*

sled /sled/ (**sleds**) N-COUNT A **sled** is the same as a **sledge**. [AM]

sledge /sledʒ/ (**sledges, sledging, sledged**) N-COUNT & V-I A **sledge** is a vehicle for travelling over snow. It consists of a frame which slides on two strips of wood or metal. If you **sledge** or go **sledging**, you ride on a sledge. [BRIT]

sleek /sliːk/ (**sleeker, sleekest**) 1 ADJ **Sleek** hair or fur is smooth and shiny and looks healthy. 2 ADJ A **sleek** person looks rich and stylish. 3 ADJ **Sleek** vehicles, furniture, or other objects look smooth, shiny, and expensive.

sleep /sliːp/ (**sleeps, sleeping, slept**) 1 N-UNCOUNT **Sleep** is the natural state of rest in which your eyes are closed, your body is inactive, and your mind does not think. ❑ *Try and get some sleep.* ❑ *Be quiet and go to sleep.* 2 V-I & N-COUNT When you **sleep**, you rest with your eyes closed and your mind and body inactive. A **sleep** is a period of sleeping. ❑ *She slept till noon.* ❑ *The pool was surrounded by sleeping sunbathers.* ❑ *I think he'll be ready for a sleep soon.* 3 V-I If one person **sleeps with** another, or if two people **sleep together**, they have sex. 4 V-T If a building or room **sleeps** a particular number of people, it has beds for that number of people. ❑ *The villa sleeps 10.* 5 PHRASE If you say that you did not **lose** any **sleep over** something, you mean that you did not worry about it at all. 6 PHRASE If a sick or injured animal **is put to sleep**, it is painlessly killed by a vet. 7 to **sleep rough** → see **rough**

→ see Word Web: **sleep**
→ see **dream**

▶ **sleep off** PHR-VERB If you **sleep off** the effects of too much drink, food, or travelling, you recover from it by sleeping. ❑ *Spend the first night of your holiday sleeping off the journey.*

▶ **sleep through** PHR-VERB If you **sleep through** a noise, it does not wake you up. ❑ *They slept right through the alarm.*

Usage

There are several verbal expressions in English which refer to the moment when you start to sleep. When you go to bed at night, you normally **go to sleep** or **fall asleep**. When you **go to sleep**, it is usually a deliberate action. ❑ *He didn't want to go to sleep.* You can **fall asleep** by accident, or at a time when you should be awake. ❑ *I've seen doctors fall asleep in the operating theatre.* If you have difficulty sleeping, you can say that you cannot **get to sleep**. ❑ *Sometimes the fever prevents the child from getting to sleep.*

Thesaurus *sleep* Also look up:

N.	nap, rest, slumber 1
V.	doze, rest; (*ant.*) awaken, wake 2

Word Partnership Use *sleep* with:

N.	sleep **deprivation**, sleep **disorder**, sleep **on the floor**, **hours of** sleep, **lack of** sleep, sleep **nights** 1
V.	**can't/couldn't** sleep, **drift off to** sleep, **get enough** sleep, **get some** sleep, **go to** sleep, **need** sleep 1
ADJ.	**deep** sleep, **good** sleep 1

sleeper /ˈsliːpə/ (**sleepers**) 1 N-COUNT You can use **sleeper** to indicate how well someone sleeps. For example, if someone is a light **sleeper**, they are easily woken up. ❑ *I'm a very heavy sleeper.* 2 N-COUNT A **sleeper** is a train with beds for passengers on overnight journeys. You can also refer to the beds themselves as **sleepers**. [BRIT] ❑ *The train has first- and second-class sleepers as well as a buffet car.*

S

ˈsleeping ˌbag (**sleeping bags**) N-COUNT A **sleeping bag** is a large warm bag for sleeping in, especially when you are camping.

sleepless /ˈsli:pləs/ **1** ADJ A **sleepless night** is one during which you do not sleep. **2** ADJ Someone who is **sleepless** is unable to sleep. ❑ *She was sitting there, sad and sleepless.* • **sleeplessness** N-UNCOUNT ❑ *He suffered from sleeplessness.*

sleepover /ˈsli:pəʊvə/ (**sleepovers**) N-COUNT A **sleepover** is an occasion when a child stays at a friend's home for the night.

sleepy /ˈsli:pi/ (**sleepier, sleepiest**) **1** ADJ If you feel **sleepy**, you feel tired and ready to go to sleep. ❑ *'Are we here?' she said in a sleepy voice.* • **sleepily** ADV ❑ *Joanna sat up, blinking sleepily.* **2** ADJ A **sleepy** place is very quiet and does not have much activity or excitement. ❑ *...a sleepy fishing village.*

sleet /sli:t/ N-UNCOUNT **Sleet** is rain that is partly frozen.
→ see **water**

sleeve /sli:v/ (**sleeves**) **1** N-COUNT The **sleeves** of a coat, shirt, or other item of clothing are the parts that cover your arms. ❑ *...a shirt with long sleeves.* **2** PHRASE If you have something **up** your **sleeve**, you have an idea or plan which you have not told anyone about. ❑ *I still have a few ideas up my sleeve.* **3** N-COUNT In British English, a record **sleeve** is the stiff envelope in which a record is kept. The usual American word is **jacket**.

sleigh /sleɪ/ (**sleighs**) N-COUNT A **sleigh** is a vehicle which can slide over snow. Sleighs are usually pulled by horses.

slender /ˈslendə/ **1** ADJ A **slender** person is thin and graceful in an attractive way. [WRITTEN] ❑ *...a tall slender woman.* ❑ *...her long slender legs.* **2** ADJ You can use **slender** to describe a situation which exists but only to a very small degree. [WRITTEN] ❑ *England had a slender lead of 20 points.*

slept /slept/ **Slept** is the past tense and past participle of **sleep**.

slew /slu:/ **Slew** is the past tense of **slay**.

slice /slaɪs/ (**slices, slicing, sliced**) **1** N-COUNT A **slice of** bread, meat, fruit, or other food is a thin piece that has been cut from a larger piece. ❑ *...a slice of lemon.* ❑ *Cut the onion into slices.* **2** V-T If you **slice** food, you cut it into thin pieces. ❑ *Slice the potatoes very finely.* ❑ *I usually buy sliced bread.* **3** V-T If something **slices through** a substance, it moves through it quickly, like a knife. [LITERARY] ❑ *The ship sliced through the water.* **4** N-COUNT If you talk about someone getting a **slice of** something, you mean that they get a part of it. ❑ *The company is trying to win a bigger slice of the international market.*
→ see **bread, cut**

S

Word Partnership Use *slice* with:

ADJ.	**small** slice, **thin** slice **1**
N.	slice **of bread**, slice **of pie**, slice **of pizza** **1**
	slice **a cake** **2**
	slice **of life** **4**
PREP.	slice **into**, slice **off**, slice **through** **2**

slick /slɪk/ (**slicker, slickest, slicks**) **1** ADJ A **slick** performance, production, or advertisement is presented in an attractive and professional way. **2** ADJ A **slick** action is done quickly and smoothly, and without any obvious effort. **3** ADJ If you describe someone as **slick**, you dislike them because they speak easily and persuasively but are not sincere. ❑ *...slick politicians.* **4** N-COUNT A **slick** is the same as an **oil slick**.

slide /slaɪd/ (**slides, sliding, slid** /slɪd/) **1** V-T/V-I When something **slides** somewhere, or when you **slide** it somewhere, it moves there smoothly over or against something else. ❑ *Tears were sliding down his cheeks.* ❑ *She slid the door open.* **2** V-I If you **slide** somewhere, you move there smoothly and quietly. ❑ *He slid into the driver's seat.* **3** N-COUNT A **slide** in a playground is a structure that has a steep slope for children to slide down. **4** V-I To **slide into** a particular mood, attitude, or situation means to gradually start to have that mood, attitude, or situation, often without intending to. ❑ *She slid into a daydream.* **5** N-COUNT A **slide** is a small piece of photographic film with a picture on it, which you can see when you shine light through it.

Word Partnership Use *slide* with:

V.	**begin to** slide, **continue to** slide **1** **2** **4**
ADJ.	**recent** slide, **steep** slide **4**

slight /slaɪt/ (**slighter, slightest, slights, slighting, slighted**) **1** ADJ Something that is **slight** is very small in degree or quantity. ❑ *Doctors say he has made a slight improvement.* ❑ *He's not the slightest bit worried.* **2** PHRASE You use **in the slightest** to emphasize a negative statement. ❑ *That doesn't interest me in the slightest.* **3** ADJ A **slight** person has a slim and delicate body. **4** V-T & N-COUNT If you **are slighted**, someone does or says something that insults you by treating you as if your views or feelings are not important. You refer to what that person does or says as a **slight**. ❑ *They felt slighted because nobody asked their opinions.*

slightly /ˈslaɪtli/ ADV **Slightly** means to some degree but not much. ❑ *His family moved to a slightly larger house.* ❑ *You can adjust it slightly.*

slim /slɪm/ (**slimmer, slimmest, slims, slimming, slimmed**) **1** ADJ A **slim** person has a thin nicely-shaped body. **2** V-I If you **are slimming**, you are trying to make yourself thinner and lighter by eating less food. • **slimmer** (**slimmers**) N-COUNT ❑ *...meals for slimmers.* • **slimming** N-UNCOUNT ❑ *We reviewed four different slimming guides.* **3** ADJ A **slim** book, wallet, or other object is thinner than usual. **4** ADJ A **slim** chance or possibility is a very small one. ❑ *The chances of your book getting published are very slim.*

▸ **slim down** PHR-VERB If a company or other organization **slims down**, or if it **is slimmed down**, it employs fewer people, in order to save money or become more efficient.

Word Partnership Use *slim* with:

ADJ.	**tall and** slim **1**
ADV.	**pretty** slim, **very** slim **1** **3**
N.	slim **chance**, slim **lead**, slim **margin** **4**

slime /slaɪm/ N-UNCOUNT **Slime** is a thick slippery substance, for example the substance which comes from a snail.

sling /slɪŋ/ (**slings, slinging, slung**) **1** V-T If you **sling** something somewhere, you throw it there carelessly. ❑ *He took off his anorak and slung it onto the back seat of the car.* **2** V-T If you **sling** something over your shoulder or over something such as a chair, you hang it there loosely. ❑ *He had a small green bag slung over one shoulder.* **3** V-T If a rope, blanket, or other object **is slung** between two points, it is hung loosely between them. ❑ *The ropes were slung between the trees.* **4** N-COUNT A **sling** is an object made of ropes, straps, or cloth that is used for carrying things. ❑ *Most babies love to be carried in a baby sling.* **5** N-COUNT A **sling** is a piece of cloth used to support an injured arm. It goes under someone's lower arm and is tied around their neck. ❑ *Next day she was back at work with her arm in a sling.*

slip /slɪp/ (**slips, slipping, slipped**) **1** V-I If you **slip**, you accidentally slide and lose your balance. ❑ *I slipped on some ice.* **2** V-I If something **slips**, it slides out of place or out of your hand. ❑ *His glasses slipped down his nose.* **3** V-I If you **slip** somewhere, you go there quickly and quietly. ❑ *Amy slipped downstairs and out of the house.* ❑ *I slipped out of bed.* **4** V-T If you **slip** something somewhere, you put it there quickly in a way that does not attract attention. ❑ *He slipped the money into his pocket.* **5** V-T If you **slip** something **to** someone, or if you **slip** someone something, you give it to them secretly. ❑ *Robert slipped her a note in school.* **6** V-I To **slip into** a particular state or situation means to pass gradually into it, in a way that is hardly noticed. ❑ *Don't slip into the habit of sleeping late.* **7** V-T/V-I If you **slip into** or **slip out of** clothes or shoes, you put them on or take them off quickly and easily. ❑ *Laila slipped into her swimsuit.* ❑ *I slipped out of my coat.* **8** N-COUNT A **slip** is a small or unimportant mistake. **9** N-COUNT A **slip of** paper is a small piece of paper.

▶ **slip up** PHR-VERB If you **slip up**, you make a small or unimportant mistake.

Thesaurus *slip* Also look up:

V.	fall, slide, trip **1**
N.	blunder, mistake **8**
	leaf, sheet, page, paper **9**

Word Partnership Use *slip* with:

ADJ.	slip **resistant** **1**
N.	slip **of paper**, **sales** slip **9**

slipper /ˈslɪpə/ (**slippers**) N-COUNT **Slippers** are loose soft shoes that you wear in the house.

slippery /ˈslɪpəri/ **1** ADJ Something that is **slippery** is smooth, wet, or greasy, making it difficult to walk on or to hold. ❑ *Motorists were warned about slippery roads.*

slit /slɪt/ (**slits, slitting, slit**) **1** V-T If you **slit** something, you make a long narrow cut in it. ❑ *He slit open the bag with a penknife.* **2** N-COUNT A **slit** is a long narrow cut or opening in something. ❑ *She watched them through a slit in the curtains.*
→ see **shark**

slither /ˈslɪðə/ (**slithers, slithering, slithered**) V-I If you **slither** somewhere, you slide along, often in an uncontrolled way. ❑ *Robert fell in the mud and slithered down the bank.*

sliver /ˈslɪvə/ (**slivers**) N-COUNT A **sliver of** something is a small thin piece or amount of it. ❑ *...slivers of glass.*

slog /slɒg/ (**slogs, slogging, slogged**) **1** V-T If you **slog through** something, you work hard and steadily through it. [INFORMAL] ❑ *She has slogged her way through ballet classes since the age of six.* **2** N-SING If you describe a task as a **slog**, you mean that it is tiring and needs a lot of effort. [INFORMAL] **3** V-I & N-SING If you **slog** somewhere, you make a long and tiring journey there, which you can refer to as a **slog**. [INFORMAL] ❑ *...a slog through the bushes to the top of the hill.*

slogan /ˈsləʊgən/ (**slogans**) N-COUNT A **slogan** is a short phrase that is easy to remember and is used in advertisements and by political parties.

slop /slɒp/ (**slops, slopping, slopped**) V-T/V-I If you **slop** liquid, or if it **slops**, it spills over the edge of a container in a messy way. ❑ *She slopped some tea into the saucer.*

slope /sləʊp/ (**slopes, sloping, sloped**) **1** N-COUNT A **slope** is a surface that is at an angle, so that one end is higher than the other. ❑ *The house was built on a slope.* **2** V-I If a surface **slopes**, it is at an angle, so that one end is higher than the other. ❑ *The bank sloped down to the river.* ● **sloping** ADJ ❑ *...the gently sloping beach.* **3** V-I If something **slopes**, it leans to the right or to the left rather than being upright. ❑ *His writing sloped backwards.* **4** N-SING The **slope** of something is the angle at which it slopes. ❑ *...a slope of ten degrees.*

sloppy /ˈslɒpi/ (**sloppier, sloppiest**) ADJ Work that is **sloppy** is messy and careless. [INFORMAL] ❑ *He hates sloppy writing and careless spelling.* ● **sloppiness** N-UNCOUNT ❑ *She won't accept any sloppiness.*

slot /slɒt/ (**slots, slotting, slotted**) **1** N-COUNT A **slot** is a narrow opening in a machine or container, for example a hole that you put coins in to make a machine work. **2** V-T/V-I When something **slots into** something else, or when you **slot** it **in**, you put it into a space where it fits. ❑ *The car seat belt slotted into place easily.* **3** N-COUNT A **slot** in a schedule or scheme is a place in it where an activity can take place. ❑ *...her daily slot on the TV programme 'Hot Chefs'.*

slouch /slaʊtʃ/ (**slouches, slouching, slouched**) V-I & N-SING If you **slouch**, or if your body is in a **slouch**, you sit, stand, or walk with your shoulders and head drooping down. ❑ *Try not to slouch when you are sitting down.* ❑ *He sat slouched over his coffee.* ❑ *He walked with a slouch.*

slow /sləʊ/ (**slower, slowest, slows, slowing, slowed**) **1** ADJ Something that is **slow** moves, happens, or is done without much speed. ❑ *The traffic is heavy and slow.* ❑ *...slow, regular breathing.* ❑ *Getting a passport can be a slow process.* ● **slowly** ADV ❑ *Chris backed slowly away.* ❑ *My love for her slowly began to die.* ● **slowness** N-UNCOUNT ❑ *The hours passed with painful slowness.* **2** V-T/V-I If something **slows**, or if you **slow** it, it starts to move or happen more slowly. ❑ *She suddenly slowed the car.* **3** ADJ AFTER LINK-V If someone is **slow to** do something or **slow in** doing something, they do it after a delay. ❑ *The government was slow to react to the crisis.* ❑ *I've been a bit slow in making up my mind.* **4** ADJ If you describe a situation, place, or activity as **slow**, you mean that it is not very exciting. ❑ *The island is too slow for her liking.* **5** ADJ If a clock or watch is **slow**, it shows a time that is earlier than the correct time. **6** ADJ Someone who is **slow** is not very clever and takes a long time to understand things.

▶ **slow down** 1 PHR-VERB If something **slows down**, or if you **slow** it **down**, it starts to move or happen more slowly. ❑ *The car slowed down.* ❑ *We cannot stop Venice sinking eventually, but we can slow the process down.* 2 PHR-VERB If someone **slows down**, they become less active. ❑ *He may be 72, but Waterhouse shows no signs of slowing down.* 3 → see also **slowdown**

▶ **slow up** PHR-VERB **Slow up** means the same as **slow down** (meaning 1). ❑ *The new working methods have slowed up the system.*

Word Partnership Use *slow* with:

ADJ. slow **acting**, slow **moving** 1
slow **but steady** 1 3
N. slow **movements**, slow **speed**, slow **traffic** 1
slow **death**, slow **growth**, slow **pace**, slow **process**, slow **progress**, slow **recovery**, slow **response**, slow **sales**, slow **start**, slow **stop** 3

Word Link *down ≈ below, lower : downfall, downhill, slowdown*

slowdown /ˈsləʊdaʊn/ (**slowdowns**) 1 N-COUNT A **slowdown** is a reduction in speed or activity. ❑ *There has been a sharp slowdown in economic growth.* 2 → see also **slow down**

ˌslow ˈmotion N-UNCOUNT When film or television pictures are shown in **slow motion**, they are shown much more slowly than normal.

sludge /slʌdʒ/ N-UNCOUNT **Sludge** is thick mud.

slug /slʌg/ (**slugs**) N-COUNT A **slug** is a small slow-moving creature, with a long slippery body, like a snail without a shell.

sluggish /ˈslʌgɪʃ/ ADJ Something that is **sluggish** moves or works much more slowly than normal. ❑ *Remember how sluggish your brain feels when you return to work after a holiday.*

slum /slʌm/ (**slums**) N-COUNT A **slum** is an area of a city where living conditions are very bad.

S

slumber /ˈslʌmbə/ (**slumbers, slumbering, slumbered**) 1 N-VAR **Slumber** is sleep. [LITERARY] ❑ *He woke Charles from his slumbers.* 2 V-I Someone who **is slumbering** is sleeping. [LITERARY]

ˈslumber ˌparty (**slumber parties**) N-COUNT A **slumber party** is an occasion when a group of young friends spend the night together at the home of one of the group. [AM]

slump /slʌmp/ (**slumps, slumping, slumped**) 1 N-COUNT & V-I If there is a **slump in** something such as the value of something, or if it **slumps**, it falls suddenly and by a large amount. ❑ *...a slump in house prices.* ❑ *Profits slumped by 41%.* 2 N-COUNT A **slump** is a time when there is a lot of unemployment and poverty. 3 V-I If you **slump** somewhere, you fall or sit down there heavily. ❑ *She slumped into a chair.*

slung /slʌŋ/ **Slung** is the past tense and past participle of **sling**.

slur /slɜː/ (**slurs, slurring, slurred**) 1 N-COUNT A **slur** is an insulting remark which could damage someone's reputation. ❑ *This is yet another slur on their neighbourhood's reputation.* 2 V-T/V-I If someone **slurs** their speech or **slurs**, they do not pronounce each word clearly, because they are drunk or sleepy. ❑ *The newsreader's words began to slur.* ● **slurred** ADJ ❑ *His left hand shook and his speech was slurred.*

sly /slaɪ/ (**slyer, slyest**) 1 ADJ A **sly** look, expression, or remark shows that you know something that other people do not know. ❑ *He gave me a sly, meaningful look.* ● **slyly** ADV ❑ *Anna grinned slyly.* 2 ADJ If you describe someone as **sly**, you mean that they are clever at deceiving people.

smack /smæk/ (**smacks, smacking, smacked**) 1 V-T & N-COUNT If you **smack** someone, or if you **give** them a **smack**, you hit them with your hand. ❑ *She smacked me on the side of the head.* ❑ *...a smack across the face.* 2 V-T If you **smack** something somewhere, you put it or throw it there so that it makes a loud sharp noise. ❑ *He took the letter out and smacked it down on the desk.* 3 V-I If something **smacks of** something that you consider bad, it reminds you of it or is like it. ❑ *We won't support anything that smacks of terrorism.*

small /smɔːl/ (**smaller, smallest**) 1 ADJ Someone or something that is **small** is not large in physical size. ❑ *She is small for her age.* ❑ *The window was too small for him to get through.* 2 ADJ A **small** group or quantity consists of only a few people or things. ❑ *...a small team of doctors and nurses.* ❑ *...a small amount of money.* 3 ADJ A **small** child is a very young child. ❑ *What were you like when you were small?* 4 ADJ You use **small** to describe something that is not significant or great in degree. ❑ *She remembered even the smallest details.* ❑ *...a relatively small problem.* 5 ADJ AFTER LINK-V If someone makes you look or feel **small**, they make you look or feel stupid. ❑ *The teachers at school always made me feel small.* 6 N-SING **The small of** your **back** is the bottom part of your back that curves inwards slightly. 7 **small wonder** → see **wonder**

Usage

You use the adjective **small** rather than **little** to draw attention to the fact that something is small. For instance, you cannot say 'The town is little' or 'I have a very little car' but you can say **'The town is small'** or **'I have a very small car'**. **Little** is a less precise word than **small**, and may be used to suggest the speaker's feelings or attitude towards the person or thing being described. For that reason, **little** is often used after another adjective. ❑ *What a nice little house you've got here!* ❑ *Be quiet, you horrible little boy!*

Thesaurus *small* Also look up:

ADJ. little, minute, petite, slight; (*ant.*) big, large 1
young 3
insignificant, minor; (*ant.*) important, major, significant 4

ˌsmall ˈprint N-UNCOUNT **The small print** of a contract or agreement is the part of it that is written in very small print.

,small-'scale ADJ A **small-scale** activity or organization is not a big or extensive one. ❑ *...small-scale projects.*

smart /smɑːt/ (**smarter, smartest, smarts, smarting, smarted**) **1** ADJ **Smart** people and things are pleasantly neat and clean in appearance. ❑ *I wore a black dress and looked very smart.* ❑ *...smart new offices.* ● **smartly** ADV ❑ *He dresses very smartly.* **2** ADJ A **smart** place or event is connected with wealthy and fashionable people. ❑ *...smart London dinner parties.* **3** ADJ You can describe someone who is clever as **smart**. ❑ *He's a smart kid.* **4** V-I If a part of your body or a wound **smarts**, you feel a sharp stinging pain in it. ❑ *Her eyes were smarting from the smoke.* **5** V-I If you **are smarting from** something such as criticism or failure, you feel upset about it. ❑ *The team was still smarting from its defeat.*

smartly /'smɑːtli/ **1** ADV If someone moves or does something **smartly**, they do it quickly and neatly. [WRITTEN] ❑ *She can move smartly when she wants to.* **2** → see also **smart**

'smart phone (**smart phones**) N-COUNT A **smart phone** is a type of cellphone that can perform many of the operations that a computer does, such as accessing the Internet.

smash /smæʃ/ (**smashes, smashing, smashed**) **1** V-T/V-I If something **smashes**, or if you **smash** it, it breaks into many pieces, for example when it is hit or dropped. ❑ *Two or three glasses fell and smashed into pieces.* ❑ *Someone smashed a bottle.* **2** V-T/V-I If you **smash through** a wall, gate, or door, you get through it by hitting and breaking it. ❑ *Demonstrators used trucks to smash through the gates.* ❑ *Soldiers smashed their way into his office.* **3** V-T/V-I If something **smashes** or **is smashed** against something solid, it moves with great force against it. ❑ *He smashed his fist into Anthony's face.* **4** N-COUNT You can refer to a car crash as a **smash**. [INFORMAL]

▸ **smash up** PHR-VERB If you **smash** something **up**, you completely destroy it by hitting it and breaking it into many pieces. ❑ *The hooligans smashed up furniture and broke windows.*

smashing /'smæʃɪŋ/ ADJ If you describe something or someone as **smashing**, you mean that you like them very much. [BRIT, DATED] ❑ *They are smashing people.*

smear /smɪə/ (**smears, smearing, smeared**) **1** V-T If you **smear** a surface **with** a substance, or if you **smear** the substance onto the surface, you spread a layer of the substance over the surface. ❑ *My sister smeared herself with suntan oil.* ❑ *Smear a little olive oil over the inside of the salad bowl.* ● **smeared** ADJ ❑ *The child's face was smeared with dirt.* **2** N-COUNT A **smear** is a dirty or greasy mark. **3** V-T & N-COUNT To **smear** someone means to spread unpleasant and untrue rumours or accusations about them in order to damage their reputation. A **smear** is an unpleasant and untrue rumour or accusation. ❑ *...a smear campaign by his political opponents.*

smell /smel/ (**smells, smelling, smelled** or **smelt**) **1** N-COUNT The **smell of** something is a quality it has which you become aware of through your nose. ❑ *...the smell of freshly baked bread.* ❑ *...horrible smells.* **2** N-UNCOUNT Your sense of **smell** is the ability that your nose has to detect things. **3** V-I If something **smells of** a particular thing, it has a particular quality which you become aware of through your nose. ❑ *The room smelled of lemons.* ❑ *It smells delicious.* **4** V-I If you say that something **smells**, you mean that it smells unpleasant. ❑ *Do my feet smell?* **5** V-T If you **smell** something, you become aware of it through your nose. ❑ *As soon as we opened the door we could smell the gas.* **6** V-T If you **smell** something, you put your nose near it and breathe in, so that you can discover its smell. ❑ *I took a rose out of the vase and smelled it.*

→ see Word Web: **smell**

→ see **taste**

Thesaurus *smell* Also look up:

N.	aroma, fragrance, odor, scent **1**	
V.	reek, stink **4**	
	breathe, inhale, sniff **5**	

smelly /'smeli/ (**smellier, smelliest**) ADJ Something that is **smelly** has an unpleasant smell. ❑ *He had extremely smelly feet.*

smelt /smelt/ (**smelts, smelting, smelted**) **1** **Smelt** is a past tense and past participle of **smell**. **2** V-T To **smelt** a substance containing metal means to process it by heating it until it melts, so that the metal is extracted and changed chemically.

→ see **mineral**

smile /smaɪl/ (**smiles, smiling, smiled**) **1** V-I & N-COUNT When you **smile**, the corners of your mouth curve outwards, usually because you are pleased or amused. The expression on your face when you smile is called a **smile**. ❑ *He loved to make people smile.* ❑ *Both of them smiled at the picture.* ❑ *She had a big smile on her face.* **2** V-T If you **smile** something, you express or say it with a smile. ❑ *'Aren't we silly?' she smiled.*

S

Word Web smell

Scientists say that the average person can recognize about 10,000 different **odours**. Until recently we didn't understand the **sense** of **smell**. Now we know that most substances send odour molecules into the air. They enter the body through the **nose**. When they reach the **nasal cavity**, they attach to **sensory** cells. The olfactory **nerve** carries the information to the brain. The brain identifies the smell. The eyes, mouth, and throat also have receptors that add to the olfactory experience. Interestingly, our sense of smell is better later in the day than it is in the morning.

Word Partnership Use *smile* with:

V. smile **and laugh**, **make** ***someone*** smile, smile **and nod**, **see** ***someone*** smile, **try to** smile 1
smile **fades**, **flash a** smile, **give** ***someone*** **a** smile 2
ADJ. **big/little/small** smile, **broad** smile, **friendly** smile, **half** smile, **sad** smile, **shy** smile, **warm** smile, **wide** smile, **wry** smile 1

smirk /smɜːk/ (**smirks, smirking, smirked**) V-I & N-COUNT If you **smirk**, or if you give a **smirk**, you smile in an unpleasant way. ❑ *Charlene smirked at Mona's dress.* ❑ *'Yeah, right,' he said with a smirk.*

smog /smɒg/ N-UNCOUNT **Smog** is a mixture of fog and smoke which occurs in some industrial cities.
→ see **ozone, pollution**

smoke /sməʊk/ (**smokes, smoking, smoked**) 1 N-UNCOUNT **Smoke** consists of gas and small bits of solid material that are sent into the air when something burns. ❑ *I can smell smoke.* 2 V-I If something **is smoking**, smoke is coming from it. ❑ *Heat the oil until it starts to smoke.* 3 V-T/V-I When someone **smokes** a cigarette, cigar, or pipe, they suck smoke from it into their mouth and blow it out again. If someone **smokes**, they regularly smoke cigarettes, cigars, or a pipe. ❑ *He sat and smoked quietly.* ● **smoker** (**smokers**) N-COUNT ❑ *He was not a heavy smoker.* ● **smoking** N-UNCOUNT ❑ *Smoking will not be allowed.* ❑ *...a no-smoking area.* 4 V-T If fish or meat **is smoked**, it is hung over burning wood so that the smoke preserves it and gives it a special flavour. ❑ *...smoked salmon.*
→ see **fire**

smoky /ˈsməʊki/ (**smokier, smokiest**) 1 ADJ A **smoky** place has a lot of smoke in the air. 2 ADJ You can use **smoky** to describe something that looks or tastes like smoke. ❑ *The tea has a special smoky flavour.* ❑ *...her smoky blue eyes.*

smolder /ˈsməʊldə/ → see **smoulder**

smooth /smuːð/ (**smoother, smoothest, smooths, smoothing, smoothed**) 1 ADJ A **smooth** surface has no roughness or holes. ❑ *Use a sheet of glass, plastic, or any smooth surface.* ● **smoothness** N-UNCOUNT ❑ *...the smoothness of her skin.* 2 ADJ A **smooth** liquid or mixture has been mixed well so that it has no lumps in it. ❑ *Mix the sauce until it is smooth.* 3 ADJ A **smooth** movement or process happens or is done evenly and steadily with no sudden changes or breaks. ❑ *He turned round in a smooth movement.* ❑ *Draw a smooth curve between the points on the graph.* ● **smoothly** ADV ❑ *She moved smoothly – gliding rather than walking.* 4 ADJ **Smooth** means successful and without problems. ❑ *His business has followed a smooth course since he started it.* ● **smoothly** ADV ❑ *So far, talks at GM have gone smoothly.* 5 ADJ If you describe a drink such as wine, whisky, or coffee as **smooth**, you mean that it is not bitter and is pleasant to drink. 6 ADJ If you describe a man as **smooth**, you mean that he is extremely smart, confident, and polite, often in a way that you find rather unpleasant. 7 V-T If you **smooth** something, or if you **smooth** it **out** or smooth it **down**, you move your hands over its surface to make it smooth and flat. ❑ *She stood up and smoothed down her dress.* ❑ *Carefully Nick smoothed a sheet of newspaper out in front of him.* 8 PHRASE If you **smooth the path** or **smooth the way** towards something, you make it easier or more likely to happen. ❑ *The meeting has smoothed the way for peace talks tomorrow.*
→ see **muscle**
▶ **smooth out** or **smooth over** PHR-VERB If you **smooth out** or **smooth over** a problem or difficulty, you make it less serious and easier to deal with, especially by talking to the people concerned. ❑ *If you think this is going to smooth out your problems with him, you're wrong.*

smother /ˈsmʌðə/ (**smothers, smothering, smothered**) 1 V-T If you **smother** a fire, you cover it with something in order to put it out. 2 V-T To **smother** someone means to kill them by covering their face with something so that they cannot breathe. 3 V-T To **smother** something **with** or **in** things is to cover it completely with them. ❑ *She gathered the baby in her arms and smothered him in kisses.* ❑ *...cakes smothered in cream and jam.* 4 V-T To **smother** someone means to give them too much love and protection. ❑ *He tends to smother his youngest daughter.*

smoulder [AM **smolder**] /ˈsməʊldə/ (**smoulders, smouldering, smouldered**) 1 V-I If something **smoulders**, it burns slowly, producing smoke but not flames. ❑ *The remains of the fire smouldered all night.* 2 V-I If a feeling **smoulders** inside you, you feel it intensely but rarely show it. ❑ *There is a smouldering anger in the community here.*
→ see **fire**

smudge /smʌdʒ/ (**smudges, smudging, smudged**) 1 N-COUNT A **smudge** is a dirty, blurred mark. 2 V-T If you **smudge** something, you make it dirty or messy by touching it. ❑ *They managed to go swimming without smudging their make-up.*

smug /smʌg/ ADJ If you say that someone is **smug**, you are criticizing the fact they seem very pleased with how good, clever, or fortunate they are. ● **smugly** ADV ❑ *The Major smiled smugly and sat down.*

smuggle /ˈsmʌgəl/ (**smuggles, smuggling, smuggled**) V-T If someone **smuggles** things or people **into** a place or **out of** it, they take them there illegally or secretly. ❑ *He smuggled papers out each day and photocopied them.* ❑ *Oskar Schindler smuggled hundreds of Jews to safety during World War II.* ● **smuggler** (**smugglers**) N-COUNT ❑ *...gun smugglers.* ● **smuggling** N-UNCOUNT ❑ *...diamond smuggling.*

snack /snæk/ (**snacks**) N-COUNT A **snack** is a small, quick meal, or something eaten between meals.
→ see **peanut**

snag /snæg/ (**snags, snagging, snagged**) 1 N-COUNT A **snag** is a small problem or disadvantage. ❑ *The snag with electric cars is that they can't go far or fast.* 2 V-T/V-I If you **snag** part of your clothing **on** a sharp or rough object or it **snags on** something, it gets caught or torn on it. ❑ *The tip of my shoe snagged on something.* ❑ *His aircraft snagged on trees as he tried to make an emergency landing.*

snail /sneɪl/ (**snails**) N-COUNT A **snail** is a small animal that has a spiral shell. It moves slowly, leaving behind a trail of slime.

snake /sneɪk/ (**snakes, snaking, snaked**) 1 N-COUNT A **snake** is a long, thin reptile with no

S

legs. **2** V-I Something that **snakes** in a particular direction goes in that direction in a line with a lot of bends. [LITERARY] ❑ *The road snaked through the mountains.*
→ see **desert**

snap /snæp/ (**snaps, snapping, snapped**) **1** V-T/V-I & N-SING If something **snaps**, or if you **snap** it, it breaks suddenly, usually with a sharp cracking noise called a **snap**. ❑ *As the plane came down, it snapped a tree in half.* ❑ *The brake pedal had just snapped off.* ❑ *The joint broke with a snap.* **2** V-T/V-I & N-SING If something **snaps** into a particular position, or if you **snap** it, it moves quickly into that position with a sharp sound called a **snap**. ❑ *The bag snapped open.* ❑ *He snapped the cap off the bottle.* ❑ *The book shut with a snap.* **3** V-T If you **snap** your **fingers**, you make a sharp sound by moving your middle finger quickly across your thumb, usually to order someone to do something. ❑ *He snapped his fingers, and Wilson produced a sheet of paper.* ❑ *She snapped her fingers at a passing waiter.* **4** V-T/V-I If someone **snaps at** you, they speak to you in a sharp, unfriendly way. ❑ *Sorry, I didn't mean to snap at you.* ❑ *'Of course I don't know her,' Roger snapped.* **5** V-I If an animal **snaps at** you, it opens and shuts its jaws quickly near you. **6** ADJ BEFORE N A **snap** decision or action is taken suddenly, without careful thought. ❑ *It's important not to make snap judgments.* **7** V-T & N-COUNT If you **snap** someone or something, or if you take a **snap** of them, you take a photograph of them. [INFORMAL] ❑ *...holiday snaps.*
▶ **snap up** PHR-VERB If you **snap** something **up**, you buy it quickly because it is a bargain or because it is just what you want. ❑ *A publisher has already snapped up the novel.*

snapshot /ˈsnæpʃɒt/ (**snapshots**) N-COUNT A **snapshot** is a photograph that is taken quickly and casually.

snare /sneə/ (**snares, snaring, snared**) **1** V-T & N-COUNT To **snare** a bird or animal means to catch it using a trap, which is called a **snare**. **2** V-T If someone **snares** something, they get it by using cleverness and cunning. ❑ *Most of all I want to snare a husband.*

snarl /snɑːl/ (**snarls, snarling, snarled**) **1** V-I & N-COUNT When an animal **snarls**, or when it gives a **snarl**, it makes a fierce, rough sound while showing its teeth. ❑ *The dogs snarled at the visitors.* ❑ *With a snarl, the dog made a dive for his heel.* **2** V-T If you **snarl** something, you say it in a fierce, angry way. ❑ *'Let go of me,' he snarled.*

snatch /snætʃ/ (**snatches, snatching, snatched**) **1** V-T/V-I If you **snatch** something, or if you **snatch at** it, you take it or pull it away quickly. ❑ *Mick snatched the cards from Archie's hand.* **2** V-T If you **snatch** an opportunity, you quickly make use of it. ❑ *She snatched a glance at him.* **3** N-COUNT A **snatch of** a conversation or a song is a very small piece of it.

sneak /sniːk/ (**sneaks, sneaking, sneaked** or [AM also] **snuck**) **1** V-I If you **sneak** somewhere, you go there quietly on foot, trying to avoid being seen or heard. ❑ *He often sneaked out of his house late at night.* **2** V-T If you **sneak** something somewhere, you take it there secretly. ❑ *I sneaked sweets into class.* **3** V-T If you **sneak** a look at someone or something, you secretly have a quick look at them. ❑ *I sneaked a quick look at my watch.*

sneaker /ˈsniːkə/ (**sneakers**) N-COUNT In American English, **sneakers** are casual shoes with rubber soles used for sports. The usual British word is **trainers**.

sneer /snɪə/ (**sneers, sneering, sneered**) V-I & N-COUNT If you **sneer at** someone or something, or if you give them a **sneer**, you express your contempt for them by what you say or by the expression on your face. ❑ *It is fashionable again to sneer at scientists.* ❑ *She sat there with a sneer on her face.*

sneeze /sniːz/ (**sneezes, sneezing, sneezed**) V-I & N-COUNT When you **sneeze**, you suddenly take in your breath and then blow it down your nose noisily, because you have a cold or because something has irritated your nose. This action is called a **sneeze**.

sniff /snɪf/ (**sniffs, sniffing, sniffed**) **1** V-T/V-I & N-COUNT When you **sniff**, or when you give a **sniff**, you breathe in air noisily through your nose, for example when you are trying not to cry, or in order to show disapproval. ❑ *She wiped her face and sniffed loudly.* ❑ *'Tourists!' she sniffed.* **2** V-T & N-COUNT If you **sniff** something, or if you take a **sniff of** it, you smell it by sniffing. ❑ *He sniffed the perfume.* ❑ *He opened it and took a sniff.*

snigger /ˈsnɪgə/ (**sniggers, sniggering, sniggered**) V-I & N-COUNT If someone **sniggers**, or if they give a **snigger**, they laugh quietly in a way which shows lack of respect. ❑ *The tourists snigger at our old-fashioned ways.*

snip /snɪp/ (**snips, snipping, snipped**) V-T If you **snip** something or if you **snip at** it, you cut part of it off with scissors in a single quick action. ❑ *I snipped all the leaves off.*

snipe /snaɪp/ (**snipes, sniping, sniped**) **1** V-I If someone **snipes at** you, they criticize you, often in an unfair or unkind way. ❑ *We watch as the country's leaders snipe at each other.* ● **sniping** N-UNCOUNT ❑ *Despite the sniping of critics, the TV show is hugely popular with the public.* **2** V-I To **snipe at** someone means to shoot at them from a hidden position. ● **sniper** (**snipers**) N-COUNT ❑ *...a sniper's bullet.* ● **sniping** N-UNCOUNT ❑ *10,069 people have been killed in the shelling and sniping.*

snippet /ˈsnɪpɪt/ (**snippets**) N-COUNT A **snippet of** information or news is a small piece of it. ❑ *...snippets of evidence.*

snob /snɒb/ (**snobs**) N-COUNT If you call someone a **snob**, you disapprove of them because they admire upper-class people and dislike lower-class people.

snobbery /ˈsnɒbəri/ N-UNCOUNT **Snobbery** is the attitude of a snob. ❑ *The show ignores the snobbery that usually exists between high art and popular culture.*

snooker /ˈsnuːkə, AM ˈsnʊk-/ N-UNCOUNT **Snooker** is a game involving balls on a large table. The players use long sticks called cues to hit a white ball, and score points by knocking coloured balls into the pockets at the sides of the table.

snoop /snuːp/ (**snoops, snooping, snooped**) V-I & N-COUNT If someone **snoops around** a place, or if they have a **snoop around** it, they secretly look around it in order to find out things. ❑ *She'd seen him snooping around Kim's hotel room.* ● **snooper** (**snoopers**) N-COUNT ❑ *They raised the wall to 10m, to stop photographers and snoopers.*

snore /snɔː/ (**snores, snoring, snored**) V-I & N-COUNT When someone who is asleep **snores**, they make a loud noise, called a **snore**, each time they breathe. ❑ *He says I snore.* ❑ *His snores keep me awake at night.*

snorkel /ˈsnɔːkəl/ (**snorkels, snorkelling, snorkelled** or [AM] **snorkeling, snorkeled**) **1** N-COUNT A **snorkel** is a tube through which a person swimming just under the surface of the sea can breathe. **2** V-I When someone **snorkels** they swim under water using a snorkel.

snort /snɔːt/ (**snorts, snorting, snorted**) V-I & N-COUNT If people or animals **snort**, or if they give a **snort**, they breathe air noisily out through their noses. People sometimes snort in order to express disapproval or amusement. ❑ *Harry snorted with laughter.* ❑ *He gave a loud snort.*

snow /snəʊ/ (**snows, snowing, snowed**) **1** N-UNCOUNT **Snow** is the soft white bits of frozen water that fall from the sky in cold weather. ❑ *The ground was covered in snow.* **2** V-I When it **snows**, snow falls from the sky.
→ see Word Web: **snow**
→ see **storm, water**

snowball /ˈsnəʊbɔːl/ (**snowballs, snowballing, snowballed**) **1** N-COUNT A **snowball** is a ball of snow. **2** V-I If something such as a campaign **snowballs**, it rapidly increases and grows. ❑ *From those early days the business has snowballed.*

snowboard /ˈsnəʊbɔːd/ (**snowboards**) N-COUNT A **snowboard** is a narrow board that you stand on in order to slide quickly down snowy slopes.

snowboarding /ˈsnəʊbɔːdɪŋ/ N-UNCOUNT **Snowboarding** is the sport or activity of travelling down snowy slopes using a snowboard.
● **snowboarder** (**snowboarders**) N-COUNT ❑ *Experienced snowboarders can get downhill amazingly fast.*

snowy /ˈsnəʊi/ (**snowier, snowiest**) ADJ A **snowy** place is covered in snow. A **snowy** day is a day when a lot of snow has fallen.

snub /snʌb/ (**snubs, snubbing, snubbed**) V-T & N-COUNT If someone **snubs** you, or if they give you a **snub**, they insult you by ignoring you or by behaving rudely towards you. ❑ *He snubbed her in public and made her feel stupid.* ❑ *This was not intended as a snub to Robbie.*

snuck /snʌk/ **Snuck** is a past tense and past participle of **sneak**. [AM]

snuff /snʌf/ (**snuffs, snuffing, snuffed**) N-UNCOUNT **Snuff** is powdered tobacco which people take by sniffing it up their nose.
▸ **snuff out** PHR-VERB If someone or something **snuffs out** something such as a rebellion or disagreement, they stop it, usually in a forceful or sudden way. ❑ *The protest was snuffed out by the president's police.*

S

snug /snʌg/ **1** ADJ If you feel **snug** or if you are in a **snug** place, you are very warm and comfortable. ❑ *I was snug and warm in bed.* **2** ADJ If something is a **snug** fit, it fits tightly. ● **snugly** ADV ❑ *The shoes fitted snugly.*

snuggle /ˈsnʌgəl/ (**snuggles, snuggling, snuggled**) V-I If you **snuggle** somewhere, you settle yourself into a warm, comfortable position, especially by moving closer to another person. ❑ *Jane snuggled up against his shoulder.*

so /səʊ/ **1** ADV You use **so** to refer back to something that has just been mentioned. ❑ *'Do you think that made much difference?'—'I think so.'* ❑ *If I want to go back home, I can do so at any time.* **2** ADV You use **so** when you are saying that something which has just been said about one person or thing is also true of another one. ❑ *They had a wonderful time and so did I.* **3** CONJ You use the structures **as...so** and **just as...so** to indicate that two events or situations are similar in a particular way. ❑ *Just as society has rules, so do schools.* **4** CONJ You use **so** and **so that** to introduce the result of the situation you have just mentioned. ❑ *I was an only child, and so had no experience of large families.* ❑ *There was snow everywhere, so that the shape of things was difficult to see.* **5** CONJ You use **so, so that**, and **so as** to introduce the reason for doing the thing you have just mentioned. ❑ *Come over here so I can see you.* ❑ *I kept my fear to myself so as not to worry my two friends.* **6** ADV You can use **so** in a conversation or an account when you are checking something, summarizing something, or moving on to a new stage. ❑ *So you're a footballer?* ❑ *So that's how I knew.* **7** ADV You can use **so** to emphasize the degree or extent of something. ❑ *He was so tired that he slept for 15 hours.* ❑ *Her hands were so wet they kept slipping off the wheel.* **8** ADV You can use **so** to intensify the meaning of an adjective, adverb, or word such as 'much' or 'many'. ❑ *John makes me so angry.* ❑ *So many children cannot read or write.* **9** ADV You can use **so** before words such as 'much' and 'many' to indicate that there is a limit to something. ❑ *There is only so much time in the day for answering letters.* ❑ *Even the greatest city can support only so many lawyers.* **10** CONVENTION You say **'So?'** and **'So what?'** to indicate that you think that what someone has said is unimportant. [INFORMAL] ❑ *'My name's Bruno.'—'So?'* ❑ *'You take a chance on the weather if you holiday in the UK.'—'So what?'* **11** **ever so** → see **ever** **12** **so far** → see **far** **13** **so long as** → see **long** **14** **so much for** → see **much** **15** **every so often** → see **often** **16** PHRASE You use **and so on** or **and so forth** at the end of a list to indicate that there are other items that you could also mention. ❑ *...health, education, tax and so on.* **17** PHRASE You use **or so** when you are giving an approximate amount. ❑ *They'll be here in the next week or so.* **18** PHRASE You use the structures **not so much** and **not so**

Word Web snow

Some people love winter. They like to watch **snowflake**s falling softly from the sky. The **snow** forms beautiful **drifts** on the ground and trees. A house with **icicle**s hanging from the roof and **frost** on the windows looks warm and cosy. But winter has a dangerous side as well. **Ice** and snow on streets and roads causes many accidents. And a **blizzard** can leave behind large amounts of snow in a single day. In the mountains, large amounts of snow can cause **avalanche**s. They usually happen when light, new snow falls on top of older, heavy snow.

Word Web soap

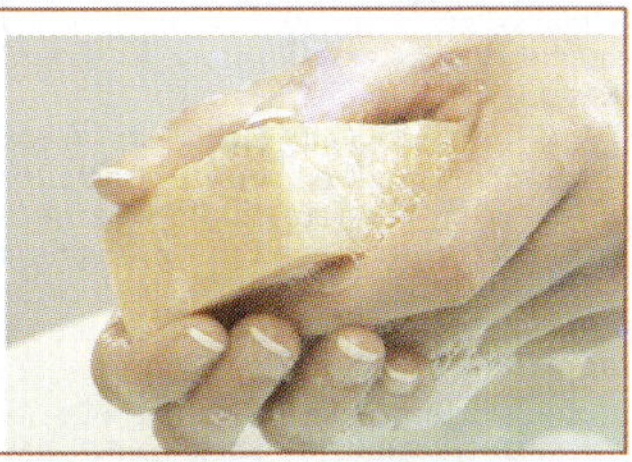

Soap is important in everyday life. We **wash** our hands before we eat. We lather up with a **bar** of soap in the **shower** or **bath**. We use liquid **detergent** to **clean** our dishes. We use **laundry** detergent to wash our clothes. But why do we use soap? How does it work? It works almost like a magnet. But soap doesn't attract metal. It attracts dirt and grease. It makes a **bubble** around the dirt, and water washes it all away.

much...as to say that something is one kind of thing rather than another kind. ❑ *This is not so much a political battle as an economic one.*

Usage

So, **very**, and **too** can all be used to intensify the meaning of an adjective, an adverb, or a word like **much** or **many**. However, they are not used in the same way. **Very** is the simplest intensifier. It has no other meaning beyond that. **So** can suggest an emotional reaction on the part of the speaker, such as pleasure, surprise, or disappointment. ❑ *John makes me so angry!* ❑ *Oh thank you so much!* **So** can also refer forward to a result clause introduced by **that**. ❑ *The cars moved along so slowly that he arrived three hours late.* **Too** suggests an excessive or undesirable amount, often so much that a particular result does not or cannot happen. ❑ *She does wear too much make-up at times.* ❑ *He was too late to save her.*

soak /səʊk/ (**soaks, soaking, soaked**) **1** V-T/V-I When you **soak** something, or when you leave it **to soak**, you put it into a liquid and leave it there. ❑ *Soak the noodles in warm water for 20 minutes.* ❑ *He left the dishes to soak.* **2** V-T When a liquid **soaks** something, it makes it very wet. ❑ *Heavy rain had soaked the road surface.* ● **soaked** ADJ ❑ *Her dress was soaked.* ● **soaking** ADJ ❑ *She was soaking wet.* **3** V-I When a liquid **soaks through** something, it passes through it. ❑ *Dark patches of sweat had soaked through the fabric.* **4** V-I & N-COUNT If someone **soaks**, or if they have a **soak**, they spend a long time in a hot bath, because they enjoy it. ❑ *I had a long soak in the bath.*
▶ **soak up** PHR-VERB When a soft or dry substance **soaks up** a liquid, the liquid goes into the substance. ❑ *Stir the wheat until it has soaked up all the water.*

ˌso-and-ˈso N-UNCOUNT You use **so-and-so** instead of a word, expression, or name when talking generally rather than giving a specific example. ❑ *They answer the phone and they say so-and-so isn't here any more.*

soap /səʊp/ (**soaps**) **1** N-VAR **Soap** is a substance that you use with water for washing yourself or sometimes for washing clothes. ❑ *...a bar of lavender soap.* ❑ *...a large packet of soap powder.* **2** N-COUNT A **soap** is the same as a **soap opera**.
→ see Word Web: **soap**

ˈsoap ˌopera (**soap operas**) N-COUNT A **soap opera** is a television drama serial about the daily lives of a group of people.

soar /sɔː/ (**soars, soaring, soared**) **1** V-I If the amount or level of something **soars**, it quickly increases by a great deal. [JOURNALISM] ❑ *The price of gas has soared.* **2** V-I If something **soars** into the air, it goes quickly up into the air. [LITERARY] ❑ *The seabirds soared and dived.*

sob /sɒb/ (**sobs, sobbing, sobbed**) V-I & N-COUNT If you **sob**, you cry in a noisy way. A **sob** is one of the noises that you make when you are crying. ❑ *I want to go home, she said, between sobs.* ● **sobbing** N-UNCOUNT ❑ *The room was silent except for her sobbing.*

sober /ˈsəʊbə/ (**sobers, sobering, sobered**) **1** ADJ When you are **sober**, you are not drunk. **2** ADJ A **sober** person is serious and thoughtful. ● **soberly** ADV ❑ *'There's a new development,' he said soberly.* **3** ADJ **Sober** colours and clothes are plain and dull. ● **soberly** ADV ❑ *The men were dressed soberly.*
▶ **sober up** PHR-VERB When someone **sobers up**, they become sober after being drunk.

sobering /ˈsəʊbərɪŋ/ ADJ You say that something is a **sobering** thought or has a **sobering** effect when a situation seems serious and makes you become serious and thoughtful. ❑ *It was a sobering experience.*

ˌso-ˈcalled **1** ADJ BEFORE N You use **so-called** in front of a word to indicate that you think that the word is incorrect or misleading. ❑ *I have no idea why my so-called friends are lying to me.* **2** ADJ BEFORE N You use **so-called** to indicate that something is generally referred to by a particular name. ❑ *She was one of the so-called Gang of Four.*

soccer /ˈsɒkə/ N-UNCOUNT In American English, **soccer** is a game played by two teams of eleven players who kick a ball around a field in an attempt to score goals. The British word is **football**.

sociable /ˈsəʊʃəbəl/ ADJ **Sociable** people enjoy meeting and talking to other people.

Word Link *soci ≈ companion : associate, social, sociology*

social /ˈsəʊʃəl/ **1** ADJ BEFORE N **Social** means relating to society. ❑ *...unemployment, low pay and other social problems.* ● **socially** ADV ❑ *The company has published a guide to socially responsible companies.* **2** ADJ BEFORE N **Social** activities are leisure activities that involve meeting other people, as opposed to activities related to work. ❑ *We ought to organize more social events.* ● **socially** ADV ❑ *We have known each other socially for a long time.*
→ see **kiss, myth**

ˌsocial exˈclusion N-UNCOUNT **Social exclusion** is the act of making certain groups of people within a society feel isolated and unimportant. ❑ *...projects aimed at tackling social exclusion.*

ˌsocial inˈclusion N-UNCOUNT **Social inclusion** is the act of making all groups of people within

S

a society feel valued and important. ❑ *This will cost money, but if social inclusion is to succeed, it must be spent.*

socialist /ˈsəʊʃəlɪst/ (**socialists**) N-COUNT & ADJ A **socialist** or a person with **socialist** beliefs believes that the state should own industries on behalf of the people and that everyone should be equal. ❑ *...members of the ruling Socialist party.* ● **socialism** N-UNCOUNT ❑ *...the battle between capitalism and socialism.*

socialize [BRIT also **socialise**] /ˈsəʊʃəlaɪz/ (**socializes, socializing, socialized**) V-I If you **socialize**, you meet other people socially. ❑ *The club is London's latest place to socialize and keep fit.*

ˈsocial ˌlife (**social lives**) N-COUNT Your **social life** consists of ways in which you spend time with your friends and acquaintances. ❑ *I don't have much of a social life.*

ˌsocial ˈscience (**social sciences**) N-VAR **Social science** is the scientific study of society. ❑ *...sociology and the other social sciences.* ❑ *...a degree in social science.*

ˌsocial seˈcurity N-UNCOUNT In Britain, **social security** is money that is paid by the government to people who are unemployed, poor, or ill. The American term is **welfare**.

ˌsocial ˈservices N-PLURAL **Social services** are services provided by the local authority to help people who have serious family problems or financial problems.

ˈsocial ˌwork N-UNCOUNT **Social work** is a job which involves giving help and advice to people with serious financial problems or family problems.

ˈsocial ˌworker (**social workers**) N-COUNT A **social worker** is a person whose job is to do social work.

society /səˈsaɪɪti/ (**societies**) **1** N-VAR **Society** consists of all the people in a country or region, considered as a group. ❑ *...Western society.* ❑ *We live in an industrial society.* **2** N-COUNT A **society** is an organization for people who have the same interest or aim. ❑ *...the Royal Geographical Society.* **3** N-UNCOUNT You can use **society** to refer to the rich, fashionable people in a particular place who meet on social occasions. ❑ *They are well-known in society.*
→ see **culture**

S

Word Link	*soci ≈ companion : associate, social, sociology*

sociology /ˌsəʊsiˈɒlədʒi/ N-UNCOUNT **Sociology** is the study of society or of the way society is organized. ● **sociological** /ˌsəʊsiəˈlɒdʒɪkəl/ ADJ ❑ *...sociological research.* ● **sociologist** (**sociologists**) N-COUNT ❑ *...her career as a sociologist.*

sock /sɒk/ (**socks**) N-COUNT **Socks** are pieces of clothing which cover your foot and ankle and are worn inside shoes.
→ see **clothing**

socket /ˈsɒkɪt/ (**sockets**) **1** N-COUNT A **socket** is a device on a piece of electrical equipment into which you can put a plug or bulb. **2** N-COUNT In British English, a **socket** is a device or point in a wall where you can connect electrical equipment to the power supply. The American word is **outlet**. **3** N-COUNT You can refer to any hollow part or opening in a structure which another part fits into as a **socket**. ❑ *Her eyes were sunk deep into their sockets.*

soda /ˈsəʊdə/ (**sodas**) **1** N-UNCOUNT **Soda** or **soda water** is fizzy water used for mixing with alcoholic drinks or fruit juice. **2** N-VAR **Soda** is a fizzy drink. A **soda** is a bottle or glass of soda. [AM]

sodden /ˈsɒdən/ ADJ Something that is **sodden** is extremely wet.

sodium /ˈsəʊdiəm/ N-UNCOUNT **Sodium** is a silvery-white chemical element which combines with other chemicals.

sofa /ˈsəʊfə/ (**sofas**) N-COUNT A **sofa** is a long, comfortable seat with a back and arms, which two or three people can sit on.

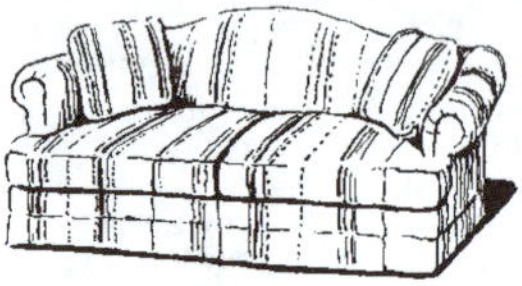

sofa

soft /sɒft, AM sɔːft/ (**softer, softest**) **1** ADJ Something that is **soft** is pleasant to touch, and not rough or hard. ❑ *...warm, soft, white towels.* ● **softness** N-UNCOUNT ❑ *The softness of the forest floor was surprising.* **2** ADJ Something that is **soft** changes shape or bends easily when you press it. ❑ *She lay down on the soft, comfortable bed.* ❑ *...soft cheese.* **3** ADJ Something that is **soft** is very gentle and has no force. For example, a **soft** sound is quiet and not harsh. A **soft** colour is pleasant to look at because it is not bright. ❑ *Soft spring rain had fallen all day.* ● **softly** ADV ❑ *She kissed the baby softly.* **4** ADJ If you are **soft on** someone, you do not treat them as severely as you should do; used showing disapproval. **5** ADJ BEFORE N **Soft drugs** are illegal drugs which many people do not consider to be strong, harmful, or addictive. **6** PHRASE If you **have a soft spot for** someone, you have a strong affection for them.

Thesaurus	*soft* Also look up:
ADJ.	fluffy, silky; *(ant.)* firm, hard, rough **1** faint, gentle, light, low; *(ant.)* clear, strong **3**

ˌsoft ˈdrink (**soft drinks**) N-COUNT A **soft drink** is a cold non-alcoholic drink such as lemonade.

soften /ˈsɒfən, AM ˈsɔːf-/ (**softens, softening, softened**) **1** V-T/V-I If something **is softened**, it becomes less hard or firm. ❑ *Fry for about 4 minutes, until the onion has softened.* **2** V-T If one thing **softens** the impact or the damaging effect of another thing, it makes it seem less severe. **3** V-T/V-I If you **soften** your position or your position **softens**, you become more sympathetic and less critical. ❑ *He said that the government was ready to soften its position on this issue.*
▶ **soften up** PHR-VERB If you **soften** someone **up**, you put them into a good mood before asking them to do something. [INFORMAL] ❑ *They only treated you well to soften you up.*

Word Link	*ware ≈ merchandise : hardware, software, warehouse*

software /ˈsɒftweə, AM ˈsɔːf-/ N-UNCOUNT Computer programs are referred to as **software**. [COMPUTING]

Word Web solar

Sources of **fossil fuel energy** are becoming scarce and expensive. They also cause **pollution**. Scientists are studying sources of energy such as **solar power**. There are two ways to use the **sun**'s **energy**. **Thermal** systems produce heat. Photovoltaic systems make electricity. Thermal systems use a **solar collector**. This is an insulated box with a clear cover. It stores the sun's energy for use in household air or water heating systems. Photovoltaic systems have thin layers of **semiconductor** materials to change the sun's heat into electricity. They are often used in calculators and solar-powered watches.

soggy /'sɒgi/ (**soggier, soggiest**) ADJ Something that is **soggy** is unpleasantly wet.

soil /sɔɪl/ (**soils, soiling, soiled**) **1** N-UNCOUNT **Soil** is the substance on the surface of the earth in which plants grow. **2** N-UNCOUNT You can use **soil** to refer to a country's territory. ❑ *Daly's last win was on British soil in 1995.* **3** V-T If you **soil** something, you make it dirty. [FORMAL] ● **soiled** ADJ ❑ *...a soiled white apron.*
→ see **erosion, farm, grassland**

solace /'sɒlɪs/ **1** N-UNCOUNT **Solace** is a feeling of comfort that makes you feel less sad. [FORMAL] ❑ *As many people do in difficult times, she found solace in her family.* **2** N-SING If something is a **solace to** you, it makes you feel less sad. [FORMAL]

solar /'səʊlə/ **1** ADJ **Solar** is used to describe things relating to the sun. ❑ *...a total solar eclipse.* **2** ADJ **Solar power** is obtained from the sun's light and heat.
→ see Word Web: **solar**
→ see **energy, greenhouse effect**

'solar system N-PROPER **The solar system** is the sun and all the planets that go round it.
→ see Picture Dictionary: **solar system**
→ see Word Web: **solar system**
→ see **galaxy**

sold /səʊld/ **Sold** is the past tense and past participle of **sell**.

soldier /'səʊldʒə/ (**soldiers**) N-COUNT A **soldier** is a person who works in an army.
→ see **war**

sole /səʊl/ (**soles**)

> In meaning 4, **sole** is both the singular and the plural form.

1 ADJ BEFORE N The **sole** thing or person of a particular type is the only one of that type. ❑ *The sole aim of these companies is to make money.* ● **solely** ADV ❑ *His decision to resign was based solely on his poor*

Picture Dictionary solar system

S

Word Web solar system

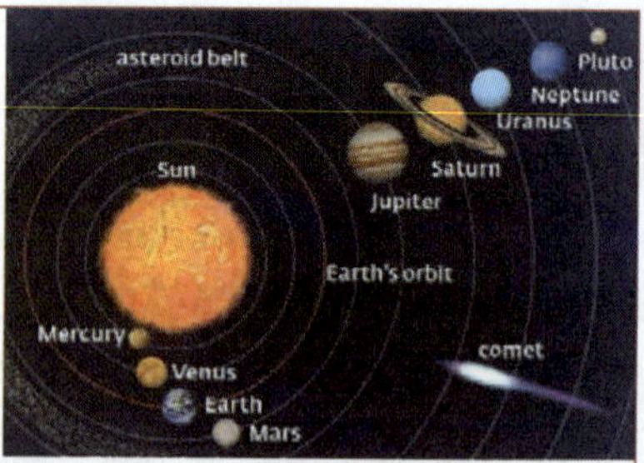

The **sun** formed when a nebula turned into a star almost five thousand million years ago. All the **planets, comets,** and asteroids in our **solar system** came from this nebula. Today they all **orbit** the sun. The four planets closest to the sun are small and rocky. The next four consist mostly of **gases**. The outermost planet, Pluto, is a dwarf planet. It is made of rock and ice. Many of the planets have **moons** orbiting them. Most asteroids have irregular shapes and are covered with **craters**. Only about 200 asteroids have diameters of over 100 kilometres.

health. **2** ADJ BEFORE N If you have **sole** charge or ownership of something, you are the only person in charge of it or who owns it. ❑ *Many women are left as the sole providers in families.* **3** N-COUNT The **sole of** your foot or **of** a shoe or sock is the underneath surface of it. ❑ *Now bring the soles of your feet together.* ❑ *...shoes with rubber soles.* **4** N-VAR A **sole** is a kind of flat fish.
→ see **foot**

solemn /ˈsɒləm/ **1** ADJ Someone or something that is **solemn** is very serious rather than cheerful or humorous. ● **solemnly** ADV ❑ *Her listeners nodded solemnly.* ● **solemnity** /səˈlemnɪti/ N-UNCOUNT ❑ *...the solemnity attached to death.* **2** ADJ A **solemn** promise or agreement is formal and sincere. ❑ *The queen has kept every one of the solemn promises she made.* ● **solemnly** ADV ❑ *The people swore solemnly to serve their Queen and their country.*

solicit /səˈlɪsɪt/ (**solicits, soliciting, solicited**) **1** V-T If you **solicit** money, help, or an opinion from someone, you ask them for it. [FORMAL] **2** V-I When prostitutes **solicit**, they offer to have sex with people in return for money. ● **soliciting** N-UNCOUNT

solicitor /səˈlɪsɪtə/ (**solicitors**) N-COUNT In Britain, a **solicitor** is a lawyer who gives legal advice, prepares legal documents and cases, and represents clients in the lower courts of law.

solid /ˈsɒlɪd/ (**solids**) **1** N-COUNT & ADJ A **solid**, or a **solid** substance or object, stays the same shape whether it is in a container or not. ❑ *Solids turn to liquids at certain temperatures.* **2** ADJ A **solid** object or mass does not have a space inside it, or holes or gaps in it. ❑ *...soft of solid rock.* ❑ *The street was packed solid with people.* **3** ADJ A **solid** structure is strong and is not likely to collapse or fall over. ● **solidly** ADV ❑ *Fortunately, their house was solidly built.* ● **solidity** /səˈlɪdɪti/ N-UNCOUNT ❑ *...the solidity of walls and floors.* **4** ADJ If you describe someone as **solid**, you mean they are very reliable and respectable. ● **solidly** ADV ❑ *Graham is so solidly consistent.* ● **solidity** N-UNCOUNT ❑ *He had the usual solidity of the English.* **5** ADJ **Solid** evidence or information is reliable because it is based on facts. **Solid** advice or work is useful and reliable. ❑ *All I am looking for is a good solid performance.* ● **solidly** ADV ❑ *She's played solidly throughout the spring.* **6** ADJ If you do something for a **solid** period of time, you do it without any pause or interruption throughout that time. ❑ *We had worked together for two solid years.* ● **solidly** ADV ❑ *For the next two hours they worked solidly on his new song.*
→ see Picture Dictionary: **solids**
→ see **matter, pattern**

solidarity /ˌsɒlɪˈdærɪti/ N-UNCOUNT If a group of people show **solidarity**, they show complete unity and support for each other, especially in political or international affairs.

solidify /səˈlɪdɪfaɪ/ (**solidifies, solidifying, solidified**) V-T/V-I When a liquid **solidifies** or you **solidify** it, it changes into a solid.

solitary /ˈsɒlɪtri, AM -teri/ **1** ADJ BEFORE N A **solitary** activity is one that you do alone. ❑ *His*

S

Picture Dictionary solids

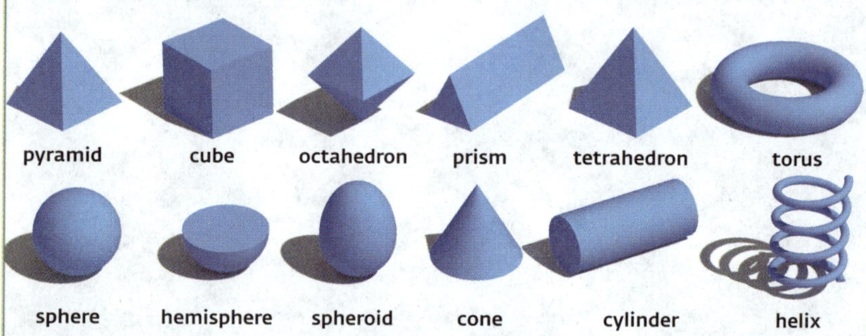

evenings were spent in solitary thought. **2** ADJ A person or animal that is **solitary** spends a lot of time alone. **3** ADJ BEFORE N A **solitary** person or object is alone and has no others nearby.

solitude /'sɒlɪtju:d, AM -tu:d/ N-UNCOUNT **Solitude** is the state of being alone, especially when this is peaceful and pleasant. ❑ *Imagine long golden beaches where you can sit in solitude.*

solo /'səʊləʊ/ (**solos**) N-COUNT & ADJ & ADV A **solo**, or a **solo** performance, especially of a piece of music, is a performance done by one person. You can also say that someone does something **solo** when they do it on their own. ❑ *He had just completed his final solo album.*

soloist /'səʊləʊɪst/ (**soloists**) N-COUNT A **soloist** is a person who performs a solo, usually a piece of music.

soluble /'sɒljʊbəl/ ADJ A substance that is **soluble** will dissolve in a liquid.

solution /sə'lu:ʃən/ (**solutions**) **1** N-COUNT A **solution to** a problem is a way of dealing with it so that the difficulty is removed. ❑ *...a peaceful solution to the crisis.* **2** N-COUNT The **solution to** a riddle or a puzzle is the answer to it. **3** N-COUNT A **solution** is a liquid in which a solid substance has been dissolved.

→ see **fraction**

Word Partnership Use *solution* with:

ADJ.	**best** solution, **peaceful** solution, **perfect** solution, **possible** solution, **practical** solution, **temporary** solution **1**
	easy solution, **obvious** solution, **simple** solution **1** **2**
PREP.	solution **to a conflict**, solution **to a crisis** **1**
	solution **to a problem** **1** **2**
V.	**propose a** solution, **reach a** solution, **seek a** solution **1**
	find a solution **1** **2**

solve /sɒlv/ (**solves, solving, solved**) V-T If you **solve** a problem or a question, you find a solution or an answer to it. ❑ *Violence won't solve anything.*

Word Partnership Use *solve* with:

N.	**ability to** solve *something*, solve **a crisis**, solve **a mystery**, solve **a problem**, solve **a puzzle**, **way to** solve *something*
V.	**attempt/try to** solve *something*, **help** solve *something*

solvent /'sɒlvənt/ (**solvents**) **1** ADJ If a person or a company is **solvent**, they have enough money to pay all their debts. **2** N-VAR A **solvent** is a liquid that can dissolve other substances.

sombre [AM **somber**] /'sɒmbə/ **1** ADJ If someone is **sombre**, they are serious, sad, or pessimistic. ● **sombrely** ADV ❑ *'I wish he'd come back,' Martha said sombrely.* **2** ADJ **Sombre** colours and places are dark and dull.

some /səm, STRONG sʌm/ **1** DET & PRON You use **some** to refer to a quantity of something or to a number of people or things, when you are not stating the quantity or number exactly. ❑ *He went to get some books.* ❑ *All the apples are ripe. We are going to pick some.* **2** DET You can use **some** to emphasize that an amount or number is fairly large. For example, if an activity takes **some** time, it takes quite a lot of time. **3** QUANT If you refer to **some of** the people or things in a group, you mean a few of them but not all of them. If you refer to **some of** a particular thing, you mean a part of it but not all of it. ❑ *Spoon some of the sauce into a bowl.* ❑ *When the chicken is cooked I'll freeze some.* **4** DET If you refer to **some** person or thing, you are referring to that person or thing vaguely, without stating exactly which one you mean. ❑ *If you are worried about some health problem, call us.* **5** ADV You can use **some** in front of a number to indicate that it is approximate. ❑ *I have kept birds for some 30 years.*

Usage

You use **not any** instead of **some** in negative sentences. ❑ *There isn't any money.* You only use **some** in questions when you expect the answer yes. ❑ *Did you buy some bread?* Otherwise you say **any**. ❑ *Did you buy any bread?*

somebody /'sʌmbədi, AM -bɑ:di/ PRON **Somebody** means the same as **someone**.

Usage

You use **not anybody**, instead of **somebody** in negative sentences. ❑ *There isn't anybody here.* You only use **somebody** in questions when you expect the answer yes. ❑ *Is somebody there?* Otherwise you say **anybody**. ❑ *Is anybody there?*

somehow /'sʌmhaʊ/ ADV You use **somehow** to say that you do not know or cannot say how something was done or will be done. ❑ *Somehow I knew he would tell me the truth.*

someone /'sʌmwʌn/ also **somebody** /'sʌmbədi, AM -bɑ:di/ **1** PRON You use **someone** or **somebody** to refer to a person without saying exactly who you mean. ❑ *I need someone to help me.* **2** PRON If you say that a person is **someone** or **somebody** in a particular kind of work or in a particular place, you mean that they are considered to be important in that kind of work or in that place. ❑ *He was somebody in the law division.*

Usage

You use **not anyone** instead of **someone** in negative sentences. ❑ *There isn't anyone here.* You only use **someone** in questions when you expect the answer yes. ❑ *Is someone there?* Otherwise you say **anyone**. ❑ *Is anyone there?*

something /'sʌmθɪŋ/ **1** PRON You use **something** to refer to a thing, situation, event, or idea, without saying exactly what it is. ❑ *He realized that there was something wrong.* ❑ *People are always watching television or busy doing something else.* **2** PRON You can use **something** in expressions like **'that's something'** when you think that a situation is not very good but is better than it might have been. ❑ *At least they are talking to her again. That's something.* **3** PRON If you say that a thing is **something of** a disappointment, you mean that it is quite disappointing. If you say that a person is **something of** an artist, you mean that they are quite good at art. ❑ *She received something of a surprise when Robert said that he was coming to New York.* **4** PRON If you say that there is **something in** an idea or suggestion, you mean that it is quite

S

good and should be considered seriously. ❑ *Could there be something in what he said?* **5** **something like** → see **like**

Usage

You use **not anything** instead of **something** in negative sentences. ❑ *There isn't anything here.* You only use **something** in questions when you expect the answer yes. ❑ *Is something wrong?* Otherwise you say **anything**. ❑ *Is anything wrong?*

sometime /ˈsʌmtaɪm/ ADV You use **sometime** to refer to a time in the future or the past that is unknown or that has not yet been decided. ❑ *Why don't you come and see me sometime.*

sometimes /ˈsʌmtaɪmz/ ADV You use **sometimes** to say that something happens on some occasions. ❑ *Have you noticed how tired he sometimes looks?*

somewhat /ˈsʌmwɒt/ ADV You use **somewhat** to indicate that something is the case to a limited extent or degree. ❑ *Conditions in the village had improved somewhat since January.*

somewhere /ˈsʌmweə/ **1** ADV You use **somewhere** to refer to a place without saying exactly where you mean. ❑ *I needed somewhere to live in London.* **2** ADV You use **somewhere** when giving an approximate amount, number, or time. ❑ *Caray is somewhere between 73 and 80 years old.* **3** PHRASE If you say that you **are getting somewhere**, you mean that you are making progress towards achieving something. ❑ *At last they were agreeing, at last they were getting somewhere.*

Usage

You use **not anywhere** instead of **somewhere** in negative sentences. ❑ *He isn't going anywhere.* You only use **somewhere** in questions when you expect the answer yes. ❑ *Are you going somewhere tonight?* Otherwise you say **anywhere**. ❑ *Are you going anywhere tonight?*

son /sʌn/ (**sons**) N-COUNT A person's **son** is their male child.
→ see **child**

sonata /səˈnɑːtə/ (**sonatas**) N-COUNT A **sonata** is a piece of classical music written for a single instrument, or for one instrument and a piano.

S

song /sɒŋ, AM sɔːŋ/ (**songs**) **1** N-COUNT A **song** is a piece of music with words and music sung together. ❑ *...a love song.* **2** N-UNCOUNT **Song** is the art of singing. ❑ *...dance, music, and song.* **3** N-VAR A bird's **song** is the pleasant musical sounds that it makes.
→ see **concert, music**

Word Partnership Use *song* with:

ADJ. **beautiful** song, **favourite** song, **old** song, **popular** song **1**
N. **hit** song, **love** song, song **lyrics**, song **music**, **pop** song, **rap** song, **theme** song, song **title**, **words of a** song **1** **bird's** song **3**
V. **hear a** song, **play a** song, **record a** song, **sing a** song, **write a** song **1**

Word Link *son ≈ sound : resonate, sonic, unison*

sonic /ˈsɒnɪk/ ADJ BEFORE N **Sonic** is used to describe things related to sound. ❑ *...the sonic boom from a supersonic aeroplane.*

ˈson-in-ˌlaw (**sons-in-law**) N-COUNT A person's **son-in-law** is the husband of their daughter.

sonnet /ˈsɒnɪt/ (**sonnets**) N-COUNT A **sonnet** is a poem with 14 lines. Each line has 14 syllables, and the poem has a fixed pattern of rhymes.

soon /suːn/ (**sooner, soonest**) **1** ADV If something is going to happen **soon**, it will happen after a short time. ❑ *This chance came sooner than I expected.* ❑ *We must catch this man, and the sooner the better.* **2** ADV If something happened **soon** after a particular time or event, it happened a short time after it. ❑ *Soon afterwards he left his wife.* **3** PHRASE If you say that something happens **as soon as** something else happens, you mean that it happens immediately after the other thing. ❑ *You'll never guess what happened as soon as I left my room.* **4** PHRASE If you say that something will happen **sooner or later**, you mean that it will happen, though it might take a long time. **5** PHRASE If you say that **no sooner** has one thing happened **than** another thing happens, you mean that the second thing happens immediately after the first thing. ❑ *No sooner had he arrived in Rome than he was kidnapped.* **6** PHRASE If you say that you **would sooner** do something, you mean that you would prefer to do it. ❑ *I'd sooner not talk about it.*

soot /sʊt/ N-UNCOUNT **Soot** is black powder which rises in the smoke from a fire and collects on the inside of chimneys.

soothe /suːð/ (**soothes, soothing, soothed**) **1** V-T If you **soothe** someone who is angry or upset, you make them calmer. ❑ *He took the child in his arms and soothed her.* ● **soothing** ADJ ❑ *...some gentle, soothing music.* **2** V-T Something that **soothes** pain makes it hurt less. ● **soothing** ADJ ❑ *Cold tea is very soothing for burns.*

Word Link *soph ≈ wise : philosopher, philosophy, sophisticated*

sophisticated /səˈfɪstɪkeɪtɪd/ **1** ADJ A **sophisticated** person is comfortable in social situations and knows about culture, fashion, and other matters that are considered socially important. **2** ADJ A **sophisticated** machine or method of doing something contains more advanced features than other things of the same type. ❑ *...a large and sophisticated new British telescope.*

Thesaurus *sophisticated* Also look up:

ADJ. cultured, experienced, refined, worldly; (*ant.*) backward, crude **1**
advanced, complex, elaborate, intricate **2**

sophistication /səˌfɪstɪˈkeɪʃən/ N-UNCOUNT **Sophistication** is the quality of being sophisticated.

soprano /səˈprɑːnəʊ, -ˈpræn-/ (**sopranos**) N-COUNT A **soprano** is a woman, girl, or boy with a high singing voice.

Word Web sound

Sound is the only form of energy we can hear. The energy makes molecules in the air **vibrate**. Fast vibrations called high **frequencies** produce high-pitched sounds. Slower vibrations produce lower frequencies. Sound vibrations travel in waves, like **waves** in water. Each wave has a **crest** and a **trough**. Amplitude measures the size of a wave. It is the vertical distance between the middle of a wave and its crest. When a **sound wave** bounces off something, it creates an **echo**. When an airplane reaches **supersonic** speed, it generates **shock waves**. As these waves move toward the ground, a **sonic boom** occurs.

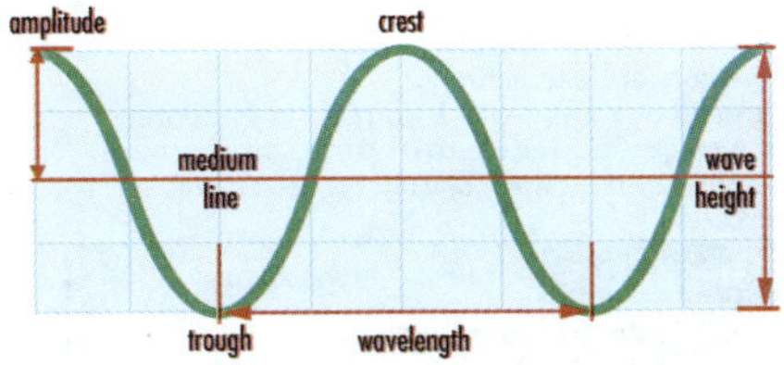

sordid /'sɔːdɪd/ **1** ADJ If you describe someone's behaviour as **sordid**, you mean that it is immoral or dishonest. ❑ *I don't want to hear the sordid details of their relationship.* **2** ADJ If you describe a place as **sordid**, you mean that it is dirty, unpleasant, or depressing. ❑ *The window of their sordid little room was dirty.*

sore /sɔː/ (**sores**) **1** ADJ If part of your body is **sore**, it causes you pain and discomfort. ❑ *...a sore throat.* **2** N-COUNT A **sore** is a painful spot on your body where the skin is infected.

sorely /'sɔːli/ ADV **Sorely** is used to emphasize that a feeling such as disappointment or need is very strong. ❑ *He will be sorely missed.*

sorrow /'sɒrəʊ/ N-UNCOUNT **Sorrow** is a feeling of deep sadness or regret. ❑ *It was a time of great sorrow.*

sorrows /'sɒrəʊz/ N-PLURAL **Sorrows** are events or situations that cause deep sadness. ❑ *...the joys and sorrows of everyday living.*

sorry /'sɒri/ (**sorrier, sorriest**) **1** CONVENTION You say **'Sorry'** or **'I'm sorry'** as a way of expressing your disappointment or sadness that something you have done or have told someone has caused them hurt or trouble. ❑ *Sorry I took so long.* ❑ *I'm really sorry if I said anything wrong.* ❑ *I'm sorry to have to tell you some bad news.* ❑ *She was very sorry about all the trouble she'd caused.* **2** ADJ AFTER LINK-V If you **feel sorry for** someone who is unhappy or in an unpleasant situation, you feel sympathy and sadness for them. ❑ *I am very sorry for the family.* **3** ADJ BEFORE N If someone or something is in a **sorry** condition, they are in a bad condition, mentally or physically. ❑ *She is a sorry sight.* **4** CONVENTION You say **'Sorry?'** when you have not heard what someone has said and you want them to repeat it.

sort /sɔːt/ (**sorts, sorting, sorted**) **1** N-COUNT A particular **sort of** something is one of its different kinds or types. ❑ *What sort of school did you go to?* **2** N-SING You describe someone as a particular **sort** when you are describing their character. ❑ *He seemed to be just the right sort for the job.* **3** V-T/V-I If you **sort** things or **sort** through things, you arrange them into different groups or places. ❑ *The students are sorted into three classes.* ❑ *He opened the box and sorted through the papers.* **4** PHRASE You use **sort of** when you want to say that your description of something is not very precise. ❑ *It just sort of happened.* **5** PHRASE If you describe something as a particular thing **of sorts**, you are suggesting that its quality or standard is poor. ❑ *He made a living of sorts selling sandwiches from a van.*
▶ **sort out** **1** PHR-VERB If you **sort out** a group of things, you organize or tidy them. ❑ *We try to sort out the truth from the lies.* **2** PHR-VERB If you **sort out** a problem, you solve it. ❑ *The computer breakdown was sorted out within 3 hours.*

soufflé also **souffle** /'suːfleɪ, AM suː'fleɪ/ (**soufflés**) N-VAR A **soufflé** is a light food made from a mixture of beaten egg whites and other ingredients that is baked in the oven.

sought /sɔːt/ **Sought** is the past tense and past participle of **seek**.

'sought-ˌafter ADJ Something that is **sought-after** is in great demand, usually because it is rare or of very good quality. ❑ *...the most sought-after prize in world sport.*

soul /səʊl/ (**souls**) **1** N-COUNT A person's **soul** is the spiritual part of them which some people believe continues existing after their body is dead. ❑ *They believe that their souls will always be together.* **2** N-COUNT You can refer to your mind, character, thoughts, and feelings as your **soul**. ❑ *I will put my heart and soul into the job.* **3** N-SING You use **soul** in negative statements to mean nobody at all. ❑ *I've never harmed a soul.* **4** N-UNCOUNT **Soul** or **soul music** is a type of pop music performed mainly by black American musicians.

sound /saʊnd/ (**sounder, soundest, sounds, sounding, sounded**) **1** N-COUNT A **sound** is something that you hear. ❑ *Liza was so frightened she couldn't make a sound.* ❑ *...the sounds of children playing.* **2** N-UNCOUNT **Sound** is what you hear when vibrations travel through air or water. ❑ *...twice the speed of sound.* **3** V-T/V-I If something such as a bell **sounds**, or if you **sound** it, it makes a noise. ❑ *A small computer bleep sounded.* **4** LINK-VERB When you are describing a noise, you can talk about the way it **sounds**. ❑ *The bang sounded like a huge explosion.* **5** LINK-VERB When you talk about the way someone **sounds**, you are describing the impression you have of them when they speak. ❑ *She sounded a bit worried.* **6** LINK-VERB & N-SING You can give your opinion about something you have just read or heard by talking about the way it **sounds**, or talking about the **sound of** it. ❑ *It sounds like a wonderful idea.* **7** ADJ You can describe a building or part of someone's mind or body as

S

sound when it is in good condition. ❑ *The walls all seem to be sound.* 8 ADJ If something such as advice is **sound**, it is reliable and sensible. 9 PHRASE If you are **sound asleep**, you are sleeping deeply.
→ see Word Web: **sound**
→ see **concert, ear, echo**
▸ **sound out** PHR-VERB If you **sound** someone **out**, you question them to find out their opinion. ❑ *The management will sound out the views of the employees.*

Thesaurus	*sound*	Also look up:
ADJ.	safe, sturdy, whole 2 logical, valid, wise; *(ant.)* illogical, unreliable 8	

soundcard /ˈsaʊndkɑːd/ (**soundcards**) N-COUNT A **soundcard** is a piece of equipment which can be put into a computer so that the computer can produce music or other sounds. [COMPUTING]

soundly /ˈsaʊndli/ 1 ADV If someone is **soundly** defeated, they are defeated thoroughly. 2 ADV If a decision, opinion, or statement is **soundly** based, there are sensible or reliable reasons behind it. 3 ADV If you sleep **soundly**, you sleep deeply.

soundtrack /ˈsaʊndtræk/ (**soundtracks**) N-COUNT The **soundtrack** of a film is its sound, speech, and especially the music.

soup /suːp/ (**soups**) N-VAR **Soup** is liquid food made by cooking meat, fish, or vegetables in water.

sour /saʊə/ (**sours, souring, soured**) 1 ADJ Something that is **sour** has a sharp taste like the taste of a lemon. ❑ *The apple was sour.* 2 ADJ **Sour** milk has an unpleasant taste because it is no longer fresh. 3 ADJ If you say that someone is **sour**, you think they are bad-tempered and unfriendly. ❑ *He gave Lane a sour look.* ● **sourly** ADV ❑ *Digby smiled sourly. 'Politics isn't pleasant.'* 4 ADJ If a situation or relationship **goes sour**, it stops being enjoyable or satisfactory. ❑ *Unfortunately, his boyhood dream turned sour.* 5 V-T/V-I If a friendship or attitude **sours**, or if something **sours** it, it becomes less friendly or hopeful. ❑ *Her mood soured a little.*
→ see **taste**

S

source /sɔːs/ (**sources**) 1 N-COUNT The **source of** something is the person, place, or thing which you get it from, or where it comes from. ❑ *...renewable sources of energy.* ❑ *Tourism is a major source of income for the city.* 2 N-COUNT A **source** is a person or book that provides information for a news story or for a piece of research. ❑ *Military sources say the boat was heading south.* 3 N-SING The **source** of a river or stream is the place where it begins.
→ see **diary**

south /saʊθ/ 1 N-SING **The south** is the direction on your right when you are looking towards the place where the sun rises. ❑ *...a warm wind from the south.* 2 N-SING & ADJ **The south of** a place, or the **south** part of a place, is the part which is towards the south. ❑ *...holidays in the south of France.* ❑ *...the south side of the valley.* 3 ADV **South** means towards the south, or positioned to the south of a place or thing. ❑ *The army moved south.* ❑ *The hurricane hit Florida just south of Miami.* 4 ADJ A **south wind** blows from the south.

ˌsouth-ˈeast 1 N-SING **The south-east** is the direction halfway between south and east. ❑ *Look towards the south-east.* 2 N-SING & ADJ **The south-east of** a place, or the **south-east** part of a place, is the part which is towards the south-east. ❑ *The suburb is seven miles south-east of Havana.* ❑ *...south-east London.* 3 ADV **South-east** means towards the south-east, or positioned to the south-east of a place or thing. ❑ *The rain should move south-east by late tomorrow.* 4 ADJ A **south-east wind** blows from the south-east.

ˌsouth-ˈeastern ADJ **South-eastern** means in or from the south-east of a region or country. ❑ *...the south-eastern edge of the United States.*

southerly /ˈsʌðəli/ 1 ADJ A **southerly** point, area, or direction is to the south or towards the south. ❑ *...the most southerly areas of Zimbabwe.* ❑ *...a southerly direction.* 2 ADJ A **southerly wind** blows from the south.

southern /ˈsʌðən/ ADJ **Southern** means in or from the south of a region or country. ❑ *...the southern hemisphere.*

southerner /ˈsʌðənə/ (**southerners**) N-COUNT A **southerner** is a person who was born in or who lives in the southern part of a place or country. ❑ *Bob Wilson is a southerner, from Texas.*

southward /ˈsaʊθwəd/ or **southwards** /ˈsaʊθwədz/ ADV & ADJ **Southward** or **southwards** means towards the south. ❑ *They flew southward.* ❑ *We decided on the southward route.*

ˌsouth-ˈwest 1 N-SING **The south-west** is the direction halfway between south and west. ❑ *Turn to the south-west to see Tor Bay.* 2 N-SING & ADJ **The south-west of** a place, or the **south-west** part of a place, is the part which is towards the south-west. ❑ *...the mountains in the south-west of the USA.* ❑ *...the south-west tip of Grenada.* 3 ADV **South-west** means towards the south-west, or positioned to the south-west of a place or thing. ❑ *Go south-west until you reach the sea.* 4 ADJ A **south-west wind** blows from the south-west.

ˌsouth-ˈwestern ADJ **South-western** means in or from the south-west of a region or country. ❑ *...south-western France.*

souvenir /ˌsuːvəˈnɪə, AM ˈsuːvənɪr/ (**souvenirs**) N-COUNT A **souvenir** is something which you buy or keep to remind you of a holiday, place, or event. ❑ *...a souvenir of the summer of 1992.*

sovereign /ˈsɒvrɪn/ (**sovereigns**) 1 ADJ A **sovereign** state or country is independent and not under the authority of any other country. 2 ADJ **Sovereign** is used to describe the person or institution that has the highest power in a country. ❑ *Nigeria's sovereign body.* 3 N-COUNT A **sovereign** is a king, queen, or other royal ruler.

sovereignty /ˈsɒvrɪnti/ N-UNCOUNT **Sovereignty** is the power that a country has to govern itself or to govern other countries. ❑ *Hong Kong is again under Chinese sovereignty.*

sow (**sows, sowing, sowed, sown**) 1 V-T /səʊ/ If you **sow** seeds, you plant them in the ground. 2 V-T If someone **sows** an undesirable feeling or situation, they cause it to begin and develop. ❑ *He cleverly sowed doubts in our minds.* 3 N-COUNT /saʊ/ A **sow** is an adult female pig.

spa /spɑː/ (**spas**) 1 N-COUNT A **spa** is a place where water with minerals in it bubbles out of the ground. 2 N-COUNT A health **spa** is a kind of hotel

where people go to do exercise and have special treatments in order to improve their health.
→ see **hotel**

space /speɪs/ (**spaces, spacing, spaced**) **1** N-VAR You use **space** to refer to an area of any size that is empty or available. ❑ *They've cut down more trees to make space for houses.* ❑ *In the spaces below, list the changes you have made.* **2** N-SING A **space of** time is a period of time. ❑ *Dramatic changes can occur in the space of a few minutes.* **3** V-T & PHR-VERB If you **space** a series of things, or if you **space** them **out**, you arrange them so that they have gaps between them. ❑ *Space the young plants a few metres apart.* ❑ *He talks quite slowly and spaces his words out.* **4** N-UNCOUNT **Space** is the vast area that lies beyond the Earth's atmosphere and surrounds the stars and planets. ❑ *...sending satellites into space.* **5** → see also **spacing**
→ see **meteor, moon, satellite**

Usage

You should use **space** or **room** to refer to an open or empty area. You do not use **place** as an uncount noun in this sense. **Room** is more likely to be used when you are talking about space inside an enclosed area. ❑ *There's not enough room in the bathroom for both of us.* ❑ *When you're driving, leave plenty of space between you and the car in front.*

spacecraft /ˈspeɪskrɑːft, -kræft/

Spacecraft is both the singular and the plural form.

N-COUNT A **spacecraft** is a rocket or other vehicle that can travel in space.

spaceship /ˈspeɪsʃɪp/ (**spaceships**) N-COUNT A **spaceship** is the same as a spacecraft.

ˈspace ˌstation (**space stations**) N-COUNT A **space station** is an object which is sent into space and then goes around the earth, and is used as a base by astronauts.
→ see **satellite**

spacing /ˈspeɪsɪŋ/ **1** N-UNCOUNT **Spacing** refers to the way that typing or printing is arranged on a page. ❑ *Write clearly in double spacing.* **2** → see also **space**

spacious /ˈspeɪʃəs/ ADJ A **spacious** room or other place is large, so that you can move around freely in it. ❑ *...spacious air-conditioned offices.*

spade /speɪd/ (**spades**) **1** N-COUNT A **spade** is a tool used for digging, with a flat metal blade and a long handle. **2** N-UNCOUNT **Spades** is one of the four suits in a pack of playing cards. Each card in the suit is called a **spade** and is marked with one or more black symbols: ♠.
→ see **garden**

spaghetti /spəˈgeti/ N-UNCOUNT **Spaghetti** is a type of pasta which looks like long pieces of string.

spam /spæm/ (**spams**) N-VAR **Spam** is unwanted e-mail that is sent to a large number of people, usually as advertising. [COMPUTING] ● **spammer** (**spammers**) N-COUNT ❑ *A spammer can send up to 200 million messages a day.*

span /spæn/ (**spans, spanning, spanned**) **1** N-COUNT A **span** is a period of time between two dates or events during which something exists or happens. ❑ *The batteries had a life span of six hours.* **2** N-COUNT Your **concentration span** or your **attention span** is the length of time you are able to concentrate on something or be interested in it. **3** V-T If something **spans** a long period of time, it lasts throughout that period of time or relates to the whole of it. ❑ *His professional career spanned 16 years.* **4** N-COUNT The **span of** something that extends or is spread out sideways is its width. ❑ *It is a very pretty butterfly, with a 2-inch wing span.* **5** V-T A bridge or other structure that **spans** something such as a river stretches right across it.
→ see **bridge**

Word Partnership Use *span* with:

N.	**life** span, **time** span	1
	attention span	2
	span **years**	3
ADJ.	**brief** span	1
	short span	1 5

spank /spæŋk/ (**spanks, spanking, spanked**) V-T If someone **spanks** a child, they punish them by hitting them on the bottom several times.

spanner /ˈspænə/ (**spanners**) N-COUNT In British English, a **spanner** is a metal tool used for tightening a nut. The American word is **wrench**.

spar /spɑː/ (**spars, sparring, sparred**) **1** V-I When boxers **spar**, they box quite gently instead of hitting each other hard, for example in training. ❑ *He could not get anyone to spar with Tyson.* **2** V-I If you **spar with** someone, you argue with them but not in an aggressive or serious way. ❑ *Then they sparred over who should apologise first.*

spare /speə/ (**spares, sparing, spared**) **1** ADJ & N-COUNT **Spare** things or **spares** are the same as things that you are already using that you are keeping ready in case others are needed. ❑ *Don't forget to take a few spare batteries.* ❑ *...two discs, with one as a spare.* **2** ADJ You use **spare** to describe something that is not being used by anyone, and is therefore available for someone to use. ❑ *They don't have much spare cash.* ❑ *...the spare bedroom.* **3** PHRASE If you have something such as time, money, or space **to spare**, you have some extra of it that you have not used or which you do not need. ❑ *He arrived with ninety seconds to spare.* **4** V-T If you **spare** time or another resource for a particular purpose, you make it available for that purpose. ❑ *She could only spare 35 minutes for our meeting.* **5** V-T To **spare** someone an unpleasant experience means to prevent them from having it. ❑ *Spare them the pain of discovering the real facts.* ❑ *So far I've been spared from injuries.*

Thesaurus *spare* Also look up:

ADJ.	additional, backup, emergency, extra, reserve	1 2

Word Partnership Use *spare* with:

N.	spare **change**, spare **equipment**	1
	spare **bedroom**	2
	a moment to spare, **time to** spare	3
	spare ***someone's* life**	5

ˌspare ˈpart (**spare parts**) N-COUNT **Spare parts** are parts that you can buy separately to replace old or broken parts in a piece of equipment.

S

spare 'time N-UNCOUNT **Your spare time** is the time during which you do not have to work when you can do whatever you like. ❑ *She read books in her spare time.*

sparing /'speərɪŋ/ ADJ If you are **sparing with** something, you use it or give it in very small quantities. ❑ *I wasn't sparing with the garlic.* ● **sparingly** ADV ❑ *We use this drug sparingly.*

spark /spɑ:k/ (**sparks, sparking, sparked**) 1 N-COUNT A **spark** is a tiny bright piece of burning material that flies up from something that is burning. 2 N-COUNT A **spark** is a flash of light caused by electricity. 3 N-COUNT A **spark of** a quality or feeling, especially a desirable one, is a small but noticeable amount of it. ❑ *You have to encourage them when they show a spark of interest.* 4 V-T & PHR-VERB If one thing **sparks** another, or if one thing **sparks off** another, the first thing causes the second thing to start happening. ❑ *The political crisis was sparked off by religious violence.*
→ see **fire**

Word Partnership	Use *spark* with:
PREP.	spark **from a fire** 1
N.	spark **conflict**, spark **debate**, spark **interest**, spark **a reaction** 4
V.	**ignite a** spark, **provide a** spark 1 4

sparkle /'spɑ:kəl/ (**sparkles, sparkling, sparkled**) V-I & N-UNCOUNT If something **sparkles**, or if it has **sparkle**, it is clear and bright and shines with a lot of very small points of light. ❑ *In the harbour, yachts sparkle in the sunshine.* ❑ *...the sparkle of coloured glass.*

sparkling /'spɑ:klɪŋ/ ADJ **Sparkling** drinks are slightly fizzy. ❑ *...a glass of sparkling water.*

sparrow /'spærəʊ/ (**sparrows**) N-COUNT A **sparrow** is a small brown bird that is common in Britain.

sparse /spɑ:s/ ADJ Something that is **sparse** is small in number or amount and spread out over an area. ❑ *He was a man of 52 with sparse hair.* ❑ *Traffic was sparse on the highway.* ● **sparsely** ADV ❑ *...the sparsely populated southern region.*

spartan /'spɑ:tən/ ADJ A **spartan** place or way of life is very simple or strict, with no luxuries. ❑ *Felicity's bedroom was spartan but bright.*

S

spasm /'spæzəm/ (**spasms**) N-VAR A **spasm** is a sudden tightening of your muscles, which you cannot control. ❑ *A lack of magnesium causes muscles to go into spasm.*

spat /spæt/ **Spat** is the past tense and past participle of **spit**.

spate /speɪt/ N-COUNT A **spate of** things, especially unpleasant things, is a large number of them that happen or appear within a short period of time. ❑ *...the recent spate of attacks on horses.*

spatial /'speɪʃəl/ ADJ BEFORE N **Spatial** is used to describe things relating to size, area, or position. ❑ *...the spatial distribution of rainfall.* ● **spatially** ADV ❑ *The music is for two spatially separated choirs.*

spatter /'spætə/ (**spatters, spattering, spattered**) V-T/V-I If a liquid **spatters** a surface, or if it **is spattered** there, drops of it fall on the surface. ❑ *Turn the fish, being careful not to spatter any hot butter on yourself.* ● **-spattered** ❑ *...the paint-spattered floor.*

speak /spi:k/ (**speaks, speaking, spoke, spoken**) 1 V-I/V-T When you **speak**, you use your voice in order to say something. ❑ *He tried to speak, but she interrupted him.* ❑ *Then I spoke these words.* ● **speaker** (**speakers**) N-COUNT ❑ *Ask questions after the speaker has stopped talking.* 2 V-I If you **speak for** a group of people, you make their views and demands known, or represent them. ❑ *I trust her to speak for me on this.* 3 V-T If you **speak** a foreign language, you know it and can use it. ❑ *He doesn't speak English.* ● **speaker** N-COUNT ❑ *A fifth of the population are Russian speakers.* 4 V-I If two people **are not speaking**, they no longer talk to each other because they have quarrelled. ❑ *My teenage daughter is not speaking to me after our most recent argument.* 5 V-I If you **speak well of** someone or **speak highly of** someone, you say good things about them. If you **speak ill of** someone, you criticize them. 6 PHRASE You use **speaking** in expressions such as **generally speaking** and **technically speaking** to indicate the way in which your statement is true or relevant. ❑ *Politically speaking, do you think that these moves have been effective?* 7 PHRASE You can say '**speaking as** a parent' or '**speaking as** a teacher', for example, to indicate that the opinion you are giving is based on your experience as a parent or as a teacher. 8 PHRASE If something **speaks for itself**, its meaning or qualities are obvious and do not need to be explained or pointed out. 9 PHRASE You can say **speaking of** something that has just been mentioned as a way of introducing a new topic which has some connection with that thing. ❑ *'I remember what you said. Forget about the past, live for the future.'—'That's right. Speaking of the future, I would like to take you to dinner tomorrow.'* 10 PHRASE **Nothing to speak of** means hardly anything or only unimportant things. ❑ *The house was nice but it had no garden to speak of.* 11 PHRASE You say **so to speak** to indicate that what you are saying is not literally true. ❑ *'We need something which will involve everyone.'—'Something to rock the boat, so to speak?'*

▸ **speak out** PHR-VERB If you **speak out** in favour of something or against something, you say publicly that you think it is good or bad. ❑ *She continued to speak out at meetings around the country.*

▸ **speak up** PHR-VERB If you ask someone to **speak up**, you are asking them to speak more loudly.

Usage

There are some differences in the way the verbs **speak** and **talk** are used. When you **speak**, you could, for example, be addressing someone or making a speech. **Talk** is more likely to be used when you are referring to a conversation or discussion. ❑ *I talked about it with my family at dinner.* ❑ *Sometimes we'd talk all night.* **Talk** can also be used to emphasize the activity of saying things, rather than the words that are spoken. ❑ *She thought I talked too much.*

Thesaurus	*speak* Also look up:
V.	articulate, communicate, declare, talk 1

Word Partnership Use *speak* with:

ADV. speak **clearly**, speak **directly**, speak **louder**, speak **slowly** 1
speak **freely**, speak **publicly** 1 2
N. **chance to** speak, **opportunity to** speak, speak **the truth** 1 2
speak **English**, speak **a (foreign) language** 3

speaker /'spi:kə/ (**speakers**) 1 N-COUNT A **speaker** is a person who makes a speech. ❑ *Bruce Wyatt will be the speaker at next month's meeting.* 2 N-COUNT A **speaker** is a piece of equipment, for example part of a radio or hi-fi system, through which sound comes out. 3 → see also **speak**

spear /spɪə/ (**spears, spearing, speared**) 1 N-COUNT A **spear** is a weapon consisting of a long pole with a sharp point. 2 V-T If you **spear** something, you push a pointed object into it. → see **army**

spearhead /'spɪəhed/ (**spearheads, spearheading, spearheaded**) V-T & N-COUNT If someone **spearheads** a campaign, or if they are involved in **the spearhead of** it, they lead it. [JOURNALISM] ❑ *He spearheaded a national campaign against bullying.*

specs /speks/ N-PLURAL A pair of **specs** is a pair of glasses. [INFORMAL]

special /'speʃəl/ 1 ADJ Someone or something that is **special** is different from normal, often in a way that makes them better or more important than other people or things. ❑ *You're very special to me, darling.* ❑ *...a special variety of strawberry.* 2 ADJ BEFORE N **Special** means relating to one particular person, group, or place. ❑ *Everyone has his or her own special problems.*

Thesaurus *special* Also look up:

ADJ. distinctive, exceptional, unique; (*ant.*) ordinary 1 2

ˌspecial efˈfect (**special effects**) N-COUNT In film, **special effects** are unusual pictures or sounds that are created by using special techniques.

specialise → see **specialize**

specialist /'speʃəlɪst/ (**specialists**) N-COUNT A **specialist** is a person who has a particular skill or knows a lot about a particular subject. ❑ *A specialist nurse will teach you how to use the medicine.*

speciality /speʃi'ælɪti/ (**specialities**) 1 N-COUNT Someone's **speciality** is the kind of work they do best or the subject they know most about. ❑ *His speciality was the history of Germany.* 2 N-COUNT In British English, a **speciality** of a place is a special food or product that is always very good there. The usual American word is **specialty**. ❑ *This pasta is a speciality of northern Italy.*

specialize [BRIT also **specialise**] /'speʃəlaɪz/ (**specializes, specializing, specialized**) V-I If you **specialize in** an area of study or a type of work, you know a lot about it and spend a lot of your time and attention on it. ● **specialization** N-UNCOUNT ❑ *...specialization in particular products.*

specialized [BRIT also **specialised**] /'speʃəlaɪzd/ ADJ Someone or something that is **specialized** is trained or developed for a particular purpose. ❑ *...specialized training in teaching reading.*

specially /'speʃəli/ 1 ADV If something has been done **specially** for a particular person or purpose, it has been done only for that person or purpose. ❑ *This soap is specially designed for sensitive skins.* 2 ADV **Specially** is used to mean more than usually or more than other things. [INFORMAL] ❑ *What was specially enjoyable about that job?*

specialty /'speʃəlti/ (**specialties**) N-COUNT A **specialty** is the same as a **speciality**. [AM]

species /'spi:ʃiz/

Species is both the singular and the plural form.

N-COUNT A **species** is a class of plants or animals whose members have the same characteristics and are able to breed with each other. → see **evolution, plant, zoo**

specific /spɪ'sɪfɪk/ 1 ADJ BEFORE N You use **specific** to emphasize that you are talking about a particular thing or subject. ❑ *Several magazines provide information on specific products.* 2 ADJ If someone is **specific**, they give a description that is exact. You can also use **specific** to describe their description. 3 ADJ Something that is **specific to** a particular thing is connected with that thing only. ❑ *...financial problems specific to students.* ● **-specific** ❑ *Most studies of trade have been country-specific.*

specifically /spɪ'sɪfɪkli/ 1 ADV You use **specifically** to emphasize that a subject is being considered separately from other subjects. ❑ *They will work out an exercise programme designed specifically for you.* 2 ADV You use **specifically** to add something more precise or exact to what you have already said. ❑ *Death frightens me, specifically my own death.* 3 ADV You use **specifically** to indicate that you are stating or describing something precisely. ❑ *I asked her to repeat specifically the words that Patti had used.*

specification /ˌspesɪfɪ'keɪʃən/ (**specifications**) N-COUNT A **specification** is a requirement which is clearly stated, for example about the necessary features in the design of something. ❑ *The jewellery can be produced to your specifications.*

specify /'spesɪfaɪ/ (**specifies, specifying, specified**) V-T If you **specify** something, you state it precisely. ❑ *Be sure to sow the seeds at the specified depth.*

specimen /'spesɪmɪn/ (**specimens**) N-COUNT A **specimen of** something is an example or small amount of it which gives an idea of the whole. ❑ *Applicants have to provide a specimen of handwriting.*

speck /spek/ (**specks**) N-COUNT A **speck** is a very small stain or mark, or a very small piece of something. ❑ *He brushed a speck of dust off his shoes.*

Word Link *spect ≈ looking : spectacle, spectacular, spectator*

spectacle /'spektəkəl/ (**spectacles**) 1 N-PLURAL Someone's **spectacles** are their glasses. [FORMAL] ❑ *...a pair of spectacles.* 2 N-COUNT A **spectacle** is an interesting or impressive sight or event. ❑ *Mahoney watched the spectacle before him.*

spectacular /spek'tækjʊlə/ (**spectaculars**) 1 ADJ Something that is **spectacular** is very impressive or dramatic. ● **spectacularly** ADV ❑ *Many of her movies were spectacularly successful.*

S

2 N-COUNT A **spectacular** is a grand and impressive show or performance. ❑ *This is one of the world's great sporting spectaculars.*

Word Link	*spect ≈ looking : spectacle, spectacular, spectator*

spectator /spek'teɪtə, AM 'spekteɪtər/ (**spectators**) N-COUNT A **spectator** is someone who watches something, especially a sporting event.

spectre [AM **specter**] /'spektə/ (**spectres**) N-COUNT You talk about **the spectre of** something unpleasant when you are frightened that it might occur. ❑ *This has raised the spectre of a full-scale war.*

spectrum /'spektrəm/ (**spectra** or **spectrums**) **1** N-SING **The spectrum** is the range of different colours produced when light passes through an object called a prism or through a drop of water. **2** N-COUNT A **spectrum** is a range of a particular type of thing. ❑ *The term 'special needs' covers a wide spectrum of problems.*

speculate /'spekjʊleɪt/ (**speculates, speculating, speculated**) **1** V-T/V-I If you **speculate** about something, you guess about its nature or identity, or about what might happen. ❑ *The reader can speculate what will happen next.* ● **speculation** (**speculations**) N-VAR ❑ *...speculation over the future of the economy.* **2** V-I When people **speculate** financially, they buy property or shares in the hope of being able to sell them at a profit. ● **speculator** (**speculators**) N-COUNT ❑ *...a property speculator.*

speculative /'spekjʊlətɪv, AM -leɪt-/ ADJ A **speculative** statement or opinion is based on guesses rather than knowledge. ❑ *A speculative report suggested that he was trying to sell the business.*

sped /sped/ **Sped** is a past tense and past participle of **speed**.

speech /spi:tʃ/ (**speeches**) **1** N-UNCOUNT **Speech** is the ability to speak or the act of speaking. ❑ *...the development of speech in children.* **2** N-SING **Your speech** is the way in which you speak. ❑ *The disease has affected his speech.* **3** N-UNCOUNT **Speech** is spoken language. ❑ *...the way these letters are usually pronounced in speech.* **4** N-COUNT A **speech** is a formal talk given to an audience.

S

Word Partnership	Use *speech* with:
ADJ.	**slurred** speech **1** **famous** speech, **major** speech, **political** speech, **recent** speech **4**
N.	**acceptance** speech, **campaign** speech, speech **writing** **4**
V.	**deliver a** speech, **give a** speech, **make a** speech, **prepare a** speech **4**

speechless /'spi:tʃləs/ ADJ If you are **speechless**, you are temporarily unable to speak, usually because something has shocked you. ❑ *Alex was speechless with fear.*

speed /spi:d/ (**speeds, speeding, sped**)

For the phrasal verb, the past tense and past participle is **speeded**.

1 N-VAR The **speed** of something is the rate at which it moves, happens, or is done. ❑ *He drove off at high speed.* ❑ *Each learner can progress at his own speed.* **2** N-UNCOUNT **Speed** is very fast movement. ❑ *People who ride horses at speed must be very brave.* **3** V-I To **speed** somewhere means to move or travel there quickly. ❑ *Trains speed through the Channel Tunnel at 186mph.* **4** V-I A motorist who **is speeding** is driving a vehicle faster than the legal speed limit. ● **speeding** N-UNCOUNT ❑ *He was fined for speeding.*

▶ **speed up** PHR-VERB When something **speeds up**, it moves, happens, or is done more quickly. ❑ *Try to speed up your breathing and stretch your legs.*

'speed ˌdating N-UNCOUNT **Speed dating** is a method of introducing unattached people to potential partners by arranging for them to meet a series of people on a single occasion. ❑ *If you're a busy person, speed dating could be for you.*

'speed ˌlimit (**speed limits**) N-COUNT The **speed limit** on a road is the maximum speed at which you are legally allowed to drive.

speedy /'spi:di/ (**speedier, speediest**) ADJ A **speedy** process, event, or action happens or is done very quickly. ❑ *We wish Bill a speedy recovery.* ● **speedily** ADV ❑ *Gerard speedily agreed.*

spell /spel/ (**spells, spelling, spelled** or [BRIT also] **spelt**) **1** V-T & PHR-VERB When you **spell** a word, or when you **spell** it **out**, you write or speak each letter in the word in the correct order. ❑ *How do you spell 'potato'?* ❑ *If I don't know a word, I ask them to spell it out for me.* **2** V-T If something **spells** a particular result, it suggests that this will be the result. ❑ *Kids love this because it spells pure, simple fun.* **3** N-COUNT A **spell of** an activity or type of weather is a short period of it. ❑ *...a long spell of dry weather.* ❑ *...a brief spell teaching English.* **4** N-COUNT A **spell** is a situation in which events are controlled by a magical power. ❑ *Brecht's singing 'put people under a magic spell'.*

▶ **spell out** **1** PHR-VERB If you **spell** something **out**, you explain it in detail. ❑ *Come on, spell out exactly how you feel.* **2** → see **spell** (meaning 1)

Word Partnership	Use *spell* with:
N.	spell **a name/word** **1** spell **the end of *something***, spell **trouble** **2**
V.	**can/can't** spell ***something*** **1** **break a** spell, **cast a** spell **4**

spellcheck /'speltʃek/ (**spellchecks, spellchecking, spellchecked**) V-T If you **spellcheck** something you have written on a computer, you use a special program to check for spelling mistakes. [COMPUTING] ❑ *This model allows you to spellcheck over 100,000 different words.*

spellchecker /'speltʃekə/ (**spellcheckers**) N-COUNT A **spellchecker** is a special program on a computer which you can use to check for spelling mistakes. [COMPUTING]

spelling /'spelɪŋ/ (**spellings**) **1** N-COUNT The **spelling** of a word is the correct sequence of letters in it. **2** N-UNCOUNT **Spelling** is the ability to spell words in the correct way. It is also an attempt to spell a word correctly. ❑ *His spelling is very bad.*

spelt /spelt/ **Spelt** is a past tense and past participle form of **spell**. [BRIT]

spend /spend/ (**spends, spending, spent**) **1** V-T When you **spend** money, you pay money for things that you want. ❑ *Every three months I spend a hundred pounds on clothes.* **2** V-T If you **spend** time or energy doing something, you use your time or effort doing it. If you **spend** time in a place, you stay there for a period of time. ❑ *Engineers spend much time developing brilliant solutions.* ❑ *She had spent 29 years as a nurse.* ❑ *We spent the night in a hotel.*

Word Partnership Use *spend* with:

N. spend **billions/millions, companies** spend, **consumers** spend, spend **money** **1** spend **an amount** **1** **2** spend **a day**, spend **energy**, spend **hours/minutes**, spend **months/weeks/years**, spend **a night**, spend **time**, spend **a weekend** **2**

V. **afford to** spend, **expect to** spend, **going to** spend, **plan to** spend **1** **2**

spent /spent/ **1** **Spent** is the past tense and past participle of **spend**. **2** ADJ **Spent** substances or containers have been used and cannot be used again. ❑ *The spent fuel is still highly radioactive.*

sperm /spɜːm/

In meaning 1, the plural is **sperm** or **sperms**.

1 N-COUNT A **sperm** is a cell produced in the sex organs of a male animal which can enter a female animal's egg and fertilize it. **2** N-UNCOUNT **Sperm** is the liquid that contains sperm when it is produced.
→ see **reproduction**

spew /spjuː/ (**spews, spewing, spewed**) V-I When things **spew** from a place, they come out in large quantities. ❑ *Bright blood spewed from his lips.*

Word Link *sphere ≈ ball : atmosphere, hemisphere, sphere*

sphere /sfɪə/ (**spheres**) **1** N-COUNT A **sphere** is an object that is perfectly round in shape like a ball. **2** N-COUNT A **sphere of** activity or interest is a particular area of activity or interest. ❑ *Our nurses work in all spheres of the health service.*
→ see **solid, volume**

spice /spaɪs/ (**spices**) N-VAR A **spice** is a part of a plant, or a powder made from that part, which you put in food to give it flavour.
→ see Word Web: **spice**

spiced /spaɪst/ ADJ When food is **spiced**, it has had spices or other strong-tasting foods added to it.

spicy /ˈspaɪsi/ (**spicier, spiciest**) ADJ **Spicy** food is strongly flavoured with spices.
→ see **spice**

spider /ˈspaɪdə/ (**spiders**) N-COUNT A **spider** is a small creature with eight legs.

spike /spaɪk/ (**spikes**) **1** N-COUNT A **spike** is a long piece of metal with a sharp point. ❑ *The 15-foot wall was topped with iron spikes.* **2** N-COUNT Some long pointed objects can be referred to as **spikes**. ❑ *Her hair stood up in spikes.*

spiked /spaɪkt/ ADJ **Spiked** things have spikes or a spike on them. ❑ *...huge iron spiked gates.*

spiky /ˈspaɪki/ (**spikier, spikiest**) ADJ Something that is **spiky** has sharp points. ❑ *...tall, spiky evergreen trees.*

spill

spill /spɪl/ (**spills, spilling, spilled** or [BRIT also] **spilt** /spɪlt/) **1** V-T & N-COUNT If you **spill** a liquid, it accidentally flows over the edge of its container. The liquid that has overflowed is called a **spill**. ❑ *I almost spilled my drink.* ❑ *Don't spill water on your suit.* ❑ *...the oil spill from the tanker.* **2** V-I If people or things **spill out** of a place, they come out in large numbers. ❑ *The crowd spilled out into the street.*

spin /spɪn/ (**spins, spinning, spun**) **1** V-T/V-I If something or someone **spins**, or if you **spin** them, they turn quickly around a central point. ❑ *He spun around, looking guilty.* ❑ *Ella spun the wheel and turned on to Main Street.* **2** V-I When someone **spins**, they make thread by twisting together pieces of a fibre such as cotton or wool. ❑ *...machinery for spinning cotton.* **3** V-T If someone **spins** a story, they give you an account of something that is untrue or only partly true.
→ see **wheel**

▶ **spin out** PHR-VERB If you **spin** something **out**, you make it last longer than it normally would.

Word Web spice

While studying the use of **spices** in cooking, scientists found that many spices can help prevent disease. Bacteria can grow quickly on food and cause serious illnesses in humans. The researchers found that many spices kill bacteria. For example, **garlic**, **onion**, allspice, and oregano kill almost all common **germs**. **Cinnamon**, tarragon, cumin, and chili **peppers** also stop about 75% of bacteria. And even common, everyday **black pepper** kills about 25% of all germs. The scientists also found that food is connected to climate. Spicy food is common in hot climates. Bland food is common in cold climates.

garlic

onion

chili pepper

ginger

black pepper

cinnamon

cloves

S

❑ *He deliberately spun out his speech.*

Word Partnership	Use *spin* with:
N.	spin **a wheel** 1
ADJ.	**positive** spin 3

spinach /ˈspɪnɪdʒ, -ɪtʃ/ N-UNCOUNT **Spinach** is a vegetable with large green leaves.
→ see **vegetable**

spinal /ˈspaɪnəl/ ADJ BEFORE N **Spinal** means relating to your spine. ❑ *...spinal injuries.*

spine /spaɪn/ (**spines**) N-COUNT Your **spine** is the row of bones down your back.

ˈspin-ˌoff (**spin-offs**) 1 N-COUNT A **spin-off** is something useful that unexpectedly happens as a result of trying to achieve something else. ❑ *Space tourism will be a spin-off from safe space transport.* 2 N-COUNT A **spin-off** is a book, film, or television series that is derived from something similar that is already successful.

spiral /ˈspaɪərəl/ (**spirals, spiralling, spiralled** or [AM] **spiraling, spiraled**) 1 N-COUNT & ADJ BEFORE N A **spiral** is a shape which winds round and round, with each curve above or outside the previous one. **Spiral** things are in the shape of a spiral. ❑ *...the spiral staircase.* 2 V-I If something **spirals** somewhere, it grows or moves in a spiral curve. ❑ *Smoke spiralled upwards from the ground.* 3 V-I If an amount or level **spirals upwards** or **downwards**, it rises or falls quickly and at an increasing rate. You can refer to this kind of change in a level or amount as a particular kind of **spiral**. ❑ *The cost of the project is spiralling out of control.* ❑ *Oil prices continue their upward spiral.*
→ see **circle**

spire /spaɪə/ (**spires**) N-COUNT The **spire** of a church is a tall cone-shaped structure on top of a tower.

spirit /ˈspɪrɪt/ (**spirits, spiriting, spirited**) 1 N-SING Your **spirit** is the part of you that is not physical and that is connected with your deepest thoughts and feelings. ❑ *She is physically weak but her spirit is very strong.* 2 N-COUNT A person's **spirit** is a part of them that is not physical and that is believed to remain alive after their death. 3 N-COUNT A **spirit** is a ghost or supernatural being. 4 N-UNCOUNT **Spirit** is courage, determination, and energy that someone shows during difficult times. ❑ *Everyone who knew her admired her spirit.* 5 N-PLURAL You can refer to your **spirits** when saying how happy or unhappy you are. For example, if your spirits are high, you are happy. ❑ *Exercise will help lift his spirits.* 6 N-SING The **spirit** in which you do something is the attitude you have when you are doing it. ❑ *Sick people with a fighting spirit are more likely to survive.* 7 N-SING **The spirit of** something such as a law or an agreement is the way that it was intended to be interpreted or applied. ❑ *We have embraced the spirit of this law and what our obligations are.* 8 V-T If someone or something **is spirited away**, they are taken from a place quickly and secretly without anyone noticing. 9 N-PLURAL In British English, **spirits** are strong alcoholic drinks such as whisky and gin. The American word is **liquor**.

spirited /ˈspɪrɪtɪd/ ADJ **Spirited** means showing great energy, confidence, or courage. ❑ *They made a decision after 12 hours of spirited debate.*

S

spiritual /ˈspɪrɪtʃʊəl/ 1 ADJ **Spiritual** means relating to people's deepest thoughts and beliefs, rather than to their bodies and physical surroundings. ● **spiritually** ADV ❑ *We were physically and spiritually exhausted.* ● **spirituality** /ˌspɪrɪtʃʊˈælɪti/ N-UNCOUNT ❑ *...the peaceful spirituality of Japanese culture.* 2 ADJ **Spiritual** means relating to people's religious beliefs. ❑ *These members were seen as spiritual leaders.*
→ see **myth**

spit /spɪt/ (**spits, spitting, spat** or [AM also] **spit**) 1 N-UNCOUNT **Spit** is the watery liquid produced in your mouth. 2 V-I/V-T If someone **spits**, they force an amount of spit out of their mouth. If you **spit** liquid or food somewhere, you force a small amount of it out of your mouth. ❑ *People were spitting and throwing stones at me.* ❑ *He spat his drink on the floor.*

spite /spaɪt/ 1 PREP You use **in spite of** to introduce a fact which makes the rest of the statement you are making seem surprising. ❑ *He hired her in spite of the fact that she had never sung on stage.* 2 PREP If you do something **in spite of yourself**, you do it although you did not really intend to or expect to. ❑ *'What's Tony's reaction to all this?' Amy asked, laughing in spite of herself.* 3 V-T & N-UNCOUNT If you do something to **spite** someone, or if you do it **out of spite**, you do it because you want to hurt or upset them. ❑ *Just to spite Loren again, Shannon kissed Brady.*

splash /splæʃ/ (**splashes, splashing, splashed**) 1 V-I & N-SING If you **splash** around in water, you hit or disturb the water in a noisy way. A **splash** is the sound made when something hits or falls into water. ❑ *Children continually splash in and out of the water.* ❑ *It hit the water with a huge splash.* 2 V-T/V-I & N-COUNT If you **splash** a liquid somewhere or if it **splashes**, it hits someone or something and scatters in a lot of small drops. A **splash of** liquid is a quantity of it that hits something in this way. ❑ *Tears splashed into her hands.* 3 PHRASE If you **make a splash**, you become noticed or become popular because of something that you have done. [INFORMAL]

▸ **splash out** PHR-VERB If you **splash out on** something, especially on a luxury, you buy it even though it costs a lot of money. [BRIT, INFORMAL] ❑ *He wanted to splash out on a new car.*

splatter /ˈsplætə/ (**splatters, splattering, splattered**) V-T/V-I If a liquid **splatters on** something or **is splattered on** it, it drops or is thrown over it. ❑ *The men were splattered with paint.*

splendid /ˈsplendɪd/ 1 ADJ If you say that something is **splendid**, you mean that it is very good. [DATED] ❑ *What a splendid idea!* ● **splendidly** ADV ❑ *We played splendidly.* 2 ADJ If you describe a building or work of art as **splendid**, you mean that it is beautiful and impressive. ❑ *...a splendid Victorian museum.* ● **splendidly** ADV ❑ *Nigel's book is splendidly illustrated.*

splendour [AM **splendor**] /ˈsplendə/ (**splendours**) N-VAR The **splendour** of something is its beautiful and impressive appearance. ❑ *...the splendour of the palace of Versailles.*

splinter /ˈsplɪntə/ (**splinters, splintering, splintered**) 1 N-COUNT A **splinter** is a very thin sharp piece of wood or glass which has broken off from a larger piece. 2 V-T/V-I If something **splinters** or **is splintered**, it breaks into splinters.

❑ *The stone flew into the glass, splintering it.*

split /splɪt/ (**splits, splitting, split**) 1 V-T/V-I If something **splits**, or if you **split** it, it is divided into two or more parts. ❑ *In the storm, the ship split in two.* ❑ *...uniting families that were split by the Korean war.* 2 V-T/V-I & N-COUNT If an organization **splits**, or if it **is split**, one group of members disagrees strongly with the other members, and may form a group of their own. You also refer to a disagreement of this kind as a **split**. ❑ *They say women priests are splitting the church.* 3 V-T/V-I If something such as wood or a piece of clothing **splits**, or if it **is split**, a long crack or tear appears in it. ❑ *I split my trousers.* 4 V-T If two or more people **split** something, they share it between them. ❑ *I was happy to split the profits with them.*

▶ **split up** 1 PHR-VERB If two people **split up**, they end their relationship or marriage. ❑ *I split up with my boyfriend.* 2 PHR-VERB If a group of people **split up**, they go away in different directions. ❑ *We decided to split up, hoping to get more done.* 3 PHR-VERB If you **split** something **up**, you divide it into a number of separate sections. ❑ *He split up the company.*

Thesaurus *split* Also look up:

V.	break, divide, part, separate; *(ant.)* combine 1 2 4
N.	crack, separation, tear 3

Word Partnership Use *split* with:

PREP.	split **into** 1
	split **over *something*** 2
	split **among**, split **between** 4
N.	split **shares**, split **wood** 1 3
	split **in a party** 2
ADV.	split **apart** 1 2

ˌsplit ˈsecond N-SING A **split second** is a very short period of time. ❑ *...a split-second decision.*

splutter /ˈsplʌtə/ (**splutters, spluttering, spluttered**) 1 V-I If someone **splutters**, they make spitting sounds and have difficulty speaking clearly, often because they are embarrassed or angry. ❑ *Mickey spluttered, and wiped his eyes with the back of his hand.* 2 V-I If something **splutters**, it makes a series of short sharp sounds. ❑ *The flame spluttered and went out.*

spoil /spɔɪl/ (**spoils, spoiling, spoiled** or [BRIT also] **spoilt**) 1 V-T If you **spoil** something, you prevent it from being successful or satisfactory. ❑ *Don't let small mistakes spoil your life.* 2 V-T If you say that someone **spoils** their children, you mean that they give their children everything they want and that this has a bad effect on their character. ● **spoilt** also **spoiled** ADJ ❑ *A spoilt child is rarely popular with other children.* 3 V-T If you **spoil yourself**, or if you **spoil** someone you love, you give yourself or them something nice, or you do something special for them. 4 N-PLURAL **The spoils of** something are things that people get as a result of winning a battle or of doing something successfully. ❑ *...the spoils of war.*

spoke /spəʊk/ (**spokes**) 1 **Spoke** is the past tense of **speak**. 2 N-COUNT The **spokes** of a wheel are the bars that join the outer ring to the centre. → see **bicycle, wheel**

spoken /ˈspəʊkən/ **Spoken** is the past participle of **speak**.

spokesman /ˈspəʊksmən/ (**spokesmen**) N-COUNT A **spokesman** is a male spokesperson.

spokesperson /ˈspəʊkspɜːsən/ (**spokespersons**) N-COUNT A **spokesperson** is a person who speaks as the representative of a group or organization.

spokeswoman /ˈspəʊkswʊmən/ (**spokeswomen**) N-COUNT A **spokeswoman** is a female spokesperson.

sponge /spʌndʒ/ (**sponges, sponging, sponged**) 1 N-UNCOUNT **Sponge** is a very light absorbent substance with lots of little holes in it. Sponge can be either man-made or natural and is capable of absorbing a lot of water. 2 N-COUNT A **sponge** is a piece of sponge that you use for washing yourself or for cleaning things. 3 V-T If you **sponge** something, you wipe it with a wet sponge. ❑ *Gently sponge your face.* 4 N-VAR A **sponge** is a light cake or pudding made from flour, eggs, sugar, and sometimes fat. ❑ *...chocolate sponge cake.*

▶ **sponge off** or **sponge on** PHR-VERB If you say that someone **sponges off** other people or **sponges on** them, you disapprove of them because they get money from others, rather than trying to support themselves. [INFORMAL]

sponsor /ˈspɒnsə/ (**sponsors, sponsoring, sponsored**) 1 V-T If an organization **sponsors** something such as an event, it pays some or all of the expenses connected with it, often in order to get publicity for itself. 2 V-T In Britain, if you **sponsor** someone who is doing something to raise money for charity, you give them a sum of money for the charity if they succeed in doing it. 3 N-COUNT A **sponsor** is a person or organization that sponsors something or someone.

sponsorship /ˈspɒnsəʃɪp/ N-UNCOUNT **Sponsorship** is financial support given by a sponsor. ❑ *...skiers in need of sponsorship.*

spontaneity /ˌspɒntəˈneɪɪti/ N-UNCOUNT **Spontaneity** is spontaneous, natural behaviour. ❑ *He had the spontaneity of a child.*

spontaneous /spɒnˈteɪniəs/ 1 ADJ **Spontaneous** acts are not planned or arranged, but are done because someone suddenly wants to do them. ❑ *I joined in the spontaneous applause.* ● **spontaneously** ADV ❑ *He was never spontaneously friendly towards us.* 2 ADJ A **spontaneous** event happens because of processes within something, rather than being caused by things outside it. ❑ *...a spontaneous explosion.* ● **spontaneously** ADV ❑ *These symptoms spontaneously disappear in a few weeks.*

spooky /ˈspuːki/ (**spookier, spookiest**) ADJ If something is **spooky**, it has a frightening and unnatural atmosphere. [INFORMAL] ❑ *It's really spooky out here.*

spool /spuːl/ (**spools**) N-COUNT A **spool** is a round object in a machine such as a sewing machine or film projector onto which thread, tape, or film is wound.

spoon /spuːn/ (**spoons, spooning, spooned**) 1 N-COUNT A **spoon** is a tool used for eating, stirring, and serving food. It is shaped like a small shallow bowl with a long handle. 2 V-T If you **spoon** food somewhere, you put it there using a

spoon. ❑ *Spoon the sauce over the meat.*
→ see **kitchen**

sporadic /spəˈrædɪk/ ADJ **Sporadic** events happen at irregular intervals. ● **sporadically** ADV ❑ *Fighting has occurred sporadically since 1988.*

spore /spɔː/ (**spores**) N-COUNT **Spores** are cells produced by fungi such as mushrooms, which can develop into new fungi. [TECHNICAL]

sport /spɔːt/ (**sports**) N-VAR **Sports** are games and other competitive activities which need physical effort and skill. ❑ *She's really good at sport.*

sporting /ˈspɔːtɪŋ/ ADJ BEFORE N **Sporting** means relating to sport or used for sport. ❑ *...sporting events.*

sportsman /ˈspɔːtsmən/ (**sportsmen**) N-COUNT A **sportsman** is a man who takes part in sports.

sportswoman /ˈspɔːtswʊmən/ (**sportswomen**) N-COUNT A **sportswoman** is a woman who takes part in sports.

sporty /ˈspɔːti/ (**sportier, sportiest**) ADJ A **sporty** person enjoys playing sport.

spot /spɒt/ (**spots, spotting, spotted**) **1** N-COUNT **Spots** are small, round, coloured areas on a surface. ❑ *The swimsuit is navy with white spots.* **2** N-COUNT **Spots** on a person's skin are small lumps or marks. **3** N-COUNT A **spot of** a substance is a small amount of it. ❑ *Spots of rain began to fall.* **4** N-COUNT You can refer to a particular place as a **spot**. ❑ *...the island's top tourist spots.* **5** V-T If you **spot** something or someone, you notice them. ❑ *We spotted smoke coming up the stairs.* **6** PHRASE If you are **on the spot**, you are at the actual place where something is happening. ❑ *You have to be on the spot to deal with any problems.* **7** PHRASE If you do something **on the spot**, you do it immediately. ❑ *He was sacked on the spot.* **8** PHRASE If you **put** someone **on the spot**, you force them to make a difficult decision or answer a difficult question. **9** to **have a soft spot for** someone → see **soft**

Word Partnership Use *spot* with:

ADJ.	**good** spot, **perfect** spot, **popular** spot, **quiet** spot, **the right** spot **4**
N.	**holiday** spot, **parking** spot **4**

spotlight /ˈspɒtlaɪt/ (**spotlights, spotlighting, spotlighted**) **1** N-COUNT A **spotlight** is a powerful light, used for example in a theatre, which can be directed so that it lights up a small area. **2** V-T To **spotlight** a particular problem or situation means to make people notice it and think about it. ❑ *Similar stories have been spotlighted in other magazines.*
→ see **concert**

spotlight

spouse /spaʊs/ (**spouses**) N-COUNT Someone's **spouse** is the person they are married to. [FORMAL]

spout /spaʊt/ (**spouts, spouting, spouted**) **1** V-T/V-I If something **spouts** liquid or fire, or if liquid or fire **spouts** out of something, it comes out very quickly with a lot of force. ❑ *The fountain spouts water 40 feet into the air.* **2** V-T If you say that someone **spouts** something, you disapprove of them because they say something which you think is wrong or insincere. ❑ *He accused Mr Brown of spouting nonsense.* **3** N-COUNT The **spout** of a kettle or teapot is the tube that the liquid comes out of.

sprain /spreɪn/ (**sprains, spraining, sprained**) **1** V-T If you **sprain** your ankle or wrist, you accidentally damage it by twisting it, for example when you fall. ❑ *...a badly sprained ankle.* **2** N-COUNT A **sprain** is the injury caused by spraining a joint.

sprang /spræŋ/ **Sprang** is the past tense of **spring**.

sprawl /sprɔːl/ (**sprawls, sprawling, sprawled**) **1** V-I If you **sprawl** somewhere, you sit or lie down with your legs and arms spread out in a careless way. ❑ *He fell and sprawled on the ground.* **2** V-I & N-UNCOUNT If a place **sprawls** over a large area of land, it completely covers that area. You can refer to this area as a **sprawl**. ❑ *...Dublin's city sprawl.*

spray /spreɪ/ (**sprays, spraying, sprayed**) **1** N-UNCOUNT **Spray** consists of a lot of small drops of water which are being splashed or forced into the air. ❑ *...the spray from the waterfall.* **2** V-T/V-I If you **spray** drops of a liquid or small pieces of something somewhere, or if they **spray** somewhere, they cover a place or shower someone. ❑ *He sprayed aftershave on his cheeks.* ❑ *The pipe split, spraying the engine with fuel.* **3** N-VAR A **spray** is a liquid kept under pressure in a container, which you can force out in very small drops. ❑ *...a can of insect spray.*

Word Partnership Use *spray* with:

PREP.	spray **with water** **2**
N.	spray **bottle**, **bug** spray, spray **can**, **hair** spray, **pepper** spray **3**

spread /spred/ (**spreads, spreading, spread**) **1** V-T If you **spread** something somewhere, you open it out or arrange it over a place or surface, so that all of it can be seen or used easily. ❑ *She spread a towel on the sand and lay on it.* **2** V-T If you **spread** your hands, arms, or legs, you move them far apart. ❑ *She spread her arms out to them in welcome.* **3** V-T If you **spread** a substance on a surface, you put a thin layer of the substance over the surface. ❑ *Spread the bread with the cheese.* **4** N-VAR A **spread** is a soft food which is put on bread. ❑ *...a salad roll with low fat spread.* **5** V-T/V-I If something **spreads**, or if it **is spread** by people, it gradually reaches or affects a larger and larger area or more and more people. ❑ *Cholera is not spreading as quickly as it did in the past.* **6** N-SING **The spread of** something is its increasing presence or occurrence. ❑ *...the spread of modern technology.* **7** V-T If something **is spread over** a period of time, it is organized so that it takes place at regular intervals over that period. ❑ *The course is spread over a five week period.* **8** N-SING A **spread of** ideas, interests, or activities is a wide variety of them. ❑ *We have an enormous spread of industries.*

▶ **spread out** **1** PHR-VERB If people, animals, or vehicles **spread out**, they move apart from each other. **2** PHR-VERB If you **spread** something **out**, you arrange it over a surface, so that all of it can be seen or used easily. ❑ *Tom spread out a map of Scandinavia.* **3** PHR-VERB If you **spread out**, you

S

relax by sitting or lying with your legs and arms stretched far apart.

Thesaurus *spread* Also look up:

V.	arrange, disperse, prepare 1
N.	range, variety 8

Word Partnership Use *spread* with:

ADV.	spread **evenly**, spread **quickly**, spread **rapidly**, spread **widely** 1 3 5
PREP.	spread **of an epidemic**, spread **of technology**, spread **of a virus** 5 6
N.	spread **fear**, **fires** spread, spread **an infection**, spread **a message**, spread **news**, spread **rumours** 5 6
V.	**continue to** spread, **prevent/stop the** spread **of *something*** 5 6

spree /spriː/ (**sprees**) N-COUNT If you go on something such as a **spending spree**, you do something such as spend money in an excessive way. ❑ *...a violent five-year crime spree.*

sprig /sprɪɡ/ (**sprigs**) N-COUNT A **sprig** is a small twig or stem with leaves on it which has been picked from a bush or plant.

spring /sprɪŋ/ (**springs, springing, sprang, sprung**) 1 N-VAR **Spring** is the season between winter and summer. In the spring the weather starts to get warmer and plants begin to grow. ❑ *The best time of year to visit Israel is in spring.* 2 N-COUNT A **spring** is a coil of wire which returns to its original shape after it is pressed or pulled. 3 N-COUNT A **spring** is a place where water comes up through the ground. ❑ *...the hot springs of Banyas de Sant Loan.* 4 V-I When a person or animal **springs**, they move suddenly upwards or forwards. ❑ *He sprang to his feet.* 5 V-I If something **springs** in a particular direction, it moves there suddenly and quickly. ❑ *The suitcase sprang open.* 6 V-I If one thing **springs from** another, the first thing is the result of the second. ❑ *The Rolls Royce company sprang from a meeting in a Manchester hotel.* 7 V-T If you **spring** some news or an event **on** someone, you tell them something that they did not expect to hear, without warning them. ❑ *The two leaders sprang a surprise yesterday by actually signing the deal.* 8 PHRASE If a boat or container **springs a leak**, liquid starts coming in or out through a hole or crack. ❑ *An oil tanker has sprung a leak.*
→ see **river**

▶ **spring up** PHR-VERB If something **springs up**, it suddenly appears or comes into existence. ❑ *Arts centres sprang up all over the country.*

Word Partnership Use *spring* with:

ADJ.	**early** spring, **last** spring, **late** spring, **next** spring 1
	cold spring, **hot** spring, **warm** spring 1 3
N.	spring **day**, spring **flowers**, spring **rains**, spring **semester**, spring **weather** 1
	spring **water** 3

sprinkle /ˈsprɪŋkəl/ (**sprinkles, sprinkling, sprinkled**) V-T If you **sprinkle** a thing **with** a substance, you scatter the substance over it. ❑ *Sprinkle the meat with salt.* ❑ *He sprinkled sand on the fire.*

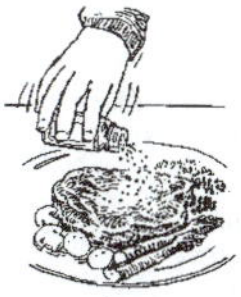
sprinkle

sprint /sprɪnt/ (**sprints, sprinting, sprinted**) 1 N-COUNT A **sprint** is a short fast race. ❑ *...the 100-metres sprint.* 2 V-I & N-SING If you **sprint** somewhere, or if you break into a **sprint**, you run as fast as you can over a short distance. ❑ *Sergeant Horne sprinted to the car.* ● **sprinter** (**sprinters**) N-COUNT ❑ *...Europe's top sprinter.*

sprout /spraʊt/ (**sprouts, sprouting, sprouted**) 1 V-I When plants, vegetables, or seeds **sprout**, they produce new shoots or leaves. ❑ *It only takes a few days for beans to sprout.* 2 V-I When leaves, shoots, or plants **sprout** somewhere, they grow there. ❑ *Mushrooms are sprouting under the trees.* 3 N-COUNT **Sprouts** are the same as **Brussels sprouts**.
→ see **tree**

spruce /spruːs/ (**spruces, sprucing, spruced**)

Spruce can also be used as the plural form.

N-VAR A **spruce** is a kind of evergreen tree. **Spruce** is the wood of this tree.

▶ **spruce up** PHR-VERB If something **is spruced up**, its appearance is improved. ❑ *We spruced ourselves up a bit and went out for dinner.*

sprung /sprʌŋ/ **Sprung** is the past participle of **spring**.

spun /spʌn/ **Spun** is the past tense and past participle of **spin**.

spur /spɜː/ (**spurs, spurring, spurred**) 1 V-T & PHR-VERB If something **spurs** you **to** do something, or if something **spurs** you **on** to do it, it encourages you to do it. ❑ *It's the money that spurs them to do it.* ❑ *I know people want me to lose but that only spurs me on.* 2 N-SING Something that acts as a **spur** encourages someone to do something or makes something happen faster or sooner. ❑ *This success has given him a spur to show the world what he can do.* 3 PHRASE If you do something **on the spur of the moment**, you do it suddenly, without planning it. ❑ *They admitted they had stolen a car on the spur of the moment.* 4 N-COUNT **Spurs** are sharp metal points attached to the heels of a rider's boots and used to make the horse go faster.

Word Partnership Use *spur* with:

N.	spur **demand**, spur **development**, spur **economic growth**, spur **the economy**, spur **interest**, spur **investment**, spur **sales** 2

spurn /spɜːn/ (**spurns, spurning, spurned**) V-T If you **spurn** something, you refuse to accept it. [FORMAL] ❑ *I spurned her offer of company and went into town on my own.* ❑ *...a spurned lover.*

spurt /spɜːt/ (**spurts, spurting, spurted**) 1 V-T/V-I & N-COUNT If something **spurts** liquid or fire, or if liquid or fire **spurts** from somewhere or something, it comes out quickly in a thin powerful stream called a **spurt**. ❑ *His wound spurted blood.* ❑ *I saw flames spurt from the roof.* ❑ *A spurt of petrol came from one pump.* 2 N-COUNT A **spurt of** activity or emotion is a sudden brief period of it.

❑ *A spurt of anger flashed through me.* **3** V-I & N-COUNT If someone or something **spurts** somewhere, or if they move there with a **spurt**, they suddenly increase their speed for a short while in order to get there. ❑ *At the end, the athletes put on a spurt.*

spy /spaɪ/ (**spies, spying, spied**) **1** N-COUNT A **spy** is a person whose job is to find out secret information about another country or organization. **2** V-I Someone who **spies for** a country or organization tries to find out secret information for them about other countries or organizations. ❑ *The agent spied for East Germany for more than twenty years.* ● **spying** N-UNCOUNT ❑ *...a ten-year sentence for spying.* **3** V-I If you **spy on** someone, you watch them secretly. ❑ *He spied on her while pretending to work in the garden.* **4** V-T If you **spy** someone or something, you notice them. [LITERARY] ❑ *He spied an old friend.*

spyware /ˈspaɪweə/ N-UNCOUNT **Spyware** is computer software that secretly records information about which websites you visit. [COMPUTING] ❑ *The publishers promise not to use spyware to grab your personal information.*

sq **sq** is used as a written abbreviation for **square** when you are giving the measurement of an area. ❑ *...2,000 sq m.*

squabble /ˈskwɒbəl/ (**squabbles, squabbling, squabbled**) V-I & N-COUNT When people **squabble**, or when they have a **squabble**, they argue about something unimportant. ❑ *The children were squabbling over the chocolate cake.*

squad /skwɒd/ (**squads**) **1** N-COUNT A **squad** is a section of a police force that is responsible for dealing with a particular type of crime. ❑ *...the Anti-Terrorist squad.* **2** N-COUNT A **squad** is a group of players from which a sports team will be chosen. **3** N-COUNT A **squad of** soldiers is a small group of them.

squadron /ˈskwɒdrən/ (**squadrons**) N-COUNT A **squadron** is a section of one of the armed forces, especially the air force.

squalid /ˈskwɒlɪd/ ADJ A **squalid** place is dirty, untidy, and in bad condition. ❑ *...living in squalid conditions.*

squalor /ˈskwɒlə/ N-UNCOUNT You can refer to squalid conditions or surroundings as **squalor**. ❑ *He was out of work and living in squalor.*

S

squander /ˈskwɒndə/ (**squanders, squandering, squandered**) V-T If you **squander** money, resources, or opportunities, you waste them. ❑ *She squandered huge sums of money on clothes and jewels.*

square /skweə/ (**squares, squaring, squared**) **1** N-COUNT A **square** is a shape with four sides of the same length and four corners that are all right angles. **2** ADJ If something is **square**, it has a shape similar to a square. ❑ *...a square table.* **3** N-COUNT In a town or city, a **square** is a flat open place, often in the shape of a square. **4** ADJ BEFORE N **Square** is used before units of length when mentioning the area of something. For example, if a rectangle is three metres long and two metres wide, its area is six square metres. **5** V-T To **square** a number means to multiply it by itself. **6** N-COUNT The **square of** a number is the number produced when you multiply that number by itself. **7** V-I If two different situations or ideas **square with** each other, they can be accepted together or they seem compatible. ❑ *That explanation squares with the facts.*
→ see **shape**

squarely /ˈskweəli/ **1** ADV **Squarely** means directly and in the middle, rather than indirectly or at an angle. ❑ *I aimed the gun squarely at his eyes.* **2** ADV If you face something **squarely**, you face it directly, without trying to avoid it.

squash /skwɒʃ/ (**squashes, squashing, squashed**) **1** V-T If someone or something **is squashed**, they are pressed or crushed with such force that they become injured or lose their shape. ❑ *Vegetables and squashed fruit lay on the ground.* **2** ADJ AFTER LINK-V If people or things are **squashed into** a place, they are put into a place where there is not enough room for them to be. ❑ *There were 2000 people squashed into her recent show.* **3** N-UNCOUNT **Squash** is a game in which two players hit a small rubber ball against the walls of a court using rackets.
→ see **vegetable**

squat /skwɒt/ (**squats, squatting, squatted**) **1** V-I & PHR-VERB If you **squat**, or if you **squat down**, you lower yourself towards the ground, balancing on your feet with your legs bent. ❑ *He squatted on his heels, looking up at the boys.* **2** ADJ If you describe someone or something as **squat**, you mean they are short and thick, usually in an unattractive way. ❑ *...squat stone houses.* **3** V-I People who **squat** occupy an unused building or unused land illegally. **4** N-COUNT A **squat** is an empty building that people are living in illegally.

squatter /ˈskwɒtə/ (**squatters**) N-COUNT A **squatter** is someone who occupies an unused building or unused land illegally.

squeak /skwiːk/ (**squeaks, squeaking, squeaked**) V-I & N-COUNT If something or someone **squeaks**, they make a short, high-pitched sound called a **squeak**. ❑ *The door squeaked open.*

squeal /skwiːl/ (**squeals, squealing, squealed**) V-I & N-COUNT If someone or something **squeals**, they make a long high-pitched sound called a **squeal**. ❑ *...a squeal of brakes.*

squeeze /skwiːz/ (**squeezes, squeezing, squeezed**) **1** V-T & N-COUNT If you **squeeze** something soft or flexible, or if you give it a **squeeze**, you press it firmly from two sides. ❑ *Dip the cloth in water, then squeeze it dry.* **2** V-T If you **squeeze** a liquid or a soft substance out of an object, you get the liquid or substance out by pressing the object. ❑ *Joe squeezed some detergent over the dishes.* **3** V-T/V-I If you **squeeze** someone or something somewhere, or if they **squeeze** there, they manage to get through or into a small space. ❑ *Mice can squeeze through a hole the size of a finger.* ❑ *He squeezed his body between the ball and the ground*

squid /skwɪd/ (**squids**)

Squid can also be used as the plural form.

N-VAR A **squid** is a sea creature with a long soft body and many tentacles. **Squid** is pieces of this creature eaten as food.

squint /skwɪnt/ (**squints, squinting, squinted**) **1** V-I If you **squint at** something, you look at it with your eyes partly closed. ❑ *The girl squinted at the photograph.* **2** N-COUNT If someone has a **squint**, their eyes look in different directions from each other.

squirm /skwɜːm/ (**squirms, squirming, squirmed**) V-I If you **squirm**, you wriggle, for example because you are nervous or uncomfortable. ❑ *We'll make him squirm.*

squirrel

squirrel /ˈskwɪrəl, AM ˈskwɜːrəl/ (**squirrels**) N-COUNT A **squirrel** is a small furry wild animal with a long bushy tail.

squirt /skwɜːt/ (**squirts, squirting, squirted**) V-T/V-I & N-COUNT If you **squirt** liquid somewhere, or if the liquid **squirts** somewhere, it is forced through a narrow opening so that it comes out in a thin fast stream called a **squirt**. ❑ *It just needs a little squirt of oil.*

St

The plural for meaning 2 is **SS**.

1 **St** is a written abbreviation for **Street**. ❑ *...116 Princes St.* 2 **St** is a written abbreviation for **Saint**. ❑ *...St Thomas.*

stab /stæb/ (**stabs, stabbing, stabbed**) 1 V-T If someone **stabs** another person, they push a knife into their body. ❑ *Stephen was stabbed to death.* 2 V-T/V-I If you **stab** something or if you **stab at** it, you push at it with your finger or with something pointed. ❑ *He stabbed at Frank with his finger.* 3 N-COUNT If you have a **stab at** something, you try to do it. [INFORMAL] ❑ *I took a stab at snowboarding.* 4 N-SING You can refer to a sudden, usually unpleasant feeling as a **stab of** that feeling. [LITERARY] ❑ *She felt a stab of pity for him.*

stabbing /ˈstæbɪŋ/ (**stabbings**) 1 N-COUNT A **stabbing** is an incident in which someone stabs someone else with a knife. 2 ADJ BEFORE N A **stabbing** pain is a sudden sharp pain.

stabilize [BRIT also **stabilise**] /ˈsteɪbɪlaɪz/ (**stabilizes, stabilizing, stabilized**) V-T/V-I If something **stabilizes**, or if someone or something **stabilizes** it, it becomes stable. ❑ *Her illness is serious but her condition is beginning to stabilize.* ●**stabilization** N-UNCOUNT ❑ *...the stabilisation of house prices.*

stable /ˈsteɪbəl/ (**stabler, stablest, stables, stabling, stabled**) 1 ADJ If something is **stable**, it is not likely to change or come to an end suddenly. ●**stability** /stəˈbɪlɪti/ N-UNCOUNT ❑ *...a time of political stability.* 2 ADJ If an object is **stable**, it is firmly fixed in position and is not likely to move or fall. 3 N-COUNT A **stable** or **stables** is a building in which horses are kept. 4 V-T When horses are **stabled**, they are put into a stable.

stack /stæk/ (**stacks, stacking, stacked**) 1 N-COUNT A **stack of** things is a neat pile of them. ❑ *There were stacks of books on the table.*

> **Usage**
>
> A **stack** of things is usually tidy, and often consists of flat objects placed directly on top of each other. ❑ *...a neat stack of dishes.* A **heap** of things is usually untidy, and often has the shape of a hill or mound. ❑ *Now, the house is a heap of stones.* A **pile** can be tidy or untidy. ❑ *...a neat pile of clothes.*

2 V-T & PHR-VERB If you **stack** a number of things, or if you **stack** them **up**, you arrange them in neat piles. ❑ *Please stack the chairs up by the wall.* 3 N-PLURAL **Stacks of** something means a lot of it. [INFORMAL] ❑ *You'll have stacks of money.* 4 PHRASE When **the odds are stacked against** someone, they are unlikely to succeed because the conditions are not favourable. ❑ *The odds are still stacked against women in business.*

stadium /ˈsteɪdiəm/ (**stadiums** or **stadia**) N-COUNT A **stadium** is a large sports ground with rows of seats all round it.

staff /stɑːf, stæf/ (**staffs, staffed**) 1 N-COUNT The **staff** of an organization are the people who work for it. **Staff** can take the singular or plural form of the verb. ❑ *The staff were very good.* 2 V-T PASSIVE If an organization **is staffed** by particular people, they are the people who work for it. ❑ *The call centre is staffed by trained nurses.* ●**staffed** ADJ ❑ *Police claim they are under-staffed.*

staffing /ˈstɑːfɪŋ, ˈstæf-/ N-UNCOUNT **Staffing** refers to the number of workers employed to work in a particular organization or building. ❑ *Staffing levels in prisons are too low.*

stag /stæg/ (**stags**) N-COUNT A **stag** is an adult male deer.

stage /steɪdʒ/ (**stages, staging, staged**) 1 N-COUNT A **stage of** an activity, process, or period is one part of it. ❑ *...the final stage of a world tour.* 2 N-COUNT In a theatre, the **stage** is an area where actors or entertainers perform. ❑ *I went on stage and did my show.* 3 N-SING You can refer to performing and the production of plays in a theatre as **the stage**. ❑ *He was the first comedian I ever saw on the stage.* 4 V-T If someone **stages** a play or other show, they organize and present a performance of it. 5 V-T To **stage** an event or ceremony means to organize it. ❑ *The film museum is staging a special exhibition.* 6 to **set the stage** → see **set**
→ see **concert, drama, theatre**

> **Word Partnership** Use *stage* with:
>
> | | |
> |---|---|
> | ADJ. | **advanced** stage, **critical** stage, **crucial** stage, **early** stage, **final** stage, **late/later** stage 1 |
> | V. | **reach a** stage 1 |
> | | **leave the** stage, **take the** stage 3 |
> | N. | stage **of development**, stage **of a disease**, stage **of a process** 1 |
> | | **actors on** stage, **centre** stage, **concert** stage, stage **fright**, stage **manager** 2 |

stagger /ˈstægə/ (**staggers, staggering, staggered**) 1 V-I If you **stagger**, you walk very unsteadily, for example because you are ill or drunk. ❑ *She staggered back to the hospital.* 2 V-T If something **staggers** you, it surprises you very much. ●**staggered** ADJ AFTER LINK-V ❑ *We have been staggered at the success of the scheme.* 3 V-T To **stagger** things means to arrange them so that they do not all happen at the same time.

staggering /ˈstægərɪŋ/ ADJ Something that is **staggering** is very surprising. ❑ *...at a staggering cost of $60 billion.* ●**staggeringly** ADV ❑ *The farmland was for sale at staggeringly low prices.*

stagnant /ˈstægnənt/ 1 ADJ **Stagnant** water is not flowing, and is therefore often dirty and

S

unhealthy. **2** ADJ If something such as a business or society is **stagnant**, there is little activity or change; used showing disapproval. ❑ *He is seeking advice on how to revive the stagnant economy.*

stagnate /stæg'neɪt, AM 'stægneɪt/ (**stagnates, stagnating, stagnated**) V-I If something such as a business or society **stagnates**, it becomes inactive or does not change; used showing disapproval. ● **stagnation** N-UNCOUNT ❑ *...the stagnation of the economy.*

staid /steɪd/ ADJ If you say that someone or something is **staid**, you mean that they are serious, dull, and rather old-fashioned. ❑ *Washington D.C. has a reputation as a very staid city.*

stain /steɪn/ (**stains, staining, stained**) **1** N-COUNT A **stain** is a mark on something that is difficult to remove. ❑ *...grass stains.* **2** V-T If a liquid **stains** something, the thing becomes coloured or marked by the liquid. ● **stained** ADJ ❑ *His clothing was stained with mud.* ● **-stained** ❑ *...ink-stained fingers.*

ˌstained 'glass N-UNCOUNT **Stained glass** consists of pieces of glass of different colours used to make decorative windows or other objects.

stainless 'steel /ˌsteɪnləs 'stiːl/ N-UNCOUNT **Stainless steel** is a metal which does not rust, made from steel and chromium.
→ see **pan**

ˌstair /steə/ (**stairs**) **1** N-PLURAL **Stairs** are a set of steps inside a building which go from one floor to another. ❑ *We walked up a flight of stairs.* **2** N-COUNT A **stair** is one of the steps in a flight of stairs. ❑ *Terry sat on the bottom stair.*

staircase /'steəkeɪs/ (**staircases**) N-COUNT A **staircase** is a set of stairs inside a house.
→ see **house**

stairway /'steəweɪ/ (**stairways**) N-COUNT A **stairway** is a flight of steps, inside or outside a building.

stake /steɪk/ (**stakes, staking, staked**) **1** PHRASE If something is **at stake**, it is being risked and might be lost or damaged if you are not successful. ❑ *The future of the planet is at stake.* **2** N-PLURAL **The stakes** involved in a risky action or a contest are the things that can be gained or lost. ❑ *The players knew exactly how high the stakes were.* **3** V-T If you **stake** something such as your money or your reputation **on** the result of something, you risk your money or reputation on it. ❑ *The government has staked its reputation on improving the health service.* **4** N-COUNT If you have a **stake in** something, its success matters to you, for example because you own part of it. ❑ *The son inherited a stake in his father's business.* **5** N-COUNT A **stake** is a pointed wooden post in the ground. **6** to **stake** your **claim** → see **claim**

S

Word Partnership Use *stake* with:

N.	**interests at** stake, **issues at** stake **1**
	stake **lives on** ***something*** **3**
	stake **in a company/firm**,
	majority/minority stake **4**
ADJ.	**controlling** stake, **personal** stake **4**

stale /steɪl/ **1** ADJ **Stale** food or air is no longer fresh. **2** ADJ AFTER LINK-V If you feel **stale**, you have no new ideas or enthusiasm for what you are doing.

stalemate /'steɪlmeɪt/ (**stalemates**) N-VAR **Stalemate** is a situation in which neither side in an argument or contest can make progress. ❑ *The war had reached a stalemate.*

stalk /stɔːk/ (**stalks, stalking, stalked**) **1** N-COUNT The **stalk** of a flower, leaf, or fruit is the thin part that joins it to the plant or tree. **2** V-T If you **stalk** a person or a wild animal, you follow them quietly and secretly in order to catch them or observe them. ❑ *I can't imagine him stalking deer or hunting rabbits.* **3** V-I If you **stalk** somewhere, you walk there in a stiff, proud, or angry way. ❑ *He got up and stalked out of the flat.* **4** V-T If someone **stalks** someone else, they keep following them or contacting them in a frightening way. ❑ *Even after their divorce he continued to stalk her.* ● **stalker** (**stalkers**) N-COUNT ❑ *A female stalker phoned him 50 times a night.*

stall /stɔːl/ (**stalls, stalling, stalled**) **1** V-T/V-I If a process **stalls**, or if someone or something **stalls** it, the process stops but may continue at a later time. ❑ *The managers had a good reason to stall the negotiations.* **2** V-T If you **stall** someone, you deliberately prevent them from doing something until later, for example by talking to them. ❑ *Brian stalled the man until the police arrived.* **3** V-I If you **stall**, you try to avoid doing something until later. ❑ *Thomas spent all week stalling over his decision.* **4** V-T/V-I If a vehicle **stalls**, or if you accidentally **stall** it, the engine stops suddenly. **5** N-COUNT A **stall** is a large table on which you put goods that you want to sell, or information that you want to give people. ❑ *...market stalls selling local fruit.* **6** N-PLURAL **The stalls** in a theatre are the seats on the ground floor in front of the stage. [BRIT]
→ see **traffic**

stallion /'stæliən/ (**stallions**) N-COUNT A **stallion** is a male horse.

stalwart /'stɔːlwət/ (**stalwarts**) N-COUNT & ADJ A **stalwart**, or someone who is **stalwart**, is a loyal and hard-working employee or supporter. ❑ *...my stalwart bodyguard.*

stamina /'stæmɪnə/ N-UNCOUNT **Stamina** is the physical or mental energy needed to do a tiring activity for a long time. ❑ *You need a lot of stamina to be a top-class dancer.*

stammer /'stæmə/ (**stammers, stammering, stammered**) V-I & N-COUNT If someone **stammers**, or if they **have** a **stammer**, they speak with difficulty, hesitating and repeating words or sounds. ❑ *He turned white and began to stammer.* ● **stammering** N-UNCOUNT ❑ *Stammering affects about 1% of adults.*

stamp /stæmp/ (**stamps, stamping, stamped**) **1** N-COUNT A **stamp** or a **postage stamp** is a small piece of paper which you stick on an envelope or parcel, to show that you have paid the cost of posting it. **2** N-COUNT A **stamp** is a small block of wood or metal with words or a design on it. You press it onto an ink pad and then onto a document in order to produce a mark on the document. The mark is also called a **stamp**. **3** V-T If you **stamp** a mark or word on an object, you press the mark or word onto the object, using a stamp. ❑ *He examined her passport and stamped it.* **4** V-T/V-I If you **stamp**, or if you **stamp** your foot, you put your foot down very hard on the ground, for example because you are angry. ❑ *Lennie stamped down the stairs.* **5** → see also **rubber stamp**

▶ **stamp out** PHR-VERB If you **stamp** something **out**, you put an end to it. ❑ *...new laws to stamp out sexual discrimination at work.*

Word Partnership	Use *stamp* with:
N.	stamp **collection**, **postage** stamp 1

ˌstamped addressed ˈenvelope → see **sae**

stampede /stæmˈpiːd/ (**stampedes, stampeding, stampeded**) V-I & N-COUNT If a group of people or animals **stampede**, or if there is a **stampede**, they run in a wild, uncontrolled way. ❑ *The crowd stampeded and many were crushed.* ❑ *There was a stampede for the exit.*

stance /stæns/ (**stances**) 1 N-COUNT Your **stance on** a particular matter is your attitude to it. ❑ *I am unlikely to change my stance on this matter.* 2 N-COUNT Your **stance** is the way that you are standing. [FORMAL] ❑ *Then his stance became more relaxed.*

Word Partnership	Use *stance* with:
PREP.	stance **against/on/toward** ***something*** 1
ADJ.	**aggressive** stance, **critical** stance, **hard-line** stance, **tough** stance 1
V.	**adopt a** stance, **take a** stance 1 2

stand /stænd/ (**stands, standing, stood**) 1 V-I & PHR-VERB When you **are standing**, or when you are **standing up**, your body is upright, your legs are straight, and your weight is supported by your feet. ❑ *They told me to stand still.* ❑ *Shop assistants have to stand up all day.* 2 V-I When someone who is sitting **stands**, or when they **stand up**, they change their position so that they are upright and on their feet. ❑ *When I walked in, they all stood up.* 3 V-I If you **stand back**, you move a short distance sideways or backwards, so that you are standing in a different place. ❑ *I stood back to let her pass.* 4 V-I If something such as a building **stands** somewhere, it is upright in that position. [WRITTEN] ❑ *The house stands alone on top of a hill.* 5 V-T If you **stand** something somewhere, you put it there in an upright position. ❑ *Stand the plant in a sunny, sheltered place.* 6 N-COUNT If you **make a stand**, or if you **take a stand**, you do something or say something in order to make it clear what your attitude to a particular thing is. ❑ *He felt the need to make a stand against racism.* 7 V-I If you ask someone **where** they **stand on** an issue, you want to know their attitude or view on it. ❑ *Where do you stand on feminism?* 8 V-I If a law, decision, or offer **stands**, it still exists and has not been changed or cancelled. ❑ *Although exceptions could be made, the rule still stands.* 9 V-I If something that can be measured **stands at** a particular level, it is at that level. ❑ *Inflation now stands at 3.6 per cent.* 10 V-T If someone or something can **stand** a situation or a test, they are strong enough to cope with it. ❑ *I just could not stand the pain.* 11 V-T If you cannot **stand** someone or something, you hate them. ❑ *He cannot stand his boss.* ❑ *You eat like a pig. I can't stand looking at you.* 12 V-T If you **stand to** gain something, you are likely to gain it. ❑ *His shops stand to lose millions of pounds.* 13 V-I In British English, if you **stand** in an election, you are a candidate in it. The American word is **run.** ❑ *She is to stand as a Member of the European Parliament.* 14 N-COUNT A **stand** is a small shop or stall, outdoors or in a large public building. ❑ *...a newspaper stand.* 15 N-COUNT A **stand** is an object or piece of furniture that is designed for supporting or holding a particular kind of thing. ❑ *...a hat stand.* ❑ *...a music stand.* 16 PHRASE You can describe someone's final attempt to defend themselves before they are defeated as their **last stand.** ❑ *This appearance could be his last stand as president.* 17 → see also **standing** 18 to **stand a chance** → see **chance** 19 to **stand firm** → see **firm** 20 to **stand on** your **own two feet** → see **foot** 21 to **stand trial** → see **trial** 22 to **stand** your **ground** → see **ground** 23 to **stand** someone **in good stead** → see **stead**
→ see **laboratory**

▶ **stand aside** → see **stand down**

▶ **stand by** 1 PHR-VERB If you **are standing by**, you are ready and waiting to provide help or to take action. ❑ *Police are at the scene and ambulances are standing by.* 2 PHR-VERB If you **stand by** and let something bad happen, you do not do anything to stop it; used showing disapproval. ❑ *We cannot stand by and watch people starve.* 3 → see also **standby**

▶ **stand down** PHR-VERB If someone **stands down**, or if someone **stands aside**, they resign from an important job. ❑ *He stood down as chairman last January.*

▶ **stand for** 1 PHR-VERB If letters **stand for** particular words, they are an abbreviation for those words. ❑ *CCTV stands for Closed Circuit Television.* 2 PHR-VERB The ideas or attitudes that someone or something **stands for** are the ones that they support or represent. ❑ *He hates us and everything we stand for.* 3 PHR-VERB If you **will not stand for** something, you will not allow it to happen or continue. ❑ *We won't stand for this any more.*

▶ **stand in** 1 PHR-VERB If you **stand in for** someone, you take their place or do their job, because they are ill or away. ❑ *He will stand in for Mr Goh when he is abroad.* 2 → see also **stand-in**

▶ **stand out** PHR-VERB If something **stands out**, it can be clearly noticed or is clearly better or more important than other similar things. ❑ *The dark shape of the castle stands out clearly on the skyline.* ❑ *He played the violin, and he stood out from all the other musicians.*

▶ **stand up** 1 PHR-VERB If something such as a claim or a piece of evidence **stands up**, it is accepted as true or satisfactory after being carefully examined. ❑ *How well does this theory stand up to close examination?* 2 → see also **stand** (meaning 2), **stand-up**

▶ **stand up for** PHR-VERB If you **stand up for** someone or something, you defend them openly; used showing approval. ❑ *Don't be afraid to stand up for yourself.*

▶ **stand up to** 1 PHR-VERB If something **stands up to** rough treatment, it remains almost undamaged. ❑ *Is this building going to stand up to the storm?* 2 PHR-VERB If you **stand up to** someone more powerful than you are, you defend yourself against their attacks or demands.

standard /ˈstændəd/ (**standards**) 1 N-COUNT A **standard** is a level of quality or achievement, especially a level that is thought to be acceptable. ❑ *Her team are setting new standards for women's* football. **2** N-PLURAL **Standards** are moral principles which affect people's attitudes and behaviour. ❑ *She sets high standards for herself.* **3** ADJ **Standard** means usual and normal. ❑ *There are two standard treatments for this disease.*

Word Partnership Use *standard* with:

V.	**become a** standard, **maintain a** standard, **meet a** standard, **raise a** standard, **set a** standard, **use a** standard **1** **2**
N.	standard **of excellence**, **industry** standard **1** **2**
	standard **English**, standard **equipment**, standard **practice**, standard **procedure** **3**

standardize [BRIT also **standardise**] /ˈstændədaɪz/ (**standardizes, standardizing, standardized**) V-T To **standardize** things means to change them so that they all have the same features. ● **standardization** N-UNCOUNT ❑ *...the standardisation of working hours in European Community countries.*
→ see **mass production**

ˌstandard of ˈliving (**standards of living**) N-COUNT Your **standard of living** is the level of comfort and wealth which you have.

standby /ˈstændbaɪ/ (**standbys**) **1** N-COUNT A **standby** is someone or something that is always ready to be used if they are needed. ❑ *We selected a standby from our second team.* **2** PHRASE If someone or something is **on standby**, they are ready to be used if they are needed. **3** ADJ BEFORE N A **standby** ticket for something such as the theatre or a plane journey is a cheap ticket that you buy just before the performance starts or the plane takes off, if there are still some seats left. ❑ *...standby flights from New York.*

ˈstand-ˌin (**stand-ins**) **1** N-COUNT A **stand-in** is a person who takes someone else's place because the other person is ill or away. **2** → see also **stand in**

standing /ˈstændɪŋ/ **1** N-UNCOUNT Someone's **standing** is their status or reputation. ❑ *...an artist of international standing.* **2** ADJ BEFORE N You use **standing** to describe something which is permanently in existence. ❑ *Elizabeth had a standing invitation to stay at their home.* **3** → see also **stand, long-standing**

ˈstand-ˌoff (**stand-offs**) N-COUNT A **stand-off** is a situation in which neither of two opposing groups will make a move until the other one does something, so nothing can happen until one of them gives way.

standpoint /ˈstændpɔɪnt/ (**standpoints**) N-COUNT If you look at an event, situation, or idea **from** a particular **standpoint**, you look at it in a particular way. ❑ *From a military standpoint, the situation is under control.*

standstill /ˈstændstɪl/ N-SING If movement or an activity comes to **a standstill**, it stops completely. ❑ *The country was brought to a standstill by the transport strikes.*

ˈstand-ˌup also **standup** **1** ADJ & N-UNCOUNT A **stand-up** comedian stands alone in front of an audience and tells jokes. **Stand-up** is stand-up comedy. **2** ADJ BEFORE N If people have a **stand-up** fight or argument, they hit or shout at each other violently.

stank /stæŋk/ **Stank** is the past tense of **stink**.

staple /ˈsteɪpəl/ (**staples, stapling, stapled**) **1** ADJ BEFORE N A **staple** food, product, or activity is one that is basic and important in people's everyday lives. ❑ *Rice is the staple food of more than half the world's population.* **2** V-T & N-COUNT If you **staple** sheets of paper together, you fasten them by putting a small piece of metal called a **staple** through all of them to hold them together.

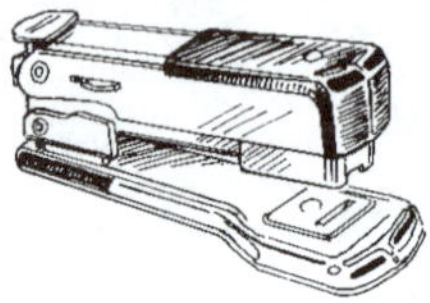
stapler

stapler /ˈsteɪplə/ (**staplers**) N-COUNT A **stapler** is a device used for putting staples into sheets of paper.

star /stɑː/ (**stars, starring, starred**) **1** N-COUNT A **star** is a large ball of burning gas in space. Stars appear to us as small points of light in the sky on clear nights. **2** N-COUNT You can refer to a shape or an object as a **star** when it has four or more points sticking out of it in a regular pattern. **3** N-COUNT Famous actors, musicians, and sports players are often referred to as **stars**. **4** V-I/V-T If an actor or actress **stars in** a play or film, he or she has one of the most important parts in it. You can also say that a play or film **stars** a famous actor or actress. ❑ *He's starred in dozens of films.* **5** N-PLURAL Your horoscope is sometimes referred to as your **stars**. [INFORMAL] ❑ *My stars said I would find love.*
→ see Word Web: **star**
→ see **galaxy, navigation**

Word Partnership Use *star* with:

ADJ.	**bright** star **1**
	bronze star, **gold** star **2**
	big star, **former** star, **rising** star **3**
N.	**basketball/football/tennis** star, **guest** star, **film/movie** star, **pop/rap** star, **porn** star, **TV** star **3**
	star **in a film/movie/show** **4**

starboard /ˈstɑːbəd/ ADJ The **starboard** side of a ship is the right side when you are facing the front.

starch /stɑːtʃ/ (**starches**) **1** N-VAR **Starch** is a carbohydrate found in foods such as bread, potatoes, and rice. **2** N-UNCOUNT **Starch** is a substance used for making cloth stiff.
→ see **rice**

starchy /stɑːtʃi/ (**starchier, starchiest**) ADJ **Starchy** foods contain a lot of starch. ❑ *You should eat more fruit, vegetables, and starchy foods.*

stardom /ˈstɑːdəm/ N-UNCOUNT **Stardom** is the state of being very famous, usually as an actor, musician, or sports player. ❑ *He admits he found stardom difficult.*

stare /steə/ (**stares, staring, stared**) V-I & N-UNCOUNT If you **stare at** someone or something, or if you give someone or something a **stare**, you look at them for a long time. ❑ *Tamara stared at him*

Word Web star

Astronomy is the oldest science. It is the study of **stars** and other objects in the **night sky**. People sometimes confuse astronomy and **astrology**. Astrology is the belief that the stars affect people's lives. Long ago people named groups of stars after gods, heroes, and imaginary animals. One of the most famous of these **constellations** is the Big Dipper. Its original name meant "the big bear." It is easy to find and it points toward the **North Star***. For centuries sailors have used the North Star to **navigate**. The best-known star in our **galaxy** is the **sun**.

North Star: the star that the earth's northern axis points toward.

angrily. ❑ *Hlasek gave him a long, cold stare.*

Usage

The verbs **stare** and **gaze** are both used to talk about looking at something for a long time. If you **stare at** something or someone, it is often because you think they are strange or shocking. ❑ *Various families came out and stared at us.* If you **gaze at** something, it is often because you think it is marvellous or impressive. ❑ *The child gazed in wonder at the bright Christmas lights.*

Word Partnership Use *stare* with:

ADJ. **blank** stare
V. **continue to** stare, **turn to** stare

stark /stɑːk/ (**starker, starkest**) **1** ADJ **Stark** choices or statements are harsh and unpleasant. ❑ *He has given a stark warning of the dangers facing the country.* ● **starkly** ADV **2** PHRASE If two things are **in stark contrast to** one another, they are very different from each other.

start /stɑːt/ (**starts, starting, started**) **1** V-T & N-COUNT If you **start to** do something, or if you make a **start** on it, you do something you were not doing before. ❑ *I started to tidy up.* ❑ *The boy started crying.* ❑ *After several starts, she read the report properly.* **2** V-T/V-I & N-SING When something **starts**, or when someone **starts** it, it takes place or begins to exist from a particular time. You can also refer to **the start of** something. ❑ *The meeting starts at 10.30.* ❑ *We started an Internet advertising company.* ❑ *...shortly before the start of the war.* ❑ *Why was she not told at the start?* **3** V-I & PHR-VERB If someone **started** or **started off** as a particular thing, their first job was as that thing. ❑ *Mr Dambar had started off as an assistant.* **4** V-T/V-I & PHR-VERB If an engine or car **starts**, or if you **start** it, or **start** it **up**, it begins to work. ❑ *The car won't start.* ❑ *The pilot started up the engine.* **5** N-COUNT A **start** is a sudden jerky movement your body makes because you are surprised or frightened. ❑ *Sylvia woke with a start.* **6** PHRASE You use **for a start** or **to start with** to introduce the first of a number of things or reasons that you want to mention or could mention. ❑ *For a start, the beach is dirty.* **7** PHRASE If you **get off to a good start**, you are successful in the early stages of doing something. If you **get off to a bad start**, you are not successful in the early stages of doing something. ❑ *The rescue got off to a slow start.* **8** → see also **head start** **9** to **get off to a flying start** → see **fly**

▶ **start off** **1** PHR-VERB If you **start off by** doing something, you do it as the first part of an activity. ❑ *I started off by setting out the facts.* **2** → see also **start** (meaning **3**)

▶ **start on** PHR-VERB If you **start on** something that needs to be done, you begin doing it. ❑ *Don't start on the washing-up yet.*

▶ **start out** **1** PHR-VERB If someone or something **starts out as** a particular thing, they are that thing at the beginning although they change later. ❑ *It started out as fun but quickly became hard work.* **2** PHR-VERB If you **start out by** doing something, you do it at the beginning of an activity or process. ❑ *I started out by bringing up my children quite strictly.*

▶ **start over** PHR-VERB If you **start over**, or if you **start** something **over**, you begin something again from the beginning. [AM] ❑ *Okay, let's start over.*

▶ **start up** **1** PHR-VERB If you **start up** something such as a new business, you create it or cause it to start. ❑ *You could start up your own newspaper.* **2** → see also **start** (meaning **4**)

Thesaurus *start* Also look up:

V. begin, commence, originate **1** **2**
establish, found, launch **2**
N. beginning, onset **2**
jump, scare, shock **5**

starter /ˈstɑːtə/ (**starters**) **1** N-COUNT A **starter** is a small quantity of food served as the first course of a meal. **2** N-COUNT The **starter** of a car is a device that starts the engine. **3** PHRASE You use **for starters** when you mention something to indicate that it is the first item or point in a series. ❑ *What do Diana Ross and Judi Dench have in common? For starters, they both sing.*

ˈstarting ˌpoint (**starting points**) N-COUNT Something that is a **starting point for** a discussion or process can be used to begin it or act as a basis for it. ❑ *He used Rilke's poem as his starting point.*

startle /ˈstɑːtəl/ (**startles, startling, startled**) V-T If something sudden and unexpected **startles** you, it surprises you and frightens you slightly. ❑ *The sound of his voice startled her.* ● **startled** ADJ ❑ *Martha gave her a startled look.*

startling /'stɑːtəlɪŋ/ ADJ Something that is **startling** is so unexpected or remarkable that people are surprised by it. ❑ *There were some startling successes.*

starve /stɑːv/ (**starves, starving, starved**) **1** V-I If people **starve**, they suffer greatly and may die from lack of food. ● **starvation** N-UNCOUNT ❑ *Up to four million people face starvation.* **2** V-T To **starve** someone means to not give them any food. ❑ *Judy decided I was starving myself.* **3** V-T If someone or something **is starved of** something they need, they are suffering because they are not getting enough of it. ❑ *...a childhood starved of friendship.*

starving /'stɑːvɪŋ/ ADJ AFTER LINK-V If you say you are **starving**, you mean you are very hungry. [INFORMAL]

stash /stæʃ/ (**stashes, stashing, stashed**) V-T & N-COUNT If you **stash** something valuable in a secret place, you store it there to keep it safe. You can then refer to it as a **stash of** something. ❑ *The weapons were stashed in a variety of locations.* ❑ *One of the world's largest stashes of gold is in India.*

state /steɪt/ (**states, stating, stated**) **1** N-COUNT You can refer to countries as **states**, particularly when you are discussing politics. ❑ *It is a recognised member state of NATO.* **2** → See note at **country** **3** ADJ BEFORE N A **state** occasion is a formal one involving the head of a country. ❑ *...a state visit to India.* **4** N-COUNT Some large countries such as the USA are divided into smaller areas called **states**. **5** N-PROPER The USA is sometimes referred to as **the States**. [INFORMAL] **6** N-SING You can refer to the government of a country as **the state**. ❑ *The majority of children were from state schools.* **7** V-T If you **state** something, you say or write it in a formal or definite way. ❑ *Please state your name.* **8** N-COUNT When you talk about the **state of** someone or something, you are referring to the condition they are in or what they are like at a particular time. ❑ *...a state of emergency.*
→ see **matter**

Thesaurus	*state* Also look up:
N.	government, land, nation, republic, sovereignty **1**
	attitude, condition, mood, situation **7**
V.	articulate, express, narrate, relate, say, tell **6**

S

stately /'steɪtli/ ADJ Something or someone that is **stately** is impressive because they look very graceful and dignified.

statement /'steɪtmənt/ (**statements**) **1** N-COUNT A **statement** is something that you say or write which gives information in a formal or definite way. ❑ *Her husband made a formal statement to the police.* ❑ *His first task was to issue a statement of apology.* **2** N-COUNT A **statement** is a printed document showing all the money paid into and taken out of a bank or building society account.

ˌstate of afˈfairs N-SING If you refer to a particular **state of affairs**, you mean the general situation and circumstances connected with someone or something. ❑ *This state of affairs needs immediate attention.*

ˈstate of mind (**states of mind**) N-COUNT Your **state of mind** is your mood or mental state at a particular time. ❑ *He's in a fairly disturbed state of mind.*

ˌstate-of-the-ˈart ADJ If you describe something as **state-of-the-art**, you mean that it is the best available because it has been made using the most modern techniques. ❑ *...state-of-the-art technology.*
→ see **technology**

statesman /'steɪtsmən/ (**statesmen**) N-COUNT A **statesman** is an important and experienced politician, especially one who is widely known and respected.

Word Link	*stat ≈ standing : static, station, stationary*

static /'stætɪk/ **1** ADJ Something that is **static** does not move or change. ❑ *Property prices remained static between February and April.* **2** N-UNCOUNT **Static** or **static electricity** is electricity which is caused by friction and which collects in things such as your body or metal objects. **3** N-UNCOUNT If there is **static** on the radio or television, you hear loud crackling noises.

station /'steɪʃən/ (**stations, stationing, stationed**) **1** N-COUNT A **station** is a building by a railway line where a train stops. **2** N-COUNT A **bus station** or **coach station** is a place where buses or coaches start a journey. **3** → see also **police station** **4** N-COUNT If you talk about a particular radio or television **station**, you are referring to the programmes broadcast by a particular radio or television company. ❑ *...an independent local radio station.* **5** V-T PASSIVE If soldiers or officials **are stationed** somewhere, they are sent there to do a job or to work for a period of time. ❑ *Hundreds of police will be stationed at airports across Britain today.*
→ see **cellphone, radio, television**

Word Partnership	Use *station* with:
N.	**railroad** station, **underground** station **1**
	radio station, **television/TV** station **3**
ADJ.	**local** station **3**

stationary /'steɪʃənri, AM -neri/ ADJ Something that is **stationary** is not moving.

Usage

You should take care not to confuse the words **stationary**, which is always an adjective and means 'not moving', and **stationery**, meaning 'paper products'.

stationery /'steɪʃənri, AM -neri/ N-UNCOUNT **Stationery** is paper, envelopes, and writing equipment.
→ see **office**

statistic /stə'tɪstɪk/ (**statistics**) **1** N-COUNT **Statistics** are facts obtained from analyzing information that is expressed in numbers. ❑ *Divorce statistics are rising.* ● **statistical** ADJ ❑ *...statistical proof.* ● **statistically** ADV ❑ *The results are not statistically significant.* **2** N-UNCOUNT **Statistics** is a branch of mathematics concerned with the study of information that is expressed in numbers.

statue /'stætʃuː/ (**statues**) N-COUNT A **statue** is a large sculpture of a person or an animal, made of stone, bronze, or some other hard material.

stature /ˈstætʃə/ **1** N-UNCOUNT Someone's **stature** is their height. ❑ *The bodies appeared to be of adults and of small stature.* **2** N-UNCOUNT Someone's **stature** is their importance and reputation. ❑ *France's international stature has suffered within the EU.*

status /ˈsteɪtəs/ **1** N-UNCOUNT Your **status** is your social or professional position. ❑ *All contestants must be of amateur status.* **2** N-UNCOUNT **Status** is the prestige and importance that someone or something has in the eyes of other people. ❑ *He has risen to gain the status of a national hero.* ❑ *Tall men tend to have a higher status in all cultures.* **3** N-UNCOUNT **Status** is an official classification which gives a person, organization, or country certain rights or advantages. ❑ *These countries officially recognise the independent status of the Baltic republics.*

Word Partnership Use *status* with:

V.	**achieve** status, **maintain/preserve** ***one's*** status **1**
N.	**celebrity** status, **wealth and** status **1** **2** **change of** status **1**-**3** **marital** status, **tax** status **3**
ADJ.	**current** status, **economic** status, **financial** status **3**

status quo /ˌsteɪtəs ˈkwəʊ/ N-SING **The status quo** is the situation that exists at a particular time. [FORMAL] ❑ *The world has a problem: the status quo is not acceptable.*

statute /ˈstætʃuːt/ (**statutes**) N-COUNT A **statute** is a rule or law which has been formally written down.

statutory /ˈstætʃʊtəri, AM -tɔːri/ ADJ **Statutory** means relating to rules or laws which have been formally written down. [FORMAL] ❑ *We had a statutory duty to report to Parliament.*

staunch /stɔːntʃ/ (**stauncher, staunchest**) ADJ A **staunch** supporter of someone or something supports them very strongly and loyally. ● **staunchly** ADV ❑ *They are staunchly opposed to this agreement.*

stave /steɪv/ (**staves, staving, staved**) PHR-VERB If you **stave off** something bad, you succeed in stopping it happening for a while. ❑ *Only dramatic action can stave off this disaster.*

stay /steɪ/ (**stays, staying, stayed**) **1** V-I If you **stay** in a place or position, you continue to be there and do not leave. ❑ *She gave up work and stayed at home to bring up her children.* ❑ *Stay away from the rocks.* **2** V-I If you **stay** in a town or hotel, or at someone's house, you live there for a short time. ❑ *We stayed the night in a little hotel.* **3** N-COUNT The time you spend in a place is referred to as your **stay** there. ❑ *He had a short stay in hospital.* **4** LINK-VERB If someone or something **stays** in a particular condition or situation, they continue to be in it. ❑ *The company could not stay ahead of its rivals.* ❑ *Nothing stays the same for long.* **5** V-I If you **stay out of** something or **stay away from** it, you do not get involved in it. ❑ *The message for young people is 'Stay away from crime.'* **6** PHRASE If you say that something is **here to stay**, you mean that people have accepted it and it has become a part of everyday life. ❑ *Satellite TV is here to stay.* **7** PHRASE If you **stay put**, you remain somewhere. ❑ *He is very happy to stay put in Lyon.*

▶ **stay in** PHR-VERB If you **stay in**, you remain at home during the evening and do not go out.

▶ **stay on** PHR-VERB If you **stay on** somewhere, you remain there after other people have left or after the time when you were going to leave. ❑ *He arranged to stay on in Adelaide.*

▶ **stay out** PHR-VERB If you **stay out**, you remain away from home at night. ❑ *I met some friends and stayed out until eleven or twelve.*

▶ **stay up** PHR-VERB If you **stay up**, you remain out of bed at a later time than normal. ❑ *I used to stay up late with my mum and watch movies.*

stead /sted/ PHRASE If something will **stand** you **in good stead**, it will be useful to you in the future. ❑ *My years of teaching stood me in good stead.*

steadfast /ˈstedfɑːst, -fæst/ ADJ If you are **steadfast in** your beliefs or opinions, you are convinced that they are right and you refuse to change them; used showing approval. ❑ *He remained steadfast in his belief that he had done the right thing.* ● **steadfastly** ADV ❑ *She steadfastly refused to look his way.*

Word Link ***stead ≈ place, stand : homestead, instead, steady***

steady /ˈstedi/ (**steadier, steadiest, steadies, steadying, steadied**) **1** ADJ Something that is **steady** continues or develops gradually without any interruptions and is unlikely to change suddenly. ❑ *They were forecasting a steady rise in sales.* ❑ *I want to find a steady job.* ● **steadily** ADV ❑ *Relax as much as possible and keep breathing steadily.* **2** ADJ If an object is **steady**, it is firm and does not move about. ❑ *Hold the camera steady.* **3** ADJ A **steady** look or voice is calm and controlled. ● **steadily** ADV ❑ *He stared steadily at Elaine.* **4** V-T/V-I If you **steady** something, or if it **steadies**, it stops shaking or moving about. ❑ *She placed her hands on the controls again and steadied the plane.* **5** V-T If you **steady yourself**, you control your voice or expression, so that people will think that you are calm. ❑ *Somehow she steadied herself.*

Thesaurus *steady* Also look up:

ADJ.	consistent, continuous, uninterrupted **1** constant, fixed, stable **2**

steak /steɪk/ (**steaks**) **1** N-VAR **Steak** is beef without much fat on it. **2** N-COUNT A fish **steak** is a large flat piece of fish.

steal /stiːl/ (**steals, stealing, stole, stolen**) **1** V-T/V-I If you **steal** something from someone, you take it away from them without their permission and without intending to return it. ❑ *He was accused of stealing a small boy's bicycle.* ❑ *We have now found the stolen car.* ❑ *Joe lied and stole.* ● **stealing** N-UNCOUNT ❑ *She was jailed for stealing.* **2** V-I If you **steal** somewhere, you move there quietly and cautiously. ❑ *They can steal away at night and join us.*

stealth /stelθ/ N-UNCOUNT If you do something with **stealth**, you do it in a slow, quiet, and secretive way. ❑ *Photographing wild animals demands stealth from the photographer.*

steam /stiːm/ (**steams, steaming, steamed**) **1** N-UNCOUNT **Steam** is the hot mist that forms

when water boils. **Steam** vehicles and machines are powered by steam. ❑ *...steam trains.* **2** V-I If something **steams**, it gives off steam. ❑ *The engine began to steam.* **3** V-T If you **steam** food, you cook it in steam. ❑ *Boil or steam the rice.* **4** → See note at **cook** **5** PHRASE If you **run out of steam**, you stop doing something because you have no more energy or enthusiasm left. [INFORMAL]
→ see **cook**

Word Partnership Use *steam* with:

ADJ.	steam **powered**, **rising** steam **1**
N.	steam **bath**, **clouds of** steam, steam **engine**, steam **locomotive**, steam **pipes**, steam **turbine** **1**

steamer /ˈsti:mə/ (**steamers**) **1** N-COUNT A **steamer** is a ship that is powered by steam. **2** N-COUNT A **steamer** is a special saucepan used for steaming food such as vegetables and fish.

steamy /ˈsti:mi/ (**steamier, steamiest**) **1** ADJ A **steamy** place is very hot and humid, usually because it is full of steam. ❑ *...a steamy kitchen.* **2** ADJ **Steamy** means erotic or passionate. [INFORMAL] ❑ *Frank began a steamy love affair with Helen.*

steel /sti:l/ (**steels, steeling, steeled**) **1** N-UNCOUNT **Steel** is a very strong metal made mainly from iron. **2** → see also **stainless steel** **3** V-T If you **steel yourself**, you prepare to deal with something unpleasant. ❑ *I had been steeling myself for something like this.*
→ see **bridge, train**

steely /ˈsti:li/ **1** ADJ You use **steely** to describe something that has a hard, greyish colour. ❑ *...the steely grey light.* **2** ADJ **Steely** is used to describe someone who is hard, strong, and determined. ❑ *'No,' she said, with a steely look in her eyes.*

steep /sti:p/ (**steeper, steepest**) **1** ADJ A **steep** slope rises at a very sharp angle and is difficult to go up. ●**steeply** ADV ❑ *The ground rose steeply.* **2** ADJ A **steep** increase is very big. ●**steeply** ADV ❑ *Unemployment is rising steeply.*

steeped /sti:pt/ ADJ AFTER LINK-V If a place or person is **steeped in** a quality or characteristic, they are surrounded by it or deeply influenced by it. ❑ *The castle is steeped in history.*

S

steer /stɪə/ (**steers, steering, steered**) **1** V-T When you **steer** a car, boat, or plane, you control it so that it goes in the direction you want. ❑ *She would often let me steer the car on the beach.* **2** V-T If you **steer** someone in a particular direction, you guide them there. ❑ *I steered him towards the door.* **3** PHRASE If you **steer clear of** someone or something, you deliberately avoid them. ❑ *Their father's advice was to steer clear of politics.*

ˈsteering wheel (**steering wheels**) N-COUNT The **steering wheel** in a vehicle is the wheel which the driver holds to steer the vehicle.

stem /stem/ (**stems, stemming, stemmed**) **1** N-COUNT The **stem** of a plant is the thin upright part on which the flowers and leaves grow. **2** N-COUNT The **stem** of a glass or vase is the long thin part which connects the bowl to the base. **3** V-T If you **stem** something that is spreading from one place to another, you stop it spreading. [FORMAL] ❑ *The authorities seem unable to stem the increasing violence.* **4** V-I If a condition or problem **stems from** something, that is what originally caused it. ❑ *Most of her problems stemmed from her childhood.*
→ see **flower**

Word Partnership Use *stem* with:

V.	stem **the flow of *something***, stem **losses**, stem **the tide of *something*** **3**
N.	**charges** stem **from *something***, **problems** stem **from *something*** **4**

stench /stentʃ/ (**stenches**) N-COUNT A **stench** is a strong, unpleasant smell. ❑ *...the stench of last week's fish.*

stencil /ˈstensəl/ (**stencils, stencilling, stencilled** or [AM] **stenciling, stenciled**) **1** N-COUNT A **stencil** is a piece of paper, plastic, or metal with a design cut out of it. You place the stencil on a surface and create the design by putting ink or paint over the cut area. **2** V-T If you **stencil** letters or designs, you print them using a stencil.

step /step/ (**steps, stepping, stepped**) **1** N-COUNT A **step** is the movement made by lifting your foot and putting it down in a different place. ❑ *I took a step back.* ❑ *He heard steps in the corridor.* **2** V-I If you **step on** something or **step** in a particular direction, you put your foot on the thing or move your foot in that direction. ❑ *He stepped on glass and cut his foot.* ❑ *Doug stepped sideways.* **3** N-COUNT A **step** is one of a series of actions that you take in order to achieve something. ❑ *This agreement is the first step towards peace.* **4** N-COUNT A **step** is a raised flat surface, often one of a series, on which you put your feet in order to walk up or down to a different level. ❑ *He sat down on the bottom step.* **5** PHRASE If you stay **one step ahead** of someone or something, you manage to achieve more than they do or avoid competition or danger from them. ❑ *The emphasis is on staying one step ahead of the terrorists.* **6** PHRASE If people are **in step with** each other, their ideas or opinions are the same. If they are **out of step with** each other, their ideas or opinions are different. ❑ *Britain is out of step with the rest of Europe on this matter.* **7** PHRASE If you do something **step by step**, you do it by progressing gradually from one stage to the next. ❑ *The police took the boy, step by step, through everything that had happened.*

▶ **step aside** → see **step down**

▶ **step back** PHR-VERB If you **step back from** a situation, you think about it in a fresh and detached way. ❑ *We stepped back from the project to look at it as a whole.*

▶ **step down** PHR-VERB If you **step down** or **step aside**, you resign from an important job or position. ❑ *Judge Ito said that if his own wife was called as a witness, he would step down as trial judge.*

▶ **step in** PHR-VERB If you **step in**, you get involved in a difficult situation, in order to help. ❑ *The referee stepped in to stop the fight.*

▶ **step up** PHR-VERB If you **step up** something, you increase it. ❑ *They have stepped up their calls for a full public enquiry.*

Word Partnership Use *step* with:

ADV. step **ahead**, step **backward**, step **closer**, step **forward**, step **outside** 1
N. **step in a** process 3
ADJ. **big** step, **bold** step, **critical** step, **giant** step, **important** step, **positive** step, **the right** step 3

stepfather also **step-father** /ˈstepfɑːðə/ (**stepfathers**) N-COUNT Your **stepfather** is the man who has married your mother after the death or divorce of your father.

stepmother also **step-mother** /ˈstepmʌðə/ (**stepmothers**) N-COUNT Your **stepmother** is the woman who has married your father after the death or divorce of your mother.

ˈstepping ˌstone (**stepping stones**) 1 N-COUNT **Stepping stones** are a line of stones which you can walk on in order to cross a shallow stream or river. 2 N-COUNT A **stepping stone** is a job or event that helps you to make progress, especially in your career. ❑ *Many students now see university as a stepping stone to a good job.*

stereo /ˈsteriəʊ/ (**stereos**) 1 ADJ **Stereo** is used to describe a recording or a system of playing music in which the sound is directed through two speakers. ❑ *...stereo headphones.* 2 N-COUNT A **stereo** is a record player with two speakers.

stereotype /ˈsteriətaɪp/ (**stereotypes, stereotyping, stereotyped**) 1 N-COUNT A **stereotype** is a fixed general image or set of characteristics representing a particular type of person or thing, but which may not be true in reality. ❑ *...the stereotype of the polite, industrious Japanese person.* 2 V-T If you **are stereotyped** as something, people form a fixed general image of you, so that it is assumed that you will behave in a particular way. ❑ *Women are stereotyped in a lot of films.*

sterile /ˈsteraɪl, AM -rəl/ 1 ADJ Something that is **sterile** is completely clean and free of germs. ❑ *...a sterile needle.* ●**sterility** /stəˈrɪlɪti/ N-UNCOUNT ❑ *...the sterility of the operating theatre.* 2 ADJ A person or animal that is **sterile** is unable to have or produce babies. ●**sterility** N-UNCOUNT ❑ *This disease causes sterility.* 3 ADJ A **sterile** situation is lacking in energy and new ideas. ❑ *Too much time has been wasted in sterile debate.* ●**sterility** N-UNCOUNT

sterilize [BRIT also **sterilise**] /ˈsterɪlaɪz/ (**sterilizes, sterilizing, sterilized**) 1 V-T If you **sterilize** a thing or place, you make it completely clean and free from germs. ❑ *Sterilize a large needle by boiling it.* 2 V-T If a person or an animal **is sterilized**, they have an operation that makes it impossible for them to have or produce babies. ●**sterilization** (**sterilizations**) N-VAR

sterling /ˈstɜːlɪŋ/ 1 N-UNCOUNT **Sterling** is the money system of Great Britain. 2 ADJ If you describe someone's work or character as **sterling**, you mean it is excellent. [FORMAL] ❑ *He reminded us of the sterling qualities of our previous headmaster.*

stern /stɜːn/ (**sterner, sternest, sterns**) 1 ADJ Someone or something that is **stern** is very serious and strict. ❑ *...a stern warning.* ●**sternly** ADV ❑ *'We will do what is necessary,' she said sternly.* 2 N-COUNT The **stern** of a boat is the back part of it.

steroid /ˈsterɔɪd, AM ˈstɪr-/ (**steroids**) N-COUNT A **steroid** is a type of chemical substance which occurs naturally in the body, and can also be made artificially.

stew /stjuː, AM stuː/ (**stews, stewing, stewed**) 1 N-VAR A **stew** is a meal made by cooking meat and vegetables in liquid at a low temperature. ❑ *...beef stew.* 2 V-T If you **stew** meat, vegetables, or fruit, you cook them slowly in liquid. ❑ *Stew the plums for about 15 minutes.*

steward /ˈstjuːəd, AM ˈstuː-/ (**stewards**) 1 N-COUNT A **steward** is a man whose job is to look after passengers on a ship, plane, or train. 2 N-COUNT A **steward** is someone who helps to organize a race, march, or other public event.

stewardess /ˌstjuːəˈdes, ˌstuː-/ (**stewardesses**) N-COUNT A **stewardess** is a woman whose job is to look after passengers on a ship, plane, or train.

stick
1 NOUN USES
2 VERB USES

stick /stɪk/ (**sticks**)
1 1 N-COUNT A **stick** is a thin branch which has fallen off a tree. ❑ *...piles of dried sticks.* 2 N-COUNT A **stick** is a long thin piece of wood which is used for a particular purpose. ❑ *...a walking stick.* ❑ *...a hockey stick.* 3 N-COUNT A **stick of** something is a long thin piece of it. ❑ *...a stick of celery.*
→ see **blog**

stick /stɪk/ (**sticks, sticking, stuck**)
2 1 V-T If you **stick** something somewhere, you put it there in a rather casual way. [INFORMAL] ❑ *He folded the papers and stuck them in his desk drawer.* 2 V-T If you **stick** a pointed object in something, you push it in. ❑ *The doctor stuck the needle in Joe's arm.* 3 V-T If you **stick** one thing to another, you attach it using glue, sticky tape, or another sticky substance. ❑ *I stuck a notice on the window saying 'Tickets'.* 4 V-I If something **sticks** somewhere, it becomes attached or fixed in one position and cannot be moved. ❑ *The rice had stuck to the pan.* 5 PHRASE If someone in an unpleasant or difficult situation **sticks it out**, they do not leave or give up. ❑ *I really didn't like New York, but I wanted to stick it out a little longer.* 6 → see also **stuck**

▸ **stick around** PHR-VERB If you **stick around**, you stay where you are. [INFORMAL] ❑ *I didn't stick around long enough to find out.*

▸ **stick by** PHR-VERB If you **stick by** someone, you continue to help or support them. ❑ *I had friends who stuck by me during the difficult times.*

▸ **stick out** 1 PHR-VERB If something **sticks out**, or if you **stick it out**, it extends beyond something else. ❑ *A newspaper was sticking out of his back pocket.* ❑ *Eve stuck her head out the window.* 2 → see also **stick** (meaning 5)

▸ **stick to** 1 PHR-VERB If you **stick to** something, you stay close to it or with it and do not change to something else. ❑ *Stick to the main road.* ❑ *I think he should stick to acting.* 2 PHR-VERB If you **stick to** a promise or agreement, you do what you said you would do.

▸ **stick together** PHR-VERB If people **stick together**, they stay with each other and support each other. ❑ *If we all stick together, we will be okay.*

▸ **stick up** 1 PHR-VERB If you **stick up** a picture or a notice, you fix it to a wall. 2 PHR-VERB If

S

something **sticks up**, it points upwards. ❑ *His hair stuck up.*
▶ **stick up for** PHR-VERB If you **stick up for** someone or something, you support or defend them strongly. ❑ *Why do you always stick up for her?*
▶ **stick with** PHR-VERB If you **stick with** someone or something, you stay with them and do not change to something else. ❑ *If you're in a job that keeps you busy, stick with it.*

sticker /ˈstɪkə/ (**stickers**) N-COUNT A **sticker** is a small piece of paper or plastic with writing or a picture on it, that you can stick onto a surface.

ˈstick ˌinsect (**stick insects**) N-COUNT A **stick insect** is an insect with a long thin body and legs.

sticky /ˈstɪki/ (**stickier, stickiest**) **1** ADJ A **sticky** substance can stick to other things. **Sticky** things are covered with a sticky substance. ❑ *...sticky paper.* ❑ *...sticky toffee.* **2** ADJ **Sticky** weather is unpleasantly hot and damp. ❑ *...an uncomfortably sticky day.* **3** ADJ A **sticky** situation is difficult or embarrassing. [INFORMAL] ❑ *We're all in a rather sticky position.*

stiff /stɪf/ (**stiffer, stiffest**) **1** ADJ Something that is **stiff** is firm and does not bend easily. ❑ *Her shoes had a stiff leather bow on top.* ● **stiffly** ADV ❑ *Moira sat stiffly upright in her chair.* **2** ADJ Something such as a drawer or door that is **stiff** does not move as easily as it should. ❑ *The brakes were very stiff.* **3** ADJ If you are **stiff**, your muscles or joints ache when you move. ● **stiffly** ADV ❑ *He climbed stiffly from the car.* ● **stiffness** N-UNCOUNT ❑ *...pain and stiffness in the neck.* **4** ADJ **Stiff** behaviour is rather formal and not relaxed. ❑ *She looked at him with a stiff smile.* ● **stiffly** ADV ❑ *...a stiffly worded letter.* **5** ADJ **Stiff** means difficult or severe. ❑ *...stiff anti-drugs laws.* **6** ADJ BEFORE N A **stiff** drink is a large amount of a strong alcoholic drink. ❑ *...a stiff whisky.* **7** ADJ A **stiff** wind blows quite strongly. **8** ADV If you are bored **stiff**, worried **stiff**, or scared **stiff**, you are extremely bored, worried, or scared. [INFORMAL] **9** **stiff upper lip** → see **lip**

stiffen /ˈstɪfən/ (**stiffens, stiffening, stiffened**) **1** V-I If you **stiffen**, you stop moving and become very tense, for example because you are afraid or angry. ❑ *His father's face stiffened with anger.* **2** V-I & PHR-VERB If your muscles or joints **stiffen**, or if they **stiffen up**, they become difficult to bend or move. ❑ *My elbow was starting to stiffen up where I'd landed on it.* **3** V-I If attitudes or behaviour **stiffen**, they become stronger or more severe, and less likely to be changed. ❑ *Canada has recently stiffened its immigration rules.* **4** V-T When something such as cloth **is stiffened**, it is made firm. ❑ *The paper has been stiffened with a kind of paste.*

S

stifle /ˈstaɪfəl/ (**stifles, stifling, stifled**) V-T To **stifle** something means to stop it happening or continuing. ❑ *Ed stifled a yawn and looked at his watch.* ❑ *This system also stifled small businesses.*

stifling /ˈstaɪfəlɪŋ/ **1** ADJ **Stifling** heat is so hot that it makes you feel uncomfortable. **2** ADJ If a situation is **stifling**, it makes you feel uncomfortable because you cannot do what you want. ❑ *Life at home with her parents and two sisters was stifling.*

stigma /ˈstɪgmə/ (**stigmas**) N-VAR If you say that something has a **stigma** attached to it, you mean that people consider it to be unacceptable or a disgrace, and you think this is unfair. ❑ *...the stigma attached to mental illness.*

stigmatize [BRIT also **stigmatise**] /ˈstɪgmətaɪz/ (**stigmatizes, stigmatizing, stigmatized**) V-T If someone or something **is stigmatized**, many people unfairly think of them as unacceptable or disgraceful.

stiletto /stɪˈletəʊ/ (**stilettos**) N-COUNT **Stilettos** are women's shoes that have high, very narrow heels.

still
1 ADVERB USES
2 NOT MOVING

still /stɪl/
1 **1** ADV If a situation that used to exist **still** exists, it has continued and exists now. ❑ *I still dream of home.* ❑ *Brian's toe is still badly swollen.* **2** ADV If something that has not yet happened could **still** happen, it is possible that it will happen. ❑ *We could still make it, but we won't get there till three.* **3** ADV You use **still** to emphasize that something remains the case or is true. ❑ *Despite the evidence, Boreham was still found guilty.* **4** ADV You use **still** before saying something that shows that you think what has just been said or mentioned is not important or is not worth worrying about. ❑ *'Any idea who is going to be there?'—'No. Still, who cares?'* **5** ADV You use **still** in expressions such as **still further**, **still another**, and **still more** to show that you find the number or quantity of things you are referring to surprising or excessive. ❑ *A storm is forecast for tomorrow and it could delay flights still further.* **6** ADV You use **still** with words such as 'better' or 'more' to indicate that something has even more of a quality than something else. ❑ *It's good to travel, but it's better still to come home.*

still /stɪl/ (**stiller, stillest**)
2 **1** ADJ If you stay **still**, you stay in the same position without moving. ❑ *He sat very still for several minutes.* **2** ADJ If something is **still**, there is no movement or activity there. ❑ *The night air was very still.* ● **stillness** N-UNCOUNT ❑ *...the beauty and stillness of the forest.*

ˌstill ˈlife (**still lifes**) N-VAR A **still life** is a painting or drawing of an arrangement of objects such as flowers or fruit. **Still life** is this type of painting or drawing.
→ see **painting**

stimulant /ˈstɪmjʊlənt/ (**stimulants**) N-COUNT A **stimulant** is a drug that increases your heart rate and makes you less likely to sleep.

stimulate /ˈstɪmjʊleɪt/ (**stimulates, stimulating, stimulated**) **1** V-T To **stimulate** something means to encourage it to begin or develop further. ❑ *This is an attempt to stimulate more interest in these events.* **2** V-T If you **are stimulated** by something, it makes you feel full of ideas and enthusiasm. ● **stimulating** ADJ ❑ *It is written in a very stimulating style.* ● **stimulation** N-UNCOUNT ❑ *...the mental stimulation of an interesting job.* **3** V-T If something **stimulates** a part of a person's body, it causes it to move or function automatically. ● **stimulation** N-UNCOUNT ❑ *...electrical stimulation of the brain.*

stimulus /ˈstɪmjʊləs/ (**stimuli** /ˈstɪmjʊlaɪ/) N-VAR A **stimulus** is something that encourages activity in people or things. ❑ *In the United States the Civil War gave a great stimulus to industrialization.*

sting /stɪŋ/ (**stings, stinging, stung**) **1** V-T/V-I If an insect or plant **stings** you, it pricks your skin, usually with poison, so that you feel a sharp pain. **2** N-COUNT The **sting** of an insect is the part that stings you. **3** V-I & N-SING If a part of your body **stings**, or if you feel a **sting**, you feel a sharp pain there. ❑ *His cheeks were stinging from the icy wind.* **4** V-T If someone's remarks **sting** you, they upset and annoy you. ❑ *Some of the criticism has stung him.* ●**stinging** ADJ ❑ *...a stinging attack on the government.*
→ see **insect**

Usage

Note that wasps and bees **sting** you, but animals, snakes, and mosquitoes **bite** you.

stink /stɪŋk/ (**stinks, stinking, stank, stunk**) **1** V-I & N-SING If something **stinks**, it smells extremely unpleasant. A **stink** is a very unpleasant smell. ❑ *The place stinks of fried onions.* **2** V-I If you say that something **stinks**, you mean that it involves ideas, feelings, or practices that you do not like. [INFORMAL] ❑ *They have done something very bad. It stinks.*

stint /stɪnt/ (**stints**) N-COUNT A **stint** is a period of time spent doing a particular job or activity. ❑ *He did a five-year stint in Hong Kong.*

stipulate /ˈstɪpjʊleɪt/ (**stipulates, stipulating, stipulated**) V-T If you **stipulate** that something must be done, you say clearly that it must be done. ❑ *The company's rules stipulate that directors must retire at 75.* ●**stipulation** (**stipulations**) N-COUNT ❑ *Clifford's only stipulation is that his clients obey his advice.*

stir /stɜː/ (**stirs, stirring, stirred**) **1** V-T When you **stir** a liquid, you mix it inside a container using something such as a spoon. ❑ *Mrs Bellingham stirred sugar into her tea.* **2** V-I If you **stir**, you move slightly, for example because you are uncomfortable or beginning to wake up. [WRITTEN] ❑ *Eileen shook him, and he started to stir.* **3** V-T If something **stirs** you or **stirs** an emotion in you, it makes you react with a strong emotion. [WRITTEN] ❑ *Amy remembered the anger he had stirred in her.* **4** N-SING If an event causes a **stir**, it causes great excitement, shock, or anger. ❑ *His film has caused a stir in America.* **5** → see also **stirring**
▶ **stir up** **1** PHR-VERB If something **stirs up** dust or mud, it causes it to move around. ❑ *First they saw a cloud of dust, then the car that was stirring it up.* **2** PHR-VERB If you **stir up** a particular mood or situation, usually a bad one, you cause it. ❑ *As usual, Harriet is stirring up trouble.*

Word Partnership Use *stir* with:

N.	stir **a mixture**, stir **in sugar** **1**
V.	**cause a** stir, **create a** stir **4**

stirring /ˈstɜːrɪŋ/ (**stirrings**) **1** ADJ A **stirring** event, performance, or account of something makes people very excited or enthusiastic. ❑ *The Prime Minister made a stirring speech.* **2** N-COUNT When there is a **stirring of** emotion, people begin to feel it. ❑ *...the first stirrings of guilt.*

stitch /stɪtʃ/ (**stitches, stitching, stitched**) **1** V-T If you **stitch** cloth, you use a needle and thread to join two pieces together or to make a decoration. ❑ *Fold the fabric and stitch the two layers together.* **2** N-COUNT **Stitches** are the pieces of thread that have been sewn in a piece of cloth. **3** N-COUNT A **stitch** is a loop made by one turn of wool around a knitting needle. **4** V-T & PHR-VERB When doctors **stitch** a wound, or when they **stitch** it **up**, they use a special needle and thread to sew the skin together. ❑ *Dr Armonson stitched up her cut wrist.* **5** N-COUNT A **stitch** is a piece of thread that has been used to stitch a wound. ❑ *He had six stitches in his head.* **6** N-SING A **stitch** is a sharp pain in your side, usually caused by laughing a lot or running.

stock /stɒk/ (**stocks, stocking, stocked**) **1** N-VAR **Stocks** are shares in the ownership of a company. A company's **stock** consists of all the shares that people have bought in it. ❑ *...the buying and selling of stocks.* **2** V-T A shop that **stocks** particular goods keeps a supply of them to sell. ❑ *The gift shop stocks Indian crafts.* **3** N-UNCOUNT A shop's **stock** is the total amount of goods which it has available to sell. **4** N-COUNT A **stock of** things is a supply of them. ❑ *...stocks of paper and ink.* **5** N-VAR **Stock** is a liquid made by boiling meat, bones, or vegetables in water. **6** PHRASE If goods are **in stock**, a shop has them available to sell. If they are **out of stock**, it does not. **7** PHRASE If you **take stock**, you pause and think about a situation before deciding what to do next. ❑ *It was time to take stock of the situation.*
▶ **stock up** PHR-VERB If you **stock up with** something or **stock up on** it, you buy a lot of it, in case you cannot get it later. ❑ *People are stocking up on fuel.*

stockbroker /ˈstɒkbrəʊkə/ (**stockbrokers**) N-COUNT A **stockbroker** is someone whose profession is buying and selling stocks and shares for clients.

stockbroking /ˈstɒkbrəʊkɪŋ/ N-UNCOUNT **Stockbroking** is the professional activity of buying and selling stocks and shares for clients.

ˈstock ˌexchange (**stock exchanges**) N-COUNT A **stock exchange** is a place where people buy and sell stocks and shares.

stockholder /ˈstɒkhəʊldə/ (**stockholders**) N-COUNT In American English, a **stockholder** is a person who owns shares in a company. The usual British word is **shareholder**.

stocking /ˈstɒkɪŋ/ (**stockings**) N-COUNT **Stockings** are items of women's clothing which fit closely over their feet and legs. Stockings are usually made of nylon or silk and are held in place by suspenders. ❑ *...a pair of silk stockings.*

stockist /ˈstɒkɪst/ (**stockists**) N-COUNT A **stockist** of a particular brand or type of goods is a person or shop that sells it. [BRIT] ❑ *Take it to your nearest Kodak Photo CD stockist.*

ˈstock ˌmarket (**stock markets**) N-COUNT **The stock market** consists of the activity of buying stocks and shares, and the people and institutions that organize it.

stockpile /ˈstɒkpaɪl/ (**stockpiles, stockpiling, stockpiled**) **1** V-T If people **stockpile** things, they store large quantities of them for future use. ❑ *People are stockpiling food for the coming winter.* **2** N-COUNT A **stockpile** is a large store of something. ❑ *...stockpiles of chemical weapons.*

stocky /ˈstɒki/ (**stockier, stockiest**) ADJ A **stocky** person has a body that is broad, solid, and short.

stoke /stəʊk/ (**stokes, stoking, stoked**) **1** V-T & PHR-VERB If you **stoke** a fire, or if you **stoke** it **up**, you put more fuel onto it. ❑ *He stoked up the fire in the hall.* **2** V-T & PHR-VERB If you **stoke** something such as a feeling, or if you **stoke** it **up**, you cause it to be felt more strongly. ❑ *These attacks are stoking fears of civil war.*

stole /stəʊl/ **Stole** is the past tense of **steal**.

stolen /ˈstəʊlən/ **Stolen** is the past participle of **steal**.

stomach /ˈstʌmək/ (**stomachs, stomaching, stomached**) **1** N-COUNT Your **stomach** is the organ inside your body where food is digested. ❑ *My stomach is completely full.* **2** N-COUNT You can refer to the front part of your body below your waist as your **stomach**. ❑ *The children lay down on their stomachs.* **3** V-T If you cannot **stomach** something, you strongly dislike it and cannot accept it. ❑ *He could not stomach violence.*

stomp /stɒmp/ (**stomps, stomping, stomped**) V-I If you **stomp** somewhere, you walk there with heavy steps, often because you are angry. ❑ *He stomped out of the room.*

stone /stəʊn/ (**stones, stoning, stoned**)

> In meaning 5, **stone** is both the singular and the plural form.

1 N-VAR **Stone** is a hard solid substance found in the ground and often used for building. ❑ *He could not tell if the floor was wood or stone.* **2** N-COUNT A **stone** is a small piece of rock. ❑ *He removed a stone from his shoe.* **3** V-T If people **stone** someone or something, they throw stones at them. ❑ *Youths burned cars and stoned police.* **4** N-COUNT In British English, the **stone** in a fruit such as a peach or plum is the large seed in the middle of it. The usual American word is **pit**. **5** N-COUNT A **stone** is a measurement of a person's weight, equal to 14 pounds or 6.35 kilograms. The plural is **stone**. [BRIT] ❑ *I weighed around 16 stone.* **6** → See note at **weight** **7** N-COUNT You can refer to a jewel as a **stone**. ❑ *...a diamond ring with three stones.* **8** PHRASE If you say that one place is **a stone's throw** from another, you mean that the places are close to each other.

S

ˈStone ˌAge N-PROPER **The Stone Age** is a very early period of human history, when people used tools and weapons made of stone, not metal.

stony /ˈstəʊni/ (**stonier, stoniest**) **1** ADJ **Stony** ground is rough and contains a lot of stones. **2** ADJ If someone's expression or behaviour is **stony**, they show no friendliness or sympathy. ❑ *He drove us home in stony silence.*

stood /stʊd/ **Stood** is the past tense and past participle of **stand**.

stool /stuːl/ (**stools**) N-COUNT A **stool** is a seat with legs but no support for your back or arms.

stoop /stuːp/ (**stoops, stooping, stooped**) **1** V-I & N-SING If you **stoop**, or if you have a **stoop**, you stand or walk with your shoulders bent forwards. ❑ *He was a tall, thin fellow with a slight stoop.* **2** V-I If you **stoop**, **stoop down**, or **stoop over**, you bend your body forwards and downwards. ❑ *Stooping down, he picked up a big stone.* **3** V-I If you say that someone **stoops to** doing something, you are criticizing them because they do something wrong or immoral that they would not normally do. ❑ *He will stoop to any level to keep this secret.* ❑ *How could anyone stoop so low?*

stop /stɒp/ (**stops, stopping, stopped**) **1** V-T/V-I If you **stop** doing something that you have been doing, you no longer do it. ❑ *He can't stop thinking about it.* ❑ *Do the politicians want to stop the fighting?* ❑ *I stopped to read the notices on the bulletin board.* **2** V-T & PHRASE If you **stop** something, or if you **put a stop to** it, you prevent it from happening or continuing. ❑ *He tried to stop the show.* ❑ *She wanted to stop us seeing each other.* ❑ *Having children won't stop me from acting.* ❑ *His daughter should have put a stop to all these rumours.* **3** V-I If an activity or process **stops**, it comes to an end. ❑ *The rain has stopped.* ❑ *They say the fighting must stop if apartheid is to be defeated.* **4** V-T/V-I If something such as a machine **stops** or you **stop** it, it is no longer moving or working. ❑ *The clock stopped at 2.12 a.m.* ❑ *Arnold stopped the engine and got out of the car.* **5** V-I & N-SING When a moving person or vehicle **stops**, or when they come to **a stop**, they no longer move. ❑ *The car failed to stop at an army checkpoint.* ❑ *He slowed the van almost to a stop.* **6** V-I & PHR-VERB If you **stop** or **stop off** somewhere on a journey, you stay there for a short while before continuing. ❑ *The president stopped off in Poland on his way to Munich.* **7** N-COUNT A **stop** is a place where buses or trains regularly stop so that people can get on and off. **8** to **stop dead** → see **dead** **9** to **stop short of** → see **short**

▶ **stop by** PHR-VERB If you **stop by** somewhere, you make a short visit to a person or place. [INFORMAL] ❑ *Perhaps I'll stop by the hospital.*

> **Usage**
>
> When an action comes to an end or stops, you say that someone **stops doing** it. ❑ *She stopped reading and closed the book.* However, if you say that someone **stops to do** something, you mean that they interrupt their movement or another activity in order to do that thing. The 'to' infinitive indicates purpose. ❑ *I stopped to have a coffee.*

stoppage /ˈstɒpɪdʒ/ (**stoppages**) N-COUNT When there is a **stoppage**, people stop working because of a disagreement with their employers.

storage /ˈstɔːrɪdʒ/ N-UNCOUNT **Storage** is the process of keeping something in a particular place until it is needed. ❑ *Some of the space will at first be used for storage.*

store /stɔː/ (**stores, storing, stored**) **1** N-COUNT A **store** is a shop. In British English, **store** is used mainly to refer to a large shop selling a variety of goods, but in American English, a **store** can be any shop. **2** V-T & PHR-VERB To **store** something or to **store** it **away** means to keep it in a place until it is needed. ❑ *The information can be stored in a computer.* ❑ *Store all medicines safely and keep them out of the reach of children.* **3** N-VAR A **store of** something is a supply of it kept in a place until it is needed. **Store** is also the word for the place where that supply is kept. ❑ *I have a store of food and water here.* ❑ *...a grain store.* **4** PHRASE If something is **in store** for you, it is going to happen at some time in the future. ❑ *We went into the night, not knowing what lay in store.* **5** → see also **department store**
→ see **city**

▶ **store away** → see **store** (meaning **2**)

Thesaurus *store* Also look up:

N. business, market, shop 1
collection, reserve, stock 3
V. accumulate, keep, save 2

storey /'stɔːri/ (**storeys**) N-COUNT The **storeys** of a building are its different floors or levels. ❑ *...a modern three-storey building.*

storm /stɔːm/ (**storms, storming, stormed**) 1 N-COUNT A **storm** is very bad weather, with heavy rain, strong winds, and often thunder and lightning. 2 N-COUNT If something causes a **storm**, it causes an angry or excited reaction from a large number of people. ❑ *Their reports caused a storm of protest in America.* 3 V-I If you **storm into** or **out of** a place, you enter or leave it quickly and noisily, because you are angry. ❑ *After a bit of an argument, he stormed out.* 4 V-T If a place that is being defended **is stormed**, a group of people attack it, usually in order to get inside it. ❑ *The refugees decided to storm the embassy.* ● **storming** N-UNCOUNT ❑ *...the storming of the Bastille.* 5 PHRASE If someone or something **takes** a place **by storm**, they are extremely successful there. ❑ *Kenya's long distance runners have taken the athletics world by storm.*
→ see Word Web: **storm**
→ see **disaster, forecast, hurricane, weather**

Word Partnership Use *storm* with:

ADJ. **gathering** storm, **heavy** storm, **severe** storm, **tropical** storm 1
N. storm **clouds**, storm **damage**, **ice/rain/snow** storm, storm **warning**, storm **winds** 1
centre of a storm, **eye of a** storm 1 2
storm **a building** 4
V. **hit by a** storm, **weather the** storm 1 2
cause a storm 2

stormy /'stɔːmi/ (**stormier, stormiest**) 1 ADJ If there is **stormy** weather, there is a strong wind and heavy rain. 2 ADJ A **stormy** situation involves a lot of angry argument or criticism. ❑ *Their working relationship was stormy at times.*

story /'stɔːri/ (**stories**) 1 N-COUNT A **story** is a description of imaginary people and events, which is written or told in order to entertain. ❑ *I shall tell you a story about four little rabbits.* 2 N-COUNT A **story** is a description or account of things that have happened. ❑ *...the story of the women's movement in Ireland.* 3 N-COUNT A news **story** is a piece of news in a newspaper or in a news broadcast. 4 PHRASE You use **a different story** to refer to a situation, usually a bad one, which exists in one set of circumstances when you have mentioned that it does not exist in another set of circumstances. ❑ *Where Marcella lives, the rents are fairly cheap, but a little further north it's a different story.* 5 PHRASE If you say it's **the same old story** or **the old story**, you mean that something unpleasant or undesirable seems to happen again and again. ❑ *It's the same old story. They want one person to do three people's jobs.* 6 PHRASE If you say that something is **only part of the story** or is **not the whole story**, you mean that the explanation or information given is not enough for a situation to be fully understood. ❑ *This may be true but it is only part of the story.* 7 PHRASE If someone tells you their **side of the story**, they tell you why they behaved in a particular way and why they think they were right, when other people think that person behaved wrongly. ❑ *He has plans for a book telling his side of the story.*
→ see **myth**

Thesaurus *story* Also look up:

N. epic, fable, fairy tale, romance, saga, tale 1
account, report 2
article, feature 3

Word Partnership Use *story* with:

N. **character in a** story, story **hour**, story **line, narrator of a** story, **title of a** story, story **writer** 1
beginning of a story, **end of a** story, **version of a** story 1-3
life story 2
front page story, **news** story 3
ADJ. **classic** story, **compelling** story, **funny** story, **good** story, **horror** story, **interesting** story 1-3
familiar story, **the full** story, **untold** story, **the whole** story 2 3
big story, **related** story, **top** story 3
V. **hear a** story, **publish a** story, **read a** story, **tell a** story, **write a** story 1

stout /staʊt/ (**stouter, stoutest**) 1 ADJ A **stout** person is rather fat. 2 ADJ **Stout** shoes, branches, or other objects are thick and strong. 3 ADJ If you use **stout** to describe someone's actions, attitudes, or beliefs, you approve of them because they are strong and determined. ● **stoutly** ADV ❑ *She stoutly*

S

Word Web storm

A bad storm is coming. How can you protect yourself and your property? Listen for warnings from the **weather** service. Strong **wind** may blow trash cans around. **Hail** may damage your car. Both should go into the garage. If you are outdoors when a storm strikes, get under cover. If you are in the open, **lightning** could hit you. Heavy **rainfall** can cause **flooding**. Do not drive on flooded roads after the rain stops. The water may be deeper than you think. Be sure to buy food and batteries before a **blizzard** because **snow** may close the roads.

defended her husband.

stove /stəʊv/ (**stoves**) N-COUNT A **stove** is a piece of equipment for heating a room or cooking. ❑ *She put the kettle on the gas stove.*

stow /stəʊ/ (**stows, stowing, stowed**) V-T & PHR-VERB If you **stow** something somewhere, or if you **stow** it **away**, you put it carefully somewhere until it is needed. ❑ *I helped her stow her bags in the boot of the car.*

straddle /ˈstrædəl/ (**straddles, straddling, straddled**) 1 V-T If you **straddle** something, you put or have one leg on either side of it. ❑ *He sat down, straddling the chair.* 2 V-T If something such as a bridge or town **straddles** a river, road, or border, it stretches across it or exists on both sides of it. ❑ *The Rumaila oilfield straddles the border between Kuwait and Iraq.* 3 V-T Someone or something that **straddles** different periods, groups, or fields of activity exists in, belongs to, or takes elements from them all. ❑ *He straddles African and Western cultures, using the best from each.*

straight /streɪt/ (**straighter, straightest**) 1 ADJ & ADV If something is **straight**, it continues in one direction or line and does not bend or curve. ❑ *Keep the boat in a straight line.* ❑ *She looked straight at me.* ❑ *He couldn't walk straight.* 2 ADV If you go **straight** to a place, you go there immediately. ❑ *We went straight to the experts for advice.* ❑ *We'll go to the meeting and come straight back.* 3 ADJ BEFORE N A **straight** choice or a **straight** fight involves only two people or things. ❑ *It's a straight choice between low-paid jobs and no jobs.* 4 ADJ & ADV If you are **straight** with someone, you speak to them honestly. ❑ *Can't you give me a straight answer?* ❑ *If you're doing something wrong, he'll tell you straight.* 5 ADJ If you describe someone as **straight**, you mean that they are heterosexual rather than homosexual. [INFORMAL] ❑ *Marty describes herself as a straight female.* 6 PHRASE If you **get** something **straight**, you make sure that you understand it properly or that someone else does. ❑ *You need to get your facts straight.* ❑ *Let's get this straight: I didn't lunch with her.* 7 **a straight face** → see **face** 8 to **set the record straight** → see **record**
→ see **hair**

Word Partnership	Use *straight* with:
V.	**drive** straight, **keep going** straight, **look** straight, **point** straight 1
N.	straight **line**, straight **nose** 1

straight a'way also **straightaway** ADV If you do something **straight away**, you do it immediately. ❑ *I knew straight away he was different.*

straighten /ˈstreɪtən/ (**straightens, straightening, straightened**) 1 V-T & PHR-VERB If you **straighten** something, or if you **straighten** it **out**, it becomes straight rather than having bends or curls in it, or being in the wrong position. ❑ *She straightened a picture on the wall.* ❑ *I had my hair straightened.* ❑ *The road twisted up the mountain then straightened out.* 2 V-I & PHR-VERB If you are bending and you then **straighten** or **straighten up**, you make your body straight and upright. ❑ *I straightened until my head hit rock.* ❑ *He straightened up and looked around.*

▸ **straighten out** 1 PHR-VERB If you **straighten out** a confused situation, you succeed in dealing with it or getting it properly organized. ❑ *We need to straighten out a couple of things.* 2 → see **straighten** (meaning 1)

straightforward /ˌstreɪtˈfɔːwəd/ 1 ADJ If something is **straightforward**, it is not complicated to do or understand. ❑ *Of course it isn't as straightforward as that!* ❑ *It seemed to be a straightforward question.* • **straightforwardly** ADV ❑ *This first problem is solved fairly straightforwardly.* 2 ADJ If you describe a person or their behaviour as **straightforward**, you approve of them because they are honest and direct, and do not try to hide their feelings. • **straightforwardly** ADV ❑ *His daughter says straightforwardly that he was not good enough.*

strain /streɪn/ (**strains, straining, strained**) 1 N-VAR If **strain** is put on a person or organization, they have to do more than they are really able to do. ❑ *The prison service is already under a lot of strain.* ❑ *...the stresses and strains of a busy career.* 2 N-UNCOUNT **Strain** is an injury to a muscle in your body, caused by using it too much or twisting it badly. ❑ *Avoid muscle strain by warming up.* 3 V-T To **strain** something means to make it do more than it is really able to do. ❑ *The number of flights is straining the air traffic control system.* 4 V-T If you **strain** a muscle, you injure it by using it suddenly or too much. 5 V-T If you **strain to** do something, you make a great effort to do it. ❑ *Several thousand voters strained to catch a glimpse of the new president.* 6 V-T When you **strain** food, you separate the liquid part of it from the solid parts.

Word Partnership	Use *strain* with:
ADJ.	**great** strain 1-5
N.	**muscle** strain, strain **a muscle** 2
	stress and strain 3

strained /streɪnd/ 1 ADJ If someone's appearance, voice, or behaviour is **strained**, they seem worried and nervous. ❑ *His laughter seemed a little strained.* 2 ADJ If relations between people are **strained**, their relationship has become difficult because they no longer like or trust each other.

strait /streɪt/ (**straits**) 1 N-COUNT You can refer to a narrow strip of sea which joins two large areas of sea as a **strait** or **the straits**. 2 N-PLURAL If someone is **in dire straits** or **in desperate straits**, they are in a very difficult situation. ❑ *Closing the company has left many small businessmen in desperate financial straits.*

strand /strænd/ (**strands, stranding, stranded**) 1 N-COUNT A **strand of** thread, wire, or hair is a thin piece of it. 2 N-COUNT A **strand of** a plan, theory, or story is one aspect of it. ❑ *She was trying to separate the different strands of the problem.* 3 V-T If you **are stranded**, you are prevented from leaving a place, for example because of bad weather. ❑ *Hundreds of motorists are preparing to spend a night stranded in their cars.*

strange /streɪndʒ/ (**stranger, strangest**) 1 ADJ **Strange** means unusual or unexpected. ❑ *I had a strange dream.* ❑ *There was something strange about his eyes: one of them was darker than the other.* • **strangely** ADV ❑ *The room suddenly seemed strangely silent.* ❑ *Strangely, the race didn't start until 8.15pm.* • **strangeness** N-UNCOUNT ❑ *There was a strangeness in her manner.* 2 ADJ BEFORE N A **strange** person or place is one that you do not know. ❑ *I ended up alone in a strange city.*

S

Thesaurus *strange* Also look up:

ADJ. bizarre, different, eccentric, odd, peculiar, unusual, weird; *(ant.)* ordinary, usual 1
exotic, foreign, unfamiliar 2

stranger /ˈstreɪndʒə/ (**strangers**) 1 N-COUNT A **stranger** is someone you have not met before or do not know at all. If two people are **strangers**, they have never met or do not know each other at all. ❑ *Telling a complete stranger about your life is difficult.* ❑ *Back then, we were strangers to each other.* 2 N-COUNT If you are a **stranger** in a place, you do not know the place at all. If you are a **stranger to** something, you have had no experience of it or do not understand it. ❑ *I'm a stranger here.* ❑ *She is no stranger to politics.*

Usage

You do not use **stranger** to talk about someone who comes from a country which is not your own. You can refer to him or her as a **foreigner**, but this word can sound rather rude. It is better to talk about **someone from abroad**.

strangle /ˈstræŋgəl/ (**strangles, strangling, strangled**) 1 V-T To **strangle** someone means to kill them by tightly squeezing their throat. 2 V-T To **strangle** something means to prevent it from developing or succeeding. ❑ *The manager said these financial problems were strangling the club.*

stranglehold /ˈstræŋgəlhəʊld/ (**strangleholds**) N-COUNT To have a **stranglehold on** something means to have control over it and prevent it being free or developing. ❑ *The troops are tightening their stranglehold on the city.* ❑ *It took the country over 40 years to break the stranglehold of the old system.*

strap /stræp/ (**straps, strapping, strapped**) 1 N-COUNT A **strap** is a narrow piece of leather, cloth, or other material. Straps are used to carry things or hold them in place. ❑ *...the strap of her handbag.* ❑ *I undid my watch strap.* 2 V-T If you **strap** something somewhere, you fasten it there with a strap.

strata /ˈstrɑːtə, AM ˈstreɪtə/ **Strata** is the plural of **stratum**.

strategic /strəˈtiːdʒɪk/ 1 ADJ **Strategic** means relating to the most important, general aspects of something such as a military operation or political policy. ❑ *...a strategic plan for reducing crime.* • **strategically** ADV ❑ *...strategically important roads.* 2 ADJ **Strategic** weapons are very powerful, long-range weapons, and the decision to use them can be made only by a political leader. 3 ADJ If you put something in a **strategic** position, you place it cleverly in a position where it will be most useful or have the most effect. • **strategically** ADV ❑ *...a strategically placed chair.*

Word Partnership Use *strategic* with:

N. strategic **decisions**, strategic **forces**, strategic **interests**, strategic **planning**, strategic **targets**, strategic **thinking** 1
strategic **missiles**, strategic **nuclear weapons** 2
strategic **location**, strategic **position** 3

strategist /ˈstrætədʒɪst/ (**strategists**) N-COUNT A **strategist** is someone who is skilled in planning the best way to achieve something, especially in war.

strategy /ˈstrætədʒi/ (**strategies**) 1 N-VAR A **strategy** is a general plan or set of plans intended to achieve something, especially over a long period. 2 N-UNCOUNT **Strategy** is the art of planning the best way to achieve something, especially in war. ❑ *...the basic rules of military strategy.*

Thesaurus *strategy* Also look up:

N. plan, policy, tactics 1

Word Partnership Use *strategy* with:

N. **campaign** strategy, **investment** strategy, **marketing** strategy, **part of a** strategy, **pricing** strategy, strategy **shift** 1
ADJ. **aggressive** strategy, **new** strategy, **political** strategy, **successful** strategy, **winning** strategy 1
military strategy 1 2
V. **adopt a** strategy, **change a** strategy, **develop a** strategy, **plan a** strategy 1
use (a) strategy 1 2

stratum /ˈstrɑːtəm, AM ˈstreɪtəm/ (**strata**) N-COUNT A **stratum of** society is a group of people in it who are similar in their social class. [FORMAL] ❑ *...the lower strata of American society.*

straw /strɔː/ (**straws**) 1 N-UNCOUNT **Straw** is the dried yellowish stalks from crops such as wheat or barley. 2 N-COUNT A **straw** is a thin tube of paper or plastic, which you use to suck a drink into your mouth. 3 PHRASE If you say that an event is **the last straw**, you mean that it is the latest in a series of unpleasant events, and makes you feel that you cannot tolerate a situation any longer.
→ see **rice**

strawberries

strawberry /ˈstrɔːbri, AM -beri/ (**strawberries**) N-COUNT A **strawberry** is a small red fruit with tiny seeds in its skin.

stray /streɪ/ (**strays, straying, strayed**) 1 V-I If someone **strays** somewhere, they wander away from where they should be. ❑ *Tourists often get lost and stray into dangerous areas.* 2 ADJ BEFORE N & N-COUNT A **stray** dog or cat has wandered away from its owner's home. A **stray** is a stray dog or cat. 3 V-I If your mind or your eyes **stray**, you do not concentrate on or look at one particular subject, but start thinking about or looking at other things. ❑ *She could not keep her eyes from straying towards him.* 4 ADJ BEFORE N **Stray** things have become separated from other similar things. ❑ *She pushed a stray hair out of her eyes.*

streak /striːk/ (**streaks, streaking, streaked**) 1 N-COUNT A **streak** is a long narrow stripe or

S

mark on something. ❑ *A streak of orange smoke shot up into the sky.* **2** V-T If something **streaks** a surface, it makes streaks on it. ❑ *His face was pale and streaked with dirt.* **3** N-COUNT If someone has a **streak of** a particular type of behaviour, they sometimes behave in that way. ❑ *There is a streak of madness in us both.* **4** V-I To **streak** somewhere means to move there very quickly. ❑ *A shooting star streaked across the sky.*

stream /striːm/ (**streams, streaming, streamed**) **1** N-COUNT A **stream** is a small narrow river. **2** N-COUNT A **stream of** things is a large number of them occurring one after another. ❑ *...a never-ending stream of jokes.* ❑ *We had a constant stream of visitors.* **3** V-I If a mass of people, liquid, or light **streams** somewhere, it enters or moves there in large amounts. ❑ *Refugees have been streaming into Travnik for months.* ❑ *Tears streamed down their faces.*
→ see **cave, river**

streamline /ˈstriːmlaɪn/ (**streamlines, streamlining, streamlined**) V-T To **streamline** an organization or process means to make it more efficient by removing unnecessary parts of it. ❑ *The zoo will have to streamline its operations if it's to survive.* ●**streamlined** ADJ ❑ *...the streamlined organisations of the future.*
→ see **mass production**

streamlined /ˈstriːmlaɪnd/ ADJ A **streamlined** object or animal has a shape that allows it to move quickly or efficiently through air or water.

street /striːt/ (**streets**) **1** N-COUNT A **street** is a road in a town or village, usually with houses along it. ❑ *He walked quickly down the street.* ❑ *...activities to keep young people off the streets.* **2** N-COUNT You can use **the street** or **the streets** when talking about activities that happen out of doors in a town rather than in a building. ❑ *Changing money on the street is illegal.* ❑ *...street theatre.* **3** PHRASE If you talk about **the man in the street**, you mean ordinary people in general. ❑ *What does all this mean for the man in the street?*

Thesaurus	*street* Also look up:
N.	avenue, drive, road **1**

streetcar /ˈstriːtkɑː/ (**streetcars**) N-COUNT In American English, a **streetcar** is an electric vehicle for carrying people which travels on rails in the streets of a town. The British word is **tram**.
→ see **transportation**

ˈstreet crime N-UNCOUNT **Street crime** refers to crimes such as vandalism, car theft and mugging that are usually committed outdoors.

strength /streŋθ/ (**strengths**) **1** N-UNCOUNT Your **strength** is the physical energy that you have, which gives you the ability to do things such as lift heavy objects. ❑ *He threw it forward with all his strength.* ❑ *You don't need strength to take part in this sport.* **2** N-UNCOUNT Someone's **strength** in a difficult situation is their courage and determination. ❑ *Something gave me the strength not to care.* ❑ *She had often shown great strength of character.* **3** N-VAR Someone's **strengths** are the qualities and abilities that they have which are an advantage to them, or which make them successful. ❑ *Take into account your own strengths and weaknesses.* ❑ *The novel's greatest strength is its dialogue.* **4** N-UNCOUNT The **strength** of an object or material is its ability to be treated roughly or to support heavy weights. ❑ *He checked the strength of the ropes.* **5** N-UNCOUNT The **strength** of a person, organization, or country is the power and influence that they have because they are successful. **6** N-UNCOUNT If you refer to **the strength of** a feeling, opinion, or belief, you are talking about how deeply it is felt or believed by people, or how much they are influenced by it. ❑ *He was surprised at the strength of his own feeling.* **7** N-UNCOUNT The **strength** of a group of people is the total number of people in it. ❑ *These soldiers make up about one-tenth of the strength of the army.* **8** PHRASE If one thing is done **on the strength of** another, it is done because of the influence of that other thing. ❑ *On the strength of those grades, he won a scholarship to Syracuse University.*
→ see **muscle**

strengthen /ˈstreŋθən/ (**strengthens, strengthening, strengthened**) V-T To **strengthen** something means to make it stronger. ❑ *Cycling strengthens all the muscles of the body.*

strenuous /ˈstrenjuəs/ ADJ A **strenuous** action or activity involves a lot of effort or energy. ❑ *Avoid strenuous exercise in the evening.* ❑ *She made strenuous efforts to pay off her debts.* ●**strenuously** ADV ❑ *Brown has always maintained his innocence strenuously.*

stress /stres/ (**stresses, stressing, stressed**) **1** V-T & N-UNCOUNT If you **stress** a point, or if you lay **stress on** it, you emphasize it because you think it is important. ❑ *He stressed that the sales department was doing well.* ❑ *...the military's stress on tradition and continuity.* **2** N-VAR If you feel under **stress**, you feel worried and tense because of difficulties in your life. ❑ *She was suffering from stress.* ❑ *...the stresses of modern living.* **3** N-VAR **Stresses** are strong physical pressures applied to an object. ❑ *Earthquakes happen when stresses in rock are suddenly released.* **4** V-T & N-VAR If you **stress** a word or part of a word when you say it, you put emphasis called **stress** on it, so that it sounds slightly louder. ❑ *The stress falls on the last syllable.*
→ see **emotion**

Word Partnership	Use *stress* with:
N.	stress **the importance of** ***something*** **1**
	anxiety and stress, **effects of** stress, **job/work-related** stress, stress **management**, stress **reduction**, **response to** stress, **symptoms of** stress, stress **test** **2**
ADJ.	**emotional** stress, **excessive** stress, **high** stress, **physical** stress, stress **related**, **severe** stress **2**
V.	**cause** stress, **cope with** stress, **deal with** stress, **experience** stress, **induce** stress, **reduce** stress, **relieve** stress **2**

stressed /strest/ ADJ If you feel **stressed**, you feel tension and anxiety because of difficulties in your life.

stressful /ˈstresfʊl/ ADJ A **stressful** situation or experience causes someone to feel stress.

stretch /stretʃ/ (**stretches, stretching, stretched**) **1** V-I Something that **stretches** over an area or distance covers or exists in the whole of

S

that area or distance. ❑ *Huge forests stretch the length of the valley.* ❑ *The procession stretched for several miles.* **2** N-COUNT A **stretch of** land or water is a length or area of it. **3** V-T/V-I When you **stretch**, or when you **stretch** your arms or legs, you put your arms or legs out straight and tighten your muscles. ❑ *He yawned and stretched.* **4** N-COUNT A **stretch** of time is a period of time. ❑ *...an 18-month stretch in the army.* **5** V-T/V-I When something soft or elastic **stretches**, or when it **is stretched**, it becomes longer or bigger as well as thinner, usually because it is pulled. ❑ *The cables are designed so that they do not stretch.* **6** V-T If something **stretches** your money or resources, it uses them up so you have hardly enough for your needs. ● **stretched** ADJ ❑ *...the company's stretched finances.*

▶ **stretch out** **1** PHR-VERB If you **stretch out**, or if you **stretch yourself out**, you lie with your legs and body in a straight line. ❑ *I stretched out in the bottom of the boat and closed my eyes.* **2** PHR-VERB If you **stretch out** a part of your body, you hold it out straight. ❑ *He stretched out his hand to grab me.*

Word Partnership Use *stretch* with:

PREP.	stretch **across** 1 3 **along a** stretch **of road, down the road a** stretch 2 **during a** stretch 3 4 **at a** stretch 4
N.	stretch **of highway/road**, stretch **of a river** 2 stretch ***your* legs** 3

stretcher /ˈstretʃə/ (**stretchers**) N-COUNT A **stretcher** is a long piece of canvas with a pole along each side, which is used to carry an injured person.

strewn /struːn/ ADJ If a place is **strewn with** things, they are scattered everywhere in it. ❑ *The room was strewn with books.* ❑ *...the rock-strewn hillside.*

stricken /ˈstrɪkən/ ADJ If a person or place is **stricken by** something such as an unpleasant feeling, illness, or natural disaster, they are severely affected by it. ❑ *...countries stricken by poverty.* ❑ *...the drought-stricken region of Tigray.*

strict /strɪkt/ (**stricter, strictest**) **1** ADJ A **strict** rule or order is very precise or severe and must be obeyed absolutely. ❑ *She gave me strict instructions not to say anything.* ● **strictly** ADV ❑ *The acceptance of new members is strictly controlled.* **2** ADJ A **strict** person does not tolerate behaviour which is not polite or obedient, especially from children. ❑ *My parents were very strict.* ● **strictly** ADV ❑ *My own mother was brought up very strictly.* **3** ADJ BEFORE N The **strict** meaning of something is its precise meaning. ❑ *It wasn't peace in the strictest sense, rather the absence of war.* ● **strictly** ADV ❑ *Actually, that is not strictly true.* ❑ *Strictly speaking, it is not one house, but three houses joined together.* **4** ADJ BEFORE N You use **strict** to describe someone who never does things that are against their beliefs. ❑ *...a strict vegetarian*

strictly /ˈstrɪktli/ ADV You use **strictly** to emphasize that something is of one particular type, or intended for one particular thing or person, rather than any other. ❑ *He seemed to like her in a strictly professional way.* ❑ *Horse racing was strictly for the rich.*

stride /straɪd/ (**strides, striding, strode**) **1** V-I If you **stride** somewhere, you walk there with quick long steps. ❑ *He turned and strode off down the corridor.* **2** N-COUNT A **stride** is a long step which you take when you are walking or running. **3** N-COUNT If you **make strides** in something that you are doing, you make rapid progress in it. ❑ *Politically, the country has made enormous strides.* **4** PHRASE In British English, if you **take** a difficult situation **in** your **stride**, you deal with it calmly and easily. The American expression is **take** something **in stride**. ❑ *She has learned to take criticism in her stride.*

Word Partnership Use *stride* with:

V.	**break *(your)*** stride, **lengthen *your*** stride 2
ADJ.	**long** stride 2

strident /ˈstraɪdənt/ **1** ADJ If you use **strident** to describe someone or the way they express themselves, you disapprove of the noticeable or persistent way that they make their feelings or opinions known. ❑ *...the strident tone of the President's remarks.* **2** ADJ A **strident** voice or sound is loud and unpleasant.

strife /straɪf/ N-UNCOUNT **Strife** is strong disagreement or fighting. ❑ *Money is a major cause of strife in many marriages.*

strike /straɪk/ (**strikes, striking, struck**) **1** N-COUNT & V-I When workers go **on strike**, or when they **strike**, they stop working for a period of time, usually to try to get better pay or conditions. ❑ *Staff at the hospital went on strike in protest.* ❑ *They shouldn't be striking for more money.* ● **striker** (**strikers**) N-COUNT ❑ *The strikers want higher wages.* **2** V-T If you **strike** someone or something, you deliberately hit them. [FORMAL] ❑ *She took a step forward and struck him across the face.* **3** V-T If something that is falling or moving **strikes** something, it hits it. [FORMAL] ❑ *His head struck the ground with a thud.* **4** V-T/V-I To **strike** someone or something means to attack them or to affect them, quickly and violently. ❑ *A powerful earthquake struck the Italian island of Sicily.* ❑ *The killer says he will strike again.* **5** N-COUNT A military **strike** is a military attack. **6** V-T If an idea or thought **strikes** you, it suddenly comes into your mind. ❑ *It suddenly struck me that I was wasting my time.* **7** V-T If something **strikes** you **as** being a particular thing, it gives you the impression of being that thing. ❑ *He struck me as a very serious but friendly person.* **8** V-T PASSIVE If you **are struck** by something, you think it is very impressive, noticeable, or interesting. ❑ *She was struck by his energy.* **9** V-T You can use **strike** to indicate that you arrive at an agreement, decision, or situation. ❑ *Try to strike a balance between work and play.* ❑ *I was struck dumb by this piece of news.* **10** V-T If something **strikes** fear or terror into people, it makes them very frightened or anxious. **11** V-T/V-I When a clock **strikes** or **strikes** the hour, its bells make a sound to indicate what the time is. ❑ *The clock struck nine.* **12** V-T If you **strike** a match, you make it produce a flame by moving it quickly against something rough. **13** V-T To **strike** oil or gold means to discover it in the ground as a result of mining or drilling.

▶ **strike down** PHR-VERB If someone **is struck down**, especially by an illness, they are killed or severely harmed. [WRITTEN] ❑ *Frank had been struck*

S

down by a massive heart attack.

▶ **strike off** PHR-VERB If a doctor or lawyer **is struck off**, their name is removed from the official register and they are not allowed to practise their profession.

▶ **strike out** 1 PHR-VERB If you **strike out** in a particular direction, you start travelling in that direction. ❑ *They left the car and struck out along the muddy track.* 2 PHR-VERB If you **strike out**, you begin to do something different, often because you want to become more independent. ❑ *She wanted me to strike out on my own.*

▶ **strike up** PHR-VERB When you **strike up** a conversation or friendship, you begin it.

striker /ˈstraɪkə/ (**strikers**) N-COUNT In football and some other team sports, a **striker** is a player whose main job is to attack and score goals.

striking /ˈstraɪkɪŋ/ 1 ADJ Something that is **striking** is very noticeable or unusual. ❑ *He bears a striking resemblance to Lenin.* ● **strikingly** ADV ❑ *The men were strikingly similar.* 2 ADJ A **striking** person is very attractive. ❑ *...the striking blond actor.* ● **strikingly** ADV ❑ *...a strikingly handsome man.*

string /strɪŋ/ (**strings, stringing, strung**) 1 N-VAR **String** is thin rope made of twisted threads, used for tying things together or tying up parcels. 2 N-COUNT A **string of** things is a number of them on a piece of string, thread, or wire. ❑ *She wore a string of pearls.* 3 N-COUNT A **string of** places or objects is a number of them that form a line. ❑ *...a string of villages.* 4 N-COUNT The **strings** on a musical instrument such as a violin or guitar are thin pieces of tightly-stretched wire or nylon. 5 N-PLURAL **The strings** are the section of an orchestra which consists of instruments played with a bow. 6 V-T If you **string** something somewhere, you hang it up between two or more objects. ❑ *He had strung a banner across the wall.* 7 PHRASE If something is offered to you **with no strings attached**, it is offered without any special conditions. ❑ *Financial help should be given to developing countries with no strings attached.*

→ see Picture Dictionary: **strings**

→ see **orchestra**

▶ **string along** PHR-VERB If you **string** someone **along**, you deceive them by letting them believe that you have the same desires, beliefs, or hopes as them. [INFORMAL] ❑ *She strung him along even after they were divorced.*

▶ **string together** PHR-VERB If you **string** things **together**, you make them into one thing by adding them to each other, one at a time. ❑ *The speaker strung together a series of jokes.*

Thesaurus *string* Also look up:

N. cord, fibre, rope 1
chain, file, line, row, sequence, series 2 3

Word Partnership Use *string* with:

N. **piece of** string 1
string **of pearls** 2
string **of attacks**, string **of bombings**, string **of losses**, string **of scandals** 3
guitar string 4

ADJ. **long** string 1 2
latest string **of** ***something***, **recent** string **of** ***something*** 3

stringent /ˈstrɪndʒənt/ ADJ **Stringent** laws, rules, or conditions are severe or are strictly controlled. [FORMAL] ❑ *...stringent controls on the possession of weapons.*

strip /strɪp/ (**strips, stripping, stripped**) 1 N-COUNT A **strip of** something is a long narrow piece of it. ❑ *These rugs are made with strips of fabric.* 2 N-COUNT A **strip of** land or water is a long narrow area of it. 3 V-T/V-I If you **strip**, or if someone **strips** you, your clothes are removed from your body. ❑ *Women residents stripped naked in protest.* 4 V-T To **strip** someone **of** their property, rights, or titles means to take those things away from them. ❑ *The soldiers stripped us of our passports.* 5 V-T To **strip** something means to remove everything that covers it. ❑ *I stripped the beds and vacuumed the carpets.* 6 N-COUNT In a newspaper or magazine, a **comic strip** is a series of drawings which tell a story.

→ see **football**

▶ **strip away** PHR-VERB To **strip away** something misleading or unnecessary means to remove it completely, so that people can see what is important or true. ❑ *Strip away the fancy packaging, and there's very little left.*

▶ **strip off** PHR-VERB If you **strip off**, or if you **strip** your clothes **off**, you take off your clothes. ❑ *He stripped off his wet clothes and stepped into the shower.*

S

Picture Dictionary strings

stripe /straɪp/ (**stripes**) N-COUNT A **stripe** is a long line which is a different colour from the areas next to it. ❑ *The walls are painted with pale blue and white stripes.*
→ see **pattern**

striped /straɪpt/ ADJ Something that is **striped** has stripes on it. ❑ *...striped wallpaper.*

stripper /ˈstrɪpə/ (**strippers**) N-COUNT A **stripper** is a person who earns money by taking off their clothes slowly and in a sexy way to music.

strive /straɪv/ (**strives, striving, strove** or **strived, striven** or **strived**) V-T/V-I If you **strive for** something or **strive to** do something, you make a great effort to get or do it. ❑ *The school strives to treat pupils as individuals.*

strode /strəʊd/ **Strode** is the past tense of **stride**.

stroke /strəʊk/ (**strokes, stroking, stroked**) 1 V-T If you **stroke** someone or something, you move your hand slowly and gently over them. ❑ *He held her quietly, his hand stroking her hair.* 2 N-COUNT If someone has a **stroke**, a blood vessel in their brain bursts or gets blocked, which may kill them or cause one side of their body to be paralysed. 3 N-COUNT The **strokes** of a pen or brush are the movements or marks you make with it when you are writing or painting. ❑ *...short, upward strokes of the pencil.* 4 N-COUNT When you are swimming or rowing, your **strokes** are the repeated movements you make with your arms or the oars. ❑ *I turned and swam a few strokes further out to sea.* 5 N-COUNT A swimming **stroke** is a particular style or method of swimming. 6 N-COUNT In sports such as tennis, cricket, and golf, a **stroke** is the action of hitting the ball. 7 N-COUNT The **strokes** of a clock are the sounds that indicate each hour. ❑ *On the stroke of 12, fireworks suddenly exploded.* 8 N-SING **A stroke of** luck is something lucky that suddenly happens. ❑ *It didn't rain, which turned out to be a stroke of luck.* 9 PHRASE If something happens **at a stroke** or **in one stroke**, it happens suddenly and completely because of one single action. ❑ *How can Britain reduce its prison population in one stroke?*

Word Partnership Use *stroke* with:

V.	**die from a** stroke, **have a** stroke, **suffer a** stroke 2
N.	**risk of a** stroke 2 stroke **of a pen** 3

stroll /strəʊl/ (**strolls, strolling, strolled**) V-I & N-COUNT If you **stroll** somewhere, or if you go for a **stroll**, you walk in a slow relaxed way. ❑ *After dinner, I took a stroll round the city.*

stroller /ˈstrəʊlə/ (**strollers**) N-COUNT In American English, a **stroller** is a small chair on wheels, in which a baby or small child can sit and be wheeled around. The British word is **pushchair**.

strong /strɒŋ, AM strɔːŋ/ (**stronger, strongest**) 1 ADJ A **strong** person is healthy with good muscles. ❑ *I'm not strong enough to carry him.* ❑ *She felt his strong hand gripping her arm.* 2 ADJ **Strong** objects or materials are not easily broken. ❑ *The flask has a strong casing, which won't crack or chip.* • **strongly** ADV ❑ *The fence was very strongly built.* 3 ADJ Someone who is **strong** is confident and determined. ❑ *She had a strong and supportive sister.* 4 ADJ If you have **strong** opinions on something or express them using **strong** words, you have extreme or very definite opinions which you are willing to express or defend. ❑ *He has strong views on the use of nuclear power.* • **strongly** ADV ❑ *I would strongly advise against it.* 5 ADJ **Strong** action is firm and severe. ❑ *The government will take strong action against strikes.* 6 ADJ **Strong** means great in degree or intensity. ❑ *His answer caused a strong reaction.* • **strongly** ADV ❑ *He is strongly influenced by Spanish painters.* 7 ADJ **Strong** is used to describe people or things that have all the qualities that make them likely to be successful. ❑ *She was a strong contender for Britain's Olympic team.* ❑ *There is a strong case for improving communication.* 8 ADJ BEFORE N Your **strong** points are the things you are good at. ❑ *Discretion is not Jeremy's strong point.* 9 ADJ You use **strong** to say how many people there are in a group. For example, a group that is twenty **strong** has twenty people in it. 10 ADJ **Strong** drinks, chemicals, or drugs contain a lot of a particular substance. ❑ *The walls were washed down with strong bleach.* 11 ADJ A **strong** colour, flavour, smell, sound, or light is intense and easily noticed. ❑ *...strong cheese.* • **strongly** ADV ❑ *He leaned over her, smelling strongly of sweat.* 12 PHRASE If someone or something is still **going strong**, they are still alive, in good condition, or popular after a long time.

Thesaurus *strong* Also look up:

ADJ.	mighty, powerful, tough; *(ant.)* weak 1 solid, sturdy 2 confident, determined; *(ant.)* cowardly 3

stronghold /ˈstrɒŋhəʊld, AM ˈstrɔːŋ-/ (**strongholds**) N-COUNT If a place is a **stronghold of** an attitude or belief, many people there have this attitude or belief. ❑ *The university was a stronghold of nationalism.*

strove /strəʊv/ **Strove** is a past tense of **strive**.

struck /strʌk/ **Struck** is the past tense and past participle of **strike**.

structural /ˈstrʌktʃərəl/ ADJ **Structural** means relating to or affecting the structure of something. ❑ *We've made some structural alterations to the house.* • **structurally** ADV ❑ *When we bought the house, it was structurally sound.*

structure /ˈstrʌktʃə/ (**structures, structuring, structured**) 1 N-VAR The **structure of** something is the way in which it is made, built, or organized. ❑ *...the structure of French education.* 2 N-COUNT A **structure** is something that is built from or consists of parts connected together in an ordered way. ❑ *The house was a handsome four-storey brick structure.* 3 V-T If you **structure** something, you arrange it in an organized pattern or system. ❑ *By structuring the course this way, we produce something valuable.* • **structured** ADJ ❑ *...a structured training programme.*

struggle /ˈstrʌgəl/ (**struggles, struggling, struggled**) 1 V-I/V-T If you **struggle** or **struggle to** do something difficult, you try hard to do it. ❑ *Those who have lost their jobs struggle to pay their supermarket bills.* 2 N-VAR A **struggle** is an attempt to obtain something or to defeat someone who is denying you something. ❑ *Life became a struggle for survival.* ❑ *...a power struggle.* 3 V-I If you **struggle** when you are being held, you twist and turn your body in order to try to get free. ❑ *I struggled, but he was a tall man.* 4 V-I & N-COUNT If two people **struggle with** each other, or if they are in a **struggle**, they fight. ❑ *He died in a struggle with prison officers.* 5 V-I If you **struggle to** move yourself or **to** move a heavy object, you manage to do it with great difficulty. ❑ *He was struggling to free himself.* ❑ *I struggled with my bags.* 6 N-SING An action or activity that is **a struggle** is very difficult for you to do. ❑ *Losing weight was a terrible struggle.*

Word Partnership Use *struggle* with:

ADJ. **bitter** struggle, **internal** struggle, **long** struggle, **ongoing** struggle, **uphill** struggle 1 2 **locked in a** struggle 1 2 4 **political** struggle 2

N. struggle **for democracy**, struggle **for equality**, struggle **for freedom/independence**, **power** struggle, struggle **for survival** 2

strum /strʌm/ (**strums, strumming, strummed**) V-T If you **strum** a guitar, you play it by moving your fingers up and down across the strings.

strung /strʌŋ/ **Strung** is the past tense and past participle of **string**.

strut /strʌt/ (**struts, strutting, strutted**) 1 V-I Someone who **struts** walks in a proud way, with their head high and their chest out; used showing disapproval. ❑ *He struts around town like he owns the place.* 2 N-COUNT A **strut** is a piece of wood or metal which strengthens or supports a building or structure.

stub /stʌb/ (**stubs, stubbing, stubbed**) 1 N-COUNT The **stub** of a cigarette or a pencil is the short piece which remains when the rest has been used. ❑ *He pulled an old pencil stub from behind his ear.* 2 N-COUNT The **stub** of a cheque or ticket is the small part that you keep. 3 V-T If you **stub** your **toe**, you hurt it by accidentally kicking something.

▸ **stub out** PHR-VERB When someone **stubs out** a cigarette, they put it out by pressing it against something hard.

S

stubble /ˈstʌbəl/ 1 N-UNCOUNT **Stubble** consists of the short stalks which are left in fields after corn or wheat has been harvested. 2 N-UNCOUNT The very short hairs on a man's face when he has not shaved recently are referred to as **stubble**. ❑ *He scratched at the stubble on his jaw.*

stubborn /ˈstʌbən/ 1 ADJ A **stubborn** person is determined to do what they want and refuses to change their mind. ❑ *...his stubborn resistance to anything new.* • **stubbornly** ADV ❑ *He stubbornly refused to tell her the truth.* • **stubbornness** N-UNCOUNT ❑ *Her refusal to talk was simple stubbornness.* 2 ADJ A **stubborn** stain is difficult to remove. ❑ *This treatment removes the most stubborn stains.*

stuck /stʌk/ 1 **Stuck** is the past tense and past participle of **stick**. 2 ADJ AFTER LINK-V If something is **stuck** in a particular position, it is fixed there and cannot move. ❑ *The tanker is stuck fast on the rocks.* 3 ADJ AFTER LINK-V If you are **stuck** in a place or in an unpleasant situation, you want to get away from it, but are unable to. ❑ *He was stuck in a line of slow-moving traffic.* 4 ADJ AFTER LINK-V If you **get stuck** when you are trying to do something, you are unable to continue doing it because it is too difficult. ❑ *They will be there to help if you get stuck.*

stud /stʌd/ (**studs**) 1 N-COUNT **Studs** are small pieces of metal which are attached to a surface for decoration. ❑ *...a black leather jacket with silver studs.* 2 N-COUNT **Studs** are small round earrings attached to a bar which goes through your ear. 3 N-UNCOUNT Horses or other animals that are kept **for stud** are kept to be used for breeding.
→ see **button**

studded /ˈstʌdɪd/ ADJ Something that is **studded** is decorated with studs. ❑ *...a gold bracelet studded with diamonds.*

student /ˈstjuːdənt, ˈstuː-/ (**students**) N-COUNT A **student** is a person who is studying at a university, college, or school. ❑ *...art students.*
→ see **graduation**

studio /ˈstjuːdiəʊ, ˈstuː-/ (**studios**) 1 N-COUNT A **studio** is a room where a designer, painter, or photographer works. ❑ *...Giorgio Armani at work in his studio.* 2 N-COUNT A **studio** is a room where radio or television programmes, records, or films are made. ❑ *...a recording studio.*
→ see **art**

Word Partnership Use *studio* with:

N. studio **album**, studio **audience**, studio **executives**, **film/movie** studio, **music** studio, **recording** studio, **television/TV** studio 2

study /ˈstʌdi/ (**studies, studying, studied**) 1 V-T/V-I & N-VAR If you **study**, or if you do a course of **study**, you spend time learning about a particular subject or subjects. ❑ *Kids would rather play than study.* ❑ *He studied History and Economics.* ❑ *Many students are forced to juggle their studies with paid employment.* 2 N-COUNT A **study of** a subject is a piece of research on it. ❑ *...the first study of English children's attitudes.* 3 N-PLURAL **Studies** are educational subjects. ❑ *...a business studies course.* 4 V-T If you **study** something, you look at it or consider it carefully. ❑ *He studied her face for a moment.* 5 N-COUNT A **study** in a house is a room used for reading, writing, and studying. 6 → see also **case study**
→ see **laboratory**

stuff /stʌf/ (**stuffs, stuffing, stuffed**) 1 N-UNCOUNT You can use **stuff** to refer to things in a general way, without mentioning the things themselves by name. ❑ *Don't tell me you still believe in all that stuff!* ❑ *...a place to buy computer stuff.* ❑ *He pointed to a duffle bag. 'That's my stuff.'* 2 V-T If you **stuff** something somewhere, you push it there quickly and roughly. ❑ *I stuffed my hands in my pockets.* 3 V-T If you **stuff** a container or space **with** something, you fill it with something or with a quantity of things until it is full. ❑ *...wallets stuffed with dollars.* 4 V-T If you **stuff** a bird such as a chicken, or a vegetable such as a pepper, you put a mixture of food inside it before cooking it. 5 V-T If a dead animal **is stuffed**, it is filled with a substance so that it can be preserved and displayed.

Thesaurus *stuff* Also look up:

N.	belongings, goods, material, substance 1
V.	crowd, fill, jam, squeeze 3

stuffing /ˈstʌfɪŋ/ (**stuffings**) 1 N-VAR **Stuffing** is a mixture of food that is put inside a bird such as a chicken before it is cooked. 2 N-UNCOUNT **Stuffing** is material that is put inside cushions or soft toys to fill them and make them firm.

stuffy /ˈstʌfi/ (**stuffier, stuffiest**) 1 ADJ If you describe a person or institution as **stuffy**, you are criticizing them for being formal and old-fashioned. [INFORMAL] ❑ *Why were grown-ups always so stuffy and slow to recognize good ideas?* 2 ADJ If a place is **stuffy**, it is unpleasantly warm and there is not enough fresh air. ❑ *...that stuffy, overheated apartment.*

stumble /ˈstʌmbəl/ (**stumbles, stumbling, stumbled**) 1 V-I If you **stumble**, you nearly fall while walking or running. ❑ *I stumbled sideways before landing flat on my back.* 2 V-I If you **stumble** while speaking, you make a mistake, and have to pause before saying the words properly. ❑ *She stumbled over her words sometimes.*

▶ **stumble across** or **stumble on** PHR-VERB If you **stumble across** something, or if you **stumble on** something, you discover it unexpectedly. ❑ *You may be lucky enough to stumble across a village fiesta.*

ˈstumbling block (**stumbling blocks**) N-COUNT A **stumbling block** is a problem which stops you from achieving something. ❑ *Money remains the main stumbling block to an agreement.*

stump /stʌmp/ (**stumps, stumping, stumped**) 1 N-COUNT A **stump** is a small part of something that remains when the rest of it has been removed or broken off. ❑ *...a tree stump.* 2 V-T If a question or problem **stumps** you, you cannot think of any solution or answer to it.

▶ **stump up** PHR-VERB If you **stump up** a sum of money, you pay the money that is required for something, often reluctantly. [BRIT, INFORMAL] ❑ *Customers do not have to stump up any cash for at least four weeks.*

stun /stʌn/ (**stuns, stunning, stunned**) 1 V-T If you **are stunned** by something, you are shocked or astonished by it and are therefore unable to speak or do anything. ❑ *Many people were stunned by the film's violent ending.* ● **stunned** ADJ ❑ *His suggestion was greeted with a stunned silence.* 2 V-T If a blow on the head **stuns** you, it makes you unconscious or confused and unsteady. 3 → see also **stunning**

stung /stʌŋ/ **Stung** is the past tense and past participle of **sting**.

stunk /stʌŋk/ **Stunk** is the past participle of **stink**.

stunning /ˈstʌnɪŋ/ ADJ A **stunning** person or thing is extremely beautiful or impressive. ❑ *The models looked stunning, as ever.* ❑ *...a stunning display of fireworks.* ● **stunningly** ADV ❑ *...stunningly beautiful countryside.*

Word Partnership Use *stunning* with:

N.	stunning **images**, stunning **views**

stunt /stʌnt/ (**stunts, stunting, stunted**) 1 N-COUNT A **stunt** is something interesting that someone does to get attention or publicity. ❑ *She turned her wedding into a publicity stunt.* 2 N-COUNT A **stunt** is a dangerous and exciting piece of action in a film. ❑ *The team will perform stunts including ramp-to-ramp jumps.* 3 V-T If something **stunts** the growth or development of a person or thing, it prevents them from growing or developing normally. ❑ *The disease stunted her growth.* ● **stunted** ADJ ❑ *...stunted trees with harsh dry leaves.*

stupid /ˈstjuːpɪd, AM ˈstuː-/ (**stupider, stupidest**) 1 ADJ If you say that someone or something is **stupid**, you mean that they show a lack of good judgement or intelligence and they are not at all sensible. ❑ *How could I have been so stupid?* ❑ *I made a stupid mistake.* ● **stupidly** ADV ❑ *We had stupidly been looking at the wrong figures.* ● **stupidity** /stjuːˈpɪdɪti, AM stuː-/ (**stupidities**) N-VAR ❑ *I stared at him, astonished by his stupidity.* 2 ADJ You say that something is **stupid** to indicate that you do not like it or that it annoys you. [INFORMAL] ❑ *Friendship is much more important to me than a stupid old ring!*

Word Partnership Use *stupid* with:

N.	stupid **idea**, stupid **man**, stupid **mistake**, stupid **people**, stupid **question** 1 stupid **things** 1 2
V.	**(don't) do anything/*something*** stupid, **feel** stupid, **look** stupid 1 **think *something* is** stupid 1 2

sturdy /ˈstɜːdi/ (**sturdier, sturdiest**) ADJ Someone or something that is **sturdy** looks strong and is unlikely to be easily injured or damaged. ❑ *She was a short, sturdy woman.* ● **sturdily** ADV ❑ *...a tall, sturdily-built man.*

stutter /ˈstʌtə/ (**stutters, stuttering, stuttered**) V-I & N-COUNT If someone **stutters**, or if they **have** a **stutter**, they have difficulty speaking because they keep repeating the first sound of a word. ❑ *He spoke with a pronounced stutter.* ● **stuttering** N-UNCOUNT ❑ *Stuttering, which usually starts in childhood, can take different forms.*

style /staɪl/ (**styles, styling, styled**) 1 N-COUNT The **style of** something is the general way it is done or presented. ❑ *His writing style is clear and straightforward.* ❑ *...American-style management.* 2 N-UNCOUNT If places or people **have style**, they are smart and elegant. ❑ *The hotel, a 20-minute drive away, has style.* 3 N-VAR The **style** of a product is its design. ❑ *Several styles of hat were available.* ❑ *Each design is very different in style.* ❑ *Guests have been asked to dress 1920s-style.* 4 V-T If something such as a car or someone's hair **is styled** in a particular way, it is designed or shaped in that way. ❑ *Her thick blond hair had been styled before the trip.* ❑ *...classically styled clothes.*

Word Partnership Use *style* with:

ADJ.	**distinctive** style, **particular** style, **personal** style 1 3
N.	**leadership** style, **learning** style, style **of life**, **management** style, **music** style, **prose** style, **writing** style 1 **differences in** style 1-3

S

stylish /'staɪlɪʃ/ ADJ Someone or something that is **stylish** is smart, elegant, and fashionable. ❑ *...the stylish shops of Buchanan Street.* • **stylishly** ADV ❑ *...stylishly dressed middle-aged women.*

stylistic /staɪ'lɪstɪk/ ADJ **Stylistic** describes things relating to the methods and techniques used in creating a piece of writing, music, or art. • **stylistically** ADV ❑ *Stylistically, this book is very different from her last.*

stylized [BRIT] also **stylised** /'staɪlaɪzd/ ADJ Something that is **stylized** uses various artistic conventions in order to create an effect. ❑ *...highly stylised furniture designs.*

suave /swɑːv/ (**suaver, suavest**) ADJ If you describe a man as **suave**, you think he is charming, polite, and elegant, but not sincere.

sub /sʌb/ (**subs**) **1** N-COUNT In team games such as football, a **sub** is a player who is brought into a match to replace another player. [BRIT] ❑ *Connell joined Hegart on the subs' bench.* **2** N-COUNT A **sub** is a **submarine.** [INFORMAL]

subcommittee also **sub-committee** /'sʌbkəmɪti/ (**subcommittees**) N-COUNT A **subcommittee** is a small committee made up of members of a larger committee.

subconscious /ˌsʌb'kɒnʃəs/ **1** N-SING **Your subconscious** is the part of your mind that can influence you even though you are not aware of it. ❑ *The memory of it all was locked deep in my subconscious.* **2** ADJ A **subconscious** feeling or action exists in or is influenced by your subconscious. ❑ *...the subconscious need for power.* • **subconsciously** ADV ❑ *Subconsciously I had known that I would not be in danger.*

Word Link	
	sub ≈ below : subculture, submarine, submerge

subculture /'sʌbkʌltʃə/ (**subcultures**) N-COUNT A **subculture** consists of the ideas, art, and way of life of a particular group within a society, which are different from those of the rest of the society. ❑ *...the violent subculture of London youth gangs.*
→ see **culture**

subdivision /ˌsʌbdɪ'vɪʒən/ (**subdivisions**) **1** N-COUNT A **subdivision** is an area or section which is a part of a larger area or section. ❑ *Months are a conventional subdivision of the year.* **2** N-COUNT A **subdivision** is an area of land for building houses on. [AM] ❑ *...a 400-home subdivision.*

S

subdue /səb'djuː, AM -'duː/ (**subdues, subduing, subdued**) V-T If soldiers or the police **subdue** a group of people, they defeat them or bring them under control by using force. ❑ *They have not been able to subdue the rebels.*

subdued /səb'djuːd, AM -'duːd/ **1** ADJ Someone who is **subdued** is quiet, often because they are sad. ❑ *The audience are strangely subdued, clapping politely after each song.* **2** ADJ **Subdued** lights, feelings, sounds, or colours are not very noticeable. ❑ *Subdued lighting helps give this bistro a relaxed and comfortable feel.*

subject (**subjects, subjecting, subjected**) **1** N-COUNT /'sʌbdʒɪkt/ The **subject of** a conversation, letter, or book is the person or thing that is being discussed or written about. ❑ *We got on to the subject of relationships.* ❑ *The battle is the subject of a new film.* ❑ *He's now the subject of an official inquiry.* **2** N-COUNT A **subject** is an area of knowledge that is studied at school, college, or university. ❑ *Mathematics was their favourite subject.* **3** N-COUNT In grammar, the **subject** of a clause is the noun group which refers to the person or thing that does the action expressed by the verb. For example, in 'My cat keeps catching birds', 'my cat' is the subject. **4** ADJ AFTER LINK-V If someone or something is **subject to** something, they are affected, or likely to be affected, by it. ❑ *Prices may be subject to change.* **5** PREP If an event will take place **subject to** a condition, it will take place only if that condition exists. ❑ *Tickets are £10 each, subject to availability.* **6** N-COUNT The people who live in or belong to a particular country, usually one ruled by a monarch, are the **subjects** of that monarch or country. ❑ *...British subjects.* **7** V-T /səb'dʒekt/ If you **subject** someone **to** something unpleasant, you make them experience it. ❑ *He subjected her to six years of bullying.*

Word Partnership	Use *subject* with:
ADJ.	**controversial** subject, **favourite** subject, **touchy** subject **1**
N.	subject **of a debate**, subject **of an investigation**, **knowledge of a** subject **research** subject **1 2**
	subject **of a sentence**, subject **of a verb** **3**
V.	**broach a** subject, **study a** subject **1 2**
PREP.	subject **to approval**, subject **to availability**, subject **to laws**, subject **to scrutiny**, subject **to a tax** **4**

subjective /səb'dʒektɪv/ ADJ Something that is **subjective** is based on personal opinions and feelings. ❑ *Taste in art is a subjective matter.* • **subjectively** ADV ❑ *She subjectively considered herself a winner.* • **subjectivity** N-UNCOUNT ❑ *...the film-maker's subjectivity.*

'subject matter N-UNCOUNT The **subject matter** of a conversation, book, or film is the thing, person, or idea that is being discussed, written about, or shown. ❑ *Artists were given greater freedom in their choice of subject matter.*

subjunctive /səb'dʒʌŋktɪv/ N-SING In English, a clause expressing a wish or suggestion can be put in **the subjunctive**, or in **the subjunctive mood**, by using the base form of a verb or 'were'. An example is 'He asked that they all be removed'.

sublime /sə'blaɪm/ ADJ & N-SING If you describe something as **sublime**, or as **the sublime**, you mean that it has a wonderful quality that affects you deeply. [LITERARY] ❑ *...the sublime view across the glittering lake.*

Word Link	
	mar ≈ sea : marine, maritime, submarine

submarine /ˌsʌbmə'riːn/ (**submarines**) N-COUNT A **submarine** is a ship that can travel below the surface of the sea.

Word Link	
	merg ≈ sinking : emerge, merge, submerge

submerge /səb'mɜːdʒ/ (**submerges, submerging, submerged**) **1** V-T/V-I If something **submerges** or **is submerged**, it goes below the surface of the water. ❑ *The river burst its banks, submerging an entire village.* **2** V-T If you **submerge yourself in** an activity, you give all your attention to it. ❑ *Vicky tried to submerge herself in her work.*

submission /səb'mɪʃən/ **1** N-UNCOUNT **Submission** is a state in which people accept that they are under the control of someone else. ❑ *They tried to terrify him into submission.* **2** N-UNCOUNT **The submission of** a proposal or application is the act of sending it to someone, so they can decide whether to accept it or not. [FORMAL]

submissive /səb'mɪsɪv/ ADJ If you are **submissive**, you behave in a quiet obedient way. ● **submissively** ADV ❑ *The troops submissively lay down their weapons.*

submit /səb'mɪt/ (**submits, submitting, submitted**) **1** V-I If you **submit to** something, you accept it reluctantly, for example because you are not powerful enough to resist it. ❑ *Mrs Jones submitted to an operation on her knee.* **2** V-T If you **submit** a proposal or application to someone, you send it to them so they can decide whether to accept it or not. ❑ *Headteachers have submitted a claim for a 9 per cent pay rise.*

subordinate (**subordinates, subordinating, subordinated**) **1** N-COUNT /sə'bɔːdɪnət/ Your **subordinate** is someone who is in a less important position than you in the organization that you both work for. **2** ADJ Something or someone who is **subordinate to** something or someone else is considered to be less important than the other thing or person. ❑ *Science became subordinate to technology.* ❑ *Women were regarded as subordinate to men.* **3** V-T /sə'bɔːdɪneɪt/ If you **subordinate** one thing **to** another, you treat it as less important than the other thing. ❑ *...subordinating their own culture to that of the host country.* ● **subordination** N-UNCOUNT ❑ *...governmental subordination to the president.*

sub,ordinate 'clause (**subordinate clauses**) N-COUNT A **subordinate clause** is a clause in a sentence which adds to the information given in the main clause. It cannot usually stand alone as a sentence.

subscribe /səb'skraɪb/ (**subscribes, subscribing, subscribed**) **1** V-I If you **subscribe to** an opinion or belief, you are one of a number of people who have this opinion or belief. ❑ *I don't subscribe to the belief that being slim is the only way to be beautiful.* **2** V-I If you **subscribe to** a service, magazine, or organization, you pay money regularly to receive the service or magazine, or to belong to or support the organization. ❑ *...computer-users who subscribe to the Internet.* ● **subscriber** (**subscribers**) N-COUNT ❑ *I have been a subscriber to Railway Magazine for many years.*

subscription /səb'skrɪpʃən/ (**subscriptions**) N-COUNT A **subscription** is an amount of money that you pay regularly to receive a service or magazine, or to belong to or support an organization.

subsequent /'sʌbsɪkwənt/ ADJ BEFORE N **Subsequent** means existing or happening after the time or event that has just been referred to. ❑ *The book was banned in the US, as were his two subsequent books.* ● **subsequently** ADV ❑ *He was born in Hong Kong where he subsequently practised as a lawyer.*

subservient /səb'sɜːviənt/ **1** ADJ If you are **subservient**, you do whatever someone wants you to do. ❑ *Women had been subservient for so long.* ● **subservience** N-UNCOUNT ❑ *...obedience and subservience to authority.* **2** ADJ AFTER LINK-V If you treat one thing as **subservient to** another, you treat it as less important than the other thing. ❑ *...the philosophy that the weak should be subservient to the strong.*

subside /səb'saɪd/ (**subsides, subsiding, subsided**) **1** V-I If a feeling or sound **subsides**, it becomes less strong or loud. ❑ *Catherine's sobs finally subsided.* **2** V-I If the ground or a building **is subsiding**, it is sinking to a lower level.

subsidiary /səb'sɪdiəri, AM -dieri/ (**subsidiaries**) **1** N-COUNT A **subsidiary** is a company which is part of a larger and more important company. ❑ *...British Asia Airways, a subsidiary of British Airways.* **2** ADJ If something is **subsidiary**, it is less important than something else with which it is connected. ❑ *All students take two main subjects and two subsidiary subjects.*

subsidize [BRIT also **subsidise**] /'sʌbsɪdaɪz/ (**subsidizes, subsidizing, subsidized**) V-T If an authority **subsidizes** something, they pay part of the cost of it. ❑ *The government continues to subsidize the production of eggs and beef.* ● **subsidized** ADJ ❑ *Subsidised tickets at £10, £15 and £20 represent a minimum saving of £17 a ticket.*

subsidy /'sʌbsɪdi/ (**subsidies**) N-VAR A **subsidy** is money paid by an authority in order to help an industry or business, or to pay for a public service. ❑ *...farming subsidies.*

subsistence /səb'sɪstəns/ N-UNCOUNT **Subsistence** is the condition of only having just enough food or money to stay alive.

substance /'sʌbstəns/ (**substances**) **1** N-COUNT A **substance** is a solid, powder, liquid, or gas. ❑ *...a soft black substance that smells like fresh soil.* **2** N-UNCOUNT **Substance** is the quality of being important or significant. [FORMAL] ❑ *They chattered away, but said nothing of any substance.* **3** N-SING **The substance of** what someone says or writes is the main thing that they are trying to say. **4** N-UNCOUNT If you say that something has no **substance**, you mean that it is not true. [FORMAL] ❑ *There is no substance in these rumours.*

Word Partnership Use *substance* with:

ADJ.	**banned** substance, **chemical** substance, **natural** substance **1**
N.	**lack of** substance **2**

substantial /səb'stænʃəl/ **1** ADJ **Substantial** means large in amount or degree. ❑ *That is a substantial improvement.* ● **substantially** ADV ❑ *The firm cut jobs substantially in the months that followed.* **2** ADJ A **substantial** building is large and strongly built. ❑ *...a substantial late Victorian house.*

Word Partnership Use *substantial* with:

ADV.	**fairly** substantial, **very** substantial
N.	substantial **amount**, substantial **changes**, substantial **difference**, substantial **evidence**, substantial **improvement**, substantial **increase**, substantial **loss**, substantial **number**, substantial **part**, substantial **progress**, substantial **savings**, substantial **support** **1**

S

substantially /səb'stænʃəli/ **1** ADV If something is **substantially** correct, it is generally correct. [FORMAL] ❑ *He checked the details and found them substantially correct.* **2** → see also **substantial**

substantiate /səb'stænʃieɪt/ (**substantiates, substantiating, substantiated**) V-T To **substantiate** a statement or a story means to supply evidence proving that it is true. [FORMAL] ❑ *There is no evidence to substantiate the claims.*

substitute /'sʌbstɪtju:t, AM -tu:t/ (**substitutes, substituting, substituted**) **1** V-T/V-I If you **substitute** one thing **for** another, you use it instead of the other thing. ❑ *Would phone conversations substitute for cosy chats over lunch?* ● **substitution** (**substitutions**) N-VAR ❑ *...the substitution of machines for human skills.* **2** N-COUNT A **substitute** is something or someone that you use instead of something or someone else. ❑ *Reduced-calorie cheese is a great substitute for cream cheese.*

Word Link	*terr ≈ earth : subterranean, terrain, territory*

subterranean /ˌsʌbtə'reɪniən/ ADJ A **subterranean** river or tunnel is underground. [FORMAL]

subtle /'sʌtəl/ (**subtler, subtlest**) **1** ADJ Something **subtle** is not immediately obvious or noticeable. ❑ *...the slow and subtle changes that take place in all living things.* ● **subtly** ADV ❑ *The truth is subtly different.* **2** ADJ **Subtle** smells, tastes, sounds, or colours are pleasantly complex and delicate. ● **subtly** ADV ❑ *...subtly coloured rugs.*

subtlety /'sʌtəlti/ (**subtleties**) **1** N-COUNT **Subtleties** are very small details or differences which are not obvious. ❑ *...the subtleties of human behaviour.* **2** N-UNCOUNT **Subtlety** is the quality of not being immediately obvious or noticeable. ❑ *African dance is vigorous, but full of subtlety.* **3** N-UNCOUNT **Subtlety** is the ability to use indirect methods to achieve something. ❑ *They were hoping to approach the topic with more subtlety.*

Word Link	*tract ≈ dragging, drawing : contract, subtract, tractor*

subtract /səb'trækt/ (**subtracts, subtracting, subtracted**) V-T If you **subtract** one number **from** another, you take the first number away from the second. ● **subtraction** (**subtractions**) N-VAR ❑ *She's learning simple addition and subtraction.*

S

Word Link	*urb ≈ city : suburb, suburbia, urban*

suburb /'sʌbɜ:b/ (**suburbs**) N-COUNT The **suburbs of** a city are the areas on the edge of it where people live.
→ see **city, transportation**

suburban /sə'bɜ:bən/ **1** ADJ BEFORE N **Suburban** means relating to a suburb. ❑ *...a suburban shopping centre.* **2** ADJ If you describe something as **suburban**, you mean that it is dull and conventional. ❑ *His clothes are very suburban.*

suburbia /sə'bɜ:biə/ N-UNCOUNT **Suburbia** is sometimes used to refer to the suburbs of cities and large towns considered as a whole. ❑ *I like British suburbia, with its neat, cared-for gardens.*

subversion /səb'vɜ:ʃən, AM -ʒən/ N-UNCOUNT **Subversion** is the attempt to weaken or destroy a political system or a government. ❑ *He was arrested on charges of subversion.*

subversive /səb'vɜ:sɪv/ (**subversives**) **1** ADJ Something that is **subversive** is intended to weaken or destroy a political system or government. ❑ *The play was banned as subversive.* **2** N-COUNT **Subversives** are people who attempt to weaken or destroy a political system or government.

Word Link	*verg, vert ≈ turning : converge, diverge, subvert*

subvert /səb'vɜ:t/ (**subverts, subverting, subverted**) V-T To **subvert** something means to destroy its power and influence. [FORMAL] ❑ *...a plot to subvert the state.*

subway /'sʌbweɪ/ (**subways**) **1** N-COUNT In British English, a **subway** is a passage for pedestrians underneath a busy road. The American word is **underpass**. **2** N-COUNT In American English, a **subway** is an underground railway. The British word is **underground**.
→ see **transportation**

succeed /sək'si:d/ (**succeeds, succeeding, succeeded**) **1** V-I To **succeed** means to achieve the result that you wanted or to perform in a satisfactory way. ❑ *We have succeeded in persuading cinemas to show the film.* ❑ *...the skills and qualities needed to succeed.* **2** V-T/V-I If you **succeed** another person, you take over their job or position when they leave. ❑ *Prince Rainier III succeeded to the throne on 9 May 1949.*

Thesaurus	*succeed* Also look up:
V.	accomplish, conquer, master; *(ant.)* fail **1**
	displace, replace; *(ant.)* precede **2**

success /sək'ses/ N-UNCOUNT **Success** is the achievement of something you have wanted to achieve. ❑ *Work was the key to success.* ❑ *We were amazed by the play's success.*

Word Partnership	Use *success* with:
N.	success **of a business, chance for/of** success, success **or failure, key to** success, **lack of** success, **measure of** success
ADJ.	**academic** success, **commercial** success, **great** success, **huge** success, **recent** success, **tremendous** success
V.	**achieve** success, success **depends on** ***something***, **enjoy** success

successful /sək'sesfʊl/ ADJ Someone or something that is **successful** achieves a desired result or performs in a satisfactory way. ❑ *How successful will this new treatment be?* ❑ *She is a successful lawyer.* ● **successfully** ADV ❑ *The doctors have successfully concluded preliminary tests.*

succession /sək'seʃən/ (**successions**) **1** N-COUNT A **succession of** things of the same kind is a number of them that exist or happen one after the other. ❑ *Adams took a succession of jobs.* ❑ *She scored three goals in quick succession.* **2** N-UNCOUNT **Succession** is the act or right of being the next person to have a particular job or position. ❑ *She is next in line of succession to the throne.*

successive /sək'sesɪv/ ADJ **Successive** means

happening or existing one after another without a break. ❑ *Tom was the winner for a second successive year.*

successor /sək'sesə/ (**successors**) N-COUNT Someone's **successor** is the person who takes their job after they have left.

suc'cess story (**success stories**) N-COUNT Someone or something that is a **success story** is very successful, often unexpectedly or in spite of unfavourable conditions.

succinct /sək'sɪŋkt/ ADJ Something that is **succinct** expresses facts or ideas clearly and in few words; used showing approval. • **succinctly** ADV ❑ *Readers are told succinctly what they need to know.*

Word Link	*ulent ≈ full of : fraudulent, opulent, succulent*

succulent /'sʌkjʊlənt/ ADJ **Succulent** food is juicy and delicious. ❑ *...succulent vegetables.*

succumb /sə'kʌm/ (**succumbs, succumbing, succumbed**) V-T If you **succumb to** persuasion or desire, you are unable to resist it. ❑ *Don't succumb to the temptation to have a dessert.*

such /sʌtʃ/ **1** PREDET & DET & PRON You use **such** to refer to the person or thing you have just mentioned or to something similar. ❑ *How can we make sense of such a story as this?* ❑ *There have been previous attacks on our members. We regard such methods as entirely unacceptable.* ❑ *We are scared to go out – such is the atmosphere here.* **2** PREDET & DET You use **such** to emphasize the degree or extent of something. ❑ *It was such a pleasant surprise.* ❑ *I have never felt such anger.* **3** PHRASE You use **such as** or **such...as** to introduce one or more examples of something. ❑ *...serious offences, such as assault.* ❑ *...such careers as teaching, nursing, hairdressing and catering.* **4** PHRASE You use **such...that** when saying what the result or consequence of something is. ❑ *He was in such a hurry that he almost pushed me over.* ❑ *We design our maps in such a way that they are both clear and usable.* **5** PHRASE You use **as such** with a negative to indicate that a word or expression is not a very accurate description of the actual situation. ❑ *I am not a learner as such – I used to ride a bike years ago.* **6** PHRASE You use **as such** after a noun to indicate that you are considering that thing on its own, separately from other things or factors. ❑ *Mr Simon said he was not against taxes as such.* **7** PHRASE You use **such and such** to refer to something without being specific. ❑ *I said, 'Well what time'll I get to Leeds?' and he said such and such a time.*

Usage

Such is followed by **a** when the noun is something that can be counted. ❑ *...such a pleasant surprise.* It is not followed by **a** when the noun is plural or something that cannot be counted. ❑ *...such beautiful women.* ❑ *...such power.* You do not use **such** when you are talking about something that is present, or about the place where you are. You need to use the phrases **like that** or **like this**. For example, if you are admiring someone's watch, you do not say 'I'd like such a watch'. You say **'I'd like a watch like that'**. Similarly, you do not say about the town where you are living 'There's not much to do in such a town'. You say **'There's not much to do in a town like this'**. **Such** in other contexts is quite formal.

suck /sʌk/ (**sucks, sucking, sucked**) **1** V-T/V-I If you **suck** something, you hold it in your mouth and pull at it with the muscles in your cheeks and tongue, for example in order to get liquid out of it. ❑ *You may prefer to give her a dummy to suck instead.* ❑ *His faced looked like he'd just sucked on a lemon.* **2** V-T If something **sucks** a liquid, gas, or object in a particular direction, it draws it there with a powerful force. ❑ *...a simple air pump that continuously sucks in the air.*

sucker /'sʌkə/ (**suckers**) **1** N-COUNT If you call someone a **sucker**, you mean that it is easy to cheat or fool them. [INFORMAL] **2** N-COUNT If you describe someone as a **sucker for** something, you mean that they find it very difficult to resist it. [INFORMAL] ❑ *I'm such a sucker for romance.* **3** N-COUNT On a plant, a **sucker** is a new growth that is sent out from the base of the plant or from its root.

suckle /'sʌkəl/ (**suckles, suckling, suckled**) **1** V-T When a mother **suckles** her baby, she feeds it by letting it suck milk from her breast. **2** V-I When a baby **suckles**, it sucks milk from its mother's breast. [FORMAL] ❑ *As the baby suckles, a supply of milk is produced.*

sudden /'sʌdən/ **1** ADJ Something that is **sudden** happens quickly and unexpectedly. ❑ *...the sudden death of her father.* • **suddenly** ADV ❑ *...David's account of why he suddenly left London.* • **suddenness** N-UNCOUNT ❑ *The enemy seemed stunned by the suddenness of the attack.* **2** PHRASE If something happens **all of a sudden**, it happens quickly and unexpectedly. ❑ *All of a sudden she fell silent.*

sue /suː/ (**sues, suing, sued**) V-T/V-I If you **sue** someone, you start a legal case against them to claim money from them because they have harmed you in some way. ❑ *She threatened to sue him for unfair dismissal.* ❑ *If I were her, I'd sue.*

suede /sweɪd/ N-UNCOUNT **Suede** is thin soft leather with a slightly rough surface.

suffer /'sʌfə/ (**suffers, suffering, suffered**) **1** V-T/V-I If you **suffer** pain or an illness, or if you **suffer from** a pain or illness, you are badly affected by it. ❑ *She began to suffer stomach cramps.* ❑ *Many team members suffered from diarrhoea.* • **sufferer** (**sufferers**) N-COUNT ❑ *...arthritis sufferers.* **2** V-T/V-I If you **suffer** or **suffer** something bad, you are in a situation in which something painful, harmful, or very unpleasant happens to you. ❑ *They suffered complete defeat.* ❑ *It is the poor who have suffered most from food shortages.* **3** V-I If something **suffers**, it becomes worse in quality or condition as a result of neglect or an unfavourable situation. ❑ *I'm not surprised that your studies are suffering.*

suffering /'sʌfərɪŋ/ (**sufferings**) N-VAR **Suffering** is serious pain which someone feels in their body or their mind. ❑ *He wanted to die in order to put an end to his suffering.*

suffice /sə'faɪs/ (**suffices, sufficing, sufficed**) V-I If something will **suffice**, it will be enough to achieve a purpose or to fulfil a need. [FORMAL] ❑ *You don't have to thank him in person; a polite letter will suffice.*

sufficient /sə'fɪʃənt/ **1** ADJ If something is **sufficient** for a particular purpose, there is as much of it as is necessary. ❑ *His savings were not*

S

sufficient to cover the cost. • **sufficiently** ADV ❑ *It was many months before I had sufficiently recovered to move about.* **2** ADJ BEFORE N If something is a **sufficient** cause or condition for something to happen, it can happen. [FORMAL] ❑ *There was not sufficient cause for such bad treatment.*

Word Link *fix ≈ fastening : fixture, prefix, suffix*

suffix /'sʌfɪks/ (**suffixes**) N-COUNT A **suffix** is a letter or group of letters added to the end of a word in order to form a different word, often of a different word class. For example, the suffix '-ly' can be added to the adjective 'quick' to form the adverb 'quickly'.

suffocate /'sʌfəkeɪt/ (**suffocates, suffocating, suffocated**) V-T/V-I If someone **suffocates**, or is **suffocated**, they die because there is no air for them to breathe. • **suffocation** N-UNCOUNT ❑ *Many of the victims died of suffocation.*

sugar /'ʃʊgə/ (**sugars**) **1** N-UNCOUNT **Sugar** is a sweet substance, often in the form of white or brown crystals, used to sweeten food and drink. **2** N-COUNT If someone takes **sugar** in their tea or coffee, they have one or more small spoonfuls of sugar in it. ❑ *How many sugars do you take?*
→ see Word Web: sugar

suggest /sə'dʒest, AM səg'dʒ-/ (**suggests, suggesting, suggested**) **1** V-T If you **suggest** something, you put forward a plan or idea for someone to consider. ❑ *I suggested we walk to the park.* ❑ *I suggested that we should charter a boat.* ❑ *I suggested to Mike that we go out for a meal.*

Usage

Note that **suggest** cannot usually be followed directly by a noun or pronoun referring to a person. You generally have to put the preposition **to** in front of it. You do not 'suggest someone something', you '**suggest something to someone**'. ❑ *John Caskey first suggested this idea to me.* Nor do you 'suggest someone to do something'. You '**suggest that someone does something**'. A subjunctive is sometimes used in the 'that' clause. ❑ *Beatrice suggested that he spend the summer at their place.*

2 V-T If you **suggest** that something is the case, you say something which you believe is the case. ❑ *I'm not suggesting that is what is happening.* **3** V-T If one thing **suggests** another, it implies it or makes you think that it is the case. ❑ *Reports suggested that a meeting would take place on Sunday.*

Word Partnership Use *suggest* with:

N. **analysts** suggest, **experts** suggest, **researchers** suggest **1**
data suggest, **findings** suggest, **results** suggest, **studies** suggest, **surveys** suggest **3**

suggestion /sə'dʒestʃən, AM səg'dʒ-/ (**suggestions**) **1** N-COUNT If you make a **suggestion**, you put forward an idea or plan for someone to think about. ❑ *John made some suggestions for improvements.* **2** N-COUNT A **suggestion** is something that someone says which implies that something is the case. ❑ *There are suggestions that jealousy drove her to murder.* **3** N-SING If there is a **suggestion of** something, there is a slight sign of it. ❑ *...the suggestion of a smile.* **4** N-UNCOUNT **Suggestion** means giving people a particular idea by associating it with other ideas. ❑ *...the power of suggestion.*

Word Partnership Use *suggestion* with:

V. **follow a** suggestion, **make a** suggestion **1**
reject a suggestion **1**

suggestive /sə'dʒestɪv, AM səg'dʒ-/ **1** ADJ AFTER LINK-V If one thing is **suggestive of** another, it gives a hint of it or reminds you of it. ❑ *...long, curving nails suggestive of animal claws.* **2** ADJ **Suggestive** remarks cause people to think about sex, often in a way that makes them feel uncomfortable. • **suggestively** ADV ❑ *She winked suggestively.*

suicidal /ˌsuːɪ'saɪdəl/ **1** ADJ People who are **suicidal** want to kill themselves. **2** ADJ If you describe an action or behaviour as **suicidal**, you mean that it is very dangerous. ❑ *It would be suicidal to attempt the climb in the dark.*

Word Link *cide ≈ killing : genocide, pesticide, suicide*

suicide /'suːɪsaɪd/ (**suicides**) **1** N-VAR People who commit **suicide** deliberately kill themselves. ❑ *...a reduction in the number of suicides.* **2** ADJ BEFORE N The people involved in a **suicide** attack, mission, or bombing do not expect to survive. ❑ *He had been*

S

Word Web sugar

Sugar cane was discovered in prehistoric New Guinea*. As people moved across the Pacific Islands and into India and China, they brought sugar cane with them. At first, people just chewed on the cane. They liked the **sweet taste**. When sugar cane reached the Middle East, people discovered how to **refine** it into **crystals**. **Brown sugar** is made by stopping the refining process earlier. This leaves some of the molasses syrup in the sugar. Today two-fifths of sugar comes from **beets**. Refined sugar is used in many **foods** and **beverages**. Too much sugar can cause many problems, such as **obesity** and **diabetes**.

New Guinea: a large island in the southern Pacific Ocean.

trained as a suicide bomber.

Word Partnership Use *suicide* with:

V. **attempt** suicide, **commit** suicide 1
N. suicide **prevention**, suicide **rate**, **risk of** suicide 2

suit /suːt/ (**suits, suiting, suited**) 1 N-COUNT A **suit** is a matching jacket and trousers, or a matching jacket and skirt. 2 N-COUNT A **suit** can be a piece of clothing worn for a particular activity. ❑ *...bathing suits.* 3 V-T If a piece of clothing or a particular style or colour **suits** you, it makes you look attractive. 4 V-T If you say that something **suits** you, you mean that it is convenient, acceptable, or appropriate for you. ❑ *Would nine o'clock suit you?* 5 N-COUNT In a court of law, a **suit** is a legal action taken by one person against another. 6 N-COUNT A **suit** is one of the four types of card in a set of playing cards. These are hearts, diamonds, clubs, and spades. 7 PHRASE If people **follow suit**, they do what someone else has just done. ❑ *I intend to avoid such companies, and I hope other people will follow suit.* 8 → see also **suited**
→ see **clothing**

Usage

You do not use the verb **suit** if clothes are simply the right size for you. The verb you need is **fit**. ❑ *Even the smallest size doesn't fit him.* ❑ *The gloves didn't fit.* You can say that something **suits** a person or place if it looks attractive on that person or in that place. However, you cannot usually say that one colour, pattern, or object **suits** another. The verb you need is **match**. ❑ *She wore a straw hat with a yellow ribbon to match her yellow dress.* ❑ *His clothes don't quite match.*

suitable /ˈsuːtəbəl/ ADJ Someone or something that is **suitable for** a particular purpose or occasion is right or acceptable for it. ❑ *She had no dress suitable for the occasion.* ❑ *...a suitable venue.* • **suitability** N-UNCOUNT ❑ *There are some who doubt his suitability for the job.* • **suitably** ADV ❑ *...suitably qualified staff.*

Word Link *cas ≈ box, hold : case, encase, suitcase*

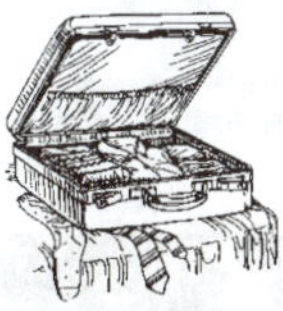
suitcase

suitcase /ˈsuːtkeɪs/ (**suitcases**) N-COUNT A **suitcase** is a case for carrying clothes when you are travelling.

suite /swiːt/ (**suites**) 1 N-COUNT A **suite** is a set of rooms in a hotel or other building. ❑ *...a new suite of offices.* 2 N-COUNT A **suite** is a set of matching furniture. ❑ *...a three-piece suite.* 3 N-COUNT A bathroom **suite** is a matching bath, basin, and toilet. ❑ *...the terrible pink suite in the bathroom.*
→ see **hotel**

suited /ˈsuːtɪd/ ADJ AFTER LINK-V If something or someone is **suited to** a particular purpose or person, they are right or appropriate for that purpose or person. ❑ *Satellites are uniquely suited to provide this information.* ❑ *As a couple they seemed ideally suited.*

Word Partnership Use *suited* with:

ADV. **ill** suited, **perfectly** suited, **uniquely** suited, **well** suited
PREP. suited **to** ***something***

suitor /ˈsuːtə/ (**suitors**) N-COUNT A woman's **suitor** is a man who wants to marry her. [DATED]

sulfur /ˈsʌlfə/ → see **sulphur**

sulk /sʌlk/ (**sulks, sulking, sulked**) V-I & N-COUNT If you **sulk**, or if you go into a **sulk**, you are silent and bad-tempered for a while because you are annoyed. ❑ *If I beat him, he goes off and has a sulk.*

sullen /ˈsʌlən/ ADJ A **sullen** person is bad-tempered and does not speak much. • **sullenly** ADV ❑ *'I've never seen it before,' Harry said sullenly.*

sulphur [AM **sulfur**] /ˈsʌlfə/ N-UNCOUNT **Sulphur** is a yellow chemical which has a strong unpleasant smell.
→ see **firework**

sultan /ˈsʌltən/ (**sultans**) N-COUNT A **sultan** is a ruler in some Muslim countries.

sultry /ˈsʌltri/ (**sultrier, sultriest**) 1 ADJ **Sultry** weather is hot and humid. 2 ADJ A **sultry** woman is attractive in a way that suggests hidden passion. [WRITTEN]

sum /sʌm/ (**sums, summing, summed**) 1 N-COUNT A **sum of** money is an amount of it. ❑ *...the relatively modest sum of £50,000.* 2 → see also **lump sum** 3 N-COUNT A **sum** is a simple calculation in arithmetic. ❑ *I can't do my sums.* 4 N-SING In mathematics, **the sum of** two numbers is the number that is obtained when they are added together. ❑ *The sum of all the angles of a triangle is 180 degrees.* 5 PHRASE You use **in sum** to introduce a statement that briefly describes a situation. [FORMAL] ❑ *In sum, this is a splendid little book.*
▶ **sum up** 1 PHR-VERB If you **sum up** or **sum** something **up**, you briefly describe the main features of something. ❑ *Well, to sum up, what is the message that you are trying to communicate?* ❑ *The atmosphere is best summed up as peaceful.* 2 → see also **summing up**

Word Partnership Use *sum* with:

ADJ. **equal** sum, **large** sum, **substantial** sum, **undisclosed** sum 1
N. sum **of money** 1

summarize [BRIT also **summarise**] /ˈsʌməraɪz/ (**summarizes, summarizing, summarized**) V-T If you **summarize** something, you give a brief description of its main points. ❑ *The article can be summarized in three sentences.* ❑ *To summarise, this is a clever approach to a common problem.*

Word Link *summ ≈ highest point : consummate, summary, summit*

summary /ˈsʌməri/ (**summaries**) 1 N-COUNT A **summary** is a short account of something giving the main points but not the details. ❑ *...a summary of the report.* 2 ADJ BEFORE N **Summary** actions are done without delay and without careful consideration. [FORMAL] ❑ *...reports of summary executions.* • **summarily** /ˈsʌmərili/ ADV ❑ *Several*

S

prisoners had been summarily executed.

summer /ˈsʌmə/ (**summers**) N-VAR **Summer** is the season between spring and autumn. In summer the weather is usually warm or hot. ❑ *The northern part of Iceland has no ice or snow in summer.*

ˈsummer ˌcamp (**summer camps**) N-COUNT In the United States, a **summer camp** is a place in the country where children can stay during the school summer holidays.

summertime also **summer time** /ˈsʌmətaɪm/ N-UNCOUNT **Summertime** is the period of time during which summer lasts. ❑ *It's a very beautiful place in summertime.*

ˌsumming ˈup (**summings up**) N-COUNT In a court of law, the **summing up** is a summary of all the evidence that has been presented at the trial.

Word Link	**summ ≈ highest point : consummate, summary, summit**

summit /ˈsʌmɪt/ (**summits**) **1** N-COUNT A **summit** is a meeting between the leaders of two or more countries to discuss important matters. ❑ *...last month's Arab summit in Baghdad.* **2** N-COUNT The **summit** of a mountain is the top of it.
→ see **mountain**

summon /ˈsʌmən/ (**summons, summoning, summoned**) **1** V-T If you **summon** someone, you order them to come to you. ❑ *Her father summoned her to his office.* **2** V-T & PHR-VERB If you **summon** the courage, energy, or strength **to** do something, or if you **summon** it **up**, you make a great effort to do it. ❑ *She tried to summon the courage to tell him.*

summons /ˈsʌmənz/ (**summonses, summonsing, summonsed**) **1** N-COUNT A **summons** is an order to come and see someone. ❑ *I received a summons to the Palace.* **2** N-COUNT & V-T If someone **receives** a **summons**, or if they **are summonsed**, they are officially ordered to appear in a court of law. ❑ *She was summonsed to appear before the magistrates.*

sumptuous /ˈsʌmptʃʊəs/ ADJ Something that is **sumptuous** is magnificent and obviously expensive. ❑ *...a variety of sumptuous fabrics.*

sun /sʌn/ (**suns**) **1** N-SING **The sun** is the ball of fire in the sky that the Earth goes round, and that gives us heat and light. ❑ *The sun was low in the sky.* **2** N-UNCOUNT You refer to the light and heat that reach us from the sun as **the sun**. ❑ *How pleasant it would be to sit in the sun.*
→ see Word Web: **sun**
→ see **astronomer, earth, eclipse, navigation, solar, solar system, star**

S

sunbathe /ˈsʌnbeɪθ/ (**sunbathes, sunbathing, sunbathed**) V-I When people **sunbathe**, they sit or lie in a place where the sun shines on them, in order to get a suntan. • **sunbathing** N-UNCOUNT ❑ *...a huge deck space for sunbathing.*

sunburn /ˈsʌnbɜːn/ N-UNCOUNT If someone **has sunburn**, their skin is red and sore because they have spent too much time in the sun.
→ see **skin**

Sunday /ˈsʌndeɪ, -di/ (**Sundays**) N-VAR **Sunday** is the day after Saturday and before Monday.

sundry /ˈsʌndri/ **1** ADJ If you refer to **sundry** people or things, you mean several people or things of various sorts. [FORMAL] ❑ *...fresh fruit and vegetables, household goods, and other sundry items.* **2** PHRASE **All and sundry** means everyone. ❑ *I made tea for all and sundry at the office.*

sunflower /ˈsʌnflaʊə/ (**sunflowers**) N-COUNT A **sunflower** is a tall plant with large yellow flowers.

sung /sʌŋ/ **Sung** is the past participle of **sing**.

sunglasses /ˈsʌnglɑːsɪz, -glæs-/ N-PLURAL **Sunglasses** are spectacles with dark lenses to protect your eyes from bright sunlight.

sunk /sʌŋk/ **Sunk** is the past participle of **sink**.

sunken /ˈsʌŋkən/ **1** ADJ BEFORE N **Sunken** ships have sunk to the bottom of a sea, ocean, or lake. ❑ *...the sunken sailing-boat.* **2** ADJ BEFORE N **Sunken** gardens, roads, or other features are below the level of their surrounding area. ❑ *The room contained a sunken bath.* **3** ADJ **Sunken** eyes or cheeks curve inwards and make you look thin and unwell. ❑ *Her eyes were sunken and black-ringed.*

sunlight /ˈsʌnlaɪt/ N-UNCOUNT **Sunlight** is the light that comes from the sun. ❑ *The calm sea glistened in the sunlight.* ❑ *...a ray of sunlight.*
→ see **habitat, rainbow, skin, sun**

sunny /ˈsʌni/ (**sunnier, sunniest**) **1** ADJ When **it is sunny**, the sun is shining brightly. ❑ *...a warm, sunny day.* **2** ADJ **Sunny** places are brightly lit by the sun. ❑ *...a sunny windowsill.*

sunrise /ˈsʌnraɪz/ (**sunrises**) **1** N-UNCOUNT **Sunrise** is the time in the morning when the sun first appears. ❑ *The rain began before sunrise.* **2** N-COUNT A **sunrise** is the colours and light that you see in the sky when the sun first appears. ❑ *There was a spectacular sunrise yesterday.*

sunscreen /ˈsʌnskriːn/ (**sunscreens**) N-VAR A **sunscreen** is a cream that protects your skin from the sun's rays in hot weather.
→ see **skin**

Word Web sun

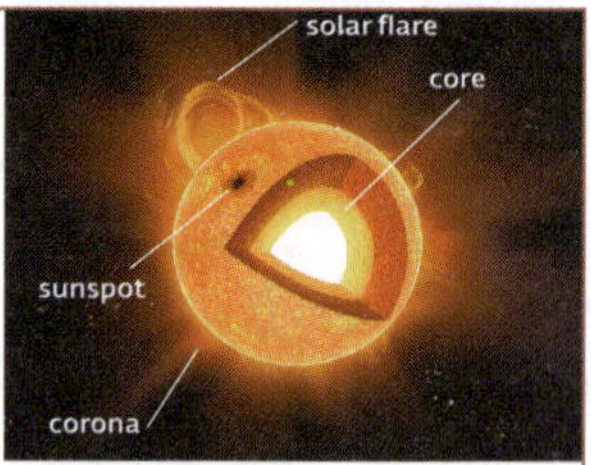

The **sun**'s core contains **hydrogen** atoms. These atoms combine to form helium. This process is called **fusion**. It makes the core very hot. The temperature is 15 million degrees Celsius. The corona is a layer of hot, glowing gases around the sun. Large flames also burn on the surface of the sun. They are called **solar flares**. **Infra-red** and **ultraviolet** light are **invisible** parts of **sunlight**. Sometimes dark patches called sunspots appear on the sun. They can appear every eleven years. Scientists believe that sunspots affect the growth of plants on Earth. They also affect radio transmissions.

sunset /'sʌnset/ (**sunsets**) 1 N-UNCOUNT **Sunset** is the time in the evening when the sun disappears. ❑ *The ceremony takes place daily at sunset.* 2 N-COUNT A **sunset** is the colours and light that you see in the sky when the sun disappears. ❑ *There was a red sunset over Paris.*

sunshine /'sʌnʃaɪn/ N-UNCOUNT **Sunshine** is the light and heat that comes from the sun. ❑ *The bay glittered in the sunshine.*

suntan /'sʌntæn/ (**suntans**) 1 N-COUNT If you **have a suntan**, the sun has turned your skin a brown colour. 2 ADJ BEFORE N **Suntan** lotion, oil, or cream protects your skin from the sun.
→ see **skin**

Word Link	*super ≈ above : super, superficial, superimpose*

super /'suːpə/ ADJ **Super** means very nice or good. [BRIT, INFORMAL] ❑ *We had a super time.*

superb /suː'pɜːb/ ADJ If something is **superb**, it is very good indeed. ❑ *Nicholson gives a superb performance as a retired police officer.* • **superbly** ADV ❑ *The orchestra played superbly.*

superficial /ˌsuːpə'fɪʃəl/ 1 ADJ If you describe someone as **superficial**, you disapprove of them because they do not think deeply, and have little understanding of anything serious or important. ❑ *...her superficial and rather silly friends.* • **superficiality** /ˌsuːpəfɪʃi'ælɪti/ N-UNCOUNT ❑ *...the superficiality of the music industry.* 2 ADJ If you describe something such as an action, feeling, or relationship as **superficial**, you mean that it includes only the simplest and most obvious aspects of that thing. ❑ *...a superficial knowledge of music.* • **superficiality** N-UNCOUNT ❑ *...the superficiality of the judgements we make when we first meet people.* • **superficially** ADV ❑ *The film touches, superficially, on these difficult questions.* 3 ADJ **Superficial** injuries are not very serious, and affect only the surface of the body. You can also describe damage to an object as **superficial**. ❑ *...four superficial wounds to his chest.* ❑ *The explosion caused superficial damage.*

superfluous /suː'pɜːflʊəs/ ADJ Something that is **superfluous** is unnecessary or is no longer needed. ❑ *Further comment was superfluous.*

superimpose /ˌsuːpərɪm'pəʊz/ (**superimposes, superimposing, superimposed**) V-T If one image **is superimposed on** or **over** another, it is put on top of it so that you can see the second image through it. ❑ *The features of different faces were superimposed over one another.*

Word Link	*ent ≈ one who does, has : dependent, resident, superintendent*

superintendent /ˌsuːpərɪn'tendənt/ (**superintendents**) N-COUNT & N-TITLE In British English, a **superintendent** is a senior police officer of the rank above an inspector. In the United States, a **superintendent** is the head of a police department. ❑ *...Superintendent Appleby.*

superior /suː'pɪəriə/ (**superiors**) 1 ADJ You use **superior** to describe someone or something that is better than other similar people or things. ❑ *...a woman greatly superior to her husband in education and sensitivity.* ❑ *...superior quality coffee.* • **superiority** /suːˌpɪəri'ɒrɪti, AM -'ɔːrɪti/ N-UNCOUNT ❑ *...the technical superiority of laser discs over tape.* 2 ADJ A **superior** person or thing has more authority or importance than another person or thing in the same organization or system. ❑ *I was taught never to question a superior officer.* 3 N-COUNT **Your superior** in an organization that you work for is a person who has a higher rank than you. 4 ADJ If you describe someone as **superior**, you disapprove of them because they behave as if they are better or more important than other people. ❑ *Finch gave a superior smile.*

Word Partnership	Use *superior* with:
ADV.	**far** superior, **morally** superior, **vastly** superior 1
N.	superior **performance**, superior **quality**, superior **service** 1

superlative /suː'pɜːlətɪv/ (**superlatives**) N-COUNT & ADJ In grammar, the **superlative** or the **superlative** form of an adjective or adverb is the form that indicates that something has more of a quality than anything else. For example, 'biggest' is the superlative form of 'big'. Compare **comparative**.

supermarket /'suːpəmɑːkɪt/ (**supermarkets**) N-COUNT A **supermarket** is a large shop which sells all kinds of food and some household goods.

supermodel /'suːpəmɒdəl/ (**supermodels**) N-COUNT A **supermodel** is a fashion model who is famous all over the world.

supernatural /ˌsuːpə'nætʃrəl/ ADJ & N-SING **Supernatural** creatures, forces, and events are believed by some people to exist or happen, although they are impossible according to scientific laws. You can refer to these things generally as **the supernatural**. ❑ *...evil spirits that possessed supernatural powers.*

superpower /'suːpəpaʊə/ (**superpowers**) N-COUNT A **superpower** is a very powerful and influential country, usually one that has nuclear weapons and is economically successful.

supersede /ˌsuːpə'siːd/ (**supersedes, superseding, superseded**) V-T If something **is superseded** by something newer, it is replaced because it has become old-fashioned or unacceptable. ❑ *Hand tools have now been superseded by machines.*

supersonic /ˌsuːpə'sɒnɪk/ ADJ BEFORE N **Supersonic** aircraft travel faster than the speed of sound.
→ see **sound**

superstar /'suːpəstɑː/ (**superstars**) N-COUNT A **superstar** is a very famous entertainer or sports player. [INFORMAL] ❑ *...a Hollywood superstar.*

superstition /ˌsuːpə'stɪʃən/ (**superstitions**) N-VAR **Superstition** is belief in things that are not real or possible, for example magic. ❑ *There are all sorts of superstitions about numbers.*

superstitious /ˌsuːpə'stɪʃəs/ ADJ People who are **superstitious** believe in things that are not real or possible, for example magic. ❑ *Jean was superstitious and believed that green brought bad luck.*

supervise /'suːpəvaɪz/ (**supervises, supervising, supervised**) V-T If you **supervise** an activity or a person, you make sure that the activity is done correctly or that the person is behaving correctly. ❑ *I supervise the packing of all orders.* • **supervision**

S

/ˌsuːpəˈvɪʒən/ N-UNCOUNT ❑ *A toddler requires close supervision.* ● **supervisor** (**supervisors**) N-COUNT ❑ *...a supervisor at a factory.*

supervisory /ˌsuːpəˈvaɪzəri/ ADJ BEFORE N **Supervisory** means concerned with the supervision of people or activities. ❑ *...supervisory staff.*

supper /ˈsʌpə/ (**suppers**) **1** N-VAR Some people refer to the main meal eaten in the early part of the evening as **supper**. ❑ *He invited me to supper.* **2** N-VAR **Supper** is a simple meal eaten just before you go to bed at night. [BRIT] **3** → See note at **meal**

supplant /səˈplɑːnt, -ˈplænt/ (**supplants, supplanting, supplanted**) V-T If one thing **supplants** another, it takes its place. [FORMAL] ❑ *By the 1930s the wristwatch had almost completely supplanted the pocket watch.*

supple /ˈsʌpəl/ **1** ADJ A **supple** object or material bends or changes shape easily without cracking or breaking. ❑ *...supple leather driving gloves.* **2** ADJ A **supple** person can move and bend their body very easily.

supplement /ˈsʌplɪmənt/ (**supplements, supplementing, supplemented**) **1** V-T If you **supplement** something, you add something to it in order to improve it. ❑ *I suggest supplementing your diet with vitamins E and A.* **2** N-COUNT A **supplement** is something which is added to another thing in order to improve it. ❑ *...a supplement to their basic pension.*

supplementary /ˌsʌplɪˈmentri, AM -teri/ ADJ **Supplementary** things are added to something in order to improve it. ❑ *Do we need to take supplementary vitamins?*

supplier /səˈplaɪə/ (**suppliers**) N-COUNT A **supplier** is a person or company that provides you with goods or equipment. ❑ *...one of the UK's biggest food suppliers.*

supply /səˈplaɪ/ (**supplies, supplying, supplied**) **1** V-T If you **supply** someone **with** something, you provide them with it. ❑ *This pipeline will supply the city with gas.* ❑ *...an agreement not to supply chemical weapons.* **2** N-PLURAL You can use **supplies** to refer to food, equipment, and other essential things that people need, especially when these are provided in large quantities. ❑ *...food and gasoline supplies.* **3** N-VAR A **supply of** something is an amount of it which is available for use. If something is **in short supply**, there is very little of it available. ❑ *The brain requires a constant supply of oxygen.* **4** N-UNCOUNT **Supply** is the quantity of goods and services that can be made available for people to buy. ❑ *Prices change according to supply and demand.*

S

Word Partnership Use *supply* with:

N.	supply **electricity**, supply **equipment**, supply **information** **1**
ADJ.	**abundant** supply, **large** supply, **limited** supply **3**

support /səˈpɔːt/ (**supports, supporting, supported**) **1** V-T & N-UNCOUNT If you **support** someone or their aims, or if you give them your **support**, you agree with them, and perhaps try to help them because you want them to succeed. ❑ *He thanked everyone who had supported the strike.* ❑ *Only 60 clubs expressed their support for the scheme.* ● **supporter** (**supporters**) N-COUNT ❑ *...supporters of the former President.* **2** N-UNCOUNT If you give **support** to someone during a difficult time, you are kind to them and help them. ❑ *...mentally ill people in need of support.* **3** V-T & N-UNCOUNT If you **support** someone, or if you give them financial **support**, you provide them with money or the things that they need. ❑ *He has a wife and two young children to support.* **4** V-T & N-UNCOUNT If a fact **supports** a statement or a theory, or if it provides **support** for it, it helps to show that it is true or correct. ❑ *History offers some support for this view.* **5** V-T If you **support** a sports team, you want them to win and perhaps go regularly to their games. ● **supporter** N-COUNT ❑ *I'm a Liverpool supporter.* **6** V-T If something **supports** an object, it is underneath the object and holding it up. ❑ *Thick wooden posts supported the ceiling.* **7** N-COUNT A **support** is a bar or other object that supports something. **8** V-T & N-UNCOUNT If something **supports** you, or if it provides you with **support**, it prevents you from falling because you are holding onto it or leaning on it. ❑ *Alice was leaning against him as if for support.*

Usage

If you dislike something very much or get very annoyed by it, you do not say 'I can't support it'. You say '**I can't bear it**' or '**I can't stand it**'. ❑ *She can't bear the new government.* ❑ *I cannot stand going shopping.*

supportive /səˈpɔːtɪv/ ADJ If you are **supportive**, you are kind and helpful to someone at a difficult time in their life. ❑ *They were always supportive of each other.*

suppose /səˈpəʊz/ (**supposes, supposing, supposed**) **1** V-T You use **suppose** or **supposing** when you are considering a possible situation or action and trying to think what effects it would have. ❑ *Suppose someone gave you a cheque for 6 million dollars or more. What would you do with it?* ❑ *Supposing it wasn't the wind that blew the door open?* **2** V-T If you **suppose that** something is true, you believe that it is probably true. ❑ *I supposed you would have a meal somewhere with Rachel.* **3** PHRASE You can say **I suppose** before stating something that you believe to be true, or something that you think you should do, when you want to express slight uncertainty or reluctance about it. [SPOKEN] ❑ *'What would you tell them?'—'The truth, I suppose.'* ❑ *I suppose I'd better do some homework.* ❑ *'Is that the right way up?'—'Yeah. I suppose so.'*

Usage

Note that when you are using the verb **suppose** with a **that** clause in order to state a negative opinion or belief, you normally make **suppose** negative, rather than the verb in the **that** clause. For instance, it is more usual to say '**I don't suppose he ever saw it**' than 'I suppose he didn't ever see it'. The same pattern applies to other verbs with a similar meaning, such as **believe, consider,** and **think**. ❑ *He didn't believe she could do it.* ❑ *I don't consider that you kept your promise.* ❑ *I don't think he saw me.*

supposed **1** ADJ /səˈpəʊzd, səˈpəʊst/ If you say that something is **supposed to** happen, you mean that it is planned or expected. Sometimes this use suggests that the thing does not really happen in this way. ❑ *Public spending is supposed to fall in the next few years.* ❑ *The first debate was supposed to be held on Tuesday.* **2** ADJ If you say that something is **supposed to** be true, you mean that people say it is true but you do not know for certain that it is true. ❑ *'The Whipping Block' has never been published, but it's supposed to be a really good poem.* **3** ADJ BEFORE N /səˈpəʊzɪd/ You can use **supposed** when you want to suggest that the following word or description is misleading, or when it is not definitely known to be true. ❑ *Her neighbour and supposed friend had told the men about her cash.* ● **supposedly** ADV ❑ *Thirty-eight women died while taking these supposedly safer pills.*

suppress /səˈpres/ (**suppresses, suppressing, suppressed**) **1** V-T If someone in authority **suppresses** an activity, they prevent it from continuing, by using force or making it illegal. ❑ *The movement was suppressed by army troops.* ● **suppression** N-UNCOUNT ❑ *...the suppression of human rights.* **2** V-T If a natural function or reaction of your body **is suppressed**, it is stopped, for example by drugs or illness. **3** V-T If you **suppress** your feelings or reactions, you do not express them, even though you might want to. ❑ *She tried to suppress her terror.* ● **suppression** N-UNCOUNT ❑ *A mother's suppression of her own feelings can cause problems.* **4** V-T If someone **suppresses** a piece of information, they prevent other people from learning it. ● **suppression** N-UNCOUNT ❑ *...the deliberate suppression of information.*

supremacy /suːˈpreməsi/ N-UNCOUNT If one group of people has **supremacy over** another group, they are more powerful. ❑ *The president has been able to assert his ultimate supremacy over the prime minister.*

supreme /suːˈpriːm/ **1** ADJ BEFORE N **Supreme** is used in a title to indicate that a person or group is at the highest level of an organization or system. ❑ *...NATO's Supreme Commander in Europe.* ❑ *...the Supreme Court.* **2** ADJ You use **supreme** to emphasize the greatness of a quality or thing. ❑ *Her approval was of supreme importance.* ● **supremely** ADV ❑ *We are supremely confident because we have so much skill and experience.*

sure /ʃʊə/ (**surer, surest**) **1** ADJ AFTER LINK-V If you are **sure** that something is true, you are certain that it is true. If you are not **sure about** something, you do not know for certain what the true situation is. ❑ *He was not sure that he was in the right job.* ❑ *It is impossible to be sure about the value of land.* **2** ADJ AFTER LINK-V If someone is **sure of** getting something, they will certainly get it. ❑ *We cannot be sure of success.* **3** ADJ AFTER LINK-V If you say that something is **sure to** happen, you are emphasizing your belief that it will happen. ❑ *They are sure to try and help you.* **4** ADJ **Sure** is used to emphasize that something such as a sign or ability is reliable or accurate. ❑ *Sharpe's shoulder began to ache, a sure sign of rain.* ❑ *It's a sure way to keep out unwanted visitors.* **5** CONVENTION **Sure** is a way of saying 'yes' or 'all right'. [INFORMAL] ❑ *'He rang you?'—'Sure. Last night.'* **6** PHRASE You say **sure enough**, especially when telling a story, to confirm that something you thought was true or would happen was really true or actually happened. ❑ *I called the hotel and asked them to check the room. Sure enough, they had found the ticket in the blankets.* **7** PHRASE If you say that something is **for sure**, or that you know it **for sure**, you mean that it is definitely true. ❑ *One thing is for sure: he is a brilliant manager.* **8** PHRASE If you **make sure** that something is done, you take action so that it is done. ❑ *Make sure that you follow the instructions carefully.* **9** PHRASE If you **make sure** that something is the way that you want or expect it to be, you check that it is that way. ❑ *He looked in the bathroom to make sure that he was alone.* **10** PHRASE If you are **sure of yourself**, you are very confident about your own abilities or opinions.

surely /ˈʃʊəli/ **1** ADV You use **surely** to emphasize that you think something should be true, and you would be surprised if it was not true. ❑ *You surely haven't forgotten Dr Walters?* **2** PHRASE If you say that something is happening **slowly but surely**, you mean that it is happening gradually but it is definitely happening.

surf /sɜːf/ (**surfs, surfing, surfed**) **1** N-UNCOUNT **Surf** is the mass of white foam formed by waves as they fall on the shore. **2** V-I If you **surf**, you ride on big waves on a special board. ● **surfer** (**surfers**) N-COUNT ❑ *Fanatical surfers travel the world looking for the perfect wave.* ● **surfing** N-UNCOUNT ❑ *The best time for surfing in Waikiki is in January.* **3** V-T If you **surf** the Internet, you move from place to place on the Internet. ● **surfer** N-COUNT ❑ *...programs and games for net surfers to download.*

surfboard

→ see **beach**

Word Link *sur ≈ above : surface, surpass, surplus*

surface /ˈsɜːfɪs/ (**surfaces, surfacing, surfaced**) **1** N-COUNT The **surface** of something is the top part of it or the outside of it. ❑ *...little waves on the surface of the water.* ❑ *Its total surface area was seven thousand square feet.* **2** V-I If someone or something under water **surfaces**, they come up to the surface of the water. ❑ *He surfaced, gasping for air.* **3** N-SING **The surface** of a situation is what can be seen easily rather than what is not immediately obvious. ❑ *Back in Britain, things appear, on the surface, simpler.* ❑ *It's brought to the surface a much bigger problem.*

Word Partnership Use *surface* with:

ADJ.	**flat** surface, **rough** surface, **smooth** surface **1**
N.	surface **area**, **Earth's** surface, surface **of the water** **1**
	surface **level** **1** **3**
V.	**break the** surface **1**
	scratch the surface **1** **3**

surge /sɜːdʒ/ (**surges, surging, surged**) **1** N-COUNT & V-I If there is a **surge** in the level or rate of something, or if the level or rate of something **surges**, there is a sudden large increase in it. ❑ *The shares surged from 43p to 163p earlier this year.* **2** N-COUNT If you feel a **surge of** a particular emotion or feeling, you experience it suddenly and powerfully. ❑ *McKee felt a sudden surge of hope.* **3** N-COUNT & V-I If there is a **surge of** a physical force such as water or electricity, or if it **surges**, there is a sudden powerful movement of it. ❑ *Thousands of volts surged through his car.*

S

4 V-I If people **surge** forward, they move forward suddenly and powerfully, usually in a crowd. ❑ *The crowd surged into the station.*

surgeon /'sɜːdʒən/ (**surgeons**) N-COUNT A **surgeon** is a doctor who performs surgery.

surgery /'sɜːdʒəri/ (**surgeries**) 1 N-UNCOUNT **Surgery** is medical treatment which involves cutting open a person's body in order to repair or remove a diseased or damaged part. ❑ *She was in good condition after surgery for a broken leg.* 2 N-COUNT A **surgery** is the room or house where a doctor or dentist works. [BRIT] 3 N-VAR A doctor's or dentist's **surgery** is the period of time each day when he or she sees patients at his or her surgery. [BRIT] ❑ *Bring him along to the morning surgery.* 4 → see also **plastic surgery**
→ see **cancer, laser**

surgical /'sɜːdʒɪkəl/ ADJ BEFORE N **Surgical** means relating to surgery. ❑ *...surgical instruments.* ❑ *...a surgical operation.* ● **surgically** ADV ❑ *Some cysts do need to be surgically removed.*

surmise /sə'maɪz/ (**surmises, surmising, surmised**) V-T If you **surmise** that something is true, you guess from the information available that it is true, but you do not know for certain. [FORMAL] ❑ *There's so little information, we can only surmise what happened.*

surname /'sɜːneɪm/ (**surnames**) N-COUNT Your **surname** is the name that you share with other members of your family.

Word Link	*sur ≈ above : surface, surpass, surplus*

surpass /sə'pɑːs, -'pæs/ (**surpasses, surpassing, surpassed**) V-T If one person or thing **surpasses** another, the first is better than, or has more of a particular quality than, the second. [FORMAL] ❑ *He was determined to surpass the achievements of his older brothers.*

surplus /'sɜːpləs/ (**surpluses**) 1 N-VAR & ADJ If there is a **surplus of** something, there is more than is needed. **Surplus** things are not needed because there are already enough of them. ❑ *Germany suffers from a surplus of teachers.* ❑ *Few people have large sums of surplus cash.* 2 N-COUNT A **surplus** refers to a situation in which a person or organization receives more than it spends.

S

surprise /sə'praɪz/ (**surprises, surprising, surprised**) 1 N-COUNT & ADJ BEFORE N A **surprise** or a **surprise** event or fact is an unexpected event or fact. ❑ *His success came as a surprise to many people.* ❑ *I have a surprise for you: we are moving to Switzerland!* ❑ *Baxter arrived here this afternoon, on a surprise visit.* 2 N-UNCOUNT **Surprise** is the feeling that you have when something unexpected happens. ❑ *They looked at her in surprise.* ❑ *To my surprise, I found I liked it.* 3 V-T If something **surprises** you, it gives you a feeling of surprise. ❑ *It surprised me that he should make those mistakes.*

Word Partnership	Use *surprise* with:
N.	surprise **announcement**, surprise **attack**, surprise **move**, surprise **visit** 1
	a bit of a surprise 1 2
	element of surprise 2
ADJ.	**big** surprise, **complete** surprise, **great** surprise, **pleasant** surprise 1 2

surprised /sə'praɪzd/ ADJ If you are **surprised at** something, you have a feeling of surprise, because it is unexpected or unusual. ❑ *She was surprised at what happened.* ❑ *Charles was surprised to find the room empty.*

surprising /sə'praɪzɪŋ/ ADJ Something that is **surprising** is unexpected or unusual and makes you feel surprised. ❑ *It is not surprising that children learn to read at different rates.* ● **surprisingly** ADV ❑ *Her voice was surprisingly good.*

surreal /sə'riːəl/ ADJ If you describe something as **surreal**, you mean that it is very strange and like a dream. ❑ *There is a surreal quality to this part of the rainforest.*

surrender /sə'rendə/ (**surrenders, surrendering, surrendered**) 1 V-I & N-VAR If you **surrender**, you stop fighting or resisting someone or something and agree that you have been beaten. **Surrender** is the act of surrendering. ❑ *He surrendered to American troops.* ❑ *...after the Japanese surrender in 1945.* 2 V-T & N-UNCOUNT If you **surrender** something you would rather keep, you give it up or let someone else have it, often after a struggle. **Surrender** is the act of surrendering something. ❑ *Nadja had to surrender all rights to her property.* ❑ *...the deadline for the surrender of weapons.*
→ see **war**

Thesaurus	*surrender* Also look up:
V.	abandon, give in, give up 1 2

surrogate /'sʌrəgeɪt, AM 'sɜːr-/ (**surrogates**) ADJ BEFORE N & N-COUNT You use **surrogate** to describe a person or thing that acts as a substitute for someone or something else. ❑ *He had been a wonderful friend to all of us; a surrogate father.* ❑ *Arms control should not be made into a surrogate for peace.*

ˌsurrogate 'mother (**surrogate mothers**) N-COUNT A **surrogate mother** is a woman who has agreed to give birth to a baby on behalf of another woman.

surround /sə'raʊnd/ (**surrounds, surrounding, surrounded**) 1 V-T If something or someone **is surrounded** by something, that thing is situated all around them. ❑ *...the fluid that surrounds the brain.* 2 V-T If you **are surrounded** by people such as soldiers or police, they spread out so that they are in positions all the way around you. ❑ *He tried to run away but found himself surrounded.* 3 V-T The circumstances, feelings, or ideas which **surround** something are those that are closely associated with it. ❑ *The boy couldn't understand the excitement surrounding the birth of his new brother.* 4 V-T If you **surround yourself with** certain people or things, you make sure that you have a lot of them near you all the time. ❑ *He surrounded himself with admirers.* ❑ *They love being surrounded by familiar possessions.*

surrounding /sə'raʊndɪŋ/ ADJ BEFORE N Something **surrounding** something else is near or around it. ❑ *...the surrounding hills.*

surroundings /sə'raʊndɪŋz/ N-PLURAL The place where someone or something is can be referred to as their **surroundings**. ❑ *...a peaceful holiday home in beautiful surroundings.*

surveillance /sə'veɪləns/ N-UNCOUNT **Surveillance** is the careful watching of someone, especially by the police or army. ❑ *The police kept Golding under surveillance.*

survey (**surveys, surveying, surveyed**)

verb /sə'veɪ/, noun /'sɜːveɪ/.

1 V-T & N-COUNT To **survey** people or organizations, or to make a **survey** of them, means to try to find out information about their opinions or behaviour by asking them questions. ❑ *The survey showed that 55.2% of Japanese people were in favour of a female monarch.* 2 V-T If you **survey** something, you look at or consider the whole of it carefully. ❑ *He pushed himself to his feet and surveyed the room.* 3 V-T & N-COUNT To **survey** a building or area of land, or to do a **survey** of it, means to examine it and measure it, usually in order to make a map of it. ❑ *...the geological survey of India.* • **surveyor** /sə'veə/ (**surveyors**) N-COUNT ❑ *...the surveyor's maps.* 4 V-T & N-COUNT If someone **surveys** a house, or if they do a **survey** of it, they examine it carefully and report on its structure. ❑ *...a structural survey done by a qualified surveyor.* • **surveyor** N-COUNT ❑ *Our surveyor warned us that the house needed totally rebuilding.*

survival /sə'vaɪvəl/ N-UNCOUNT **Survival** is the fact of continuing to live or exist in spite of great danger or difficulty. ❑ *An animal's sense of smell is necessary to its survival.* ❑ *...companies which have been struggling for survival.*

Word Link *viv ≈ living : revival, survive, vivid*

survive /sə'vaɪv/ (**survives, surviving, survived**) 1 V-T/V-I If someone **survives** in a dangerous situation, they do not die. ❑ *These drugs can help people survive heart attacks.* • **survivor** (**survivors**) N-COUNT ❑ *There were no survivors of the plane crash.* 2 V-T/V-I If you **survive** in difficult circumstances, you manage to continue in spite of them. ❑ *...people who are struggling to survive without jobs.* ❑ *Can the company survive a recession?* • **survivor** N-COUNT ❑ *...female survivors of domestic violence.* 3 V-T If you **survive** someone, you continue to live after they have died. ❑ *Most women will survive their partners.*

susceptible /sə'septɪbəl/ 1 ADJ AFTER LINK-V If you are **susceptible to** something or someone, you are likely to be influenced by them. ❑ *Young people are the most susceptible to advertisements.* 2 ADJ AFTER LINK-V If you are **susceptible to** a disease or injury, you are likely to be affected by it. 3 ADJ BEFORE N A **susceptible** person is very easily influenced emotionally.

suspect (**suspects, suspecting, suspected**) 1 V-T /sə'spekt/ If you say that you **suspect** that something is true, you mean that you believe it is probably true, but you want to make it sound less strong or direct. ❑ *I suspect they were right.* ❑ *Do women really like these jokes? We suspect not.* 2 V-T If you **suspect** that something dishonest or unpleasant has been done, you believe that it has probably been done. ❑ *They suspected that he knew the thief.* 3 N-COUNT /'sʌspekt/ A **suspect** is a person who the police think may be guilty of a crime. 4 ADJ If something is **suspect**, it cannot be trusted or regarded as genuine. ❑ *The whole affair has been highly suspect.*

suspend /sə'spend/ (**suspends, suspending, suspended**) 1 V-T If you **suspend** something, you delay or stop it for a while. ❑ *The union suspended strike action this week.* 2 V-T If someone **is suspended** from their job, they are prevented from doing it for a fixed period of time, usually as a punishment. ❑ *Julie was suspended from her job shortly after the incident.* 3 V-T If something **is suspended** from a high place, it is hung from that place. ❑ *A map of Europe was suspended from the ceiling.*

suspenders /sə'spendəz/ N-PLURAL In American English, **suspenders** are a pair of straps that go over someone's shoulders and are fastened to their trousers at the front and at the back to prevent the trousers from falling down. The British word is **braces**.

suspense /sə'spens/ N-UNCOUNT **Suspense** is a state of excitement or anxiety about something that is going to happen very soon. ❑ *There was genuine suspense before Wilson was named the winner.*

suspension /sə'spenʃən/ (**suspensions**) 1 N-UNCOUNT The **suspension of** something is the act of delaying or stopping it for a while. ❑ *...the suspension of flights between London and Manchester.* 2 N-VAR Someone's **suspension** is their removal from a job for a period of time, usually as a punishment. ❑ *...a two-year suspension from international skiing competitions.* 3 N-UNCOUNT A vehicle's **suspension** consists of the springs and other devices, which give a smooth ride over bumps in the road.
→ see **bridge**

suspicion /sə'spɪʃən/ (**suspicions**) 1 N-VAR **Suspicion** is a belief or feeling that someone has committed a crime or done something wrong. ❑ *He was arrested on suspicion of robbery.* 2 N-VAR If there is **suspicion** of someone or something, people do not trust them or consider them to be reliable. ❑ *I was regarded with a certain amount of suspicion.* 3 N-COUNT A **suspicion** is a feeling that something is probably true or is likely to happen. ❑ *I had a sneaking suspicion she was enjoying herself.*

suspicious /sə'spɪʃəs/ 1 ADJ If you are **suspicious of** someone or something, you do not trust them. ❑ *He was suspicious of all journalists.* • **suspiciously** ADV ❑ *'What's the matter with you?' Jake asked suspiciously.* 2 ADJ If you describe someone or something as **suspicious**, you mean that there is some aspect of them which makes you think that they are involved in a crime or a dishonest activity. ❑ *Police last night found a suspicious package.* • **suspiciously** ADV ❑ *...suspiciously large sums of money.*

sustain /sə'steɪn/ (**sustains, sustaining, sustained**) 1 V-T If you **sustain** something, you continue it or maintain it for a period of time. ❑ *...how to get enough food to sustain life.* 2 V-T If you **sustain** something such as a defeat, loss, or injury, it happens to you. [FORMAL] ❑ *He had sustained a cut on his left eyebrow.* 3 V-T If something **sustains** you, it supports you by giving you help, strength, or encouragement. [FORMAL] ❑ *He'll have lots of great memories to sustain him when he's away.*

sustainable /sə'steɪnəbəl/ ADJ A **sustainable** plan, method, or system can be continued at the same pace or level of activity without harming its efficiency and the people affected by it. ❑ *...an efficient and sustainable transport system.*

swab /swɒb/ (**swabs**) N-COUNT A **swab** is a small piece of cotton wool used for cleaning a wound.

swagger /'swægə/ (**swaggers, swaggering, swaggered**) V-I & N-SING If you **swagger**, or if you walk with a **swagger**, you walk in a proud way, holding your body upright and swinging your hips. ❑ *Weber swaggered into the room.*

swallow /ˈswɒləʊ/ (**swallows, swallowing, swallowed**) **1** V-T/V-I & N-COUNT When you **swallow** something, or when you take a **swallow**, you cause something to go from your mouth down into your stomach. ❑ *You are asked to swallow a capsule containing vitamin B.* ❑ *Jim chewed, swallowed and nodded.* ❑ *Jan lifted her glass and took a quick swallow.* **2** V-T If someone **swallows** a story or a statement, they believe it completely. ❑ *I too found this story a little hard to swallow.* **3** V-T If you **swallow** your feelings, you do not express them, although you want to very much. ❑ *Gordon swallowed his anger.* **4** N-COUNT A **swallow** is a small bird with pointed wings and a forked tail.

swam /swæm/ **Swam** is the past tense of **swim**.

swamp /swɒmp/ (**swamps, swamping, swamped**) **1** N-VAR A **swamp** is an area of wet land with wild plants growing in it. **2** V-T If something **swamps** a place or object, it fills it with water. ❑ *The river burst its banks, swamping a caravan park.* **3** V-T If you **are swamped** by things or people, you have more of them than you can deal with. ❑ *The railway station was swamped with thousands of families.*

swan /swɒn/ (**swans**) N-COUNT A **swan** is a large white bird with a long neck that lives on rivers and lakes.

swap also **swop** /swɒp/ (**swaps, swapping, swapped**) **1** V-T/V-I & N-COUNT If you **swap** something **with** someone, or if you do a **swap**, you give it to them and receive something else in exchange. ❑ *I wouldn't swap jobs with her.* ❑ *Next week they will swap places.* ❑ *He read one half of the book and I read the other. Then we swapped.* ❑ *Do you fancy a job swap?* **2** V-T If you **swap** one thing **for** another, you remove the first thing and replace it with the second. ❑ *He'd swapped his overalls for a suit and tie.* **3** V-T When you **swap** stories or opinions with someone, you tell each other stories or give each other your opinions. ❑ *They all sat together at table, laughing and swapping stories.*

swarm /swɔːm/ (**swarms, swarming, swarmed**) **1** N-COUNT A **swarm of** bees or other insects is a large group of them flying together. **2** V-I When bees or other insects **swarm**, they move or fly in a large group. **3** V-I When people **swarm** somewhere, they move there quickly in a large group. ❑ *People swarmed to the shops, buying up everything in sight.* **4** V-I If a place **is swarming with** people, it is full of people moving about in a busy way. ❑ *Within minutes the area was swarming with officers.* **5** N-COUNT A **swarm of** people is a large group of them moving about quickly.

swat /swɒt/ (**swats, swatting, swatted**) V-T If you **swat** an insect, you hit it with a quick, swinging movement.

swathe also **swath** /sweɪð, AM swɑːð/ (**swathes, swathing, swathed**) **1** N-COUNT A **swathe of** land is a long strip of land. ❑ *The army took over another swathe of territory.* **2** V-T To **swathe** someone or something **in** cloth means to wrap them in it completely. ❑ *She swathed her body in thin black fabric.*

sway /sweɪ/ (**sways, swaying, swayed**) **1** V-I When people or things **sway**, they lean or swing slowly from one side to the other. ❑ *The people swayed back and forth.* **2** V-T If you **are swayed** by someone or something, you are influenced by them. ❑ *Don't ever be swayed by fashion.* **3** PHRASE If someone or something **holds sway**, they have great power or influence over a particular place or activity. ❑ *...ideas that held sway for centuries.*

swear /sweə/ (**swears, swearing, swore, sworn**) **1** V-I If someone **swears**, they use language that is considered to be rude or offensive. ❑ *They swore at us and ran off.* **2** V-T If you **swear to** do something, you solemnly promise that you will do it. ❑ *We have sworn to fight cruelty.* ❑ *Alan swore that he would do everything in his power to help us.* ❑ *He swore allegiance to the U.S. government.* **3** V-T/V-I If you **swear** that something is true, or if you say that you can **swear to** it, you say very firmly that it is true. ❑ *I swear I've told you all I know.* **4** V-T If someone **is sworn to** secrecy or silence, they promise another person that they will not reveal a secret. ❑ *She was bursting to announce the news but was sworn to secrecy.* **5** → see also **sworn**

▶ **swear by** PHR-VERB If you **swear by** something, you believe that it can be relied on to have a particular effect. ❑ *Many people swear by vitamin C's ability to ward off colds.*

▶ **swear in** PHR-VERB When someone **is sworn in**, they promise to fulfil the duties of a new job or appointment.

Word Partnership	Use *swear* with:
N.	swear **words** 1 swear **allegiance**, swear **an oath** 2
ADV.	**solemnly** swear 3

sweat /swet/ (**sweats, sweating, sweated**) **1** N-UNCOUNT **Sweat** is the salty colourless liquid which comes through your skin when you are hot, ill, or afraid. ❑ *He wiped the sweat off his face.* **2** V-I When you **sweat**, sweat comes through your skin. ● **sweating** N-UNCOUNT ❑ *...symptoms such as sweating, anxiety and depression.* **3** PHRASE If someone is **in a sweat** or **in a cold sweat**, they are sweating a lot, especially because they are afraid or ill. ❑ *The thought brought me out in a cold sweat.*

sweater /ˈswetə/ (**sweaters**) N-COUNT A **sweater** is a warm knitted piece of clothing which covers the upper part of your body and your arms. → see **clothing**

sweatshirt /ˈswetʃɜːt/ (**sweatshirts**) N-COUNT A **sweatshirt** is a loose warm piece of casual clothing, usually made of thick cotton, which covers the upper part of your body and your arms. → see **clothing**

sweaty /ˈsweti/ (**sweatier, sweatiest**) ADJ If your clothing or body is **sweaty**, it is soaked or covered with sweat.

sweep /swiːp/ (**sweeps, sweeping, swept**) **1** V-T If you **sweep** an area of ground, you push dirt or rubbish off it with a broom. ❑ *She was in the kitchen sweeping crumbs into a dust pan.* **2** V-T If you **sweep** things off something, you push them off with a quick smooth movement of your arm. ❑ *She swept the cards from the table.* **3** V-T If a strong force **sweeps** you along, it moves you quickly along. ❑ *The landslides buried homes and swept cars into the sea.* **4** V-T/V-I If events or ideas **sweep** or **sweep through** a place, they spread quickly through it.

S

❑ *A flu epidemic is sweeping through Moscow.* ❑ *...the wave of nationalism sweeping the country.* **5** V-T To **sweep** something **away** or **aside** means to remove it quickly and completely. ❑ *Mr Prentice swept aside rumours that he planned to retire soon.* **6** V-T If your gaze or a light **sweeps** an area, it moves over it. ❑ *Helicopters with searchlights swept the park.* **7** PHRASE If someone **sweeps** something bad or wrong **under the carpet**, they try to prevent people from hearing about it.

▶ **sweep up** PHR-VERB If you **sweep up** dirt or rubbish, you push it together with a brush and then remove it. ❑ *Get a broom and sweep up that broken glass.*

sweeping /'swi:pɪŋ/ **1** ADJ If someone makes a **sweeping** statement or generalization, they make a firm definite statement although they have not considered the relevant facts or details carefully; used showing disapproval. ❑ *You can't make sweeping generalizations about young people of today.* **2** ADJ **Sweeping** changes or reforms are large in scale and have very important or significant results.

sweet /swi:t/ (**sweeter, sweetest, sweets**) **1** ADJ **Sweet** food or drink contains a lot of sugar. ❑ *...a mug of sweet tea.* ● **sweetness** N-UNCOUNT ❑ *Florida oranges have a natural sweetness.* **2** N-COUNT In British English, **sweets** are sweet things such as toffees, chocolates, or mints. In American English, sweets are referred to as **candy**. **3** N-COUNT A **sweet** is something sweet, such as fruit or a pudding, that you eat at the end of a meal. [BRIT] **4** ADJ A **sweet** smell is pleasant and fragrant. ❑ *...the sweet smell of her shampoo.* **5** ADJ A **sweet** sound is pleasant, smooth, and gentle. ❑ *...the sweet sounds of Mozart.* ● **sweetly** ADV ❑ *He sang much more sweetly than he has before.* **6** ADJ If you describe something as **sweet**, you mean that it gives you great pleasure and satisfaction. [WRITTEN] ❑ *It was sweet revenge for the Warriors, who beat the Titans 42-19.* **7** ADJ If you describe someone as **sweet**, you mean that they are pleasant, kind, and gentle towards other people. ❑ *How sweet of you to think of me!* ● **sweetly** ADV ❑ *I just smiled sweetly.* **8** ADJ If you describe a small person or thing as **sweet**, you mean that they are attractive in a child-like way. [INFORMAL] ❑ *...a sweet little baby girl.*
→ see **sugar, taste**

sweetcorn /'swi:tkɔ:n/ N-UNCOUNT **Sweetcorn** consists of the yellow seeds of the maize plant, which are eaten as a vegetable.

sweeten /'swi:tən/ (**sweetens, sweetening, sweetened**) V-T If you **sweeten** food or drink, you add sugar, honey, or another sweet substance to it.

sweetener /'swi:tənə/ (**sweeteners**) N-VAR A **sweetener** is an artificial substance that can be used instead of sugar.

sweetheart /'swi:thɑ:t/ (**sweethearts**) **1** N-VOC You call someone **sweetheart** if you are affectionate towards them. ❑ *Happy birthday, sweetheart.* **2** N-COUNT Your **sweetheart** is your boyfriend or girlfriend. [DATED]

swell /swel/ (**swells, swelling, swelled, swollen**)

> The forms **swelled** and **swollen** are both used as the past participle.

1 V-T/V-I If the amount or size of something **swells**, or **is swelled** or **is swollen**, it becomes larger than it was before. ❑ *His bank balance has swelled by £222,000.* ❑ *Cairo's population has swollen to more than 15 million.* **2** V-I & PHR-VERB If something such as a part of your body **swells**, or if it **swells up**, it becomes larger and rounder than normal. ❑ *The limbs swell to an enormous size.* ❑ *The glands in the neck swell up.* **3** V-I If you **swell with** a feeling, you are suddenly full of that feeling. [LITERARY] ❑ *She could see her two sons swell with pride.* **4** → see also **swollen**

swelling /'swelɪŋ/ (**swellings**) N-VAR A **swelling** is a raised curved shape on the surface of your body which appears as a result of an injury or an illness. ❑ *...painful swellings of the big toe joint.* ❑ *The cyst was causing swelling.*

sweltering /'sweltərɪŋ/ ADJ If the weather is **sweltering**, it is very hot. ❑ *In LA it's sweltering – 98 degrees in the shade.* ❑ *...a day of sweltering heat.*

swept /swept/ **Swept** is the past tense and past participle of **sweep**.

swerve /swɜ:v/ (**swerves, swerving, swerved**) V-T/V-I & N-COUNT If a vehicle or other moving thing **swerves**, or if a driver **swerves** it, it suddenly changes direction, often in order to avoid colliding with something else. This movement is called a **swerve**. ❑ *Her car swerved off the road.* ❑ *Ned swerved the truck.* ❑ *That swerve saved Malone's life.*

swift /swɪft/ (**swifter, swiftest**) **1** ADJ A **swift** event or process happens very quickly or without delay. ❑ *The police were swift to act.* ❑ *We wish him a swift recovery.* ● **swiftly** ADV ❑ *The police failed to act swiftly enough.* ● **swiftness** N-UNCOUNT ❑ *...the secrecy and swiftness of the invasion.* **2** ADJ Something that is **swift** moves very quickly. ❑ *With a swift movement, she reached into the cot.*

swim /swɪm/ (**swims, swimming, swam, swum**) **1** V-I & N-SING When you **swim**, or when you **go for a swim**, you move through water by making movements with your arms and legs. ❑ *I swim a mile a day.* ❑ *When can we go for a swim?* ● **swimmer** (**swimmers**) N-COUNT ❑ *I'm a good swimmer.* **2** V-I If objects **swim**, they seem to be moving backwards and forwards, usually because you are ill. ❑ *He felt too hot and the room was swimming.* **3** V-I If your **head is swimming**, you feel dizzy.

swimming /'swɪmɪŋ/ N-UNCOUNT **Swimming** is the activity of swimming, especially as a sport or for pleasure. ❑ *It was too chilly for swimming.* ❑ *I now go swimming five times a week.*

'swimming pool (**swimming pools**) N-COUNT A **swimming pool** is a place that has been built for people to swim in. It consists of a large hole that has been tiled and filled with water.

swimsuit /'swɪmsu:t/ (**swimsuits**) N-COUNT A **swimsuit** is a piece of clothing that is worn for swimming, especially by women and girls.

swindle /'swɪndəl/ (**swindles, swindling, swindled**) V-T & N-COUNT If someone **swindles** a person or an organization, or if someone is involved in a **swindle**, they deceive the person or organization in order to get money from them. ❑ *A City businessman swindled investors out of millions of pounds.* ❑ *...a tax swindle.* ● **swindler** (**swindlers**) N-COUNT ❑ *...an insurance swindler.*

swing /swɪŋ/ (**swings, swinging, swung**) **1** V-T/V-I & N-COUNT If something **swings**, or if you **swing** it, it moves backwards and forwards or from side to side from a fixed point, once or several times. You can refer to this movement as a **swing**. ❑ *The pendulum slowly started to swing.* ❑ *Mary Rose came* *back into the room, swinging her handbag.* ❑ *Roy swung his legs carefully off the couch.* ❑ *...walking with a slight swing to her hips.* **2** V-T/V-I If a vehicle **swings** in a particular direction, or if a driver **swings** his or her vehicle in a particular direction, he or she turns it suddenly in that direction. ❑ *He got into Margie's car and swung out onto the road.* ❑ *He swung the car off the road.* **3** V-I & N-COUNT If you **swing at** someone or something, or if you take a **swing at** them, you try to hit them. ❑ *She picked up his baseball bat and swung at the man's head.* ❑ *I often want to take a swing at someone.* **4** N-COUNT A **swing** is a seat hanging by two ropes or chains from a metal frame or tree. You can sit on the seat and move backwards and forwards through the air. **5** V-I & N-COUNT If people's opinions, attitudes, or feelings **swing**, or if there is a **swing** in them, they change significantly. ❑ *The mood amongst members was swinging away from their leader.* ❑ *...violent mood swings.* **6** PHRASE If something is **in full swing**, it is operating fully and is no longer in its early stages. ❑ *The international rugby season is in full swing.*

Word Partnership Use *swing* with:

N.	swing **a bat**, **golf** swing **1**
	swing **at a ball** **3**
	porch swing **4**
	voters swing **5**
ADJ.	**in full** swing **6**

swipe /swaɪp/ (**swipes, swiping, swiped**) V-I & N-COUNT If you **swipe at** a person or thing, or if you **take** a **swipe at** them, you try to hit them, making a swinging movement with your arm. ❑ *She swiped at Rusty as though he was a fly.* ❑ *She took a swipe at the ball.*

'swipe ˌcard (**swipe cards**) N-COUNT A **swipe card** is a plastic card with a magnetic strip on it containing information that can be read by a machine.

swirl /swɜːl/ (**swirls, swirling, swirled**) **1** V-T/V-I If you **swirl** something liquid or flowing, or if it **swirls**, it moves round and round quickly. ❑ *She swirled the ice-cold liquid around in her glass.* ❑ *The black water swirled around his legs.* **2** N-COUNT A **swirl** is a pattern made by moving something round and round quickly. ❑ *...small swirls of chocolate cream.*

swish /swɪʃ/ (**swishes, swishing, swished**) V-I & N-COUNT If something **swishes**, it moves quickly through the air, making a soft sound. This action is called a **swish**. ❑ *A car swished by.* ❑ *She turned with a swish of her skirt.*

S

switch /swɪtʃ/ (**switches, switching, switched**) **1** N-COUNT A **switch** is a small control for an electrical device which you use to turn the device on or off. ❑ *...a light switch.*

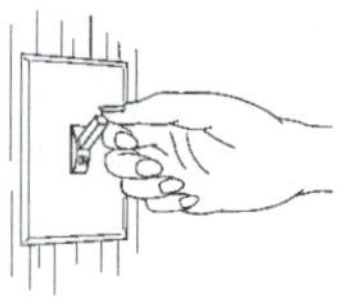
switch

2 V-I & N-COUNT If you **switch to** something different, for example to a different system, task, or subject of conversation, or if there is a **switch to** it, you change to it from what you were doing or saying before. ❑ *The law encourages companies to switch from coal to cleaner fuels.* ❑ *A friend encouraged Chris to switch jobs.* ❑ *New technology made a switch to oil possible.* **3** V-T If you **switch** two things, you replace one with the other. ❑ *The documents have been switched.*

▸ **switch off** **1** PHR-VERB If you **switch off** an electrical device, you stop it working by operating a switch. ❑ *The driver switched off the headlights.* **2** PHR-VERB If you **switch off**, you stop paying attention to something. [INFORMAL] ❑ *You've got so many things to think about that it's difficult to switch off.*

▸ **switch on** PHR-VERB If you **switch on** an electrical device, you make it start working by operating a switch. ❑ *We switched on the radio.*

Word Partnership Use *switch* with:

N.	**ignition** switch, **light** switch,
	power switch **1**
	switch **sides** **2**
V.	**flick a** switch, **flip a** switch,
	turn a switch **1**
	make a switch **2**

switchboard /ˈswɪtʃbɔːd/ (**switchboards**) N-COUNT A **switchboard** is a place in a large office or business where all the telephone calls are connected. ❑ *He was connected to the central switchboard.*

swivel /ˈswɪvəl/ (**swivels, swivelling, swivelled** or [AM] **swiveling, swiveled**) V-T/V-I If someone or something **swivels**, or if you **swivel** them, they turn around a central point so that they are facing in a different direction. ❑ *He swivelled round to face Sarah.* ❑ *She swivelled her chair round.*

swollen /ˈswəʊlən/ **1** **Swollen** is a past participle of **swell**. **2** ADJ If a part of your body is **swollen**, it is larger and rounder than normal, usually as a result of injury or illness. ❑ *Her glands were swollen and painful.*

swoop /swuːp/ (**swoops, swooping, swooped**) **1** V-I & N-COUNT If police or soldiers **swoop on** a place, or if they carry out a **swoop on** a place, they go there suddenly and quickly, usually in order to arrest someone or to attack the place. ❑ *Police swooped on the property, taking away computers and documents.* ❑ *...a swoop on a German lorry.* **2** V-I When a bird or aeroplane **swoops**, it suddenly moves downwards through the air in a smooth curving movement. ❑ *More than 20 helicopters began swooping in low.*

swop /swɒp/ → see **swap**

sword

sword /sɔːd/ (**swords**) N-COUNT A **sword** is a weapon with a handle and a long blade.
→ see **army**

swore /swɔː/ **Swore** is the past tense of **swear**.

sworn /swɔːn/ **1** **Sworn** is the past participle of **swear**. **2** ADJ BEFORE N If you make a **sworn** statement or declaration, you swear that everything that you have said in it is true. ❑ *...sworn legal statements.*

swum /swʌm/ **Swum** is the past participle of **swim**.

swung /swʌŋ/ **Swung** is the past tense and past participle of **swing**.

syllable /ˈsɪləbəl/ (**syllables**) N-COUNT A

syllable is a part of a word that contains a single vowel-sound and that is pronounced as a unit. For example, 'book' has one syllable, and 'reading' has two syllables.

syllabus /ˈsɪləbəs/ (**syllabuses**) N-COUNT You can refer to the subjects that are studied in a particular course as the **syllabus**. ❑ *...the history syllabus.*

symbol /ˈsɪmbəl/ (**symbols**) 1 N-COUNT A **symbol of** something such as an idea is a shape or design that is used to represent it. ❑ *A dove is a symbol of peace.* 2 N-COUNT A **symbol for** an item in a calculation or formula is a number, letter, or shape that represents the item. ❑ *'What's the chemical symbol for mercury?'—'Hg.'*
→ see **myth**

symbolic /sɪmˈbɒlɪk/ 1 ADJ If you describe an event, action, or procedure as **symbolic**, you mean that it represents an important change, although it has little practical effect. ❑ *The President's visit is full of symbolic significance.* ● **symbolically** ADV ❑ *It was a simple gesture, but symbolically important.* 2 ADJ **Symbolic** is used to describe things involving or relating to symbols. ❑ *...symbolic representations of landscape.* ● **symbolism** /ˈsɪmbəlɪzəm/ N-UNCOUNT ❑ *The film was praised for its visual symbolism.*

symbolize [BRIT also **symbolise**] /ˈsɪmbəlaɪz/ (**symbolizes, symbolizing, symbolized**) V-T If one thing **symbolizes** another, it is used or regarded as a symbol of it. ❑ *The fall of the Berlin Wall symbolised the end of the Cold War.*

symmetrical /sɪˈmetrɪkəl/ ADJ If something is **symmetrical**, it has two halves which are exactly the same, except that one half is the mirror image of the other. ❑ *...rows of perfectly symmetrical windows.* ● **symmetrically** ADV ❑ *The food was arranged symmetrically on the plate.*

symmetry /ˈsɪmɪtri/ (**symmetries**) N-VAR Something that has **symmetry** is symmetrical in shape, design, or structure. ❑ *...the incredible beauty and symmetry of a snowflake.*

sympathetic /ˌsɪmpəˈθetɪk/ 1 ADJ If you are **sympathetic to** someone who has had a misfortune, you are kind to them and show that you understand how they are feeling. ❑ *She was very sympathetic to the problems of students.* ❑ *...a sympathetic friend.* ● **sympathetically** ADV ❑ *She nodded sympathetically.* 2 ADJ If you are **sympathetic to** a proposal or action, you approve of it and are willing to support it. ❑ *A number of senior members were sympathetic to the idea.*

sympathize [BRIT also **sympathise**] /ˈsɪmpəθaɪz/ (**sympathizes, sympathizing, sympathized**) 1 V-I If you **sympathize with** someone who has had a misfortune, you show that you are sorry for them. ❑ *Anyone who has had a similar experience will sympathise with Sue.* ❑ *He sympathized but he didn't understand.* 2 V-I If you **sympathize with** someone's feelings, you understand them and are not critical of them. ❑ *Vicky sympathized with his need to feel in control of the business.* 3 V-I If you **sympathize with** a person or group, you approve of their actions or proposals. ❑ *Most of the people there sympathized with the workers.* ● **sympathizer** (**sympathizers**) N-COUNT ❑ *Fuchs was a communist sympathiser.*

Word Link *path ≈ feeling : apathy, empathy, sympathy*

Word Link *sym ≈ together : sympathy, symphony, symposium*

sympathy /ˈsɪmpəθi/ (**sympathies**) 1 N-UNCOUNT If you have **sympathy for** someone who has had a misfortune, you are sorry for them, and show this in the way you behave towards them. ❑ *We expressed our sympathy for her loss.* ❑ *I have had very little help and no sympathy at all.* 2 N-VAR If you have **sympathy with** someone's ideas or opinions, you agree with them. ❑ *I have some sympathy with this point of view.* 3 N-UNCOUNT If you take some action **in sympathy with** someone else, you do it in order to show that you support them. ❑ *The union has called for a nationwide strike in sympathy with the KBS workers.*

Word Partnership Use *sympathy* with:
ADJ. **deep** sympathy, **great** sympathy, **public** sympathy 1
V. **express** sympathy, **feel** sympathy, **gain** sympathy, **have** sympathy 1 2

Word Link *phon ≈ sound : microphone, symphony, telephone*

symphony /ˈsɪmfəni/ (**symphonies**) N-COUNT A **symphony** is a piece of music written to be played by an orchestra, usually in four parts.
→ see **music, orchestra**

ˈsymphony orchestra (**symphony orchestras**) N-COUNT A **symphony orchestra** is a large orchestra that plays classical music.

symposium /sɪmˈpəʊziəm/ (**symposiums**) N-COUNT A **symposium** is a conference in which experts or scholars discuss a particular subject.

symptom /ˈsɪmptəm/ (**symptoms**) 1 N-COUNT A **symptom** of an illness is something wrong with your body that is a sign of the illness. ❑ *...patients with flu symptoms.* 2 N-COUNT A **symptom of** a bad situation is something that happens which is considered to be a sign of this situation. ❑ *Your difficulties are just a symptom of a larger problem.*
→ see **diagnosis, illness**

symptomatic /ˌsɪmptəˈmætɪk/ ADJ AFTER LINK-V If something is **symptomatic of** something else, especially something bad, it is a sign of it. [FORMAL] ❑ *The city's problems are symptomatic of the crisis that is spreading through the country.*

synagogue /ˈsɪnəgɒg/ (**synagogues**) N-COUNT A **synagogue** is a building where Jewish people worship.

Word Link *syn ≈ together : synchronize, syndicate, synthesis*

synchronize [BRIT also **synchronise**] /ˈsɪŋkrənaɪz/ (**synchronizes, synchronizing, synchronized**) V-T If you **synchronize** two activities, processes, or movements, you cause them to happen at the same time and speed as each other. ❑ *You may want to synchronize your breathing with the movements of the exercise.*

syndicate /ˈsɪndɪkət/ (**syndicates**) N-COUNT A **syndicate** is an association of people or

S

organizations that is formed for business purposes or to carry out a project. ❑ *...a major crime syndicate.*

syndrome /ˈsɪndrəʊm/ (**syndromes**) **1** N-COUNT A **syndrome** is a medical condition that is characterized by a particular group of symptoms. ❑ *...sudden infant death syndrome.* **2** N-COUNT You can refer to an undesirable condition that is characterized by a particular type of activity or behaviour as a **syndrome**. ❑ *Scientists call this the 'look at me now' syndrome.*

Word Link	*onym ≈ name : acronym, anonymous, synonym*

synonym /ˈsɪnənɪm/ (**synonyms**) N-COUNT A **synonym** is a word or expression which means the same as another one. For example, 'sad' and 'unhappy' are synonyms.

synonymous /sɪˈnɒnɪməs/ **1** ADJ **Synonymous** words or expressions have the same meaning as each other. **2** ADJ If you say that one thing is **synonymous with** another, you mean that the two things are very closely associated with each other. ❑ *Paris has always been synonymous with elegance.*

Word Link	*syn ≈ together : synchronize, syndicate, synthesis*

synthesis /ˈsɪnθɪsɪs/ (**syntheses** /ˈsɪnθɪsiːz/) N-COUNT A **synthesis of** different ideas or styles is a mixture or combination of them. [FORMAL] ❑ *...a synthesis of feminism and socialism.*

synthesize [BRIT also **synthesise**] /ˈsɪnθɪsaɪz/ (**synthesizes, synthesizing, synthesized**) V-T If you **synthesize** different ideas, facts, or experiences, you combine them to develop a single idea or impression. [FORMAL] ❑ *The movement synthesised various different elements of modern art.*

synthetic /sɪnˈθetɪk/ ADJ **Synthetic** products are made from chemicals or artificial substances rather than from natural ones. ❑ *...synthetic rubber.*

syphon /ˈsaɪfən/ (**syphons**) → see **siphon**

syringe /sɪˈrɪndʒ/ (**syringes**) N-COUNT A **syringe** is a small tube with a fine hollow needle, used for injecting drugs or for taking blood from someone's body.

syrup /ˈsɪrəp/ (**syrups**) N-VAR **Syrup** is a sweet liquid made by cooking sugar with water or fruit juice.

system /ˈsɪstəm/ (**systems**) **1** N-COUNT A **system** is a way of working, organizing, or doing something which follows a fixed plan or set of rules. ❑ *...the present system of funding for higher education.* **2** N-COUNT You use **system** to refer to a set of equipment, parts, or devices. ❑ *...powerful computer systems..* ❑ *...a central heating system.* ❑ *...the body's digestive system.* **3** N-COUNT You use **system** to refer to a whole institution or aspect of society that is organized in a particular way. ❑ *...the British legal system.* ❑ *...Australia's road and rail system.* **4** N-COUNT A **system** is a set of rules, especially in mathematics or science, which is used to count or measure things. ❑ *...the decimal system of metric weights.* **5** N-SING People sometimes refer to the government or administration of a country as **the system**. ❑ *Dickens wrote about the fight of ordinary people against the system.* **6** → see also **immune system, nervous system, solar system**

systematic /ˌsɪstəˈmætɪk/ ADJ Something that is done in a **systematic** way is done according to a fixed plan, in a thorough and efficient way. ❑ *They began a systematic search.* ● **systematically** ADV ❑ *They have systematically destroyed the country's oil fields.*

Tt

tab /tæb/ (**tabs**) **1** N-COUNT A **tab** is a small piece of cloth or paper that is attached to something, usually with information about that thing written on it. **2** PHRASE If someone **keeps tabs on** you, they make sure that they always know where you are and what you are doing, often in order to control you. [INFORMAL] **3** PHRASE If you **pick up the tab**, you pay a bill on behalf of a group of people or provide the money that is needed for something.

table /'teɪbəl/ (**tables, tabling, tabled**) **1** N-COUNT A **table** is a piece of furniture with a flat top that you put things on or sit at. ❑ *...the kitchen table.* **2** N-COUNT A **table** is a set of facts or figures arranged in columns and rows. **3** PHRASE If you **turn the tables on** someone who is causing you problems, you change the situation completely so that you cause problems for them instead. **4** V-T If someone **tables** a proposal or motion, they say formally that they want it to be discussed at a meeting. [BRIT] ❑ *They've tabled a proposal criticising the Government.*

tablecloth /'teɪbəlklɒθ, AM -klɔːθ/ (**tablecloths**) N-COUNT A **tablecloth** is a large piece of material used to cover a table, especially during a meal.

tablespoon /'teɪbəlspuːn/ (**tablespoons**) N-COUNT A **tablespoon** is a fairly large spoon used for serving food and in cookery. A **tablespoon** of food or liquid is the amount that a tablespoon will hold.

tablet /'tæblət/ (**tablets**) N-COUNT A **tablet** is a small, solid, round mass of medicine which you swallow. ❑ *I take herbal sleeping tablets.*

tabloid /'tæblɔɪd/ (**tabloids**) N-COUNT A **tabloid** is a newspaper with small pages, often with short articles and lots of photographs.

taboo /tæ'buː/ (**taboos**) N-COUNT & ADJ If there is a **taboo** on a subject or activity, or if it is **taboo**, it is a social custom to avoid doing that activity or talking about that subject, because people find it embarrassing or offensive. ❑ *The subject of addiction remains a taboo.* ❑ *Cancer is a taboo subject.*

tacit /'tæsɪt/ ADJ If someone gives their **tacit** agreement or approval, they agree to something or approve it without actually saying so. ❑ *He gave tacit support to terrorists.* ● **tacitly** ADV ❑ *He tacitly admitted that the government had broken the law.*

tack /tæk/ (**tacks, tacking, tacked**) **1** N-COUNT A **tack** is a short nail with a broad flat head. **2** V-T If you **tack** something to a surface, you pin it there with tacks. ❑ *He had tacked this note to her door.* **3** N-UNCOUNT If you change **tack** or try a different **tack**, you try a different method for dealing with a situation. ❑ *This report takes a different tack from the last one.*

▶ **tack on** PHR-VERB If you say that something **is tacked on to** something else, you think that it is added in a hurried and unsatisfactory way. ❑ *A small kitchen is tacked on to the back of the beautiful stone house.*

tackle /'tækəl/ (**tackles, tackling, tackled**) **1** V-T If you **tackle** a difficult task, you start dealing with it in a determined way. ❑ *They will need help to tackle the crisis.* **2** V-T & N-COUNT If you **tackle** someone in a game such as football, you try to take the ball away from them. This action is called a **tackle**. **3** V-T If you **tackle** someone about a difficult matter, you speak to them frankly about it, usually in order to get something changed or done. **4** N-UNCOUNT **Tackle** is the equipment that you need for an activity, especially fishing.

tacky /'tæki/ (**tackier, tackiest**) ADJ If you describe something as **tacky**, you dislike it because it is cheap and badly made or vulgar. [INFORMAL] ❑ *...tacky red sunglasses.*

tact /tækt/ N-UNCOUNT **Tact** is the ability to avoid upsetting or offending people by being careful not to say or do things that would hurt their feelings. ❑ *You tend to say exactly what you mean when it might be better to exercise a little tact.*

tactful /'tæktfʊl/ ADJ If you describe someone as **tactful**, you approve of them because they are careful not to say or do anything that would offend or upset other people. ❑ *Sometimes it's more tactful not to ask for the truth.* ● **tactfully** ADV ❑ *Tactfully, she turned away as I changed my clothes.*

Word Link	*tact ≈ touching : contact, intact, tactic*

tactic /'tæktɪk/ (**tactics**) N-COUNT **Tactics** are the methods that you choose in order to achieve what you want. ❑ *...delaying tactics.*

tactical /'tæktɪkəl/ **1** ADJ A **tactical** action or plan is intended to help someone achieve what they want in the future, rather than immediately. ❑ *Public seminars were arranged to discuss the tactical management of the prison service.* ● **tactically** ADV ❑ *Many people will vote tactically to prevent Robertson getting back in power.* **2** ADJ **Tactical** means relating to tactics. ❑ *He's made a tactical error.*

tag /tæg/ (**tags, tagging, tagged**) **1** N-COUNT A **tag** is a small piece of card or cloth which is attached to an object and has information about that object on it. ❑ *The jackets still had their price tags attached.* **2** V-T If you **tag** something, you attach something to it or mark it so that it can be identified later.

▶ **tag along** PHR-VERB If you **tag along with** someone, you go with them, especially because you are interested in what they are doing. ❑ *He said we could tag along with them, to find out about his work.*

tail /teɪl/ (**tails, tailing, tailed**) **1** N-COUNT The **tail** of an animal is the part extending beyond the

end of its body. **2** N-COUNT You can use **tail** to refer to the end or back of something, especially something long and thin. ❑ *...the tail of the plane.* **3** V-T To **tail** someone means to follow close behind them and watch what they do. [INFORMAL] ❑ *The police have been tailing the gang for weeks.*
→ see **horse**
▶ **tail off** PHR-VERB If something **tails off**, it gradually becomes less, and perhaps ends completely. ❑ *Wolf's success tailed off as the 60s ended.*

tailor /'teɪlə/ (**tailors, tailoring, tailored**) **1** N-COUNT A **tailor** is a person who makes clothes, especially for men. **2** V-T If you **tailor** something such as a plan or system **to** someone's needs or purposes, you make it suitable for them by changing the details of it. ❑ *The system is tailored to meet the needs of every student.*

ˌtailor-'made ADJ Something that is **tailor-made for** a person or purpose is very suitable or was specially designed for them. ❑ *The music was tailor-made for her voice.*

taint /teɪnt/ (**taints, tainting, tainted**) **1** V-T If you say that something or someone **is tainted** by something undesirable or corrupt, you mean that their status or reputation is harmed by it. ❑ *The place has not been tainted by modern culture.* ● **tainted** ADJ ❑ *...tainted evidence.* **2** N-SING A **taint** is an undesirable quality in something which spoils it. ❑ *Her government never got rid of the taint of corruption.*

take

1 USED WITH NOUNS DESCRIBING ACTIONS
2 OTHER VERB AND NOUN SENSES
3 PHRASES
4 PHRASAL VERBS

take /teɪk/ (**takes, taking, took, taken**)
1 **1** V-T You can use **take** to say that someone does something. ❑ *Take a look at this.* ❑ *Betty took a photograph of us.* **2** V-T You can use **take** with nouns instead of using a more specific and often more formal verb. ❑ *The Party took power after a three-month civil war.*

take /teɪk/ (**takes, taking, took, taken**)
2 **1** V-T If you **take** something, you reach for it and hold it. ❑ *Let me take your coat.* ❑ *Opening a drawer, she took out a letter.* **2** V-T If you **take** something with you when you go somewhere, you carry it with you. ❑ *I'll take these papers home and read them.* **3** V-T If you **take** something from its owner, you steal it. **4** V-T If a person, vehicle, or path **takes** someone somewhere, they transport or lead them there. ❑ *She took me to a Mexican restaurant.* **5** V-T To **take** something or someone means to win or capture them from an enemy or opponent. ❑ *The army went in, taking 15 prisoners.* **6** V-T If you **take** something that is offered to you, you accept it. ❑ *When I took the job I thought I could change the system.* **7** V-T If you **take** a road or route, you choose to travel along it. ❑ *Take the Chester Road to the outskirts of town.* **8** V-T If you **take** a car, train, bus, or plane, you use it to go from one place to another. ❑ *She took the train to New York.* **9** V-T If you **take** a particular size in shoes or clothes, that size fits you. ❑ *I take a size five shoe.* **10** V-T If someone **takes** a drug or medicine, they swallow it. **11** V-T If you **take** an event or piece of news well or badly, you react to it well or badly. ❑ *No one took my messages seriously.* **12** V-T If something **takes** a certain amount of time, you need that amount of time in order to do it. ❑ *The sauce takes 25 minutes to prepare.* **13** V-T If something **takes** a particular quality or thing, it requires it. ❑ *Walking across the room took all her strength.* **14** V-T If you cannot **take** something unpleasant, you cannot bear it. ❑ *Don't ever ask me to look after those kids again. I just can't take it!* **15** V-T If you **take** a subject or course at school or university, you choose to study it. ❑ *Students are allowed to take European history and American history.* **16** V-T If you **take** an exam, you do it or take part in it. **17** → See note at **exam** **18** V-T The teacher who **takes** a class for a subject teaches the class that subject. [BRIT]

Usage

Take and **bring** are both used to talk about carrying something or accompanying someone somewhere, but **take** is used to suggest movement away from the speaker and **bring** is used to suggest movement towards the speaker. ❑ *We could not bring it here because it is rather heavy.* ❑ *Anna took the book to bed with her.* In the first sentence, **bring** suggests that we are coming to the same place as the speaker, that is, the speaker is here too. In the second sentence, **took** suggests that Anna moved away from the speaker when she went to bed, or alternatively that the speaker is merely reporting something that he or she was not involved in. The difference between **bring** and **take** is equivalent to that between **come** and **go**. **Bring** and **come** suggest movement towards the speaker, while **take** and **go** suggest movement away.

Thesaurus *take* Also look up:

v.	grab, grasp, hold ② 1
	steal ② 3
	drive, escort, transport ② 4
	capture, seize ② 5

take /teɪk/ (**takes, taking, took, taken**)
3 **1** PHRASE You can say **'I take it'** to someone in order to confirm that you have understood their meaning or understood a situation. ❑ *I take it that you don't read 'The Times'.* **2** PHRASE If you say to someone **'take it or leave it'**, you are telling them that they can accept something or not accept it, but that you are not prepared to discuss any other alternatives.

take /teɪk/ (**takes, taking, took, taken**)
4 ▶ **take after** PHR-VERB If you **take after** a member of your family, you look or behave like them. ❑ *He takes after his dad.*
▶ **take apart** PHR-VERB If you **take** something **apart**, you separate it into its different parts.
▶ **take away** **1** PHR-VERB If you **take** something **away from** someone, you remove it from them. ❑ *If you don't like it, we'll take it away for free.* **2** → see also **takeaway**
▶ **take back** **1** PHR-VERB If you **take** something **back**, you return it. ❑ *I once took back a pair of shoes that fell apart after a week.* **2** PHR-VERB If you **take back** something that you said, you admit that it was wrong. ❑ *Take back what you said about Jeremy!*
▶ **take down** **1** PHR-VERB When people **take**

down a structure, they separate it into pieces and remove it. ❑ *They took down the wall between the living room and the kitchen.* 2 PHR-VERB If you **take down** information, you write it down. ❑ *I took down his comments in my notebook.*

▶ **take in** 1 PHR-VERB If you **take** someone **in**, you allow them to stay in your house or country, especially when they are homeless or in trouble. ❑ *The church has taken in 26 refugees.* 2 PHR-VERB If you **are taken in** by someone or something, you are deceived or fooled by them. ❑ *They were taken in by his lies.* 3 PHR-VERB If you **take** something **in**, you pay attention to it and understand it when you hear or read it. ❑ *Robert took it all in without needing a second explanation.*

▶ **take off** 1 PHR-VERB When an aircraft **takes off**, it leaves the ground and starts flying. 2 → see also **takeoff** 3 PHR-VERB If something such as a product, an activity, or someone's career **takes off**, it suddenly becomes very successful. ❑ *In 1985, he met Madonna, and his career took off.* 4 PHR-VERB If you **take off** something that you are wearing, you move it off your body. ❑ *She took off her hat and scarf.* 5 → See note at **wear** 6 PHR-VERB If you **take** time **off**, you do not go to work. ❑ *She took two days off work.*

▶ **take on** 1 PHR-VERB If you **take on** a job or responsibility, you accept it. ❑ *Don't take on more responsibilities than you can manage.* 2 PHR-VERB If you **take on** someone more powerful than you, you fight them or compete against them. 3 PHR-VERB If you **take** someone **on**, you give them a job. ❑ *The company has been taking on new staff.* 4 PHR-VERB If something **takes on** a new appearance or quality, it develops that appearance or quality. ❑ *Bess's face took on a worried look at once.*

▶ **take out** 1 PHR-VERB If you **take out** something such as a loan or insurance policy, a company agrees to let you have it. 2 PHR-VERB If you **take** someone **out**, you take them to an enjoyable place, and you pay for both of you. ❑ *Rachel took me out to lunch.* 3 PHR-VERB If you **take** your unhappiness or anger **out on** someone, you behave in an unpleasant way towards them, even though it is not their fault that you feel upset. ❑ *Just because you've had a bad day at work, there's no need to take it out on us.* 4 → see also **takeout**

▶ **take over** 1 PHR-VERB To **take over** something such as a company or country means to gain control of it. ❑ *A British newspaper says British Airways plan to take over Trans World Airways.* 2 → see also **takeover** 3 PHR-VERB If you **take over** a job, or if you **take over**, you start doing the job after someone else has stopped doing it. ❑ *In 1966, Pastor Albertz took over as mayor.*

▶ **take to** 1 PHR-VERB If you **take to** someone or something, you like them immediately. ❑ *My wife and I immediately took to Alan.* 2 PHR-VERB If you **take to** doing something, you begin to do it regularly. ❑ *They had taken to wandering through the streets.*

▶ **take up** 1 PHR-VERB If you **take up** an activity or job, you start doing it. ❑ *The girls were encouraged to take up a hobby.* 2 PHR-VERB If you **take** someone **up on** an offer that they have made, you accept their offer. ❑ *When she offered to babysit, I took her up on it.* 3 PHR-VERB If you **take up** a matter, you start to deal with it or discuss how you are going to deal with it. ❑ *Dr Mahathir intends to take up the proposal with the prime minister.*

▶ **take upon** PHR-VERB If you **take it upon yourself to** do something, you do it even though it is not your duty. ❑ *Knox had taken it upon himself to choose the wine.*

takeaway /ˈteɪkəweɪ/ (**takeaways**) N-COUNT In British English, a **takeaway** is a shop or restaurant which sells hot food to be eaten elsewhere. A meal that you buy there is also called a **takeaway**. The American word is **takeout**.

taken /ˈteɪkən/ 1 **Taken** is the past participle of **take**. 2 ADJ AFTER LINK-V If you are **taken with** something or someone, you find them attractive and interesting. ❑ *She seems very taken with the idea.*

takeoff /ˈteɪkɒf, AM -ɔːf/ (**takeoffs**) N-VAR **Takeoff** is the beginning of a flight, when an aircraft leaves the ground. ❑ *The plane was waiting for takeoff.*

takeout /ˈteɪkaʊt/ (**takeouts**) → see **takeaway**

takeover /ˈteɪkəʊvə/ (**takeovers**) 1 N-VAR A **takeover** is the act of gaining control of a company by buying a majority of its shares. ❑ *...the proposed takeover of Midland Bank.* 2 N-COUNT A **takeover** is the act of taking control of a country, political party, or movement by force. ❑ *There's been a military takeover of some kind.*

taker /ˈteɪkə/ (**takers**) N-COUNT If there are no **takers** or few **takers** for an offer or challenge, hardly anyone is willing to accept it.

takings /ˈteɪkɪŋz/ N-PLURAL The **takings** of a business such as a shop or cinema consist of the amount of money it gets from selling its goods or tickets during a certain period. [BRIT]

tale /teɪl/ (**tales**) 1 N-COUNT A **tale** is a story, especially one involving adventure or magic. 2 N-COUNT You can refer to an interesting, exciting, or dramatic account of a real event as a **tale**. ❑ *...tales of horror and loss resulting from Monday's earthquake.* 3 → see also **fairy tale**

talent /ˈtælənt/ (**talents**) N-VAR **Talent** is the natural ability to do something well. ❑ *Both her children have a talent for music.* ❑ *It is important to use people's talents to the full.*

Thesaurus	*talent* Also look up:
N.	ability, aptitude, gift

Word Partnership	Use *talent* with:
ADJ.	**great** talent, **musical** talent, **natural** talent
V.	**have (a)** talent, **have got** talent
N.	talent **pool**, talent **search**

talented /ˈtæləntɪd/ ADJ Someone who is **talented** has a natural ability to do something well. ❑ *Howard is a talented pianist.*

talisman /ˈtælɪzmən/ (**talismans**) N-COUNT A **talisman** is an object which you believe has magic powers to protect you or bring you luck.

talk /tɔːk/ (**talks, talking, talked**) 1 V-I & N-VAR When you **talk**, you say things to someone. **Talk** is the things you say. ❑ *They were talking about American food.* ❑ *A teacher reprimanded a girl for talking in class.* ❑ *We had a long talk about her father.* 2 V-I & N-COUNT If you **talk**, or if you give a **talk on** or **about** something, you make an informal speech about

t

it. ❑ *He intends to talk to young people about the dangers of AIDS.* **3** V-I & N-PLURAL When different sides in a dispute or negotiation **talk**, or when they have **talks**, they have formal discussions. ❑ *The two sides still aren't prepared to talk to each other.* ❑ *...peace talks.* **4** V-I If someone **talks** when they are being held by police or soldiers, they reveal important or secret information, usually unwillingly. **5** V-T If you **talk** politics or sport, for example, you discuss it. ❑ *...middle-aged men talking business.*

▶ **talk down** PHR-VERB If someone **talks** something **down**, they reduce its value or importance by saying bad things about it. ❑ *I will not accept anybody talking down my country.*

▶ **talk into** PHR-VERB If you **talk** someone **into** doing something, you persuade them to do it.

▶ **talk out of** PHR-VERB If you **talk** someone **out of** doing something, you persuade them not to do it.

▶ **talk over** PHR-VERB If you **talk** something **over**, you discuss it thoroughly and honestly. ❑ *He always talked things over with his friends.*

▶ **talk through** PHR-VERB To **talk through** a problem is the same as to **talk** it **over**. ❑ *That's how we cope, by talking things through.*

▶ **talk up** PHR-VERB If someone **talks up** a particular thing, they increase its value, success, or importance by saying exaggerated things about it. ❑ *The area is talked up as a cool and fabulous place to live.*

Usage

There are some differences in the way the verbs **talk** and **speak** are used. **Talk** is more likely to be used when you are referring to a conversation or discussion. ❑ *I talked about it with my family at dinner.* ❑ *Sometimes we'd talk all night.* Talk can also be used to emphasize the activity of saying things, rather than the words that are spoken. ❑ *She thought I talked too much.* When you **speak**, however, you could, for example, be addressing someone or making a speech.

Thesaurus *talk* Also look up:

V. chat, discuss, gossip, say, share, speak, tell; *(ant.)* listen **1**

N. argument, chat, conversation, dialogue, discussion, interview, negotiation; *(ant.)* silence **1**

T

Word Link *er ≈ more : bigger, louder, taller*

tall /tɔːl/ (**taller, tallest**) **1** ADJ Someone or something that is **tall** is above average height. ❑ *He was very tall.* **2** ADJ You use **tall** to ask or talk about the height of someone or something. ❑ *How tall are you?* ❑ *I'm only 5ft tall.* **3** PHRASE If something is **a tall order**, it is very difficult. ❑ *Paying for your studies may seem like a tall order.* **4** → See note at **high**

tally /ˈtæli/ (**tallies, tallying, tallied**) **1** N-COUNT A **tally** is a record of amounts or numbers which you keep changing and adding to as the activity which affects it progresses. ❑ *The final tally was 817 votes for Mrs King and 731 for Mr Lee.* **2** V-I If two numbers or statements **tally**, they agree with each other or are exactly the same. ❑ *This description didn't seem to tally with what we saw.*

tame /teɪm/ (**tamer, tamest, tames, taming, tamed**) **1** ADJ A **tame** animal or bird is not afraid of humans. **2** ADJ If you say that something or someone is **tame**, you are criticizing them for being weak and boring. ❑ *Some of today's political demonstrations look rather tame.* ● **tamely** ADV ❑ *He tamely did what someone else told him.* **3** V-T If someone **tames** a wild animal or bird, they train it not to be afraid of humans.

tamper /ˈtæmpə/ (**tampers, tampering, tampered**) V-I If someone **tampers with** something, they interfere with it or try to change it when they have no right to do so. ❑ *He found his computer had been tampered with.* ● **tampering** N-UNCOUNT ❑ *The police arrested the teenager for tampering with the van.*

tampon /ˈtæmpɒn/ (**tampons**) N-COUNT A **tampon** is a firm piece of cotton wool that a woman puts inside her vagina when she has a period, in order to absorb the blood.

tan /tæn/ (**tans, tanning, tanned**) **1** N-COUNT If you have a **tan**, your skin has become darker than usual because you have been in the sun. **2** V-T/V-I If a part of your body **tans** or if you **tan** it, your skin becomes darker than usual because you spend time in the sun. ● **tanned** ADJ ❑ *He is very tanned.*

tandem /ˈtændəm/ (**tandems**) **1** N-COUNT A **tandem** is a bicycle designed for two riders. **2** PHRASE If two things happen or are done **in tandem**, they happen or are done together.
→ see **bicycle**

Word Link *tang ≈ touching : entangle, intangible, tangible*

tangible /ˈtændʒɪbəl/ ADJ If something is **tangible**, it is clear enough to be easily seen, felt, or noticed. ❑ *Involve her in activities with tangible results, such as cooking.*

tangle /ˈtæŋgəl/ (**tangles, tangling, tangled**) **1** N-COUNT A **tangle of** something is a mass of it twisted together in a confusing manner. ❑ *...a tangle of wires.* **2** V-T & PHR-VERB If something **is tangled**, or if it **is tangled up**, it becomes twisted into a confusing mass that is difficult to separate into its original form. ❑ *Animals get tangled in fishing nets and drown.*

tank /tæŋk/ (**tanks**) **1** N-COUNT A **tank** is a large container for holding liquid or gas. ❑ *...a tank full of goldfish.* **2** N-COUNT A **tank** is a military vehicle covered with armour and equipped with guns or rockets.

tanker /ˈtæŋkə/ (**tankers**) N-COUNT A **tanker** is a ship or truck used for transporting large quantities of gas or liquid, especially oil.
→ see **oil, ship**

tanned /tænd/ → see **tan**

tantalize [BRIT also **tantalise**] /ˈtæntəlaɪz/ (**tantalizes, tantalizing, tantalized**) V-T If something or someone **tantalizes** you, they make you feel hopeful and excited about something, usually before disappointing you. ❑ *...the dreams that have tantalized them.* ● **tantalizing** ADJ ❑ *...a tantalising aroma of roast beef.*

tantamount /ˈtæntəmaʊnt/ ADJ AFTER LINK-V If you say that one thing is **tantamount to** a second, more serious thing, you are emphasizing how bad or unfortunate the first thing is by saying it is almost the same as the second. [FORMAL] ❑ *Slowing down can seem tantamount to admitting you're weak.*

tantrum /'tæntrəm/ (**tantrums**) N-COUNT If a child has a **tantrum**, it suddenly loses its temper in a noisy and uncontrolled way.

tap /tæp/ (**taps, tapping, tapped**) **1** N-COUNT A **tap** is a device that controls the flow of a liquid or gas from a pipe or container. ❑ *She turned on the tap and splashed her face with cold water.* **2** V-T/V-I & N-COUNT If you **tap** something, or if you **tap on** it, you hit it with a quick light blow or a series of quick light blows. This kind of blow is called a **tap**. ❑ *O'Leary tapped the pavement with his foot.* ❑ *A tap on the door interrupted him.* **3** V-T If you **tap** a resource, you make use of it. ❑ *The book took six years to complete, and tapped the minds of 1,000 experts.* **4** V-T & N-COUNT If someone **taps** your telephone, they attach a special device called a **tap** to the line so that they can secretly listen to your conversations. → see **bathroom, dance**

Word Partnership Use *tap* with:

N.	**cold/hot water** tap **1** tap **on a door**, tap **your feet**, tap ***someone* on the shoulder** **2** tap **a (tele)phone** **4**
V.	**turn on a** tap **1**

tape /teɪp/ (**tapes, taping, taped**) **1** N-UNCOUNT **Tape** is a narrow plastic strip covered with a magnetic substance. It is used to record sounds, pictures, and computer information. ❑ *Some students did not wish to be interviewed on tape.* **2** N-COUNT A **tape** is a cassette with magnetic tape wound round it. **3** V-T If you **tape** music, sounds, or television pictures, you record them using a tape recorder or a video recorder. ● **taping** (**tapings**) N-VAR ❑ *...an unauthorized taping.* **4** N-VAR A **tape** is a strip of cloth used to tie things together or to identify who a piece of clothing belongs to. ❑ *...name tapes.* **5** N-UNCOUNT **Tape** is a sticky strip of plastic used for sticking things together. ❑ *...adhesive tape.* **6** V-T If you **tape** one thing to another, you attach it using sticky tape. ❑ *The envelope was taped shut.* **7** → see also **red tape** → see **office**

▶ **tape up** PHR-VERB If you **tape** something **up**, you fasten tape around it firmly, in order to protect it or hold it in a fixed position.

Word Partnership Use *tape* with:

N.	**piece of** tape, **roll of** tape **1** **cassette** tape, **music** tape, tape **player** **3** tape **a conversation**, tape **an interview**, **reel of** tape, tape **a show** **3**
V.	**listen to a** tape, **make a** tape, **play a** tape, **watch a** tape **3**

tape measure

'tape ˌmeasure (**tape measures**) N-COUNT A **tape measure** is a strip of metal, plastic, or cloth with marks on it, used for measuring, especially for clothes and DIY.

taper /'teɪpə/ (**tapers, tapering, tapered**) V-T/V-I If something **tapers**, or if you **taper** it, it gradually becomes thinner at one end. ❑ *...a beard that tapered to a sharp point.* ● **tapered** ADJ ❑ *...the elegantly tapered legs of the dressing-table.*

▶ **taper off** PHR-VERB If something **tapers off**, it gradually reduces in amount, number, or size. ❑ *The storm is expected to taper off today.*

'tape ˌrecorder (**tape recorders**) N-COUNT A **tape recorder** is a machine used for recording and playing music, speech, or other sounds.

tapestry /'tæpɪstri/ (**tapestries**) N-VAR A **tapestry** is a piece of heavy, good quality cloth with a picture or pattern sewn on it.

tar /tɑː/ N-UNCOUNT **Tar** is a thick, black, sticky substance used in making roads.

target /'tɑːgɪt/ (**targets, targeting, targeted**) **1** N-COUNT A **target** is something that someone is trying to hit with a weapon or other object. ❑ *Both his kicks missed the target.* ❑ *The airport could be a target for attack.* **2** V-T If someone **targets** someone or something, they decide to attack or criticize them. ❑ *He targets the economy as the cause of the violence.* **3** N-COUNT The **target of** an attack or a criticism is the person or thing being attacked or criticized. ❑ *They have been the target of racist abuse.* **4** N-COUNT A **target** is a result that you are trying to achieve. ❑ *...the park's annual target of 11 million visitors.* **5** PHRASE If someone or something is **on target**, they are making good progress and are likely to achieve the result that is wanted. **6** V-T If you **target** a particular group of people, you try to appeal to those people or affect them. ❑ *The organization was particularly keen to target young people.*

Word Partnership Use *target* with:

V.	**attack a** target, **hit a** target, **miss a** target **1**
ADJ.	**easy** target, **moving** target **1** **intended** target, **likely** target, **possible** target, **prime** target **1** **3**
N.	target **practice** **1** target **of criticism**, target **of an investigation** **3** target **date** **4** target **audience**, target **group**, target **population** **6**

tariff /'tærɪf/ (**tariffs**) **1** N-COUNT A **tariff** is a tax on goods coming into a country. **2** N-COUNT A **tariff** is the rate at which you are charged for something. [BRIT]

tarmac /'tɑːmæk/ N-UNCOUNT **Tarmac** is a material used for making road surfaces, consisting of crushed stones mixed with tar. **Tarmac** is a trademark. [BRIT]

tarnish /'tɑːnɪʃ/ (**tarnishes, tarnishing, tarnished**) **1** V-T If something **tarnishes** a person's reputation, it damages it and causes people to lose respect for that person. ● **tarnished** ADJ ❑ *He wants to improve the tarnished image of his country.* **2** V-T/V-I If metal **tarnishes**, or if something **tarnishes** it, it becomes stained and loses its brightness. ● **tarnished** ADJ ❑ *...brown surfaces of tarnished brass.*

tart /tɑːt/ (**tarts, tarter, tartest**) **1** N-VAR A **tart** is a shallow pastry case with a filling of sweet food

t

or fruit. ❑ *...jam tarts.* **2** ADJ If something such as fruit is **tart**, it has a sharp slightly bitter taste.

tartan /'tɑːtən/ ADJ **Tartan** cloth, which traditionally comes from Scotland, has different coloured stripes crossing each other.
→ see **pattern**

task /tɑːsk, tæsk/ (**tasks**) N-COUNT A **task** is an activity or piece of work which you have to do. ❑ *Waterman had the unpleasant task of breaking the bad news to Harris.* ❑ *...administrative tasks.*

Thesaurus *task* Also look up:

N. assignment, job, responsibility

Word Partnership Use *task* with:

V. **accomplish a** task, **assign** ***someone*** **a** task, **complete a** task, **face a** task, **give** ***someone*** **a** task, **perform a** task
ADJ. **complex** task, **difficult** task, **easy** task, **enormous** task, **important** task, **impossible** task, **main** task, **simple** task

taste /teɪst/ (**tastes, tasting, tasted**) **1** N-UNCOUNT Your sense of **taste** is your ability to recognize the flavour of things with your tongue. **2** N-COUNT The **taste** of something is the flavour that it has, for example whether it is sweet or salty. ❑ *I like the taste of chocolate.* **3** V-I If food or drink **tastes of** something, it has that particular flavour. ❑ *The tea tasted of lemon.* ❑ *The pizza tastes delicious.* **4** V-T & N-SING If you **taste** some food or drink, or if you have a **taste of** it, you try a small amount of it in order to see what its flavour and texture is like. **5** V-T If you can **taste** something that you are eating or drinking, you are aware of its flavour. ❑ *You can taste the chilli in the dish.* **6** V-T & N-SING If you **taste** something such as a way of life or a pleasure, or if you have a **taste of** it, you experience it for a short period of time. **7** N-SING If you have a **taste for** something, you enjoy it. ❑ *That gave me a taste for reading.* **8** N-UNCOUNT & N-PLURAL A person's **taste** is their choice in the things that they like or buy, for example their clothes, possessions, or favourite music. ❑ *There was music for all ages and all tastes.* **9** PHRASE If you say that something that is said or done is **in bad taste** or **in poor taste**, you mean that it is offensive because it is inappropriate for the situation. ❑ *He doesn't think his film is in bad taste.*
→ see Word Web: **taste**
→ see **sugar**

Word Partnership Use *taste* with:

N. **sense of** taste **1**
ADJ. **bitter/salty/sour/sweet** taste **2**
taste **bitter/salty/sour/sweet**, taste **good** **4**
acquired taste **9**
bad/good/poor taste, **in bad/good/poor** taste **9**
V. **like the** taste **of** ***something*** **2**
get a taste **of** ***something*** **7**
ADV. taste **like** ***something*** **3**

tasteful /'teɪstfʊl/ ADJ If you describe something as **tasteful**, you mean that it is attractive and elegant. ❑ *...a tasteful linen suit.*
● **tastefully** ADV ❑ *...a large and tastefully decorated home.*

tasteless /'teɪstləs/ **1** ADJ If you describe something as **tasteless**, you mean that it is vulgar and unattractive. **2** ADJ If you describe something such as a remark or joke as **tasteless**, you mean that it is offensive. **3** ADJ If you describe food or drink as **tasteless**, you mean that it has very little or no flavour.

tasty /'teɪsti/ (**tastier, tastiest**) ADJ If you say that food, especially savoury food, is **tasty**, you mean that it has a pleasant and fairly strong flavour which makes it good to eat.

tattered /'tætəd/ ADJ If something such as clothing is **tattered**, it is torn or crumpled, especially because it is old and has been used a lot.

tatters /'tætəz/ **1** N-PLURAL Clothes that are **in tatters** are badly torn in several places. **2** N-PLURAL If you say that something such as a plan or relationship is **in tatters**, you are emphasizing that it is weak and has suffered a lot of damage.

tattoo /tæ'tuː/ (**tattoos, tattooing, tattooed**) **1** N-COUNT A **tattoo** is a design on someone's skin, made by pricking little holes and filling them with coloured dye. **2** V-T If someone **tattoos** you, they draw a design on your skin by pricking little holes and filling them with coloured dye. ❑ *He had 'Mother' tattooed on his arm.*

Word Web taste

What we think of as **taste** is mostly **odour**. The sense of **smell** controls about 80% of the experience. We taste only four **sensations**: **sweet**, **salty**, **sour**, and **bitter**. We experience sweetness and saltiness through **taste buds** near the tip of the **tongue**. We sense sourness at the sides and bitterness at the back of the tongue. Some people have more taste buds than others. Scientists have discovered some "supertasters" with 425 taste buds per square centimetre. Most of us have about 184 and some "nontasters" have only about 96.

Word Web tea

Do you want to **brew** a good cup of **tea**? Don't use a **tea bag**. For the best taste, use fresh **tea leaves**. First, boil water in a **teakettle**. Use some of the water to warm the inside of a china **teapot**. Empty the pot, and add the tea leaves. Pour in more boiling water. Let the tea steep for at least five minutes. Serve the tea in thin china **cups**. Add milk and sugar if you wish.

taught /tɔːt/ **Taught** is the past tense and past participle of **teach**.

taunt /tɔːnt/ (**taunts, taunting, taunted**) 1 V-T If someone **taunts** you, they try to upset or annoy you by saying unkind or insulting things to you, especially about your weaknesses or failures. 2 N-COUNT A **taunt** is an unkind or insulting comment that is intended to upset or annoy you. ❑ *...racist taunts.*

taut /tɔːt/ (**tauter, tautest**) ADJ Something that is **taut** is stretched very tight.

tax /tæks/ (**taxes, taxing, taxed**) 1 N-VAR **Tax** is an amount of money that you have to pay to the government so that it can pay for public services. ❑ *...the basic rate of income tax.* 2 V-T When a person or company **is taxed**, they have to pay a part of their income or profits to the government. When goods **are taxed**, a percentage of their price has to be paid to the government. ❑ *Biscuits and ice cream are taxed at 11 percent.* 3 V-T If something **taxes** your strength, your patience, or your resources, it uses nearly all of them, so that you have great difficulty in carrying out what you are trying to do. 4 → see also **taxing**
→ see **citizenship**

taxable /ˈtæksəbəl/ ADJ **Taxable** income is income on which you have to pay tax.

taxation /tækˈseɪʃən/ 1 N-UNCOUNT **Taxation** is the system by which a government takes money from people so that it can use it to pay for public services. 2 N-UNCOUNT **Taxation** is the amount of money that people have to pay in taxes. ❑ *The result will be higher taxation.*

ˌtax-ˈfree ADJ **Tax-free** is used to describe income on which you do not have to pay tax. ❑ *...a tax-free savings plan.*

taxi /ˈtæksi/ (**taxis, taxiing, taxied**) 1 N-COUNT A **taxi** is a car driven by a person whose job is to take people where they want to go in return for money. 2 V-I When an aircraft **taxis** along the ground, it moves slowly along it before taking off or after landing.

taxi

taxing /ˈtæksɪŋ/ ADJ A **taxing** task or problem requires a lot of mental or physical effort.

taxpayer /ˈtækspeɪə/ (**taxpayers**) N-COUNT **Taxpayers** are people who pay a percentage of their income to the government as tax.

TB /ˌtiː ˈbiː/ N-UNCOUNT **TB** is a very serious infectious disease that affects someone's lungs and other parts of their body. **TB** is an abbreviation for 'tuberculosis'.

tea /tiː/ (**teas**) 1 N-VAR **Tea** is a drink made by pouring boiling water on the chopped dried leaves of a plant called the tea bush. ❑ *Would you like a cup of tea?* 2 N-VAR **Tea** is the chopped dried leaves that you use to make tea. ❑ *...a packet of tea.* 3 N-VAR Drinks such as mint **tea** are made by pouring boiling water on the dried leaves of the particular plant or flower. ❑ *...herbal teas.* 4 N-VAR **Tea** is a meal some people eat in the late afternoon, especially in Britain. It consists of food such as sandwiches and cakes, with tea to drink. 5 N-VAR Some people refer to the main meal that they eat in the early part of the evening as **tea**. [BRIT] 6 → See note at **meal**
→ see Word Web: **tea**

teach /tiːtʃ/ (**teaches, teaching, taught**) 1 V-T If you **teach** someone something, you give them instructions so that they know about it or know how to do it. ❑ *George had taught him how to ride a horse.* ❑ *She taught Julie to read.* 2 V-T To **teach** someone something means to show them how to think, feel, or act in a new or different way. ❑ *We have to teach drivers to respect cyclists.* 3 V-T/V-I If you **teach** or **teach** a subject, your job is to help students to learn about a subject by explaining it or showing them how to do it. ❑ *Ingrid is currently teaching mathematics at Shimla Public School.* ● **teacher** (**teachers**) N-COUNT ❑ *...her chemistry teacher.* ● **teaching** N-UNCOUNT ❑ *...the teaching of English in schools.* 4 to **teach** someone **a lesson** → see **lesson**

Thesaurus *teach* Also look up:

V. educate, school, train 1 2 3

Word Partnership Use *teach* with:

ADV. teach ***someone*** **how** 1
N. teach ***someone*** **a skill**, teach **students** 1
teach **children** 1–3
teach ***someone*** **a lesson** 2
teach **classes**, teach **courses**, teach **English/history/reading/science**, teach **school** 3
V. **try to** teach 1–3

teaching /ˈtiːtʃɪŋ/ (**teachings**) N-COUNT The **teachings** of a particular person, school of thought, or religion are all the ideas and principles that they teach.

teak /tiːk/ N-UNCOUNT **Teak** is a very hard wood grown in South-East Asia which is used to make furniture.

team /tiːm/ (**teams, teaming, teamed**) 1 N-COUNT A **team** is a group of people who play together against another group in a sport or game. **Team** can take the singular or plural form of the verb. ❑ *The team is close to bottom of the League.* ❑ *The men's team are now out of the competition.* **2** N-COUNT You can refer to any group of people who work together as a **team**. **Team** can take the singular or plural form of the verb. ❑ *...a team of doctors.*

▸ **team up** PHR-VERB If you **team up with** someone, you join them in order to work together for a particular purpose. ❑ *Elton teamed up with Eric Clapton to make the record.* ❑ *A friend suggested that we team up for a working holiday in Europe.*

'team-mate (**team-mates**) N-COUNT In a game or sport, your **team-mates** are the other members of your team.

teamwork /'ti:mwɜ:k/ N-UNCOUNT **Teamwork** is the ability that a group of people have to work well together.

teapot /'ti:pɒt/ (**teapots**) N-COUNT A **teapot** is a container with a lid, a handle, and a spout, used for making and serving tea.

→ see **tea**

tear
1 CRYING
2 DAMAGING OR MOVING

tear /tɪə/ (**tears**)
1 **1** N-COUNT **Tears** are the drops of liquid that come out of your eyes when you are crying.
2 N-PLURAL You can use **tears** in expressions such as **in tears**, **burst into tears**, and **close to tears** to indicate that someone is crying or is almost crying. ❑ *He was in floods of tears.*

→ see **cut, cry**

tear /teə/ (**tears, tearing, tore, torn**)
2 **1** V-T & N-COUNT If you **tear** something such as paper or cloth, you pull it into two pieces or you pull it so that a hole appears in it. A **tear** in something is a hole that has been made in it. ❑ *Mary Ann tore the edge off her paper napkin.* ❑ *Nancy quickly tore open the envelope.* ❑ *His trousers had a tear in one knee.* **2** V-T To **tear** something from somewhere means to remove it violently. ❑ *She tore the windscreen wipers from his car.* **3** V-I If you **tear** somewhere, you move there very quickly, often in an uncontrolled or dangerous way. ❑ *The door flew open and Miranda tore into the room.*

▸ **tear apart** PHR-VERB If something **tears** people **apart**, it causes them to quarrel or to leave each other. ❑ *The quarrel tore the couple apart.*

T

▸ **tear away** PHR-VERB If you **tear** someone **away from** a place or activity, you force them to leave the place or stop doing the activity, even though they want to remain there or carry on. ❑ *She couldn't tear herself away from the radio.*

▸ **tear down** PHR-VERB If you **tear** something **down**, you destroy it or remove it completely. ❑ *They tore the school down some years later.*

▸ **tear off** PHR-VERB If you **tear off** your clothes, you take them off quickly in a rough way.

▸ **tear up** PHR-VERB If you **tear up** a piece of paper, you tear it into a lot of small pieces. ❑ *Don't you dare tear up her ticket.* ❑ *...a torn up photograph.*

tearful /'tɪəfʊl/ ADJ If someone is **tearful**, their face or voice shows signs that they have been crying or that they want to cry.

tear gas /'tɪəgæs/ N-UNCOUNT **Tear gas** is a gas that causes your eyes to sting and fill with tears. It is used by the police to control violent crowds.

tease /ti:z/ (**teases, teasing, teased**) V-T To **tease** someone means to laugh at them or make jokes about them in order to embarrass, annoy, or upset them. ❑ *'You must be expecting a young man,' she teased.*

Thesaurus *tease* Also look up:
V. aggravate, bother, provoke

teaspoon /'ti:spu:n/ (**teaspoons**) **1** N-COUNT A **teaspoon** is a small spoon that you use to put sugar into tea or coffee. **2** N-COUNT A **teaspoon of** food or liquid is the amount that a teaspoon will hold. ❑ *He wants three teaspoons of sugar in his coffee.*

Word Link ***techn** ≈ art, skill : technical, technician, technique*

technical /'teknɪkəl/ **1** ADJ **Technical** means involving the sorts of machines, processes, and materials used in industry, transport, and communications. ❑ *A number of technical problems will have to be solved.* ❑ *...jobs that require technical knowledge.* **2** ADJ You use **technical** to describe the practical skills and methods used to do an activity such as an art, a craft, or a sport. ❑ *Their technical ability is exceptional.* • **technically** ADV ❑ *While Sade's voice isn't technically brilliant, it has a beautiful quality.* **3** ADJ **Technical** language involves using special words to describe the details of a specialized activity. ❑ *...a technical term.*

Word Partnership Use *technical* with:
N. technical **knowledge** **1**
technical **assistance**, technical **difficulties**, technical **expertise**, technical **experts**, technical **information**, technical **issues**, technical **problems**, technical **services**, technical **skills**, technical **support**, technical **training** **2**
ADV. **highly** technical **1** **2**

technicality /ˌteknɪ'kælɪti/ (**technicalities**) **1** N-PLURAL The **technicalities of** a process or activity are the detailed methods used to do it. ❑ *...the technicalities of classroom teaching.* **2** N-COUNT A **technicality** is a point based on a strict interpretation of a law or a set of rules. ❑ *The murderers were allowed to go free on a technicality.*

technically /'teknɪkli/ ADV If something is **technically** true or possible, it is true or possible according to a strict interpretation of the facts, laws, or rules, but may not be important or relevant in a particular situation. ❑ *Technically, the two sides have been in a state of war ever since 1949.*

technician /tek'nɪʃən/ (**technicians**) N-COUNT A **technician** is someone whose job involves skilled practical work with scientific equipment, for example in a laboratory.

technique /tek'ni:k/ (**techniques**) **1** N-COUNT A **technique** is a particular method of doing an activity, usually a method that involves practical skills. ❑ *...the techniques of modern agriculture.* **2** N-UNCOUNT **Technique** is skill and ability in an

Word Web technology

Innovative technologies affect everything in our lives. In new homes, **state-of-the-art** computer systems control heating, lighting, communication, and entertainment systems. **Gadgets** such as **digital** music players are small and easy to carry. But high technology has a serious side, too. **Biotechnology** may help us cure diseases. It also raises many ethical questions. **Cutting-edge** biometric technology is replacing old-fashioned security systems. Soon your ATM will check your identity by scanning the iris of your eye and your laptop will scan your fingerprint.

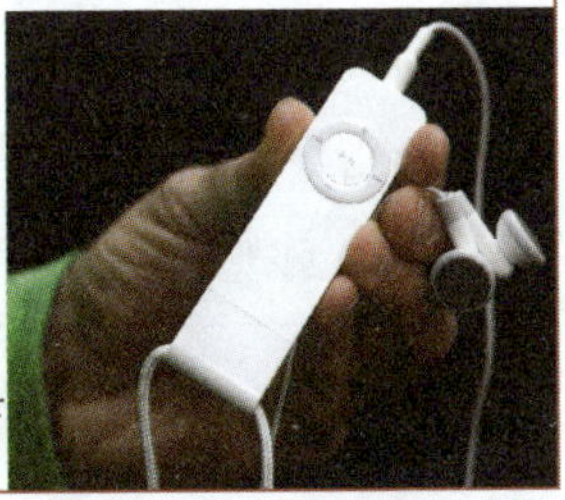

artistic, sporting, or other practical activity that is developed through training and practice. ❑ *...the band's lack of technique.*

Word Link ***techn ≈ art, skill : technical, technician, technology***

technology /tek'nɒlədʒi/ (**technologies**) N-VAR **Technology** refers to things which are the result of scientific knowledge being used for practical purposes. ❑ *Personal computing and mobile telephone are technologies which once represented the future.* ❑ *...technologies like microwave ovens and contact lenses.* ● **technological** /ˌteknə'lɒdʒɪkəl/ ADJ BEFORE N ❑ *...an era of very rapid technological change.* ● **technologically** /ˌteknə'lɒdʒɪkli/ ADV ❑ *...technologically advanced aircraft.*
→ see Word Web: **technology**

Word Partnership Use *technology* with:

ADJ. **advanced** technology, **available** technology, **educational** technology, **high** technology, **latest** technology, **medical** technology, **modern** technology, **new** technology, **sophisticated** technology, **wireless** technology

N. **computer** technology, **information** technology, **science and** technology

teddy /'tedi/ (**teddies**) N-COUNT A **teddy** or a **teddy bear** is a soft toy that looks like a bear.

tedious /'ti:diəs/ ADJ If you describe something such as a job or a situation as **tedious**, you mean it is boring and frustrating. ● **tediously** ADV ❑ *These first chapters are tediously repetitive.*

teem /ti:m/ (**teems, teeming, teemed**) V-I If a place **is teeming with** people or animals, there are a lot of people or animals moving around in it. ❑ *The area is teeming with tourists.* ❑ *...the teeming streets of Calcutta.*

teen /ti:n/ (**teens**) **1** N-PLURAL If you are **in** your **teens**, you are between thirteen and nineteen years old. ❑ *I first met John in my late teens.* **2** ADJ BEFORE N **Teen** is used to describe films, magazines, music, or activities that are aimed at or done by teenagers. ❑ *...a teen movie.*

teenage /'ti:neɪdʒ/ ADJ BEFORE N **Teenage** children are aged between thirteen and nineteen years old. ❑ *Almost one in four teenage girls are on a diet.* ❑ *...'Smash Hits', a teenage magazine.*

Word Link ***teen ≈ plus ten, from 13-19 : eighteen, seventeen, teenager***

teenager /'ti:neɪdʒə/ (**teenagers**) N-COUNT A **teenager** is someone between thirteen and nineteen years of age.
→ see **age, child**

teeter /'ti:tə/ (**teeters, teetering, teetered**) **1** V-I **Teeter** is used in expressions such as **teeter on the brink** to emphasize that something seems to be in a very unstable situation or position. ❑ *The country teetered on the edge of war.* **2** V-I If someone or something **teeters**, they shake in an unsteady way, and seem to be about to lose their balance and fall over. ❑ *He watched the cup teeter before it fell.*

teeth /ti:θ/ **Teeth** is the plural of **tooth**.
→ see Word Web: **teeth**
→ see **face**

TEFL /'tefəl/ N-UNCOUNT **TEFL** is the teaching of English to people whose first language is not English, especially people from a country where

Word Web teeth

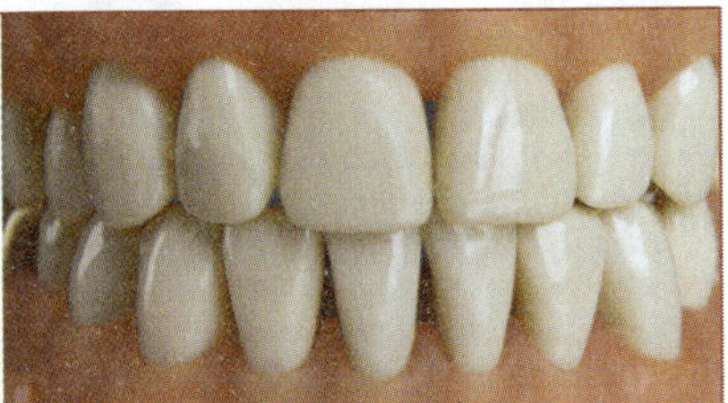

Dentists say **brushing** and flossing every day helps prevent **cavities**. Brushing removes food from the surface of the **teeth**. Flossing removes **plaque** from between teeth and **gums**. In many places, the water supply contains fluoride which also helps keep teeth healthy. If **tooth decay** does develop, a dentist can use a metal or plastic **filling** to repair the tooth. A badly damaged or broken tooth may require a **crown**. Orthodontists use **braces** to straighten uneven rows of teeth. Occasionally, a dentist must remove all of a patient's teeth. Then **dentures** take the place of natural teeth.

English is not spoken. **TEFL** is an abbreviation for 'teaching English as a foreign language'.

telecommunications /ˌtelɪkəmjuːnɪˈkeɪʃənz/ N-UNCOUNT **Telecommunications** is the technology of sending signals and messages over long distances using electronic equipment, for example by radio and telephone.

Word Link *gram ≈ writing : diagram, program, telegram*

telegram /ˈtelɪɡræm/ (**telegrams**) N-COUNT A **telegram** is a message that is sent by electricity or radio and then printed and delivered to someone's home or office.

telemarketing /ˈtelɪˌmɑːkɪtɪŋ/ N-UNCOUNT **Telemarketing** is the selling of a company's products or services by telephone.

Word Link *tele ≈ distance : telepathy, telephone, telescope*

telepathy /tɪˈlepəθi/ N-UNCOUNT **Telepathy** is the direct communication of thoughts and feelings between people's minds, without the need to use speech or writing. ● **telepathic** /ˌtelɪˈpæθɪk/ ADJ ❑ *They had a telepathic understanding.*

telephone /ˈtelɪfəʊn/ (**telephones, telephoning, telephoned**) **1** N-UNCOUNT **The telephone** is an electrical system used to talk to someone in another place by dialling a number on a piece of equipment and speaking into it. ❑ *She wanted to speak to him on the telephone.* ❑ *He made a telephone call to his wife.* **2** N-COUNT A **telephone** is the piece of equipment used to talk to someone by telephone. ❑ *He got up and answered the telephone.* **3** V-T/V-I If you **telephone** or **telephone** someone, you dial their telephone number and speak to them by telephone. ❑ *They usually telephone first to see if she is at home.* **4** PHRASE If you are **on the telephone**, you are speaking to someone by telephone. ❑ *Linda remained on the telephone for three hours.* **5** PHRASE If someone is **on the telephone**, they have a telephone in their house or office which is connected to the rest of the telephone system. ❑ *He's not on the telephone.*

ˈtelephone ˌbox (**telephone boxes**) N-COUNT In British English, a **telephone box** is a small shelter in the street in which there is a public telephone. The American term is **phone booth**.

telesales /ˈtelɪseɪlz/ N-UNCOUNT **Telesales** means the same as **telemarketing**.

Word Link *scope ≈ looking : horoscope, microscope, telescope*

telescope /ˈtelɪskəʊp/ (**telescopes**) N-COUNT A **telescope** is an instrument shaped like a tube. It has lenses inside it that make distant things seem larger and nearer when you look through it.
→ see Word Web: **telescope**

televise /ˈtelɪvaɪz/ (**televises, televising, televised**) V-T If an event **is televised**, it is filmed and shown on television. ❑ *The game was televised live in front of 2,000 supporters.*

Word Link *vid, vis ≈ seeing : television, videotape, visible*

television /ˈtelɪvɪʒən, -ˈvɪʒ-/ (**televisions**) **1** N-COUNT A **television** or a **television set** is a piece of electrical equipment consisting of a box with a screen on which you can watch programmes with pictures and sounds. **2** N-UNCOUNT **Television** is the system of sending pictures and sounds by electrical signals over a distance so that people can receive them on a television set. ❑ *They have begun promoting their products on television.*
→ see Word Web: **television**

tell /tel/ (**tells, telling, told**) **1** V-T If you **tell** someone something, you give them information. ❑ *They told us the dreadful news.* ❑ *I told people what he had been doing.* **2** V-T If you **tell** someone **to** do something, you order, instruct, or advise them to do it. ❑ *A passer-by told the driver to move his car.* **3** V-T If facts or events **tell** you something, they reveal certain information to you through ways other than speech. ❑ *The facts tell us that this is not true.* ❑ *The photographs tell a different story.* **4** V-T If you can **tell** what is happening or what is true, you are able to judge correctly what is happening or what is true. ❑ *You never can tell what life is going to bring you.* ❑ *You can tell he's joking.* **5** V-I If an unpleasant or tiring experience begins to **tell**, it begins to have a serious effect. ❑ *The pressure of the job is beginning to tell on the prime minister.*

▶ **tell apart** PHR-VERB If you cannot **tell** people or things **apart**, you are not able to recognize the differences between them and cannot therefore

T

Word Web telescope

Once, there were only two types of **telescopes**. Refracting telescopes had lenses. **Reflecting** telescopes had a concave **mirror**. The lenses and the mirror had the same purpose. They **focused light rays** and made a clear **image**. Today scientists use **radio telescopes** to study the **universe**. These telescopes can detect **X-rays**, gamma rays, and other types of invisible light **waves**. But sometimes a person makes important discoveries without fancy tools. Robert Evans is an amateur **astronomer** in Australia. He has discovered more supernovas than anyone else in the world. And he uses a very simple 16-inch reflecting telescope set up in his back garden.

Word Web television

For many years, all **televisions** had cathode-ray **tubes**. These tubes made the picture. They shot a stream of **electrons** at a **screen**. When the electrons hit the screen, they made a tiny lighted area. This area is called a pixel. The average cathode ray TV screen has about 200,000 pixels. Today, **high definition** TV is popular. Ground **stations**, **satellites**, and **cables** still supply the TV **signal**. But high definition television uses **digital** information. It produces the picture on a flat screen. Digital **receivers** can show two million pixels per square inch. So they produce a much clearer **image**.

identify them individually. ❑ *The twins are so physically similar that even DNA testing cannot tell them apart.*

▶ **tell off** PHR-VERB If you **tell** someone **off**, you speak to them angrily or seriously because they have done something wrong. ❑ *I'm always getting told off for being late.*

Usage

Note that the verb **tell** is usually followed by a direct object indicating the person who is being addressed. ❑ *He told Alison he was suffering from cancer.* ❑ *What did she tell you?* 'What did she tell to you?' is wrong. With the verb **say**, however, if you want to mention the person who is being addressed, you should use the preposition **to**. 'What did she say you?' is wrong. '**What did she say to you?**' is correct. **Tell** is used to report information that is given to someone. ❑ *He told me that the product did not contain nuts.* **Tell** can also be used with a 'to' infinitive to report an order or instruction. ❑ *My mother told me to shut up and eat my dinner.* **Say** is the most general verb for reporting the words that someone speaks.

teller /telə/ (**tellers**) N-COUNT A **teller** is someone who works in a bank.

telling /'telɪŋ/ 1 ADJ If something is **telling**, it shows the true nature of a person or situation. ❑ *The laughter was a telling sign of the mood of the audience.* ● **tellingly** ADV ❑ *Tellingly, fewer than 1.1 percent of people living there have university qualifications.* 2 PHRASE You use **there's no telling** to introduce a statement when you want to say that it is impossible to know what will happen in a situation. ❑ *There's no telling how long the talks could go on.*

telly /'teli/ (**tellies**) N-VAR **Telly** means the same as **television**. [BRIT, INFORMAL] ❑ *I've seen him on the telly.*

temper /'tempə/ (**tempers, tempering, tempered**) 1 N-VAR If you say that someone has a **temper**, you mean that they become angry very easily. ❑ *I hope he can control his temper.* 2 PHRASE If you **lose** your **temper**, you become very angry. ❑ *I've never seen him get angry or lose his temper.* 3 N-VAR If someone is **in** a particular type of **temper**, that is the way they are feeling. ❑ *Lee left the field in a furious temper.* 4 V-T To **temper** something means to make it less extreme. [FORMAL] ❑ *He had to learn to temper his enthusiasm and high spirits.*

Word Partnership

Use *temper* with:

ADJ.	**bad** temper, **explosive** temper, **quick** temper, **short** temper, **violent** temper 1
N.	temper **tantrum** 1
V.	**control your** temper, **have a** temper 1 **lose your** temper 2

temperament /'temprəmənt/ (**temperaments**) 1 N-VAR Your **temperament** is your basic nature, especially as it is shown in the way that you react to situations or to people. ❑ *His fiery temperament often got him into difficulties.* 2 N-UNCOUNT **Temperament** is a tendency to behave in an uncontrolled, bad-tempered, or unreasonable way. ❑ *Some of the models were given to fits of temperament.*

temperamental /ˌtemprə'mentəl/ 1 ADJ If you say that someone is **temperamental**, you are criticizing them for having moods that change often and suddenly. ❑ *He often has temperamental outbursts.* 2 ADJ If you describe something such as a machine or car as **temperamental**, you mean that it often does not work properly. ❑ *Old cars can be temperamental.*

temperate /'tempərɪt/ ADJ A **temperate** climate or place is one that is never extremely hot or extremely cold. ❑ *The Nile Valley keeps a temperate climate throughout the year.*

temperature /'temprətʃə/ (**temperatures**) 1 N-VAR The **temperature** of something is how hot or cold it is. ❑ *Winter closes in and the temperature drops below freezing.* 2 N-COUNT Your **temperature** is the temperature of your body. ❑ *His temperature continued to rise.* 3 PHRASE If someone **takes** your **temperature**, they use a thermometer to measure your temperature. ❑ *He will probably take your child's temperature too.* 4 PHRASE If you **have a temperature**, your temperature is higher than it usually is and you feel ill. ❑ *David had a temperature and a terrible headache.*

→ see **calories, climate, cook, forecast, greenhouse effect, habitat, wind**

Usage

In Britain, two different scales are commonly used for measuring temperature. On the **Celsius** (formerly **Centigrade**) scale, water freezes at zero degrees and boils at 100 degrees. On the **Fahrenheit** scale, water freezes at 32 degrees and boils at 212 degrees.

t

Word Partnership Use *temperature* with:

ADJ. **average** temperature, **high/low** temperature, **normal** temperature 1
V. **reach a** temperature 1
N. **changes in/of** temperature, temperature **increase**, **ocean** temperature, **rise in** temperature, **room** temperature, **surface** temperature, **water** temperature 1
body temperature 2

template /'templeɪt, AM -plɪt/ (**templates**) N-COUNT A **template** is a thin piece of metal or plastic which is cut into a particular shape. It is used to help you cut wood, paper, metal, or other materials accurately, or to reproduce the same shape many times.

temple /'tempəl/ (**temples**) 1 N-COUNT A **temple** is a building used for the worship of a god or gods, especially in the Buddhist and Hindu religions. 2 N-COUNT Your **temples** are the flat parts on each side of the front part of your head, near your forehead.

tempo /'tempəʊ/ (**tempos**) 1 N-SING The **tempo** of an event is the speed at which it happens. ❑ *He was dissatisfied with the tempo of political change.* 2 N-VAR The **tempo** of a piece of music is the speed at which it is played.

Word Link *tempo ≈ time : contemporary, temporal, temporary*

temporary /'tempərəri, AM -reri/ ADJ Something that is **temporary** lasts for only a limited time. ❑ *His job here is only temporary.* ❑ *...a temporary loss of memory.* ● **temporarily** ADV ❑ *The airport was temporarily closed.*

tempt /tempt/ (**tempts, tempting, tempted**) V-T Something that **tempts** you attracts you and makes you want it, even though it may be wrong or harmful. ❑ *These young people may be easily tempted into crime.* ❑ *Don't be tempted into buying something you can't afford.* ● **tempting** ADJ ❑ *...Raoul's tempting offer of the Palm Beach trip.*

Word Link *tempt ≈ trying : attempt, temptation, tempted*

temptation /temp'teɪʃən/ (**temptations**) N-VAR **Temptation** is the state you are in when you want to do or have something, although you know it might be wrong or harmful. ❑ *Will they be able to resist the temptation to buy?*

T

tempted /'temptɪd/ ADJ AFTER LINK-V If you say that you are **tempted to** do something, you mean that you would like to do it. ❑ *I'm very tempted to sell my house.*

ten /ten/ (**tens**) NUM **Ten** is the number 10.

tenacious /tɪ'neɪʃəs/ ADJ A **tenacious** person is very determined and does not give up easily. ❑ *...a tenacious and persistent interviewer.* ● **tenaciously** ADV ❑ *In spite of his illness, he clung tenaciously to his job.*

tenacity /tɪ'næsɪti/ N-UNCOUNT If you have **tenacity**, you are very determined and do not give up easily. ❑ *Hard work and tenacity are necessary for career success.*

tenancy /'tenənsi/ (**tenancies**) N-VAR **Tenancy** is the use that you have of land or property belonging to someone else, for which you pay rent. ❑ *His father took over the tenancy of the farm.*

tenant /'tenənt/ (**tenants**) N-COUNT A **tenant** is someone who pays rent for the place they live in, or for land or buildings that they use.

tend /tend/ (**tends, tending, tended**) 1 V-T If something **tends to** happen, it usually happens or it happens often. ❑ *I tend to forget things.* 2 V-I If someone or something **tends towards** a particular characteristic, they often display that characteristic. ❑ *The local cuisine tends towards boiled meat dishes.* 3 V-T/V-I If you **tend** someone or something, or **tend to** them, you do what is necessary to keep them in a good condition. [FORMAL] ❑ *He tends the flower beds and bushes.*

Word Partnership Use *tend* with:

V. tend **to avoid**, tend **to become**, tend **to develop**, tend **to forget**, tend **to happen**, tend **to lose**, tend **to stay** 1
tend **to agree**, tend **to blame**, tend **to feel**, tend **to think** 1 3
N. **children/men/women** tend, **people** tend 1 2

tendency /'tendənsi/ (**tendencies**) N-COUNT A **tendency** is a worrying or unpleasant habit or action that keeps occurring. ❑ *Her suicidal tendencies continued.* ❑ *These sweaters have a tendency to be itchy.*

tender /'tendə/ (**tenderer, tenderest, tenders, tendering, tendered**) 1 ADJ A **tender** person expresses gentle and caring feelings. ● **tenderly** ADV ❑ *Mr White tenderly embraced his wife.* ● **tenderness** N-UNCOUNT ❑ *She smiled, politely rather than with tenderness.* 2 ADJ BEFORE N If someone is at a **tender** age, they are young and inexperienced. 3 ADJ Meat or other food that is **tender** is easy to cut or chew. 4 ADJ If a part of your body is **tender**, it is sensitive and painful when it is touched. 5 V-I & N-VAR If a company **tenders for** something, or if they put in a **tender for** it, it makes a formal offer to supply goods or do a job for a particular price. 6 V-T If you **tender** something such as a suggestion or money, you formally offer or present it. [FORMAL] ❑ *She quickly tendered her resignation.*
→ see **cook**

tendon /'tendən/ (**tendons**) N-COUNT A **tendon** is a strong cord of tissue in your body joining a muscle to a bone.

tenement /'tenəmənt/ (**tenements**) N-COUNT A **tenement** is a large old terraced building divided into a lot of flats, also called **tenements**.

tenet /'tenɪt/ (**tenets**) N-COUNT The **tenets of** a theory or belief are the principles on which it is based. [FORMAL] ❑ *Non-violence and patience are the central tenets of their faith.*

tennis /'tenɪs/ N-UNCOUNT **Tennis** is a game played by two or four players on a rectangular court with a net across the middle. The players use rackets to hit a ball over the net.
→ see Picture Dictionary: **tennis**

tenor /'tenə/ (**tenors**) 1 N-COUNT A **tenor** is a male singer with a fairly high voice. 2 ADJ A **tenor** musical instrument has a range of notes of fairly low pitch. 3 N-SING The **tenor of** something is the general meaning or mood that it

Picture Dictionary tennis

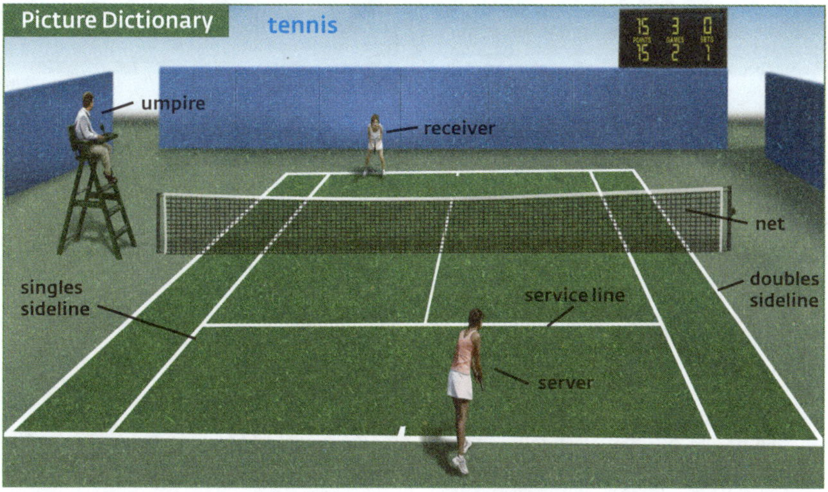

expresses. [FORMAL] ❑ *The whole tenor of discussions has changed.*

tense /tens/ (**tenser, tensest, tenses, tensing, tensed**) **1** ADJ If you are **tense**, you are worried and nervous, and cannot relax. ❑ *She had never seen him so tense.* **2** ADJ If your body is **tense**, your muscles are tight and not relaxed. **3** V-I & PHR-VERB If your muscles **tense**, or if they **tense up**, they become tight and stiff, often because you are anxious or frightened. ❑ *Jane tensed up her muscles to stop them from shaking.* **4** N-VAR The **tense** of a verb is the form which shows whether you are referring to past, present, or future time.

Word Partnership Use *tense* with:

N.	tense **atmosphere**, tense **moment**, tense **mood**, tense **situation** 1 **muscles** tense 3
ADV.	**very** tense 1–3
V.	**feel** tense 2 3
ADJ.	**future/past/perfect/present** tense 4

tension /ˈtenʃən/ (**tensions**) **1** N-VAR **Tension** is a feeling of fear or nervousness produced before a difficult, dangerous, or important event. ❑ *The tension between the two countries is likely to remain.* **2** N-UNCOUNT **Tension** is a feeling of worry and nervousness which makes it difficult for you to relax. ❑ *Laughing actually relieves tension.* **3** N-UNCOUNT The **tension** in a rope or wire is how tightly it is stretched.
→ see **anger**

Word Partnership Use *tension* with:

V.	**ease** tension, tension **grows**, tension **mounts**, **relieve** tension 1 2
N.	**source of** tension 1 2
ADJ.	**racial** tension 1

tent /tent/ (**tents**) N-COUNT A **tent** is a shelter made of canvas or nylon and held up by poles and ropes, used mainly by people who are camping.

tent

tentacle /ˈtentəkəl/ (**tentacles**) N-COUNT The **tentacles** of an animal such as an octopus are the long thin parts used for feeling, holding things, and moving.

tentative /ˈtentətɪv/ **1** ADJ **Tentative** agreements or plans are not definite or certain, but have been made as a first step. ❑ *...a tentative agreement to hold a conference.* **2** ADJ If someone is **tentative**, they are cautious and not very confident because they are uncertain or afraid. ❑ *He gave a tentative smile.* ● **tentatively** ADV ❑ *I tentatively suggested an alternative route.*

tenth /tenθ/ (**tenths**) ORD The **tenth** item in a series is the one that you count as number ten.

tenuous /ˈtenjʊəs/ ADJ If you describe something such as a connection, a reason, or someone's position as **tenuous**, you mean that it is very uncertain or weak. ❑ *This decision puts the President in a rather tenuous position.*

tenure /ˈtenjə/ **1** N-UNCOUNT **Tenure** is the legal right to live in a place or to use land or buildings for a period of time. **2** N-UNCOUNT **Tenure** is the period of time during which someone holds an important job. ❑ *...during his tenure as foreign minister.*

tepid /ˈtepɪd/ **1** ADJ A **tepid** liquid is slightly warm. **2** ADJ If you describe a feeling or reaction as **tepid**, you mean that it lacks enthusiasm or liveliness. ❑ *...tepid applause.*

term /tɜːm/ (**terms, terming, termed**) **1** PHRASE If you talk about something **in** particular **terms**, or **in terms of** a particular thing, you are specifying which aspect of it you are discussing. ❑ *Hunting is a good way for fathers to bond with their sons, and, in practical terms, it's a way to feed the family.* ❑ *Our goods compete in terms of product quality.* **2** N-COUNT A **term** is a word or expression with a specific meaning. ❑ *'Myocardial infarction' is the medical term for a heart attack.* **3** V-T If you say that something **is termed** a particular thing, you mean that that is what people call it or that is their opinion of it. ❑ *He termed the war a nightmare.* **4** N-VAR A **term** is one of the periods of time that a school, college, or university year is divided into. ❑ *...the last day of term.* **5** N-COUNT A **term** is a period of time that someone spends doing a particular job or in a particular place. ❑ *Felipe Gonzalez won a fourth term of office.* ❑ *...a seven-year prison term.* **6** N-PLURAL The **terms** of an agreement or arrangement are the conditions that have been accepted by the people involved in it. **7** PHRASE If you **come to terms with** something difficult or unpleasant, you learn to accept it. ❑ *It was hard to come to terms with her death.* **8** PHRASE If two people are treated **on equal terms** or **on the same terms**, neither of them has an advantage over the other. **9** PHRASE If two people are **on good terms** or **on friendly terms**, they are friendly with each other. **10** PHRASE You use the expressions **in the long term, in the short term**, and **in the medium term** to talk about what will happen over that period of time. ❑ *In the long term the company hopes to open in Moscow.* **11** PHRASE If you say you are **thinking in terms of** doing something or **talking in terms of** doing it, you mean that you are considering it. ❑ *United should be thinking in terms of winning the European Cup.* **12** **a contradiction in terms** → see **contradiction** **13** **in real terms** → see **real** **14** **in no uncertain terms** → see **uncertain**

Word Link	*term, termin ≈ limit, end : determine, terminal, terminate*

terminal /'tɜːmɪnəl/ (**terminals**) **1** ADJ A **terminal** illness or disease cannot be cured and eventually causes death. ● **terminally** ADV ❑ *The patient is terminally ill.* **2** N-COUNT A **terminal** is a place where vehicles, passengers, or goods begin or end a journey. **3** N-COUNT A computer **terminal** is a piece of equipment consisting of a keyboard and a screen connected to a computer. [COMPUTING]

terminate /'tɜːmɪneɪt/ (**terminates, terminating, terminated**) **1** V-T/V-I When something **terminates**, or when you **terminate** it, it ends completely. [FORMAL] ❑ *His contract terminates at the season's end.* ● **termination** N-UNCOUNT ❑ *...the abrupt termination of trade.* **2** V-I When a train or bus **terminates** somewhere, it ends its journey there.

T

terminology /ˌtɜːmɪ'nɒlədʒi/ (**terminologies**) N-VAR The **terminology** of a subject is the set of special words and expressions used in connection with it. ❑ *...football terminology.*

termite /'tɜːmaɪt/ (**termites**) N-COUNT **Termites** are small white insects that eat wood.

terrace /'terɪs/ (**terraces**) **1** N-COUNT A **terrace** is a row of similar houses joined together by their side walls. [BRIT] **2** N-COUNT A **terrace** is a flat area of stone or grass next to a building where people can sit. ❑ *...a garden terrace.*

ˌterraced 'house (**terraced houses**) ADJ A **terraced house** or a **terrace house** is one of a row of similar houses joined together by their side walls. [BRIT]

terracotta /ˌterə'kɒtə/ N-UNCOUNT **Terracotta** is a brownish-red clay that has been baked but not glazed and that is used for making things such as flower pots and tiles.

Word Link	*terr ≈ earth : subterranean, terrain, territory*

terrain /tə'reɪn/ N-UNCOUNT The **terrain** in an area is the type of land that is there. ❑ *...flat desert terrain.*

terrible /'terɪbəl/ **1** ADJ **Terrible** means extremely bad. ❑ *Her French is terrible.* ● **terribly** ADV ❑ *My son has suffered terribly.* **2** ADJ BEFORE N You use **terrible** to emphasize the great extent or degree of something. ❑ *Her death is a terrible waste.* ● **terribly** ADV ❑ *I'm terribly sorry to bother you.*

terrific /tə'rɪfɪk/ **1** ADJ If you describe something or someone as **terrific**, you are very pleased with them or very impressed by them. [INFORMAL] ❑ *You look terrific, Ann.* **2** ADJ BEFORE N **Terrific** means very great in amount, degree, or intensity. ❑ *There was a terrific bang.*

terrify /'terɪfaɪ/ (**terrifies, terrifying, terrified**) V-T If something **terrifies** you, it makes you feel extremely frightened. ❑ *The idea of death terrified me.* ● **terrified** ADJ ❑ *He was terrified of heights.*

terrifying /'terɪfaɪɪŋ/ ADJ If something is **terrifying**, it makes you very frightened. ❑ *Crime is increasing at a terrifying rate.*

territorial /ˌterɪ'tɔːriəl/ ADJ **Territorial** means concerned with the ownership of a particular area of land or water. ❑ *Some dogs are territorial and protective of their homes.*

Word Link	*ory ≈ place where something happens: conservatory, factory, territory*

territory /'terətri, AM -tɔːri/ (**territories**) **1** N-VAR **Territory** is land which is controlled by a particular country or ruler. ❑ *Pakistan has fought three wars with India, two over the territory of Kashmir.* **2** N-UNCOUNT You can use **territory** to refer to an area of knowledge or experience. ❑ *Her first film covers the familiar territory of her experiences growing up in Margate.* **3** N-COUNT **Territory** is land with a particular character. ❑ *...mountainous territory.*

Word Partnership	Use territory with:
N.	**enemy** territory, **part of a** territory 1 2
ADJ.	**vast** territory 1 3
	controlled territory, **disputed** territory 1
	familiar territory 3

terror /'terə/ (**terrors**) **1** N-VAR **Terror** is very great fear. ❑ *I shook with terror.* ❑ *He had a terror of being caught.* **2** **reign of terror** → see **reign**

terrorism /'terərɪzəm/ N-UNCOUNT **Terrorism** is the use of violence in order to achieve political aims or to force a government to do something. ❑ *They are ready to join us in the fight against terrorism.*

terrorist /'terərɪst/ (**terrorists**) N-COUNT A **terrorist** is a person who uses violence in order to achieve political aims. ❑ *...terrorist attacks.*

terrorize [BRIT also **terrorise**] /'terəraɪz/ (**terrorizes, terrorizing, terrorized**) V-T If someone **terrorizes** you, they frighten you by making it seem likely that they will attack you. ❑ *...elderly* *people terrorised by neighbours.*

terse /tɜːs/ (**terser, tersest**) ADJ A **terse** comment or statement is brief and unfriendly. ● **tersely** ADV ❑ *'It's too late,' he said tersely.*

tertiary /ˈtɜːʃəri, AM -ʃieri/ ADJ BEFORE N **Tertiary** education is education at university or college level.
→ see **colour**

test /test/ (**tests, testing, tested**) **1** V-T & N-COUNT When you **test** something, or when you conduct a **test** on it, you try using it in order to find out what it is, what condition it is in, or how well it works. ❑ *The company needed to test the drug in several different countries.* ❑ *Experts will carry out tests of the air and water supply around the school.* **2** V-T & N-COUNT If you **test** someone, or if you give them a **test**, you ask them questions to find out how much they know about something. ❑ *...an arithmetic test.* **3** N-COUNT If an event or situation is a **test of** a person or thing, it reveals their qualities or effectiveness. ❑ *Next season will be a real test of his coaching skills.* **4** V-T If you **are tested for** a particular disease or medical condition, you are examined in order to find out whether you have that disease or condition. ❑ *My doctor wants me to be tested for diabetes.* **5** N-COUNT A medical **test** is an examination of your body in order to check that you are healthy. **6** PHRASE If you **put** something **to the test**, you find out how useful or effective it is by using it. ❑ *It appears that the system has never been put to the test.*
→ see **experiment**

Word Partnership Use *test* with:

N.	test **a drug**, test **a hypothesis** **1**
	achievement test, **aptitude** test, **crash** test, test **data/results**, **flight** test, **intelligence** test, test **items**, **math/reading** test, test **preparation**, test **scores**, **standardized** test, **strength** test, **stress** test, test **takers** **2**
	blood test, **drug** test, **HIV** test, **pregnancy** test **4**
ADJ.	**nuclear** test **1**
	test **negative/positive** **4**
	diagnostic test **5**
V.	**administer a** test, test **drive**, **fail a** test, **give *someone* a** test, **pass a** test, **study for a** test, **take a** test **2**

testament /ˈtestəmənt/ (**testaments**) N-VAR If one thing is a **testament to** another thing, it shows that the other thing exists or is true. [FORMAL] ❑ *It is a testament to his strength of will that he has recovered so quickly.*

ˈtest ˌcase (**test cases**) N-COUNT A **test case** is a legal case which becomes an example for deciding other similar cases.

testicle /ˈtestɪkəl/ (**testicles**) N-COUNT A man's **testicles** are the two sex glands that produce sperm.

testify /ˈtestɪfaɪ/ (**testifies, testifying, testified**) **1** V-T/V-I When someone **testifies** in a court of law, they give a statement of what they saw someone do or what they know of a situation, after having promised to tell the truth. **2** V-I If one thing **testifies to** another, it supports the belief that the second thing is true. [FORMAL] ❑ *The blood stains near her house testified to the brutal nature of the attack.*

Word Link ***mony** ≈ **resulting state** : **ceremony**, **harmony**, **testimony***

testimony /ˈtestɪməni, AM -məʊni/ (**testimonies**) **1** N-VAR In a court of law, someone's **testimony** is a formal statement that they make about what they saw someone do or what they know of a situation, after having promised to tell the truth. **2** N-UNCOUNT If one thing is **testimony to** another, it shows that the second thing has a particular quality. ❑ *It was a decisive victory and a testimony to his talent and determination.*
→ see **trial**

testosterone /teˈstɒstərəʊn/ N-UNCOUNT **Testosterone** is a hormone found in higher levels in men than in women.

tether /ˈteðə/ (**tethers, tethering, tethered**) **1** PHRASE If you are **at the end of** your **tether**, you are so worried or tired because of your problems that you feel you cannot cope. **2** V-T If you **tether** an animal or object **to** something, you attach it there with a rope or chain.

text /tekst/ (**texts, texting, texted**) **1** N-VAR **Text** is any written material. ❑ *A CD-ROM can store more than 250,000 pages of typed text.* **2** N-COUNT A **text** is a book or other piece of writing, especially one connected with science or education. ❑ *His early plays are set texts in universities.* **3** N-COUNT A **text** is the same as a **text message**. ❑ *He sent me about 20 texts.* **4** V-T If you **text** someone, you send them a text message on a mobile phone. ❑ *Mary texted me when she got home.*
→ see **diary**

textbook /ˈtekstbʊk/ (**textbooks**) N-COUNT A **textbook** is a book about a particular subject that is intended for students.

textile /ˈtekstaɪl/ (**textiles**) **1** N-COUNT **Textiles** are types of woven cloth. **2** N-PLURAL **Textiles** are the industries concerned with making cloth. ❑ *75,000 jobs will be lost in textiles and clothing.*
→ see **industry, quilt**

texting /ˈtekstɪŋ/ N-UNCOUNT **Texting** means the same as **text messaging**.

ˈtext ˌmessage (**text messages**) N-COUNT A **text message** is a message that you send using a mobile phone.

ˈtext ˌmessaging N-UNCOUNT **Text messaging** is the sending of written messages using a mobile phone.

texture /ˈtekstʃə/ (**textures**) N-VAR The **texture** of something is the way that it feels when you touch it. ❑ *His face had the texture of old leather.*

than /ðən, STRONG ðæn/ **1** PREP & CONJ You use **than** to link two parts of a comparison or contrast. ❑ *The package was smaller than a shoe box.* ❑ *It contains less than 1 per cent fat.* ❑ *He could have helped her more than he did.* ❑ *She was more a dictator than a leader.* **2** **less than** → see **less** **3** **more than** → see **more** **4** **more often than not** → see **often** **5** **other than** → see **other** **6** **rather than** → see **rather**

thank /θæŋk/ (**thanks, thanking, thanked**) **1** CONVENTION You say **thank you** or, more

t

informally, **thanks** to express your gratitude or acknowledgement when someone does something for you or gives you something. ❑ *Thank you very much for your call.* ❑ *Thanks for the information.* ❑ *'Would you like another piece of cake?'—'No thank you.'* **2** V-T & N-PLURAL When you **thank** someone, or when you give them your **thanks**, you express your gratitude to them for something. ❑ *I thanked them for their long and loyal service.* ❑ *May I say a word of thanks to all the people who helped me.* **3** CONVENTION You can use **thank you** to say firmly that you do not want someone's help or to tell them that you do not like the way they are behaving towards you. ❑ *I can stir my own tea, thank you.* **4** PHRASE You say **'Thank God'**, **'Thank Goodness'**, or **'Thank heavens'** when you are very relieved about something. ❑ *Thank heavens we have you here.* **5** PHRASE If something happens **thanks to** someone or something, they are responsible for it or caused it to happen. ❑ *Thanks to recent research, effective treatments are available.*

thankful /'θæŋkfʊl/ ADJ When you are **thankful**, you feel happy and relieved that something has happened. ❑ *I'm just thankful that I've got a job.* ● **thankfully** ADV ❑ *Simon thankfully slipped off his uniform and relaxed.*

thankfully /'θæŋkfʊli/ ADV You use **thankfully** to express approval and relief about a statement that you are making. ❑ *Thankfully, she was not injured.*

thanks /θæŋks/ → see **thank**

Thanksgiving /ˌθæŋks'gɪvɪŋ/ N-UNCOUNT In the United States, **Thanksgiving** or **Thanksgiving Day** is a public holiday on the fourth Thursday in November.

that

❶ DEMONSTRATIVE USES
❷ CONJUNCTION AND RELATIVE PRONOUN USES

that /ðæt/

❶ **1** PRON & DET You use **that** to refer back to an idea, situation, or period of time that you have referred to previously. ❑ *You wanted to talk to me. Why was that?* ❑ *'I've never been to Paris.'—'That's a pity.'* ❑ *She returned to work later that week.* **2** DET & PRON You use **that** when you are referring to someone or something which is a distance away from you, especially when you indicate or point to them. ❑ *You see that man over there?* ❑ *What's that you're writing?* ❑ *That looks heavy.* **3** ADV If something is not **that** bad, funny, or expensive, for example, it is not as bad, funny, or expensive as it might be or as has been suggested. ❑ *Do I look that stupid?* **4** PHRASE You use **that is** or **that is to say** to indicate that you are about to explain something more clearly, more specifically, or in more detail. ❑ *Productivity – that is, the output of every employee – has not increased.* **5** PHRASE You use **that's that** or **that's it** to indicate that there is nothing more to be done or said, or that the end has been reached. ❑ *I'm staying here, and that's that.* ❑ *When he left the office, that was it, the working day was over.* **6** → see also **those** **7** **this and that** → see **this**

that /ðət, STRONG ðæt/

❷ **1** CONJ You use **that** after many verbs, nouns, and adjectives to introduce a clause. ❑ *He said that he did not want to be seen.* ❑ *...breaking the news that someone has died.* ❑ *It's obvious that you need more time.* **2** PRON You use **that** immediately after a noun to introduce a clause which gives more information about the noun. ❑ *...a car that won't start.* ❑ *...a man that Maddock has known for nearly 20 years.* **3** CONJ You use **that** after expressions with 'so' and 'such' in order to introduce the result or effect of something. ❑ *She came towards me so quickly that she knocked a chair over.*

thatched /θætʃd/ ADJ A **thatched** house has a roof made of straw or reeds.

that's /ðæts/ **That's** is a spoken form of 'that is'.

thaw /θɔː/ (**thaws, thawing, thawed**) **1** V-T/V-I When something frozen **thaws**, or when you **thaw** it, it melts. ❑ *It's so cold the snow doesn't get a chance to thaw.* ❑ *Always thaw frozen meat thoroughly.* **2** N-COUNT A **thaw** is a period of warmer weather when the snow and ice melt. **3** V-T & N-SING If something **thaws** relations between people, or if there is a **thaw** in relations, people become friendly again after a period of tension. ❑ *It took up to Christmas for political relations to thaw.*

the

The is pronounced /ðə/ before a consonant and /ði/ before a vowel, but pronounced /ðiː/ when you are emphasizing it.

1 DET **The** is the definite article. You use **the** at the beginning of noun groups to refer to someone or something when they are generally known about or when it is clear which particular person or thing you are referring to. ❑ *Amy sat outside in the sun.* ❑ *Who was that on the phone?* ❑ *I patted him on the head.* **2** DET You can use **the** in front of a singular noun to refer to all people or things of that type. ❑ *The computer has made considerable advances in recent years.* **3** DET You use **the** in front of an adjective when you are referring to a particular thing that is described by that adjective. ❑ *He's wishing for the impossible.* **4** DET You can use **the** in front of adjectives and plural nouns to refer to all people of a particular type or nationality, or to a couple or family with a particular name. ❑ *...care for the elderly.* ❑ *The Germans and the French both have identity-card systems.* ❑ *...the Browns.* **5** DET You use **the** in front of numbers that refer to days and dates. ❑ *The meeting should take place on the fifth of May.* ❑ *...how bad things were in the thirties.* **6** DET You use **the** in front of superlative adjectives and adverbs. ❑ *Brisk daily walks are still the best exercise.* **7** DET You use **the** in front of two comparative adjectives or adverbs to describe how one amount or quality changes in relation to another. ❑ *The more confidence you build up, the greater your chances of success.* **8** DET **The** is used in rates, prices, and measurements to refer to a single unit, which is related or compared to a number of units of a different kind. ❑ *The exchange rate will soon be $2 to the pound.*

theatre [AM **theater**] /'θiːətə/ (**theatres**) **1** N-COUNT A **theatre** is a building with a stage on which plays and other entertainments are performed. ❑ *We went to the theatre.* **2** N-UNCOUNT **Theatre** is entertainment involving the performance of plays. ❑ *...theatre for children.* **3** N-COUNT In American English, a **theater** or a **movie theater** is a place where people go to watch films. The British word is **cinema**. **4** N-COUNT In a hospital, a **theatre** is a room where surgeons

T

carry out operations.
→ see Word Web: **theatre**
→ see **drama, city**

theatrical /θiˈætrɪkəl/ **1** ADJ BEFORE N **Theatrical** means relating to the theatre. ❑ *...an outstanding theatrical performance.* **2** ADJ **Theatrical** behaviour is deliberately exaggerated and unnatural. ❑ *...her big, theatrical gestures.* ● **theatrically** ADV ❑ *He looked theatrically at his watch.*

theft /θeft/ (**thefts**) N-VAR **Theft** is the criminal act of stealing. ❑ *...the theft of documents from a car.*
→ see **crime**

their /ðeə/ **1** DET You use **their** to indicate that something belongs or relates to the group of people, animals, or things you are talking about. ❑ *Janis and Kurt have announced their engagement.* ❑ *The trees shed their leaves.* **2** DET You use **their** instead of 'his or her' to indicate that something belongs or relates to a person without saying whether that person is a man or a woman. Some people think this use is incorrect. ❑ *Has anyone taken their coat off yet?*

theirs /ðeəz/ **1** PRON You use **theirs** to indicate that something belongs or relates to the group of people, animals, or things that you are talking about. ❑ *...at the table next to theirs.* ❑ *Theirs had been a happy marriage.* **2** PRON You use **theirs** instead of 'his or hers' to indicate that something belongs or relates to a person without saying whether that person is a man or a woman. Some people think this use is incorrect. ❑ *I don't know whose book it is. Somebody must have left theirs.*

them /ðəm, STRONG ðem/ **1** PRON **Them** is used as the object of a verb or preposition. You use **them** to refer to a group of people, animals, or things. ❑ *The Beatles – I never get tired of listening to them.* ❑ *The dark socks had a stripe on them.* **2** PRON You use **them** instead of 'him or her' to refer to a person without saying whether that person is a man or a woman. Some people think this use is incorrect. ❑ *It takes great courage to face your child and tell them the truth.*

theme /θiːm/ (**themes**) N-COUNT A **theme** in a piece of writing, a discussion, or a work of art is an important idea or subject in it. ❑ *The book's central theme is power.*
→ see **myth**

Word Partnership Use *theme* with:

ADJ.	**central** theme, **common** theme, **dominant** theme, **main** theme, **major** theme, **new** theme, **recurring** theme
N.	theme **of a book/movie/story**, **campaign** theme, theme **music**, theme **song**, theme **and variations**

themselves /ðəmˈselvz/ **1** PRON You use **themselves** to refer to people, animals, or things when the object of a verb or preposition refers to the same people or things as the subject of the verb. ❑ *They all seemed to be enjoying themselves.* ❑ *The men talked amongst themselves.* **2** PRON You use **themselves** to emphasize the people or things that you are referring to. ❑ *The islands themselves are not inhabited.* **3** PRON You use **themselves** instead of 'himself or herself' to refer back to the person who is the subject of sentence without saying whether it is a man or a woman. Some people think this use is incorrect. ❑ *What can a patient with heart disease do to help themselves?*

then /ðen/ **1** ADV **Then** means at a particular time in the past or in the future. ❑ *Things were simpler and clearer then.* ❑ *Since then, Knowles has published around 50 titles.* ❑ *I'm coming up on Friday so I can give it to you then.* **2** ADV You use **then** to say that one thing happens after another, or is after another on a list. ❑ *He thought a bit and then answered.* ❑ *He'll speak first, then Robert's mother, then me.* **3** ADV You use **then** to introduce a summary or conclusion to what you have just said, or to end a conversation. ❑ *By 1931, then, France was a country of massive immigration.* ❑ *He stood up. 'That's settled then.'* ❑ *Bye bye then.* **4** ADV You use **then** with words like 'now', 'well', and 'okay', to introduce a new topic or a new point of view. ❑ *Well then, I'll put the kettle on.* **5** ADV You use **then** to introduce the second part of a sentence which begins with 'if'. The first part of the sentence describes a possible situation, and **then** introduces the result of the situation. ❑ *If the answer is 'yes', then we must decide what to do.* **6** ADV You use **then** at the beginning of a sentence or after 'and' or 'but' to introduce a comment or an extra piece of information. ❑ *He sounded sincere, but then, he always did.* **7** **now and then** → see **now** **8** **there and then** → see **there**

theologian /ˌθiːəˈləʊdʒən/ (**theologians**) N-COUNT A **theologian** is someone who studies religion and the nature of God.

t

Word Web theatre

It only takes two hours to watch a **play**. It takes a lot of time, money, and work before the curtain rises on the **stage**. First, a **playwright** writes an interesting story. Then, a **producer** gets the money for the **production** and finds a **theatre**. **Actors audition** for the play. The **director casts** the actors in the **roles**. **Rehearsals** sometimes go on for months. The **set**, **lighting**, and **costumes** all have to be designed and made. Special **props** and **make-up** are usually necessary. A **band** or an **orchestra** is needed if the play is a **musical**. It takes a large **crew** to do all these things.

A scene from the Broadway play, Les Miserables

theology /θiˈɒlədʒi/ N-UNCOUNT **Theology** is the study of religion and the nature of God. • **theological** /ˌθiːəˈlɒdʒɪkəl/ ADJ ❑ *...a theological college.*

theoretical /ˌθiːəˈretɪkəl/ ADJ **Theoretical** means based on or using the ideas and abstract principles of a subject, rather than the practical aspects of it. ❑ *...a lecturer in theoretical physics.*

theoretically /ˌθiːəˈretɪkəli/ ADV You use **theoretically** to say that although something is supposed to be true or to exist in the way stated, it may not in fact be true or exist in that way. ❑ *Theoretically, the price should be marked.* ❑ *No one believes it will happen. But it is theoretically possible.*

theorize [BRIT also **theorise**] /ˈθiːəraɪz/ (**theorizes, theorizing, theorized**) V-T/V-I If you **theorize** that something is true, or if you **theorize about** something, you develop a set of abstract ideas about it in order to explain it. ❑ *By studying the way people behave, we can theorize about what is going on in their mind.* • **theorist** (**theorists**) N-COUNT ❑ *...a leading theorist of the French Communist Party.*

theory /ˈθɪəri/ (**theories**) 1 N-COUNT A **theory** is a formal idea or set of ideas intended to explain something. ❑ *...Darwin's theory of evolution.* 2 N-COUNT If you have a **theory** about something, you have your own opinion about it which you cannot prove but which you think is true. ❑ *My theory is that there are too many of us in the city.* 3 N-UNCOUNT The **theory of** a practical subject or skill is the set of rules and principles that form the basis of it. ❑ *...the theory and practice of educational management.* 4 PHRASE You use **in theory** to say that although something is supposed to be true or to happen in the way stated, it may not in fact be true or happen in that way. ❑ *In theory I'm available day and night.*
→ see **evolution, experiment, science**

Word Partnership Use *theory* with:

N.	**evidence for a** theory, **support for a** theory 1 3
	conspiracy theory 2
	learning theory, theory **and practice** 3
ADJ.	**scientific** theory 1
	economic theory, **literary** theory 3
V.	**advance a** theory, **propose a** theory 1–3
	develop a theory, **test a** theory 1 3

T

therapeutic /ˌθerəˈpjuːtɪk/ 1 ADJ If something is **therapeutic**, it helps you to feel happier and more relaxed. ❑ *Yoga is very therapeutic.* 2 ADJ **Therapeutic** treatment is designed to treat a disease or to improve a person's health. [TECHNICAL] ❑ *...therapeutic drugs.*

therapist /ˈθerəpɪst/ (**therapists**) N-COUNT A **therapist** is a person skilled in a type of therapy.

therapy /ˈθerəpi/ N-UNCOUNT **Therapy** is the treatment of mental or physical illness without the use of drugs or operations. ❑ *...group therapy sessions for teenagers.*
→ see **cancer**

there

There is pronounced /ðə, STRONG ðeə/ for meanings 1 and 2, and /ðeə/ for all other meanings.

1 PRON You use **there** as the subject of the verb 'be' to say that something exists or does not exist, or to draw attention to it. ❑ *There must be another way of doing this.* ❑ *There's no way we can afford to buy a house.* ❑ *There are no cars on some of the islands.* 2 ADV If something is **there**, it exists or is available. ❑ *The old buildings are still there today.* ❑ *The book is there for people to read.* 3 ADV You use **there** to refer to a place that has already been mentioned. ❑ *Durrell was born in India; his family had lived there for generations.* 4 ADV You say **there** to indicate a place that you are pointing to or looking at. ❑ *The toilets are over there.* ❑ *Where did I put it? – Oh there it is.* 5 ADV You use **there** when speaking on the telephone to ask if someone is available to speak to you. ❑ *Hello, is Gordon there please?* 6 ADV You use **there** to refer to a point that someone has made in a conversation. ❑ *I think you're right there, John.* 7 ADV You use **there** to refer to a stage that has been reached in an activity or process. ❑ *We are making further investigations and will take the matter from there.* 8 ADV You can use **there** in expressions such as **there you go** or **there we are** when accepting that an unsatisfactory situation cannot be changed. [SPOKEN] ❑ *The wages are not generous, but there you are.* 9 ADV You can use **there** in expressions such as **there you go** and **there we are** when emphasizing that something proves that you were right. [SPOKEN] ❑ *'There you are, you see!' she exclaimed. 'I knew you'd say that!'* 10 PHRASE You use **there again** to introduce an extra piece of information which either contradicts what has been said or gives an alternative to it. ❑ *You may be lucky and find someone to help you, but, there again, you might not.* 11 PHRASE If something happens **there and then** or **then and there**, it happens immediately. 12 PHRASE You say **'there you are'** or **'there you go'** when you are offering something to someone. ❑ *There you are, Lennie, you take the biscuit.*

Usage

There is normally followed by a plural form of the verb **be** when it is used to introduce a count noun in the plural. ❑ *There were policemen everywhere.* However, when it introduces a series of nouns in the singular, linked by **and**, a singular form of the verb **be** is normally used. ❑ *There is a time and a place for everything.* ❑ *There was a street fair and a brass band.* Do not confuse the spelling of **there** with **their** as a possessive pronoun.

thereafter /ˌðeərˈɑːftə, -ˈæftə/ ADV **Thereafter** means after the event or date mentioned. [FORMAL] ❑ *In 1954 he met Simone Forti, and shortly thereafter they married.*

thereby /ˌðeəˈbaɪ/ ADV You use **thereby** to introduce a result or consequence of the event or action just mentioned. [FORMAL] ❑ *Our bodies sweat, thereby losing heat.*

therefore /ˈðeəfɔː/ ADV You use **therefore** to introduce a logical result or conclusion. ❑ *The process is much quicker and therefore cheaper.*

therein /ˌðeərˈɪn/ 1 ADV **Therein** means in the place just mentioned. [FORMAL] ❑ *His gaze fell to the paper, to the notice therein.* 2 ADV When you say **therein** lies a situation or problem, you mean that an existing situation has caused that situation or problem. [DATED, FORMAL] ❑ *The village is barely mentioned in guidebooks; therein lies its charm.*

Word Web thermometer

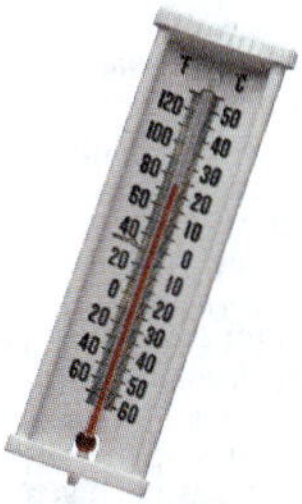

The first scientist to **measure** heat was Galileo. He invented a simple water **thermometer** in 1593. But his thermometer did not have a **scale** to show exact **temperatures.** In 1714, a German named Daniel Fahrenheit invented a **mercury** thermometer. In 1724, he added the **Fahrenheit scale** of temperatures with 32°F* as the **freezing** temperature of water. On this scale, water **boils** at 212°F. In 1742, **Anders Celsius** invented the **centigrade** scale. Centigrade means 'divided into 100 **degrees**'. On this scale, water freezes at 0°C* and boils at 100° C.

32°F = thirty-two degrees Fahrenheit
0°C = zero degrees Celsius or zero degrees centigrade

thermal /'θɜːməl/ 1 ADJ BEFORE N **Thermal** means relating to heat or caused by heat. ❑ *...thermal power stations.* 2 ADJ BEFORE N **Thermal** clothes are specially designed to keep you warm. ❑ *...thermal underwear.*
→ see **solar**

Word Link *meter ≈ measuring : diameter, perimeter, thermometer*

thermometer /θə'mɒmɪtə/ (**thermometers**) N-COUNT A **thermometer** is an instrument for measuring the temperature of a room or of a person's body.
→ see Word Web: **thermometer**

these /ðiːz/ 1 DET & PRON You use **these** to refer to people or things that have been mentioned. ❑ *Set up a monthly gym membership. Most gyms now offer these.* ❑ *Please bring any medicines that you are taking. These must be handed to the nurse.* 2 DET & PRON You use **these** to introduce people or things that you are going to talk about. ❑ *If you're looking for a builder, these phone numbers will be useful.* ❑ *These are some of the things you can do.* 3 DET People use **these** to introduce people or things into a story. [INFORMAL, SPOKEN] ❑ *I was on my own and these men came along.* 4 PRON You use **these** when you are identifying someone or asking about their identity. ❑ *These are my children.* 5 DET & PRON You use **these** to refer to people or things that are near you, especially when you touch them or point to them. ❑ *These scissors are very sharp.* ❑ *These are the only CDs we have.* 6 PHRASE If you say that **these days** something happens, you mean that at the present time it happens, in contrast to in the past. ❑ *Families do not eat together often enough these days.*

thesis /'θiːsɪs/ (**theses** /'θiːsiːz/) 1 N-COUNT A **thesis** is an idea or theory that is expressed as a statement and discussed in a logical way. 2 N-COUNT A **thesis** is a long piece of writing based on your own ideas and research that you do as part of a university degree.
→ see **graduation**

they /ðeɪ/ 1 PRON You use **they** to refer to a group of people, animals, or things. ❑ *The Beatles' success meant that they often missed out on normal activities.* 2 PRON You use **they** instead of 'he or she' to refer to a person without saying whether that person is a man or a woman. Some people think this use is incorrect. ❑ *The teacher is not responsible for the student's success or failure. They are only there to help the student learn.* 3 PRON You use **they** in expressions such as 'they say' or 'they call it' when you want to refer vaguely to what people in general say, think, or do. ❑ *They say there are plenty of opportunities.*

they'd /ðeɪd/ **They'd** is the usual spoken form of 'they had', especially when 'had' is an auxiliary verb. **They'd** is also a spoken form of 'they would'. ❑ *They'd both lived in this road all their lives.* ❑ *They agreed that they'd visit her.*

they'll /ðeɪəl/ **They'll** is the usual spoken form of 'they will'.

they're /ðeə, ðeɪə/ **They're** is the usual spoken form of 'they are'.

they've /ðeɪv/ **They've** is the usual spoken form of 'they have', especially when 'have' is an auxiliary verb. ❑ *They've gone out.*

thick /θɪk/ (**thicker, thickest**) 1 ADJ Something that is **thick** has a large distance between its two opposite surfaces. ❑ *...a thick stone wall.* ● **thickly** ADV ❑ *Slice the meat thickly.* 2 ADJ You can use **thick** to talk or ask about how wide or deep something is. ❑ *The folder was two inches thick.* ❑ *How thick are these walls?* ❑ *...a plant with a thick brown root.* ● **thickness** (**thicknesses**) N-VAR ❑ *The size of the fish will determine the thickness of the steaks.* 3 ADJ If something that consists of several things is **thick**, it has a large number of them very close together. ❑ *Our father has thick, wavy hair.* ● **thickly** ADV ❑ *The trees grew thickly here by the river.* 4 ADJ **Thick** smoke, fog, or cloud is difficult to see through. 5 ADJ **Thick** liquids are fairly stiff and solid and do not flow easily. ❑ *They had to battle through thick mud.* 6 ADJ If you describe someone as **thick**, you think that they are stupid. [BRIT, INFORMAL] 7 PHRASE If things happen **thick and fast**, they happen very quickly and in large numbers. ❑ *The rumours have been coming thick and fast.* 8 PHRASE If you are **in the thick of** an activity or situation, you are very involved in it. ❑ *The company was in trouble, and Naomi was in the thick of it.*

Word Partnership Use *thick* with:

N.	thick **glass**, thick **ice**, thick **layer**, thick **lips**, thick **neck**, thick **slice**, thick **wall** 1 thick **carpet**, **feet/inches** thick 2 thick **beard**, thick **fur**, thick **grass**, thick **hair** 3 thick **air**, thick **clouds**, thick **fog**, thick **smoke** 4
ADV.	**so** thick, **too** thick, **very** thick 1 3 4 5

thicken /'θɪkən/ (**thickens, thickening, thickened**) V-T/V-I If something **thickens**, or if you **thicken** it, it becomes thicker. ❑ *The crowds around*

t

him began to thicken. ❑ *Thicken the sauce by adding the cream.*

thief /θiːf/ (**thieves**) N-COUNT A **thief** is a person who steals something from another person.

thigh /θaɪ/ (**thighs**) N-COUNT Your **thighs** are the top parts of your legs, between your knees and your hips.
→ see **body**

thin /θɪn/ (**thinner, thinnest, thins, thinning, thinned**) **1** ADJ If something is **thin**, there is a small distance between its two opposite surfaces. ❑ *...a thin cable.* ❑ *The material was too thin.* ● **thinly** ADV ❑ *Peel and thinly slice the onion.* **2** ADJ A **thin** person or animal has no extra fat on their body. **3** ADJ **Thin** liquids are weak and watery. **4** V-I & PHR-VERB If something **thins** or **thins out**, it becomes less crowded because people or things have been removed from it. ❑ *By midnight the crowd had thinned.* ❑ *Thin out plants if they become crowded.* **5** PHRASE If you say that people or things are **thin on the ground**, you mean that there are not very many of them and so they are hard to find. ❑ *Good managers are often thin on the ground.*

Thesaurus *thin* Also look up:

ADJ.	flimsy, transparent; *(ant.)* dense, solid, thick **1**
	lean, skinny, slender, slim, underweight; *(ant.)* fat, heavy **2**
	watery, weak; *(ant.)* thick **3**

Word Partnership Use *thin* with:

N.	thin **face**, thin **fingers**, thin **legs**, thin **line**, thin **lips**, thin **mouth**, thin **smile**, thin **strips** **1**
	thin **body**, thin **man/woman** **2**
	thin **film**, thin **ice**, thin **layer**, **razor** thin, thin **slice** **3**
ADJ.	**long and** thin **1**
	tall and thin **2**
ADV.	**extremely** thin, **too** thin, **very** thin **1 2 3**

thing /θɪŋ/ (**things**) **1** N-COUNT You use **thing** as a substitute for another word when you are unable to be more precise, or you do not need or want to be more precise. ❑ *What's that thing in the middle of the fountain?* ❑ *...crisps and peanuts and things like that.* ❑ *Give up? Now that's a thing I would never do.* **2** N-SING **Thing** is often used instead of the pronouns 'anything,' or 'everything' in order to emphasize what you are saying. ❑ *Don't you worry about a thing.* **3** N-COUNT A **thing** is a physical object that is considered as having no life of its own. ❑ *It's not a thing; it's a human being!* **4** N-COUNT You can call a person or an animal a particular **thing** when you are expressing your feelings towards them. [INFORMAL] ❑ *Oh you lucky thing!* **5** N-PLURAL Your **things** are your clothes or possessions. ❑ *Sara told him to take all his things and not to return.* **6** N-PLURAL **Things** can refer to life in general and the way it affects you. ❑ *How are things going?* **7** PHRASE If you do something **first thing**, you do it at the beginning of the day, before you do anything else. If you do it **last thing**, you do it at the end of the day. ❑ *I always do it last thing on a Saturday.* **8** PHRASE If you **have a thing about** someone or something, you have very strong positive or negative feelings about them. [INFORMAL] ❑ *He's got a thing about ties.* **9** PHRASE You say **for one thing** when you give only one reason for something, but want to indicate that there are other reasons. ❑ *She was unable to sell it because for one thing, it was too big.* **10** PHRASE If you **do** your **own thing**, you live or behave in the way you want to, without paying attention to convention or depending on other people. **11** PHRASE You can say **'The thing is'** to introduce an explanation or opinion relating to something that has just been said. ❑ *I'm starting a college course next week. The thing is, I don't think I want to do it any more.*

think /θɪŋk/ (**thinks, thinking, thought**) **1** V-T/V-I If you **think** that something is the case, you have the opinion that it is the case. ❑ *I certainly think I would enjoy it.* ❑ *What do you think of my theory?* ● **thinking** N-UNCOUNT ❑ *What's your thinking on the subject of climate change?* **2** V-T If you **think** that something is true or will happen, you believe that it is true or will happen, although you are not certain of the facts. ❑ *Nora thought he was seventeen years old.* ❑ *The storm is thought to be responsible for four deaths.*

Usage

Note that when you are using the verb **think** with a **that** clause in order to state a negative opinion or belief, you normally make **think** negative, rather than the verb in the **that** clause. For instance, it is more usual to say '**I don't think he saw me**' than 'I think he didn't see me'. The same pattern applies to other verbs with a similar meaning, such as **believe**, **consider**, and **suppose**. ❑ *He didn't believe she could do it.* ❑ *I don't consider that you kept your promise.* ❑ *I don't suppose he ever saw it.*

3 V-T/V-I If you **think** highly or a lot of someone or something, you admire them. ❑ *People at the club think very highly of him.* **4** V-I & N-SING When you **think about** ideas or problems, or when you have **a think about** them, you make a mental effort to consider them or solve them. ❑ *She closed her eyes for a moment, trying to think.* ❑ *I'll have a think about that.* ● **thinking** N-UNCOUNT ❑ *...quick thinking.* **5** V-T/V-I When you **think of** something, you remember it or it comes into your mind. ❑ *Nobody could think of anything to say.* ❑ *I was trying to think what else we had to do.* **6** V-T When you **are thinking** something, you have words or ideas in your mind without saying them out loud. ❑ *I remember thinking how lovely he looked.* **7** V-I If you **are thinking of** doing something, you are considering doing it. ❑ *After 37 years in politics, he was thinking of retiring.* **8** → see also **thought** **9** PHRASE You can use **'I think'** as a way of being polite when you are explaining or suggesting something, giving your opinion, or responding to an offer. ❑ *I think he means 'at' rather than 'to'.* ❑ *'Would you like to do that another time.'—'Yes I think so.'* **10** PHRASE If you say that someone would **think nothing of** doing something difficult or strange, you mean that they would do it and not think that it was difficult or strange at all. ❑ *I thought nothing of betting £1,000 on a horse.*

▶ **think back** PHR-VERB If you **think back**, you remember things that happened in the past. ❑ *I thought back to my time as a reporter in Liverpool.*

T

▶ **think over** PHR-VERB If you **think** something **over**, you consider it carefully before making a decision.
▶ **think through** PHR-VERB If you **think** a problem or situation **through**, you consider it thoroughly. ❑ *I didn't think through the consequences of promotion.*
▶ **think up** PHR-VERB If you **think** something **up**, for example an idea or plan, you invent it using mental effort. ❑ *Julian has been thinking up new ways of raising money.*

Thesaurus	*think* Also look up:
v.	believe, consider, feel, judge, understand 1 analyze, evaluate, meditate, reflect, study 4 recall, remember; *(ant.)* forget 5

thinker /ˈθɪŋkə/ (**thinkers**) N-COUNT A **thinker** is a person who spends a lot of time thinking deeply about important things, especially a philosopher who is famous for thinking of new ideas.
thinking /ˈθɪŋkɪŋ/ 1 → see **think** 2 → see also **wishful thinking**
third /θɜːd/ (**thirds**) 1 ORD The **third** item in a series is the one that you count as number three. 2 N-COUNT A **third** is one of three equal parts of something.
thirdly /ˈθɜːdli/ ADV You use **thirdly** when you are about to mention the third thing in a series of items. ❑ *First of all, there are not many of them, secondly, they have little money and, thirdly, they have few big businesses.*
ˌthird ˈparty (**third parties**) N-COUNT A **third party** is someone who is not one of the two main people or groups involved in a business or legal matter, but who becomes involved in a minor way.
ˌThird ˈWorld N-PROPER Some of the countries of Africa, Asia, and South America are sometimes referred to as the **Third World**. These countries are also sometimes referred to as the **developing world**.
thirst /θɜːst/ (**thirsts**) 1 N-VAR **Thirst** is the feeling that you need to drink something. ❑ *Drink water to quench your thirst.* 2 N-UNCOUNT **Thirst** is the condition of not having enough to drink. ❑ *They died of thirst.* 3 N-SING **A thirst for** something is a very strong desire for it. ❑ *Children show a real thirst for learning.*
thirsty /ˈθɜːsti/ (**thirstier, thirstiest**) ADJ If you are **thirsty**, you feel a need to drink something.
thirteen /ˌθɜːˈtiːn/ NUM **Thirteen** is the number 13.
thirteenth /ˌθɜːˈtiːnθ/ ORD The **thirteenth** item in a series is the one that you count as number thirteen.
thirtieth /ˈθɜːtiəθ/ ORD The **thirtieth** item in a series is the one that you count as number thirty.
thirty /ˈθɜːti/ (**thirties**) NUM **Thirty** is the number 30. For examples of how numbers such as thirty and eighty are used see **eighty**.
this /ðɪs/ 1 DET & PRON You use **this** to refer to a person or thing that has been mentioned. ❑ *The President has long prepared for this challenge.* ❑ *I had been on many film sets, but never one like this.* 2 PRON & DET You use **this** to introduce someone or something that you are going to talk about. ❑ *This is what I will do. I will telephone Anna and explain.* ❑ *This report is from our Jerusalem correspondent, Gerald Butt.* 3 PRON & DET You use **this** to refer to a person or thing that is near you now, or to the present time. When there are two or more people or things near you, **this** refers to the nearest one. ❑ *Is this what you were looking for?* ❑ *This is my colleague, Mr Arnold Landon.* ❑ *This place is run like a hotel.* 4 PRON You use **this** when you refer to a situation which is happening or has just happened and which you feel involved in. ❑ *Tim, this is awful.* ❑ *Is this what you want to do with the rest of your life?* 5 DET You use **this** to refer to the next occurrence of a particular day, month, season, or festival. ❑ *...this Sunday's 7.45 performance.* ❑ *We're getting married this June.* 6 PRON You use **this** in order to say who you are when you are speaking on the telephone, radio, or television. ❑ *'Hello, is this Raymond Brown?'—'Yeah, who's this?'* 7 PHRASE You can refer to a variety of things that you are doing or talking about as **this and that** or **this, that and the other**. ❑ *'And what are you doing now?'—'Oh this and that.'*

thorn

thorn /θɔːn/ (**thorns**) N-COUNT **Thorns** are the sharp points on some plants and trees such as roses and holly.
thorny /ˈθɔːni/ (**thornier, thorniest**) 1 ADJ A **thorny** plant or tree is covered with thorns. 2 ADJ A **thorny** problem or question is difficult to deal with.
thorough /ˈθʌrə, AM ˈθɜːrəʊ/ 1 ADJ A **thorough** action is done very carefully and methodically. ❑ *We are making a thorough investigation.* ● **thoroughly** ADV ❑ *Food that is being offered hot must be reheated thoroughly.* ● **thoroughness** N-UNCOUNT ❑ *I have no doubt about the thoroughness of her work.* 2 ADJ Someone who is **thorough** does things in a careful and methodical way. ● **thoroughness** N-UNCOUNT ❑ *I commend the authors for their thoroughness and accuracy.* 3 ADJ You can use **thorough** for emphasis. ❑ *The management has got itself into a thorough mess.* ● **thoroughly** ADV ❑ *I thoroughly enjoy your programme.*
those /ðəʊz/ 1 DET & PRON You use **those** to refer to people, things, or situations which have already been mentioned. ❑ *Most of those crimes are committed by young people.* ❑ *Waterfalls always attract tourists, and those at the Falls of Clyde are no exception.* 2 DET & PRON You use **those** when you are referring to people or things that are a distance away from you in position or time, often when you indicate or point to them. ❑ *What are those buildings?* ❑ *Those are nice shoes.* 3 PRON You use **those** to mean 'people'. ❑ *He caused a lot of worry to those around him.*
though /ðəʊ/ 1 CONJ & ADV You use **though** to introduce a fact or comment which contrasts with something else that is being said, or makes it seem surprising. ❑ *They went to the same school, though they never met there.* ❑ *I like him. He sometimes makes me angry, though.* 2 **as though** → see **as**
thought /θɔːt/ (**thoughts**) 1 **Thought** is the past tense and past participle of **think**. 2 N-COUNT A **thought** is an idea or opinion. ❑ *I hate the thought of someone suffering.* ❑ *...his thoughts on love and*

t

fatherhood. **3** N-UNCOUNT **Thought** is the activity of thinking, especially deeply, logically, or with concentration. ❑ *After much thought I decided to end my marriage.* **4** N-UNCOUNT **Thought** is the group of ideas and beliefs or way of thinking which belongs, for example, to a particular religion or political party. ❑ *...the history of the development of religious thought.* **5** → see also **second thoughts**

thoughtful /ˈθɔːtfʊl/ **1** ADJ If you are **thoughtful**, you are quiet and serious because you are thinking about something. • **thoughtfully** ADV ❑ *Daniel nodded thoughtfully.* **2** ADJ If you describe someone as **thoughtful**, you approve of them because they remember what other people want, need, or feel, and try not to upset them. • **thoughtfully** ADV ❑ *He had thoughtfully brought flowers to the party.*

thoughtless /ˈθɔːtləs/ ADJ If you describe someone as **thoughtless**, you are critical of them because they forget or ignore other people's wants, needs, or feelings. • **thoughtlessly** ADV ❑ *They thoughtlessly planned a picnic without him.*

thousand /ˈθaʊzənd/ (**thousands**) **1** NUM **A thousand** or **one thousand** is the number 1,000. **2** N-PLURAL & PRON If you refer to **thousands of** things or people, you are emphasizing that there are very many of them. **Thousands** means very many. ❑ *I've driven past that place thousands of times.*

thousandth /ˈθaʊzənθ/ ORD The **thousandth** item in a series is the one you count as number one thousand.

thrash /θræʃ/ (**thrashes, thrashing, thrashed**) **1** V-T If one player or team **thrashes** another in a game or contest, they defeat them easily. [INFORMAL] • **thrashing** (**thrashings**) N-COUNT ❑ *...his team's 5-0 thrashing of the home team.* **2** V-T If someone **thrashes** you, they hit you several times as a punishment. • **thrashing** N-COUNT ❑ *If Sarah caught her, she would get a thrashing.* **3** V-I If someone **thrashes about**, they move in a wild or violent way, often hitting against something. ❑ *Jimmy fell on the floor, thrashing about.*

▸ **thrash out** PHR-VERB If people **thrash out** something such as a problem or a plan, they discuss it in detail until a solution is reached. ❑ *...an effort by two people to thrash out differences.*

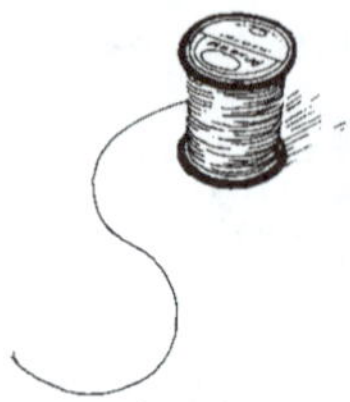
thread

thread /θred/ (**threads, threading, threaded**) **1** N-VAR & V-T **Thread** or a **thread** is a long, thin piece of cotton, silk, nylon, or wool. When you **thread** a needle, you put a piece of thread through the hole in the top of the needle. **2** V-T If you **thread** small objects such as beads onto a string, you join them together by pushing the string through them. ❑ *Wipe the mushrooms clean and thread them on a string.* **3** N-COUNT The **thread** of a story or a situation is an aspect of it that connects all the different parts together. ❑ *He lost the thread of the story.* **4** V-T If you **thread** your **way** through a group of people or things, you move through it carefully. ❑ *Anna threaded her way through the crowded room towards the buffet.*

threat /θret/ (**threats**) **1** N-VAR A **threat to** someone or something is a danger that something unpleasant might happen to them. A **threat** is also the cause of this danger. ❑ *They saw her as a threat to their relationship.* ❑ *Africa's lions are under threat from hunters.* **2** N-SING A **threat** is a statement by someone that they will do something unpleasant, especially if you do not do what they want. ❑ *He may be forced to carry out his threat to resign.*

Word Partnership Use *threat* with:

N.	threat **to** ***someone's*** **health** **1**
	threat **of attack**, **death** threat, threat **to peace**, threat **to stability**, threat **of a strike**, **terrorist** threat, threat **of violence**, threat **of war** **1** **2**
ADJ.	**biggest** threat, **greatest** threat, **major** threat **1**
	credible threat, **potential** threat, **real** threat, **serious** threat, **significant** threat **1** **2**

threaten /ˈθretən/ (**threatens, threatening, threatened**) **1** V-T If someone **threatens to** do something unpleasant to you, or if they **threaten** you, they say or imply that they will do something unpleasant to you, especially if you do not do what they want. • **threatening** ADJ ❑ *...a threatening phone call.* **2** V-T If something **threatens** people or things, it is likely to harm them. ❑ *Many reptiles, birds, and fish are currently threatened with extinction.* **3** V-T If something unpleasant **threatens to** happen, it seems likely to happen. ❑ *The fighting is threatening to turn into war.*

Word Partnership Use *threaten* with:

N.	threaten **safety**, threaten **security**, threaten **stability**, threaten **survival** **2**

three /θriː/ (**threes**) NUM **Three** is the number 3.

ˌthree-diˈmensional ADJ A **three-dimensional** object is solid rather than flat, because it can be measured in three dimensions, usually the height, depth, and width.

ˌthree-ˈquarters QUANT **Three-quarters** is an amount that is three out of four equal parts of something. ❑ *Three-quarters of the country's workers took part in the strike.* ❑ *Road deaths have increased by three-quarters.*

threshold /ˈθreʃhəʊld/ (**thresholds**) **1** N-COUNT The **threshold** of a building or room is the floor in the doorway, or the doorway itself. **2** N-COUNT A **threshold** is an amount, level, or limit on a scale. ❑ *She has a low threshold of boredom.* **3** PHRASE If you are **on the threshold of** something exciting or new, you are about to experience it. ❑ *We are on the threshold of a new era in astronomy.*

threw /θruː/ **Threw** is the past tense of **throw**.

thrift /θrɪft/ N-UNCOUNT **Thrift** is the quality and practice of being careful with money and not wasting things.

thrill /θrɪl/ (**thrills, thrilling, thrilled**) V-T & N-COUNT If something **thrills** you, or if something gives you a **thrill**, it gives you a feeling of great pleasure or excitement. ❑ *He still gets a thrill from acting in the theatre.*

thrilled /θrɪld/ ADJ AFTER LINK-V If you are **thrilled** about something, you are pleased and excited about it. ❑ *I was so thrilled to get a good report.*

thriller /ˈθrɪlə/ (**thrillers**) N-COUNT A **thriller** is a book, film, or play that tells an exciting story about something such as criminal activities or spying.

thrilling /ˈθrɪlɪŋ/ ADJ Something that is **thrilling** is very exciting and enjoyable. ❑ *...a thrilling adventure movie.*

thrive /θraɪv/ (**thrives, thriving, thrived**) V-I If someone or something **thrives**, they do well and are successful, healthy, or strong. ❑ *Her business is thriving.* ❑ *He thrives on pressure.*

throat /θrəʊt/ (**throats**) 1 N-COUNT Your **throat** is the back of your mouth and the top part of the tubes that go down into your stomach and your lungs. 2 N-COUNT Your **throat** is the front part of your neck. 3 PHRASE If you **clear** your **throat**, you cough once in order to make it easier to speak or to attract people's attention.

throb /θrɒb/ (**throbs, throbbing, throbbed**) 1 V-I & N-SING If a part of your body **throbs**, you feel a series of strong and usually painful beats there. You can refer to this feeling as a **throb**. ❑ *His head throbbed.* 2 V-I & N-SING If something **throbs**, it vibrates and makes a rhythmic noise, called a **throb**. [LITERARY] ❑ *The music throbbed with a strong beat.*

throne /θrəʊn/ (**thrones**) 1 N-COUNT A **throne** is an ornate chair used by a king, queen, or emperor on important occasions. 2 N-SING You can talk about **the throne** as a way of referring to the position of being king, queen, or emperor. ❑ *...the heir to the throne.*

throng /θrɒŋ, AM θrɔːŋ/ (**throngs, thronging, thronged**) 1 N-COUNT A **throng** is a large crowd of people. 2 V-T/V-I When people **throng** somewhere, they go there in great numbers. ❑ *Millions of people thronged into the capital.* • **thronged** ADJ AFTER LINK-V ❑ *The streets are thronged with people.*

throttle /ˈθrɒtəl/ (**throttles, throttling, throttled**) 1 V-T To **throttle** someone means to kill or injure them by holding them tightly by the throat so that they cannot breathe. 2 N-COUNT The **throttle** of a motor vehicle or aircraft is a device that controls the quantity of fuel entering the engine and is used to control the vehicle's speed.

through /θruː/ 1 PREP & ADV To move, cut, or travel **through** something, means to move, cut, or travel from one side or end to the other. ❑ *Go straight through that door under the EXIT sign.* ❑ *He went straight through to the kitchen.* ❑ *The exhaust pipe had been cut through.* 2 PREP If you can see, hear, or feel something **through** a particular thing, that thing is between you and the thing you can see, hear, or feel. ❑ *They could hear music pulsing through the walls of the house.* 3 PREP & ADV If something happens **through** a period of time, it happens from the beginning until the end. ❑ *He worked hard right through the summer.* 4 PREP If you go **through** a particular experience or event, you experience it. ❑ *We have been going through a bad time.* 5 ADJ AFTER LINK-V If you are **through with** something or if it is **through**, you have finished doing it and will never do it again. If you are **through with** someone, you do not want to have anything to do with them again. ❑ *I'm through with women.* 6 PREP If something happens because of something else, you can say that it happens **through** it. ❑ *Geoff had to retire early through ill health.* 7 PREP & ADV If someone gets **through** an examination or a round of a competition, they succeed or win. 8 PREP If you go **through** or look **through** a lot of things, you deal with them one after another. ❑ *Try working through the exercises in this chapter.*

throughout /θruːˈaʊt/ 1 PREP & ADV If something happens **throughout** a particular period of time, it happens during the whole of that period. ❑ *The school runs cookery courses throughout the year.* ❑ *It was an absorbing contest throughout.* 2 PREP & ADV If something happens or exists **throughout** a place, it happens or exists in all parts of it. ❑ *The hospital is well lit throughout.*

throw /θrəʊ/ (**throws, throwing, threw, thrown**) 1 V-T If you **throw** an object that you are holding, you move your hand quickly and let go of the object, so that it moves through the air. ❑ *He spent hours throwing a tennis ball against a wall.* ❑ *He threw Brian a rope.* 2 V-T To **throw** something into a place or position means to cause it to fall there. ❑ *David threw his coat on the nearest chair.* ❑ *He threw me to the ground.* 3 V-T If you **throw** a part of your body somewhere, you move it there suddenly and with a lot of force. ❑ *She threw her hands into the air.* ❑ *He threw himself on his bed.* 4 V-T If a horse **throws** its rider, it makes the rider fall off. 5 V-T If a person or thing **is thrown** into an unpleasant situation or state, something causes them to be in it. ❑ *She was thrown into a panic at the thought of an evening alone.* 6 V-T If you **throw yourself**, your energy, or your money into a particular job or activity, you become involved in it very enthusiastically. 7 V-T If someone **throws** a fit or tantrum, they are suddenly very angry and start to behave in an uncontrolled way. 8 V-T When someone **throws** a party, they organize one. [INFORMAL] 9 V-T If something such as a remark or an experience **throws** you, it confuses you because it is unexpected. ❑ *That reporter really threw me.*

▸ **throw away** 1 PHR-VERB If you **throw away** or **throw out** something you do not want, you get rid of it. ❑ *I never throw anything away.* 2 PHR-VERB If you **throw away** something good that you have, you waste it. ❑ *The Government has thrown away a chance of becoming a world leader in engineering.*

▸ **throw in** PHR-VERB If someone who is selling or offering something **throws in** something else, they add it to what they are selling or offering for no extra charge. ❑ *...a weekend break in Paris – with free meals thrown in.*

▸ **throw off** PHR-VERB If you **throw off** something that is restricting you or making you unhappy, you get rid of it. ❑ *The royal family needs to throw off its outdated image.*

▸ **throw out** 1 → see **throw away** (meaning 1) 2 PHR-VERB If you **throw** someone **out**, you force them to leave. ❑ *I was so cross with him that I threw him out of the house.* 3 PHR-VERB If a court or committee **throws out** a case, proposal, or request, they reject it.

▸ **throw up** PHR-VERB To **throw up** means to vomit. [INFORMAL]

Word Partnership	Use *throw* with:
N.	throw **a ball**, throw **a pass**, throw **a pitch**, throw **a rock/stone** 1

t

thrown /θrəʊn/ **Thrown** is the past participle of **throw**.

thrush /θrʌʃ/ (**thrushes**) N-COUNT A **thrush** is a small brown bird with small marks on its chest.

thrust /θrʌst/ (**thrusts, thrusting, thrust**) **1** V-T & N-COUNT If you **thrust** something somewhere, or if you make a **thrust** with it, you push or move it there quickly with a lot of force. ❑ *They thrust him into the back of a car.* ❑ *...knife thrusts.* **2** N-SING **The thrust of** an activity or idea is the main or essential things it involves. ❑ *The main thrust of the research will be the study of the early universe.*

thud /θʌd/ (**thuds, thudding, thudded**) N-COUNT & V-I A **thud** is a dull sound, usually made by a solid, heavy object hitting something soft. If something **thuds** somewhere, it makes this sound as it hits it. ❑ *She tripped and fell with a sickening thud.* ❑ *She ran up the stairs, her bare feet thudding on the wood.*

thug /θʌg/ (**thugs**) N-COUNT If you refer to someone as a **thug**, you disapprove of them and think they are violent or a criminal.

thumb /θʌm/ (**thumbs, thumbing, thumbed**) N-COUNT Your **thumb** is the short, thick digit on the side of your hand next to your first finger.
→ see **hand**

▶ **thumb through** PHR-VERB If you **thumb through** a book or magazine, you glance at the pages quickly rather than reading them carefully.

thump /θʌmp/ (**thumps, thumping, thumped**) **1** V-T/V-I & N-COUNT If you **thump** someone or something, or if you give them a **thump**, you hit them hard with your fist. ❑ *I'll thump you.* ❑ *I heard you thumping on the door.* ❑ *He felt a thump on his shoulder.* **2** V-T/V-I & N-COUNT If you **thump** something somewhere, or if it **thumps** there, it hits something else with a loud, dull sound called a **thump**. ❑ *He thumped the can down on the table.* **3** V-I When your heart **thumps**, it beats strongly and quickly, usually because you are afraid or excited.

thunder /ˈθʌndə/ (**thunders, thundering, thundered**) **1** N-UNCOUNT & V-I **Thunder** is the loud noise that you hear from the sky after a flash of lightning. When it **thunders**, you hear thunder. **2** N-UNCOUNT & V-I **The thunder of** something such as traffic is the loud, deep, continuous noise it makes. If something **thunders**, it makes this noise. ❑ *...the thunder of the sea on the rocks.*

thunderous /ˈθʌndərəs/ ADJ A **thunderous** noise is very loud and deep. ❑ *...thunderous applause.*

thunderstorm /ˈθʌndəstɔːm/ (**thunderstorms**) N-COUNT A **thunderstorm** is a storm in which there is thunder, lightning, and heavy rain.
→ see **erosion**

Thursday /ˈθɜːzdeɪ, -di/ (**Thursdays**) N-VAR **Thursday** is the day after Wednesday and before Friday.

thus /ðʌs/ **1** ADV You use **thus** to introduce the consequence or conclusion of something that you have just mentioned. [FORMAL] ❑ *They didn't watch the news. Thus Caroline only heard of John's death when Peter telephoned.* ❑ *Some people will be more capable and thus better paid than others.* **2** ADV If you say that something is **thus** or happens **thus**, you mean that it is, or happens, as you describe. [FORMAL] ❑ *Joanna was pouring the drink. While she was thus engaged, Charles sat on one of the sofas.*

thwart /θwɔːt/ (**thwarts, thwarting, thwarted**) V-T If you **thwart** someone or **thwart** their plans, you prevent them from doing or getting what they want. ❑ *The security forces were doing all they could to thwart terrorists.*

thyme /taɪm/ N-UNCOUNT **Thyme** is a type of herb.

tick /tɪk/ (**ticks, ticking, ticked**) **1** N-COUNT In British English, a **tick** is a written mark like a V with the right side extended. You use it to show that something is correct or has been dealt with. The usual American word is **check**. ❑ *Place a tick in the appropriate box.* **2** V-T If you **tick** something that is written on a piece of paper, you put a tick next to it. ❑ *Please tick this box if you do not wish to receive such mailings.* **3** V-I & N-COUNT When a clock or watch **ticks**, it makes a regular series of short sounds as it works. The **tick** of a clock is this series of short sounds. ● **ticking** N-UNCOUNT ❑ *...the endless ticking of clocks.* **4** V-I If you talk about what makes someone **tick**, you are talking about the reasons for their character and behaviour. [INFORMAL] ❑ *Their parents simply don't understand what makes them tick.*
→ see **answer**

▶ **tick away** or **tick by** PHR-VERB If you say that the clock or time is **ticking away** or **ticking by**, you mean that time is passing, especially when there is something urgent that needs to be done or when someone is waiting for something to happen.

▶ **tick off** **1** PHR-VERB If you **tick off** an item on a list, you put a tick by it to show that it has been dealt with. **2** PHR-VERB If you **tick** someone **off**, you speak to them angrily because they have done something wrong. [INFORMAL] ❑ *Harry will be ticked off for being careless.* ● **ticking off** (**tickings off**) N-COUNT ❑ *They got a ticking off from the police.*

▶ **tick over** PHR-VERB Something that **is ticking over** is working or operating steadily, but not producing very much or making much progress. ❑ *Eating little and often keeps your metabolism ticking over.*

ticket

ticket /ˈtɪkɪt/ (**tickets**) **1** N-COUNT A **ticket** is an official piece of paper or card which shows that you have paid for a journey or have paid to enter a place of entertainment. **2** → see also **season ticket** **3** N-COUNT If you get a **ticket**, you are given a piece of paper which orders you to pay a fine or to appear in court because you have committed a driving or parking offence. ❑ *...the money she owed on an unpaid parking ticket.*

Word Partnership Use *ticket* with:

N.	ticket **agent**, ticket **booth**, ticket **counter**, ticket **holder**, **lottery** ticket, **plane** ticket, ticket **price** **1** **parking** ticket, **speeding** ticket **2**
ADJ.	**free** ticket, **winning** ticket **1**
V.	**buy/pay for a** ticket, **get a** ticket **1** **2**

T

Word Web tide

The **gravitational** pull of the **moon** on the earth's **oceans** causes **tides**. It moves the water in the earth's oceans. **High tides** occur twice a day at any given point on the earth's surface. Then the water **ebbs** gradually. After six hours, **low tide** occurs. In some places tidal energy powers hydroelectric **plants**. Riptides cause the deaths of hundreds of swimmers each year. But a riptide is not really a tide. It is a strong ocean **current**.

tickle /'tɪkəl/ (**tickles, tickling, tickled**) **1** V-T When you **tickle** someone, you move your fingers lightly over their body, often in order to make them laugh. **2** V-T/V-I If something **tickles** or **tickles** you, it causes an irritating feeling by lightly touching a part of your body. ❑ *A beard doesn't scratch, it just tickles.*

tidal /'taɪdəl/ ADJ **Tidal** means relating to or produced by tides. ❑ *...tidal energy.*

'tidal ˌwave (**tidal waves**) **1** N-COUNT A **tidal wave** is a very large wave, often caused by an earthquake. **2** N-COUNT A **tidal wave of** emotions, things, or people is a very large number of them all occurring at the same time. ❑ *A report in this morning's paper shows a tidal wave of job losses.*

tide /taɪd/ (**tides, tiding, tided**) **1** N-COUNT The **tide** is the regular change in the level of the sea on the shore. ❑ *The tide was going out.* **2** N-COUNT The **tide of** opinion or fashion is what the majority of people think or do at a particular time. ❑ *The tide of opinion seems to be in his favour.*
→ see Word Web: **tide**
→ see **ocean**

▶ **tide over** PHR-VERB If someone or something **tides** you **over**, they help you to get through a period when you are having difficulties, especially by providing you with money. ❑ *He's doing extra work for people to tide him over.*

tidy /'taɪdi/ (**tidier, tidiest, tidies, tidying, tidied**) **1** ADJ Something that is **tidy** is neat and arranged in an orderly way. ❑ *...a tidy desk.* • **tidily** ADV ❑ *...books and magazines stacked tidily on shelves.* • **tidiness** N-UNCOUNT ❑ *...the tidiness of his apartment.* **2** ADJ **Tidy** people keep their things tidy. ❑ *She's obsessively tidy.* • **tidiness** N-UNCOUNT ❑ *I'm very impressed by your tidiness.* **3** V-T When you **tidy** a place, you make it neat by putting things in their proper places. ❑ *He tidied his garage.* **4** ADJ BEFORE N A **tidy** amount of money is a large amount. [INFORMAL] ❑ *He has made a tidy profit.*

▶ **tidy away** PHR-VERB When you **tidy** something **away**, you put it in a cupboard or drawer so that it is not in the way. ❑ *McMinn tidied away the glasses and tea-cups.*

▶ **tidy up** PHR-VERB When you **tidy up** or **tidy** a place **up**, you put things back in their proper places so that everything is neat. ❑ *Kelly spent an hour tidying up the shop.*

tie /taɪ/ (**ties, tying, tied**) **1** V-T & PHR-VERB If you **tie** two things together, or if you **tie** them **up**, you fasten them together with a knot. ❑ *They tied the ends of the bags securely.* ❑ *He tied up the bag and took it outside.* **2** V-T & PHR-VERB If you **tie** someone or something in a place or position, or if you **tie** them **up**, you put them in that place or position and fasten them there using rope or string. ❑ *He tied her hands behind her back.* ❑ *He had tied the dog to one of the trees.* **3** V-T If you **tie** a piece of string or cloth around something, you put a piece of string or cloth around it and fasten the ends together in a knot or bow. ❑ *Roll the meat and tie it with string.* **4** V-T If you **tie** something in a knot or bow, you fasten the ends together in a knot or bow. ❑ *She tied a knot in the ribbon.* **5** N-COUNT A **tie** is a long narrow piece of cloth that is worn round the neck under a shirt collar and tied in a knot at the front. This item of clothing is usually worn by men. **6** V-T If one thing **is tied to** another, the two things have a close connection or link. ❑ *Their income is tied to the company's profits.* **7** N-COUNT **Ties** are the connections you have with people or a place. ❑ *...France's close ties with the Arab world.* **8** V-I & N-COUNT If two people **tie** in a competition or game, or if there is a **tie** between them, they have the same number of points or the same degree of success. ❑ *Ronan Rafferty had tied with Frank Nobilo.* ❑ *The first game ended in a tie.*
→ see **clothing**

tier /tɪə/ (**tiers**) N-COUNT A **tier** is a row or layer of something that has other layers above or below it. ❑ *...the tiers of seats around the stadium.*

tiger /'taɪgə/ (**tigers**) N-COUNT A **tiger** is a large fierce animal belonging to the cat family. Tigers are orange with black stripes.

tight /taɪt/ (**tighter, tightest**) **1** ADJ **Tight** clothes or shoes fit very closely. ❑ *...her tight black jeans.* • **tightly** ADV ❑ *He buttoned his collar tightly round his thick neck.* **2** ADV & ADJ If you hold someone or something **tight**, you hold them firmly. ❑ *Hold on tight!* ❑ *He kept a tight hold of her arm.* • **tightly** ADV ❑ *She wrapped the sheet tightly round her body.* **3** ADJ **Tight** controls or rules are very strict. • **tightly** ADV ❑ *The media were tightly controlled by the government during the war.* **4** ADJ Skin, cloth, or string that is **tight** is stretched or pulled so that it is smooth or straight. • **tightly** ADV ❑ *Her pale skin was drawn tightly across the bones of her face.* **5** ADJ **Tight** is used to describe an amount of something or a group of things that is closely packed together. ❑ *She curled up in a tight ball.* • **tightly** ADV ❑ *Many animals travel in tightly packed lorries.* **6** ADJ A **tight** schedule or budget allows very little time or money for unexpected events or expenses. ❑ *Financially, things are a bit tight.* **7** to **sit tight** → see **sit**

t

Word Partnership Use *tight* with:

N.	tight **dress/jeans/pants** 1 tight **fit** 1 4 tight **grip**, tight **hold** 2 tight **control**, tight **security** 3 tight **lips**, tight **muscles**, tight **smile**, tight **squeeze** 5
ADV.	**extremely** tight, **a little** tight, **so** tight, **too** tight, **very** tight 1 2 4 6

tighten /'taɪtən/ (**tightens, tightening, tightened**) 1 V-T/V-I If you **tighten** your grip on something, or if your grip on something **tightens**, you hold it more firmly or securely. ❑ *I could feel him tighten his grip on the stick.* 2 V-T/V-I If you **tighten** a rope or chain, or if a rope or chain **tightens**, it stretches until it is straight. 3 V-T & PHR-VERB When you **tighten** a screw, nut, or other device, or when you **tighten** it **up**, you turn it or move it so that it is more firmly in place or holds something more firmly. ❑ *I used my fingers to tighten the screw.* ❑ *It's important to tighten up the wheels properly.* 4 V-T To **tighten** rules or controls means to make them stricter. ❑ *...an attempt by management to tighten the rules.* ❑ *You need to tighten control of your finances.* 5 to **tighten** your **belt** → see **belt**

tights /taɪts/ N-PLURAL **Tights** are a piece of clothing made of thin material such as nylon that covers your hips and each of your legs and feet separately. ❑ *...a new pair of tights.*

tile /taɪl/ (**tiles**) N-VAR **Tiles** are flat square pieces of baked clay, carpet, cork, or other substance, which are fixed as a covering onto a floor, wall, or roof.

tiled /taɪld/ ADJ A **tiled** surface is covered with tiles. ❑ *...the hard tiled floor.*

till /tɪl/ (**tills**) 1 PREP & CONJ **Till** is often used instead of **until**. ❑ *They had to wait till Monday.* ❑ *They slept till the alarm woke them.* 2 N-COUNT In a shop or other place of business, a **till** is a counter or cash register where money is kept, and where customers pay for what they have bought. [BRIT]

tilt /tɪlt/ (**tilts, tilting, tilted**) V-T/V-I If you **tilt** an object, or if it **tilts**, you change its position so that one end or side is higher than the other. ❑ *Leonard tilted his chair back on two legs.*

timber /'tɪmbə/ N-UNCOUNT In British English, **timber** is wood used for building houses and making furniture. The American word is **lumber**. → see **forest**

T

time /taɪm/ (**times, timing, timed**) 1 N-UNCOUNT **Time** is what we measure in minutes, hours, days, and years. ❑ *...a two-week period of time.* ❑ *Time passed, and still Ma did not appear.* ❑ *Religion has changed over time.* 2 N-SING You use **time** to ask or talk about a specific point in the day, which can be stated in hours and minutes and is shown on clocks. ❑ *'What time is it?'—'Eight o'clock.'* ❑ *He asked me the time.* 3 N-COUNT The **time** when something happens is the point in the day when it happens or is supposed to happen. ❑ *Departure times are 0815 from St Quay, and 1815 from St Helier.* 4 N-UNCOUNT & PHRASE You use **time** to refer to the period that someone spends doing something or when something has been happening. If something happens **all the time**, it happens continually. ❑ *Adam spent a lot of time in his grandfather's office.* ❑ *I haven't got much time.* ❑ *We can't be together all the time.* 5 N-SING If you say that something happens **for a time**, you mean that it happens for a fairly long period of time. ❑ *He stayed for quite a time.* 6 N-COUNT You use **time** or **times** to talk about a period of time. ❑ *We were in the same college, which was male-only at that time.* ❑ *During the time I was married I tried to be the perfect wife.* ❑ *Homes are more affordable than at any time in the past five years.* ❑ *...one of the most severe storms in modern times.* 7 N-COUNT When you describe the **time** that you had on a particular occasion or during a particular part of your life, you are describing the sort of experience that you had then. ❑ *I had a great time while the kids were away.* 8 N-UNCOUNT If you say it is **time for** something, you mean that this thing ought to happen or be done now. ❑ *It was time for him to go to work.* ❑ *This was no time to make a speech.* 9 N-COUNT When you talk about a **time** when something happens, you are referring to a specific occasion when it happens. ❑ *The last time I saw her was about sixteen years ago.* 10 N-COUNT You use **time** after numbers to say how often something happens. ❑ *It was her job to make tea three times a day.* ❑ *How many times has your mother told you?* 11 N-PLURAL You use **times** after numbers when comparing one thing to another and saying, for example, how much bigger, smaller, better, or worse it is. ❑ *...an area five times the size of Britain.* 12 PREP You use **times** in arithmetic to link numbers or amounts that are multiplied together. ❑ *Four times six is 24.* 13 V-T If you **time** something, you plan or decide to do it or cause it to happen at a particular time. ❑ *We had timed our visit for March 7.* ❑ *He had timed his arrival well.* 14 V-T If you **time** an action or activity, you measure how long it lasts. ❑ *He timed each performance with a stop-watch.* 15 → see also **timing** 16 PHRASE If you say it is **about time** that something was done, or that it is **high time** that something was done, you are emphasizing that it should be done now, and really should have happened or been done sooner. ❑ *It's about time he learnt to behave properly.* 17 PHRASE If someone is **ahead of** their **time** or **before** their **time**, they have new ideas a long time before other people start to think in the same way. 18 PHRASE If you say that someone or something is, for example, the best writer **of all time**, or the most successful film **of all time**, you mean that they are the best or most successful that there has ever been. 19 PHRASE If something is the case **for the time being**, it is the case, but only until something else becomes possible or happens. ❑ *The situation is calm for the time being.* 20 PHRASE If you are **in time for** a particular event, or if you are **on time**, you are not late. ❑ *I arrived just in time for my flight.* ❑ *Their planes usually arrive on time.* 21 PHRASE If something will happen **in time**, it will happen eventually. ❑ *He would sort out his own problems, in time.* 22 PHRASE If you say that something will happen, for example, **in** a week **'s time**, you mean that it will happen a week from now. 23 PHRASE **Once upon a time** is used at the beginning of children's stories to indicate that something happened or existed a long time ago or in an imaginary world. ❑ *'Once upon a time,' he began, 'there was a man who had everything.'* 24 PHRASE If you say that something was the case **at one time**, you mean that it was

Picture Dictionary time

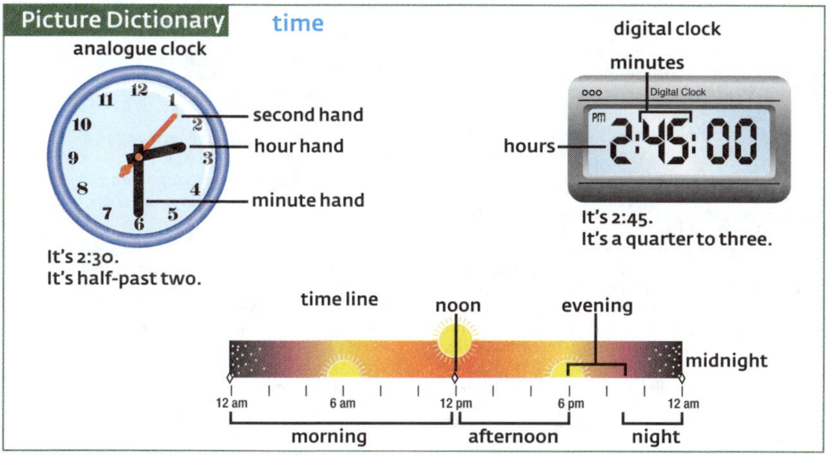

the case during a particular period in the past. ❑ *At one time 400 men, women and children lived in the village.* 25 PHRASE You use **at the same time** to introduce a statement that contrasts with the previous statement. ❑ *I was afraid of her, but at the same time I really liked her.* 26 PHRASE If you **take** your **time** doing something, you do it slowly and do not hurry. 27 PHRASE If you say that something will **take time**, you mean that it will take a long time. ❑ *Change will come, but it will take time.* 28 PHRASE If you do something **from time to time**, you do it occasionally. 29 → see also **timing** 30 **time and again** → see **again**
→ see Picture Dictionary: **time**

Usage

You do not say 'one time a year' or 'two times a year'; you say **'once a year'** or **'twice a year'**. You also do not say 'two times as much'; you say **'twice as much'**.

ˈtime-ˌhonoured ADJ BEFORE N A **time-honoured** tradition or way of doing something is one that has been used and appreciated for a very long time. ❑ *Made by time-honoured methods, Edam cheese is high in protein.*

timeless /ˈtaɪmləs/ ADJ If you describe something as **timeless**, you mean that it is so good or beautiful that it cannot be affected by changes in society or fashion. ❑ *There is a timeless quality to his best work.*

timely /ˈtaɪmli/ ADJ If you describe an event as **timely**, you mean that it happens at exactly the right moment. ❑ *Disaster was only avoided by the timely arrival of the police.*

timetable /ˈtaɪmteɪbəl/ (**timetables**) 1 N-COUNT A **timetable** is a plan of the times when particular events are to take place. ❑ *We will send you a detailed timetable and information about the activities.* 2 N-COUNT A **timetable** is a list of the times when trains, boats, buses, or aeroplanes arrive at or depart from a place.

timid /ˈtɪmɪd/ (**timider, timidest**) ADJ **Timid** people are shy, nervous, and don't have much self-confidence. ● **timidly** ADV ❑ *The little boy stepped forward timidly.* ● **timidity** /tɪˈmɪdɪti/ N-UNCOUNT ❑ *He appeared to have more timidity than his wife.*

timing /ˈtaɪmɪŋ/ 1 N-UNCOUNT **Timing** is the skill or action of judging the right moment in a situation or activity at which to do something. ❑ *His photo has caught the happy moment with perfect timing.* 2 N-UNCOUNT You can refer to the time at which something happens or is planned to happen as its **timing**. ❑ *The minister was criticized for the timing of his announcement.* 3 → see also **time**

tin /tɪn/ (**tins**) 1 N-UNCOUNT **Tin** is a soft silvery-white metal. 2 N-COUNT In British English, a **tin** is a sealed metal container filled with food. The usual American word is **can**. ❑ *...a tin of tomatoes.* 3 N-COUNT A **tin** is a metal container with a lid. ❑ *Store the cookies in an airtight tin.* 4 N-COUNT A baking **tin** is a metal container used for baking things such as cakes and bread in an oven.
→ see **pan**

tinge /tɪndʒ/ (**tinges**) N-COUNT A **tinge** of a colour, feeling, or quality is a small amount of it. ❑ *His skin had an unhealthy greyish tinge.* ❑ *...a tinge of guilt.*

tinged /tɪndʒd/ ADJ If something is **tinged with** a colour, feeling, or quality, it has a small amount of it. ❑ *Her arrival was tinged with sadness.* ● **-tinged** ❑ *...pink-tinged flowers.*

tingle /ˈtɪŋgəl/ (**tingles, tingling, tingled**) 1 V-I When a part of your body **tingles**, you feel a slight prickly sensation there. ● **tingling** N-UNCOUNT ❑ *A sensation of burning or tingling may be experienced in the hands.* 2 V-I & N-COUNT If you **tingle with** a feeling such as excitement, or if you feel a **tingle** of that feeling, you feel it very strongly. ❑ *She tingled with excitement.* ❑ *When I think about him I tingle all over.* ❑ *...a sudden tingle of excitement.*

tinker /ˈtɪŋkə/ (**tinkers, tinkering, tinkered**) V-I If you **tinker with** something, you make some small alterations to it in order to repair or improve it. ❑ *They tinkered with the engine.*

tinned /tɪnd/ ADJ In British English, **tinned** food has been preserved by being sealed in a tin. The usual American word is **canned**. ❑ *...tinned fish.*

tint /tɪnt/ (**tints, tinting, tinted**) **1** N-COUNT A **tint** is a small amount of a colour. ❑ *...the unusual green tint of these glass bottles.* **2** V-T If something **is tinted**, it has a small amount of a particular colour or dye in it. ❑ *Eyebrows can be tinted with black dye.* ● **-tinted** ❑ *He wore green-tinted glasses.*

tiny /ˈtaɪni/ (**tinier, tiniest**) ADJ Someone or something that is **tiny** is extremely small. ❑ *She was tiny, but she had a very loud voice.*

tip /tɪp/ (**tips, tipping, tipped**) **1** N-COUNT The **tip of** something long and narrow is the end of it. ❑ *...the tips of his fingers.* ❑ *...the southern tip of Florida.* **2** PHRASE If you say that a problem is **the tip of the iceberg**, you mean that it is one small part of a much larger problem. ❑ *The above complaints are, I suspect, just the tip of the iceberg.* **3** V-T/V-I If an object or part of your body **tips**, or if you **tip** it, it moves into a sloping position with one end or side higher than the other. ❑ *She had to tip her head back to see him.* **4** V-T If you **tip** something somewhere, you pour it there. ❑ *Tip the vegetables into a bowl.* ❑ *Tip away the salt and wipe the pan.* **5** N-COUNT A **tip** is a place where rubbish is left. [BRIT] **6** N-COUNT & V-T If you give someone such as a waiter a **tip**, or if you **tip** them, you give them some money for their services. ❑ *She tipped the barmen 10 dollars.* **7** N-COUNT A **tip** is a useful piece of advice. ❑ *A good tip is to buy the most expensive lens you can afford.* **8** V-T If a person **is tipped to** do something or **is tipped for** success at something, experts or journalists believe that they will do that thing or achieve that success. ❑ *He is tipped to be the country's next prime minister.*

▶ **tip off** PHR-VERB If someone **tips** you **off**, they give you information about something that has happened or is going to happen. ● **tip-off** (**tip-offs**) N-COUNT ❑ *The man was arrested at his home after a tip-off to police.*

▶ **tip over** PHR-VERB If something **tips over**, it falls over or turns over.

Word Partnership	Use *tip* with:
N.	**tip of your finger/nose** 1
ADJ.	**northern/southern** tip **of an island** 1
	anonymous tip 7

tiptoe /ˈtɪptəʊ/ (**tiptoes, tiptoeing, tiptoed**) V-I & PHRASE If you **tiptoe** somewhere, or if you walk somewhere **on tiptoe**, you walk there very quietly without putting your heels on the floor. ❑ *She slipped out of bed and tiptoed to the window.*

T

tirade /taɪˈreɪd/ (**tirades**) N-COUNT A **tirade** is a long angry speech criticizing someone or something.

tire /taɪə/ (**tires, tiring, tired**) **1** V-T & PHR-VERB If something **tires** you, or if it **tires** you **out**, it uses a lot of your energy, leaving you very tired and needing to rest. ❑ *The afternoon heat had quite tired him out.* **2** V-I If you **tire of** something, you become bored with it. ❑ *He would never tire of international cricket.* **3** → see also **tyre**
→ see **bicycle**

tired /taɪəd/ (**tireder, tiredest**) **1** ADJ If you are **tired**, you feel that you want to rest or sleep. ❑ *She was too tired to take a shower.* ● **tiredness** N-UNCOUNT ❑ *He felt half dead with tiredness.* **2** ADJ AFTER LINK-V If you are **tired of** something, you do not want it to continue because you are bored with it. ❑ *I was tired of being an accountant.*
→ see **sleep**

Word Partnership	Use *tired* with:
V.	**look** tired 1
	feel tired 1 2
	be tired, **get** tired, **grow** tired 1 2
ADJ.	tired **and hungry** 1
	sick and tired **of** ***something*** 2
ADV.	**a little** tired, **(just) too** tired,
	very tired 1 2

tireless /ˈtaɪələs/ ADJ If you describe someone or their efforts as **tireless**, you approve of the fact that they put a lot of hard work into something, and refuse to give up. ● **tirelessly** ADV ❑ *He worked tirelessly for the cause of health and safety.*

tiresome /ˈtaɪəsəm/ ADJ If you describe someone or something as **tiresome**, you mean that you find them irritating or boring. ❑ *I had the tiresome habit of developing very bad colds.*

tiring /ˈtaɪərɪŋ/ ADJ If you describe something as **tiring**, you mean that it makes you tired so that you want to rest or sleep. ❑ *Travelling is tiring.* ❑ *...a long and tiring day.*

tissue /ˈtɪʃuː, ˈtɪsjuː/ (**tissues**) **1** N-VAR In animals and plants, **tissue** consists of cells that are similar in appearance and function. ❑ *...muscle tissue.* **2** N-UNCOUNT **Tissue** or **tissue paper** is thin paper used for wrapping things that are easily damaged. **3** N-COUNT A **tissue** is a piece of thin soft paper that you use as a handkerchief.
→ see **cancer**

title /ˈtaɪtəl/ (**titles**) **1** N-COUNT The **title** of a book, play, film, or piece of music is its name. **2** N-COUNT Someone's **title** is a word such as 'Lord' or 'Mrs' that is used before their name to show their status or profession. ❑ *She has been awarded the title of Professor.* **3** N-COUNT A **title** in a sports competition is the position of champion. ❑ *He has retained his title as world chess champion.*
→ see **graph**

titled /ˈtaɪtəld/ ADJ Someone who is **titled** has a name such as 'Lord', 'Lady', 'Sir', or 'Princess' before their own name showing that they are a member of the aristocracy. ❑ *...a titled lady.*

to
1 PREPOSITION AND ADVERB USES
2 USED BEFORE THE BASE FORM OF A VERB

to

To is usually pronounced /tə/ before a consonant and /tʊ/ before a vowel, but pronounced /tuː/ when you are emphasizing it.

1 **1** PREP You use **to** when indicating the place that someone or something visits, moves towards, or points at. ❑ *Ramsay made a second visit to Italy.* ❑ *She went to the window and looked out.* ❑ *He pointed to a chair.* **2** PREP If you go **to** an event, you go where it is taking place. ❑ *We went to a party at the leisure centre.* **3** PHRASE If someone moves **to and fro**, they move repeatedly from one place to another and back again. ❑ *She stood up and began to pace to and fro.* **4** PREP If something is attached **to**

something larger or fixed **to** it, the two things are joined together. ❑ *There was a piece of cloth tied to the dog's collar.* **5** PREP You use **to** when indicating the position of something. For example, if something is **to** your left, it is nearer your left side than your right. ❑ *Atlanta was only an hour's drive to the north.* **6** PREP When you give something **to** someone, they receive it. **7** PREP You use **to** to indicate who or what an action or a feeling is directed towards. ❑ *...troops loyal to the government.* ❑ *...repairs to the house.* **8** PREP You use **to** when indicating someone's reaction to something. ❑ *To his surprise, the bedroom door was locked.* **9** PREP You use **to** when indicating the person whose opinion you are stating. ❑ *It was clear to me that he respected his boss.* **10** PREP You use **to** when indicating the state that someone or something gradually starts to be in. ❑ *The old farm has been converted to a nature centre.* ❑ *He made a return to international rugby this summer.* **11** PREP You use **to** when indicating the last thing in a range of things. ❑ *I read everything from fiction to history and science.* **12** PREP You sometimes use **to** when you are stating a time. For example, 'five to eight' means five minutes before eight o'clock. **13** PREP You use **to** in ratios and rates. ❑ *...a mixture of one part milk to two parts water.* **14** ADV If you push a door **to**, you close it but do not shut it completely. ❑ *He slipped out, pulling the door to.*

to
❷ **1** You use **to** with an infinitive when indicating the purpose of an action. ❑ *...programs set up to save animals.* **2** You use **to** with an infinitive when commenting on your attitude or intention in making a statement. ❑ *I'm disappointed, to be honest.* **3** You use **to** with an infinitive in various other constructions when talking about an action or state. ❑ *The management wanted to know.* ❑ *Nuclear plants are expensive to build.* ❑ *...advice about how to do her job.* ❑ *The Foreign Minister is to visit China.*

toad /təʊd/ (**toads**) N-COUNT A **toad** is an animal like a frog, but with a drier skin.

toast /təʊst/ (**toasts, toasting, toasted**) **1** N-UNCOUNT **Toast** is slices of bread heated until they are brown and crisp. ❑ *...a piece of toast.* **2** V-T When you **toast** bread, you heat it so that it becomes brown and crisp. **3** → See note at **cook** **4** N-COUNT & V-T When you drink a **toast to** someone, or when you **toast** them, you wish them success or good health, and then drink some alcoholic drink.
→ see **cook**

toaster /'təʊstə/ (**toasters**) N-COUNT A **toaster** is a piece of electric equipment used to toast bread.

tobacco /tə'bækəʊ/ (**tobaccos**) N-VAR **Tobacco** is the dried leaves of a plant which people smoke in pipes, cigars, and cigarettes.

today /tə'deɪ/ **1** ADV & N-UNCOUNT **Today** means the day on which you are speaking or writing. ❑ *How are you feeling today?* ❑ *Today is Friday.* **2** ADV & N-UNCOUNT You can refer to the present period of history as **today**. ❑ *We wanted to make this product suitable for today's consumer.* ❑ *...the Africa of today.*

toddler /'tɒdlə/ (**toddlers**) N-COUNT A **toddler** is a young child who has only just learnt to walk.
→ see **age, child**

toe /təʊ/ (**toes, toeing, toed**) **1** N-COUNT Your **toes** are the five movable parts at the end of each foot. **2** N-COUNT The **toe** of a shoe or sock is the part that covers the end of your foot. **3** PHRASE If you **toe the line**, you behave in the way that people in authority expect you to. ❑ *...politicians that wouldn't toe the party line.*
→ see **foot**

toenail /'təʊneɪl/ (**toenails**) N-COUNT Your **toenails** are the thin hard areas at the end of each of your toes.
→ see **foot**

toffee /'tɒfi, AM 'tɔːfi/ (**toffees**) N-VAR A **toffee** is a sweet made by boiling sugar and butter together with water.

together /tə'geðə/ **1** ADV If people do something **together**, they do it with each other. ❑ *We went on long bicycle rides together.* ❑ *They all live together in a large house.* ❑ *Together they swam to the ship.* **2** ADV If two things happen **together**, they happen at the same time. ❑ *Three horses crossed the finish line together.* **3** ADV If things are joined **together**, they are joined to each other so that they touch or form one whole. ❑ *Mix the ingredients together thoroughly.* ❑ *She clasped her hands together on her lap.* **4** ADV If things or people are situated **together**, they are in the same place and very near to each other. ❑ *The trees grew close together.* ❑ *We gathered our things together.* **5** ADV You use **together** when you are adding two or more amounts or things to each other in order to consider a total amount or effect. ❑ *The two parties together won 29.8 per cent of the vote.* **6** PREP **Together with** something means as well as that thing. ❑ *Return the completed questionnaire, together with your cheque for £60.*

Word Partnership Use *together* with:

V.	**live** together, **play** together, **spend time** together, **work** together **1**
	come together **1–4**
	get together **1**
	act together, **go** together **1** **3**
	fit together, **glue** together, **join** together, **lump** together, **mix** together, **string** together, **stuck** together, **tied** together **2** **3**
	bring together, **keep** together, **stay** together **1** **4** **6**
	gather together, **sit** together, **stand** together **1**
	hold together **3**
	stick together **3** **4**
ADJ.	**bound** together **3**
	close together **4**

toil /tɔɪl/ (**toils, toiling, toiled**) V-I & N-UNCOUNT If you say that people **toil**, or if you describe their work as **toil**, you mean that they work hard doing unpleasant or tiring tasks. [LITERARY] ❑ *Workers toiled long hours.* ❑ *Hours of toil paid off in the end.*

toilet /'tɔɪlət/ (**toilets**) **1** N-COUNT A **toilet** is a large bowl connected to the drains which you use when you want to get rid of urine or faeces from your body. ❑ *She flushed the toilet and went back in the bedroom.* **2** N-COUNT In British English, a **toilet** is a small room containing a toilet. The American word is **bathroom**.
→ see **bathroom**

'toilet ˌpaper N-UNCOUNT **Toilet paper** is paper that you use to clean yourself after getting rid of urine or faeces from your body.

toiletries /'tɔɪlətriz/ N-PLURAL **Toiletries** are products such as soap and toothpaste that you use when cleaning or taking care of your body.

token /'təʊkən/ (**tokens**) 1 N-COUNT A **token** is a piece of paper, plastic, or metal which can be used instead of money. ❑ *...a £10 book token.* ❑ *...subway tokens.* 2 N-COUNT If you give something to someone as a **token of** your feelings for them, you give it as a way of expressing those feelings. ❑ *The ring was given as a token of love.* 3 ADJ BEFORE N You use **token** to describe things or actions which show your intentions or feelings but are small or unimportant. ❑ *...token gestures of force.* 4 PHRASE You use **by the same token** to introduce a statement that you think is true for the same reasons that were given for a previous statement. ❑ *If you give up exercise, your muscles shrink and fat increases. By the same token, if you expend more energy you will lose fat.*

told /təʊld/ 1 **Told** is the past tense and past participle of **tell**. 2 PHRASE You can use **all told** to indicate a summary, generalization, or total. ❑ *All told, he went to 14 different schools.*

tolerable /'tɒlərəbəl/ ADJ If something is **tolerable**, it is acceptable or bearable, but not pleasant or good. ❑ *The pain was tolerable.* ● **tolerably** ADV ❑ *Their captors treated them tolerably well.*

tolerant /'tɒlərənt/ ADJ If you are **tolerant**, you let other people say and do what they like, even if you do not agree with it or approve of it. ❑ *Society is becoming more tolerant of difference.* ● **tolerance** N-UNCOUNT ❑ *...religious tolerance.*

tolerate /'tɒləreɪt/ (**tolerates, tolerating, tolerated**) 1 V-T If you **tolerate** things that you do not agree with or approve of, you allow them to exist or happen. ❑ *We will not tolerate such behaviour.* 2 V-T If you can **tolerate** something unpleasant or painful, you are able to bear it. ❑ *Women tolerate pain better than men.*

toll /təʊl/ (**tolls, tolling, tolled**) 1 V-I When a bell **tolls**, it rings slowly and repeatedly, often as a sign that someone has died. 2 N-COUNT A **toll** is a sum of money that you have to pay in order to use a particular bridge or road. 3 PHRASE If something **takes a toll** or **takes its toll**, it has a bad effect on someone or something, or causes a lot of suffering. ❑ *The cold weather can take its toll on your health.* 4 → see also **death toll**

T

tomato /tə'mɑːtəʊ, AM -'meɪ-/ (**tomatoes**) N-VAR A **tomato** is a small, soft, red fruit that is used in cooking as a vegetable or eaten raw in salads.
→ see **vegetable**

tomb /tuːm/ (**tombs**) N-COUNT A **tomb** is a stone structure containing the body of a dead person.

tombstone /'tuːmstəʊn/ (**tombstones**) N-COUNT A **tombstone** is a large flat piece of stone on someone's grave, with their name written on it.

tomorrow /tə'mɒrəʊ, AM -'mɔːr-/ 1 ADV & N-UNCOUNT **Tomorrow** refers to the day after today. ❑ *The results will be announced tomorrow.* ❑ *Tomorrow is her thirteenth birthday.* 2 ADV & N-UNCOUNT You can refer to the future as **tomorrow**. ❑ *What is education going to look like tomorrow?* ❑ *...a preview of tomorrow's computer industry.*

ton /tʌn/ (**tons**) 1 N-COUNT A non-metric **ton** is a unit of weight equal to 2,240 pounds in Britain and 2,000 pounds in the United States. 2 N-COUNT A metric **ton** is a unit of weight equal to 1,000 kilograms.

tone /təʊn/ (**tones, toning, toned**) 1 N-COUNT The **tone** of a sound is its particular quality. ❑ *They began speaking in low tones.* ❑ *...the clear tone of the bell.* 2 N-COUNT Someone's **tone** is a quality in their voice which shows what they are feeling or thinking. ❑ *I still didn't like his tone of voice.* ❑ *Her tone implied that her patience was limited.* 3 N-UNCOUNT The **tone** of a speech or piece of writing is its style and the feelings expressed in it. ❑ *The tone of the letter was very friendly.* ❑ *His comments to reporters were cautious in tone.* 4 V-T & PHR-VERB Something that **tones** or **tones up** your body makes it firm and strong. ❑ *Massage tones up the muscles.*
▸ **tone down** PHR-VERB If you **tone down** something that you have written or said, you make it less forceful, severe, or offensive. ❑ *It would help if you toned down your language.*

Word Partnership Use *tone* with:

ADJ.	**clear** tone, **low** tone 1
	different tone 2
	serious tone 2 3
V.	**change your** tone 2
	set a tone 3
N.	tone **of voice** 2
	muscle tone 4

tongue /tʌŋ/ (**tongues**) 1 N-COUNT Your **tongue** is the soft movable part inside your mouth that you use for tasting, licking, and speaking. 2 N-COUNT A **tongue** is a language. [LITERARY] ❑ *English is not her native tongue.* 3 PHRASE A **tongue-in-cheek** remark is made as a joke, and is not serious or sincere. 4 to **bite** your **tongue** → see **bite**
→ see **diagnosis, face, taste**

Word Partnership Use *tongue* with:

ADJ.	**pink** tongue 1
	native tongue 3
V.	**bite your** tongue, **stick out your** tongue 1

tonic /'tɒnɪk/ (**tonics**) 1 N-VAR **Tonic** or **tonic water** is a colourless, fizzy drink that has a slightly bitter flavour. ❑ *...a delicious new blend of fruit juice and tonic water.* 2 N-COUNT You can refer to anything that makes you feel stronger or more cheerful as a **tonic**. ❑ *Seeing Marcus at that moment was a great tonic.*

tonight /tə'naɪt/ ADV & N-UNCOUNT **Tonight** refers to the evening or night that will come at the end of today. ❑ *What are you doing tonight?* ❑ *Tonight is the opening night of the opera.*

tonne /tʌn/ (**tonnes**) N-COUNT A **tonne** is a unit of weight equal to 1,000 kilograms.

too /tuː/ 1 ADV You use **too** after mentioning another person, thing, or aspect that a previous statement applies to or includes. ❑ *'Nice to talk to* *you.'—'Nice to talk to you too.'* ❑ *'I've got a great feeling about it.'—'Me too.'* ❑ *Depression may be expressed physically too.* ❑ *He doesn't want to meet me. I, too, have been afraid to talk to him.* 2 ADV You use **too** after adding a piece of information or a comment to a statement, in order to emphasize it. ❑ *We did learn to read, and quickly too.* ❑ *'That money's mine.'—'Of course it is, and quite right too.'* 3 ADV You use **too** to indicate that there is more of a thing or quality than is desirable or acceptable. ❑ *Eggs shouldn't be kept in the fridge; it's too cold.* ❑ *She was drinking too much.* ❑ *We have too much to do today.* 4 ADV You can use **too** to make a negative opinion politer or more cautious. ❑ *She wasn't too keen to leave her beloved country.* ❑ *I wasn't too happy with what I'd written so far.* 5 **too bad** → see **bad** 6 **none too** → see **none** 7 PHRASE You use **all too** or **only too** to emphasize that something happens to a greater degree than is pleasant or desirable. ❑ *She remembered it all too well.* ❑ *The letter spoke only too clearly of his worries.*

Usage

Too can be used to intensify the meaning of an adjective, an adverb, or a word like **much** or **many**. **Too**, however, also suggests an excessive or undesirable amount, often so much that a particular result does not or cannot happen. ❑ *She does wear too much make-up at times.* ❑ *He was too late to save her.* **Too** is not generally used to modify an adjective inside a noun group. For instance, you cannot say 'the too heavy boxes' or 'too expensive jewellery'. There is one exception to this rule, which is when the noun group begins with **a** or **an**. Notice the word order in the following examples. ❑ *...if the products have been stored at too high a temperature.* ❑ *He found it too good an opportunity to miss.* ❑ *It was too long a drive for one day.*

took /tʊk/ **Took** is the past tense of **take**.

tool /tuːl/ (**tools**) 1 N-COUNT A **tool** is any instrument or simple piece of equipment, for example a hammer or a knife, that you hold in your hands and use to do a particular kind of work. 2 N-COUNT You can refer to anything that you use for a particular purpose as a particular type of **tool**. ❑ *The Internet is a useful tool for speeding up business communications.*
→ see Picture Dictionary: **tools**

Word Partnership Use *tool* with:

N.	tool **belt** 1 **communication** tool, **learning** tool, **management** tool, **marketing** tool, **teaching** tool 2
V.	**use a** tool 1 2
ADJ.	**effective** tool, **important** tool, **valuable** tool 1 2 **powerful** tool 2

toolbar /ˈtuːlbɑː/ (**toolbars**) N-COUNT A **toolbar** is a strip across a computer screen containing pictures which represent different computer functions. [COMPUTING]

tooth /tuːθ/ (**teeth**) 1 N-COUNT Your **teeth** are the hard, white objects in your mouth that you use for biting and chewing. 2 N-PLURAL The **teeth** of a comb, saw, or zip are the parts that stick out in a row. 3 to **grit** your **teeth** → see **grit**
→ see **teeth**

toothbrush /ˈtuːθbrʌʃ/ (**toothbrushes**) N-COUNT A **toothbrush** is a small brush used for cleaning your teeth.

toothpaste /ˈtuːθpeɪst/ (**toothpastes**) N-VAR **Toothpaste** is a thick substance which you use to clean your teeth.

top /tɒp/ (**tops, topping, topped**) 1 N-COUNT The **top of** something is its highest point or part. ❑ *I waited at the top of the stairs.* ❑ *Don't fill it up to the top.* 2 ADJ BEFORE N The **top** thing or level in a series of things or layers is the highest one. ❑ *Our new flat was on the top floor.* 3 PHRASE If one thing is **on top of** another, it is on its highest part. ❑ *...the fairy on top of the Christmas tree.* ❑ *...hot chocolate with whipped cream on top.* 4 N-COUNT The **top** of a bottle, jar, or tube is its cap or lid. 5 ADJ BEFORE N You can use **top** to describe the highest level of a scale or measurement. ❑ *The vehicles have a top speed of 80 kilometres per hour.* 6 ADJ & N-SING If someone is **top of** a table or league, or if they are **at the top of** it, their performance is better than that of all the other people involved. ❑ *She came top in French and second in maths.* ❑ *The United States will be at the top of the medal table.* 7 N-SING & ADJ BEFORE N If someone is **at the top of** an organization or career, they are among the most senior, important, or successful people in it. You can also refer to the

Picture Dictionary tools

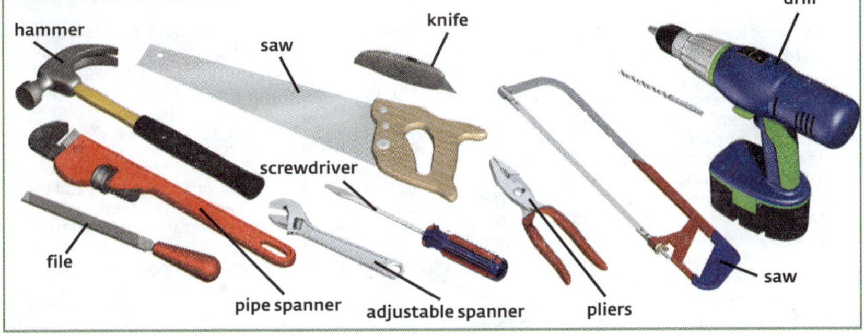

t

top people in an organization or career. ❑ *...the managers at the top of the company.* ❑ *He has got to the top on natural talent.* ❑ *...a top model.* **8** → see also **topped** **9** PHRASE **On top of** other things means in addition to them. ❑ *An extra 700 jobs are being cut on top of the 2,000 lost last year.* **10** PHRASE If you are **on top of** a task, you are dealing with it successfully. **11** PHRASE If you say that something is **over the top**, you mean that it is unacceptable because it is too extreme. [BRIT, INFORMAL] ❑ *Her paintings are over the top.*
→ see **hat**

▶ **top up** PHR-VERB If you **top up** a container, you fill it again when it has been partly emptied. ❑ *He topped her glass up.*

Thesaurus	**top** Also look up:
N.	peak, summit; (*ant.*) base, bottom **1**
ADJ.	best, finest **7**

ˌtop ˈclass ADJ **Top class** means amongst the finest of its kind. ❑ *You have to have a lot of energy to be a top-class dancer.*

topic /ˈtɒpɪk/ (**topics**) N-COUNT A **topic** is a particular subject that you write about or discuss. ❑ *The weather is a constant topic of conversation in Britain.*

topical /ˈtɒpɪkəl/ ADJ **Topical** means relating to events that are happening at the time when you are speaking or writing. ❑ *The aim of the magazine is to discuss topical issues.*

topless /ˈtɒpləs/ ADJ If a woman goes **topless**, she does not wear anything to cover her breasts. ❑ *...a topless dancer.*

topped /tɒpt/ ADJ If something is **topped by** or **with** another thing, the other thing is on top of it. ❑ *...hot scones topped with fresh cream.*

topple /ˈtɒpəl/ (**topples, toppling, toppled**) **1** V-I If someone or something **topples** somewhere, or if they **topple over**, they become unsteady and fall over. ❑ *His foot slipped and he toppled into the boat head first.* **2** V-T To **topple** a government or leader means to cause them to lose power. [JOURNALISM] ❑ *...the revolution which toppled the old regime.*

ˌtop ˈsecret ADJ **Top-secret** information or activity is intended to be kept completely secret. ❑ *...a top-secret military mission.*

torch /tɔːtʃ/ (**torches**) **1** N-COUNT In British English, a **torch** is a small, battery-powered electric light which you carry in your hand. The American word is **flashlight**. **2** N-COUNT A **torch** is a long stick with burning material at one end, used to provide light or to set things on fire.

T

tore /tɔː/ **Tore** is the past tense of **tear**.

torment (**torments, tormenting, tormented**) **1** N-VAR /ˈtɔːment/ **Torment** is extreme suffering, usually mental suffering. ❑ *He spent years in torment going from one psychiatrist to another.* ❑ *...the torments of being a writer.* **2** V-T /tɔːˈment/ If something **torments** you, it causes you extreme mental suffering. ❑ *He had been awake all night, tormented by jealousy.* **3** V-T To **torment** a person or animal means to annoy them in a playful, rather cruel way, for your own amusement.

torn /tɔːn/ **Torn** is the past participle of **tear**.

tornado /tɔːˈneɪdəʊ/ (**tornadoes** or **tornados**) N-COUNT A **tornado** is a violent storm with strong circular winds.

torpedo /tɔːˈpiːdəʊ/ (**torpedoes, torpedoing, torpedoed**) **1** N-COUNT A **torpedo** is a bomb shaped like a tube that travels underwater. **2** V-T If a ship **is torpedoed**, it is hit, and usually sunk, by a torpedo.

torrent /ˈtɒrənt, AM ˈtɔːr-/ (**torrents**) **1** N-COUNT A **torrent** is a lot of water falling or flowing rapidly or violently. ❑ *Torrents of water gushed into the boat.* ❑ *The rain came down in torrents.* **2** N-COUNT A **torrent of** abuse or questions is a lot of insults or questions directed continuously at someone.

torrential /təˈrenʃəl, AM tɔːr-/ ADJ **Torrential** rain falls very fast and very heavily.

torso /ˈtɔːsəʊ/ (**torsos**) N-COUNT Your **torso** is the main part of your body, excluding your head, arms, and legs. [FORMAL]

tortoise /ˈtɔːtəs/ (**tortoises**) N-COUNT A **tortoise** is a slow-moving animal with a shell into which it can pull its head and legs for protection.

tortuous /ˈtɔːtʃʊəs/ **1** ADJ A **tortuous** road is full of bends and twists. [FORMAL] **2** ADJ A **tortuous** process is long and complicated. [FORMAL]

torture /ˈtɔːtʃə/ (**tortures, torturing, tortured**) V-T & N-VAR If someone **is tortured**, or if they are subjected to **torture**, another person deliberately causes them great pain, in order to punish them or make them reveal information. ❑ *Many died under torture, others committed suicide.* ❑ *Prisoners continue to be tortured.*

Tory /ˈtɔːri/ (**Tories**) ADJ & N-COUNT In Britain, a **Tory** politician or voter is a member of, or votes for, the Conservative Party. A **Tory** is a member of, or votes for, the Conservative Party.

toss /tɒs, AM tɔːs/ (**tosses, tossing, tossed**) **1** V-T If you **toss** something somewhere, you throw it there lightly and carelessly. ❑ *She tossed her suitcase onto one of the beds.* ❑ *He tossed Malone a bar of chocolate.* **2** V-T If you **toss** your head, you move it backwards quickly and suddenly, often as a way of expressing anger or contempt. **3** V-T & N-COUNT In sports and informal situations, if you decide something by **tossing** a coin, or by **the toss of** a coin, you spin a coin into the air and guess which side of the coin will face upwards when it lands. **4** V-T If something such as the wind or sea **tosses** an object, it causes it to move from side to side or up and down. ❑ *The sea tossed the small boat like a cork.*

total /ˈtəʊtəl/ (**totals, totalling, totalled** or [AM] **totaling, totaled**) **1** N-COUNT & ADJ BEFORE N A **total** is the number that you get when you add several numbers together or when you count how many things there are in a group. ❑ *The companies have a total of 1,776 employees.* ❑ *The total cost of the project would be more than $240 million.* **2** PHRASE If there are a number of things **in total**, there are that number of them when you count or add them all together. ❑ *I worked there for eight years in total.* **3** V-T If several numbers **total** a certain figure, that is the figure you get when all the numbers are added together. ❑ *They will compete for prizes totalling nearly £3000.* **4** ADJ **Total** means complete. ❑ *I have total confidence that things will change.* ● **totally** ADV ❑ *...something totally different.* ❑ *The fire totally* destroyed the top floor and roof.

Word Partnership Use *total* with:

ADJ.	**grand** total 1 3
N.	total **area**, total **population**, **sum** total 1 total **amount**, total **cost**, total **expenses**, total **sales**, total **savings**, total **value** 1 3

totter /'tɒtə/ (**totters, tottering, tottered**) V-I When someone **totters** somewhere, they walk there in an unsteady way.

touch /tʌtʃ/ (**touches, touching, touched**) 1 V-T & N-SING If you **touch** something, or if you give it a **touch**, you put your fingers or hand on it. ❑ *Kate leaned forward and touched his hand reassuringly.* ❑ *Don't touch that knife.* ❑ *...a gentle touch on the hand.* 2 V-T/V-I When two things **touch**, or when one thing **touches** another, their surfaces come into contact with each other. ❑ *Their knees were touching.* ❑ *Annie lowered her legs until her feet touched the floor.* 3 N-UNCOUNT Your sense of **touch** is your ability to tell what something is like when you feel it with your hands. ❑ *The heater should feel hot to the touch.* 4 V-I If you **touch on** a particular subject, you mention it briefly. 5 V-T If something that someone says or does **touches** you, it affects you emotionally, often because that person is suffering or is being very kind. • **touched** ADJ AFTER LINK-V ❑ *He was touched that we came.* • **touching** ADJ ❑ *...a touching tale of love and romance.* 6 N-COUNT A **touch** is a detail which is added to something to improve it. ❑ *The dish has a great aroma and the olives are a nice touch.* 7 QUANT A **touch of** something is a very small amount of it. ❑ *He performed well, and had a touch of luck too.* 8 N-UNCOUNT If you are **in touch with** someone, you write, phone, or visit each other regularly. ❑ *We will be in touch with you shortly.* ❑ *We have to keep in touch by phone.* ❑ *We lost touch for many years.* 9 PHRASE If you say that something is **touch and go**, you mean that it is uncertain whether it will happen or succeed. ❑ *It was touch and go whether we'd get home that night.* 10 PHRASE If you are **in touch with** a subject or situation, you know the latest information about it. If you are **out of touch with** it, your knowledge of it is out of date.

▶ **touch down** PHR-VERB When an aircraft **touches down**, it lands.

Word Partnership Use *touch* with:

ADJ.	**gentle** touch, **light** touch 1 **finishing** touch, **nice** touch, **personal** touch, **soft** touch 6

'touch-ˌscreen (**touch-screens**) N-COUNT A **touch-screen** is a computer screen that allows the user to give commands to the computer by touching parts of the screen rather than by using the keyboard or mouse.

touchy /'tʌtʃi/ (**touchier, touchiest**) 1 ADJ **Touchy** people are easily upset or irritated. 2 ADJ A **touchy** subject is one that needs to be dealt with carefully, because it might upset or offend people.

tough /tʌf/ (**tougher, toughest**) 1 ADJ A **tough** person has a strong character and can tolerate difficulty or hardship. • **toughness** N-UNCOUNT ❑ *Mrs Potter has won a reputation for toughness and determination.* 2 ADJ A **tough** substance is strong, and difficult to break or cut. ❑ *...dark brown beans with a rather tough skin.* 3 ADJ A **tough** task or way of life is difficult or full of hardship. ❑ *She had a tough childhood.*

Word Partnership Use *tough* with:

N.	tough **guy** 1 tough **conditions**, tough **going**, tough **luck**, tough **situation**, tough **time** 3
V.	**get** tough, **talk** tough 1 **make the** tough **decisions** 3

toughen /'tʌfən/ (**toughens, toughening, toughened**) 1 V-T/V-I If you **toughen** something, or if it **toughens**, you make it stronger so that it will not break easily. ❑ *...toughened glass.* 2 V-T & PHR-VERB If an experience **toughens** you, or if it **toughens** you **up**, it makes you stronger in character. ❑ *He thinks boxing is good for kids, that it toughens them up.*

tour /tʊə/ (**tours, touring, toured**) 1 V-I & N-VAR When people such as musicians, politicians, or theatre companies **tour**, or when they go **on tour**, they go to several different places, stopping to meet people or perform. ❑ *He toured for nearly two years.* ❑ *The band will be going on tour.* ❑ *Their British tour was a virtual sell-out.* 2 N-COUNT A **tour** is a trip or journey to an interesting place or around several interesting places. 3 V-T If you **tour** a place, you go on a journey or trip round it.

Word Partnership Use *tour* with:

N.	**concert** tour, **farewell** tour, **world** tour 1 tour **bus**, tour **guide**, **walking** tour 2 **museum** tour 3
V.	**begin a** tour, **finish a** tour 2 **take a** tour 2

tourism /'tʊərɪzəm/ N-UNCOUNT **Tourism** is the business of providing services for people on holiday.

→ see **industry**

tourist /'tʊərɪst/ (**tourists**) N-COUNT A **tourist** is a person who is visiting a place for pleasure, especially when they are on holiday.

→ see **city**

tournament /'tʊənəmənt/ (**tournaments**) N-COUNT A **tournament** is a sports competition in which players who win a match continue to play further matches until just one person or team is left.

tout /taʊt/ (**touts, touting, touted**) 1 V-T If someone **touts** something, they try to sell it or convince people that it is good; used showing disapproval. ❑ *The product is touted as being completely natural.* 2 V-I If someone **touts for** business or custom, they try to obtain it. [BRIT] 3 N-COUNT A **tout** is someone who unofficially sells tickets outside a sports ground or theatre, often for more than their original value. [BRIT]

tow /təʊ/ (**tows, towing, towed**) 1 V-T If one vehicle **tows** another, the first vehicle pulls the second along behind it. ❑ *They threatened to tow away my car.* 2 PHRASE If you have someone **in tow**, they are following you closely because you are looking after them or you are leading them somewhere. [INFORMAL] ❑ *There she was on my*

t

doorstep with child in tow.

towards /tə'wɔːdz, AM tɔːrdz/

> The form **toward** is also used and is the more usual form in American English.

1 PREP If you move or look **towards** something or someone, you move or look in their direction. ❑ *Caroline leant across the table towards him.* 2 PREP If people move **towards** a particular situation, that situation becomes nearer in time or more likely to happen. ❑ *She began moving toward a different lifestyle.* 3 PREP If you have a particular attitude **towards** something or someone, you feel like that about them. ❑ *Not everyone in the world will be kind and caring towards you.* 4 PREP If something happens **towards** a particular time, it happens just before that time. ❑ *The Channel tunnel was due to open towards the end of 1993.* 5 PREP If something is **towards** part of a place or thing, it is near that part. ❑ *The house was up Gloucester Road, towards the top of the hill.* 6 PREP If you give money **towards** something, you give it to help pay for that thing. ❑ *He gave them £50,000 towards a house.*

towel /taʊəl/ (**towels, towelling, towelled** or [AM] **toweling, toweled**) 1 N-COUNT A **towel** is a piece of thick, soft cloth that you use to dry yourself with. 2 V-T If you **towel** something, you dry it with a towel. ❑ *I towelled myself dry.* 3 PHRASE If you **throw in the towel**, you stop trying to do something because you realize that you cannot succeed.
→ see **bathroom**

tower /taʊə/ (**towers, towering, towered**) 1 N-COUNT A **tower** is a tall narrow structure, that is often part of a church or castle. 2 V-I Someone or something that **towers over** surrounding people or things is a lot taller than they are.
→ see **computer**

towering /'taʊərɪŋ/ ADJ BEFORE N If you describe something such as a mountain or cliff as **towering**, you mean that it is very high and therefore impressive. [LITERARY]

town /taʊn/ (**towns**) 1 N-COUNT A **town** is a place with many streets and buildings where people live and work. 2 N-UNCOUNT You use **town** in order to refer to the town where you live. ❑ *She left town.*

ˌtown 'hall also **Town Hall** (**town halls**) N-COUNT The **town hall** in a town is a large building owned and used by the town council, often as its headquarters.

T

township /'taʊnʃɪp/ (**townships**) N-COUNT In South Africa, a **township** was a town where only black people lived.

toxic /'tɒksɪk/ ADJ A **toxic** substance is poisonous. • **toxicity** /tɒk'sɪsɪti/ (**toxicities**) N-VAR ❑ *...the toxicity of chemicals in food.*
→ see **cancer**

toy /tɔɪ/ (**toys, toying, toyed**) N-COUNT A **toy** is an object that children play with, for example a doll or a model car.

▸ **toy with** 1 PHR-VERB If you **toy with** an idea, you consider it casually, without making any decisions about it. 2 PHR-VERB If you **toy with** an object or with your food, you keep moving it around but do not use it properly or eat it, especially because you are thinking about something else.

trace /treɪs/ (**traces, tracing, traced**) 1 V-T If you **trace** someone or something, you find them after looking for them. ❑ *They traced the van to a car rental agency.* 2 V-T & PHR-VERB If you **trace** the origin or development of something, or if you **trace** it **back**, you find out or describe how it started or developed. ❑ *He traced his jealousy back to something that happened when he was two.* 3 V-T If you **trace** a picture, you copy it by covering it with a piece of transparent paper and drawing over the lines underneath. 4 N-COUNT A **trace** is a sign which shows that someone or something has been in a place. ❑ *...traces of chemicals in food and water.*
→ see **draw, fossil**

> **Word Partnership** Use *trace* with:
>
> N. trace ***your* ancestry/origins/roots**, trace **the history of *something***, trace **the origins/roots of *something*** 1
> trace **of an accent**, trace **amount**, trace **minerals** 4

track /træk/ (**tracks, tracking, tracked**) 1 N-COUNT A **track** is a narrow road or path. 2 N-COUNT A **track** is a piece of ground that is used for races. 3 N-COUNT Railway **tracks** are the rails that a train travels along. 4 N-PLURAL Animal **tracks** are the footprints that animals make. 5 V-T If you **track** animals or people, you try to find them by following their footprints or other signs. 6 PHRASE If a place is **off the beaten track**, it is in a quiet and isolated area. 7 PHRASE If you **keep track of** a situation or a person, you have accurate information about them all the time. If you **lose track of** them, you no longer know where they are or what is happening. ❑ *It's easy to lose track of who's playing who.* 8 PHRASE If you are **on the right track**, you are acting or progressing in a way that is likely to result in success.
→ see **fossil, transportation**

▸ **track down** PHR-VERB If you **track down** someone or something, you find them after a long and difficult search. ❑ *It took two years to track him down.*

> **Word Partnership** Use *track* with:
>
> N. **dirt** track 1 2
> track **meet**, track **team** 2
> **train** track 3

ˌtrack 'record (**track records**) N-COUNT If you talk about the **track record** of a person, company, or product, you are referring to their past achievements or failures.

tracksuit /'træksuːt/ (**tracksuits**) N-COUNT A **tracksuit** is a loose, warm suit consisting of trousers and a top, worn mainly when exercising.

> **Word Link** ***tract ≈ dragging, drawing : contract, subtract, tractor***

tractor /'træktə/ (**tractors**) N-COUNT A **tractor** is a farm vehicle that is used for pulling farm machinery.
→ see **barn**

trade /treɪd/ (**trades, trading, traded**) V-I & N-UNCOUNT When people or countries **trade**, they buy, sell, or exchange goods or services. This

Word Web traffic

Boston's Southeast Expressway opened in 1959. It was built to handle 75,000 **vehicles** a day. But it wasn't enough and **commuter traffic** crawled. Sometimes it **stalled** completely. The 27 entrance **ramps** and no **breakdown lanes** caused frequent **gridlock**. By the 1990s, **traffic congestion** was even worse. Nearly 200,000 cars were using the **highway** every day and there were constant **traffic jams**. In 1994, a ten-year **road** construction project called the Big Dig began. The project built underground roadways, six-**lane** bridges, and improved **tunnels**. As a result of the project, traffic **flows** more smoothly through the city.

activity is called **trade**. ❑ *Texas has a long history of trade with Mexico.* ●**trading** N-UNCOUNT ❑ *...trading on the stock exchange.*

Thesaurus *trade* Also look up:

V. barter, exchange, swap

trademark /ˈtreɪdmɑːk/ (**trademarks**) N-COUNT A **trademark** is a name or symbol that a company uses on its products and that cannot legally be used by another company.

trader /ˈtreɪdə/ (**traders**) N-COUNT A **trader** is a person whose job is to trade in goods or stocks.

ˌtrade ˈunion also **trades union** (**trade unions**) N-COUNT A **trade union** is an organization formed by workers in order to represent their rights and interests to their employers.

ˌtrade ˈunionist also **trades unionist** (**trade unionists**) N-COUNT A **trade unionist** is an active member of a trade union.

tradition /trəˈdɪʃən/ (**traditions**) N-VAR A **tradition** is a custom or belief that has existed for a long time. ❑ *...the rich traditions of Afro-Cuban music.* ●**traditional** ADJ ❑ *...traditional teaching methods.* ●**traditionally** ADV ❑ *This dish was traditionally eaten as a wedding breakfast.*

Thesaurus *tradition* Also look up:

N. culture, custom, practice, ritual

Word Link *tra ≈ across : traffic, travel, travesty*

traffic /ˈtræfɪk/ (**traffics, trafficking, trafficked**) 1 N-UNCOUNT **Traffic** refers to all the vehicles that are moving along the roads in an area. ❑ *Traffic was unusually light for that time of day.* 2 N-UNCOUNT **Traffic** refers to the movement of ships, trains, or aircraft between one place and another. ❑ *Air traffic had returned to normal.* 3 V-I & N-UNCOUNT If someone **traffics in** illegal or stolen goods, or if they are involved in the **traffic** of such goods, they buy and sell them illegally. ❑ *Traffic in illicit drugs was now worth some $500 thousand million a year.* ●**trafficking** N-UNCOUNT ❑ *...charges of drug trafficking.* ●**trafficker** (**traffickers**) N-COUNT ❑ *Mexican police have arrested a powerful drug trafficker.*
→ see Word Web: **traffic**

Word Partnership Use *traffic* with:

ADJ. **heavy** traffic, **light** traffic, **stuck in** traffic 1

N. traffic **accident**, **city** traffic, traffic **congestion**, traffic **flow**, traffic **pollution**, traffic **problems**, **rush hour** traffic, traffic **safety**, traffic **signals**, traffic **violation** 1
air traffic, **Internet** traffic, **network** traffic 2
drug traffic 3

ˈtraffic ˌcircle (**traffic circles**) N-COUNT In American English, a **traffic circle** is a circle at a place where several roads meet. The British word is **roundabout**.

ˈtraffic jam (**traffic jams**) N-COUNT A **traffic jam** is a long line of vehicles that cannot move because there is too much traffic, or because the road is blocked.

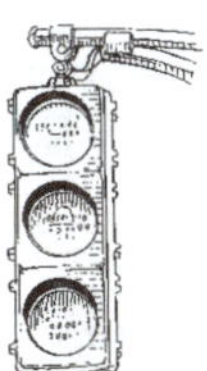

traffic light

ˈtraffic ˌlight (**traffic lights**) N-COUNT **Traffic lights** are the coloured lights at road junctions which control the flow of traffic.

tragedy /ˈtrædʒɪdi/ (**tragedies**) 1 N-VAR A **tragedy** is an extremely sad event or situation. ❑ *They have suffered an enormous personal tragedy.* 2 N-VAR **Tragedy** is a type of serious drama, often ending in the death of the main character.

tragic /ˈtrædʒɪk/ 1 ADJ Something that is **tragic** is extremely sad, usually because it involves death or suffering. ❑ *It was just a tragic accident.* ●**tragically** ADV ❑ *He died tragically young.* 2 ADJ BEFORE N **Tragic** is used to refer to literary tragedy. ❑ *...Shakespearean tragic heroes.*

trail /treɪl/ (**trails, trailing, trailed**) 1 N-COUNT A **trail** is a rough path across open country or through forests. 2 N-COUNT A **trail** is a series of marks or other signs left by someone or something as they move along. ❑ *He left a trail of clues at the scenes of his crimes.* 3 PHRASE If you are **on the trail of** a person or thing, you are trying to find them. ❑ *...on the trail of the jewel thief.* 4 V-T If you **trail** someone or something, you follow them secretly. ❑ *I trailed her to a shop in Kensington.*

5 V-T If you **trail** something, it hangs down loosely behind you as you move along. ❑ *He trailed his fingers in the water.* **6** V-I If someone **trails** somewhere, they move there slowly and without enthusiasm. ❑ *He trailed through the wet Manhattan streets.* **7** V-I In a contest, if someone **is trailing**, they are behind their opponents. ❑ *They trailed by nine points to six at half-time.*

▶ **trail away** or **trail off** PHR-VERB If a speaker's voice **trails off** or **trails away**, their voice becomes quieter and they hesitate until they stop speaking completely.

Word Partnership Use *trail* with:

N.	**hiking** trail **1**
V.	**follow a** trail **1–2**
	leave a trail, **pick up a** trail **2**

trailer /ˈtreɪlə/ (**trailers**) **1** N-COUNT A **trailer** is a vehicle without an engine which is pulled by a car or lorry. In American English, a **trailer** is also the same as a **caravan**. **2** N-COUNT A **trailer** for a film or television programme is a set of short extracts which are shown to advertise it.

ˈtrailer ˌpark also **trailer court** (**trailer parks**) N-COUNT In American English, a **trailer park** is an area where people can pay to park their trailers and live in them. The usual British term is **caravan site**.

train /treɪn/ (**trains, training, trained**) **1** N-COUNT A **train** is a number of carriages or trucks pulled by a railway engine. ❑ *He arrived in Shenyang by train.* **2** N-COUNT A **train of thought** or a **train of events** is a connected series of thoughts or events. ❑ *He lost his train of thought for a moment.* **3** V-T If you **train to** do something, or if someone **trains** you **to** do it, they teach you the skills that you need in order to do it. ❑ *Stavros was training to be a priest.* ❑ *They train teachers in counselling skills.* ❑ *I'm a trained nurse.* ● **-trained** ❑ *...an American-trained lawyer.* ● **trainer** (**trainers**) N-COUNT ❑ *...teacher trainers.* ● **training** N-UNCOUNT ❑ *Robertson had no formal training as a decorator.* **4** V-T/V-I If you **train for** an activity such as a race, or if someone **trains** you **for** it, you prepare for it by doing particular physical exercises. ● **trainer** N-COUNT ❑ *She went to the gym with her trainer.* ● **training** N-UNCOUNT ❑ *He will soon be back in training for next year's National.* **5** V-T If you **train** something such as a gun, a camera, or a light **on** someone or something, you keep it pointing steadily towards them. ❑ *There is a camera trained on the nest from another tree.*

→ see Word Web: **train**

→ see **transportation**

trainee /treɪˈniː/ (**trainees**) N-COUNT A **trainee** is a junior employee who is being taught how to do a job.

trainer /ˈtreɪnə/ (**trainers**) N-COUNT In British English, **trainers** are shoes with rubber soles used for sports. The usual American word is **sneakers**.

→ see **clothing, shoe**

trainspotter /ˈtreɪnspɒtə/ (**trainspotters**) **1** N-COUNT A **trainspotter** is someone who is very interested in trains and spends time going to stations and recording the numbers of the trains that they see. [BRIT] **2** N-COUNT A **trainspotter** is someone who other people think is boring because they want to know every detail about a particular subject; used showing disapproval. [BRIT]

trainspotting /ˈtreɪnspɒtɪŋ/ N-UNCOUNT **Trainspotting** is the hobby of going to railway stations and recording the numbers of the trains that you see. [BRIT]

trait /treɪt, treɪ/ (**traits**) N-COUNT A **trait** is a characteristic, quality, or tendency that someone or something has. ❑ *Creativity is a human trait.*

→ see **culture**

traitor /ˈtreɪtə/ (**traitors**) N-COUNT A **traitor** is someone who betrays their country or a group of which they are a member by helping their enemies.

tram /træm/ (**trams**) N-COUNT In British English, a **tram** is a public transport vehicle, usually powered by electricity, which travels along rails laid in the surface of a street. The usual American word is **streetcar**.

→ see **transportation**

tramp /træmp/ (**tramps, tramping, tramped**) **1** N-COUNT A **tramp** is a person with no home or job who travels around and gets money by doing occasional work or by begging. **2** V-I If you **tramp** somewhere, you walk with slow heavy footsteps, for a long time. ❑ *She spent all day yesterday tramping around.*

trample /ˈtræmpəl/ (**tramples, trampling, trampled**) **1** V-I To **trample on** someone's rights or values means to deliberately ignore or disregard them. ❑ *With this new law, the government is trampling on our rights.* **2** V-T If someone **is trampled**, they are injured or killed by being trodden on

T

Word Web train

In sixteenth-century Germany, a **railway** was a **horse-drawn wagon** traveling along wooden **rails**. By the 19th century, **steam locomotives** and **steel rails** had replaced the older system. At first, railroads operated only **freight lines**. Later, they began to run **passenger** trains. And soon Pullman cars were added to make overnight trips more comfortable. Today, Japan's bullet trains carry people at speeds up to 300 miles per hour. This type of train doesn't have an engine or use tracks. Instead, an electromagnetic field allows the **cars** to float just above the ground. This electromagnetic field also pushes the train ahead.

A Japanese Bullet Train

by animals or people. **3** V-I If you **trample on** something, you tread heavily on it and damage it. ❑ *They don't want people trampling on the grass.*

Word Link *ance ≈ quality, state : performance, resistance, trance*

trance /trɑːns, træns/ (**trances**) N-COUNT If someone is **in a trance**, they seem to be asleep, but they can see and hear things and respond to commands.

tranquil /'træŋkwɪl/ ADJ **Tranquil** means calm and peaceful. ●**tranquillity** N-UNCOUNT ❑ *He enjoyed the tranquillity of village life.*

Word Link *ize ≈ making : finalize, normalize, tranquillize*

tranquillize [BRIT also] **tranquillise** [AM also] **tranquilize** /'træŋkwɪlaɪz/ (**tranquillizes, tranquillizing, tranquillized**) V-T To **tranquillize** a person or an animal means to make them become calm, sleepy, or unconscious by means of a drug.

tranquillizer [BRIT also] **tranquilliser** [AM also] **tranquilizer** /'træŋkwɪlaɪzə/ (**tranquillizers**) N-COUNT A **tranquillizer** is a drug that is used to tranquillize people or animals.

transaction /træn'zækʃən/ (**transactions**) N-COUNT A **transaction** is a business deal.

Word Partnership Use *transaction* with:
N. **cash** transaction, transaction **costs**, transaction **fee**
V. **complete a** transaction

transatlantic /ˌtrænzət'læntɪk/ **1** ADJ BEFORE N **Transatlantic** flights or signals go across the Atlantic Ocean, usually between the United States and Britain. ❑ *Many transatlantic flights land there.* **2** ADJ BEFORE N **Transatlantic** is used to refer to something that happens, exists, or originates in the United States. [BRIT] ❑ *...transatlantic fashions.*

transcend /træn'send/ (**transcends, transcending, transcended**) V-T Something that **transcends** normal limits or boundaries goes beyond them, because it is more significant than them. ❑ *Human rights transcend age, class and race.*

Word Link *scrib ≈ writing : inscribe, scribble, transcribe*

transcribe /træn'skraɪb/ (**transcribes, transcribing, transcribed**) V-T If you **transcribe** something that is spoken or written, you write it down, copy it, or change it into a different form of writing.

Word Link *script ≈ writing : manuscript, scripture, transcript*

transcript /'trænskrɪpt/ (**transcripts**) N-COUNT A **transcript of** something that is spoken is a written copy of it.

Word Link *trans ≈ across : transfer, transition, translate*

transfer (**transfers, transferring, transferred**)
verb /træns'fɜː/, noun /'trænsfɜː/.
1 V-T & N-VAR If you **transfer** something or someone **from** one place **to** another, they go from the first place to the second. The **transfer of** something or someone is the act of transferring them. ❑ *He wants to transfer some money to her account.* ❑ *Arrange for the transfer of medical records to your new doctor.* **2** V-T & N-VAR If you **are transferred** to a different place or job, or if you get a **transfer**, you move to a different place or job within the same organization. ❑ *Two senior members of staff had been transferred.*

transform /træns'fɔːm/ (**transforms, transforming, transformed**) V-T To **transform** someone or something means to change it completely. ❑ *A big, happy smile transformed her face.* ●**transformation** (**transformations**) N-VAR ❑ *...the transformation of an attic room into a study.*

transfusion /træns'fjuːʒən/ (**transfusions**) N-COUNT A blood **transfusion** is a process in which blood is injected into the body of a person who is badly injured or ill.

transient /'trænziənt, AM -nʃənt/ (**transients**) **1** ADJ Something that is **transient** does not last very long or is constantly changing. [FORMAL] ❑ *In most cases, pain is transient.* ●**transience** /'trænziəns, AM -nʃəns/ N-UNCOUNT ❑ *The charm of real flowers is their transience.* **2** N-COUNT **Transients** are people who stay in a place for only a short time and do not have a fixed home. [FORMAL]

transistor /træn'zɪstə/ (**transistors**) **1** N-COUNT A **transistor** is a small electronic component in something such as a television or radio, which is used to amplify or control electronic signals. **2** N-COUNT A **transistor** or a **transistor radio** is a small portable radio. [DATED]

transit /'trænzɪt/ **1** N-UNCOUNT & PHRASE **Transit** is the carrying of goods or people by vehicle from one place to another. People or things that are **in transit** are travelling or being taken from one place to another. ❑ *...goods lost in transit.* **2** ADJ BEFORE N A **transit** area or building is a place where people wait or where goods are kept between different stages of a journey. ❑ *...a transit lounge at Moscow airport.* **3** N-UNCOUNT In American English, a **transit** system is a system for moving people or goods from one place to another, for example on buses or trains. The usual British word is **transport**. ❑ *...the Chicago Transit Authority.*
→ see **transportation**

transition /træn'zɪʃən/ (**transitions**) N-VAR **Transition** is the process in which something changes from one state to another. ●**transitional** ADJ ❑ *...the transitional stage between the old and new methods.*

transitive /'trænzɪtɪv/ ADJ A **transitive** verb has an object. For example in the sentence 'I love you', 'love' is the transitive verb and 'you' is the object.

translate /trænz'leɪt/ (**translates, translating, translated**) **1** V-T If something that someone has said or written **is translated**, it is said or written again in a different language. ❑ *Martin Luther translated the Bible into German.* ●**translation** N-UNCOUNT ❑ *The papers have been sent to Saudi Arabia for translation.* ●**translator** (**translators**) N-COUNT ❑ *To work as a translator, you need fluency in at least one foreign language.* **2** V-T To **translate** one thing **into** another means to convert it into something else. ❑ *Your decision must be translated into specific, concrete actions.*

Word Web transport

Mass transport began more than 200 years ago. By 1830, there were **horse-drawn trams** in New York City and New Orleans. They ran on **rails** built into the right of way of city streets. The first electric **tram** opened in Berlin in 1881. Later, **buses** became more popular because they didn't require **tracks**. Today, **commuter trains** link **suburbs** to cities everywhere. Many large cities also have an underground train system. It may be called the **subway, metro,** or **tube**. In cities with steep hills, funiculars and **cable cars** are a popular form of mass **transit**.

translation /trænz'leɪʃən/ (**translations**) N-COUNT A **translation** is a piece of writing or speech that has been translated from a different language.

Word Link *luc ≈ light : hallucination, lucid, translucent*

translucent /trænz'lu:sənt/ ADJ If a material is **translucent**, some light can pass through it. ❑ *...translucent plastic sheeting.*
→ see **pottery**

transmission /trænz'mɪʃən/ (**transmissions**) **1** N-UNCOUNT The **transmission** of something involves passing or sending it to a different place or person. ❑ *...the fax machine and other forms of electronic data transmission.* **2** N-UNCOUNT The **transmission** of television or radio programmes is the broadcasting of them. **3** N-COUNT A **transmission** is a television or radio broadcast. **4** N-VAR A vehicle's **transmission** is the system of gears by which the power from the engine reaches and turns the wheels.

transmit /trænz'mɪt/ (**transmits, transmitting, transmitted**) **1** V-T When a message or electronic signal **is transmitted**, it is sent by wires, radio waves, or satellite. ❑ *This is currently the most efficient way to transmit electronic mail.* **2** V-T To **transmit** something to a different place or person means to pass or send it to the place or person. [FORMAL] ❑ *...transmitting the infection through operations.*

transmitter /trænz'mɪtə/ (**transmitters**) N-COUNT A **transmitter** is a piece of equipment used for broadcasting television or radio programmes.
→ see **cellphone, radio**

transparency /træns'pærənsi, AM -'per-/ (**transparencies**) **1** N-COUNT A **transparency** is a small piece of photographic film in a frame which can be projected onto a screen. **2** N-UNCOUNT **Transparency** is the quality that an object or substance has if you can see through it.

transparent /træns'pærənt, AM -'per-/ **1** ADJ If an object or substance is **transparent**, you can see through it. ❑ *...a sheet of transparent plastic.* **2** ADJ If a situation, system, or activity is **transparent**, it is easily understood or recognized. ● **transparently** ADV ❑ *He had been transparently honest with her.*
→ see **glass**

transpire /træn'spaɪə/ (**transpires, transpiring, transpired**) **1** V-T When it **transpires that** something is the case, people discover that it is the case. [FORMAL] ❑ *It transpired that there was something wrong with the roof.* **2** V-I When something **transpires**, it happens. [FORMAL]
→ see **water**

transplant (**transplants, transplanting, transplanted**) **1** N-VAR /'trænsplɑ:nt, -plænt/ A **transplant** is a surgical operation in which a part of a person's body is replaced because it is diseased. ❑ *...a heart transplant.* **2** V-T /træns'plɑ:nt, -'plænt/ To **transplant** someone or something means to move them to a different place. ❑ *Marriage had transplanted Rebecca from London to Manchester.*
→ see **donor, hospital**

transport (**transports, transporting, transported**) **1** N-UNCOUNT /'trænspɔ:t/ **Transport** refers to any type of vehicle that you can travel in. ❑ *Have you got your own transport?* ❑ *...public transport.* **2** N-UNCOUNT **Transport** is the moving of goods or people from one place to another. ❑ *The transport of soldiers and equipment now is complete.* **3** V-T /træns'pɔ:t/ When goods or people **are transported from** one place **to** another, they are moved there.
→ see Word Web: **transport**

transportation /ˌtrænspɔ:'teɪʃən/ N-UNCOUNT **Transportation** is the same as **transport**. [AM]

trap /træp/ (**traps, trapping, trapped**) **1** N-COUNT & V-T A **trap** is a device for catching animals. If you **trap** animals, you catch them using a trap. **2** V-T & N-COUNT If someone **traps** you, they trick you so that you do or say something which you did not want to. A **trap** is a trick that is intended to catch or deceive someone. ❑ *Were you trying to trap her into making an admission?* **3** V-T If you **are trapped** somewhere, something falls onto you or blocks your way, preventing you from moving. ❑ *One man was trapped under the car and another inside it.*

Word Partnership Use *trap* with:

V. **avoid a** trap, **caught in a** trap, **fall into a** trap, **set a** trap **1** **2**

trapped /træpt/ ADJ If you feel **trapped**, you are in an unpleasant situation in which you lack freedom, and you feel you cannot escape from it. ❑ *Gordon found himself trapped in a boring job.*

trappings /ˈtræpɪŋz/ N-PLURAL **The trappings of** power or wealth are the extra things, such as decorations and luxury items, that go with it; used showing disapproval.

trash /træʃ/ N-UNCOUNT In American English, **trash** consists of unwanted things or waste material such as old food. The British word is **rubbish**.

Usage

In American English, the words **trash** and **garbage** are most commonly used to refer to waste material that is thrown away. ❑ *...the smell of rotting garbage.* ❑ *She threw the bottle into the trash.* In British English, **rubbish** is the usual word. **Garbage** and **trash** are sometimes used in British English, but only informally and metaphorically. ❑ *I don't have to listen to this garbage.* ❑ *The book was trash.*

Thesaurus *trash* Also look up:

N. debris, garbage, junk, litter

trauma /ˈtrɔːmə, AM ˈtraʊmə/ (**traumas**) N-VAR **Trauma** is a very severe shock or very upsetting experience, which may cause psychological damage. ❑ *...the trauma of divorce.*

traumatic /trɔːˈmætɪk, AM traʊ-/ ADJ A **traumatic** experience is very shocking or upsetting, and may cause psychological damage.

Word Link *tra ≈ across : traffic, travel, travesty*

travel /ˈtrævəl/ (**travels, travelling, travelled** or [AM] **traveling, traveled**) **1** V-I If you **travel**, you go from one place to another, often to a place that is far away. ❑ *I've been travelling all day.* **2** N-UNCOUNT **Travel** is the act of travelling. ❑ *Information on travel in New Zealand is available at the hotel.* **3** N-PLURAL Someone's **travels** are the journeys they make to places a long way from their home. ❑ *He collects things for the house on his travels abroad.* **4** V-I When light, sound, or news from one place reaches another, you say that it **travels** to the other place. ❑ *When sound travels through water, strange things can happen.*

Usage

The noun **travel** is used to talk about the general activity of travelling. It is either uncount or plural. You cannot say 'a travel'. If you want to talk about a particular instance of someone going somewhere, you should refer to it as a **journey**. ❑ *...a journey by train from Berlin.* You should use **trip** to refer to the whole business of going somewhere, staying there and returning. ❑ *He suggested I cancel my trip to China.* **Voyage** is a more literary word, and is used only when you are talking about travelling by ship or spacecraft.

Thesaurus *travel* Also look up:

V. explore, trek, visit **1**

N. expedition, journey, trip **2** **3**

ˈtravel ˌagent (**travel agents**) **1** N-COUNT A **travel agent** or **travel agent's** is a shop where you can arrange a holiday or journey. **2** N-COUNT A **travel agent** is a person or business that arranges holidays and journeys.

traveller [AM **traveler**] /ˈtrævələ/ (**travellers**) N-COUNT A **traveller** is a person who is making a journey or who travels a lot.

ˈtraveller's ˌcheque [AM **traveler's check**] (**traveller's cheques**) N-COUNT **Traveller's cheques** are special cheques that you can exchange for local currency when you are abroad.

traverse /ˈtrævɜːs, trəˈvɜːs/ (**traverses, traversing, traversed**) V-T If someone or something **traverses** an area of land or water, they go across it. [FORMAL] ❑ *...the muddy path that traversed the field.*

travesty /ˈtrævəsti/ (**travesties**) N-COUNT If you describe something as a **travesty of** something else, you mean that it is a very bad representation of the other thing. ❑ *The judgment was a travesty of justice.*

trawler /ˈtrɔːlə/ (**trawlers**) N-COUNT A **trawler** is a fishing boat with large nets that are dragged along the bottom of the sea.

tray /treɪ/ (**trays**) N-COUNT A **tray** is a flat piece of wood, plastic, or metal that has raised edges and that is used for carrying food or drinks.

treacherous /ˈtretʃərəs/ **1** ADJ If you describe someone as **treacherous**, you think they are likely to betray you. [FORMAL] **2** ADJ If you say that something is **treacherous**, you mean that it is dangerous and unpredictable. ❑ *Blizzards had made the roads treacherous.*

treachery /ˈtretʃəri/ N-UNCOUNT **Treachery** is behaviour in which someone betrays their country or betrays a person who trusts them. [FORMAL]

tread /tred/ (**treads, treading, trod, trodden**) **1** V-I If you **tread on** something, you put your foot on it when you are walking or standing. ❑ *Oh, sorry, I didn't mean to tread on your foot.* **2** V-I If you **tread** in a particular way, you walk that way. [LITERARY] ❑ *He trod softly up the stairs.* **3** N-SING Someone's **tread** is the sound made by their feet as they walk. [WRITTEN] ❑ *She had heard the sound of his heavy tread on the stairs.* **4** V-I If you **tread** carefully, you behave with caution. **5** N-COUNT The **tread** of a tyre is the pattern of grooves on it.

treadmill /ˈtredmɪl/ (**treadmills**) N-COUNT You can refer to a task or a job as a **treadmill** when you have to keep doing it although it is unpleasant.

treason /ˈtriːzən/ N-UNCOUNT **Treason** is the crime of betraying your country.

treasure /ˈtreʒə/ (**treasures, treasuring, treasured**) **1** N-UNCOUNT In children's stories, **treasure** is a collection of valuable old objects, such as gold coins and jewels. **2** N-COUNT **Treasures** are valuable objects, especially works of art and items of historical value. ❑ *...stolen art treasures.* **3** V-T If you **treasure** something that you have, you keep it carefully because it gives you great pleasure and you think it is very special. ❑ *She treasures her memories of those happy days.*
● **treasured** ADJ BEFORE N ❑ *...my most treasured possessions.*

treasurer /ˈtreʒərə/ (**treasurers**) N-COUNT The **treasurer** of a society or organization is the person

t

in charge of its finances.

Treasury /'treʒəri/ N-PROPER In Britain, the United States, and some other countries, **the Treasury** is the government department that deals with the country's finances.

treat /tri:t/ (**treats, treating, treated**) **1** V-T If you **treat** someone or something in a particular way, you behave towards them in that way. ❑ *Stop treating me like a child.* ❑ *All faiths should be treated with respect.* **2** V-T When a doctor **treats** a patient or an illness, he or she tries to make the patient well again. ❑ *The boy was treated for a minor head injury.* **3** V-T If something **is treated with** a particular substance, the substance is put onto or into it, for example in order to clean it. ❑ *Treat your lawn regularly with weed-killer.* **4** N-COUNT & V-T If you give someone a **treat**, or if you **treat** them, you buy or arrange something special for them which they will enjoy. ❑ *Sometimes as a special treat my grandfather took me to the zoo.* ❑ *Go on, treat yourself to a new dress.*

Word Partnership Use *treat* with:

ADV.	treat **differently**, treat **equally**, treat **fairly**, treat **well** 1
PREP.	treat **with contempt/dignity/respect** 1
N.	treat **people**, treat **women** 1 2
	treat **AIDS**, treat **cancer**, treat **a disease**, **doctors** treat 2

treatment /'tri:tmənt/ (**treatments**) **1** N-VAR **Treatment** is medical attention given to a sick or injured person or animal. ❑ *There are two standard treatments for this disease.* **2** N-UNCOUNT Your **treatment of** someone is the way you behave towards them. ❑ *Ginny was angry at his treatment of Chris.* ❑ *We don't want any special treatment.*
→ see **cancer, illness**

Word Partnership Use *treatment* with:

V.	**get/receive** treatment, **give** treatment, **undergo** treatment 1
N.	treatment **of addiction**, **AIDS** treatment, **cancer** treatment, treatment **centre**, treatment **of an illness** 1
	treatment **of prisoners** 2
ADJ.	**effective** treatment, **medical** treatment 1
	better treatment, **equal/unequal** treatment, **fair** treatment, **humane** treatment 2
	special treatment 2

treaty /'tri:ti/ (**treaties**) N-COUNT A **treaty** is a written agreement between countries.

treble /'trebəl/ (**trebles, trebling, trebled**) V-T/V-I If something **trebles**, or if you **treble** it, it becomes three times greater in number or amount. ❑ *The number of claims has almost trebled this year.*

tree /tri:/ (**trees**) N-COUNT A **tree** is a tall plant with a hard trunk, branches, and leaves.
→ see Word Web: **tree**
→ see **forest, plant**

trek /trek/ (**treks, trekking, trekked**) V-I & N-COUNT If you **trek** somewhere, or if you go on a **trek**, you go on a long journey across difficult terrain, usually on foot. ❑ *...trekking through the jungle.*

Word Link *trem ≈ shaking : **trem**ble, **trem**endous, **trem**or*

tremble /'trembəl/ (**trembles, trembling, trembled**) **1** V-I If you **tremble**, you shake slightly, usually because you are frightened or cold. ❑ *I was trembling with fear.* **2** V-I If something **trembles**, it shakes slightly. [LITERARY] ❑ *He felt the earth tremble under him.*

tremendous /trɪ'mendəs/ **1** ADJ You use **tremendous** to emphasize how strong a feeling or quality is, or how large an amount is. ❑ *I felt a tremendous pressure on my chest.* ❑ *...a tremendous amount of information.* • **tremendously** ADV ❑ *I enjoyed it tremendously.* **2** ADJ You can describe someone or something as **tremendous** when you think they are very impressive.

tremor /'tremə/ (**tremors**) **1** N-COUNT A **tremor** is a small earthquake. **2** N-COUNT A **tremor** is a shaking of your body or voice that you cannot control. ❑ *Winslow felt a little tremor of excitement.*

trench /trentʃ/ (**trenches**) N-COUNT A **trench** is a long narrow channel dug in the ground.

trend /trend/ (**trends**) N-COUNT A **trend** is a change towards something different. ❑ *...the growing trend towards online shopping.*

Thesaurus *trend* Also look up:

N.	craze, fad, style

Word Partnership Use *trend* with:

ADJ.	**current** trend, **disturbing** trend, **growing** trend, **latest** trend, **new** trend, **overall** trend, **recent** trend, **warming** trend
V.	**continue a** trend, **reverse a** trend, **start a** trend

trendy /'trendi/ (**trendier, trendiest**) ADJ If you say that something or someone is **trendy**, you mean that they are very fashionable and modern. [INFORMAL] ❑ *...a trendy London restaurant.*

trepidation /,trepɪ'deɪʃən/ N-UNCOUNT **Trepidation** is fear or anxiety about something that you are going to do or experience. [FORMAL] ❑ *They will await the result with some trepidation.*

trespass /'trespəs/ (**trespasses, trespassing, trespassed**) V-I If you **trespass on** someone's land, you go onto it without their permission. • **trespasser** (**trespassers**) N-COUNT ❑ *Trespassers will be prosecuted.*

trial /traɪəl/ (**trials**) **1** N-VAR & PHRASE A **trial** is the legal process in which a judge and jury listen to evidence and decide whether a person is guilty of a crime. You say that the person being judged is **on trial** or that they **stand trial**. ❑ *He was giving evidence at the trial of Gary Hart, aged 37.* **2** N-VAR & PHRASE A **trial** is an act of testing something or someone to see how well they perform a task. You say that the thing or person being tested is **on trial**. ❑ *The vaccine is about to go on trial in the US.* **3** PHRASE If you do something **by trial and error**, you try different ways of doing it until you find

T

Word Web tree

Trees are one of the oldest living things. They are also the largest **plant**. Some scientists believe that the largest living thing on Earth is a coniferous giant redwood tree named General Grant. Other scientists think that a huge **grove** of **deciduous** aspen trees known as Pando is the oldest. This grove is a single plant because all of the trees grow from the root system of just one tree. Pando covers more than 106 acres. Some aspen trees **germinate** from seeds, but most come from natural cloning. In this process the parent tree sends up new **sprouts** from its root system. Fossil records show tree clones may live up to a million years.

the best one.
→ see Word Web: **trial**

Word Link *tri ≈ three : **tri**angle, **tri**logy, **tri**llion*

triangle /'traɪæŋgəl/ (**triangles**) N-COUNT A **triangle** is a shape with three straight sides. ● **triangular** /traɪ'æŋgjʊlə/ ADJ ❑ *...the triangular frame.*
→ see **circle**, **shape**

tribe /traɪb/ (**tribes**) N-COUNT **Tribe** is sometimes used to refer to a group of people of the same race, language, and customs, especially in a developing country. Some people disapprove of this use. **Tribe** can take the singular or plural form of the verb. ❑ *...the Xhosa tribe of South Africa.* ● **tribal** ADJ ❑ *...tribal lands.*

tribulation /ˌtrɪbjʊ'leɪʃən/ (**tribulations**) N-VAR You can refer to the suffering or difficulty that you experience in a particular situation as **tribulations**. [FORMAL] ❑ *...the trials and tribulations of everyday life.*

tribunal /traɪ'bju:nəl/ (**tribunals**) N-COUNT A **tribunal** is a special court or committee that is appointed to deal with particular problems. **Tribunal** can take the singular or plural form of the verb. ❑ *...an industrial tribunal.*

tribute /'trɪbju:t/ (**tributes**) **1** N-VAR A **tribute** is something that you say or do to show your admiration and respect for someone. ❑ *He paid tribute to his manager.* **2** N-SING If one thing is a **tribute to** another, it is the result of the other thing and shows how good it is. ❑ *Their success is a tribute to their hard work.*

'tribute ˌband (**tribute bands**) N-COUNT A **tribute band** is a pop group that plays the music and copies the style of another, much more famous, pop group. ❑ *...a Beatles tribute band, the Prefab Four.*

trick /trɪk/ (**tricks, tricking, tricked**) **1** V-T & N-COUNT If someone **tricks** you, or if they **play** a **trick on** you, they deceive you, often in order to make you do something. ❑ *His family tricked him into going to Pakistan.* **2** N-COUNT A **trick** is a clever or skilful action that someone does in order to entertain people. ❑ *...card tricks.* **3** N-COUNT A **trick** is a special way of doing something. ❑ *There is a trick to installing it properly.* **4** PHRASE If something **does the trick**, it achieves what you wanted. [INFORMAL] ❑ *Sometimes a few sympathetic words will do the trick.*

Word Partnership Use *trick* with:

ADJ.	**cheap** trick, **clever** trick, **neat** trick, **old** trick **1** **2** **3**
V.	**play a** trick, **pull a** trick **try to** trick ***someone*** **1** **do the** trick **4**
N.	**card** trick **2**

trickle /'trɪkəl/ (**trickles, trickling, trickled**) **1** V-I & N-COUNT If a liquid **trickles** somewhere,

t

Word Web trial

Many countries have **trial** by jury. The **judge** begins by explaining the **charges** against the **defendant**. Next the defendant **pleads guilty** or not guilty. Then the **attorneys** for the **plaintiff** and the defendant present **evidence**. Both **attorneys** interview **witnesses**. They can also question each other's **clients**. Sometimes the lawyers go back and **cross-examine** witnesses about **testimony** they gave earlier. When they finish, the **jury** meets to **deliberate**. They deliver their **verdict** and the judge **pronounces** the **sentence**. At this point, the plaintiff may be able to **appeal** the verdict and request a new trial.

or if there is a **trickle of** it, it flows slowly in a thin stream. ❑ *A tear trickled down the old man's cheek.* ❑ *...a trickle of water.* **2** V-I & N-COUNT If people or things **trickle** somewhere, or if there is a **trickle of** them to that place, they move there slowly in small amounts. ❑ *We've had a steady trickle of customers.*

tricky /ˈtrɪki/ (**trickier, trickiest**) ADJ A **tricky** task or problem is difficult to deal with.

tried /traɪd/ **Tried** is the past tense and past participle of **try**.

trifle /ˈtraɪfəl/ (**trifles**) **1** PHRASE You can use **a trifle** to mean slightly. ❑ *He seemed a trifle annoyed.* **2** N-COUNT **Trifles** are things that are not considered important. ❑ *She always took people's problems seriously, even when they were trifles and easily solved.* **3** N-VAR **Trifle** is a cold dessert made of layers of sponge cake, fruit, jelly, and custard.

trigger /ˈtrɪgə/ (**triggers, triggering, triggered**) **1** N-COUNT The **trigger** of a gun is the small lever which you pull to fire it. **2** V-T To **trigger** a bomb or system means to cause it to work. ❑ *The thieves triggered the alarm.* **3** V-T & PHR-VERB If something **triggers** an event, or if it **triggers off** an event, it causes the event to happen. ❑ *It is still not clear what triggered the demonstrations.* **4** N-COUNT If something acts as a **trigger for** another thing, the first thing causes the second thing to begin. ❑ *Stress may act as a trigger for these illnesses.*

Word Link *tri ≈ three : triangle, trilogy, trillion*

trillion /ˈtrɪljən/ NUM A **trillion** is a million million.

trilogy /ˈtrɪlədʒi/ (**trilogies**) N-COUNT A **trilogy** is a series of three books, plays, or films with the same characters or subject.

trim /trɪm/ (**trimmer, trimmest, trims, trimming, trimmed**) **1** ADJ Something that is **trim** is neat and attractive. ❑ *The neighbours' gardens were trim and tidy.* **2** ADJ If someone has a **trim** figure, they are slim. ❑ *...a trim woman in her forties.* **3** V-T & N-COUNT If you **trim** something, or if you give it a **trim**, you cut off small amounts of it to make it look neater. ❑ *His hair needed a trim.* **4** V-T If something such as a piece of clothing **is trimmed with** a type of material or design, it is decorated with it, usually along its edges. ❑ *...a white dress trimmed with blue bows.* **5** N-VAR The **trim** on something such as a piece of clothing is a decoration along its edges in a different colour or material. ❑ *...black leather boots with fur trim.*

T

▸ **trim off** PHR-VERB If you **trim off** parts of something, you cut them off, because they are not needed. ❑ *Trim the fat off the ham.*

trimming /ˈtrɪmɪŋ/ (**trimmings**) **1** N-VAR The **trimming** on something such as a piece of clothing is the decoration along its edges in a different colour or material. ❑ *...the lace trimming on her nightdress.* **2** N-PLURAL **Trimmings** are extra things that can be added to something or included in something. ❑ *...roast turkey with all the trimmings.*

trio /ˈtriːəʊ/ (**trios**) N-COUNT A **trio** is a group of three people, especially musicians or singers.

trip /trɪp/ (**trips, tripping, tripped**) **1** N-COUNT A **trip** is a journey that you make to a place and back again. ❑ *We went out on a day trip.* ❑ *...a business trip.* **2** → see also **round trip** **3** V-I & PHR-VERB If you **trip** when you are walking, or if you **trip up**, you knock your foot against something and fall over. ❑ *He was just coming down the ramp when he tripped up.* **4** V-T & PHR-VERB If you **trip** someone who is walking, or if you **trip** them **up**, you put your foot or something else in front of them so that they knock their own foot against it and fall. **5** N-COUNT If you say that someone is, for example, on a power **trip**, a guilt **trip**, or a nostalgia **trip**, you mean that their behaviour is motivated by power, guilt, or nostalgia. [INFORMAL] ❑ *The biggest power trip must be having a private plane.*

Word Partnership Use *trip* with:

N.	**boat** trip, **bus** trip, **business** trip, **camping** trip, **field** trip, trip **home**, **return** trip, **shopping** trip, **train** trip **1**
V.	**cancel a** trip, **make a** trip, **plan a** trip, **return from a** trip, **take a** trip **1**
ADJ.	**free** trip, **last** trip, **long** trip, **next** trip, **recent** trip, **safe** trip, **short** trip **1**

triple /ˈtrɪpəl/ (**triples, tripling, tripled**) **1** ADJ BEFORE N **Triple** means consisting of three things or parts. ❑ *...a triple gold medallist.* **2** V-T/V-I If something **triples**, or if you **triple** it, it becomes three times greater in size or number. ❑ *The exhibition has tripled in size since last year.*

triplet /ˈtrɪplət/ (**triplets**) N-COUNT **Triplets** are three children born at the same time to the same mother.

tripod /ˈtraɪpɒd/ (**tripods**) N-COUNT A **tripod** is a stand with three legs, used to support something such as a camera.

triumph /ˈtraɪʌmf/ (**triumphs, triumphing, triumphed**) **1** N-VAR A **triumph** is a great success or achievement. ❑ *The building is a triumph of modern design.* **2** N-UNCOUNT **Triumph** is a feeling of great satisfaction when you win or achieve something. ❑ *The feeling of triumph was short-lived.* **3** V-I If you **triumph**, you win a victory or succeed in overcoming something. ❑ *The film is about good triumphing over evil.*

triumphant /traɪˈʌmfənt/ ADJ If you are **triumphant**, you feel very happy because you have won a victory or achieved something. • **triumphantly** ADV ❑ *They marched triumphantly into the capital.*

trivia /ˈtrɪviə/ N-UNCOUNT **Trivia** consists of unimportant facts or details. ❑ *The two men chatted about such trivia as their favourite kinds of fast food.*

trivial /ˈtrɪviəl/ ADJ If you describe something as **trivial**, you think that it is unimportant and not serious. ❑ *...trivial details.*

triviality /ˌtrɪviˈælɪti/ (**trivialities**) N-VAR If you refer to something as a **triviality**, you think it is unimportant.

trod /trɒd/ **Trod** is the past tense of **tread**.

trodden /ˈtrɒdən/ **Trodden** is the past participle of **tread**.

trolley /ˈtrɒli/ (**trolleys**) **1** N-COUNT A **trolley** is a small cart on wheels that you use to carry things such as shopping or luggage. [BRIT] ❑ ...*supermarket trolleys.* **2** N-COUNT A **trolley** is a small table on wheels on which food and drinks can be carried. [BRIT] **3** N-COUNT In American English, a **trolley** is an electric vehicle which travels on rails along a street.

trombone /trɒm'bəʊn/ (**trombones**) N-COUNT A **trombone** is a long brass musical instrument which you play by blowing into it and sliding part of it backwards and forwards.
→ see **orchestra**

troop /truːp/ (**troops, trooping, trooped**) **1** N-PLURAL **Troops** are soldiers. ❑ ...*more than 35,000 troops from a dozen countries.* **2** N-COUNT A **troop** is a group of soldiers within a cavalry or armoured regiment. **3** V-I If people **troop** somewhere, they walk there in a group. ❑ *They all trooped back to the house.*
→ see **army**

trooper /'truːpə/ (**troopers**) **1** N-COUNT A **trooper** is a soldier of low rank in the cavalry or in an armoured regiment in the army. **2** N-COUNT In the United States, a **trooper** is a police officer in a state police force.

trophy /'trəʊfi/ (**trophies**) N-COUNT A **trophy** is a prize such as a cup, given to the winner of a competition.

tropical /'trɒpɪkəl/ ADJ **Tropical** means belonging to or typical of the tropics. ❑ ...*tropical diseases.* ❑ ...*tropical weather.*
→ see **habitat, hurricane**

tropics /'trɒpɪks/ N-PLURAL The **tropics** are the hottest parts of the world, near the equator.

trot /trɒt/ (**trots, trotting, trotted**) **1** V-I & N-SING When an animal such as a horse **trots**, or when it breaks into a **trot**, it moves fairly fast, taking quick small steps. ❑ *Pete got on his horse and started trotting across the field.* **2** V-I If you **trot** somewhere, you move fairly fast, taking small quick steps. ❑ *I trotted down the steps.* **3** PHRASE If several things happen **on the trot**, they happen one after the other, without a break. [INFORMAL] ❑ *She lost five games on the trot.*
▶ **trot out** PHR-VERB If you say that someone **is trotting out** old ideas or information, you mean that they are repeating them in a boring way.

trouble /'trʌbəl/ (**troubles, troubling, troubled**) **1** N-VAR You can refer to problems or difficulties as **trouble**. ❑ *I had trouble parking.* ❑ ...*financial troubles.* **2** N-SING If you say that one aspect of a situation is **the trouble**, you mean that it is the aspect which is causing problems. ❑ *The trouble is that these symptoms have remained.* **3** V-T If something **troubles** you, it makes you feel worried. ❑ *He was troubled by the lifestyle of his son.* • **troubling** ADJ ❑ ...*troubling chest pains.* **4** N-UNCOUNT If you have back **trouble**, for example, there is something wrong with your back. **5** N-UNCOUNT If there is **trouble**, people are quarrelling or fighting. ❑ *There was some trouble on the subway tonight.* **6** PHRASE If someone is **in trouble**, they have broken a rule or law and are likely to be punished by someone in authority. ❑ *He was in trouble with his teachers.* **7** PHRASE If you **take the trouble to** do something, you do it although it requires some time or effort.

Word Partnership Use *trouble* with:

V.	**run into** trouble **1** **have** trouble **1** **4** **cause** trouble, **make** trouble, **spell** trouble, **start** trouble **1** **5** **get in/into** trouble, **get out of** trouble, **stay out of** trouble **5**
N.	**engine** trouble **1** **sign of** trouble **1** **2**
ADJ.	**financial** trouble **1** **big** trouble, **deep** trouble, **real** trouble, **serious** trouble **1** **5** **heart** trouble **4**
ADV.	trouble **ahead** **1** **5**
PREP.	trouble **with** **1** **2** **5** **in** trouble **5**

troubled /'trʌbəld/ ADJ **Troubled** means worried or full of problems. ❑ *Rose sounded deeply troubled.* ❑ ...*this troubled country.*

troublemaker /'trʌbəlmeɪkə/ (**troublemakers**) N-COUNT A **troublemaker** is someone who causes trouble.

Word Link *some* ≈ *causing: awesome, fearsome, troublesome*

troublesome /'trʌbəlsəm/ ADJ Someone or something that is **troublesome** causes problems or difficulties. ❑ ...*a troublesome back injury.*

trough /trɒf, AM trɔːf/ (**troughs**) **1** N-COUNT A **trough** is a long container from which farm animals drink or eat. **2** N-COUNT A **trough** is a low point in a pattern that has regular high and low points. ❑ *Share prices have risen by 60% since the trough last October.*
→ see **sound**

troupe /truːp/ (**troupes**) N-COUNT A **troupe** is a group of actors, singers, or dancers who work together.

trousers /'traʊzəz/ N-PLURAL In British English, **trousers** are a piece of clothing that you wear over your body from the waist downwards, and that cover each leg separately. You can also say **a pair of trousers**. The usual American word is **pants**. ❑ ...*a blue blouse and white trousers.* ❑ *Alexander rolled up his trouser legs.*
→ see **clothing**

trout /traʊt/ (**trouts**) N-VAR A **trout** is a kind of fish that lives in rivers and streams. **Trout** is the flesh of this fish eaten as food.

truant /'truːənt/ (**truants**) **1** N-COUNT A **truant** is a child who stays away from school without permission. **2** PHRASE If children **play truant**, they stay away from school without permission.

truce /truːs/ (**truces**) N-COUNT A **truce** is an agreement between two people or groups to stop fighting or quarrelling for a short time.

truck /trʌk/ (**trucks**) **1** N-COUNT In American English a **truck** is a large vehicle that is used to transport goods by road. The usual British word is **lorry**. **2** N-COUNT A **truck** is an open vehicle used for carrying goods on a railway. [BRIT]

trudge /trʌdʒ/ (**trudges, trudging, trudged**) V-I & N-SING If you **trudge** somewhere, you walk there with slow heavy steps. This way of walking is called a **trudge**. ❑ *...the long trudge home.*

true /tru:/ (**truer, truest**) **1** ADJ If something is **true**, it is based on facts and is not invented or imagined. ❑ *Is it true that businessmen make bad politicians?* ❑ *The film is based on a true story.* **2** ADJ BEFORE N **True** means real, genuine, or typical. ❑ *This country claims to be a true democracy.* ❑ *The true cost is often higher.* **3** PHRASE If a dream, wish, or prediction **comes true**, it actually happens. **4** PHRASE If a general statement **holds true** in particular circumstances, or if your previous statement **holds true** in different circumstances, it is true or valid in those circumstances. ❑ *The nearer the cinema, the worse the restaurant. This rule holds true across most of London.*

Word Partnership Use *true* with:

N.	true **identity**, true **meaning**, **opposite/reverse is** true, true **statement**, true **story** 1 true **believer**, true **feelings**, true **love** 2
ADV.	**absolutely** true, **always** true, **certainly** true, **not necessarily** true, **partly** true, **probably** true, **quite** true, **really** true 1
V.	**remain** true 1

truly /'tru:li/ **1** ADV **Truly** means completely and genuinely. ❑ *Not all doctors truly understand the disease.* ❑ *Believe me, Susan, I am truly sorry.* **2** ADV You can use **truly** in order to emphasize your description of something. ❑ *They were truly appalling.* **3** ADV You can use **truly** to emphasize that what you are saying is true. ❑ *I do not expect there to be a war. Truly I do not.* **4** CONVENTION You can write **Yours truly** before your signature at the end of a letter to someone you do not know very well. **5** **well and truly** → see **well**

trump /trʌmp/ (**trumps**) **1** N-UNCOUNT In a game of cards, **trumps** is the suit which is chosen to have the highest value in a particular game. **2** PHRASE Your **trump card** is the most powerful thing that you can use or do to gain an advantage. ❑ *They took their appeal to the Supreme Court; this, they believed, would be their trump card.*

trumpet /'trʌmpɪt/ (**trumpets**) N-COUNT A **trumpet** is a brass wind instrument.
→ see **orchestra**

trumpeter /'trʌmpɪtə/ (**trumpeters**) N-COUNT A **trumpeter** is someone who plays a trumpet.

T

trundle /'trʌndəl/ (**trundles, trundling, trundled**) **1** V-I If a vehicle **trundles** somewhere, it moves there slowly. ❑ *The train eventually trundled in at 7.54.* **2** V-T If you **trundle** something somewhere, especially an object with wheels, you move or roll it along slowly. ❑ *The old man lifted the barrow and trundled it away.*

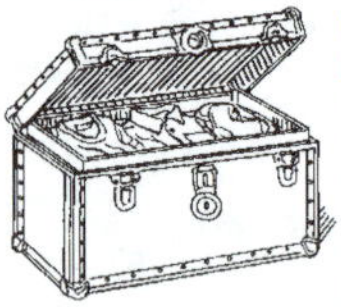
trunk

trunk /trʌŋk/ (**trunks**) **1** N-COUNT The **trunk** of a tree is the large main stem from which the branches grow. **2** N-COUNT A **trunk** is a large strong case or box used for storing things or for taking on a journey. **3** N-COUNT An elephant's **trunk** is its long nose. **4** N-COUNT In American English, the **trunk** of a car is a covered space at the back or front that is used for luggage. The usual British word is **boot**.

trust /trʌst/ (**trusts, trusting, trusted**) **1** V-T & N-UNCOUNT If you **trust** someone, or if you have **trust in** them, you believe that they are honest and will not deliberately do anything to harm you. ❑ *I don't trust you anymore.* ❑ *He destroyed my trust in men.* ❑ *You've betrayed their trust.* **2** V-T If you **trust** someone **to** do something, you believe that they will do it. ❑ *I knew I could trust him to get the job done.* **3** V-T If you **trust** someone **with** something, you allow them to look after it or deal with it. ❑ *I wouldn't trust him with my child.* **4** N-UNCOUNT **Trust** is responsibility that you are given to deal with important, valuable, or secret things. ❑ *This is a position of trust which is generously paid.* **5** V-T If you do not **trust** something, you feel that it is not safe or reliable. ❑ *He didn't trust his legs to hold him up.* **6** V-T If you **trust** someone's judgment or advice, you believe that it is good or right. **7** N-VAR A **trust** is a financial arrangement in which an organization keeps and invests money for someone. ❑ *They've set up a trust fund for their son.* ❑ *The money will be put in trust until she is 18.*

Word Partnership Use *trust* with:

V.	**build** trust, **create** trust, **learn to** trust, **place** trust **in** ***someone*** 1
ADJ.	**mutual** trust 1 **charitable** trust 7
N.	trust ***your*** **instincts**, trust ***someone's*** **judgment** 6 **investment** trust 7

trustee /trʌ'sti:/ (**trustees**) N-COUNT A **trustee** is someone with legal control of money or property that is kept or invested for another person.

trusting /'trʌstɪŋ/ ADJ A **trusting** person believes that people are honest and sincere and do not intend to harm him or her.

trustworthy /'trʌstwɜ:ði/ ADJ A **trustworthy** person is reliable, responsible, and can be trusted completely.

truth /tru:θ/ (**truths**) **1** N-UNCOUNT The **truth** about something is all the facts about it, rather than things that are imagined or invented. ❑ *We all want to know the truth about what happened to him.* ❑ *I want you to tell me the truth.* **2** N-UNCOUNT If you say that there is some **truth** in a statement or story, you mean that it is true, or partly true. ❑ *There is some truth in the criticisms.* **3** N-COUNT A **truth** is something that is generally accepted to be true. ❑ *...universal truths.*

Word Partnership Use *truth* with:

V.	**accept the** truth, **find the** truth, **know the** truth, **learn the** truth, **search for the** truth, **tell the** truth 1
N.	**a grain of** truth, **the** truth **of the matter** 1
ADJ.	**the awful** truth, **the plain** truth, **the sad** truth, **the simple** truth, **the whole** truth 1 **absolute** truth 1 3

truthful /'tru:θfʊl/ ADJ If a person or their comments are **truthful**, they are honest and do not tell any lies. • **truthfully** ADV ❑ *I answered all their questions truthfully.* • **truthfulness** N-UNCOUNT ❑ *...qualities such as honesty and truthfulness.*

try /traɪ/ (**tries, trying, tried**) **1** V-T/V-I & N-COUNT If you **try to** do something, or if you have a **try** at doing something, you make an effort to do it. ❑ *I tried to persuade him to stay.* ❑ *I must try to see him.* ❑ *I tried calling him when I got here but he wasn't at home.* ❑ *After a few tries Patrick gave up.* **2** V-T & N-COUNT If you **try** something new or different, or if you give it a **try**, you use it or do it in order to find out how useful, effective, or enjoyable it is. ❑ *You could try a little cheese melted on the top.* **3** V-T If you **try** a particular place or person, you go to that place or person because you think they may be able to provide you with what you want. ❑ *Have you tried the local music shops?* **4** V-T When a person **is tried**, they appear in court and are found innocent or guilty after the judge and jury have heard the evidence. **5** N-COUNT In the game of rugby, a **try** is the action of scoring by putting the ball down behind the goal line of the opposing team. **6** to **try** your **hand** → see **hand** **7** to **try** your **luck** → see **luck**

▶ **try on** PHR-VERB If you **try on** a piece of clothing, you put it on to see if it fits you or if it looks nice.

▶ **try out** PHR-VERB If you **try** something **out**, you test it in order to find out how useful or effective it is. ❑ *London Transport hopes to try out the system in September.*

Usage

Try and is often used instead of **try to** in spoken English, but you should avoid it in writing. ❑ *Just try and stop me!* Notice also the difference between **try to** and **try** with the -ing form of the verb. **Try to** means 'attempt to', whereas **try** with the -ing form of the verb is used for making suggestions. ❑ *I'm going to try to open the door.* ❑ *Try opening the windows to freshen the air.*

trying /'traɪɪŋ/ ADJ Someone or something that is **trying** is difficult to deal with and makes you feel impatient or annoyed. ❑ *The whole business has been very trying.*

'T-ˌshirt also **tee-shirt** (**T-shirts**) N-COUNT A **T-shirt** is a cotton shirt with short sleeves and no collar or buttons.
→ see **clothing**

tub /tʌb/ (**tubs**) **1** N-COUNT A **tub** is a deep container of any size. ❑ *...four tubs of ice cream.* **2** N-COUNT In American English, a **tub** is a container which you fill with water and sit in while you wash your body. The British word is **bath**.
→ see **soap**

tube /tju:b, AM tu:b/ (**tubes**) **1** N-COUNT A **tube** is a long hollow cylinder. ❑ *They feed him through a tube that enters his nose.* **2** N-COUNT A **tube of** paste is a long thin container which you squeeze in order to force the paste out. ❑ *...a tube of toothpaste.* **3** N-SING **The Tube** is the underground railway system in London. [BRIT] ❑ *He travelled by tube to work every day.*
→ see **container, laboratory, transportation**

tuberculosis /tju:ˌbɜ:kjʊ'ləʊsɪs, AM tu:-/ N-UNCOUNT **Tuberculosis**, or **TB**, is a serious infectious disease that affects the lungs.

tubing /'tju:bɪŋ, AM 'tu:-/ N-UNCOUNT **Tubing** is plastic, rubber, or other material made in the shape of a tube.

tuck /tʌk/ (**tucks, tucking, tucked**) V-T If you **tuck** something somewhere, you put it there so that it is safe, comfortable, or neat. ❑ *He tried to tuck his shirt inside his trousers.*

▶ **tuck away** **1** PHR-VERB If you **tuck away** something such as money, you store it in a safe place. ❑ *I tucked the box away in the drawer.* **2** PHR-VERB If someone or something **is tucked away**, they are well hidden in a quiet place where very few people go. ❑ *His home is tucked away in the forest.*

▶ **tuck in** **1** PHR-VERB If you **tuck in** a piece of material, you secure it in position by placing the edge of it behind or under something else. ❑ *Tuck the sheets in firmly.* ❑ *Straighten your cap and tuck your shirt in.* **2** PHR-VERB If you **tuck** a child **in** bed, or if you **tuck** them **in**, you make them comfortable by straightening the sheets and blankets and pushing the loose ends under the mattress.

▶ **tuck into** or **tuck in** PHR-VERB If someone **tucks into** a meal, or if they **tuck in**, they start eating enthusiastically or hungrily. [BRIT, INFORMAL] ❑ *Tuck in while it's hot.*

Tuesday /'tju:zdeɪ, -di, AM 'tu:z-/ (**Tuesdays**) N-VAR **Tuesday** is the day after Monday and before Wednesday.

tug /tʌg/ (**tugs, tugging, tugged**) **1** V-T/V-I & N-COUNT If you **tug** something, if you **tug at** it, or if you give it a **tug**, you give it a quick pull. ❑ *Anna tugged at Martha's arm. 'Look,' she said.* **2** N-COUNT A **tug** is a small powerful boat which pulls large ships, usually when they come into a port.

tuition /tjʊ'ɪʃən, AM tʊ-/ N-UNCOUNT If you are given **tuition** in a particular subject, you are taught about that subject, especially on your own or in a small group. ❑ *At school, he was given extra tuition for two hours a week.*

tulip /'tju:lɪp, AM 'tu:-/ (**tulips**) N-COUNT **Tulips** are garden flowers that grow in the spring.

tumble /'tʌmbəl/ (**tumbles, tumbling, tumbled**) V-I & N-COUNT If someone or something **tumbles**, or if they take a **tumble**, they fall with a rolling or bouncing movement. ❑ *The gun tumbled out of his hand.* ❑ *He injured himself in a tumble from his horse.*

tummy /'tʌmi/ (**tummies**) N-COUNT Your **tummy** is your stomach. [INFORMAL]

tumour [AM **tumor**] /'tju:mə, AM 'tu:-/ (**tumours**) N-COUNT A **tumour** is a mass of diseased or abnormal cells that has grown in someone's body.

tumultuous /tju:'mʌltʃʊəs, AM tu:-/ **1** ADJ **Tumultuous** feelings or events are very exciting or confusing. ❑ *...the tumultuous changes in Eastern Europe.* **2** ADJ A **tumultuous** reaction to something is very noisy, because the people involved are very happy or excited. ❑ *...tumultuous applause.*

tuna /'tju:nə, AM 'tu:nə/

The plural is **tuna** or **tunas**.

N-VAR A **tuna** or a **tuna fish** is a large fish that lives in warm seas. **Tuna** or **tuna fish** is the flesh of this fish eaten as food.

Word Web tunnel

The Egyptians built the first **tunnels** as entrances to tombs. Later the Babylonians* built a tunnel under the Euphrates River*. It connected the royal palace with the Temple of Jupiter*. The Romans **dug** tunnels when **mining** for gold. By the late 1600s, **explosives** had replaced **digging**. Gunpowder was used to build the **underground** section of a canal in France in 1679. Nitroglycerin explosions helped create a railroad tunnel in Massachusetts in 1867. The longest continuous tunnel in the world is the Delaware Aqueduct. It carries water from the Catskill Mountains* to New York City and is 105 miles long.

Babylonians: people who lived in the ancient city of Babylon.
Euphrates River: a large river in the Middle East.
Temple of Jupiter: a religious building.
Catskill Mountains: a mountain range in the northeastern U.S.

tune /tjuːn, AM tuːn/ (**tunes, tuning, tuned**) 1 N-COUNT A **tune** is a series of musical notes that is pleasant to listen to. ❑ *...a merry little tune.* 2 V-T When someone **tunes** or **tunes up** a musical instrument, they adjust it so that it produces the right notes. 3 V-T If your radio or television **is tuned to** a particular broadcasting station, you are listening to or watching the programmes being broadcast on that station. 4 PHRASE A person or musical instrument that is **in tune** produces exactly the right notes. 5 PHRASE If you say that someone **has changed** their **tune**, you are criticizing them because they have changed their opinion or way of doing things. 6 PHRASE **To the tune of** a particular amount means to the extent of that amount. ❑ *The family suddenly found itself in debt to the tune of some $5,000.*

▶ **tune in** PHR-VERB If you **tune in to** a particular television or radio station or programme, you watch or listen to it.

tunic /ˈtjuːnɪk, AM ˈtuː-/ (**tunics**) N-COUNT A **tunic** is a loose garment that is worn on the top part of your body.

tunnel /ˈtʌnəl/ (**tunnels, tunnelling, tunnelled** or [AM] **tunneling, tunneled**) 1 N-COUNT A **tunnel** is a long passage which has been made under the ground, usually through a hill or under the sea. 2 V-I To **tunnel** somewhere means to make a tunnel there. ❑ *The prisoners tunnelled out of the jail.*
→ see Word Web: **tunnel**
→ see **traffic**

T

turbine /ˈtɜːbaɪn, AM -bɪn/ (**turbines**) N-COUNT A **turbine** is a machine or engine which uses a stream of air, gas, water, or steam to turn a wheel and produce power.
→ see **electricity, wheel**

turbulent /ˈtɜːbjʊlənt/ 1 ADJ A **turbulent** time, place, or relationship is one in which there is a lot of change and confusion. ❑ *...six turbulent years of conflict.* ● **turbulence** N-UNCOUNT ❑ *...a region often affected by political turbulence.* 2 ADJ **Turbulent** water or air contains strong currents which change direction suddenly. ● **turbulence** N-UNCOUNT ❑ *His plane encountered severe turbulence.*

turf /tɜːf/ (**turfs, turfing, turfed**) N-UNCOUNT **Turf** is short, thick, even grass.

▶ **turf out** PHR-VERB If someone **is turfed out of** a place or position, they are forced to leave. [BRIT, INFORMAL] ❑ *She should have been turfed out of her job years ago.*

turkey

turkey /ˈtɜːki/ (**turkeys**) 1 N-COUNT A **turkey** is a large bird that is kept on a farm for its meat. 2 N-UNCOUNT **Turkey** is the meat of a turkey eaten as food.

turmoil /ˈtɜːmɔɪl/ N-UNCOUNT **Turmoil** is a state of confusion or great anxiety. ❑ *...the political turmoil of 1989.* ❑ *Her marriage was in turmoil.*

turn
1 TO CHANGE IN DIRECTION OR NATURE
2 YOUR TIME OR OCCASION TO DO SOMETHING
3 PHRASAL VERBS

turn /tɜːn/ (**turns, turning, turned**) 1 1 V-T/V-I To **turn** means to move in a different direction or to move into a different position. **Turn around** or **turn round** means the same as **turn**. ❑ *He turned his head left and right.* ❑ *She had turned the bedside chair to face the door.* ❑ *Kate turned to see a woman standing there.* 2 V-I & N-COUNT When you **turn** in a particular direction, you change the direction in which you are moving or travelling. A **turn** is a change of direction. ❑ *Now turn right to follow West Ferry Road.* ❑ *You can't do a right-hand turn here.* 3 → see also **turning** 4 V-I If you **turn to** a particular page in a book, you open it at that page. 5 V-T/V-I If you **turn** your attention or thoughts **to** a particular person or thing, you start thinking about them or discussing them. ❑ *We turn now to the British news.* 6 V-I If you **turn to** someone, you ask for their help or advice. ❑ *There was no one to turn to.* 7 V-T/V-I When something **turns into** something else, or when you **turn** it **into** something else, it becomes something different. ❑ *The government plans to turn the country into a democracy.* 8 N-COUNT If a situation or trend takes a particular kind of **turn**, it changes so that it starts developing in a different or opposite way. ❑ *...the latest turn in the fighting.* 9 to **turn** your **back** → see **back** 10 to **turn the tables** → see **table**

turn /tɜːn/ (**turns**)
② 1 N-COUNT If it is your **turn to** do something, you now have the right or duty to do it, when other people have done it before you or will do it after you. ❑ *Tonight it's my turn to cook.* 2 PHRASE You use **in turn** to refer to actions or events that are in a sequence one after the other, for example because one causes the other. ❑ *Cuba buys rice from China which in turn buys sugar from Cuba.* 3 PHRASE If two or more people **take turns to** do something or **take it in turns to** do it, they do it one after the other several times, rather than doing it together.

Thesaurus	*turn* Also look up:
V.	bend, pivot, revolve, rotate, spin, twist ① 1 2
	become ① 6
N.	chance, opportunity ②

turn /tɜːn/ (**turns, turning, turned**)
③ ▶ **turn against** PHR-VERB If you **turn against** someone or something, or if something **turns** you **against** them, you stop supporting them, trusting them, or liking them. ❑ *Even his formerly loyal supporters turned against him.*

▶ **turn around** or **turn round** 1 → see **turn** (meaning 1) 2 PHR-VERB If you **turn** something **around**, or if it **turns around**, it is moved so that it faces the opposite direction. ❑ *I turned the car around and went south.*

▶ **turn away** PHR-VERB If you **turn** someone **away**, you reject them or send them away. ❑ *These colleges are being forced to turn away students.*

▶ **turn back** PHR-VERB If you **turn back**, or if someone **turns** you **back** when you are going somewhere, you change direction and go towards where you started from. ❑ *Police attempted to turn back protesters.*

▶ **turn down** 1 PHR-VERB If you **turn down** a person or their request or offer, you refuse their request or offer. ❑ *After careful consideration I turned the invitation down.* 2 PHR-VERB When you **turn down** a radio, heater, or other piece of equipment, you reduce the amount of sound or heat being produced, by adjusting the controls. ❑ *He kept turning the central heating down.*

▶ **turn off** 1 PHR-VERB If you **turn off** the road or path you are going along, you start going along a different road or path which leads away from it. ❑ *Turn off at the sign to Walton.* 2 PHR-VERB When you **turn off** a piece of equipment or a supply of something, you stop heat, sound, or water being produced by adjusting the controls. ❑ *The light's a bit too bright. You can turn it off.*

▶ **turn on** 1 PHR-VERB When you **turn on** a piece of equipment or a supply of something, you cause heat, sound, or water to be produced by adjusting the controls. ❑ *She asked them why they hadn't turned the lights on.* 2 PHR-VERB If someone **turns on** you, they attack you or speak angrily to you.

▶ **turn out** 1 PHR-VERB If something **turns out** a particular way, it happens in that way or has the result or degree of success indicated. ❑ *I was positive things were going to turn out fine.* 2 PHR-VERB If something **turns out** to be a particular thing, it is discovered to be that thing. ❑ *The smell turned out to be beefburgers and chips.* 3 PHR-VERB When you **turn out** something such as a light or gas, you move the device that controls it so that it stops giving out light or heat. ❑ *Turn the lights out.* 4 PHR-VERB If people **turn out** for a particular event or activity, they go and take part in it or watch it. 5 → see also **turnout**

▶ **turn over** 1 PHR-VERB If you **turn** something **over**, or if it **turns over**, it is moved so that the top part is now facing downwards. ❑ *He turned over the card and laid it on the table.* 2 PHR-VERB If you **turn** something **over** in your mind, you think carefully about it. 3 PHR-VERB If you **turn** something **over to** someone, you give it to them when they ask for it, because they have a right to it. ❑ *I turned the evidence over to the police.* 4 → see also **turnover**

▶ **turn round** → see **turn around**

▶ **turn up** 1 PHR-VERB If you say that someone or something **turns up**, you mean that they arrive, often unexpectedly or after you have been waiting a long time. ❑ *We waited for the bus, but it never turned up.* 2 PHR-VERB When you **turn up** a radio, heater, or other piece of equipment, you increase the amount of sound, heat, or power being produced. ❑ *I turned the volume up.*

turning /ˈtɜːnɪŋ/ (**turnings**) 1 N-COUNT If you take a particular **turning**, you go along a road which leads away from the side of another road. ❑ *Take the next turning on the right.* 2 → see also **turn**

ˈturning ˌpoint (**turning points**) N-COUNT A **turning point** is a time at which an important change takes place which affects the future of a person or thing. ❑ *The turning point came when we joined a parents' group.*

turnip /ˈtɜːnɪp/ (**turnips**) N-VAR A **turnip** is a round vegetable with a green and white skin.

turnout also **turn-out** /ˈtɜːnaʊt/ (**turnouts**) N-COUNT The **turnout** at an event is the number of people who go to it. ❑ *It was a marvellous afternoon with a huge turnout of people.*

turnover /ˈtɜːnəʊvə/ 1 N-UNCOUNT The **turnover** of a company is the value of goods or services sold during a particular period of time. ❑ *The zoo has an annual turnover of £7 million.* 2 N-UNCOUNT The **turnover** of people in an organization is the rate at which people leave and are replaced. ❑ *At 22 per cent, NHS staff turnover is well above the national average.*

turquoise /ˈtɜːkwɔɪz/ (**turquoises**) ADJ & N-VAR Something that is **turquoise** is greenish-blue in colour. ❑ *I glanced out at the turquoise sea.*

turtle

turtle /ˈtɜːtəl/ (**turtles**) N-COUNT A **turtle** is a large reptile with a thick shell which lives in the sea.

tusk /tʌsk/ (**tusks**) N-COUNT The **tusks** of an elephant or wild boar are its two very long pointed teeth.

tussle /ˈtʌsəl/ (**tussles, tussling, tussled**) V-I & N-COUNT If one person **tussles with** another, or if they **tussle**, they grab hold of and struggle with each other. A **tussle** is a struggle in which people grab hold of each other.

t

tutor /ˈtjuːtə, AM ˈtuːt-/ (**tutors, tutoring, tutored**) **1** N-COUNT A **tutor** is a teacher at a British university or college. **2** N-COUNT A **tutor** is someone who gives private lessons to a pupil or a small group of pupils. **3** V-T If someone **tutors** a person or subject, they teach that person or subject. ❑ *She was tutored at home by her parents.* ❑ *He still tutors medical students in anatomy.*

tutorial /tjuːˈtɔːriəl, AM ˈtuːt-/ (**tutorials**) N-COUNT In a university or college, a **tutorial** is a regular meeting between a tutor and one or several students for discussion of a subject that is being studied.

tuxedo /tʌkˈsiːdəʊ/ (**tuxedos**) N-COUNT A **tuxedo** is a black or white jacket worn by men for formal social events.

TV /ˌtiː ˈviː/ (**TVs**) N-VAR **TV** means the same as **television**. ❑ *I prefer going to the cinema to watching TV.* ❑ *...a brand-new TV.*

tweed /twiːd/ (**tweeds**) N-VAR **Tweed** is a thick woollen cloth, often woven from different coloured threads.

twelfth /twelfθ/ (**twelfths**) **1** ORD The **twelfth** item in a series is the one that you count as number twelve. **2** N-COUNT A **twelfth** is one of twelve equal parts of something.

twelve /twelv/ (**twelves**) NUM **Twelve** is the number 12.

twentieth /ˈtwentiəθ/ ORD The **twentieth** item in a series is the one that you count as number twenty.

twenty /ˈtwenti/ (**twenties**) NUM **Twenty** is the number 20. For examples of how numbers such as twenty and eighty are used see **eighty**.

24-7 or **twenty-four seven** /ˌtwentifɔːˈsevən/ ADV & ADJ If something happens **24-7**, it happens all the time without ever stopping. **24-7** means twenty-four hours a day, seven days a week. [AM, INFORMAL] ❑ *I feel like sleeping 24-7.* ❑ *...a 24-7 radio station.*

Word Link *twi ≈ two : twice, twilight, twin*

twice /twaɪs/ **1** ADV If something happens **twice**, it happens two times. ❑ *I've visited Africa twice.* ❑ *Try to do this exercise at least twice a day.* **2** ADV & PREDET If one thing is, for example, **twice as** big or old **as** another thing, or if it is **twice the** size or age **of** another thing, it is two times as big or old as the other thing. ❑ *Your toenails take twice as long to grow as your fingernails.* ❑ *Unemployment in Northern Ireland is twice the national average.*

T

twig /twɪg/ (**twigs**) N-COUNT A **twig** is a very small thin branch of a tree or bush.

twilight /ˈtwaɪlaɪt/ **1** N-UNCOUNT **Twilight** is the time after sunset when it is just getting dark. ❑ *They returned at twilight.* **2** N-UNCOUNT **Twilight** is the dim light that there is outside just after sunset. ❑ *...the deepening autumn twilight.*

twin /twɪn/ (**twins**) **1** N-COUNT If two people are **twins**, they have the same mother and were born on the same day. ❑ *...her twin sister.* **2** ADJ BEFORE N **Twin** is used to describe a pair of things that look the same and are close together. ❑ *The fourth bedroom has twin beds.* ❑ *...the world's largest twin-engined aircraft.*
→ see **clone**

twinkle /ˈtwɪŋkəl/ (**twinkles, twinkling, twinkled**) **1** V-I If a star or a light **twinkles**, it shines with an unsteady light which rapidly and constantly changes from bright to faint. **2** V-I & N-SING If you say that someone's eyes **twinkle**, or that there is a **twinkle** in their eye, you mean that their face expresses good humour, amusement, or mischief.

twirl /twɜːl/ (**twirls, twirling, twirled**) **1** V-T/V-I If you **twirl** something, or if it **twirls**, it turns round and round with a smooth fairly fast movement. ❑ *Bonnie twirled her empty glass in her fingers.* **2** V-I If you **twirl**, you move round and round rapidly, for example when you are dancing. ❑ *She jumped out of bed and twirled around the room on her toes.*

twist /twɪst/ (**twists, twisting, twisted**) **1** V-T If you **twist** something, you turn it to make a spiral shape, for example by turning the two ends of it in opposite directions. ❑ *Her hands began to twist the handles of the bag.* ❑ *She twisted her hair into a bun.* **2** V-T/V-I If you **twist** something, especially a part of your body, or if it **twists**, it moves into a strange, uncomfortable, or distorted shape or position. ❑ *He twisted her arms behind her back.* ❑ *...the twisted wreckage of a train.* **3** V-T/V-I If you **twist** part of your body such as your head or your shoulders, you turn that part while keeping the rest of your body still. ❑ *She twisted her head sideways.* ❑ *Susan twisted round in her seat.* **4** V-T If you **twist** a part of your body such as your ankle or your wrist, you injure it by turning it too sharply or in an unusual direction. ❑ *I twisted my knee last year playing tennis.* **5** V-T If you **twist** something, you turn it so that it moves around in a circular direction. ❑ *He takes out a jar and twists the lid off.* **6** V-T If someone **twists** what you say, they repeat it in a way that changes its meaning, in order to harm you or benefit themselves. ❑ *You're twisting my words.* **7** N-COUNT A **twist** in something is an unexpected and significant development. ❑ *The long-running battle took a new twist last night.*

Word Partnership Use *twist* with:

ADV.	twist **around** 1 3
V.	twist **and turn** 4
	plot twist, **story** twist 7
ADJ.	**added** twist, **bizarre** twist, **interesting** twist, **latest** twist, **new** twist, **unexpected** twist 7

twisted /ˈtwɪstɪd/ ADJ If you describe a person as **twisted**, you dislike them because you think they are strange in an unpleasant way.

twitch /twɪtʃ/ (**twitches, twitching, twitched**) V-I & N-COUNT If a part of your body **twitches**, it makes a little jerking movement, called a **twitch**. ❑ *He saw the corners of Alex's mouth twitch.* ❑ *He developed a nervous twitch.*

two /tuː/ (**twos**) NUM **Two** is the number 2.

ˌtwo-ˈthirds also **two thirds** QUANT **Two-thirds** is an amount that is two out of three equal parts of something. ❑ *Two-thirds of families in Britain already own their homes.* ❑ *Profits have fallen by two-thirds.*

ˌtwo-ˈway ADJ **Two-way** means moving or working in two opposite directions. ❑ *The bridge is now open to two-way traffic.* ❑ *We all carry two-way radios.*

tycoon /taɪ'kuːn/ (**tycoons**) N-COUNT A **tycoon** is a person who is successful in business and so has become rich and powerful.

type
1 SORT OR KIND
2 WRITING AND PRINTING

type /taɪp/ (**types**)
1 1 N-COUNT A **type of** something is a group of those things that have particular features in common. ❑ *...several types of lettuce.* ❑ *In 1990, 25% of households were of this type.* 2 N-COUNT If you refer to a particular thing or person as a **type of** something more general, you are considering that thing or person as an example of that more general group. ❑ *Have you done this type of work before?* ❑ *I am a very determined type of person.* 3 N-COUNT If you refer to a person as a particular **type**, you mean that they have that particular appearance, character, or type of behaviour. ❑ *I was rather an outdoor type.* ❑ *She was certainly not the type to murder her husband.*
→ see **printing**

type /taɪp/ (**types, typing, typed**)
2 V-T/V-I If you **type**, or **type** something, you use a typewriter or word processor to write it. ❑ *I had never really learnt to type properly.* ● **typing** N-UNCOUNT ❑ *He learnt shorthand and typing.*
▶ **type in** or **type into** PHR-VERB If you **type** information **into** a computer, you press keys on the keyboard so that the computer stores or processes the information.
▶ **type up** PHR-VERB If you **type up** a handwritten text, you produce a typed copy of it.

typewriter /'taɪpraɪtə/ (**typewriters**) N-COUNT A **typewriter** is a machine with keys which are pressed in order to print letters, numbers, or other characters onto paper.

typhoon /taɪ'fuːn/ (**typhoons**) N-COUNT A **typhoon** is a very violent tropical storm.
→ see **disaster, hurricane**

typical /'tɪpɪkəl/ 1 ADJ You use **typical** to describe someone or something that shows the most usual characteristics of a particular type of person or thing, and is therefore a good example of that type. ❑ *Aaron was brought up as a typical American child.* ❑ *A typical day begins at 8.30.* 2 ADJ If a particular action or feature is **typical of** someone or something, it shows their usual qualities or characteristics. ❑ *She is typical of the sort of people who live round here.*

typically /'tɪpɪkəli/ 1 ADV You use **typically** to say that something usually happens in the way that you are describing it. ❑ *The day typically begins with exercises and swimming.* 2 ADV You use **typically** to say that something shows all the most usual characteristics of a particular type of person or thing. ❑ *Ashley's pretty bedroom looks typically English.* 3 ADV You use **typically** to indicate that someone has behaved in the way that they normally do. ❑ *Typically, he took the criticism in good humour.*

typify /'tɪpɪfaɪ/ (**typifies, typifying, typified**) V-T To **typify** something means to be a typical example of it. ❑ *The county includes coastal scenery typified by beautiful beaches, bays, and fishing ports.*

typist /'taɪpɪst/ (**typists**) N-COUNT A **typist** is someone who works in an office typing letters and other documents.

tyranny /'tɪrəni/ N-UNCOUNT **Tyranny** is cruel and unjust rule by a person or small group of people.

tyrant /'taɪərənt/ (**tyrants**) N-COUNT A **tyrant** is someone who treats the people they have authority over in a cruel and unfair way.

tyre [AM **tire**] /taɪə/ (**tyres**) N-COUNT A **tyre** is a thick ring of rubber filled with air and fitted round the wheel of a vehicle.

Uu

ubiquitous /juːˈbɪkwɪtəs/ ADJ If you describe something as **ubiquitous**, you mean that it seems to be everywhere at the same time. ❑ *The mobile phone has become ubiquitous.*

ugly /ˈʌgli/ (**uglier, ugliest**) 1 ADJ If you say that someone or something is **ugly**, you mean that they are unattractive and unpleasant to look at. ❑ *...an ugly little hat.* ● **ugliness** N-UNCOUNT ❑ *...the ugliness of her home town.* 2 ADJ If you refer to a situation as **ugly**, you mean that it is very unpleasant, usually because it involves violence. ❑ *...ugly confrontations between workers and police.*

Thesaurus *ugly* Also look up:

ADJ.	hideous, unattractive; (*ant.*) beautiful 1
	disagreeable, offensive, unpleasant 2

ulcer /ˈʌlsə/ (**ulcers**) N-COUNT An **ulcer** is a sore area on or inside a part of your body which is very painful and may bleed.

Word Link ***ultim** ≈ end, last : penultimate, ultimate, ultimatum*

ultimate /ˈʌltɪmət/ 1 ADJ BEFORE N You use **ultimate** to describe the final result or the original cause of a long series of events. ❑ *It is not possible to estimate the ultimate result.* 2 ADJ BEFORE N You use **ultimate** to describe the most important or extreme thing of a particular kind. ❑ *The president is still the ultimate authority.* 3 PHRASE **The ultimate in** something is the best or most advanced thing of its kind. ❑ *This hotel is the ultimate in luxury.*

Word Partnership Use *ultimate* with:

N.	ultimate **aim/goal/objective**, ultimate **outcome** 1
	ultimate **authority**, ultimate **decision**, ultimate **power**, ultimate **weapon** 2
	ultimate **experience** 2 3

ultimately /ˈʌltɪmətli/ 1 ADV **Ultimately** means finally, after a long series of events. ❑ *I think they will ultimately succeed.* 2 ADV You use **ultimately** to emphasize that what you are saying is the most important point in a discussion. ❑ *Ultimately, the problem lies with employers.*

ultimatum /ˌʌltɪˈmeɪtəm/ (**ultimatums**) N-COUNT An **ultimatum** is a warning that unless someone acts in a particular way within a particular time limit, action will be taken against them. ❑ *Workers have given the government an ultimatum.*

ultrasound /ˈʌltrəsaʊnd/ (**ultrasounds**) 1 N-UNCOUNT **Ultrasound** refers to sound waves which travel at such a high frequency that they cannot be heard by humans. 2 N-COUNT An **ultrasound** or an **ultrasound scan** is a medical test in which ultrasound waves are used to form a picture of the inside of someone's body.

ultraviolet /ˌʌltrəˈvaɪələt/ ADJ **Ultraviolet** light or radiation causes your skin to darken after you have been in sunlight.
→ see **ozone, skin, sun, wave**

umbrella /ʌmˈbrelə/ (**umbrellas**) 1 N-COUNT An **umbrella** is an object which you use to protect yourself from the rain. It consists of a long stick with a folding frame covered in cloth. 2 N-SING **Umbrella** refers to a single idea or group that includes a lot of different ideas or groups. ❑ *...an umbrella group of human rights organisations.*

umbrella

umpire /ˈʌmpaɪə/ (**umpires, umpiring, umpired**) 1 N-COUNT An **umpire** is a person whose job is to make sure that a sports match or contest is played fairly and that the rules are not broken. 2 V-T/V-I If you **umpire**, or **umpire** a game, you do the job of an umpire.

unable /ʌnˈeɪbəl/ ADJ If you are **unable to** do something, it is impossible for you to do it. ❑ *I was unable to accept the invitation.*

Word Partnership Use *unable* with:

ADV.	**physically** unable
V.	unable **to afford**, unable **to agree**, unable **to attend**, unable **to control**, unable **to cope**, unable **to decide**, unable **to explain**, unable **to find**, unable **to hold**, unable **to identify**, unable **to make**, unable **to move**, unable **to pay**, unable **to perform**, unable **to reach**, unable **to speak**, unable **to walk**, unable **to work**

unacceptable /ˌʌnəkˈseptəbəl/ ADJ If you describe something as **unacceptable**, you strongly disapprove of it or object to it and feel that it should not be allowed to happen or continue. ❑ *It is totally unacceptable for children to swear.*

unaffected /ˌʌnəˈfektɪd/ 1 ADJ AFTER LINK-V If someone or something is **unaffected by** an event, they are not changed by it in any way. ❑ *She seemed totally unaffected by the news.* 2 ADJ If you describe someone as **unaffected**, you approve of them because they are natural and genuine in their behaviour.

unanimity /ˌjuːnəˈnɪmɪti/ N-UNCOUNT When there is **unanimity** among a group of people, they all agree about something. [FORMAL]

Word Link *anim ≈ alive, mind : animal, animated, unanimous*

unanimous /juːˈnænɪməs/ ADJ When a group of people or their opinion is **unanimous**, they all agree about something. ● **unanimously** ADV ❑ *The committee voted unanimously against the new plans.*

unannounced /ˌʌnəˈnaʊnst/ ADJ If someone arrives or does something **unannounced**, they do it unexpectedly and without telling anyone about it beforehand. ❑ *He arrived unannounced from South America.*

unanswered /ʌnˈɑːnsəd, -ˈæns-/ ADJ Something such as a question or letter that is **unanswered** has not been answered. ❑ *The most important questions remain unanswered.*

unarmed /ˌʌnˈɑːmd/ ADJ If a person or vehicle is **unarmed**, they are not carrying any weapons.

unashamed /ˌʌnəˈʃeɪmd/ ADJ If you describe someone's behaviour or attitude as **unashamed**, you mean that they are open and honest about things that other people might find embarrassing or shocking. ● **unashamedly** /ˌʌnəˈʃeɪmɪdli/ ADV ❑ *...an unashamedly old-fashioned tradition.*

unattractive /ˌʌnəˈtræktɪv/ **1** ADJ **Unattractive** people and things are unpleasant in their appearance. **2** ADJ If you describe something as **unattractive**, you mean that people do not like it and do not want to be involved with it. ❑ *The Church is unattractive to many young people.*

unauthorized [BRIT also **unauthorised**] /ˌʌnˈɔːθəraɪzd/ ADJ If something is **unauthorized**, it has been produced or is happening without official permission. ❑ *They were arrested for taking unauthorized photographs.*

unavailable /ˌʌnəˈveɪləbəl/ ADJ When things or people are **unavailable**, you cannot obtain them, meet them, or talk to them. ❑ *Mr Hicks is out of the country and unavailable for meetings.*

unavoidable /ˌʌnəˈvɔɪdəbəl/ ADJ If something bad is **unavoidable**, it cannot be avoided or prevented. ❑ *Stress is an unavoidable part of life for most people.*

Word Link *war ≈ watchful : aware, beware, unaware*

unaware /ˌʌnəˈweə/ ADJ AFTER LINK-V If you are **unaware of** something, you do not know about it. ❑ *She appeared to be unaware of the dangers.*

Word Partnership Use *unaware* with:

ADV. **apparently** unaware, **blissfully** unaware, **completely** unaware, **totally** unaware

unbalanced /ʌnˈbælənst/ **1** ADJ If you describe someone as **unbalanced**, you mean that they appear to be very disturbed or upset, and perhaps mentally ill. ❑ *He is mentally unbalanced.* **2** ADJ If you describe something such as a report or argument as **unbalanced**, you think that it is unfair or inaccurate because it emphasizes some things and ignores others.

unbearable /ʌnˈbeərəbəl/ ADJ If you describe something as **unbearable**, you mean that it is so unpleasant, painful, or upsetting that you feel unable to accept it or deal with it. ❑ *War has made life almost unbearable for us.* ● **unbearably** ADV ❑ *It was unbearably hot.*

unbeatable /ˌʌnˈbiːtəbəl/ ADJ If you describe something as **unbeatable**, you mean that it is the best thing of its kind. ❑ *Holiday resorts in Spain are unbeatable in terms of price.*

unbeaten /ˌʌnˈbiːtən/ ADJ In sport, if a person or their performance is **unbeaten**, nobody has ever beaten them. ❑ *He's unbeaten in 20 fights.*

unbelievable /ˌʌnbɪˈliːvəbəl/ **1** ADJ If you say that something is **unbelievable**, you are emphasizing that it is very extreme, impressive, or shocking. ❑ *The pressure we were under was unbelievable.* ❑ *It was an unbelievable moment when Chris won.* ● **unbelievably** ADV ❑ *What you did was unbelievably stupid.* **2** ADJ If an idea or theory is **unbelievable**, it is so unlikely or so illogical that you cannot believe it. ❑ *I know it sounds unbelievable but I never wanted to cheat.* ● **unbelievably** ADV ❑ *Lainey was, unbelievably, pregnant again.*

Thesaurus *unbelievable* Also look up:

ADJ. astounding, incredible, remarkable **1** inconceivable, preposterous, unimaginable **3**

unborn /ˌʌnˈbɔːn/ ADJ & N-PLURAL An **unborn** child is still inside its mother's womb or is going to be born in the future. **The unborn** are children who are not born yet. ❑ *At 16 weeks, the mother can feel the unborn child move.*

unbroken /ˌʌnˈbrəʊkən/ ADJ If something is **unbroken**, it is continuous or complete. ❑ *We've had ten days of almost unbroken sunshine.*

uncanny /ˌʌnˈkæni/ ADJ If something is **uncanny**, it is strange and difficult to explain. ❑ *I had this uncanny feeling that I was seeing the future.* ● **uncannily** ADV ❑ *The night was uncannily quiet.*

uncertain /ʌnˈsɜːtən/ **1** ADJ If you are **uncertain about** something, you do not know what to do. ❑ *He was uncertain about his brother's plans.* ❑ *They were uncertain how to proceed.* ● **uncertainly** ADV ❑ *He entered the room and stood uncertainly.* **2** ADJ If something is **uncertain**, it is not known or not definite. ❑ *It's uncertain whether they will agree.* **3** PHRASE If you say that someone tells a person something **in no uncertain terms**, you are emphasizing that they say it firmly and clearly so that there is no doubt about what they mean.

Word Partnership Use *uncertain* with:

PREP. uncertain **about** ***something*** **1**
V. **be** uncertain, **remain** uncertain **1** **2**
ADV. **highly** uncertain, **still** uncertain **1** **2**

U

uncertainty /ʌnˈsɜːtənti/ (**uncertainties**) N-VAR **Uncertainty** is a state of doubt about the future or about what is the right thing to do. ❑ *...uncertainties about the future of the company.*

unchallenged /ˌʌnˈtʃælɪndʒd/ ADJ When something is **unchallenged**, people accept it without questioning whether it is right or wrong. ❑ *This new research has gone unchallenged.*

unchanged /ˌʌnˈtʃeɪndʒd/ ADJ Something that is **unchanged** has stayed the same during a period of time. ❑ *Prices have remained largely unchanged over* the past six months.

uncharacteristic /ˌʌnkærɪktəˈrɪstɪk/ ADJ If an action or mood is **uncharacteristic of** someone, it is not their usual type of behaviour. ❑ *It was uncharacteristic of her father to disappear like this.* • **uncharacteristically** ADV ❑ *Owen has been uncharacteristically silent.*

unchecked /ˌʌnˈtʃekt/ ADJ If something undesirable is left **unchecked**, it keeps growing without anyone trying to stop it. ❑ *The fighting continued unchecked for seven days.*

uncle /ˈʌŋkəl/ (**uncles**) N-COUNT Your **uncle** is the brother of your mother or father, or the husband of your aunt.
→ see **family**

unclear /ˌʌnˈklɪə/ **1** ADJ If something is **unclear**, it is not known or not certain. ❑ *It is unclear how much money they have.* **2** ADJ AFTER LINK-V If you are **unclear about** something, you do not understand it properly or are not sure about it. ❑ *He is still unclear about his own future.*

uncomfortable /ˌʌnˈkʌmftəbəl/ **1** ADJ If you are **uncomfortable**, you are not physically relaxed, and feel slight pain or discomfort. • **uncomfortably** ADV ❑ *When he awoke he found himself lying uncomfortably on the floor.* **2** ADJ If you are **uncomfortable**, you are slightly worried or embarrassed, and not relaxed and confident. • **uncomfortably** ADV ❑ *Dr Willcox pulled uncomfortably at his tie.* **3** ADJ Something that is **uncomfortable** makes you feel slight pain or physical discomfort when you experience it or use it. ❑ *...an uncomfortable chair.*

Thesaurus *uncomfortable* Also look up:

ADJ.	awkward, embarrassed, troubled; *(ant.)* comfortable **2**
	irritating, painful **1** **3**

uncomplicated /ˌʌnˈkɒmplɪkeɪtɪd/ ADJ **Uncomplicated** things are simple and straightforward. ❑ *...his uncomplicated sense of humour.*

uncompromising /ˌʌnˈkɒmprəmaɪzɪŋ/ ADJ If you describe someone as **uncompromising**, you mean that they are determined not to change their opinions or aims in any way. ❑ *...a tough and uncompromising politician.*

unconcerned /ˌʌnkənˈsɜːnd/ ADJ If someone is **unconcerned about** something, they are not interested in it or not worried about it. ❑ *Sue is unconcerned about her health.*

U

unconditional /ˌʌnkənˈdɪʃənəl/ ADJ Something that is **unconditional** is done or given to someone freely, without anything being required in return. ❑ *Children need unconditional love.* • **unconditionally** ADV ❑ *The prisoners were released unconditionally.*

unconfirmed /ˌʌnkənˈfɜːmd/ ADJ If a report or rumour is **unconfirmed**, there is not yet any definite proof that it is true.

unconnected /ˌʌnkəˈnektɪd/ ADJ If two things are **unconnected with** each other, they are not related to each other in any way. ❑ *Her personal problems are unconnected with her marriage.*

unconscious /ˌʌnˈkɒnʃəs/ **1** ADJ Someone who is **unconscious** is in a state similar to sleep, as a result of a shock, accident, or injury. ❑ *He was beaten unconscious by two men.* • **unconsciousness** N-UNCOUNT ❑ *He slipped into unconsciousness.* **2** ADJ If you are **unconscious of** something, you are unaware of it. Similarly, if feelings or attitudes are **unconscious**, you are unaware of them. ❑ *Mr Battersby was quite unconscious of their presence in the room.* ❑ *...an unconscious fear of being abandoned.* • **unconsciously** ADV ❑ *Rachel watched the dancing, unconsciously tapping her foot in time to the music.* **3** N-SING In psychology, **the unconscious** is the part of your mind which contains feelings and ideas that you do not know about or cannot control.
→ see **dream**

unconstitutional /ˌʌnkɒnstɪˈtjuːʃənəl, AM -ˈtuː-/ ADJ Something that is **unconstitutional** is against the rules of an organization or political system. ❑ *The parliament declared the elections unconstitutional.*

uncontrollable /ˌʌnkənˈtrəʊləbəl/ ADJ If something such as an emotion is **uncontrollable**, you can do nothing to prevent it or control it. ❑ *He burst into uncontrollable laughter.* • **uncontrollably** ADV ❑ *I started shaking uncontrollably.*

uncontrolled /ˌʌnkənˈtrəʊld/ ADJ If something such as a feeling or activity is **uncontrolled**, no attempt is made to stop or restrain it. ❑ *The children have uncontrolled use of the television.*

unconventional /ˌʌnkənˈvenʃənəl/ ADJ If someone is **unconventional**, they do not behave in the same way as most other people in their society. ❑ *He had rather unconventional work habits, preferring to work through the night.*

unconvincing /ˌʌnkənˈvɪnsɪŋ/ ADJ If you describe a statement, argument, or explanation as **unconvincing**, you do not believe it is true or valid. ❑ *Her reasons were unconvincing.* • **unconvincingly** ADV ❑ *'Yes, I like it,' he said, unconvincingly.*

ˌuncount ˈnoun (**uncount nouns**) N-COUNT An **uncount noun** or an **uncountable noun** is a noun such as 'gold' or 'information' which does not have a plural and can be used without a determiner.

uncover /ˌʌnˈkʌvə/ (**uncovers, uncovering, uncovered**) **1** V-T If you **uncover** something secret, you find out about it. ❑ *The army uncovered evidence of war crimes.* **2** V-T To **uncover** something means to remove a cover from it.

Word Partnership Use *uncover* with:

N.	uncover **a plot**, uncover **evidence**, uncover **the truth** **1**
V.	**help** uncover ***something*** **1** **2**

undaunted /ˌʌnˈdɔːntɪd/ ADJ If you are **undaunted**, you are confident about dealing with something that would frighten or worry most people. ❑ *He seems undaunted by his problems.*

Word Link ***un ≈ not : undecided, undressed, unfair***

undecided /ˌʌndɪˈsaɪdɪd/ ADJ If you are **undecided** about something, you have not yet made a decision about it. ❑ *She was undecided about what to wear.*

Word Link *demo ≈ people : democracy, democratically, undemocratic*

undemocratic /ˌʌndeməˈkrætɪk/ ADJ In an **undemocratic** system, decisions are made by a small number of powerful people without consulting all the people who are affected; used showing disapproval.

undeniable /ˌʌndɪˈnaɪəbəl/ ADJ If something is **undeniable**, it is definitely true or definitely exists. ❑ *Her talent is undeniable.* ● **undeniably** ADV ❑ *Bringing up a baby is undeniably hard work.*

under /ˈʌndə/ 1 PREP If something is **under** something else, it is directly below or beneath it. ❑ *I put my head under the blanket.* ❑ *A boat passed under the bridge.* 2 PREP & ADV If something or someone is **under** a particular age or amount, they are less than that age or amount. ❑ *This year the company spent just under £15 billion.* ❑ *This is a film for children aged six and under.* 3 PREP If something happens **under** particular circumstances or conditions, it happens when those circumstances or conditions exist. ❑ *Under normal circumstances, the men would never have met.* ❑ *They worked under pressure.* 4 PREP If people live or work **under** a particular person, that person is their ruler, boss, or teacher. ❑ *I am the new manager and you will be working under me.* ❑ *The artists studied under Beuys.* 5 PREP If you do something **under** a particular name, you use that name instead of your real name. ❑ *Mrs Collins is a novelist, writing under the name Claire Hunter.* 6 PREP You use **under** to say which section of a list, book, or system something is classified in. ❑ *This study is described under 'General Diseases of the Eye'.* ❑ *'Where will it be?'—'Filed under C, second drawer down.'*
→ see **location**

underclass /ˈʌndəklɑːs, -klæs/ (**underclasses**) N-COUNT The **underclass** consists of people who are poor, and who have little chance of improving their situation.

undercover /ˌʌndəˈkʌvə/ ADJ **Undercover** work involves secretly obtaining information for the government or the police. ❑ *...an undercover investigation.*

undercurrent /ˈʌndəkʌrənt, -kɜːr-/ (**undercurrents**) N-COUNT If there is an **undercurrent of** a feeling, the feeling exists in a weak form, and may become powerful later. ❑ *...a growing undercurrent of fear.*

undercut /ˌʌndəˈkʌt/ (**undercuts, undercutting, undercut**) V-T If a business **undercuts** its competitors or their prices, it sells a product more cheaply than its competitors.

underdeveloped /ˌʌndədɪˈveləpt/ ADJ An **underdeveloped** country does not have modern industries, and usually has a low standard of living. Some people prefer to use the term **developing**.

underdog /ˈʌndədɒg, AM -dɔːg/ (**underdogs**) N-COUNT The **underdog** in a contest is the person who seems least likely to succeed or win.

underestimate /ˌʌndərˈestɪmeɪt/ (**underestimates, underestimating, underestimated**) 1 V-T If you **underestimate** something, you do not realize how large it is or will be. ❑ *They underestimated how much work they needed to do.* 2 V-T If you **underestimate** someone, you do not realize what they are capable of doing. ❑ *Don't make the mistake of underestimating him.*

undergo /ˌʌndəˈgəʊ/ (**undergoes, undergoing, underwent, undergone**) V-T If you **undergo** something necessary or unpleasant, it happens to you. ❑ *New recruits have been undergoing training.* ❑ *He recently underwent brain surgery.*

undergraduate /ˌʌndəˈgrædʒʊət/ (**undergraduates**) N-COUNT An **undergraduate** is a student at a university or college who is studying for his or her first degree. ❑ *...a 21-year-old history undergraduate.*

Word Link *ground ≈ bottom : background, groundwork, underground*

underground

adverb /ˌʌndəˈgraʊnd/; noun and adjective /ˈʌndəgraʊnd/.

1 ADV & ADJ BEFORE N Something that is **underground** is below the surface of the ground. ❑ *The tourists were trapped underground for nine days.* ❑ *...an underground car park.* 2 N-SING In British English, **the underground** in a city is the railway system in which electric trains travel below the ground in tunnels. The American word is **subway**. 3 ADJ BEFORE N **Underground** political activities take place secretly, and are directed against the government. ❑ *...underground political groups.*
→ see **tunnel**

undergrowth /ˈʌndəgrəʊθ/ N-UNCOUNT **Undergrowth** consists of bushes and plants growing closely together under trees. [BRIT] ❑ *He pushed his way through the undergrowth.*

underlie /ˌʌndəˈlaɪ/ (**underlies, underlying, underlay, underlain**) V-T If something **underlies** a feeling or situation, it is the cause or basis of it. ❑ *Try to figure out what underlies your anger.*

underline /ˌʌndəˈlaɪn/ (**underlines, underlining, underlined**) 1 V-T In British English, if a person or event **underlines** something, they draw attention to it and emphasize its importance. The American word is **underscore**. ❑ *The Second World War underlined the importance of science and technology.* 2 V-T In British English, if you **underline** a word or sentence, you draw a line underneath it. The American word is **underscore**.

Word Partnership Use *underline* with:

N. underline **the need for *something*** 1
underline **passages**, underline **text**, underline **titles**, underline **words** 2

underlying /ˌʌndəˈlaɪɪŋ/ ADJ BEFORE N The **underlying** aspects of an event or situation are the aspects that are not obvious but that have great significance or effect. ❑ *To solve a problem you have to understand its underlying causes.*

undermine /ˌʌndəˈmaɪn/ (**undermines, undermining, undermined**) V-T To **undermine** someone or something means to make them less certain or less secure. ❑ *He felt that she was trying to undermine his authority.*

Word Partnership Use *undermine* with:

N. undermine **authority**, undermine **confidence**, undermine **government**, undermine **peace**, undermine **security**
V. **threaten to** undermine, **try to** undermine

underneath /ˌʌndəˈniːθ/ 1 PREP & ADV If one thing is **underneath** another, it is directly below or beneath it. ❑ *I was lying with my arm underneath me, and I couldn't move.* 2 ADV & N-SING The part of something which is **underneath** is the part which normally touches the ground or faces towards the ground. **The underneath of** something is the part which is underneath. ❑ *Look underneath the chair.* ❑ *I know what the underneath of a car looks like.* 3 ADV & PREP You use **underneath** when you are talking about feelings and emotions that people do not show in their behaviour. ❑ *Underneath her calm manner was a growing sense of panic.*
→ see **location**

underpants /ˈʌndəpænts/ N-PLURAL **Underpants** are a piece of underwear with two holes for your legs and elastic around the waist. In British English, **underpants** refers only to men's underwear. In American English it refers to both men's and women's underwear.

underrate /ˌʌndəˈreɪt/ (**underrates, underrating, underrated**) V-T If you **underrate** someone, you do not realize how clever, able, or important they are. ● **underrated** ADJ ❑ *He is a very underrated poet.*

underscore /ˌʌndəˈskɔː/ (**underscores, underscoring, underscored**) 1 V-T In American English, if a person or an event **underscores** something, they draw attention to it and emphasize its importance. The British word is **underline**. ❑ *The recent violence underscores how serious the problems are.* 2 V-T In American English, if you **underscore** a word or a sentence, you draw a line underneath it. The British word is **underline**. 3 N-COUNT You say **underscore** to refer to a line that underlines letters or words. For example, if you are giving the email address 'Dave_Sims@hotmail.com' you say 'Dave underscore Sims at hotmail dot com'.

underside /ˈʌndəsaɪd/ (**undersides**) N-COUNT The **underside of** something is the part of it which normally faces towards the ground.

understand /ˌʌndəˈstænd/ (**understands, understanding, understood**) 1 V-T If you **understand** someone, or if you **understand** what they are saying, you know what they mean. ❑ *I don't understand what you are talking about.* ❑ *She could not understand a word of English.* 2 V-T To **understand** someone means to know how they feel and why they behave in the way that they do. ❑ *My husband and I understand each other very well.* 3 V-T You say that you **understand** something when you know why or how it happens. ❑ *They are too young to understand what is going on.* 4 V-T If you say that you **understand** that something is true, you mean that you think it is the truth because you have heard or read that it is. [FORMAL] ❑ *I understand that he's just retired.*
→ see **philosophy**

U

Thesaurus	*understand*	Also look up:
V.	catch on, comprehend, get, grasp; (*ant.*) misunderstand 1	

understandable /ˌʌndəˈstændəbəl/ ADJ If you describe someone's behaviour or feelings as **understandable**, you mean that they have reacted to a situation in a natural way or in the way you would expect. ❑ *It is understandable that Mr Khan wants to go home.* ● **understandably** ADV ❑ *Most organizations are, quite understandably, suspicious of new ideas.*

understanding /ˌʌndəˈstændɪŋ/ (**understandings**) 1 N-SING & N-UNCOUNT If you have an **understanding of** something, you know how it works or what it means. ❑ *They need to have a basic understanding of computers.* ❑ *Mr Smith has little understanding of how the system works.* 2 ADJ If you are **understanding** towards someone, you are kind and forgiving. ❑ *John has a very understanding wife.* 3 N-UNCOUNT If there is **understanding between** people, they are friendly towards each other and trust each other. ❑ *The organization promotes understanding between people of different religions.* 4 N-COUNT An **understanding** is an informal agreement about something. ❑ *We had an understanding that we would meet up in the summer.*

Word Partnership	Use *understanding* with:
V.	**develop** understanding, **difficulty** understanding, **have trouble** understanding, **lack** understanding 1
ADV.	**basic** understanding, **clear** understanding, **complete** understanding 1
	better understanding, **deep/deeper** understanding, **greater** understanding 1-3
	mutual understanding 3 4

understate /ˌʌndəˈsteɪt/ (**understates, understating, understated**) V-T If you **understate** something, you describe it in a way that suggests that it is less important or serious than it really is. ❑ *The figures understate the extent of the problem.*

understated /ˌʌndəˈsteɪtɪd/ ADJ BEFORE N If you describe a style, colour, or effect as **understated**, you like it because it is not obvious. ❑ *...understated elegance.*

understatement /ˈʌndəsteɪtmənt/ (**understatements**) N-VAR An **understatement** is a statement which does not fully express the extent to which something is true. ❑ *To say I'm disappointed is an understatement.*

understood /ˌʌndəˈstʊd/ **Understood** is the past tense and past participle of **understand**.

undertake /ˌʌndəˈteɪk/ (**undertakes, undertaking, undertook, undertaken**) 1 V-T When you **undertake** a task or job, you start doing it and accept responsibility for it. [FORMAL] ❑ *She undertook a major reorganization of the legal department.* ● **undertaking** (**undertakings**) N-COUNT ❑ *Organizing the show has been a massive undertaking.* 2 V-T If you **undertake to** do something, you promise that you will do it. [FORMAL] ❑ *He undertook to write the report himself.* ● **undertaking** N-COUNT ❑ *Frank gave an undertaking to be a good parent.*

undertaker /ˈʌndəteɪkə/ (**undertakers**) N-COUNT In British English, an **undertaker** is a person whose job is to deal with the bodies of people who have died and to arrange funerals. The American word is **mortician**.

undertook /ˌʌndəˈtʊk/ **Undertook** is the past tense of **undertake**.

undervalue /ˌʌndəˈvæljuː/ (**undervalues, undervaluing, undervalued**) V-T If you **undervalue** something, you fail to recognize how valuable or important it is. ❑ *We must never undervalue freedom.*

underwater /ˌʌndəˈwɔːtə/ ADV & ADJ BEFORE N Something that exists or happens **underwater** exists or happens below the surface of the sea, a river, or a lake. ❑ *Scuba divers spend hours underwater at temperatures just above freezing.* ❑ *...underwater photography.*

underway /ˌʌndəˈweɪ/ ADJ AFTER LINK-V If an activity gets **underway**, it starts. If an activity is **underway**, it has already started. ❑ *Talks are underway in Washington.*

underwear /ˈʌndəweə/ N-UNCOUNT **Underwear** is clothing which you wear next to your skin under your other clothes, such as a **bra**, a **vest** and **underpants**.

underwent /ˌʌndəˈwent/ **Underwent** is the past tense of **undergo**.

underworld /ˈʌndəwɜːld/ N-SING The **underworld** consists of organized crime and the people involved in it. ❑ *...a wealthy businessman with underworld connections.*

undesirable /ˌʌndɪˈzaɪərəbəl/ ADJ If you describe something or someone as **undesirable**, you think they will have harmful effects. ❑ *These drugs can have undesirable side-effects.*

undid /ʌnˈdɪd/ **Undid** is the past tense of **undo**.

undisclosed /ˌʌndɪsˈkləʊzd/ ADJ **Undisclosed** information has not been revealed to the public. ❑ *She was paid an undisclosed sum by her former employer.*

Word Link	*put ≈ thinking : computer, dispute, undisputed*

undisputed /ˌʌndɪˈspjuːtɪd/ ADJ If you describe something as **undisputed**, you mean that everyone accepts that it exists or is true. ❑ *Many people see Madonna as the undisputed queen of pop music.*

undisturbed /ˌʌndɪˈstɜːbd/ **1** ADJ Something that remains **undisturbed** has not been touched, moved, or changed. ❑ *The desk looked undisturbed.* **2** ADJ If you are **undisturbed** in something that you are doing, you are able to continue doing it and are not affected by something that is happening. ❑ *He was able to work undisturbed.*

Word Link	*un ≈ reversal : untie, undo, unwrap*

undo /ʌnˈduː/ (**undoes, undoing, undid, undone**) **1** V-T If you **undo** something, you unfasten, loosen, or untie it. ❑ *She undid the buttons of her jacket.* **2** V-T To **undo** something that has been done means to reverse its effect. ❑ *It will be difficult to undo the damage.*

undoing /ʌnˈduːɪŋ/ N-SING If you say that something is someone's **undoing**, you mean that it is the cause of their failure. ❑ *His lack of experience may prove to be his undoing.*

undoubted /ʌnˈdaʊtɪd/ ADJ You can use **undoubted** to emphasize that something exists or is true. ❑ *The event was an undoubted success.* ● **undoubtedly** ADV ❑ *He is undoubtedly a very talented player.*

Word Link	*un ≈ not : undecided, undressed, unfair*

undress /ʌnˈdres/ (**undresses, undressing, undressed**) **1** V-T/V-I When you **undress**, you take off your clothes. If you **undress** someone, you take off their clothes. ● **undressed** ADJ ❑ *He got undressed in the bathroom.* **2** → See note at **wear**

undue /ʌnˈdjuː, AM -ˈduː/ ADJ BEFORE N If you describe something bad as **undue**, you mean that it is greater or more extreme than you think is reasonable. ❑ *We do not wish to cause any undue suffering.* ● **unduly** ADV ❑ *The report was unduly complicated.*

Word Partnership	Use *undue* with:
N.	undue **attention**, undue **burden**, undue **delay**, undue **emphasis**, undue **hardship**, undue **influence**, undue **interference**, undue **pressure**, undue **risk**

undulating /ˈʌndʒʊleɪtɪŋ/ ADJ **Undulating** means having gentle curves or slopes, or moving gently and slowly up and down or from side to side. [LITERARY] ❑ *...gently undulating hills.*

unearth /ʌnˈɜːθ/ (**unearths, unearthing, unearthed**) V-T If someone **unearths** something hidden or secret, they discover it. ❑ *Researchers have unearthed documents from the 1600s.*

unease /ʌnˈiːz/ N-UNCOUNT If you have a feeling of **unease**, you feel that something is wrong and you are anxious or uncomfortable about it. ❑ *The atmosphere on the streets was one of unease.*

uneasy /ʌnˈiːzi/ **1** ADJ If you are **uneasy**, you feel that something is wrong and you are anxious or uncomfortable about it. ❑ *I started to feel uneasy about my new career.* ● **uneasily** ADV ❑ *Meg shifted uneasily on her chair.* ● **uneasiness** N-UNCOUNT ❑ *I felt a great uneasiness about meeting her again.* **2** ADJ If you describe a situation or relationship as **uneasy**, you mean that it is not settled and may not continue. ❑ *An uneasy calm has settled over Los Angeles.*

unemployed /ˌʌnɪmˈplɔɪd/ ADJ & N-PLURAL Someone who is **unemployed** does not have a job although they want one. **The unemployed** are people who are unemployed.

unemployment /ˌʌnɪmˈplɔɪmənt/ N-UNCOUNT **Unemployment** is the fact that people who want jobs cannot get them. ❑ *...the highest unemployment rate in western Europe.*

unequivocal /ˌʌnɪˈkwɪvəkəl/ ADJ If you describe someone's attitude as **unequivocal**, you mean that it is very clear and firm. [FORMAL] ❑ *The message to him was unequivocal: 'Get out'.* ● **unequivocally** ADV ❑ *He stated unequivocally that the French were ready to go to war.*

unethical /ʌnˈeθɪkəl/ ADJ If you describe someone's behaviour as **unethical**, you think it is morally wrong. [FORMAL] ❑ *It is unethical to record people's conversations without telling them.*

uneven /ʌnˈiːvən/ **1** ADJ An **uneven** surface is not level or smooth. ❑ *...the uneven surface of the car park.* **2** ADJ Something that is **uneven** is not regular or consistent. ❑ *Her breathing was uneven.*

Thesaurus *uneven* Also look up:
ADJ. jagged, rough; *(ant.)* even 1
inconsistent, irregular 2

unexpected /ˌʌnɪk'spektɪd/ ADJ Something that is **unexpected** surprises you because you did not think it was likely to happen. ❑ *His death was totally unexpected.* ● **unexpectedly** ADV ❑ *Mr Kirk had arrived unexpectedly early.*

Thesaurus *unexpected* Also look up:
ADJ. startling, surprising

unexplained /ˌʌnɪk'spleɪnd/ ADJ If something is **unexplained**, the reason for it or the cause of it is unclear or is not known. ❑ *...the unexplained death of their leader.*

Word Link *un ≈ not : undecided, undressed, unfair*

unfair /ˌʌn'feə/ ADJ Something that is **unfair** is not right or not just. ❑ *It was unfair that he suffered so much.* ● **unfairly** ADV ❑ *She claims she was unfairly treated.* ● **unfairness** N-UNCOUNT ❑ *He was angry at the unfairness of life.*

ˌunfair disˈmissal N-UNCOUNT If an employee claims **unfair dismissal**, they begin a legal action against their employer in which they claim that they were dismissed from their job unfairly.

unfaithful /ˌʌn'feɪθfʊl/ ADJ If someone is **unfaithful to** their lover or to the person they are married to, they have a sexual relationship with someone else. ❑ *James had been unfaithful to her many times.* ❑ *...his unfaithful wife.*

unfamiliar /ˌʌnfə'mɪlɪə/ ADJ If something is **unfamiliar to** you, or if you are **unfamiliar with** it, you know very little about it and have not seen or experienced it before. ❑ *She is unfamiliar with Japanese culture.*

unfashionable /ˌʌn'fæʃənəbəl/ ADJ If something is **unfashionable**, it is not approved of or done by most people. ❑ *Wearing fur became deeply unfashionable.*

unfavourable [AM **unfavorable**] /ˌʌn'feɪvərəbəl/ 1 ADJ **Unfavourable** conditions or circumstances cause problems and reduce the chance of success. ❑ *...unfavourable conditions for British industry.* 2 ADJ If you have an **unfavourable** reaction **to** something, you do not like it. ● **unfavourably** ADV ❑ *The report compares the UK unfavourably with other European countries.*

U

unfinished /ˌʌn'fɪnɪʃt/ ADJ If something is **unfinished**, it has not been completed. ❑ *...Jane Austen's unfinished novel.*

unfit /ˌʌn'fɪt/ 1 ADJ If you are **unfit**, your body is not in good condition because you have not been taking regular exercise. 2 ADJ If someone or something is **unfit for** a particular purpose, they are not suitable or not of a good enough quality. ❑ *The doctor said she was mentally unfit for work.*

unfold /ˌʌn'fəʊld/ (**unfolds, unfolding, unfolded**) 1 V-I When a situation or story **unfolds**, it develops and becomes known or understood. ❑ *The facts started to unfold before them.* 2 V-T/V-I If someone **unfolds** something which has been folded or if it **unfolds**, it is opened out and becomes flat. ❑ *He quickly unfolded the blankets.*

Word Link *fore ≈ before : forecast, foresight, unforeseen*

unforeseen /ˌʌnfə'siːn/ ADJ An **unforeseen** event happens unexpectedly. ❑ *Her office was shut due to unforeseen circumstances.*

unforgettable /ˌʌnfə'getəbəl/ ADJ If something is **unforgettable**, it is so impressive that you are likely to remember it for a long time. ❑ *A visit to the British Museum is an unforgettable experience.*

unfortunate /ʌn'fɔːtʃʊnət/ 1 ADJ If you say that someone is **unfortunate**, you mean that something unpleasant or unlucky has happened to them. ❑ *He was one of those unfortunate people who put on weight very easily.* 2 ADJ If you say that something that has happened is **unfortunate**, you mean that it is a pity that it happened. ❑ *I would like to apologise to all concerned in this unfortunate incident.*

unfortunately /ʌn'fɔːtʃʊnətli/ ADV You can use **unfortunately** to express regret about what you are saying. ❑ *Unfortunately, my time is limited.* ❑ *I received a C for accounts and maths, but unfortunately I failed geography.*

unfounded /ˌʌn'faʊndɪd/ ADJ If you say that a belief is **unfounded**, you mean that it is wrong, and is not based on facts or evidence. ❑ *The stories in the newspapers are unfounded.*

unfriendly /ˌʌn'frendli/ ADJ If you describe someone as **unfriendly**, you mean that they behave in an unkind or hostile way. ❑ *The staff in the café are slow and unfriendly.*

unfulfilled /ˌʌnfʊl'fɪld/ 1 ADJ You say that a hope is **unfulfilled** when the thing that you hoped for has not happened. ❑ *Do you have any unfulfilled ambitions?* 2 ADJ If someone feels **unfulfilled**, they feel dissatisfied with life or with their achievements.

unfurl /ˌʌn'fɜːl/ (**unfurls, unfurling, unfurled**) V-T/V-I If you **unfurl** something such as a flag or umbrella, or if it **unfurls**, you unroll or unfold it so that it is flat or open and can be seen or used. ❑ *The protesters unfurled a banner saying 'Stop the cuts!'*

unhappy /ʌn'hæpi/ (**unhappier, unhappiest**) 1 ADJ If you are **unhappy**, you are sad and depressed. ● **unhappily** ADV ❑ *...an unhappily married woman.* ● **unhappiness** N-UNCOUNT ❑ *There was a lot of unhappiness during my teenage years.* 2 ADJ AFTER LINK-V If you are **unhappy about** something, you are not pleased about it or not satisfied with it. ❑ *The public is unhappy that the government isn't doing more.* ● **unhappiness** N-UNCOUNT ❑ *...his unhappiness with the decision.* 3 ADJ BEFORE N An **unhappy** situation is not satisfactory or desirable. ❑ *This event is part of the unhappy state of British politics.*

Thesaurus *unhappy* Also look up:
ADJ. depressed, miserable, sad; *(ant.)* happy 1

unharmed /ˌʌn'hɑːmd/ ADJ If someone or something is **unharmed** after an accident or violent incident, they are not hurt or damaged in any way. ❑ *His daughter was unharmed in the attack.*

unhealthy /ʌn'helθi/ (**unhealthier, unhealthiest**) 1 ADJ Something that is

unhealthy is likely to cause illness or poor health. ❑ *...unhealthy foods such as chips.* 2 ADJ If you are **unhealthy**, you are not very fit or well.

ˌun'heard of ADJ You can say that an event or situation is **unheard of** when it never happens, or has never happened before. ❑ *Working women with children were almost unheard of in those days.*

unhelpful /ˌʌn'helpfʊl/ ADJ If you say that someone or something is **unhelpful**, you mean that they do not help you or improve a situation, and may even make things worse. ❑ *The criticism is both unfair and unhelpful.*

unhurt /ˌʌn'hɜːt/ ADJ If someone who has been attacked, or involved in an accident, is **unhurt**, they are not injured. ❑ *The lorry driver escaped unhurt, but a pedestrian was injured.*

> **Word Link** *ident ≈ same : identical, identification, unidentified*

unidentified /ˌʌnaɪ'dentɪfaɪd/ ADJ If you describe someone or something as **unidentified**, you mean that nobody knows who or what they are. ❑ *The man was shot by an unidentified gunman in the street.*

unification /ˌjuːnɪfɪ'keɪʃən/ N-UNCOUNT **Unification** is the process by which two or more countries join together and become one country.

> **Word Link** *uni ≈ one : uniform, unilateral, union*

uniform /'juːnɪfɔːm/ (**uniforms**) 1 N-VAR A **uniform** is a special set of clothes which some people wear to work in, and which some children wear at school. ❑ *Philip was in uniform.* 2 ADJ If something is **uniform**, it does not vary, but is even and regular throughout. ❑ *Chips should be cut into uniform size.* ● **uniformity** /ˌjuːnɪ'fɔːmɪti/ N-UNCOUNT ❑ *...uniformity of colour.* ● **uniformly** ADV ❑ *...a uniformly blue sky.* 3 ADJ If you describe a number of things as **uniform**, you mean that they are all the same. ❑ *...a uniform row of boring houses.* ● **uniformity** N-UNCOUNT ❑ *...the dull uniformity of the architecture.* ● **uniformly** ADV ❑ *The teachers uniformly agreed.*

uniform

uniformed /'juːnɪfɔːmd/ ADJ **Uniformed** people such as police officers wear a uniform while doing their job. ❑ *Three uniformed men knocked at the door early in the morning.*

unify /'juːnɪfaɪ/ (**unifies, unifying, unified**) V-T/V-I If someone **unifies** different things or parts, or if the things or parts **unify**, they are brought together to form one thing. ❑ *West and East Germany were unified in 1990.* ● **unified** ADJ ❑ *...a unified system of education.*

unilateral /ˌjuːnɪ'lætərəl/ ADJ A **unilateral** decision or action is taken by only one of the groups or countries involved in a particular situation, without the agreement of the others. ❑ *They ended the unilateral ceasefire on September 1 2000.*

unimaginable /ˌʌnɪ'mædʒɪnəbəl/ ADJ If you describe something as **unimaginable**, you are emphasizing that it is difficult to imagine or understand properly, because it is not part of people's normal experience. ❑ *The children here have experienced unimaginable horrors.* ● **unimaginably** ADV ❑ *The prisons here are unimaginably bad.*

unimportant /ˌʌnɪm'pɔːtənt/ ADJ If you describe something or someone as **unimportant**, you mean that they do not have much effect or value, and are therefore not worth considering.

unimpressed /ˌʌnɪm'prest/ ADJ AFTER LINK-V If you are **unimpressed by** something or someone, you do not think they are particularly good or important.

uninhibited /ˌʌnɪn'hɪbɪtɪd/ ADJ If you describe a person as **uninhibited**, you mean that they express their opinions and feelings openly, and behave as they want to, without worrying what other people think.

uninstall /ˌʌnɪn'stɔːl/ (**uninstalls, uninstalling, uninstalled**) V-T If you **uninstall** a computer program, you remove it permanently from your computer. [COMPUTING]

unintentional /ˌʌnɪn'tenʃənəl/ ADJ Something that is **unintentional** is not done deliberately, but happens by accident. ● **unintentionally** ADV ❑ *The film is an unintentionally funny adaptation of 'Dracula'.*

uninterrupted /ˌʌnɪntə'rʌptɪd/ ADJ If something is **uninterrupted**, it continues without any breaks or interruptions. ❑ *...an uninterrupted night's sleep.*

union /'juːnjən/ (**unions**) 1 N-COUNT A **union** is the same as a **trade union**. 2 N-UNCOUNT When the **union** of two or more things occurs, they are joined together and become one thing. ❑ *Britain should move towards closer union with its neighbours.*
→ see **empire, factory**

unionist /'juːnjənɪst/ (**unionists**) N-COUNT A **unionist** is someone who believes in the set of political principles based on the idea that two or more political or national units should be joined or remain together.

unique /juː'niːk/ 1 ADJ Something that is **unique** is the only one of its kind. ❑ *Each person's signature is unique.* ● **uniquely** ADV ❑ *Wilfred Owen's poetry is uniquely British.* ● **uniqueness** N-UNCOUNT ❑ *I like the uniqueness of the flavours in Australian cooking.* 2 ADJ AFTER LINK-V If something is **unique to** one thing or person, it concerns or belongs only to that thing or person. ❑ *This animal is unique to Borneo.* ● **uniquely** ADV ❑ *The problem is uniquely American.* 3 ADJ Some people use **unique** to mean very unusual and special. ❑ *Kauffman was a woman of unique talent.* ● **uniquely** ADV ❑ *...this uniquely beautiful city.*

> **Thesaurus** *unique* Also look up:
> ADJ. different, special; *(ant.)* common, standard, usual 1 3

> **Word Link** *son ≈ sound : resonate, sonic, unison*

unison /'juːnɪsən, -zən/ PHRASE If a group of people do something **in unison**, they all do it together at the same time.

unit /'juːnɪt/ (**units**) 1 N-COUNT If you consider something as a **unit**, you consider it as

a single complete thing. ❑ *...the basic family unit.* **2** N-COUNT A **unit** is a group of people who work together at a specific job, often in a particular place, for example in the army. ❑ *...the BBC's Natural History Unit.* **3** N-COUNT A **unit** is a small machine which has a particular function, often part of a larger machine. ❑ *The unit plugs into any TV set.* **4** N-COUNT A **unit** of measurement is a fixed, standard length, quantity, or weight. The litre, the centimetre, and the ounce are all units.
→ see **graph**

unite /juːˈnaɪt/ (**unites, uniting, united**) V-T/V-I If a group of people or things **unite**, or if someone or something **unites** them, they join together and act as a group. ❑ *Only the president can unite the people.*

united /juːˈnaɪtɪd/ **1** ADJ When people are **united** on something, they agree about it and act together. ❑ *The government was totally united on this issue.* **2** ADJ **United** is used to describe a country which has been formed from two or more countries or states. ❑ *...a united Germany.*

U͵nited ˈNations N-PROPER **The United Nations** is a worldwide organization which most countries belong to. Its role is to encourage international peace, cooperation, and friendship.

unity /ˈjuːnɪti/ **1** N-UNCOUNT **Unity** is the state of different areas or groups being joined together to form a single country or organization. ❑ *...European economic unity.* **2** N-UNCOUNT When there is **unity**, people are in agreement and act together for a particular purpose. ❑ *The choice created an impression of party unity.*

universal /͵juːnɪˈvɜːsəl/ ADJ Something that is **universal** relates to everyone in the world or to everyone in a particular group or society. ❑ *...a universal symbol of life and good luck.* ● **universally** ADV ❑ *...a universally accepted point of view.*

universe /ˈjuːnɪvɜːs/ (**universes**) N-COUNT **The universe** is the whole of space, and all the stars, planets, and other forms of matter and energy in it.
→ see **galaxy, telescope**

university /͵juːnɪˈvɜːsɪti/ (**universities**) N-VAR A **university** is an institution where students study for degrees and where academic research is done. ❑ *They want their daughter to go to university.*

unjust /͵ʌnˈdʒʌst/ ADJ If you describe an action, system, or law as **unjust**, you think that it treats a person or group badly in a way that they do not deserve. ● **unjustly** ADV ❑ *She was unjustly accused of stealing money.*

U

unjustified /ʌˈndʒʌstɪfaɪd/ ADJ If you describe a belief or action as **unjustified**, you think that there is no good reason for having it or doing it. ❑ *The men listened to a lot of unjustified criticism.*

unkind /ʌnˈkaɪnd/ (**unkinder, unkindest**) ADJ If someone is **unkind**, they behave in an unpleasant, unfriendly, or slightly cruel way. ❑ *I think it's very unkind of you to make up stories about him.* ● **unkindly** ADV ❑ *He never spoke unkindly of anyone.* ● **unkindness** N-UNCOUNT ❑ *He realized the unkindness of the comment.*

Thesaurus *unkind* Also look up:

ADJ.	harsh, mean, unfriendly; *(ant.)* kind

unknown /͵ʌnˈnəʊn/ (**unknowns**) **1** ADJ & N-COUNT If something or someone is **unknown to** you, you do not know what or who they are. An **unknown** is something that you do not know. ❑ *An unknown number of men were arrested.* ❑ *The length of the war is one of the biggest unknowns.* **2** ADJ & N-COUNT An **unknown** person is not famous or publicly recognized. You can refer to a person like this as an **unknown**. ❑ *...a film starring unknowns Jonathan Byrne and Alex Reid.* **3** N-SING **The unknown** refers generally to things or places that people do not know about or understand. ❑ *...fear of the unknown.*

unlawful /͵ʌnˈlɔːfʊl/ ADJ If something is **unlawful**, the law does not allow you to do it. [FORMAL] ❑ *...unlawful killings.* ● **unlawfully** ADV ❑ *The government acted unlawfully.*

unleaded /͵ʌnˈledɪd/ ADJ & N-UNCOUNT **Unleaded** fuels contain a reduced amount of lead in order to reduce the pollution caused when they are burned. You can refer to such fuels as **unleaded**. ❑ *All the cars here run on unleaded petrol.*

unleash /͵ʌnˈliːʃ/ (**unleashes, unleashing, unleashed**) V-T If you say that someone or something **unleashes** a powerful movement or feeling, you mean that it starts suddenly and has an immediate strong effect. ❑ *The British Air Force unleashed a terrible attack on the city of Dresden in 1945.*

unless /ʌnˈles/ CONJ You use **unless** to introduce the only circumstances in which an event you are mentioning will not take place or in which a statement you are making is not true. ❑ *I'm not happy unless I drive my car every day.*

unlike /͵ʌnˈlaɪk/ **1** PREP If one thing is **unlike** another thing, the two things have different features from each other. ❑ *This pudding is unlike anything I've had before.* **2** PREP You can use **unlike** to contrast two people or things and show how they are different. ❑ *Unlike aerobics, walking is free and you can do it whenever you want.* **3** PREP If you describe something that someone has done as **unlike** them, you mean that it is not typical of their normal behaviour. ❑ *It was so unlike him to say something like that.*

unlikely /ʌnˈlaɪkli/ (**unlikelier, unlikeliest**) **1** ADJ If you say that something is **unlikely to** happen or **unlikely to** be true, you believe that it will not happen or that it is not true, although you are not completely sure. ❑ *He is unlikely to arrive before Sunday.* **2** ADJ BEFORE N If you describe someone or something as **unlikely**, you mean it is surprising that they have a particular role or have done a particular thing. ❑ *Businessman Mr Trump has become an unlikely television star.*

Word Partnership Use *unlikely* with:

N.	unlikely **event** 1
V.	unlikely **to change**, unlikely **to happen**, **seem** unlikely 1
ADV.	**extremely** unlikely, **highly** unlikely, **most** unlikely, **very** unlikely 2

unlimited /ʌnˈlɪmɪtɪd/ ADJ If there is an **unlimited** quantity of something, you can have as much of it as you want. ❑ *You have unlimited access to the swimming pool.*

unload /͵ʌnˈləʊd/ (**unloads, unloading, unloaded**) V-T If you **unload** goods from a vehicle, or if you **unload** a vehicle, you remove the goods from the vehicle. ❑ *She unloaded her shopping from the car.*

unlock /ˌʌn'lɒk/ (**unlocks, unlocking, unlocked**) V-T If you **unlock** something such as a door, a room, or a container, you open it using a key. ❑ *He unlocked the car.* ❑ *...the key that unlocks their solid oak door.*

unlucky /ʌn'lʌki/ (**unluckier, unluckiest**) **1** ADJ If you are **unlucky**, you have bad luck. ❑ *They were unlucky not to reach the World Cup Final.* **2** ADJ **Unlucky** is used to describe something that is thought to cause bad luck. ❑ *The number four is considered unlucky by the Chinese.*

Word Link	*mark ≈ boundary, sign : bookmark, landmark, unmarked*

unmarked /ˌʌn'mɑːkt/ **1** ADJ Something that is **unmarked** has no marks of damage or injury on it. ❑ *Her shoes are still white and unmarked.* **2** ADJ Something that is **unmarked** has no signs on it which identify what it is or whose it is. ❑ *...an unmarked police car.*

unmistakable also **unmistakeable** /ˌʌnmɪs'teɪkəbəl/ ADJ If you describe something as **unmistakable**, you mean that it is so obvious that it cannot be mistaken for anything else. ❑ *He didn't give his name, but the voice was unmistakable.* ● **unmistakably** ADV ❑ *The name was unmistakably French.*

unmoved /ˌʌn'muːvd/ ADJ AFTER LINK-V If you are **unmoved by** something, you are not emotionally affected by it.

unnamed /ˌʌn'neɪmd/ ADJ **Unnamed** people or things are talked about but their names are not mentioned. ❑ *The cash comes from an unnamed source.*

unnatural /ʌn'nætʃərəl/ **1** ADJ If you describe something as **unnatural**, you mean that it is strange and often frightening, because it is different from what you normally expect. ❑ *The plane climbed with unnatural speed.* ● **unnaturally** ADV ❑ *The house was unnaturally silent.* **2** ADJ If you describe someone's behaviour as **unnatural**, you mean that it does not seem normal or spontaneous. ❑ *She gave him a smile which seemed unnatural.* ● **unnaturally** ADV ❑ *Try to avoid shouting or speaking unnaturally.*

unnecessary /ʌn'nesəsri, AM -seri/ ADJ If you describe something as **unnecessary**, you mean that it is not needed or does not have to be done. ❑ *Diana was making an unnecessary fuss.* ● **unnecessarily** ADV ❑ *I didn't want to upset my husband unnecessarily.*

unnerve /ˌʌn'nɜːv/ (**unnerves, unnerving, unnerved**) V-T If something **unnerves** you, it frightens, worries, or startles you. ❑ *The news about Dermot unnerved me.* ● **unnerving** ADJ ❑ *He has always found flying to be an unnerving experience.*

unnoticed /ˌʌn'nəʊtɪst/ ADJ If something happens or passes **unnoticed**, it is not seen or noticed by anyone. ❑ *I tried to climb the stairs unnoticed.*

unobtrusive /ˌʌnəb'truːsɪv/ ADJ If you describe something or someone as **unobtrusive**, you mean that they are not easily noticed or do not draw attention to themselves. [FORMAL] ❑ *The coffee table is made of glass, to be as unobtrusive as possible.* ● **unobtrusively** ADV ❑ *They slipped away unobtrusively.*

unofficial /ˌʌnə'fɪʃəl/ ADJ An **unofficial** action is not authorized, approved, or organized by a person in authority. ❑ *...an unofficial request.* ● **unofficially** ADV ❑ *The painting was unofficially valued at nearly £500.*

Word Link	*dox ≈ opinion : orthodox, paradox, unorthodox*

unorthodox /ʌn'ɔːθədɒks/ ADJ If you describe someone's behaviour, beliefs, or customs as **unorthodox**, you mean that they are different from what is generally accepted. ❑ *...his unorthodox management style.*

unpack /ˌʌn'pæk/ (**unpacks, unpacking, unpacked**) V-T/V-I When you **unpack**, or **unpack** a suitcase, box, or bag, or when you **unpack** the things inside it, you take the things out of it. ❑ *I unpacked as soon as I got home.*

unpaid /ˌʌn'peɪd/ **1** ADJ BEFORE N If you do **unpaid** work, you do a job without receiving any money for it. **2** ADJ **Unpaid** taxes or bills have not been paid yet.

unpalatable /ʌn'pælɪtəbəl/ ADJ If you describe an idea as **unpalatable**, you mean that you find it unpleasant and difficult to accept. [FORMAL] ❑ *I began to learn the unpalatable truth about John.*

unparalleled /ʌn'pærəleld/ ADJ If you describe something as **unparalleled**, you are emphasizing that it is, for example, bigger, better, or worse than anything else of its kind. ❑ *The country is facing a crisis unparalleled since the Second World War.* ❑ *Hong Kong has an unparalleled advantage in its geographic location in relation to its key markets.*

unpleasant /ʌn'plezənt/ **1** ADJ If something is **unpleasant**, it gives you bad feelings, for example by making you feel upset or uncomfortable. ❑ *The symptoms of a cold can be uncomfortable and unpleasant.* ● **unpleasantly** ADV ❑ *The smell was unpleasantly strong.* **2** ADJ An **unpleasant** person is unfriendly and rude. ● **unpleasantly** ADV ❑ *Melissa laughed unpleasantly.*

unplug /ˌʌn'plʌg/ (**unplugs, unplugging, unplugged**) V-T If you **unplug** a piece of electrical equipment, you take its plug out of the socket.

unpopular /ˌʌn'pɒpjʊlə/ ADJ If something or someone is **unpopular**, most people do not like them. ❑ *He was unpopular at school.* ● **unpopularity** N-UNCOUNT ❑ *...the unpopularity of the new tax.*

unprecedented /ʌn'presɪdentɪd/ **1** ADJ If something is **unprecedented**, it has never happened before. ❑ *The BBC made an unprecedented apology on the national news.* **2** ADJ If you describe something as **unprecedented**, you are emphasizing that it is very great in quality, amount, or scale. ❑ *...an unprecedented success.*

unpredictable /ˌʌnprɪ'dɪktəbəl/ ADJ If someone or something is **unpredictable**, you cannot tell what they are going to do or how they are going to behave. ❑ *The weather in Britain is unpredictable.* ● **unpredictability** N-UNCOUNT ❑ *I love the unpredictability of sport.*

unprepared /ˌʌnprɪ'peəd/ **1** ADJ If you are **unprepared for** something, you are not ready for it, and are therefore surprised or at a disadvantage when it happens. ❑ *She was totally unprepared for the terrible news.* **2** ADJ If you are **unprepared to** do

U

something, you are not willing to do it. ❑ *He was unprepared to answer the reporter's questions.*

unproductive /ˌʌnprəˈdʌktɪv/ ADJ Something that is **unproductive** does not produce anything useful. ❑ *...unproductive land.* ❑ *...a busy but unproductive day at work.*

unprofitable /ˌʌnˈprɒfɪtəbəl/ ADJ An industry, company, or product that is **unprofitable** does not make enough profit.

unprotected /ˌʌnprəˈtektɪd/ **1** ADJ An **unprotected** person or place is not looked after or defended, and so they may be harmed or attacked. ❑ *The soldiers ran towards the unprotected camp.* **2** ADJ If something is **unprotected**, it is not covered or treated with anything, and so it may easily be damaged. ❑ *Skin that is unprotected from the sun will burn.*

unpublished /ˌʌnˈpʌblɪʃt/ ADJ An **unpublished** book, letter, or report has never been published.

unqualified /ˌʌnˈkwɒlɪfaɪd/ **1** ADJ If you are **unqualified**, you do not have any qualifications, or do not have the right qualifications for a particular job. **2** ADJ **Unqualified** means total, unlimited, and complete. ❑ *The event was an unqualified success.*

unquestionable /ʌnˈkwestʃənəbəl/ ADJ If you describe something as **unquestionable**, you are emphasizing that it is so obviously true or real that nobody can doubt it. ❑ *Her love for the King was unquestionable.* • **unquestionably** ADV ❑ *The next two years were unquestionably the happiest of his life.*

unravel /ʌnˈrævəl/ (**unravels, unravelling, unravelled** or [AM] **unraveling, unraveled**) V-T/V-I If you **unravel** a mystery or puzzle, or if it **unravels**, it gradually becomes clearer and you can work out the answer to it. ❑ *Carter was still trying to unravel the truth of the woman's story.*

unreal /ˌʌnˈriːl/ ADJ AFTER LINK-V If you say that a situation is **unreal**, you mean that it is so strange that you find it difficult to believe it is happening. • **unreality** /ˌʌnriˈælɪti/ N-UNCOUNT ❑ *The weekend had a strange feeling of unreality.*

unrealistic /ˌʌnriəˈlɪstɪk/ ADJ If you say that someone is being **unrealistic**, you mean that they do not recognize the truth about a situation, especially about the difficulties involved. ❑ *...their unrealistic view of parenthood.*

unreasonable /ʌnˈriːzənəbəl/ **1** ADJ If you say that someone is being **unreasonable**, you mean that they are behaving in a way that is not fair or sensible. • **unreasonably** ADV ❑ *We unreasonably expect our children to behave perfectly.* **2** ADJ An **unreasonable** decision, action, price, or amount seems unfair and difficult to justify. • **unreasonably** ADV ❑ *The banks' charges are unreasonably high.*

U

unrelated /ˌʌnrɪˈleɪtɪd/ ADJ If one thing is **unrelated to** another, there is no connection between them. ❑ *My work is unrelated to politics.* ❑ *The two incidents are unrelated.*

unrelenting /ˌʌnrɪˈlentɪŋ/ **1** ADJ If you describe someone's behaviour as **unrelenting**, you mean that they are continuing to do something in a very determined way. ❑ *He showed unrelenting commitment to the team.* **2** ADJ If you describe something unpleasant as **unrelenting**, you mean that it is continuing without stopping. ❑ *The violence was unrelenting.*

unreliable /ˌʌnrɪˈlaɪəbəl/ ADJ If you describe a person, machine, or method as **unreliable**, you mean that you cannot trust them to do or provide what you want. ❑ *The car was slow and unreliable.*

unremarkable /ˌʌnrɪˈmɑːkəbəl/ ADJ If you describe someone or something as **unremarkable**, you mean that they do not have many exciting, original, or attractive qualities. ❑ *The man was tall and thin, with an unremarkable face.*

unrepentant /ˌʌnrɪˈpentənt/ ADJ If you are **unrepentant**, you are not ashamed of your beliefs or actions. ❑ *He is unrepentant about his violent past.*

unresolved /ˌʌnrɪˈzɒlvd/ ADJ If a problem or difficulty is **unresolved**, no satisfactory solution has been found to it. [FORMAL]

unrest /ʌnˈrest/ N-UNCOUNT If there is **unrest** in a particular place or society, people are expressing anger and dissatisfaction, often by demonstrating or rioting. [JOURNALISM] ❑ *There is growing unrest among students in several major cities.*

unrestricted /ˌʌnrɪˈstrɪktɪd/ ADJ If an activity is **unrestricted**, you are free to do it in the way that you want, without being limited by any rules.

unrivalled [AM **unrivaled**] /ʌnˈraɪvəld/ ADJ If you describe something as **unrivalled**, you are emphasizing that it is better than anything else of the same kind. ❑ *He has an unrivalled knowledge of Saudi Arabian society.*

unruly /ʌnˈruːli/ (**unrulier, unruliest**) **1** ADJ If you describe people as **unruly**, you mean that they behave badly and are difficult to control. **2** ADJ **Unruly** hair is difficult to keep tidy.

unsafe /ˌʌnˈseɪf/ **1** ADJ If a building, machine, activity, or area is **unsafe**, it is dangerous. ❑ *The stadium is unsafe for major sporting events.* **2** ADJ AFTER LINK-V If you are **unsafe**, you are in danger of being harmed. ❑ *I felt very unsafe.*

unsatisfactory /ˌʌnsætɪsˈfæktəri/ ADJ If you describe something as **unsatisfactory**, you mean that it is not as good as it should be, and cannot be considered acceptable. ❑ *He received unsatisfactory answers to his questions.*

unsavoury [AM **unsavory**] /ʌnˈseɪvəri/ ADJ If you describe someone or something as **unsavoury**, you mean that you find them unpleasant or morally unacceptable. ❑ *'I don't mix with unsavoury characters,' he said.*

unscathed /ʌnˈskeɪðd/ ADJ If you are **unscathed** after a dangerous experience, you have not been injured or harmed by it.

unscrupulous /ʌnˈskruːpjʊləs/ ADJ If you describe a person as **unscrupulous**, you are critical of the fact that they are prepared to act in a dishonest or immoral way in order to get what they want.

unseen /ˌʌnˈsiːn/ ADJ You use **unseen** to describe things that you cannot see or have not seen. ❑ *The two boys escaped unseen.*

unsettled /ˌʌnˈsetəld/ **1** ADJ In an **unsettled** situation, there is a lot of uncertainty about what will happen. ❑ *...Britain's unsettled political situation.* **2** ADJ AFTER LINK-V If you are **unsettled**, you cannot concentrate on anything, because you are worried. ❑ *To tell the truth, I'm a bit unsettled tonight.*

unsettling /ˌʌnˈsetəlɪŋ/ ADJ If you describe something as **unsettling**, you mean that it causes you to feel restless or rather worried. ❑ *His sense of* *humour was really unsettling.*

unsightly /ʌn'saɪtli/ (**unsightlier, unsightliest**) ADJ If you describe something as **unsightly**, you mean that it is unattractive to look at. ❑ *There was an unsightly hole in the garden.*

unskilled /ˌʌn'skɪld/ **1** ADJ People who are **unskilled** do not have any special training for a job. ❑ *He worked as an unskilled labourer.* **2** ADJ **Unskilled** work does not require any special training. ❑ *...low-paid, unskilled jobs.*

unsolicited /ˌʌnsə'lɪsɪtɪd/ ADJ Something that is **unsolicited** is given without being asked for and may not have been wanted. ❑ *...unsolicited advice.*

unsolved /ˌʌn'sɒlvd/ ADJ An **unsolved** problem or mystery has never been solved.

unspeakable /ʌn'spiːkəbəl/ ADJ If you describe something as **unspeakable**, you are emphasizing that it is extremely unpleasant. ❑ *...the unspeakable horrors of the First World War.* ● **unspeakably** ADV ❑ *The book was unspeakably boring.*

unspecified /ʌn'spesɪfaɪd/ ADJ You say that something is **unspecified** when you are not told exactly what it is. ❑ *He was sent to an unspecified British jail.*

unspoiled /ˌʌn'spɔɪld/ [BRIT also **unspoilt**] /ˌʌn'spɔɪlt/ ADJ If you describe a place as **unspoilt**, you think it is beautiful because it has not been changed or built on for a long time. ❑ *...the unspoiled island of Kefalonia.*

unspoken /ˌʌn'spəʊkən/ ADJ If your thoughts or feelings are **unspoken**, you do not speak about them.

unstable /ˌʌn'steɪbəl/ **1** ADJ You can describe something as **unstable** if it is likely to change suddenly, especially if this creates difficulty. ❑ *The situation is unstable and dangerous.* **2** ADJ **Unstable** objects are likely to move or fall. ❑ *...an unstable cliff with deep cracks in it.* **3** ADJ If people are **unstable**, their emotions and behaviour keep changing because their minds are disturbed. ❑ *He was emotionally unstable.*

unsteady /ʌn'stedi/ **1** ADJ If you are **unsteady**, you have difficulty doing something because you cannot completely control your body. ❑ *Deng was unsteady on his feet and his left hand shook.* ● **unsteadily** ADV ❑ *She pulled herself unsteadily from the bed.* **2** ADJ If you describe something as **unsteady**, you mean that it is not regular or stable. ❑ *When he spoke, his voice was unsteady.* **3** ADJ **Unsteady** objects are not held, fixed, or balanced securely. ❑ *...a slightly unsteady piece of furniture.*

unsubscribe /ˌʌnsəb'skraɪb/ (**unsubscribes, unsubscribing, unsubscribed**) V-I If you **unsubscribe** from an online service, you send a message saying that you no longer wish to receive that service. [COMPUTING]

unsubstantiated /ˌʌnsəb'stænʃieɪtɪd/ ADJ An **unsubstantiated** statement or story has not been proved true.

unsuccessful /ˌʌnsək'sesfʊl/ **1** ADJ Something that is **unsuccessful** does not achieve what it was intended to achieve. ❑ *...a second unsuccessful operation on his knee.* ● **unsuccessfully** ADV ❑ *He tried unsuccessfully to sell the business.* **2** ADJ Someone who is **unsuccessful** does not achieve what they intended to achieve. ❑ *Boris was unsuccessful in getting a job.*

unsuitable /ˌʌn'suːtəbəl/ ADJ Someone or something that is **unsuitable for** a particular purpose or situation does not have the right qualities for it. ❑ *Amy's shoes were unsuitable for walking.*

unsure /ˌʌn'ʃʊə/ **1** ADJ If you are **unsure of yourself**, you don't have much confidence. ❑ *He made her feel awkward and unsure of herself.* **2** ADJ AFTER LINK-V If you are **unsure about** something, you feel uncertain about it. ❑ *Fifty-two per cent of people were unsure about the idea.*

unsuspecting /ˌʌnsə'spektɪŋ/ ADJ You can use **unsuspecting** to describe someone who is not aware of something that is happening or going to happen. ❑ *...his unsuspecting victim.*

unsympathetic /ˌʌnsɪmpə'θetɪk/ **1** ADJ If someone is **unsympathetic**, they are not kind or helpful to a person in difficulties. ❑ *Her husband was unsympathetic and she felt she had no one to talk to.* **2** ADJ An **unsympathetic** person is unpleasant and difficult to like. ❑ *...a very unsympathetic main character.*

untenable /ˌʌn'tenəbəl/ ADJ An argument or position that is **untenable** cannot be defended successfully against criticism or attack. ❑ *After his team lost several matches, his position was untenable.*

unthinkable /ʌn'θɪŋkəbəl/ **1** ADJ & N-SING If you say that something is **unthinkable**, you mean that it cannot possibly be accepted or imagined as a possibility. **The unthinkable** is something that is unthinkable. ❑ *Any thought of divorce was unthinkable.* ❑ *The unthinkable had happened – a power failure.* **2** ADJ You can use **unthinkable** to describe a situation or event which is extremely unpleasant to imagine or remember. ❑ *Life without you would be unthinkable.*

untidy /ʌn'taɪdi/ (**untidier, untidiest**) **1** ADJ Something that is **untidy** is messy, and not neatly arranged. ❑ *She threw her clothes into an untidy heap.* ● **untidily** ADV ❑ *Her long hair fell untidily around her shoulders.* **2** ADJ If you describe a person as **untidy**, you mean that they do not care about whether things are neat and well arranged. ❑ *He's very untidy, but he's also the kindest man I've ever met.*

Word Link ***un ≈ reversal : untie, undo, unwrap***

untie /ˌʌn'taɪ/ (**unties, untying, untied**) **1** V-T If you **untie** something that is tied to another thing, or if you **untie** two things that are tied together, you remove the string or rope that holds them. ❑ *Just untie my hands.* **2** V-T If you **untie** something such as string or rope, you undo the knot in it.

until /ʌn'tɪl/ **1** PREP & CONJ If something happens **until** a particular time, it happens during the period before that time and stops at that time. ❑ *She lived in Canada until 2004.* ❑ *I waited until it got dark.* **2** PREP & CONJ If something does not happen **until** a particular time, it does not happen before that time and only happens after it. ❑ *The baby is not due until the end of July.*

Usage

Note that you only use **until** or **till** when you are talking about time. You do not use these words to talk about place or position. Instead, you should use **as far as** or **up to**. ❑ *You can come with us as far as the village.* ❑ *We walked up to where his bicycle was.*

untold /ˌʌnˈtəʊld/ **1** ADJ BEFORE N You can use **untold** to emphasize how unpleasant something is. ❑ *This might do untold damage to her health.* **2** ADJ BEFORE N You can use **untold** to emphasize that an amount or quantity is very large, especially when you are not sure how large it is. ❑ *An Olympic gold medal can lead to untold riches for an athlete.*

untouched /ˌʌnˈtʌtʃt/ **1** ADJ Something that is **untouched** has not been changed or damaged in any way. ❑ *The island is still untouched by tourism.* ❑ *There was one building that remained untouched.* **2** ADJ If food or drink is **untouched**, none of it has been eaten or drunk. ❑ *The coffee was untouched.*

untrained /ˌʌnˈtreɪnd/ **1** ADJ Someone who is **untrained** has not been taught the skills that they need for a particular job. **2** ADJ You use **untrained** with words like 'eye' and 'ear' to describe how something seems to someone who is not an expert. ❑ *They don't look very different to the untrained eye.*

untreated /ˌʌnˈtriːtɪd/ **1** ADJ If an injury or illness is left **untreated**, it is not given medical treatment. **2** ADJ **Untreated** materials, water, or chemicals are harmful and have not been made safe.

untrue /ˌʌnˈtruː/ ADJ Something that is **untrue** is not true. ❑ *Such comments are both unkind and untrue.*

unused **1** ADJ /ʌnˈjuːzd/ Something that is **unused** has not been used or is not being used at the moment. ❑ *The car has been standing unused for months.* **2** ADJ AFTER LINK-V /ʌnˈjuːst/ If you are **unused to** something, you have not often done it or experienced it. ❑ *He was unused to speaking in public.*

unusual /ʌnˈjuːʒʊəl/ ADJ If something is **unusual**, it does not happen very often or you do not see it or hear it very often. ❑ *It's very unusual for him to make a mistake.* ❑ *...rare and unusual plants.* ● **unusually** ADV ❑ *...an unusually cold winter.*

Thesaurus	*unusual*	Also look up:
ADJ.	abnormal, different, interesting, strange, unconventional; *(ant.)* usual	

unveil /ˌʌnˈveɪl/ (**unveils, unveiling, unveiled**) **1** V-T If someone **unveils** something such as a new statue or painting, they draw back the curtain which is covering it, in a special ceremony. **2** V-T If you **unveil** something that has been kept secret, you make it known to the public. ❑ *The company unveiled plans to open 100 new stores.*

U

unwanted /ˌʌnˈwɒntɪd/ ADJ You say that something is **unwanted** when someone does not want it. ❑ *...unwanted gifts.* ❑ *Every year thousands of unwanted animals are abandoned.*

unwarranted /ʌnˈwɒrəntɪd, AM -ˈwɔːr-/ ADJ Something that is **unwarranted** is not justified or deserved. [FORMAL] ❑ *She was upset by the unwarranted criticism.*

unwelcome /ʌnˈwelkəm/ **1** ADJ An **unwelcome** experience is one that you do not like and did not want. ❑ *...unwelcome attention from men.* **2** ADJ If a visitor is **unwelcome**, you did not want them to come. ❑ *She made him feel unwelcome.*

unwell /ˌʌnˈwel/ ADJ AFTER LINK-V If you are **unwell**, you are ill. ❑ *Mrs Pringle was too unwell to go with him to the supermarket.*

unwieldy /ʌnˈwiːldi/ (**unwieldier, unwieldiest**) **1** ADJ An **unwieldy** object is difficult to move or carry because it is big or heavy. **2** ADJ An **unwieldy** system does not work well because it is too large or is badly organized. ❑ *...Britain's unwieldy health service.*

unwilling /ˌʌnˈwɪlɪŋ/ ADJ If you are **unwilling to** do something, you do not want to do it. ❑ *He was unwilling to discuss the problem.* ● **unwillingly** ADV ❑ *Unwillingly, she stood up.* ● **unwillingness** N-UNCOUNT ❑ *...his unwillingness to spend money.*

unwind /ˌʌnˈwaɪnd/ (**unwinds, unwinding, unwound**) **1** V-I When you **unwind** after working hard, you relax. ❑ *Tavira is the perfect place to unwind.* **2** V-T/V-I If you **unwind** something that is wrapped round something else, you undo it. If something **unwinds**, it stops being wrapped round something else and becomes straight again.

unwise /ˌʌnˈwaɪz/ ADJ Something that is **unwise** is foolish. ❑ *It would be unwise to expect too much.* ● **unwisely** ADV ❑ *She had acted unwisely.*

unwitting /ʌnˈwɪtɪŋ/ ADJ If you describe a person or their actions as **unwitting**, you mean that the person does something or is involved in something without realizing it. ❑ *The report discusses unwitting racism at work.* ● **unwittingly** ADV ❑ *The woman had unwittingly bought a stolen car.*

unworkable /ˌʌnˈwɜːkəbəl/ ADJ If an idea or plan is **unworkable**, it cannot succeed. ❑ *This proposal is unworkable.*

unworthy /ʌnˈwɜːði/ (**unworthier, unworthiest**) **1** ADJ If someone is **unworthy of** something, they do not deserve it. [LITERARY] ❑ *She felt unworthy of any respect.* **2** ADJ If you say that an action is **unworthy of** someone, you mean that it is not a nice thing to do and someone with their reputation or position should not do it. ❑ *His behaviour that night was unworthy of a future king.*

unwound /ˌʌnˈwaʊnd/ **Unwound** is the past tense and past participle of **unwind**.

Word Link	*un ≈ reversal : untie, undo, unwrap*

unwrap /ˌʌnˈræp/ (**unwraps, unwrapping, unwrapped**) V-T When you **unwrap** something, you take off the paper or covering that is around it.

unwritten /ˌʌnˈrɪtən/ ADJ **Unwritten** things have not been printed or written down. ❑ *The book he wanted to write remained unwritten.*

unzip /ˌʌnˈzɪp/ (**unzips, unzipping, unzipped**) **1** V-T To **unzip** an item of clothing or a bag means to unfasten its zip. ❑ *She unzipped her coat.* **2** V-T To **unzip** a computer file means to open a file that has been compressed. [COMPUTING] ❑ *How do you unzip a compressed file?*

up

① PREPOSITION, ADVERB, AND ADJECTIVE USES
② VERB USES

up /ʌp/ (**ups**)
① **1** PREP & ADV **Up** means towards a higher place, or in a higher place. ❑ *I ran up the stairs.* ❑ *The Newton Hotel is halfway up a steep hill.* ❑ *He put his hand up.* **2** ADV If someone stands **up**, they move so that they are standing. ❑ *He stood up and*

went out into the garden. 3 ADV **Up** means in the north or towards the north. ❑ *Mark travelled up to London from Dover by train.* 4 PREP If you go **up** something such as a road or river, you go along it. ❑ *Three cars came up the road.* 5 ADV If you go **up to** something or someone, you move to the place where they are and stop there. ❑ *The girl ran up to the car.* 6 ADJ AFTER LINK-V If you are **up**, you are not in bed. ❑ *He was already up at 6am.* 7 ADV If an amount goes **up**, it increases. If an amount of something is **up**, it is at a higher level than it was. ❑ *The price of property has gone up again.* 8 ADJ AFTER LINK-V If a period of time is **up**, it has come to an end. ❑ *When the six weeks were up, everybody was sad that she had to leave.* 9 PHRASE If you move **up and down**, you move repeatedly in one direction and then in the opposite direction. ❑ *Her son started to jump up and down.* ❑ *I walked up and down waiting for the taxi.* 10 PHRASE If you have **ups and downs**, you experience a mixture of good things and bad things. ❑ *Every relationship has a lot of ups and downs.* 11 PHRASE If you are **up against** something, you have a difficult situation or problem to deal with. ❑ *They were up against a good team but did very well.* 12 PHRASE If someone or something is **up for** discussion, election, or review, they are about to be considered or judged. ❑ *The whole question of education is up for discussion.* 13 PHRASE You use **up to** to say how large something can be or what level it has reached. ❑ *It could be up to two years before the building is finished.* 14 PHRASE If you do not feel **up to** doing something, you do not feel well enough to do it. 15 PHRASE If you say that it is **up to** someone to do a particular thing, you mean that it is their responsibility to do it. ❑ *It is up to you to tell them.* 16 PHRASE If something happens **up to** or **up until** a particular time, it happens until that time. ❑ *Please feel free to call me any time up until half past nine.*

up /ʌp/ (**ups, upping, upped**)
❷ V-T If you **up** something such as the amount of money you are offering for something, you increase it. ❑ *We talked about upping her pay.*

ˌup-and-ˈcoming ADJ BEFORE N **Up-and-coming** people are likely to be successful in the future. An **up-and-coming** area is an area which is becoming more popular as a place to live. ❑ *Their daughter is an up-and-coming tennis player.* ❑ *...a house in an up-and-coming area of London.*

upbeat /ˈʌpbiːt/ ADJ If you describe someone as **upbeat**, you mean they are cheerful and optimistic about a situation. [INFORMAL] ❑ *Ann was in an upbeat mood.*

upbringing /ˈʌpbrɪŋɪŋ/ N-SING Your **upbringing** is the way your parents treat you and the things that they teach you when you are growing up. ❑ *Her son had a good upbringing.*

upcoming /ˈʌpkʌmɪŋ/ ADJ BEFORE N **Upcoming** events will happen in the near future.

update (**updates, updating, updated**) 1 V-T /ʌpˈdeɪt/ If you **update** something, you make it more modern, usually by adding newer parts to it. ❑ *The travel guide was updated last year.* 2 N-COUNT /ˈʌpdeɪt/ An **update** is a news item which has been rewritten so that it includes the latest developments in a situation.

ˌup ˈfront also **upfront** 1 ADV If a payment is made **up front**, it is made in advance, so that the person being paid can be sure that they will be paid. ❑ *You have to pay up front and claim the money back later.* 2 ADJ If you are **up front about** something, you act openly or publicly so that people know what you are doing or what you believe. ❑ *He's upfront about his personal life.*

upgrade /ˌʌpˈgreɪd/ (**upgrades, upgrading, upgraded**) V-T & N-COUNT To **upgrade** something, or to give it an **upgrade**, means to change it so that it is more important or better. ❑ *The company upgraded the canteen.* ❑ *...an upgrade of the sports facilities.*
→ see **hotel**

upheaval /ʌpˈhiːvəl/ (**upheavals**) N-VAR An **upheaval** is a big change which causes a lot of trouble and confusion. ❑ *They wanted to film in my garden, but I didn't want all the upheaval.*

upheld /ʌpˈheld/ **Upheld** is the past tense and past participle of **uphold**.

uphill /ˌʌpˈhɪl/ 1 ADV & ADJ If you go **uphill**, you go up a slope. ❑ *We walked uphill for twenty minutes.* ❑ *...a long, uphill journey.* 2 ADJ BEFORE N If you refer to something as an **uphill** struggle, you mean that it requires a great deal of effort and determination.

uphold /ʌpˈhəʊld/ (**upholds, upholding, upheld**) V-T If you **uphold** a law, principle, or decision, you support and maintain it. ❑ *...upholding the right to freedom of speech.*

upholstery /ʌpˈhəʊlstəri/ N-UNCOUNT **Upholstery** is the soft covering on chairs and sofas that makes them comfortable.

upkeep /ˈʌpkiːp/ 1 N-UNCOUNT The **upkeep** of a building or place is the continual process of keeping it in good condition. ❑ *We are responsible for the general upkeep of the park.* 2 N-UNCOUNT The **upkeep** of a group of people or services is the process of providing them with the things that they need. ❑ *He pays £100 a month towards his son's upkeep.*

uplifting /ʌpˈlɪftɪŋ/ ADJ If something is **uplifting**, it makes you feel cheerful and happy. ❑ *...a very uplifting experience.*

upmarket /ˌʌpˈmɑːkɪt/ ADJ **Upmarket** places or products are intended to appeal to people with sophisticated and expensive tastes. [BRIT] ❑ *...an upmarket hotel.*

upon /əˈpɒn/ 1 PREP If one thing is **upon** another, it is on it. [FORMAL] ❑ *He set the tray upon the table.* 2 PREP You use **upon** when mentioning an event that is followed immediately by another. ❑ *Upon leaving the club, he fell over.* 3 PREP You use **upon** between two occurrences of the same noun in order to say that there are large numbers of the thing mentioned. ❑ *...row upon row of books.* 4 PREP If an event is **upon** you, it is just about to happen. ❑ *The football season is upon us.*

upper /ˈʌpə/ 1 ADJ You use **upper** to describe something that is above something else. ❑ *...a smart restaurant on the upper floor.* 2 ADJ The **upper** part of something is the higher part. ❑ *...the upper shelves of the kitchen cupboards.* 3 PHRASE If you have **the upper hand** in a situation, you have more power than the other people involved and can make decisions about what happens.

ˌupper ˈclass (**upper classes**) N-COUNT & ADJ **The upper class** or **the upper classes** are the group of people in a society who own the most property and have the highest social status. You say people like this are **upper class**. ❑ *...wealthy, upper-class families.*

upright /'ʌpraɪt/ 1 ADJ If you are sitting or standing **upright**, you have your back straight and are not bending or lying down. ❑ *The wind was so strong I couldn't stand upright.* 2 ADJ You can describe people as **upright** when they are careful to follow acceptable rules of behaviour and behave in a moral way. ❑ *...an upright citizen.*

uprising /'ʌpraɪzɪŋ/ (**uprisings**) N-COUNT When there is an **uprising**, a group of people start fighting against the people who are in power in their country.

uproar /'ʌprɔː/ 1 N-UNCOUNT & N-SING An **uproar** is a lot of shouting and noise because people are very angry or upset about something. 2 N-UNCOUNT & N-SING An **uproar** is a lot of public criticism and debate about something that has made people angry. ❑ *The book caused uproar when it was published in France in 1949.*

uproot /ʌp'ruːt/ (**uproots, uprooting, uprooted**) 1 V-T If you **uproot yourself**, or if you **are uprooted**, you leave or are made to leave a place where you have lived for a long time. ❑ *He did not want to uproot his family from the Midlands.* 2 V-T If someone **uproots** a tree or plant, or if the wind **uproots** it, it is pulled out of the ground.

upset (**upsets, upsetting, upset**)

verb and adjective /ʌp'set/, noun /'ʌpset/.

1 ADJ If you are **upset**, you are unhappy or disappointed because something unpleasant has happened. ❑ *They are terribly upset by their parents' divorce.* 2 V-T If something **upsets** you, it makes you feel worried or unhappy. ❑ *I'm sorry if I've upset you.* ● **upsetting** ADJ ❑ *The whole experience was very upsetting.* 3 V-T If events **upset** something such as a procedure or a state of affairs, they cause it to go wrong. ❑ *Political problems could upset the peace process.* 4 N-COUNT & ADJ BEFORE N If you have a **stomach upset**, or if you have an **upset stomach**, you have a slight illness in your stomach caused by an infection or by something that you have eaten.

→ see **anger**

Thesaurus *upset* Also look up:

ADJ.	disappointed, hurt, unhappy; *(ant.)* happy 1
	ill, sick, unsettled 4
V.	overturn, spill, topple 3

Word Partnership Use *upset* with:

PREP.	upset **about/by/over** ***something*** 1
ADV.	**visibly** upset 1
	really upset, **so** upset, **very** upset 1 2
N.	**stomach** upset (*or* upset **stomach**) 4
V.	**become** upset, **feel** upset, **get** upset 1 4

ˌupside ˈdown also **upside-down** 1 ADV & ADJ If something has been put **upside down**, it has been turned round so that the part that is usually lowest is above the part that is usually highest. ❑ *The painting was hung upside down.* ❑ *...an upside-down map of Britain.* 2 PHRASE If you **turn** a place **upside down**, you move everything around and make it untidy, because you are looking for something.

upstage /ˌʌp'steɪdʒ/ (**upstages, upstaging, upstaged**) V-T To **upstage** someone is to draw attention away from them by being more attractive or interesting.

upstairs /ˌʌp'steəz/ 1 ADV If you go **upstairs** in a building, you go up a staircase towards a higher floor. ❑ *Maureen ran upstairs to her bedroom.* 2 ADV & ADJ If something or someone is **upstairs** in a building, they are on a floor that is higher than the ground floor. ❑ *There is another bar upstairs.* ❑ *...the upstairs flat.* 3 N-SING **The upstairs** of a building is the floor or floors that are higher than the ground floor.

upstart /'ʌpstɑːt/ (**upstarts**) N-COUNT You can refer to someone as an **upstart** when they behave as if they are important, but you think that they are too new in a place or job to be treated as important.

upstream /ˌʌp'striːm/ ADV & ADJ Something that is moving **upstream** is moving along a river towards the source of the river. Something that is **upstream** is towards the source of a river. ❑ *He lives about 60 miles upstream from here.*

upsurge /'ʌpsɜːdʒ/ N-SING If there is an **upsurge in** something, there is a sudden large increase in it. [FORMAL] ❑ *...the upsurge in house prices.*

uptight /ˌʌp'taɪt/ ADJ If someone is **uptight**, they are very tense, because they are worried or annoyed about something. [INFORMAL]

ˌup-to-ˈdate also **up to date** 1 ADJ If something is **up-to-date**, it is the newest thing of its kind. ❑ *...Germany's most up to date electric power station.* 2 ADJ If you are **up-to-date with** something, you have the latest information about it.

uptown /ˌʌp'taʊn/ ADV & ADJ BEFORE N If you go **uptown**, or go to a place **uptown**, you go away from the centre of a town or city towards one of its suburbs. [AM] ❑ *Susan continued to live uptown.* ❑ *...uptown New Orleans.*

upturn /'ʌptɜːn/ (**upturns**) N-COUNT If there is an **upturn in** the economy or in a company or industry, it becomes more successful.

upwards /'ʌpwədz/

In British English, **upwards** is an adverb and **upward** is an adjective. In formal British English and in American English, **upward** is both an adjective and an adverb.

1 ADV & ADJ BEFORE N If you move or look **upwards**, you move or look up towards a higher place. ❑ *They climbed upwards along the steep cliffs surrounding the village.* ❑ *She started once again on the steep upward climb.* 2 ADV If an amount or rate moves **upwards**, it increases. ❑ *The price is likely to leap upwards.* 3 PREP A quantity that is **upwards of** a particular number is more than that number. ❑ *...projects worth upwards of £200 million.*

uranium /jʊ'reɪniəm/ N-UNCOUNT **Uranium** is a radioactive metal that is used to produce nuclear energy and weapons.

Word Link *urb ≈ city : suburb, suburbia, urban*

urban /'ɜːbən/ ADJ **Urban** means belonging to, or relating to, a town or city. ❑ *...the urban population.*

→ see **city**

U

urge /ɜːdʒ/ (**urges, urging, urged**) **1** V-T If you **urge** someone **to** do something, you try hard to persuade them to do it. ❑ *He urged her to come to Ireland.* ❑ *'Now read,' I urged.* **2** N-COUNT If you have an **urge to** do or have something, you have a strong wish to do or have it. ❑ *The urge to have children was beginning to take over her life.*
▶ **urge on** PHR-VERB If you **urge** someone **on**, you encourage them to do something. ❑ *Urged on by his mother, he decided to become a doctor.*

Word Partnership Use *urge* with:

N.	urge **action**, urge **caution**, **leaders/officials** urge, urge **people**, urge **restraint**, urge **support**, urge **voters** 1
ADV.	**strongly** urge 1
V.	**feel an** urge, **fight an** urge, **get an** urge, **resist an** urge 2

urgent /ˈɜːdʒənt/ **1** ADJ If something is **urgent**, it needs to be dealt with as soon as possible. ❑ *...an urgent need for food and water.* ❑ *He had urgent business in New York.* ● **urgency** N-UNCOUNT ❑ *It is a matter of utmost urgency.* ● **urgently** ADV ❑ *A new road is urgently needed.* **2** ADJ If you speak in an **urgent** way, you show that you are anxious for people to notice something or do something. ● **urgency** N-UNCOUNT ❑ *She was surprised at the urgency in his voice.* ● **urgently** ADV ❑ *'Are you still there?' Jerrold asked urgently.*

Word Partnership Use *urgent* with:

N.	urgent **action**, urgent **business**, urgent **care**, urgent **matter**, urgent **meeting**, urgent **mission**, urgent **need**, urgent **problem** 1
	urgent **appeal**, urgent **message** 2

urinate /ˈjʊərɪneɪt/ (**urinates, urinating, urinated**) V-I When you **urinate**, you get rid of urine from your body.

urine /ˈjʊərɪn/ N-UNCOUNT **Urine** is the liquid that you get rid of from your body when you go to the toilet.

URL /juː ɑːr ˈel/ (**URLs**) N-COUNT A **URL** is an address that shows where a particular page can be found on the World Wide Web. **URL** is an abbreviation for 'Uniform Resource Locator'. [COMPUTING] ❑ *The URL for Collins is http://www.collins.co.uk.*

urn /ɜːn/ (**urns**) **1** N-COUNT An **urn** is a container like a large vase, especially one in which the ashes of a cremated person are kept. **2** N-COUNT An **urn** is a metal container used for making a large quantity of tea or coffee and keeping it hot.

us /əs, STRONG ʌs/ PRON A speaker or writer uses **us** to refer to a group of people which includes himself or herself. ❑ *Neither of us forgot about it.* ❑ *He told us we had to leave Delhi by 7am.*

usable /ˈjuːzəbəl/ ADJ If something is **usable**, it is in a good enough state or condition to be used. ❑ *The castle has twelve usable bedrooms.*

usage /ˈjuːsɪdʒ/ **1** N-UNCOUNT **Usage** is the way in which words are actually used in particular contexts, especially with regard to their meanings. ❑ *...an Australian Guide to Modern English Usage.* **2** N-UNCOUNT **Usage** is the degree to which something is used or the way in which it is used. ❑ *The motor wore out from constant usage.*

USB /juː es ˈbiː/ (**USBs**) N-COUNT A **USB** or a **USB port** on a computer is a place where you can attach another piece of equipment, for example a printer. **USB** is an abbreviation for 'Universal Serial Bus'. [COMPUTING]

use
1 VERB USES
2 NOUN USES

use /juːz/ (**uses, using, used**)
1 **1** V-T If you **use** a particular thing, you do something with it in order to do a job or to achieve something. ❑ *May I use your phone?* ❑ *Use a very sharp knife to cut the beef.* ❑ *He had never used violence.* **2** V-T & PHR-VERB If you **use** a supply of something, or if you **use** it **up**, you finish it so that none of it is left. ❑ *Did you use up the milk?* **3** V-T If you **use** a particular word or expression, you say or write it. **4** V-T If you say that someone **uses** people, you disapprove of them because they are only interested in other people when they can benefit from them.

use /juːs/ (**uses**)
2 **1** N-UNCOUNT Your **use of** something is the action or fact of your using it. ❑ *...the use of mobile phones.* **2** N-COUNT If something has a particular **use**, it is intended for a particular purpose. ❑ *The Internet has many uses.* ❑ *They both loved the fabric, but couldn't find a use for it.* **3** N-UNCOUNT If you have the **use of** something, you have permission or the ability to use it. ❑ *They had regular use of a car.* ❑ *He lost the use of his legs during the war.* **4** N-COUNT A **use of** a word is a particular meaning that it has or a particular way in which it can be used. **5** PHRASE If something such as a technique, building, or machine is **in use**, it is used regularly. If it has gone **out of use**, it is no longer used regularly. **6** PHRASE If you **make use of** something, you do something with it in order to do a job or achieve something. ❑ *I shall make use of this time and do the washing.* **7** PHRASE You use expressions such as **it's no use**, **there's no use** and **what's the use** to indicate that an action will not achieve anything. ❑ *There's no use arguing with him when he's in a mood like this.*

used
1 MODAL USES AND PHRASES
2 ADJECTIVE USES

used /juːst/
1 **1** MODAL If something **used to** be done or **used to** be the case, it was done regularly in the past or was the case in the past. ❑ *People used to come and visit him every day.* ❑ *The gallery in north London used to be a shop.* **2** PHRASE If you **are used to** something, you are familiar with it because you have done it or experienced it many times before. If you **get used to** something, you become familiar with it. ❑ *Norman's used to getting up early.* ❑ *'You're famous, Maurice.—Get used to it.'*

used /juːzd/
2 **1** ADJ A **used** handkerchief, glass, or other object is dirty or spoiled because it has been used.

U

Picture Dictionary kitchen utensils

2 ADJ A **used** car has already had one or more owners.

useful /'juːsfʊl/ **1** ADJ If something is **useful**, you can use it to do something or to help you. ❑ *...useful information.* ● **usefully** ADV ❑ *This leaflet usefully explains how to build it.* ● **usefulness** N-UNCOUNT ❑ *...the usefulness of his work.* **2** PHRASE If an object or skill **comes in useful**, it can help you achieve something in a particular situation.

Word Partnership Use *useful* with:

ADV.	**also** useful, **especially** useful, **extremely** useful, **less/more** useful, **particularly** useful, **very** useful **1**
N.	useful **information**, useful **knowledge**, useful **life**, useful **purpose**, useful **strategy**, useful **tool** **1**

useless /'juːsləs/ **1** ADJ If something is **useless**, you cannot use it. ❑ *Their money was useless in this country.* **2** ADJ If a course of action is **useless**, it does not achieve anything. ❑ *She knew it was useless to argue.* **3** ADJ If you say that someone or something is **useless**, you mean that they are no good at all. [INFORMAL] ❑ *He was useless at sport.*

user /'juːzə/ (**users**) N-COUNT The **users** of a product, machine, service, or place are the people who use it. ❑ *Beach users have complained about the dogs.*
→ see **Internet**

U

ˌuser-'friendly ADJ If you describe something such as a machine or system as **user-friendly**, you mean that it is well designed and easy to use.

usher /'ʌʃə/ (**ushers, ushering, ushered**) **1** V-T If you **usher** someone somewhere, you show them where they should go, often by going with them. ❑ *I ushered him into the office.* **2** N-COUNT An **usher** is a person who shows people where to sit, for example at a wedding or a concert.
▶ **usher in** PHR-VERB If a person or event **ushers in** an important change, they help make it happen. [JOURNALISM] ❑ *The development will usher in a new generation of super powerful computers.*

usual /'juːʒʊəl/ **1** ADJ **Usual** is used to describe what happens or what is done most often in a particular situation. ❑ *The policeman asked the usual questions.* ❑ *The winter has been colder than usual.* ❑ *It is usual to give waiters a tip.* **2** PHRASE You use **as usual** to indicate that you are describing something that normally happens or that is normally the case. ❑ *As usual, Owen saved the match with a last-minute goal.* **3** PHRASE If something happens **as usual**, it happens in the way that it normally does. ❑ *When somebody died everything went on as usual.*

Word Partnership Use *usual* with:

ADV.	**less/more than** usual, **longer than** usual
N.	usual **place**, usual **routine**, usual **self**, usual **stuff**, usual **suspects**, usual **way**

usually /'juːʒʊəli/ ADV If something **usually** happens, it is the thing that most often happens in a particular situation. ❑ *We usually eat in here.*

usurp /juː'zɜːp/ (**usurps, usurping, usurped**) V-T If you say that someone **usurps** a job, role, title, or position, you mean that they take it from someone when they have no right to do this. [FORMAL]

utensil /juː'tensəl/ (**utensils**) N-COUNT **Utensils** are tools or other objects that you use when you are cooking or doing other tasks in your home. ❑ *...cooking utensils.*
→ see Picture Dictionary: **kitchen utensils**

uterus /'juːtərəs/ (**uteruses**) N-COUNT A woman's **uterus** is the part of her body where a baby grows. It is also called a **womb**. [TECHNICAL]

utilise /'juːtɪlaɪz/ → see **utilize**

utility /juː'tɪlɪti/ (**utilities**) **1** N-COUNT A **utility** is an important service such as water, electricity, or gas that is provided for everyone, and that everyone pays for. **2** N-UNCOUNT The **utility of** something is its usefulness. [FORMAL] ❑ *He questioned the utility of his work.*

utilize [BRIT also **utilise**] /'juːtɪlaɪz/ (**utilizes, utilizing, utilized**) V-T If you **utilize** something, you use it. [FORMAL] ❑ *She wants a job where she can utilize her skills and experience.* ● **utilization** N-UNCOUNT ❑ *...the utilization of technology.*

Word Link *most ≈ superlative degree : almost, foremost, utmost*

utmost /ˈʌtməʊst/ 1 ADJ BEFORE N You can use **utmost** to emphasize the importance or seriousness of something or to emphasize the way that it is done. [FORMAL] ❑ *I have a matter of the utmost importance to discuss with you.* 2 N-SING If you say that you are doing your **utmost to** do something, you are emphasizing that you are trying as hard as you can to do it. ❑ *He will try his utmost to help them.*

utopia /juːˈtəʊpiə/ (**utopias**) N-VAR If you refer to an imaginary situation as a **utopia**, you mean that it is one in which society is perfect and everyone is happy, but which you feel is not possible.

utopian /juːˈtəʊpiən/ ADJ If you describe a plan or idea as **utopian**, you are criticizing it because it is unrealistic and shows a belief that things can be improved much more than is possible.

utter /ˈʌtə/ (**utters, uttering, uttered**) 1 V-T If someone **utters** sounds or words, they say them. [LITERARY] ❑ *They left without uttering a word.* 2 ADJ BEFORE N You use **utter** to emphasize the great degree or amount of something bad. ❑ *This is utter nonsense.* ❑ *...his utter lack of interest in the subject.*

utterance /ˈʌtərəns/ (**utterances**) N-COUNT Someone's **utterances** are the things that they say. [FORMAL] ❑ *...the Queen's public utterances.*

utterly /ˈʌtəli/ ADV You use **utterly** to emphasize the great degree or amount of something bad. ❑ *The new laws are utterly ridiculous.*

ˈU-ˌturn (**U-turns**) 1 N-COUNT If you make a **U-turn** when you are driving or cycling, you turn in a half circle in one movement, so that you are then going in the opposite direction. 2 N-COUNT When a government or other decision maker does a **U-turn**, it abandons a policy and does something completely different.

U-turn

Vv

V, v /viː/ **V** or **v** is an abbreviation of **versus.** It is used to indicate that two teams are competing against each other. ❑ *...Manchester United v Chelsea.*

vacancy /ˈveɪkənsi/ (**vacancies**) **1** N-COUNT A **vacancy** is a job or position which has not been filled. ❑ *We have a vacancy for a secretary.* **2** N-COUNT If there are **vacancies** at a hotel, there are rooms still available for people to stay in.

Word Link	*vac ≈ empty : evacuate, vacant, vacate*

vacant /ˈveɪkənt/ **1** ADJ If something is **vacant**, it is not being used by anyone. ❑ *She sat down on a vacant seat.* **2** ADJ If a job or position is **vacant**, it has not yet been filled, and people can apply for it. ❑ *The post of headteacher has been vacant since June.* **3** ADJ A **vacant look** suggests that someone does not understand or that they are not concentrating. ● **vacantly** ADV ❑ *He looked vacantly out of the window.*

vacate /veɪˈkeɪt, AM ˈveɪkeɪt/ (**vacates, vacating, vacated**) V-T If you **vacate** a place or a job, you leave it and make it available for other people. [FORMAL] ❑ *He vacated the house and went to stay with a friend.*

vacation /vəˈkeɪʃən, AM veɪ-/ (**vacations**) **1** N-VAR In American English, a **vacation** is a period of time when you are not working and are away from home for relaxation. The British word is **holiday.** ❑ *We went on vacation to Puerto Rico.* **2** N-COUNT A **vacation** is a period of the year when universities or colleges are officially closed. ❑ *During his summer vacation he visited Russia.*

vaccinate /ˈvæksɪneɪt/ (**vaccinates, vaccinating, vaccinated**) V-T If a person or animal **is vaccinated**, they are given a vaccine, usually by injection, to prevent them from getting a disease. ❑ *Has your child been vaccinated against measles?* ● **vaccination** (**vaccinations**) N-VAR ❑ *We recommend vaccination against hepatitis B.*

V

vaccine /ˈvæksiːn, AM vækˈsiːn/ (**vaccines**) N-VAR A **vaccine** is a substance containing the germs that cause a disease. It is given to people to prevent them getting the disease.
→ see **hospital**

vacuum /ˈvækjuːm, -juːəm/ (**vacuums, vacuuming, vacuumed**) **1** N-COUNT If someone or something creates a **vacuum**, they leave a place or position which then needs to be filled by someone or something else. ❑ *They say major news events create a vacuum and make other things appear unimportant by comparison.* **2** N-COUNT A **vacuum** is a space that contains no air or other gas. **3** V-T/V-I If you **vacuum** something, you clean it using a vacuum cleaner.

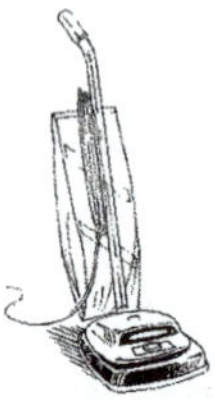
vacuum cleaner

ˈvacuum cleaner (**vacuum cleaners**) N-COUNT A **vacuum cleaner** or a **vacuum** is an electric machine which sucks up dust and dirt from carpets.

vagary /ˈveɪgəri/ (**vagaries**) N-COUNT **The vagaries of** something are the unexpected and unpredictable changes in it. [FORMAL] ❑ *...the vagaries of the weather.*

vagina /vəˈdʒaɪnə/ (**vaginas**) N-COUNT A woman's **vagina** is the passage connecting her outer sex organs to her womb. ● **vaginal** ADJ BEFORE N ❑ *...vaginal infections.*

vague /veɪg/ (**vaguer, vaguest**) **1** ADJ If something is **vague**, it is not clear, distinct, or definite. You can also say that someone is **vague** about something. ❑ *The description was pretty vague.* ❑ *Keith is quite vague about dates.* ● **vaguely** ADV ❑ *Judith vaguely remembered what her mother had said.* **2** ADJ If you describe someone as **vague**, you mean that they do not seem to be thinking clearly. ● **vaguely** ADV ❑ *He looked vaguely around the room.* **3** ADJ A **vague** shape or outline is not clear or easy to see.

vaguely /ˈveɪgli/ **1** ADV **Vaguely** means to a small degree. ❑ *The voice on the phone was vaguely familiar.* **2** → see also **vague**

vain /veɪn/ (**vainer, vainest**) **1** ADJ BEFORE N & PHRASE A **vain** attempt to do something does not succeed. If you do something **in vain**, what you do has no effect. ❑ *She made a vain attempt at a smile.* ❑ *It became obvious that all her complaints were in vain.* ● **vainly** ADV ❑ *He hunted vainly through his pockets for some money.* **2** ADJ If you describe someone as **vain**, you disapprove of them because they are too proud of their appearance.

valiant /ˈvæliənt/ ADJ **Valiant** means very brave. ● **valiantly** ADV ❑ *They fought valiantly to defend their country.*

valid /ˈvælɪd/ **1** ADJ A **valid** reason or argument is logical and reasonable, and therefore worth taking seriously. ❑ *He recognized the valid points that both sides were making.* ● **validity** /væˈlɪdɪti/ N-UNCOUNT ❑ *This argument has lost much of its validity.* **2** ADJ If a ticket or document is **valid**, it can be used and will be accepted by people in authority. ❑ *You will need a valid passport to travel abroad.*

validate /ˈvælɪdeɪt/ (**validates, validating, validated**) V-T To **validate** a statement or claim means to prove that it is true or correct. ❑ *An independent judge validated the company's actions.*

● **validation** (**validations**) N-VAR ❑ *There must be independent validation of these claims.*

valley /ˈvæli/ (**valleys**) N-COUNT A **valley** is a low area of land between hills, often with a river flowing through it.
→ see **river**

valuable /ˈvæljʊəbəl/ **1** ADJ Something that is **valuable** is very useful. ❑ *Her comments are a valuable contribution to the debate.* **2** ADJ **Valuable** objects are worth a lot of money. ❑ *...valuable books.*

Thesaurus *valuable* Also look up:

ADJ.	helpful, important, useful; *(ant.)* useless **1**
	costly, expensive, priceless; *(ant.)* worthless **2**

Word Partnership Use *valuable* with:

V.	**learn a** valuable **lesson** **1**
N.	valuable **experience**, valuable **information**, valuable **lesson**, **time is** valuable **1**
	valuable **asset**, valuable **resource** **1** **2**
	valuable **property** **2**
ADV.	**extremely** valuable, **less** valuable, **very** valuable **1** **2**

valuables /ˈvæljʊəbəlz/ N-PLURAL **Valuables** are things that you own that are worth a lot of money, especially small objects such as jewellery.

valuation /ˌvæljʊˈeɪʃən/ (**valuations**) N-VAR A **valuation** is a judgement about how much money something is worth. ❑ *...an independent valuation of the company.*

value /ˈvælju:/ (**values, valuing, valued**) **1** N-UNCOUNT The **value** of something such as a quality or a method is its importance or usefulness. ❑ *Some people dispute the value of this research.* **2** V-T If you **value** someone or something, you think that they are important and you appreciate them. ❑ *She values his opinion and advice.* **3** N-VAR The **value** of something is the amount of money it is worth. ❑ *The company's market value rose to $5.5 billion.* ❑ *Italy's currency went down in value by 3.5 per cent.* ❑ *...land of little value.* **4** V-T When experts **value** something, they decide how much money it is worth. ❑ *The aid - valued at $740,000 - will be used to buy medical supplies.* **5** N-UNCOUNT A thing's **value** is its worth in relation to the money that it costs. ❑ *This holiday is excellent value for money, with all flights, accommodation and meals included in the price.* **6** N-PLURAL The **values** of a person or group are their moral principles and beliefs. ❑ *...traditional family values.* **7** → see also **face value**

Thesaurus *value* Also look up:

N.	importance, merit, usefulness **1**
	cost, price, worth **3**
V.	admire, honour, respect **2**
	appraise, estimate, price **4**

Word Partnership Use *value* with:

V.	**decline in** value, **increase in** value, **lose** value **1** **3**
ADJ.	**actual** value, **artistic** value, **equal** value, **great** value **1** **3**
	estimated value **3**
N.	**cash** value, value **of an investment**, **market** value, **pound** value **3**

valve /vælv/ (**valves**) N-COUNT A **valve** is a device which controls the flow of a gas or liquid, for example in a pipe or tube.
→ see **engine**

vampire /ˈvæmpaɪə/ (**vampires**) N-COUNT In horror stories, **vampires** are creatures who come out of their graves at night and suck the blood of living people.

van /væn/ (**vans**) N-COUNT A **van** is a medium-sized road vehicle that is used for carrying goods.
→ see **car**

vandal /ˈvændəl/ (**vandals**) N-COUNT A **vandal** is someone who deliberately damages things, especially public property.

vandalism /ˈvændəlɪzəm/ N-UNCOUNT **Vandalism** is the deliberate damaging of things, especially public property.

vandalize [BRIT also **vandalise**] /ˈvændəlaɪz/ (**vandalizes, vandalizing, vandalized**) V-T If something **is vandalized** by someone, they deliberately damage it. ❑ *The walls were vandalized with spray paint.*

vanguard /ˈvæŋgɑ:d/ N-SING If someone is **in the vanguard of** something such as a revolution or an area of research, they are involved in the most advanced part of it.

vanilla /vəˈnɪlə/ N-UNCOUNT **Vanilla** is a flavouring used in ice cream and other sweet food.

vanish /ˈvænɪʃ/ (**vanishes, vanishing, vanished**) V-I If someone or something **vanishes**, they disappear suddenly or cease to exist altogether. ❑ *The missing woman vanished from her home last Wednesday.* ❑ *Tigers have vanished from south-east Asian countries.*

vanity /ˈvænɪti/ N-UNCOUNT If you refer to someone's **vanity**, you disapprove of them because they are too interested in their own appearance, or in other good qualities they believe they possess. ❑ *All his achievements are spoiled by his vanity.*

vantage point /ˈvɑ:ntɪdʒpɔɪnt, ˈvænt-/ (**vantage points**) N-COUNT A **vantage point** is a place from which you can see a lot of things. ❑ *From his hidden vantage point, he saw a car arrive.*

vapour [AM **vapor**] /ˈveɪpə/ (**vapours**) N-VAR **Vapour** consists of tiny drops of water or other liquids in the air, which appear as mist.
→ see **greenhouse effect, lake, water**

variable /ˈveəriəbəl/ (**variables**) **1** ADJ Something that is **variable** is likely to change at any time. ❑ *The weather is extremely variable at the moment.* ● **variability** N-UNCOUNT ❑ *...the variability in the climate.* **2** N-COUNT A **variable** is a factor in a situation that can change. ❑ *There is no such thing as a certainty in sailing - there are too many variables.*
→ see **experiment**

variance /ˈveəriəns/ PHRASE If one thing is **at**

V

variance with another, the two things seem to contradict each other. [FORMAL] ❑ *His statements are at variance with the facts.*

variant /ˈveəriənt/ (**variants**) N-COUNT A **variant of** something has a different form from the usual one. ❑ *Coca-Cola is to launch a lime-flavoured variant of its cola drink in the United States.* ❑ *Many words have variant spellings.*

variation /ˌveəriˈeɪʃən/ (**variations**) 1 N-COUNT A **variation on** something is the same thing presented in a different form. ❑ *This dish is a variation on an omelette.* 2 N-VAR A **variation** is a difference in a level, amount, or quantity. ❑ *...a wide variation in the prices charged for school meals.*

varied /ˈveərid/ 1 ADJ Something that is **varied** consists of things of different types, sizes, or qualities. ❑ *It is essential that your diet is varied and balanced.* 2 → see also **vary**

variety /vəˈraɪɪti/ (**varieties**) 1 N-UNCOUNT If something has **variety**, it consists of things which are different from each other. ❑ *Variety is the key to a healthy diet.* 2 N-SING A **variety of** things is a number of different kinds or examples of the same thing. ❑ *This area has a variety of good shops and supermarkets.* 3 N-COUNT A **variety of** something is a type of it. ❑ *She has 12 varieties of rose in her garden.*

Word Partnership Use *variety* with:

N. variety **of activities**, variety **of colours**, variety **of foods**, variety **of issues**, variety **of problems**, variety **of products**, variety **of reasons**, variety **of sizes**, variety **of styles**, variety **of ways** 2

V. **choose a** variety, **offer a** variety, **provide a** variety 2

various /ˈveəriəs/ ADJ If you say that there are **various** things, you mean there are several different things of the type mentioned. ❑ *Various countries will be represented at the conference.* ❑ *Definitions of the word 'love' are many and various.*

variously /ˈveəriəsli/ ADV You can use **variously** to introduce a number of different ways in which something is described. ❑ *He is variously described as a designer, a stylist, and a photographer.*

varnish /ˈvɑːnɪʃ/ (**varnishes, varnishing, varnished**) 1 N-VAR **Varnish** is an oily liquid which is painted onto wood to give it a hard, clear, shiny surface. 2 V-T If you **varnish** something, you paint it with varnish.

vary /ˈveəri/ (**varies, varying, varied**) 1 V-I If things **vary**, they are different in size, amount, or degree. ❑ *As the necklaces are handmade, each one varies slightly.* ❑ *The amount of sleep we need varies from person to person.* 2 V-T/V-I If something **varies**, or if you **vary** it, it becomes different or it changes. ❑ *The amount of food that a dog needs varies according to its age.* 3 → see also **varied**

Word Partnership Use *vary* with:

N. **prices** vary, **rates** vary, **styles** vary 1
vary **by location**, vary **by size**, vary **by state**, vary **by store** 1 2

ADV. vary **considerably**, vary **greatly**, vary **slightly**, vary **widely** 1 2

V

vase /vɑːz, AM veɪs/ (**vases**) N-COUNT A **vase** is a jar used for holding cut flowers or as an ornament. → see **glass**

vast /vɑːst, væst/ ADJ Something that is **vast** is extremely large. ❑ *...vast stretches of land.*

Word Partnership Use *vast* with:

N. vast **amounts**, vast **distance**, vast **expanse**, vast **knowledge**, vast **majority**, vast **quantities**

vastly /ˈvɑːstli, ˈvæst-/ ADV **Vastly** means to an extremely great degree or extent. ❑ *...two vastly different accounts of what happened.*

vault /vɔːlt/ (**vaults, vaulting, vaulted**) 1 N-COUNT A **vault** is a secure room where money and other valuable things can be kept safely. ❑ *...bank vaults.* 2 N-COUNT A **vault** is a room underneath a church or in a cemetery where people are buried. 3 N-COUNT A **vault** is an arched roof or ceiling. 4 V-T/V-I If you **vault** something or **vault over** it, you jump over it, putting one or both of your hands on it. ❑ *He vaulted over the wall.*

VCR /ˌviː siː ˈɑː/ (**VCRs**) N-UNCOUNT A **VCR** is a machine that can be used to record television programmes or films onto video tapes. **VCR** is an abbreviation for 'video cassette recorder'.

VDU /ˌviː diː ˈjuː/ (**VDUs**) N-COUNT A **VDU** is a machine with a screen which is used to display information from a computer. **VDU** is an abbreviation for 'visual display unit'. [COMPUTING]

veal /viːl/ N-UNCOUNT **Veal** is meat from a calf.

veer /vɪə/ (**veers, veering, veered**) V-I If something **veers** in a particular direction, it suddenly moves in that direction. ❑ *The plane veered off the runway.*

vegetable /ˈvedʒtəbəl/ (**vegetables**) N-COUNT **Vegetables** are edible plants such as cabbages, potatoes, and onions.
→ see Picture Dictionary: **vegetables**
→ see **vegetarian**

Word Link ***arian** ≈ believing in, having :*
humanitarian, totalitarian, vegetarian

vegetarian /ˌvedʒɪˈteəriən/ (**vegetarians**) N-COUNT & ADJ A **vegetarian** is someone who does not eat meat or fish. ❑ *...a strict vegetarian diet.*
→ see Word Web: **vegetarian**

vegetation /ˌvedʒɪˈteɪʃən/ N-UNCOUNT **Vegetation** is plants, trees and flowers. [FORMAL]
→ see **erosion, habitat**

vehement /ˈviːəmənt/ ADJ **Vehement** feelings and opinions are strongly held and forcefully expressed. ● **vehemence** N-UNCOUNT ❑ *He spoke with great vehemence.* ● **vehemently** ADV ❑ *Some people vehemently hated her, some adored her.*

vehicle /ˈviːɪkəl/ (**vehicles**) 1 N-COUNT A **vehicle** is a machine with an engine, for example a car, that carries people or things from place to place. 2 N-COUNT You can use **vehicle** to refer to something that you use in order to achieve a particular purpose. ❑ *Her art became a vehicle for her political beliefs.*
→ see **car, traffic**

veil /veɪl/ (**veils**) 1 N-COUNT A **veil** is a piece of thin soft cloth that women sometimes wear

Picture Dictionary **vegetables**

veil

over their heads and which can also cover their face. **2** N-COUNT You can refer to something that hides a situation or activity as a **veil**. ❑ *A veil of silence surrounded the meeting.*

veiled /veɪld/ **1** ADJ BEFORE N A **veiled** comment is expressed in a disguised form rather than directly and openly. ❑ *His words were a thinly-veiled threat.* **2** ADJ A **veiled** person is wearing a veil.

vein /veɪn/ (**veins**) **1** N-COUNT Your **veins** are the tubes in your body through which your blood flows towards your heart. **2** N-COUNT The **veins** on a leaf are the thin lines on it. **3** N-UNCOUNT Something that is written or spoken **in** a particular **vein** is written or spoken in that style or mood. ❑ *The girl smiled and replied to him in similar vein.*

velocity /vɪˈlɒsɪti/ (**velocities**) N-VAR **Velocity** is the speed at which something moves. [TECHNICAL]

velvet /ˈvelvɪt/ N-UNCOUNT **Velvet** is a soft fabric with a thick layer of short cut threads on one side.

vendetta /venˈdetə/ (**vendettas**) N-VAR If one person has a **vendetta against** another, the first person wants revenge for something the second person did to them in the past.

vendor /ˈvendə/ (**vendors**) N-COUNT A **vendor** is someone who sells things such as newspapers or hamburgers from a small stall or cart. ❑ *...ice-cream vendors.*

veneer /vɪˈnɪə/ N-SING If you refer to the pleasant way that someone behaves or that something appears as a **veneer**, you are critical of them because you believe that their true nature is unpleasant, and this is being hidden. ❑ *He fooled people with his veneer of compassion.*

venerable /ˈvenərəbəl/ **1** ADJ **Venerable** people deserve respect because they are old and wise. **2** ADJ **Venerable** things are impressive because they are old and historically important. ❑ *Yale University is a venerable institution.*

vengeance /ˈvendʒəns/ **1** N-UNCOUNT **Vengeance** is the act of harming someone because they have harmed you. ❑ *He swore vengeance on everyone involved in the murder.* **2** PHRASE If you say that something happens **with a vengeance**, you are emphasizing that it happens to a great extent. ❑ *It began to rain again with a vengeance.*

venison /ˈvenɪzən/ N-UNCOUNT **Venison** is the meat of a deer.

venom /ˈvenəm/ **1** N-UNCOUNT **Venom** is a feeling of great bitterness or anger towards someone. ❑ *There was venom in his voice.* **2** N-UNCOUNT The **venom** of certain snakes, spiders, or other creatures is the poison that they inject into animals, insects, or people when they bite or sting them.

vent /vent/ (**vents, venting, vented**) **1** N-COUNT A **vent** is a hole in something which allows air to come in and smoke, gas, or smells to go out. ❑ *There was a small air vent in the ceiling.* **2** V-T If you **vent** your feelings, you express them forcefully. ❑ *The students tried to vent their anger on the police.*

ventilate /ˈventɪleɪt/ (**ventilates, ventilating, ventilated**) V-T If you **ventilate** a room or building, you allow fresh air to get into it. ❑ *When you use this paint, ventilate the room.* • **ventilation** N-UNCOUNT ❑ *The only ventilation in this room comes from tiny windows.*

venture /ˈventʃə/ (**ventures, venturing, ventured**) **1** N-COUNT A **venture** is a new project or activity which is exciting and difficult because it involves the risk of failure. ❑ *...his latest money-making venture.* **2** V-I If you **venture into** an activity, you do something that involves the risk of failure because it is new and different. ❑ *He had little success when he ventured into business.* **3** V-I If you **venture** somewhere, you go there, although it might be dangerous. ❑ *People were afraid to venture out for fear of attack.*

venue /ˈvenjuː/ (**venues**) N-COUNT The **venue** for an event or activity is the place where it will happen. ❑ *The Embassy was the venue for a New Year's Eve party.*
→ see **concert**

veranda also **verandah** /vəˈrændə/ (**verandas**) N-COUNT A **veranda** is a platform with a roof along the outside wall of a house.

veranda

verb /vɜːb/ (**verbs**) N-COUNT A **verb** is a word such as 'sing' or 'feel' which is used to say what someone or something does or what happens to them, or to give information about them.

> **Word Link** *verb ≈ word : adverb, proverb, verbal*

verbal /ˈvɜːbəl/ **1** ADJ You use **verbal** to indicate that something is expressed in speech rather than in writing or action. ❑ *We have a verbal agreement with her.* ● **verbally** ADV ❑ *We complained both verbally and in writing.* **2** ADJ You use **verbal** to indicate that something is connected with words and the use of words. ❑ *She has a great sense of humour, imagination and verbal skill.*

> **Word Link** *ver ≈ truth : verdict, verify, version*

verdict /ˈvɜːdɪkt/ (**verdicts**) **1** N-COUNT In a law court, a **verdict** is the decision that is given by the jury or judge at the end of a trial. ❑ *The jury returned a unanimous guilty verdict.* **2** N-COUNT Someone's **verdict on** something is their opinion of it, after thinking about it or investigating it. ❑ *The critics gave their verdict on the show.*
→ see **trial**

verge /vɜːdʒ/ (**verges, verging, verged**) **1** PHRASE If you are **on the verge of** something, you are going to do it or it is about to happen. ❑ *Carole was on the verge of tears.* **2** N-COUNT The **verge** of a road is the narrow strip of grassy ground at the side. [BRIT]
▶ **verge on** PHR-VERB If someone or something **verges on** a particular state or quality, they are almost the same as that state or quality. ❑ *His fury verged on madness.*

V

verify /ˈverɪfaɪ/ (**verifies, verifying, verified**) V-T If you **verify** something, you check or confirm that it is true. ❑ *The clerk verified that the payment and invoice amount matched.* ● **verification** /ˌverɪfɪˈkeɪʃən/ N-UNCOUNT ❑ *You need to provide independent verification of your claims.*

veritable /ˈverɪtəbəl/ ADJ You can use **veritable** to emphasize the size or nature of something. ❑ *It was a veritable feast of Indian, Russian, and Thai food.*

vernacular /vəˈnækjʊlə/ (**vernaculars**) N-COUNT **The vernacular** is the language or dialect that is most widely spoken by ordinary people in a region or country. ❑ *...books or plays written in the vernacular.*

> **Word Link** *vers ≈ turning : reversal, versatile, version*

versatile /ˈvɜːsətaɪl, AM -təl/ **1** ADJ If you say that a person is **versatile**, you approve of them because they have many different skills. ❑ *...one of the game's most versatile athletes.* ● **versatility** /ˌvɜːsəˈtɪlɪti/ N-UNCOUNT ❑ *She is an actress of incredible versatility.* **2** ADJ A **versatile** activity, material, or machine can be used for many different purposes. ❑ *Metal is a very versatile material: it can be twisted and beaten into all manner of forms.* ● **versatility** N-UNCOUNT ❑ *It is his versatility that will make this French actor an international star.*

verse /vɜːs/ (**verses**) **1** N-UNCOUNT **Verse** is writing arranged in lines which have rhythm and which often rhyme at the end. ❑ *Several lines of verse were written on the piece of paper.* **2** N-COUNT A **verse** is one of the parts into which a poem, a song, or a chapter of the Bible or Koran is divided.

version /ˈvɜːʃən, -ʒən/ (**versions**) **1** N-COUNT A **version of** something is a form of it in which some details are different from earlier or later forms. ❑ *...an updated version of his book.* **2** N-COUNT Someone's **version of** an event is their personal account of it.

versus /ˈvɜːsəs/ **1** PREP You use **versus** to say that two ideas or things are opposed. ❑ *...the dilemma of career versus motherhood.* **2** PREP **Versus** is used to indicate that two people or teams are competing against each other in a sporting event. ❑ *He scored the winning goal in a Scotland versus England game.*

vertebra /ˈvɜːtɪbrə/ (**vertebrae** /ˈvɜːtɪbreɪ/) N-COUNT **Vertebrae** are the small circular bones that form your backbone.

vertical /ˈvɜːtɪkəl/ ADJ Something that is **vertical** stands or points straight upwards. ❑ *...a vertical wall of rock.* ● **vertically** ADV ❑ *Cut each apple in half vertically.*
→ see **graph**

very /ˈveri/ **1** ADV **Very** is used to give emphasis to an adjective or adverb. ❑ *The problem and the answer are very simple.* ❑ *Thank you very much.* **2** ADJ BEFORE N You use **very** with certain nouns in order to specify an extreme position or extreme point in time. ❑ *I turned to the very end of the book, to read the final words.* ❑ *He was wrong from the very beginning.* **3** ADJ BEFORE N You use **very** with nouns to emphasize that something is exactly the right one or exactly the same one. ❑ *She lived in this very house.* **4** CONVENTION **Very well** is used to say that you agree to do something or you accept someone's answer, even though you might not be completely satisfied with it. ❑ *'I still don't agree.'—'Very well, we won't argue about it.'* **5** PHRASE The expression **very much so** is an emphatic way of answering 'yes' to something or saying that it is true or correct. ❑ *'Are you enjoying your holiday?'—'Very much so.'*

Usage

Very, **so**, and **too** can all be used to intensify the meaning of an adjective, an adverb, or a word like **much** or **many**. However, they are not used in the same way. **Very** is the simplest intensifier. It has no other meaning beyond that. **So** can suggest an emotional reaction on the part of the speaker, such as pleasure, surprise, or disappointment. ❑ *John makes me so angry!* ❑ *Oh thank you so much!* **So** can also refer forward to a result clause introduced by **that**. ❑ *The procession was forced to move so slowly that he arrived three hours late.* **Too** suggests an excessive or undesirable amount, often so much that a particular result does not or cannot happen. ❑ *She does wear too much make-up at times.* ❑ *He was too late to save her.*

Thesaurus *very* Also look up:

ADV. absolutely, extremely, greatly, highly 1

vessel /ˈvesəl/ (**vessels**) 1 N-COUNT A **vessel** is a ship or a large boat. [FORMAL] ❑ *...a US naval vessel.* 2 N-COUNT A **vessel** is a bowl or other container in which liquid is kept. [FORMAL] ❑ *...storage vessels.* 3 → see also **blood vessel**
→ see **ship**

vest /vest/ (**vests, vesting, vested**) 1 N-COUNT A **vest** is a piece of underwear which is worn to keep the top part of your body warm. [BRIT] 2 N-COUNT In American English, a **vest** is a sleeveless piece of clothing with buttons which people usually wear over a shirt. The British word is **waistcoat**. 3 V-T If something **is vested in** you, or if you **are vested with** it, it is given to you as a right or responsibility. [FORMAL] ❑ *Ultimate power was vested in the King.*

ˌvested ˈinterest (**vested interests**) N-COUNT If you have a **vested interest in** something, you have a very strong reason for acting in a particular way, for example to protect your money or reputation. ❑ *They are a truly national company with no vested interest in one area of the country.*

vestige /ˈvestɪdʒ/ (**vestiges**) N-COUNT The **vestiges of** something are the small parts that still remain after most of it has gone. ❑ *I lost the last vestiges of religious faith at nineteen.*

vet /vet/ (**vets, vetting, vetted**) 1 N-COUNT A **vet** is someone who is qualified to treat sick or injured animals. [BRIT] 2 V-T If someone or something **is vetted**, that person or thing is checked carefully to make sure that they reach certain standards, particularly standards of morality or trust. [BRIT] ❑ *He is not allowed to read any book until his mother has vetted it.* ● **vetting** N-UNCOUNT ❑ *There were demands for even tighter vetting of people who work with children.*

veteran /ˈvetərən/ (**veterans**) 1 N-COUNT A **veteran** is someone who has served in the armed forces of their country, especially during a war. 2 N-COUNT A **veteran** is someone who has been involved in a particular activity for a long time. ❑ *...Tony Benn, the veteran Labour MP and former Cabinet minister.*

veterinary /ˈvetərənəri, AM -neri/ ADJ BEFORE N **Veterinary** is used to describe the work of a person whose job is to treat sick or injured animals, or to describe the medical treatment of animals. ❑ *...a veterinary surgeon.*

veto /ˈviːtəʊ/ (**vetoes, vetoing, vetoed**) 1 V-T & N-COUNT If someone in authority **vetoes** something, or if they put a **veto** on it, they forbid it, or stop it being put into action. ❑ *The Education Secretary vetoed the scheme.* ❑ *The plan was unacceptable to the White House and the President threatened a veto.* 2 N-UNCOUNT **Veto** is the right that someone in authority has to forbid something. ❑ *...the President's power of veto.*

vex /veks/ (**vexes, vexing, vexed**) V-T If someone or something **vexes** you, they make you feel annoyed. ❑ *Everything about her vexed him.* ● **vexed** ADJ ❑ *Farmers are vexed and blame the government.* ● **vexing** ADJ ❑ *It was a vexing problem.*

via /vaɪə, ˈviːə/ 1 PREP If you go somewhere **via** a particular place, you go through that place on the way to your destination. ❑ *She returned home via Britain and France.* 2 PREP If you do something **via** a particular means or person, you do it by making use of that means or person. ❑ *She sent us the photo via e-mail.*

viable /ˈvaɪəbəl/ ADJ Something that is **viable** is capable of doing what it is intended to do. ❑ *They were confident that their business plan was viable.* ● **viability** N-UNCOUNT ❑ *We are confident of our business's long-term viability.*

vibrant /ˈvaɪbrənt/ 1 ADJ Something or someone that is **vibrant** is full of energy and enthusiasm. ❑ *...her vibrant personality.* ● **vibrancy** N-UNCOUNT ❑ *She was a woman with extraordinary vibrancy.* 2 ADJ **Vibrant** colours are very bright and clear. ❑ *The grass was a vibrant green.* ● **vibrantly** ADV ❑ *...vibrantly coloured rugs.*

vibrate /vaɪˈbreɪt, AM ˈvaɪbreɪt/ (**vibrates, vibrating, vibrated**) V-T/V-I If something **vibrates**, or if you **vibrate** it, it shakes with repeated small quick movements. ❑ *The noise made the table vibrate.* ● **vibration** (**vibrations**) N-VAR ❑ *The vibration of the traffic rattled the shop windows.*
→ see **ear, sound**

vicar /ˈvɪkə/ (**vicars**) N-COUNT A **vicar** is a priest in the Church of England.

vice /vaɪs/ (**vices**)

The spelling **vise** is used in American English for meaning 3.

1 N-COUNT A **vice** is a habit which is regarded as a weakness in someone's character, but not usually as a serious fault. ❑ *I spend too much on clothes; that's my only vice.* 2 N-UNCOUNT **Vice** refers to criminal activities connected with pornography or prostitution. 3 N-COUNT A **vice** or **vise** is a tool with a pair of jaws that hold an object tightly while you do work on it.

vice versa /ˌvaɪsəˈvɜːsə/ PHRASE **Vice versa** is used to indicate that the reverse of what you have said is also true. For example, 'Women may bring their husbands with them, and vice versa' means that men may also bring their wives with them.

vicinity /vɪˈsɪnɪti/ N-SING If something is **in the vicinity of** a place, it is in the nearby area. ❑ *There are a hundred hotels in the vicinity of the station.*

vicious /ˈvɪʃəs/ 1 ADJ A **vicious** person is violent and cruel. ● **viciously** ADV ❑ *She was viciously attacked with a hammer.* ● **viciousness** N-UNCOUNT ❑ *...the intensity and viciousness of these attacks.* 2 ADJ

V

A **vicious** remark is cruel and intended to upset someone. ● **viciously** ADV ❑ *'He deserves to suffer,' said Penelope viciously.*

Thesaurus	*vicious* Also look up:
ADJ.	brutal, cruel, violent; *(ant.)* nice 1

ˌvicious 'circle N-SING A **vicious circle** is a problem or difficult situation that has the effect of creating new problems which then cause the original problem or situation to occur again.

victim /'vɪktɪm/ (**victims**) N-COUNT A **victim** is someone who has been hurt or killed by someone or something. ❑ *...the victims of violent crime.*

victimize [BRIT also **victimise**] /'vɪktɪmaɪz/ (**victimizes, victimizing, victimized**) V-T If someone **is victimized**, they are deliberately treated unfairly. ❑ *The students were victimized because they opposed the government.* ● **victimization** N-UNCOUNT ❑ *This artist protests against society's victimization of women.*

victor /'vɪktə/ (**victors**) N-COUNT The **victor** in a contest or battle is the person who wins. [LITERARY]

Victorian /vɪk'tɔːriən/ (**Victorians**) 1 ADJ **Victorian** means belonging to, connected with, or typical of Britain in the middle and last parts of the 19th century, during the reign of Queen Victoria. ❑ *...a Victorian house.* 2 N-COUNT The **Victorians** were the people who lived in the reign of Queen Victoria.

Word Link	*vict, vinc ≈ conquering : convince, invincible, victorious*

victorious /vɪk'tɔːriəs/ ADJ You use **victorious** to describe someone who has won a victory in a struggle, war, or competition. ❑ *...a member of the victorious British team.*

victory /'vɪktəri/ (**victories**) N-VAR A **victory** is a success in a war or a competition. ❑ *The New Democracy party claimed victory.*

Thesaurus	*victory* Also look up:
N.	conquest, success, win; *(ant.)* defeat

video /'vɪdiəʊ/ (**videos, videoing, videoed**) 1 N-COUNT A **video** is a film or television programme recorded on videotape. 2 N-UNCOUNT **Video** is the recording and showing of films and events, using a video recorder, videotapes, and a television set. ❑ *She watched the race on video.* 3 N-COUNT A **video** is the same as a **VCR**. 4 V-T If you **video** something, you record it on magnetic tape, either by using a video recorder or camera.

V

'video game (**video games**) N-COUNT A **video game** is a computer game that you play on your television set or on a similar device.

'video recorder (**video recorders**) N-COUNT A **video recorder** or a **video cassette recorder** is the same as a **VCR**.

Word Link	*vid, vis ≈ seeing : television, videotape, visible*

videotape /'vɪdiəʊteɪp/ (**videotapes**) N-VAR **Videotape** is magnetic tape that is used to record pictures and sounds to be shown on television.

vie /vaɪ/ (**vies, vying, vied**) V-I If one person **vies with** another **to** do something, or if they **vie to** do it, they both try hard to do it sooner or better than the other person. [FORMAL] ❑ *The brothers vied with each other to offer their help.*

view
1 OPINIONS
2 BEING ABLE TO SEE THINGS

view /vjuː/ (**views, viewing, viewed**)
1 1 N-COUNT Your **views on** something are the opinions or beliefs that you have about it. ❑ *We have similar views on the matter.* ❑ *I take the view that she should resign as soon as possible.* ❑ *In my view things won't change.* 2 N-SING Your **view of** a particular subject is the way that you understand and think about it. ❑ *...a Christian-centred view of religion.* 3 → see also **point of view** 4 V-T If you **view** something in a particular way, you think of it in that way. ❑ *We will view any proposals with interest.* 5 PREP You use **in view of** when you are taking into consideration facts that have just been mentioned or are just about to be mentioned. ❑ *In view of his injury, he was offered only a short-term contract.* 6 PHRASE If you do something **with a view to** a particular result, you do it to achieve that result. ❑ *The Prime Minister called a meeting, with a view to forming a new government.*

view /vjuː/ (**views, viewing, viewed**)
2 1 N-COUNT The **view** from a particular place is everything you can see from that place, especially when it is considered to be beautiful. 2 N-SING If you have a **view** of something, you can see it. ❑ *He stopped in the doorway, blocking her view.* 3 N-UNCOUNT You use **view** in expressions to do with being able to see something. For example, if something is **in view**, you can see it. If something is **in full view of everyone**, everyone can see it. ❑ *No one was in view.* 4 V-T If you **view** something, you inspect it or look at it for a particular purpose. [FORMAL] ❑ *Hundreds of people came to view the paintings.* 5 PHRASE If something such as a work or art is **on view**, it is being exhibited in public.

viewer /'vjuːə/ (**viewers**) N-COUNT **Viewers** are people who watch television.

viewpoint /'vjuːpɔɪnt/ (**viewpoints**) N-COUNT Someone's **viewpoint** is the way they think about things in general or about a particular thing. ❑ *The novel is written from the girl's viewpoint.*

Word Link	*vig ≈ awake, strong : invigorating, vigil, vigilant*

vigil /'vɪdʒɪl/ (**vigils**) N-COUNT A **vigil** is a period of time when people remain quietly in a place, especially at night, for example because they are praying or are making a political protest. ❑ *Protesters are holding a twenty-four hour vigil.*

vigilant /'vɪdʒɪlənt/ ADJ Someone who is **vigilant** gives careful attention to a particular problem or situation and concentrates on noticing any danger or trouble that there might be. ❑ *Storms are forecast for the weekend and motorists should be vigilant.* ● **vigilance** N-UNCOUNT ❑ *Courage and vigilance averted a catastrophe aboard this flight to Miami.*

vigilante /ˌvɪdʒɪ'lænti/ (**vigilantes**) N-COUNT **Vigilantes** are people who organize themselves into an unofficial group to protect their community and to catch and punish criminals.

vigor → see **vigour**

vigorous /'vɪgərəs/ ADJ **Vigorous** actions involve using a lot of energy and enthusiasm. ❑ *...the benefits of vigorous exercise.* ● **vigorously** ADV ❑ *He shook his head vigorously.* ❑ *She vigorously denies the allegation.*

vigour [AM **vigor**] /'vɪgə/ N-UNCOUNT **Vigour** is physical or mental energy and enthusiasm. ❑ *The election was fought with vigour.*

vile /vaɪl/ (**viler, vilest**) ADJ If you say that someone or something is **vile**, you mean that they are extremely unpleasant.

villa /'vɪlə/ (**villas**) N-COUNT A **villa** is a fairly large house, especially one that is used for holidays in Mediterranean countries.

village /'vɪlɪdʒ/ (**villages**) N-COUNT A **village** consists of a group of houses, together with other buildings such as a church and school, in a country area.

villager /'vɪlɪdʒə/ (**villagers**) N-COUNT You refer to the people who live in a village as the **villagers**.

villain /'vɪlən/ (**villains**) 1 N-COUNT A **villain** is someone who deliberately harms other people or breaks the law in order to get what he or she wants. 2 N-COUNT The **villain** in a novel, film, or play is the main bad character.

vindicate /'vɪndɪkeɪt/ (**vindicates, vindicating, vindicated**) V-T If a person **is vindicated**, they are proved to be correct, after people have said that they were wrong. [FORMAL] ❑ *He was vindicated in court and damages of $100,000 were awarded.* ● **vindication** (**vindications**) N-VAR ❑ *He will receive some degree of vindication from the report.*

vindictive /vɪn'dɪktɪv/ ADJ Someone who is **vindictive** deliberately tries to upset or cause trouble for people who they think have done them harm. ● **vindictiveness** N-UNCOUNT ❑ *He let vindictiveness get in the way of his judgment.*

vine /vaɪn/ (**vines**) N-COUNT A **vine** is a climbing or trailing plant, especially one which produces grapes.

vinegar /'vɪnɪgə/ N-UNCOUNT **Vinegar** is a sharp-tasting liquid, usually made from sour wine or malt, which is used to make things such as salad dressing.

vineyard /'vɪnjəd/ (**vineyards**) N-COUNT A **vineyard** is an area of land where grape vines are grown in order to produce wine.

vintage /'vɪntɪdʒ/ (**vintages**) 1 N-COUNT The **vintage** of a good quality wine is the year and place that it was made. 2 ADJ BEFORE N **Vintage** wine is good quality wine that has been stored for several years in order to improve its quality. 3 ADJ BEFORE N **Vintage** cars or aeroplanes are old but are admired because they are considered to be the best of their kind.

vinyl /'vaɪnɪl/ N-UNCOUNT **Vinyl** is a strong plastic used for making things such as floor coverings and furniture.

viola /vi'əʊlə/ (**violas**) N-COUNT A **viola** is a musical instrument which looks like a violin but is slightly larger.
→ see **orchestra, string**

violate /'vaɪəleɪt/ (**violates, violating, violated**) 1 V-T If someone **violates** an agreement, law, or promise, they break it. ❑ *Doctors who violate the law could face two years in prison.* ● **violation** (**violations**) N-VAR ❑ *I believe that the use of violence against prisoners is a violation of human rights.* 2 V-T If you **violate** someone's privacy or peace, you disturb it. [FORMAL] 3 V-T If someone **violates** a special place, for example a tomb, they damage it or treat it without respect. ● **violation** N-VAR ❑ *...the violation of the graves.*

violence /'vaɪələns/ 1 N-UNCOUNT **Violence** is behaviour which is intended to hurt or kill people. ❑ *Twenty people were injured in the violence.* 2 N-UNCOUNT If you do or say something with **violence**, you use a lot of force and energy in doing or saying it, often because you are angry. [LITERARY] ❑ *There was such violence in her voice that he was startled.*

violent /'vaɪələnt/ 1 ADJ If someone is **violent**, or if they do something which is **violent**, they use physical force or weapons to hurt or kill other people. ❑ *We all know violent crime is on the increase.* ● **violently** ADV ❑ *He was violently attacked by an elderly lady with an umbrella.* 2 ADJ A **violent** event happens suddenly and with great force. ❑ *With a sudden violent movement, his father threw down his newspaper.* ● **violently** ADV ❑ *The volcano erupted violently.* 3 ADJ If you describe something as **violent**, you mean that it is said, done, or felt with great force and energy. ❑ *He had violent stomach pains.* ● **violently** ADV ❑ *Other experts violently disagree.*

violet /'vaɪəlɪt/ (**violets**) 1 N-COUNT A **violet** is a small purple or white flower that blooms in the spring. 2 ADJ & N-VAR Something that is **violet** in colour is bluish-purple.
→ see **colour, rainbow**

violin /ˌvaɪə'lɪn/ (**violins**) N-COUNT A **violin** is a musical instrument with four strings stretched over a shaped hollow box. You hold a violin under your chin and play it with a bow. ● **violinist** (**violinists**) N-COUNT ❑ *...the famous jazz violinist.*
→ see **orchestra, string**

VIP /ˌviː aɪ 'piː/ (**VIPs**) N-COUNT A **VIP** is someone who is given better treatment than ordinary people because he or she is famous or important. **VIP** is an abbreviation for 'very important person'.

virgin /'vɜːdʒɪn/ (**virgins**) 1 N-COUNT A **virgin** is someone who has never had sex. ● **virginity** /və'dʒɪnɪti/ N-UNCOUNT ❑ *She lost her virginity when she was 20.* 2 ADJ You use **virgin** to describe something such as land that has never been used or spoiled. ❑ *...a field of virgin snow.*

Word Link	***vir** ≈ man : **vir**ile, **vir**ility, **vir**tue*

virile /'vɪraɪl, AM -rəl/ ADJ If you describe a man as **virile**, you mean he has the qualities that a man is traditionally expected to have, such as strength and sexuality. ● **virility** /vɪ'rɪlɪti/ N-UNCOUNT ❑ *At what age does a man begin to feel uncertain about his virility?*

virtual /'vɜːtʃʊəl/ ADJ BEFORE N 1 You can use **virtual** to indicate that something is so nearly true that for most purposes it can be regarded as being true. ❑ *The men say that they were held in virtual slavery and paid nothing for their work.* ● **virtually** ADV ❑ *The task looks virtually impossible now.* 2 ADJ **Virtual** objects and activities are generated by a computer to simulate real objects and activities.

[COMPUTING] ❑ *The company is planning to create a virtual shopping centre on the Internet.*

virtual re'ality N-UNCOUNT **Virtual reality** is an environment which is produced by a computer and seems very like reality to the person experiencing it. [COMPUTING]

Word Link	*vir ≈ man : virile, virility, virtue*

virtue /'vɜːtʃuː/ (**virtues**) 1 N-UNCOUNT **Virtue** is thinking and doing what is right, and avoiding what is wrong. 2 N-COUNT A **virtue** is a good quality or way of behaving. ❑ *His virtue is patience.* 3 N-VAR The **virtue** of something is an advantage or benefit that it has, especially in comparison with something else. ❑ *The other great virtue of this material is its hard-wearing quality.* 4 PREP You use **by virtue of** to explain why something happens or is true. [FORMAL] ❑ *Mr Olaechea has British residency by virtue of his marriage.*

virtuoso /ˌvɜːtʃʊ'əʊzəʊ/ (**virtuosos** or **virtuosi** /ˌvɜːtʃʊ'əʊzi/) 1 N-COUNT A **virtuoso** is someone who is exceptionally good at playing a musical instrument. 2 ADJ A **virtuoso** performance or display shows exceptional skill.

virtuous /'vɜːtʃʊəs/ 1 ADJ A **virtuous** person behaves in a moral and correct way. ❑ *...virtuous people who obey the rules and are nice to others.* 2 ADJ If you describe someone as **virtuous**, you mean that they feel very pleased with their own good behaviour; often used showing disapproval. ❑ *I cleaned the flat, which left me feeling virtuous.* ● **virtuously** ADV ❑ *'I've already done that,' said Ronnie virtuously.*

Word Link	*vir ≈ poison : virulent, virus, virulence*

virulent /'vɪrjʊlənt/ 1 ADJ **Virulent** feelings or actions are extremely bitter and hostile. ❑ *He faced virulent attacks from the media.* ● **virulently** ADV ❑ *The talk was virulently hostile.* ● **virulence** N-UNCOUNT ❑ *The virulence of his anger appalled her.* 2 ADJ A **virulent** disease or poison is extremely powerful and dangerous. ● **virulence** N-UNCOUNT ❑ *...the virulence of the disease.*

virus /'vaɪərəs/ (**viruses**) 1 N-COUNT A **virus** is a kind of germ that can cause disease. 2 N-COUNT In computer technology, a **virus** is a program that alters or destroys the information stored in a system. [COMPUTING]
→ see **illness**

visa /'viːzə/ (**visas**) N-COUNT A **visa** is an official document or a stamp put in your passport which allows you to enter or leave a particular country.

vise /vaɪs/ → see **vice**

V **visibility** /ˌvɪzɪ'bɪlɪti/ N-UNCOUNT **Visibility** is how far or how clearly you can see in particular weather conditions. ❑ *Visibility was poor.*

Word Link	*vid, vis ≈ seeing : television, videotape, visible*

visible /'vɪzɪbəl/ 1 ADJ If an object is **visible**, it can be seen. ❑ *The mainland is clearly visible from their island.* 2 ADJ You use **visible** to describe something or someone that people notice or recognize. ❑ *He made a visible effort to control his temper.* ● **visibly** ADV ❑ *They were visibly distressed.*
→ see **wave**

Word Partnership	Use *visible* with:
N.	visible **to the naked eye** 1
ADV.	**barely** visible, **clearly** visible, **highly** visible, **less** visible, **more** visible, **still** visible, **very** visible 1 2
V.	**become** visible 1 2

vision /'vɪʒən/ (**visions**) 1 N-COUNT Your **vision of** a future situation or society is what you imagine or hope it would be like, if things were very different from the way they are now. ❑ *I have a vision of a society that is free of injustice.* 2 N-UNCOUNT Your **vision** is your ability to see clearly with your eyes. ❑ *The disease causes serious loss of vision.*

Word Partnership	Use *vision* with:
V.	**have a** vision, **see a** vision, **share a** vision 1
N.	vision **of the future**, vision **of peace**, vision **of reality** 1
	colour vision, **field of** vision 2
ADJ.	**blurred** vision, **clear** vision 2

visionary /'vɪʒənri, AM -neri/ (**visionaries**) 1 N-COUNT A **visionary** is someone who has strong original ideas about how things might be different in the future, especially about how things might be improved. 2 ADJ You use **visionary** to describe the strong original ideas of a visionary. ❑ *...the visionary architecture of Etienne Boullée.*

visit /'vɪzɪt/ (**visits, visiting, visited**) 1 V-T & N-COUNT If you **visit** someone, or if you **pay** them a **visit**, you go to see them and spend time with them. ❑ *She visited her sister in hospital over the weekend.* ❑ *Helen recently paid him a visit.* 2 V-T & N-COUNT If you **visit** a place, or if you make a **visit to** a place, you go to see it. ❑ *...the Pope's visit to Canada.*
▶ **visit with** PHR-VERB If you **visit with** someone, you go to see them and spend time with them. [AM] ❑ *I visited with him in San Francisco.*

Thesaurus	*visit* Also look up:
V.	call on, go, see, stop by 1

Word Partnership	Use *visit* with:
N.	visit **family/relatives**, visit **friends**, visit ***your*** **mother** 1
	weekend visit 1 2
	visit **a museum**, visit **a restaurant** 2
V.	**come to** visit, **go to** visit, **invite** ***someone*** **to** visit, **plan to** visit 1 2
ADJ.	**brief** visit, **last** visit, **next** visit, **recent** visit, **short** visit, **surprise** visit 1 2
	foreign visit, **official** visit 2

visitor /'vɪzɪtə/ (**visitors**) N-COUNT A **visitor** is someone who is visiting a person or place.

vista /'vɪstə/ (**vistas**) 1 N-COUNT A **vista** is a view, especially a beautiful view from a high place. ❑ *I looked out on a vista of hills and rooftops.* 2 N-COUNT A **vista** is a vision of a situation or of a range or possibilities. ❑ *...a vista of a future without hope.*

visual /ˈvɪʒʊəl/ ADJ **Visual** means relating to sight, or to things that you can see. ❑ *The film's visual effects are impressive.* ❑ *...careers in the visual arts.* ● **visually** ADV ❑ *...visually impaired children*

Word Partnership Use *visual* with:

N. visual **arts**, visual **effects**, visual **information**, visual **memory**, visual **perception**

visualize [BRIT also **visualise**] /ˈvɪʒʊəlaɪz/ (**visualizes, visualizing, visualized**) V-T If you **visualize** something, you imagine what it is like by forming a mental picture of it. ❑ *He could not visualize her as old.* ❑ *Visualize how you want to hit the ball.*

Word Link *vita ≈ life : revitalize, vital, vitality*

vital /ˈvaɪtəl/ 1 ADJ If something is **vital**, it is necessary or very important. ❑ *It is vital that action is taken quickly.* ❑ *...vital information.* ● **vitally** ADV ❑ *Lesley's career is vitally important to her.* 2 ADJ **Vital** people, organizations, or activities are very energetic and full of life. ❑ *He is a vital and funny man.*

Thesaurus *vital* Also look up:

ADJ. crucial, essential, necessary; *(ant.)* unimportant 1

Word Partnership Use *vital* with:

ADV. **absolutely** vital 1
N. vital **importance**, vital **information**, vital **interests**, vital **link**, vital **organs**, vital **part**, vital **role** 1

vitality /vaɪˈtælɪti/ N-UNCOUNT If someone or something has **vitality**, they have great energy and liveliness. ❑ *He has enormous vitality.* ❑ *...the financial vitality of the business.*

vitamin /ˈvɪtəmɪn, AM ˈvaɪt-/ (**vitamins**) N-COUNT **Vitamins** are organic substances in food which you need in order to remain healthy. ❑ *...vitamin D.* ❑ *...vitamin supplements.*

Word Link *viv ≈ living : revival, survive, vivid*

vivid /ˈvɪvɪd/ 1 ADJ **Vivid** memories and descriptions are very clear and detailed. ❑ *...a very vivid dream.* ● **vividly** ADV ❑ *I remember the phone call vividly.* 2 ADJ Something that is **vivid** is very bright in colour. ❑ *...a vivid blue sky.* ● **vividly** ADV ❑ *...vividly coloured birds.*

Word Link *voc ≈ speaking: advocate, vocabulary, vocal*

vocabulary /vəʊˈkæbjʊləri, AM -leri/ (**vocabularies**) 1 N-VAR Your **vocabulary** is the total number of words you know in a particular language. ❑ *...people with a limited vocabulary.* 2 N-SING The **vocabulary** of a language is all the words in it. ❑ *...a new word in the German vocabulary.* → see **English**

Word Partnership Use *vocabulary* with:

N. **part of *someone's*** vocabulary 1
vocabulary **development** 1 2
V. **learn** vocabulary 1 2
ADJ. **specialized** vocabulary, **technical** vocabulary 2

vocal /ˈvəʊkəl/ 1 ADJ You say that people are **vocal** when they speak forcefully and with feeling about something. ❑ *She was very vocal in expressing her objections.* 2 ADJ BEFORE N **Vocal** means involving the use of the human voice, especially in singing.

vocalist /ˈvəʊkəlɪst/ (**vocalists**) N-COUNT A **vocalist** is a singer who sings with a pop group. ❑ *...the band's lead vocalist.*

vocals /ˈvəʊkəlz/ N-PLURAL In a pop song, the **vocals** are the singing, in contrast to the playing of instruments.

vocation /vəʊˈkeɪʃən/ (**vocations**) N-VAR If you have a **vocation**, you have a strong feeling that you are especially suited to a particular job or role in life. You can also call your job a **vocation** if you feel like this about it. ❑ *He sees social work as a vocation.*

vocational /vəʊˈkeɪʃənəl/ ADJ **Vocational** training and skills are the training and skills needed for a particular job or profession. ❑ *Newer universities tend to offer more vocational courses.*

vociferous /vəˈsɪfərəs, AM vəʊs-/ ADJ If you describe someone as **vociferous**, you mean that they speak with great energy and determination, because they want their views to be heard. [FORMAL] ❑ *He was a vociferous opponent of Conservatism.* ● **vociferously** ADV ❑ *The Prime Minister campaigned vociferously for this result.*

vodka /ˈvɒdkə/ (**vodkas**) N-VAR **Vodka** is a strong clear alcoholic drink.

vogue /vəʊg/ 1 N-SING If there is a **vogue for** something, it is very popular and fashionable. ❑ *...the vogue for herbal tea.* 2 PHRASE If something is **in vogue**, is very popular and fashionable. If it **comes into vogue**, it becomes very popular and fashionable.

voice /vɔɪs/ (**voices, voicing, voiced**) 1 N-COUNT When someone speaks or sings, you hear their **voice**. ❑ *'The police are here,' she said in a low voice.* 2 N-COUNT You can use **voice** to refer to someone's opinion on a particular topic. ❑ *All voices must be heard, both pro and con.* 3 N-SING If you have a **voice in** something, you have the right to express an opinion on it. ❑ *Workers should have a voice in decisions that affect their jobs.* 4 V-T If you **voice** an opinion or an emotion, you say what you think or feel. ❑ *Scientists have voiced concern that the disease could be passed on to humans.* 5 N-SING In grammar, if a verb is in **the active voice**, the person who performs the action is the subject of the verb. For example, 'The man feeds the dog' is in the active voice. If a verb is in **the passive voice**, the thing or person affected by the action is the subject of the verb. For example, 'The dog is fed by the man' is in the passive voice.

void /vɔɪd/ (**voids**) 1 N-COUNT If you describe a situation or a feeling as a **void**, you mean that it seems empty because there is nothing interesting or worthwhile about it. ❑ *His death left a very deep void in my life.* 2 N-COUNT You can describe a large

Word Web volcano

The world's most famous **volcano** is Mount Vesuvius, near Naples, Italy. This mountain sits in the middle of the much older **volcanic cone** of Mount Somma. In 79 AD the sleeping volcano **erupted**, and magma rose to the surface. The people of the nearby city of Pompeii were terrified. Huge black clouds of **ash** and pumice came rushing toward them. The clouds blocked out the sun. They smothered thousands of people. Pompeii was buried under hot ash and **molten lava**. Centuries later the remains of the people and town were found. The discovery made this active volcano famous.

or frightening space as a **void**. ❑ *The ship moved silently through the black void.* **3** ADJ AFTER LINK-V Something that is **void** is officially considered to have no value or authority. ❑ *The vote was declared void.*

volatile /'vɒlətaɪl, AM -təl/ **1** ADJ A **volatile** situation is likely to change suddenly and unexpectedly. ❑ *The political situation remained volatile across the country yesterday.* **2** ADJ A **volatile** person is someone whose moods or attitudes change quickly and frequently.

volcanic /vɒl'kænɪk/ ADJ **Volcanic** means coming from or created by volcanoes. ❑ *St Vincent is a lush, volcanic island.*
→ see **volcano**

volcano /vɒl'keɪnəʊ/ (**volcanoes**) N-COUNT A **volcano** is a mountain from which hot melted rock, gas, steam and ash sometimes burst. ❑ *The volcano erupted last year killing many people.*
→ see Word Web: **volcano**

volley /'vɒli/ (**volleys, volleying, volleyed**) **1** N-COUNT A **volley of** gunfire is a lot of bullets that are fired at the same time. ❑ *A volley of shots rang out.* **2** V-T & N-COUNT In sports such as tennis and football, if someone **volleys** the ball, they hit or kick it before it touches the ground. A **volley** is a shot like this. ❑ *He volleyed the ball into the far corner of the net.*

volleyball /'vɒlibɔːl/ N-UNCOUNT **Volleyball** is a sport in which two teams use their hands to hit a large ball over a high net.

volt /vəʊlt/ (**volts**) N-COUNT A **volt** is a unit used to measure the force of an electric current.

voltage /'vəʊltɪdʒ/ (**voltages**) N-VAR The **voltage** of an electrical current is its force measured in volts. ❑ *...high-voltage power lines.*

volume /'vɒljuːm/ (**volumes**) **1** N-COUNT The **volume of** something is the amount of it that there is. ❑ *The volume of sales has increased slightly.* ❑ *...the huge volume of traffic.* **2** N-COUNT The **volume** of an object is the amount of space that it contains or occupies. ❑ *Place the rice in a pan with four times its volume of salted water.* **3** N-COUNT A **volume** is one book in a series of books. ❑ *...the first volume of his autobiography.* **4** N-UNCOUNT The **volume** of a radio, TV, or sound system is how loud it is. ❑ *He turned down the volume.*
→ see Picture Dictionary: **volume**

voluntary /'vɒləntri, AM -teri/ **1** ADJ **Voluntary** is used to describe actions and activities that you

Picture Dictionary volume

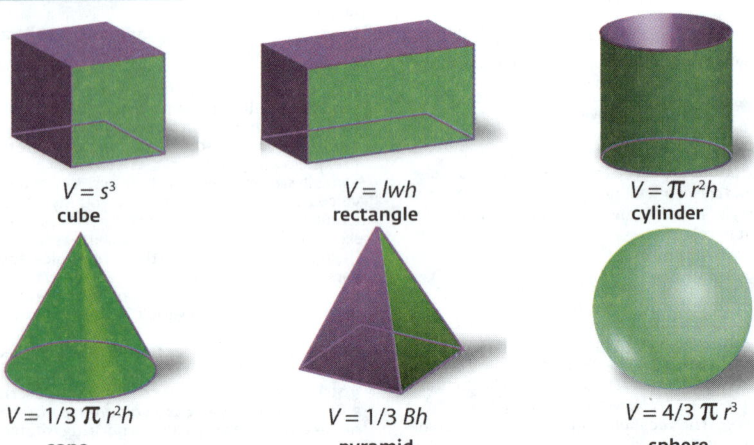

do because you choose them, rather than because you have to do them. ❑ *...classes where attendance is voluntary.* • **voluntarily** ADV ❑ *He asked people to surrender their weapons voluntarily.* **2** ADJ **Voluntary** work is work which people do not get paid for, but which they do to help an organization such as a charity. **3** ADJ BEFORE N A **voluntary** organization, for example a charity, is controlled by the people who have chosen to work for it, often without being paid.
→ see **muscle**

Word Partnership Use *voluntary* with:

N. voluntary **action**, voluntary **basis**, voluntary **compliance**, voluntary **contributions**, voluntary **programme**, voluntary **retirement**, voluntary **test** **1**
voluntary **organizations** **3**

Word Link *eer ≈ one who does : auctioneer, engineer, volunteer*

Word Link *vol ≈ will : benevolent, involuntary, volunteer*

volunteer /ˌvɒlənˈtɪə/ (**volunteers, volunteering, volunteered**) **1** N-COUNT A **volunteer** is someone who does work without being paid for it, especially for an organization such as a charity. ❑ *She now helps in a local school as a volunteer.* **2** N-COUNT A **volunteer** is someone who offers to do a particular task without being forced to do it. ❑ *Thirty-five volunteers are necessary to make the project a success.* **3** N-COUNT A **volunteer** is someone who chooses to join the armed forces, especially in wartime, as opposed to someone who is forced to join by law. **4** V-T/V-I If you **volunteer to** do something, you offer to do it without being forced to do it. ❑ *Mary volunteered to clean up the kitchen.* ❑ *He volunteered for overseas service.* **5** V-T If you **volunteer** information, you tell someone something without being asked. [FORMAL] ❑ *No one volunteered any further information.* ❑ *'Where's the kid?' Lucas asked.—'I'll get him,' Jones volunteered.*

Word Partnership Use *volunteer* with:

N. **community** volunteer **1**
volunteer **organization**, volunteer **programme**, volunteer **work** **1** **2**
volunteer **for the army**, volunteer **for service** **3**
volunteer **information** **5**
V. **need a** volunteer **1** **2** **3**
volunteer **to help**, volunteer **to work** **4**

vomit /ˈvɒmɪt/ (**vomits, vomiting, vomited**) **1** V-I If you **vomit**, food and drink comes back up from your stomach and out through your mouth. **2** N-UNCOUNT **Vomit** is partly digested food and drink that comes out of someone's mouth when they vomit.

voracious /vəˈreɪʃəs, AM vɔːr-/ ADJ If you describe a person, or their appetite for something, as **voracious**, you mean that they want a lot of it. [FORMAL] ❑ *She was a voracious reader.*

vote /vəʊt/ (**votes, voting, voted**) **1** N-COUNT A **vote** is a choice made by a particular person or group in a meeting or an election. ❑ *He walked to the local polling centre to cast his vote.* ❑ *Mr Reynolds was re-elected by 102 votes to 60.* ❑ *They took a vote and decided not to do it.* **2** N-SING **The vote** is the total number of votes or voters in an election, or the number of votes received or cast by a particular group. ❑ *The vote was strongly in favour of the Democratic Party.* ❑ *...a huge majority of the white male vote.* **3** N-SING If you have **the vote** in an election, or have **a vote** in a meeting, you have the legal right to indicate your choice. ❑ *In Italy women did not get the vote until 1945.* **4** V-T/V-I When you **vote**, you indicate your choice officially at a meeting or in an election, for example by raising your hand or writing on a piece of paper. ❑ *Who are you going to vote for?* ❑ *The parliament voted to allow greater political and religious freedoms.* • **voting** N-UNCOUNT ❑ *Voting began about two hours ago.* • **voter** (**voters**) N-COUNT ❑ *Voters have two votes, one for an individual and one for a party.*
→ see **citizenship**

voucher /ˈvaʊtʃə/ (**vouchers**) N-COUNT A **voucher** is a piece of paper that can be used instead of money to pay for something. ❑ *...a voucher for a pair of cinema tickets.*

vow /vaʊ/ (**vows, vowing, vowed**) **1** V-T If you **vow to** do something, you make a promise or decision that you will do it. ❑ *She vowed to avenge his death.* ❑ *I vowed that some day I would return to live in Europe.* ❑ *'I'll kill him,' she vowed.* **2** N-COUNT A **vow** is a promise. ❑ *I made a silent vow to be more careful in the future.* ❑ *I took my marriage vows and kept them.*

vowel /vaʊəl/ (**vowels**) N-COUNT A **vowel** is a sound such as the ones represented in writing by the letters 'a', 'e' 'i', 'o' and 'u', which you pronounce with your mouth open, allowing the air to flow through it.

voyage /ˈvɔɪɪdʒ/ (**voyages**) **1** N-COUNT A **voyage** is a long journey on a ship or in a spacecraft. [LITERARY] ❑ *...Columbus's voyage to the West Indies.* **2** → See note at **travel**

vs. **vs.** is a written abbreviation for **versus**. ❑ *What happened in the Broncos vs. Canberra game?*

vulgar /ˈvʌlgə/ **1** ADJ If you describe something as **vulgar**, you think it is in bad taste or of poor artistic quality. ❑ *I think it's a very vulgar house.* ❑ *...a vulgar display of wealth.* • **vulgarity** N-UNCOUNT ❑ *I hate the vulgarity of this room.* **2** ADJ If you describe someone or something as **vulgar**, you dislike them because they use bad language, or because they refer to sex or the body in an unpleasant way. ❑ *'Don't be vulgar,' she reprimanded.* ❑ *...vulgar jokes.* • **vulgarity** N-UNCOUNT ❑ *It's his vulgarity that I can't stand.*

vulnerable /ˈvʌlnərəbəl/ **1** ADJ If someone or something is **vulnerable to** something, they have some weakness or disadvantage which makes them more likely to be harmed or affected by that thing. ❑ *Men, like women, are more vulnerable to breast cancer as they get older.* ❑ *...attacks on vulnerable targets.* • **vulnerability** /ˌvʌlnərəˈbɪlɪti/ N-UNCOUNT ❑ *All good drivers are aware of the vulnerability of cyclists.* **2** ADJ A **vulnerable** person is weak and without protection, with the result that they are easily hurt physically or emotionally. ❑ *Old people are particularly vulnerable members of our society.* • **vulnerability** N-UNCOUNT ❑ *...the emotional vulnerability of childhood.*

V

Word Partnership Use *vulnerable* with:

N.	vulnerable **to attack**, vulnerable **children/people/women** 1 2
V.	**become** vulnerable, **feel** vulnerable, **remain** vulnerable 1 2
ADV.	**especially** vulnerable, **extremely** vulnerable, **highly** vulnerable, **particularly** vulnerable, **so** vulnerable, **too** vulnerable, **very** vulnerable 1 2

vulture /ˈvʌltʃə/ (**vultures**) 1 N-COUNT A **vulture** is a large bird which lives in hot countries and eats the flesh of dead animals. 2 N-COUNT If you describe a person as a **vulture**, you disapprove of them because you think they are trying to gain from another person's troubles. ❑ *When the company's share price began to fall, the vultures started to circle.*

vulva /ˈvʌlvə/ (**vulvas**) N-COUNT The **vulva** is the outer part of a woman's sexual organs.

vying /ˈvaɪɪŋ/ **Vying** is the present participle of **vie**.

Ww

wacky also **whacky** /ˈwæki/ (**wackier, wackiest**) ADJ If you describe something or someone as **wacky**, you mean that they are eccentric, unusual, and often funny. [INFORMAL] ❑ *...a wacky new television comedy series.*

wad /wɒd/ (**wads**) N-COUNT A **wad of** something such as paper or banknotes is a thick, tightly packed bundle of it. ❑ *...a thick wad of banknotes.*

waddle /ˈwɒdəl/ (**waddles, waddling, waddled**) **1** V-I If someone **waddles** somewhere, they walk there with short, quick steps, swinging slightly from side to side. ❑ *He pushed himself out of the chair and waddled to the window.*

wade /weɪd/ (**wades, wading, waded**) V-I If you **wade** through mud or water, you walk through it with difficulty.

▶ **wade in** or **wade into** PHR-VERB If someone **wades in**, or if they **wade into** something, they intervene in something in a very determined and forceful way, often without thinking about the consequences. ❑ *Powell waded in with his fists.*

▶ **wade through** PHR-VERB If you **wade through** a difficult book or document, you spend a lot of time and effort reading it. ❑ *Managers have no time to wade through these reports.*

wafer /ˈweɪfə/ (**wafers**) N-COUNT A **wafer** is a thin crisp biscuit, often eaten with ice cream.

waffle /ˈwɒfəl/ (**waffles, waffling, waffled**) **1** V-I & N-UNCOUNT If someone **waffles**, they talk or write a lot without saying anything clear or important. You can call what they say or write **waffle**. ❑ *He had nothing to say, but couldn't stop waffling.* ❑ *We had 15 seconds of comment and 15 minutes of waffle.* **2** N-COUNT A **waffle** is a type of thick pancake.

waft /wɒft, wæft/ (**wafts, wafting, wafted**) **1** V-T/V-I & N-COUNT If sounds or scents **waft** through the air, or if something **wafts** them, they move gently through the air. You can call a sound or scent which has been carried on the air a **waft**. ❑ *A breeze wafted the heavy scent of flowers past her.* ❑ *...the waft of fresh coffee.*

wag /wæg/ (**wags, wagging, wagged**) **1** V-T/V-I When a dog **wags** its tail, or when its tail **wags**, its tail moves repeatedly from side to side. ❑ *The dog was biting, growling and wagging its tail.* **2** V-T If you **wag** your finger, you shake it repeatedly and quickly from side to side, usually because you are scolding someone. ❑ *He wagged a disapproving finger at her.*

wage /weɪdʒ/ (**wages, waging, waged**) **1** N-COUNT Someone's **wages** are the amount of money that is regularly paid to them for the work that they do. ❑ *His wages have gone up.* **2** V-T To **wage** a campaign or war means to start it and carry it on over a period of time. ❑ *Peter waged an unsuccessful 17-month legal battle to fight the move.*
→ see **factory**

Usage

Pay is a general word which you can use to refer to the money you get from your employer for doing your job. Manual workers are paid **wages**, or **a wage**. The plural is more common than the singular, especially when you are talking about the actual cash that someone receives. ❑ *Every week he handed all his wages in cash to his wife.* Wages are usually paid, and quoted, as an hourly or a weekly sum. ❑ *...a starting wage of five dollars an hour.* Professional people and office workers receive a **salary**, which is paid monthly. However, when talking about someone's salary, you usually give the annual figure. ❑ *I'm paid a salary of £25,000 a year.* Your income consists of all the money you receive from all sources, including your pay.

Thesaurus *wage* Also look up:

N. earnings, pay, salary **1**

Word Partnership Use *wage* with:

ADJ. **average** wage, **high/higher** wage, **hourly** wage, **low/lower** wage **1**
V. **offer a** wage, **pay a** wage, **raise a** wage **1**
N. wage **cuts**, wage **earners**, wage **increases**, wage **rates** **1**
wage **a campaign**, wage **war** **2**

wager /ˈweɪdʒə/ (**wagers, wagering, wagered**) V-I & N-COUNT If you **wager on** the result of a horse race, football match, or other event, or if you have a **wager on** it, you bet money on the result.

wagon [BRIT also **waggon**] /ˈwægən/ (**wagons**) N-COUNT A **wagon** is a strong vehicle with four wheels which is used for carrying heavy loads, and which is usually pulled by a horse or tractor.
→ see **train**

wail /weɪl/ (**wails, wailing, wailed**) **1** V-I & N-COUNT If you **wail**, or if you let out a **wail**, you cry loudly. ❑ *The baby began to wail again.* ❑ *Alice let out a wail of terror.* **2** V-I & N-COUNT If something such as a police siren **wails**, or if it makes a **wail**, it makes long, high-pitched, piercing sounds. ❑ *...the wail of sirens.*

waist /weɪst/ (**waists**) **1** N-COUNT Your **waist** is the middle part of your body, above your hips. **2** N-COUNT The **waist** of a garment such as a dress or pair of trousers is the part of it which covers the middle part of your body.
→ see **body**

waistcoat /'weɪstkəʊt, 'weskət/ (**waistcoats**) N-COUNT In British English, a **waistcoat** is a sleeveless piece of clothing with buttons, usually worn over a shirt. The American word is **vest**.

wait /weɪt/ (**waits, waiting, waited**) 1 V-I If you **wait**, you spend some time, usually doing very little, before something happens. ❑ *Stop waiting for things to happen. Make them happen.* ❑ *I waited to see how she responded.* ❑ *We will have to wait a week before we know the result.* ● **waiting** ADJ ❑ *She went towards the waiting car.* 2 N-COUNT A **wait** is a period of time in which you do very little, before something happens. ❑ *...the four-hour wait for the result.* 3 V-I If something **is waiting for** you, it is ready for you to use, have, or do. ❑ *When we came home we had a meal waiting for us.* 4 V-I If you say that something **can wait**, you mean that it can be dealt with later. ❑ *I want to talk to you, but it can wait.* 5 V-T **Wait** is used in expressions such as **wait a minute** and **wait a moment** to interrupt someone when they are speaking, for example because you object to what they are saying or because you want them to repeat something. 6 PHRASE If you **can't wait to** do something, or **can hardly wait to** do it, you are very excited about it and eager to do it. [SPOKEN]
▶ **wait around** or **wait about** PHR-VERB If you **wait around**, or if you **wait about**, you stay in the same place, usually doing very little, because you cannot act before something happens or before someone arrives. ❑ *The attacker had been waiting around for an opportunity.*

Thesaurus *wait* Also look up:

V.	anticipate, expect, hold on, stand by; *(ant.)* carry out, go ahead 1
N.	delay, halt, hold-up, pause 2

Word Partnership Use *wait* with:

V.	**(can't) afford to** wait, **can/can't/couldn't** wait, **can hardly** wait 6 **have to** wait, wait **to hear**, wait **to say**, **will/won't/wouldn't** wait 1 4
N.	wait **for an answer**, wait **days/hours**, wait **a long time**, wait ***your* turn** 1 wait **a minute**, wait **until tomorrow** 1 5
ADV.	wait **forever**, wait **here**, wait **outside**, wait **patiently** 1 **just** wait 1 5
ADJ.	**worth the** wait 2

waiter /'weɪtə/ (**waiters**) N-COUNT A **waiter** is a man who serves food and drink in a restaurant.

'waiting list (**waiting lists**) N-COUNT A **waiting list** is a list of people who have asked for something which they cannot receive immediately, for example medical treatment or housing, and so who must wait until it is available. ❑ *There were 20,000 people on the waiting list.*

'waiting-room (**waiting-rooms**) N-COUNT A **waiting-room** is a room in a place such as a railway station or a doctor's surgery, where people can sit and wait.

waitress /'weɪtrəs/ (**waitresses**) N-COUNT A **waitress** is a woman who serves food and drink in a restaurant.

waive /weɪv/ (**waives, waiving, waived**) 1 V-T If you **waive** your right to something, for example legal representation, or if someone else **waives** it, you no longer have the right to receive it. 2 V-T If someone **waives** a rule, they decide not to enforce it. ❑ *The museum waives admission charges on Sundays.*

waiver /'weɪvə/ (**waivers**) N-COUNT A **waiver** is an agreement by a person, government, or organization to give up a right or claim or to not enforce a particular rule or law. ❑ *Non-members do not qualify for the tax waiver.*

Word Link *wak ≈ being awake : awake, awakening, wake*

wake /weɪk/ (**wakes, waking, woke, woken**)

The form **waked** is used in American English for the past tense.

1 V-I & PHR-VERB When you **wake**, or when you **wake up**, you become conscious again after being asleep. ❑ *She woke to find the room lit by flashing lights.* ❑ *It's lovely to wake up every morning and see a blue sky.* 2 N-COUNT A **wake** is a gathering of people who have collected together to mourn someone's death. 3 N-COUNT The **wake** of a boat is the track of waves that it makes behind it as it moves through the water. 4 PHRASE If one thing follows **in the wake of** another, it happens after the other thing is over, often as a result of it. ❑ *The decision was delayed in the wake of the attacks.* 5 PHRASE If you leave something **in** your **wake**, you leave it behind you as you go. ❑ *Adam left a trail of devastation in his wake.*
▶ **wake up** 1 → see **wake** (meaning 1) 2 PHR-VERB If you **wake up to** something, you become aware of it. ❑ *We must wake up to the truth.*

Word Partnership Use *wake* with:

PREP-P.	wake **up during the night**, wake **up in the middle of the night**, wake **up in the morning** 1
ADV.	wake ***(someone)* up** 1

walk /wɔːk/ (**walks, walking, walked**) 1 V-I & N-SING When you **walk**, or when you move at a **walk**, you move along by putting one foot in front of the other on the ground. ❑ *They would stop the car and walk a few steps.* ❑ *When I was your age I walked to school.* ❑ *She slowed to a steady walk.* 2 N-COUNT A **walk** is an outing made by walking. ❑ *He often took long walks in the hills.* 3 N-SING A **walk** of a particular distance is the distance which a person has to walk to get somewhere. ❑ *The hotel is a short walk from the Empire State Building.* 4 V-T If you **walk** someone somewhere, you walk there with them. ❑ *I walked her to the car.* 5 V-T If you **walk** your dog, you take it for a walk in order to keep it healthy.
▶ **walk off with** 1 PHR-VERB If someone **walks off with** something that does not belong to them, they take it without permission. [INFORMAL] 2 PHR-VERB If you **walk off with** something such as a prize, you win it very easily. [JOURNALISM]
▶ **walk out** 1 PHR-VERB If you **walk out of** a meeting, performance, or unpleasant situation, you leave it suddenly, usually to show that you

are angry or bored. ❑ *Several people walked out of the meeting in protest.* ● **walkout** (**walkouts**) N-COUNT ❑ *The protest included a walkout by the U.S. representative.* 2 PHR-VERB If someone **walks out** on their family or their partner, they leave them suddenly. 3 PHR-VERB If workers **walk out**, they go on strike. ● **walkout** N-COUNT ❑ *Employees staged a one-day walkout today.*

Thesaurus *walk* Also look up:

V.	amble, hike, stroll 1
N.	hike, march, parade, stroll 1 2

Word Partnership Use *walk* with:

ADV.	walk **alone**, walk **away**, walk **back**, walk **home**, walk **slowly** 1
V.	**begin to** walk, **start to** walk 1 **go for a** walk, **take a** walk 2 3
ADJ.	**(un)able to** walk 1 **brisk** walk, **long** walk, **short** walk 2 3
N.	walk **a dog** 5

walker /ˈwɔːkə/ (**walkers**) N-COUNT A **walker** is a person who walks, especially in the countryside for pleasure.

walking /ˈwɔːkɪŋ/ N-UNCOUNT **Walking** is the activity of going for walks in the country. ❑ *I've started to do a lot of walking and cycling.*

ˌwalk of ˈlife (**walks of life**) N-COUNT The **walk of life** that you come from is the position that you have in society and the kind of job you have. ❑ *...people from all walks of life.*

walkway /ˈwɔːkweɪ/ (**walkways**) N-COUNT A **walkway** is a path or passage for pedestrians, especially one which is raised above the ground.

wall /wɔːl/ (**walls**) 1 N-COUNT A **wall** is one of the vertical sides of a building or room. ❑ *...the bedroom walls.* 2 N-COUNT A **wall** is a long narrow vertical structure made of stone or brick that surrounds or divides an area of land. ❑ *He climbed over a garden wall to steal apples.* 3 N-COUNT The **wall** of something hollow is its side. ❑ *...the stomach wall.*

Word Partnership Use *wall* with:

N.	**back to the** wall, **brick** wall, **concrete** wall, **glass** wall, **stone** wall 1 2
PREP.	**against a** wall, **along a** wall, **behind a** wall, **near a** wall, **on a** wall 1 2
V.	**build a** wall, **climb a** wall, **lean against/on a** wall 1 2

walled /wɔːld/ ADJ A **walled** area of land is surrounded by a wall. ❑ *...a walled rose garden.*

wallet /ˈwɒlɪt/ (**wallets**) N-COUNT A **wallet** is a small flat folded case where you can keep banknotes and credit cards.

wallow /ˈwɒləʊ/ (**wallows, wallowing, wallowed**) 1 V-I If you say that someone **is wallowing in** an unpleasant situation or feeling, you are criticizing them for being deliberately unhappy. ❑ *He was wallowing in self-pity.* 2 V-I When an animal **wallows** in mud or water, it lies or rolls about in it slowly.

wallpaper /ˈwɔːlpeɪpə/ (**wallpapers, wallpapering, wallpapered**) 1 N-VAR **Wallpaper** is thick coloured or patterned paper that is used to decorate the walls of rooms. 2 V-T If someone **wallpapers** a room, they cover the walls with wallpaper. 3 N-UNCOUNT **Wallpaper** is the background on a computer screen. [COMPUTING]

walnut /ˈwɔːlnʌt/ (**walnuts**) N-COUNT **Walnuts** are light brown edible nuts which have a wrinkled shape and a very hard round shell.

waltz /wɔːlts/ (**waltzes, waltzing, waltzed**) 1 N-COUNT A **waltz** is a piece of music with a rhythm of three beats in each bar, which people can dance to. 2 N-COUNT & V-I When two people do a **waltz**, or when they **waltz**, they dance a waltz together. ❑ *Couples waltzed round the dance floor.* 3 V-I If you **waltz** into a place, you enter in a quick confident way that makes other people notice you. [INFORMAL] ❑ *Suddenly this guy waltzed in, and asked me my name.*

wander /ˈwɒndə/ (**wanders, wandering, wandered**) 1 V-I & N-SING If you **wander** around a place, or if you take a **wander** round it, you walk around in no special direction. ❑ *I went out and wandered around the halls looking for him.* ❑ *Take a wander around the market.* 2 V-I If a person or animal **wanders** from a place where they are supposed to stay, they move away from the place without going in a particular direction. ❑ *He has wandered off somewhere.* 3 V-I If your mind **wanders** or your thoughts **wander**, you stop concentrating on something and start thinking about other things.

wane /weɪn/ (**wanes, waning, waned**) 1 V-I If a condition, attitude, or emotion **wanes**, it becomes weaker, often so that it eventually disappears. ❑ *His interest in these sports began to wane.* ● **waning** ADJ ❑ *...her mother's waning strength.* 2 PHRASE If a condition, attitude, or emotion is **on the wane**, it is becoming weaker. ❑ *The party's influence was clearly on the wane.*

want /wɒnt/ (**wants, wanting, wanted**) 1 V-T If you **want** something, you feel a desire or a need for it. ❑ *I want a drink.* ❑ *People wanted to know who this talented designer was.* ❑ *He wanted his power recognised.* ❑ *Do you want another cup of coffee?* 2 V-T If you say that something **wants** doing, you think that it needs to be done. [INFORMAL] ❑ *The windows wanted cleaning.* 3 V-T If you tell someone that they **want to** do a particular thing, you are advising them to do it. [INFORMAL] ❑ *You want to be careful what you say.* 4 V-T If someone **is wanted** by the police, the police are searching for them. ● **wanted** ADJ BEFORE N ❑ *He is one of the most wanted criminals in Europe.* 5 N-SING A **want of** something is a lack of it. [FORMAL] ❑ *If they fail, it is not through a want of effort.* 6 PHRASE You say **if you want** when you are making or agreeing to an offer or suggestion in a casual way. ❑ *Mary says you're welcome to stay the night if you want.* 7 PHRASE If you do something **for want of** something else, you do it because the other thing is not available or not possible. ❑ *He had taken the job for want of anything better to do.*

Thesaurus *want* Also look up:

V.	covet, desire, long, need, require, wish 1

Word Web **war**

The Hague Conventions* and the Geneva Convention* are rules for **war**. They try to make war more humane. First, they say countries should avoid **armed conflict**. They suggest a **neutral mediator** or a 30-day "time out." A country must **declare** war before **combat** can begin. Sneak **attacks** are forbidden. The rules for **firearms** are simple. One rule states it is illegal to **kill** or **injure** a person who **surrenders**. **Wounded soldiers, prisoners,** and **civilians** must get medical care immediately. And countries must not use **biological** and **chemical weapons**.

Hague Conventions: agreements between many nations on rules to limit warfare and weapons.
Geneva Convention: an agreement between most nations on treatment of prisoners of war and the sick, injured, or dead.

wanting /ˈwɒntɪŋ/ ADJ If you find something **wanting**, or if it proves **wanting**, it is not as good as you think it should be. ❑ *He analysed his technique and found it wanting.*

WAP /wæp/ N-UNCOUNT **WAP** is a system which allows devices such as mobile phones to connect to the Internet. **WAP** is an abbreviation for 'Wireless Application Protocol'. [COMPUTING]

war /wɔː/ (**wars**) **1** N-VAR A **war** is a period of fighting between countries. ❑ *They've been at war for the last fifteen years.* **2** N-VAR **War** is intense economic competition between countries or organizations. ❑ *...a trade war.* **3** → see also **civil war** **4** PHRASE If two people, countries, or organizations have a **war of words**, they criticize each other because they strongly disagree about something. [JOURNALISM]
→ see Word Web: **war**
→ see **army, history**

ward /wɔːd/ (**wards, warding, warded**) **1** N-COUNT A **ward** is a room in a hospital which has beds for many people, often people who need similar treatment. **2** N-COUNT A **ward** is a district which forms part of a political constituency or local council. **3** N-COUNT Someone's **ward** is a child who they are responsible for as their appointed guardian.
→ see **hospital**

▶ **ward off** PHR-VERB To **ward off** a danger or illness means to do something to prevent it from affecting you or harming you. ❑ *...the ability of vitamin C to ward off colds.*

warden /ˈwɔːdən/ (**wardens**) **1** N-COUNT A **warden** is an official who is responsible for a particular place or thing, and for making sure that certain laws are obeyed. ❑ *...a safari park warden.* **2** N-COUNT In British English, a **warden** is someone who works in a prison supervising the prisoners. The American word is **guard**.

W

warder /ˈwɔːdə/ (**warders**) N-COUNT A **warder** is the same as a prison **warden**. [BRIT]

wardrobe /ˈwɔːdrəʊb/ (**wardrobes**) **1** N-COUNT A **wardrobe** is a tall cupboard in which you hang your clothes. **2** N-COUNT Someone's **wardrobe** is the total collection of clothes that they own. ❑ *If your wardrobe is all black, everything matches.*

ware /weə/ (**wares**) **1** **Ware** is used to form nouns that refer to objects that are made of a particular material, or that are used for a particular purpose. ❑ *...porcelain cooking ware.* **2** N-PLURAL Someone's **wares** are the things that they sell, usually in the street or in a market. [DATED]

Word Link *ware ≈ merchandise : hardware, software, warehouse*

warehouse /ˈweəhaʊs/ (**warehouses**) N-COUNT A **warehouse** is a large building where raw materials or manufactured goods are stored before they are taken to a shop.

warfare /ˈwɔːfeə/ N-UNCOUNT **Warfare** is the activity of fighting a war. ❑ *...the threat of chemical warfare.*

warhead /ˈwɔːhed/ (**warheads**) N-COUNT A **warhead** is the front end of a bomb or missile, where the explosives are carried.

warm /wɔːm/ (**warmer, warmest, warms, warming, warmed**) **1** ADJ Something that is **warm** has some heat but not enough to be hot. ❑ *It was warm during the day, but the nights were cold.* ❑ *...warm water.* **2** → See note at **hot** **3** ADJ **Warm** clothes and blankets are made of a material such as wool which protects you from the cold. ● **warmly** ADV ❑ *Remember to wrap up warmly on cold days.* **4** ADJ A **warm** person is friendly and affectionate. ● **warmly** ADV ❑ *He greeted me warmly.* **5** V-T If you **warm** a part of your body, or if something hot **warms** it, it stops feeling cold and starts to feel hotter. ❑ *She warmed her hands by the fire.* **6** V-I If you **warm to** a person or an idea, you become fonder of the person or more interested in the idea. ❑ *We began to warm to his openness and honesty.*

▶ **warm up** **1** PHR-VERB If you **warm** something **up**, or if it **warms up**, it gets hotter. ❑ *Have you warmed the milk up, Mum?* ❑ *The weather had warmed up.* **2** PHR-VERB If you **warm up** for an event such as a race, you prepare yourself for it by doing exercises or by practising just before it starts. ● **warm-up** (**warm-ups**) N-COUNT ❑ *She broke her ankle during the warm-up.* **3** PHR-VERB When an engine **warms up**, it becomes ready for use a little while after being switched on or started. ❑ *We waited five minutes while the pilot warmed up the engines.*

Word Partnership Use *warm* with:

ADJ.	warm **and sunny** 1 warm **and cozy**, warm **and dry** 1 2 **soft and** warm 2 warm **and friendly** 3
N.	warm **air**, warm **bath**, warm **breeze**, warm **hands**, warm **water**, warm **weather** 1 warm **clothes** 2 warm **smile**, warm **welcome** 3

warmth /wɔːmθ/ 1 N-UNCOUNT The **warmth** of something is the heat that it has or produces. ❑ *...the warmth of the fire.* 2 N-UNCOUNT The **warmth** of something such as a garment or blanket is the protection that it gives you against the cold. 3 N-UNCOUNT Someone who has **warmth** is friendly and enthusiastic in their behaviour towards others.

warn /wɔːn/ (**warns, warning, warned**) 1 V-T/V-I If you **warn** someone **about** a possible danger or problem, you tell them about it so that they are aware of it. ❑ *UN officials warn of disease and famine.* ❑ *Friends had warned me that children were expensive.* 2 V-T If you **warn** someone **not to** do something, you advise them not to do it in order to avoid possible danger or punishment. ❑ *Mrs Blount warned me not to go.* ❑ *'Don't do anything yet,' he warned.* ❑ *Officials warned people against eating or picking mushrooms.*

Thesaurus *warn* Also look up:

V.	alert, caution, notify 1

warning /ˈwɔːnɪŋ/ (**warnings**) N-VAR A **warning** is something which is said or written to tell people of a possible danger, problem, or other unpleasant thing that might happen. ❑ *They issued a warning that recovery is likely to be slow.* ❑ *The soldiers opened fire without warning.*

Word Partnership Use *warning* with:

ADJ.	**stern** warning
N.	**advance** warning, warning **of danger**, **early** warning, **hurricane** warning, warning **labels**, warning **signs**, **storm** warning
V.	**give (a)** warning, **ignore a** warning, **receive (a)** warning, **send a** warning

warp /wɔːp/ (**warps, warping, warped**) 1 V-T/V-I If something **warps** or **is warped**, it becomes damaged by bending or curving, often because of the effect of heat or water. ❑ *The wood had started to warp.* ● **warped** ADJ ❑ *The door was warped.* 2 V-T If something **warps** someone's character or mind, it damages them or influences them in a bad way. ● **warped** ADJ ❑ *...a terrible crime committed by a warped mind.*

warrant /ˈwɒrənt, AM ˈwɔːr-/ (**warrants, warranting, warranted**) 1 V-T If something **warrants** a particular action, it makes the action seem necessary or appropriate. ❑ *Your son's behavious warrants him being removed from school.* 2 N-COUNT A **warrant** is an official document signed by a judge or magistrate, which gives the police special permission to do something such as arrest someone or search their house.

warranty /ˈwɒrənti, AM ˈwɔːr-/ (**warranties**) N-COUNT A **warranty** is a written guarantee which enables you to get a product repaired or replaced free of charge within a certain period of time. ❑ *The equipment is still under warranty.*

warrior /ˈwɒriə, AM ˈwɔːr-/ (**warriors**) N-COUNT A **warrior** is a fighter or soldier, especially one in former times who was very brave and experienced in fighting.

warship /ˈwɔːʃɪp/ (**warships**) N-COUNT A **warship** is a ship with guns that is used for fighting in wars.
→ see **ship**

wart /wɔːt/ (**warts**) N-COUNT A **wart** is a small lump which grows on your skin and which is usually caused by a virus.

wartime /ˈwɔːtaɪm/ N-UNCOUNT **Wartime** is a period of time when there is a war. ❑ *...his wartime experiences in France.*

wary /ˈweəri/ ADJ If you are **wary of** someone or something, you are cautious because you do not know much about them and you believe they may be dangerous or cause problems. ❑ *She warned them to be wary of strangers.* ❑ *They were very wary about giving him a contract.* ● **warily** ADV ❑ *She studied me warily.*

was /wəz, STRONG wɒz, AM wʌz/ **Was** is the first and third person singular of the past tense of **be**.

wash /wɒʃ/ (**washes, washing, washed**) 1 V-T & N-COUNT If you **wash** something, or if you give it a **wash**, you clean it using water and soap or detergent. ❑ *It took a long time to wash the mud out of his hair.* ❑ *Rub down the door and wash off the dust.* ❑ *That coat could do with a wash.* 2 V-T/V-I & N-COUNT If you **wash**, or if you **have a wash**, you clean part of your body using soap and water. ❑ *She washed her face with cold water.* ❑ *You are going to have your dinner, get washed, and go to bed.* ❑ *She had a wash and changed her clothes.* 3 N-SING **The wash** is all the clothes, sheets and other things that are washed together at one time. ❑ *His grey socks were in the wash.* 4 V-T/V-I If a sea or river or something carried by a sea or river **washes** somewhere or **is washed** there, it flows there gently. ❑ *The force of the water washed him back into the cave.* 5 to **wash** your **hands of** something → see **hand** 6 → see also **washing**
→ see **soap**

▶ **wash away** PHR-VERB If rain or floods **wash away** something, they destroy it and carry it away. ❑ *Flood waters washed away one of the main bridges.*

▶ **wash down** PHR-VERB If you **wash** something **down with** a drink, you swallow it and then drink the drink, for example to make it easier to swallow or digest. ❑ *...a beef sandwich washed down with a glass of water.*

▶ **wash up** 1 PHR-VERB If you **wash up**, you wash the pans, plates, cups, and cutlery which have been used in cooking and eating a meal. [BRIT] ❑ *I made breakfast and then washed up the plates.* 2 PHR-VERB If something **is washed up** on a piece of land, it is carried there by a river or the sea and left there. 3 → see also **washing-up**

Thesaurus *wash* Also look up:

V. clean, rinse, scrub 1
bathe, clean 2

Word Partnership Use *wash* with:

N. wash **a car**, wash **clothes**, wash **dishes** 1
wash ***your*** **face/hair/hands** 2

washable /ˈwɒʃəbəl/ ADJ **Washable** clothes or materials can be washed without being damaged. ❑ *...washable sofa covers.*

washbasin also **wash basin** /ˈwɒʃbeɪsən/ (**washbasins**) N-COUNT A **washbasin** is a large bowl for washing your hands and face. It is usually fixed to a wall, with taps for hot and cold water.

washer /ˈwɒʃə/ (**washers**) 1 N-COUNT A **washer** is a thin flat ring of metal or plastic, which is placed over a bolt before the nut is screwed on. 2 N-COUNT A **washer** is the same as a **washing machine**. [INFORMAL]

washing /ˈwɒʃɪŋ/ N-UNCOUNT **Washing** is clothes, sheets, and other things that need to be washed, are being washed, or have just been washed. ❑ *They brought the washing in before it rained.*

ˈwashing machine (**washing machines**) N-COUNT A **washing machine** is a machine that you use to wash clothes in.

ˌwashing-ˈup N-UNCOUNT To **do the washing-up** means to wash the pans, plates, cups, and cutlery which have been used in cooking and eating a meal. [BRIT]

wasn't /ˈwɒzənt, AM ˈwʌz-/ In informal English, **wasn't** is the usual spoken form of 'was not'.

wasp /wɒsp/ (**wasps**) N-COUNT A **wasp** is a small insect with a painful sting. It has yellow and black stripes across its body.

waste /weɪst/ (**wastes, wasting, wasted**) 1 V-T & N-SING If you **waste** something such as time, money, or energy, you use too much of it doing something that is not important or necessary, or is unlikely to succeed. You can say that doing this is a **waste of** time, money, or energy. ❑ *She didn't want to waste time looking at old cars.* ❑ *I resolved not to waste money on a hotel.* ❑ *It was just a waste of government money.* ❑ *I thought the meeting was a waste of time.* 2 V-T If you **waste** an opportunity, you do not take advantage of it when it is available. 3 N-UNCOUNT & N-PLURAL **Waste** or **wastes** is material which has been used and is no longer wanted, for example because the valuable or useful part has been removed. ❑ *...industrial waste.* 4 ADJ **Waste** land is land which is not used or looked after by anyone. 5 N-PLURAL **Wastes** are a large area of land, for example a desert, in which there are very few people, plants, or animals. ❑ *...the frozen wastes of Siberia.*

▶ **waste away** PHR-VERB If someone **wastes away**, they become extremely thin and weak because they are ill or are not eating properly.

Thesaurus *waste* Also look up:

V. misuse, squander 1

W

Word Partnership Use *waste* with:

N. waste **energy**, waste **money**, waste **time**, waste **water** 1
V. **recycle** waste, **reduce** waste 3
ADJ. **hazardous** waste, **human** waste, **industrial** waste, **nuclear** waste, **toxic** waste 3

wasteful /ˈweɪstfʊl/ ADJ Action that is **wasteful** uses too much of something valuable such as time, money, or energy. ❑ *The whole process is thoroughly wasteful.*

wasteland /ˈweɪstlænd/ (**wastelands**) N-VAR A **wasteland** is an area of land which cannot be used, for example because it is infertile or because it has been misused by people.

watch
1 LOOKING AND PAYING ATTENTION
2 INSTRUMENT THAT TELLS THE TIME

watch /wɒtʃ/ (**watches, watching, watched**)
1 1 V-T/V-I If you **watch** someone or something, you look at them, usually for a period of time. ❑ *Two girls stood watching.* ❑ *They had been sitting watching television.* 2 V-T If you **watch** a situation, you pay attention to it or you are aware of it, but are not participating in it. ❑ *Human rights groups have been closely watching the case.* 3 V-T If you tell someone to **watch** a particular person or thing, you are warning them to be careful that the person or thing does not get out of control or do something unpleasant. ❑ *You really need to watch people like that.*

Usage

If you want to say that someone is paying attention to something they can see, you say that they **are watching** it or **are looking at** it. In general, you **watch** something that is moving or changing, while you **look at** something that is not moving. ❑ *He watched Blake run down the stairs.* ❑ *I asked him to look at the picture above his bed.* You use **see** to talk about things that you are aware of because a visual impression reaches your eyes. You often use **can** in this case. ❑ *I can see the fax here on the desk.*

4 PHRASE You say **'watch it'** in order to warn someone to be careful. [INFORMAL] 5 PHRASE If someone **keeps watch**, they look around all the time, usually when other people are asleep, so that they can warn the others of danger or an attack. 6 PHRASE If you **keep watch on** events or a situation, you pay attention to what is happening, so that you can take action at the right moment.

▶ **watch for** or **watch out for** PHR-VERB If you **watch for** something, or if you **watch out for** it, you pay attention so that you notice it, either because you do not want to miss it or because you want to avoid it. ❑ *We'll be watching for any developments.* ❑ *Watch out for hidden sugar in food by reading the label carefully.*

▶ **watch out** PHR-VERB If you tell someone to **watch out**, you are warning them to be careful, because something unpleasant might happen

to them or they might get into difficulties. ❑ *You have to watch out - there are dangers everywhere.*
▸ **watch out for** → see **watch for**

watch /wɒtʃ/ (**watches**)
❷ N-COUNT A **watch** is a small clock which you wear on a strap on your wrist or on a chain.
→ see **jewellery**

Word Partnership Use *watch* with:

ADV.	watch **carefully**, watch **closely** ① 1 3
N.	watch **a DVD**, watch **a film/movie**, watch **fireworks**, watch **a game**, watch **the news**, watch **people**, watch **television/TV**, watch **a video** ① 1 watch **children** ① 3
V.	**check *your*** watch, **glance at *your*** watch, **look at *your*** watch ② 1

watchdog /ˈwɒtʃdɒg, AM -dɔːg/ (**watchdogs**) N-COUNT A **watchdog** is a person or committee whose job is to make sure that companies do not act illegally or irresponsibly. ❑ *...the head of Britain's gas industry watchdog.*

watchful /ˈwɒtʃfʊl/ ADJ Someone who is **watchful** is careful to notice everything that is happening. ❑ *They had been alert and watchful, but had seen nothing unusual.*

water /ˈwɔːtə/ (**waters, watering, watered**)
1 N-UNCOUNT **Water** is a clear thin liquid that has no colour or taste when it is pure. It falls from clouds as rain. ❑ *Please could I have a glass of water?* 2 N-UNCOUNT & N-PLURAL When people are talking about a large area of water, for example a lake or sea, they sometimes call it **the water** or **the waters**. ❑ *Monique ran down to the water's edge.* ❑ *...the icy waters of the South Atlantic.* 3 N-PLURAL A country's **waters** consist of the area of sea which is near it and which is regarded as belonging to it. ❑ *...ferries operating in British waters.* 4 V-T If you **water** plants, you pour water into the soil to help them to grow. 5 V-I If your eyes **are watering**, you have tears in them because they are sore or because you are upset. 6 V-I If you say that your mouth **is watering**, you mean that you can smell or see some appetizing food.
→ see Word Web: **water**
→ see **erosion, glacier, greenhouse effect, habitat, lake**
▸ **water down** 1 PHR-VERB If you **water down** a substance, for example food or drink, you add water to it to make it weaker. ❑ *You can water down a glass of fruit juice and make it last twice as long.* 2 PHR-VERB If something, especially a proposal, speech, or statement **is watered down**, it is made much weaker and less forceful or less controversial.

watercolour [AM **watercolor**] /ˈwɔːtəkʌlə/ (**watercolours**) 1 N-PLURAL **Watercolours** are coloured paints, used for painting pictures, which you apply with a wet brush or dissolve in water first. 2 N-COUNT A **watercolour** is a picture which has been painted using watercolours.

waterfall /ˈwɔːtəfɔːl/ (**waterfalls**) N-COUNT A **waterfall** is a place where water flows over the edge of a steep cliff or rocks and falls into a pool below, such as Niagara Falls and Victoria Falls.

waterfront /ˈwɔːtəfrʌnt/ (**waterfronts**) N-COUNT A **waterfront** is a street or piece of land which is next to an area of water, for example a harbour or the sea. ❑ *...a two-bedroom apartment on the waterfront.*

waterproof /ˈwɔːtəpruːf/ ADJ Something that is **waterproof** does not let water pass through it. ❑ *...waterproof clothing.*

watershed /ˈwɔːtəʃed/ (**watersheds**) N-COUNT If something such as an event is a **watershed** in the history or development of something, it is very important because it represents the beginning of a new stage in it. ❑ *The election of a woman president in 1990 was a watershed in Irish politics.*

watertight /ˈwɔːtətaɪt/ 1 ADJ Something that is **watertight** does not allow water to pass through it, for example because it is tightly sealed. ❑ *The batteries are safely enclosed in a watertight compartment.* 2 ADJ A **watertight** case or agreement is one that nobody can disprove or find fault with. ❑ *The police had a watertight case.*

waterway /ˈwɔːtəweɪ/ (**waterways**) N-COUNT A **waterway** is a canal, river, or narrow channel of sea which ships or boats can sail along.

watery /ˈwɔːtəri/ 1 ADJ Something that is **watery** is weak or pale. ❑ *A watery light began to show through the branches.* 2 ADJ **Watery** food or drink contains too much water or is thin and tasteless like water. ❑ *...a plateful of watery soup.* 3 ADJ Something that is **watery** contains, resembles, or consists of water. ❑ *Emma's eyes went red and watery.*

watt /wɒt/ (**watts**) N-COUNT A **watt** is a unit of measurement of electrical power. ❑ *...a 100-watt light-bulb.*

Word Web water

Water changes its form in the hydrologic **cycle**. The sun warms oceans, lakes, and rivers. Some water **evaporates**. Evaporation creates a gas called **water vapour**. Plants also give off water vapour through **transpiration**. Water vapour rises into the **atmosphere**. It hits cooler air and **condenses** into drops of water. These drops form **clouds**. When these drops get heavy enough, they begin to fall. They form different types of **precipitation**. Rain forms in warm air. Cold air creates **freezing rain**, **sleet**, and **snow**.

W

wave /weɪv/ (**waves, waving, waved**) **1** V-T/V-I & N-COUNT If you **wave** or **wave** your hand, or if you give a **wave**, you move your hand from side to side in the air, usually in order to say hello or goodbye to someone. ❑ *He smiled and waved to journalists.* ❑ *Paddy spotted Mary Ann and gave her a cheery wave.* **2** V-T If you **wave** someone somewhere, you make a movement with your hand to indicate that they should move in a particular direction. ❑ *He tried to speak to her, but she waved him away.* **3** V-T If you **wave** something, you hold it up and move it rapidly from side to side. ❑ *More than 4000 people waved flags and sang nationalist songs.* **4** N-COUNT A **wave** is a raised mass of water on the sea or a lake, caused by the wind or the tide. **5** N-COUNT A **wave** is a sudden increase in a particular feeling, activity, or type of behaviour, especially an undesirable or unpleasant one. ❑ *...the current wave of violence.* ❑ *The loneliness and grief comes in waves.* **6** N-COUNT **Wave** is used to refer to the way in which things such as sound, light, and radio signals travel. ❑ *Radio waves have a certain frequency.* **7** → see also **new wave, shock wave, tidal wave**
→ see Word Web: **wave**
→ see **beach, ear, earthquake, echo, ocean, radio, sound**

Word Partnership Use *wave* with:

N.	wave ***your* hand** **1**
	wave **a flag** **3**
	crest of a wave **4**
	radio wave **6**
	wave **of attacks/bombings**, wave **of violence** **5**
V.	**smile and** wave **1**
	ride a wave **4**

wavelength /ˈweɪvleŋθ/ (**wavelengths**) **1** N-COUNT A **wavelength** is the distance between the same point on two waves of energy such as light or sound that are next to each other. ❑ *Blue light has a shorter wavelength than red.* **2** N-COUNT A **wavelength** is the size of radio wave which a particular radio station uses to broadcast its programmes. **3** PHRASE If two people are **on the same wavelength**, they find it easy to understand each other and they tend to agree, because they share similar interests or opinions.

waver /ˈweɪvə/ (**wavers, wavering, wavered**) **1** V-I If you **waver**, you are uncertain or indecisive about something. ❑ *He never wavered in his belief.* **2** V-I If something **wavers**, it shakes with very slight movements or changes. ❑ *Shadows wavered and settled on the walls.*

wavy /ˈweɪvi/ (**wavier, waviest**) **1** ADJ **Wavy** hair is not straight or curly, but curves slightly. **2** ADJ A **wavy** line has a series of regular curves along it. ❑ *The boxes were decorated with a wavy gold line.*

wax /wæks/ N-UNCOUNT **Wax** is a solid, slightly shiny substance made of fat or oil which is used to make candles and polish.

way /weɪ/ (**ways**) **1** N-COUNT If you refer to a **way of** doing something, you are referring to how you can do it, for example the method you can use to achieve it. ❑ *Another way of making new friends is to go to an evening class.* ❑ *I can't think of a better way to spend my time.* **2** N-COUNT You can refer to the **way** that an action is done to indicate the quality that it has. ❑ *She smiled in a friendly way.* **3** N-PLURAL The **ways** of a particular person or group of people are their customs or their usual behaviour. ❑ *She will never change her ways.* **4** N-COUNT If a general statement or description is true **in** a particular **way**, that is a particular manner or form that it takes in a specific case. ❑ *She was afraid in a way that was quite new to her.* ❑ *In some ways, it's nice working from home.* **5** N-SING The **way** you feel about something is your attitude to it or your opinion about it. ❑ *I'm terribly sorry, I had no idea you felt that way.* **6** N-COUNT **The way** to a particular place is the route that you must take in order to get there. ❑ *Does anybody know the way to the bathroom?* ❑ *We'll go out the back way.* ❑ *This is the way in.* **7** N-SING You use **way** to indicate the direction or position of something. ❑ *As he went into the kitchen, he passed Pop coming the other way.* ❑ *Turn the cake the right way up.* **8** N-SING If someone or something is **in the way**, they prevent you from moving freely or from seeing clearly. ❑ *I couldn't see it because a truck was in the way.* ❑ *Get out of my way!* **9** N-SING You use **way** in expressions such as **push** your **way** and **make** your **way** to indicate movement or progression, especially when this is difficult or slow. ❑ *He pushed his way to the bar.* ❑ *Fergus sat at the desk working his way through a pile of papers.* **10** N-SING You use **way** in expressions such as **a long way** and **a little way** to say how far away something is. ❑ *We've a long way to go yet.* **11** N-SING You use **way** in expressions such as **all the way, most of the way**, and **half the way** to refer to the extent to which an action has been completed. ❑ *Did you listen to the CD all the way through?* **12** ADV You can use **way** to emphasize, for

Word Web wave

THE ELECTROMAGNETIC SPECTRUM

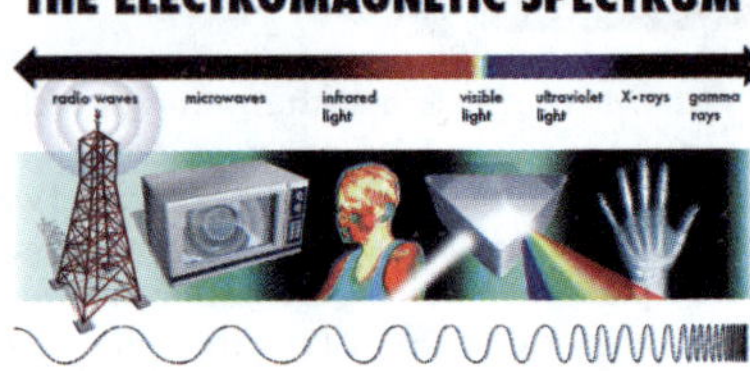

As **wind** blows across water, it makes **waves**. It does this by transferring energy to the water. If the waves meet an object, they bounce off it. Light also moves in waves and acts the same way. We can see an object only if light waves bounce off it. Light waves differ in **frequency**. Wave frequency is usually the measure of the number of waves per second. **Radio waves** and **microwaves** are examples of low-frequency light waves. **Visible light** is made of medium-frequency light waves. **Ultraviolet radiation** and **X-rays** are high-frequency light waves.

example, that something is a great distance away or is very much below or above a particular level or amount. ❑ *Way down in the valley is the town of Freiburg.* ❑ *I have to plan it way in advance.* **13** PHRASE If an object that is supporting something **gives way**, it breaks or collapses. ❑ *He fell when a ledge gave way beneath him.* **14** PHRASE If you **give way to** someone or something that you have been resisting, you stop resisting and allow yourself to be persuaded or controlled by them. ❑ *The President has given way to pressure from the public.* **15** PHRASE If a moving person or a vehicle or its driver **gives way**, they slow down or stop in order to allow other people or vehicles to pass in front of them. [BRIT] **16** PHRASE If you **lose** your **way**, you become lost when you are trying to go somewhere. **17** PHRASE If one person or thing **makes way for** another, the first is replaced by the second. ❑ *The building will be demolished in January to make way for new offices.* **18** PHRASE If you **go out of** your **way to** do something, you make a special effort to do it. ❑ *She went out of her way to make him feel comfortable.* **19** PHRASE If you **keep out of** someone's **way**, you avoid them. **20** PHRASE When something **is out of the way**, it is over or you have dealt with it. ❑ *We will get the next race out of the way before making any further plans.* **21** PHRASE If an activity or plan is **under way**, it has begun and is now taking place. ❑ *Peace talks are under way.* **22** PHRASE If someone **gets** their **way** or **has** their **way**, nobody stops them doing what they want to do. You can also say that someone **gets** their **own way** or **has** their **own way**. ❑ *As long as she gets her own way, she can be a delightful child.* **23** PHRASE If someone says that you **can't have it both ways**, they mean that you have to choose between two things and cannot do or have them both. **24** PHRASE If you say that someone or something **has a way of** doing a particular thing, you mean they often do it. ❑ *Bosses have a way of always finding out about such things.* **25** PHRASE You say **by the way** when you add something to what you have said, especially something that you have just thought of. [SPOKEN] ❑ *By the way, how is your back?* **26** PHRASE You use **in a way** to indicate that your statement is true to some extent or in one respect. ❑ *In a way, I suppose I'm frightened of failing.*

ˌway of ˈlife (**ways of life**) N-COUNT Someone's **way of life** consists of their habits and daily activities.

wayward /ˈweɪwəd/ ADJ A **wayward** person is likely to change suddenly, and is therefore difficult to control.

we /wɪ, STRONG wiː/ PRON **We** is used as the subject of a verb. A speaker or writer uses **we** to refer to a group of people which includes himself or herself. ❑ *We ordered some pizza.* ❑ *We students respect her tremendously.*

weak /wiːk/ (**weaker, weakest**) **1** ADJ If someone is **weak**, they do not have very much strength or energy. ● **weakly** ADV ❑ *Sharon shook her head weakly.* ● **weakness** N-UNCOUNT ❑ *Symptoms of infection include weakness, nausea and vomiting.* **2** ADJ Something that is **weak** is not strong or good, and is likely to break or fail. ❑ *...the weak structure of the buildings.* ❑ *She had a weak heart.* **3** ADJ If you describe someone as **weak**, you mean that they are not very confident or determined, so that they are often frightened or worried, or easily influenced by other people. ● **weakness** N-UNCOUNT ❑ *Many people felt that admitting to stress was a sign of weakness.* **4** ADJ If something such as an argument or case is **weak**, it is not convincing or there is little evidence to support it. ❑ *The evidence against him was weak.* **5** ADJ A **weak** drink, chemical, or drug contains very little of a particular substance, for example because it has been diluted with a lot of water. ❑ *...a cup of weak tea.*

→ see **muscle**

Thesaurus	*weak*	Also look up:
ADJ.	feeble, frail; (*ant.*) strong **1**	
	cowardly, insecure; (*ant.*) strong **3**	

Word Partnership	Use *weak* with:
ADV.	**relatively** weak, **still** weak, **too** weak, **very** weak **1**-**5**

weaken /ˈwiːkən/ (**weakens, weakening, weakened**) **1** V-T/V-I To **weaken** something means to make it less strong or less powerful. ❑ *The crisis has weakened so many firms.* ❑ *Family structures are weakening and breaking up.* **2** V-T/V-I If someone **weakens**, they become less certain about a decision they have made. ❑ *Jennie weakened, and finally gave in.* ❑ *The result hasn't weakened his determination.*

weakness /ˈwiːknəs/ (**weaknesses**) **1** N-COUNT If you have a **weakness for** something, you like it very much. ❑ *Stephen had a weakness for cats.* **2** → see also **weak**

wealth /welθ/ **1** N-UNCOUNT **Wealth** is a large amount of money or property owned by someone, or the possession of it. ❑ *His own wealth increased.* **2** N-SING A **wealth of** something means a very large amount of it. [LITERARY] ❑ *The city offers a wealth of beautiful churches.*

Thesaurus	*wealth*	Also look up:
N.	affluence, funds, money; (*ant.*) poverty **1**	

wealthy /ˈwelθi/ (**wealthier, wealthiest**) ADJ & N-PLURAL **Wealthy** people have a large amount of money or property. You can call people like this **the wealthy**.

wean /wiːn/ (**weans, weaning, weaned**) **1** V-T When a mother **weans** her baby, she stops feeding it with milk from her breast and starts giving it other food. **2** V-T If you **wean** someone **off** a bad habit, you gradually make them stop doing it or liking it. ❑ *...a programme to wean people off chips and fast food.*

weapon /ˈwepən/ (**weapons**) N-COUNT A **weapon** is an object such as a gun, knife, or missile. ❑ *...armed with automatic weapons.*

→ see **army, war**

weaponry /ˈwepənri/ N-UNCOUNT **Weaponry** is all the weapons that a group or country has or that are available to it.

ˌweapons of ˌmass deˈstruction N-PLURAL **Weapons of mass destruction** are biological, chemical, or nuclear weapons.

wear /weə/ (**wears, wearing, wore, worn**) **1** V-T When you **wear** clothes, shoes, or jewellery, you have them on your body. ❑ *He was wearing a brown uniform.* **2** V-T If you **wear** your hair in a particular way, it is cut or styled in that way. ❑ *She wore her hair in a long braid.* **3** N-UNCOUNT You can use **wear** to refer to clothes that are suitable for a particular time or occasion. ❑ *...an extensive range of beach wear.* **4** N-UNCOUNT **Wear** is the amount or type of use that something has over a period of time. ❑ *You'll get more wear out of a dark-coloured hat.* **5** V-I & N-UNCOUNT If something **wears**, or if it shows signs of **wear**, it becomes thinner or weaker from constant use. ❑ *Your horse needs new shoes if the shoe has worn thin or smooth.* ❑ *...a large armchair which showed signs of wear.* **6** → see also **worn**

▶ **wear away** PHR-VERB If you **wear** something **away**, it becomes thin and eventually disappears because it is used a lot or rubs a lot. ❑ *The softer rock wears away.*

▶ **wear down** **1** PHR-VERB If you **wear** something **down**, it becomes flatter or smoother as a result of constantly rubbing against something else. **2** PHR-VERB If someone **wears** you **down**, they weaken you by continually attacking or criticizing you, or by trying to persuade you to do something. ❑ *They hoped the waiting would wear me down.*

▶ **wear off** PHR-VERB If a feeling or sensation **wears off**, it slowly disappears. ❑ *The shock was wearing off, and now he was in great pain.*

▶ **wear out** **1** PHR-VERB When something **wears out**, it is used so much that it becomes thin or weak and cannot be used any more. ❑ *He wore out his shoes walking around Mexico City.* **2** → see also **worn-out** **3** PHR-VERB If something **wears** you **out**, it makes you feel extremely tired. [INFORMAL]

Usage

After you get up in the morning, you **get dressed**, or you **dress**, by **putting on** your clothes. ❑ *He put on his shoes and socks.* Small children and sick people may be unable to **dress themselves**, so someone else has to **dress** them. When you **are dressed**, you **are wearing** your clothes, or you **have** them **on**. ❑ *Edith had her hat on.* ❑ *They should stop walking round the house with nothing on.* During the day you might want to **get changed**, or to **change**, or to **change** your clothes. ❑ *She returned having changed from trousers and a pullover into a short-sleeved blouse and a skirt.* ❑ *Adams changed his shirt twice a day.* Before you go to bed, you **get undressed**, or you **undress**, by **taking off** your clothes. ❑ *He won't take his clothes off in front of me.* See also the note at **clothes**.

Word Partnership Use *wear* with:

N.	wear **black/red/white**, wear **clothes**, wear **contact lenses**, wear **glasses**, wear **gloves**, wear **a hat/helmet**, wear **a jacket**, wear **jeans**, wear **make up**, wear **a mask**, wear **a suit**, wear **a uniform** **1**
ADJ.	**casual** wear, **day** wear, **evening** wear **3**

weary /ˈwɪəri/ (**wearier, weariest, wearies, wearying, wearied**) **1** ADJ If you are **weary**, you are very tired. • **wearily** ADV ❑ *I sighed wearily.* • **weariness** N-UNCOUNT ❑ *Despite his weariness, Bertie gave a weak smile.* **2** V-I & ADJ AFTER LINK-V If you **weary of** something, or if you are **weary of** it, you become tired of it. ❑ *He had wearied of teaching in universities.* ❑ *She was weary of being alone.*

weather /ˈweðə/ (**weathers, weathering, weathered**) **1** N-UNCOUNT The **weather** is the condition of the atmosphere in an area at a particular time, for example, if it is raining, hot, or windy. ❑ *The weather was bad.* ❑ *...cold weather.* **2** V-T/V-I If something such as rock or wood **weathers**, or if something **weathers** it, it changes colour or shape as a result of the effects of wind, sun, rain, or frost. **3** V-T If you **weather** a difficult time, you survive it. ❑ *The company has weathered the crisis.*

→ see Word Web: **weather**

→ see **forecast**, **storm**

Word Partnership Use *weather* with:

ADJ.	**bad** weather, **clear** weather, **cold** weather, **cool** weather, **dry** weather, **fair** weather, **good** weather, **hot** weather, **inclement** weather, **mild** weather, **nice** weather, **rainy** weather, **rough** weather, **severe** weather, **stormy** weather, **sunny** weather, **warm** weather, **wet** weather **1**
N.	weather **conditions**, weather **prediction**, weather **report**, weather **service** **1**
V.	weather **permitting** **1**

weave /wiːv/ (**weaves, weaving, wove, woven**)

The form **weaved** is used for the past tense and past participle for meaning 3.

1 V-T If you **weave** cloth, you make it by crossing threads over and under each other using a machine called a loom. • **weaver** (**weavers**) N-COUNT ❑ *...a linen weaver from Ireland.* • **weaving** N-UNCOUNT ❑ *I studied weaving.* **2** N-COUNT The **weave** of a cloth is the way in which the threads are arranged. ❑ *Fabrics with a close weave.* **3** V-T If you **weave** your **way** somewhere, you move between and around things as you go there. ❑ *He weaves his way through a crowd.*

→ see **industry**

web /web/ (**webs**) **1** N-COUNT A spider's **web** is the thin net which it makes from the sticky substance it produces in its body. **2** N-COUNT A **web** is a complicated pattern of connections or relationships, often considered as an obstacle or a danger. ❑ *They accused him of weaving a web of lies.* **3** → see also **World-Wide Web**

→ see **blog**

webcam also **Webcam** /ˈwebkæm/ (**webcams**) N-COUNT A **webcam** is a video camera that takes pictures which can be viewed on a website. The pictures are often of something that is happening while you watch. [COMPUTING]

webcast also **Webcast** /ˈwebkɑːst, -kæst/ (**webcasts**) N-COUNT A **webcast** is an event such as a concert which you can watch on the Internet. [COMPUTING]

weblog or **Web log, web log** /ˈweblɒg/ (**weblogs**) N-COUNT A **weblog** is a website containing a diary or journal on a particular subject. [COMPUTING]

W

Word Web weather

Researchers believe the **weather** affects our bodies and minds. The barometric **pressure** drops before a **storm**. The difference in pressure may change the blood flow in the brain. Some people get migraine headaches. In **damp**, **humid** weather people have problems with arthritis. A sudden **heat wave** can produce heatstroke. People get seasonal affective disorder or SAD in the winter. They feel depressed during the short, **gloomy** days. As the word "sad" suggests, people with this condition feel depressed. The bitter cold of a **blizzard** can cause frostbite. The **hot**, **dry** Santa Ana winds* in southern California create confusion and depression in some people.

Santa Ana winds: strong, hot, dry winds that blow in southern California in autumn and early spring.

webmaster also **Webmaster** /'webmɑːstə, -mæs-/ (**webmasters**) N-COUNT A **webmaster** is someone who is in charge of a website, especially someone who does that as their job. [COMPUTING]
→ see **Internet**

'web page also **Web page** (**web pages**) N-COUNT A **web page** is a set of data or information which is designed to be viewed as part of a website. [COMPUTING]
→ see **Internet**

Word Link *site, situ ≈ position, location : campsite, situation, website*

website also **Web site** also **web site** /'websaɪt/ (**websites**) N-COUNT A **website** is a set of data and information about a particular subject which is available on the Internet. [COMPUTING]
→ see **blog**, **Internet**

webspace /'webspeɪs/ N-UNCOUNT **Webspace** is computer memory that you can use to create web pages. [COMPUTING]

wed /wed/ (**weds**, **wedding**, **wedded**)

The form **wed** is used in the present tense and is the past tense. The past participle can be either **wed** or **wedded**.

V-T/V-I If one person **weds** another or if two people **wed**, they get married. [JOURNALISM]

we'd /wɪd, wiːd/ **We'd** is the usual spoken form of 'we would' or 'we had', especially when 'had' is an auxiliary verb. ❑ *I don't know how we'd manage without her!*

wedding /'wedɪŋ/ (**weddings**) N-COUNT A **wedding** is a marriage ceremony and the celebration that often takes place afterwards.
→ see Word Web: **wedding**

wedge /wedʒ/ (**wedges**, **wedging**, **wedged**) **1** N-COUNT A **wedge** is an object with one pointed edge and one thick edge, which you put under a door to keep it firmly in position. **2** V-T If you **wedge** something such as a door or window, you keep it firmly in position by pushing a wedge or a similar object between it and the surface next to it. ❑ *We wedged the gate shut with bits of wood.* **3** V-T If you **wedge** something somewhere, you fit it there tightly. ❑ *Wedge the plug into the hole.* **4** PHRASE If someone **drives a wedge between** two people who are close, they cause ill feelings between them in order to weaken their relationship.

Wednesday /'wenzdeɪ, -di/ (**Wednesdays**) N-VAR **Wednesday** is the day after Tuesday and before Thursday.

wee /wiː/ ADJ **Wee** means small or little; used especially in Scotland. ❑ *...a wee child.*

weed /wiːd/ (**weeds**, **weeding**, **weeded**) **1** N-COUNT A **weed** is a wild plant growing where it is not wanted, for example in a garden. **2** V-T/V-I If you **weed**, or if you **weed** an area, you remove the weeds from it. ❑ *You're probably busy weeding and planting.*
▸ **weed out** PHR-VERB If you **weed out** things or people that are not wanted in a group, you find them and get rid of them. ❑ *Some are better than others, and we intend to weed out the weak ones.*

Word Web wedding

Some **weddings** are fancy, like the one in this picture. Most weddings have a similar group of attendants. The maid of honour or matron of honor helps the **bride** get ready for the ceremony. She also signs the **marriage certificate** as a legal **witness**. The **bridesmaids** plan the bride's wedding hen party. The best man plans the stag party. He also helps the groom dress for the wedding. After the **ceremony**, the guests go to a **reception**. When the party is over, many couples leave on a **honeymoon** trip.

week /wiːk/ (**weeks**) **1** N-VAR A **week** is a period of seven days, which is often considered to start on Monday and end on Sunday. ❑ *I had a letter from my mother last week.* ❑ *Her mother stayed for another two weeks.* **2** N-COUNT Your working **week** is the hours that you spend at work during a week. ❑ *The law fixes a maximum 35-hour working week.* **3** N-SING **The week** is the part of the week that does not include Saturday and Sunday. ❑ *...looking after the children during the week.*
→ see **year**

weekday /ˈwiːkdeɪ/ (**weekdays**) N-COUNT A **weekday** is any day of the week except Saturday and Sunday.

weekend /ˌwiːkˈend/ (**weekends**) N-COUNT A **weekend** is Saturday and Sunday. ❑ *I'll phone you at the weekend.*

weekly /ˈwiːkli/ (**weeklies**) **1** ADJ BEFORE N & ADV **Weekly** is used to describe something that happens or appears once a week. ❑ *...a weekly newspaper.* ❑ *The group meets weekly.* **2** N-COUNT A **weekly** is a newspaper or magazine that is published once a week.

weep /wiːp/ (**weeps, weeping, wept**) V-T/V-I & N-SING If someone **weeps** or if they have a **weep**, they cry. ❑ *She wept uncontrollably over the loss of her baby.* ❑ *There are times when I sit down and have a good weep.*
→ see **cry**

weigh /weɪ/ (**weighs, weighing, weighed**) **1** V-T If someone or something **weighs** a particular amount, that is how heavy they are. ❑ *He weighs 19 stone.* **2** V-T If you **weigh** someone or something, you measure how heavy they are. **3** V-T & PHR-VERB If you **weigh** the facts about a situation, or if you **weigh** them **up**, you consider them very carefully before you decide or say anything. ❑ *She weighed her options.* ❑ *I've been weighing up all the alternatives.* **4** V-I If a problem **weighs on** you, it makes you worried or unhappy. ❑ *The separation weighed on both of them.*

▸ **weigh down** **1** PHR-VERB If something that you are wearing or carrying **weighs** you **down**, it stops you moving easily because it is heavy. ❑ *...soldiers weighed down by their heavy packs.* **2** PHR-VERB If you **are weighed down by** something, it makes you very worried or causes you great problems. ❑ *She was weighed down with misery and disappointment.*

Word Partnership Use *weigh* with:

ADV.	weigh **less**, weigh **more** **1**
	weigh **carefully** **2** **3**
N.	weigh **10 pounds** **1**
	weigh **alternatives**, weigh **benefits**, weigh **costs**, weigh **the evidence**, weigh **risks** **3**

weight /weɪt/ (**weights, weighting, weighted**) **1** N-VAR The **weight** of a person or thing is how heavy they are, measured in units such as kilos or pounds. ❑ *What is your height and weight?* ❑ *This reduced the weight of the load.* **2** N-COUNT **Weights** are metal objects which weigh a known amount. ❑ *I was in the gym lifting weights.* **3** N-COUNT You can refer to a heavy object as a **weight**. ❑ *...laws protecting workers who lift heavy weights.* **4** N-SING If you feel a **weight** on you, you have a worrying problem or responsibility. ❑ *A great weight lifted from me.* ❑ *I feel great weight of responsibility in my job.* **5** PHRASE If someone is not **pulling** their **weight**, they are not working as hard as everyone else who is involved in the same task. **6** PHRASE If you **throw** your **weight behind** a person or a plan, you use all your influence and do everything you can to support them.
→ see **diet**

▸ **weight down** PHR-VERB If you **weight** something **down**, you put something heavy on it or in it, often so that it cannot move easily.

Usage

In British English, a person's weight is normally measured in **stones** and **pounds**. A **stone** is equivalent to 14 pounds, or 6.35 kilograms. When you are mentioning someone's weight, you often omit the word **pounds. Stone** usually has a singular form although its meaning is plural. ❑ *Jodie confessed she now weighed 9 stone 12.* In American English, only **pounds** are used. ❑ *I weigh 110 pounds.*

Word Partnership Use *weight* with:

V.	**add** weight, **gain/lose** weight, **put on** weight **1**
N.	**body** weight, weight **gain/loss**, **height and** weight **1**
	size and weight, weight **training** **1**
ADJ.	**excess** weight, **healthy** weight, **ideal** weight, **normal** weight **1**

weighted /ˈweɪtɪd/ ADJ A system that is **weighted** in favour of a person or group is organized so that this person or group has an advantage. ❑ *The system seems to be weighted against the poor.*

weightlifting also **weight-lifting** /ˈweɪtˌlɪftɪŋ/ N-UNCOUNT **Weightlifting** is a sport in which the competitor who can lift the heaviest weight wins.

ˈweight ˌtraining N-UNCOUNT **Weight training** is a kind of exercise in which people lift or push heavy weights with their arms and legs.

weighty /ˈweɪti/ (**weightier, weightiest**) ADJ **Weighty** issues seem serious or important. [FORMAL] ❑ *He discusses such weighty matters as life, death and the family.*

weir /wɪə/ (**weirs**) N-COUNT A **weir** is a low dam built across a river to control the flow of water.

weird /wɪəd/ (**weirder, weirdest**) ADJ **Weird** means strange and peculiar. ❑ *It must be weird to suddenly become rich.* ● **weirdly** ADV ❑ *...men who dressed weirdly.*

welcome /ˈwelkəm/ (**welcomes, welcoming, welcomed**) **1** V-T & N-COUNT If you **welcome** someone or if you give them a **welcome**, you greet them in a friendly way when they arrive. ❑ *She was there to welcome him home.* ❑ *There would be a fantastic welcome awaiting him.* **2** CONVENTION You can say **'Welcome'** to someone who has just arrived. ❑ *Welcome to Washington.* ❑ *Welcome back, Deborah – it's good to have you here.* **3** ADJ If you say that someone is **welcome** in a particular place, you are encouraging them to go there by assuring them that they will be accepted. ❑ *New members are always* *welcome.* **4** PHRASE If you **make** someone **welcome** or **make** them **feel** welcome, you make them feel happy and accepted in a new place. **5** V-T & ADJ If you **welcome** an action or decision, or if you say it is **welcome**, you approve of it and support it. ❑ *Papon's lawyers welcomed the decision.* ❑ *It's a welcome change to see something more creative.* **6** ADJ AFTER LINK-V If you tell someone that they are **welcome to** do something, you are encouraging them to do it. ❑ *Guests are welcome to use the restaurant.* **7** CONVENTION You can acknowledge someone's thanks by saying **'You're welcome'**. ❑ *'Thank you for the information.'—'You're welcome.'*

Word Partnership Use *welcome* with:

N.	welcome **guests**, welcome **visitors** 1 6
ADV.	welcome **home** 2
	always welcome 3-6
ADJ.	**warm** welcome 1 3 4

weld /weld/ (**welds, welding, welded**) **1** V-T If you **weld** one piece of metal to another, you join them by heating their edges and putting them together so that they cool and harden into one piece. **2** N-COUNT A **weld** is a join where two pieces of metal have been welded together.

welfare /'welfeə/ **1** N-UNCOUNT The **welfare** of a person or group is their health, comfort, and prosperity. ❑ *I do not think he is considering Emma's welfare.* **2** ADJ **Welfare** services are provided to help with people's living conditions and financial problems. ❑ *He wants to deal with problems in the welfare system.* **3** N-UNCOUNT In American English, **welfare** is money that is paid by the government to people who are unemployed, poor, or ill. The British term is **social security**.

Word Partnership Use *welfare* with:

ADJ.	**public** welfare, **social** welfare 1
N.	**animal** welfare, **health and** welfare 1
	child welfare, welfare **programmes**, welfare **reform**, welfare **system** 2
	welfare **benefits**, welfare **cheques** 3

,welfare 'state N-SING In Britain and some other countries, **the welfare state** is a system in which the government uses money collected from taxes to provide social services such as health and education and give money to people when they are unable to work.

well

1 DISCOURSE USES
2 ADVERB USES
3 PHRASES
4 ADJECTIVE USE
5 NOUN USES
6 VERB USE

well /wel/

Well is used mainly in spoken English.

1 **1** ADV You say **well** to indicate that you are about to say something else, especially when you are hesitating, when you are trying to make your statement less strong, when you are about to correct a statement, or when you are changing the topic. ❑ *Well, I thought she was a bit unfair about me.* ❑ *There was a note. Well, not really a note.* **2** CONVENTION You say **oh well** to indicate that you accept a situation or that someone else should accept it, even though you or they are not very happy about it. ❑ *Oh well, it could be worse.* **3** **very well** → see **very**

→ see **oil**

well /wel/ (**better, best**)

2 **1** ADV If you do something **well**, you do it to a high standard or to a great extent. ❑ *All the Indian batsmen played well.* ❑ *He speaks English better than I do.* ❑ *People live longer nowadays, and they are better educated.* ❑ *I don't really know her very well.* **2** ADV If you do something **well**, you do it thoroughly and completely. ❑ *Mix all the ingredients well.* **3** ADV You use **well** to ask or talk about the extent or standard of something. ❑ *How well do you remember your mother, Franzi?* ❑ *He wasn't dressed any better than me.* **4** ADV You use **well** in front of prepositions and a few adjectives in order to emphasize them. ❑ *Franklin did not arrive until well after midnight.* ❑ *The show is well worth a visit.* **5** ADV You use **well** after verbs such as 'may' and 'could' when you are saying what you think is likely to happen. ❑ *The murderer may well live nearby.*

well /wel/

3 **1** PHRASE If one thing is involved and another thing is involved **as well**, the second thing is also involved. ❑ *Most of my friends have got kids, and I want to include them as well.* **2** PHRASE If one thing is involved **as well as** another, the first thing is involved in addition to the second. ❑ *Jim Morrison was a poet as well as a singer.* **3** PHRASE If you say that something that has happened **is just as well**, you mean that it is fortunate that it happened in the way it did. ❑ *It's just as well she wasn't there, considering what happened.* **4** PHRASE If you say that you **might as well** do something, or that you **may as well** do it, you mean that you will do it although you do not have a strong desire to do it and may even feel slightly reluctant about it. ❑ *Now you're here, you might as well stay.* **5** PHRASE If you say that something is **well and truly** over, you are emphasizing that it is completely finished or gone. ❑ *The war is well and truly over.*

well /wel/

4 ADJ If you are **well**, you are healthy and not ill. ❑ *I'm not very well today.*

well /wel/ (**wells**)

5 **1** N-COUNT A **well** is a hole in the ground where a supply of water is kept. **2** N-COUNT A **well** is an oil well.

well /wel/ (**wells, welling, welled**)

6 V-I & PHR-VERB If tears **well** in your eyes, or if they **well up** in your eyes, they come to the surface. ❑ *Tears well up in her eyes when she speaks of her husband's death.*

we'll /wɪl, STRONG wiːl/ **We'll** is the usual spoken form of 'we shall' or 'we will'. ❑ *We'll come over tonight for a chat.*

,well-'balanced **1** ADJ Someone who is **well-balanced** is sensible and does not have many emotional problems. **2** ADJ If you describe something that is made up of several parts as **well-balanced**, you mean that there is a good mixture of each part. ❑ *...a well-balanced diet.*

'well-being also **wellbeing** N-UNCOUNT

Someone's **well-being** is their health and happiness. ❑ *Singing can create a sense of wellbeing.*

ˌwell ˈdone 1 CONVENTION You say **'Well done'** to indicate that you are pleased that someone has got something right or done something good. 2 ADJ If meat is **well done**, it has been cooked thoroughly.

ˌwell-ˈdressed ADJ Someone who is **well-dressed** is wearing smart or elegant clothes.

ˌwell-esˈtablished ADJ If something is **well-established**, it has existed for quite a long time and is successful. ❑ *...well-established companies.*

ˌwell-inˈformed ADJ Someone who is **well-informed** knows a lot about many different subjects or about one particular subject.

ˌwell-inˈtentioned ADJ **Well-intentioned** means the same as **well-meaning**.

ˌwell-ˈknown 1 ADJ Something or someone that is **well-known** is famous or familiar. ❑ *She was a very well-known author.* 2 → See note at **famous**

ˌwell-ˈmeaning ADJ Someone who is **well-meaning** tries to be helpful, but is usually unsuccessful or causes unfortunate results.

ˌwell-ˈoff ADJ Someone who is **well-off** is rich enough to be able to do and buy most of the things that they want.

ˌwell-ˈpaid ADJ If you say that a person or their job is **well-paid**, you mean that they receive a lot of money for the work that they do.

ˌwell-to-ˈdo ADJ **Well-to-do** means the same as **well-off**.

went /went/ **Went** is the past tense of **go**.

wept /wept/ **Wept** is the past tense and past participle of **weep**.

were /wə, STRONG wɜː/ 1 **Were** is the plural and the second person singular of the past tense of **be**. 2 **Were** is sometimes used instead of 'was' in certain structures, for example in conditional clauses or after the verb 'wish'. [FORMAL] ❑ *They were treating her as if she were a child.* ❑ *He wished he were back in Washington.*

we're /wɪə/ **We're** is the usual spoken form of 'we are'. ❑ *We're going to win the World Cup.*

weren't /wɜːnt/ **Weren't** is the usual spoken form of 'were not'. ❑ *We weren't totally happy with the way things sounded.*

west /west/ 1 N-SING **The west** is the direction in which you look to see the sun set. 2 N-SING & ADJ **The west of** a place, or the **west** part of a place, is the part which is towards the west. ❑ *...a house in the west of the city.* ❑ *He's from the west coast of Africa.* 3 ADV **West** means towards the west, or positioned to the west of a place or thing. ❑ *We'll drive west to Kanchanaburi.* ❑ *They're planning to build a film studio just west of London.* 4 ADJ A **west** wind blows from the west. 5 N-SING **The West** is used to refer to the United States, Canada, and the countries of Western, Northern, and Southern Europe.

westerly /ˈwestəli/ 1 ADJ A **westerly** point, area, or direction is to the west or towards the west. ❑ *They set out in a westerly direction along the riverbank.* 2 ADJ A **westerly** wind blows from the west.

western /ˈwestən/ (**westerns**) 1 ADJ **Western** means in or from the west of a region or country. 2 ADJ **Western** means coming from or associated with the societies of the United States, Canada, and the countries of Western, Northern, and Southern Europe. 3 N-COUNT A **western** is a film or book about the life of cowboys.

westerner /ˈwestənə/ (**westerners**) N-COUNT A **westerner** is a person who was born in or who lives in the United States, Canada, or Western, Northern, or Southern Europe.

westward /ˈwestwəd/ also **westwards** /ˈwestwədz/ ADV & ADJ **Westward** or **westwards** means towards the west. ❑ *...the ship on which Cook sailed westwards from New Zealand.* ❑ *...the one-hour westward flight over the Andes to Lima.*

wet /wet/ (**wetter, wettest, wets, wetting, wetted**)

> The forms **wet** and **wetted** are both used as the past tense and past participle of the verb.

1 ADJ If something is **wet**, it is covered in water or another liquid. ❑ *My gloves were soaking wet.* 2 V-T To **wet** something means to cause it to have water or another liquid on it. ❑ *Wet the hair before applying the product.* 3 ADJ When the weather is **wet**, it is raining. ❑ *It was very wet and windy, the day I went to Millend.* 4 ADJ If something such as paint or cement is **wet**, it is not yet dry. 5 V-T If someone **wets** their bed or clothes, or if they **wet themselves**, they urinate in their bed or clothes because they cannot control their bladder.

Word Partnership Use *wet* with:

V.	**get** wet 1
ADJ.	**soaking** wet 1
	cold and wet 1 3
N.	wet **clothes**, wet **feet**, wet **grass**, wet **hair**, wet **sand** 1
	wet **snow**, wet **weather** 3
	wet **the bed** 5

we've /wɪv, STRONG wiːv/ **We've** is the usual spoken form of 'we have', especially when 'have' is an auxiliary verb. ❑ *Hello, I don't think we've met.*

whack /wæk/ (**whacks, whacking, whacked**) V-T If you **whack** someone or something, you hit them hard. [INFORMAL] ❑ *Someone whacked him on the head.*

whacky → see **wacky**

whale /weɪl/ (**whales**) N-COUNT A **whale** is a very large sea mammal.
→ see Word Web: **whale**

whaling /ˈweɪlɪŋ/ N-UNCOUNT **Whaling** is the activity of hunting and killing whales. ❑ *...commercial whaling.*

wharf /wɔːf/ (**wharves**) N-COUNT A **wharf** is a platform by a river or the sea where ships can be tied up.

what /wɒt/ 1 PRON & DET You use **what** in questions when you are asking for information. ❑ *What do you want?* ❑ *'Has something happened?'—'Indeed it has.'—'What?'* ❑ *Hey! What are you doing?* ❑ *What kind of poetry does he like?* 2 CONJ & DET You use **what** after certain words, especially verbs and adjectives, when you are referring to a situation that is unknown or has not been specified. ❑ *I*

Word Web whale

Whales belong to a group of animals called cetaceans. This group also includes **dolphins** and porpoises. Whales live in the water, but they are **mammals**. They breathe air and are warm-blooded. Whales are adapted to life in the **ocean**. They have a 2-inch thick layer of blubber under their skin. This insulates them from the cold ocean water. They sing beautiful songs that can be heard miles away. Blue whales are the largest animals in the world. They can become almost 100 feet long and weigh up to 145 tons.

want to know what happened to Norman. ❑ *She was very embarrassed when she realized what she had done.* **3** CONJ You use **what** at the beginning of a clause in structures where you are changing the order of the information to give special emphasis to something. ❑ *What she does remember is that her mother was always there for her.* **4** CONJ & DET You use **what** to indicate that you are talking about the whole of an amount. ❑ *He drank what was left in his glass.* ❑ *They spent what money they had.* **5** PREDET & DET You use **what** to express your opinion of something, for example when you are surprised by it. ❑ *What a horrible thing to do.* ❑ *What ugly things; throw them away.* **6** CONVENTION You say **'What?'** when you want someone to repeat something because you did not hear it properly. 'What' is not as polite as 'pardon' or 'sorry'. ❑ *'They could paint this place,' she said. 'What?' he asked.* **7** CONVENTION You can say **'What'** to express surprise or disbelief. ❑ *'We've won the money!'—'What?'* **8** PHRASE You use **what about** when you are making a suggestion or offer. ❑ *What about a cup of tea?* **9** PHRASE You use **what if** at the beginning of a question about the consequences of something, especially something undesirable. ❑ *What if this doesn't work out?* **10** PHRASE If you know **what's what**, you know the important things that need to be known about a situation. **11** PHRASE You say **what with** to introduce the reasons for a situation, especially an undesirable one. ❑ *Maybe they are tired, what with all the sleep they're losing.* **12** **what's more** → see **more**

whatever /wɒt'evə/ **1** CONJ & DET You use **whatever** to refer to anything or everything of a particular type. ❑ *Franklin was free to do whatever he pleased.* ❑ *Whatever doubts he might have had about Ingrid were all over now.* **2** CONJ You use **whatever** when you are indicating that you do not know the precise identity, meaning, or value of the thing just mentioned. ❑ *'I love you,' he said.—'Whatever that means,' she said.* **3** CONJ You use **whatever** to say that something is the case in all circumstances. ❑ *We will love you whatever happens.* ❑ *People will judge you whatever you do.* **4** ADV You use **whatever** after a noun group to emphasize a negative statement. ❑ *I have nothing whatever to say.* **5** ADV You use **whatever** to ask in an emphatic way about something which you are very surprised about. ❑ *Whatever is the matter with you both?*

what's /wɒts/ **What's** is the usual spoken form of 'what is' or 'what has', especially when 'has' is an auxiliary verb.

whatsoever /ˌwɒtsəʊ'evə/ ADV You use **whatsoever** after a noun group in order to emphasize a negative statement. ❑ *I've nothing whatsoever to say on the subject.*

wheat /wi:t/ N-UNCOUNT **Wheat** is a cereal crop grown for its grain, which is ground into flour to make bread.
→ see **grain**

wheel /wi:l/ (**wheels, wheeling, wheeled**) **1** N-COUNT A **wheel** is a circular object which turns round on a rod attached to its centre. Wheels are fixed underneath vehicles so that they can move along. ❑ *The car wheels spun and slipped on some oil.* **2** N-COUNT A **wheel** is the same as a **steering wheel**. **3** V-T If you **wheel** an object that has wheels somewhere, you push it along. ❑ *He wheeled his bike into the alley.*
→ see Word Web: **wheel**
→ see **bicycle, colour**

▶ **wheel around** PHR-VERB If you **wheel around**, you turn round suddenly. ❑ *He wheeled around to face her.*

Word Partnership Use *wheel* with:

N.	wheel **of a car/lorry/vehicle** **1**
V.	**grip the** wheel, **slide behind the** wheel, **spin the** wheel, **turn the** wheel

Word Web wheel

In about 5000 BC the **wheel** was invented in Mesopotamia, part of modern-day Iraq. That's when someone first **spun** a **potter's wheel** to make a clay jar. About 1500 years later, people put wheels on an axle and made a chariot. These first wheels were solid wood and were very heavy. However, in about 2000 BC the Egyptians invented much lighter wheels with **spokes**. The wheel has driven the development of all kinds of modern technology. The waterwheel, **spinning wheel**, and **turbine** were important to the Industrial Revolution. Even the propeller and jet engine are based on the wheel.

wheelchair /'wi:ltʃeə/ (**wheelchairs**) N-COUNT A **wheelchair** is a chair with wheels that sick or disabled people use in order to move about.
→ see **disability**

wheeze /wi:z/ (**wheezes, wheezing, wheezed**) V-I If you **wheeze**, you breathe with difficulty, making a hissing or whistling sound.

when /wen/ **1** ADV You use **when** to ask questions about the time at which things happen. ❑ *When did you get married?* ❑ *'I'll be there this afternoon.'—'When?'* **2** CONJ You use **when** to introduce a clause where you refer to the time at which something happens. ❑ *I asked him when he'd be back to pick me up.* ❑ *I don't know when the decision was made.* ❑ *He was a student when we met.* ❑ *She remembered that day when she'd gone exploring the town.* **3** CONJ You use **when** to introduce the reason for an opinion or question. ❑ *How can you understand, when you don't have kids?* **4** CONJ You use **when** in order to introduce a fact or comment which makes the other part of the sentence rather surprising or unlikely. ❑ *They think it's an easy job, when in fact, it's a lot of hard work.*

whenever /wen'evə/ CONJ You use **whenever** to refer to any time or every time that something happens or is true. ❑ *She always called in to see us whenever she was in the area.* ❑ *Avoid processed foods whenever possible.*

where /weə/ **1** ADV You use **where** to ask questions about the place something is in, or is coming from or going to. ❑ *Where did you meet him?* ❑ *'You'll never guess where I'm going.'—'Where?'* **2** CONJ & PRON You use **where** to specify or refer to the place in which something is situated or happens. ❑ *People looked across to see where the noise was coming from.* ❑ *He knew where Henry Carter had gone.* ❑ *Is this the travel agency where you booked your holiday?* **3** CONJ & PRON & ADV You use **where** when you are referring to or asking about a situation, a stage in something, or an aspect of something. ❑ *It's easy to see where she got the idea.* ❑ *The government is at a stage where it is willing to talk.* ❑ *Where will it all end?* **4** CONJ **Where** is used to introduce a clause which contrasts with what is said in the main clause. ❑ *Sometimes a teacher will be listened to, where a parent might not.*

whereabouts **1** N-SING /'weərəbaʊts/ The **whereabouts** of a person or thing is the place where they are. ❑ *...a map showing the whereabouts of local castles.* **2** ADV /ˌweərə'baʊts/ You use **whereabouts** in questions when you are asking precisely where something is. ❑ *Whereabouts in Liverpool are you from?*

whereas /weər'æz/ CONJ You use **whereas** to introduce a comment which contrasts with what is said in the main clause. ❑ *She shows her feelings, whereas I don't.*

whereby /weə'baɪ/ PRON A system or action **whereby** something happens is one that makes that thing happen. [FORMAL] ❑ *...a deal whereby the youngest child flies, stays and eats free.*

W

whereupon /ˌweərə'pɒn/ CONJ You use **whereupon** to say that one thing happens immediately after another thing and usually as a result of it. [FORMAL] ❑ *'Well, get on with it then,' said Dobson, whereupon Davies started to explain.*

wherever /weər'evə/ **1** CONJ You use **wherever** to say that something happens or is true in any place or situation. ❑ *Some people enjoy themselves wherever they are.* **2** CONJ You use **wherever** to indicate that you do not know where a place or person is. ❑ *She wanted to turn and run for the exit, wherever that was.*

whether /'weðə/ **1** CONJ You use **whether** to talk about a choice or doubt between two or more alternatives. ❑ *They now have two weeks to decide whether or not to buy.* **2** CONJ You use **whether** to say that something is true in any of the circumstances you mention. ❑ *We're in this together, whether we like it or not.*

which /wɪtʃ/ **1** PRON & DET You use **which** to ask questions when there are two or more possible answers or alternatives. ❑ *Which is your cabin ?* ❑ *Which woman or man do you most admire?* **2** DET & PRON You use **which** to refer to a choice between two or more possible answers or alternatives. ❑ *I wanted to know which school you went to.* ❑ *There are so many different dictionaries, how do you know which to choose?* **3** PRON You use **which** at the beginning of a relative clause that specifies the thing you are talking about or that gives more information about it. ❑ *He was a passenger in a car which was hit by a train.* **4** PRON & DET You use **which** to refer back to what has just been said. ❑ *I play tennis and go riding, which doesn't interest him.* ❑ *It could be an infection, in which case she needs to see a doctor.*

whichever /wɪtʃ'evə/ **1** DET & CONJ You use **whichever** to indicate that it does not matter which of the possible alternatives happens or is chosen. ❑ *Whichever way you look at it, it's a mess.* ❑ *You can make your pizzas round or square, whichever you prefer.* **2** DET & CONJ You use **whichever** to specify which of a number of possibilities is the right one or the one you mean. ❑ *...learning to relax by whichever method suits you best.* ❑ *Fishing is from 6am to nightfall or 10.30pm, whichever is sooner.*

whiff /wɪf/ (**whiffs**) **1** N-COUNT If there is a **whiff of** something, there is a slight smell of it. ❑ *He caught a whiff of her perfume.* **2** N-COUNT A **whiff of** something bad or harmful is a slight sign of it. ❑ *There's a whiff of trouble in the air.*

while /waɪl/ (**whiles, whiling, whiled**) **1** CONJ If one thing happens **while** another thing is happening, the two things happen at the same time. ❑ *I unwrapped the package while he watched.* ❑ *Her parents help with child care while she works.* **2** CONJ You use **while** to introduce a clause which contrasts with the other part of the sentence. ❑ *The first two treatments are free, while the third costs £35.00.* **3** CONJ You use **while** in a clause to say that although something is the case, it does not affect the truth of the other part of the sentence. ❑ *While the news so far has been good, there may be days ahead when it is bad.* **4** N-SING A **while** is a period of time. ❑ *They walked on in silence for a while.* ❑ *He was married a little while ago.* **5** to be **worth** your **while** → see **worth** **6** PHRASE You use **all the while** in order to say that something happens continually or that it happens throughout the time when something else is happening. ❑ *All the while the people at the next table watched me eat.* **7** PHRASE If something happens **once in a while**, it happens occasionally.

▶ **while away** PHR-VERB If you **while away** the time in a particular way, you spend time in that way because you are waiting for something or because you have nothing else to do. ❑ *They whiled* *away the hours telling stories.*

whilst /waɪlst/ CONJ **Whilst** means the same as **while** when it is used as a conjunction. [BRIT, FORMAL] ❑ *The girls met four years ago whilst singing with a local band.*

whim /wɪm/ (**whims**) N-VAR A **whim** is a sudden desire to do or have something without any particular reason. ❑ *We decided, on a whim, to sail to Morocco.*

whimper /ˈwɪmpə/ (**whimpers, whimpering, whimpered**) V-I & N-COUNT If someone **whimpers**, they make quiet unhappy or frightened sounds called **whimpers**, as if they are about to start crying. ❑ *She lay at the bottom of the stairs, whimpering in pain.* ❑ *David's crying subsided to a whimper.*

whimsical /ˈwɪmzɪkəl/ ADJ Something that is **whimsical** is unusual and slightly playful, and is not trying to make a serious point. ❑ *...his gentle and whimsical humour.*

whine /waɪn/ (**whines, whining, whined**) **1** V-I & N-COUNT If something or someone **whines**, they make a long, high-pitched noise called a **whine**, which often sounds sad or unpleasant. ❑ *The dog started to whine with impatience.* ❑ *...the whine of jet engines.* **2** V-I If someone **whines about** something, they complain about it in an annoying way.

whinge /wɪndʒ/ (**whinges, whingeing, whinged**) V-I & N-COUNT If you say that someone **is whingeing** or having a **whinge**, you mean that they are complaining in an annoying way about something unimportant. [BRIT, INFORMAL] ❑ *I'm tired of listening to everybody's whinges.*

whip /wɪp/ (**whips, whipping, whipped**) **1** N-COUNT A **whip** is a long thin piece of leather or rope fastened to a handle. It is used for hitting animals or people. **2** V-T If someone **whips** an animal or person, they hit them with a whip. • **whipping** (**whippings**) N-COUNT ❑ *He threatened to give her a whipping.* **3** V-T If you **whip** something **out** or **whip** something off, you take it out or take it **off** very quickly and suddenly. ❑ *Bob whipped out his notebook.* ❑ *He whipped off his jacket and placed it round her shoulders.* **4** V-T If you **whip** cream or eggs, you stir them very quickly to make them thick or stiff. ❑ *Serve warm or cold with whipped cream.*
▶ **whip up** PHR-VERB If someone **whips up** an emotion such as hatred, they deliberately cause and encourage people to feel that emotion. ❑ *He accused the media of whipping up hatred and fear.*

whir /wɜː/ → see **whirr**

whirl /wɜːl/ (**whirls, whirling, whirled**) **1** V-T/V-I If something or someone **whirls around**, or if you **whirl** them **around**, they move round or turn round very quickly. ❑ *He whirled around and began to run back down the alley.* ❑ *...whirling snow.* **2** N-COUNT You can refer to a lot of intense activity as a **whirl of** activity.

whirlwind /ˈwɜːlwɪnd/ (**whirlwinds**) N-COUNT A **whirlwind** is a tall column of air which spins round and round very fast and moves across the land or sea.

whirr also **whir** /wɜː/ (**whirrs, whirring, whirred**) V-I & N-COUNT If something such as a machine **whirrs**, it makes a series of low sounds so quickly that they seem like one continuous sound. This sound is called a **whirr**. ❑ *...the constant whirr of his electric fan.*

whisk /wɪsk/ (**whisks, whisking, whisked**) **1** V-T If you **whisk** someone or something somewhere, you take them there quickly. ❑ *I was whisked away in a police car.* **2** V-T If you **whisk** eggs or cream, you stir air into them very fast. **3** N-COUNT A **whisk** is a kitchen tool used for whisking eggs or cream.
→ see **kitchen**

whisker

whisker /ˈwɪskə/ (**whiskers**) **1** N-COUNT The **whiskers** of an animal such as a cat or mouse are the long stiff hairs that grow near its mouth. **2** N-PLURAL People sometimes refer to the hair on a man's face as his **whiskers**.

whiskey /ˈwɪski/ (**whiskeys**) N-VAR **Whiskey** is whisky made in Ireland or the United States.

whisky /ˈwɪski/ (**whiskies**) N-VAR **Whisky** is a strong alcoholic drink made, especially in Scotland, from grain such as barley or rye.

whisper /ˈwɪspə/ (**whispers, whispering, whispered**) V-T/V-I & N-COUNT If you **whisper** something, or if you say it in a **whisper**, you say it very quietly, using only your breath and not your voice. ❑ *He whispered the message to David.* ❑ *Don't whisper. It's rude.* ❑ *They spoke in whispers.*

whistle /ˈwɪsəl/ (**whistles, whistling, whistled**) **1** V-T/V-I When you **whistle**, you make sounds by forcing your breath out between your lips or teeth. ❑ *He whistled a tune.* ❑ *He whistled, surprised but not shocked.* **2** V-I If something such as a train or a kettle **whistles**, it makes a loud, high sound. ❑ *Somewhere a train whistled.* **3** V-I If something such as the wind **whistles** somewhere, it moves there, making a loud high sound. ❑ *The wind whistled through the trees.* **4** N-COUNT A **whistle** is a small metal tube which you blow in order to produce a loud sound and attract someone's attention.

ˈwhistle-blowing N-UNCOUNT **Whistle-blowing** is the act of telling the authorities or the public that the organization you are working for is doing something immoral or illegal.

white /waɪt/ (**whiter, whitest, whites**) **1** ADJ & N-VAR Something that is **white** is the colour of snow or milk. **2** ADJ & N-COUNT A **white** person has a pale skin and belongs to a race of European origin. **Whites** are white people. ❑ *He was white, with brown shoulder-length hair.* ❑ *...a law that has kept blacks and whites apart.* **3** ADJ **White** wine is wine of a pale yellowish colour. **4** ADJ **White** coffee contains milk or cream. [BRIT] **5** N-VAR The **white** of an egg is the transparent liquid surrounding the yolk. **6** N-COUNT The **white** of your eye is the white part of your eyeball.
→ see **colour**

ˌwhite-ˈcollar ADJ BEFORE N **White-collar** workers work in offices rather than doing manual work in industry.

ˈWhite House N-PROPER **The White House** is the official home in Washington DC of the President of the United States. You can also use **White House** to refer to the President of the United States and his or her officials.

whitewash /'waɪtwɒʃ/ **1** N-UNCOUNT **Whitewash** is a mixture of lime or chalk and water used for painting walls white. **2** N-SING A **whitewash** is an attempt to hide the unpleasant facts about something from the public in order to make a situation look less serious than it really is. ❑ *He has described the investigation as a whitewash.*

whittle /'wɪtəl/ (**whittles, whittling, whittled**) ▶ **whittle away** or **whittle down** PHR-VERB To **whittle** something **away** or to **whittle** it **down** means to make it smaller or less effective. ❑ *He had whittled eight applicants down to two.*

whizz /wɪz/ (**whizzes, whizzing, whizzed**) V-I If something **whizzes** somewhere, it moves there very fast. [INFORMAL] ❑ *He felt a bullet whizz past his face.*

who /hu:/ **1** PRON You use **who** when asking questions about the name or identity of a person or group of people. ❑ *Who's there?* ❑ *Who did you ask?* ❑ *Who do you work for?* ❑ *'You reminded me of somebody.'—'Who?'* **2** CONJ You use **who** to introduce a clause where you talk about the identity of a person or a group of people. ❑ *I was suddenly curious and asked who she was.* ❑ *They haven't found out who did it.* **3** PRON You use **who** at the beginning of a relative clause when specifying the person or group of people you are talking about or when giving more information about them. ❑ *The woman, who needs constant attention, is cared for by relatives.* ❑ *The man gave himself up to police, who are now questioning him.*

Usage

Who is now commonly used as the object where in the past it was only considered to be correct to use **whom**. **Who**, however, cannot be used directly after a preposition; for example, you cannot say 'the woman to who I spoke'. Instead you say '**the woman to whom I spoke**' or '**the woman I spoke to**'. There are some types of sentence, for example when you are talking about quantities, in which **who** cannot be used: ❑ *...twenty masked prisoners, many of whom are armed.*

who'd /hu:d/ **Who'd** is the usual spoken form of 'who had', especially when 'had' is an auxiliary verb. **Who'd** is also a spoken form of 'who would'.

whoever /hu:'evə/ **1** PRON You use **whoever** to refer to someone when their identity is not yet known. ❑ *Whoever was responsible for this crime is a very dangerous person.* ❑ *Whoever wins this year is going to be famous for life.* **2** CONJ You use **whoever** to indicate that the actual identity of the person who does something will not affect a situation. ❑ *You can have whoever you like to visit you.* ❑ *People should respect each other, whoever they are, and whatever their race.*

W

whole /həʊl/ **1** QUANT If you refer to **the whole of** something, you mean all of it. ❑ *I was cold through the whole of my body.* ❑ *We spent the whole summer in Italy.* **2** N-SING A **whole** is a single thing which contains several different parts. ❑ *How do the separate parts work together to form a whole?* **3** ADJ AFTER LINK-V If something is **whole**, it is in one piece and is not broken or damaged. ❑ *Most of the building was ruined, but the front was whole.* ❑ *He took an ice cube from the glass and swallowed it whole.* **4** ADJ BEFORE N You use **whole** to emphasize what you are saying. [INFORMAL] ❑ *...a whole new way of doing business.* ❑ *There's a whole group of friends he wants you to meet.* **5** PHRASE If you refer to something **as a whole**, you are referring to it generally and as a single unit. ❑ *For the group as a whole, sales are down by 2 per cent.* **6** PHRASE You say **on the whole** to indicate that what you are saying is only true in general and may not be true in every case. ❑ *The cheeses they make are, on the whole, of a high standard.*

Usage

Whole is often used to mean the same as **all** but when used in front of plurals, **whole** and **all** have different meanings. For example, if you say '**Whole buildings have been destroyed**', you mean that some buildings have been destroyed completely. If you say '**All the buildings have been destroyed**', you mean that every building has been destroyed.

wholehearted /ˌhəʊl'hɑ:tɪd/ ADJ If you support something or agree to something in a **wholehearted** way, you support or agree to it enthusiastically and completely. ❑ *He has my wholehearted support.* ● **wholeheartedly** ADV ❑ *I agree wholeheartedly with you.*

wholesale /'həʊlseɪl/ **1** ADJ & ADV **Wholesale** goods or goods that are bought **wholesale** are bought cheaply in large quantities and then sold again to shops. ❑ *Wholesale prices have fallen over the past year.* ❑ *Each tablet is sold wholesale for just 2p or 3p.* **2** ADJ BEFORE N & ADV You use **wholesale** to describe something undesirable or unpleasant that is done to an excessive extent. ❑ *...a campaign to stop the wholesale destruction of villages.*

wholesaler /'həʊlseɪlə/ (**wholesalers**) N-COUNT A **wholesaler** is a person whose business is buying large quantities of goods and selling them in smaller amounts to shops.

wholesome /'həʊlsəm/ **1** ADJ If you describe something as **wholesome**, you approve of it because you think it will have a positive influence on people, especially because it does not involve anything sexually immoral. ❑ *...good, wholesome fun.* **2** ADJ If you describe food as **wholesome**, you approve of it because you think it is good for your health.

who'll /hu:l/ **Who'll** is a spoken form of 'who will' or 'who shall'.

wholly /'həʊlli/ ADV **Wholly** means completely. ❑ *This is a wholly new approach.*

whom /hu:m/

Whom is used in formal or written English instead of 'who' when it is the object of a verb or preposition.

1 PRON You use **whom** in questions when you ask about the name or identity of a person or group of people. ❑ *'I want to send a telegram.'—'Fine, to whom?'* ❑ *Whom did he expect to answer his phone?* **2** CONJ You use **whom** to introduce a clause where you talk about the name or identity of a person or a group of people. ❑ *He asked me whom I'd seen.* ❑ *They may appoint whom they like.* **3** PRON You use **whom** at the beginning of a relative clause when specifying the person or people you are talking about, or when giving more information about them. ❑ *One writer in whom I was interested was Immanuel Velikovsky.* ❑ *The workers whom I knew had little money and little free* *time.* **4** → See note at **who**

whoop /wuːp, AM huːp/ (**whoops, whooping, whooped**) V-I & N-COUNT If you **whoop**, or if you let out a **whoop**, you shout loudly in a very happy or excited way. [WRITTEN] ❑ *Harry whooped with delight.* ❑ *...loud whoops and yells.*

whore /hɔː/ (**whores**) N-COUNT A **whore** is the same as a **prostitute**.

who're /ˈhuːə/ **Who're** is a spoken form of 'who are'.

who's /huːz/ **Who's** is the usual spoken form of 'who is' or 'who has', especially when 'has' is an auxiliary verb.

whose /huːz/ **1** PRON You use **whose** at the beginning of a relative clause to indicate that something belongs to or is associated with the person or thing mentioned in the previous clause. ❑ *A man was shouting at a driver whose car was blocking the street.* **2** PRON & DET You use **whose** in questions to ask about the person or thing that something belongs to or is associated with. ❑ *Whose was the better performance?* ❑ *Whose is this?* ❑ *Whose daughter is she?* **3** DET & CONJ You use **whose** to introduce a clause where you talk about the person or thing that something belongs to or is associated with. ❑ *I can't remember whose idea it was.* ❑ *It doesn't matter whose it is.*

who've /huːv/ **Who've** is the usual spoken form of 'who have,' especially when 'have' is an auxiliary verb.

why /waɪ/ **1** ADV You use **why** when asking questions about the reason for something. ❑ *Why hasn't he brought the car?* ❑ *'I just want to see him.'—'Why?'* ❑ *Why should I leave?* **2** CONJ & ADV You use **why** at the beginning of a clause in which you talk about the reason for something. ❑ *Experts wonder why the government is not taking action.* ❑ *I don't know why.* ❑ *Here's why.* **3** ADV You use **why** with 'not' to introduce a suggestion in the form of a question. ❑ *Why not give Claire a call?* ❑ *Why don't we talk it through?* **4** CONVENTION You say **why not** in order to agree with what someone has suggested. ❑ *'Want to spend the afternoon with me?'—'Why not?'*

wicked /ˈwɪkɪd/ **1** ADJ You use **wicked** to describe someone or something that is very bad in a way that is deliberately harmful to people. ❑ *She described the shooting as a wicked attack.* ● **wickedness** N-UNCOUNT ❑ *...the wickedness of nuclear weapons.* **2** ADJ If you describe someone or something as **wicked**, you mean that they are mischievous in a way that you find enjoyable. ❑ *She had a wicked sense of humour.* ● **wickedly** ADV ❑ *...a wickedly funny story.*

wicker /ˈwɪkə/ N-UNCOUNT **Wicker** is material made by weaving canes or twigs together, which is used to make baskets and furniture.

wide /waɪd/ (**wider, widest**) **1** ADJ Something that is **wide** measures a large distance from one side to the other. ❑ *...long, wide streets.* ❑ *The explosion could be heard over a wide area.* **2** ADV If you open or spread something **wide**, you open or spread it to its fullest extent. ❑ *Open your mouth wide.* ❑ *'It was huge,' he announced, spreading his arms wide.* **3** ADJ You use **wide** to talk or ask about how much something measures from one side or edge to the other. ❑ *The road is only one track wide.* ❑ *...a desk that was almost as wide as the room.* **4** ADJ You use **wide** to describe something that includes a large number of different things or people. ❑ *...a wide choice of hotels.* ❑ *...a wide range of topics.* ● **widely** ADV ❑ *She published widely in scientific journals.* **5** ADJ BEFORE N **Wider** is used to describe something relating to the most important or general parts of a situation rather than the details. ❑ *He was concerned about the wider issue of safety.* **6** ADJ A **wide** shot or punch does not hit its target. ❑ *Nearly half the missiles landed wide.* **7** **far and wide** → see **far** **8** **wide of the mark** → see **mark**

Thesaurus *wide* Also look up:

ADJ. broad, large; (*ant.*) narrow **1** **4**

Word Partnership Use *wide* with:

N. wide **shoulders** **1**
wide **grin/smile** **1**
arms/eyes/mouth open wide **2**
wide **array**, wide **audience**, wide **margin**, wide **selection**, wide **variety** **4**

ˈwide-eyed **1** ADJ If you describe someone as **wide-eyed**, you mean that they seem inexperienced, and perhaps don't have common sense. ❑ *...a wide-eyed boy ready to explore.* **2** ADJ & ADV If someone is **wide-eyed**, their eyes are more open than usual, especially because they are surprised or frightened. ❑ *...an expression of wide-eyed amazement.* ❑ *Trevor was staring wide-eyed at me.*

widen /ˈwaɪdən/ (**widens, widening, widened**) **1** V-T/V-I If you **widen** something, or if it **widens**, it becomes bigger from one side or edge to the other. ❑ *The river widens considerably as it begins to turn east.* **2** V-T/V-I If something **widens**, or if you **widen** it, it becomes greater in range, size, or variety or affects a larger number of people or things. ❑ *The search for my brother widened.* ❑ *...the widening gap between Britain's best and worst paid.*

ˌwide-ˈranging ADJ If something is **wide-ranging**, it affects or deals with a great variety of different things. ❑ *The team of investigators has wide-ranging powers.*

widescreen /ˈwaɪdskriːn/ ADJ A **widescreen** television has a screen that is wide in relation to its height.

Word Link *wide ≈ extending throughout : nationwide, widespread, worldwide*

widespread /ˈwaɪdspred/ ADJ Something that is **widespread** exists or happens over a large area or to a very great extent. ❑ *Food shortages are widespread.*

widow /ˈwɪdəʊ/ (**widows**) N-COUNT A **widow** is a woman whose husband has died.

widowed /ˈwɪdəʊd/ ADJ If someone **is widowed**, their husband or wife has died.

widower /ˈwɪdəʊə/ (**widowers**) N-COUNT A **widower** is a man whose wife has died.

width /wɪdθ/ (**widths**) N-VAR The **width of** something is the distance that it measures from one side to the other. ❑ *Measure the full width of the window.* ❑ *The road was reduced to 4 metres in width.*

wield /wiːld/ (**wields, wielding, wielded**) **1** V-T If you **wield** a weapon or tool, you carry it and use it. ❑ *...a gang member wielding a knife.* **2** V-T If someone **wields power**, they have it and are able to use it. ❑ *He remains chairman, but wields little power at the company.*

wife /waɪf/ (**wives**) N-COUNT A man's **wife** is the woman he is married to.
→ see **family, love**

wig /wɪɡ/ (**wigs**) N-COUNT A **wig** is a mass of false hair which is worn on your head.

wiggle /ˈwɪɡəl/ (**wiggles, wiggling, wiggled**) V-T/V-I & N-COUNT If you **wiggle** something, or if it **wiggles**, it moves around with small, quick movements, called **wiggles**. ❑ *Your baby will try to shuffle or wiggle along the floor.* ❑ *...a wiggle of the hips.*

wild /waɪld/ (**wilder, wildest, wilds**) **1** ADJ **Wild** animals and plants live or grow in natural surroundings and are not looked after by people. **2** ADJ **Wild** land is natural and not cultivated. ❑ *...forests and other wild areas.* **3** N-PLURAL **The wilds** are remote areas, far away from towns. **4** ADJ **Wild** behaviour is uncontrolled, excited, or energetic. ❑ *As George came on stage, the crowd went wild.* ● **wildly** ADV ❑ *The crowd clapped wildly.* **5** ADJ BEFORE N A **wild** idea or guess is unusual or made without much thought. ● **wildly** ADV ❑ *'Thirteen?' he guessed wildly.* **6** PHRASE If something or someone **runs wild**, they behave in a natural, free or uncontrolled way. ❑ *Molly lets that girl run wild.*

Thesaurus *wild* Also look up:

ADJ. desolate, natural, overgrown **2**
excited, rowdy, uncontrolled **4**

Word Partnership Use *wild* with:

N. wild **animal**, wild **beasts/creatures**, wild **game**, wild **horse**, wild **mushrooms** **1**
wild **bowl**, wild **swing** **4**
V. **run** wild **6**
go wild **4** **5**
ADJ. wild-**eyed** **4** **6**

wilderness /ˈwɪldənes/ (**wildernesses**) N-COUNT A **wilderness** is an area of natural land which is not cultivated. ❑ *...one of the largest wilderness areas in North America.*

wildlife /ˈwaɪldlaɪf/ N-UNCOUNT You can use **wildlife** to refer to animals and other living things that live in the wild. ❑ *Pets or wildlife could be affected by the disease.*
→ see **zoo**

wildly /ˈwaɪldli/ **1** ADJ You use **wildly** to emphasize the degree, amount, or intensity of something. ❑ *The two victims have wildly different stories of what happened.* ❑ *The island's hotels vary wildly.* **2** → see also **wild**

W

wilful [AM **willful**] /ˈwɪlfʊl/ **1** ADJ BEFORE N **Wilful** actions or attitudes are done or expressed deliberately, especially with the intention of hurting someone. ❑ *He admitted wilful neglect of the baby.* ● **wilfully** ADV ❑ *...those who cannot pay and those who wilfully refuse to pay.* **2** ADJ A **wilful** person is obstinate and determined to get what they want. ❑ *He is a wilful and rather unpleasant young man.*

will

❶ MODAL VERB USES
❷ WANTING SOMETHING TO HAPPEN

will /wɪl/

The usual spoken form of **will not** is **won't**.

❶ **1** MODAL You use **will** to indicate that you hope, think, or have evidence that something is going to happen in the future. ❑ *The airport will have to be upgraded.* ❑ *Will you ever feel at home here?* **2** MODAL You use **will** to talk about someone's intention to do something. ❑ *'Dinner's ready.'—'Thanks, Carrie, but we'll have a drink first.'* ❑ *What will you do next?* ❑ *Will you be remaining in the city?* **3** MODAL You use **will** to say that someone or something is able to do something in the future. ❑ *How will I recognize you?* **4** MODAL You use **will** when making offers, invitations, or requests. ❑ *Will you stay for supper?* ❑ *Won't you sit down?* **5** MODAL You use **will** to say that someone is willing to do something. You use **will not** or **won't** to indicate that someone refuses to do something. ❑ *All right, I'll forgive you.* ❑ *I'll answer the phone.* ❑ *I won't let you pay for a taxi.*

will /wɪl/ (**wills, willing, willed**)
❷ **1** N-VAR **Will** is the determination to do something. ❑ *He lost his will to live.* ❑ *It's a constant battle of wills with your children.* **2** → see also **free will** **3** N-SING If something is **the will of** a person or group of people with authority, they want it to happen. ❑ *He has given himself up to the will of God.* ❑ *The law should reflect the will of the people.* **4** V-T If you **will** something **to** happen, you try to make it happen using mental rather than physical effort. ❑ *I looked at the telephone, willing it to ring.* **5** N-COUNT A **will** is a legal document stating what you want to happen to your money and property when you die. **6** PHRASE If you can do something **at will**, you can do it whenever you want. ❑ *...to be able to slow down your heart rate at will.*

willful → see **wilful**

willing /ˈwɪlɪŋ/ **1** ADJ If someone is **willing to** do something, they do not mind doing it or have no objection to doing it. ● **willingly** ADV ❑ *I am glad you have come here so willingly.* ● **willingness** N-UNCOUNT ❑ *I had to prove my willingness to work hard.* **2** ADJ If you describe someone as **willing**, you mean that they are eager and enthusiastic. ❑ *He was a natural and willing pupil.*

willow /ˈwɪləʊ/ (**willows**) N-COUNT A **willow** is a tree with long narrow leaves and branches that hang down.

willpower or **will-power** or **will power** /ˈwɪlpaʊə/ N-UNCOUNT **Willpower** is a very strong determination to do something. ❑ *I couldn't go on a diet. I don't have the willpower.*

wilt /wɪlt/ (**wilts, wilting, wilted**) V-I If a plant **wilts**, it gradually bends downwards and becomes weak, because it needs more water or is dying.

wily /ˈwaɪli/ (**wilier, wiliest**) ADJ **Wily** people are clever and cunning. ❑ *...the wily old gentleman.*

wimp /wɪmp/ (**wimps**) N-COUNT If you call someone a **wimp**, you disapprove of them because they lack confidence or determination, or because they are often afraid of things. [INFORMAL]

win /wɪn/ (**wins, winning, won**) **1** V-T/V-I &

N-COUNT If you **win** a fight, game, or argument, you defeat your opponent, or you do better than everyone else involved. You can also talk about a **win**. ❑ *I don't think they'll win the match.* ❑ *...eight games without a win.* **2** V-T If you **win** a prize or medal, you get it because you have defeated everyone else in a competition, or you have been very successful at something. ❑ *The first correct entry wins the prize.* ❑ *He won a silver medal at the 1994 World Championships.* **3** V-T If you **win** something that you want or need, you succeed in getting it. ❑ *The company has won an order worth $340 million.* **4** → see also **winning**

▶ **win over** or **win round** PHR-VERB If you **win** someone **over** or **win** them **round**, you persuade them to support you or agree with you. ❑ *Not all my staff agree but I am winning them over.*

Thesaurus *win* Also look up:

V.	conquer, succeed, triumph; *(ant.)* lose **1**
N.	conquest, success, victory; *(ant.)* defeat **1**

wince /wɪns/ (**winces, wincing, winced**) V-I & N-COUNT If you **wince**, or if you give a **wince**, the muscles of your face tighten suddenly because you are in pain or have experienced something unpleasant. ❑ *Just reading about it makes you wince.*

winch /wɪntʃ/ (**winches, winching, winched**) **1** N-COUNT A **winch** is a machine for lifting heavy objects. It consists of a cylinder around which a rope or chain is wound. **2** V-T If you **winch** an object or person somewhere, you lift or lower them using a winch.

wind
❶ AIR
❷ TURNING OR WRAPPING

wind /wɪnd/ (**winds, winding, winded**) ❶ **1** N-VAR A **wind** is a current of air moving across the earth's surface. ❑ *There was a strong wind blowing.* ❑ *A gust of wind had blown the pot over.* **2** V-T If you **are winded** by something such as a blow, you have difficulty breathing for a short time. ❑ *Two kicks in the kidneys winded him.* **3** N-UNCOUNT **Wind** is the air that you sometimes swallow with food or drink, or gas that is produced in your intestines, which causes an uncomfortable feeling.
→ see Word Web: **wind**
→ see **beach, erosion, storm, wave**

wind /waɪnd/ (**winds, winding, wound**) ❷ **1** V-I If a road, river, or line of people **winds** in a particular direction, it goes in that direction with a lot of bends or twists in it. ❑ *The road wound through the mountains.* **2** V-T When you **wind** something **around** something else, you wrap it round it several times. ❑ *She wound the bandage around his knee.* **3** V-T When you **wind** a mechanical device, for example a watch, you turn a key or handle on it round and round in order to make it operate. ❑ *I wound the watch and listened to it tick.*

▶ **wind down** PHR-VERB If someone **winds down** a business or activity, they gradually reduce the amount of work that is done or the number of people that are involved. ❑ *He was simply winding down his career.*

▶ **wind up** PHR-VERB If someone **winds up** a business or activity, they close it down or finish it. ❑ *Could we wind up this meeting as quickly as possible?*

Thesaurus *wind* Also look up:

N.	air, current, gust ① **1**
V.	bend, loop, twist; *(ant.)* straighten ② **2**

Word Partnership Use *wind* with:

ADJ.	**cold** wind, **hot** wind, **howling** wind, **icy** wind, **warm** wind ① **1**
N.	**desert** wind, **gust of** wind, wind **power**, **winter** wind ① **1**
V.	wind **blows, blown/driven by the** wind, wind **whips** ① **1**

windfall /ˈwɪndfɔːl/ (**windfalls**) N-COUNT A **windfall** is a sum of money that you receive unexpectedly.

windmill /ˈwɪndmɪl/ (**windmills**) N-COUNT A **windmill** is a tall building with sails which turn as the wind blows. Windmills are used to grind grain or pump water.

windmill

window /ˈwɪndəʊ/ (**windows**) **1** N-COUNT A **window** is a space in the wall of a building or in the side of a vehicle, which has glass in it so that light can pass through and people can see in or out. ❑ *He looked out of the window. It was a lovely day.* **2** N-COUNT On a computer screen, a **window** is one of the work areas that the screen can be divided into. [COMPUTING]
→ see **glass**

Word Web wind

The earth's surface **temperature** isn't the same everywhere. This temperature difference causes **air** to move from one area to another. We call this airflow **wind**. As warm air expands and rises, air pressure goes down. Then denser cool air **blows** in. The amount of difference in air pressure determines how strong the wind will be. It can be anything from a **breeze** to a **gale**. The earth's geography creates **prevailing winds**. For example, air in the warmer areas near the Equator is always rising, and cooler air from polar regions is always flowing in to take its place.

Word Partnership Use *window* with:

ADJ. **broken** window, **dark** window, **large/small** window, **narrow** window, **open** window 1
V. **close/open a** window, **look in/out a** window, **peer in/into/out/through a** window, **watch through a** window 1
N. **car** window, window **curtains**, window **display**, **kitchen** window, window **screen**, **shop** window, **store** window, window **treatment** 1

windscreen /ˈwɪndskriːn/ (**windscreens**) N-COUNT In British English, the **windscreen** of a car or other vehicle is the glass window at the front through which the driver looks. The usual American word is **windshield**.

windshield /ˈwɪndʃiːld/ (**windshields**) → see **windscreen**

windy /ˈwɪndi/ (**windier, windiest**) ADJ If it is **windy**, the wind is blowing a lot.

wine /waɪn/ (**wines**) N-VAR **Wine** is an alcoholic drink, usually made from grapes.

ˈwine bar (**wine bars**) N-COUNT A **wine bar** is a place where people can buy and drink wine, and sometimes eat food as well.

wing /wɪŋ/ (**wings**) 1 N-COUNT The **wings** of a bird or insect are the parts of its body that it uses for flying. 2 N-COUNT The **wings** of an aeroplane are the long flat parts at each side which support it while it is flying. 3 N-COUNT A **wing** of a building is a part of it which sticks out from the main part. ❑ *...the east wing of the palace.* 4 N-COUNT A **wing** of an organization is a group within it which has a particular function or has particular beliefs. ❑ *...the military wing of the African National Congress.* 5 → see also **left-wing, right-wing** 6 N-COUNT The **wings** of a car are the parts around the wheels. [BRIT] 7 N-PLURAL In a theatre, **the wings** are the sides of the stage which are hidden from the audience by curtains or scenery.
→ see **bird, insect**

Word Partnership Use *wing* with:

N. **aircraft** wing 2
ADJ. **military/political** wing 4

winged /wɪŋd/ ADJ A **winged** insect or other creature has wings.

wink /wɪŋk/ (**winks, winking, winked**) V-I & N-COUNT If you **wink at** someone, or if you give them a **wink**, you look towards them and close one eye very briefly, usually as a signal that something is a joke or a secret.

W

winner /ˈwɪnə/ (**winners**) N-COUNT The **winner** of a prize, race, or competition is the person, animal, or thing that wins it.

winning /ˈwɪnɪŋ/ (**winnings**) 1 ADJ BEFORE N You can use **winning** to describe a person or thing that wins something such as a competition, game, or election. ❑ *Donovan scored the winning goal.* 2 ADJ BEFORE N **Winning** is used to describe actions or qualities that please people and make them feel friendly towards you. ❑ *...his winning personality.*

winnings /ˈwɪnɪŋz/ N-PLURAL You can refer to the money that someone wins in a competition or by gambling as their **winnings**.

winter /ˈwɪntə/ (**winters**) N-VAR **Winter** is the season between autumn and spring. In winter the weather is usually cold. ❑ *Dried fruit is eaten in winter, when fresh fruit is not available.*

wipe /waɪp/ (**wipes, wiping, wiped**) 1 V-T & N-COUNT If you **wipe** something, or if you give it a **wipe**, you rub its surface to remove dirt or liquid from it. ❑ *He began to wipe the floor clean.* ❑ *Lainey wiped her hands on the towel.* ❑ *I'm going to give the toys a good wipe.* 2 V-T If you **wipe** dirt or liquid from something, you remove it, for example by using a cloth or your hand. ❑ *Nancy wiped the sweat from her face.* 3 N-COUNT A **wipe** is a small moist cloth for cleaning things and is designed to be used only once. ❑ *...antiseptic wipes.*
▶ **wipe out** PHR-VERB To **wipe out** a place or a group of people or animals means to destroy it completely. ❑ *...the disease that wiped out thousands of seals in Europe.*

Word Partnership Use *wipe* with:

ADJ. wipe ***something*** **clean** 1
N. wipe **blood**, wipe ***your*** **eyes**, wipe ***someone's*** **face**, wipe **tears** 2

wire /waɪə/ (**wires, wiring, wired**) 1 N-VAR A **wire** is a long thin piece of metal that is used to fasten things or to carry electric current. ❑ *...fine copper wire.* 2 → see also **barbed wire**
→ see **metal**
▶ **wire up** PHR-VERB If you **wire up** something such as a building or piece of equipment, you install or connect wires inside it so that electricity or signals can pass into or through it. ❑ *I wired up the alarm system.*

Word Link *less* ≈ *without* : *careless, endless, wireless*

wireless /ˈwaɪələs/ (**wirelesses**) 1 ADJ **Wireless** technology uses radio waves rather than electricity and therefore does not require any wires. ❑ *...the wireless communication market.* 2 N-COUNT A **wireless** is a radio. [DATED]
→ see **cellphone**

wiring /ˈwaɪərɪŋ/ N-UNCOUNT The **wiring** in a building or machine is the system of wires that supply electricity to the different parts of it.

wiry /ˈwaɪəri/ (**wirier, wiriest**) 1 ADJ Someone who is **wiry** is rather thin but is also strong. 2 ADJ Something such as hair or grass that is **wiry** is stiff and rough to touch.

Word Link *dom* ≈ *state of being* : *boredom, freedom, wisdom*

wisdom /ˈwɪzdəm/ 1 N-UNCOUNT **Wisdom** is the ability to use your experience and knowledge to make sensible decisions and judgments. ❑ *...the patience and wisdom that comes from old age.* 2 N-SING If you talk about **the wisdom of** an action or decision, you are talking about how sensible it is. ❑ *I have to question the wisdom of allowing the visit to go ahead.*

wise /waɪz/ (**wiser, wisest**) ADJ A **wise** person is able to use their experience and knowledge to make sensible decisions and judgments. ❑ *He took his brother's wise advice.* ● **wisely** ADV ❑ *They've invested their money wisely.*

wish /wɪʃ/ (**wishes, wishing, wished**) **1** N-COUNT A **wish** is a desire for something. ❑ *Her wish is to be in films.* **2** V-T If you **wish to** do something, you want to do it. [FORMAL] ❑ *I wish to leave a message.* **3** V-T If you **wish** that something were the case, you would like it to be the case, even though it is impossible or unlikely. ❑ *I wish I could paint like that.* **4** V-I & N-COUNT If you **wish for** something, or if you make a **wish**, you express the desire for something silently to yourself. In fairy stories, when someone wishes for something, it often happens by magic. ❑ *What did you wish for?* **5** V-T If you **wish** someone something such as luck or happiness, you express the hope that they will be lucky or happy. ❑ *I wish you both a very good journey.* **6** N-PLURAL If you express your good **wishes** towards someone, you are politely expressing your friendly feelings towards them and your hope that they will be successful or happy. ❑ *Please give him my best wishes.*

Word Partnership Use *wish* with:

V.	**get your** wish, **grant a** wish, **have a** wish, **make a** wish **1** **4**
	I wish **I knew** **3**
	wish **come true** **4**
N.	wish ***someone*** **the best**, wish ***someone*** **luck** **5**

ˌwishful ˈthinking N-UNCOUNT If a hope or wish is **wishful thinking**, it is unlikely to come true. ❑ *It is wishful thinking to imagine that things will improve.*

wistful /ˈwɪstfʊl/ ADJ If someone is **wistful**, they are sad because they want something and know they cannot have it. ❑ *He looked a little wistful.* ● **wistfully** ADV ❑ *'I wish I had a little brother,' said Daphne wistfully.*

wit /wɪt/ (**wits**) **1** N-UNCOUNT **Wit** is the ability to use words or ideas in an amusing and clever way. ❑ *He writes beautifully and with great wit.* **2** N-PLURAL You can refer to someone's ability to think quickly in a difficult situation as their **wits**. ❑ *She needs to keep her wits about her.*

witch /wɪtʃ/ (**witches**) N-COUNT A **witch** is a woman who is believed to have magic powers, especially evil ones.

witchcraft /ˈwɪtʃkrɑːft, -kræft/ N-UNCOUNT **Witchcraft** is the use of magic powers, especially evil ones.

ˈwitch-hunt (**witch-hunts**) N-COUNT A **witch-hunt** is an attempt to find and punish a particular group of people who are being blamed for something, often simply because of their opinions and not because they have actually done anything wrong; used showing disapproval. ❑ *He accused the police of conducting a witch hunt against the former Communists.*

with /wɪð, wɪθ/ **1** PREP If one thing or person is **with** another, they are together in one place. ❑ *She is currently staying with her father.* ❑ *He walked with her to the front door.* **2** PREP If you discuss something **with** someone, or if you fight or argue **with** someone, you are both involved in a discussion, fight, or argument. ❑ *We didn't even discuss it with each other.* ❑ *I argued with him for fifteen minutes.* ❑ *The war with Spain was over.* **3** PREP If you do something **with** a particular tool, object, or substance, you do it using that tool or object. ❑ *Wipe the mushrooms with a damp cloth.* ❑ *She wasn't allowed to eat with her fingers.* **4** PREP If someone stands or goes somewhere **with** something, they are carrying it. ❑ *A man came round with a tray of chocolates.* **5** PREP Someone or something **with** a particular feature or possession has that feature or possession. ❑ *She was six feet tall with red hair.* ❑ *...a single-storey house with a flat roof.* **6** PREP If something is filled or covered **with** a substance or **with** things, it has that substance or those things in it or on it. ❑ *His legs were covered with dried mud.* **7** PREP You use **with** to indicate what a state, quality, or action relates to, involves, or affects. ❑ *He still has a serious problem with money.* ❑ *He is always kind and patient with children.* **8** PREP You use **with** when indicating the way something is done or the feeling that someone has when they do something. ❑ *He listened with great care.* ❑ *She accepted, but with regret.* **9** PREP You use **with** when indicating a sound, gesture, or facial expression that is made at the same time as an action. ❑ *'Broken again,' Jane said with a sigh.* ❑ *The front door closed with a crash.* **10** PREP You use **with** to indicate the feeling that makes someone behave in a particular way. ❑ *She was shaking with anger.* **11** PREP You use **with** when mentioning the position or appearance of someone or something at the time that they do something, or what someone else is doing at that time. ❑ *Joanne stood with her hands on the table.* ❑ *She walked back to the bus stop, with him following.* **12** PREP You use **with** to introduce a current situation that is a factor affecting another situation. ❑ *With all the problems we've been having, I forgot to tell you about it.*

Word Link ***with*** **≈ *against, away* :** ***withdraw, withhold, withstand***

withdraw /wɪðˈdrɔː/ (**withdraws, withdrawing, withdrew, withdrawn**) **1** V-T If you **withdraw** something from a place, you remove it or take it away. [FORMAL] ❑ *He reached into his pocket and withdrew a sheet of notepaper.* **2** V-T/V-I When troops **withdraw**, or when someone **withdraws** them, they leave the place where they are fighting or where they are based and return nearer home. **3** V-T If you **withdraw** money from a bank account, you take it out of that account. ❑ *He withdrew £750 from his account.* **4** V-I If you **withdraw from** an activity or organization, you stop taking part in it. ❑ *They threatened to withdraw from the talks.* **5** V-T If you **withdraw** a remark or statement you have made, you say that you want people to ignore it. [FORMAL] ❑ *I demand that the Prime Minister withdraw that remark.*

Word Partnership Use *withdraw* with:

N.	withdraw **an offer**, withdraw **support** **1**
	decision to withdraw **1**-**5**
	deadline to withdraw, **forces/troops** withdraw **2**
	withdraw **money** **3**

withdrawal /wɪðˈdrɔːəl/ (**withdrawals**) **1** N-VAR **The withdrawal of** something is the act or process of removing it or ending it. [FORMAL]

❑ *...the withdrawal of American troops from South Vietnam.* **2** N-UNCOUNT Someone's **withdrawal** from an activity or an organization is their decision to stop taking part in it. ❑ *...his withdrawal from government in 1946.* **3** N-COUNT If you make a **withdrawal** from your bank account, you take money out of it. **4** N-UNCOUNT **Withdrawal** is the period during which someone feels ill after they have stopped taking a drug which they were addicted to. ❑ *These vitamins help addicts with the first stages of withdrawal.* **5** N-UNCOUNT **Withdrawal** is behaviour in which someone prefers to be alone and does not want to talk to other people. ❑ *Her periods of withdrawal and mental illness increased.*

withdrawn /wɪð'drɔːn/ **1** **Withdrawn** is the past participle of **withdraw**. **2** ADJ AFTER LINK-V Someone who is **withdrawn** is quiet and shy.

withdrew /wɪð'druː/ **Withdrew** is the past tense of **withdraw**.

wither /'wɪðə/ (**withers, withering, withered**) **1** V-I If something **withers away**, it becomes weaker until it no longer exists or is no longer effective. ❑ *He predicts that religion will eventually wither away.* **2** V-T/V-I If a plant **withers**, or if something **withers** it, it shrinks, dries up, and dies.

withered /'wɪðəd/ ADJ If a person or a part of their body is **withered**, their skin is very wrinkled and dry, and looks old. ❑ *...a withered old man.*

Word Link	***with ≈ against, away : withdraw, withhold, withstand***

withhold /wɪð'həʊld/ (**withholds, withholding, withheld**) V-T If you **withhold** something that someone wants, you do not let them have it. [FORMAL] ❑ *The Council gave no reason for withholding these documents.*

within /wɪ'ðɪn/ **1** PREP & ADV If something is **within** a place, area, or object, it is inside it or surrounded by it. [FORMAL] ❑ *She lives in one of the quiet villages within the forest.* ❑ *A small voice called from within. 'Yes, just coming.'* **2** PREP & ADV Something that happens or exists **within** a society, organization, or system, happens or exists inside it or to something that is part of it. ❑ *Are you keen to work within a large organization?* ❑ *Why not join the enemy and destroy it from within?* **3** PREP & ADV If you have a feeling, you can say that it is **within** you. [LITERARY] ❑ *She could almost feel fresh life and hope rising within her.* ❑ *...a sense of loneliness deep within.* **4** PREP If something is **within** a particular limit, it does not go beyond that limit. ❑ *The film will be finished within its budget.* **5** PREP If you are **within** a particular distance of a place, you are less than that distance from it. ❑ *The man was within a few feet of him.* ❑ *It was within easy walking distance of the hotel.* **6** PREP **Within** a particular length of time means before that length of time has passed. ❑ *And within twenty-four hours I'd got the money.* **7** PREP If something is **within sight, within earshot** or **within reach**, you can see it, hear it, or reach it.

W

without /wɪ'ðaʊt/ **1** PREP You use **without** to indicate that someone or something does not have or use the thing mentioned. ❑ *No one recognized him without his beard.* ❑ *...a meal without tomato sauce.* **2** PREP If one thing happens **without** another thing, or if you do something **without** doing something else, the second thing does not happen or occur. ❑ *They worked without a break until about eight in the evening.* ❑ *Alex had done this without consulting her.* **3** PREP If you do something **without** a particular feeling, you do not have that feeling when you do it. ❑ *'Hello, Swanson,' he said without surprise.* **4** PREP If you do something **without** someone else, they are not with you when you do it. ❑ *We would never go anywhere without you.* **5** → see also **do without, go without**

withstand /wɪð'stænd/ (**withstands, withstanding, withstood** /wɪð'stʊd/) V-T To **withstand** a force or action means to survive it or not to give in to it. [FORMAL] ❑ *The toys are designed to withstand a lot of rough treatment.*

witness /'wɪtnəs/ (**witnesses, witnessing, witnessed**) **1** N-COUNT A **witness to** an event such as an accident or crime is a person who saw it. **2** V-T & PHRASE If you **witness** something, or if you **are witness to** it, you see it happen. ❑ *Anyone who witnessed the attack should call the police.* **3** N-COUNT A **witness** is someone who appears in a court of law to say what they know about a crime or other event. ❑ *Eleven witnesses will be called to testify.* **4** N-COUNT A **witness** is someone who writes their name on a document that you have signed, to confirm that it really is your signature. **5** V-T If someone **witnesses** your signature, they write their name after it, to confirm that it really is your signature. **6** PHRASE If something or someone **bears witness to** something else, they show or say that it exists or happened. [FORMAL] ❑ *Many of these poems bear witness to his years spent in India.*

→ see **trial, wedding**

witty /'wɪti/ (**wittier, wittiest**) ADJ Someone or something that is **witty** is amusing in a clever way. ❑ *His plays were very good, very witty.*

wives /waɪvz/ **Wives** is the plural of **wife**.

wizard /'wɪzəd/ (**wizards**) **1** N-COUNT In legends and fairy stories, a **wizard** is a man who has magic powers. **2** N-COUNT If you say that someone is a **wizard** at a particular kind of activity, you mean that they are very good at it. ❑ *...a financial wizard.* **3** N-COUNT A **wizard** is a computer program that guides you through the stages of a particular task. [COMPUTING]

→ see **fantasy**

WMD /ˌdʌbljʊˌem'diː/ N-PLURAL **WMD** is an abbreviation for **weapons of mass destruction**.

wobble /'wɒbəl/ (**wobbles, wobbling, wobbled**) V-I If someone or something **wobbles**, they make small movements from side to side, for example because they are unsteady. ❑ *...a cyclist who wobbled into my path.*

wobbly /'wɒbli/ (**wobblier, wobbliest**) **1** ADJ If something is **wobbly**, it moves unsteadily from side to side. ❑ *I was sitting on a wobbly plastic chair.* **2** ADJ If you feel **wobbly**, or if your legs feel **wobbly**, you feel weak and have difficulty standing up, especially because you are afraid, ill, or exhausted.

woe /wəʊ/ (**woes**) **1** N-UNCOUNT **Woe** is very great sadness. [LITERARY] ❑ *He listened to my tale of woe.* **2** N-PLURAL You can refer to someone's problems or misfortunes as their **woes**. [WRITTEN]

woeful /'wəʊfʊl/ ADJ You can use **woeful** to emphasize that something is very bad or undesirable. ❑ *...the woeful state of the economy.*

● **woefully** ADV ❑ *We are woefully short of trained staff.*

woke /wəʊk/ **Woke** is the past tense of **wake**.

woken /ˈwəʊkən/ **Woken** is the past participle of **wake**.

wolf

wolf /wʊlf/ (**wolves, wolfs, wolfing, wolfed**) **1** N-COUNT A **wolf** is a wild animal that looks like a large dog. **2** V-T & PHR-VERB If someone **wolfs** their food, or if they **wolf** it **down**, they eat it all very quickly and greedily. [INFORMAL] ❑ *Pitt wolfed down a cheese sandwich.*

Word Link *man ≈ human being : human, humanity, woman*

woman /ˈwʊmən/ (**women**) N-COUNT A **woman** is an adult female human being.
→ see **age**

womanhood /ˈwʊmənhʊd/ N-UNCOUNT **Womanhood** is the state of being a woman rather than a girl, or the period of a woman's adult life.

womb /wuːm/ (**wombs**) N-COUNT A woman's **womb** is the part inside her body where a baby grows before it is born.

women /ˈwɪmɪn/ **Women** is the plural of **woman**.

won /wʌn/ **Won** is the past tense and past participle of **win**.

wonder /ˈwʌndə/ (**wonders, wondering, wondered**) **1** V-T If you **wonder** about something, you think about it and try to guess or understand more about it. ❑ *I wondered what that noise was.* ❑ *'Why does she want to get in there?' Pete wondered.* **2** V-I If you **wonder at** something, you are surprised and amazed about it. ❑ *He liked to sit and wonder at all that had happened.* **3** N-SING If you say that it is a **wonder** that something happened, you mean it is very surprising that it happened. ❑ *It's a wonder that it took almost ten years.* **4** N-UNCOUNT **Wonder** is a feeling of surprise and amazement. ❑ *'That's right!' Bobby exclaimed in wonder.* **5** N-COUNT A **wonder** is something remarkable that people admire. ❑ *...the wonders of space and space exploration.* **6** PHRASE If you say **'no wonder'**, **'little wonder'**, or **'small wonder'**, you mean that you are not surprised by something that has happened. ❑ *No wonder my brother wasn't feeling well.* **7** PHRASE If you say that something or someone **works wonders** or **does wonders**, you mean that they have a very good effect on something.

wonderful /ˈwʌndəfʊl/ ADJ If you describe something or someone as **wonderful**, you think they are extremely good. ❑ *The cold, misty air felt wonderful on his face.* ❑ *It's wonderful to see you.* ● **wonderfully** ADV ❑ *It's a system that works wonderfully well.*

won't /wəʊnt/ **Won't** is the usual spoken form of 'will not'.

woo /wuː/ (**woos, wooing, wooed**) **1** V-T If you **woo** people, you try to get them to help or support you. ❑ *They wooed customers by offering special deals.* **2** V-T If a man **woos** a woman, he spends time with her and tries to persuade her to marry him. [DATED]
→ see **love**

wood /wʊd/ (**woods**) **1** N-VAR **Wood** is the material which forms the trunks and branches of trees. ❑ *Their dishes were made of wood.* **2** N-COUNT A **wood** is a large area of trees growing near each other. You can refer to one or several of these areas as **woods**. ❑ *...a walk in the woods.*
→ see **energy, fire, forest**

wooded /ˈwʊdɪd/ ADJ A **wooded** area is covered in trees. ❑ *...a wooded valley.*

wooden /ˈwʊdən/ ADJ A **wooden** object is made of wood. ❑ *...handmade wooden toys.*

woodland /ˈwʊdlənd/ (**woodlands**) N-VAR **Woodland** is land covered with trees.

woodwork /ˈwʊdwɜːk/ **1** N-UNCOUNT You can refer to the doors and other wooden parts of a house as the **woodwork**. ❑ *...fresh paint on the woodwork.* **2** N-UNCOUNT **Woodwork** is the activity or skill of making things out of wood.

woodwork

wool /wʊl/ (**wools**) **1** N-UNCOUNT **Wool** is the hair that grows on sheep and on some other animals. **2** N-VAR **Wool** is a material made from animal's wool. It is used for making clothes, blankets, and carpets. **3** → see also **cotton wool**

woollen [AM **woolen**] /ˈwʊlən/ ADJ **Woollen** clothes are made from wool. ❑ *...woollen socks.*

woolly [AM **wooly**] /ˈwʊli/ (**woollier, woolliest, woollies**) **1** ADJ Something that is **woolly** is made of wool or looks like wool. ❑ *...a woolly hat.* **2** ADJ If you describe people or their ideas as **woolly**, you are criticizing them for being inconsistent or confused. ❑ *He hates woolly thinking.*

word /wɜːd/ (**words, wording, worded**) **1** N-COUNT A **word** is a single unit of language in writing or speech. In English, a word has a space on either side of it when it is written. ❑ *He didn't understand the words, but that didn't matter.* **2** N-SING If you have **a word with** someone, you have a short conversation with them, usually in private. [SPOKEN] ❑ *It's time you had a word with him.* ❑ *James, could I have a word?* **3** N-COUNT If you offer someone a **word of** warning, advice, or praise, you warn, advise, or praise them. ❑ *May I also say a word of thanks to all the people who sent letters.* **4** N-SING If you say that someone does not hear, understand, or say **a word**, you are emphasizing that they hear, understand, or say nothing at all. ❑ *Not a word was spoken.* **5** N-UNCOUNT If there is **word** of something, people receive news or information about it. ❑ *We have had no word from my son. It is a very anxious time.* **6** N-SING If you give your **word**, you promise to do something. ❑ *She gave her word that the boy would be supervised.* **7** V-T To **word** something in a particular way means to choose or use particular words to express it. ❑ *If I had written the letter, I might have worded it differently.* ● **-worded** ❑ *...a carefully-worded speech.* **8** PHRASE If one person **has words with** another, they have a serious discussion or argument, especially because one has complained about the other's behaviour. ❑ *We had words and she left the restaurant.* **9** PHRASE You say **in a word** to indicate that you

are summarizing what you have just been saying. ❑ *Victor, in a word, got increasingly annoyed.* 10 PHRASE If you **have the last word** in an argument, you make the comment that finishes it and defeats the other person. 11 PHRASE You say **in other words** when introducing a simpler or clearer explanation of something that has just been said. ❑ *The service has been reorganised – in other words, it's been reduced.* 12 PHRASE If you say that someone has said something, but **not in so many words**, you mean that they said it or expressed it, but in an indirect way. ❑ *'And has she agreed to go with you?'—'Not in so many words.'* 13 PHRASE If you repeat something **word for word**, you repeat it exactly as it was originally said or written. ❑ *I don't try to learn speeches word for word.*
→ see **English**

wording /'wɜːdɪŋ/ N-UNCOUNT The **wording** of a piece of writing or a speech is the words that are used in it, especially when these are chosen to have a particular effect. ❑ *The wording is so vague that no one actually knows what it means.*

ˌword ˈprocessing N-UNCOUNT **Word processing** is the work or skill of producing printed material using a word processor. [COMPUTING]

ˌword ˈprocessor (**word processors**) N-COUNT A **word processor** is a computer which is used to produce printed material such as letters and books. [COMPUTING]

wore /wɔː/ **Wore** is the past tense of **wear**.

work /wɜːk/ (**works, working, worked**) 1 V-I People who **work** have a job, usually one which they are paid to do. ❑ *Weiner works for the US Department of Transport.* ❑ *He worked as an electrician.* 2 N-UNCOUNT People who have **work**, or who are **in work**, have a job, usually one which they are paid to do. ❑ *Fewer and fewer people are in work.* ❑ *I was out of work at the time.* ❑ *What kind of work do you do?* 3 V-I When you **work**, you do tasks which your job involves, or a task that needs to be done. ❑ *We work really hard and we get the lowest pay.* ❑ *...people like me who were working 24 hours a day to survive.* 4 N-UNCOUNT **Work** consists of the tasks which your job involves, or any tasks which need to be done. ❑ *I've got work to do.* ❑ *There are days when I finish work at 2pm.* 5 N-UNCOUNT **Work** is the place where you do your job. ❑ *Many people travel to work by car.* 6 N-COUNT A **work** is something such as a painting, book, or piece of music. ❑ *...the complete works of Shakespeare.* 7 V-I If a machine or piece of equipment **works**, it operates and performs its function. ❑ *The bed was dirty and the shower didn't work.* 8 V-I If an idea, method, or system **works**, it is successful. ❑ *95 per cent of these diets do not work.* ❑ *A gentle approach works best.* 9 V-T If you **work** a machine or piece of equipment, you operate it. ❑ *He could never work the fax machine; I had to do it.* 10 → see also **working, social work** 11 PHRASE If you **work** your **way** somewhere, you move or progress there slowly, and with a lot of effort or work. ❑ *Many personnel managers started as secretaries and worked their way up.* 12 PHRASE If you say that you will **have** your **work cut out to** do something, you mean that it will be a very difficult task. ❑ *He will have his work cut out to get into the team.*
→ see **factory**

▶ **work into** PHR-VERB If you **work** one substance **into** another, or if you **work** it **in**, you add it to the other substance and mix the two together thoroughly. ❑ *Work the liquid into the flour with a wooden spoon.*

▶ **work off** PHR-VERB If you **work off** energy or anger, you get rid of it by doing something that requires a lot of physical effort. ❑ *If I've had a bad day I'll work it off by cooking.*

▶ **work out** 1 PHR-VERB If you **work out** a solution to a problem or mystery, you find the solution by thinking or talking about it. ❑ *They are planning to meet later today to work out a solution.* 2 PHR-VERB If something **works out at** a particular amount, it is calculated to be that amount. ❑ *It will probably work out cheaper to hire a van and move your own things.* 3 PHR-VERB If a situation **works out**, it happens or progresses in a satisfactory way. ❑ *The deal just isn't working out the way we hoped.* 4 PHR-VERB If you **work out**, you go through a physical exercise routine. 5 → see also **workout**

▶ **work up** 1 PHR-VERB If you **work yourself up**, you make yourself very upset or angry about something. ❑ *She worked herself up into a state.* • **worked up** ADJ AFTER LINK-V ❑ *Steve shouted at her. He was really worked up.* 2 PHR-VERB If you **work up** the enthusiasm or courage **to** do something, you gradually make yourself feel it. ❑ *She had never worked up the courage to tell anyone.*

Usage

The verb **work** has a different meaning in the continuous tenses than it does in the simple tenses. You use the continuous tenses, with the '-ing' form, to talk about a temporary job, but the simple tenses to talk about a permanent job. For example, if you say **'I'm working in London'**, this suggests that the situation is temporary and you may soon move to a different place. If you say **'I work in London'**, this suggests that London is your permanent place of work. The verb **live** behaves in a similar way. You use the continuous tenses, with the '-ing' form, to talk about a temporary home, but the simple tenses to talk about a permanent home.

Thesaurus *work* Also look up:

V.	labour 3
	function, go, operate, perform, run 7
N.	business, craft, job, occupation, profession, trade, vocation; *(ant.)* entertainment, fun, pastime 4

workable /'wɜːkəbəl/ ADJ A **workable** idea or system is realistic and practical, and likely to be effective.

worker /'wɜːkə/ (**workers**) 1 N-COUNT **Workers** are people who are employed in industry or business and who are not managers. 2 N-COUNT You can use **worker** to say how well or badly someone works. ❑ *He is a hard worker.*
→ see **factory**

Thesaurus *worker* Also look up:

N.	employee, help, labourer 1

workforce /'wɜːkfɔːs/ (**workforces**) 1 N-COUNT The **workforce** is the total number of people in a

W

country or region who are physically able to do a job and are available for work. **2** N-COUNT The **workforce** is the total number of people who are employed by a particular company.

working /ˈwɜːkɪŋ/ (**workings**) **1** ADJ BEFORE N **Working** people have jobs which they are paid to do. ❑ *Working women everywhere buy these prepared foods.* **2** ADJ BEFORE N A **working** day or week is the number of hours that you work during a day or a week. ❑ *...a shorter, more flexible working week.* **3** ADJ BEFORE N If you have a **working knowledge** of a subject, you have a useful but not very thorough knowledge of it. **4** N-PLURAL The **workings** of a piece of equipment, an organization, or a system are the ways in which it operates. **5** **in working order** → see **order** **6** → see also **work**

ˌworking ˈclass (**working classes**) N-COUNT & ADJ **The working class** or **the working classes** are the people in a society who do not own much property, who have low social status, and whose work involves physical skills rather than intellectual skills. You can also say that someone is from a **working class** background.

workload /ˈwɜːkləʊd/ (**workloads**) N-COUNT Your **workload** is the amount of work that you have to do. ❑ *Wilson has had a heavy workload this season.*

workman /ˈwɜːkmən/ (**workmen**) N-COUNT A **workman** is a man who works with his hands, for example a builder or plumber.

ˌwork of ˈart (**works of art**) **1** N-COUNT A **work of art** is a painting or piece of sculpture of high quality. **2** N-COUNT You can refer to something that has been skilfully produced as a **work of art**. ❑ *The chocolate cake was a work of art.*
→ see **blog**

workout /ˈwɜːkaʊt/ (**workouts**) N-COUNT A **workout** is a period of physical exercise or training. ❑ *...a 35-minute workout.*
→ see **muscle**

workplace /ˈwɜːkpleɪs/ (**workplaces**) N-COUNT Your **workplace** is the place where you work. ❑ *...the difficulties facing women in the workplace.*

workshop /ˈwɜːkʃɒp/ (**workshops**) **1** N-COUNT A **workshop** is a room or building containing tools or machinery for making or repairing things. **2** N-COUNT A **workshop** is a period of discussion or practical work on a particular subject in which a group of people share their knowledge or experience. ❑ *...a writers' workshop.*

workstation /ˈwɜːksteɪʃən/ (**workstations**) N-COUNT A **workstation** is a computer. [COMPUTING]

world /wɜːld/ (**worlds**) **1** N-SING **The world** is the planet that we live on. ❑ *It's a beautiful part of the world.* ❑ *More than anything, I'd like to travel around the world.* **2** N-COUNT A **world** is a planet. ❑ *...the possibility of life on other worlds.* **3** ADJ BEFORE N You can use **world** to describe someone or something that is one of the most important or significant of its kind on earth. ❑ *China has once again become a world power.* ❑ *...a world authority on heart diseases.* **4** N-COUNT Someone's **world** is the life they lead, the people they have contact with, and the things they experience. ❑ *I lost my job and my world fell apart.* **5** N-SING You can use **world** to refer to a particular field of activity, and the people involved in it. ❑ *...the latest news from the world of finance.* **6** N-SING You can use **world** to refer to a particular group of living things, for example **the animal world, the plant world**, and **the insect world**. **7** PHRASE **The world over** means throughout the world. ❑ *Some problems are the same the world over.* **8** PHRASE If you say that someone has **the best of both worlds**, you mean that they have the benefits of two things and none of the disadvantages. ❑ *Her living room provides the best of both worlds, with an office at one end and comfortable sofas at the other.* **9** PHRASE You can use **the outside world** to refer to all the people who do not live in a particular place or who are not involved in a particular situation. ❑ *For many, the post office is the only link with the outside world.*

Word Partnership Use *world* with:

N.	world **history**, world **peace**, world **premiere** 1
	world **record** 3
	world **of** ***something*** 5 6
V.	**travel the** world 1
PREP.	**all over the** world, **anywhere in the** world, **around the** world 1

ˌworld-ˈclass ADJ A **world-class** competitor in a sporting event is one of the best in the world at what they do. [JOURNALISM]

ˌworld-ˈfamous ADJ Someone or something that is **world-famous** is known about by people all over the world. ❑ *...the world-famous Oxford Street.*

worldly /ˈwɜːldli/ (**worldlier, worldliest**) **1** ADJ **Worldly** is used to talk about the ordinary things of life, especially things like possessions, rather than spiritual things. [LITERARY] ❑ *He hadn't left many worldly goods behind him.* **2** ADJ Someone who is **worldly** is experienced, practical, and knowledgeable about life.

ˌworld ˈview (**world views**) N-COUNT A person's **world view** is the way they see and understand the world, especially regarding issues such as politics, philosophy, and religion.

ˌworld ˈwar (**world wars**) N-VAR A **world war** is a war involving countries from all over the world.

Word Link ***wide ≈ extending throughout*** ***: nationwide, widespread, worldwide***

worldwide /ˌwɜːldˈwaɪd/ ADJ & ADV **Worldwide** means happening throughout the world. ❑ *The band enjoyed worldwide success in the 1990s.* ❑ *His books have sold more than 20 million copies worldwide.*

ˌWorld-Wide ˈWeb N-PROPER **The World-Wide Web** is a system which links documents and pictures into an information database that is stored in computers in many different parts of the world and which can be accessed with a single program. **World-Wide Web** is often abbreviated to **the Web**.
→ see **Internet**

worm /wɜːm/ (**worms, worming, wormed**) **1** N-COUNT A **worm** is a small thin animal without bones or legs which lives in the soil. **2** N-PLURAL If animals or people have **worms**, worms are living as parasites in their intestines. **3** V-T If you **worm** an animal, you give it medicine in order to kill the worms that are living in its intestines. **4** V-T If you **worm** your **way** somewhere, you move there slowly and with difficulty.

worn /wɔːn/ **1** **Worn** is the past participle of **wear**. **2** ADJ **Worn** things are damaged or thin because they are old and have been used a lot. ❑ *...a worn blue carpet.* **3** ADJ AFTER LINK-V If someone looks **worn**, they look old and tired.

ˌworn-ˈout **1** ADJ **Worn-out** things are too old, damaged, or thin from use to be used any more. ❑ *...his worn-out shoes.* **2** ADJ If you are **worn-out**, you are extremely tired.

worry /ˈwʌri, AM ˈwɜːri/ (**worries, worrying, worried**) **1** V-I If you **worry**, you keep thinking about a problem or about something unpleasant that might happen. ❑ *Don't worry; your luggage will come on afterwards by taxi.* ❑ *I worry about her constantly.* ● **worried** ADJ ❑ *I'm worried about what is going to happen to us.* **2** V-T If someone or something **worries** you, they cause you to worry. ❑ *'Why didn't you tell us?'—'I didn't want to worry you.'* **3** N-UNCOUNT **Worry** is the state or feeling of anxiety and unhappiness caused by the problems that you have or by thinking about unpleasant things that might happen. ❑ *It's a wonderful life, except for the financial worry.* **4** N-COUNT A **worry** is a problem that you keep thinking about and that makes you unhappy. ❑ *My main worry was that she would still be there.*

Word Partnership	Use *worry* with:
N.	**analysts** worry, **experts** worry, **people** worry **1** **no need to** worry **1** **2**
V.	**begin to** worry, **don't** worry, **have things/nothing to** worry **about**, **not going to** worry **1** **2**

worrying /ˈwʌriɪŋ, AM ˈwɜːriɪŋ/ ADJ If something is **worrying**, it causes people to worry. ❑ *This is a very worrying incident.*

worse /wɜːs/ **Worse** is the comparative of **bad** and **badly**. **1** PHRASE If a situation **goes from bad to worse**, it becomes even more unpleasant or unsatisfactory. ❑ *For the past couple of years my life has gone from bad to worse.* **2** PHRASE If a situation changes **for the worse**, it becomes more unpleasant or more difficult. ❑ *The grandparents sigh and say how things have changed for the worse.* **3** PHRASE If you tell someone that they **could do worse than** do a particular thing, you are advising them that it would be quite a good thing to do. ❑ *You could do worse than consider a career in medicine.*

worsen /ˈwɜːsən/ (**worsens, worsening, worsened**) V-T/V-I If a situation **worsens**, or if something **worsens** it, it becomes more difficult, unpleasant, or unacceptable. ❑ *The security forces prevented the situation from worsening.* ❑ *Talking to them would actually worsen the problem.*

W

worship /ˈwɜːʃɪp/ (**worships, worshipping, worshipped** or [AM] **worshiping, worshiped**) **1** V-T/V-I & N-UNCOUNT To **worship** God or a god means to show your respect to God or a god, for example by saying prayers. The act of showing respect in this way is called **worship**. ❑ *...Jews worshipping at the Wailing Wall.* ❑ *...places of worship.* ● **worshipper** (**worshippers**) N-COUNT ❑ *The mosque will hold 1,000 worshippers.* **2** V-T If you **worship** someone or something, you love them or admire them very much. ❑ *He worships his father.*

worst /wɜːst/ **1** **Worst** is the superlative of **bad** and **badly**. **2** N-SING **The worst** is the most unpleasant or unfavourable thing that could happen or does happen. ❑ *The country has survived the worst of the crisis.* **3** PHRASE You use **at worst** when considering a situation in the most unfavourable or most pessimistic way. ❑ *At best Nella would be unable to walk; at worst she would die.* **4** PHRASE If someone is **at** their **worst**, they are behaving as unpleasantly or doing something as unsuccessfully as it is possible for them to do. ❑ *This was their mother at her worst.*

worth /wɜːθ/ **1** PREP If something is **worth** an amount of money, it can be sold for that amount or has that value. ❑ *These books might be worth £80 or £90 or more to a collector.* **2** **Worth** combines with amounts of money, so that when you talk about a particular amount of money's **worth of** something, you mean the quantity of it that you can buy for that amount of money. ❑ *I bought about six dollars' worth of potato chips.* **3** N-UNCOUNT Someone's **worth** is their value, usefulness, or importance. ❑ *These highly skilled people have already proved their worth.* **4** PREP You use **worth** to say that something is so enjoyable or useful that it is a good thing to do or have. ❑ *This restaurant is well worth a visit.* ❑ *He's decided to look at the house and see if it's worth buying.* **5** PHRASE If an action or activity is **worth** your **while**, it will be helpful or useful to you. ❑ *It might be worth your while to ask for the agreement to be changed.*

Word Partnership	Use *worth* with:
N.	worth **five pounds**, worth **a fortune**, worth **money**, worth **the price** **1** worth **the effort**, worth **the risk**, worth **the trouble**, worth **a try** **4**
V.	worth **buying**, worth **having** **4** worth **fighting for**, worth **remembering**, worth **saving**, worth **watching** **5**

worthless /ˈwɜːθləs/ ADJ Something that is **worthless** is of no real use or value. ❑ *...a worthless piece of rubbish.*

worthwhile /ˌwɜːθˈwaɪl/ ADJ If something is **worthwhile**, it is enjoyable or useful, and worth the time, money, or effort spent on it. ❑ *...a worthwhile movie that you will want to watch again.* ❑ *It might be worthwhile to consider buying a new car.*

Thesaurus	*worthwhile* Also look up:
ADJ.	beneficial, helpful, useful; *(ant.)* worthless

worthy /ˈwɜːði/ (**worthier, worthiest**) ADJ If someone or something is **worthy of** something, they deserve it because they have the qualities or abilities required. [FORMAL] ❑ *The bank might think you're worthy of a loan.* ❑ *Agassi was a worthy winner.*

would /wəd STRONG wʊd/

In spoken English, **would** is often abbreviated to **'d**.

1 MODAL You use **would** when you are saying what someone believed, hoped, or expected to happen or be the case. ❑ *Would he always be like this?*

❑ *The report said unemployment would continue to rise.* **2** MODAL You use **would** when you are referring to the result or effect of a possible situation. ❑ *It would be fun to be taken to expensive restaurants.* **3** MODAL You use **would** to say that someone was willing to do something. You use **would not** to indicate that someone refused to do something. ❑ *She promised that she would help her husband.* ❑ *He wouldn't say where he had obtained the information.* **4** MODAL You use **would**, especially with verbs such as 'like', 'love', and 'wish' when saying that someone wants to do or have something or wants something to happen. ❑ *She asked me what I would like to do.* ❑ *She would love to become pregnant again.* ❑ *Anne wouldn't mind going to Italy or France to live.* **5** MODAL You use **would** in polite questions and requests. ❑ *Would you like a drink?* ❑ *Do you think it would be all right if I opened the window?* **6** MODAL You say that someone **would** do something when it is or was typical of them. ❑ *I was amazed to be told, 'Well, you would say that: you're a man.'* ❑ *Sunday mornings my mother would bake. I'd stand in the kitchen and help.* **7** MODAL You use **would** or **would have** to express your opinion about something that you think is true. ❑ *I think you'd agree he's a very respected politician.* ❑ *I would have thought it was obvious what he wanted.* **8** MODAL If you talk about what **would have** happened if a possible event had occurred, you are talking about the result or effect of that event. ❑ *If they had done that, then we would have called the police.* **9** MODAL If you say that someone **would have** liked or preferred something, you mean that they wanted to do it or have it but were unable to. ❑ *I would have liked a bit more time.*

'would-be ADJ BEFORE N You use **would-be** to describe what someone wants to do or become. ❑ *...a would-be writer.*

wouldn't /'wʊdənt/ **Wouldn't** is the usual spoken form of 'would not'.

would've /wʊdəv/ **Would've** is a spoken form of 'would have', especially when 'have' is an auxiliary verb.

wound (**wounds, wounding, wounded**) **1** /waʊnd/ **Wound** is the past tense and past participle of **wind**, 2. **2** N-COUNT /wuːnd/ A **wound** is an injury to your body, especially a cut or hole caused by a gun, knife, or similar weapon. **3** V-T If a weapon or something sharp **wounds** you, it injures your body. ❑ *The bomb killed six people and wounded another five.* ❑ *...two wounded men.* **4** V-T If you **are wounded** by what someone says or does, they make you feel hurt and upset.

Usage

Note that when someone is hurt accidentally, for example in a car crash or when they are playing sport, you do not say that they **are wounded** or that they receive a **wound**. You say that they **are injured** or that they receive an **injury**. In more formal English, **injury** can also be an uncount noun. ❑ *A man and his baby were injured in the explosion.* ❑ *Many of the deaths that occur in cycling are due to head injuries.* ❑ *They escaped serious injury when their car went out of control.* **Wound** is normally restricted to soldiers who are injured in battle, or to deliberate acts of violence against a particular person. ❑ *...stab wounds.*

Word Partnership Use *wound* with:

N.	**bullet** wound, **chest** wound, **gunshot** wound, **head** wound **2**
V.	**die from a** wound, wound **heals**, **inflict a** wound **2**
ADJ.	**fatal** wound, **open** wound **2**

wound up /waʊnd 'ʌp/ ADJ If someone is **wound up**, they are very tense and nervous or angry. [INFORMAL]

wove /wəʊv/ **Wove** is the past tense of **weave**.

woven /'wəʊvən/ **Woven** is the past participle of **weave**.

wow /waʊ/ EXCLAM You can say **'wow'** when you are very impressed, surprised, or pleased. [INFORMAL] ❑ *Wow, this is so exciting.*

wrangle /'ræŋgəl/ (**wrangles, wrangling, wrangled**) V-I & N-COUNT If two people **are wrangling over** something, or if they are involved in a **wrangle over** it, they are arguing angrily for a long time about it. ❑ *...legal wrangles over contracts.* • **wrangling** (**wranglings**) N-VAR ❑ *Their decision follows months of wrangling.*

wrap /ræp/ (**wraps, wrapping, wrapped**) **1** V-T & PHR-VERB If you **wrap** something, or if you **wrap** it **up**, you fold paper or cloth tightly round it to cover it. ❑ *I'll take the opportunity to wrap up some presents.* **2** V-T If you **wrap** something such as a piece of paper or cloth **around** another thing, you put it around it. ❑ *She wrapped a handkerchief around her bleeding hand.* **3** V-T If you **wrap** your arms, fingers, or legs **around** something, you put them tightly around it. ❑ *He wrapped his arms around her and held her for half a minute.* **4** → see also **wrapping**
▶ **wrap up** **1** PHR-VERB If you **wrap up**, you put warm clothes on. ❑ *It can be breezy, so wrap up well.* **2** PHR-VERB If you **wrap up** something such as a job or an agreement, you complete it in a satisfactory way. ❑ *The deal was wrapped up in just 24 hours.* **3** → see also **wrap** (meaning 1)

,wrapped 'up ADJ AFTER LINK-V If someone is **wrapped up in** something or someone, they spend nearly all their time thinking about them, so that they forget about other things which may be important. ❑ *They were totally wrapped up in their own problems.*

wrapper /'ræpə/ (**wrappers**) N-COUNT A **wrapper** is a piece of paper, plastic, or foil which covers and protects something that you buy, especially food.

wrapping /'ræpɪŋ/ (**wrappings**) N-VAR **Wrapping** is something such as paper or plastic which is used to cover and protect something. ❑ *I tore off the wrapping and opened the box.*

wrath /rɒθ, AM ræθ/ N-UNCOUNT **Wrath** means anger. [LITERARY]

wreak /riːk/ (**wreaks, wreaking, wreaked** or **wrought**) **1** V-T Something or someone that **wreaks** havoc or destruction causes a great amount of disorder or damage. [JOURNALISM] ❑ *Heavy rain wreaked havoc on the south coast yesterday.* **2** V-T If you **wreak** revenge or vengeance on someone, you do something to harm them, because they have harmed you. [LITERARY] **3** → see also **wrought**

wreath /riːθ/ (**wreaths**) N-COUNT A **wreath** is

wreath

a ring of flowers and leaves which is put onto a grave as a sign of remembrance for the dead person.

wreck /rek/ (**wrecks, wrecking, wrecked**) **1** V-T To **wreck** something means to completely destroy or ruin it. ❑ *Twenty-one people were killed and 50 houses wrecked.* ❑ *...the injuries which nearly wrecked his career.* **2** N-COUNT A **wreck** is something such as ship, car, plane, or building which has been destroyed, usually in an accident.

wreckage /'rekɪdʒ/ N-UNCOUNT When a plane, car, or building has been destroyed, you can refer to what remains as the **wreckage**.

wren /ren/ (**wrens**) N-COUNT A **wren** is a very small brown bird.

wrench /rentʃ/ (**wrenches, wrenching, wrenched**) **1** V-T If you **wrench** something, usually something that is in a fixed position, you pull or twist it violently. ❑ *He felt two men wrench the suitcase from his hand.* ❑ *She wrenched herself from his grasp.* **2** V-T If you **wrench** a limb or one of your joints, you twist it and injure it. **3** N-SING If you say that leaving someone or something is **a wrench**, you feel very sad about it. **4** N-COUNT A **wrench** is an adjustable metal tool used for tightening or loosening nuts and bolts. The British term is **spanner**. [AM]
→ see **tool**

wrestle /'resəl/ (**wrestles, wrestling, wrestled**) **1** V-I If you **wrestle with** a difficult problem or situation, you try to solve it. **2** V-I If you **wrestle with** someone, you fight them by forcing them into painful positions or throwing them to the ground, rather than by hitting them. Some people wrestle as a sport.

wrestler /'reslə/ (**wrestlers**) N-COUNT A **wrestler** is someone who wrestles as a sport.

wrestling /'reslɪŋ/ N-UNCOUNT **Wrestling** is a sport in which two people wrestle and try to throw each other to the ground.

wretched /'retʃɪd/ **1** ADJ You describe someone as **wretched** when you feel sorry for them because they are in an unpleasant situation or have suffered unpleasant experiences. [FORMAL] ❑ *...wretched people who had to sell their homes or starve.* **2** ADJ If you describe something or someone as **wretched**, you think that they are very bad. [SPOKEN] ❑ *The food was wretched.* ❑ *'Wretched woman,' he thought, 'why can't she wait?'*

wriggle /'rɪgəl/ (**wriggles, wriggling, wriggled**) V-T/V-I If you **wriggle**, or if you **wriggle** a part of your body, you twist and turn your body with quick movements. ❑ *Janey wriggled out of her father's arms.* ❑ *She pulled off her shoes and wriggled her toes.*

W

▸ **wriggle out of** PHR-VERB If you **wriggle out of** doing something that you do not want to do, you manage to avoid doing it. [INFORMAL] ❑ *I had wriggled out of the washing up.*

wring /rɪŋ/ (**wrings, wringing, wrung**) V-T If you **wring** something **out of** someone, you manage to make them give it to you even though they do not want to.

▸ **wring out** PHR-VERB When you **wring out** a wet cloth or a wet piece of clothing, you squeeze the water out of it by twisting it strongly.

wrinkle /'rɪŋkəl/ (**wrinkles, wrinkling, wrinkled**) **1** N-COUNT **Wrinkles** are lines which form on someone's face as they grow old. **2** V-T/V-I When you **wrinkle** your nose or forehead, or when it **wrinkles**, you tighten the muscles in your face so that the skin folds. ❑ *Jack wrinkled his nose at that unpleasant thought.*
→ see **skin**

wrinkled /'rɪŋkəld/ **1** ADJ Someone who has **wrinkled** skin has a lot of wrinkles. ❑ *...the old man's wrinkled face.* **2** ADJ **Wrinkled** clothes have lots of small untidy folds or lines in them. ❑ *His white uniform was dirty and wrinkled.*

wrist /rɪst/ (**wrists**) N-COUNT Your **wrist** is the part of your body between your hand and arm which bends when you move your hand.
→ see **body, hand**

writ /rɪt/ (**writs**) N-COUNT A **writ** is a legal document that orders a person to do a particular thing.

write /raɪt/ (**writes, writing, wrote, written**) **1** V-T/V-I When you **write** something on a surface, you use something such as a pen or pencil to produce words, letters, or numbers on it. ❑ *They were still trying to teach her to read and write.* ❑ *She took a card out and wrote an address on it.* **2** V-T If you **write** something such as a book, a poem, or a piece of music, you create it and record it on paper or perhaps on a computer. ❑ *She writes for many papers, including the Sunday Times.* **3** V-T/V-I When you **write to** someone, or when you **write** them a letter, you give them information, ask them something, or express your feelings in a letter. In American English, you can also **write** someone. ❑ *She had written him a note a week earlier.* ❑ *The next day I wrote to the manager.* **4** V-T & PHR-VERB When someone **writes** something such as a cheque, receipt, or prescription, or when they **write** it **out**, they put the necessary information on it and usually sign it. ❑ *I'll write you a cheque in a moment.* ❑ *My wife will write you out a receipt before you leave.* **5** → see also **writing, written**

▸ **write down** PHR-VERB When you **write** something **down**, you record it on a piece of paper using a pen or pencil. ❑ *I wrote down exactly what I thought.*

▸ **write in** PHR-VERB If you **write in to** an organization, you send them a letter. ❑ *Please write in to tell about your childhood experiences.*

▸ **write into** PHR-VERB If a rule or detail **is written into** a law or agreement, it is included in it when the law or agreement is made.

▸ **write off** **1** PHR-VERB If you **write off to** a company or organization, you send them a letter asking for something. ❑ *He wrote off to the government for these booklets.* **2** PHR-VERB If you **write off** an amount of money you have lost, you accept that you will never get it back. ❑ *He had long since written off the money.* **3** PHR-VERB If you **write** someone or something **off**, you decide that they are unimportant or useless and that they are not worth further serious attention. ❑ *He has had enough of people writing him off because of his age.* **4** PHR-VERB If someone **writes off** a vehicle, they have a crash in it and it is so badly damaged that it is not worth repairing. ❑ *One of Pete's friends wrote his car off there.* **5** → see also **write-off**

▸ **write out** → see **write** (meaning **4**)

▶ **write up** PHR-VERB If you **write up** something that has been done or said, you record it on paper in a neat and complete form, usually using notes that you have made. ❑ *He wrote up his experiences in Railway Magazine.*

'write-off (**write-offs**) N-COUNT If a vehicle is a **write-off**, it is so badly damaged in an accident that it is not worth repairing.

Word Link	*er, or ≈ one who does, that which does: astronomer, author, writer*

writer /raɪtə/ (**writers**) 1 N-COUNT A **writer** is a person whose job is writing books, stories, or articles. 2 N-COUNT The **writer** of a story or other piece of writing is the person who wrote it.

writhe /raɪð/ (**writhes, writhing, writhed**) V-I If you **writhe**, you twist and turn your body violently backwards and forwards, usually because you are in great pain.

writing /'raɪtɪŋ/ (**writings**) 1 N-UNCOUNT **Writing** is something that has been written or printed. ❑ *Joe tried to read the writing on the opposite page.* ❑ *If you have a complaint, please inform us in writing.* 2 N-UNCOUNT You can refer to any piece of written work as **writing**, especially when you are considering the style of language used in it. ❑ *It was such a brilliant piece of writing.* 3 N-UNCOUNT **Writing** is the activity of writing, especially of writing books for money. 4 N-UNCOUNT Your **writing** is the way the words that you write down look when you see them on paper. ❑ *It was a little difficult to read your writing.*

written /'rɪtən/ 1 **Written** is the past participle of **write**. 2 ADJ A **written** test or piece of work is one which involves writing rather than doing something practical or giving spoken answers. 3 ADJ BEFORE N A **written** agreement or law has been officially written down. ❑ *We're waiting for written confirmation from the Americans.*

wrong /rɒŋ, AM rɔːŋ/ (**wrongs, wronging, wronged**) 1 ADJ AFTER LINK-V If you say that there is something **wrong**, you mean that there is something unsatisfactory about the situation, person, or thing you are talking about. ❑ *Pain is the body's way of telling us that something is wrong.* ❑ *The relationship felt wrong from the start.* ❑ *What's wrong with him?* 2 ADJ BEFORE N & ADV **Wrong** means not correct or not suitable. ❑ *The wrong man had been punished.* ❑ *I really made the wrong decision there.* ❑ *You've done it wrong.* ● **wrongly** ADV ❑ *She was wrongly blamed for breaking a vase.* 3 ADJ AFTER LINK-V If you are **wrong about** something, what you say or think about it is not correct. ❑ *I admit I may have been wrong about that.* ● **wrongly** ADV ❑ *They believed wrongly that we were lying.* 4 ADJ AFTER LINK-V If you say that something someone does is **wrong**, you mean that it is bad or immoral. ❑ *She was wrong to leave her child alone.* ❑ *We don't consider we did anything wrong.* 5 N-UNCOUNT **Wrong** is used to refer to actions that are bad or immoral. ❑ *He can't tell the difference between right and wrong.* 6 N-COUNT A **wrong** is an unjust action or situation. ❑ *The judge said a terrible wrong had been done.* 7 V-T If someone **wrongs** you, they treat you in an unfair way. [LITERARY] 8 PHRASE If something **goes wrong**, it stops working or is no longer successful. ❑ *Something went wrong with the lift.* ❑ *My marriage started to go wrong.* 9 PHRASE If someone who is involved in an argument or dispute is **in the wrong**, they have behaved in a way which is morally or legally wrong.

Thesaurus	*wrong*	Also look up:
ADJ.	incorrect; (*ant.*) right 2	
	corrupt, immoral, unjust 4	
N.	abuse, offence, sin 5	

wrongdoing /'rɒŋduːɪŋ, AM 'rɔːŋ-/ (**wrongdoings**) N-VAR **Wrongdoing** is behaviour that is illegal or immoral. ❑ *The bank has denied any wrongdoing.*

wrote /rəʊt/ **Wrote** is the past tense of **write**.

wrought /rɔːt/ 1 V-T If something has **wrought** a change, it has caused it. [LITERARY] ❑ *Events in Paris wrought a change in British opinion towards France.* 2 **Wrought** is a past tense and past participle of **wreak**.

wrung /rʌŋ/ **Wrung** is the past tense and past participle of **wring**.

wry /raɪ/ ADJ If someone responds to a bad or difficult situation with a **wry** remark or facial expression, it shows that they find a bad or difficult situation slightly amusing or ironic. ❑ *There is a wry sense of humour in his work.* ● **wryly** ADV ❑ *She turned and smiled wryly.*

wuss /wʊs/ (**wusses**) N-COUNT If you call someone a **wuss**, you are criticizing them for being afraid; used showing disapproval. [INFORMAL, SPOKEN]

WWW /ˌdʌbljuː dʌbljuː 'dʌbljuː/ **WWW** is an abbreviation for 'World-Wide Web'. It appears at the beginning of website addresses in the form **www.** [COMPUTING] ❑ *Check out our website at www.harpercollins.co.uk.*

W

Xx

xenophobia /ˌzenəˈfəʊbiə/ N-UNCOUNT **Xenophobia** is fear or strong dislike of people from other countries. • **xenophobic** ADJ ❑ *The man was obsessively xenophobic.*

Xerox /ˈzɪərɒks/ (**Xeroxes, Xeroxing, Xeroxed**) **1** N-COUNT A **Xerox** is a machine that can make copies of pieces of paper which have writing or other marks on them. **Xerox** is a trademark. The British term is **photocopier**. **2** V-T & N-COUNT If you **Xerox** a document, or if you make a **Xerox** of it, you make a copy of it using a Xerox machine. The British term is **photocopy**.

ˈX-ray (**X-rays, X-raying, X-rayed**) **1** N-COUNT An **X-ray** is a type of radiation that can pass through most solid materials. X-rays are used by doctors to examine the bones or organs inside your body, and at airports to see inside people's luggage. **2** N-COUNT An **X-ray** is a picture made by sending X-rays through something. **3** V-T If someone or something **is X-rayed**, an X-ray picture is taken of them.
→ see **telescope, wave**

Yy

yacht

yacht /jɒt/ (**yachts**) N-COUNT A **yacht** is a large boat with sails or a motor, used for racing or for pleasure trips.

yachting /ˈjɒtɪŋ/ N-UNCOUNT **Yachting** is the sport or activity of sailing a yacht.

yank /jæŋk/ (**yanks, yanking, yanked**) V-T & N-COUNT If you **yank** something somewhere, or if you give it a **yank**, you pull it suddenly with a lot of force. ❑ *She yanked open the drawer.* ❑ *Grabbing his hair, Shirley gave it a yank.*

yard /jɑːd/ (**yards**) **1** N-COUNT A **yard** is a unit of length equal to 36 inches or approximately 91.4 centimetres. **2** N-COUNT A **yard** is a flat area of concrete or stone that is next to a building and often has a wall around it. **3** N-COUNT You can refer to a large open area where a particular type of work is done as a **yard**. ❑ *...a ship repair yard.* **4** N-COUNT In American English, a **yard** is an area of land next to a house, with plants, trees, and grass. The usual British word is **garden**.
→ see **measurement**

yardstick /ˈjɑːdstɪk/ (**yardsticks**) N-COUNT If you use someone or something as a **yardstick**, you use them as a standard for comparison when you are judging other people or things. ❑ *These models become the yardstick against which we weigh and measure ourselves.*

yarn /jɑːn/ (**yarns**) **1** N-VAR **Yarn** is thread that is used for knitting or making cloth. **2** N-COUNT A **yarn** is a story that someone tells, often with invented details which make it more interesting.

yawn /jɔːn/ (**yawns, yawning, yawned**) V-I & N-COUNT When you **yawn**, you open your mouth wide and breathe in more air than usual, often when you are tired. A **yawn** is an act of yawning. ❑ *She yawned and stretched lazily.* ❑ *He rubbed his eyes, then gave a huge yawn.*
→ see **sleep**

yd (**yds**) N-COUNT **yd** is a written abbreviation for **yard.** ❑ *...200 yds further on.*

yeah /jeə/ CONVENTION **Yeah** is used in written English to represent the way yes is pronounced in informal speech. ❑ *'Can I have a word with you, Mick?'—'Yeah, yeah. What's it about?'*

year /jɪə/ (**years**) **1** N-COUNT A **year** is a period of twelve months, beginning on the first of January and ending on the thirty-first of December. **2** N-COUNT A **year** is any period of twelve months. ❑ *These museums attract more than a million visitors a year.* **3** N-COUNT A period of the year which is connected with schools or business can be called a school **year** or a business **year**. **4** N-PLURAL You can use **years** to emphasize that you are referring to a very long time. ❑ *I haven't laughed so much in years.* **5** PHRASE If something happens **all year round**, it happens continually throughout the year. **6** → see also **New Year**
→ see Word Web: **year**
→ see **season**

yearly /ˈjɪəli/ **1** ADJ BEFORE N & ADV A **yearly** event happens once a year or every year. ❑ *...their yearly meeting in London.* ❑ *Clients normally pay fees in advance, monthly, quarterly, or yearly.* **2** ADJ BEFORE N & ADV You use **yearly** to describe something such as an amount that relates to a period of one year. ❑ *...a yearly salary of $43,000.* ❑ *Tourism is worth £4bn yearly to Ireland's economy.*

yearn /jɜːn/ (**yearns, yearning, yearned**) V-T/V-I If someone **yearns for** something, they want it very much. ❑ *He yearned for freedom.* ❑ *I yearned to be a movie actor.* • **yearning** (**yearnings**) N-VAR ❑ *...a yearning for a child of my own.*

-year-old (**-year-olds**) **-year-old** combines with numbers to form adjectives and nouns that indicate the age of people or things. ❑ *She has a six-year-old daughter.* ❑ *...a ski school for 3- to 6-year-olds.*

yeast /jiːst/ (**yeasts**) N-VAR **Yeast** is a kind of fungus which is used to make bread rise, and in making alcoholic drinks such as beer.
→ see **fungus**

Word Web year

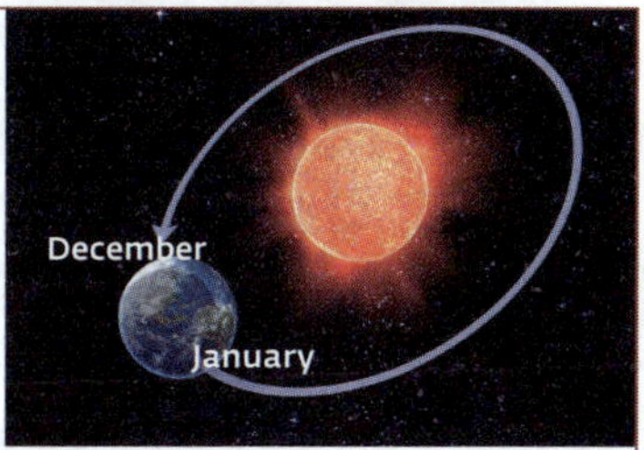

The earth takes a **year** to orbit the sun. It is about 365 **days**. The exact time is 365.242199 days. To make years come out even, every four years there is a leap year. It has 366 days. The **months** on a **calendar** are based on the phases of the moon. The Greeks had a 10-month calendar. About 60 days were left over. So the Romans added two months. The idea of seven-day **weeks** came from the Bible. The Romans named the days. We still use three of these names: Sunday (sun day), Monday (moon day), and Saturday (Saturn day).

yell /jel/ (**yells, yelling, yelled**) V-I & N-COUNT If you **yell** or **yell out**, or if you give a **yell**, you shout loudly, usually because you are excited, angry, or in pain. ❑ *I'm sorry I yelled at you last night.* ❑ *'Are you going out?' they yelled at him.* ❑ *He let out a yell.*

Thesaurus	*yell* Also look up:
V.	cry, scream, shout; *(ant.)* whisper

yellow /ˈjeləʊ/ (**yellows, yellowing, yellowed**) **1** ADJ & N-VAR Something that is **yellow** is the colour of lemons or egg yolks. ❑ *...the soft yellows of the desert sands.* **2** V-I If something **yellows**, it becomes yellow in colour, often because it is old. → see **colour, rainbow**

ˌyellow ˈcard (**yellow cards**) N-COUNT In football or rugby, the **yellow card** is a card that the referee shows to a player to warn them that if they break the rules again they will have to leave the pitch.

yen /jen/

Yen is both the singular and the plural form.

N-COUNT The **yen** is the unit of currency used in Japan.

yes /jes/ **1** CONVENTION You use **yes** to give a positive response to a question, or when you are saying that something is true, accepting an offer or request, or giving permission. ❑ *'Are you a friend of Nick's?'—'Yes.'* ❑ *'That flower is a rose, isn't it?'—'Yes, it is a rose.'* ❑ *'Can I ask you something?'—'Yes, of course.'* **2** CONVENTION You can use **yes** when disagreeing with something that someone says. ❑ *'I don't know what you're talking about.'—'Yes, you do.'*

yesterday /ˈjestədeɪ, -di/ ADV & N-UNCOUNT You use **yesterday** to refer to the day before today. ❑ *She left yesterday.* ❑ *...yesterday's meeting.*

yet /jet/ **1** ADV You use **yet** in negative statements to indicate that something has not happened up to the present time, although it probably will happen. You also use **yet** in questions to ask if something has happened up to the present time. ❑ *No decision has yet been made.* ❑ *He knew that Billy was not yet here.* ❑ *Have you got satellite TV yet?*

Usage

In British English, **yet** and **already** are usually used with the present perfect tense. ❑ *Have they said sorry yet?* ❑ *I have already started knitting baby clothes.* In American English, a past tense is commonly used. ❑ *I didn't get any sleep yet.* ❑ *She already told the neighbors not to come.* This usage is becoming more common in British English.

2 ADV If you say that something should not or cannot be done **yet**, you mean that it should not or cannot be done now, although it will have to be done at a later time. ❑ *Don't get up yet.* **3** ADV You use **yet** to say that there is still a possibility that something will happen. ❑ *An agreement might yet be possible.* **4** ADV You use **yet** after an expression referring to a period of time, when you want to say how much longer a situation will continue. ❑ *Unemployment will go on rising for some time yet.* **5** ADV If you say that you have **yet to** do something, you mean that you have never done it. ❑ *He has been nominated three times for the Oscar but has yet to win.* **6** CONJ You can use **yet** to introduce a fact which seems rather surprising after the previous fact you have just mentioned. ❑ *I don't eat much, yet I am overweight.* **7** ADV You can use **yet** to emphasize a word, especially when you are saying that something is surprising because it is more extreme than previous things of its kind, or a further case of them. ❑ *I saw yet another doctor.*

yield /jiːld/ (**yields, yielding, yielded**) **1** V-I If you **yield** to someone or something, you stop resisting them. ❑ *She yielded to pressure and told the truth.* ❑ *She finally yielded and agreed to marry Craig.* **2** V-T If you **yield** something that you have control of or responsibility for, you allow someone else to have control or responsibility. ❑ *The President is now under pressure to yield power to the republics.* **3** V-I If something **yields**, it breaks or moves position because pressure has been put on it. ❑ *He reached the massive door of the barn and pushed. It yielded.* **4** V-T & N-COUNT When something **yields** an amount of something such as food or money, it produces that amount. The amount produced is called a **yield**. ❑ *The vineyard yields 200 tonnes of grapes annually.* ❑ *A yield of more than 7 per cent is expected from the shares.*

Word Partnership	Use *yield* with:
N.	yield **to pressure**, yield **to temptation** **1** yield **information**, yield **results** **2** yield **a profit** **4**
V.	**refuse to** yield **2**
ADJ.	**annual** yield, **expected** yield, **high/higher** yield **4**

yoga /ˈjəʊgə/ N-UNCOUNT **Yoga** is a type of exercise in which you move your body into various positions in order to become more fit or flexible, to improve your breathing, and to relax your mind.

yogurt also **yoghurt** /ˈjɒgət, AM ˈjəʊ-/ (**yogurts**) N-VAR **Yogurt** is a slightly sour thick liquid made by adding bacteria to milk. A **yogurt** is a small pot of yogurt.

yoke /jəʊk/ (**yokes, yoking, yoked**) N-SING If you say that people are under **the yoke of** something or someone bad, you mean they are forced to live in a difficult or unhappy state because of that thing or person. [LITERARY] ❑ *People are still suffering under the yoke of slavery.*

yolk /jəʊk/ (**yolks**) N-VAR The **yolk** of an egg is the yellow part in the middle.

you /juː/ **1** PRON A speaker or writer uses **you** to refer to the person or people that he or she is speaking to. ❑ *When I saw you across the room I knew I'd met you before.* **2** PRON A speaker or writer sometimes uses **you** to refer to people in general. ❑ *In those days you did what you were told.*

you'd /juːd/ **You'd** is the usual spoken form of 'you had', especially when 'had' is an auxiliary verb. **You'd** is also a spoken form of 'you would'. ❑ *I think you'd better tell us why you're asking these questions.*

you'll /juːl/ **You'll** is the usual spoken form of 'you will'.

young /jʌŋ/ (**younger, youngest**) **1** ADJ & N-PLURAL A **young** person, animal, or plant has not lived or existed for long and is not yet mature. You can refer to people who are young as **the young**. ❑ *...his younger brother.* **2** N-PLURAL The **young** of an animal are its babies. → see **age, mammal**

Y

Thesaurus *young* Also look up:

ADJ. childish, immature, youthful; *(ant.)* mature, old 1
N. family, litter 2

Word Link *ster ≈ one who does : gangster, mobster, youngster*

youngster /ˈjʌŋstə/ (**youngsters**) N-COUNT Young people, especially children, are sometimes referred to as **youngsters**.

your /jɔː, jʊə/ 1 DET A speaker or writer uses **your** to indicate that something belongs or relates to the person or people that he or she is talking or writing to. ❑ *Emma, I trust your opinion.* ❑ *I left all of your messages on your desk.* 2 DET A speaker or writer sometimes uses **your** to indicate that something belongs or relates to people in general. ❑ *Pain-killers are very useful in small amounts to bring your temperature down.*

you're /jɔː, jʊə/ **You're** is the usual spoken form of 'you are'.

yours /jɔːz, jʊəz/ 1 PRON A speaker or writer uses **yours** to refer to something that belongs or relates to the person or people that he or she is talking or writing to. ❑ *I'll take my coat upstairs. Shall I take yours, Roberta?* ❑ *I believe Paul was a friend of yours.* 2 CONVENTION People write **Yours**, **Yours sincerely**, or **Yours faithfully** at the end of a letter before they sign their name. ❑ *With best regards, Yours, George.* ❑ *Yours faithfully, Michael Moore, London Business School.*

yourself /jɔːˈself, jʊə-/ (**yourselves**) 1 PRON A speaker or writer uses **yourself** to refer to the person that he or she is talking or writing to. **Yourself** is used when the object of a verb or preposition refers to the same person as the subject of the verb. ❑ *Why don't you go out and enjoy yourselves?* 2 PRON You use **yourself** to emphasize the person that you are referring to. ❑ *You can't convince others if you yourself aren't convinced.*

youth /juːθ/ (**youths** /juːðz/) 1 N-UNCOUNT Someone's **youth** is the period of their life when they are a child, before they are a fully mature adult. ❑ *In my youth I wanted to be an inventor.* 2 N-UNCOUNT **Youth** is the quality or state of being young and perhaps immature or inexperienced. ❑ *The team is now a good mixture of experience and youth.* 3 N-COUNT Journalists often refer to young men as **youths**. ❑ *Gangs of youths broke windows and looted shops.* 4 N-PLURAL **The youth** are young people considered as a group. ❑ *He represents the opinions of the youth of today.*

Word Partnership Use *youth* with:

N. youth **centre**, youth **culture**, youth **groups**, youth **organizations**, youth **programmes**, youth **services** 4

youthful /ˈjuːθfʊl/ ADJ Someone who is **youthful** behaves as if they are young or younger than they really are. ❑ *She's a very youthful 50.*

you've /juːv/ **You've** is the usual spoken form of 'you have', especially when 'have' is an auxiliary verb.

yr (**yrs**) N-COUNT **Yr** is a written abbreviation for **year**.

yuppie /ˈjʌpi/ (**yuppies**) N-COUNT A **yuppie** is a young middle-class person with a well-paid job, who likes to have an expensive lifestyle; used showing disapproval.

Zz

zany /'zeɪni/ (**zanier, zaniest**) ADJ **Zany** humour or a **zany** person is strange or eccentric in an amusing way. [INFORMAL] ❑ *... the zany humour of the Marx Brothers.*

zap /zæp/ (**zaps, zapping, zapped**) V-T To **zap** someone or something means to kill, destroy, or hit them, usually using a gun, spray, or laser. [INFORMAL] ❑ *She had her spots zapped with a laser.*

zapper /zæpə/ (**zappers**) N-COUNT A **zapper** is a small device that you use to control a television, DVD player, or stereo from a distance. [INFORMAL] ❑ *She changed channels with the zapper.*

zeal /ziːl/ N-UNCOUNT **Zeal** is great enthusiasm, especially in connection with work, religion, or politics. ❑ *He set about his task with zeal.*

zealous /'zeləs/ ADJ Someone who is **zealous** spends a lot of time or energy supporting something that they believe in very strongly, especially a political or religious ideal. ● **zealously** ADV ❑ *This company zealously guards the privacy of its customers.*

zebra /'zebrə, 'ziː-/

The plural can be **zebra** or **zebras**.

N-COUNT A **zebra** is an African wild horse which has black and white stripes.

zebra

zero /'zɪərəʊ/ (**zeros** or **zeroes**) **1** NUM **Zero** is the number 0. **2** N-UNCOUNT **Zero** is freezing point on the Centigrade scale. It is often written as 0°C. ❑ *... thirty degrees below zero.* **3** ADJ You can use **zero** to say that there is none at all of the thing mentioned. ❑ *His chances are zero.*

→ see Word Web: **zero**

Usage

As a number, **zero** is used mainly in scientific contexts, or when you want to be precise. In spoken British English, **nought** is much more common. ❑ *'I'll show you how fast the car can go from nought to 60.'—'No thanks. Speed kills.'* However, when you are stating a telephone number, you say **o** (/əʊ/). In some sports contexts, especially football scores, **nil** is used. ❑ *England beat Poland two-nil at Wembley.* In tennis, **love** is the usual word. ❑ *He won the first set and took a two-games-to-love lead in the second.*

Thesaurus *zero* Also look up:

NUM. none, nothing **3**

zest /zest/ **1** N-UNCOUNT **Zest** is a feeling of pleasure and enthusiasm. ❑ *... a lovable girl with a zest for life.* **2** N-UNCOUNT **Zest** is a quality in an activity or situation which you find exciting. ❑ *There's a real zest to the film's chase scenes.* **3** The **zest of** a lemon, orange, or lime is the outer skin when it is used to give flavour to something such as a cake or drink.

zigzag also **zig-zag** /'zɪgzæg/ (**zigzags, zigzagging, zigzagged**) **1** N-COUNT A **zigzag** is a line with a series of angles in it, like a continuous series of 'W's. **2** V-T/V-I If you **zigzag**, you move forward by going at an angle first to one side then to the other. ❑ *He zigzagged his way across the field.*

zinc /zɪŋk/ N-UNCOUNT **Zinc** is a bluish-white metal which is used to make other metals such as brass or to cover other metals such as iron to stop them rusting.

zip /zɪp/ (**zips, zipping, zipped**) **1** N-COUNT In British English, a **zip** is a device used to open and close parts of clothes and bags. It consists of two rows of metal or plastic teeth which separate or fasten together as you pull a small tag along them.

Word Web zero

The **number zero** developed after the other numbers. At first, ancient peoples first used numbers for real objects. They counted two children or four sheep. Over time they moved from "four sheep" to "four things" to the concept of "four." The idea of a **place** holder like zero came from the Babylonians*. Originally, they wrote numbers like 23 and 203 the same way. The reader had to figure out the difference based on the context. Later, they used zero to represent the idea of null value. It shows that there is no amount of something. For example, the number 203 shows that there are 2 hundreds, no tens, and 3 ones.

Babylonians: people who lived in the ancient city of Babylon.

The usual American word is **zipper**. ❑ *He pulled the zip of his jacket down.* **2** V-T & PHR-VERB When you **zip** something, or when you **zip up** something, you close it using a zip. ❑ *He zipped up his jeans.* **3** V-T + PHR-VERB To **zip** or **zip up** a computer file means to compress it so that it needs less space for storage on disk and can be transmitted more quickly. [COMPUTING] ❑ *These files have been zipped up to take up less disk space.*
→ see **button**

zipper /ˈzɪpə/ (**zippers**) N-COUNT A **zipper** is the same as a **zip**. [AM] ❑ *...the metal zipper on his jacket.*

zodiac /ˈzəʊdiæk/ N-SING **The zodiac** is a diagram used by astrologers to represent the positions of the planets and stars. It is divided into twelve sections, each with a special name and symbol. ❑ *There are twelve signs of the zodiac.*

zone /zəʊn/ (**zones, zoning, zoned**) **1** N-COUNT A **zone** is an area that has particular features or characteristics. ❑ *The area has been declared a disaster zone.* ❑ *Many people have stayed behind in the war zone.* **2** V-T If an area of land **is zoned**, it is formally set aside for a particular purpose. ❑ *The area is zoned for both residential and commercial use.* ● **zoning** N-UNCOUNT ❑ *The state imposed a strict zoning plan to protect public land.*

Thesaurus	*zone* Also look up:
N.	area, region, section **1**

zoo /zuː/ (**zoos**) N-COUNT A **zoo** is a park where live animals are kept so that people can look at them.
→ see Word Web: **zoo**

zoology /zuːˈɒlədʒi, zəʊ-/ N-UNCOUNT **Zoology** is the scientific study of animals. ❑ *...the Cambridge Museum of Zoology.* ● **zoological** ADJ BEFORE N ❑ *...zoological research.* ● **zoologist** (**zoologists**) N-COUNT ❑ *...a famous zoologist and writer.*

zoom /zuːm/ (**zooms, zooming, zoomed**) V-I If you **zoom** somewhere, you go there very quickly. [INFORMAL] ❑ *We zoomed through the countryside.*
▸ **zoom in** PHR-VERB If a camera **zooms in on** something that is being filmed or photographed, it gives a close-up picture of it. ❑ *The camera zoomed in on the number plate of the van.*

zucchini /zuːˈkiːni/

> The plural can be **zucchini** or **zucchinis**.

N-VAR In American English, **zucchini** are long thin green vegetables of the marrow family. The British word is **courgette**.

Word Web zoo

At **zoos** people enjoy looking at animals. But zoos are important for another reason, too. More and more **species** are becoming extinct. Zoos help preserve **biological diversity**. They use educational programmes, **breeding** programmes, and **research** studies to do this. One example is the Smithsonian National Zoological Park in Washington, DC. It trains **wildlife** managers from 80 different countries. A breeding programme at the Wolong Reserve in China has produced 38 **pandas** since 1991. And the Tama Zoo in Hino, Japan, does research. It studies **chimpanzee** behavior. One chimp has even learned to use a vending machine.

Contents

abate **1** VERB to abate here means to lessen or diminish ❑ *There lives within the very flame of love/A kind of wick or snuff that will abate it* (*Hamlet* 4.7) **2** VERB to abate here means to shorten ❑ *Abate thy hours* (*A Midsummer Night's Dream* 3.2) **3** VERB to abate here means to deprive ❑ *She hath abated me of half my train* (*King Lear* 2.4)

abjure VERB to abjure means to renounce or give up ❑ *this rough magic I here abjure* (*Tempest* 5.1)

abroad ADV abroad means elsewhere or everywhere ❑ *You have heard of the news abroad* (*King Lear* 2.1)

abrogate VERB to abrogate means to put an end to ❑ *so it shall praise you to abrogate scurrility* (*Love's Labours Lost* 4.2)

abuse **1** NOUN abuse in this context means deception or fraud ❑ *What should this mean? Are all the rest come back?/ Or is it some abuse, and no such thing?* (*Hamlet* 4.7) **2** NOUN an abuse in this context means insult or offence ❑ *I will be deaf to pleading and excuses/Nor tears nor prayers shall purchase our abuses* (*Romeo and Juliet* 3.1) **3** NOUN an abuse in this context means using something improperly ❑ *we'll digest/Th'abuse of distance* (*Henry II Chorus*) **4** NOUN an abuse in this context means doing something which is corrupt or dishonest ❑ *Come, bring them away: if these be good people in a commonweal that do nothing but their abuses in common houses, I know no law: bring them away.* (*Measure for Measure* 2.1)

abuser NOUN the abuser here is someone who betrays, a betrayer ❑ *I ... do attach thee/For an abuser of the world* (*Othello* 1.2)

accent NOUN accent here means language ❑ *In states unborn, and accents yet unknown* (*Julius Caesar* 3.1)

accident NOUN an accident in this context is an event or something that happened ❑ *think no more of this night's accidents* (*A Midsummer Night's Dream* 4.1)

accommodate VERB to accommodate in this context means to equip or to give someone the equipment to do something ❑ *The safer sense will ne'er accommodate/His master thus.* (*King Lear* 4.6)

according ADJ according means sympathetic or ready to agree ❑ *within the scope of choice/Lies my consent and fair according voice* (*Romeo and Juliet* 1.2)

account NOUN account often means judgement (by God) or reckoning ❑ *No reckoning made, but sent to my account/With all my imperfections on my head* (*Hamlet* 1.5)

accountant ADJ accountant here means answerable or accountable ❑ *his offence is... /Accountant to the law* (*Measure for Measure* 2.4)

ace NOUN ace here means one or first referring to the lowest score on a dice ❑ *No die, but an ace, for him; for he is but one./Less than an ace, man; for he is dead; he is nothing.* (*A Midsummer Night's Dream* 5.1)

acquit VERB here acquit means to be rid of or free of. It is related to the verb quit ❑ *I am glad I am so acquit of this tinderbox* (*The Merry Wives of Windsor* 1.3)

afeard ADJ afeard means afraid or frightened ❑ *Nothing afeard of what thyself didst make* (*Macbeth* 1.3)

affiance NOUN affiance means confidence or trust ❑ *O how hast thou with jealousy infected/The sweetness of affiance* (*Henry V* 2.2)

affinity NOUN in this context, affinity means important connections, or relationships with important people ❑ *The Moor replies/That he you hurt is of great fame in Cyprus,/And great affinity* (*Othello* 3.1)

agnize VERB to agnize is an old word that means that you recognize or acknowledge something ❑ *I do agnize/ A natural and prompt alacrity I find in hardness* (*Othello* 1.3)

ague NOUN an ague is a fever in which the patient has hot and cold shivers one after the other ❑ *This is some monster of the isle with four legs, who hath got ... an ague* (*The Tempest* 2.2)

alarm, alarum NOUN an alarm or alarum is a call to arms or a signal for soldiers to prepare to fight ❑ *Whence cometh this alarum and the noise?* (*Henry VI part I* 1.4)

Albion NOUN Albion is another word for England ❑ *but I will sell my dukedom,/To buy a slobbery and a dirty farm In that nook-shotten isle of Albion* (*Henry V* 3.5)

all of all PHRASE all of all means everything, or the sum of all things ❑ *The very all of all* (*Love's Labours Lost* 5.1)

amend VERB amend in this context means to get better or to heal ❑ *at his touch... They presently amend* (*Macbeth* 4.3)

anchor VERB if you anchor on something you concentrate on it or fix on it ❑ *My invention ... Anchors on Isabel* (*Measure for Measure* 2.4)

anon ADV anon was a common word for soon ❑ *You shall see anon how the murderer gets the love of Gonzago's wife* (*Hamlet* 3.2)

antic **1** ADJ antic here means weird or strange ❑ *I'll charm the air to give a sound/ While you perform your antic round* (*Macbeth* 4.1) **2** NOUN in this context antic means a clown or a strange, unattractive creature ❑ *If black, why nature, drawing an antic,/Made a foul blot* (*Much Ado About Nothing* 3.1)

apace ADV apace was a common word for quickly ❑ *Come apace* (*As You Like It* 3.3)

apparel NOUN apparel means clothes or clothing ❑ *one suit of apparel* (*Hamlet* 3.2)

appliance NOUN appliance here means cure ❑ *Diseases desperate grown/By desperate appliance are relieved* (*Hamlet* 4.3)

argument NOUN argument here means a topic of conversation or the subject ❑ *Why 'tis the rarest argument of wonder that hath shot out in our latter times* (*All's Well That Ends Well* 2.3)

arrant ADJ arrant means absolute, complete. It strengthens the meaning of a noun ❑ *Fortune, that arrant whore* (*King Lear* 2.4)

arras NOUN an arras is a tapestry, a large cloth with a picture sewn on it using coloured thread ❑ *Behind the arras I'll convey myself/To hear the process* (*Hamlet* 3.3)

art **1** NOUN art in this context means knowledge ❑ *Their malady convinces/The great essay of art* (*Macbeth* 4.3) **2** NOUN art can also mean skill as it does here ❑ *He ... gave you such a masterly report/For art and exercise in your defence* (*Hamlet* 4.7) **3** NOUN art here means magic ❑ *Now I want/Spirits to enforce, art to enchant* (*The Tempest* 5 Epilogue)

assay **1** NOUN an assay was an attempt, a try ❑ *Make assay./Bow, stubborn knees* (*Hamlet* 3.3) **2** NOUN assay can also mean a test or a trial ❑ *he hath made assay of her virtue* (*Measure for Measure* 3.1)

attend (on/upon) VERB attend on means to wait for or to expect ❑ *Tarry I here, I but attend on death* (*Two Gentlemen of Verona* 3.1)

auditor NOUN an auditor was a member of an audience or someone who listens ❑ *I'll be an auditor* (*A Midsummer Night's Dream* 3.1)

aught NOUN aught was a common word which meant anything ❑ *if my love thou holdest at aught* (Hamlet 4.3)

aunt **1** NOUN an aunt was another word for an old woman and also means someone who talks a lot or a gossip ❑ *The wisest aunt telling the saddest tale* (A Midsummer Night's Dream 2.1) **2** NOUN aunt could also mean a mistress or a prostitute ❑ *the thrush and the jay/Are summer songs for me and my aunts/While we lie tumbling in the hay* (The Winter's Tale 4.3)

avaunt EXCLAM avaunt was a common word which meant go away ❑ *Avaunt, you curs!* (King Lear 3.6)

aye ADV here aye means always or ever ❑ *Whose state and honour I for aye allow* (Richard II 5.2)

baffle VERB baffle meant to be disgraced in public or humiliated ❑ *I am disgraced, impeached, and baffled here* (Richard II 1.1)

bald ADJ bald means trivial or silly ❑ *I knew 'twould be a bald conclusion* (The Comedy of Errors 2.2)

ban NOUN a ban was a curse or an evil spell ❑ *Sometimes with lunatic bans... Enforce their charity* (King Lear 2.3)

barren ADJ barren meant empty or hollow ❑ *now I let go your hand, I am barren.* (Twelfth Night 1.3)

base ADJ base is an adjective that means unworthy or dishonourable ❑ *civet is of a baser birth than tar* (As You Like It 3.2)

base **1** ADJ base can also mean of low social standing or someone who was not part of the ruling class ❑ *Why brand they us with 'base'?* (King Lear 1.2) **2** ADJ here base means poor quality ❑ *Base cousin,/Darest thou break first?* (Two Noble Kinsmen 3.3)

bawdy NOUN bawdy means obscene or rude ❑ *Bloody, bawdy villain!* (Hamlet 2.2)

bear in hand PHRASE bear in hand means taken advantage of or fooled ❑ *This I made good to you In our last conference, passed in probation with you/ How you were borne in hand* (Macbeth 3.1)

beard VERB to beard someone was to oppose or confront them ❑ *Com'st thou to beard me in Denmark?* (Hamlet 2.2)

beard, in one's PHRASE if you say something in someone's beard you say it to their face ❑ *I will verify as much in his beard* (Henry V 3.2)

beaver NOUN a beaver was a visor on a battle helmet ❑ *O yes, my lord, he wore his beaver up* (Hamlet 1.2)

become VERB if something becomes you it suits you or is appropriate to you ❑ *Nothing in his life became him like the leaving it* (Macbeth 1.4)

bed, brought to PHRASE to be brought to bed means to give birth ❑ *His wife but yesternight was brought to bed* (Titus Andronicus 4.2)

bedabbled ADJ if something is bedabbled it is sprinkled ❑ *Bedabbled with the dew, and torn with briers* (A Midsummer Night's Dream 3.2)

Bedlam NOUN Bedlam was a word used for Bethlehem Hospital which was a place the insane were sent to ❑ *The country give me proof and precedent/ Of Bedlam beggars* (King Lear 2.3)

bed-swerver N a bed-swerver was someone who was unfaithful in marriage, an adulterer ❑ *she's/A bed-swerver* (Winter's Tale 2.1)

befall **1** VERB to befall is to happen, occur or take place ❑ *In this same interlude it doth befall/That I present a wall* (A Midsummer Night's Dream 5.1) **2** VERB to befall can also mean to happen to someone or something ❑ *fair befall thee and thy noble house* (Richard III 1.3)

behoof NOUN behoof was an advantage or benefit ❑ *All our surgeons/Convent in their behoof* (*Two Noble Kinsmen* 1.4)

beldam NOUN a beldam was a witch or old woman ❑ *Have I not reason, beldams as you are?* (*Macbeth* 3.5)

belike ADV belike meant probably, perhaps or presumably ❑ *belike he likes it not* (*Hamlet* 3.2)

bent **1** NOUN bent means a preference or a direction ❑ *Let me work,/For I can give his humour true bent,/And I will bring him to the Capitol* (*Julius Caesar* 2.1) **2** ADJ if you are bent on something you are determined to do it ❑ *for now I am bent to know/By the worst means the worst.* (*Macbeth* 3.4)

beshrew VERB beshrew meant to curse or wish evil on someone ❑ *much beshrew my manners and my pride/If Hermia meant to say Lysander lied* (*A Midsummer Night's Dream* 2.2)

betime (s) ADV betime means early ❑ *To business that we love we rise betime* (*Antony and Cleopatra* 4.4)

bevy NOUN bevy meant type or sort, it was also used to mean company ❑ *many more of the same bevy* (*Hamlet* 5.2)

blazon VERB to blazon something meant to display or show it ❑ *that thy skill be more to blazon it* (*Romeo and Juliet* 2.6)

blind ADJ if you are blind when you do something you are reckless or do not care about the consequences ❑ *are you yet to your own souls so blind/That two you will war with God by murdering me* (*Richard III* 1.4)

bombast NOUN bombast was wool stuffing (used in a cushion for example) and so it came to mean padded out or long-winded. Here it means someone who talks a lot about nothing in particular ❑ *How now my sweet creature of bombast* (*Henry IV part I* 2.4)

bond **1** NOUN a bond is a contract or legal deed ❑ *Well, then, your bond, and let me see* (*Merchant of Venice* 1.3) **2** NOUN bond could also mean duty or commitment ❑ *I love your majesty/According to my bond* (*King Lear* 1.1)

bottom NOUN here bottom means essence, main point or intent ❑ *Now I see/The bottom of your purpose* (*All's Well That Ends Well* 3.7)

bounteously ADV bounteously means plentifully, abundantly ❑ *I prithee, and I'll pay thee bounteously* (*Twelfth Night* 1.2)

brace **1** NOUN a brace is a couple or two ❑ *Have lost a brace of kinsmen* (*Romeo and Juliet* 5.3) **2** NOUN if you are in a brace position it means you are ready ❑ *For that it stands not in such warlike brace* (*Othello* 1.3)

brand VERB to mark permanantly like the markings on cattle ❑ *the wheeled seat/Of fortunate Caesar ... branded his baseness that ensued* (*Anthony and Cleopatra* 4.14)

brave ADJ brave meant fine, excellent or splendid ❑ *O brave new world/That has such people in't* (*The Tempest* 5.1)

brine NOUN brine is sea-water ❑ *He shall drink nought brine, for I'll not show him/Where the quick freshes are* (*The Tempest* 3.2)

brow NOUN brow in this context means appearance ❑ *doth hourly grow/Out of his brows* (*Hamlet* 3.3)

burden **1** NOUN the burden here is a chorus ❑ *I would sing my song without a burden* (*As You Like It* 3.2) **2** NOUN burden means load or weight (this is the current meaning) ❑ *the scarfs and the bannerets about thee did manifoldly dissuade me from believing thee a vessel of too great a burden* (*All's Well that Ends Well* 2.3)

buttons, in one's PHRASE this is a phrase that means clear, easy to see ❑ *Tis in his buttons he will carry't* (*The Merry Wives of Windsor* 3.2)

cable NOUN cable here means scope or reach ❑ *The law ... Will give her cable* (*Othello* 1.2)

cadent ADJ if something is cadent it is falling or dropping ❑ *With cadent tears fret channels in her cheeks* (*King Lear* 1.4)

canker VERB to canker is to decay, become corrupt ❑ *And, as with age his body uglier grows,/So his mind cankers* (*The Tempest* 4.1)

canon, from the PHRASE from the canon is an expression meaning out of order, improper ❑ *Twas from the canon* (*Coriolanus* 3.1)

cap-a-pie ADV cap-a-pie means from head to foot, completely ❑ *I am courtier cap-a-pie* (*The Winter's Tale* 4.4)

carbonadoed ADJ if something is carbonadoed it is cut or scored (scratched) with a knife ❑ *it is your carbonadoed* (*All's Well That Ends Well* 4.5)

carouse VERB to carouse is to drink at length, party ❑ *They cast their caps up and carouse together* (*Anthony and Cleopatra* 4.12)

carrack NOUN a carrack was a large old ship, a galleon ❑ *Faith, he tonight hath boarded a land-carrack* (*Othello* 1.2)

cassock NOUN a cassock here means a military cloak, long coat ❑ *half of the which dare not shake the snow from off their cassocks lest they shake themselves to pieces* (*All's Well That Ends Well* 4.3)

catastrophe NOUN catastrophe here means conclusion or end ❑ *pat he comes, like the catastrophe of the old comedy* (*King Lear* 1.2)

cautel NOUN a cautel was a trick or a deceptive act ❑ *Perhaps he loves you now/ And now no soil not cautel doth besmirch* (*Hamlet* 1.2)

celerity NOUN celerity was a common word for speed, swiftness ❑ *Hence hath offence his quick celerity/When it is borne in high authority* (*Measure for Measure* 4.2)

chafe NOUN chafe meant anger or temper ❑ *this Herculean Roman does become/The carriage of his chafe* (*Anthony and Cleopatra* 1.3)

chanson NOUN chanson was an old word for a song ❑ *The first row of the pious chanson will show you more* (*Hamlet* 2.2)

chapman NOUN a chapman was a trader or merchant ❑ *Not uttered by base sale of chapman's tongues* (*Love's Labours Lost* 2.1)

chaps, chops NOUN chaps (and chops) was a word for jaws ❑ *Which ne'er shook hands nor bade farewell to him/Till he unseamed him from the nave to th' chops* (*Macbeth* 1.2)

chattels NOUN chattels were your moveable possessions. The word is used in the traditional marriage ceremony ❑ *She is my goods, my chattels* (*The Taming of the Shrew* 3.3)

chide VERB if you are chided by someone you are told off or reprimanded ❑ *Now I but chide, but I should use thee worse* (*A Midsummer Night's Dream* 3.2)

chinks NOUN chinks was a word for cash or money ❑ *he that can lay hold of her/Shall have the chinks* (*Romeo and Juliet* 1.5)

choleric ADJ if something was called choleric it meant that they were quick to get angry ❑ *therewithal unruly waywardness that infirm and choleric years bring with them* (*King Lear* 1.1)

chuff NOUN a chuff was a miser, someone who clings to his or her money ❑ *ye fat chuffs* (*Henry IV part I* 2.2)

cipher NOUN cipher here means nothing ❑ *Mine were the very cipher of a function* (*Measure for Measure* 2.2)

circummured ADJ circummured means that something is surrounded with a wall ❑ *He hath a garden circummured with brick* (*Measure for Measure* 4.1)

civet NOUN a civet is a type of scent or perfume ❑ *Give me an ounce of civet* (*King Lear* 4.6)

clamorous ADJ clamorous means noisy or boisterous ❑ *Be clamorous and leap all civil bounds* (*Twelfth Night* 1.4)

clangour, clangor NOUN clangour is a word that means ringing (the sound that bells make) ❑ *Like to a dismal clangour heard from far* (*Henry VI part III* 2.3)

cleave VERB if you cleave to something you stick to it or are faithful to it ❑ *Thy thoughts I cleave to* (*The Tempest* 4.1)

clock and clock, 'twixt PHRASE from hour to hour, without stopping or continuously ❑ *To weep 'twixt clock and clock* (*Cymbeline* 3.4)

close ADJ here close means hidden ❑ *Stand close; this is the same Athenian* (*A Midsummer Night's Dream* 3.2)

cloud NOUN a cloud on your face means that you have a troubled, unhappy expression ❑ *He has cloud in's face* (*Anthony and Cleopatra* 3.2)

cloy VERB if you cloy an appetite you satisfy it ❑ *Other women cloy/The appetites they feed* (*Anthony and Cleopatra* 2.2)

cock-a-hoop, set PHRASE if you set cock-a-hoop you become free of everything ❑ *You will set cock-a-hoop* (*Romeo and Juliet* 1.5)

colours NOUN colours is a word used to describe battle-flags or banners. Sometimes we still say that we nail our colours to the mast if we are stating which team or side of an argument we support ❑ *the approbation of those that weep this lamentable divorce under her colours* (*Cymbeline* 1.5)

combustion NOUN combustion was a word meaning disorder or chaos ❑ *prophesying ... Of dire combustion and confused events* (*Macbeth* 2.3)

comely ADJ if you are or something is comely you or it is lovely, beautiful, graceful ❑ *O, what a world is this, when what is comely/Envenoms him that bears it!* (*As You Like It* 2.3)

commend VERB if you commend yourself to someone you send greetings to them ❑ *Commend me to my brother* (*Measure for Measure* 1.4)

compact NOUN a compact is an agreement or a contract ❑ *what compact mean you to have with us?* (*Julius Caesar* 3.1)

compass **1** NOUN here compass means range or scope ❑ *you would sound me from my lowest note to the top of my compass* (*Hamlet* 3.2) **2** VERB to compass here means to achieve, bring about or make happen ❑ *How now shall this be compassed?/Canst thou bring me to the party?* (*Tempest* 3.2)

comptible ADJ comptible is an old word meaning sensitive ❑ *I am very comptible, even to the least sinister usage.* (*Twelfth Night* 1.5)

confederacy NOUN a confederacy is a group of people usually joined together to commit a crime. It is another word for a conspiracy ❑ *Lo, she is one of this confederacy!* (*A Midsummer Night's Dream* 3.2)

confound VERB if you confound something you confuse it or mix it up; it also means to stop or prevent

❑ *A million fail, confounding oath on oath.* (A Midsummer Night's Dream 3.2)

contagion N contagion is an old word for disease or poison ❑ *hell itself breathes out/Contagion to this world* (Hamlet 3.2)

contumely NOUN contumely is an old word for an insult ❑ *the proud man's contumely* (Hamlet 3.1)

counterfeit **1** VERB if you counterfeit something you copy or imitate it ❑ *Meantime your cheeks do counterfeit our roses* (Henry VI part I 2.4) **2** VERB in this context counterfeit means to pretend or make believe ❑ *I will counterfeit the bewitchment of some popular man* (Coriolanus)

coz NOUN coz was a shortened form of the word cousin ❑ *sweet my coz, be merry* (As You Like It 1.2)

cozenage NOUN cozenage is an old word meaning cheating or a deception ❑ *Thrown out his angle for my proper life,/ And with such coz'nage* (Hamlet 5.2)

crave VERB crave used to mean to beg or request ❑ *I crave your pardon* (The Comedy of Errors 1.2)

crotchet NOUN crotchets are strange ideas or whims ❑ *thou hast some strange crotchets in thy head now* (The Merry Wives of Windsor 2.1)

cuckold NOUN a cuckold is a man whose wife has been unfaithful to him ❑ *As there is no true cuckold but calamity* (Twelfth Night 1.5)

cuffs, go to PHRASE this phrase meant to fight ❑ *the player went to cuffs in the question* (Hamlet 2.2)

cup VERB in this context cup is a verb which means to pour drink or fill glasses with alcohol ❑ *cup us til the world go round* (Anthony and Cleopatra 2.7)

cur NOUN cur is an insult meaning dog and is also used to mean coward ❑ *Out, dog! out, cur! Thou drivest me past the bounds/Of maiden's patience* (A Midsummer Night's Dream 3.2)

curiously ADV in this context curiously means carefully or skilfully ❑ *The sleeves curiously cut* (The Taming of the Shrew 4.3)

curry VERB curry means to flatter or to praise someone more than they are worth ❑ *I would curry with Master Shallow that no man could better command his servants* (Henry IV part II 5.1)

custom NOUN custom is a habit or a usual practice ❑ *Hath not old custom made this life more sweet/Than that of painted pomp?* (As You Like It 2.1)

cutpurse NOUN a cutpurse is an old word for a thief. Men used to carry their money in small bags (purse) that hung from their belts; thieves would cut the purse from the belt and steal their money ❑ *A cutpurse of the empire and the rule* (Hamlet 3.4)

dainty ADJ dainty used to mean splendid, fine ❑ *Why, that's my dainty Ariel!* (Tempest 5.1)

dally VERB if you dally with something you play with it or tease it ❑ *They that dally nicely with words may quickly make them wanton* (Twelfth Night 3.1)

damask COLOUR damask is a light-red or pink colour ❑ *Twas just the difference/ Betwixt the constant red and mingled damask* (As You Like It 3.5)

dare **1** VERB dare means to challeng or, confront ❑ *He goes before me, and still dares me on* (A Midsummer Night's Dream 3.3) **2** VERB dare in this context means to present, deliver or inflict ❑ *all that fortune, death, and danger dare* (Hamlet 4.4)

darkly ADV darkly was used in this context to mean secretly or cunningly

❑ *I will go darkly to work with her* (*Measure for Measure* 5.1)

daw NOUN a daw was a slang term for idiot or fool (after the bird jackdaw which was famous for its stupidity) ❑ *Yea, just so much as you may take upon a knife's point and choke a daw withal* (*Much Ado About Nothing* 3.1)

debile ADJ debile meant weak or feeble ❑ *And debile minister great power* (*All's Well That Ends Well* 2.3)

deboshed ADJ deboshed was another way of saying corrupted or debauched ❑ *Men so disordered, deboshed and bold* (*King Lear* 1.4)

decoct VERB to decoct was to heat up, warm something ❑ *Can sodden water,/ A drench for sur-reained jades ... Decoct their cold blood to such valiant heat?* (*Henry V* 3.5)

deep-revolving ADJ deep-revolving here uses the idea that you turn something over in your mind when you are thinking hard about it and so means deep-thinking, meditating ❑ *The deep-revolving Buckingham/No more shall be the neighbour to my counsels* (*Richard III* 4.2)

defect NOUN defect here means shortcoming or something that is not right ❑ *Being unprepared/Our will became the servant to defect* (*Macbeth* 2.1)

degree **1** NOUN degree here means rank, standing or station ❑ *Should a like language use to all degrees,/And mannerly distinguishment leave out/Betwixt the prince and beggar* (*The Winter's Tale* 2.1) **2** NOUN in this context, degree means extent or measure ❑ *her offence/Must be of such unnatural degree* (*King Lear* 1.1)

deify VERB if you deify something or someone you worship it or them as a God ❑ *all.. deifying the name of Rosalind* (*As You Like It* 3.2)

delated ADJ delated here means detailed ❑ *the scope/Of these delated articles* (*Hamlet* 1.2)

delicate ADJ if something was described as delicate it meant it was of fine quality or valuable ❑ *thou wast a spirit too delicate* (*The Tempest* 1.2)

demise VERB in this context demise means to transmit, give or convey ❑ *what state ... Canst thou demise to any child of mine?* (*Richard III* 4.4)

deplore VERB to deplore means to express with grief or sorrow ❑ *Never more/Will I my master's tears to you deplore* (*Twelfth Night* 3.1)

depose VERB if you depose someone you make them take an oath, or swear something to be true ❑ *Depose him in the justice of his cause* (*Richard II* 1.3)

depositary NOUN a depositary is a trustee ❑ *Made you ... my depositary* (*King Lear* 2.4)

derive **1** VERB to derive means to comes from or to descend (it usually applies to people) ❑ *No part of it is mine,/ This shame derives itself from unknown loins.* (*Much Ado About Nothing* 4.1) **2** VERB if you derive something from someone you inherit it ❑ *Treason is not inherited ...Or, if we derive it from our friends/What's that to me?* (*As You Like It* 1.3)

descry VERB to see or catch sight of ❑ *The news is true, my lord. He is descried* (*Anthony and Cleopatra* 3.7)

desert **1** NOUN desert means worth or merit ❑ *That dost in vile misproson shackle up/My love and her desert* (*All's Well That Ends Well* 2.3) **2** ADJ desert is used here to mean lonely or isolated ❑ *if that love or gold/Can in this desert place buy entertainment* (*As You LIke It* 2.4)

design **1** VERB to design means to indicate or point out ❑ *we shall see/*

Justice design the victor's chivalry (*Richard II* 1.1) **2** NOUN a design is a plan, an intention or an undertaking ❑ *hinder not the honour of his design* (*All's Well That Ends Well* 3.6)

designment NOUN a designment was a plan or undertaking ❑ *The desperate tempest hath so bang'd the Turks,/That their designment halts* (*Othello* 2.1)

despite VERB despite here means to spite or attempt to thwart a plan ❑ *Only to despite them I will endeavour anything* (*Much Ado About Nothing* 2.2)

device NOUN a device is a plan, plot or trick ❑ *Excellent, I smell a device* (*Twelfth Night* 2.3)

disable VERB to disable here means to devalue or make little of ❑ *he disabled my judgement* (*As You Like It* 5.4)

discandy VERB here discandy means to melt away or dissolve ❑ *The hearts ... do discandy, melt their sweets* (*Anthony and Cleopatra* 4.12)

disciple VERB to disciple is to teach or train ❑ *He ...was/Discipled of the bravest* (*All's Well That Ends Well* 1.2)

discommend VERB if you discommend something you criticize it ❑ *my dialect which you discommend so much* (*King Lear* 2.2)

discourse NOUN discourse means conversation, talk or chat ❑ *which part of it I'll waste/With such discourse as I not doubt shall make it/Go quick away* (*The Tempest* 5.1)

discover VERB discover used to mean to reveal or show ❑ *the Prince discovered to Claudio that he loved my niece* (*Much Ado About Nothing* 1.2)

disliken VERB disguise, make unlike ❑ *disliken/The truth of your own seeming* (*The Winter's Tale* 4.4)

dismantle VERB to dismantle is to remove or take away ❑ *Commit a thing so monstrous to dismantle/So many folds of favour* (*King Lear* 1.1)

disponge VERB disponge means to pour out or rain down ❑ *The poisonous damp of night dispongeupon me* (*Anthony and Cleopatra* 4.9)

distrain VERB to distrain something is to confiscate it ❑ *My father's goods are all distrained and sold* (*Richard II* 2.3)

divers ADJ divers is an old word for various ❑ *I will give out divers schedules of my beauty* (*Twelfth Night* 1.5)

doff VERB to doff is to get rid of or dispose ❑ *make our women fight/To doff their dire distresses* (*Macbeth* 4.3)

dog VERB if you dog someone or something you follow them or it closely ❑ *I will rather leave to see Hector than not to dog him* (*Troilus and Cressida* 5.1)

dotage NOUN dotage here means infatuation ❑ *Her dotage now I do begin to pity* (*A Midsummer NIght's Dream* 4.1)

dotard NOUN a dotard was an old fool ❑ *I speak not like a dotard nor a fool* (*Much Ado About Nothing* 5.1)

dote VERB to dote is to love, cherish, care without seeing any fault ❑ *And won her soul; and she, sweet lady, dotes,/ Devoutly dotes, dotes in idolatry* (*A Midsummer Night's Dream* 1.1)

doublet NOUN a doublet was a man's close-fitting jacket with short skirt ❑ *Lord Hamlet, with his doublet all unbraced* (*Hamlet* 2.1)

dowager NOUN a dowager is a widow ❑ *Like to a step-dame or a dowage* (*A Midsummer Night's Dream* 1.1)

dowdy NOUN a dowdy was an ugly woman ❑ *Dido was a dowdy* (*Romeo and Juliet* 2.4)

dower NOUN a dower (or dowery) is the riches or property given by the father of a bride to her husband-to-be ❑ *Thy truth then by they dower* (*King Lear* 1.1)

dram NOUN a dram is a tiny amount ❑ *Why, everything adheres together that no dram of a scruple* (*Twelfth Night* 3.4)

drift NOUN drift is a plan, scheme or intention ❑ *Shall Romeo by my letters know our drift* (*Romeo and Juliet* 4.1)

dropsied ADJ dropsied means pretentious ❑ *Where great additions swell's and virtues none/It is a dropsied honour* (*All's Well That Ends Well* 2.3)

drudge NOUN a drudge was a slave, servant ❑ *If I be his cuckold, he's my drudge* (*All's Well That Ends Well* 1.3)

dwell VERB to dwell sometimes meant to exist, to be ❑ *I'd rather dwell in my necessity* (*Merchant of Venice* 1.3)

earnest ADJ an earnest was a pledge to pay or a payment in advance ❑ *for an earnest of a greater honour/He bade me from him call thee Thane of Cawdor* (*Macbeth* 1.3)

ecstasy NOUN madness ❑ *This is the very ecstasy of love* (*Hamlet* 2.1)

edict NOUN law or declaration ❑ *It stands as an edict in destiny.* (*A Midsummer Night's Dream* 1.1)

egall ADJ egall is an old word meaning equal ❑ *companions/Whose souls do bear an egall yoke of love* (*Merchant of Venice* 2.4)

eisel NOUN eisel meant vinegar ❑ *Woo't drink up eisel?* (*Hamlet* 5.1)

eke, eke out VERB eke meant to add to, to increase. Eke out nowadays means to make something last as long as possible – particularly in the sense of making money last a long time ❑ *Still be kind/And eke out our performance with your mind* (*Henry V Chorus*)

elbow, out at PHRASE out at elbow is an old phrase meaning in poor condition – as when your jacket sleeves are worn at the elbow which shows that it is an old jacket ❑ *He cannot, sir. He's out at elbow* (*Measure for Measure* 2.1)

element NOUN elements were thought to be the things from which all things were made. They were: air, earth, water and fire ❑ *Does not our lives consist of the four elements?* (*Twelfth Night* 2.3)

elf VERB to elf was to tangle ❑ *I'll ... elf all my hairs in knots* (*King Lear* 2.3)

embassy NOUN an embassy was a message ❑ *We'll once more hear Orsino's embassy.* (*Twelfth Night* 1.5)

emphasis NOUN emphasis here means a forceful expression or strong statement ❑ *What is he whose grief/Bears such an emphasis* (*Hamlet* 5.1)

empiric NOUN an empiric was an untrained doctor sometimes called a quack ❑ *we must not ... prostitute our past-cure malady/To empirics* (*All's Well That Ends Well* 2.1)

emulate ADJ emulate here means envious ❑ *pricked on by a most emulate pride* (*Hamlet* 1.1)

enchant VERB to enchant meant to put a magic spell on ❑ *Damn'd as thou art, thou hast enchanted her,/For I'll refer me to all things of sense* (*Othello* 1.2)

enclog VERB to enclog was to hinder something or to provide an obstacle to it ❑ *Traitors enscarped to enclog the guitless keel* (*Othello* 1.2)

endure VERB to endure was to allow or to permit ❑ *and will endure/Our setting down before't.* (*Macbeth* 5.4)

enfranchise VERB if you enfranchised something you set it free ❑ *Do this or this;/Take in that kingdom and enfranchise that;/Perform't, or else we damn thee.'* (*Anthony and Cleopatra* 1.1)

engage VERB to engage here means to pledge or to promise ❑ *This to be true I do engage my life* (*As You Like It* 5.4)

engaol VERB to lock up or put in prison ❑ *Within my mouth you have engaoled my tongue* (*Richard II* 1.3)

engine NOUN an engine was a plot, device or a machine ❑ *their promises, enticements, oaths, tokens, and all these engines, of lust, are not the things they go under* (*All's Well That Ends Well* 3.5)

englut VERB if you were engulfed you were swallowed up or eaten whole ❑ *For certainly thou art so near the gulf,/ Thou needs must be englutted.* (*Henry V* 4.3)

enjoined ADJ enjoined describes people joined together for the same reason ❑ *Of enjoined penitents/There's four or five* (*All's Well That Ends Well* 3.5)

entertain **1** VERB to entertain here means to welcome or receive ❑ *Approach, rich Ceres, her to entertain.* (*The Tempest* 4.1) **2** VERB to entertain in this context means to cherish, hold in high regard or to respect ❑ *and I quake,/ Lest thou a feverous life shouldst entertain/ And six or seven winters more respect/Than a perpetual honour.* (*Measure for Measure* 3.1) **3** VERB to entertain means here to give something consideration ❑ *But entertain it,/And though you think me poor, I am the man/Will give thee all the world.* (*Anthony and Cleopatra* 2.7) **4** VERB to entertain here means to treat or handle ❑ *your highness is not entertained with that ceremonious affection as you were wont* (*King Lear* 1.4)

envious ADJ envious meant spiteful or vindictive ❑ *he shall appear to the envious a scholar* (*Measure for Measure* 3.2)

ere PREP ere was a common word for before ❑ *ere this I should ha' fatted all the region kites* (*Hamlet* 2.2)

err VERB to err means to go astray, to make a mistake ❑ *And as he errs, doting on Hermia's eyes* (*A Midsummer Night's Dream* 1.1)

erst ADV erst was a common word for once or before ❑ *that erst brought sweetly forth/The freckled cowslip* (*Henry V* 5.2)

eschew VERB if you eschew something you deliberately avoid doing it ❑ *What cannot be eschewed must be embraced* (*The Merry Wives of Windsor* 5.5)

escote VERB to escote meant to pay for, support ❑ *How are they escoted?* (*Hamlet* 2.2)

estimable ADJ estimable meant appreciative ❑ *I could not with such estimable wonder over-far believe that* (*Twelfth Night* 2.1)

extenuate VERB extenuate means to lessen ❑ *Which by no means we may extenuate* (*A Midsummer Night's Dream* 1.1)

fain ADV fain was a common word meaning gladly or willingly ❑ *I would fain prove so* (*Hamlet* 2.2)

fall NOUN in a voice or music fall meant going higher and lower ❑ *and so die/ That strain again! it had a dying fall* (*Twelfth Night* 1.1)

false ADJ false was a common word for treacherous ❑ *this is counter, you false Danish dogs!* (*Hamlet* 4.5)

fare VERB fare means to get on or manage ❑ *I fare well* (*The Taming of the Shrew Introduction* 2)

feign VERB to feign was to make up, pretend or fake ❑ *It is the more like to be feigned* (*Twelfth Night* 1.5)

fie EXCLAM fie was an exclamation of disgust ❑ *Fie, that you'll say so!* (*Twelfth Night* 1.3)

figure VERB to figure was to symbolize or look like ❑ *Wings and no eyes, figure unheedy haste* (*A Midsummer Night's Dream* 1.1)

filch VERB if you filch something you steal it ❑ *With cunning hast thou filch'd my daughter's heart* (*A Midsummer Night's Dream* 1.1)

flout VERB to flout something meant to scorn it ❑ *Why will you suffer her to flout me thus?* (*A Midsummer Night's Dream* 3.2)

fond ADJ fond was a common word meaning foolish ❑ *Shall we their fond pageant see?* (*A Midsummer Night's Dream* 3.2)

footing **1** NOUN footing meant landing on shore, arrival, disembarkation ❑ *Whose footing here anticipates our thoughts/A se'nnight's speed.* (*Othello* 2.1) **2** NOUN footing also means support ❑ *there your charity would have lacked footing* (*Winter's Tale* 3.3)

forsooth ADV in truth, certainly, truly ❑ *I had rather, forsooth, go before you like a man* (*The Merry Wives of Windsor* 3.2)

forswear VERB if you forswear you lie, swear falsely or break your word ❑ *he swore a thing to me on Monday night, which he forswore on Tuesday morning* (*Much Ado About Nothing* 5.1)

freshes NOUN a fresh is a fresh water stream ❑ *He shall drink nought brine, for I'll not show him/Where the quick freshes are.* (*Tempest* 3.2)

furlong NOUN a furlong is a measure of distance. It is the equivalent on one eight of a mile ❑ *Now would I give a thousand furlongs of sea for an acre of barren ground* (*Tempest* 1.1)

gaberdine NOUN a gaberdine is a cloak ❑ *My best way is to creep under his gaberdine* (*Tempest* 2.2)

gage NOUN a gage was a challenge to duel or fight ❑ *There is my gage, Aumerle, in gage to thine* (*Richard II* 4.1)

gait NOUN your gait is your way of walking or step ❑ *I know her by her gait* (*Tempest* 4.1)

gall VERB to gall is to annoy or irritate ❑ *Let it not gall your patience, good Iago,/ That I extend my manners* (*Othello* 2.1)

gambol NOUN frolic or play ❑ *Hop in his walks, and gambol in his eyes* (*A Midsummer Night's Dream* 3.1)

gaskins NOUN gaskins is an old word for trousers ❑ *or, if both break, your gaskins fall.* (*Twelfth Night* 1.5)

gentle ADJ gentle means noble or well-born ❑ *thrice-gentle Cassio!* (*Othello* 3.4)

glass NOUN a glass was another word for a mirror ❑ *no woman's face remember/ Save from my glass, mine own* (*Tempest* 3.1)

gleek VERB to gleek means to make a joke or jibe ❑ *Nay, I can gleek upon occasion* (*A Midsummer Night's Dream* 3.1)

gust NOUN gust meant taste, desire or enjoyment. We still say that if you do something with gusto you do it with enjoyment or enthusiasm ❑ *the gust he hath in quarrelling* (*Twelfth Night* 1.3)

habit NOUN habit means clothes ❑ *You know me by my habit* (*Henry V* 3.6)

heaviness NOUN heaviness means sadness or grief ❑ *So sorrow's heaviness doth heavier grow/For debt that bankrupt sleep doth sorrow owe* (*A Midsummer Night's Dream* 3.2)

heavy ADJ if you are heavy you are said to be sad or sorrowful ❑ *Away from light steals home my heavy son* (*Romeo and Juliet* 1.1)

hie VERB to hie meant to hurry ❑ *My husband hies him home* (*All Well That Ends Well* 4.4)

hollowly ADV if you did something hollowly you did it insincerely ❑ *If hollowly invert/What best is boded me to mischief!* (*Tempest* 3.1)

holy-water, court PHRASE if you court holy water you make empty promises, or make statements which sound good but have no real meaning ❑ *court holy-water in a dry house is better than this rain-water out o'door* (*King Lear* 3.2)

howsoever ADV howsoever was often used instead of however ❑ *But howsoever strange and admirable* (*A Midsummer Night's Dream* 5.1)

humour NOUN your humour was your mood, frame of mind or temperament ❑ *it fits my humour well* (*As You Like It* 3.2)

ill ADJ ill means bad ❑ *I must thank him only,/Let my remembrance suffer ill report* (*Antony and Cleopatra* 2.2)

indistinct ADJ inseparable or unable to see a difference ❑ *Even till we make the main and the aerial blue/An indistinct regard.* (*Othello* 2.1)

indulgence NOUN indulgence meant approval ❑ *As you from crimes would pardoned be,/Let your indulgence set me free* (*The Tempest Epilogue*)

infirmity NOUN infirmity was weakness or fraility ❑ *Be not disturbed with my infirmity* (*The Tempest* 4.1)

intelligence NOUN here intelligence means information ❑ *Pursue her; and for this intelligence/If I have thanks* (*A Midsummer Night's Dream* 1.1)

inwards NOUN inwards meant someone's internal organs ❑ *the thought whereof/Doth like a poisonous mineral gnaw my inwards* (*Othello* 2.1)

issue **1** NOUN the issue of a marriage are the children ❑ *To thine and Albany's issues,/Be this perpetual* (*King Lear* 1.1) **2** NOUN in this context issue means outcome or result ❑ *I am to pray you, not to strain my speech,/To grosser issues* (*Othello*)

kind NOUN kind here means situation or case ❑ *But in this kind, wanting your father's voice,/The other must be held the worthier.* (*A Midsummer Night's Dream* 1.1)

knave NOUN a knave was a common word for scoundrel ❑ *How absolute the knave is!* (*Hamlet* 5.1)

league NOUN A distance. A league was the distance a person could walk in one hour ❑ *From Athens is her house remote seven leagues* (*A Midsummer Night's Dream* 1.1)

lief, had as ADJ I had as lief means I should like just as much ❑ *I had as lief the town crier spoke my lines* (*Hamlet* 1.2)

livery NOUN livery was a costume, outfit, uniform usually worn by a servant ❑ *You can endure the livery of a nun* (*A Midsummer Night's Dream* 1.1)

loam NOUN loam is soil containing decayed vegetable matter and therefore good for growing crops and plants ❑ *and let him have some plaster, or some loam, or some rough-cast about him, to signify wall* (*A Midsummer Night's Dream* 3.1)

lusty ADJ lusty meant strong ❑ *and oared/Himself with his good arms in lusty stroke/To th' shore* (*The Tempest* 2.1)

maidenhead NOUN maidenhead means chastity or virginity ❑ *What I am, and what I would, are as secret as maidenhead* (*Twelfth Night* 1.5)

mark VERB mark means to note or pay attention to ❑ *Where sighs and groans,/ Are made not marked* (*Macbeth* 4.3)

marvellous ADJ very or extremely ❑ *here's a marvellous convenient place for our rehearsal* (*A Midsummer Night's Dream* 3.1)

meet ADJ right or proper ❑ *tis most meet you should* (*Macbeth* 5.1)

merely ADV completely or entirely ❑ *Love is merely a madness* (*As You Like It* 3.2)

misgraffed ADJ misgraffed is an old word for mismatched or unequal ❑ *Or else misgraffed in respect of years* (*A Midsummer Night's Dream* 1.1)

misprision NOUN a misprision meant an error or mistake ❑ *Misprision in the highest degree!* (*Twelfth Night* 1.5)

mollification NOUN mollification is appeasement or a way of preventing someone getting angry ❑ *I am to hull here a little longer. Some mollification for your giant* (*Twelfth Night* 1.5)

mouth, cold in the PHRASE a well-known saying of the time which meant to be dead ❑ *What, must our mouths be cold?* (*The Tempest* 1.1)

murmur NOUN murmur was another word for rumour or hearsay ❑ *and then 'twas fresh in murmur* (*Twelfth Night* 1.2)

murrain NOUN murrain was another word for plague, pestilence ❑ *A murrain on your monster, and the devil take your fingers!* (*The Tempest* 3.2)

neaf NOUN neaf meant fist ❑ *Give me your neaf, Monsieur Mustardseed* (*A Midsummer Night's Dream* 4.1)

nice **1** ADJ nice had a number of meanings here it means fussy or particular ❑ *An therefore, goaded with most sharp occasions,/Which lay nice manners by, I put you to/The use of your own virtues* (*All's Well That Ends Well* 5.1) **2** ADJ nice here means critical or delicate ❑ *We're good... To set so rich a man/On the nice hazard of one doubtful hour?* (*Henry IV part 1*) **3** ADJ nice in this context means carefully accurate, fastidious ❑ *O relation/Too nice and yet too true!* (*Macbeth* 4.3) **4** ADJ trivial, unimportant ❑ *Romeo .. Bid him bethink/ How nice the quarrel was* (*Romeo and Juliet* 3.1)

nonpareil NOUN if you are nonpareil you are without equal, peerless ❑ *though you were crown'd/The nonpareil of beauty!* (*Twelfth Night* 1.5)

office NOUN office here means business or work ❑ *Speak your office* (*Twelfth Night* 1.5)

outsport VERB outsport meant to overdo ❑ *Let's teach ourselves that honorable stop,/Not to outsport discretion.* (*Othello* 2.2)

owe VERB owe meant own, possess ❑ *Lend less than thou owest* (*King Lear* 1.4)

paragon **1** VERB to paragon was to surpass or excede ❑ *he hath achieved a maid/That paragons description and wild fame* (*Othello* 2.1) **2** VERB to paragon could also mean to compare with ❑ *I will give thee bloody teeth If thou with Caesar paragon again/My man of men* (*Anthony and Cleopatra* 1.5)

pate NOUN pate is another word for head ❑ *Back, slave, or I will break thy pate across* (*The Comedy of Errors* 2.1)

paunch VERB to paunch someone is to stab (usually in the stomach). Paunch is still a common word for a stomach ❑ *Batter his skull, or paunch him with a stake* (*The Tempest* 3.2)

peevish ADJ if you are peevish you are irritable or easily angered ❑ *Run after that same peevish messenger* (*Twelfth Night* 1.5)

peradventure ADV perhaps or maybe ❑ *Peradventure this is not Fortune's work* (*As You Like It* 1.2)

perforce **1** ADV by force or violently ❑ *my rights and royalties,/Plucked from my arms perforce* (*Richard II* 2.3) **2** ADV necessarily ❑ *The hearts of men, they must perforce have melted* (*Richard II* 5.2)

personage NOUN personage meant your appearance ❑ *Of what personage and years is he?* (*Twelfth Night* 1.5)

pestilence NOUN pestilience was a common word for plague or disease ❑ *Methought she purg'd the air of pestilence!* (*Twelfth Night* 1.1)

physic NOUN physic was medicine or a treatment ❑ *tis a physic/That's bitter to sweet end* (*Measure for Measure* 4.6)

place NOUN place means a person's position or rank ❑ *Sons, kinsmen, thanes,/ And you whose places are the nearest* (*Macbeth* 1.4)

post NOUN here a post means a messenger ❑ *there are twenty weak and wearied posts/Come from the north* (*Henry IV part II* 2.4)

pox NOUN pox was a word for any disease during which the victim had blisters on the skin. It was also a curse, a swear word ❑ *The pox of such antic, lisping, affecting phantasims* (*Romeo and Juliet* 2.4)

prate VERB to prate means to chatter ❑ *if thou prate of mountains* (*Hamlet* 5.1)

prattle VERB to prattle is to chatter or talk without purpose ❑ *I prattle out of fashion, and I dote In mine own comforts* (*Othello* 2.1)

precept NOUN a precept was an order or command ❑ *and my father's precepts I therein do forget.* (*The Tempest* 3.1)

present ADJ present here means immediate ❑ *We'll put the matter to the present push* (*Hamlet* 5.1)

prithee EXCLAM prithee is the equivalent of please or may I ask – a polite request ❑ *I prithee, and I'll pay thee bounteously* (*Twelfth Night* 1.2)

prodigal NOUN a prodigal is someone who wastes or squanders money ❑ *he's a very fool, and a prodigal* (*Twelfth Night* 1.3)

purpose NOUN purpose is used here to mean intention ❑ *understand my purposes aright* (*King Lear* 1.4)

quaff VERB quaff was a common word which meant to drink heavily or take a big drink ❑ *That quaffing and drinking will undo you* (*Twelfth Night* 1.3)

quaint **1** ADJ clever, ingenious ❑ *with a quaint device* (*The Tempest* 3.3) **2** ADJ cunning ❑ *I'll... tell quaint lies* (*Merchant of Venice* 3.4) **3** ADJ pretty, attractive ❑ *The clamorous owl, that nightly hoots and wonders/At our quaint spirit* (*A Midsummer Night's Dream* 2.2)

quoth VERB an old word which means say ❑ *Tis dinner time.' quoth I* (*The Comedy of Errors* 2.1)

rack NOUN a rack described clouds or a cloud formation ❑ *And, like this insubstantial pageant faded,/Leave not a rack behind* (*The Tempest* 4.1)

rail VERB to rant or swear at. It is still used occasionally today ❑ *Why do I rail on thee* (*Richard II* 5.5)

rate NOUN rate meant estimate, opinion ❑ *My son is lost, and, in my rate, she too* (*The Tempest* 2.1)

recreant NOUN recreant is an old word which means coward ❑ *Come, recreant, come, thou child* (*A Midsummer Night's Dream* 3.2)

remembrance NOUN remembrance is used here to mean memory or recollection ❑ *our remembrances of days foregone* (*All's Well That Ends Well* 1.3)

resolute ADJ firm or not going to change your mind ❑ *You are resolute, then?* (*Twelfth Night* 1.5)

revels NOUN revels means celebrations or a party ❑ *Our revels now are ended* (*The Tempest* 4.1)

rough-cast NOUN a mixture of lime and gravel (sometimes shells too) for use on an outer wall ❑ *and let him have some plaster, or some loam, or some rough-cast about him, to signify wall* (*A Midsummer Night's Dream* 3.1)

sack NOUN sack was another word for wine ❑ *My man-monster hath drowned his tongue in sack.* (*The Tempest* 3.2)

sad ADJ in this context sad means serious, grave ❑ *comes me the Prince and Claudio... in sad conference* (*Much Ado About Nothing* 1.3)

sampler NOUN a piece of embroidery, which often showed the family tree ❑ *Both on one sampler, sitting on one cushion* (*A Midsummer Night's Dream* 3.2)

saucy ADJ saucy means rude ❑ *I heard you were saucy at my gates* (*Twelfth Night* 1.5)

schooling NOUN schooling means advice ❑ *I have some private schooling for you both.* (*A Midsummer Night's Dream* 1.1)

seething ADJ seething in this case means boiling – we now use seething when we are very angry ❑ *Lovers and madmen have such seething brains* (*A Midsummer Night's Dream* 5.1)

semblative ADJ semblative means resembling or looking like ❑ *And all is semblative a woman's part.* (*Twelfth Night* 1.4)

several ADJ several here means separate or different ❑ *twenty several messengers* (*Anthony and Cleopatra* 1.5)

shrew NOUN An annoying person or someone who makes you cross ❑ *Bless you, fair shrew.* (*Twelfth Night* 1.3)

shroud VERB to shroud is to hide or shelter ❑ *I will here, shroud till the dregs of the storm be past* (*The Tempest* 2.2)

sickleman NOUN a sickleman was someone who used a sickle to harvest crops ❑ *You sunburnt sicklemen, of August weary* (*The Tempest* 4.1)

soft ADV soft here means wait a moment or stop ❑ *But, soft, what nymphs are these* (*A Midsummer Night's Dream* 4.1)

something ADV something here means somewhat or rather ❑ *Be something scanter of your maiden presence* (*Hamlet* 1.3)

sooth NOUN truly ❑ *Yes, sooth; and so do you* (*A Midsummer Night's Dream* 3.2)

spleen NOUN spleen means fury or anger ❑ *That, in a spleen, unfolds both heaven and earth* (*A Midsummer Night's Dream* 1.1)

sport NOUN sport means recreation or entertainment ❑ *I see our wars/ Will turn unto a peaceful comic sport* (*Henry VI part I* 2.2)

strain NOUN a strain is a tune or a musical phrase ❑ *and so die/That strain again! it had a dying fall* (*Twelfth Night* 1.1)

suffer VERB in this context suffer means perish or die ❑ *but an islander that hath lately suffered by a thunderbolt.* (*The Tempest* 2.2)

suit NOUN a suit is a petition, request or proposal (marriage) ❑ *Because she will admit no kind of suit* (*Twelfth Night* 1.2)

sup VERB to sup is to have supper ❑ *Go know of Cassio where he supped tonight* (*Othello* 5.1)

surfeit NOUN a surfeit is an amount which is too large ❑ *If music be the food of love, play on;/Give me excess of it, that, surfeiting,/The appetite may sicken* (*Twelfth Night* 1.1)

swain NOUN a swain is a suitor or person who wants to marry ❑ *take this transformed scalp/From off the head of this Athenian swain* (*A Midsummer Night's Dream* 4.1)

thereto ADV thereto meant also ❑ *If she be black, and thereto have a wit* (*Othello* 2.1)

throstle NOUN a throstle was a name for a song-bird ❑ *The throstle with his note so true* (*A Midsummer Night's Dream* 3.1)

tidings NOUN tidings meant news ❑ *that upon certain tidings now arrived, importing the mere perdition of the Turkish fleet* (*Othello* 2.2)

transgress VERB if you transgress you break a moral law or rule of behaviour ❑ *Virtue that transgresses is but patched with sin* (*Twelfth Night* 1.5)

troth, by my PHRASE this phrase means I swear or in truth or on my word ❑ *By my troth, Sir Toby, you must come in earlier o' nights* (*Twelfth Night* 1.3)

trumpery NOUN trumpery means things that look expensive but are worth nothing (often clothing) ❑ *The trumpery in my house, go bring it hither/For stale catch these thieves* (*The Tempest* 4.1)

twink NOUN In the wink of an eye or no time at all ❑ *Ay, with a twink* (*The Tempest* 4.1)

undone ADJ if something or someone is undone they are ruined, destroyed, brought down ❑ *You have undone a man of fourscore three* (*The Winter's Tale* 4.4)

varlets NOUN varlets were villains or ruffians ❑ *Say again: where didst thou leave these varlets?* (*The Tempest* 4.1)

vaward NOUN the vaward is an old word for the vanguard, front part or earliest ❑ *And since we have the vaward of the day* (*A Midsummer Night's Dream* 4.1)

visage NOUN face ❑ *when Phoebe doth behold/Her silver visage in the watery glass* (*A Midsummer Night's Dream* 1.1)

voice NOUN voice means vote ❑ *He has our voices* (*Coriolanus* 2.3)

waggish ADJ waggish means playful ❑ *As waggish boys in game themselves forswear* (*A Midsummer Night's Dream* 1.1)

wane VERB to wane is to vanish, go down or get slighter. It is most often used to describe a phase of the moon ❑ *but, O, methinks, how slow/This old moon wanes* (*A Midsummer Night's Dream* 1.1)

want VERB to want means to lack or to be without ❑ *a beast that wants discourse of reason/Would have mourned longer* (*Hamlet* 1.2)

warrant VERB to assure, promise, guarantee ❑ *I warrant your grace* (*As You Like It* 1.2)

welkin NOUN welkin is an old word for the sky or the heavens ❑ *The starry welkin cover thou anon/With drooping fog as black as Acheron* (*A Midsummer Night's Dream* 3.2)

wench NOUN wench is an old word for a girl ❑ *Well demanded, wench* (*The Tempest* 1.2)

whence ADV from where ❑ *Whence came you, sir?* (*Twelfth Night* 1.5)

wherefore ADV why ❑ *Wherefore, sweetheart? what's your metaphor?* (*Twelfth Night* 1.3)

wide-chopped ADJ if you were wide-chopped you were big-mouthed ❑ *This wide-chopped rascal* (*The Tempest* 1.1)

wight NOUN wight is an old word for person or human being ❑ *She was a wight, if ever such wight were* (*Othello* 2.1)

wit NOUN wit means intelligence or wisdom ❑ *thou didst conclude hairy men plain dealers, without wit* (*The Comedy of Errors* 2.2)

wits NOUN wits mean mental sharpness ❑ *we that have good wits have much to answer for* (*As You Like It* 4.1)

wont ADJ to wont is to be in the habit of doing something regularly ❑ *When were you wont to use my sister thus?* (*The Comedy of Errors* 2.2)

wooer NOUN a wooer is a suitor, someone who is hoping to marry ❑ *and of a foolish knight that you brought in one night here to be her wooer* (*Twelfth Night* 1.3)

wot VERB wot is an old word which means know or learn ❑ *for well I wot/Thou runnest before me* (*A Midsummer Night's Dream* 3.2)

Text Messaging and Emoticons

Texting Abbreviations

1	used to replace "*-one*": *NE1* = anyone
2	**to** or **too**: *it's up 2* U = it's up to you; *me 2* = me too used to replace "**to-**": *2day* = today
2DAY	**today**
2MORO	**tomorrow**
2NITE	**tonight**
4	**for**: *4* U = for you used to replace "**-fore**": *B4* = before
411	**information**: *TNX 4 the 411*
8	used to replace "**-ate**" or "**-eat**": *GR8* = great; *C U L8R* = see you later
86	discard, get rid of:
AFAIK	**as far as I know**
B	**be**: used to replace "**be-**" in other words: *B4* = before
B4	**before**
B4N	**bye for now**
BRB	**be right back**
BTW	**by the way**
C	**see**: *C U 2moro* = see you tomorrow
CID	**consider it done**
CU	**see you**
CUL8R	**call you later**
D8	**date**
EZ	**easy**
FWIW	**for what it's worth**: used for saying that someone may or may not be interested in what you have to say
FYI	**for your information**: used as a way of introducing useful information
GR8	**great**
G2G	**got to go**
HHIS	**hanging head in shame**: used for showing that you are embarassed
IB	**I'm back**
IYSS	**if you say so**
K	**OK**
L8	**late**
L8R	**later**: *CUL8R* =see you later
LOL	**laughing out loud**: used for showing that you think something is funny
MSG	**message**
MYOB	**mind your own business**: for telling people not to ask questions about something that you do not want them to know about
NE	**any**
NE1	**anyone**
NO1	**no one**
NETHING	**anything**
OIC	**Oh, I see**
OTOH	**on the other hand**
PCM	**please call me**
PLS	**please**
prolly	**probably**
R	**are**: *RU free 2nite* = Are you free tonight?
RUCMNG	**Are you coming?**
RUOK?	**Are you OK?**
SPK	**speak**
SRY	**sorry**
THNQ	**thank you**: *THNQ for visiting my home page.*
THX/TX	**thanks**: *THX 4 the info.*
TTUL/TTYL	**talk to you later**
U	**you**: *CUL8R* = see you later
URW	**You're welcome.**
W8	**wait**
WAN2	**want to**
WRK	**work**
XLNT	**excellent**
YR	**your**
ZZZZ	**sleeping**

EMOTICONS HORIZONTAL →

:-)	smiling; agreeing
:-D	laughing
|-)	hee hee
|-D	ho ho
‘-) or ;-)	winking; just kidding
:*)	clowning
:-(	frowning; sad
:(	sad
:’-(	crying and really sad
>:-< or :-||	angry
:-@	screaming
:-V	shouting
:-p or :-r	sticking tongue out
|-O	yawning
: *	kiss
((((name))))	hug
@-{----	rose
<3	heart
</3	broken heart

EMOTICONS VERTICAL ↓

(^_^)	smiling
(`_^) or (^_~)	winking
(>_<)	angry, or ouch
(-_-)zzz	sleeping
\(^o^)/	very excited (raising hands)
(-_-;) or (^_^’)	nervous, or sweatdrop (embarrassed; semicolon can be repeated)
d-_-b title.mp3	listening to music, labeling title afterwards
\m/	rocker fingers
\m/(>_<)\m/	rocker dude

Defining Vocabulary

a
abandon
ability
able
abortion
about
above
abroad
absence
absolute
absolutely
abuse
academic
accept
acceptable
accepted
access
accident
accompany
accord
according to
account
accurate
accuse
achieve
achievement
acid
acknowledge
acquire
acquisition
acre
across
act
action
active
activist
activity
actor
actress
actual
actually
ad
add
addition
address
adequate
adjust
administration
admire
admit
adopt
adult
advance
advanced
advantage
advertise
advice
advise
adviser
advocate
affair
affect
afford
afraid
African
after
afternoon
afterwards
again
against
age
agency
agenda
agent
aggressive
ago
agree
agreement
agriculture
ahead
ahead of
aid
AIDS
aim
air
aircraft
air force
airline
airport
alarm
album
alcohol
alert
alive
all
allegation
alliance
allied
allow
all right
ally
almost
alone
along
alongside
already
also
alter
alternative
although
altogether
always
amateur
amazing
ambassador
ambition
amendment
American
amid
among
amount
analysis
analyst
ancient
and
anger
angle
angry
animal
anniversary
announce
announcement
annual
another
answer
antique
anxiety
anxious
any
anybody
anyone
anything
anyway
anywhere
apart
apartheid
apartment
apparent
apparently
appeal
appear
appearance
apple
application
apply
appoint
appointment
appreciate
approach
appropriate
approval
approve
April
area
argue
argument
arise
arm
armed
armed forces
army
around
arrange
arrangement
arrest
arrival
arrive
art
article
artist
as
Asian
aside
ask
aspect
assault
assembly
assess
asset
assist
assistance
assistant
associate
association
assume
assumption
assured
at
athlete
atmosphere
attach
attack
attempt
attend
attention
attitude
attorney
attract
attractive
auction
audience
August
aunt
author
authority
automatic
autumn
available
average
avoid
await
award
aware
away
awful

baby
back
background
backing
bad
badly
bag
bake
balance
ball
ballot
ban
band
bank
banker
banking
bar
bare
barely
bargain
barrel
barrier
base
baseball
basic
basically
basis
bass
bat
bath
bathroom
battle
bay
be
beach
bean
bear
bearing
beat
beautiful
beauty
because
become
bed
bedroom
beer
before
begin
beginning
behalf
behave
behaviour
behind
being
belief
believe
bell
belong
below
belt
bend
beneath
benefit
beside
besides
best
bet
better
between
beyond
bid
big
bike
bill
billion
bird
birth
birthday
bit
bite
bitter
black
blame
blast
blind
block
blood
bloody
blow

blue
board
boat
body
boil
bomb
bond
bone
book
boom
boost
boot
border
bore
born
borrow
boss
both
bother
bottle
bottom
bound
bowl
box
boy
brain
branch
brand
brave
bread
break
breakfast
breast
breath
breathe
breed
bridge
brief
bright
brilliant
bring
British
broad
broadcast
broker
brother
brown
brush
budget
build
building
bunch
burden
burn
burst
bury
bus
business
businessman
busy
but
butter
button
buy
by
bye

cabinet
cable
cake
call
calm
camera
camp
campaign
can
cancel
cancer
candidate
cap
capable
capacity
capital
captain
caption
capture
car
carbon
card
care
career
careful
caring
carrier
carry
case
cash
cast
castle
casualty
cat
catch
category
Catholic
cause
cautious
cave
CD
cease
ceasefire
celebrate
cell
central
centre
century
ceremony
certain
certainly
chain
chair
chairman
challenge
chamber
champion
championship
chance
change
channel
chaos
chapter
character
characteristic
charge
charity
chart
charter
chase
chat
cheap
check
cheer
cheese
chemical
chest
chicken
chief
child
childhood
chip
chocolate
choice
choose
chop
Christian
Christmas
church
cigarette
cinema
circle
circuit
circumstance
cite
citizen
city
civil
civilian
civil rights
civil war
claim
clash
class
classic
classical
clean
clear
clever
client
climate
climb
clinic
clock
close
clothes
clothing
cloud
club
coach
coal
coalition
coast
coat
code
coffee
cold
collapse
colleague
collect
collection
collective
college
colonel
colour
coloured
column
combat
combination
combine
come
comedy
comfort
comfortable
coming
command
commander
comment
commentator
commerce
commercial
commission
commissioner
commit
commitment
committee
common
communicate
communication
communist
community
company
compare
compared
comparison
compensation
compete
competition
competitive
competitor
complain
complaint
complete
complex
complicated
component
comprehensive
compromise
computer
concede
concentrate
concentration
concept
concern
concert
concession
conclude
conclusion
concrete
condemn
condition
conduct
conference
confidence
confident
confirm
conflict
confront
confrontation
Congress
connection
conscious
consciousness
consequence
conservative
consider
considerable
consideration
considering
consist
consistent
constant
constitution
construction
consult
consultant
consumer
contact
contain
contemporary
content
contest
context
continent
continue
contract
contrast
contribute
contribution
control
controversial
controversy
convention
conventional
conversation
convert
convict
conviction
convince
cook
cooking
cool
co-operate
cope
copy
core
corner
corporate

corporation
correct
correspondent
corruption
cost
cottage
cotton
cough
could
council
counsel
count
counter
counterpart
country
countryside
county
coup
couple
courage
course
court
cousin
cover
coverage
cow
crack
craft
crash
crazy
cream
create
creative
credit
crew
cricket
crime
criminal
crisis
critic
critical
criticism
criticize
crop
cross
crowd
crown
crucial
cruise
cry
crystal
cue
cultural
culture
cup
cure
curious
currency
current
curtain
customer
cut
cutting
cycle

dad
daily
damage
dance
danger
dangerous
dare
dark
data
date
daughter
day
dead
deadline
deal
dear
death
debate
debt
debut
decade
December
decide
decision
deck
declaration
declare
decline
decorate
deep
defeat
defence
defend
deficit
define
definitely
definition
degree
delay
delegate
delegation
deliberate
delight
delighted
deliver
delivery
demand
democracy
democrat
democratic
demonstrate
deny
department
departure
depend
deposit
depression
depth
deputy
describe
description
desert
deserve
design
designer
desire
desk
desperate
despite
destroy
detail
detailed
detective
determine
determined
develop
development
device
dialogue
diary
die
diet
difference
different
difficult
difficulty
dig
dinner
diplomat
diplomatic
direct
direction
director
dirty
disappear
disappointed
disaster
discipline
discount
discover
discovery
discuss
discussion
disease
dish
dismiss
display
dispute
distance
distribution
district
divide
dividend
division
divorce
do
doctor
document
dog
dollar
domestic
dominate
done
door
double
doubt
down
dozen
Dr
draft
drag
drain
drama
dramatic
draw
dream
dress
dressed
drift
drink
drive
drop
drug
drum
dry
due
dump
during
dust
duty

each
eager
ear
earlier
early
earn
earnings
earth
ease
easily
east
eastern
easy
eat
echo
economic
economics
economist
economy
edge
edit
edition
editor
editorial
education
effect
effective
efficient
effort
egg
eight
eighteen
eighteenth
eighth
eightieth
eighty
either
elderly
elect
election
electoral
electric
electricity
electronic
elegant
element
eleven
eleventh
eliminate
else
elsewhere
embassy
emerge
emergency
emotion
emotional
emphasis
emphasize
empire
employ
employee
employer
employment
empty
enable
encounter
encourage
end
enemy
energy
engage
engine
engineer
engineering
English
enhance
enjoy
enormous
enough
ensure
enter
enterprise
entertain
entertainment
enthusiasm
entire
entirely
entitle
entrance
entry
environment
equal
equally
equipment
equivalent
era
error
escape
especially

essential
essentially
establish
establishment
estate
estimate
etc
ethnic
EU
European
European Union
even
evening
event
eventually
ever
every
everybody
everyone
everything
everywhere
evidence
evil
exact
exactly
examination
examine
example
excellent
except
exception
excerpt
excess
exchange
exchange rate
exciting
excuse
execute
executive
exercise
exhaust
exhibition
exile
exist
existence
existing
expand
expect
expectation
expense
expensive
experience
experiment
expert
explain
explanation
explode
exploit
explore
explosion
export
expose
exposure
express
expression
extend
extensive
extent
extra
extraordinary
extreme
eye

fabric
face
facility
fact
faction
factor
factory
fade
fail
failure
fair
fairly
faith
fall
false
familiar
family
famous
fan
fancy
fantasy
far
fare
farm
farmer
fashion
fast
fat
fate
father
fault
favour
favourite
fear
feature
February
federal
federation
fee
feed
feel
feeling
fellow
female
fence
festival
few
field
fierce
fifteen
fifteenth
fifth
fiftieth
fifty
fight
fighter
figure
file
fill
film
final
finally
finance
financial
find
fine
finger
finish
fire
firm
first
fiscal
fish
fishing
fit
five
fix
fixed
flag
flash
flat
flavour
flee
fleet
flexible
flight
float
flood
floor
flow
flower
fly
focus
fold
folk
follow
following
food
fool
foot
football
for
force
forecast
foreign
foreigner
forest
forget
form
form
formal
former
formula
forth
fortieth
fortune
forty
forward
found
foundation
founder
four
fourteen
fourteenth
fourth
frame
fraud
free
freedom
freeze
frequent
fresh
Friday
friend
friendly
friendship
from
front
fruit
frustrate
fry
fuel
fulfil
full
fully
fun
function
fund
fundamental
funny
furniture
further
future

gain
gallery
game
gang
gap
garden
gas
gate
gather
gay
gear
gene
general
general election
generally
generate
generation
generous
gentle
gentleman
genuine
gesture
get
giant
gift
girl
give
give
given
glad
glance
glass
global
go
goal
god
going
gold
golden
golf
gone
good
goods
got
govern
government
governor
grab
grade
graduate
grain
grand
grant
grass
grave
great
green
grey
grip
gross
ground
group
grow
growth
guarantee
guard
guerrilla
guess
guest
guide
guilty
guitar
gun
guy

habit
hair
half
hall
halt
hand
handle
hang
happen
happy
harbour
hard
hardly

harm
hat
hate
have
he
head
headline
headquarters
heal
health
healthy
hear
hearing
heart
heat
heaven
heavy
height
helicopter
hell
hello
help
her
here
hero
herself
hi
hide
high
highlight
highly
hill
him
himself
hint
hip
hire
his
historic
historical
history
hit
HIV
hold
holder
hole
holiday
holy
home
homeless
homosexual
honest
honour
hook
hope
horror
horse
hospital
host
hostage
hot
hotel
hour

house
household
housing
how
however
huge
human
"human rights
humour
hundred
hundredth
hunt
hunter
hurt
husband

I
ice
idea
ideal
identify
identity
if
ignore
ill
illegal
illness
illustrate
image
imagination
imagine
immediate
immediately
immigrant
immigration
immune
impact
implement
implication
imply
import
important
impose
impossible
impress
impression
impressive
improve
in
inch
incident
include
including
income
increase
increasingly
incredible
indeed
independent
index
indicate
indication
individual

industrial
industry
inevitable
infect
infection
inflation
influence
inform
information
ingredient
initial
initially
initiative
injured
injury
inner
innocent
inquiry
inside
insist
inspect
inspector
install
instance
instant
instead
institute
institution
instruction
instrument
insurance
integrate
intellectual
intelligence
intelligent
intend
intense
intention
interest
interested
interesting
interim
interior
internal
international
interview
into
introduce
invasion
invest
investigate
investment
invitation
invite
involve
involved
involvement
iron
Islam
island
issue
it
item

its
itself

jacket
jail
January
jazz
jersey
jet
Jew
Jewish
job
join
joint
joke
journal
journalist
journey
joy
judge
judgment
juice
July
jump
June
junior
jury
just
justice
justify

keen
keep
key
kick
kid
kill
killer
kilometre
kind
king
kiss
kitchen
knee
knife
knock
know
knowledge

label
laboratory
labour
lack
lad
lady
lake
land
landscape
lane
language
lap
large
largely

last
late
later
latest
latter
laugh
laughter
launch
law
lawyer
lay
layer
lead
leader
leadership
leading
leaf
league
leak
lean
leap
learn
lease
least
leather
leave
lecture
left
leg
legal
legislation
lend
length
lens
lesbian
less
lesson
let
let's
letter
level
liberal
liberate
liberty
library
licence
lie
life
lift
light
like
likely
limit
limited
line
link
lip
list
listen
literary
literature
little
live

living
load
loan
lobby
local
location
lock
long
long-time
look
loose
lord
lose
loss
lost
lot
loud
love
lovely
lover
low
lower
Ltd
luck
lucky
lunch
luxury

machine
mad
magazine
magic
mail
main
mainly
maintain
major
majority
make
maker
make-up
male
man
manage
management
manager
manner
manufacture
manufacturer
many
map
march
March
margin
marine
mark
marked
market
marriage
married
marry
mask
mass
massive
master
match
mate
material
matter
maximum
may
May
maybe
mayor
me
meal
mean
meaning
means
meanwhile
measure
meat
mechanism
medal
media
medical
medicine
medium
meet
meeting
member
membership
memory
mental
mention
merchant
mere
merely
merger
mess
message
metal
method
metre
middle
middle class
Middle East
midnight
might
mild
mile
militant
military
milk
mill
million
millionth
mind
mine
minimum
minister
ministry
minor
minority
minute
mirror
miss
missile
missing
mission
mistake
mix
mixed
mixture
mm
mobile
model
moderate
modern
modest
moment
Monday
monetary
money
monitor
month
monthly
mood
moon
moral
more
moreover
morning
mortgage
most
mostly
mother
motion
motivate
motor
mount
mountain
mouth
move
movement
movie
MP
Mr
Mrs
Ms
much
mum
murder
muscle
museum
music
musical
musician
Muslim
must
mutual
my
myself
mystery
myth

name
narrow
nation
national
nationalist
native
natural
naturally
nature
naval
navy
near
nearby
nearly
neat
necessarily
necessary
neck
need
negative
negotiate
negotiation
neighbour
neither
nerve
nervous
net
network
never
nevertheless
new
newly
news
news agency
newspaper
next
nice
night
nightmare
nine
nineteen
nineteenth
ninetieth
ninety
ninth
no
nobody
nod
noise
none
no one
nor
normal
normally
north
north-east
northern
north-west
nose
not
note
noted
nothing
notice
notion
novel
November
now
nowhere
nuclear
number
numerous
nurse

object
objective
observe
observer
obtain
obvious
obviously
occasion
occasional
occupation
occupy
occur
ocean
o'clock
October
odd
of
of course
off
offence
offensive
offer
office
officer
official
often
oh
oil
okay
old
Olympic
on
once
one
one's
online
only
onto
open
opening
opera
operate
operation
operator
opinion
opponent
opportunity
oppose
opposed
opposite
opposition
opt
optimistic
option
or

orange
order
ordinary
organization
organize
organized
origin
original
other
otherwise
ought
our
ourselves
out
outcome
outline
output
outside
outstanding
over
overall
overcome
overnight
overseas
overwhelming
owe
own
owner
ownership

pace
pack
package
pact
page
pain
painful
paint
painting
pair
palace
pale
pan
panel
panic
paper
parent
park
parliament
parliamentary
part
participate
particular
particularly
partly
partner
partnership
party
pass
passage
passenger
passion
past
path
patient
pattern
pause
pay
payment
peace
peaceful
peak
peer
peg
pen
penalty
penny
pension
people
pepper
per
per cent
percentage
perfect
perform
performance
perhaps
period
permanent
permission
permit
person
personal
personality
personally
personnel
perspective
persuade
pet
phase
philosophy
phone
phone call
photo
photograph
photographer
phrase
physical
pick
picture
piece
pile
pill
pilot
pin
pink
pipe
pit
pitch
place
plain
plan
plane
planet
planning
plant
plastic
plate
platform
play
player
pleasant
please
pleased
pleasure
pledge
plenty
plot
plunge
plus
PM
pocket
poem
poet
poetry
point
point of view
pole
police
policeman
police officer
policy
political
politician
politics
poll
pollution
pool
poor
pop
popular
population
port
portrait
pose
position
positive
possibility
possible
possibly
post
pot
potato
potential
pound
pour
poverty
power
powerful
pp.
practical
practice
praise
precisely
predict
prefer
pregnant
premier
premium
preparation
prepare
prepared
presence
present
preserve
presidency
president
presidential
press
pressure
presumably
pretty
prevent
previous
previously
price
pride
priest
primary
prime
Prime Minister
prince
princess
principal
principle
print
prior
priority
prison
prisoner
private
privatize
prize
probably
problem
procedure
proceed
process
produce
product
production
profession
professional
professor
profile
profit
program
programme
progress
project
prominent
promise
promote
prompt
proof
proper
property
proportion
proposal
propose
prosecution
prospect
protect
protection
protein
protest
proud
prove
provide
province
provision
provoke
psychological
pub
public
publication
publicity
publish
publisher
publishing
pull
pump
punch
pupil
purchase
pure
purple
purpose
pursue
push
put

qualified
qualify
quality
quantity
quarter
queen
question
quick
quiet
quite
quote

race
racial
racing
radical
radio
rage
raid
rail
railway
rain
raise
rally
range
rank
rape
rapid
rare
rarely
rate
rather
rating

raw
ray
reach
react
reaction
read
reader
reading
ready
real
reality
realize
really
rear
reason
reasonable
rebel
recall
receive
recent
recently
recession
reckon
recognition
recognize
recommend
record
recording
recover
recovery
recruit
red
reduce
reduction
reel
refer
reference
referendum
reflect
reform
refugee
refuse
regard
regime
region
register
regret
regular
regulation
regulator
reject
relate
related
relation
relationship
relative
relax
release
reliable
relief
religion
religious
reluctant
rely
remain
remaining
remark
remarkable
remember
remind
remote
remove
renew
rent
repair
repeat
replace
replacement
reply
report
reporter
reporting
represent
representative
republic
republican
reputation
request
require
requirement
rescue
research
reserve
resident
resign
resignation
resist
resistance
resolution
resolve
resort
resource
respect
respond
response
responsibility
responsible
rest
restaurant
restore
result
resume
retail
retain
retire
retirement
retreat
return
reveal
revenue
reverse
review
revolution
revolutionary
reward
rhythm
rice
rich
rid
ride
rider
right
ring
riot
rise
risk
rival
river
road
rock
rocket
role
roll
romantic
roof
room
root
rose
rough
round
route
routine
row
royal
rugby
ruin
rule
ruling
rumour
run
runner
running
rural
rush

sack
sacrifice
sad
safe
safety
sail
saint
sake
salary
sale
salt
same
sample
sanction
sand
satellite
satisfied
Saturday
sauce
save
say
scale
scandal
scene
schedule
scheme
school
science
scientific
scientist
score
scream
screen
script
sea
seal
search
season
seat
second
secret
secretary
Secretary of State
section
sector
secure
security
see
seed
seek
seem
segment
seize
select
selection
self
sell
Senate
senator
send
senior
sense
sensible
sensitive
sentence
separate
September
series
serious
seriously
servant
serve
service
session
set
settle
settlement
set-up
seven
seventeen
seventeenth
seventh
seventieth
seventy
several
severe
sex
sexual
shade
shadow
shake
shall
shame
shape
shaped
share
shareholder
sharp
she
shed
sheet
shell
shelter
shift
ship
shirt
shock
shoe
shoot
shop
shopping
shore
short
shortage
shortly
short-term
shot
should
shoulder
shout
show
shut
sick
side
sigh
sight
sign
signal
significant
silence
silent
silver
similar
simple
simply
since
sing
singer
single
sink
sir
sister
sit
site
situation
six
sixteen
sixteenth
sixth

sixtieth
sixty
size
ski
skill
skin
sky
sleep
slice
slide
slight
slightly
slim
slip
slow
small
smart
smash
smell
smile
smoke
smooth
snap
snow
so
so-called
soccer
social
socialist
society
soft
software
soil
soldier
solicitor
solid
solution
solve
some
somebody
somehow
someone
something
sometimes
somewhat
somewhere
son
song
soon
sophisticated
sorry
sort
soul
sound
source
south
south-east
southern
south-west
space
spare
spark
speak
speaker
special
specialist
specialize
species
specific
specifically
spectacular
speculate
speech
speed
spell
spend
spin
spirit
spiritual
spite
split
spokesman
sponsor
sport
spot
spray
spread
spring
spur
squad
square
squeeze
stable
stadium
staff
stage
stake
stamp
stand
standard
star
stare
start
state
statement
station
statistic
status
stay
steady
steal
steam
steel
stem
step
sterling
stick
still
stimulate
stir
stock
stock exchange
stock market
stomach
stone
stop
store
storm
story
straight
strain
strange
strategic
strategy
stream
street
strength
strengthen
stress
stretch
strict
strike
striking
string
strip
stroke
strong
structure
struggle
student
studio
study
stuff
stupid
style
subject
subsequent
subsidy
substance
substantial
substitute
succeed
success
successful
such
sudden
suffer
sufficient
sugar
suggest
suggestion
suicide
suit
suitable
sum
summer
summit
sun
Sunday
super
superb
superior
supply
support
suppose
supposed
supreme
sure
surely
surface
surgery
surplus
surprise
surprised
surprising
surrender
surround
survey
survival
survive
suspect
suspend
suspicion
sustain
sweep
sweet
swim
swing
switch
symbol
sympathy
symptom
system

table
tackle
tactic
tail
take
takeover
tale
talent
talk
tall
tank
tap
tape
target
task
taste
tax
tea
teach
teaching
team
tear
technical
technique
technology
teenager
telephone
television
tell
temperature
temple
temporary
ten
tend
tendency
tennis
tension
tenth
term
terrible
territory
terrorism
terrorist
test
text
than
thank
that
the
theatre
their
them
theme
themselves
then
theory
therapy
there
therefore
these
they
thick
thin
thing
think
thinking
third
Third World
thirteen
thirteenth
thirtieth
thirty
this
thorough
those
though
thought
thousand
threat
threaten
three
throat
through
throughout
throw
Thursday
thus
ticket
tide
tie
tight
till
time
tiny
tip
tired
tissue
title
to
today
together

tomorrow
ton
tone
tonight
too
tool
tooth
top
torture
total
touch
tough
tour
tourist
tournament
towards
tower
town
toy
trace
track
trade
trader
tradition
traffic
tragedy
trail
train
transaction
transfer
transform
transition
transport
trap
travel
traveller
treat
treatment
treaty
tree
tremendous
trend
trial
trick
trigger
trip
triumph
troop
trouble
truck
true
truly
trust
truth
try
tube
Tuesday
tune
tunnel
turn
TV
twelfth
twelve
twentieth
twenty
twice
twin
twist
two
type
typical

ultimate
ultimately
unable
uncle
under
undermine
understand
understanding
unemployment
unexpected
unfair
unfortunately
unhappy
unidentified
uniform
union
unique
unit
United Nations
unity
universe
university
unknown
unless
unlike
unlikely
until
unusual
up
upon
upper
upset
urban
urge
urgent
us
use
used
useful
user
usual
usually

valley
valuable
value
van
variety
various
vary
vast
vegetable
vehicle
venture
venue
verdict
version
very
vessel
veteran
via
vice
victim
victimize
victory
video
view
village
violate
violence
violent
virus
visible
vision
visit
visitor
vital
vitamin
voice
volume
voluntary
volunteer
vote
vulnerable

wage
wait
wake
walk
wall
want
war
warm
warn
warning
wash
waste
watch
water
wave
way
we
weak
weaken
wealth
weapon
wear
weather
website
wedding
Wednesday
week
weekend
weekly
weigh
weight
welcome
welfare
well
well-known
west
western
wet
what
whatever
wheel
when
whenever
where
whereas
whether
which
while
whilst
whip
whisper
white
who
whole
whom
whose
why
wide
widespread
wife
wild
will
willing
win
wind
window
wine
wing
winner
winning
winter
wipe
wire
wise
wish
with
withdraw
withdrawal
within
without
witness
woman
wonder
wonderful
wood
wooden
word
work
worker
working
world
world war
worldwide
worry
worth
would
wound
wrap
write
writer
writing
written
wrong
WWW

X

yacht
yard
yeah
year
yellow
yes
yesterday
yet
yield
you
young
youngster
your
yours
yourself
youth

zone

Academic Word List

This list contains the head words of the families in the Academic Word List. The numbers indicate the sublist of the Academic Word List, with Sublist 1 containing the most frequent words, Sublist 2 the next most frequent and so on. For example, *abandon* and its family members are in Sublist 8 of the Academic Word List.

abandon	8
abstract	6
academy	5
access	4
accommodate	9
accompany	8
accumulate	8
accurate	6
achieve	2
acknowledge	6
acquire	2
adapt	7
adequate	4
adjacent	10
adjust	5
administrate	2
adult	7
advocate	7
affect	2
aggregate	6
aid	7
albeit	10
allocate	6
alter	5
alternative	3
ambiguous	8
amend	5
analogy	9
analyze	1
annual	4
anticipate	9
apparent	4
append	8
appreciate	8
approach	1
appropriate	2
approximate	4
arbitrary	8
area	1
aspect	2
assemble	10
assess	1
assign	6
assist	2
assume	1
assure	9
attach	6
attain	9
attitude	4
attribute	4
author	6
authority	1
automate	8
available	1
aware	5
behalf	9
benefit	1
bias	8
bond	6
brief	6
bulk	9
capable	6
capacity	5
category	2
cease	9
challenge	5
channel	7
chapter	2
chart	8
chemical	7
circumstance	3
cite	6
civil	4
clarify	8
classic	7
clause	5
code	4
coherent	9
coincide	9
collapse	10
colleague	10
commence	9
comment	3
commission	2
commit	4
commodity	8
communicate	4
community	2
compatible	9
compensate	3
compile	10
complement	8
complex	2
component	3
compound	5
comprehensive	7
comprise	7
compute	2
conceive	10
concentrate	4
concept	1
conclude	2
concurrent	9
conduct	2
confer	4
confine	9
confirm	7
conflict	5
conform	8
consent	3
consequent	2
considerable	3
consist	1
constant	3
constitute	1
constrain	3
construct	2
consult	5
consume	2
contact	5
contemporary	8
context	1
contract	1
contradict	8
contrary	7
contrast	4
contribute	3
controversy	9
convene	3
converse	9
convert	7
convince	10
cooperate	6
coordinate	3
core	3
corporate	3
correspond	3
couple	7
create	1
credit	2
criteria	3
crucial	8
culture	2
currency	8
cycle	4
data	1
debate	4
decade	7
decline	5
deduce	3
define	1
definite	7
demonstrate	3
denote	8
deny	7
depress	10
derive	1
design	2
despite	4
detect	8
deviate	8
device	9
devote	9
differentiate	7
dimension	4
diminish	9
discrete	5
discriminate	6
displace	8
display	6
dispose	7
distinct	2
distort	9
distribute	1
diverse	6
document	3
domain	6
domestic	4
dominate	3
draft	5
drama	8
duration	9
dynamic	7
economy	1

edit	6
element	2
eliminate	7
emerge	4
emphasis	3
empirical	7
enable	5
encounter	10
energy	5
enforce	5
enhance	6
enormous	10
ensure	3
entity	5
environment	1
equate	2
equip	7
equivalent	5
erode	9
error	4
establish	1
estate	6
estimate	1
ethic	9
ethnic	4
evaluate	2
eventual	8
evident	1
evolve	5
exceed	6
exclude	3
exhibit	8
expand	5
expert	6
explicit	6
exploit	8
export	1
expose	5
external	5
extract	7
facilitate	5
factor	1
feature	2
federal	6
fee	6
file	7
final	2
finance	1
finite	7
flexible	6
fluctuate	8
focus	2
format	9
formula	1
forthcoming	10
foundation	7
found	9
framework	3
function	1
fund	3
fundamental	5
furthermore	6
gender	6
generate	5
generation	5
globe	7
goal	4
grade	7
grant	4
guarantee	7
guideline	8
hence	4
hierarchy	7
highlight	8
hypothesis	4
identical	7
identify	1
ideology	7
ignorance	6
illustrate	3
image	5
immigrate	3
impact	2
implement	4
implicate	4
implicit	8
imply	3
impose	4
incentive	6
incidence	6
incline	10
income	1
incorporate	6
index	6
indicate	1
individual	1
induce	8
inevitable	8
infer	7
infrastructure	8
inherent	9
inhibit	6
initial	3
initiate	6
injure	2
innovate	7
input	6
insert	7
insight	9
inspect	8
instance	3
institute	2
instruct	6
integral	9
integrate	4
integrity	10
intelligence	6
intense	8
interact	3
intermediate	9
internal	4
interpret	1
interval	6
intervene	7
intrinsic	10
invest	2
investigate	4
invoke	10
involve	1
isolate	7
issue	1
item	2
job	4
journal	2
justify	3
label	4
labor	1
layer	3
lecture	6
legal	1
legislate	1
levy	10
liberal	5
license	5
likewise	10
link	3
locate	3
logic	5
maintain	2
major	1
manipulate	8
manual	9
margin	5
mature	9
maximize	3
mechanism	4
media	7
mediate	9
medical	5
medium	9
mental	5
method	1
migrate	6
military	9
minimal	9
minimize	8
minimum	6
ministry	6
minor	3
mode	7
modify	5
monitor	5
motive	6
mutual	9
negate	3
network	5
neutral	6
nevertheless	6
nonetheless	10
norm	9
normal	2
notion	5
notwithstanding	10
nuclear	8
objective	5
obtain	2
obvious	4
occupy	4
occur	1
odd	10
offset	8
ongoing	10
option	4
orient	5
outcome	3
output	4

overall	4
overlap	9
overseas	6
panel	10
paradigm	7
paragraph	8
parallel	4
parameter	4
participate	2
partner	3
passive	9
perceive	2
percent	1
period	1
persist	10
perspective	5
phase	4
phenomenon	7
philosophy	3
physical	3
plus	8
policy	1
portion	9
pose	10
positive	2
potential	2
practitioner	8
precede	6
precise	5
predict	4
predominant	8
preliminary	9
presume	6
previous	2
primary	2
prime	5
principal	4
principle	1
prior	4
priority	7
proceed	1
process	1
professional	4
prohibit	7
project	4
promote	4
proportion	3
prospect	8
protocol	9
psychology	5
publication	7
publish	3
purchase	2
pursue	5
qualitative	9
quote	7
radical	8
random	8
range	2
ratio	5
rational	6
react	3
recover	6
refine	9
regime	4
region	2
register	3
regulate	2
reinforce	8
reject	5
relax	9
release	7
relevant	2
reluctance	10
rely	3
remove	3
require	1
research	1
reside	2
resolve	4
resource	2
respond	1
restore	8
restrain	9
restrict	2
retain	4
reveal	6
revenue	5
reverse	7
revise	8
revolution	9
rigid	9
role	1
route	9
scenario	9
schedule	8
scheme	3
scope	6
section	1
sector	1
secure	2
seek	2
select	2
sequence	3
series	4
sex	3
shift	3
significant	1
similar	1
simulate	7
site	2
so-called	10
sole	7
somewhat	7
source	1
specific	1
specify	3
sphere	9
stable	5
statistic	4
status	4
straightforward	10
strategy	2
stress	4
structure	1
style	5
submit	7
subordinate	9
subsequent	4
subsidy	6
substitute	5
successor	7
sufficient	3
sum	4
summary	4
supplement	9
survey	2
survive	7
suspend	9
sustain	5
symbol	5
tape	6
target	5
task	3
team	9
technical	3
technique	3
technology	3
temporary	9
tense	8
terminate	8
text	2
theme	8
theory	1
thereby	8
thesis	7
topic	7
trace	6
tradition	2
transfer	2
transform	6
transit	5
transmit	7
transport	6
trend	5
trigger	9
ultimate	7
undergo	10
underlie	6
undertake	4
uniform	8
unify	9
unique	7
utilize	6
valid	3
vary	1
vehicle	8
version	5
via	8
violate	9
virtual	8
visible	7
vision	9
visual	8
volume	3
voluntary	7
welfare	5
whereas	5
whereby	10
widespread	8

This list shows the spelling and pronunciation of geographical names. If a country has different words for the country, adjective, and person, these are all shown. Inclusion in this list does not imply status as a sovereign nation.

Af|ghani|stan /æfgænɪstæn/; Af|ghan, Af|ghani /æfgæn/, /æfgæni, -gɑni/

Af|ri|ca /æfrɪkə/; Af|ri|can /æfrɪkən/

Al|ba|nia /ælbeɪniə/; Al|ba|ni|an /ælbeɪniən/

Al|ge|ria /ældʒɪəriə/; Al|ge|ri|an /ældʒɪəriən/

An|dor|ra /ændɔrə/; An|dor|ran /ændɔrən/

An|go|la /æŋgoʊlə/; An|go|lan /æŋgoʊlən/

Ant|arc|ti|ca /æntɑrktɪkə, -ɑrtɪ-/; Ant|arc|tic /æntɑrktɪk, -ɑrtɪk/

An|ti|gua and Bar|bu|da /æntigə ən bɑrbudə/; An|ti|guan, Bar|bu|dan /æntigən/, /bɑrbudən/

(the) Arc|tic Ocean /(ði) ɑrktɪk oʊʃən, ɑrtɪk/; Arc|tic /ɑrktɪk, ɑrtɪk/

Ar|gen|ti|na /ɑrdʒəntinə/; Ar|gen|tine, Ar|gen|tin|ian, or Ar|gen|tin|ean /ɑrdʒəntin, -taɪn/, /ɑrdʒəntɪniən/

Ar|me|nia /ɑrminiə/; Ar|me|nian /ɑrminiən/

A|sia /eɪʒə/; A|sian /eɪʒən/

(the) Atlantic Ocean /(ði) ætlæntɪk oʊʃən/

Aus|tral|ia /ɔstreɪlyə/; Aus|tral|ian /ɔstreɪlyən/

Aus|tria /ɔstriə/; Aus|trian /ɔstriən/

Azer|bai|jan /æzərbaɪdʒɑn, ɑzər-/; Azer|bai|jani, Azeri /æzərbaɪdʒɑni, ɑzər-/, /əzɛri/

(the) Ba|ha|mas /(ðə) bəhɑməz/; Ba|ha|mian /bəheɪmiən, -hɑ-/

Bah|rain /bareɪn/; Bah|raini /bareɪni/

Ban|gla|desh /bɑŋglədɛʃ, bæŋ-/; Ban|gla|deshi /bɑŋglədɛʃi, bæŋ-/

Bar|ba|dos /bɑrbeɪdoʊs/; Bar|ba|dian /bɑrbeɪdiən/

Bela|rus /bɛlərus, byɛl-/; Bela|rus|sian /bɛlərʌʃən, byɛl-/

Bel|gium /bɛldʒəm/; Bel|gian /bɛldʒən/

Be|lize /bəliz/; Be|liz|ean /bəliziən/

Be|nin /bənin/; Be|ni|nese /bɛnɪniz/

Bhu|tan /butɑn, -tæn/; Bhu|tani, Bhu|ta|nese /butɑni, -tæni/, /butᵊniz/

Bo|liv|ia /bəlɪviə/; Bo|liv|ian /bəlɪviən/

Bos|nia and Her|ze|go|vina /bɒzniə ən hɛrtsəgoʊvinə/; Bosnian, Her|ze|go|vinian /bɒzniən/, /hɛrtsəgoʊviniən/

Bot|swana /bɒtswɑnə/; Mot|swana (person), Bat|swana (people) /mɒtswɑnə/, /bɑtswɑnə/

Bra|zil /brəzɪl/; Bra|zil|ian /brəzɪlyən/

Bru|nei Da|rus|salam /brunaɪ dɑrusɑləm/; Bru|nei, Bru|nei|an /brunaɪ/, /brunaɪən/

Bul|garia /bʌlgɛəriə/; Bul|gar|ian /bʌlgɛəriən/

Bur|kina Faso /bərkinə fɑsoʊ/; Bur|kin|abe, Bur|kinese /bɜrkɪnɑbeɪ/, /bɜrkɪniz/

Bur|ma--See Myanmar /bɜrmə/; Bur|mese—/bɜrmiz/

Bu|rundi /burʊndi/; Bu|run|dian /burʊndiən/

Cam|bo|dia /kæmboʊdiə/; Cam|bo|dian /kæmboʊdiən/

Cam|eroon /kæmərun/; Cam|eroo|nian /kæməruniən/

Can|ada /kænədə/; Ca|na|dian /kəneɪdiən/

Cape Verde /keɪp vɜrd/; Cape Ver|dean /keɪp vɜrdiən/

Cen|tral Af|ri|can Re|pub|lic /sɛntrəl æfrɪkən rɪpʌblɪk/; Cen|tral Af|ri|can /sɛntrəl æfrɪkən/

Chad /tʃæd/; Chad|ian /tʃædiən/

Chi|le /tʃɪli, -leɪ/; Chil|ean /tʃɪliən, tʃɪleɪ-/

Chi|na /tʃaɪnə/; Chi|nese /tʃaɪniz/

Co|lom|bia /kəlʌmbiə/; Co|lom|bian /kəlʌmbiən/

Co|mo|ros /kɒmərouz/; Co|mor|an /kəmɔrən/

Co|sta Ri|ca /kɒstə rikə/; Co|sta Ri|can /kɒstə rikən/

Côte d'Ivoire /koʊt divwɑr/; Ivoir|ian /ivwɑriən/

Croa|tia /kroʊeɪʃə/; Croatian /kroʊeɪʃən/

Cu|ba /kyubə/; Cu|ban /kyubən/

Cy|prus /saɪprəs/; Cyp|riot /sɪpriət/

(the) Czech Re|pub|lic /(ðə) tʃɛk rɪpʌblɪk/; Czech /tʃɛk/

Demo|cratic Re|pub|lic of the Congo, or (the) Congo /dɛməkrætɪk rɪpʌblɪk əv ðə kɒŋgoʊ/, /(ðə) kɒŋgoʊ/; Con|go|lese /kɒŋgəliz, -lis/

Den|mark /dɛnmɑrk/; Da|nish, Dane /deɪnɪʃ/, /deɪn/

Dji|bouti /dʒɪbuti/; Dji|bou|tian /dʒɪbutiən/

Domi|nica /dɒmɪnikə, dəmɪnɪkə/; Domi|ni|can /dɒmɪnikən/

(the) Do|mi|ni|can Re|pub|lic /(ðə) dəmɪnɪkən rɪpʌblɪk/ Dominican /dəmɪnɪkən/

East Ti|mor /ist timɔr/; East Ti|mor|ese /ist timɔriz/

Ecua|dor /ɛkwədɔr/; Ecua|dor|ian /ɛkwədɔriən/

Egypt /idʒɪpt/; Egyp|tian /ɪdʒɪpʃən/

El Sal|va|dor /ɛl sælvədɔr/; Sal|va|do|ran, Sal|va|do|rean /sælvədɔrən/, /sælvədɔriən/

Eng|land /ɪŋglənd/; Eng|lish /ɪŋglɪʃ/

Equi|to|rial Guinea /ɛkwɪtɔriəl gɪni/; Equi|to|rial Guin|ean, Equito|guinean /ɛkwɪtɔriəl gɪniən/, /ɛkwɪtoʊgɪniən/

Eri|trea /ɛrɪtriə/; Eri|trean /ɛrɪtriən/

Es|to|nia /estoʊniə/; Es|to|nian /ɛstoʊniən/

Ethio|pia /iθioʊpiə/; Ethio|pian /iθioʊpiən/

Eu|rope /yʊərəp/; Euro|pean /yʊərəpiən/

Fiji /fidʒi/; Fi|jian /fidʒiən, fiji-/
Fin|land /fɪnlənd/; Fin|nish, Finn, Fin|lander /fɪnɪʃ/, /fɪn/, /fɪnləndər, -lændər/
France /fræns/; French /frɛntʃ/
Ga|bon /gaboun/; Gabo|nese /gæbəniz/
(the) Gam|bia /(ðə) gæmbiə/; Gam|bian /gæmbiən/
Geor|gia /dʒɔrdʒə/; Geor|gian /dʒɔrdʒən/
Ger|many /dʒɜrməni/; Ger|man /dʒɜrmən/
Ghana /ganə/; Gha|naian /ganiən, gəneɪən/
Greece /gris/; Greek /grik/
Gre|nada /grɪneɪdə/; Gre|nadian /grɪneɪdiən/
Gua|temala /gwatəmalə/; Gua|temalan /gwatəmalən/
Guinea /gɪni/; Guin|ean /gɪniən/
Guinea-Bissau /gɪni bɪsau/; Guin|ean /gɪniən/
Guy|ana /gaɪænə, -anə/; Guy|anese /gaɪəniz/
Haiti /heɪti/; Hai|tian /heɪʃən/
Hon|du|ras /hɒnduərəs/; Hon|du|ran /hɒnduərən/
Hungary /hʌŋgəri/; Hungarian /hʌŋgɛəriən/
Ice|land /aɪslənd/; Ice|lan|dic, Ice|lander /aɪslændɪk/, /aɪsləndər, -lændər/
In|dia /ɪndiə/; In|dian /ɪndiən/
(the) In|dian Ocean /(ði) ɪndiən oʊʃən/
In|do|ne|sia /ɪndəniʒə/; In|do|ne|sian /ɪndəniʒən/
Iran /ɪran, ɪræn, aɪræn/; Ira|nian, Irani /ɪreɪniən, ɪra-, aɪreɪ-/, /ɪrani/
I|raq /ɪræk, ɪrak/; I|raqi /ɪræki, ɪraki/
Ire|land /aɪərlənd/; Ir|ish /aɪrɪʃ/
Is|rael /ɪzriəl, -reɪəl/; Is|raeli /ɪzreɪli/
Ita|ly /ɪtəli/; Ital|ian /ɪtælyən/
Ja|maica /dʒəmeɪkə/; Ja|mai|can /dʒəmeɪkən/
Ja|pan /dʒəpæn/; Japa|nese /dʒæpəniz/
Jor|dan /dʒɔrdən/; Jor|danian /dʒɔrdeɪniən/
Kaza|khstan /kazakstan, -stæn/; Kaza|khstani, Kazakh /kazakstani, -stæni/, /kazak, kəzæk/
Kenya /kɛnyə, kin-/; Ken|yan /kɛnyən, kin-/
Kiri|bati /kɪərəbati, -bæs/; I-Kiri|bati /i kɪərəbati, -bæs/
Ko|rea, South Ko|rea, North Ko|rea /kəriə, kɔ-/, /soʊθ kəriə, kɔ-/, /nɔrθ kəriə, kɔ-/; Ko|rean /kəriən, kɔ-/, /soʊθ kəriən, kɔ-/, /nɔrθ kəriən, kɔ/
Ku|wait /kuweɪt/; Ku|waiti /kuweɪti/
Kyr|gyz|stan /kɪərgɪstan, -stæn/; Kyr|gyz|stani /kɪərgɪstani, -stæni/
Laos /laoʊs, laʊs/; Lao, Laotian /laoʊ, laʊ/, /leɪoʊʃən/
Lat|via /lætviə, lat-/; Lat|vian /lætviən, lat-/
Leba|non /lɛbənən, -nɒn/; Leba|nese /lɛbəniz/
Le|so|tho /ləsoutoʊ, -sutu/ Sotho, Mo|so|tho (person), Ba|so|tho (people) /soutoʊ, sutu/, /mɔsoutoʊ, -sutu/, /basoutoʊ, -sutu/
Li|beria /laɪbɪəriə/; Li|berian /laɪbɪəriən/
Libya /lɪbiə/; Lib|yan /lɪbiən/
Liech|ten|stein /lɪktənstaɪn/; Liech|ten|stein, Liech|ten|steiner /lɪktənstaɪn/, /lɪktənstaɪnər/
Lithua|nia /lɪθueɪniə/; Lithua|nian /lɪθueɪniən/
Luxem|bourg /lʌksəmbɜrg/; Luxem|bourg, Luxem|bourger /lʌksəmbɜrg/, /lʌksəmbɜrgər/
Mac|edo|nia /mæsɪdouniə/; Mac|edo|nian /mæsɪdouniən/
Mad|agas|car /mædəgæskər/; Mada|gas|can, Mala|gasy /mædəgæskən/, /mæləgæsi/
Ma|lawi /məlawi/; Ma|la|wian /məlawiən/
Ma|lay|sia /məleɪʒə/; Ma|lay|sian /məleɪʒən/
Mal|dives /mɔldivz, -daɪvz/; Mal|div|ian /mɔldɪviən/
Mali /mali/; Ma|lian /maliən/
Malta /mɔltə/; Mal|tese /mɔltiz/
(the) Marshall Islands /(ðə) marʃəl aɪləndz/; Marshallese /marʃəliz/
Mau|ri|ta|nia /mɔrɪteɪniə/; Mau|ri|ta|nian /mɔrɪteɪniən/
Mau|ri|tius /mɔrɪʃəs/; Mau|ri|tian /mɔrɪʃən/
Mexi|co /mɛksɪkoʊ/; Mexi|can /mɛksɪkən/
Mi|cro|nesia /maɪkrəniʒə/; Mi|cro|nesian /maɪkrəniʒən/
Mol|dova /mɔldouvə/; Mol|do|van /mɔldouvən/
Mon|aco /mɒnəkoʊ/; Mon|acan, Mon|egasque /mɒnəkən/, /mɒnɪgæsk/
Mon|go|lia /mɒŋgouliə/; Mon|go|lian /mɒŋgouliən/
Mo|rocco /mərɒkoʊ/; Mo|roc|can /mərɒkən/
Mo|zam|bique /mouzæmbik, -zəm-/; Mo|zam|bi|can /mouzæmbikən, -zəm-/
Myan|mar (Burma) /myanmar (bɜrmə)/; Bur|mese /bərmiz/
Na|mibia /nəmɪbiə/; Na|mib|ian /nəmɪbiən/
Na|uru /nauru/; Na|uruan /nauruən/
Ne|pal /nəpɔl/; Nepa|lese /nɛpəliz/
(the) Nether|lands /(ðə) nɛðərləndz/; Dutch /dʌtʃ/
New Zea|land /nu zilənd/; New Zea|land, New Zea|lander /nu zilənd/, /nu ziləndər/
Nica|ra|gua /nɪkəragwə/; Nica|ra|guan /nɪkəragwən/
Ni|ger /naɪdʒər, niʒɛər/; Ni|ge|rien, Nigerois /naɪdʒɪəriən, niʒɛryɛn/, /niʒɛrwa/
Ni|geria /naɪdʒɪəriə/; Ni|gerian /naɪdʒɪəriən/
Nor|way /nɔrweɪ/; Nor|we|gian /nɔrwidʒən/
Oman /ouman/; Omani /oumani/
(the) Pa|cific Ocean /(ðə) pəsɪfɪk oʊʃən/
Paki|stan /pækɪstæn, pakɪstan/; Paki|stani /pækɪstæni, pakɪstani/
Pa|lau /palau, pə-/; Pa|lauan /palauən, pə-/
Pan|ama /pænəma, -mɔ/; Pan|ama|nian /pænəmeɪniən/

Pap|ua New Guinea /pæpyuə nu gɪni, pɑpuɑ/; Pap|ua New Guin|ean, Pap|uan /pæpyuə nu gɪniən, pɑpuɑ/, pæpyuən, pɑpuən/

Para|guay /pærəgwaɪ, -gweɪ/; Para|guayan /pærəgwaɪən, -gweɪən/

Peru /pəru/; Pe|ru|vian /pəruviən/

(the) Phil|ip|pines /(ðə) fɪlɪpinz/; Phil|ip|pine, Fili|pino, Fili|pina /fɪlɪpin/, /fɪlɪpinoʊ/, /fɪlɪpinə/

Po|land /poʊlənd/; Po|lish, Pole /poʊlɪʃ/, /poʊl/

Por|tu|gal /pɔrchəgəl/; Por|tu|guese /pɔrchəgiz/

Qa|tar /kətɑr/; Qa|tari /kətɑri/

Ro|ma|nia /roʊmeɪniə/; Ro|ma|nian /roʊmeɪniən/

Rus|sia /rʌʃə/; Rus|sian /rʌʃən/

Rwanda /ruɑndə/; Rwan|dan /ruɑndən/

Saint Kitts-Ne|vis /seɪnt kɪts nivɪs/; Kittitian, Ne|visian /kɪtɪʃən/, /nɪvɪʒən/

Saint Lu|cia /seɪnt luʃə/; Saint Lu|cian /seɪnt luʃən/

Saint Vin|cent and the Grena|dines /seɪnt vɪnsənt ən ðə grɛnədinz/; Saint Vin|cen|tian, Vin|cen|tian /seɪnt vɪnsɛnʃən/, /vɪnsɛnʃən/

Sa|moa /səmoʊə/; Sa|moan /səmoʊən/

San Ma|rino /sæn mərinoʊ/; Sam|mari|nese, San Mari|nese /sæmmærɪniz/, /sæn mærɪniz/

Sao Tome and Prin|cipe /soʊn təmeɪ ən prɪnsɪpi/; Sao Tomean /soʊn təmeɪən/

Saudi Arabia /soʊdi əreɪbiə/; Saudi Arabian /soʊdi əreɪbiən/

Scot|land /skɒtlənd/; Scot|tish, Scot(s) /skɒtɪʃ/, /skɒts/

Sen|egal /sɛnɪgəl, -gɑl/; Sen|egal|ese /sɛnɪgəliz/

Ser|bia and Mon|te|negro /sɜrbiə ən mɒntɪnɛgroʊ/ Ser|bian, Serb, Mon|te|negrin /sɜrbiən/, /sɜrb/, /mɒntɪnɛgrɪn/

(the) Sey|chelles /(ðə) seɪʃɛlz/; Sey|chel|lois /seɪʃɛlwɑ/

Si|erra Le|one /siɛrə lioʊn/; Si|erra Le|onean /siɛrə lioʊniən/

Sin|ga|pore /sɪŋəpɔr, sɪŋgə-/; Sin|ga|porean /sɪŋəpɔriən, sɪŋgə-/

Slo|va|kia /sloʊvɑkiə, -vækiə/; Slo|vak, Slo|va|kian /sloʊvæk/, /sloʊvɑkiən, -væk-/

Slo|ve|nia /sloʊviniə/; Slo|ve|nian /sloʊviniən/

Solo|mon Is|lands /sɒləmən aɪləndz/; Solo|mon Is|lander /sɒləmən aɪləndər/

So|ma|lia /səmɑliə, soʊ-/; So|ma|li, So|ma|lian /səmɑli, soʊ-/, /səmɑliən, soʊ-/

South Af|rica /soʊθ æfrɪkə/; South Af|ri|can /soʊθ æfrɪkən/

(the Re|pub|lic of) Spain (ðə rɪpʌblɪk əv) /speɪn/; Span|ish, Span|iard /spænɪʃ/, /spænyərd/

Sri Lanka /sri lɑŋkə, ʃri/; Sri Lan|kan /sri lɑŋkən, ʃri/

Su|dan /sudæn, -dɑn/; Su|da|nese /sudᵊniz/

Su|ri|name /sʊərɪnɑm/; Su|ri|na|mer, Su|ri|na|mese /sʊərɪnɑmər/, /sʊərɪnəmiz/

Swazi|land /swɑzilænd/; Swazi /swɑzi/

Swe|den /swidᵊn/; Swe|dish, Swede /swidɪʃ/, /swid/

Switzer|land /swɪtsərlənd/; Swiss /swɪs/

Syria /sɪəriə/; Syr|ian /sɪəriən/

Tai|wan /taɪwɑn/; Tai|wan|ese /taɪwɑniz/

Ta|jiki|stan /tɑdʒɪkɪstæn, -stɑn/; Ta|jiki|stani, Tajik /tɑdʒɪkɪstæni, -stɑni/, /tɑdʒɪk, -dʒik/

Tan|za|nia /tænzəniə/; Tan|za|nian /tænzəniən/

Thai|land /taɪlænd, -lənd/; Thai /taɪ/

Togo /toʊgoʊ/; To|go|lese /toʊgəliz/

Tonga /tɒŋgə/; Ton|gan /tɒŋgən/

Trini|dad and To|bago /trɪnɪdæd ən təbeɪgoʊ/; Trini|dadian, To|bago|nian /trɪnɪdeɪdiən/, /toʊbəgoʊniən/

Tu|ni|sia /tuniʒə/; Tu|ni|sian /tuniʒən/

Tur|key /tɜrki/; Tur|kish, Turk /tɜrkɪʃ/, /tɜrk/

Turk|meni|stan /tərkmɛnɪstæn, -stɑn/; Turk|men /tɜrkmɛn, -mən/

Tu|valu /tuvɑlu, tuvəlu/; Tu|va|luan /tuvəluən/

Uganda /yugændə, ugɑn-/; Ugan|dan /yugændən, ugɑn-/

Ukraine /yukreɪn/; Ukran|ian /yukreɪniən/

(the) United Arab Emir|ates /(ðə) yunaɪtɪd ærəb ɛmərɪts, -əreɪts/; Emir|ati /ɛmərɑti/

(the) United King|dom of Great Brit|ain and North|ern Ire|land /(ðə) yunaɪtɪd kɪŋdəm əv greɪt brɪtᵊn ən nɔrðərn aɪərlənd/; Brit|ish /brɪtɪʃ/

(the) United States of America /(ðə) yunaɪtɪd steɪts əv əmɛrɪkə/; Ameri|can /əmɛrɪkən/

Uru|guay /yʊərəgweɪ, -gwaɪ/; Uru|guayan /yʊərəgweɪən, -gwaɪən/

Uz|beki|stan /ʊzbɛkɪstæn, -stɑn, uz-/; Uz|beki|stani, Uz|bek /ʊzbɛkɪstæni, -stɑni, uz-/, /ʊzbɛk, uz-/

Van|uatu /vænwɑtu/; Ni-Van|uatu /ni vænwɑtu/

Vat|ican City /vætɪkən sɪti/

Ven|ezuela /vɛnɪzweɪlə/; Ven|ezue|lan /vɛnɪzweɪlən/

Vi|et|nam /viɛtnɑm, vyɛt-/; Vi|et|nam|ese /viɛtnəmiz, vyɛt-/

Wales /weɪlz/; Welsh /wɛlʃ/

Yemen /yɛmən/; Yem|eni, Yem|en|ite /yɛməni/, /yɛmənaɪt/

Zam|bia /zæmbiə/; Zam|bian /zæmbiən/

Zim|ba|bwe /zɪmbɑbweɪ, -wi/; Zim|ba|bwean /zɪmbɑbweɪən, -wiən/

Credits

Illustrations:

Higgins Bond: pp. 155, 258, 289, 295, 318, 353, 371, 400, 453, 560, 577, 701,853; © Higgins Bond/Anita Grien

Richard Carbajal: pp. 28, 136, 233, 289, 473 (top), 504, 552, 711, 770, 809,860 (bottom); © Richard Carbajal/illustrationOnLine.com

Ron Carboni: pp. 97, 116, 145, 224, 306, 427 (bottom), 477 (top), 548, 703, 729 (bottom),809;© Ron Carboni/Anita Grien

Todd Daman: pp. 18, 63; © Todd Daman/illustrationOnLine.com

Dick Gage: pp. 83, 236 (top); © Dick Gage/illustrationOnLine.com

Patrick Gnan: pp. 248 (bottom), 416, 499, 529 (right), 662; © Patrick Gnan/illustrationOnLine.com

Sharon and Joel Harris: pp. 77, 180, 203, 298 (bottom), 349, 513, 649 (fetus), 652,717; © Sharon and Joel Harris/illustrationOnLine.com

Philip Howe: pp. 101, 130, 270, 506, 553, 681, 883; © Philip Howe/illustrationOnLine.com

Robert Kayganich: pp. 70, 84, 200,236 (bottom), 316, 325, 365, 483, 685, 749, 772,895; © Robert Kayganich/illustrationOnLine.com

Robert Kemp: pp. 156, 167, 245, 336,527; © Robert Kemp/illustrationOnLine.com

Stephen Peringer: pp. 133, 160, 199, 239, 298 (top), 321; © Stephen Peringer/illustrationOnLine.com

Alan Reingold: pp. 172, 225, 346; © Alan Reingold/Anita Grien

Mark Ryan: pp.699, 730 (bottom), 860 (top); © Mark Ryan/illustrationOnLine.com

Simon Shaw: pp. 68, 241, 445, 623; © Simon Shaw/illustrationOnLine.com

Daniel M. Short: pp. 249; © Daniel M. Short

Gerard Taylor: pp. 16, 61, 274, 406, 733, 869, 870; © Gerard Taylor/illustrationOnLine.com

Ralph Voltz: pp. 38, 276, 299, 331, 374, 473 (bottom), 478, 538, 716, 795; © Ralph Voltz/illustrationOnLine.com

Cam Wilson: pp. 162, 212, 238 (top), 296, 304, 327, 338, 360, 422, 431, 466, 730 (top), 762; © Cam Wilson/illustrationOnLine.com

Photos:

Cover image: Earth taken by Apollo 17 astronauts ©NASA/National Space Science Data Center

40: (right) © Burstein Collection/CORBIS, (left) © ArchivoIconografico, S.A./ CORBIS
45: © Louie Psihoyos/CORBIS
87: AM Corporation / Alamy
102: Craig Lovell / Eagle Visions Photography / Alamy
104: Phil Talbot / Alamy
122: Robert Harding Picture Library Ltd / Alamy
124: © William Manning/Corbis
124: (far left) © David Turnley/Corbis, (middle left) © David McNew/Getty Images, (middle) © Anne Rippy/ Getty Images, (middle right) © Royalty-Free/ Corbis, (far right) © Masterfile Royalty Free (RF)
129: © Jonathan Blair/CORBIS
146: Redferns Music Picture Library / Alamy;
161: Imageshop / Alamy
171: © Tim Wright/CORBIS
176: Blend Images / Alamy
178: (right) BananaStock / Alamy , (center) Kimball Hall / Alamy, (left) Digital Archive Japan / Alamy
182: © Bettmann/CORBIS
183 (bottom): (top left) © Comstock/Corbis, (top middle) © Gail Mooney/ CORBIS, (top right) © Robbie Jack/Corbis, (bottom left) © Mario Tama/Getty Images, (bottom middle) © Masterfile Royalty Free (RF), (bottom right) © Julie Lemberger/Corbis
205: BananaStock / Alamy
208: Frances Roberts / Alamy
209: Dinodia Images / Alamy
221: Owe Andersson /Alamy
234: (bottom) David Butow/CORBIS SABA
253: © Herbert Spichtinger/zefa/Corbis
271: © CORBIS
300: Dennis MacDonald/ Alamy
301: Bill Marsh Royalty Free Photography / Alamy
311: (apple) © age fotostock / SuperStock, (orange segment) © Envision/ Corbis, (pear, fig) © Getty Royalty Free, (pineapple, lemon, grapes, banana, kiwi, watermelon, orange)
© PhotoObjects
313: nagelestock.com / Alamy
326: Janine Wiedel Photolibrary / Alamy
335: Medioimages / Alamy
337: David Noton Photography / Alamy
345: (far left) © Don Mason/Corbis, (left) © Bert Leidmann/zefa/Corbis, (right) © J. A. Kraulis/ Masterfile, (far right) © Frans Lanting/Corbis

347: Image Source / Alamy
361: © Alexander Burkatovski/ CORBIS
372: BananaStock / Alamy
373: Jeff Greenberg / Alamy
394: (left) image100 / Alamy, (right top) Trevor Smithers ARPS / Alamy
424: © CORBIS
427: (top): © Bettmann/CORBIS
429: MONSERRATE J. SCHWARTZ / Alamy;
443: Dynamic Graphics Group / IT Stock Free / Alamy
458: © Royalty-Free/Corbis
463: ImageState / Alamy
472: © Hulton DeutschCollection/CORBIS
494: (right) Craig Lovell / Eagle Visions Photography / Alamy
496: © NASA/Roger Ressmeyer/CORBIS
498: numb / Alamy
503: BananaStock / Alamy
510: (right) Comstock Images / Alamy
548: © Reuters/CORBIS
562: Nikreates / Alamy
569: © Bill Ross/CORBIS
570: (left) © Araldo de Luca/CORBIS, (center) © The Art Archive/Corbis (right) © Bettmann/CORBIS
571: Stockbyte Platinum / Alamy
577: Wildscape / Alamy
584: oote boe / Alamy
600: © Bettmann/CORBIS
621: © Bohemian Nomad Picturemakers/CORBIS
624: AM Corporation / Alamy
649: (far left) © Matthias Kulka/zefa/Corbis, (left) © Yorgos Nikas/ Getty Images, (right) © Neil Harding/ Getty Images, (far right) © Thinkstock/Corbis
658: Food Features / Alamy
700: ImageState / Alamy
702: Stock Connection Distribution / Alamy
719: Blend Images / Alamy
726: © Freeman Patterson/ Masterfile
757: Jon Arnold Images / Alamy
788: STOCK IMAGE/PIXLAND / Alamy
791: (top): © Kim Kulish/Corbis
792: Mark Hamilton / Alamy
793: (right): Rex Argent / Alamy
793: (left): Leslie Garland Picture Library / Alamy
799: North Wind Picture Archives / Alamy
799: © Susanna Raab/Sygma/Corbis
801: © Masterfile Royalty Free (RF)
807: © Richard T. Nowitz/CORBIS
818: © HASHIMOTO NOBORU/CORBIS SYGMA

820: © Bettmann/CORBIS
823: (bottom): Comstock Images / Alamy
828: Digital Archive Japan / Alamy
866: © Stapleton Collection/CORBIS
873: (bottom) Purestock / Alamy
877: (top) Stephen Frink Collection / Alamy
899: John Sturrock / Alamy

Photos on the following pages are from JUPITER IMAGES. © 2006 Jupiterimages Corporation: 27, 28, 59 (top), 119 (bottom), 177, 183 (top), 204, 244, 288 (bottom), 377, 433, 446, 465, 475, 482, 494, 510(left, center), 529 (left), 531, 551, 589, 676, 732, 727, 729 (top), 739, 789

Photos on the following pages are from IndexOpen. © 2006 IndexOpen: 37, 104, 111, 219 (top), 288 (top), 477 (bottom), 487, 873 (top), 877 (bottom)